Annotated Teacher's Edition

HOLT
ELEMENTS OF LITERATURE

Sixth Course
ESSENTIALS OF BRITISH AND WORLD LITERATURE

HOLT, RINEHART AND WINSTON
A Harcourt Education Company
Orlando • Austin • New York • San Diego • Toronto • London

EDITORIAL
Editorial Vice President: Laura Wood
Project Directors: Kathleen Daniel, Mescal Evler
Executive Editors: Kristine E. Marshall, Laura Mongello
Senior Editors: John Haffner Layden, Susan Lynch, Kathryn Rogers, Jennifer Tench, Hester Weeden
Managing Editor: Marie Price
Senior Product Manager: Don Wulbrecht
Editorial Staff: Abraham Chang, Steven Fechter, Christine Han, Jennifer Schwan, Crystal Wirth, Michael Zakhar
Copyediting Manager: Michael Neibergall
Copyediting Supervisor: Mary Malone
Copyeditors: Christine Altgelt, Elizabeth Dickson, Emily Force, Leora Harris, Anne Heausler, Julia Thomas Hu, Kathleen Scheiner, Nancy Shore
Associate Managing Editors: Lori De La Garza, Elizabeth LaManna
Editorial Support: Christine Degollado, Danielle Greer, Erik Netcher
Editorial Permissions: Carrie Jones, Susan Lowrance, Erik Netcher

ART, DESIGN, AND PRODUCTION
Director: Athena Blackorby
Senior Design Director: Betty Mintz
Design: Preface, Inc.
Composition and PrePress: TSI Graphics, Inc.
Production Manager: Carol Trammel

COVER
(Inset) *Garrowby Hill* (1998) by David Hockney. Oil on canvas. Juliana Cheney Edwards Collection, Seth K. Sweetser Fund, and Tompkins Collection, 1998.56 © 2003 Museum of Fine Arts, Boston. (Background) Homes and farmland. © Freeman Paterson/Masterfile.

Copyright © 2005 by Holt, Rinehart and Winston

All rights reserved. No part of this publication may be reproduced or transmitted in any form or by any means, electronic or mechanical, including photocopy, recording, or any information storage and retrieval system, without permission in writing from the publisher.

Requests for permission to make copies of any part of the work should be mailed to the following address: Permissions Department, Holt, Rinehart and Winston, 10801 N. MoPac Expressway, Building 3, Austin, Texas 78759-5415.

Acknowledgments appear on pages 1255–1257 and 1283, which are extensions of the copyright page.

Printed in the United States of America

ISBN 0-03-068388-2

2 3 4 5 6 048 06 05 04 03

Sixth Course Program Organization

	Collection 1 The Anglo-Saxons 449–1066	Collection 2 The Middle Ages 1066–1485	Collection 3 The Renaissance 1485–1660	Collection 4 The Restoration and the Eighteenth Century 1660–1800
Literary Response	Evaluate the historical influences of the Anglo-Saxon era. Analyze characteristics of the epic. Analyze archetypes drawn from myth and tradition. Analyze and compare themes. Compare works from different literary periods.	Evaluate the historical influences of the Middle Ages. Analyze characteristics of subgenres of poetry and prose. Compare frame stories from different cultures and literary periods. Analyze the use of verbal and situational irony. Analyze different methods of characterization. Compare works from different literary periods.	Evaluate the historical influences of the Renaissance. Analyze the characteristics of subgenres of poetry, drama, and prose. Analyze the use of poetic and literary devices. Analyze political points of view on a topic. Analyze patterns of organization. Analyze an author's style. Compare works from different literary periods.	Evaluate the historical influences of the Restoration and the eighteenth century. Analyze verbal irony, diction, antithesis, epigrams, and tone. Compare satires from different cultures. Analyze characteristics of subgenres of poetry and prose. Compare wisdom literature from different countries. Analyze political points of view on a topic. Compare works from different literary periods.
Reading Public Documents and Informational Text			Analyze an author's argument.	Analyze persuasive techniques. Analyze rhetorical devices in public documents. Analyze an author's argument.
Vocabulary	Understand and identify Anglo-Saxon roots and affixes. Create semantic maps. Use context clues to determine word meanings.	Create semantic maps with antonyms. Understand etymologies and multiple-meaning words. Complete word analogies.	Identify word relationships. Understand scientific and mathematical terms derived from Greek and Latin. Understand and use synonyms.	Compare word meanings. Analyze word analogies. Create etymology maps. Understand the meanings and origins of words.
Writing, Listening, and Speaking	Write a descriptive essay.	Write a literary research report. Present literary research.	Write an analysis of literature. Present a recitation of literature.	Write a literary essay. Present a literary response.

Sixth Course Program Organization

	Collection 5 The Romantic Period 1798–1832	Collection 6 The Victorian Period 1832–1901	Collection 7 The Modern World 1900–Present
Literary Response	Evaluate the historical influences of the Romantic period. Analyze an author's style. Analyze theme. Analyze the use of poetic devices. Compare and contrast poetry from different cultures. Analyze characteristics of subgenres of poetry. Compare works from different literary periods.	Evaluate the historical influences of the Victorian period. Analyze the use of poetic devices. Analyze characteristics of subgenres of poetry and short stories. Analyze an author's style. Compare realist works. Analyze the way characters affect plot. Compare works from different literary periods. Analyze theme.	Evaluate the historical influences of the Modern era. Analyze the use of poetic and literary devices. Analyze political points of view on a topic. Analyze characteristics of subgenres of prose and poetry. Analyze theme. Analyze point of view. Analyze an author's style. Analyze the use of foreshadowing and flashback. Compare works from different cultures and literary periods.
Reading Public Documents and Informational Text			Compare main ideas across texts. Evaluate an author's beliefs and assumptions. Identify and critique an argument.
Vocabulary	Understand word analogies. Use context clues. Understand multiple-meaning words.	Understand connotations. Analyze word analogies. Identify antonyms.	Use synonyms and antonyms. Clarify word meanings. Understand the etymology of political, scientific, and historical terms. Analyze context clues. Create semantic charts. Analyze word analogies.
Writing, Listening, and Speaking	Write a reflective essay. Present a reflection.	Write an essay comparing and contrasting literature.	Write a persuasive essay. Write an analysis of nonfiction. Write a short story. Analyze and use media. Present and analyze speeches.

Program Scope and Sequence

LITERARY SKILLS	Grade 6	Grade 7	Grade 8	Grade 9	Grade 10	Grade 11	Grade 12
Alexandrine							■
Allegory				■	■	■	■
Alliteration	■	■	■	■	■	■	■
Allusion	■	■	■	■	■	■	■
Ambiguity				■	■	■	
American Indian oratory						■	
Analogy		■	■	■	■	■	■
Anecdote	■	■	■			■	■
Antagonist			■	■	■		■
Anticlimax							■
Antithesis							■
Aphorism						■	■
Apostrophe							■
Approximate rhyme			■	■	■	■	
Archetype						■	■
Argument					■	■	
Arthurian legend		■			■		■
Aside				■	■		
Assonance			■	■		■	■
Atmosphere		■	■	■	■	■	■
Autobiography	■	■	■	■	■	■	■
Ballad			■	■	■	■	■
Biography	■	■	■	■	■	■	■
Blank verse				■	■	■	■
Cadence						■	
Caesura							■
Carpe diem							■
Catalog poem				■		■	
Character	■	■	■	■	■	■	■
Character interactions		■		■	■		
Character traits	■	■	■	■	■		

T5

Program Scope and Sequence

LITERARY SKILLS	Grade 6	Grade 7	Grade 8	Grade 9	Grade 10	Grade 11	Grade 12
Characterization	■	■	■	■	■	■	■
Chronological order	■	■	■	■	■	■	
Classicism							■
Climax	■	■	■	■	■	■	■
Comedy			■	■	■	■	■
Comic devices			■			■	
Comparing texts	■	■	■	■	■	■	■
Conceit							■
Conflict	■	■	■	■	■	■	■
Connotation	■	■	■	■	■	■	■
Contradiction				■	■		
Couplet		■	■	■	■	■	■
Deism						■	■
Denotation	■	■	■	■	■	■	■
Denouement				■	■	■	■
Description	■	■	■	■	■	■	■
Dialect	■	■	■	■	■	■	■
Dialogue	■	■	■	■	■	■	■
Diction			■	■	■	■	■
Didactic literature	■	■	■				■
Direct characterization	■	■	■	■	■		
Drama	■	■	■	■	■		■
Dramatic irony			■	■	■	■	■
Dramatic monologue				■	■	■	■
Elegy		■	■			■	■
End rhyme	■	■	■	■	■		
Epic			■	■			■
Epic conventions							■
Epic hero			■	■			■
Epic simile							■
Epigram							■

Program Scope and Sequence

LITERARY SKILLS	Grade 6	Grade 7	Grade 8	Grade 9	Grade 10	Grade 11	Grade 12
Epiphany							■
Epitaph							■
Essay	■	■	■	■	■	■	■
Exposition		■	■	■	■	■	■
Extended metaphor	■	■	■	■	■	■	■
External conflict	■	■	■	■	■	■	■
Fable	■	■	■	■	■		■
Farce					■		
Fiction	■	■	■				
Figurative language	■	■	■	■	■	■	■
First-person narrator	■	■		■	■	■	■
First-person point of view	■	■	■	■	■	■	■
Flashback	■	■	■	■	■	■	■
Flash-forward		■		■	■		
Flat character				■	■		
Foil				■	■		
Folk tale	■	■	■	■			
Foreshadowing	■	■	■	■	■	■	■
Frame story						■	■
Free verse	■	■	■	■	■	■	■
Gothic tale						■	■
Haiku	■			■			■
Harlem Renaissance	■		■			■	
Historical context	■			■	■	■	■
Historical fiction		■	■				
Humanism							■
Hyperbole	■					■	■
Iambic pentameter		■	■	■	■	■	■
Idiom	■	■	■	■	■	■	
Imagery	■	■	■	■	■	■	■
Implied metaphor			■	■	■	■	

Program Scope and Sequence

LITERARY SKILLS	Grade 6	Grade 7	Grade 8	Grade 9	Grade 10	Grade 11	Grade 12
Indirect characterization		■	■	■	■		
Interior monologue						■	
Internal conflict	■	■	■	■	■	■	■
Internal rhyme	■	■	■	■	■	■	
Inversion			■		■	■	
Irony	■	■	■	■	■	■	■
Kenning							■
Legend	■	■	■		■		
Literary criticism	■	■	■	■	■	■	■
Lyric poetry		■	■	■	■	■	■
Magic realism					■	■	■
Main idea	■	■	■	■	■	■	■
Memoir	■	■				■	■
Metamorphosis	■	■	■			■	
Metaphor	■	■	■	■	■	■	■
Metaphysical poetry							■
Meter	■	■	■	■	■	■	■
Metonymy							■
Mock epic			■				■
Modernism						■	■
Mood	■	■	■	■	■	■	■
Motif	■	■	■				■
Motivation	■	■	■	■	■	■	■
Myth	■	■	■	■	■	■	■
Narration	■	■	■	■	■	■	■
Narrative	■	■	■			■	
Narrative poem	■	■	■	■	■	■	
Narrator	■	■	■		■	■	■
Naturalism						■	
Neoclassicism							■
Nonfiction	■	■	■	■	■	■	■

Program Scope and Sequence

LITERARY SKILLS	Grade 6	Grade 7	Grade 8	Grade 9	Grade 10	Grade 11	Grade 12
Objective writing		■	■		■	■	
Ode	■	■	■		■		■
Omniscient narrator		■		■	■	■	■
Omniscient point of view		■	■	■	■	■	■
Onomatopoeia	■	■	■	■	■	■	■
Ottava rima							■
Oxymoron							■
Parable					■	■	■
Paradox						■	
Parallelism				■	■	■	■
Parody						■	■
Pastoral							■
Persona				■	■		
Personification	■	■	■	■	■	■	■
Persuasion	■	■		■	■	■	■
Plain style						■	
Plot	■	■	■	■	■	■	■
Poetry	■	■	■	■	■	■	■
Point of view	■	■	■	■	■	■	■
Postmodernism						■	■
Protagonist	■	■	■	■	■		■
Proverb						■	■
Rationalism						■	■
Realism						■	■
Refrain	■	■	■	■	■	■	■
Regionalism						■	
Renaissance							■
Repetition	■	■	■	■	■	■	
Resolution	■	■	■	■	■	■	■
Rhyme	■	■	■	■	■	■	■
Rhyme scheme	■	■	■	■	■	■	■

Program Scope and Sequence

LITERARY SKILLS	Grade 6	Grade 7	Grade 8	Grade 9	Grade 10	Grade 11	Grade 12
Rhythm	■	■	■	■	■	■	■
Romance					■	■	■
Romanticism						■	■
Round character				■	■		
Satire			■	■	■	■	■
Scene design			■	■	■		
Setting	■	■	■	■	■	■	■
Short story	■	■	■	■	■	■	■
Simile	■	■	■	■	■	■	■
Situational irony			■	■	■	■	■
Slant rhyme		■				■	
Soliloquy			■	■	■		■
Sonnet		■	■	■	■	■	■
Sound effects	■	■		■	■	■	
Speaker	■	■	■	■	■	■	■
Speech		■	■	■	■	■	■
Spenserian stanza							■
Stanza	■	■	■				
Static character		■	■	■	■		
Stereotype						■	
Stock character					■	■	
Stream of consciousness						■	■
Style			■	■	■	■	■
Subjective writing		■	■		■	■	
Subplots			■				
Surprise ending	■			■			
Suspense	■	■	■	■	■		
Symbol	■	■	■	■	■	■	■
Synesthesia						■	■
Tall tale	■	■	■			■	
Tanka					■		■

Program Scope and Sequence

LITERARY SKILLS	Grade 6	Grade 7	Grade 8	Grade 9	Grade 10	Grade 11	Grade 12
Teleplay	■	■	■				
Terza rima							■
Theme	■	■	■	■	■	■	■
Third-person-limited point of view	■	■		■	■		
Title	■	■	■	■	■	■	
Tone	■	■	■	■	■	■	■
Tragedy			■	■	■		■
Tragic hero				■			
Transcendentalism						■	
Understatement			■			■	■
Universal themes			■	■	■		
Unreliable narrator			■	■	■		
Verbal irony			■	■	■	■	
Vernacular						■	■
Villanelle						■	■
Voice				■	■		

READING SKILLS	Grade 6	Grade 7	Grade 8	Grade 9	Grade 10	Grade 11	Grade 12
Anachronism					■		
Analogy		■	■	■	■	■	■
Application forms	■	■					
Argument		■		■	■	■	■
Assertions	■				■		
Author's opinion				■	■	■	■
Author's purpose	■	■	■	■	■	■	■
Bias		■		■	■		■
Cause and effect	■	■	■	■	■	■	
Chronological order	■	■	■	■	■		■
Claim				■	■	■	■
Coherence			■	■	■	■	■

T11

Program Scope and Sequence

READING SKILLS	Grade 6	Grade 7	Grade 8	Grade 9	Grade 10	Grade 11	Grade 12
Comparing texts	■	■	■	■	■	■	■
Comparison and contrast	■	■	■	■	■	■	■
Connotation	■	■	■	■	■	■	■
Consumer documents		■	■	■	■		
Context clues	■	■	■	■	■	■	■
Credibility				■	■	■	■
Denotation	■	■	■	■	■	■	■
Drawing conclusions	■	■	■	■	■	■	■
Emotional appeals	■	■	■	■	■	■	■
Evaluating evidence	■	■	■	■	■	■	■
Evaluating historical accuracy			■				
Evidence	■	■	■	■	■	■	■
Fact	■	■	■	■	■		
Fallacious reasoning	■	■	■	■	■	■	■
Generalizations	■	■	■	■	■	■	■
Generating research questions				■	■		
Graphic features	■	■	■	■	■	■	■
Graphic organizers	■	■	■	■	■	■	■
Graphs	■	■	■	■	■	■	■
Historical context	■	■	■	■	■	■	■
Idiom	■	■	■	■	■		
Inferences	■	■	■	■	■	■	■
Informative texts	■	■	■	■	■	■	■
Internet sources	■	■	■	■	■	■	■
Inversion				■		■	
Judgments			■				
Logic	■	■	■	■	■	■	■
Logical appeals	■	■		■	■	■	■
Logical order			■	■	■	■	■
Main idea	■	■	■	■	■	■	■
Maps	■	■	■	■	■	■	■

Program Scope and Sequence

READING SKILLS	Grade 6	Grade 7	Grade 8	Grade 9	Grade 10	Grade 11	Grade 12
Monitor reading	■	■	■	■	■	■	■
Note taking	■	■	■	■	■	■	■
Objective writing		■	■		■	■	
Opinion	■	■	■	■	■	■	■
Outlining	■	■	■	■	■	■	■
Paraphrasing	■	■	■	■	■	■	
Persuasion	■	■	■	■	■	■	■
Predictions	■	■	■	■	■	■	■
Previewing			■				
Primary sources				■	■	■	■
Prior knowledge	■	■	■			■	
Propaganda	■	■					
Proposition and support			■				
Public documents		■	■	■	■	■	■
Purpose of texts	■	■	■				
Questioning			■				
Reading for details	■	■	■	■	■	■	■
Reading for information	■	■	■	■	■	■	■
Reading poetry	■	■	■	■	■	■	■
Reading rate	■	■		■	■	■	■
Researching information	■			■	■		
Retelling	■	■	■			■	
Rhetorical devices						■	■
Secondary sources				■	■	■	
Stereotyping		■	■				
Subjective writing		■			■	■	
Summarizing	■	■	■	■	■	■	■
Syntax				■	■		
Synthesizing sources				■	■		
Text structures	■	■	■	■	■	■	■
Vernacular						■	

Program Scope and Sequence

WRITING SKILLS	Grade 6	Grade 7	Grade 8	Grade 9	Grade 10	Grade 11	Grade 12
Biographical narrative					■	■	
Business letter				■	■		
Compare and contrast media genres				■	■		
Compare and contrast two literary works							■
Comparison-contrast essay	■	■	■				
Descriptive essay	■	■		■	■	■	■
Editorial						■	
Historical research report						■	
Informative report		■	■				
Literary research paper							■
Minutes of a meeting				■			
Personal narrative	■	■	■				
Persuasive cause-and-effect essay				■			
Persuasive essay	■	■	■	■	■		■
Problem-solution essay	■	■	■		■		
Reflective essay						■	■
Report	■						
Research paper				■	■		
Short story	■	■	■	■	■	■	■
Technical documents					■		
WRITING PROCESS							
Prewriting							
Choose topic	■	■	■	■	■	■	■
Identify purpose	■	■	■	■	■	■	■
Identify audience	■	■	■	■	■	■	■
Generate ideas	■	■	■	■	■	■	■
Gather information	■	■	■	■	■	■	■
Organize information	■	■	■	■	■	■	■
Draft thesis statement	■	■	■	■	■	■	■

Program Scope and Sequence

WRITING SKILLS	Grade 6	Grade 7	Grade 8	Grade 9	Grade 10	Grade 11	Grade 12
Writing a draft							
State main point	■	■	■	■	■	■	■
Include relevant support	■	■	■	■	■	■	■
Include elaboration	■	■	■	■	■	■	■
Follow plan of elaboration	■	■	■	■	■	■	■
Revising							
Revise for content	■	■	■	■	■	■	■
Revise for style	■	■	■	■	■	■	■
Publishing							
Proofread for grammar, usage, and mechanics	■	■	■	■	■	■	■
Publish or share writing	■	■	■	■	■	■	■
Reflect on the writing experience	■	■		■	■	■	■

LISTENING and SPEAKING SKILLS	Grade 6	Grade 7	Grade 8	Grade 9	Grade 10	Grade 11	Grade 12
LISTENING AND SPEAKING MODE							
Debate an issue				■	■	■	■
Informative speech	■	■	■				
Multimedia presentation	■			■	■		
Oral autobiographical narrative				■	■		■
Oral descriptive essay				■		■	■
Oral interpretation of a poem				■		■	
Oral narrative	■	■	■	■		■	
Oral problem-solution essay	■						
Oral recitation of literature		■	■	■	■	■	■
Oral reflective essay						■	■
Oral research report				■	■	■	■
Oral response to a literary work	■		■	■	■	■	■
Persuasive speech	■	■	■	■	■	■	■

Program Scope and Sequence

LISTENING and SPEAKING SKILLS	Grade 6	Grade 7	Grade 8	Grade 9	Grade 10	Grade 11	Grade 12
LISTENING AND SPEAKING PROCESS							
Analyze a documentary		■					
Analyze and evaluate a speech	■	■	■	■	■	■	■
Analyze content	■	■	■	■	■	■	■
Analyze delivery	■	■	■	■	■	■	■
Analyze electronic journalism		■					
Analyze organization	■	■	■	■	■	■	■
Analyze strategies used by media	■		■	■	■	■	■
Plan and organize speech or presentation	■	■	■	■	■	■	■
Rehearse and deliver speech or presentation	■	■	■	■	■	■	■
Understand and identify logical fallacies				■		■	■
Understand and identify propaganda techniques	■			■		■	■
Use rhetorical techniques				■		■	■
Use verbal and nonverbal techniques	■	■	■	■	■	■	■

MEDIA SKILLS	Grade 6	Grade 7	Grade 8	Grade 9	Grade 10	Grade 11	Grade 12
Analyze a documentary		■					
Analyze and use media	■	■	■	■	■	■	■
Analyze electronic journalism		■					
Analyze strategies used by media	■		■	■	■	■	■
Compare and contrast media genres				■	■		
Create graphics for technical documents			■				
Multimedia presentation	■			■	■	■	■
Use electronic texts to locate information	■						

SIXTH COURSE MINIMUM COURSE OF STUDY

	Literature	Political Points of View	Writing Workshop	Media/Listening and Speaking Workshops
Collection 1	• from *Beowulf,* Part One • from *Beowulf,* Part Two			
Collection 2	• "Lord Randall" • "Get Up and Bar the Door" • The Prologue to *The Canterbury Tales*		• Reporting Literary Research	
Collection 3	• "The Passionate Shepherd to His Love" • "The Nymph's Reply to the Shepherd" • "Sonnet 29" • "Sonnet 116" • "Death be not proud" • "The Fall of Satan" from *Paradise Lost*			
Collection 4	• "A Modest Proposal" • from *Don Quixote*	Women's Rights • from "A Vindication of the Rights of Woman" • "To the Ladies" • from "The Education of Women"		
Collection 5	• "The Tyger" • "The Lamb" • "Lines Composed a Few Miles Above Tintern Abbey" • "Kubla Khan" • "The Rime of the Ancient Mariner" • "Ozymandias" • "Jade Flower Palace" • "Ode on a Grecian Urn"			

SIXTH COURSE MINIMUM COURSE OF STUDY

	Literature	Political Points of View	Writing Workshop	Media/Listening and Speaking Workshops
COLLECTION 6	• "The Lady of Shalott" • "My Last Duchess" • "Dover Beach" • "To an Athlete Dying Young" • "How Much Land Does a Man Need?"		• Comparing and Contrasting Literature	
COLLECTION 7	A World at War • "Dulce et Decorum Est" • "Blood, Sweat, and Tears" • "In the Shadow of War" Clashes of Culture • "Shakespeare's Sister" from *A Room of One's Own* Discoveries and Transformations • "The Second Coming" • "Araby" • "B. Wordsworth" Ourselves Among Others • "Do Not Go Gentle into That Good Night" • "Sonnet 79/Soneto 79" • "Games at Twilight"	The Holocaust • "On the Bottom" from *Survival in Auschwitz* • from *The War* • "Never Shall I Forget" Colonialism • "No Witchcraft for Sale"	• Writing a Persuasive Essay	• Analyzing and Using Media • Presenting and Analyzing Speeches

Program Authors

Kylene Beers established the reading pedagogy for *Elements of Literature*. A former middle-school teacher, Dr. Beers has turned her commitment to helping readers having difficulty into the major focus of her research, writing, speaking, and teaching. Dr. Beers is currently Senior Reading Researcher at the Child Study Center of the School Development Program at Yale University and was formerly a Research Associate Professor at the University of Houston. Dr. Beers is also currently the editor of the National Council of Teachers of English journal *Voices from the Middle*. She is the author of *When Kids Can't Read: What Teachers Can Do* and co-editor of *Into Focus: Understanding and Creating Middle School Readers*. Dr. Beers is the 2001 recipient of the Richard Halle Award from the NCTE for outstanding contributions to middle-level literary education. She has served on the review boards of the *English Journal* and *The Alan Review*. Dr. Beers currently serves on the board of directors of the International Reading Association's Special Interest Group on Adolescent Literature.

Lee Odell helped establish the pedagogical framework for writing, listening, and speaking for *Elements of Literature*. Dr. Odell is Professor of Composition Theory and Research and, since 1996, Director of the Writing Program at Rensselaer Polytechnic Institute. He began his career teaching English in middle and high schools. More recently he has worked with teachers in grades k–12 to establish a program that involves students from all disciplines in writing across the curriculum and for communities outside their classrooms. Dr. Odell's most recent book (with Charles R. Cooper) is *Evaluating Writing: The Role of Teacher's Knowledge About Text, Learning, and Culture*. He is past chair of the Conference on College Composition and Communication and of NCTE's Assembly for Research. Dr. Odell is currently working on a college-level writing textbook.

Writers

John Malcolm Brinnin, author of six volumes of poetry that have received many prizes and awards, was a member of the American Academy and Institute of Arts and Letters. He was a critic of poetry, a biographer of poets, and for a number of years, director of New York's famous Poetry Center. His teaching career included terms at Vassar College, the University of Connecticut, and Boston University, where he succeeded Robert Lowell as Professor of Creative Writing and Contemporary Letters. In addition to other works, Mr. Brinnin wrote *Dylan Thomas in America: An Intimate Journal* and *Sextet: T. S. Eliot & Truman Capote & Others*.

Claire Miller Colombo received a doctorate in English from the University of Texas at Austin and has taught English at both college and secondary levels. She has been a freelance writer of educational materials since 1990. She is currently at work on a collection of poetry.

Robert DeMaria, Jr., is the Henry Noble MacCracken Professor of English Literature at Vassar College, where he has taught since receiving his doctorate from Rutgers University in 1975. He is an expert on eighteenth-century British literature and has edited the college text *British Literature 1640–1789: An Anthology* (Second Edition, 2001). He has also written three books about Samuel Johnson. Most recently Dr. DeMaria has edited an edition of *Gulliver's Travels;* he is now writing a book about Jonathan Swift.

Donald Gray is Professor Emeritus of English at Indiana University, Bloomington. Dr. Gray has written essays on Victorian poetry and culture and has served as editor of *College English*.

Harley Henry was Professor of English at Macalester College in St. Paul, Minnesota. He has also been a senior Fulbright lecturer in Zimbabwe and a Redfield Visiting Professor at the University of Chicago. In addition to the Romantic period, his teaching specialties include the literature of Zimbabwe, William Faulkner, American fiction from 1945 to 1960, and fiction about baseball.

Rose Sallberg Kam holds a master's in English from California State University, Sacramento, and a master's in biblical studies from the Graduate Theological Union, Berkeley. She taught secondary English for seventeen years, has been a freelance writer of educational materials for nineteen years, and is the author of *Their Stories, Our Stories: Women of the Bible*.

David Adams Leeming was for many years a Professor of English and Comparative Literature at the University of Connecticut. He is the author of several books on mythology, including *Mythology: The Voyage of the Hero; The World of Myth;* and *Encyclopedia of Creation Myths*. For several years, Dr. Leeming taught English at Robert College in Istanbul, Turkey. He also served as secretary and assistant to the writer James Baldwin in New York and Istanbul. He has published the biographies *James Baldwin* and *Amazing Grace: A Life of Beauford Delaney*.

John Leggett is a novelist, biographer, and former teacher. He went to the Writers' Workshop at the University of Iowa in the spring of 1969. In 1970, he assumed temporary charge of the program, and for the next seventeen years he was its director. Mr. Leggett's novels include *Wilder Stone, The Gloucester Branch, Who Took the Gold Away?, Gulliver House,* and *Making Believe*. He is also the author of the highly acclaimed biography *Ross and Tom: Two American Tragedies* and of a biography of William Saroyan, *A Daring Young Man*. Mr. Leggett lives in Napa Valley, California.

C. F. Main was for many years Professor of English at Rutgers University in New Brunswick, New Jersey. He was the editor of *Poems: Wadsworth Handbook and Anthology* and wrote reviews and articles on sixteenth-, seventeenth-, and eighteenth-century literature.

Mairead Stack has a master's degree in English from New York University. A former teacher, she has edited and written educational materials for literature and language arts for more than twenty years.

Senior Program Consultant

Carol Jago is the editor of CATE's quarterly journal, *California English*. She teaches English at Santa Monica High School, in Santa Monica, and directs the California Reading and Literature Project at UCLA. She writes a weekly education column for the *Los Angeles Times*. She is the author of several books, including three in a series on contemporary writers in the classroom: *Alice Walker in the Classroom*; *Nikki Giovanni in the Classroom*; and *Sandra Cisneros in the Classroom*. She is also the author of *With Rigor for All: Teaching the Classics to Contemporary Students*; *Beyond Standards: Excellence in the High School English Classroom*; and *Cohesive Writing: Why Concept Is Not Enough*.

ADVISORS

Cynthia A. Arceneaux
Administrative Coordinator
Office of Deputy Superintendent, Instructional Services
Los Angeles Unified School District
Los Angeles, California

Dr. Julie M. T. Chan
Director of Literacy Instruction
Newport-Mesa Unified School District
Costa Mesa, California

Al Desmarais
English Department Chair and Curriculum Specialist in Language Arts
El Toro High School
Saddleback Valley Unified School District
Lake Forest, California

José M. Ibarra-Tiznado
ELL Program Coordinator
Bassett Unified School District
La Puente, California

Dr. Ronald Klemp
Instructor
California State University, Northridge
Northridge, California

Fern M. Sheldon
K–12 Curriculum and Instruction Specialist
Rowland Unified School District
Rowland Heights, California

Jim Shields
Instructor
El Toro High School
Saddleback Valley Unified School District
Lake Forest, California

CRITICAL REVIEWERS

Elmire C. Budak
Lynwood High School
Lynwood, California

Paulette Dewey
Toledo Public High School
Toledo, Ohio

Matthew Falk
John A. Rowland High School
Rowland Unified School District
Rowland Heights, California

R. E. Fisher
Westlake High School
Atlanta, Georgia

Janice Gauthier
Everett High School
Everett, Massachusetts

Victor Jaccarino
Herricks High School
New Hyde Park, New York

Diane M. Jackson
Washington Preparatory High School
Los Angeles, California

Barbara Kimbrough
Kane Area High School
Kane, Pennsylvania

Dr. Louisa Kramer-Vida
Oyster Bay-East Norwich SD
Oyster Bay, New York

Martin P. Mushik
Covina High School
Covina, California

Mary Ellen Snodgrass
Hickory High School
Hickory, North Carolina

Elaine Sorrell
Marina High School
Huntington Beach, California

David Trimble
Norwin High School
N. Huntingdon, Pennsylvania

Donna Walthour
Greensburg Salem High School
Greensburg, Pennsylvania

John R. Williamson
Highlands High School
Fort Thomas, Kentucky

FIELD-TEST PARTICIPANTS

Barbara A. Briggs
Barberton High School
Barberton, Ohio

Annette Dade
West Orange High School
West Orange, New Jersey

Robert Gardner
John A. Rowland High School
Rowland Unified School District
Rowland Heights, California

Bobbye Sykes-Perkins
Luther Burbank High School
Sacramento, California

John R. Williamson
Highlands High School
Fort Thomas, Kentucky

CONTENTS IN BRIEF

COLLECTION 1
The Anglo-Saxons 449–1066 1
Connecting to World Literature Epics: Stories on a Grand Scale ... 44
Writing Workshop Writing a Descriptive Essay 74

COLLECTION 2
The Middle Ages 1066–1485 89
Connecting to World Literature The Frame Story:
A Tale Linking Tales 169
Writing Workshop Reporting Literary Research 204

COLLECTION 3
The Renaissance 1485–1660 233
Political Points of View Education and Equality 322
Connecting to World Literature
Worlds of Wisdom: Wisdom Literature 346
Writing Workshop Analyzing Literature 390

COLLECTION 4
The Restoration and the Eighteenth Century 1660–1800 407
Connecting to World Literature The Sting of Satire 462
Political Points of View Women's Rights 482
Writing Workshop Writing a Literary Essay 500

COLLECTION 5
The Romantic Period 1798–1832 517
Connecting to World Literature Tanka and Haiku 565
Connecting to World Literature
The Golden Age of Chinese Poetry 627
Writing Workshop Writing a Reflective Essay 656

COLLECTION 6

The Victorian Period 1832–1901 673
Connecting to World Literature The Rise of Realism 746
Writing Workshop Comparing and Contrasting Literature 784

COLLECTION 7

The Modern World: 1900 to the Present 799

A WORLD AT WAR 819
Political Points of View The Holocaust 832
Mini-Workshop Writing a Persuasive Essay 883

CLASHES OF CULTURE 885
Political Points of View Colonialism 896
Mini-Workshop Analyzing Nonfiction 941

DISCOVERIES AND TRANSFORMATIONS 943
Mini-Workshop Writing a Short Story 1031

OURSELVES AMONG OTHERS 1033
Political Points of View Human Rights 1088
Media Workshop Analyzing and Using Media 1112

RESOURCE CENTER
Reading Matters 1133
The World of Work 1147
Writer's Handbook 1153
Test Smarts 1165
Handbook of Literary and Historical Terms 1181
Language Handbook 1205
Glossary 1243
Spanish Glossary 1249

Maps
The British Isles A44
Map of the World A46

Collection 1

The Anglo-Saxons
449–1066
Songs of Ancient Heroes

	SCOPE AND SEQUENCE / RESOURCE MANAGER	**1A–D**
	Time Line	2
	Political and Social Milestones	4
	Introduction to the Literary Period:	
	The Anglo-Saxons by David Adams Leeming	6
	Beowulf (Introduction)	18
	from **Beowulf** translated by Burton Raffel .... EPIC	20
	The Battle with Grendel	21
	The Monster's Mother	26
John Gardner	CONNECTION / *from* **Grendel** .... NOVEL	29
Howard G. Chua-Eoan	CONNECTION / **Life in 999:**	
	A Grim Struggle .... MAGAZINE ARTICLE	30
	from **Beowulf** translated by Seamus Heaney .... EPIC	
	The Final Battle	33
Ellen Ashdown	CONNECTION / **The Fury of the Northmen** .... ARTICLE	39

Connecting to World Literature

	Epics: Stories on a Grand Scale *by* David Adams Leeming	44
MESOPOTAMIA	*from* **Gilgamesh: A Verse Narrative**	
	retold by Herbert Mason .... EPIC	47
Homer GREECE	**the Iliad**, *from* **Book 22: The Death of Hector** *translated by* Robert Fagles .... EPIC	56
C. W. Ceram	CONNECTION / Trojan Gold *from* **Gods, Graves, and Scholars** .... HISTORY	67

Read On FOR INDEPENDENT READING 73

Writing Workshop Writing a Descriptive Essay 74

COLLECTION 1: SKILLS REVIEW

Comparing Literature
from The Seafarer *by* Anonymous Anglo-Saxon
translated by Burton Raffel .... POEM 82
Break, Break, Break *by* Alfred, Lord Tennyson .... POEM 84
Vocabulary Skills 86
Writing Skills 87

Collection 2

THE MIDDLE AGES 1066–1485

The Tales They Told

SCOPE AND SEQUENCE / RESOURCE MANAGER   88A–H

Time Line	90
Political and Social Milestones	92

Introduction to the Literary Period:
The Middle Ages by David Adams Leeming 94

Lord Randall	BALLAD	108
Get Up and Bar the Door	BALLAD	110

The Canterbury Tales: Snapshot of an Age
(Introduction) 115

Geoffrey Chaucer   *from* **The Canterbury Tales**
translated by Nevill Coghill .... NARRATIVE POEM

The Prologue	118
from **The Pardoner's Tale**	145
from **The Wife of Bath's Tale**	155

T28   Contents

Connecting to World Literature
The Frame Story: A Tale Linking Tales
by David Adams Leeming 169

| Panchatantra
INDIA | **Right-Mind and Wrong-Mind**
translated by Arthur William Ryder . . . . FABLE 172 |

| The Thousand and
One Nights
ARABIA | *from* **The Third Voyage of Sindbad the Sailor**
translated by N. J. Dawood . . . . STORY 179 |

| Giovanni Boccaccio
ITALY | **Federigo's Falcon** *from the* **Decameron**
translated by Mark Musa and Peter Bondanella . . . . STORY 186 |

Sir Thomas Malory   *from* **The Day of Destiny** *from* **Le Morte d'Arthur**
retold by Keith Baines . . . . ROMANCE NARRATIVE 193

Read On FOR INDEPENDENT READING 203

Writing Workshop Reporting Literary Research 204

Listening and Speaking Workshop Presenting Literary Research 224

COLLECTION 2: SKILLS REVIEW

Comparing Literature
The Twa Corbies *by* Anonymous Scottish .... BALLAD 226
Raven doth to raven fly *by* Alexander Pushkin
translated by Walter Arndt .... POEM 227

Vocabulary Skills 230

Writing Skills 231

Collection 3

The Renaissance
1485-1660

A Flourish of Genius

	SCOPE AND SEQUENCE / RESOURCE MANAGER	**232A–L**
	Time Line	234
	Political and Social Milestones	236
	Introduction to the Literary Period: The Renaissance by C. F. Main	238
Christopher Marlowe	The Passionate Shepherd to His Love ...... POEM	257
Sir Walter Raleigh	The Nymph's Reply to the Shepherd ...... POEM	261
Robert Herrick	To the Virgins, to Make Much of Time ...... POEM	263
Andrew Marvell	To His Coy Mistress ...... POEM	267
Joseph Papp *and* Elizabeth Kirkland	**CONNECTION / Give Us This Day Our Daily Bread** ... HISTORY	269
	Shakespeare's Sonnets: The Mysteries of Love *(Introduction)*	275
Francesco Petrarch	Sonnet 42 *translated by* Joseph Auslander ...... SONNET	276
William Shakespeare	Sonnet 18 ...... SONNET	277
	Sonnet 29 ...... SONNET	278
	Sonnet 30 ...... SONNET	280
	Sonnet 71 ...... SONNET	281
	Sonnet 73 ...... SONNET	282
	Sonnet 116 ...... SONNET	283
	Sonnet 130 ...... SONNET	284

Louise Labé	**Sonnet 23** *translated by* Willis Barnstone	SONNET	285
William Shakespeare	**Blow, Blow, Thou Winter Wind**	SONG	286
	Fear No More the Heat o' the Sun	SONG	288
	Full Fathom Five	SONG	290
	FAMOUS SHAKESPEAREAN SPEECHES		
	To be, or not to be *from* Hamlet	SOLILOQUY	292
	Tomorrow, and tomorrow, and tomorrow *from* Macbeth	SOLILOQUY	295
	Saint Crispin's Day Speech *from* Henry V	SPEECH	296
	Our revels now are ended *from* The Tempest	SPEECH	298
John Donne	**Song**	POEM	301
	A Valediction: Forbidding Mourning	POEM	304
	Meditation 17	MEDITATION	307
	Death be not proud	SONNET	312
Margaret Edson	**CONNECTION** / *from* W;t	DRAMA	314
Ben Jonson	**On My First Son**	POEM	318
	Song: To Celia	POEM	320

Political Points of View Education and Equality 322

Main Reading

Francis Bacon **Of Studies** .... ESSAY 324

PRIMARY SOURCE / **Axioms** *from* **the Essays**
by Francis Bacon .... AXIOMS 327

Connected Readings

■ PUBLIC DOCUMENT

Queen Elizabeth I **Tilbury Speech** .... SPEECH 330

■ PUBLIC DOCUMENT

Margaret Cavendish,
duchess of Newcastle *from* **Female Orations** .... DEBATE 332

King James Bible **The King James Bible (1611):**
A Masterpiece by a Committee (*Introduction*) 336
Psalms: Worship Through Poetry (*Introduction*) 337
Psalm 23 .... PSALM 338
Psalm 137 .... PSALM 340
The Parable of the Prodigal Son .... PARABLE 342

Connecting to World Literature

Worlds of Wisdom: Wisdom Literature 346

Koran
ARABIA **Night** translated by N. J. Dawood .... SACRED TEXT 349

Bhagavad-Gita
INDIA *from* **Philosophy and Spiritual Discipline**
translated by Barbara Stoler Miller .... SACRED TEXT 351

Buddhist Traditional
JAPAN **Zen Parables** compiled by Paul Reps .... PARABLES 353

Confucius
CHINA *from* **The Analects of Confucius**
translated and annotated by Arthur Waley .... MAXIMS 355

Laotzu
CHINA *from the* **Tao Te Ching**
translated by Stephen Mitchell .... SACRED TEXT 356

Tao Traditional
CHINA **Taoist Anecdotes**
translated and edited by Moss Roberts .... ANECDOTES 357

Saadi
PERSIA **Sayings of Saadi**
translated by Idries Shah .... AXIOMS 358

AFRICA **African Proverbs**
compiled by Charlotte and Wolf Leslau .... PROVERBS 359

	Paradise Lost: Milton's Epic (Introduction)	363
John Milton	**The Fall of Satan** *from* **Paradise Lost** .... EPIC	365
	When I consider how my light is spent ...... SONNET	379
John Bunyan	*from* **The Pilgrim's Progress** .... ALLEGORY	383
	Read On FOR INDEPENDENT READING	389
	Writing Workshop Analyzing Literature	390
	Listening and Speaking Workshop Reciting Literature	398

COLLECTION 3: SKILLS REVIEW

Comparing Literature
When You Are Old *by* Pierre de Ronsard
translated by Humbert Wolfe .... POEM 400
When You Are Old *by* William Butler Yeats .... POEM 401

Vocabulary Skills 404

Writing Skills 405

Collection 4

The Restoration and the EIGHTEENTH CENTURY
1660–1800

The Best of All Possible Worlds

	SCOPE AND SEQUENCE / RESOURCE MANAGER	**406A–H**
	Time Line	408
	Political and Social Milestones	410
	Introduction to the Literary Period: The Restoration and the Eighteenth Century by C. F. Main	412
Jonathan Swift	**A Modest Proposal** .... ESSAY	428
T. Coraghessan Boyle	CONNECTION / **Top of the Food Chain** .... SHORT STORY	438
Alexander Pope	**Heroic Couplets** .... COUPLETS	446
	from **An Essay on Man** .... PHILOSOPHICAL POEM	449
	from **The Rape of the Lock** .... MOCK EPIC	451

Connecting to World Literature

	The Sting of Satire by Robert DeMaria, Jr.	462
Voltaire FRANCE	from **Candide** translated by Richard Aldington .... NOVEL	466
Miguel de Cervantes SPAIN	from **Don Quixote** translated by Samuel Putnam .... NOVEL	474

	Political Points *of* **View** Women's Rights	482
	Main Reading	
	■ PUBLIC DOCUMENT	
Mary Wollstonecraft	*from* **A Vindication of the Rights of Woman** .... PLATFORM	485
	Connected Readings	
Mary, Lady Chudleigh	**To the Ladies** .... POEM	494
Daniel Defoe	*from* **The Education of Women** .... ESSAY	495

Read On FOR INDEPENDENT READING 499

Writing Workshop Writing a Literary Essay 500

Listening and Speaking Workshop
Presenting a Literary Response 508

COLLECTION 4: SKILLS REVIEW

Comparing Literature
from The Burning of Rome *from* The Annals *by* Tacitus
translated by George Gilbert Ramsay .... ANNAL 510
from The Diary of Samuel Pepys *by* Samuel Pepys .... DIARY 511

Vocabulary Skills 514
Writing Skills 515

Collection 5

The Romantic Period
1798–1832

The Quest for Truth and Beauty

	SCOPE AND SEQUENCE / RESOURCE MANAGER	**516A–J**
	Time Line	518
	Political and Social Milestones	520
	Introduction to the Literary Period: The Romantic Period *by* Harley Henry	522
William Blake	Blake's Poems: Innocence to Experience *(Introduction)*	535
	The Tyger .... POEM	536
	PRIMARY SOURCE / "Blake Is a Real Name..." *by* Charles Lamb .... LETTER	538
	The Lamb .... POEM	539
	The Chimney Sweeper *from* Songs of Innocence .... POEM	541
	The Chimney Sweeper *from* Songs of Experience .... POEM	543
	■ **PUBLIC DOCUMENT** PRIMARY SOURCE / *from* **Evidence Given Before the Sadler Committee** *by* Peter Smart .... TESTIMONY	544
	A Poison Tree .... POEM	547

William Wordsworth	**Lines Composed a Few Miles Above Tintern Abbey** .... POEM 551
	Composed upon Westminster Bridge .... SONNET 559
	The World Is Too Much with Us .... SONNET 561

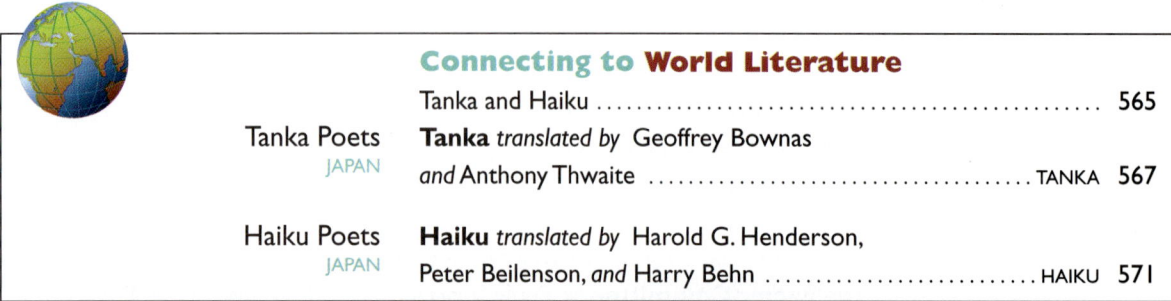

Connecting to World Literature

Tanka and Haiku 565

Tanka Poets — JAPAN: **Tanka** *translated by* Geoffrey Bownas *and* Anthony Thwaite .... TANKA 567

Haiku Poets — JAPAN: **Haiku** *translated by* Harold G. Henderson, Peter Beilenson, *and* Harry Behn .... HAIKU 571

Samuel Taylor Coleridge	**Kubla Khan**	POEM	574
	The Rime of the Ancient Mariner	NARRATIVE POEM	578
	PRIMARY SOURCE / **Coleridge Describes His Addiction** by Samuel Taylor Coleridge	LETTER	603
Bruce Chatwin	CONNECTION / from **In Patagonia**	TRAVEL BOOK	604
George Gordon, Lord Byron	**She Walks in Beauty**	POEM	610
	from **Childe Harold's Pilgrimage, Canto IV**	NARRATIVE POEM	612
Percy Bysshe Shelley	**Ozymandias**	SONNET	618
	Ode to the West Wind	ODE	621

Connecting to World Literature
The Golden Age of Chinese Poetry 627

Tu Fu CHINA	**Jade Flower Palace** translated by Kenneth Rexroth	POEM	631
	Night Thoughts Afloat translated by Arthur Cooper	POEM	633
Li Po CHINA	**Quiet Night Thoughts** translated by Arthur Cooper	POEM	636
	Question and Answer Among the Mountains translated by Robert Kotewall and Norman L. Smith	POEM	637
	Letter to His Two Small Children translated by Arthur Cooper	POEM	638

John Keats	**On First Looking into Chapman's Homer**	SONNET	641
	When I Have Fears	SONNET	643
	PRIMARY SOURCE / **Keats's Last Letter** by John Keats	LETTER	645
	Ode to a Nightingale	ODE	646
	Ode on a Grecian Urn	ODE	651

Read On FOR INDEPENDENT READING 655

Writing Workshop Writing a Reflective Essay 656

Listening and Speaking Workshop
Presenting a Reflection 664

COLLECTION 5: SKILLS REVIEW

Comparing Literature
London by William Blake .... POEM 666
The Virgins by Derek Walcott .... POEM 667

Vocabulary Skills 670

Writing Skills 671

Collection 6

The VICTORIAN PERIOD
1832–1901
Paradox and Progress

	SCOPE AND SEQUENCE / RESOURCE MANAGER		**672A–H**
	Time Line		674
	Political and Social Milestones		676
	Introduction to the Literary Period: The Victorian Period *by* Donald Gray		678
Alfred, Lord Tennyson	The Lady of Shalott	NARRATIVE POEM	695
	Ulysses	POEM	703
Robert Browning	My Last Duchess	DRAMATIC MONOLOGUE	708
Julia Markus	CONNECTION / Scenes from a Modern Marriage	NEWS FEATURE	711
Elizabeth Barrett Browning	Sonnet 43	SONNET	714
Gerard Manley Hopkins	Pied Beauty	POEM	717
Matthew Arnold	Dover Beach	POEM	721
A. E. Housman	To an Athlete Dying Young	POEM	726
Daniel Pool	CONNECTION / Death and Other Grave Matters	HISTORY	728
Rudyard Kipling	The Mark of the Beast	SHORT STORY	731

Connecting to World Literature
The Rise of Realism 746

Leo Tolstoy — **How Much Land Does a Man Need?** .... SHORT STORY 750
RUSSIA
translated by Louise *and* Aylmer Maude

Anton Chekhov — **The Bet** *translated by* Constance Garnett .... SHORT STORY 766
RUSSIA

Guy de Maupassant — **The Jewels** *translated by* Roger Colet .... SHORT STORY 775
FRANCE

Read On FOR INDEPENDENT READING 783

Writing Workshop Comparing and Contrasting Literature 784

COLLECTION 6: SKILLS REVIEW

Comparing Literature
Drummer Hodge *by* Thomas Hardy .... POEM 792
The Sleeper of the Valley *by* Arthur Rimbaud
translated by Ludwig Lewisohn .... POEM 793

Vocabulary Skills 796

Writing Skills 797

Collection 7

The Modern World 1900 to the Present

A Remarkable Diversity

SCOPE AND SEQUENCE / RESOURCE MANAGER	**798A–R**
Time Line	800
Political and Social Milestones	802
Introduction to the Literary Period: **The Modern World: 1900 to the Present** by John Leggett *and* David Adams Leeming	804

A WORLD AT WAR

Wilfred Owen ENGLAND	**Dulce et Decorum Est**	POEM	821
Siegfried Sassoon ENGLAND	CONNECTION / The Rear-Guard	POEM	823
T. S. Eliot AMERICA / ENGLAND	**The Hollow Men**	POEM	826

T42 Contents

Political Points of View The Holocaust 832

Main Reading

Primo Levi
ITALY
On the Bottom *from* **Survival in Auschwitz**
translated by Stuart Woolf .... MEMOIR 834

Connected Readings

Marguerite Duras
FRANCE
from **The War** translated by Barbara Bray .... MEMOIR 840

Elie Wiesel
ROMANIA
Never Shall I Forget .... POEM 844

The United States Holocaust Memorial Museum
CONNECTION / **Kristallnacht** .... WEB PAGE 846

	■ PUBLIC DOCUMENT		
Winston Churchill ENGLAND	**Blood, Sweat, and Tears**	SPEECH	849
Yasunari Kawabata JAPAN	**The Silver Fifty-Sen Pieces** translated by Lane Dunlop and J. Martin Holman	SHORT STORY	854
Graham Greene ENGLAND	**The Destructors**	SHORT STORY	862
Ben Okri NIGERIA	**In the Shadow of War**	SHORT STORY	875
Wisława Szymborska POLAND	CONNECTION / The End and the Beginning translated by Stanislaw Baranczak and Clare Cavanagh	POEM	880
	Mini-Workshop Writing a Persuasive Essay		883

CLASHES OF CULTURE

Virginia Woolf ENGLAND	**Shakespeare's Sister** from **A Room of One's Own**	ESSAY	887
	Political Points of View Colonialism		896
	Main Readings		
George Orwell ENGLAND	**Shooting an Elephant**	ESSAY	898
Doris Lessing ZIMBABWE	**No Witchcraft for Sale**	SHORT STORY	908
	Connected Readings		
	■ PUBLIC DOCUMENT		
Joseph Chamberlain ENGLAND	"I Believe in a British Empire"	SPEECH	916
	■ PUBLIC DOCUMENT		
Jawaharlal Nehru INDIA	"The Noble Mansion of Free India"	SPEECH	919
Nadine Gordimer SOUTH AFRICA	**Once upon a Time**	SHORT STORY	923
Chinua Achebe NIGERIA	**Marriage Is a Private Affair**	SHORT STORY	930
Wole Soyinka NIGERIA	**Telephone Conversation**	POEM	938
	Mini-Workshop Analyzing Nonfiction		941

DISCOVERIES AND TRANSFORMATIONS

William Butler Yeats IRELAND	**The Second Coming**	POEM	945
	The Lake Isle of Innisfree	POEM	948
	The Wild Swans at Coole	POEM	951
Rainer Maria Rilke CZECHOSLOVAKIA / AUSTRIA	**CONNECTION** / **The Swan** *translated by* Robert Bly	POEM	953
James Joyce IRELAND	**Araby**	SHORT STORY	956
D. H. Lawrence ENGLAND	**The Rocking-Horse Winner**	SHORT STORY	968
	PRIMARY SOURCE / **D. H. Lawrence on Money** *by* D. H. Lawrence	LETTER	980
Anna Akhmatova RUSSIA	**Lot's Wife** *translated by* Richard Wilbur	POEM	983
	All the unburied ones *translated by* Judith Hemschemeyer	POEM	985
	I am not one of those who left the land *translated by* Stanley Kunitz	POEM	985
Elizabeth Bowen IRELAND	**The Demon Lover**	SHORT STORY	988
Julio Cortázar ARGENTINA	**Axolotl** *translated by* Paul Blackburn	SHORT STORY	999
Jorge Luis Borges ARGENTINA	**The Book of Sand** *translated by* Andrew Hurley	SHORT STORY	1007
V. S. Naipaul TRINIDAD	**B. Wordsworth**	SHORT STORY	1015
Naguib Mahfouz EGYPT	**Half a Day** *translated by* Denys Johnson-Davies	SHORT STORY	1023
Seamus Heaney IRELAND	**Digging**	POEM	1028
	Mini-Workshop Writing a Short Story		1031

OURSELVES AMONG OTHERS

Katherine Mansfield NEW ZEALAND	**The Doll's House**	SHORT STORY 1035
W. H. Auden ENGLAND / AMERICA	**Musée des Beaux Arts**	POEM 1046
Gabriela Mistral CHILE	**Fear** translated by Doris Dana	POEM 1049
Dylan Thomas WALES	**Fern Hill** **Do Not Go Gentle into That Good Night**	POEM 1053 POEM 1056
Pablo Neruda CHILE	**Sonnet 79** translated by Stephen Tapscott **Soneto 79**	SONNET 1060 SONETO 1060
R. K. Narayan INDIA	**Like the Sun**	SHORT STORY 1064
Anita Desai INDIA	**Games at Twilight**	SHORT STORY 1071
Penelope Lively ENGLAND	**Next Term, We'll Mash You**	SHORT STORY 1081

Political Points *of* View Human Rights 1088

Main Reading

Ha Jin CHINA	**Saboteur**	SHORT STORY 1090

Connected Readings

■ PUBLIC DOCUMENT

United Nations Commission on Human Rights	*from the* **Universal Declaration of Human Rights**	POLITICAL STATEMENT 1100

■ PUBLIC DOCUMENT

Desmond Tutu SOUTH AFRICA	*from* **The Question of South Africa**	SPEECH 1102

■ PUBLIC DOCUMENT

Aung San Suu Kyi MYANMAR	*from* **Towards a True Refuge**	SPEECH 1106

Read On FOR INDEPENDENT READING 1111

Media Workshop Analyzing and Using Media 1112

Listening and Speaking Workshop
Presenting and Analyzing Speeches 1120

COLLECTION 7: SKILLS REVIEW

Comparing Literature
The Lorelei *by* Heinrich Heine
translated by Louis Untermeyer .... POEM 1124
Siren Song *by* Margaret Atwood .... POEM 1125

Vocabulary Skills 1128

Writing Skills 1129

Resource Center

Reading Matters *by* Kylene Beers 1133
    When the Text Is Tough 1133
    Improving Your Comprehension 1134
    Improving Your Reading Rate 1143
    Vocabulary Development 1145

The World of Work 1147
    Reading 1147
    Informative Documents 1147
        Consumer Documents 1147
        Workplace Documents 1148
    Persuasive Documents 1149
        Critiquing Persuasive Documents 1149

    Writing 1150
    Job Applications and Résumés 1150
    Workplace Documents 1151
    Word-Processing Features 1151
        Integrating Databases, Graphics, and Spreadsheets 1151
        Résumé Format 1151

Writer's Handbook 1153
    The Writing Process 1153
    Paragraphs 1155
    The Writer's Language 1159
    Designing Your Writing 1161

Test Smarts *by* Flo Ota De Lange *and* Sheri Henderson 1165
    Strategies for Taking Multiple-Choice Tests 1165
    Strategies for Taking Writing Tests 1174

Handbook of Literary and Historical Terms 1181

Language Handbook 1205
    The Parts of Speech 1206
    Agreement 1207
    Using Verbs 1209
    Using Pronouns 1211
    Using Modifiers 1213
    Phrases 1214
    Clauses 1216
    Sentence Structure 1217
    Sentence Style 1220
    Sentence Combining 1223
    Capitalization 1224
    Punctuation 1227, 1230
    Spelling 1235
    Glossary of Usage 1237

Glossary 1243

Spanish Glossary 1249

Acknowledgments 1255

Picture Credits 1258

Index of Skills 1261
    Literary Skills 1261
    Vocabulary Skills 1263
    Reading Skills 1264
    Writing Skills 1265
    Language (Grammar, Usage, and Mechanics) Skills 1270
    Listening and Speaking Skills 1271
    Independent Reading 1273

Index of Art 1274

Index of Authors and Titles 1280

SKILLS, WORKSHOPS, AND FEATURES

SKILLS

LITERARY SKILLS

Epic Hero	20, 44
Alliteration	41, 574, 717, 948, 950
Kennings	41
Foil	47
Epic Simile	56
Epic Conventions	71
Ballad	108, 111
Character	118, 144
Frame Story	118, 169
Imagery	144, 567, 636, 1071
Irony	145, 186, 428, 618, 898, 930, 965, 1064, 1090
Narrator	155
Couplets	167, 726
Fable	172
Archetype	179
Romance Hero	193
Pastoral	257
Carpe Diem	263
Sonnet	275, 278, 641, 714
Dramatic Song	286
Monologue and Soliloquy	292
Metaphysical Poetry	301, 303
Metaphysical Conceits	304
Tone	307, 485
Paradox	312, 1007
Epigram	318, 450
Parallelism	324, 338, 541
Parable	342
Didactic Literature	346, 349
Style	365, 376
Allusion	379, 561, 826
Allegory	383, 750
Connotations	443
Antithesis	446
Mock Epic	451
Satire	462, 466, 938
Parody	474
Symbol	536, 923, 951, 968, 1035
Theme	547, 703, 766, 775, 854, 908, 945, 983, 1081
Blank Verse	551
Personification	559
Romantic Lyric	563
Literary Ballad	578
Simile	610
Apostrophe	612, 626
Ode	621
Terza Rima	626
Mood	631, 721
Synesthesia	646

T50 Skills, Workshops, and Features

Metaphor	651, 1028, 1060
Word Music	695
Dramatic Monologue	708
Assonance	717, 948, 950
Conflict	731
Figures of Speech	821
Memoir	834
Setting	862, 1015
Point of View	875
Essay	887
Epiphany	956
Flashback	988
Magic Realism	999
Foreshadowing	1023
Modern Short Story	1043
Diction	1046
Refrain	1049
Lyric Poetry	1053
Elegy	1056
Villanelle	1058

READING SKILLS

Analyzing Style: Details	118
Interpreting Character	155
Evaluating Historical Context	186, 834, 908
Drawing Inferences	322, 708, 775, 854
Analyzing Arguments	324, 495, 827, 849
Milton's Style	365
Recognizing Persuasive Techniques	428
Identifying the Writer's Stance	446, 898
Analyzing Rhetorical Devices	483
Noting Patterns of Organization	485, 551
Reading Archaic Words	578
Reading Rhyme and Rhythm	612
Reading Inverted Syntax	641
Visualizing Imagery	651
Identifying Contrasting Images	695
Identifying Conflicts and Resolutions	731
Making Predictions	766, 876, 988, 1007
Comparing Main Ideas	832, 896, 1088
Implicit and Explicit Beliefs	840, 887
Inferring Motives	862
Identifying Language Structures	923
Comparing and Contrasting	956
Identifying Point of View	999
Analyzing Details	1071
Identifying Political Influences	1090

READING MATTERS

When the Text Is Tough	1133
Improving Your Comprehension	1134
Improving Your Reading Rate	1143
Vocabulary Development	1145

VOCABULARY SKILLS

Anglo-Saxon Legacy: Words and Word Parts	43
Antonyms	144, 782, 839, 1099
Distinguishing Multiple Meanings of Words	168
Analogies	177, 444, 514, 607, 745, 852, 928, 1005, 1069, 1079
Semantic Mapping	184

SKILLS, WORKSHOPS, AND FEATURES

Etymologies 191, 201, 461, 906

Words Derived From Greek and
Latin Roots and Affixes 377

Context Clues 608, 915, 1027, 1042

Synonyms 839, 1099

WORKSHOPS

WRITING WORKSHOPS

Writing a Descriptive Essay 74

Reporting Literary Research 204

Analyzing Literature 390

Writing a Literary Essay 500

Writing a Reflective Essay 656

Comparing and Contrasting Literature 784

MINI-WORKSHOPS

Writing a Persuasive Essay 883

Analyzing Nonfiction 941

Writing a Short Story 1031

LISTENING AND SPEAKING WORKSHOPS

Presenting Literary Research 224

Reciting Literature 398

Presenting a Literary Response 508

Presenting a Reflection 664

Presenting and Analyzing Speeches 1120

MEDIA WORKSHOP

Analyzing and Using Media 1112

FEATURES

A CLOSER LOOK

Women in Anglo-Saxon Culture 12

"A Terrible Worm in an Iron Cocoon" 98

Money, Gunpowder, and the Middle Class:
The End of an Era 104

Places of Pilgrimage 128

The Archetype of Arthur 198

The Glass of Fashion 255

Life Among the Haves 416

. . . and Life Among the Have-Nots 418

The Lure of the Gothic 530

An Irresistible Bad Boy:
The Byronic Hero 615

An Age in Need of Heroines:
Reform in Victorian Britain 682

The Pre-Raphaelite Brotherhood:
Challenging Artistic Authority 684

Victorian Drama: From Relief to Realism 690

The Age of Empire 736

Votes for Women! 893

CONNECTING TO WORLD LITERATURE

Epics: Stories on a Grand Scale
by David Adams Leeming 44

SKILLS, WORKSHOPS, AND FEATURES

The Frame Story: A Tale Linking Tales
by David Adams Leeming 169

Worlds of Wisdom: Wisdom Literature 346

The Sting of Satire
by Robert DeMaria, Jr. 462

Tanka and Haiku 565

The Golden Age of Chinese Poetry 627

The Rise of Realism 746

CRITICAL COMMENTS

Shelley and the Ode 625

Dialogue with the Soul 650

The Arc of Experience 654

Escaping a World of Shadows 701

Love Is Itself a Faith 723

The Influence of James Joyce 962

PRIMARY SOURCES

Axioms *from the* Essays   Francis Bacon 327

"Blake Is a Real Name..."
Charles Lamb 538

from Evidence Given Before
the Sadler Committee   Peter Smart 544

Coleridge Describes His Addiction
Samuel Taylor Coleridge 603

Keats's Last Letter   John Keats 645

D. H. Lawrence on Money
D. H. Lawrence 980

GRAMMAR LINK

Make It Clear: Sentence Fragments and
Run-on Sentences 72

Linking It Up: Combining Sentences
with Coordinating and
Subordinating Conjunctions 202

Appropriate Additions: Adjective Clauses
and Adverb Clauses 311

Make Sure It Agrees:
Subject-Verb Agreement 493

The Right Tense for Sense:
Verb Tense Consistency 549

Choosing the Right Reference: Pronoun
and Antecedent Agreement 764

Effective Sentences:
The Power of Parallelism 860

The Wrong Place at the Wrong Time:
Dangling Modifiers 936

Building Coherence: Connecting Ideas 997

Active-Voice Verbs and
Passive-Voice Verbs 1044

LANGUAGE HANDBOOK

The Parts of Speech 1206

Agreement 1207

Using Verbs 1209

Using Pronouns 1211

Using Modifiers 1213

Phrases 1214

Clauses 1216

Sentence Structure 1217

Sentence Style 1220

Sentence Combining 1223

Capitalization 1224

Punctuation 1227, 1230

Spelling 1235

Glossary of Usage 1237

SKILLS, WORKSHOPS, AND FEATURES

SKILLS REVIEW

Comparing Literature 82, 226, 400, 510, 666, 792, 1124

Vocabulary 86, 230, 404, 514, 670, 796, 1128

Writing 87, 231, 405, 515, 671, 797, 1129

THE WORLD OF WORK

Reading 1147

Informative Documents 1147

Persuasive Documents 1149

Writing 1150

Job Applications and Résumés 1150

Workplace Documents 1151

Word-Processing Features 1151

WRITER'S HANDBOOK

The Writing Process 1153

Paragraphs 1155

The Writer's Language 1159

Designing Your Writing 1161

TEST SMARTS

Strategies for Taking
Multiple-Choice Tests 1165

Strategies for Taking Writing Tests 1174

SELECTIONS BY GENRE

FICTION

ALLEGORY

from **The Pilgrim's Progress**
John Bunyan 383

ANECDOTES

Taoist Anecdotes 357

DEBATE

from **Female Orations**
Margaret Cavendish, duchess of Newcastle 332

FABLE

Right-Mind and Wrong-Mind
from the **Panchatantra** 172

NOVEL EXCERPTS

from **Grendel**
John Gardner 29

from **Candide**
Voltaire 466

from **Don Quixote**
Miguel de Cervantes 474

PARABLES

The Parable of the Prodigal Son 342

Zen Parables 353

ROMANCE NARRATIVE

from **The Day of Destiny**
from **Le Morte d'Arthur**
Sir Thomas Malory 193

TALES / SHORT STORIES

from **The Third Voyage of Sindbad the Sailor**
from **The Thousand and One Nights** 179

Federigo's Falcon from the **Decameron**
Giovanni Boccaccio 186

Top of the Food Chain
T. Coraghessan Boyle 438

The Mark of the Beast
Rudyard Kipling 731

How Much Land Does a Man Need?
Leo Tolstoy 750

The Bet
Anton Chekhov 766

The Jewels
Guy de Maupassant 775

The Silver Fifty-Sen Pieces
Yasunari Kawabata 854

The Destructors
Graham Greene 862

In the Shadow of War
Ben Okri 875

No Witchcraft for Sale
Doris Lessing 908

Once upon a Time
Nadine Gordimer 923

Marriage Is a Private Affair
Chinua Achebe 930

Araby
James Joyce 956

The Rocking-Horse Winner
D. H. Lawrence 968

The Demon Lover
Elizabeth Bowen 988

SELECTIONS BY GENRE

Axolotl
Julio Cortázar 999

The Book of Sand
Jorge Luis Borges 1007

B. Wordsworth
V. S. Naipaul 1015

Half a Day
Naguib Mahfouz 1023

The Doll's House
Katherine Mansfield 1035

Like the Sun
R. K. Narayan 1064

Games at Twilight
Anita Desai 1071

Next Term, We'll Mash You
Penelope Lively 1081

Saboteur
Ha Jin 1090

DRAMATIC EXCERPTS

To be, or not to be from **Hamlet**
William Shakespeare 292

Tomorrow, and tomorrow, and tomorrow
from **Macbeth**
William Shakespeare 295

Saint Crispin's Day Speech from **Henry V**
William Shakespeare 296

Our revels now are ended from **The Tempest**
William Shakespeare 298

from **W;t**
Margaret Edson 314

POETRY

BALLADS

Lord Randall 108

Get Up and Bar the Door 110

The Twa Corbies 226

Raven doth to raven fly
Alexander Pushkin 227

DRAMATIC MONOLOGUE

My Last Duchess
Robert Browning 708

EPICS

from **Beowulf**
  The Battle with Grendel 21
  The Monster's Mother 26
  The Final Battle 33

from **Gilgamesh: A Verse Narrative** 47

the **Iliad**, from **Book 22: The Death of Hector**
Homer 56

The Fall of Satan from **Paradise Lost**
John Milton 365

SELECTIONS BY GENRE

HAIKU

Haiku 571

LYRICS

Break, Break, Break
Alfred, Lord Tennyson 84

The Passionate Shepherd to His Love
Christopher Marlowe 257

The Nymph's Reply to the Shepherd
Sir Walter Raleigh 261

To the Virgins, to Make Much of Time
Robert Herrick 263

To His Coy Mistress
Andrew Marvell 267

Song
John Donne 301

A Valediction: Forbidding Mourning
John Donne 304

On My First Son
Ben Jonson 318

Song: To Celia
Ben Jonson 320

When You Are Old
Pierre de Ronsard 400

When You Are Old
William Butler Yeats 401

To the Ladies
Mary, Lady Chudleigh 494

The Tyger
William Blake 536

The Lamb
William Blake 539

The Chimney Sweeper
from **Songs of Innocence**
William Blake 541

The Chimney Sweeper
from **Songs of Experience**
William Blake 543

A Poison Tree
William Blake 547

Lines Composed a Few Miles Above Tintern Abbey
William Wordsworth 551

Kubla Khan
Samuel Taylor Coleridge 574

She Walks in Beauty
George Gordon, Lord Byron 610

Jade Flower Palace
Tu Fu 631

Night Thoughts Afloat
Tu Fu 633

Quiet Night Thoughts
Li Po 636

Question and Answer Among the Mountains
Li Po 637

Letter to His Two Small Children
Li Po 638

London
William Blake 666

The Virgins
Derek Walcott 667

Ulysses
Alfred, Lord Tennyson 703

Pied Beauty
Gerard Manley Hopkins 717

Dover Beach
Matthew Arnold 721

To an Athlete Dying Young
A. E. Housman 726

Drummer Hodge
Thomas Hardy 792

SELECTIONS BY GENRE

The Sleeper of the Valley
Arthur Rimbaud 793

Dulce et Decorum Est
Wilfred Owen 821

The Rear-Guard
Siegfried Sassoon 823

The Hollow Men
T. S. Eliot 826

Never Shall I Forget
Elie Wiesel 844

The End and the Beginning
Wisława Szymborska 880

Telephone Conversation
Wole Soyinka 938

The Second Coming
William Butler Yeats 945

The Lake Isle of Innisfree
William Butler Yeats 948

The Wild Swans at Coole
William Butler Yeats 951

The Swan
Rainer Maria Rilke 953

Lot's Wife
Anna Akhmatova 983

All the unburied ones
Anna Akhmatova 985

I am not one of those who left the land
Anna Akhmatova 985

Digging
Seamus Heaney 1028

Musée des Beaux Arts
W. H. Auden 1046

Fear
Gabriela Mistral 1049

Fern Hill
Dylan Thomas 1053

Do Not Go Gentle into That Good Night
Dylan Thomas 1056

The Lorelei
Heinrich Heine 1124

Siren Song
Margaret Atwood 1125

MOCK EPIC

from **The Rape of the Lock**
Alexander Pope 451

NARRATIVE POETRY

from **The Seafarer** 82

from **The Canterbury Tales**
Geoffrey Chaucer
   The Prologue 118
   from **The Pardoner's Tale** 145
   from **The Wife of Bath's Tale** 155

The Rime of the Ancient Mariner
Samuel Taylor Coleridge 578

from **Childe Harold's Pilgrimage, Canto IV**
George Gordon, Lord Byron 612

The Lady of Shalott
Alfred, Lord Tennyson 695

ODES

Ode to the West Wind
Percy Bysshe Shelley 621

Ode to a Nightingale
John Keats 646

Ode on a Grecian Urn
John Keats 651

PHILOSOPHICAL VERSE

Heroic Couplets
Alexander Pope 446

SELECTIONS BY GENRE

from **An Essay on Man**
Alexander Pope 449

PSALMS

Psalm 23 338

Psalm 137 340

SONGS

Blow, Blow, Thou Winter Wind
William Shakespeare 286

Fear No More the Heat o' the Sun
William Shakespeare 288

Full Fathom Five
William Shakespeare 290

SONNETS

Sonnet 42
Francesco Petrarch 276

Sonnet 18
William Shakespeare 277

Sonnet 29
William Shakespeare 278

Sonnet 30
William Shakespeare 280

Sonnet 71
William Shakespeare 281

Sonnet 73
William Shakespeare 282

Sonnet 116
William Shakespeare 283

Sonnet 130
William Shakespeare 284

Sonnet 23
Louise Labé 285

Death be not proud
John Donne 312

When I consider how my light is spent
John Milton 379

Composed upon Westminster Bridge
William Wordsworth 559

The World Is Too Much with Us
William Wordsworth 561

Ozymandias
Percy Bysshe Shelley 618

On First Looking into Chapman's Homer
John Keats 641

When I Have Fears
John Keats 643

Sonnet 43
Elizabeth Barrett Browning 714

Sonnet 79 / Soneto 79
Pablo Neruda 1060

TANKA

Tanka 567

NONFICTION AND INFORMATIONAL TEXT

AXIOMS AND MAXIMS

Axioms *from the* **Essays**
Francis Bacon 327

from **The Analects of Confucius** 355

Sayings of Saadi
Saadi 358

CRITICAL COMMENTS

Shelley and the Ode 625

Dialogue with the Soul 650

SELECTIONS BY GENRE

The Arc of Experience 654
Escaping a World of Shadows 701
Love Is Itself a Faith 723
The Influence of James Joyce 962

CULTURAL COMMENTARY

Women in Anglo-Saxon Culture 12
"A Terrible Worm in an Iron Cocoon" 98
Money, Gunpowder, and the Middle Class:
The End of an Era 104
Places of Pilgrimage 128
The Archetype of Arthur 198
The Glass of Fashion 255
Life Among the Haves 416
...and Life Among the Have-Nots 418
The Lure of the Gothic 530
An Irresistible Bad Boy:
The Byronic Hero 615
An Age in Need of Heroines:
Reform in Victorian Britain 682
The Pre-Raphaelite Brotherhood:
Challenging Artistic Authority 684
Victorian Drama:
From Relief to Realism 690
The Age of Empire 736
Votes for Women! 893

DIARY

from **The Diary of Samuel Pepys**
Samuel Pepys 511

ESSAYS

Of Studies
Francis Bacon 324

A Modest Proposal
Jonathan Swift 428

from **The Education of Women**
Daniel Defoe 495

Shakespeare's Sister
from **A Room of One's Own**
Virginia Woolf 887

Shooting an Elephant
George Orwell 898

HISTORIES

The Fury of the Northmen
Ellen Ashdown 39

Trojan Gold from **Gods, Graves, and Scholars**
C. W. Ceram 67

Give Us This Day Our Daily Bread
Joseph Papp and Elizabeth Kirkland 269

from **The Burning of Rome** from **The Annals**
Tacitus 510

Death and Other Grave Matters
Daniel Pool 728

LETTERS

"Blake Is a Real Name..."
Charles Lamb 538

Coleridge Describes His Addiction
Samuel Taylor Coleridge 603

Keats's Last Letter
John Keats 645

D. H. Lawrence on Money
D. H. Lawrence 980

SELECTIONS BY GENRE

MAGAZINE AND NEWSPAPER ARTICLES

Life in 999: A Grim Struggle
Howard G. Chua-Eoan 30

Scenes from a Modern Marriage
Julia Markus 711

MEDITATION

Meditation 17
John Donne 307

MEMOIRS

On the Bottom from **Survival in Auschwitz**
Primo Levi 834

from **The War**
Marguerite Duras 840

PROVERBS

African Proverbs 359

SACRED TEXTS

Night from the **Koran** 349

from **Philosophy and Spiritual Discipline**
from **Bhagavad-Gita** 351

from the **Tao Te Ching**
Laotzu 356

TRAVEL BOOK

from **In Patagonia**
Bruce Chatwin 604

WEB PAGE

Kristallnacht Web page from **The United States Holocaust Memorial Museum** 846

PUBLIC DOCUMENTS

DEBATE

from **Female Orations**
Margaret Cavendish, duchess of Newcastle 332

PLATFORM

from **A Vindication of the Rights of Woman**
Mary Wollstonecraft 485

POLITICAL STATEMENT

from the **Universal Declaration of Human Rights**
United Nations Commission on Human Rights 1100

SPEECHES

Tilbury Speech
Queen Elizabeth I 330

Blood, Sweat, and Tears
Winston Churchill 849

"I Believe in a British Empire"
Joseph Chamberlain 916

"The Noble Mansion of Free India"
Jawaharlal Nehru 919

from **The Question of South Africa**
Desmond Tutu 1102

from **Towards a True Refuge**
Aung San Suu Kyi 1106

TESTIMONY

from **Evidence Given Before the Sadler Committee**
Peter Smart 544

SELECTIONS BY REGION

AFRICA

African Proverbs 359

In the Shadow of War
Ben Okri 875

No Witchcraft for Sale
Doris Lessing 908

Once upon a Time
Nadine Gordimer 923

Marriage Is a Private Affair
Chinua Achebe 930

Telephone Conversation
Wole Soyinka 938

Half a Day
Naguib Mahfouz 1023

from **The Question of South Africa**
Desmond Tutu 1102

ASIA

from **Gilgamesh: A Verse Narrative** 47

Right-Mind and Wrong-Mind
from the **Panchatantra** 172

from **The Third Voyage of Sindbad the Sailor**
from **The Thousand and One Nights** 179

Night from the **Koran** 349

from **Philosophy and Spiritual Discipline**
from the **Bhagavad-Gita** 351

Zen Parables 353

from **The Analects of Confucius** 355

from the **Tao Te Ching**
Laotzu 356

Taoist Anecdotes 357

Sayings of Saadi
Saadi 358

Tanka 567

Haiku 571

Jade Flower Palace
Tu Fu 631

Night Thoughts Afloat
Tu Fu 633

Quiet Night Thoughts
Li Po 636

Question and Answer Among the Mountains
Li Po 637

Letter to His Two Small Children
Li Po 638

The Silver Fifty-Sen Pieces
Yasunari Kawabata 854

"The Noble Mansion of Free India"
Jawaharlal Nehru 919

Like the Sun
R. K. Narayan 1064

Games at Twilight
Anita Desai 1071

Saboteur
Ha Jin 1090

from **Towards a True Refuge**
Aung San Suu Kyi 1106

EUROPE

the **Iliad**, *from* **Book 22: The Death of Hector**
Homer 56

Federigo's Falcon *from the* **Decameron**
Giovanni Boccaccio 186

Raven doth to raven fly
Alexander Pushkin 227

Sonnet 42
Francesco Petrarch 276

Sonnet 23
Louise Labé 285

When You Are Old
Pierre de Ronsard 400

When You Are Old
William Butler Yeats 401

A Modest Proposal
Jonathan Swift 428

from **Candide**
Voltaire 466

from **Don Quixote**
Miguel de Cervantes 474

from **The Burning of Rome** *from* **The Annals**
Tacitus 510

How Much Land Does a Man Need?
Leo Tolstoy 750

The Bet
Anton Chekhov 766

The Jewels
Guy de Maupassant 775

The Sleeper of the Valley
Arthur Rimbaud 793

On the Bottom *from* **Survival in Auschwitz**
Primo Levi 834

from **The War**
Marguerite Duras 840

Never Shall I Forget
Elie Wiesel 844

The End and the Beginning
Wisława Szymborska 880

The Second Coming
William Butler Yeats 945

The Lake Isle of Innisfree
William Butler Yeats 948

The Wild Swans at Coole
William Butler Yeats 951

The Swan
Rainer Maria Rilke 953

Araby
James Joyce 956

Lot's Wife
Anna Akhmatova 983

All the unburied ones
Anna Akhmatova 985

I am not one of those who left the land
Anna Akhmatova 985

The Demon Lover
Elizabeth Bowen 988

Digging
Seamus Heaney 1028

The Lorelei
Heinrich Heine 1124

GREAT BRITAIN

from **Beowulf** 20

from **The Seafarer** 82

Break, Break, Break
Alfred, Lord Tennyson 84

The Prologue *from* **The Canterbury Tales**
Geoffrey Chaucer 118

from **The Pardoner's Tale**
Geoffrey Chaucer 145

SELECTIONS BY REGION

from **The Wife of Bath's Tale**
Geoffrey Chaucer 155

from **The Day of Destiny**
from **Le Morte d'Arthur**
Sir Thomas Malory 193

The Twa Corbies 226

The Passionate Shepherd to His Love
Christopher Marlowe 257

The Nymph's Reply to the Shepherd
Sir Walter Raleigh 261

To the Virgins, to Make Much of Time
Robert Herrick 263

To His Coy Mistress
Andrew Marvell 267

Sonnet 18
William Shakespeare 277

Sonnet 29
William Shakespeare 278

Sonnet 30
William Shakespeare 280

Sonnet 71
William Shakespeare 201

Sonnet 73
William Shakespeare 282

Sonnet 116
William Shakespeare 283

Sonnet 130
William Shakespeare 284

Blow, Blow, Thou Winter Wind
William Shakespeare 286

Fear No More the Heat o' the Sun
William Shakespeare 288

Full Fathom Five
William Shakespeare 290

To be, or not to be *from* **Hamlet**
William Shakespeare 292

Tomorrow, and tomorrow, and tomorrow
from **Macbeth**
William Shakespeare 295

Saint Crispin's Day Speech *from* **Henry V**
William Shakespeare 296

Our revels now are ended
from **The Tempest**
William Shakespeare 298

Song
John Donne 301

A Valediction: Forbidding Mourning
John Donne 304

Meditation 17
John Donne 307

Death be not proud
John Donne 312

On My First Son
Ben Jonson 318

Song: To Celia
Ben Jonson 320

Of Studies
Francis Bacon 324

Tilbury Speech
Queen Elizabeth I 330

from **Female Orations**
Margaret Cavendish, duchess of Newcastle 332

Psalm 23 338

Psalm 137 340

The Parable of the Prodigal Son 342

The Fall of Satan *from* **Paradise Lost**
John Milton 365

When I consider how my light is spent
John Milton 379

from **The Pilgrim's Progress**
John Bunyan 383

Heroic Couplets
Alexander Pope 446

from **An Essay on Man**
Alexander Pope 449

from **The Rape of the Lock**
Alexander Pope 451

SELECTIONS BY REGION

from A Vindication of the Rights of Woman
Mary Wollstonecraft 485

To the Ladies
Mary, Lady Chudleigh 494

from The Education of Women
Daniel Defoe 495

from The Diary of Samuel Pepys
Samuel Pepys 511

The Tyger
William Blake 536

"Blake Is a Real Name ..."
Charles Lamb 538

The Lamb
William Blake 539

The Chimney Sweeper
from **Songs of Innocence**
William Blake 541

The Chimney Sweeper
from **Songs of Experience**
William Blake 543

from Evidence Given Before the Sadler Committee
Peter Smart 544

A Poison Tree
William Blake 547

Lines Composed a Few Miles Above Tintern Abbey
William Wordsworth 551

Composed upon Westminster Bridge
William Wordsworth 559

The World Is Too Much with Us
William Wordsworth 561

Kubla Khan
Samuel Taylor Coleridge 574

The Rime of the Ancient Mariner
Samuel Taylor Coleridge 578

Coleridge Describes His Addiction
Samuel Taylor Coleridge 603

from In Patagonia
Bruce Chatwin 604

She Walks in Beauty
George Gordon, Lord Byron 610

from Childe Harold's Pilgrimage, Canto IV
George Gordon, Lord Byron 612

Ozymandias
Percy Bysshe Shelley 618

Ode to the West Wind
Percy Bysshe Shelley 621

On First Looking into Chapman's Homer
John Keats 641

When I Have Fears
John Keats 643

Keats's Last Letter
John Keats 645

Ode to a Nightingale
John Keats 646

Ode on a Grecian Urn
John Keats 651

London
William Blake 666

The Lady of Shalott
Alfred, Lord Tennyson 695

Ulysses
Alfred, Lord Tennyson 703

My Last Duchess
Robert Browning 708

Sonnet 43
Elizabeth Barrett Browning 714

Pied Beauty
Gerard Manley Hopkins 717

Dover Beach
Matthew Arnold 721

To an Athlete Dying Young
A. E. Housman 726

The Mark of the Beast
Rudyard Kipling 731

Drummer Hodge
Thomas Hardy 792

SELECTIONS BY REGION

Dulce et Decorum Est
Wilfred Owen 821

The Rear-Guard
Siegfried Sassoon 823

The Hollow Men
T. S. Eliot 826

Blood, Sweat, and Tears
Winston Churchill 849

The Destructors
Graham Greene 862

Shakespeare's Sister
from **A Room of One's Own**
Virginia Woolf 887

Shooting an Elephant
George Orwell 898

"I Believe in a British Empire"
Joseph Chamberlain 916

The Rocking-Horse Winner
D. H. Lawrence 968

D. H. Lawrence on Money
D. H. Lawrence 980

Musée des Beaux Arts
W. H. Auden 1046

Fern Hill
Dylan Thomas 1053

Do Not Go Gentle into That Good Night
Dylan Thomas 1056

Next Term, We'll Mash You
Penelope Lively 1081

NORTH AMERICA

Life in 999: A Grim Struggle
Howard G. Chua-Eoan 30

The Fury of the Northmen
Ellen Ashdown 39

Trojan Gold from **Gods, Graves, and Scholars**
C. W. Ceram 67

Give Us This Day Our Daily Bread
Joseph Papp and Elizabeth Kirkland 269

from **W;t**
Margaret Edson 314

Top of the Food Chain
T. Coraghessan Boyle 438

Scenes from a Modern Marriage
Julia Markus 711

Death and Other Grave Matters
Daniel Pool 728

Siren Song
Margaret Atwood 1125

NEW ZEALAND

The Doll's House
Katherine Mansfield 1035

SOUTH AMERICA

Axolotl
Julio Cortázar 999

The Book of Sand
Jorge Luis Borges 1007

Fear
Gabriela Mistral 1049

Sonnet 79 / Soneto 79
Pablo Neruda 1060

WEST INDIES

The Virgins
Derek Walcott 667

B. Wordsworth
V. S. Naipaul 1015

Elements of Literature on the Internet

TO THE STUDENT

At the *Elements of Literature* Internet site, you can analyze the work of professional writers and learn the inside stories behind your favorite authors. You can also build your word power and analyze messages in the media. As you move through *Elements of Literature*, you will find the best online resources at **go.hrw.com**.

Here's how to log on:

1. Start your Web browser, and enter **go.hrw.com** in the Address or Location field.

2. Note the keyword in your textbook.

3. Enter the keyword, and click "go."

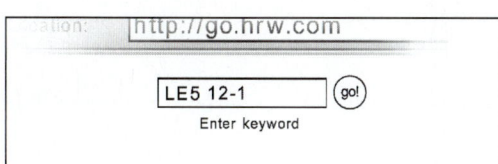

FEATURES OF THE SITE

More About the Writer
Author biographies provide the inside stories behind the lives and works of great writers.

More Writer's Models
Interactive Writer's Models present annotations and reading tips to help you with your own writing. Printable Professional Models and Student Models provide you with quality writing by real writers and students across the country.

Interactive Reading Model
Interactive Reading Workshops guide you through high-interest informational articles and allow you to share your opinions through pop-up questions and polls.

Vocabulary Practice
Interactive vocabulary-building activities help you build your word power.

Projects and Activities
Projects and activities help you extend your study of literature through writing, research, art, and public speaking.

Speeches
Video clips from historical speeches provide you with the tools you need to analyze elements of great speechmaking.

Media Tutorials
Media tutorials help you dissect messages in the media and learn to create your own multimedia presentations.

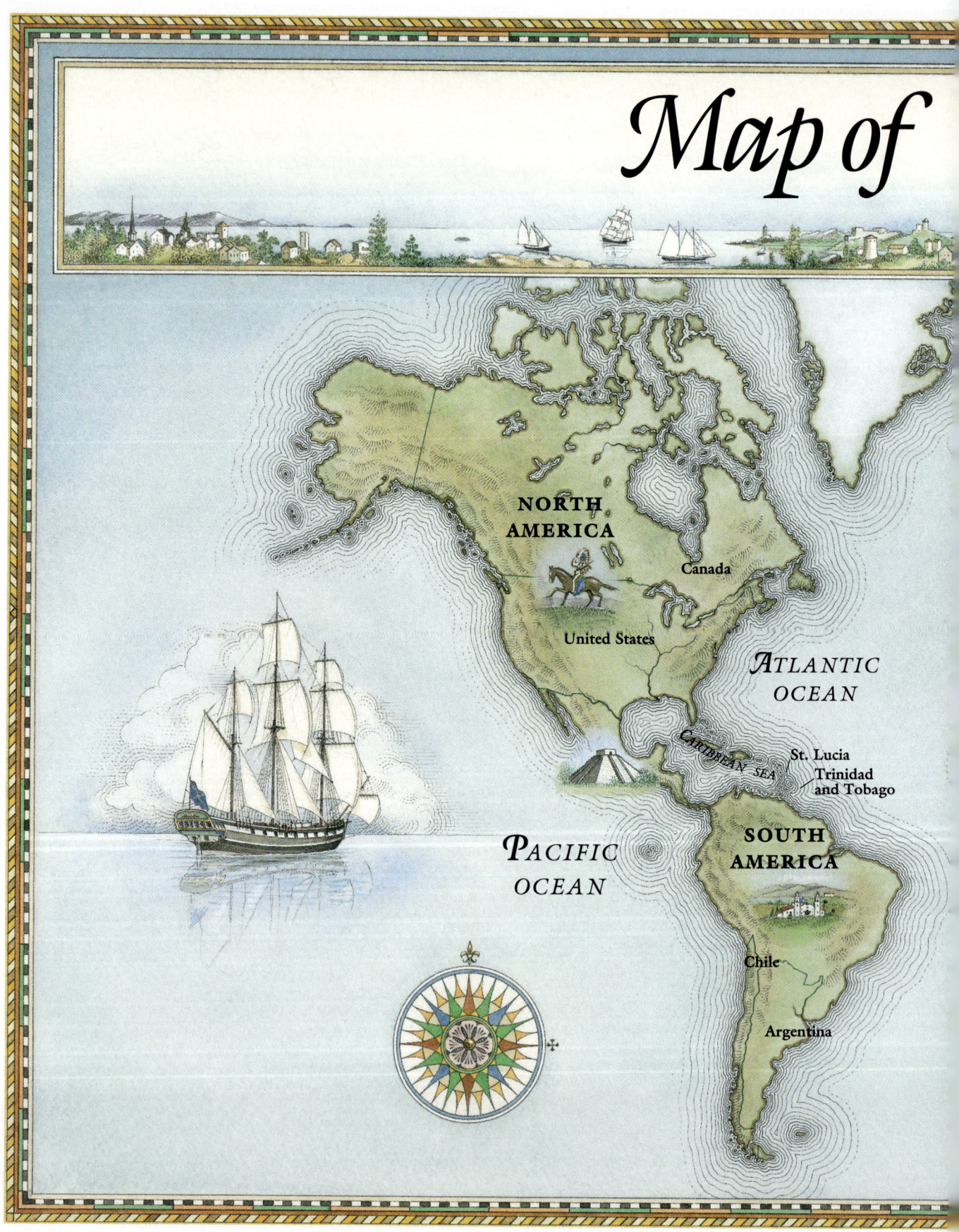

the World

A Walk Through *Elements of Literature*

The *Elements of Literature* Student Edition is the primary tool for building knowledge and understanding of literature and language skills. Opportunities for practice and remediation, reteaching, and assessing are offered throughout the program.

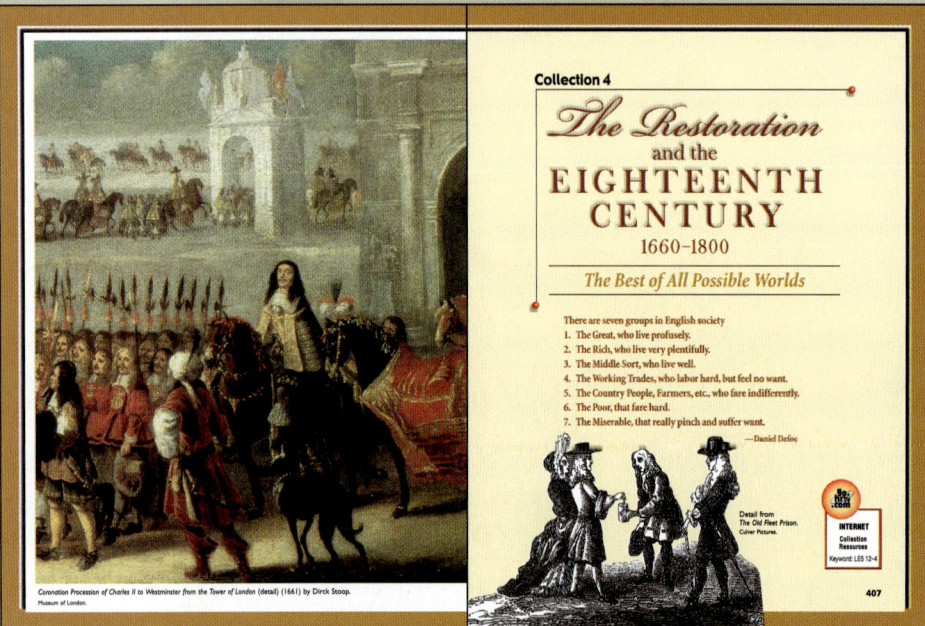

Collections

The collections in *Elements of Literature* are organized chronologically to cover each literary period's historical, political, and social contexts. Informational texts include introductions to literary periods, public documents, and features such as Social and Political Milestones, Political Points of View, and A Closer Look. Opportunities are provided for students to compare pieces of literature, including British and world literature in the Sixth Course. Each collection offers multiple opportunities for students to master each skill, as well as a review section.

Introduction to the Literary Period

Introduction to the Literary Period gives students an understanding of the literary period and the historical forces that shaped it. It includes a Political and Social Milestones section as well as a detailed Time Line.

Walk Through

Author Biography
An **author biography** appears before each literature selection, providing students with comprehensive background on the author.

Alexander Pope
(1688–1744)

Alexander Pope and Dog Bounce (detail) (c. 1718) attributed to Jonathan Richardson. Hagley Hall, Worcestershire, England.

Alexander Pope, the most important poet of the early eighteenth century, was a child prodigy. As a very little boy, he later admitted, he "lisped in numbers." That is, he could speak in meter even before he could pronounce English properly. Such a talented youth would ordinarily be educated at Cambridge or Oxford. Pope's family was Roman Catholic, however, and therefore prohibited from attending these universities, as well as from voting, from holding public office, and even from practicing their religion.

Pope's father, a retired linen merchant, could afford to educate his son at home, which was perhaps the best place for Pope since his health was very delicate. Early in life he contracted a kind of tuberculosis that stunted his growth and disfigured his body, so that eventually his servants had to lace him into a canvas brace before he could sit upright. Since he continually suffered pains in his head, bones, and joints, it is no wonder he spoke of his life as "this long disease."

In spite of all of this, Pope led a remarkably busy and productive life. When he was twenty-three, he published *An Essay on Criticism*, a poem inspired in part by the Latin poet Horace's *Art of Poetry*. At twenty-four, he published a miniature classical epic, *The Rape of the Lock*. During his thirties he translated into English two enormous Greek epics, Homer's *Iliad* and, with the help of two assistants, Homer's *Odyssey*. In these works, Pope was not at all limited by his classical models, but used them to make works that were fresh and original. For this reason, he is sometimes referred to as a neoclassical (that is, new classical) poet.

Pope's early, brilliant successes inspired envy in lesser writers, who ridiculed him. To defend himself he turned to satire, a kind of writing highly suited to his temperament. The great satires of Pope's maturity include *The Dunciad* (1728, enlarged and revised in 1743), which attacks dull, uninteresting writers of all kinds and shows the forces of stupidity, ignorance, and folly taking over the world; and the *Moral Essays* (1731–1735), which pass judgment on certain immoral men and women as well as on very rich people who lack common sense and good taste.

As a man Pope was, and still is, both loved and hated. In his lifetime and long after, he had a reputation for cruelty, malice, and ill nature. But Pope had a large circle of friends, men and women, including some of the best writers of the day, who found him good-natured, generous, and brilliant in conversation. His agreeable manners, his large expressive eyes, and his way of dressing elegantly in bright colors charmed his friends. Pope became rich and famous; as for the people who raged against him, most of them are remembered today only because they disliked Alexander Pope.

Alexander Pope 445

Before You Read

from The Rape of the Lock

Make the Connection
Quickwrite
If you look at the newspapers and magazines displayed at a supermarket checkout, you'll probably agree that many Americans like to read about rich and famous people—those who have made it big in politics, sports, business, and entertainment. Many readers find it especially interesting to read about the trivial problems and petty quarrels of these well-known people. *The Rape of the Lock* tells the story of a petty quarrel among members of the eighteenth-century nobility. Take a few minutes to think about why people today (and people in the eighteenth century) are fascinated by the lives of the rich and famous. Has the appeal of "celebrity gossip" changed very much since Pope's day? Why or why not? Write down your thoughts.

Literary Focus
Mock Epic
The Rape of the Lock is a **mock epic**. Its comedy arises from the discrepancy between its trivial subject matter (the snipping of a curl) and its grandiose treatment. (In mock epics, cracked teacups become major catastrophes.) Pope achieves this comic discrepancy by putting all the traditional devices found in serious epics (like Homer's *Iliad*, Virgil's *Aeneid*, and Milton's *Paradise Lost*) into a tame, domestic context where little is at risk. For instance, the classical epics all have gods and goddesses who intervene in human affairs. Following these models, Pope creates tiny, airy spirits (called "sylphs") who try, in vain, to prevent the "rape" of Belinda's curl. Similarly, Pope includes a hotly contested game of cards and an outburst of temper to satisfy the requirement that every epic contain battles.

A **mock epic** is a comic narrative poem, written in dignified language, that parodies the serious epic genre by treating a trivial subject in a lofty, grand manner.

For more on Mock Epic, see the Handbook of Literary and Historical Terms.

Background
The title of Pope's comic masterpiece means "the violent theft of a lock of hair." The poem is based on a real incident. The lock in question belonged to a certain rich and fashionable young lady named Arabella Fermor. The theft in question was committed by a certain rich and fashionable young man named Robert, Lord Petre. When Robert snipped a curl from Arabella's hairdo, he set off a quarrel between the Fermor and the Petre families. Had the two families been less sensible, their row might have escalated into bitter hatred. As it turned out, the feud subsided into laughter—thanks to Alexander Pope.

Vocabulary Development
exulting (eg·zult′ĭŋ) v. used as adj.: rejoicing.
repast (rĭ·past′) n.: meal.
desist (dĭ·zist′) v.: stop.
recesses (rē′ses·ĭz) n. pl.: secluded or hidden places.
titillating (tĭt′l·āt′ĭŋ) v. used as adj.: exciting; stimulating.
dejects (dē·jekts′) v.: casts down; dispirits.

 INTERNET
Vocabulary Practice
Keyword: LE5 12-4

 SKILLS FOCUS
Literary Skills
Understand the characteristics of a mock epic.

Alexander Pope 451

Before You Read

Before You Read precedes every selection, giving students adequate prereading information, motivation, and a purpose for reading. The **skills focus** is listed on the page so students know what skills they will be learning.

Make the Connection asks students to think or write about issues they will encounter in the literature they are about to read.

Literary Focus enables students to learn about or review a key literary element in the selection.

Reading Skills introduces a skill that will help students' reading comprehension, such as making inferences, summarizing, or making predictions.

Background provides students with necessary information that will help them understand the context of the literature.

Vocabulary Development lists the **key vocabulary words** from the selection and their definitions.

T73

Walk Through

Pope's poem is divided into five sections called **cantos**. Canto I begins like a proper epic, with a statement of the subject and an invocation to the Muse—a female deity who was supposed to inspire poets and other artists. Pope, however, clearly signals his comic intentions in the very first couplet:

> What dire offense from amorous causes springs,
> What mighty contests rise from trivial things,
> I sing—

In Canto II, Belinda and her friends take a boat up the river Thames to a party. All who see her admire the two beautiful curled locks that hang down her back. And despite the small army of sprites (spirits) assigned to protect Belinda's beautiful hair, the Baron resolves to possess these locks.

from *The Rape of the Lock*
Alexander Pope

from Canto III

Close by those meads, forever crowned with flowers,
Where Thames with pride surveys his rising towers,
There stands a structure° of majestic frame,
Which from the neighboring Hampton takes its name.
5 Here Britain's statesmen oft the fall foredoom
Of foreign tyrants, and of nymphs° at home;
Here thou, great Anna!° whom three realms obey,
Dost sometimes counsel take—and sometimes tea.
Hither the heroes and the nymphs resort,
10 To taste awhile the pleasures of a court;
In various talk th' instructive hours they passed,
Who gave the ball, or paid the visit last;
One speaks the glory of the British queen,
And one describes a charming Indian screen;
15 A third interprets motions, looks, and eyes;
At every word a reputation dies.

---
3. structure *n.*: Hampton Court, a royal residence on the river Thames, upstream from London.
6. nymphs *n. pl.*: young ladies.
7. Anna: Queen Anne (1665–1714), who ruled England, Ireland, and Scotland.

1–16. In lines 1–8, notice how Pope juxtaposes, or places side by side, the grandiose and the trivial: At Hampton Court, statesmen discuss the fall of tyrants—and also of young ladies. Meanwhile, Queen Anne is sometimes served political counsel—and at other times, tea.
❓ What does line 16 tell you about life at Hampton Court?

Alexander Pope 453

Directed-Reading questions appear throughout many of the selections. They model the thinking and questioning strategies students need to build strong reading skills.

Response and Analysis

A **Response and Analysis** page guides comprehension. Questions clearly assess the skills focus and reading skills taught with the selection.

Reading Check questions tap students' basic comprehension of the selection.

Thinking Critically includes interpretive and analytical discussion questions that explore the students' deeper understanding of the selection.

Extending and Evaluating offers questions that encourage students to find personal or real-world applications for key concepts they have discovered in their reading.

Literary Criticism gives students the opportunity to interpret and comment on critics' opinions of literary works.

Writing assignments give students the opportunity to use the selection as a springboard for imaginative assignments. They also provide opportunities for analysis, comparison and contrast, and other higher-level thinking skills.

Response and Analysis

Reading Check
1. Summarize the main events of Pope's poem in **chronological** order. Be sure to include all the main events that lead up to and follow the theft of the lock of hair.

Thinking Critically
2. Who, if anyone, do you think is victorious at the end of the poem? Cite lines from the poem to support your opinion.
3. In the satirical passage that opens Canto III (lines 1–18), what seems to be Pope's **tone**—his attitude toward the queen and her courtiers? Is he scornful or amused? How can you tell?
4. The world outside the poem and the world inside it come together in Canto III (lines 7–8). What is the effect of the three words after the dash?
5. In Canto III (line 86), Pope juxtaposes—that is, places side by side—dying husbands and dying lapdogs. What is the effect of this juxtaposition? Find other surprising juxtapositions in the poem, and describe their effects.
6. A **mock epic** amusingly parodies the style and conventions of the serious epic. Ever since Homer, a hallmark of the epic has been the elaborate **epic simile**, or extended comparison between two unlike things. What things are being compared in Canto III (lines 57–58 and 85–88) and Canto V (lines 31–32)?
7. In the complete poem, Pope frequently makes **satirical** remarks about the world outside the privileged ranks to which Belinda and her friends belong. Examples of such remarks occur in Canto III (lines 21–22 and 45–46). Who or what are Pope's targets in these **couplets**?
8. Belinda's victory at cards in Canto III (lines 23–28) and her cries of triumph are ironic because her happiness is so momentary; it's about to be shattered by the theft of her lock. Since **irony** always involves a discrepancy of some kind, explain how Belinda's victory over the Baron in Canto V (lines 13–22) also might be considered ironic.
9. Based on the extracts you have read, how would you state Pope's **theme**—his central message—in this mock epic? Who or what are the objects of his satire?
10. Does the epic apply in any way to any aspects of contemporary life? Can you find passages that could serve as satiric commentaries on people's behavior today? Be sure to review your Quickwrite notes before you answer.

WRITING
Mocking Epics
In a brief **essay, compare and contrast** Pope's **mock epic** with a serious epic: *Beowulf* (see page 21), Homer's *Iliad* (see page 57), Milton's *Paradise Lost* (see page 367), or, if you know it well, Homer's *Odyssey*. Consider these elements of the epic: invocations to the Muse, statement of subject, intervention of gods and goddesses, epic battles, a hero or heroine who reflects the values of a particular society, and use of elevated language. What aspects of Pope's mock epic most successfully parody the great epics of the past?

Your Mock-Heroic Style
In Canto III, Pope describes making and drinking coffee in rich, elevated, and roundabout language (lines 33–40). This mock-heroic writing style breaks the elementary rule that says writers must try to use simple, direct language when describing simple activities. As an exercise in mock-heroic writing, write a prose **description** of a common activity (such as riding a bicycle or cooking and eating a hamburger), using inflated language and rich images.

King Charles Spaniels (1845) (detail) by Sir Edwin Henry Landseer.
© Tate Gallery, London/Art Resource, New York.

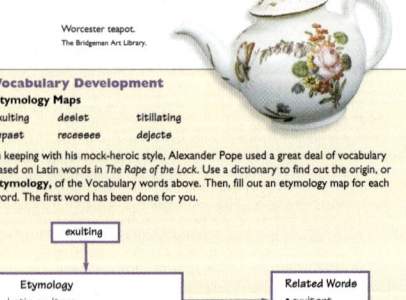
Worcester teapot.
The Bridgeman Art Library.

Vocabulary Development
Etymology Maps

exulting desist titillating
repast recesses dejects

In keeping with his mock-heroic style, Alexander Pope used a great deal of vocabulary based on Latin words in *The Rape of the Lock*. Use a dictionary to find out the origin, or **etymology**, of the Vocabulary words above. Then, fill out an etymology map for each word. The first word has been done for you.

```
              exulting
                 │
      ┌──────────┴──────────┐
      ▼                     ▼
  Etymology           Related Words
  Latin exultare;     • exultant
  ex- = "out; up" +   • exultation
  saltare = "to leap"
      │                     ▲
      ▼                     │
  Meanings             Sentences
  • rejoice greatly    • Mom exults over my success.
  • be jubilant or     • We exulted over winning the game.
    triumphant
```

460 Collection 4 The Restoration and the Eighteenth Century

Alexander Pope 461

Walk Through

Vocabulary Development

Vocabulary Development focuses on the skills students need to build strong vocabularies and includes exposition and practice exercises.

Grammar Links

Grammar Links provide instruction and practice on common errors in usage, mechanics, and style.

Connecting to World Literature

Connecting to World Literature features address various subgenres or topics that are pertinent to the historical period. Each feature begins with an introductory essay and is followed by selections from various regions of the world. Questions ask students to compare the world literature selections with each other and with British literature selections.

Walk Through

Introducing Political Points of View
Women's Rights

Main Reading
Mary Wollstonecraft . . . . . from **A Vindication of the Rights of Woman** . . . 487

Connected Readings
Mary, Lady Chudleigh . . . . **To the Ladies** 494
Daniel Defoe . . . . from **The Education of Women** 495

You will be reading the three selections listed above in this Political Points of View feature on women's rights. In the top corner of the pages in this feature, you'll find three stars. Smaller versions of the stars appear next to the questions on page 492 that focus on women's rights. At the end of the feature (page 498), you'll compare the various points of view expressed in the selections.

Examining the Issue: Women's Rights
The women's rights movement, an ongoing series of political movements aimed at attaining educational, social, and political equality for women, arose primarily in England and the United States. Its roots lay both in humanistic thought (see page 242) and in the Industrial Revolution of the eighteenth and nineteenth centuries—two important influences that, in very different ways, contributed to the creation of a more democratic society.

According to the dictates of both theology and law, married women of the eighteenth century still could not own property, run a business, or control their own lives or those of their children. Social critics (both male and female) began to contrast this state of affairs with the ideal of freedom that inspired the American and French Revolutions of the late eighteenth century. Since then, there have been countless advances and setbacks in campaigns for the rights of women to study, to own property, to vote, to pursue a career, and, in general, to control their own lives. The readings in this Political Points of View feature present some of the earliest shots fired in the battle for women's rights.

Make the Connection
Quickwrite
The basic concept behind the issue of women's rights is that women and men are equally human and should have equal stature in society. Few westerners now challenge that concept, yet many dislike or reject such labels as "feminism," preferring instead to speak of "human rights" or "women's rights." What do these three labels mean to you? Write a brief explanation of which term you find most meaningful and why you prefer it over the other two terms.

Political Points of View

Political Points of View features throughout the book provide opportunities for students to examine different political points of view on issues pertinent to the historical period. The selections included in these features span a variety of genres, including public documents, informational text, poetry, and prose.

Public Documents

Public Documents give students an opportunity to examine and critique the arguments on an issue of public concern. These documents include speeches, essays, policy statements, interviews, and newspaper articles.

from A Vindication of the Rights of Woman
Mary Wollstonecraft

Introduction

After considering the historic page, and viewing the living world with anxious **solicitude**, the most melancholy emotions of sorrowful indignation have depressed my spirits, and I have sighed when obliged to confess, that either nature has made a great difference between man and man, or that the civilization which has hitherto taken place in the world has been very **partial**. I have turned over various books written on the subject of education, and patiently observed the conduct of parents and the management of schools; but what has been the result?—a profound conviction that the neglected education of my fellow-creatures is the grand source of the misery I **deplore**; and that women, in particular, are rendered weak and wretched by a variety of concurring causes, originating from one hasty conclusion. The conduct and manners of women, in fact, evidently prove that their minds are not in a healthy state; for, like the flowers which are planted in too rich a soil, strength and usefulness are sacrificed to beauty; and the flaunting leaves, after having pleased a **fastidious** eye, fade, disregarded on the stalk, long before the season when they ought to have arrived at maturity.—One cause of this barren blooming I attribute to a false system of education, gathered from the books written on this subject by men who, considering females rather as women than human creatures, have been more anxious to make them alluring mistresses than affectionate wives and rational mothers;

> In the first paragraph, Wollstonecraft sets up her argument by asserting that women are denied proper educations.
> What loaded words does she use in this opening paragraph?

Vocabulary
solicitude (sə·lis′ə·tōōd′) n.: care; concern.
partial (pär′shəl) adj.: biased.
deplore (dē·plôr′) v.: regret; strongly disapprove of.
fastidious (fa·stid′ē·əs) adj.: picky; overly fussy.

Connection

A number of selections are followed by a **Connection** feature: an additional work, often in a different genre, that makes a pertinent literary connection to the main selection. Newspaper articles, poems, and essays appear as **Connection** features, enabling students to compare and contrast different treatments of a theme and make relevant personal connections.

CONNECTION / SHORT STORY

Top of the Food Chain
T. Coraghessan Boyle

The thing was, we had a little problem with the insect vector[1] there, and believe me, your tamer stuff, your Malathion and pyrethrum[2] and the rest of the so-called environmentally safe products, didn't begin to make a dent in it, not a dent, I mean it was utterly useless—we might as well have been spraying Chanel No. 5 for all the good it did. And you've got to realize these people were literally covered with insects day and night—and the fact that they hardly wore any clothes just compounded the problem. Picture if you can, gentlemen, a naked little two-year-old boy so black with flies and mosquitoes it looks like he's wearing long johns, or the young mother so racked with the malarial shakes she can't even lift a Diet Coke to her lips—it was pathetic, just pathetic, like something out of the Dark Ages.... Well, anyway, the decision was made to go with DDT.[3] In the short term. Just to get the situation under control, you understand.

Yes, that's right, Senator, *DDT*: Dichlorodiphenyltrichloroethane.

Yes, I'm well aware of that fact, sir. But just because *we* banned it domestically, under pressure from the bird-watching contingent and the hopheads down at the EPA, it doesn't necessarily follow that the rest of the world—especially the developing world—was about to jump on the bandwagon. And that's the key word here, Senator: developing. You've got to realize this is Borneo we're talking about here, not Port Townsend or Enumclaw. These people don't know from square one about sanitation, disease control, pest eradication. It rains a hundred and twenty inches a year, minimum.[4] They dig up roots in the jungle. They've still got headhunters along the Rajang River, for god's sake.

And please don't forget they *asked* us to come in there, practically begged us—and not only the World Health Organization but the Sultan of Brunei and the government in Sarawak too. We did what we could to accommodate them and reach our objective in the shortest period of time and by the most direct and effective means.

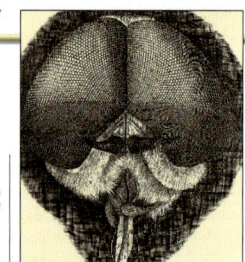

Eye of a Fly by Robert Hooke, from *Micrographia* (1665).
Rare Books and Manuscripts Division, The New York Public Library, Astor, Lenox and Tilden Foundations.

1. **vector** n.: bearer or carrier of disease.
2. **Malathion** (mal′ə·thī′än′) **and pyrethrum** (pī·rēth′rəm): insecticides made from organic substances. Though they are less toxic than synthetic insecticides, their safety is still debated.
3. **DDT**: synthetic compound first discovered to be an insecticide in 1939. Widely used during World War II, DDT was later found to cause such toxic effects in other animal populations that its use was severely restricted in the United States in 1972.
4. **hundred and twenty inches ... minimum**: In comparison, the average yearly rainfall in most of the United States is less than half this figure.

Walk Through

READ ON: FOR INDEPENDENT READING

DRAMA

The Rogue and the Recluse
The French playwright Molière had a remarkable genius for exposing and satirizing the ills of society. In Richard Wilbur's translations of *Tartuffe* and *The Misanthrope*, you'll meet two men whom Molière considered representative of his age: one a roguish hypocrite who charms everyone he meets and the other an eccentric recluse who shuns hypocrisy at a great cost to himself. Molière's comedies of manners, so relevant when they were first written, have lost none of their potency and humor today.

FICTION
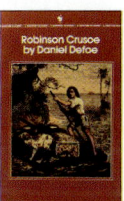
Diary of a Castaway
Since its publication in 1719, Daniel Defoe's *Robinson Crusoe* has spawned countless imitations and adaptations. Perhaps the story contained in Crusoe's fictional autobiography has endured because it poses age-old questions. How might we react if we were plucked from our ordinary lives and set on a barren island? Could we face the physical hardships and mental isolation of such an extraordinary new life?

NONFICTION

Pioneer of Science
Restoration England was an age marked by avid amateur experimentation and heated public debates about the mysteries of science. Sir Isaac Newton single-handedly unraveled many of the world's great puzzles: He invented calculus, formulated the three laws of motion, and realized, as no one else had, that gravity accounts for both orbiting planets and falling apples. You can read about the man and his works in *Isaac Newton and the Scientific Revolution* by Gale E. Christianson.

FICTION

Down on the Farm
Like Pope and Swift, George Orwell uses satire to reveal the absurdities of human nature. In his famous novel *Animal Farm* (1945), Orwell satirizes the problems of a supposedly equal society. The animals of Manor Farm revolt against their incompetent owner and install the "Seven Commandments of Animalism," which the sheep simply remember as "four legs good, two legs bad." The pigs Napoleon and Snowball eventually disagree about the future of the farm, and a rivalry for power ensues.

This title is available in the HRW Library.

Read On 499

Read On

At the end of each collection, **Read On** provides students with suggestions for independent reading of **fiction** and **nonfiction**. The recommended books have themes or subjects similar to those in the collection.

Writing Workshops

Writing Workshops at the end of each collection guide students through the writing process. Each workshop covers a different mode of writing, such as narration, persuasion, description, or exposition, and is a logical extension of the literary and informational selections covered in the collection.

Prewriting provides step-by-step instruction to help students get started and think about the audience they want to reach.

Writer's Framework shows students how to structure their papers.

Writer's Model demonstrates the workshop assignment with annotations to help students understand the structure and development of an essay.

Editor in Charge offers a three-step process with specific actions for students to take to locate and correct weaknesses in their papers.

Style Guidelines encourage students to revise their papers a second time for precise and effective language.

Writing Workshop

Writing a Literary Essay

Writing Assignment
Write a literary essay that shows how multiple works reflect the same literary trend.

Because they reflect universal human feelings and experiences, great works of literature such as Miguel de Cervantes' *Don Quixote* transcend time. Yet every work of literature is shaped by the era in which it is produced. In this workshop you'll write a **literary essay** that analyzes three works from the same literary period to discover how they reflect the literary trends of the time in which they were written.

Prewriting

Choose a Topic

A Trendy Topic Start by choosing a literary period on which to focus. You may want to investigate the literary period of one of your favorite authors or works, or you might get ideas about important literary periods by talking to your teacher or school librarian. Below is a list of literary periods you might consider.

- Renaissance (1485–1660)
- Victorian Period (1832–1901)
- Romantic Period (1798–1832)
- Twentieth Century (1901–2000)

Once you've chosen a literary period, do research to identify the **literary trends**, such as changes in style or the development of new literary genres, of that period and the works that reflect those trends. Find information about literary periods and works by looking through this textbook—particularly at the introduction to the literary period you've chosen—or by checking out library books that discuss the literary period.

Select one literary trend and three works by three different writers that reflect that trend. If the works you choose are long works, such as novels or epic poems, you will probably need to deal with a single section of each work to provide a thorough analysis in a 1,500-word essay. For example, one student who selected the eighteenth century as the focus of his literary essay chose to write about "A Voyage to Laputa" from Jonathan Swift's *Gulliver's Travels*, Book I of Alexander Pope's *The Dunciad*, and all of Voltaire's short novel *Candide* to show how they reflect a dominant trend in eighteenth-century literature—satire.

Analyze Literary Works

The Evidence Will Show . . . Through your research, you already know that your three works reflect a literary trend. Now you'll demonstrate *how* each work reflects that trend. To do that, read each work critically, following the guidelines on the next page.

Writing Skills
Write an essay analyzing works of literature.

500 Collection 4 The Restoration and the Eighteenth Century

T77

Walk Through

Listening and Speaking Workshop

Some collections feature a **Listening and Speaking Workshop** that guides students in delivering focused, coherent presentations and in evaluating a variety of oral and media communications.

Each **Listening and Speaking Workshop** is tied to a **Writing Workshop** and focuses on a different kind of presentation, such as narration, exposition, persuasion, research, and response to literature.

Practice and Apply encourages students to follow easy steps to help them construct, deliver, and evaluate a presentation.

Skills Review

A **Skills Review** at the end of each collection provides standardized-test practice for the vocabulary and writing skills taught in the collection. Students also compare and contrast two literary works from different time periods, completing both **multiple-choice** questions and an **essay**.

Walk Through

Reading Matters

Reading Matters is a handbook that offers students strategies designed to improve their reading skills. It focuses on issues such as reading comprehension and reading rate.

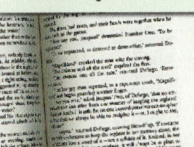

The World of Work

World of Work

World of Work includes information about and examples of **consumer documents** (such as warranties), **workplace documents** (such as memos), and **public documents** (such as policy statements). It also includes guidelines for writing resumes and completing job applications.

Test Smarts

Test Smarts is a handbook that gives students strategies for taking multiple-choice tests and writing tests. It includes questions for reading comprehension, vocabulary, and analogies.

T79

Walk Through

Language Handbook

The **Language Handbook** is a quick reference guide that gives students an overview of important issues in **grammar, usage,** and **mechanics.**

Handbook of Literary and Historical Terms

The **Handbook of Literary and Historical Terms** serves as a reference guide to the important literary and historical terms and concepts students will encounter throughout the text.

T80

Program Resources

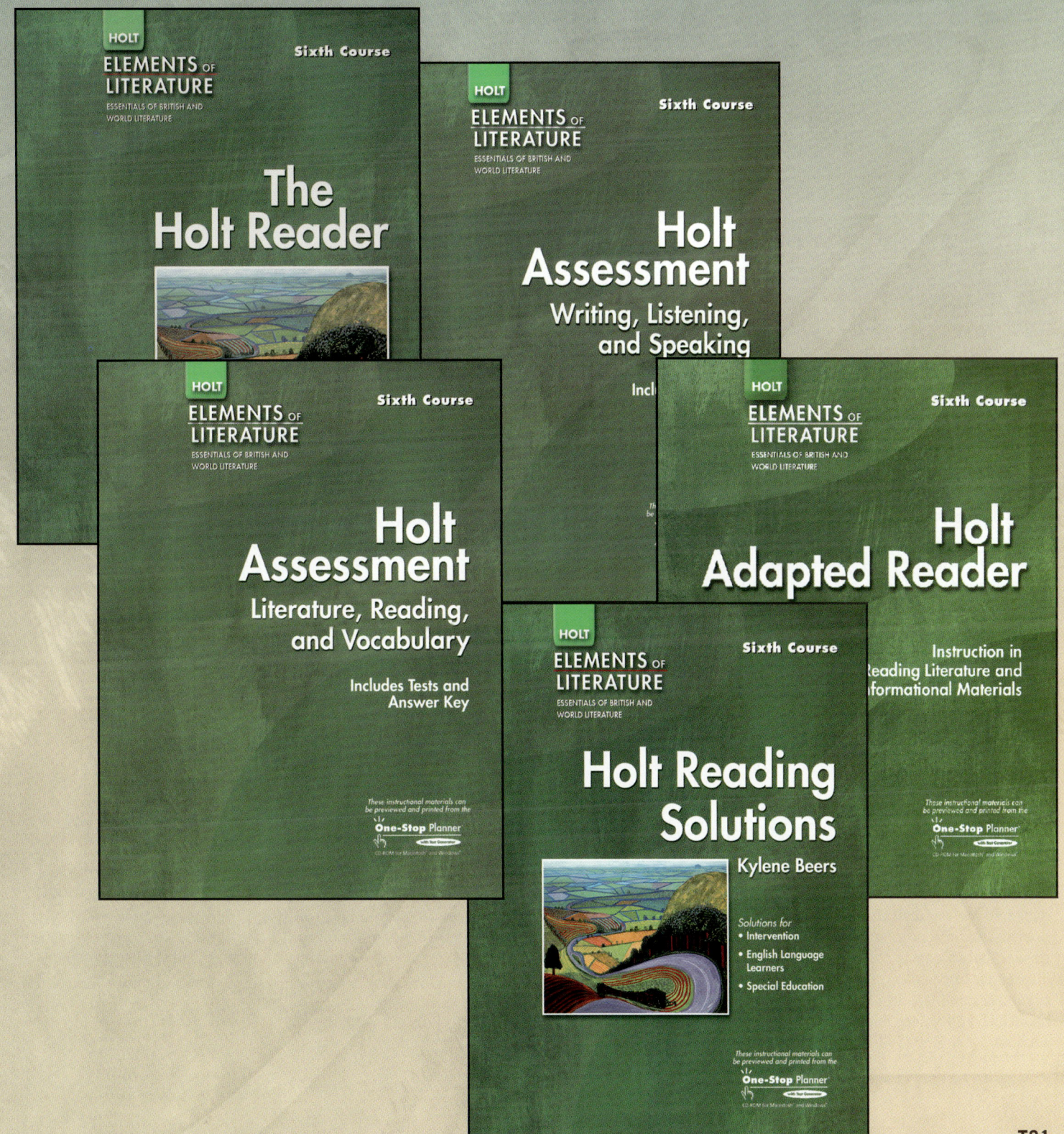

Program Resources

Planning

Annotated Teacher's Edition
This planning and teaching tool offers
- Specific questions to help reinforce and evaluate reading and literary skills for each selection
- Special approaches for learners having difficulty, English-language learners, and advanced learners
- Planning charts in the interleaf pages for each collection that provide information about the collection's scope and sequence of skills, core content, and resources
- Specific sequencing suggestions to ensure coverage of grade-level skills, effective testing, and remediation and reteaching opportunities

One-Stop Planner CD-ROM with ExamView Test Generator
This time-saving planning software contains print-based teaching resources, clips from the video program, and valuable assessment tools. The *One-Stop Planner* also
- Simplifies lesson planning and management
- Includes all the teaching resources for *Elements of Literature*
- Includes printable program resources and an easy-to-use test generator
- Offers previews of all teaching resources, including assessments and worksheets linked to the **Student Edition**
- Launches directly to the **go.hrw.com** Web site

PowerNotes for Literature and Reading
- Contains fully editable instructional PowerPoint® presentations that teach literary elements and reading skills and that introduce literary periods
- Includes teacher's notes with discussion questions and student note-taking worksheets with graphic organizers for each presentation

Professional Development

Web-Based Professional Development
Teaching Literacy to All Students, Grades 6–12, is a 9-module online professional development program that is ideal for all subject areas. *Teaching Reading to All Students, Grades 6–8*, is a 16-module online professional development program designed for middle school language arts teachers. Each module provides video demonstrations of best teaching practices tied to web-based content that includes explanations and examples, interactive applications to the teacher's own classroom, graphic organizers and lesson-planning templates, printable classroom handouts, and assessment instruments. The modules cover topics such as

- Planning schoolwide literacy programs
- Using assessment data to drive instruction
- Modifying instruction for English language learners
- Helping struggling readers with comprehension and fluency
- Integrating standards-based instruction

Face-to-Face Professional Development
Holt, Rinehart and Winston provides customized, comprehensive teacher training to assist school districts and individual teachers in the effective implementation of *Elements of Literature*.
- The training is facilitated by highly qualified professional development providers with language arts and reading expertise.
- Training institute and workshop topics include effective teaching practices, evidence-based research, and standards-based instruction.

Differentiating Instruction

The Holt Reader
This worktext includes alternative direct instruction and additional practice for the skills taught in each collection of *Elements of Literature*. The consumable format offers students' an interactive, hands-on approach to building reading, vocabulary, and literary analysis skills. Students circle, underline, and write responses in the margins of the selections.
- **Part 1** contains key literary selections from *Elements of Literature* and additional literary selections that extend student's practice. Instruction is focused on vocabulary, literary elements, and reading skills.
- **Part 2** contains informational texts such as magazine and newspaper articles, editorials, and essays. Also offered are vocabulary exercises and standardized-test practice.

Holt Adapted Reader
This consumable worktext contains the literary and informational adaptations found in *Holt Reading Solutions*. With scaffolded instruction that provides guided support, the *Holt Adapted Reader* can be used with struggling readers while other students in the class read the same selection in *The Holt Reader* or the **Student Edition**.
- Adaptations are within the reading range of English-language learners, special education students, and reluctant readers
- "Here's How" annotations model vocabulary, literary analysis, and reading comprehension skills; "Your Turn" annotations ask students to answer a question using the skill just modeled
- Graphic organizers help students review and consolidate what they've learned

Program Resources

Reading/Literature/Vocabulary

The Holt Reader
This worktext includes alternative direct instruction and additional practice for the skills taught in each collection of *Elements of Literature*. The consumable format offers students an interactive, hands-on approach to building reading, vocabulary, and literary analysis skills. Students circle, underline, and write responses in the margins of the selections.
- **Part 1** contains key literary selections from *Elements of Literature* and additional literary selections that extend student's practice. Instruction is focused on vocabulary, literary elements, and reading skills.
- **Part 2** contains informational texts such as magazine and newspaper articles, editorials, and essays. Also offered are vocabulary exercises and standardized-test practice.

Holt Adapted Reader
This consumable worktext contains the literary and informational adaptations found in *Holt Reading Solutions*. With scaffolded instruction that provides guided support, the *Holt Adapted Reader* can be used with struggling readers while other students in the class read the same selection in *The Holt Reader* or the *Student Edition*.
- Adaptations are within the reading range of English-language learners, special education students, and reluctant readers
- "Here's How" annotations model vocabulary, literary analysis, and reading comprehension skills; "Your Turn" annotations ask students to answer a question using the skill just modeled
- Graphic organizers help students review and consolidate what they've learned

Holt Reading Solutions
This book pulls together all of the reading resources in the *Elements of Literature* program to create a powerful tool for intervention and whole-class instruction. It includes
- Diagnostic assessment tools
- Lesson plans for English-language learners and special education students
- Adaptations of selected reading selections
- Vocabulary and comprehension worksheets
- Information on phonics and decoding
- Additional instruction and practice in remedial reading skills and strategies

Vocabulary Development
- Includes copying master worksheets that expand on students' ability to define and use the Vocabulary words identified in the *Student Edition*
- Includes cumulative reviews that reinforce students' mastery of the Vocabulary words

Holt Reading Solutions
This book pulls together all of the reading resources in the *Elements of Literature* program to create a powerful tool for intervention and whole-class instruction. It includes
- Diagnostic assessment tools
- Lesson plans for English-language learners and special education students
- Adaptations of selected reading selections
- Vocabulary and comprehension worksheets
- Information on phonics and decoding
- Additional instruction and practice in remedial reading skills and strategies

Supporting Instruction in Spanish
Provides the following Spanish-language materials as extra support for students who are making the transition from Spanish to English:
- Summaries of selections in *Elements of Literature*
- Criteria for major writing modes
- Definitions and examples of key grammar terms and concepts
- Introductions and summaries of Visual Connections segments

Audio CD Library
- Includes dramatic readings by professional actors that bring to life nearly every reading selection in *Elements of Literature*

Audio CD Library, Selections and Summaries in Spanish
- Includes Spanish translations of key selections in *Elements of Literature* that assist students in reading and developing their own sense of a selection
- Includes recordings of summaries in Spanish of virtually every selection in *Elements of Literature* that serve as a valuable tool for English-language learners

Workshop Resources: Writing, Listening, and Speaking
Supports instruction and assignments in the **Student Edition**
- Includes worksheets for each Writing Workshop and each Listening and Speaking Workshop
- Includes exercises and lesson plans with alternative teaching strategies for English-language learners and special education students

Family Involvement Activities in English and Spanish
- Offers a selection of letters written for the parents or guardians of students using *Elements of Literature*
- Suggests activities that can be completed at home to extend the material in the **Student Editions**
- Allows parents or guardians to participate in students' education and helps foster an atmosphere in the home that encourages academic success

Program Resources

HRW Library
- Offers a comprehensive selection of the best novels, works of nonfiction, anthologies, and connected readings, with selections drawn from a variety of cultures
- Includes Study Guides that help motivate students and enhance their appreciation and understanding of classic and contemporary literature

Writing/Grammar and Language/Listening and Speaking

Workshop Resources: Writing, Listening, and Speaking
Supports instruction and assignments in the **Student Edition**
- Includes worksheets for each Writing Workshop and each Listening and Speaking Workshop
- Includes exercises and lesson plans with alternative teaching strategies for English-language learners and special education students

Language Handbook Worksheets
- Includes practice and reinforcement worksheets that cover the material presented in the Language Handbook section of *Elements of Literature*
- Includes tests at the end of each section of the booklet that can be used either for assessment or as end-of-section reviews

Daily Language Activities
A notebook of transparencies that reinforce skills in reading, writing, grammar, usage, and mechanics that are covered in *Elements of Literature*. Transparencies are grouped into the following categories:
- Proofreading Warm-ups
- Vocabulary
- Analogies
- Sentence Combining
- Critical Reading

Assessment

Holt Assessment: Literature, Reading, and Vocabulary
Contains diagnostic, progress, and summative assessment tests, as follows:
- An Entry-Level Test and diagnostic tests for each collection assess students' level of preparation
- Tests for every reading selection provide ongoing evaluation of students' skill development
- Summative tests for each collection and an End-of-Year Test then offer cumulative assessment opportunities

Holt Assessment: Writing, Listening, and Speaking
- Includes assessment of writing, listening, and speaking skills in a variety of test formats, including standardized tests
- Provides scales and rubrics for each workshop assignment

Holt Online Assessment
- Includes entry-level and summative assessments
- Provides tools to monitor student progress through tracking student mastery and recording and analyzing scores

One-Stop Planner CD-ROM with ExamView Test Generator
Time-saving planning software that includes a printable version of all the tests from *Holt Assessment: Reading, Literature, and Vocabulary* and *Holt Assessment: Writing, Listening, and Speaking* as well as an easy-to-use test generator.

Holt Online Essay Scoring
- Provides writing prompts for the types of writing most common in state assessments
- Instantly scores and gives holistic and analytic feedback on student essays
- Provides writing tips, activities, and model essays geared to students' results

Technology
Internet

Elements of Literature Basic Online Edition
A Web-based version of the print edition of *Elements of Literature*, this "digital textbook"
- Delivers the content of the textbook in an online format that lightens the load students carry in their backpacks
- Enables students to complete homework online
- Includes access to an online notebook for storing student work, taking notes, and responding to the same questions and activities that appear in the student book

Elements of Literature Enhanced Online Edition
In addition to all the features of the Basic Online Edition described above, the Enhanced Online Edition includes a number of selections from the student text that are enhanced with various interactive features. The Enhanced Online Edition
- Provides point-of-use interactive critical thinking and literary response questions that pop up in the Notebook, where students can type responses, edit, save, and print their work
- Includes audio excerpts from the selection in both English and Spanish
- Features vocabulary links in English and Spanish, with accompanying audio
- Delivers links to high-interest video clips that enhance students' understanding of selections and build their prior knowledge

Program Resources

- Provides Spanish summaries of selections, in audio
- Includes highlighting and annotation tools for use by both students and teachers
- Features an Image Gallery where students can click to see art and graphics from their textbook

AuthorSpace

A Web environment available on *Elements of Literature* **Enhanced Online Edition** that provides students opportunities to dig deeper into the lives and works of various authors

- Uses a variety of interactive features such as timelines, maps, and illustrated "webs of influence" to help students gain a more detailed understanding of an author's life and his or her place in literary history
- Gives students a chance to read additional literary works, as well as primary source documents, by featured authors

go.hrw.com

At **go.hrw.com** students put their reading, writing, listening, and speaking skills into action in real-world situations. The GO Site

- Reinforces the study of literature through additional biographical information about authors, a variety of cross-curricular projects connected to the literature in the student textbook, and literary elements activities
- Includes interactive reading workshops that guide students through informational texts
- Includes interactive writers' models that illustrate various types of writing
- Includes vocabulary-building activities, through which students explore synonyms, antonyms, etymologies, and multiple meanings

Holt Online Assessment

- Includes entry-level and summative assessments
- Provides tools to monitor student progress through tracking student mastery and recording and analyzing scores

Holt Online Essay Scoring

- Provides writing prompts for the types of writing most common in state assessments
- Instantly scores and gives holistic and analytic feedback on student essays
- Provides writing tips, activities, and model essays geared to students' results

Teaching Literacy to All Students, Grades 6–12

This online professional development program provides video demonstrations of best teaching practices combined with interactive exercises, graphic organizers, and lesson-planning templates; printable classroom handouts; and assessment instruments. The program contains 9 lesson-segments covering literacy topics such as

- Schoolwide literacy programs
- Assessment driving instruction
- English language learners and intensive learners
- Comprehension and fluency
- Strategies in language arts

Media

Visual Connections Videocassette Program

- Consists of author biographies, interviews, historical summaries, and cross-curricular connections that motivate students and enrich and extend learning

Fine Art Transparencies

- Features stunning examples of classic and contemporary art to complement the literature selections in *Elements of Literature*
- Helps students explore literary characters and ideas through visual representations
- Encourages students to make cross-curricular connections

One-Stop Planner CD-ROM with ExamView Test Generator

- Time-saving planning software that contains print-based teaching resources, clips from the video program, and valuable assessment tools

PowerNotes for Literature and Reading

- Fully editable instructional PowerPoint presentations that teach literary elements and reading skills and that introduce literary periods

Audio CD Library

- Includes dramatic readings by professional actors that bring to life nearly every reading selection in *Elements of Literature*

Audio CD Library, Selections and Summaries in Spanish

- Includes Spanish translations of key selections in *Elements of Literature*
- Includes recordings of summaries in Spanish of virtually every selection in *Elements of Literature*

Diagnosis and Prescription

Diagnosis and Prescription: Tracking Student Mastery

The Entry-Level and End-of-Year tests can be used to inform instructional planning, chart student progress, and provide individual and group snapshots of core language arts skills proficiency.

CORE SKILLS	Entry-Level Test	End-of-Year Test	Collection Diagnostic Test	Collection Summative Test	Reteaching	Remediation
Collection 1						
Epic			Items 1–3	Item 11	• *The Holt Reader,* Collection 1	*Holt Reading Solutions* • Lesson Plans (ELL) • Special Ed Lesson Plans • Adapted Readings *Holt Adapted Reader*
Foil			Item 7		• *The Holt Reader,* Collection 1	*Holt Reading Solutions* • Lesson Plans (ELL) • Special Ed Lesson Plans • Adapted Readings *Holt Adapted Reader*
Archetypes	Item 9		Item 4	Item 12	• *ATE,* Reteaching Lessons	
Visualizing imagery	Items 4, 7		Item 6	Items 13–14	• *The Holt Reader,* Collection 1	*Holt Reading Solutions* • Lesson Plans (ELL) • Special Ed Lesson Plans • Adapted Readings *Holt Adapted Reader*
Vocabulary	Items 31–40	Items 9, 15, 31–40	Item 10	Items 1–5	• *The Holt Reader,* Collection 1	
Collection 2						
Characterization	Items 2, 3, 6	Items 3, 5	Item 2	Items 6–12	• *The Holt Reader,* Collection 2	*Holt Reading Solutions* • Lesson Plans (ELL) • Special Ed Lesson Plans • Adapted Readings • MiniReads *Holt Adapted Reader*
Situational irony			Item 4	Item 16	• *The Holt Reader,* Collection 2 • *ATE,* Reteaching Lessons	*Holt Reading Solutions* • Lesson Plans (ELL) • Special Ed Lesson Plans • Adapted Readings *Holt Adapted Reader*
Analyzing key details	Items 5, 14, 18, 28, 29	Items 1, 2, 6, 12, 14, 16–21		Item 11	• *The Holt Reader,* Collection 2	*Holt Reading Solutions* • Lesson Plans (ELL) • Special Ed Lesson Plans • Adapted Readings *Holt Adapted Reader*
Evaluating historical context		Item 13		Items 13, 15	• *The Holt Reader,* Collection 2	*Holt Reading Solutions* • Lesson Plans (ELL) • Special Ed Lesson Plans • Adapted Readings *Holt Adapted Reader*
Vocabulary	Items 31–40	Items 9, 15, 31–40	Items 9, 10	Items 1–5	• *The Holt Reader,* Collection 2	

Diagnosis and Prescription

CORE SKILLS	Entry-Level Test	End-of-Year Test	Collection Diagnostic Test	Collection Summative Test	Reteaching	Remediation
Collection 3						
Shakespearean sonnet			Item 1	Items 6–10, 12–15	• *The Holt Reader,* Collection 3	*Holt Reading Solutions* • Lesson Plans (ELL) • Special Ed Lesson Plans
Monologue and soliloquy			Item 2		• *The Holt Reader,* Collection 3	*Holt Reading Solutions* • Lesson Plans (ELL) • Special Ed Lesson Plans
Tone	Item 6		Item 3	Item 11	• *The Holt Reader,* Collection 3 • *ATE,* Reteaching Lessons	*Holt Reading Solutions* • Lesson Plans (ELL) • Special Ed Lesson Plans • Adapted Readings *Holt Adapted Reader*
Drawing inferences	Items 2–3, 5, 8, 20, 24	Items 1–3, 5–8, 18–20		Items 6–10	• *The Holt Reader,* Collection 3	*Holt Reading Solutions* • Lesson Plans (ELL) • Special Ed Lesson Plans • Adapted Readings • MiniReads *Holt Adapted Reader*
Vocabulary	Items 31–40	Items 9, 15, 31–40	Items 9, 10	Items 1–5	• *The Holt Reader,* Collection 4	
Collection 4						
Verbal irony			Item 1	Items 13–14	• *The Holt Reader,* Collection 4	*Holt Reading Solutions* • Lesson Plans (ELL) • Special Ed Lesson Plans • Adapted Readings *Holt Adapted Reader*
Satire			Item 3	Items 13–14		
Parody			Item 4		• *The Holt Reader,* Collection 4	*Holt Reading Solutions* • Lesson Plans (ELL) • Special Ed Lesson Plans • Adapted Readings *Holt Adapted Reader*
Recognizing persuasive techniques	Items 13–14, 25		Items 8–9	Item 11	• *The Holt Reader,* Collection 4	*Holt Reading Solutions* • Lesson Plans (ELL) • Special Ed Lesson Plans
Identifying the writer's stance	Items 14, 17, 20, 24	Items 7–8, 18, 23		Item 12	• *The Holt Reader,* Collection 4	*Holt Reading Solutions* • Lesson Plans (ELL) • Special Ed Lesson Plans
Analyzing an argument	Items 13–15		Items 8–9		• *The Holt Reader,* Collection 4 • *ATE,* Reteaching Lessons	
Vocabulary	Items 31–40	Items 9, 15, 31–40	Item 10	Items 1–5	• *The Holt Reader,* Collection 4	*Holt Reading Solutions* • Lesson Plans (ELL) • Special Ed Lesson Plans

Diagnosis and Prescription

CORE SKILLS	Entry-Level Test	End-of-Year Test	Collection Diagnostic Test	Collection Summative Test	Reteaching	Remediation
Collection 5						
Symbolism			Item 1	Items 13, 15	• *The Holt Reader,* Collection 5	*Holt Reading Solutions* • Lesson Plans (ELL) • Special Ed Lesson Plans • Adapted Readings *Holt Adapted Reader*
Irony		Item 5			• *The Holt Reader,* Collection 5 • *ATE,* Reteaching Lessons	*Holt Reading Solutions* • Lesson Plans (ELL) • Special Ed Lesson Plans
Sonnet				Items 8–9	• *The Holt Reader,* Collection 5	*Holt Reading Solutions* • Lesson Plans (ELL) • Special Ed Lesson Plans
Metaphor				Items 13, 14	• *The Holt Reader,* Collection 5	*Holt Reading Solutions* • Lesson Plans (ELL) • Special Ed Lesson Plans • MiniReads
Recognizing patterns of organization	Item 17	Item 30	Item 6		• *The Holt Reader,* Collection 5 • *ATE,* Reteaching Lessons	*Holt Reading Solutions* • Lesson Plans (ELL) • Special Ed Lesson Plans
Vocabulary	Items 31–40	Items 9, 15, 31–40	Items 9, 10	Items 1–5	• *The Holt Reader,* Collection 5	
Collection 6						
Theme	Item 10	Items 7, 11	Item 2	Items 10, 12	• *The Holt Reader,* Collection 6 • *ATE,* Reteaching Lessons	*Holt Reading Solutions* • Lesson Plans (ELL) • Special Ed Lesson Plans • Adapted Readings • MiniReads *Holt Adapted Reader*
Dramatic monologue			Item 3		• *The Holt Reader,* Collection 6	*Holt Reading Solutions* • Lesson Plans (ELL) • Special Ed Lesson Plans
Petrarchan sonnet			Item 4		• *The Holt Reader,* Collection 6	*Holt Reading Solutions* • Lesson Plans (ELL) • Special Ed Lesson Plans
Mood		Items 2, 19, 21	Item 5	Items 6, 13	• *The Holt Reader,* Collection 6	*Holt Reading Solutions* • Lesson Plans (ELL) • Special Ed Lesson Plans • Adapted Readings *Holt Adapted Reader*
Drawing inferences from textual clues	Items 2–3, 5, 8, 20, 24	Items 1–3, 5–8, 18–20		Item 11	• *The Holt Reader,* Collection 6	*Holt Reading Solutions* • Lesson Plans (ELL) • Special Ed Lesson Plans • MiniReads
Vocabulary	Items 31–40	Items 9, 15, 31–40	Item 10	Items 1–5	• *The Holt Reader,* Collection 6	

Diagnosis and Prescription

CORE SKILLS	Entry-Level Test	End-of-Year Test	Collection Diagnostic Test	Collection Summative Test	Reteaching	Remediation
Collection 7						
Allusion			Item 2		• *The Holt Reader,* Collection 7	*Holt Reading Solutions* • Lesson Plans (ELL) • Special Ed Lesson Plans
Point of view		Items 22, 23	Item 5	Items 7, 8	• *The Holt Reader,* Collection 7	*Holt Reading Solutions* • Lesson Plans (ELL) • Special Ed Lesson Plans • Adapted Readings *Holt Adapted Reader*
Lyric poetry			Item 15	Item 14	• *The Holt Reader,* Collection 7 • *ATE,* Reteaching Lessons	*Holt Reading Solutions* • Lesson Plans (ELL) • Special Ed Lesson Plans
Identifying and critiquing an author's argument	Items 13–15, 20		Items 17, 18		• *The Holt Reader,* Collection 7 • *ATE,* Reteaching Lessons	*Holt Reading Solutions* • Lesson Plans (ELL) • Special Ed Lesson Plans
Identifying the author's beliefs	Items 14, 17, 20, 24	Items 7–8, 18, 23	Item 16	Item 15	• *The Holt Reader,* Collection 7 • *ATE,* Reteaching Lessons	*Holt Reading Solutions* • Lesson Plans (ELL) • Special Ed Lesson Plans
Vocabulary	Items 31–40	Items 9, 15, 31–40	Items 19, 20	Items 1–5	• *The Holt Reader,* Collection 7	

Research Base

Best Practices in Writing

Harvey A. Daniels
Professor of Education
National-Louis University
Evanston, IL

RESEARCH

Atwell, N. 2002.
In the Middle: New Understandings About Writing, Reading, and Learning.
Portsmouth: Heinemann Educational Books.

Graves, D. 1983.
Writing: Teachers and Children at Work.
Portsmouth: Heinemann Educational Books.

Newman, F. 1996.
Authentic Achievement: Restructuring Schools for Intellectual Quality.
San Francisco: Jossey-Bass.

National Council of Teachers of English/ International Reading Association. 1999.
Standards for the English Language Arts.
Newark: NCTE/IRA.

Zemelman, S., H. Daniels, and A. Hyde. 1998.
Best Practice: New Standards for Teaching and Learning in America's Schools, 2nd ed.
Portsmouth: Heinemann Educational Books.

"There is a process to follow. There is a process to learn. That's the way it is with a craft, whether it be teaching or writing. There is a road, a journey to travel, and there is someone to travel with us, someone who has already made the trip." —Donald Graves

The Process of Writing

Over the past twenty-five years, the "process" model of writing has been strongly validated by educational research. A generation ago, many viewed writing as a somewhat magical act in which flawless texts flowed from the pens of a few muse-blessed artists. Today, we understand that writing is not so much a rare talent but a definable series of cognitive operations that can be learned by anyone who can read. For even the most skilled writer, composing is a sequential process of constructing meaning: gathering information, organizing material, trying out ideas in draft, revising and restructuring text, proofreading and editing, and sharing text with readers and using their feedback for further refinement. No, these stages aren't linear and lockstep; indeed, recursive and even idiosyncratic approaches are normal and useful. But the underlying cognitive reality remains: Just like reading, writing is a staged cognitive process of building up meaning.

New Teacher Roles

Once we understand that writing is more craft than magic, we can recast the teacher as a master craftsperson, helping apprentices to learn a trade. Process-writing teachers model, mentor, and coach; they create a classroom workshop where students build a repertoire of strategies for starting, developing, and polishing written products over a wide range of genres. The teacher's first job is to show how writing gets made, by serving as a live example of an adult writer at work. This doesn't mean teachers must be paragons or professionals, just journeyman composers eager to share their own writings and explain their own strategies. Then they can add rich literary models, bathing the workshop in fine literature, so students have great writers to learn from. That's why the *Elements of Literature* series includes collections of great and varied literature, followed by activities that help students draw directly upon these models to create their own original pieces.

Instructional Implications

Young writers need plenty of writing practice. In the workshop approach, students start many pieces, save all materials in a portfolio, and gradually develop selected drafts to a highly polished and public form. At the core of this work is deep revision: Students are constantly helped to re-see ideas and rethink organization, as well as to follow carefully the conventions of written language. Where possible, writing is not just graded, but shared with real audiences. This makes the work more rhetorically genuine and provides authentic feedback that can help writers grow. All these features of writing-process instruction remind us that—when the trade secrets are revealed, explained, and practiced—writing is not a mysterious practice reserved for the gifted, but a trade that's open to all.

Research Base

Effective Vocabulary Instruction

Kylene Beers, Ph.D.
Senior Reading Researcher
Child Study Center
Youth Development Program
Yale University
New Haven, CT

RESEARCH

Beers, K. 2002.
When Kids Can't Read—What Teachers Can Do.
Portsmouth: Heinemann.

Blachowicz, C. L. Z., and Fisher, P. 2000.
"Vocabulary Instruction." *Handbook of Reading Research.* Eds. P. D. Pearson, R. Barr, M. Kamil, and P. Mosenthal.
White Plains: Longman. 503–524.

Tierney, R., and Cunningham, J. 1984.
"Research on Teaching Reading Comprehension." *Handbook of Reading Research.* Eds. P. D. Pearson, R. Barr, M. Kamil, and P. Mosenthal.
White Plains: Longman. 609–656.

"Preteaching vocabulary . . . requires that the words to be taught must be key words, . . . be taught in semantically and topically related sets, . . . and that only a few words be taught per lesson." —Tierney and Cunningham

Preteaching Vocabulary

When students don't know the meaning of words that are used in a text, their ability to understand that text is diminished. They can use the context as a clue to get the gist of the meaning, but sometimes the context doesn't provide enough information and other times the gist isn't helpful enough. In those cases, we must preteach the vocabulary. To do so effectively, focus on which words you teach, the number that you teach, and how you teach them.

The Right Words and the Right Number

Deciding which words to teach is linked to deciding how many to teach. Twenty new words per week are probably too many for struggling readers, especially when you consider that the list of twenty is just for English class. The more vocabulary words we give students to learn weekly, the less chance they have of learning a word to the level needed to move it from short term to long term memory. Keeping the number between five and ten means students have a better chance of retaining that word beyond the end of the week (Beers, 2002).

Consequently, choose wisely the words to be taught. Avid readers benefit by studying rare words—those highly unusual ones—because they already have a solid vocabulary of the more common ones. Struggling readers, however, benefit by focusing on high-utility words—those more common words that they are likely to see in other contexts. So, in this sentence, "The boys banked the canoe to the lee side of the rock," the inclination might be to teach the word *lee*, a rare word. However, if students don't know what *banked* means in this context or don't know the word *canoe*, it matters little what *lee* means. For struggling readers, a focus on high-utility words is more beneficial than a focus on rare words.

The Right Instructional Approach

Tierney and Cunningham (1984) explain that offering students a list of vocabulary words with their definitions is not as effective as placing each word within a semantic context. Students learn how to use words as they read or hear them used correctly. *Elements of Literature* provides a short list of words on the "Before You Read" page of each selection that are defined and then used in a sentence. It is this semantic placement that most helps students learn words. Choosing the right number of the right words and presenting words in a semantic context helps students build their vocabulary and, as a consequence, improve their comprehension.

Research Base

Kylene Beers, Ph.D.
Senior Reading Researcher
Child Study Center
Youth Development Program
Yale University
New Haven, CT

RESEARCH

Baumann, J. 1984.
"Effectiveness of a Direct Instruction Paradigm for Teaching Main Idea Comprehension." *Reading Research Quarterly*, 20: 93–108.

Beers, K. 2002.
When Kids Can't Read—What Teachers Can Do. Portsmouth: Heinemann.

Dole, J., Brown, K., and Trathen, W. 1996.
"The Effects of Strategy Instruction on the Comprehension Performance of At-risk Students." *Reading Research Quarterly*, 31: 62–89.

Duffy, G. 2002.
"The Case for Direct Explanation of Strategies." *Comprehension Instruction: Research-Based Best Practices*. Eds. C. Block and M. Pressley. New York: Guilford Press. 28–41.

Pearson, P. D. 1984.
"Direct Explicit Teaching of Reading Comprehension." *Comprehension Instruction: Perspectives and Suggestions.* Eds. G. Duffy, L. Roehler, and J. Mason. New York: Longman. 222–233.

Teaching Comprehension

"Comprehension is both a product and a process, something that requires purposeful, strategic effort on the reader's part as he or she predicts, visualizes, clarifies, questions, connects, summarizes, and infers."
—Kylene Beers

When the Text Is Tough

"Comprehension is only tough when you can't do it," explained the eleventh-grader. I almost dismissed his words until I realized what truth they offered. We aren't aware of all the thinking we do to comprehend a text until faced with a difficult text. Then, all too clearly, we're aware of what words we don't understand, what syntax seems convoluted, what ideas are beyond our immediate grasp. As skilled readers, we know what to do: We slow our pace, re-read, ask questions, connect whatever we do understand to what we don't understand, summarize what we've read thus far, make inferences about what the author is saying. In short, we make that invisible act of comprehension visible as we consciously push our way through the difficult text. At those times, we realize that, indeed, comprehension is tough.

Reading Strategies for Struggling Readers

It's even tougher if you lack strategies that would help you through the difficult text. Many struggling readers believe they aren't successful readers because that's just the way things are (Beers, 2002); they believe successful readers know some secret that they haven't been told (Duffy, 2002). While we don't mean to keep comprehension a secret, at times we do. For instance, though we tell students to "re-read," we haven't shown them how to alter their reading. We tell them to "make inferences" or "make predictions," but we haven't taught them how to do such things. In other words, we tell them what to do, but don't show them how to do it, in spite of several decades of research showing the benefit of direct instruction in reading strategies to struggling readers. (Baumann, 1984; Pearson, P. D., 1984; Dole, et al., 1996; Beers, 2002).

Direct Instruction

Direct instruction means telling students what you are going to teach them, modeling it for them, providing assistance as they practice it, then letting them practice it on their own. It's not saying, "Visualize while you read," but instead explaining, "Today, I'm going to read this part aloud to you. I'm going to focus on seeing some of the action in my mind as I read. I'm going to stop occasionally and tell you what I'm seeing and what in the text helped me see that." When we directly teach comprehension strategies to students via modeling and repeated practice, we show students that good readers don't *just* get it. They work hard to get it. *Elements of Literature* takes the secret out of comprehension as it provides teachers the support they need to reach struggling readers.

The Technology Connection

Nancy Patterson, Ph.D.
Assistant Professor, School of Education
Grand Valley State University
Grand Rapids, MI

RESEARCH

Bolter, Jay David.   1991.
Writing Space: The Computer, Hypertext, and the History of Writing.
Mahwah: Lawrence Erlbaum Associates.

Henderson, Kathryn.   1995.
"The Visual Culture of Engineers."
The Cultures of Computing. Ed. Susan Leigh Star. Cambridge: Blackwell Publishers. 196–218.

Joyce, Michael.   1995.
Of Two Minds: Hypertext Pedagogy and Poetics.
Ann Arbor: University of Michigan Press.

Snyder, Ilana.   1997.
Hypertext: The Electronic Labyrinth.
New York: New York University Press.

Weaver, Constance.   1994.
Reading Process and Practice: From Socio-Psycholinguistics to Whole Language, 2nd ed.
Portsmouth: Heinemann.

"Reading comprehension is a process that involves the orchestration of the reader's prior experience and knowledge about the world and about language."   —Bartoli and Botel

Technology Promotes Thinking Skills

Without technology, there would be no reading. It takes technology to create text. Whether that technology has been the invention of the scroll, the moveable printing press, or e-books, each new innovation in text-creation technology brings new challenges for readers and writers. Computer technology is no exception, especially when it comes to helping readers access, and even create, the necessary prior knowledge needed for efficient reading.

Michael Joyce (1995) believes that Internet technology offers the possibility for students to use the same thinking skills "that experts routinely, subtly, and self-consciously apply in accomplishing intellectual tasks"—as it "promises to unlock these skills for novice learners and to empower and enfranchise their learning." The Internet offers this promise because it allows readers to act physically on the associations or mental connections they make when reading. Hyperlinks effectively placed in a piece of online text can help students make connections between what they are reading and what they already know. Hyperlinks support students' thinking by prompting them through the wording of the links, and when they activate a link, allowing them to immediately learn more information about a given topic.

Webbed Text and Thinking

Constance Weaver (1994) explains that prior knowledge develops through our experience with the world. Readers create some of those experiences through active participation with webbed texts. So, when the appropriate prior knowledge does not exist, students can gain knowledge via hyperlinks associated with a selection.

Jay Bolter (1991) believes that webbed texts bring the usually unconscious transaction between reader and writer to the forefront. The writer invites the reader to choose paths—or click on links. The reader considers the author's invitations and follows various paths through the links-as-invitation. Students experience the satisfaction of physically clicking on a link that addresses the same topic they may have been thinking about as they read. Those connections to more information increase their prior knowledge.

But webbed text can provide more than just information. We cannot ignore the importance of visual literacy in our culture today. In a world where images convey so much meaning, students must understand how images affect meaning. The more they are able to construct meaning with images, the better they will become at that mode of meaning construction (Henderson, 196). The effective combination of text and visually rich images on many Web pages, coupled with reflections on those elements, can help students build the literacies they need in this complex world.

Research Base

Dale Allender
Associate Executive Director
National Council of Teachers of English
Urbana, IL

RESEARCH

Allender, D.   2002
"The Myth Ritual Theory and the Teaching of Multicultural Literature."
English Journal 5: 52–55.

Barthes, R.   1981
"Theory of the Text." *Untying the Text: A Poststructuralist Reader.* Ed. R Young.
London: Routledge.

Bloome, D. and Egan-Robertson, A.   1993
"The Social Construction of Intertextuality in Classroom Reading and Writing Lessons."
Reading Research Quarterly 28: 304–333.

Callahan, Meg   2002
"Intertextual Composition: The Power of the Digital Pen." *English Education* 35: 46–64.

Spears-Bunton, L.   1999
"Calypso, Jazz, Reggae, and Salsa: Literature Response and the African Diaspora." *Reader Response in Secondary and College Classrooms.*
Ed. N. Karolides.
Mahway, New Jersey: Lawrence Erlbaum Associates.

Multicultural Literacy

"Inherent in the theory of text is the notion of intertextuality."
—Meg Callahan

Finding a Way In

Multicultural literature affirms and celebrates the rich diversity of our classrooms. That very same literature, however, can be a source of confusion and frustration for some readers, as it often contains unfamiliar references and unfamiliar words or phrases. We can overcome these surface problems by using intertextual readings.

Intertextual Reading

At first glance, intertextual reading looks like paired reading via novel sets or themed reading. However, it is far more. It is an activity for before, during, and after reading; and it can be led by the teacher or students. When reading intertextually, teachers and students read widely within and across genres, canons and eras as a way of exploring one novel, short story or poem (Barthes 1981; Bloome and Egan-Robinson, 1993). This is a particularly helpful strategy when the core selection represents a nonwhite cultural group. Students begin to build an understanding of the core selection by reading various other selections. Some students will read primary-source documents from the era of the literary work; others will look at contemporary media with related content. Still others will look at student-produced research papers, Web sites, CDs, or poetry. Everything is fair game, as long as it has some relationship to the literature the whole class is reading. It is helpful if the additional material is short—a newspaper article, letter, poem, video clip, song, or excerpt from a reference book. Short pieces allow students to read and re-read quickly and not get bogged down in something intended to help with the primary reading task.

From Text to Talk

All of the additional reading can then be discussed in relation to the primary work as a way of illuminating, challenging, or affirming it through various reading, writing, and speaking activities. For example, students might use a Venn diagram to compare information in a newspaper account of a historic event to the representation of that event in the literature. Or they can interview each other about the literature in light of the related reading. They might ask a partner who read an article or studied a photograph how the literature shapes or expresses the event in a different way from the image or article. They might ask if the literature adds colorful language or if it changes facts and information. Such intertextual reading will help students understand multicultural literature. In fact, such reading extends the meaning of reading multiculturally so that now it includes reading multiple sources about a diversity of experiences and communities. *Elements of Literature,* with its thematic grouping of literature and its wide variety of genres, offers readers repeated opportunities for intertextual reading.

Research Base

Literary Analysis: Beyond Response

Carol Jago
English Teacher
Santa Monica High School
Santa Monica, CA
and
Director
California Reading and Literature Project
University of California,
Los Angeles, CA

RESEARCH

Emig, J. 1990.
"Our Missing Theory." *Conversations: Contemporary Critical Theory and the Teaching of Literature.* Eds. C. Moran and E.F. Penfield. Urbana: National Council of Teachers of English. 87–96.

Greene, M. 1988.
The Dialectic of Freedom.
New York: Teachers College Press.

Rosenblatt, L. 1968.
Literature as Exploration. 2nd ed.
New York: Noble & Noble.

Scholes, R. 1985.
Textual Power: Literary Theory and the Teaching of English.
New Haven: Yale University Press.

"When there is active participation in literature—the reader living through, reflecting on, and criticizing his own responses to the text—there will be many kinds of benefits." —**Louise Rosenblatt**

Literary Analysis

Literary analysis is hard work that begins with readers' initial response to a literary work and deepens as readers measure that response against the richness of the text. That richness includes ideas presented in the text, symbols embedded in the text, and persuasive devices the author offers throughout the text. As readers do as Rosenblatt suggested and live through, reflect on, and criticize their own responses to the text, there are indeed many benefits. Those benefits become most evident when analysis follows response. As Robert Scholes explains in *Textual Power*, reading "requires both interpretation and criticism for completion."

Reading Stances

During the process of reading, readers take a series of stances toward the text. A reader's initial stance is a first impression including surface features of a text such as genre, content, and language. Moving through the text, the reader becomes caught up in the story or is carried along by a persuasive argument. Upon completion, readers step back and reflect on their own experience and prior knowledge. The text may cause them to rethink what they know. Finally, readers step back from their reading and reflect upon the context within which this piece of literature was created. Sometimes this stance includes thinking about the reading experience itself. These stances are not a hierarchy of skills, nor are they ever really independent of one another. Each adds a different dimension to the reader's understanding.

Critical Literary Stances

A stance can also refer to the point of view a reader adopts towards a text. Formal approaches to teaching literary analysis include psychological theories: psychoanalytic criticism drawing on the theories of Sigmund Freud, biographical approaches exploring the influence of the author's life upon the text, reader response approaches focusing upon what the reader brings to the text, and archetypal approaches examining universal responses to text. Other critical stances that readers may adopt include Marxist readings, new historicist readings, cultural readings, postcolonial readings, feminist readings, gender readings, and deconstructionist readings.

Maxine Greene argues that, "Learning to look through multiple perspectives, young people may be helped to build bridges among themselves; attending to a range of human stories, they may be provoked to heal and to transform." Throughout **Elements of Literature**, students are given the tools to build those bridges as they read texts and form initial responses and deepen them as they consider texts from multiple perspectives, examine literary techniques, and recognize the author's biases and purposes.

Collection 1
The Anglo-Saxons: 449–1066

About Collection 1
In Collection 1, students will master the following skills:
- **Literary Skills:** Evaluate the philosophical, political, religious, ethical, and social influences of a historical period; analyze archetypes, universal themes, epic poetry, epic similes, and the epic; compare and contrast literary forms of different historical periods.
- **Vocabulary Skills:** Understand and identify Anglo-Saxon words and affixes; create semantic maps; use context clues to determine the meaning of words.
- **Writing Skills:** Develop, write, and revise a descriptive essay.

Minimum Course of Study
Most skills can be taught with a minimum number of selections and features. In the chart to the right, lessons **highlighted in green** constitute the minimum course of study that provides coverage of the skills taught in Collection 1.

Resource Manager
(see pp. 1C–1D)
Lesson and workshop resources are referenced in the Resource Manager on the pages that follow. These resources can be used to reinforce the skills taught in Collection 1, remediate students who are having difficulty, and provide supporting activities for English-language learners.

Scope and Sequence

Selection ▪ Feature	Literary Skills
The Anglo-Saxons: 449–1066 by David Adams Leeming	• Evaluate the philosophical, political, religious, ethical, and social influences of a historical period
from **Beowulf, Part One** translated by Burton Raffel ↔ *at grade level*	• Analyze the archetype of the epic hero
from **Beowulf, Part Two** translated by Seamus Heaney ↑ *above grade level*	• Analyze the universal themes of epic poetry • Understand and analyze alliteration and kennings
Connecting to World Literature: Epics: Stories on a Grand Scale by David Adams Leeming	• Understand the epic and the archetype of the epic hero in ancient and modern literature • Compare literary forms of major literary periods
from **Gilgamesh: A Verse Narrative** retold by Herbert Mason ↔ *at grade level*	• Analyze the use of a foil • Analyze the epic and the archetype of the epic hero in ancient and modern literature • Compare literary forms of major literary periods
from **Book 22: The Death of Hector** *from the* **Iliad** by Homer ↑ *above grade level*	• Analyze the epic simile • Understand the conventions of epic poetry • Compare epics from different literary periods
Writing Workshop: *Writing a Descriptive Essay*	
Skills Review: *Literary Skills Vocabulary Skills Writing Skills*	• Compare and contrast works from different literary periods

Reading Skills	Vocabulary Skills	Writing ■ Grammar and Language ■ Listening and Speaking Skills
	• Demonstrate word knowledge • Understand and identify Anglo-Saxon words and affixes	• Write a character-analysis essay • Write a descriptive essay • Present a dramatic reading
	• Demonstrate word knowledge	• Write an interior monologue
	• Create semantic maps	• Write an essay comparing and contrasting epic heroes • Identify and correct sentence fragments and run-on sentences
		• Write a descriptive essay
	• Use context clues to determine the meaning of words	• Write a descriptive essay

1B

Resource Manager

Selection • Feature	Planning	Differentiating Instruction • Lesson Plans with ELL Strategies and Practice	Reading • Vocabulary
The Anglo-Saxons: 449–1066 by David Adams Leeming	• PowerNotes: The Anglo-Saxons	• Holt Adapted Reader	• Holt Adapted Reader
from **Beowulf, Part One** translated by Burton Raffel *from* **Beowulf, Part Two** translated by Seamus Heaney	• One-Stop Planner with ExamView Test Generator • PowerNotes: Alliteration and Kennings	• The Holt Reader, pp. 10–18 • Holt Adapted Reader • Holt Reading Solutions, pp. 31–33 • Supporting Instruction in Spanish, pp. 3–4 • Audio CD Library, disc 1 • Audio CD Library, Selections and Summaries in Spanish	• The Holt Reader • Holt Adapted Reader • Holt Reading Solutions • Vocabulary Development, p. 1
Connecting to World Literature: Epics: Stories on a Grand Scale by David Adams Leeming			
from **Gilgamesh: A Verse Narrative** retold by Herbert Mason *from* **Book 22: The Death of Hector** *from the* **Iliad** by Homer	• One-Stop Planner with ExamView Test Generator	• The Holt Reader, pp. 19–43 • Holt Adapted Reader • Holt Reading Solutions, pp. 37–45 • Supporting Instruction in Spanish, p. 5 • Audio CD Library, disc 1 • Audio CD Library, Selections and Summaries in Spanish	• The Holt Reader • Holt Adapted Reader • Holt Reading Solutions • Vocabulary Development, pp. 2, 3
Writing Workshop: *Writing a Descriptive Essay*	• One-Stop Planner with ExamView Test Generator	• Workshop Resources: Writing, Listening, and Speaking, pp. 1–8 • Family Involvement Activities in English and Spanish • Supporting Instruction in Spanish, p. 67	
Skills Review: *Literary Skills* *Vocabulary Skills* *Writing Skills*			

The Holt Reader

The Holt Reader is a consumable paperback book that can be used alone or to accompany *Elements of Literature*. It offers guided support throughout the reading process and encourages students to become active readers by circling, underlining, questioning, and jotting down responses as they read. *The Holt Reader* works well for homework, students who have missed class, additional instructional time, reteaching, and remediation.

Holt Reading Solutions (HRS)

Holt Reading Solutions pulls together reading resources in the *Elements of Literature* program to create a powerful tool for intervention and whole-class instruction. *HRS* includes diagnostic assessment tools, lesson plans for English-language learners and special education students, adaptations of selected reading selections, vocabulary and comprehension worksheets, information on phonics and decoding, and additional instruction and practice in remedial reading skills.

Writing · Grammar and Language · Listening and Speaking	Assessment
• Daily Language Activities	• Holt Assessment: Literature, Reading, and Vocabulary • Holt Online Assessment • One-Stop Planner with ExamView Test Generator
• Daily Language Activities • Language Handbook Worksheets, pp. 80, 82, 83	• Holt Assessment: Literature, Reading, and Vocabulary • Holt Online Assessment • One-Stop Planner with ExamView Test Generator
• Daily Language Activities • Workshop Resources: Writing, Listening, and Speaking, pp. 1–8	• Holt Assessment: Writing, Listening, and Speaking • Holt Online Assessment • One-Stop Planner with ExamView Test Generator
	• Holt Assessment: Writing, Listening, and Speaking • One-Stop Planner with ExamView Test Generator

Technology

INTERNET

- go.hrw.com
- Holt Online Assessment
- Holt Online Essay Scoring
- Elements of Literature Online

MEDIA
 • One-Stop Planner with ExamView Test Generator

 • PowerNotes

 • Audio CD Library, disc 1

• Audio CD Library, Selections and Summaries in Spanish

• Visual Connections Videocassette Program, Segments 1 and 2

• Fine Art Transparencies, 1 and 2

 Transparency   Video

 CD-ROM   Audio CD

One-Stop Planner with ExamView Test Generator

The *One-Stop Planner* CD-ROM contains electronic versions of print-based teaching resources, clips from the video program, and valuable assessment tools. The *One-Stop Planner* resources are presented in easy-to-follow, point-and-click menu formats. To preview resources or print out worksheets and tests, you simply make a selection and click.

One-Stop Planner CD-ROM

Collection 1

INTRODUCING THE COLLECTION

When students think of a hero, they may think of a real person, such as Abraham Lincoln, or a fictional character, such as Superman. The selections in this collection will familiarize students with the classic heroes of Anglo-Saxon and world literature. By reading stories of legendary figures such as Beowulf and Gilgamesh, students will learn the characteristics of the archetypal hero. The collection concludes with an opportunity for students to write a descriptive essay about a character they hold dear.

VIEWING THE ART

This image is in a manuscript produced by monks. Point out that the image lacks the illusion of three dimensions or a sense of perspective. The artist, however, tried to create a sense of depth by stacking the objects one upon the other. This approach was taken because the technique of perspective was not invented until the Renaissance.

Activity. Have the students describe what is taking place in the scene. [The boats are crowded with warriors, most of whom wield spears and shields. Their anxious expressions convey a sense of urgency. The men are obviously getting ready for battle.]

Invasion of Danes under Hinguar (Ingvar) and Hubba (detail). Page from *Life, Passion, and Miracles of St. Edmund* (c. 1130). M.736.f.9v. © The Pierpont Morgan Library, New York.

COLLECTION 1 RESOURCES: READING

Planning
- *One-Stop Planner* CD-ROM with ExamView Test Generator

Differentiating Instruction
- *Holt Reading Solutions*
- *The Holt Reader*
- *Holt Adapted Reader*
- *Family Involvement Activities in English and Spanish*

- *Supporting Instruction in Spanish*
- *Audio CD Library, Selections and Summaries in Spanish*

Vocabulary
- *Vocabulary Development*

Grammar and Language
- *Language Handbook Worksheets*
- *Daily Language Activities*

Assessment
- *Holt Assessment: Literature, Reading, and Vocabulary*
- *One-Stop Planner* CD-ROM with ExamView Test Generator
- *Holt Online Assessment*

Internet
- go.hrw.com (Keyword: LE5 12-1)
- *Elements of Literature Online*

Collection 1 The Anglo-Saxons

Collection 1

The Anglo-Saxons
449–1066
Songs of Ancient Heroes

And sometimes a proud old soldier
Who had heard songs of the ancient heroes
And could sing them all through, story after story,
Would weave a net of words...

—from *Beowulf*, translated by Burton Raffel

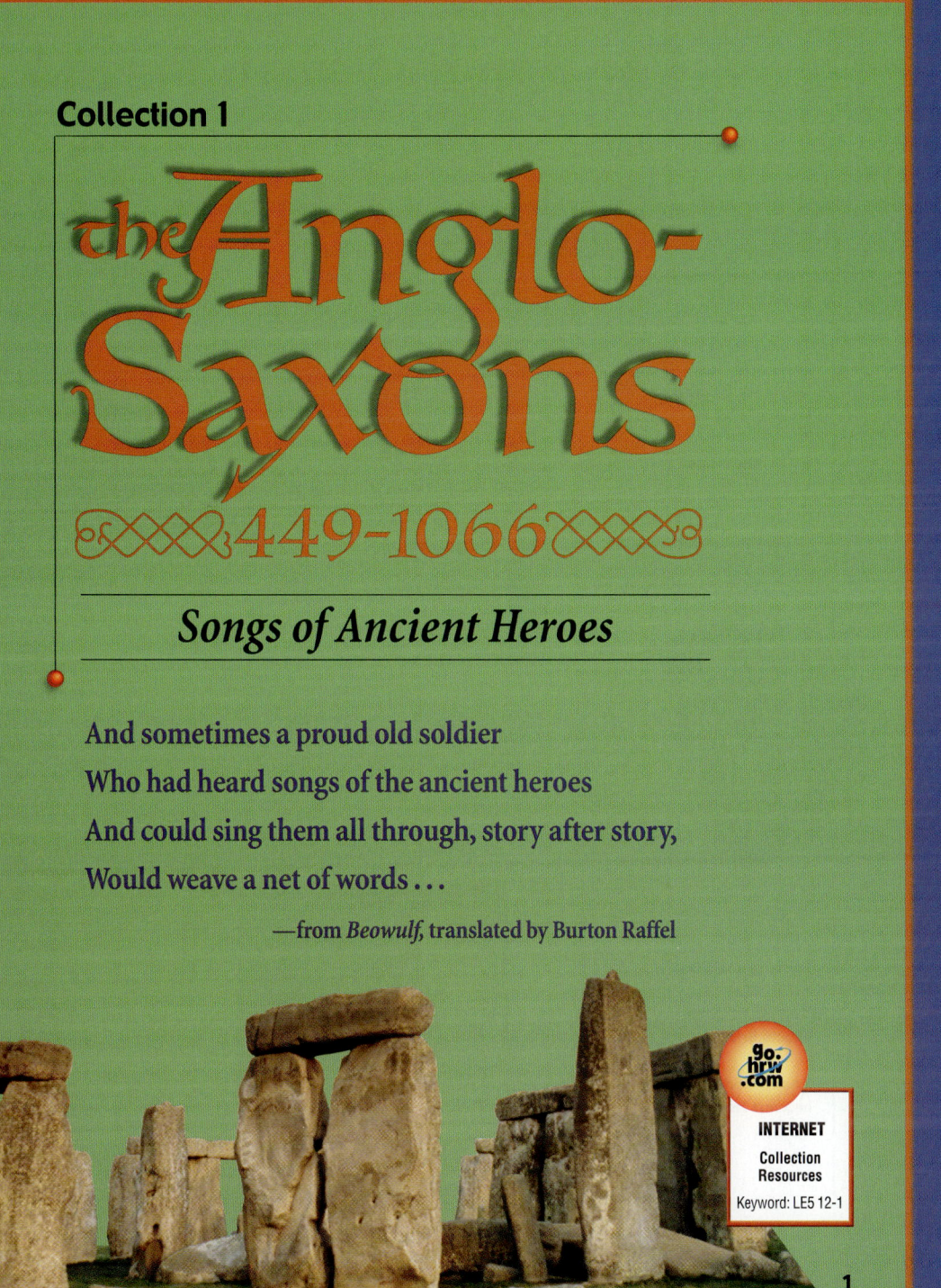

THE QUOTATION

What do you think these lines from *Beowulf* reveal about the role of storytelling in Anglo-Saxon society? [Possible responses: Anglo-Saxon men could be poets as well as warriors, creating their own retellings of heroic deeds. Both roles, soldier and poet, were important to the Anglo-Saxons.] What heroes and heroines do we celebrate in poems, songs, and folk tales today? Are they usually warriors? [Possible responses: Hercules; Ulysses; King Arthur; Charlemagne; Mulan; Joan of Arc; Paul Revere; Paul Bunyan; John Henry; Johnny Appleseed; Martin Luther King, Jr.; Rosa Parks; Nelson Mandela. Some of these heroes and heroines are warriors, but most are heroic in some other way.]

Media
- Audio CD Library
- Audio CD Library, Selections and Summaries in Spanish
- Fine Art Transparencies
- Visual Connections Videocassette Program
- PowerNotes

Time Line

■ c. 1300 B.C.
Epic of *Gilgamesh*

The epic of *Gilgamesh* tells the adventures of a Mesopotamian king who was part god and part human. These tales about Gilgamesh were written down in cuneiform script on eleven clay tablets that were rediscovered during the nineteenth century. They were among some 25,000 tablets found among the ruins at Nineveh in the library of a powerful Assyrian king, Assurbanipal, who ruled during the seventh century B.C.

■ c. 50
London

The Romans established Londinium as a trading center. After the Romans withdrew from Britain in A.D. 409, London did not regain its importance until 866, under King Alfred. Present-day London encompasses approximately 620 square miles along both sides of the Thames River and is one of the world's leading financial, cultural, and commercial centers.

■ 552
Buddhism in Japan

The native religion of Japan is Shinto, which involves the worship of ancestors and gods found in nature. Buddhism originated in India (c. 525 B.C.) and came to Japan by way of Korea and China during the sixth century A.D. Today, about 75 percent of the Japanese practice Buddhism.

■ late 500s
Chinese Bookmaking

The Chinese had been writing books on bamboo by 1000 B.C. They had already invented paper in A.D. 105 and were printing books by 591. By about 1045, they had gone beyond the carved wooden blocks and ink of the sixth century to create movable type, about four hundred years before Gutenberg.

The Anglo-Saxon Period

LITERARY EVENTS
1300 B.C.–A.D. 299   **A.D. 300**

- **c. 1300 B.C.** *Gilgamesh* epic is written down
- **c. 700 B.C.** Homer writes the *Iliad*
- **307 B.C.** Alexandria is center of Greek learning; library under Ptolemy is begun
- **70 B.C.** Roman poet Virgil is born
- **c. A.D. 5** Roman poet Ovid writes *Metamorphoses*
- **c. 360** Throughout Europe, scrolls begin to be replaced by vellum books
- **late 500s** Books are printed in China

Seated Buddha (c. 650). Chinese sculpture from the T'ang dynasty.
The Metropolitan Museum of Art, Rogers Fund, 1919 (19.186). Photograph by Lynton Gardiner. © 1989 The Metropolitan Museum of Art, New York.

POLITICAL AND SOCIAL EVENTS
1300 B.C.–A.D. 299   **A.D. 300**

- **c. 50** Londinium (present-day London) is founded by Romans as a supply port
- **61** Queen Boadicea leads her eastern British tribe in an uprising against the Romans
- **300s B.C.** Celts called Brythons live in Britain
- **55 B.C.** Julius Caesar invades Britain
- **51 B.C.** Cleopatra VII becomes last queen of Egypt
- **c. 313** Christianity is proclaimed lawful religion in the Roman Empire
- **409** Roman legions withdraw from Britain
- **c. 449** Angles, Saxons, and Jutes invade Britain
- **476** Roman Empire falls to Germanic tribes
- **c. 516** Semilegendary King Arthur rules Celtic tribe
- **537** King Arthur dies at Battle of Camlann
- **547** Widespread plague reaches Britain from Europe
- **552** Buddhism is introduced to Japan
- **597** Saint Augustine converts Anglo-Saxon King Ethelbert and establishes monastery at Canterbury

Roman helmet.
© British Museum, London.

Comes Litoris Saxon per Britaniam (c. 950). Anglo-Saxon map.
Bibliothèque municipale, Rouen, France. The Bridgeman Art Library, New York.

Using the Time Line

Activity. Have students use a print or non-print encyclopedia to place the following events in science, mathematics, and literature on the time line.

- Euclid publishes *The Elements of Geometry*. [c. 300 B.C.]
- Li Po writes poetry during China's "golden age of literature." [A.D. 701–762]
- The Maya, during their classical period, devise an extremely accurate calendar system consisting of 260 ritual days in a 365-day year that is part of a longer cycle of 52 years. [A.D. 320–900]
- In India, Aryabhata calculates the value of *pi* to four decimal places and the length of the solar year to 365.3586805 days. [c. A.D. 500]

449–1066

Kingston brooch (6th or 7th century).
City of Liverpool Museum, England.
The Bridgeman Art Library, New York.

700 — **1066**

600s Lyric poetry of the T'ang period promotes everyday use of Chinese language

640 At Alexandria, Arabs discover the famous library with 300,000 papyrus scrolls

c. 670 Caedmon, the earliest English Christian poet, writes hymns

c. 700 *Beowulf* is first recorded

730 The Venerable Bede, an English cleric, writes the *Ecclesiastical History of the English People*

c. 759 *Manyoshu (Collection of Ten Thousand Leaves)*, Japanese anthology of about 4,500 poems, is compiled

760 Monks begin the Book of Kells, an illuminated manuscript of Latin Gospels

c. 850 The *Poetic Edda*, a famous cycle of Norse mythological poems, is composed

900 The Arabian tales *The Thousand and One Nights* are begun

c. 975 *The Exeter Book*, a collection of English poetry, is first copied

c. 1000 In Japan, Lady Murasaki Shikibu writes the world's first novel, *The Tale of Genji*

700 — **1066**

618 Golden age of T'ang dynasty begins in China

c. 625 Mohammed (b. 570), founder of Islam, begins to dictate the Koran

664 Synod of Whitby unites British Christian Church with Roman Church

Coronation of Charlemagne by Pope Leo III. Miniature.
Bibliothèque de l'arsenal, Paris. © Scala/Art Resource, New York.

711 Moors invade Spain

793 Vikings invade Britain, beginning a century of invasions

800 In France, Charlemagne is crowned emperor of the West by Pope Leo III

c. 800 Incas build fortress-city of Machu Picchu in Peru

c. 810 Algebra is devised in Persia

813 School of astronomy is founded at Baghdad

871 Alfred the Great (849–899) becomes king of England

878 Alfred forces the Danes from Wessex

900s Kingdom of Ghana, in Africa, flourishes

1066 Normans defeat Saxons; William the Conqueror becomes English king

Danes attacking an East Anglian town.
The Pierpont Morgan Library, NY.

Mayan figure holding tortillas.

■ 711
The Moors

The Moors of northwestern Africa (called the Mauri by the Romans) were a Berber people, many of whom spoke Arabic in addition to their own language. Converted to Islam, they conquered Spain with the Arabs in the early 700s and ruled during the Middle Ages, establishing a Moorish civilization. After losing most of their Spanish holdings by the 1200s, the Moors settled primarily in North Africa.

■ 730
The Venerable Bede

A monk and a scholar, Bede (673–735) is the man most responsible for our knowledge of England during the eighth century. The purpose of his *Ecclesiastical History* is to show how the Church brought unity to England, ending an era of violence and barbarism.

■ 871–899
King Alfred

In addition to being the only ruler able to successfully resist Danish (Viking) invasions, Alfred the Great was a patron of learning who furthered the education of his people. He invited scholars to his court, and he himself translated scholarly works.

■ c. 975
The Exeter Book

The Exeter Book, a manuscript of miscellaneous poems dating from around A.D. 940, is our chief source of Anglo-Saxon poetry. The manuscript is now preserved at Exeter Cathedral in England.

Activity. Ask students to examine the time line and then answer the following questions:
- What four peoples invaded Britain in the period covered by this time line? [the Romans in 55 B.C.; the Angles, Saxons, and Jutes c. 449; the Vikings in 793; and the Normans in 1066]
- What effects might a series of invasions—one every three hundred to five hundred years—have on a culture? [Possible responses: Such a history might make a culture adaptable; people would learn to live with and absorb the influences of those who spoke a different language or practiced a different religion. Some students might suggest that a history of invasion would make a culture become militaristic.]

Political and Social

Political and Social Milestones

Roman Occupation, 55 B.C.–A.D. 409

The Roman Empire occupied not only the British Isles, but also most of Europe, Asia Minor, the Middle East, and North Africa—including what is now Italy, France, Germany, Switzerland, Belgium, Holland, Spain, Portugal, Armenia, parts of southern Russia, western Romania, Greece, Turkey, Persia, Syria, Jordan, Palestine, Egypt, Tunisia, Algeria, and Morocco. Students who are interested in history might wish to explore the many interpretations that have been proposed to explain Rome's conquest and domination of so much of the world. (The Romans themselves argued that they fought only "just wars," meaning only when they were provoked.) Students may also wish to explore the various theories purporting to explain the decline and fall of the Roman Empire, as well as how that fall has been used as a cautionary tale for other powerful nations, including the United States.

Anglo-Saxon Invasion, A.D. 449

According to the sixth-century British writer Gildas, these groups were first actually invited to Britain by a British king, Vortigern, to help him fight the Picts and the Scots. Later waves of settlers and invaders were not so welcome, and for a while their advance was stopped by native resistance. By the end of the sixth century, however, after a new wave of Anglo-Saxon invasions, the Britons were defeated.

Roman Occupation, 55 B.C.–A.D. 409

Roman conquerors arrived with Julius Caesar and remained in Britain for more than four hundred years. They built roads throughout the island and Hadrian's Wall, a seventy-three-mile-long fortification that kept invaders out for several centuries. But when the Romans withdrew completely, in A.D. 409, Britain was left with no government—and again it was vulnerable to invasion.

Hadrian's Wall, a seventy-three-mile defensive barrier (built c. A.D. 122).
© Sandro Vannini/CORBIS.

Anglo-Saxon Invasion, A.D. 449

In the fifth century the Angles and Saxons, from Germany, and the Jutes, from Denmark, drove the Britons to the perimeter of the country and imposed their

Milestones 449–1066

language and warrior culture on most of Britain. The Anglo-Saxons brought with them a fierce loyalty to their tight-knit communities and to their grim religion. They also greatly esteemed the scops, the storytellers of their society. The scops played the invaluable role of community preservationists, celebrating the heroes of Anglo-Saxon culture through poetic songs.

Divided at first into clans and principalities and later harassed by invading Danes, the Anglo-Saxons were eventually united under King Alfred the Great of Wessex in the ninth century.

(Opposite) Dragon ship. Detail from a manuscript.
By permission of The British Library, London.

The Spread of Christianity, A.D. 400–A.D. 699

Christianity was introduced to Britain during the Roman occupation, but centuries passed before it became the dominant religion of the country. Starting in the early fifth century, Ireland's Christian monks, along with missionaries from Rome and elsewhere on the Continent, began to settle parts of Britain and spread their beliefs. Christian monasteries and Anglo-Saxon culture coexisted for many years. By the late seventh century, however, Christianity had virtually replaced the British pagan religions.

Celtic cross in Cornwall, England.
© Michael Nicholson/CORBIS.

The Spread of Christianity, A.D. 400–A.D. 699

These missionaries from Rome were sent by Pope Gregory I and led by a Benedictine prior named Augustine (later called Saint Augustine of Canterbury and the apostle of England). In 597, Augustine's delegation of about forty monks landed on an island off the southeast coast of England. He was welcomed by King Ethelbert of Kent, whom he converted to Christianity, along with thousands of his subjects. Augustine built a monastery and a cathedral at Canterbury, and in 601, he became the first archbishop of Canterbury (the highest-ranking cleric in England).

The Norman Invasion, 1066

William the Conqueror (1027?–1087) was the illegitimate son of Robert I, duke of Normandy (a province of France). When his father died in 1035, the young boy became duke and then struggled to establish his power, both because of his youth and his illegitimacy. William's interest in England seems to have begun because of a family connection: Two of his cousins had reigned in turn as kings of England, the second of whom, Edward the Confessor, apparently promised William to make him his heir. When Edward died (childless) and his brother-in-law—Harold, earl of Wessex—was crowned king instead, William decided to invade England. This invasion, often called the Norman Conquest, is considered one of the pivotal events in world history.

The Norman Invasion, 1066

William the Conqueror crossed the English Channel in 1066 and defeated the Anglo-Saxon armies at the Battle of Hastings. Thus was ended the dominance of Anglo-Saxon culture in the island kingdom.

The battle in which King Harold is killed, from the Bayeux Tapestry (detail) (c. 11th century).
Musée de la tapisserie, Bayeux, France.

SKILLS FOCUS, pp. 6–17

Grade-Level Skills

■ **Literary Skills**
Evaluate the philosophical, political, religious, ethical, and social influences of a historical period.

Preview

Think About . . .
Suggest to students that before they begin reading this introduction, they first make a list of all the essay's subheadings and then read the Fast Facts box on p. 14.

DIRECT TEACHING

A **Content-Area Connections**

Geography: Great Britain
You might wish to point out to students that Great Britain, or Britain, is an island comprising England, Scotland, and Wales. The modern nation known as the United Kingdom includes Great Britain and Northern Ireland (the northern part of the neighboring island of Ireland) plus several smaller islands. Collectively this group of large and small islands is also known as the British Isles.

B **Exploring the Historical Period**
IBERIANS
The earliest settlers in Britain were called Iberians because it is thought they originally came from the Iberian Peninsula (the peninsula of present-day Portugal and Spain).

The Anglo-Saxons 449–1066
by David Adams Leeming

PREVIEW

Think About...
The United States would not be what it is today without its British legacy—in law, literature, and language.

As you read about this period, look for answers to the following questions:

- What specifically did America inherit from Britain in terms of our political system, law, and language?
- What was the influence of Christianity on Britain?
- What was the heroic ideal of Anglo-Saxon Britain?

SKILLS FOCUS
Collection introduction (pages 4–17) covers
Literary Skills
Evaluate the philosophical, political, religious, ethical, and social influences of a historical period.

A Isolated from the European continent, rain-drenched and often fogged in but also green and dotted with thatched cottages, quaint stone churches, and mysterious stone ruins, the island of Great Britain seems made for elves, legends, and poets. If this land of mystery, beauty, and melancholy weather has produced Stonehenge, Robin Hood, and Shakespeare, it has also produced the theory of gravity, the Industrial Revolution, radar, penicillin, and the Beatles.

The British Legacy

We tend to associate the British with their monarchy and their former empire. We should also remember, however, that while most of the world suffered under various forms of tyranny, the British from the time of the Magna Carta (1215) were gradually creating a political system "by and for the people" that remains today a source of envy and inspiration for many nations. Although Americans rebelled against British rule in 1776, the United States would not be what it is today without the legacy of British common law—with its emphasis on personal rights and freedom. Nor would the United States be what it is today without the British parliamentary government, British literature, and the English language.

B This relatively small island of Great Britain has been invaded and settled many times: first by ancient people we call the Iberians, then by the Celts (kelts), by the Romans, by the Angles and Saxons, by the Vikings, and by the Normans. Whatever we think of as British today owes something to each of these invaders.

6 Collection 1 The Anglo-Saxons

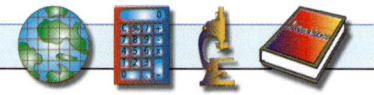

CONTENT-AREA CONNECTIONS

Culture: Ancient Civilizations
Students may need to be reminded that ancient civilizations, some of which were quite advanced, had arisen in other parts of the world well before the time period discussed in this essay. For example, the great pyramids had already been built along the Nile. City-states had risen and fallen in Mesopotamia. Persia had already united many lands, and China was a unified, powerful empire. The beginnings of democracy had already come and gone in Greece. By contrast, Britain was a green, dark, isolated, sleepy island where civilization and empire had yet to bloom.

The Spirit of the Celts

When Greek travelers visited what is now Great Britain in the fourth century B.C., they found an island settled by tall blond warriors who called themselves Celts. Among these island Celts was a group called Brythons—Britons—who left their permanent stamp in one of the names eventually adopted for the land they settled (Britain).

The religion of the Celts seems to have been a form of **animism,** from the Latin word for "spirit." The Celts saw spirits everywhere—in rivers, trees, stones, ponds, fire, and thunder. These spirits, or gods, controlled all aspects of existence, and they had to be constantly satisfied. Priests, called Druids, acted as intermediaries between the gods and the people. Sometimes ritual dances were called for, sometimes even human sacrifice. Some think that Stonehenge—that array of huge stones on Salisbury Plain in Wiltshire—was used by the Druids for religious rites having to do with the lunar and solar cycles.

> *All the Britons dye their bodies with woad, which produces a blue color, and this gives them a more terrifying appearance in battle. They wear their hair long, and shave the whole of their bodies except the head and the upper lip.*
>
> —Julius Caesar

Stonehenge, consisting of large sandstone blocks and smaller bluestone pillars.

History: Stonehenge

Built in three stages, Stonehenge (c. 3100–1100 B.C.) is the best known of many ancient stone sites in the British Isles. The name comes from the Saxon, combining *stone* and *henge,* "hang"—thus, a place of hanging stone. Stonehenge stands at the top of a gentle slope among the dry grasslands of the Salisbury Plain, in southern England. Why these huge stones were arranged in their positions and how they were moved to their present location has been a great mystery. (Some of the pillars, which weigh up to four tons, are made of a type of bluestone believed to have been transported 240 miles from southwestern Wales.) Today, most archaeologists believe that the site served as a ceremonial gathering place for ancient religious functions and that the stones were arranged to facilitate the observation of astronomical events, such as the solstices.

DIRECT TEACHING

C Exploring the Culture
THE CELTS AND THEIR DESCENDANTS

From about 700 B.C., the Celts dominated most of western and central Europe. Skilled artisans, they introduced the use of iron to the rest of Europe. They also had a highly developed religion and a legal system that specified individual rights. The language of the Celts was dominant in Britain until around the fifth century A.D. Descendants of the Celts still live in Cornwall, the highlands of Scotland, Ireland, Wales, and Brittany (in northwest France). Welsh, Scots Gaelic, and Irish are forms of the Celtic language that may still be heard today. The Welsh refer to themselves as *cymry,* meaning "fellow countrymen," emphasizing their role as the true native Britons. Cymraeg, the language of Wales, shares origins with languages still spoken in geographic areas that range from the Hebrides in the northwest Atlantic to Brittany.

D Exploring the Culture
THE DRUIDS

Druids are known to have existed since the third century B.C. The word *druid* means "knowing the oak tree" and may derive from the fact that these Celtic priests seem to have performed their religious ceremonies in oak groves. They considered oak trees sacred, as well as the mistletoe that grows on oaks. (The custom of kissing under mistletoe apparently originated with the Druids.) The Druids constituted a priestly upper class within Celtic society. They may have studied to become priests for as long as twenty years, learning great numbers of religious verses by heart. Responsible for educating the young, the Druids taught a doctrine of transmigration of souls—the belief that the soul was immortal, passing in death from one person to another.

DIRECT TEACHING

A Exploring the Historical Period
BOADICEA

In *Roman History*, Dio Cassius described Boadicea like this: "She was very tall, the glance of her eye most fierce; her voice harsh. A great mass of the reddest hair fell down to her hips. Around her neck was a large golden necklace, and she always wore a tunic of many colors over which she fastened a thick cloak with a broach. Her appearance was terrifying."

B Content-Area Connections

Literature: Irish Myths and Folk Tales

Irish folk tales are also full of fairies, the good folk, and the wee people. These tales reflect the ancient Celtic storytelling tradition and love of magic. You might ask students to read an Irish or Celtic tale and then report on the kinds of characters, plot elements, and motifs they find.

C Exploring the Historical Period
ROMAN ROADS AND WALLS

The five thousand miles of stone roads the Romans built in Britain linked tribal capitals and towns, especially London, York, and Winchester. These roads facilitated trade, the collection of taxes, and the movement of troops. The great defensive wall referred to in this text is Hadrian's Wall, a seventy-three-mile wall that linked the North Sea and the Atlantic near the present-day border between England and Scotland. Hadrian's Wall held back the marauding Picts and Scots for 250 years. Along this wall were seventeen large stone forts used to house the Roman legions that were guarding the frontier.

A Boadicea, queen of a Briton tribe, was flogged by the Romans after they had plundered her dead husband's property. She led the Britons in a fierce retaliation.

Boadicea found herself at the head of a numerous army, and nearly all the Britons within reach rallied to her standard. There followed an up-rush of hatred from the abyss, which is a measure of the cruelty of the conquest. It was a scream of rage against invincible oppression. . . . Her monument on the Thames Embankment opposite Big Ben reminds us of the harsh cry of liberty or death which has echoed down the ages.

—Winston S. Churchill

The Celtic Heroes and Heroines: A Magical World

The mythology of the Celts has influenced British and Irish writers to this day. Sir Thomas Malory (see page 192), in the fifteenth century, having time on his hands while in jail, gathered together the Celtic legends about a warrior named Arthur. He mixed these stories generously with chivalric legends from the Continent and produced *Le Morte d'Arthur,* about the king who ultimately became the very embodiment of British values.

Early in the twentieth century, William Butler Yeats used the Celtic myths in his poetry and plays in an attempt to make the Irish aware of their lost heroic past.

B The Celtic stories are very different from the Anglo-Saxon tales that came later (see page 21), although it is the Anglo-Saxon myths that we tend to study in school. Unlike the male-dominated Anglo-Saxon stories, the Celtic legends are full of strong women, like the tall and fierce and very beautiful Queen Maeve of Connacht (kân'ôt) in Ireland. Maeve once led her troops in an epic battle over the ownership of a fabulous white bull whose back was so broad fifty children could play upon it. Celtic stories, unlike the later, brooding Anglo-Saxon stories, leap into the sunlight (no matter how much blood is spilled). Full of fantastic animals, passionate love affairs, and incredible adventures, the Celtic myths take you to enchanted lands where magic and the imagination rule.

The Romans: The Great Administrators

Beginning with an invasion led by Julius Caesar in 55 B.C. and culminating in one organized by Emperor Claudius about a hundred years later, the Celts were finally conquered by the legions of Rome. Using the administrative genius that enabled them to hold dominion over much of the known world, the Romans provided the armies and organization that prevented further serious invasions of Britain for several hundred years. **C** They built a network of roads (some still used today) and a great defensive wall seventy-three miles long. During Roman rule, Christianity, which would later become a unifying force, gradually took hold under the

A god, perhaps with sacrificial victims, from the Gundestrup caldron (detail) (c. 100 B.C.). Silver. National Museum, Copenhagen. © Erich Lessing/Art Resource, NY.

CONTENT-AREA CONNECTIONS

Literature: Storytellers from Other Cultures

Like the Greek bards or rhapsodes before them, the Irish *ollamhs* were both historians and entertainers who preserved their culture's myths and legends. They studied philosophy, astronomy, and magic and had to know 250 basic tales plus hundreds of variations. The Irish *shanachies,* the tellers of tales of history, were entrusted with 178 accounts.

Other cultures have their traditional storytellers, too. These include Navajo singers, who recite stories in Blessingway ceremonies that last for days, and the Inuit of the far north, who use whalebone knives to trace scenes from their traditional stories in the snow and mud. All these storytellers preserve oral traditions and in the end influence the written literature of their people.

King Sweyn and his Danish troops arrive in England, from a manuscript (c. 14th century).
The British Library, London.

leadership of European missionaries. The old Celtic religion began to vanish.

If the Romans had stayed, Londoners today might speak Italian. But the Romans had troubles at home. By A.D. 409, they had evacuated their troops from Britain, leaving roads, walls, villas, and great public baths, but no central government. Without Roman control, Britain was a country of separate clans. The resulting weakness made the island ripe for a series of successful invasions by non-Christian peoples from the Germanic regions of continental Europe.

The Anglo-Saxons Sweep Ashore

This time the attack came from the north. In the middle of the fifth century, the invaders, Angles and Saxons from Germany and Jutes from Denmark, crossed the North Sea. They drove out the old Britons and eventually settled the greater part of Britain. The language of the Anglo-Saxons became the dominant language in the land that was to take a new name—Engla land, or England—from the Angles.

The Anglo-Saxons 9

DIRECT TEACHING

VIEWING THE ART

This illustration of King Sweyn's eleventh-century invasion of England is notable for its lack of historical accuracy. The illustrator has made no attempt to represent Sweyn's Viking ship and the soldiers' armor as they were. Instead, he has drawn a boat and soldiers that resemble the boats and soldiers that he would have been familiar with in his own century.

Activity. Ask what the illustration's lack of historical accuracy suggests about the medieval approach to history. [Medieval artisans were not concerned with how customs changed from one historical period to another.]

D Reading Skills
Monitoring comprehension.
Make sure students understand that the "old Britons" and the "Celts" are the same people. The terms are being used interchangeably.

E Exploring the Historical Period
TACITUS ON THE ANGLES
At the height of the Roman Empire, the Roman historian Tacitus (c. 56–c. 120) described the Germanic tribes of the North, including the Angles, as having these positive attributes: love of freedom, chaste women, and lack of public extravagance.

DIFFERENTIATING INSTRUCTION

Learners Having Difficulty
Take time to go over the way this essay is organized, pointing out the subheads, the preview section, the boxed list of key ideas (p. 11), the boxed mini-essay (p. 12), the boxed Fast Facts lists, and the review feature.

English-Language Learners
Help students understand the idioms in the essay, using these examples: "who *left their permanent stamp* in one of the names" (p. 7); "Christianity . . . gradually *took hold*" (p. 8); and "Warfare was *the order of the day*" (p. 12).

Special Education Students
For lessons designed for special education students, see *Holt Reading Solutions*.

Advanced Learners
Enrichment. Ask students to think about what they would and would not have liked about living in Anglo-Saxon times; they may develop their ideas into an essay or poem.

The Anglo-Saxons 9

DIRECT TEACHING

A Content-Area Connections

Literature: King Arthur
Students may read more about King Arthur in Sir Thomas Malory's treatment of the Arthur legend, *Le Morte d'Arthur* (c. 1469); Alfred, Lord Tennyson's *Idylls of the King* (1859–1885); or T. H. White's novel *The Once and Future King* (1958).

B Exploring the Historical Period

KING ALFRED THE GREAT
King Alfred truly deserves the appellation "the great." Not only did he help save Wessex and other kingdoms in England from the Danes, but he also helped create a cohesive English society from a collection of small, fractious kingdoms. In addition, he restored cities destroyed during invasions and revived interest in learning and in the English language.

VIEWING THE ART

The Alfred jewel shows an enameled figure of a man holding two scepters. The inscription around the edge reads: "Alfred ordered me to be made."

Activity. Ask students what symbolic significance the two scepters might have. [Possible response: They symbolized the political unity Alfred was trying to achieve.]

Reconstructed Anglo-Saxon village in West Stow, Suffolk, England. The communal hall is at the right.

The latest newcomers did not have an easy time of it. The Celts put up a strong resistance before they retreated into Wales, in the far west of the country. There traces of their culture, especially their language, can still be found. One of the heroic Celtic leaders was a **A** Welsh chieftain called Arthur, who developed in legend as Britain's "once and future king."

Unifying Forces: Alfred the Great and Christianity

At first, Anglo-Saxon England was no more politically unified than Celtic Britain had been. The country was **B** divided into several independent principalities, each with its own "king." It was not until King Alfred of Wessex (reigned 871–899), also known as Alfred the Great, led the Anglo-Saxons against the invading Danes that England became in any true sense a nation. The Danes were one of the fierce Viking peoples who crossed the cold North

Gold and enamel jewel (9th century) thought to have belonged to King Alfred, possibly the handle to a pointer used for following manuscript text.
Ashmolean Museum, Oxford, England.

Primary and Secondary Sources

The Historian's View
Here is how a modern historian, C. Warren Hollister, describes King Alfred the Great: "Like all successful leaders of the age, Alfred was an able warrior. But more than that, he was a brilliant, imaginative organizer who systematized military recruitment and founded the English navy, seeing clearly that Christian Europe could not hope to drive back the Vikings without challenging them on the seas. He filled his land with fortresses which served both as defensive strongholds and as places of sanctuary for the agrarian population in time of war. . . . Alfred clarified and rationalized the laws of his people, enforced them strictly, and ruled with an authority such as no Anglo-Saxon king had exercised before his time.

"King Alfred was also a scholar and a patron of learning. . . . By Alfred's time, Latin—the key to classical Christian culture—was almost

Sea in their dragon-prowed boats in the eighth and ninth centuries. Plundering and destroying everything in their path, the Danes eventually took over and settled in parts of northeast and central England.

It is possible that even King Alfred would have failed to unify the Anglo-Saxons had it not been for the gradual reemergence of Christianity in Britain. Irish and Continental missionaries converted the Anglo-Saxon kings, whose subjects converted also. Christianity provided a common faith and common system of morality and right conduct; it also linked England to Europe. Under Christianity and Alfred, Anglo-Saxons fought to protect their people, their culture, and their church from the ravages of the Danes. Alfred's reign began the shaky dominance of Wessex kings in southern England. Alfred's descendants—Ethelfleda, a brilliant military leader and strategist, and her brother Edward—carried on his battle against the Danes.

The battle continued until both the Anglo-Saxons and the Danes were defeated in 1066 by William, duke of Normandy, and his invading force of Normans from northwestern France.

Anglo-Saxon Life: The Warm Hall, the Cold World

In 1939, in Sutton Hoo (in Suffolk, England), archaeologists discovered a treasure that had been under the earth for thirteen hundred years. This enormous ship-grave contained the imprint of a huge wooden ship and a vast treasure trove—all of which had been buried with a great king or noble warrior. There was no trace of the king or warrior himself, but his sword lay there, along with other

What Does "Anglo-Saxon England" Mean?

Here are some key features of this age of warriors:

- Anglo-Saxon society developed from kinship groups led by a strong chief.
- The people farmed, maintained local governments, and created fine crafts, especially metalwork.
- Christianity eventually replaced the old warrior religion, linking England to continental Europe.
- Monasteries served as centers of learning and preserved works from the older oral tradition.
- English—not just the Church's Latin—gained respect as a written language.

The coronation of King Harold, from the Bayeux Tapestry (detail) (11th century).
Musée de la tapisserie, Bayeux, France.

unknown in England. [He] gathered scholars from far and wide—England, Wales, the continent—and set them to work teaching Latin and translating Latin classics into the Anglo-Saxon language. . . . Alfred's intellectual revival . . . was a salvage operation rather than an outburst of originality. He was both modest and accurate when he described himself as one who wandered through a great forest collecting timber with which others could build."

The King's View

In the preface to Boethius's *Consolation of Philosophy* (which King Alfred translated from the Latin), the king describes his own philosophy of leadership: "To be brief, I may say that it has always been my wish to live honorably, and after my death to leave to those who come after me my memory in good works."

DIRECT TEACHING

A Exploring the Culture
ANGLO-SAXON SOCIAL CLASSES

An agricultural, seminomadic people, the Anglo-Saxons had a two-class society: the *thanes*, or earls, who ruled and were related to the leader of the tribe, and the *churls*, or bondservants, whose ancestors had been captured by the tribe. Although they admired their warriors, the Anglo-Saxons insisted on a social organization based on more than courage, a society with strict laws and a sense of obligation to others. An absolute ruler and mighty warrior, the Anglo-Saxon king nevertheless consulted with the *witan* ("wise men"), an assembly of respected earls. The churls provided the hard labor for this society and were bound to the earls' service unless they could earn possessions and special royal favor to become freemen (independent landholders).

A CLOSER LOOK

This feature discusses the property rights and religious opportunities of women in Anglo-Saxon society.

B Exploring the Culture
THE ROLE OF WOMEN

An upper-class woman (the wife of an earl, or *thane*) would supervise the weaving and dyeing of clothes, the slaughter of livestock, and (most important) the brewing of mead—an alcoholic beverage made from fermented honey and water. Because honey was so essential, beekeeping was also an important chore.

C Background
Whitby Abbey

Hild, sometimes called Saint Hilda, originally founded Whitby Abbey for both monks and nuns. Until it was destroyed by the Vikings in 867, the abbey was the chief school of learning in the north.

Helmet fragment (7th century) from the Sutton Hoo ship treasure, Suffolk, England.
The Bridgeman Art Library, New York/British Museum, London.

meticulously decorated treasures of gold, silver, and bronze—his purse, coins, helmet, buckle, serving vessels, and harp. This grave can't help but remind us of the huge burial mound erected in memory of the king Beowulf.

As these Sutton Hoo ship treasures show, the Anglo-Saxons were not barbarians, though they are frequently depicted that way. However, they did not lead luxurious lives either, nor were their lives dominated by learning or the arts. Warfare was the order of the day. As *Beowulf* shows, law and order, at least in the early days, were the responsibility of the leader in any given group, whether family, clan, tribe, or kingdom. Fame and success, even survival, were gained only through loyalty to the leader, especially during war, and success was measured in gifts from the leader. Beowulf, as you will see in the story that follows, makes his name and gains riches by defeating the monsters who try to destroy King Hrothgar.

A CLOSER LOOK: SOCIAL INFLUENCES

Women in Anglo-Saxon Culture

INFORMATIONAL TEXT

Anglo-Saxon culture, with its emphasis on warfare, sounds as if it would be an inhospitable place for women. In fact, women had rights in this society, rights that were sharply curtailed after the Norman Conquest in 1066.

Evidence from wills first used during the later Anglo-Saxon period shows that women inherited and held property. Even when married, women still retained control over their own property. In fact, a prospective husband had to offer a woman a substantial gift (called the *morgengifu*, "morning-gift") of money and land. The woman (not her family or her husband) had personal control over this gift: She could give it away, sell it, or bequeath it as she chose.

Christianity also offered opportunities for women. Women joined religious communities, and some women became powerful abbesses. These abbesses, usually women from noble families, were in charge of large double houses that included both a monastery and a nunnery. Hild (614–680), the abbess of Whitby (in present-day Yorkshire), was one of the most famous of these women. Hild accumulated an immense library and turned Whitby into a center of learning. Vikings sacked Whitby Abbey in the ninth century. The ruins of a monastery later founded at the same site still stand today, high atop cliffs overlooking the wild, gray North Sea.

The ruins of Whitby Abbey, Yorkshire, England.
The Bridgeman Art Library. Private Collection.

12 Collection 1 The Anglo-Saxons

Conducting a Historical Investigation

The role of women. Students who are interested in the role of women in Anglo-Saxon society might do additional research on the topic. A good resource to start with is the book *Women in Anglo-Saxon England and the Impact of 1066,* by Christine E. Fell (Bloomington: Indiana University Press, 1984). You might also give students tips on how to conduct a Web search on this topic (for example, they might use the keywords *Anglo-Saxon women*). Students can present the results of their research in the form of a written report, an oral presentation, a visual display, or even a skit with other students.

This pattern of loyal dependency was basic to Anglo-Saxon life. Such loyalty grew out of a need to protect the group from the terrors of an enemy-infested wilderness—a wilderness that became particularly frightening during the long, bone-chilling nights of winter. In most of England, the Anglo-Saxons tended to live close to their animals in single-family homesteads, wooden buildings that surrounded a communal court or a warm, fire-lit chieftain's hall. This cluster of buildings was protected by a wooden stockade fence. The arrangement contributed to a sense of security and to the close relationship between leader and followers. It also encouraged the Anglo-Saxon tendency to participate in community discussion and rule by consensus.

Three standing figures (Odin, Thor, and Freyr) in tunics, from a Viking tapestry (12th century).
Statens Historiska Museet, Stockholm.

The god Odin being eaten by the wolf Fenrir, from a Viking stone carving.
Manx Museum, Isle of Man, England. © Werner Forman/Art Resource, New York.

DIRECT TEACHING

VIEWING THE ART

In medieval Europe, pictures were an important means of recording and communicating information. Thus, tapestries were probably used as a means of educating people and keeping records of important events.

Activity. Ask students to speculate about why Norse gods are featured in this tapestry. [Possible response: Perhaps the Vikings wanted to pay homage to their gods through art or to depict a story about them.]

D Exploring the Culture
CHIEFTAINS AND FOLLOWERS

The chieftain and his followers were bound to each other until death. If the lord was killed, his warriors had to avenge his death or die beside him. After a battle, the warriors gathered in the mead hall of the lord and feasted at trestle tables and mead benches studded with gold.

CONTENT-AREA CONNECTIONS

Art: Anglo-Saxon Workmanship

Many gifts from a chieftain to his loyal followers were decorative objects. In fact, the art of the Anglo-Saxons was functional art—drinking horns, buckles, clasps, purses, and above all, beautifully engraved weapons. Weapons such as swords were sometimes engraved with runes, letters from an alphabet known as the *futhark*, thought to provide magical protection from harm. This runic alphabet, however, was used strictly for ornamental inscriptions, not for lengthy written communication. (A fine example of a runic inscription can be seen in the photograph of the Franks casket on p. 28.)

DIRECT TEACHING

A **Exploring the Historical Period**
SAINT PATRICK

A famous legend about Saint Patrick concerns the shamrock, the three-leaf plant that is the national flower and symbol of Ireland. Patrick supposedly used the shamrock to explain the doctrine of the holy Trinity (the three-person godhead of Christianity).

B **Exploring the Historical Period**
IRISH CIVILIZATION

The golden age of Irish civilization was eventually disrupted by the arrival of Scandinavian invaders near the end of the eighth century.

C **Reading Skills**
Recognizing cultural assumptions. Some students may be offended by this view of Christianity as a force of light gleaming against "the darkness." Ask students to think about what kinds of cultural assumptions Churchill's words reflect.

VIEWING THE ART

Written and illuminated during the seventh century in the Monastery of Lindisfarne on Holy Island (off the northwest coast of Northumbria, England), the Lindisfarne Gospels demonstrate the monks' interest not only in biblical studies but also in artistry. The designs are influenced by Celtic art, and the marginal notes, which were added later, are written in the Anglo-Saxon language.

Activity. What does the Lindisfarne Gospels' mixture of Celtic design and Anglo-Saxon marginal notes suggest about early medieval Christianity? [Possible response: The spread of Christianity in Europe encouraged cross-cultural exchange.]

A Light from Ireland

Ireland had historical good luck in the fifth century. Unlike England and the rest of Europe, Ireland, isolated and surrounded by wild seas, was not overrun by the Germanic invaders. Then, in 432, the whole of Celtic Ireland was converted to Christianity by a Romanized Briton named Patricius (Patrick). Patrick had been seized by Irish slave traders when he was a teenager and had been held in bondage by a sheepherder in Ireland for six years. He escaped captivity, became a bishop, and returned to convert his former captors. His success was speedy and undying. From 432 to 750, while Europe and England sank into constant warfare, confusion, and ignorance, Ireland experienced a golden age. The Irish monks founded monasteries that became sanctuaries of learning for refugee scholars from Europe and England. Thus it was in Ireland that Christianity, in the words of Winston Churchill, "burned and gleamed through the darkness."

Opening of *St. Matthew's Gospel,* from the Lindisfarne Gospels (7th century). Note the scribe's comments in the margins.
The British Library, London.

The Christian Monasteries: The Ink Froze

In the death-shadowed world of the Anglo-Saxons, the poets or bards provided one element of hope: the possibility that heroic deeds might be enshrined in the society's memory. Another element of hope was supplied by Christianity. The monasteries served as centers of learning in this period, just as they would in the Middle Ages. In England the cultural and spiritual influence of monasteries existed right alongside the older Anglo-Saxon religion. In fact, the monasteries preserved not only the Latin and Greek classics but also some of the great works of popular literature, such as *Beowulf.*

Conducting a Historical Investigation

Non-Christian civilizations. Some students might be interested in researching what various non-Christian cultures throughout the world were accomplishing during the Irish golden age of Christianity (see annotation B above). They can report back to the class in an oral presentation or prepare an illustrated time line showing some of the artistic, mathematical, and scientific achievements of these civilizations.

Monks assigned to the monastery's scriptorium, or writing room, probably spent almost all their daylight hours copying manuscripts by hand. (Printing was still eight hundred years away in England.) The scriptorium was in a covered walkway (the cloister) open to a court. Makeshift walls of oiled paper or glass helped somewhat, but the British Isles in winter are cold; the ink could freeze. Picture a shivering scribe, hunched over sheepskin "paper," called vellum, pressing with a quill pen, obeying a rule of silence: That's how seriously the Church took learning.

The Rise of the English Language

Latin alone remained the language of serious study in England until the time of King Alfred. During his reign, Alfred instituted the *Anglo-Saxon Chronicle,* a lengthy running history of England that covered the earliest days and continued until 1154. Partly because of King Alfred's efforts, English began to gain respect as a language of culture. Only then did the Old English stories and poetry preserved by the monks come to be recognized as great works of literature.

Page from the *Anglo-Saxon Chronicle* (detail).
By permission of The British Library, London.

REVIEW

Talk About . . .

Turn back to the Think About questions at the beginning of this introduction to the Anglo-Saxon period (page 6). Write down your responses, and get together with a classmate to compare and discuss your views.

Write About . . .

Contrasting Literary Periods

Heroism, then and now. The mythology and literature of the early Celts and Anglo-Saxons were filled with larger-than-life heroes. The Anglo-Saxon heroes were exclusively male, but Celtic history and mythology record some powerful female warriors. How do these ancient views of heroism compare with today's notions of personal greatness? In a brief essay, discuss the ways in which individuals gain fame and fortune today. How are their accomplishments celebrated and remembered?

DIRECT TEACHING

D Exploring the Historical Period
MONASTERIES
Before Henry VIII destroyed the English monasteries in the early sixteenth century, there were, in Yorkshire alone, twenty-eight abbeys, twenty-six priories, twenty-three convents, thirty friaries, and thirteen cells. All are in ruins today.

E Exploring the Historical Period
ANGLO-SAXON CHRONICLE
This chronicle, kept by generations of anonymous scribes, tells of weak kings, greedy abbots, and proud barons. It also chronicles various natural events of the period. Although it is kept in the British Library, an electronic edition is available on the Internet. This chronicle was the first important prose work in English.

Review

Talk About . . .
Modeling. You might model answering the first bulleted question on p. 6 as follows: "After reading the first page of this essay, I see it states that America inherited British common law with its emphasis on personal rights, British parliamentary government, and the English language."

Primary Source

The English Language
In his preface to the English translation of Bede's *Historia Ecclesiastica,* King Alfred explains his emphasis on English: "Therefore it seems better to me . . . that we should all translate certain books which are most necessary for all men to know, into the language that we can all understand, and also arrange it . . . so that all the youth of freemen . . . are able to read English writing as well."

Check Test: True-False
1. Celtic and Anglo-Saxon stories are so similar that they are often confused. [F]
2. The Roman occupation provided several hundred years of stability for Britain. [T]
3. When the Anglo-Saxons conquered Britain, renaming it England, the Celts retreated to Ireland. [F]
4. *Scop* is another word for "warrior." [F]

SKILLS FOCUS, pp. 18–43

Grade-Level Skills

■ **Literary Skills**

Analyze archetypes, including the epic hero.

■ **Literary Skills**

Analyze the way the theme of a selection represents a comment on life, using evidence from the text to support your claim.

■ **Literary Skills**

Understand and analyze alliteration and kennings.

More About *Beowulf*

Background. An epic is sometimes called a heroic poem. *Beowulf,* the *Iliad,* and the *Odyssey* are all heroic poems or epics. They are long narratives about the adventures of larger-than-life characters. Epics tend to have these characteristics:

- The hero is a great leader who is identified strongly with a particular people or society.
- The setting is broad and often includes supernatural realms, especially the land of the dead.
- The hero does great deeds in battle or undertakes an extraordinary journey or quest.
- Sometimes gods or other supernatural or fantastic beings take part in the action.
- The story is told in heightened language.

VIEWING THE ART

The Sutton Hoo helmet was found in fragments and reassembled. The face mask visible on this unfinished reconstruction is made of bronze eyebrows that are inlaid with silver wire. Gilded bronze boar's heads—symbols of strength and courage—decorate the ends of the eyebrows. Two dragon heads lie nose to nose in the center. The nose, eyebrows and dragon form a bird, probably a bird of prey, with outstretched wings. For more about the treasure of Sutton Hoo, see p. 24 of the Teacher's Edition.

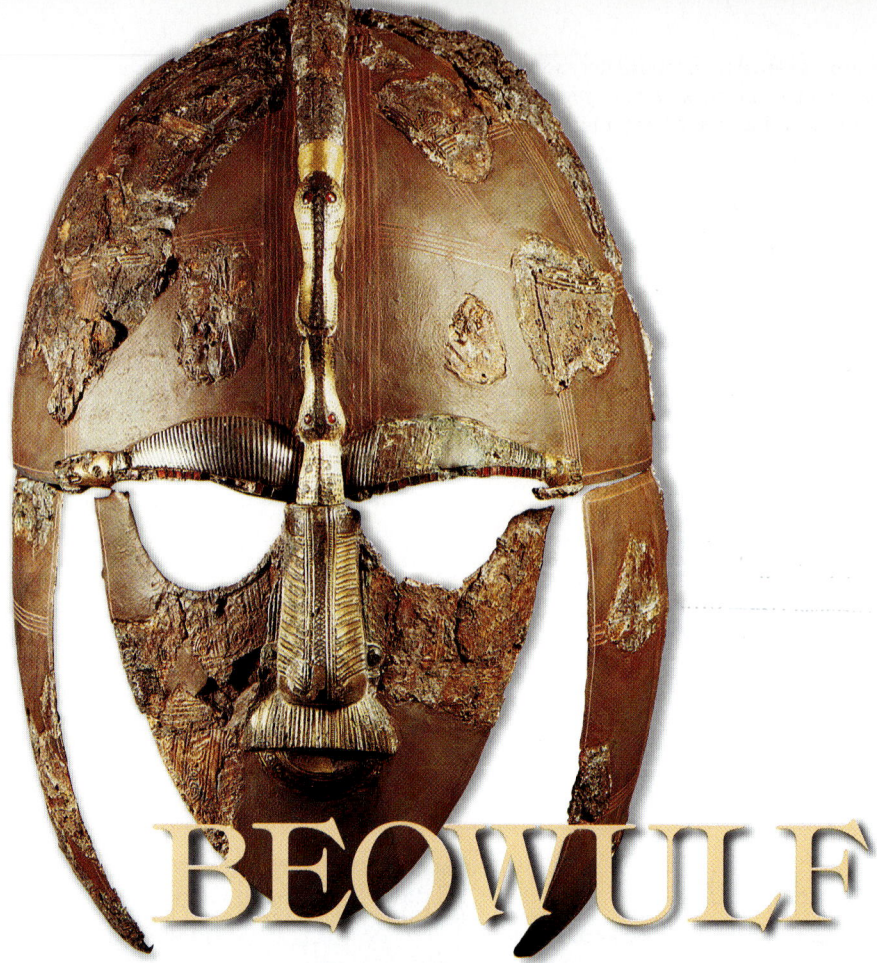

BEOWULF

Sutton Hoo helmet (7th century), from the Sutton Hoo ship treasure, Suffolk, England
British Museum, London.

Beowulf is to England what Homer's *Iliad* (see page 57) and *Odyssey* are to ancient Greece: It is the first great work of the English national literature—the mythical and literary record of a formative stage of English civilization. It is also an epic of the heroic sources of English culture. As such, *Beowulf* uses a host of traditional **motifs,** or recurring elements, associated with heroic literature all over the world.

The epic tells of Beowulf (his name may mean "bear"), a Geat from Sweden who crosses the sea to Denmark in a quest to rescue King Hrothgar's people from the demonic monster Grendel. Like most early heroic literature, *Beowulf* is an oral epic. It was handed down, with changes and embellishments, from one minstrel to another. The stories of *Beowulf,* like those of all oral epics, are traditional, familiar to the audiences who crowded around the harpist-bards in the communal halls at night. They are the stories

RESOURCES: READING

Planning
- One-Stop Planner CD-ROM with ExamView Test Generator

Differentiating Instruction
- Holt Reading Solutions
- The Holt Reader
- Holt Adapted Reader
- Supporting Instruction in Spanish

- Audio CD Library, Selections and Summaries in Spanish

Vocabulary
- Vocabulary Development

Grammar and Language
- Daily Language Activities

Assessment
- Holt Assessment: Literature, Reading, and Vocabulary

of dream and legend, archetypal tales of monsters and god-fashioned weapons, of descents to the underworld and fights with dragons, of the hero's quest and a community threatened by the powers of evil.

The Sources of *Beowulf*

By the standards of Homer, whose epics run to nearly 15,000 lines, *Beowulf* is short—approximately 3,200 lines. It was composed in Old English, probably in Northumbria, in northeastern England, sometime between 700 and 750. The world it depicts, however, is much older, that of the early sixth century. Much of the poem's material is based on early folk legends—some Celtic, some Scandinavian. Since the scenery described is the coast of Northumbria, not Scandinavia, it has been assumed that the poet who wrote the version that has come down to us was Northumbrian. Given the Christian elements in the epic, it is thought that this poet may have been a monk.

The only manuscript of *Beowulf* we have dates from the year 1000 and is now in the British Museum in London. Burned and stained, it was discovered in the eighteenth century: Somehow it had survived Henry VIII's destruction of the monasteries two hundred years earlier.

The Translations of *Beowulf*

Part One of the text you are about to read is from Burton Raffel's popular 1963 translation of the epic. Part Two is from the Irish poet Seamus Heaney's award-winning, bestselling translation of the work, published in 2000.

Prow of the Oseberg ship.
University Museum of National Antiquities, Oslo, Norway.

People, Monsters, and Places

Beowulf: a Geat, son of Edgetho (Ecgtheow) and nephew of Higlac (Hygelac), king of the Geats.

Grendel: man-eating monster who lives at the bottom of a foul mere, or mountain lake. His name might be related to the Old Norse *grindill,* meaning "storm," or *grenja,* "bellow."

Herot: golden guest hall built by King Hrothgar, the Danish ruler. It was decorated with the antlers of stags; the name means "hart [stag] hall." Scholars think Herot might have been built near Lejre on the coast of Zealand, in Denmark.

Hrothgar: king of the Danes, builder of Herot. He had once befriended Beowulf's father. His father was called Healfdane (which probably means "half Dane").

Wiglaf: a Geat warrior, one of Beowulf's select band and the only one to help him in his final fight.

More About *Beowulf*

Background. The *Beowulf* manuscript is part of a volume, or codex, that also contains four other works in Old English: *The Passion of St. Christopher, The Wonders of the East, Alexander's Letter to Aristotle,* and a fragment of *Judith.* Interestingly, Beowulf is the only character who is not also found in earlier legends or in actual history. The Grendel character, for instance, almost surely has his roots in the Old Norse stories of the *draugar,* or dead men of supernatural strength who walked at night, spreading evil and terror. Often a *draugar* had a mother even more terrible than he—a *ketta,* or "she-cat."

VIEWING THE ART

The Oseberg ship, unearthed in 1904, may have been the burial ship of Asa, a Viking queen whose active life belied the passive role that women were believed to have played at this time in history. Married against her will to a Norwegian king, Asa had her husband killed and ruled alone until her death in 850. Accompanying Asa on her voyage to the afterlife were the body of a maidservant, priceless gold and gems (which subsequently were stolen by looters), and objects such as sleds and a wagon. These would permit Asa to travel in the afterlife as much as the Vikings enjoyed traveling while living.

Activity. Ask students how funerals for great leaders are conducted today.

- *One-Stop Planner* CD-ROM with ExamView Test Generator
- Holt Online Assessment

Internet
- go.hrw.com (Keyword: LE5 12-1)
- Elements of Literature Online

Media
- Audio CD Library
- Audio CD Library, Selections and Summaries in Spanish
- Fine Art Transparencies

PRETEACHING

Summary ⬆ *above grade level*

The monster Grendel arrives at Herot, the home of the Danish King Hrothgar. He breaks down the door, devours one Geat, and then grabs Beowulf. Beowulf's men find their weapons useless against Grendel's magic; all they can do is look on as their leader and the monster grapple in a symbolic battle between good and evil. With God's help, Beowulf finally rips off Grendel's arm. Mortally wounded, Grendel retreats to his marsh. Beowulf hangs the monster's arm from the rafters of Hrothgar's hall. Everyone rejoices at Beowulf's bravery and their deliverance from Grendel's raids.

To face Grendel's vengeful mother, Beowulf dives to the bottom of the lake where she lives. She attacks him but cannot penetrate his chain-mail shirt. When Beowulf discovers that his sword is useless against her, he continues the fight with his bare hands. Finally, he finds a magic sword, "hammered by giants," and kills Grendel's mother with one fierce blow. He then locates Grendel's body and cuts off the head in revenge for the men whom the monster killed.

Skills Starter

Build prerequisite skills. Have students name any characters in books, movies, or TV programs that can be described as one of the following types: a wise and brave leader, a loyal companion, a mysterious stranger, a villain who plots the downfall of a person or group of people, or a naive young person seeking to become an adult. Explain that these are some of the basic types of characters in literature, called archetypes, that appear in literary traditions around the world.

Before You Read

from Beowulf

Make the Connection
Quickwrite ✏️

This is a story about a hero from the misty reaches of the British past, a hero who faces violence, horror, and even death to save a people in mortal danger. The epic's events took place many centuries ago, but this story still speaks to people today, perhaps because so many of us are in need of a rescuer, a hero.

Take a moment to write about a contemporary hero, real or fictional, and the challenges he or she faces. Describe your hero, and then briefly analyze him or her using these questions:

- What sort of evil or oppression does your hero confront?
- Why does he or she confront evil? What's the motivation?
- For whom does your hero confront evil?
- What virtues does your hero represent?

Literary Focus
The Epic Hero

Beowulf is ancient England's hero, but he is also an **archetype**, or perfect example, of an **epic hero**. In other times, in other cultures, the hero has taken the shape of King Arthur or Gilgamesh (see page 48), or Sundiata or Joan of Arc. In modern America the hero may be a real person, like Martin Luther King, Jr., or a fictional character, like Shane in the western novel of the same name. The hero archetype in *Beowulf* is the dragon slayer, representing a besieged community facing evil forces that lurk in the cold darkness. Grendel, the monster lurking in the depths of the lagoon, may represent all of those threatening forces.

Beowulf, like all epic heroes, possesses superior physical strength and supremely ethical standards. He embodies the highest ideals of Anglo-Saxon culture. In his quest he must defeat monsters that embody dark, destructive powers. At the end of the quest, he is glorified by the people he has saved. If you follow current events, particularly stories concerning people who have gained freedom after years of oppression, you will still see at work this impulse to glorify those people who have set them free. You might also see this impulse in the impressive monuments—and great tourist attractions—in Washington, D.C.

> The **epic hero** is the central figure in a long narrative that reflects the values and heroic ideals of a particular society. An **epic** is a quest story on a grand scale.
>
> *For more on the Epic, see the Handbook of Literary and Historical Terms.*

Vocabulary Development

resolute (rez′·ə·lōōt′) *adj.*: determined.

vehemently (vē′·ə·mənt·lē) *adv.*: violently.

infallible (in·fal′·ə·bəl) *adj.*: unable to fail or be wrong.

furled (furld) *v.*: rolled up.

lavish (lav′ish) *adj.*: extravagant.

assail (ə·sāl′) *v.*: attack.

extolled (ek·stōld′) *v.*: praised.

Viking coin minted in England (10th–11th century). Most such coins consist of precious metals extorted from the British as tribute.
British Museum, London.

INTERNET Vocabulary Practice Keyword: LE5 12-1

SKILLS FOCUS
Literary Skills Understand the archetype of the epic hero.

20 Collection 1 The Anglo-Saxons

Previewing Vocabulary

Have students read the definitions of the Vocabulary words on p. 20 and express each definition in their own words. Then, have students complete the following sentences with the correct Vocabulary word or words.

1. When Jenny was awarded the music scholarship, her parents _____ her for the accomplishment. [extolled]

2. The generals argued quite _____ about the best way to _____ the fortress. [vehemently, assail]

3. Won't you admit your mistake? After all, no one is _____. [infallible]

4. After securing the boat at the dock, I _____ its sail. [furled]

5. The king was _____ in his plan to change his _____ habits and live more simply. [resolute, lavish]

from Beowulf
Part One, translated by Burton Raffel

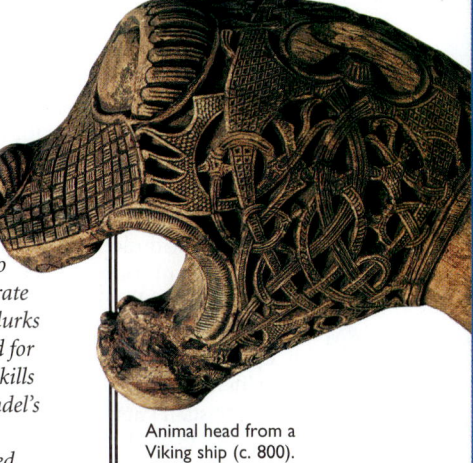

Animal head from a Viking ship (c. 800).
University Museum of National Antiquities, Oslo, Norway.

(Background) First page of *Beowulf* manuscript (c. 1000).
The Art Archive/British Library, London.

As the epic begins, we are introduced to King Hrothgar, a revered and successful leader who has ruled the Danes for many years. He has recently built the mead hall Herot to commemorate his many victories. As Hrothgar's men celebrate and enjoy life in Herot, however, a monster called Grendel lurks in the swamps nearby, seething with resentment and hatred for humans. Eventually Grendel attacks Herot and mercilessly kills thirty of Hrothgar's men. This marks the beginning of Grendel's reign of terror over the Danes, which lasts for twelve years.

Rescue finally comes in the form of a great warrior named Beowulf who hails from the land of the Geats (Sweden). Beowulf hears of Hrothgar's troubles and decides to journey to Denmark with some of his strongest men to do battle with Grendel. Once he arrives, he meets with Hrothgar and boasts of his numerous past achievements, which qualify him to challenge Grendel. Beowulf then announces that he will fight the monster that night without weapons. A celebratory feast ensues. As it ends, Beowulf and his men take the place of Hrothgar's followers and lie down to sleep in Herot. Beowulf, however, is wakeful, eager to meet his enemy. He is not kept waiting long.

THE BATTLE WITH GRENDEL

1

Out from the marsh, from the foot of misty
Hills and bogs, bearing God's hatred,
Grendel came, hoping to kill
Anyone he could trap on this trip to high Herot.
5   He moved quickly through the cloudy night,
Up from his swampland, sliding silently
Toward that gold-shining hall. He had visited Hrothgar's
Home before, knew the way—

Lines have been renumbered and do not correspond to the New American Library edition or the Farrar, Straus, and Giroux edition.

DIRECT TEACHING

A Literary Focus
Rhyme. These lines demonstrate how translators (Burton Raffel, in this case) can use rhyme in surprising ways. There is no end rhyme, but *hot* and *thought* and *know* and *gnaw* are examples of approximate rhyme, and *crowded* and *rows* (ll. 19–20) are an example of eye rhyme. Students may better appreciate the rhymes—and the effect of these lines upon an audience—by reading the lines aloud.

B Reading Skills
Making inferences. Why do you think Beowulf allows Grendel to slaughter one of the Geats before taking action? [Possible responses: Perhaps Beowulf is taking time to formulate a plan of attack; perhaps Grendel simply moves too quickly for Beowulf to stop him.]

VIEWING THE ART

Point out the intricate carvings on the dragonhead horse collar here.

Activity. Have students speculate about why people would decorate such an object. [Possible response: Art was put to practical purposes. The Norse people valued useful objects and lovingly decorated bowls, pins, drinking horns, and swords.]

Responses to Margin Questions

Lines 25–27. This time Beowulf is waiting for him—and this time Grendel will not survive.

Lines 44–56. Beowulf has "harder" hands than anyone else whom Grendel has met, and he is holding onto Grendel with a grip that cracks the mighty monster's claws.

But never, before nor after that night,
10 Found Herot defended so firmly, his reception
So harsh. He journeyed, forever joyless,
Straight to the door, then snapped it open,
Tore its iron fasteners with a touch,
And rushed angrily over the threshold.
15 He strode quickly across the inlaid
Floor, snarling and fierce: His eyes
Gleamed in the darkness, burned with a gruesome
Light. Then he stopped, seeing the hall
Crowded with sleeping warriors, stuffed
20 With rows of young soldiers resting together.
And his heart laughed, he relished the sight,
Intended to tear the life from those bodies
By morning; the monster's mind was hot
With the thought of food and the feasting his belly
25 Would soon know. But fate, that night, intended
Grendel to gnaw the broken bones
Of his last human supper. Human
Eyes were watching his evil steps,
Waiting to see his swift hard claws.
30 Grendel snatched at the first Geat
He came to, ripped him apart, cut
His body to bits with powerful jaws,
Drank the blood from his veins, and bolted
Him down, hands and feet; death
35 And Grendel's great teeth came together,
Snapping life shut. Then he stepped to another
Still body, clutched at Beowulf with his claws,
Grasped at a strong-hearted wakeful sleeper
—And was instantly seized himself, claws
40 Bent back as Beowulf leaned up on one arm.
    That shepherd of evil, guardian of crime,
Knew at once that nowhere on earth
Had he met a man whose hands were harder;
His mind was flooded with fear—but nothing
45 Could take his talons and himself from that tight
Hard grip. Grendel's one thought was to run
From Beowulf, flee back to his marsh and hide there:
This was a different Herot than the hall he had emptied.
But Higlac's follower remembered his final
50 Boast and, standing erect, stopped
The monster's flight, fastened those claws
In his fists till they cracked, clutched Grendel
Closer. The infamous killer fought
For his freedom, wanting no flesh but retreat,
55 Desiring nothing but escape; his claws

Dragonhead from a Viking horse collar (detail) (10th century). Denmark.
National Museum, Copenhagen.

25–27. These lines **foreshadow**, or hint at, the outcome of the battle between Grendel and Beowulf.
? *Grendel has been attacking Herot successfully for years. What will be different about this visit to Herot?*

44–56. "Higlac's follower" is Beowulf. He had earlier sworn to kill Grendel with his bare hands.
? *What details in these lines demonstrate Beowulf's superhuman strength?*

DIFFERENTIATING INSTRUCTION

Advanced Learners
Enrichment. After students have read a portion of the text, have one student ask another questions about the content, about related information from the introductory essays, or about style and language. Then, have students reverse the roles.

Had been caught, he was trapped. That trip to Herot
Was a miserable journey for the writhing monster!
   The high hall rang, its roof boards swayed,
And Danes shook with terror. Down
60 The aisles the battle swept, angry
And wild. Herot trembled, wonderfully
Built to withstand the blows, the struggling
Great bodies beating at its beautiful walls;
Shaped and fastened with iron, inside
65 And out, artfully worked, the building
Stood firm. Its benches rattled, fell
To the floor, gold-covered boards grating
As Grendel and Beowulf battled across them.
Hrothgar's wise men had fashioned Herot
70 To stand forever; only fire,
They had planned, could shatter what such skill had put
Together, swallow in hot flames such splendor
Of ivory and iron and wood. Suddenly
The sounds changed, the Danes started
75 In new terror, cowering in their beds as the terrible
Screams of the Almighty's enemy sang
In the darkness, the horrible shrieks of pain
And defeat, the tears torn out of Grendel's
Taut throat, hell's captive caught in the arms
80 Of him who of all the men on earth
Was the strongest.

2

   That mighty protector of men
Meant to hold the monster till its life
Leaped out, knowing the fiend was no use
To anyone in Denmark. All of Beowulf's
85 Band had jumped from their beds, ancestral
Swords raised and ready, determined
To protect their prince if they could. Their courage
Was great but all wasted: They could hack at Grendel
From every side, trying to open
90 A path for his evil soul, but their points
Could not hurt him, the sharpest and hardest iron
Could not scratch at his skin, for that sin-stained demon
Had bewitched all men's weapons, laid spells
That blunted every mortal man's blade.
95 And yet his time had come, his days
Were over, his death near; down
To hell he would go, swept groaning and helpless
To the waiting hands of still worse fiends.

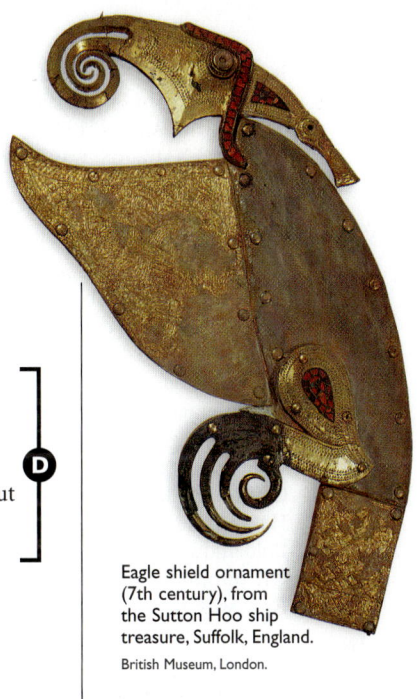

Eagle shield ornament (7th century), from the Sutton Hoo ship treasure, Suffolk, England.
British Museum, London.

76–81. The "Almighty's enemy"—God's enemy—in line 76 refers to Grendel. Earlier in the epic, Grendel's origin is explained: He is the offspring of one of the descendants of Cain, the son of Adam and Eve who killed his brother, Abel, and became the first murderer. Cain was eternally cursed by God and, according to legend, fathered all the evil beings that plague humankind: monsters, demons, and evil spirits.

? *In what ways is this battle between Grendel and Beowulf really a battle between good and evil? What details in the description of the battle make this clear?*

? *88–94. According to these lines, why can't Beowulf's men harm Grendel?*

Beowulf   23

DIRECT TEACHING

C Learners Having Difficulty

Reading inverted sentences. In many sentences in this narrative, the subject is preceded by one or more descriptive phrases. Model for students how to change the clause that begins on l. 64 so that the subject comes first. [The building—shaped and fastened with iron, inside and out, artfully worked—stood firm.] Have students make a similar change to the sentence beginning "Down the aisles the battle swept" (ll. 59–61). [The battle, angry and wild, swept down the aisles.]

D Content-Area Connections

History: Herot
Archaeologists have confirmed that Herot was built of wood held together with iron bands. The gabled roof was overlaid with gold, and the floor was inlaid.

E Advanced Learners

Enrichment. Ask students to explain how this passage shows a tension between the paganism of Beowulf's day and the Christianity of the recorder's day. [Possible response: Grendel is "sin-stained" but also has the power to bewitch and cast spells, suggestive of pagan rites. These lines also say that Grendel is doomed to hell.]

Responses to Margin Questions

Lines 76–81. Beowulf represents humanity and its virtues; Grendel represents hatred and the powers of darkness. The kennings used to describe Grendel—*shepherd of evil, guardian of crime,* and *the infamous killer,* for example—help highlight the distinction.

Lines 88–94. Grendel has put a spell on their weapons. Beowulf then proves his status by using his own hands to battle and best the monster.

CONTENT-AREA CONNECTIONS

Culture: Anglo-Saxon Values
Many cultures have produced poems to celebrate their heroes and to express the values and customs of their civilizations. In *Beowulf,* these ideas include the following items:
- honoring courage over long life
- enjoying feasting, storytelling, and music
- viewing life fatalistically, even within the Christian tradition
- admiring physical strength more than intelligence
- valuing loyalty to the lord or king above all

Individual activity. As students read through *Beowulf,* urge them to note lines or narrative details that suggest these ideas.

DIRECT TEACHING

A Literary Focus

? Epic hero. As this episode ends, what details remind us that Beowulf is a hero of epic proportions, able to represent a people and their values? [Possible response: By rescuing the Danes from evil, Beowulf has fulfilled his promise and covered himself with new glory.]

B Content-Area Connections

History: The Geats
The Geats lived in what is now southwestern Sweden. Higlac, king of the Geats and Beowulf's kinsman, was killed during a raid on the Franks in A.D. 521. The complete epic of *Beowulf* forecasts the Geats' defeat by the Swedes.

Responses to Margin Questions

Lines 99–108. Beowulf rips off Grendel's arm, causing a fatal wound.

Lines 123–126. He hangs the monster's arm from Herot's rafters. The act is a gesture of triumph and an assurance to all at Herot that Grendel will trouble the hall no more.

Lines 131–142. Grendel's slow bleeding to death is suggested by the steaming, boiling water of the lake, evoking the fires of hell. Finally, Grendel dies "in murky darkness."

---

100 Now he discovered—once the afflictor
     Of men, tormentor of their days—what it meant
     To feud with Almighty God: Grendel
     Saw that his strength was deserting him, his claws
     Bound fast, Higlac's brave follower tearing at
105 His hands. The monster's hatred rose higher,
     But his power had gone. He twisted in pain,
     And the bleeding sinews deep in his shoulder
     Snapped, muscle and bone split
     And broke. The battle was over, Beowulf
110 Had been granted new glory: Grendel escaped,
     But wounded as he was could flee to his den,
     His miserable hole at the bottom of the marsh,
     Only to die, to wait for the end
     Of all his days. And after that bloody
115 Combat the Danes laughed with delight.
     He who had come to them from across the sea,
     Bold and strong-minded, had driven affliction
     Off, purged Herot clean. He was happy,
     Now, with that night's fierce work; the Danes
120 Had been served as he'd boasted he'd serve them; Beowulf,
     A prince of the Geats, had killed Grendel,
     Ended the grief, the sorrow, the suffering
     Forced on Hrothgar's helpless people
     By a bloodthirsty fiend. No Dane doubted
125 The victory, for the proof, hanging high
     From the rafters where Beowulf had hung it, was the monster's
     Arm, claw and shoulder and all.

3

     And then, in the morning, crowds surrounded
     Herot, warriors coming to that hall
     From faraway lands, princes and leaders
130 Of men hurrying to behold the monster's
     Great staggering tracks. They gaped with no sense
     Of sorrow, felt no regret for his suffering,
     Went tracing his bloody footprints, his beaten
     And lonely flight, to the edge of the lake
135 Where he'd dragged his corpselike way, doomed
     And already weary of his vanishing life.
     The water was bloody, steaming and boiling
     In horrible pounding waves, heat
     Sucked from his magic veins; but the swirling
140 Surf had covered his death, hidden
     Deep in murky darkness his miserable
     End, as hell opened to receive him.

Detail of three-ringed gold collar (6th century).
Statens Historiska Museer, Stockholm.

? 99–108. How does Beowulf defeat Grendel?

? 123–126. How does Beowulf prove his victory over Grendel? Why might he do this?

? 131–142. What has happened to Grendel?

Secondary Source

Anglo-Saxon Artistry

Anglo-Saxon artistry was confirmed by the 1939 discovery of a burial mound at Sutton Hoo in East Anglia. Believed to be the burial site of a King Raedwald, Sutton Hoo yielded items of silver and gold and thousands of intricately mounted garnets. Prior to this find, scholars had doubted that Anglo-Saxon artisans were capable of creating the magnificent treasures described in *Beowulf*. Yet, as Rupert Bruce-Mitford of the British Museum writes, the Sutton Hoo objects "reveal . . . a completely unexpected school of art, and a supreme one. It is pagan Saxon art in its final flower, overloaded, but not decadent. The gold jewelry is brimming with novel and daring ideas. It shows an overflowing exuberance and displays the highest level of craftsmanship, excelling anything known in this medium from the rest of Europe in its era."

Then old and young rejoiced, turned back
From that happy pilgrimage, mounted their hard-hooved
145 Horses, high-spirited stallions, and rode them
Slowly toward Herot again, retelling
Beowulf's bravery as they jogged along.
And over and over they swore that nowhere
On earth or under the spreading sky
150 Or between the seas, neither south nor north,
Was there a warrior worthier to rule over men.
(But no one meant Beowulf's praise to belittle
Hrothgar, their kind and gracious king!) . . .

Grendel's monstrous mother, in grief for her son, next attacks Herot, and in her dripping claws she carries off one man—Hrothgar's closest friend. The monster also carries off Grendel's arm, which Beowulf had hung high from the rafters. Beowulf is awakened and called for again. In one of the most famous verses in the epic, the old king describes where Grendel and his mother live.

4

. . . "They live in secret places, windy
155 Cliffs, wolf-dens where water pours
From the rocks, then runs underground, where mist
Steams like black clouds, and the groves of trees
Growing out over their lake are all covered
With frozen spray, and wind down snakelike
160 Roots that reach as far as the water
And help keep it dark. At night that lake
Burns like a torch. No one knows its bottom,
No wisdom reaches such depths. A deer,
Hunted through the woods by packs of hounds,
165 A stag with great horns, though driven through the forest
From faraway places, prefers to die
On those shores, refuses to save its life
In that water. It isn't far, nor is it
A pleasant spot! When the wind stirs
170 And storms, waves splash toward the sky,
As dark as the air, as black as the rain
That the heavens weep. Our only help,
Again, lies with you. Grendel's mother
Is hidden in her terrible home, in a place
175 You've not seen. Seek it, if you dare! Save us,
Once more, and again twisted gold,
Heaped-up ancient treasure, will reward you
For the battle you win!"

Anglo-Saxon gold buckle (7th century), from the Sutton Hoo ship treasure, Suffolk, England.
British Museum, London.

172–178. What is Hrothgar asking Beowulf to do?

Beowulf 25

DIRECT TEACHING

C Literary Focus

? Epic hero. Point out that many princes and leaders travel to Herot after Beowulf's victory. How does this add to Beowulf's status as an epic hero? [Possible response: It shows that Beowulf is heroic by anyone's standards (not just the Geats' or the Danes'). An archetypal hero would be recognized by a variety of cultures, and this passage—with the visitors' homage and subsequent retelling of his bravery—suggests that Beowulf is achieving that status.]

D Literary Focus

? Imagery. What images in the description of Grendel's lair associate Grendel with death and darkness? [Possible response: Associations of death and darkness stem from images of windy cliffs, secret dens, swirling mists, and a burning, bottomless lake that strikes fear in animals.]

Response to Margin Question

Lines 172–178. Hrothgar is asking Beowulf to find and kill Grendel's mother.

Literary Criticism

Critic's Commentary: Beowulf as Archetype

Scholar Alvin A. Lee comments that "*Beowulf* is not about an individual as such but about a man of archetypal proportions, whose significance, in the broadest and deepest sense, is social. The poem is an imaginative vision of two kinds of society: one symbolized by generosity, loyalty, and love, the other by monsters of darkness and bloodshed who prey on the ordered, light-filled world man desires and clings to. . . . [The characters in *Beowulf*] are all functionaries playing out their roles as long as *wyrd* (fate) permits, not images of real people but exemplars of human types. . . ." Discuss how the society of Herot could be said to represent "generosity, loyalty, and love." Then, ask students to apply Lee's comment about functionaries to Beowulf himself. See if their responses change when they read Part Two (p. 33).

DIRECT TEACHING

A Learners Having Difficulty

Re-reading. Remind students to re-read when they lose track of the action or setting. Ask students, "What can you learn about the setting by re-reading ll. 197–203?" [Possible response: Beowulf seems still to be underwater, but Grendel's mother has taken him into a heat-resistant structure with a high-arching roof.]

B Literary Focus

Epic hero. What characteristics of an epic hero does Beowulf display during his fight with Grendel's mother? [Possible responses: Beowulf exhibits superhuman strength; nothing stops him in his quest to defeat the powers of darkness; he stays focused on "fame," which for him means triumph in a good cause.]

VIEWING THE ART

Brooches were used by the Anglo-Saxons to fasten clothing. One historian calls them "glorified versions of our old friend the safety pin, but with a spring on both sides of the head." This extraordinarily fine brooch is inlaid with amber.

Response to Margin Question

Lines 179–203. Fully armed, Beowulf descends to the bottom of the lake—a journey that takes hours. No ordinary man could stay underwater that long. In addition, when Beowulf finds himself in the monster's lair, he is bathed in a supernatural light that protects him.

Carrying the sword Hrunting, Beowulf goes to the lake where Grendel's mother has her underwater lair. Then, fully armed, he dives to the depths of this watery hell.

THE MONSTER'S MOTHER

5

```
        . . . He leaped into the lake, would not wait for anyone's
180     Answer; the heaving water covered him
        Over. For hours he sank through the waves;
        At last he saw the mud of the bottom.
        And all at once the greedy she-wolf
        Who'd ruled those waters for half a hundred
185     Years discovered him, saw that a creature
        From above had come to explore the bottom
        Of her wet world. She welcomed him in her claws,
        Clutched at him savagely but could not harm him,
        Tried to work her fingers through the tight
190     Ring-woven mail on his breast, but tore
        And scratched in vain. Then she carried him, armor
        And sword and all, to her home; he struggled
        To free his weapon, and failed. The fight
        Brought other monsters swimming to see
195     Her catch, a host of sea beasts who beat at
        His mail shirt, stabbing with tusks and teeth
        As they followed along. Then he realized, suddenly,
        That she'd brought him into someone's battle-hall,
        And there the water's heat could not hurt him,
200     Nor anything in the lake attack him through
        The building's high-arching roof. A brilliant
        Light burned all around him, the lake
        Itself like a fiery flame.
                                  Then he saw
        The mighty water witch, and swung his sword,
205     His ring-marked blade, straight at her head;
        The iron sang its fierce song,
        Sang Beowulf's strength. But her guest
        Discovered that no sword could slice her evil
        Skin, that Hrunting could not hurt her, was useless
210     Now when he needed it. They wrestled, she ripped
        And tore and clawed at him, bit holes in his helmet,
        And that too failed him; for the first time in years
        Of being worn to war it would earn no glory;
        It was the last time anyone would wear it. But Beowulf
215     Longed only for fame, leaped back
```

179–203. Describe how Beowulf comes to the lair of Grendel's mother. What details remind you that Beowulf is not an ordinary man?

Silver and gold brooch with amber ornaments (9th century). Roscrea, County Tipperary.
National Museum of Ireland, Dublin.

READING MINI-LESSON

Developing Word-Attack Skills

Tell students that breaking words with prefixes and suffixes into their component parts is often a good strategy for decoding unfamiliar words, but with some words, this strategy can lead to mispronunciations. Use the selection word *infamous* as an example. It is made up of the prefix *in–* and the adjective *famous*, but it is not pronounced like a combination of *in* and *famous*. The stress shifts to the first syllable, and the word is pronounced /in′fə•məs/.

Explain that a shift in stress often accounts for the fact that a word does not sound the way it looks. In other instances, words simply are not what they appear to be. Use the word *weary* as an example. Someone unfamiliar with the word might think it was a combination of

Into battle. He tossed his sword aside,
Angry; the steel-edged blade lay where
He'd dropped it. If weapons were useless he'd use
His hands, the strength in his fingers. So fame
220 Comes to the men who mean to win it
And care about nothing else! He raised
His arms and seized her by the shoulder; anger
Doubled his strength, he threw her to the floor.
She fell, Grendel's fierce mother, and the Geats'
225 Proud prince was ready to leap on her. But she rose
At once and repaid him with her clutching claws,
Wildly tearing at him. He was weary, that best
And strongest of soldiers; his feet stumbled
And in an instant she had him down, held helpless.
230 Squatting with her weight on his stomach, she drew
A dagger, brown with dried blood and prepared
To avenge her only son. But he was stretched
On his back, and her stabbing blade was blunted
By the woven mail shirt he wore on his chest.
235 The hammered links held; the point
Could not touch him. He'd have traveled to the bottom of
    the earth,
Edgetho's son, and died there, if that shining
Woven metal had not helped—and Holy
God, who sent him victory, gave judgment
240 For truth and right, Ruler of the Heavens,
Once Beowulf was back on his feet and fighting.

6

Then he saw, hanging on the wall, a heavy
Sword, hammered by giants, strong
And blessed with their magic, the best of all weapons
245 But so massive that no ordinary man could lift
Its carved and decorated length. He drew it
From its scabbard, broke the chain on its hilt,°
And then, savage, now, angry
And desperate, lifted it high over his head
250 And struck with all the strength he had left,
Caught her in the neck and cut it through,
Broke bones and all. Her body fell
To the floor, lifeless, the sword was wet
With her blood, and Beowulf rejoiced at the sight.
255   The brilliant light shone, suddenly,
As though burning in that hall, and as bright as Heaven's

216–241. What details in this description of the battle between Grendel's mother and Beowulf add to your suspense about the outcome? At what point do you think Beowulf may not be successful? What saves him?

Dragon-shaped brooch (2nd century) from the Romano-British period.
© British Museum, London.

247. scabbard . . . hilt: A scabbard is a case that holds the blade of a sword; a hilt is a sword's handle.

242–254. How does Beowulf kill Grendel's mother?

Beowulf   27

DIRECT TEACHING

A Reading Skills

? Evaluating plot. Do you think that Beowulf's search for the body of Grendel and his beheading of it add anything to the story? Why or why not? [Possible responses: Yes, it shows a final victory over the Danes' enemies; no, Grendel has already been killed and proof of his death presented.] Point out that in *Gilgamesh*, the next epic students will read, the hero also beheads the enemy he kills.

Response to Margin Question

Lines 257–274. Beowulf's final revenge occurs when he beheads the body of Grendel.

VIEWING THE ART

The scenes carved on this whalebone box derive from three different cultures: The front of the box displays a Germanic legend on the left and the Christian story of the wise men's visit to the newborn Christ on the right; scenes depicting Roman history are carved into the left-hand end and on the back. Another scene from Germanic legend appears on the right-hand end and on the lid.

Activity. What conclusions can you draw about the eighth-century culture that produced this casket? [Possible response: While the culture had been Christianized, biblical lore had not completely superceded the belief in pagan legends.]

Own candle, lit in the sky. He looked
At her home, then following along the wall
Went walking, his hands tight on the sword,
260 His heart still angry. He was hunting another
Dead monster, and took his weapon with him
For final revenge against Grendel's vicious
Attacks, his nighttime raids, over
And over, coming to Herot when Hrothgar's
265 Men slept, killing them in their beds,
Eating some on the spot, fifteen
Or more, and running to his loathsome moor
With another such sickening meal waiting
In his pouch. But Beowulf repaid him for those visits,
270 Found him lying dead in his corner,
Armless, exactly as that fierce fighter
Had sent him out from Herot, then struck off
His head with a single swift blow. The body
Jerked for the last time, then lay still. . . .

? 257–274. What is Beowulf's final revenge against Grendel? What action of Beowulf's provides a **resolution**, or wrapping up, of the episode?

(Left) the Germanic hero Weland at his forge and (right) the adoration of the Magi (8th century), from the Franks casket. Whalebone.
British Museum. © Michael Holford.

28 Collection 1 The Anglo-Saxons

SKILLS REVIEW

Analyzing an author's assumptions and beliefs. *Beowulf* is a work that developed over many years and was influenced by the views of its many tellers. Have small groups of students use the following questions to discuss the philosophical assumptions and beliefs suggested in the text.

- When the first teller of *Beowulf* prepared to share the tale, what assumptions do you think he (or she) made about the purpose of the story? [It was to entertain an audience and convey Anglo-Saxon values.]
- How do you think the storytellers' beliefs about the intended audience—men gathered in mead halls—affected the content of the story? [Storytellers may have added gory details to please their audience.]
- If indeed a monk recorded *Beowulf*, how do you think his views may have changed the story? Consider what he might have taken out or added. [He may have eliminated favorable references to pagan gods and practices and may have added more references to Christian beliefs.]

CONNECTION/NOVEL

In his novel Grendel *(1971), the American writer John Gardner (1933–1982) retells part of* Beowulf *from the point of view of the monster. In this excerpt, Grendel tells his own version of one of his raids on Hrothgar's hall.*

from Grendel
John Gardner

And so I come through trees and towns to the lights of Hrothgar's meadhall. I am no stranger here. A respected guest. Eleven years now and going on twelve I have come up this clean-mown central hill, dark shadow out of the woods below, and have knocked politely on the high oak door, bursting its hinges and sending the shock of my greeting inward like a cold blast out of a cave. "Grendel!" they squeak, and I smile like exploding spring. The old Shaper, a man I cannot help but admire, goes out the back window with his harp at a single bound, though blind as a bat. The drunkest of Hrothgar's thanes come reeling and clanking down from their wall-hung beds, all shouting their meady, outrageous boasts, their heavy swords aswirl like eagles' wings. "Woe, woe, woe!" cries Hrothgar, hoary with winters, peeking in, wide-eyed, from his bedroom in back. His wife, looking in behind him, makes a scene. The thanes in the mead-hall blow out the lights and cover the wide stone fireplace with shields. I laugh, crumple over; I can't help myself. In the darkness, I alone see clear as day. While they squeal and screech and bump into each other, I silently sack up my dead and withdraw to the woods. I eat and laugh and eat until I can barely walk, my chest-hair matted with dribbled blood, and then the roosters on the hill crow, and dawn comes over the roofs of the houses, and all at once I am filled with gloom again.

"This is some punishment sent us," I hear them bawling from the hill.

My head aches. Morning nails my eyes.

"Some god is angry," I hear a woman keen. "The people of Scyld and Herogar and Hrothgar are mired in sin!"

My belly rumbles, sick on their sour meat. I crawl through bloodstained leaves to the eaves of the forest, and there peak out. The dogs fall silent at the edge of my spell, and where the king's hall surmounts the town, the blind old Shaper, harp clutched tight to his fragile chest, stares futilely down, straight at me. Otherwise nothing. Pigs root dully at the posts of a wooden fence. A rumple-horned ox lies chewing in dew and shade. A few men, lean, wearing animal skins, look up at the gables of the king's hall, or at the vultures circling casually beyond. Hrothgar says nothing, hoarfrost-bearded, his features cracked and crazed. Inside, I hear the people praying—whimpering, whining, mumbling, pleading—to their numerous sticks and stones. He doesn't go in. The king has lofty theories of his own.

"Theories," I whisper to the bloodstained ground. So the dragon once spoke. ("They'd map out roads through Hell with their crackpot theories!" I recall his laugh.)

Then the groaning and praying stop, and on the side of the hill the dirge-slow shoveling begins. . . .

Beowulf 29

Connection

Summary *at grade level*

In an interior monologue, Grendel describes one of his raids on Hrothgar's mead hall. With grim humor, he remembers the panic that his appearance incited at Herot and boasts of his superiority to humans. Still, Grendel's self-confidence wavers: Though he delights in killing humans, their meat makes him sick, and he seems troubled by Hrothgar's "theories" about religion.

DIRECT TEACHING

A Literary Focus
Verbal irony. What words and expressions indicate that Grendel is using irony in his storytelling? What does the irony suggest about his personality? [Ironic words and expressions include *A respected guest, knocked politely,* and *greeting;* the response of the people of Herot makes it clear that the opposite is true. Students may suggest that the irony shows that Grendel has a sense of humor and is proud of himself.]

B Literary Connections
Scop: Anglo-Saxon Storyteller The "old Shaper" refers to a storyteller. Since the days of the bard Homer, who was rumored to be blind, storytellers are often depicted as blind harpists.

C Reading Skills
Hypothesizing. What are Hrothgar's "theories"? Explain. [Possible response: They are theories about a more "lofty" religion than that of Hrothgar's subjects, who pray in fear "to their numerous sticks and stones." This religion might be Christianity.]

Comparing and Contrasting Texts

Call on volunteers to identify the opinions that Grendel expresses in this excerpt. Then, discuss the following questions:

- In relation to the excerpts of *Beowulf* that you are reading, where does this excerpt from *Grendel* fall? [It comes before the first excerpt, because that excerpt tells of Grendel's final, fatal visit to Herot. Based on what Grendel says here about Hrothgar, Beowulf has not yet appeared on the scene.]

- The old Shaper does not appear in the excerpts of *Beowulf* that you are reading. In Gardner's version, what does he symbolize? [Possible response: He may symbolize literary tradition, and Grendel's admiration of him suggests that Gardner is not only manipulating a classic tale but also making a comment about art.]

Connection

Summary ⇔ at grade level

This article describes life in Europe in A.D. 999. At that time, European society was rather primitive. Life for most people was short and marked by poverty, poor health, and virtually no chance of improving one's circumstances.

DIRECT TEACHING

Ⓐ Reading Informational Text

? Characterizing the historical period. Why might a writer use the concept of speed to define a particular historical age? [Possible response: The pace of life often reflects the age. Today, for example, people grow impatient during a five-minute wait at a supermarket checkout; in A.D. 999, however, obtaining food could be an entire day's work.]

Ⓑ Content-Area Connections

Culture: Salt
So crucial was salt to people's lives long ago that the word *salary* referred to the money paid to Roman soldiers so that they could buy it.

Ⓒ Reading Informational Text

? Finding supporting details. The main idea of this paragraph is that life expectancy in the Anglo-Saxon age was short. What details does the author cite to prove this point? [Many women died in childbirth before the age of 30; diseases were rampant; 50 was considered old.]

CONNECTION/MAGAZINE ARTICLE

Life in 999: A Grim Struggle

INFORMATIONAL TEXT

Howard G. Chua-Eoan

from *Time*, October 15, 1992

Ⓐ Today's world is measured in light-years and Mach speed and sheathed in silicon and alloy. In the world of 999, on the eve of the first millennium, time moved at the speed of an oxcart or, more often, of a sturdy pair of legs, and the West was built largely on wood. Europe was a collection of untamed forests, countless mile upon mile of trees and brush and brier, dark and inhospitable. Medieval chroniclers used the word *desert* to describe their arboreal world, a place on the cusp of civilization where werewolves and bogeymen still lunged out of the shadows and bandits and marauders maintained their lairs.

Yet the forests, deep and dangerous as they were, also defined existence. Wood kindled forges and kept alive the hearths of the mud-and-thatch huts of the serfs. Peasants fattened their hogs on forest acorns (pork was crucial to basic subsistence in the cold of winter), and wild berries helped supplement the meager diet. In a world without sugar, honey from forest swarms provided the only sweetness for food or drink. The pleasures of the serfs were few and simple: earthy lovemaking and occasional dances and fests.

Ⓑ Feudal lords ruled over western Europe, taking their share of the harvests of primitive agriculture and making the forests their private hunting grounds. Poaching was not simply theft (usually punishable by imprisonment) but a sin against the social order. Without the indulgence of the nobility, the peasants could not even acquire salt, the indispensable ingredient for preserving meat and flavoring a culinary culture that possessed few spices. Though a true money economy did not exist, salt could be bought with poorly circulated coin, which the lord hoarded in his castle and dispensed to the poor only as alms.

It was in the lord's castle too that peasants and their flocks sought refuge from wolf packs and barbarian invaders. In 999, however, castles, like most other buildings in Europe, were made of timber, far from the granite bastions that litter today's imagined Middle Ages. The peasants, meanwhile, were relegated to their simple huts, where everyone—including the animals—slept around the hearth. Straw was scattered on the floors to collect scraps as well as human and animal waste. Housecleaning consisted of sweeping out the straw.

Ⓒ Illness and disease remained in constant residence. Tuberculosis was endemic, and so were scabrous skin diseases of every kind: abscesses, cankers, scrofula, tumors, eczema, and erysipelas. In a throwback to biblical times, lepers constituted a class of pariahs living on the outskirts of villages and cities. Constant famine, rotten flour, and vitamin deficiencies afflicted huge segments of society with blindness, goiter, paralysis, and bone malformations that created hunchbacks and cripples. A man was lucky to survive 30, and 50 was a ripe old age. Most women, many of them succumbing to the ravages of childbirth, lived less than 30 years. There was no time for what is now considered childhood; children of every class had to grow up immediately and be useful as soon as possible. Emperors were leading armies in their teens; John XI became Pope at the age of 21.

While the general population was growing faster than it had in the previous five cen-

---

Comparing and Contrasting Texts

Have students summarize the article; then, discuss the following questions:

- How does *Beowulf* reflect the idea that humanity lived "on the cusp of civilization"? [Possible response: Hrothgar rules from Herot, but his hall is near Grendel's lair.]
- How well does Hrothgar fit the article's description of a feudal lord? [Possible response: We do not see Hrothgar interacting with peasants, but we are told that he is a revered ruler. He does not seem to be the kind of self-centered leader that the article discusses; rather, he seeks out help and is quick to reward Beowulf for his efforts.]
- Read the headnote on p. 33. How old is Beowulf when he faces the dragon? How old would he have seemed by the standards of his time? [He is more than fifty years old, probably in his late sixties; very old.]

February, from *The Grimani Breviary* (prayer book) (detail).
Biblioteca Marciana, Venice. © Scala/Art Resource, New York.
© 1992 Time Inc. Reprinted by permission.

turies, there was still a shortage of people to cultivate the fields, clear the woodlands, and work the mills. Local taxes were levied on youths who did not marry upon coming of age. Abortion was considered homicide, and a woman who terminated a pregnancy was expelled from the church.

The nobility spent its waking hours battling foes to preserve its prerogatives, the clergy chanting prayers for the salvation of souls, the serfs laboring to feed and clothe everyone. Night, lit only by burning logs or the rare taper, was always filled with danger and terror. The seasons came and went, punctuated chiefly by the occurrence of plentiful church holidays. The calendar year began at different times for different regions; only later would Europe settle on the Feast of Christ's Circumcision, January 1, as the year's beginning.

Thus there was little panic, not even much interest, as the millennium approached in the final months of 999. For what terrors could the apocalypse hold for a continent that was already shrouded in darkness? Rather Europe—illiterate, diseased, and hungry—seemed grimly resigned to desperation and impoverishment. It was one of the planet's most unpromising corners, the Third World of its age.

Response and Analysis

Reading Check

1. Describe what happens to Grendel when he raids Herot and encounters Beowulf.
2. What prevents Beowulf's men from helping Beowulf in his battle with Grendel?
3. How do the Danes feel about Beowulf after his battle with Grendel?
4. What obstacle does Beowulf face in his confrontation with Grendel's mother? How does he overcome the obstacle?

Thinking Critically

5. What significance can you find in the fact that Grendel attacks at night?
6. **Images** are words that help us see something, and often hear it, smell it, taste it, and touch it as well. Identify images describing Grendel that associate him with death or darkness. How are these images supposed to make you feel about Grendel?
7. Why do you think it's important to Beowulf and to his image as an **epic hero** that he face Grendel without a weapon? What **symbolism** do you see in the uselessness of human-made weapons against Grendel?
8. What details describe Grendel's mother and her lair? What might Grendel and his mother represent for the Anglo-Saxons?
9. How does Gardner's depiction of Grendel differ from the epic's depiction of him? (See the **Connection** on page 29.) Did Gardner make you sympathize with Grendel? Explain.
10. The **Connection** on page 30, "Life in 999: A Grim Struggle," describes daily life in late Anglo-Saxon England. What details in this picture of daily life relate to what you've read so far in *Beowulf*? How does life in 999 compare with life today?

Extending and Evaluating

11. Beowulf is the **archetype** of the dragon slayer, the hero who faces death in order to save a threatened community. Does Beowulf remind you of any heroes in real life, in fiction, or in the movies today? What characteristics do the heroes share?

INTERNET
Projects and Activities
Keyword: LE5 12-1

Literary Skills Analyze the archetype of the epic hero.

Detail of picture stone from Gotland, Sweden.

32 Collection 1 The Anglo-Saxons

INDEPENDENT PRACTICE

Response and Analysis

Reading Check

1. Beowulf seizes him with a mighty grip and tears off his arm. The monster, mortally wounded, flees.
2. Grendel has put a spell on their weapons and so cannot be hurt by them.
3. They laugh with delight, rejoice at the monster's defeat, and praise Beowulf.
4. Beowulf's sword is useless against the monster. At first he fights her with his bare hands, protected by God and his chain-mail shirt; then he finds an ancient sword that has magic of its own and uses it to kill her.

Thinking Critically

5. Darkness is associated with death and destruction, so it is an appropriate time for Grendel to prowl at night.
6. Images include "shepherd of evil," "the Almighty's enemy," and "hell's captive." The images are designed to create revulsion in readers.
7. As an epic hero, Beowulf must show both superior physical strength and high ethics, including abandoning his sword to avoid taking unfair advantage of Grendel. The symbolism suggests that this is a spiritual battle between right and wrong.
8. Grendel's mother is called a "she-wolf," and there are several references to her claws. Her lair is deep underwater, in a building with a high-arched roof and an ancient sword mounted on one wall. The two monsters might represent social disorder and/or the supernatural powers of darkness.
9. Gardner depicts Grendel as a creature with human feelings. The monster uses verbal irony, is moody, and suffers from physical ailments like stomachaches. Most important, the monster reasons and philosophizes. Many students will say they did sympathize with Grendel.
10. Beowulf lives in a grim and desperate world of forests, wild animals, and marauders. Wooden castles offer little protection from danger. In 999, life was harsh and short; life is easier today.

Extending and Evaluating

11. Beowulf may remind students of movie action heroes, community leaders, military leaders, or sports figures. The heroes may share qualities such as courage, selflessness, loyalty, great strength, and leadership.

from Beowulf
Part Two, translated by Seamus Heaney

Beowulf carries Grendel's head to King Hrothgar and then returns gift-laden to the land of the Geats, where he succeeds to the throne. After fifty winters pass, Beowulf, now an old man, faces his final task: He must fight a dragon who, angry because a thief has stolen a jeweled cup from the dragon's hoard of gold, is laying waste to the Geats' land. Beowulf and eleven warriors are guided to the dragon's lair by the thief who stole the cup. For Beowulf the price of this last victory will be great.

Shoulder clasp (7th century), from the Sutton Hoo ship treasure, Suffolk, England.
British Museum, London/Photograph © Michael Holford.

THE FINAL BATTLE

7

275 Then he addressed each dear companion
one final time, those fighters in their helmets,
<u>resolute</u> and high-born: "I would rather not
use a weapon if I knew another way
to grapple with the dragon and make good my boast
280 as I did against Grendel in days gone by.
But I shall be meeting molten venom
in the fire he breathes, so I go forth
in mail-shirt and shield. I won't shift a foot
when I meet the cave-guard: what occurs on the wall
285 between the two of us will turn out as fate,
overseer of men, decides. I am resolved.
I scorn further words against this sky-borne foe.

"Men at arms, remain here on the barrow,°
safe in your armour, to see which one of us
290 is better in the end at bearing wounds
in a deadly fray. This fight is not yours,
nor is it up to any man except me

[margin note: goes to battle alone]

275–287. Throughout *Beowulf*, there are many references to the pagan notion of fate (see line 285) as an impersonal force that predetermines the outcome of events in a person's life. This concept, known as *wyrd*, was central to Anglo-Saxon beliefs.
? How is this older Beowulf different from the Beowulf who slew Grendel and his mother?

288. barrow *n.*: a hill.

Vocabulary
resolute (rez′ə·lōōt′) *adj.*: determined.

PRETEACHING

Summary ⇔ at grade level

Many years into his reign as king of the Geats, Beowulf resolves to fight a fire-breathing dragon that threatens his people. Fate will not give Beowulf glory in this battle, however. His sword angers but does not kill the dragon, which advances upon Beowulf and lays him low with its fiery breath. A true Anglo-Saxon hero, Beowulf accepts his fate without complaint while all but one of his companions run off in fear. Wiglaf alone remembers the duties due to his kinsman and berates those who run. After Wiglaf and Beowulf kill the dragon, Wiglaf brings the dragon's treasure hoard to the dying king, who thanks God that he can leave such wealth to his people. Then Beowulf commissions Wiglaf to look after them and to build a memorial to him. After giving Wiglaf his armor, Beowulf dies. His ashes are placed in a tower by the sea, and twelve loyal followers mourn his loss and praise him for his great character and deeds.

DIRECT TEACHING

Response to Margin Question
Lines 275–287. The older and wiser Beowulf realizes that he cannot meet this fire-breathing enemy barehanded.

CONTENT-AREA CONNECTIONS

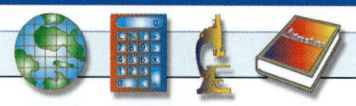

Literature: Beowulf and Ulysses
Beowulf often has been compared to an even more ancient archetypal epic hero—Odysseus, or Ulysses, who faces a variety of challenges as he attempts to bring a band of his followers home and rejoin his own family. Like Beowulf, Odysseus is an older man; like Beowulf, he represents his culture.

Whole-class activity. In the poem "Ulysses" (p. 704), Alfred, Lord Tennyson, explores an aging hero's need for one final adventure. Have students read the poem and identify a statement by Ulysses that they think also rings true for Beowulf. [Possible response: The final six lines of "Ulysses" could have been spoken easily by Beowulf.]

DIRECT TEACHING

VIEWING THE ART

The Vikings were excellent blacksmiths who used hammers to beat molten iron into weapons such as swords and shields.

Activity. Ask students to comment on how the designs on the weapons compare with the Vikings' behavior toward other people. [The designs are elegant and sensitive, yet the Vikings' behavior was sometimes brutal.]

A Reading Skills

❓ **Tracing recurring motifs.** Beowulf insists upon going into battle alone. When has he done so in the past? [Possible response: He fought Grendel and Grendel's mother alone.] What does this motif suggest? [Possible responses: the importance of an individual's battle against evil; the virtue of self-sacrifice; the need for courage in an epic hero.]

B Vocabulary Development

❓ **Anglo-Saxon affixes.** The words *unscathed* (l. 307) and *unburdened* (l. 310) share something as Anglo-Saxon as the story in which they are used: They share the Anglo-Saxon prefix *un–*, which means "not," "lack of," or "the opposite of." What do these two words mean? [Possible response: *unscathed*—"not harmed"; *unburdened*—"not weighed down."] Name two other *un–* words that you think describe Beowulf or this battle. [Possible responses: *unafraid, unfailing, unrelenting,* and *unrestrained*.]

Response to Margin Question

Lines 288–296. Despite his misgivings, he is willing to battle the dragon to the death in order to save his people. His selflessness adds to his heroic stature.

Viking sword handles, embellished with Viking Age motifs.
Statens Historiska Museer, Stockholm.

A
```
        to measure his strength against the monster
        or to prove his worth. I shall win the gold
   295  by my courage, or else mortal combat,
        doom of battle, will bear your lord away."

        Then he drew himself up beside his shield.
        The fabled warrior in his warshirt and helmet
        trusted in his own strength entirely
   300  and went under the crag. No coward path.
        Hard by the rock-face that hale° veteran,
        a good man who had gone repeatedly
        into combat and danger and come through,
        saw a stone arch and a gushing stream
   305  that burst from the barrow, blazing and wafting
        a deadly heat. It would be hard to survive
        unscathed near the hoard, to hold firm
        against the dragon in those flaming depths.
```

B
```
        Then he gave a shout. The lord of the Geats
   310  unburdened his breast and broke out
        in a storm of anger. Under grey stone
        his voice challenged and resounded clearly.
        Hate was ignited. The hoard-guard recognized
        a human voice, the time was over
   315  for peace and parleying.° Pouring forth
        in a hot battle-fume, the breath of the monster
        burst from the rock. There was a rumble under ground.
        Down there in the barrow, Beowulf the warrior
        lifted his shield: the outlandish thing
   320  writhed and convulsed and vehemently
```

❓ **288–296.** How does Beowulf's acceptance of fate show his deep sense of responsibility to his people?

301. hale *adj.*: healthy and energetic.

315. parleying *v.* used as *n.*: discussing.

Vocabulary
vehemently (vē′ə·mənt·lē) *adv.*: violently.

SKILLS REVIEW

Using sounds to evoke readers' emotions. Before it was ever written down, *Beowulf* was meant to be heard. Devices of sound, therefore, are an important part of its storytelling style. In his translation, Seamus Heaney often uses words whose sounds imitate or suggest their meaning—that is, onomatopoeia. Invite students to comment on the ways in which the following onomatopoeic words from this section enhance the narrative.

1. burst (l. 305)
2. rumble (l. 317)
3. writhed (l. 320)
4. gliding (l. 328)
5. slashed (l. 337)

turned on the king, whose keen-edged sword,
an heirloom inherited by ancient right,
was already in his hand. Roused to a fury,
each antagonist struck terror in the other.
325 Unyielding, the lord of his people loomed
by his tall shield, sure of his ground,
while the serpent looped and unleashed itself.
Swaddled in flames, it came gliding and flexing
and racing towards its fate. Yet his shield defended
330 the renowned leader's life and limb
for a shorter time than he meant it to:
that final day was the first time
when Beowulf fought and fate denied him
glory in battle. So the king of the Geats
335 raised his hand and struck hard
at the enamelled scales, but scarcely cut through:
the blade flashed and slashed yet the blow
was far less powerful than the hard-pressed king
had need of at that moment. The mound-keeper
340 went into a spasm and spouted deadly flames:
when he felt the stroke, battle-fire
billowed and spewed. Beowulf was foiled°
of a glorious victory. The glittering sword,
infallible before that day,
345 failed when he unsheathed it, as it never should have.
For the son of Ecgtheow, it was no easy thing
to have to give ground like that and go
unwillingly to inhabit another home
in a place beyond; so every man must yield
the leasehold of his days.

350 　　　　　　　　　It was not long
until the fierce contenders clashed again.
The hoard-guard took heart, inhaled and swelled up
and got a new wind; he who had once ruled
was furled in fire and had to face the worst.
355 No help or backing was to be had then
from his high-born comrades; that hand-picked troop
broke ranks and ran for their lives
to the safety of the wood. But within one heart
sorrow welled up: in a man of worth
360 the claims of kinship cannot be denied.

Vocabulary
infallible (in·fal′ə·bəl) *adj.*: unable to fail or be wrong.
furled (furld) *v.*: rolled up.

318–329. The image of a lone hero standing up to a fire-breathing dragon or other giant monster is one of the most **archetypal** images in Western heroic literature. *How does the dragon compare with Grendel and Grendel's mother?*

329–350. In lines 329–345, what goes wrong during Beowulf's battle with the dragon? In lines 346–350, what are you led to believe about Beowulf's ultimate fate?

342. foiled *v.*: prevented from.

355–358. How do Beowulf's men react to the sight of the dragon gaining victory over Beowulf?

Beowulf 35

8

His name was Wiglaf, a son of Weohstan's,
a well-regarded Shylfing warrior
related to Aelfhere. When he saw his lord
tormented by the heat of his scalding helmet,
365 he remembered the bountiful gifts bestowed on him,
how well he lived among the Waegmundings,
the freehold° he inherited from his father before him.
He could not hold back: one hand brandished
the yellow-timbered shield, the other drew his sword— . . .

370 Sad at heart, addressing his companions,
Wiglaf spoke wise and fluent words:
"I remember that time when mead was flowing,
how we pledged loyalty to our lord in the hall,
promised our ring-giver we would be worth our price,
375 make good the gift of the war-gear,
those swords and helmets, as and when
his need required it. He picked us out
from the army deliberately, honoured us and judged us
fit for this action, made me these lavish gifts—
380 and all because he considered us the best
of his arms-bearing thanes.° And now, although
he wanted this challenge to be one he'd face
by himself alone—the shepherd of our land,
a man unequaled in the quest for glory
385 and a name for daring—now the day has come
when this lord we serve needs sound men
to give him their support. Let us go to him,
help our leader through the hot flame
and dread of the fire. As God is my witness,
390 I would rather my body were robed in the same
burning blaze as my gold-giver's body
than go back home bearing arms.
That is unthinkable, unless we have first
slain the foe and defended the life
395 of the prince of the Weather-Geats. I well know
the things he has done for us deserve better.
Should he alone be left exposed
to fall in battle? We must bond together,
shield and helmet, mail-shirt and sword."

367. **freehold** *n.*: estate.

370–399. What arguments does Wiglaf use to convince the men that they must fight with Beowulf?

381. thanes *n. pl.*: in Anglo-Saxon England, group of men who held land of the king in exchange for military service.

Bronze stag atop ceremonial scepter (detail) (7th century), from the Sutton Hoo ship treasure, Suffolk, England.
© British Museum, London.

Vocabulary
lavish (lav′ish) *adj.*: extravagant.

Together Beowulf and the young Wiglaf kill the dragon, but the old king is fatally wounded. Beowulf, thinking of his people, asks to see the monster's treasure. Wiglaf enters the dragon's cave and finds a priceless hoard of jewels and gold.

9

400 . . . Wiglaf went quickly, keen to get back,
excited by the treasure; anxiety weighed
on his brave heart, he was hoping he would find
the leader of the Geats alive where he had left him
helpless, earlier, on the open ground.
405 So he came to the place, carrying the treasure,
and found his lord bleeding profusely,
his life at an end; again he began
to swab his body. The beginnings of an utterance
broke out from the king's breast-cage.
410 The old lord gazed sadly at the gold.

"To the everlasting Lord of All,
to the King of Glory, I give thanks
that I behold this treasure here in front of me,
that I have been thus allowed to leave my people
415 so well endowed on the day I die.
Now that I have bartered my last breath
to own this fortune, it is up to you
to look after their needs. I can hold out no longer.
Order my troop to construct a barrow
420 on a headland on the coast, after my pyre has cooled.
It will loom on the horizon at Hronesness
and be a reminder among my people—
so that in coming times crews under sail
will call it Beowulf's Barrow, as they steer
425 ships across the wide and shrouded waters."

Then the king in his great-heartedness unclasped
the collar of gold from his neck and gave it
to the young thane, telling him to use
it and the warshirt and the gilded helmet well.

430 "You are the last of us, the only one left
of the Waegmundings. Fate swept us away,

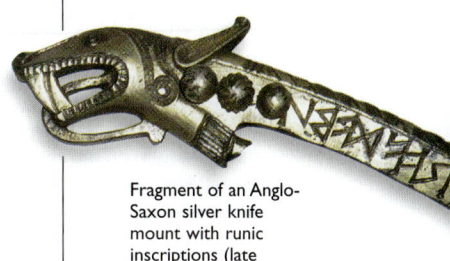

Fragment of an Anglo-Saxon silver knife mount with runic inscriptions (late 8th century).
C. M. Dixon.

411–418. The ultimate purpose of the **epic hero** is to leave something of lasting value to his culture.
❓ What has Beowulf left to his people?

419–425. What are Beowulf's final wishes?

The great ax, with depiction of bird-animal (10th century), from Jutland, Denmark.
National Museum of Copenhagen, Denmark. © Werner Forman/Art Resource, New York.

Beowulf 37

DIRECT TEACHING

A Literary Focus

? Epic hero. The early Anglo-Saxons did not believe strongly in the afterlife but in the glory or fame that lived on after death. According to this belief, how should people remember a hero who has died? [Possible response: They should praise the hero's accomplishments and exemplary character, and they should hold dear the hero's memory.]

VIEWING THE ART

A warrior's shield and sword were among his most precious possessions. However, this particular shield, scholars conjecture, was thrown into the Thames as an offering to a river god. It was found in 1857 in a section of the Thames that runs through London's old Battersea district. Approximately two thousand years old, the shield is made of copper alloy and inlaid with red glass; it measures about thirty inches in length.

Activity. Ask students to solve the following Anglo-Saxon riddle. "I am by nature solitary, scarred by spear and wounded by sword, weary of battle. I frequently see the face of war and fight hateful enemies. What am I?" [a shield]

Response to Margin Question

Lines 438–451. He performed great deeds and was gracious, fair-minded, and kind—and the most determined to be remembered.

---

sent my whole brave high-born clan
to their final doom. Now I must follow them."
That was the warrior's last word.
435 He had no more to confide. The furious heat
of the pyre would assail him. His soul fled from his breast
to its destined place among the steadfast ones.

Wiglaf berates the faithless warriors who did not go to the aid of their king. With sorrow the Geats cremate the corpse of their greatest king. They place his ashes, along with all of the dragon's treasure, in a huge burial tower by the sea, where it can be seen by voyagers.

10

Then twelve warriors rode around the tomb,
chieftains' sons, champions in battle,
440 all of them distraught, chanting in dirges,
mourning his loss as a man and a king.
They extolled his heroic nature and exploits
and gave thanks for his greatness; which was the proper thing,
for a man should praise a prince whom he holds dear
445 and cherish his memory when that moment comes
when he has to be convoyed from his bodily home.
So the Geat people, his hearth companions,
sorrowed for the lord who had been laid low.
They said that of all the kings upon the earth
450 he was the man most gracious and fair-minded,
kindest to his people and keenest to win fame.

Vocabulary
assail (ə·sāl′) *v.*: attack.
extolled (ek·stōld′) *v.*: praised.

438–451. The closing lines of *Beowulf* serve as a kind of **elegy**—a poem that mourns the death of a person or laments something lost.
? *According to these elegiac final lines of the epic, what qualities made Beowulf a great hero?*

A Celtic shield, found in Battersea, near the Thames River, perhaps thrown in the river as an offering to the river god.
Courtesy of the Trustees of the British Museum, London.

38 Collection 1 The Anglo-Saxons

DIFFERENTIATING INSTRUCTION

Advanced Learners
Enrichment. Encourage students to complete one of these group activities on *Beowulf*.
Activity. Have students choose a passage from *Beowulf* and prepare it for a reader's theater presentation. One or two group members should give a summary of the action to the rest of the class while other group members act out the scenes, using dialogue from the poem and perhaps some dialogue that they write themselves.
Activity. Have students prepare a special-edition newspaper about *Beowulf*. Copy might include news stories on Beowulf's battles, an editorial on heroism, an interview with Wiglaf, and a *Beowulf*-themed puzzle. Other group members can do computer entry, layout, and artwork.

CONNECTION / ARTICLE **INFORMATIONAL TEXT**

The Fury of the Northmen

Ellen Ashdown

When the fearsome Vikings began raiding England at the end of the eighth century, the church added a new prayer: "God, deliver us from the fury of the Northmen." Were these Scandinavian warriors—descended from the peoples of *Beowulf*—really such berserk destroyers? The fiercest ones were, indicated by the word *berserk* itself: In Old Norse, a *berserkr* was a "frenzied Norse warrior," so wild and fearless even his comrades kept clear.

Bear or bare?

Berserkr literally means either "bear shirt" or "bare shirt," suggesting that these warriors wore bearskins or perhaps fought "bare"—without armor. Some say the berserkers were religious madmen, followers of Odin, god of death and war. Some say they ate mind-altering plants. Both may be true, because the berserker entered battle in a kind of fit, biting his shield, taunting death, and, like Beowulf, "If weapons were useless he'd use / His hands. . . . So fame / Comes to the men who mean to win it / And care about nothing else!" (lines 218–221).

Sigurd kills the dragon. Detail of carved portal of Hylestad stave church (12th century).

Dragons from the sea.

The Viking Age spanned the ninth through eleventh centuries, the European continent, and the Atlantic Ocean. Pushed by overpopulation, Vikings from Sweden, Norway, and Denmark struck out for new land. They were farmers at home, but they were a warrior culture too, and they devastated England with nightmarish hit-and-run attacks. Even the name "Viking" comes from a telling phrase: For the Scandinavians, *to go a-viking* meant "to fight as a warrior or pirate."

The Vikings' extraordinary seafaring and shipbuilding skills, honed in their watery land of fiords, or narrow ocean inlets, gave them the advantage of making surprise attacks. The unique Viking warships were long (up to ninety-five feet, manned by thirty rowers), light and swift (to go farther on their provisions), and steady (built with a keel). Shallow-drafted, these dragon-prowed ships could be pulled onto a river shore, swiftly disgorging warriors wielding swords.

Unafraid of the unknown.

But though the Vikings conquered peoples as far away as Spain and Russia (*Rus* was the Slavic word for "Swedes"), their motive was pure wanderlust as much as bloodlust. Expert in navigating by sun, stars, landmarks, and bird flights, the Vikings settled Iceland and Greenland and even explored North America—five hundred years before Columbus. That's why the United States once named a spacecraft *Viking*: to honor the human spirit that dared uncharted seas in the ninth century, and dares uncharted Mars in the twentieth.

CONTENT-AREA CONNECTIONS

Geography: Viking Travels
Have students research the places where Vikings settled, raided, or traded, and have them create a map to show these locations. The type of interaction could be indicated by color coding. (Maps should show Viking settlements in England, France, Germany, Ireland, and the Netherlands. Raiding and trading occurred in Italy, Spain, Russia, and even in North Africa.)

Science: Navigational Tools
The Vikings did not have the concept of longitude. They traveled by using the *husan-otra*, which was a stick used for measuring latitude based on the location of the stars. Have students research this and other early methods of navigation, including the use of "sun stones" and the practice of gauging the color of the water.

Connection

Summary at grade level

This article provides background about the Vikings, the seafaring marauders who descended from Beowulf's people and ranged from Russia to North America during the ninth to eleventh centuries.

DIRECT TEACHING

A **Content-Area Connections**

History: Viking Raids
Violence and widespread destruction were the hallmarks of a Viking raid. The warriors raped women, slaughtered monks and children, and often killed men by slitting their backbone so that their ribs sprang out, exposing their heart. Consequently, the Vikings were greatly feared and hated by the early people of what is now Great Britain. Their main targets were monasteries. The Vikings first attacked the monastery in Lindisfarne in A.D. 793 and moved quickly onto the church at Jarrow; by A.D. 795, they had also plundered Columba's monastery on Iona. The Vikings preyed upon these settlements because the monasteries had accumulated great treasure. Until A.D. 851, most Viking raids were hit-and-run. However, in that year, according to the *Anglo-Saxon Chronicles,* 350 ships destroyed Canterbury and caused more carnage than had ever been heard of. The Vikings remained in Canterbury throughout that winter.

Although ruthless and violent, the Vikings also had a softer side. They loved their *eddas,* or epic sagas, so much that they often brought their *skalds,* or court poets, to their battles to read verses for luck. In addition, they created beautiful gold and inlaid jewelry and fine tapestries.

INDEPENDENT PRACTICE

Response and Analysis

Reading Check

1. Only Wiglaf helps Beowulf, out of a bond of loyalty—*comitatus*.
2. The funeral of Beowulf and the raising of his burial mound conclude the epic.
3. The treasure is buried with Beowulf's ashes.

Thinking Critically

4. Although Beowulf fought the dragon to give its treasure hoard to his people, the hoard is returned to the earth, signaling the coming destruction of Beowulf's people.
5. Details describing the dragon as a serpent and being coiled, fiery, and scaly occur in ll. 304–308, 315–316, 327–329, 336, and 340–342. The dragon may symbolize evil, death, or Satan.
6. Since the society was built upon loyalty to a lord or protector, the men's panicked retreat is ominous for the future of the kingdom.
7. Among the words and images that students may mention are *distraught, dirges,* and *loss* in ll. 440–441 and *sorrowed* and *laid low* in l. 448.
8. Students may identify the Anglo-Saxon values of courage, loyalty, fighting prowess, and fatalism. Universal themes include "loyalty and self-sacrifice as admirable traits," "the triumph of good over evil (albeit at a painful cost)," and "the achievement of fame through great deeds."
9. *Beowulf* paints an idealized picture of life in Viking culture. The epic emphasizes the obligations and duties of the tribal leader and glorifies fighting that occurs in defense of the tribe rather than fighting that occurs as part of a raid.

Response and Analysis

Reading Check

1. Who comes to Beowulf's aid in Beowulf's final battle with the dragon? Why does he help Beowulf?
2. What sad scene concludes the epic?
3. What happens to the dragon's hoard?

Thinking Critically

4. A hoarded treasure in Old English literature is usually a **symbol** of spiritual death or damnation. How does this fact add significance to Beowulf's last fight with the dragon?
5. What details does the poet use to describe the dragon? Keeping those details in mind, explain what the dragon might **symbolize** as Beowulf's final foe.
6. Given what you know about the structure of Anglo-Saxon society, explain what is especially ominous about the behavior of Beowulf's men during the final battle. What does it suggest about the future of the kingdom?
7. The epic closes on a somber, elegiac note—a note of mourning. What words or **images** contribute to this **tone**?
8. Epic poetry usually embodies the attitudes and ideals of an entire culture. What values of Anglo-Saxon society does *Beowulf* reveal? What universal themes does it also reveal? Use specific examples from the poem to support your answer.
9. The **Connection** on page 39 describes the culture of the Vikings. How does this picture of Viking society relate to what you've read in *Beowulf*?

Literary Criticism

10. **Philosophical approach.** Although the story of Beowulf is set in a pre-Christian era among a people who worshiped stern gods and saw little to hope for beyond the grave, many modern readers see definite strains of a Christian outlook. Review the selections from *Beowulf*. Which passages might reflect a specifically Anglo-Saxon philosophy of life? Which passages might reflect a Christian outlook?

WRITING

Analyzing the Monster

In an **essay**, analyze the monster Grendel, focusing on the character's nature. Begin your **character analysis** of the monster with a sentence stating your general assessment of Grendel as a character. Then, support your assessment with details from the epic. Before you write, organize your details in a chart like the following one:

Character Name	Details from Epic
Actions	
Motives	
Words describing character	
People's responses	
Setting	
Does the character symbolize anything?	

Describe the Mom

In a brief **essay,** describe Grendel's mother. Base your description on the details you find in the text, and add details of your own. Tell what she looked like, how her voice sounded, how she smelled, how she walked. Describe her home. Describe what she ate and how she passed her time. Use as many sensory details as you can: You want your readers to feel they are meeting the monster face to face. How do you want your

---

SKILLS FOCUS

Pages 40–42 cover
Literary Skills Analyze the universal themes of epic poetry. Understand and analyze alliteration and kennings.
Writing Skills Write a character-analysis essay. Write a descriptive essay.
Listening and Speaking Skills Present a dramatic reading.
Vocabulary Skills Demonstrate word knowledge.

Literary Criticism

10. Possible answers:
Part One—Lines 25–27 express an Anglo-Saxon view of fate; ll. 95–101, the Christian concept of hell and the authority of "Almighty God."

Part Two—Lines 291–296 express the Anglo-Saxon idea of a hero who is both strong and virtuous; ll. 411–415, a Christian hymn of praise to a God who is greater than any king and who has helped Beowulf.

readers to feel about the monster? Do you want horror, or are you interested in making her somewhat sympathetic? The words you choose will make the difference.

▶ Use "Writing a Descriptive Essay," pages 74–81, for help with this assignment.

LISTENING AND SPEAKING
Being a Bard

Choose any excerpt from the portions of *Beowulf* you have just read, and present a dramatic reading to your classmates as though you were an Anglo-Saxon bard. Choose a section that you feel has particular emotional intensity and suspense, and practice reading it several times before you deliver your reading to the class. Try to find various ways of involving your listeners in the act of storytelling: Vary the rate and pitch of your delivery, make dramatic pauses, and use gestures and even sound effects. For example, a guitar could be used to strike chords at dramatic moments.

Vocabulary Development
Which Word?

resolute   furled   extolled
vehemently lavish
infallible assail

Put your knowledge of the selection Vocabulary to work by answering the following questions with the correct word from the list above:

1. Which word is often used in reference to a flag?
2. Which word describes someone who is stubborn?
3. Which word describes how someone might argue about a subject he or she feels strongly about?
4. Which word is a synonym for *praised*?
5. Which word describes someone who cannot fail?
6. Which word describes someone who gives very generous gifts?
7. Which word is another way of saying *attack*?

Vocabulary Development

1. furled
2. resolute
3. vehemently
4. extolled
5. infallible
6. lavish
7. assail

Literary Focus: Alliteration and Kennings

Write a line or two from *Beowulf* (especially Part One) on the chalkboard. Identify alliteration and kennings one at a time, demonstrating their use. After reading the feature, students might work in groups to respond to the listed questions.

Literary Focus

Alliteration and Kennings: Taking the Burden off the Bard

The Anglo-Saxon oral poet was assisted by two poetic devices, alliteration and the kenning.

Alliteration. Alliteration is the repetition of consonant sounds in words close to one another. Anglo-Saxon poetry is often called alliterative poetry. Instead of rhyme unifying the poem, the verse line is divided into two halves separated by a rhythmic pause, or **caesura**. In the first half of the line before the caesura, two words alliterate; in the second half, one word alliterates with the two from the first half. Many lines, however, have only two alliterative words, one in each half. Notice the alliterative *g* and the four primary stresses in this Old English line from *Beowulf*:

Gód mid Géatum Gréndles daéda

Literary Focus: Alliteration and Kennings

Analyzing the Text

1. This passage contains the kennings *warshirt, rock-face, hoard-guard, battle-fume, mound-keeper,* and *battle-fire.*
2. *Hyphenated compounds*—"gold-shining" (l. 7, means "glorious"); "a strong-hearted wakeful sleeper" (l. 38, refers to brave Beowulf); "that sin-stained demon" (l. 92, refers to Grendel). *Prepositional phrases*—"shepherd of evil, guardian of crime" (l. 41, refers to Grendel); "That mighty protector of men" (l. 81, refers to Beowulf); "the afflictor / Of men, tormentor of their days" (ll. 99–100, refers to Grendel). *Possessives*—"Higlac's follower" (l. 49, refers to Beowulf); "the Almighty's enemy" (l. 76, refers to Grendel); "Higlac's brave follower" (l. 103, refers to Beowulf); "that night's fierce work" (l. 118, refers to the battle).
3. Examples might include *big bird* for *airplane* and *top dog* for *boss*.
4. Raffel's translation more often keeps the caesura while Heaney's line tends to be longer. Students may feel that the style of Heaney's translation is more colloquial, more detailed.
5. *Figures of speech*—"mead was flowing" (Heaney); "trusting our swords" (Raffel). *Kennings*—"ring-giver" (Heaney); "mead-hall" (Raffel). *Alliteration*—"make good the gift of the war-gear" (Heaney); "boasting of how brave we'd be when Beowulf" (Raffel).

Kennings. The kenning, a special metaphor made of compound words, is a staple of Anglo-Saxon literature that also has a place in our language today. *Gas guzzler* and *headhunter* are two modern-day kennings you are likely to have heard.

The earliest and simplest kennings are compound words formed from two common nouns: *sky-candle* for *sun*, *battle-dew* for *blood,* and *whale-road* for *sea.* Later, kennings grew more elaborate, and compound adjectives joined the compound nouns. A ship became a *foamy-throated ship*, then a *foamy-throated sea-stallion,* and finally a *foamy-throated stallion of the whale-road.* Once a kenning was coined, it was used by the singer-poets over and over again.

In their original languages, kennings are almost always written as simple compounds, with no hyphens or spaces between the words. In translation, however, kennings are often written as hyphenated compounds (*sky-candle*, *foamy-throated*), as prepositional phrases (*wolf of wounds*), or as possessives (*the sword's tree*).

The work of kennings. Scholars believe that kennings filled three needs: (1) Old Norse and Anglo-Saxon poetry depended heavily on alliteration, but neither language had a large vocabulary. Poets created the alliterative words they needed by combining existing words. (2) Because the poetry was oral and had to be memorized, bards valued ready-made phrases. Such phrases made finished poetry easier to remember, and they gave bards time to think ahead when they were composing new poetry on the spot during a feast or ceremony. (3) The increasingly complex structure of the kennings must have satisfied the early Norse and Anglo-Saxon peoples' taste for elaboration.

Analyzing the text. As you examine these poetic devices, be sure to listen to the way they sound.

1. Read aloud the account of Beowulf's challenge to the dragon (lines 297–343), and listen for the effects of the alliteration. What **kennings** can you identify?
2. Look back over lines 1–126. Locate at least two examples of kennings written as **hyphenated compounds,** two written as **prepositional phrases,** and two written as **possessives.** What does each kenning refer to?
3. Compile a list of modern-day kennings, such as *headhunter*.
4. Here is an additional passage from Burton Raffel's translation. How does it compare with the corresponding lines (372–381) in Seamus Heaney's translation (page 36)?

> "I remember how we sat in the
>   mead-hall, drinking
> And boasting of how brave we'd be
>   when Beowulf
> Needed us, he who gave us these
>   swords
> And armor: All of us swore to repay
>   him,
> When the time came, kindness for
>   kindness
> —With our lives, if he needed
>   them. He allowed us to join
>   him,
> Chose us from all his great army,
>   thinking
> Our boasting words had some
>   weight, believing
> Our promises, trusting our swords.
>   He took us
> For soldiers, for men."

5. Now that you've read excerpts from two translations of *Beowulf,* think about the similarities and differences you see and hear between them. How does each translator use **figures of speech,** such as **kennings** and **alliteration**?

Vocabulary Development

Anglo-Saxon Legacy: Words and Word Parts

Words from Anglo-Saxon. English has borrowed words from most of the world's languages, but many words in our basic vocabulary come to us from Anglo-Saxon, or Old English. Simple, everyday words, such as the names of numbers (*an* for "one," *twa* for "two," *threo* for "three," *feower* for "four"), words designating family relationships (*fæder* for "father," *modor* for "mother," *sunu* for "son," *dohtor* for "daughter"), names for parts of the body (*heorte* for "heart," *fot* for "foot") and common, everyday things and activities (*æppel* for "apple," *hund* for "hound," *wefan* for "weave") are survivors of Old English words.

Anglo-Saxon affixes. Many English-language conventions can be traced back to Anglo-Saxon times. Both making nouns plural by adding *s* and creating the possessive of a noun by adding *'s* come to us from Old English. Old English has also given us the vowel changes in some irregular verbs like *sing, sang, sung* (*singan, sang, sungen*) and the regular endings for the past tense and past participles of regular verbs (as in *healed, has healed*). The word endings we use to create degrees of comparison with adjectives (as in *darker, darkest*) are also of Anglo-Saxon origin.

Anglo-Saxon has also contributed many important word parts—prefixes and suffixes—to the English language. Some of these affixes just change the tense, person, or number of a word, such as a verb. Others change the entire meaning of a word, and often its part of speech.

Prefixes from Anglo-Saxon	Meanings	Examples
a–	in; on; of; up; to	ashore, aside
be–	around; about; treat as	behind, befriend
for–	away; off; from	forsake, forget
mis–	badly; not; wrongly	misspell, misfire
over–	above; excessive	overtake, oversee
un–	not; reverse of	untrue, unknown

Suffixes from Anglo-Saxon	Meanings	Examples
–en	made of; like	golden, molten
–dom	state; rank; condition	wisdom, kingdom
–ful	full of; marked by	wonderful, useful
–hood	state; condition	brotherhood, neighborhood
–ish	suggesting; like	selfish, childish
–less	lacking; without	hopeless, helpless
–like	like; similar	dreamlike, childlike
–ly	like; characteristic of	friendly, cowardly
–ness	quality; state	kindness, tenderness
–some	apt to; showing	handsome, tiresome
–ward	in the direction of	forward, skyward
–y	showing; suggesting	wavy, hilly, salty

PRACTICE

List examples of modern English words that use each of the Anglo-Saxon prefixes and suffixes shown above.

SKILLS FOCUS
Vocabulary Skills
Understand and identify Anglo-Saxon words and affixes.

Gundestrup caldron.
National Museum, Copenhagen.

ASSESSING

Assessment
- Holt Assessment: *Literature, Reading, and Vocabulary*

RETEACHING

For lessons reteaching theme, meaning, and archetypes, see **Reteaching**, p. 1129A.

Connecting to World Literature

SKILLS FOCUS, pp. 44–45

Grade-Level Skills

■ **Literary Skills**

Analyze archetypes, including the epic hero.

■ **Literary Skills**

Compare literary forms of major literary periods.

Literary Focus: Epics

Before assigning this introduction, review with students the definition of *epic* on p. 44. Then, ask a volunteer to locate ancient Mesopotamia and Greece on a map.

DIRECT TEACHING

Ⓐ Literary Connections

Sundiata

An exciting blend of fact and legend, *Sundiata* is the best-known African epic. It tells the story of Sundiata Keita of the Mandingo people of the West African kingdom of old Mali some eight hundred years ago.

Ⓑ Reading Skills

❓ **Finding the main idea.** What connection does the author make between the epic and cultural identity? [The epic was conceived as a "national literature" that would explore and define the identity of that particular culture.]

Ⓒ Literary Connections

Hercules

Hercules is one of these special human heroes. The son of the god Jupiter and a mortal, he was worshiped in both ancient Greece and Rome. Hercules slew ferocious monsters, battled Amazons and giants, and descended to the underworld to do penance for the crime of killing his own children in a fit of madness.

Connecting to World Literature

Epics: Stories on a Grand Scale
by David Adams Leeming

> You have just read an excerpt from the Anglo-Saxon epic *Beowulf*. In this Connecting to World Literature feature, you will read excerpts from the following epics from around the world:
>
> from **Gilgamesh: A Verse Narrative** . . (ancient Mesopotamia) . . . 48
>
> from the **Iliad** by **Homer** . . . . (ancient Greece) . . . 57

A.D. 700
Beowulf first recorded

700 B.C.
Homer writes the *Iliad* and the *Odyssey*

1300 B.C.
The epic of *Gilgamesh* is put into complete form

Ⓐ "I teach kings the history of their ancestors," declares the narrator of the African epic *Sundiata*, "for the world is old, but the future springs from the past." These same words could be applied to epics from all times and places, for an **epic**—a long narrative poem about the exploits of a national hero—is a bridge from the past to the future. Epics carry Ⓑ a culture's history, values, myths, legends, and traditions from one generation to the next.

The Epic Hero: An Eternal Archetype

Whereas the old religious stories, or myths, tended to emphasize the deeds of the gods, epic poems emphasize the deeds of a special kind of human being related to the gods: the **epic hero.** From Gilgamesh to Achilles, epic heroes carry the images and super-Ⓒ natural energies of the gods within themselves. Yet these heroic figures are also, like all of us, subject to the joys and hardships of the human condition.

No matter what the differences may be between epics of different cultures or times, the epic hero remains constant. It is as if each hero wears the particular costume of his or her culture but is really the same figure underneath, facing the same kinds of challenges and ordeals. While the heroes of the Mesopotamian *Gilgamesh* epic, the Greek *Iliad*, and the Anglo-

Pages 44–45 cover **Literary Skills** Understand the epic and the archetype of the epic hero in ancient and modern literature. Compare literary forms of major literary periods.

44 Collection 1 The Anglo-Saxons

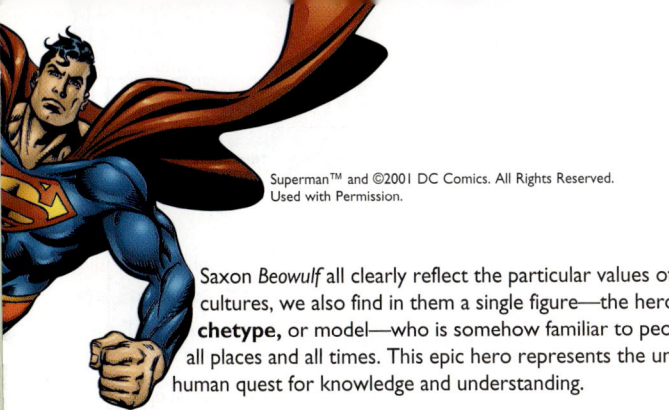

Superman™ and ©2001 DC Comics. All Rights Reserved. Used with Permission.

Saxon *Beowulf* all clearly reflect the particular values of their cultures, we also find in them a single figure—the heroic **archetype**, or model—who is somehow familiar to people of all places and all times. This epic hero represents the universal human quest for knowledge and understanding.

The Hero's Journey

The epic hero's adventures always involve trials and temptations. As in our own journey through life, there are always obstacles that stand in the way of the hero's goals. Like Gilgamesh, we all have our hopeless desires; like Achilles, we all have our potentially fatal weaknesses; like Beowulf, we must fight our own Grendels and dragons—our inner and outer demons. It is the epic hero's belief in himself (traditionally, epic heroes have always been male) and his own powers that make his success possible in spite of the obstacles.

The Epic Lives On

Today, the epic hero and his quest are alive and well in our own popular culture. In movies, comic books, fantasy novels, television programs, and video games, we meet an endless procession of larger-than-life, sometimes superhuman heroes—both male and female—whom we recognize as descendants of the ancient world's epic heroes. The archetype endures because it is, quite simply, universal and always relevant, a symbol of some of the most deeply held values of humankind. The stories of the epic hero address every aspect of the human experience—its joys, its agonies, its accomplishments, its failures, its sense of its relation to the mysteries of the universe. In Gilgamesh's journey from arrogant kingship to humbled returning pilgrim, in Achilles' passage from pouting adolescent to experienced warrior humbled by the ancient Priam, and in Beowulf's movement from self-seeking adventure to heroic but humble death, we discover a dramatic record of the personal and collective human quest.

Hercules slaying the centaur Eurytion. Detail of a marble sculpture.
Ali Meyer/CORBIS.

> An **epic** is a long narrative poem that narrates the great deeds of a larger-than-life hero who embodies the most deeply held values of a particular society.

> **The Features of an Epic**
> - Takes the form of a long narrative poem about a quest, told in formal, elevated language
> - Narrates the exploits of a larger-than-life hero who embodies the values of a particular culture
> - Begins with a statement of subject and theme and, sometimes, a prayer to a deity
> - Deals with events on a large scale
> - Uses many of the conventions of oral storytelling, such as repetition, sound effects, figures of speech, and stock epithets
> - Often includes gods and goddesses as characters
> - Mixes myth, legend, and history

DIRECT TEACHING

D **Exploring the Culture**
WOMEN IN EPICS
Although some of the goddesses that show up in epic poetry are extremely warlike, human female characters in traditional epics are usually presented as the property of the epic heroes—either as prizes to be won (or defended) or as family members.

E **Literary Focus**
Epic hero. Can you think of a person in literature, film, or real life who is perceived by some people to exemplify the values of American culture? [Possible response: John Wayne.] Do you agree with that perception? [Answers will vary.]

F **Literary Focus**
The epic. Almost all epic heroes have to face death, the ultimate human experience; some heroes even visit the land of the dead. This convention is often used to make the point that human beings must accept their mortality and their place in the larger scheme of things.

G **Literary Focus**
The epic. The high style of the figures of speech used in epics—as indicated especially in the Homeric, or epic, simile (see p. 56)—never obscures the reality of human life. In a Homeric simile a noble deed might be compared to the crackling of a piece of sausage in a frying pan. Apollo's destruction of a city wall is compared to a boy's destruction of a sand castle. Such comparisons to ordinary life enabled the audience to identify deeply with the events of the epic.

Epics: Stories on a Grand Scale **45**

DIRECT TEACHING

VIEWING THE ART

This relief represents Gilgamesh as a subduer of lions, a role assumed by many heroes. The lion is a contradictory figure because it symbolizes both kingship (civilization) and savagery (civilization's opposite).

Activity. Ask students to describe Gilgamesh and the lion. Are the proportions realistic? What conclusion can be drawn about Gilgamesh? [Gilgamesh looks powerful and serene; the lion looks small but menacing. Gilgamesh is larger than life: an ordinary person would not be able to hold a lion with one arm.]

A Literary Focus

? The epic. What reasons for fighting Humbaba does Gilgamesh give in this speech? [He wants to prove that his people should not fear Humbaba and that the gods can be defied. He also wants to inspire the youth of Uruk with his deeds.] How do the elders react to Gilgamesh's plan? [Possible response: Their wish for glory overcomes their fear.]

B Literary Focus

? The epic. How would you summarize Gilgamesh's attitude toward death? [Possible response: Unlike the gods, all humans die; your actions are not important, so fear of losing your life is not justified. However, if you die in battle against a worthy enemy, you will be remembered and praised.]

---

from Gilgamesh
A Verse Narrative

retold by **Herbert Mason**

Why are you worried about death?
Only the gods are immortal anyway,
Sighed Gilgamesh.
What men do is nothing, so fear is never
5 Justified. What happened to your power
That once could challenge and equal mine?
I will go ahead of you, and if I die
I will at least have the reward
Of having people say: He died in war
10 Against Humbaba. You cannot discourage me
With fears and hesitations.
I will fight Humbaba,
I will cut down his cedars.
Tell the armorers to build us two-edged swords
15 And double shields and tell them
I am impatient and cannot wait long.

Thus Gilgamesh and Enkidu went
Together to the marketplace
To notify the Elders of Uruk
20 Who were meeting in their senate.
They too were talking of Humbaba,
As they often did,
Edging always in their thoughts
Toward the forbidden.

25 The one you speak of, Gilgamesh addressed them,
I now must meet, I want to prove
Him not the awesome thing we think he is
And that the boundaries set up by gods
Are not unbreakable. I will defeat him
30 In his cedar forest. The youth of Uruk
Need this fight. They have grown soft
And restless.

The old men leaned a little forward
Remembering old wars. A flush burned on

Gilgamesh holding a lion. Relief from the palace of Sargon II (8th century B.C.), Khorsabad, Iraq.
Louvre, Paris.

(Top left) detail of mosaic from the Turkish palace of Attalos II (3rd century B.C.).
Pergamon Museum, Berlin. The Bridgeman Art Library.

DIFFERENTIATING INSTRUCTION

Learners Having Difficulty
Some students may have difficulty following the plot of this story in verse. Have students work in pairs to read the selection aloud. Ask them to stop every ten lines or so to summarize what is happening to the characters.

Invite learners having difficulty to read *Gilgamesh* in interactive format in *The Holt Reader* and to use the sidenotes as aids to understanding the selection.

English-Language Learners
Since Mason does not use quotation marks to distinguish dialogue, students may need help understanding which character is speaking throughout the poem. Have students form small groups, and give each student a photocopy of the selection. Each group should go through the selection, placing quotation marks around the dialogue and noting in the margin which character is speaking.

Then have each group read the selection aloud as a play, with students taking the parts of Gilgamesh, Enkidu, and sections of the part of the narrator who also voices Humbaba and the elders and people of Uruk.

35 Their cheeks. It seemed a little dangerous
    And yet they saw their king
    Was seized with passion for this fight.
    Their voices gave the confidence his friend
    Had failed to give; some even said
40 Enkidu's wisdom was a sign of cowardice.
    You see, my friend, laughed Gilgamesh,
    The wise of Uruk have outnumbered you.

    Amidst the speeches in the hall
    That called upon the gods for their protection,
45 Gilgamesh saw in his friend that pain
    He had seen before and asked him what it was
    That troubled him.

    Enkidu could not speak. He held his tears
    Back. Barely audibly he said:
50 It is a road which you have never traveled.

    The armorers brought to Gilgamesh his weapons
    And put them in his hand. He took his quiver,
    Bow and ax, and two-edged sword,
    And they began to march.

55 The Elders gave their austere blessing
    And the people shouted: Let Enkidu lead,
    Don't trust your strength, he knows the forests,
    The one who goes ahead will save his friend.
    May Shamash° bring you victory. . . .

60 After three days they reached the edge
    Of the forest where Humbaba's watchman stood.
    Suddenly it was Gilgamesh who was afraid,
    Enkidu who reminded him to be fearless.
    The watchman sounded his warning to Humbaba.
65 The two friends moved slowly toward the forest gate.

    When Enkidu touched the gate his hand felt numb,
    He could not move his fingers or his wrist,
    His face turned pale like someone's witnessing
                                                 a death,
    He tried to ask his friend for help
70 Whom he had just encouraged to move on,

Vocabulary
austere (ô·stir′) *adj.*: restrained; spare; very plain.

Gilgamesh between two demigods supporting the sun. Detail from a stone monument (9th century B.C.), Tell Halaf, Syria.
Archaeological Museum, Aleppo, Syria/Dagli Orti. The Art Archive.

59. Shamash (shä′mäsh): god associated with the sun and human laws.

Gilgamesh: A Verse Narrative   49

DIRECT TEACHING

VIEWING THE ART

Votive figures like this one were made for religious purposes and were left at temples to offer prayers to the Sumerian gods. Notice the figure's stiff, formal stance, with hands clasped and eyes wide open, apparently in a state of awe.

A Literary Focus

? The epic. What might the dark forest represent? [Possible responses: The forest might represent the great unknown that everyone must face; it might represent aspects of the epic hero's personality that he has not yet dealt with; it might represent heaven or hell.]

B Reading Skills

? Tracing recurring themes. Enkidu's fear and pain during the night are exacerbated by having to face them alone, as Gilgamesh is sleeping. What theme recurs in this passage? [Possible responses: the importance of friendship; people are stronger together than they are alone.]

C Content-Area Connections

Literature: Enkidu and the Courtesan
After Enkidu's creation by the gods, he lives among animals in the wilderness. News of the wild man comes to Gilgamesh, who sends a temple courtesan to teach Enkidu the ways of civilization. The prostitute teaches Enkidu about love, clothing, and proper manners and brings him back to Uruk. As Enkidu lies sleepless in the cedar forest, the monsters of his imagination seem much more dreadful than any creature he saw as a wild man.

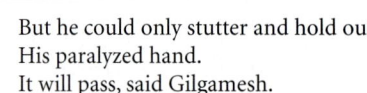

<pre>
        But he could only stutter and hold out
        His paralyzed hand.
        It will pass, said Gilgamesh.
        Would you want to stay behind because of that?
75   We must go down into the forest together.
        Forget your fear of death. I will go before you
        And protect you. Enkidu followed close behind
        So filled with fear he could not think or speak.
        Soon they reached the high cedars.

80   They stood in awe at the foot
        Of the green mountain. Pleasure
        Seemed to grow from fear of Gilgamesh.
        As when one comes upon a path in woods
        Unvisited by men, one is drawn near
85   The lost and undiscovered in himself;
        He was revitalized by danger.
        They knew it was the path Humbaba made.
        Some called the forest "Hell," and others "Paradise";
        What difference does it make? said Gilgamesh.
90   But night was falling quickly
        And they had no time to call it names,
        Except perhaps "The Dark,"
        Before they found a place at the edge of the forest
        To serve as shelter for their sleep.

95   It was a restless night for both. One snatched
        At sleep and sprang awake from dreams. The other
        Could not rest because of pain that spread
        Throughout his side. Enkidu was alone
        With sights he saw brought on by pain
100   And fear, as one in deep despair
        May lie beside his love who sleeps
        And seems so unafraid, absorbing in himself the phantoms
        That she cannot see—phantoms diminished for one
        When two can see and stay awake to talk of them
105   And search out a solution to despair,
        Or lie together in each other's arms,
        Or weep and in exhaustion from their tears
        Perhaps find laughter for their fears.
        But alone and awake the size and nature
110   Of the creatures in his mind grow monstrous,
        Beyond resemblance to the creatures he had known
        Before the prostitute had come into his life.
</pre>

Figure of a man from the Square Temple at Tell Asmar (c. 2750–2600 B.C.), Iraq.
National Museum, Damascus.
© Giraudon/Art Resource, New York.

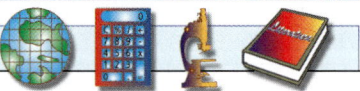

CONTENT-AREA CONNECTIONS

Literature: The Story of Gilgamesh
If you do not assign advanced learners to research and present a summary of the entire story, the rest of the epic of *Gilgamesh* can be summarized as follows:

After their victory in the cedar forest, Gilgamesh and Enkidu return to Uruk. Gilgamesh refuses to wed Ishtar, goddess of love and war, because she has turned many of her previous lovers into animals. In a rage, Ishtar causes the Bull of Heaven to be set loose upon Uruk, where it slays many of the people, but Gilgamesh and Enkidu succeed in killing the bull. Enkidu then has a dream that a council of the gods discusses the disrespectful deeds of the two heroes and decrees that Enkidu is the one who must die in atonement. Enkidu falls ill and dies, leaving Gilgamesh grief-stricken.

Gilgamesh (center) depicted on a Chaldean seal.
Bettmann/CORBIS.

> He cried aloud for them to stop appearing over him
> Emerging from behind the trees with phosphorescent° eyes
> 115 Brought on by rain. He could not hear his voice
> But knew he screamed and could not move his arms
> But thought they tried to move
> As if a heavy weight he could raise
> Or wriggle out from underneath
> 120 Had settled on his chest,
> Like a turtle trapped beneath a fallen branch,
> Each effort only added to paralysis.
> He could not make his friend, his one companion, hear.
>
> Gilgamesh awoke but could not hear
> 125 His friend in agony, he still was captive to his dreams
> Which he would tell aloud to exorcise:°
> I saw us standing in a mountain gorge,
> A rockslide fell on us, we seemed no more
> Than insects under it. And then
> 130 A solitary graceful man appeared
> And pulled me out from under the mountain.
> He gave me water and I felt released.
>
> Tomorrow you will be victorious,
> Enkidu said, to whom the dream brought chills
> 135 (For only one of them, he knew, would be released)
> Which Gilgamesh could not perceive in the darkness
> For he went back to sleep without responding
> To his friend's interpretation of his dream.

114. phosphorescent (fäs′fə·res′ənt) *adj.*: giving off light after being exposed to heat.

126. exorcise *v.*: to drive out.

Understanding his own mortality for the first time, Gilgamesh sets off to search for immortality. He seeks his ancestor Utnapishtim, the Mesopotamian Noah, who survived a great flood that killed the rest of humanity and was rewarded with eternal life. Gilgamesh travels through the gate to the afterlife and eventually enters the garden of the gods. He meets there several gods who discourage him in his quest, but finally finds Utnapishtim, who tells the hero, "There is no permanence." Finally, Utnapishtim is persuaded to tell Gilgamesh of the existence of an underwater plant that will renew youth. Gilgamesh finds the plant, but in a moment of carelessness, he allows it to be eaten by a serpent. His chance for immortality gone, Gilgamesh returns to Uruk sadder but wiser, and he lives out the rest of his days as a kind and just ruler.

DIRECT TEACHING

A Literary Focus

Foil. What do Enkidu's responses to Gilgamesh's dreams reveal about his character? [He is thoughtful and holds his feelings inside. He attaches more importance to Gilgamesh's well-being than to his own fear.] What do Gilgamesh's responses to his own dreams reveal about his character? [He is impulsive and tells Enkidu everything he is thinking. He is never afraid for long.]

B Literary Focus

The epic. Epic heroes often have rather ambiguous relationships with the gods. Part human and part god, epic heroes may offend the gods one moment and appeal to them for aid the next, as Gilgamesh does here.

C Literary Focus

Figurative language. What figures of speech are used to describe Humbaba? [Similes are used to compare Humbaba's head to that of a water buffalo and his shoulders to those of a porter weighed down by building stones.] What characteristics do these comparisons emphasize? [Humbaba's strength and size]

D Reading Skills

Identifying cause and effect. Why does Gilgamesh first feel pity for Humbaba but then quickly change his mind? [Possible response: Humbaba is a slave to the gods, but the gods never notice him. He seems pitiable to both Enkidu and Gilgamesh, but when he strikes Enkidu, the warriors' pity turns to rage.]

    Did you call me? Gilgamesh sat up again.
140 Why did I wake again? I thought you touched me.
    Why am I afraid? I felt my limbs grow numb
    As if some god passed over us drawing out our life.
    I had another dream:
    This time the heavens were alive with fire, but soon
145 The clouds began to thicken, death rained down on us,
    The lightning flashes stopped, and everything
    Which rained down turned to ashes.
    What does this mean, Enkidu?

    That you will be victorious against Humbaba,
150 Enkidu said, or someone said through him
    Because he could not hear his voice
    Or move his limbs although he thought he spoke,
    And soon he saw his friend asleep beside him.

    At dawn Gilgamesh raised his ax
155 And struck at the great cedar.
    When Humbaba heard the sound of falling trees,
    He hurried down the path that they had seen
    But only he had traveled. Gilgamesh felt weak
    At the sound of Humbaba's footsteps and called to Shamash
160 Saying, I have followed you in the way decreed;
    Why am I abandoned now? Suddenly the winds
    Sprang up. They saw the great head of Humbaba
    Like a water buffalo's bellowing down the path,
    His huge and clumsy legs, his flailing arms
165 Thrashing at phantoms in his precious trees.
    His single stroke could cut a cedar down
    And leave no mark on him. His shoulders,
    Like a porter's° under building stones,
    Were permanently bent by what he bore;
170 He was the slave who did the work for gods
    But whom the gods would never notice.
    Monstrous in his contortion, he aroused
    The two almost to pity.
    But pity was the thing that might have killed.
175 It made them pause just long enough to show
    How pitiless he was to them. Gilgamesh in horror saw
    Him strike the back of Enkidu and beat him to the ground
    Until he thought his friend was crushed to death.
    He stood still watching as the monster leaned to make

Man carrying a goat, from a Sam'al basalt bas-relief (c. 730 B.C.).
Pergamon Museum, Berlin. The Bridgeman Art Library.

168. porter *n.*: person who carries things for other people.

Vocabulary

decreed (dē·krēd′) *v.*: ordered; commanded.
contortion (kən·tôr′shən) *n.*: twisted shape or motion.

READING MINI-LESSON

Developing Word-Attack Skills

Use the selection word *enveloping* to explore words that are pronounced differently depending on their part of speech. Compare the spelling and pronunciation of the verb *envelop* (en·vel′əp) and the noun *envelope* (än′və·lōp′). Point out that in the case of *envelop* and *envelope*, the presence or absence of final *e* provides a clue to how the words are pronounced. In most cases, particularly with words that end with *–ate*, sentence context and part of speech are the only clues. Write these sentences on the chalkboard, underlining *articulate* in each sentence:

- It's often hard to articulate ideas.
- Even articulate people sometimes have difficulty.

180 His final strike against his friend, unable
To move to help him, and then Enkidu slid
Along the ground like a ram making its final lunge
On wounded knees. Humbaba fell and seemed
To crack the ground itself in two, and Gilgamesh,
185 As if this fall had snapped him from his daze,
Returned to life
And stood over Humbaba with his ax
Raised high above his head watching the monster plead
In strangled sobs and desperate appeals
190 The way the sea contorts under a violent squall.
I'll serve you as I served the gods, Humbaba said;
I'll build you houses from their sacred trees.

Enkidu feared his friend was weakening
And called out: Gilgamesh! Don't trust him!
195 As if there were some hunger in himself
That Gilgamesh was feeling
That turned him momentarily to yearn
For someone who would serve, he paused;
And then he raised his ax up higher
200 And swung it in a perfect arc
Into Humbaba's neck. He reached out
To touch the wounded shoulder of his friend,

And late that night he reached again
To see if he was yet asleep, but there was only
205 Quiet breathing. The stars against the midnight sky
Were sparkling like mica° in a riverbed.
In the slight breeze
The head of Humbaba was swinging from a tree.

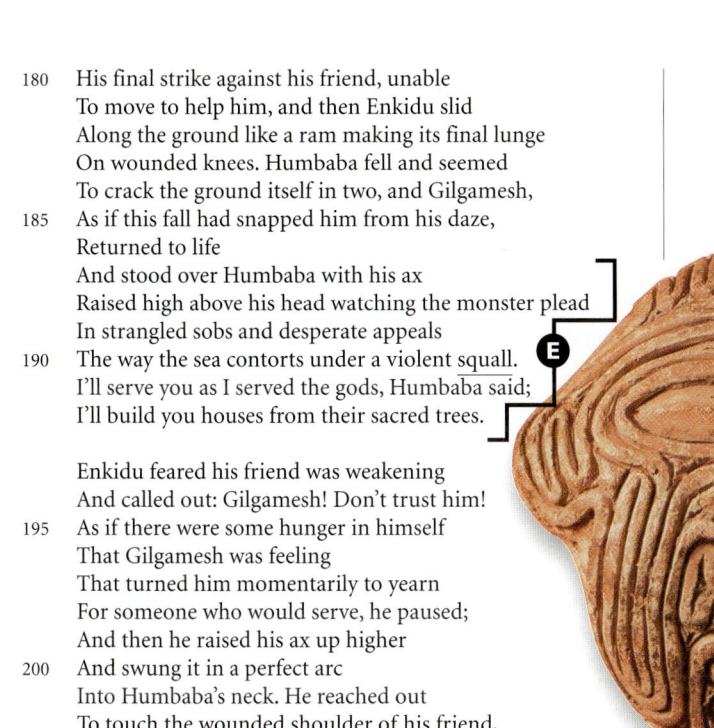

Babylonian sculpture of head of Humbaba carved to resemble intestines (c. 1800–1600 B.C.).
British Museum, London. The Bridgeman Art Library.

206. **mica** *n.*: kind of thin, crystalline mineral.

Vocabulary
squall (skwôl) *n.*: violent storm that doesn't last very long.

INDEPENDENT PRACTICE

Response and Analysis

Reading Check

1. The elders give Gilgamesh their support.
2. Humbaba strikes down Enkidu. When Humbaba falls, Gilgamesh starts to cut off the giant's head. Humbaba pleads for his life, but Enkidu warns his friend not to listen, and so Humbaba dies. Contrary to Gilgamesh's expectations, he comes close to letting the giant live, and Enkidu is wounded.

Thinking Critically

3. Enkidu is cautious and afraid of death, and he places the safety of his friend and himself before the pursuit of fame; we therefore see more clearly that Gilgamesh is impulsive and heedless of danger; he values excitement, glory, and absolute power more than safety.
4. They encourage each other to be brave and help each other in battle. Gilgamesh causes Enkidu's injury by bringing him along on the expedition and then by not defending him from Humbaba. Students' Quickwrite comparisons will vary.
5. Gilgamesh views him as a slave of the gods. Humbaba's shoulders are bent by the work he performs for them, but the gods are indifferent to him.
6. *Figures of speech*—"The great head of Humbaba like a water buffalo's"; "His shoulders, like a porter's under building stones." They arouse fear because they suggest Humbaba's size and strength.

Extending and Evaluating

7. Students may say that Gilgamesh is too thoughtless and power hungry to be admirable. He needs to learn humility.

Response and Analysis

Reading Check

1. How do the elders of Uruk respond to Gilgamesh's plan?
2. Summarize what happens in the cedar forest. Do events unfold exactly as Gilgamesh anticipated? Explain.

Thinking Critically

3. Enkidu acts as a **foil** to Gilgamesh. What do you learn about Gilgamesh's strengths and weaknesses by contrasting him with Enkidu?
4. How do Gilgamesh and Enkidu help each other on their adventure? Are there any ways in which they hurt each other? Compare their experiences with those of the friends you wrote about in your Quickwrite notes. ✏️
5. Enkidu repeatedly associates Humbaba with death. How does Gilgamesh characterize Humbaba? What are we told about Humbaba's relationship with the gods?
6. Find specific **figures of speech** that describe Humbaba. How do these descriptions make you feel about Humbaba?

Extending and Evaluating

7. After reading this excerpt, do you see Gilgamesh as a hero worthy of unqualified admiration? What lessons, if any, do you think he still needs to learn if he is to be a true **epic hero**?

Comparing Literature

8. How does Humbaba compare with the monster figures in the *Beowulf* epic?
9. How is Gilgamesh like and unlike the epic hero Beowulf? What elements of Gilgamesh's battle with Humbaba are similar to Beowulf's battles with his monsters?

SKILLS FOCUS

Literary Skills Analyze the use of a foil. Analyze the epic and the archetype of the epic hero in ancient and modern literature. Compare literary forms of major literary periods.
Writing Skills Write an interior monologue.
Vocabulary Skills Demonstrate word knowledge.

WRITING

The Inner Quest
Even though the great early epics are full of action, they also show keen psychological insight. Gilgamesh and Enkidu are guided by internal needs and plagued by inner fears and doubts. These are revealed in the characters' dialogue and in their dreams. Imagine what Gilgamesh or Enkidu is thinking and feeling after the battle with Humbaba. Write an **interior monologue** that expresses what is going through the mind of one of them. Use the first-person pronoun *I*.

> **Vocabulary Development**
> **Question and Answer**
> Answer the following questions to test your understanding of the underlined Vocabulary words.
> 1. What is the opposite of an <u>austere</u> room?
> 2. What type of person would have <u>decreed</u> something?
> 3. What could a <u>contortion</u> look like?
> 4. What is the difference between a light drizzle and a <u>squall</u>?

Sumerian bull's head in bronze, from a musical instrument or piece of furniture (c. 2500 B.C.).
Pergamon Museum, Berlin. The Bridgeman Art Library.

Comparing Literature

8. Like the *Beowulf* monsters, Humbaba is evil, pitiless, and hostile to humans. Unlike them, the giant is depicted as pitiable.
9. Both are brave, strong, and nobly born, and both seek fame and glory. Gilgamesh is more defiant of the gods and depends on his friend Enkidu, while Beowulf is mainly self-sufficient. Each severs the head of his opponent.

Vocabulary Development

1. a luxurious room
2. a king
3. a person twisted up
4. A squall is more forceful.

Homer and the *Iliad*

Europe's first and most enduring literary epics, the *Iliad* (il′ē·əd) and the *Odyssey* (äd′i·sē), were composed sometime between 900 and 700 B.C. We know little about Homer, the author of these epics. He was probably a native of the Greek district of Ionia on the western coast of Asia Minor. The name *Homer* may mean "hostage," suggesting that the poet may have been a slave or descended from slaves. Homer belonged to a class of bards who played a vitally important role in Greek society, serving as both oral historians and entertainers. Tradition says Homer was blind, a detail probably based more on convention than on fact: In Greek culture, physical blindness was often a metaphor for profound insight.

The Legend of the Trojan War

Both the *Iliad* and the *Odyssey* tell stories about the heroes and events of the Trojan War. According to oral tradition, the war began not with a battle but with a beauty contest—an unusual beauty contest. Three goddesses—Aphrodite, Athena, and Hera—decided to compete for a golden apple that was inscribed "To the Fairest." The gods, smart enough not to get involved in a potentially hazardous situation, chose a mortal to judge the most beautiful goddess. Paris, a young and handsome but naive prince of Troy, was selected. Each goddess in turn tried to bribe Paris in order to get his vote. The bribe Paris finally accepted was Aphrodite's, for she offered him the most appealing gift of all—marriage to the world's most beautiful woman, Helen, the wife of King Menelaus of Greece. Paris took Helen from Menelaus, and the two sailed for Troy. Outraged by the abduction of Helen, the Greek chieftains, bound by oaths of loyalty, banded together under the leadership of Menelaus's brother, Agamemnon, and attacked Troy. The war party laid siege to Troy, beginning a conflict that would drag on for ten years before the Greeks would finally succeed in sacking Troy and recapturing Helen—thanks to the wiles of the clever hero Odysseus.

Background to the *Iliad*

The *Iliad* opens as the Trojan War enters its tenth year, and it closes several weeks later. The story revolves around two main characters: Achilles, the bravest and handsomest warrior in the Greek army, and his enemy Hector, the honorable warrior-prince of the Trojans. In Book 22 of the epic, the conflict between these two antagonists reaches its tragic climax.

The tragedy that is at the heart of the *Iliad* is set into motion by a human emotion: the anger of Achilles. Human beings are the epic's combatants, but gods and goddesses take sides and profoundly affect the outcome. The Greeks saw their deities as immortal and powerful but in many ways just like humans: interested in human events and actions and capable of the same weaknesses as people—rivalry, jealousy, anger, and pettiness. The Greek gods and goddesses could and did involve themselves in human affairs and could either help or hinder individual people. Ultimately, though, as Homer's epic demonstrates, a person's fate was based as much on his or her own character and actions as on a proper relationship with the gods.

Homer 55

DIRECT TEACHING

A Content-Area Connections
Literature: The *Odyssey*
The *Odyssey* takes place in the aftermath of the events of the *Iliad*. The ten-year siege of Troy finally over, Odysseus, one of the Greek generals, sets out for his home on the island of Ithaca. The poem relates his fantastic adventures on the long voyage home. Odysseus tangles with the Sirens, the Cyclops, the witch Calypso, and the sea god Poseidon, among others; loses his ship and all his men; and is washed ashore in various parts of the Mediterranean before finally making it home to his wife and son in Ithaca. As you might guess, the English word *odyssey*, meaning "an epic journey," comes from the name Odysseus.

B Exploring the Historical Period
THE TROJAN WAR
Evidence from excavations carried out at the archaeological site of Troy (in Turkey) points to a real war that took place around 1200 B.C.—three hundred to five hundred years before Homer—between the Greeks and the people of Troas (Troy). The conflict may have been over the control of the Dardanelles and Black Sea trade.

C Content-Area Connections
Culture/Literature: Helen
Helen was the offspring of Zeus and Leda, a queen of Sparta. Zeus came to Leda in the form of a swan. In some versions of the legend, Leda laid two eggs, from which were hatched Helen and Pollux in one egg and Clytemnestra (later the wife of King Agamemnon, leader of the Athenians) and Castor in the other.

CONTENT-AREA CONNECTIONS

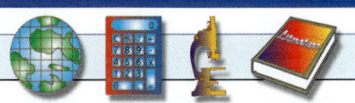

Archaeology: The Discovery of Troy
The historical city of Troy was discovered by the German archaeologist Heinrich Schliemann (1822–1890) in 1871 at what is now Hissarlik in Turkey. Schliemann deduced Troy's location from clues in the texts of the *Iliad* and the *Odyssey*; the archaeological world was dumbfounded when Schliemann announced that he had found the fabled city of ancient Troy. To date nine cities have been detected in the archaeological strata, the earliest dating from around 3000 B.C. Troy VIIa is probably the city sacked by the historical equivalent of Achilles' army; it appears to have been destroyed by enemy attack around 1200 B.C., close to the legendary date of the fall of Troy.

Individual activity. Have students research information regarding the archaeological findings at the site of Troy. To begin, have them read the Connection on p. 67.

Homer 55

SKILLS FOCUS, pp. 56–72

Grade-Level Skills

- **Literary Skills**

Analyze epic similes.

- **Literary Skills**

Compare literary forms of major literary periods.

PRETEACHING

Summary *above grade level*

The Trojan forces have retreated into the city, but Hector, their general and son of King Priam and Queen Hecuba, remains alone before the gates of the city, waiting to challenge the mighty Greek warrior Achilles. The king and queen implore their son to return to safety, but Hector stands fast. Achilles approaches at a run, raging at Hector's disrespectful treatment of the body of Patroclus, Achilles' friend; Hector loses his courage and flees. Achilles pursues the Trojan three times around the walls of Troy. Zeus, king of the gods, favors Hector and wishes to help him, but Athena, goddess of wisdom, is on the side of the Greeks. She protests that Hector's doom is already sealed, and Zeus agrees.

(continued)

Before You Read

from Book 22: The Death of Hector

Make the Connection
Quickwrite

The *Iliad* is essentially a war story, and its heroes are warriors, but men like Achilles and Hector are not just bloodthirsty killers eager for the next fight. Homer's warriors strive to achieve *arete*, or personal honor and excellence. In their eyes it is honorable to fight bravely for one's king and comrades and dishonorable to seek safety for oneself when one's friends are threatened. To die at the hands of a more powerful enemy is far preferable to them than living with the dishonor of having fled a fight or failed to give one's all in battle. What do the concepts of honor and personal excellence mean to you? How can an ideal of honor make a better society? (Could it also harm a society?) Take some notes on contemporary ideals of honor and how they compare and contrast with the *arete* of Homer's heroes.

Literary Focus
The Epic Simile

One of the most important features of the *Iliad* is Homer's use of extended comparisons called **epic similes** (also known as **Homeric similes**). Homer's comparisons often extend over many lines and make use of the words *like* and *as*. These complex figures of speech usually compare extraordinary, heroic actions to simple, everyday events that Homer's audience could easily understand. For example, in lines 1–3 of this excerpt from Book 22, Achilles, in hot pursuit of Hector, is compared to a hunting dog: "nonstop / as a hound in the mountains starts a fawn from its lair, / hunting him down the gorges, down the narrow glens." By using the familiar image of a hunt, Homer makes it easy for his listeners to imagine Achilles racing headlong after Hector.

INTERNET
Vocabulary Practice
•
More About Homer
•
Keyword: LE5 12-1

SKILLS FOCUS
Literary Skills
Understand the epic simile.

An **epic**, or **Homeric, simile** is a long, elaborate comparison of two events, one unusual and heroic, the other familiar and ordinary.

For more on the Epic, see the Handbook of Literary and Historical Terms.

Background

As the *Iliad* begins, the war between the Greeks and the Trojans has been a stalemate for nearly ten years. Each army has fought bravely, and each has received the help of the gods. Apollo assists Hector and the Trojans, and Athena aids Achilles and the Greeks (who are also referred to as the Achaeans or the Argives). Prior to Book 22, Hector kills Patroclus, Achilles' dearest friend, and strips the corpse of its armor, leaving the body exposed and unburied. Because the Greeks believed that a soul could not find rest until certain burial rites had been performed, Achilles is enraged at Hector and seeks revenge.

Vocabulary Development

groveling (gräv′əl·iŋ) *v.* used as *adj.*: crawling; humiliating oneself in front of authority.

gallant (gal′ənt) *adj.*: noble; brave.

scourge (skʉrj) *n.*: means of inflicting severe punishment. Usually the word refers to a whip.

fawning (fôn′iŋ) *v.* used as *adj.*: cringing and pleading.

56   Collection 1   The Anglo-Saxons

RESOURCES: READING

Planning
- *One-Stop Planner* CD-ROM with ExamView Test Generator

Differentiating Instruction
- *Holt Reading Solutions*
- *The Holt Reader*
- *Supporting Instruction in Spanish*
- *Audio CD Library, Selections and Summaries in Spanish*

Vocabulary
- *Vocabulary Development*

Grammar and Language
- *Daily Language Activities*
- *Language Handbook Worksheets*

Assessment
- *Holt Assessment: Literature, Reading, and Vocabulary*
- *Holt Online Assessment*

- *One-Stop Planner* CD-ROM with ExamView Test Generator

Internet
- go.hrw.com (Keyword: LE5 12-1)
- *Elements of Literature Online*

Media
- *Audio CD Library, Selections and Summaries in Spanish*
- *Fine Art Transparencies*

the Iliad

from Book 22: The Death of Hector
Homer
translated by **Robert Fagles**

The Characters in the *Iliad*

The Greeks

Achilles (ə·kil′ēz′): son of a mortal king, Peleus, and the sea goddess Thetis; king of the Myrmidons; mightiest of the Greek warriors.

Patroclus (pə·trō′kləs): Greek warrior and dearest friend of Achilles.

The Trojans

Hector (hek′tər): son of King Priam and Queen Hecuba; commander of the Trojan forces.

Paris (par′is): son of King Priam and Queen Hecuba; also known as Alexandros.

Priam (prī′əm): king of Troy; father of Hector and Paris.

Gods and Goddesses

Apollo (ə·päl′ō): god of poetry, music, and prophecy; often referred to only as the son of Zeus and Leto, the daughter of Titans. Apollo sides with the Trojans.

Athena (ə·thē′nə): goddess of wisdom. Athena takes the Greeks' side in the conflict.

Zeus (zo͞os): father-god. Zeus remains more or less neutral throughout the conflict.

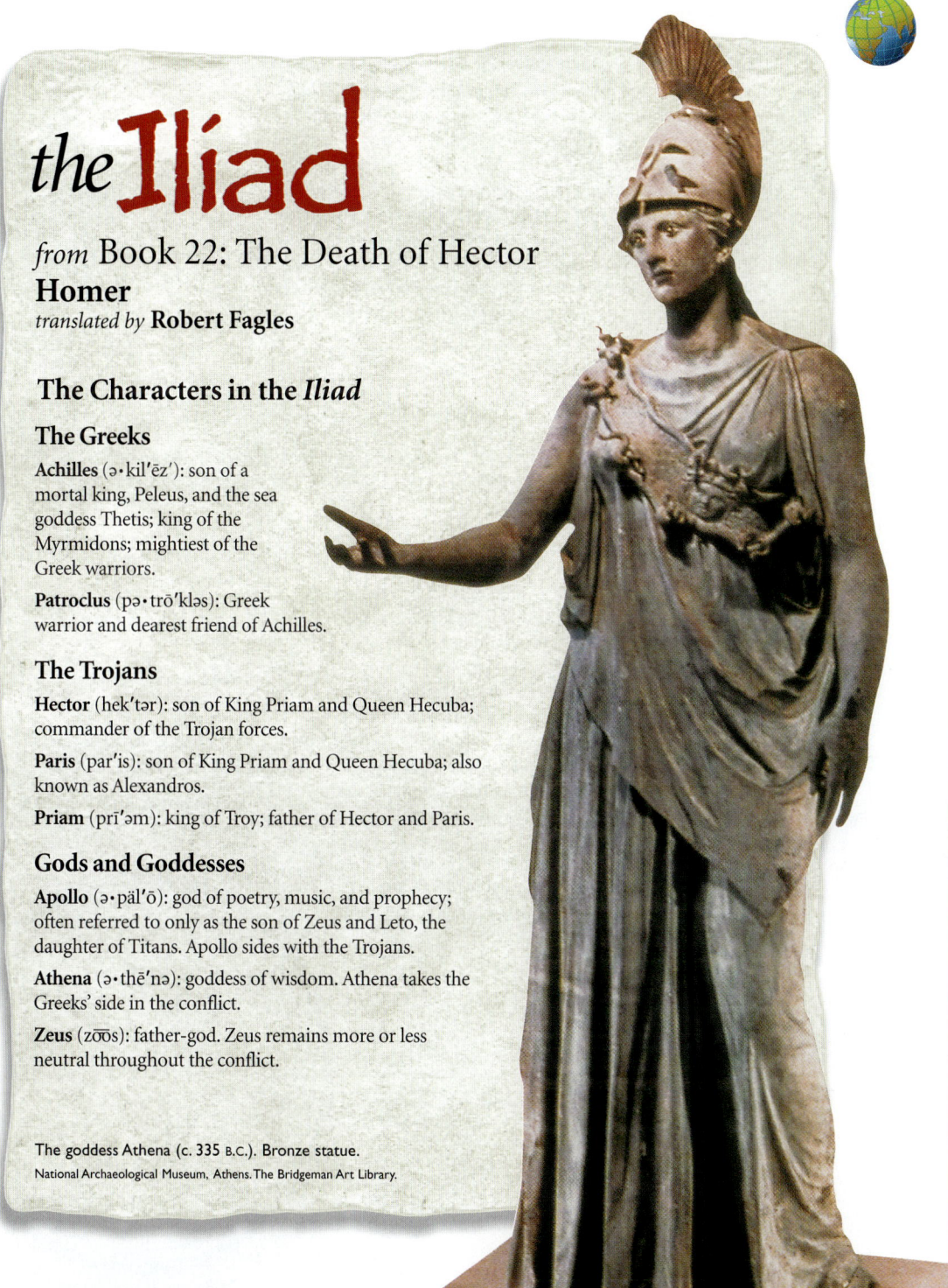

The goddess Athena (c. 335 B.C.). Bronze statue.
National Archaeological Museum, Athens. The Bridgeman Art Library.

Previewing Vocabulary

Have students complete each of the following sentences with the correct Vocabulary word from p. 56.

1. The _____ dog whined pitifully from the other side of the fence. [fawning]
2. The _____ firefighter saved the occupants from the burning building. [gallant]
3. The students felt that their professor's vicious exams were a _____. [scourge]
4. I made _____ apologies to Rita for standing her up. [groveling]

(continued)

Athena tricks Hector by assuming the form of his brother Deiphobus and then deserting him as soon as he turns to fight Achilles. The Greek strikes the Trojan down. The dying Hector begs Achilles to return his body to his parents for honorable burial, but Achilles refuses. The Greeks marvel at the body of the great Hector; they gloat and stab his body numerous times. His anger still unappeased, Achilles ties the body by the ankles to the back of his chariot and drives back to the Greek lines, the noble head of Hector dragging in the dust.

Skills Starter

Build prerequisite skills. Remind students that writers use figurative language to compare one thing to another. Have students review the definition of the term *epic simile* on p. 56 before reading the selection.

VIEWING THE ART

Athena was primarily the goddess of wisdom and of civilization. When she assisted warriors, it was usually in defense of civilized values. She was said to have sprung from the head of Zeus fully grown and clad for battle. She is often depicted, as here, with a helmet and sometimes a spear and shield.

Activity. As students read the *Illiad,* have them consider how the Greeks' recapturing of Helen might be considered a defensive act, the only kind of warfare that Athena would support. [Helen was the wife of Greek King Menelaus, so the Trojan War could be regarded as a defense of Greek honor.]

Homer 57

DIRECT TEACHING

A Content-Area Connections

Literature: Hubris in the *Iliad*
Students should understand that Hector has placed himself in mortal danger because of pride. The Trojan army has been crippled because Hector arrogantly ignored the good advice of Polydamas, and now Hector feels himself bound to try to rectify that mistake by killing Achilles single-handedly. Excessive pride, or hubris, is an important theme throughout the *Iliad*.

B Literary Focus

? The epic. Hector decides that there is no point in trying to negotiate with Achilles. Unlike Gilgamesh's and Beowulf's enemies, Hector's enemy is a hero, rather than an irredeemable monster. Do you think Hector is making a mistake in not talking to Achilles? [Possible responses: Students may say that Achilles is so angry that negotiations would surely fail. Others may say that one should always try to negotiate first and that maybe negotiations could have prevented the war from lasting ten years.]

Response to Margin Question

Lines 1–18. The simile in ll. 1–6 compares Achilles to a hound intent on pursuing a fawn, its quarry. The simile in ll. 14–18 compares Achilles' pursuit of Hector to a chase in a dream in which one man endlessly pursues another—one unable to escape and the other unable to capture. The terms *swift racer* and *swift Achilles*, and words such as *dash* and *sprinting*, also emphasize the heroes' speed.

A As Book 22 opens, the exhausted Trojans take refuge behind the walls of their city, but Hector remains outside the gates. As Achilles races toward Troy, Hector's parents urge their son to come back inside the city walls. But Hector resolves to stay exposed outside the gates. After an inner struggle in which he considers simply bargaining with Achilles peacefully, Hector decides to fight to the death. As Achilles bears down on him, though, Hector panics and flees in fear. An epic chase around the walls of Troy begins. Looking down from Mount Olympus, Zeus considers saving Hector from certain death. Athena protests vehemently, however, and Zeus allows her to do as she wishes. Athena races down from Olympus to help Achilles, her favorite. Hector's fate is sealed.

B

And swift Achilles kept on coursing Hector, nonstop
as a hound in the mountains starts a fawn from its lair,
hunting him down the gorges, down the narrow glens
and the fawn goes to ground, hiding deep in brush
5 but the hound comes racing fast, nosing him out
until he lands his kill. So Hector could never throw
Achilles off his trail, the swift racer Achilles—
time and again he'd make a dash for the Dardan Gates,°
trying to rush beneath the rock-built ramparts, hoping
10 men on the heights might save him, somehow, raining spears
but time and again Achilles would intercept him quickly,
heading him off, forcing him out across the plain
and always sprinting along the city side himself—
endless as in a dream . . .
15 when a man can't catch another fleeing on ahead
and he can never escape nor his rival overtake him—
so the one could never run the other down in his speed

1–18. Achilles repeatedly prevents Hector from nearing the city gates, where his comrades might supply him with extra weapons.
? *What words and comparisons emphasize Achilles' speed?*

8. Dardan Gates: gates of Troy. Dardania, a city built near the foot of Mount Ida, became part of Troy.

Hector and Menelaus fight over the body of Euphorbos (c. 600 B.C.).
The British Museum, London.
The Bridgeman Art Library, New York.

DIFFERENTIATING INSTRUCTION

Learners Having Difficulty
Some students may have difficulty with the archaic, image-rich language of the *Iliad*. Have students work in small groups to read the selection aloud, ten lines at a time. After each section is read, students should help each other to summarize what just happened and to whom.

Invite learners having difficulty to read the *Iliad* in interactive format in *The Holt Reader* and to use the sidenotes as aids to understanding the selection.

English-Language Learners
Before reading the selection, review with students the list of characters on p. 57. Briefly discuss each character's history and affiliation

nor the other spring away. And how could Hector have fled
the fates of death so long? How unless one last time,
one final time Apollo had swept in close beside him,
driving strength in his legs and knees to race the wind?
And brilliant Achilles shook his head at the armies,
never letting them hurl their sharp spears at Hector—
someone might snatch the glory, Achilles come in second.
But once they reached the springs for the fourth time,
then Father Zeus held out his sacred golden scales:
in them he placed two fates of death that lays men low—
one for Achilles, one for Hector breaker of horses—
and gripping the beam mid-haft the Father raised it high
and down went Hector's day of doom, dragging him down
to the strong House of Death—and god Apollo left him.
Athena rushed to Achilles, her bright eyes gleaming,
standing shoulder-to-shoulder, winging orders now:
"At last our hopes run high, my brilliant Achilles—
Father Zeus must love you—
we'll sweep great glory back to Achaea's fleet,
we'll kill this Hector, mad as he is for battle!
No way for him to escape us now, no longer—
not even if Phoebus the distant deadly Archer
goes through torments, pleading for Hector's life,
groveling over and over before our storming Father Zeus.
But you, you hold your ground and catch your breath
while I run Hector down and persuade the man
to fight you face-to-face."
                                So Athena commanded
and he obeyed, rejoicing at heart—Achilles stopped,
leaning against his ashen spearshaft barbed in bronze.
And Athena left him there, caught up with Hector at once,
and taking the build and vibrant voice of Deiphobus°
stood shoulder-to-shoulder with him, winging orders:
"Dear brother, how brutally swift Achilles hunts you—
coursing you round the city of Priam in all his lethal speed!
Come, let us stand our ground together—beat him back."

"Deiphobus!"—Hector, his helmet flashing, called out to her—
"dearest of all my brothers, all these warring years,
of all the sons that Priam and Hecuba produced!
Now I'm determined to praise you all the more,
you who dared—seeing me in these straits—
to venture out from the walls, all for *my* sake,
while the others stay inside and cling to safety."

25–31. How does Zeus decide the fates of Hector and Achilles? What is the final judgment?

Athena. Silver coin (c. 324–323 B.C.).
Fitzwilliam Museum, Cambridge, England. The Art Archive/Dagli Orti.

48. Deiphobus (dē·if′ō·bəs): one of Hector's brothers.

34–52. What does Athena tell Achilles she is going to do? How does Athena trick Hector?

Vocabulary
groveling (gräv′əl·iŋ) *v.* used as *adj.*: crawling; humiliating oneself in front of authority.

DIRECT TEACHING

A Literary Focus

? Epic hero. Both Hector and Achilles are wearing full bronze body armor and helmets, and each carries a sword, shield, and spear. Homer has described the two men running full speed around and around the walls of Troy—presumably no small distance as shown on the map here. Does this feat of extraordinary physical prowess remind you of any of Beowulf's exploits? [Possible response: Beowulf dove down to Grendel's mother's lair while wearing chain mail and carrying a sword. This dive took many hours and would have been impossible for an ordinary human being.]

VIEWING THE ART

This illustration attempts to demonstrate the strategic advantage that the Trojans had over the Greeks. Troy looks out over the plain on which the Greeks were obliged to camp, and a wall protects the city from attack.

Activity. Ask students to consider why having a clear view of the Greek camps would help the Trojans. [They would be able to see the Greek's preparation for any attack.]

Response to Margin Question

Lines 73–79. Hector vows to stand and fight. He believes he has the support of his brother and is ready to accept whatever fate may bring.

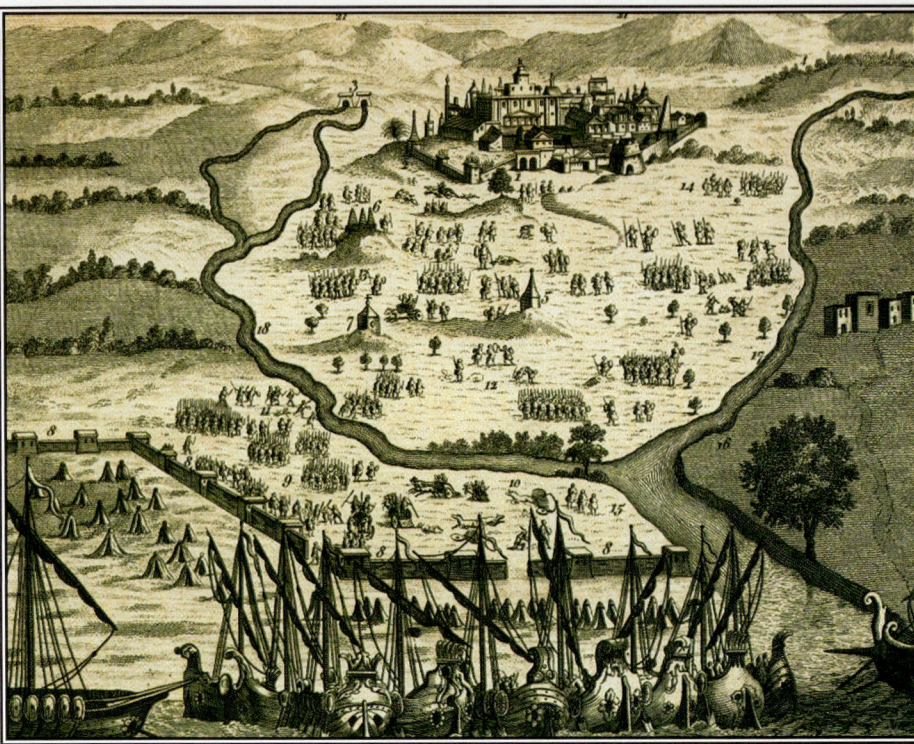

Map of ancient Troy. The Greek ships and encampments are shown outside the walled city.
Bettmann/CORBIS.

60   The goddess answered quickly, her eyes blazing,
"True, dear brother—how your father and mother both
implored me, time and again, clutching my knees,
and the comrades round me begging me to stay!
Such was the fear that broke them, man for man,
65   but the heart within me broke with grief for you.
Now headlong on and fight! No letup, no lance spared!
So now, now we'll *see* if Achilles kills us both
and hauls our bloody armor back to the beaked ships
or *he* goes down in pain beneath your spear."

70   Athena luring him on with all her immortal cunning—
and now, at last, as the two came closing for the kill
it was tall Hector, helmet flashing, who led off:
"No more running from you in fear, Achilles!
Not as before. Three times I fled around
75   the great city of Priam—I lacked courage then
to stand your onslaught. Now my spirit stirs me
to meet you face-to-face. Now kill or be killed!
Come, we'll swear to the gods, the highest witnesses—
the gods will oversee our binding pacts. I swear

? 73–79. What does Hector vow? Why does he now have courage?

60   Collection 1   The Anglo-Saxons

CONTENT-AREA CONNECTIONS

Culture: *Moira* and Hubris
The concepts of *moira*, or fate, and hubris, excessive pride, are fundamental to the Greek heroic view of life. The Greeks believed that each person had an assigned fate and that the boundaries of that fate should not be challenged. Unlike the Mesopotamian Gilgamesh, who attempted to change his fate by seeking immortality, the Greeks believed that one should try to bear the limitations of the human condition with dignity and proper pride. A Greek hero should gain as much fame and glory as possible, but only within the boundaries of his *moira*. Transgressing those boundaries invariably results in divine vengeance.

80   I will never mutilate you—merciless as you are—
     if Zeus allows me to last it out and tear your life away.
     But once I've stripped your glorious armor, Achilles,
     I will give your body back to your loyal comrades.
     Swear you'll do the same."
                                 A swift dark glance
85   and the headstrong runner answered, "Hector, stop!
     You unforgivable, you . . . don't talk to me of pacts.
     There are no binding oaths between men and lions—
     wolves and lambs can enjoy no meeting of the minds—
     they are all bent on hating each other to the death.
90   So with you and me. No love between us. No truce
     till one or the other falls and gluts with blood
     Ares who hacks at men behind his rawhide shield.
     Come, call up whatever courage you can muster.
     Life or death—now prove yourself a spearman,
95   a daring man of war! No more escape for you—
     Athena will kill you with my spear in just a moment.
     Now you'll pay at a stroke for all my comrades' grief,
     all you killed in the fury of your spear!"
                                           With that,
     shaft poised, he hurled and his spear's long shadow flew
100 but seeing it coming glorious Hector ducked away,
     crouching down, watching the bronze tip fly past
     and stab the earth—but Athena snatched it up
     and passed it back to Achilles
     and Hector the gallant captain never saw her.
105 He sounded out a challenge to Peleus' princely son:
     "You missed, look—the great godlike Achilles!
     So you knew nothing at all from Zeus about my death—
     and yet how sure you were! All bluff, cunning with words,
     that's all you are—trying to make me fear you,
110 lose my nerve, forget my fighting strength.
     Well, you'll never plant your lance in my back
     as I flee *you* in fear—plunge it through my chest
     as I come charging in, if a god gives you the chance!
     But now it's for you to dodge *my* brazen spear—
115 I wish you'd bury it in your body to the hilt.
     How much lighter the war would be for Trojans then
     if you, their greatest scourge, were dead and gone!"

     Shaft poised, he hurled and his spear's long shadow flew
     and it struck Achilles' shield—a dead-center hit—

Vocabulary
gallant (gal′ənt) *adj.*: noble; brave.
scourge (skurj) *n.*: means of inflicting severe punishment. Usually the word refers to a whip.

> **78–98.** What pact has Hector offered Achilles? Why does Achilles refuse the pact?

> **106–117.** Hector is emboldened by Achilles' unsuccessful attack.
> What do Hector's words suggest about the relationship between mortals and gods? What is Hector unaware of?

Homer   61

DIRECT TEACHING

A Literary Focus

❓ Epic simile. What simile does the poet use in ll. 139–144 to describe Hector's charge? ["... [H]e swooped like a soaring eagle / launching down from the dark clouds to earth / to snatch some helpless lamb or trembling hare."] What does this simile imply about Hector's attitude in the face of death? [Possible response: Now that his death is assured, Hector shows heroic bravery. Instead of being the pursued, Hector swoops eagerly upon his pursuer.]

Responses to Margin Questions

Lines 123–139. Hector realizes that the gods have taken Achilles' side and that he, Hector, is about to die at the hands of the Greek. Hector decides to die with a glorious struggle against Achilles.

Lines 146–155. "[B]ursting with rage, barbaric"; "guarding his chest with the well-wrought blazoned shield"; "head tossing his gleaming helmet, four horns strong"; "golden plumes shook"; "Bright as that star amid the stars in the night sky, / star of the evening, brightest star that rides the heavens."

Lines 156–165. Achilles drives his spear through Hector's throat, the one spot unprotected by Patroclus's armor.

---

120 but off and away it glanced and Hector seethed,
his hurtling spear, his whole arm's power poured
in a wasted shot. He stood there, cast down . . .
he had no spear in reserve. So Hector shouted out
to Deiphobus bearing his white shield—with a ringing shout
125 he called for a heavy lance—
         but the man was nowhere near
     him, vanished—
         yes and Hector knew the truth in his heart
and the fighter cried aloud, "My time has come!
At last the gods have called me down to death.
I thought he was at my side, the hero Deiphobus—
130 he's safe inside the walls, Athena's tricked me blind.
And now death, grim death is looming up beside me,
no longer far away. No way to escape it now. This,
this was their pleasure after all, sealed long ago—
Zeus and the son of Zeus, the distant deadly Archer—
135 though often before now they rushed to my defense.
So now I meet my doom. Well let me die—
but not without struggle, not without glory, no,
in some great clash of arms that even men to come
will hear of down the years!"
         And on that resolve
140 he drew the whetted sword that hung at his side,
tempered, massive, and gathering all his force
A he swooped like a soaring eagle
launching down from the dark clouds to earth
to snatch some helpless lamb or trembling hare.
145 So Hector swooped now, swinging his whetted sword
and Achilles charged too, bursting with rage, barbaric,
guarding his chest with the well-wrought blazoned shield,
head tossing his gleaming helmet, four horns strong
and the golden plumes shook that the god of fire
150 drove in bristling thick along its ridge.
Bright as that star amid the stars in the night sky,
star of the evening, brightest star that rides the heavens,
so fire flared from the sharp point of the spear Achilles
brandished high in his right hand, bent on Hector's death,
155 scanning his splendid body—where to pierce it best?
The rest of his flesh seemed all encased in armor,
burnished, brazen—*Achilles'* armor that Hector stripped
from strong Patroclus when he killed him—true,
but one spot lay exposed,
160 where collarbones lift the neckbone off the shoulders,
the open throat, where the end of life comes quickest—*there*
as Hector charged in fury brilliant Achilles drove his spear
and the point went stabbing clean through the tender neck

123–139. What truth does Hector now realize? What does he decide to do?

146–155. What descriptive words does Homer use to create a vivid image of Achilles' charge?

156–165. Here we are reminded that Hector is wearing Achilles' old armor. Achilles had given the armor to his dear friend Patroclus, whom Hector had killed. How does Achilles mortally wound Hector?

62   Collection 1   The Anglo-Saxons

READING MINI-LESSON

Developing Word-Attack Skills
Use the selection word *groveling* to explore the sounds of vowels that precede the letter *v*. Explain that the number of consonant letters or sounds that follow a vowel can signal if the vowel sound is short or long. Illustrate this using the words *blazoned* and *blizzard*. In *blazoned*, where the first vowel is followed by a single *z*, the vowel sound is long: /blā′zənd/.

In *blizzard*, where the first vowel is followed by two *zz*'s, the vowel sound is short: /bliz′ərd/.

Explain that in a word like *groveling*, however, the single *v* is not a clue that the first vowel sound is long because double *v* rarely occurs in English words. Compare the first vowel sounds in *cloven* and *grovel* and in *graven*

Chariot race depicted on black-figured amphora with white glaze (6th century B.C.). Louvre, Paris. © Erich Lessing/Art Resource, New York.

but the heavy bronze weapon failed to slash the windpipe—
165　Hector could still gasp out some words, some last reply . . .
　　he crashed in the dust—
　　　　　　　　godlike Achilles gloried over him:
　　"Hector—surely you thought when you stripped Patroclus'
　　　　armor
　　that you, you would be safe! Never a fear of me—
　　far from fighting as I was—you fool!
170　Left behind there, down by the beaked ships
　　his great avenger waited, a greater man by far—
　　that man was I, and I smashed your strength! And you—
　　the dogs and birds will maul you, shame your corpse
　　while Achaeans bury my dear friend in glory!"

175　　Struggling for breath, Hector, his helmet flashing,
　　said, "I beg you, beg you by your life, your parents—
　　don't let the dogs devour me by the Argive ships!
　　Wait, take the princely ransom of bronze and gold,
　　the gifts my father and noble mother will give you—
180　but give my body to friends to carry home again,
　　so Trojan men and Trojan women can do me honor
　　with fitting rites of fire once I am dead."

175–182. This exchange between Hector and Achilles emphasizes the importance the Greeks and Trojans placed on a proper burial. Without "fitting rites," both men believed, the soul of the departed would never find rest.
? *What does Hector plead?*

Homer　63

DIRECT TEACHING

A Literary Focus

The epic. Achilles' anger has been described by the poet as extreme and intemperate, but in ll. 185–186, the hero says he wishes that his rage could be even greater so that he could eat Hector's raw flesh. Achilles believes that Hector's crime against Patroclus is so horrible that no punishment is too barbaric.

VIEWING THE ART

In the image on this drinking vessel, Achilles is lying on a couch with a table before him and Hector's corpse profanely thrown beneath him. As Priam approaches from the left to beg for the corpse, Achilles looks toward the right, toward his cupbearer, who stands with a ladle and a wine sieve.

Activity. Ask students to consider the symbolic significance of the contrast between Priam and the cupbearer in the picture. Note that Achilles sits between them, looking toward the cupbearer, but he is about to turn toward Priam. [The contrast is between a father, or a figure of authority, and the cupbearer, a figure of pleasure. Achilles turning from the one figure to the other signifies his turn to pious thoughts.]

Response to Margin Question

Lines 183–194. Achilles spurns Hector's plea with anger and says that "dogs and birds will rend you—blood and bone!"

Staring grimly, the proud runner Achilles answered,
"Beg no more, you <u>fawning</u> dog—begging me by my parents!
185 Would to god my rage, <u>my</u> fury would drive me now
to hack your flesh away and eat you raw—
such agonies you have caused me! Ransom?
No man alive could keep the dog-packs off you,
not if they haul in ten, twenty times that ransom
190 and pile it here before me and promise fortunes more—
no, not even if Dardan Priam should offer to weigh out
your bulk in gold! Not even then will your noble mother
lay you on your deathbed, mourn the son she bore . . .
The dogs and birds will rend you—blood and bone!"

195 At the point of death, Hector, his helmet flashing,
said, "I know you well—I see my fate before me.
Never a chance that I could win you over . . .
Iron inside your chest, that heart of yours.

Vocabulary
fawning (fôn′iŋ) v. used as *adj.*: cringing and pleading.

? 183–194. How does Achilles react to Hector's plea?

Priam begging Achilles to give him the body of Hector (which lies beneath Achilles' couch). Detail from Greek drinking vessel (c. 490 B.C.).
Kunsthistorisches Museum, Vienna. © Erich Lessing/Art Resource, New York.

64 Collection 1 The Anglo-Saxons

　　　　But now beware, or my curse will draw god's wrath
200　upon your head, that day when Paris and lord Apollo—
　　　for all your fighting heart—destroy you at the Scaean Gates!"° **B**

　　　　Death cut him short. The end closed in around him.
　　　Flying free of his limbs
　　　his soul went winging down to the House of Death,
205　wailing his fate, leaving his manhood far behind,
　　　his young and supple strength. But brilliant Achilles
　　　taunted Hector's body, dead as he was, "Die, die!
　　　For my own death, I'll meet it freely—whenever Zeus
　　　and the other deathless gods would like to bring it on!"

210　　With that he wrenched his bronze spear from the corpse,
　　　laid it aside and ripped the bloody armor off the back.
　　　And the other sons of Achaea, running up around him,
　　　crowded closer, all of them gazing wonder-struck
　　　at the build and marvelous, lithe beauty of Hector.
215　And not a man came forward who did not stab his body,
　　　glancing toward a comrade, laughing: "Ah, look here—
　　　how much softer he is to handle now, this Hector,
　　　than when he gutted our ships with roaring fire!"

　　　　Standing over him, so they'd gloat and stab his body.
220　But once he had stripped the corpse the proud runner Achilles
　　　took his stand in the midst of all the Argive troops
　　　and urged them on with a flight of winging orders:
　　　"Friends—lords of the Argives, O my captains!
　　　Now that the gods have let me kill this man
225　who caused us agonies, loss on crushing loss—
　　　more than the rest of all their men combined—
　　　come, let us ring their walls in armor, test them,
　　　see what recourse the Trojans still may have in mind.
　　　Will they abandon the city heights with this man fallen?
230　Or brace for a last, dying stand though Hector's gone?
　　　But wait—what am I saying? Why this deep debate?
　　　Down by the ships a body lies unwept, unburied—
　　　Patroclus . . . I will never forget him,
　　　not as long as I'm still among the living
235　and my springing knees will lift and drive me on.
　　　Though the dead forget their dead in the House of Death,
　　　I will remember, even there, my dear companion.
　　　　　　　　　　　　　　　　　　　　　　　　　　Now,
　　　come, you sons of Achaea, raise a song of triumph!

200–201. Paris . . . Gates: Hector is foretelling Achilles' ultimate fate. Achilles will later be slain by Paris, who will shoot an arrow into Achilles' heel, the only vulnerable part of his body.

212–218. Achilles' comrades gather around the great warrior and the body of his victim.
? *What do the Greek soldiers do to Hector's body?*

232–237. In the midst of his victory cry, Achilles pauses to remember his dear friend Patroclus, whose death has now been avenged.

DIRECT TEACHING

B Literary Focus
The epic. In l. 202, Hector uses the phrase "for all your fighting heart" to mean that even a hero of Achilles' stature cannot escape the limits of the human condition.

C Content-Area Connections
Literature: Achilles' Heel Students have probably heard the expression "an Achilles heel," which means a point of weakness or vulnerability. Achilles' mother, Thetis, knew the destiny in store for him and tried to protect him by dipping him at birth in the waters of the River Styx, one of the rivers of Hades. This made Achilles' body invulnerable—with the exception of the one heel by which Thetis held him. Just as Hector prophesies, Achilles' fate is to be slain by Paris before the Scaean Gates. Apollo, still on the Trojans' side, guides Paris's arrow to strike the vulnerable heel.

Response to Margin Question
Lines 212–218. The Greek soldiers marvel at the physical beauty of Hector, and they gloat and stab his body numerous times as a sign of disrespect.

Conducting a Historical Investigation

Both *Gilgamesh* and the *Iliad* are explorations of ideals that spring from specific historical contexts. Have students write an essay comparing and contrasting the relationships of the poems to their historical contexts. Students might focus on one aspect, such as religion, government, history, or geography, or they might synthesize several aspects to present a broader view.

DIRECT TEACHING

VIEWING THE ART

This vase dates from a period near the conjectured date of the Trojan War (c. 1200 B.C.). The figures on the vase may seem crude in comparison to later Greek art, but there is an attempt here to achieve realism.

Activity. Why does this vase appear to be an artifact from a warrior culture? [The vase shows the soldiers' weapons and armor accurately.]

A Literary Focus

The epic. Re-read ll. 242–253. How do you think the poet feels about the shaming of Hector's body? [Possible response: The poet describes the scene as an "outrage," and uses the word *defiled*, so it seems he disapproves of Achilles' actions.]

Response to Margin Question

Lines 242–253. Hector's body is transported from the scene of death by being dragged behind Achilles' chariot. Most students will say that they feel pity for Hector, and some may say that they also feel disgust for Achilles.

GUIDED PRACTICE

Monitoring students' progress. Have students create Venn diagrams, graphic organizers with two overlapping circles. One circle should be labeled "Achilles" and the other "Hector." Ask students to fill in the circles with characteristics for each hero; the overlapping section of the circles should be filled in with characteristics the heroes share.

Warriors depicted on Mycenaen ceramic vase (detail) (c. 1300–1100 B.C.).
National Archaeological Museum, Athens.
© Scala/Art Resource, New York.

> Down to the ships we march and bear this corpse on high—
> 240   we have won ourselves great glory. We have brought
> magnificent Hector down, that man the Trojans
> glorified in their city like a god!"
>   So he triumphed
> and now he was bent on outrage, on shaming noble Hector.
> Piercing the tendons, ankle to heel behind both feet,
> 245   he knotted straps of rawhide through them both,
> lashed them to his chariot, left the head to drag
> and mounting the car, hoisting the famous arms° aboard,
> he whipped his team to a run and breakneck on they flew,
> holding nothing back. And a thick cloud of dust rose up
> 250   from the man they dragged, his dark hair swirling round
> that head so handsome once, all tumbled low in the dust—
> since Zeus had given him over to his enemies now
> to be defiled in the land of his own fathers.

247. **famous arms:** Hector's armor.

242–253. Achilles' wrath is so great that he cannot stop at merely killing Hector.
How is Hector's body transported from the scene of death? How do you feel as you read this description?

66   Collection 1   The Anglo-Saxons

CONNECTION / HISTORY

For centuries people thought that Homer's great stories in the Iliad were just that—stories, with no basis in historical fact. Then a self-taught German named Heinrich Schliemann (1822–1890) came along. Schliemann had been fascinated with Homer's stories since he was a child. When he was forty-six years old, he abandoned his successful business career and went off to Greece. He wanted to see if he could find evidence that the heroes he loved—Achilles, Patroclus, Hector— had really existed.

Incredibly, Schliemann was successful. Where Troy had once stood, Schliemann and his workers unearthed seven buried cities. The question was now: Which of these ancient cities was the Troy of the Iliad?

Trojan Gold
from Gods, Graves, and Scholars

INFORMATIONAL TEXT

C. W. Ceram

Schliemann dug and searched. In the second and third levels from the bottom he found traces of fire, the remains of massive walls, and the ruins of a gigantic gate. He was sure that these walls had once enclosed the palace of Priam, and that he had found the famous Scaean Gate.

He unearthed things that were treasures from the scientific point of view. Part of this material he shipped home, part he gave over to experts for examination, material that yielded a detailed picture of the Trojan epoch, the portrait of a people.

It was Heinrich Schliemann's triumph, and the triumph, too, of Homer. He had succeeded, the enthusiastic amateur, in demonstrating the actual existence of what had always counted as mere saga and myth, a figment of the poetic fancy.

A wave of excitement coursed through the intellectual world. Schliemann, whose workers had moved more than 325,000 cubic yards of earth, had earned a breathing spell. Presently, his interests meanwhile having turned to other projects, he set June 15, 1873 as the date for the termination of the diggings. On the day before the last shovelful of earth was to be turned, he found a treasure that crowned his labors with a golden splendor, to the delight of the watching world.

It happened dramatically. Even today, reading about this amazing discovery takes one's breath away. The discovery was made during the early hours of a hot morning. Schliemann, accompanied by his wife, was supervising the excavation. Though no longer seriously expectant of finding anything, nevertheless out of habit he was still keeping close watch on the workmen's every move. They were down twenty-eight feet, at the lower level of the masonry that

---

Connection

Summary  at grade level

This excerpt describes how archaeologist Heinrich Schliemann, on the second-to-last day of his dig at Troy, was working on what he thought was Priam's palace when he discovered gold. He quickly sent his workers home before they too saw the treasure. Until the end of his life, Schliemann was convinced he had found Priam's cache of gold, but later archaeologists proved that this treasure belonged to an earlier king.

DIRECT TEACHING

A Content-Area Connections
Archaeology: Heinrich Schliemann
After his explorations at Troy, Schliemann went to Mycenae on the Peloponnesus, where he looked for artifacts from King Agamemnon's realm. He also bought land on the island of Crete, but unfortunately he passed away before he could start any excavations.

B Reading Informational Text
❓ **Sequence of information.** In providing accounts of expeditions and excavations, scientific writers often try to maintain readers' interest by building up suspense. How does C. W. Ceram do this in the excerpt? [He delays telling readers exactly what Schliemann discovered that hot morning.]

Direct Teaching

A Reading Informational Text

❓ **Surprise ending.** The truth about Schliemann's remarkable discovery is not revealed until the last three sentences. What mistake had he and his team made? [They had dug through the ruins of Troy and arrived at an earlier layer.]

B Reading Informational Text

❓ **Finding the main idea.** How would you evaluate Schliemann's contributions? [Although he misidentified the gold, he did find Troy, and he proved that Homeric literature could be a good guide for archaeologists.]

VIEWING THE ART

Troy, the archaeologist Heinrich Schliemann proved in the nineteenth century, is not only the mythical city in which Homer and other ancient Greek writers situated the legendary Trojan War, but also an actual city-fortress located in what is today Turkey (near the entrance to the Dardanelles). Archaeologists have since discovered that the city was rebuilt several times. The illustration here is from the book in which Schliemann revealed to the world that he had fulfilled his lifelong ambition and unearthed the city of Greek myth and history.

Activity. What does the discovery of the real Troy tell us about Greek legend? [Greek legend functioned as a sort of history.]

Schliemann identified with Priam's palace. Suddenly his gaze was held spellbound. He began to act as if under compulsion. No one can say what the thievish workers would have done if they had seen what met Schliemann's astonished eyes. He seized his wife by the arm. "Gold!" he whispered. She looked at him in amazement. "Quick," he said. "Send the men home at once." The lovely Greek [Schliemann's wife] stammered a protest. "No buts," he told her. "Tell them anything you want. Tell them today is my birthday, that I've just remembered, and that they can all have the rest of the day off. Hurry up, now, hurry!"

The workers left. "Get your red shawl!" Schliemann said to his wife as he jumped down into the hole. He went to work with his knife like a demon. Massive blocks of stone, the debris of millennia, hung perilously over his head, but he paid no attention to the danger. "With all possible speed I cut out the treasure with a large knife," he writes. "I did this by dint of strenuous effort, and in the most frightful danger of losing my life; for the heavy citadel wall, which I had to dig under, might have crashed down on me at any moment. But the sight of so many immeasurably priceless objects made me foolhardy and I did not think of the hazards."

There was the soft sheen of ivory, the jingle of gold. Schliemann's wife held open the shawl to be filled with Priam's treasure. It was the golden treasure of one of the mightiest kings of prehistory, gathered together in blood and tears, the ornaments of a godlike people, buried for three thousand years until dug from under the ruined walls of seven vanished kingdoms. Not for one moment did Schliemann doubt that he had found Priam's treasure-trove. And not until shortly before his death was it proved that Schliemann had been misled in the heat of enthusiasm. Troy lay neither in the second nor in the third layer from the bottom, but in the sixth. The treasure had belonged to a king who had antedated Priam by a thousand years.

Upper part of buildings discovered below a temple of Athena, illustration from Heinrich Schliemann's *Troy and Its Remains* (1875).
The Art Archive.

Response and Analysis

Reading Check
1. How does Athena deceive Hector? Why does Zeus decline to save Hector?
2. What is Hector's dying request, and how does Achilles respond to it?
3. How is Hector's body abused by the Greeks?

Thinking Critically
4. In two extended similes, Hector and Achilles are compared to animals. Find these **epic similes** and others in this part of the story. What comparisons are made in each simile?
5. Achilles and Hector are rival warriors, but are they both heroes? Discuss your opinion of each character in terms of the Greek view of *arete,* or honor, and of your own view of it. You may want to consult the Quickwrite notes you made on contemporary ideals of honor.
6. Homer is concerned with the relationship between *moira,* or fate, and a person's character. Do you feel that Hector was doomed by his noble character, by fate, or by both? Explain.
7. Consider the role of the gods in Book 22. How do they direct or influence events? Do you think their intervention turns the human characters into puppets, or do the humans still make choices that affect their fate? Give reasons for your answer.
8. One of the moving parts of this story is Hector's request that his body be left unmutilated. What episodes in actual wars today, or in movies or stories about war, show that we have this same concern for the bodies of our fallen soldiers?

Extending and Evaluating
9. The *Iliad* is primarily a war epic. In your view, is the *Iliad* a condemnation of the brutality of war, a celebration of the heroism that war can inspire, or an evenly developed examination of both of these aspects? Justify your answer with examples from the epic and from life.
10. The **Connection** on page 67 shows that archaeologists have uncovered physical evidence of a walled city where Troy was said to have stood. Do you suppose some of the details in the *Iliad* could be historical? Which events might have happened? Which are definitely fictional?

Literary Criticism
11. **Philosophical approach.** The critic David Denby made the following statement about the *ethos,* or attitudes and ethical beliefs, of the Greek and Trojan warriors of Homer's epic:

> Accepting death in battle as inevitable, the Greek and Trojan aristocrats of the *Iliad* experience the world not as pleasant or unpleasant, nor as good and evil, but as glorious or shameful.

Discuss how the worldview that Denby describes helps to account for, and make sense of, the violent and vengeful elements of Homer's *Iliad* that may seem cruel and immoral to a contemporary reader.

SKILLS FOCUS

Pages 69–71 cover
Literary Skills Analyze the epic simile. Understand conventions of epic poetry. Compare epics from different literary periods.
Writing Skills Write an essay comparing and contrasting epic heroes.
Vocabulary Skills Create semantic maps.

Homer 69

INDEPENDENT PRACTICE

Response and Analysis
Thinking Critically
4. The speed of Achilles is compared to that of a hound on the chase in ll. 1–18. Their endless chase is compared to that in a dream (l. 14). The charge of Hector is compared to an eagle sweeping down on a hare or lamb in ll. 142–144.
5. Some students may say that Hector fails to uphold *arete* when he flees from Achilles, but that he regains it when he decides to fight. Others may say that Achilles' determination to avenge Patroclus upholds *arete,* but that his defilement of Hector's body goes too far.
6. Some students may say that Hector's pride led to his death by causing him to ignore his parents' advice. Others may say that both Hector's character and his *moira* were instrumental in his doom.
7. Athena and Apollo take sides in the conflict between the Greeks and the Trojans and actively intervene at various times. Zeus interests himself in the war, although more at a distance, when he allows fate to take its course. Most students will say that although the humans are affected by the actions of the gods, both Greeks and Trojans affect their own fate when they fall victim to excessive pride.
8. Stories by writers such as Tim O'Brien show the importance of fallen soldiers.

(continued)

Reading Check
1. Athena deceives Hector by assuming the form of Deiphobus and pretending that she will help Hector against Achilles. Zeus does not save Hector because Athena persuades her father that he should not change the fate of a mortal.
2. Hector's dying request is that Achilles will return his body to the Trojans to be honored in death. Achilles refuses because he is still angry at the dishonor done to the body of Patroclus.
3. The Greeks stab Hector's body repeatedly, and Achilles drags him by his heels to the Greek ships.

Homer 69

Extending and Evaluating

9. Most students will argue that the *Iliad* addresses both the brutality and the heroism of war, citing specific examples such as Achilles' mutilation of Hector's body and the repeated characterization of Achilles and Hector as glorious champions.

10. The siege probably occurred; the conversations are invented.

Literary Criticism

11. Most students will think that the two heroes' actions and motivations make more sense in the context of such a worldview: Hector's facing Achilles alone is an honorable way to reverse a shameful defeat; Achilles' desecration of Hector's body is Achilles' solution to the dishonor done to Patroclus.

Comparing Literature

12. Gilgamesh hesitates over killing Humbaba, and Enkidu warns him against the desire for power; Gilgamesh realizes that his friendship with Enkidu is more important than his own desire for heroic glory. Achilles' devotion to Patroclus drives him to ignore the siege against Troy until he succeeds in avenging Patroclus's dishonor.

13. The battle scenes in the *Iliad* are full of magnificent, taunting speeches; flashing armor; and leaping, charging, and running heroes. The battle scenes in *Beowulf* also combine exciting action with heroic language, while the fight scene in *Gilgamesh* is shorter and described in less glorious terms. All describe specific bodily damage from weapons. Both Beowulf and Achilles are supremely confident, even joyful, in the heat of battle. Gilgamesh alternates between heroic confidence and paralyzing fear. Hector is afraid of death but fights bravely for the sake of his honor. Students' answers will vary as to the relative heroism of these characters.

Comparing Literature

12. The theme of friendship is important in both the *Iliad* and the Sumerian epic *Gilgamesh*. Achilles is fiercely loyal to his dead friend Patroclus, and Gilgamesh stands by Enkidu in the gravest danger. Discuss how the specific actions of these epic heroes are influenced by their deeply meaningful friendships.

13. How do the battle scenes in the *Iliad* compare with those in *Beowulf* and *Gilgamesh*? How does each epic hero respond to the sometimes fatal violence that he faces in battle? Are they all equally heroic in their behavior? Explain.

WRITING

Mirror Images?
Consider Achilles and Hector as ideals of the hero in ancient Greece. What special qualities does each hero exhibit? In what ways do they mirror each other? Are their limitations and weaknesses the same, or are they different? Is one hero more "human" than the other? Write a brief essay in which you **compare and contrast** Achilles and Hector as heroes. Cite evidence from the epic to support your findings.

Vocabulary Development
Word Charts

groveling   scourge
gallant   fawning

This chart organizes some basic information about the word *gallant*. Using a dictionary, make similar charts for the other Vocabulary words listed above.

gallant
• **Meaning:** noble; brave
• **Origin:** Old English *galaunt*, meaning "merry; brave"
• **Examples:** a very courteous man is *gallant*; knights are *gallant*; a person who is sick and does not complain is *gallant*.

The charioteer of Delphi (detail) (c. 478 B.C.). Bronze statue.
Archaeological Museum, Delphi, Greece.
© Nimatallah/Art Resource, New York.

Vocabulary Development
Sample Chart
groveling. Meaning—crawling; humiliating oneself in front of authority. *Origin*—Middle English *grufelinge*, meaning "on the face." *Examples*—The king's attendants were <u>groveling</u>, trying to secure his favor; the prisoner used <u>groveling</u> as a last resort.

Literary Focus

Epic Conventions

Certain features of Homer's work were so widely imitated in later written epics, such as Virgil's *Aeneid* and Milton's *Paradise Lost* (see page 367), that they became recognizable characteristics, or **conventions,** of the epic genre. The origins of many of these conventions lie in the oral tradition that gave birth to the *Iliad*. The oral poets used formulas that allowed them to summarize past events rapidly or sketch characters in the epic quickly. Here are some of the epic conventions that occur in the *Iliad*:

1. **Invocation.** The *Iliad* begins with an **invocation,** or formal plea for aid, to the Muse Calliope (kə·lī′ə·pē), one of the nine goddesses who presided over the arts and sciences. The Greeks believed that this "immortal one" spoke through mortal epic poets. The invocation also serves to state the epic's subject and theme. This invocation from the *Iliad* is one of the most famous invocations in all of literature.

> Rage—Goddess, sing the rage of
>   Peleus' son Achilles,
> murderous, doomed, that cost the
>   Achaeans countless losses,
> hurling down to the House of
>   Death so many sturdy souls,
> great fighters' souls, but made
>   their bodies carrion,
> feasts for the dogs and birds,
> and the will of Zeus was moving
>   toward its end.
> Begin, Muse, when the two first
>   broke and clashed,
> Agamemnon lord of men and
>   brilliant Achilles.
>
> —translated by Robert Fagles

2. ***In medias res.*** The epic plunges us into the middle of the action—that is, *in medias res* (in mā′dē·äs′res′), a Latin term meaning "into the midst of things." **Flashbacks** are then used to inform the audience of events that took place before the narrative's current time.

3. **Epic similes.** One of the most striking features of the language of the *Iliad* is Homer's use of extended, elaborate comparisons, called **epic,** or **Homeric, similes.** Some epic similes are developed over many lines. Such similes compare heroic events to simple, everyday events—events that Homer's audience could easily understand. For example, in another part of Book 22, when Achilles chases Hector, his pursuit is compared to "the wild mountain hawk, the quickest thing on wings, / launching smoothly, swooping down on a cringing dove." Homer's listeners would have been familiar with the image of the birds; this simile would help them understand the epic's action.

4. **Stock epithets.** Another figure of speech that occurs frequently in the *Iliad* is the **stock epithet,** a descriptive adjective or phrase that is repeatedly used with—or in place of—a noun or proper name. Thus, the audience hears of Zeus referred to as "Lord of the lightning" and Athena as "third-born of the gods." The repetition of these kinds of epithets helped the audience follow the narrative; the repetition also helped the rhapsode as he improvised the poem in performance.

Finding epic conventions. Look through the excerpt of the *Iliad* you've just read. Try to find examples of as many of the conventions listed above as possible. How do these conventions add to or detract from the *Iliad*'s appeal?

Grammar Link

Make It Clear: Sentence Fragments and Run-on Sentences

Sentence fragments. What would you think if you came across the following group of words in your reading?

> After Agamemnon dishonors Apollo's priest by refusing to surrender Chryseis.

You might be confused by this **sentence fragment** because it does not express a complete thought. Instead, it leaves you wondering: "What happens after Agamemnon dishonors the priest?" A sentence fragment is a group of words that does not express a complete thought but is punctuated as though it were a sentence. Complete sentences, unlike the fragment above, express complete thoughts.

> After Agamemnon dishonors Apollo's priest by refusing to surrender Chryseis, <u>Apollo punishes the Greeks by sending the plague.</u>

Run-on sentences. In the following sentence it is difficult to tell where one complete thought ends and another begins:

> Paris, a prince of Troy, was chosen by the gods to judge the beauty contest, he was offered bribes by each goddess in turn.

A **run-on sentence,** like the example above, contains two or more complete sentences run together as if they were one sentence. You can correct a run-on by separating the two sentences with a period.

> Paris, a prince of Troy, was chosen by the gods to judge the beauty contest. He was offered bribes by each goddess in turn.

Here is another run-on sentence:

> Achilles' mother, Thetis, tried to protect Achilles by dipping him in the River Styx, however, she held him by the heel, making him still vulnerable to attack.

You can correct the run-on by separating the two sentences with a semicolon.

> Achilles' mother, Thetis, tried to protect Achilles by dipping him in the River Styx; however, she held him by the heel, making him still vulnerable to attack.

SKILLS FOCUS
Grammar Skills
Identify and correct sentence fragments and run-on sentences.

PRACTICE

Identify each of the following items as a run-on or a fragment. Then, revise each item to make it a complete sentence.

1. Agamemnon wanted Achilles' prize, Achilles refused to give up any part of his spoils.
2. To break up the dispute. Athena grabbed the golden-red hair of Achilles.
3. Because *homer* may mean "hostage" in Greek. Historians have assumed Homer was a slave or descended from slaves.
4. As king of the gods. Zeus remained neutral through much of the battle.
5. Hera was the queen of the gods she was an enemy of the Trojans.

Apply to Your Writing

Review a writing assignment you are working on now or have already completed. Are there any fragments? Are there any run-on sentences? Revise them to make them complete sentences.

▶ For more help, see Sentence Fragments, 9d, and Run-on Sentences, 9e, in the Language Handbook.

Writing

Writing a Descriptive Essay

A Writer's Framework

Introduction
- Begin with an attention-grabbing opener.
- Give the title of the poem, and include necessary background information.
- Include a clear thesis statement.

Body
- Use narrative details—actions and reactions, speech, and thoughts and feelings.
- Add descriptive details—sensory details, figurative language, and information about physical appearance.

Conclusion
- Review the importance of the chosen scene and character.
- Restate your thesis in an interesting way.
- Close with a dramatic statement.

A Writer's Model

Run, Hector, Run

"Whatever you do," Hector mutters to himself as he spits in the dust, "don't act like a Greek—those cowards." High above him, on the walls of the city, the citizens and soldiers of the city crowd around, talking and calling down to him. His parents—Priam and Hecuba, king and queen of Troy—scream in fear, begging him to come inside the safety of the Trojan gates. Hector, a hero of Homer's the *Iliad*, refuses to obey them, so angry is he over this seemingly endless ten-year-old war between the Trojans and the Greeks.

"Don't they realize what this moment means?" he asks himself. "What should I do?" he thinks, "Go inside the walls, or offer a treasure to Achilles if he and the Greeks will just go away, or stand and fight?" As Hector readies himself for the approach of Achilles, his appearance, actions, and thoughts and feelings show how even the most noble of all Trojan warriors fears death.

"Be quiet!" Hector yells up to their pleas. Usually, his resolve is fixed on war. However, something today in the heat and dust has made him nervous. He looks off to his left, over to the tower where inside his beautiful wife is weaving and his young son is sleeping. Hector's craggy face softens, and a dreamy look comes over it. He can almost see Andromache at her loom shuttling the golden threads through the red cloth. Then, he remembers his enemy Achilles, and his eyes harden and his fist curls around his spear. As a stray dog snuffs for food around his sandals, Hector pulls at the armor he took

(continued)

INTRODUCTION
Attention grabber

Reactions

Background information

Thoughts

Thesis statement

BODY/Speech
Thoughts and feelings

Sensory details
Figurative language
Physical appearance

RETEACHING

Body
Since the concept of "showing" versus "telling" is often difficult for students to understand, you might use the statement *Joe is a nice man* to show that *nice man* means different things to different readers. However, writing *Joe is a genuine and caring man who consistently puts others' needs before his own* shows exactly what the writer means.

DIRECT TEACHING

Body
Remind students to use transitions to make clear to their readers the organization of their descriptive essays.

CRITICAL THINKING
Tell students that it will help them in their own writing if they analyze **A Writer's Model** for its use of descriptive language. Divide the chalkboard into three columns. Label the first column "Sensory Details," the second "Figurative Language," and the third "Information About Physical Appearance." Then, have student volunteers read the model to the class, and call on students to write examples from the narrative of each element of description in the appropriate column. Direct students to p. 75 of the Student Edition if they need help defining descriptive elements.

DIFFERENTIATING INSTRUCTION

Advanced Learners
Enrichment. Flashbacks in literature can present unique organizational challenges. Lead a round table discussion about how to incorporate information revealed through flashbacks into an essay. Ask whether information learned in flashbacks should be discussed in the order in which it occurs in the poem or when it occurs chronologically. Encourage students to identify changes in a character's personality from the period presented in the flashback to the current events of the poem. Has the character changed significantly? What was his or her motivation to change? Was the change for better or worse?

CORRECTING MISCONCEPTIONS

Students may think that quotations used to describe their characters should be lengthy or used in isolation. Point out the effective use of several short, descriptive phrases taken from the poem and incorporated into **A Writer's Model**.

PRACTICE & APPLY 2

Guided and Independent Practice

Monitor student progress by having each student turn in a written thesis. Evaluate each thesis to determine if it is specific to the character and poem, realistic in its scope—not too broad or too narrow—and supportable. Return thesis statements with brief comments, and have students complete **Practice and Apply 2** independently.

(continued)

Actions	from his enemy, Patroclus, loosening it from around his huge neck and biceps. "That Greek dog," he thinks. He paces up and down, testing his spear, checking his sword, his sandals scuffing in the dust.
Exact words from the poem	He is, after all, Hector, "breaker of horses" (194), "tall Hector" (295), "glorious Hector" (323), "noble Hector" (466), Hector of the "splendid body" (378, 438). He is a Trojan warrior. He is THE Trojan warrior. As he turns to squint into the sun again toward the Greek ships, he sees Achilles, and Hector's mouth goes dry.
Reactions / Actions	Achilles strides along the sand away from the sea, with the sun reflecting off his brilliant bronze armor breastplate. Hector stands
Figurative language / Physical appearance	frozen, staring at Achilles, his memory of earlier battle victories as dull as the blue mist rolling in from the sea. Hector stands, all six feet four inches of him, and feels his knees tremble. His eyes widen in terror; he
Sensory details	looks to the right, to the left; the dog near his feet begins to bark. The sounds from the wall—spears clanking, people calling—grow louder
Reactions	and louder. As Achilles seems to glow brighter and more brilliant in the heat, Hector feels his feet, almost in slow motion, begin to churn in the hot, dry dust. He backs up three or four steps toward the city's gate and
Thoughts / Actions / Figurative language	hears a voice somewhere within him urging, "Run, you fool, RUN!" Hector does run, three times around the city walls, his escape into the city always blocked by Achilles, who harries him like a hound after a rabbit. Hector hears all the noises swelling in his head until one voice sings out louder than the rest—the voice of his old friend Deiphobus calling encouragement. At that, Hector swings around to face Achilles, the one last soldier in the long line of Greeks that Hector has faced and defeated.
Speech / Exact words from the poem	"No more running from you, Achilles!" Hector says. "You'll never plant your lance in my back as I flee you in fear!" (334–335)
CONCLUSION	
Importance of scene for the character	Hector's dramatic turnaround erases any charge of cowardice against him, especially when his actions are compared to those of Achilles. Hector—not Achilles—begins the last fight, by swooping down "like a soaring eagle" swinging his whetted, tempered, massive sword. (365, 363, 364).
Reference to thesis / Final statement	In his last actions and words, Hector's fear and flight of moments before have been cancelled. He is again the awesome, heroic "noble Hector."

INTERNET
More Writer's Models
Keyword: LE5 12-1

PRACTICE & APPLY 2 Using the framework and Writer's Model on these pages as your guide, write the first draft of your descriptive essay.

Revising

Evaluate and Revise Your Descriptive Essay

Retakes Sometimes screenwriters must revise their film treatments several times to make sure that they have fully described the character in a scene. You also should look over your descriptive essay and double-check that you have described the character and scene effectively. Use the guidelines below as a think sheet to help you evaluate and revise the content and organization of your descriptive essay. Then, use the guidelines on the next page to revise for style.

▶ **First Reading: Content and Organization** Use the chart below to improve the content and organization of your descriptive essay. As you consider the evaluation questions, take into account your essay's intended audience and your purpose for writing the essay. Use the Tips column to help you mark your essay, and then make the revisions suggested in the Revision Techniques column.

PEER REVIEW
Before you revise, exchange your essay with a peer. Have the student read your paper and make suggestions about using sensory details and figurative language.

Rubric: Writing a Descriptive Essay

Evaluation Questions	Tips	Revision Techniques
❶ Does the introduction name the character, mention the title of the poem, and state the thesis?	▶ **Circle** the character's name and the title of the poem. **Highlight** the thesis statement.	▶ **Add** a sentence that names the character. **Add** the title of the poem. **Add** a sentence that conveys the thesis.
❷ Does the essay include exact words and phrases from the poem?	▶ **Bracket** any exact words and phrases from the poem.	▶ **Add** exact words or phrases. Cite line numbers in parentheses.
❸ Does the essay include narrative and descriptive details?	▶ **Underline** the narrative details. **Double underline** the descriptive details.	▶ **Elaborate** with the character's actions, speech, and thoughts and feelings. **Add** sensory details and figurative language.
❹ Is there an obvious, easy-to-follow organizational pattern?	▶ **Label** important ideas, using numbers for sequence or importance or *top, left,* etc. for location.	▶ **Rearrange** ideas in a consistent pattern. **Add** transitions if necessary.
❺ Does the conclusion explain why the chosen scene is important for the character? Does the conclusion restate the thesis and close with a dramatic final statement?	▶ **Put a check** by the sentence that reviews the scene's importance for the character. **Draw a star** by the sentence that restates the thesis. **Draw a box** around the final statement.	▶ **Reword** the conclusion to include a sentence that reviews the importance of the scene for the character. **Add** a sentence that restates the thesis. **Add** a final interesting statement.

DIRECT TEACHING

First Reading: Content and Organization

An additional way for students to check for an obvious organizational pattern in their or their peers' essays is to look for transitions that signal a pattern. Students should **circle** the transitions that show organization when revising for content and organization.

Elaboration

To elaborate further in their essays, have students complete these two steps. First, have them identify and tally the specific references they have used in these three categories: character's actions, speech, and thoughts and feelings. Second, if they have not used equal numbers of references for those three categories, have them find specific additional references to even out the categories.

DIFFERENTIATING INSTRUCTION

Learners Having Difficulty

One strategy for revising a draft is to have someone else read it aloud while others listen critically. Have students work in groups of three with one student reading a draft aloud, another asking for clarification and pointing out any problems with the guidelines on this page, and the writer of the draft taking notes. Students should rotate through each role until each draft has been read.

TECHNOLOGY TIP

If students have access to computers, have them use the search or find command to find commonly used, general, or vague adjectives—such as *nice, bad,* or *awesome*—so that they can replace these adjectives with specific adjectives or with words and phrases that convey more vivid pictures.

GUIDED PRACTICE

Responding to the Revision Process

Answers

1. The specific sounds described, *clanking* and *calling,* help create the scene in the reader's mind.
2. The reference to heat appeals to another sense, the sense of touch, and helps create a more vivid image of the scene. *Bad* dust has no real meaning. *Hot* and *dry* add to sensory impressions.
3. The added quote helps show, rather than tell, Hector's thoughts and actions.

PRACTICE & APPLY 3

Independent Practice
Have students follow these two steps as they check their essays for the use of unnecessarily repetitive adjectives.

1. **Circle** all pairs of adjectives (adjectives joined by a comma or by *and* or *but*). Revise any circled pair having almost the same meaning.
2. **Cut** one of the adjectives from a pair, or replace one with a contrasting adjective and change the connecting word *and* to *but*.

▶ **Second Reading: Style** After reviewing your essay's content and organization, you can focus on your writing style. You may have used some adjectives that are vague or less precise than they could be. For example, describing someone or something as "nice," "bad," or "awesome" doesn't convey as much information as saying, for example, that the "nice" person is "well-mannered and kind." The following chart explains how to replace vague adjectives with more precise words and phrases.

Style Guidelines

Evaluation Question	Tip	Revision Technique
● Does the essay include general or vague adjectives, such as "nice," "bad," or "awesome"?	▶ **Draw a line** through adjectives that don't convey much information.	▶ **Replace** vague adjectives with specific adjectives or with words and phrases that convey a more vivid picture.

ANALYZING THE REVISION PROCESS
Study these revisions, and answer the questions that follow.

> *—spears clanking, people calling—*
> **add** The sounds from the wall grow louder and louder.
>
> As Achilles seems to glow brighter and more brilliant in the
>
> heat, Hector feels his feet, almost in slow motion, begin to
> *hot, dry*
> **replace** churn in the ~~bad~~ dust. He backs up three or four steps toward
> *hears a voice somewhere within him*
> **elaborate** the city's gate and ~~runs~~. *urging, "Run, you fool, RUN!"*

Responding to the Revision Process

1. Why do you think the writer expanded the word *sounds* with sensory details in sentence one? What is the effect of such additions?
2. What is the effect of replacing *bad* with *hot, dry* in sentence two?
3. Why do you think the writer added information to sentence three? What is the effect of the addition?

SKILLS FOCUS
Writing Skills
Revise for content and style.

PRACTICE & APPLY 3
Using the guidelines on these two pages, revise the content, organization, and style of your descriptive essay. Remember to eliminate vague adjectives.

80 Collection 1 The Anglo-Saxons

DIFFERENTIATING INSTRUCTION

English-Language Learners
Depending on their levels of proficiency, some students will not yet have developed the requisite skills to proofread for errors in grammar, usage, and mechanics. You may pair English-proficient students with English-Language Learners to proofread their essays. Once they have proofread the papers together, note the areas in which most errors occur. Provide students with further explanation and extra practice in their particular problem areas.

Publishing

Proofread and Publish Your Essay

Last Cut A careful proofreading will ensure that your final paper follows the **conventions** of good writing and is free of errors in grammar, usage, and mechanics. Check through your final paper and correct errors if you find them.

Distribution Rights Now that you have written your descriptive essay, you may want to share it with others. Here are some methods for publishing your essay.

- Adapt your essay into a film or video presentation. Dress your actors to match the descriptions of the characters in your essay, and add a soundtrack that helps bring out the actions and thoughts of your main character.

- Gather several classmates to read and comment on each other's essays.

- E-mail your essay to a Web site for student film productions, or for student screenplays. Ask for your essay to be posted on the Web site, and request feedback from readers.

- Add several illustrations of the narrative poem's scene and character to the text of your descriptive essay. Use illustrations you have drawn, collected from other sources, or generated by computer. Submit your essay to your school's literary magazine.

TIP To make sure that your essay follows the **conventions** of American English, look carefully at the proper names of any characters or places in your description and make sure that you have capitalized them correctly. For more on **capitalization,** see Capitalization, 11a–f, in the Language Handbook.

Reflect on Your Essay

Box Office Receipts Look back over your work on the descriptive essay. To evaluate what you have done, ask yourself the following questions.

- How did your work on this descriptive essay help you understand how screenwriters might create a character for a film based on a narrative poem?

- What was your biggest challenge in adapting the character from the narrative poem to the descriptive essay? Explain why.

- If you were to write a descriptive essay from the perspective of another character in the narrative poem, what changes would you make and why?

PRACTICE & APPLY 4 Use the information on this page to proofread, publish, and reflect on your essay describing a character from a narrative poem.

Writing Skills
Proofread, especially for correct capitalization.

Collection 1: Skills Review

Comparing Literature

SKILLS FOCUS, pp. 82–85

Grade-Level Skills

■ **Literary Skills**
Compare literary forms of major literary periods.

INTRODUCING THE SKILLS REVIEW

Use this review to assess students' ability to contrast works from different literary periods.

DIRECT TEACHING

A **Reading Skills**

? Characterizing the speaker. What do the first fifteen lines of this poem tell you about the speaker? [Possible response: He has spent his life enduring the hardships of the sea.]

B **Reading Skills**

? Comparing and contrasting. What two ways of life is the speaker contrasting? [Possible response: He contrasts the lonely, harsh life of the sea to the warmth and intimacy of life at home and at the mead hall.]

Collection 1: Skills Review
Comparing Literature

Test Practice

The following two poems were written more than nine hundred years apart in two vastly different periods of English history. "The Seafarer," an anonymous Anglo-Saxon poem, was written in the tenth century. "Break, Break, Break" is a highly polished poem by the great poet laureate of Victorian England, Alfred, Lord Tennyson (1809–1892) (see page 694). Both poets chose the sea as a central image to express a recurring human yearning that knows no boundaries of time, place, or social circumstance.

DIRECTIONS: Read the following two poems. Then, read each multiple-choice question that follows, and write the letter of the best response.

from The Seafarer
translated by Burton Raffel

This tale is true, and mine. It tells
How the sea took me, swept me back
And forth in sorrow and fear and pain,
Showed me suffering in a hundred ships,
5 In a thousand ports, and in me. It tells
Of smashing surf when I sweated in the cold
Of an anxious watch, perched in the bow
As it dashed under cliffs. My feet were cast
In icy bands, bound with frost,
10 With frozen chains, and hardship groaned
Around my heart. Hunger tore
At my sea-weary soul. No man sheltered
On the quiet fairness of earth can feel
How wretched I was, drifting through winter
15 On an ice-cold sea, whirled in sorrow,
Alone in a world blown clear of love,
Hung with icicles. The hailstorms flew.
The only sound was the roaring sea,
The freezing waves. The song of the swan
20 Might serve for pleasure, the cry of the sea-fowl,
The death-noise of birds instead of laughter,
The mewing of gulls instead of mead.
Storms beat on the rocky cliffs and were echoed
By icy-feathered terns° and the eagle's screams;

24. **terns** *n. pl.*: seabirds related to gulls.

Pages 82–85 cover
Literary Skills
Compare and contrast works from different literary periods.

82   Collection 1   The Anglo-Saxons

READING MINI-LESSON

Reviewing Word-Attack Skills
Activity. Display these pairs of words. The first word will reappear in the second word. Have students underline the syllable said with greatest stress in each word. Have them consult a dictionary to check their work. Answers are underlined.

1. mo<u>ment</u>   mo<u>men</u>tous
2. po<u>si</u>tion   depo<u>si</u>tion
3. <u>su</u>per   su<u>per</u>lative
4. <u>mag</u>net   mag<u>net</u>ic
5. <u>tro</u>phy   <u>at</u>rophy
6. <u>se</u>quence   <u>sub</u>sequence

82   Collection 1   The Anglo-Saxons

Collection 1: Skills Review

25   No kinsman could offer comfort there,
     To a soul left drowning in desolation.
            And who could believe, knowing but
     The passion of cities, swelled proud with wine
     And no taste of misfortune, how often, how wearily,
30   I put myself back on the paths of the sea.
     Night would blacken; it would snow from the north;
     Frost bound the earth and hail would fall,
     The coldest seeds. And how my heart
     Would begin to beat, knowing once more
35   The salt waves tossing and the towering sea!
     The time for journeys would come and my soul
     Called me eagerly out, sent me over
     The horizon, seeking foreigners' homes.
            But there isn't a man on earth so proud,
40   So born to greatness, so bold with his youth,
     Grown so brave, or so graced by God,
     That he feels no fear as the sails unfurl,
     Wondering what Fate has willed and will do.
     No harps ring in his heart, no rewards,
45   No passion for women, no worldly pleasures,
     Nothing, only the ocean's heave;
     But longing wraps itself around him.
     Orchards blossom, the towns bloom,
     Fields grow lovely as the world springs fresh,
50   And all these admonish° that willing mind
     Leaping to journeys, always set
     In thoughts traveling on a quickening tide.
     So summer's sentinel, the cuckoo, sings
     In his murmuring voice, and our hearts mourn
55   As he urges. Who could understand,
     In ignorant ease, what we others suffer
     As the paths of exile stretch endlessly on?
            And yet my heart wanders away,
     My soul roams with the sea, the whales'
60   Home, wandering to the widest corners
     Of the world, returning ravenous° with desire,
     Flying solitary, screaming, exciting me
     To the open ocean, breaking oaths
     On the curve of a wave. . . .

50. **admonish** *v.:* scold mildly.

61. **ravenous** *adj.:* very hungry.

DIRECT TEACHING

C Reading Skills

? Analyzing motivation. Why does the seafarer return to the sea time after time? [Possible responses: He may feel more at home at sea than on land. He may feel fated to this way of life. He may be unable to resist the lure of the sea.]

D Reading Skills

? Recognizing philosophical attitudes. What common Anglo-Saxon attitude does this line reflect? [the Anglo-Saxon acceptance of fate]

E Reading Skills

? Speculating. What oaths do you think the speaker may have broken? [Possible response: promises made to a wife, lover, son, or daughter never to return to the sea]

Activity. The same word appears in each pair of sentences below. Have students tell in which sentence the word is pronounced with a long *a* in the final syllable. Answers are checked.

1. Please <u>duplicate</u> this document. √
   Keep the <u>duplicate</u> in the files.
2. This newspaper is part of a <u>syndicate</u>.
   They will <u>syndicate</u> the new comic strip. √
3. The new strip will <u>alternate</u> with another one. √
   The two will appear on <u>alternate</u> days.

Activity. Have volunteers read the first word in each set and identify which of the following words has the same first vowel sound. Answers are underlined.

1. clavichord   <u>cavern</u>   craven
2. shiver   <u>shrivel</u>   thrive
3. lavish   slavish   lavender
4. maverick   <u>haversack</u>   favorable
5. clover   glover   <u>plover</u>
6. bovine   covenant   <u>jovial</u>

Collection 1: Skills Review

Direct Teaching

A Reading Skills

Comparing and contrasting. To understand the two poems, readers will need to compare and contrast the speakers and their relationships to the sea. What does the first stanza reveal about the location of the speaker? [Unlike the speaker of "The Seafarer," he is on the shore.] What do the adjectives *cold* and *gray* suggest about the speaker's feelings toward the sea? [He views the sea as cheerless and indifferent to his feelings.]

B Literary Focus

Alliteration. What examples of alliteration can you find in ll. 9–10? ["stately ships" and "haven under the hill"] Where else in the poem does Tennyson use this same sound device? ["Break, break, break"; "shouts with his sister"; "boat on the bay"; "day that is dead"]

C Literary Focus

Mood. What word choices in the last two lines of the poem give clues to the speaker's mood? [The words *dead* and *never* suggest that the speaker is feeling a profound sadness from which he does not expect to recover.] How does this mood compare to the mood of "The Seafarer"? [Both are mournful, although the speaker in "The Seafarer" moves on with life while the speaker in Tennyson's poem seems more passive.]

Test-Taking Tips

Advise students to read all the answer items before attempting to choose the correct one.
 For more instruction on how to answer multiple-choice items, refer students to **Test Smarts**.

Break, Break, Break
Alfred, Lord Tennyson

A
Break, break, break,
 On thy cold gray stones, O Sea!
And I would that my tongue could utter
 The thoughts that arise in me.

5 O, well for the fisherman's boy,
 That he shouts with his sister at play!
O, well for the sailor lad,
 That he sings in his boat on the bay!

B
And the stately ships go on
10 To their haven under the hill;
But O for the touch of a vanished hand,
 And the sound of a voice that is still!

C
Break, break, break,
 At the foot of thy crags, O Sea!
15 But the tender grace of a day that is dead
 Will never come back to me.

---

1. In "The Seafarer" the dominant impression of the speaker's life at sea is one of —
   A warm companionship
   B physical hardship
   C exciting adventure
   D mind-numbing routine

2. In "The Seafarer," the compound word "whales' home" (lines 59–60) is an example of an Anglo-Saxon figure of speech called —
   F pentameter
   G alliteration
   H kenning
   J elegy

84 Collection 1   The Anglo-Saxons

Answers and Model Rationales

1. **B** Throughout the poem, the speaker gives many specific details of his long, hard life at sea.

2. **H** Since this metaphorical compound phrase is not alliterative and is too short to have meter or constitute an elegy, it must be an example of kenning.

84 Collection 1 The Anglo-Saxons

Collection 1: Skills Review

3. Lines 33–35 of "The Seafarer" contain examples of which literary element?
   A alliteration
   B kennings
   C foils
   D allusions

4. In the third stanza of "Break, Break, Break," the speaker grieves over —
   F a sunken ship
   G the loss of a loved one
   H his inability to move on
   J the fisherman's boy

5. What aspect of the sea is emphasized by the repetition of the word *break* in Tennyson's poem?
   A its ability to transform
   B its tender fragility
   C its relentless violence
   D its stark beauty

6. The hardships experienced by the speaker of "Break, Break, Break" differ from those felt by the seafarer in that they —
   F are physical rather than emotional
   G prevent him from sailing again
   H are easily forgotten
   J are emotional rather than physical

7. What attitude toward the sea do the speakers of both poems have in common?
   A Both love the sea and cannot leave it.
   B Both connect the sea with hardship and loss.
   C Both condemn the sea's destructiveness.
   D Both see the sea as the source of life.

8. How does the Anglo-Saxon speaker of "The Seafarer" differ from the Victorian speaker of "Break, Break, Break"?
   F The Anglo-Saxon speaker refuses to mention his hardships.
   G He is bitter about all that he has suffered.
   H He has never longed for love or companionship.
   J He chooses to remain active rather than observe life from a distance.

Essay Question

Both "The Seafarer" and "Break, Break, Break" are elegies, or sorrowful poems that lament loss and the inevitable passage of time. In an essay, compare and contrast the source of each speaker's sorrow. Discuss how the language and imagery in each poem convey the sorrowful mood of an elegy. Use details from each poem to support your response.

---

3. **A** Line 34, "begin to beat," and l. 35, "tossing and the towering sea," are examples of alliteration.
4. **G** "The touch of a vanished hand" and "the sound of a voice that is still" indicate that the speaker has lost a beloved companion.
5. **C** The repetition of the hard *b* and *k* sounds echoes the constant, harsh pounding of waves on the shore.
6. **J** Tennyson's speaker mentions neither physical hardships nor being prevented from sailing again; he focuses on the psychic pain which his thoughts and memories bring him—memories not easily forgotten.
7. **B** The Anglo-Saxon speaker connects the sea with physical hardship and loss of comfort while Tennyson's speaker associates it with nature's indifference to his personal loss.
8. **J** The Anglo-Saxon speaker chooses again and again to return to the sea while the Victorian speaker stands on the shore, thinking and watching but not actively participating in life.

Essay Question
The Anglo-Saxon speaker bemoans the loss of the comforts and pleasures of home on land, while the Victorian speaker longs for "the tender grace" of the time spent with his lost friend. The language and imagery in "The Seafarer" is active, physical, and robust while that of "Break, Break, Break" is contemplative, emotional, and restrained.

ASSESSING

Assessment
- Holt Assessment: Literature, Reading, and Vocabulary

Using Academic Language

Review of Literary Terms
Ask students to look back through the collection to find the meanings of the terms listed at right. Then, have students show their grasp of the terms by citing passages from the collection that illustrate the meanings of those terms.

Archetype (p. 20); **Epic Hero** (pp. 20, 44); **Epic** (pp. 20, 44, 45); **Alliteration** (p. 41); **Kennings** (p. 42); **Foil** (p. 47); **Epic Similes** (p. 56).

Collection 1: Skills Review

Vocabulary Skills

Context Clues

Modeling. Model the thought process of a good reader getting the answer to item 1 by saying, "Since the context sentence is describing the attack of an angry beast, it is unlikely that such an attacker would be behaving in the mild ways suggested by A, B, and D. Therefore, C is correct."

Answers and Model Rationales

1. **C** See rationale above.
2. **J** The phrase "deserving of praise" restates and explains the meaning of the word *extolled*.
3. **B** The first part of the sentence that describes Beowulf as confident in his ability to kill rules out A, C, and D.
4. **F** The examples of the gifts given rule out H and J since swords and helmets are neither insignificant nor pointless to soldiers. The inclusion of the word *rings* also rules out G.
5. **B** The context does not describe Humbaba as angry or beautiful, ruling out C and D. Since A creates a redundancy, "twisted shape" is the one choice that corresponds with "permanently stooped."
6. **G** The context clues "still sane" and "under strain" indicate a stressed but still functioning mental state.
7. **A** The context clue "begs" indicates that the action described is "humbling oneself in front of authority."

Collection 1: Skills Review

Vocabulary Skills

Test Practice

Context Clues

DIRECTIONS: Choose the answer that gives the best definition of the underlined word.

1. As Beowulf lifted his shield, the angry beast flailed and thrashed and vehemently attacked the king.
   Vehemently means —
   A calmly
   B timidly
   C violently
   D feebly

2. After Beowulf's death the Geats extolled the heroic deeds of their fallen king, proclaiming that no other man was so deserving of praise.
   Extolled means —
   F criticized
   G condemned
   H exploited
   J praised

3. Beowulf never expresses uncertainty about his ability to kill Grendel; he is both proud and resolute.
   Resolute means —
   A uncertain
   B determined
   C fearful
   D angry

4. Wiglaf encourages his fellow soldiers to join the battle against the dragon by reminding them of the lavish gifts, such as rings and swords and helmets, that Beowulf has given them.
   Lavish means —
   F extravagant
   G useful
   H insignificant
   J pointless

5. Because Humbaba has huge, flailing limbs and is permanently stooped, he is described as "monstrous in his contortion."
   Contortion means —
   A monstrosity
   B twisted shape
   C anger
   D beauty

6. King Priam declares that although he is still sane, he is under strain and is harrowed from having suffered so much.
   Harrowed means —
   F youthful
   G mentally distressed
   H incapacitated
   J helpless

7. Athena tells Achilles that Hector can no longer escape them, not even if the Archer begs for Hector's life, groveling in front of Zeus.
   Groveling means —
   A humbling oneself in front of authority
   B demanding something of an inferior
   C escaping for one's life
   D refusing to give up

SKILLS FOCUS

Vocabulary Skills
Use context clues to determine the meanings of words.

86 Collection 1 The Anglo-Saxons

Vocabulary Review

Use this activity to assess whether students have retained the collection Vocabulary. Ask students to complete each of the sentences with a Vocabulary word from the box.

| decreed | assail | furled |
| scourge | infallible | |

1. Although Beowulf was a wise ruler, his judgment was not _____. [infallible]
2. Gilgamesh had the courage to _____ the giant Humbaba with an ax. [assail]
3. When the enemy was defeated, the king _____ a period of feasting. [decreed]
4. The marauding Grendel was the _____ of Hrothgar's warriors. [scourge]
5. As night fell, the encamped soldiers _____ their flags and lit fires. [furled]

Collection 1: Skills Review
Writing Skills

Test Practice — DIRECTIONS: Read the following paragraph from a draft of a student's descriptive essay. Then, answer the questions below it.

(1) In Hrothgar's dark and silent mead hall, Beowulf pulls his cloak around his cold vest of hammered chain mail and looks curiously at his hands, which are growing warmer in the cold, reflecting the heat and fire from the hearth. (2) The mead halls here in Herot are much colder than those in Beowulf's faraway home. (3) He flexes his fingers, then clasps and unclasps his hands on his sword in front of him, remembering that even in battle with sea monsters in the frigid ocean surf, his hands had been warm. (4) Then, in the dark, he hears something. (5) Suddenly, leaning up on one arm, Beowulf stretches out his right hand and seizes Grendel's claws, bending them back in his fierce grip.

1. Which sentence could be added to show thoughts and feelings after sentence 1?
   A Beowulf used to feel embarrassed about his hands.
   B "Take care of your hands," his mother had always advised him.
   C The Geats all thought, "Beowulf is too protective of his hands."
   D Nobody in Herot remembered the stories about Beowulf's hands.

2. Which sentence could be deleted to improve the paragraph's organization?
   F 2
   G 3
   H 4
   J 5

3. How could sentence 4 be rewritten to include sensory details?
   A Because it is quiet in the dark, Beowulf has no trouble hearing something that sounds strange.
   B Then, in the very dark hall, he hears something awesome.
   C Then, while Beowulf listens in the dark, he hears a sound.
   D Then, in the dark, he hears the shadow monster snapping the bones of a fellow Geat.

4. Which reference to the poem could be added after sentence 5 to show a character's feelings?
   F Beowulf, "who of all the men on earth/Was the strongest," held the monster fast (lines 80–81).
   G Beowulf, the "mighty protector of men," held the monster fast (line 81).
   H In fierce pain, Grendel "fought / For his freedom" (lines 53–54).
   J In fierce pain, Grendel's "mind was flooded with fear" (line 44).

5. How would you describe the writer's tone in this passage?
   A hateful
   B apathetic
   C suspenseful
   D joyous

SKILLS FOCUS

Writing Skills Write a descriptive essay.

Collection 1: Skills Review
Writing Skills

Answers
1. A
2. F
3. D
4. J
5. C

APPLICATION

The Illustrated Hero

For homework, have students create a suitable character for a narrative poem. Students should use their knowledge of narrative poetry, such as *Beowulf,* to spark their imagination. After determining the physical characteristics of the character, students should draw or paint a large, detailed, life-sized image of the character. Around the drawing students should write descriptive phrases about the character's personality, using the language of traditional epic poetry—for example, "swift-footed Achilles."

EXTENSION

A Poetic Tribute

Have students think again about a person whose qualities they admire. Have students research the person to find an important event in the person's life that illustrates the person's best qualities. Then, have students write a poem about the event. The poem should be written in the tradition of the narrative poetry students have read. You may ask students to read their poems to the class.

RESOURCES: WRITING

Assessment
- *Holt Assessment: Writing, Listening, and Speaking*
- *One-Stop Planner* CD-ROM with ExamView Test Generator

Internet
- *Holt Online Assessment*
- *Holt Online Essay Scoring*

Collection 2
The Middle Ages: 1066–1485

About Collection 2
In Collection 2, students will master the following skills:
- **Literary Skills:** Evaluate the philosophical, political, religious, ethical, and social influences of a historical period; analyze ballads, frame stories, narrators, fables, archetypes, characterization, imagery, verbal and situational irony, couplets and the use of rhymes; compare and contrast works of major literary periods.
- **Reading Skills:** Analyze style using key details; interpret character; evaluate historical context; compare influences of different historical periods.
- **Vocabulary Skills:** Create semantic maps with antonyms; understand etymologies and multiple-meaning words; complete word analogies.
- **Writing Skills:** Develop, write, and revise a literary research paper.
- **Listening and Speaking Skills:** Present a literary research paper.

Minimum Course of Study
Most skills can be taught with a minimum number of selections and features. In the chart to the right, lessons **highlighted in green** constitute the minimum course of study that provides coverage of the skills taught in Collection 2.

Resource Manager
(see pp. 88E–88H)
Lesson and workshop resources are referenced in the Resource Manager on the pages that follow. These resources can be used to reinforce the skills taught in Collection 2, remediate students who are having difficulty, and provide supporting activities for English-language learners.

Scope and Sequence

Selection ■ Feature	Literary Skills
The Middle Ages: 1066–1485 by David Adams Leeming	• Evaluate the philosophical, political, religious, ethical, and social influences of a historical period
Ballads: • **Lord Randall** • **Get Up and Bar the Door** ↔ *at grade level*	• Analyze the characteristics of ballads
The Prologue to The Canterbury Tales by Geoffrey Chaucer ↔ *at grade level*	• Analyze characterization • Analyze characteristics of a frame story • Analyze imagery in characterization
from **The Pardoner's Tale** by Geoffrey Chaucer ↔ *at grade level*	• Analyze irony, including verbal and situational irony
from **The Wife of Bath's Tale** by Geoffrey Chaucer ↔ *at grade level*	• Analyze the characteristics of a narrator • Analyze couplets and the use of rhymes
Connecting to World Literature: **The Frame Story: A Tale Linking Tales** by David Adams Leeming	• Understand the characteristics of frame stories • Compare frame stories from different cultures and literary periods
Right-Mind and Wrong-Mind *from the* **Panchatantra** ↔ *at grade level*	• Analyze the characteristics of fables • Compare frame stories
from **The Third Voyage of Sindbad the Sailor** *from* **The Thousand and One Nights** ↓ *below grade level*	• Analyze the characteristics of an archetype
Federigo's Falcon *from the* **Decameron** by Giovanni Boccaccio ↔ *at grade level*	• Analyze situational irony

Reading Skills	Vocabulary Skills	Writing ▪ Grammar and Language ▪ Listening and Speaking Skills
		• Retell a ballad as a news story • Give an oral performance of a ballad
• Analyze style using key details	• Create semantic maps with antonyms	• Write a prologue to a modern frame story
	• Demonstrate word knowledge	• Write a character analysis
• Interpret character	• Demonstrate word knowledge • Understand etymologies and multiple-meaning words	• Write a historical research report
	• Complete word analogies	• Give an oral performance of a fable
	• Create semantic maps	• Write a story that contains an archetypal hero
• Evaluate historical context • Compare influences of different historical periods	• Understand etymologies	• Write an essay comparing and contrasting two literary characters

(continued)

88B

Scope and Sequence

Selection • Feature	Literary Skills	Reading Skills
from **The Day of Destiny** from **Le Morte d'Arthur** by Sir Thomas Malory ↔ at grade level	• Analyze the archetype of the romance hero	
Writing Workshop: Reporting Literary Research		
Listening and Speaking Workshop: Presenting Literary Research		
Skills Review: Literary Skills Vocabulary Skills Writing Skills	• Compare and contrast works of major literary periods	

Vocabulary Skills	Writing ▪ Grammar and Language ▪ Listening and Speaking Skills
• Understand etymologies	• Write an essay comparing and contrasting archetypal heroes • Combine sentences using coordinating and subordinating conjunctions
	• Write a literary research paper
	• Present a literary research paper
• Understand multiple-meaning words	• Write a historical research paper

Resource Manager

Selection • Feature	Planning	Differentiating Instruction • Lesson Plans with ELL Strategies and Practice	Reading • Vocabulary
The Middle Ages: 1066–1485 *by* David Adams Leeming	• PowerNotes: The Middle Ages	• Holt Adapted Reader	• Holt Adapted Reader
Ballads: Lord Randall Get Up and Bar the Door	• One-Stop Planner with ExamView Test Generator • PowerNotes: Ballads	• Supporting Instruction in Spanish, p. 7 • Audio CD Library, disc 2 • Audio CD Library, Selections and Summaries in Spanish	
The Prologue to The Canterbury Tales *by* Geoffrey Chaucer	• One-Stop Planner with ExamView Test Generator • PowerNotes: The Language of Geoffrey Chaucer	• The Holt Reader, pp. 53–68 • Holt Adapted Reader • Holt Reading Solutions, pp. 51–53 • Supporting Instruction in Spanish, p. 8 • Audio CD Library, disc 2 • Audio CD Library, Selections and Summaries in Spanish	• The Holt Reader • Holt Adapted Reader • Holt Reading Solutions • Vocabulary Development, p. 6
from **The Pardoner's Tale** *by* Geoffrey Chaucer	• One-Stop Planner with ExamView Test Generator • PowerNotes: The Language of Geoffrey Chaucer	• Supporting Instruction in Spanish, p. 8 • Audio CD Library, disc 2 • Audio CD Library, Selections and Summaries in Spanish	• Vocabulary Development, p. 7
from **The Wife of Bath's Tale** *by* Geoffrey Chaucer	• One-Stop Planner with ExamView Test Generator • PowerNotes: The Language of Geoffrey Chaucer	• Supporting Instruction in Spanish, p. 9 • Audio CD Library, disc 2 • Audio CD Library, Selections and Summaries in Spanish	• Vocabulary Development, p. 8
Connecting to World Literature: The Frame Story: A Tale Linking Tales *by* David Adams Leeming			
Right Mind and Wrong Mind *from the* **Panchatantra** *from* **The Third Voyage of Sindbad the Sailor** *from* **The Thousand and One Nights** **Federigo's Falcon** *from the* **Decameron** *by* Giovanni Boccaccio	• One-Stop Planner with ExamView Test Generator	• The Holt Reader, pp. 69–79 • Holt Adapted Reader • Holt Reading Solutions, pp. 57–59 • Supporting Instruction in Spanish, pp. 9–11 • Audio CD Library, disc 3 • Audio CD Library, Selections and Summaries in Spanish	• The Holt Reader • Holt Adapted Reader • Holt Reading Solutions • Vocabulary Development, pp. 9, 10, 11

Writing ■ Grammar and Language ■ Listening and Speaking	Assessment
• Daily Language Activities	• Holt Assessment: Literature, Reading, and Vocabulary • Holt Online Assessment • One-Stop Planner with ExamView Test Generator
• Daily Language Activities	• Holt Assessment: Literature, Reading, and Vocabulary • Holt Online Assessment • One-Stop Planner with ExamView Test Generator
• Daily Language Activities	• Holt Assessment: Literature, Reading, and Vocabulary • Holt Online Assessment • One-Stop Planner with ExamView Test Generator
• Daily Language Activities	• Holt Assessment: Literature, Reading, and Vocabulary • Holt Online Assessment • One-Stop Planner with ExamView Test Generator
• Daily Language Activities	• Holt Assessment: Literature, Reading, and Vocabulary • Holt Online Assessment • One-Stop Planner with ExamView Test Generator

(continued)

Technology

INTERNET
- go.hrw.com
- Holt Online Assessment
- Holt Online Essay Scoring
- Elements of Literature Online

MEDIA

- One-Stop Planner with ExamView Test Generator

- PowerNotes
- Audio CD Library, discs 2 and 3
- Audio CD Library, Selections and Summaries in Spanish
- Visual Connections Videocassette Program, Segment 3
- Fine Art Transparencies, 3

 Transparency   Video

 CD-ROM   Audio CD

Resource Manager

Selection • Feature	Planning	Differentiating Instruction • Lesson Plans with ELL Strategies and Practice	Reading • Vocabulary
from **The Day of Destiny** from **Le Morte d'Arthur** by Sir Thomas Malory	• One-Stop Planner with ExamView Test Generator	• Supporting Instruction in Spanish, p. 12 • Audio CD Library, disc 3 • Audio CD Library, Selections and Summaries in Spanish	• Vocabulary Development, p. 12
Writing Workshop: *Reporting Literary Research*	• One-Stop Planner with ExamView Test Generator	• Workshop Resources: Writing, Listening, and Speaking, pp. 9–16 • Family Involvement Activities in English and Spanish • Supporting Instruction in Spanish, p. 67	
Listening and Speaking Workshop: *Presenting Literary Research*	• One-Stop Planner with ExamView Test Generator	• Workshop Resources: Writing, Listening, and Speaking, pp. 17–22 • Supporting Instruction in Spanish, p. 109	
Skills Review: *Literary Skills* *Vocabulary Skills* *Writing Skills*			

The Holt Reader

The Holt Reader is a consumable paperback book that can be used alone or to accompany *Elements of Literature*. It offers guided support throughout the reading process and encourages students to become active readers by circling, underlining, questioning, and jotting down responses as they read. *The Holt Reader* works well for homework, students who have missed class, additional instructional time, reteaching, and remediation.

Holt Reading Solutions (HRS)

Holt Reading Solutions pulls together reading resources in the *Elements of Literature* program to create a powerful tool for intervention and whole-class instruction. *HRS* includes diagnostic assessment tools, lesson plans for English-language learners and special education students, adaptations of selected reading selections, vocabulary and comprehension worksheets, information on phonics and decoding, and additional instruction and practice in remedial reading skills.

Writing ▪ Grammar and Language ▪ Listening and Speaking	Assessment
• Daily Language Activities • Language Handbook Worksheets, p. 76	• Holt Assessment: Literature, Reading, and Vocabulary • Holt Online Assessment • One-Stop Planner with ExamView Test Generator
• Daily Language Activities • Workshop Resources: Writing, Listening, and Speaking, pp. 9–16	• Holt Assessment: Writing, Listening, and Speaking • Holt Online Assessment • One-Stop Planner with ExamView Test Generator
• Daily Language Activities • Workshop Resources: Writing, Listening, and Speaking, pp. 17–22	• Holt Assessment: Writing, Listening, and Speaking • Holt Online Assessment • One-Stop Planner with ExamView Test Generator
	• Holt Assessment: Writing, Listening, and Speaking • One-Stop Planner with ExamView Test Generator

Technology

INTERNET
- go.hrw.com
- Holt Online Assessment
- Holt Online Essay Scoring
- Elements of Literature Online

MEDIA
 • One-Stop Planner with ExamView Test Generator
 • PowerNotes
- Audio CD Library, discs 2 and 3
- Audio CD Library, Selections and Summaries in Spanish
- Visual Connections Videocassette Program, Segment 3
- Fine Art Transparencies, 3

 Transparency   Video

 CD-ROM   Audio CD

One-Stop Planner with ExamView Test Generator

The *One-Stop Planner* CD-ROM contains electronic versions of print-based teaching resources, clips from the video program, and valuable assessment tools. The *One-Stop Planner* resources are presented in easy-to-follow, point-and-click menu formats. To preview resources or print out worksheets and tests, you simply make a selection and click.

Collection 2

INTRODUCING THE COLLECTION

In this collection, students will become familiar with the works of major writers of the Middle Ages. They will learn about the major literary forms, such as the ballad and the romance, used by writers of the time. The centerpiece of Collection 2 is selections from *The Canterbury Tales* by Geoffrey Chaucer. In addition to reading background material on the tales, students will analyze Chaucer's use of imagery, irony, and characterization. The collection concludes by giving students the opportunity to write a literary research paper on a topic of their choice and to present their research to an audience.

VIEWING THE ART

This image is from a book that is now known as the *Golf Book of Hours* because one of its illustrations shows men playing a game similar to the modern sport of golf. The book is particularly interesting because it shows both peasants and the nobility playing a variety of sports. Here we see peasants taking a break from their work in the fields.

Activity. What elements in the illustration suggest that it is a romanticized view of peasant life? [Possible responses: the peasants' clothing is neat; the peasants do not seem fatigued from hard work; the mood of the scene is peaceful and serene.] What message might this image have with respect to daily religious devotion—the purpose of a book of hours? [Possible response: Religious life and daily life are inseparable.]

Scene from *Golf Book of Hours* (detail) (c. 1500).
British Library, London. The Bridgeman Art Library.

COLLECTION 2 RESOURCES: READING

Planning
- *One-Stop Planner* CD-ROM with ExamView Test Generator

Differentiating Instruction
- Holt Reading Solutions
- The Holt Reader
- Holt Adapted Reader
- Family Involvement Activities in English and Spanish
- Supporting Instruction in Spanish
- Audio CD Library, Selections and Summaries in Spanish

Vocabulary
- Vocabulary Development

Grammar and Language
- Language Handbook Worksheets
- Daily Language Activities

Collection 2

THE MIDDLE AGES
1066–1485
The Tales They Told

The medieval world we know was far from perfect. Life expectancy was short, and disease was mostly incontestable. It was a world burdened by royal autocracy and social hierarchy inherited from ancient times. Its piety and devotion were affected by fanaticism and a potential for persecution. Its intellectuals were given to too abstract and not enough practical thinking. But it exhibited as elevated a culture, as peaceful a community, as benign a political system, as high-minded and popular a faith as the world has ever seen.

—Norman F. Cantor

INTERNET
Collection Resources
Keyword: LE5 12-2

THE QUOTATION

A professor at New York University, Norman F. Cantor has written extensively about the Middle Ages. His works, known for their lively way of presenting scholarly information, include *Inventing the Middle Ages, Medieval Lives: Eight Charismatic Men and Women in the Middle Ages,* and *Encyclopedia of the Middle Ages.* You might ask students if Cantor's description fits our stereotyped image of the Middle Ages. You might also discuss how one would support Cantor's assertion that the medieval world displayed positive traits comparable to those of any culture that ever existed.

Assessment
- *Holt Assessment: Literature, Reading, and Vocabulary*
- *One-Stop Planner* CD-ROM with ExamView Test Generator
- *Holt Online Assessment*

Internet
- go.hrw.com (Keyword: LE5 12-2)
- *Elements of Literature Online*

Media
- *Audio CD Library*
- *Audio CD Library, Selections and Summaries in Spanish*
- *Fine Art Transparencies*
- *Visual Connections Videocassette Program*
- *PowerNotes*

Time Line

Before looking at individual items on the time line, discuss why many of the dates on it are marked *c.* (for *circa,* or "approximately"). [Possible response: Record keeping was not commonplace in this era.] Note that greater historical documentation moves away from anonymous or group authorship and toward attributed authorship.

■ 1100
The Heroic Poem

One of the most important literary forms of the Middle Ages was the *chanson de geste* ("song of deeds"), or heroic poem, a long narrative poem on a serious subject strongly rooted in one society. The heroic poem centers on a legendary figure whose actions affect the well-being of an entire group. The greatest French heroic poem is the *Song of Roland,* which recounts a legendary campaign of the Holy Roman Emperor Charlemagne and his knights. True to form, the hero Roland, a knight, embodies the chivalrous and Christian virtues of his time.

■ 1095–1270
Effects of the Crusades

Knights who joined the Crusades had a number of goals: They wanted to free Jerusalem from Turkish control, fight a holy war, and perhaps return home with gold and other riches. Although they had only limited success, the Crusades changed European culture in many ways. They helped bring to the West the fruits of Islamic scholarship, technology, and medicine. The Crusades weakened feudalism by causing the deaths of many knights and the destruction of the nobles' manor houses at home. The weakening of the nobles increased the power of the kings. In addition, the increase in trade stimulated the growth of towns, where people could live outside the feudal order.

The Middle Ages   1066–1485

LITERARY EVENTS

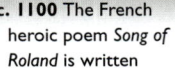

- **c. 1100** The French heroic poem *Song of Roland* is written
- **1131** Omar Khayyám, Persian poet and astronomer, dies
- **c. 1150** In Spain, paper is first mass-produced
- **c. 1170s** In France, Chrétien de Troyes writes *Lancelot*
- **1179** Hildegard of Bingen, German abbess, mystic, and poet, dies
- **c. 1200** The German epic poem the *Nibelungenlied* is begun
- **1213** Persian poet **Saadi** is born
- **c. 1216** Marie de France, first known European woman to write narrative poetry, dies

Scene from the *Song of Roland*. Stained-glass window, Chartres Cathedral, France (13th century).

Marie de France. Bibliothèque Nationale de France.

POLITICAL AND SOCIAL EVENTS

- **1066** King Edward the Confessor dies without heir
- **1066** Duke of Normandy invades England
- **1086** Domesday Book, a record of all land-ownership in England, is first compiled
- **1095** Crusades to free Jerusalem from Turkish control begin
- **c. 1119** Knights Templar, a religious order whose mission was to protect pilgrims to the Holy Land, is founded
- **1163** Construction of Cathedral of Notre Dame in Paris begins
- **1170** Thomas à Becket is murdered
- **1171** Henry II invades Ireland, beginning nearly eight hundred years of British domination
- **1192** Minamoto Yoritomo becomes first shogun (military ruler) of Japan
- **1211** Mongol leader Genghis Khan invades China
- **1215** English barons force King John to sign the Magna Carta
- **c. 1232** Pope Gregory IX begins the Inquisition

Domesday Book (c. 1085–1086).
© Michael Freeman/CORBIS.

A man and his wife on horseback, from a book of hours (c. 1500).
By permission of the British Library, London.

Using the Time Line

Activity. Have students use print or nonprint sources to place the following events on the time line and to explain their significance.

- **The kingdom of Mali emerges.** [c. 1235: Sundiata takes over the kingdom of Ghana, promotes agriculture, and renews the gold-salt trade.]
- **The Model Parliament is held.** [1295: When Edward I needs to raise taxes for his war against the French, he calls together burgesses and knights to serve as a legislative group. This assembly becomes a "model" for representative government.]
- **Ibn Battuta visits most of the countries of the Islamic world.** [mid-1300s: Born in Tangier, Ibn Battuta becomes an early historian of the African Islamic world.]

Timeline 1250–1485

1266–1273 Thomas Aquinas writes *Summa Theologica*

c. 1307 Dante Alighieri begins writing *The Divine Comedy*

1341 Petrarch is crowned poet laureate in Italy

c. 1342 Julian of Norwich, one of the first English women of letters, is born

c. 1343 Geoffrey Chaucer is born

1349–1353 Giovanni Boccaccio writes the *Decameron*

c. 1373 Margery Kempe, author of first autobiography in English, is born

c. 1378 Legendary hero Robin Hood appears in *Piers Plowman*

1380 Entire Bible is translated into English for first time, by followers of John Wycliffe

c. 1387 Chaucer begins *The Canterbury Tales*

1400 Chaucer dies

1455 Gutenberg prints first book with movable type

c. 1475 William Caxton prints first book in English

1485 Thomas Malory's *Le Morte d'Arthur* is first printed by Caxton

From *Hours of the Duchess of Burgundy* (c.1450).
Musée Condé, Chantilly, France.

c. 1250 First commoners are allowed in British Parliament

1270 Crusades end

1275 Venetian traveler Marco Polo visits court of Kublai Khan in China

1296 Edward I invades Scotland and declares himself king

1300s Zimbabwe emerges as major trading empire

1325 Aztecs begin to establish empire in Mexico

1337 Hundred Years' War, between England and France, begins

1348 Black Death strikes England

1368 Ming dynasty begins three-hundred-year rule of China

1381 Peasants' Revolt takes place in England

1399 King Richard II is deposed

1400s Benin Kingdom in West Africa flourishes

1431 In France, Joan of Arc is burned at the stake by the English

c. 1438 Incan Empire is established in Peru

1455–1485 War between the Houses of York and Lancaster (also called the Wars of the Roses) is fought

1473 Nicolaus Copernicus, Polish astronomer, is born

1485 First Tudor king, Henry VII, is crowned

Marco Polo in Beijing.
Bibliothèque Nationale de France, Paris.

Chinese porcelain jar, Xuande period, Ming dynasty (15th century).
The Metropolitan Museum of Art, Gift of Robert E. Tod, 1936. (37.191.1)

▪ 1266–1273
Summa Theologica

This work by Thomas Aquinas is important because it applies the reasoning of the ancient Greeks, especially Aristotle, to Christian doctrine.

▪ 1307
Dante's *Divine Comedy*

Dante Alighieri was one of the greatest writers of the Middle Ages. His *Divine Comedy* ranks with the works of Shakespeare and Homer.

▪ 1373–1475
The Rise of the English Language

❓ What two literary events on this time line demonstrate that English was beginning to be accepted as a written language? [The Bible was translated into English in 1380; William Caxton produced the first book in English printed with movable type in 1475.]

▪ 1368–1485
The Ming in China

At the beginning of the fifteenth century, a Ming emperor named Yonglo launched great exploratory missions, led by a Muslim admiral, to learn about the outside world. Yonglo also built the palace known as the Forbidden City, where no foreigner or commoner was allowed to enter without special permission.

▪ 1431
Joan of Arc

As a teenager who commanded French troops and led them to several victories during the Hundred Years' War, Joan of Arc was scarcely the typical woman of the Middle Ages. After capturing her, the English army turned her over to an ecclesiastical court, which found her guilty of crimes ranging from wearing men's clothes to witchcraft and burned her at the stake.

Political and Social Milestones

■ Norman Conquest, 1066

William the Conqueror was crowned king of England on Christmas Day, 1066, following the Battle of Hastings. For the next several years he had to deal with numerous rebellions by the Saxons. By 1086, resistance had died out, and most of the landholdings were in the hands of Norman nobles. In that year, William secured the loyalty of those nobles in a unique way: He summoned them to a meeting on the Salisbury plain, and there he ordered them to swear their allegiance directly to him (rather than to their immediate superiors). According to *The Anglo-Saxon Chronicle,* William "was met by his councilors; and all the landsmen that were of any account over all England became this man's vassals as they were; and they all bowed themselves before him, and became his men, and swore him oaths of allegiance that they would against all other men be faithful to him."

VIEWING THE ART

The bishop of Bayeux, France, commissioned this tapestry to commemorate the Norman conquest of England. The tapestry, woven on coarse linen, depicts not just the Norman invasion but also a coronation, a feast, and other events. In this scene, William the Conqueror's invading army sails across the English Channel.

Activity. This detail of the tapestry shows the Normans crossing the channel. How does the artist convey a sense of movement? [A sense of motion is created by the curved sails, the wavy lines of the sea, and the placement of the ships.]

Political and Social

Norman Conquest, 1066

William the Conqueror and his powerful Norman army defeated the English king, Harold, at the Battle of Hastings in 1066. William then installed himself as king of England and divided the land among Norman barons loyal to him alone. This feudal system of landownership that William implemented created a social structure in which every man and woman had a place in a fixed hierarchy, or class system.

William the Conqueror's invasion fleet, from the Bayeux Tapestry (detail) (11th century).
By special permission of the City of Bayeux.

Milestones 1066–1485

A master with his carpenter and stonemason.
British Library, London. The Bridgeman Art Library.

The Age of Feudalism

Feudalism was a system that assigned an economic, political, and social position to every individual at birth. All land was bestowed on lords or barons by the lord over all, the king. Lesser lords, knights, vassals, and serfs served the landowning lords in turn, each with specific obligations to those above them on the feudal ladder. Knights, for instance, were professional warriors who fought their lord's battles, usually against the knights of rival lords. Serfs or peasants, the lowest of the social orders, were bound to the land they tilled and gave most of what they grew to their lord in return for his protection from war and starvation.

The Decline of Feudalism

The tight feudal order gradually broke down as the English people were exposed to other influences and as opportunities arose for them to make money outside the web of feudal obligations. Increased trade with the East created a merchant class. The growth of cities provided people with alternative means of supporting themselves: The growing cities needed carpenters, stonemasons, and other skilled workers. This new, urban middle class was emerging at the same time that the old feudal warriors—the knights—were being replaced by an army made up of yeomen (the class of small landowners). These yeomen used longbows that could even pierce the knights' iron armor.

Two men observe the construction of a house, with formal gardens in the background (15th century).
British Library, London. The Bridgeman Art Library.

■ The Age of Feudalism

The basic economic unit of feudalism, as a property system, was the manor. The lord of the manor and the serfs who worked it participated in an economic exchange. The lord provided the serfs with land, simple housing, and protection from wandering bandits. The serfs provided services to their lord, including maintaining the estate and giving him a portion of what they grew. After paying what they owed to the lord, serfs also had to pay money to the Church. Like slaves, serfs could not leave the land that they worked; unlike slaves, they could not be bought and sold. Theirs was a life of hard labor and few comforts.

■ The Decline of Feudalism

The growth of cities increased the demand for skilled workers, including builders (who physically expanded the cities) and craftspeople (who helped supply the citizens' needs). In the mid-1300s, however, the arrival of the Black Death, or bubonic plague (see page 106), dramatically reduced the ranks of skilled workers in England. Because of the tradition of long apprenticeships, those workers were difficult to replace. One solution to the problem proved to be the increased participation of women. Wives and daughters of merchants and artisans learned the skills of their husbands and fathers. Women worked in family businesses and often kept the businesses going when the heads of households died. Women also developed their own cottage industries (trades in which production could be done at home)—and were so successful that they gave the English language such family names as *Baxter* (literally, "female baker") and *Webster* (literally, "female weaver").

SKILLS FOCUS, pp. 94–107

Grade-Level Skills

■ **Literary Skills**

Evaluate the philosophical, political, religious, ethical, and social influences of the historical period.

Preview

Think About . . .

The questions listed in Think About can serve as a guide for reading this essay. You might also suggest that students concentrate first upon the main text (possibly using the subheadings to guide their progress) and leave the features (A Closer Look, for example, and the marginal lists of information) for later reading.

DIRECT TEACHING

 Exploring the Historical Period
THE LOOK OF A CONQUEROR

William of Malmesbury, one of the greatest of English chroniclers, describes William the Conqueror this way: "He was of just stature, extraordinary corpulence, fierce countenance: his forehead bare of hair; of such strength of arm that it was often a matter of surprise that no one was able to draw his bow which he himself could bend when his horse was on full gallop: he was majestic whether sitting or standing, although the protuberance of his belly deformed his royal person."

The Middle Ages 1066–1485
by David Adams Leeming

PREVIEW

Think About . . .

Anglo-Saxon England was permanently changed by the invasion of the Norman French, led by William the Conqueror in 1066. Despite his name, however, William wished to govern the Anglo-Saxon English, not to conquer them. The Anglo-Norman England that developed under William and his barons combined the older, more democratic Anglo-Saxon traditions with the new social system of the Norman invaders: feudalism.

As you read about this period, look for answers to these questions:

- What effects did the Norman invasion have on the way the English were governed?
- What were the main features of feudalism? How did feudalism change the social structure of Anglo-Saxon England?
- What developments in the fourteenth and fifteenth centuries began to undermine the feudal system?

SKILLS FOCUS

Collection introduction (pages 92–107) covers **Literary Skills** Evaluate the philosophical, political, religious, ethical, and social influences of a historical period.

In October 1066, a daylong battle near Hastings, England, changed the course of history. There, just ten miles from the channel dividing England from France, Duke William of Normandy, France, defeated and killed King Harold of England, the last of the Anglo-Saxon kings. So began the Norman Conquest, an event that radically affected English history, the English character, and the English language. Unlike the Romans, the Normans never withdrew from England.

William the Conqueror and the Norman Influence

Who was this William the Conqueror? He was the illegitimate son of the previous duke of Normandy, who was in turn a cousin of the English king called Edward the Confessor. Edward had died childless earlier in 1066, and Harold, the earl of Wessex, had been crowned the following day. William claimed, however, that the old king had promised the throne to him. Determined to seize what he considered rightfully his, William sailed across the English Channel with an enormous army.

Secondary Source

An Alternate History
According to the scholar Morris Bishop, "October 14, 1066, was one of the decisive days of history. The battle itself was nip and tuck; the shift only of a few elements here or there, a gift of luck could have given the victory to the Anglo-Saxons. If Harold had won at Hastings and had survived, William would have had no choice but to renounce his adventure. There is little likelihood that anyone would have attempted a serious invasion of England during the next millennium—by water, at least. England would have strengthened its bonds with Scandinavia while remaining distrustful of the western Continent—even more distrustful than it is today. The native Anglo-Saxon culture would have developed in unimaginable ways, and William the Conqueror would be dimly known in history only as William the Bastard."

Norman horsemen chasing defeated English soldiers after the Battle of Hastings, from the Bayeux Tapestry (detail) (11th century).
Musée de la tapisserie, Bayeux, France/Dagli Orti/The Art Archive.

DIRECT TEACHING

VIEWING THE ART

The Bayeux Tapestry, which is composed of a series of connected panels 231 feet long and about 18 inches high, tells the story of the Norman invasion in a graphic form. The image here is from the very last panel, which shows the Briton's fleeing the victorious Norman invasion army at the Battle of Hastings. The story seems to end in the middle of things. The Normans have not really assumed control of England; they haven't really even finished the battle they are fighting.

Activity: What is the effect of ending the story on the tapestry in the middle of things? [The tapestry suggests that the struggle to control England is not over even though the Normans have won the war.]

DIFFERENTIATING INSTRUCTION

Learners Having Difficulty
Encourage students to use the art accompanying this introductory essay to make some generalizations about life in the Middle Ages. You might remind students, however, that art throughout the ages has often been produced by or for those with the greatest advantages and does not always reflect the full range of social classes, human activity, or day-to-day life.

English-Language Learners
For a lesson designed for intermediate and advanced English-language learners, see *Holt Reading Solutions*.

Special Education Students
For a lesson designed for special education students, see *Holt Reading Solutions*.

DIRECT TEACHING

A Exploring the Historical Period
THE DOMESDAY BOOK

This massive survey, written in Latin in red and black ink, was significant because it helped to solidify the feudal system. The survey was managed by seven or eight panels of commissioners who compiled detailed accounts by geographical area of the manors, serfs, huts, mills, fishponds, and streams. The nobles resented this survey, but it established a social hierarchy that was recognized for centuries. Today, the Domesday Book is on display at the Public Record Office, in Chancery Lane, London.

B Exploring the Historical Period
ARISTOCRATIC TITLES

After the Norman Conquest, any noble person who held lands granted by the king was called a baron. This term could also refer to higher nobles, such as earls, and members of the royal family called dukes. The wife of any nobleman was referred to as a lady.

VIEWING THE ART

During the Middle Ages, battering rams were used to break down the walls and gates of castles if those within could not be forced to surrender by other means. During such attacks, those defending the castle rained missiles, hot oil, and other items down upon the attackers, who tried to protect themselves with huge wicker shields covered with wood or hide. Besiegers also used movable wooden towers to raise themselves to the same level as those atop the castle walls.

Activity. Ask students to identify the objects of war depicted in this image. [Among the items are battering rams, movable towers, wicker shields, and a catapult.]

William was an efficient and ruthless soldier, but he wanted to rule the Anglo-Saxons, not eliminate them. Today, as a result, rather than a Norman, French-speaking England (and United States), we find a culture and a language that combine Norman and Anglo-Saxon elements. To the Anglo-Saxons' more democratic and artistic tendencies, the Normans brought administrative ability, an emphasis on law and order, and cultural unity.

One of William's great administrative feats was an inventory of nearly every piece of property in England—land, cattle, buildings—in the Domesday Book. (The title suggests a comparison between William's judgment of his subjects' financial worth and God's final judgment of their moral worth.) For the first time in European history, taxes were based on what people owned.

The Normans Change England

Although the Normans did not erase Anglo-Saxon culture, they did bring significant changes to England. William and many of his successors remained dukes of Normandy as well as kings of England. The powerful Anglo-Norman entity they molded brought England into mainstream European civilization in a new way. For example, William divided the holdings of the fallen English landowners among his own followers. These men and their families brought to England not only a new language—French—but also a new social system—feudalism—which displaced the old Nordic social structure described in *Beowulf*.

Coin depicting William the Conqueror (11th century).
British Museum, London.
The Bridgeman Art Library.

An attack on a fortress, from a French manuscript (detail) (13th–14th century).
MS Fr. 1604, fol. 57v. © cliché Bibliothèque Nationale de France, Paris.

Scene from a French manuscript of *Romance of the Rose* (15th century).
By permission of the British Library, London.

Feudal Relationships

- **king:** all-powerful overlord and landowner.
- **vassal:** aristocratic dependent tenant who received land (a fief) from a lord in exchange for military service and other expressions of loyalty. Vassals could simultaneously serve higher lords and serve as lords themselves by distributing portions of the land they had been allotted.
- **lord:** noble who had the power to grant land to vassals. Lords could also be vassals to other lords.
- **knight:** armored warrior. Vassals had to provide their lords with military service—in the form of knights—for a certain period of time. The larger the fief, the more knights a vassal had to supply.
- **serfs:** peasants who worked on and were bound to vassals' lands. Serfs were not involved in the complicated oaths of loyalty between vassals and lords.

Feudalism: From the Top Down

More than simply a social system, **feudalism** was also a caste system, a property system, and a military system. Ultimately it was based on a religious concept of rank, with God as the supreme overlord. In this sense even a king held land as a **vassal**—a dependent tenant—by "divine right." A king as powerful as William the Conqueror could stand firmly at the top of the pyramid. He could appoint certain barons as his immediate vassals, allotting them portions of his land in return for their economic or military allegiance—or both. In turn, the barons could appoint vassals of their own. The system operated all the way down to the landless knights and to the **serfs,** who were not free to leave the land they tilled. The historian Morris Bishop describes the relationship between lord and vassal in this way:

DIRECT TEACHING

C Exploring the Historical Period
CENTRALIZED GOVERNMENT

By requiring that the nobles swear loyalty to him, William was establishing in England the principle of centralized government. Over time the power of the king in England would diminish as the role of Parliament grew, but the importance of a centralized government would endure.

VIEWING THE ART

The *Romance of the Rose* is one of the most important medieval **allegories** (stories in which the characters, settings, and events represent abstract or moral concepts). Written in France, it enjoyed enormous success both there and in England, where Geoffrey Chaucer translated part of it. In this dream poem, the poet goes to the Garden of Delight, where he meets Rose, his love. Allegorical characters include Idleness, Pleasure, Shame, and Evil Tongue.

Activity. Have students describe what they see in this exquisite garden scene. Then, ask them to look for these colors: green, which signifies new love, and blue, which symbolizes fidelity. The enclosed garden symbolizes virginity. Point out the fruit on the trees, symbolizing fertility.

Primary Source

Voices from Turbulent Times

One of the most interesting views of feudalism from the late Middle Ages is the correspondence of the three generations of Pastons, a wealthy family in Norfolk, England. The letters, which date from 1422 to 1509, chronicle the family's attempts to acquire and defend land and to increase their social and political prestige. Margaret Paston was one of the family's leading correspondents. Her letters describe ways in which others did not honor feudal obligations, attacks on her own manor, and uncertainty about her future and the safety of her lands and possessions. The Pastons' letters have been included in several collections of medieval historical and literary writings.

DIRECT TEACHING

A Reading Skills

? Analyzing symbolism. According to Bishop, a vassal taking the oath of fealty would place his clasped hands within the hands of his lord. What do you think that action represented for the vassal? for the lord? [Possible response: The clasped hands suggest prayer, perhaps meaning that the vassal held the lord in high regard and depended upon his help. The lord's placing his hands around those of his vassal may have represented his acceptance of the vassal's pledge and a promise to protect the vassal.]

A CLOSER LOOK

This feature describes changes in the manufacture and use of armor during the Middle Ages.

B Background
The Hauberk

The hauberk was originally made of small metal discs sewn on linen. Eventually it was replaced by chain mail, which was composed of interlocking iron rings.

C Reading Skills

? Making inferences. What physical qualities would a person who frequently wore full-scale armor need? Explain. [Possible response: The person would have to be strong enough to function despite the weight of the armor, flexible enough to overcome the armor's restrictions in battle, and generally healthy enough to endure the heat and lack of ventilation within the armor.]

Granting of land to two knights, from *Life of the Noble Princes of Hainaut* by Jacques de Guise (15th century).
© Giraudon/Art Resource, New York.

A " The bond between lord and vassal was affirmed or reaffirmed by the ceremony of homage. The vassal knelt, placed his clasped hands within those of his master, declared, 'Lord, I become your man,' and took an oath of fealty. The lord raised him to his feet and bestowed on him a ceremonial kiss. The vassal was thenceforth bound by his oath 'to love what his lord loved and loathe what he loathed, and never by word or deed do aught that should grieve him.' "

The feudal system did not always work. Secure in a well-fortified castle, a vassal might choose not to honor his obligations to a weak overlord. The ensuing battles between iron-clad knights around moated castles account for one of the enduring images of the Middle Ages.

The feudal system carried with it a sense of form and manners that influenced all aspects of the life, art, and literature of the Middle Ages. This sense of formalism came to life most fully in the

A CLOSER LOOK: SOCIAL INFLUENCES

"A Terrible Worm in an Iron Cocoon"

When we hear the term *medieval period*, we inevitably think of knights and their magnificent suits of armor. During the early Middle Ages, armor consisted of a **B** helmet, a shield, and a relatively flexible mail shirt, or *hauberk*, made of countless riveted or welded iron rings. With the crossbow, however, came the need for more protection, so the knight was forced to compromise flexibility and mobility for the sake of heavier armor.

A burden in battle. Held together by rivets, leather straps, hinges, turning pins, buckles, and pegs, a suit of armor replaced mail as the warrior's chief protection. Knights wore a heavily padded undergarment of leather and a mail shirt under the armor, in addition to plate arm, leg, and foot pieces. Mail covered the neck, elbows, and other joints, and gauntlets constructed of linked plates covered the hands. Some suits of armor weighed 120 pounds and contained 200 custom-fitted iron plates. The knight also carried a variety of weapons: lance, dagger, sword, battle-ax, and club-headed mace.

The threat of death in battle was bad enough, but the armor itself could also be fatal—causing death from suffocation, heart failure, even drowning. Battle during hot weather was particularly difficult. Since small slits in the helmet allowed only a limited line of vision and little ventilation, heatstroke—often deadly for the knight—was common. **C** One anonymous poem describes the armored knight as "a terrible worm in an iron cocoon."

Protection at a price. Only aristocratic knights could afford the huge cost of armor, a war horse, packhorses, a mount to ride when not in battle, and servants. The armor's weight and the complex fittings required to piece it together meant that a knight couldn't dress himself for battle. In fact,

---

SKILLS REVIEW

Evaluating an informative text. After students have read A Closer Look, ask them to evaluate it.

1. Ask students to identify the purpose of the essay. [to inform]
2. With students, brainstorm a list of criteria that might be used to evaluate the essay, such as accuracy, organization, clarity of ideas and language, thoroughness of coverage, readability, and use of visuals. You might suggest that the criteria be phrased as questions and that students be prepared to explain their answers when they meet in groups. (See item 3 below.)
3. Have students work in small groups to apply the criteria to the essay. Each group should provide a detailed analysis of the essay in relation to each criterion, as well as an overall judgment.

institution of knighthood and in the related practice, or code, of chivalry. **D**

Knights in Shining Armor

We cannot think of the medieval period without thinking of knights. Since the primary duty of males above the serf class was military service to their lords, boys were trained from an early age to become warriors. Often their training took place in houses other than their own, to be sure that the training was strict. When a boy's training was

A medieval knight in armor.
MS 42130, fol. 202v. By permission of the British Library, London.

INFORMATIONAL TEXT

battles were usually scheduled to allow the warring knights time to be dressed. Servants stood by during battle in case the knight was unhorsed. An armored knight on his back was like an upside-down turtle trying to get on its feet. In this position the knight was vulnerable to his adversary. If he fell into a body of water, he could drown.

From combatant to courtier.
During the fifteenth century the knight and his horse were considered invulnerable. This role changed dramatically when the longbow and, later, the musket ball came into warfare. When his armor could no longer protect him in battle, the knight in shining armor became more of a courtier than a combatant. In the last years of their existence, knights participated solely in exhibitions.

Arming a man for fighting on foot. Detail from a manuscript page from *Ordinances of Armory* (15th century). England.
M.775, F.122v. © The Pierpont Morgan Library, New York.

DIRECT TEACHING

D Exploring the Culture
CHIVALRY
The word *chivalry* is related to *cheval,* the French word for "horse." In French, *chevalier* refers to a knight who rides a horse. In England as well as France, riding was an important skill—but chivalry was about more than horseback riding, or even skill in battle. Chivalry was a code of conduct. The knight's first obligation was to defend his lord, the king, and the Christian faith; but the code also covered how to treat a lady, how to help others, and how to resist the urge to run away if captured.

E Exploring the Historical Period
FROM BOY TO KNIGHT
Although there was a great demand for knights, not every boy could become a knight. For one thing, his parents had to be rich enough to buy him a horse, armor, and weapons. Knights were often the sons of nobles. (Chaucer, though born into a middle-class family, was educated as a knight in a noble household.) A knight's education began at about the age of seven, with instruction in good manners and social skills, such as singing, dancing, and playing chess. Young boys also began to learn to use a sword and shield at this time. At about the age of fourteen, a boy became a squire, a kind of personal servant to a knight. In the Prologue to *The Canterbury Tales,* students will meet a knight who is traveling with his son, a squire.

CONTENT-AREA CONNECTIONS

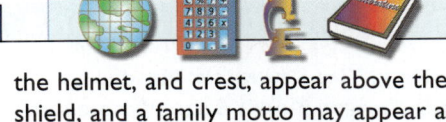

Humanities: Coats of Arms
The tradition of armorial bearings, or coats of arms, developed as a way of identifying knights wearing suits of armor. Originally a cloth tunic worn over the armor, the coat of arms is a highly stylized record of family descent, alliances, property, or profession. The escutcheon, or shield, is divided into nine points (sections) and split into a sinister (left) and dexter (right) side. In a heraldic emblem the helmet, and crest, appear above the shield, and a family motto may appear above the crest or below the shield. Colors used in heraldry are red, blue, black, green, purple, gold, and silver.

Paired activity. Have pairs of students make a poster showing a coat of arms, labeled with the specialized terms and the various colors. Help students prepare a display of the finished coats of arms.

DIRECT TEACHING

VIEWING THE ART

Pages 99–101 present examples of illustrated manuscript, one of the most important art forms of the Middle Ages. These four examples are typical of Gothic illustration, in which people and their surroundings usually take precedence over fantasy figures.

Activity. In the pieces of art on these pages, how do the roles of medieval women and men differ? [Possible response: The women are helping the men prepare for battle, going off to work, and watching a joust. The upper-class women stay out of the fray, but the peasant woman shares the center of the scene with her husband (who, it must be added, is doing the pushing while his wife sits and holds the wine).]

A Reading Skills

Interpreting. What was the role of a woman in medieval society, according to these lines? [Possible response: Women were to devote all their energies to serving men.] What is the speaker's attitude toward women's lot? Explain. [Possible response: The comment about a woman's life of "care and woe" suggests that the speaker finds this a cruel fate.]

B Exploring the Culture
WOMEN'S STATUS AND THE CHURCH

The Church also regarded women as inferior to men. Women had no authority in the Church and could not serve at the altar. During the Middle Ages, the Church took further steps to diminish women's status by reclaiming convents and monasteries that had been founded or supported by noblewomen.

> A woman is a worthy wight:
> She serveth a man both daye and nyght;
> Thereto she putteth all her might,
> And yet she hathe but care and woe.
> —Anonymous (fifteenth century)

completed, he was dubbed, or ceremonially tapped on his shoulder (originally a hard blow to test the boy's courage). Once knighted, the youth became a man with the title "Sir" and the full rights of the warrior caste.

Knighthood was grounded in the feudal ideal of loyalty, and it was based on a complex system of social codes. Breaking any one of those codes would undermine not only the knight's position but also the very institution of knighthood.

Women in Medieval Society: No Voice, No Choice

Since they were not soldiers, women had no political rights in a system that was primarily military. A woman was always subservient to a man, whether husband, father, or brother. Her husband's or father's social standing determined the degree of respect she commanded. For peasant women, life was a ceaseless round of childbearing, housework, and hard fieldwork. Women of higher stations were occupied with childbearing and household supervision. Such women might even manage entire estates while their men were away on business or at war, but the moment the men returned, the women had to give up their temporary powers.

Off for a day of haying, a peasant pushes his wife to work in a wheelbarrow.
MS Lat. 1173, fol. 4v. © cliché Bibliothèque Nationale de France, Paris.

Chivalry and Courtly Love: Ideal but Unreal

Chivalry was a system of ideals and social codes governing the behavior of knights and gentlewomen. The rules of chivalry included taking an oath of loyalty to the overlord and observing certain rules of warfare, such as never attacking an unarmed opponent. In addition, adoring a particular lady (not necessarily one's wife) was seen as a means of self-improvement.

The idea that adoring a lady would make a knight braver and nobler was central to one aspect of chivalry, courtly love. **Courtly love** was, in its ideal form, nonsexual. A knight might wear his lady's colors in battle, he might glorify her in words and be inspired by her, but the lady always remained pure and out of reach. She was set above her admirer, just as the feudal lord was set above his vassal. The fact that such a concept flew in the face of human nature provided a perfect dramatic vehicle for poets and storytellers, as the King Arthur sagas illustrate. When Sir Lancelot and Queen Guinevere, for example, cross the line between courtly

---

CONTENT-AREA CONNECTIONS

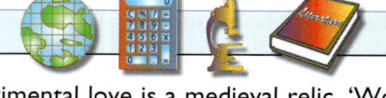

Psychology: The Chivalric Mind
In *The Middle Ages*, Morris Bishop (also quoted on p. 98) describes the way the system of chivalry continues to influence human attitudes and behavior: "In time the chivalric code was modified, but it has never died. It set a standard for upper-class behavior, especially in the Victorian era. Our esteem for sentimental love is a medieval relic. 'Women and children come first' is a chivalric motto. When the *Titanic* sank and the gentlemen bowed the ladies into the lifeboats, they were 'verray parfit gentil knights.'"

Whole-class activity. Have the class list other social customs that may have originated from the chivalric code.

and physical love, the whole social system represented by Arthur's Round Table collapses. Camelot crumbles because the sexual code was broken.

The Rise of the Romance

Chivalry brought about an idealized attitude toward women, but it did little to improve their actual position. A woman's perceived value remained tied to the value of the lands she brought to a marriage. Chivalry did give rise to a new form of literature, the **romance** (see page 193). The greatest English example of the romance is *Sir Gawain and the Green Knight*. The romance hero—who often has the help of magic—undertakes a quest to conquer an evil enemy. J. R. R. Tolkien's *The Lord of the Rings* trilogy shows that the romance is still alive and well today.

The New City Classes: Out from Under the Overlords

For the most part, medieval society centered on the feudal castle, but as the population grew, an increasing number of people lived in towns and cities. Eventually, those population centers would make the feudal system obsolete.

The development of the city classes—lower, middle, and upper middle—is evident in the works of Geoffrey Chaucer (see page 113). Many of his characters make their livings outside the feudal system. Their horizons are defined not by any lord's manor but by such cities as London and Canterbury.

More important, the emerging merchant class had its own tastes in the arts and the ability to pay for what it wanted. As a result, much medieval art is not aristocratic; it is middle class, even "people's art." The people of the cities were free, tied neither to the land nor to knighthood and chivalry. Their point of view was expressed in the **ballads** sung in alehouses and at firesides (see page 108), in the mystery and miracle plays performed outdoors by the new guilds, or craft unions, and even in the great cathedrals and municipal buildings that are synonymous with England to so many people today.

Noblewomen watching a tournament, from a German manuscript (c. 14th century).
Cod. Pal. Germ. 848, Codex Manesse, fol. 52v. Universitätsbibliothek, Heidelberg, Germany.

February: Man warming himself, from Ermangol de Beziers, *Breviaire d'amour* (13th century) France.
Provencal codex, fol. 58v. © Giraudon/Art Resource, New York.

The Middle Ages 101

DIRECT TEACHING

C Correcting Misconceptions

How romantic! When students hear the word *romance*, they may think of contemporary tales of romance. Emphasize that that is not the meaning of *romance* here: Although the medieval romance genre included stories of courtly love, that love was relatively distant and idealized.

D Content-Area Connections

Culture: City Life, Medieval Style What was life like in the growing medieval cities?

- Most shops opened at 6:00 A.M. and closed around 3:00 P.M. Merchants advertised by shouting out to—and sometimes grabbing—passersby.
- News came primarily from the town crier, who would ring a bell as he walked about, calling out timely information.
- Pigs owned by citizens roamed freely, adding to the filth from open drains that often ran down the middle of streets.

E Literary Connections

Medieval Drama
Not surprisingly, medieval drama originated in the Church: In an era when most of the population could not read, plays provided religious instruction. Typical medieval plays include the miracle plays, based on the legends of the saints; mystery plays, based on biblical history; and morality plays, dramatizations of allegorical stories.

CONTENT-AREA CONNECTIONS

Architecture: Urban Buildings
Individual activity. With the rise of cities came the rise of urban architecture. Have students report on Durham Cathedral, Winchester Cathedral, and the Tower of London, as well as the wooden buildings that housed most of the populace and were consumed in the Great Fire of London in 1666.

Social Studies: Social Pyramids
Small-group activity. Have students work in groups of three or four to create visual representations of society in the Middle Ages. Each group should create a social pyramid, with serfs at its base, other classes in its middle layers, and the king at the top. Ask students to create an image or icon for each layer of the pyramid.

SKILLS FOCUS, pp. 108–112

Grade-Level Skills
- Literary Skills

Analyze the characteristics of sub-genres of poetry, including ballads.

PRETEACHING

Summary ⇔ *at grade level*

Told in Scottish dialect, this ballad takes the form of a conversation between a mother and her son, Lord Randall, who has returned from hunting wanting nothing more than to lie down. The mother voices suspicions about where her son has been and what has happened to him. She learns that he has dined with his "true love" and that his hunting hounds are dead. In the final stanza, the mother finally admits her fear that he has been poisoned. The son replies that he has indeed been poisoned; he implies that his "true love" did the deed.

Skills Starter

Build review skills. As you introduce the ballad as a subgenre, relate the discussion to narrative songs with which students may be familiar from popular music, such as country, rock, blues, and reggae.

Before You Read

Ballads

Make the Connection

THREE DEAD SONS VISIT MOTHER FOR DINNER…SLIGHTED WOMAN SPURNS LOVER'S DEATHBED REQUEST…MAIDEN HEADED FOR GALLOWS; FAMILY REFUSES HELP.

These aren't the latest tabloid headlines or current soap-opera summaries; they're the plots of medieval ballads. In the Middle Ages, just as today, certain forms of popular entertainment tended toward the sensational.

Ballads were the poetry of the people, just as popular songs are today, and their subjects were predictably popular—domestic tragedy, false love, true love, the absurdity of husband-wife relationships, and the supernatural. Unlike today's music, ballads were not copyrighted by a composer but were passed down orally from singer to singer. Using a strong beat and repetition, ballads were a gift of story passed from performer to performer, from generation to generation.

Literary Focus
Ballad

Ballads are songs or songlike poems that tell stories in simple, rhythmic language. Virtually every ballad includes certain predictable features, or conventions, including sensational or tragic subject matter, omitted details, supernatural events, and a **refrain**—a repeated word, line, or group of lines. (For more on ballads, see pages 111–112.)

> A **ballad** is a song or songlike poem that tells a story in a regular pattern of rhythm and rhyme and uses simple, direct language.
>
> *For more on Ballads, see the Handbook of Literary and Historical Terms.*

Background

The word *ballad* is derived from an Old French word meaning "dancing song." Although the English ballads' connection with dance has been lost, it is clear from their meter and their structure that the original ballads were composed to be sung to music.

The ballads as we know them today probably took their form in the fifteenth century, but they were not printed until Sir Thomas Percy published a number of them in 1765. Inspired by Percy, Sir Walter Scott and others traveled around the British Isles and collected the songs from the people who still sang them.

Young musician, from *De Musica* (On Music) (14th century) by Anicius Boetius (c. 450–524).
Folio 47R. Biblioteca Nazionale, Naples. The Art Archive/Dagli Orti.

SKILLS FOCUS

Literary Skills Understand the characteristics of ballads.

RESOURCES: READING

Planning
- One-Stop Planner CD-ROM with ExamView Test Generator

Differentiating Instruction
- Supporting Instruction in Spanish
- Audio CD Library, Selections and Summaries in Spanish

Grammar and Language
- Daily Language Activities

Assessment
- Holt Assessment: Literature, Reading, and Vocabulary
- One-Stop Planner CD-ROM with ExamView Test Generator
- Holt Online Assessment

Internet
- go.hrw.com (Keyword: LE5 12-2)
- Elements of Literature Online

Media
- Audio CD Library
- Audio CD Library, Selections and Summaries in Spanish

108 Collection 2 The Middle Ages

This ballad is sung in different versions in several countries. The basic story of the song varies little, but Randall is variously known as Donald, Randolph, Ramsay, Ransome, and Durango. Sometimes his last meal consists of fish, sometimes snakes. The dialect of this version is Scottish. This ballad, like many others, is sung entirely as a conversation in a question-and-answer format that builds suspense.

Lord Randall

"O where hae ye been, Lord Randall, my son?
O where hae ye been, my handsome young man?"
"I hae been to the wild wood; mother, make my bed soon,
For I'm weary wi' hunting, and fain° wald lie down."

5 "Where gat ye your dinner, Lord Randall, my son?
Where gat ye your dinner, my handsome young man?"
"I din'd wi' my true-love; mother, make my bed soon,
For I'm weary wi' hunting, and fain wald lie down."

"What gat ye to your dinner, Lord Randall, my son?
10 What gat ye to your dinner, my handsome young man?"
"I gat eels boil'd in broo;° mother, make my bed soon,
For I'm weary wi' hunting, and fain wald lie down."

"What became of your bloodhounds, Lord Randall, my son?
What became of your bloodhounds, my handsome young man?"
15 "O they swell'd and they died; mother, make my bed soon,
For I'm weary wi' hunting, and fain wald lie down."

"O I fear ye are poison'd, Lord Randall, my son!
O I fear ye are poison'd, my handsome young man!"
"O yes! I am poison'd; mother, make my bed soon,
20 For I'm sick at the heart, and I fain wald lie down."

---

4. **fain** *adv.*: gladly.
11. **broo** *n.*: archaic form of "broth."

A knight and his lady feeding a falcon, detail from a German manuscript (c. 14th century).
Cod. Pal. Germ. 848, Codex Manesse, fol. 249v.
Universitätsbibliothek, Heidelberg, Germany.

Ballads 109

PRETEACHING

Summary ⇔ at grade level

In a humorous twist on the age-old theme of the battle of the sexes, a husband and wife bicker over who will get up and bar (lock) the door. They finally agree that the next one to speak will have to bar the door. Later two intruders arrive. They eat the food prepared by the wife; then they discuss shaving off the man's beard and kissing the woman. The man leaps up, protesting, and his wife jumps for joy: Since her husband has spoken first, he will have to get up and bar the door.

DIRECT TEACHING

A Literary Focus

? The ballad. What story elements are introduced in these first three stanzas? [Possible response: the main characters—a husband and wife; the setting—at home, before a holiday, when there is plenty to do; the situation—the door needs to be barred (locked); the conflict—husband versus wife, over who will bar the door.]

B Reading Skills

? Drawing conclusions. What does this pact reveal about the man and woman? [Possible response: Both of them are very stubborn.]

C Content-Area Connections

History: Gentlemanly Prerogatives
The behavior of the "gentlemen" reveals two facts of life about the Middle Ages: (1) The times were often lawless, and citizens were at the mercy of bandits and thieves; and (2) members of the upper classes could mistreat members of the lower classes with little fear of punishment.

The story in this ballad exists in many versions in Europe, Asia, and the Middle East—perhaps illustrating the universal theme called the battle of the sexes. Goodman and goodwife are terms once applied to married men and women, something like Mr. and Mrs. today.

The story takes place around November 11—Martinmas, or the feast of Saint Martin of Tours, which was usually celebrated with a big meal.

Get Up and Bar the Door

The Chef (15th century). Woodcut.

A
It fell about the Martinmas time,
    And a gay time it was then,
When our goodwife got puddings° to make,
    And she's boild them in the pan.

5 The wind sae cauld blew south and north,
    And blew into the floor;
Quoth our goodman to our goodwife,
    "Gae out and bar the door."

"My hand is in my hussyfskap,°
10   Goodman, as ye may see;
An° it should nae be barrd this hundred year,
    It's no be barrd for me."

B
They made a paction tween them twa,
    They made it firm and sure,
15 That the first word whaeer should speak,
    Should rise and bar the door.

Then by there came two gentlemen,
    At twelve o clock at night,
And they could neither see house nor hall,
20   Nor coal nor candle-light.

"Now whether is this a rich man's house,
    Or whether it is a poor?"
But neer a word ane° o them speak,
    For barring of the door.

---
3. **puddings** *n. pl.*: sausages made with blood.
9. **hussyfskap** (hu′zif·skəp) *n.*: archaic word meaning "household chores."
11. **an** *conj.*: archaic word for "if."
23. **ane** *adj.*: archaic word for "one."

C
25 And first they ate the white puddings,
    And then they ate the black;
Tho muckle° thought the goodwife to hersel,
    Yet neer a word she spake.

Then said the one unto the other,
30   "Here, man, tak ye my knife;
Do ye tak aff the auld man's beard,
    And I'll kiss the goodwife."

"But there's nae water in the house,°
    And what shall we do than?"
35 "What ails ye at the pudding-broo,°
    That boils into the pan?"

O up then started our goodman,
    An angry man was he:
"Will ye kiss my wife before my een,
40   And scad° me wi pudding-bree?"°

Then up and started our goodwife,
    Gied three skips on the floor:
"Goodman, you've spoken the foremost word,
    Get up and bar the door."

---
27. **muckle** *adj.*: archaic word meaning "much."
33. **but . . . house:** He probably wants water to soften the husband's beard.
35. **what . . . pudding-broo:** What's wrong with using the pudding broth?
40. **scad** *v.*: archaic word meaning "scald." **bree** *n.*: archaic word meaning "broth."

GUIDED PRACTICE

Monitoring students' progress. Guide the class in answering these questions.

Short Answer

1. What does Lord Randall keep telling his mother that he wants to do, and why? [He says that he wants to lie down because he is tired from hunting.]
2. To what two places has he gone? [to the woods and to his true love's house]
3. In "Get Up and Bar the Door," what excuse does the wife give for not barring the door? [She says she is too busy.]

Response and Analysis

Reading Check
1. What has happened to Lord Randall?
2. In "Get Up and Bar the Door," what do the husband and wife argue about? What pact do they make?

Thinking Critically
3. What is the emotional effect of the **refrain's** variation in the fifth stanza of "Lord Randall"?
4. "Lord Randall" provides a good example of **incremental repetition**—the repetition of lines with a new element introduced each time to advance the story until the climax is reached. At what point in this ballad did you discover what is wrong with Lord Randall? How does the incremental repetition increase your suspense?
5. Typical of ballads, "Lord Randall" omits details and ends with only half the story told. Do you think the young man's lover has poisoned him? Explain why or why not. What other questions regarding the **plot** are left unanswered?
6. What prominent parts do puddings or sausages play in the **plot** of "Get Up and Bar the Door"?
7. How is the possibility of violence combined with **ironic** humor in "Get Up and Bar the Door"?
8. As you read "Get Up and Bar the Door," did you find yourself siding with the husband, the wife, or neither? Explain your views.

Extending and Evaluating
9. People often criticize today's media for glorifying violence. Do you think these ballads also glorify violence? Is the issue the same? Explain your responses.

WRITING
Late-Breaking News!
Take one of the basic situations in these ballads, and retell it as a contemporary **news story.** Like a reporter, be sure to tell *what* happened, *where* and *when* it happened, to *whom* it happened, *why* it happened, and *how* it happened. Present your news story in print form, complete with headlines.

LISTENING AND SPEAKING
Bring a Ballad to Life
With a small group, select a traditional or contemporary ballad (or write your own), and prepare to perform it. Have an audience evaluate your first performance according to criteria you all agree on (such as clarity of story, use of ballad conventions, aesthetic effect, and so on). Make sure your performance demonstrates an understanding of the meaning of the ballad you choose. Use your audience's evaluations to perfect your final performance.

INTERNET
Projects and Activities
Keyword: LE5 12-2

Literary Focus

Ballads: Popular Poetry
Ballads come from an oral tradition, so there are no strict rules dictating their form. However, a number of characteristics have come to be associated with ballads, and every ballad reflects at least some of them: **supernatural events; sensational, sordid, or tragic subject matter;** a **refrain;** and the **omission of details.** The ballad singers also used some of the following conventions:

- **incremental repetition** to build up suspense. A phrase or sentence is repeated with a new element added each time until the climax is reached.
- **a question-and-answer format** in which the facts of a story are gleaned little

Pages 111–112 cover
Literary Skills
Analyze the characteristics of ballads.

Writing Skills
Retell a ballad as a news story.

Listening and Speaking Skills
Give an oral performance of a ballad.

Ballads 111

INDEPENDENT PRACTICE

Response and Analysis

5. Most students will suspect Lord Randall's lover, since he is feeling sick after having just eaten with her. Students may speculate that someone else poisoned him at that meal (perhaps a man who wanted the woman for himself). Students may want to know more about the circumstances under which the dogs died; they will probably want to know if Lord Randall actually dies and if the person who poisoned him is ever identified and punished.
6. Possible answer: The fact that the sausages have been cooking shows that the woman is busy. When the intruders eat the sausages, the woman is bothered, but she keeps silent—a sign of her determination not to lose in the pact. When the intruders talk about scalding the husband with the water in which the sausages have been cooking, the man protests—bringing the story to its climax and making his wife the winner.
7. Possible answer: The gentlemen's threats to kiss the wife and humiliate the husband are menacing. Ironically, the wife is concerned more about the pact of silence than about the danger.
8. Answers will vary and may be split along gender lines. Some students may side with neither, pointing out that although the wife wins, both she and her husband have been robbed and humiliated by the intruders.

Extending and Evaluating
9. Answers will vary. Discuss whether honestly depicting violence is different from glorifying it.

Reading Check
1. His dogs have died, and he has been poisoned, presumably by the woman he loved.
2. They argue about who should get up and bar the door. They agree that whoever speaks first will have to do it.

Thinking Critically
3. Possible answer: The variation expresses tragic sadness: Lord Randall is dying, heartbroken at the treachery of his lover.
4. Possible answer: In l. 17, Lord Randall's mother expresses fear that he has been poisoned. The insistence implied by the refrain that ends each stanza signals that something is wrong; the hints dropped along the way—the fact that Lord Randall dined with his true love, the death of his hounds—help build both suspense and suspicion in the reader's mind.

Ballads 111

Literary Focus

Ballads

If you referred to more recent narrative songs while discussing "Lord Randall" and "Get Up and Bar the Door," invite students to discuss differences in style or in structure between the songs of the different periods. Then, as you work your way through this page and the next, have students decide which ballad in the text best exemplifies each convention. (Students will probably choose "Lord Randall" for the first two conventions but may cite examples from either ballad for the third and fourth.)

A Book of Ballads

You may wish to reserve some relevant books or recordings in the school library before making this assignment; also, encourage students (working either individually or collaboratively) to explore resources at the public library or on the Internet.

VIEWING THE ART

Martin Le Franc's *The Nine Muses* depicts the sisters Calliope (muse of epic poetry), Clio (muse of history), Erato (muse of love poetry), Euterpe (muse of music), Melpomene (muse of tragedy), Polyhymnia (muse of sacred poetry), Terpsichore (muse of dance), Thalia (muse of comedy), and Urania (muse of astronomy).

Activity. Point out that all the muses except one are playing musical instruments. Ask students to identify the instruments. [Possible responses: dulcimers, recorder, lute, oboe, horn, drum, flute, organ.] If possible, show illustrations of muses in ancient Greek art, and have students make comparisons between the Greek images and those of the Middle Ages.

---

by little from the answers. Again, this device builds suspense.

- **conventional phrases** understood by listeners to have meaning beyond their literal ones. "Make my bed soon" in "Lord Randall" is an example. Whenever a character in a ballad asks someone to make his bed or to make her bed narrow, it means that the speaker is preparing for death.

- **a strong, simple beat** with verse forms that are relatively uncomplicated. Ballads were sung for a general audience, not an elitist one. Only later, in the era of so-called literary ballads (more sophisticated poems that artfully evoked the atmosphere of the originals), did the rhyme scheme (*abcb*) and meter (a quatrain in which lines of four stresses alternate with lines of three stresses) of the ballad stanza become standard.

Collect a book of ballads. Collect at least three traditional ballads from any culture (including American), or find three variations of the same ballad ("Lord Randall" is supposed to have 103 known variations), and present them in a printed form that can be kept in the classroom for future reference. Write a brief introduction to each ballad, telling what you have learned about its origins and pointing out the conventions it shares with other ballads. If your ballads are not from the English tradition, explain how they are like and unlike traditional British ballads.

The Nine Muses (15th century) by Martin Le Franc.
Bibliothèque de Grenoble, France. The Bridgeman Art Library.

112 Collection 2   The Middle Ages

Geoffrey Chaucer
(c. 1343–1400)

Geoffrey Chaucer (1400).

Geoffrey Chaucer, often called the father of English poetry, made the English language respectable.

Ordinary people in Chaucer's England spoke the Anglo-Norman composite now called Middle English, a language that became the ancestor of Modern English. But in Chaucer's time the languages of literature, science, diplomacy, and religion were still Latin and French. Before Chaucer it was not fashionable for serious poets to write in English. People felt that English couldn't possibly convey all the nuances and complexities of serious literature.

By composing in the **vernacular**—the everyday language spoken in London and the East Midlands—Chaucer lent respectability to a language that would develop into the medium for one of the world's greatest bodies of literature. In this sense he is indeed the father of English poetry.

Friends in High Places

Not a great deal is known of Chaucer's life. He was born into a middle-class family in London in the early 1340s, not long after the beginning of the Hundred Years' War. We are told that his father was a wine merchant who had enough money to provide his son with some education. The young Chaucer read a great deal and had some legal training. He became a page to an eminent family from whom he received the finest training in good manners. As he advanced in his government career, he became attached to several noble patrons.

We know, too, that Chaucer was captured in France while serving as a soldier during the Hundred Years' War and that he was important enough to have the king contribute to his ransom. We also know that he married Philippa and had at least two children and that he was on several occasions sent to Europe as the king's ambassador. In 1367, he was awarded the first of several pensions for his services to the Crown. (On April 23, 1374, he was granted the promise of a daily pitcher of wine.) In 1385, he was appointed justice of the peace in the county of Kent, later becoming a member of Parliament. He continued to serve and to enjoy the king's protection.

Writing and Holding a Job

It seems clear that Chaucer was a relatively important government servant and that his work took precedence over his writing. (It would be as if a prominent adviser to the U.S. president were also a highly acclaimed poet.) Yet Chaucer wrote a great deal and sometimes for personal advancement. In about 1369, for example, he composed his first important poem, *The Book of the Duchess,* in memory of his patron's wife, who had just died of the plague.

Despite his government responsibilities, between 1374 and 1386, Chaucer managed to create several great allegorical poems, including *House of Fame* and *Parliament of Fowls,* and his love story *Troilus and Criseyde.*

More About the Writer

Background. As students read *The Canterbury Tales,* they may question whether Chaucer was, as John Gardner asserts in his quotation, "full of faith." According to Gardner, Chaucer "was religious . . . all his life: from his first long poem on, he shows his deep and comfortable Christianity, his firm belief in God's love and mercy, and his doubt that acquisitive real-life friars and Popes have much to do with a sinner's reaching heaven. From the beginning to the end of his poetic career, Chaucer's position is clear and unvarying. He defends one virtue, *charity:* the good man's willingness to give the benefit of the doubt, to find some nobility in even the most wretched and deplorable of men. . . . Chaucer's specific interests change but the theme never changes: God is love, and so is man at his best."

The Italian Connection

In 1372 and 1378, Chaucer traveled in Italy, where he was very likely influenced by the poems of Dante and Petrarch and by the stories of Giovanni Boccaccio (see page 185). The connection between Boccaccio's collection of tales called the *Decameron* (c. 1348–1353) and Chaucer's *The Canterbury Tales* (c. 1387–1400) is evident. Both use a framing device within which the characters tell their tales, and both include tales based on similar old plots.

Chaucer began writing *The Canterbury Tales* in 1387, during a few years of unemployment when his patron was out of the country. Perhaps because he felt that he had lost his ability to find rhymes, he never completed all the stories. In spite of this, the collection must be considered one of the greatest works in the English language. *The Canterbury Tales* alone—even the Prologue alone, in which each traveler is described—would have been sufficient to place Chaucer in the company of Shakespeare and Milton.

The Force of Personality

What is so great about *The Canterbury Tales?* In part, its greatness lies in Chaucer's language. It also comes from the sheer strength of Chaucer's spirit and personality. John Gardner, one of Chaucer's many biographers, offers a tribute to Chaucer's lasting power:

> In a dark, troubled age, as it seems to us, he was a comfortable optimist, serene, full of faith. For all his delight in irony—and all his poetry has a touch of that—he affirmed this life, to say nothing of the next, from the bottom of his capacious heart. Joy—satisfaction without a trace of sentimental simple-mindedness—is still the effect of Chaucer's poetry and of Chaucer's personality as it emerges from the poems. It is not the simple faith of a credulous man in a credulous age: No poet has ever written better on the baffling complexity of things. But for all the foggy shiftings of the heart and mind, for all the obscurity of God's huge plan, to Chaucer life was a magnificent affair, though sadly transient; and when we read him now, six centuries later, we are instantly persuaded.

The End of the Old Alliterative Anglo-Saxon World

Chaucer used several metrical forms and some prose in *The Canterbury Tales,* but the dominant meter is based on ten syllables, with an unstressed syllable followed by a stressed syllable. We call this meter **iambic pentameter.** It is a rhythm that most closely matches the way English is spoken. You might hear this rhythm if you read aloud this line in Middle English. (*Bathed* is pronounced with two syllables, bäth′ed; *swich* means "sweet"):

And bathed every veyne in swich licour

When we read a line such as this, we experience a version of the meter that was to become the most popular metrical line in English. At a stroke we have abandoned the old, alliterative world of the Anglo-Saxons and entered the modern world of Shakespeare, Wordsworth, and even Robert Frost.

The Father in the Family Vault

Chaucer died on October 25, 1400, if we are to believe the date on his tombstone (which an admirer erected in Westminster Abbey in 1556). Chaucer was the very first of those many famous English writers who would be gathered into what we know as the Poets' Corner in Westminster Abbey—one of the great tourist sights in London today. "The Father of English poetry," notes Nevill Coghill, "lies in his family vault."

THE CANTERBURY TALES:
SNAPSHOT OF AN AGE

The Canterbury Tales gives us a collection of good stories and a snapshot, a picture of life in the Middle Ages frozen in time. To include the complete range of medieval society in the same picture, Chaucer places his characters on a pilgrimage, a religious journey made to a shrine or holy place. These pilgrims, like a group of people on tour today, are from many stations and stages of life. Together they travel on horseback from London to the shrine of the martyr Saint Thomas à Becket at Canterbury Cathedral, about fifty-five miles to the southeast.

Setting up the frame. The *Tales* begin with a general Prologue, the first lines of which establish that this pilgrimage takes place in the spring, the time of new life and awakening. Fifty-five miles is a long journey by horseback, especially along muddy tracks that would hardly pass as roads today. An inn was always a welcome oasis, even if it provided few luxuries. The poet-pilgrim narrator, whom many consider to be Chaucer himself, starts out at the Tabard Inn in Southwark, a borough in the south of London. There he meets twenty-nine other pilgrims also bound for Canterbury. It is the host of the Tabard who suggests to the pilgrims, as they sit around the fire after dinner, that they exchange tales to pass the time along the way to Canterbury and back to London. The host's suggestion sets up Chaucer's **frame story**—the main story of the pilgrimage that includes each pilgrim's story.

Page from *The Canterbury Tales*, from the Ellesmere manuscript (15th century). The man on the horse is thought to be Chaucer.

DIRECT TEACHING

A **Exploring the Historical Period**
PILGRIMAGES
In Chaucer's day, almost everyone from every social class made at least one pilgrimage. In a single year in the early fifteenth century, one hundred thousand people from throughout Europe are believed to have made a pilgrimage to Canterbury.

B **Exploring the Historical Period**
THOMAS À BECKET
Canterbury Cathedral was the most sacred pilgrimage destination in England because it housed the shrine of Thomas à Becket, who was killed defending the rights of the English Church against King Henry II (see p. 103).

C **Exploring the Historical Period**
THE ROUTE TO CANTERBURY
The pilgrims' route from London to Canterbury was originally a Roman road. You can still travel on this road south from Southwark to Dover, but it bears little resemblance to the road that passed through hayfields and forests in Chaucer's day.

D **Literary Connections**
Chaucer's Original Plan
According to the Host's plan, each pilgrim is to tell two tales on the way to Canterbury and two on the way back—for a total of a hundred and twenty tales. In fact, Chaucer wrote only twenty-four of the tales (two of which are unfinished) and the Prologue before he died. Donald R. Howard argues that we can't assume that Chaucer intended to write all these tales.

Secondary Source

Murder in the Cathedral
In *Medieval Europe,* the historian C. Warren Hollister explains what happened after Becket's murder: "This dramatic crime made a deep impact on the age. Becket was regarded as a martyr; miracles were alleged to have occurred at his tomb, and he was quickly canonized. For the remainder of the Middle Ages, Canterbury was a major pilgrimage center and the cult of St. Thomas enjoyed immense popularity. Henry, who had not ordered the killing but whose anger had prompted it, suffered acute embarrassment. He was obliged to do penance by walking barefoot through the streets of Canterbury and submitting to a flogging by the Canterbury monks." Nevertheless, Henry ultimately managed to achieve his goal and "succeeded in bringing the English Church under tight rein."

DIRECT TEACHING

VIEWING THE ART

This engraving is based on Blake's painting of Chaucer's pilgrims, which was exhibited in 1809. The style of the engraving is old-fashioned, but Blake's intent was not to create a historical piece. Blake thought that Chaucer's characters were universal types, not individuals, and his engraving is meant to suggest their universality.

Activity. As students read the selections from *The Canterbury Tales,* have them look at this illustration and try to identify the Pardoner and the Wife of Bath and the characteristics of each that Blake captured in his illustration.

Ⓐ Exploring the Historical Period
THE ELLESMERE MANUSCRIPT

About ninety manuscripts of *The Canterbury Tales* exist, but some are incomplete. The Ellesmere manuscript, now at the Huntington Library in San Marino, California, is considered the best. Because it was unusual for a secular manuscript to be so elaborately illustrated (see p. 115 and the illustrations of the pilgrims throughout the Prologue), scholars assume that an aristocrat commissioned this work.

Ⓑ Exploring the Historical Period
PILGRIMAGES AND SHRINES

The Church believed that Becket's body and blood had the power to cure. Thus, many pilgrims went to his shrine to be healed, but some went for other reasons. For example, Chaucer's Knight is on a pilgrimage to give thanks for his successful military campaigns (see p. 122, ll. 79–80).

Ⓐ Figure thought to be Chaucer, from the Ellesmere manuscript.

Fol. 153v. By permission of The Huntington Library, San Marino, California.

A pageant of medieval life. As the Prologue progresses and we are introduced to the pilgrims, Chaucer's brilliant picture of life in late medieval England comes into focus. Here is what Nevill Coghill, one of Chaucer's translators, says about the Prologue:

> In all literature there is nothing that touches or resembles the *Prologue*. It is the concise portrait of an entire nation, high and low, old and young, male and female, lay and clerical, learned and ignorant, rogue and righteous, land and sea, town and country, but without extremes. Apart from the stunning clarity, touched with nuance, of the characters presented, the most noticeable thing about them is their normality. They are the perennial progeny of men and women. Sharply individual, together they make a party.

Ⓑ At its most basic level, Chaucer's great work operates on several levels. As a pilgrimage story, it is one of the world's many quest narratives, and it moves from images of spring and awakening at the beginning of the Prologue to images of penance, death, and eternal life in the Parson's tale at the end of the work. The storytellers themselves are pilgrims in search of renewal at the shrine of Thomas à Becket. Coming as they do from all walks of life and all social classes, they cannot help but represent "everyman," or all of us, on our universal pilgrimage through life.

Chaucer's Middle English is here translated into Modern English by Nevill Coghill. While Coghill's version is true to the spirit of Chaucer's original poem, you might attempt to read at least bits of the *Tales* in the wonderfully musical original. (See the beginning of the Prologue in its original Middle English on page 119.)

Literary Criticism

Critic's Commentary: Chaucer's Fiction

It is true that *The Canterbury Tales* forms a remarkable snapshot of an age, but the Chaucer scholar E. T. Donaldson reminds the reader that it is a work of fiction: "Too many readers, too much influenced by Chaucer's brilliant verisimilitude, tend to regard his famous pilgrimage to Canterbury as significant not because it is great fiction, but because it seems to be a remarkable record of a fourteenth-century pilgrimage. A remarkable record it may be, but if we treat it too narrowly as such there are going to be certain casualties among the elements that make up the fiction. Perhaps first among these elements is the fictional reporter, Chaucer the pilgrim, and the role he plays." Donaldson goes on to say that Chaucer plays different roles in telling his story: He is at times Chaucer the man, Chaucer the pilgrim, and Chaucer the poet.

Chaucer's Canterbury Pilgrims (1810) by William Blake. Engraving.
Private Collection/The Bridgeman Art Library.

Brief Pronunciation Guide to Middle English

Vowels
a: *ah,* as in *father.*
ai, ay, ei, ey: a long *a,* as in *pay.*
au, aw: *ow,* as in *house.*
oo: *oh,* as in *oat.*
e: at times, like a long *a,* as in *mate.* When a double *e* is used, it is always long. *Eek* is pronounced āk.
e: at times, like a short *e,* as in *men.*
The final *e* in Middle English is a separate syllable sounded like a final *ah: soote* rhymes with *soda.* But when the final *e* precedes a word that starts with a vowel or an *h,* it is not sounded. In "droghte of March," the final *e* in *droghte* is silent.

Consonants
g: hard *g,* as in *go,* except before *e* or *i* (in words borrowed from French) where it is sounded like *zh,* as in *garage. Pilgrimage* rhymes with *garage.*
gh, ch: like the German *ch,* as in *nicht.* (These sounds are usually silent in Modern English.) *Knight* is pronounced k•nicht'.
–tion, –cial: The *t* and *c* in such words are not blended with the *i* as they are in Modern English (as in the words *condition* and *special*). The *i* is sounded as a separate syllable. *Special* would have three syllables and *condition* four: kon•di•sē•ôn'. (*C* has the sound of *s* when it comes before *i.*)

DIRECT TEACHING

C Literary Connections
Rhymes and Pronunciation
Rhymes help historians learn how English once sounded. Scholars of Middle English believe that Chaucer was thought to have been meticulous about his rhymes. Linguists have used them to determine which sound distinctions existed in Chaucer's day and which have emerged or disappeared since then.

CONTENT-AREA CONNECTIONS

Language: Middle English
The Norman Conquest of 1066 altered the English language forever. Over the generations, English lost most inflectional endings and much of its Germanic flavor. Although many Old English (Anglo-Saxon) words, such as *cwene* (queen), *tempel* (temple), and *lytel* (little) survived the transition into Middle English, many Latin and French words were added to the vocabulary. Chaucer's East Midland dialect of Middle English was the dialect spoken in London, which eventually evolved into Modern English. Thus, students reading *The Canterbury Tales* in the original will be able to recognize many of Chaucer's words, though they might be at a loss as to how to pronounce them.

PRETEACHING

Summary at grade level

The Prologue introduces the twenty-nine pilgrims who, along with the narrator, are on their way to the shrine of Saint Thomas à Becket in Canterbury. The time is April, and the place is the Tabard Inn in Southwark, just outside London, where the pilgrims are staying overnight. The narrator describes the pilgrims, revealing their personalities through direct and indirect characterization, sharp images, and figurative comparisons. (Chaucer's descriptions of dress and appearance are particularly revealing of psychological traits.) The pilgrims generally fall into the three major divisions of medieval society: the feudal order (the Knight and his Squire), the church (the Monk and the Prioress), and the merchant or professional class (the Miller and the Doctor). The narrator then says that he will repeat what he has seen and heard, no matter how offensive. Finally he describes the Host's proposal that each pilgrim tell two tales on the way to Canterbury and two on the return trip. Whoever tells the best story will be treated to a meal at the inn, but anyone who backs out of the plan will have to pay the entire cost of the journey. The pilgrims agree to the Host's proposal, and he says he will join the pilgrimage and serve as a guide and judge of the tales.

Skills Starter

Motivate. Ask students to think of a modern book or movie that uses the device of a frame story—an introductory outer story that sets the stage for one or more inner stories. For example, Amy Tan's novel *The Joy Luck Club* has a frame story that links multiple tales. The movie *Titanic* has a frame story with a single inner story.

Before You Read

The Prologue to *The Canterbury Tales*

Make the Connection

If you went on a tour today, what types of people would you expect to meet? Most of Chaucer's pilgrims are the kinds of people he would have known and perhaps even observed many times riding toward Canterbury on the old pilgrimage road.

Literary Focus

Characterization

To create the portraits of his pilgrims, Chaucer uses the same methods of **characterization** that writers still use today. He reveals his characters by telling us
- how the character looks and dresses
- how the character speaks and acts
- what the character thinks and feels
- how others respond to the character

He also may tell us directly what the character's nature is—virtuous, vain, clever, and so on.

Frame Story

When Chaucer chooses to have each of his pilgrims tell a story on the way to Canterbury, he is using a popular literary device called the frame story. A **frame story** is a story within a story. Chaucer uses the outer story of the pilgrimage to unite his travelers' individual tales, but the tales themselves also have thematic unity.

INTERNET
Vocabulary Practice
•
More About Geoffrey Chaucer
•
Keyword: LE5 12-2

SKILLS FOCUS

Literary Skills Understand characterization. Understand the characteristics of a frame story.

Reading Skills Analyze style using key details.

> **Characterization** is the process by which the writer reveals the personality of a character. A **frame story** is a story that serves to bind together several different narratives.
>
> For more on Character and the Frame Story, see the Handbook of Literary and Historical Terms.

Reading Skills

Analyzing Style: Key Details

With twenty-nine pilgrims to introduce in the Prologue, Chaucer could not develop any one character at great length. Instead, he had to provide a few well-chosen details that would make each character stand out vividly.

As you read the descriptions of each pilgrim in the Prologue, jot down striking details of dress, appearance, and behavior that give you an immediate impression of what the character is really like. Note that these telling details often undermine what the characters think of themselves or would like others to think about them.

Vocabulary Development

agility (ə·jil′ə·tē) *n.*: ability to move quickly and easily.

eminent (em′ə·nənt) *adj.*: high-standing; great.

accrue (ə·krōō′) *v.*: increase over time.

arbitrate (är′bə·trāt′) *v.*: settle or decide by listening to both sides of an argument.

benign (bi·nīn′) *adj.*: kind; gracious.

guile (gīl) *n.*: sly dealings; skill in deceiving.

obstinate (äb′stə·nət) *adj.*: unreasonably stubborn.

frugal (frōō′gəl) *adj.*: thrifty; careful with money.

duress (dŏŏ·res′) *n.*: pressure.

(Opposite) The opening lines of the Prologue to *The Canterbury Tales*, in the original Middle English.

118   Collection 2   The Middle Ages

Previewing Vocabulary

To reinforce understanding of the Vocabulary words, have students complete the following sentences with the correct word or words.

1. It was difficult to _____ the disagreement because Anna and Joe were both so _____. [arbitrate; obstinate]

2. Lily's grandmother is an _____ judge on the Supreme Court. [eminent]

3. A good basketball player must possess speed, endurance, and _____. [agility]

4. Because Pat is _____, she has been able to _____ savings over time. [frugal; accrue]

5. Under _____ the executives admitted that they had made their profits through _____ and deception. [duress; guile]

6. The king was a fair and _____ ruler. [benign]

118   Collection 2   The Middle Ages

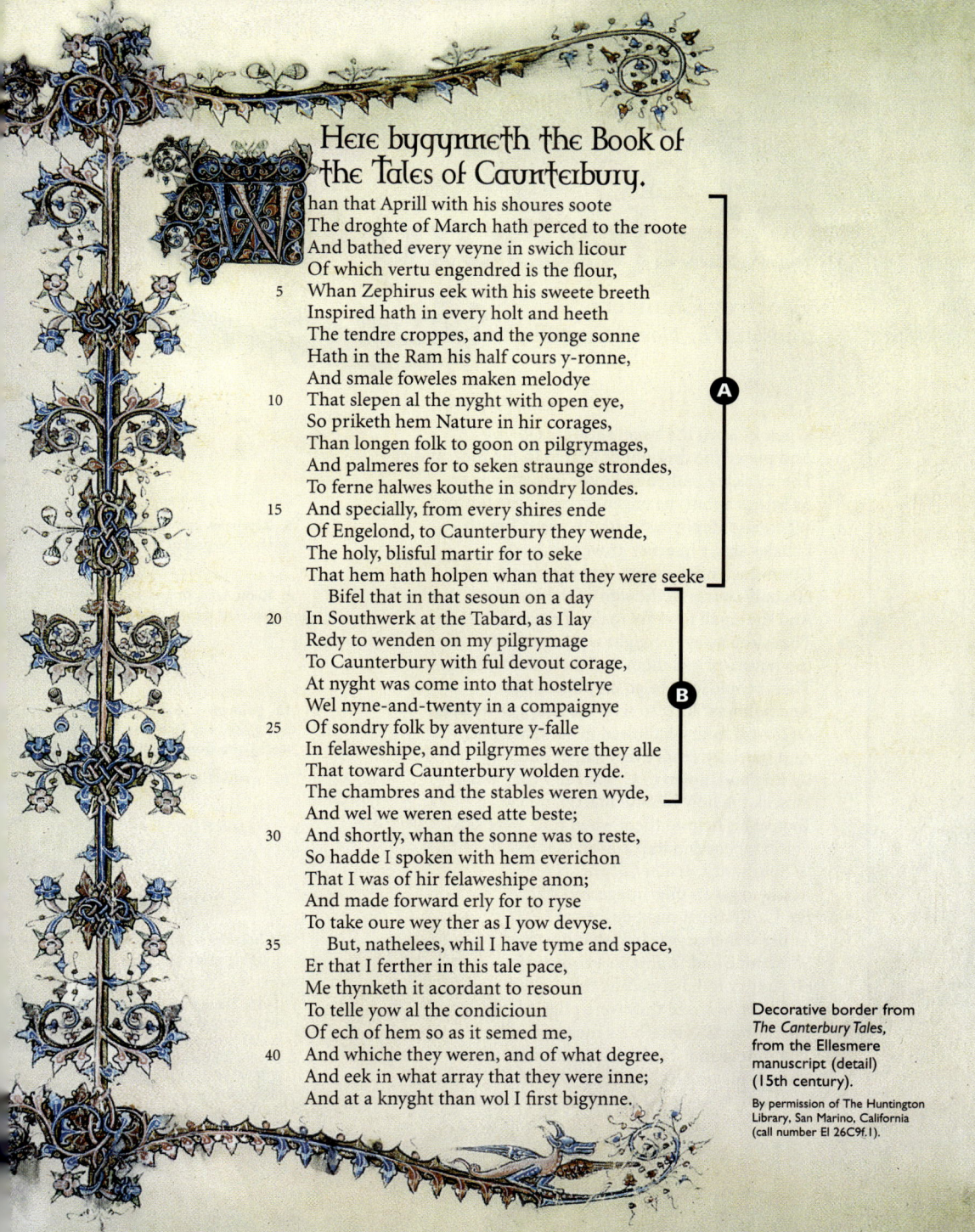

Here bygynneth the Book of the Tales of Caunterbury.

Whan that Aprill with his shoures soote
The droghte of March hath perced to the roote
And bathed every veyne in swich licour
Of which vertu engendred is the flour,
5   Whan Zephirus eek with his sweete breeth
Inspired hath in every holt and heeth
The tendre croppes, and the yonge sonne
Hath in the Ram his half cours y-ronne,
And smale foweles maken melodye
10 That slepen al the nyght with open eye,
So priketh hem Nature in hir corages,
Than longen folk to goon on pilgrymages,
And palmeres for to seken straunge strondes,
To ferne halwes kouthe in sondry londes.
15 And specially, from every shires ende
Of Engelond, to Caunterbury they wende,
The holy, blisful martir for to seke
That hem hath holpen whan that they were seeke.
    Bifel that in that sesoun on a day
20 In Southwerk at the Tabard, as I lay
Redy to wenden on my pilgrymage
To Caunterbury with ful devout corage,
At nyght was come into that hostelrye
Wel nyne-and-twenty in a compaignye
25 Of sondry folk by aventure y-falle
In felaweshipe, and pilgrymes were they alle
That toward Caunterbury wolden ryde.
The chambres and the stables weren wyde,
And wel we weren esed atte beste;
30 And shortly, whan the sonne was to reste,
So hadde I spoken with hem everichon
That I was of hir felaweshipe anon;
And made forward erly for to ryse
To take oure wey ther as I yow devyse.
35   But, nathelees, whil I have tyme and space,
Er that I ferther in this tale pace,
Me thynketh it acordant to resoun
To telle yow al the condicioun
Of ech of hem so as it semed me,
40 And whiche they weren, and of what degree,
And eek in what array that they were inne;
And at a knyght than wol I first bigynne.

Decorative border from *The Canterbury Tales,* from the Ellesmere manuscript (detail) (15th century).
By permission of The Huntington Library, San Marino, California (call number El 26C9f.1).

DIRECT TEACHING

A Literary Focus

Iambic pentameter. Chaucer wrote *The Canterbury Tales* in iambic pentameter, a meter that captures the natural rhythms of spoken English. However, though the iambic pentameter line is usually ten syllables, sometimes Chaucer's lines have an eleventh syllable at the end, as in l. 2. That's because many Middle English words end with a final *e* that is pronounced rather than silent, as in *roote.* This final *e* can also supply an unstressed syllable within the line, as in *smale* in l. 9. (See the pronunciation guide on p. 117 for the rules on when to pronounce the final *e.*)

Play the CD recording of the first eighteen lines of the Prologue in Middle English from the *Audio CD Library,* and encourage students to learn at least some of the Middle English pronunciations. Remind students that Chaucer's East Midland dialect of Middle English was the most common colloquial language of his day; it became the basis of modern English.

B Literary Focus

Rhyme scheme. Chaucer's iambic pentameter lines are also rhyming couplets. Yet they manage to avoid the singsong quality often associated with this rhyme scheme because they are not always end-stopped— the complete thought doesn't always end when the couplet does but may run on to the next line, couplet, or series of couplets. Also, a sentence might end in the middle of a couplet (as in ll. 27–28), so that the rhyme is broken up. Chaucer's use of open couplets creates a highly crafted poetry that still sounds like natural speech.

DIFFERENTIATING INSTRUCTION

Learners Having Difficulty
Invite learners having difficulty to read the Prologue in interactive format in *The Holt Reader* and to use the sidenotes as aids to understanding the selection. The interactive version provides additional instruction, practice, and assessment of the literary skill taught in the Student Edition. Monitor students' responses to the selection, and correct any misconceptions that arise.

English-Language Learners
To engage English-language learners, have them listen to the description of each pilgrim on the recording in the *Audio CD Library.*

Geoffrey Chaucer   119

DIRECT TEACHING

A Reading Skills

❓ Finding the main idea. The first eighteen lines of the Prologue are among the most famous passages in English literature. (High school and college students are often required to memorize them in the original Middle English.) These lines make up a single sentence. After two adverbial clauses (each beginning with *When*) that describe the time of year, the narrator introduces his main idea. What is it? [People long to go on pilgrimages in April, the beginning of spring, when all nature begins to be revive.]

B Learners Having Difficulty

❓ Breaking down difficult text. Students may have trouble with those of Chaucer's sentences that are long and complex, with multiple clauses and phrases. (Reassure them that few sentences are as long as the first!) Help students break down these difficult sentences, section by section, to identify the main idea. Begin with ll. 19–27: Where is the narrator (speaker), and why is he there? [He is at the Tabard Inn in Southwark. He is about to go on a pilgrimage to Canterbury.] **Who arrives at the inn?** [Twenty-nine other pilgrims who are also planning to go to Canterbury.] **What is the main idea of the sentence?** [Twenty-nine pilgrims arrive at the Tabard Inn, where the narrator is staying, to go on a pilgrimage to Canterbury.]

Response to Margin Question

Lines 1–18. They long to go on pilgrimages.

---

from The Canterbury Tales

Geoffrey Chaucer
translated by **Nevill Coghill**

The Prologue

A
When in April the sweet showers fall
And pierce the drought of March to the root, and all
The veins are bathed in liquor of such power
As brings about the engendering of the flower,
5 When also Zephyrus° with his sweet breath
Exhales an air in every grove and heath
Upon the tender shoots, and the young sun
His half-course in the sign of the *Ram*° has run,
And the small fowl are making melody
10 That sleep away the night with open eye
(So nature pricks them and their heart engages)
Then people long to go on pilgrimages
And palmers° long to seek the stranger strands
Of far-off saints, hallowed in sundry lands,
15 And specially, from every shire's end
Of England, down to Canterbury they wend°
To seek the holy blissful martyr, quick
To give his help to them when they were sick.

B
  It happened in that season that one day
20 In Southwark, at *The Tabard,* as I lay
Ready to go on pilgrimage and start
For Canterbury, most devout at heart,
At night there came into that hostelry°
Some nine and twenty in a company
25 Of sundry folk happening then to fall
In fellowship, and they were pilgrims all
That towards Canterbury meant to ride.
The rooms and stables of the inn were wide;
They made us easy, all was of the best.

---

5. Zephyrus (zef′ə·rəs): in Greek mythology, god of the west wind.

8. Ram: Aries, first sign of the zodiac. The time is mid-April.

13. palmers *n. pl.:* people who had visited the Holy Land and wore palm fronds to show it.

16. wend *v.:* go; travel.

23. hostelry *n.:* inn. *The Tabard* is a lodging place.

1–18. These lines consist of a single, long sentence that is built on this structure: "When *x* occurs, then *y* happens."
❓ When spring brings new life, then—according to the narrator—what do people long to do?

---

120 Collection 2 The Middle Ages

DIFFERENTIATING INSTRUCTION

English-Language Learners
For lessons designed for intermediate and advanced English-language learners, see *Holt Reading Solutions.*

Special Education Students
For lessons designed for special education students, see *Holt Reading Solutions.*

Advanced Learners
Enrichment. Have students read literary criticism of the Prologue. They might begin with a few of the excerpts included here in the bottom margins and then follow up on an issue or theme that interests them.

John Lydgate and the Canterbury pilgrims leaving Canterbury, from a volume of Lydgate's poems (early 16th century).
MS Royal 18 D II, fol. 148. British Library, London.

30 And, briefly, when the sun had gone to rest,
    I'd spoken to them all upon the trip
    And was soon one with them in fellowship,
    Pledged to rise early and to take the way
    To Canterbury, as you heard me say.
35   But none the less, while I have time and space,
    Before my story takes a further pace,
    It seems a reasonable thing to say
    What their condition was, the full array
    Of each of them, as it appeared to me,
40 According to profession and degree,
    And what apparel they were riding in;
    And at a Knight I therefore will begin.

DIRECT TEACHING

A Content-Area Connections

History: "Holy" Wars
The Knight fought in wars that spanned forty years and fell into three categories: against the Moors in Spain and North Africa; against the Arabs and Turks in Egypt, Turkey, and Armenia; and against the Tatars and other peoples along the Russian border. All the wars Chaucer mentions were considered holy wars rather than political ones; they were fought in defense of Christianity against non-Christians, whom the Church called infidels or heathens. The Knight is thus presented as a spiritual man rather than simply a brave warrior.

B Reading Skills

? Analyzing key details. What qualities does the Knight possess that are different from those you might expect to find in a veteran soldier? [Possible response: He is modest, considerate, and well-mannered. He embodies the ideal of chivalry rather than our image of a tough, crusty, battle-hardened soldier.]

C Literary Focus

? Characterization. When the narrator presents details about the Knight's equipment and clothing, rather than directly stating his qualities (as in ll. 69–74), he is using indirect characterization. What do these details reveal about the Knight's character? [Possible response: His coarse, worn, stained clothing suggests a plain, modest man who cares little about impressing others.]

The Knight

There was a *Knight*, a most distinguished man,
Who from the day on which he first began
45 To ride abroad had followed chivalry,
Truth, honor, generousness, and courtesy.
He had done nobly in his sovereign's war
And ridden into battle, no man more,
As well in Christian as in heathen° places,
50 And ever honored for his noble graces.
  When we took Alexandria,° he was there.
He often sat at table in the chair
Of honor, above all nations, when in Prussia.
In Lithuania he had ridden, and Russia,
55 No Christian man so often, of his rank.
When, in Granada, Algeciras sank
Under assault, he had been there, and in
North Africa, raiding Benamarin;
In Anatolia he had been as well
60 And fought when Ayas and Attalia fell,
For all along the Mediterranean coast
He had embarked with many a noble host.
In fifteen mortal battles he had been
And jousted for our faith at Tramissene
65 Thrice in the lists, and always killed his man.
This same distinguished knight had led the van
Once with the Bey of Balat, doing work
For him against another heathen Turk;
He was of sovereign value in all eyes.
70 And though so much distinguished, he was wise
And in his bearing modest as a maid.
He never yet a boorish thing had said
In all his life to any, come what might;
He was a true, a perfect gentle-knight.
75   Speaking of his equipment, he possessed
Fine horses, but he was not gaily dressed.
He wore a fustian° tunic stained and dark
With smudges where his armor had left mark;
Just home from service, he had joined our ranks
80 To do his pilgrimage and render thanks.

The Squire

He had his son with him, a fine young *Squire*,
A lover and cadet, a lad of fire
With locks as curly as if they had been pressed.
He was some twenty years of age, I guessed.

---

43. Notice that *Knight* appears in italics; so will each new character's designation as the character is introduced.

? As you read, you might wish to create a list of all the characters introduced in the Prologue.

49. heathen *n.*: pagan. Chaucer here is referring to non-Christians.
51. Alexandria: city in Egypt captured by the Crusaders in 1365. In the next few lines, Chaucer is indicating the knight's distinguished and extensive career.

The Knight, from the Ellesmere manuscript.
Fol. 10r. By permission of The Huntington Library, San Marino, California.

77. fustian (fus'chən) *adj.*: coarse cloth made of linen and cotton.

---

122 Collection 2 The Middle Ages

Literary Criticism

Critic's Commentary: The Perfect Knight

According to E. T. Donaldson, "By beginning his portraits with the ideal knight, Chaucer sets up a pattern of perfection against which all the other pilgrims may be measured. At the same time he is beginning with the dominant figure of his own age, which was still the Age of Chivalry however degenerate actual knighthood may have become.... Just as the wars in which he [the Knight] has fought are not political but religious, so his personality as it appears in the Prologue is less that of an experienced veteran than that of a perfect knight."

The Squire, from the Ellesmere manuscript.
Fol. 115v. By permission of The Huntington Library, San Marino, California.

85 In stature he was of a moderate length,
With wonderful agility and strength.
He'd seen some service with the cavalry
In Flanders and Artois and Picardy
And had done valiantly in little space
90 Of time, in hope to win his lady's grace.
He was embroidered like a meadow bright
And full of freshest flowers, red and white.
Singing he was, or fluting° all the day;
He was as fresh as is the month of May.
95 Short was his gown, the sleeves were long and wide;
He knew the way to sit a horse and ride.
He could make songs and poems and recite,
Knew how to joust and dance, to draw and write.
He loved so hotly that till dawn grew pale
100 He slept as little as a nightingale.
Courteous he was, lowly and serviceable,
And carved to serve his father at the table.

The Yeoman

There was a *Yeoman* with him at his side,
No other servant; so he chose to ride.
105 This Yeoman wore a coat and hood of green,
And peacock-feathered arrows, bright and keen
And neatly sheathed, hung at his belt the while
—For he could dress his gear in yeoman style,
His arrows never drooped their feathers low—
110 And in his hand he bore a mighty bow.
His head was like a nut, his face was brown.
He knew the whole of woodcraft up and down.
A saucy brace was on his arm to ward
It from the bow-string, and a shield and sword
115 Hung at one side, and at the other slipped
A jaunty dirk,° spear-sharp and well-equipped.
A medal of St. Christopher° he wore
Of shining silver on his breast, and bore
A hunting-horn, well slung and burnished clean,
120 That dangled from a baldrick° of bright green.
He was a proper forester, I guess.

Vocabulary
agility (ə·jil′ə·tē) *n.*: ability to move quickly and easily.

93. **fluting** *v.*: whistling.

87–102. Summarize the narrator's description of the Squire. In what ways does the Squire appear to embody the code of chivalry? (See page 100 for a review of chivalry.)

The Canon Yeoman, from the Ellesmere manuscript.
Fol. 194r. By permission of The Huntington Library, San Marino, California.

116. **dirk** *n.*: long dagger.
117. **St. Christopher**: patron saint of travelers.

120. **baldrick** (bôl′drik′) *n.*: belt slung over the shoulder and chest to hold a sword.

Literary Criticism

Two Critics' Commentaries: Generation Gap

Muriel Bowden notes that the Squire's clothing stresses his youth and frivolity: "Short, embroidered gowns and long, wide sleeves were the marks of the ultrafashionable in the late fourteenth century . . . ; short coats were denounced as 'indecent'; embroidery was called unnecessarily expensive."

John Gardner argues that the Squire is not the man his father is: "Whereas his father is humble and self-effacing, the buoyant young Squire is vain perhaps to the point of putting curlers in his hair. . . . Nevertheless, the Squire is not to be laughed away. . . . Chaucer makes it clear that he likes his Squire; he praises the young man's accomplishments and ends with a couplet proving the Squire's good manners and knowledge of his place."

DIRECT TEACHING

A Content-Area Connections

Religion: Nuns
A nun is a woman who lives in a convent and takes a vow of poverty, obedience, and chastity (she is married to Christ). As mother superior of a convent, a prioress is under oath not to leave her charges. As students read this description of the Prioress, ask them to notice whether her attitudes and behavior are appropriate for a nun.

B Literary Focus

Irony. It is ironic that the Prioress swears by Saint Loy—a saint known for his refusal to swear. Her name, Eglantyne, is also ironic because it is the name of several romantic heroines in literature and thus is not appropriate for a nun. (It is also a type of clinging rose.) As students continue reading the portrait of the Prioress, tell them to look for other ways in which she is presented as a romantic rather than a religious figure.

C Literary Focus

Diction. The poet's choice of the word *counterfeit* reveals his attitude toward the Prioress. Though amiable and attractive, there is something fake about her. According to the critic Donald R. Howard, her attempt to seem dignified shows that she is preoccupied with social status rather than religion.

Response to Margin Question

Lines 122–145. Though she speaks French, her French is not the real thing (as spoken in Paris). Her table manners are "well taught," but seem overly studied; she is "straining to counterfeit a courtly kind of grace."

The Nun

There also was a *Nun*, a Prioress,°
Her way of smiling very simple and coy.
Her greatest oath was only "By St. Loy!"°
125 And she was known as Madam Eglantyne.
And well she sang a service, with a fine
Intoning through her nose, as was most seemly,
And she spoke daintily in French, extremely,
After the school of Stratford-atte-Bowe;°
130 French in the Paris style she did not know.
At meat her manners were well taught withal;
No morsel from her lips did she let fall,
Nor dipped her fingers in the sauce too deep;
But she could carry a morsel up and keep
135 The smallest drop from falling on her breast.
For courtliness she had a special zest,
And she would wipe her upper lip so clean
That not a trace of grease was to be seen
Upon the cup when she had drunk; to eat,
140 She reached a hand sedately for the meat.
She certainly was very entertaining,
Pleasant and friendly in her ways, and straining
To counterfeit a courtly kind of grace,
A stately bearing fitting to her place,
145 And to seem dignified in all her dealings.
As for her sympathies and tender feelings,
She was so charitably solicitous
She used to weep if she but saw a mouse
Caught in a trap, if it were dead or bleeding.
150 And she had little dogs she would be feeding

122. Prioress: head of a convent of nuns.

124. St. Loy: Saint Eligius, known for his perfect manners.

129. Stratford-atte-Bowe: Benedictine convent near London where inferior French was spoken.

122–145. What details in the description of the Prioress thus far suggest that the narrator thinks she is putting on airs—that is, trying to appear more refined and "high class" than she really is?

The Prioress, from the Ellesmere manuscript.
Fol. 148v. By permission of The Huntington Library, San Marino, California.

The Nun's Priest, from the Ellesmere manuscript.
Fol. 179r. By permission of The Huntington Library, San Marino, California.

124 Collection 2 The Middle Ages

Literary Criticism

A Critic's Commentary: Counterfeit Class

According to the Chaucer scholar Donald R. Howard, the Prioress (along with the Monk and the Friar) exemplifies "the fundamental flaw in the practice of the religious life" during the Middle Ages: "that its values and ideals were contaminated by secular—and chiefly aristocratic—ones." Not having renounced "the world," as members of religious orders were expected to, she remains "class conscious," with her phony refinement. "It is not clear whether the Prioress is the daughter of a noble house or, as seems more likely, from the *haute bourgeoisie* or the 'gentry': one rather assumes that in the circles where high social rank was taken for granted such manners and bearing were second nature—a lady of such a background wouldn't need to 'countrefete' them."

With roasted flesh, or milk, or fine white bread.
And bitterly she wept if one were dead
Or someone took a stick and made it smart;
She was all sentiment and tender heart.
155 Her veil was gathered in a seemly way,
Her nose was elegant, her eyes glass-gray;
Her mouth was very small, but soft and red,
Her forehead, certainly, was fair of spread,
Almost a span° across the brows, I own;
160 She was indeed by no means undergrown.
Her cloak, I noticed, had a graceful charm.
She wore a coral° trinket on her arm,
A set of beads, the gaudies tricked in green,°
Whence hung a golden brooch of brightest sheen
165 On which there first was graven a crowned A,
And lower, *Amor vincit omnia.*°
  Another *Nun,* the secretary at her cell,°
Was riding with her, and *three Priests* as well.

The Monk

  A *Monk* there was, one of the finest sort
170 Who rode the country; hunting was his sport.
A manly man, to be an Abbott able;
Many a dainty horse he had in stable.
His bridle, when he rode, a man might hear
Jingling in a whistling wind as clear,
175 Aye, and as loud as does the chapel bell
Where my lord Monk was Prior of the cell.
The Rule of good St. Benet or St. Maur°
As old and strict he tended to ignore;
He let go by the things of yesterday
180 And took the modern world's more spacious way.
He did not rate that text at a plucked hen
Which says that hunters are not holy men
And that a monk uncloistered is a mere
Fish out of water, flapping on the pier,
185 That is to say a monk out of his cloister.
That was a text he held not worth an oyster;
And I agreed and said his views were sound;
Was he to study till his head went round
Poring over books in cloisters? Must he toil
190 As Austin° bade and till the very soil?
Was he to leave the world upon the shelf?
Let Austin have his labor to himself.
  This Monk was therefore a good man to horse;
Greyhounds he had, as swift as birds, to course.°
195 Hunting a hare or riding at a fence

159. span *n.:* nine inches. A span was supposed to be the distance between the extended thumb and little finger.
162. coral *adj.:* In the Middle Ages, coral was a defense against worldly temptations—but it was also a love charm.
163. a set of beads . . . green: Beads are a rosary, or a set of prayer beads and a crucifix on a string or chain. Every eleventh bead is a gaud, a large bead indicating when the Lord's Prayer is to be said.
166. Amor vincit omnia (ä′môr′ vin′chit ôm′nē·ä′): Latin for "Love conquers all."
167. cell *n.:* small convent connected to a larger one.

177. St. Benet or St. Maur: Saint Benet is Benedict (c. 480–c. 547), who founded numerous monasteries and wrote a famous code of regulations for monastic life. Saint Maur is Maurice, a follower of Benedict.

190. Austin: Saint Augustine (354–430), bishop of Hippo in North Africa. He criticized lazy monks and suggested they do hard manual labor.
194. course *v.:* cause to chase game.

Geoffrey Chaucer **125**

DIRECT TEACHING

D Reading Skills

Analyzing key details. Nuns were not supposed to keep pets, because the money required for their care was meant for the poor. What does this detail about her dogs suggest about the Prioress? [She is concerned more with worldly luxuries than with the poor.]

E Reading Skills

Analyzing key details. In Chaucer's time physical characteristics were thought to reveal a person's inner nature. In this description of the Prioress one such revealing detail is her high forehead, considered a sign of intelligence and good breeding. However, a nine-inch brow would be most unusual. Why do you think Chaucer exaggerates this feature? [Possible response: He is gently mocking the Prioress's pretensions to good breeding.] Why might the narrator use understatement to describe her figure (l. 160)? [Possible response: It adds to the gentle mockery; she must be plump or perhaps very tall.]

F Reading Skills

Analyzing key details. Many critics have noted that the inscription on the Prioress's brooch, meaning "Love conquers all," can be interpreted in either a secular or a religious way. What can we infer about the Prioress from this key detail? [Possible response: She may be devoted to either the divine ideal of God's love, or to the secular ideal of romantic love.]

G Literary Focus

Unreliable narrator. Tell students to look for clues that this portrait is ironic—that the narrator's attitude toward the Monk is not the same as the poet's.

Literary Criticism

Two Critics' Commentaries: Willful Worldliness

John Gardner sees the Monk, like the Prioress, as a "delightfully dim-witted" character who is "flawed" but "not thoroughly corrupt." Yet he "is worse than the Prioress in that his worldliness is willful." Though less delighted by the Monk's stupidity, E. T. Donaldson agrees that Chaucer is harder on him than on the Prioress: "His masterful personality quite overwhelms the narrator, as, in a different way, the Prioress' charming femininity had done. But brute force is less attractive than charm, and the poet subjects it to more emphatic satire. We are never sure that the Prioress fully knows what she is doing, but the Monk knows and even boasts about his failure to behave as a monk should."

DIRECT TEACHING

A Reading Skills

? Analyzing key details. How do the details in this portrait of the Monk imply that he is not serious about his vocation? [Possible response: He ignores Saint Benedict's Rule. He doesn't think a monk needs to study, do manual labor, or stay in his cloister. He indulges in luxuries: He rides a fine horse, races greyhounds, hunts, wears fancy clothes and jewelry, and eats delicacies.] You might point out that monks were not supposed to hunt (just as nuns were not supposed to keep pets), because hunting was considered a sinful waste of time and money.

B Literary Focus

? Irony. In the Middle Ages, fatness was a sign of wealth, because people didn't always have enough to eat. Why is it ironic that the Monk is fat? [Possible response: A monk has taken a vow of poverty and should not be so well-fed.]

C Literary Focus

? Characterization. One of a friar's main duties was to hear people's confessions and absolve, or forgive, their sins after imposing a penance, or penalty—usually prayers or good works to be performed. The Friar offers "pleasant absolution" (l. 226), or light penance, in exchange for money. What does this reveal about his character? [He is greedy and corrupt.]

Response to Margin Question

Lines 193–211. They are both worldly, enjoying fine food, clothing, and other luxuries. Chaucer hints that both have been tempted by love (her gold brooch, his gold pin like a lover's knot).

The Friar, from the Ellesmere manuscript.
Fol. 76v. By permission of The Huntington Library, San Marino, California.

Was all his fun, he spared for no expense.
I saw his sleeves were garnished at the hand
With fine gray fur, the finest in the land,
And on his hood, to fasten it at his chin
200 He had a wrought-gold, cunningly fashioned pin;
Into a lover's knot it seemed to pass.
His head was bald and shone like looking-glass;
So did his face, as if it had been greased.
He was a fat and personable priest;
205 His prominent eyeballs never seemed to settle.
They glittered like the flames beneath a kettle;
Supple his boots, his horse in fine condition.
He was a prelate fit for exhibition,
He was not pale like a tormented soul.
210 He liked a fat swan best, and roasted whole.
His palfrey° was as brown as is a berry.

? 193–211. In what ways does the description of the Monk remind you of the Prioress?

211. **palfrey** (pôl′frē) *n.:* horse.

The Friar

There was a *Friar*, a wanton one and merry,
A Limiter,° a very festive fellow.
In all Four Orders° there was none so mellow,
215 So glib with gallant phrase and well-turned speech.
He'd fixed up many a marriage, giving each
Of his young women what he could afford her.
He was a noble pillar to his Order.
Highly beloved and intimate was he
220 With County folk within his boundary,
And city dames of honor and possessions;
For he was qualified to hear confessions,
Or so he said, with more than priestly scope;
He had a special license from the Pope.
225 Sweetly he heard his penitents° at shrift°
With pleasant absolution,° for a gift.
He was an easy man in penance-giving
Where he could hope to make a decent living;
It's a sure sign whenever gifts are given
230 To a poor Order that a man's well shriven,°
And should he give enough he knew in verity
The penitent repented in sincerity.
For many a fellow is so hard of heart
He cannot weep, for all his inward smart.
235 Therefore instead of weeping and of prayer
One should give silver for a poor Friar's care.
He kept his tippet° stuffed with pins for curls,
And pocket-knives, to give to pretty girls.
And certainly his voice was gay and sturdy,

213. **Limiter:** friar having the exclusive right to beg and preach in an assigned (limited) district.
214. **Four Orders:** The four orders of mendicant (beggar) friars are the Franciscans, the Dominicans, the Carmelites, and the Augustinians.

225. **penitents** *n. pl.:* people seeking the sacrament of confession so that their sins can be forgiven. **shrift** *n.:* confession.
226. **absolution** *n.:* formal forgiveness of sins, given by a priest.

230. **well shriven:** well confessed and absolved (or forgiven) of sins.

237. **tippet** *n.:* hood or long sleeve (of a robe).

126 Collection 2 The Middle Ages

SKILLS REVIEW

The unreliable narrator. Some readers, unprepared for Chaucer's ironic humor, may take the narrator's characterizations of the pilgrims at face value. Point out that Chaucer (as pilgrim) is a classic example of an unreliable narrator—a narrator who can't be completely trusted. Some narrators are untrustworthy because they aren't telling the truth, but others are unreliable because they are naive—they don't fully understand what they are describing. Naive narrators create dramatic irony because they understand less than the reader does.

Activity. When the narrator tells the Monk that his views are "sound" (l. 187), he means that they are correct, but he unwittingly implies that they are merely empty words. As students read the portrait of the Friar, ask them to notice how Chaucer gets us to distrust the narrator.

240 For he sang well and played the hurdy-gurdy.°
     At sing-songs he was champion of the hour.
     His neck was whiter than a lily-flower
     But strong enough to butt a bruiser down.
     He knew the taverns well in every town
245 And every innkeeper and barmaid too
     Better than lepers, beggars and that crew,
     For in so eminent a man as he
     It was not fitting with the dignity
     Of his position, dealing with a scum
250 Of wretched lepers; nothing good can come
     Of commerce with such slum-and-gutter dwellers,
     But only with the rich and victual-sellers.°
     But anywhere a profit might accrue
     Courteous he was and lowly of service too.
255 Natural gifts like his were hard to match.
     He was the finest beggar of his batch,
     And, for his begging-district, paid a rent;
     His brethren did no poaching where he went.
     For though a widow mightn't have a shoe,
260 So pleasant was his holy how-d'ye-do
     He got his farthing° from her just the same
     Before he left, and so his income came
     To more than he laid out. And how he romped,
     Just like a puppy! He was ever prompt
265 To arbitrate disputes on settling days°
     (For a small fee) in many helpful ways,
     Not then appearing as your cloistered scholar
     With threadbare habit hardly worth a dollar,
     But much more like a Doctor or a Pope.
270 Of double-worsted° was the semi-cope°
     Upon his shoulders, and the swelling fold
     About him, like a bell about its mould
     When it is casting, rounded out his dress.
     He lisped a little out of wantonness°
275 To make his English sweet upon his tongue.
     When he had played his harp, or having sung,
     His eyes would twinkle in his head as bright
     As any star upon a frosty night.
     This worthy's name was Hubert, it appeared.

Vocabulary
eminent (em′ə·nənt) *adj.*: high-standing; great.
accrue (ə·krōō′) *v.*: increase over time.
arbitrate (är′bə·trāt′) *v.*: settle or decide by listening to both sides of an argument.

---

240. **hurdy-gurdy** *n.*: lutelike instrument played by turning a crank.

252. **victual-sellers**: merchants, especially of food.

256–279. What details in these lines show the Friar's love of luxury? How does this Friar compare with your expectations of a religious figure?

261. **farthing** (fär′t͟hiŋ) *n.*: former British coin worth one fourth of a penny.

265. **settling days**: days on which disputes could be settled out of court by independent negotiators. Though friars often acted as negotiators (for a fee), they were officially forbidden to do so.

270. **double-worsted**: a high-quality woven wool. **semi-cope** *n.*: capelike garment.

274. **wantonness** *n.*: here, pretense.

Geoffrey Chaucer **127**

DIRECT TEACHING

D Literary Focus
Characterization. In Chaucer's day, people believed that certain physical characteristics revealed a person's true nature. What character trait do you think a lily-white neck might reveal? [Possible response: a taste for luxury and easy living.]

E Content-Area Connections
Religion: Friars
The Franciscan order of friars was founded by Saint Francis for the express purpose of ministering to the poorest and least fortunate—the very people the Friar considers beneath his notice.

F Literary Focus
Naive narrator. What does the reader realize that the narrator does not? [Possible response: The Friar is a scoundrel whose "gifts" consist in the ability to talk people out of their money.]

Response to Margin Question
Lines 256–279. He is greedy and corrupt. He begs money from poor widows and settles disputes for a fee (though friars were forbidden to do so). He dresses in expensive clothing despite his vow of poverty. Previous lines reveal that he sells his absolution and considers himself too dignified to associate with the poor and sick. He is the antithesis of what a religious figure should be.

READING SKILLS REVIEW

Archaic usage. Although this is a modern translation of Chaucer's Middle English, the translator has preserved an old-fashioned flavor through his choice of words. For example, the word *dainty*, as used in l. 172 to describe the Monk's horses, means "fine," but that meaning is now archaic: It is no longer used in ordinary speech or writing. Today the most common definition of *dainty* is "delicate."

Activity. Have students look up the meaning of each underlined word.
1. "And jousted . . . / . . . in the lists" (ll. 64–65). [tournament grounds]
2. "Must he toil / As Austin bade" (ll. 189–190)? [commanded]
3. "He had a wrought-gold, cunningly fashioned pin" (l. 200). [skillfully]

DIRECT TEACHING

A Reading Skills

Analyzing key details. Once again, the narrator undermines his own credibility. Why does the reader distrust the characterization of the Merchant as "an excellent fellow"? [Possible response: Because the narrator has already revealed the Merchant's hypocrisy: He acts as if he were rich, but in fact, he's in debt.]

B Reading Skills

Analyzing key details. The Merchant may be hiding his identity so that his creditors can't find him.

A CLOSER LOOK

This feature discusses important religious pilgrimage sites around the world: Rome; Jerusalem; the Kaaba in Mecca, Saudi Arabia; the Golden Temple in Varanasi, India; and the Grand Shrine of Ise in Mie Prefecture, Japan.

C Reading Informational Text

Recognizing patterns of organization. What information does each paragraph present? [Each paragraph discusses a pilgrimage site or sites of a different religion: Christianity, Judaism, Islam, Hinduism, and Shinto.]

The Merchant

280 There was a *Merchant* with a forking beard
     And motley° dress; high on his horse he sat,
     Upon his head a Flemish beaver hat
     And on his feet daintily buckled boots.
     He told of his opinions and pursuits
285 In solemn tones, he harped on his increase
     Of capital; there should be sea-police
     (He thought) upon the Harwich-Holland ranges;°
     He was expert at dabbling in exchanges.
     This estimable Merchant so had set
290 His wits to work, none knew he was in debt,
     He was so stately in administration,
     In loans and bargains and negotiation.
     He was an excellent fellow all the same;
     To tell the truth I do not know his name.

281. motley (mät′lē) *adj.*: multi-colored.

287. Harwich-Holland ranges: sea route between Harwich (a port city on the southeastern coast of England) and Holland.

A CLOSER LOOK: RELIGIOUS INFLUENCES

PLACES OF PILGRIMAGE

INFORMATIONAL TEXT

Chaucer's pilgrims are hardly alone in their faith that visiting a holy site will have spiritual benefits. Besides Canterbury, many Christians of Chaucer's time made pilgrimages to Rome and Jerusalem, both sites that the Wife of Bath, something of a professional pilgrim, had visited. Today Christian pilgrims still travel to Jerusalem and Rome.

In ancient times Jews also made pilgrimages to Jerusalem, during three major festivals: Pesach (Passover), Shavuot (Pentecost), and Sukkot (Tabernacles). These pilgrimages, associated with festivals that mark the Jews' escape from Egypt and journey to Israel, were expected of Jewish men.

For a follower of Islam, no place is more sacred than Mecca, located near the Red Sea in western Saudi Arabia. Mecca is the site of the Kaaba, a sacred, cube-shaped stone building around which Muslim pilgrims must walk. Mohammed, the founder of Islam, decreed that all Muslims who are physically and financially able to make the trip must journey to Mecca at least once in their lifetime.

Varanasi, a city on the Ganges River in India and the site of fifteen hundred temples, is visited by more than one million Hindu pilgrims each year. The Golden Temple, the main Hindu shrine there, is dedicated to the god Shiva. Pilgrims who worship at the Ganges at Varanasi believe they gain special merit in this life, and Hindus who die in Varanasi believe they are guaranteed release from endless rebirths.

The Grand Shrine of Ise, the most sacred site of Japanese Shinto pilgrimages, is located at Ise in Mie Prefecture, Japan. The shrines there are viewed as the dwelling place of two deities, the sun goddess Amaterasu and the agricultural god Toyuke. The history of Ise shrine dates back some two thousand years, but the actual buildings are always fairly new. By tradition the shrines must be rebuilt in the same style every twenty-one years.

128   Collection 2   The Middle Ages

CONTENT-AREA CONNECTIONS

History: Commerce

In Chaucer's day, it was illegal to charge interest on a loan, but the practice still went on. E. T. Donaldson explains that "to inspire confidence in one's reliability was even more important for a merchant in the Middle Ages than it is today," because a merchant who was considered financially unsound would have to pay a higher interest rate. "If, like Shakespeare's Antonio, the merchant of Venice, he found himself in real need of cash while all his own capital was known to be tied up in merchandise still at sea, he might be unmercifully squeezed by the moneylender." A merchant would therefore "be particularly careful to hide his indebtedness." If his ships didn't return home in time for him to repay his debts, he might need to leave town suddenly (perhaps on the pretext of a pilgrimage).

The Clerk of Oxford, from the Ellesmere manuscript.
Fol. 88r. By permission of The Huntington Library, San Marino, California.

The Oxford Cleric

295 An *Oxford Cleric*, still a student though,
One who had taken logic long ago,
Was there; his horse was thinner than a rake,
And he was not too fat, I undertake,
But had a hollow look, a sober stare;
300 The thread upon his overcoat was bare.
He had found no preferment in the church
And he was too unworldly to make search
For secular employment. By his bed
He preferred having twenty books in red
305 And black, of Aristotle's° philosophy,
Than costly clothes, fiddle, or psaltery.°
Though a philosopher, as I have told,
He had not found the stone for making gold.°
Whatever money from his friends he took
310 He spent on learning or another book
And prayed for them most earnestly, returning
Thanks to them thus for paying for his learning.
His only care was study, and indeed
He never spoke a word more than was need,
315 Formal at that, respectful in the extreme,
Short, to the point, and lofty in his theme.
A tone of moral virtue filled his speech
And gladly would he learn, and gladly teach.

The Lawyer

A *Sergeant at the Law* who paid his calls,
320 Wary and wise, for clients at St. Paul's°
There also was, of noted excellence.
Discreet he was, a man to reverence,
Or so he seemed, his sayings were so wise.
He often had been Justice of Assize
325 By letters patent,° and in full commission.
His fame and learning and his high position
Had won him many a robe and many a fee.
There was no such conveyancer° as he;
All was fee-simple° to his strong digestion,
330 Not one conveyance could be called in question.
Though there was nowhere one so busy as he,
He was less busy than he seemed to be.
He knew of every judgment, case, and crime

---

305. Aristotle's (ar′is·tät″lz): reference to the Greek philosopher (384–322 B.C.).
306. psaltery (sôl′tər·ē) *n.*: stringed instrument that is plucked.
308. stone...gold: Alchemists at the time were searching for a stone that was supposed to turn ordinary metals into gold.

295–318. Which details in the sketch of the Oxford Cleric match the stereotype of the starving student? In what significant ways is the Oxford Cleric different from the Prioress, the Monk, and the Friar?

320. St. Paul's: London cathedral. Lawyers often met outside it to discuss their cases when courts were closed.
325. letters patent: letters from the king permitting people to act as judges at the Assizes, court sessions held periodically.
328. conveyancer *n.*: person who draws up documents transferring ownership of land. The Lawyer is transferring the ownership to himself.
329. fee-simple *n.* used as *adj.*: absolute ownership of real property; in other words, he took absolute possession of everything.

Geoffrey Chaucer 129

Direct Teaching

A Reading Skills

Drawing conclusions. What conclusions can you draw from the fact that the Sergeant at the Law pretends to be busier than he is and dresses in expensive clothing? (A parti-colored coat and a silk belt were signs of wealth.) [Possible responses: He has gotten rich without working hard (perhaps through buying up land); perhaps he knows the value of appearing prosperous and busily employed—just as he "seems" to be "a man to reverence." (l. 322).]

B Content-Area Connections

History: Medieval Meals
Medieval Britons usually ate only two meals a day: a midmorning dinner and an early-evening supper. The Franklin also eats a breakfast of sop, a mixture of wine, almond milk, ginger, sugar, and spices poured over good bread.

C Literary Focus

Characterization. Although the Franklin is clearly a pleasure-loving man, he is not depicted in a negative way. What good points can we infer about his character? [Possible response: He is a generous host and neighbor.]

D Literary Focus

Characterization. In addition to being a good neighbor, the Franklin is a good citizen who has held several public offices. E. T. Donaldson points out that "he seems to be one of the relatively few pilgrims who are capable of disinterested conduct."

---

335 Ever recorded since King William's time.
He could dictate defenses or draft deeds;
No one could pinch a comma from his screeds°
And he knew every statute off by rote.
He wore a homely parti-colored° coat,
340 Girt with a silken belt of pin-stripe stuff;
Of his appearance I have said enough.

The Franklin

There was a *Franklin*° with him, it appeared;
White as a daisy-petal was his beard.
A sanguine° man, high-colored and benign,
He loved a morning sop of cake in wine.
345 He lived for pleasure and had always done,
For he was Epicurus'° very son,
In whose opinion sensual delight
Was the one true felicity in sight.
As noted as St. Julian° was for bounty
350 He made his household free to all the County.
His bread, his ale were finest of the fine
And no one had a better stock of wine.
His house was never short of bake-meat pies,
Of fish and flesh, and these in such supplies
355 It positively snowed with meat and drink
And all the dainties that a man could think.
According to the seasons of the year
Changes of dish were ordered to appear.
He kept fat partridges in coops, beyond,
360 Many a bream and pike were in his pond.
Woe to the cook unless the sauce was hot
And sharp, or if he wasn't on the spot!
And in his hall a table stood arrayed
And ready all day long, with places laid.
365 As Justice at the Sessions° none stood higher;
He often had been Member for the Shire.°
A dagger and a little purse of silk
Hung at his girdle, white as morning milk.
As Sheriff he checked audit, every entry.
370 He was a model among landed gentry.

Vocabulary
benign (bi·nīn′) *adj*.: kind; gracious.

336. **screeds** *n. pl.*: tiresome, lengthy writings.
338. **parti-colored** *adj.*: multi-colored.

341. **Franklin:** well-to-do landowner who is not of the nobility.
343. **sanguine** (saŋ′gwin) *adj*.: ruddy-complexioned. In Chaucer's day this was considered a sign of a cheerful temperament; today the word signifies optimism.
346. **Epicurus':** Epicurus (341–270 B.C.), an ancient Greek philosopher, taught that the goal of life is pleasure, which is achieved through virtue and moderation. Most people came to think of Epicureans as pleasure seekers.
349. **St. Julian:** patron saint of hospitality.

365. **Justice at the Sessions:** judge at a court meeting.
366. **Member for the Shire:** county representative in Parliament.

The Franklin, from the Ellesmere manuscript.
Fol. 123v. By permission of The Huntington Library, San Marino, California.

DEVELOPING FLUENCY

Model reading part of the Prologue aloud to students. As you do, discuss ways to use pitch, volume, pauses, expression, body language, and even eye contact with the audience to achieve fluency and add dramatic effect. Remind students to use punctuation and meaning to decide when to pause, rather than simply stopping mechanically at the end of every line. (You might want to review the discussion of open couplets in annotation B, p. 119.) Discuss how students can use expression and tone of voice to convey their interpretation of the narrator's (or the poet's) attitude toward a particular character.

Paired activity. Have students work in pairs to practice their own oral reading skills on selected passages. After they have practiced a few times, have them listen to the same passage on the *Audio CD Library* and then present their readings to the whole class.

The Cook, from the Ellesmere manuscript.
Fol. 47r. By permission of The Huntington Library, San Marino, California.

The Guildsmen

A *Haberdasher,*° a *Dyer,* a *Carpenter,*
A *Weaver,* and a *Carpet-maker* were
Among our ranks, all in the livery°
Of one impressive guild-fraternity.
375 They were so trim and fresh their gear would pass
For new. Their knives were not tricked out with brass
But wrought with purest silver, which avouches°
A like display on girdles and on pouches.
Each seemed a worthy burgess,° fit to grace
380 A guild-hall with a seat upon the dais.
Their wisdom would have justified a plan
To make each one of them an alderman;°
They had the capital and revenue,
Besides their wives declared it was their due.
385 And if they did not think so, then they ought;
To be called "*Madam*" is a glorious thought,
And so is going to church and being seen
Having your mantle carried, like a queen.

The Cook

They had a *Cook* with them who stood alone
390 For boiling chicken with a marrow-bone,
Sharp flavoring-powder and a spice for savor.
He could distinguish London ale by flavor,
And he could roast and seethe and broil and fry,
Make good thick soup, and bake a tasty pie.
395 But what a pity—so it seemed to me,
That he should have an ulcer on his knee.
As for blancmange,° he made it with the best.

The Skipper

There was a *Skipper* hailing from far west;
He came from Dartmouth, so I understood.
400 He rode a farmer's horse as best he could,
In a woollen gown that reached his knee.
A dagger on a lanyard° falling free

---

371. **Haberdasher** (hab′ər·dash′ər): seller of men's clothing and accessories.

373. **livery** *n.*: traditional uniform associated with a particular trade.

377. **avouches** (ə·vouch′iz) *v.*: guarantees.

379. **burgess** *n.*: citizen.

382. **alderman** *n.*: head of a guild and therefore a town-council member.

371–388. Whose characters do you learn more about in these lines: the characters of the guildsmen or the characters of their wives? Explain.

397. **blancmange** (blə·mônzh′) *n.*: French for "white food." In Chaucer's day this was a sweet dish containing diced chicken, milk, sugar, and almonds.

402. **lanyard** (lan′yərd) *n.*: cord.

Geoffrey Chaucer   131

Literary Criticism

Critic's Commentary: Mouthwatering?
James L. Matterer notes that the Cook "was actually based on a real London cook known to Chaucer, a Roger Ware. . . . Chaucer obviously intended for his London readers to recognize this poor cook with the sore on his knee." From the descriptions of his culinary specialties, we might conclude that Roger Ware was an excellent cook. However, "another description of his abilities occurs in the Cook's prologue to his tale, but is far from complimentary. The host of the pilgrimage accuses Roger of not only selling warmed over and stale pasties, but of having so many flies in his shop that they often end up in the food. His poor, stubble-fed geese were so badly prepared that the host tells him, 'From many a pilgrim hast thou Christ's curse.'"

DIRECT TEACHING

A Reading Skills
Analyzing key details. Make sure students understand that while transporting wine from Bordeaux, France, the Skipper siphons off some from the barrels, thus stealing from the merchant who owns the wine.

B Vocabulary Development
Multiple meanings. Be sure students understand that the word *nice* has several meanings, including "subtle; requiring discernment."

C Literary Focus
Irony. The name of the ship is a variant of "Magdalene." Mary Magdalene was a Christian saint who by tradition typifies the repentant sinner. Why is the ship's name ironic? [There is nothing saintly or repentant about the Skipper.]

D Reading Skills
Analyzing key details. What does this detail reveal about the Doctor's character? [Possible response: He is greedy and dishonest; he prescribes medicines and gets a kickback from the apothecaries.]

Response to Margin Question
Lines 408–410. He sends them to their death (by drowning). Clearly, killing prisoners is not exactly observing the "nicer rules of conscience."

Hung from his neck under his arm and down.
The summer heat had tanned his color brown,
405 And certainly he was an excellent fellow.
Many a draught of vintage, red and yellow,
He'd drawn at Bordeaux, while the trader snored.
The nicer rules of conscience he ignored.
If, when he fought, the enemy vessel sank,
410 He sent his prisoners home; they walked the plank.
As for his skill in reckoning his tides,
Currents, and many another risk besides,
Moons, harbors, pilots, he had such dispatch
That none from Hull to Carthage was his match.
415 Hardy he was, prudent in undertaking;
His beard in many a tempest had its shaking,
And he knew all the havens as they were
From Gottland to the Cape of Finisterre,
And every creek in Brittany and Spain;
420 The barge he owned was called *The Maudelayne*.

The Doctor

A Doctor too emerged as we proceeded;
No one alive could talk as well as he did
On points of medicine and of surgery,
For being grounded in astronomy,
425 He watched his patient closely for the hours
When, by his horoscope, he knew the powers
Of favorable planets, then ascendent,
Worked on the images for his dependent.
The cause of every malady you'd got
430 He knew, and whether dry, cold, moist, or hot;°
He knew their seat, their humor and condition.
He was a perfect practicing physician.
These causes being known for what they were,
He gave the man his medicine then and there.
435 All his apothecaries° in a tribe
Were ready with the drugs he would prescribe
And each made money from the other's guile;
They had been friendly for a goodish while.
He was well-versed in Aesculapius° too
440 And what Hippocrates and Rufus knew
And Dioscorides, now dead and gone,
Galen and Rhazes, Hali, Serapion,

Vocabulary
guile (gīl) *n.*: sly dealings; skill in deceiving.

 **408–410.** Read these lines carefully. What does "sent his prisoners home" actually mean? How does this fit in with the narrator's observation about the Skipper: "The nicer rules of conscience he ignored"?

The Physician, from the Ellesmere manuscript.
Fol. 133r. By permission of The Huntington Library, San Marino, California.

430. dry...hot: People of the time believed that one's physical and mental conditions were influenced by the balance of four major humors, or fluids, in the body—blood (hot and wet), yellow bile (hot and dry), phlegm (cold and wet), and black bile (cold and dry).
435. apothecaries: (ə·päth′ə·ker′ēz) *n. pl.*: pharmacists.
439. Aesculapius: in Greek and Roman mythology, the god of medicine. The names that follow were early Greek, Roman, Middle Eastern, and medieval medical authorities.

READING MINI-LESSON

Developing Word-Attack Skills
Write the selection words *sanguine* and *guile* on the board, and compare the sounds represented by *gu* in each word. Point out that in *sanguine* the *u* has the consonant sound /w/ (saŋ′gwin), whereas in *guile* the *u* is silent (gīl). Then, compare the sound of *u* in *squire* and *liquor*, pointing out that *u* has the sound /w/ in *squire* (skwīr) but is silent in *liquor* (lik′ər).

Activity. Have students assign the label *s* to words in which the *u* is silent and the label *w* to words in which it stands for /w/.

quay [s]   roguish [s]   guardian [s]
unrequited [w]   beguile [s]   guava [w]
antique [s]   disguise [s]   bequeath [w]
marquee [s]   guild [s]   linguistics [w]
guacamole [w]   antiquated [w]   query [w]

Averroes, Avicenna, Constantine,
Scotch Bernard, John of Gaddesden, Gilbertine.
445 In his own diet he observed some measure;
There were no superfluities° for pleasure,
Only digestives, nutritives and such.
He did not read the Bible very much.
In blood-red garments, slashed with bluish gray
450 And lined with taffeta, he rode his way;
Yet he was rather close as to expenses
And kept the gold he won in pestilences.
Gold stimulates the heart, or so we're told.
He therefore had a special love of gold.

446. **superfluities:** (sōō′pər·flōō′ə·tēz) *n. pl.:* excesses.

451–454. How did the Doctor get his gold?

The Wife of Bath

455   A worthy *woman* from beside *Bath* city
Was with us, somewhat deaf, which was a pity.
In making cloth she showed so great a bent
She bettered those of Ypres and of Ghent.°
In all the parish not a dame dared stir
460 Towards the altar steps in front of her,
And if indeed they did, so wrath was she
As to be quite put out of charity.
Her kerchiefs were of finely woven ground;°
I dared have sworn they weighed a good ten pound,
465 The ones she wore on Sunday, on her head.
Her hose were of the finest scarlet red
And gartered tight; her shoes were soft and new.
Bold was her face, handsome, and red in hue.
A worthy woman all her life, what's more
470 She'd had five husbands, all at the church door,
Apart from other company in youth;
No need just now to speak of that, forsooth.
And she had thrice been to Jerusalem,
Seen many strange rivers and passed over them;
475 She'd been to Rome and also to Boulogne,
St. James of Compostella and Cologne,
And she was skilled in wandering by the way.
She had gap-teeth,° set widely, truth to say.
Easily on an ambling horse she sat
480 Well wimpled° up, and on her head a hat
As broad as is a buckler or a shield;
She had a flowing mantle that concealed
Large hips, her heels spurred sharply under that.
In company she liked to laugh and chat
485 And knew the remedies for love's mischances,
An art in which she knew the oldest dances.

458. **Ypres** (ē′pr′) **and of Ghent:** Flemish centers of the wool trade.

463. **ground** *n.:* type of cloth.

455–486. Does the Wife of Bath remind you of any comic female stereotypes? Explain.

478. **gap-teeth:** In Chaucer's time, gap-teeth on a woman were considered a sign of boldness and were said to indicate an aptitude for love and travel.
480. **wimpled** *adj.:* A wimple is a linen covering for the head and neck.

Geoffrey Chaucer 133

DIRECT TEACHING

A Literary Focus
Characterization. As students read this portrait, encourage them to note the many details the narrator uses to present the Parson in idealized terms, as he did the Knight.

B Content-Area Connections
History: The Medieval Church
Unlike other priests, the Parson doesn't threaten to excommunicate parishioners who haven't paid their tithes—taxes owed to the Church consisting of one tenth of their income.

C Reading Skills
? Monitoring comprehension.
Line 507 means that he practiced what he preached. "This figure" means a figure of speech. How would you explain the Parson's metaphor in ll. 510–512? [Possible response: He is comparing a priest to gold (a pure metal) and "a common man" to iron (a baser metal that rusts easily). In other words, he is asking, "If a priest does not set a good example, how can his parishioners be expected to act virtuously?"]

D Content-Area Connections
History: The Medieval Church
E. T. Donaldson explains that the plague "so depopulated the country that many rural parishes could no longer support their priests. As a result, priests often rented their parishes to vicars even needier than themselves and migrated to the larger cities where money was still to be had."

Response to Margin Question
Lines 487–538. Unlike the Monk and the Friar, the Parson is honest, poor, learned, and dedicated to serving God and his parishioners.

The Parson

A holy-minded man of good renown
There was, and poor, the *Parson* to a town,
Yet he was rich in holy thought and work.
490 He also was a learned man, a clerk,
Who truly knew Christ's gospel and would preach it
Devoutly to parishioners, and teach it.
Benign and wonderfully diligent,
And patient when adversity was sent
495 (For so he proved in much adversity)
He hated cursing to extort a fee,
Nay rather he preferred beyond a doubt
Giving to poor parishioners round about
Both from church offerings and his property;
500 He could in little find sufficiency.
Wide was his parish, with houses far asunder,
Yet he neglected not in rain or thunder,
In sickness or in grief, to pay a call
On the remotest, whether great or small,
505 Upon his feet, and in his hand a stave.°
This noble example to his sheep° he gave
That first he wrought, and afterward he taught;
And it was from the Gospel he had caught
Those words, and he would add this figure too,
510 That if gold rust, what then will iron do?
For if a priest be foul in whom we trust
No wonder that a common man should rust;
And shame it is to see—let priests take stock—
A shitten shepherd and a snowy flock.
515 The true example that a priest should give
Is one of cleanness, how the sheep should live.
He did not set his benefice to hire°
And leave his sheep encumbered in the mire
Or run to London to earn easy bread
520 By singing masses for the wealthy dead,
Or find some Brotherhood and get enrolled.°
He stayed at home and watched over his fold
So that no wolf should make the sheep miscarry.
He was a shepherd and no mercenary.°
525 Holy and virtuous he was, but then
Never contemptuous of sinful men,
Never disdainful, never too proud or fine,
But was discreet in teaching and benign.
His business was to show a fair behavior
530 And draw men thus to Heaven and their Savior,

The Parson, from the Ellesmere manuscript.
Fol. 206v. By permission of The Huntington Library, San Marino, California.

505. stave *n.*: staff.
506. sheep *n. pl.*: his parishioners.

? 487–538. Contrast the Parson with the Monk and Friar described earlier. Which of the three characters does the narrator present as a true man of God?

517. He . . . benefice to hire: He did not hire someone else to perform his duties.

521. find . . . enrolled: He did not take a job as a paid chaplain to a guild.

524. mercenary *n.*: someone who will agree to do anything for money.

134 Collection 2 The Middle Ages

Literary Criticism

Critic's Commentary: Chaucer Stops Winking
Explaining the role of the naive narrator, David Williams says that the irony we perceive "is produced by a kind of flash of communication we get with Chaucer the Author over the head of Pilgrim Chaucer. The author catches our eye, so to speak, and winks." But when the narrator describes the Parson, that irony disappears: "In contrast to the corrupt Monk, . . . the Parson . . . is the epitome of simple virtue, a credit to his profession and a witness to man's moral perfectibility. The Narrator lists his virtues with an unusual reverence, and the complete absence of irony suggests that for once, at least, Pilgrim Chaucer and Chaucer the Author see things in exactly the same way."

Unless indeed a man were obstinate;
And such, whether of high or low estate,°
He put to sharp rebuke, to say the least.
I think there never was a better priest.
535 He sought no pomp or glory in his dealings,
No scrupulosity had spiced his feelings.
Christ and His Twelve Apostles and their lore
He taught, but followed it himself before.

The Plowman

There was a *Plowman* with him there, his brother;
540 Many a load of dung one time or other
He must have carted through the morning dew.
He was an honest worker, good and true,
Living in peace and perfect charity,
And, as the gospel bade him, so did he,
545 Loving God best with all his heart and mind
And then his neighbor as himself, repined
At no misfortune, slacked for no content,
For steadily about his work he went
To thrash his corn, to dig or to manure
550 Or make a ditch; and he would help the poor
For love of Christ and never take a penny
If he could help it, and, as prompt as any,
He paid his tithes in full when they were due
On what he owned, and on his earnings too.
555 He wore a tabard smock° and rode a mare.
    There was a *Reeve*,° also a *Miller*, there,
A College *Manciple*° from the Inns of Court,
A papal *Pardoner*° and, in close consort,
A Church-Court *Summoner*,° riding at a trot,
560 And finally myself—that was the lot.

The Miller

The *Miller* was a chap of sixteen stone,°
A great stout fellow big in brawn and bone.
He did well out of them, for he could go
And win the ram at any wrestling show.
565 Broad, knotty, and short-shouldered, he would boast
He could heave any door off hinge and post,
Or take a run and break it with his head.
His beard, like any sow or fox, was red
And broad as well, as though it were a spade;

Vocabulary
obstinate (äb′stə·nət) *adj.*: unreasonably stubborn.

---

532. **estate** *n.*: rank; social standing.

The Miller, from the Ellesmere manuscript.
Fol. 34v. By permission of The Huntington Library, San Marino, California.

539–555. *How is the Plowman like his brother, the Parson? How can you tell that the narrator approves of him?*

555. **tabard** (tab′ərd) **smock:** short jacket.
556. **Reeve:** serf who was the steward of a manor. A reeve saw that the estate's work was done and that everything was accounted for.
557. **Manciple** (man′sə·pəl): minor employee whose principal duty was to purchase provisions for a college or law firm.
558. **Pardoner:** minor member of the Church who bought and sold pardons for sinners.
559. **Summoner:** low-ranking officer who summoned people to appear in church court.
561. **sixteen stone:** 224 pounds.

DIRECT TEACHING

D Reading Skills
Interpreting. The Parson leads by example and is compassionate rather than disdainful toward sinners. But when someone stubbornly persists in wrongdoing, the Parson is not afraid to speak his mind, even if that person is highborn and powerful.

E Content-Area Connections
Literature: Poetic Influences Chaucer's idealized Plowman may owe something to another fourteenth-century poem. In William Langland's *Piers Plowman,* the hero is portrayed as an instrument of salvation for his community.

F Literary Focus
Allusion. These lines are an allusion to the Bible: "And thou shalt love the Lord thy God with all thine heart, and with all thy soul, and with all thy might" (Deut. 6:5) and "thou shalt love thy neighbor as thyself" (Lev. 19:18). Jesus cites these as the two greatest commandments of all (Mark 12:28–31; Matt. 22:37–40).

Response to Margin Question
Lines 539–555. They are both poor, hardworking, honest, pious, and devoted to helping their neighbors. The narrator makes no disparaging or ironic remarks about him.

Geoffrey Chaucer   135

CONTENT-AREA CONNECTIONS

History: The Peasants' Revolt

In June 1381, six years before Chaucer began writing *The Canterbury Tales,* a mob of angry peasants descended on London to demand improvements in their lives. According to F. E. Halliday, "The underlying causes [of the Peasants' Revolt] were serfdom and low wages, but the immediate cause was a poll-tax that fell more heavily on the poor than the rich." The rebellion was put down, with fourteen-year-old King Richard II promising to abolish serfdom and redress the peasants' grievances. But when the rebellion was over, the government reneged on the king's promises. "Thousands of rebels were executed, and a period of savage repression followed."

Chaucer must have been an eyewitness to the rioting, because he was in London the week it took place. According to John Gardner, he must have hated the revolt because he "believed in degree, acceptance of duties, submission to authority, convinced to the soles of his feet that if authority became corrupt—as he knew it was during most of his life—it was not the business of peasants to correct things but the business of authority to correct itself."

DIRECT TEACHING

A Content-Area Connections
History: The Miller
A miller's fee was a percentage of the grain he ground for the customer. Thus, if he increased the weight of the grain, he increased his fee. Here Chaucer seems to be playing on the medieval proverb "An honest miller has a golden thumb."

B Reading Skills
Monitoring comprehension. Make sure students understand that the Manciple is actually cheating the lawyers he works for. He "watches the market" not so that he can keep down his employers' expenses but so that he can pocket the savings on bargains.

C Vocabulary Development
Multiple meanings. Here the word *peer* is a noun meaning "English nobleman." (A *peer of the realm* is a peer who is a member of the House of Lords.) To "live on what he had" means to live on his income, which many nobles had a hard time doing.

Response to Margin Question
Lines 568–575. No. He is compared to a sow or fox, a spade, an old sow's ear, and a furnace door. These comparisons suggest that he is wily, uncouth, dirty, brutish, and fierce.

The Manciple, from the Ellesmere manuscript.
Fol. 203r. By permission of The Huntington Library, San Marino, California.

The Reeve, from the Ellesmere manuscript.
Fol. 42r. By permission of The Huntington Library, San Marino, California.

570 And, at its very tip, his nose displayed
　　　A wart on which there stood a tuft of hair
　　　Red as the bristles in an old sow's ear.
　　　His nostrils were as black as they were wide.
　　　He had a sword and buckler at his side,
575　His mighty mouth was like a furnace door.
　　　A wrangler and buffoon, he had a store
　　　Of tavern stories, filthy in the main.
　　　His was a master-hand at stealing grain.
　　　He felt it with his thumb and thus he knew
580　Its quality and took three times his due—
　　　A thumb of gold, by God, to gauge an oat!°
　　　He wore a hood of blue and a white coat.
　　　He liked to play his bagpipes up and down
　　　And that was how he brought us out of town.

The Manciple

585　The *Manciple* came from the Inner Temple;°
　　　All caterers might follow his example
　　　In buying victuals; he was never rash
　　　Whether he bought on credit or paid cash.
　　　He used to watch the market most precisely
590　And got in first, and so he did quite nicely.
　　　Now isn't it a marvel of God's grace
　　　That an illiterate fellow can outpace
　　　The wisdom of a heap of learned men?
　　　His masters—he had more than thirty then—
595　All versed in the abstrusest° legal knowledge,
　　　Could have produced a dozen from their College
　　　Fit to be stewards in land and rents and game
　　　To any Peer in England you could name,
　　　And show him how to live on what he had

568–575. Are any of the comparisons that the narrator makes flattering to the character of the Miller? Explain.

581. thumb ... oat: In other words, he pressed on the scale with his thumb to increase the weight of the grain.

585. Inner Temple: one of the four legal societies in London comprising the Inns of Court. Only the Inns were permitted to license lawyers.

595. abstrusest (ab·strōōs′est) *adj.:* most complex; hardest to understand.

136　Collection 2　The Middle Ages

CONTENT-AREA CONNECTIONS

History: Shops, Shopkeepers, and Food
As a steward, or food buyer, for a society of lawyers, the Manciple would have frequented the local shops in London. These shops, which were really workshops, usually had a stall out front where goods were displayed. In most cases, merchants who sold the same type of goods clustered together onto streets called rows, as in Fishmongers' Row. Shopkeepers hung the symbol of their trade outside their store, but there were few written signs, since most customers couldn't read. As a food buyer, the Manciple would have shopped for venison, mutton, pork, or seafood (but not horsemeat, which was forbidden by the Church). Seafood included porpoise, whale, haddock, cod, lamprey, tuna, and eel. Popular vegetables were onions, peas, beans, and cabbage (but not tomatoes, potatoes, or corn, which were not imported from the Americas until the 1500s).

Small-group activity. Students interested in learning more about daily life in the Middle Ages might do one of the following projects:
- Research medieval trade symbols, and design shop signs displaying the symbols.
- Research the kinds of food eaten during the Middle Ages, and prepare a medieval feast.

600 Debt-free (unless of course the Peer were mad)
Or be as frugal as he might desire,
And make them fit to help about the Shire
In any legal case there was to try;
And yet this Manciple could wipe their eye.°

The Reeve

605   The *Reeve* was old and choleric° and thin;
His beard was shaven closely to the skin,
His shorn hair came abruptly to a stop
Above his ears, and he was docked° on top
Just like a priest in front; his legs were lean,
610 Like sticks they were, no calf was to be seen.
He kept his bins and garners° very trim;
No auditor could gain a point on him.
And he could judge by watching drought and rain
The yield he might expect from seed and grain.
615 His master's sheep, his animals and hens,
Pigs, horses, dairies, stores, and cattle-pens
Were wholly trusted to his government.
He had been under contract to present
The accounts, right from his master's earliest years.
620 No one had ever caught him in arrears.°
No bailiff,° serf, or herdsman dared to kick,
He knew their dodges, knew their every trick;
Feared like the plague he was, by those beneath.
He had a lovely dwelling on a heath,
625 Shadowed in green by trees above the sward.°
A better hand at bargains than his lord,
He had grown rich and had a store of treasure
Well tucked away, yet out it came to pleasure
His lord with subtle loans or gifts of goods,
630 To earn his thanks and even coats and hoods.
When young he'd learnt a useful trade and still
He was a carpenter of first-rate skill.
The stallion-cob° he rode at a slow trot
Was dapple-gray and bore the name of Scot.
635 He wore an overcoat of bluish shade
And rather long; he had a rusty blade
Slung at his side. He came, as I heard tell,
From Norfolk, near a place called Baldeswell.
His coat was tucked under his belt and splayed.
640 He rode the hindmost of our cavalcade.

604. **wipe their eye:** outdo them. This medieval idiom means something like "steal their thunder" or "show them up."
605. **choleric** (käl′ər·ik) *adj.:* having too much choler, or yellow bile, and thus (supposedly) bad-tempered.
608. **docked** *adj.:* clipped short.

611. **garners** *n. pl.:* granaries.

620. **in arrears:** behind schedule in paying back debts.
621. **bailiff** *n.:* here, farm manager.

625. **sward** (swôrd) *n.:* lawn.

633. **stallion-cob:** stocky male riding horse.

Vocabulary
frugal (frōō′gəl) *adj.:* thrifty; careful with money.

DIRECT TEACHING

A Reading Skills

Analyzing key details. The children are afraid of the Summoner because of his appearance—but perhaps also because of his job (see "Content-Area Connections" below). Some critics have suggested that the Summoner's skin problems result from venereal disease; others have suggested that they are caused by what he eats and drinks.

B Reading Skills

? Monitoring comprehension. The Summoner knows only a few Latin phrases. How would you explain the metaphor in ll. 662–663? [Possible response: The Summoner's wits, or mind, are being compared to a bag. The metaphor is saying that if you looked inside his mind, trying to find more knowledge of Latin, you'd find it empty.]

C Reading Skills

Monitoring comprehension. A concubine is a mistress, and adultery was grounds for excommunication. The Summoner is running a protection racket, extorting bribes from those he allows to keep mistresses and blackmailing those he discovers committing the offense. The narrator says that he's kind because his bribes are so reasonable—a mere quart of wine.

Response to Margin Question

Lines 641–666. His physical appearance is disgusting, and so is his character. The boils and pimples on his face symbolize his inner corruption and moral decay, which can't be cleaned up or cured. Lines 665–666 are ironic because the Summoner is clearly neither noble nor kind.

The Summoner

> There was a *Summoner*° with us at that Inn,
> His face on fire, like a cherubim,°
> For he had carbuncles.° His eyes were narrow,
> He was as hot and lecherous as a sparrow.
> 645 Black scabby brows he had, and a thin beard.
> Children were afraid when he appeared.
> No quicksilver, lead ointment, tartar creams,
> No brimstone, no boracic, so it seems,
> Could make a salve that had the power to bite,
> 650 Clean up, or cure his whelks° of knobby white
> Or purge the pimples sitting on his cheeks.
> Garlic he loved, and onions too, and leeks,
> And drinking strong red wine till all was hazy.
> Then he would shout and jabber as if crazy,
> 655 And wouldn't speak a word except in Latin
> When he was drunk, such tags as he was pat in;
> He only had a few, say two or three,
> That he had mugged up out of some decree;
> No wonder, for he heard them every day.
> 660 And, as you know, a man can teach a jay°
> To call out "Walter" better than the Pope.
> But had you tried to test his wits and grope
> For more, you'd have found nothing in the bag.
> Then "*Questio quid juris*"° was his tag.
> 665 He was a noble varlet° and a kind one,
> You'd meet none better if you went to find one.
> Why, he'd allow—just for a quart of wine—
> Any good lad to keep a concubine
> A twelvemonth and dispense him altogether!
> 670 And he had finches of his own to feather:°
> And if he found some rascal with a maid
> He would instruct him not to be afraid
> In such a case of the Archdeacon's curse
> (Unless the rascal's soul were in his purse)
> 675 For in his purse the punishment should be.
> "Purse is the good Archdeacon's Hell," said he.
> But well I know he lied in what he said;
> A curse should put a guilty man in dread,
> For curses kill, as shriving brings, salvation.
> 680 We should beware of excommunication.
> Thus, as he pleased, the man could bring duress
> On any young fellow in the diocese.

Vocabulary

duress (doo·res′) *n.*: pressure.

---

641. Summoner: A summoner delivers summonses that call people to appear in church courts.
642. cherubim *n.*: in medieval art, a little angel with a rosy face.
643. carbuncles (kär′bun·kəlz) *n. pl.*: pus-filled skin inflammations, something like boils.

650. whelks *n. pl.*: pus-filled sores.

? 641–666. How does the Summoner's physical appearance (lines 642–651) match his inner character? How do you know that Chaucer is being ironic in lines 665–666?

660. jay *n.*: type of bird.

664. *Questio quid juris* (kwest′ē·ō kwid yoo′ris): Latin for "I ask what point of the law [applies]." The Summoner uses this phrase to stall and dodge the issue.
665. varlet (vär′lit) *n.*: scoundrel.

670. finches . . . feather: a maxim that means roughly the same as "feathering one's nest"—taking care of one's own interests.

The Summoner, from the Ellesmere manuscript.
Fol. 81r. The Huntington Library, San Marino, CA.

CONTENT-AREA CONNECTIONS

History: Civil and Ecclesiastical Law

In Europe during the Middle Ages, there were two types of courts: civil (administered by the government) and ecclesiastical (administered by the Church). The Summoner works for the ecclesiastical court, whose jurisdiction included not only offenses against the Church (such as failure to pay one's tithe) but also moral offenses (such as adultery). By Chaucer's time the local summoner had become a dreaded figure; not only did he serve summonses (like modern subpoenas) requiring the accused to appear in court, he also spied on people and then blackmailed them by threatening to report their offenses to the archdeacon, who presided over the ecclesiastical court. Summoners were also widely believed to extort money from the innocent by threatening them with false charges.

The Pardoner, from the Ellesmere manuscript.
Fol. 138r. By permission of The Huntington Library,
San Marino, California.

He knew their secrets, they did what he said.
He wore a garland set upon his head
685 Large as the holly-bush upon a stake
Outside an ale-house, and he had a cake,
A round one, which it was his joke to wield
As if it were intended for a shield.

The Pardoner

He and a gentle *Pardoner* rode together,
690 A bird from Charing Cross of the same feather,
Just back from visiting the Court of Rome.
He loudly sang *"Come hither, love, come home!"*
The Summoner sang deep seconds° to this song,
No trumpet ever sounded half so strong.
695 This Pardoner had hair as yellow as wax,
Hanging down smoothly like a hank of flax.
In driblets fell his locks behind his head
Down to his shoulders which they overspread;
Thinly they fell, like rat-tails, one by one.
700 He wore no hood upon his head, for fun;
The hood inside his wallet had been stowed,
He aimed at riding in the latest mode;
But for a little cap his head was bare
And he had bulging eye-balls, like a hare.
705 He'd sewed a holy relic° on his cap;
His wallet lay before him on his lap,
Brimful of pardons° come from Rome, all hot.
He had the same small voice a goat has got.
His chin no beard had harbored, nor would harbor,
710 Smoother than ever chin was left by barber.
I judge he was a gelding, or a mare.
As to his trade, from Berwick down to Ware
There was no pardoner of equal grace,
For in his trunk he had a pillow-case
715 Which he asserted was Our Lady's veil.
He said he had a gobbet° of the sail
Saint Peter had the time when he made bold
To walk the waves, till Jesu Christ took hold.
He had a cross of metal set with stones
720 And, in a glass, a rubble of pigs' bones.
And with these relics, any time he found
Some poor up-country parson to astound,
In one short day, in money down, he drew

693. deep seconds: harmonies.

A Pardoner dispensed pardons granted by the pope.
689–704. How do such details as "driblets," "like rat-tails," "yellow as wax," and "bulging eye-balls, like a hare" affect the way you feel about this man?

705. relic *n.*: remains of a saint.

707. pardons *n. pl.*: small strips of parchment with papal seals attached. They were sold as indulgences (pardons for sins), with the proceeds supposedly going to a religious house.

716. gobbet *n.*: fragment.

714–734. These lines depict the Pardoner as a scam artist. Why do people fall for his tricks?

Geoffrey Chaucer   139

CONTENT-AREA CONNECTIONS

Religion: Relics

Relics are body parts or other objects associated with a saint or other holy figure or event. Saying a prayer while holding a relic was thought to bring an indulgence, or respite from the suffering a person would have to undergo in Purgatory before reaching Heaven. Relics were highly valued in medieval society, not only by pilgrims but also by the churches and shrines where they were kept. Sometimes one church would steal relics from another in hopes of attracting more pilgrims. Once a pilgrim reached a holy site, he or she would try to buy a relic to bring home (like a souvenir). Relics owned by laypeople were usually kept in reliquaries in the form of necklaces or rings. Many relics were fake—like the pigs' bones the Pardoner is passing off as a saint's bones—yet they were easy to sell to credulous people.

DIRECT TEACHING

D Content-Area Connections

History: Medieval Taverns
The sign for a tavern was a garland of holly hanging from a pole that stuck out from the front of the building.

E English-Language Learners

Idioms. Explain that the expression "birds of a feather" refers to people who have a lot in common (from the saying "Birds of a feather flock together"). Ask students to predict what the Summoner and the Pardoner have in common. [Possible response: They may both be corrupt and dishonest.]

F Content-Area Connections

Religion: Relics
The Middle English identifies this relic as a Veronica—a handkerchief belonging to Saint Veronica, said to show the image of Jesus's face because she had wiped his brow with it while he carried the cross.

G Reading Skills

Making inferences. A gelding is a neutered horse. The narrator is hinting that the Pardoner is a eunuch.

Responses to Margin Questions

Lines 689–704. These are all unappealing images that make him seem unwholesome and repugnant.

Lines 714–734. They fall for his tricks because, like many con artists, he is an eloquent, charismatic speaker with a gift for telling a story.

Direct Teaching

A Reading Skills

? Making inferences. How does the narrator imply that the Pardoner's relics are fake? [Possible response: The word "asserted" in l. 715 on p. 139 suggests that he doubts the Pardoner's claim about the pillow-case. He directly states that the glass contains pigs' (not saint's) bones. He says the Pardoner "made monkeys" of the priest and congregation.]

B Reading Skills

Recognizing organizational patterns. The narrator now takes us back to the Tabard Inn and goes on to explain how he will organize the rest of his narrative.

C Literary Focus

? Naive narrator. Here the narrator clearly assumes the stance of the naive witness and reporter. First he apologizes for the candor he is about to show in reporting the sometimes bawdy content of the pilgrims' tales. Then he offers the excuse that he is "short of wit." What does Chaucer gain by using the device of the naive narrator? [Possible response: It adds humor and irony when the narrator admires pilgrims the reader sees as unworthy. It also allows the poet to say what he wants without being held accountable.]

Responses to Margin Questions

Lines 740–744. He will report on the rest of the pilgrimage as it happened, that is, chronologically.

Lines 745–766. He is apologizing for being about to speak frankly, relating everything the pilgrims said and did, even if their words were offensive.

A (725)
More than the parson in a month or two,
And by his flatteries and prevarication°
Made monkeys of the priest and congregation.
But still to do him justice first and last
In church he was a noble ecclesiast.°
How well he read a lesson or told a story!
(730) But best of all he sang an Offertory,°
For well he knew that when that song was sung
He'd have to preach and tune his honey-tongue
And (well he could) win silver from the crowd.
That's why he sang so merrily and loud.

B (735)
  Now I have told you shortly, in a clause,
The rank, the array, the number, and the cause
Of our assembly in this company
In Southwark, at that high-class hostelry
Known as *The Tabard*, close beside *The Bell*.
(740) And now the time has come for me to tell
How we behaved that evening; I'll begin
After we had alighted at the Inn,
Then I'll report our journey, stage by stage,
All the remainder of our pilgrimage.
(745) But first I beg of you, in courtesy,
Not to condemn me as unmannerly
If I speak plainly and with no concealings
And give account of all their words and dealings,
Using their very phrases as they fell.
(750) For certainly, as you all know so well,
He who repeats a tale after a man
Is bound to say, as nearly as he can,
Each single word, if he remembers it,
However rudely spoken or unfit,
(755) Or else the tale he tells will be untrue,
The things pretended and the phrases new.
He may not flinch although it were his brother,
He may as well say one word as another.
And Christ Himself spoke broad in Holy Writ,
(760) Yet there is no scurrility° in it,
And Plato says, for those with power to read,
"The word should be as cousin to the deed."
Further I beg you to forgive it me

C
If I neglect the order and degree
(765) And what is due to rank in what I've planned.
I'm short of wit as you will understand.

725. prevarication (pri·var′i·kā′shən) *n.*: telling lies.

728. ecclesiast (e·klē′zē·ast) *n.*: practitioner of church ritual.

730. Offertory *n.*: hymn sung while offerings are collected in church.

? 740–744. How will the narrator organize the rest of his narrative?

? 745–766. What is the narrator apologizing for in advance?

760. scurrility (skə·ril′ə·tē) *n.*: indecency.

Literary Criticism

Critic's Commentary: An Archetypal Figure

The critic Donald R. Howard argues that "Chaucer points up the Pardoner's evil trickery—his false relics, his preaching for gain—but reminds us that he was a brilliant orator, an actor, an evil genius with an artist's gifts and instincts. We are meant to be overwhelmed by the cleverness of his oratory and the fascination of his tale, are meant to be amused by his candor in admitting that he preaches only for gain, that his relics are counterfeits, that he can make people repent though he cares nothing for their souls. We are meant to be horrified at the extent of his evil—horrified and fascinated. . . . The Pardoner is an archetypal figure, one of those figures we encounter in our dreams . . . whose evil reveals to us, like a mirror, the evil in ourselves and warns us of its punishment."

The Host

Our *Host* gave us great welcome; everyone
Was given a place and supper was begun.
He served the finest victuals you could think,
770 The wine was strong and we were glad to drink.
A very striking man our Host withal,
And fit to be a marshal in a hall.
His eyes were bright, his girth a little wide;
There is no finer burgess in Cheapside.°
775 Bold in his speech, yet wise and full of tact,
There was no manly attribute he lacked,
What's more he was a merry-hearted man.
After our meal he jokingly began
To talk of sport, and, among other things
780 After we'd settled up our reckonings,
He said as follows: "Truly, gentlemen,
You're very welcome and I can't think when
—Upon my word I'm telling you no lie—
I've seen a gathering here that looked so spry,
785 No, not this year, as in this tavern now.
I'd think you up some fun if I knew how.
And, as it happens, a thought has just occurred
To please you, costing nothing, on my word.
You're off to Canterbury—well, God speed!
790 Blessed St. Thomas answer to your need!
And I don't doubt, before the journey's done
You mean to while the time in tales and fun.
Indeed, there's little pleasure for your bones
Riding along and all as dumb as stones.
795 So let me then propose for your enjoyment,
Just as I said, a suitable employment.
And if my notion suits and you agree
And promise to submit yourselves to me
Playing your parts exactly as I say
800 Tomorrow as you ride along the way,
Then by my father's soul (and he is dead)
If you don't like it you can have my head!
Hold up your hands, and not another word."
   Well, our opinion was not long deferred,
805 It seemed not worth a serious debate;
We all agreed to it at any rate
And bade him issue what commands he would.
"My lords," he said, "now listen for your good,
And please don't treat my notion with disdain.
810 This is the point. I'll make it short and plain.
Each one of you shall help to make things slip
By telling two stories on the outward trip

774. **Cheapside:** district of medieval London.

771–779. What do you learn about the Host in these lines? How do you think the narrator feels about the Host?

781–803. What do words like *fun* (line 786), *pleasure* (line 793), and *enjoyment* (line 795) suggest about the Host's character?

Geoffrey Chaucer 141

Direct Teaching

A Literary Focus

Frame story. Although the Host has declared himself the judge of the storytelling contest, in reality it is the reader who will judge. Now that we have met all the pilgrims and begun to make judgments about them (on the basis of the narrator's portraits), we are ready to listen to their tales.

Guided Practice

Monitoring students' progress. Guide the class in answering these comprehension questions.

Short Answer

1. Where are the pilgrims traveling from, and where are they headed? [from Southwark, just outside London, to Canterbury]
2. What month of the year is it? [April]
3. Which of the pilgrims described by the narrator are women? [the Prioress and the Wife of Bath]
4. Which pilgrims are father and son? [the Knight and the Squire]
5. Which pilgrims are brothers? [the Parson and the Plowman]

Response to Margin Question

Lines 811–829. The Host will choose the best tale—the most enjoyable and morally instructive one—and the prize will be a free supper at the tavern, paid for by all the other pilgrims. Anyone who refuses to tell a tale will have to pay the entire cost of the journey.

  To Canterbury, that's what I intend,
  And, on the homeward way to journey's end
815 Another two, tales from the days of old;
  And then the man whose story is best told,
  That is to say who gives the fullest measure
  Of good morality and general pleasure,
  He shall be given a supper, paid by all,
820 Here in this tavern, in this very hall,
  When we come back again from Canterbury.
  And in the hope to keep you bright and merry
  I'll go along with you myself and ride
  All at my own expense and serve as guide.
825 I'll be the judge, and those who won't obey
  Shall pay for what we spend upon the way.
  Now if you all agree to what you've heard
  Tell me at once without another word,
  And I will make arrangements early for it."
830   Of course we all agreed, in fact we swore it
  Delightedly, and made entreaty° too
  That he should act as he proposed to do,
  Become our Governor in short, and be
  Judge of our tales and general referee,
835 And set the supper at a certain price.
  We promised to be ruled by his advice
  Come high, come low; unanimously thus
  We set him up in judgment over us.
  More wine was fetched, the business being done;
840 We drank it off and up went everyone
  To bed without a moment of delay.
   Early next morning at the spring of day
  Up rose our Host and roused us like a cock,
  Gathering us together in a flock,
845 And off we rode at slightly faster pace
  Than walking to St. Thomas' watering-place;
  And there our Host drew up, began to ease
  His horse, and said, "Now, listen if you please,
  My lords! Remember what you promised me.
850 If evensong and matins will agree°
  Let's see who shall be first to tell a tale.
  And as I hope to drink good wine and ale
  I'll be your judge. The rebel who disobeys,
  However much the journey costs, he pays.
855 Now draw for cut° and then we can depart;
  The man who draws the shortest cut shall start."

811–829. Summarize the rules the Host proposes for the storytelling competition. What's the prize? Who will be the judge?

825. By "those who won't obey," the Host means those who won't play the game of telling a story when it's their turn. Lines 853–854 further clarify their penalty: Those who won't obey must pay the cost of the entire journey.

831. entreaty *n.:* urgent request.

850. If . . . agree: in other words, if you feel the same way in the evening (at evensong, or evening prayers) as you do in the morning (at matins, or morning prayers).
855. draw for cut: in other words, draw straws.

Response and Analysis

Reading Check

1. When do people "long to go on pilgrimages"?
2. Where is the narrator at the very beginning of the Prologue? Who joins him, and for what purpose?
3. Place each pilgrim within one of these three groups that comprised medieval society: the feudal system (related to the land), the Church, and the city (merchants and professionals).
4. What plan (which becomes the basis of the **frame story**) does the Host propose to the pilgrims? How do the pilgrims respond to his proposal?

Thinking Critically

5. Chaucer is a master at using physical details—eyes, hair, complexion, body type, clothing—to reveal **character.** Describe at least three pilgrims whose inner natures are revealed by their appearance. Refer to your reading notes for help.
6. Clearly Chaucer **satirizes** the Church of his time. Show how this is true by analyzing two characters connected with the Church. What "good," or honorable, Church people does Chaucer include to balance his satire?
7. What aspects of medieval society does Chaucer **satirize** in his portrayals of the Merchant? of the Franklin? of the Doctor? of the Miller?
8. Which pilgrims do you think Chaucer idealizes?
9. In describing the pilgrims, what has Chaucer as the pilgrim-narrator revealed about his own personality, biases, and values?
10. Which of the pilgrims' professions or trades have survived and exist in society today? Which of Chaucer's character types can be seen today in airports, on pulpits, on farms, in classrooms, on city streets, or in small towns?

WRITING

A Frame Story

Write your own prologue to a modern frame story. Set your frame story in an airport or a bus station where people are waiting or on a tour or a pilgrimage like the ones described in the Closer Look on page 128. Or you might choose to establish your frame by using people stranded by a storm or waiting for rescue from an accident. You will have to decide who your narrator will be and who the travelers will be and what their professions are. Model your prologue on Chaucer's, and describe your travelers in such a way that their inner natures are revealed.

INTERNET
Projects and Activities
Keyword: LE5 12-2

Pages 143–144 cover

Literary Skills
Analyze characterization.
Analyze characteristics of a frame story.
Analyze imagery in characterization.

Reading Skills
Analyze style using key details.

Writing Skills
Write a prologue to a modern frame story.

Vocabulary Skills
Create semantic maps with antonyms.

Figure thought to be Chaucer; from the Ellesmere manuscript.
Fol. 153v. By permission of The Huntington Library, San Marino, California.

INDEPENDENT PRACTICE

Response and Analysis

Thinking Critically

5. One example is the Knight, whose stained tunic reveals his disregard for outward show. Other pilgrims with revealing physical details include the Squire, Prioress, Monk, Miller, Wife of Bath, Summoner, and Pardoner.
6. Students could analyze the satiric descriptions of the Prioress, Monk, Friar, Summoner, and Pardoner. Chaucer presents the Oxford Cleric and the Parson as good.
7. Merchant—self-important hypocrites; Franklin—the gentry's excessive devotion to pleasure; Doctor—the greed (and perhaps ignorance) of those in the profession; Miller—dishonest businesspeople.
8. He idealizes the Knight, Oxford Cleric, Parson, and Plowman.
9. As pilgrim-narrator, Chaucer portrays himself as good-natured and somewhat impressionable (he seemingly admires characters whom we see as unworthy). He values honesty, modesty, simplicity, indifference to money, and genuine piety. He condemns cheating and fraud, yet he doesn't always seem to recognize it.
10. Surviving occupations include nun, priest, monk, merchant, lawyer, doctor, merchant, cook, and ship's captain. Examples of all of Chaucer's character types—rogues, hypocrites, gallant soldiers, status seekers, hedonists, devoted scholars—can still be found today.

Reading Check

1. They long to go on pilgrimages in April.
2. The narrator is at the Tabard, an inn. He is joined by twenty-nine other pilgrims, who are also on their way to Canterbury.
3. *Feudal system*—Knight, Squire, Yeoman, Franklin, Plowman, Reeve, Miller. *Church*—Prioress, Nun's Priests, Monk, Friar, Oxford Cleric, Parson, Summoner, Pardoner. *City*—Merchant, Sergeant at the Law, Guildsmen, Cook, Skipper, Doctor, Wife of Bath, Manciple, narrator (Chaucer).
4. The Host proposes that each pilgrim will tell two stories on the way to Canterbury and two on the way back. The pilgrims respond enthusiastically to this plan.

Vocabulary Development

Sample Answers

agility. Sentence with word—The Squire is young and active, possessing great strength and <u>agility</u>. Antonym—clumsiness. Sentence with antonym—Chaucer's poetry sounds natural, with none of the singsong <u>clumsiness</u> often found in rhyming couplets.

eminent. Sentence with word—The Sergeant at the Law is not as wise and <u>eminent</u> as he appears. Antonym—lowly. Sentence with antonym—The Friar prefers not to deal with those he considers <u>lowly</u>.

guile. Sentence with word—The Pardoner uses <u>guile</u> to get people to buy his relics. Antonym—innocence. Sentence with antonym—the <u>innocence</u> of Chaucer's narrator is mostly a literary device.

obstinate. Sentence with word—The Parson is compassionate toward sinners unless they are <u>obstinate</u> in refusing to change their ways. Antonym—flexible. Sentence with antonym—The Prioress is quite <u>flexible</u> in her idea of what constitutes appropriate behavior for a nun.

frugal. Sentence with word—The Knight is a <u>frugal</u> man who doesn't care for outward show. Antonym—extravagant. Sentence with antonym—The Prioress and the Monk are <u>extravagant</u> in their tastes.

duress. Sentence with word—Under <u>duress</u> the young men of the diocese pay the Summoner bribes to avoid punishment. Antonym—freedom. Sentence with antonym—Unlike the Wife of Bath, most medieval women did not have the <u>freedom</u> to go on pilgrimages.

Vocabulary Development

Antonym Map

agility   guile
eminent   obstinate
accrue   frugal
arbitrate   duress
benign

Create an antonym map like the one below for each Vocabulary word. First, choose an appropriate antonym for each word in the list. Then, write two sentences based on the Prologue or your responses to it. In the first sentence, use the Vocabulary word. In the second sentence, use the antonym you chose.

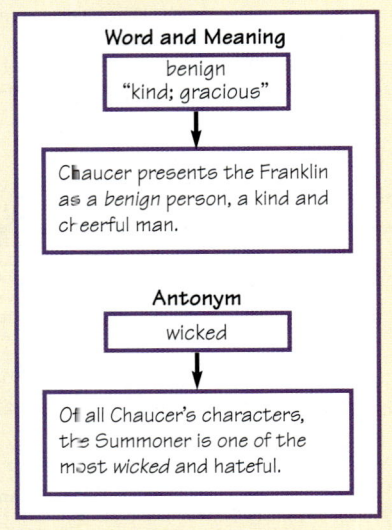

Literary Focus

Imagery and Character

Chaucer is a master of **imagery**, language that appeals to the senses. Most images are visual, but imagery can also appeal to our sense of hearing, smell, taste, or touch. In a few vivid words, sometimes using figures of speech, Chaucer creates a cast of characters as real to us as the characters in the latest novel—more real, perhaps, because Chaucer's pilgrims exhibit all the essentials of human nature.

Chaucer relies on his readers' knowledge of physiognomy. Based on some of Aristotle's treatises, physiognomy compares varieties of people with animals and asserts that certain physical characteristics reveal one's true character. Thus, when Chaucer's contemporaries read that the Wife of Bath had "gap-teeth, set widely, truth to say," they knew that the physiognomists believed that a gap between a woman's two front teeth indicated not only that she would travel far but also that she was bold and amorous.

Analyzing Chaucer's imagery. Below is a list of a few physical characteristics and their corresponding physiognomic interpretations. Choose a pilgrim who exhibits each characteristic. How does the physiognomic interpretation reinforce what you already know about the character's nature?

- ramlike appearance = strength
- flaring nostrils = anger
- foxlike appearance = slyness
- high forehead = intelligence
- infected sores = lechery

How do writers reveal character types today? In stories or movies, do any physical features automatically suggest something about character?

Literary Focus

Imagery and Character
Analyzing Chaucer's Imagery

- ramlike appearance = strength. The Miller is capable of great feats of strength.
- flaring nostrils = anger. The Miller is a brawler.
- foxlike appearance = slyness. The Miller steals grain.
- high forehead = intelligence. The Prioress has exaggerated manners and sensitivity.
- infected sores = lechery. The Summoner is described as "hot and lecherous."

Before You Read

from The Pardoner's Tale

Make the Connection

The story in "The Pardoner's Tale" has roots that are old and widespread. Greed as the root of evil is a theme that appears in stories the world over. Starting from the Latin saying *"Radix malorum est cupiditas"*—translated loosely as "The love of money is the root of all evil"—the Pardoner presents us with an **exemplum,** an anecdote that teaches a moral lesson. As in all the tales, Chaucer fits the story to the character of the storyteller. (You may wish to review the description of the Pardoner in lines 689–734 of the general Prologue.)

Literary Focus

Irony

Chaucer is a master of both verbal and situational irony. You use both types of irony yourself all the time. You use **verbal irony** when you say one thing but mean something else. When a friend asks how you liked spending three hours cleaning your room, you might answer, "It was just great." You both know that was not the case, of course. In **situational irony,** what actually happens is different from what you expect. Situational irony occurs when it rains on the weather forecasters' picnic or when the police officer's son robs the bank.

> **Irony** is a contrast or a discrepancy between expectations and reality—between what is said and what is meant, between what is expected and what happens, or between what appears to be true and what actually is true.
>
> *For more on Irony, see the Handbook of Literary and Historical Terms.*

Background

In the medieval Church, a pardoner was a member of the clergy who had been given power by the pope to forgive sins and grant indulgences. Even when their sins were forgiven in this earthly life, however, many believed that punishment for their sinful deeds awaited them in the next life. Indulgences could help alleviate this problem: They were promises made by the Church to reduce the length and severity of punishments due after death. Forgiving sins and granting indulgences were powers the Church gave the clergy for the spiritual benefit of believers. Such benefits were not supposed to be bought and sold, but greedy clergy sometimes took advantage of people's fear of punishment to demand money. Some, like Chaucer's Pardoner, went so far as to keep the money for themselves instead of turning it over to the Church.

Vocabulary Development

avarice (av′ə·ris) *n.*: too great a desire for wealth.

abominable (ə·bäm′ə·nə·bəl) *adj.*: disgusting; hateful.

superfluity (soo′pər·floo′ə·tē) *n.*: excess.

grisly (griz′lē) *adj.*: terrifying.

adversary (ad′vər·ser′ē) *n.*: enemy.

pallor (pal′ər) *n.*: paleness.

prudent (proo′dənt) *adj.*: careful; cautious.

transcend (tran·send′) *v.*: exceed; surpass.

credentials (kri·den′shəlz) *n.*: evidence of a person's position.

absolve (ab·zälv′) *v.*: forgive; make free from blame.

INTERNET
Vocabulary Practice
•
More About Geoffrey Chaucer
•
Keyword: LE5 12-2

Literary Skills Understand irony, including verbal and situational irony.

Geoffrey Chaucer 145

SKILLS FOCUS, pp. 145–154

Grade-Level Skills

- **Literary Skills**

Analyze the way a writer uses irony to achieve specific rhetorical or aesthetic purposes.

PRETEACHING

Summary  *at grade level*

> After a prologue in which he brags about his own avarice, the unscrupulous Pardoner tells a moral tale illustrating the consequences of greed. As three young men sit in a tavern, a coffin passes, bearing the body of a man who they learn has been murdered by a thief called Death. The three decide to find Death and kill him. They set out and meet an old man who says that Death waits under a nearby tree. They go there and find a stash of gold coins, which they decide to steal. While the youngest is in town getting supplies, the other two decide to kill him and share the gold. But the youngest plots to get rid of the other two by poisoning the wine. When he returns, his two accomplices kill him, drink the wine, and die.

Selection Starter

Build background. Most of Chaucer's tales are based on older stories. The earliest known version of the Pardoner's Tale is found in the Hindu collection *Vedabbha Jataka.*

RESOURCES: READING

Planning
- One-Stop Planner CD-ROM with ExamView Test Generator

Differentiating Instruction
- Supporting Instruction in Spanish
- Audio CD Library, Selections and Summaries in Spanish

Vocabulary
- Vocabulary Development

Grammar and Language
- Daily Language Activities

Assessment
- Holt Assessment: Literature, Reading, and Vocabulary
- One-Stop Planner CD-ROM with ExamView Test Generator

- Holt Online Assessment

Internet
- go.hrw.com (Keyword: LE5 12-2)
- Elements of Literature Online

Media
- Audio CD Library
- Audio CD Library, Selections and Summaries in Spanish

from The Pardoner's Tale

Geoffrey Chaucer
translated by **Nevill Coghill**

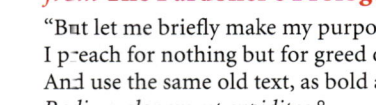

The Pardoner, from the Ellesmere manuscript.
Fol. 138r. By permission of The Huntington Library, San Marino, California.

from The Pardoner's Prologue

"But let me briefly make my purpose plain;
I preach for nothing but for greed of gain
And use the same old text, as bold as brass,
Radix malorum est cupiditas.°
5 And thus I preach against the very vice
I make my living out of—avarice.
And yet however guilty of that sin
Myself, with others I have power to win
Them from it, I can bring them to repent;
10 But that is not my principal intent.
Covetousness° is both the root and stuff
Of all I preach. That ought to be enough.
'Well, then I give examples thick and fast
From bygone times, old stories from the past.
15 A yokel° mind loves stories from of old,
Being the kind it can repeat and hold.
What! Do you think, as long as I can preach
And get their silver for the things I teach,
That I will live in poverty, from choice?
20 That's not the counsel of my inner voice!
No! Let me preach and beg from kirk° to kirk
And never do an honest job of work,
No, nor make baskets, like St. Paul, to gain
A livelihood. I do not preach in vain.
25 There's no apostle I would counterfeit;
I mean to have money, wool and cheese and wheat
Though it were given me by the poorest lad

4. *Radix malorum est cupiditas* (rā′diks ma·lō′rum est kōō·pi′di·tas): literally, "The root of evil is desire" (1 Timothy 6:10). The Pardoner has been telling the pilgrims about his preaching methods.

11. **Covetousness** (kuv′ət·əs·nis) *n*.: quality of craving wealth or possessions; greed.

15. **yokel** *n*. used as *adj*.: rustic; of the country.

21. **kirk** *n*.: Scottish for "church."

Vocabulary
avarice (av′ə·ris) *n*.: too great a desire for wealth.

Or poorest village widow, though she had
A string of starving children, all agape.°
30 No, let me drink the liquor of the grape
And keep a jolly wench in every town!
   "But listen, gentlemen; to bring things down
To a conclusion, would you like a tale?
Now as I've drunk a draft of corn-ripe ale,
35 By God it stands to reason I can strike
On some good story that you all will like.
For though I am a wholly vicious° man
Don't think I can't tell moral tales. I can!
Here's one I often preach when out for winning;
40 Now please be quiet. Here is the beginning."

The Pardoner's Tale

In Flanders once there was a company
Of youngsters haunting vice and ribaldry,°
Riot and gambling, stews and public-houses
Where each with harp, guitar, or lute carouses,°
45 Dancing and dicing° day and night, and bold
To eat and drink far more than they can hold,
Doing thereby the devil sacrifice
Within that devil's temple of cursed vice,
Abominable in superfluity,
50 With oaths so damnable in blasphemy°
That it's a grisly thing to hear them swear.
Our dear Lord's body they will rend and tear.°...
It's of three rioters° I have to tell
Who, long before the morning service bell,
55 Were sitting in a tavern for a drink.
And as they sat, they heard the hand-bell clink
Before a coffin going to the grave;
One of them called the little tavern-knave°
And said "Go and find out at once—look spry!—
60 Whose corpse is in that coffin passing by;
And see you get the name correctly too."
"Sir," said the boy, "no need, I promise you;
Two hours before you came here I was told.
He was a friend of yours in days of old,
65 And suddenly, last night, the man was slain,
Upon his bench, face up, dead drunk again.
There came a privy° thief, they call him Death,

29. **agape** *adj.*: open-mouthed.

37. **vicious** *adj.*: here, possessing many faults.

42. **ribaldry** (rib′əl·drē) *n.*: vulgar language or humor.
44. **carouses** (kə·rouz′ez) *v.*: drinks and celebrates noisily.
45. **dicing** *v.*: gambling (throwing dice).

50. **blasphemy** (blas′fə·mē) *n.*: mockery of God.
52. **Our...tear:** Their oaths refer to "God's arms" and "God's blessed bones."
53. **rioters** *n. pl.*: people living a wild, unrestrained lifestyle.

58. **tavern-knave:** serving boy.

67. **privy** (priv′ē) *adj.*: archaic usage meaning "secretive; furtive."

Vocabulary
abominable (ə·bäm′ə·nə·bəl) *adj.*: disgusting; hateful.
superfluity (sōō′pər·flōō′ə·tē) *n.*: excess.
grisly (griz′lē) *adj.*: terrifying.

Who kills us all round here, and in a breath
He speared him through the heart, he never stirred.
And then Death went his way without a word.
He's killed a thousand in the present plague,° [70]
And, sir, it doesn't do to be too vague
If you should meet him; you had best be wary.
Be on your guard with such an adversary,
Be primed to meet him everywhere you go,
That's what my mother said. It's all I know." [75]
    The publican° joined in with, "By St. Mary,
What the child says is right; you'd best be wary,
This very year he killed, in a large village
A mile away, man, woman, serf at tillage,°
Page in the household, children—all there were. [80]
Yes, I imagine that he lives round there.
It's well to be prepared in these alarms,°
He might do you dishonor." "Huh, God's arms!"
The rioter said, "Is he so fierce to meet?
I'll search for him, by Jesus, street by street. [85]
God's blessed bones! I'll register a vow!
Here, chaps! The three of us together now,
Hold up your hands, like me, and we'll be brothers
In this affair, and each defend the others,
And we will kill this traitor Death, I say! [90]
Away with him as he has made away
With all our friends. God's dignity! Tonight!"
    They made their bargain, swore with appetite,
These three, to live and die for one another [95]
As brother-born might swear to his born brother.
And up they started in their drunken rage
And made towards this village which the page
And publican had spoken of before.
Many and grisly were the oaths they swore, [100]
Tearing Christ's blessed body to a shred;
"If we can only catch him, Death is dead!"
    When they had gone not fully half a mile,
Just as they were about to cross a stile,°
They came upon a very poor old man [105]
Who humbly greeted them and thus began,
"God look to you, my lords, and give you quiet!"
To which the proudest of these men of riot
Gave back the answer, "What, old fool? Give place!
Why are you all wrapped up except your face? [110]
Why live so long? Isn't it time to die?"

Vocabulary

adversary (ad′vər·ser′ē) *n.*: enemy.

---

71. present plague: the Black Death, which killed nearly one third of the population of England during the mid–fourteenth century.

77. publican *n.*: tavern keeper; from *public house,* an inn or tavern.

80. tillage *n.*: working the land.

83. alarms *n. pl.*: here, anxious times.

104. stile *n.*: steps used for climbing over a wall.

The old, old fellow looked him in the eye
And said, "Because I never yet have found,
Though I have walked to India, searching round
115 Village and city on my pilgrimage,
One who would change his youth to have my age.
And so my age is mine and must be still
Upon me, for such time as God may will.
"Not even Death, alas, will take my life;
120 So, like a wretched prisoner at strife
Within himself, I walk alone and wait
About the earth, which is my mother's gate,°
Knock-knocking with my staff from night to noon
And crying, 'Mother, open to me soon!
125 Look at me, mother, won't you let me in?
See how I wither, flesh and blood and skin!
Alas! When will these bones be laid to rest?
Mother, I would exchange—for that were best—
The wardrobe in my chamber, standing there
130 So long, for yours! Aye, for a shirt of hair°
To wrap me in!' She has refused her grace,
Whence comes the pallor of my withered face.
"But it dishonored you when you began
To speak so roughly, sir, to an old man,
135 Unless he had injured you in word or deed.
It says in holy writ,° as you may read,
'Thou shalt rise up before the hoary° head
And honor it.' And therefore be it said,
'Do no more harm to an old man than you,
140 Being now young, would have another do
When you are old'—if you should live till then.
And so may God be with you, gentlemen,
For I must go whither I have to go."
"By God," the gambler said, "you shan't do so,
145 You don't get off so easy, by St. John!
I heard you mention, just a moment gone,
A certain traitor Death who singles out
And kills the fine young fellows hereabout.
And you're his spy, by God! You wait a bit.
150 Say where he is or you shall pay for it,
By God and by the Holy Sacrament!
I say you've joined together by consent
To kill us younger folk, you thieving swine!"
"Well, sirs," he said, "if it be your design
155 To find out Death, turn up this crooked way

Vocabulary
pallor (pal′ər) n.: paleness.

122. **mother's gate:** The old man is personifying Death as a mother, her house surrounded by a gate (the earth). Thus, "mother's gate" is the entrance to the grave.

130. **shirt of hair:** Coarse shirts of woven horsehair were worn as penance. Here, the old man refers to such a shirt used to wrap his body for burial.

136. **holy writ:** the Bible.
137. **hoary** adj.: white.

The Three Living, the Three Dead, from the *Psalter and Prayer Book of Bonne of Luxembourg, Duchess of Normandy* (14th century). Grisaille, color, gilt, and brown ink on vellum (4 15/16″ × 3 9/16″).
Fol. 321v–322r. The Metropolitan Museum of Art. The Cloisters Collection, 1969 (69.86). Photograph © 1991 The Metropolitan Museum of Art.

Geoffrey Chaucer   149

Literary Criticism

Critic's Commentary: Christian Imagery
Chaucer scholar Robert P. Miller regards the "brother" rioters as "Cain-like" and finds the story illustrative of a vast array of Christian imagery. For example, he notes that Death "lies up the 'crooked way,' the opposite of the straight and narrow; 'in that grove,' that is, in the false paradise of cupidity; and 'under a tree,' where Adam and Eve lost their true Eden and found Death first. In terms of medieval Christian imagery, this is surely the way to find Death, but not the way to slay him." Miller adds that "the oak tree under which the gold is discovered literally exemplifies the words of [the] text, *Radix malorum est cupiditas*. For this tree may itself be regarded as the tree of evil (or of death) whose root is cupidity symbolized by the golden earthly treasure."

DIRECT TEACHING

E Literary Focus
Irony. What is ironic about the attitudes of the rioters and the old man toward Death? [Possible responses: Most people fear Death and try to avoid it, but the old man seeks release through Death. The rioters also seek Death, but their purpose is to challenge it. Furthermore, the old man tells the rioters where to find Death, but he has not yet found Death himself.]

F Literary Focus
Personification. What does personification of Death as a mother suggest? [Possible response: This image suggests that Death is a comforter, providing a home and relief from suffering.]

G Content-Area Connections
Culture: Biblical Allusion
The old man has created his own variation of the biblical injunction "Therefore all things whatsoever ye would that men should do to you, do ye even so to them" (Matthew 7:12).

H Reading Skills
Hypothesizing. Why does the old man add "if you should live till then"? [Possible responses: He knows for sure what will happen to the rioters, or he can guess, based on his observation of their recklessness; he may simply be observing that in this time of plague, people cannot count on living to an old age.]

DIRECT TEACHING

A Literary Focus

? Irony. What is ironic about this line? [The young men no longer seek Death, but they probably have found the instrument of their own Death in the gold coins.]

B Literary Focus

? Personification. What does the capital *F* in *Fortune* tell you? What have the young men forgotten? [Fortune is personified here. The men have forgotten that they were told Death awaited under the tree (Death is their Fortune), or they have forgotten that Fortune can be good or bad.]

C English-Language Learners

Understanding informal usage. *Chaps*, meaning "fellows" or "boys" (today we might say "guys"), is an example of informal language. Although occasionally used in American English, the word is most frequently used in British English. (The word *chaps* is the translator's, not Chaucer's.)

D Literary Focus

? Characterization. In this example of indirect characterization, what do the speaker's words reveal about him? [Possible responses: He thinks quickly. He is a schemer. He is greedily protecting his interests.]

Towards that grove, I left him there today
Under a tree, and there you'll find him waiting.
He isn't one to hide for all your prating.°
You see that oak? He won't be far to find.
160   And God protect you that redeemed mankind,
Aye, and amend° you!" Thus that ancient man.
      At once the three young rioters began
To run, and reached the tree, and there they found
A pile of golden florins° on the ground,
165   New-coined, eight bushels of them as they thought.
No longer was it Death those fellows sought,
For they were all so thrilled to see the sight,
The florins were so beautiful and bright,
That down they sat beside the precious pile.
170   The wickedest spoke first after a while.
"Brothers," he said, "you listen to what I say.
I'm pretty sharp although I joke away.
It's clear that Fortune has bestowed this treasure
To let us live in jollity and pleasure.
175   Light come, light go! We'll spend it as we ought.
God's precious dignity! Who would have thought
This morning was to be our lucky day?
      "If one could only get the gold away,
Back to my house, or else to yours, perhaps—
180   For as you know, the gold is ours, chaps—
We'd all be at the top of fortune, hey?
But certainly it can't be done by day.
People would call us robbers—a strong gang,
So our own property would make us hang.
185   No, we must bring this treasure back by night
Some prudent way, and keep it out of sight.
And so as a solution I propose
We draw for lots and see the way it goes;
The one who draws the longest, lucky man,
190   Shall run to town as quickly as he can
To fetch us bread and wine—but keep things dark°—
While two remain in hiding here to mark
Our heap of treasure. If there's no delay,
When night comes down we'll carry it away,
195   All three of us, wherever we have planned."
      He gathered lots and hid them in his hand
Bidding them draw for where the luck should fall.
It fell upon the youngest of them all,
And off he ran at once towards the town.

158. **prating** *n.:* chattering.

161. **amend** *v.:* improve.

164. **florins** *n. pl.:* coins worth twenty-four pence. *Pence* is the British plural of *penny*.

191. **keep things dark:** do it in secret.

Vocabulary
prudent (prōō′dənt) *adj.:* careful; cautious.

DIFFERENTIATING INSTRUCTION

Learners Having Difficulty
These students must be able to follow what happens in the Pardoner's narrative before they will be able to extract its moral or understand its ironies. To help students track the plot, show them how to construct a time line illustrating the chain of events that leads to the rioters' deaths. Write in the first event for them: "Rioters decide to kill Death." Then, have students work on their own.

English-Language Learners
Provide these students with a photocopy of the tale, on which they can record their own dialogue with the text. Encourage students to write down their questions, predictions, and emotional reactions to as many lines or sections as possible. Then, have them share their notes with a partner and work with that partner to answer questions and compare responses.

200   As soon as he had gone the first sat down
      And thus began a parley° with the other:
      "You know that you can trust me as a brother;
      Now let me tell you where your profit lies;
      You know our friend has gone to get supplies
205   And here's a lot of gold that is to be
      Divided equally among us three.
      Nevertheless, if I could shape things thus
      So that we shared it out—the two of us—
      Wouldn't you take it as a friendly act?"
210   "But how?" the other said. "He knows the fact
      That all the gold was left with me and you;
      What can we tell him? What are we to do?"
      "Is it a bargain," said the first, "or no?
      For I can tell you in a word or so
215   What's to be done to bring the thing about."
      "Trust me," the other said, "you needn't doubt
      My word. I won't betray you, I'll be true."
      "Well," said his friend, "you see that we are two,
      And two are twice as powerful as one.
220   Now look; when he comes back, get up in fun
      To have a wrestle; then, as you attack,
      I'll up and put my dagger through his back
      While you and he are struggling, as in game;
      Then draw your dagger too and do the same.
225   Then all this money will be ours to spend,
      Divided equally of course, dear friend.
      Then we can gratify our lusts and fill
      The day with dicing at our own sweet will."
      Thus these two miscreants° agreed to slay
230   The third and youngest, as you heard me say.
         The youngest, as he ran towards the town,
      Kept turning over, rolling up and down
      Within his heart the beauty of those bright
      New florins, saying, "Lord, to think I might
235   Have all that treasure to myself alone!
      Could there be anyone beneath the throne
      Of God so happy as I then should be?"
         And so the Fiend,° our common enemy,
      Was given power to put it in his thought
240   That there was always poison to be bought,
      And that with poison he could kill his friends.
      To men in such a state the Devil sends
      Thoughts of this kind, and has a full permission
      To lure them on to sorrow and perdition;°
245   For this young man was utterly content
      To kill them both and never to repent.

201. **parley** *n.*: discussion.

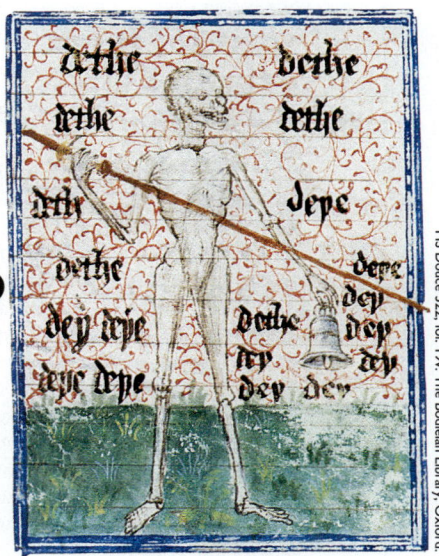

Death with his spear, from "The Pardoner's Tale."

229. **miscreants** (mis′krē·ənts) *n. pl.*: criminals; literally, "unbelievers."

238. **Fiend**: the devil.

244. **perdition** (pər·dish′ən) *n.*: damnation.

Geoffrey Chaucer   **151**

DIRECT TEACHING

A Literary Focus

Irony. What is ironic about the reason the young man gives for buying poison? [Possible responses: He wants it for "vermin that destroy a man by night." Ironically, the "vermin" he plans to kill are planning to "destroy a man"—him. In addition, the young man fits his own definition of vermin.]

B Literary Focus

Style. Note how a great deal of action is described in a few sentences in this section. How does this device affect the story? [Possible responses: The compressed action and heightened pace reinforces the drama and suspense.]

C Literary Focus

Characterization. The phrase "this devil's clay" is in apposition to the subject. This is an example of direct characterization, yet it is essentially a metaphor. What does the author mean by "this devil's clay"? [Possible response: The rioter's character was molded, like clay, by the devil. He is like clay: changeable, easily manipulated, and without moral integrity.]

D Literary Focus

Irony. What is the irony implicit in the narrator's question? [The Pardoner's story is an exemplum, or moral anecdote, of the kind frequently used in sermons. The Pardoner is saying he will *not* make a sermon of his tale. However, that is what he intends to do for his own gain.]

And on he ran, he had no thought to tarry,
Came to the town, found an apothecary°
And said, "Sell me some poison if you will,
250 I have a lot of rats I want to kill
And there's a polecat too about my yard
That takes my chickens and it hits me hard;
But I'll get even, as is only right,
With vermin that destroy a man by night."
255 The chemist answered, "I've a preparation
Which you shall have, and by my soul's salvation
If any living creature eat or drink
A mouthful, ere° he has the time to think,
Though he took less than makes a grain of wheat,
260 You'll see him fall down dying at your feet;
Yes, die he must, and in so short a while
You'd hardly have the time to walk a mile,
The poison is so strong, you understand."
This cursed fellow grabbed into his hand
265 The box of poison and away he ran
Into a neighboring street, and found a man
Who lent him three large bottles. He withdrew
And deftly poured the poison into two.
He kept the third one clean, as well he might,
270 For his own drink, meaning to work all night
Stacking the gold and carrying it away.
And when this rioter, this devil's clay,
Had filled his bottles up with wine, all three,
Back to rejoin his comrades sauntered° he.
275 Why make a sermon of it? Why waste breath?
Exactly in the way they'd planned his death
They fell on him and slew him, two to one.
Then said the first of them when this was done,
"Now for a drink. Sit down and let's be merry,
280 For later on there'll be the corpse to bury."
And, as it happened, reaching for a sup,
He took a bottle full of poison up
And drank; and his companion, nothing loth,°
Drank from it also, and they perished both.
285 There is, in Avicenna's° long relation
Concerning poison and its operation,
Trust me, no ghastlier section to <u>transcend</u>
What these two wretches suffered at their end.
Thus these two murderers received their due,
290 So did the treacherous young poisoner too. . . .

248. **apothecary** (ə·päth′ə·ker′ē) *n.*: druggist. Formerly apothecaries prescribed drugs.

258. **ere** *prep.*: before.

274. **sauntered** (sôn′tərd) *v.*: strolled.

283. **loth** (lōth) *adj.*: reluctant; unwilling; alternative spelling of *loath*.

285. **Avicenna's** (av′i·sen′əz): Avicenna (A.D. 980–1037), a famous Islamic philosopher and doctor, wrote several medical books.

Vocabulary
transcend (tran·send′) *v.*: exceed; surpass.

DEVELOPING FLUENCY

Whole-class activity. Encourage students to prepare an oral reading of the tale to help them follow its intricate narrative structure. Have them begin by working together to decide who is speaking in each major segment of the selection. Help them to discover that the Pardoner speaks the Prologue and narrates the tale in which specific characters, such as the publican and the rioters, engage in dialogue. Have the students mark these instances of dialogue within the tale (alert them to look for quotation marks) and choose individuals to read each character's exact words. Finally, call their attention to the final thirteen lines of the selection, and be sure they understand that this is a return to the frame story in which the general narrator is speaking. After students have prepared their script, have them rehearse reading aloud with attention to expressiveness.

"One thing I should have mentioned in my tale,
Dear people. I've some relics in my bale°
And pardons too, as full and fine, I hope,
As any in England, given me by the Pope.
295 If there be one among you that is willing
To have my absolution° for a shilling°
Devoutly given, come! and do not harden
Your hearts but kneel in humbleness for pardon;
Or else, receive my pardon as we go.
300 You can renew it every town or so
Always provided that you still renew
Each time, and in good money, what is due.
It is an honor to you to have found
A pardoner with his credentials sound
305 Who can absolve you as you ply the spur°
In any accident that may occur.
For instance—we are all at Fortune's beck°—
Your horse may throw you down and break your neck.
What a security it is to all
310 To have me here among you and at call
With pardon for the lowly and the great
When soul leaves body for the future state!
And I advise our Host here to begin,
The most enveloped of you all in sin.
315 Come forward, Host, you shall be the first to pay,
And kiss my holy relics right away.
Only a groat.° Come on, unbuckle your purse!"
    "No, no," said he,° "not I, and may the curse
Of Christ descend upon me if I do! . . ."

320 The Pardoner said nothing, not a word;
He was so angry that he couldn't speak.
"Well," said our Host, "if you're for showing pique,°
I'll joke no more, not with an angry man."
    The worthy Knight immediately began,
325 Seeing the fun was getting rather rough,
And said, "No more, we've all had quite enough.
Now, Master Pardoner, perk up, look cheerly!
And you, Sir Host, whom I esteem so dearly,
I beg of you to kiss the Pardoner.
330 Come, Pardoner, draw nearer, my dear sir.
Let's laugh again and keep the ball in play."°
They kissed, and we continued on our way.

292. relics in my bale: Relics are the supposedly holy remains of a saint—bones, teeth, hair, or clothing. A bale is a bundle of goods. In the Middle Ages, many relics were faked.
296. absolution (ab·sə·lōō′shən) *n.:* forgiveness. **shilling** *n.:* coin worth twelve pence.

305. ply the spur: In today's terms, this idiom means something like "rev it up" or "put on speed." It refers to the action of a rider digging his spurs into a horse to make it go faster.
307. beck *n.:* summons; in other words, subject to Fortune's will.

317. groat *n.:* silver coin worth four pence.
318. he: the Host.

322. pique (pēk) *n.:* resentment and ill humor.

331. keep the ball in play: continue.

Vocabulary
credentials (kri·den′shəlz) *n.:* evidence of a person's position.
absolve (ab·zälv′) *v.:* forgive; make free from blame.

Geoffrey Chaucer   153

SKILLS REVIEW

Determining character traits. Remind students that readers learn about characters' traits from what the narrator of a story says about the characters, as well as what the characters reveal about themselves in monologues and dialogue. Then, have students look back at the text of "The Pardoner's Tale" to answer the following questions:

- What does the Pardoner reveal about his own character in the Prologue to his tale? [He admits that he will do anything for money except honest work, that he enjoys wine and women, and that he feels no sympathy for those he swindles.]
- Does the Pardoner's behavior after telling his tale support or challenge his self-assessment in the Prologue? [His behavior confirms his self-assessment since he attempts to sell pardons as soon as he finishes his tale.]

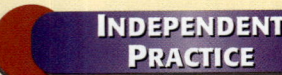

Response and Analysis

Reading Check

1. He admits he is corrupt and greedy.
2. They want to kill him.
3. He tells them to look under a nearby oak tree; they treat him disrespectfully.
4. The youngest rioter will go to town while the other two stay with the treasure. The two left behind plot to murder the youngest; the youngest plans to kill the other two with poisoned wine. When the youngest returns, the other two kill him, drink the wine, and die also.

Thinking Critically

5. The tavern-knave calls Death a "privy thief," and the publican says that Death probably lives near the village where many people have died. The rioters show how foolish and arrogant they are when they decide to "kill" Death.
6. He may symbolize Death or the futility of resisting death.
7. The rioters seek to kill Death; they expect to find Death under the tree but instead find the gold, which ironically brings about their death.
8. Possible answers: The Pardoner admits that he is motivated by avarice, the very sin he preaches against. He is a professional swindler who routinely manipulates his audience to make money, as demonstrated by the fact that he frankly admits his motives before telling his tale but after telling it immediately seeks to extract money. The Pardoner appears to cheat automatically.
9. Chaucer is satirizing greedy clerics who deceive the faithful.
10. The Pardoner's moral is that greed can lead to death. Chaucer's moral may be to beware of hypocrites.

Response and Analysis

Reading Check

1. How does the Pardoner describe his own character and morals in the Prologue to his tale?
2. According to "The Pardoner's Tale," why are the three young rioters looking for Death?
3. Where does the old man tell the rioters to look for Death? How do they treat him?
4. Describe the rioters' plan for the gold and how it proves fatal to all three of them.

Thinking Critically

5. How do the descriptions given by the tavern-knave and the publican **personify** Death? What does the rioters' response to the description of Death tell you about their characters?
6. What do you think the poor old man **symbolizes**?
7. **Irony** is a discrepancy between expectations and reality. What is the central irony in "The Pardoner's Tale"? (What do the rioters *expect* to find under the tree? What do they *actually* find?)
8. Explain the **irony** in the fact that the Pardoner preaches a story with this particular moral. How do you account for the psychology of the Pardoner? Is he truly evil, simply drunk, or so used to cheating that he does it automatically?
9. What aspects of medieval society (and human nature in general) do you think Chaucer is **satirizing** in "The Pardoner's Tale"?
10. What **moral** does the Pardoner want us to draw from his tale? How is it different from the moral you think Chaucer wants you to draw from "The Pardoner's Tale"?
11. Do people with the Pardoner's ethics exist today—in all sorts of professions? Explain your response.

INTERNET
Projects and Activities
Keyword: LE5 12-2

SKILLS FOCUS

Literary Skills Analyze irony, including verbal and situational irony.

Writing Skills Write a character analysis.

Vocabulary Skills Demonstrate word knowledge.

154 Collection 2 The Middle Ages

12. *Is* greed or desire the root of all evil? Discuss the Pardoner's moral.

WRITING

What Makes the Pardoner Tick?

Write a **character analysis** of the Pardoner. Consider in your analysis the Pardoner's Prologue, his tale, and the description of the Pardoner in the general Prologue (see pages 139–140). Before you write, gather details for your analysis in a cluster diagram like the following one:

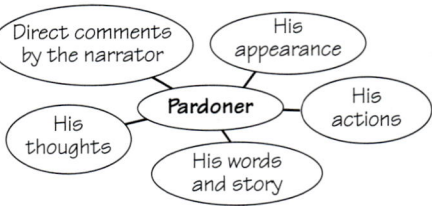

Be sure to quote directly from the text to support your character analysis. If you are so inspired, supply your own illustration (or a cartoon) of the Pardoner.

Vocabulary Development
Question and Answer

Demonstrate your understanding of the underlined Vocabulary words by answering the following questions.

1. Might a person guilty of <u>avarice</u> have a <u>superfluity</u> of possessions?
2. Why might running into an <u>adversary</u> bring a <u>pallor</u> to someone's complexion?
3. Who could <u>absolve</u> a person of an <u>abominable</u> <u>crime</u>?
4. What could you do to <u>transcend</u> your fears if you were faced with a <u>grisly</u> sight?
5. When would it be <u>prudent</u> to check someone's <u>credentials</u>?

---

11. The Pardoner is an example of someone who does not practice what he preaches. Students should be able to cite examples of people like the Pardoner (or behavior like his) in several professions.
12. Many students may be familiar with the saying "Money is the root of all evil" and agree with it. Others may feel that pride is the most basic sin.

Vocabulary Development

Sample Answers

1. Greedy people often gather an excessive number of possessions.
2. Meeting an enemy unexpectedly might cause anyone to turn pale.

Before You Read

from The Wife of Bath's Tale

Make the Connection
Quickwrite

No one on the road to Canterbury is more recognizable than the Wife of Bath (a married woman from the city of Bath, west of London). She is Chaucer's most vibrant and lively character. Having outlived five husbands (and possibly looking for a sixth on the pilgrimage), she is witty, intelligent, opinionated, and sensual. The tale that she tells belongs to the "marriage group," several tales that explore what men and women expect from and ought to do in marriage. In the tale, a knight must find the answer to the question "What is the thing that women most desire?" How would *you* answer this question? Jot down your thoughts before you read.

Literary Focus
Narrator

Every **narrator,** or person who tells a story, has a distinct voice or character that is revealed through the subject matter of the story, the story's tone, and the language that sets that tone. It's important not to confuse a story's narrator with its author, especially when the narrator is not an obvious presence. In the case of the tale you're about to read, it's impossible not to notice the narrator. Chaucer is a master at matching his narrators and their stories. The Wife of Bath, for example, reveals as much about herself in her tale as she does about medieval society or the desires of women.

> A **narrator** is one who tells, or narrates, a story.
>
> For more on Narrator, see the Handbook of Literary and Historical Terms.

Reading Skills
Interpreting Character

The Wife of Bath is an opinionated woman with very definite ideas about women, men, and marriage. We cannot be sure that her views represent those of Chaucer or of the majority of women of her day, but we do get a very clear picture of what *she* believes. As you read, jot down details that reveal the Wife of Bath's views on women, marriage, and true gentility or goodness. Then, think about how her views relate to her character. In other words, do you think she practices what she preaches?

Vocabulary Development

reprove (ri·prōōv') *v.*: disapprove of.

concede (kən·sēd') *v.*: grant.

extort (eks·tôrt') *v.*: get by threats or violence.

disperses (di·spʉrs'iz) *v.*: breaks up.

contemptuous (kən·temp'chōō·əs) *adj.*: scornful.

bequest (bē·kwest') *n.*: gift left by means of a will.

prowess (prou'is) *n.*: outstanding ability.

temporal (tem'pə·rəl) *adj.*: limited to this world; not spiritual.

capacity (kə·pas'i·tē) *n.*: ability to absorb.

pestilence (pes'tə·ləns) *n.*: plague.

INTERNET

Vocabulary Practice
•
More About Geoffrey Chaucer

Keyword: LE5 12-2

Literary Skills
Understand the characteristics of a narrator.

Reading Skills
Interpret character.

Geoffrey Chaucer 155

SKILLS FOCUS, pp. 155–168

Grade-Level Skills

■ **Literary Skills**
Understand the characteristics of a narrator.

■ **Literary Skills**
Analyze characteristics of subgenres of poetry, including couplets.

■ **Reading Skills**
Interpret character.

PRETEACHING

Summary *at grade level*

The Wife of Bath narrates a story about a knight sentenced to death for rape. The queen promises to spare his life if he can discover in a year and a day what women most desire. He sets out to find the answer. He gets unsatisfactory responses until he meets an ugly, old woman who promises to give him the answer if he will grant her the first thing she asks for. He agrees, and she explains that what women want most is power over men. The knight gives this answer at court; all agree that it is correct. The old woman requires that he marry her. Very reluctantly agreeing, the knight is lectured by his new wife on the attributes of a good wife. She offers him a choice between a beautiful, faithless wife or an ugly, faithful one. Recognizing her desire for power, the knight allows her to make the choice, and she rewards him by becoming young, beautiful, *and* faithful.

RESOURCES: READING

Planning
■ One-Stop Planner CD-ROM with ExamView Test Generator

Differentiating Instruction
■ Supporting Instruction in Spanish
■ Audio CD Library, Selections and Summaries in Spanish

Vocabulary
■ Vocabulary Development

Grammar and Language
■ Daily Language Activities

Assessment
■ Holt Assessment: Literature, Reading, and Vocabulary
■ One-Stop Planner CD-ROM with ExamView Test Generator

■ Holt Online Assessment

Internet
■ go.hrw.com (Keyword: LE5 12-2)
■ Elements of Literature Online

Media
■ Audio CD Library
■ Audio CD Library, Selections and Summaries in Spanish

Geoffrey Chaucer 155

from The Wife of Bath's Tale

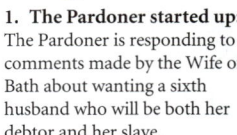

The Wife of Bath, from the Ellesmere manuscript.
Fol. 72r. By permission of The Huntington Library, San Marino, California.

from The Wife of Bath's Prologue

The Pardoner started up,° and thereupon
"Madam," he said, "by God and by St. John,
That's noble preaching no one could surpass!
I was about to take a wife; alas!
5 Am I to buy it on my flesh so dear?
There'll be no marrying for me this year!"
   'You wait,' she said, "my story's not begun.
You'll taste another brew before I've done;
You'll find it doesn't taste as good as ale;
10 And when I've finished telling you my tale
Of tribulation° in the married life
In which I've been an expert as a wife,
That is to say, myself have been the whip.
So please yourself whether you want to sip
15 At that same cask of marriage I shall broach.
Be cautious before making the approach,
For I'll give instances, and more than ten.
And those who won't be warned by other men,
By other men shall suffer their correction,
20 So Ptolemy° has said, in this connection.
You read his *Almagest*;° you'll find it there."
   "Madam, I put it to you as a prayer,"
The Pardoner said, "go on as you began!
Tell us your tale, spare not for any man.
25 Instruct us younger men in your technique."
"Gladly," she said, "if you will let me speak,
But still I hope the company won't reprove me
Though I should speak as fantasy may move me,
And please don't be offended at my views;
30 They're really only offered to amuse." . . .

1. **The Pardoner started up:** The Pardoner is responding to comments made by the Wife of Bath about wanting a sixth husband who will be both her debtor and her slave.

11. **tribulation** *n.*: distress; suffering.

20. **Ptolemy** (tăl′ə·mē) (A.D. 100?–165?): ancient geographer, astronomer, and mathematician from Alexandria, Egypt.
21. **Almagest:** word meaning "the greatest"; another title for Ptolemy's major work, *Mathematical Composition,* in which he argues that the earth is the center of the universe, a view held in Europe until 1543.

Vocabulary
reprove (ri·prōōv′) *v.*: disapprove of.

The Wife of Bath's Tale

When good King Arthur ruled in ancient days
(A king that every Briton loves to praise)
This was a land brim-full of fairy folk.
The Elf-Queen and her courtiers° joined and broke
35   Their elfin dance on many a green mead,°
Or so was the opinion once, I read,
Hundreds of years ago, in days of yore.
But no one now sees fairies any more.
For now the saintly charity and prayer
40   Of holy friars seem to have purged the air;
They search the countryside through field and stream
As thick as motes° that speckle a sun-beam,
Blessing the halls, the chambers, kitchens, bowers,
Cities and boroughs, castles, courts and towers,
45   Thorpes,° barns and stables, outhouses and dairies,
And that's the reason why there are no fairies.
Wherever there was wont° to walk an elf
To-day there walks the holy friar himself
As evening falls or when the daylight springs,
50   Saying his matins° and his holy things,
Walking his limit round from town to town.
Women can now go safely up and down
By every bush or under every tree;
There is no other incubus° but he,
55   So there is really no one else to hurt you
And he will do no more than take your virtue.
    Now it so happened, I began to say,
Long, long ago in good King Arthur's day,
There was a knight who was a lusty liver.°
60   One day as he came riding from the river
He saw a maiden walking all forlorn
Ahead of him, alone as she was born.
And of that maiden, spite of all she said,
By very force he took her maidenhead.°
65   This act of violence made such a stir,
So much petitioning to the king for her,
That he condemned the knight to lose his head
By course of law. He was as good as dead
(It seems that then the statutes° took that view)
70   But that the queen, and other ladies too,
Implored the king to exercise his grace
So ceaselessly, he gave the queen the case
And granted her his life, and she could choose
Whether to show him mercy or refuse.
75   The queen returned him thanks with all her might,
And then she sent a summons to the knight

---

34. **courtiers** (kôrt′ē·ərz) *n. pl.*: attendants.
35. **mead** *n.*: meadow.

42. **motes** *n. pl.*: dust particles.

45. **thorpes** *n. pl.*: villages.

47. **wont** (wänt) *adj.*: accustomed.

50. **matins** (mat″nz) *n. pl.*: morning prayers.

54. **incubus** (in′kyə·bəs) *n.*: evil spirit believed to descend on a sleeping woman and make her pregnant.

59. **liver** *n.*: In medieval times, the liver—not the heart—was believed to be the source of all desires and emotions.

64. **maidenhead** *n.*: virginity.

69. **statutes** *n. pl.*: laws.

Geoffrey Chaucer   157

DIRECT TEACHING

A Learners Having Difficulty

? Paraphrasing. Lines 78–82 express key ideas in the plot, yet you may find the interrupted movement, archaic usage, and unusual word order confusing. Can you paraphrase these lines? [Possible response: As things stand, it is not certain that you will live. You shall survive if you can answer the question of what women want most, but if you do not fulfill that requirement, your head will be cut off.]

B Content-Area Connections

Literature: The Riddle Archetype
? What other stories do you know in which a character must solve a riddle in order to save his or her own life? [Possible responses: the tale of Rumpelstiltskin; Tolkien's tale of the Hobbit and Gollum; the myth of Oedipus.]

C Literary Focus

? Narrator. Chaucer has the Wife of Bath digress in her narration here. Why do you think she strays from her story at this point? [Possible responses: She is more interested in the question of what women want than in advancing the plot of her story; she wants to heighten her listeners' curiosity and create suspense.]

D Literary Focus

? Narrator. Of all the possible answers suggested so far to the Knight's question, which one does the Wife of Bath think is the best? [She believes that women like to be flattered and fussed over.]

At her convenience, and expressed her will:
"You stand, for such is the position still,
In no way certain of your life," said she,
80 "Yet you shall live if you can answer me:
What is the thing that women most desire?
Beware the axe and say as I require.
"If you can't answer on the moment, though,
I will concede you this: You are to go
85 A twelvemonth and a day to seek and learn
Sufficient answer, then you shall return.
I shall take gages° from you to extort
Surrender of your body to the court."
Sad was the knight and sorrowfully sighed,
90 But there! All other choices were denied,
And in the end he chose to go away
And to return after a year and day
Armed with such answer as there might be sent
To him by God. He took his leave and went.
95 He knocked at every house, searched every place,
Yes, anywhere that offered hope of grace.
What could it be that women wanted most?
But all the same he never touched a coast,
Country, or town in which there seemed to be
100 Any two people willing to agree.
Some said that women wanted wealth and treasure,
"Honor," said some, some "Jollity and pleasure,"
Some "Gorgeous clothes" and others "Fun in bed,"
"To be oft widowed and remarried," said
105 Others again, and some that what most mattered
Was that we should be cossetted° and flattered.
That's very near the truth, it seems to me;
A man can win us best with flattery.
To dance attendance on us, make a fuss,
110 Ensnares us all, the best and worst of us.
Some say the things we most desire are these:
Freedom to do exactly as we please,
With no one to reprove our faults and lies,
Rather to have one call us good and wise.
115 Truly there's not a woman in ten score°
Who has a fault, and someone rubs the sore,
But she will kick if what he says is true;
You try it out and you will find so too.
However vicious we may be within

Vocabulary
concede (kən·sēd′) v.: grant.
extort (eks·tôrt′) v.: get by threats or violence.

87. **gages** n. pl.: pledges.

Man and woman, from a fifteenth-century manuscript of Virgil's *Aeneid*.

106. **cossetted** (käs′it·id) v.: pampered.

115. **ten score:** two hundred. A score is twenty.

158 Collection 2 The Middle Ages

READING MINI-LESSON

Developing Word-Attack Skills
Remind students that *The Canterbury Tales* was written in iambic pentameter and in rhyming couplets. Each line has five feet, called iambs. Each foot has an unaccented syllable and an accented syllable. The last words in every pair of lines rhyme. Explain that the modern English translation that students are reading replicates the rhythm and rhyme of the original. Use these lines from "The Wife of Bath's Tale" to illustrate this:

At last he said, with all the care in life,
"My lady and my love, my dearest wife. . . ."

Point out that the rhythm and rhyme of the work can help students read unfamiliar words they encounter. Direct attention to ll. 213–214 in "The Wife of Bath's Tale."

120 We like to be thought wise and void of sin.
     Others assert we women find it sweet
     When we are thought dependable, discreet
     And secret, firm of purpose and controlled,
     Never betraying things that we are told.
125 But that's not worth the handle of a rake;
     Women conceal a thing? For Heaven's sake!
     Remember Midas°? Will you hear the tale?
        Among some other little things, now stale,
     Ovid° relates that under his long hair
130 The unhappy Midas grew a splendid pair
     Of ass's ears; as subtly as he might,
     He kept his foul deformity from sight;
     Save for his wife, there was not one that knew.
     He loved her best, and trusted in her too.
135 He begged her not to tell a living creature
     That he possessed so horrible a feature.
     And she—she swore, were all the world to win,
     She would not do such villainy and sin
     As saddle her husband with so foul a name;
140 Besides to speak would be to share the shame.
     Nevertheless she thought she would have died
     Keeping this secret bottled up inside;
     It seemed to swell her heart and she, no doubt,
     Thought it was on the point of bursting out.
145   Fearing to speak of it to woman or man,
     Down to a reedy marsh she quickly ran
     And reached the sedge.° Her heart was all on fire
     And, as a bittern° bumbles in the mire,
     She whispered to the water, near the ground,
150 "Betray me not, O water, with thy sound!
     To thee alone I tell it: It appears
     My husband has a pair of ass's ears!
     Ah! My heart's well again, the secret's out!
     I could no longer keep it, not a doubt."
155 And so you see, although we may hold fast
     A little while, it must come out at last,
     We can't keep secrets; as for Midas, well,
     Read Ovid for his story;° he will tell.
        This knight that I am telling you about
160 Perceived at last he never would find out
     What it could be that women loved the best.
     Faint was the soul within his sorrowful breast,
     As home he went, he dared no longer stay;
     His year was up and now it was the day.
165   As he rode home in a dejected mood
     Suddenly, at the margin° of a wood,

127. **Midas:** mythical king. Everything he touched turned to gold.
129. **Ovid** (43 B.C.–c. A.D. 17): Roman poet. Ovid's *Metamorphoses*, a collection of tales, includes one version of the Midas story.

147. **sedge** *n.:* grasslike plant.
148. **bittern** *n.:* type of wading bird.

158. **Read ... story:** In Ovid's version, it is Midas's barber, not his wife, who tells the secret to a hole in the ground. Reeds grow up from the spot and whisper the secret whenever the wind rustles them.

166. **margin** *n.:* edge.

Direct Teaching

A Reading Skills

? Evaluating plot details. The "four and twenty ladies" mysteriously vanish. Do you think this is an irrelevant detail? How would the story be different if the knight simply noticed an old woman sitting at the edge of the wood? [Possible responses: The disappearance of the ladies suggests that something magical or unpredictable is happening. The story might have been different because the discouraged knight might not have stopped to hear the opinion of one old woman.]

B English-Language Learners

Understanding archaic usage. Point out that students will encounter some of the archaic language used here in other early literature. Examples include *nay* in l. 168, *ere* in l. 170, *lo* in l. 171, and *alack* in l. 181. Then, ask students to use context clues to guess the meaning of these words. [*Nay* means "no"; *ere*, "before"; *lo* is an expression of surprise or wonder, meaning "look"; *alack* is an expression of dismay, meaning "alas."]

C Vocabulary Development

? Distinguishing between multiple meanings. What meaning of the noun *court* is Chaucer using here? [the place where a sovereign presides over his or her subjects] What other meanings does the word have? [Possible responses: an expanse of open ground surrounded by walls; the attendants of a sovereign; a body of persons assembled to try cases; the building where cases are tried.] Could the word be used in more than one sense here? [Yes, because the knight is also facing judgment and possible punishment in this court.]

He saw a dance upon the leafy floor
Of four and twenty ladies, nay, and more.
Eagerly he approached, in hope to learn
170 Some words of wisdom ere he should return;
But lo! Before he came to where they were,
Dancers and dance all vanished into air!
There wasn't a living creature to be seen
Save one old woman crouched upon the green.
175 A fouler-looking creature I suppose
Could scarcely be imagined. She arose
And said, "Sir knight, there's no way on from here.
Tell me what you are looking for, my dear,
For peradventure° that were best for you;
180 We old, old women know a thing or two."
     "Dear Mother," said the knight, "alack the day!
I am as good as dead if I can't say
What thing it is that women most desire;
If you could tell me I would pay your hire."
185 "Give me your hand," she said, "and swear to do
Whatever I shall next require of you
—If so to do should lie within your might—
And you shall know the answer before night."
"Upon my honor," he answered, "I agree."
190 "Then," said the crone, "I dare to guarantee
Your life is safe; I shall make good my claim.
Upon my life the queen will say the same.
Show me the very proudest of them all
In costly coverchief or jeweled caul°
195 That dare say no to what I have to teach.
Let us go forward without further speech."
And then she crooned her gospel in his ear
And told him to be glad and not to fear.
     They came to court. This knight, in full array,
200 Stood forth and said, "O Queen, I've kept my day
And kept my word and have my answer ready."
     There sat the noble matrons and the heady
Young girls, and widows too, that have the grace
Of wisdom, all assembled in that place,
205 And there the queen herself was throned to hear
And judge his answer. Then the knight drew near
And silence was commanded through the hall.
     The queen gave order he should tell them all
What thing it was that women wanted most.
210 He stood not silent like a beast or post,
But gave his answer with the ringing word
Of a man's voice and the assembly heard:

179. peradventure *adv.:* perhaps.

194. coverchief . . . caul (kôl): women's headgear. The coverchief covered the entire head; the caul, a small, netted cap, was sometimes ornamented.

The Knight and the Old Lady.
© The Bodleian Library, University of Oxford, England. MS. Douce.195, Fol. 105r.

160 Collection 2 The Middle Ages

Literary Criticism

Critic's Commentary: The Wife's Heresy
Edwin J. Howard reminds readers that the Wife of Bath is on her way to Canterbury to seek salvation. Yet in her tale, she is "dealing with a matter of religion: sovereignty in the family; and she [is] utterly heretical in her views, as the Bible very definitely states that woman is to be subject to her husband. All the members of the clergy on the pilgrimage would shudder to hear her bold denial of Holy Writ."

Activity. Have students evaluate the Wife of Bath's feminist perspective. Does she differ from feminist thinkers today? If so, how?

"My liege° and lady, in general," said he,
"A woman wants the self-same sovereignty°
215 Over her husband as over her lover,
And master him; he must not be above her.
That is your greatest wish, whether you kill
Or spare me; please yourself. I wait your will."
 In all the court not one that shook her head
220 Or contradicted what the knight had said;
Maid, wife, and widow cried, "He's saved his life!"
 And on the word up started the old wife,
The one the knight saw sitting on the green,
And cried, "Your mercy, sovereign lady queen!
225 Before the court disperses, do me right!
'Twas I who taught this answer to the knight,
For which he swore, and pledged his honor to it,
That the first thing I asked of him he'd do it,
So far as it should lie within his might.
230 Before this court I ask you then, sir knight,
To keep your word and take me for your wife;
For well you know that I have saved your life.
If this be false, deny it on your sword!"
 "Alas!" he said, "Old lady, by the Lord
235 I know indeed that such was my behest,°
But for God's love think of a new request,
Take all my goods, but leave my body free."
"A curse on us," she said, "if I agree!
I may be foul, I may be poor and old,
240 Yet will not choose to be, for all the gold
That's bedded in the earth or lies above,
Less than your wife, nay, than your very love!"
 "My love?" said he. "By heaven, my damnation!
Alas that any of my race and station
245 Should ever make so foul a misalliance!"°
Yet in the end his pleading and defiance
All went for nothing, he was forced to wed.
He takes his ancient wife and goes to bed.
 Now peradventure some may well suspect
250 A lack of care in me since I neglect
To tell of the rejoicings and display
Made at the feast upon their wedding-day.
I have but a short answer to let fall;
I say there was no joy or feast at all,
255 Nothing but heaviness of heart and sorrow.
He married her in private on the morrow

213. **liege** (lēj) *n*.: lord.
214. **sovereignty** (sä v′rən·tē) *n*.: power.

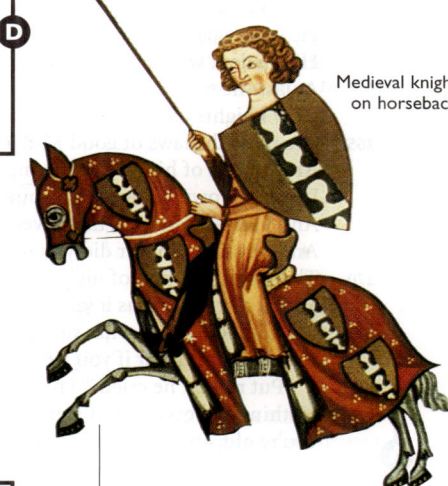
Medieval knight on horseback.

235. **behest** *n*.: command; order.

245. **misalliance** (mis·ə·lī′əns) *n*.: here, a marriage that is unsuitable or inappropriate.

Vocabulary
disperses (di·spurs′iz) *v*.: breaks up.

Geoffrey Chaucer 161

DIRECT TEACHING

A Learners Having Difficulty

❓ Paraphrasing. This passage expresses a rather simple idea about poverty in a complex way. In your own words, what is the old woman saying about her poverty? [Possible response: You criticize my poverty, but God himself—whom we follow and believe in and by whose will we exist—chose a life of poverty, and everyone knows that God would never choose to do anything shameful.]

B Reading Skills

❓ Evaluating arguments. What arguments does the old woman present in favor of poverty? [The poor don't have to worry about thievery; poverty promotes hard work, helps people to attain wisdom, precludes envy and slander, brings the poor closer to God, and permits true knowledge of oneself and one's true friends.] Urge students to evaluate her arguments and to present counterarguments.

"Reflect how noble (says Valerius)°
Was Tullius surnamed Hostilius,°
Who rose from poverty to nobleness.
And read Boethius,° Seneca° no less,
345 Thus they express themselves and are agreed:
'Gentle is he that does a gentle deed.'
And therefore, my dear husband, I conclude
That even if my ancestors were rude,
Yet God on high—and so I hope He will—
350 Can grant me grace to live in virtue still,
A gentlewoman only when beginning
To live in virtue and to shrink from sinning.

   'As for my poverty which you reprove,
Almighty God Himself in whom we move,
355 Believe, and have our being, chose a life
Of poverty, and every man or wife
Nay, every child can see our Heavenly King
Would never stoop to choose a shameful thing.
No shame in poverty if the heart is gay,
360 As Seneca and all the learned say.
He who accepts his poverty unhurt
I'd say is rich although he lacked a shirt.
But truly poor are they who whine and fret
And covet what they cannot hope to get.
365 And he that, having nothing, covets not,
Is rich, though you may think he is a sot.°

   "True poverty can find a song to sing.
Juvenal° says a pleasant little thing:
'The poor can dance and sing in the relief
370 Of having nothing that will tempt a thief.'
Though it be hateful, poverty is good,
A great incentive to a livelihood,
And a great help to our capacity
For wisdom, if accepted patiently.
375 Poverty is, though wanting in estate,
A kind of wealth that none calumniate.°
Poverty often, when the heart is lowly,
Brings one to God and teaches what is holy,
Gives knowledge of oneself and even lends
380 A glass by which to see one's truest friends.
And since it's no offense, let me be plain;
Do not rebuke my poverty again.

   "Lastly you taxed me, sir, with being old.
Yet even if you never had been told

Vocabulary
capacity (kə·pas′i·tē) *n.:* ability to absorb.

---

341. Valerius (və·lir′ē·əs): first-century A.D. Roman writer who collected historical anecdotes that public speakers could use.
342. Tullius (tul′ē·əs) **surnamed Hostilius** (hos·til′ē·əs): Tullius Hostilius, legendary king of Rome who rose from humble origins.
344. Boethius (bō·ē′thē·əs) (c. A.D. 480–c. 524): Roman philosopher. In his *Consolation of Philosophy*, he argues that rank is no guarantee of honorable conduct. **Seneca** (sen′i·kə) (c. 4 B.C.–A.D. 65): Roman philosopher whose works were popular in the Middle Ages.

366. sot *n.:* fool.

368. Juvenal (jōō′və·n'l) (c. A.D. 60–c. 140): Roman satirist.

376. calumniate (kə·lum′nē·āt′) *v.:* slander.

Connecting to World Literature

The Frame Story: A Tale Linking Tales
by David Adams Leeming

> You have just read excerpts from Chaucer's *The Canterbury Tales,* an example of a frame story. In this Connecting to World Literature feature you will read excerpts from these other frame stories:
> **Right-Mind and Wrong-Mind** . . . . (India) 173
> *from* **The Third Voyage of Sindbad the Sailor** . . . (Arabia) . . . 180
> Giovanni Boccaccio . . . **Federigo's Falcon** . . . . (Italy) 187

Many—perhaps most—of the tales told by Chaucer's pilgrims in *The Canterbury Tales* did not originate with Chaucer. Instead, they were based on older stories that Chaucer was familiar with—some from the ancient folklore of other cultures. For example, the tale the Pardoner tells (see page 146) is a variation of a story that appears in cultures as diverse as Persia and Tibet.

The Collecting Bug
In the Middle Ages, there was a deliberate effort to collect beloved stories from the oral tradition. These were stories that had formerly been flying about the world by word-of-mouth—from one village and town to the other and even from one country and one continent to the other. These popular tales—fairy tales, legends, moral tales—were the direct ancestors of what we know today as the short story.

The Unifying Frame
How could a grouping of well-told but completely unrelated stories best be collected into one book? The answer came in the form of the **frame story.** We can trace the frame story back at least to the Indian collection of tales called the *Panchatantra* (*pancha* means "five" and *tantra* means "books"), which probably dates from around A.D. 300. A frame story was a means by which a collection of tales could be held together by a common element. Instead of just moving from one unrelated story to another, an outer story (the frame) provided a rationale for the collection.

A Frame to Set Them In
Writers found a variety of ways to frame their collections. The *Panchatantra* is unified by a frame story in which a Hindu wise man, Vishnusharman (vish′nōō·shär′mən), uses a series of fables—stories with a moral—to teach proper behavior to three ignorant and unruly sons of a king. In *The Canterbury Tales,* the frame is the story of pilgrims agreeing to tell tales to kill time on their way to and from Canterbury.

1387
Chaucer begins to write *The Canterbury Tales*

1348–1353
Boccaccio writes the *Decameron*

c. 850
The stories of *The Thousand and One Nights* begin to be collected

100 B.C.– A.D. 500
Stories of the *Panchatantra* are collected

A

Pages 169–170 cover
Literary Skills
Understand the characteristics of frame stories. Compare frame stories from different cultures and literary periods.

The Frame Story: A Tale Linking Tales **169**

SKILLS FOCUS,
pp. 169–170

Grade-Level Skills

■ **Literary Skills**
Analyze characteristics of subgenres, including frame stories.

■ **Literary Skills**
Compare major literary forms of different historical periods.

Elements of Literature: The Frame Story

Ask students to scan the subheadings of this introductory essay and to note that those subheadings all relate to the structure and the history of the frame story—a time-honored and practical invention for bringing many tales together under one literary umbrella.

DIRECT TEACHING

A Literary Connections
Folklore
Ask students to volunteer their own definitions of the word *folklore.* Emphasize that folklore is a widely inclusive term that encompasses prose and poetry, fiction and nonfiction versions, and oral and written works. Examples of folklore include folk tales, legends, fairy tales, tall tales, fables, nursery rhymes, ballads, limericks, proverbs, and in contemporary times urban legends. Generally, folklore is the creation of people who are not professional writers and artists, although sometimes professional writers have collected and given permanent form to works of folklore that might otherwise have been lost to posterity.

The Frame Story: A Tale Linking Tales **169**

DIRECT TEACHING

VIEWING THE ART

While all the stories in *The Thousand and One Nights* are told by Scheherazade (whose own story provides a frame for the tales), the three Sindbad tales are themselves framed by the story of Sindbad's relating tales of his voyages. The image here illustrates Sindbad in the act of telling his story.

Activity. Have students identify elements in the picture that suggest Sindbad's status. [He's sitting on a thronelike seat; the setting is opulent; he is obviously a person of high rank, perhaps even royalty.] Ask how this image compares to those of heroes in other artworks that students have seen. [Heroes are often portrayed as knights and aristocrats; they are not usually poor or unkempt.]

A Literary Connections
Contemporary Frame Stories
One contemporary writer who has made delightful postmodern use of the frame story is the Italian novelist Italo Calvino. In Calvino's *The Castle of Crossed Destinies* (1973), a group of men and women meet by chance at a castle in a dark wood and proceed to relate their amazing stories by commenting on tarot cards. In another vein the American novelist John Barth created his own unique take on *The Thousand and One Nights*. In Barth's *Chimera* (1972), the opening section is titled "Dunyazadiad"—a rather risqué tale told by Dunyazade, the exuberant younger sister of Scheherazade (affectionately referred to as "Sherry").

Just before Chaucer's time, in Italy, the writer Giovanni Boccaccio created a frame story in which ten young people flee to a hill town to avoid the Great Plague of 1348 (the Black Death). To while away the ten days of their isolation, they agree to tell ten stories each—hence the title of the collection, the *Decameron* (from the Greek *deca* meaning "ten" and *hemera* meaning "day"). *The Thousand and One Nights* (also known as *The Arabian Nights*), is a famous ninth-century Arabic collection of Indian, Persian, and Arabian tales (finally collected in their present form in about 1450). The frame for this collection is provided by the storytelling of Scheherazade, a wife of the evil sultan, Shahriyar. The sultan is so disgusted by the unfaithfulness of one of his wives that he takes a new bride every day and has her killed at dawn. However, the latest bride, Scheherazade, is such a gifted storyteller that she is able to postpone her death each day by withholding the end of her story until the next night. The sultan doesn't kill her because he can't bear to miss the endings of her stories. What better testament to the power of storytelling?

Sindbad the Sailor entertains a group with stories of his seven fantastic voyages, from *The Thousand and One Nights*.

K.T.C.102.b.2. By permission of the British Library, London. Reproduced by permission of Hodder and Stoughton Limited.

Panchatantra
(c. 300)

The *Panchatantra* (pun′chə·tun′trə) began in ancient India as a tool for teaching statecraft to young princes. The anonymous work consists of a series of **fables,** or brief stories that teach practical lessons about life. The stories are contained within a larger outer story, a narrative framework that gives the tales a thematic unity.

In the outer story, the **frame,** a Brahman priest named Vishnusharman (vish′no͞o·shär′mən) tries to teach the art of rulership to three rather dimwitted young princes. The lessons take the form of a series of fables, presented in five sections: how one loses friends, how one wins friends, how one should handle international relations, how one may lose profits and possessions, and how hasty actions can have harmful consequences.

The central theme that runs through the *Panchatantra* is the idea of *niti* (ni′tē), which means "worldly wisdom." A person needs five things in order to achieve *niti*: physical security, freedom from want, resolute action, good friends, and intelligence. A person with *niti* is the sort of person who can triumph over evil or dishonest people by turning the tables on them.

The *Panchatantra* is among the most well-known collections of fables in the world. It was translated into Persian as early as the sixth century. During the Middle Ages it was translated into Arabic, Greek, Hebrew, Latin, German, and Italian. The classic Indian fables have influenced works as diverse as *The Thousand and One Nights* (see page 180), Geoffrey Chaucer's *The Canterbury Tales* (see page 115), and Giovanni Boccaccio's *Decameron* (see page 187). All three of those works, like the *Panchatantra,* rely on a frame story to establish overall unity.

Elephant painting.
City Palace Museum, Udaipur Rajasthan, India. Earl & Nazima Kowall/CORBIS.

SKILLS FOCUS, pp. 171–177

Grade-Level Skills
- **Literary Skills**

Analyze the characteristics of sub-genres of prose, including fables.

- **Literary Skills**

Compare major literary forms of different historical periods.

Review Skills
- **Literary Skills**

Compare and contrast similar themes across genres.

More About the Translator
Background. Arthur William Ryder's translation of the *Panchatantra* (1925) was one of the earliest English translations made directly from the Sanskrit. Educated at Harvard University and the University of Leipzig, Ryder was professor of Sanskrit at the University of California for many years before his death in 1938. He not only translated Sanskrit works into English, but also composed original poetry in Sanskrit.

In the introduction to his translation, Ryder explains that the *Panchatantra* is actually a "textbook of *niti*," a guide to the wise conduct of life. He also notes that although the stories are charming, it is the wit and wisdom of the verses that raise the collection to the higher level of philosophical art. Ryder also mentions that he has supplied all the titles of the stories, since in the original the stories do not have individual titles.

RESOURCES: READING

Planning
- One-Stop Planner CD-ROM with ExamView Test Generator

Differentiating Instruction
- Supporting Instruction in Spanish
- Audio CD Library, Selections and Summaries in Spanish

Vocabulary
- Vocabulary Development

Grammar and Language
- Daily Language Activities

Assessment
- Holt Assessment: Literature, Reading, and Vocabulary
- One-Stop Planner CD-ROM with ExamView Test Generator
- Holt Online Assessment

Internet
- go.hrw.com (Keyword: LE5 12-2)
- Elements of Literature Online

Media
- Audio CD Library
- Audio CD Library, Selections and Summaries in Spanish

PRETEACHING

Summary 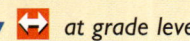 at grade level

Two friends return from a journey with a thousand dinars. They each take a hundred dinars and bury the rest. Soon wasting his hundred, Wrong-Mind proposes that each take another hundred, which they do. Wrong-Mind then steals the rest and blames Right-Mind for the theft. In court, Wrong-Mind says that the goddess of the forest will prove Right-Mind guilty. He plans to have his father hide in a tree and, in the voice of the goddess, accuse Right-Mind. The father thinks the plan is foolish, and he relates the fable of the herons who are eaten by the mongoose that they thought would save them from a snake; however, he agrees to the plan. The magistrates are fooled, but Right-Mind sets fire to the tree and smokes the father out. Wrong-Mind is hanged, and Right-Mind is rewarded.

Selection Starter

Build background. The importance of friendship is at the heart of the *Panchatantra*. The larger framework of the first section, "The Loss of Friends," is the story of the bull Lively and the lion Rusty. They meet in the forest and become friends. However, a jackal, feeling left out, tells both the bull and the lion that his friend is plotting against him. A battle ensues in which Lively is killed and the jackal enjoys the results of his maneuverings. Within this framework there are thirty-four stories, most of them told by two jackals, Victor and Cheek. In this case, Cheek tells the story "Right-Mind and Wrong-Mind" to Victor.

Before You Read

Right-Mind and Wrong-Mind

Make the Connection

Today, if we want to teach someone a moral or practical lesson about life, how do we go about it? Do some people take a direct approach and ask the person to listen to a lecture or to read a self-help manual? Do others try to get the point across in a less direct way—by telling a story, for instance? In your opinion, which way of delivering a lesson is more effective?

Literary Focus
Fable

A **fable** is a brief story in prose or verse that teaches a moral or offers a practical lesson about life. The characters in most fables are animals that speak or act like human beings; this kind of fable is often called a "beast fable." Occasionally, however, the characters in fables are human beings. Whether humans or animals, though, characters in fables often represent abstract qualities—stupidity, trickery, honesty, innocence.

INTERNET
Vocabulary Practice
Keyword: LE5 12-2

A **fable** is a brief story in prose or verse that teaches a moral or gives a practical lesson about life.

For more on Fable, see the Handbook of Literary and Historical Terms.

SKILLS FOCUS
Literary Skills
Understand the characteristics of fables.

Background

The fable "Right-Mind and Wrong-Mind" is taken from "The Loss of Friends," the first section of the *Panchatantra*, and it illustrates two important literary elements of that ancient Indian collection of fables. The first is the use of the **frame story**, or story-within-a-story device. In this case, the inner story "A Remedy Worse Than the Disease" is used to emphasize the lesson being taught in the main fable, "Right-Mind and Wrong-Mind."

The second literary element is the use of epigrams, which are interspersed throughout the prose narrative. **Epigrams** are brief, clever verses that contain moral or practical advice. In addition to summarizing the lessons of the fables, epigrams add color and flavor to the narratives.

Vocabulary Development

duplicity (d$\overline{oo}$·plis′ə·tē) *n.*: cunning; treachery.

residue (rez′ə·d$\overline{oo}$′) *n.*: leftover portion; remainder.

preliminary (prē·lim′ə·ner′ē) *adj.*: preparing for the main event; introductory.

initiative (i·nish′ə·tiv) *n.*: action of making the first move.

discern (di·surn′) *v.*: recognize (the difference); make out clearly.

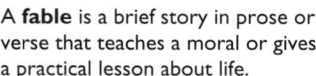

Previewing Vocabulary

Have students read the words and definitions in Vocabulary Development on p. 172. Then, have them demonstrate understanding of the definitions by answering the following questions:

1. Who demonstrates duplicity—a friend who sticks by you or someone who pretends to support you while secretly plotting against you?

2. What do you usually do with the residue of a big dinner?

3. Name three acts that are preliminary to taking a standardized test.

4. Why do you think employers are looking for people with initiative?

5. How do experts discern the difference between real money and counterfeit money?

Right-Mind and Wrong-Mind

from the Panchatantra
translated by Arthur William Ryder

In a certain city lived two friends, sons of merchants, and their names were Right-Mind and Wrong-Mind. These two traveled to another country far away in order to earn money. There the one named Right-Mind, as a consequence of favoring fortune, found a pot containing a thousand dinars,[1] which had been hidden long before by a holy man. He debated the matter with Wrong-Mind, and they decided to go home, since their object was attained. So they returned together.

When they drew near their native city, Right-Mind said: "My good friend, a half of this falls to your share. Pray take it, so that, now that we are at home, we may cut a brilliant figure before our friends and those less friendly."

But Wrong-Mind, with a sneaking thought of his own advantage, said to the other: "My good friend, so long as we two hold this treasure in common, so long will our virtuous friendship suffer no interruption. Let us each take a hundred dinars, and go to our homes after burying the remainder. The decrease or increase of this treasure will serve as a test of our virtue."

Now Right-Mind, in the nobility of his nature, did not comprehend the hidden duplicity of his friend, and agreed to the proposal. Each then took a certain sum of money. They carefully hid the residue in the ground, and made their entrance into the city.

---

1. **dinars** (di·närz′) *n.:* A dinar was originally a Roman coin (*denarius*). This currency of varying values was used in many parts of the Mediterranean and the Middle East.

Vocabulary
duplicity (d⁻o͞o·plis′ə·tē) *n.:* cunning; treachery.
residue (rez′ə·d⁻o͞o) *n.:* leftover portion; remainder.

Shah Jahan, who ruled India during the Mughal dynasty, from 1628 to 1658. Jahan designed the Taj Mahal to immortalize his favorite wife.
Victoria and Albert Museum, London. The Bridgeman Art Library.

DIRECT TEACHING

A Literary Focus
? Fable. What has Wrong-Mind done so far that proves he is living up to his name? [He has wasted his share of the money and has stolen the remainder.]

B Reading Skills
Paraphrasing. Restate in your own words the message of Right-Mind's epigrammatic verse. [Possible response: The righteous person does not covet the possessions of others, does not commit adultery, and respects all living things as he respects himself.]

C Learners Having Difficulty
? Interpreting. According to Wrong-Mind's verse, in what order should evidence be relied on? [The best evidence is written statements; next is oral statements by witnesses; last is ordeals—grueling tests given to accused people to determine their innocence or guilt.]

D Literary Focus
Fable. Point out to students that gods, goddesses, and various nature spirits are usually features of myths, not fables. However, especially in the most ancient fables, divine spirits may play a role. The goddess of the wood in this fable would probably be the equivalent of a Greek dryad, or wood nymph.

Before long, Wrong-Mind exhausted his preliminary portion because he practiced the vice of unwise expenditure and because his predetermined fate offered vulnerable points. He therefore made a second division with Right-Mind, each taking a second hundred. Within a year this, too, had slipped in the same way through Wrong-Mind's fingers. As a result, his thoughts took this form: "Suppose I divide another two hundred with him, then what is the good of the remainder, a paltry four hundred, even if I steal it? I think I prefer to steal a round six hundred." After this meditation he went alone, removed the treasure, and leveled the ground.

A mere month later, he took the initiative, going to Right-Mind and saying: "My good friend, let us divide the rest of the money equally." So he and Right-Mind visited the spot and began to dig. When the excavation failed to reveal any treasure, that impudent Wrong-Mind first of all smote his own head with the empty pot, then shouted: "What became of that good lucre?[2] Surely, Right-Mind, you must have stolen it. Give me my half. If you don't, I will bring you into court."

"Be silent, villain!" said the other. "My name is Right-Mind. Such thefts are not in my line. You know the verse:

> A man right-minded sees but trash,
> Mere clods of earth, in others' cash;
> A mother in his neighbor's wife;
> In all that lives, his own dear life."

So together they carried their dispute to court and related the theft of the money. And when the magistrates[3] learned the facts, they decreed an ordeal[4] for each. But Wrong-Mind said: "Come! This judgment is not proper. For the legal dictum[5] runs:

> Best evidence is written word;
> Next, witnesses who saw and heard;
> Then only let ordeals prevail
> When witnesses completely fail.

In the present case, I have a witness, the goddess of the wood. She will reveal to you which one of us is guilty, which not guilty." And they replied: "You are quite right, sir. For there is a further saying:

> To meanest witnesses, ordeals
>   Should never be preferred;
> Of course much less, if you possess
>   A forest goddess's word.

Now we also feel a great interest in the case. You two must accompany us tomorrow morning to that part of the forest." With this they accepted bail from each and sent them home.

Then Wrong-Mind went home and asked his father's help. "Father dear," said he, "the dinars are in my hand. They only require one little word from you. This very night I am going to hide you out of sight in a hole in the mimosa[6] tree that grows near the spot where I dug out the treasure before. In the morning you must be my witness in the presence of the magistrates."

"Oh, my son," said the father, "we are both lost. This is no kind of scheme. There is wisdom in the old story:

> The good and bad of given schemes
>   Wise thought must first reveal:
> The stupid heron saw his chicks
>   Provide a mongoose meal."

"How was that?" asked Wrong-Mind. And his father told the story of

---

2. **lucre** (loo′kər) *n.*: riches; money.
3. **magistrates** *n. pl.*: officials with judicial powers.
4. **ordeal** *n.*: here, a form of trial in which guilt or innocence is determined by subjecting the accused to painful or dangerous tests.
5. **dictum** *n.*: formal pronouncement.
6. **mimosa** *n.*: flowering tree.

Vocabulary
preliminary (prē·lim′ə·ner′ē) *adj.*: introductory.
initiative (i·nish′ə·tiv) *n.*: action of making the first move.

CONTENT-AREA CONNECTIONS

Linguistics: Sanskrit
Remind students that this tale was originally written in Sanskrit. In India's ancient literary tradition, Sanskrit is considered a sacred language, the language spoken by the gods and goddesses. As such, Sanskrit was seen as the only appropriate form of expression for the noblest literary works—epics, court poems, and dramas, among others. Although India claims more than fourteen major languages and hundreds of regional dialects, Sanskrit has given an amazing cohesiveness to Indian literature over the past 3,500 years. Poets, novelists, and dramatists, writing in various Indian languages, have drawn much of their inspiration from the classical tradition represented in Sanskrit texts, which are known for their beauty and intellectual subtlety.

Peacocks and cranes beside a river. Illustration from the *Baburnama* (*The Memoirs of Babur*) (1589–1590). Mughal School.

National Museum of India, New Delhi. The Bridgeman Art Library.

A Remedy Worse Than the Disease

A flock of herons once had their nests on a fig tree in a part of a forest. In a hole in the tree lived a black snake who made a practice of eating the heron chicks before their wings sprouted.

At last one heron, in utter woe at seeing the young ones eaten by a snake, went to the shore of the pond, shed a flood of tears, and stood with downcast face. And a crab who noticed him in this attitude, said: "Uncle, why are you so tearful today?" "My good friend," said the heron, "what am I to do? Fate is against me. My babies and the youngsters belonging to my relatives have been eaten by a snake that lives in a hole in the fig tree. Grieved at their grief, I weep. Tell me, is there any possible device for killing him?"

Panchatantra 175

DIRECT TEACHING

A Learners Having Difficulty

? Paraphrasing. How would you restate the verse proverb in your own words? [Possible response: Talk smoothly and be hardhearted: Provoke your enemy to do things that will lead him and his followers to destruction.]

B Learners Having Difficulty

? Interpreting. What lesson is Wrong-Mind's father trying to teach through this fable? [His point is that sometimes a solution to a problem can be worse than the problem itself, so one should consider one's course of action carefully.]

C Literary Focus

? Character and theme. What does Right-Mind's action tell you about his character? [Possible response: His setting fire to the tree indicates that he is a clearthinking man of action.] What theme or message does his action convey? [Possible response: Taking simple decisive action can break through deception and solve problems.]

D Literary Focus

? Fable. In your opinion, does this story teach a moral lesson or a practical one? Explain your response. [Possible responses: The story teaches a moral lesson about not stealing because Wrong-Mind is hanged for his crime. The story teaches two practical lessons: Be wary of trusting people, especially when large sums of money are involved, and take decisive action to cut through hypocrisy and fraud.]

On hearing this, the crab reflected: "After all, he is a natural-born enemy of my race. I will give him such advice—a kind of true lie—that other herons may also perish. For the proverb says:

> Let your speech like butter be;
> Steel your heart remorselessly:
> Stir an enemy to action
> That destroys him with his faction."

And he said aloud: "Uncle, conditions being as they are, scatter bits of fish all the way from the mongoose burrow to the snake's hole. The mongoose will follow that trail and will destroy the villainous snake."

When this had been done, the mongoose followed the bits of fish, killed the villainous snake, and also ate at his leisure all the herons who made their home in the tree.

"And that is why I say:

> The good and bad of given schemes, . . .
> and the rest of it."

But Wrong-Mind disdained the paternal warning, and during the night he hid his father out of sight in the hole in the tree. When morning came, the scamp took a bath, put on clean garments, and followed Right-Mind and the magistrates to the mimosa tree, where he cried in piercing tones:

> "Earth, heaven, and death, the feeling mind,
> Sun, moon, and water, fire and wind,
> Both twilights, justice, day and night
> Discern man's conduct, wrong or right.

O blessed goddess of the wood, which of us two is the thief? Speak."

Then Wrong-Mind's father spoke from his hole in the mimosa: "Gentlemen, Right-Mind took that money." And when all the king's men heard this statement, their eyes blossomed with astonishment, and they searched their minds to discover the appropriate legal penalty for stealing money, in order to visit it on Right-Mind.

Meanwhile, Right-Mind heaped inflammable matter about the hole in the mimosa and set fire to it. As the mimosa burned, Wrong-Mind's father issued from the hole with a pitiful wail, his body scorched and his eyes popping out. And they all asked: "Why, sir! What does this mean?"

"It is all Wrong-Mind's doing," he replied. Whereupon the king's men hanged Wrong-Mind to a branch of the mimosa, while they commended Right-Mind and caused him satisfaction by conferring upon him the king's favor and other things. ■

Vocabulary
discern (di·surn′) v.: recognize (the difference); make out clearly.

Tamarind tree (detail) (1590) by Mirza Abd al-Rahim. Mughal school.
The Art Archive/British Library, London.

176 Collection 2 The Middle Ages

FAMILY/COMMUNITY ACTIVITY

Have students canvass family and community members to gather, assemble, and present a collection of favorite proverbs, epigrams, and maxims that convey "worldly wisdom." Students can record the proverbs and ask each contributor for a comment or an anecdote explaining why each proverb is so meaningful.

ASSESSING

Assessment
- *Holt Assessment: Literature, Reading, and Vocabulary*

Response and Analysis

Reading Check

1. What do Right-Mind and Wrong-Mind agree to do with their treasure?
2. How does Wrong-Mind break their agreement?
3. Why does Wrong-Mind hide his father in the mimosa tree?
4. How does Right-Mind expose Wrong-Mind's scheme?

Thinking Critically

5. What **moral lessons** about rulership can be learned from the **fable** "Right-Mind and Wrong-Mind"?
6. What kind of person does the character Wrong-Mind seem to stand for in the fable?
7. How does the story-within-a-story, "A Remedy Worse Than the Disease," connect to the **moral** of "Right-Mind and Wrong-Mind"?
8. An **epigram** is a brief, clever, and often memorable statement. Which of the four-line epigrammatic verses best sums up the overall moral of the fable?
9. Do the lessons taught in "Right-Mind and Wrong-Mind" relate at all to people and their problems today? Think especially in terms of arguments over money and the use of courts to settle disputes. Use examples from the fable to support your opinions.
10. In what other situations could the "remedy" be "worse than the disease"?

Comparing Literature

11. How do these stories from India compare with the stories you've read from *The Canterbury Tales*? Consider these three story elements:
    - characterization
    - use of a frame story
    - use of moral lessons

LISTENING AND SPEAKING

Performing the Fable

Prepare "Right-Mind and Wrong-Mind" for an oral presentation to an audience. You will have to decide how many readers you will need and which parts of the fable you will assign to which reader. Before you present your fable to an audience, try it out before a group of classmates. Have your critics evaluate your performance in terms of clarity, dramatic interest, and originality. Use their evaluation as you make final adjustments in your presentation for the real performance.

Vocabulary Development
Analogies

duplicity   preliminary   discern
residue   initiative

In an **analogy** two pairs of words have the same relationship. They may be antonyms or synonyms, or they may share some other relationship. Work with a partner to complete each analogy below with a Vocabulary word from above.

1. SUM : TOTAL :: residue : remainder
2. SWEET : SOUR :: _____ : final
3. NOISE : SILENCE :: _____ : laziness
4. WISDOM : KNOWLEDGE :: _____ : dishonesty
5. WALK : AMBLE :: _____ : figure out

Literary Skills
Analyze the characteristics of fables. Compare frame stories.

Listening and Speaking Skills
Give an oral performance of a fable.

Vocabulary Skills
Complete word analogies.

Panchatantra 177

INDEPENDENT PRACTICE

Response and Analysis

6. Possible answers: Wrong-Mind represents greed, avarice, hypocrisy, fraud, and betrayal. He is someone who would do anything for money, even rob from his friends and implicate his family in his crimes.
7. The characters in the story-within-a-story act hastily, depend upon advice from untrustworthy sources, and fail to consider the consequences of their actions, as Wrong-Mind does himself.
8. Possible answer: The moral is best conveyed by the verse that begins "The good and bad of given schemes."
9. Modern audiences should still heed these moral lessons about the dangers of greed, the dangers of lying to cover up crimes, and the difficulty of uncovering the truth in a trial setting. Students may cite examples such as Wrong-Mind's scheme, which leads to his own death, or the fateful outcome of the heron's unwise decision to accept the advice of the crab.
10. Some medical treatments make you feel sicker than the illness itself.

Comparing Literature

11. Possible answers: The characters in the frame story of *The Canterbury Tales* are much more developed than the abstract characters in "Right-Mind and Wrong-Mind." Both tales provide a number of moral lessons that still hold true today.

Vocabulary Development

2. preliminary
3. initiative
4. duplicity
5. discern

Reading Check

1. They agree to take one hundred dinars each and bury the rest of the money.
2. After they each take another hundred dinars, Wrong-Mind steals the rest of the money.
3. Wrong-Mind wants his father to pretend to be the goddess of the wood and falsely accuse Right-Mind of the theft.
4. Right-Mind sets fire to the tree, forcing Wrong-Mind's father to come out.

Thinking Critically

5. Possible answers: Be on guard against fraud and advice from unreliable sources. Consider all possible outcomes and consequences of a plan.

SKILLS FOCUS, pp. 178–184

Grade-Level Skills

■ **Literary Skills**

Analyze the characteristics of archetypes drawn from myth and tradition.

Review Skills

■ **Literary Skills**

Compare works that express a universal theme and provide evidence to support that theme.

More About the Translator

Background. The first translation of *The Thousand and One Nights* into a European language was Antoine Galland's 1704 French version, which led to an English translation in 1706. Since then, many Western authors, including Alexander Pope and William Wordsworth, have been inspired by the marvelous tales. N. J. Dawood was born in Baghdad in 1927 and is a businessman, publisher, and consultant for Middle Eastern and Arab affairs. His 1956 translation of the Koran won him international critical acclaim.

The Thousand and One Nights
(c. 850–c. 1500)

Ever since the writer Antoine Galland translated *The Thousand and One Nights*—or *The Arabian Nights' Entertainments*—into French in the early eighteenth century, this collection of tales has been the best-known and most widely read work of Arabic literature in the West. The often fantastic adventures of the characters Ali Baba, Aladdin, and Sindbad are known throughout the world today.

The original stories in *The Thousand and One Nights* came from many oral and written sources including such collections as the Indian *Panchatantra* (see page 171) and tales brought by travelers from China, India, and every part of the Middle East. Scholars have identified sources for many of the stories, but the true origins of many others remain unknown because they exist in more than one version and in more than one language.

The earliest references to *The Thousand and One Nights* appear in manuscripts from as early as the ninth century. Kept alive by Arab storytellers throughout the Middle Ages, the collection grew and changed. By the mid–sixteenth century, an unknown Egyptian had put the stories into the form we know today. The tales were first published in Arabic in 1548.

The tales in the collection are loosely held together by a **frame story.** In the frame story a sultan, Shahriyar, is enraged at his wife's unfaithfulness and orders her executed. He then takes a new wife each day but has her killed at dawn the next day because he believes that no woman can ever be faithful. The supply of potential wives is running low when the sultan takes Scheherazade (shə·her′ə·zäd′) as his wife.

Scheherazade is a spellbinding storyteller and a clever woman besides. Each night she entertains the sultan with a new tale, but she delays revealing the ending until the following night. The captivated sultan keeps postponing her execution in order to hear the end of each story. After one thousand and one nights of tales, he abandons his plans to kill Scheherazade, and the couple remains happily married.

The Princess in the Kitchens by Edmund Dulac. Illustration for a 1911 edition of *The Arabian Nights*. Lithograph.
Private Collection/The Bridgeman Art Library. Reproduced by permission of Hodder and Stoughton Limited.

MEDIEVAL ARABIA

RESOURCES: READING

Planning
■ *One-Stop Planner* CD-ROM with ExamView Test Generator

Differentiating Instruction
■ Supporting Instruction in Spanish
■ Audio CD Library, Selections and Summaries in Spanish

Vocabulary
■ Vocabulary Development

Grammar and Language
■ Daily Language Activities

Assessment
■ Holt Assessment: Literature, Reading, and Vocabulary
■ *One-Stop Planner* CD-ROM with ExamView Test Generator
■ Holt Online Assessment

Internet
■ go.hrw.com (Keyword: LE5 12-2)
■ Elements of Literature Online

Media
■ Audio CD Library
■ Audio CD Library, Selections and Summaries in Spanish

Before You Read

from The Third Voyage of Sindbad the Sailor

Make the Connection
Think of monsters you might find in popular stories and movies today. What qualities do these monsters usually have? What does a typical monster or villain look like? What are his or her habits? How does he or she feel about other people? Where do these monsters live—that is, what settings are associated with them?

Literary Focus

Archetypes

An **archetype** is a very old pattern used in storytelling. An archetype can be a plot, a character, a setting, or even just an object. One of the most universal archetypes is the "monster-slaying story." If you have read Homer's *Odyssey*, you might even recognize the monster in this Middle Eastern story. This is a characteristic of archetypes: They cross borders and cultures. In storytelling, archetypes seem to satisfy or excite the most basic human needs and longings.

> An **archetype** is the basic pattern or model of a character, a plot, a setting, or an object that recurs in storytelling.
>
> For more on Archetype, see the Handbook of Literary and Historical Terms.

Background
Sindbad is a rich young man from Baghdad (now the capital of Iraq) who goes to sea to regain his fortune after recklessly spending all his wealth. His marvelous adventures at sea are the subjects of the three Sindbad stories that form a story cycle in *The Thousand and One Nights*. Some scholars believe the tales originated in Baghdad, but others argue persuasively that they came from Oman (a country on the southeast coast of the Arabian Peninsula) and only later became associated with Baghdad.

Vocabulary Development

disconsolately (dis·kän′sə·lit·lē) *adv.*: dejectedly; unhappily.

corpulent (kôr′pyōō·lənt) *adj.*: fat.

approbation (ap′rə·bā′shən) *n.*: approval.

nimbly (nim′blē) *adv.*: in a quick, light way.

contrived (kən·trīvd′) *v.*: managed.

Sindbad the Sailor being carried by a sea monster, from *One Thousand and One Nights* (18th century).
Archivo Iconografico, S.A./CORBIS.

Literary Skills Understand the characteristics of an archetype.

PRETEACHING

Summary below grade level

The narrator, Sindbad, explains that, bored with idleness, he again sets off, looking for profit and adventure. After trading at many ports, he and his merchant companions approach an island from which swarm apelike dwarfs who overrun the ship and maroon the merchants. On the island they discover a huge palace, in which they find a heap of bones, an open oven, and enormous pots. In the evening a monstrous giant appears, roasts and devours the captain, and falls asleep. In the morning the giant wakes and leaves the men cowering. They lament their fate and search the island for a place to hide. Finding none, they return to the palace in the evening. The giant returns, eats another merchant, sleeps all night, and leaves again the next morning. The remaining merchants agree that they must at least try to kill the monster. Following Sindbad's proposal, they build a raft for escape and leave it ready on the shore. That night the giant returns, eats another merchant, and again falls asleep. The merchants heat two iron spits in the fire and plunge them into the giant's eyes. Blinded and enraged, the giant gropes in vain for the men and staggers outside. The men rush to the shore, board the raft, and push off. The giant, however, guided by a giant hag, throws enormous boulders at them. All but two of Sindbad's companions are drowned, and the three survivors manage to paddle away.

Previewing Vocabulary

Have students express the definition of each Vocabulary item in their own words. Then, have students complete each of the following sentences with the correct Vocabulary word from p. 179.

1. The basketball star seldom committed fouls because he moved so _____. [nimbly]
2. The human shapes in the painting ranged from the scrawny to the _____. [corpulent]
3. She reported _____ that she had failed the chemistry test. [disconsolately]
4. Nevertheless, she _____ to stay on the honor roll. [contrived]
5. With the _____ of his supervisor, he was given much more responsibility. [approbation]

from The Third Voyage of Sindbad the Sailor

from **The Thousand and One Nights**

translated by **N. J. Dawood**

Know, my friends, that for some time after my return I continued to lead a happy and tranquil life, but I soon grew weary of my idle existence in Baghdad and once again longed to roam the world in quest of profit and adventure. Unmindful of the dangers of ambition and worldly greed, I resolved to set out on another voyage. I provided myself with a great store of goods and, after taking them down the Tigris,[1] set sail from Basrah,[2] together with a band of honest merchants.

The voyage began prosperously. We called at many foreign ports, trading profitably with our merchandise. One day, however, whilst we were sailing in midocean, we heard the captain of our ship, who was on deck scanning the horizon, suddenly burst out in a loud lament. He beat himself about the face, tore his beard, and rent his clothes.

"We are lost!" he cried, as we crowded round him. "The treacherous wind has driven us off our course toward that island which you see before you. It is the isle of the Zughb, where dwell a race of dwarfs more akin to apes than men, from whom no voyager has ever escaped alive!"

Scarcely had he uttered these words when a multitude of apelike savages appeared on the beach and began to swim out toward the ship. In a few moments they were upon us, thick as a swarm of locusts. Barely four spans[3] in height, they were the ugliest of living creatures, with little gleaming yellow eyes and bodies thickly covered with black fur. And so numerous were they that we did not dare to provoke them or attempt to drive them away, lest they should set upon us and kill us to a man by force of numbers.

They scrambled up the masts, gnawing the cables with their teeth and biting them to shreds. Then they seized the helm and steered the vessel to their island. When the ship had run ashore, the dwarfs carried us one by one to the beach, and, promptly pushing off again, climbed on board and sailed away.

<u>Disconsolately</u> we set out to search for food and water, and by good fortune came upon some fruit trees and a running stream. Here we refreshed ourselves, and then wandered about the island until at length we saw far off among the trees a massive building, where we hoped to pass the night in safety. Drawing nearer, we found that it was a towering palace surrounded by a lofty wall, with a great ebony door which stood wide open. We entered the spacious courtyard, and to our surprise found it deserted. In one corner lay a great heap of bones, and on the far side we saw a broad bench, an open oven, pots and pans of enormous size, and many iron spits for roasting.

---

1. **Tigris** (tī′gris): river in southwest Asia, flowing from Turkey through Iraq.
2. **Basrah** (bus′rə): port at the head of the Shatt-al-Arab Channel, where the Tigris and Euphrates rivers join.
3. **spans** *n. pl.*: A span was a measurement equal to nine inches, based on the distance between the extended thumb and little finger.

Vocabulary
disconsolately (dis·kän′sə·lit·lē) *adv.*: dejectedly; unhappily.

Colossus by Francisco de Goya y Lucientes.
© Scala/Art Resource, New York.

Exhausted and sick at heart, we lay down in the courtyard and were soon overcome by sleep. At sunset we were awakened by a noise like thunder. The earth shook beneath our feet and we saw a colossal black giant approaching from the doorway. He was a fearsome sight—tall as a palm tree, with red eyes burning in his head like coals of fire; his mouth was a dark well, with lips that drooped like a camel's loosely over his chest, whilst his ears, like a pair of large round discs, hung back over his shoulders: his fangs were as long as the tusks of a boar and his nails were like the claws of a lion.

The sight of this monster struck terror to our hearts. We cowered motionless on the ground as we watched him stride across the yard and sit down on the bench. For a few moments he eyed us one by one in silence; then he rose and, reaching out toward me, lifted me up by the neck and began feeling my body as a butcher would a lamb. Finding me little more than skin and bone, however, he flung me to the ground and, picking up each of my companions in turn, pinched and prodded them and set them down until at last he came to the captain.

DIRECT TEACHING

VIEWING THE ART

Francisco de Goya y Lucientes (1746–1828) belongs to a group of nineteenth-century artists who sought to expose people's pretensions to being rational creatures. Goya and his Romantic contemporaries were particularly interested in painting images of physical and emotional violence, madness, and struggle.

Activity. How does this image illustrate Goya's interest in the irrational? [The colossus himself is an image of the irrational, since he is monstrous, but he also provokes derangement in the people and other creatures at the bottom of the image.]

E Literary Focus

Archetype. Identify the similes and the metaphor used to describe the giant. [*Similes*—noise like thunder; tall as a palm tree; eyes like coals; lips like a camel's; ears like discs; fangs like tusks; nails like lion's claws. *Metaphor*—His mouth was a dark well.] What image do they evoke? [They evoke an image of an enormous monster with a strange amalgam of human and animal-like features.]

F Literary Focus

Frame story. At this point in the story, we have forgotten about Scheherazade and are caught up in Sindbad's narration. In what way does having Sindbad as the narrator affect the suspense of his story? [Possible response: Because he is narrating, we know that he will not be killed.]

CONTENT-AREA CONNECTIONS

Music: *Scheherazade*

Whole-class activity. Many people associate *The Thousand and One Nights* with the themes of the symphonic suite *Scheherazade* by Russian composer Nikolai Rimsky-Korsakov (1844–1908). With its Romantic feeling and scintillating orchestration, *Scheherazade* paints unforgettable musical pictures of four scenes in "The Sea and Sinbad's Ship," "The Story of the Kalender Prince," "The Young Prince and the Young Princess," and "Festival in Baghdad. . . ." Many recordings of this classic work are available, and students might especially enjoy Rimsky-Korsakov's dramatic storm and shipwreck scenes.

DIRECT TEACHING

A Reading Skills

❓ Recognizing philosophical assumptions. What does this exclamation reveal about the beliefs of Sindbad and his fellow merchants? [Possible response: They believe that their fates are determined by Allah. Nevertheless, they take practical action.]

B Literary Focus

❓ Irony. How does the ironic understatement "prepared his supper" heighten the grim tone of the scene? [By saying "prepared his supper" instead of describing the horrible death of one of his companions, the narrator implies that the scene is too gruesome to describe and shows that he is toughening his own mind and heart against the loss.]

Now the captain was a <u>corpulent</u> fellow, tall and broad-shouldered. The giant seemed to like him well. He gripped him as a butcher grips a fatted ram and broke his neck under his foot. Then he thrust an iron spit through his body from mouth to backside and, lighting a great fire in the oven, carefully turned his victim round and round before it. When the flesh was finely roasted, the ogre tore the body to pieces with his fingernails as though it were a pullet,[4] and devoured it limb by limb, gnawing the bones and flinging them against the wall. The monster then stretched himself out on the bench and soon fell fast asleep. His snores were as loud as the grunts and gurgles that issue from the throat of a slaughtered beast.

Thus he slept all night, and when morning came he rose and went out of the palace, leaving us half-crazed with terror.

A As soon as we were certain that the monster had gone we began lamenting our evil fortune. "Would that we had been drowned in the sea or killed by the apes!" we cried. "That would surely have been better than the foul death which now awaits us. But that which Allah has ordained must surely come to pass."

We left the palace to search for some hiding place, but could find no shelter in any part of the island, and had no choice but to return to the palace in the evening. Night came, and with it the black giant, announcing his approach by a noise like thunder. No sooner had he entered than he snatched up one of the merchants and **B** prepared his supper in the same way as the night before. Then, stretching himself out to sleep, he snored the night away.

Next morning, when the giant had gone, we discussed our desperate plight.

"By Allah," cried one of the merchants, "let us rather throw ourselves into the sea than remain alive to be roasted and eaten!"

"Listen, my friends," said another. "We must kill this monster. For only by destroying him can we end his wickedness and save good Muslims from his barbarous cruelty."

This proposal was received with general <u>approbation</u>; so I rose in my turn and addressed the company. "If we are all agreed to kill this monster," I said, "let us first build a raft on which we can escape from this island as soon as we have sent his soul to damnation. Perchance our raft will take us to some other island, where we can board a ship bound for our country. If we are drowned, we shall at least escape roasting and die a martyr's death."

"By Allah," cried the others, "that is a wise plan."

Setting to work at once, we hauled several logs from the great pile of wood stacked beside the oven and carried them out of the palace. Then we fastened them together into a raft, which we left ready on the seashore.

In the evening the earth shook beneath our feet as the black giant burst in upon us, barking and snarling like a mad dog. Once more he seized upon the stoutest of my companions and prepared his meal. When he had eaten his fill, he stretched himself upon the bench as was his custom and soon fell fast asleep.

Noiselessly we now rose, took two of the great iron spits from the oven, and thrust them into the fire. As soon as they were red-hot we carried them over to the snoring monster and plunged their sharpened ends deep into his eyes, exerting our united weight from above to push them home. The giant gave a deafening shriek which filled our hearts with terror and cast us back on the ground many yards away. Totally blinded, he leapt up from the bench groping for us with outstretched hands, while we <u>nimbly</u> dodged his frantic clutches. In despair he felt his way to the ebony door and

---

Vocabulary

corpulent (kôr′pyōō·lənt) *adj.*: fat.
approbation (ap′rə·bā′shən) *n.*: approval.
nimbly (nim′blē) *adv.*: in a quick, light way.

---

4. **pullet** *n.*: chicken.

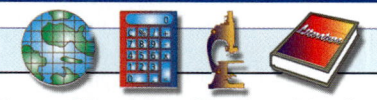

CONTENT-AREA CONNECTIONS

Literature: Homer's *Odyssey*
Paired activity. Have students research the episode of Odysseus and the Cyclops in Homer's *Odyssey*. Ask them to explain to the rest of the class how Homer's story and the tale of Sindbad and the giant are similar and different. What do these two tales reveal about the archetype of the monster-slaying story?

Culture: Monster-Slaying Stories
Individual activity. Encourage students from other cultures to discuss archetypal characters, plots, and settings of monster-slaying adventure stories from their own cultures. Have them make a list on the chalkboard of characters, plots, and settings that they remember and compare them to the elements found in "The Third Voyage of Sindbad the Sailor."

DEVELOPING FLUENCY

Whole-class activity. Have students take turns reading parts of Sindbad's adventure aloud. Students should practice reading with emotion and intensity, paying special attention to clues such as "cried out" and the use of exclamation points. Remind students, however, that intensity does not always require volume; sometimes a whisper is more effective than a shout.

Illustration by Edmund Dulac from *Sindbad the Sailor and Other Stories*.
Harry Ransom Humanities Research Center, The University of Texas at Austin. Reproduced by permission of Hodder and Stoughton Limited.

staggered out of the yard, groaning in agonies of pain.

Without losing a moment we made off toward the beach. As soon as we reached the water we launched our raft and jumped aboard; but scarcely had we rowed a few yards when we saw the blind savage running toward us, guided by a foul hag of his own kind. On reaching the shore they stood howling threats and curses at us for a while, and then caught up massive boulders and hurled them at our raft with stupendous force. Missile followed missile until all my companions, save two, were drowned; but we three who escaped soon contrived to paddle beyond the range of their fury. ■

Vocabulary
contrived (kən·trīvd') *v.*: managed.

The Thousand and One Nights 183

INDEPENDENT PRACTICE

Response and Analysis

Reading Check

1. *Basic situation and conflict*—Sindbad, a captain, and some merchants sail near an island, are overtaken by apelike dwarfs, are marooned, and encounter a man-eating giant. *Main events*—The giant roasts and devours the captain and two merchants. *Climax*—Sindbad and the remaining merchants blind the giant by thrusting heated iron spits into his eyes. *Resolution*—The survivors escape on a raft they have built; however, the giant throws boulders at them and all drown except Sindbad and two companions.

Thinking Critically

2. The giant resembles other inhuman, bestial, surly, ferocious, and menacing creatures in monster-slaying stories.

3. He compares the giant's distorted eyes, lips, ears, and so on, to those of animals. The giant's cannibalism violates a strict human taboo against eating human flesh.

4. Possible answer: Many sci-fi and action movie-makers adapt the monster archetype by creating an evil alien creature that assumes the shape of a human.

Literary Criticism

5. Possible answer: The tales have remained popular because they appeal to a universal interest in fantasy and heroism; they are among the archetypes of heroic adventures.

Comparing Literature

6. The giant resembles Humbaba in his immensity and Grendel in his appetite for human flesh.

Response and Analysis

Reading Check

1. Like all folk tales, this one is built on a simple **plot** structure. Show the story's structure by filling out a chart like the following. (The number of main events may vary.)

Basic situation and conflict	
Main events	
Climax	
Resolution	

Thinking Critically

2. **Archetypes** are very old patterns found in stories across the ages, from many diverse cultures. Archetypes can be characters (the superhuman hero), plots (monster-slaying stories), or places (paradises and hells). How is the giant in this story an example of the archetypal monster who threatens a hero and his people?

3. Storytellers often make the hero's enemy only partly human. How does the storyteller in Sindbad's story make the giant particularly disgusting? Why do you think cannibalism makes an enemy seem especially evil?

4. How do storytellers today (including moviemakers) use the old monster **archetype** found in Sindbad's story?

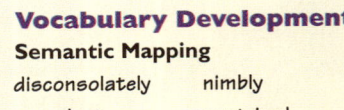

Literary Skills Analyze the characteristics of an archetype.
Writing Skills Write a story that contains an archetypal hero.
Vocabulary Skills Create semantic maps.

Literary Criticism

5. Some Arab scholars have dismissed *The Thousand and One Nights* as mere popular entertainment that is far from being great literature. These scholars have argued that the stories have crude and simplistic plots and no depth of characterization or theme. If this is true, why do you think *The Thousand and One Nights* has remained popular for hundreds of years?

Comparing Literature

6. How does this monster compare with the monsters that challenge Beowulf (see page 21) and Gilgamesh (see page 48)?

WRITING

Fantastic Foe

Write your own episode about an adventure-seeking hero and his encounter with a monster. You may wish to follow the pattern of the Sindbad story you have just read, but change the details enough so that your story is unique. Before you begin, try mapping out the story details you will include. If you wish, illustrate your story.

Vocabulary Development
Semantic Mapping

disconsolately   nimbly
corpulent   contrived
approbation

Make a **semantic map** like the following for the Vocabulary words listed above. Be sure to locate the word in the story to determine its meaning in context.

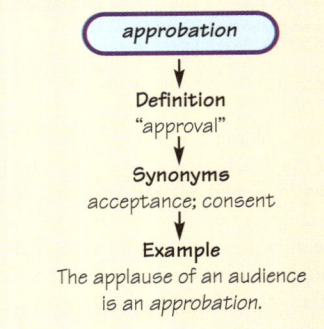

Vocabulary Development
Sample Answer

- *disconsolately.* Definition—dejectedly. Synonyms—unhappily; sorrowfully. Example—Having lost the game, he answered the reporter *disconsolately.*

Giovanni Boccaccio
(1313–1375)

Giovanni Boccaccio (bō·käch′ē·ō′) was born in the summer of 1313, perhaps in Florence or possibly in Certaldo, a small Tuscan town twenty miles outside the city. The illegitimate son of an unknown Frenchwoman and a Florentine merchant banker, Boccaccio spent his boyhood with his father. At the age of fourteen, however, he was sent to Naples, where his father had arranged for him to be a clerk in one of his banks.

After finishing his apprenticeship at the bank, Boccaccio entered the University of Naples and earned a degree in law. In 1340, when Boccaccio's father suffered a financial setback, he asked his son to return to Florence. There Boccaccio met Francesco Petrarch, the great Italian poet, who became a lifelong friend and literary advisor. In Florence, too, Boccaccio experienced the most catastrophic event of his lifetime when the Black Death struck the city in 1348. During this plague three out of four Florentines died a gruesome death. The streets of the city were piled high with swollen, reeking corpses covered with black splotches.

Boccaccio used the plague as the backdrop for his masterpiece, the *Decameron*. Written in vernacular Italian—the Italian of everyday speech—instead of Latin, the *Decameron*'s one hundred tales deal with two great subjects: love and the corruption of the clergy. Many of the *Decameron*'s stories are adaptations of popular folk tales, fables, anecdotes, and even jokes that Boccaccio might have overheard on the bustling streets of medieval Florence.

Completed about 1353, the *Decameron* established Boccaccio's literary reputation. Boccaccio, however, did not consider the *Decameron* to be his best work. In fact, he considered it trifling and unimportant. Nevertheless, the *Decameron* has survived the test of time. Geoffrey Chaucer, William Shakespeare, John Milton, and many other writers have used Boccaccio's work as both a model and a source.

Boccaccio (15th century) by Andrea del Castagno.
Uffizi, Florence, Italy.

SKILLS FOCUS, pp. 185–191

Grade-Level Skills

■ **Literary Skills**
Analyze the way a writer uses irony to achieve specific rhetorical or aesthetic purposes.

■ **Reading Skills**
Evaluate historical context.

■ **Reading Skills**
Compare influences of different historical periods.

More About the Writer

Background. The illegitimate son of a banker, Boccaccio had an unhappy childhood; furthermore, his father educated him for a business career that did not appeal to him. As a very young man, Boccaccio found some happiness in Naples, where he saw some remnants of medieval chivalry, a subject that figured significantly in his early writing. At one point in his writing career, Boccaccio suffered through a creative slump and was tempted to burn some of his earlier works. Fortunately, his friend and mentor Petrarch persuaded him to save the writings. Boccaccio continued to devote himself to writing throughout his life, despite his struggle to make a living at it.

RESOURCES: READING

Planning
■ *One-Stop Planner* CD-ROM

Differentiating Instruction
■ Holt Reading Solutions
■ The Holt Reader
■ Holt Adapted Reader
■ Supporting Instruction in Spanish
■ Audio CD Library, Selections and Summaries in Spanish

Vocabulary
■ Vocabulary Development

Grammar and Language
■ Daily Language Activities

Assessment
■ Holt Assessment: Literature, Reading, and Vocabulary
■ *One-Stop Planner* CD-ROM with ExamView Test Generator

■ Holt Online Assessment

Internet
■ go.hrw.com (Keyword: LE5 12-2)
■ Elements of Literature Online

Media
■ Audio CD Library
■ Audio CD Library, Selections and Summaries in Spanish
■ Fine Art Transparencies

PRETEACHING

Summary at grade level

The nobleman Federigo is so deeply in love with Monna Giovanna, a virtuous married woman, that he becomes poor trying to impress her. He is forced to move to a small farm, with only one valuable possession—a magnificent falcon. After Monna Giovanna's husband dies, she and her son move to a farm nearby, and the boy grows fond of Federigo's falcon. He becomes ill and begs his mother to bring him the creature. Monna Giovanna reluctantly goes to Federigo and offers to dine with him. Deeply honored, Federigo kills the falcon to serve a meal worthy of her. After they have eaten, Monna Giovanna stuns Federigo by making her request for the falcon; despairing, he reveals why he cannot help her. The sad irony of the situation is intensified when Monna Giovanna's son dies. However, the tale ends on a happy note: Pressured by her brothers to marry, Monna Giovanna chooses Federigo, whose noble gesture has won her heart.

Selection Starter

Motivate. Ask students if they have ever had a possession they prized so much that they could not imagine giving it up under any circumstances. Have student volunteers tell the class how they got these possessions, why they treasured them so much, and what eventually became of them.

Before You Read

Federigo's Falcon

Make the Connection

Few experiences are more painful than falling in love with someone who doesn't care about you. We get over it—most of us—and it never (well, almost never) does us serious damage. At the most painful moments, when you think that things can't possibly get worse, they very well might. Or they might, surprisingly, turn around. . . .

Literary Focus
Situational Irony

Situational irony occurs when what actually happens in a story is the opposite of what is expected or appropriate. For example, in Greek mythology, the story of King Midas is loaded with situational irony. Midas, who values wealth above all else, is granted the power to turn anything he touches into gold, but he soon discovers that his touch also turns food, drink, and even his beloved daughter to gold. Thus, far from making him happy, as he expected, Midas's golden touch makes him miserable. Situational irony always produces an unexpected turn of events.

INTERNET
Vocabulary Practice
•
More About Giovanni Boccaccio
•
Keyword: LE5 12-2

> Situational irony occurs when what actually happens is the opposite of what is expected or appropriate.
>
> For more on Irony, see the Handbook of Literary and Historical Terms.

Reading Skills
Evaluating Historical Context

Relations between men and women in the Middle Ages were shaped by the social, economic, and ethical realities of the era. Medieval women could not marry without the permission of their male relatives, and family money was usually passed down from male to male. The values of the courtly love tradition required women to be virtuous and withholding, yet capable of inspiring devoted service in a noble man.

Boccaccio may have experienced courtly love firsthand. In his first prose romance, he describes meeting—and immediately falling in love with—a woman named Fiammetta. Fiammetta reappears in many of Boccaccio's works, and it is she who tells the story of Federigo's falcon in the *Decameron*.

As you read Boccaccio's love story, jot down notes on how the historical context affects the plot of the story.

Background

In the **frame story** of the *Decameron*, ten wealthy young Florentines flee to a villa outside the city to escape the ravages of the plague. To pass the time, the young people decide that for each of ten days they will name a king or queen, who, in turn, will choose a theme upon which the others must tell a story. "Federigo's Falcon" is the ninth story told on the fifth day, a day devoted to telling stories with happy endings.

SKILLS FOCUS

Literary Skills Understand situational irony.
Reading Skills Evaluate historical context.

Vocabulary Development

dire (dīr) *adj*.: extreme; desperate.
compensate (käm′pən·sāt′) *v*.: repay; make up (for or to).
presumption (prē·zump′shən) *n*.: act of taking too much for granted.
console (kən·sōl′) *v*.: comfort.
reproached (ri·prōcht′) *v*.: expressed disapproval.

Previewing Vocabulary

To reinforce students' understanding of the Vocabulary words on p. 186, have partners answer the following questions:

1. Mention strategies you might use to <u>compensate</u> for a poor sense of direction.
2. Would the prediction of a <u>dire</u> outcome make you happy or sad?
3. What would you do to <u>console</u> a child who lost a favorite toy?
4. Explain how an army's <u>presumption</u> of victory might actually lead to defeat.
5. How might a person feel when <u>reproached</u> by someone he or she respects?

Federigo's Falcon

from the Decameron
Giovanni Boccaccio

translated by **Mark Musa** *and* **Peter Bondanella**

There was once in Florence a young man named Federigo, the son of Messer[1] Filippo Alberighi, renowned above all other men in Tuscany for his prowess in arms and for his courtliness. As often happens to most gentlemen, he fell in love with a lady named Monna[2] Giovanna, in her day considered to be one of the most beautiful and one of the most charming women that ever there was in Florence; and in order to win her love, he participated in jousts and tournaments, organized and gave feasts, and spent his money without restraint; but she, no less virtuous than beautiful, cared little for these things done on her behalf, nor did she care for him who did them. Now, as Federigo was spending far beyond his means and was taking nothing in, as easily happens he lost his wealth and became poor, with nothing but his little farm to his name (from whose revenues he lived very meagerly) and one falcon which was among the best in the world.

More in love than ever, but knowing that he would never be able to live the way he wished to in the city, he went to live at Campi,[3] where his farm was. There he passed his time hawking whenever he could, asked nothing of anyone, and endured his poverty patiently. Now, during the time that Federigo was reduced to dire need, it happened that the husband of Monna Giovanna fell ill, and realizing death was near, he made his last will. He was very rich, and he made his son, who was growing up, his heir, and, since he had loved Monna Giovanna very much, he made her his heir should his son die without a legitimate heir; and then he died.

Detail from Frederick II's *Treatise on Falconry*.
Ms. Pal. Lat. 1071, fol. 5v. Apostolic Library, Vatican City, Rome.

1. **Messer** (mes′ər): title of address similar to *sir*.
2. **Monna** (mō′nə): In Italian, *Monna* is an abbreviation for *Madonna* (mə·dän′ə), a formal title for a woman, similar to *madam*.
3. **Campi** (käm′pē): small town set in the mountains northwest of Florence. *Campi* literally means "fields."

Vocabulary
dire (dīr) *adj.:* extreme; desperate.

Giovanni Boccaccio   187

Direct Teaching

A Literary Focus

? Situational irony. What is ironic about the fact that Monna Giovanna needs Federigo now? [Possible response: When he was wealthy, nothing he did could win her favor. The reader might expect his poverty to increase the gap between them. However, the opposite has happened: Federigo's poverty has brought him in contact with her, and Federigo's falcon is the one thing that she needs.]

B Reading Skills

? Making predictions. How do you think Federigo will respond to the request that Monna Giovanna plans to make? [Possible responses: He will be overjoyed that he can finally give her something she wants; he may be torn between his love for her and his desire to keep his falcon.]

C Reading Skills

? Evaluating the historical context. How does Federigo's behavior reflect the medieval conventions of courtly love? [Possible response: In stories about courtly love, a handsome young noble falls in love with a beautiful, unattainable woman who is usually married. The lover, suffering because she refuses to consider him, tries to win her by performing bold or generous deeds in her name.]

D Reading Skills

? Evaluating the historical context. How does this exchange reflect the historical context of the story? [Possible response: It is formal and extremely polite, and it follows the conventions of courtly love in which a woman grants a man a small favor and the man cherishes his suffering on her account because it has ennobled him.]

Monna Giovanna was now a widow, and as is the custom among our women, she went to the country with her son to spend a year on one of her possessions very close by to Federigo's farm, and it happened that this young boy became friends with Federigo and began to enjoy birds and hunting dogs; and after he had seen Federigo's falcon fly many times, it pleased him so much that he very much wished it were his own, but he did not dare to ask for it, for he could see how dear it was to Federigo. And during this time, it happened that the young boy took ill, and his mother was much grieved, for he was her only child and she loved him enormously. She would spend the entire day by his side, never ceasing to comfort him, and often asking him if there was anything he desired, begging him to tell her what it might be, for if it were possible to obtain it, she would certainly do everything possible to get it. After the young boy had heard her make this offer many times, he said:

"Mother, if you can arrange for me to have Federigo's falcon, I think I would be well very soon."

When the lady heard this, she was taken aback for a moment, and she began to think what she should do. She knew that Federigo had loved her for a long while, in spite of the fact that he never received a single glance from her, and so, she said to herself:

"How can I send or go and ask for this falcon of his which is, as I have heard tell, the best that ever flew, and besides this, his only means of support? And how can I be so insensitive as to wish to take away from this gentleman the only pleasure which is left to him?"

And involved in these thoughts, knowing that she was certain to have the bird if she asked for it, but not knowing what to say to her son, she stood there without answering him. Finally the love she bore her son persuaded her that she should make him happy, and no matter what the consequences might be, she would not send for the bird, but rather go herself for it and bring it back to him; so she answered her son:

"My son, take comfort and think only of getting well, for I promise you that the first thing I shall do tomorrow morning is to go for it and bring it back to you."

The child was so happy that he showed some improvement that very day. The following morning, the lady, accompanied by another woman, as if going for a stroll, went to Federigo's modest house and asked for him. Since it was not the season for it, Federigo had not been hawking for some days and was in his orchard, attending to certain tasks. When he heard that Monna Giovanna was asking for him at the door, he was very surprised and happy to run there. As she saw him coming, she greeted him with feminine charm, and once Federigo had welcomed her courteously, she said:

"Greetings, Federigo!" Then she continued: "I have come to <u>compensate</u> you for the harm you have suffered on my account by loving me more than you needed to; and the compensation is this: I, along with this companion of mine, intend to dine with you—a simple meal—this very day."

To this Federigo humbly replied: "Madonna, I never remember having suffered any harm because of you. On the contrary, so much good have I received from you that if ever I have been worth anything, it has been because of your merit and the love I bore for you; and your generous visit is certainly so dear to me that I would spend all over again that which I spent in the past; but you have come to a poor host."

And having said this, he received her into his home humbly, and from there he led her into his garden, and since he had no one there to keep her company, he said:

"My lady, since there is no one else, this good woman here, the wife of this workman, will keep you company while I go to set the table."

Though he was very poor, Federigo, until now, had never before realized to what extent he had wasted his wealth; but this morning, the fact that he found nothing with which he could honor the lady for the love of whom he had once entertained countless men in the past gave him cause

Vocabulary

compensate (käm′pən·sāt′) v.: repay; make up (for or to).

188   Collection 2   The Middle Ages

DIFFERENTIATING INSTRUCTION

Advanced Learners

Enrichment. Encourage interested students to learn more about falconry, such as the kinds of birds used, their various physical and performance traits, how they are trained, and the history of the sport. Explain that Federigo probably used his falcon for sport when he was wealthy, but after he became poor he may have depended on the bird's hunting for his supply of meat.

DEVELOPING FLUENCY

Whole-class activity. Have students read the dialogue exchanges aloud. Although they may find the language and syntax a little stilted since it echoes a much earlier time, ask them to read as naturally as they can. After they have finished, discuss how it would feel to talk like this all the time.

to reflect. In great anguish, he cursed himself and his fortune and, like a man beside himself, he started running here and there, but could find neither money nor a pawnable[4] object. The hour was late and his desire to honor the gracious lady was great, but not wishing to turn for help to others (not even to his own workman), he set his eyes upon his good falcon, perched in a small room; and since he had nowhere else to turn, he took the bird, and finding it plump, he decided that it would be a worthy food for such a lady. So, without further thought, he wrung its neck and quickly gave it to his servant girl to pluck, prepare, and place on a spit to be roasted with care; and when he had set the table with the whitest of tablecloths (a few of which he still had left), he returned, with a cheerful face, to the lady in his garden, saying that the meal he was able to prepare for her was ready.

The lady and her companion rose, went to the table together with Federigo, who waited upon them with the greatest devotion, and they ate the good falcon without knowing what it was they were eating. And having left the table and spent some time in pleasant conversation, the lady thought it time now to say what she had come to say, and so she spoke these kind words to Federigo:

"Federigo, if you recall your past life and my virtue, which you perhaps mistook for harshness and cruelty, I do not doubt at all that you will be amazed by my presumption when you hear what my main reason for coming here is; but if you had children, through whom you might have experienced the power of parental love, it seems certain to me that you would, at least in part, forgive me. But, just as you have no child, I do have one, and I cannot escape the common laws of other mothers; the force of such laws compels me to follow them, against my own will and against good manners and duty, and to ask of you a gift which I know is most precious to you; and it is naturally so, since your extreme condition has left you no other delight, no other pleasure, no other

---

4. **pawnable** *adj.*: able to be given as security in return for a loan of money or goods.

August: Departure for the Hunt with Falcons, from the calendar for the *Très riches heures du duc de Berry* by the Limbourg brothers.
Ms. 65/1284, fol. 8v. Musée Condé, Chantilly, France.

consolation; and this gift is your falcon, which my son is so taken by that if I do not bring it to him, I fear his sickness will grow so much worse that I may lose him. And therefore I beg you, not because of the love that you bear for me, which does not oblige you in the least, but because of your own nobility, which you have shown to be greater

Vocabulary
presumption (prē·zump′shən) *n.*: act of taking too much for granted.

DIRECT TEACHING

E Literary Focus

? Situational irony. What is the situational irony in Federigo's decision to kill his falcon and serve it for dinner? [In his attempt to please Monna Giovanna with something trivial—a nice meal—Federigo has unwittingly prevented himself from doing her a much greater favor.]

F Literary Focus

? Characterization. What seems to be Monna Giovanna's attitude toward Federigo, as revealed in her speech? [Possible responses: She uses humble and dignified language that expresses admiration and respect for Federigo and compassion for his reduced circumstances. She does not seem to return his love, however.]

VIEWING THE ART

The three **Limbourg brothers** were commissioned by the Duke de Berry in 1415 to illustrate a book of hours, which was a collection of prayers to be recited at set times during the day. *Très riches heures du duc de Berry* that the Limbourgs produced is considered the finest illuminated manuscript in existence.

Activity. Ask students what they can learn about medieval life from this August scene. [Possible responses: Both men and women from the nobility hunted with falcons; the towns were walled, probably to protect people from outlaws and enemies; poorer people worked in the fields; during summer, people went swimming in the river, apparently naked and in plain sight.]

Comparing and Contrasting Texts

Notions of nobility. In "The Wife of Bath's Tale" (p. 156), the old woman argues that gentility is not the result of noble birth but of noble actions. After students have finished the Boccaccio story, ask them to consider which characters in "Federigo's Falcon" would agree with the old woman, and which would disagree. [Possible response: Monna Giovanna would agree, because she is influenced not by Federigo's social position but by his last act of generosity. Her brothers, however, accept Federigo only because of his noble birth. It is possible that Federigo himself would have assumed that nobility comes with birth.]

Direct Teaching

A Literary Focus

Situational irony. Why is Monna Giovanna's plea particularly ironic? [Possible response: After ignoring all that he did to please her, she begs for a favor that he cannot grant, for he has just killed his falcon. Now he is brokenhearted.]

B Learners Having Difficulty

Breaking down difficult text. How many sentences can you find in this long speech? [two] Re-read each sentence clause by clause; then, restate the main idea of each sentence in your own words. [Possible response: Fortune has worked against me before, but never so much as now. I've just honored you the best way I could, by feeding you my falcon, and now I'm sad because I can't give you the falcon to take to your son."]

C Literary Focus

Situational irony. Irony is not always sad; sometimes the ironic twist can be a happy one. How is this happy ending ironic? [Possible response: Ironically, Federigo's generosity in killing his falcon ultimately leads to his marriage to Monna Giovanna, and having lost his fortune courting his lady, Federigo gets her and her fortune in the end.]

Assessing

- Holt Assessment: Literature, Reading, and Vocabulary

Reteaching

For a lesson reteaching author's tone and style, see **Reteaching**, p. 1129A.

than that of all others in practicing courtliness, that you be pleased to give it to me, so that I may say that I have saved the life of my son by means of this gift, and because of it I have placed him in your debt forever."

When he heard what the lady requested and knew that he could not oblige her since he had given her the falcon to eat, Federigo began to weep in her presence, for he could not utter a word in reply. The lady, at first, thought his tears were caused more by the sorrow of having to part with the good falcon than by anything else, and she was on the verge of telling him she no longer wished it, but she held back and waited for Federigo's reply after he stopped weeping. And he said:

"My lady, ever since it pleased God for me to place my love in you, I have felt that Fortune has been hostile to me in many things, and I have complained of her, but all this is nothing compared to what she has just done to me, and I must never be at peace with her again, thinking about how you have come here to my poor home where, while it was rich, you never deigned to come, and you requested a small gift, and Fortune worked to make it impossible for me to give it to you; and why this is so I shall tell you briefly. When I heard that you, out of your kindness, wished to dine with me, I considered it fitting and right, taking into account your excellence and your worthiness, that I should honor you, according to my possibilities, with a more precious food than that which I usually serve to other people; therefore, remembering the falcon that you requested and its value, I judged it a food worthy of you, and this very day I had it roasted and served to you as best I could; but seeing now that you desired it in another way, my sorrow in not being able to serve you is so great that I shall never be able to console myself again."

And after he had said this, he laid the feathers, the feet, and the beak of the bird before her as proof. When the lady heard and saw this, she first reproached him for having killed such a falcon to serve as a meal to a woman; but then to herself she commended the greatness of his spirit, which no poverty was able or would be able to diminish; then, having lost all hope of getting the falcon and, perhaps because of this, of improving the health of her son as well, she thanked Federigo both for the honor paid to her and for his good will, and she left in grief, and returned to her son. To his mother's extreme sorrow, either because of his disappointment that he could not have the falcon, or because his illness must have necessarily led to it, the boy passed from this life only a few days later.

After the period of her mourning and bitterness had passed, the lady was repeatedly urged by her brothers to remarry, since she was very rich and was still young; and although she did not wish to do so, they became so insistent that she remembered the merits of Federigo and his last act of generosity—that is, to have killed such a falcon to do her honor—and she said to her brothers:

"I would prefer to remain a widow, if that would please you; but if you wish me to take a husband, you may rest assured that I shall take no man but Federigo degli Alberighi."

In answer to this, making fun of her, her brothers replied:

"You foolish woman, what are you saying? How can you want him; he hasn't a penny to his name?"

To this she replied: "My brothers, I am well aware of what you say, but I would rather have a man who needs money than money that needs a man."

Her brothers, seeing that she was determined and knowing Federigo to be of noble birth, no matter how poor he was, accepted her wishes and gave her in marriage to him with all her riches. When he found himself the husband of such a great lady, whom he had loved so much and who was so wealthy besides, he managed his financial affairs with more prudence than in the past and lived with her happily the rest of his days. ∎

Vocabulary

console (kən·sōl′) v.: comfort.
reproached (ri·prōcht′) v.: expressed disapproval.

190 Collection 2 The Middle Ages

Guided Practice

True-False

1. Federigo has always been poor and has always loved Monna Giovanna. [F]
2. Monna Giovanna moves to the country because she, like Federigo, has become poor after her husband dies. [F]
3. Monna Giovanna makes her request for the falcon after the bird is killed but before it has been eaten. [F]
4. Monna Giovanna's brothers accept Federigo because he comes from the noble class. [T]

Response and Analysis

Reading Check

1. How does the young Federigo try to win Monna Giovanna's love? What are the results of his efforts?
2. What does Monna Giovanna do when she learns what Federigo has made for supper?
3. When her brothers urge her to remarry, what does Monna Giovanna remember?

Thinking Critically

4. Why do you think Monna Giovanna does not return Federigo's love at the beginning of the story?
5. How does Federigo's sacrifice change Monna Giovanna's opinion of him? Why will she "take no man but Federigo"?
6. Explain how Monna Giovanna fits the image of the virtuous woman in the medieval courtly love tradition. How does Federigo fit the image of the chivalrous lover? Are there any ways in which these characters depart from the conventional images?
7. The unexpected visit of Monna Giovanna to Federigo after he has lost all his money is an example of **situational irony**. What did you expect would happen? What actually happens?
8. Cite two other examples of situational irony in the story. How is the falcon central to these ironic events?

Comparing Literature

9. What influences of the medieval period help to shape the plots, characters, and themes of the selections you have read from *The Canterbury Tales* and the *Decameron*? How might these stories change if they were set in the twenty-first century? Consult your reading notes.

WRITING

Two Medieval Women

How does Monna Giovanna compare with Chaucer's famous character the Wife of Bath (see page 156)? In an essay, **compare** these medieval female characters. Consider the following:

- their social classes
- their attitudes toward men
- their attitudes toward love and marriage

Vocabulary Development

Etymologies

dire   console
compensate reproached
presumption

Use a good dictionary to research the origin, or **etymology,** of each Vocabulary word listed above. Use a chart like the one below, which shows the etymology of *dire*, to organize your findings.

Word	Language of Origin	Original Word
dire	Latin (L)	*dirus,* meaning "fearful"

SKILLS FOCUS

Literary Skills Analyze situational irony.

Reading Skills Evaluate historical context. Compare influences of different historical periods.

Writing Skills Write an essay comparing and contrasting two literary characters.

Vocabulary Skills Understand etymologies.

Giovanni Boccaccio 191

INDEPENDENT PRACTICE

Response and Analysis

6. Monna Giovanna is beautiful, virtuous, and unattainable. Federigo is courtly, handsome, noble, brave, and deeply in love. They depart from these conventional images when adversity strikes.
7. You expect Federigo to gladly give his falcon to the lady but unfortunately he kills it to serve her for supper.
8. Other ironies include the lady choosing to marry Federigo because of his sacrifice and the fact that in the end they are both happy and rich. The sacrifice of the falcon leads to the main characters' being united.

Comparing Literature

9. The plots, characters, and themes are shaped in part by historical details such as tournaments, feasts, pilgrimages, chivalry, religious pardoning, falconry, bequeathing property to sons rather than to wives, a widow's secluded period of mourning—all of which would change if the stories were set today.

Vocabulary Development

- **compensate.** Language of Origin—Latin (L). Original Word—*compensare,* meaning "to weigh one thing against another."
- **presumption.** Language of Origin—Latin (L). Original Word—*praesumptio,* meaning "a taking beforehand."
- **console.** Language of Origin—Latin (L). Original Word—*consolari* from *com–,* "with," plus *solari,* "to comfort."
- **reproached.** Language of Origin—Latin (L). Original Word—*re–,* meaning "back," plus *prope,* meaning "near."

Reading Check

1. by spending his money, giving feasts, and participating in tournaments; she did not care for Federigo or his exploits
2. First she scolds him for sacrificing so much just to give her dinner; however, she silently commends his "greatness of spirit." Finally, she thanks Federigo for his kindness.
3. Federigo's merits and his generous sacrifice

Thinking Critically

4. She may love her husband; she may be repelled by Federigo's ostentatious attempts to impress her.
5. His sacrifice makes Monna Giovanna see the nobility in his heart, as opposed to his showy displays when he was courting her. She knows no other man who would be so generous.

Sir Thomas Malory
(c. 1405–1471)

The historical identity of Sir Thomas Malory, the author of Britain's most famous work on King Arthur, is almost as uncertain as the identity of the hero of his *Le Morte d'Arthur* (*The Death of Arthur*). All we know for sure about Malory is that he was a knight familiar with chivalric romances who was writing in the years 1469–1470. We know this from a sort of postscript that appears in the manuscript of Malory's work that William Caxton printed in 1485. In this postscript, Malory asks his readers to pray for his deliverance, suggesting that he was in prison during some of the time he was writing his stories about Arthur.

Since the fifteenth century, scholars have been trying to find out more about the actual person who wrote the work Caxton entitled *Le Morte d'Arthur*. At one time as many as five different "historical" Malorys were proposed. However, most scholars have come to accept the Thomas Malory born in Warwickshire as the most likely author of *Le Morte d'Arthur*.

This Warwickshire Malory served in France during the Hundred Years' War and apparently fought at the siege of Calais in 1436. A few years later he married a woman named Elizabeth, who bore him a son. Sir Thomas was elected to Parliament at least once and died in 1471, perhaps from the plague.

The record of this aristocratic war hero, however, also contains a series of arrests for theft, burglary, and assault, including the robbing of an abbey in which he supposedly broke eighteen doors and roughed up the monks.

But the charges against Malory were merely accusations, and there is no record of any trials or convictions. The late fifteenth century was a time of great political partisanship and civil disorder, so it is very possible that Malory's imprisonment was politically motivated. He might simply have backed the wrong side in a political conflict.

The Arthur in Malory's work is not the historical sixth-century general who helped his fellow Britons defend themselves against the invading Saxons. No, Malory's Arthur is a consolidation of later legends that developed in England and on the Continent. Using Celtic and Continental sources, Malory created a mythic Arthur who later became the very embodiment of British values.

Le Morte d'Arthur, coming as it does at the end of the fifteenth century, serves as a kind of literary swan song to the feudal order of the Middle Ages, with its castles, knights, and chivalric codes. Malory's readers lived in a different world. Cities were growing, and money and competition were replacing the old feudal ways of barter and mutual obligation. Something in the chivalric order that Malory portrayed, however, seems to have answered a longing in his audience for a more orderly world.

Detail from fifteenth-century French manuscript of *Le roman du roi Arthur et les compagnons de la Table Ronde* by Chrétien de Troyes.
The Art Archive/Biblioteca Nazionale Turin/Dagli Orti.

Before You Read

from The Day of Destiny

Make the Connection

People hate to let go of their heroes. In fact, many cultures tell stories in which the hero promises to return in an hour of need to help the people once again. How do we try to keep our heroes alive? We build statues to them and record their portraits on canvas, coins, and film. Most of all, though, we tell their stories—stories that we hope will keep our heroes and the values they respect alive in the memories of future generations.

Literary Focus

The Romance Hero

From the thirteenth century onward *romance* was a term applied to a verse narrative that traces the adventures of a brave knight or other hero who has to overcome danger for the love of a noble lady or some other high ideal. The typical medieval romance is a narrative set in a world in which the ordinary laws of nature are suspended and idealized heroes fight, and almost always conquer, the forces of evil.

Malory's Arthur is in many ways the archetypal, or typical, romance hero—the medieval descendent of the epic hero. The **romance hero** is usually born under mysterious circumstances, grows up in obscurity, and undergoes a childhood initiation involving a magic weapon. In his maturity he fights to defeat evil and promote peace. Throughout his life he is aided by magic weapons and wise mentors. Mysterious events surround his departure from this world, suggesting that he may return when his people need him the most.

Background

Malory's *Le Morte d'Arthur* contains a series of tales about the birth, education, adventures, and death (or disappearance) of King Arthur. In the early tales, Arthur persuades his knights to unite in the fellowship of the Round Table and to dedicate themselves to the chivalric code of honor. For a while, Arthur's vision is realized, and justice prevails in the kingdom. But human frailties, including Arthur's own, gradually corrupt the fellowship of the Round Table. Arthur becomes vulnerable to evil forces, personified by Sir Modred, who is Arthur's own illegitimate son.

In this last episode, Arthur is about to meet his wicked son in battle.

> **Vocabulary Development**
>
> **righteous** (rī′chəs) *adj.*: morally right.
> **prevailed** (prē·vāld′) *v.*: gained the desired effect.
> **dissuade** (di·swād′) *v.*: advise against.
> **brandishing** (bran′dish·iŋ) *v.* used as *adj.*: shaking in a threatening way.
> **piteous** (pit′ē·əs) *adj.*: deserving of pity.

INTERNET
Vocabulary Practice
Keyword: LE5 12-2

A **romance hero** is a larger-than-life figure, usually of mysterious origins, who performs extraordinary deeds with the aid of magic.

For more on the Romance, see the Handbook of Literary and Historical Terms.

Literary Skills
Understand the archetype of the romance hero.

Sir Thomas Malory   193

Previewing Vocabulary

To reinforce students' understanding of the Vocabulary words on p. 193, have partners answer the following questions:

1. Why would it be difficult for a chronic liar to prove that he or she is <u>righteous</u>?
2. Why would a man <u>brandishing</u> a weapon be considered a threat?
3. When would you try to <u>dissuade</u> a friend from taking a dangerous risk?
4. Why did everyone celebrate when the home team <u>prevailed</u> in the game?
5. What <u>piteous</u> state might someone be in after waving a red flag at a bull?

PRETEACHING

Summary ⇔ *at grade level*

In a dream the dead Sir Gawain warns King Arthur not to go to war with his illegitimate son and enemy, Modred. Arthur heeds this warning, but just as a treaty is about to be arranged, a knight, startled by a snake, draws his sword. This launches the gathered armies into a sad, bloody battle, which only Arthur, Modred, and the brothers Bedivere and Lucas survive. Arthur mortally wounds Modred; however, before he dies, Modred manages to wound Arthur badly. Sir Lucas dies soon after. Weakening quickly, Arthur gives his bejeweled sword to Bedivere and orders him to throw it into the lake. Twice Bedivere fails to obey because he covets the beautiful sword. Finally, shamed by the king, he throws the sword into the water, where it is caught by a mysterious hand that waves the sword three times and disappears. Arthur then departs for Avalon on a barge piloted by lamenting women. The next day at Glastonbury, Bedivere notices a new grave. Told by the Archbishop of Canterbury of the arrival of a company of ladies bearing a dead man, Bedivere concludes that the grave is Arthur's. He spends the rest of his life tending the grave.

Selection Starter

Motivate. Ask students to name people they regard as heroes. Students' heroes could be famous or unknown, but the students should be able to explain what makes these people heroic. Discuss why people need heroes and whether different times need different kinds of heroes.

Sir Thomas Malory   193

DIRECT TEACHING

A Literary Focus

? Romance hero. What elements in this opening present Arthur as a romance hero? [Possible responses: his strange, portentous dream full of dragons and sea serpents; his gold clothing; his squires; his vision of Sir Gawain and the beautiful ladies.]

B Reading Skills

? Making predictions. What future events might these dreams foretell? [Possible responses: Arthur's death; treachery against him; a last-minute rescue from a horrible fate.]

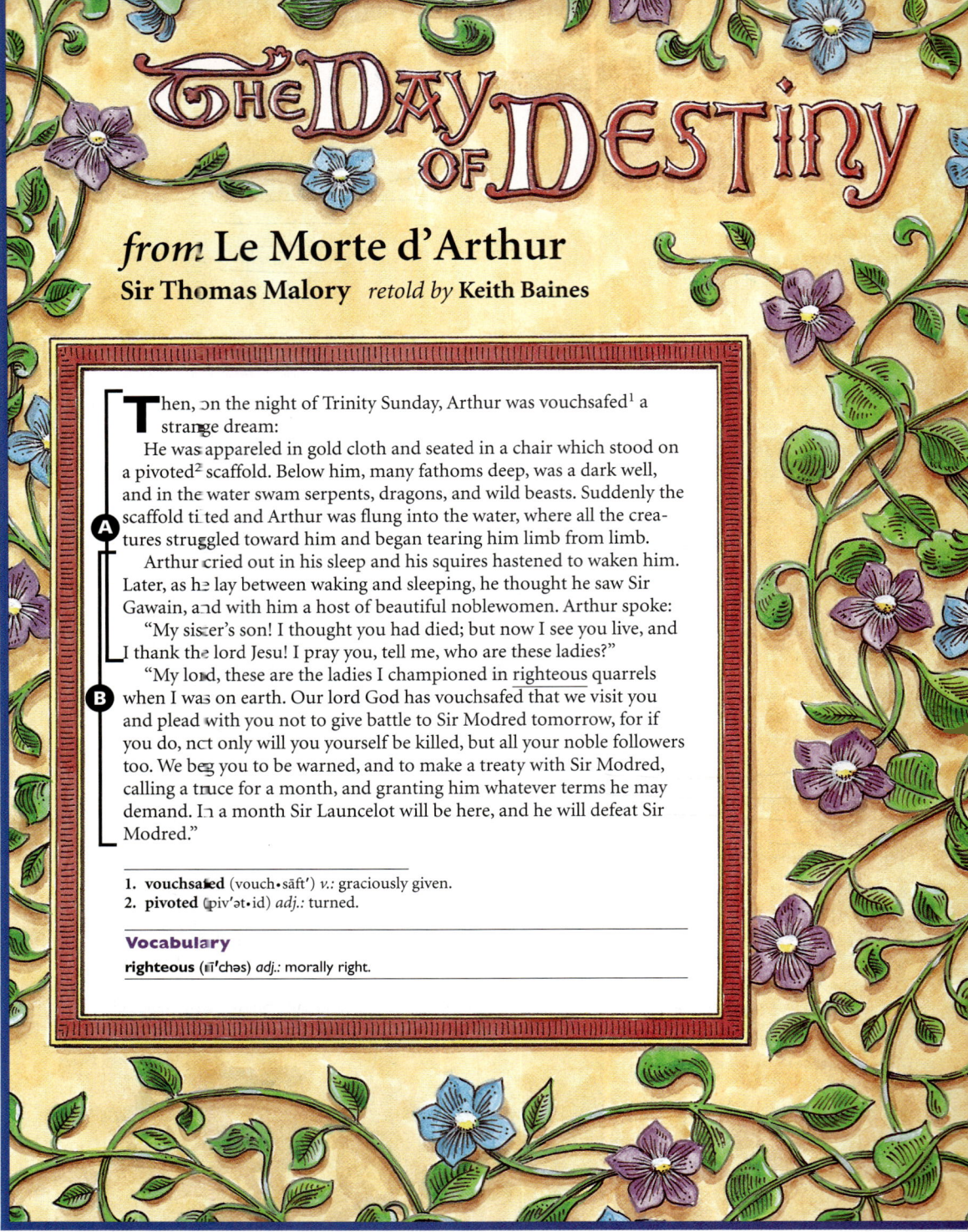

The Day of Destiny

from Le Morte d'Arthur

Sir Thomas Malory *retold by* **Keith Baines**

Then, on the night of Trinity Sunday, Arthur was vouchsafed[1] a strange dream:

He was appareled in gold cloth and seated in a chair which stood on a pivoted[2] scaffold. Below him, many fathoms deep, was a dark well, and in the water swam serpents, dragons, and wild beasts. Suddenly the scaffold tilted and Arthur was flung into the water, where all the creatures struggled toward him and began tearing him limb from limb.

Arthur cried out in his sleep and his squires hastened to waken him. Later, as he lay between waking and sleeping, he thought he saw Sir Gawain, and with him a host of beautiful noblewomen. Arthur spoke:

"My sister's son! I thought you had died; but now I see you live, and I thank the lord Jesu! I pray you, tell me, who are these ladies?"

"My lord, these are the ladies I championed in righteous quarrels when I was on earth. Our lord God has vouchsafed that we visit you and plead with you not to give battle to Sir Modred tomorrow, for if you do, not only will you yourself be killed, but all your noble followers too. We beg you to be warned, and to make a treaty with Sir Modred, calling a truce for a month, and granting him whatever terms he may demand. In a month Sir Launcelot will be here, and he will defeat Sir Modred."

---

1. **vouchsafed** (vouch·sāft′) *v.:* graciously given.
2. **pivoted** (piv′ət·id) *adj.:* turned.

Vocabulary
righteous (rī′chəs) *adj.:* morally right.

DIFFERENTIATING INSTRUCTION

Learners Having Difficulty
Before they read the excerpt, have students work together to list the characters involved in *Le Morte d'Arthur,* identifying each briefly and noting any relationships between them. Then, as they read, have students make a time line showing the major events of the story, noting which characters are involved in each event.

English-Language Learners
Explain that this excerpt is a modernized translation of an original that was written in Middle English, which most people find very difficult to read. Have English-language learners pair up with fluent English-speakers to find two to three examples of words and phrases that seem old-fashioned. Fluent English-speakers can help the English-language learners understand the meanings of such terms.

Advanced Learners
Enrichment. Encourage interested students to compare this version of Arthur's last days with other versions, in particular, Tennyson's *Idylls of the King* and T. H. White's *The Once and Future King.* On what points do the different versions agree and disagree? What view of Arthur does each create?

Battle between King Arthur and Modred, from *St. Alban's Chronicle* (late 15th century).
Ms. 6, fol. 66v. Lambeth Palace Library, London/The Bridgeman Art Library.

Thereupon Sir Gawain and the ladies vanished, and King Arthur once more summoned his squires and his counselors and told them his vision. Sir Lucas and Sir Bedivere were commissioned to make a treaty with Sir Modred. They were to be accompanied by two bishops and to grant, within reason, whatever terms he demanded.

The ambassadors found Sir Modred in command of an army of a hundred thousand and unwilling to listen to overtures of peace. However, the ambassadors eventually prevailed on him, and

Vocabulary
prevailed (prē·vāld') v.: gained the desired effect.

DIRECT TEACHING

VIEWING THE ART

This image illustrates the significance of knights on the medieval battlefield. During a battle a knight's death would be regarded as a significant loss, and two knights could decide the outcome of a battle before it began by fighting in single combat. In this image, two knights are engaged in combat while their armies look on. Perhaps there has been an agreement to grant the victory to the army of the successful knight, or perhaps this combat symbolizes the whole battle.

Activity. What does the prominence of the knights in this illustration imply about their status in medieval battles and in society in general? [Possible responses: They were battle leaders; their fate determined the fate of battles; they held high status in the society.]

C Literary Focus

Romance hero. In what way does this passage present Arthur as a romance hero? [Possible responses: He has had a prophetic dream, or vision, about his death and other future events, such as the coming of Launcelot. Arthur acts in accordance with his vision, suggesting that he expects supernatural powers to be aligned with him.]

DEVELOPING FLUENCY

Small-group activity. Have groups of students work together to read predetermined portions of the selection. Each student will read aloud for exactly one minute, with a student who is not reading at the time serving as timekeeper. After reading, students will write down the number of lines and portions of lines they managed to read in that minute. Encourage them to chart their progress in a line graph. The activity should last long enough to enable everyone to read three or four times, and all students should see some increase in the number of lines they can read in a minute. Stress that students should not expect to read at the same rates, since different passages present different challenges. Also emphasize that the goal of the exercise is to read more smoothly, but not so fast as to be unintelligible. Encourage group members to support each other in the quest to read more fluently; for example, acknowledge clarity of pronunciation and overall progress made by individuals and groups.

DIRECT TEACHING

A Reading Skills

? Interpreting. What might be the significance of the way the battle begins—as a misunderstanding involving a snake? [Possible responses: The snake suggests the Garden of Eden and the Fall of Man and, therefore, signifies doom for both sides; the snake also recalls Arthur's dream, which included snakes; snakes symbolize treachery.]

B Literary Focus

? Theme. What view of war does this passage communicate? [Possible response: This particular fight seems a futile, destructive activity.]

C Literary Focus

? Romance hero. In this "heartless" battle, in which both armies are destroyed, does King Arthur still seem like a romance hero? Why or why not? [Possible responses: No, the pointlessness of the battle undercuts Arthur's heroism; yes, Arthur still manages to act bravely, even though he is pursuing a lost cause.]

D Reading Skills

? Making judgments. Who is right in this argument between Arthur and Lucas? [Possible responses: Lucas is right, because Arthur may still benefit from the prophecy in the dream and declare victory, since Modred is powerless without his army; Arthur is right, because Modred is evil and Arthur has nothing left to lose anyway.]

in return for the truce granted him suzerainty[3] of Cornwall and Kent, and succession to the British throne when King Arthur died. The treaty was to be signed by King Arthur and Sir Modred the next day. They were to meet between the two armies, and each was to be accompanied by no more than fourteen knights.

Both King Arthur and Sir Modred suspected the other of treachery, and gave orders for their armies to attack at the sight of a naked sword. When they met at the appointed place, the treaty was signed and both drank a glass of wine.

A Then, by chance, one of the soldiers was bitten in the foot by an adder which had lain concealed in the brush. The soldier unthinkingly drew his sword to kill it, and at once, as the sword flashed in the light, the alarums were given, trumpets sounded, and both armies galloped into the attack.

"Alas for this fateful day!" exclaimed King Arthur, as both he and Sir Modred hastily mounted and galloped back to their armies. **B** There followed one of those rare and heartless battles in which both armies fought until they were destroyed. King Arthur, with his customary valor, led squadron after squadron of cavalry into the attack, and Sir Modred encountered **C** him unflinchingly. As the number of dead and wounded mounted on both sides, the active combatants continued dauntless until nightfall, when four men alone survived.

King Arthur wept with dismay to see his beloved followers fallen; then, struggling toward him, unhorsed and badly wounded, he saw Sir Lucas the Butler and his brother, Sir Bedivere.

"Alas!" said the king, "that the day should come when I see all my noble knights destroyed! I would prefer that I myself had fallen. But what has become of the traitor Sir Modred, whose evil ambition was responsible for this carnage?"

Looking about him King Arthur then noticed Sir Modred leaning with his sword on a heap of the dead.

"Sir Lucas, I pray you give me my spear, for I have seen Sir Modred."

---
3. **suzerainty** (sōō′zə·rin′tē) *n.*: position of feudal lord.

"Sire, I entreat you, remember your vision—how Sir Gawain appeared with a heaven-sent message to dissuade you from fighting Sir Modred. Allow this fateful day to pass; it is ours, **D** for we three hold the field, while the enemy is broken."

"My lords, I care nothing for my life now! And while Sir Modred is at large I must kill him: there may not be another chance."

"God speed you, then!" said Sir Bedivere.

Vocabulary

dissuade (di·swād′) *v.*: advise against.

READING MINI-LESSON

Developing Word-Attack Skills
Compare the two selection words *righteous* and *piteous*. Both are adjectives and end with the letters –*eous*, but the sounds of these letters are different. In *righteous*, the letter *e* does not have its own sound. All the vowel letters together become the unaccented vowel sound /ə/, the preceding consonant sound becomes /ch/, and *righteous* is pronounced as a two-syllable word: /rī′chəs/. In *piteous*, the letter *e* has the long *e* sound, and the word is pronounced in three syllables: /pit′ē·əs/.

In a similar way, compare the adjectives *insidious* and *rebellious*. Both end with the letters –*ious*, but the sounds of these letters are different in each word. In *insidious*, the second *i* stands for the sound /ē/, and the word is

Arthur is mortally wounded, from *Roman du Saint Graal* (detail) (early 14th century). The British Library, London.

When Sir Modred saw King Arthur advance with his spear, he rushed to meet him with drawn sword. Arthur caught Sir Modred below the shield and drove his spear through his body; Sir Modred, knowing that the wound was mortal, thrust himself up to the handle of the spear, and then, brandishing his sword in both hands, struck Arthur on the side of the helmet, cutting through it and into the skull beneath; then he crashed to the ground, gruesome and dead.

King Arthur fainted many times as Sir Lucas and Sir Bedivere struggled with him to a small chapel nearby, where they managed to ease his wounds a little. When Arthur came to, he thought he heard cries coming from the battlefield.

"Sir Lucas, I pray you, find out who cries on the battlefield," he said.

Wounded as he was, Sir Lucas hobbled painfully to the field, and there in the moonlight saw the camp followers stealing gold and jewels from the dead, and murdering the wounded. He returned to the king and reported to him what he had seen, and then added:

"My lord, it surely would be better to move you to the nearest town?"

Vocabulary
brandishing (brăn′dĭsh•ĭng) *v.* used as *adj.*: shaking in a threatening way.

Sir Thomas Malory 197

DIRECT TEACHING

VIEWING THE ART

This image of the mortally wounded Arthur is striking in its compositional disorder. The medieval view of the cosmos was a highly ordered one, and medieval art generally reflects this—especially in the portrayal of kings, who, ruling by divine right, were thought to bring order to the world.

Activity. Ask students to identify the elements that seem disordered in the illustration and to discuss their significance. [The horses, knights, and King Arthur are juxtaposed in a chaotic, blood-splashed, collagelike arrangement, reflecting the disruption to the social order resulting from war and the death of the king.]

E Learners Having Difficulty

Paraphrasing. Have students rephrase in their own words what happens in this extremely important and vivid passage. [Possible response: Modred and Arthur began to fight, Arthur with his spear and Modred with his sword. Arthur plunged his spear into Modred's body; Modred knew he was about to die and pushed Arthur's spear deeper into his body so that only the handle protruded in front, in order to get closer to his enemy. Swinging his sword with both hands, Modred managed to hit Arthur so hard that he cut through his helmet. Then Modred dropped dead.]

---

pronounced in four syllables: /ĭn•sĭd′ē•əs/. In *rebellious,* the letter *i* stands for the consonant sound /y/, and the word is pronounced in three syllables: /rĭ•bĕl′yəs/.

Activity. Display these words. Each ends with *–eous* or *–ious.* Have students group the words according to whether *–eous* or *–ious* is pronounced as one syllable or two.

beauteous [2]	egregious [1]	gorgeous [1]
bounteous [2]	facetious [1]	harmonious [2]
copious [2]	fictitious [1]	herbaceous [1]
courageous [1]	fractious [1]	hideous [2]
courteous [2]	furious [2]	invidious [2]
notorious [2]	obsequious [2]	outrageous [1]
prodigious [1]	pretentious [1]	vicious [1]

DIRECT TEACHING

Ⓐ Correcting Misconceptions

Explain that the king is repenting the bitter quarrel he and Sir Launcelot had over Queen Guinevere. He wishes Sir Launcelot had been with him in this battle.

A CLOSER LOOK

This essay on the archetype of Arthur traces this "once and future king" through the Victorian era and into the 1960s.

Ⓑ Content-Area Connections

Culture: Camelot
In a touching scene at the end of the popular musical *Camelot* about King Arthur, Thomas Malory makes an anachronistic appearance as a young man called Tom of Warwick whom King Arthur charges with the mission of keeping the memory of Camelot's "one brief shining moment" alive. Point out that Thomas Malory, whoever he was, lived centuries after King Arthur—if he ever existed—so the meeting could never have taken place.

Ⓒ Reading Informational Text

❓ Making inferences. When does interest in the Arthur archetype usually resurge, based on the information in this essay? [during times of uncertainty and social disorder]

Ⓐ "My wounds forbid it. But alas for the good Sir Launcelot! How sadly I have missed him today! And now I must die—as Sir Gawain warned me I would—repenting our quarrel with my last breath."

Sir Lucas and Sir Bedivere made one further attempt to lift the king. He fainted as they did so. Then Sir Lucas fainted as part of his intestines broke through a wound in the stomach. When the king came to, he saw Sir Lucas lying dead with foam at his mouth.

"Sweet Jesu, give him succor!"[4] he said. "This noble knight has died trying to save my life—alas that this was so!"

Sir Bedivere wept for his brother.

"Sir Bedivere, weep no more," said King

---

4. **succor** (suk′ər) *n.:* help.

A CLOSER LOOK: SOCIAL INFLUENCES

The Archetype of Arthur

INFORMATIONAL TEXT

If you remember your old myths and fairy tales, you'll recognize many of the same elements in Arthur's story. Even movies and cartoons today use these **archetypes** of the romance hero. (For more about the heroic archetype, see pages 44–45.)

In Malory's mythic form, Arthur has the mysterious birth typical of the romance hero. His childhood points to his kinship with such mythic and romance heroes as the Greek Theseus and the German Siegfried. His strange death, departure, and promised return also place him among other "once and future kings"—heroes whose return is always hoped for.

The Arthurian tales were carried into the Elizabethan age. They were resurrected in the nineteenth century by Alfred, Lord Tennyson (see page 694), in his group of poems called *Idylls of the King*. Tennyson brought Arthur and his knights back at a time when the English nation, embarked upon building an empire, needed a reminder of its heroic past and special destiny.

The Arthurian legend was revived yet again in the twentieth century by T. H. White in his bestselling book *The Once and Future King* (1958). Though White's treatment of the Arthurian material is ironic (in keeping with an ironic age), it still inspired the 1960s musical Ⓑ Ⓒ play and movie *Camelot*, which capture the romantic imagination of another generation struggling with disillusion and social disorder.

The Lady of the Lake, from *Morte d'Arthur*, illustrated by Aubrey Beardsley (1872–1898).
The Art Archive.

CONTENT-AREA CONNECTIONS

Culture: The Arthurian Legend
A number of sources contributed to the Arthurian legend at different times during the Middle Ages. In some early accounts, which appeared around the ninth century, Arthur was a fifth- or sixth-century Christian British chieftain who successfully fought the Romans in the Battle of Mount Badon in 518 and died in the Battle of Camlann in 539. Arthur also appears as a heroic king in very old Welsh poems surfacing later in the thirteenth-century collection *The Black Book of Carmarthen*. Some of these early poems mention certain knights, including Gawain, Kay, and Bedivere. Geoffrey of Monmouth was the first to tell Arthur's story at length, in his *Historia regum Britanniae*; his account includes many of the details still associated with Arthur's legend, especially those describing his birth. The French romance writers of the thirteenth century enriched

Arthur, "for you can save neither your brother nor me; and I would ask you to take my sword Excalibur⁵ to the shore of the lake and throw it in the water. Then return to me and tell me what you have seen."

"My lord, as you command, it shall be done."

Sir Bedivere took the sword, but when he came to the water's edge, it appeared so beautiful that he could not bring himself to throw it in, so instead he hid it by a tree, and then returned to the king.

"Sir Bedivere, what did you see?"

"My lord, I saw nothing but the wind upon the waves."

"Then you did not obey me; I pray you, go swiftly again, and this time fulfill my command."

Sir Bedivere went and returned again, but this time too he had failed to fulfill the king's command.

"Sir Bedivere, what did you see?"

"My lord, nothing but the lapping of the waves."

"Sir Bedivere, twice you have betrayed me! And for the sake only of my sword: it is unworthy of you! Now I pray you, do as I command, for I have not long to live."

This time Sir Bedivere wrapped the girdle around the sheath and hurled it as far as he could into the water. A hand appeared from below the surface, took the sword, waved it thrice, and disappeared again. Sir Bedivere returned to the king and told him what he had seen.

"Sir Bedivere, I pray you now help me hence, or I fear it will be too late."

Sir Bedivere carried the king to the water's edge, and there found a barge in which sat many beautiful ladies with their queen. All were wearing black hoods, and when they saw the king, they raised their voices in a piteous lament.

"I pray you, set me in the barge," said the king.

Sir Bedivere did so, and one of the ladies laid the king's head in her lap; then the queen spoke to him:

"My dear brother, you have stayed too long: I fear that the wound on your head is already cold."

Thereupon they rowed away from the land and Sir Bedivere wept to see them go.

"My lord King Arthur, you have deserted me! I am alone now, and among enemies."

"Sir Bedivere, take what comfort you may, for my time is passed, and now I must be taken to Avalon⁶ for my wound to be healed. If you hear of me no more, I beg you pray for my soul."

The barge slowly crossed the water and out of sight while the ladies wept. Sir Bedivere walked alone into the forest and there remained for the night.

In the morning he saw beyond the trees of a copse a small hermitage.⁷ He entered and found a hermit kneeling down by a fresh tomb. The hermit was weeping as he prayed, and then Sir Bedivere recognized him as the Archbishop of Canterbury, who had been banished by Sir Modred.

"Father, I pray you, tell me, whose tomb is this?"

"My son, I do not know. At midnight the body was brought here by a company of ladies. We buried it, they lit a hundred candles for the service, and rewarded me with a thousand bezants."⁸

"Father, King Arthur lies buried in this tomb."

Sir Bedivere fainted when he had spoken, and when he came to he begged the Archbishop to allow him to remain at the hermitage and end his days in fasting and prayer.

"Father, I wish only to be near to my true liege."⁹

"My son, you are welcome; and do I not recognize you as Sir Bedivere the Bold, brother to Sir Lucas the Butler?"

---

5. **Excalibur:** Arthur's sword, given to him by the mysterious Lady of the Lake.
6. **Avalon:** legendary island, sometimes identified with the earthly Paradise.
7. **hermitage** (hur′mə•tij) *n.*: secluded home.
8. **bezants** (bez′ənts) *n. pl.*: gold coins of Byzantium.
9. **liege** (lēj) *n.*: lord or sovereign.

Vocabulary
piteous (pit′ē•əs) *adj.*: deserving of pity.

---

the legend by threading in other characters who had been legendary figures themselves—Launcelot, Merlin, and Tristram. Arthur became a kind of linchpin holding together a number of romances of knightly or magical doings.

Culture: Morgan le Fay
Point out that the queen on the barge may be Morgan le Fay. According to some sources, she was Arthur's half sister. In some legends, Morgan had tricked the young Arthur into sleeping with her and so gave birth to Arthur's illegitimate son Modred, who was one cause of Arthur's downfall. In another portion of Malory's text, Morgan tries to kill Arthur. It is unclear why Malory might have her lead the ladies who bear him off to Avalon. In fact, one writer has called Malory's attitude toward Morgan "ambivalent."

DIRECT TEACHING

D Literary Focus

Romance hero. How might Arthur's request to Sir Bedivere reinforce Arthur's image as a romance hero? [Possible responses: Arthur's request is a strange, mysterious one, in keeping with the mystery of a romance hero; the mystery is heightened (and Arthur's heroic power underscored) because he expects something to happen when Bedivere throws the sword in the lake.]

E Literary Focus

Romance hero. How does Arthur's response here contribute to his role as a romance hero? [Possible response: Arthur has superhuman powers that enable him to know that something will happen when his sword is thrown in the lake; consequently, he knows Bedivere is not telling the truth. His commandment to Bedivere seems godlike.]

F Literary Focus

Romance hero. How do these details suggest that the sword is part of the legend of a romance hero? [Possible response: Bedivere throws the sword in the lake only on his third try and the arm shakes the sword three times, echoing the number-three motif often found in other legends and fairy tales. Also, the arm that grabs the sword is strange and wonderful in itself, suggesting another heroic or supernatural being.]

Bedivere returning Excalibur to the lake upon the death of Arthur, from *Roman du Saint Graal* (early 14th century).
The British Library, London.

Thus the Archbishop and Sir Bedivere remained at the hermitage, wearing the habits of hermits and devoting themselves to the tomb with fasting and prayers of contrition.[10]

Such was the death of King Arthur as written down by Sir Bedivere. By some it is told that there were three queens on the barge: Queen Morgan le Fay, the Queen of North Galys, and the Queen of the Waste Lands; and others include the name of Nyneve, the Lady of the Lake who had served King Arthur well in the past, and had married the good knight Sir Pelleas.

In many parts of Britain it is believed that King Arthur did not die and that he will return to us and win fresh glory and the Holy Cross[11] of our Lord Jesu Christ; but for myself I do not believe this, and would leave him buried peacefully in his tomb at Glastonbury, where the Archbishop of Canterbury and Sir Bedivere humbled themselves, and with prayers and fasting honored his memory. And inscribed on his tomb, men say, is this legend:

HIC IACET ARTHURUS, REX QUONDAM REXQUE FUTURUS.[12] ■

---

10. **contrition** (kən·trish′ən) *n.*: here, remorse for having offended God.

11. **Holy Cross:** cross on which Jesus was crucified.
12. Latin for "Here lies Arthur, the once and future King."

Response and Analysis

Reading Check

1. What does King Arthur dream of on Trinity Sunday?
2. What is Sir Lucas's advice to Arthur? What does Arthur do?
3. What happens when Arthur and Sir Modred meet?
4. Where does Sir Bedivere take the wounded king? What happens to Bedivere?

Thinking Critically

5. "The Day of Destiny" includes many romance motifs, or **archetypes,** that often occur in epics, legends, myths, and folk tales. Fill in this graphic organizer to show how each of the archetypes listed appears in the story of Arthur.

Romance Motif	Arthur Story
Faithful follower	
Wise old man	
Dreams	
Number 3	
Magic	
Testing of follower	
Betrayal	

6. Over the centuries many people have searched for Arthur's grave. According to this old story, what should archaeologists look for in their search for the tomb?
7. What mysterious details surround Arthur's last hours? How could these details—combined with the inscription on Arthur's tomb—suggest that Arthur did not die?

WRITING

Comparing Heroes

In a brief essay, discuss the ways in which King Arthur is like the ancient epic heroes who preceded him—heroes like Gilgamesh (see page 48), Achilles (see page 57), and, especially, the first archetypal British hero, Beowulf (see page 21). How is Arthur unlike such heroes? Use specific examples from the texts to back up your ideas. Before you write, gather information from the texts about these details that pertain to heroes:

- is a leader of the people
- has devoted followers
- has superhuman strength
- is courageous
- fights evil
- has magic weapons
- encounters supernatural elements

Vocabulary Development

Etymologies

righteous   dissuade   piteous
prevailed   brandishing

For each Vocabulary word listed above, look up its **etymology** in a dictionary. If a word has a prefix or suffix, look up its meaning as well. Make a chart like the one below for each word. Remember that prefixes and suffixes are defined separately in the dictionary.

Word	Prefix or suffix	Origin
righteous	–ous, "full of; characterized by"	(OE) *rihtwis,* meaning "right"

INTERNET
Projects and Activities
Keyword: LE5 12-2

SKILLS FOCUS

Literary Skills
Analyze the archetype of the romance hero.

Writing Skills
Write an essay comparing and contrasting archetypal heroes.

Vocabulary Skills
Understand etymologies.

Sir Thomas Malory   201

Reading Check

1. King Arthur dreams of Sir Gawain, who warns that the king will die if he does battle with Modred. Gawain advises Arthur to negotiate a peace treaty and wait for Launcelot to reinforce his army.
2. Sir Lucas advises Arthur not to attack Modred when he finds him at the end of the battle. However, Arthur ignores the advice and attacks Modred.
3. Arthur's spear penetrates Modred's body, causing a mortal wound. However, Modred pushes the spear in deeper until only the handle protrudes so that he can strike Arthur one more time, giving him a severe head wound. Then Modred dies.
4. He takes Arthur near a lake, where the king is placed on a barge full of lamenting women. The next day Bedivere sees a new grave at Glastonbury, concludes that it is Arthur's, and spends the rest of his life tending it.

Response and Analysis

Thinking Critically

5. Possible answers: *Faithful follower*—Bedivere. *Wise old man*—Archbishop / hermit. *Dreams*—Arthur's dream about the serpents, wild beasts, and Gawain. *Number 3*—Bedivere throws the sword into the lake on his third try; the hand that comes from the lake shakes the sword three times. *Magic*—Arthur's knowledge that something will happen when the sword is thrown into the lake and the mysterious appearance of the hand. *Testing of follower*—Bedivere's temptation to keep the sword and his eventual compliance with Arthur's command. *Betrayal*—Modred's killing of Arthur.
6. Possible answers: the ruins of a small hermitage, perhaps near a lake or a stream; a skull with a gash in it.
7. The return of the sword to the lake sets the supernatural tone for Arthur's last hours. Arthur says that he is going to Avalon to heal his wound, hinting at immortality. No one actually sees Arthur die. The sanctity of Arthur's supposed burial place and the mystery regarding his fate echo Christ's death, as does the reference to Arthur as "the once and future King," since Christ is also predicted to reappear at the end of the world.

Vocabulary Development

Sample answer:
Word—prevailed. *Prefix or suffix*—*pre–,* "before." *Origin*—(L) *valere,* meaning "to be strong"

Grammar Link

Linking It Up: Combining Sentences with Coordinating and Subordinating Conjunctions

Read these sentences aloud. How could they be improved?

> Then King Arthur summoned his knights. King Arthur told them to assemble his noble lords and bishops. He was ready to meet with Modred.

When two or more sentences express related ideas that are equally important, you may be able to combine them with a kind of connective word called a **coordinating conjunction**. Coordinating conjunctions—*and, but, for, nor, or, so,* and *yet*—enable you to combine subjects, verbs, objects, or even entire sentences.

> Then King Arthur summoned his knights and told them to assemble his noble lords and bishops, for he was ready to meet with Modred.

How could you improve these sentences?

> All the black-hooded women in the barge saw Arthur. They wailed piteously.

When two or more sentences express related ideas that are of unequal importance, you can combine the sentences by making the more important sentence a main, or independent, clause and the less important idea a subordinate, or dependent, clause. To show the relationship between the clauses, you must use a connective word called a **subordinating conjunction,** which begins a subordinate clause and connects it to a main clause. Among the most commonly used subordinating conjunctions are *after, although, as, because, before, how, if, since, then, that, though, unless, until, when, where,* and *while*. A subordinating conjunction may appear between the clauses it connects, or it can come at the beginning of a sentence to add emphasis or sentence variety.

> All the black-hooded women in the barge wailed piteously when they saw King Arthur.
>
> When they saw King Arthur, all the black-hooded women in the barge wailed piteously.

Grammar Skills
Combine sentences using coordinating and subordinating conjunctions.

PRACTICE

Combine each of the following sentences into one sentence by using coordinating or subordinating conjunctions or a combination of the two, as appropriate. You can combine subjects, verbs, objects, or entire sentences. You may have to add, change, or delete words and punctuation to make the resulting combined sentence read smoothly and make sense. Bear in mind that the sentences can be combined in a number of ways.

1. Sir Gawain appeared to King Arthur in a dream. He warned of Arthur's impending death.
2. King Arthur told his men to consider the treaty broken if they saw any sword drawn. Sir Modred told his men to do the same.
3. Sir Bedivere threw Excalibur into the lake. A hand appeared out of the lake. The hand caught the sword.

Apply to Your Writing

Read over a writing assignment you are working on now or have already completed. Are there any short, choppy sentences that have a clear relationship to one another? (It is often easier to determine this if you read your work aloud.) Where appropriate, use coordinating and subordinating conjunctions to combine any such sentences.

▶ For more help, see Coordinating Ideas and Subordinating Ideas, 9a and 9b, in the Language Handbook.

202 Collection 2 The Middle Ages

DIFFERENTIATING INSTRUCTION

Learners Having Difficulty
Write the following sentences on the chalkboard. Have students combine them by eliminating words and adding coordinating or subordinating conjunctions.

1. A barge full of lamenting women approached. The barge took Arthur away. [A barge full of lamenting women approached and took Arthur away.]
2. Sir Bedivere saw a new grave. The grave was being tended by a hermit. [Sir Bedivere saw a new grave that was being tended by a hermit.]
3. The hermit said that the grave was for a man. The man had arrived on a barge. Bedivere concluded that Arthur was buried there. [The hermit said that the grave was for a man; Bedivere concluded that Arthur was buried there, since the man had arrived on a barge.]

Answers
1. Sir Gawain appeared to King Arthur in a dream and warned of Arthur's impending death.
2. King Arthur and Sir Modred told their men to consider the treaty broken if they saw any sword drawn.
3. When Sir Bedivere threw Excalibur into the lake, a hand appeared and caught the sword.

ASSESSING

Assessment
- Holt Assessment: Literature, Reading, and Vocabulary

RETEACHING

For a lesson reteaching archetypes, see **Reteaching**, p. 1129A.

READ ON: FOR INDEPENDENT READING

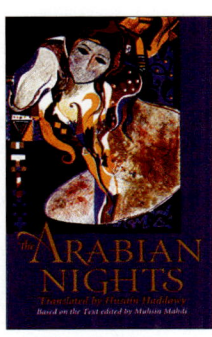

FICTION
Stories That Save a Life
Perhaps you have been entranced by the story of Sindbad's fantastic voyages—just one of the many tales in *The Arabian Nights* (translated by Husain Haddawy), a framework of stories that date back to the ninth century. Princess Scheherazade, whose husband intends to murder her, saves her own life by telling a dazzling variety of tales but stopping each night at the most suspenseful moment, thereby postponing her death.

NONFICTION
Within Castle Walls
The romance of the medieval castle lives on in literature, in film, and in our collective impression of what life in a castle entails. We think of creaking drawbridges, dungeons, sword fights, and grand dinners for ravenous knights. In Joseph and Frances Gies's *Life in a Medieval Castle,* the romance is tempered with a truth more interesting than fiction.

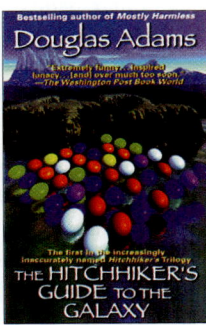

FICTION
Pilgrims in Outer Space
Join Earthling Arthur Dent and his trusty sidekick from Betelgeuse, Ford Prefect, on a cosmic (and comic) quest through the galaxy. In *The Hitchhiker's Guide to the Galaxy,* by Douglas Adams, you may "finally learn once and for all the plain and simple answer to all those nagging little problems of Life, the Universe, and Everything!"

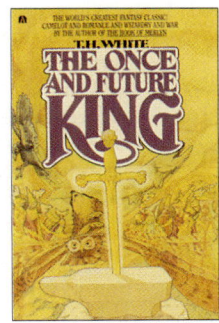

FICTION
A Lasting Hero
The English writer T. H. White wrote his version of the Arthurian legend, *The Sword in the Stone,* before World War II, when England was in need of a hero to bolster its national pride. He later expanded this story into a four-part novel, *The Once and Future King,* that explores the problems of war, justice, and national identity. Though White views Arthur's quest as a tragedy, he balances this somber theme with humorous characters and comic fun.

Read On 203

DIFFERENTIATING INSTRUCTION

Estimated Word Counts and Reading Levels of Read On Books:

Fiction
The Arabian Nights	↓	193,200
The Once and Future King	↔	273,200
The Hitchhiker's Guide to the Galaxy	↓	42,100

Nonfiction
Life in a Medieval Castle	↔	54,800

KEY: ↑ above grade level ↔ at grade level ↓ below grade level

Read On
For Independent Reading
If students enjoyed the themes and topics explored in this collection, you might recommend the following titles for independent reading.

Assessment Options
The following projects can help you evaluate and assess your students' outside reading.

- **Write and illustrate a children's book.** Students could work together to write and illustrate a children's book (or several books) based on *The Arabian Nights* stories or the King Arthur legend. Before starting their project, students should examine some children's books to find ways of appealing to children visually. The intended audience's age range should be clearly specified. Research on the stories should be meticulous: The aim is to retell the stories in language that children can grasp while remaining as true as possible to the original versions.

- **A report on the hitchhikers as questers.** Have students write an analysis of Douglas Adams's popular book, focusing on its use of the quest archetype. The analysis should include plot, characters, themes, and settings and should conclude with a statement of how the reader feels about the book.

- **Castle models.** Students who read *Life in a Medieval Castle* should be encouraged to create models of medieval castles or of special features in medieval castles. Using information from the book as well as from literature in this chapter, they could focus on the kitchen, the chapel, the grand hall, or perhaps just the keep. Students might find useful information and illustrations in children's books such as *Castle Diary: The Journal of Tobias Burgess, Page* by Richard Platt.

Writing Workshop

Reporting Literary Research

Writing Assignment
Write a formal research paper of at least 1,500 words on a topic that links literature and historical investigation.

To what extent did the clergy of Chaucer's *The Canterbury Tales* represent the clergy of the fourteenth century? Was Malory's King Arthur based, at least in part, on an actual historical figure? **Literary research** arises from questions such as these and involves a study not only of works of literature but also of sources that illuminate the literature, such as scholarly writings on history. By researching such sources, you can expand your understanding of the literary work, its author, and the culture that produced it.

Prewriting

Choose and Narrow a Research Topic

My Kingdom for a Topic Literary research is a labor-intensive process that can be intensely rewarding for what it tells you about a literary subject. If a research topic that fascinates you doesn't immediately come to mind, scan your textbook, searching for authors and works that look intriguing. Jot down a list of several possibilities, and do a little preliminary research in your textbook, in general reference works like encyclopedias, and on the Internet to gather some information on the works and authors on your list. Then, from your list choose a general literary topic, such as Chaucer's *The Canterbury Tales,* for your research. You'll have the opportunity to narrow your topic later.

Once you've chosen a general topic, decide on an appropriate historical approach you'd like to take in your research. You might need to do some more preliminary research to get an idea of the historical significance of the topic you've chosen. Here are some examples of topics appropriate for literary and historical investigation.

- Investigate how Geoffrey Chaucer's life as a civil servant in fourteenth-century England influenced his writing.
- Investigate how accurately *Beowulf* reflects the history and culture of the ancient Germanic tribes who populate its pages.
- Investigate how Christianity spread among the Angles, Saxons, and Jutes of England and influenced their literature.
- Investigate how the writing of John Stuart Mill or Charles Dickens influenced social and economic reforms of the Victorian period.

SKILLS FOCUS
Writing Skills
Write a literary research paper.

Tailor to Fit Narrow your subject so that you can cover it adequately. For example, the cultural history of England as reflected in Geoffrey Chaucer's *The Canterbury Tales* is much too broad for a research paper of 1,500 words. To narrow a topic, keep challenging

204 Collection 2 The Middle Ages

technical accuracy of a passage. Enclose the passage in quotation marks. Since your paper should be a synthesis of information you derive from outside sources and your own analysis and conclusions, avoid using too many direct quotations and long quotations.

When you do use direct quotations in your paper, smoothly integrate them into your sentences and paragraphs. If you need only part of a quotation, you might need to use ellipsis points to show omissions from quoted text. If you need to insert your words into a quotation to clarify or explain it, put brackets around those insertions. (For more on the use of **ellipsis points** and **brackets** with quotations, see 13e and 13o in the Language Handbook.)

- **Paraphrase** When you want to use material from a source without directly quoting the source, paraphrase the information. Paraphrasing means that you completely rewrite a passage in your own words and style. A paraphrase is usually about the same length as the original.

- **Summary** When you want to use the general idea presented in a source, summarize the information. A typical summary is highly condensed—one fourth to one third the length of the original passage.

TIP Avoid **plagiarizing**, or failing to give credit to an author whose words or ideas you have used, by completely rewriting the passages. Simply substituting synonyms for some of the words from your source is not enough.

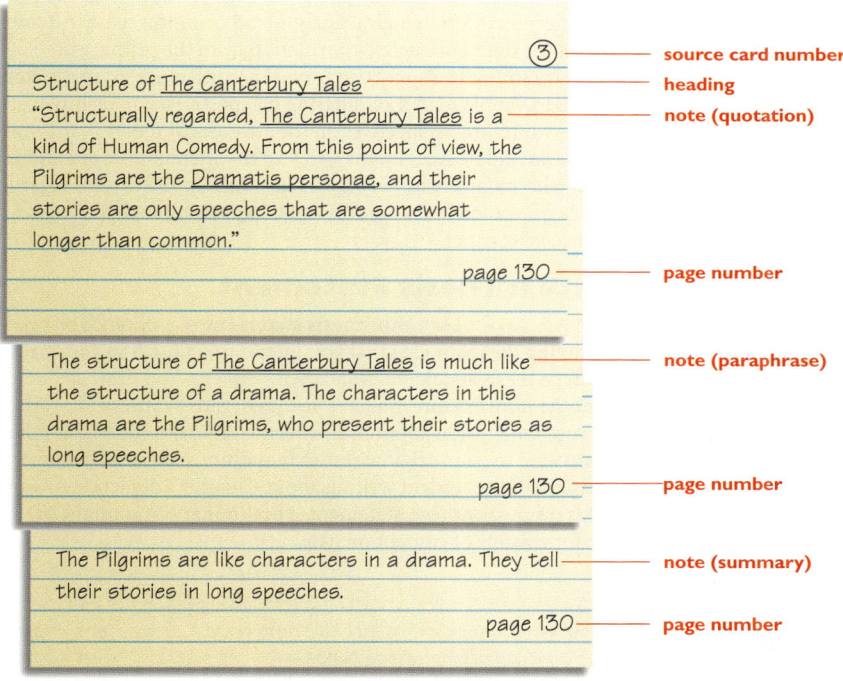

CORRECTING MISCONCEPTIONS

Students may omit important information from their note cards, neglect to enclose direct quotations in quotation marks, or use abbreviations they make up on the spot, all under the assumption they will remember the circumstances in which they made their note cards. Point out to students that a research project often involves investigating a number of sources. Students should not assume they will remember anything about any source they use. Their note cards should be thorough and accurate.

RETEACHING

Summary

To help reteach the skill of summarizing, give students a paragraph from any book or article. Then, ask students to write down the main idea and the major supporting details in as few words as possible. To review paraphrasing, give students the same paragraph to rewrite as a paraphrase. Finally, discuss how the two skills differ and where they might be used in the research process.

Analyze Research Information

The Good, the Bad, and the Useless Analyze the information you uncovered to see if it is relevant and useful for your topic and to account for any differences in scholarly records. Start by dividing your notes into categories based on their headings. The student writing about Chaucer's female characters, for example, first divided her cards into two stacks, one each for the Prioress and the Wife of Bath. Then she subdivided each set on the basis of what aspect of each character the note dealt with, discarding notes that turned out to be irrelevant to her topic as she did so. Her notes became the source of the specific examples and supporting details she used to develop the main ideas in her paper. Her method of organizing became the basis of her formal outline.

Next, analyze the notes, both for consistency of factual information and for interpretation of factual information. If two sources are inconsistent in their presentation of facts, check each source for reliability and validity by using the suggestions on page 207. Use the information from the most reliable and valid source or the information that is verified in other reputable sources.

If two reliable sources disagree on an interpretation of facts, subject both interpretations to logical analysis and common sense. Attempt to **explain** the difference using information from the primary or secondary source to support your point. A difference in interpretation might be a simple matter of differing perspectives. For example, scholars' differing perspectives on the attitudes of men toward women during the Middle Ages might well lead to different interpretations of the female characters in *The Canterbury Tales* or of customs regarding the role of women in the Middle Ages. Explaining such differences will enhance your paper.

> **TIP** Your teacher may require that you develop two or more main ideas from your information. Keep in mind that if you use only two main ideas, each one must be fully elaborated in your research paper.

Write a Thesis Statement

Assert Yourself Your **thesis statement** is a sentence or two identifying the main idea that you intend to set forth in your paper. Writing a thesis statement is an act of *synthesis*. You draw a conclusion about the information you have analyzed, thus synthesizing your topic and your conclusion about it. In effect, your thesis statement reflects the answers to your original research questions. Here is the thesis statement of the student writing about Chaucer's depiction of women. At this point, any thesis statement is preliminary. You might change it later for reasons of content or style.

Writing Skills
Analyze information. Write a thesis statement.

> Chaucer reflects the social changes taking place for women by creating complex, often inconsistent female characters who echo the contradictions of the times.

DIRECT TEACHING

Write a Thesis Statement
To help students get immediate feedback on their thesis statements, have them meet in groups of no more than four to check one another's work. Each student can read his or her thesis statement aloud and then ask the group members what information they expect the paper to include. The writer will then know whether or not the thesis is clear. For example, if a student reads a thesis statement like "*Beowulf* is an example of heroic literature," others might suggest that the writer be more specific. The thesis could be revised to "Many traditional motifs associated with heroic literature appear in *Beowulf*."

Make an Outline

Mapping the Territory Create an outline by taking your note cards and arranging them according to the main-idea headings you put on them. Keep rearranging them until you find an order that makes sense. You will probably end up using a combination of organizational patterns—chronological order, order of importance, and logical order—for both your main ideas and your specific examples and supporting details.

- **Chronological order** can be used to discuss events in an author's or character's life in the order in which they occurred.

- **Order of importance** can be used to discuss main ideas about an author's work. The most important idea is often discussed last.

- **Logical order** groups ideas by the relationships among them—for example, cause-and-effect or comparison-contrast.

Organizing your notes paves the way for a **formal outline,** which, in its final form, can also serve as a table of contents for the finished paper. Follow standard outline format, as shown below in the partial outline of the Writer's Model on page 216.

```
II. The Prioress: Spiritual Concerns and Worldly Concerns
    A. Appearance
       1. Fine forehead
          a. Takes pride in forehead
          b. Shows forehead despite conventions of the time
       2. Jewelry
          a. Wears green-beaded rosary
          b. Has gold brooch with motto
    B. Interests/pleasures
       1. French language
       2. Aristocratic manners
       3. Animal lover
          a. Keeps dogs
          b. Feeds dogs from the table
```

 TIP You can also use the major divisions of your outline as **headings** within the paper to make it easier to follow, as the writer of the model on page 216 did.

Document Sources

Reveal Your Sources To document a paper means to identify the sources from which the information in your paper came. Although the rules for *how* to document sources are clearly set forth in whichever style guide you follow, the rules about *what* to document are not so distinct. In general, document all but the most widely known quotations; all theories, ideas, and opinions other than your own; all data from surveys, research studies, and interviews conducted by

SKILLS FOCUS

Writing Skills
Make an outline.

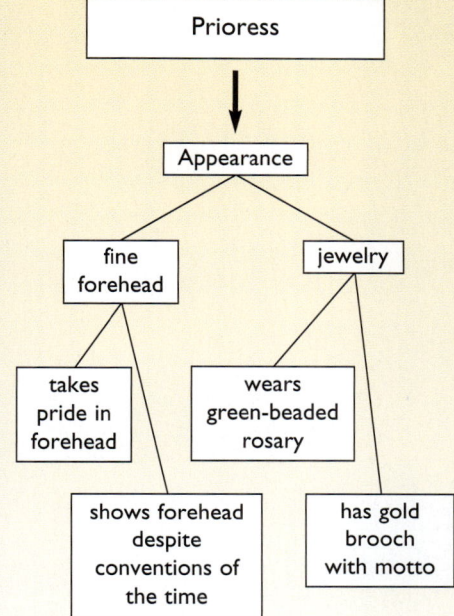

TECHNOLOGY TIP

You may want to point out to students the footnoting capabilities of most word-processing programs. These capabilities can save time and reduce frustration.

TIP Your teacher may prefer a style of documentation different from parenthetical citations, such as footnotes or endnotes. **Footnotes** are placed at the bottom of the same page where you used the source information. **Endnotes** are identical to footnotes but are compiled in a list at the end of the paper.

someone other than you; and all obscure information represented as factual. You don't need to document common knowledge—information that can be found in several sources or standard reference works.

Point the Way Place **parenthetical citations** (sources enclosed in parentheses) within the body of your paper as close as possible to the information they document. They direct readers to the *Works Cited* list at the end of your paper for more complete information on each source.

Parenthetical citations should be as brief as possible. For most citations, use the last name of the author and the page number. If you name the author in the sentence, give only the page number in parentheses. The chart below gives guidelines for citing sources.

GUIDELINES FOR GIVING CREDIT WITHIN A PAPER

Types of Sources	Content of Citation/Example
Sources with one author	Author's last name and a page reference, if any (Chaucer 25)
Separate passages in a single source	Author's last name and page references, if any (Bishop 37, 39)
Sources with more than one author	All authors' last names; if over three, use first author's last name and *et al.* ("and others") (Thompson and Johnson 322) (Anderson, et al. 313)
Multivolume sources	Author's last name, plus volume and page reference (Prucha 2: 214–15)
Sources with a title only	Full title (if short) or shortened version and page (*World Almanac* 38)
Literary sources published in many editions	Author's last name, title, and division references (act, scene, canto, book, chapter, part, and line numbers) in place of page numbers (Shakespeare, *The Tempest* 3.2.51–52)
Indirect sources	Abbreviation *qtd. in* (quoted in) before the source (qtd. in Blamires 29)
More than one source in the same citation	Citations separated with semicolons (Chute 30; Sheehan 64)

Parenthetical citations are usually inserted near the end of the information they are documenting. The following sample passage contains information from three sources.

Writing Skills
Include a *Works Cited* list.

> Although their status was changing dramatically (Bishop 37), women were paid less for doing the same work as their husbands (Gies and Gies, *Women* 181), and within marriages husbands still expected the same compliance that seemed "natural" to the medieval male (Kittredge 143).

Other Sources

Personal Interview
Landow, Charles. Personal interview. 20 Oct. 2002.

Telephone Interview
Barnes, Elaine. Telephone interview. 17 Aug. 2002.

Published Interview with Title
Midgeley, Abigail. "Men Always Made the Big Decisions." <u>Generations: A Century of Women Speak About Their Lives</u>. By Myriam Miedzian and Alisa Malinovich. New York: Atlantic Monthly P, 1997. 241–45.

Broadcast or Recorded Interview with Title
Campbell, Joseph. "Love and the Goddess." <u>The Power of Myth</u>. Prod. Joan Konner and Alvin H. Perlmutter. Videocassette. Mystic Fire, 1988.

Published Letter
Paston, Margaret. "To Her Husband, John Paston." 14 Dec. 1441. Letter in <u>Women's Lives in Medieval Europe: A Sourcebook</u>. Ed. Emilie Amt. New York: Routledge, 1993. 170–71.

Personal Letter or E-Mail Message
Grau, Katherine. Letter to the author. 22 Jan 2002.
Rodholm, Kai. E-mail to the author. 9 July 2001.

Sound Recording
Dyson, George. <u>The Canterbury Pilgrims</u>. Perf. Yvonne Kenny, Robert Tear, and Stephen Roberts. London Symphony Chorus. Cond. Malcolm Hicks. London Symphony Orch. Cond. Richard Hickox. Chandos, 1997.

Film or Video Recording
NOTE: Always include the title, director (if known) distributor, and year. You may include the producer. For video recordings, add a description of the medium (*Videotape* or *Videocassette*) before the distributor's name.

<u>"The Wife of Bath" by Geoffrey Chaucer</u>. Videocassette. Films for the Humanities and Sciences, 1996.

Material Accessed Through the Internet
"Courtly Love." <u>Geoffrey Chaucer Page</u>. Harvard U. 31 Jan. 2002. <http://icg.fas.harvard.edu/~chaucer/special/lifemann/love>.

Article from a CD-ROM Reference Work
Miller, Robert P. "Chaucer, Geoffrey." <u>The 1998 Grolier's Multimedia Encyclopedia</u>. CD-ROM. Danbury: Grolier Interactive Inc., 1998.

Full-Text Magazine, Newspaper, or Journal Article from a CD-ROM Database
"Middle Ages." <u>History Today</u> Apr. 1998: 51. <u>MAS FullTEXT Select Version 5.0</u>. CD-ROM. EBSCO Publishing, 1996.

PRACTICE & APPLY 1
Using the preceding instructions, select a topic for your literary research paper. Then, locate and record information from primary and secondary sources. Write a thesis statement and plan your paper's documentation. Be sure to follow the guidelines for making source cards (page 207) and taking notes (page 208).

Writing

Literary Research Paper

A Writer's Framework

Introduction
- Hook your readers with an intriguing opening.
- Provide background information about the author, his or her work(s), and the period in which he or she wrote.
- Include a clear thesis statement.

Body
- Choose one or a combination of organizational patterns.
- Develop each main idea that supports your thesis.
- Add facts, details, and examples from your research.
- Use sources offering different perspectives.

Conclusion
- Restate your thesis.
- Bring your paper to a close by providing a final insight into your research.

A Writer's Model

Chaucer's Female Characters: A Reflection of Change

INTRODUCTION
Intriguing opening
Primary source

In the Prologue to Geoffrey Chaucer's *The Canterbury Tales*, the Prioress wears a gold brooch inscribed with the motto "*Amor Vincit Omnia*" (Chaucer 25)—"Love Conquers All"—a motto that could mean spiritual love or romantic love. If the Prioress represents nuns in general in the late fourteenth century, then the motto is ironic. Later in the Prologue, Chaucer introduces the independent and gregarious Wife of Bath, proud widow of five husbands. She, too, seems to represent an ironic version of fourteenth-century wives in general.

Direct quotation
Secondary source
Background information

Chaucer, "one of the most wonderful observers in the whole of English literature" (Power 94), reports everything he observes about people with accuracy—even if he sees contradictions. His ability to "tell a good story" with "vivid and familiar" character types and a "wickedly modern sense of irony" is well known to contemporary readers ("Remembering Geoffrey Chaucer"). The last half of the fourteenth century was a time of contradictions (Thompson and Johnson 863). Most of the traditional relationships of society were changing, and "the times were filled with war, plague, suffering, and anger" (Bishop 334). Amid all this upheaval, the relation of women to society was also changing. By creating complex, often inconsistent female characters who echo the contradictions of the times, Chaucer reflects the social changes taking place for women.

Source by two authors

Thesis statement

The Prioress: Spiritual Concerns and Worldly Concerns

    The Prioress (Madame Eglantine) appears in the General Prologue as both a woman of the Church and a vain woman with worldly interests. Her simple but coy smile seems an affectation, and her graceful manner calls attention to herself. She takes pride in her "well-shaped head, / Almost a span across the brows" (Chaucer 25). Madame Eglantine does not hesitate to show off one of her finest features, even though, as Eileen Power points out, "The nuns were supposed to wear their veils pinned tightly down to their eyebrows, so that their foreheads were completely hidden" (89). The Prioress also has "a set of beads, the gaudies tricked in green," from which hangs the gold brooch that proclaims her faith in the power of love (Chaucer 25); yet she coyly refrains from specifying whether that love is spiritual or romantic.

    Her interests range further than devotion to God and singing "the service" (Chaucer 24) or the medieval hymn "Angelus ad Virginem" (Wood). She speaks good French and has the perfect manners of an aristocratic lady. She goes to great lengths to make sure that no crumb falls from her lips and that no trace of grease appears on her drinking cup. In addition, she has a tender sympathy for animals, weeping for a mouse caught in a trap. She feeds several dogs "roasted flesh, or milk and fine white bread" from the table (Chaucer 25). In all these ways, she indulges her taste in the pleasures of the world and gives more than a usual sympathy for animals, rather than in the practices of self-denial and attention to human need, as might be expected of a nun.

    Chaucer's picture of the Prioress seemingly matches the lives of nuns at this time. Morris Bishop comments that in the late Middle Ages nuns often entered convents not because they have a spiritual calling but because they were "surplus or unmarriageable daughters of the noble and bourgeois classes." He calls the convents "aristocratic spinsters' clubs" (174). They were aristocratic because, although not formally required, a payment to the convent was necessary before a girl would be accepted as a novitiate (Gies and Gies, <u>Women</u> 64). Under these conditions of admission, many of the nuns were not devoted to a spiritual life and were openly rebellious toward the restrictions that the Church tried to impose on them.

    Among the Church's prohibitions were pets, which the bishops believed interfered with discipline. Such a ruling, however, did not rid the convent of animals (Power 90). Like Chaucer's Prioress, the nuns enjoyed having pets and kept them as companions. Life in the convent was limited even further because nuns were not supposed to travel.

(continued)

RETEACHING

A Writer's Model

To help students visualize the concise and logical overall organization of **A Writer's Model,** have small groups of students outline the section of the essay dealing with the Wife of Bath. Tell students that the outline on p. 211 will get them started. Have groups present their outlines to the class. Point out ways students can use a similar organization to make their essays more logical and concise.

(continued)

Ellipsis within quotation
Writer's conclusion

In 1300, a Papal Bull, a special decree or edict from the Pope, ordered that nuns be confined in the convents except under the most exceptional of circumstances. In response, the nuns of one convent chased the bishop who brought the order to the gate of the nunnery and "when he was riding away . . . threw the Bull at his head, screaming that they would never obey it" (Power 93). The model for Chaucer's Prioress, then, is rooted in history: Nuns may be devoted to the Church but also strongly interested in worldly affairs.

Heading
Second main idea

The Wife of Bath: Dominance and Dependence

For the Wife of Bath, the conflict is between a desire for dominance and a desire for a strong husband; she wants power, but she also wants a conventional marriage relationship (Patterson 142). Chaucer describes her in the Prologue as an independent woman, yet always refers to her, as she always refers to herself, as a "Wife" (Patterson 136). She has had five husbands, and she says, in introducing her tale, "Welcome the sixth, whenever he appears" (Chaucer 218).

Writer's conclusion

From her friendly manner and engaging conversation she appears to have joined the other pilgrims to Canterbury to look for another husband.

Summary of primary source

The Wife of Bath, a weaver by trade, is a woman with money and the respect of society. She has wealth enough to travel three times to Jerusalem and through Italy and France. She makes her social position obvious by her clothing, especially the kerchiefs she wears as a headdress, which "weighed a good ten pound, / The ones she wore on Sunday" (Chaucer 34). Such clothing denoted status (Carroll).

Online source

Although she wants to be admired and respected for her money and position, ironically she does not want to "change the system" completely (Patterson 142).

Writer's conclusion

She wants to be a special kind of wife—an understandable desire when considered within her historical context.

Information from secondary sources

In the two centuries before Chaucer, conditions for women had been oppressive and unchangeable (Thompson and Johnson 322). Women were expected both by custom and by law to be subservient to their husbands and were valued in some cases for little else than their ability to bear children (Thompson and Johnson 322) and do menial work (Bishop 37). One commentary of the Middle Ages proposed that if God had intended women to be equal to men, Eve would have been derived from Adam's head instead of his rib (Coulton 190). The men of the time agreed that "women were inferior beings" (Rowling 72).

Writer's conclusion

However, comparing the Wife of Bath to the accepted social conventions of marriage produces surprising results. Because the Wife of Bath has outlived five husbands, she is not physically inferior. Because she has independent wealth, she is not financially inferior. She is an ironic representation of the traditional woman of the times.

In fact, Chaucer's Wife of Bath argues to readjust the system. She wants to be married, but she wants power over men within the home and an end to men's control, particularly economic control, of women. She does not advocate independence from men. She understands that in marriage "sovereignty is synonymous with economic control" and that by achieving economic independence, she gains "independence of spirit, the freedom to give freely" (Carruthers). Once she feels she has "sovereignty in wedlock," she is "as kind to him / As any wife from Denmark to the rim / Of India, and as true" (Chaucer 237).

Historically, women during Chaucer's time, like the Wife of Bath, could be in "business for themselves and were considered legally capable of controlling funds for their business and of answering for that business in borough court" (Sheehan 32). Moreover, a woman could work with her husband, and "when a man die[d] his widow carrie[d] on the trade" (Gies and Gies, Life 53). However, women were paid less for doing the same work as their husbands (Gies and Gies, Women 181), and within marriages husbands still expected the same compliance that seemed "natural" to the medieval male (Kittredge 143). Georges Duby says that women were almost nonexistent in a social sense unless they had husbands (98). The irony about the Wife of Bath is her *managing* so many husbands.

In the prologue to Chaucer's dream-vision poem, *The Legend of Good Women,* the god of love punishes Chaucer by having him write only about stereotypically good women instead of stereotypically bad (Lumiansky). A decade later, in *The Canterbury Tales,* using his keen powers of observation, Chaucer creates women who escape both stereotypical molds, women who are real people, mirroring the contradictory times in which they lived. In the Prioress and the Wife of Bath, Chaucer focuses our attention on women whose complexity parallels the complexity of the times. Since these characters are not at all simple, they remain still fresh and alive after six hundred years.

Analysis of primary source

Online source

Connection of history and literature

Brackets within quotations

Paraphrase

Writer's conclusion

CONCLUSION
Primary source

Restatement of thesis

Final insight

Works Cited

Bishop, Morris. The Middle Ages. New York: American Heritage P, 1970.

Carroll, Sharon. "Women's Clothing in the Middle Ages." Millersville U. 10 May 2001 <http://www.millersv.edu/~english/homepage/duncan/medfem/cloth.html>.

(continued)

TIP Research reports and *Works Cited* lists are normally double-spaced. See a double-spaced Writer's Model at go.hrw.com.

DIRECT TEACHING

A Writer's Model
Point to the sample conclusion to show how writers avoid using the words *I, me, my, you,* or *your.* Explain that even though they are expressing personal opinions and recommendations, good writers avoid using first- and second-person pronouns in order to achieve a more formal tone.

(continued)

Carruthers, Mary. "The Wife of Bath and the Painting of Lions." Geoffrey Chaucer Page. Harvard U. 10 May 2001 <http://icg.fas.harvard.edu/~chaucer/canttales/wbpro/carruth.htm>.

Chaucer, Geoffrey. The Canterbury Tales. Trans. Nevill Coghill. New York: Penguin Classics, 1977.

Coulton, G. G. Chaucer and His England. London: Methuen, 1963.

Duby, Georges. Love and Marriage in the Middle Ages. Trans. Jane Dunnett. Chicago: U of Chicago P, 1994.

Gies, Joseph, and Frances Gies. Life in a Medieval City. New York: Harper, 1969.

---. Women in the Middle Ages. New York: Harper, 1978.

Kittredge, George Lyman. "Chaucer's Discussion of Marriage." Chaucer Criticism: The Canterbury Tales. Ed. Richard J. Schoeck and Jerome Taylor. Vol. 1. Notre Dame: U of Notre Dame P, 1960. 130–59.

Lumiansky, R. M. "Chaucer, Geoffrey." Encyclopaedia Britannica Online. 10 May 2001. <http://www.eb.com:180>.

Patterson, Lee. "'Experience woot well it is nought so': Marriage and the Pursuit of Happiness in the Wife of Bath's Prologue and Tale." Geoffrey Chaucer: The Wife of Bath. Ed. Peter G. Beidler. Case Studies in Contemporary Criticism. Boston: Bedford Books of St. Martin's, 1996. 133–54.

Power, Eileen. Medieval People. New York: Barnes, 1968.

"Remembering Geoffrey Chaucer." All Things Considered. Host. Linda Wertheimer. Nat'l. Public Radio. KUT, Austin. 27 October 2000.

Rowling, Marjorie. Life in Medieval Times. New York: Capricorn, 1973.

Sheehan, Michael M. "The Wife of Bath and Her Four Sisters: Reflections on a Woman's Life in the Age of Chaucer." Medievalia et Humanistica. Ed. Paul M. Clogan. New Ser. 13. Totowa, NJ: Rowman & Allanheld, 1985. 23–42.

Thompson, James Westfall, and Edgar Nathaniel Johnson. An Introduction to Medieval Europe 300–1500. New York: Norton, 1937.

Wood, Carol. "Angelus ad Virginem." The Chaucer Songbook. Audio CD. Mel Bay Publications, Inc., 2000.

INTERNET
More Writer's Models
Keyword: LE5 12-2

PRACTICE & APPLY 2

Guided and Independent Practice

Guide the drafting of student essays by having students answer the following questions about their rough drafts.

- Does your thesis clearly state the focus of your research?
- Does the information in the body of your essay support the thesis?
- Have you provided a variety of sources, quotations, paraphrases, and summaries?
- Does your essay contain internal documentation?
- Does your conclusion restate your thesis?
- Does the end of your essay include a *Works Cited* list? Point out to students that while conducting research on a classic work of literature like *The Canterbury Tales,* they are likely to encounter sources that are quite old but considered to be classic works of scholarship. They may use such classic works in their own *Works Cited* lists.

Then, have students complete **Practice and Apply 2** as independent practice.

PRACTICE & APPLY 2 Use the framework and the Writer's Model to draft and document your literary research paper and to create a *Works Cited* list for it.

Revising

Evaluate and Revise Your Literary Research Paper

The Best It Can Be Because doing all that a research paper entails is difficult and time-consuming, you want your paper to be as good as you can make it. Therefore, take the time to revise it. Careful revisions can turn a run-of-the-mill research paper into a superior paper. Read your paper at least twice. First, evaluate and revise the content and organization of your paper. Second, evaluate and revise its style.

PEER REVIEW
Before you revise, trade papers with a peer. He or she may be able to point out ideas in your paper that need more or better supporting details.

▶ **First Reading: Content and Organization** Use the guidelines in the following chart to evaluate and revise the content and organization of your research paper. To answer the evaluation questions in the first column, use the tips in the second column. Then, if necessary, use the revision techniques suggested in the third column.

Rubric: Reporting Literary Research

Evaluation Questions	Tips	Revision Techniques
❶ Does the introduction hook the reader's attention, give background information, and clearly state the thesis?	**Circle** the hook, **underline** background information, and **bracket** the thesis statement.	**Add** a quotation or interesting detail to hook readers. **Add** necessary background. **Add** a thesis statement.
❷ Does the body include only main ideas and supporting details that are relevant to the thesis?	With a colored marker, **highlight** the main ideas. **Number** supporting details for each.	**Delete** irrelevant ideas and details. **Add** details to support ideas with fewer than three supporting details.
❸ Are facts and ideas stated mainly in the writer's own words?	**Star** sentences containing direct quotations. If more than one third of the sentences are starred, revise.	**Replace** unnecessary direct quotations with paraphrases and summaries.
❹ Are sources credited when necessary? Are citations correctly placed and punctuated?	**Place check marks** by material from outside sources that requires documentation.	**Add** parenthetical citations. **Correct** placement and punctuation of citations.
❺ Does the conclusion restate the thesis? Is the *Works Cited* list complete and correctly formatted?	**Bracket** the restatement of the thesis. **Place an X** beside *Works Cited* entries of each source cited in the body of the paper.	**Add** a sentence or two restating the thesis. **Add** and **correct** *Works Cited* entries.

DIRECT TEACHING

Rubric: Reporting Literary Research

Advise students to use the **Rubric** chart on this page as a think sheet by having them answer the questions in their notebooks. Explain to students that using think sheets to summarize their notes allows them to place their thoughts, observations, and questions on paper, which, in turn, helps improve the content and organization of their research papers.

Elaboration

Be sure students elaborate on key ideas that support the thesis. Suggest that they add a sentence or two of explanation to help the reader see the connection between the thesis and a key idea. Students could further elaborate by adding a sentence or two that return the reader to the purpose of the research.

GUIDED PRACTICE

Responding to the Revision Process
Answers
1. The example "such as the relationship between knight and lord" does not support the discussion of Chaucer's female characters. The adverb phrase was added to the second sentence to show a clear connection to the first sentence and to show when the change was taking place.
2. The last sentence was rearranged to vary the sentence patterns.

PRACTICE & APPLY 3

Independent Practice
Guide students by making sure they follow the suggestions in the Tips column of the **Rubric** chart on p. 221. Check student work for circles and brackets, underlining, numbered sources, and check marks. Encourage students to seek peer review to show where essays need revision. Then, have students complete **Practice and Apply 3** as independent practice.

▶ **Second Reading: Style** To keep your readers' attention fixed firmly on the ideas in your paper, avoid long series of sentences that follow the same pattern. For example, avoid beginning every sentence with the same subject-verb pattern. Instead, use a variety of sentence patterns to keep your style fresh and lively. The guidelines below will help you improve **sentence variety** in your paper.

Style Guidelines

Evaluation Question	Tip	Revision Technique
● Do many of the sentences begin in the same familiar subject-verb pattern?	▶ **Underline** the first five words of each sentence. If three sentences in a row begin with the subject-verb pattern, revise.	▶ **Rearrange** or **combine** sentences to place dependent clauses at the beginning. Rephrase when necessary.

ANALYZING THE REVISION PROCESS
Study these revisions, and answer the questions that follow.

> Most of the traditional relationships of society, ~~such as the relationship between knight and lord~~, were changing, and "the times were filled with war, plague, suffering and anger" (Bishop 334). *Amid all this upheaval,* The relation of women to society was also changing. Chaucer reflects the social changes taking place *for women.* by creating complex, often inconsistent female characters who echo the contradictions of the times.

delete / *add* / *rearrange*

Responding to the Revision Process
1. Why did the writer delete information from the first sentence and add information to the second sentence?
2. Why did the writer rearrange the last sentence?

Writing Skills
Revise for content and style.

▶ **PRACTICE & APPLY 3** Using the guidelines in this section, first evaluate and revise the content and organization of your research paper. Then, evaluate and revise the style of your paper, particularly the way you begin your sentences.

Publishing

Proofread and Publish Your Paper

Polish the Prose When you went to all the trouble to research and write a literary research paper, you became an authority on your topic. Don't allow careless errors in grammar, usage, and mechanics to destroy your credibility as an authority. Instead, finish the job by proofreading your paper very carefully. Meticulously correct every error you find. While good content, organization, and style are the most impressive aspects of a paper, an error-free paper is also impressive.

Publish Your Essay

Share the Wealth (of Knowledge) Your research paper is a synthesis of a great deal of information, the conclusions you have drawn about that research, and your interpretations and insights. Don't let it go to waste after sharing it with your teacher and classmates. Make it available to others. Consider these publishing ideas.

- Save your literary research project as a writing sample to submit for a college or job application.
- If the topic is one that would be of interest to students in another class, offer to present the report to the class, complete with appropriate **visuals** and **graphics**.
- If your school has a Web site, or you know of a Web site on a topic related to your paper, submit the paper to the creators of the site for possible inclusion.

Reflect on Your Essay

Consider the Road You've Traveled Responding to the following questions will help you think about what this research project has meant to you and what you've learned about yourself as a writer. Keep your answers along with a copy of your paper, and refer to both the next time you write a research paper.

- What was the most intriguing discovery your research produced? Why?
- What questions did your research answer that you had not asked or anticipated? Describe them.
- What passage in your paper was the most effective combination of research and conclusions drawn from that research? Why?

PRACTICE & APPLY 4 Following the guidelines in this section, first proofread your research paper to correct any errors. Then, publish your essay in an appropriate source and reflect on your literary research paper.

TIP As you proofread, be sure to see that you have followed the **conventions** of standard American English. Look in particular for dangling modifiers, modifiers that do not clearly and sensibly modify a word or group of words in a sentence. It is easy to write a dangling modifier when you explain complex ideas, as you often do in research papers. For more on **dangling modifiers,** see Placement of Modifiers, 5h, in the Language Handbook.

COMPUTER TIP

If you have access to a computer and advanced publishing software, consider using those tools to design and format graphics and visuals to enhance the content of your research paper. For more on **graphics** and **visuals,** see *Designing Your Writing* in the Writer's Handbook.

SKILLS FOCUS

Writing Skills
Proofread, especially for correct use of modifiers. Design and format a research paper, including visuals and graphics.

Listening & Speaking Workshop

PRETEACHING

Motivate. Ask students to consider a time when someone gave them too much factual information. Were they able to remember things clearly? As students prepare their research for oral presentation, encourage them to keep their presentation style simple.

DIFFERENTIATING INSTRUCTION

English-Language Learners

Some students may need help using certain grammatical constructions correctly. Others might need help finding the appropriate technical vocabulary or idiomatic phrases to express their ideas clearly. Ask each student to read the first draft of his or her speech to a native speaker of English. Have the partner point out passages that are unclear and suggest alternate ways of phrasing these concepts.

DIFFERENTIATING INSTRUCTION

Advanced Learners

Enrichment. Challenge students to adapt their speeches for two different audiences and two different occasions—in other words, for two different purposes and two different tones. Both verbal strategies and nonverbal strategies should be adapted to meet the needs of the listeners. For example, a student might prepare a speech for delivery to a class of younger students currently studying the literary subject of the speech. Then, the student could prepare a second speech for a meeting of a local library or literary association. Ask students to brainstorm two different audiences and occasions for their topics.

Presenting Literary Research

Speaking Assignment
Adapt your literary research paper for an oral presentation to an audience.

Scholars in various fields—science, history, literature, anthropology—put the results of their research into the forms of books and articles, which are published in scholarly or professional journals. No doubt you ran across many such writings in your research. These same scholars also make oral presentations of the results of their research before their peers at various meetings and conferences. In this workshop you will do the same—adapt your written report for an oral presentation to your peers.

Adapt Your Literary Research Paper

Adapt to Your Environment The **purpose** of your oral report will be to share the results of your literary research with an **audience**—in this case, your classmates. Because your listeners will not be able to stop and think about or re-read information, you may need to simplify and clarify the material from your paper. Try the following suggestions for adapting your literary research paper.

- Liven up your **introduction.** Look for an interesting fact or an intriguing quotation to seize the immediate attention of your audience.

- State your **thesis** clearly in the introduction, perhaps even repeating important parts for emphasis, to focus the attention of your audience.

- Make the most of your **conclusion** by hammering home your thesis. Communicate a final insight into your topic with a relevant anecdote or a compelling quotation.

- Simplify your vocabulary, and break up long sentences into shorter ones. Doing both these things will make your oral presentation easier to understand. Also, maintain a combination of **exposition, narration,** and **description** from your written report to support your thesis and to make your report both informative and entertaining.

- Include information from as many of the **primary** and **secondary sources** you used in your written report as your time allows. Be sure to include information from all **relevant perspectives** on the topic. Explain the differences in information from your sources.

- Do not cite sources except to identify the author of important quotations or striking facts or conclusions. To integrate an important quotation into your oral presentation, you might say, "According to Eileen Power, Chaucer was 'one of the most wonderful observers in the whole of English literature.'" At the beginning of your presentation, tell your audience that you will be using information from a variety of sources.

SKILLS FOCUS
Listening and Speaking Skills
Present a literary research paper.

224 Collection 2 The Middle Ages

COLLECTION 2 RESOURCES: LISTENING & SPEAKING

Planning
- *One-Stop Planner* CD-ROM with ExamView Test Generator

Differentiating Instruction
- *Workshop Resources: Writing, Listening, and Speaking*
- *Family Involvement Activities in English and Spanish*
- *Supporting Instruction in Spanish*

Listening and Speaking
- *Workshop Resources: Writing, Listening, and Speaking*
- *Daily Language Activities*
- *Language Handbook Worksheets*

Assessment
- *Holt Assessment: Writing, Listening, and Speaking*

Rehearse Your Presentation

Formally Speaking Since you will be speaking as an authority on the subject of your presentation, deliver your presentation **extemporaneously.** This means that you'll rehearse your presentation until you are thoroughly familiar and comfortable with your material, but you will not memorize it. Maintain a formal, objective tone suitable for a research presentation. Create note cards with reminders of important points and the full text of important quotations. Be sure to arrange your note cards in the order of your presentation.

Perfect Practice Once you are comfortable with the content of your presentation, start rehearsals to perfect it. Try one or more of these rehearsal strategies: videotape your presentation, practice in front of a mirror, or present your report to your family or friends. As you rehearse, pay attention not only to the content of your presentation but also to performance details such as those presented in the chart below.

PERFORMANCE TECHNIQUES

Technique	Tips
Diction	• Use standard American English, and speak clearly. • Define any technical terms for your audience. • Avoid the use of informal expressions.
Emphasis	Emphasize important points by changing the volume or tone of your voice.
Pauses	• Pause to give your audience time to think about what you have just said. • Pause to emphasize the point you are about to make.
Facial Expressions	Make your facial expressions complement the content of your presentation—serious expressions for serious content and lively ones for light content.
Gestures	Use natural, relaxed gestures, and don't be afraid to move around as you speak.
Eye Contact	Engage your audience by making eye contact with as many people as possible.

The Eyes Have It Perhaps your presentation is one that could be enhanced through the use of **visuals**—charts, graphs, photographs, or exhibits. If so, think carefully about how you want to present your visuals and include them in your rehearsals. Visuals should be large enough for the audience to see clearly and obviously relevant to the part of the oral presentation you're making at the time you use them. Direct your audience's attention to your visuals, if necessary.

 Follow the instructions in this workshop to adapt your literary research paper for an oral presentation. Rehearse your presentation thoroughly before presenting it to your class.

Listening and Speaking Skills
Rehearse effective performance techniques.

- *One-Stop Planner* CD-ROM with ExamView Test Generator

Internet
- go.hrw.com (Keyword: LE5 12-2)
- *Elements of Literature Online*

Collection 2: Skills Review

Comparing Literature

SKILLS FOCUS, pp. 226–229

Grade-Level Skills

- Literary Skills

Compare literary works of different historical periods.

INTRODUCING THE SKILLS REVIEW

Use this review to assess students' ability to contrast forms, techniques, and characteristics of works of different literary periods.

DIRECT TEACHING

A Reading Skills

Understanding dialect. Explain that this poem consists of an overheard conversation in Scottish dialect between "twa corbies," or "two ravens."

B Literary Focus

? Tone. How would you describe the tone of this ballad? [Possible responses: The tone is tragic because the unfeeling scavenger birds are pecking at a dead knight, who will not even be given a proper burial by those who loved him. The tone may be ironic because to the birds the knight is no more than nesting material.]

Collection 2: Skills Review

Comparing Literature

Test Practice

The two poems that follow tell essentially the same story. The first, "The Twa Corbies," is an anonymous medieval Scottish folk ballad passed down orally. The second poem is a literary ballad, carefully constructed in 1828 by the great Russian poet Alexander Pushkin. Like many Romantic poets of his day, Pushkin admired the songs and stories of the common people, both inside and outside of Russia. He freely borrowed from such popular sources as ballads and folk tales when composing his own poetry.

DIRECTIONS: Read the following poems. Then, read each multiple-choice question that follows, and write the letter of the best response.

The Twa Corbies

Anonymous

As I was walking all alane
I heard twa corbies making a mane;°
The tane unto the t'other say,
'Where sall we gang and dine today?'

5 '—In behint yon auld fail dyke,°
I wot° there lies a new-slain Knight;
And naebody kens° that he lies there,
But his hawk, his hound, and lady fair.

'His hound is to the hunting gane,
10 His hawk to fetch the wild-fowl hame,
His lady's ta'en another mate,
So we may mak our dinner sweet.

'Ye'll sit on his white hause-bane,°
And I'll pick out his bonny blue een:°
15 Wi' ae lock o' his gowden hair
We'll theek° our nest when it grows bare.

'Mony a one for him makes mane,
But nane sall ken where he is gane;
O'er his white banes, when they are bare,
20 The wind sall blaw for evermair.'

SKILLS FOCUS

Pages 226–229 cover **Literary Skills** Compare and contrast works of major literary periods.

2. **mane** *n.*: moan.
5. **fail dyke:** earth bank.
6. **wot** *v.:* know.
7. **kens** *v.:* knows.

13. **hause-bane:** neck-bone.
14. **een** *n. pl.*: eyes.
16. **theek** *n.*: thatch.

226 Collection 2 The Middle Ages

READING MINI-LESSON

Reviewing Word-Attack Skills

Activity. Display these pairs of words. Have students identify the word in which *u* stands for the sound /w/. Answers are underlined.

1. beguile — <u>bequest</u>
2. iniquity — <u>unique</u>
3. mannequin — <u>sequin</u>
4. languid — <u>languor</u>
5. league — <u>segue</u>

6. trilingual — <u>intrigue</u>
7. disquiet — <u>disguise</u>
8. banquet — <u>baguette</u>

Activity. Rhyming words must have the same final sounds and the same stress pattern. Have students read these words and identify the rhyming words in each set. Encourage them to check a dictionary if they are unsure of a pronunciation. Answers are underlined.

1. valiant — <u>defiant</u> — <u>reliant</u>
2. outrageous — <u>contagious</u> — gorgeous
3. finial — <u>denial</u> — infantile
4. dalliance — <u>misalliance</u> — defiance
5. comestible — survival — archival
6. mercenary — wary — plenary

226 Collection 2 The Middle Ages

Raven doth to raven fly

Alexander Pushkin

translated by Walter Arndt

Raven doth to raven fly,
Raven doth to raven cry:
Raven, where is fallen meat?
What shall be the morning's treat? **C**

Raven answers raven thus:
Well I know of meat for us;
On the fallow, by the willow
Lies a knight, a clod his pillow.

Why he died, who dealt the blow,
That his hawk alone can know,
And the sable mare that bore him,
And his bride who rode before him. **D**

But the hawk now sails the air,
And the foe bestrode the mare,
And the bride a wreath is wreathing
For a new love, warm and breathing.

DIRECT TEACHING

C Literary Focus

Comparing works. What similarities do you see between this verse and the opening verse of "The Twa Corbies"? [They both are quatrains with an *aabb* rhyme scheme. Both involve a raven that poses a question to another raven about where to find meat.]

D Literary Focus

Universal themes. What universal theme do both of these poems convey? [Possible responses: After death, life goes on; death is part of the natural cycle of things; nature does not care about human concerns; ultimately, everyone returns to nature.]

Activity. Have students identify the two words in each set in which *–eous* or *–ious* stands for the same sounds. Answers are underlined.

1. <u>piteous</u> <u>insidious</u> factious
2. <u>gracious</u> <u>herbaceous</u> instantaneous
3. <u>hideous</u> <u>odious</u> precocious
4. invidious <u>litigious</u> <u>prodigious</u>

Collection 2: Skills Review

Answers and Model Rationales

1. **C** Only C mentions "nest," which is associated with birds. Any person and many animals can moan (A); many animals might sit on the neck of a body (B). Both people and animals eat dinner (D).

2. **J** Line 4 means "Where shall we go and dine today?" F is wrong because "gang" is dialect for "go," not a group of friends. G and H are wrong because in this stanza the bird does not mention either a mate or a knight.

3. **A** Line 11 explicitly states the answer. B is wrong because the hawk and hound are hunting, not killed. C is wrong because the lady's grief is not mentioned. D is wrong because the lady takes another mate and does not search forever.

4. **H** The birds make a "dinner sweet" of the Knight. F is wrong because they show no regret. G is wrong because they say no one will remember him. J is wrong because they show no pity.

5. **C** A, B, and D are wrong because they are all natural events.

6. **F** In each first stanza, one bird asks about eating and the other bird answers by mentioning a dead knight.

---

1. In "The Twa Corbies," which of the following phrases *most* helps you realize that the *corbies* are birds?
   A "I heard the twa corbies making a mane"
   B "Ye'll sit on his white hause-bane"
   C "We'll theek our nest when it grows bare"
   D "So we may mak our dinner sweet"

2. In "The Twa Corbies," what question does one corbie ask the other in the first stanza?
   F Where is the rest of our gang?
   G Where will I find a faithful mate?
   H Where is the slain Knight?
   J Where shall we go and dine today?

3. In "The Twa Corbies," the lady reacts to the Knight's death by —
   A taking another mate
   B killing his hawk and hound
   C becoming grief-stricken
   D searching for him forever

4. In "The Twa Corbies," what is the attitude of the corbies toward the dead Knight?
   F They regret that he died so young.
   G They believe he will be remembered forever.
   H They are pleased to make a meal of him.
   J They pity those who are left behind to grieve.

5. Which of the following is a supernatural element found in "The Twa Corbies"?
   A birds feasting on a dead Knight
   B the lady taking another mate
   C talking birds
   D a hound hunting fowl

6. What is similar about the first two stanzas of both ballads?
   F The first stanza poses a question, and the second one answers it.
   G Both stanzas are written in dialect.
   H Each stanza has an *abcb* rhyme scheme.
   J The speaker of each stanza is a knight.

Collection 2: Skills Review

7. What does the third stanza of "Raven doth to raven fly" imply about how the knight died?
   A He fell off his horse.
   B He was slain by an enemy.
   C His bride poisoned him.
   D He died in a hunting accident.

8. Unlike "The Twa Corbies," the last stanza of "Raven doth to raven fly" emphasizes —
   F the knight's decay
   G the lady's lack of grief
   H the corbies' meal
   J the hound's hunting activities

9. A theme common to both ballads is —
   A the beauty of nature
   B the peacefulness of death
   C the importance of friendship
   D the failure of love

10. What word *best* describes the tone of both ballads?
    F warmhearted
    G unsentimental
    H humorous
    J romantic

Essay Question

These two ballads tell similar stories about the death of a knight. Both are told from the point of view of the birds that are about to devour the dead man. Yet for all their similarities, there are differences in details that subtly distinguish each ballad. Write an essay in which you point out the differences between the ballads. Be sure to describe the emotional effect of each ballad.

---

7. **B** "Who dealt the blow" implies an enemy. A is wrong because no mention is made of falling off a horse. C is wrong because he died of a blow, not poison. D is wrong because, although the knight may have been hunting when he died, that would tell you about *when* he died, not *how*.

8. **G** F is wrong because the stanza does not mention the knight's decay. H is wrong because the stanza does not mention the corbies. J is wrong because the stanza does not mention the hound.

9. **D** D is correct because both ballads mention a lady taking a new lover. A is wrong because nature is portrayed as indifferent, not beautiful. B is wrong because the knights' deaths are not peaceful. C is wrong because friendship is not mentioned in the poems.

10. **G** Both poems portray nature as indifferent and the ladies as unfeeling. F is wrong because no one is warmhearted except for the ladies with their new lovers. H is wrong because neither poem is comic. J is wrong because both poems puncture romantic ideals of pure love and chivalrous loyalty.

Essay Question

Encourage students to list the characteristics of the poems (such as use of dialect, tone, and theme) and to discuss their emotional impact. Point out that they should note not only what is said but also what is not said.

Test-Taking Tips

For information on answering multiple-choice items, refer students to **Test Smarts**.

ASSESSING

Assessment

- Holt Assessment: *Literature, Reading, and Vocabulary*

Using Academic Language

Review of Literary Terms
Ask students to look back through the collection to find the meanings of the terms listed at right. Then, have students show their grasp of these terms by citing passages from the collection that illustrate the meanings of those terms.

Ballad (p. 108); **Refrain** (p. 108); **Characterization** (p. 118); **Frame Story** (pp. 118, 169, 172); **Imagery** (p. 144); **Verbal Irony** (p. 145); **Situational Irony** (pp. 145, 186); **Narrator** (p. 155); **Couplet** (p. 167); **Half Rhymes** (p. 167); **Fable** (p. 172); **Epigrams** (p. 172); **Archetype** (p. 179); **Romance Hero** (p. 193).

Collection 2: Skills Review

Vocabulary Skills

Multiple-Meaning Words

Modeling. Model the thought process of a good reader getting the answer to item 1 by saying, " 'Silent like a beast or *post*' indicates that *post* is a noun meaning something that stands and is silent. So A, in which *post* is a verb, is clearly wrong. In B, *post* is an assigned position, and in D, *post* is a job—neither has anything to do with being silent. C is correct because the post of an old barn stands silently."

Answers and Model Rationales

1. **C** See model rationale above.
2. **J** In J, *plain* means "clear." F uses *plain* as a noun, and in G and H, *plain* means "unflavored" and "not handsome," respectively.
3. **B** Only B uses *gain* as a noun meaning "increase of wealth." A, C, and D use it as a verb meaning "to add or acquire."
4. **G** A "general referee" would be the overall referee. F refers to a military rank. In H, *general* means "unspecialized," and in J, it means "in most cases." In G, *general* means an "overall or predominant" feeling. Therefore, G is correct.
5. **B** In "set the supper at a certain price," *set* means "to establish according to a rule." In A, *set* means "to devote oneself to something." In C, *set* means "predetermined." D refers to a theatrical stage design. Only B uses *set* to refer to establishment of a fee according to a rule.

230 Collection 2 The Middle Ages

Collection 2: Skills Review

Vocabulary Skills

Test Practice

Words with Multiple Meanings

DIRECTIONS: Choose the answer in which the underlined word is used in the same way as it is used in the lines from *The Canterbury Tales*.

1. "He stood not silent like a beast or <u>post</u>,
   But gave his answer with the ringing word . . ."
   A The student planned to <u>post</u> an ad.
   B The soldier would not leave her <u>post</u>.
   C All that's left of that old barn is a rotted <u>post</u>.
   D She gladly accepted the <u>post</u> when her boss offered it to her.

2. "But let me briefly make my purpose <u>plain</u> . . ."
   F The wind-swept <u>plain</u> stretched far and wide.
   G I prefer <u>plain</u> yogurt.
   H He's not handsome; his face is very <u>plain</u>.
   J I thought she had made it <u>plain</u> that she would be leaving tomorrow.

3. "I preach for nothing but for greed of <u>gain</u> . . ."
   A The doctor will <u>gain</u> nothing but respect for all her charity work.
   B Too many crimes have been committed for petty <u>gain</u>.
   C If I could just <u>gain</u> their interest, I know they'd hire me.
   D We could probably <u>gain</u> more speed if we shift gears.

4. "Become our Governor in short, and be Judge of our tales and <u>general</u> referee . . ."
   F In the armed forces, a <u>general</u> ranks higher than a colonel.
   G There's a <u>general</u> feeling that we're being too strict.
   H He buys his supplies at the <u>general</u> store.
   J In <u>general</u>, the salesperson preferred to work weekends.

5. "And <u>set</u> the supper at a certain price."
   A Once Mira has <u>set</u> her mind on a goal, there's no way to stop her.
   B The fine was <u>set</u> at five hundred dollars.
   C Is there a <u>set</u> number of players needed for this game?
   D We need help getting this <u>set</u> ready for the play.

Vocabulary Skills Understand multiple-meaning words.

230 Collection 2 The Middle Ages

Vocabulary Review

Use this activity to assess whether students have retained the collection Vocabulary.

piteous	adversary	dire
initiative	approbation	

Activity. Ask students to complete the sentences with the correct Vocabulary word.

1. She demonstrated great _____ in getting the huge project rolling. [initiative]
2. The trade of the star outfielder did not meet with the fans' _____. [approbation]
3. The prisoner of war was in _____ circumstances with no food. [dire]
4. The sick kitten moaned in a _____ manner. [piteous]
5. His _____ in the boxing ring was a seasoned professional. [adversary]

Collection 2: Skills Review
Writing Skills

Test Practice

DIRECTIONS: Read the following paragraph from a draft of a student's historical research paper. Then, answer the questions below it.

(1) Anglo-Saxon literature has similarities with the literature of the Middle Ages. (2) Because the English epic *Beowulf* tells a story that predates the arrival of Christianity in England, it is saturated with pagan ideas and symbolism. (3) However, it also contains Christian themes and references to Christian symbols. (4) In fact, some scholars believe that monks may have added Christian elements to the original *Beowulf* story. (5) By the Middle Ages, Christian themes in literature had largely replaced pagan themes. (6) *Beowulf* is also effective as an exciting adventure story.

1. Which sentence states the main idea of the passage better than sentence 1?
   - A *Beowulf* is an example of Anglo-Saxon literature that combines pagan and Christian elements.
   - B Christian themes are dominant in the most enduring literature of the Middle Ages.
   - C *Beowulf* and *The Canterbury Tales* are the literary high points of their respective ages.
   - D Anglo-Saxon literature reflects paganism, but medieval literature reflects Christianity.

2. To strengthen support for the main idea, the writer could
   - F discuss the history of the medieval Christian church
   - G mention a differing opinion from a secondary source
   - H include an analysis of *Beowulf's* pagan and Christian themes
   - J contrast the religious beliefs of various medieval writers

3. Which sentence, if added, would support the idea in sentence 5?
   - A Grendel, the monster in *Beowulf*, is a pagan symbol.
   - B *The Canterbury Tales* depicts the perfect Christian knight.
   - C During the Middle Ages, feudal themes dominated literature.
   - D The Church's influence on medieval literature was extensive.

4. Which sentence should be deleted to improve the passage's organization?
   - F 2
   - G 3
   - H 5
   - J 6

5. While presenting this passage in an oral presentation, the speaker could
   - A pause to emphasize important ideas
   - B avoid making eye contact in order to focus on the message
   - C stand perfectly still while speaking
   - D speak softly so others may practice their presentations

Writing Skills
Write a historical research paper.

Collection 2: Skills Review
Writing Skills

Answers
1. A
2. H
3. D
4. J
5. A

APPLICATION

My Hometown

Have students identify and research a historical site, a local celebrity, or a regional legend or tall tale and prepare an audio or audiovisual presentation. The presentation should include interviews with people who have firsthand knowledge of the topic if possible. Students may want to ask a peer to perform any needed narration.

EXTENSION

Make a Poster

For homework, have students design a poster that teaches one aspect of writing the research paper. Subjects for posters might include how to prepare an annotated bibliography or how to prepare an alternative to a formal outline.

RESOURCES: WRITING

Assessment
- *One-Stop Planner* CD-ROM with ExamView Test Generator
- *Holt Assessment: Writing, Listening, and Speaking*

Internet
- Holt Online Assessment
- Holt Online Essay Scoring

Collection 3
The Renaissance: 1485–1660

About Collection 3
In Collection 3, students will master the following skills:

- **Literary Skills:** Evaluate the philosophical, political, religious, ethical, and social influences of a historical period; analyze pastoral poems, *carpe diem* poetry, Shakespearean sonnets, dramatic songs, monologue, soliloquy, metaphysical poetry, metaphysical conceits, tone, paradox, epigrams, political points of view on a topic, parallelism, didactic literature, epic similes, blank verse, allusion, allegory; compare and contrast works from different cultures and literary periods.
- **Reading Skills:** Draw inferences; analyze arguments; and understand Milton's style.
- **Vocabulary Skills:** Identify word relationships; understand and use words derived from Greek and Latin; and understand and use synonyms.
- **Writing Skills:** Develop, write, and revise a literary analysis of a poem.
- **Listening and Speaking Skills:** Present a recitation of a poem, speech, or dramatic soliloquy.

Minimum Course of Study
Most skills can be taught with a minimum number of selections and features. In the chart to the right, lessons **highlighted in green** constitute the minimum course of study that provides coverage of the skills taught in Collection 3.

Scope and Sequence

Selection • Feature	Literary Skills
The Renaissance: 1485–1660 by C. F. Main	• Evaluate the philosophical, political, religious, ethical, and social influences of a historical period
The Passionate Shepherd to His Love by Christopher Marlowe **The Nymph's Reply to the Shepherd** by Sir Walter Raleigh ↔ at grade level	• Analyze the characteristics of pastoral poems
To the Virgins, to Make Much of Time by Robert Herrick **To His Coy Mistress** by Andrew Marvell ↔ at grade level	• Analyze *carpe diem* poetry
Sonnets 29,* 30, 71, 73, 116,* 130 by William Shakespeare ↔ at grade level *minimum course of study	• Analyze the characteristics of Shakespearean sonnets
Songs from Shakespeare: • Blow, Blow, Thou Winter Wind • Fear No More the Heat o' the Sun • Full Fathom Five by William Shakespeare ↔ at grade level	• Analyze the characteristics of dramatic songs
Famous Shakespearean Speeches: • To be, or not to be • Tomorrow, and tomorrow, and tomorrow • Saint Crispin's Day Speech • Our revels now are ended by William Shakespeare ↔ at grade level	• Analyze the uses of monologue and soliloquy in drama
• **Song** ↔ at grade level • **A Valediction: Forbidding Mourning** ↑ above grade level • **Meditation 17** ↔ at grade level	• Analyze the characteristics of metaphysical poetry • Analyze metaphysical conceits • Analyze the use of tone

Resource Manager
(see pp. 232G–232L)
Lesson and workshop resources are referenced in the Resource Manager on the pages that follow. These resources can be used to reinforce the skills taught in Collection 3, remediate students who are having difficulty, and provide supporting activities for English-language learners.

Reading Skills	Vocabulary Skills	Writing ■ Grammar and Language ■ Listening and Speaking Skills
		• Write a comparison-contrast essay
		• Write lyrics for a *carpe diem* song • Write an essay comparing and contrasting two poems
		• Write a sonnet • Write an essay comparing and contrasting two sonnets • Write a response to a sonnet
		• Write a character interpretation • Present an oral interpretation of a sonnet and a dramatic song
		• Write a paraphrase of a monologue or soliloquy • Give an oral performance of a monologue or soliloquy
		• Write an imitation of a metaphysical poem • Write a letter • Write an essay explaining the author's use of metaphors • Understand and use adjective clauses and adverb clauses

(continued)

Scope and Sequence

Selection ■ Feature	Literary Skills	Reading Skills
Death be not proud by John Donne ↔ *at grade level*	• Analyze the use of paradox	
• **On My First Son** • **Song: To Celia** by Ben Jonson ↔ *at grade level*	• Analyze the characteristics of epigrams	
Introducing Political Points of View: Education and Equality	• Analyze and compare political points of view on a topic	• Draw inferences

Main Reading:
Of Studies
by Francis Bacon
↑ *above grade level*
 	
Connected Readings:
• **Tilbury Speech**
  by Queen Elizabeth I
• *from* **Female Orations**
  by Margaret Cavendish, duchess of Newcastle
↔ *at grade level*
	• Analyze the use of parallelism	• Analyze arguments

• **Psalms 23 and 137** • **The Parable of the Prodigal Son** *from the* **King James Bible** ↔ *at grade level*	• Analyze the use of parallelism • Analyze the characteristics of parables	
Connecting to World Literature: Worlds of Wisdom: Wisdom Literature ↔ *at grade level*		

• **Night**
  from the **Koran**
• *from* **Philosophy and Spiritual Discipline**
  from the **Bhagavad-Gita**
• **Zen Parables**
• *from* **The Analects of Confucius**
• *from the* **Tao Te Ching**
  by Laotzu
• **Taoist Anecdotes**
• **Sayings of Saadi**
• **African Proverbs**
	• Compare wisdom literature from different cultures and literary periods
	• Analyze the characteristics of didactic literature
	• Compare wisdom literature from different countries	

The Fall of Satan *from* **Paradise Lost** by John Milton ↑ *above grade level*	• Analyze the use of style • Analyze epic similes, irregular syntax and blank verse	• Understand Milton's style

232C

Vocabulary Skills	Writing ■ Grammar and Language ■ Listening and Speaking Skills
	• Write an essay comparing and contrasting personification in two poems
	• Write a letter to the poet • Give an oral presentation of a poem
	• Write a letter to one of the writers
• Demonstrate word knowledge	• Write a response essay
	• Write an essay comparing and contrasting two versions of a psalm • Write a modern parable
	• Write an essay comparing different views of life • Write a modern proverb
• Identify word relationships • Understand and use words derived from Greek and Latin	• Write an essay analyzing a passage from the selection • Write a paraphrase of a speech from the selection

(continued)

Scope and Sequence

Selection • Feature	Literary Skills	Reading Skills
When I consider how my light is spent by John Milton ↑ *above grade level*	• Analyze the use of allusion	
from **The Pilgrim's Progress** by John Bunyan ↔ *at grade level*	• Analyze the use of allegory	
Writing Workshop: *Analyzing Literature*		
Listening and Speaking Workshop: *Reciting Literature*		
Skills Review: *Literary Skills* *Vocabulary Skills* *Writing Skills*	• Compare and contrast works from different literary periods	

Vocabulary Skills	Writing ▪ Grammar and Language ▪ Listening and Speaking Skills
	• Write an essay analyzing a line of a sonnet • Recite a sonnet that has two speakers
• Understand and use synonyms	• Write an allegory
	• Write a literary analysis of a poem
	• Present a recitation of a poem, speech, or dramatic soliloquy
• Use synonyms	• Write a literary analysis of a poem

Resource Manager

Selection • Feature	Planning	Differentiating Instruction • Lesson Plans with ELL Strategies and Practice	Reading • Vocabulary
The Renaissance: 1485–1660 *by* C. F. Main	• PowerNotes: The Renaissance	• Holt Adapted Reader	• Holt Adapted Reader
The Passionate Shepherd to His Love *by* Christopher Marlowe **The Nymph's Reply to the Shepherd** *by* Sir Walter Raleigh	• One-Stop Planner with ExamView Test Generator	• Audio CD Library, disc 4 • Audio CD Library, Selections and Summaries in Spanish	
To the Virgins, to Make Much of Time *by* Robert Herrick **To His Coy Mistress** *by* Andrew Marvell	• One-Stop Planner with ExamView Test Generator	• Audio CD Library, disc 4 • Audio CD Library, Selections and Summaries in Spanish	
Sonnets 29, 30, 71, 73, 116, 130 *by* William Shakespeare **Songs from Shakespeare:** • Blow, Blow, Thou Winter Wind • Fear No More the Heat o' the Sun • Full Fathom Five *by* William Shakespeare **Famous Shakespearean Speeches:** • To be, or not to be • Tomorrow, and tomorrow, and tomorrow • Saint Crispin's Day Speech • Our revels now are ended *by* William Shakespeare	• One-Stop Planner with ExamView Test Generator	• The Holt Reader, pp. 93–99 • Holt Reading Solutions, p. 71 • Supporting Instruction in Spanish, pp. 14–16 • Audio CD Library, disc 4 • Audio CD Library, Selections and Summaries in Spanish	• The Holt Reader • Holt Reading Solutions • PowerNotes: Reading Shakespeare
• Song • A Valediction: Forbidding Mourning • Meditation 17 • Death be not proud *by* John Donne	• One-Stop Planner with ExamView Test Generator	• The Holt Reader, pp. 102–109 • Holt Adapted Reader • Holt Reading Solutions, pp. 75–78 • Supporting Instruction in Spanish, pp. 17–18 • Audio CD Library, disc 4 • Audio CD Library, Selections and Summaries in Spanish	• The Holt Reader • Holt Adapted Reader • Holt Reading Solutions

Writing ■ Grammar and Language ■ Listening and Speaking	Assessment
• Daily Language Activities	• Holt Assessment: Literature, Reading, and Vocabulary • Holt Online Assessment • One-Stop Planner with ExamView Test Generator
• Daily Language Activities	• Holt Assessment: Literature, Reading, and Vocabulary • Holt Online Assessment • One-Stop Planner with ExamView Test Generator
• Daily Language Activities	• Holt Assessment: Literature, Reading, and Vocabulary • Holt Online Assessment • One-Stop Planner with ExamView Test Generator
• Daily Language Activities • Language Handbook Worksheets, pp. 53, 88, 59	• Holt Assessment: Literature, Reading, and Vocabulary • Holt Online Assessment • One-Stop Planner with ExamView Test Generator

Technology

INTERNET
- go.hrw.com
- Holt Online Assessment
- Holt Online Essay Scoring
- Elements of Literature Online

MEDIA
- One-Stop Planner with ExamView Test Generator
- PowerNotes
- Audio CD Library, discs 4, 5, and 6
- Audio CD Library, Selections and Summaries in Spanish
- Visual Connections Videocassette Program, Segments 4 and 5
- Fine Art Transparencies, 4 and 5

 Transparency   Video

 CD-ROM   Audio CD

(continued)

Resource Manager

Selection • Feature	Planning	Differentiating Instruction • Lesson Plans with ELL Strategies and Practice	Reading • Vocabulary
• On My First Son • Song: To Celia *by* Ben Jonson	• One-Stop Planner with ExamView Test Generator	• Supporting Instruction in Spanish, p. 18 • Audio CD Library, disc 4 • Audio CD Library, Selections and Summaries in Spanish	
Introducing Political Points of View: **Education and Equality**			• PowerNotes: Making Inferences
Main Reading: **Of Studies** *by* Francis Bacon **Connected Readings:** • Tilbury Speech *by* Queen Elizabeth I • *from* Female Orations *by* Margaret Cavendish, duchess of Newcastle	• One-Stop Planner with ExamView Test Generator	• The Holt Reader, pp. 111–112 • Holt Reading Solutions, pp. 82–87 • Holt Adapted Reader • Supporting Instruction in Spanish, p. 19 • Audio CD Library, disc 4 • Audio CD Library, Selections and Summaries in Spanish	• The Holt Reader • Holt Adapted Reader • Holt Reading Solutions • Vocabulary Development, p. 15
• Psalms 23 and 137 • The Parable of the Prodigal Son *from the* King James Bible	• One-Stop Planner with ExamView Test Generator	• Holt Adapted Reader • Supporting Instruction in Spanish, pp. 20–21 • Audio CD Library, disc 4 • Audio CD Library, Selections and Summaries in Spanish	• Holt Adapted Reader
Connecting to World Literature: Worlds of Wisdom: **Wisdom Literature** • Night *from the* Koran • *from* Philosophy and Spiritual Discipline *from the* Bhagavad-Gita • Zen Parables • *from* The Analects of Confucius • *from the* Tao Te Ching *by* Laotzu • Taoist Anecdotes • Sayings of Saadi • African Proverbs	• One-Stop Planner with ExamView Test Generator	• Supporting Instruction in Spanish, pp. 21–23 • Audio CD Library, disc 5 • Audio CD Library, Selections and Summaries in Spanish	

Writing ■ Grammar and Language ■ Listening and Speaking	Assessment
• Daily Language Activities • Language Handbook Worksheets, pp. 53, 88, 59	• Holt Assessment: Literature, Reading, and Vocabulary • Holt Online Assessment • One-Stop Planner with ExamView Test Generator
• Daily Language Activities	• Holt Assessment: Literature, Reading, and Vocabulary • Holt Online Assessment • One-Stop Planner with ExamView Test Generator
• Daily Language Activities	• Holt Assessment: Literature, Reading, and Vocabulary • Holt Online Assessment • One-Stop Planner with ExamView Test Generator
• Daily Language Activities	• Holt Assessment: Literature, Reading, and Vocabulary • Holt Online Assessment • One-Stop Planner with ExamView Test Generator

(continued)

Technology

INTERNET

- go.hrw.com
- Holt Online Assessment
- Holt Online Essay Scoring
- Elements of Literature Online

MEDIA

 • One-Stop Planner with ExamView Test Generator

 • PowerNotes

 • Audio CD Library, discs 4, 5, and 6

 • Audio CD Library, Selections and Summaries in Spanish

 • Visual Connections Videocassette Program, Segments 4 and 5

 • Fine Art Transparencies, 4 and 5

 Transparency   Video

 CD-ROM   Audio CD

Resource Manager

Selection ■ Feature	Planning	Differentiating Instruction ■ Lesson Plans with ELL Strategies and Practice	Reading ■ Vocabulary
• The Fall of Satan *from* **Paradise Lost** • When I consider how my light is spent *by* John Milton	• One-Stop Planner with ExamView Test Generator	• The Holt Reader, pp. 114–115 • Holt Reading Solutions, p. 88 • Supporting Instruction in Spanish, pp. 23–24 • Audio CD Library, disc 6 • Audio CD Library, Selections and Summaries in Spanish	• The Holt Reader • Holt Reading Solutions • Vocabulary Development, p. 16
from **The Pilgrim's Progress** *by* John Bunyan	• One-Stop Planner with ExamView Test Generator	• Supporting Instruction in Spanish, p. 24 • Audio CD Library, disc 6 • Audio CD Library, Selections and Summaries in Spanish	• Vocabulary Development, p. 17
Writing Workshop: *Analyzing Literature*	• One-Stop Planner with ExamView Test Generator	• Workshop Resources: Writing, Listening, and Speaking, pp. 23–29 • Supporting Instruction in Spanish, p. 68	
Listening and Speaking Workshop: *Reciting Literature*	• One-Stop Planner with ExamView Test Generator	• Workshop Resources: Writing, Listening, and Speaking, pp. 30–35 • Supporting Instruction in Spanish, p. 109	
Skills Review: *Literary Skills* *Vocabulary Skills* *Writing Skills*			

The Holt Reader

The Holt Reader is a consumable paperback book that can be used alone or to accompany *Elements of Literature*. It offers guided support throughout the reading process and encourages students to become active readers by circling, underlining, questioning, and jotting down responses as they read. *The Holt Reader* works well for homework, students who have missed class, additional instructional time, reteaching, and remediation.

Holt Reading Solutions (HRS)

Holt Reading Solutions pulls together reading resources in the *Elements of Literature* program to create a powerful tool for intervention and whole-class instruction. *HRS* includes diagnostic assessment tools, lesson plans for English-language learners and special education students, adaptations of selected reading selections, vocabulary and comprehension worksheets, information on phonics and decoding, and additional instruction and practice in remedial reading skills.

Writing ■ Grammar and Language ■ Listening and Speaking	Assessment
• Daily Language Activities	• Holt Assessment: Literature, Reading, and Vocabulary • Holt Online Assessment • One-Stop Planner with ExamView Test Generator
• Daily Language Activities	• Holt Assessment: Literature, Reading, and Vocabulary • Holt Online Assessment • One-Stop Planner with ExamView Test Generator
• Daily Language Activities • Workshop Resources: Writing, Listening, and Speaking, pp. 23–29	• Holt Assessment: Writing, Listening, and Speaking • Holt Online Assessment • One-Stop Planner with ExamView Test Generator
• Workshop Resources: Writing, Listening, and Speaking, pp. 30–35	• Holt Assessment: Writing, Listening, and Speaking • One-Stop Planner with ExamView Test Generator
	• Holt Assessment: Writing, Listening, and Speaking • One-Stop Planner with ExamView Test Generator

Technology

INTERNET
- go.hrw.com
- Holt Online Assessment
- Holt Online Essay Scoring
- Elements of Literature Online

MEDIA
- One-Stop Planner with ExamView Test Generator
- PowerNotes
- Audio CD Library, discs 4, 5, and 6
- Audio CD Library, Selections and Summaries in Spanish
- Visual Connections Videocassette Program, Segments 4 and 5
- Fine Art Transparencies, 4 and 5

 Transparency   Video

 CD-ROM   Audio CD

One-Stop Planner with ExamView Test Generator

The *One-Stop Planner* CD-ROM contains electronic versions of print-based teaching resources, clips from the video program, and valuable assessment tools. The *One-Stop Planner* resources are presented in easy-to-follow, point-and-click menu formats. To preview resources or print out worksheets and tests, you simply make a selection and click.

Collection 3

INTRODUCING THE COLLECTION

Collection 3 features the distinctive authors of the Renaissance. Students will examine the stylistic flourishes of Shakespeare, Milton, and Marlowe. They will also learn the characteristics of the favored genres of the time: Marlowe's pastorals, Donne's metaphysical poetry, and the Shakespearean sonnet. In the Political Points of View feature, students will read several articles about the importance of education. Collection 3 concludes by giving the students the opportunity to analyze a poem of their choice.

VIEWING THE ART

Hans Holbein the Younger (c. 1497–1543) was born into a family of German artists. He gained a reputation in England and Switzerland as one of the most important portrait painters in northern Europe. The ambassadors in Holbein's painting are posed at a table bearing objects representing the highest achievements of Renaissance learning—instruments and documents related to astronomy, mathematics, and music. The ambassadors, it is suggested, have mastered these disciplines. The value of their achievement, however, is undercut by the elongated object that can be seen at the ambassadors' feet. Viewed from an extreme angle on the right, the object can be seen as a skull, a symbol of death. The specter of death thereby casts its shadow over the very accomplishments that Holbein seems to be celebrating.

Activity. If you are in a position to properly see the skull, the rest of the painting becomes incoherent. What does this suggest about the significance of death? [In the face of death, our accomplishments are meaningless.]

The Ambassadors (1533) by Hans Holbein the Younger. Oil on canvas. The ambassadors are Jean de Dintville and Georges de Selve, from the court of King Henri II of France. The objects on the table represent the arts and sciences.
National Gallery, London, Great Britain. © Photograph by Erich Lessing/Art Resource, New York.

COLLECTION 3 RESOURCES: READING

Planning
- One-Stop Planner CD-ROM with ExamView Test Generator

Differentiating Instruction
- Holt Reading Solutions
- The Holt Reader
- Holt Adapted Reader
- Family Involvement Activities in English and Spanish

- Supporting Instruction in Spanish
- Audio CD Library, Selections and Summaries in Spanish

Vocabulary
- Vocabulary Development

Grammar and Language
- Language Handbook Worksheets
- Daily Language Activities

Collection 3

The Renaissance
1485–1660

A Flourish of Genius

O England! model to thy inward greatness,

Like little body with a mighty heart . . .

—William Shakespeare

Grammar students with their teacher (c. 1330–1338) by Andrea Pisano. Bas relief.
The Art Archive/Duomo Florence/Dagli Orti (A).

INTERNET
Collection Resources
Keyword: LE5 12-3

Assessment
- Holt Assessment: Literature, Reading, and Vocabulary
- One-Stop Planner CD-ROM with ExamView Test Generator
- Holt Online Assessment

Internet
- go.hrw.com (Keyword: LE5 12-3)
- Elements of Literature Online

Media
- Audio CD Library
- Audio CD Library, Selections and Summaries in Spanish
- Fine Art Transparencies
- Visual Connections Videocassette Program
- PowerNotes

THE QUOTATION
These lines are from the Prologue to Act II of *Henry V*. Ask students what Shakespeare is saying about England. [Possible response: He is saying that although England is small in size, it has a large heart. This relationship of a small body to a large heart is analogous to the relationship of a small country to its "greatness" or importance in the world.]

Time Line

1485–1515
Age of Exploration

Students may need help making the connection between the age of exploration—which increased humans' knowledge of the world, opened up vast new opportunities for colonization, and created wealth—and the changing world-views of the Renaissance.

1540–1566
Sonnets

In 1557, the year before Elizabeth became queen, a printer named Richard Tottel put out an important collection of poems titled *Songs and Sonnets*. The best poems in this book, which is commonly called *Tottel's Miscellany*, had been written some years earlier by Sir Thomas Wyatt and Henry Howard, the earl of Surrey. Both Wyatt and Howard were inspired by the Italian scholar and poet Petrarch and were responsible for introducing Petrarch's work into England.

1566–1590
Golden Age in the East

During these years, the Mogul leader Akbar reigned during a golden age in what is now India. He defended religious freedom and presided over a cultural flowering that still impresses those who study examples of it in India's great miniature paintings and architecture. Meanwhile, beginning in 1588, Shah Abbas led the Safavid dynasty, in what is now Iran, through a similar period of greatness.

The Renaissance 1485–1660

LITERARY EVENTS

1485 | 1515 | 1540 | 1566

- **1513** Niccolò Machiavelli writes *The Prince*
- **1516** Thomas More's *Utopia* is published
- **1538** Book-licensing laws are introduced in England
- **1557** *Tottel's Miscellany* (including poems of Wyatt and Surrey) is published
- **1564 William Shakespeare**, the Bard of Avon, is born
- **1572** In France, Montaigne begins his *Essais*
- **c. 1586** Okuni, a former priestess, forms first kabuki theater company in Japan
- **1590** Edmund Spenser publishes first three books of *The Faerie Queene*

Martin Luther's sermon (detail) (16th century), from a triptych by Lucas Cranach the Elder.
Church of St. Marien, Wittenberg.

Portrait of Queen Elizabeth I within the Armada jewel (16th century) by Nicholas Hilliard.
The Victoria and Albert Museum, London.

POLITICAL AND SOCIAL EVENTS

1485 | 1515 | 1540 | 1566

- **1485** Richard III is killed in battle
- **1492** Christopher Columbus reaches the Americas
- **1498** Vasco da Gama reaches India via Cape of Good Hope
- **c. 1503** Leonardo da Vinci paints *Mona Lisa*
- **1509** Henry VIII is crowned king of England
- **1513** Balboa crosses Isthmus of Panama and sights Pacific Ocean
- **1517** Martin Luther posts his ninety-five theses on a church door in Wittenburg, Germany, beginning the Protestant Reformation
- **1517** First Africans are taken to Americas as slaves
- **1519–1521** Magellan leads first expedition to circumnavigate the globe
- **1521** Hernando Cortés conquers Mexico, destroying Aztec Empire
- **c. 1534** With the Supremacy Act, Henry VIII proclaims himself head of Church of England
- **1543** Polish astronomer Nicolaus Copernicus publishes theory that planets orbit the sun
- **1553–1558** Mary Tudor—"Bloody Mary"—reigns, restoring papal authority in England
- **1558** Elizabeth I becomes queen of England
- **1588** English navy defeats Spanish Armada

English astrolabe (1559), a navigational instrument, made for Queen Elizabeth I by Thomas Gemini.
Museum of the History of Science, University of Oxford.

234   Collection 3   The Renaissance

Using the Time Line

Activity. Have students use a print or nonprint encyclopedia or a database to place the following events in science, geography, literature, the arts, and diplomacy on the time line.
- Botticelli paints *The Birth of Venus*. [c. 1485]
- Leonardo da Vinci draws the human figure in a circle to show proportions. [c. 1486–1490]
- Michelangelo sculpts his marble *David*, which is seventeen feet tall. [1501–1504]
- Diplomat Baldassare Castiglione publishes *The Courtier*, a book about polite society. [1528]
- Cabeza de Vaca publishes *La Relación*, an account of one of his journeys in the New World. [1542]
- Gerardus Mercator designs a projection of the round earth onto a flat map. [1569]
- Johannes Kepler discovers that the orbits of the planets are elliptical. [1609]

Nicolaus Copernicus (detail) (1575). German School. Museum of Torun, Poland.

1590	1610	1640	1660
1593–1594 In London, outbreak of plague forces theaters to close	**1610–1611** John Donne writes *Holy Sonnets*	**1642–1660** Puritans close all theaters in England	
1599 Globe Theatre is built in London	**1611** King James Bible is published	**1650** American poet Anne Bradstreet's *The Tenth Muse Lately Sprung Up in America* is published in London	
1605 Cervantes publishes Part I of *Don Quixote* (Part II is published in 1615)	**1621** Newspapers are first published in London	**c. 1658** John Milton begins *Paradise Lost*	
1605–1606 Shakespeare writes *King Lear* and *Macbeth*			
1609 Shakespeare's sonnets (written c. mid-1590s) are published			

1610		1640	1660
1600 British East India Company founded for trade with Asia	**1620** The *Mayflower* lands at Plymouth Rock, Massachusetts	**1642–1651** English Civil Wars are fought	**1660** Puritan Commonwealth ends; monarchy is restored with Charles II
1605 Gunpowder Plot, an attempt by Guy Fawkes and others to blow up Parliament and assassinate James I, is averted	**1628** English physician William Harvey explains the circulation of blood	**1649** Charles I is beheaded	
1607 First permanent English settlement in North America is established at Jamestown, Virginia	**c. 1632–1649** Taj Mahal is built near Agra, India	**1652** Dutch establish settlement in South Africa	
1609 In Italy, Galileo is first to study sky with telescope	**1639** Japan expels all Europeans except the Dutch	**1653–1658** Oliver Cromwell rules England as lord protector	
		1655 Jews are legally readmitted to England (after being expelled in 1290)	

The world map (c. 1540), from the *Portolan Atlas of the World* by Battista Agnese of Venice. Royal Geographic Society, London.

Hernando Cortés (1485–1547), Spanish explorer, meeting Montezuma II (c. 1480–1520), Aztec emperor.

The Renaissance 235

■ 1590–1610
Galileo

Galileo Galilei (1564–1642) made discoveries that challenged the official teaching of the Roman Catholic Church. Galileo's Copernican view that the earth revolved around the sun, rather than the opposite, was denounced by the Church as heresy in 1616 because it contradicted the Bible and displaced humanity as the center of the universe. Galileo was ordered not to spread his theory. In 1632, however, he published *Dialogue on Two Chief World Systems*. He was again summoned by the Church and this time knelt in public to recant his view. He is said, however, to have muttered on arising, "Eppur si muove" ("But still it [Earth] moves"). He spent the last eight years of his life under house arrest. In 1992, Pope John Paul II officially announced that the Church had been wrong in its condemnation of Galileo.

■ 1610–1640
Francis Bacon and the Scientific Method

Another scientific thinker of the Renaissance was Francis Bacon, who championed experimentation instead of relying on the conclusions of ancient thinkers. Modern scientific methods are based not only on Bacon's thinking but also on that of René Descartes, a French mathematician of the Renaissance.

Activity. Have students identify the entries that refer to voyages of discovery. Then, ask them to mark the route of each explorer on a copy of a world map.

Activity. Ask students to read through the time line and pick an entry that they find intriguing. Then, have each student research the significance of his or her event and give a three-minute oral report.

Activity. Have students choose an event, such as Henry VIII's establishment of the Church of England, and create a focused time line that traces the major consequences or results of this event. Students may select events already listed on this time line, or they may fill in key related dates from their reading of the introduction and from independent research.

Political and Social Milestones

Humanism: A New Intellectual Movement

During the 1500s, the educational philosophy known as humanism became widespread in boarding schools and among the tutors who educated the sons of upper-class and noble families in Europe. Unlike earlier educators, who had emphasized rote memorization, humanists stressed insight and reasoning. Humanists advocated studying human thoughts and achievements from a historical perspective, so they eagerly unearthed long-forgotten classical Greek and Latin texts, thereby bringing about a revival of classical learning. Humanists also established universities and libraries in order to foster the spread of classical studies; by the 1500s, there were about eighty universities in Europe.

Henry VIII Breaks with the Roman Catholic Church, 1534

In November of 1534, the Act of Supremacy gave King Henry VIII the title of Supreme Head of the Church of England, severing English Christians from the Church of Rome. This law stated that all church matters were now the responsibility of the English king, who regarded himself, not the pope, as God's deputy on earth. Between 1535 and 1539, King Henry VIII closed all Roman Catholic monasteries and convents in England; he sold or gave their lands to members of the middle and upper classes. This dissolution of church property replenished Henry's coffers and provided the English gentry with much-desired land.

Political and Social

Humanism: A New Intellectual Movement

During the Renaissance educated people began to embrace an intellectual movement known as humanism. The movement took its name from the *studia humanitatis* (humane studies)—the fields of study we today call the humanities, such as philosophy, history, languages, and the arts. Humanists looked not only to the Bible but also to the Latin and Greek classics for wisdom and knowledge. They combined classical ideals with traditional Christian thought in order to teach people how to live and rule. The invention of the printing press helped spread this new emphasis on the humanities, as more books became available to more people than ever before.

St. Jerome in His Study (detail) (1480) by Domenico Ghirlandaio. Chiesa di Ognissanti, Florence, Italy.

Milestones 1485–1660

Henry VIII Breaks with the Roman Catholic Church, 1534

The pope refused to grant Henry VIII an annulment of his marriage to his first wife, Catherine of Aragon. In response, Henry denied the authority of the pope and declared himself head of the Church in England. This marked the beginning of the Protestant Reformation in England. Many of Henry's subjects viewed his bold move as an opportunity to achieve much-needed reform of the Church. They wished to put an end to the widespread corruption among the clergy and to the political power that Rome and its ally Spain wielded over English affairs. Some of Henry's subjects remained loyal to the Roman Catholic Church, however, and many of them lost their lives or their property by refusing to recognize Henry as head of the new Church of England.

(Opposite) *King Henry VIII* (1542) by Hans Holbein the Younger. Oil and tempura on oak. This portrait was painted after Catherine Howard's execution.
From the Castle Howard Collection, York, England.

Always interested in theology, King Henry in his later years devoted much time to church doctrines. To the end of his life, he considered himself a devout Catholic, worshiping in the traditional fashion. He deplored Martin Luther (see p. 246) and generally worked to block religious reforms urged by English Protestants.

The English Navy Defeats the Spanish Armada, 1588

The most decisive event in England's emergence as a naval power and independent political force in northern Europe was the defeat of the great armada of Spanish ships by the Royal Navy in 1588. (An *armada* is a fleet of warships.) Never again would the Spanish Empire be the undisputed ruler of the oceans of the known world.

Launch of Fireships Against the Armada (16th century). Netherlands School.
© National Maritime Museum Picture Library.

The English Navy Defeats the Spanish Armada, 1588

In the religious conflicts of the 1500s, Spain saw itself as the defender of the Roman Catholic faith against the growing forces of Protestantism in England, Germany, and Holland. Spain was at the time the world's most powerful nation militarily. It was also the wealthiest—its colonies provided a steady supply of gold and silver. English sea captains, such as Sir Francis Drake and Sir John Hawkins, preyed on richly loaded Spanish vessels in the West Indies and off the coast of South America. As a result of these exploits, war eventually broke out between England and Spain. In July of 1588, the 130-ship Spanish Armada sailed into the English Channel with 30,000 men aboard. In the opening battle the smaller and more maneuverable English ships inflicted considerable damage on the galleons of the Armada. Later the English set fire to eight ships and let them drift down toward the Armada, scattering the Spanish fleet. Then heavy winds wrecked many Spanish ships off the coast of Ireland. In the end only sixty-seven ships and six thousand men returned to Spain.

The Renaissance 1485–1660
by C. F. Main

PREVIEW

Think About...

The Renaissance era in Europe and in England was marked by a change in the way people thought about themselves and the world. No longer content with the fixed religious beliefs of the Middle Ages, people became more interested in expanding their knowledge of history, art, science, and especially the classic texts of ancient Greece and Rome. The Roman Catholic Church was challenged on a number of fronts. By the end of the sixteenth century, the Church had lost its position as the supreme moral and political power in Europe.

As you read about this period, look for answers to these questions:

- What questions interested the humanist thinkers?
- What social and economic developments during the Renaissance fostered a growing interest in reading and learning?
- What forces led people to challenge the power of the Roman Catholic Church in England and on the Continent?

Collection introduction (pages 236–256) covers **Literary Skills** Evaluate the philosophical, political, religious, ethical, and social influences of a historical period.

What do you think people living a hundred years from now will call the age we live in today? Will they say we lived in the space age, the age of computers, the age of anxiety, the age of violence? We might be given a label we can't even imagine.

Just as we don't know what people of the future will think of us, the people of Europe living in the 1400s, 1500s, and 1600s didn't know that they were living in the Renaissance. Historical periods—the Middle Ages, the Renaissance, the Romantic period—are historians' inventions, useful labels for complex phenomena. The Middle Ages in England did not end on a certain night in 1485, when King Richard III's naked body, trussed up like a turkey, was thrown into an unmarked grave. The English Renaissance did not begin the moment a Tudor nobleman was crowned King Henry VII. The changes in people's values, beliefs, and behavior that marked the emerging Renaissance occurred gradually. Much that could be called medieval lingered on long after the period known as the

(Opposite) *A Marriage Fête at Bermondsey* (c. 1570) by J. Hoefnagel. Oil on panel.
Hatfield House, Hertfordshire, England. © Marquess of Salisbury Collection.

238 Collection 3 The Renaissance

VIEWING THE ART

As a young man, **Joris Hoefnagel** (1545–1601), the son of a Belgian diamond merchant, traveled through Europe with his family and made drawings. On their way home the family lost everything to Spanish plunderers and fled to Bavaria, where Hoefnagel was befriended by a patron who employed him to illustrate four books on natural history. Hoefnagel became an engraver as well as a printer and made maps, including some for a book on world history.

Activity. Ask students to make inferences about the various people shown in this picture. What are they doing? What classes do they come from? How do they live? [Possible responses: The title of the painting and the food table set up in an open-air hall suggest that the black-garbed people on the right are attending a party. These people may be from the upper class, merchant class, or landed class—people with time for leisure. The other people—people working in the baker's shop and those providing entertainment in the foreground—are likely from a lower class.]

The Renaissance   239

Advanced Learners

Encourage advanced learners to find a topic in this introduction that they would like to explore further. Students may wish, for example, to learn more about Thomas More, Erasmus, Elizabeth I, or some aspect of everyday life in England during the Renaissance. As you proceed with the chapter, have advanced students share the information they gather.

DIRECT TEACHING

A Literary Connections
The Term *Renaissance*
The term *Renaissance* was first used in the eighteenth century to characterize the changes that began at the end of the Middle Ages and continued through the fifteenth or sixteenth century. Historians now describe the period as marked by a series of renaissances, rather than one overarching transformation.

B Exploring the Historical Period
THE BOOK
These early books were actually handwritten manuscripts, preserved by Byzantine and Islamic scholars. With the invention of the printing press in the fifteenth century, however, what we know as the book became a reality and a working tool for scholars. By 1500, printers—particularly Italian printers—had published in book form the works of most of the important Latin authors.

VIEWING THE ART

Paulus Vredeman de Vries (1567–c. 1630), a Flemish painter, continued the tradition of painting architectural scenes with figures developed by his father, Hans Vredeman de Vries (1527–c. 1606).
Activity. Have students discuss an aspect of the painting that reveals something about the customs of the times.

Sir Francis Bacon.

Some books are to be tasted, others to be swallowed, and some few to be chewed and digested.
—Francis Bacon (1625)

Middle Ages was past. Historical periods cannot be rigidly separated from one another, but they can be distinguished.

Rediscovering Ancient Greece and Rome

The term *renaissance* is a French word meaning "rebirth." It refers particularly to renewed interest in classical learning—the writings of ancient Greece and Rome. During the long period of the Middle Ages, most European scholars had forgotten the Greek language, and they used a form of Latin that was very different from the Latin of ancient Rome. Few ordinary people could read. Those who could read were encouraged to study texts explaining Church doctrine. In the Renaissance, however, people discovered the marvels of old Greek and Latin classics—books that had been tucked away on the cobweb-covered shelves of monasteries for hundreds of years. Now people learned to read Greek once more and reformed the Latin that they read, wrote, and spoke.

The Spirit of Rebirth

Some people became more curious about themselves and their world than people generally had been in the Middle Ages, so that gradually there was a renewal of the human spirit—a renewal of curiosity and creativity. New energy seemed to be available for creating beautiful things and thinking new, even daring thoughts.

Ladies and Gentlemen Dancing in a Sumptuous Interior by Paulus Vredeman de Vries (1567–c. 1630). Christie's, London.

READING SKILLS REVIEW

Making generalizations. Review making generalizations, emphasizing that a generalization is a rule or statement that applies to many different situations or events. Ask students to form generalizations or recall generalizations they've heard about familiar items, such as cars, clothes, and teenagers.
Activity. Lead students in discussing how they would answer the question posed in the essay's first paragraph (p. 238). Ask, "What label best defines the modern age?" Then, encourage students to list characteristics that best describe the late twentieth and early twenty-first centuries. Have students rank the listed items in an order of importance that captures the spirit of the age. Finally, have students use the list as the basis for a label and general statement about our historical period.

Primary Source

The following explanation of creation by the humanist Giovanni Pico della Mirandola (1463–1494) of Florence represents the new thinking of the Renaissance: "God made man and woman at the close of the creation, to know the laws of the universe, to love its beauty, and to admire its greatness. He bou his human creatures to no fixed place, to no prescribed form of work, and by no iron

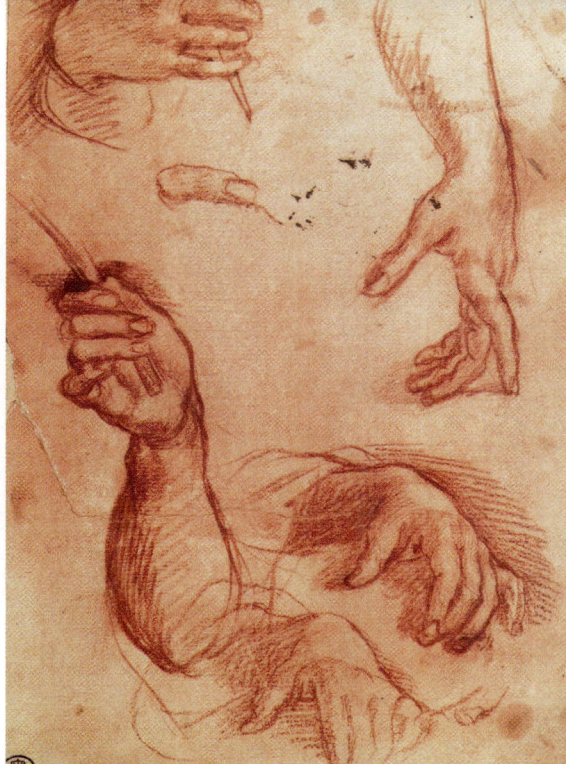

Study of Hands (16th century) by Andrea del Sarto.
© Scala/Art Resource, New York.

Today we still use the term *Renaissance person* for an energetic and productive human being who is interested in science, literature, history, art, and other subjects. (In America, Virginia's Thomas Jefferson, author of the Declaration of Independence, is referred to as a Renaissance man.)

It All Began in Italy: A Flourish of Genius

The new energy and creativity started in Italy, where considerable wealth had been generated from banking and trade with the East. The Renaissance began in Italy in the fourteenth century and lasted into the sixteenth. Thinking about just a few of the extraordinary people who flourished in this period—artists such as Leonardo da Vinci and Michelangelo, explorers such as Christopher Columbus, or scientists such as Galileo—reminds us how remarkably rich this period was and how much we owe to it.

Almost everyone in Europe and Britain at this time was Roman Catholic, in name anyway, so the Church was very rich and powerful, even in political affairs, in ways we would probably object to today. Many of the popes were lavish patrons of artists, architects, and scholars. Pope Julius II, for example, commissioned the artist

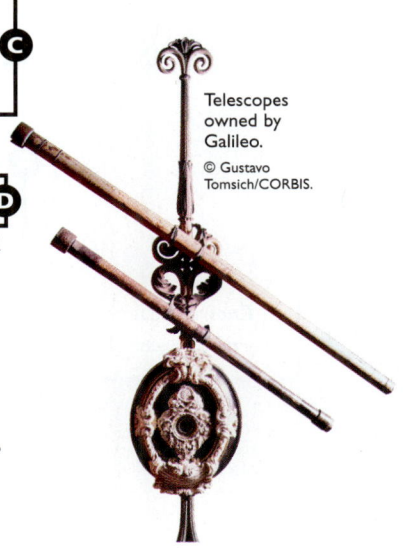

Telescopes owned by Galileo.
© Gustavo Tomsich/CORBIS.

necessity, but gave them freedom to will and to love. 'I have set thee,' says the Creator, 'in the midst of the world, that thou mayest the more easily behold and see all that is therein. I created thee a being neither heavenly nor earthly, neither mortal nor immortal only that thou mightest be free to shape and to overcome thyself. Thous mayest sink into a beast or be born anew to the divine likeness. To thee alone is given a growth and a development depending on thine own free will.'"
Activity. Invite students to discuss how this version of creation differs from the biblical version. [Possible response: This version does not dwell on sin; it emphasizes freedom of choice.]

DIRECT TEACHING

VIEWING THE ART

The Renaissance was not simply an age in which people rediscovered classical texts; it was also an age in which people sought to learn about their world through observation. They began to question what was said about the human body in ancient medical books by Galen (A.D. c. 130–c. 200) and to look at real bodies in anatomy theaters. In the visual arts the interest in observable phenomenon translated into a desire to draw things as they appeared in the world, rather than as they appeared in previous paintings.

Activity. Why did Andrea del Sarto (1486–1530) draw hands from various angles as he did in this study? [He was perfecting his ability to draw hands realistically.]

C Content-Area Connections

Humanities: Renaissance Man
Leonardo da Vinci (1452–1519) was probably the ultimate Renaissance man. A master painter, he pioneered new techniques such as sfumato, a way of softening lines. He was also a scientist who explored everything from the movement of water to human anatomy. In addition, he was an engineer who designed various kinds of machines, including some for military use.

D Content-Area Connections

History: Renaissance Wealth
Ask students to identify the event on the time line (p. 234) that helped open up new sources of wealth from the East. [Vasco da Gama's voyage to India in 1498]

DIRECT TEACHING

VIEWING THE ART

Michelangelo Buonarroti (1475–1564) always insisted that he was primarily a sculptor, but the Italian artist was also a painter, an architect, and a poet—a true Renaissance man. He labored for four years on the arduous task of painting the Sistine Chapel ceiling. The panel on which these hands appear was inspired by the account of humanity's creation as told in Genesis; it shows God touching Adam.

Activity. What is the significance of God's touching Adam's hand? [It depicts God giving Adam life.]

A Exploring the Culture
THE SISTINE CHAPEL
The Sistine Chapel is named after Pope Sixtus IV, who commissioned its construction (1473–1481). The chapel's interior walls feature frescoes depicting events from the lives of Christ and Moses, painted by a number of artists. The biblical stories on the ceiling and *The Last Judgment* on the wall behind the altar are the work of Michelangelo.

B Content-Area Connections
Humanities: The Humanities
The humanists not only studied the subjects related to a classical education—history, literature, philosophy, and more—but they made these subjects popular again. Hence, the collective term for these subjects became the *humanities*.

The creation of Adam (detail), from the Sistine Chapel ceiling (16th century) by Michelangelo.
© Scala/Art Resource, New York.

A Michelangelo to paint gigantic scenes from the Bible on the ceiling of the Sistine Chapel, a small church in the pope's "city" that was called, as it is today, the Vatican. Lying on his back on a scaffold, Michelangelo painted the Creation, the Fall of Man and Woman, the Flood, and other biblical subjects. His bright, heroic figures, which are still admired by thousands of visitors to Rome each year, show individual human beings who are noble and capable of perfection. This optimistic view of humanity was expressed by many other Renaissance painters and writers as well.

Knowledge is power.
—Francis Bacon (1597)

Humanism: Questions About the Good Life

B Refreshed by the classics, the new writers and artists were part of an intellectual movement known as **humanism.** The humanists went to the old Latin and Greek classics to discover new answers to such questions as "What is a human being?" "What is a good life?" and "How do I lead a good life?" Of course, Christianity provided complete answers to these questions, answers that the Renaissance humanists accepted as true. Renaissance humanists found no essential conflicts between the teachings of the Church and those of an ancient Roman moralist

---

Secondary Source

Humanists
William Manchester writes, "We picture the eminent scholars . . . wearing their distinctive outsized berets, the floppy brims hooding their ears, bowed over desks tilted toward them, pen and ink at hand. Poring over manuscripts and proofs in several languages, reliving the glories of the ancient past, half lost in the life of the mind, they were exalted by the awareness that they were rekindling flames extinguished in the glorious past. They cannot have been unaware of the recognition of their contemporaries. Each was a personage, admired beyond the borders of his own state, a man of substance in whom his compatriots took pride. . . . The peasant, the tradesman, the ordinary townsman lacked the feeblest grasp of the source for the scholars' fame . . . but he doffed his cap and tugged his forelock in the presence of such towering humanists. . . ."

like Cicero. They sought instead to harmonize these two great sources of wisdom: the Bible and the classics. Their aim was to use the classics to strengthen, not discredit, Christianity.

The humanists' first task was to recover accurate copies of these ancient writings. Their searches through Italian monasteries turned up writers and works whose very existence had been forgotten. Their next task was to share their findings. So they became teachers, especially of the young men who would become the next generation's rulers—wise and virtuous rulers, they hoped. From the Greek writer Plutarch, for instance, these humanist teachers would learn that the aim of life is to attain virtue, not success or money or fame, because virtue is the best possible human possession and the only source of true happiness.

The New Technology: A Flood of Print

The computer has radically transformed how we get information today. Similarly, the printing press transformed the way information was exchanged during the Renaissance. Before this all books were laboriously written out by hand—you can imagine how difficult and expensive this was and how few books were available.

The inventor of printing with movable type was a German named Johannes Gutenberg (1400?–1468). He printed the first complete

Printing Shop (1580s) by Jan van der Straet. Engraving.

By permission of The Folger Shakespeare Library, Washington, D.C.

DIRECT TEACHING

A Exploring the Historical Period
THE PRINTING PRESS
Spain, Hungary, and Poland also had their first printing presses between 1473 and 1476; Denmark and Sweden were equipped by 1482 to 1489. By 1500, forty thousand titles had been printed, totaling about twenty million books.

VIEWING THE ART

Hans Holbein the Younger (see p. 232) had the reputation of a master portraitist who could capture lifelike details of skin, clothing, and hair. He was often asked to produce likenesses of royalty. Henry VIII and most of his wives sat for Holbein portraits. The king admired Holbein and pardoned him for pushing an earl down some stairs. (The earl had insisted on visiting Holbein's art studio.) Holbein died in London during a plague.

Activity. Encourage students to compare Holbein's portraits with others in this book. They can also note what the subjects of Holbein's portraits are holding or wearing and why these details are significant. (More is wearing the chain of office.)

book, an immense Latin Bible, at Mainz, Germany, around 1455. From there the art and craft of printing spread to other cities in Germany, the Low Countries (the Netherlands, Belgium, and Luxembourg), and northern Italy. By 1500, relatively inexpensive books were available throughout western Europe. In 1476, printing reached England, then regarded as an island remote from the centers of civilization. In that year, William Caxton (1422?–1491), a merchant, diplomat, and writer who had been living in the Low Countries, set up a printing press in Westminster (now part of London). In all, Caxton's press issued about one hundred different titles, initiating a flood of print in English that is still increasing.

Two Friends—Two Humanists

When you hear people speak of humanism, you may hear the name Erasmus. Desiderius Erasmus (1466?–1536) is today perhaps the best known of all the Renaissance humanists. Erasmus was a Dutch monk, but he lived outside the monastery and loved to travel, visit-

Sir Thomas More (detail) (16th century) by Hans Holbein the Younger.
© The Frick Collection, New York.

Erasmus of Rotterdam (detail) (c. 1523) by Hans Holbein the Younger. Oil on wood (42 cm × 32 cm).
Louvre, Paris.

244 Collection 3 The Renaissance

DIFFERENTIATING INSTRUCTION

Learners Having Difficulty
Have students work in small groups to confer Renaissance Man or Renaissance Woman awards on people of today who exemplify the spirit and values of the Renaissance. In a brief awards ceremony, have students explain their choices, summarizing the achievements and interests of the award winners.

English-Language Learners
Invite students to keep a list of questions and comments that occur to them as they read this essay. When they have finished reading, invite them to write a self-assessment about how well they understood the essay.

Advanced Learners
Sir Thomas More's novel about a utopia (see p. 245) ironically inspired a new literary genre, the dystopian novel, which usually depicts a negative utopia. Interested students could give oral reports on More's *Utopia* and some of its dystopian descendants, such as George Orwell's *1984* and Aldous Huxley's *Brave New World*.

Bird's-eye view of London, from *Atlas Civitatis Orbis Terrarum* (c. 1574) by Georg Braun.
Map L85c 27. By permission of The Folger Shakespeare Library, Washington, D.C.

DIRECT TEACHING

B Exploring the Historical Period
EDUCATION FOR WOMEN
Defying custom, More taught Latin to his daughter Meg; few women in Renaissance Europe were given any kind of higher education.

C Literary Connections
More's *Utopia*
Book I of Thomas More's *Utopia* is a dialogue analyzing the social, economic, penal, and moral problems in England. Book II is a narrative describing Utopia. More coined the word *utopia* from the Greek words *ou*, meaning "not," and *topos*, meaning "place." Etymologically, therefore, *utopia* means "nowhere." In Utopia, which is nowhere or nonexistent, poverty, crime, injustice, and other problems do not exist.

ing many of the countries in Europe, including Italy, France, Germany, and England. He belonged, then, to all Europe. Because he wrote in Latin, he could address his many writings to all the educated people of western Europe.

On his visits to England, Erasmus taught Greek at Cambridge University and became friendly with a number of important people, among them a young lawyer named Thomas More (1477?–1535). More and Erasmus had much in common: They both loved life, laughter, and classical learning, and they both were dedicated to the Church, though they were impatient with some of the Church's corrupt practices at that time.

Like Erasmus, More wrote in Latin—poems, pamphlets, biographies, and his famous treatise on human society, *Utopia* (yōō·tō′pē·ə) (1516). *Utopia* became immediately popular, and it has been repeatedly translated into English and many other languages. Hundreds of writers have imitated or parodied it, and it has given us a useful adjective for describing impractical social schemes: *utopian*. More himself was far from impractical; he held a number of impor-

Secondary Source

More's Conflict with King Henry VIII
Historian Francis Hackett offers this assessment of Thomas More's motivations for opposing King Henry VIII: "The conflict between Henry and Thomas More was a conflict of civilizations, a conflict of principles, a conflict of wills. A new ferment, that of nationalism and commerce and the possibilities of economic individualism, was beginning to work in society, and was breaking up the medieval mind. Thomas More had been a humanist . . . ; he had criticized Rome until he saw that it was in danger of falling and in its collapse dragging down the precious spiritual tradition of a society governed from above. But when this danger was present, when the alternative to the papal religion of Christ, which Luther assailed, was the willfulness of Henry . . . then More forgot his zeal to reform the Church in a greater zeal to love his Master, to praise him, and to serve him."

DIRECT TEACHING

A Exploring the Historical Period
THE CATHOLIC REFORMATION

Students should know that this was a time of internal reform in the Church as well as a time of criticism by those who chose to break away. Pope Paul III, for example, convened the Council of Trent in 1545 to investigate the selling of indulgences, or religious pardons.

B Exploring the Historical Period
PROTESTANTISM

Luther founded the Lutheran church. Soon other faiths, including the Anglican, Calvinist, and Anabaptist churches, sprang up. These faiths and the denominations that developed from them (such as Episcopalian, Methodist, and Presbyterian) have come to be called Protestant.

C Literary Connections
Erasmus on Ethics

In 1509, Erasmus wrote his satire, *The Praise of Folly*. In this work he not only suggests that people return to a simple code of Christian ethics but also makes fun of greedy merchants and mincing scholars. Clerics who failed to live a life of humility were also a special target of his biting wit.

---

tant offices, rose to the very top of his profession, was knighted, and as lord chancellor became one of the king's chief ministers. More continues to fascinate people today. The play and film *A Man for All Seasons*, by Robert Bolt, is about More and his tragic standoff with King Henry VIII over a matter of law (see page 247).

The Reformation: Breaking with the Church

While the Renaissance was going on throughout Europe, there occurred in some countries another important series of events, called the **Reformation**. In England these two vast movements were closely related, and their forces were felt by all English writers. Although the exact nature of the Reformation varied from country to country, one feature was common to all Reformers: They rejected the authority of the pope and the Italian churchmen. In England, conflicts with the papacy had occurred off and on over the centuries, but adjustments had always been made on both sides. By the 1530s, an open break with the Roman Catholic Church could no longer be avoided.

By then a number of circumstances made such a break possible. Strong feelings of patriotism and national identity made the English people resent the financial burdens imposed on them by the Vatican—the pope, after all, was a foreign power in far-off Italy. Moreover, new religious ideas were coming into England from the Continent, especially from Germany. There, a monk named Martin Luther (1483–1546) had founded a new kind of Christianity, based not on what the pope said but on a personal understanding of the Bible. Like any institution that has been around for a long time and has ignored corruption within its ranks, the Church needed reform. Right at home in England, humanists like More and Erasmus were ridiculing old superstitions, as well as the ignorance and idleness of monks and the loose living and personal wealth of priests and bishops.

Martin Luther (1529) by Lucas Cranach the Elder.
Galleria degli Uffizi, Florence, Italy/The Bridgeman Art Library.

> *Superstition, idolatry, and hypocrisy have ample wages, but truth goes a-begging.*
> —Martin Luther
> from *Table Talk* (1569)

King Versus Pope: All for an Heir

The generations-old conflict between the pope and the king of England came to a climax when Henry VIII wanted to get rid of his wife of twenty-four years. Divorce was not allowed, especially for kings (until recently that was still true in Britain), so Henry needed a loophole. He asked Pope Clement VII to declare that he, Henry, was not properly married to his Spanish wife, Catherine of Aragon, because she had previously been wedded—for all of five months—to his older brother Arthur, now dead. (It was against Church law to marry a dead sibling's spouse; the biblical basis for the law is in Leviticus.)

Henry had two motives for wanting to get rid of Catherine. First, although she had borne him a princess, she was too old to give him

246 Collection 3 The Renaissance

READING SKILLS REVIEW

Using text organizers. Remind students that headings, glosses, boxed call-out quotations, and sidenotes can help them identify main ideas and details in an essay.

Activity. Have students identify the italicized call-out quotations on pp. 246 and 247. What important ideas do they present? Then, have students explain the purpose of the side margin features of p. 253.

An Allegory of the Tudor Succession: The Family of Henry VIII (c. 1589–1595). British School, possibly after Lucas de Heere. Oil on panel (45″ × 71¾″). Yale Center for British Art, Paul Mellon Collection, New Haven, Connecticut.

the male heir that he thought he must have. (Catherine had lost five babies.) What is more, another, younger woman had won Henry's dangerous affections: The king now wished to marry Anne Boleyn, who had been his "favorite" for several years. (Henry had earlier seduced Anne's sister.) The pope was not able to grant Henry the annulment of his marriage, even if he had wanted to, because the pope was controlled by Queen Catherine's nephew, the emperor of Spain. So, upon receiving the pope's refusal in 1533, Henry appointed a new archbishop of Canterbury, who obligingly declared Henry's marriage to Catherine invalid. In 1534, Henry concluded the break with Rome by declaring himself head of the English Church.

The Protestant Reformation

With Catherine packed away under house arrest—since she refused to accept the annulment of her marriage—Henry closed all of England's monasteries and sold the rich buildings and lands to his subjects. While the vast majority of his subjects agreed with Henry's changes in the Church, some of them did not. The best known of those who remained loyal to the pope was Sir Thomas More, now the lord chancellor of England. More felt he could not legally recognize his friend Henry as head of the Church. For More's stubbornness, Henry ordered that his lord chancellor be beheaded.

Anne Boleyn (detail), from *Memoirs of the Court of Queen Elizabeth* by Sarah, countess of Essex.
© Stapleton Collection/CORBIS.

Reminding us of a point in astronomy, which is that the longer the days are the farther off is the sun and yet the hotter; so is it with our love, for although by absence we are parted it nevertheless keeps its fervency, at least in my case and hoping the like of yours . . .

—King Henry VIII, from a letter to Anne Boleyn (1528)

DIRECT TEACHING

VIEWING THE ART

This painting is a political allegory designed to justify Elizabeth's sovereignty. The seated monarch is Henry VIII. Henry hands a sword to the boy, who is King Edward VI (Henry's son by Jane Seymour). On the left are the hated Mary and her husband, the Spanish King Philip II (the English always depicted the Spanish in melancholic black clothing). The god of war stands behind them. On the right, Elizabeth stands with the goddesses of peace and plenty behind her.

Activity. What details about this scene suggest that it was painted during the reign of Elizabeth I? [Attention is directed toward Elizabeth in the foreground dressed in light colors.] What might be the painting's message regarding Elizabeth's attitude toward her reign? [Elizabeth's position in the painting asserts her place in the succession, as well as her ability to bring peace and plenty to her country.]

DIRECT TEACHING

A Content-Area Connections
Culture: Protestantism
The word *Protestant* was first used in April 1529. At that time, it was applied to a number of German protesters who disagreed with the Catholic majority's decision to have Lutheranism condemned. Later, the word came to refer to anyone vocally "*protest*-ant" or to those who belonged to a Christian church or sect other than the Catholic or Orthodox Church.

B Exploring the Historical Period
EFFECTS OF THE WARS OF THE ROSES
The Wars of the Roses began in 1455 and were fought by the rival families of York and Lancaster. By the time the struggle ended in 1485, the ranks of the aristocracy were diminished. Henry VII became a king by usurping the throne.

It wasn't the first—or the last—time that Henry would execute a friend.

This was the very beginning of Protestantism in England. Many people were dissatisfied with the new church for reasons just the opposite of More's. They felt that it was not reformed enough, that it was merely a copy of Catholicism, as in some respects it was. These people later became known as Puritans, Baptists, Presbyterians, Dissenters, and Nonconformists. All of them wanted to get rid of many things they called "popish," such as the bishops, the prayer book, the priest's vestments, and even the church bells and the stained-glass windows. Some of them said that religion was solely a matter between the individual and God. This idea, which is still the foundation of most Protestant churches, is directly traceable to the teachings of those Renaissance humanists who emphasized the freedom of all human beings.

Henry VIII: Renaissance Man and Executioner

The five Tudor rulers of England are easy to remember: They consist of a grandfather, a father, and three children. The grandfather was Henry VII (1457–1509), a Welsh nobleman who seized the throne after England was exhausted by the long struggle called the Wars of the Roses. (Both factions involved used a rose as their emblem, one red, one white.) Henry VII was a shrewd, patient, and stingy man who restored peace and order to the kingdom; without these there could never have been a cultural Renaissance.

The Great Harry (detail) (1546) from the Anthony Roll manuscript.
The Pepys Library, Magdalene College, Cambridge, England.

Secondary Source

Henry VIII
What was Henry VIII's greatest accomplishment? According to historian John Burke, it was the creation of what would become the modern Admiralty, the government department in charge of the navy. Burke writes that Henry VIII also "extended the royal dockyards and encouraged the construction of faster ships with superior firepower. He laid, as it were, the keels of that future navy which was to thwart the ambitions of one greedy enemy after another." Burke also credits Henry VIII with the creation or development of many beautiful buildings and praises his concern for at least some forms of the law.

His son Henry VIII (reigned 1509–1547) had six wives: After Catherine of Aragon and Anne Boleyn, there were Jane Seymour, Anne of Cleves, Catherine Howard, and Catherine Parr. The fates of these unfortunate women are summarized in a jingle:

> Divorced, beheaded, died,
> Divorced, beheaded, survived.

The sexual intrigues of the court trapped two of Henry's wives: The king could play around, but he couldn't tolerate any suspicion of his wives' fidelity. The price paid by two young wives was heavy: Like Thomas More, Anne Boleyn and Catherine Howard lost their heads on the chopping block.

Despite his messy home life, Henry VIII was an important figure. He created the Royal Navy, which put a stop to foreign invasions of England and provided the means for this island kingdom to spread its political power, language, and literature all over the globe. If we overlook his use of the sword against his enemies (and friends), Henry VIII himself deserves the title Renaissance man. He wrote poetry and played many musical instruments well; he was a champion athlete and a hunter; and he supported the new humanistic learning. In his old age, however, Henry was also coarse, dissolute, arrogant, and a womanizer. He died without knowing that the child he ignored because she was female would become the greatest ruler England ever had.

The Boy King and Bloody Mary

Henry VIII was survived by three children: Mary, daughter of the Spanish princess Catherine of Aragon; Elizabeth, daughter of Anne Boleyn, a lady-in-waiting at the court; and Edward, son of the noblewoman Jane Seymour, who died twelve days after her son's birth. According to the laws of succession, a son had to be crowned first, and so at age nine the son of Henry and Jane Seymour became Edward VI (reigned 1547–1553). An intelligent but sickly boy, he ruled in name only while his relatives wielded the actual power.

When Edward died (of tuberculosis) he was followed by his half-Spanish half-sister Mary (reigned 1553–1558). Mary was a devout, strong-willed Catholic determined to avenge the wrongs done to her mother. She restored the pope's power in England and ruthlessly hunted down Protestants.

Had she lived longer and had she exercised better judgment, Mary might have undone all her father's accomplishments.

Catherine of Aragon (16th century) by M. Sittou.
Kunsthistorisches Museum, Vienna.

Mary Tudor (16th century).
Musée Condé, Chantilly, France.

DIRECT TEACHING

VIEWING THE ART

Michael Sittou (1469–1525) worked for royalty in Spain, Flanders, London, and Copenhagen and developed a cosmopolitan painting style.

Activity. Catherine's hair was blond and long, and as the portrait shows, she was pretty. Her piety and dignity in the face of the humiliation she endured at the hands of her husband earned her the everlasting love of the English people. Ask students to contrast Catherine's portrait with that of her daughter, her only surviving child, whose portrait by an unknown artist appears below. Students may compare physical features and styles of dress as well as facial expressions. [Possible response: Catherine looks less regal and more humble than her daughter.]

C Exploring the Historical Period
THE ETHNOCENTRIC ENGLISH

Henry, like many an Englishman before and after him, was ethnocentric: He believed in the superiority of the English. In *The Civilization of Europe in the Renaissance*, John Hale presents this Renaissance Italian description of the English: "The English are great lovers of themselves and everything belonging to them; they think there are no other men than themselves, and no other world but England. . . ."

CONTENT-AREA CONNECTIONS

Writing: Applying Models

Have students consider how they could use elements of this essay as models for their own writing on historical or factual topics. Bring up the following items:

- Ask students to identify aspects of structure and organization they could use. [Students could use headings. They could organize by means of chronological order or cause-and-effect analysis.]

- Ask students to identify in this model the "extras" (especially visual extras) that they could provide in their own writing. [Students could provide illustrations, as well as other graphic organizers, such as a time line. They could incorporate and amplify through dramatic placement some quotations and key facts.]

- Ask students how they might imitate the style of this piece. [Students might use a serious style appropriate to the subject, yet display a witty attitude toward their subject through word choice and phrases such as "With Catherine packed away under house arrest . . ."]

DIRECT TEACHING

Ⓐ Exploring the Historical Period
THE VIRGIN QUEEN

On the fascinating phenomenon of a virgin queen, Elizabethan expert A. L. Rowse has this to say: "Ordinary mortals, especially at the beginning, could not understand it; they grew to accept it, and in the end to find inspiration in it. Some people, then and since, have thought there was something wrong with her. Those in the best position to know . . . did not think so. Common sense was a sufficient warning as to the danger of childbearing at the time, and there were the fearful examples of her sister and her mother to bring it home to her. It is fairly clear to a perceptive eye that she did not intend to marry. The Scotch ambassador, Melville, saw well enough that her deepest passion was to rule and that she would never give herself a master—as any sixteenth-century woman did by marrying."

Ⓑ Reading Skills

❓ **Making inferences.** What do you think this quotation is about? [Possible response: Walter Raleigh had a love interest in Elizabeth I. He is saying he'd like to approach her, yet he fears doing so—probably because she is queen. She replies, wittily and in verse, that if Raleigh has to wonder about whether he has sufficient courage to woo her, then he shouldn't bother trying.]

VIEWING THE ART

George Gower (c. 1540–1596) was one of the most accomplished painters in Elizabethan England.

Activity. Have students notice the depiction of the destruction of the Spanish Armada in the small right-hand window behind the queen. Ask students to identify symbols of power and authority in the portrait. [Possible responses: the crown; the globe.]

The Armada portrait of Elizabeth I (c. 1588) attributed to George Gower.
Woburn Abbey, Bedfordshire, UK/The Bridgeman Art Library.

> Ⓑ *Fain would I climb, yet fear I to fall.*
> —Sir Walter Raleigh to Elizabeth I, scratched on a windowpane
>
> *If thy heart fails thee, climb not at all.*
> —Elizabeth's reply, scratched underneath

She made a strategic error, however, when she burned about three hundred of her subjects at the stake. She further lost the support of her people when she married Philip II, king of Spain, a country England was beginning to fear and hate. (Mary was thirty-seven and Philip only twenty-six.) Mary's executions earned her the name Bloody Mary. The queen died of a fever. Because she was childless, she was succeeded by her sister Elizabeth.

Ⓐ Elizabeth: The Virgin Queen

Elizabeth I (reigned 1558–1603) was one of the most brilliant and successful monarchs in history. Since she inherited a kingdom torn by fierce religious feuds, her first task was to restore law and order. She reestablished the Church of

Secondary Source

Economic Effects of Excommunication

Historian Lisa Jardine notes an important economic effect of the pope's excommunication of England. "Officially outlawed by the Pope, [the English merchants] were free to take advantage of prohibited trade with the 'infidel' market in the East. The papal edict banning the export of munitions and foodstuffs from Christendom to the Islamic territories had been enforced by many popes. . . . Following their excommunication, the English merchants considered themselves free to export cloth for soldiers' uniforms and metal for arms. . . . In spite of their relatively late arrival on the eastern trading scene, the English merchant companies were now in a position to pursue their trading profit, in an entirely secular commercial context, free from the operating constraints of international religious law."

England and again rejected the pope's authority. The pope excommunicated her. To keep Spain happy, she pretended that she just might marry her widowed brother-in-law, King Philip.

Philip was the first of a long procession of noblemen, both foreign and English, who wanted to wed her. However, Elizabeth resisted marriage all her life and officially remained "the Virgin Queen" (thereby giving the American colony Virginia its name). She knew that her strength lay in her independence and in her ability to play one suitor off against another. "I am your anointed Queen," she told a group from Parliament who urged her to marry. "I will never be by violence constrained to do anything. I thank God I am endued with such qualities that if I were turned out of the realm in my petticoat, I were able to live in any place in Christendom."

A True Daughter

A truly heroic person, Elizabeth survived many plots against her life. Several of these plots were initiated by her cousin, another Mary—Mary Stuart, Queen of Scots. As Elizabeth

> Then she, lying very still upon the block, one of the executioners holding her slightly with one of his hands, she endured two strokes of the other executioner with an axe, she making very small noise or none at all, and not stirring any part of her from the place where she lay: and so the executioner cut off her head, saving one little gristle, which being cut asunder, he lift up her head to the view of all the assembly and bade God save the Queen. Then, her dress of lawn falling from off her head, it appeared as gray as one of threescore and ten years old, polled very short, her face in a moment being so much altered from the form she had when she was alive, as few could remember her by her dead face. Her lips stirred up and down a quarter of an hour after her head was cut off.
>
> —Robert Wynkfielde, eyewitness to the execution of Mary, Queen of Scots (1587)

Execution of Mary, Queen of Scots (detail) (16th century) by a Dutch artist.
Scottish National Portrait Gallery, Edinburgh.

DIRECT TEACHING

C Exploring the Historical Period
MARY STUART

Mary Stuart (1542–1587), Elizabeth's cousin, should not be confused with "Bloody Mary," who was Mary Tudor (1516–1558), Elizabeth's half sister. Mary Stuart was the daughter of a French mother and Henry VIII's nephew, James V. Married as a young girl to the aged Francis II of France, Mary returned to Scotland in 1560, after her husband's death, to claim the throne of Scotland, which was still independent from England. Mary Stuart's ties to France and Spain through family and religion made her a powerful threat to Elizabeth's England. Elizabeth had her cousin beheaded at Fotheringay on February 8, 1587.

VIEWING THE ART

This drawing does not accurately show the exact moment of Mary's execution. Mary, for instance, is shown giving away her crucifix just as the executioner raises his ax above his head; in fact, she gave away her crucifix before she placed her head on the block.

Activity. Ask students to consider the effect created by placing activities from different moments into a single picture. [The technique allows an artist to condense a sequence of events into one image.]

English Ships and the Spanish Armada, August 1588 (detail). English School. Oil. National Maritime Museum, London.

DIRECT TEACHING

VIEWING THE ART

In 1588, the Spanish Armada was the largest fleet of ships that had ever been assembled; consequently, the Spanish expected to defeat the English fleet, which was composed of fewer and smaller ships. The English ships, however, were faster, so the English strategy was to scatter the Spanish fleet in order to gain an advantage. The English set ablaze eight small frigates and sailed them into the Armada, thereby scattering the Spanish ships and forcing them to retreat.

Activity. The painting manages to represent the imposing quality of a Spanish ship, while still emphasizing the importance of the English actions. How does it do so? [Placing the Spanish ship (red flag with yellow cross) in the foreground makes it look bigger. However, the position of the English warship (white flag with red cross) in the painting suggests the English ship's ability to outmaneuver the Spanish ships.]

Ⓐ Literary Connections
Maxwell Anderson
The American dramatist Maxwell Anderson explored the conflict between the two monarchs in his verse plays *Elizabeth the Queen* (1930) and *Mary of Scotland* (1933).

As for her face, it is and appears to be very aged. It is long and thin and her teeth are very yellow and unequal, compared with what they were formerly, so they say, and on the left side less than on the right. Many of them are missing so that one cannot understand her easily when she speaks quickly. Her figure is fair and tall and graceful in whatever she does; so far as may be she keeps her dignity...
—André Hurault, French ambassador, writing about Elizabeth I (1597)

had no children, Mary was heir to England's throne because she too was a direct descendant of Henry VII. A Catholic, Mary was eventually deposed from her throne in Protestant Scotland. Put under house arrest, she lived as a royal exile in England, carefully watched by her cousin Elizabeth. Elizabeth endured Mary and her plots for twenty years and then, a true daughter of her father, sent her Scottish cousin to the chopping block.

The Spanish Armada Sinks: A Turning Point in History

King Philip of Spain, ever watchful for an opportunity to hammer at England, used Mary's execution as an excuse to invade England. He assembled a vast fleet of warships for that purpose: the famous Spanish Armada. In 1588, England's Royal Navy, assisted greatly by nasty weather in the Irish Sea, destroyed the Armada. This victory assured England's and all of northern Europe's independence from the powerful Catholic countries of the Mediterranean. It was a great turning point in history and Elizabeth's finest moment. If Spain had prevailed, history would have been quite different: All of North America, like most of South America, might be speaking Spanish instead of English.

A Flood of Literature

What is the connection between these political events and English literature? With their own religious and national identity firmly established, the English started writing as never before. After the defeat of the Armada, Elizabeth became a beloved symbol of peace, security, and prosperity to her subjects, and she provided inspiration to scores of English authors. They represented her mythologically in poetry, drama, and fiction—as Gloriana, Diana, the Faerie Queene, and Cynthia. Literary works that did not directly represent her were dedicated to her because authors knew she was a connoisseur of literature, a person of remarkably wide learning, and something of a writer herself.

A Dull Man Succeeds a Witty Woman

Elizabeth died childless. She was succeeded by her second cousin, James VI of Scotland. James was the son of Elizabeth's cousin Mary, whom Elizabeth had beheaded years before. As James I of England (reigned 1603–1625), he lacked Elizabeth's ability to resolve (or postpone) critical issues, especially religious and economic ones. James was a spendthrift where Elizabeth had been thrifty; he was thick tongued and goggle-eyed where she had been glamorous and witty; he was essentially a foreigner where she had been a complete Englishwoman.

James I tried hard. He wrote learned books in favor of the divine right of kings and against tobacco; he patronized Shakespeare; he sponsored a new translation of the Bible; and he was in many respects an admirable man and a benevolent, peaceful ruler. Yet his relationship with many of his subjects, especially with pious, puritanically minded merchants, went from bad to worse.

The Decline of the Renaissance

The difficulties of James's reign became the impossibilities of his son's. Charles I (reigned 1625–1649) turned out to be remote, autocratic, and self-destructive. Some of his most powerful subjects had him beheaded in 1649. For the next eleven years, England was ruled by Parliament and the Puritan dictator Oliver Cromwell, not by an anointed king. When Charles's self-indulgent son came to power eleven years later, in 1660, England had changed in many important ways.

> *All my possessions for a moment of time.*
> —Elizabeth I's last words (1603)

FAST FACTS

Philosophical Views
- Intellectuals who are part of the humanist movement use Latin and Greek classics along with the Bible to teach people a better way to live and rule.
- Strong feelings of patriotism and new ideas coming from the Continent encourage people to question the authority of the Catholic Church and to object to the financial burdens imposed on them by the pope in Rome.

Political Highlights
- The Protestant Reformation begins in 1534, when King Henry VIII rejects the authority of the pope and declares himself head of the English Church.
- Henry's daughter Elizabeth I succeeds to her father's throne in 1558 and reestablishes the Church of England.
- In 1588, the Royal Navy defeats the Spanish Armada.

Primary Source

Counterblaste to Tobacco
King James was an early opponent of smoking, a habit that had become increasingly common during his reign due to imports of tobacco from the new English colony in Virginia. *Counterblaste to Tobacco,* published anonymously in 1604, was widely known to be the work of James I himself. *Counterblaste,* a lengthy pamphlet, concludes with "A custome loathsome to the eye, hatefull to the Nose, harmefull to the braine, dangerous to the Lungs, and in the blacke stinking fume thereof, neerest resembling the horrible Stigian smoke of that pit that is bottomelesse." Others at the time expressed antismoking views in verse: "Tobacco, that outlandish weed, / It spends the brain and spoils the seed. / It dulls the sprite, it dims the sight, / It robs a woman of her right."

DIRECT TEACHING

B Literary Connections
Elizabeth as a Literary Symbol
The names Gloriana, Cynthia, and Faerie Queene come from Edmund Spenser's epic poem *The Faerie Queene*. The name Cynthia was also used by Sir Walter Raleigh in his poem "The Ocean to Cynthia." Cynthia is also another name for Diana, the virgin goddess of the moon.

C Exploring the Historical Period
JAMES AND JACOBEAN ENGLAND
James VI was the only son of Mary, Queen of Scots, and her second husband, an English nobleman named Lord Darnley. When James succeeded his mother's cousin Elizabeth as sovereign of England and of Scotland, he was called King James I because he was the first James to rule the newly formed Great Britain. The reign of James is called the Jacobean period. (Jacobus is the Latin form of James.)

D Exploring the Historical Period
KING CHARLES AND OLIVER CROMWELL
By the time Charles I came to the throne, the Puritans had risen to prominence and their parliamentary party had gained power. By 1642, England was embroiled in a civil war that pitted the parliamentary party, led by Oliver Cromwell, against the king's party, or Royalists. Cromwell's followers killed the king, and Cromwell (now considered the foremost military and political strategist of his time) wielded power and asserted England's primacy in world affairs in ways reminiscent of the reign of Elizabeth I.

Review

Talk About...

- **Modeling.** You might model answering the first bulleted question on p. 238 as follows: "Under the heading 'Humanism: Questions About the Good Life' on p. 242, the essay explains that the humanists were interested in questions such as 'What is a human being?' 'What is a good life?' and 'How do I lead a good life?' The humanists studied the classics of ancient Rome and Greece and the teachings of Christianity to find answers to these questions."

- The introduction of the printing press and of movable type around 1455 fostered a growing interest in reading and learning by making books more available and relatively inexpensive.

- Strong feelings of patriotism and national identity led some European countries to reject the authority of the pope and to resent the financial burdens imposed by Rome. Some scholars cited the shortcomings of Church authorities and called for reforms. Others, such as Martin Luther, founded new forms of Christianity based on their personal understanding of the Bible. In England, King Henry VIII broke with the pope in order to end a marriage.

Write About...

- **Revolutions in reading, then and now.** Encourage students to look for print and online articles that predict the future of electronic books in the twenty-first century. Have commentators maintained one position, or is opinion divided on the subject, and if so, how?

FAST FACTS

Social and Economic Influences

- The invention of the printing press in Germany in the mid-1400s makes books more widely available than ever and fosters an explosion of learning.
- The rise of a rich merchant and banking class provides the wealth that makes possible the growth in art, literature, and learning.

Of course the Renaissance did not end in 1660 when Charles II returned from exile in France, just as it had not begun on a specific date. Renaissance values, which were primarily moral and religious, gradually eroded, and Renaissance energies gradually gave out. The last great writer of the English Renaissance was John Milton, who lived on into an age in which educated people were becoming more worldly in their outlook. Scientific truths were soon to challenge long-accepted religious beliefs.

The English Renaissance was over.

REVIEW

Talk About...

Turn back to the Think About questions posed at the start of this introduction to the Renaissance (see page 238). Discuss these questions with a group of classmates.

Write About...

Contrasting Literary Periods

Revolutions in reading, then and now. Gutenberg's invention of the printing press in Germany in the mid-1400s made it possible for people in Europe to obtain and read a greater variety of books and printed materials than ever before. In time this invention revolutionized people's view of the world and created a desire for even more books on a wider range of subjects. In the contemporary world the inventions of the computer and the Internet have also created an explosion of access to information and a demand for even greater access. At the same time there are predictions that the printed book as we know it will soon disappear and that literacy itself may suffer. Compare and contrast these two great technological revolutions—printing and the computer. Discuss the impact of each technology on literature and the pursuit of knowledge.

Check Test: True-False

Monitoring students' progress. Guide the class in answering these questions.

1. The term *Renaissance* refers to a rebirth of interest in the writings of classical Greece and Rome. [T]
2. New creativity in the arts during this era appeared first in Italy. [T]
3. Renaissance humanists rejected the Bible. [F]
4. The invention of the printing press helped make classical texts more readily available. [T]
5. In the countries where the Reformation occurred, a key element was the rejection of the authority of the pope. [T]

A CLOSER LOOK: SOCIAL INFLUENCES

The Glass of Fashion

INFORMATIONAL TEXT

They displayed their new costumes from ten o'clock in the morning till noon, strolling up and down the center aisle of St. Paul's Church. They insisted on rich fabrics: velvet, taffeta, gold brocade, and fur. They wore the finest silk stockings and cork platform shoes. They curled their hair, perfumed their gloves, and (if daring) wore makeup. They showed off favorite jewels—pearls, perhaps—in earrings, bracelets, and designs sewn all over their clothes. The men in the Renaissance were peacocks indeed!

Exquisite excess. Women also dressed flamboyantly in the Renaissance. Elizabeth I herself owned eighty wigs and three thousand gowns at her death.

In the 1580s and 1590s, the Renaissance silhouette was ridiculously exaggerated. Starched linen neck ruffs stretched from shoulder to shoulder. Shoulders themselves were extended with "wings" that make even the most exaggerated of today's shoulder pads look like cotton balls. Hoop skirts (called farthingales) could be four feet wide at the hips, and men's full, thigh-length pants were padded to what critics called "monstrous and outrageous greatness."

Women corseted their waists to produce a

Portrait of Elizabeth Vernon, countess of Southampton (c. 1610).
By permission of the duke of Buccleuch, Kettering, England.

Portrait of a lady said to be Lady Style (detail) (16th century) by the circle of William Larkin.
Christie's, London.

Portrait of a nobleman in garter robes, said to be the seventh earl of Shrewsbury (detail) (16th century) by Paul van Somer.
Christie's, London.

A CLOSER LOOK

This feature explores the extravagances of Renaissance fashion—both the exaggerated styles the upper classes preferred and the ways in which they augmented their figures.

DIRECT TEACHING

A English-Language Learners

Multiple meanings. One of the meanings of *glass* is "mirror." Explain that a mirror was once called a looking glass, just as something to drink from was frequently called a drinking glass. Remind students of Lewis Carroll's *Through the Looking-Glass,* the sequel to *Alice's Adventures in Wonderland*.

B Exploring the Culture
ROYAL WARDROBES

James I spent an astonishing £36,377 per year on his wardrobe for the five years of his reign. By contrast, Elizabeth I's yearly wardrobe expenses for the last four years of her reign were only £9,535 per year.

C Reading Informational Text

Recognizing organizational structure. In the following text, identify at least two examples that justify the writer's use of the heading "Exquisite excess" to introduce the section. [The number of wigs Elizabeth owned, the complexity of ruffs, the four-foot width of skirts across hips, and "a painful narrowness" are four examples of "exquisite excess."]

Primary Source

Courtly Fashions

English Puritans strongly condemned what they viewed as excesses and abuses of courtly fashions. Phillip Stubbes in *The Anatomie of Abuses* attacks many aspects of culture, including fashions such as the ruff. "No pen is able to well to discribe it, as the eye is to vilify it. . . . [The ruffs have] three or foure degrees of minor ruffes, placed by degree, step by step, one beneath the others; and all under the Maister devil ruffe; the skyrts, then, of these great ruffes are long and wide every way, pleated and crested ful curiously, God wot. Then last of all they are either clogged with golde, silver or silk lace of stately price, wrought all over with needle woork, speckled and sparkled here and there with the sonne, the moone, the stares, and many other antiquities straunge to beholde. Some are wrought with . . . purled lace so cloyed, and other gew gawes. . . ."

The Renaissance 255

DIRECT TEACHING

A CLOSER LOOK

A Exploring the Culture
THE BIG-BELLY LOOK

The peascod belly (or peasecod belly or goose belly) was a look that began in Spain. The goal was to create a big belly, usually by stuffing horsehair into doublets. Evidently, fat was in for men (it suggested prosperity). For women, however, the opposite seems to have been true. Women of the sixteenth century wore bodices called "stomachers," which were often worn over corsets ribbed with bones that made women's bodies rigid.

B Reading Informational Text

? Analyzing implicit assumptions. In this paragraph, what does "a must" and "to peek" suggest about the author's attitude toward the way Renaissance men and women dressed? [Possible response: The author seems to be smiling while suggesting that there is no accounting for taste in dress.]

Mary Denton, née Martyn, age fifteen in 1573 (detail) (16th century) by the circle of George Gower.
York City Art Gallery, York, England.

painful narrowness while men stiffened doublets (an upper garment) with pasteboard and stuffed them with horsehair, rags, or even bran to achieve what was called a peascod belly. A man's silhouette was narrowest at the bottom, where stockings and garters, worn above the knee, made even shapely legs look better.

Symbols and signals. In the Renaissance intricate pattern (like poetry's "artificiality") was also a must. Braids, bows, spangles, and lace covered the luxurious fabrics, and slashed sleeves and doublets allowed embroidered underclothes to peek through. Colors were rich and bold—red, gold, black, and white were a favorite combination.

Colors and designs also had symbolic meanings: Green meant love, white and tawny together showed patience in adversity, a pansy represented sadness, a snake flattery, and so on. Queen Elizabeth often wore white and black together—both colors symbolized chastity. Whole treatises were devoted to color and to defining "emblems" such as rainbows, clouds, worms, and flies.

Reading T-shirts. How will historians of dress read the clothes we wear today? Are bodices embroidered with flies so strange when viewed against the sort of printed T-shirts sold by the hundreds in any shopping mall? What messages do our clothes send out to the world, and what will they tell the future?

Gilbert Talbot, seventh earl of Shrewsbury, age forty (detail) (16th century) by William Seger.
Christie's, London.

Lettice Knollys, daughter of Sir Henry Knollys, wife of the fourth Lord Paget (detail) (16th century). English School.
Manor House, Stanton Harcourt, Oxon, England.

CONTENT-AREA CONNECTIONS

History: Trade with the East
The Elizabethan court was not the only one of its day parading about in rich fabrics and ornate costumes. During this time, the Ming dynasty (1368–1644) of China displayed its opulence in costume as well. In Elizabethan England, a person's costume revealed whether he or she was wealthy or noble, although it did not exactly signify rank. In China during the Ming dynasty, however, the decoration or embroidery on a robe was a clear indication of the wearer's social status or official rank.

Culture: Tudor Architecture
Individual activity. During Tudor times in England (1485–1603), a distinctive style of architecture developed. Ask students to find out what a Tudor house looks like and to determine some of its characteristic features. Students should draw or photocopy an illustration. They should also speculate on why homes (at least for the upper classes) were becoming so much larger and more comfortable at this time.

Before You Read

The Passionate Shepherd to His Love
The Nymph's Reply to the Shepherd

Make the Connection
You've heard it before. On the radio or in a music video, a singer passionately appeals to a woman to be his love. Although the specific lyrics may vary, the message is always the same. What you may not know is that people have heard this message for centuries. The "invitation to love" is an old poetic tradition. It was especially common in Renaissance England, and it lives on today—not only in the lyrics of popular music but also in the letters, poems, and e-mails that people write to those whose love they seek.

Literary Focus
The Pastoral
Marlowe's poem is a **pastoral**, from the Latin word *pastor*, meaning "shepherd." Pastoral poems are set in an idealized countryside inhabited by handsome shepherds and beautiful nymphs (young women) all living in harmony with nature. Although the characters in the Elizabethan pastorals are presented as simple country people, the diction, imagery, and arguments of these rustic speakers are highly sophisticated. This gives pastoral poems an elegance and an artificiality that do not really correspond to their naive, uncomplicated characters and settings. Many pastorals express a longing or nostalgia for simpler, more innocent times.

> **Pastoral** poems depict country life in idyllic, idealized terms. The characters in pastoral poems are naive and innocent yet express themselves with poetic sophistication.
>
> *For more on the Pastoral, see the Handbook of Literary and Historical Terms.*

A woman, possibly personifying Summer (detail) (late 17th century). Satin embroidered with silk, metal thread, and beads.
By Courtesy of the Board of Trustees of the Victoria and Albert Museum, London.

Literary Skills Understand the characteristics of pastoral poems.

SKILLS FOCUS, pp. 257–262

Grade-Level Skills
- **Literary Skills**

Analyze characteristics of subgenres of poetry, including pastoral poems.

Review Skills
- **Literary Skills**

Analyze the importance of setting to the mood, tone, and meaning of the text.

RESOURCES: READING

Planning
- *One-Stop Planner* CD-ROM with ExamView Test Generator

Differentiating Instruction
- Supporting Instruction in Spanish
- Audio CD Library, Selections and Summaries in Spanish

Grammar and Language
- Daily Language Activities

Assessment
- Holt Assessment: Literature, Reading, and Vocabulary
- *One-Stop Planner* CD-ROM with ExamView Test Generator
- Holt Online Assessment

Internet
- go.hrw.com (Keyword: LE5 12-3)
- Elements of Literature Online

Media
- Audio CD Library
- Audio CD Library, Selections and Summaries in Spanish

PRETEACHING

More About the Writer

Background. Many of the theories about Marlowe's death are conspiracy theories. One critic has suggested that by substituting the corpse of a sailor for his own body, Marlowe faked death and succeeded in escaping to the Continent. Other critics have maintained that Marlowe was killed to prevent him from testifying against an important figure in the spy network of Queen Elizabeth's government.

Summary ⟷ at grade level

> "Come live with me," urges the speaker, describing some of the simple pleasures—but none of the hardships—of life in the country. He lists the wondrous things he will make for his love, including beds of roses and slippers with gold buckles, and promises that young shepherd boys will dance and sing for her delight each May morning.

Selection Starter

Build background. Students may read this poem more attentively if you tell them that when it was set to music in the 1580s, Marlowe came close to achieving the fame of a modern-day rock star. One critic called the song one of the rages of the 1580s and said that it resulted in great commercial acclaim for its author.

Christopher Marlowe
(1564–1593)

Marlowe belonged to the first generation of Elizabethan dramatists. His career ended about the time Shakespeare's began, although he was only two months older than Shakespeare. The son of a Canterbury shoemaker, Marlowe won scholarships to the King's School in Canterbury and then to Cambridge University. While still a student, he translated some love poems by Ovid, the Roman poet. The poems were declared too erotic by the bishop of London, who had the books burned.

In 1537, before completing his studies, Marlowe apparently became a spy. Elizabeth's government maintained an elaborate espionage system to keep track of Roman Catholics, but just what spying Marlowe did for the government remains uncertain. It *is* certain that Marlowe had only six more years to live when, at twenty-three, he came down to London from Cambridge. He associated with a number of other recent university graduates living near the London theaters and supporting themselves by writing plays and pamphlets. Excitement and danger were part of their lives. Marlowe himself was jailed for his involvement in a street fight that ended with one man murdered.

Another brush with the law came when Marlowe's roommate, a fellow dramatist named Thomas Kyd, accused him of making scandalous, seditious, and atheistic speeches. Marlowe was arrested. A few days before the case was to be heard, he went with some rather shady characters down the Thames, to a tavern in Deptford. After supper the men got into a violent fight over the bill; Marlowe was stabbed above the eye and died instantly. The court acquitted his assailant on the grounds of self-defense, though it is very possible that all the testimony in this case was fabricated and that Marlowe was assassinated for reasons not yet discovered. Theories about Marlowe's life and death are abundant; there are even a few people today who believe, without any evidence, that Marlowe wasn't murdered but lived on to write all of Shakespeare's plays for him.

Today Marlowe's most famous play is probably *The Tragicall History of Dr. Faustus*, about the man who makes a bargain with Satan. Faustus and all of Marlowe's other tragic heroes have been called overreachers: self-driven, power-hungry men who refuse to recognize either their limitations as human beings or their responsibilities to God and their fellow creatures. Marlowe's heroes all want to be more than mere men, and only death can put an end to their monstrous ambitions. To express these grandiose themes, Marlowe created wild and soaring poetry, like nothing ever heard before on the stage. Although Marlowe did not write Shakespeare's plays, he showed Shakespeare what was possible in dramatic poetry.

Reputed portrait of Christopher Marlowe (1585).
French School. Oil.
The Master and Fellows of Corpus Christi College,
Cambridge, England.

DIFFERENTIATING INSTRUCTION

Learners Having Difficulty
Explain that at the time of the Renaissance, English-speakers used the pronoun *thou* to address close friends and family. *Thee* is the objective form and *thy* or *thine* the possessive. *Thou* and *thee* later gave way to *you* and *thy* or *thine* to *your*.

English-Language Learners
Students will benefit from following along in their books as they listen to the audio recording of the poem or to a fluent reader reading the poem aloud. Draw attention to rhyming pairs of words—*love, prove,* and *move, love*—that are pronounced differently than they are in modern English.

This poem is part of two literary traditions. It is an example of a **pastoral** *poem (it is, in fact, probably the most famous of the English pastorals), and it is part of the* carpe diem *tradition. The* **carpe diem** *poem (see page 263) is a call to "seize the day"—live life to the fullest in the here and now. Marlowe's poem has often been set to music, and several poets have written answers or sequels to it. (The most famous reply to this poem, by Sir Walter Raleigh, follows on page 261.)*

The Passionate Shepherd to His Love

Christopher Marlowe

Young man leaning against a tree among roses, by Nicholas Hilliard. Miniature.
© Victoria and Albert Museum, London/Art Resource, New York.

Come live with me, and be my love,
And we will all the pleasures prove°
That valleys, groves, hills, and fields,
Woods, or steepy mountain yields.

5 And we will sit upon the rocks,
Seeing the shepherds feed their flocks
By shallow rivers, to whose falls
Melodious birds sing madrigals.°

And I will make thee beds of roses,
10 And a thousand fragrant posies,
A cap of flowers, and a kirtle,°
Embroidered all with leaves of myrtle.

A gown made of the finest wool
Which from our pretty lambs we pull,
15 Fair linèd slippers for the cold,
With buckles of the purest gold.

A belt of straw and ivy buds,
With coral clasps and amber studs,
And if these pleasures may thee move,
20 Come live with me, and be my love.

The shepherd swains° shall dance and sing
For thy delight each May morning.
If these delights thy mind may move,
Then live with me, and be my love.

2. **prove** *v.*: experience.

8. **madrigals** (ma′dri·gəlz) *n. pl.*: complicated songs for several voices.

11. **kirtle** (kurt″l) *n.*: archaic word for "dress," "gown," or "skirt."

21. **swains** *n. pl.*: young boys.

DIRECT TEACHING

A Literary Focus
❓ **Carpe diem.** How can you tell that the speaker wants his love to comply with his request right now—to "seize the day"? [The imperative *Come* suggests urgency.]

B Learners Having Difficulty
Reading inverted sentences. Students may need help to understand that the birds are singing madrigals to the waterfalls.

C Literary Focus
❓ **Refrain.** What is the effect of the repetition of l. 1? [It creates a songlike rhythm and emphasizes the speaker's urgency.]

D Reading Skills
❓ **Expressing an opinion.** Do you find the speaker persuasive? Why or why not? [Possible responses: No, the life he depicts is unrealistic; yes, his vision is sensitive and passionate.]

CONTENT-AREA CONNECTIONS

Music: The Sounds of the Renaissance

The sweet madrigals of the English Renaissance complement the themes in this poem. Students might find examples of songs and airs by Renaissance composers such as Thomas Tallis, Orlando Gibbons, John Dowland, and William Byrd. Have them analyze how the words, the sounds of the characteristic instruments (lute and viol), and the tunes evoke the pastoral atmosphere expressed by Marlowe.

PRETEACHING

More About the Writer

Background. As biographer Robert Lacey writes, "[Raleigh] was one of the most handsome men at court." Scholars A. D. Wraight and Virginia F. Stern note that "Raleigh always cut a splendid figure at Court in his subtle satins and brocades, a single jewel in his ear. . . ." He could not save himself from death, but he could go nobly to his fate. When it came time for him to be executed, he checked the ax to see if it was sharp.

VIEWING THE ART

Nicholas Hilliard (1547–1619) was an Elizabethan portrait painter with an eye for detail.

Activity. Students might speculate about what Raleigh would say regarding today's fashions.

Summary *at grade level*

The nymph asserts that not every shepherd tells the truth. She ridicules the shepherd's promises by painting a realistic view of each. She ends by saying that she might accept the shepherd's invitation if youth and love lasted forever.

Skills Starter

Build prerequisite skills. Remind students that the speaker—here, a young woman—is not the poet.

Sir Walter Raleigh
(c. 1552–1618)

Ralegh (also spelled Ralegh) is one of the most colorful figures of a very colorful age. A handsome, expensively dressed, and probably arrogant man, at the peak of his success he was Queen Elizabeth's confidential secretary and captain of her guard. He fought brilliantly for England in France, Spain, Ireland, and America. He was passionately devoted to the cause of colonizing the Americas, and to advertise its products, he became one of the first bold Englishmen to smoke tobacco and grow potatoes.

In his rise to power, Raleigh made many enemies, some of whom saw their chance to destroy him when the queen died. They poisoned King James's mind against him, and—on trumped-up evidence—he was convicted of treason. Raleigh was sentenced to death in 1603, though his execution was not carried out until 1618.

Imprisoned in the Tower of London during this long interval, he conducted chemical experiments and wrote a *History of the World* that runs from Adam and Eve to the establishment of the Roman Empire. He also dreamed of another expedition to Guiana, a region on the northern coast of South America; he had explored Guiana earlier in his life and believed it contained vast hoards of gold and jewels. In 1617, still under a death sentence, he was allowed to undertake his last voyage to Guiana. It was a disaster. The English obtained no treasure, and the Spanish killed many of Raleigh's men, including his beloved son. Very ill with fever, Raleigh sailed home to face a certain and shameful death. According to the verdict of history, however, the shame is King James's, not Raleigh's. Raleigh was sacrificed to satisfy the Spanish, who were clamoring for his death as a condition for maintaining peaceful relations with England.

In his speech on the scaffold, Raleigh described himself as "a seafaring man, a soldier, and a courtier." He did not think of himself as a writer. He was carefree with his poems; only about thirty-five of them have survived, and they have been slowly assembled by literary researchers over the past four centuries. His most ambitious poem is the *Ocean to Cynthia,* one of the hundreds of literary works that Queen Elizabeth's subjects wrote to express their love and devotion. It survives only in fragments. This is unfortunate, because Raleigh's poems have considerable merit. They are powerful, outspoken, even blunt, and suffused with the courage of a man who was always ready to accept without self-pity whatever life might bring him. He could have been thinking of himself when he wrote in his *History,* "There is no man so assured of his honor, of his riches, health, or life, but that he may be deprived of either or all, the very next hour or day to come."

Sir Walter Raleigh (16th century) by Nicholas Hilliard.
By Courtesy of the National Portrait Gallery, London.

260 Collection 3 The Renaissance

DIFFERENTIATING INSTRUCTION

Learners Having Difficulty
Explain to students that the speaker in this poem is the young woman who was addressed by the speaker of Marlowe's poem. Suggest that they watch especially for references to time and change.

English-Language Learners
Explain that ll. 21–22 of the final stanza contain two conditional statements expressed in unusual ways. Suggest that students insert the word *if* in these lines and reorder the words this way: *If youth could last . . .* and *If joys had no date. . . .*

Advanced Learners
Enrichment. As the headnote explains, *nymph* means "young woman," but Raleigh was aware also that *nymph* comes from the Greek word that means "bride" and that in Greek and Roman mythology a nymph was a nature spirit. Ask how these meanings apply. [Possible response: A human bride cannot foretell the future; a spirit would be aware of the effects time has on all living things.]

Here is Raleigh's reply to Marlowe's "Passionate Shepherd." Elizabethan London was a small place, and Raleigh's and Marlowe's paths must have crossed more than once. Other poets, including John Donne and Robert Herrick, replied to Marlowe, but Raleigh wrote the best answer. His speaker is identified as a nymph, which means a young woman. Like her creator, she has a strong character.

The Nymph's Reply to the Shepherd

Sir Walter Raleigh

Embroidered wall hanging (detail) (1601).
Schweizerisches Landesmuseum, Zurich, Switzerland.

If all the world and love were young,
And truth in every shepherd's tongue,
These pretty pleasures might me move
To live with thee and be thy love.

5 But Time drives flocks from field to fold,°
When rivers rage and rocks grow cold,
And Philomel° becometh dumb;
The rest complains of cares to come.

The flowers do fade, and wanton° fields
10 To wayward winter reckoning yields;
A honey tongue, a heart of gall°
Is fancy's spring, but sorrow's fall.

Thy gowns, thy shoes, thy beds of roses,
Thy cap, thy kirtle, and thy posies.
15 Soon break, soon wither, soon forgotten,
In folly ripe, in reason rotten.

Thy belt of straw and ivy buds,
Thy coral clasps and amber studs,
All these in me no means can move
20 To come to thee and be thy love.

But could youth last and love still breed,
Had joys no date, nor age no need,
Then these delights my mind might move
To live with thee and be thy love.

---

5. **fold** *n.:* pen where sheep are kept in winter.

7. **Philomel:** the nightingale.

9. **wanton** *adj.:* luxuriant.

11. **gall** *n.:* bitter substance.

PRETEACHING

More About the Writer

Background. Herrick doesn't sound like a traditional man of the cloth, and that discrepancy held true in other aspects of his life as well. He called Devonshire "dull" and "loathèd" and admitted to being bored there. He kept a tame pig and taught it to drink from a tall drinking mug. He once threw his sermon book at a congregation that had the audacity to look bored.

Summary  *at grade level*

> Herrick's lyric may be the most famous of all *carpe diem* poems, and its first line is a coda or summary of the "live for today" philosophy. The speaker warns that time flies and youth fades. For these reasons, he says, young women should marry quickly—before losing the chance.

Selection Starter

Motivate. Discuss with students how their perception of time has changed as they've grown. Has the notion that "time flies" taken on added meaning as they approach the end of their time in high school? Do they think this is the best time of their lives, or are better times ahead?

Robert Herrick
(1591–1674)

Robert Herrick (18th century) by Schiavonetti. By Courtesy of the National Portrait Gallery, London.

We first hear of Herrick as an apprentice to his uncle, a London goldsmith and jeweler; it is pleasant to think that the future poet may have acquired his taste for small, beautiful things in his uncle's workshop. Herrick apparently lacked ambition and drive, since he did not enter a university until he was twenty-two, a very late age in those days, and he did not leave it until he was twenty-nine. For the next few years he had no regular occupation but enjoyed himself in London as a member of the playwright Ben Jonson's circle of young friends (see page 317). At some point he was ordained a priest, but the serious part of Herrick's life did not begin until he was thirty-nine.

Herrick was then called to a parish in Dean Prior, in Devonshire, far from London, in the West Country, which Londoners habitually regarded as wretched and barbaric. According to some of Herrick's poems, this was an intolerable exile; according to others, it was heaven on earth. At any rate, Herrick's stay in Dean Prior came abruptly to an end in 1647 with the arrival of Cromwell's army, which deprived him of his parish and substituted in his place a clergyman of a more puritanical stripe. (It would not be easy to find a less puritanical priest than Herrick.) When the king was restored some thirteen years later, so was Herrick, and he lived on at Dean Prior until he died, at the age of eighty-three.

While deprived of his parish and living in London, Herrick published a fat little volume containing about fourteen hundred poems. The book was called *Hesperides, or the Works Both Human and Divine of Robert Herrick, Esq.*

(1648). Less than a fourth of the poems fit into the "divine" category, and these are mainly witty verses on biblical characters and events. All the rest of the poems are definitely "human," though the book's last line—"Jocund his Muse was; but his Life was chaste"—suggests that Herrick's life was a bit less lively than his poetry. The word *Hesperides* in the title is borrowed from classical mythology; it is the collective name for the nymphs who live in a garden where they watch over a tree that bears golden apples. The title implies that Herrick's book is a garden full of precious things.

Herrick borrowed more than his title from classical antiquity. He was so steeped in Latin poetry that he frequently wrote his poems as if he were an ancient Roman, imposing pagan customs, creeds, and rituals on the English countryfolk and his own household. He imitated the Latin love poets, especially Catullus, when he addressed poems to beautiful women with such classical names as Julia, Corinna, Perilla, Anthea, and Electra.

Herrick also wrote about his small house, his spaniel named Tracy, the royal family in far-off London—whatever came into his mind. Altogether his poems give us a picture of "Merrie England," which is not so much the England of any particular time or place but an ideal, pastoral state where sadness is momentary and pleasure innocent. It is only recently that scholars have started to see, behind the seeming innocence of Herrick's joyful poems, that the "jocund" poet often hid his political views behind the harmless guise of pastoral poetry.

264 Collection 3 The Renaissance

DIFFERENTIATING INSTRUCTION

Learners Having Difficulty
Have students divide a piece of paper into four columns. After they read the poem once, ask them to rate their comprehension from 1 to 10, with 1 being the lowest. Next, have them jot down in the first column any questions about the meaning of the poem. Then, have them re-read the poem, rate their comprehension again, and repeat the process two more times. After the fourth reading, discuss the results.

English-Language Learners
Ask students to identify sayings in their native language that reflect the idea of *carpe diem*.

Advanced Learners
Enrichment. Have students compare the poem's *carpe diem* message with the worldview in this political epigram by Herrick:

Moderation
In things a moderation keep,
Kings ought to shear, not skin, their sheep.

264 Collection 3 The Renaissance

The first line of this little lyric, Herrick's most popular poem, has been a metaphorical part of our language ever since the nineteenth century, when Herrick was "discovered" by people interested in Renaissance literature. Instead of courting one woman, as in most **carpe diem** *poems, Herrick addresses all "virgins," or young women. As you read, remember that Herrick was a priest.*

To the Virgins, to Make Much of Time

Robert Herrick

Gather ye rosebuds while ye may,
    Old Time is still a-flying;
And this same flower that smiles today,
    Tomorrow will be dying.

5 The glorious lamp of heaven, the sun,
    The higher he's a-getting,
The sooner will his race be run,
    And nearer he's to setting.

That age is best which is the first,
10 When youth and blood are warmer;
But being spent, the worse, and worst
    Times still° succeed the former.

Then be not coy,° but use your time;
    And while ye may, go marry:
15 For having lost but once your prime,
    You may forever tarry.°

12. **still** *adv.:* always.
13. **coy** *adj.:* cold; inaccessible; aloof.
16. **tarry** *v.:* delay; linger.

Spring (detail) (1595) by Lucas van Valkenborch.
Victoria and Albert Museum, London.

PRETEACHING

More About the Writer

Background. In his later years, Marvell hated Charles II so much that some friends feared he would get them into trouble with the king. Because Marvell had many political foes, at his death a rumor arose that he had been poisoned; it is more likely that he died during a fever from lack of medical care. Some scholars think that if "Mary Marvell" had not devised her publishing scheme, Marvell's lyrics might have been lost forever.

Summary ⇔ at grade level

In ll. 1–20, the speaker uses hyperbole to describe the extreme lengths to which he would go to express his love if only there were time enough to do so. In ll. 21–32, he employs the famous "wingèd chariot hurrying near" to stress the brevity of life. In ll. 33–46, in a challenging and defiant tone, he urges his mistress "therefore" to "tear our pleasures" from life, for time cannot be made to stand still.

Selection Starter

Build background. The word *coy* comes from the Latin word *quietus*, meaning "to become quiet." Acknowledge that today *coy* suggests a certain deliberate flirtatiousness, a meaning Marvell would not have employed.

Andrew Marvell
(1621–1678)

Andrew Marvell (c. 1655–1660). Oil on canvas (23½" × 18½").
By Courtesy of the National Portrait Gallery, London.

Marvell, whose very English name should be accented on its first syllable, like *marvelous*, was the son of a clergyman, who sent him to Cambridge University. There he must have received an excellent education, because the poet John Milton (see page 361), who was not easily impressed by other men's learning, said that Marvell was "well read in the Greek and Latin classics." After receiving his bachelor's degree, Marvell traveled for several years in Holland, France, Italy, and Spain. There is, surprisingly, no record of Marvell's having been involved in the great upheaval of the 1640s. He seems to have survived the Civil Wars without allying himself with either the Royalists or the Parliamentarians. About 1650, he became a tutor to Mary Fairfax, an heiress and a daughter of Sir Thomas Fairfax, who had served as lord general of the Parliamentary armies. The Fairfaxes had several large estates, one of them at a place called Nun Appleton, and there Marvell wrote a remarkable long poem, "Upon Appleton House." However, he did not publish this or any of the other poems that are so highly regarded today. In the best Renaissance fashion, he wrote only for his friends' and his own entertainment.

After leaving the Fairfax household, where presumably he wrote his best poems, Marvell became tutor to a ward of Oliver Cromwell, the lord protector and virtual dictator of England in the 1650s. Then, in 1657, he became assistant to Cromwell's secretary of state, having been strongly recommended for the post by his friend and fellow poet John Milton. Marvell became active in politics, serving as a member of Parliament for his native city, Hull, from 1659 until his death. When King Charles II was restored and the Commonwealth government dissolved in 1660, Marvell somehow had enough influence with the Royalists to save Milton's life. At this point in his career, Marvell began to publish verse satires of his political opponents and prose pamphlets on issues of the day. Still, his lyric poems remained in manuscript until after his death, when his housekeeper, calling herself Mary Marvell and claiming to be his wife, sold them to a publisher, who brought them out.

Marvell's posthumous volume, called *Miscellaneous Poems*, made little impression when it appeared in 1681. Styles in poetry had changed after 1660, so that Marvell's witty, ingenious metaphors must have seemed old-fashioned to readers who admired the lucid, rational poems of the Restoration writers. Today we are in a better position to appreciate Marvell. To many judicious critics his poems sum up much that is admirable in Renaissance lyric poetry. He is a master craftsman, always in control of his materials. His poems have precision, urbanity, and lightness of touch. Many of Marvell's poems are also, under their graceful surfaces, deep and thoughtful, like those of John Donne (see page 300). No wonder Marvell is sometimes called the "most major" of the minor poets in English.

266 Collection 3 The Renaissance

DIFFERENTIATING INSTRUCTION

Learners Having Difficulty

Explain that the speaker's argument has three main parts:
- Lines 1–20: If we had time enough, we could (and should) court each other for an eternity.
- Lines 21–32: But time is short and old age and death come very soon.
- Lines 33–46: So let us make the most of the time we have.

Pause at the end of each section, and have students paraphrase the speaker's ideas. For ll. 45–46, explain the biblical allusion to Joshua 10:13, in which the Lord made the sun stop for the children of Israel.

English-Language Learners

Go through the sidenotes with students before they read the poem.

This poem is the most famous invitation to love in English. Nobody has ever assumed that Marvell, a bachelor, was writing to a particular woman, yet the poem is much deeper than others of its kind. Its speaker dwells on the details of human mortality with morbid precision, to make his beloved feel that even immoral behavior while alive is preferable to being good but dead. The title could be rephrased as "To his cold, standoffish girlfriend"; at the time, mistress *did not mean a sexual partner.*

To His Coy Mistress
Andrew Marvell

    Had we but world° enough, and time,
This coyness,° Lady, were no crime.
We would sit down, and think which way
To walk, and pass our long love's day.
5 Thou by the Indian Ganges' side
Shouldst rubies find; I by the tide
Of Humber° would complain.° I would
Love you ten years before the Flood,°
And you should, if you please, refuse
10 Till the conversion of the Jews.°
My vegetable° love should grow
Vaster than empires and more slow;
An hundred years should go to praise
Thine eyes, and on thy forehead gaze;
15 Two hundred to adore each breast,
But thirty thousand to the rest;
An age at least to every part,
And the last age should show your heart.
For, Lady, you deserve this state,°
20 Nor would I love at lower rate.
    But at my back I always hear
Time's wingèd chariot hurrying near;
And yonder all before us lie
Deserts of vast eternity.
25 Thy beauty shall no more be found,
Nor, in thy marble vault, shall sound
My echoing song; then worms shall try
That long-preserved virginity,
And your quaint honor turn to dust,

1. **world** *n.*: geographical space.
2. **coyness** *n.*: reluctance to make a commitment.

7. **Humber:** muddy river in Marvell's hometown of Hull; here, ironically compared to the grand Ganges in India.
complain *v.*: utter complaints about not being loved.
8. **Flood:** biblical flood, described in Genesis.
10. **conversion of the Jews:** Christians once believed that all Jews would be converted to Christianity immediately before the Last Judgment.
11. **vegetable** *adj.*: plantlike; having the power to grow very large, like oak trees.
19. **state** *n.*: ceremony.

DIRECT TEACHING

A Reading Skills
Finding the main idea. What is the speaker's main idea in the first section? [If time were limitless, he would devote much of it to complimenting his lady's attributes.] What figure of speech does he use to show the intensity of his feelings? [He uses hyperbole, or overstatement.]

B Literary Focus
Personification. How is time personified here? [Time is depicted as a charioteer pursuing the speaker.]

Literary Criticism

Imagery
Among the many critics who have admired Marvell's "To His Coy Mistress" is T. S. Eliot, who praised the "variety and order" of Marvell's images, noting the "high speed, the succession of concentrated images," and the way each image magnifies the original idea. Even without his complimentary words, however, it would be quite clear that Eliot liked the poem, for he took Marvell's words "Let us roll all our strength and all / Our sweetness up into one ball" (ll. 41–42) and in his poem "The Love Song of J. Alfred Prufrock" wrote, "To have squeezed the universe into a ball / To roll it towards some overwhelming question. . . ."

DIRECT TEACHING

A Literary Focus

Diction. How does Marvell's word choice in this couplet create a striking contrast? [The words *fine* and *private* in l. 31 dignify death; the understated "none . . . do there embrace" in l. 32 dismisses that soothing sentiment.]

B Literary Focus

Carpe diem. What tells you that this is a *carpe diem* poem? [Possible responses: the poem's message that there is not time to "languish," delay pleasure, or miss opportunities; its emphasis on the fading of beauty, the inevitability of death, and the vastness of eternity.]

GUIDED PRACTICE

Monitoring students' progress. Guide the class in answering these questions.

True-False

To the Virgins . . .

1. Herrick's poem is about picking flowers and maintaining a garden. [F]
2. The speaker in Herrick's poem thinks women should remain single. [F]

To His Coy Mistress

3. Marvell's speaker says he has enough time to praise his love. [F]
4. Marvell's speaker says that he and his love must outrun time. [T]

Two lovers (detail) (15th century), from an Italian plate.
© British Museum, London.

> 30 And into ashes all my lust:
> A The grave's a fine and private place,
>   But none, I think, do there embrace.
>   Now therefore, while the youthful hue
>   Sits on thy skin like morning dew,
> 35 And while thy willing soul transpires°
>   At every pore with instant fires,
>   Now let us sport us while we may,
>   And now, like amorous birds of prey,
>   Rather at once our time devour
> B 40 Than languish in his slow-chapped° power.
>   Let us roll all our strength and all
>   Our sweetness up into one ball,
>   And tear our pleasures with rough strife
>   Through the iron gates of life;
> 45 Thus, though we cannot make our sun
>   Stand still, yet we will make him run.

35. transpires *v.*: breathes out.

40. slow-chapped: slow-jawed. Time is seen as consuming life.

268 Collection 3   The Renaissance

DEVELOPING FLUENCY

Small-group activity. Have each group choose either Herrick's or Marvell's poem to present to the class as a choral reading. Students should work together to come up with an arrangement that suits the poem's diction, rhythm, and theme. Among the questions they will want to consider are these: Which lines, if any, should go to soloists or to just two or three group members and which to the whole group? Should music accompany the presentation? If so, what instrument(s) will enhance the presentation without being intrusive? Provide time for the groups to present their readings, and discuss the effectiveness of the various presentations.

CONNECTION / HISTORY

Most young people of Marlowe's and Marvell's time—those who didn't come from wealthy families or didn't acquire generous patrons—had difficult, exhausting lives. For them witty conceits praising adored ladies were as foreign as the moon—and life was consumed with making ends meet.

INFORMATIONAL TEXT

Give Us This Day Our Daily Bread
from Shakespeare Alive!

Joseph Papp *and* Elizabeth Kirkland

You are living in England in the late years of the sixteenth century. Like most people, you live with your family in the countryside, eking out a meager existence as best you can. If you're lucky, your father is a yeoman farmer who owns enough land to support his family, or a "husbandman" who has less property but supplements his income by wage earning.

The land you live in is full of contradictions. A woman, Queen Elizabeth, rules the nation, while within the family, men still rule women. A highly educated elite enjoys the fruits of literature, while many people can't even read. The government invests huge sums of money in voyages of exploration and wars with other nations, while science and medicine remain in an appallingly primitive state. In London, the royal court glitters with jewels and finery, while misery reigns in rural hovels. Rich young men wander around Europe for fun, while in England, thousands of homeless people wander from parish to parish, begging and stealing to survive.

The gap between the rich and the poor seems to have widened in the 1570s and 1580s; wealth and power are concentrated in the hands of the few, and many people can't even find a job. You come from a family of laborers. You don't have much land at all, hardly even a vegetable garden you can call your own, and you are completely dependent on whatever wages you can get by harvesting other people's crops and doing odd jobs around the village. There is no money for such "extras" as education or nice clothes or red meat. In fact, your father's daily income, even when combined with yours, barely covers the cost of feeding you and your brothers and sisters; thank goodness your mother is able to bring in a few extra pennies from her spinning.

Your dependent status as a tenant makes your perch in life still more precarious. To an unjust and unscrupulous landlord, profit is more important than principles, and yours feels no obligation to look out for your best interests. If he decides to "enclose" the land—to stop using it for farming and turn it into grazing pastures for sheep—he has endless means of forcing you out: He might make you give up your lease, or renew it only at great expense, or, most commonly, charge you exorbitant rent.

Three Peasants (detail) (16th or 17th century) by Albrecht Dürer. Oil on panel.
Kunsthistorisches Museum, Vienna.

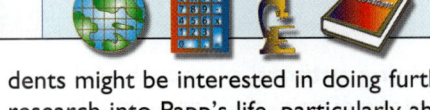

CONTENT-AREA CONNECTIONS

Literature: Joseph Papp
Joseph Papp was a well-known theater impresario in New York City. For years he directed productions of Shakespeare in the Park and ran the Public Theater. Papp also brought the world *A Chorus Line* and *Hair*. He died in 1991.
Individual activity. Interested students might obtain a copy of *Shakespeare Alive!*, the book from which this essay is excerpted, and write a critical review of the work. Other students might be interested in doing further research into Papp's life, particularly about his work with the Shakespeare in the Park productions.

Connection

Summary *at grade level*

The authors transport the reader back in time to experience what life was like for most young people in sixteenth-century England. Poverty, squalor, and injustice were widespread and became worse as the population grew. As jobs and food grew scarce, starvation was the grim outcome for many.

DIRECT TEACHING

A Reading Skills
Interpreting allusions. Explain that the title of this essay is a line from the Lord's Prayer, which Jesus Christ taught his disciples.

B Reading Informational Text
? Recognizing patterns of organization. How is each paragraph of the essay organized? [The first sentence of each paragraph is the topic sentence, which states the paragraph's main idea.] How does this pattern affect your ability to understand the essay? [It makes the progression of ideas easy to follow.]

DIRECT TEACHING

A Content-Area Connections
Economics: Mercantilism
The depletion of the population of Europe, brought about by the plague in the fourteenth century, influenced the rise of mercantilism—a doctrine popular between the sixteenth and eighteenth centuries. Mercantilism held that a large and growing population was necessary for a wealthy and powerful nation. Many mercantilists were not concerned about the harmful results of population growth.

B Reading Skills
Interpreting allusions. "Getting and spending" is an allusion to a line from Wordsworth's sonnet "The World Is Too Much with Us" (see p. 562), in which the speaker laments the effects of materialism. Writing approximately 250 years after the time discussed here, Wordsworth idealized the effects of nature that led to much suffering in the late 1500s.

C Reading Informational Text
? Making reasonable assertions about the authors' argument. How does the essay's title, "Give Us This Day Our Daily Bread," connect to the authors' argument? [The title underscores their idea that many people were unable to meet their basic needs. In this essay the line from the prayer is not metaphorical; it is literal.]

D Reading Informational Text
? Analyzing the authors' style. What effect does the use of the second person have on your response to the essay? [Most students will probably say that it drew them into the essay.]

A While your family has been struggling against these odds and worrying about how to make ends meet from day to day, larger forces have been at work that are going to affect you drastically. First, England has been undergoing a huge increase in population. The two-and-a-half million English people who were alive when your grandparents were born will practically have doubled by the time your grandchildren die. This unprecedented population growth is already being translated into inflated prices, as too many people chase after scarce resources. It also means that wages stay unacceptably low; with so many laborers on the job market, farmers and other employers can easily find people willing to work for the pathetically low wages they offer if you're not interested.

B Getting and spending have been a constant battle, and staying on the winning side has depended on plentiful harvests, which bring the twofold benefit of jobs and low grain prices. But in recent years the battle has become a losing one: The heavy rains of the last two summers have ruined the harvests, the population has been growing faster than the crops, and famine has begun to cast its long, thin shadow across your life.

C Grain—whether you eat the oatmeal cakes of northern England or the coarse wheat bread of the southerners—is a staple of your diet and, if you have no land and have to buy all your grain on the market, your single biggest expense. When prices shoot up, as they do in bad harvest years, it spells disaster for many a citizen; the Carriers in Shakespeare's *Henry IV Part 1* remember a comrade who "never joyed since the price of oats rose. It was the death of him." You try to find cheaper kinds of grain than your usual wheat, supplementing your diet with stomach-filling peas and beans—but even the prices of these are rising now, and you begin to realize, horrifying though it is, that there aren't many alternatives. Starvation seems inevitable.

D You wonder how you and your family are going to cope with the steady advance of such hunger, the hair falling out and the skin turning gray and the bleak prospect of watching your fellow villagers "starving and dying in our streets and in the fields [because] of lack of bread," as a contemporary in the northern town of Newcastle writes.

To make matters worse, there has been an economic recession too, mainly because of a slump in the cloth trade that your mother had been depending on for her livelihood. Many people rely on the cloth and wool trades for their living, and now, "the deadness of that trade and want of money is such that they are for the most part without work, and know not how to live," as an official of one parish reports.

Summer (detail) (16th century) by Jorg Breu the Elder.

Comparing and Contrasting Texts

Determining authors' purposes. Ask students how the picture of life presented in "Give Us This Day Our Daily Bread" compares with those presented in the preceding pastoral poems and what might account for the differences. [Possible responses: The speakers in the poems, seemingly unconcerned about making a living, focus on pleasure (in the case of Raleigh's poem, on the fact that it cannot last); the less well-off people described in Papp and Kirkland's essay have no time to think of pleasure, only survival. The essayists' purpose was to provide background information for people reading or watching Shakespeare's works, while the pastoral poets' purposes were to entertain and to display their skills.]

Response and Analysis

To the Virgins, to Make Much of Time
To His Coy Mistress

Thinking Critically

1. In "To the Virgins, to Make Much of Time" and "To His Coy Mistress," what do Herrick and Marvell say about time and its effects on youth and beauty?

2. A famous **image** of time appears in couplet form in Marvell's "To His Coy Mistress," in lines 21–22. To what does he compare time? What does this image make you see?

3. What does the **speaker** in Herrick's "To the Virgins" say about marriage? How do you think the speaker in Marvell's "To His Coy Mistress" feels about marriage?

4. Marvell's "To His Coy Mistress" contains both **hyperbole**, or exaggeration, and **understatement**. Find examples of each rhetorical device.

5. The image of the sun appears in both "To the Virgins" (line 5) and "To His Coy Mistress" (line 45). How does each poet use the reference to the sun? How would you **paraphrase** the last two lines of Marvell's "To His Coy Mistress"?

Extending and Evaluating

6. In two or three sentences, explain how the difficult existence described in "Give Us This Day Our Daily Bread" (see the **Connection** on page 269) corresponds to your previous notion of life in the late 1500s. In light of this information, what is surprising—or, perhaps, *not* surprising—about the visions of life presented in the pastoral poems you have just read?

7. Herrick, in "To the Virgins," and Marvell, in "To His Coy Mistress," have similar objectives but different approaches. Is one poet more persuasive than the other? How are their arguments both similar and different?

WRITING

Carpe Diem Song

Write **lyrics** for your own *carpe diem* song in any style. You might try to imitate the melancholic, romantic tone of the poems you've read, or you might adopt the more modern style of today's songs, which are sometimes romantic, sometimes plaintive, sometimes humorous.

Carpe Diem Comparison

In a short essay, **compare and contrast** any two of the four *carpe diem* poems you have read by Marlowe, Raleigh, Herrick, and Marvell. Include in your essay your own response to the poems. Use a chart like the following to gather details for your essay.

	Poem 1	Poem 2
Tone		
Images		
Figures of speech		
Theme		
Setting		
My response:		

INTERNET
Projects and Activities
Keyword: LE5 12-3

Literary Skills
Analyze *carpe diem* poetry.

Writing Skills
Write lyrics for a *carpe diem* song. Write an essay comparing and contrasting two poems.

INDEPENDENT PRACTICE

Response and Analysis

To the Virgins, to Make Much of Time
To His Coy Mistress

Thinking Critically

1. *Herrick*—Time brings death and diminishes a girl's chances of marrying. *Marvell*—Time brings death, loss of beauty, and decay.

2. Marvell compares time to a winged chariot. Students may picture horses pulling a winged carriage across the sky.

3. Herrick's speaker says that women should marry young while they still have the chance. Marvell's speaker doesn't mention marriage, but he would agree with the advice to marry young.

4. Lines 5–18 contain examples of hyperbole regarding the Ganges River, biblical flood, and time. Lines 31–32 are an understatement concerning death.

5. Herrick uses the sun to warn that life is finite; Marvell uses it to challenge his mistress to join him in outrunning time. Possible paraphrase: We can't stop time, but we can live as if we could elude it.

Extending and Evaluating

6. Possible answers: Students may say that based on books and movies, they believed the 1500s to be more generally prosperous. They may be surprised that well-educated and politically aware poets either didn't know or didn't care about the struggles of rural people.

7. Possible answer: Herrick is more persuasive because he is more direct and doesn't introduce the image of human death. Both recommend seizing the day; Herrick's speaker sounds like a kindly advisor, while Marvell's is a passionate lover.

ASSESSING

Assessment

- *Holt Assessment: Literature, Reading, and Vocabulary*

William Shakespeare
(1564–1616)

William Shakespeare, attributed to John Taylor (d. 1651). By courtesy of the National Portrait Gallery, London.

Every literate person has heard of Shakespeare, the author of more than thirty-six remarkable plays and more than 150 poems. Over the centuries these literary works have made such a deep impression on the human race that all sorts of fancies, legends, and theories have been invented about their author. Some critics claim that somebody other than Shakespeare wrote the works that bear his name, although they cannot agree on who, among a dozen candidates, this other author actually was. Controversy about the authorship of Shakespeare's plays rests on two assumptions. First, some people assume that someone with Shakespeare's modest education (he was not a university graduate) could not possibly have written plays that show such a wide range of knowledge. Second, some people assume that we do not know much about Shakespeare. They say that a great number of contemporary references would have been made about a man who wrote such successful plays.

In fact, Shakespeare's life is better documented than the life of any other dramatist of the time, except perhaps Ben Jonson (see page 317), a writer who seems almost modern in the way he publicized himself. Jonson was an honest, blunt, and outspoken man who knew Shakespeare well; for a time the two dramatists wrote for the same theater company, and Shakespeare even acted in Jonson's plays. Often severe in his judgments of other writers, Jonson published a poem praising Shakespeare, asserting that he was superior to all Greek, Roman, and English dramatists, predicting that he would be "not of an age, but for all time." Jonson's judgment is now commonly accepted, and his prophecy has come true.

The Years in Stratford-on-Avon

Shakespeare was born in Stratford-on-Avon, a historic and prosperous market town in Warwickshire, and was christened in the parish church there on April 26, 1564. His father was John Shakespeare, a glovemaker who was active in the town government; his mother—born Mary Arden—came from a prominent family in the county. Presumably, for seven years or so, Shakespeare attended the King's New School, where he obtained an excellent education in Latin and the Bible. (Little English was taught except when students had to translate Latin works into English and then back into Latin.) After leaving school, Shakespeare may have become a teacher himself, but because he shows in his plays very detailed knowledge of many different crafts and trades, speculators have proposed a number of different occupations that he could have had.

At eighteen, Shakespeare married Anne Hathaway, the twenty-six-year-old daughter of a farmer living near Stratford. They had three children, a daughter named Susanna and twins named Hamnet and Judith. We don't know how the young Shakespeare supported his family, but his needs and ambitions soon drew him to London. The two daughters grew up and eventually married; the son died when he was eleven.

The "Upstart Crow"

How did Shakespeare first become interested in the theater? Presumably by seeing plays. We know that traveling acting companies frequently visited Stratford, and we assume that he attended their performances and that he also went to the nearby city of Coventry, where a famous cycle of religious plays was put on every year. To be a dramatist, however, one had to be in London, where theater was flourishing in the 1580s. Exactly when Shakespeare left his family and moved to London (there is no evidence that his wife was ever in the city) is uncertain; scholars say that he probably arrived there in 1587. It is certain that he was busy and successful in the London theater by 1592, when a fellow dramatist named Robert Greene attacked him in print and ridiculed a passage in his early play *Henry VI*. Greene, a down-and-out Cambridge graduate, warned other university men then writing plays to beware of this mere actor who was writing plays—an "upstart crow beautified with our feathers." Greene died of dissipation just as his ill-natured attack was being published, but a friend of his named Henry Chettle immediately apologized in print to Shakespeare and commended Shakespeare's acting and writing abilities and his personal honesty.

Actor and Author

From 1592 on, there is ample documentation of Shakespeare's life and works. We know where he lived in London, at least approximately when his plays were produced and printed, and even how he spent his money. From 1594 until his retirement in about 1613, he was a member of one company, which also included the great tragic actor Richard Burbage and the popular clown Will Kemp. Although actors and others connected with the theater had a very low status legally, in practice they enjoyed the patronage of noblemen and even royalty. It is a mistake to think of Shakespeare as an obscure actor who somehow wrote great plays; he was well-known even as a young man.

Rubbing Shoulders with the Aristocracy

By 1596, Shakespeare was beginning to prosper. He had his father apply to the Heralds' College for a coat of arms that the family could display, signifying that they were "gentlefolk," or people of high social standing. On Shakespeare's family crest is a falcon shaking a spear. To support this claim to gentility, Shakespeare bought New Place, a handsome house and grounds in Stratford, a place so spacious and elegant that the queen of England once stayed there after Shakespeare's daughter Susanna inherited it. Shakespeare also, in 1599, joined with a few other members of his company, called the Lord Chamberlain's Men, to finance a new theater—the famous Globe—on the south side of the Thames. The "honey-tongued Shakespeare," as he was called in a book about English literature published in 1598, was now earning money as a playwright, an actor, and a shareholder in a theater. By 1600, Shakespeare was regularly associating with members of the aristocracy, and six of his plays had been given command performances at the court of Queen Elizabeth.

The King's Men

Shakespeare prospered even more under Elizabeth's successor, King James of Scotland. Fortunately for Shakespeare's company, as it turned out, James's royal entry into London in 1603 had to be postponed for several months because the plague was raging in the city. While waiting for the epidemic to subside, the royal court stayed in various palaces outside

---

Primary Source

Henry Chettle's Apology

Henry Chettle, the partner of a printer, had been instrumental in publishing Robert Greene's attack on Shakespeare. Chettle's apology, appearing in his pamphlet *Kind-Hart's Dream,* reads in part, "I am sorry as if the originall fault a had been by [my?] fault, because my selfe haue seene his [Shakespeare's] demeanor no less ciuill than he exelent in the qualities he professes: Besides, diuers of worship [that is, various highly situated people], haue reported, his vprightness of dealing, which argues his honesty, and his facetious grace in writting, that aproues his Art."

Activity. Write the quotation on the chalkboard, and encourage students to translate Chettle into modern English. For example, "my selfe haue seene . . ." can be expressed as "I have seen that he is as civil in demeanor as he is excellent at his profession."

DIRECT TEACHING

A Exploring the Culture
GROOMS OF THE CHAMBER

Becoming grooms of the royal chamber meant that the players were considered members of the royal household. This position did not guarantee them a fixed salary, as they were not usually in attendance. However, each man did receive four and a half yards of scarlet red cloth for his livery from Sir George Home, Master of the Great Wardrobe. The costume was probably worn by the King's Men on public occasions. In addition, James rewarded the players generously at each performance. No troupe gave more performances before James than his own men.

B More About the Writer
Background. Shakespeare contracted a fever in mid-March of 1616. On March 25, seeming to recognize that he was seriously ill, Shakespeare executed a detailed will. Within a month, despite his family's careful nursing, he was dead. Several scholars suggest that his fever was typhoid, which had apparently struck Stratford in the early spring of 1616 after an unseasonably warm winter.

For Independent Reading

If students choose to read the plays, encourage them to view live or filmed performances as well. Watching performances will minimize hurdles that might come from reading Shakespeare's English on the page.

London. Shakespeare's company took advantage of this situation and, since the city theaters were closed, performed several plays for the court and the new king. Shakespeare's plays delighted James, for he loved literature and was starved for pleasure after the grim experience of ruling Scotland for many years. He immediately took the company under his patronage, renamed it the King's Men, gave it patents to perform anywhere in the realm, provided the men with special clothing for state occasions, increased their salaries, and appointed their chief members, including Shakespeare, to serve as grooms of the royal chamber. All this patronage brought such prosperity to Shakespeare that he was able to make some very profitable real estate investments in Stratford and London.

An Active Retirement

In about 1610, Shakespeare decided that, having made a considerable sum from his plays and theatrical enterprises, he would retire to his handsome house in Stratford, a place he had never forgotten, though he seems to have kept his life there rather separate from his life in London. His retirement was not complete, for the records show that after he returned to Stratford, he still took part in the management of the King's Men and their two theaters: the Globe, an octagonal building opened in 1599 and used for performances in good weather, and the Blackfriars, acquired in 1608 and used for indoor performances. Shakespeare's works in this period show no signs of diminished creativity, except that in some years he wrote one play instead of the customary two, and they continue to illustrate the great diversity of his genius.

The Last Years

Shakespeare's last recorded visit to London was made with his son-in-law Dr. John Hall in November 1614, though he may have gone down to the city afterward because he continued to own property there, including a building very near the Blackfriars theater. Probably, though, he spent most of the last two years of his life at New Place, with his daughter Susanna Hall (and his granddaughter Elizabeth) living nearby. He died on April 23, 1616, and was buried under the floor of Stratford Church, with this epitaph warning posterity not to dig up his remains and transfer them to the graveyard outside the church—a common practice in those days to make room for newer corpses:

> Good friend, for Jesus' sake forbear
> To dig the dust enclosèd here!
> Blest be the man that spares these stones,
> And curst be he that moves my bones.

For Independent Reading

These plays by Shakespeare are recommended:
- *A Midsummer Night's Dream* (comedy)
- *Hamlet* (tragedy)
- *Othello* (tragedy)
- *Macbeth* (tragedy)
- *The Tempest* (comedy)

Christopher Walken (top) and Raul Julia in *Othello*, performed for the New York Shakespeare Festival (1991).

Conducting a Historical Investigation

With the goal of learning more about what Shakespeare experienced and what he thought, have students form small groups to produce and present a feature piece on him in the format of a television show. Suggest that students include a dramatized fictional segment in which Shakespeare and some of his contemporaries are interviewed. Each group may use this essay as a foundation and do additional research as necessary. Each person in the group should have one or more functions to perform as a member of the team. After the features have been developed, ask each group to present its piece to the class, either in person or on videotape.

Shakespeare's Sonnets: The Mysteries of Love

Shakespeare. The name calls to mind the great plays whose characters have come to life on stages around the world: *Hamlet, Macbeth, Romeo and Juliet, Othello.* Yet had Shakespeare written no plays at all, his reputation as a poet, as the author of the *Sonnets* (1609), would still have been immense. There are 154 sonnets altogether; their speaker is male, and their chief subject is love. Beyond those three points, however, there is little agreement, only questions:

- Is the sonnets' speaker a dramatic character invented by Shakespeare, like Romeo, Macbeth, or Hamlet, or is he the poet himself?

- If the sonnets are about the real man Shakespeare, then who are the real people behind the characters the sonnets mention?

- Is the order in which the sonnets were originally published (probably without Shakespeare's consent) the correct or the intended sequence? Could they be arranged to tell a more coherent story? *Should* they be so arranged?

- In the 1609 publication, who is the "Mr. W. H." mentioned as the "only begetter" of the sonnets: the young man? someone else?

These and dozens of other questions about the sonnets have been asked and answered over and over again—but never to everybody's satisfaction. We have hundreds of conflicting theories but no absolutely convincing answers.

About the individual sonnets, though, if not the whole sequence, agreement is perfect: They are among the supreme utterances in English. They say profound things about important human experiences, and they say them with great art.

Emblems and Devices of Love (detail) (early 16th century), a French text by Pierre Sala.
Stowe 955 fol. 12b–13.
British Library, London.

William Shakespeare 275

DIRECT TEACHING

A Background
Sonnets in Elizabethan England
Since Elizabethans appreciated complex patterns, the sonnet form, popularized by Italy's Petrarch (1304–1374), had long appealed to their literary tastes. (See p. 276.) As a boy, Shakespeare probably heard or read popular sonnets by Sir Thomas Wyatt (1503–1542) and Henry Howard, earl of Surrey (1517–1547). As an adult, Shakespeare read translations of sonnets by the French poets Pierre de Ronsard (1524–1585) and Joachim du Bellay (1522–1560). Sir Philip Sidney's acclaimed sonnet sequence *Astrophel and Stella* appeared in London in 1591 and Edmund Spenser's *Amoretti* in 1595. By this time, Shakespeare had probably already begun his own sonnet series.

B Exploring the Culture
LIVING BY THE PEN
Shakespeare the playwright worked under constant pressure to meet deadlines and to please the public. However, Shakespeare the sonneteer avoided both constraints. He withheld some of his sonnets from publication for at least ten years, gaining the freedom to please himself: to revise and polish, rework and rethink.

DIRECT TEACHING

A Content-Area Connections

Literature: English Sonnets
Shakespeare refined the sonnet form that bears his name, but he did not invent it. George Gascoigne defined the form in a 1575 publication: ". . . I can beste allowe to call those Sonets which are of fourteene lynes, every line conteyning tenne syllables. The firste twelve do ryme in staves of foure lines by crosse meetre, and the last twoo ryming togither do conclude the whole." The earl of Surrey had used a version of this form for sonnets printed in *Tottel's Miscellany* in 1557, seven years before Shakespeare's birth.

The Sonnet in the Renaissance

The word *sonnet* is derived from the Italian word *sonetto,* meaning "little sound; song." A **sonnet** is a fourteen-line lyric poem that conforms to strict patterns of rhythm and rhyme.

In Italy the sonnet form was perfected by Francesco Petrarca, known in English as Petrarch. The form he popularized is called the **Italian,** or **Petrarchan, sonnet.** The Petrarchan sonnet has two parts: an eight-line section, called the **octave,** followed by a six-line section, called the **sestet.** This form makes the Italian sonnet perfectly suited for a two-part statement: question-answer, problem-solution, or theme-comment. The transition between the two parts, called the **volta,** or turn, is usually found in the ninth line—the beginning of the sestet—as in Petrarch's Sonnet 42, below.

SONNET 42
PETRARCH

The spring returns, the spring wind softly blowing	a
Sprinkles the grass with gleam and glitter of showers,	b
Powdering pearl and diamond, dripping with flowers,	b
Dropping wet flowers, dancing the winters going;	a
The swallow twitters, the groves of midnight are glowing	a
With nightingale music and madness; the sweet fierce powers	b
Of love flame up through the earth; the seed-soul towers	b
And trembles; nature is filled to overflowing . . .	a
The spring returns, but there is no returning	c
Of spring for me. O heart with anguish burning!	c
She that unlocked all April in a breath	d
Returns not . . . And these meadows, blossoms, birds	e
These lovely gentle girls—words, empty words	e
As bitter as the black estates of death!	d

Lines 1–8: Octave
Lines 9–10: Volta
Lines 9–14: Sestet

Translated by Joseph Auslander

The Shakespearean Sonnet Form

Each of Shakespeare's sonnets has its formal organization, established by the rules of the sonnet form. Each sonnet also has a logical organization of ideas, also established by the sonnet form.

A In the English sonnet form known as the **Shakespearean sonnet,** the fixed requirements are fourteen iambic pentameter lines divided into three quatrains and a couplet, with the rhyme scheme *abab cdcd efef gg.* Here is how Shakespeare structured Sonnet 18 to make these two organizations cooperate in a way that seems natural, not forced.

SONNET 18
WILLIAM SHAKESPEARE

LOGICAL ORGANIZATION			FORMAL ORGANIZATION
A question and tentative answers	Shall I compare thee to a summer's day? Thou art more lovely and more temperate. Rough winds do shake the darling buds of May, And summer's lease hath all too short a date.	a b a b	First quatrain
	Sometime too hot the eye of heaven shines, And often is his gold complexion dimmed; And every fair from fair sometime declines, By chance, or nature's changing course untrimmed.	c d c d	Second quatrain
The turn	But thy eternal summer shall not fade, Nor lose possession of that fair thou owest, Nor shall Death brag thou wander'st in his shade When in eternal lines to time thou grow'st.	e f e f	Third quatrain
A final answer	So long as men can breathe, or eyes can see, So long lives this, and this gives life to thee.	g g	Couplet

The logical organization of ideas, of course, varies from sonnet to sonnet. In Sonnet 18, the first line's question is followed by negative answers: The speaker's beloved does bear some resemblances to a summer's day, but only superficial ones. The first two quatrains concentrate on the summer day's imperfections rather than on the loved one.

Then in line 9 comes the **turn**—a shift in focus or thought. The speaker turns from the faulty summer's day to the beloved, and by the end of the third quatrain, the speaker has entirely abandoned the opening comparison. Like most literary terms, the word *turn* is a metaphor; the speaker, figuratively speaking, is turning from one thing to another.

Sonnet 18, with its turn after line 8, follows the pattern of the Petrarchan sonnet; in an English sonnet the final couplet is often a second turn of great impact: a final summary or explanation of all that came before. In this sonnet the couplet says, perhaps with some exaggeration, that by being addressed in this poem, the beloved person has become immortal.

DIRECT TEACHING

B Exploring the Historical Period
SHAKESPEARE'S SUMMER
Summer begins in agricultural Europe on the day of the summer solstice, just as spring begins on the day of the spring equinox. Shakespeare probably loosely used the word *summer* to mean "spring and summer."

C Content-Area Connections
Literature: Conceits
A conceit is a fanciful and extended poetic comparison of two things that appear to have little in common. The last two lines of Sonnet 18 provide an example of the convention called the eternizing conceit, which suggests that the sonnet itself immortalizes, or eternizes, human love.

D Content-Area Connections
Literature: Petrarchan Sonnets
A good example of a Petrarchan sonnet appears on p. 285 following the treatment of six sonnets by Shakespeare.

PRETEACHING

Selection Starter

Motivate. You might bring in (or ask students to bring in) and play recordings of popular love songs. Have students identify themes. Then, tell students to look for similar themes in the sonnets.

Summary ⇔ *at grade level*

The speaker describes ugly feelings of self-pity, envy, and self-loathing, which he then banishes by recalling that in love, he is richer than kings.

VIEWING THE ART

Nicholas Hilliard (c. 1547–1619), a famous sixteenth-century miniature portrait painter, wrote *The Arte of Limning* (c. 1600), the first known writing by an artist of the English Renaissance. Unlike larger paintings, miniatures were intended to be held and kept close to the owner. Indeed, they had a very personal meaning. From the sixteenth century until the mid-nineteenth century, these small portraits were intimately connected to the lives of those who owned them.

Activity. What social value do you imagine miniatures had? [Miniatures may have been memorials of friendship or love, like some photographs are today.]

Before You Read

Sonnets 29, 30, 71, 73, 116, 130

Make the Connection

What is it that makes us happy, that lets us look back over years receding into the past, and ahead to the inevitable conclusion, without sorrow or despair? Wealth hasn't answered the question satisfactorily for many people. Power always seems to dwindle or be wrenched out of our hands in an instant. Fame evaporates faster than the early-morning dew. If there is any answer to this question, for many people it is love. Time passes and death is inescapable, but love, if we are fortunate enough to find it or create it, sustains us through it all.

In these six sonnets, Shakespeare speculates on what love is and what it does to us and for us.

Literary Focus

Shakespearean Sonnet

English poets, limited by their "rhyme-poor" language, created the **English,** or **Shakespearean, sonnet,** which allows more rhymes than the Petrarchan sonnet. The Shakespearean sonnet is fourteen lines long and uses three four-line units, called **quatrains,** followed by a final two-line **couplet.** The organization of thought in the sonnet usually corresponds to this structure: The three quatrains often express related ideas, and the couplet sums up the poet's message. The Shakespearean sonnet is written in a particular **meter,** or rhythmic pattern, called **iambic pentameter,** with each line consisting of five unstressed syllables alternating with five stressed syllables. The typical rhyme scheme of the Shakespearean sonnet is *abab cdcd efef gg.*

INTERNET
More About
William Shakespeare
Keyword: LE5 12-3

SKILLS FOCUS
Literary Skills
Understand the characteristics of Shakespearean sonnets.

The **Shakespearean sonnet** is written in iambic pentameter and has three four-line units, or **quatrains,** followed by a concluding two-line unit, or **couplet.**

For more on the Shakespearean Sonnet, see Sonnet *in the Handbook of Literary and Historical Terms.*

Background

Shakespeare's greatest nondramatic poetry is in a group of 154 sonnets. In addition to their richness of language and imagery, Shakespeare's sonnets have an unusual depth of perception and feeling, extending beyond the conventional subject of love to a contemplation of the beauty of life and the mortality of man. In his first 126 sonnets, Shakespeare celebrates his devoted friendship with a young man, which he presents as a higher, less selfish relationship than his passionate love for a particular woman (the "dark lady"), who is the subject of the remaining twenty-eight sonnets. The identities of the young man and the dark lady to whom the sonnets are addressed have never been determined with certainty.

Portrait by Nicholas Hilliard. Miniature on vellum.
© Victoria and Albert Museum, London/Art Resource, New York.

DIFFERENTIATING INSTRUCTION

Learners Having Difficulty

Play the audio version of Sonnet 29 as students read along silently. Next, you might say, "Here's the worst-possible paraphrase: 'When I feel blue, I think of you; you pull me through.'" Point out that the paraphrase rhymes and more or less conveys the meaning; then, ask students, "What gets lost?" Elicit students' ideas of memorable images, striking sound effects, and thought-provoking implications from the sonnet. Point out that Shakespeare's artistry lies, in part, in these aspects of the sonnet. Suggest that students create paraphrases (rhymed or unrhymed) of the other sonnets in order to grasp the meanings, and then ask themselves, "What gets lost?" to explore the artistry.

Invite learners having difficulty to read Sonnet 29 in interactive format in *The Holt Reader* and to use the sidenotes as aids to understanding the selection.

English-Language Learners

Shakespeare's now-archaic vocabulary and diction will challenge English-language learners. You might ease students into each sonnet by first guiding them in identifying, pronouncing, and defining the rhyming phrases at the ends of the lines.

In this sonnet the speaker describes how he rids himself of such ugly emotions as envy, self-pity, self-hatred, and the dismal belief that everybody else is luckier than he is.

Sonnet 29

William Shakespeare

When, in disgrace° with Fortune and men's eyes,
I all alone beweep my outcast state,
And trouble deaf heaven with my bootless° cries,
And look upon myself and curse my fate,
5 Wishing me like to one more rich in hope,
Featured like him, like him° with friends possessed,
Desiring this man's art,° and that man's scope,°
With what I most enjoy contented least;
Yet in these thoughts myself almost despising,
10 Haply° I think on thee, and then my state,
    Like to the lark° at break of day arising
    From sullen° earth, sings hymns at heaven's gate;
        For thy sweet love remembered such wealth brings
        That then I scorn to change my state with kings.

1. **disgrace** *n.*: loss of favor.
3. **bootless** *adj.*: useless; futile.
5–6. **one ... him ... him**: three men whom the speaker envies.
7. **art** *n.*: literary ability.
   scope *n.*: power.
10. **haply** *adv.*: by chance.
11. **lark** *n.*: English skylark, a bird whose song seems to pour down from the sky.
12. **sullen** *adj.*: gloomy.

Response and Analysis

Thinking Critically

1. Like many of Shakespeare's sonnets, Sonnet 29 is actually a single sentence. In the long introductory clause, what does the speaker say he envies?
2. The main clause begins the **turn**. In what line does the turn occur? What remembrance changes the speaker's state of mind?
3. How does the speaker's **tone**, or attitude, change after the turn?
4. What **simile** does the speaker use in lines 11–12 to describe his new state of mind? Does this simile strike you as a good description of joy?
5. Do you think that love has this power to transform our feelings? Discuss your responses to the poem.

WRITING

Solace from a Sonnet

In Sonnet 29, Shakespeare describes how he overcomes feelings of despair and failure by remembering his love. People today also experience temporary periods of depression when they feel their looks, possessions, friends, or accomplishments don't measure up. Write a modern version of Shakespeare's Sonnet 29, either following the sonnet form or writing the poem entirely in couplets. To get ideas for your **poem**, consider these questions: What might people today envy in their neighbors? What might help a modern person feel more satisfied?

SKILLS FOCUS

Literary Skills
Analyze the characteristics of Shakespearean sonnets.

Writing Skills
Write a sonnet.

William Shakespeare   279

DIRECT TEACHING

A Literary Focus

Shakespearean sonnet. Many of Shakespeare's sonnets are complaints, which are poems conveying laments of unrequited lovers. What laments does the speaker list in ll. 1–4? [He says he's unlucky, disliked, and alone.]

B Reading Skills

Interpreting. What causes the speaker's spirits to rise? [Possible response: the thought of his beloved's love.]

INDEPENDENT PRACTICE

Response and Analysis

Thinking Critically

1. He envies anyone who has reason to hope, is handsome, has friends, or has ability and power.
2. The turn begins at l. 9. The remembrance of his love for the person addressed in the sonnet changes his state of mind.
3. In l. 10, the tone changes from self-pity to delight.
4. He compares himself to a lark.
5. Students may agree that love can lift one's spirits, as evidenced by their own experiences and observations. The sonnet's happy ending may appeal to students.

ASSESSING

Assessment

- *Holt Assessment: Literature, Reading, and Vocabulary*

Special Education Students
For lessons designed for special education students, see *Holt Reading Solutions*.

Advanced Learners
Enrichment. Encourage students to choose one artwork and one musical composition, from any era, that might accompany each sonnet. Ask students to describe their choices and to explain why they find these choices appropriate. What qualities do the art and music share with the sonnets in form, content, or impact?

William Shakespeare   279

Summary  at grade level

Using images of legal procedures and fines, the speaker describes his ruminations on bereavements, failed loves, and old grievances—and finds that having one "dear friend" cancels out all his losses.

DIRECT TEACHING

A Literary Focus

? Shakespearean sonnet. In ll. 6–9 of Sonnet 30, what sorrows trouble the speaker? [bereavement at the death of friends, regret for lost loves, and bitterness over old grievances] What change occurs in the final couplet? [Thinking of his "dear friend" ends his sorrows.]

INDEPENDENT PRACTICE

Response and Analysis

Thinking Critically

1. He remembers unmet goals, time's damage, dead friends, lost loves.
2. thoughts of the friend he is addressing
3. The turn occurs in l. 13.
4. The metaphors *summon up remembrance; canceled woe; expense of . . . sight; grievances foregone; tell o'er / the sad account; Which I new pay as if not paid before; losses are restored* all evoke matters of law.
5. Repeated *s* sounds occur in ll. 1–3; *w*, in l. 4; and *d*, in ll. 5–6.
6. Both sonnets express the healing power of love.

Shakespeare's best sonnets are remarkable for their original, imaginative **metaphors**—their comparisons of two unlike things. Sonnet 30 begins with such a metaphor: Periods of quiet meditation are called sessions, as though they were court trials in which one's thoughts come to the bar of justice to hear their cases tried. Notice how line 2 continues the legal metaphor.

Sonnet 30
William Shakespeare

When to the sessions of sweet silent thought
I summon up remembrance of things past,
I sigh the lack of many a thing I sought,
And with old woes new wail° my dear time's waste.°
5 Then can I drown an eye (unused to flow)
For precious friends hid in death's dateless° night,
And weep afresh love's long since canceled woe,
And moan th' expense° of many a vanished sight.°
Then can I grieve at grievances foregone,
10 And heavily from woe to woe tell° o'er
The sad account of fore° bemoanèd moan,
Which I new pay as if not paid before.
   But if the while I think on thee, dear friend,
   All losses are restored and sorrows end.

4. **new wail:** again lament.
my . . . waste: the damage that time has done to things dear to me.
6. **dateless** *adj.:* endless.
8. **expense** *n.:* loss.
vanished sight: things gone, such as dead friends.
10. **tell** *v.:* count.
11. **fore** *adv.:* already.

Response and Analysis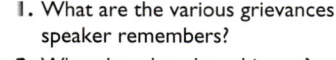

Literary Skills
Analyze the characteristics of Shakespearean sonnets.

Thinking Critically

1. What are the various grievances the speaker remembers?
2. What thoughts cheer him up?
3. Where does the **turn** take place in this sonnet?
4. What **metaphors** in this sonnet compare the speaker's sadness to things having to do with law? (Look for legal terms like *summon, canceled, expense, grievances, account, pay*.)
5. Point out where in this sonnet Shakespeare uses **alliteration**—the repetition of consonant sounds. Read the sonnet aloud to hear the effect of these repeated sounds.
6. What similarities can you find in the main ideas expressed in Sonnet 30 and Sonnet 29?

ASSESSING

Assessment

- Holt Assessment: Literature, Reading, and Vocabulary

RETEACHING

For a lesson reteaching poetic devices, see **Reteaching**, p. 1129A.

In several of Shakespeare's sonnets, the speaker emphasizes the difference between his age and his beloved's: He is much older, and so presumably he will die first. This sonnet says, surprisingly, that he does not want his loved one to remember him at all. "Forget me," he says, "as soon as you hear my funeral bell."

Sonnet 71
William Shakespeare

No longer mourn for me when I am dead
Than you shall hear the surly sullen bell
Give warning to the world that I am fled
From this vile world, with vilest worms to dwell.
5   Nay, if you read this line, remember not
The hand that writ it; for I love you so
That I in your sweet thoughts would be forgot
If thinking on me then should make you woe.
O, if, I say, you look upon this verse
10   When I, perhaps, compounded am with clay,
Do not so much as my poor name rehearse,
But let your love even with my life decay,
   Lest the wise world should look into your moan
   And mock you with me after I am gone.

A man aged twenty-four, by Nicholas Hilliard.
© Victoria and Albert Museum, London/Art Resource, New York.

Response and Analysis

Thinking Critically

1. What does the speaker tell his loved one to do after he has died?
2. What two reasons does the speaker give for wanting his beloved to forget about him?
3. The shift in **mood** in Sonnet 71 is more subtle than that in the preceding sonnets. Where does the **turn** occur? What mood does the speaker shift into?
4. Where in this sonnet do you hear **alliteration**—the repetition of consonant sounds?
5. How does the speaker use **irony** in line 13 when he calls the world "wise"?
6. Think about the **tone** of this sonnet—the speaker's attitude toward his subject, which is his own death. How would you describe his tone?
7. What does this speaker imply about the way in which the world views him?

SKILLS FOCUS

Literary Skills Analyze the characteristics of Shakespearean sonnets.

William Shakespeare   281

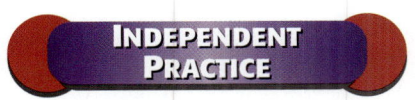

Response and Analysis

Thinking Critically

1. He tells his beloved to forget him.
2. He wants to spare his beloved a sense of longing, and he wants to forestall others' judgmental comments about the relationship.
3. In ll. 5–6, the speaker shifts from bitter negativity about both life and death to deep tenderness toward his beloved.
4. Lines 1 and 14 repeat *m* sounds; l. 2, *s* sounds; ll. 3, 4, and 13, *w* sounds; and ll. 12–13, *l* sounds.
5. The phrase "wise world" is ironic because the speaker sees the world as "vile" (l. 4). A world that mocks a bereaved lover (ll. 13–14) is mindless and cruel, not wise.
6. Possible answer: His tone suggests regret about his death but greater concern about his beloved's welfare.
7. He implies that the world scorns him.

As in Sonnet 71, the speaker of Sonnet 73 dwells on his advanced years. This sonnet is rich in striking metaphors, with each quatrain developing a single metaphor.

Sonnet 73

William Shakespeare

A That time of year thou mayst in me behold
When yellow leaves, or none, or few, do hang
Upon those boughs which shake against the cold,
Bare ruined choirs° where late the sweet birds sang.
B 5 In me thou see'st the twilight of such day
As after sunset fadeth in the west,
Which by and by black night doth take away,
Death's second self, that seals up all in rest.
In me thou see'st the glowing of such fire,
10 That on the ashes of his youth doth lie
As the deathbed whereon it must expire,
Consumed with that which it was nourished by.°
C   This thou perceivest, which makes thy love more strong,
  To love that well which thou must leave ere long.

4. **choirs** *n. pl.*: parts of a church or cathedral in which services are held. The landscape of Shakespeare's England was dotted with church ruins, a result of Henry VIII's destruction of monasteries.

12. **consumed ... nourished by:** choked by the ashes of the wood that once fed its flame.

Response and Analysis

Thinking Critically

1. What three **metaphors** does this speaker use to describe himself? What contrast between the speaker and his beloved is implied?
2. What seasonal **images** do you see in this poem? How do these images contribute to the poem's **tone** of loss and sadness?
3. Find the **turn** in this sonnet. What does the speaker tell his beloved in the final couplet?
4. The idea in line 12 is somewhat compressed. **Paraphrase** it in your own words, after you have thought about what originally fed ("nourished") the speaker's fires—fires that are now choked ("consumed").
5. How do you feel about the main idea of this sonnet, expressed in the last couplet?

Literary Skills Analyze the characteristics of Shakespearean sonnets.

Writing Skills Write an essay comparing and contrasting two sonnets.

WRITING

Tone Poems

Both Sonnet 71 and Sonnet 73 have particular tones and moods. In a brief **essay, compare and contrast** the sonnets by focusing on each speaker's **tone.** Discuss how word choice, figurative language, imagery, and sound effects work together to create a very specific tone in each poem.

Perhaps the most famous of Shakespeare's sonnets, Sonnet 116 defines true love metaphorically as "the marriage of true minds." Such love is completely firm against all "impediments," a word taken from the priest's remarks to those attending a Church of England wedding service: "If any of you know cause or just impediment why these persons should not be joined together..."

Sonnet 116

William Shakespeare

> Let me not to the marriage of true minds
> Admit impediments. Love is not love
> Which alters when it alteration finds,
> Or bends with the remover to remove.
> 5 Oh no! It is an ever-fixèd mark°
> That looks on tempests and is never shaken.
> It is the star to every wandering bark,°
> Whose worth's unknown, although his height be taken.°
> Love's not Time's fool, though rosy lips and cheeks
> 10 Within his bending sickle's compass° come.
> Love alters not with his brief hours and weeks,
> But bears it out° even to the edge of doom.
>   If this be error and upon me proved,
>   I never writ, nor no man ever loved.

5. **mark** *n.:* seamark; a prominent object on shore that serves as a guide to sailors.
7. **bark** *n.:* boat.
8. **height be taken:** altitude measured to determine a ship's position.
10. **compass** *n.:* range; reach.
12. **bears it out:** survives.

Summary at grade level

The speaker offers an idealistic definition of love: Love stays constant despite the passage of time or the fading of beauty. If he is wrong, he claims, then he is no writer and no one ever loved.

DIRECT TEACHING

A Literary Focus
Shakespearean sonnet. In ll. 9–10, the speaker alludes to the medieval image of time as the grim reaper, who cuts off life with the sweep of a sickle. In ll. 7–8, he alludes to Polaris, the North Star.

INDEPENDENT PRACTICE

Response and Analysis

Thinking Critically

1. *Metaphors*—"It is an ever-fixèd mark" (l. 5). "It is the star to every wandering bark" (l. 7).
2. Lines 2–4, 9, and 11 define love by telling what love is *not* and what it does *not* do.
3. Time is a grim reaper who cuts down youth (ll. 9–10).
4. The turn comes between ll. 13 and 14. Line 13 might be spoken in a direct, emphatic tone and l. 14 in an ironic tone.
5. The sonnet emphasizes love's constancy.
6. Love goes deeper than superficial matters of age.
7. Most will agree, perhaps saying that a reminder of the eternity of love is appropriate anytime.

Response and Analysis

Thinking Critically

1. What **metaphors** in this sonnet describe the steadiness of love?
2. Where does the speaker define love by what it is *not* and by what it does *not* do?
3. How is time **personified** in this poem?
4. Where does the **turn** in this sonnet take place? How do you think the speaker's voice might change as he speaks this line?
5. What single quality of true love does this sonnet emphasize?
6. How could this sonnet be used to justify a difference in the lovers' ages?
7. This poem is read at both weddings and funerals. Do you think the poem is equally appropriate for either occasion? Explain why or why not.

SKILLS FOCUS

Literary Skills
Analyze the characteristics of Shakespearean sonnets.

DIFFERENTIATING INSTRUCTION

Learners Having Difficulty
Invite learners having difficulty to read Sonnet 116 in interactive format in *The Holt Reader* and to use the sidenotes as aids to understanding the selection. The interactive version provides additional instruction, practice, and assessment of the literary skill taught in the Student Edition. Monitor students' responses to the selection, and correct any misconceptions that arise.

ASSESSING

Assessment
- *Holt Assessment: Literature, Reading, and Vocabulary*

Summary ⇔ at grade level

The speaker of Sonnet 130 describes the object of his love with humorous frankness: She is far from the idealized damsel of conventional love poems; instead, she is an ordinary mortal. Yet, he stresses, he can love such a woman as much as he scorns hackneyed poetic convention.

DIRECT TEACHING

A Literary Focus

? Shakespearean sonnet. How might ll. 1–8 surprise readers who expect a conventional love poem? [The speaker describes his beloved's lack of beauty.] Where and how does the speaker create a second surprise? [In ll. 9 and 13–14, he says he loves her regardless.]

B Reading Skills

? Determining author's purpose. What, in your opinion, was Shakespeare's purpose in writing Sonnet 130? [Possible responses: to amuse readers by mocking trite conceits; to affirm that love exists between real—not idealized—men and women.]

INDEPENDENT PRACTICE

Response and Analysis

Thinking Critically

1. Possible answers: No, the speaker is just mocking convention. Yes, though the speaker does not seem to mind.
2. The speaker reverses the conventional romantic conceits by using unflattering comparison and understatement.
3. It affirms his love for his mistress and his dislike of overused conceits.

4. Some students will see the hyperbole of wiry hair and bad breath as humorous. Some may find such remarks unacceptable in today's world and therefore may not see the humor.

ASSESSING

Assessment

- Holt Assessment: Literature, Reading, and Vocabulary

This sonnet ridicules the fashionable, exaggerated metaphors some of Shakespeare's fellow poets were using to describe the women they loved: Your eyes are suns that set me on fire, your cheeks are roses, your breasts are white as snow. Such metaphors, known as **conceits**, are traceable to Petrarch, but by 1600 they had become, through overuse, tiresome or laughable. (Note that the word *mistress* in this poem simply meant "girlfriend" in the Renaissance.)

Sonnet 130
William Shakespeare

My mistress' eyes are nothing like the sun,
Coral is far more red than her lips' red.
If snow be white, why then her breasts are dun,°
If hairs be wires, black wires grow on her head.
5 I have seen roses damasked,° red and white,
But no such roses see I in her cheeks.
And in some perfumes is there more delight
Than in the breath that from my mistress reeks,
I love to hear her speak, yet well I know
10 That music hath a far more pleasing sound.
I grant I never saw a goddess go,
My mistress, when she walks, treads on the ground.
    And yet, by Heaven, I think my love as rare
    As any she belied° with false compare.

3. **dun** *adj.*: dull, grayish brown.

5. **damasked** *v.*: variegated in two colors.

14. **belied** *v.*: misrepresented.

The Lady with the Ermine (15th century) by Leonardo da Vinci.
Czartoryski Museum, Krakow, Poland/The Bridgeman Art Library.

Response and Analysis

Thinking Critically

SKILLS FOCUS

Literary Skills Analyze the characteristics of Shakespearean sonnets.

Writing Skills Write a response to a sonnet. Write an essay comparing and contrasting two sonnets.

1. Do you think the speaker's loved one in Shakespeare's Sonnet 130 is actually unattractive? Why or why not?
2. Sonnet 130 could have been written by someone who had read too many **Petrarchan sonnets.** What details in the sonnet poke fun at sonnet conventions?
3. Why is the **couplet** absolutely necessary to keep Shakespeare's Sonnet 130 from being misunderstood?
4. Which remarks in Shakespeare's sonnet did you find humorous?

WRITING

A Reply

Suppose you are the beloved of the speaker of Shakespeare's Sonnet 130. Write a **response** to his description of you, or write a comic **description** of another beloved who falls short of perfection.

284   Collection 3   The Renaissance

Literary Criticism

Critic's Commentary: Influences
Shakespeare biographer Park Honan offers confirmation that Petrarchan conceits were considered trite in Shakespeare's time. Honan quotes Renaissance author George Gascoigne: "If I should undertake to wryte in praysse of a gentlewoman, I would neither praise hir christal eye, nor hir cherrie lippe, &c. For these things are *trita & obvia* . . . I would

Louise Labé's Sonnet 23 is written in the style of Petrarch and responds to the conceits that Shakespeare mocks in Sonnet 130. Labé (1524?–1566), a wealthy and well-educated Frenchwoman, was married to an elderly manufacturer. Two unhappy love affairs might explain the tone of her sonnet.

Sonnet 23

Louise Labé

translated by **Willis Barnstone**

What good is it to me if long ago
you eloquently praised my golden hair,
compared my eyes and beauty to the flare
of two suns where, you say, love bent the bow,
5   sending the darts that needled you with grief?
Where are your tears that faded in the ground?
Your death? by which your constant love is bound
in oaths and honor now beyond belief?
Your brutal goal was to make *me* a slave
10   beneath the ruse° of being served by you.
Pardon me, friend, and for once hear me through:
I am outraged with anger and I rave.
Yet I am sure, wherever you have gone,
your martyrdom is hard as my black dawn.

10. **ruse** *n.:* trick.

Portrait of a Young Woman (1569) (detail).
Tate Gallery, London/Art Resource, New York.

WRITING

Sonnets Side by Side

How does Louise Labé's sonnet compare with Shakespeare's Sonnet 130? To gather details for your **comparison,** fill out a chart like the following one. Use the block method to write your comparison: First, tell how Shakespeare uses the following elements of poetry; then, tell how Labé uses them.

	Shakespeare	Labé
Speaker		
Person addressed		
Images		
Tone		
Message		
Sonnet form		

▶ Use "Comparing and Contrasting Literature," pages 784–791, for help with this assignment.

INTERNET
Projects and Activities
Keyword: LE5 12-3

Summary ⟷ *at grade level*

In Labé's Sonnet 23, the speaker bitterly describes her "black dawn"—her awakening to the idea that a lover seeming to serve her (through tears, vows, and compliments) was really gaining power over her. Now he is gone, and she is furious.

DIRECT TEACHING

A Literary Focus

❓ **Petrarchan sonnet.** In the octave, or first eight lines, the speaker reminds a former lover of his extravagant flattery and vows of love to her. How would you describe the speaker's tone, or attitude, toward him now? [Possible responses: sarcastic; angry; reproachful; ironic; mocking.]

B Literary Focus

❓ **Petrarchan sonnet.** In the metaphor in the last line, what do you think the speaker is comparing to a "black dawn"? [Possible response: her angry awakening to the fact that she has been manipulated]

---

undertake to aunswere for any imperfection that shee hath, and thereupon rayse the prayse of hir commendacion." Invite students to re-read Shakespeare's Sonnet 18 (p. 277) and Sonnet 130. Ask students to find specific examples in these sonnets that suggest Shakespeare shared Gascoigne's ideas.

Comparing and Contrasting Texts

Comparing themes. Labé's Sonnet 23 and Shakespeare's Sonnet 130 both use irony to mock trite conceit. Labé's speaker rages at insincere words of love ("What good is it to me . . ."), and Shakespeare's speaker denounces as "false" the exaggerations in most love poetry. Ask students to compare how the final couplets of each sonnet are different in meaning.

PRETEACHING

Summary at grade level

"Blow, Blow, Thou Winter Wind," sung by the outcast Amiens, compares ingratitude and disloyalty to winter cold. The tone is upbeat, with the chorus calling life "most jolly" despite human failings.

In "Fear No More the Heat o' the Sun," the brothers Guiderius and Arviragus tenderly mourn their sister Imogen. They list earthly cares from which her apparent death has freed her and wish her an undisturbed rest. The chorus stresses that all humans must eventually "come to dust."

In "Full Fathom Five," Ariel describes the drowning of Prince Ferdinand's father as a magical transformation.

Skills Starter

Motivate. Invite students to recite their favorite song lyrics from a movie soundtrack. You might encourage students to bring in recordings and play them for the class. Discuss the characteristics of the words and music in relation to the functions that they serve in the film: to enhance characterization or setting, to intensify a mood, or to advance action.

Before You Read

Songs from Shakespeare

Make the Connection

In Shakespeare's time, when people went to the Globe, the Swan, or any other London theater, they expected not only to see a tragedy or comedy performed but also to hear music, both vocal and instrumental. Shakespeare included a great variety of songs in his plays: some melancholy, some comic, some thoughtful. Each song is particularly adapted to the play and scene in which it appears and to the character who performs it.

Think of the ways songs and instrumental music are used in films, television programs, and plays today. What various purposes—dramatic and otherwise—do such songs serve in the context of the larger work?

Literary Focus
Dramatic Song

The **songs** in Shakespeare's plays are the best of this kind that have come down to us, for Shakespeare excelled in lyric and dramatic poetry. Shakespeare's songs serve a variety of dramatic purposes: Some advance the play's action; some help establish the mood of a scene; some reveal character. The songs, which use a variety of poetic techniques, rely heavily on **onomatopoeia**, language that sounds like what it means.

INTERNET
More About William Shakespeare
Keyword: LE5 12-3

SKILLS FOCUS

Literary Skills
Understand the characteristics of dramatic songs.

A **dramatic song** is a type of poem found in many of Shakespeare's plays. The songs serve to advance the action, create a mood, or reveal character. Like most songs, the dramatic songs rely on a variety of poetic techniques.

For more on Dramatic Song, see the Handbook of Literary and Historical Terms.

Background

Although many of Shakespeare's songs are written for female characters, all the women's roles in the plays were filled by boys. These were boys who had been trained to sing as well as act and who probably sang in high, pure voices that sounded very feminine. Unfortunately, most of the original music for the songs has been lost, but just as the plays themselves have inspired many composers of music for opera, orchestra, and ballet, so have the songs from the plays been set to music by many composers, right up to the present time.

Couple courting, from a Bible manuscript said to have been owned by Pope John XXII (15th century).
The Art Archive/Musée Atger Montpellier/Dagli Orti.

286 Collection 3 The Renaissance

DIFFERENTIATING INSTRUCTION

Learners Having Difficulty

Play the audio versions of Shakespeare's songs for students. Then you might go over the songs line by line, examining unfamiliar words and phrasings. Encourage students to identify the main ideas expressed in each song and the mood that each creates.

English-Language Learners

After students have listened to the audio versions of the songs, you might have students read aloud as you play the audio versions a second or third time. Encourage students to identify the rhymes, alliteration, and assonance that they hear.

A character named Amiens sings this song in As You Like It *(Act II, Scene 7), a comedy about a group of sophisticated courtiers exiled from their palaces and living in a very comfortable wilderness, the Forest of Arden. This song makes a playful comment on a common human failing: ingratitude. In comparison with people's ungrateful behavior, the cruel winter weather seems kind.*

Blow, Blow, Thou Winter Wind

William Shakespeare

    Blow, blow, thou winter wind,°
    Thou art not so unkind
        As man's ingratitude;
    Thy tooth is not so keen,
5   Because thou art not seen,
        Although thy breath be rude.
Heigh-ho! Sing, heigh-ho! Unto the green holly:
Most friendship is feigning, most loving mere folly:
        Then, heigh-ho, the holly!
10 This life is most jolly.

    Freeze, freeze, thou bitter sky,
    That dost not bite so nigh
        As benefits forgot:
    Though thou the waters warp°
15 Thy sting is not so sharp
        As friend remembered not.
Heigh-ho! Sing, heigh-ho! Unto the green holly:
Most friendship is feigning, most loving mere folly:
        Then, heigh-ho, the holly!
20 This life is most jolly.

1. **wind** *n.:* pronounced to rhyme with *find.*
14. **warp** *v.:* make rough by freezing.

Winter by William Blake.
© Tate Gallery, London/Art Resource, New York.

DIRECT TEACHING

A Literary Focus
Dramatic song. This verse personifies the winter wind as keen of tooth, rude of breath, and unkind—but what, according to the singer, is even more unkind? ["man's ingratitude"]

B Literary Focus
Dramatic song. In the chorus, what statements does the singer make about friendship and love? [Most friendship is phony; most love is foolishness.] Which words show his attitude toward human failings? [He says, "Heigh-ho" and "life is most jolly," suggesting an attitude of cheerful acceptance.]

C Literary Focus
Dramatic song. Where in the chorus do you find alliteration? [with the words *heigh-ho* and *holly*; *friendship, feigning,* and *folly*; *loving* and *life*] Notice that this melodic sound effect adds to the light tone.

D Literary Focus
Dramatic song. In *As You Like It,* two power-hungry characters turn against family and friends such as Amiens. Which words in the second verse directly refer to this unpleasant behavior? ["benefits forgot"; "friend remembered not"]

Advanced Learners
Enrichment. You might encourage students to read the specific acts in *As You Like It, Cymbeline,* and *The Tempest* in which the songs appear (see citations on Student Edition pages). By reading the acts, students will gain a deeper understanding of the characters who sing the songs, the action surrounding the songs, and the settings in which the songs are presented.

DIRECT TEACHING

A Literary Focus

? Dramatic song. The brothers do not yet know that they are princes, but the heartfelt sorrow of their dirge would have suggested to Elizabethan audiences that the brothers were nobly born. Which ideas from this verse have you heard in funeral speeches of our own time? [Possible responses: the idea that death is a release from fear or suffering, an end to work on earth, a return home, a time to reap rewards.]

B Content-Area Connections

History: Child Labor
In Renaissance Europe, impoverished parents might apprentice children as young as four or five to chimney sweeps. The youngsters, poorly cared for so that they would stay small, were forced down the tightest chimneys, inhaling soot as they worked. Their lives contrasted starkly with those of the "golden lads and girls" of the aristocracy.

C Literary Focus

? Dramatic song. From which difficult aspects of society is the dead person now free? [from the need to fear those in power; from worries about food and clothing]

This song in Shakespeare's late play *Cymbeline* (Act IV, Scene 2) is recited, not sung, by two young princes, Guiderius and Arviragus. They claim they cannot sing because their voices have suddenly "got the mannish crack" or, as we would say, have started to change. So they take turns reciting the lines, as indicated, over the body of their sister Imogen, who looks very dead but as it turns out later has only drunk a sleeping potion.

The song is an **elegy**—a kind of poem lamenting the dead and consoling the living. When such a poem is designed to be sung or performed at a funeral, it is usually called a **dirge**. Some of the content of this particular dirge is traditional. One of its themes, that of "death the leveler," makes the point that we all—high and low, rich and poor—die. Its other theme is called the consolation theme. It recounts unpleasant experiences in life from which the dead person is free.

Fear No More the Heat o' the Sun

William Shakespeare

Guiderius Fear no more the heat o' the sun
 Nor the furious winter's rages;
 Thou thy worldly task hast done,
 Home art gone, and ta'en thy wages.
5 Golden lads and girls all must,
 As° chimney sweepers, come to dust.

Arviragus Fear no more the frown o' the great;
 Thou art past the tyrant's stroke.
 Care no more to clothe and eat;
10 To thee the reed° is as the oak.
 The scepter, learning, physic, must
 All follow this and come to dust.

Guiderius Fear no more the lightning flash—
Arviragus Nor th' all-dreaded thunderstone;°
15 **Guiderius** Fear not slander, censure rash;

6. **as** *prep.:* like.

10. **reed** *n.:* proverbially frail plant.

14. **thunderstone** *n.:* type of stone, formerly associated with the noise of thunder.

288 Collection 3 The Renaissance

Literary Criticism

Critic's Commentary: Park Honan
Critic and biographer Park Honan maintains that "Fear No More . . ." provides a fitting elegy for Shakespeare himself: "A sufferer with typhoid fever knows . . . terrible thirst and discomfort. The features begin to shrivel. Whatever the cause of his own fever, Shakespeare's face in the effigy at Holy Trinity seems to be modeled on a death-mask. His eyes stare, the face is heavy, and the nose is small and sharp. Because of the shrinkage of the muscles . . . the upper lip is elongated. . . . But his sufferings were over, and the speeches of the exiled brothers, Arviragus and Guiderius, in Act IV of *Cymbeline,* might well do for his epitaph. . . ."

Encourage students to re-read Shakespeare's biography on pp. 272–274 and to identify events and details in his life to which phrases from "Fear No More . . ." might apply.

Arviragus	Thou hast finished joy and moan.
Both	All lovers young, all lovers must Consign to° thee and come to dust.
Guiderius	No exorciser° harm thee!
20 **Arviragus**	Nor no witchcraft charm thee!
Guiderius	Ghost unlaid° forbear thee!
Arviragus	Nothing ill come near thee!
Both	Quiet consummation° have, And renowned be thy grave!

18. **consign to:** agree with.
19. **exorciser** *n.:* conjurer; magician.
21. **unlaid** *v.:* not properly laid to rest in the grave, condemned to walk the earth forever.
23. **consummation** *n.:* finality.

Time (c. 1500–1510). French tapestry (338.9 cm × 739.1 cm). Tapestry weave: wool and silk. The inscription, translated from the French, reads, "Sometimes we see Time adorned with green foliage, as pleasant as an angel; and then suddenly he changes and becomes very strange. Never does Time persist in one state."
© The Cleveland Museum of Art, 2002, Gift from Various Donors and by Exchange, 1960.176.3.

DIRECT TEACHING

A Learners Having Difficulty

❓ **Reading inverted sentences.** Lines 1 and 2 invert standard English sentence order. How might you paraphrase these lines, using standard order and more familiar wording? (Hint: *Full fathom five* means "at the bottom of the sea.") [Possible response: Your father lies at the bottom of the sea; coral is being made from his bones.]

B Literary Focus

❓ **Dramatic song.** What changes is death bringing about, according to Ariel? [The dead person is turning into jewels.] How does this view of death differ from that expressed in the chorus of "Fear No More . . ."? [In "Fear No More . . . ," the chorus says that death reduces everyone to dust, whereas here death transforms a person into treasure.]

C English-Language Learners

❓ **Building background knowledge.** Sea nymphs are beautiful, imaginary ocean creatures. What does his reference to them suggest about Ariel? [Possible responses: He is playful and magical; he likes fanciful ideas.]

D Literary Focus

❓ **Dramatic song.** What sound effects do you notice here? [*Ding-dong* is onomatopoeic; *hark* and *hear* show alliteration.]

Ariel, the "airy spirit" of The Tempest, *sings this brief song in Act I, Scene 2, to Prince Ferdinand, who has lost his father at sea in the dreadful storm that opens the play. But the father is not really dead. Unknown to Ferdinand, he has been washed up onto the island on which the play takes place.*

Full Fathom Five
William Shakespeare

    A Full fathom five thy father lies;
        Of his bones are coral made:
      Those are pearls that were his eyes:
    B   Nothing of him that doth fade,
5 But doth suffer a sea change
      Into something rich and strange.
    C Sea nymphs hourly ring his knell:°
        Ding-dong.
    D Hark! I hear them—Ding-dong, bell.

7. **knell** (nel) *n.:* tolling of bells at a funeral.

DEVELOPING FLUENCY

Mixed-ability group activity. Shakespeare's songs are ideal for choral reading. Place students in mixed-ability groups to plan, practice, and present their readings. You might assign one song to each group. Have groups start by choosing the mood they want to create. Then, have them decide which lines will be read by one person, which by two or more, which words and phrases to emphasize, where to pause, and so on. Students might select background music to accompany their readings. If possible, videotape or tape-record their presentations.

Response and Analysis

Songs from Shakespeare

Thinking Critically

1. What aspects of human nature does the singer of "Blow, Blow" criticize?
2. How does man's bite compare with winter's in "Blow, Blow"?
3. The song "Blow, Blow" is sung by a character named Amiens. What would you say this song reveals about Amiens's **character**?
4. **Personification** is when a nonhuman thing or quality is talked about as if it were human. What details personify the wind and the sky in "Blow, Blow"?
5. How does the merry-sounding chorus of "Blow, Blow" affect the impression created by the preceding verses?
6. According to the dirge "Fear No More," what are the advantages of being dead? What are the dangers?
7. Identify the lines in "Fear No More" that convey the **theme** of death as a leveler—a force that makes all people equal in the end.
8. Re-read the famous **simile** in lines 5–6 of "Fear No More." How are the "golden lads and girls" different from "chimney sweepers"? How are these two types of people also the same?
9. When the singer of "Fear No More" refers to *scepter, learning,* and *physic* in line 11, he is using a figure of speech called **metonymy** (mə·tän′ə·mē)—something closely related to a person or thing is substituted for the person or thing itself. When we say, "The White House vetoed the bill," we are using metonymy. We are substituting something closely associated with the president (the White House) for the president himself. What professions do the words in line 11 refer to?
10. "Thy father"—the subject of "Full Fathom Five"—is King Alonso, a thoroughly bad man who, in the course of the play, becomes a good man. What other "sea changes" are identified in this dirge?
11. Which lines of "Full Fathom Five" suggest that Ariel has a playful and cheerful character?
12. Identify the **alliteration** in the first line of "Full Fathom Five." What other **sound effects** do you hear in this song?
13. Think about the subjects of these three songs. Do songs today deal with these same subjects? Could these songs be put in modern musical settings? Discuss your responses.

WRITING
Song Sense

"Blow, Blow" is probably one of the first dramatic songs to characterize the singer. Since Shakespeare's day this practice has been commonplace in musicals and operas—even rock operas. Find the lyrics of a song from a musical that is sung by a particular character and reveals something about that character's personality or nature. Write a brief **interpretation** of the character based on the song's lyrics. If you can find a recording of the song, play it for the class, and then share your interpretation.

LISTENING AND SPEAKING
Sounds Like Shakespeare

Select one of these songs and one of the sonnets, and prepare them for a performance before a group of classmates. You will have to decide if you want to do a solo reading, a group reading, or a choral reading. The refrains, for example, could be read by a chorus. Be sure to think carefully about how you will use your voice, where you will speak loudly or softly, and where you will pause or come to a full stop. What words or lines in the poems do you think should receive emphasis?

Literary Skills
Analyze the characteristics of dramatic songs.

Writing Skills
Write a character interpretation.

Listening and Speaking Skills
Present an oral interpretation of a sonnet and a dramatic song.

INDEPENDENT PRACTICE

Response and Analysis

8. "Golden lads and girls" are wealthy and pampered; "chimney sweepers" are exploited and poor. Both groups "must . . . come to dust."
9. *Scepter* stands for a monarch; *learning*, for a scholar; and *physic*, for a specialist in medicine.
10. Alonso's bones turn into coral, and his eyes turn into pearls.
11. Lines 7–9, with their fanciful image of a death knell rung by sea nymphs, suggest Ariel's cheerful and playful nature.
12. The words *full, fathom, five,* and *father* alliterate. Other sound effects include more alliteration (*s* and *ch* sounds in ll. 5–6), rhyme (*change* and *strange*), assonance (long *i* in *five, thy, lies*), and onomatopoeia ("Ding-dong, bell").
13. Students will probably conclude that songs today also deal with unfaithfulness, coming to terms with death, and inexplicable changes.

ASSESSING

Assessment
- Holt Assessment: Literature, Reading, and Vocabulary

Thinking Critically

1. The singer criticizes ingratitude, feigned friendship, insincere love, and forgetfulness.
2. Man's bite is harsher.
3. Amiens sees human failings realistically but is lighthearted; some students may say he seems sarcastic.
4. The wind has a keen "tooth" and rude "breath"; the sky can "bite."
5. The merry chorus contrasts with the bitter verse and lightens it.
6. *Advantages*—freedom from cares about weather, whims of rulers, food, clothing, slander, censure. *Dangers*—magicians, witchcraft, ghosts.
7. The theme of death as a leveler appears in ll. 5–6, 11–12, and 17–18.

PRETEACHING

Summary ⇔ at grade level

In "To be, or not to be," the overburdened young prince considers whether to avenge his father's murder and whether to go on living at all. Death seems a relief until he reflects that conscience might torment him, even in the grave.

In "Tomorrow, and tomorrow, and tomorrow," the king responds to his approaching doom by reflecting on the meaningless of life: "a life . . . Signifying nothing."

In the Saint Crispin's Day Speech, Henry rallies his outnumbered, exhausted troops by inspiring courage and stressing honor even over victory.

In "Our revels now are ended," Prospero comments on a pageant that he conjured but then caused to vanish. Using theater as a metaphor, he suggests that life, like a play, is "gorgeous" and "solemn," yet fleeting and insubstantial.

Selection Starter

Build background. You might point out that monologues often mark turning points in plays. To help students grasp the power inherent in dramatic monologue, remind them of the impact that real-life speeches have had on modern history. Mention, for example, Churchill's "Blood, Sweat, and Tears" speech or King's "I Have a Dream" speech, and discuss the effects on the audience.

Before You Read

Famous Shakespearean Speeches

Make the Connection

What do you do when you want to think through a personal problem or experience or analyze your feelings? Do you talk to a friend or relative, write an e-mail, or sit down with your journal? In drama, characters often express their thoughts and conflicts in long speeches, called soliloquies and monologues.

Literary Focus
Monologue and Soliloquy

Most of the words spoken in a play occur in conversation, or verbal exchange between characters—that is, in dialogue. Renaissance playwrights frequently used two other devices for revealing to an audience a dramatic character's thoughts and feelings: monologues and soliloquies. A **monologue** is a long, usually formal speech spoken by one character to another character or the audience. A **soliloquy** (sə·lil′ə·kwē) is a meditative kind of monologue in which the speaker, usually alone onstage, shares his or her true inner thoughts and feelings directly with the audience.

INTERNET
More About William Shakespeare
Keyword: LE5 12-3

SKILLS FOCUS

Literary Skills
Understand the uses of monologue and soliloquy in drama.

A **monologue** is a long speech made by one character in a play to another character or the audience.

In the type of monologue known as a **soliloquy,** a single character, usually alone onstage, speaks directly to the audience about his or her private thoughts and feelings.

For more on Monologue and Soliloquy, see the Handbook of Literary and Historical Terms.

Background

The Elizabethan soliloquy, or solo speech, derives from classical sources, particularly the Latin orations that Shakespeare and his contemporaries studied as schoolboys and later imitated when writing their plays. It was Shakespeare, however, who developed the art of the soliloquy far beyond anything his predecessors or contemporaries accomplished. Particularly in his great tragedies, he overcame the natural artificiality of the soliloquy (people do not usually speak their thoughts out loud in poetic, formal language). He did this by making the words and rhythms fit his characters and their situations, so that the speeches sound completely natural.

An actor stepping to the front of the stage to deliver a soliloquy, at the new Globe Theatre on London's South Bank.

DIFFERENTIATING INSTRUCTION

Learners Having Difficulty
Tell students that some lines from these speeches are famous because speakers and writers have quoted or alluded to them so often over the centuries. You might read the lines aloud, write them on the chalkboard, and then have students identify them in context as they read. Use ll. 1, 3, 10, and 28 from "To be, or not to be"; ll. 1, 6–8, and 8–10 from "Tomorrow, and tomorrow, and tomorrow"; ll. 11–12 and 43 from Saint Crispin's Day speech; and ll. 11–13 from "Our revels now are ended."

Invite learners having difficulty to read Saint Crispin's Day speech in interactive format in *The Holt Reader* and to use the sidenotes as aids to understanding the selection.

English-Language Learners
To build students' background knowledge, take extra time to go over the headnote for each speech. Discuss unfamiliar terms and idioms. You might ask students to paraphrase the headnotes. If possible, show video clips of modern actors giving the speeches. The actors' gestures, intonations, and phrasing will help to demystify Shakespeare's English.

Hamlet, the young prince of Denmark, has been told by the ghost of his father (the elder Hamlet) that his uncle, Claudius, now married to Hamlet's mother, murdered the elder Hamlet. The prince is plagued by doubts, conflicting impulses, and confusing emotions. He both desires and fears to take revenge on his uncle. In this most famous of Shakespearean soliloquies, Hamlet weighs the case for action against inaction. The soliloquy is from Hamlet, *Act III, Scene 1.*

To be, or not to be
William Shakespeare

Hamlet.
To be, or not to be—that is the question.
Whether 'tis nobler in the mind to suffer
The slings and arrows of outrageous° fortune,
Or to take arms against a sea of troubles,
5   And by opposing end them. To die, to sleep—
No more, and by a sleep to say we end
The heartache and the thousand natural shocks
That flesh is heir to. 'Tis a consummation°
Devoutly to be wished. To die, to sleep,
10   To sleep—perchance to dream. Aye, there's the rub,°
For in that sleep of death what dreams may come
When we have shuffled off this mortal coil°
Must give us pause. There's the respect
That makes calamity of so long life.°
15   For who would bear the whips and scorns of time,
The oppressor's wrong, the proud man's contumely,°
The pangs of despised love, the law's delay,
The insolence of office, and the spurns
That patient merit of the unworthy takes,°
20   When he himself might his quietus° make
With a bare bodkin?° Who would fardels° bear,
To grunt and sweat under a weary life,
But that the dread of something after death,
The undiscovered country from whose bourn
25   No traveler returns, puzzles the will,
And makes us rather bear those ills we have
Than fly to others that we know not of?

3. **outrageous** *adj.:* cruel.

8. **consummation** *n.:* ending.

10. **rub** *n.:* obstacle.

12. **coil** *n.:* turmoil (but also life's entanglements).
13–14. **the respect...life:** the reason that makes living so long a calamity; also, the reason that makes calamity so long-lived.
16. **contumely** *n.:* insult.
18–19. **the spurns...takes:** the insults from the unworthy that people of merit must endure patiently.
20. **quietus** (kwī·ēt′əs) *n.:* release.
21. **bare bodkin:** mere dagger (less likely meaning is "unsheathed dagger"). **fardels** *n. pl.:* burdens.

DIRECT TEACHING

A Literary Focus

? Monologue and soliloquy. Hamlet is considering the dangerous act of attacking the king, his uncle. How does the possibility of death affect his attempt to decide, according to these lines? [It weakens his resolve and forestalls his taking action.]

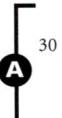

Thus conscience does make cowards of us all,
And thus the native hue° of resolution
30 Is sicklied o'er with the pale cast° of thought,
And enterprises of great pitch and moment
With this regard their currents turn awry
And lose the name of action. . . .°

29. **native hue:** reddish complexion.
30. **cast** *n.:* color.
32–33. **with...action:** Brooding on this thought causes great enterprises to be diverted from their course and left undone.

Kevin Kline as Hamlet, performed for the New York Shakespeare Festival.
Martha Swope/Timepix.

DEVELOPING FLUENCY

Paired activity. Pair students, and ask each pair to prepare two oral readings of "To be, or not to be": one suggesting that Hamlet, in the course of the soliloquy, decides to try to kill his uncle, and the other suggesting that Hamlet decides not to. Remind students that variations in timing, voice pitch and volume, posture, and facial expression can help to convey underlying thoughts and feelings. Have each pair of students present both readings to the class, and challenge the class to guess which is which.

This scene, from Act V, Scene 5, of Macbeth, *occurs after a long series of betrayals and murders, set in motion by Macbeth and his wife. Now, having gained the throne of Scotland through violence and treachery, the two are racked with guilt and fear of their enemies. Lady Macbeth, sleepless and haunted, takes her own life. Preoccupied with the approach of the rightful heirs to the throne and their armed allies, Macbeth, alone in his castle, reacts to the news of his wife's death with this soliloquy.*

Tomorrow, and tomorrow, and tomorrow

William Shakespeare

Macbeth.
Tomorrow, and tomorrow, and tomorrow
Creeps in this petty pace from day to day,
To the last syllable of recorded time;
And all our yesterdays have lighted fools
5 The way to dusty death. Out, out, brief candle!
Life's but a walking shadow, a poor player
That struts and frets his hour upon the stage
And then is heard no more. It is a tale
Told by an idiot, full of sound and fury,
10 Signifying nothing.

Raul Julia as Macbeth, performed for the New York Shakespeare Festival.
Martha Swope/Timepix.

DIRECT TEACHING

A Literary Focus

Monologue and soliloquy. What examples do you find in ll. 1–5 of repetition and alliteration? [*Repetition:* tomorrow; day, (yester)day. *Alliteration:* petty and pace; day, dusty, and death.] Notice how these sound effects give the soliloquy a musical quality. It is almost as much a dirge as a speech.

B Literary Focus

Monologue and soliloquy. To what does Macbeth compare life in l. 5? [a candle]

C Literary Focus

Monologue and soliloquy. What feeling about his own life is Macbeth expressing in these lines? [Possible responses: despair; indifference; disgust.]

D Content-Area Connections

Literature: Echoes of Shakespeare
In 1929, William Faulkner published a novel showing the degeneration of a once-great family in the American South. A large part of the novel uses stream of consciousness to represent the thoughts of a man of very low intelligence. Alluding to Macbeth's soliloquy, Faulkner titled this novel *The Sound and the Fury*.

CONTENT-AREA CONNECTIONS

History: Shakespeare's Sources
The characters Macbeth and Henry V (pp. 295, 296) are based on real people, though Shakespeare shaped the historical facts to suit his dramatic purposes. One of his sources of information was *Chronicles of England, Scotland, and Ireland,* by Raphael Holinshead, first published in 1577.
Mixed-ability group activity. Invite students to brainstorm questions they would like to ask about the real Macbeth and Henry V. [Possible questions: Why did Macbeth usurp the throne of Scotland? What finally happened to him? Did King Henry and his troops win at Agincourt? What else happened during his reign?] Then, place students in mixed-ability groups. Have each group choose and research a question and present findings to the class.

William Shakespeare

DIRECT TEACHING

A Literary Focus
Monologue and soliloquy. King Henry addresses the earl of Westmorland, but Westmorland stands among other officers, one of whom is accompanied by all his troops; thus, the speech reaches the ears of a great many English soldiers.

B Literary Focus
❓ **Monologue and soliloquy.** According to Henry, what are the advantages of having so few soldiers? [If they die, their deaths will indeed be a loss to England but not so great as would be if their number were greater. If they live, they will each earn more honor than they would if there were many more of them.]

C Literary Focus
❓ **Monologue and soliloquy.** What does Henry say he values above all else? [honor] In the rest of the speech, look for evidence that he is an honorable person.

D Literary Focus
❓ **Monologue and soliloquy.** How will the king deal with English soldiers who want to avoid the battle? [He will let them leave, with money and a passport.] How do you think the king's offer might affect disheartened soldiers? [Possible response: It might come as a relief, shame them, or rally them.]

Young Prince Hal assumes the throne of England at the death of his father and becomes King Henry V. To consolidate his power at home, the new king decides to cross the English Channel and seize the French crown, which he believes rightfully belongs to England. Under Henry's able leadership the small but brave English army defeats the French forces at Harfleur. Now sick, tired, and underfed, Henry's troops face a much larger French force at Agincourt.

A noble has just wished aloud that the English had more fighting men. This is the king's answer, from *Henry V*, Act IV, Scene 3.

Saint Crispin's Day Speech
William Shakespeare

King.
What's° he that wishes so?
My cousin Westmorland? No, my fair cousin.
If we are marked to die, we are enough
To do our country loss; and if to live,
5   The fewer men, the greater share of honor.
God's will, I pray thee, wish not one man more.
By Jove, I am not covetous for gold,
Nor care I who doth feed upon my cost;
It yearns° me not if men my garments wear;
10   Such outward things dwell not in my desires.
But if it be a sin to covet honor
I am the most offending soul alive.
No, faith, my coz, wish not a man from England.
God's peace, I would not lose so great an honor
15   As one man more, methinks, would share from me
For the best hope I have. O, do not wish one more!
Rather proclaim it, Westmorland, through my host°
That he which hath no stomach to this fight,
Let him depart; his passport shall be made
20   And crowns for convoy put into his purse.
We would not die in that man's company
That fears his fellowship to die with us.

1. **what's:** who's.

9. **yearns** *v.:* saddens.

17. **host** *n.:* army.

296   Collection 3   The Renaissance

READING MINI-LESSON

Developing Word-Attack Skills
Direct students' attention to ll. 40–42 in the Saint Crispin's Day speech from *Henry V*: "And Crispin Crispian shall ne'er go by, / From this day to the ending of the world, / But we in it shall be rememberèd...." Read the lines, and note that *–ed* in *rememberèd* is pronounced as a separate syllable: /ri•mem´bər•id/ instead of /ri•mem´bərd/. In some editions there is an accent mark over the e that indicates how to pronounce the syllable to fit the rhythm of the line.

Remind students that *–ed* usually adds the sound /d/ or /t/ to a word. It is pronounced as a separate syllable only in words that end with /d/ or /t/ in their base form, such as *minded* and *waited*. There are some words that don't

This day is called the Feast of Crispian.°
He that outlives this day and comes safe home
25 Will stand a-tiptoe when this day is named
And rouse him at the name of Crispian.
He that shall see this day and live old age
Will yearly on the vigil feast his neighbors
And say, "Tomorrow is Saint Crispian."
30 Then will he strip his sleeve and show his scars,
And say, "These wounds I had on Crispin's Day."
Old men forget; yet all shall be forgot,
But he'll remember with advantages°
What feats he did that day. Then shall our names,
35 Familiar in his mouth as household words—
Harry the King, Bedford and Exeter,
Warwick and Talbot, Salisbury and Gloucester—
Be in their flowing cups freshly remembered.
This story shall the good man teach his son;
40 And Crispin Crispian shall ne'er go by,
From this day to the ending of the world,
But we in it shall be rememberèd—
We few, we happy few, we band of brothers.
For he today that sheds his blood with me
45 Shall be my brother; be he ne'er so vile,
This day shall gentle his condition.°
And gentlemen in England now abed
Shall think themselves accursed they were not here,
And hold their manhoods cheap whiles any speaks
50 That fought with us upon Saint Crispin's Day.

23. **Feast of Crispian:** Saint Crispin's Day, October 25. Crispinus and Crispianus were martyrs who fled Rome in the third century. Because they worked as shoemakers, they became that craft's patron saints after they were martyred.

33. **advantages** *n. pl.:* additions of his own.

46. **gentle his condition:** bring him up to the position of gentleman.

Andre Braugher as Henry V, performed for the New York Shakespeare Festival (1996).

fit this pattern—that is, words in which final *–ed* is pronounced as a separate syllable even though the base words do not end with /d/ or /t/. These words are usually adjectives. *Wicked* is an example.
Activity. Have students identify the word in each sentence in which *–ed* is pronounced as a separate syllable. Answers are underlined.

1. The <u>wicked</u> merchant tricked everyone.
2. He <u>unashamedly</u> claimed his elixir possessed miraculous powers.
3. It turned fools into <u>learned</u> men.
4. Limbs that looked weak and <u>crooked</u> were made strong.
5. With brash and <u>dogged</u> boldness, he bragged that it could cure any ill.

Portrait of a lady with a large ruff. The armillary sphere in the background was used to teach the concepts of astronomy (16th century). English School.

Johnny van Haeften Gallery, London.

Song

John Donne

Go, and catch a falling star,
    Get with child a mandrake° root,
Tell me, where all past years are,
    Or who cleft° the devil's foot,
5 Teach me to hear mermaids° singing,
Or to keep off envy's stinging,
        And find
        What wind
Serves to advance an honest mind.

10 If thou be'st born to strange sights,
    Things invisible to see,
Ride ten thousand days and nights,
    Till age snow white hairs on thee,
Thou, when thou return'st, wilt tell me
15 All strange wonders that befell thee,
        And swear
        Nowhere
Lives a woman true, and fair.

If thou find'st one, let me know,
20   Such a pilgrimage were sweet;
Yet do not, I would not go,
    Though at next door we might meet,
Though she were true, when you met her,
And last, till you write your letter,
25   Yet she
       Will be
False, ere I come, to two, or three.

2. **mandrake** *n.*: plant whose forked root is said to resemble a human being's torso and legs.
4. **cleft** *v.*: split.
5. **mermaids** *n. pl.*: sirens of Greek mythology. The song of these sea nymphs lured sailors and led them to crash their ships on rocky shores.

Response and Analysis

Thinking Critically

1. To whom is this **speaker** talking? What do you think might have occasioned the writing of the poem?
2. In the second stanza, what does the speaker say his listener will discover about a woman both "true, and fair"?
3. In the last stanza, what does the speaker say he will not do? Why?
4. What **hyperbole**, or exaggeration, does the speaker use to make his points?
5. How would you describe the speaker's **tone**? List at least three words that reveal his attitude. Do you think he is being serious?

WRITING

Coining Commands

Imitate the first stanza of "Song" by constructing some **exaggerated** commands of your own to show the impossibility of something. You might want to respond to the points Donne raises in "Song."

Literary Focus

Metaphysical Poetry

In the nineteenth century, Samuel Coleridge (see page 573) described Donne's inventiveness as a "forge and fire-blast" that could twist "iron pokers into true-love knots." In the 1590s, when Donne started writing, this blazing poetic style was truly revolutionary. Most poets then aimed for sweet, smooth, musical-sounding verse. Donne would have none of that. "I sing not siren-like, to tempt, for I am harsh," he says in one poem. The new style he forged came to be called, by later critics, **metaphysical poetry**—a term that reflected its intensity of intellect, its self-conscious invention, and its bold emotion.

For the most part, Donne based the rhythm and sounds of his poems on colloquial—that is, spoken—English. "For God's sake hold your tongue and let me love," he begins one poem. The speaker in his poems frequently sounds blunt and angry, or he broods to himself, or he seems to be thinking out loud. At times the speaker almost seems to be lecturing the woman he is addressing.

Whatever his tone, Donne's speaker is always using his brains and bringing into the poems ideas from scholarly disciplines, especially philosophy and theology. He also brings in images from everyday activities and trades and from learned disciplines like law, medicine, and science. Reading a metaphysical poem is frequently like figuring out the solution to a riddle—or trying to untangle a complicated knot.

To their critics, metaphysical poets were showoffs. They were accused of writing poems just to display their learning and wit.

Responding to the metaphysical poets. The seventeenth-century poet and critic John Dryden, who disliked it, said metaphysical poetry "perplexed the minds of the fair sex with nice [here meaning 'paltry' or 'foolish'] speculations of philosophy." How do you feel about this kind of intellectual poetry? Can you see a connection between the metaphysical poets' imagery and the art by Escher on page 301? Explain.

Literary Skills
Analyze the characteristics of metaphysical poetry.

Writing Skills
Write an imitation of a metaphysical poem.

INDEPENDENT PRACTICE

Response and Analysis

Thinking Critically

1. The speaker may be talking to a male friend or to men in general. An unhappy romance might have prompted the poem.
2. The listener will discover that no such woman exists.
3. He will not go see the "true, fair" woman if his friend finds her, because even if she lives next door, she will be false to other men before he gets there.
4. The commands in the first stanza, "ten thousand days and nights" in l. 12, and the exaggeration in ll. 25–27 are used to make the speaker's points.
5. Possible answers: A cynical or offensive tone comes through in the statement "Nowhere / Lives a woman true, and fair." Words and phrases that reveal a fanciful or dramatic tone include *mermaids, mandrake root,* and *ten thousand days*. Students may conclude that the speaker does not care about literal truth; he simply wants to point out the rareness of his ideal.

ASSESSING

Assessment

■ *Holt Assessment: Literature, Reading, and Vocabulary*

RETEACHING

For a lesson reteaching author's tone and style, see **Reteaching,** p. 1129A.

PRETEACHING

Summary ⬆ above grade level

The first eight lines urge the wife to behave with quiet dignity when they part, just as virtuous people die without drama or display. The speaker uses elegant metaphysical imagery to describe the relationship as a union of souls so complete that distance cannot separate them.

Skills Starter

Motivate. Have students recall scenes from movies or novels in which partners separate. Have them recall what made these scenes poignant and to note promises the couple made or keepsakes they exchanged.

Selection Starter

Background. Lines 9–16 reflect the cosmology, or worldview, of many Christians in the 1600s. The view held that Earth was the center of the universe and the other heavenly bodies encircled it. Perfection existed only in the heavenly spheres beyond the moon. Life on Earth was "sublunary"—beneath the sphere of the moon—and thus inferior.

VIEWING THE ART

Other portraits by Hans Holbein appear on pp. 232, 236, and 244.
Activity. The ring on the top indicates this portrait is to be worn on a chain. Ask how we remember loved ones today.

Before You Read

A Valediction: Forbidding Mourning

Make the Connection
Quickwrite

Leaving someone you love for a long time is never easy. If this poem is autobiographical—as Izaak Walton, Donne's friend and biographer, claimed—Donne was trying to ease a parting of great pain. The poem is typical of Donne's work in that it is set on a particular dramatic occasion. The speaker, a man about to take a long journey, says goodbye ("valediction") to the woman he loves, telling her not to cry or feel sad ("forbidding mourning").

If you were leaving for a long time, what would you say to someone you love whom you were leaving behind? If you were the one left behind, what would you want to hear? Take notes on your thoughts.

Literary Focus
Metaphysical Conceits

This poem contains the most famous of all **metaphysical conceits.** These are odd and surprising figures of speech in which one thing is compared to another thing that is very much unlike it. The metaphysical poets—as their name suggests—used such conceits for an analytic and psychological investigation of love and life. Here are some examples of these unusual conceits: A lover's tears are newly minted coins; the king's court is a bowling alley; a man is a world; lovers are holy saints. In this poem, the lovers are compared to the two prongs of a compass (the kind used to draw circles in geometry).

> **Metaphysical conceits** are especially complex and clever figures of speech that make surprising connections between two seemingly dissimilar things.
>
> *For more on Conceits, see the Handbook of Literary and Historical Terms.*

Background

Walton said Donne wrote this poem for his wife when he left for a diplomatic mission to France. She urged him not to go because she was pregnant and unwell, but he felt obligated to the mission's leader, Sir Robert Drury. Two days after arriving in Paris, Donne had a vision which he described to Sir Robert: "I have seen my dear wife pass twice by me through this room, with her hair hanging about her shoulders, and a dead child in her arms." A messenger sent back to England returned with the news that "Mrs. Donne . . . after a long and dangerous labor . . . had been delivered of a dead child" on the very day Donne had the vision.

go.hrw.com
INTERNET
More About John Donne
Keyword: LE5 12-3

SKILLS FOCUS
Literary Skills
Understand metaphysical conceits.

Mrs. Pemberton (16th century) by Hans Holbein the Younger.
The Victoria and Albert Museum, London.

304 Collection 3 The Renaissance

DIFFERENTIATING INSTRUCTION

Learners Having Difficulty
Invite learners having difficulty to read "A Valediction: Forbidding Mourning" in interactive format in *The Holt Reader* and to use the sidenotes as aids to understanding the selection. The interactive version provides additional instruction, practice, and assessment of the literary skill taught in the Student Edition. Monitor students' responses to the selection, and correct any misconceptions that arise.

English-Language Learners
Because of the difficulty of this poem, pair English-language learners with advanced learners. Go over the glosses with each pair to be sure they understand them. Then, preteach these idioms and archaic expressions:
- l. 1: *pass . . . away,* meaning "die"
- l. 3: *whilst,* meaning "while"
- l. 7: *'twere,* meaning "it were"
- l. 10: *reckon,* meaning "guess, figure out"
- l. 31: *hearkens,* meaning "listens attentively"

304 Collection 3 The Renaissance

A Valediction: Forbidding Mourning

John Donne

As virtuous men pass mildly away,
    And whisper to their souls, to go,
Whilst some of their sad friends do say,
    The breath goes now, and some say, no:

5 So let us melt, and make no noise,
    No tear-floods, nor sigh-tempests move,
'Twere profanation° of our joys
    To tell the laity° our love.

Moving of th' earth° brings harms and fears,
10   Men reckon what it did and meant,°
But trepidation of the spheres,°
    Though greater far, is innocent.°

Dull sublunary° lovers' love
    (Whose soul° is sense°) cannot admit
15 Absence, because it doth remove
    Those things which elemented° it.

But we by a love, so much refined,
    That ourselves know not what it is,
Interassurèd of the mind,
20   Care less eyes, lips, and hands to miss.

Our two souls therefore, which are one,
    Though I must go, endure not yet
A breach,° but an expansion,
    Like gold to airy thinness beat.

25 If they be two, they are two so
    As stiff twin compasses are two,
Thy soul the fixed foot, makes no show
    To move, but doth, if th' other do.

And though it in the center sit,
30   Yet when the other far doth roam,
It leans, and hearkens after it,
    And grows erect, as that comes home.

Such wilt thou be to me, who must
    Like th' other foot, obliquely° run;
35 Thy firmness° makes my circle just,°
    And makes me end, where I begun.

---

7. **profanation** *n.*: lack of reverence.
8. **laity** *n.*: laypersons; here, those unable to understand the "religion" of true love.
9. **moving of th' earth**: earthquake.
10. **meant**: "What does it mean?" was a question ordinarily asked of any unusual phenomenon.
11. **trepidation of the spheres**: irregularities in the movements of remote heavenly bodies.
12. **innocent** *adj.*: unobserved and harmless compared with earthquakes.
13. **sublunary** *adj.*: under the moon, therefore subject to change.
14. **soul** *n.*: essence. **sense** *n.*: the body with its five senses; that is, purely physical rather than spiritual.
16. **elemented** *v.*: comprised; composed.

23. **breach** *n.*: break; split.

34. **obliquely** *adv.*: off course.
35. **firmness** *n.*: fidelity. **just** *adj.*: perfect. A circle symbolizes perfection, hence wedding rings.

DIRECT TEACHING

A Reading Skills

Inferring. Why does the speaker urge his wife to part from him quietly? [It would spoil the sacredness of their love to display their feelings publicly.]

B Literary Focus

Simile. What comparison does Donne use in the sixth stanza to express the separation of the lovers' souls? [The souls are compared to a lump of gold beaten thinner than paper. Their separation does not resemble a division but instead an expansion into a thin golden foil.]

C Literary Focus

Metaphysical conceit. What comparison do ll. 25–28 make? [These lines compare the husband and wife to the two legs of a compass. The lines suggest that one point remains fixed, while the other circles around it.] Why is this comparison a metaphysical conceit? [It is a clever, complex, and original comparison.]

D Reading Skills

Analyzing. What makes the use of the word *circle* such a perfect choice at the end of this poem? [Possible response: Like perfect love, a circle has no beginning and no end. It is continuous and everlasting. The circle harks back not only to the compass image but also to the orbit of the heavenly bodies, which Donne refers to earlier.]

Special Education Students
For lessons designed for special education students, see *Holt Reading Solutions*.

Advanced Learners
Donne expected his readers to enjoy dissecting a difficult text. Have students identify three challenging stanzas, lines, or metaphors in the poem and offer their own interpretations of them.

Literary Criticism

Critic's Commentary: Metaphysical Conceit
James Winny discusses the metaphysical conceit in ll. 23–24: "No other literary mode . . . could have enabled a poet to describe spiritual being in terms so concrete and yet so closely sympathetic to his argument."

Activity. Have students suggest other ways that Donne could have described "spiritual being."

INDEPENDENT PRACTICE

Response and Analysis

Thinking Critically

1. Paraphrase: Like virtuous men who die peacefully and silently, we should part without tears and rely on the strength of our sacred love. The simile evokes confidence, security.

2. Other couples must be in proximity to each other, but the love between the speaker and his wife can survive separation.

3. The reference to earthquakes underscores the trauma that lovers feel during separation. The separation of the speaker and his wife is like "trepidation of the spheres," movements in the cosmos that go unnoticed on earth.

4. The speaker compares himself and his wife to the two legs of a compass. She leans toward him when he moves away, but he always returns to her at her fixed position in the center of his life. The nature of love, as defined by this conceit, is constancy even as it allows for movement and physical separation.

5. He does so to emphasize their union, harmony, and trust.

6. The references and images of the specialized movements of the planets, the goldsmith's art, and the movements of the parts of the compass all mark this as a metaphysical poem. The surprising comparisons of the poet's love to the movements of the planets and the movements of the compass evoke feelings of awe and certainty.

7. Possible answers: He is passionate and intellectual.

Literary Criticism

8. Be sure students understand the levels of meaning in these conceits before they judge them.

Response and Analysis

Thinking Critically

1. How would you paraphrase the **simile** in lines 1–8? What emotions does this figure of speech evoke?

2. The **speaker** tells his wife that their love is different from that of other couples. What difference does he see, and how does he express it?

3. Why do you think Donne refers to irregular events on earth and in the heavens in lines 9–12? What kind of event is like the separation of lovers?

4. How would you explain the **conceit** Donne uses in lines 25–36? What does it suggest about the nature of love?

5. Why does the speaker insist that the lovers—obviously two people—are actually one?

6. What unusual **images** and references to specialized fields of knowledge mark this as a metaphysical poem? What emotions do these images evoke?

7. What impression of the speaker did you form as you read and discussed this poem? What sort of man does he seem to be?

Literary Criticism

8. The eighteenth-century writer Samuel Johnson disapproved of metaphysical conceits. He described them as "the discovery of occult [hidden] resemblances in things apparently unlike.... The most heterogeneous [dissimilar] ideas are yoked by violence together." Do you think Donne's conceits are forced (or violent)? Do you think they work—that is, can you draw meaning from the connections they make between such dissimilar things? Explain your own responses to Donne's poetry.

WRITING

Your Own Valediction

Suppose that you, like Donne, are leaving a loved one behind for a long, possibly dangerous journey. Write your own "valediction" in a brief **letter.** Be sure to refer to the thoughts you wrote down for the Quickwrite on page 304.

SKILLS FOCUS

Literary Skills Analyze metaphysical conceits.

Writing Skills Write a letter.

A Wooded Landscape at Evening (detail) (19th century) by Carl Bondel.
Bonhams, London.

ASSESSING

Assessment
- Holt Assessment: Literature, Reading, and Vocabulary

RETEACHING

For a lesson reteaching poetic devices, see **Reteaching,** p. 1129A.

Before You Read

Meditation 17

Make the Connection
There is one farewell that everyone must make, one parting and passage that time holds in store for all of us, whether we prepare ourselves for the journey or not. In 1624, prompted by a serious illness, Donne wrote a series of meditations—thoughtful reflections on a topic or theme. The opening of Meditation 17 refers to the practice, in Donne's time, of ringing church bells to announce the death of a church member.

Literary Focus
Tone
Writers deliberately express certain attitudes toward or feelings about a subject. For instance, one writer may express an idealistic attitude on the subject of love and another a bitter and disillusioned view. The writer's attitude toward or feelings about the subject, the reader, or a character constitute the **tone** of a work. Writers convey their tone by the words, images, and details they choose. In Meditation 17, Donne's tone reinforces his solemn and sad message.

> **Tone** is the attitude a writer takes toward the reader, the subject, or a character in a work.
>
> *For more on Tone, see the Handbook of Literary and Historical Terms.*

(Opposite and right) Marble effigy of John Donne in his shroud, from St. Paul's Cathedral, London.
© Woodmansterne Limited Watford.

INTERNET
More About John Donne
Keyword: LE5 12-3

Literary Skills
Understand the use of tone.

PRETEACHING

Summary ⇔ at grade level
This deeply religious meditation on the meaning of death and suffering begins with a Latin quotation that sums up Donne's main idea: A funeral bell tolling for one person is a reminder to everyone else that we must all die. Donne uses a series of extended analogies to illustrate the interconnectedness of all human beings as creatures of God: People are part of a book authored by God; they are part of a continent that is diminished by the loss of any one person. Finally, referring to a Christian belief, Donne equates affliction with treasure that can secure the sufferer a place in heaven.

Skills Starter
Motivate. Tell students that alienation and isolation are often cited as problems that people face today. Invite volunteers to share their understanding of these terms and to give examples of occurrences from modern society. Ask students to consider how Donne addresses these issues in the next selection.

Selection Starter
Build background. Donne's religious struggles did not have to do with faith, or believing, but in believing rightly and acting accordingly. His sermons tried to establish a finite person's relations with an infinite God.

DIFFERENTIATING INSTRUCTION

Learners Having Difficulty
Invite learners having difficulty to read Meditation 17 in interactive format in *The Holt Reader* and to use the sidenotes as aids to understanding the selection. The interactive version provides additional instruction, practice, and assessment of the literary skill taught in the Student Edition. Monitor students' responses to the selection, and correct any misconceptions that arise.

Special Education Students
For lessons designed for special education students, see *Holt Reading Solutions*.

Meditation 17

John Donne

*Nunc lento
sonitu dicunt,
Morieris.*

Now, this bell tolling softly
for another, says to me,
Thou must die.

Perchance he for whom this bell tolls, may be so ill, as that he knows not it tolls for him; and perchance I may think myself so much better than I am, as that they who are about me, and see my state, may have caused it to toll for me, and I know not that. The Church is catholic, universal, so are all her actions; all that she does belongs to all. When she baptizes a child, that action concerns me; for that child is thereby connected to that Head[1] which is my Head too, and engrafted into that body, whereof I am a member. And when she buries a man, that action concerns me: All mankind is of one Author, and is one volume; when one man dies, one chapter is not torn out of the book, but translated[2] into a better language; and every chapter must be so translated; God employs several translators; some pieces are translated by age, some by sickness, some by war, some by justice; but God's hand is in every translation; and his hand shall bind up all our scattered leaves[3] again, for that Library where every book shall lie open to one another: As therefore the bell that rings to a sermon, calls not upon the preacher only, but upon the congregation to come; so this bell calls us all: but how much more me, who am brought so near the door by this sickness. There was a contention as far as a suit[4] (in which both piety and dignity, religion and estimation,[5] were mingled), which of the religious orders should ring to prayers first in the morning; and it was determined, that they should ring first that rose earli-

---

1. **Head:** Christ.
2. **translated** *v.:* spiritually carried across from one realm to another.
3. **leaves** *n. pl.:* pages.
4. **contention . . . suit:** argument that went as far as a lawsuit.
5. **estimation** *n.:* self-esteem.

est. If we understand aright the dignity of this bell that tolls for our evening prayer, we would be glad to make it ours, by rising early, in that application, that it might be ours, as well as his, whose indeed it is. The bell doth toll for him that thinks it doth; and though it intermit[6] again, yet from that minute, that that occasion wrought upon him, he is united to God. Who casts not up his eye to the sun when it rises? but who takes off his eye from a comet when that breaks out?[7] Who bends not his ear to any bell, which upon any occasion rings? but who can remove it from that bell, which is passing a piece of himself out of this world? No man is an island, entire of itself; every man is a piece of the continent, a part of the main;[8] if a clod be washed away by the sea, Europe is the less, as well as if a promontory were, as well as if a manor of thy friends or of thine own were; any man's death diminishes me, because I am involved in mankind; and therefore never send to know for whom the bell tolls; it tolls for thee. ❷ Neither can we call this a begging of misery or a borrowing of misery, as though we were not miserable enough of ourselves, but must fetch in more from the next house, in taking upon us the misery of our neighbors. Truly it were an excusable covetousness if we did; for affliction[9] is a treasure, and scarce any man hath enough of it. No man hath affliction enough that is not matured, and ripened by it, and made fit for God by that affliction. If a man carry treasure in bullion, or in a wedge of gold, and have none coined into current monies, his treasure will not defray[10] him as he travels. Tribulation is treasure in the nature of it, but it is not current money in the use of it, except we get nearer and nearer our home, Heaven, by it. Another man may be sick too, and sick to death, and this affliction may lie in his bowels, as gold in a mine, and be of no use to him; but this bell, that tells me of his affliction, digs out, and applies that gold to me; if by this consideration of another's danger I take mine own into contemplation, and so secure myself by making my recourse[11] to my God, who is our only security. ❸ ■

---

❷ In this mystical passage, Donne suggests that all human souls are connected and that when one soul passes from this world to the next, all souls lose a measure of life.

? *In your opinion, what phrase from this passage best captures its main idea?*

❸ Donne's logic here is this: We must take upon ourselves the pain of our dying neighbor, because this pain, while no longer of use to the neighbor, might motivate us to improve our lives by strengthening our relationship with God.

? *What effect does Donne achieve with the repetition of the word* affliction *in this passage? Do you agree or disagree that suffering can, in one sense, be thought of as "gold"?*

---

6. **intermit** *v.:* cease.
7. **comet … out:** Comets were regarded as signs of disaster to come.
8. **main** *n.:* mainland.
9. **affliction** *n.:* suffering.
10. **defray** *v.:* pay for.
11. **making my recourse:** turning for aid.

John Donne 309

DIRECT TEACHING

C Literary Focus

? **Tone.** What tone is conveyed by the images in this famous passage? [Possible response: The images help create the solemn yet hopeful tone that is characteristic of the meditation and is in keeping with Donne's faith in a beneficent creator and heavenly afterlife.]

D Literary Focus

? **Theme.** According to Donne, how can people profit from the suffering of others? [They can see suffering as a reminder that pain and death will also come to them. Suffering can give them an opportunity to turn to God.]

Responses to Boxed Questions

2. Students might suggest that the expression "The bell doth toll for him that thinks it doth" best captures the main idea that all people are connected.

3. Students might suggest that the repetition of the word *affliction* forces us to recognize that pain and suffering are indeed a constant part of life. Students might suggest that meditating on the suffering and affliction that we see all around us will give us a new perspective on our lives and motivate us to focus on what is most important.

CONTENT-AREA CONNECTIONS

Music: *The Lamentations of Jeremiah*
The most influential composer of the Tudor era, Thomas Tallis (1510?–1585) served as organist for four English monarchs beginning with Henry VII. In this stormy period in England's religious history, it is a testament to Tallis's talent (as well as to Elizabeth's tolerance when not provoked) that although he remained a Roman Catholic, he was not demoted from his position when England returned to the Protestant faith after Queen Mary died and her half sister Elizabeth was crowned. As a composer, Tallis is noted for sacred choral music. *The Lamentations of Jeremiah* (inspired by the biblical book of Jeremiah, which is a lament for the fall of Jerusalem) is considered one of his finest works.

Individual activity. After students read Donne's Meditation 17, have them listen to Part I of Tallis's *The Lamentations of Jeremiah*. Then, ask them to write a paragraph or two comparing the spirit and fervor of Donne's writing with the emotions expressed in Tallis's composition.

INDEPENDENT PRACTICE

Response and Analysis

Thinking Critically

1. The speaker begins his meditation on hearing a church bell toll to signify a person's death.

2. People form part of a body that has Christ as its head; pages in a book whose translation God oversees; pieces of the continent. These metaphors imply that God joins Christians or all humanity together in society.

3. Affliction is a treasure because it helps people get nearer to God. Like money, tribulation has little worth when hoarded but is valuable when used to help others turn to God.

4. He is saying that everyone must die and that another's death should remind people of their own mortality.

5. We are interconnected; we all must die; we should welcome suffering, for it helps us get to heaven. Students will agree that everyone must die but may argue about humanity's interdependence, the role of suffering, and an afterlife.

6. The tone is dignified and optimistic, characterized by words such as *universal*, *piety*, and *affliction* and reflecting profound religious values.

7. The dignity and optimism of Donne's tone are fitting because Donne wants his audience to realize they too can feel dignified and optimistic if they follow his advice.

8. Students may note that many people today would be responsive to Donne's call for connections among all people.

Response and Analysis

Thinking Critically

1. What sound prompts the speaker to begin his meditation?

2. Several of Donne's **metaphors** suggest something about the relationship of people to one another. Identify two of those metaphors. What do they imply about society?

3. Why does the speaker feel that affliction is a treasure? In what ways is tribulation like money?

4. How would you explain what Donne means by saying, "The bell . . . tolls for thee"?

5. What do you think Donne's **main ideas** are in this meditation? Do you agree with them all? Explain why or why not.

6. How would you describe the speaker's **tone**: solemn, sad, depressed, angry, resigned, or something else? Which words in the meditation reinforce this tone?

7. **Rhetoric** refers to the art of using words effectively to communicate. How does Donne's **tone** in this meditation support the point he is trying to make?

8. Do any lines from this meditation have particular relevance to our lives today? Explain your response.

WRITING

Meditation on Metaphors

In a brief **essay**, take two of the **metaphors** from Meditation 17, and show how Donne uses them to make his points. Explain the comparisons the metaphors are based on. Show how Donne extends the metaphors. Describe the emotions that each metaphor evokes.

SKILLS FOCUS

Literary Skills
Analyze the use of tone.

Writing Skills
Write an essay explaining the author's use of metaphors.

310 Collection 3 The Renaissance

READING SKILLS REVIEW

Using context clues. Remind students that context clues take several forms, including appositives (that define unfamiliar words), synonyms, and antonyms.

Activity. Invite students to locate each of the following words in Meditation 17. Ask students to use context clues to figure out what each word means. Then, have them check their guesses in a dictionary.

1. perchance
2. catholic
3. engrafted
4. promontory
5. aright
6. wrought
7. covetousness
8. bullion

Grammar Link

Appropriate Additions: Adjective Clauses and Adverb Clauses

How can you combine short, choppy sentences to form sentences that flow smoothly? Try using adjective and adverb clauses. An **adjective clause** modifies a noun or a pronoun and usually begins with *who, whom, whose, which, that,* or *where*. Here are two choppy sentences:

> John Donne became the dean of St. Paul's Cathedral. St. Paul's Cathedral is in London.

By turning one of these sentences into an adjective clause, we can combine the two choppy sentences.

> John Donne became the dean of St. Paul's Cathedral, which is in London.

If an adjective clause is not essential to the meaning of a sentence, it is a **nonrestrictive clause** (as in the sentence above) and must be set off from the rest of the sentence with a comma or commas.

If an adjective clause is essential to the meaning of a sentence, it is a **restrictive clause** (*The poem that I like the best is "Song."*), and no commas are necessary.

An **adverb clause** modifies a verb, an adjective, or an adverb. An adverb clause begins with a subordinating conjunction, such as *after, although, because, before, if, since, until, when,* or *while*. Here are two more choppy sentences:

> John Donne studied at Oxford. He was only twelve years old.

By turning one of these sentences into an adverb clause, you can combine the choppy sentences.

> When John Donne was only twelve years old, he studied at Oxford.

When you place an adverb clause at the beginning of a sentence, separate it from the independent clause with a comma.

PRACTICE

Combine each pair of sentences that follows by using either an adjective clause or an adverb clause. Identify the kind of clause that you use for each item.

1. John Donne was related to Sir Thomas More. Sir Thomas More was beheaded by Henry VII in 1535.
2. John Donne was jailed for marrying Anne More. He had not asked her father's permission.
3. In Meditation 17, Donne compares humanity to chapters in a book. The chapters have been authored by God.
4. John Donne became private secretary to Sir Thomas Egerton. He had had many adventures.

Apply to Your Writing

Take out a writing assignment you are working on now or have already completed. Are there any short, choppy sentences? Add variety to your writing by combining those sentences using adjective or adverb clauses.

▶ For more help, see The Adjective Clause, 7d, and The Adverb Clause, 7f, in the Language Handbook.

Grammar Skills
Understand and use adjective clauses and adverb clauses.

Grammar Link

Practice

Possible Answers

1. John Donne was related to Sir Thomas More, who was beheaded by Henry VII in 1535. (adjective clause)
2. John Donne was jailed for marrying Anne More because he had not asked her father's permission. (adverb clause)
3. In Meditation 17, Donne compares humanity to chapters in a book that have been authored by God. (adjective clause)
4. After John Donne had had many adventures, he became private secretary to Sir Thomas Egerton. (adverb clause)

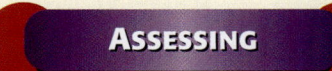

Assessment
- Holt Assessment: *Literature, Reading, and Vocabulary*

For a lesson reteaching author's tone and style, see **Reteaching, p. 1129A**.

DIFFERENTIATING INSTRUCTION

Learners Having Difficulty

Write the following sentences on the chalkboard. Have students combine each pair by using an adjective clause or an adverb clause.

1. Most anthologies of English literature include a few pieces by John Donne. He was a metaphysical poet and a preacher. [Most anthologies of English literature include a few pieces by John Donne, who was . . . ; Most anthologies of English literature include a few pieces by John Donne because he was . . .]
2. John Gunther was a twentieth-century American writer. He borrowed a title from Donne. [John Gunther, who was a twentieth-century American writer, borrowed a title from Donne.]
3. Many people use the sentence "No man is an island." They may not know Donne's work. [Many people use the sentence "No man is an island," even though they may not know Donne's work.]

PRETEACHING

Summary ⇔ *at grade level*

> In this sonnet the speaker taunts Death, asserting that Death does not kill and will itself die—because it is the soul's deliverance into eternal life. Death is also the slave of "fate, chance, kings, and desperate men." Therefore, Death can inflict only a temporary "sleep"; the soul will awaken, live eternally, and defeat Death.

Skills Starter

Motivate. Invite students to share what they have heard about "near-death experiences" of people who have been in accidents or who were brought close to death by illness. Ask students to discuss unexpected or unusual reactions that these people have expressed about their experiences.

Selection Starter

Background. Death was one of the most common themes of Donne's poetry, even his love poems, and the complex syntax of "Death be not proud" reflects Donne's ongoing struggle with the meaning of life and death. The poem is similar to a Shakespearean, or English, sonnet, with three quatrains and a concluding couplet. The rhyme scheme of the quatrains is *abba abba cddc*.

Before You Read

Death be not proud

Make the Connection
Quickwrite

Although death is inescapable, it is not, for everyone, unconquerable. For those who believe in the immortality of the soul—as Donne firmly did—death is merely a station on the soul's journey, the moment of its delivery from the confines of the body to the bliss of eternal life.

Write the labels "Defeat" and "Triumph" at the top of two columns. Under each label, list ways in which you think death can be seen as either a triumph or a defeat. For example, dying to save someone's life may be triumph and dying in a needless accident may be defeat.

Literary Focus
Paradox

A **paradox** is a statement that at first glance seems impossible or illogical ("The child is the father of the man") but, when looked at more closely, expresses a deeper truth than was immediately apparent ("What we are as adults is very much influenced by our childhood experiences"). Paradoxes are useful because they capture our attention and force us to think more deeply about issues we might otherwise take for granted.

INTERNET
More About
John Donne
Keyword: LE5 12-3

> A **paradox** is a seeming contradiction that is actually true.
>
> *For more on Paradox, see the Handbook of Literary and Historical Terms.*

SKILLS FOCUS

Literary Skills Understand the use of paradox.

Background

In Donne's collected poems, which are grouped by type, "Death be not proud" is one of nineteen Holy Sonnets included in the category of "Divine Poems." Because Donne never published the Holy Sonnets and because they are arranged in different ways in contemporary manuscripts and in books printed after his death, we do not know the order in which he wanted us to read them.

Italian Landscape (18th century) by Hubert Robert.
Musée Calvet, Avignon, France/Peter Willi/
The Bridgeman Art Library.

312 Collection 3   The Renaissance

DIFFERENTIATING INSTRUCTION

Learners Having Difficulty
Students may find the direct address and the imperative voice in the title confusing. Add a comma after *Death,* and explain that Death is being addressed as if it were a person. Then, ask students to supply a modern translation of "be not proud." [Don't be proud.] You might model a paraphrase of the title such as "Death, don't think you're so great."

English-Language Learners
Encourage students to rearrange and substitute words as they read. For example, they might paraphrase "From rest and sleep, which but thy pictures be, / Much pleasure" as "We get a lot of pleasure from rest and sleep, which look a lot like death."

Advanced Learners
Invite students to find and read another of Donne's Holy Sonnets and to compare and contrast its structure, tone, and poetic elements with those in "Death be not proud."

The Ruins of Holyrood Chapel (c. 1824) by Louis Jacques Mandé Daguerre.
Board of Trustees of the National Museums and Galleries on Merseyside (Walker Art Gallery), Liverpool, England.

Death be not proud

John Donne

Death be not proud, though some have callèd thee
Mighty and dreadful, for thou art not so,
For those whom thou think'st thou dost overthrow,
Die not, poor Death, nor yet canst thou kill me.
5 From rest and sleep, which but thy pictures° be,
Much pleasure,° then from thee, much more must flow,
And soonest our best men with thee do go,
Rest of their bones, and soul's delivery.°
Thou art slave to fate, chance, kings, and desperate men,
10 And dost with poison, war, and sickness dwell,
And poppy,° or charms° can make us sleep as well,
And better than thy stroke; why swell'st° thou then?
One short sleep past, we wake eternally,
And death shall be no more; Death, thou shalt die.

5. **pictures** *n. pl.:* images. A sleeping person can resemble a dead person.
6. **much pleasure:** That is, rest and sleep give much pleasure.
8. **rest . . . delivery:** Death gives the body rest and delivers the soul from the bondage of the body.
11. **poppy** *n.:* opium. **charms** *n. pl.:* magic; hypnotism.
12. **swell'st** *v.:* swell with pride.

Literary Criticism

Critic's Commentary: A Departure?
The critic William Harmon explains how Donne's Holy Sonnets differ from traditional English sonnets of the period: "Donne's nineteen 'Holy Sonnets,' written around 1610–1620, are in some ways a part and a culmination of a fashion in sonnet-writing that had been going on for about seventy-five years; but there are many ways in which a 'holy sonnet' is a pronounced departure from fashion and convention.

"As practiced by Wyatt, Surrey, Shakespeare, Sidney, and Spenser, the sonnet was relatively 'unholy'; it was a secular love lyric that could become intensely erotic and also lightheartedly satirical. And it could exploit love's capacity for exaggeration and paradox. . . .

"In his 'Holy Sonnets,' Donne lifted the level of love from secular to sacred, but he kept the dramatic emphasis on paradox. . . . He also kept much of the physical, erotic imagery from secular love lyrics."
Activity. Invite students to make their own comparisons and contrasts of sonnets by Donne and by other English sonneteers.

INDEPENDENT PRACTICE

Response and Analysis

Thinking Critically

1. Death does not kill anyone. It serves "fate, chance, kings, and desperate men."

2. Possible answers: In rest and sleep a person is often motionless, as in death; according to Donne, a person rises from rest and sleep, as from death, renewed, freed from pain and worldly cares.

3. The speaker starts with a stern warning to Death, moves on to pretended sympathy and ridicule of Death, drops to a hushed tone with talk of rest and sleep, and ends with a striking judgment of Death.

4. The paradoxes are resolved by the assumption or belief that there is an afterlife.

5. Possible response: The tone is primarily defiant. Words that reveal the tone include "though some have callèd thee / Mighty and dreadful, . . . thou art not so," and "Death, thou shalt die."

6. Responses will vary. Students might say that Donne's mockery of Death seems original for its boldness.

7. Answers will vary.

8. The sonnet is Shakespearean. It has three quatrains, each with a regular rhyme scheme, and a concluding rhyming couplet.

Extending and Evaluating

9. Students should indicate that a comma represents only a brief pause, while a semicolon indicates a stop almost as long as a period. Students might agree with the professor: The comma makes Death less substantial, by suggesting that it is a mere breath away; the use of the semicolon, by contrast, sets Death off more distinctly, making it seem of greater consequence.

Response and Analysis

Still Life—Vanitas (1623) by Pieter Claesz. Oil on wood.

The Metropolitan Museum of Art, Rogers Fund, 1949 (49.107).
Photograph ©1979 The Metropolitan Museum of Art, New York.

Thinking Critically

1. According to the poem, why shouldn't Death be proud? Whom must Death serve as a slave?

2. Explain how rest and sleep are the "pictures" of Death (line 5).

3. Show how, as the sonnet develops, the speaker shifts the grounds of his attack on Death.

4. How does the sonnet resolve its **paradoxes**: that those who die do not die and that Death itself will die?

5. What is the speaker's **tone** in this poem—how does he feel toward Death? What words reveal his attitude?

6. Did you find any of your Quickwrite ideas in Donne's poem? Did any of his taunts of Death seem especially original to you? Explain.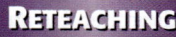

7. Donne **personifies** Death—that is, he speaks of Death as if Death were a person. How does this poem make you feel about Death? (Does it make Death less frightening? Does it give you a new way of looking at Death?)

8. Is this a **Shakespearean** or a **Petrarchan sonnet** (see pages 275–277)? Demonstrate how you arrived at your answer.

Extending and Evaluating

9. The last line of this version of "Death be not proud" is punctuated differently from the version that the professor in the **Connection** on page 314 prefers. Is there any important difference between the use of a comma and the use of a semicolon in the last line? What feeling might the semicolon subtly evoke?

WRITING

Death Personified

In "Death be not proud," Donne forcefully **personifies** Death. How does Donne's image differ from that of the personified Death in Chaucer's "The Pardoner's Tale" (see page 146)?

In an **essay, compare and contrast** the two portrayals of Death. Consider these points:

- Death's characteristics and power
- how people respond to Death

SKILLS FOCUS

Literary Skills Analyze the use of paradox.

Writing Skills Write an essay comparing and contrasting personification in two poems.

ASSESSING

Assessment
■ Holt Assessment: Literature, Reading, and Vocabulary

RETEACHING

For a lesson reteaching poetic devices, see **Reteaching**, p. 1129A.

Ben Jonson
(1572?–1637)

Benjamin Jonson (early 17th century) after Abraham van Blyenberch. Oil on canvas (18½" × 16½").
By Courtesy of the National Portrait Gallery, London.

Although Jonson was christened Benjamin, he was, and is, always known as Ben. He was probably born in the same year as his friend John Donne, and if his friend William Shakespeare had never existed, Jonson would probably be regarded as the chief dramatist of the age.

Ben's father died before he was born. His stepfather, a bricklayer, intended to make him a bricklayer too, but while still a boy, Jonson became acquainted with William Camden, a scholar and headmaster of the superb Westminster School. Camden enrolled young Ben in his school and educated him at his own expense.

Jonson never attended a university, but he had an immense knowledge of Latin literature and a small acquaintance with Greek. He was no mere pedant or bookish recluse. After leaving Westminster, Ben joined the English army and fought against the Spanish in Flanders. There, while the two massed armies watched, he engaged in single combat with the Spanish champion and killed him. Back in England he became a playwright and an actor, specializing in loud and roaring parts. He had two brushes with the law: once when he killed a fellow actor in a duel and escaped hanging by demonstrating that he could read; once when he went to prison for making derogatory remarks about Scotland in a play. In short, Jonson was very much a part of the tough, violent life of the time—a complete Londoner, holding forth at the Mermaid Tavern, where his witty combats with Shakespeare and others are mentioned in contemporary writings.

Gradually Jonson became known as a dramatist. He was particularly good at devising masques (elaborate, expensively mounted productions) for the court of King James. Jonson also wrote tragedies and comedies for the public theaters.

Jonson's attitude toward his writing was different from Donne's and Shakespeare's; Jonson was more like today's writers, who are, for the most part, eager for public notice. In 1616, Jonson astonished the reading public by publishing a number of his plays and poems under the title *Works*, a label traditionally reserved for more intellectual subjects, such as theology and history. Jonson believed that poems and plays are serious works of art, as serious in their own way as history and theology and as worthy of high regard.

At the height of his career, Jonson was a sort of literary dictator in London—opinionated and crusty but admired by a number of younger writers, who became known as the tribe of Ben or the sons of Ben. They stood by Jonson in his old age, when he was sick and poor and neglected because his blunt and forthright manner had made him many enemies. Jonson was buried near Chaucer in Westminster Abbey, in what later became known as the Poets' Corner. His inscription required only four words: "O rare Ben Jonson."

For Independent Reading

You may want to read these poems by Jonson:
- "Song: Still to Be Neat"
- "On My First Daughter"

PRETEACHING

Summary ⇔ at grade level

"On My First Son" begins with a farewell to a dead son. The speaker regrets having forgotten that his child was merely lent to him by God. He consoles himself with the thought that his son is now free of the pains of living and of growing old. In the last lines, the speaker offers an epitaph for his son, calling him "his best piece of poetry." He concludes with a vow never again to "like too much" what he loves.

Skills Starter

Motivate. Ask students whether they have ever been at a funeral or memorial service and heard a moving eulogy, or short oration meant to honor one who has died. Encourage them to list reasons for marking the passing of a loved one in this way.

Selection Starter

Build background. Ben Jonson knew that *poetry* is derived from a word that means "things made" or "products." By a reversible conceit, therefore, Jonson could speak of his poems as children and his children as poems.

Before You Read

On My First Son
Song: To Celia

Make the Connection
When you hear the word *love*, do you first think of romantic love? If you do, this is a natural response. However, the ties of love bind us powerfully to family, friends, mentors, even pets—not just to the objects of our romantic affection. One of love's ironies is that a strong bond of love, so strengthening and fulfilling—even inspiring—also opens us to crushing heartache when the bond is cut. The two poems by Ben Jonson that follow explore two very different kinds of love—and two very different outcomes for love.

Literary Focus
The Epigram
Both of the following Ben Jonson poems were published in his collection *Epigrams* (1616). The **epigram**—a brief, cleverly worded, memorable statement, usually in rhymed verse—was a classical form Jonson favored in contrast to both Elizabethan romanticism and the metaphysical complexity of a John Donne poem (see page 301). For the ancients an epigram was written to give permanence to an event or observation; it was pointed, polished, and striking—like an engraved motto on a monument. Jonson's epigrams take the form of short poems, often with a two-part structure: The first part establishes the mood or the event; the second makes a concise point.

> An **epigram** is a brief, clever, and usually memorable poem or short verse.
>
> For more on Epigram, see the Handbook of Literary and Historical Terms.

Background
Jonson once said that he always wrote out his poems in prose before turning them into verse, just as his headmaster Camden had taught him to. At times, it must be admitted, the prose that he versified was not his own but someone else's. For example, the poem "Song: To Celia" was crafted out of five different prose passages that Jonson found in the *Epistles* of the Greek philosopher Philostratus (A.D. 170?–245).

Throughout most of his life, Jonson's enemies taunted him for once having been a bricklayer. In a sense he remained a bricklayer all his creative life, a builder whose tiniest literary construction is solid and seamless.

Details from *The Grimani Breviary*.
Archivo Iconographico, S.A./CORBIS.

SKILLS FOCUS
Literary Skills
Understand the characteristics of epigrams.

318 Collection 3 The Renaissance

Literary Criticism

Critic's Commentary: Epigrams
In *Lives of the Poets,* Michael Schmidt has this to say about Ben Jonson's use of epigrams: "In classical times, an 'epigram' was the inscription on a tombstone, usually in elegiac verse. But like the term 'elegy,' 'epigram' outgrew its original sense. For Jonson it named the short and not so short occasional poem with a single mood or idea: satirical, amatory, dedicatory or elegiac. He and the 'sons of Ben' developed it to high perfection. His long poems tend to 'epigram' in the newer sense of 'pithy brief statement': couplets and other passages detach themselves and catch like burrs in the mind."

Activity. Invite students to name some passages from songs or poems that have caught in their minds "like burrs." Ask them whether they would consider these lines epigrams.

*This poem is about Ben Jonson's son, Benjamin, who died of the plague on his seventh birthday. (Jonson and his wife also lost a daughter, Mary, in infancy.) The name Benjamin in Hebrew means "child of the right hand" and, ironically, connotes a "lucky, clever child." Pay special attention to the famous **epitaph**, or inscription on a grave, that appears in quotation marks at the end of the poem.*

On My First Son

Ben Jonson

Farewell, thou child of my right hand, and joy;
   My sin was too much hope of thee, loved boy:
Seven years thou wert lent to me, and I thee pay,°
   Exacted° by thy fate, on the just° day.
5 Oh, could I lose all father° now! for why
   Will man lament the state he should envy—
To have so soon 'scaped world's and flesh's rage,
   And if no other misery, yet age?
Rest in soft peace, and asked, say, "Here doth lie
10   Ben Jonson his best piece of poetry;
For whose sake henceforth all his vows be such
   As what he loves may never like too much."

3. **thee pay:** pay thee back.
4. **exacted** *v.:* forced. **just** *adj.:* exact. Loans were often made for exactly seven years.
5. **father** *n.:* sense of fatherhood; the need to mourn like a father.

Portrait of a boy (16th century) by Robert Peake the Elder.
Christie's, London.

DIRECT TEACHING

A Reading Skills

Inferring. Why do you suppose the speaker calls hope a sin? [Possible response: Perhaps he feels that his son's death is God's punishment for his caring too much about his child; perhaps he had such high hopes for his son that he forgot how fragile life is.]

B Literary Focus

Metaphor. Ask students how Jonson uses this idea as a metaphor. [He compares his son to a loan from God that came due after seven years.]

C Reading Skills

Finding the main idea. What view of death is expressed in these three lines? [Jonson suggests that Heaven is the goal of life, and death is welcome inasmuch as it is an escape from the suffering of the world.] Do you think this view comforts Jonson? [Despite the assurances that Heaven seems to offer, Jonson's pain comes through very clearly.]

D Literary Focus

Epigrams. Samuel Taylor Coleridge defined an epigram this way: "What is an epigram? A dwarfish whole / Its body brevity, and wit its soul." Consider this definition and the one in the text (p. 318), and discuss why these lines are an epigram. [Possible responses: It is a short rhymed verse; its language is pointed and concise; it makes a clear point.]

SKILLS REVIEW

Analyzing epigrams. To help students understand the epigram, introduce this poem, written by Sarah Cleghorn in 1917.

The Golf Links

The golf links lie so near the mill
   That almost every day
The laboring children can look out
   And see the men at play.

Note how economically the poet expresses the irony of men at play and children at work; just four lines speak volumes.

Activity. Ask students to answer the following question about the epigram: What point does the poet want to make about her society? [A society that allows children to work while men play has questionable values.]

PRETEACHING

Summary ⇄ *at grade level*

The speaker praises a woman, saying that he prefers her kiss to wine and would not exchange it even for a drink that would make him immortal.

DIRECT TEACHING

Ⓐ Vocabulary Development

❓ Multiple meanings. How do both meanings of *pledge*—"promise" and "drink to the health of; salute"—work in the poem? [The speaker talks about both promising love and toasting his love.]

Ⓑ English-Language Learners

Understanding archaic language. Explain that *doth* means "does" and that *sup* (related to *sip*) means "take a mouthful." Help students paraphrase ll. 5–8. [Possible response: The thirst that rises from the soul / Asks for a divine drink; / But even if I could sip Jove's nectar, / I would not trade it for yours.]

Ⓒ Literary Focus

❓ Paradox. What paradox does Jonson present about the wreath? What deeper truth might this suggest? [Possible response: By claiming that the wreath now grows rather than fading, the poet is suggesting that the woman rejuvenates him.]

This poem has a very famous tune that many people still know. Thomas Arne (1710–1778), who also composed the British national anthem, "Rule, Britannia," created music for Ben Jonson's poem and called it "Drink to Me Only with Thine Eyes." The song can still be found in many old songbooks.

Song: To Celia

Ben Jonson

Ⓐ Drink to me only with thine eyes,
   And I will pledge with mine;
Or leave a kiss but in the cup,
   And I'll not look for wine.
Ⓑ 5 The thirst that from the soul doth rise
   Doth ask a drink divine;
But might I of Jove's nectar° sup,
   I would not change° for thine.
I sent thee late a rosy wreath,
10   Not so much honoring thee
As giving it a hope, that there
   It could not withered be.
Ⓒ But thou thereon didst only breathe,
   And sent'st it back to me;
15 Since when it grows, and smells, I swear,
   Not of itself but thee.

7. **Jove's nectar:** Jove, more commonly called Jupiter, is the supreme god in Roman mythology. Nectar was the drink that kept the gods immortal.
8. **change** *v*.: exchange.

320   Collection 3   The Renaissance

CONTENT-AREA CONNECTIONS

History: The Plague
Ben Jonson's beloved son died of the plague. During the 1590s, the plague wreaked havoc in London. Encourage students to research the history of the plague in the city from 1518 to 1636. Students might be interested to learn that doctors recommended hollowing a large onion and filling it with fig, rue (a medicinal herb), and treacle as a way to ward off the plague.

Music: "Drink to Me Only with Thine Eyes"
Encourage students to find Thomas Arne's original music for Jonson's "Song: To Celia," which is listed in many old songbooks as "Drink to Me Only with Thine Eyes." Encourage students to listen to the music and then compose their own melody for the selection.

Response and Analysis

On My First Son
Song: To Celia

Thinking Critically

1. According to line 2 of "On My First Son," what was the speaker's (Jonson's) "sin"? What do you think he means by this declaration?
2. Explain the **metaphor** Jonson uses in lines 3–4 of "On My First Son." What does this comparison tell you about how Jonson views life?
3. In lines 7–8 of "On My First Son," what comfort does Jonson suggest is possible? Do you feel that he, the speaker, is comforted by this idea? Explain, using evidence from the text.
4. What does Jonson vow at the end of "On My First Son"?
5. Jonson borrowed some of the features of "On My First Son" from Latin works: The direct address to the dead boy in line 9 and the first three words of the **epitaph**, or inscription, "Here doth lie . . ." are straight out of Latin classics. However, the ideas contained in the epitaph are original to Jonson, especially the central **metaphor** in line 10. To what does Jonson compare his son? What do you think of this comparison?
6. In "Song: To Celia," what do you think it means to "drink" and "pledge" with the eyes?
7. What does "thine" refer to in line 8 of "Song: To Celia"?
8. How would you **paraphrase** lines 9–16 of "Song: To Celia"?

WRITING

On Love and Loss

In "On My First Son," Jonson resolves never again to love so strongly, because his loss is so unbearable. What do you think of Jonson's resolution? What effect could a vow like this have on someone? In a **letter** to the writer, explain what you think of his vow to never again love too much.

LISTENING AND SPEAKING

Reciting a Poem

Choose either of the Jonson poems you have just read, and prepare an oral reading. Before you begin, be sure to mark copies of the poems with appropriate pauses and stopping points so that you can read the poem in a natural, convincing way. Be sure that the **tone** of your reading—whether it is exuberant or restrained, grave or lively—matches the tone of the poem you have chosen. Recite your poem for the class, and ask for critiques of your delivery.

Motets (16th century) by Richard Sampson. Canon, with circular staves and rose at center.
Roy 11 E XI fol. 2v. British Library, London.

SKILLS FOCUS

Literary Skills
Analyze the characteristics of epigrams.

Writing Skills
Write a letter to the poet.

Listening and Speaking Skills
Give an oral presentation of a poem.

Thinking Critically

1. According to l. 2, the speaker's sin was having too much hope, or too many high expectations, for his son. The speaker might consider this a sin because he took too much pride in his own creation, his son.
2. In this metaphor, Jonson compares his son to a seven-year loan that has come due; that is, Jonson sees his son as being "on loan" to him from God. This metaphor suggests that Jonson takes a somewhat fatalistic view of life in which all events are ordained by God.
3. His son is now free from the cares of the world and physical decay. Students may suggest that the speaker is not really comforted by this thought but is trying to rationalize his loss.
4. The speaker vows never to "like too much" those people and things he loves; that is, he promises himself not to cling too tightly to loved ones, since they, like his son, may be taken from him.
5. Jonson compares his son to a poem. The comparison is original and somewhat humble, suggesting that none of Jonson's work is as wonderful as this boy was. The comparison might have given Jonson a new perspective on what is most important in life, leading him to place family and friends above his literary work.
6. Traditionally, the meeting of lovers' eyes conveys much more than spoken words. Here eyes pledge faithfulness.
7. It refers to the lady's nectar, which is a symbol for her love.
8. Possible answer: I recently sent you a wreath in the hope that it would not die. You sent it back alive, growing and sweet with your fragrance.

Assessment

- Holt Assessment: Literature, Reading, and Vocabulary

Political Points of View

SKILLS FOCUS, pp. 322–335

Grade-Level Skills

■ **Literary Skills**

Analyze political points of view in a selection of literary works on a topic.

■ **Reading Skills**

Draw inferences.

Political Issue: Education and Equality

Explain to students that education usually reflects the values of a society. Also tell them that the word *education* comes from a Latin word meaning "lead out." Then, use these questions to guide a class discussion:

- What does *education* mean today?
- Toward what is education meant to lead people?
- How does modern education reflect the values of our society?

Skills Starter

Build review skills. Have students work in groups to write a definition of *assumption* and to think of three assumptions that many people hold. Afterward, have the groups share their definitions. Then, help students see that a political assumption is a basic belief about how society should be organized and governed.

Introducing Political Points of View

Education and Equality

Main Reading		
Francis Bacon	**Of Studies**	325
Connected Readings		
Queen Elizabeth I	**Tilbury Speech**	330
Margaret Cavendish	from **Female Orations**	332

You will be reading the three selections listed above in this Political Points of View feature on education and equality. In the top corner of the pages in this feature, you'll find three stars. Smaller versions of these stars appear next to the questions on page 328 that focus on education and equality. On page 335, you'll compare the points of view expressed in the selections.

Examining the Issue: Education and Equality

With the advent of humanism, education was no longer restricted to the clergy. In fact, men of the privileged classes were now expected to study a wide array of subjects, from philosophy and economics to music and science. Education for Renaissance women, however, was a different story. Only women of noble birth had access to education, and the goal of education was to produce better wives and mothers, since education was linked to growth in moral virtue and since women directed the early education of their children.

Although education was held up as a primary good during the Renaissance, it was certainly not available to all—and its goal was not to create equality, either between classes or between men and women.

Make the Connection

Quickwrite

Jot down your ideas about the role of education in bringing women closer to equality with men. Does the struggle for equality between the sexes continue today? What other kinds of equality can education help to create?

Reading Skills

Drawing Inferences

When you read thoughtfully, you make **inferences**—you draw certain conclusions from a text based on the evidence. The selections that follow differ greatly in purpose and subject matter, but they are all firmly rooted in their authors' times. From what these writers say—and how they say it—you can draw inferences about the social and political realities of their time. Take careful notes as you read.

Pages 322–335 cover
Literary Skills
Analyze political points of view on a topic.
Reading Skills
Draw inferences.

322 Collection 3 The Renaissance

Francis Bacon
(1561–1626)

From his earliest days, Francis Bacon knew that he was an important person. When he was about nine, Queen Elizabeth asked him how old he was, and he is said to have replied, "Two years younger than your Majesty's happy reign." A boy who speaks like this will go far, and Bacon went far. He rose in his chosen profession, the law, until he reached the very top and became lord chancellor and keeper of the great seal, an office that his father, Sir Nicholas Bacon, had also held. He was elevated to the peerage, the British nobles who could govern as members of the House of Lords, and he amassed a large fortune, though he was often in debt because of his extravagant lifestyle. At the height of his political career, he was found guilty of taking bribes and was removed from office. Bacon retired to his country estate, where he devoted himself full time to thinking and writing about new ways to discover knowledge.

In a now famous letter to his uncle, Lord Burghley, Elizabeth's secretary of state, Bacon wrote, "I have taken all knowledge to be my province." Of course, he did not master all knowledge, but he did make important contributions to many different branches of knowledge: political science, economics, biology, physics, music, architecture, botany, constitutional law, industrial development, philosophy, theology, mythology, astronomy, chemistry, landscape gardening, and literature. He is most famous, however, for his vision of humanity's future, when knowledge would be based on verifiable experimentation and science would be separate from theology.

Bacon's best-known literary works, the *Essays*, are intended to help people get ahead in life. Bacon was the first Englishman to use the word *essay* to designate a brief discourse in prose. He took the word from the French writer Montaigne (män·tān′), whose delightful *essais* are mainly about a fascinating person, Montaigne himself. Bacon writes instead about humanity in general.

Bacon had embarked on a new career as a practicing scientist when death overtook him. One wintry day he descended from his carriage carrying a dead chicken, intending to freeze it in the snow and thereby test the preservative powers of cold. Today this seems like a painfully obvious thing to do, but nobody had tried it in a systematic way before 1626. Suddenly, in the midst of the experiment, Bacon took a chill. His servants carried him into nearby Highgate, the house of the earl of Arundel. In poor health most of his life, Bacon died there of complications resulting from exposure.

In all his works, Bacon's aim was to make the world better. As the destroyer of old Aristotelian ways of thinking and as the stimulator of "modern" ones, Bacon has no equal.

Sir Francis Bacon, Viscount of St. Albans (detail) (late 16th–early 17th century) by Paul van Somer. Oil.
Private Collection.

SKILLS FOCUS, pp. 323–328

Grade-Level Skills

- **Literary Skills**

Analyze political points of view on a topic.

- **Literary Skills**

Analyze the way patterns of organization, such as parallelism, affect the meaning of a text.

- **Reading Skills**

Analyze arguments.

Review Skills

- **Literary Skills**

Analyze the way a work of literature relates to the themes and issues of its historical period.

More About the Writer

Background. Bacon was instrumental in introducing the scientific method to England. In *New Atlantis*, a short utopian fantasy, he describes an assembly of scholars devoted to scientific study and research. This concept inspired the chartering of the British scientific academy known as the Royal Society in 1660, more than thirty years after Bacon's death. Although this intellectual institution was later satirized by Jonathan Swift in *Gulliver's Travels* (1726), it boasts a distinguished history and remains in existence today.

RESOURCES: READING

Planning
- One-Stop Planner CD-ROM with ExamView Test Generator

Differentiating Instruction
- Supporting Instruction in Spanish
- Audio CD Library, Selections and Summaries in Spanish

Grammar and Language
- Daily Language Activities

Vocabulary
- Vocabulary Development

Assessment
- Holt Assessment: Literature, Reading, and Vocabulary
- One-Stop Planner CD-ROM with ExamView Test Generator
- Holt Online Assessment

Internet
- go.hrw.com (Keyword: LE5 12-3)
- Elements of Literature Online

Media
- Audio CD Library
- Audio CD Library, Selections and Summaries in Spanish

DIRECT TEACHING

A Literary Focus

❓ Analyzing parallel structure. What are the parallel adjectives and the adjective phrase in this sentence? ["wise," "witty," "subtle," "deep," "grave," and "able to contend"]

B Reading Skills

❓ Analyzing clarity of meaning. How does the repetitive style help the reader anticipate the comparison Bacon goes on to make? [Possible response: Bacon's listing of several physical ailments and remedies leads the reader to guess that he will also name some mental ailments and recommend study as an antidote.]

Response to Boxed Question

4. Studies are to the mind as exercise is to the body.

GUIDED PRACTICE

Monitoring students' progress. Guide the class in answering the following questions.

True-False

1. According to Bacon, you can feel secure if you make judgments based only on what you have studied. [F]
2. Bacon says that you do not need to read every book thoroughly. [T]
3. In Bacon's view, mental pursuits are superior to physical ones, such as walking and riding. [F]
4. According to Bacon, study offers a cure for every weakness of the intellect. [T]

A Histories make men wise; poets witty;[14] the mathematics subtle; natural philosophy deep; moral grave; logic and rhetoric able to contend. *Abeunt studia in mores.*[15] Nay, there is no stond[16] or impediment in the wit but may be wrought[17] out by fit studies: like as diseases of the body may have appropriate exercises. Bowling is good

B for the stone and reins;[18] shooting for the lungs and breast; gentle walking for the stomach; riding for the head; and the like. So if a man's wit be wandering, let him study the mathematics; for in demonstrations, if his wit be called away never so little, he must begin again: If his wit be not apt to distinguish or find differences, let him study the Schoolmen;[19] for they are *cymini sectores:*[20] If he be not apt to beat over[21] matters, and to call one thing to prove and illustrate another, let him study the lawyers' cases; so every defect of the mind may have a special receipt.[22] ❹ ■

---

14. **witty** *adj.:* imaginative.   15. **Abeunt...mores:** Latin for "Studies help form character," from *Heroides* by Ovid (43 B.C.–c. A.D. 17).   16. **stond** *n.:* stoppage.   17. **wrought** *v.:* worked.   18. **stone and reins:** archaic for "kidney stones and the kidneys."   19. **schoolmen** *n. pl.:* medieval philosophers.   20. **cymini sectores:** Latin for "hairsplitters"; literally, dividers of the cumin seed.   21. **beat over:** thoroughly discuss.   22. **receipt** *n.:* remedy.

Vocabulary

impediment (im·ped′ə·mənt) *n.:* obstacle; stumbling block.

---

❹ Bacon uses an extended analogy to argue the value of "fit studies."
❓ Summarize Bacon's analogy: Studies are to the mind as _____ is to _____

A Still Life with Books (detail) (17th century) by Charles E. Bizet d'Annonay.
Musée de l'Ain, Bourg-en-Bresse, France.

DIFFERENTIATING INSTRUCTION

Advanced Learners

Enrichment. After they read the axioms on the following page, have students formulate a contemporary axiom that captures a piece of practical wisdom in a few words. The axiom should respond in some way to an idea in Bacon's essay. Tell students that they may present their axioms in the form of bumper stickers, T-shirt designs, or advertisements, and display their work in the classroom.

PRIMARY SOURCE / AXIOMS

Bacon's essays are written in a terse, compressed style that demands a reader's full attention. For the most part, Bacon does not develop his ideas in paragraphs. Instead, he writes a sentence containing one idea, then follows it with a sentence containing another idea. While the sentences are all related to the topic of the essay, they are related in different ways—and they could be rearranged without much damage to the whole. The effect is like a string of beads all the same size.

Many of the sentences contain nuggets of wisdom known as **axioms** or adages. Like proverbs, axioms do not argue or explain but merely make positive statements. Here is a sampling of some of Bacon's most memorable axioms.

Axioms
from the Essays

Francis Bacon

Musée de l'Ain, Bourg-en-Bresse, France.

Men fear death as children fear to go in the dark; and as that natural fear in children is increased with tales, so is the other.
—"Of Death"

Revenge is a kind of wild justice, which the more man's nature runs to, the more ought law to weed it out.
—"Of Revenge"

The virtue of prosperity is temperance; the virtue of adversity is fortitude.
—"Of Adversity"

He that hath wife and children hath given hostages to fortune.
—"Of Marriage and Single Life"

There was never proud man thought so absurdly well of himself as the lover doth of the person loved: And therefore it was well said, *That it is impossible to love and to be wise.*
—"Of Love"

They that deny a God destroy man's nobility, for certainly man is of kin to the beasts by his body, and if he be not of kin to God by his spirit, he is a base and ignoble creature.
—"Of Atheism"

A principal fruit of friendship is the ease and discharge of the fullness and swellings of the heart.
—"Of Friendship"

As the baggage is to an army, so is riches to virtue.
—"Of Riches"

No man prospers so suddenly as by others' errors.
—"Of Fortune"

There is no excellent beauty that hath not some strangeness in the proportion.
—"Of Beauty"

It were better to have no opinion of God at all than such an opinion as is unworthy of him.
—"Of Superstition"

Francis Bacon 327

INDEPENDENT PRACTICE

Response and Analysis

Reading Check

1. Studies can lead to sloth or affectation.
2. Reading should be used for delight, for ornament, and for ability. Reading should not be used just to feed disputes, to assume the author's beliefs, or to have something to talk about.
3. Histories make men wise; poetry makes men creative; mathematics makes men subtle; natural philosophy breeds depth; moral philosophy breeds seriousness; logical rhetoric helps men argue.

Thinking Critically

4. Possible response: Studies are a vital element of human experience. They enable people to develop their natures fully. They should be balanced with engagement in the real world and performed for a purpose. Students' quotes should logically connect to the main idea.
5. The paradox is that someone can study too much, without putting knowledge to work in the real world. Most students will probably agree with Bacon, but some may feel that knowledge does not need to have an immediate application.
6. Examples include the sentences beginning "So if a man's wit" and "If he be not apt . . ."
7. Students are likely to cite Bacon's first sentence. The remaining sentences support this idea.

Extending and Evaluating

8. Students may cite the sentences beginning "To spend too much time," "Crafty men contemn studies," and "Reading maketh a full man." Parallelism emphasizes the important points and helps make the essay powerful and persuasive.
9. Most students will agree that Bacon's basic points are still valid.

Response and Analysis

Reading Check

1. What are some of the ways in which studies can be misused?
2. What should reading be used for? What should it *not* be used for?
3. What do these kinds of readings do for us: histories, poems, mathematics, natural philosophy, moral philosophy, logical rhetoric?

Thinking Critically

4. In no more than three sentences, state what you think is Bacon's **main idea** in "Of Studies." Then, quote **details** from the essay that support your statement of its main idea.
5. Bacon says that too much studying is "sloth"—laziness. Do you agree? Explain how this **paradox,** or seeming contradiction, can be true.
6. Bacon had the reputation of being a hard, ambitious man, and his essays are frequently said to be cynical and lacking in warmth. Find remarks in "Of Studies" that could support this view.
7. Which sentence from the essay best sums up Bacon's views on the value of study? Cite reasons and examples he offers to support his argument. Has Bacon convinced you of his **point of view**? Explain. You may want to consult your reading notes.

SKILLS FOCUS

Literary Skills Analyze political points of view on a topic. Analyze the use of parallelism.
Reading Skills Analyze arguments.
Writing Skills Write a response essay.
Vocabulary Skills Demonstrate word knowledge.

Extending and Evaluating

8. Bacon's fondness for **parallelism** and balanced sentences is apparent in "Of Studies," which uses parallel structures to state, restate, and elaborate his main idea. For example, "Some books are to be tasted, others to be swallowed, and some few to be chewed and digested."

Find other examples of parallelism in the essay, and explain how it improves the essay's clarity.

9. "Of Studies" was written almost four hundred years ago. Do you think Bacon's views are still relevant today? Are any of his points dated? Do you disagree with anything Bacon says? Explain. Consult your Quickwrite notes.

WRITING

Talking Back to Bacon

Write an **essay** of your own in response to Bacon's reflections on studies or in response to one of the axioms in the *Primary Source* on page 327. Your response to Bacon may range from total disagreement to total approval of all he says. In your opening statement, tell what the topic of your essay will be. Be sure to bring in examples and experiences from real life to support or refute Bacon. Give your essay a title that uses the word *Of.*

Vocabulary Development
Stating Opinions

discourse   diligence
sloth   impediment
affectation

Use each of the words above to state an opinion or make an assertion that could be argued in a persuasive essay. One has been done for you below.

> Children who show signs of sloth will grow up to be lazy adults.

---

328 Collection 3 The Renaissance

Vocabulary Development
Students' assertions will vary.

Assessment
- Holt Assessment: Literature, Reading, and Vocabulary

For a lesson reteaching clarity of meaning, see **Reteaching,** p. 1129A.

Connected Readings

Education and Equality

Queen Elizabeth I .... **Tilbury Speech**
Margaret Cavendish .... *from* **Female Orations**

You have just read Sir Francis Bacon's persuasive essay "Of Studies," which praises the virtues of reading and learning and expresses a solidly Renaissance view of the value of knowledge and education. The next two selections you will be reading—a speech by Queen Elizabeth I and a selection of dramatic monologues in the form of a literary debate by Margaret Cavendish—also shed light (in both direct and indirect ways) on Renaissance views of the value of education. Although immense emphasis was placed on education during the Renaissance, formal education of the type extolled by Sir Francis Bacon was not available to the majority of the population, and particularly not to women. It was, however, available to women of the privileged classes—and some of these women took full advantage of the opportunity, becoming as intellectually accomplished as their male peers.

After you have read these selections, answer the questions on page 335, which ask you to compare all three selections—and to consider the relationship between education and equality today.

Education and Equality   329

Connected Readings

Summary ⇨ *at grade level*

The selections in this feature present views on the different standards of behavior for men and women in Renaissance society. Students should find the texts engaging and provocative.

DIRECT TEACHING

A Background
The "Woman Question"
Public debate about women intensified during this period. The vigor of the debate reflected a growing consciousness of women as a significant segment of society.

B Background
Learned Women of the Renaissance

- **Lady Jane Grey** (1537–1554), known as England's "nine day queen," ruled briefly before Mary claimed the throne in 1553. Although this—and her subsequent beheading—is Grey's primary claim to fame, she was also an accomplished scholar. Her intense education began when she was only three, and by the age of fifteen, Grey had acquired an impressive range of knowledge.

- **Mary Sidney Herbert, Countess of Pembroke** (1561–1621) is best known as the sister of the poet Sir Philip Sidney, but she was also a skilled translator and poet in her own right. Her home, Wilton House, was widely known as an informal center of learning and debate. Herbert's best-known work is a series of English translations of the psalms of the Bible, regarded by both her contemporaries and modern-day scholars as a stylistic masterpiece.

DIFFERENTIATING INSTRUCTION

Advanced Learners
Enrichment. Have students investigate the life of Jane Grey, Mary Sidney Herbert, or one of the following women of the European Renaissance:

- Margaret Peutinger (Germany)
- Katarina Jagellonica (Sweden)
- Vittoria Colonna (Italy)
- Olympia Morata (Italy)
- Elena Cornaro-Piscopia (Italy)

Invite students to share with the class one or two interesting facts about each woman.

Education and Equality   329

Connected Reading

Summary ⇔ at grade level

In this speech, Elizabeth affirms her faith in her subjects, declares her willingness to die for her country, likens her courage and strength of will to those of a king, and promises to reward her people for their readiness to do their duty.

DIRECT TEACHING

A Reading Skills

Recognizing persuasive technique. Why might Queen Elizabeth compliment her subjects in this way? [Possible responses: to inspire their loyalty; to bolster their confidence and prepare them for battle.]

B Reading Skills

Analyzing political assumptions. What assumption does Elizabeth hold about the nature of leadership? [Possible responses: that leadership requires sacrifice and selflessness.]

C Political Issues

Education and equality. With typical rhetorical finesse, Elizabeth throws a sop to those who regard women as weak while asserting her own power—and, by extension, that of other women. Explain how she does this. [She admits that her body is less strong than a man's but claims that her courage and spirit are those of a king.]

Political Points of View

Before You Read

King Henry VIII appointed humanist scholars to tutor both his son and his daughters. His younger daughter eventually became Queen Elizabeth I (1533–1603), the most influential of England's educated women. She could translate Greek and Latin classics into polished English, and she spoke and read six languages. She was also proficient in areas common to most gentlewomen—riding, music, astronomy, geography, philosophy, mathematics, and needlepoint. As queen, Elizabeth dazzled poets, dramatists, and court ambassadors with her superb literary training and political and diplomatic skills. One of her tutors, Roger Ascham, went so far as to exclaim, "It is your shame (I speak to you all, you young gentlemen of England) that one maid should go beyond you all in excellency of learning and knowledge of diverse tongues."

Many of Elizabeth's aristocratic countrywomen also gained excellent educations, yet what could they do with their knowledge? No professorships were open to them, nor could they join the ranks of the clergy. Aside from the personal satisfaction available from study, few women found themselves in a position where they could actually make use of their education.

Queen Elizabeth I wrote poems, letters, prayers, sermons, and translations—at the same time that she governed the country, conducted foreign policy, fostered the arts, and dedicated herself fervently to the new religion of her reign. She also wrote masterful speeches and political addresses. One of her best-known orations is the Tilbury Speech, given in 1588 before news of the destruction of the Spanish Armada reached England. Elizabeth's goal was to rouse her land forces to defend England against Spanish invasion.

SPEECH

Tilbury Speech
Queen Elizabeth I

My loving people: We have been persuaded by some that are careful of our safety to take heed how we commit ourself to armed multitudes for fear of treachery, but I assure you I do not desire to live to distrust my faithful and loving people. Let tyrants fear. I have always so behaved myself that, under God, I have placed my chiefest strength and safeguard in the loyal hearts and goodwill of my subjects. And therefore I am come amongst you, as you see, at this time, not for my recreation and disport, but being resolved in the midst and heat of the battle to live or die amongst you all, to lay down for my God, and for my kingdom, and for my people, my honor and my blood, even in the dust. I know I have the body but of a weak and feeble woman, but I have the heart and stomach of a king—and of a king of England too—and think foul scorn that Parma, or Spain, or any prince of Europe should dare to invade the borders of my realm. To which, rather than any dishonor shall grow by me, I myself will take up arms, I myself will be your general, judge, and rewarder of every one of your virtues in the field. I know already for your forwardness you have deserved rewards and crowns, and we do assure you, in the word of a prince, they shall be duly paid you.

—Elizabeth I

RESOURCES: READING

Planning
- One-Stop Planner CD-ROM with ExamView Test Generator

Differentiating Instruction
- Holt Reading Solutions
- The Holt Reader
- Holt Adapted Reader
- Supporting Instruction in Spanish

- Audio CD Library, Selections and Summaries in Spanish

Grammar and Language
- Daily Language Activities

Assessment
- Holt Assessment: Literature, Reading, and Vocabulary
- One-Stop Planner CD-ROM with ExamView Test Generator

- Holt Online Assessment

Internet
- go.hrw.com (Keyword: LE5 12-3)
- Elements of Literature Online

Media
- Audio CD Library
- Audio CD Library, Selections and Summaries in Spanish

The Rainbow Portrait (c. 1600) of Elizabeth I, attributed to Isaac Oliver. The inscription next to the rainbow reads *"Non sine sole iris,"* which means "No rainbow without the sun." Elizabeth would have been the sun. Note the eyes and ears embroidered on her gown.

DIRECT TEACHING

VIEWING THE ART

The "Rainbow" portrait (c. 1600) illustrates the ways artists flattered Elizabeth. The most obvious element of flattery in the picture is the queen's youthful appearance. Elizabeth was around sixty-seven when the portrait was painted. Less obvious to twenty-first-century observers is the Renaissance iconography that the painter uses. The serpent on Elizabeth's sleeve is a symbol of wisdom, and its presence is meant to indicate that Elizabeth is wise. The eyes, ears, and mouths on the gown suggest that Elizabeth is able to hear and see all that is going on in her realm. The rainbow in Elizabeth's hand and the words *Non sine sole iris* ("No rainbow without the sun") indicate Elizabeth's importance.

Activity. What is suggested about Elizabeth by the relationship between her and the rainbow in the portrait? [If there can be no rainbow without the sun, then the sun in the picture must be Elizabeth. She is England's sun.]

DIFFERENTIATING INSTRUCTION

Learners Having Difficulty
Invite students to read "The Tilbury Speech" in interactive format in *The Holt Reader* and to use the sidenotes as aids to understanding the selection. The interactive version provides additional instruction, practice, and assessment of the literary skill taught in the Student Edition. Monitor students' responses to the selection, and correct any misconceptions that arise.

English-Language Learners
For lessons designed for intermediate and advanced English-language learners, see *Holt Reading Solutions*.

Special Education Students
For lessons designed for special education students, see *Holt Reading Solutions*.

CONTENT-AREA CONNECTIONS

Film Studies: Elizabeth I
Individual activity. Elizabeth I has been dramatized in films including *Fire Over England* (1936), *The Sea Hawk* (1940), *The Private Lives of Elizabeth and Essex* (1939), *The Virgin Queen* (1955), *Shakespeare in Love* (1998), and *Elizabeth* (1998). Ask students to view one of these films and then hold a panel discussion to compare and contrast the film character with the historical figure.

Connected Reading

Summary ⇔ *at grade level*

> In each section of this fictional debate, a different speaker expresses her view on women, their lives, and their nature.

Selection Starter

Build background. The child of an English nobleman and his wife, Margaret Cavendish began writing books as a teenager. She later received informal instruction in science and philosophy from her husband, Sir William Cavendish, and wrote several books on these subjects. She also wrote plays, works of science fiction, and an autobiography.

Ⓐ Reading Skills

❓ **Analyzing political assumptions.** What assumptions does this speaker hold about women, women's rights, and achieving those rights? [Possible response: Women are not as "free, happy, and famous" as men but have a right to be; to win their rights, women must unite.]

Ⓑ Reading Skills

❓ **Analyzing rhetorical language.** Why is this simile particularly surprising and effective, given the audience? [Possible response: Comparing houses and beds to graves is effective—and startling—because the female members of the audience have been trained to think of the home as a place of safety, security, and repose.]

Response to Boxed Question

1. The speaker says women are miserable because they lack the freedom, pleasure, wealth, power, and fame enjoyed by men.

Political Points of View

Before You Read

Margaret Cavendish, duchess of Newcastle (1623–1673), was an eccentric gentlewoman who reached adulthood some decades after Elizabeth's death and the troubled times that followed. As a member of the aristocracy, Cavendish had both access to education and the freedom to write what she pleased. Although she was viewed as an oddity, she openly tackled such controversial topics as the situation of women in a male-dominated society. Some called her "the crazy duchess." Despite this kind of criticism, however, Cavendish published many unique works of prose and poetry during her lifetime—a time when women were considered daring if they wrote anything at all.

Female Orations is a fictional debate between women, representing a range of viewpoints on the role of women in society. Cavendish's speculations on the meaning of femininity are unusually sophisticated in their insight into the complexity of women's cultural situation in the mid–seventeenth century.

DEBATE

from Female Orations
Margaret Cavendish, duchess of Newcastle

I

Ⓐ Ladies, gentlewomen, and other inferior women, but not less worthy: I have been industrious to assemble you together, and wish I were so fortunate as to persuade you to make frequent assemblies, associations, and combinations amongst our own sex, that we may unite in prudent counsels, to make ourselves as free, happy, and famous as men; whereas now we live and die as if we were produced from beasts, rather than from men; for men are happy, and we women are miserable; they possess all the ease, rest, pleasure, wealth, power, and fame; whereas women are restless with labor, easeless with pain, melancholy for want of pleasures, helpless for want of power, and die in oblivion, for want of fame. ❶ Nevertheless, men are so unconscionable[1] and cruel against us Ⓑ that they endeavor to bar us of all sorts of liberty, and will not suffer us freely to associate amongst our own sex; but would fain[2] bury us in their houses or beds, as in a grave. The truth is, we live like bats or owls, labor like beasts, and die like worms.

---
1. **unconscionable** (un·kän'shən·ə·bəl) *adj.*: not fair.
2. **fain** *adv.*: eagerly; gladly.

> ❶ The first speaker in the debate welcomes the participants and expresses her wish that women would assemble for such discussion and debate more frequently.
> ❓ How does this speaker contrast the situation of women with that of men?

DIFFERENTIATING INSTRUCTION

Learners Having Difficulty

Explain to students that the writing style of Cavendish—and of many others during this time—is characterized by long, multipart sentences. These sentences are usually made up of two or more independent clauses, joined by semicolons. Before students begin reading, have them skim the text and note where one clause ends and another begins. Then, have them read the orations aloud in small groups, with each student reading only one segment of a sentence (stopping at the semicolon or period). After reading each segment, the student should clarify its meaning by restating it in his or her own words.

II

Ladies, gentlewomen, and other inferior women: The lady that spoke to you hath spoken wisely and eloquently, in expressing our unhappiness; but she hath not declared a remedy, or showed us a way to come out of our miseries; but, if she could or would be our guide, to lead us out of the labyrinth[3] men have put us into, we should not only praise and admire her, but adore and worship her as our goddess: but alas! men, that are not only our tyrants but our devils, keep us in the hell of subjection, from whence I cannot perceive any redemption or getting out; we may complain and bewail our condition, yet that will not free us; we may murmur and rail against men, yet they regard not what we say. In short, our words to men are as empty sounds; our sighs, as puffs of winds; and our tears, as fruitless showers; and our power is so inconsiderable, that men laugh at our weakness.

III

Ladies, gentlewomen, and other inferior women: The former orations were exclamations against men, repining[4] at their condition and mourning for our own; but we have no reason to speak against men, who are our admirers and lovers; they are our protectors, defenders, and maintainers; they admire our beauties, and love our persons; they protect us from injuries, defend us from dangers, are industrious for our subsistence, and provide for our children; they swim great voyages by sea, travel long journeys by land, to get us rarities and curiosities; they dig to the center of the earth for gold for us; they dive to the bottom of the sea for jewels for us: they build to the skies houses for us: they hunt, fowl, fish, plant, and reap for food for us. All which, we could not do ourselves; and yet we complain of men, as if they were our enemies, whenas[5] we could not possibly live without them, which shows we are as ungrateful as inconstant. But we have more reason to murmur against Nature, than against men, who hath made men more ingenious, witty, and wise than women; more strong, industrious, and laborious than women; for women are witless and strengthless, and unprofitable creatures, did they not bear children.

Wherefore, let us love men, praise men, and pray for men; for without men, we should be the most miserable creatures that Nature hath made or could make....

---
3. **labyrinth** *n.*: maze.
4. **repining** *v.* used as *adj.*: complaining.
5. **whenas:** *conj.*: while on the other hand.

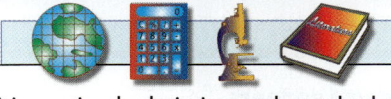

Margaret Cavendish, duchess of Newcastle (17th century). English School. Engraving.
Private Collection/The Bridgeman Art Library.

History: Cavendish and the Royal Society

In 1667, Margaret Cavendish asked for permission to attend a meeting of the Royal Society of London, founded in 1660 to support and advance the natural sciences. The request was hotly debated, for women were not typically admitted to such gatherings, nor were they encouraged to study the sciences. In the end, Cavendish, along with several of her ladies-in-waiting, gained admission and watched with interest while scientist Robert Boyle performed his latest experiments.

Individual activity. Have students research the Royal Society of London. What kinds of experiments might Robert Boyle have presented? When was the first woman admitted as a member of the Society?

DIRECT TEACHING

A Political Issue
? **Education and equality.**
Why might the speaker consider "scholastical studies . . . and disputes" a waste? [Possible response: They do not have immediate, practical applications in women's lives.]
What is ironic about this speaker's opinion? [The speaker is herself engaged in an intellectual dispute.]

B Content-Area Connections
History: Oppression
? **Nature and oppression.**
What other groups of people have been oppressed on the basis of assumptions about their nature? [Possible response: The institution of slavery was based on the belief that people of color were naturally inferior to whites.]

Responses to Boxed Questions

4. She is eloquent and gracious. Unlike the other speakers, she omits any reference to "inferior" women.

5. The parallel structure emphasizes the advantages that the speaker claims for women.

6. The speaker claims that women are so much more favorably endowed by nature that men are forced to admire them.

7. The seventh speaker asserts that to rule over men, women need only embrace the attributes nature has given them. She says that women should not aspire to be masculine but rather should exercise the power of their superior femininity. Some students may agree with the speaker's argument that women's situation is better than men's. Others may feel that the benefits described by the speaker do not compensate for the drawbacks of inequality.

Woman reading *Tristan und Isolde* by W. Hauschild.
The Art Archive/Neuschwanstein Castle, Germany/Dagli Orti (A).

Several other viewpoints are expressed as the debate continues in parts IV–VI. Part VII, which follows, is the last section of the debate.

VII

Noble ladies, honorable gentlewomen, and worthy female-commoners: ❹ The former oratoress's speech was to persuade us out of ourselves and to be that which Nature never intended us to be, to wit, masculine. But why should we desire to be masculine, since our own sex and condition is far the better? For if men have more courage, they have more danger; and if men have more strength, they have more labor than women have; if men are more eloquent in speech, women are more harmonious in voice; if men be more active, women are more graceful; if men have more liberty, women have more safety; ❺ for we never fight duels nor battles; nor do we go long travels or dangerous voyages; we labor not in building nor digging in mines, quarries, or pits, for metal, stone, or coals; neither do we waste or shorten our lives with university or scholastical studies, questions, and disputes; we burn not our faces with smiths' forges or chemists' furnaces; and hundreds of other actions which men are employed in; for they would not only fade the fresh beauty, spoil the lovely features, and decay the youth of women, causing them to appear old, when they are young; but would break their small limbs, and destroy their tender lives. Wherefore women have no reason to complain against Nature or the god of Nature, for although the gifts are not the same as they have given to men, yet those gifts they have given to women are much better; for we women are much more favored by Nature than men, in giving us such beauties, features, shapes, graceful demeanor, and such insinuating[6] and enticing attractives, that men are forced to admire us, love us, and be desirous of us; ❻ insomuch that rather than not have and enjoy us, they will deliver to our disposals their power, persons, and lives, enslaving themselves to our will and pleasures; also, we are their saints, whom they adore and worship; and what can we desire more than to be men's tyrants, destinies, and goddesses? ❼

6. **insinuating** v. used as adj.: suggestive.

❹ What can you infer about the seventh and final speaker from the way she addresses her audience? (Review the way the first three speakers opened their comments.)

❺ What is the effect of this speaker's repeated use of an "If . . . then" parallel structure in these sentences?

❻ Why, according to this speaker, do women have no reason to complain?

❼ How would you summarize this speaker's argument? Do you agree or disagree with her? Explain.

DIFFERENTIATING INSTRUCTION

Advanced Learners
Using *Female Orations* as a springboard, have students discuss in small groups the "nature" of women and men. Is one sex naturally stronger? smarter? more adventurous? more nurturing? more analytical? more emotional? Or are people taught from birth to behave in certain ways so that these behaviors *seem* more natural than others? After the small-group discussions, divide the class into two teams, define the point of view that each team represents, and organize a formal debate on the topic. Encourage students to use material from *Female Orations* to defend their position and to refute that of the other team.

Analyzing Political Points of View

Education and Equality

The questions on this page ask you to analyze the views on education and equality in the preceding three selections.

Francis Bacon .... **Of Studies**
Queen Elizabeth I .... **Tilbury Speech**
Margaret Cavendish .... from **Female Orations**

Comparing Political Assumptions

1. In light of the selections you've just read, how do you think Francis Bacon intended to use the word *man* throughout "Of Studies"? Was he using it to mean any human being, male or female, or did he intend to apply his ideas only to males? What evidence from Renaissance history—or simply the essay itself—supports your conclusion?

2. In the Tilbury Speech, Queen Elizabeth says that she has the body of "a weak and feeble woman" but "the heart and stomach of a king." What **inference** can you draw about implicit and explicit ideas and assumptions of her time toward women—and men? (An **implicit** idea is one that is not stated directly and must be inferred from details. An **explicit** idea is stated directly.) Why do you think she finds it necessary to mention her gender? Consult your reading notes from page 322.

3. Review the excerpts from Margaret Cavendish's *Female Orations*. Characterize the speaker of each section. What arguments does each speaker present? What assumptions about women may have been valid in the seventeenth century but are no longer valid today?

4. In the sixteenth and seventeenth centuries, an "inferior" was someone of lower social status than an aristocrat or a noble. Even when you know the meaning of this word, what effect does Cavendish's repeated use of the phrase "Ladies, gentlewomen, and other inferior women" have on you as a modern reader? Why do you think Cavendish has her first three speakers use this opening address?

WRITING

Letter to the Past

Write a letter to Queen Elizabeth I or to Margaret Cavendish, duchess of Newcastle, in which you express your thoughts about their writings and attitudes. Begin by explaining that you have just read something the writer wrote more than three centuries ago. Identify the work, and tell the writer how attitudes or realities have changed since her time. (See your Quickwrite notes from page 322 for ideas.) Explain to her our contemporary views on education and equality. Conclude by telling the writer what you think of her achievements.

Pages 322–335 cover
Literary Skills
Analyze and compare political points of view on a topic.

Reading Skills
Draw inferences.

Writing Skills
Write a letter to one of the writers.

Analyzing Political Points of View

INDEPENDENT PRACTICE

3. The first speaker argues that women lead miserable, subservient lives. The second speaker agrees but asserts that it is futile to entertain notions of liberation. The third speaker defends men as protectors and providers; she considers women naturally weak and unintelligent. The last speaker argues that nature has given different gifts to each sex and that woman's chief gift—her beauty—should be celebrated for the power it gives women over men. The assumption that women are naturally feeble while men are strong and adventurous is no longer valid today.

4. Answers will vary, but most students will find the phrase offensive. Some may feel that the phrase reveals Cavendish's complicity with the biases of her time. Others may point out that Cavendish has the last speaker use the phrase "worthy female-commoners," perhaps as an implicit criticism of the other speakers' attitudes.

ASSESSING

Assessment
- *Holt Assessment: Literature, Reading, and Vocabulary*

Comparing Political Assumptions

1. Bacon most likely intended the word *man* to refer only to males. Although some upper-class women were educated, their knowledge was never applied in the world of business or politics—in the "marshaling of affairs" for the sake of which Bacon recommends study.

2. Elizabeth's words suggest that most people considered women too weak to conduct public affairs, let alone govern a nation. Elizabeth mentions her sex probably to reassure her subjects of her ability to govern in spite of her sex.

The King James Bible (1611): A Masterpiece by a Committee

One of the first acts of James I after he was crowned king of England was to sponsor a new translation of the Bible. There were many translations of the Bible available, but the king, like others, disliked the interpretive comments included in the existing translations. Moreover, Renaissance scholarship had made people more historically minded and sensitive to textual inaccuracies. The new translation would be checked against the most authoritative Hebrew and Greek texts available.

The King's Scholars

To produce the translation, the king appointed a team of fifty-four learned clergymen. They broke up into groups, each with a section of the Scriptures to translate and each with a pair of scholars to check the work. Seven years later, after a committee of bishops gave it a final review, the new translation was published. It has become known variously as the King James Bible, because James sponsored it; as the Authorized Version, because the Anglican Church authorized its use; and simply as the English Bible, because it has been so important to the civilization and literature of all English-speaking countries.

The Influence of the English Bible

If English-speaking people living before our time read anything, they read the English Bible. And if they read nothing themselves, they regularly heard the Bible read in church. For nearly four centuries most writers in English have been influenced, consciously or unconsciously, by the English Bible. They have quoted it, echoed it, paraphrased it, alluded to it, imitated it, and retold its fascinating stories over and over.

Everyday English speech is full of words and phrases from the English Bible: "lovingkindness," "tender mercy," "long-suffering." We "cast pearls before swine" and "wait until the eleventh hour" before acting. We speak of the "wisdom of Solomon" and the "patience of Job." Many biblical words (such as *scapegoat*) are by now so embedded in our language that we use them without knowing we are using biblical language.

Today, the King James Bible stands with Shakespeare as an exemplar of English when the language was, as many people believe, more flexible and eloquent than at any other time, and more capable of stirring people's hearts and minds.

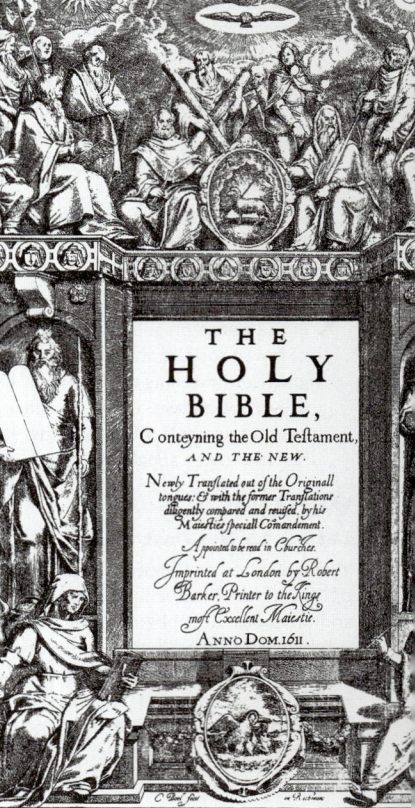

Title page from the King James Bible (1611). Printed by Robert Barker, London.
The Pierpont Morgan Library, NY.

Psalms: Worship Through Poetry

Illuminated *P* (detail) (c. 1500) from a Flemish Bible.
Victoria and Albert Museum, London.

The Bible is full of poetry. Every book of it contains poems or fragments of poems inserted into the prose, and much of the prose itself is highly rhythmical. One book, Psalms, consists entirely of poems, some of which were set to music and sung during worship services in the ancient Temple in Jerusalem. The Book of Psalms preserves 150 of these songs, a fraction of the total number that the ancient Hebrews knew and sang. Psalms were used as hymnals and included songs appropriate for many types of worship: thanksgiving, lament, praise, and devotion. Modern scholars now agree that the psalms were written by many authors over many centuries, but seventy-three of the psalms are said to be "for David" or "concerning David," the heroic Hebrew king.

Faithful to the source. In English a collection of psalms is called a psalter (the *p* is silent in both *psalm* and *psalter*). (In Hebrew the name for the collection is *Tehillim,* or "songs of praise.") There have been dozens of English psalters besides the one in the King James Bible, but none of them has lasted so well and so long. King James's translators did not try to impose rhyme on their versions because there is no rhyme in the originals. Instead, they imitated such Hebrew poetic devices as **repetition** and **parallel structure** (the use of sentences or phrases similar in structure):

> Let the floods clap their hands,
> Let the hills be joyful together.
> —Psalm 98:8

The psalmists were fond of saying essentially the same thing twice, in different words ("thy rod and thy staff" in Psalm 23). The King James Bible uses the numbering of the ancient Hebrew manuscripts; some other Bibles use a different numbering system, derived from a Greek translation of the Hebrew, and these Bibles have an extra psalm, number 151.

Ancient yet modern. Biblical poetry, then, is much like modern free verse in that it does not have rhyme and meter but it does have other patterns of repetition, balance, antithesis, and parallelism. Metaphors and similes abound, and so do images drawn from nature and everyday experience:

> My God, in him will I trust.
> Surely he shall deliver thee from the snare of the fowler,
> And from the noisome pestilence.
> He shall cover thee with his feathers,
> And under his wings shalt thou trust:
> His truth shall be thy shield and buckler.
> Thou shalt not be afraid for the terror by night;
> Nor for the arrow that flieth by day;
> Nor for the pestilence that walketh in darkness;
> Nor for the destruction that wasteth at noonday.
> —Psalm 91:2–6

DIRECT TEACHING

C Content-Area Connections
Library Skills: Biblical Resources
Make sure students know that there are reference books called *concordances* for locating biblical passages. Two widely used concordances for the King James Bible are *Strong's Exhaustive Concordance of the Bible* and *Young's Analytical Concordance.*

D Content-Area Connections
Literature: Poetry in the Bible
Poetic writing can be found in David's lament for Saul and Jonathan in 2 Samuel 1:19–27, Mary's "Magnificat" in Luke 1:46–55, and throughout Job, Proverbs, the Song of Solomon, Ecclesiastes, Isaiah, and Jeremiah.

E Content-Area Connections
History: Bible Publication
Historically, the Psalms and the Gospels have been published as separate volumes more often than any other books of the Bible. *The Bay Psalm Book* (1640) was the first book published in the American Colonies.

READING SKILLS REVIEW

Analyzing implicit and explicit philosophical assumptions

Read aloud the following quotation from the translators' preface to the King James Bible: "Translation it is that openeth the window, to let in the light; that breaketh the shell, that we may eat the kernel; that putteth aside the curtain, that we may look into the most holy place; that removeth the cover of the well, that we may come by the water; even as Jacob rolled away the stone from the mouth of the well, by which means the flocks of Laban were watered. Indeed without translation into the vulgar tongue, the unlearned are but like children at Jacob's well (which was deep) without a bucket or something to draw with." Elicit students' responses to this statement and comments on the quality of other translations they have read.

PRETEACHING

Summary ↔ at grade level

The psalms, hymns to or about God, are collected in the Book of Psalms in the Old Testament.

- **Psalm 23.** The speaker of the lyric Psalm 23 uses two extended metaphors: The first compares God to a shepherd; the second compares God to a generous host. The figurative language creates a picture of a benevolent God who guides, comforts, and provides for those in his care, in spite of life's dangers. The tone of the poem is serene and trusting, an equilibrium created as much by the rhythmic repetition of words and parallel grammatical elements as by the imagery.

- **Psalm 137.** The speaker of Psalm 137 is one of the Israelites taken captive by foreign conquerors, the Babylonians, and forced to leave their beloved Jerusalem. The tone of the psalm progresses from mournfulness to resolution to anger and finally to vengefulness. The natural images of water and willows suggest weeping, loss, and longing, and the setting is "a strange land" far from home. Singing and laughter are unnatural for a people in exile. Memories of home and the hope of destroying the destroyers sustain the displaced speaker, much as repetition and parallelism sustain the rhythm of this lament.

Selection Starter

Build background. A culture's images for God usually reflect the values and ways of life of the people. The images of Psalm 23, for example, echo the pastoral, or sheepherding, way of life of the Israelite people for whom the songs were originally written.

Before You Read

Psalms 23 and 137

Make the Connection

You may be familiar with one or both of the following psalms. Psalm 23 is a song of trust that affirms the speaker's confidence in God. Psalm 137 is a cry from the heart of the speaker, a captive Israelite in Babylon who is experiencing life's perils firsthand.

What troubling events in modern history might inspire people to seek the comforting presence of God?

Literary Focus

Parallelism

Parallelism is the repetition of words, phrases, or sentences that have the same grammatical structure or restate a similar idea. Parallelism is common in literature meant to be sung or recited, such as the poems in the Bible's Book of Psalms. Instead of relying on rhyme, meter, or other modern poetic devices, the psalms use parallel structure to create a sense of rhythm, balance, and order; to show the relationships among ideas; and to heighten emotional impact.

> **Parallelism** is the repetition of words, phrases, or sentences that have the same grammatical structure or restate a similar idea.
>
> *For more on Parallelism, see the Handbook of Literary and Historical Terms.*

Literary Skills Understand the use of parallelism.

Background

The Book of Psalms is the Bible's songbook. The Greek word *psalmos*, which means "plucking of strings," tells us that the poems were sung to musical accompaniment. The Hebrew title of the book, *Tehillim,* means "songs of praise." The book's 150 lyric poems express not only praise, however, but a wide range of emotions. They evoke everything from the heights of joy and gratitude to the depths of anguish and bitterness.

Some, like Psalm 137, connect directly to the history of the people of Israel. In the sixth century B.C., King Nebuchadnezzar of Babylonia conquered Jerusalem and deported many Israelites to his own capital, Babylon. (Ancient Babylon is now a ruin; it lies on the Euphrates River south of Baghdad, in Iraq.)

Nebuchadnezzar admires the Hanging Gardens of Babylon. Illustration by E. Wallcousins from *Myths of Babylonia and Assyria.*
Mary Evans Picture Library.

338   Collection 3   The Renaissance

DIFFERENTIATING INSTRUCTION

Learners Having Difficulty
Have students rewrite one of the psalms in prose. This exercise will help them make inferences and identify main ideas and themes.

English-Language Learners
To help students struggling with the archaic language, have them work with others to rewrite the psalms in the language of today. Divide the class into small groups, and have each group prepare their version to read aloud.

Psalm 23 is probably the best-known religious poem in the Western world. The opening verses, comparing God to a shepherd, use the kind of pastoral imagery found throughout the Bible. (This song was sung by a pastoral people, so the comparison of the Lord to a shepherd is particularly appropriate.) Then the metaphors in the psalm change, and the Lord becomes a host providing a banquet for the speaker, whose enemies watch him enviously as he eats, not daring to harm him. Among the images of the poem, there is also a suggestion of the speaker as a pilgrim traveling through a dangerous world.

Shepherds. Bas-relief on the lintel over the west portal of Chartres Cathedral in France.
Chartres Cathedral, France.

Psalm 23

The Lord is my shepherd; I shall not want.
He maketh me to lie down in green pastures:
He leadeth me beside the still waters.
He restoreth my soul:
5 He leadeth me in the paths of righteousness for his name's sake.°
Yea, though I walk through the valley of the shadow of death,
I will fear no evil: For thou art with me;
Thy rod and thy staff they comfort me.
Thou preparest a table before me in the presence of mine enemies:
10 Thou anointest my head with oil; my cup runneth over.
Surely goodness and mercy shall follow me all the days of my life:
And I will dwell in the house of the Lord forever.

5. **his name's sake:** That is, he will live up to his name as shepherd.

King James Bible

DIRECT TEACHING

A English-Language Learners
Archaic language. Explain that the ending *–eth* is the archaic equivalent of the modern third-person present-tense *–s* ending. Have students restate the words *maketh, leadeth,* and *restoreth* using modern endings. [*makes, leads, restores*]

B Literary Focus
Parallelism. What grammatical structure is repeated in ll. 2–5? [The subject-verb-object pattern "He maketh me," "He leadeth me," etc.] How does the repetition of this structure reflect or emphasize the psalm's message? [The repetition has a soothing, reassuring effect and suggests the speaker's faith in God.]

C Reading Skills
Speculating. What kinds of experiences might be described as "walk[ing] through the valley of the shadow of death"? [Possible responses: dealing with a life-threatening illness or injury; living with depression; being a victim of a violent crime.]

D Learners Having Difficulty
Identifying details. Whom does the speaker address in these lines? [God] Whom does the speaker address in ll. 1–5? [a human audience]

DIFFERENTIATING INSTRUCTION

Advanced Learners
Enrichment. Suggest these activities to interested students. Have them present their findings in a format of their own choosing:

- Research sheepherding around the world in the past and present. Try to find out what characteristics would make some shepherds more effective than others.

- Do research to find out why the city of Jerusalem is so important to the speaker of Psalm 137. Speculate on what the city meant to him in the past and why it occupies his thoughts now.

DEVELOPING FLUENCY

Using different editions of the Bible, photocopy several translations of these psalms, and distribute them to students. Have students read the various translations aloud in small groups. Afterward, have them decide which translation they found most poetic, which was easiest to understand, and which was hardest to understand.

King James Bible 339

DIRECT TEACHING

A Literary Focus

Imagery. What feelings are suggested by "harps / Upon the willows"? How do those feelings relate to the speaker's situation? [Possible response: The image suggests the speaker's feelings of sorrow and longing for what has been lost.]

B Literary Focus

Parallelism. What structure is repeated in ll. 10–14? [Clauses beginning with "If I"; the first two are followed by a main clause beginning with "Let my."] How does this repetition help you understand the speaker's feelings? [Possible responses: It reflects the speaker's distress over his captivity and his fear that he will never see his homeland again. The repetition is a kind of verbal wailing.]

C Reading Skills

Reading aloud. Read this line aloud, and emphasize *thy*. What does the emphasis help you understand? [Possible responses: It suggests that the speaker has seen his own children dashed to death.]

GUIDED PRACTICE

Monitoring students' progress. Guide the class in answering the following questions.

True-False

1. The speaker of Psalm 23 is afraid. [F]
2. Psalm 23 is a cry for help. [F]
3. In Psalm 137 the captors have asked the captives to sing. [T]
4. The speaker of Psalm 137 longs to forget his homeland. [F]

Clusters of stone ruins from ancient Babylon, now Iraq.
Nik Wheeler/Black Star Publishing/Picture Quest.

This is a song of entreaty on the occasion of a national catastrophe: Many Israelites are being held captive in Babylon. This lament over a remembered home has been recited by many captives in the thousands of years since it was first sung in ancient Babylon.

The speaker of Psalm 137 is a captive Israelite, bitterly lamenting his people's exile. The Babylonians have asked their captives to sing to entertain them, but what do the captives have to sing about?

Psalm 137

By the rivers of Babylon, there we sat down, yea, we wept,
When we remembered Zion.°
We hanged our harps
Upon the willows in the midst thereof.
5 For there they that carried us away captive required of us a song;
And they that wasted us required of us mirth,
Saying, "Sing us one of the songs of Zion."
How shall we sing the Lord's song
In a strange land?
10 If I forget thee, O Jerusalem,
Let my right hand forget her cunning.
If I do not remember thee,
Let my tongue cleave° to the roof of my mouth;
If I prefer not Jerusalem above my chief joy.
   Remember, O Lord, the children of Edom° in the day of
15   Jerusalem;
Who said, "Raze it,° raze it, even to the foundation thereof."
O daughter of Babylon,° who art to be destroyed;
Happy shall he be, that rewardeth thee
As thou hast served us.
20 Happy shall he be, that taketh
And dasheth thy little ones against the stones.

2. **Zion:** a hill in Jerusalem that is often a symbol for the whole of Israel.

13. **cleave** *v.*: adhere; stick.

15. **children of Edom:** The Edomites, neighbors of the Israelites, rejoiced when the Israelites' kingdom was conquered and most of its population was deported.
16. **Raze it:** Level it to the ground.
17. **daughter of Babylon:** the Babylonian people.

340   Collection 3   The Renaissance

CONTENT-AREA CONNECTIONS

Music: Sounds of the Psalms
Over the centuries, many composers have set psalms to music. Among them is the Austrian composer Franz Schubert (1797–1828), who began his musical career as a singer in the Imperial Chapel Choir while he attended the Royal Seminary in Vienna.

Whole-class activity. After students have read Psalm 23, let them listen to Schubert's musical setting of the psalm and comment on the feelings it evokes. Interested students might research some contemporary settings of the psalms, such as the English composer John Rutter's version of Psalm 23 (from *Requiem*), pop/rock versions of Psalm 137 by Don McLean on his 1971 album *American Pie* ("Babylon"), and by Manfred Mann and the Earth Band's 1976 album *The Roaring Silence* ("The Road to Babylon").

Response and Analysis

Thinking Critically

1. An **extended metaphor** is a comparison that is developed at length, perhaps over several lines of writing or even an entire work, such as a poem. In Psalm 23, how does the speaker extend the metaphor that compares God to a shepherd? What feeling does this metaphor evoke?

2. The second **metaphor** in Psalm 23 compares God to a generous host. (In the ancient Middle East, it was a sign of hospitality to anoint a guest's head and dusty feet with oil.) How does the speaker extend this metaphor of God as a gracious host, with the speaker as his guest?

3. Which lines of Psalm 23 hint at the idea that life is a perilous journey?

4. Psalm 23 is often read at funerals or memorial services. Why might people find the images in the psalm consoling?

5. The speaker in Psalm 137 is both homesick and vengeful. Which lines convey each of these emotions? How do you react to the final line of the psalm?

6. On what occasion might Psalm 137 be sung? Does the text of the psalm have any relevance for people today?

7. Both psalms contain examples of **parallelism**, or parallel structure—places where the same grammatical structure is repeated or an idea is restated in different words. Read aloud at least one example of parallelism in each psalm.

WRITING

Psalm Similarities

The version of Psalm 23 that follows appeared in a psalter translated by the Massachusetts Puritans and published in the *Bay Psalm Book* (1640). In a brief **essay, compare and contrast** this version with the version in the King James Bible. Tell which version you prefer and why, using examples from each text.

Psalm 23

The Lord to me a shepherd is;
    want therefor shall not I.
He in the folds of tender grass
    doth cause me down to lie.
To waters calm me gently leads,
    restore my soul doth he;
He doth in paths of righteousness for his name's sake lead me.
5 Yea, though in valley of death's
    shade I walk, none ill I'll fear,
Because thou art with me; thy rod
    and staff my comfort are.
For me a table thou hast spread in
    presence of my foes;
Thou dost anoint my head with
    oil; my cup it overflows.
Goodness and mercy surely shall
    all my days follow me.
And in the Lord's house I shall
10   dwell so long as days shall be.

Before you begin writing, gather your details in a chart like the following one.

	King James	Bay Psalms
Images		
Main idea		
Sound effects		
Syntax (sentence patterns)		

Literary Skills
Analyze the use of parallelism.

Writing Skills
Write an essay comparing and contrasting two versions of a psalm.

INDEPENDENT PRACTICE

Response and Analysis

Thinking Critically

1. The speaker describes the "green pastures" and "still waters" to which God leads him (sheep do not drink from rapidly moving water); he speaks of the shepherd's rod and staff. The metaphor evokes comfort.

2. The speaker describes the host's graciousness in preparing a table for him and providing an overflowing cup.

3. Lines 6, 7, and 9 suggest that life has dangers.

4. Possible answers: The psalm might remind survivors of God's love for them; the images of the "valley of the shadow of death" and "the house of the Lord" suggest the hope that the mourners, as well as the deceased, will be welcomed into heaven.

5. Homesickness is conveyed strongly in ll. 1–2 and 10–14, as is revenge in ll. 15–21. Some students may be appalled by this violent image.

6. Possible answer: Psalm 137 would have special meaning for any group facing literal or figurative captivity. Its continuing relevance resides in the emotions expressed—love of one's homeland, despair in exile, and a desire to see wrongs avenged.

7. Examples of parallelism in Psalm 23 include ll. 2–5, l. 8, and ll. 9–10. These repetitions create a soothing, reassuring effect that mirrors the theme of the psalm. Examples of parallelism in Psalm 137 include ll. 5–6, 10–14, and 18–21. These repetitions suggest the speaker's mournful bitterness, his homesickness, and his preoccupation with revenge.

ASSESSING

Assessment
- Holt Assessment: *Literature, Reading, and Vocabulary*

RETEACHING

For a lesson reteaching author's tone and style, see **Reteaching**, p. 1129A.

PRETEACHING

Summary 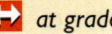 at grade level

This parable, from the Gospel of Luke, concerns a father and his two sons. The younger son asks the father for his share of the inheritance, and the father obliges him. The young man leaves home, travels to a distant land, and squanders the money. After suffering hunger during a famine and being given degrading employment, the son decides to return to his father, beg for mercy, and ask to be received as a servant. He does so and is greeted warmly by his father, who showers him with gifts and orders that a lavish feast be prepared. The older son resentfully complains that his steadfast service has never brought him such rewards. The father reassures the older son of his affection but maintains that the return of a lost son is truly an occasion for rejoicing. Jesus' original audience, firmly committed to the principles of justice and retribution, would have been challenged by the moral lesson of the parable: that the mercy and spiritual riches of God are available to all those who seek him—even those deemed unworthy by other people.

Skills Starter

Build prerequisite skills. Remind students that the characters in an allegory—and thus in a parable—are often two-dimensional. That is, rather than being fully fleshed-out characters, they represent one or two common personality traits or tendencies, such as greed, wastefulness, or loyalty. They may also symbolize a larger idea or entity, such as good or evil. As students read, have them look beyond the literal words and actions of the main characters to the character traits or the ideas they represent.

Before You Read

The Parable of the Prodigal Son

Make the Connection
Quickwrite

The Bible contains about forty **parables**, or moral lessons, which occur in all four Gospels. They are attributed to Jesus, who, like other Jewish teachers, used them to make his messages clear. The parables of Jesus tend to be down-to-earth and easy to grasp on a literal level. They involve ordinary events that people of his time could relate to: a shepherd searching for a sheep that has strayed from the flock; sleeping bridesmaids who are unprepared for the arriving bridal party; a poor woman who loses a coin. The underlying messages of these parables concern deep truths about conduct and morality.

Jot down brief notes about a modern situation that would make a good parable—an anecdote that teaches a lesson about life. It may be something you have experienced or something you have heard about.

Literary Focus
Parable

A **parable** is a short, allegorical story that teaches a moral or religious lesson about life. The word *parable* comes from a Greek word meaning "comparison; analogy." Parables convey their lessons about life through the use of **allegory**: The simple characters, places, and events in the story symbolize broader, more complex concepts. Because symbols can be interpreted in multiple ways, even a brief allegory can yield more than one meaning. The biblical parables draw their lessons from characters and situations that would have been familiar to people of Jesus' time: a shepherd and his lost sheep, a problem son, a victim of a highway robbery.

Literary Skills Understand the characteristics of parables.

A **parable** is a short, allegorical story that teaches a moral lesson about life.

For more on Parable, see the Handbook of Literary and Historical Terms.

Background

In ancient Israel—Jesus' homeland—the oldest son in a family would inherit a double share of his father's wealth and become the head of the family upon his father's death. In this parable we encounter a family situation that would have been common: The elder son is set to receive two thirds of his father's estate, and the younger son, one third. During his lifetime a father was under no obligation to divide up his estate or cash in any part of it for the sake of his sons.

You may notice that the word *prodigal*, used for centuries to identify this parable, never occurs in the story itself. The word usually means "recklessly extravagant; wasteful," but it can also mean "lavish; abundant." As you read "The Parable of the Prodigal Son," keep these different meanings in mind. Determine which characters could be called prodigal and why.

342   Collection 3   The Renaissance

DIFFERENTIATING INSTRUCTION

Learners Having Difficulty
Because the parable is short, students can read it aloud. Have students take turns reading paragraphs. After each paragraph, ask a student to paraphrase what was read.

English-Language Learners
Before students read the parable, define for them the following words: *substance, riotous,*

perish, and *transgressed.* Help students use context clues to determine the meanings of other unfamiliar words.

Advanced Learners
Enrichment. Have students write an analysis of the parable that includes a key to the parable's symbolism. Then, have students compare their analyses.

The Prodigal Son (1975–1976) by Marc Chagall.
© Scala/Art Resource, New York. © 2003 Artists Rights Society (ARS), New York/ADAGP, Paris.

DIRECT TEACHING

VIEWING THE ART

Marc Chagall (1887–1985) is one of the few modern artists to focus on religious themes. This image shows the prodigal son being embraced by his father. The crowd in the background may be those who were invited to the feast given by the father upon the return of his son.

Activity. Ask students to list adjectives that describe the mood of Chagall's painting. [Possible response: Like the parable, Chagall's painting seems tender and joyous.]

The Parable of the Prodigal Son

And he[1] said, A certain man had two sons:

And the younger of them said to his father, Father, give me the portion of goods that falleth to me. And he divided unto them his living.

And not many days after the younger son gathered all together, and took his journey into a far country, and there wasted his substance with riotous living.

And when he had spent all, there arose a mighty famine in that land; and he began to be in want.

And he went and joined himself to a citizen of that country; and he sent him into his fields to feed swine.[2]

And he would fain have filled his belly with the husks that the swine did eat: and no man gave unto him.

And when he came to himself, he said, How many hired servants of my father's have bread enough and to spare, and I perish with hunger!

I will arise and go to my father, and will say unto him, Father, I have sinned against heaven, and before thee,

And am no more worthy to be called thy son: make me as one of thy hired servants.

And he arose, and came to his father. But when he was yet a great way off, his father saw him, and had compassion, and ran, and fell on his neck, and kissed him.

And the son said unto him, Father, I have sinned against heaven, and in thy sight, and am no more worthy to be called thy son.

But the father said to his servants, Bring forth the best robe, and put it on him; and put a ring on his hand, and shoes on his feet:

And bring hither the fatted calf, and kill it; and let us eat, and be merry:

For this my son was dead, and is alive again; he was lost, and is found. And they began to be merry.

Now his elder son was in the field: and as he came and drew nigh to the house, he heard musick and dancing.

And he called one of the servants, and asked what these things meant.

And he said unto him, Thy brother is come; and thy father hath killed the fatted calf, because he hath received him safe and sound.

And he was angry, and would not go in: therefore came his father out, and intreated him.

And he answering said to his father, Lo, these many years do I serve thee, neither transgressed I at any time thy commandment: and yet thou never gavest me a kid,[3] that I might make merry with my friends:

But as soon as this thy son was come, which hath devoured thy living with harlots,[4] thou hast killed for him the fatted calf.

And he said unto him, Son, thou art ever with me, and all that I have is thine.

It was meet that we should make merry, and be glad: for this thy brother was dead, and is alive again; and was lost, and is found.

—Luke 15:11–32

---

1. **he:** Jesus.

2. **swine** *n.*: pigs. The ancient Israelites considered swine ritually taboo, or unclean, and they avoided any contact with them. Tending pigs would thus have been considered degrading work.

The Prodigal Son (detail) (1975–1976) by Marc Chagall.
© Scala/Art Resource, New York.
© 2003 Artists Rights Society (ARS), New York/ADAGP, Paris.

3. **kid** *n.*: baby goat.

4. **harlots** *n. pl.*: prostitutes.

Response and Analysis

Reading Check
1. How does the younger son acquire his money? How does he then lose it?
2. Why does the younger son decide to return home?
3. What is his father's reaction to the younger son's return? What is his brother's reaction?

Thinking Critically
4. At the end of the **parable,** whose position do you understand better, that of the father or that of the elder son? Why?
5. As an **allegory** this parable can be understood on both a literal and a symbolic level. The literal level concerns two sons, an inheritance, and a loving father. On that level, state in your own words the **theme** of the story—the comment it makes about life.
6. On a **symbolic** level this parable carries religious messages about God, sin, and forgiveness. On that level the father symbolizes God, and his welcoming attitude symbolizes forgiveness. What do the following elements of the allegory most probably symbolize?
    - the younger son
    - working as a swineherd
    - the elder son's resentment
7. What contemporary situations could this parable apply to?

Literary Criticism
8. Some commentators point out that the title "The Parable of the Prodigal Son" is misleading—because the plot hinges on the actions of a prodigal *father* who gives lavishly of his goods and love to *both* of his sons. Consider all of the meanings of the word *prodigal*. How do they apply to the father? Do they apply more to the son than to the father? How might readers' perceptions of the story change if it were called "The Parable of the Prodigal Parent"?

WRITING
Plotting a Parable
Using your Quickwrite notes as a basis, write a modern **parable.** To be sure that the characters and plot of your parable carry both literal and symbolic meanings, make a chart of each element of the story and its symbolic meaning before you write.

You may want to rewrite "The Parable of the Prodigal Son" instead, using language, situations, and references that a modern reader would understand. For example, your setting might be a high school, your characters might be female instead of male, and so on. To plan your update, make a chart like the one below, listing the features of the original parable, their allegorical meanings, and the features of the updated parable. The allegorical meanings should remain the same when you update the various features.

Features of Original Parable	Allegorical Meaning	Features of Updated Parable
Characters:		Characters:
Places:		Places:
Events:		Events:

SKILLS FOCUS

Literary Skills
Analyze the characteristics of parables.

Writing Skills
Write a modern parable.

King James Bible 345

SKILLS FOCUS, pp. 346–360

Grade-Level Skills

■ **Literary Skills**

Compare literary forms from different cultures and historical periods.

■ **Literary Skills**

Analyze characteristics of subgenres of prose, including didactic literature.

DIRECT TEACHING

Time Line

■ **651–652**

Around 600, Mohammed began to preach a new monotheistic religion (Islam), based on his interpretation of Judaism and Christianity. After Mohammed died (632), his followers continued to spread the religion. By about 750, Muslims ruled an area from Spain in the west to northern India in the east.

■ **1000–100 B.C.**

Many books of the Jewish scriptures were first written down during the sixth century B.C. About the same time, Confucius, Buddha, Laotzu, and others founded religions and schools of philosophy.

A Literary Connections

Didactic Literature

One of the earliest forms of didactic literature in English is the morality play, popular during the fifteenth and sixteenth centuries. The characters are personified abstractions, with names such as Everyman, Fellowship, Kindred, and Goods.

B Reading Skills

❓ **Making generalizations.**

What generalizations can we make about literature that is in the oral tradition? [Possible responses: The written texts are probably not the exact words of the person who originally spoke. Ideas may have been changed slightly.]

Connecting to World Literature
Worlds of Wisdom: Wisdom Literature

c. 1213–1292
Saadi lives

1191
Zen is introduced to Japan

651–652
The Koran is written

c. 300 B.C.–c. A.D. 300
The Bhagavad-Gita is written

c. 400–c. 100 B.C.
Taoist anecdotes are created

479 B.C.
Confucius dies

c. 571 B.C.
Laotzu is born

1000–100 B.C.
Hebrew Bible is written and assembled

You have just read two psalms and a parable from the King James Bible. In this Connecting to World Literature feature, you will read excerpts from wisdom literature from around the world:

Night from the ***Koran*** .... Arabia 350
from **Philosophy and Spiritual Discipline**
from the ***Bhagavad-Gita*** .... India 351
Zen Parables .... Japan 353
from ***The Analects of Confucius*** .... China 355
from the ***Tao Te Ching*** .... China 356
Taoist Anecdotes .... China 357
Sayings of Saadi .... Persia 358
African Proverbs .... Africa 359

From age to age and culture to culture, people have wrestled with the same fundamental questions: What is the meaning of life? How can I become my truest self? What is justice? What is my place in the grand scheme of things?

Society after society has distilled its answers to such questions to create "wisdom literature"—poems, stories, and sayings that provide guidance on everything from rearing children to preparing for the afterlife. Wisdom literature thus serves a **didactic,** or instructional, purpose: It teaches people how to live.

Oral Roots, Sacred Roots

The literary forms represented in this feature—fable, parable, scripture, anecdote, and proverb—spring from the **oral tradition.** Just as Jesus wrote no books, neither did the Taoist teachers, Confucius, or the masters of Zen Buddhism. Their disciples wrote down their teachings for later ages and, in doing so, retained many features of their masters' oral styles. Thus you will find wisdom literature rich in rhetorical techniques, such as **parallelism, repetition,** and **figures of speech.**

Like the wisdom literature in the Bible, many of these selections have a **sacred,** or religious, context. For example, the Arabic Koran, the holy book of the Islamic faith, contains didactic writings that teach people how to relate to God and how to live a moral life.

SKILLS FOCUS

Literary Skills
Compare wisdom literature from different cultures and literary periods.

Using the Time Line

Activity. Have students use reference sources to place the following events on the time line:

■ Most of the Christian scriptures are written. [50–100]
■ Jerusalem comes under Muslim rule. [638]
■ Crusaders capture Jerusalem. [1099]
■ The last Christian stronghold in Palestine (Acre) falls, ending the Crusades. [1291]

Scene from the life of Confucius and his disciples (early 18th century). Ink, watercolor, and sepia wash.
Bibliothèque Nationale, Paris, France/Giraudon-Bridgeman Art Library.

Revealed Truths and Hidden Meanings

Both sacred and secular wisdom may be taught indirectly through stories. A **parable**—from a Greek word meaning "comparison; analogy"—is a brief allegorical story that teaches a moral, or lesson, about life. (See page 342.) Jesus and the twelfth-century masters of Zen Buddhism often taught by means of parables.

An **anecdote** is another type of brief story. An anecdote usually focuses on a single interesting incident or event, often one that reveals the character of an important person. Taoist teachers in China and Sufi masters in Persia often taught by means of anecdotes.

Witty Wisdom

Much of the world's wisdom is condensed into witty one-liners. **Proverbs, aphorisms, axioms,** and **maxims** are all brief sayings—sometimes blunt and to the point, sometimes poetic and obscure. These sayings are widely accepted as true—for example, "Don't cry over spilled milk." Similar proverbs pop up the world over. For instance, English speakers say, "A bird in the hand is worth two in the bush," while the Ashanti people of Ghana say, "One bird in your hand is worth ten birds in the sky." Proverbs sometimes contradict one another: "Absence makes the heart grow fonder" and "Out of sight, out of mind" offer totally opposing views, yet taken separately, each proverb expresses a truth about human nature.

Reflecting its roots, wisdom literature—especially the proverb—employs a variety of catchy oral techniques and literary devices, such as **metaphor**

Worlds of Wisdom 347

A **Literary Connections**

The Tao and Zen of Practically Everything

Interest in the classics of Eastern philosophy has spawned a number of books relating Eastern thought to modern concerns. One of the most popular is *The Tao of Pooh,* which explains Taoism through Winnie the Pooh and Winnie the Pooh through Taoism. Other titles include *The Tao of Physics, The Tao of Divorce, Zen and the Art of Motorcycle Maintenance, Zen in the Art of Archery,* and *Zen and the Art of the Internet.*

A teacher and his pupil, from the Coburg Pentateuch, copied by Simhah ben Samuel Halevi (1395).
British Library, London, UK/ The Bridgeman Art Library.

("The squeaky wheel gets the grease"), **alliteration** ("It takes two to tango"), **parallelism** ("The bigger they are, the harder they fall"), and **rhyme** ("Birds of a feather flock together").

Lasting Legacy

 Many classics of Eastern wisdom, from Islamic Sufi poetry to Zen parables, have gained immense popularity in the West. The Chinese *Tao Te Ching* and the Indian *Bhagavad-Gita,* along with the Bible, have been translated more often than any other books in the world. How do these works manage to transcend barriers of place, time, and culture? A partial answer lies in the beauty of their expression: The sayings, poems, and stories speak timeless truths in timeless voices.

A deeper answer lies in the sheer commonality of human experience. In the sixth century B.C., Confucius taught, "Never do to others what you would not like them to do to you." In the first century B.C., Rabbi Hillel of Israel taught, "What is hateful to you, do not do to your neighbor." Christians attribute another version of the same teaching to Jesus and call it the golden rule: "Do unto others as you would have them do unto you."

SKILLS REVIEW

Analyzing Metaphors Review with students the definition of *metaphor* and the way a metaphor adds meaning to a text. Then, discuss the appeal of metaphors.

Activity. The metaphorical proverb given in the text ("The squeaky wheel gets the grease," on p. 348) is an implied metaphor. In other words, the comparison being made—between a squeaky wheel and a complaining person—is not stated directly. Have students list other proverbs containing implied metaphors—for example, "A rolling stone gathers no moss." Have them determine what comparison is implied in each proverb. Then, have students invent and illustrate proverbs containing implied metaphors.

Before You Read

Worlds of Wisdom

Make the Connection

Probably every society that has ever existed on earth has developed its own sets of instructions for how to lead a good life: how we should conduct ourselves in everyday life, how we should deal with the difficulties that confront us, how we can find meaning and purpose in our existence. Where do we look today for answers to these and other profound human questions? What is the wisdom literature of contemporary life? How is it different from—or the same as—the wisdom literature that has come down to us from the past?

Literary Focus

Didactic Literature

A literary work that is meant to instruct, give advice, or convey a philosophy or a moral message is known as **didactic literature**. A great deal of the world's wisdom literature—works as diverse as the Taoist anecdotes and the biblical parables—comes in the form of sacred texts. Secular works such as proverbs, fables, anecdotes, folk tales, and maxims can also serve as didactic literature. Most didactic literature ultimately derives from an oral tradition.

> **Didactic literature** is literature that instructs or conveys a philosophy or moral message.
>
> For more on Didactic Literature, see the Handbook of Literary and Historical Terms.

The Ascent of the Prophet Mohammed to Heaven, from a sixteenth-century manuscript. Gouache, ink, and gold on paper.
Art Resource, New York.

Literary Skills Understand the characteristics of didactic literature.

PRETEACHING

Selection Starter

Motivate. Ask students to write for five minutes on one of the following topics: "The best advice I ever got" or "The wisest statement I ever heard." Ask for volunteers to share what they wrote. Then, instruct students to look for connections between their notes and the selections they are about to read.

VIEWING THE ART

The gold and lapis lazuli that Muslim artists used to make their paints gave their work a luminous quality similar to that of the illuminated manuscripts made by medieval Christian monks. This picture is unusual because Muslim artists rarely painted human figures in religious scenes. When they did, they usually left Mohammed's face blank. Muslim artists in Persia and India sometimes bent these rules.

Activity. Have students research how medieval Islamic art differs from medieval Christian art. [Christian artists most often represented religious scenes, and they always put a face on sacred figures.]

Worlds of Wisdom 349

DIFFERENTIATING INSTRUCTION

Learners Having Difficulty
Have students pause after reading each selection and discuss with a partner anything that they do not understand. Suggest that they write down the main idea of each selection and look for ways in which the ideas in two or more of the selections are related. An alternative strategy is described on p. 350.

English-Language Learners
Ask students to recite proverbs, aphorisms, axioms, or maxims in their native language and to express them, if they can, in English. Encourage students to identify any similarities between the selections they read and sayings from their native culture.

Advanced Learners
Suggest that students read additional proverbs, aphorisms, axioms, or maxims in the sources from which these selections are taken (for example, the Koran, the *Bhagavad-Gita,* and collections of African proverbs). Challenge students to compile a book of wise sayings for each day of the week. Have them share their collections with the class.

Worlds of Wisdom 349

DIRECT TEACHING

VIEWING THE ART

This colorful painting shows Krishna and Arjuna at the beginning of the battle in the *Bhagavad-Gita*. The blue figure of Krishna is mounted on the horse that pulls the chariot bearing Arjuna as they face Arjuna's opponents. Note the symmetry of the composition: Arjuna and his armies are mirrored by figures that appear almost identical to him, representing his relatives, the Kauravas.

Activity. What are the smaller figures surrounding Arjuna and Krishna? [They represent the armies of Arjuna and his opponents.]

A Learners Having Difficulty

Using graphic aids. Have students make a flow chart showing the chain of events that leads to ruin, according to Krishna. [Thinking about sensuous objects→attachment to them→desire→anger→confusion→memory lapses→loss of understanding→ruin.]

Arjuna and His Charioteer Lord Krsna Confront Carna (detail) Indian, Darhwal School.
Philadelphia Museum of Art: Purchased: Edith H. Bell Fund (1975-23-1).

Sensuous objects fade
when the embodied self abstains from
    food;
the taste lingers, but it too fades
20 in the vision of higher truth.

Even when a man of wisdom
tries to control them, Arjuna,
the bewildering senses
attack his mind with violence.

25 Controlling them all,
with discipline he should focus on me;
when his senses are under control,
his insight is sure.

Brooding about sensuous objects
30 makes attachment to them grow;
from attachment desire arises,
from desire anger is born.

From anger comes confusion;
from confusion memory lapses;
from broken memory understanding is
35   lost;
from loss of understanding, he is ruined.

But a man of inner strength
whose senses experience objects
without attraction and hatred,
40 in self-control, finds serenity.

352 Collection 3   The Renaissance

Comparing and Contrasting Texts

Comparing aesthetics of style. All of the wisdom literature in this section, including the Bible, has been translated from the original. Have students compare the aesthetic appeal of the King James translation of Psalms 23 and 137 with that of the translation of the *Bhagavad-Gita*. Encourage them to compare techniques used in each (such as parallelism) as well as the overall effect on the reader.

The parables illustrating the insights of Zen Buddhism are drawn from an austere philosophical and religious tradition within Buddhism that originated in China and then flowered in Japan starting in the twelfth century. The object of Zen is to free the mind of everyday, conventional logic through meditation. Instead of imparting facts in a clear and logical way, the Zen master first tries to confuse his students, to force them to abandon all preconceived notions of what knowledge is. He might, for example, ask a nonsensical question that has no answer, such as "What is the sound of one hand clapping?" or "What did your face look like before you were born?" This technique prepares the students to understand the lessons inherent in these deceptively simple **parables,** *or brief allegorical stories that teach lessons or morals about life.*

Zen Parables
compiled by **Paul Reps**

The Moon Cannot Be Stolen

Ryokan, a Zen master, lived the simplest kind of life in a little hut at the foot of a mountain. One evening a thief visited the hut only to discover there was nothing in it to steal.

Ryokan returned and caught him. "You may have come a long way to visit me," he told the prowler, "and you should not return empty-handed. Please take my clothes as a gift."

The thief was bewildered. He took the clothes and slunk away.

Ryokan sat naked, watching the moon. "Poor fellow," he mused, "I wish I could give him this beautiful moon."

Temper

A Zen student came to Bankei and complained: "Master, I have an ungovernable temper. How can I cure it?"

"You have something very strange," replied Bankei. "Let me see what you have."

"Just now I cannot show it to you," replied the other.

"When can you show it to me?" asked Bankei.

"It arises unexpectedly," replied the student.

"Then," concluded Bankei, "it must not be your own true nature. If it were, you could show it to me at any time. When you were born, you did not have it, and your parents did not give it to you. Think that over."

The Gates of Paradise

A soldier named Nobushige came to Hakuin, and asked: "Is there really a paradise and a hell?"

"Who are you?" inquired Hakuin.

"I am a samurai," the warrior replied.

"You, a soldier!" exclaimed Hakuin. "What kind of ruler would have you as his guard? Your face looks like that of a beggar."

Nobushige became so angry that he began to draw his sword, but Hakuin continued: "So you have a sword! Your weapon is probably much too dull to cut off my head."

As Nobushige drew his sword, Hakuin remarked: "Here open the gates of hell!"

At these words the samurai, perceiving the master's discipline, sheathed his sword and bowed.

"Here open the gates of paradise," said Hakuin.

Direct Teaching

A English-Language Learners

Homonyms. Point out that *principle* means "fundamental truth" and that the homonym *principal* may mean "most important" or "head of a school."

B Literary Focus

? Didactic literature. What is irony, and how is it used here to teach a lesson? [Possible response: Irony is a discrepancy between what is expected and what actually happens. The expectation is that the best results are produced when people work slowly and painstakingly and heed criticism. But in reality the master produces his best work when he does it hurriedly, without worrying about criticism. Irony is used here to suggest that people work best when they feel at ease and are not trying to please others.]

A The First Principle

When one goes to Obaku temple in Kyoto, he sees carved over the gate the words "The First Principle." The letters are unusually large, and those who appreciate calligraphy° always admire them as being a masterpiece. They were drawn by Kosen two hundred years ago.

When the master drew them he did so on paper, from which workmen made the larger carving in wood. As Kosen sketched the letters, a bold pupil was with him who had made several gallons of ink for the calligraphy and who never failed to criticize his master's work.

"That is not good," he told Kosen after the first effort.

"How is that one?"

"Poor. Worse than before," pronounced the pupil.

Kosen patiently wrote one sheet after another until eighty-four First Principles had accumulated, still without the approval of the pupil.

B Then, when the young man stepped outside for a few moments, Kosen thought: "Now is my chance to escape his keen eye," and he wrote hurriedly, with a mind free from distraction:

"The First Principle."

"A masterpiece," pronounced the pupil. ■

° **calligraphy** *n.:* the art of beautiful handwriting.

354 Collection 3 The Renaissance

Conducting a Historical Investigation

Comparing historical contexts. Instruct students to choose the wisdom literature of a culture other than England in the seventeenth century. Have them research the time and place in which the literature was written and the time and place in which the Christian scriptures were written. Then, have them compare the historical conditions that gave rise to the wisdom literature. What conditions might have influenced the teachings in each text?

Confucius, the founder of an important and lasting Chinese philosophical system, left no written works. After his death, in around 479 B.C., his disciples gathered his sayings in a collection known as The Analects—"selected sayings." The sayings in The Analects range from brief statements, or **maxims,** to more extended dialogues between Confucius and his students. Confucius, who followed the ancient "way of goodness," believed that studying ancient teachings enabled people to join the continuous chain of minds from the past to their own time.

In The Analects, Confucius—called "the Master"—speaks about the concept of chung-yung, usually translated as "the golden mean," an ideal of universal moral and social harmony. The Analects instructs the individual on how to achieve moderation in all things through moral education, the building of a harmonious family life, and the development of virtues such as loyalty, obedience, and integrity. Confucius also emphasizes filial piety—the carrying out of basic obligations to one's living parents or dead ancestors.

from The Analects of Confucius

translated and annotated by **Arthur Waley**

The Master said, "Yu, shall I teach you what knowledge is? When you know a thing, to recognize that you know it, and when you do not know a thing, to recognize that you do not know it. That is knowledge."

The Master said, "Even when walking in a party of no more than three I can always be certain of learning from those I am with. There will be good qualities that I can select for imitation and bad ones that will teach me what requires correction in myself."

Tzu-kung asked, saying, "Is there any single saying that one can act upon all day and every day?" The Master said, "Perhaps the saying about consideration: 'Never do to others what you would not like them to do to you.'" ∎

A portrait of Confucius carved on a stone stele, from the Tang dynasty (618–906).
© Werner Forman/Art Resource, New York.

The poet Saadi, whose real name was Musharrif Od-Din Muslih Od-Din, lived in thirteenth-century Persia (now Iran). As a follower of Sufism (sōō′fĭz′əm), a mystical sect of Islam, he believed in the holiness of all creation. His witty, practical sayings and lush lyrics made him one of Persia's best-loved poets.

For Sufis, Sufism is not only a religion or a philosophy, but also a way of life. Sufi mystics withdrew from the material world and devoted themselves to a stark, homeless existence, begging for their living and wandering from place to place as they meditated on God's love. Even today, Sufis are not attached to belongings and places, and they are not driven by concerns of time, money, or achievement. They concentrate instead on the development of the human mind and on reaching a higher plane of understanding through a gradual process of thought and practice.

Sayings of Saadi

translated by **Idries Shah**

The Unfed Dervish

When I see the poor dervish° unfed
My own food is pain and poison to me.

Information and Knowledge

However much you study, you cannot know
    without action.
A donkey laden with books is neither an
    intellectual nor a wise man.
Empty of essence, what learning has he—
Whether upon him is firewood or book?

The Elephant Keeper

Make no friendship with an elephant keeper
If you have no room to entertain an elephant.

° **dervish** *n.:* Muslim monk dedicated to a life of poverty.

Safety and Riches

Deep in the sea are riches beyond compare.
But if you seek safety, it is on the shore.

The Fox and the Camels

A fox was seen running away in terror. Someone asked what was troubling it. The fox answered: "They are taking camels for forced labor." "Fool!" he was told, "the fate of camels has nothing to do with you, who do not even look like one." "Silence!" said the fox, "for if an intriguer were to state that I was a camel, *who* would work for my release?" ■

Turkish portrait of a dervish (early 17th century). Colors on paper (8 5/8″ × 4 3/16″).
The Metropolitan Museum of Art, New York. The Cora Timken Burnett Collection of Persian Miniatures and Other Persian Art Objects. Bequest of Cora Timken Burnett, 1956 (57.51.30).

*In the oral literatures of Africa, **proverbs** represent a poetic form that achieves great depth of meaning using very few words. In cultures that have no written literature, proverbs function as the distilled essence of a people's values and knowledge. They are used to settle legal disputes, resolve ethical dilemmas, and teach children the philosophy of their people. Because proverbs often contain puns, rhymes, and clever allusions, they also provide entertainment. Like poetry, they compress complicated ideas into a few thoughtfully crafted words. The following proverbs are from several different African cultures.*

African Proverbs

compiled by **Charlotte** and **Wolf Leslau**

An Ashanti head. The Ashanti are famous for their goldwork.
Werner Forman Archive, Wallace Collection, London/Art Resource, New York.

Only when you have crossed the river, can you say the crocodile has a lump on his snout.
—Ashanti

When a man is wealthy, he may wear an old cloth.
—Ashanti

The ruin of a nation begins in the homes of its people.
—Ashanti

He who cannot dance will say: "The drum is bad."
—Ashanti

It is the fool's sheep that break loose twice.
—Ashanti

No one tests the depth of a river with both feet.
—Ashanti

Wood may remain ten years in the water, but it will never become a crocodile.
—Zaire

Evil enters like a needle and spreads like an oak tree.
—Ethiopia

The witness of a rat is another rat.
—Ethiopia

The frog wanted to be as big as the elephant, and burst.
—Ethiopia

When the heart overflows, it comes out through the mouth.
—Ethiopia

When spider webs unite, they can tie up a lion.
—Ethiopia

Confiding a secret to an unworthy person is like carrying grain in a bag with a hole.
—Ethiopia

I have a cow in the sky, but cannot drink her milk.
—Ethiopia

If you offend, ask for pardon; if offended, forgive.
—Ethiopia

A fool and water will go the way they are diverted.
—Ethiopia

Worlds of Wisdom 359

INDEPENDENT PRACTICE

Response and Analysis

Thinking Critically

1. A person should do good works for the sake of Allah. Those who do not will burn in a blazing fire.
2. The third and fourth stanzas begin with *when* clauses and end with the words "his insight is sure." Lines 31–36 express a causal chain in which each line begins with the word *from*.
3. Possible answer: A person blinded by an obsession is unable to see the consequences of his or her actions.
4. Confucius's saying is phrased in negative terms: "Never do to others what you would not like them to do to you." The Bible's golden rule counsels positive action.
5. Possible answer: Both water and the Tao nourish all things without trying to and are content with the low places that people disdain. To gain respect, you must be yourself.
6. Possible answers: He means that people learn from their experiences. Information is facts. Knowledge is the ability to use facts in a meaningful way.
7. Students may name any of the pieces; all of them are relevant today.

Extending and Evaluating

8. Possible answers: Some students will say that metaphor illuminates because it puts abstract ideas into concrete form. Others will maintain that metaphor obscures because it takes attention away from the actual teaching.

Response and Analysis

Thinking Critically

1. According to "Night," a sura from the Koran, what kind of life should a person live? What will happen to those who live otherwise?
2. **Parallelism,** or **parallel structure,** is the repetition of words or phrases that have the same grammatical structure. For example, lines 5–7 of the excerpt you read from "Philosophy and Spiritual Discipline" illustrate a parallel arrangement of words in each line. How does the poet use parallelism throughout the rest of the excerpt?
3. How would you summarize the lesson taught in the Taoist anecdote "Gold, Gold"?
4. Across cultures we find many similar ideas expressed in religious and philosophical texts. What is the main difference between Confucius's saying and the Bible's golden rule, "Do unto others as you would have them do unto you"?
5. In the passage you read from the *Tao Te Ching,* in what two ways is water described as being like the *Tao*? What must one do to gain people's respect?
6. In Saadi's saying "Information and Knowledge," what does the speaker mean by "you cannot know without action"? How would you sum up the difference between information and knowledge?
7. Name at least three of these pieces of wisdom literature that directly relate to our lives today. Think about family life, love, relationships, wisdom, and responsibility.

Literary Skills
Analyze the characteristics of didactic literature. Compare and contrast wisdom literature from different countries.

Writing Skills
Write an essay comparing and contrasting different views of life. Write a modern proverb.

Extending and Evaluating

8. Didactic literature often uses **metaphor** and conveys its moral or message indirectly. Do you think using metaphor illuminates the message more clearly or obscures it? Explain.

Comparing Literature

9. As with Jesus' **parables** in the Bible, readers must draw their own lessons or meanings from the Zen parables. While some of the morals are obvious, many of these parables have more than one level of meaning. Compare and contrast the lessons of the Zen parables with "The Parable of the Prodigal Son" (see page 344) or other biblical parables you are familiar with. Which parables do you find easier to understand? Why?

WRITING

Worldly Wisdom

Some of the didactic literature you have just read may express attitudes toward life that you find surprising, baffling, or in conflict with your own views and beliefs. Other pieces may strike you as accurately reflecting your beliefs. Choose one piece of wisdom literature that either expresses a view quite different from your own or reflects your own beliefs. Then, write a brief **essay** explaining the similarities or differences between your view of life and the view you find reflected in the selection.

Proverbial Truths

The most memorable proverbs stand the test of time because they address general truths. Think of a general truth of modern life, and write it in the form of a **proverb.** If you can't think of a fresh topic, try updating a well-known proverb.

360 Collection 3 The Renaissance

Comparing Literature

9. Possible answers: The lessons of the Zen parables are concerned with knowing oneself and taking the right approach to life. "The Parable of the Prodigal Son" has two levels of meaning. On the literal level it is about the relationships in a family, but on a symbolic level it is about the relationship between people and God.

Assessment

- *Holt Assessment: Literature, Reading, and Vocabulary*

John Milton
(1608–1674)

John Milton (1670) by William Faithorne. Colored engraving.
The Granger Collection, New York.

Early in his life, John Milton resolved to be a great poet. His teachers and his parents encouraged him in this ambition because they believed, as Milton said later in his life, that he "might perhaps leave something so written to aftertimes as they should not willingly let it die." Time has confirmed his parents' and his teachers' confidence: Milton's *Paradise Lost*, his major epic, is one of the most brilliant achievements in English poetry and perhaps the richest and most intricately beautiful poem in the world. Posterity has not let *Paradise Lost* die.

Fortunate Beginnings

Milton was fortunate in his parents. His father, a musician and prosperous businessman, had Milton educated at St. Paul's School (which he loved) and Cambridge University (which he hated). Indulged in every way by his parents, Milton spent the next eight years after college (1632–1640) continuing his education by himself, since he firmly believed that a poet must be a person of learning, familiar with ancient and contemporary philosophy, history, languages, and literatures.

Political Activity: Intelligent Devotion

In the 1640s, an ongoing struggle between King Charles and his Parliament came to a head. Milton, believing that a poet must be active in the life of his time, entered the paper warfare that accompanied the conflict and started publishing prose works—some of them very elaborate and a few of them very insulting—in support of the Parliamentary party. For this reason some people have referred to Milton as a Puritan, but this is a label that has only limited application to a person of Milton's stature. If he shared some of the Puritans' ideas and attitudes, such as their extreme dislike of kings and bishops, he also differed greatly from them in other important ways. For instance, he advocated divorce for incompatible married couples, and he argued that the press should be free from government censorship and interference. Although we take these freedoms for granted, most people in the seventeenth century, particularly most Puritans, considered them dangerously radical.

During part of this period, Milton served in the government of England under Oliver Cromwell, who, with the title of lord protector, ruled England after the Parliamentary party had won the Civil Wars and executed King Charles. As Latin secretary to the Council of State, Milton was responsible for translating all correspondence with foreign countries, Latin then being the language of diplomacy.

Milton's eyesight was gradually failing. By 1652, he could only distinguish day from night; otherwise, by the age of forty-four, before

More About the Writer

Background. In June 1642, Milton married Mary Powell, only seventeen at the time, who left him within six weeks to return to her parents' home. After three years they reconciled, and she subsequently gave birth to three daughters. Their only son died in infancy; Mary herself died after giving birth in 1652. Milton married Katherine Woodcock in 1656. She also died from complications related to childbirth, two years later. In 1663, Milton—now blind and discredited—married Elizabeth Minshull, who survived him by many years.

---

he had finished his life's work, Milton was totally blind.

All for Nothing: Milton the Traitor

To Milton the ideal government was a republic in which the most capable, intelligent, and virtuous men would serve as leaders. To establish and maintain such a government in England, he had devoted most of his intelligence and energy for twenty years. Then suddenly, in 1660, the cause for which he had worked so hard became totally discredited; the English recalled their dead king's son from exile and crowned him as King Charles II. Overnight Milton found himself stripped of his possessions and under arrest as a traitor. Fortunately influential friends, including the poet Andrew Marvell (see page 266), intervened, and Milton was allowed to go into retirement rather than to the scaffold. From then on, he lived in seclusion with his three daughters and his third wife, his first two wives and only son having died. By reading aloud to him, his daughters enabled him to carry on the studies he thought necessary for a poet.

A Subject Fit for an Epic

Being a poet, in Milton's view, meant imitating the great writers of antiquity, the epic poets Homer and Virgil and the Greek dramatists Aeschylus, Sophocles, and Euripides. Because those writers chose subjects drawn from their own nations' histories, Milton first pondered various English subjects for his works, especially King Arthur and the knights of the Round Table. After years of thinking and reading, however, Milton decided that King Arthur's exploits were mainly fictitious, and so he settled on subjects drawn from the Bible.

Paradise Lost: The Work of a Lifetime

Milton published *Paradise Lost* twice: first in a ten-book version in 1667 and then in twelve books in 1674, the year of his death. It's no exaggeration to say that Milton in one way or another worked on this epic all his life. He made many different plans and even once thought of it as a tragedy with Satan, the fallen archangel transformed into the chief devil, as its protagonist. In the finished poem, Satan is still very conspicuous. The first two books are devoted mainly to him, he appears frequently in Books III–X, and Milton lavishes on him some of his most glorious writing. It's not surprising, then, that many readers have regarded Satan as the secret hero of the poem, especially since he receives no such grand treatment in the Bible. Milton was "of the Devil's party without knowing it," asserted the poet and artist William Blake (see page 534). Yet this argument is convincing only to those who concentrate on certain parts of the poem and ignore the rest of it. Moreover, in literary works, evil frequently seems more interesting than good, and if any part of *Paradise Lost* fails from a literary point of view, it is Milton's portrayal of God.

A Profound Work of Art

In *Paradise Lost*, Milton took relatively few verses from the Bible, mainly Genesis, and developed them into a 10,565-line poem. He used the conventions and devices of the classical epic to make the poem a work of art; he used his great learning and wide experience of human affairs to make the poem profound. Although the poem ranges back and forth between Hell and Heaven, the most important action takes place on Earth, where the first human beings, Adam and Eve, are given the choice of obeying or disobeying God. They choose to disobey, and having done so, they accept their punishment and make the best of the life that is left to them. They are the heroes of Milton's epic, and they represent us all.

Primary Source

The Poet as Father

One reliable early biographer of Milton was Edward Phillips, the poet's nephew and pupil. His comments about Milton's daughters indicate that tending to their brilliant father was not easy: "Yet excusing only the eldest daughter by reason of her bodily infirmity, and difficult utterance of speech (which to say truth I doubt was the principal cause of excusing her), the other two were condemned to the performance of reading, and exactly pronouncing of all the languages of whatever book he should at one time or another think fit to peruse; viz., the Hebrew (and I think the Syriac), the Greek, the Latin, the Italian, Spanish, and French. All which sorts of books, to be confined to reading without understanding one word, must needs be a trial of patience, almost beyond endurance; yet it was endured by both for a long time; yet the irksomeness of this employment could not always be concealed, but broke out more and more into expressions of uneasiness; so that at length they were all (even the eldest also) sent out to learn some curious and ingenious sorts of manufacture that are proper for women . . . , particularly embroideries in gold and silver."

The Fallen Angels Entering Pandemonium, an illustration by John Martin for *Paradise Lost,* Book I, (exhibited 1841). Tate Gallery, London/Art Resource, New York.

Paradise Lost: Milton's Epic

At the very beginning of *Paradise Lost,* Milton describes the content of his epic as "things unattempted yet in prose or rhyme" (line 16). His allusions to Homer, Virgil, Dante, and a host of lesser epic poets leave no doubt that Milton wanted *Paradise Lost* to sum up and also surpass all previous epics. To write his great literary epic (a **literary epic,** as distinguished from an epic from the oral tradition, is the product of the imagination of an individual writer), Milton followed the examples of the past by using the conventions of the epic. He begins with an invocation to the Muse, he starts the action *in medias res* ("in the middle of things"), and he writes about a grand subject. Above all, Milton follows the epic tradition by casting his poem in an **elevated style** suited to the grand events he is describing, using ornate

DIRECT TEACHING

VIEWING THE ART

The English painter **John Martin** (1789–1854), known as "Mad Martin," is remembered more for his extravagant plans to improve London's sanitation system than for his artwork. Martin's eccentricity is reflected in his paintings, such as *The Fallen Angels Entering Pandemonium,* in which the angels are practically obscured by the grandeur of Pandemonium. In his paintings of burning cities and natural disasters, Martin strove for physical immensity on the canvas. Eventually the public tired of his colossal spectacles. In Milton's epic, Pandemonium is the capital of Hell, established by Satan. The word comes from the Greek words *pan,* meaning "all," and *daimon,* meaning "demon."

Activity. Call students' attention to the lake of fire. How does Martin use color to heighten the emotion of his subject matter? [Possible responses: The fiery red immediately draws the viewer's eye to the molten lake. The dark rocks that border the lake are also streaked with red, as if they are about to melt. The red represents all-consuming fire but also suggests blood and destruction. In contrast, the cool blues and grays and the dim white light in the upper half of the painting make Heaven seem calm and serene.]

Literary Criticism

Critics' Commentary: Johnson and Lamb

Two of the best-known remarks about Milton's *Paradise Lost* come from the critic Samuel Johnson (1709–1784) and the essayist Charles Lamb (1775–1834). Johnson admired *Paradise Lost* but also quipped that "nobody ever wished it longer." Later Lamb wrote a rejoinder to Johnson: "'We read the *Paradise Lost* as a task,' says Dr. Johnson. Nay, rather as a celestial recreation, of which the dullard mind is not at all hours alike recipient. 'Nobody ever wished it longer';—nor the moon rounder, he might have added. Why, 'tis the perfectness and completeness of it, which makes us imagine that not a line could be added to it, or diminished from it, with advantage."

Whole-class activity. Ask students to name contemporary critics who have disagreed about a recently published book or a new recording or film.

DIRECT TEACHING

A Content-Area Connections
Literature: Epic Invocation Homer's *Iliad* begins "Sing, goddess, the anger of Peleus's son Achilles." The opening words of his *Odyssey* are "Sing in me, Muse, and through me tell the story." Ask interested students to read the opening invocations of Homer's epics in their entirety and to compare them with Milton's invocation at the beginning of *Paradise Lost.* You might also suggest that they read the invocations of Virgil's *Aeneid* and Dante's *Divine Comedy* and compare them with Milton's opening lines.

B Literary Focus
Iambic pentameter. Review the rules of meter with the class before they begin reading "The Fall of Satan." Remind students that iambic pentameter is a line of verse containing five iambs. (An iamb is a metrical foot consisting of two syllables, the first unstressed and the second stressed).

---

language, complex syntax, multiple **allusions**, and elaborate comparisons called **epic similes**. (For more about epic conventions, see page 71.) The quality that would set Milton's epic apart, of course, was that it dealt with great deeds on a cosmic scale at the dawn of Creation—rather than with earthly matters.

A Grand Subject
There is a formal, set way to begin an epic. At the outset, an epic poet does two things: The speaker invokes the Muse (one of the nine Greek goddesses who inspire poets and other practitioners of the arts and sciences) to speak or sing through the poet; and the speaker states the subject of the poem. Milton does both these things in the first, complicated sentence (lines 1–16) of *Paradise Lost*. Grammatically, this sentence begins in line 6 with the command, "Sing, Heavenly Muse." "Sing," says Milton, and now we move back to line 1, "Of man's first disobedience," which is Adam and Eve's first act of disobedience against God, who has forbidden them to eat the fruit of a particular tree in Eden. The result, or "fruit," of their disobedience is expulsion from and loss of Paradise, another name for the Garden of Eden. Yet all is not lost, because a "greater Man" (line 4), Jesus Christ, has restored the possibility of Paradise for the human race.

Milton's Great Argument
Milton calls this argument "great" (line 24), for he is attempting to resolve a dilemma that has puzzled many people throughout the ages. On the one hand, we are told that through his Eternal Providence (line 25) God takes loving care of Creation; on the other hand, we know that there are many very bad things in the world, such as war, crime, poverty, disease, oppression, and injustice. In *Paradise Lost,* Milton asserts that God is not responsible for these evils; instead, Adam and Eve's disobedience to God "Brought death into the world, and all our woe" (line 3). God gave Adam and Eve the freedom to choose between good and evil, and the strength to resist evil; yet they chose evil, and their offspring—all of us—have suffered the effects of their choice ever since.

This explanation is not original to Milton; many Christians have accepted it for centuries. Yet a reader need not accept this traditional explanation of the evil in the world in order to enjoy and admire the poem. (Indeed, some readers have found evidence in the poem that Milton himself did not really believe it.) The poem is rich enough to provide support for many different interpretations.

Reading *Paradise Lost*
Milton decided to write his epic in his native language and in Shakespeare's meter, which is **blank verse**, or unrhymed iambic pentameter. Though blank verse was the usual meter in dramatic poetry, it was not used at all for nondramatic poems in Milton's day and for long after. Most of Milton's sentences are long, and many of them are not in normal word order (subject-verb-object). Also, his vocabulary includes words not used in ordinary prose today. (Unfamiliar proper nouns are explained in the notes, but they still have to be understood in their context.)

Paradise Within
In Milton's heroic, optimistic view of life, goodness was not goodness unless it resulted from a struggle to overcome evil. God purposely let Satan escape from Hell and establish himself on Earth, not only so that Satan's deeds would damn him further but also so that human beings would have something to fight against—and with God's help triumph over. In one of his prose tracts, *Areopagitica* (1644), Milton describes life as a race in which good must compete with bad. Virtue, he says, is not virtue unless it is won in the "dust and heat" of the conflict with evil. And so, when Adam and Eve lose Paradise, they also gain something: the opportunity to prove themselves in the real world. The Archangel Michael, who comes to turn them out of their perfect garden, tells them how to live in the new, imperfect world. Practice good deeds, he says, and patience, temperance, faith, and love, and

> then wilt thou be not loath
> To leave this Paradise, but shalt possess
> A Paradise within thee, happier far.
> —Book XII, lines 585–587

Before You Read

The Fall of Satan

Make the Connection
Why does evil exist? What is the source of its power to fascinate? The struggle of good versus evil is central to *Paradise Lost*—in this case, the conflict exists on a truly epic scale, as Satan first rebels against God (in Book I) and then ensnares Adam and Eve to do likewise (in Book IX). In Milton's epic and in the Bible, this original choice of evil over good explains the sufferings and the burdens of humanity and our fateful tendencies to misuse reason and freedom, to let pride override fear of God.

Literary Focus
Style

The unique manner in which writers use language to express their ideas is called **style**. An author's style is closely connected to **diction**, or word choice, and **syntax**, or the way sentences are constructed. A writer's style can be categorized as formal or casual, plain or ornate, abstract or concrete—or by any of a number of other descriptive words.

> **Style** is the unique manner in which writers use language to express their ideas. Two of the main aspects of style are diction and syntax.
>
> *For more on Style, see the Handbook of Literary and Historical Terms.*

Reading Skills
Milton's Style

Milton wrote in the 1600s, and on first reading you may be daunted by his style. As you read Milton, you will find it helpful to identify areas of difficulty and apply strategies to deal with them. If you are stalled by an unfamiliar word, try using **context clues** to figure it out. Make use of the **side glosses** that are provided to help you with unfamiliar names and terms. Read and answer the **reading stop** annotations and questions for help understanding key ideas as you go along.

Milton is challenging—just as many good things are. Once you have solved the puzzles posed by Milton's style, though, you should be hooked by this story of the primal battle between the forces of good and the forces of evil.

Vocabulary Development

transgress (trans·gres′) v.: sin against; violate a limit.

infernal (in·fur′nəl) adj.: hellish; fiendish.

guile (gīl) n.: cunning.

affliction (ə·flik′shən) n.: suffering.

contention (kən·ten′shən) n.: struggle.

ignominy (ig′nə·min′ē) n.: dishonor; disgrace.

impetuous (im·pech′ōō·əs) adj.: forceful; violent.

desolation (des′ə·lā′shən) n.: utter misery; extreme loneliness.

reiterated (rē·it′ə·rāt′id) v. used as adj.: repeated.

malice (mal′is) n.: ill will; evil intentions.

INTERNET
Vocabulary Practice
•
More About John Milton
•
Keyword: LE5 12-3

Literary Skills Understand the use of style.
Reading Skills Understand Milton's style.

PRETEACHING

Summary *above grade level*

This excerpt comes from the beginning of Milton's literary epic *Paradise Lost*. Milton's purpose in writing this monumental work was to answer the question of why God permits his human creations to suffer and die. In l. 26, Milton says his goal is to "justify the ways of God to men." Milton also set out to write an epic that was at least equal in gravity and grace to the towering works of Homer and Virgil.

Milton begins with an account of how Satan, known in Heaven as Lucifer, led a group of rebellious angels to defy God. The rebels lost and so were thrown into Hell. Milton stresses the pride and willfulness that motivated Satan to revolt. In fact, Milton's portrait of Satan's character is so compelling that some critics consider Satan, not Adam, the epic's hero and the main focus. Milton paints vivid pictures of two settings, Heaven and Hell, using imagery of light and darkness to contrast the glory of Heaven with the horror of Hell. In a dialogue with Beelzebub, another fallen angel, Satan vows to avenge himself on God by tempting Adam and Eve to do evil and thus disrupt God's plans for Creation. Beelzebub, less audacious than his leader, wonders whether the fallen angels might still be God's subjects in Hell, a possibility adamantly rejected by Satan. In Milton's view, Satan is doomed to lose in his cosmic battle with God because Satan's will to do evil operates only with God's permission and so ultimately serves God's ends.

Previewing Vocabulary

Have pairs of students complete this activity.

1. If you <u>transgress</u> a school rule, what punishment can you expect?
2. What feelings would the sight of an <u>infernal</u> landscape produce in the viewer?
3. How might someone use <u>guile</u> to avoid a vicious guard dog?
4. Why is love a "delightful <u>affliction</u>"?
5. If you found yourself in <u>contention</u> with a friend in an election, what would you do?
6. What circumstances might cause someone to experience <u>ignominy</u>?
7. Describe a setting in which an <u>impetuous</u> movement would be dangerous.
8. Describe the attitude of someone who feels complete <u>desolation</u>.
9. Who needs to hear instructions <u>reiterated</u>?
10. What might be an example of <u>malice</u> shown toward someone?

DIRECT TEACHING

VIEWING THE ART

This painting by **William Blake** (1757–1827) shows Adam and Eve shortly after their fall. Before the fall, Adam and Eve were naked; they had no need for clothes because, without the knowledge of good and evil, they felt no shame over their nakedness.

Activity. What elements of Blake's painting demonstrate the shame felt by Adam and Eve in their fallen state? [Adam and Eve are both blushing, and they both look down to avoid the eyes of the angel.] How would you interpret the angel's gesture and facial expression? [Possible response: Though Adam and Eve have sinned, the angel's embrace suggests compassion; his face conveys sorrow, wisdom, and forgiveness.]

DIFFERENTIATING INSTRUCTION

Learners Having Difficulty
Encourage students to paraphrase Milton's text as they read along, line by line, without worrying about reading quickly. Make sure they check the glosses for a particular line before trying to paraphrase it.

English-Language Learners
To help students with Milton's difficult syntax, pair them with more advanced students whose first language is English. Advise them to focus on identifying subjects and verbs in Milton's long sentences. You might suggest that students create a graphic organizer to analyze the sentences. Also make sure that students answer the margin questions.

The Fall of Satan
from Paradise Lost
John Milton

    Of man's first disobedience, and the fruit
Of that forbidden tree, whose mortal taste
Brought death into the world, and all our woe,
With loss of Eden, till one greater Man°
5 Restore us, and regain the blissful seat,
Sing, Heavenly Muse,° that on the secret top
Of Oreb, or of Sinai,° didst inspire
That shepherd,° who first taught the chosen seed°
In the beginning how the Heavens and Earth
10 Rose out of Chaos; or if Sion hill°
Delight thee more, and Siloa's brook° that flowed
Fast by the oracle of God, I thence
Invoke thy aid to my adventurous song,
That with no middle flight intends to soar
15 Above the Aonian mount,° while it pursues
Things unattempted yet in prose or rhyme.
And chiefly thou, O Spirit,° that dost prefer
Before all temples the upright heart and pure,
Instruct me, for thou know'st; thou from the first
20 Wast present, and with mighty wings outspread
Dove-like sat'st brooding on the vast abyss
And mad'st it pregnant: what in me is dark
Illumine, what is low raise and support;
That to the height of this great argument
25 I may assert Eternal Providence,
And justify the ways of God to men.
    Say first, for Heaven hides nothing from thy view,
Nor the deep tract of Hell, say first what cause
Moved our grand parents° in that happy state,
30 Favored of Heaven so highly, to fall off
From their Creator, and transgress his will
For one restraint,° lords of the world besides?°
Who first seduced them to that foul revolt?
The infernal Serpent;° he it was, whose guile,

Vocabulary
transgress (trans·gres′) v.: sin against; violate a limit.
infernal (in·fur′nəl) adj.: hellish; fiendish.
guile (gīl) n.: cunning.

(Opposite) *The Angel of Divine Presence* (detail) by William Blake. Watercolor.
Fitzwilliam Museum, University of Cambridge, UK/The Bridgeman Art Library.

4. **one greater Man:** Christ.

6. **Heavenly Muse:** Urania, muse of astronomy and sacred poetry. Milton hopes to be inspired by Urania, just as Moses was inspired to receive God's word for the Hebrews.
7. **Oreb . . . Sinai:** names for the mountain where Moses received God's inspiration.
8. **shepherd** n.: Moses. **chosen seed:** the Hebrews.
10. **Sion hill:** Zion, a hill near Jerusalem.
11. **Siloa's brook:** stream that flowed past the Temple, "the oracle of God," on Mount Zion.
15. **Aonian mount:** in Greek mythology, Mount Helicon, the home of the Muses.
17. **Spirit:** Holy Spirit; divine inspiration.

> **1–16.** *Paraphrase the first sentence of the epic. What will the subject of Milton's story be? (See lines 1–5.)*

29. **grand parents:** Adam and Eve.

32. **one restraint:** the command not to eat of the fruit of the tree of knowledge. **besides** adv.: in every other way.
34. **Serpent:** Milton is referring to Satan's final form.

> **26.** *According to line 26, what is Milton's purpose? State this purpose in your own words.*

Direct Teaching

A Literary Focus

Alliteration. How does alliteration make this statement vivid? [Possible response: The repeated *h* sounds—*Him, Hurled headlong, hideous*—emphasize the sudden, explosive quality of the event.]

B Reading Skills

Making predictions. What would you expect to hear in a speech from a person filled with "obdurate pride and steadfast hate"? [Possible responses: anger; self-justification; complaints about injuries; threats; refusal to listen to reason.] Look for those characteristics in the words of Satan, beginning in l. 84.

C Literary Focus

Allusion. Explain that this description echoes the inscription over the entrance to Hell in the *Inferno* by Dante (1265–1321): "Abandon all hope ye who enter here."

Responses to Margin Questions

Lines 53–56. He is tormented by the loss of eternal happiness and the prospect of eternal pain.

Lines 61–77. The images include a dark, horrible dungeon; a furnace that belches darkness; sights of misery; a flood of fire.

---

35 Stirred up with envy and revenge, deceived
The mother of mankind, what time his pride
Had cast him out from Heaven, with all his host
Of rebel angels, by whose aid aspiring
To set himself in glory above his peers,°
40 He trusted to have equaled the Most High,
If he opposed; and with ambitious aim
Against the throne and monarchy of God,
Raised impious war in Heaven and battle proud
With vain attempt. Him the Almighty Power
45 Hurled headlong flaming from the ethereal° sky
With hideous ruin and combustion down
To bottomless perdition,° there to dwell
In adamantine° chains and penal° fire,
Who durst° defy the Omnipotent to arms.
50 Nine times the space that measures day and night
To mortal men, he with his horrid crew
Lay vanquished, rolling in the fiery gulf,
Confounded though immortal. But his doom
Reserved him to more wrath; for now the thought
55 Both of lost happiness and lasting pain
Torments him; round he throws his baleful eyes,
That witnessed huge affliction and dismay
Mixed with obdurate° pride and steadfast hate.
At once as far as angels ken° he views
60 The dismal situation waste and wild:
A dungeon horrible on all sides round
As one great furnace flamed, yet from those flames
No light, but rather darkness visible
Served only to discover sights of woe,
65 Regions of sorrow, doleful shades, where peace
And rest can never dwell, hope never comes
That comes to all; but torture without end
Still urges,° and a fiery deluge, fed
With ever-burning sulfur unconsumed:
70 Such place Eternal Justice had prepared
For those rebellious, here their prison ordained
In utter darkness, and their portion set
As far removed from God and light of Heaven
As from the center thrice to the utmost pole.°
75 O how unlike the place from whence they fell!
There the companions of his fall, o'erwhelmed
With floods and whirlwinds of tempestuous fire,
He soon discerns, and weltering° by his side

Vocabulary
affliction (ə·flik′shən) *n.*: suffering.

---

39. peers *n. pl.*: equals; the other archangels.

45. ethereal *adj.*: heavenly.

47. perdition *n.*: damnation.
48. adamantine (ad′ə·man′tin) *adj.*: unbreakable. **penal** *adj.*: punishing.
49. durst *v.*: dared.

53–56. Milton explains that the archangel Satan, jealous of God's power, has rebelled against the Almighty and thus been expelled from Heaven. The action of the poem begins at this point, *in medias res* ("in the middle of things")—the customary starting point of classical epics.
What most torments Satan in Hell?

58. obdurate *adj.*: stubborn; unrepentant.
59. ken *n.*: range of view.

68. still urges: always afflicts.

61–77. What images does Milton use to describe Hell?

74. center ... pole: three times the distance from Earth, or "center," to the outermost point in the universe. In Milton's cosmos, Earth is the center of ten concentric spheres.
78. weltering *v.*: used as *adj.*: rolling about.

---

368 Collection 3 The Renaissance

SKILLS REVIEW

Analyzing context clues. Remind students that using context clues means figuring out the meaning of an unfamiliar word by examining the words or sentences surrounding it. Milton often embeds synonyms and appositives—words and phrases that explain or define other words—in his sentences.

Activity. Have students use context clues to arrive at the meaning of *baleful* (l. 56). Ask them to list the words in the sentence (beginning in l. 53) that describe Satan's mental and emotional state (*wrath, lost happiness, pain, torments, affliction, dismay, hate*) and then imagine what the eyes of a person with these feelings would look like.

The Fallen Angels on the Wing by Gustave Doré. Engraving. Culver Pictures.

One next himself in power, and next in crime,
80 Long after known in Palestine, and named
Beelzebub.° To whom the Arch-Enemy,
And then in Heaven called Satan,° with bold words
Breaking the horrid silence thus began:
    "If thou beest he—but O how fallen! how changed
85 From him, who in the happy realms of light
Clothed with transcendent brightness didst outshine
Myriads though bright—if he whom mutual league,
United thoughts and counsels, equal hope
And hazard in the glorious enterprise,
90 Joined with me once, now misery hath joined
In equal ruin: into what pit thou seest
From what height fallen! so much the stronger proved
He with his thunder;° and till then who knew
The force of those dire arms? Yet not for those,
95 Nor what the potent Victor in his rage
Can else inflict, do I repent or change,
Though changed in outward luster, that fixed mind
And high disdain, from sense of injured merit,
That with the Mightiest raised me to contend,
100 And to the fierce <u>contention</u> brought along
Innumerable force of spirits armed

Vocabulary
contention (kən·ten'shən) *n.*: struggle.

81. **Beelzebub** (bē·el'zə·bub'): next in power to Satan; described as prince of the devils in Matthew 12:24.
82. **Satan**: Hebrew for "adversary; opposer."

93. **He . . . thunder:** God.

93–124. In this speech, Satan claims that although he has been defeated by God (the "potent Victor"), he will not surrender.
❓ *What details in Satan's speech show that he sees himself and God as the generals of two opposing armies? What is Satan's attitude toward his defeat?*

John Milton   369

DIRECT TEACHING

VIEWING THE ART

Although inspired by Milton's writing, Blake was not entirely satisfied with Milton's vision of Heaven and Hell. In Blake's view, Milton was both "a true Poet and of the Devil's party without knowing it." This image suggests the difficulties that Blake saw in Milton's representation of Satan.

Activity. Describe the expression on Satan's face. What feeling might this expression evoke in someone observing it? [Satan's expression of terror may compel the viewer to sympathize with him.]

A Literary Focus

Theme. Here Satan introduces the idea of "the unconquerable will." What does he suggest about God's will, compared with his own? [Possible response: God's will is not as strong as Satan's. Satan believes that God's confidence was shaken by the rebellion and that he was uncertain about the outcome of the battle in Heaven.]

B Literary Focus

Style. What is the effect of Satan's oratory here, and what techniques contribute to that effect? [Possible response: His words are an eloquent, compelling cry of defiance. His oratorical techniques include parallelism, repetition, and the use of a string of punchy, one-syllable words: "What though the field be lost? / All is not lost."]

The Angel Michael Binding Satan (c. 1805) by William Blake. Watercolor, ink, and graphite.

Courtesy of the Fogg Art Museum, Harvard University Art Museums, Gift of W. A. White. © President and Fellows of Harvard College.

> That durst dislike his reign, and, me preferring,
> His utmost power with adverse power opposed
> In dubious battle on the plains of Heaven,
> 105 And shook his throne. What though the field be lost?
> All is not lost; the unconquerable will,
> And study° of revenge, immortal hate,
> And courage never to submit or yield:
> And what is else not to be overcome?
> 110 That glory never shall his wrath or might
> Extort from me. To bow and sue for grace
> With suppliant° knee, and deify his power
> Who from the terror of this arm so late
> Doubted° his empire, that were low indeed,
> 115 That were an ignominy and shame beneath
> This downfall; since by fate the strength of gods

107. **study** *n.:* pursuit.

112. **suppliant** *adj.:* humble.

114. **doubted** *v.:* archaic for "feared for."

Vocabulary
ignominy (ig′nə•min′ē) *n.:* dishonor; disgrace.

370   Collection 3   The Renaissance

READING MINI-LESSON

Developing Word-Attack Skills
Activity. Remind students that *ea* and *ee* are two ways to spell /ē/. Have students think of words that illustrate these letter-sound relationships and write them on the chalkboard. [Possible responses: *eat, easy, heal, team, bee, seed.*]

Display the following words from the selection: *ethereal, vengeance, Beelzebub.* Discuss the sounds represented by *ea* or *ee* in each word.

- In *ethereal, ea* stands for two vowel sounds, /ē/ and the unstressed vowel sound /ə/; /ē•thir′ē•əl/.

And this empyreal substance° cannot fail,
Since through experience of this great event,
In arms not worse, in foresight much advanced,
120 We may with more successful hope resolve
To wage by force or guile eternal war
Irreconcilable to our grand Foe,
Who now triumphs, and in the excess of joy
Sole reigning holds the tyranny of Heaven."
125   So spake the apostate° Angel, though in pain,
Vaunting° aloud, but racked with deep despair;
And him thus answered soon his bold compeer:°
    "O Prince, O Chief of many thronèd Powers,
That led the embattled Seraphim° to war
130 Under thy conduct, and in dreadful deeds
Fearless, endangered Heaven's perpetual King,
And put to proof his high supremacy,
Whether upheld by strength, or chance, or fate;
Too well I see and rue the dire event,°
135 That with sad overthrow and foul defeat
Hath lost us Heaven, and all this mighty host
In horrible destruction laid thus low,
As far as gods and heavenly essences
Can perish: for the mind and spirit remains
140 Invincible, and vigor soon returns,
Though all our glory extinct, and happy state
Here swallowed up in endless misery.
But what if he our Conqueror (whom I now
Of force° believe almighty, since no less
145 Than such could have o'erpowered such force as ours)
Have left us this our spirit and strength entire
Strongly to suffer and support our pains,
That we may so suffice° his vengeful ire,
Or do him mightier service as his thralls°
150 By right of war, whate'er his business be,
Here in the heart of Hell to work in fire,
Or do his errands in the gloomy deep?
What can it then avail,° though yet we feel
Strength undiminished, or eternal being
155 To undergo eternal punishment?"
    Whereto with speedy words the Arch-Fiend replied:
"Fallen Cherub, to be weak is miserable,
Doing or suffering:° But of this be sure,
To do aught° good never will be our task,

117. **empyreal** (em·pir′ē·əl) **substance:** heavenly—and therefore indestructible—substance of which all angels (including Satan) are made.

125. **apostate** *adj.*: guilty of abandoning one's beliefs. Satan is an apostate.
126. **vaunting** *v.* used as *adj.*: boasting.
127. **compeer** *n.*: companion; equal. Now Beelzebub speaks.
129. **Seraphim:** highest order of angels.

134. **event** *n.*: archaic for "outcome."

143–145. What does Beelzebub admit about God? How is his attitude different from Satan's?

144. **of force:** of necessity.

148. **suffice** *v.*: archaic for "satisfy."
149. **thralls** *n. pl.*: slaves.

153. **avail** *v.*: be of help or advantage.

158. **doing or suffering:** whether active or passive.
159. **aught** *n.* used as *adj.*: anything; whatever.

John Milton 371

DIRECT TEACHING

A Literary Focus

Style. How does the syntax of ll. 159–160 reflect the content of Satan's argument? [Possible response: Satan portrays his own evil as equal to God's goodness. The use of parallel structure in this sentence (the repetition of the phrase *to do* and the pairings *never/ever* and *good/ill*) reflects the content of his argument.] Encourage students to look for other parallel structures in which Satan sets himself in opposition to God, such as the one in ll. 162–165.

B English-Language Learners

Paraphrase. Restate "disturb / His inmost counsels from their destined aim" in your own words. [Possible response: "interfere with God's plans."]

C Reading Skills

Making predictions. How do you suppose Satan will prevent God's "inmost counsels" from reaching their "destined aim"? [Possible responses: He will introduce evil into the world; he will tempt Adam and Eve.]

Responses to Margin Questions

Lines 156–168. Satan vows never to do good, to thwart any effort by God to do good, and to turn anything good into evil. His intention is the essence of evil in that his commitment to evil is uncompromising.

Lines 192–210. Possible response: Satan is compared to the Leviathan, a sea monster that tricked sailors into believing it was an island. The comparison underlines Satan's size and power.

A 160 But ever to do ill our sole delight,
         As being the contrary to his high will
         Whom we resist. If then his providence
         Out of our evil seek to bring forth good,
         Our labor must be to pervert that end,
    165 And out of good still° to find means of evil;
         Which ofttimes may succeed, so as perhaps
B   Shall grieve him, if I fail not, and disturb
         His inmost counsels from their destined aim.
C   But see the angry Victor° hath recalled
    170 His ministers of vengeance and pursuit
         Back to the gates of Heaven; the sulfurous hail
         Shot after us in storm, o'erblown hath laid
         The fiery surge, that from the precipice
         Of Heaven received us falling, and the thunder,
    175 Winged with red lightning and impetuous rage,
         Perhaps hath spent his shafts, and ceases now
         To bellow through the vast and boundless deep.
         Let us not slip° the occasion, whether scorn
         Or satiate° fury yield it from our Foe.
    180 Seest thou yon dreary plain, forlorn and wild,
         The seat of desolation, void of light,
         Save what the glimmering of these livid flames
D   Casts pale and dreadful? Thither let us tend
         From off the tossing of these fiery waves,
    185 There rest, if any rest can harbor there,
         And reassembling our afflicted powers,
         Consult how we may henceforth most offend
         Our Enemy, our own loss how repair,
         How overcome this dire calamity,
    190 What reinforcement we may gain from hope,
         If not, what resolution from despair."
            Thus Satan talking to his nearest mate
         With head uplift above the wave, and eyes
E   That sparkling blazed; his other parts besides,
    195 Prone on the flood, extended long and large,
         Lay floating many a rood,° in bulk as huge
         As whom the fables name of monstrous size,
         Titanian or Earth-born, that warred on Jove,
         Briareos or Typhon,° whom the den
    200 By ancient Tarsus held, or that sea-beast
         Leviathan,° which God of all his works
         Created hugest that swim the ocean stream:

Vocabulary

impetuous (im·pech′ōō·əs) *adj.*: forceful; violent.
desolation (des′ə·lā′shən) *n.*: utter misery; extreme loneliness.

156–168. What does Satan vow? In what ways might this be considered the essence of evil?

165. still *adv.*: always.

169. angry Victor: God.

178. slip *v.*: lose.
179. satiate *v.* used as *adj.*: satisfied

192–210. Milton uses an epic simile to describe Satan lying in repose on the lake of fire (lines 196–209). *To what is Satan being compared? What does this comparison suggest about Satan?*

196. rood *n.*: old unit of measure varying locally from about six to eight yards.
198–200. Titanian... Typhon: In an epic simile, Milton compares Satan to the Titans and giants of Greek mythology. Briareos, a hundred-handed giant, helped Zeus (Jove) battle the Titans. Typhon, a hundred-headed serpent-monster from Cilicia (near Tarsus), attacked heaven and was imprisoned by Zeus.
201. Leviathan: biblical sea monster, either a reptile or a whale.

Satan in His Original Glory by William Blake. Watercolor. Tate Gallery, London.

> Him haply slumbering on the Norway foam,
> The pilot of some small night-foundered° skiff,
> 205 Deeming some island, oft, as seamen tell,
> With fixèd anchor in his scaly rind
> Moors by his side under the lee, while night
> Invests° the sea, and wishèd morn delays:
> So stretched out huge in length the Arch-Fiend lay
> 210 Chained on the burning lake; nor ever thence
> Had risen or heaved his head, but that the will
> And high permission of all-ruling Heaven
> Left him at large to his own dark designs,
> That with reiterated crimes he might
> 215 Heap on himself damnation, while he sought
> Evil to others, and enraged might see
> How all his malice served but to bring forth
> Infinite goodness, grace, and mercy shown
> On man by him seduced, but on himself
> 220 Treble confusion, wrath, and vengeance poured.
>   Forthwith upright he rears from off the pool
> His mighty stature; on each hand the flames

204. night-foundered: overtaken by night.

208. invests *v.:* covers.

214–220. Milton reminds his readers that Satan remains at the mercy of God and that God plans to use Satan's evil to bring good into the world.
? Why has God left Satan "to his own dark designs"? Paraphrase what Milton says in lines 214–220.

Vocabulary
reiterated (rē·it′ə·rāt′id) *v.* used as *adj.:* repeated.
malice (mal′is) *n.:* ill will; evil intentions.

John Milton   373

Direct Teaching

A **Advanced Learners**
Enrichment. Encourage these students to note Milton's frequent use of light/dark contrasts. Such images are common throughout literature, but since Milton was blind, it is quite possible that he was moved in a special way by the idea of losing light.

B **Reading Skills**
❓ **Making inferences.** Why is Satan so proud of possessing his infernal world? [Possible response: He believes that having his own kingdom proves he is God's equal.] Does his pride seem genuine? [Possible responses: Yes, he is glad to be far from God and to rule his own kingdom; no, he is bitter at being thrown out of Heaven and realizes that his kingdom is a horrible place.]

C **Reading Skills**
❓ **Making connections.** How does the saying "Misery loves company" apply here? [Possible responses: Satan is eager to rally his forces so that they can share with him "their part / In this unhappy mansion." He needs their support to pursue revenge against God. He may believe that sharing his torment with others will alleviate his pain.]

Responses to Margin Questions

Lines 221–238. Possible responses: He is compared to destructive winds and to Mount Etna, a volcano in Sicily. Satan stretches his wings and flies to dry land. The comparison portrays Satan as a mighty and destructive force that weighs the air down.

Lines 254–255. Possible response: It doesn't matter where you are physically; your attitude toward your surroundings matters more than the surroundings themselves. The mind can create joy or misery in any setting.

Driven backward slope their pointing spires, and rolled
In billows, leave in the midst a horrid vale.
225 Then with expanded wings he steers his flight
Aloft, incumbent° on the dusky air
That felt unusual weight, till on dry land
He lights, if it were land that ever burned
With solid, as the lake with liquid fire;
230 And such appeared in hue, as when the force
Of subterranean wind transports a hill
Torn from Pelorus,° or the shattered side
Of thundering Etna,° whose combustible
And fueled entrails thence conceiving fire,
235 Sublimed° with mineral fury, aid the winds,
And leave a singèd bottom all involved°
With stench and smoke: such resting found the sole
Of unblest feet. Him followed his next mate,
Both glorying to have scaped the Stygian° flood
240 As gods, and by their own recovered strength,
Not by the sufferance° of supernal° power.
      "Is this the region, this the soil, the clime,"
Said then the lost Archangel, "this the seat
That we must change for Heaven, this mournful gloom
245 For that celestial light? Be it so, since he
Who now is sovereign can dispose and bid
What shall be right: farthest from him is best,
Whom reason hath equaled, force hath made supreme
Above his equals. Farewell, happy fields,
250 Where joy forever dwells! Hail, horrors! hail,
Infernal world! and thou, profoundest° Hell,
Receive thy new possessor; one who brings
A mind not to be changed by place or time.
The mind is its own place, and in itself
255 Can make a Heaven of Hell, a Hell of Heaven.
What matter where, if I be still the same,
And what I should be, all but less than he
Whom thunder hath made greater? Here at least
We shall be free; the Almighty hath not built
260 Here for his envy, will not drive us hence:
Here we may reign secure, and in my choice
To reign is worth ambition, though in Hell:
Better to reign in Hell than serve in Heaven.
But wherefore let we then our faithful friends,
265 The associates and copartners of our loss,
Lie thus astonished° on the oblivious° pool,
And call them not to share with us their part
In this unhappy mansion, or once more
With rallied arms to try what may be yet
270 Regained in Heaven, or what more lost in Hell?"

---

226. incumbent *adj.*: lying.

❓ **221–238.** To what natural forces is Satan compared? Paraphrase the actions of Satan described in these lines. What impression of Satan does Milton create here?

232. Pelorus: headland in Sicily, Italy; now called Cape Faro.
233. Etna: volcano in Sicily, Italy.
235. sublimed *v.* used as *adj.*: vaporized.
236. involved *adj.*: enveloped.
239. Stygian (stij'ē·ən): of or like the river Styx; infernal; hellish. In Greek mythology the river Styx encircles the underworld.
241. sufferance *n.*: permission. **supernal** *adj.*: heavenly.

251. profoundest *adj.*: lowest; deepest.

254–255. Satan accepts his fate, bids farewell to Heaven, and declares himself the sovereign ruler of Hell.
❓ How would you paraphrase what Satan says in these lines? In what ways is his declaration true? In what ways is it false?

266. astonished *v.* used as *adj.*: dazed. **oblivious** *adj.*: causing forgetfulness.

Check Test: True-False

Monitoring students' progress. Guide the class in answering these questions.

1. Satan had been one of God's favored angels. [T]
2. Satan rebels because God made him a slave. [F]
3. Satan was very ugly, with red skin and horns. [F]
4. Satan is a bolder leader than Beelzebub. [T]
5. When Satan says "[f]arthest from him is best" (l. 247), he means that the rebels can do as they please when they are away from God. [T]

Response and Analysis

Reading Check

1. Whom does Milton call upon at the beginning of his epic (lines 6–16)? What question does he ask about Adam and Eve (lines 27–33)?
2. What is Milton's purpose in writing this epic poem (lines 24–26)?
3. Why was Satan cast out of Heaven (lines 41–43)?
4. In his first speech, what does Satan tell Beelzebub that he will never do (line 96)? What course does he favor instead (lines 105–124)?
5. According to lines 210–220, who allows Satan the freedom to pursue his evil intentions?
6. In his last speech (lines 258–264), what does Satan claim are the advantages of life in Hell?

Thinking Critically

7. According to Milton, how is the rebellion of Satan and the angels against God connected to "man's first disobedience" and the origin of evil in the world? How does Milton explain the existence of evil in a world created by a loving God?
8. Re-read Milton's first description of Hell in lines 53–74. How is Hell both a psychological state and a physical place? What do you make of the poet's use of an **oxymoron** in the phrase "darkness visible" (line 63)? (An oxymoron is a figure of speech that relies on a **paradox**, or a self-contradictory idea.)
9. In his opening speech, Satan vows never to "repent or change" (line 96). Nevertheless, where can you catch hints that the angel longs for his former state? How might this yearning relate to Milton's mention of "the thought . . . of lost happiness" in lines 54–55?
10. In lines 210–220, the speaker offers a solemn assurance that despite all Satan's power and grandeur, the devil is still subject to God's purposes. How do these lines contribute a level of **dramatic irony** to Satan's ringing assertion of freedom in lines 242–270?
11. How do people today still use the arguments and rationalizations used by Satan and his old crony Beelzebub in lines 143–168?

Extending and Evaluating

12. Judging by this excerpt from *Paradise Lost*, does Milton succeed in explaining the causes of evil and suffering in this world? Explain your thinking.

Literary Criticism

13. Many critics see Satan as the real hero of *Paradise Lost*. Like many literary villains, Satan is a compelling figure—but can he really be considered a heroic figure from any perspective? Use evidence from the text—including descriptions of Satan's appearance, his words, his actions, and his effect on others—to support your point of view.

WRITING

True Words?

Among the most famous passages in *Paradise Lost* are these words from Satan's last speech (lines 254–255):

> The mind is its own place,
>   and in itself
> Can make a Heaven of Hell,
>   a Hell of Heaven.

In a brief **essay**, explain what these words mean and whether they address something that is true about the human condition. In your opinion, are Satan's words an accurate description of what the mind can do? Draw from your own knowledge and experience to find examples of ways in which these words are (or are not) true in everyday life.

SKILLS FOCUS

Pages 375–376 cover
Literary Skills Analyze the use of style. Analyze epic similes, irregular syntax, and blank verse.
Reading Skills Understand Milton's style.
Writing Skills Write an essay analyzing a passage from the selection. Write a paraphrase of a speech from the selection.
Vocabulary Skills Identify word relationships.

INDEPENDENT PRACTICE

Response and Analysis

Thinking Critically

7. Possible answer: Out of vengefulness, Satan plans to corrupt God's original plan for humanity, his latest creation. According to Milton, God allows evil to exist in order that good may arise from it.
8. Possible answers: Hell is a place of physical torment because it is fiery yet dark. Words and phrases such as "doom," "Lost happiness" and "dismay" suggest psychological pain. The oxymoron "Darkness visible" hints at the character of Hell—a state of horror beyond human comprehension.
9. Satan's tone is mournful when he laments Beelzebub's lost glory and when he compares the sight of Hell to the memory of Heaven. His greatest sorrow is losing his happiness and status in Heaven.
10. Possible answer: Satan's assertions of independence contrast sharply with Milton's statement that his actions are allowed by "high permission of all-ruling Heaven." Since he exists only with God's consent and is driven by hostility toward him, he can never be free of God. This situation is an example of dramatic irony: The reader grasps this fact, while Satan does not.
11. Possible answer: Some people believe that evil is as much under God's control as is good—that God created both and that anything good has a potential for evil, and vice versa.

(Answers continued on p. 376.)

Reading Check

1. He calls upon the Heavenly Muse. He asks why Adam and Eve violated God's one restriction on their freedom.
2. His purpose is to affirm God's benevolence and to explain God's treatment of humanity.
3. He led a rebellion of angels against God.
4. He will never "repent or change." He seeks revenge by thwarting God's plans and mounting another attack against Heaven.
5. "All-ruling Heaven"—that is, God.
6. He and his angels are assured freedom there.

Extending and Evaluating

12. Possible answer: Milton's explanation is logical and satisfying, assuming one believes in God. Other explanations for the existence of evil and suffering tend toward chaos and randomness, which some people may find more believable than Milton's orderly, purposeful worldview.

Literary Criticism

13. Possible answer: Satan's words and actions are compelling and make him the most interesting character in the excerpt. However, being compelling and interesting are not defining qualities in a hero. Satan's fierce determination to oppose his foe—God—merely establishes him as the ultimate villain, not as a hero. He wins no battles, achieves no noble goals, and performs no great deeds.

Vocabulary Development

1. *infernal*—fiendish. *impetuous*—forceful; violent. *contention*—struggle. Relationship—These words all describe the behavior of the angels who defied God.

2. *reiterated*—repeated. *guile*—cunning. Relationship—In the poem, God allows Satan to have his own kingdom where the fallen angel's cunning behavior (guile) can be reiterated.

3. *ignominy*—disgrace. *desolation*—utter misery. *affliction*—suffering. Relationship—These words all describe the miserable conditions Satan endures in Hell.

4. *malice*—ill will. *transgress*—sin against. Relationship—These words illustrate a cause-and-effect relationship that explains Satan's behavior: Satan's malice causes him to transgress.

Literary Focus

1. Satan's body is compared to the bodies of the giants Briareas and Typhon and to the sea creature Leviathan. These creatures are huge and terrifying.

Paraphrase a Speech

Write a **paraphrase** of one of the long speeches in this text. You might try Satan's speech in lines 84–124, Beelzebub's speech in lines 157–191, or Satan's speech in lines 242–270. In your paraphrase, make the text very clear by following these guidelines:

- Put Milton's sentences in subject-verb-complement order.
- Provide words missing in Milton's text.
- Rephrase figures of speech to be sure you understand them.
- Replace archaic, or old-fashioned, words with modern words.

Imagine that you are writing a paraphrase to explain the text to a reader who is having trouble understanding it.

Vocabulary Development
Identifying Word Relationships

1. infernal, impetuous, contention
2. reiterated, guile
3. ignominy, desolation, affliction
4. malice, transgress

On a separate sheet of paper, write down the meanings of the Vocabulary words in each set above. Then, explain what relationship the words in each set share. Sometimes a word may have to be considered as it appears in the context of the poem.

Literary Focus

Milton's Poetic Style

Analyzing epic similes. The word *as* in Milton's epic tells us that a simile is coming, an elaborate **epic simile** in which something in the poem is compared to something quite outside the poem—often an animal, sometimes a human being or a human action. These epic similes allow Milton to bring to his epic a variety of nonbiblical material. Note the **analogies,** or similarities between two unlike things, that the similes are based on.

1. What epic similes are used to describe Satan's bulk in lines 196–208? What is compared to what? How are these things alike?

2. What epic simile describes Satan's landing on dry land in lines 230–237? What is compared to what? How are these things alike?

Reading irregular syntax. To accommodate the demands of his meter, Milton often **omits words** and **inverts syntax,** wrenching some of his sentences out of the usual subject-verb-complement order. If you are having problems finding the **subject** and **verb** in one of his long or inverted sentences, re-read the sentence until you can locate these core sentence parts.

3. In lines 76–78, what are the **subject,** the **verb,** and the **direct object**? What additional words should be supplied in lines 78–81 to make sense of the rest of this sentence?

4. Using normal English syntax, how would you rephrase lines 157–162?

Reading blank verse. Milton uses **blank verse,** or unrhymed iambic pentameter, to give his epic an exalted tone. In iambic pentameter each line of a poem has ten syllables, with five strong stresses alternating with five weaker stresses (the lines begin with an unstressed syllable and end with a stressed one). An **iamb** is an unstressed syllable followed by a stressed one, as in the word *refer*.

5. Choose a passage to read aloud so that you can hear the beat of the iambs. Where does Milton vary the meter to give his verse variety and to prevent a singsong rhythm?

---

2. Satan's landing is compared to the smashing of a hill or to a volcano torn from its original site by a blast and carried by the wind. These explosive actions are alike in their enormous force.

3. *He / discerns / comparisons.* To clarify, repeat the verb or supply a synonym. (He discerns his companions and sees Beelzebub by his side.)

4. Possible answer: Fallen Cherub, weakness is miserable. Let us be strong in avoiding good; let us delight in acting contrary to God.

5. Answers will vary.

Vocabulary Development

Scientific and Mathematical Words Derived from Greek and Latin

Many of the scientific and mathematical terms that we use today are derived from ancient Greek and Latin, the classical languages that were rediscovered and embraced by scholars during the Renaissance. Developing a knowledge of Greek and Latin roots and affixes can help you feel more at home in the world of complex scientific and mathematical words. If you become a scientist or a mathematician yourself, you might go to Greek and Latin when you need to make up names for your discoveries.

Words are built on a base, or **root,** which contains the core of the word's meaning. The root –*bio*–, for instance, comes from a Greek word meaning "life." The words *biorhythm, biome,* and *biodegradable* contain this root. These words also contain **affixes**—word parts added to the beginning (prefixes) or end (suffixes) of a root to change its meaning. For instance, by adding the **suffix** –*logy*, meaning "study of," to the root –*bio*–, the word *biology*—"the study of life"—is formed. The **prefix** *micro*– added to *biology* creates the word *microbiology*, "the study of very small [*microscopic*] life-forms."

Some common roots, prefixes, and suffixes from Greek and Latin are listed in the charts below. Knowing these word parts will help you determine the meanings of unfamiliar scientific and mathematical terms when you come across them in various texts.

Greek and Latin Roots	Meaning	Example
–aero–	air; gas	aerobic; aerial
–anthr–, –anthrop–, –andro–	human	anthropology; androgyny
–baro–	weight	barometric
–cal–, –calor–	heat	calorie; calorimeter
–geo–	earth; ground	geography; geology
–gon–	angle	polygon; pentagon; trigonometry
–hydr–, –hydro–	water	hydrogen; hydrate
–iso–	alike; equal	isosceles; isometric
–morph–	shape; form	morphology; polymorphous
–patho–	disease	pathology; pathological
–psych–	mind	psychology; psychoanalysis
–zo–	life; animal	zoology; protozoa

Pages 377–378 cover **Vocabulary Skills** Understand and use words derived from Greek and Latin.

Vocabulary Development

Practice

1. *anthropomorphic.* Possible guess—having a human shape or form. Definition—regarded as having human qualities. Derivation——*anthrop*–, "human"; –*morph*–, "shape; form."

2. *aerobiology.* Possible guess—study of organisms living in the air. Definition—study of airborne materials such as microorganisms. Derivation— –*aero*–, "air"; –*bio*–, "life."

3. *pathogen.* Possible guess—something that causes disease. Definition—agent of disease. Derivation— –*patho*–, "disease"; –*gen*, "making; causing."

4. *psychopathology.* Possible guess—study of diseased minds. Definition—study of mental disorders. Derivation— –*psych*–, "mind"; –*patho*–, "disease."

5. *metamorphosis.* Possible guess—change in shape. Definition—change in form, shape, or structure. Derivation— –*meta*–, "change"; –*morph*–, "shape."

6. *transcontinental.* Possible guess—across a continent. Definition—that crosses a continent. Derivation— –*trans*– "across."

ASSESSING

Assessment

- Holt Assessment: Literature, Reading, and Vocabulary

RETEACHING

For a lesson reteaching author's tone and style, see **Reteaching**, p. 1129A.

Greek and Latin Affixes	Meaning	Example
ana–	upward; throughout; similar to	analysis; analog
anti–	against	antibiotic; antidote
–gen	something that produces or is produced	oxygen; hydrogen
hemi–	half	hemisphere
hypo–	under; below; too little	hypodermic
meta–	change; over; through	metastasis
–osis	state; condition; formation	meiosis; mitosis; symbiosis
–quadro–, quadr–	four	quadratic; quadruped
sub–	under	subtract; suborbital
–tomy	cutting	anatomy
trans–	across; over; beyond	transversal; transduce
tri–	three	triangle

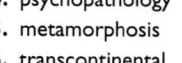

Each of the following words is used in mathematical or scientific fields of study. Use the charts above and your own knowledge of words to guess as best you can each word's meaning, based on its root or affixes. Then, check your guess by looking up the definition of the word in a dictionary. Write down how the root or affix of each word helped you determine the word's meaning.

1. anthropomorphic
2. aerobiology
3. pathogen
4. psychopathology
5. metamorphosis
6. transcontinental

DIFFERENTIATING INSTRUCTION

Learners Having Difficulty
Remind students that a sonnet consists of fourteen lines with one of several rhyme schemes. Explain that a sonnet often starts by expressing a problem and then proposes a solution to that problem. Have students paraphrase the poem and express its main idea in a sentence or two.

Before You Read

When I consider how my light is spent

Make the Connection
Quickwrite

Our lives are filled with turning points—successes and failures, tests and triumphs, beginnings and endings. Sometimes we recognize the turning points only in hindsight. In the sonnet that follows, Milton writes about a turning point in his life: the onset of blindness during middle age.

People of every era, at any age, often face questions similar to the ones Milton ponders: "Where do I go from here?" and "Now that tragedy has struck, how can I possibly go on?" Jot down four or five critical turning points that a person might face during his or her life, and list the questions that those events might force a person to consider.

Literary Focus
Allusion

An **allusion** is a reference to a statement, person, place, event, or thing that is known from literature, history, religion, mythology, politics, sports, science, or popular culture.

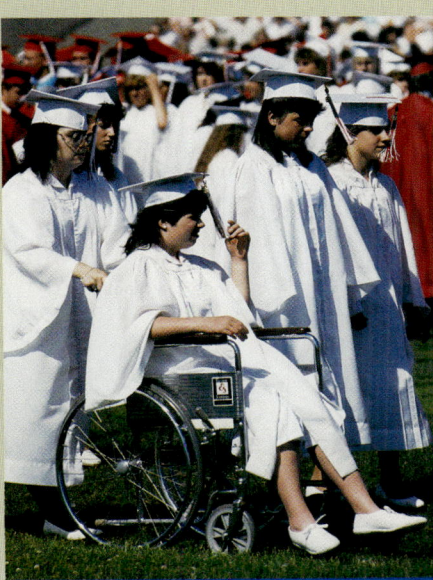

In ordinary conversation we may allude to a famous figure by calling an intelligent person an Einstein or a good baseball player a Babe Ruth. We might allude to a parable in the Gospel of Luke in the Bible by calling someone who has helped us change a flat tire a good Samaritan. Literary works frequently allude to past literary classics: Ernest Hemingway's novel *For Whom the Bell Tolls* takes its title from John Donne's Meditation 17 (see page 308), and the title of John Steinbeck's novel *The Grapes of Wrath* comes from the "Battle Hymn of the Republic." As you saw in "The Fall of Satan" from *Paradise Lost,* Milton himself took delight in alluding to everything from geographic locations to biblical passages.

> An **allusion** is a reference to a statement, a person, a place, an event, or a thing that is known from literature, history, religion, mythology, politics, sports, science, or popular culture.
>
> *For more on Allusion, see the Handbook of Literary and Historical Terms.*

Background
Altogether Milton wrote eighteen sonnets in English and five in Italian. In both form and subject matter, his sonnets differ from those of his English predecessors, Sidney, Spenser, and Shakespeare. Milton's sonnets closely follow the Italian, or Petrarchan, sonnet form and are about events and persons in his own public and private life. In "When I consider how my light is spent," however, he introduces a variation into the Petrarchan sonnet by making the turn, or change, before line 9. (For more information about the Petrarchan sonnet, see page 276.)

INTERNET
More About
John Milton
Keyword: LE5 12-3

SKILLS FOCUS
Literary Skills
Understand the use of allusion.

John Milton 379

PRETEACHING

Summary *at grade level*

In "When I consider how my light is spent," Milton grieves for his lost sight and expresses his fear that he will never use his abilities as he had hoped to. However, he finds consolation in the thought that patiently bearing his burden and waiting to serve God's will advance the divine plan as much as completing the heroic works of which he dreamed.

Invite learners having difficulty to read "When I consider how my light is spent" in interactive format in *The Holt Reader* and to use the sidenotes as aids to understanding the selection.

English-Language Learners
Help these students break down the sentences, identifying subjects and verbs.

Advanced Learners
Ask students to find and read "How soon hath Time," another famous sonnet by Milton on the theme of passages. Encourage students to comment on the views of time and the speaker's sense of his role in the world as expressed in "How soon hath Time" in comparison with the views in "When I consider how my light is spent."

The Blind Milton Dictating
Paradise Lost *to His Daughters*
(1877) by Mihály Munkácsy.
Collection of the New York Public Library. Astor, Lenox and Tilden Foundations.

In "When I consider how my light is spent," sometimes titled "On His Blindness," Milton dramatizes a calamity that hit him in middle age: blindness. Long before he had accomplished his life's work, he lost his sight. Deeply religious and believing firmly that everyone is accountable to God, Milton asks in the first part of the sonnet, "How can I continue to do the work that God expects of me?" He proposes an answer in the remainder of the sonnet.

When I consider how my light is spent

John Milton

When I consider how my light is spent
Ere half my days in this dark world and wide,
And that one talent° which is death to hide
Lodged with me useless, though my soul more bent
5   To serve therewith my Maker, and present
My true account, lest He returning chide,
"Doth God exact day-labor, light denied?"
I fondly° ask. But Patience, to prevent
That murmur, soon replies, "God doth not need
10   Either man's work or His own gifts. Who best
Bear His mild yoke, they serve Him best. His state
Is kingly: Thousands° at His bidding speed,
And post o'er land and ocean without rest;
They also serve who only stand and wait."

3. **talent** *n.*: reference to the parable of the talents (Matthew 25:14–30), in which a servant is scolded for burying his one talent, or coin, in the earth instead of putting it to good use.
8. **fondly** *adv.*: foolishly.

12. **thousands**: of angels.

Response and Analysis

Thinking Critically

1. What question does the speaker ask of God in the first eight lines? How would you paraphrase this question—that is, how would you restate it in your own words?

2. The answer to the question indicates the turn in this sonnet. What is Patience's reply to the question in the last six lines? How would you paraphrase that answer in your own words?

3. The word *talent* in line 3 is both a pun and an **allusion** to a biblical **parable** that Milton's readers would have recognized instantly. In Matthew 25:14–30, three servants are given coins called talents. The first two servants invest their talents and double their value, while the third is punished for burying the one talent he received, accomplishing nothing at all. What is Milton's "one talent"? How is his situation similar to or different from that of the third servant in the parable?

4. The phrase "mild yoke" in line 11 refers to the words of Jesus in Matthew 11:30: "For my yoke is easy, and my burden is light." What is Milton's "yoke," or burden? By making such an **allusion**, what is Milton saying about his situation?

5. In this sonnet, how well does Milton answer the fundamental questions, "Where do I go from here?" and "How can I go on, now that tragedy has struck?" Would his answers have satisfied people of his own time? How well does the sonnet speak to people of today? Be sure to explain your responses. You may want to consult your Quickwrite notes for help.

WRITING

Those Who Stand and Wait

In a brief **essay**, explore the ways in which the quotation "They also serve who only stand and wait," might apply to your life. Think of some situations in which it would be appropriate to stand and wait. What dangers, or pitfalls, do you also see in the statement? That is, how might people use it to avoid doing something that is demanded by justice or fairness? What do you think Milton meant by the phrase?

LISTENING AND SPEAKING

Two Speakers

Present this sonnet using two speakers, one to present the problem in the octave and the other to present the response in the sestet. Before you present the poem, be sure you understand the structure of Milton's sentences. Then, determine exactly where you must pause and when you must make full stops. It will help to write or print the poem out first. On the copy, write directions for your oral reading.

Literary Skills
Analyze the use of allusion.

Writing Skills
Write an essay analyzing a line of a sonnet.

Listening and Speaking Skills
Recite a sonnet that has two speakers.

DIRECT TEACHING

VIEWING THE ART

The stages in Christian's journey to the Celestial City are depicted in this cleverly conceived Victorian etching. Though the style of the etching may strike us as quaint or even naive, it nevertheless compresses the message of *The Pilgrim's Progress* into a form that a child could grasp.

Activity. Have students identify some of the temptations depicted in the engraving. Then, have them design a map showing the temptations someone might face today on the road from the City of Destruction to the Celestial City.

Ⓐ Literary Focus

❓ **Allegory.** Readers and viewers of *The Wizard of Oz* usually sense its allegorical dimensions. Dorothy is a kind of Everyperson on a journey, beset by evildoers and accompanied by three friends on their own quests. What other allegorical elements can you identify in *The Wizard of Oz*? [Possible responses: the alluring Emerald City; the wizard who rules through deception and fear; the Tin Man's quest for a heart; the Lion's quest for courage.] What structural similarity do *The Pilgrim's Progress* and *The Wizard of Oz* have? [Both are related as dreams.]

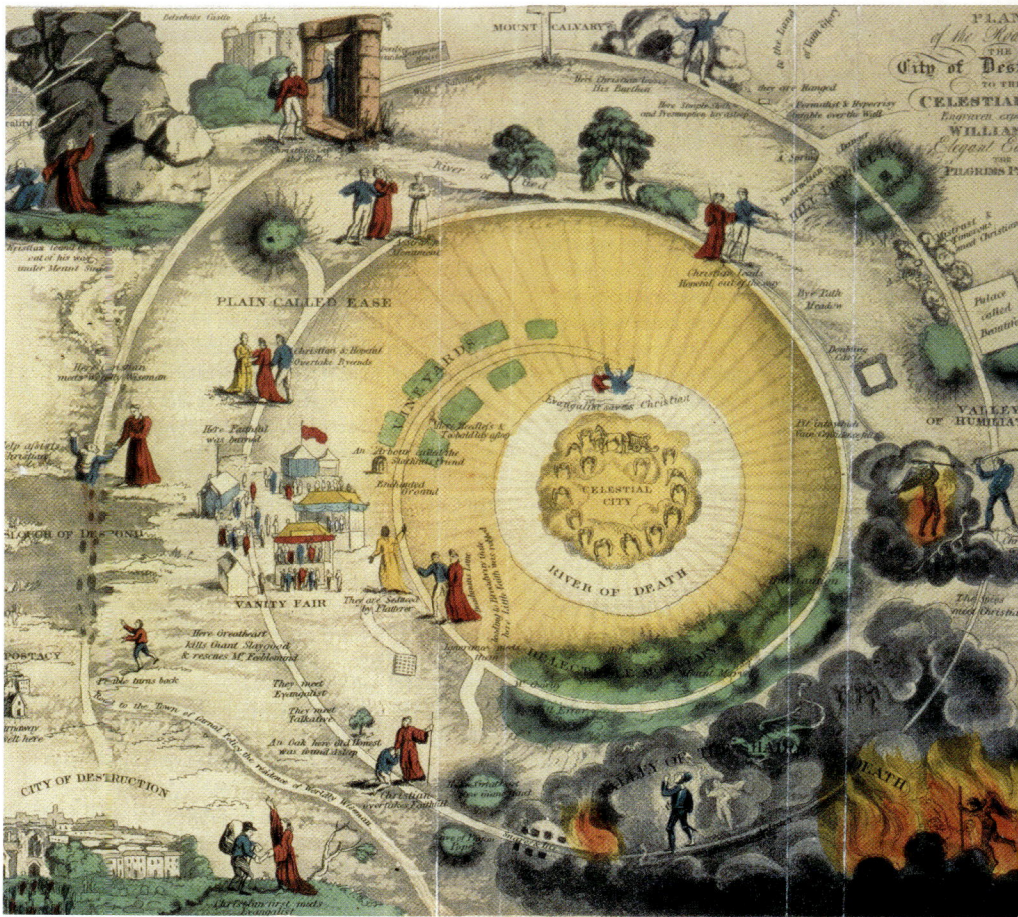

Plan of the road from the City of Destruction to the Celestial City, from *The Pilgrim's Progress* (19th century). Engraving.
Private Collection/The Bridgeman Art Library.

from The Pilgrim's Progress
John Bunyan

Bunyan tells the story of Christian's journey as if he, the narrator, were recounting his own dream. At this point in the story, Christian and his traveling companion, Faithful, enter a town called Vanity in which the local fair, or outdoor market, is in full swing. In Bunyan's day, merchants from all over Europe would sell their wares at such events, and the buying and selling would be accompanied by eating, drinking, sport, and general merriment.

384   Collection 3   The Renaissance

DIFFERENTIATING INSTRUCTION

Learners Having Difficulty
To help students understand the twofold nature of allegory, have them discuss the character of Faithful in this excerpt. Ask them to define *faithfulness* and explain how someone would demonstrate faithfulness. Then, have them identify whom and what Bunyan's character is faithful to.

English-Language Learners
Be sure students understand the meanings of *pilgrim*: its common meaning, "traveler," and its religious meaning, "someone who travels to a holy place." Point out that the Pilgrims were the band of Puritans who founded Plymouth Colony in 1620.

Advanced Learners
Encourage students to read parts of Dante Alighieri's *Divine Comedy*, the medieval poem that consists of the *Inferno*, *Purgatorio*, and *Paradiso*. Have them compare and contrast Dante's themes, characters, style, and tone to those of John Bunyan.

Then I saw in my dream that when they were got out of the wilderness they presently saw a town before them, and the name of that town is Vanity; and at the town there is a fair kept called Vanity-Fair. It is kept all the year long; it beareth the name of Vanity-Fair, because the town where 'tis kept is lighter than vanity; and also, because all that is there sold, or that cometh thither, is Vanity. As is the saying of the wise, *All that cometh is vanity*.

This Fair is no new erected business, but a thing of ancient standing; I will show you the original of it.

Almost five thousand years agone, there were pilgrims walking to the Celestial City, as these two honest persons are; and Beelzebub, Apollyon, and Legion,[1] with their companions, perceiving by the path that the Pilgrims made that their way to the City lay through this town of Vanity, they contrived here to set up a fair; a fair wherein should be sold of all sorts of vanity, and that it should last all the year long. Therefore at this Fair are all such merchandise sold, as houses, lands, trades, places, honours, preferments,[2] titles, countries, kingdoms, lusts, pleasures, and delights of all sorts, as whores, bawds, wives, husbands, children, masters, servants, lives, blood, bodies, souls, silver, gold, pearls, precious stones, and what not.

And moreover, at this Fair there is at all times to be seen jugglings, cheats, games, plays, fools, apes, knaves, and rogues, and that of all sorts.

Here are to be seen too, and that for nothing, thefts, murders, adulteries, false-swearers, and that of a blood-red colour.

And as in other fairs of less moment there are the several rows and streets under their proper names, where such and such wares are vended: so here likewise, you have the proper places, rows, streets (*viz.*[3] countries and kingdoms), where the wares of this Fair are soonest to be found: here is the Britain Row, the French Row, the Italian Row, the Spanish Row, the German Row, where several sorts of vanities are to be sold. But as in other fairs, some one commodity is as the chief of all the fair, so the ware of Rome and her merchandise is greatly promoted in this Fair: only our English nation, with some others, have taken a dislike thereat.

Now, as I said, the way to the Celestial City lies just through this town, where this lusty Fair is kept; and he that will go to the City, and yet not go through this town, must needs go out of the world. The Prince of Princes himself, when here, went through this Town[4] to his own country, and that upon a fair-day too. Yea, and as I think it was Beelzebub, the chief lord of this Fair, that invited him to buy of his vanities; yea, would have made him lord of the Fair, would he but have done him reverence as he went through the town. Yea, because he was such a person of honour, Beelzebub had him from street to street, and showed him all the kingdoms of the world in a little time, that he might if possible allure that Blessed One, to cheapen[5] and buy some of his vanities. But he had no mind to the merchandise, and therefore left the town without laying out so much as one farthing upon these vanities. This Fair therefore is an ancient thing, of long standing, and a very great Fair.

Now these pilgrims, as I said, must needs go through this Fair: well, so they did; but behold, even as they entered into the Fair, all the people in the Fair were moved, and the town itself as it were in a hubbub about them; and that for several reasons: for,

First, the pilgrims were clothed with such kind of raiment as was diverse from the raiment of any that traded in that Fair. The people therefore of the Fair made a great gazing upon them: Some

---

1. **Beelzebub** (bē·el′zə·bub′): here, Satan. **Apollyon** (ə·päl′yən): in the book of Revelation, the angel of the bottomless pit. **Legion**: unclean spirits or devils.
2. **preferments** *n. pl.*: appointments to political or religious positions.
3. *viz. adv.*: namely.
4. **The Prince of Princes . . . Town**: reference to the temptation of Christ (Matthew 4:1–11).
5. **cheapen** *v.*: ask the price of.

Vocabulary
allure (ə·loor′) *v.*: tempt; attract.

John Bunyan   385

Direct Teaching

A Content Area Connections
Humanities: Etymology
Point out that the men of the Fair and the pilgrims seem like barbarians to each other because they speak different languages. The word *barbarian* comes from the ancient Greeks, who used the word *barbaros* to refer to anyone whose language was not Greek. To the Greeks, all foreign speakers seemed only to be saying "ba-ba."

B Literary Focus
❓ Allegory and irony. Why is Mr. Blind-man's name allegorical? Why is his statement ironic?
[Possible responses: Allegorically, he represents spiritual blindness but says he can see clearly.]

---

said they were fools, some they were bedlams,[6] and some 'They are outlandish-men.'[7]

A Secondly, and as they wondered at their apparel so they did likewise at their speech; for few could understand what they said; they naturally spoke the language of Canaan;[8] but they that kept the Fair, were the men of this world: so that from one end of the Fair to the other, they seemed barbarians each to the other.

Thirdly, but that which did not a little amuse the merchandisers was that these pilgrims set very light by all their wares, they cared not so much as to look upon them; and if they called upon them to buy, they would put their fingers in their ears, and cry, *Turn away mine eyes from beholding vanity*; and look upwards, signifying that their trade and traffic was in Heaven.

One chanced mockingly, beholding the carriages of the men, to say unto them, 'What will ye buy?' but they, looking gravely upon him, said, 'We buy the truth.' At that there was an occasion taken to despise the men the more; some mocking, some taunting, some speaking reproachfully, and some calling upon others to smite them. At last things came to a hubbub and great stir in the Fair; insomuch that all order was confounded. Now was word presently brought to the great one of the Fair, who quickly came down and deputed some of his most trusty friends to take these men into examination about whom the Fair was almost overturned....

The townspeople at Vanity Fair are immediately suspicious of Christian and Faithful, and they arrest the two pilgrims and bring them to trial. Three witnesses, Envy, Superstition, and Pick-thank, a favor-seeker, testify against Faithful. His fate is turned over to a jury of townspeople.

Then went the jury out, whose names were Mr. Blind-man, Mr. No-good, Mr. Malice, Mr. Love-lust, Mr. Live-loose, Mr. Heady, Mr. High-mind, Mr. Enmity, Mr. Liar, Mr. Cruelty, Mr. Hate-light, and Mr. Implacable, who every one gave in his private verdict against him among themselves, and afterwards unanimously concluded to bring **B** him in guilty before the Judge. And first Mr. Blind-man, the foreman, said, "I see clearly that this man is an heretic." Then said Mr. No-good, "Away with such a fellow from the earth." "Ay," said Mr. Malice, "for I hate the very looks of him." Then said Mr. Love-lust, "I could never endure him."

---

6. **bedlams** *n. pl.*: mental patients from Bethlehem Hospital, the notorious hospital for the insane in London.
7. **outlandish-men:** foreigners.
8. **Canaan:** Promised Land. The "language of Canaan" is the language of the Bible.

Vocabulary
reproachfully (ri·prōch′fəl·ē) *adv.*: accusingly.
confounded (kən·foun′did) *adj.*: confused.
implacable (im·plak′ə·bəl) *adj.*: unchangeable; fixed.

Comparing and Contrasting Texts

Comparing styles. John Bunyan and John Milton were contemporaries, and both wrote about religious faith. However, there is a world of difference in their writing styles. Have students compare this excerpt from *The Pilgrim's Progress* with the excerpt from *Paradise Lost* (see pp. 367–374). Ask them to identify at least three stylistic differences, supporting their statements with examples from the texts. Suggest that students use a chart like the following one to organize their material.

Stylistic Differences

	Bunyan	Milton
Vocabulary	simple	elevated
Syntax	straightforward	complex
Literary elements	allegory	epic simile

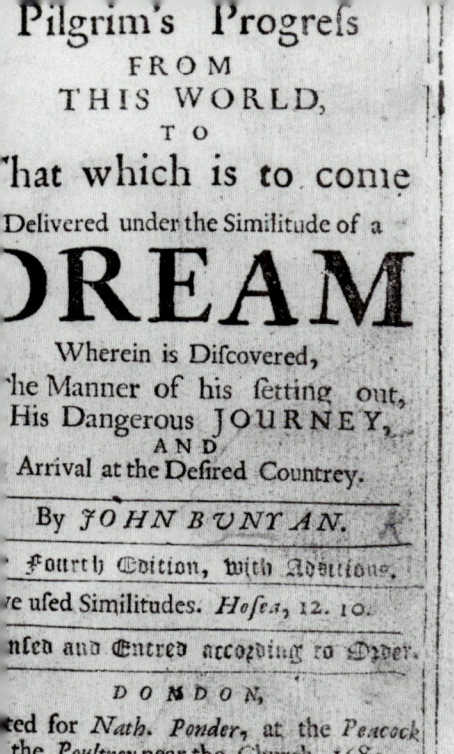

Frontispiece of *The Pilgrim's Progress* (1680) by John Bunyan. English School. Engraving.

"Nor I," said Mr. Live-loose, "for he would always be condemning my way." "Hang him, hang him," said Mr. Heady. "A sorry scrub," said Mr. High-mind. "My heart riseth against him," said Mr. Enmity. "He is a rogue," said Mr. Liar. "Hanging is too good for him," said Mr. Cruelty. "Let's dispatch him out of the way," said Mr. Hate-light. Then said Mr. Implacable, "Might I have all the world given me, I could not be reconciled to him, therefore let us forthwith bring him in guilty of death." And so they did, therefore he was presently condemned to be had from the place where he was, to the place from whence he came, and there to be put to the most cruel death that could be invented.

They therefore brought him out to do with him according to their law; and first they scourged him, then they buffeted him, then they lanced his flesh with knives; after that they stoned him with stones, then pricked him with their swords; and last of all they burned him to ashes at the stake. Thus came Faithful to his end. Now, I saw that there stood behind the multitude a chariot and a couple of horses, waiting for Faithful, who (so soon as his adversaries had dispatched him) was taken up into it, and straightway was carried up through the clouds, with sound of trumpet, the nearest way to the Celestial Gate. But as for Christian, he had some respite, and was remanded back to prison; so he there remained for a space: but he that over-rules all things, having the power of their rage in his own hand, so wrought it about that Christian for that time escaped them, and went his way. . . .

Christian continues on his journey and finds another companion, the convert Hopeful. After more trials and tests of faith, the two reach their long-awaited destination: the Gates of the Celestial City.

Now I saw in my dream, that these two men went in at the Gate; and lo, as they entered they were transfigured, and they had raiment put on that shone like gold. There was also that met them with harps and crowns, and gave them to them, the harp to praise withal, and the crowns in token of honour. Then I heard in my dream, that all the bells in the City rang again for joy; and that it was said unto them, "*Enter ye into the joy of your Lord.*" I also heard the men themselves, that they sang with a loud voice, saying, "*Blessing, honour, glory, and power, be to him that sitteth upon the throne, and to the Lamb for ever and ever.*"

Now just as the Gates were opened to let in the men, I looked in after them; and behold, the City shone like the sun, the streets also were paved with gold, and in them walked many men with crowns on their heads, palms in their hands, and golden harps to sing praises withal. ∎

Vocabulary
respite (res′pit) *n.*: postponement; reprieve.
transfigured (trans · fig′yərd) *v.*: changed the form of.

INDEPENDENT PRACTICE

Response and Analysis

Reading Check

1. Vanity Fair offers all the material goods of the world, as well as all forms of entertainment and pleasure.
2. They are disturbed by the pilgrims' dress, language, and disdain for the wares and values of Vanity Fair.
3. Faithful is tortured and burned.
4. He escapes and continues his journey.

Thinking Critically

5. Possible answer: Details include the array of merchandise at the fair, the juggling and games, the bluntness and mockery of the townspeople, and the prison.
6. To reach Heaven, one must reject worldly temptations.
7. Possible answer: They cannot endure the presence of saintly people amid their own corruption.
8. Possible answer: They want him destroyed. Each juror's name and words reflect his immoral attitude.
9. Possible answers: Cartoons, movies, and video games may be the most likely sources.
10. Possible answers: Bunyan wants to teach that worldliness is empty and an obstacle to salvation. Opinions on the applicability of the lesson today will vary.

Extending and Evaluating

11. Opinions will vary.

Literary Criticism

12. Possible answer: Bunyan's appeal may lie in the simplicity of his approach to morality and faith. He uses the archetype of the quest as a basis for his religious message, and even those who are not Christian can recognize and identify with the human desire to reach an eternal paradise.

388 Collection 3 The Renaissance

Response and Analysis

Reading Check

1. What is offered at Vanity Fair?
2. What characteristics of the two pilgrims disturb the people at Vanity Fair?
3. What happens to Faithful after he is arrested and tried?
4. What becomes of Christian after his imprisonment?

Thinking Critically

5. True to the spirit of **allegory,** Vanity Fair is both a **literal** and a **symbolic** place. What are some of the concrete details that give Bunyan's creation the feel of an actual English marketplace?
6. What is the **allegorical,** or symbolic, significance of the town of Vanity Fair in Christian's spiritual journey?
7. What do you think is the main reason the townspeople arrest Christian and Faithful? What really upsets them?
8. What attitude toward Faithful do all the members of the jury have in common? How do their names and their words reveal their **characters**?
9. Who or what are the modern counterparts to the allegorical characters on Faithful's jury and to the challenges that the two pilgrims face in Vanity Fair?
10. What does Bunyan wish to teach by means of the Vanity Fair episode? Do you think this lesson still has meaning in the modern world? Explain your response.

Extending and Evaluating

11. Is **allegory** an effective way of getting a moral message across today? Why or why not?

Literary Criticism

12. Biblical characters, cosmology, and quotations abound in *The Pilgrim's Progress,* yet the work has been translated widely and read by people of many cultures and religions. In fact, next to the Bible itself, it has been the most widely read of all English books. Discuss how Bunyan's narrative transcends its Christian framework to achieve universal appeal.

WRITING

The Jury Is In

One of the most enjoyable parts of the Vanity Fair episode is the commentary of the delightfully named jurors. Try writing your own **allegory** by expanding this scene. Invent other allegorical characters that might have appeared in the courtroom that day. Give your characters names, and write dialogue for them that reflects their names. Like Bunyan, you may want to use humor and satire.

SKILLS FOCUS

Literary Skills Analyze the use of allegory.
Writing Skills Write an allegory.
Vocabulary Skills Understand and use synonyms.

Vocabulary Development
Venn Diagrams

allure	implacable
reproachfully	respite
confounded	transfigured

Using a dictionary or the definitions on page 383, find a synonym for each Vocabulary word listed above. Then, explore the similarities among and the differences between the two synonymous words by making a Venn diagram like the one below. In the overlapping area, write the meanings that apply to both words.

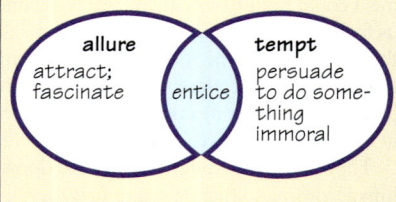

388 Collection 3 The Renaissance

Vocabulary Development

Sample answers:
Reproachfully means "disapprovingly."
Accusingly means "in a condemnatory way."
Both mean "in a critical way."

READ ON: FOR INDEPENDENT READING

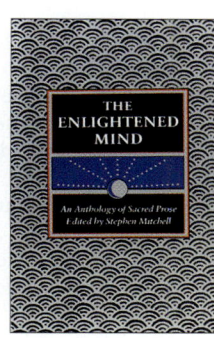

NONFICTION
Wisdom Through the Ages

If you're looking for an eye-opener, *The Enlightened Mind: An Anthology of Sacred Prose*, edited by Stephen Mitchell, might be just the book for you. This inspiring compilation highlights sacred writings from many cultures and traditions. It includes essays, sermons, and aphorisms from such diverse writers and thinkers as Plato, the Zen masters, and the Renaissance poet George Herbert.

NONFICTION
Motorcycle Meditations

Part travelogue, part meditation, part rambling discourse, Robert Pirsig's *Zen and the Art of Motorcycle Maintenance* is above all an inquiry into human values. While taking an extended motorcycle trip, Pirsig pursues the same questions that intrigued Francis Bacon and John Milton: What is the nature of the universe, and what is our place in it? How should we conduct our lives?

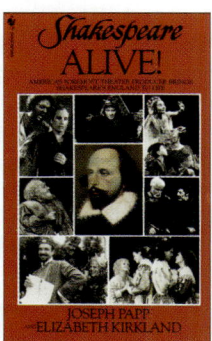

NONFICTION
The Bard's Background and Playground

People flocked in droves to Renaissance London, where the theater was a major attraction. Shakespeare was an integral part of this world, but there's been a tendency to divorce the man from his background. *Shakespeare Alive!* by Joseph Papp and Elizabeth Kirkland helps bring the legend back to life, placing Shakespeare in the theatrical and social context where he thrived.

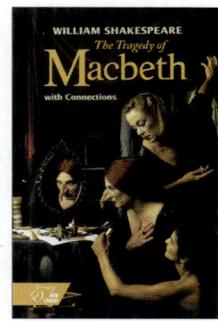

PLAY
Crime and Consequence

Have you ever wondered how a single act could affect the entire course of your life? In William Shakespeare's play *Macbeth,* a brave and intelligent Scotsman, tempted by the promise of ambition and power, commits a horrible crime that changes his life catastrophically. Although based on a true story, Shakespeare's Macbeth transcends the historical Macbeth, resulting in a play that features riveting action and intense psychological depth.

This title is available in the HRW Library.

DIFFERENTIATING INSTRUCTION

Estimated Word Counts and Reading Levels of Read On Books:

Nonfiction		
The Enlightened Mind	↑	60,000
Zen and the Art of Motorcycle Maintenance	↑	68,900
Shakespeare Alive!	↓	60,500

Play		
Macbeth	↔	112,400

KEY: ↑ above grade level   ↔ at grade level   ↓ below grade level

---

Read On

For Independent Reading

If students enjoyed the themes and topics explored in this collection, you might recommend the titles listed on p. 389 for independent reading.

Assessment Options

Use the following projects to evaluate and assess your students' outside reading.

- **Create an anthology.** Have students collect their favorite prose passages, poems, proverbs, or quotations that convey a spiritual message or traditional wisdom. Encourage students to follow Stephen Mitchell's example and draw on a wide range of cultures as sources. Suggest to students that they include drawings and create original covers for their books.

- **Make a collage.** Have students use magazine pictures, photos, and drawings to make a collage based on the physical and spiritual journey described in *Zen and the Art of Motorcycle Maintenance.*

- **Create a museum exhibit.** Have students set up a museum exhibit depicting the life and times of Shakespeare. They might build a model of the Globe, for example, and display photographs and original artwork that present a picture of the writer and his times. Students can find more information in *Shakespeare Alive!* and the film *Shakespeare in Love.*

- **Write a review.** Have students write a review of one of the film versions of *Macbeth*. Several are available, including Orson Welles's 1948 version and Akira Kurosawa's 1957 samurai version, *Throne of Blood.* Encourage students to compare and contrast a staged or filmed version of the play with the original written version.

Writing Workshop

Analyzing Literature

PRETEACHING

Skills Starter

Motivate. To help students begin thinking about the use of literary elements in poetry, write on the chalkboard this list of terms: *alliteration, allusion, couplet, imagery, metaphor, personification, rhyme,* and *simile.* Using two or three of the elements, students should compose original lines or phrases in which they describe or comment upon their current school year. For example, for *couplet* a student may write:

> My teachers hurl challenges in my direction,
> And I've managed to meet each new expectation.

After students have had time to compose, allow volunteers to share some of their examples. Tell students that in this workshop they will write an analysis in which they discuss the literary elements in a poem of their choosing.

DIRECT TEACHING

A Work of Substance

You may want to suggest these Renaissance poems, which can be found in many literature textbooks, for students to analyze:
- Sir Thomas Wyatt: "Whoso List to Hunt"
- Edmund Spenser: "Sonnet 30," "Sonnet 75"
- Sir John Suckling: "Why So Pale and Wan, Fond Lover?"
- Richard Lovelace: "To Lucasta, On Going to the Wars," "To Althea, from Prison"

Writing Assignment
Write an essay in which you analyze the literary elements of a poem.

When you read the literary selections in this collection, your initial responses, whether positive or negative, enthusiastic or indifferent, were personal and subjective. You're not required to defend your first thoughts and feelings about a work. However, when you dig deeper and begin to analyze a work of literature, you must become more critical and objective because you must be able to support your conclusions. When you write a **literary analysis,** you examine a selection's parts, or literary elements, and how they work together to produce an overall effect. In this workshop you will focus your critical attention on the elements of a poem.

Prewriting

Choose and Analyze a Poem

A Work of Substance To begin your analysis, choose a poem of moderate length, approximately ten to twenty lines. Because your literary analysis should be at least 1,500 words long, the poem should be rich in meaning and complex enough to require careful analysis. To find a suitable poem, re-read poems you have enjoyed in the past. Also, page through this book, or ask your teacher, a librarian, family members, or friends to recommend poems that they've found especially memorable or moving.

I Spy with a Critical Eye . . . After you've chosen a poem, read it carefully, examining the poem critically to discover its unique aspects—what distinguishes it from other poems. Read it as many times as it takes to feel comfortable in your understanding of the ideas it expresses. The following chart explains the basic **literary elements** you'll find in poetry and provides analysis questions for each.

LITERARY ELEMENTS

Element	Analysis Questions
Speaker is the imaginary voice, or persona, assumed by a writer.	Who is the speaker? Is his or her voice immediately identifiable? Is the speaker speaking about himself or herself or about others? Is the speaker speaking to someone? Is the speaker describing a scene or emotion or is the speaker narrating a story?

(continued)

COLLECTION 3 RESOURCES: WRITING

Planning
- *One-Stop Planner* CD-ROM with ExamView Test Generator

Differentiating Instruction
- *Workshop Resources: Writing, Listening, and Speaking*
- *Family Involvement Activities in English and Spanish*
- *Supporting Instruction in Spanish*

Writing and Language
- *Workshop Resources: Writing, Listening, and Speaking*
- *Daily Language Activities*
- *Language Handbook Worksheets*

Stylistic devices are the techniques a writer uses to control **language** to create effects.	How does **diction** (word choice) affect the poem's tone? What effects does the poet create through **rhythm, rhyme, alliteration,** and **onomatopoeia**? Does the poet use **figurative language,** such as similes or metaphors, to suggest feelings or ideas? Does the poet use **imagery** that appeals to readers' senses? How do these images affect the mood of the poem?
Theme is the central idea or insight of a work of literature.	What main idea does the poem express about its subject? Does the poem examine a universal theme, common problem, or life experience? Does it reveal any insight into the human condition?
Tone is the attitude a poet takes toward the reader or subject of the poem.	What's the poet's attitude toward the subject? sarcastic? reverent? What's the speaker's attitude toward the audience? intimate? condescending? What words and details convey the tone? How does the tone affect your response to the poem?

Repeat the process of critical reading until you have a comprehensive understanding of the **significant ideas** in the poem and a firm grip on the elements that help communicate those ideas. Because there are often many elements working at once to create a poem's overall effect, plan to focus your essay on just one or two elements. In poems of ten to twenty lines, one or two elements usually dominate.

Digging Deeper A deep, thoughtful literary analysis identifies the **ambiguities, nuances,** and **complexities** of a work and elaborates on their impact on the poem. The chart below provides definitions of these characteristics as well as student examples based on Shakespeare's "Sonnet 73" (page 282).

AMBIGUITIES, NUANCES, AND COMPLEXITIES

Definitions	Examples
Ambiguities are lines or words that lend themselves to more than one interpretation.	The word "consumed" in the third quatrain is ambiguous. It can mean that the speaker's youth has been destroyed by a metaphorical fire. It could also mean that he has wastefully spent his youth or that he's engrossed or obsessed with thinking about his youth.
Nuances are changes in the tone or meaning of the poem.	"Sonnet 73" begins with a somber tone in the first three quatrains and ends with a happier, hopeful tone in the final couplet.
Complexities result when a poem is rich in meaning but difficult to interpret.	The first quatrain of "Sonnet 73" uses a complex metaphor, going beyond the traditional association between winter and old age to create the image of an elderly person whose thin arms and legs (boughs, or limbs) shake in the cold.

Assessment
- *Holt Assessment: Writing, Listening, and Speaking*
- *One-Stop Planner* CD-ROM with ExamView Test Generator
- *Holt Online Assessment*
- *Holt Online Essay Scoring*

Internet
- go.hrw.com (Keyword: LE5 12-3)
- *Elements of Literature Online*

DIRECT TEACHING

State Your Thesis and Gather Support

Remind students that they should write about the one or two most significant elements in the poem. This means that they should focus on the elements that matter most to the poem's overall effect rather than the elements that simply appear most often.

The Importance of Being Orderly

You may wish to have students combine organizational methods by arranging the elements by order of importance, then tracing the development of each element chronologically.

CORRECTING MISCONCEPTIONS

Students might not realize that sections of a poem can be quoted more than once for different purposes. For example, a line could be quoted once as an example of the poet's use of metaphor; later, it could be quoted again because of the contribution it makes to the understanding of the poem's theme.

PRACTICE & APPLY 1

Guided and Independent Practice

Have students locate poems in reliable sources such as a textbook or an anthology edited by a respected poet or poetry scholar. Explain to students that poems found in many popular magazines, written by acquaintances, or printed in vanity anthologies (in which the author pays to have work published) may not stand up to serious analysis.

TIP Use the **literary present** tense whenever you summarize the plot or subject matter of a literary work or refer to an author's relationship to his or her work; for example, " 'Sonnet 73' **begins** with a somber tone" and "Shakespeare **writes** about the universal theme of love and loss."

State Your Thesis and Gather Support

A Statement of Intent Review your notes, and pull together all your information to determine what your essay will say about the poem. To do this, ask yourself the following questions.

- Do one or two literary elements stand out as more interesting or significant than others?
- What overall effect do the elements create?

DO THIS

Using your answers to these questions, draft a **thesis statement,** like the student example below, that identifies the one or two elements you have chosen to analyze and states your main idea about their effects.

> In "Sonnet 73" Shakespeare develops a solemn metaphor for old age, leading up to a final statement of the poem's hope-filled theme: Love grows strong in the face of approaching death.

TIP You may also wish to consult professional or academic analyses of the poem for evidence others have gathered. If you quote or paraphrase any of these analyses in your essay, be sure to document them appropriately. For more on **documenting sources,** see page 211.

The Evidence Will Show Your literary analysis is an interpretation, your unique viewpoint, that you must support through evidence and elaboration. Select three to five **key points**—the ideas about the literary elements you are discussing that are most important to proving your thesis. Support your key points by gathering **literary evidence**—direct quotations and paraphrases of lines or passages. You may need to review the poem repeatedly to find accurate and detailed **references** from the text of the poem that support your key points and thesis. **Elaborate** on the evidence you find by explaining its meaning and tying it to your thesis statement.

The Importance of Being Orderly A strong thesis and compelling evidence won't convince readers that your interpretation is valid if your essay's organization is hard to follow. Your essay's focus will help you determine how you organize your ideas. If your essay focuses on a single literary element, you may want to use **chronological order,** tracing the development of the element from its first appearance in the poem to its last. If it focuses upon two literary elements, you may want to organize them by **order of importance,** from most important to least, or vice versa.

Writing Skills Write a literary analysis of a poem. Assess, organize, and analyze information. Draft a thesis statement.

PRACTICE & APPLY 1 Analyze a poem by critically examining the poet's use of literary elements. Develop a thesis, gather your support, and organize your analysis.

Writing

Analyzing Literature

A Writer's Framework

Introduction
- Create an engaging opening with an interesting quotation or a bold statement.
- Introduce the poem you're analyzing by title and author.
- State a clear thesis that identifies the literary elements and your main idea about their effects.

Body
- Discuss the key points of your analysis.
- Provide literary evidence from the text of the poem.
- Elaborate on your evidence.
- Organize your essay by order of importance or by chronological order.

Conclusion
- Restate your thesis in a memorable way.
- Leave readers with a closing thought to consider.

A Writer's Model

Metaphor and Theme in Shakespeare's "Sonnet 73"

There's an old saying: "You don't miss the water, 'til the well runs dry." We often do not appreciate what we have until it is gone. However, what happens when we foresee an approaching loss? In "Sonnet 73" Shakespeare considers this question by discussing aging and dying. He develops a solemn metaphor for old age, leading up to a final statement of the poem's hope-filled theme: Love grows strong in the face of approaching death.

First, in the opening quatrain, the speaker compares himself to a tree in winter, a tree whose "yellow leaves, or none, or few, do hang / Upon those boughs which shake against the cold" (lines 2–3). Beginning this poem on a somber note, this complex metaphor goes beyond the traditional association between winter and old age to create the image of an elderly person whose thin arms and legs (boughs, or limbs) shake in the cold. The metaphor suggests that death is natural.

Next, in the second quatrain, the speaker compares himself to the twilight of the day, that time of day just before dark, "after sunset fadeth in the west" (6). This metaphor suggests that the speaker is very near the end of his life because "by and by black night" (7) will take away all remaining light. Shakespeare enriches the metaphor by

(continued)

INTRODUCTION
Engaging opener

Title and author
Thesis statement

BODY
First key point
Evidence: quotation
Complexity

Elaboration

Second key point
Chronological order
Evidence: quotations

DIFFERENTIATING INSTRUCTION

English-Language Learners
Some students may run into difficulty when trying to create an engaging opening because, for example, they may not be familiar with English-language sayings like the one that begins **A Writer's Model.** Pair these students with native speakers of English. The English-Language Learner can share his or her idea for an opening, and the native English speaker can help come up with a saying that fits the need. If the English-Language Learner has a saying from his or her native language in mind, the native speaker can help translate it or identify a comparable English saying.

DIRECT TEACHING

A Writer's Model
This model is based on an analysis of Shakespeare's "Sonnet 73," which you can find on p. 282.

TECHNOLOGY TIP

Students may find it useful to save a set of prewriting notes or an outline in electronic-text form. As they develop their drafts, students can use the multiple-window feature of their word-processing program to view their notes and their outlines at the same time.

CRITICAL THINKING

Pair students, and have them use the guidelines in **A Writer's Framework** on p. 393 to come up with three compliments for the author of the analysis. Also, ask students to identify one question they wish they could ask the writer and to brainstorm possible replies.

PRACTICE & APPLY 2

Guided and Independent Practice

Guide the writing process by allotting a half-hour or more of class time for students to begin their rough drafts. Use this time to help students avoid frustration by dealing with questions and difficulties immediately. You may also wish to schedule at least one more day in class for writing, based on student progress and their questions and problems with the assignment. They will then be in a good position to complete **Practice and Apply 2** independently.

(continued)

Elaboration

personifying death and night, "Death's second self" (8). Again, Shakespeare takes advantage of traditional associations between the cycle of the day and the cycle of life to emphasize that death is an inevitable and natural part of life.

Third key point

Then, in the third quatrain, Shakespeare develops a complex metaphor of fire to suggest the progression through life to death. The speaker compares himself to the ember stage of a fire. The fire, the

Evidence: quotation
Elaboration
Evidence: paraphrase

"deathbed whereon [the speaker] must expire" (11), is now a bed of ashes. The ashes represent all the years the speaker has lived up to this point. Ultimately, then, the speaker will be consumed by what once nourished him, the wood—now ash—that will finally suffocate the last

Elaboration

glowing embers of life. The association of the life cycle with the natural phenomenon of fire paints death as merely the last step in a natural process. This metaphor has a degree of ambiguity, as well. Shakespeare

Ambiguity
Elaboration

uses the word *consumed* (12), which has many meanings. Readers should assume the primary definition, which is that the speaker's youth has been destroyed by fire. However, to appreciate the richness of the metaphor, readers should also consider the other definitions: Perhaps the speaker's youth has been spent wastefully or the speaker is engrossed or obsessed with thoughts of his youth. With any of these definitions, the image and tone remains somber.

Fourth key point
Evidence: paraphrase

Finally, in the concluding couplet, the speaker shifts from metaphors about aging to his theme. The speaker addresses his friend, saying that the friend clearly sees that the speaker's death is fast approaching, but that the effect of this knowledge is to make "thy love

Evidence: quotation

more strong, / To love that well which thou must leave ere long"

Elaboration
Nuance

(13–14). The speaker seems to say that his friend's love grows stronger as he or she realizes that death will soon separate them. His tone, then, shifts from the somber tone of the first three quatrains to a happier, more hopeful tone in the closing couplet.

CONCLUSION
Thesis restated
Closing thought

Shakespeare's metaphors lead the reader to a universal truth of human existence: As death nears, the bonds of friendship are strengthened and intensified. Perhaps the intensity of emotion we feel for someone we love at the approach of the inevitable and natural end of life is nature's way of telling us to cherish the people we love while we can.

INTERNET
More Writer's Models
Keyword: LE5 12-3

 **PRACTICE & APPLY 2** Refer to the framework on page 393 and the Writer's Model that begins on the same page as you write the first draft of your literary analysis of a poem.

394   Collection 3   The Renaissance

Revising

Evaluate and Revise Your Analysis

In Pursuit of Perfection Like artists who paint multiple versions of their subjects, good writers know that their work can always be improved upon. A word, sentence, paragraph, or even the whole organizational structure may need adjusting. When you begin the revision process, start by evaluating and revising the content and organization of your analysis, using the guidelines below. Then, evaluate and revise the sentence style of your analysis using the guidelines on the next page.

PEER REVIEW
Before you begin revising, ask a peer to read your paper and offer constructive criticism. He or she may be able to point out places where you need more evidence from the poem's text to support your ideas.

▶ **First Reading: Content and Organization** Use the chart below to look for ways to improve the content and organization of your literary analysis.

Rubric: Analyzing Literature

Evaluation Questions	Tips	Revision Techniques
❶ Does the introduction engage the reader's interest and introduce the subject of the analysis?	**Put parentheses** around the engaging opening. **Circle** the title of the poem and the name of the author.	If necessary, **add** a quotation or a bold statement. **Add** the name of the poem and author.
❷ Does the introduction include a thesis statement that clearly identifies the literary elements and states a main idea about their effects?	**Highlight** the thesis statement. **Bracket** the literary elements and the main idea about their effects.	If needed, **add** a thesis statement that identifies the poem's literary elements and states your main idea about their effects.
❸ Are the key points clear? Do they support the thesis?	**Underline** the key points. **Draw an arrow** from the key points to the thesis.	**Rewrite** key points that are not clearly expressed. **Replace** key points that don't support the thesis with ones that do.
❹ Does literary evidence support all key points about the thesis? Does the essay elaborate upon all evidence?	**Put a check mark** by each direct quotation or paraphrase from the poem. **Put an X** by elaboration of literary evidence.	If necessary, **add** literary evidence for key points, or **add** elaboration to all evidence.
❺ Are the key points arranged logically so that they are easy to follow?	**Review** the underlined key points to see if their arrangement is logical.	**Rearrange** key points by order of importance or by chronological order.
❻ Does the conclusion restate the thesis? Does it include a thought-provoking closing thought?	**Highlight** the sentence restating the thesis. **Underline** the sentence or sentences containing the closing thought.	**Add** a sentence restating the thesis or a closing thought, if either are needed.

Writing Workshop: Analyzing Literature 395

MODELING AND DEMONSTRATION

In Pursuit of Perfection

To model how students can avoid terms such as *I, me, my,* and *mine* by rewording statements or by using the pronoun *one*, write these sentences on the chalkboard.

1. I didn't understand the sonnet's resolution. [The sonnet's resolution was unclear.]
2. I expected the ending to be happier. [One might have expected the ending to be happier.]

Revise the first sentence to eliminate the first-person pronoun. Then, have a student volunteer demonstrate understanding by revising the second sentence on the chalkboard.

DIRECT TEACHING

Rubric: Analyzing Literature

Advise students to use the **Rubric** chart on this page as a think sheet by answering the questions in their notebooks. Explain to students that using think sheets to summarize their notes allows them to place their thoughts, observations, and questions on paper—which in turn helps improve the content and organization of their literary analyses.

RETEACHING

Elaboration

If students have difficulty identifying areas of their analyses that need more elaboration, remind them that their most complex ideas (often the ones based on ambiguities, nuances, and complexities in the poem) will require the most elaboration. Students may need to write several sentences to introduce the point and provide evidence from the text, and several more to tie the idea to the thesis.

Writing Workshop: Analyzing Literature 395

GUIDED PRACTICE

Responding to the Revision Process

Answers

1. The word *Then* indicates that the writer is presenting evidence in a logical order and is now moving on to the next point. The writer also pinpoints the location of the next quote.
2. The writer has clarified the metaphor by quoting the actual lines.
3. The writer needed one more sentence to explain fully the meaning of the metaphor.

PRACTICE & APPLY 3

Independent Practice

Prepare students to be good peer editors by discussing appropriate ways to make suggestions for revisions.

Using the **Rubric: Analyzing Literature** and **Style Guidelines** charts on pp. 395 and 396, suggest specific statements that students can use when pointing out portions of the paper in need of revision. For example, a student who wanted to encourage a peer to revise the introduction to make it more engaging might say, "I wonder if there is a way to make this introduction even more engaging." If key points are in need of revision, the peer editor could say, "Can you tell me more? I don't understand how this point relates to the thesis."

This type of responsible, respectful editing should contribute to improved essays.

Second Reading: Style Once you've revised *what* you say in your analysis, you can concentrate on *how* you say it—your writing style. Since a literary analysis can often be complex and difficult to follow, you can improve the sentence style of your essay by using **transitional words and phrases** to connect your ideas and to guide readers through your analysis.

To show chronology in your analysis, use transitions such as *first, next, then,* and *finally*. To show order of importance, use such transitions as *most important, last,* and *mainly*. To help you add transitional words and phrases to your analysis, use the guidelines in the chart below.

Style Guidelines

Evaluation Question	Tip	Revision Technique
● Does the essay include transitional words and phrases that guide the reader?	▶ **Draw a box** around transitional words and phrases. If there are none, revise.	▶ **Add** transitional words and phrases to make the connection of ideas in the analysis clear.

ANALYZING THE REVISION PROCESS

Study these revisions, and answer the questions that follow.

> add → *Then, in the third quatrain,* Shakespeare develops a complex metaphor of fire to suggest the progression through life to death. The speaker compares
> add → *, the "deathbed whereon [the speaker] must expire" (11),* himself to the ember stage of a fire. The fire is now a bed of
> add → ashes. *The ashes represent all the years the speaker has lived up to this point.*

Responding to the Revision Process

1. How does adding the transition to the first sentence help the reader understand the flow of the ideas?
2. How does the added quotation improve the passage?
3. Why do you think the writer added the sentence at the end of this passage?

Writing Skills
Revise for content and style.

PRACTICE & APPLY 3

Following the guidelines on this page and the previous one, evaluate and revise the content, organization, and style of your analysis. If possible, collaborate with a classmate throughout the revision process.

Publishing

Proofread and Publish Your Analysis

Bottom of the Ninth Before you publish your analysis, proofread it and make any last-minute changes. Search for and eliminate errors in grammar, usage, and mechanics. Such errors can distract your readers from your message, lessening the impact of your analysis and making all your hard work less meaningful.

Share Your Expertise Analyzing the poem you chose has made you something of an authority on that particular poem. Now you can share with others the knowledge and insight you have gained from writing your analysis. Here are some ideas for publishing your work.

- If the poem you analyzed is by a living poet, send a copy of your analysis to him or her and ask for feedback.

- Around the world, people celebrate the birthdays of noteworthy poets. Create a pamphlet about the poet whose work you've studied. Include graphics (such as a drawing or photo of the poet), some background information about him or her, plus the poem you analyzed and your analysis. Distribute the pamphlet to friends, family, and classmates on the poet's birthday.

- Search the Internet for Web sites devoted to the poet whose work you have analyzed. If the site or sites you find accept submissions, send them your analysis for possible posting.

- Present a memorized recitation of the poem you have analyzed. After the recitation, share with your audience the insights about the poem that you've gained through analyzing it. For more on **reciting literature,** see page 398.

Reflect on Your Analysis

Look Back for the Future Use the following questions to determine what lessons you've learned from writing a literary analysis and how those lessons might benefit your future writing efforts.

- How did writing a literary analysis help you to better understand the poem? How will this new understanding help you approach reading other poems?

- Do you think the skills you used in writing a literary analysis will carry over to other types of writing? Why or why not?

PRACTICE & APPLY 4 Following the guidelines on this page, first proofread your analysis for errors in grammar, usage, and mechanics. Then, publish your analysis for a wider audience and reflect on the writing experience.

> **TIP** Proofreading will help ensure that your literary analysis follows the **conventions** of standard American English. For example, identify and correct punctuation errors you've made in incorporating direct quotations from the poem. For more on **quotation marks,** see Quotation Marks, 13c–d, in the Language Handbook.

> **COMPUTER TIP**
> If you have access to publishing software and design programs, you can use them to make a more professional-looking pamphlet. For more on **page design, type,** and **visuals,** see *Designing Your Writing* in the Writer's Handbook.

SKILLS FOCUS

Writing Skills
Proofread, especially for correct use of quotation marks.

DIRECT TEACHING

Share Your Expertise
You need to be aware that Internet resources are sometimes public forums, and that their content may be unpredictable.

PRACTICE & APPLY 4

Guided and Independent Practice

To guide the proofreading process, have pairs of students exchange papers to check for correct use of pronouns. Have partners mark each pronoun in the essay and then draw an arrow to its antecedent. They should then determine whether each pronoun agrees with its antecedent in number, gender, and person. As they are checking each others' papers, move about the room to answer questions. Then, have students complete **Practice and Apply 4** as independent practice.

PRETEACHING

Motivate. Ask a student who is involved in drama to present a well-known soliloquy to your class. Prepare your students for the soliloquy by briefly identifying the play, author, and context from which it is taken. After the presentation, ask students to discuss the techniques that made the delivery effective. Encourage students to "cut loose" dramatically as they present.

DIFFERENTIATING INSTRUCTION

Advanced Learners

Enrichment. Challenge students to create a how-to or behind-the-scenes video that presents a detailed look at how they selected, prepared, and rehearsed their pieces for recitation. This video should be detailed enough so that other students could view it as a teaching tool.

DIRECT TEACHING

Choose a Text

Point out that students should consider time constraints when selecting a text to recite. The material should not be too long to be recited in the given time. If reading an excerpt from a longer poem, students should be sure that it can stand alone, with little or no background information.

Listening & Speaking Workshop

Reciting Literature

Speaking Assignment
Prepare and present a recitation of a poem, a speech, or a dramatic soliloquy.

Reading and analyzing poetry on paper is certainly a rewarding challenge. Yet some people believe that poetry is not fully experienced unless it is read or listened to aloud. Through the ages, people have gathered to hear Shakespeare's plays and poetry brought to life through performance and recitations. Literary readings still attract attentive audiences today. When you present a memorized **recitation** of a literary work, you can enrich your understanding of the work and make it live and breathe for your listeners.

Prepare Your Recitation

Choose a Text Start by finding an appropriate poem, speech, or dramatic soliloquy—one that you find meaningful or moving, that will appeal to your audience, and that you can recite in the amount of time your teacher allows. Browse through this book, literary magazines, and anthologies of collected works for possible selections. Select the literary work that best fits the following criteria.

SELECTION CRITERIA FOR A RECITATION

Criteria	Questions
Aptness	Are the content and tone appropriate for your audience and the occasion?
Artistic merit	Does the selection use precise, vivid language? Are ideas clearly expressed? Will the selection appeal to the listeners' emotions as well as their intellects?
Originality	Does the selection present a unique perspective on life or human nature?
Relevance	Does the selection deal with universal themes such as life and death, love, justice, or personal identity?

Analyze the Text A good recitation is more than just a display of your memorization skills: It's an **interpretation**—an expression of your personal understanding of the selection's meaning. The following tips will help you analyze the text in order to create your interpretation.

- **Identify** the selection's speaker, including his or her motivations.
- **Look up** the definitions and pronunciations of any unfamiliar words.
- **Paraphrase** to check your understanding of the text by restating the ideas in your own words.
- **Research** to clarify material that you don't understand. Check for historical allusions in an encyclopedia. Look up classical or literary allusions in an unabridged or specialized dictionary.

Listening and Speaking Skills
Present a recitation of a poem, speech, or dramatic soliloquy.

398   Collection 3   The Renaissance

COLLECTION 3 RESOURCES: LISTENING & SPEAKING

Planning
- *One-Stop Planner* CD-ROM with ExamView Test Generator

Differentiating Instruction
- *Workshop Resources: Writing, Listening, and Speaking*
- *Family Involvement Activities in English and Spanish*

- *Supporting Instruction in Spanish*

Listening and Speaking
- *Workshop Resources: Writing, Listening, and Speaking*
- *Daily Language Activities*
- *Language Handbook Worksheets*

Assessment
- *Holt Assessment: Writing, Listening, and Speaking*
- *One-Stop Planner* CD-ROM with ExamView Test Generator

Internet
- go.hrw.com (Keyword: LE5 12-3)
- *Elements of Literature Online*

Deliver Your Recitation

Rehearse Your Material A recitation should deliver your interpretation clearly and forcefully while creating an aesthetic effect through skillful **artistic staging**. Practice your presentation until you achieve a comfortable command of the text. Experiment with various ways of expressing the selection's meaning with your voice and body. If possible, research and analyze professional recitations for models of how you can effectively vocalize and use body language yourself. The following strategies will help you polish your delivery.

- **Stress** or **pause** to emphasize certain words or phrases.
- Vary the **pitch** and **tone** of your voice to reveal the speaker's feelings. A rising tone often suggests uncertainty, while a falling tone expresses conviction.
- Vary your **rate of speaking** to convey the mood of the passage. A slower rate can suggest contemplation or hesitation; a quicker pace may signal excitement, nervousness, anger, or joy.
- Use **facial expressions** and natural **gestures** and **movements** to convey the meaning and mood of the material. A smile and a flourish with the hand may suggest a lighter mood, while a snarl and a raised fist may hint at anger in the speaker.

Mark up a double-spaced copy of the text with notes on the decisions you make during rehearsals. This marked copy can help you commit your delivery strategies to memory. Here are markings you can use to translate textual cues into a meaningful interpretation.

TIP Give your listeners a brief introduction to your selection. Along with the title and the author's name, include background information and reasons why you chose the selection.

MARKING TEXT FOR DELIVERY

Markings	Interpretive Technique
Draw a single slash (/) after each comma or semicolon. **Draw a double slash (//)** after each colon, dash, and period.	Pause for each single slash; pause longer for each double slash.
Underline italicized words.	Stress or speak these words more loudly.
Draw an arrow with a rising curve over each question mark.	Speak with a rising tone.
Highlight significant words, phrases, or lines.	Adjust pitch, volume, or rate for emphasis.

PRACTICE & APPLY 5 Using the directions in this workshop, prepare a recitation of a poem, speech, or dramatic soliloquy. Pay close attention to performance details. Present your final recitation to an audience, such as your classmates or family.

SKILLS FOCUS
Listening and Speaking Skills
Rehearse and deliver your presentation.

Listening and Speaking Workshop: Reciting Literature 399

RETEACHING

Tip

If students have trouble putting together an introduction to their chosen selections, write on the chalkboard or overhead projector these three headings: *Poem, Speech,* and *Dramatic Soliloquy.* Have students suggest the information that must be provided to ensure that each type of piece is placed in a context for listeners. For example, under *Poem,* the students might suggest author, title, date of composition, and specific events or people referred to in the poem. Tell students to consult these lists as they prepare their recitations.

DIFFERENTIATING INSTRUCTION

Learners Having Difficulty

Encourage students who are having difficulty to record a dress rehearsal on audiotape or videotape. This will allow those who are anxious about performing to increase their confidence through focused practice, and to evaluate and refine the details of their recitation that need further work.

PRACTICE & APPLY 5

Guided and Independent Practice

To guide the fine-tuning of student presentations, provide this evaluation chart:

Criteria	Yes	No
The introduction prepares the listener.		
The performer speaks clearly and smoothly.		
The performer varies volume, pitch, and rate of speech.		
The performer uses gestures and facial expressions.		

Collection 3: Skills Review

Comparing Literature

SKILLS FOCUS, pp. 400–403

Grade-Level Skills

■ **Literary Skills**
Compare major literary forms from different historical periods.

Introducing the Skills Review

Use this review to assess students' ability to contrast works from different literary periods.

DIRECT TEACHING

A Reading Skills

? Recognizing philosophical assumptions. The themes of love and time appear throughout the world's literature, just as they do in life. What are the speaker's fundamental beliefs about love? [Possible response: Love is essential and life-giving; it outlasts time.] What does the speaker believe about time? [Possible response: Time passes inexorably for everyone—for those who love and those who don't.]

B Literary Focus

Theme. Summarize the speaker's advice to the lady. [Possible response: Nobody knows what the future may bring, so grab as much pleasure as you can every day.]

Collection 3: Skills Review
Comparing Literature

Test Practice

The subject of love, with its great joys and deep sorrows, has engaged lyric poets of every age. Renaissance poets, so keenly aware of the individual in the here and now, were particularly fascinated by the tension between the urgency of love and the shortness of time. The French poet Pierre de Ronsard (1524–1585) explored this theme in his sonnet "When You Are Old," one of a collection of poems addressed to a lady, Helene, who apparently rejected the aging poet. Three centuries later the young Irish poet William Butler Yeats (1865–1939) found in Ronsard's poignant clause a suitable beginning for his own address to another reluctant woman.

DIRECTIONS: Read the poems that follow. Then, read each multiple-choice question that follows, and write the letter of the best response.

When You Are Old

Pierre de Ronsard
translated by Humbert Wolfe

When you are old, at evening candle-lit
   beside the fire bending to your wool,
read out my verse and murmur, "Ronsard writ
   this praise for me when I was beautiful."
5 And not a maid but, at the sound of it,
   though nodding at the stitch on broidered stool,
will start awake, and bless love's benefit
   whose long fidelities bring Time to school.
I shall be thin and ghost beneath the earth
10 by myrtle shade in quiet after pain,
but you, a crone,° will crouch beside the hearth
   mourning my love and all your proud disdain.
And since what comes tomorrow who can say?
Live, pluck the roses of the world today.

---
11. **crone** *n.*: old woman.

Pages 400–403 cover
Literary Skills
Compare and contrast works from different literary periods.

400   Collection 3   The Renaissance

READING MINI-LESSON

Reviewing Word-Attack Skills
Activity. Have students decide which of the underlined words in each sentence is pronounced as a two- or three-syllable word.

1. The playful puppy <u>fetched</u> a <u>wretched</u> old teddy bear. [wretched]
2. He <u>dragged</u> the <u>ragged</u> toy by a tattered ear across the floor. [ragged]
3. Yipping and pouncing, he <u>waged</u> playful war on the <u>aged</u> bear. [aged]
4. Then he <u>shoved</u> the <u>beloved</u> plaything under the coach. [beloved]

Activity. Have students read the following words and state the number of syllables heard in each one. Remind them that every vowel sound is a syllable.

Collection 3: Skills Review

When You Are Old
William Butler Yeats

When you are old and grey and full of sleep,
And nodding by the fire, take down this book,
And slowly read, and dream of the soft look
Your eyes had once, and of their shadows deep;

5 How many loved your moments of glad grace,
And loved your beauty with love false or true,
But one man loved the pilgrim soul in you,
And loved the sorrows of your changing face;

And bending down beside the glowing bars,
10 Murmur, a little sadly, how Love fled
And paced upon the mountains overhead
And hid his face amid a crowd of stars.

C Reading Skills

? Interpreting details. How did the speaker's love differ from the love of all the others? [Possible response: The others focused on the woman's beauty and grace, but he loved her soul, her spiritual questing, even her sorrow.]

D Literary Focus

Tone. Compare the tones of the two poems. [Possible response: Ronsard's speaker perseveres in his pursuit, although he has been rejected. He is gallant and worldly, a man who still believes in the seductive power of poetry. Yeats's speaker is more subdued, mourning his lost love now and projecting his mourning into the future. He is dreamy, nostalgic, and full of regret.]

---

1. beatific [4]
2. beanery [3]
3. rearrangement [4]
4. oread [3]
5. treacle [2]
6. demeanor [3]
7. spirea [3]
8. zealot [2]
9. preamble [3]
10. feasible [3]
11. cereal [3]
12. surreal [2]

Activity. The letters of the shorter words appear in each of the longer words. Have students underline the short word whose sounds are heard in the longer word. Students may consult a dictionary.

1. here — red — hereditary
2. line — mental — lineamental
3. male — cent — maleficent
4. line — ate — delineate
5. dime — men — dimensional
6. pot — ate — potentiate

Answers and Model Rationales

1. **D** The titles indicate that D is correct. A is wrong: Neither woman is imagined happy. B is incorrect: The poets admit that beauty passes. C is incorrect: Forgetting the women is not an issue.

2. **F** *Carpe diem,* or "seize the day," is equivalent to "pluck the roses." G, a midline break, is wrong. H is wrong: The lines contain no complex image. J is a type of metaphor.

3. **B** He is trying to persuade her to take the opportunity to love him; thus, B is correct. A implies vengefulness, which he does not exhibit. C may be true, but it is not his main purpose. D is false: She is not pursuing him.

4. **H** The roses stand for beauty that passes—thus opportunities to be seized. F is wrong: No promises were made. G is wrong: Roses *are* flowers. J is wrong: He wants her to seize his love itself.

5. **A** The sonnet (A) has the rhyme scheme *abab abab cdcd ee.* It is not an epic (B). The rhyme scheme of the octet isn't *abbaabba* (C). The poem does not tell a story (D).

6. **G** "Pilgrim soul" indicates the quest for spiritual values (G). The poet does not love her for wandering (F). *Pilgrim* is used in a religious sense in H. The poet loves her questing, not any certainty in her (J).

Collection 3: Skills Review

1. The speaker in both poems is asking the woman he is addressing to imagine that she —
   A is happy in her solitude
   B is still beautiful in old age
   C has not been forgotten
   D is old and reading his poetry

2. The last two lines of Ronsard's poem are an example of the literary theme known as —
   F *carpe diem*
   G caesura
   H metaphysical conceit
   J kenning

3. What do the last two lines of Ronsard's poem reveal about the speaker's purpose in addressing the woman?
   A He wishes to get even with her for rejecting him.
   B He is trying to persuade her to marry him now.
   C He wishes to immortalize her in a love poem.
   D He is trying to stop her from pursuing him.

4. The roses in the last line of Ronsard's poem symbolize —
   F broken promises
   G flowers
   H opportunities
   J compliments

5. Ronsard's poem is an example of which poetic form?
   A Shakespearean sonnet
   B literary epic
   C Petrarchan sonnet
   D ballad

6. In Yeats's poem the image "pilgrim soul" in line 7 suggests that the woman the speaker loves is —
   F homeless
   G a restless seeker after truth
   H a religious dissenter
   J logical and sure of herself

402 Collection 3 The Renaissance

Using Academic Language

Review of Literary Terms
Ask students to look back through the collection to find the meanings of the terms listed in the next column. Then, have students show their grasp of the terms by citing passages from the collection that illustrate the meanings of those terms.

Pastoral (p. 257); **Carpe Diem poems** (p. 263); **Shakespearean Sonnet** (pp. 277, 278); **Quatrains** (p. 278); **Couplet** (p. 278); **Meter** (p. 278); **Iambic Pentameter** (p. 278); **Dramatic Song** (p. 286); **Onomatopoeia** (p. 286); **Monologue** (p. 292); **Soliloquy** (p. 292); **Metaphysical Poetry** (pp. 301, 303); **Metaphysical**

Collection 3: Skills Review

7. What emotion do both poets hope to evoke in the women they are addressing?
   A pity
   B revenge
   C regret
   D joy

8. The attitude of Yeats's speaker toward the woman differs from that of Ronsard's speaker in that Yeats's speaker —
   F desires revenge
   G has not given up on the possibility of winning her
   H is more sad than angry
   J is more offended by her rejection

9. How does the attitude toward time expressed in Ronsard's poem reflect Renaissance attitudes on that subject?
   A Ronsard's speaker is acutely aware of the brevity of youth, beauty, and earthly life.
   B Ronsard's speaker is focused on the afterlife rather than earthly life.
   C Ronsard's speaker feels he has more than enough time to accomplish what he wants in life.
   D Ronsard's speaker expects that time inevitably will bring greater happiness.

10. Which statement about these poems is *not* true?
    F Both poems use rhyme.
    G Both poems follow a regular meter.
    H Each speaker asks a woman to read his verses.
    J Both poems are bitter in tone.

Essay Question

In a brief essay, compare and contrast these two poems. Focus on how each poet uses each of these elements: speaker, person addressed, message, tone, key word or phrase, and form and structure (use of sound effects, meter, figurative language). Arrange your essay in the block style: First, tell how Ronsard uses these elements; then, tell how Yeats uses them.

Collection 3: Skills Review   403

---

7. **C** They are not begging to be pitied (A). Revenge is too fierce an emotion for aspiring lovers (B). Both realize that joy may come, but it is not the immediate emotion they hope to create (D).

8. **H** Yeats's speaker focuses on his sorrow over his loss. F is wrong: He would never hurt her. G is wrong: He knows love has fled. J is wrong: He is hurt but not offended.

9. **A** Renaissance humanism focused on mortality. B is wrong: He wants his beloved to "seize the day." C is wrong: It is the opposite of A. D is wrong: He says that no one knows what time may bring.

10. **J** Ronsard's speaker, but not Yeats's, may be bitter. F is wrong: Both use rhyme. G is wrong: Both are regular. H is wrong: Both do ask.

Essay Question

Sample elements for the Ronsard poem:
The speaker, Ronsard, addresses a woman who has spurned his advances, asking her in her old age to reconsider his love. The tone is regretful but with a final optimistic *carpe diem* note. Key words and phrases include "When you are old," "when I was beautiful," "love's benefit," "you, a crone, . . . / mourning my love," "pluck the roses of the world today." The form is a Shakespearean sonnet, but the meter is not consistently iambic. The poem includes some alliteration. The roses are a symbol.

Conceits (p. 304); **Tone** (p. 307); **Paradox** (p. 312); **Epigram** (p. 318); **Parable** (p. 342); **Anecdote** (p. 347); **Didactic Literature** (p. 348); **Literary Epic** (p. 362); **Elevated Style** (p. 362); **Epic Similes** (p. 362); **Style** (p. 364); **Diction** (p. 364); **Syntax** (p. 364); **Allusion** (p. 378); **Allegory** (p. 382).

Review of Informational Terms
Ask students to look back through the collection to find the meanings of the terms listed below. Then, have students use those terms to explain how clarity of meaning is affected by the patterns of organization in a text.
Parallel Structure or **Parallelism** (pp. 324, 338).

Collection 3: Skills Review

Vocabulary Skills

Synonyms

Modeling. Model the thought process of a good reader arriving at the answer to item 1 by saying, "To transgress is to cross a boundary. Crossing the boundary of a law means breaking it; therefore, B is the right answer. Questioning, explaining, and applying a law have nothing to do with crossing its boundaries."

Answers and Model Rationales

1. **B** See rationale above.
2. **H** An impetuous person rushes into things without much thought, so H (*impulsive*) is a synonym.
3. **A** An impediment is something that obstructs (A).
4. **J** People use guile when they want to deceive someone (J).
5. **B** An implacable foe is one who never gives up (B).
6. **G** An ignominious defeat brings shame or disgrace (G).
7. **D** *Diligence* is a positive quality. *Persevering* comes the closest. A, B, and C are negative qualities.
8. **H** *Reproach* is blame.
9. **A** *Allure* is a quality that attracts attention, so *fascinating* is correct.
10. **H** To *reiterate* is to say or do again. Thus, *repeat* is the synonym.

ASSESSING

Assessment
- Holt Assessment: Literature, Reading, and Vocabulary

Collection 3: Skills Review

Vocabulary Skills

Test Practice

Synonyms

DIRECTIONS: Words that have similar meanings are called **synonyms.** For example, *benign* and *kind* are synonyms. In the sentences below, choose the word or group of words whose meaning is most similar to the meaning of the underlined word.

1. To <u>transgress</u> a law is to —
   A question it
   B break it
   C explain it
   D apply it

2. An <u>impetuous</u> person is —
   F overly helpful
   G dangerously manipulative
   H extremely impulsive
   J unreasonably stubborn

3. An <u>impediment</u> is —
   A an obstacle
   B an architectural feature
   C a commandment
   D a plea

4. <u>Guile</u> is the same as —
   F innocence
   G bitterness
   H awe
   J deceit

5. Someone who is <u>implacable</u> is —
   A fearful
   B relentless
   C vigilant
   D confused

6. <u>Ignominy</u> means —
   F ignorance
   G disgrace
   H aggression
   J retaliation

7. A person who studies with <u>diligence</u> is —
   A inconsistent
   B careless
   C unfocused
   D persevering

8. Someone who looks at you <u>reproachfully</u> is —
   F studying you
   G admiring you
   H blaming you
   J afraid of you

9. Something with <u>allure</u> is —
   A fascinating
   B flattering
   C repulsive
   D threatening

10. If you have <u>reiterated</u> a statement, you have —
    F denied it
    G explained it
    H repeated it
    J contradicted it

Vocabulary Skills
Use synonyms.

404 Collection 3 The Renaissance

Vocabulary Review

Ask students to complete each of the analogies below with a Vocabulary word from the box. The first pair in each analogy also contains a Vocabulary word.

| affliction | guile | ignominy |
| respite | sloth | |

1. ATTRACTION : RESISTANCE :: diligence : _____. [sloth]

2. FRIENDLINESS : MALICE :: enjoyment : _____. [affliction]

3. RESOLUTION : CONTENTION :: honor : _____. [ignominy]

4. IMPEDIMENT : SOLUTION :: toil : _____. [respite]

5. NATURALNESS : AFFECTATION :: straightforwardness : _____. [guile]

Collection 3: Skills Review
Writing Skills

Test Practice

DIRECTIONS: Read the following paragraph from a draft of a student's analysis of a poem. Then, answer the questions below it.

(1) The speaker in Andrew Marvell's poem "To His Coy Mistress" urges his lady to accept his love by gradually changing the tone of his requests. (2) He begins with an idealistic tone, describing how extravagant his love would be if time were not an issue. (3) Soon his tone admonishes her, trying to frighten her into accepting his advances before it is too late. (4) He describes "Time's wingèd chariot hurrying near" (line 22) to show that there is little time left for them to act. (5) The winged chariot is an allusion to Greek mythology. (6) The tone becomes urgent by the poem's end as the speaker persuades his lady to "tear our pleasures with rough strife / Through the iron gates of life" (lines 43–44).

1. Which of these transitions could be added to the beginning of sentence 2?
   A However,
   B As a result,
   C For example,
   D Additionally,

2. Which reference could the student add to support the ideas in sentence 2?
   F He predicts "The grave's a fine and private place, / But none, I think, do there embrace" (lines 31–32).
   G He offers to spend a hundred years "to praise / Thine eyes, and on thy forehead gaze" (lines 13–14).
   H The speaker tries to persuade her by saying, "Now let us sport us while we may" (line 37).
   J He insists that she act "while the youthful hue / Sits on thy skin like morning dew" (lines 33–34).

3. The best way to add depth to the passage would be to
   A compare courtship practices of Marvell's time to those of today
   B relate other stylistic devices to the nuances in tone
   C add an overview of the interesting facts of Andrew Marvell's life
   D elaborate on the allusions to the Ganges and Humber rivers

4. Which sentence should be deleted to improve the passage's organization?
   F 2   H 4
   G 3   J 5

5. To recite Marvell's poem orally, the student should
   A elaborate on any metaphors the listeners might not understand
   B read directly from a marked-up copy of the poem
   C briefly introduce the poem to explain its context
   D deliver each line with the same pitch and tone

SKILLS FOCUS
Writing Skills
Write a literary analysis of a poem.

Collection 3: Skills Review 405

RESOURCES: WRITING

Assessment
- One-Stop Planner CD-ROM with ExamView Test Generator
- Holt Assessment: Writing, Listening, and Speaking

Internet
- Holt Online Assessment
- Holt Online Essay Scoring

Collection 3: Skills Review
Writing Skills

Answers
1. C
2. G
3. B
4. J
5. C

APPLICATION

Poetry Primer
For homework, have students select a specific poetic element, such as metaphor, and construct a booklet that defines the element and presents at least five poems that contain several examples of the element. The poems can be by different authors and have different forms and themes. Each occurrence of the element being presented should be highlighted or otherwise identified and briefly explained.

EXTENSION

Poetic Interpretation
Though the sound of poetry is important, students may gain a deeper appreciation of poetry by focusing on the sense of a poem—in other words, a poem's meaning or imagery. Students should select a poem similar in length to the one they selected for their analysis. Then, they should choose one of the following three means for presenting the poem.

1. Present the poem using American Sign Language (ASL) and concentrating on a fluid, artistic delivery.
2. Choreograph and present an interpretive dance.
3. Create a video or slide presentation about the poem using no audio.

Collection 3: Skills Review 405

Collection 4
The Restoration and the Eighteenth Century: 1660–1800

About Collection 4
In Collection 4, students will master the following skills:

- **Literary Skills:** Evaluate the philosophical, political, religious, ethical, and social influences of a historical period; analyze verbal irony, diction, connotations, antithesis, epigrams, mock epic, satire, parody, tone; compare and contrast works from different cultures and literary periods.
- **Reading Skills:** Analyze persuasive techniques (logical, emotional, and ethical appeals), the writer's stance, rhetorical devices, patterns of organization, and a writer's argument.
- **Vocabulary Skills:** Compare word meanings; analyze connotations, word analogies, the meanings and origins of words; create etymology maps.
- **Writing Skills:** Develop, write, and revise an essay analyzing works of literature.
- **Listening and Speaking Skills:** Deliver an oral response to literature.

Minimum Course of Study
Most skills can be taught with a minimum number of selections and features. In the chart to the right, lessons **highlighted in green** constitute the minimum course of study that provides coverage of the skills taught in Collection 4.

Scope and Sequence

Selection ▪ Feature	Literary Skills
The Restoration and the Eighteenth Century: 1660–1800 by C. F. Main	• Evaluate the philosophical, political, religious, ethical, and social influences of a historical period
A Modest Proposal by Jonathan Swift ↔ *at grade level*	• Analyze verbal irony, diction, and connotations
• **Heroic Couplets** • *from* **An Essay on Man** by Alexander Pope ↔ *at grade level*	• Analyze antithesis and epigrams
from **The Rape of the Lock** by Alexander Pope ↔ *at grade level*	• Analyze the characteristics of a mock epic
Connecting to World Literature: The Sting of Satire by Robert DeMaria, Jr.	• Understand the characteristics of satire • Compare satires from different cultures and literary periods
from **Candide** by Voltaire ↔ *at grade level*	• Analyze the characteristics of satire • Compare satires from different cultures and literary periods
from **Don Quixote** by Miguel de Cervantes ↔ *at grade level*	• Analyze the characteristics of parody • Compare works from different cultures and literary periods
Introducing Political Points of View: Women's Rights	• Analyze and compare political points of view on a topic

Resource Manager
(see pp. 406E–406H)
Lesson and workshop resources are referenced in the Resource Manager on the pages that follow. These resources can be used to reinforce the skills taught in Collection 4, remediate students who are having difficulty, and provide supporting activities for English-language learners.

Reading Skills	Vocabulary Skills	Writing ■ Grammar and Language ■ Listening and Speaking Skills
• Analyze persuasive techniques (logical, emotional, and ethical appeals)	• Compare word meanings • Analyze word analogies	• Write an ironic proposal • Generate research topics
• Analyze the writer's stance		• Write an essay comparing literary works • Present an oral interpretation of a poem
	• Create etymology maps	• Write an essay comparing and contrasting epics • Write a description in mock-heroic style
	• Understand the meanings and origins of words	• Write an essay analyzing a literary work • Write a brief play
	• Demonstrate word knowledge	• Write a parody
• Understand and analyze rhetorical devices		• Write an essay explaining a political philosophy

(continued)

406B

406D

Scope and Sequence

| Selection ■ Feature | Literary Skills | Reading Skills |

Collection 4

INTRODUCING THE COLLECTION

Jonathan Swift, Alexander Pope, and other writers of their period were not only trying to create lasting works of art but also trying to raise awareness of societal problems. By reading the selections in this collection, students will become familiar with how writers viewed life during the Restoration and the eighteenth century. They will also learn how writers of this period used parody, satire, and other rhetorical devices to make their points. Students will gain additional familiarity with this time period by reading historical essays and the selections in the Political Points of View feature. The collection concludes by giving students an opportunity to write an essay focusing on a literary period of their choosing.

VIEWING THE ART

The Dutch painter **Dirck Stoop** (c. 1610–1686) often painted scenes of cavalry engagements, hunting, and seaports. He also captured several important events in the life of King Charles II, including the restoration of the king to the British throne.

Activity. Call attention to the way Stoop gives his painting depth by making the horses and people in the background smaller and smaller. (This technique, called linear perspective, was a Renaissance innovation in Western art.) In what ways is Stoop's depiction of this event idealized? [The procession moves in a stately, majestic way through an empty, stylized cityscape; there are no spectators, a highly unlikely circumstance.]

Coronation Procession of Charles II to Westminster from the Tower of London (detail) (1661) by Dirck Stoop. Museum of London.

COLLECTION 4 RESOURCES: READING

Planning
- One-Stop Planner CD-ROM

Differentiating Instruction
- Holt Reading Solutions
- The Holt Reader
- Holt Adapted Reader
- Family Involvement Activities in English and Spanish
- Supporting Instruction in Spanish
- Audio CD Library, Selections and Summaries in Spanish

Vocabulary
- Vocabulary Development

Grammar and Language
- Language Handbook Worksheets
- Daily Language Activities

Collection 4

The Restoration and the EIGHTEENTH CENTURY
1660–1800

The Best of All Possible Worlds

There are seven groups in English society
1. The Great, who live profusely.
2. The Rich, who live very plentifully.
3. The Middle Sort, who live well.
4. The Working Trades, who labor hard, but feel no want.
5. The Country People, Farmers, etc., who fare indifferently.
6. The Poor, that fare hard.
7. The Miserable, that really pinch and suffer want.

—Daniel Defoe

Detail from *The Old Fleet Prison.* Culver Pictures.

INTERNET
Collection Resources
Keyword: LE5 12-4

THE QUOTATION

Students will learn more about Daniel Defoe (1660–1731) when they read an excerpt from his essay "On the Education of Women" later in this collection. For now, explain that Defoe wrote on a variety of subjects but is probably best known as the author of *The Life and Adventures of Robinson Crusoe* (1719).

Ask students what conclusions they can draw about eighteenth-century English society from Defoe's quotation. [Possible response: There is an enormous gap between the rich and the poor and a number of levels in between, including three groups (the "Middle Sort," the "Working Trades," and the "Country People") that modern readers might consider middle class.] **Invite students to compare the society Defoe describes with American society today.** [Students may mention the reduced numbers of "Country People" and may combine some groups but will probably find Defoe's categories generally applicable.]

Assessment
- *Holt Assessment: Literature, Reading, and Vocabulary*
- *One-Stop Planner* CD-ROM with ExamView Test Generator
- Holt Online Assessment

Internet
- go.hrw.com (Keyword: LE5 12-4)
- Elements of Literature Online

Media
- *Audio CD Library*
- *Audio CD Library, Selections and Summaries in Spanish*
- *Fine Art Transparencies*
- *Visual Connections Videocassette Program*
- PowerNotes

The Restoration and the

Time Line

■ 1666
Molière

Molière's plays, such as *The Misanthrope,* satirized the upper class and the newly rich, setting the standard for European comedies: witty, urbane, fast-paced plays that depicted relationships between men and women.

■ 1673
The Test Acts

The Test Acts, passed by Parliament in 1673 and 1678, restricted the liberties of people who were not members of the Anglican Church. The law required all people holding civilian or military positions to swear allegiance to the English Crown and to take Communion in the Church of England. A series of laws passed between 1828 and 1871 finally repealed the Test Acts.

■ 1685–1688
James II

James II, a devout Catholic and believer in "the divine right of kings," alienated many people by torturing the followers of the duke of Monmouth, who had led a rebellion against him, and by dispensing with the laws barring Catholics from high office.

■ 1687
Sir Isaac Newton

Newton discovered the law of gravity and the law of the composition of light and developed calculus.

LITERARY EVENTS

1660
- **1660** Samuel Pepys begins his diary
- **1650s** London theaters reopen; actresses appear onstage for the first time
- **1666** In France, Jean Baptiste Molière's *The Misanthrope* is first performed

Opening page of Samuel Pepys's *Diary* (1659–1660). The Pepys Library, Magdalene College, Cambridge, England.

1670
- **1678** John Bunyan publishes *The Pilgrim's Progress,* Part 1 (Part 2 appears in 1684)
- **1680s** Poems of **Bashō** help popularize haiku poetry in Japan
- **1688** Aphra Behn publishes *Oroonoko,* an early antislavery novel

1690
- **1691** In Mexico, Sor Juana Inés de la Cruz publishes *Respuesta a Sor Filotea (Reply to Sister Philotea),* a defense of women's intellectual rights
- **1709** First issue of Addison and Steele's *The Tatler* is printed (*The Spectator* is begun in 1711)

1710
- **1712** Alexander **Pope** publishes part of *The Rape of the Lock*
- **1719** Daniel Defoe publishes *Robinson Crusoe*
- **1726** Jonathan Swift publishes *Gulliver's Travels*
- **1729** Swift publishes *A Modest Proposal,* protesting English treatment of Irish poor

Gold turtle-shaped Ashanti emblem (17th or 18th century) from Ghana.

POLITICAL AND SOCIAL EVENTS

1660
- **1660** Charles II is proclaimed king of England (crowned in 1661)
- **1665** Plague claims more than 68,000 people in London
- **1666** Great Fire destroys much of London

1670
- **c. 1670s** Ashanti Empire is formed in Africa
- **1673** English Test Act bans Roman Catholics from public office
- **1685–1688** James II, king of England, tries to reestablish Catholic Church
- **1687** Newton publishes *Mathematical Principles of Natural Philosophy*
- **1688–1689** Glorious (Bloodless) Revolution: James II is succeeded by Protestant rulers William and Mary

The Great Fire of London (17th century).

1690
- **1690** John Locke publishes *An Essay Concerning Human Understanding*
- **1695** English Parliament enacts Penal Laws, depriving Irish Catholics of civil rights
- **1707** England, Wales, and Scotland are politically unified as Great Britain

1710
- **1714** George I, a German who could not speak English, becomes king of England
- **1718** In England, Lady Mary Wortley Montagu introduces Turkish practice of inoculation against smallpox

Signature of Charles II. The *R* stands for *Rex,* Latin for "king." The Bridgeman Art Library.

Using the Time Line

Activity. Have students use print or nonprint sources to place the following events in world history on the time line.

- William and Mary sign the English Bill of Rights, transferring some royal powers to the elected members of Parliament. [1689]
- Parliament passes the Habeas Corpus Act, which reaffirms and strengthens the prohibition on holding people in jail for indefinite periods without trial. [1679]
- The British Museum is founded in London. [1753]
- Adam Smith publishes the economic treatise *The Wealth of Nations.* [1776]
- Wolfgang Amadeus Mozart composes the opera *The Marriage of Figaro.* [1786]
- The Swedish scientist Anders Celsius invents the centigrade thermometer. [1742]
- James Hargreaves invents the spinning jenny, which spurs the Industrial Revolution. [1764]
- Louis XIV commissions the building of the Palace at Versailles. [1661]

Collection 4 The Restoration and the Eighteenth Century

Eighteenth Century 1660–1800

1740 Samuel Richardson publishes *Pamela, or Virtue Rewarded*

1755 Samuel Johnson publishes his *Dictionary of the English Language*

1759 In France, **Voltaire** publishes *Candide*

1773 African American poet Phillis Wheatley's *Poems on Various Subjects, Religious and Moral* is published in London

1789 Olaudah Equiano, once held in slavery in Colonial America, publishes his autobiography in Britain

1791 James Boswell's *The Life of Samuel Johnson* is published

1792 Mary Wollstonecraft publishes *A Vindication of the Rights of Woman*

1798 Wordsworth and **Coleridge** publish *Lyrical Ballads*

Frontispiece of Phillis Wheatley's *Poems on Various Subjects, Religious and Moral* (1773).

An Early London Coffeehouse (detail) (c. 1705) signed A. S. British Museum, London.

French Revolution button (c. 1789–1793). The motto may be translated as "Liberty or Death." Brass with miniatures painted on ivory.

1752 Benjamin Franklin invents the lightning rod

1760 George III is crowned king of England; becomes known as the king who lost the American Colonies

1762 Catherine II (Catherine the Great) becomes czarina of Russia

1765 British Parliament passes Stamp Act for taxing American Colonies

1765 Mozart writes *Symphony No. 1* at age nine

1773 Boston Tea Party occurs

1775 American Revolution begins

1789 French Revolution begins with storming of the Bastille

1798 British crush Irish nationalist rebellion led by Theobald Wolfe Tone

1799 Rosetta stone (key to deciphering Egyptian hieroglyphics) is found in Egypt

1799 Napoleon heads revolutionary government in France

■ 1760
The British in North America

Following their victory in the French and Indian War, the British took almost all French territory in Canada and all French possessions east of the Mississippi River except New Orleans. The war, which began in 1754, arose from disputes between Britain and France over North American territories. George III's mismanagement of these vast territories led the colonists to revolt.

■ 1762
Catherine II of Russia

Catherine II (1729–1796), a German princess, became empress of Russia when she overthrew her husband, Peter. She became interested in the liberal ideas of the Age of Reason and promoted European culture in Russia. Personally extravagant, Catherine also spent money on schools and hospitals.

■ 1789
The French Revolution

Many of the philosophical underpinnings of the French Revolution, which began in 1789, lay in the writings of Jean-Jacques Rousseau (1712–1778), one of the most influential thinkers of the Age of Reason. Rousseau advocated government by common consent and a legal system that expresses the general will of the people. He believed that humans in their natural state are good but that society brings out their aggression and selfishness.

■ 1798
Lyrical Ballads

William Wordsworth (1770–1850) and Samuel Taylor Coleridge (1772–1834) collaborated on *Lyrical Ballads,* considered the foundation of English Romantic poetry.

Activity. Ask students to think about the following questions.

- What connection can you see between James II's attempt to reestablish the Catholic Church and the ascension of William and Mary in 1688? [The English wanted to maintain the Protestant status quo.]
- How might the Penal Laws of 1695 have led to Jonathan Swift's *A Modest Proposal*? [Swift may have seen the sufferings of the Irish firsthand.]
- Why might Equiano have published his autobiography in England rather than in the American Colonies? [England already had an antislavery literary tradition, begun by Aphra Behn.]

Political and Social Milestones

1660–1800

The Restoration of Charles II, 1660

With the death of Oliver Cromwell in 1658, and the general dissatisfaction with the rule of his successor, his son Richard, restoration of the monarchy seemed possible. Parliament contacted Charles in his exile in Breda, the Netherlands; Charles responded with a letter praising Parliament and a declaration that included promises of religious tolerance and amnesty for his opponents. Delighted at the ease of the negotiations, Parliament quickly issued Charles an invitation to return and renamed the ship sent to bring him home the *Royal Charles*.

The common people of Britain welcomed the return of the Stuarts in the person of Charles II. They also relished the return of such English pastimes and traditions as bull-baiting, bear-baiting, horse racing, cockfighting, and dancing around the maypole. Puritan zeal had exhausted itself; even Cromwell's sons were indifferent to it.

The Bloodless Revolution, 1688

When William and Mary assumed the throne, more than the Protestant succession was secured. The Bloodless Revolution also increased the status and power of Parliament. Since that time Parliament has played a prominent part in British politics and has exercised a democratizing influence on the monarchy.

Political and Social

The Restoration of Charles II, 1660

When the Stuart King Charles II was returned to the throne in 1660, the Church of England regained its power. The life of the aristocratic courtier became the model for a sophisticated age of taste, refinement, and luxury. London theaters reopened, and censorship of the arts declined. However, religious persecution became increasingly widespread, causing many dissenters to immigrate to other countries in search of religious freedom.

The Return of Charles II to Whitehall in 1660 (1867) by Alfred Barron Clay. Oil on canvas.
The Bridgeman Art Library.

An Early London Coffeehouse (detail) (c. 1705) signed A. S.
British Museum, London.

The Bloodless Revolution, 1688

When Charles II died, in 1685, without a legitimate heir, his brother James II, a Roman Catholic, became king. Protestant English political leaders, fearing domination by Rome, acted quickly to transfer power to James's Protestant daughter Mary. Mary's Dutch husband, William of Orange, then attacked England and

Milestones 1660–1800

forced King James to flee. Parliament invited William and Mary to assume the English throne. They accepted and were installed in 1689 without a drop of blood having been shed. Thus, the Protestant succession to the throne of England was secured in what has come to be called the Glorious (Bloodless) Revolution.

> OATS. n. s. [aten, Saxon.] A grain, which in England is generally given to horses, but in Scotland supports the people.
>
> Definition from Samuel Johnson's *A Dictionary of the English Language*.

The Growth of a New Reading Public

As the eighteenth century progressed, more and more writers were focusing on values and concerns associated with middle-class rather than upper-class life. These concerns included thrift, work, domestic relations, and social respectability. Writers like Daniel Defoe, Richard Steele, and Joseph Addison began practicing a new profession, journalism, in which they not only reported on contemporary social and political events but also urged improvement in public manners and morals. Other new literary forms, such as the novel, also found an eager audience in the middle classes, especially among women.

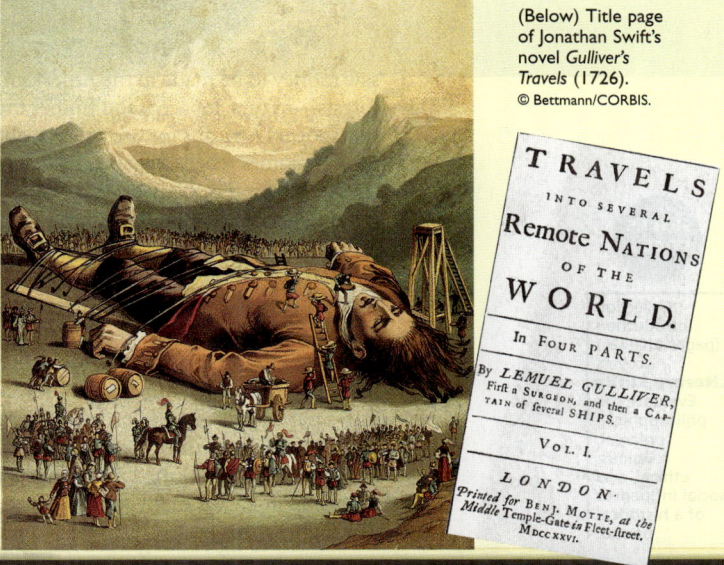

Gulliver awakens in Lilliput, where everyone is about the size of a finger. Illustration.

(Below) Title page of Jonathan Swift's novel *Gulliver's Travels* (1726).
© Bettmann/CORBIS.

The Growth of a New, Middle-Class Reading Public

Women as well as men swelled the ranks of new readers in Great Britain. It is estimated that in the 1670s, only about 22 percent of women were literate (as defined by the ability to read and write their own name); by the 1690s, the figure had risen to about 48 percent. Literacy also depended somewhat upon one's line of work. In seventeenth-century London, for example, virtually all merchants were considered literate, but only about 71 percent of sailors, 65 percent of butchers, and 60 percent of carpenters had the most basic reading and writing skills.

The rise of journalism was reflected in the variety of newspapers available to the English reader. Today a city might have one or two large daily papers, whose revenues come primarily from advertising. During this era, cities such as London had a range of newspapers, each with its own agenda or point of view. Many had a circulation of no more than three thousand copies, and their revenues came primarily from the purchase price. Almost all the great eighteenth-century British writers wrote for periodicals from time to time.

VIEWING THE ART

> Immediately upon publication, Jonathan Swift's book *Gulliver's Travels* was a sensational success. Gulliver was so convincing that some people went about claiming that they had met him. Gulliver and his amazing adventures were, of course, products of Swift's imagination.

DIRECT TEACHING

A Background
AUGUSTUS

Augustus presided over the golden age of Roman literature and architecture; he boasted that he had "found Rome brick and left it marble." (Students may recognize Caesar Augustus as the emperor whose decree "that all the world should be taxed" led to Jesus Christ's being born in Bethlehem—the city where Joseph had to register his family. [Luke 2].) After his death, the Romans worshiped Augustus as a god.

B Exploring the Historical Period
CROMWELL AND CHARLES II

One reason Charles II was restored to power was the failures of Oliver Cromwell's rule. Cromwell had begun by taking democratic measures: He abolished the monarchy and the House of Lords, he instituted the commonwealth (a republican form of government), and he oversaw the drafting of a constitution for England. Beset with problems, however, Cromwell set aside the constitution and imposed military rule. He also instituted a strict Puritan morality, which made illegal such leisure-time activities as attending the theater.

The stress of governing England weighed heavily on Cromwell. In 1658, not long before he died, he told Parliament, "I would have been glad to have lived under my woodside, and to have kept a flock of sheep, rather than to have undertaken this government."

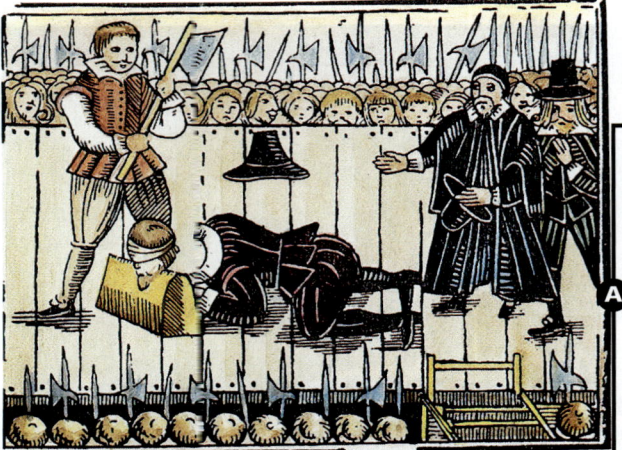

The Execution of King Charles I at Whitehall, London, January 30, 1649. Woodcut.
The Granger Collection, New York.

A emperor Octavian (63 B.C.–A.D. 14). When he became emperor, Octavian was given the high-sounding name *Augustus,* meaning "the exalted one." Augustus restored peace and order to Rome after Julius Caesar's assassination. Similarly, the Stuart monarchs of England restored peace and order to England after the civil wars that led to the execution of King Charles I in 1649—wars that continued even after the king was dead.

The people of both Rome and England were weary of war, suspicious of revolutionaries and radicals, and ready to settle down, make money, and enjoy life. The Roman Senate had hailed Augustus as the second founder of Rome; in 1660, the English people brought back the son of Charles I from his exile in France, crowned him King Charles II, and hailed him as their savior. **B** As a warning to revolutionaries, they dug up the corpse of Oliver Cromwell, who had ruled England between Charles I and Charles II, and cut off its head. The monarchy was restored without shedding a drop of blood in warfare.

In this age, many English writers consciously modeled their works on the old Latin classics, which they had studied in school and university. These writings that imitate Latin works were called **neoclassical**—"new classical." The classics, it was generally agreed, were valuable because they represented what was permanent and universal in human experience. All educated people knew the Latin classics better than they knew their own English literature.

Reason and Enlightenment: From Why? to How?

Labels like the "Age of Reason" and the "Enlightenment" reveal how people were gradually changing their view of themselves and the world. For instance, Shakespeare, the greatest writer of the Renaissance, expressed a commonly held view when he described the unusual events that preceded the assassination of Julius Caesar— "a tempest dropping fire" and "blue lightning." These unnatural events, says a character in the play *Julius Caesar,* are "instruments of fear and warning." For centuries, people had believed that before a great public disaster like the assassination of a ruler, the earth and

> We, therefore, the Representatives of the United States of America, in General Congress, Assembled, . . . do, in the Name, and by Authority of the good People of these Colonies, solemnly Publish and Declare, . . . that all political Connection between them and the State of Great Britain, is and ought to be totally dissolved. . . .
> — Declaration of Independence, Philadelphia (July 4, 1776)
>
> Nothing of importance happened today.
> — Diary entry reportedly made by King George III (July 4, 1776)

CONTENT-AREA CONNECTIONS

Music: The Neoclassical Style
Consistent with the period's philosophy and literature was the balanced, elegant music composed and performed during the period. Outstanding examples of the style include *Dido and Aeneas* by Henry Purcell (1659–1695) and *Julius Caesar* and *Xerxes* by George Frideric Handel (1685–1759).

Mixed-ability group activity. Ask interested students to create a radio program devoted to baroque music. Programming for a fifteen- or thirty-minute segment should include a playlist (with excerpts from longer works), introductory comments, and an interview with a record reviewer or musician. Invite students to present their program in class.

sky gave warnings. People believed that unusual events such as earthquakes, comets, and even babies born with malformations had some kind of meaning, and that they were sent as punishments for past misdoings or as warnings of future troubles. People did not ask, "*How* did this unusual event take place?" but "*Why* did this unusual event take place, and what does it *mean*?"

Throughout the Enlightenment, people gradually stopped asking *why?* questions and started asking *how?* questions, and the answers to those questions—about everything from the workings of the human body to the laws of the universe—became much less frightening and superstitious. For instance, the astronomer Edmond Halley (1656–1742) took the terror out of celestial phenomena by calculating when they were going to occur. He computed, with "immense labor," he said, the orbit of the comet that still bears his name. He predicted it would appear in 1758, 1834, 1910, and 1986—and it did. And how did he know it would reappear at seventy-six-year intervals? Because that was the time it took to complete its orbit. This reasonable explanation made no connection between the comet and human affairs.

> *The truth is, the science of Nature has been already too long made only a work of the brain and the fancy: It is now high time that it should return to the plainness and soundness of observations on material and obvious things.*
> —Robert Hooke

Interior of Henry VII's Chapel, Westminster Abbey (c. 1750) by Canaletto.
Museum of London.

Literary Criticism

Critic's Commentary: Pathetic Fallacy
Shakespeare's descriptions of unusual natural events quoted on p. 414 are examples of the **pathetic fallacy**, the attribution of human emotions to nature. The term, which is closely related to personification, was introduced by the English writer John Ruskin (1819–1900) in a discussion of these lines from Charles Kingsley's *The Sands of Dee:* "They rowed her in across the rolling foam—The cruel, crawling foam." "The foam is not cruel," wrote Ruskin, "neither does it crawl. The state of mind which attributes to it these characters of a living creature is one in which the reason is unhinged by grief. All violent feelings have the same effect. They produce in us a falseness in all our impressions of external things, which I would generally characterize as the 'pathetic fallacy.'" The fallacy lies in "the difference between the ordinary, proper, and true appearance of things to us; and the extraordinary, or false appearances, when we are under the influence of emotion of contemplative fancy."

DIRECT TEACHING

Content-Area Connections
Science: The Scientific Method
Francis Bacon, Lord Chancellor of England (1561–1626), was the first to endorse the scientific method, the slow, careful process of examining physical evidence, performing experiments, and evaluating various hypotheses against the results of these experiments. His writings set the stage for the growth in scientific knowledge that occurred in the mid-1600s.

Background
Robert Hooke
Robert Hooke (1635–1703) was one of the greatest scientists of the seventeenth century. Like Leonardo da Vinci, however, he often failed to fully develop his ideas. (For example, he anticipated some of the ideas about gravity that Sir Isaac Newton would later formulate.) Known for his study of elasticity as well as his work on watches and clocks, Hooke contributed to many fields of science. Two of his biological drawings appear on pp. 438 and 439.

VIEWING THE ART

The real name of the Italian painter **Canaletto** (1697–1768) was Giovanni Antonio Canal. Known for his scenes of Venice, Canaletto captures here the soaring verticality of Westminster Abbey's nave.

Activity. Westminster Abbey is the most famous church and prime symbol of Christianity in England. Ask students to speculate on Canaletto's attitude toward the church, judging from the details in this painting. [Possible response: The light that illuminates the soaring Gothic arches suggests an attitude of reverence toward the Abbey.]

DIRECT TEACHING

A Exploring the Culture
DEISM

A product of the Enlightenment, Deism was a spiritual belief based on reason and the observation of nature. The French philosophers Jean-Jacques Rousseau and Voltaire and the German philosopher Immanuel Kant embraced Deism. Strains of Deism also appear in the U.S. Declaration of Independence (as in "They are endowed by their creator with certain inalienable rights"), the contents of which were influenced by leading colonial Deists, including Benjamin Franklin, Thomas Jefferson, and Thomas Paine.

A CLOSER LOOK

This feature discusses the fashions and leisure-time activities of England's upper class during this era.

B Reading Informational Text

? Verifying facts. How could you prove the accuracy of this description? [Possible responses: by examining portraits and other paintings of the period; by reading letters or essays from that time in which fashion is discussed.]

Newton's reflecting telescope (1688).
Royal Society, London.

Changes in Religion: More Questions

The new scientific and rational explanations of phenomena gradually began to affect some people's religious views. If comets were not sent by God to warn people, perhaps God didn't interfere at all in human affairs. Perhaps the universe was like an immense piece of clockwork, set in motion by a Creator who more or less withdrew from this perfect mechanism and let it run by itself. Such a view, part of an ideology known as deism, could make people feel self-satisfied and complacent, especially if they believed, as Alexander Pope (see page 445) noted, that "Whatever is, is right." Some philosophers even argued that "in this best of all possible worlds, . . . all is for the best"—a view that the French writer Voltaire ridiculed in his novel *Candide* (1759). (See page 467.) But other than a tiny minority of "enlightened" rationalists and materialists,

A CLOSER LOOK: SOCIAL INFLUENCES

Life Among the Haves . . .

According to the law, all men were equal, but some were more equal than others—especially England's wealthy, during the Restoration and the eighteenth century. Famous for its excesses this artificial age offered extreme luxuries to those known as "quality" or "polite" society—the rich.

Gossip and gambling. Greatly influenced by the French in manners, dress, furniture, gardens, and recreation, the elite gathered regularly at London's fashionable coffeehouses—numbering three thousand by the early eighteenth century. These centers of news, gossip, and gambling were places to see and to be seen in. Another meeting place, the city's formal gardens, offered illuminated groves, dining, and fireworks.

Powder and plumage. Whatever their haunt, both men and women devoted themselves to colorful and extravagant fashion. Men carried snuffboxes and wore velvet or satin coats, lace ruffles, silk knee breeches, high-heeled shoes with gold or silver buckles, and broad-brimmed hats decorated with feathers. Women wore low-cut silk dresses with hoops made from whalebones. Their elaborate petticoats were fashioned from colorful silk, velvet, or chintz, often quilted or trimmed with silver.

By 1664, wigs and makeup were the rage for men and women. Powdered and stuffed with horsehair, women's headdresses grew to enormous proportions. Jewels, flowers, ribbons, plumage, and even fruit decorated these monstrous structures—reaching two to three feet in height. Men also wore their hair in pigtails—tied with a bow and powdered. In 1795, a tax was created to generate income from the rich—a guinea on every powdered head. Cosmetics were made from ingredients such as borax, vinegar, bread, eggs, and pigeon wings. Black patches, or fake beauty marks, were an important fashion accessory.

INFORMATIONAL TEXT

SKILLS REVIEW

Identifying idioms. Explain that an *idiom* is an expression whose meaning is different from the literal meanings of its words taken together. Examples include *stuck up*, *all of a sudden*, and *taken for granted*.
Activity. Have students interpret the following idioms from this essay.

1. "they also saw money to be made" (p. 412) [they realized that they could become rich]
2. "settle down" (p. 414) [adopt a calmer, more responsible lifestyle]
3. "take place" (p. 415) [happen]
4. "places to see and to be seen in" (p. 416) [places where one could look at interesting things and where one hopes to be noticed and admired by others]

most people, including great philosophers and scientists like Sir Isaac Newton (1642–1727) and John Locke (1632–1704), remained religious. Christianity in its various forms continued to exercise an undiminished power over almost all Europeans in this period, just as it had in the Middle Ages and the Renaissance.

Religion and Politics: Repression of Minority Sects

Religion determined people's politics in this period. Charles II reestablished the Anglican Church as the official church of the country, which it continues to be in England to this day. (In the United States it is called the Episcopal Church.) With the approval of Parliament, the king attempted to outlaw all the various Puritan and Independent sects—dozens of them, all happily disagreeing

Alexander Pope.

Nature and Nature's laws lay hid in night: God said, Let Newton be! and all was light.
—Alexander Pope, epitaph intended for Sir Isaac Newton

Cartoon mocking the huge wigs worn by rich women (1771). Lithograph.
© Historical Picture Archive/CORBIS.

The pursuit of pleasure. The wealthy divided the year between London residences, country estates, and fashionable spas. A whirlwind of masked balls, dances, and formal dinner parties, known as the London season, ended by the first week in June. Summers were often spent in seaside towns and at freshwater springs. Daniel Defoe described one trendy spa: "[The attendants] present you with a little floating dish like a basin, in which the lady puts her handkerchief and a nosegay, of late the snuffbox is added, and some patches; through the bath occasioning a little perspiration, the patches do not stick as kindly as they should."

It was a careless, pleasure-seeking time centered on dancing, dining, drinking, theatergoing, card playing, and gambling. As is always the case with fashion, change was inevitable. By the end of the eighteenth century, the lifestyle of the wealthy leaned toward simplicity and sobriety.

DIRECT TEACHING

C Exploring the Culture
RATIONALISM AND MATERIALISM

Rationalism is a philosophy in which reason is regarded as the proper basis for making decisions. In the seventeenth century philosophical rationalism held that reason is more powerful than sensory experience and that through reason, humans can understand the nature of reality. In the eighteenth century cultural rationalism emphasized reason over faith in explaining human destiny. Thomas Paine, author of *The Age of Reason* (1793), was a prominent figure in this movement.

Materialism holds that everything is a state of matter. Even human consciousness itself arises from processes involving matter. This philosophy can be traced to the fifth century B.C., when the Greek philosophers Leucippus and Democritus developed *atomism*, the notion that indivisible particles (atoms) make up everything that exists. The spread of Christianity caused interest in materialism to wane for several centuries. However, the rise of modern science during the 1600s renewed discussion of materialism.

D Reading Skills
❓ Interpreting. What did Alexander Pope mean by this comment about Sir Isaac Newton? [Possible responses: People understood little about nature until Newton came along; Newton taught the world about the composition of light.]

E Reading Informational Text
❓ Analyzing philosophical assumptions. Charles II once said, "God will never damn a man for allowing himself a little pleasure." How does his comment relate to this feature? [It illustrates the prevailing attitude of the "haves," for whom pleasure was a high priority.]

CONTENT-AREA CONNECTIONS

Science: Comets
Individual activity. Ask students whether they have ever seen a comet. Some students may recall Hale-Bopp in 1998, for instance. Then, have students re-read "Reason and Enlightenment: From Why? to How?" on pp. 414–415. Afterward, have volunteers research and explain the mathematical principles behind Edmond Halley's calculations of parabolic orbits.

Culture: Fashion
Mixed-ability group activity. Have students who are interested in fashion create a collage showing eighteenth-century styles and styles modeled on or resembling them from other periods. For example, students could show a powdered wig worn by a woman of this era next to a 1960s beehive hairdo.

The Restoration and the Eighteenth Century 423

eighteenth-century life is illustrated in the paintings and engravings

> 7   Hope springs eternal in the human breast:
>   Man never is, but always to be blest.
>   —*An Essay on Man,* Epistle I, lines 95–96
>
> 8   'Tis education forms the common mind,
>   Just as the twig is bent, the tree's inclined.
>   —*Moral Essays,* Epistle I, lines 149–150
>
> 9   But when to mischief mortals bend their will,
>   How soon they find fit instruments of ill!
>   —*The Rape of the Lock,* Canto III, lines 125–126
>
> 10 Satire's my weapon, but I'm too discreet
>   To run amuck, and tilt[4] at all I meet.
>   —*Imitations of Horace, Satire I,* Book II, lines 69–70

4. **tilt** *v.:* charge at or thrust a weapon toward an opponent.

View Across Greenwich Park Toward London (detail) (18th century) by Jean Rigaud.
Roy Miles Gallery, London.

Primary Source

Pope on Poetry Versus Prose
In a preface to *An Essay on Man,* Alexander Pope offered this explanation for why he chose to express his philosophical ideas in poetry, not prose: "I chose verse, and even rhyme for two reasons. The one will appear obvious; that principles, maxims, or precepts, so written, both strike the reader more strongly at first, and are more easily retained by him afterwards; the other may seem odd, but it is true; I found I could express them more shortly this way than in prose itself; and nothing is more certain than that much of the force as well as grace of arguments or instructions depends on their conciseness."

Whole-class activity. Ask students to debate the pros and cons of expressing ideas in poetry or prose. Do they agree that ideas can be stated more concisely in poetry?

DIRECT TEACHING

A Literary Focus

? Style. What is the purpose of the comma in the second line? [Possible response: It indicates a pause and emphasizes the antithesis between actually being "blest" and hoping to be "blest."]

B Reading Skills

? Identifying the writer's stance. Based on this couplet, what view did Pope take toward his fellow human beings? [Possible response: People are all too apt to make trouble; being "difficult" is quite easy for most people.]

C Reading Skills

? Evaluating. In the first line, Pope uses a metaphor to compare satire to a weapon. Is the comparison effective? Why or why not? [Possible responses: Yes, because words can be sharp; words can "cut." No, because the comparison seems like a cliché.]

VIEWING THE ART

Jean Rigaud (1700–?) a French painter, completed several English landscapes during his career.

Activity. Ask students if they can explain the geographical significance of Greenwich, England. [Greenwich, a borough of London, is the site of an imaginary line designated as zero longitude. All other longitudes—and the world's time zones—are calculated from this line.]

An *Essay on Man* is Pope's long (1,304 lines) philosophical poem, published when he was forty-five. A lifetime of reading, in both English and foreign languages, contributed to its composition. The poem is concerned not only with "man," by which Pope means the whole human race, but with the entire universe as well. It's important to know that the ideas in the poem are not merely the private notions of Pope and his friends, but that they come from many authors, including Plato, Aristotle, St. Thomas Aquinas, Dante, Erasmus, Shakespeare, Bacon, and Milton.

from An Essay on Man
Alexander Pope

Know then thyself,° presume not God to scan;°
The proper study of mankind is man.
Placed on this isthmus of a middle state,°
A being darkly wise, and rudely great:
With too much knowledge for the skeptic° side,
With too much weakness for the Stoic's pride,°
He hangs between; in doubt to act, or rest;
In doubt to deem himself a god, or beast;
In doubt his mind or body to prefer;
Born but to die, and reasoning but to err;
Alike in ignorance, his reason such,
Whether he thinks too little, or too much:
Chaos of thought and passion, all confused;
Still° by himself abused, or disabused;°
Created half to rise, and half to fall;
Great lord of all things, yet a prey to all;
Sole judge of truth, in endless error hurled:
The glory, jest, and riddle of the world!

1. **Know...thyself:** moral precept of Socrates and other ethical philosophers. **scan** *v.:* pry into; speculate about.
3. **middle state:** that is, having the rational intellect of angels and the physical body of beasts.
5. **skeptic** *n.* used as *adj.:* The ancient Skeptics doubted that humans can gain accurate knowledge of anything. They emphasized the limitations of human knowledge.
6. **Stoic's pride:** The ancient Stoics' ideal was a calm acceptance of life and an indifference to both pain and pleasure. Stoics are called proud because they refused to recognize human limitations.
14. **still** *adv.:* always; continually. **disabused** *v.:* undeceived.

Alexander Pope.
Portrait in oil.
Bryn Mawr College,
Bryn Mawr, Pennsylvania.

PRETEACHING

Summary at grade level

This excerpt, written in heroic couplets, is rich in antithesis as Pope explores his paradoxical view of humanity, which, he says is the "glory, jest, and riddle of the world."

DIRECT TEACHING

A Reading Skills

Analyzing philosophical assumptions. What assumptions does Pope reveal in this couplet? [Pope assumes that God exists but human beings can never understand Him and that people should instead spend time learning about humanity.]

B Reading Skills

Identifying the writer's stance. What does Pope's choice of the word *isthmus* reveal about the place of humankind in the universe? [Possible response: An isthmus is a small strip of land connecting two larger bodies of land and bordered on both sides by water. Through this comparison, Pope is suggesting that human beings form a link between the spiritual world of heaven above and the physical world of animals below.]

C Literary Focus

Antithesis. What antithesis do you see in l. 4? ["Darkly wise" and "rudely great" are grammatically and structurally parallel: Both consist of two-syllable adverbs preceding single-syllable adjectives. Each phrase also offers contrasts: We associate wisdom with light, not darkness, and greatness with refinement, not rudeness.]

DIFFERENTIATING INSTRUCTION

Learners Having Difficulty
Invite learners having difficulty to read from *An Essay on Man* in interactive format in *The Holt Reader* and to use the sidenotes as aids to understanding the selection.

English-Language Learners
For lessons designed for English-language learners and special education students, see *Holt Reading Solutions.*

Response and Analysis

Heroic Couplets
from An Essay on Man

Thinking Critically

1. What explicit value or point of view does Pope directly express in each of the heroic couplets? **Paraphrase** or express each couplet in your own words. You may want to refer to your reading notes.

2. Think of some examples of how a little learning could be a dangerous thing (couplet 2).

3. Pope habitually uses **antithesis** to focus and clarify his meaning. List all the antitheses you can find in the heroic couplets. What parallel elements can you find?

4. In almost every sentence in this excerpt from *An Essay on Man,* Pope says something flattering about the human race, only to follow it with something critical. What characteristics does he think we should be proud of? ashamed of?

5. In what ways do you think human beings could be seen as the "glory" of this world? as its "jest"? as its "riddle" (line 18 of the *Essay*)?

Extending and Evaluating

6. Do you disagree with any of Pope's opinions and pronouncements—in the couplets or in the *Essay?* Explain.

7. Which opinions of Pope's do you think are most true or most valuable—even in the world today?

WRITING

Pope Versus Shakespeare

In an **essay,** compare Pope's view of humanity with the view expressed by William Shakespeare's *Hamlet* in the following lines:

What a piece of work is a man! how noble in reason! how infinite in faculties! in form and moving how express and admirable! in action how like an angel! in apprehension how like a god! the beauty of the world, the paragon of animals!

—*Hamlet,* Act II, Scene 2

Conclude your analysis by stating which point of view is closer to your own. Cite a few reasons to support your response.

LISTENING AND SPEAKING

Read Aloud: A Pope Performance

Present "Two Minutes of Pope" to the class. Read a selection of couplets aloud to feel the effect of **antitheses, rhymes,** and **alliteration.** Be sure to practice alternative readings before you make your presentation.

Literary Focus

Epigrams

Pope had a dog named Bounce, one of whose puppies he gave to his friend Frederick, Prince of Wales, who lived in Kew. Pope had an epigram engraved on the puppy's collar. An **epigram** is a short poem, often satirical, that ends in a witticism or clever turn of thought. To whom do you think the epigram is addressed? (Don't say "the prince," because surely the prince knows his own dog.)

> **Epigram Engraved on the Collar of a Dog**
>
> I am his Highness's dog at Kew;
> Pray tell me sir, whose dog are you?

Skills Focus

Literary Skills Analyze antithesis and epigrams.

Reading Skills Analyze the writer's stance.

Writing Skills Write an essay comparing literary works.

Listening and Speaking Skills Present an oral interpretation of a poem.

450   Collection 4   The Restoration and the Eighteenth Century

Before You Read

from The Rape of the Lock

Make the Connection
Quickwrite

If you look at the newspapers and magazines displayed at a supermarket checkout, you'll probably agree that many Americans like to read about rich and famous people—those who have made it big in politics, sports, business, and entertainment. Many readers find it especially interesting to read about the trivial problems and petty quarrels of these well-known people. *The Rape of the Lock* tells the story of a petty quarrel among members of the eighteenth-century nobility. Take a few minutes to think about why people today (and people in the eighteenth century) are fascinated by the lives of the rich and famous. Has the appeal of "celebrity gossip" changed very much since Pope's day? Why or why not? Write down your thoughts.

Literary Focus
Mock Epic

The Rape of the Lock is a **mock epic**. Its comedy arises from the discrepancy between its trivial subject matter (the snipping of a curl) and its grandiose treatment. (In mock epics, cracked teacups become major catastrophes.) Pope achieves this comic discrepancy by putting all the traditional devices found in serious epics (like Homer's *Iliad*, Virgil's *Aeneid*, and Milton's *Paradise Lost*) into a tame, domestic context where little is at risk. For instance, the classical epics all have gods and goddesses who intervene in human affairs. Following these models, Pope creates tiny, airy spirits (called "sylphs") who try, in vain, to prevent the "rape" of Belinda's curl. Similarly, Pope includes a hotly contested game of cards and an outburst of temper to satisfy the requirement that every epic contain battles.

A **mock epic** is a comic narrative poem, written in dignified language, that parodies the serious epic genre by treating a trivial subject in a lofty, grand manner.

For more on Mock Epic, see the Handbook of Literary and Historical Terms.

Background
The title of Pope's comic masterpiece means "the violent theft of a lock of hair." The poem is based on a real incident. The lock in question belonged to a certain rich and fashionable young lady named Arabella Fermor. The theft in question was committed by a certain rich and fashionable young man named Robert, Lord Petre. When Robert snipped a curl from Arabella's hairdo, he set off a quarrel between the Fermor and the Petre families. Had the two families been less sensible, their row might have escalated into bitter hatred. As it turned out, the feud subsided into laughter—thanks to Alexander Pope.

Vocabulary Development

exulting (eg·zult′iŋ) v. used as *adj.*: rejoicing.

repast (ri·past′) n.: meal.

desist (di·zist′) v.: stop.

recesses (rē′ses·iz) n. pl.: secluded or hidden places.

titillating (tit″l·āt′iŋ) v. used as *adj.*: exciting; stimulating.

dejects (dē·jekts′) v.: casts down; dispirits.

INTERNET
Vocabulary Practice
Keyword: LE5 12-4

SKILLS FOCUS

Literary Skills
Understand the characteristics of a mock epic.

Alexander Pope 451

Previewing Vocabulary

Go over the definitions of the Vocabulary words on p. 451 with students. Then, have them match each Vocabulary word with its antonym. Encourage them to use a dictionary or a thesaurus, if necessary.

1. exulting [b]   a. continue
2. titillating [d]   b. sorrowing
3. desist [a]   c. uplifts
4. recesses [e]   d. boring
5. dejects [c]   e. protuberances
6. repast [f]   f. fast

PRETEACHING

Summary *at grade level*

By Canto III of this mock epic, the fair Belinda has joined friends at a gathering at Hampton Court. There, she and others of wealth and leisure, including the Baron, sip coffee, gossip, flirt, and play cards. The Baron schemes to shear a lock of Belinda's hair and finally does so despite the defensive efforts of the sylphs, or sprites. Using a volley of snuff and a hairpin, the outraged Belinda engages the Baron in battle. When the Baron shows no remorse, Belinda concedes her loss. Her consolation, the speaker suggests, is that her lock of hair will rise into heaven as a star, an absurd parody of a classical metamorphosis.

Selection Starter

Motivate. Ask volunteers to suggest some of the ways in which the battle of the sexes is played out in their everyday lives. Also inquire whether they think the battle of the sexes has an impact on the values of American society. Explain that in *The Rape of the Lock*, Alexander Pope takes an amusing look at the battle of the sexes in eighteenth-century England.

Skills Starter

Build background. In the 794 lines of *The Rape of the Lock*, Alexander Pope manages to mock most of the typical elements that his readers would have expected to find in a classical epic. For the epic battle, Pope substitutes a card game. A pinch of snuff and a hairpin serve for the epic stratagem. In this mock epic, the "arming" of the hero takes place at Belinda's dressing table. Indeed, Pope's choice of a female protagonist was meant to mock the traditional male hero. Finally, for the gods and goddesses who typically intervene in an epic, Pope substituted an array of airy sprites called sylphs.

Alexander Pope 451

DIRECT TEACHING

VIEWING THE ART

Thomas Gainsborough (1727–1788) was an accomplished painter of portraits, especially those of elegant women. With its fine brushwork, use of color, attention to detail, and display of elegance, this portrait shows off Gainsborough's style particularly well.

Activity. Encourage students to make inferences about the lady's character based on this portrait. [She seems very concerned with fashion and her appearance.]

A Woman in Blue (Portrait of the Duchess of Beaufort) (late 1770s) by Thomas Gainsborough.
Hermitage, St. Petersburg. The Bridgeman Art Library.

DIFFERENTIATING INSTRUCTION

Learners Having Difficulty
In this mock epic, Pope is making fun of the lifestyle of the aristocracy, and he assumes the reader has a lot of background knowledge. For instance, "gave the ball" in l. 12 refers to holding a social dance; "Indian screen" in l. 14 denotes a fire screen made in India, often used to protect ladies from sparks; the "board" in l. 33 is an archaic word for dining table; the "nosegay" in l. 69 is a corsage, and "peer" in l. 75 means "nobleman." Have students work in pairs to find references they do not understand. Help students clarify any confusing passages.

Invite learners having difficulty to read "from *The Rape of the Lock*" in interactive format in *The Holt Reader* and to use the sidenotes as aids to understanding the selection.

Pope's poem is divided into five sections called **cantos.** Canto I begins like a proper epic, with a statement of the subject and an invocation to the Muse—a female deity who was supposed to inspire poets and other artists. Pope, however, clearly signals his comic intentions in the very first couplet:

> What dire offense from amorous causes springs,
> What mighty contests rise from trivial things,
> I sing—

In Canto II, Belinda and her friends take a boat up the river Thames to a party. All who see her admire the two beautiful curled locks that hang down her back. And despite the small army of sprites (spirits) assigned to protect Belinda's beautiful hair, the Baron resolves to possess these locks.

from
The Rape of the Lock
Alexander Pope

from Canto III

    Close by those meads, forever crowned with flowers,
Where Thames with pride surveys his rising towers,
There stands a structure° of majestic frame,
Which from the neighboring Hampton takes its name.
5 Here Britain's statesmen oft the fall foredoom
Of foreign tyrants, and of nymphs° at home;
Here thou, great Anna!° whom three realms obey,
Dost sometimes counsel take—and sometimes tea.
    Hither the heroes and the nymphs resort,
10 To taste awhile the pleasures of a court;
In various talk th' instructive hours they passed,
Who gave the ball, or paid the visit last;
One speaks the glory of the British queen,
And one describes a charming Indian screen;
15 A third interprets motions, looks, and eyes;
At every word a reputation dies.

---

3. **structure** *n.:* Hampton Court, a royal residence on the river Thames, upstream from London.
6. **nymphs** *n. pl.:* young ladies.
7. **Anna:** Queen Anne (1665–1714), who ruled England, Ireland, and Scotland.

> **1–16.** In lines 1–8, notice how Pope juxtaposes, or places side by side, the grandiose and the trivial: At Hampton Court, statesmen discuss the fall of tyrants—and also of young ladies. Meanwhile, Queen Anne is sometimes served political counsel—and at other times, tea.
> *What does line 16 tell you about life at Hampton Court?*

DIRECT TEACHING

A Literary Focus

❓ Antithesis. Why is l. 30 an example of antithesis? ["Too soon dejected" and "too soon elate" are structurally parallel and show the paradoxical tendency of humankind to both despair and rejoice prematurely.]

VIEWING THE ART

Romantic painter **J.M.W. Turner** (1775–1851) revolutionized landscape painting by using sweeping brushstrokes and areas of color to portray natural forms and processes. According to William Hazlitt, a nineteenth-century literary and art critic, Turner was more interested in his manner of painting than in the subjects he painted.

Activity. Is Turner's approach to artistic representation the same as Pope's? [No. Pope wanted people to see things clearly as they are.]

Responses to Margin Questions

Lines 21–22. Judges and jury members get hungry around dinnertime, so they quickly finish up their work, signing papers that will result in hangings, so they can rush home to eat on time. The couplet is witty because it expresses a sad truth about human selfishness and inhumanity in an elegant way.

Lines 23–28. Belinda "burns to encounter" knights; her ambition is to have young men fall in love with her and then to reject them.

    Snuff,° or the fan,° supply each pause of chat,
    With singing, laughing, ogling, and all that.
       Meanwhile, declining from the noon of day,
20 The sun obliquely shoots his burning ray;
    The hungry judges soon the sentence sign,
    And wretches hang that jurymen may dine....
    Belinda now, whom thirst of fame invites,
    Burns to encounter two adventurous knights,
25 At omber° singly to decide their doom;
    And swells her breast with conquests yet to come....
    The nymph <u>exulting</u> fills with shouts the sky;
    The walls, the woods, and long canals reply.
       Oh thoughtless mortals! ever blind to fate,
A 30 Too soon dejected and too soon elate.
    Sudden, these honors shall be snatched away,

---

17. **snuff** *n.:* powdered tobacco product sniffed or rubbed on the teeth and gums. **fan** *n.:* standard equipment for a lady.
25. **omber** *n.:* card game for three players, popular in the eighteenth century.

Vocabulary
exulting (eg·zult′iŋ) *v.* used as *adj.:* rejoicing.

21–22. These clever lines have been quoted for centuries.
❓ *What do these two lines mean?*

23–28. ❓ *What is Belinda's ambition? How does Pope describe Belinda?*

View of Hampton Court, Herefordshire (c. 1806) by J.M.W. Turner.
The Bridgeman Art Library. Yale Center for British Art, Paul Mellon Collection, New Haven, Connecticut.

DIFFERENTIATING INSTRUCTION

Learners Having Difficulty
Have groups of five students play the characters of Belinda, the Baron, Clarissa, Ariel, and Belinda's friend (the "virago" of Canto V, l.1). In a discussion of the poem's plot, have the characters sum up what they have done and said so far and how they feel about what has happened.

English-Language Learners
Invite students to sketch a drawing or cartoon of one or more scenes from the poem. Encourage students to show their sketches and explain the actions being portrayed.

Advanced Learners
Enrichment. Students may take special interest in the poem's many allusions. Have them keep a list as they read. Then, using a good classical or mythological dictionary, students should explain how each allusion deepens the meaning or increases the satire of the poem.

And cursed forev[...]
    For lo! the bo[...]
The berries° cra[...]
35 On shining alta[...]
The silver lamp;[...]
From silver spou[...]
While China's ea[...]
At once they gra[...]
40 And frequent cu[...]
Straight hover r[...]
Some, as she sip[...]
Some o'er her lap then careful p[...]
Trembling, and conscious of the rich brocade.
45 Coffee (which makes the politician wise,
And see through all things with his half-shut eyes)
Sent up in vapors to the Baron's brain
New stratagems, the radiant lock to gain.
Ah, cease, rash youth! desist ere 'tis too late,
50 Fear the just gods, and think of Scylla's fate!°
Changed to a bird, and sent to flit in air,
She dearly pays for Nisus' injured hair!
    But when to mischief mortals bend their will,
How soon they find fit instruments of ill!
55 Just then, Clarissa drew with tempting grace
A two-edged weapon from her shining case:
So ladies in romance assist their knight,
Present the spear, and arm him for the fight.
He takes the gift with reverence, and extends
60 The little engine° on his fingers' ends;
This just behind Belinda's neck he spread,
As o'er the fragrant steams she bends her head.
Swift to the lock a thousand sprites repair,
A thousand wings, by turns, blow back the hair;

---

34. **berries** *n. pl.*: coffee beans. **mill** *n.*: coffee grinder.
35. **altars of Japan:** small lacquered tables.
38. **China's earth:** cups made of earthenware. **smoking tide:** coffee.
50. **Scylla's fate:** In Greek mythology, Scylla (sil′ə) is turned into a seabird by the gods after she betrays her father Nisus by cutting off his purple lock of hair, on which his life and kingdom depend.
60. **engine** *n.*: instrument.

Vocabulary
repast (ri·past′) *n.*: meal.
desist (di·zist′) *v.*: stop.

[Margin notes:]
In this verse paragraph, Pope sets the scene for the grand offense. The rich are gathered in a sitting room at Hampton Court, drinking endless cups of coffee.

? What are Belinda's companions doing? What is the Baron doing?

? 55–62. What action is described in these lines?

Alexander Pope 455

DIRECT TEACHING

A Learners Having Difficulty

? Paraphrasing. Why couldn't the sprites protect Belinda from the advancing Baron? [Ariel, the chief sprite, discerns that Belinda actually loves the Baron, and the sprites are powerless to block the course of true love.]

B Literary Focus

? Antithesis. In ll. 75–76, what is particularly clever about the use of antithesis in the description of the scissors? [The Baron "spreads" the scissors to enclose the lock of hair, and he "joins" the scissors to separate the lock from Belinda's head. The verbs name contradictory actions but work together to produce a unified description.]

C Literary Focus

? Mock epic. What grandiose account does Pope give of Belinda's reaction to the Baron's act? [Living lightning flashes from her eyes; her cries rend the heavens.] Why is this extraordinary reaction comic under the circumstances? [All the Baron has done is snip one of her curls.]

Responses to Margin Questions

Lines 75–82. Although a sylph is cut in two trying to protect the lock, the Baron succeeds in snipping a curl of Belinda's hair with the scissors.

Lines 83–88. Belinda's shrieks are compared to those that might be heard when a husband or a lapdog dies or when an expensive piece of china breaks.

---

65 And thrice they twitched the diamond in her ear;
    Thrice she looked back, and thrice the foe drew near.
    Just in that instant, anxious Ariel° sought
    The close <u>recesses</u> of the virgin's thought;
    As on the nosegay in her breast reclined,
70 He watched th' ideas rising in her mind,
    Sudden he viewed, in spite of all her art,
    An earthly lover lurking at her heart.°
    Amazed, confused, he found his power expired,
    Resigned to fate, and with a sigh retired.
75   The peer now spreads the glittering *forfex*° wide,
    T' enclose the lock; now joins it, to divide.
    Even then, before the fatal engine closed,
    A wretched sylph too fondly interposed;
    Fate urged the shears, and cut the sylph in twain,
80 (But airy substance soon unites again).
    The meeting points the sacred hair dissever
    From the fair head, forever, and forever!
        Then flashed the living lightning from her eyes,
    And screams of horror rend th' affrighted skies.
85 Not louder shrieks to pitying Heaven are cast,
    When husbands, or when lapdogs breathe their last;
    Or when rich china vessels fallen from high,
    In glittering dust, and painted fragments lie!
        "Let wreaths of triumph° now my temples twine,"
90 The victor cried, "the glorious prize is mine!
    While fish in streams, or birds delight in air,
    Or in a coach and six° the British fair,
    As long as *Atalantis*° shall be read,
    Or the small pillow grace a lady's bed,
95 While visits shall be paid on solemn days,
    When numerous wax lights in bright order blaze,
    While nymphs take treats, or assignations give,

---

67. **Ariel:** chief of the heavenly sprites sent to protect Belinda.
72. **earthly lover . . . heart:** If in her heart Belinda wants the Baron to succeed, the sprites cannot protect her.
75. ***forfex:*** Latin for "scissors."
89. **wreaths of triumph:** like the ones worn by athletic and military heroes in ancient times.
92. **coach and six:** coach with six horses.
93. ***Atalantis:*** *The New Atalantis* (1709), a fashionable novel by Mrs. Delarivière Manley that thinly disguises some contemporary scandals.

Vocabulary
recesses (rē′sĕs·ĭz) *n. pl.:* secluded or hidden places.

63–74. Having been armed by an accomplice, the Baron advances toward Belinda's back and then retreats three times in rapid sequence. This comical image mimics the rhythms of fencing.

? 75–82. How is the theft of the lock accomplished?

83–88. Belinda screams in horror at the abduction of her lock.
? What three kinds of shrieks is Belinda's shriek compared to?

Primary Source

Pope to Belinda
Share with students this passage from a letter Pope wrote to Arabella Fermor, the young woman on whom Belinda is based: "As to the following cantos, all the passages of them are as fabulous as the vision at the beginning, or the transformation at the end (except the loss of your hair, which I always mention with reverence). The human persons are as fictitious as the airy ones; and the character of Belinda as it is now managed, resembles you in nothing but in beauty."

Activity. Ask students to comment on the purpose and tone of this letter. [Some students may find the letter a straightforward explanation of Pope's work. Some may see the letter as an attempt to forestall Arabella's anger with flattery. Others may see some mild mockery of her.]

456 Collection 4 The Restoration and the Eighteenth Century

So long my honor, name, and praise shall live!
What time would spare, from steel receives its date,°
100 And monuments, like men, submit to fate!"...

In Canto IV, Pope describes an incident that occurs in all proper epics: a descent into the underworld. Just as Virgil had Aeneas travel down to Hades, Pope has Umbriel, a "melancholy sprite," fly down to a dismal, imaginary place called the Cave of Spleen. (Spleen was the eighteenth century's name for what we call depression; rich, idle people were particularly subject to spleen in Pope's day.) In the cave, Umbriel obtains a vial of "soft sobs, melting griefs, and flowing tears," as well as an immense bag full of "sighs, sobs, and passions," which somewhat resembles the bag of unfavorable winds in Homer's Odyssey, given to Odysseus to keep tightly closed so his ship won't be blown off course. Umbriel then returns to the earth's surface and empties the contents of the bag and vial over Belinda and her girlfriend, who is even angrier than Belinda. The canto ends with Belinda lamenting to the Baron:

"O, hadst thou, cruel! been content to seize
Hairs less in sight, or any hairs but these!"

The others in Belinda's tea-party audience shed tears of pity, but the Baron ignores her pleas: "Fate and Jove had stopped the Baron's ears."

89–100. Like a victorious epic hero, the Baron sings of his mighty conquest, observing that while men and monuments shall pass away, his name shall live forever.

? Why is the Baron's attitude amusing? How long will the Baron's reputation really last—and how can you tell?

from **Canto V**

..."To arms, to arms!" the fierce virago° cries,
And swift as lightning to the combat flies.
All side in parties, and begin th' attack;
Fans clap, silks rustle, and tough whalebones° crack;
5 Heroes' and heroines' shouts confus'dly rise,
And bass and treble voices strike the skies.
No common weapons in their hands are found,
Like gods they fight, nor dread a mortal wound.°...
    See, fierce Belinda on the Baron flies,
10 With more than usual lightning in her eyes:
Nor feared the chief th' unequal fight to try,

? **1–8.** What is being described in these lines?

---

99. **date** *n.*: destruction.
1. **virago** *n.*: ferocious woman; here, Belinda's girlfriend, who leads the attack on the Baron and his friends.
4. **whalebones** *n. pl.*: Whalebones were used to shape and stiffen women's clothing.
8. **like gods ... mortal wound:** Like gods, who are immortal and have no fear of physical wounds, these fighters do not fear the wounds inflicted by words.

Alexander Pope   457

DIRECT TEACHING

A Literary Focus
? Mock epic. What other revenge does Belinda threaten to take? [She threatens to stab the Baron with a hairpin.]

B Literary Focus
? Mock epic. What scene from a classical epic does this speech parody? [It parodies the typical speech of a brave warrior who has performed well in battle but suffered a mortal wound.]

C Reading Skills
? Comparing and contrasting. Based on the information in the gloss, why does Pope compare Belinda's cries to those of Othello? [He mocks Belinda by equating her hurt feelings over a snipped curl with Othello's anguish at his wife's supposed betrayal.]

D Reading Skills
? Interpreting. What do you think Pope is saying about the intelligence of beaux in ll. 41–42? [Possible responses: Pope implies that the gentlemen are unintelligent (since their wits fit into such small boxes); or that a society that develops such elaborate cases for snuff and tweezers must be vain and frivolous.]

Responses to Margin Questions
Lines 9–20. In a true epic, the main characters would clash together in a fight to the death; in this mock battle, the weapons are snuff and a hairpin, and Belinda's victory takes the form of making the Baron sneeze.

Lines 29–38. Belinda cries for her lock to be replaced, but fate (or Heaven) determines that it is too precious for ordinary humans to keep.

Who sought no more than on his foe to die.
But this bold lord with manly strength endued,
She with one finger and a thumb subdued:
15 Just where the breath of life his nostrils drew,
A charge of snuff the wily virgin threw;
The gnomes direct, to every atom just,
The pungent grains of titillating dust.
Sudden with starting tears each eye o'erflows,
20 And the high dome re-echoes to his nose.
"Now meet thy fate," incensed Belinda cried,
And drew a deadly bodkin° from her side. . . .
"Boast not my fall," he cried, "insulting foe!
Thou by some other shalt be laid as low.
25 Nor think, to die dejects my lofty mind:
All that I dread is leaving you behind!
Rather than so, ah, let me still survive,
And burn in Cupid's flames—but burn alive."
"Restore the lock!" she cries; and all around
30 "Restore the lock!" the vaulted roofs rebound.
Not fierce Othello° in so loud a strain
Roared for the handkerchief that caused his pain.
But see how oft ambitious aims are crossed,
And chiefs contend till all the prize is lost!
35 The lock, obtained with guilt, and kept with pain,
In every place is sought, but sought in vain:
With such a prize no mortal must be blessed,
So Heaven decrees! with Heaven who can contest?
Some thought it mounted to the lunar sphere,
40 Since all things lost on earth are treasured there.
There heroes' wits are kept in ponderous vases,
And beaux'° in snuffboxes and tweezer cases.
There broken vows and deathbed alms are found,
And lovers' hearts with ends of riband bound. . . .
45 But trust the Muse—she saw it upward rise,
Though marked by none but quick, poetic eyes: . . .

---

22. **bodkin** *n.:* long, ornamental hairpin shaped like a dagger.
31. **Othello:** Shakespeare's tragic hero Othello gave his wife a handkerchief, which his enemy stole and then used as false evidence of the wife's unfaithfulness.
42. **beaux':** fashionable gentlemen's.

Vocabulary
titillating (tit″l·āt′iŋ) *v.* used as *adj.:* exciting; stimulating.
dejects (dē·jekts′) *v.:* casts down; dispirits.

9–20. Belinda revenges herself on the Baron by throwing snuff in his face to make him sneeze.
? How is this silly action in keeping with the **mock-epic** genre?

29–38. Paraphrase this verse paragraph. Why, according to the speaker, is the lock unable to be found?

458 Collection 4 The Restoration and the Eighteenth Century

Secondary Source

Mack on Pope's Mock Epic

In his biography *Alexander Pope,* Maynard Mack notes that the poet's description of aristocratic society in *The Rape of the Lock* "never allows us to forget that in such a world ethical judgments have reached a sad disarray. Hearts and necklaces, lapdogs and lovers, statesmanship and tea, queens and Indian screens, the hunger of jurymen and justice, Bibles and billets-doux: his verse entangles the trifling and the serious to reflect a similar entanglement in the society's mind. And it is just here, in the presentation of moral muddle, that the mock-heroic structure proves itself invaluable. By juxtaposing the contemporary with the heroic, the poet can emphasize both the epic proportions to which this society has magnified its trifles (such as the estrangement of families over a lock of hair) and also their real triviality. Furthermore, by the contrast

Sir Plume Demands the Restoration of the Lock (1854) by C. R. Leslie. Oil.
Private Collection.

A sudden star, it shot through liquid air,
And drew behind a radiant trail of hair.°. . .
   Then cease, bright nymph! to mourn thy ravished hair,
50 Which adds new glory to the shining sphere!
Not all the tresses that fair head can boast,
Shall draw such envy as the lock you lost.
For, after all the murders° of your eye,
When, after millions slain, yourself shall die;
55 When those fair suns shall set, as set they must,
And all those tresses shall be laid in dust,
This lock, the Muse shall consecrate to fame,
And midst the stars inscribe Belinda's name.

---

48. **trail of hair:** The word *comet* derives from a Greek word for "long-haired."
53. **murders** *n. pl.:* Just as Belinda's eyes are said to "eclipse the day" (Canto I, line 14), here they are said to murder the young men who admire her. Both compliments are ancient and overused in love poetry.

between the social ephemera that his verse licks up as it flows along—watches, sedan chairs, cosmetics, curling irons, men, monkeys, parrots, snuff boxes, bodkins—and the quite different world of heroic activity evoked through the epic parodies and the high style, he can remind us of the inexorable conditions of life, death, and self-giving that not even the most glittering civilization can afford to ignore."

PRETEACHING

Summary ⬌ at grade level

In this excerpt from the first two chapters of *Candide,* the reader meets the main character, Candide, who is growing up on the estate of Baron Thunder-ten-tronckh. When Candide is caught expressing amorous interest in the baron's daughter, Cunegonde, he is expelled from the estate. At first he wanders aimlessly, but he is soon captured by the Bulgarians, impressed into military service, and severely punished after his attempt at desertion.

Selection Starter

Motivate. Ask students to discuss what attitudes and institutions they think need to be reformed today. Encourage them to notice, as they read, if any of the same attitudes and institutions appear as objects of satire in *Candide.*

Skills Starter

Build prerequisite skills. Review with students the use of exaggeration and understatement as literary techniques and common logical fallacies, such as overgeneralization. If possible, bring in examples of political cartoons that use these and other satirical techniques.

Before You Read

from Candide

Make the Connection
Voltaire's *Candide* tells the tale of the woes that befall a naive young man named Candide. The novel's subtitle, "Optimism," reflects the fact that Candide is brought up to believe that his world is the best of all possible worlds. (Many people liked to believe this during the Enlightenment.) Candide and his beloved, Cunegonde, suffer a series of disasters, which Voltaire narrates with verve and wit. Yet the humor never obscures Voltaire's deeper messages: Optimism is foolish in a world where people's lives are all too often shaped by cruel social forces, and humankind and its social institutions stand in need of reform.

Literary Focus
Satire

Satire is a kind of writing that ridicules human weakness, vice, or folly in order to bring about social reform. Satires often try to persuade the reader to do or believe something by showing the opposing view as absurd, vicious, or inhumane. Expert satirists use a variety of tools to undermine their opponents' beliefs. As you read the excerpts from *Candide,* look for five techniques in particular: outrageous exaggerations, deadpan understatements, warped logic (absurdities dressed up as common sense), improbable situations, and ridiculous names.

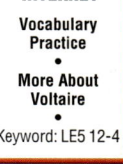

INTERNET
Vocabulary Practice
•
More About Voltaire
Keyword: LE5 12-4

SKILLS FOCUS

Literary Skills
Understand the characteristics of satire.

> **Satire** is a kind of writing that ridicules human weakness, vice, or folly in order to bring about social reform.
>
> *For more on Satire, see the Handbook of Literary and Historical Terms.*

Background
In the tumultuous social climate of eighteenth-century Europe, writers, scientists, and philosophers questioned accepted truths in ways they never had before. Yet direct challenges to authority can be dangerous. Thus satire, with its indirect criticism and deflating humor, became for many the weapon of choice. In *Candide,* Voltaire satirizes the calamities that befall Candide, an innocent who has been schooled by the repellent Doctor Pangloss to believe that everything happens for the best. In the first two chapters, Voltaire holds up for ridicule the castle and the army—two of the most important social institutions of eighteenth-century Europe. He also targets the theories of the German philosopher Gottfried Leibniz, who believed that a rational God made a rational world in which everything, including evil, has a place and a purpose. Voltaire's Doctor Pangloss directly echoes Leibniz every time he proclaims, "In this best of all possible worlds, . . . all is for the best."

Vocabulary Development

endowed (en·doud′) *v.* used as *adj.:* provided with.

candor (kan′dər) *n.:* honesty; directness.

pensive (pen′siv) *adj.:* reflective; thoughtful.

vivacity (vī·vas′ə·tē) *n.:* liveliness; high-spiritedness.

consternation (kän′stər·nā′shən) *n.:* bewilderment; dismay.

prodigy (präd′ə·jē) *n.:* someone gifted from childhood with an exceptional quality or talent.

clemency (klem′ən·sē) *n.:* mercy; leniency.

466 Collection 4 The Restoration and the Eighteenth Century

Previewing Vocabulary

To reinforce students' understanding of the Vocabulary words on p. 466, have them write responses to the following questions. (Possible responses are given.)

1. What does a person who is <u>endowed</u> with a sense of humor do? [He or she laughs a lot.]

2. When might a friend's <u>vivacity</u> be most welcome? [It might be welcome when a person is feeling sad or depressed.]

3. When does a person need <u>clemency</u>? [when he or she has done something wrong]

4. Why is <u>candor</u> a positive trait in a politician? [Voters want to know what a politician really thinks about issues.]

5. In what field was Mozart a <u>prodigy</u>? [He was a musical prodigy.]

6. What kind of facial expression would a <u>pensive</u> person have? [He or she would have a serious facial expression.]

7. Do <u>consternation</u> and joy go hand in hand? [No, they are opposites.]

from Candide

Voltaire
translated by Richard Aldington

Chapter I

How Candide was brought up in a noble castle and how he was expelled from the same

In the castle of Baron Thunder-ten-tronckh in Westphalia[1] there lived a youth, endowed by Nature with the most gentle character. His face was the expression of his soul. His judgment was quite honest and he was extremely simple-minded; and this was the reason, I think, that he was named Candide. Old servants in the house suspected that he was the son of the Baron's sister and a decent honest gentleman of the neighborhood, whom this young lady would never marry

---

1. **Westphalia** (west·fā′lē·ə): region in western Germany noted for its excellent ham. In a letter to his niece, Voltaire described Westphalia as "vast, sad, sterile, detestable."

Vocabulary
endowed (en·doud′) *v.* used as *adj.*: provided with.

Candide (played by Mark Baker) and his beloved Cunegonde (played by Maureen Brennan) in the 1974 Broadway revival of the musical *Candide*. © Martha Swope/TimePix.

DIRECT TEACHING

A Literary Focus

Satire. How is satire used in this passage? [Possible responses: Voltaire satirizes the notion of liberty, or free will, in a situation in which a person must choose between two evils. He also employs comic exaggeration in details such as running even twice (let alone thirty-six times) through a gauntlet composed of two thousand men and surviving four thousand strokes.]

B Literary Focus

Satire. What group is Voltaire satirizing in this passage, and how does he satirize them? [Possible response: He is satirizing philosophers. He says that Candide was ignorant in worldly matters because he was a metaphysician, but a metaphysician studies the nature of reality.]

GUIDED PRACTICE

Monitoring students' progress. Guide the class in answering these comprehension questions.

True-False

1. Candide is a deceptive person who tries to outwit the Baron. [F]
2. Dr. Pangloss is the tutor at the castle. [T]
3. Because Candide falls in love with the Baroness, he is sent away forever. [F]
4. Candide volunteers to serve in the Bulgarian army. [F]
5. Candide survives four thousand strokes as he runs the gauntlet. [T]

Dr. Pangloss (played by Lewis J. Stadlen), the greatest philosopher in the universe, in the 1974 Broadway revival of the musical *Candide*.

a choice; by virtue of that gift of God which is called liberty, he determined to run the gauntlet[10] thirty-six times and actually did so twice. There were two thousand men in the regiment. That made four thousand strokes which **A** laid bare the muscles and nerves from his neck to his backside. As they were about to proceed to a third turn, Candide, utterly exhausted, begged as a favor that they would be so kind as to smash his head; he obtained this favor; they bound his eyes and he was made to kneel down. At that moment the King of the Bulgarians came by and inquired the victim's crime, and as this King was possessed of a vast genius, he perceived from what he **B** learned about Candide that he was a young metaphysician[11] very ignorant in worldly matters, and therefore pardoned him with a clemency which will be praised in all newspapers and all ages. An honest surgeon healed Candide in three weeks with the ointments recommended by Dioscorides.[12] He had already regained a little skin and could walk when the King of the Bulgarians went to war with the King of the Abares.[13] ■

10. **run the gauntlet:** run between two rows of soldiers who strike the victim with clubs or other weapons.
11. **metaphysician** (met′ə·fə·zish′ən) *n.*: philosopher who studies the nature of reality and the origin and structure of the universe.
12. **Dioscorides** (dī′əs·kôr·ə·dēz′): Greek army physician who wrote a treatise on medicine in the first century A.D. Even in Voltaire's day, Dioscorides' work was out-of-date.
13. **Abares** (a·bär′): that is, the French, who fought against the "Bulgarians," or Prussians, in the Seven Years' War (1756–1763).

Vocabulary
clemency (klem′ən·sē) *n.*: mercy; leniency.

470   Collection 4   The Restoration and the Eighteenth Century

Comparing and Contrasting Texts

Tracing recurring themes. The theme of most satires is the folly and venality of human beings. Pope's *The Rape of the Lock* is in the tradition of Horace's gentle satire that pokes fun at human nature. Swift's *A Modest Proposal* is harsher, closer to the tradition of Juvenal's criticisms of society. Have students discuss the tone in *Candide*. To which tradition does it seem closer? Or is it a blend of the two?

Response and Analysis

Reading Check
1. Who is Candide and what do we know of his background and character? (Where did his name come from?)
2. What is Doctor Pangloss's philosophy?
3. Why is Candide expelled from the Baron's castle?
4. How does Candide become a soldier in the Bulgarian army?
5. Why is Candide sentenced to run the gauntlet?

Thinking Critically
6. **Satire** relies on many techniques usually associated with comedy. Five such techniques are exaggeration, understatement, warped logic, improbable situations, and ridiculous names. On a sheet of paper, draw a chart like the one below and list as many examples of each technique as you can find in this excerpt from *Candide*. Your list will be very long!

Exaggeration	
Understatement	
Warped Logic	
Improbable Situations	
Ridiculous Names	

7. Do people like Doctor Pangloss still exist in today's worlds of education, politics, or religion? Where and why do you still hear people saying things like "It's all for the best"?
8. How does Voltaire use **exaggeration** in Chapter II to satirize disciplinary practices in the Prussian Army? What point do you think he is trying to make?
9. As Chapter II illustrates, Candide suffers every time he exercises what he believes to be his free will. According to Voltaire, what forces get in the way of a person's exercise of free will?
10. What details of character and plot in *Candide* **parody,** or mock, the popular romances that still appear on today's bestseller lists or in the movies or on TV soap operas? Why do you think such romances continue to appeal to many people?

Extending and Evaluating
11. Voltaire wrote *Candide* more than 230 years ago. In your opinion, how well has his satire held up? What value, if any, does *Candide* hold for someone growing up in today's world? Does Voltaire's underlying message against intolerance, cruelty, and smugness still apply? Explain your response.

A cleric (played by Joe Palmieri) in the 1974 Broadway revival of the musical *Candide*.
© Martha Swope/TimePix.

SKILLS FOCUS

Literary Skills
Analyze the characteristics of satire. Compare satires from different cultures and literary periods.

Writing Skills
Write an essay analyzing a literary work. Write a brief play.

Vocabulary Skills
Understand the meanings and origins of words.

INDEPENDENT PRACTICE

Response and Analysis

Thinking Critically

6. Possible answers: *Exaggeration*—the family tree of the rejected suitor of the Baron's sister. *Understatement*—Dr. Pangloss's lesson in "experimental physics" to the maid. *Warped Logic*—Since this is the best of all possible worlds, the Baron's castle is the best of all castles. *Improbable Situations*—a military leader choosing soldiers by height. *Ridiculous Names*—Baron Thunder-ten-tronckh; Waldberghoff-trarbk-dikdorff.
7. Possible answers: Some politicians say it's all for the best when they can't solve a problem; some clergy say it's all for the best when they can't explain why bad things happen; some teachers say it's all for the best when students fail because the students will try harder.
8. Possible answer: Voltaire exaggerates the choices Candide is given (death or 72,000 lashes). His point is that military discipline is too harsh.
9. Institutions such as the military prevent people from exercising their free will.
10. The scenes in which Candide and Cunegonde meet, first outside the castle and then behind the screen, parody love scenes in popular romances. Such romances are appealing because they provide an escape from day-to-day life.

Extending and Evaluating

11. *Candide* is relevant today because there are still those who think they are better than others based on the circumstances of their birth; there are still institutions that punish instead of rehabilitate offenders.

Reading Check

1. Candide is a young man who lived in the castle of the Baron Thunder-ten-tronckh. He is rumored to be the son of the Baron's sister and a gentleman whom she refused to marry because of his genealogy. He is honest and simple-minded, and that is why he was named Candide.
2. There is no effect without a cause, and this is the best of all possible worlds.
3. He and Cunegonde, the Baron's daughter, are caught in an amorous embrace.
4. Two soldiers pay for his meal, make him drink to the King of Bulgaria, and then impress him into the Bulgarian army.
5. He is forced to choose between death and running the gauntlet after he tries to desert.

Comparing Literature

12. Possible answer: *Candide* and *The Rape of the Lock* are similar in that both use humor and irony to target the foolish attitudes and behaviors of the rich and powerful. *The Rape of the Lock* exaggerates the aristocracy's vanity by calling the cutting of a lock of hair a rape, while *Candide* exaggerates the injustices of society by making the "hero" a victim of its excesses. Pope uses ironic juxtaposition ("Dost sometimes counsel take—and sometimes tea") to belittle the rich, while Voltaire uses ridiculous names to the same end. Pope's tone is more lighthearted than Voltaire's, and his main goal appears to be to amuse in a witty way. Voltaire also appears to want to entertain his readers, but in addition, he wishes to expose society's ills.

Vocabulary Development

- **candor.** Meaning—honesty. Origin—L., *candere*, "to shine." Related Words—candid (adj.), candidly (adv.). Examples—direct answers, honest statements.
- **pensive.** Meaning—seriously thoughtful. Origin—L., *pensare*, "to consider." Related Words—pensively (adv.), pensiveness (n.). Examples—a person can look pensive.
- **vivacity.** Meaning—liveliness. Origin—L., *vivere*, "to live." Related Words—vivacious (adj.), vivaciously (adv.), vivaciousness (n.). Examples—people and animals can exhibit vivacity.
- **consternation.** Meaning—bewilderment; dismay. Origin—L., *consternere*, "to terrify." Related Words—consternate (v.). Examples—unusual behavior, unexpected natural phenomena.
- **prodigy.** Meaning—a child of unusual talent or genius. Origin—L., *pro-*, "before" + *agiom*, "a thing said." Related Words—prodigious (adj.), prodigiously (adv.), prodigiousness (n.). Examples—"Blind Tom" Bethune was a musical prodigy.

Comparing Literature

12. In what ways is Voltaire's satire like Alexander Pope's in *The Rape of the Lock* (see page 453)? Consider these techniques of satire as you compare the two texts:
- target of the satire
- use of humor
- use of exaggeration
- use of improbable situations
- use of ridiculous names
- expression of tone (lighthearted or bitter?)

WRITING

Analyzing Humor

Refer to the chart you filled out for question number 6 on page 471. Use the details you gathered on that chart to write a brief **analysis** of Voltaire's humor. When you analyze something, you take it apart and examine its elements to see how it works. The chart will show you many techniques used by Voltaire to ridicule his characters and to make us laugh. At the end of your essay, describe the targets of Voltaire's satire.

▶ Use "Writing a Literary Essay," pages 500–507, for help with this assignment.

Candide Onstage

In 1956, Leonard Bernstein and Richard Wilbur brought their musical comedy based on *Candide* to the Broadway stage. (The photographs in the text are from a later production of that musical.) Try your hand at adapting these two chapters of *Candide* as a **play** for the stage. You will have to identify your main characters and the sets. You can pick up a great deal of your dialogue from the text itself.

Program from a 1996 production of *Candide* at Arena Stage, Washington, D.C.
Illustration by Scott McKowen.

- **clemency.** Meaning—mercy; leniency. Origin—L., *clemens*, "merciful." Related Words—clement (adj.), clemently (adv.). Examples—a judge can show clemency.

Vocabulary Development

Word Information Charts

endowed	consternation
candor	prodigy
pensive	clemency
vivacity	

Using a dictionary, make a chart of basic information about each Vocabulary word listed above. The first one has been done for you.

endowed
• Meaning: "provided with"
• Origin: Old French *en-*, "in," and *dotare*, "to endow"
• Related Words: *endow* (v.); *endowment* (n.)
• Examples (things that can be endowed): money, talent, scholarships

ASSESSING

Assessment

- Holt Assessment: Literature, Reading, and Vocabulary

472 Collection 4 The Restoration and the Eighteenth Century

Miguel de Cervantes
(1547–1616)

Miguel de Cervantes.

Miguel de Cervantes (sər·vän'tēz'), son of a wandering apothecary, or druggist, was born near Madrid, Spain, in 1547. In 1569, Cervantes, seeing no prospects at home, enlisted in the army, fought valiantly, and was wounded at the Battle of Lepanto in 1571. His left hand was crippled, earning him the nickname *el manco de Lepanto*—"the one-handed man of Lepanto."

Cervantes hoped to be promoted to an army captain after the war, but his plans were ruined when he was captured by Barbary pirates and held as a slave for five years in Algeria. He returned to Spain in 1580, jobless, in debt, and without any hope of regaining his army career. Over the years he worked as a playwright, bureaucrat, and tax collector before finally landing in jail for failure to pay his debts. Many of those debts had accrued as a result of his family's scraping together the ransom money to buy his freedom from the pirates.

According to legend, it was while he was in jail that the idea for *Don Quixote* came to Cervantes. His hero, Don Quixote, is a poor, aging landowner who reads nothing but romantic tales of chivalry. As he teeters on the edge of insanity, the old man becomes convinced that he is a knight-errant, even though the age of knights is long past.

The Ingenious Gentleman Don Quixote of La Mancha was published in January of 1605 and immediately caused a sensation. Once the first edition sold out, pirated (illegally printed) copies began to appear. Six editions were issued in the first year, and translations into French and English appeared within ten years. It seemed that everyone in Spain, and soon everyone in Europe, was laughing at the adventures of the ridiculous knight Don Quixote.

Cervantes, at the age of fifty-eight, was now a famous author, but he was still poor. As was common until the nineteenth century, authors were at the mercy of publishers and were seldom able to retain the copyrights on their books. Thus, *Don Quixote*'s publisher, not Cervantes, reaped the lion's share of the book's profits. Spain's greatest writer died in poverty on April 22, 1616—one day before Shakespeare. To his family, Cervantes left many debts. To the world he left a comic masterpiece that earned him the title of father of the modern novel.

PRETEACHING

Summary ↔ at grade level

In this excerpt from Chapter 8, Don Quixote, whose quest for adventures has been inspired by his reading of medieval romances, fearlessly engages in "righteous warfare" with windmills that he perceives as "lawless giants." Badly battered by the first windmill's whirling vanes, Don Quixote brushes off the outcome of the encounter as "the fortunes of war" and attributes it to a non-existent magician. Aching but undeterred, he remounts the equally battered Rocinante and rides on in search of more adventures, the loyal Sancho Panza at his side.

Selection Starter

Build background. Review with students what they learned about chivalry and the chivalric code in Collection 2, and explain that by the time Cervantes wrote *Don Quixote*, chivalry was no longer important to most of Western Europe. The rise of the middle class, with its emphasis on commercial values; the emergence of nation-states; the growth of Protestantism; and the use of artillery in war were just four of many elements that cut down the flower of knighthood. Only in Spain did the aristocracy cling to the old values, and it is this reluctance to face reality and change that Cervantes mocks in the figure of Don Quixote.

Before You Read

from Don Quixote

Make the Connection

Don Quixote is a comic lampoon of the medieval romances that audiences of Cervantes's era continued to devour. But beneath the parody, *Don Quixote* makes a poignant comment on universal human qualities. Even as we laugh at Don Quixote, we realize that there is something of him in all of us. Like Don Quixote, who wished he had lived in an earlier age, and like Cervantes himself, who wished he were a military hero, most of us cherish unlikely dreams. In *Man of La Mancha*, Dale Wasserman's musical adaptation of *Don Quixote* for the stage, Quixote sings of his need "to dream the impossible dream." We can no more relinquish our dreams than he could, without giving up an important part of our inner selves.

The "impossible dream" aspect of Cervantes's novel led to a new adjective in English: *quixotic* (kwik·sät′ik). The word describes a dreamer who is well-intentioned but impractical. What quixotic heroes can you think of—from movies, comic strips, television shows, or books? What traits do they share? What keeps them going, no matter what happens?

Literary Focus

Parody

A literary **parody** is an imitation of a work of literature for amusement or instruction. Parodies often make the characteristics of someone or something seem ridiculous by transferring them to a ridiculous subject. To achieve this, parodies use exaggeration, verbal irony (saying one thing and meaning another), incongruity (deliberately pairing things that don't belong together), and humorously twisted imitation. Cervantes pokes fun at every aspect of the medieval romance and its heroic knights. Quixote sees himself as a knight of old, but his armor is rusty, his horse is a nag, and the giants he battles turn out to be windmills.

> **Parody** is the imitation of a work of literature for amusement or instruction.
>
> *For more on Parody, see the Handbook of Literary and Historical Terms.*

Background

Initially, Cervantes intended *Don Quixote* to lampoon tales of chivalry and courtly romances, stories from the medieval period about romantic love and knightly adventure, which were still eagerly read by the audience of Cervantes's time. In these stories, idealized knights fought villains, dragons, and monsters, and embarked on quests in honor of ladies to whom they had sworn their love. Such heroes stood for military values such as honor, courage, and loyalty, combined with Christian values such as piety, courtesy, and chastity.

> **Vocabulary Development**
>
> **succor** (suk′ər) *v.*: help in time of distress.
>
> **enmity** (en′mə·tē) *n.*: hostility.
>
> **victuals** (vit″lz) *n. pl.*: provisions; pieces of food.
>
> **vigil** (vij′əl) *n.*: staying watchfully awake.
>
> **flaccid** (flas′id) *adj.*: limp; flabby.
>
> **disposition** (dis′pə·zish′ən) *n.*: natural qualities of personality.

INTERNET
Vocabulary Practice
•
More About Miguel de Cervantes
•
Keyword: LE5 12-4

SKILLS FOCUS
Literary Skills
Understand the characteristics of parody.

474 Collection 4 The Restoration and the Eighteenth Century

Previewing Vocabulary

Have pairs of students take turns reading aloud the definitions of the Vocabulary words on p. 474. Then, have them work together on the following exercises to reinforce their understanding of the words.

1. Name a community organization whose volunteers <u>succor</u> others. [the Red Cross]

2. Suggest two ways people can avoid provoking their neighbors' <u>enmity</u>. [Don't play loud music; return borrowed items.]

3. List three of your favorite <u>victuals</u>. [corn on the cob; mashed potatoes; roasted chicken]

4. Describe a situation in which you might take part in a <u>vigil</u>. [staying awake until midnight on New Year's eve]

5. How would you try to revive a <u>flaccid</u> houseplant? [by watering it]

6. Suggest a nickname for someone with a cheerful <u>disposition</u>. [Sunny]

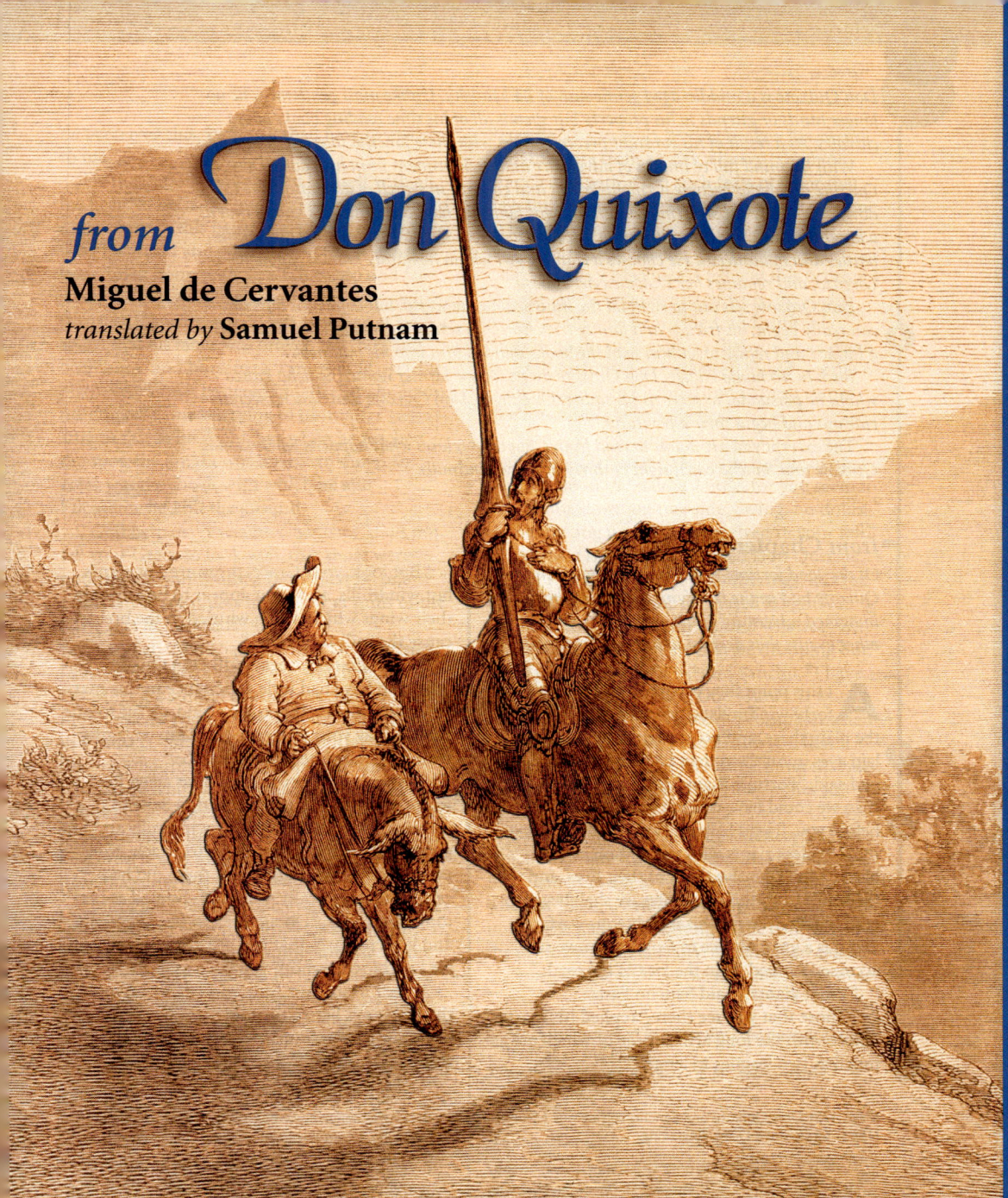

from Don Quixote

Miguel de Cervantes
translated by **Samuel Putnam**

DIRECT TEACHING

VIEWING THE ART

Gustave Doré (1832–1883) engraved many illustrations to accompany literature. This engraving depicts Don Quixote and his squire, Sancho Panza. Don Quixote believes he lives in a world that mirrors the one described in medieval romances. The world in which Don Quixote lives is very different from the one described in the romances, yet he always seems to see the world that he expects to see—the medieval world of romance.

Activity. What elements in the picture show the difference between Don Quixote's view of the world and Sancho Panza's? How do the images of Don Quixote and Sancho Panza compare to those of the Knight and the Squire in Blake's depiction of pilgrims from *The Canterbury Tales* on p. 122? [Don Quixote is dressed as a knight in shining armor and is riding a healthy-looking horse. This image reflects his idealistic, romantic nature. Sancho Panza is dressed as who he is (a poor farmer), indicating his more realistic view of the world.

Chaucer's Knight and Squire are both depicted as gallant and authentic. Unlike Don Quixote, Chaucer's Knight fights in real battles during the Crusades, rather than imaginary ones against windmills.]

DIFFERENTIATING INSTRUCTION

Learners Having Difficulty
Check students' comprehension of the selection paragraph by paragraph. Point out that this excerpt begins with a conversation between Don Quixote and Sancho Panza about the windmills. If students need help following the dialogue, label each speech with the appropriate character's name. Be sure students understand that Sancho Panza calls his master "your Grace."

Invite learners having difficulty to read from *Don Quixote* in interactive format in *The Holt Reader* and to use the sidenotes as aids to understanding the selection.

English-Language Learners
Remind students that Don Quixote imagines himself as a knight-errant. As such, he carries a shield and a lance, a fourteen-foot wooden spear tipped with steel that was used for jousting or tilting with the enemy.

Advanced Learners
Enrichment. Encourage students to read and discuss additional chapters of *Don Quixote*. They might also read Mark Twain's *A Connecticut Yankee in King Arthur's Court* (1889) and compare and contrast these parodies of romance literature written nearly three centuries apart.

Miguel de Cervantes

DIRECT TEACHING

VIEWING THE ART

Doré's engraving of the windmill episode illustrates Quixote's folly by confirming Sancho's perspective.

Activity. How does Doré's illustration confirm Sancho's perspective? [He shows Don Quixote being whacked by the windmill vane as Sancho observes the event with resigned quietude.]

The adventure with the windmills (c. 1868) by Gustave Doré. Engraving.
The Bridgeman Art Library.

Literary Criticism

Critic's Commentary: Contrasts in Don Quixote

The critic Gerald Brenan, in his essay on Cervantes, points out that "... there is the contrast between the actual situation and what it appears to be to Don Quixote, there is that between his noble and exalted way of feeling and Sancho's peasant shrewdness and self-interest; and ... that between the knight's wise and sane ratiocinations and the violent fantasies whenever the subject of Chivalry enters his head. Every situation that turns up brings at least two of these into play, and the reader is kept in suspense until he knows precisely how it will be decided. By this means, the weakness inherent in the picaresque form—a chain of events loosely strung together—is overcome and the greatest concentration brought to bear on each incident. Note too—a stylistic contrast—that this madness of the principal character has a language of its own. The archaic magniloquence of the books of Chivalry provides a sort of upper floor of pomp and imagery ... rising out of the plain and habitable level of Cervantes' prose."

Activity. As students read, have them look for contrasts that tie the various scenes of the episode together.

to eat. The knight replied that he himself had no need of food at the moment, but his squire might eat whenever he chose. Having been granted this permission, Sancho seated himself as best he could upon his beast, and, taking out from his saddlebags the provisions that he had stored there, he rode along leisurely behind his master, munching his victuals and taking a good, hearty swig now and then at the leather flask in a manner that might well have caused the biggest-bellied tavern-keeper of Málaga to envy him. Between drafts he gave not so much as a thought to any promise that his master might have made him, nor did he look upon it as any hardship, but rather as good sport, to go in quest of adventures however hazardous they might be.

The short of the matter is, they spent the night under some trees, from one of which Don Quixote tore off a withered bough to serve him as a lance, placing it in the lance head from which he had removed the broken one. He did not sleep all night long for thinking of his lady Dulcinea; for this was in accordance with what he had read in his books, of men of arms in the forest or desert places who kept a wakeful vigil, sustained by the memory of their ladies fair. Not so with Sancho, whose stomach was full, and not with chicory water.[4] He fell into a dreamless slumber, and had not his master called him, he would not have been awakened either by the rays of the sun in his face or by the many birds who greeted the coming of the new day with their merry song.

Upon arising, he had another go at the flask, finding it somewhat more flaccid than it had been the night before, a circumstance which grieved his heart, for he could not see that they were on the way to remedying the deficiency within any very short space of time. Don Quixote did not wish any breakfast; for, as has been said, he was in the habit of nourishing himself on savorous memories. They then set out once more along the road to Puerto Lápice, and around three in the afternoon they came in sight of the pass that bears that name.

"There," said Don Quixote as his eyes fell upon it, "we may plunge our arms up to the elbow in what are known as adventures. But I must warn you that even though you see me in the greatest peril in the world, you are not to lay hand upon your sword to defend me, unless it be that those who attack me are rabble and men of low degree, in which case you may very well come to my aid; but if they be gentlemen, it is in no wise permitted by the laws of chivalry that you should assist me until you yourself shall have been dubbed a knight."

"Most certainly, sir," replied Sancho, "your Grace shall be very well obeyed in this; all the more so for the reason that I myself am of a peaceful disposition and not fond of meddling in the quarrels and feuds of others. However, when it comes to protecting my own person, I shall not take account of those laws of which you speak, seeing that all laws, human and divine, permit each one to defend himself whenever he is attacked."

"I am willing to grant you that," assented Don Quixote, "but in this matter of defending me against gentlemen you must restrain your natural impulses."

"I promise you I shall do so," said Sancho. "I will observe this precept as I would the Sabbath day...." ∎

Vocabulary

victuals (vit″lz) *n. pl.*: provisions; food.
vigil (vij′əl) *n.*: staying watchfully awake.
flaccid (flas′id) *adj.*: limp; flabby.
disposition (dis′pə·zish′ən) *n.*: natural qualities of personality.

---

4. **chicory water:** inexpensive coffee substitute.

Miguel de Cervantes 479

INDEPENDENT PRACTICE

Response and Analysis

Reading Check

1. He says the magician Frestón transformed the giants to deprive him of a glorious victory.
2. Don Quixote ignores the need for food, drink, and sleep. Sancho Panza eats heartily, drinks his fill, and sleeps soundly.

Thinking Critically

3. Possible answers: *exaggeration*—some of the windmills' vanes are "two leagues in length"; *verbal irony*—Don Quixote laughs at Sancho's "simplicity" as if Sancho were the ridiculous one, when the servant seems far more sensible than Don Quixote; *incongruity*— the pairing of Don Quixote and Sancho Panza; *humorous imitation*—Rocinante, a far cry from a noble steed.
4. Possible answers: Knights may not complain of their wounds; they should go without food or sleep, surviving on memories of their courtly love; a squire may not defend his knight against gentlemen.
5. Possible answer: Don Quixote is an idealist, as shown by his passionate commitment to the chivalric code and his penchant for seeing the world as he wants it to be (windmills as giants). Sancho Panza is a realist, as shown by his commitment to self-preservation and his practicality in seeing the world as it is (windmills as windmills).
6. Don Quixote is ascetic, depriving himself of food and sleep; he is motivated by glory and service, seeking to demonstrate his nobility by defeating the "lawless." Sancho Panza is sybaritic, freely indulging his appetites for food, drink, and sleep; he is motivated by a thirst for adventure but is determined to protect himself from harm.

Response and Analysis

Reading Check

1. After being knocked down by the windmill, how does Don Quixote explain the fact that he has not killed a giant?
2. What natural human needs does Don Quixote ignore? How does Sancho Panza, in contrast, satisfy those same needs?

Thinking Critically

3. In his **parody**, Cervantes uses the techniques of **exaggeration, verbal irony, incongruity,** and **humorous imitation.** List one example of each technique used in this selection.
4. Cervantes directly pokes fun at the medieval romance every time Don Quixote obeys one of the rules of knighthood, or "ordinances of chivalry," as he understands them. List three such "rules" that Don Quixote cites.
5. Put simply, an idealist, or romantic, views the world as he or she thinks it ought to be; a realist views the world as it is. Is Don Quixote an idealist or a realist? Which role does Sancho Panza fit? Cite evidence from the text to support your conclusions.
6. A **foil** is a character who is used as a contrast to another character. In what ways is Sancho Panza a foil to Don Quixote? Identify the behaviors of the two men that suggest they are opposites.

SKILLS FOCUS

Literary Skills Analyze the characteristics of parody. Compare works from different cultures and literary periods.

Writing Skills Write a parody.

Vocabulary Skills Demonstrate word knowledge.

Comparing Literature

7. How does Don Quixote's optimism and idealism compare with Candide's (see page 467)? Do both of these characters "tilt at windmills," or do they manifest their philosophies in profoundly different ways? Explain your responses.
8. Cervantes parodies the medieval romance in *Don Quixote*, and Alexander Pope mocks the literary epic in *The Rape of the Lock* (see page 453). What satiric techniques do these two lampoons share?

Don Quixote and the windmill (detail) by Gustave Doré.
Giraudon/Art Resource, New York.
Bibliothèque Nationale, Paris, France.

Comparing Literature

7. Possible answer: The two protagonists are actually quite different. Unlike Candide, Don Quixote is well aware of the existence of evil in the world; indeed, Don Quixote is so intent on righting wrongs that his senses deceive him, as when he mistakes the windmills for "lawless giants." His optimism, the result of reading too many romances, takes the form of believing that he is invincible; Candide's optimism, the result of Pangloss's logically warped teachings, takes the form of naiveté, which gradually gives way to wisdom as he learns through experience that this is not "the best of all possible worlds."
8. Possible answer: Both writers use exaggeration, understatement, verbal irony, incongruity, and twisted imitation.

WRITING

A Modern-Day Parody

Imagine Cervantes writing a parody today. Select some form of written communication that you imagine he would relish lampooning, and then write a **parody** of your own. You may choose from such forms of writing as the multiple-choice test, the memoir, the business memo, the advice-column letter, or the political-campaign speech. Before you begin writing your parody, decide what the target of your satire will be. Then, use one or more of Cervantes's tools—exaggeration, verbal irony, incongruity, humorous imitation—to write a parody of your own.

Vocabulary Development
Question and Answer Charts

succor   victuals   flaccid
enmity   vigil   disposition

Work with a group or alone to find out what you know about the meanings of the Vocabulary words listed above. Make up two questions about each word, and organize your answers in a chart. After you've completed charts for all the words, invite someone else to answer your questions. The first word has been done for you.

succor	
Questions	Answers
How would you succor someone who has been injured?	• get medical help • try to make him or her comfortable
In what situations might you be required to succor someone?	• when someone falls off a horse • when someone faints

Vocabulary Development

- **enmity**. Questions—If you felt enmity for someone, how would you get over it? If someone felt enmity for you, how would you appease the person?

- **victuals**. Questions—What are your favorite victuals? What restaurant serves those victuals?

- **vigil**. Questions—If you were keeping a vigil, whom would you want with you? Where might you keep a vigil?

- **flaccid**. Questions—If you were hiking in the desert, why wouldn't you want your water canteen to be flaccid? How might you improve flaccid muscles in your body?

- **disposition**. Questions—How would you describe your disposition? Whose disposition do you admire most?

ASSESSING

Assessment
- Holt Assessment: Literature, Reading, and Vocabulary

Political Points of View

SKILLS FOCUS, pp. 482–498

Grade-Level Skills

■ **Literary Skills**
Analyze political points of view in a selection of literary works on a topic.

■ **Reading Skills**
Analyze the way authors use the features and rhetorical devices of public documents.

Political Issue: Women's Rights

You might point out that today women's rights vary by country, including the rights to attend school, work outside the home, to own property, to vote, to choose a marriage partner, and to divorce. Invite students to share what they know about these variations.

Skills Starter

Build prerequisite skills. To help students identify political assumptions, remind them that an assumption is an underlying idea that a speaker or writer accepts as needing no proof. Ask students what assumptions about laws might underlie the following statements:

- You'd better not do that because it's against the law. [Disobeying the law is undesirable.]
- It's all right to discriminate against certain groups if the law doesn't prohibit it. [Any behavior not prohibited by law is acceptable.]

Introducing Political Points of View

Women's Rights

Main Reading
Mary Wollstonecraft ..... from **A Vindication of the Rights of Woman** ... 487

Connected Readings
Mary, Lady Chudleigh .... **To the Ladies** 494
Daniel Defoe .... from **The Education of Women** 495

You will be reading the three selections listed above in this Political Points of View feature on women's rights. In the top corner of the pages in this feature, you'll find three stars. Smaller versions of the stars appear next to the questions on page 492 that focus on women's rights. At the end of the feature (page 498), you'll compare the various points of view expressed in the selections.

Examining the Issue: Women's Rights

The women's rights movement, an ongoing series of political movements aimed at attaining educational, social, and political equality for women, arose primarily in England and the United States. Its roots lay both in humanistic thought (see page 242) and in the Industrial Revolution of the eighteenth and nineteenth centuries—two important influences that, in very different ways, contributed to the creation of a more democratic society.

According to the dictates of both theology and law, married women of the eighteenth century still could not own property, run a business, or control their own lives or those of their children. Social critics (both male and female) began to contrast this state of affairs with the ideal of freedom that inspired the American and French Revolutions of the late eighteenth century. Since then, there have been countless advances and setbacks in campaigns for the rights of women to study, to own property, to vote, to pursue a career, and, in general, to control their own lives. The readings in this Political Points of View feature present some of the earliest shots fired in the battle for women's rights.

Pages 482–498 cover
Literary Skills Analyze political points of view on a topic.
Reading Skills Understand and analyze rhetorical devices.

Make the Connection
Quickwrite
The basic concept behind the issue of women's rights is that women and men are equally human and should have equal stature in society. Few westerners now challenge that concept, yet many dislike or reject such labels as "feminism," preferring instead to speak of "human rights" or "women's rights." What do these three labels mean to you? Write a brief explanation of which term you find most meaningful and why you prefer it over the other two terms.

482 Collection 4 The Restoration and the Eighteenth Century

Reading Skills

Analyzing Rhetorical Devices

Rhetorical devices are methods writers or speakers use to make their language more effective or to reinforce a particular point. Rhetorical devices are particularly important in any kind of communication that seeks to win the reader over to a writer's point of view. Speeches, policy statements, debates, political and religious tracts, arguments, persuasive essays, and many other kinds of public documents freely employ a variety of rhetorical devices, such as the following:

- **rhetorical question:** The writer, for effect, asks a question for which an answer is not expected—usually because the writer expects that the audience will agree with the opinion being expressed.
- **argument by analogy:** The writer points out a parallel between two subjects or situations in order to make a point.
- **historical allusion:** The writer cites a person, a place, or an event from history that relates to the topic at hand.
- **repetition** or **restatement:** The writer repeats the main idea in different ways.
- **counterargument:** The writer anticipates the audience's objections or concerns and openly addresses them.
- **appeal to authority:** The writer cites the opinions of experts on the subject.
- **illustrative anecdote or example:** The writer uses a brief story or cites a particular case in order to support his or her point.

In the following selections on the topic of women's rights, be alert for various rhetorical devices. How does each writer use them to reinforce his or her main points?

The Art Class (late 19th century) by Arturo Ricci.
© Christie's Images/CORBIS.

VIEWING THE ART

Arturo Ricci (1854–1919) was a late-Victorian artist who looked to the eighteenth century, rather than the artistic fashions of his day, for inspiration. Here he uses a touch of satire in his depiction of a group of fashionably dressed men and women taking an art class.

Activity. Identify satirical elements in the picture. [Possible response: the students' formal, elaborate attire and the flirtation taking place at the left, which suggest dilettantism and a lack of seriousness.]

Women's Rights 483

SKILLS FOCUS, pp. 484–493

Grade-Level Skills

Literary Skills

Analyze the way an author's tone and use of connotations achieves specific rhetorical purposes.

Reading Skills

Analyze the way patterns of organization, repetition of main ideas, and word choice affect the meaning of a text.

More About the Writer

Background. Intelligent, warm, and courageous, Mary Wollstonecraft lived briefly but intensely. Her diverse circle of London friends included radical theologian and chemist Joseph Priestley, first to isolate oxygen; poet and artist William Blake (see pp. 534–547); and artist Henry Fuseli (Johann Heinrich Füssli)—all progressive thinkers and innovators. During the French Revolution, Wollstonecraft moved to Paris, where she earned the respect of political leaders but began a disastrous relationship with American adventurer Gilbert Imlay. In 1794, Wollstonecraft and Imlay returned to England together, where she continued writing, and her fame grew. Within two years, however, Imlay had deserted her. In 1797, Wollstonecraft married William Godwin, although neither believed in marriage. That year she bore their daughter Mary, contracted septicemia, and died at age thirty-eight.

Mary Wollstonecraft
(1759–1797)

Mary Wollstonecraft Godwin (c. 1797) by John Opie. Engraving after painting.
The Granger Collection, New York.

English feminism begins with Mary Wollstonecraft, who demanded "JUSTICE for one half of the human race"—that is, women. The last place Wollstonecraft felt she would ever find justice in eighteenth-century England was in the institution of marriage. "I will not marry," she announced, a decision born from years of emotionally and physically protecting her mother from the abuse and anger of a husband and father who had squandered his fortune in futile attempts to become a successful gentleman farmer. Wollstonecraft's upbringing had left her with good reason to distrust the bond of marriage.

Nineteen and self-educated, Wollstonecraft left home to work in some of the few occupations legally available to single women. Eventually, she became a governess for a wealthy Irish family and witnessed the "dissipated lives the women of quality lead," with their single-minded obsession with "matrimony and dress."

Wollstonecraft left Ireland and moved to London to work as an editorial assistant. There she met some of the radical political thinkers of the day, including Thomas Paine, an American agitator and patriot, and William Godwin, a political philosopher. (At a dinner party, Wollstonecraft and Godwin disagreed with each other on every topic discussed.)

In 1789, the French Revolution erupted, an upheaval that terrified monarchs in Europe and thrilled radicals with its slogan "liberty, equality, fraternity." Wollstonecraft published *A Vindication of the Rights of Men* (1790), which vigorously defended the principles of human equality underlying the French Revolution. She then topped that with her masterpiece, *A Vindication of the Rights of Woman* (1792), an impassioned criticism of social and economic institutions that sanctioned women's inequality. Critics—especially those who refused to read her book or answer her arguments—attacked her swiftly; one critic called her "a hyena in petticoats."

Eventually—and ironically—Wollstonecraft became romantically involved with William Godwin, the dinner companion with whom she had argued vehemently years before. Godwin had spent years arguing for the abolition of all institutions, especially government, organized religion, and marriage. The two put aside their objections, however, and married, discovering to their delight that they were very happy with each other.

Such domestic joy, however, was short-lived; eleven days after giving birth to their daughter, Mary Wollstonecraft died from septicemia, the result of a botched operation to correct a complication from her pregnancy. Daughter Mary survived, grew up to marry the poet Percy Bysshe Shelley, and wrote the famous novel *Frankenstein* (1818). William Godwin erected a stone at Wollstonecraft's grave with the inscription: "Mary Wollstonecraft Godwin, Author of *A Vindication of the Rights of Woman*." No other words were necessary.

RESOURCES: READING

Planning
- *One-Stop Planner* CD-ROM with ExamView Test Generator

Differentiating Instruction
- Supporting Instruction in Spanish
- Audio CD Library
- Audio CD Library, Selections and Summaries in Spanish

Vocabulary
- Vocabulary Development

Grammar and Language
- Language Handbook Worksheets
- Daily Language Activities

Assessment
- Holt Assessment: Literature, Reading, and Vocabulary
- Holt Online Assessment

- *One-Stop Planner* CD-ROM with ExamView Test Generator

Internet
- go.hrw.com (Keyword: LE5 12-4)
- Elements of Literature Online

Media
- Audio CD Library
- Audio CD Library, Selections and Summaries in Spanish

Before You Read

from *A Vindication of the Rights of Woman*

Political Points of View

In much of today's world, the same educational opportunities are available to both genders. Women share the vote with men, and women may study for and pursue virtually any career they wish. These opportunities, often taken for granted, were not always available to women. In England, during the Restoration, the educated woman was the exception to the rule, and women were not allowed to vote. Keep these facts in mind as you read this excerpt from a famous feminist's essay. How much of what she says still rings true today? How far have we—or haven't we—come since the late 1700s?

Literary Focus

Tone

Tone is the attitude a writer takes toward the reader or toward his or her topic. Writers establish tone through the careful choice of details and words. One way that writers control tone is through the use of words with specific **connotations**—those associations and emotions that have come to be attached to a word through usage. For example, the words *economical* and *frugal* are both synonyms for *thrifty*, but *economical* connotes that a person is simply managing expenditures so as to avoid wasting money, while *frugal* connotes that a person has cut down on all but necessary expenses and is counting every penny. Be alert to Wollstonecraft's choice of "loaded" words—words with strong connotations.

> **Tone** is the attitude a writer takes toward the reader, the subject, or a character.
>
> *For more on Tone, see the Handbook of Literary and Historical Terms.*

Reading Skills

Noting Patterns of Organization

Persuasive arguments, like the ones in this famous essay, usually state a position, clarify that position, offer supporting arguments for it, and conclude by restating the position or making recommendations or judgments based upon it. The excerpt that follows is the introduction to Wollstonecraft's essay. Introductions typically prepare the reader for the text that follows, by explaining why the text is called for and presenting its arguments in brief form. As you read the introduction, take note of sections that explain why the essay as a whole is necessary and sections that present an overview of the arguments the essay will propose.

The word *vindication* is used here to mean "justification."

Vocabulary Development

solicitude (sə·lis′ə·tōōd′) *n*.: care; concern.

partial (pär′shəl) *adj*.: biased.

deplore (dē·plôr′) *v*.: regret; strongly disapprove of.

fastidious (fa·stid′ē·əs) *adj*.: picky; overly fussy.

specious (spē′shəs) *adj*.: showy but false; lacking genuineness.

abrogated (ab′rə·gāt′id) *v*. used as *adj*.: abolished; repealed.

cursory (kʉr′sə·rē) *adj*.: hasty; superficial.

vitiate (vish′ē·āt) *v*.: impair; weaken; spoil.

insipid (in·sip′id) *adj*.: dull; flat.

propensity (prə·pen′sə·tē) *n*.: natural inclination or tendency.

INTERNET
Vocabulary Practice
•
More About Mary Wollstonecraft
•
Keyword: LE5 12-4

SKILLS FOCUS

Literary Skills Analyze political points of view on a topic. Understand tone and connotations.

Reading Skills Understand patterns of organization.

Mary Wollstonecraft 485

PRETEACHING

Summary ⬆ *above grade level*

> Mary Wollstonecraft's words sparkle with wit, her satirical tone combining irony and impassioned sincerity. In this introduction to her essay on women's rights, Wollstonecraft focuses on women as wives and mothers and on educational equality, in keeping with the political realities of her time. She first posits the essay's main idea: denying women an education impairs their "usefulness" as well as their happiness. She then sketches the essay's organization, noting that she will consider women as human beings first, females second, and that she will differentiate between the situations of upper-class and middle-class women. She also summarizes her arguments: conventional notions of femininity rob women of integrity and dignity; strength of character is women's greatest need (education can provide it); people fear women's gaining "too much courage or fortitude," but women's relative physical weakness makes that unlikely; and if men are "chaste and modest," women will be also.

Skills Starter

Build prerequisite skills. Remind students that they can describe tone with the same words they use to describe attitudes: *sincere, facetious, bitter, respectful,* and so on. Ask students to list more words that can describe tone and to apply the words to the selections they have recently read.

Previewing Vocabulary

After discussing the Vocabulary words on p. 485, have students use them to solve the following acrostics. Letters with double underlines will spell a key issue in Wollstonecraft's essay.

1. d e _ l _ _ _ _ [deplore]
2. _ _ s t _ _ _ o _ _ [fastidious]
3. _ _ r _ _ _ y [cursory]
4. _ p _ _ _ o _ s [specious]
5. _ b _ _ g _ _ e _ [abrogated]
6. v _ _ i _ _ _ [vitiate]
7. _ a _ _ _ _ l [partial]
8. _ r _ p _ n _ _ _ y [propensity]
9. i _ _ i _ _ d [insipid]
10. _ o _ _ c _ _ u d _ [solicitude]

[Hidden word: *education*]

Mary Wollstonecraft 485

VIEWING THE ART

John Highmore (1692–1780) painted twelve scenes based on Samuel Richardson's *Pamela, or Virtue Rewarded* (1744), a novel in which Pamela, a servant girl, wards off the advances of her master, Mr. B. The novel takes the form of letters between the characters and of Pamela's journal, which Mr. B reads without her permission. Ultimately, Mr. B proposes marriage, Pamela accepts, and her virtue is thus rewarded with social advancement. The novel suggests that women who keep in their place will be rewarded for doing so.

Activity. Invite students to make up a dialogue between Pamela and Mr. B to accompany the painting. Then, ask students to discuss what Mary Wollstonecraft might have thought of Richardson's story.

Mr. B. Finds Pamela Writing (18th century) by Joseph Highmore. Illustration for *Pamela, or Virtue Rewarded* (1740) by Samuel Richardson. Oil on canvas.
Pamela is the servant of Mr. B's mother. The novel involves Mr. B's dishonorable pursuit of Pamela.
The Bridgeman Art Library.

486 Collection 4 The Restoration and the Eighteenth Century

READING MINI-LESSON

Developing Word-Attack Skills
Display this sentence from the essay:

One cause of this barren blooming I <u>attribute</u> to a false system of education.

Ask students what part of speech *attribute* is and how it is pronounced. (verb; /ə·trib′yōōt/) Then, display this sentence:

False refinement is hardly a desirable <u>attribute</u>.

Ask students to tell what part of speech *attribute* is in this sentence and how it is pronounced. (noun; /a′trə·byōōt′/)

Explain that many words are pronounced differently depending on their part of speech.
Activity. Have students pronounce each underlined word correctly and give its part of speech.

1. How should girls <u>conduct</u> themselves? [/kən·dukt′/ verb]

   The rules of <u>conduct</u> have changed. [/kän′dukt′/ noun]

2. Indignation is <u>precedent</u> to change. [/prē·sēd′nt/; adjective]

   Women's suffrage set a <u>precedent</u>. [/pres′ə·dənt/; noun]

3. They never <u>deviate</u> from their goal. [/dē′vē·āt/; verb]

   Take a <u>deviate</u> route. [/dē′vē·it/; adjective]

486 Collection 4 The Restoration and the Eighteenth Century

from A Vindication of the Rights of Woman

Mary Wollstonecraft

Introduction

After considering the historic page, and viewing the living world with anxious solicitude, the most melancholy emotions of sorrowful indignation have depressed my spirits, and I have sighed when obliged to confess, that either nature has made a great difference between man and man, or that the civilization which has hitherto taken place in the world has been very partial. I have turned over various books written on the subject of education, and patiently observed the conduct of parents and the management of schools; but what has been the result?—a profound conviction that the neglected education of my fellow-creatures is the grand source of the misery I deplore; and that women, in particular, are rendered weak and wretched by a variety of concurring causes, originating from one hasty conclusion. The conduct and manners of women, in fact, evidently prove that their minds are not in a healthy state; for, like the flowers which are planted in too rich a soil, strength and usefulness are sacrificed to beauty; and the flaunting leaves, after having pleased a fastidious eye, fade, disregarded on the stalk, long before the season when they ought to have arrived at maturity. —One cause of this barren blooming I attribute to a false system of education, gathered from the books written on this subject by men who, considering females rather as women than human creatures, have been more anxious to make them alluring mistresses than affectionate wives and rational mothers;

> In the first paragraph, Wollstonecraft sets up her argument by asserting that women are denied proper educations.
>
> **?** What loaded words does she use in this opening paragraph?

Vocabulary

solicitude (sə·lis′ə·tōōd′) *n.*: care; concern.
partial (pär′shəl) *adj.*: biased.
deplore (dē·plôr′) *v.*: regret; strongly disapprove of.
fastidious (fa·stid′ē·əs) *adj.*: picky; overly fussy.

DIRECT TEACHING

A English-Language Learners

❓ **Archaic language.** In eighteenth-century English, *the sex* meant "women." What does this clause say about women? [Possible response: Women have been misled into valuing male adoration over respect for "nobler" abilities.]

B Political Issue

❓ **Women's rights.** Here the author discusses her purposes in writing. What issue does she say she does not intend to "agitate"? [the issue of women's equality or inferiority to men]

C Literary Focus

❓ **Tone.** What irony do you find in the author's denial of a desire to stir up controversy about gender equality? [Possible response: The irony is that in the preceding paragraph, she has begun to attack the issue of equality, and she continues her attack after denying that she intends to do so.]

D Reading Skills

❓ **Rhetorical question.** Here she poses the rhetorical question *Where are the masculine women?* What is her point? [She is saying that women should try to attain nobility of character, presumably a masculine trait.]

Responses to Boxed Questions

2. Women are physically weaker than men, and men weaken women's minds by treating women as objects.

3. She understands *masculine* to mean "having 'those talents and virtues, the exercise of which ennobles the human character.'" Her underlying assumption is that most men have these talents and virtues.

A and the understanding of the sex has been so bubbled[1] by this specious homage, that the civilized women of the present century, with a few exceptions, are only anxious to inspire love, when they ought to cherish a nobler ambition, and by their abilities and virtues exact[2] respect.

In a treatise, therefore, on female rights and manners, the works which have been particularly written for their improvement must not be overlooked; especially when it is asserted, in direct terms, that the minds of women are enfeebled by false refinement; that the books of instruction, written by men of genius, have had the same tendency as more frivolous productions; and that, in the true style of Mahometanism,[3] they are treated as a kind of subordinate beings, and not as a part of the human species, when improvable[4] reason is allowed to be the dignified distinction which raises men above the brute creation, and puts a natural scepter[5] in a feeble hand.

B Yet, because I am a woman, I would not lead my readers to suppose that I mean violently to agitate the contested question respecting the equality or inferiority of the sex; but as the subject lies in my way, and I cannot pass it over without subjecting the main tendency of my reasoning to misconstruction,[6] I shall stop a moment to deliver, in a few words, my opinion. ❷ —

> ❷ In this paragraph and the next, Wollstonecraft asserts that she will acknowledge and draw upon the work of other people who share her view, but that it is her primary intention to express her own opinions.
>
> ❓ What two opinions does Wollstonecraft then express?

1. **bubbled** *v.*: be deluded with "bubbles," that is, flimsy evidence.
2. **exact** *v.*: demand; require.
3. **Mahometanism:** Islam, the religion of Muslims. Europeans mistakenly thought that the Koran teaches that women have no souls. On the contrary, the Koran teaches that women are to be treated as equals to men.
4. **improveable** *adj.*: capable of being improved.
5. **scepter** (sep'tər) *n.*: ornamental staff symbolizing a monarch's authority.
6. **misconstruction** *n.*: misunderstanding.

In the government of the physical world it is observable that the female in point of strength is, in general, inferior to the male. This is the law of nature; and it does not appear to be suspended or abrogated in favor of woman. A degree of physical superiority cannot, therefore, be denied—and it is a noble prerogative![7] But **C** not content with this natural pre-eminence, men endeavor to sink us still lower, merely to render us alluring objects for a moment; and women, intoxicated by the adoration which men, under the influence of their senses, pay them, do not seek to obtain a durable interest in their hearts, or to become the friends of the fellow creatures who find amusement in their society.

I am aware of an obvious inference:—from every quarter have I heard exclamations against masculine women; but where are they to be found? If by this appellation[8] men mean to inveigh[9] against their ardour in hunting, shooting, and gaming, I shall most cordially join in the cry; but if it be against the imitation of manly virtues, or, more properly speaking, the **D** attainment of those talents and virtues, the exercise of which ennobles the human character, and which raise females in the scale of animal being, when they are comprehensively termed mankind;—all those who view them with a philosophic eye must, I should think, wish with me, that they may every day grow more and more masculine. ❸

> ❸ In this paragraph Wollstonecraft anticipates her readers' concerns and presents a counterargument explaining why women should aspire to be "masculine."
>
> ❓ What does Wollstonecraft understand the word *masculine* to mean? What implicit assumptions underlie her use of the word?

7. **prerogative** *n.*: privilege.
8. **appellation** *n.*: name.
9. **inveigh** *v.*: complain loudly.

Vocabulary

specious (spē'shəs) *adj.*: showy but false; lacking genuineness.

abrogated (ab'rə·gāt'id) *v.* used as *adj.*: abolished; repealed.

488 Collection 4 The Restoration and the Eighteenth Century

DIFFERENTIATING INSTRUCTION

Advanced Learners

Enrichment. Tell students that for nearly a century after Wollstonecraft's call for equality in education, universities in Europe and the United States remained closed to women. Not until the 1870s and 1880s did these institutions admit their first female students. (One exception, Oberlin College in Ohio, accepted women from its founding in 1833.) Invite students to learn more about historical obstacles to higher education for women in various parts of the world.

This discussion naturally divides the subject. I shall first consider women in the grand light of human creatures, who, in common with men, are placed on this earth to unfold their faculties; and afterwards I shall more particularly point out their peculiar designation.

> **4** How will the writer divide her subject?

I wish also to steer clear of an error which many respectable writers have fallen into; for the instruction which has hitherto been addressed to women, has rather been applicable to *ladies,* if the little indirect advice, that is scattered through Sandford and Merton,[10] be excepted; but, addressing my sex in a firmer tone, I pay particular attention to those in the middle class, because they appear to be in the most natural state. Perhaps the seeds of false refinement, immorality, and vanity, have ever been shed by the great. Weak, artificial beings, raised above the common wants and affections of their race, in a premature unnatural manner, undermine the very foundation of virtue, and spread corruption through the whole mass of society! As a class of mankind they have the strongest claim to pity; the education of the rich tends to render them vain and helpless, and the unfolding mind is not strengthened by the practice of those duties which dignify the human character.—They only live to amuse themselves, and by the same law which in nature invariably produces certain effects, they soon only afford barren amusement.

> **5** Why will Wollstonecraft focus on middle-class women?

But as I purpose[11] taking a separate view of the different ranks of society, and of the moral character of women in each, this hint is, for the present, sufficient; and I have only alluded to the subject, because it appears to me to be the very essence of an introduction to give a cursory account of the contents of the work it introduces.

My own sex, I hope, will excuse me, if I treat them like rational creatures, instead of flattering their *fascinating* graces, and viewing them as if they were in a state of perpetual childhood, unable to stand alone. I earnestly wish to point out in what true dignity and human happiness consists—I wish to persuade women to endeavor to acquire strength, both of mind and body, and to convince them that the soft phrases, susceptibility of heart, delicacy of sentiment, and refinement of taste, are almost synonymous with epithets[12] of weakness, and that those beings who are only the objects of pity and that kind of love, which has been termed its sister, will soon become objects of contempt.

> **6** This and the next paragraph contain a rough sketch of Wollstonecraft's essay.
>
> What is Wollstonecraft trying to persuade her readers of?

Dismissing then those pretty feminine phrases, which the men condescendingly use to soften our slavish dependence, and despising that weak elegancy of mind, exquisite sensibility, and sweet docility of manners, supposed to be the sexual characteristics of the weaker vessel, I wish to shew[13] that elegance is inferior to virtue, that the first object of laudable[14] ambition is to obtain a character as a human being, regardless of the distinction of sex; and that secondary views should be brought to this simple touchstone.[15]

This is a rough sketch of my plan; and should I express my conviction with the energetic emotions that I feel whenever I think of the subject,

---

10. **Sandford and Merton:** reference to *The History of Sandford and Merton,* a children's book. A character in the book often cites the moral superiority of a poor boy over a rich one.
11. **purpose** *v.:* intend.
12. **epithets** (ep′ə·thets′) *n. pl.:* names.
13. **shew** *v.:* archaic spelling of *show.*
14. **laudable** *adj.:* praiseworthy.
15. **touchstone** *n.:* criterion; originally a stone used for testing the quality of gold and silver alloys by the color of the streak produced by rubbing them upon it.

Vocabulary
cursory (kʉr′sə·rē) *adj.:* hasty; superficial.

Mary Wollstonecraft **489**

DIRECT TEACHING

E Literary Focus

Tone. In earlier English, *ladies* meant "upper-class women." How would you describe the author's attitude toward them? [Possible responses: harsh, scornful, disgusted.] Which loaded words help to establish this tone? [Possible responses: *false, artificial, unnatural, immorality, vanity, weak, helpless, undermine, corruption, barren.*]

F Reading Skills

Analyzing patterns of organization. What does Wollstonecraft think an introduction should do? [Possible response: It should give a brief overview of the work it introduces and examine its organization.]

G Literary Focus

Tone. These characteristics of women are examples of the "*fascinating* graces" that the author mentions above. What is her attitude toward these graces? [She really considers these qualities degrading.]

Responses to Boxed Questions

4. She divides her subject into two topics: women as human beings and women as females.
5. They are more natural than the degenerate women of the aristocracy.
6. She plans to convince women that dignity and happiness come from mental and physical strength; that traditional femininity sabotages them; and that above all, women must develop their characters as human beings.

CONTENT-AREA CONNECTIONS

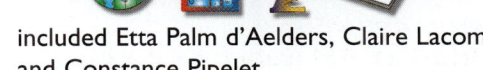

History: Women's Rights
French contemporaries of Wollstonecraft struggled for women's rights during the French Revolution. In 1791, a year before Wollstonecraft's *A Vindication of the Rights of Woman,* Olympe de Gouges published *Declaration of the Rights of Woman.* (Gouges was guillotined in 1793.) Other writers supporting women's rights during the 1790s included Etta Palm d'Aelders, Claire Lacombe, and Constance Pipelet.

Individual activity. Invite interested students to read works by the French authors mentioned above and to report on them to the class. Students might enter the authors' names, or *French Revolution* and *women's rights,* as keywords in an Internet search engine.

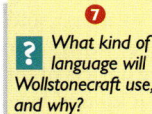

the dictates of experience and reflection will be felt by some of my readers. Animated by this important object, I shall disdain to cull[16] my phrases or polish my style;—I aim at being useful, and sincerity will render me unaffected; for, wishing rather to persuade by the force of my arguments, than dazzle by the elegance of my language, I shall not waste my time in rounding periods, or in fabricating the turgid bombast[17] of artificial feelings, which, coming from the head, never reach the heart.—I shall be employed about things, not words!—and, anxious to render my sex more respectable members of society, I shall try to avoid that flowery diction which has slided from essays into novels, and from novels into familiar letters and conversation.

7. What kind of language will Wollstonecraft use, and why?

These pretty superlatives,[18] dropping glibly from the tongue, vitiate the taste, and create a kind of sickly delicacy that turns away from simple unadorned truth; and a deluge of false sentiments and overstretched feelings, stifling the natural emotions of the heart, render the domestic pleasures insipid, that ought to sweeten the exercise of those severe duties, which educate a rational and immortal being for a nobler field of action.

The education of women has, of late, been more attended to than formerly; yet they are still reckoned a frivolous sex, and pitied or ridiculed by the writers who endeavor by satire or instruction to improve them. It is acknowledged that they spend many of the first years of their lives in acquiring a smattering of accomplishments; meanwhile strength of body and mind are sacrificed to libertine[19] notions of beauty, to the desire of establishing themselves,—the only way women can rise in the world,—by marriage. And this desire making mere animals of them, when they marry they act as such children may be expected to act:—they dress; they paint, and nickname God's creatures.—Surely these weak beings are only fit for a seraglio![20]—Can they be expected to govern a family with judgment, or take care of the poor babes whom they bring into the world?

8. What, according to Wollstonecraft, is women's main ambition in life?

If then it can be fairly deduced from the present conduct of the sex, from the prevalent fondness for pleasure which takes place of ambition and those nobler passions that open and enlarge the soul; that the instruction which women have hitherto received has only tended, with the constitution[21] of civil society, to render them insignificant objects of desire—mere propagators[22] of fools!—if it can be proved that in aiming to accomplish them, without cultivating their understandings, they are taken out of their sphere of duties, and made ridiculous and useless when the short-lived bloom of beauty is over,* I presume that *rational* men will excuse me for endeavoring to persuade them to become more masculine and respectable.

9. This paragraph consists of a single sentence. Break it down by locating the two if statements in the sentence. Then, paraphrase both of them, as well as the implied then statement in the final clause.

Indeed the word masculine is only a bugbear:[23] there is little reason to fear that

---

*A lively writer, I cannot recollect his name, asks what business women turned of forty have to do in the world?

---

20. **seraglio** (si·ral′yō) *n.:* place in a Muslim house where wives live; a harem.
21. **constitution** *n.:* composition.
22. **propagators** *n. pl.:* spreaders.
23. **bugbear** *n.:* anything causing needless fear.

Vocabulary
vitiate (vish′ē·āt) *v.:* impair; weaken; spoil.
insipid (in·sip′id) *adj.:* dull; flat.

---

16. **cull** *v.:* sort out.
17. **turgid bombast:** pompous rant or utterance.
18. **superlatives** *n.:* exaggerations.
19. **libertine** *adj.:* sensual.

Marriage à la Mode: The Marriage Contract (c. 1743) by William Hogarth. Oil on canvas.

women will acquire too much courage or fortitude; for their apparent inferiority with respect to bodily strength, must render them, in some degree, dependent on men in the various relations of life; but why should it be increased by prejudices that give a sex to virtue, and confound simple truths with sensual reveries?[24]

Women are, in fact, so much degraded by mistaken notions of female excellence, that I do not mean to add a paradox when I assert, that this artificial weakness produces a propensity to tyrannize, and gives birth to cunning, the natural opponent of strength, which leads them to play off those contemptible infantine airs that undermine esteem even whilst they excite desire. Let men become more chaste and modest, and if women do not grow wiser in the same ratio, it will be clear that they have weaker understandings. It seems scarcely necessary to say, that I now speak of the sex in general. Many individuals have more sense than their male relatives; and, as nothing preponderates[25] where there is a constant struggle for equilibrium, without it has naturally more gravity, some women govern their husbands without degrading themselves, because intellect will always govern.

> Wollstonecraft points out a curious **paradox,** or seeming contradiction, that has occurred as a result of women's oppression.
>
> **?** What is this paradox?

---

24. **reveries** *n. pl.*: musings.
25. **preponderates** *v.*: predominates.

Vocabulary
propensity (prə·pen′sə·tē) *n.*: natural inclination or tendency.

INDEPENDENT PRACTICE

Response and Analysis

Reading Check

1. See p. 485 in the Teacher's Edition for a summary of the essay's main points.
2. She proposes that if she can prove that women's lack of education renders them useless, then readers must agree that educating women would be worthwhile.

Thinking Critically

3. She accepts the roles of wife and mother. She feels that better education would allow women to be more helpful, affectionate, and interesting wives and more rational and effective mothers.
4. Men—strength, reason, dignity, virtue, independence, respectability, usefulness, courage. Women—beauty, weakness, frivolity, dependence, docility, uselessness, vanity, childishness. The author satirically says that she would join men in complaining against women who enjoy "hunting, shooting, and gaming."
5. The writer outlines her essay on the necessity of educating women by saying that she will first discuss women as human beings, then women in contrast to men; she will examine differences between upper-class and middle-class women; she will persuade women to develop mental and physical strength rather than to aim solely at pleasing men.
6. She says that women's lack of power forces them to use cunning and makes them want to tyrannize others. Her solution is for men to become "more chaste and modest" and to offer women better training.

Response and Analysis

Reading Check

1. Outline the main points of this essay, and show the details the writer uses to support them. Your answers to the questions posed in the text will guide you in making your outline.
2. In the final four paragraphs (beginning "The education of women..."), what test does the author propose for judging the value of educating women?

Thinking Critically

3. Overall, what basic roles for women does the author continue to accept? In her view, how would better education help women fulfill these roles?
4. The author uses wit and **satire** throughout the essay whenever she discusses the qualities conventionally assigned to men and to women. List some of those qualities. How does the writer satirize the belief that educating women will make them masculine?
5. In paragraphs five through nine, how does the author outline her topic? You might want to refer to your reading notes for help.
6. In her concluding paragraph, how does Wollstonecraft explain women's use of cunning to get their way? What solution does she propose?
7. How would you describe the **tone** of Wollstonecraft's text? What particular words, phrases, or longer passages contribute to this tone?

Literary Criticism

8. **Political approach.** Explain the basic political viewpoint that Wollstonecraft advances regarding the education of middle-class women. In what way is her view a radical one for the time in which she lived? Are there any ways in which her argument is limited by the political realities of her time?

WRITING

Then and Now

In a brief **essay**, evaluate the relevance of Wollstonecraft's essay to our time. Do her observations about the role of women hold true today, or are her arguments limited to the social realities of the eighteenth century? Which, if any, of her observations about men and women remain valid in the twenty-first century? Use details from the text and examples from real life to support your response.

SKILLS FOCUS

Literary Skills Analyze political points of view on a topic. Analyze tone.
Reading Skills Analyze patterns of organization.
Writing Skills Write an essay.
Vocabulary Skills Demonstrate word knowledge.
Grammar Skills Use correct subject-verb agreement.

Vocabulary Development

Question and Answer

Be prepared to justify your answer to each question.

1. Name something that a parent would feel **solicitude** for.
2. What is the opposite of a **partial** juror?
3. What word is the opposite of **deplore**?
4. What is the opposite of a **fastidious** person?
5. Why would you reject a **specious** argument?
6. If you have **abrogated** your responsibilities, have you abandoned them or embraced them?
7. What is the opposite of a **cursory** investigation?
8. If you **vitiate** an argument, do you strengthen it or weaken it?
9. What is the opposite of an **insipid** argument?
10. If you have a **propensity** for lying, how would people react to you?

---

7. The tone is impassioned ("... should I express my conviction with the energetic emotions that I feel..."), sincere ("I earnestly wish to point out..."), and sometimes satirical ("My own sex, I hope, will excuse me, if I treat them like rational creatures...").

Literary Criticism

8. She proposes that middle-class women and men receive equal educations, a radical view when women were considered inferior to men. Since political realities precluded women's voting or sharing political power with men, she focuses on women as wives and mothers.

Grammar Link

Make Sure It Agrees: Subject-Verb Agreement

Read the following paragraph about Mary Wollstonecraft.

Doubts about the institution of marriage was always uppermost in Mary Wollstonecraft's mind. Marriage, along with domestic life, were a kind of slavery to her. To her great surprise, however, she found a true soul mate in William Godwin. Wollstonecraft and Godwin was in some ways an unlikely couple. Neither Wollstonecraft nor Godwin were "the marrying kind." Yet they found solace and support in each other. One of their favorite pastimes were exchanging witty notes.

The writer has trouble with some tricky subject-verb combinations. In many English sentences and clauses the subject comes right before the verb. When you vary this standard sentence pattern, however, agreement problems can occur. These problems can be solved and mastered.

1. Subject-verb agreement means that a singular verb takes a singular subject and plural subjects take plural verbs. A subject's number is not changed by a following phrase or clause.

   Doubts about the institution of marriage were always uppermost in Mary Wollstonecraft's mind.

2. In formal usage, a singular subject followed by a parenthetical phrase such as *along with ...*, *as well as ...*, or *in addition to ...* remains singular.

   Marriage, along with domestic life, was a kind of slavery to her.

3. A compound subject is two or more subjects having the same verb. A compound subject joined by *and* usually takes a plural verb, even if one subject is singular.

   Wollstonecraft and Godwin were in some ways an unlikely couple.

4. When a compound subject is joined by *or* or *nor*, the verb agrees with the subject closer to the verb.

   Neither Wollstonecraft nor Godwin was "the marrying kind."

5. When a singular indefinite pronoun is the subject, it takes a singular verb.

   One of their favorite pastimes was exchanging witty notes.

PRACTICE

On a separate sheet of paper, correct any problems with subject-verb agreement in the following sentences. If the subject and verb agree, write *correct*.

1. Women who rise to the upper class lives only to amuse themselves, according to Wollstonecraft.
2. Marriage to wealthy men were the only way women could improve their status.
3. One of Wollstonecraft's early novels were partly autobiographical.
4. Wollstonecraft thought that neither beauty nor weakness make women attractive.
5. The goal of Wollstonecraft's writings is to educate and bring about social reform.

Apply to Your Writing

Review a writing assignment you are working on now or have already completed. Are there any sentences in which the subjects and verbs do not agree? Revise to correct the subject-verb agreement.

▶ For more help, see Agreement of Subject and Verb, 2a–i, in the Language Handbook.

Vocabulary Development

Possible Answers
1. an infant
2. an unbiased juror
3. praise
4. a slob
5. It has fallacies.
6. abandoned them
7. a thorough investigation
8. weaken it
9. a lively argument
10. They would disbelieve you.

Grammar Link

Practice
1. Women who rise to the upper class live only to amuse themselves, according to Wollstonecraft.
2. Marriage to wealthy men was the only way women could improve their status.
3. One of Wollstonecraft's early novels was partly autobiographical.
4. Wollstonecraft thought that neither beauty nor weakness makes women attractive.
5. correct

ASSESSING

Assessment
- *Holt Assessment: Literature, Reading, and Vocabulary*

RETEACHING

For lessons reteaching clarity of meaning, and author's tone and style, see **Reteaching**, p. 1129A.

DIFFERENTIATING INSTRUCTION

Learners Having Difficulty

Write the following sentences on the chalkboard. For each sentence, ask students to choose the verb form that agrees with the subject.

1. Mary Wollstonecraft, with her progressive views, (has, have) earned the respect of later generations. [has]
2. Wollstonecraft or her daughter (is, are) famous for writing *Frankenstein*. [is]
3. One of her beliefs (was, were) that girls should learn Greek and Latin. [was]
4. Political leaders who shaped modern France (was, were) among Wollstonecraft's friends. [were]
5. One of her essays (suggest, suggests) ideas a century ahead of her time. [suggests]

Connected Reading

Summary ⇔ *at grade level*

"To the Ladies" argues that since a wife's position is little better than a servant's, women should avoid marriage and instead develop personal pride.

More About the Writer
Background. Mary, Lady Chudleigh grew up in an upper-class family. Although she did not learn Latin and Greek, which were standard subjects for boys, she did read English translations of the classics.

DIRECT TEACHING

Ⓐ Political Issue

❓ **Women's rights.** What political issue do the first eight lines raise? [women's rights in marriage]

Ⓑ Reading Skills

❓ **Rhetorical devices: Analogy.** In l. 9 the speaker begins an analogy, extending it through l. 19. To what does she compare a husband? [a haughty Eastern prince]

Ⓒ Literary Focus

❓ **Tone.** The use of hyperbole is one mark of a satirical tone. In ll. 13–19, where do you notice hyperbole? [Possible responses: "Like Mutes she Signs alone must make, / And never any Freedom take"; "And fear her Husband as her God."]

Connected Readings

Mary, Lady Chudleigh ...... **To the Ladies**
Daniel Defoe .... from **The Education of Women**

You have just read an excerpt from Mary Wollstonecraft's persuasive essay *A Vindication of the Rights of Woman* and considered the views it expresses about women's rights. Each of the next two selections you will be reading presents another point of view on women's rights. As you read, ask yourself how these views are alike and how they are different. After you have read these selections, answer the questions on page 498, which ask you to compare all three selections.

Political Points *of* View
Before You Read

The poems and essays of Mary, Lady Chudleigh (1656–1710), addressed the concerns of women of her time and explored a philosophy of how to live a peaceful life. She adamantly opposed the idea that wives should submit to the will of their husbands, and she expressed this view in many of her works. While none of her writings were published until 1701, Chudleigh wrote for members of her London literary circle for years. Even though four of her children died at a very young age and she herself suffered years of excruciating rheumatism that ultimately caused her death, her poems and essays demonstrate that she had the time and freedom to acquire an impressive knowledge of philosophy, science, and history.

"To the Ladies" is Chudleigh's most anthologized poem; it appeared in print in 1703 and was so popular that it has been found copied onto the flyleaves of other books. Chudleigh's marriage may have been somewhat unrewarding and may have contributed to the bitter tone in this poem.

POEM

To the Ladies
Mary, Lady Chudleigh

    Wife and Servant are the same,
    But only differ in the Name:
    For when that fatal Knot is ty'd,
    Which nothing, nothing can divide:
5 When she the word *obey* has said,
    And Man by Law supreme has made,
    Then all that's kind is laid aside,
    And nothing left but State° and Pride:
    Fierce as an Eastern Prince he grows,
10 And all his innate Rigor shows:
    Then but to look, to laugh, or speak,
    Will the Nuptial Contract break.
    Like Mutes she Signs alone must make,
    And never any Freedom take:
15 But still be govern'd by a Nod,
    And fear her Husband as her God:
    Him still must serve, him still obey,
    And nothing act, and nothing say,
    But what her haughty Lord thinks fit,
20 Who with the Pow'r, has all the Wit.
    Then shun, oh! shun that wretched State,
    And all the fawning Flatt'rers hate:
    Value your selves, and Men despise,
    You must be proud, if you'll be wise.

8. **State** *n.*: ostentation; pretentiousness.

RESOURCES: READING

Media
- Audio CD Library

DIFFERENTIATING INSTRUCTION

Learners Having Difficulty
Tell students that restatement is one rhetorical device used by all three writers in this lesson. Point out that writers seldom repeat themselves exactly; instead they restate their ideas in different words. In "To the Ladies," for example, ll. 7 and 9–10 restate the same idea. As students read, remind them to look for other examples of restatement.

Advanced Learners
Enrichment. Ask students to comment on Chudleigh's poem "The Wish."
"... One pious, lib'ral, just, and brave,
And to his passions not a slave ...
In whom I safely may confide,
And with him all my cares divide ...
Who charm'd with Wit, and inward
  Graces,

Political Points of View

Before You Read

Daniel Defoe (1660–1731) was at various times a businessman and a spy, but he was always a man who wrote and wrote and wrote—more than five hundred works in all, on every conceivable subject, from the choice of a wife to the history of the devil to the manufacture of glass. He wrote in every literary form: political pamphlets, treatises on economic theory, satiric verse, popular novels, and journalistic accounts of sensational events. During Defoe's lifetime, his political writings led to notoriety, arrests, public punishment, and even jail time. It is a great irony of literary history that the prolific Defoe is now primarily remembered as the author of only one book, a novel about a survivor—a shipwrecked sailor named *Robinson Crusoe* (1719).

Reading informational materials: analyzing an argument. In order to convince audiences to think or act in a certain way, writers use **argument,** a form of persuasion that appeals to reason, rather than to emotion. Underlying any argument is the writer's **point of view,** an attitude shaped by the writer's background and values. No matter how logical and well-reasoned an argument is, the careful reader can often discern a particular leaning, or **bias,** on the part of a writer—a value judgment or preference that prevents the author from being completely impartial.

Daniel Defoe (1706).
The Granger Collection, New York.

Connected Reading

Summary ⬆ *above grade level*

In this essay from the early 1700s, Defoe advocates educating women to make them better wives. He argues that denying them education is unfair and irrational; he suggests that they learn music, dance, speaking skills, history, and modern languages; and he assures readers that this education will not cause women to "encroach" on men's domains.

More About the Writer

Background. Ironically, Defoe himself did not receive the standard education for young gentlemen of his era. His parents were Dissenters, Protestants who disapproved of the Church of England, and so he was barred from attending either Oxford or Cambridge. Instead, he studied history, law, economics, geography, and natural science at an alternative academy. When he was around twenty, he set himself up as a merchant, trading in haberdashery, brandy, wool, real estate, and at one point civet cats. By the time he married, at twenty-four, he was already writing and publishing. "The Education of Women" is one of his numerous pamphlets on religious and political controversies. Some of his contemporaries apparently found him an annoying gadfly: Jonathan Swift wrote in 1708, "there is no enduring him," and Joseph Addison in 1713 called him "a false, shuffling, prevaricating rascal—unqualified to give his testimony in a Court of Justice."

ESSAY

from The Education of Women
Daniel Defoe

I have often thought of it as one of the most barbarous customs in the world, considering us as a civilized and a Christian country, that we deny the advantages of learning to women. ❶ We reproach the sex every day with folly and impertinence; while I am confident, had they the advantages of education equal to us, they would be guilty of less than ourselves.

One would wonder, indeed, how it should happen that women are conversible at all; since they are only beholden to natural parts, for all their knowledge. Their youth is spent to teach them to stitch and sew or make baubles. They are taught to read, indeed, and perhaps to write their names, or so; and that is the height of a woman's education. And I would but ask

> ❶ What is Defoe's central claim?

SKILLS FOCUS

Reading Skills
Analyze a writer's argument.

Despises Fools with tempting Faces;
And still a beauteous Mind does prize
Above the most enchanting Eyes. . . ."

RESOURCES: READING

Media
- Audio CD Library

Reading
- *The Holt Reader*

DIRECT TEACHING

Response to Boxed Question

1. Defoe's central claim is that women should receive education.

VIEWING THE ART

Jean-Baptiste Chardin (1699–1779) celebrated simplicity in a flamboyant age. Chardin painted images of ordinary objects and everyday life. He was particularly interested in representing scenes of domestic simplicity.

Activity. Ask students to consider why the figures in *The Young Schoolmistress* might be seen as images of "domestic simplicity." [The figures in the painting are dressed plainly, and they are working in a bare room on an ordinary piece of furniture.]

DIRECT TEACHING

A Learners Having Difficulty

? Paraphrasing. In Defoe's time, *gentleman* meant "man of the upper class"; *estate* meant "social standing"; *parts* meant "character traits"; *figure* meant "impression"; and *for want of* meant "without." How would you state the main point that Defoe makes in this sentence? [Possible response: Even if a man had high social status and good character traits, he would make a poor impression without any education.]

B Reading Skills

Analyzing an argument. Help students to see that Defoe's basic argument is as follows: If education improves the soul, then women, as beings with souls, should be educated.

Responses to Boxed Questions

2. soul
3. Possible paraphrases: Ignorance is attractive; a wise woman is a problem; women do not deserve education; education will only increase their pride and impertinence; women are too foolish for education.

The Young Schoolmistress (1740) by Jean-Baptiste Chardin. Oil on canvas.
The Bridgeman Art Library.

A any who slight the sex for their understanding, what is a man (a gentleman, I mean) good for, that is taught no more? I need not give instances, or examine the character of a gentleman, with a good estate, or a good family, and with tolerable parts; and examine what figure he makes for want of education.

B The soul is placed in the body like a rough diamond; and must be polished, or the luster of it will never appear. And 'tis manifest, that as the rational soul distinguishes us from brutes; so education carries on the distinction, and makes some less brutish than others. ❷ This is too evident to need any demonstration. But why then should women be denied the benefit of instruction? If knowledge and understanding had been useless additions to the sex, GOD Almighty would never have given them capacities; for he made nothing needless. Besides, I would ask such, What they can see in ignorance, that they should think it a necessary ornament to a woman? or how much worse is a wise woman than a fool? or what has the woman done to forfeit the privilege of being taught? Does she plague us with her pride and impertinence? Why did we not let her learn, that she might have had more wit? Shall we upbraid women with folly, when 'tis only the error of this inhuman custom, that hindered them from being made wiser? ❸

> ❷ Defoe uses an analogy to advance his argument.
> **?** In the analogy, *polish* is to *diamond* as *educate* is to _____.

> ❸ In a series of rhetorical questions, Defoe explores (and implicitly dismisses) several reasons why women are kept in ignorance.
> **?** Paraphrase two of these reasons.

496 Collection 4 The Restoration and the Eighteenth Century

DIFFERENTIATING INSTRUCTION

Advanced Learners

Enrichment. Suggest to students that Defoe's "The Education of Women" may have been one of the "books of instruction, written by men of genius," that Mary Wollstonecraft refers to in her *A Vindication of the Rights of Woman*. Ask students, as they read Defoe's essay, to look for material justifying Wollstonecraft's assertions that these writers regard women as "a kind of subordinate species" and that "[Women] are still reckoned a frivolous sex, and ridiculed or pitied by the writers who endeavour by satire or instruction to improve them."

The capacities of women are supposed to be greater, and their senses quicker than those of the men; and what they might be capable of being bred to, is plain from some instances of female wit, which this age is not without. Which upbraids us with Injustice, and looks as if we denied women the advantages of education, for fear they should *vie* with the men in their improvements....

[They] should be taught all sorts of breeding suitable both to their genius and quality. And in particular, Music and Dancing; which it would be cruelty to bar the sex of, because they are their darlings. But besides this, they should be taught languages, as particularly French and Italian: and I would venture the injury of giving a woman more tongues than one. They should, as a particular study, be taught all the graces of speech, and all the necessary air of conversation; which our common education is so defective in, that I need not expose it. They should be brought to read books, and especially history; and so to read as to make them understand the world, and be able to know and judge of things when they hear of them.

To such whose genius would lead them to it, I would deny no sort of learning; but the chief thing, in general, is to cultivate the understandings of the sex, that they may be capable of all sorts of conversation; that their parts and judgments being improved, they may be as profitable in their conversation as they are pleasant.

Women, in my observation, have little or no difference in them, but as they are or are not distinguished by education. Tempers, indeed, may in some degree influence them, but the main distinguishing part is their Breeding....

The great distinguishing difference, which is seen in the world between men and women, is in their education; and this is manifested by comparing it with the difference between one man or woman, and another.

And herein it is that I take upon me to make such a bold assertion, That all the world are mistaken in their practice about women. For I cannot think that GOD Almighty ever made them so delicate, so glorious creatures; and furnished them with such charms, so agreeable and so delightful to mankind; with souls capable of the same accomplishments with men: and all, to be only Stewards of our Houses, Cooks, and Slaves.

Not that I am for exalting the female government in the least: but, in short, *I would have men take women for companions, and educate them to be fit for it.* A woman of sense and breeding will scorn as much to encroach upon the prerogative of man, as a man of sense will scorn to oppress the weakness of the woman. But if the women's souls were refined and improved by teaching, that word would be lost. To say, the *weakness* of the sex, as to judgment, would be nonsense; for ignorance and folly would be no more to be found among women than men.

I remember a passage, which I heard from a very fine woman. She had wit and capacity enough, an extraordinary shape and face, and a great fortune: but had been cloistered up all her time; and for fear of being stolen, had not had the liberty of being taught the common necessary knowledge of women's affairs. And when she came to converse in the world, her natural wit made her so sensible of the want of education, that she gave this short reflection on herself: "I am ashamed to talk with my very maids," says she, "for I don't know when they do right or wrong. I had more need go to school, than be married."...

'Tis a thing will be more easily granted than remedied.... ■

Analyzing Political Points of View

Comparing Political Assumptions

1. Men of the period might resent equating wives with servants. Details appear in ll. 3–20: wives cannot divorce, must give up freedom, must endure harshness and irrationality, and have no recourse if men break vows.

2. He suggests history, modern Romance languages, music, dance, rhetoric, and social skills to develop women's souls.

3. His argument that educated women will be better companions for men sounds outdated because women are no longer viewed merely as potential or actual wives. Also outdated is Defoe's argument that educated women will not usurp male "prerogatives."

4. Both writers advocate education to make women better wives, and both deny that educated women will pose a threat to men. Only Wollstonecraft argues that education will make women happier; only Defoe argues that women should not be granted more power.

5. The last lines of the poem advise women to shun marriage and to develop self-respect. Defoe's last lines suggest that the woman would have gained more self-respect through education than through marriage.

6. All three use illustrative examples, analogies, and restatement. Wollstonecraft and Defoe also use counterargument and rhetorical questions. Wollstonecraft criticizes authorities; Defoe's "if God hadn't wanted" might be called an appeal to authority. Some students may select Wollstonecraft's essay for its satirical comments and analogies. Others may choose the poem for its memorable, rhymed examples. Still others may choose Defoe's essay for its incisive rhetorical questions.

Analyzing Political Points of View

Women's Rights

The questions on this page ask you to analyze the views on women's rights in the preceding three selections.

Mary Wollstonecraft . . . from **A Vindication of the Rights of Woman**
Mary, Lady Chudleigh . . **To the Ladies**
Daniel Defoe . . . . from **The Education of Women**

Comparing Political Assumptions

1. Why would readers of the eighteenth century have found the opening line of Lady Chudleigh's poem somewhat shocking? What details of the poem support the meaning of this line?

2. In his essay "The Education of Women," what types of learning does Defoe particularly recommend for women? Why?

3. Which of Defoe's arguments sound outdated today? Why?

4. Compare Defoe's essay with Wollstonecraft's. What arguments are advanced by both writers for granting women "the advantages of learning"? What arguments are advanced only by one writer or the other?

5. Compare the second to last sentence of Defoe's essay—"'I had more need go to school, than be married'"—with the last two lines of Chudleigh's poem. How are the ideas related?

6. Each of these writings makes strong claims about the rights of women. Discuss the effectiveness of each text, not only for *what* it says, but for *how* it gets its message across. What **rhetorical devices** do these writers use? Which writer, in your opinion, creates the most powerful and memorable argument? You may want to refer to your reading notes from page 483.

SKILLS FOCUS

Pages 482–498 cover
Literary Skills Analyze and compare political points of view on a topic.
Reading Skills Analyze rhetorical devices.
Writing Skills Write an essay explaining a political philosophy.

WRITING

Defining a Philosophy

In a short paper, summarize your understanding of the philosophical stance that underlies women's rights movements. Then, discuss appropriate names for that philosophy. Was *feminism* originally a good name for it? Is it still a suitable name, or would some other phrase or title speak more clearly to people of the twenty-first century? See your Quickwrite notes for ideas.

Conducting a Historical Investigation

Researching views on women's rights. Other English women writing during the Restoration and eighteenth century included Aphra Behn (1640–1689), whose fiction influenced Defoe's novels, and Lady Mary Wortley Montagu (1689–1762), who introduced the smallpox vaccine into Britain from Turkey. Ask students to use library or Internet resources to locate works by these authors. Have students read selections by either author, and then write short essays comparing the views on women's rights in works by Behn or Montagu with the views in works by Defoe, Chudleigh, or Wollstonecraft.

READ ON: FOR INDEPENDENT READING

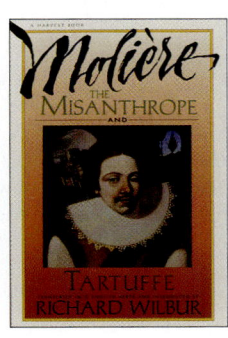

DRAMA
The Rogue and the Recluse
The French playwright Molière had a remarkable genius for exposing and satirizing the ills of society. In Richard Wilbur's translations of *Tartuffe* and *The Misanthrope*, you'll meet two men whom Molière considered representative of his age: one a roguish hypocrite who charms everyone he meets and the other an eccentric recluse who shuns hypocrisy at a great cost to himself. Molière's comedies of manners, so relevant when they were first written, have lost none of their potency and humor today.

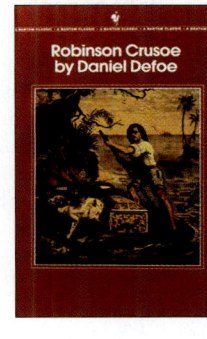

FICTION
Diary of a Castaway
Since its publication in 1719, Daniel Defoe's *Robinson Crusoe* has spawned countless imitations and adaptations. Perhaps the story contained in Crusoe's fictional autobiography has endured because it poses age-old questions. How might we react if we were plucked from our ordinary lives and set on a barren island? Could we face the physical hardships and mental isolation of such an extraordinary new life?

NONFICTION
Pioneer of Science
Restoration England was an age marked by avid amateur experimentation and heated public debates about the mysteries of science. Sir Isaac Newton single-handedly unraveled many of the world's great puzzles: He invented calculus, formulated the three laws of motion, and realized, as no one else had, that gravity accounts for both orbiting planets and falling apples. You can read about the man and his works in *Isaac Newton and the Scientific Revolution* by Gale E. Christianson.

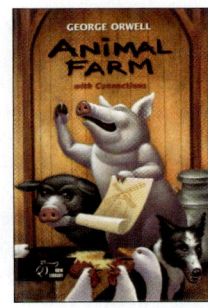

FICTION
Down on the Farm
Like Pope and Swift, George Orwell uses satire to reveal the absurdities of human nature. In his famous novel *Animal Farm* (1945), Orwell satirizes the problems of a supposedly equal society. The animals of Manor Farm revolt against their incompetent owner and install the "Seven Commandments of Animalism," which the sheep simply remember as "four legs good, two legs bad." The pigs Napoleon and Snowball eventually disagree about the future of the farm, and a rivalry for power ensues.

This title is available in the HRW Library.

Read On
For Independent Reading
If students enjoyed the themes and topics explored in this collection, you might recommend the following titles for independent reading.

Assessment Options
The following projects can help you evaluate and assess your students' outside reading.

- **Stage a scene.** Have students who read the Molière works collaborate on planning and staging a scene from one of the plays for the rest of the class. Students should first select a scene, discuss their interpretations of it, and choose a director. The director can then coordinate the casting and other tasks.
- **Write a review.** Students who read *Robinson Crusoe* and have seen the film *Cast Away* (2000) might compare and contrast the different treatments of the theme of isolation in the two works.
- **Present a monologue.** Have students who read the biography of Isaac Newton prepare and present a monologue in which Newton responds to the biographer.
- **Analyze the allegory.** Ask those who read *Animal Farm* to work as a group to research the Russian Revolution and prepare a display on the parallels between the characters and plot of the novel and actual historical figures and events.

DIFFERENTIATING INSTRUCTION

Estimated Word Counts and Reading Levels of Read On Books:

Drama			Nonfiction		
The Misanthrope and Tartuffe	⬆	25,400	Isaac Newton and the Scientific Revolution	⬇	32,100
Fiction					
Robinson Crusoe	⬌	112,800			
Animal Farm	⬇	39,600			

KEY: ⬆ above grade level ⬌ at grade level ⬇ below grade level

PRETEACHING

Skills Starter
Motivate. Ask students if they have watched older films and noticed particular styles in previous decades' clothing, architecture, or music fashions. Have students give examples from specific times such as the 1940s and 1960s, and discuss with students how literature changes styles over time as well.

DIRECT TEACHING

Choose a Topic
As students begin researching a literary period in which they are interested, alert them to consider the important historical events of the time period when selecting works to compare, as the events may have some bearing on the literature of those specific years.

MODELING AND DEMONSTRATION

Analyze Literary Works
To help students discern a trend their chosen literary work reflects, have them choose works that are frequently mentioned together in critical discussions of the literature of the era. Model this process by reading aloud a section from a textbook's or anthology's introduction to eighteenth-century literature in which Swift, Pope, and Voltaire are mentioned together. Ask volunteers to identify a trend by sharing their own resources with the class and giving an idea of the direction they expect their essays will take.

Writing Workshop

Writing a Literary Essay

Writing Assignment
Write a literary essay that shows how multiple works reflect the same literary trend.

Because they reflect universal human feelings and experiences, great works of literature such as Miguel de Cervantes' *Don Quixote* transcend time. Yet every work of literature is shaped by the era in which it is produced. In this workshop you'll write a **literary essay** that analyzes three works from the same literary period to discover how they reflect the literary trends of the time in which they were written.

Prewriting

Choose a Topic

A Trendy Topic Start by choosing a literary period on which to focus. You may want to investigate the literary period of one of your favorite authors or works, or you might get ideas about important literary periods by talking to your teacher or school librarian. Below is a list of literary periods you might consider.

- Renaissance (1485–1660)
- Victorian Period (1832–1901)
- Romantic Period (1798–1832)
- Twentieth Century (1901–2000)

Once you've chosen a literary period, do research to identify the **literary trends,** such as changes in style or the development of new literary genres, of that period and the works that reflect those trends. Find information about literary trends and works by looking through this textbook—particularly at the introduction to the literary period you've chosen—or by checking out library books that discuss the literary period.

Select one literary trend and three works by three different writers that reflect that trend. If the works you choose are long works, such as novels or epic poems, you will probably need to deal with a single section of each work to provide a thorough analysis in a 1,500-word essay. For example, one student who selected the eighteenth century as the focus of his literary essay chose to write about "A Voyage to Laputa" from Jonathan Swift's *Gulliver's Travels,* Book I of Alexander Pope's *The Dunciad,* and all of Voltaire's short novel *Candide* to show how they reflect a dominant trend in eighteenth-century literature—satire.

Analyze Literary Works

The Evidence Will Show . . . Through your research, you already know that your three works reflect a literary trend. Now you'll demonstrate *how* each work reflects that trend. To do that, read each work critically, following the guidelines on the next page.

Writing Skills
Write an essay analyzing works of literature.

500 Collection 4 The Restoration and the Eighteenth Century

COLLECTION 4 RESOURCES: WRITING

Planning
- *One-Stop Planner* CD-ROM with ExamView Test Generator

Differentiating Instruction
- *Workshop Resources: Writing, Listening, and Speaking*
- *Family Involvement Activities in English and Spanish*
- *Supporting Instruction in Spanish*

Writing and Language
- *Workshop Resources: Writing, Listening, and Speaking*
- *Daily Language Activities*
- *Language Handbook Worksheets*

Assessment
- *Holt Assessment: Writing, Listening, and Speaking*

- First, as you read each work, ask yourself, "What **evidence** shows that this work illustrates the literary trend I've chosen?" Jot down your responses to this question.
- Next, once you've read and responded to one work, analyze your responses to see what **major point** most of the evidence supports.

When you've gone through this process for each work, you should have the major points you'll discuss in your essay and the evidence supporting them. The partial chart below shows one student's major point about Swift's work and the literary evidence that led him to it.

Evidence	Major Point
Members of the Laputian nobility regard themselves as scientists; their heads are tilted and their eyes are strangely arranged; tailors take measurements with scientific instruments, but the clothes they make don't fit.	Swift uses satire to ridicule the impractical ideas and practices of some of the scientists of his time.

TIP Consider including historical background information about your chosen period as part of your major points, thesis, or elaboration. You can find historical information on most literary periods in this book; however, you may also wish to check your history textbook or other works for additional information.

Write a Thesis Statement

Tying the Knot Now that you've analyzed each work and identified the major points you will discuss in your essay, you can tie those points together in a **thesis statement**—a sentence or two that expresses the main idea of your essay. Your thesis statement should also identify the literary period, the literary trend, and the authors whose works you'll discuss. Remember, it's likely that you'll revise your thesis statement—for reasons of content or style—by the time you write your final draft. Here is one student's working thesis statement.

Jonathan Swift, Alexander Pope, and Voltaire used satire to ridicule the intellectual folly of the eighteenth century.

Elaborate on the Evidence

Building Your Case A compelling case in a literary essay consists of the major points that support your thesis, plus at least two pieces of **literary evidence** that support each major point. Use **precise and relevant examples** as support; however, don't merely state a major point and then follow it with only literary evidence from the work in question. Instead, **elaborate** upon the evidence by interpreting it for your readers. In other words, explain precisely how the evidence supports the major point. Look at how one student structured part of his argument about Pope in the notes on the next page. Notice how he wrote down a **parenthetical citation**, showing where in the work he found the quote; then, he elaborated on this literary evidence.

Writing Skills
Analyze works of literature.
Write a thesis statement.
Support ideas with references to the text.

DIFFERENTIATING INSTRUCTION

Advanced Learners

Enrichment. Challenge students to choose three works of the same era from three different countries and/or from three different literary genres. It may be more difficult to compare disparate literary works, but students could also find that their similarities stand out more clearly. Students will probably discover, however, that analyzing such a spectrum of work gives them a more complete picture of the era.

English-Language Learners

Students may not understand the rationale behind the use of the literary present when writing about literature. Explain to students that one helpful definition of *literature* is that it is "news that stays news," that is, writing that will always offer insight into the human condition. Accordingly, when writing about literature, one discusses humanity's *present* condition. You may want to advise students not to worry too much about the literary present in the drafting stage but to set aside one revision pass for verb tenses only.

PRACTICE & APPLY 1

Guided and Independent Practice

Guide students' analyses of literary works by offering these strategies:

- Is there any common ground in the themes of the three works?
- Do the works share stylistic methods or quirks?
- What other similarites can you find among the works' literary elements? Consider especially tone, characters, plot, and setting.

Reference Note
For more on **parenthetical citations,** see page 212.

TIP When writing about literature, use the **literary present tense.** The characters and actions depicted in literature are forever unfolding for new readers. For example, instead of writing "In *Gulliver's Travels*, Swift used satire...," you would write "In *Gulliver's Travels*, Swift uses satire...."

Writing Skills
Use a clear structure and system of organization.

Major Point: Pope uses satire to chastise writers who create dull, nonsensical works.

Literary Evidence: In a prayer to the goddess Dulness, the poet Bays asks her to "spread a healing mist before the mind" and to replace reason with cobwebs (I, 174).

Elaboration: Bays wants a mist, or fog, to obscure his vision. He wants cobwebs instead of reason in his mind. This is an ironic contrast to what we expect writers to want—clear vision and clear reason. Pope uses irony—the contrast between expectation and reality—to satirize writers who create illogical works.

TIP Writers from every period use **stylistic devices**—figurative language, irony, imagery, diction—that suit their purposes. Some styles of literature require certain stylistic devices—so much so that the literary style and the device can hardly be separated. Such is the case with irony and satire, the literary style that holds human vice and folly up to ridicule. If part of your literary evidence involves a writer's use of a stylistic device, be sure to explain the relationship between the stylistic device and the trend. For more on **stylistic devices,** see page 391.

Organize Your Essay

Setting Forth Plan to **structure** your arguments and ideas in a sustained way. Since this essay deals with three works by different writers, plan to discuss one work at a time, starting with the one published first and ending with the one published last. By organizing the works chronologically, you can show how each not only reflects the literary trend you're discussing, but also contributes to establishing that trend. Here is part of a student's working outline for an essay on satire in the works of Swift, Pope, and Voltaire.

—Introduction
   —Background information
   —Thesis statement
—Swift on scientists
   —Major point
     —First example of literary evidence
       —Elaboration
     —Second example of literary evidence
       —Elaboration

PRACTICE & APPLY 1

Follow the guidelines in this section to analyze three works from one literary period. Find literary evidence to support your major points, elaborate on your evidence, and organize your essay chronologically.

Writing

Writing a Literary Essay

A Writer's Framework

Introduction
- Introduce the literary period and provide background information about that period.
- In a thesis statement, identify the literary period, the literary trend, and the authors discussed in the essay.

Body
- Develop the major points that support the thesis.
- Use at least two pieces of fully elaborated literary evidence to support each point.
- Organize the essay in chronological order.

Conclusion
- Restate, but don't repeat, your thesis.
- Close with a final observation on the literary works or on the literary period.

A Writer's Model

Satire in the Eighteenth Century

The eighteenth century was known as the Enlightenment and the Age of Reason for its emphasis on reason and common sense. Some scientists, writers, and philosophers, however, divorced reason from common sense. The result was reason carried to ludicrous extremes. Jonathan Swift, Alexander Pope, and Voltaire—three of the most important writers of the eighteenth century—used satire to ridicule the intellectual folly of the day.

In *Gulliver's Travels,* Swift uses satire to present a humorous characterization of scientists and to expose some of their impractical ideas. Swift creates a fictional island, Laputa, where members of the nobility regard themselves as scientists. These Laputians' heads are always tilted to one side as if they are in deep thought. In addition, their eyes are strangely arranged—one of them turns inward, and the other turns straight up to show that their thoughts are fixed on themselves and on higher ideas. Swift turns the mental characteristics of the Laputians into humorous physical characteristics. The position of their heads suggests that they are lost in thought and cannot look at anything straight on. In addition, due to the position of their eyes, they cannot see the ground and so they are not down to earth. As evidence of the Laputians' impracticality, the tailor sent to make clothes for Gulliver takes measurements with scientific instruments made for other tasks. Ironically, the result is that Gulliver's new clothes don't fit.

(continued)

INTRODUCTION
Literary period and background information

Thesis statement

BODY
Major point

Evidence: summary

Elaboration

Evidence: summary

RETEACHING

A Writer's Framework

To help students present their thesis statements, point out to them that their statements will answer a form of the question *How?*, such as: "How do the authors you have chosen reflect or use the literary trend to respond to their specific time?" Students can use the question to make sure their thesis statements include all the necessary elements.

For their final observations, encourage students to connect the topics of their essays with the present time: "What about the writers' themes and trends still applies to the present day? How do the writers' works still remain 'news'?"

CRITICAL THINKING

After students have read **A Writer's Model,** ask them to think of other ways the essay could have been organized. Ask: "Could the essay have presented similar points from the three different authors in the body paragraphs, instead of treating the major points in block style? Could the body paragraphs have been organized instead by area of knowledge: science, philosophy, and literature?"

Have students consider alternatives and discuss the benefits and drawbacks. Lead students to see that the organization of the model is probably the best way to present the information clearly and completely to the reader.

DIRECT TEACHING

A Writer's Model
Citations in **A Writer's Model** come from these sources:

Pope:
The Complete Poetical Works of Pope. Boston: Houghton-Mifflin, 1931.

Voltaire:
Voltaire. *Candide.* New York: Bantam, 1959.

PRACTICE & APPLY 2

Guided and Independent Practice
Guide students by reviewing with them **A Writer's Framework** on p. 503, and the method of citation you would prefer they use for their papers. Direct them to ask these questions to help them evaluate the support they give for their main points:

- Is the evidence relevant to the main point?
- Is the evidence from a reliable or reputable source?
- Is the evidence the best I can find in the text?
- Have I elaborated on the evidence enough so that the reader will see its meaning and significance?

The answer to every question for students should be "yes." Have students complete **Practice and Apply 2** as independent practice.

(continued)

Elaboration — Like the scientists of the eighteenth century, the Laputians have become so carried away with knowledge for its own sake that they have lost sight of common sense.

Major point
Evidence: summary
Elaboration — Alexander Pope satirizes the literature of the time in his long poem *The Dunciad,* which praises a goddess named Dulness. The title *The Dunciad* makes fun of poems written by stupid people—dunces. The goddess named Dulness implies that these poets are inspired by dullness. In other words, Pope is saying that the poets of his day value dullness and write boring poems. His character, a poet named Bays,

Evidence: quotation
Elaboration — prays to Dulness, asking her to "spread a healing mist before the mind" and to replace reason with cobwebs (I, 174). Instead of asking for his mind to be sharp and clear, as one would expect, Bays wants the opposite. Pope uses the stylistic device of irony to ridicule the dull and dimwitted writers of his day.

Major point
Evidence: summary — In *Candide,* Voltaire makes fun of eighteenth-century philosophers who teach that the world is a rational, perfect place. To ridicule this kind of thinking, Voltaire creates a character named Pangloss, who is a philosopher. Pangloss teaches the young Candide a popular philosophy

Evidence: quotation/summary — of the day: In this "best of all possible worlds," everything happens for the best (20). However, when Candide goes out to experience this "best of all possible worlds," he encounters one misfortune after another—he is kicked out of his home, separated from the woman he loves, kidnapped, forced to take part in a brutal war, beaten, nearly killed and eaten, cheated, robbed, shipwrecked, and caught in an earthquake. As Candide suffers, he echoes Pangloss's ridiculous teachings to others who suffer terrible misfortunes, making this

Elaboration — philosophy seem more and more ridiculous. The novel's irony is the contrast between the optimistic philosophy of some eighteenth-century thinkers and Candide's actual experience.

CONCLUSION
Restatement of thesis
Final observation — Just as the best scientists, writers, and philosophers of the eighteenth century exposed superstitions to the light of reason, Swift, Pope, and Voltaire exposed the misguided reasoning of lesser scientists, writers, and philosophers. In doing so, they established the trend of using satire to fight folly.

INTERNET
More Writer's Models
Keyword: LE5 12-4

PRACTICE & APPLY 2 Using the framework on page 503 and the Writer's Model above as guides, write the first draft of your literary essay. Be sure to cite all literary evidence used in your essay.

504 Collection 4 The Restoration and the Eighteenth Century

Revising

Evaluate and Revise Your Draft

Polish Your Prose A literary essay is a sophisticated piece of writing that requires much effort. To be sure that your essay is as clearly developed and organized as you want it to be, read through your draft at least twice. On your first reading, consider the content and organization of your essay. On your second, consider the style.

PEER REVIEW
Before you revise, trade papers with a peer. He or she may be able to offer advice on how to improve your elaboration of literary evidence.

▶ **First Reading: Content and Organization** Use the following chart to help you evaluate and revise the content and organization of your literary essay. Answer the questions in the left-hand column by using the tips in the middle column. If revisions are necessary, use the revision techniques in the right-hand column.

Rubric: Writing a Literary Essay

Evaluation Questions	Tips	Revision Techniques
❶ Does the introduction introduce the literary period and give necessary background information?	**Box** the literary period. **Bracket** background information about the literary period.	**Add** sentences that introduce the literary period and give necessary background information.
❷ Does the introduction contain a thesis statement that identifies the literary period, the literary trend, and the authors being discussed?	**Underline** the thesis statement. **Double underline** the mention of the literary period, the literary trend, and the authors.	**Add** information to identify the literary period, the literary trend, and the authors whose works the essay discusses.
❸ Are the major points that support the thesis clear? Are the works organized chronologically?	**Star** the major points that support the thesis statement. **List** each work's publication date in the margin.	**Add** major points, or **rewrite** them so they clearly support the thesis statement. **Rearrange** major points to put works in chronological order.
❹ Is each major point supported by at least two pieces of literary evidence? Is the evidence fully elaborated through explanations and interpretation?	**Circle** each piece of literary evidence. **Highlight** sentences or parts of sentences that elaborate upon the literary evidence.	**Add** literary evidence, if necessary. **Elaborate** upon literary evidence by explaining how it supports a significant idea and by interpreting the evidence.
❺ Does the conclusion restate the thesis and make a final observation about the literary works or period?	**Draw a squiggly line** under the restatement of the thesis. **Double underline** the final observation.	**Add** a sentence that restates the thesis. **Add** a final observation about the literary works or period.

▶ **Second Reading: Style** The second time you read your draft, focus on evaluating and revising your style—the way you express yourself. One way to improve your style is to **introduce quotations** gracefully so that a reader doesn't hesitate or stumble. Look at the examples below, and then use the style guidelines in the chart to improve the style of your essay.

Awkward Pangloss stands by his philosophy even when faced with his own misfortune. He says that "it would be unbecoming for me to recant" (136).

Smooth Even when faced with his own misfortune, Pangloss clings to his optimistic philosophy, saying "it would be unbecoming for me to recant" (136).

Style Guidelines

Evaluation Question	Tip	Revision Technique
● Are quotations introduced smoothly so that they don't interrupt the flow of thought?	▶ **Highlight** the introductions to all quotations.	▶ **Add** introductory phrases to quotations or **combine** quotations with other sentences.

ANALYZING THE REVISION PROCESS
Study these revisions, and answer the questions that follow.

combine   His character, a poet named Bays, prays to Dulness, ~~Bays says,~~ *, asking her to*
"Spread a healing mist before the mind" *and* to replace reason with
elaborate   cobwebs (I, 174), *Instead of asking for his mind to be sharp* Pope uses the stylistic device of irony to
and clear, as one would expect, Bays wants the opposite.
ridicule the dull and dimwitted writers of his day.

Responding to the Revision Process
1. Why did the writer combine the first two sentences?
2. How does the writer's elaboration of the literary evidence contained in this passage improve the draft?

Writing Skills
Revise for content and style.

PRACTICE & APPLY 3 Using the guidelines on pages 505 and 506, first evaluate and revise the content and organization of your literary essay. Then, evaluate and revise its style, introducing quotations gracefully.

Publishing

Proofread and Publish Your Essay

Say What You Mean Errors in basic grammar, usage, and mechanics can ruin the value of an otherwise excellent literary essay. To ensure that your audience will focus on your ideas and not on your mistakes, proofread your essay with care before you submit your final draft.

Far and Wide In your literary essay, you collected and interpreted information that might be of interest to other readers. With a classmate, brainstorm imaginative publishing ideas, or try one of these suggestions to share your essay with a wider audience.

- With classmates, create a Web site that contains your essays along with links that lead to a variety of sites related to the literary works and periods you discussed.
- Submit your essay to one of the many online literary magazines published by high school students.
- Ask a history teacher who teaches the period that your essay examines to make your essay available to his or her classes.
- Adapt your essay into an oral response to literature, and present it to an audience of your classmates. For more on **presenting a literary response**, see page 508.

Reflect on Your Literary Essay

Know Yourself You've created a complex analysis. Take a few minutes now to reflect on your essay in order to grasp how much you've accomplished—how much you learned about your topic and about your writing process. Write responses to the following questions, and include them with a final copy of your essay.

- Did your thesis change by the time you wrote your final draft? If so, explain how and why.
- What major revisions did you make to your draft? How did they improve the essay?
- Did writing the essay deepen your understanding of the works and the literary period you chose? Why or why not?
- What kinds of resources were helpful to you in developing your topic? For what other types of assignments, for this class and others, might resources such as these also be useful? Explain your response.

PRACTICE & APPLY 4 Proofread the final draft of your essay for errors in the conventions of grammar, usage, and mechanics. Then, publish and reflect on your literary essay using the suggestions and questions above.

> **TIP** As you proofread, make sure your essay follows the **conventions** of standard American English. Look in particular to see that you use quotation marks and italics correctly in punctuating the titles of the literary works you discuss. For more on **punctuating titles,** see Italics, 13b, and Quotation Marks, 13d, in the Language Handbook.

Writing Skills
Proofread, especially for correct punctuation of titles.

DIRECT TEACHING

Proofread and Publish Your Essay

If students decide to publish their essays on a Web site, you need to be aware that the World Wide Web sometimes functions as a public forum and that Internet content can be unpredictable.

PRACTICE & APPLY 4

Guided and Independent Practice

Monitor students' progress by using these steps:

1. Ask students to write a short list of grammar, usage, and mechanics errors they commonly find when proofreading their papers.
2. Have them list strategies for correcting these errors.
3. After briefly checking students' lists, take a quick poll to make sure each student has an idea for publishing his or her essay.

Then, have students complete **Practice and Apply 4** for independent practice.

Listening & Speaking Workshop

Presenting a Literary Response

Speaking Assignment
Adapt your literary essay for an oral response to literature, and present it to your class.

Writing a literary essay about a specific literary period probably helped you understand that period better. You can share that understanding with your classmates by adapting your literary essay for an **oral response to literature** and delivering it to your class.

Adapt Your Written Essay

Go with the Flow You can follow the same basic organization of your written essay, but you might need to adjust the introduction, body, and conclusion to make your oral presentation effective.

- The **introduction** to an oral presentation needs to be more dramatic than a written introduction so your listeners won't tune you out before you get started. Consider beginning with one of the **unique aspects** of the works you'll discuss. For example, a unique aspect of *The Dunciad* is Alexander Pope's use of the mock-epic genre to ridicule some poets of his day. End your introduction with a strong but simple **thesis statement** that leaves listeners with no misconceptions about the literary period, literary trend, or authors whose works you plan to discuss.

- The **body** of your oral presentation should cover the main points of your essay as well as the **literary evidence**—quotations and detailed references to the works—and elaboration that interprets or explains the evidence. Make clear the significant ideas in the works. Explain for listeners the effects of any **stylistic devices,** such as imagery or language, that the authors use. Be especially thorough in your explanation of the **ambiguities** (events or passages subject to more than one interpretation), **nuances** (subtle shades of meaning), and **complexities** (passages rich in meaning, but difficult to understand). Remember, listeners must immediately understand the ideas you present, so explain these challenging elements simply and clearly.

- The **conclusion** for your oral response serves the same purpose as your written conclusion: It wraps up your ideas. To impress listeners, it should also be memorable. Consider using a **rhetorical device** such as a rhetorical question, repetition, or parallelism when restating your thesis. When you make a final observation about your topic, consider framing it in terms of the **universal themes** shared by the works you are discussing. For example, a universal theme in the works of Swift, Pope, and Voltaire is that human beings are capable of reform, despite their foolishness.

SKILLS FOCUS
Listening and Speaking Skills
Deliver an oral response to literature.

Rehearse and Deliver Your Oral Response

Naturally Speaking Because you want your presentation to sound natural and relaxed, don't memorize it. Instead, speak **extemporaneously.** Make **concise notes** to use now as you rehearse and later when you deliver your presentation. On note cards, write key words or phrases about main points and brief reminders of evidence you'll use in your presentation. Write quotations out word for word so you can present them accurately. Arrange the note cards in the order in which you want to present the information on them.

A Polished Performance Merely standing up, staring straight ahead, and delivering the content of your presentation in a natural sounding voice will not make your presentation effective. You must use certain delivery techniques, too, including those in the chart below.

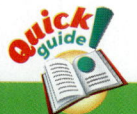

DELIVERY TECHNIQUES

Technique	Tips
Pronunciation and enunciation	Pronounce the words you are using correctly, clearly, and distinctly. Don't slur words.
Emphasis	Emphasize important points by changing the volume or tone of your voice.
Pauses	Pause to give your audience time to think about what you have just said and to emphasize the point you are about to make.
Facial expressions	Make your facial expressions complement the content of your presentation—serious expressions for serious content and light expressions for light content.
Gestures	Use natural, relaxed gestures, and don't be afraid to move around as you speak.
Eye contact	Engage your audience by making eye contact with as many people as possible.

TIP Be sure to use **standard American English** when you deliver your presentation. Avoid using slang and colloquialisms in an oral response to literature. Your listeners could misunderstand nonstandard language.

Stand and Deliver Rehearse your presentation until you are thoroughly familiar and comfortable with the content and the delivery techniques you intend to use when you actually present your response. If possible, rehearse in front of an audience of friends or family, and ask for feedback on how you might improve your presentation.

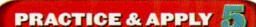 Use the instructions in this workshop to adapt your written literary essay for an oral presentation. Speak extemporaneously, and use delivery techniques effectively as you present your oral response to literature.

Listening and Speaking Skills
Use effective verbal and nonverbal techniques.

Collection 4: Skills Review

Comparing Literature

SKILLS FOCUS, pp. 510–513

Grade-Level Skills

■ **Literary Skills**
Compare and contrast the major literary forms of different historical periods.

INTRODUCING THE SKILLS REVIEW
Use this review to assess students' ability to contrast works from different periods.

DIRECT TEACHING

A Literary Focus

❓ **Style.** How would you describe Tacitus's diction, or word choice, in this passage? [Possible responses: It is elegant but not stuffy or ornate; it includes many words with multiple syllables.]

B Literary Focus

❓ **Style.** How does the use of parallel structure here contribute to the mood of this scene? [The linking of opposites—the aged and the young, the hurrying and the lingering—emphasizes the extent of the chaos.]

Collection 4: Skills Review
Comparing Literature

Test Practice

The following excerpts provide two accounts of disastrous fires that occurred over sixteen hundred years apart. The fire described by the Roman historian Tacitus (c. A.D. 56–c. 117) in "The Burning of Rome" occurred in A.D. 64. It is perhaps best remembered as the occasion when Emperor Nero, a particularly heartless, despotic ruler, "fiddled while Rome burned." Samuel Pepys (1633–1703; pronounced "peeps"), the most famous diarist of the English Restoration, kept a secret, multivolume diary from 1660 to 1669. He recorded "The First Day of the Great Fire of London" alongside entries describing his public and private experiences in daily life. The Great Fire, which occurred in 1666, was a horrible national disaster for England.

DIRECTIONS: Read the following excerpts. Then, read each multiple-choice question that follows, and write the letter of the best response.

from The Burning of Rome
from The Annals
Tacitus
translated by **George Gilbert Ramsay**

A And now came a calamitous fire—whether it was accidental or purposely contrived by the Emperor remains uncertain for on this point authorities are divided—more violent and destructive than any that ever befell our city. It began in that part of the Circus[1] which adjoins the Palatine and Caelian hills.[2] Breaking out in shops full of inflammable merchandise, it took hold and gathered strength at once; and being fanned by the wind soon embraced the entire length of the Circus, where there were no mansions with protective walls, no temple-enclosures, nor anything else to arrest its course. Furiously the destroying flames swept on, first over the level ground, then up the heights, then again plunging into the hollows, with a rapidity which outstripped all efforts to cope with them, the ancient city lending itself to their progress by its narrow tortuous streets and its misshapen blocks of buildings. **B** The shrieks of panic-stricken women; the weakness of the aged, and the helplessness of the young; the efforts of some to save themselves, of others to help their neighbors; the hurrying of those who dragged their sick along, the lingering of those who waited for them—all made up a scene of inextricable confusion.

Many persons, while looking behind them, were enveloped from the front or from the side; or having escaped to the nearest place of safety, found this, too, in posses-

---

Pages 510–513 cover **Literary Skills** Compare and contrast works from different literary periods.

1. **Circus:** Circus Maximus, a great arena used for chariot races.
2. **Palatine** (pa'lə·tīn') **and Caelian** (sē'lē·ən) **hills:** two of seven hills of ancient Rome.

510 Collection 4 The Restoration and the Eighteenth Century

READING MINI-LESSON

Reviewing Word-Attack Skills

Activity. Have students read each set of words and identify the two words in which the underlined letters stand for the same sounds.

1. sp<u>e</u>cies   sp<u>e</u>cious   sp<u>e</u>cific
   [species, specious]
2. abr<u>o</u>gate   interr<u>o</u>gatory   der<u>o</u>gatory
   [interrogatory, derogatory]
3. <u>i</u>nfinite   f<u>i</u>nale   f<u>i</u>nality
   [infinite, finale]
4. l<u>i</u>terate   <u>i</u>lliterate   obl<u>i</u>terate
   [literate, illiterate]
5. n<u>eu</u>tral   n<u>eu</u>trality   n<u>eu</u>tralize
   [neutral, neutralize]
6. hi<u>nd</u>rance   hi<u>nd</u>sight   hi<u>nd</u>most
   [hindsight, hindmost]
7. frater<u>n</u>ity   frater<u>n</u>al   frater<u>n</u>ize
   [fraternity, fraternal]
8. gra<u>d</u>ation   gra<u>d</u>ual   gra<u>d</u>ient
   [gradation, gradient]
9. var<u>i</u>ance   var<u>i</u>etal   var<u>i</u>egated
   [variance, variegated]
10. gen<u>u</u>s   ingen<u>u</u>ous   gen<u>u</u>ine
    [ingenuous, genuine]

510 Collection 4 The Restoration and the Eighteenth Century

Collection 4: Skills Review

sion of the flames, and even places which they had thought beyond their reach in the same plight with the rest. At last, not knowing where to turn, or what to avoid, they poured into the roads or threw themselves down in the fields: some having lost their all, not having even food for the day; others, though with means of escape open to them, preferred to perish for love of the dear ones whom they could not save. And none dared to check the flames; for there were many who threatened and forced back those who would extinguish them, while others openly flung in torches, saying that *they had their orders;*—whether it really was so, or only that they wanted to plunder undisturbed.

from The Diary of Samuel Pepys
Samuel Pepys

SEPTEMBER 2, 1666
The First Day of the Great Fire of London

Lord's Day. Some of our maids sitting up late last night to get things ready against our feast today, Jane called us up, about three in the morning, to tell us of a great fire they saw in the City.[1] So I rose, and slipped on my nightgown and went to her window, and thought it to be on the backside of Mark Lane at the furthest; but being unused to such fires as followed, I thought it far enough off, and so went to bed again and to sleep. About seven rose again to dress myself, and there looked out at the window and saw the fire not so much as it was, and further off. So to my closet[2] to set things to rights after yesterday's cleaning. By and by Jane comes and tells me that she hears that above three hundred houses have been burned down tonight by the fire we saw, and that it was now burning down all Fish Street by London Bridge. So I made myself ready presently, and walked to the Tower[3] and there got up upon one of the high places, Sir J. Robinson's little son going up with me; and there I did see the houses[4] at that end of the bridge all on fire, and an infinite great fire on this and the other side of the end of the bridge—which, among other people, did trouble me for poor little Michell and our Sarah[5] on the bridge. So down, with my heart full of trouble, to the Lieutenant of the Tower, who tells me that it begun this morning in the King's baker's house in Pudding Lane, and that it hath burned down St. Magnes Church and most part of Fish Street

---

1. **City:** London. The Great Fire started in a bakery, raged for four days and four nights, and destroyed some 13,000 residences. It leveled four fifths of the city and left about 100,000 people homeless.
2. **closet** *n.:* private room.
3. **Tower:** Tower of London, a short walk from Pepys's house.
4. **houses** *n. pl.:* Shops and dwellings were built on London Bridge.
5. **Sarah:** maid whom Mrs. Pepys discharged on December 5, 1662. Pepys wrote: "The wench cried, and I was ready to cry too."

Activity. Have students identify the prefix in each of these words.

1. intermittent [*inter–*]
2. interminable [*in–*]
3. protrusive [*pro–*]
4. prototype [*proto–*]
5. unilateral [*uni–*]
6. unidiomatic [*un–*]
7. retrogress [*retro–*]
8. remember [*re–*]
9. intractable [*in–*]
10. intracutaneous [*intra–*]

Activity. Have students identify the syllable said with greatest stress in each underlined word.

1. She worked to perfect her backhand. [second syllable]
   Now her form is perfect. [first syllable]
2. Persistence is a valuable attribute. [first syllable]
   We attribute success to determination. [second syllable]
3. Sometimes it's necessary to combat discouragement. [second syllable]
   This sort of mental combat pays off. [first syllable]

Collection 4: Skills Review

DIRECT TEACHING

A Literary Focus

? Imagery. To what senses do the images in this passage appeal? [They appeal to the senses of sight and touch and contribute to the sense of panic and confusion.]

B Literary Focus

? Style. Notice that this passage consists of a single sentence. What effect does this long, packed sentence have? [Possible responses: It conveys the great urgency Pepys felt; it shows how his mind was racing; it creates an almost unbearable tension.]

Answers and Model Rationales

1. **A** B is wrong because the efforts of some to help others is included merely as a detail to support his main point—the confusion. The scene is anything but orderly, and there is no anticipation—the effects of the fire are experienced immediately. Thus, C and D are wrong.

2. **J** The author's use of parallel structure (F) and words with strong connotations (G) is evident in every paragraph, and the excerpt begins and ends with examples of two different explanations for an event (H). Therefore, *all of the above* (J), is correct.

---

already. So I down to the waterside and there got a boat and through bridge, and there saw a lamentable fire. Poor Michell's house, as far as the Old Swan,[6] already burned that way and the fire running further, that in a very little time it got as far as the Steelyard while I was there. Everybody endeavoring to remove their goods, and flinging into the river or bringing them into lighters[7] that lay off. Poor people staying in their houses as long as till the very fire touched them, and then running into boats or clambering from one pair of stair by the waterside to another. And among other things, the poor pigeons I perceive were loath to leave their houses, but hovered about the windows and balconies till they were some of them burned, their wings, and fell down.

---

6. **Michell's house . . . Old Swan:** Betty Michell, a former sweetheart of Pepys, lost her house in the fire. The Old Swan was a tavern on Thames Street, near London Bridge.
7. **lighters** *n. pl.:* large, open barges.

Having stayed, and in an hour's time seen the fire rage every way, and nobody to my sight endeavoring to quench it, but to remove their goods and leave all to the fire; and having seen it get as far as the Steelyard, and the wind mighty high and driving it into the City, and everything, after so long a drought, proving combustible, even the very stones of churches, and among other things, the poor steeple by which pretty Mrs. —— lives, and whereof my old schoolfellow Elborough is parson, taken fire in the very top and there burned till it fall down—I to Whitehall with a gentleman with me who desired to go off from the Tower to see the fire in my boat—to Whitehall, and there up to the King's closet in the chapel, where people came about me and I did give them an account dismayed them all; and word was carried in to the King, so I was called for and did tell the King and Duke of York what I saw, and that unless his Majesty did command houses to be pulled down, nothing could stop the fire. . . .

---

1. Tacitus describes the scene of the fire as being one of —
    A confusion
    B heroism
    C orderliness
    D anticipation

2. A distinctive feature of Tacitus's style is his —
    F use of parallel structure
    G use of words with strong connotations
    H offering of two different causes or explanations for an event
    J all of the above

Using Academic Language

Review of Literary Terms

Ask students to look back through the collection to find the meanings of the terms listed at right. Then, have students show their grasp of these terms by citing passages from the collection that illustrate the meanings of those terms.

Verbal Irony (p. 428); **Antithesis** (p. 446); **Epigram** (p. 450); **Mock Epic** (p. 451); **Satire** (pp. 462, 466); **Parody** (p. 474); **Tone** (p. 485).

Review of Informational Terms

Ask students to look back through the collection to find the meanings of the terms listed below. Then, have students use those terms to explain the ways in which authors use rhetorical devices.

Rhetorical Question (p. 483); **Argument by Analogy** (p. 483); **Historical Allusion** (p. 483); **Repetition** (p. 483); **Counterargument** (p. 483); **Appeal to Authority** (p. 483); **Illustrative Anecdote** (p. 483).

Collection 4: Skills Review

3. Which of the following is true of both "The Burning of Rome" and "The First Day of the Great Fire of London"?
   A Both express contempt for the victims.
   B Both describe scenes of beauty.
   C Both describe people making the fire worse on purpose.
   D Both describe the power of the fire.

4. What word best describes Tacitus's tone?
   F enthusiastic
   G critical
   H sentimental
   J neutral

5. In which of the following ways does Pepys's literary technique differ from Tacitus's?
   A Pepys describes the fire scene.
   B Pepys writes in the third person.
   C Pepys romanticizes the beauty of the fire.
   D Pepys describes his personal feelings.

6. According to Pepys's diary entry, after he first sees the fire from a window, he goes back to sleep because —
   F he is too terrified to go outdoors
   G the fire seems far away
   H he thinks it is a dream
   J he is ill

7. Pepys's descriptions of the "lamentable fire" and the "poor pigeons" typify his tone of —
   A cynicism
   B superiority
   C disgust
   D compassion

8. What is Pepys's reaction to the fire?
   F He finds the sight worrisome.
   G He wishes the flames were bigger.
   H He becomes enraged.
   J He has no reaction at all.

9. One aspect of Restoration life depicted in Pepys's account is —
   A commercialism
   B a clear-cut class system
   C the popularity of satire
   D vast scientific progress

Essay Question

The excerpts you have read are accounts of great tragedies recounted by two very different writers from very different time periods—a historian from ancient Rome and a diarist from Restoration England. In a short essay, compare and contrast the texts. In your essay consider these elements of each text:
- audience
- purpose
- writer's perspective
- use of personal details
- tone

3. **D** Only Tacitus mentions people making the fire worse on purpose. Neither account expresses contempt for the victims (A) or describes scenes of beauty (B). Therefore, D is correct.

4. **G** The best answer is G because Tacitus criticizes those who fan the flames. The author is not enthusiastic (F) or sentimental (H); his criticism negates choice J.

5. **D** Writing in the first person, Pepys describes his horror and his concern for Londoners.

6. **G** Students can eliminate F, H, and J because Pepys makes no mention of being afraid or ill or of thinking he was dreaming.

7. **D** Since *lamentable* means "heartbreaking" and *poor* means "worthy of pity," Pepys's tone is clearly compassionate. He shows no trace of being cynical, superior, or disgusted.

8. **F** He is alarmed by the fire, which eliminates G; anger plays no part in his thinking, eliminating H; and he is clearly deeply moved, which rules out J.

9. **A** Pepys mentions the baker, a pub, and the Steelyard, all commercial enterprises. His access to the king rules out B; he mentions neither satire nor scientific progress, eliminating C and D.

ASSESSING

Assessment
- Holt Assessment: Literature, Reading, and Vocabulary

Essay Question

Pepys's plain, colloquial language, his use of the first person, and his disregard for language conventions create an informal, conversational style. His use of long, free-form sentences gives his writing a breathless quality that conveys both the urgency of the events and the depth of his compassion and concern. His detailed, unfiltered account would probably have been welcomed by the Londoners of his day as a vivid eyewitness report by a skillful observer.

Like Pepys's tone, Tacitus's overall tone is compassionate, although that tone is undercut somewhat by the cynicism of the alternate explanations for the origin of the fire and the motives of those making it worse. The excerpt's style is considerably more formal, primarily because it contains elevated language, is written in the third person, and is highly structured (particularly in its use of parallel structure). Writing for scholars of future generations, Tacitus wants his prose to be as lucid as possible.

Resource Manager

Selection • Feature	Planning	Differentiating Instruction Lesson Plans with ELL Strategies and Practice	Reading • Vocabulary
The Romantic Period: 1798–1832 by Harley Henry	• PowerNotes: The Romantic Period	• Holt Adapted Reader	• Holt Adapted Reader
• The Tyger • The Lamb • The Chimney Sweeper, from Songs of Innocence • The Chimney Sweeper, from Songs of Experience • A Poison Tree by William Blake	• One-Stop Planner with ExamView Test Generator	• Supporting Instruction in Spanish, pp. 29–30 • Audio CD Library, disc 9 • Audio CD Library, Selections and Summaries in Spanish	
• Lines Composed a Few Miles Above Tintern Abbey • Composed upon Westminster Bridge • The World Is Too Much with Us by William Wordsworth	• One-Stop Planner with ExamView Test Generator	• The Holt Reader, pp. 168–175 • Holt Adapted Reader • Holt Reading Solutions, p. 115 • Supporting Instruction in Spanish, pp. 30–31 • Audio CD Library, disc 9 • Audio CD Library, Selections and Summaries in Spanish	• The Holt Reader • Holt Adapted Reader • Holt Reading Solutions
Connecting to World Literature: Tanka and Haiku **Tanka** by Princess Nukada; Oshikochi Mitsune; Ki Tsurayuki; Ono Komachi; Priest Saigyo **Haiku** by Matsuo Bashō; Uejima Onitsura; Taniguchi Buson; Kobayashi Issa	• One-Stop Planner with ExamView Test Generator	• Supporting Instruction in Spanish, p. 31 • Audio CD Library, disc 9 • Audio CD Library, Selections and Summaries in Spanish	
Kubla Khan **The Rime of the Ancient Mariner** by Samuel Taylor Coleridge	• One-Stop Planner with ExamView Test Generator	• The Holt Reader, pp. 176–180 • Holt Adapted Reader • Holt Reading Solutions, p. 118 • Supporting Instruction in Spanish, pp. 32–33 • Audio CD Library, disc 9 • Audio CD Library, Selections and Summaries in Spanish	• The Holt Reader • Holt Adapted Reader • Holt Reading Solutions • Vocabulary Development, p. 27
She Walks in Beauty from *Childe Harold's Pilgrimage*, Canto IV by George Gordon, Lord Byron	• One-Stop Planner with ExamView Test Generator	• Supporting Instruction in Spanish, p. 33 • Audio CD Library, disc 10 • Audio CD Library, Selections and Summaries in Spanish	

Collection 5

The Romantic Period
※ 1798–1832 ※

The Quest for Truth and Beauty

The divine arts of imagination:
imagination, the real & eternal world
of which this vegetable universe
is but a faint shadow.
—William Blake

Brickmakers (1821) by Sir John Gilbert.
© Getty Images.

INTERNET
Collection Resources
Keyword: LE5 12-5

THE QUOTATION

As the Industrial Revolution progressed, the Romantics confronted a "vegetable universe" undergoing dramatic changes. The quotation, from a letter written by Blake, focuses on the importance of what the Romantics called "the imagination," as opposed to the intellect, in coping with these changes. Ask students whether they agree that the imagination forms the "real world" and the visible world is just a shadow. [Possible responses: Yes, the imagination can be richer and more "real" than reality; no, the real world is the material "vegetable universe."]

Assessment
- Holt Assessment: Literature, Reading, and Vocabulary
- One-Stop Planner CD-ROM with ExamView Test Generator
- Holt Online Assessment

Internet
- go.hrw.com (Keyword: LE5 12-5)
- Elements of Literature Online

Media
- Audio CD Library
- Audio CD Library, Selections and Summaries in Spanish
- Fine Art Transparencies
- Visual Connections Videocassette Program
- PowerNotes

The Romantic Period 1798–1832

Time Line

1789
The French Revolution

The revolutionaries who stormed the Bastille limited the power of King Louis XVI, established the 1789 Declaration of the Rights of Man, and set up a constitutional monarchy. By September 1792, however, the more radical Jacobins were in control and were calling for the king's head.

1804
Napoleon Bonaparte

Napoleon Bonaparte (1769–1821) rose to power in France in an astonishingly short period of time. In 1785, the young Napoleon was a new army officer; by 1799, he had become the military dictator of France by virtue of a coup. Shortly after, he had himself crowned emperor, and by 1810, he ruled most of Europe. After France's defeat at Waterloo, he was exiled to the island of St. Helena, where he died in 1821.

1812
The Brothers Grimm

Jakob Ludwig Karl Grimm (1785–1863) and Wilhelm Karl Grimm (1786–1859) were German brothers whose collections of folk songs and folk tales gave rise to folklore as a science.

1811
The Luddites

The Luddites, named after the probably mythical Ned Ludd, were a group of artisans who attacked weaving machines throughout northern England. In 1812, many Luddites were shot under orders of a factory owner named Horsfall (who was murdered in reprisal). The movement dissolved in 1813 after many of its members were hanged in York. The word *Luddite* survives today to denote someone who opposes the development and spread of technology.

LITERARY EVENTS

1786 Robert Burns publishes *Poems, Chiefly in the Scottish Dialect*

1789 William Blake publishes *Songs of Innocence*

1792 Mary Wollstonecraft critiques female educational restrictions in *A Vindication of the Rights of Woman*

1794 Ann Radcliffe's *The Mysteries of Udolpho* popularizes the Gothic novel

1798 William Wordsworth and Samuel Taylor Coleridge publish *Lyrical Ballads*

1800 Maria Edgeworth's *Castle Rackrent*, the first historical novel in English, satirizes absentee landowners in Ireland

1807 Charles and Mary Lamb publish *Tales from Shakespeare*

1808 Johann Wolfgang von Goethe publishes Part I of *Faust*

1812 Charles Dickens is born

1812 Lord Byron publishes first two cantos of *Childe Harold's Pilgrimage*

1812 Brothers Grimm begin to publish *Grimm's Fairy Tales*

1813 Jane Austen publishes *Pride and Prejudice*

Jane Austen (c. 1790). The Granger Collection, New York.

POLITICAL AND SOCIAL EVENTS

Marie Antoinette, queen of France, being led to execution. Drawing (late 18th century) by Jacques-Louis David. Bettmann/CORBIS.

1789 French Revolution begins with storming of Bastille

1793 King Louis XVI of France is beheaded

1793 France declares war on England

1800 Thomas Jefferson is elected U.S. president

1800 Napoleon conquers parts of Italy

1801 Act of Union creates United Kingdom of Great Britain and Ireland

1802 Workday of pauper children is limited to twelve hours in England

1803 United States purchases Louisiana Territory from France

1804 Napoleon crowns himself emperor in France

1805 Egypt gains independence from Ottoman Turks

1805 Lord Nelson defeats Napoleon's navy at Battle of Trafalgar

1806 Construction begins on Arc de Triomphe

1808 United States bans importation of slaves from Africa

1810 Simón Bolívar begins series of South American rebellions against Spain

1811 Venezuela declares independence from Spain

1811 English artisans called Luddites riot and destroy textile machines, fearing that industrialism threatens their livelihoods

1812 Napoleon invades Russia

1812 United States declares war on Great Britain

Napoleon in his study (19th century) by Hippolyte (Paul) Delaroche. Agnew & Sons, London. The Bridgeman Art Library.

Using the Time Line

Activity. Ask students to choose five familiar events or publications from the time line. Then, have them share what they know about the events or publications and look for connections that may reveal something about the Romantic period. Encourage students to make a statement about the spirit of the times based on how they might have felt if they had lived in the Romantic era. Students can use a chart like the following to organize their observations and ideas.

Event or Publication	What I Know	Its Relation to Other Events	Spirit of the Time
[Children's workday limited to 12 hrs.]	[Eventually child labor became illegal.]	[Dickens wrote about this.]	[People began to question the use of child labor.]

Timeline 1814–1833

1814 Noted actor Edmund Kean debuts as Shylock in Shakespeare's *The Merchant of Venice*

1818 Mary Shelley, daughter of **Mary Wollstonecraft**, publishes *Frankenstein*

1819 Sir Walter Scott publishes *Ivanhoe*

1819 John Keats writes his greatest poems between January and September

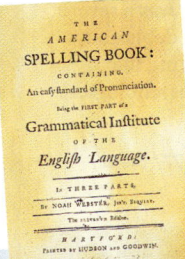

Title page of the first known edition of Noah Webster's *The American Spelling Book* (1788). The Granger Collection, New York.

1823 Alexander Pushkin begins his novel in verse, *Eugene Onegin*

1826 James Fenimore Cooper publishes *The Last of the Mohicans*

1827 John James Audubon begins publishing *The Birds of America*

1828 Noah Webster publishes *An American Dictionary of the English Language*

1830 Emily Dickinson is born in Amherst, Massachusetts

1831 Victor Hugo publishes *The Hunchback of Notre Dame*

Scarlet Ibis by John James Audubon. Collection of New-York Historical Society (Acc. No. 1863.17.397).

1814 British forces burn Washington, D.C.

1815 Allied British, Dutch, and German forces defeat Napoleon at Waterloo

1815 German confederation is created to replace Holy Roman Empire

1819 One of a series of ineffective Factory Acts prohibits employment of all children under nine

1819 First steamship, the *Savannah*, crosses the Atlantic in twenty-nine days

1820 Antarctica is sighted by Russian, British, and American ships

1820 George III, mentally unstable since 1810, dies

1821 Cherokee system of writing is created by Sequoyah

1821 Mexico declares its independence from Spain

1822 Liberia is founded as home for former U.S. slaves

1822 Rosetta stone is deciphered, allowing Egyptian hieroglyphics to be read

1823 In the United States, Monroe Doctrine closes the Americas to further European colonization

1824 First labor unions are permitted in Great Britain

1829 Catholic Emancipation Act allows British Roman Catholics to hold public office

1831 Charles Darwin serves as naturalist on HMS *Beagle* during expedition along the coast of South America

1831 Nat Turner leads slave rebellion in Virginia

1832 Reform Act extends voting rights in Britain to upper-middle-class men

1833 Slavery is abolished in British Empire

HMS *Beagle*. The Granger Collection, New York.

Sequoyah (19th century). Lithograph printed by Lehman and Duval after a painting by Charles Bird King (1785–1862). Philadelphia Museum of Art, Philadelphia. Given by Miss William Adger.

■ 1818
Frankenstein

In her novel *Frankenstein*, Mary Shelley calls into question the aims and methods of science: A scientist tries to imitate God and create life. Still, one of the novel's many ironies is that the creature, although monstrous, is somehow more human than its creator.

■ 1819
Sir Walter Scott

Scott (1771–1832) was already a famous poet when he began publishing novels anonymously. By 1827, he had written more than twenty-five books, including the medieval romance *Ivanhoe*, which is still read by high-school students today. The popularity of Scott's books was an indication of the strength of the Romantic movement.

■ 1831
Charles Darwin

Darwin (1809–1882) spent five years as a naturalist aboard HMS *Beagle* on its way to the Galapagos Islands. After he returned to England, he spent twenty years assimilating his observations and developing his theories of evolution. Darwin's theories, published in *On the Origin of Species by Means of Natural Selection* (1859), have had a powerful impact on Western thought and society.

■ 1832
The Right to Vote

The Reform Bill of 1832 began a series of changes in voting rights that continued in Britain for one hundred years, resulting in suffrage for a majority of Britain's population by 1918. As a start, the Reform Bill gave some well-to-do middle-class men the right to vote. It also changed the formula for electing members of Parliament, giving more weight to new industrial cities, such as Manchester.

Activity. Model how to analyze this time line by posing the following questions based on it:
- What political upheavals occurred during the Romantic era? [Possible responses: the French Revolution; Egyptian rebellion against the Turks; Bolivar's rebellion against Spain; Venezuela's independence from Spain; Nat Turner's revolt against slavery.] What generalization can you draw from these events? [Possible response: Many people fought for political freedom during this era.]
- What two social reforms in Britain were aimed at improving the lives of working people? [The Factory Acts of 1819 and the formation of labor unions in 1824] What can you infer from these events? [Possible response: Friction between workers and owners grew as reformers tried to improve workers' quality of life.]

Encourage students to form similar questions and generalizations about events.

Political and Social

Political and Social Milestones

The American Revolution, 1776–1783

According to the British historian G. M. Trevelyan, the American Revolution decided the fate not only of the United States but also of the British monarchy. It was a war begun and prolonged by the stubbornness of the British monarch, George III. When Britain lost the war and the colonies, government by the personal power of the king came to an end in England. Trevelyan suggests that if this had not been the case, the British reform movements of the next century would have become antiroyalist and republican and might have brought about the downfall of the British monarchy.

The French Revolution and the Era of Napoleon, 1789–1815

The French Revolution was sparked by a meeting of the Estates-General called by the financially troubled King Louis XVI in May 1789. At the meeting, the king and the first two estates (clergy and nobles) refused to write a constitution, whereupon representatives of the third estate (peasants and the middle class) declared themselves the National Assembly of France and vowed not to disband until they had written a constitution. Parisians then stormed the Bastille, while peasants rose up against nobles in the countryside. Between August 1789 and September 1791, the National Assembly instituted a number of reforms and wrote a constitution establishing France as a limited monarchy. Believing the revolution to be over, the Assembly disbanded. Louis XVI continued to oppose the new government, however, and was eventually imprisoned, tried for treason, and executed.

Over time, the revolution grew more violent. Its leaders, the Jacobins, declared a policy of terrorizing anyone who disputed their authority. Eventually the Jacobins quarreled among themselves, and a new government was formed, called the Directory. Plagued by war, economic problems, and the continued opposition of both royalists and Jacobins, the Directory was overthrown by Napoleon on November 9, 1799. The revolution was over.

The American Revolution, 1776–1783

The beginning of the end of the worldwide British Empire began with the revolt of the thirteen American Colonies. Britain's defeat in the American War of Independence was a severe economic blow, leaving the country with massive war debts and without the American revenue which had been enriching the British economy. The loss of the Colonies was also a psychological blow to England.

The Death of General Mercer at the Battle of Princeton, January 3, 1777 (detail) (c. 1789–1831) by John Trumbull.
© Francis G. Mayer/CORBIS.

The French Revolution and the Era of Napoleon, 1789–1815

In July of 1789, an angry crowd of Frenchmen stormed the Bastille, a prison in Paris, to protest the oppressive policies of the French monarchy. This event marked the first step in a long series of violent political upheavals and radical changes in the French national government. These revolutionary experiments, which were intended to introduce "liberty, fraternity, and equality" into French society, instead often resulted in a loss of freedom, civility, and safety. Events

Milestones 1798–1832

The guillotine.
Musée de la Ville de Paris, Musée Carnavalet, Paris. © Giraudon/Art Resource, New York.

such as the massacre of clergy and nobility in September of 1792, the execution of King Louis XVI in 1793, and finally the rise to power of Napoleon (a military dictator with world-conquering ambitions) dashed the hopes of British liberals and strengthened the conservative side. The British liberals had initially looked to revolutionary France for new models of political freedom, but now rich and powerful British conservatives could point a finger at French excesses to justify their repressive policies.

The Motto of the Republic of France (18th century).
Musée de la Revolution Française, Vizille, France. The Bridgeman Art Library.

Interior of a coal mine in South Staffordshire, England.
Ironbridge Gorge Museum, Telford, Shropshire, England. The Bridgeman Art Library.

The Industrial Revolution in England

With the invention of efficient machines to do work formerly done at home by hand, nineteenth-century England began moving from a traditional rural, agricultural society to a more modern, urban, and industrialized state. Masses of landless people now had no choice but to move to crowded cities and work in squalid, dangerous factories for low wages. The wealthy owners of these new factories and mills embraced the hands-off economic theory of *laissez faire* (les′ā fer′)—"let people do as they please"—to justify doing nothing to improve the appalling conditions in which their labor force lived and worked. This laissez-faire approach was even applied to rationalize the use of young children of the poor for back-breaking labor.

Child working in a brick factory.
Bettmann/CORBIS.

■ The Industrial Revolution in England

The Industrial Revolution, which eventually spread to other countries, began in England. The two main reasons for this are that England had the natural resources (coal and iron) necessary for early industrialization and that England ruled an empire. Its colonies not only supplied raw materials but also provided markets for finished products. Before the Industrial Revolution, goods were produced on a small scale by workers living in cottages on farms and in villages. Merchants distributed raw materials to these workers and collected the finished products. This system was called the domestic system. In the late eighteenth century, an increase in demand for English products forced merchants to compete for raw materials and labor. Competition increased production costs, which in turn cut into profits. Seeking more efficient means of production, merchants began turning to machinery. Machines could be efficient only on a large scale. Thus the factory system was born, bringing workers out of their homes to work with machines in factories and under the direct control of the merchants.

SKILLS FOCUS, pp. 534–549

Grade-Level Skills

■ **Literary Focus**

Analyze the way the author's style, including the use of parallelism, achieves specific rhetorical or aesthetic purposes.

■ **Literary Focus**

Analyze the way in which the theme of a selection represents a comment on life, using evidence from the text to support your claim.

Review Skills

■ **Literary Skills**

Analyze various literary devices, including symbolism.

More About the Writer

Background. Today William Blake is known as much for his art as for his poetry. Using a technique he invented called "illuminated printing" (revealed to him, he claimed, by his dead brother in a vision), Blake engraved the text and illustrations of his books himself. He first printed each page in monochrome from an engraved plate of both text and illustration, produced by a type of relief etching. Then, with the help of his wife, he handcolored the prints with watercolor. Most of Blake's works were laboriously "published" in this way, ensuring that only a limited audience saw them during the artist's lifetime. Single-minded and unworldly, Blake did not seek fame; he and his wife lived in poverty and obscurity for much of their lives, aided by the generosity and dedication of a handful of friends, patrons, and collectors.

In one of his volumes of poetry, William Wordsworth offers an explanation of the poetic process, which begins, "The powers requisite for the production of poetry are, first, those of observation and description. . . . 2dly, Sensibility." In the margin of his copy, Blake wrote, "One Power alone makes a Poet: Imagination, The Divine Vision." Blake's poetry is strongly visionary, and he makes no apologies for locating its source in the divine.

William Blake
(1757–1827)

William Blake (detail) (1807) by Thomas Phillips. Oil on canvas (35¼" × 17¼").
The Granger Collection, New York.

William Blake's life is not as "romantic" or "poetic" as the lives of Coleridge, Shelley, and Keats were. By all accounts, he was somewhat happily married to the same woman for much of his life. He never traveled, and he lived outside London for only three years (1800–1803). He began his artistic training at ten, when his father, a London shopkeeper, sent him to one of the best drawing schools. Apprenticed to an engraver at fourteen, Blake worked steadily at his craft as an engraver and as a professional artist throughout a long life.

During his lifetime, Blake's work received very little attention, and a great deal of his poetry was never published in the sense of being public. When his work was noticed, readers and viewers too often decided that it, and therefore Blake himself, was weird, confused, or mad. What we really know of Blake—from the enormous energy and variety of his poetry, paintings, drawings, and engravings—is that he was quite simply a great artist in the fullest sense.

A woman at a gathering is said to have asked Blake where he had come upon the scene he had just vividly described to her. "Here, madam," he said, pointing his finger at his forehead. To paraphrase Blake, if we see with imagination, we see all things in the infinite. But if we see only with reason, we see only ourselves. "I know that this world is a world of imagination & vision," he wrote.

The history of Blake the poet cannot really be separated from that of Blake the visual artist. Not only did he provide illustrations for most of his poems, but he also printed much of his poetry himself (and sometimes only for himself), using engraving methods he himself had created. According to Blake's nineteenth-century biographer Alexander Gilchrist, "the poet and his wife did everything in making the book [*Songs of Innocence* (1789)]—writing, designing, printing, engraving—everything except manufacturing the paper; the very ink, or color rather, they did make. Never before surely was a man so literally the author of his own book."

A good deal of what Blake wrote other than his poems is cryptic and needs illumination from his art. But one characteristic of the man himself shines through clearly—the optimism sustained by his continuous joy in the "one continued vision" of his art. As one acquaintance described Blake, "He was a man without a mask; his aim single, his path straightforward, and his wants few; so he was free, noble, and happy."

534 Collection 5 The Romantic Period

RESOURCES: READING

Planning
- One-Stop Planner CD-ROM with ExamView Test Generator

Differentiating Instruction
- Supporting Instruction in Spanish
- Audio CD Library, Selections and Summaries in Spanish

Grammar and Language
- Daily Language Activities
- Language Handbook Worksheets

Assessment
- Holt Assessment: Literature, Reading, and Vocabulary
- One-Stop Planner CD-ROM with ExamView Test Generator
- Holt Online Assessment

Blake's Poems: Innocence to Experience

William Blake first published *Songs of Innocence* in 1789. In 1794, this collection and *Songs of Experience* were issued together in one volume, the title page promising a demonstration of "the two Contrary States of the Human Soul."

Innocence and experience. Blake conceived the first of these states, "Innocence," as a state of genuine love and naive trust toward all humankind, accompanied by unquestioned belief in Christian doctrine. Though a firm believer in Christianity, Blake thought that its doctrines were being used by the English Church and other institutions as a form of social control: to encourage among the people passive obedience and acceptance of oppression, poverty, and inequality. Recognition of this marks what Blake called the state of "Experience," a profound disillusionment with human nature and society. One entering the state of "Experience" sees cruelty and hypocrisy only too clearly but is unable to imagine a way out. Blake also conceived of a third, higher state of consciousness that he called "Organized Innocence," which is expressed in his later works. In this state, one's sense of the divinity of humanity coexists with oppression and injustice, though involving continued recognition of and active opposition to them.

Reading Blake. When reading *Songs of Innocence* and, to a lesser extent, *Songs of Experience*, it is important to remember that Blake intended them not as simple expressions of religious faith. The poems are demonstrations of viewpoints that are necessarily limited or distorted by each narrator's or speaker's state of consciousness.

The Ghost of Samuel Appearing to Saul (1800) by William Blake. Pen and ink with watercolor over graphite (12 5/16" × 13 1/2").

Rosenwald Collection, © 2003 Board of Trustees, National Gallery of Art, Washington, D.C.

DIRECT TEACHING

VIEWING THE ART

According to the Bible, Samuel (c. 1050 B.C.) was the last judge of Israel. Saul was the first king of Israel, anointed by Samuel, but he incurred God's displeasure. Just before a crucial battle against the Philistines, Saul asked the Witch of Endor (the figure on the right) to invoke the ghost of Samuel to foretell the future. Samuel appeared and declared that God would deliver Saul into the hands of the enemy. Saul and his sons perished in battle the next day.

Activity. What techniques does Blake employ to make the appearance of Samuel dramatic? [Possible response: The sweeping line of Samuel's body and his flying white hair create the impression that he has suddenly risen out of the ground, causing Saul to fall back and fling up his hands in self-defense. The witch's pose and wind-swept hair show the powerful forces that she is commanding. Blake's use of light and dark adds to the figure's impact.]

CONTENT-AREA CONNECTIONS

Internet
- go.hrw.com (Keyword: LE5 12-5)
- *Elements of Literature Online*

Media
- *Audio CD Library*
- *Audio CD Library, Selections and Summaries in Spanish*

Humanities: Engraving

Engraving is a technique that involves incising a design into a metal (usually copper) plate, applying ink to the incisions, and then printing the image on paper. In this way, multiple exact reproductions can be made of the same image, although eventually the plate will begin to degrade. Invented in the fifteenth century by German and Italian goldsmiths, engraving permitted more subtle and varied effects than the earlier woodcut, in which the design was laboriously carved into a block of wood.

PRETEACHING

Summary ↔ at grade level

In a well-known apostrophe, the speaker in "The Tyger" asks the tiger what immortal being, divine or demonic, could have created such a powerful and fearsome creature, and how. Those questions remain unanswered.

In "The Lamb" the speaker also asks who made the subject of the poem, but this time answers the question: Christ the Redeemer made the lamb. The speaker identifies himself as a child, linking his own innocence and that of the lamb to the innocence and purity of Christ.

Skills Starter

Build prerequisite skills. Before students read the two poems, ask them to brainstorm symbolic meanings that they associate with the tiger and the lamb. Write students' responses on the chalkboard.

Before You Read

The Tyger
The Lamb

Make the Connection

William Blake's poetry and art reflect his fascination with the Bible and his struggle to find answers to questions that profoundly disturbed him: What is the source of evil in the world? Why does God allow the innocent to suffer? Can evil be transformed or transcended?

One of Blake's early conclusions about the problem of good and evil was that "without contraries is no progression." To Blake, "The Tyger" and "The Lamb" reflect "two contrary states of the human soul," both of which are as essential to humanity as joy and sadness, innocence and experience.

Literary Focus
Symbol

A **symbol** is a person, place, animal, thing, or event that stands for both itself and something more than itself. In literature, symbols function on two levels: They have a literal, or exact, meaning and a figurative, or metaphorical, one. The metaphorical meaning involves states, feelings, and experiences that are hard to articulate yet are of great importance to people, such as love, death, danger, or hope.

The meanings of some symbols are widely recognized, such as the dove as a sign of peace, but poets and writers often create new symbols whose meaning can only be discovered by exploring the structure, language, and imagery of the works in which they appear.

Literary Skills
Understand symbols.

A **symbol** is a person, place, animal, thing, or event that stands for itself and for something beyond itself.

For more on Symbol, see the Handbook of Literary and Historical Terms.

Background

Blake's poems have a surface simplicity that masks a very complex view of human life and of Christianity. As a religious visionary, Blake saw the entire material world as a set of signs or symbols representing religious or mystical realities. In addition, any one of Blake's symbols—the "tyger," for instance—has such a rich array of meanings that we cannot expect ever to understand fully what such a symbol meant to him.

Elohim Creating Adam (1795–1805) by William Blake.
Tate Gallery, London.

DIFFERENTIATING INSTRUCTION

Learners Having Difficulty
Before students read the two poems on their own, go over the first stanza of "The Tyger" and the first couplet of "The Lamb" with them. Make sure they understand that in each poem the subject—the tiger or the lamb—is being addressed in apostrophe, as if speaker and subject were face to face. Ask students to focus on the questions the speaker asks each animal and the answers he imagines. Be sure students see that Blake is concerned with the relationship between good and evil, innocence and experience.

English-Language Learners
The rhyming couplets, short lines, and repetition of words may help these students grasp the rhythm of these poems. You may want to play the audio recording of the poems and have students follow along as they listen.

While almost everyone agrees that "The Tyger" is one of the most powerful of Blake's Songs of Experience, *there has been much disagreement about the meaning of the poem's central* **symbol,** *the tiger itself. One possibility is that the tiger represents a strong revolutionary energy that can enlighten and transform society—a positive but volatile force Blake believed was operating in the French Revolution. The poem's speaker, at any rate, cannot comprehend such a startling energy, and can only wonder whether it is demonic or godlike.*

The Tyger
from Songs of Experience
William Blake

The Tyger (1793) by William Blake, from his book *Songs of Experience.* Hand-colored etching.
Library of Congress, Washington, D.C.

Tyger! Tyger! burning bright
In the forests of the night,
What immortal hand or eye
Could frame thy fearful symmetry?

5   In what distant deeps or skies
Burnt the fire of thine eyes?
On what wings dare he aspire?
What the hand dare seize the fire?

And what shoulder, and what art,
10   Could twist the sinews of thy heart?
And when thy heart began to beat,
What dread hand? and what dread feet?

What the hammer? what the chain?
In what furnace was thy brain?
15   What the anvil? what dread grasp
Dare its deadly terrors clasp?

When the stars threw down their spears,°
And watered heaven with their tears,
Did he smile his work to see?
20   Did he who made the Lamb make thee?

Tyger! Tyger! burning bright
In the forests of the night,
What immortal hand or eye,
Dare frame thy fearful symmetry?

17. **stars . . . spears:** reference to the angels who fell with Satan and threw down their spears after losing the war in heaven.

William Blake   **537**

Primary Source

The essayist and critic Charles Lamb had a wide circle of literary friends that included Samuel Taylor Coleridge and Leigh Hunt. He held Wednesday evening meetings with a number of these people—meetings that became deservedly famous and at which Lamb exhibited his eloquence and wit. As a Romantic essayist, Lamb aimed not to cover a subject fully but rather to re-create a particular feeling, character, or moment. This letter is written in the easy, intimate style that characterizes his essays. Lamb paraphrases one of Blake's comments on his own painting ability: "I do not pretend to Paint better than Rafael or Mich. Angelo or Julio Romano or Alb. Durer, but I do Pretend to Paint finer than Rubens or Rembt. or Correggio or Titian."

DIRECT TEACHING

A Content-Area Connections
Art: Line More Than Color
Blake's dislike of Rubens, Rembrandt, Correggio, and Titian (among others) stemmed from his belief in the primacy of line over color. He felt himself to be bitterly at odds with the contemporary taste for such artists and their painterly brushwork, indistinct contours, and atmospheric effects of light and shade. In the *Descriptive Catalogue,* which accompanied an 1809 exhibit of his artwork, Blake stated that "the great and golden rule of art, as well as of life, is this: That the more distinct, sharp, and wirey the bounding line, the more perfect the work of art: and the less keen and sharp, the greater is the evidence of weak imitation." Although Blake shows himself in many works to be a lyrical and sensuous colorist, his sinewy line remains the dominant element in his compositions.

PRIMARY SOURCE / LETTER

Charles Lamb (1775–1834), perhaps the most accomplished Romantic essayist, sings the praises of William Blake in a letter to Bernard Barton.

"Blake Is a Real Name . . ."

Blake is a real name, I assure you, and a most extraordinary man, if he be still living. He is the Robert [William] Blake, whose wild designs accompany a splendid folio edition of the *Night Thoughts,* which you may have seen, in one of which he pictures the parting of soul and body by a solid mass of human form floating off, God knows how, from a lumpish mass (facsimile to itself) left behind on the dying bed. He paints in watercolors marvelous strange pictures, visions of his brain, which he asserts that he has seen. They have great merit. He has *seen* the old Welsh bards on Snowden—he has seen the beautifulest, the strongest, and the ugliest man, left alone from the massacre of the Britons by the Romans, and has painted them from memory (I have seen his paintings), and asserts them to be as good as the figures of Raphael and Angelo, but not better, as they had precisely the same retrovisions and prophetic visions with himself. The painters in oil (which he will have it that neither of them practiced) he affirms to have been the ruin of art, and affirms that all the while he was engaged in his water paintings, Titian was disturbing him, Titian the III Genius of Oil Painting. His pictures—one in particular, the *Canterbury Pilgrims* (far above Stothard's)—have great merit, but hard, dry, yet with grace. He has written a catalogue of them with a most spirited criticism on Chaucer, but mystical and full of vision. His poems have been sold hitherto only in manuscript. I never read them; but a friend at my desire procured the Sweep Song. There is one to a tiger, which I have heard recited, beginning:

> Tiger, Tiger, burning bright,
> Thro' the desarts of the night,

which is glorious. But, alas! I have not the book; for the man is flown, whither I know not, to Hades or a madhouse—But I must look on him as one of the most extraordinary persons of the age.

—Charles Lamb

The Agony in the Garden (c. 1799–1800) (detail) by William Blake.
Tate Gallery, London.

DIFFERENTIATING INSTRUCTION

Advanced Learners
Enrichment. The inspiration for nearly all of Blake's poetry and artwork is Christianity—in an unorthodox form. He was a firm believer in the Christian God despite his antipathy toward organized religion, and he rejected the philosophies of rationalism and Deism that were popular in the late eighteenth century. Ask students to write a short paper discussing whether Blake should be included among the Romantics, and why.

One of the Songs of Innocence, *this poem has often been read as a statement of Christian faith. However, we know that Blake's other writings show Christ as an active fighter against injustice, not the "meek" and "mild" lamb—a common symbol for Christ—with which this innocent speaker identifies. The speaker's viewpoint is thus an incomplete representation of Blake's beliefs—just one aspect of Blake's worldview.*

The Lamb
from Songs of Innocence
William Blake

The Lamb (c. 1789–1794) by William Blake, from his book *Songs of Innocence and of Experience*. Relief etching finished in pen and watercolor.
Fitzwilliam Museum, University of Cambridge, England.

    Little Lamb, who made thee?
    Dost thou know who made thee?
    Gave thee life, and bid thee feed
    By the stream and o'er the mead,°
5 Gave thee clothing of delight,
    Softest clothing, wooly, bright;
    Gave thee such a tender voice,
    Making all the vales° rejoice?
        Little Lamb, who made thee?
10   Dost thou know who made thee?

    Little Lamb, I'll tell thee,
    Little Lamb, I'll tell thee:
    He° is called by thy name,
    For He calls himself a Lamb.
15 He is meek, and he is mild;
    He became a little child.
    I a child, and thou a lamb,
    We are called by his name.
        Little Lamb, God bless thee!
20   Little Lamb, God bless thee!

4. **mead** *n.:* meadow.

8. **vales** *n. pl.:* valleys.

13. **He:** Christ.

CONTENT-AREA CONNECTIONS

Religion: The Lamb as a Religious Symbol

The lamb is an important symbol in the Judeo-Christian tradition. The Bible compares humans to sheep watched over by God. The lamb also represents sacrifice. The Passover holiday commemorates the freeing of the Israelites (Exodus 12) from Egypt after God sent an angel to slay the firstborn sons of the Egyptians. The Israelites marked their doors with the blood of a lamb to signal the angel to "pass over" their homes. A sacrificial animal in many Middle Eastern religious rites, the lamb was adopted by early Christians as a symbol of Jesus' sacrifice, which redeems humanity. John 1:29 identifies Jesus as "the lamb of God"; in Revelation 14:1, the Redeemer is a triumphant lamb on Judgment Day.

DIRECT TEACHING

A English-Language Learners
Archaic language. Explain that *bid* means "command or order" and that *thee* is an archaic form of *you*. What other word contains the root *bid*? [Possible response: forbid.]

B Literary Focus
Imagery. What emotions does Blake's description of the lamb evoke in you? [Possible responses: joy; tenderness; protectiveness.] What words and phrases evoke those emotions? [Possible responses: the image of the lamb's wool as "clothing of delight, / Softest clothing, wooly, bright"; "tender voice"; vales that "rejoice."]

C Reading Skills
Using context and glosses. The word *he* is glossed. What context clues in the poem help you confirm the definition given? [Possible responses: Since the speaker is answering his question, "He" must refer to the creator of the lamb; in l. 14, "He" is capitalized, following the tradition of Christians referring to God or Jesus.]

D Literary Focus
Symbol. Where in the second stanza does Blake make explicit the Christian symbolism of his poem? [Possible response: According to the speaker, the creator calls himself a lamb and became a human child (referring to God's incarnation as Jesus). Thus, the lamb being addressed and the child speaker symbolize their creator's innocence and purity.]

INDEPENDENT PRACTICE

Response and Analysis

Thinking Critically

1. The speaker asks the tiger who its creator was; the implied answer is that the creator is either God or the devil.
2. The speaker wonders in ll. 4–8 whether God created the tiger. The imagery in ll. 9–10 of twisting the animal's heart could suggest a demonic creator. The tools and furnace suggest a human creator.
3. Possible answers: The image of the tiger "burning bright" suggests both enlightenment and revolutionary violence.
4. Possible answer: Blake means that the tiger is both beautiful and frightening in its markings, movement, and match of form to function as a predator.
5. In the first stanza, Blake wonders who *could* be powerful enough to create the tiger; in the last, he wonders who would *dare*. The change suggests that creation is a dangerous act.
6. There is something both magnificent and frightening about the ferocity of a tiger.
7. He gives the lamb life, food, clothing, and a gentle voice.
8. The speaker answers; he names God.
9. The speaker says that he is a child. The speaker may be naive.
10. He may sacrifice himself for the good of others.
11. The speaker in "The Lamb" is an innocent child; the speaker in "The Tyger" is an adult, with an awareness of the world's complexity. The first accepts simple answers; the second sees that there are no easy answers to complex questions.
12. Answers will vary. Students may choose humans—perhaps a revolutionary and a saint—as symbols; they may choose other animals—perhaps a lion and a dolphin.

540 Collection 5 The Romantic Period

Response and Analysis

The Tyger
The Lamb

Thinking Critically

1. What question does the speaker of "The Tyger" ask over and over? What answer is implied?
2. Where in the poem does the speaker wonder if the tiger may have been created by God? What **imagery** tells us that the speaker also suspects that the tiger could be a demonic creation? List the images that suggest a human creator—like a blacksmith or a goldsmith.
3. What **imagery** suggests that the tiger could be a force of enlightenment? of revolutionary violence?
4. What do you think Blake means by the tiger's "fearful symmetry"? (Picture a tiger's stripes.)
5. The last stanza of "The Tyger" virtually repeats the first. What is the significance of the one word changed in the last stanza?
6. How does "The Tyger" represent people's simultaneous attraction toward and repulsion from evil?
7. What does the creator do for his creation in the first stanza of "The Lamb"?
8. How does the second stanza of "The Lamb" respond to the questions asked in the first stanza?
9. What are you told directly about the **speaker** of "The Lamb"? What inferences can you draw from this information?
10. Christ called himself a lamb because, like the Passover lamb slain to save the people of Israel, he sacrificed himself for the people. What might this imply about the fate of the young **speaker** in this poem?

Literary Skills
Analyze symbols.

Writing Skills
Compare and contrast the early draft with the final version of a poem.

11. How do you think the voice of the speaker in "The Lamb" is different from the voice of the speaker in "The Tyger"? Why do you think the questions in "The Lamb" get answers?
12. If you had to choose your own symbols for the qualities represented by Blake's tiger and lamb, what would they be? Explain.

Extending and Evaluating

13. Why do human beings commit evil? Why does God allow innocent children to suffer? Such questions profoundly disturbed Blake. One of his early conclusions about the problem of good and evil is his idea that "Without contraries [opposites] there is no progression [growth]." How do "The Tyger" and "The Lamb" reflect what Blake termed "two contrary states of the human soul"? In what sense are these contrasting states essential to human beings?

WRITING

Second-Guessing Blake

In an early draft of "The Tyger," Blake inserted the following lines after the third stanza:

> Could fetch it from the furnace deep
> And in thy horrid ribs dare steep
> In the well of sanguine wee
> In what clay and in what mold
> Were thy eyes of fury rolled

This early version also lacked the fifth stanza of the final version. In a brief **essay**, **compare and contrast** the early draft with the final version of "The Tyger," commenting on why you think Blake made the changes he made.

Extending and Evaluating

13. Possible answer: The tiger may represent the power of human experience, including evil; the lamb, the innocence into which humans are born. The two are essential because humans develop from innocence to experience, retaining aspects of each as they mature.

ASSESSING

Assessment
- Holt Assessment: Literature, Reading, and Vocabulary

Before You Read

The Chimney Sweeper from Songs of Innocence
The Chimney Sweeper from Songs of Experience

Make the Connection
Quickwrite

In these two poems, the first from *Songs of Innocence* and the second from *Songs of Experience,* Blake speaks for the poor children of his day who were forced to do backbreaking labor. In Blake's London, buildings were heated by coal- or wood-burning fireplaces, so every house had at least one chimney that had to be cleaned regularly. Poor children were often used to do this dirty and hazardous work because they could fit into the narrow chimney passages. In fact, some parents were so poverty stricken that they sold their children to "masters" who managed crews of young sweepers. The work was dangerous, and the children were badly treated by masters concerned only with profits.

If you could cry out against an evil of our day—and get people to listen—which social injustice would you protest? Take a few minutes to jot down your thoughts.

Literary Focus
Parallelism

When words, phrases, or sentences are arranged in balanced grammatical structures, they are said to be **parallel.** Poets, dramatists, preachers, and speechwriters (whose work is meant to be spoken aloud) are particularly likely to employ parallelism because the repetition it introduces enhances the rhythmic and emotional effect of their lines and makes them easier to understand and remember. Blake's use of parallelism contributes to the childlike simplicity of the surface of his poems.

> **Parallelism** is the repetition of words, phrases, or sentences that have the same grammatical structure or that restate a similar idea.
>
> *For more on Parallelism, see the Handbook of Literary and Historical Terms.*

Background

In the late 1700s, prices increased sharply and work became scarce. Blake saw starving people rooting through garbage, homeless families sleeping in doorways, and children begging on the streets or working at horrible jobs. Most members of the upper class believed that they deserved their comfortable stations in life, and that the poor must be innately evil, deserving the hunger and appalling conditions that they endured.

Blake was said to be mad, not only because he saw visions, but also because his poems cry out against the social problems he saw all around him: the growing division between classes, the wretched working conditions, and child labor. No one should go hungry, he said, in a land as green and wealthy as England.

SKILLS FOCUS

Literary Skills Understand parallelism.

A row of rooftops above a street of terraced houses in Britain.

William Blake 541

PRETEACHING

Summary ⇔ *at grade level*

In "The Chimney Sweeper," from *Songs of Innocence,* the speaker is a young boy whose father sold him to work as a chimney sweeper. The boy innocently tries to cheer himself and a fellow chimney sweep, Tom Dacre. Tom has a dream in which an angel appears and reveals God to be a loving father who will reward the children with endless joy in heaven if they do their duty on earth. Despite their desperate plight, the speaker and Tom naively profess their trust in God.

In "The Chimney Sweeper," from *Songs of Experience,* another young chimney sweeper weeps in the snow while his parents are at church. He says they made him a sweep because he was happy, and now, because he still appears happy, they think they have not hurt him. The system of church and government, he says, rationalizes his misery and creates a heaven for the ruling classes out of the misery of the poor.

Selection Starter

Motivate. After students read the background note on p. 541, ask them to consider the situation of the homeless in our society today. Encourage them to explore how much society has or has not changed since Blake's time, two hundred years ago.

DIFFERENTIATING INSTRUCTION

Learners Having Difficulty
Help students recognize the first-person point of view of the speaker in the first poem, indicated by the pronouns "my" and "I." Draw students' attention to the storylike structure of the poem. Also define the word "sport," used in l. 18 to mean "play." Invite student pairs to read the poems aloud to each other, alternating stanzas.

English-Language Learners
One way to help students understand the poem is having them paraphrase lines in which Blake used inverted word order, such as ll. 13 [And an angel came by] and 15 [Then they run down a green plain, leaping and laughing]. Point out that the speaker in the first stanza of the second "Chimney Sweeper" is not the same as the speaker in the remaining stanzas.

William Blake 541

DIRECT TEACHING

A Literary Focus

Parallelism. What are some examples of parallelism in this poem? [Possible responses: The first nine lines contain three instances of main clauses beginning with "so"; the last line of the poem repeats this construction.] What purposes do these parallel elements serve? [Possible responses: The clauses beginning with "so," as well as the frequent use of "and," suggest the rhythmic, singsong quality of a children's song, reinforcing the characterization of the speaker and heightening the contrast with his too-adult circumstances.]

B Literary Focus

Symbol. What might the "coffins of black" symbolize besides death? [Possible responses: the dark lives of the children; the narrow confines of their lives; the death of innocence and childhood]

C Literary Focus

Dramatic irony. The innocent speaker expresses optimism about the future if "all do their duty." Why does the speaker's simple faith make the final lines sting? [Possible response: The reader knows what the speaker does not—that all will not turn out well.]

This poem from Songs of Innocence *features a child speaker who tries to cheer himself and his fellow chimney sweep, Tom Dacre, with the thought that the oppression and poverty they endure will be compensated for by endless joy in heaven.*

The Chimney Sweeper
from Songs of Innocence

William Blake

Drawing depicting a young English chimney sweep covered with soot (1850).
MANSELL/TimePix.

When my mother died I was very young,
And my father sold me while yet my tongue
Could scarcely cry "'weep! 'weep! 'weep! 'weep!"°
So your chimneys I sweep, and in soot I sleep.

5   There's little Tom Dacre, who cried when his head,
That curled like a lamb's back, was shaved: so I said
"Hush, Tom! never mind it, for when your head's bare
You know that the soot cannot spoil your white hair."

And so he was quiet, and that very night,
10 As Tom was a-sleeping, he had such a sight!—
That thousands of sweepers, Dick, Joe, Ned, and Jack,
Were all of them locked up in coffins of black.

And by came an Angel who had a bright key,
And he opened the coffins and set them all free;
15 Then down a green plain leaping, laughing, they run,
And wash in a river, and shine in the Sun.

Then naked and white, all their bags left behind,
They rise upon clouds and sport in the wind;
And the Angel told Tom, if he'd be a good boy,
20 He'd have God for his father, and never want° joy.

And so Tom awoke; and we rose in the dark,
And got with our bags and our brushes to work.
Though the morning was cold, Tom was happy and warm;
So if all do their duty they need not fear harm.

3. "'weep . . . 'weep": the child's attempt at the chimney sweepers' cry of "Sweep! Sweep!"

20. **want** *v.*: lack.

CONTENT-AREA CONNECTIONS

History: Child Labor

The new technologies and social dislocation of the Industrial Revolution meant that young children were working harder and with less protection than ever before. Tending factory machines required manual dexterity and alertness more than experience, so employers hired young children and unskilled women as laborers for very low wages. At that time local parishes were required by law to provide for orphans or children whose parents could not care for them by apprenticing the children to a trade. During the Industrial Revolution, however, many thousands of unprotected children were simply turned over to factory owners by local officials and became little more than slaves. Many children were also employed in the coal mines that fueled the industrial explosion. Ragged and malnourished children as young as five years

The Chimney Sweeper
from Songs of Experience

William Blake

A little black thing among the snow
Crying "'weep, 'weep," in notes of woe!
"Where are thy father and mother? say?"
"They are both gone up to the church to pray.

5 "Because I was happy upon the heath,
And smil'd among the winter's snow;
They clothed me in the clothes of death,
And taught me to sing the notes of woe.

"And because I am happy, and dance and sing,
10 They think they have done me no injury,
And are gone to praise God and his Priest and King,
Who make up a heaven of our misery."

"The Chimney Sweeper," plate 37 from *Songs of Innocence and of Experience*, copy AA (c. 1815–26), by William Blake. Etching, ink, and watercolor.
Fitzwilliam Museum, University of Cambridge, England. The Bridgeman Art Library.

Primary Source

Michael Sadler was a Leeds businessman and the Conservative member of Parliament for Newick between 1829 and 1832. Over a three-month period, Sadler's committee interviewed forty-eight people who had worked in textile factories as children. When he discovered that at least six of those who had given testimony had subsequently lost their jobs, Sadler concentrated on interviewing doctors instead.

This selection is from the testimony of Peter Smart, a textile mill laborer. He describes the inhumane conditions he endured as a child laborer, indentured between the ages of eleven and seventeen. He then tells of becoming an overseer at another mill, where, in order to satisfy his master's production demands, he inflicted the same cruelty upon the child workers that he had suffered himself.

DIRECT TEACHING

A Content-Area Connections

History: Child Labor Laws
Today such conditions seem barbarous, but they were an improvement over what had existed previously. The Industrial Revolution also brought child labor problems to the United States, where far-reaching national legislation to protect children from commercial exploitation was not enacted and upheld until 1938. The Fair Labor Standards Act, also known as the Wages and Hours Act, is still the basic child-labor act in this country. Employers engaged in interstate commerce may not employ workers under sixteen or in hazardous occupations under eighteen. Children between the ages of fourteen and sixteen may in some circumstances work outside of school hours.

PRIMARY SOURCE / TESTIMONY

In 1831, Michael Sadler (1780–1835) introduced a bill in Parliament that proposed limiting the hours of workers under eighteen years of age to ten hours a day. Parliament did not pass this bill, but in April of 1832, it established a committee to investigate the conditions of children working in textile factories. With Sadler as chairman, this committee interviewed factory owners, workers, and doctors who treated people who worked in the factories. After the Sadler Committee's report was published, Parliament passed the Factory Act of 1833. This act limited working hours to twelve hours a day for textile workers aged thirteen to seventeen, and eight hours a day for those aged nine to twelve. The interview printed here is representative of the kinds of testimony heard by the Sadler Committee. The examiner's questions are followed by Peter Smart's answers, which are indicated by dashes.

A

from Evidence Given Before the Sadler Committee

Peter Smart, called in; and Examined.
You say you were locked up night and day?
—Yes.

Do the children ever attempt to run away?
—Very often.

Were they pursued and brought back again?
—Yes, the overseer pursued them, and brought them back.

Did you ever attempt to run away?
—Yes, I ran away twice.

And you were brought back?
—Yes; and I was sent up to the master's loft, and thrashed with a whip for running away.

Were you bound[1] to this man?
—Yes, for six years.

By whom were you bound?
—My mother got 15s.[2] for the six years.

1. **bound** *v.*: legally obliged to work for.
2. **s.**: one shilling was equal to one twentieth of a pound.

Do you know whether the children were, in point of fact, compelled to stop during the whole time for which they were engaged?
—Yes, they were.

By law?
—I cannot say by law; but they were compelled by the master; I never saw any law used there but the law of their own hands.

To what mill did you next go?
—To Mr. Webster's, at Battus Den, within eleven miles of Dundee.

In what situation did you act there?
—I acted as overseer.

At 17 years of age?
—Yes.

Did you inflict the same punishment that you yourself had experienced?
—I went as overseer; not as a slave, but as a slave-driver.

544 Collection 5 The Romantic Period

Primary Source

Social Science: Desperate Times
Students may be shocked that Peter Smart's mother would sell her own child into virtual slavery. In a speech before the House of Commons, Michael Sadler described the heartbreaking predicament facing many desperately poor families: "The parents rouse [their children] in the morning and receive them tired and exhausted after the day has closed; they see them droop and sicken, and, in many cases, become cripples and die, before they reach their prime; and they do all this, because they must otherwise starve. It is a mockery to contend that these parents have a choice. They choose the lesser evil, and reluctantly resign their offspring to the captivity and pollution of the mill."

What were the hours of labor in that mill?
—My master told me that I had to produce a certain quantity of yarn; the hours were at that time fourteen; I said that I was not able to produce the quantity of yarn that was required; I told him if he took the timepiece out of the mill I would produce that quantity, and after that time I found no difficulty in producing the quantity.

How long have you worked per day in order to produce the quantity your master required?
—I have wrought nineteen hours.

Was this a water-mill?
—Yes, water and steam both.

To what time have you worked?
—I have seen the mill going till it was past 12 o'clock on the Saturday night.

So that the mill was still working on the Sabbath morning?
—Yes.

Were the workmen paid by the piece, or by the day?
—No, all had stated wages.

Did not that almost compel you to use great severity to the hands then under you?
—Yes; I was compelled often to beat them, in order to get them to attend to their work, from their being over-wrought.

Were not the children exceedingly fatigued at that time?
—Yes, exceedingly fatigued.

Were the children bound in the same way in that mill?
—No; they were bound from one year's end to another, for twelve months.

Did you keep the hands locked up in the same way in that mill?
—Yes, we locked up the mill; but we did not lock the bothy.[3]

Did you find that the children were unable to pursue their labor properly to that extent?
—Yes; they have been brought to that condition, that I have gone and fetched up the doctor to them, to see what was the matter with them, and to know whether they were able to rise or not able to rise; they were not at all able to rise; we have had great difficulty in getting them up.

When that was the case, how long have they been in bed, generally speaking?
—Perhaps not above four or five hours in their beds.

Children at work in a cotton factory (1839). Engraving.
MANSELL/TimePix.

3. **bothy** *n.*: hut.

INDEPENDENT PRACTICE

Response and Analysis

Thinking Critically

1. The speaker's mother died when he was young, and his father sold him off as a chimney sweeper. His life is one of drudgery.

2. The angel promises Tom that if he is good, he will have God as his father and will always be happy. The speaker draws the moral lesson that if all do their duty on earth, they will be rewarded in heaven.

3. In the dream, Tom is clean and carefree; he plays happily in the sunshine. In reality, he slaves in dark, filthy conditions.

4. The child bitterly tells the adult that his parents are in church praising the system that justifies his exploitation. Possible answer: The "clothes of death" may refer to the child's probable future.

5. Possible answer: My parents have gone to praise the very system that subjects us to misery.

6. The tone of the second poem is bitter. Whereas the speaker of the first poem accepts his situation without question, the speaker of the second poem understands and resents his situation.

7. Possible answer: In the first poem, parallelism creates the effect of a child's song, heightening the pathos of the speaker's situation. In the second poem, the repetition of the phrase "notes of woe" reinforces the visceral impact of the sweep's cry, a child's wail of misery.

8. Answers will vary. Students may say that the mispronunciation reveals the extreme youth of the children; that insight may evoke an emotional reaction in addition to their intellectual reaction to the subject.

546 Collection 5 The Romantic Period

Response and Analysis

The Chimney Sweeper from **Songs of Innocence**
The Chimney Sweeper from **Songs of Experience**

Thinking Critically

1. What details of the speaker's history do you learn in the first poem? What is his present life like?

2. In the first poem, how does the angel reassure Tom Dacre in his dream? What **moral lesson** does the speaker in the first poem draw from Tom's dream?

3. How does Tom Dacre's dream contrast with the actual conditions of his daily life?

4. In the second poem, how does the young chimney sweeper answer the adult's question? What do you think are his "clothes of death"?

5. How would you **paraphrase** the last two lines of the second poem?

6. How would you describe the **tone** of the second poem? How does this sweeper's attitude toward his life and his parents contrast with the attitude of the sweeper in the first poem?

7. How does Blake's use of **parallelism** in both poems add to their emotional effect? Discuss specific examples of parallelism in the poems.

8. In each poem, what is the emotional effect of the child's mispronunciation of the chimney sweeper's cry?

9. Do people today sometimes take the attitude expressed by the speaker of the first poem: If you are good, if you do your duty, you need not fear harm? Expand on your response.

10. Do these poems remind you of any cases of exploitation or injustice in modern life? Consult your Quickwrite notes.

SKILLS FOCUS

Literary Skills Analyze parallelism.
Writing Skills Write part of a prose narrative.

546 Collection 5 The Romantic Period

WRITING

Down the Chimney

Based on details from both "The Chimney Sweeper" poems, the information in the *Primary Source* on page 544, and any other research materials you want to use, write the opening or closing paragraphs of a prose narrative that tells about the daily life of a child laborer in Blake's London. You may want to write in the first person, as if for an autobiography.

Engraving depicting a young English chimney sweep sitting on top of a chimney, reading (1800).
MANSELL/TimePix.

9. Answers will vary. Possible answer: Yes, some people, perhaps fearing the consequences of standing up for themselves, accept unfair burdens.

10. Answers will vary, but most students will probably be able to suggest some instances of modern-day exploitation.

ASSESSING

Assessment
- *Holt Assessment: Literature, Reading, and Vocabulary*

Before You Read

A Poison Tree

Make the Connection
Quickwrite

What happens to anger that is allowed to grow and fester; anger that is nurtured and held dear? In this poem, one of Blake's *Songs of Experience*, the speaker describes what happens when anger is left unresolved. As you read, notice the images Blake uses to describe anger and how it works on the individual psychologically. Before you begin, jot down some notes describing the ways anger can be destructive, not only to the object of the anger, but also to the person feeling it.

Literary Focus
Theme

The **theme** of a work of literature is its central idea or main insight about human nature or human life. The theme of a work is not the same as its subject; rather, the theme is the writer's point of view on the subject. In the case of "A Poison Tree," Blake's subject is anger, and his theme is his insight into what anger is and does. In poetry the theme is rarely stated directly. More often, it is implied by all the details, images, and symbols of the poem and must be deciphered by the reader.

> The **theme** of a work of literature is the main idea or central insight into human nature or human life that the writer conveys either directly or indirectly.
>
> For more on Theme, see the Handbook of Literary and Historical Terms.

A Poison Tree
from Songs of Experience

William Blake

I was angry with my friend:
I told my wrath, my wrath did end.
I was angry with my foe:
I told it not, my wrath did grow. **A**

5   And I watered it in fears,
Night and morning with my tears;
And I sunned it with smiles, **B**
And with soft deceitful wiles.° **C**

And it grew both day and night,
10 Till it bore an apple bright;
And my foe beheld it shine,
And he knew that it was mine,

And into my garden stole
When the night had veiled the pole:
15 In the morning glad I see
My foe outstretched beneath the tree.

---
8. **wiles** *n. pl.:* cunning tricks.

Literary Skills Understand theme.

William Blake 547

PRETEACHING

Summary ⇔ *at grade level*

> The speaker relates how he hides his anger from an enemy and secretly cultivates it. The anger grows into a tree that bears a poisonous apple, which the speaker's foe steals and eats. The foe dies, and the speaker is glad; he, too, has been poisoned by his secret anger.

Skills Starter

Motivate. Before students read the poem, have them discuss ways people deal with anger.

DIRECT TEACHING

A Reading Skills
Expressing an opinion. Do you agree with the implication in l. 4 about the effect of repressing anger? Why or why not? [Possible responses: Yes, the only way to get rid of anger is to express it. No, expressing anger may cause pain or generate more anger; wait until anger cools before expressing it.]

B Literary Focus
Imagery. How does Blake compare the speaker's anger to a tree? [He has the speaker tend his anger as he would a tree; the speaker feeds it with fears, tears, and deceit.]

C Literary Focus
Theme. How would you restate this poem's comment on the effects of anger? [Possible response: Anger that is not expressed will increase and harm both the person who is angry and the object of anger.]

DIFFERENTIATING INSTRUCTION

Learners Having Difficulty
Most students will understand the idea of repressed anger; they may have difficulty with the image of anger as a living thing, like a tree, that is nourished by repression. Guide students, as necessary, in grasping the concept that the fruit of the tree is both attractive and poisonous to the speaker's foe and poisonous to the speaker's spirit.

Advanced Learners
Have students compare Blake's use of a tree as a metaphor in this poem to his use of plants as metaphors in other poems, such as "The Sick Rose," "Ah! Sun-Flower," and "The Garden of Love."

INDEPENDENT PRACTICE

Response and Analysis

Thinking Critically

1. The two methods are expressing anger, which ends the anger, and suppressing anger, which causes the anger to grow. In the first situation the anger is directed at a friend; in the second the anger is directed at an enemy.

2. Blake uses the image of a poisonous tree, which the speaker carefully tends, "watering" and "sunning" it with malicious thoughts and deceitfulness.

3. The speaker's foe eats the poisonous apple and dies. He is a victim of the speaker; he is also responsible himself, since ll. 11–13 suggest that he stole the apple.

4. Possible answer: The apple symbolizes a harmful or evil action taken by the speaker; the tree symbolizes the anger and malice that motivate the action.

5. The speaker is consumed and harmed by his anger. Students may say that his forgiveness of his friend shows him to be good, but that the pleasure he takes in killing his enemy shows him to be evil as well.

6. Possible answer: Repressed anger poisons both the person who harbors it and its object. The comment on human nature might be that even a good person is capable of evil when clinging to hatred, as shown by the speaker's actions toward friend and foe.

7. Blake alludes to the Tree of Knowledge, traditionally an apple tree, whose fruit God forbade Adam and Eve to eat.

8. Answers will vary depending on Quickwrite notes.

Response and Analysis

Thinking Critically

1. What two ways of handling anger are mentioned in the poem? What is different about the two situations?
2. What **imagery** is used to describe the second way in which the speaker handles anger?
3. What happens to the speaker's foe in the last stanza? Of whom or what is he a victim?
4. What do you think the "apple bright" (line 10) **symbolizes**? What is the "poison tree"?
5. How is the speaker of the poem a victim? Do you see the speaker as good or evil or both? Give examples from the poem.
6. What do you see as the **theme** of the poem? How does this theme comment on human nature? Give specific details from the poem to support your interpretation.
7. What is Blake alluding to in his reference to forbidden fruit in the third stanza?
8. Does the poem describe ways in which anger can be destructive that are similar to the ways you wrote about in your Quickwrite notes? Does it offer any insights on anger that you did not consider? ✏️

INTERNET
Projects and Activities
Keyword: LE5 12-5

SKILLS FOCUS

Literary Skills Analyze theme.
Writing Skills Write an essay analyzing a poem.
Grammar Skills Use verb tenses consistently.

Extending and Evaluating

9. Blake's use of **parallel structure** and simple diction gives "A Poison Tree" an air of straightforward, even childlike, simplicity. Do you think this tone supports or undercuts the points being made about anger and its consequences? Explain.

WRITING
Contrary States

Blake's two groups of poems, *Songs of Innocence* and *Songs of Experience,* depict two contrary states of the human soul. The speakers in *Songs of Innocence* are usually children or childlike. The speakers in *Songs of Experience* are usually adults. In an **essay**, analyze "A Poison Tree." Tell what you believe its theme is and explain why the poem is an appropriate *Song of Experience* and not a *Song of Innocence*. What comment does the poem make on the cosmos of "Mercy, Pity, Peace, and Love," which Blake describes for *Songs of Innocence*?

A Poison Tree (1794) by William Blake, from his book *Songs of Experience*. Relief etching with watercolor and pen additions.
Private Collection.

Extending and Evaluating

9. Students may say that the simplicity of Blake's style makes the presentation of his theme clear and effective. Others may say that the childlike tone makes the outcome seem less serious.

Grammar Link

The Right Tense for Sense: Verb Tense Consistency

You use tenses to show when something happened. Unnecessarily changing verb tense in midsentence can create awkwardness and confusion. When you write about events occurring at the same time, use verbs that are in the same tense. Use different tenses only to indicate that events occur at different times.

Two events occurring at the same time:

INCORRECT   Blake began writing poetry at the age of twelve, but he intends to become a painter.

CORRECT   Blake began writing poetry at the age of twelve, but he intended to become a painter.

Two events occurring at different times:

UNCLEAR   By the time Blake was twenty-seven, he published his first work of poetry.

CLEAR   By the time Blake was twenty-seven, he had published his first work of poetry. [This sentence makes it clear that Blake published his work before he turned twenty-seven.]

"Auguries of Innocence" by William Blake (transcribed c. 1807) from the Pickering, or Ballads, manuscript.
The Pierpont Morgan Library, NY.

PRACTICE

Check for consistency of verb tenses in the following sentences. If the tenses are consistent, write *correct*. If the tenses are not consistent, rewrite the sentence with the correct verb tense.

1. Blake not only wrote his poetry, but he illustrates it as well.
2. Blake was an innovative artist; he invented many of his own printing techniques.
3. In his own time, Blake's art fails to attract attention, but now, his art is appreciated by many people worldwide.
4. By the time Blake died in 1827, he illustrated the works of many famous authors, including John Milton, Thomas Gray, and Edward Young.

Apply to Your Writing

Review a writing assignment you are working on now or have already completed. Are there any sentences with unnecessary shifts in verb tense? Correct these shifts to avoid awkwardness and confusion.

▶ For more help, see Tenses and Their Uses, 3b–c, in the Language Handbook.

Grammar Link
Practice

1. Blake not only wrote his poetry, but he <u>illustrated</u> it as well.
2. correct
3. In his own time, Blake's art <u>failed</u> to attract attention, but now, his art is appreciated by many people worldwide.
4. By the time Blake died in 1827, he <u>had illustrated</u> the works of many famous authors, including John Milton, Thomas Gray, and Edward Young.

ASSESSING

Assessment
- Holt Assessment: *Literature, Reading, and Vocabulary*

RETEACHING

For a lesson reteaching theme and meaning, see **Reteaching,** p. 1129A.

DIFFERENTIATING INSTRUCTION

Learners Having Difficulty

Write the following sentences on the chalkboard. Have students replace the incorrect verb or verb phrase underlined in each sentence with the correct verb or verb phase.

1. After his brother Robert died, Blake <u>had seen</u> him in a vision. [saw]
2. Blake invented a technique called illuminated printing, which he <u>claims</u> Robert had revealed to him in the vision. [claimed]
3. Using this exacting technique, Blake <u>has worked</u> slowly and made very little money. [worked]
4. Today Blake is respected as a great artist and poet, and his "illuminated books" <u>were considered</u> works of art. [are considered]

SKILLS FOCUS, pp. 550–564

Grade-Level Skills

■ **Literary Skills**
Analyze the way the author's style, including the use of blank verse, achieves specific rhetorical or aesthetic purposes.

■ **Literary Skills**
Analyze ways poets use poetic devices, including personification and allusion.

■ **Literary Skills**
Analyze characteristics of subgenres of poetry, including sonnets, odes, and meditative poems.

■ **Reading Skills**
Recognize patterns of organization in a text.

Review Skills

■ **Literary Skills**
Identify the literary devices that define a writer's style.

More About the Writer

Background. During the years 1797–1805, Wordsworth produced his greatest poetry, including the poems on pp. 552, 560, and 562, as well as *The Prelude*, his masterpiece. After 1805, Wordsworth's poetic powers declined. As his poetry lost its energy and his political opinions grew more conservative, Wordsworth found himself attacked by younger Romantics, who felt he had betrayed his ideals. Yet even as Wordsworth's creative powers waned, his importance grew, and he became a cultural icon. In 1843, he was named England's poet laureate.

William Wordsworth
(1770–1850)

William Wordsworth (1842) by Benjamin Robert Haydon. Oil on canvas (49" × 39").
By Courtesy of the National Portrait Gallery, London.

Surveying Wordsworth's life can be like walking around a large statue, awed by its presence and puzzled by its apparent importance. Sometimes Wordsworth must have felt the same way. As he thought about his early life and re-created it in his autobiographical poem *The Prelude*, Wordsworth said he felt as if he were "two consciousnesses"—one remembering, the other one remembered.

When Wordsworth's mother died in 1778, he and his three brothers were sent to school at Hawkshead in the Lake District. His sister, Dorothy, aged seven, had to live with relatives. When their father died in 1783, the children were placed under the guardianship of two uncles. William managed to get a degree from Cambridge in 1791. As an educated man with no title, wealth, or head for business, he had little interest in the few careers open to him—the main one being the Church. In late 1791, Wordsworth went to France to learn the language and, as it turned out, discovered the bliss of being young in that time of birth and rebirth known as the French Revolution. Thus began a decade of painful growth, as he searched for and eventually found his vocation as a poet.

After he returned from France in 1792, war broke out between France and England. Wordsworth was sickened by the war, and he gradually became deeply disillusioned about his hopes for change. Late in 1793, he went on a long walking tour. This experience—and the collapse of his radical hope of perfecting society—drove him to poetry.

In 1795, his fortunes began to change. He was reunited with his sister, Dorothy, who became a constant companion and inspiration.

When he inherited some money from a friend, he and Dorothy took up residence in a rent-free cottage, and the poet Samuel Taylor Coleridge suddenly burst upon their lives. By June 1797, when he and Dorothy moved to a country house four miles from the village where Coleridge lived, Wordsworth had produced a good deal of new poetry, none yet published, including a play and some stark narratives. Coleridge and Wordsworth quickly became powerful influences on each other's work. *Lyrical Ballads* (1798) was the fruit of their friendship and mutual influence. During the following decade, Wordsworth wrote many of his most widely read works.

The distinguishing quality of Wordsworth's best lyric poetry comes from his simple delight in the nature of experience itself and in the mind's capacity to shape everyday experience into something lasting and poetic. Poetry, he wrote in the Preface to *Lyrical Ballads*, is the "spontaneous overflow of powerful feelings"; but, he added, poems of lasting value are produced only by someone who has "thought long and deeply." The marriage of feeling and thought, as Coleridge recognized, made Wordsworth "the best poet of the age."

550 Collection 5 The Romantic Period

RESOURCES: READING

Planning
■ One-Stop Planner CD-ROM

Differentiating Instruction
■ Holt Reading Solutions
■ The Holt Reader
■ Holt Adapted Reader
■ Supporting Instruction in Spanish
■ Audio CD Library, Selections and Summaries in Spanish

Grammar and Language
■ Daily Language Activities

Assessment
■ Holt Assessment: Literature, Reading, and Vocabulary
■ One-Stop Planner CD-ROM with ExamView Test Generator
■ Holt Online Assessment

Internet
■ go.hrw.com (Keyword: LE5 12-5)
■ Elements of Literature Online

Media
■ Audio CD Library
■ Audio CD Library, Selections and Summaries in Spanish
■ Fine Art Transparencies

Before You Read

Lines Composed a Few Miles Above Tintern Abbey

Make the Connection
William Wordsworth loved nature in all of its forms, and he believed that nature helped him to "see into the life of things." Loving nature, he writes in this poem, quiets his mind, lightens his mood, guides him to kind acts, and brings him closer to God.

Literary Focus
Blank Verse
Wordsworth composed poetry in his head while he walked—"his jaws working the whoal time," recalled a person in the country who observed him. He spoke the words aloud to memorize them and to get the rhythm right. When Wordsworth was a child, under the direction of his father, he memorized and recited long passages in **blank verse** (unrhymed iambic pentameter) from the works of Shakespeare and Milton. In "Tintern Abbey," Wordsworth uses for the first time a less formal, "conversational" blank verse that gives his poem the flowing rhythm of natural speech.

> **Blank verse** is poetry written in unrhymed **iambic pentameter.** Each line contains five iambs; each iamb, or metrical foot, is an unstressed syllable followed by a stressed syllable.
>
> *For more on Blank Verse, see the Handbook of Literary and Historical Terms.*

Reading Skills
Recognizing Patterns of Organization
Before you read this poem aloud, look for the end punctuation and the indents that signal the end of one stanza and the beginning of another. (How many stanzas are in the poem?) Then, as you read, make notes on how Wordsworth uses these stanzas to organize his ideas.

Background
"Tintern Abbey" (which refers to the ruined abbey mentioned only in the title) is one of the most important short lyric works in English literature. A major step forward in Wordsworth's writing and a definitive statement of some of the Romantics' ideas, it has inspired and guided many poets since. The ease with which Wordsworth wrote it is therefore even more astonishing. In July 1798, Wordsworth and his sister, Dorothy, went on a vigorous walking tour in southern Wales. Shortly after leaving the Wye River Valley, Wordsworth, by his own account, began to compose this poem about revisiting the valley, finishing it "just as I was entering Bristol in the evening after a ramble of four or five days. . . . Not a line of it was altered, and not any part of it written down till I reached Bristol. It was published almost immediately after."

Wordsworth had learned something important from Coleridge: the use of a flowing blank verse and the easy maneuvering of the meditative poem.

go.hrw.com
INTERNET
More About William Wordsworth
Keyword: LE5 12-5

Literary Skills
Understand blank verse.

Reading Skills
Recognize patterns of organization.

PRETEACHING

Summary ⬆ *above grade level*

This lyric poem is a meditation on what nature means to the speaker. He describes the physical beauty of a valley that he is seeing after an absence, and asserts that the mere memory of this landscape has given him solace, lifting his spirits and inspiring him to acts of kindness and love. Next he explains how the passionate relationship he had with nature in his youth has given way to a deeper, more spiritual appreciation, a sense of a sublime presence that connects all things, including the human mind. In his maturity, nature has become the center of his "moral being" (l. 111). Finally the speaker addresses his sister. He tells her that seeing the landscape through her youthful eyes makes it even more precious to him. He hopes that she will take comfort from his memory when he is dead and recall the pleasure he had in seeing the valley with her.

Selection Starter
Build background. Wordsworth was exploring a new form known as the conversation poem—usually a deeply personal meditation addressed to a silent listener or a loved one who is absent or asleep (see l. 114). Point out that although the language of the poem does not sound like colloquial speech to our ears, we nevertheless seem to be hearing a spontaneous utterance of the speaker's thoughts and feelings.

DIFFERENTIATING INSTRUCTION

Learners Having Difficulty
Invite learners having difficulty to read "Lines Composed a Few Miles Above Tintern Abbey" in interactive format in *The Holt Reader* and to use the sidenotes as aids to understanding the selection. The interactive version provides additional instruction, practice, and assessment of the literary skill taught in the Student Edition. Monitor students' responses to the selection, and correct any misconceptions that arise.

English-Language Learners
Help students break down difficult passages into short sentences.

Lines Composed a Few Miles Above Tintern Abbey

On Revisiting the Banks of the Wye During a Tour. July 13, 1798

William Wordsworth

Five years have past; five summers, with the length
Of five long winters! and again I hear
These waters, rolling from their mountain springs
With a soft inland murmur.—Once again
5   Do I behold these steep and lofty cliffs,
That on a wild secluded scene impress
Thoughts of more deep seclusion; and connect
The landscape with the quiet of the sky.
The day is come when I again repose
10 Here, under this dark sycamore, and view
These plots of cottage ground, these orchard tufts,
Which at this season, with their unripe fruits,
Are clad in one green hue, and lose themselves
'Mid groves and copses.° Once again I see
15 These hedgerows,° hardly hedgerows, little lines
Of sportive wood run wild: these pastoral° farms,
Green to the very door; and wreaths of smoke
Sent up, in silence, from among the trees!
With some uncertain notice, as might seem
20 Of vagrant dwellers in the houseless woods,
Or of some Hermit's cave, where by his fire
The Hermit sits alone.
                         These beauteous forms,
Through a long absence, have not been to me
As is a landscape to a blind man's eye:
25 But oft, in lonely rooms, and 'mid the din
Of towns and cities, I have owed to them
In hours of weariness, sensations sweet,
Felt in the blood, and felt along the heart;
And passing even into my purer mind,
30 With tranquil restoration:—feelings too
Of unremembered pleasure: such, perhaps,

1–22. The speaker describes a beloved place in nature to which he has returned after five years. *Look for the verbs* hear, behold, view, *and* see. *What does the speaker hear? What does he see?*

14. copses *n. pl.:* areas densely covered with shrubs and small trees.
15. hedgerows *n. pl.:* rows of bushes, shrubs, and small trees that serve as fences.
16. pastoral *adj.:* relating to herds or flocks, pasture land, and country life.

Tintern Abbey (1834) by J.M.W. Turner.
British Museum, London.

As have no slight or trivial influence
On that best portion of a good man's life,
His little, nameless, unremembered acts
35 Of kindness and of love. Nor less, I trust,
To them I may have owed another gift,
Of aspect more sublime; that blessed mood,
In which the burden of the mystery,
In which the heavy and the weary weight
40 Of all this unintelligible world,
Is lightened:—that serene and blessed mood,
In which the affections° gently lead us on,—
Until, the breath of this corporeal° frame
And even the motion of our human blood
45 Almost suspended, we are laid asleep
In body, and become a living soul:
While with an eye made quiet by the power

> **23–41.** According to the speaker, how have memories of this beloved landscape affected him?

42. **affections** *n. pl.*: feelings.
43. **corporeal** *adj.*: bodily.

William Wordsworth 553

CONTENT-AREA CONNECTIONS

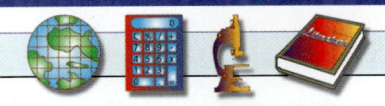

History: The Wye Valley

In *The Hidden Wordsworth,* Kenneth R. Johnston outlines a debate among modern critics. It "turns . . . on the 'uncertain notice' that Wordsworth gives to the smoke rising from the trees, since we know that smoke was rising from the thriving, around-the-clock iron industry of small forges in the wooded hills above the abbey, and from the kilns which burnt these trees to produce the charcoal needed for the forges. . . . Furthermore, Wordsworth's tentative suggestion that the smoke 'might seem' to come from 'vagrant dwellers in the houseless woods' touches with extreme delicacy on a fact known to everybody who visited the abbey: that it was the shelter and resort for many beggars and vagabonds, who made their living by cadging from the well-to-do tourists who came to visit it, under the pretext of offering them 'tours.'" In the standard guidebook of the region, the author describes the "poverty and wretchedness" of these beggars. But Wordsworth and Dorothy "had not gone up the Wye valley to see the iron works, still less to see beggars squatting in the abbey. They went there . . . to enjoy the scenery and for a respite from the noisy city. They went for relief in nature—and they found instead more human misery, which Wordsworth almost but not quite excluded from his poem."

William Wordsworth 553

Direct Teaching

A Reading Skills
Interpreting. According to the critic John L. Mahoney, in ll. 41–49 the speaker "sums up the greatest of all the blessings he has experienced in his five years away from . . . the River Wye. . . . Seeing into the life of things, intuiting value at moments of unsuspected openness to the life-giving powers of nature—these are part of a strong pull in the poet toward a secular faith . . . that is at the root of his prayer of reminiscence" in ll. 55–57.

B Learners Having Difficulty
Monitoring comprehension. Make sure students understand what "this" refers to: the description in the previous stanza of the way the speaker's memories of the Wye Valley have affected him (restoring his balance, making him a better person, giving him insight into the meaning of life). He is saying that even if this assertion is merely a "vain belief"—in other words, even if he is exaggerating the transformative power of his memories—his spirit has often turned to his memories of this place for solace.

C Reading Skills
Recognizing patterns of organization. Point out to students that this stanza (ll. 49–57) is much shorter than the other stanzas. In blank verse, stanzas don't have to be of a fixed length (as they do in other verse forms). Also point out that the first line of the next stanza is *not* a continuation of the last line of the previous stanza (as it is for every other stanza transition).

Response to Margin Question

Line 49. An indentation and a split line are generally used to show where one stanza ends and another begins. The speaker now addresses the river directly: "O sylvan Wye! thou wanderer" (l. 56). He is back in the present.

Landscape (detail) (19th century) by Patrick Nasmyth.
Roy Miles Fine Painting, London, UK.

>   Of harmony, and the deep power of joy,
>   We see into the life of things.
>   If this
> 50 Be but a vain belief, yet, oh! how oft—
>   In darkness and amid the many shapes
>   Of joyless daylight; when the fretful stir
>   Unprofitable, and the fever of the world,
>   Have hung upon the beatings of my heart—
> 55 How oft, in spirit, have I turned to thee,
>   O sylvan° Wye! thou wanderer through the woods,
>   How often has my spirit turned to thee!

49. What visual clue signals that a new stanza is beginning here? How does the speaker's focus or emphasis change in the new stanza?

56. sylvan *adj.*: associated with the forest or woodlands.

SKILLS REVIEW

The untraditional pastoral. The pastoral is a subgenre of poetry in which rural life is depicted in an idealized way. The term comes from the Latin word for "shepherd": Pastorals were originally about shepherds and nymphs. The most famous traditional English pastoral poem is Marlowe's "The Passionate Shepherd to His Love" (p. 259), which Raleigh satirized in "The Nymph's Reply to the Shepherd" (p. 261). The term has gradually come to have a broader meaning, describing any work that expresses reverence for the rustic life or nostalgia for a lost age or place of innocence.

Activity. "Tintern Abbey" has been called an untraditional pastoral—untraditional in that its subject is not shepherds. Ask students to look for elements of setting, tone, and theme that place the poem in the broad tradition of the pastoral.

      And now, with gleams of half-extinguished thought,
      With many recognitions dim and faint,
60   And somewhat of a sad perplexity,
      The picture of the mind° revives again:
      While here I stand, not only with the sense
      Of present pleasure, but with pleasing thoughts
      That in this moment there is life and food
65   For future years. And so I dare to hope,
      Though changed, no doubt, from what I was when first
      I came among these hills; when like a roe°
      I bounded o'er the mountains, by the sides

61. picture of the mind: primarily the picture in the mind, but also the picture the individual mind has of itself.

67. roe *n.:* deer.

Literary Criticism

Critic's Commentary: Why No Abbey?
In *The Song of the Earth,* the critic Jonathan Bate points out, "The ruined abbey at Tintern was always regarded as the high point of the Wye tour" because it was considered picturesque. (In the eighteenth century the word *picturesque* described a landscape that looked as if it had come out of a picture and tended to include such elements as harmoniously placed ruins, colorful peasants, and dilapidated cottages.) Given the conventional attitude of tourists to the Wye River Valley, "the title of Wordsworth's poem would have come as a surprise to readers educated in the picturesque. . . . Where previous visitors stood amidst the abbey ruins and reflected on mortality, Wordsworth pointedly locates his poem at an unspecified spot several miles upstream and makes his subject not death but 'the life of things' [l. 49]. . . . The absence of the abbey from the poem has two main effects. First, it critiques the picturesque assumption that 'artificial' features such as ruins . . . may be classed as part of nature. . . . The second effect of the absence is the transfer of religious sentiment from Christianity to nature." According to Bate, Wordsworth rejects the notion of the picturesque: "Though he is himself on a tour through the Wye valley, he attempts to overcome the . . . tourist's status as gazer" and instead seeks to have an "'immediate apprehension of nature.'"

Composed upon Westminster Bridge

September 3, 1802

William Wordsworth

Earth has not anything to show more fair:
Dull would he be of soul who could pass by
A sight so touching in its majesty:
This City now doth, like a garment, wear
5   The beauty of the morning; silent, bare,
Ships, towers, domes, theaters, and temples lie
Open unto the fields, and to the sky;
All bright and glittering in the smokeless air.
Never did sun more beautifully steep
10 In his first splendor, valley, rock, or hill;
Ne'er saw I, never felt, a calm so deep!
The river glideth at his own sweet will:
Dear God! the very houses seem asleep;
And all that mighty heart is lying still!

Westminster Bridge, London (detail)
(late 19th or early 20th century)
by Louis H. Grimshaw.

Response and Analysis

Thinking Critically

1. What details and features of the city are mentioned by the speaker?
2. What details **personify** the city? How does this personification make you feel?
3. What **paradox**, or seeming contradiction, do you find in the poem's last line?
4. What quality, or characteristic, of the scene seems to move the speaker most deeply?
5. What seems to be the **mood** of the speaker in this poem?

SKILLS FOCUS

Literary Skills
Analyze personification.

Writing Skills
Write a description using personification.

Extending and Evaluating

6. How do the **themes** and **images** of this poem classify Wordsworth as a typical Romantic poet?

WRITING

A City as a Person

Write a **description,** in prose or verse, of a city or town that you know well. Use **personification** to characterize your city or town. You might open with Wordsworth's first line: "Earth has not anything to show more fair."

Before You Read

The World Is Too Much with Us

Make the Connection
Quickwrite
The "world" is sometimes thought of as the world of material objects—the world of money and status symbols, the world of power, competition, and ambition. In seeking out the pleasures of this material world, what could a person lose? Jot down some answers to this question.

Literary Focus
Allusion
An **allusion** is a reference to a person, place, thing, or event that is recognizable from literature, history, religion, mythology, politics, sports, science, or popular culture. Allusions are often used to lend deeper meaning to a literary passage or work. In Wordsworth's poem "The World Is Too Much with Us," the poet alludes to two sea gods from Greek mythology—Proteus and Triton. By making reference to these gods, Wordsworth underscores an earlier sentiment in the poem. Look for this connection as you read.

> An **allusion** is a reference to something from literature, history, religion, mythology, politics, sports, science, or popular culture.
>
> *For more on Allusion, see the Handbook of Literary and Historical Terms.*

Background
Wordsworth wrote his final draft of this sonnet in 1804, at a time when he realized that his imaginative powers were beginning to fail. Although he continued to compose new works and to edit *The Prelude,* a long poem published after his death, he knew he was no longer responding to nature with the youthful passion that had inspired his earlier poems.

This sonnet counterattacks the ferocious criticism that Wordsworth was receiving from conservative reviewers, especially Francis Jeffrey in the *Edinburgh Review.* Jeffrey accused Wordsworth of using unpoetic language, but, even more, of conspiring against society, brooding needlessly over problems "instead of contemplating the wonders and pleasures which civilization has created for mankind." Jeffrey considered Wordsworth an enemy of progress because of his "idle discontent with the existing institutions of society" and his yearning for an earlier, less civilized time when people lived in harmony with nature.

Mosaic of Tritons, Nereids, and a sea antelope (1st century) from Ostia, Italy.
Museo Ostiense, Ostia, Italy.

INTERNET
More About William Wordsworth
Keyword: LE5 12-5

SKILLS FOCUS
Literary Skills
Understand allusion.

William Wordsworth 561

PRETEACHING

Summary — at grade level

> This sonnet in the Italian mode laments our tendency to get caught up in material considerations (the "world") at the expense of the soul, or deeper self. In the octave—the first eight lines—and the first half of l. 9, the speaker's tone is one of restrained disapproval as he states his theme: "we are out of tune" with nature. In the middle of l. 9 the tone suddenly changes (as signaled by the exclamation "Great God!"), and the speaker passionately proclaims that he would rather be a pagan than remain cut off from nature and life's true meaning.

Selection Starter
Build background. Point out that the pagan gods were often associated with natural phenomena, such as thunder, rain, wind, and fire. (Ask students to name some of these gods from Greek, Roman, African, Native American, Norse, or any other culture's mythology.) Thus, a pagan would see divinity in nature without needing to strain to make the connection.

VIEWING THE ART

> In Greek mythology the name Triton is often used to refer to a group of sea gods (mermen) who serve Poseidon, the head sea god and brother of Zeus. The Nereids are sea nymphs.
>
> **Activity.** Ask students to contrast modern mosaics they've seen with this first-century example. [Possible response: Modern mosaics are generally less detailed.]

DIFFERENTIATING INSTRUCTION

Learners Having Difficulty
Ask students how they reconnect to basic values when they feel overwhelmed by the material world.

English-Language Learners
Make sure students understand the expression "out of tune" (l. 8)—in both its literal and its figurative sense.

Advanced Learners
Enrichment. Have students compare this poem with Wordsworth's "London, 1802" (p. 526).

William Wordsworth 561

DIRECT TEACHING

VIEWING THE ART

Romantic artists like Wordsworth and **John Constable** (1776–1837) believed that industrialization alienated people from nature. These artists sought unity with nature—a unity they eventually found almost impossible to achieve.

Activity. How does Constable use color to show people's alienation from or unity with nature in this painting? [The bright red coat separates the man on the road from the color of the background, while the colors of the woman's dress cause her figure to blend in with her surroundings.]

A Reading Skills

? Analyzing. What does the speaker mean by "getting and spending"? [earning money and buying things]

B Literary Focus

? Irony. Why is the exclamation "Great God!" ironic, considering the content of ll. 10–14? [Possible response: It's ironic that the speaker calls out to God that he'd rather be a pagan—a believer in many gods.]

C Learners Having Difficulty

? Monitoring comprehension. What does "suckled in a creed outworn" mean? [Possible response: brought up in an obsolete religion.]

A Country Road with Trees and Figures by John Constable.
Victoria and Albert Museum, London. The Bridgeman Art Library.

The World Is Too Much with Us

William Wordsworth

> The world is too much with us; late and soon,
> **A** Getting and spending, we lay waste our powers:
> Little we see in Nature that is ours;
> We have given our hearts away, a sordid boon!°
> 5 This Sea that bares her bosom to the moon;
> The winds that will be howling at all hours,
> And are up-gathered now like sleeping flowers;
> For this, for everything, we are out of tune;
> **B** It moves us not.—Great God! I'd rather be
> **C** 10 A Pagan suckled in a creed outworn;
> So might I, standing on this pleasant lea,°
> Have glimpses that would make me less forlorn;
> Have sight of Proteus° rising from the sea;
> Or hear old Triton° blow his wreathèd horn.

4. **sordid boon:** foul gift. That is, the act of giving our hearts away is shameful.

11. **lea** *n.*: meadow.
13. **Proteus** (prō′tē·əs): in Greek mythology, a sea god who can change shape at will.
14. **Triton** (trī′tən): in Greek mythology, a sea god who controls the waves by blowing a conch shell. (See the mosaic on page 561.)

562 Collection 5 The Romantic Period

Literary Criticism

Critic's Commentary: Visions of Myth
Here is John L. Mahoney's analysis of the sonnet's sestet: "Then . . . the voice of the speaker . . . explodes with a guttural apostrophe, 'Great God,' . . . as he . . . exclaims almost blasphemously, . . . I'd rather abandon every traditional religious belief, every pious dogma if I might return to the primitive awe, reverence, amazement, worship of nature's beauties. . . . 'So might I,' he says, just a bit calmer, but still caught up in the intensity of his response, 'Have glimpses that would make me less forlorn' (l. 12). . . . And what glimpses they are, evoking a world and a time when it was possible to believe in myth, in the imaginative view of reality, in the presence of the divine in the midst of the vicissitudes of everyday reality. . . . It is a powerful sonnet, a sonnet keenly attuned to a culture out of tune with the vivifying energies of nature, the comforting visions of myth."

Response and Analysis

Thinking Critically

1. What does the speaker mean by the "world"? What do you think the speaker means when he says, "We have given our hearts away" (line 4)? Explain why you agree or disagree with the speaker.
2. Why do you think the speaker would "rather be / A Pagan" (lines 9–10)?
3. What is Wordsworth's purpose in alluding to mythology in the last lines of the poem? What emotions do these **allusions** evoke?
4. Identify the two parts of this sonnet. How is the **tone** of the second part different from the tone of the first part? How does this difference affect the meaning of the poem?
5. Identify the central **theme** of the poem. Does Wordsworth state this theme directly, or is it implied? How does the **personification** of the sea and the wind contribute to the theme?
6. How are the ideas about materialism and progress in this poem relevant to today's world? You may want to refer to your Quickwrite notes.

Extending and Evaluating

7. What is your reaction to the speaker's attack on modern life? Do you agree with Wordsworth that if people were in tune with nature they would be happier and less materialistic? Explain why or why not.

WRITING

Typically Romantic

In a brief **essay**, identify the elements in "The World Is Too Much with Us" that make the poem "typically Romantic"—that is, representative of Romantic lyric poetry. Consider the **allusions** and **images** Wordsworth uses, as well as the **theme** of the poem. Be sure to quote specific lines from the poem to support your points.

Literary Focus

Romantic Lyric Forms

The poems in this section represent a number of lyric forms—from variations on traditional sonnet schemes and experiments with the ode to the distinctive Romantic lyric form, the "meditative poem."

Sonnet. The sonnet was popular in Romantic poetry as a traditional type of occasional poem written on an important subject, public or private. Milton, for example, had used the sonnet in this way. But for the Romantics the sonnet was also used for experimentation. Coleridge's early sonnets, called "effusions" to excuse their looseness, helped him create the meditative poem. Keats's sonnets shaped the stanza forms for his odes. The main sonnet form was the **Italian,** or **Petrarchan,** composed of an octave (eight lines) and a sestet (six lines). But the Romantics also used the **Shakespearean sonnet** of three quatrains (four lines) and a couplet (two lines) form.

Ode. The Romantic ode was a self-conscious use of a classical form that had been brought into English literature in the seventeenth and eighteenth centuries. The structure of the Romantic ode was certainly influenced by the Romantic meditative poem. Sometimes a poem in the manner of an ode was called a "hymn." A traditional ode has two distinctive features: (1) It uses heightened, impassioned language, and (2) it addresses some object. The ode may speak to, or **apostrophize,** objects (an urn), creatures (a nightingale), and presences or powers (the west wind). The speaker invokes the object and then creates a relationship with it, through praise or prayer.

Meditative poem. The Romantics developed the meditative poem and passed it on to later generations of poets. It is the best

Literary Skills
Analyze allusion.
Analyze Romantic lyric forms (sonnet, ode, meditative poem).

Writing Skills
Write an essay identifying the Romantic elements in a poem.

INDEPENDENT PRACTICE

Response and Analysis

5. Possible answer: The theme of the poem is implied: We have given up our most important gift—our connection to nature—in exchange for material goods and the benefits of civilization. The personification of the sea and the wind reinforces the idea of a personal connection to nature.
6. Students may argue that people today are even more materialistic and estranged from nature than they were in Wordsworth's time and that we are not just ignoring nature but actively destroying it.

Extending and Evaluating

7. Students should be prepared to back up their opinions about how important harmony with nature is to human happiness. Students might also discuss the expensive gear used by many nature lovers (hikers, canoeists, cyclists, skiers, snowboarders, climbers) today. Is it still possible to enjoy nature without all this equipment?

Thinking Critically

1. By the "world," the speaker means the world of material things. He thinks that people have given up their values in the pursuit of material wealth.
2. The speaker believes that pagans recognize and worship the divine in nature.
3. The use of mythology dramatizes the connection to nature. These allusions evoke feelings of longing for a time when people were in greater awe of nature.
4. The first part is the octave, ll. 1–8, and the first part of l. 9. The sestet begins with "Great God!" The tone of the octave is disillusioned, sad, and even angry. The tone of the sestet is passionate, filled with longing and regret and finally awe. The difference in tone highlights the contrast the speaker sees between the material world he is denouncing and the world of nature and natural divinity.

INDEPENDENT PRACTICE

Literary Focus
Romantic Lyric Forms
Accept any pairings of speakers and poems students suggest if they can justify it by pointing to words or lines in each poem.

ASSESSING

Assessment
- Holt Assessment: Literature, Reading, and Vocabulary

RETEACHING

For a lesson reteaching poetic devices, see **Reteaching**, p. 1129A.

VIEWING THE ART

John Constable (see p. 562) believed that in landscape painting the sky was "the key note, the standard scale, and the chief organ of sentiment." Of Constable's paintings, the art historian H. W. Janson says, "Often . . . the land serves as no more than a foil for the ever-changing drama of wind, sunlight, and clouds."

Activity. Invite students to compare *Study of Sky and Trees* with *A Country Road with Trees and Figures,* on p. 562, with regard to theme, composition, use of color, and overall effect. Ask students to form their own conclusions about Constable's style and its relevance to the aims of the Romantic poets.

---

example of the artful illusion of the lyric in which we are to imagine a person speaking. The perfect example of the form—Wordsworth's "Tintern Abbey"—is in a flowing **blank verse** in which the stanzas are the equivalent of paragraphs, beginning and ending where sense, rather than strict form, dictates. The tone of these lyrics is much easier and more colloquial than the tone of the odes. Coleridge called one of his meditative lyrics a "conversation poem."

Recognizing speakers and tone. Re-read Wordsworth's lyrics aloud, paying attention to the voices you hear. As you read, think about the speakers: the bard or prophet who speaks about matters of great concern; the wanderer who happens upon something that turns out to be revealing; and the lover of poetic experiences who finds beauty in all the details of life. Which of these **speakers** do you see in each of Wordsworth's poems?

Study of Sky and Trees by John Constable.
Victoria and Albert Museum. © Scala/Art Resource, New York.

564 Collection 5 The Romantic Period

DEVELOPING FLUENCY

Individual activity. Have students pick one of the Wordsworth poems included in this collection and prepare an oral reading that emphasizes the speaker, tone, and form of that lyric. For example, a student reading "The World Is Too Much with Us" might emphasize the speaker's disillusionment, anger, and sense of loss, as well as the dramatic change in tone that occurs at the beginning of the sestet. A student reading "Tintern Abbey" (or a section of it) might focus on conveying the speaker's reflective, conversational tone, and the fact that he is addressing a silent listener. Suggest that students work in pairs to prepare their oral readings.

Connecting to World Literature
Tanka and Haiku

You have just read Romantic poems by William Blake and William Wordsworth. In this Connecting to World Literature feature, you will read two very different forms of poetry—Japanese tanka and haiku—that, like Romantic poetry, use images of nature. Unlike Romantic poetry, however, these Japanese forms are concise and rigidly structured.

Tanka . . . . (Japan) 569
Haiku . . . . (Japan) 571

The **tanka** (tän′kə) and the **haiku** (hī′kōō′) are two of the most beloved forms of Japanese poetry. Both are very old, tanka dating from the eighth century A.D. and haiku from the thirteenth and fourteenth centuries. Both forms of poetry demand the compression of ideas and images into the space of a few words.

Borrowed Words, New Beginnings
In early times, Japanese was exclusively a spoken language; there was no system for writing it down. The earliest Japanese poets wrote in Chinese. Between the fifth and eighth centuries, a system for writing Japanese was developed: Chinese letters, or characters, were adapted to represent Japanese sounds. These phonetic characters came to be known as kana (kä′nə), meaning "borrowed names."

Toward the end of this period—during the eighth century—a collection of poems called the *Manyoshu* (man′yō·shū), or *Collection of Ten Thousand Leaves*, appeared. By this time, Japanese poets had begun to appreciate the lyrical power of their own language. Indeed, the Japanese view the *Manyoshu* as the beginning of a written literature that they could call entirely their own.

The Origin of Tanka
It is in the *Manyoshu* that the earliest-known tanka appear. **Tanka,** meaning "short songs," are brief and lyrical. Like other lyric poems, each tanka expresses a private emotion or thought, often on the theme of change, solitude, or love. The traditional tanka consists of exactly thirty-one syllables divided among five lines. Three of the poem's lines have seven syllables, and the other two have five.

Lovers composed and exchanged tanka as expressions of affection. Aristocrats amused themselves by playing a game in which one person would invent the first three lines of a tanka and another would finish it.

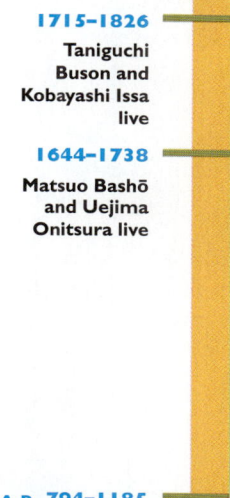

1715–1826
Taniguchi Buson and Kobayashi Issa live

1644–1738
Matsuo Bashō and Uejima Onitsura live

A.D. 794–1185
Tanka thrives during Heian period

SKILLS FOCUS

Literary Skills
Understand tanka and haiku. Compare and contrast Japanese poetry with Romantic poetry.

Tanka and Haiku 565

Using the Time Line
Activity. Have students use information from an encyclopedia or this textbook to place the following events on the time line:
- Chaucer begins writing *The Canterbury Tales.* [1387]
- *Beowulf* is first written down. [c. 700]
- Wordsworth and Coleridge publish *Lyrical Ballads.* [1798]
- Shakespeare writes *Hamlet.* [1600–1601]

DIRECT TEACHING

A Literary Connections
The Origins of Haiku
Haiku has roots in another Japanese poetic form, a linked-verse poem called a renga. Originally the three-line haiku served as the opening stanza of the renga, establishing its tone. As time passed, however, haiku began to be composed as free-standing poems.

B Literary Connections
American Haiku
American poets who have experimented with the haiku form include Ezra Pound, Amy Lowell, William Carlos Williams, Richard Wright, and Gary Snyder.

C Literary Focus
Imagery. Donald Keene, a scholar of Japanese literature, compares this imaginative connection to the leap of a spark between two electric poles.

D Literary Connections
Translation
A traditional haiku consists of two images, one suggesting timelessness and the other suggesting change, usually divided by a kireji, or "cutting word." Even if they don't translate the kireji, translators usually try to convey the tension or revelation produced by the word.

Haiku Happenings

Eventually, tanka inspired an even more condensed poetic form—the haiku. A **haiku** is a brief, unrhymed, three line poem. In Japanese, the first and last lines have five syllables each and the middle line has seven.

Examples of short verses similar to haiku have been found in thirteenth- and fourteenth-century Japanese literature. However, the art of haiku was not perfected until later in the seventeenth century, when the greatest of the classical haiku poets, Matsuo Bashō (ba'shō), lived. When English authors such as John Milton were composing epic, intricate poems, Bashō and his pupils were writing strikingly pure, compressed verses only a few words long. In the centuries since Bashō, the haiku form has been adopted by poets all over the world.

Unlike many Western poets, the classical haiku masters do not present similes, metaphors, or other figures of speech. Rather, haiku poets present simple, unadorned images, and the reader must make an imaginative leap to understand the connection between them.

To Say or Not to Say?

By their precision, their simple beauty, and their economy of words, tanka and haiku embody an important principle of Japanese art and culture: What is *not* said is often as important as what *is* said. Understandably, this principle creates certain challenges for translators of both haiku and tanka.

One difficulty faced by translators is that the Japanese language differs greatly from English. For example, it has no articles and rarely uses pronouns. To accommodate these differences, the English translators of tanka and haiku sometimes choose to make their English versions rhyme, though this is not in keeping with Japanese tradition. In other cases, the English translations do not have the exact number of syllables per line as prescribed by the Japanese form.

Although form must sometimes be sacrificed, the main work of translating any poem is to preserve its essence—the transcendent quality that stretches across the miles and the years to connect a single author and a single reader at any given moment. This essence of Japanese poetry is summarized by Ki Tsurayuki (kē tsōō·rä·yōō′kē), one of the editors of the great tenth-century tanka anthology, *Kokinshu*, in his preface to the collection:

> ❝ When we hear the notes of the nightingale among the blossoms, when we hear the frog in the water, we know that every living being is capable of song. Poetry, without effort, can move heaven and earth, can touch the gods and spirits . . . it turns the hearts of man and woman to each other and it soothes the soul of the fierce warrior. ❞

Though his comments were written over a thousand years ago, they still hold true for much of Japanese verse.

Birds on a Snowy Plum Bough by Muryu.
British Library, London, UK/ The Bridgeman Art Library.

READING SKILLS REVIEW

Comparing and contrasting translations. A haiku may be translated in a variety of ways. Consider this famous haiku by Bashō. Harold G. Henderson's translation is a literal version of the Japanese:

> Old pond:
>   frog jump-in
>   water-sound

Harry Behn's translation retains the seventeen syllables of the original:

> An old silent pond . . .
> A frog jumps into the pond,
>   splash! Silence again.

A looser translation by Asatarō Miyamori captures the essential images but abandons the three-line form:

> The ancient pond!
> A frog plunged—splash!

Activity. Ask students which translation of the haiku they prefer, and why. What differences do they notice among the three versions, other than those of form? Which translation creates the sharpest tension between the images of the pond and the frog?

Before You Read

Tanka and Haiku

Make the Connection
Quickwrite

Tanka and haiku are highly visual poetic forms, presenting subtle images of nature and the changing seasons to suggest a variety of moods and emotions, from quiet joy to bittersweet reflection. The best tanka and haiku use simple sensory images—tree branches, streams, the stirrings of an autumn breeze—to imply far more than they state directly. How would you suggest a mood through a single image? If you were a photographer, what scenes or objects would you photograph to convey the following moods: loneliness, nostalgia, contentment? Freewrite for a few minutes, describing in detail the images you would photograph, and explaining your reasons for choosing these images.

Literary Focus
Imagery

Imagery is language that appeals to the senses—to sight, hearing, smell, touch, and taste. The Japanese tanka and haiku writers relied on imagery—often from nature—to subtly and indirectly suggest moods and themes. What is left out is as important as what is included, and it is up to the reader to make the connection between the images and the emotions they imply. Thus, the image of a fallen cherry blossom may suggest the brevity of love or even of life itself, and the image of the full moon may prompt philosophical musings about change and eternity. The reader must ponder the images in order to grasp the meaning of the poem.

> **Imagery** is language that appeals to the senses of sight, hearing, smell, touch, and taste.
>
> *For more on Imagery, see the Handbook of Literary and Historical Terms.*

Background

The five tanka you will read (see page 569) were composed by five different Japanese poets over a period of five centuries, yet they share a similar form and similar themes. Although each poem reflects its author's individual age, social position, and philosophy of life, all evoke equally strong images and emotions.

Because all the tanka presented here are translations from the Japanese, they necessarily differ from the originals. For example, only one of the five translated poems actually follows the traditional tanka formula of thirty-one syllables. The translated poems also do not have the same rhythm or cadence as the Japanese originals. Yet in other respects the translated poems are faithful to the traditions of Japanese tanka. They are unrhymed, for instance, which is in keeping with classical tanka style, and they make use of **assonance,** the repetition of similar vowel sounds in nearby words.

The first three haiku you will read are by the greatest seventeenth-century haiku master, Bashō. In all three poems, Bashō finds beauty in seemingly insignificant or ordinary objects or events. This practice is inspired by the Buddhist belief that, through contemplation, anyone can find great significance in even the humblest of things.

Literary Skills Understand imagery.

SKILLS FOCUS, pp. 567–572

Grade-Level Skills
- **Literary Skills**

Analyze ways poets use poetic devices, including imagery.

PRETEACHING

Summary ↔ *at grade level*

> Each tanka presents a moment—when the speaker is waiting for a lover, stopping during a journey, wondering what a friend is thinking, feeling adrift, watching the moon—and an image that captures that moment. Each haiku also presents an image or juxtaposes two images: a crow on a withered branch, a village where bells don't ring at dusk, a time for putting flowers in rice bowls, a celebration of cherry blossoms, a woman reading in the moonlight near a pear tree in bloom, a hut covered with vines.

Skills Starter

Motivate. Ask students to think about the kinds of images they're used to seeing in English-language poetry. Tell them that they will see very different kinds of images in the tanka and haiku.

RESOURCES: READING

Planning
- One-Stop Planner CD-ROM with ExamView Test Generator

Differentiating Instruction
- Supporting Instruction in Spanish
- Audio CD Library, Selections and Summaries in Spanish

Grammar and Language
- Daily Language Activities

Assessment
- Holt Assessment: Literature, Reading, and Vocabulary
- One-Stop Planner CD-ROM with ExamView Test Generator
- Holt Online Assessment

Internet
- go.hrw.com (Keyword: LE5 12-5)
- Elements of Literature Online.

Media
- Audio CD Library
- Audio CD Library, Selections and Summaries in Spanish
- Fine Art Transparencies

PRETEACHING

Summary *at grade level*

In "Kubla Khan," Coleridge sets forth a fantastic vision. His speaker states that Kubla Khan has built a majestic pleasure dome in Xanadu, with gardens, forests, and winding streams. Deep in a chasm a fountain bursts forth, sending the sacred river Alph into a motionless ocean. Amid the noise of the river, the Khan hears voices prophesying war. The speaker then describes a vision of an Abyssinian (Ethiopian) woman. He claims that if he could recapture her music, he could rebuild the pleasure dome at Xanadu, arousing fear and awe in the people.

Selection Starter

Motivate. Share with students the anecdote of the poet at a public reading who, after reading a poem, was asked by an audience member what the poem meant. In answer, the poet proceeded to read the entire poem again. In effect, he was implying that the poem *is* its meaning. Ask students how they make sense of a poem. Must a poem be reduced to a logical statement in order to make sense?

Before You Read

Kubla Khan

Make the Connection
Quickwrite

The poem you are about to read may challenge the limits of your imagination. Fantastical and strange, it is like a vivid yet incomprehensible dream. Coleridge, in fact, suggested that the poem came to him in a dream. Like a dream, the poem contains allusions to the deepest human desires—for pleasure, order, beauty, even chaos and war. It also holds within it the moment when, upon waking, the vividness and the supposed logic of the dream are suddenly—perhaps forever—lost to the dreamer.

Think about some dreams that you have had. Then, jot down some notes that describe how dreams seem to work. Are they logical or illogical? How do they progress? Do they tell coherent stories or do they consist mostly of images and fragments of stories? As you read, think about how the poem may imitate or reproduce this process.

Literary Focus
Alliteration

Alliteration—the repetition of a consonant sound in words that are close to one another—can have several effects. Coleridge uses alliteration throughout "Kubla Khan" to help create the poem's enchanted mood. Alliteration can impart a musical quality to a poem, emphasize a particular line or idea, or help establish a rhythm. As in lines 25–26 of "Kubla Khan," alliteration can also suggest a certain kind of movement: "Five *m*iles *m*eandering with a *m*azy *m*otion, / Through wood and dale the sacred river ran. . . ." Here the repeated *m* sound evokes and imitates the lazy, serpentine flow of the river. As you read the poem, look for—and listen to—other examples of alliteration.

INTERNET
More About
Samuel Taylor
Coleridge
Keyword: LE5 12-5

Literary Skills
Understand alliteration.

Alliteration is the repetition of a consonant sound in words that are close to one another.
For more on Alliteration, see the Handbook of Literary and Historical Terms.

Background

"Kubla Khan" has a lyrical tone and manner that resemble a meditative ode. Full of mystery and dread, "Kubla Khan" was composed at about the same time (late 1797 or early 1798) as *The Rime of the Ancient Mariner.*

"Kubla Khan" has always intrigued readers, including the poet Byron, who, after reading it in manuscript, apparently persuaded Coleridge to publish it in 1816. At the time, Coleridge added a prose introduction that offered a rational account of the poem's origins. He claimed it was written in a reverie brought on by opium taken after he had read a provocative passage in a seventeenth-century travel book. Coleridge asserted that he woke from his dream and was interrupted by a visitor while composing the poem. After the visitor departed an hour later, a mere fragment of his dream-poem could be reproduced, he claimed.

Kubla Khan (c. 1216–1294), the grandson of Genghis Khan, was the Mongol conqueror of China.

Kublai Khan, from the Yüan dynasty, China.
National Palace Museum, Taipei Taiwan, Republic of China.

574   Collection 5   The Romantic Period

DIFFERENTIATING INSTRUCTION

Learners Having Difficulty
Invite learners having difficulty to read "Kubla Khan" in interactive format in *The Holt Reader* and to use the s denotes as aids to understanding the selection. The interactive version provides additional instruction, practice, and assessment of the literary skill taught in the Student Edition. Monitor students' responses to the selection, and correct any misconceptions that arise.

English-Language Learners
Point out the use of the suffix *–less,* and help students define the words ending in *–less* in the poem: *measureless, sunless, ceaseless, lifeless.*

Special Education Students
For lessons designed for English-language learners and special education students, see *Holt Reading Solutions.*

574   Collection 5   The Romantic Period

Palace of Kublai Khan at Peking (14th century). Miniature from the *Livre des Merveilles*.
(MS Fr. 2810, fol. 37) © Bibliothèque Nationale de France, Paris.

Kubla Khan

Samuel Taylor Coleridge

In Xanadu did Kubla Khan
A stately pleasure-dome decree:
Where Alph,° the sacred river, ran
Through caverns measureless to man
5 Down to a sunless sea.
So twice five miles of fertile ground
With walls and towers were girdled round:
And there were gardens bright with sinuous rills,°
Where blossomed many an incense-bearing tree;
10 And here were forests ancient as the hills,
Enfolding sunny spots of greenery.

But oh! that deep romantic chasm which slanted
Down the green hill athwart a cedarn cover!°
A savage place! as holy and enchanted

3. **Alph:** probably a reference to the Greek river Alpheus, which flows into the Ionian Sea, and whose waters are fabled to rise up again in Sicily.

8. **sinuous** (sin′yo͞o·əs) **rills:** winding streams.

13. **athwart a cedarn cover:** crossing diagonally under a covering growth of cedar trees.

DIRECT TEACHING

A Learners Having Difficulty
Re-reading. What change in imagery and tone occurs here? [The imagery becomes frightening; the tone becomes sinister, a Romantic combination of bright and dark.]

B Reading Skills
Paraphrasing. What is described here? [A fountain gushes out of a chasm, spraying a hail of rocks and forming a river. The river flows for five miles, reaching the caverns and sinking into a lifeless sea.]

C Reading Skills
Interpreting imagery. What does the flow of the sacred river represent to Coleridge? [Possible response: the flow of the imagination—born of nature, active for a short time, and finally sinking into oblivion.]

D Literary Focus
Symbol. How would you explain the contradictory qualities of the dome? [Possible response: The dome is imaginary and dreamlike; dream images often contain contradictory features.]

E Literary Focus
Alliteration. What examples of alliteration can you find in ll. 37–45? What effect do they create? [*d* sounds in "damsel," "dulcimer," and "deep delight"; *s* sounds in "once," "saw," "symphony," and "song"; *l* sounds in "loud" and "long." Possible response: The alliteration creates a musical effect, evoking the beauty of the young woman's song.]

F Reading Skills
Interpreting. What does the speaker long to do? [to "build that dome in air" (with music)] What effect would this have? [He would be regarded with fear and awe.]

---

15 As e'er beneath a waning moon was haunted
By woman wailing for her demon-lover!
And from this chasm, with ceaseless turmoil seething,
As if this earth in fast thick pants were breathing,
A mighty fountain momently° was forced:
20 Amid whose swift half-intermitted burst
Huge fragments vaulted like rebounding hail,
Or chaffy grain beneath the thresher's flail:°
And 'mid these dancing rocks at once and ever
It flung up momently the sacred river.
25 Five miles meandering with a mazy° motion
Through wood and dale the sacred river ran,
Then reached the caverns measureless to man,
And sank in tumult to a lifeless ocean:
And 'mid this tumult Kubla heard from far
30 Ancestral voices prophesying war!
    The shadow of the dome of pleasure
    Floated midway on the waves;
    Where was heard the mingled measure°
    From the fountain and the caves.
35 It was a miracle of rare device,
A sunny pleasure-dome with caves of ice!

    A damsel with a dulcimer°
    In a vision once I saw:
    It was an Abyssinian° maid,
40   And on her dulcimer she played,
    Singing of Mount Abora.°
    Could I revive within me
    Her symphony and song,
    To such a deep delight 'twould win me,
45 That with music loud and long,
I would build that dome in air,
That sunny dome! those caves of ice!
And all who heard should see them there,
And all should cry, Beware! Beware!
50 His flashing eyes, his floating hair!
Weave a circle round him thrice,
And close your eyes with holy dread,
For he on honeydew hath fed,
And drunk the milk of Paradise.

---

19. momently *adv.*: at each moment.

22. thresher's flail: heavy, whiplike tool used to thresh, or beat, grain in order to separate the kernels from their chaff, or husks.
25. mazy *adj.*: like a maze; having many turns.

33. measure *n.*: rhythmic sound.

37. dulcimer *n.*: musical instrument that is often played by striking the strings with small hammers.
39. Abyssinian: Ethiopian. Ethiopia is in northeast Africa.
41. Mount Abora: probably a reference to John Milton's (1608–1674) *Paradise Lost,* in which Mount Amara, in Ethiopia, is a mythical, earthly paradise.

CONTENT-AREA CONNECTIONS

Humanities: Orientalism
The image of Eastern culture that developed in the West has been the subject of study by cultural critics. Among the most notable is Edward Said, whose book *Orientalism* (1978) explores Western stereotypes of the East.
Individual activity. Ask students to research the effects of the Romantic interest in the "exotic" and the way it has shaped current attitudes toward the East.

DEVELOPING FLUENCY

Help students improve their pronunciation and intonation by having them read the poem in unison. Divide the class into small groups including both English-language learners and English-proficient peers.

Response and Analysis

Thinking Critically

1. In the first stanza, what **images** create pictures of the pleasure-dome that Kubla Khan decrees?
2. Why is the "deep romantic chasm" of line 12 called a "savage" place? What ominous note is introduced toward the end of the second stanza?
3. In the third stanza, what does the speaker see in a vision? What does the speaker say he wants to do?
4. The speaker in the poem has been interpreted as being an artist, perhaps a poet. Why would the "damsel with a dulcimer" be important to the speaker?
5. What could the "dome in air" which the speaker wants to create **symbolize**?
6. Many ancient cultures regarded poets as seers who had a special relationship with the gods and thus were to be treated with reverence. How might Coleridge be alluding to such beliefs in the closing lines of the last stanza?
7. How could this poem be about the creation of a poem?
8. Describe the **rhyme scheme** and **meter** of the poem. What examples of **alliteration** add to the poem's music?

Extending and Evaluating

9. The power of the imagination is often exalted in Romantic poetry. In your opinion, does "Kubla Khan" celebrate the imagination or caution against its indulgence? Support your response with evidence from the poem.

WRITING

The Stuff of Dreams

Review the Quickwrite notes you made earlier describing dreams. How do your thoughts on the way dreams work compare to the dreamlike flow of "Kubla Khan"? Use your notes to **evaluate** Coleridge's claim that the poem began as a dream. Explain whether "Kubla Khan" reads like a dream, using examples from the poem as evidence. Then, draw your own conclusion about Coleridge's claim. Do you think the poem is in fact the product of a dream?

INTERNET
Projects and Activities
Keyword: LE5 12-5

Literary Skills
Analyze alliteration.

Writing Skills
Evaluate a poet's claim.

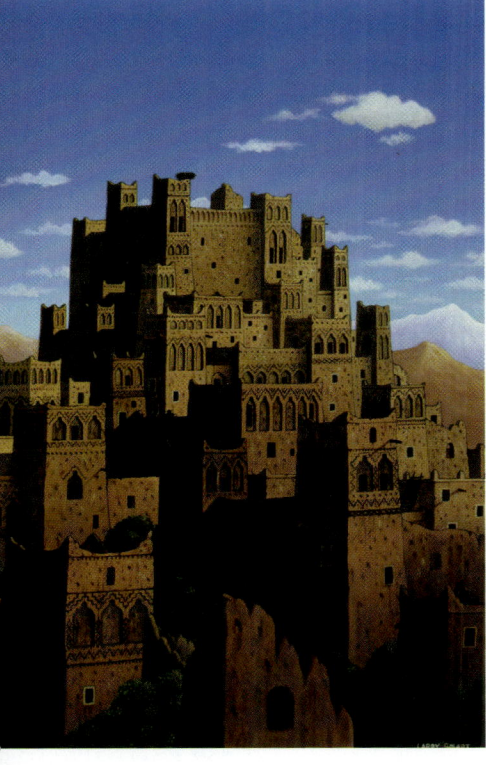

Beyond the Valley of the Kasbahs.
The Bridgeman Art Library/Getty Images.

INDEPENDENT PRACTICE

Response and Analysis

5. Possible answer: It symbolizes mysterious, miraculous creation.
6. The people use a ritual to protect themselves from the poet (l. 51); they regard him with fear and awe because he has "drunk the milk of Paradise."
7. Possible answer: The poem itself has been created from air—with words—to give us vivid images and a new way to look at creativity and the imagination.
8. The rhyme scheme in the first stanza is *abaabccdbdb*; it varies in the later stanzas. The meter is iambic, with varying numbers of feet in each line. Line 25 contains alliteration, in "miles meandering with a mazy motion," suggesting the course of the river. Lines 19, 27, and 50 also include examples of alliteration.

Extending and Evaluating

9. Possible answer: The poem celebrates the power of the imagination, but it warns of the "tumult" that exists outside of the imagination's "pleasure-dome."

ASSESSING

Assessment
- Holt Assessment: Literature, Reading, and Vocabulary

RETEACHING

For a lesson reteaching poetic devices, see **Reteaching**, p. 1129A.

Thinking Critically

1. In the first stanza we learn that a sacred river runs through the deep caverns of the dome to a sea unlit by the sun. Inside walls and towers stand gardens with streams, sweet-smelling trees, and green forests on which the sun shines.
2. Within the chasm, water churns, finally bursting from the earth in a fountain. In l. 30, voices warn of war.
3. He sees a young woman with a dulcimer. He says that he wants to re-create the pleasure dome in the air.
4. Possible answer: The young woman represents imagination, the power or "song" that will enable the speaker to rebuild the dome.

PRETEACHING

Summary ⇔ at grade level

This literary ballad is a harrowing exploration of the torments that guilt can inflict on the human soul and the terrible expiation required of those who sin against nature. The setting is apparently medieval, and the principal characters are the ancient Mariner—an old, weary sailor—and the Wedding Guest, to whom he tells his tale. The Mariner describes how his ship set sail under a good wind, heading toward the South Pole. On the way, he commits a senseless crime: killing an albatross that the sailors believe to be a good omen. As a result, the Polar Spirit—apparently a spirit of nature itself—pursues the ship, and suffering and punishment descend on the vessel. Two specters, Death and Life-in-Death, play dice for the crew; all die except the Mariner, who has been won by Life-in-Death. Only when the Mariner recognizes the beauty of a passing group of water snakes and blesses them does the curse of the albatross, which has been hung around his neck, begin to abate. The Mariner then falls asleep. When he awakens, he finds that the ship is being sailed by the reanimated corpses of the crew. Eventually the Mariner realizes that a troop of angels is in control of the ship. He falls into a trance, during which the ship magically arrives back at his own country. The curse has been expiated, but as the harbor Pilot comes out to the ship, the battered vessel sinks in a violent whirlpool. The Mariner rows the Pilot's boat to shore and finally reaches land, where he confesses his sin to a holy Hermit. As his penance, the Mariner must wander the earth for the rest of his life, telling his fantastic tale to passing strangers.

Before You Read

The Rime of the Ancient Mariner

Make the Connection
Quickwrite
Have you ever done something on impulse, knowing even while you were doing it that you would regret it later? The ancient Mariner's strange tale turns on just such an action. And the dreadful consequences of his impulsive deed are as hypnotizing to us as they are to the Mariner's spellbound listener. As you read, try to chart your responses to the Mariner's story. When do you feel sympathy for him—or sorrow or fear? When does his story seem true, and when is it hopelessly distorted by guilt?

The Mariner's tale is essentially a confession. Jot down a few of your own ideas about the act of confession. What purpose does confession have for the teller and the listener? Why do you think the act of confession plays such an important role in law and religion?

Literary Focus
Literary Ballad
Coleridge's **literary ballad** imitates the traditional **folk ballad** in both subject matter and form. Like the old folk ballads (see page 108), his sensational narrative blends real with supernatural events. It also uses simple language, a good deal of repetition, and strong patterns of rhythm and rhyme. Coleridge was a skilled poet, and to avoid monotony, he often varies his **meter** and **rhyme scheme.** He also uses sophisticated sound devices like **internal rhyme** ("The guests are *met*, the feast is *set*") and **assonance** ("'Tis sweeter far to me"). To give his ballad an archaic sound, he uses language that was old-fashioned for his day.

INTERNET
Vocabulary Practice
•
More About Samuel Taylor Coleridge
•
Keyword: LE5 12-5

SKILLS FOCUS

Literary Skills Understand the characteristics of a literary ballad.
Reading Skills Understand archaic words.

A **literary ballad,** a songlike poem that tells a story, is written in imitation of the folk ballad, which springs from a genuine oral tradition.
For more on the Ballad, see the Handbook of Literary and Historical Terms.

Reading Skills
Reading Archaic Words
To give his ballad an antique flavor, Coleridge used many words that were **archaic,** or out of date.

As you read, you will find the meanings of many of these words in the margin of the page. However, you may not want to interrupt the powerful rhythm of the verse to stop and check a word's meaning. If not, try reading several stanzas at once, pausing only occasionally to check words you didn't understand. Some of the words' meanings will be suggested by context clues, as in "Nor dim nor red, like God's own head, / The glorious Sun *uprist.*" Here, the prefix *up–*, in addition to your own knowledge about the sun, might lead you to guess correctly that the meaning of *uprist* is "rose." As you read, jot down any archaic words, or parts of words, that are still in use today.

Background
Coleridge wrote *The Rime of the Ancient Mariner* as part of the collaboration with Wordsworth in 1797–1798 that culminated in *Lyrical Ballads.* As Coleridge later recalled, some of the poems in this volume were intended to present ordinary people and events in a fresh and interesting way.

578 Collection 5 The Romantic Period

Previewing Vocabulary

To reinforce students' understanding of the Vocabulary words on p. 579, have them respond to the following questions.

1. Describe the most <u>ghastly</u> Halloween costume you've ever seen.
2. What options do people suffering under a <u>tyrannous</u> government have other than violent revolution?
3. What effect does <u>dismal</u> weather have on your ability to study?
4. Which historical event has most <u>wrenched</u> our nation?
5. Do you think the pressure on the younger generation to succeed has increased or <u>abated</u>? Explain.

Others, such as *Ancient Mariner,* were to present supernatural characters and events, yet in such a way that would induce the reader to "procure for these shadows of imagination that willing suspension of disbelief for the moment, which constitutes poetic faith."

The Rime of the Ancient Mariner was the first poem in the 1798 edition of *Lyrical Ballads.* In part because of Wordsworth's discomfort with the disparity between it and the other poems in the volume, Coleridge revised the poem for later editions, modernizing many of the deliberately old-fashioned words he had used. The marginal notes were added in 1817.

It is helpful in reading this narrative to keep one or two things in mind. First, the poem gives no explanation for the killing of the albatross. The results of the act, rather than the act itself, are important. Second, all the objects and events described in the story are being seen through the eyes of the Mariner, whose frame of mind is constantly shifting. This unstable perspective makes it difficult—perhaps impossible—for the reader to tell what really happened.

Vocabulary Development

tyrannous (tir′ə·nəs) *adj.:* harsh; oppressive.

dismal (diz′məl) *adj.:* gloomy.

ghastly (gast′lē) *adj.:* dreadful; ghostly.

abated (ə·bāt′id) *v.:* lessened.

wrenched (rencht) *v.:* anguished; grief-stricken.

"With my crossbow / I shot the ALBATROSS."

PRETEACHING

Selection Starter

Motivate. Coleridge had never been to sea when he wrote this poem, and some critics have complained that it lacks verisimilitude. Coleridge also seems to have known little about albatrosses. Realism, however, was never his objective. Urge students to suspend their disbelief and to have, in Coleridge's words, "poetic faith."

Build background. Coleridge remarked that the poem has too much and yet too little of a moral; that is, the moral is obtrusive and yet inadequate. Throughout his life, Coleridge was wracked with feelings of failure and guilt, feelings that link him closely to the character of the Mariner.

VIEWING THE ART

The renowned nineteenth-century French engraver **Gustave Doré** (1832–1883) created the illustrations on these pages (except the one on p. 580). Doré illustrated many classics, including the Bible, Milton's *Paradise Lost,* Tennyson's *Idylls of the King,* and Dante's *Divine Comedy.* Doré is known for the bizarre and grotesque scenes in much of his work.

Activity. Ask students to preview the illustrations for the ballad and record their predictions of what will happen in the poem.

DIFFERENTIATING INSTRUCTION

Learners Having Difficulty
Modeling. Model the skill of dealing with archaic words by saying: "If, as I'm reading, I notice a word I don't know or a word that seems out of place, I use the context to try to figure out the meaning. If that doesn't work, I look to see whether the word is glossed in the margin; if it is, it may be an archaic word or a word being used in an archaic sense." Encourage students to ask themselves, "Is this word archaic? Is it a word being used in an archaic sense?"

English-Language Learners
Explain that in most cases, Coleridge's marginal notes sum up the action. (One notable exception occurs in the description of the Polar Spirit.) Encourage students to make notes in their notebooks summarizing other passages.

Advanced Learners
Coleridge's criticism and philosophy have been just as influential as his poetry. Have students read excerpts from *Biographia Literaria* (1817), perhaps Chapter 13 (on imagination) and Chapter 14 (on defining prose and poetry), which appear in *The Portable Coleridge.* Students can share insights about Coleridge during discussions of the ballad.

DIRECT TEACHING

VIEWING THE ART

Caspar David Friedrich (1774–1840) is now considered the greatest German Romantic painter, but he attained only modest fame during his lifetime. Art historians have described some of his paintings as melancholy, a word that might also be applied to Coleridge's poetry. (See also the painting on p. 531.)

Activity. Encourage students to identify elements in the painting that create a sense of melancholy. [Possible responses: the darkness of the images; the stillness of the ships.]

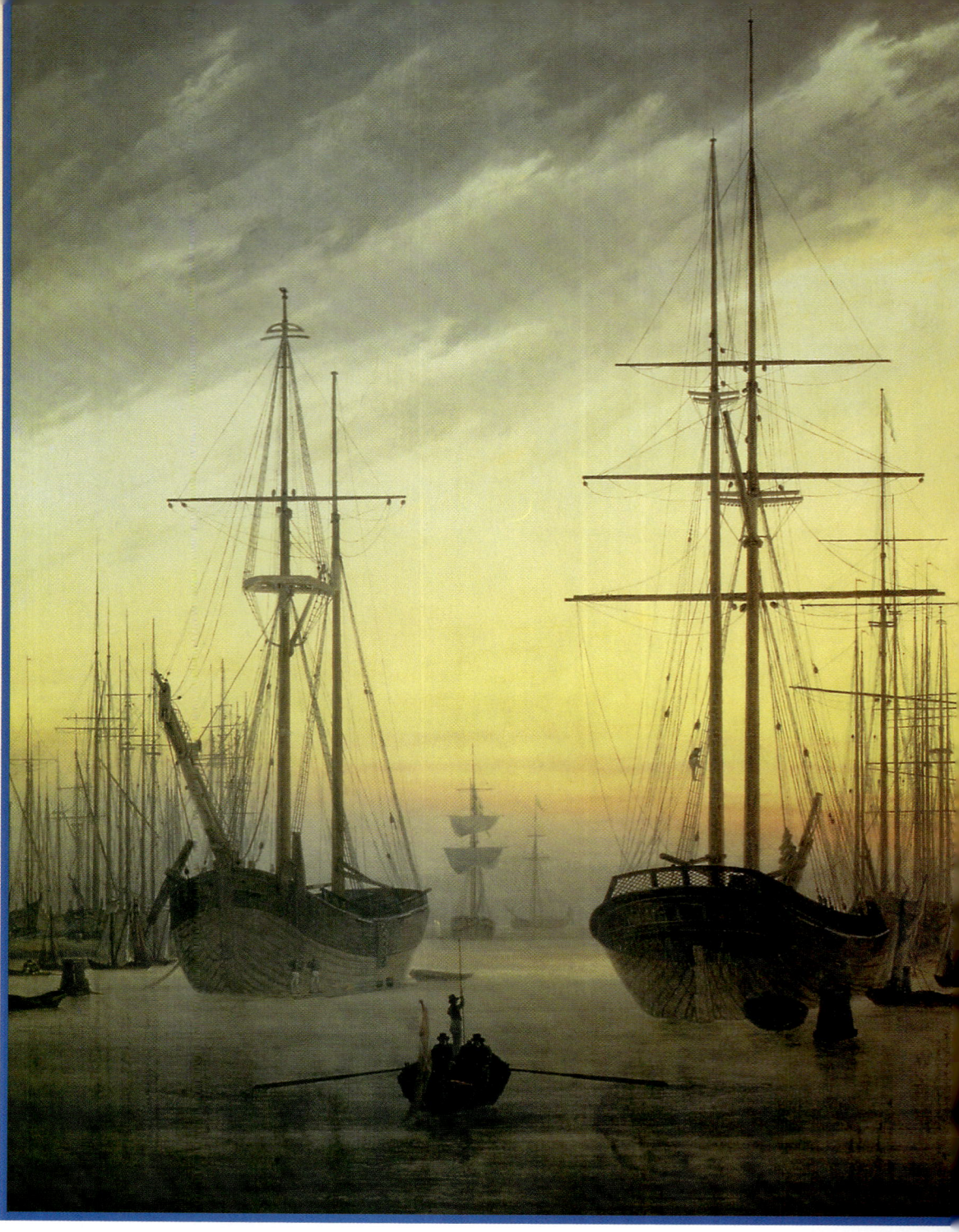

The Rime of the Ancient Mariner

Samuel Taylor Coleridge

Argument
How a Ship having passed the Line was driven by storms to the cold Country toward the South Pole; and how from thence she made her course to the tropical Latitude of the Great Pacific Ocean; and of the strange things that befell; and in what manner the Ancient Mariner came back to his own Country.

Part I

It is an ancient Mariner,
And he stoppeth one of three.
"By thy long gray beard and glittering eye,
Now wherefore stopp'st thou me?

5 The Bridegroom's doors are opened wide,
And I am next of kin;
The guests are met, the feast is set:
May'st hear the merry din."

He holds him with his skinny hand,
10 "There was a ship," quoth he.
"Hold off! unhand me, gray-beard loon!"
Eftsoons° his hand dropt he.

An ancient Mariner meeteth three Gallants bidden to a wedding feast, and detaineth one.

12. **eftsoons:** archaic for "at once."

(Opposite) *View of a Harbour* (1815–1816) by Caspar David Friedrich. Oil on canvas.
Schloss Sanssouci, Potsdam, Germany. The Bridgeman Art Library.

Direct Teaching

A Content-Area Connections

History: Mesmerizers
In the late 1700s, Franz Anton Mesmer developed a method of hypnotism that he claimed involved a magnetic force that redirected invisible fluids through the body. Many people believed that mesmerizers could "fix" and immobilize a victim with an "evil eye." Mesmerizers played on the Romantics' love of the Gothic and were popular attractions in theaters in both England and the United States.

VIEWING THE ART

Activity. Ask students to identify and discuss elements in the engraving that convey the character of the Mariner and his effect on the three guests. [Possible response: The Mariner's appearance—his disheveled clothing and wild-eyed expression—and his imperative gesture inspire fear in the three guests and suggest that the Mariner is mad and possibly dangerous.]

He holds him with his glittering eye—
The Wedding Guest stood still,
15 And listens like a three years' child:
The Mariner hath his will.

The Wedding Guest sat on a stone:
He cannot choose but hear;
And thus spake on that ancient man,
20 The bright-eyed Mariner.

The Wedding Guest is spellbound by the eye of the old seafaring man, and constrained to hear his tale.

"It is an ancient Mariner, And he stoppeth one of three."

Literary Criticism

Critic's Commentary: Wordsworth
These are William Wordsworth's reminiscences on his contribution to this ballad: "Much the greatest part of the story was Mr. Coleridge's invention, but certain parts I suggested; for example, some crime was to be committed which should bring upon the Old Navigator, as Coleridge afterwards delighted to call him, the spectral persecution, as a consequence of that crime and his own wanderings. . . . 'Suppose,' said I, 'you represent him as having killed one of these [albatrosses] on entering the South Sea, and that the tutelary spirits of these regions take upon them to avenge the crime.' . . . I also suggested the navigation of the ship by the dead men, but do not recollect that I had anything more to do with the scheme of the poem."

"The ship was cheered, the harbor cleared,
Merrily did we drop
Below the kirk,° below the hill,
Below the lighthouse top.

25 The Sun came up upon the left,
Out of the sea came he!
And he shone bright, and on the right
Went down into the sea.

Higher and higher every day,
30 Till over the mast at noon°—"
The Wedding Guest here beat his breast,
For he heard the loud bassoon.

The bride hath paced into the hall,
Red as a rose is she;
35 Nodding their heads before her goes
The merry minstrelsy.°

The Wedding Guest he beat his breast,
Yet he cannot choose but hear;
And thus spake on that ancient man,
40 The bright-eyed Mariner.

"And now the STORM-BLAST came, and he
Was tyrannous and strong:
He struck with his o'ertaking wings,
And chased us south along.

45 With sloping masts and dipping prow,
As who° pursued with yell and blow
Still° treads the shadow of his foe,
And forward bends his head,
The ship drove fast, loud roared the blast,
50 And southward aye° we fled.

And now there came both mist and snow,
And it grew wondrous cold:
And ice, mast-high, came floating by,
As green as emerald.

---

23. kirk *n.*: church.

The Mariner tells how the ship sailed southward with a good wind and fair weather, till it reached the Line.

30. over...noon: The ship has reached the equator, here called the Line.

The Wedding Guest heareth the bridal music; but the Mariner continueth his tale.

36. minstrelsy (min′strəl·sē) *n.*: group of musicians.

The ship driven by a storm toward the South Pole.

46. who *pron.*: one.
47. still *adv.*: archaic for "always."

50. aye *adv.*: archaic for "continually."

Vocabulary
tyrannous (tir′ə·nəs) *adj.*: harsh; oppressive.

DIRECT TEACHING

B Literary Focus
Imagery. What is the Mariner describing in ll. 22–24? What effect do these lines create? [Possible responses: He is describing the departure of the ship and the way it seems to drop from view because of the curvature of the earth's surface, which adds a sense of mystery or doom to the departure.]

C Reading Skills
Evaluating. What is the effect of interrupting the Mariner's account with a description of the bassoon and the revelry of the wedding? [Possible responses: The interruption creates suspense; the joy of the celebration contrasts with the somber tone of the Mariner's tale.]

D Literary Focus
Literary ballad. What is the effect of the repetition in ll. 20 and 40? [Possible response: It reminds us that this is a ballad, a song form in which repetition is often used.]

E Literary Focus
Personification. To what does Coleridge compare the ship as it is caught up in the stormy blast? [Possible response: He compares the ship to a person leaning forward as he flees a pursuing enemy.]

CONTENT-AREA CONNECTIONS

Psychology: The Sea
Why did Coleridge set this tale at sea? The sea is a source of mystery and has often served as a setting for tales of the supernatural. In addition, many writers of the Romantic period, including Coleridge and Herman Melville, believed that human beings have an elemental attraction to the sea. In the words of Rachel Carson, a historian of the sea, "All at last return to the sea, to Oceanus, the ocean river, like the ever-flowing stream of time, the beginning and the end."

Whole-class activity. Encourage students to comment on the theory that we are attracted to the sea because it represents a beginning and an end—a place of origin and a destination.

Direct Teaching

A Content-Area Connections
Literature: Coleridge's Sources
Coleridge apparently based many of his images of the ice and snow on descriptions in travel books about the Antarctic. Details of the ship's route may have come from the reports of sailors who traveled through the Strait of Magellan. See pp. 604–605 for more information.

B Content-Area Connections
Science: Ornithology
Albatrosses cannot perch ("And round and round it flew") because their webbed toes have no backward extension.

C Reading Skills
Speculating. Why are the sailors happy to see the albatross? [Possible response: After being at sea in an ice storm, they are happy to see a bird because birds are usually a sign that land is near.] Note the Christian references associated with the bird: The albatross "crosses" the ship; the sailors greet it as if it had a Christian soul; the bird flies over to the ship during evening prayers.

D Reading Skills
Speculating. Why do you think the Mariner shoots the albatross? [Possible responses: He is bored; he is showing off; he is annoyed or maddened by the bird's presence; "the fiends" cause him to do it.] Notice that the lack of a clear motive adds mystery to the poem.

E Learners Having Difficulty
Summarizing. How would you summarize the events in Part I? [An old Mariner stops a Wedding Guest and tells him how he and his shipmates sailed to the South Pole. The ship is followed by an albatross, which the Mariner shoots with his crossbow.]

---

55 And through the drifts° the snowy cliffs°
Did send a dismal sheen:
Nor shapes of men nor beasts we ken°—
The ice was all between.

The ice was here, the ice was there,
60 The ice was all around:
It cracked and growled, and roared and howled,
Like noises in a swound!°

At length did cross an Albatross,
Through the fog it came;
65 As if it had been a Christian soul,
We hailed it in God's name.

It ate the food it ne'er had eat,
And round and round it flew.
The ice did split with a thunder fit;
70 The helmsman steered us through!

And a good south wind sprung up behind;
The Albatross did follow,
And every day, for food or play,
Came to the mariner's hollo!

75 In mist or cloud, on mast or shroud,°
It perched for vespers° nine;
Whiles all the night, through fog-smoke white,
Glimmered the white Moonshine."

"God save thee, ancient Mariner!
80 From the fiends, that plague thee thus!—
Why look'st thou so?"—With my crossbow
I shot the ALBATROSS.

Part II

The Sun now rose upon the right:
Out of the sea came he,
85 Still hid in mist, and on the left
Went down into the sea.

The land of ice, and of fearful sounds where no living thing was to be seen.
55. **drifts** *n. pl.*: windblown snow and fog. **cliffs** *n. pl.*: icebergs.
57. **ken** *v.*: archaic for "saw."

62. **swound** *n.*: swoon.

Till a great seabird, called the Albatross, came through the snow fog, and was received with great joy and hospitality.

And lo! the Albatross proveth a bird of good omen, and followeth the ship as it returned northward through fog and floating ice.

75. **shroud** *n.*: support rope that stretches from the top of the mast to the side of the ship.
76. **vespers** *n. pl*: evenings; also, evening prayers.

The ancient Mariner inhospitably killeth the pious bird of good omen.

Vocabulary
dismal (diz'məl) *adj.*: gloomy.

584   Collection 5   The Romantic Period

CONTENT-AREA CONNECTIONS

Geography: Tracking a Voyage
Small-group or paired activity. As students read, ask them to think about the probable route of the Mariner's ship. Then, have students work in pairs or small groups to create a rough map showing the route and noting places where key events occurred. Tell students to support their speculations with textual references. For instance, the word "kirk,"  which is Scottish in origin, suggests that the voyage begins in Scotland.

And the good south wind still blew behind,
But no sweet bird did follow,
Nor any day for food or play
90 Came to the mariner's hello!

And I had done a hellish thing,
And it would work 'em woe:
For all averred,° I had killed the bird
That made the breeze to blow.
95 Ah wretch! said they, the bird to slay,
That made the breeze to blow!

Nor dim nor red, like God's own head,
The glorious Sun uprist:
Then all averred, I had killed the bird
100 That brought the fog and mist.
'Twas right, said they, such birds to slay,
That bring the fog and mist.

The fair breeze blew, the white foam flew,
The furrow° followed free;
105 We were the first that ever burst
Into that silent sea.

Down dropt the breeze, the sails dropt down,
'Twas sad as sad could be;
And we did speak only to break
110 The silence of the sea!

All in a hot and copper sky,
The bloody Sun, at noon,
Right up above the mast did stand,
No bigger than the Moon.

115 Day after day, day after day,
We stuck, nor breath nor motion;
As idle as a painted ship
Upon a painted ocean.

Water, water, everywhere,
120 And all the boards did shrink;
Water, water, everywhere,
Nor any drop to drink.

The very deep did rot: O Christ!
That ever this should be!
125 Yea, slimy things did crawl with legs
Upon the slimy sea.

His shipmates cry out against the ancient Mariner, for killing the bird of good luck.
93. averred (ə·vurd′) *v.:* asserted; claimed.

But when the fog cleared off, they jusified the same, and thus make themselves accomplices in the crime.

The fair breeze continues; the ship enters the Pacific Ocean, and sails northward, even till it reaches the Line.
104. furrow *n.:* ship's wake.

The ship hath been suddenly becalmed.

And the Albatross begins to be avenged.

Samuel Taylor Coleridge   585

DIRECT TEACHING

A Literary Focus

Allusion. These lines allude to Act I, Scene 3, of *Macbeth*. In this scene three witches pronounce a curse on a sailor, sending storms to batter his ship, then declare in unison:

> The weird sisters, hand in hand,
> Posters of the sea and land,
> Thus do go about, about.

What mood does this allusion build? [Possible response: It builds an ominous, foreboding mood.]

B Literary Focus

Literary ballad. What do this passage and its marginal gloss reveal about the cause of the sailors' plight? [Possible response: It reveals that something supernatural is pursuing and plaguing the ship.]

C English-Language Learners

Idiom. The word *albatross* is often used to refer to a heavy burden (a usage that stems from this poem). In reality, an albatross is too large to be hung around a person's neck.

D Learners Having Difficulty

Summarizing. How would you summarize the events in Part II? [Possible response: At first the crew condemn the Mariner for shooting the bird. Then the fog and mist lift; the crew now declare that he was right to shoot the albatross, which they blame for the bad weather. Suddenly, however, the ship is becalmed, and the sailors grow thirsty. They turn on the Mariner, blaming him for their situation, and hang the dead bird around his neck.]

About, about, in reel and rout°
The death-fires° danced at night;
The water, like a witch's oils,
130   Burnt green, and blue and white.

And some in dreams assured were
Of the Spirit that plagued us so;
Nine fathom deep he had followed us
From the land of mist and snow.

135   And every tongue, through utter drought,
Was withered at the root;
We could not speak, no more than if
We had been choked with soot.

Ah! welladay!° what evil looks
140   Had I from old and young!
Instead of the cross, the Albatross
About my neck was hung.

Part III

There passed a weary time. Each throat
Was parched, and glazed each eye.
145   A weary time! a weary time!
How glazed each weary eye,
When looking westward, I beheld
A something in the sky.

At first it seemed a little speck,
150   And then it seemed a mist;
It moved and moved, and took at last
A certain shape, I wist.°

A speck, a mist, a shape, I wist!
And still it neared and neared:
155   As if it dodged a water sprite,
It plunged and tacked and veered.°

With throats unslaked,° with black lips baked,
We could not laugh nor wail;
Through utter drought all dumb we stood!
160   I bit my arm, I sucked the blood,
And cried, A sail! a sail!

A Spirit had followed them; one of the invisible inhabitants of this planet, neither departed souls nor angels; concerning whom the learned Jew, Josephus, and the Platonic Constantinopolitan, Michael Psellus, may be consulted. They are very numerous, and there is no climate or element without one or more.

127. reel and rout: violent, whirling movement.
128. death-fires *n. pl.*: firelike, luminous glow that is said to be seen over dead bodies.

The shipmates, in their sore distress, would fain throw the whole guilt on the ancient Mariner: in sign whereof they hang the dead seabird round his neck.

139. welladay *interj.*: archaic for "alas," an exclamation of sorrow.

The ancient Mariner beholdeth a sign in the element afar off.

152. wist *v.*: archaic for "knew."

156. tacked and veered: turned toward and then away from the wind.

At its nearer approach, it seemeth him to be a ship; and at a dear ransom, he freeth his speech from the bonds of thirst.

157. unslaked *v.*: unrelieved of thirst.

CONTENT-AREA CONNECTIONS

Science: Explaining the Strange
Explain that many of the strange phenomena the Mariner recounts have scientific explanations. The "death-fires" in l. 128 may be Saint Elmo's fire, an electrical discharge that sometimes appears on ships' masts during storms; some sailors regard it as a good omen. The oily, iridescent appearance of the water is probably caused by plankton, microscopic plant and animal life that floats in massive drifts in ocean currents. Some plankton is bioluminescent and glows white and green in the dark. The slimy creatures mentioned in ll. 125–126 may be polychaetes, a type of worm that has appendages resembling legs and lives in the sea.

Individual activity. Have students research one of these phenomena in depth and present their findings to the class.

With throats unslaked, with black lips baked,
Agape° they heard me call:
Gramercy!° they for joy did grin,
And all at once their breath drew in,
As they were drinking all.

See! see! (I cried) she tacks no more!
Hither to work us weal;°
Without a breeze, without a tide,
She steadies with upright keel!

The western wave was all aflame.
The day was well nigh done!
Almost upon the western wave
Rested the broad bright Sun;
When that strange shape drove suddenly
Betwixt us and the Sun.

163. **agape** *adv.*: with mouths wide open in wonder or fear.
A flash of joy;
164. **gramercy** (grə·mur′sē) *interj.*: from Middle French *grand merci*, an exclamation of great thanks.
And horror follows. For can it be a ship that comes onward without wind or tide?
168. **work us weal:** do us good.

"Through utter drought all dumb we stood!"

DIRECT TEACHING

A Literary Focus

Literary ballad. What literary devices does Coleridge use to convey the joy the Mariner feels at approaching his home? [Possible response: The alliteration of the "s" sound and the assonance in "sweetly," "breeze," and "me" mimic the soft wind and create a sense of harmony and joy.]

B Advanced Learners

Enrichment. What earlier scene do these lines recall? (You may want to refer students to ll. 22–24.) [Possible response: They return to the scene of the ship's departure, referring to the same landmarks.] What is their purpose? [They bring the reader full circle, emphasizing the Mariner's joy at returning to the familiar.]

C Reading Skills

Reading archaic words. What archaic usage and spelling appear in this line? ["Mine" is archaic for *my*; "countree" is an archaic spelling of *country*.] At one time, *mine* was the form used before words beginning with vowels and *my* was the form used before words beginning with consonants.

VIEWING THE ART

As he beholds his native country, the Mariner is filled with hope; yet in Doré's interpretation, the scene is not altogether welcoming. **Activity.** How does Doré capture the ambiguity of the Mariner's homecoming here? [Possible responses: The scene is both calm and eerie; the sky is clear and the moon is bright, but the shadows are dark and ominous; there are no people in view.]

But soon there breathed a wind on me,
Nor sound nor motion made:
Its path was not upon the sea,
455　In ripple or in shade.

It raised my hair, it fanned my cheek
Like a meadow gale of spring—
It mingled strangely with my fears,
Yet it felt like a welcoming.

460　Swiftly, swiftly flew the ship,
Yet she sailed softly too:
Sweetly, sweetly blew the breeze—
On me alone it blew.

Oh! dream of joy! is this indeed
465　The lighthouse top I see?
Is this the hill? is this the kirk?
Is this mine own countree?

We drifted o'er the harbor bar,
And I with sobs did pray—
470　O let me be awake, my God!
Or let me sleep alway.

The harbor bay was clear as glass,
So smoothly it was strewn!°
And on the bay the moonlight lay,
475　And the shadow of the Moon.

The rock shone bright, the kirk no less,
That stands above the rock:
The moonlight steeped in silentness
The steady weathercock.°

480　And the bay was white with silent light,
Till rising from the same,
Full many shapes, that shadows were,
In crimson colors came.

A little distance from the prow
485　Those crimson shadows were:
I turned my eyes upon the deck—
Oh, Christ! what saw I there!

"And on the bay the moonlight lay,
And the shadow of the Moon."

And the ancient Mariner beholdeth his native country.

473. strewn *v.*: stretched out; calmed.

479. weathercock *n.*: rooster-shaped weather vane.

The angelic spirits leave the dead bodies,

And appear in their own forms of light.

596　Collection 5　The Romantic Period

CONTENT-AREA CONNECTIONS

Music and Literature: Wagner and Scott

The Rime of the Ancient Mariner recalls the legend of the Flying Dutchman, a story from the European maritime tradition. In this story a spectral ship is doomed to wander forever because of the captain's rash pledge to sail around the Cape of Good Hope in a storm. In his 1843 opera *The Flying Dutchman,* Richard Wagner offers the captain salvation: The curse is lifted when a woman agrees to be faithful to him.

Another version of the legend puts the ship in the North Sea. Sir Walter Scott uses this setting in his 1813 narrative poem *Rokeby*, in which a ship is banned from every harbor. **Individual activity.** Interested students could compare these works with Coleridge's *Rime.*

Each corse lay flat, lifeless and flat,
And, by the holy rood!°
490 A man all light, a seraph man,°
On every corse there stood.

This seraph band, each waved his hand:
It was a heavenly sight!
They stood as signals to the land,
495 Each one a lovely light;

This seraph band, each waved his hand,
No voice did they impart—
No voice; but oh! the silence sank
Like music on my heart.

500 But soon I heard the dash of oars,
I heard the Pilot's cheer;
My head was turned perforce away
And I saw a boat appear.

489. **rood** *n.:* crucifix.
490. **seraph man:** angel of the highest rank.

"Full many shapes, that shadows were,
In crimson colors came."

DIRECT TEACHING

D Learners Having Difficulty

❓ Identifying the main idea. What is happening now? [Possible response: The Mariner sees a seraph on the "corse," or body, of every sailor. Each seraph is waving a hand and shining like a beacon to the land.]

E Content-Area Connections

Theology: Angels
In Christian theology the nine orders of angels are the Seraphim, Cherubim, and Thrones, in the first circle; the Dominions, Virtues, and Powers, in the second circle; and the Principalities, Archangels, and Angels, in the third circle. The word *angel* comes from the Greek *angelos,* meaning "messenger." Some of the orders are named from references in the Bible (Ephesians 1:21 and Colossians 1:16).

F Literary Focus

❓ Literary ballad. What elements of a literary ballad can you identify in this stanza? [Possible response: This stanza contains internal rhymes and end rhymes, alliteration, assonance, and supernatural characters.]

VIEWING THE ART

This illustration shows the seraphs on the bay.

Activity. Ask students to point out distinctively Romantic elements in this illustration. [Possible responses: The angels are fantastic, mysterious beings emerging from a shadowy world; the moon and the nighttime setting are eerily evocative; there are no humans present in the illustration.]

CONTENT-AREA CONNECTIONS

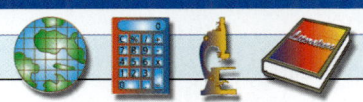

Music: Folk Ballads
Among the many supernatural legends of seafaring peoples are the tales of silkies (also spelled *selkies* and *selchies,* and sometimes called Finns or roane), enchanted creatures that take the form of seals at sea and of humans on land. Francis Child's famous collection of British ballads includes a dramatic tale about one of these creatures: "The Great Silkie of Sule Skerry." (A skerry is a small, rocky isle.) The ballad, which has several variants, originated in the Orkney or Shetland Islands, between Scotland and Norway.

Whole-class activity. After students read *The Rime of the Ancient Mariner,* have them listen to the folk ballad "The Great Silkie." Ask them to discuss the similarities and differences between the two works.

Samuel Taylor Coleridge **597**

Direct Teaching

A Reading Skills

Evaluating. Is the shift in focus to the Hermit effective? Why or why not? [Possible responses: Yes, the Hermit seems to represent all that the Mariner should be—pious, wholesome, joyful; no, the Hermit seems unrelated to the story, an intrusion or a distraction.] The presence of the Hermit, a stock figure in medieval literature, is one of many details that suggest the Mariner's tale is set in the Middle Ages.

B Learners Having Difficulty

Summarizing. How would you summarize the events in Part VI? [Possible response: A supernatural force drives the ship homeward. The Mariner awakens from his trance to find the eyes of the dead crew fixed on him. Finally he is able to tear his glance away, and he feels a gentle breeze blowing on him. As the ship comes into the harbor, an angel stands over every corpse and sends a beacon to the land. The beacons are answered by a boat rowed by a Pilot and the Pilot's boy.]

The Pilot and the Pilot's boy,
505 I heard them coming fast:
Dear Lord in Heaven! it was a joy
The dead men could not blast.

I saw a third—I heard his voice:
It is the Hermit good!
510 He singeth loud his godly hymns
That he makes in the wood.
He'll shrieve° my soul, he'll wash away
The Albatross's blood.

512. shrieve (shrēv) v.: archaic for "release from guilt after hearing confession."

 Part VII

This Hermit good lives in that wood
515 Which slopes down to the sea.
How loudly his sweet voice he rears!
He loves to talk with marineres
That come from a far countree.

The Hermit of the Wood,

He kneels at morn, and noon, and eve—
520 He hath a cushion plump:
It is the moss that wholly hides
The rotted old oak stump.

The skiff boat° neared: I heard them talk,
"Why, this is strange, I trow!°
525 Where are those lights so many and fair,
That signal made but now?"

523. skiff boat: rowboat.
524. trow v.: archaic for "believe."

"Strange, by my faith!" the Hermit said—
"And they answered not our cheer!
The planks looked warped! and see those sails,
530 How thin they are and sere!
I never saw aught° like to them,
Unless perchance it were

Approacheth the ship with wonder.

531. aught pron.: anything.

Brown skeletons of leaves that lag°
My forest brook along;
535 When the ivy tod° is heavy with snow,
And the owlet whoops to the wolf below,
That eats the she-wolf's young."

533. lag v.: drift; move more slowly than the current.
535. ivy tod: clump of ivy.

"Dear Lord! it hath a fiendish look—
(The Pilot made reply)
540 I am afeared"—"Push on, push on!"
Said the Hermit cheerily.

598 Collection 5 The Romantic Period

Literary Criticism

Critic's Commentary: Art and Life
According to the critic Martin Gardner, Coleridge was a compulsive talker. This description is supported by one of Coleridge's contemporaries, the essayist Charles Lamb. Lamb once imagined himself being button-holed by Coleridge and escaping by snipping off the button, then returning five hours later to find Coleridge, eyes closed, still holding the button and talking eloquently. Ask students how this portrait of Coleridge connects to the character of the ancient Mariner.

Students might also be interested to know that a group of Coleridge's poems are referred to as his "conversation" poems. These include "The Aeolian Harp," "Frost at Midnight," "To William Wordsworth," and "Dejection: An Ode."

The boat came closer to the ship,
But I nor spake nor stirred;
The boat came close beneath the ship,
545 And straight° a sound was heard.

Under the water it rumbled on,
Still louder and more dread:
It reached the ship, it split the bay;
The ship went down like lead.

550 Stunned by that loud and dreadful sound,
Which sky and ocean smote,°
Like one that hath been seven days drowned
My body lay afloat;
But swift as dreams, myself I found
555 Within the Pilot's boat.

545. straight *adv.*: straightaway; at once.

The ship suddenly sinketh.

The ancient Mariner is saved in the Pilot's boat.
551. smote *v.*: struck.

"It reached the ship, it split the bay;
The ship went down like lead."

DIRECT TEACHING

A Literary Focus

? **Literary ballad.** What elements of the popular ballad do you find here? [Possible responses: The whirling of the rowboat in the wake of the sinking ship creates a feeling of doom; the shrieking, praying, and insane laughter of those in the boat create a mood of high drama; the Pilot's boy assumes that the Mariner is the Devil, a stock character in folk ballads; the lines generate suspense and a sense of the unpredictable and the uncanny; the stanza includes end rhymes, inverted syntax, alliteration, and internal rhyme.]

"Upon the whirl, where sank the ship,
The boat spun round and round."

"'Ha! ha!' quoth he, 'full plain I see,
The Devil knows how to row.'"

Upon the whirl, where sank the ship,
The boat spun round and round;
And all was still, save that the hill
Was telling of the sound.

560   I moved my lips—the Pilot shrieked
And fell down in a fit;
The holy Hermit raised his eyes,
And prayed where he did sit.

I took the oars: the Pilot's boy,
565   Who now doth crazy go,
Laughed loud and long, and all the while
His eyes went to and fro.
"Ha! ha!" quoth he, "full plain I see,
The Devil knows how to row."

570   And now, all in my own countree,
I stood on the firm land!
The Hermit stepped forth from the boat,
And scarcely he could stand.

575 "O shrieve me, shrieve me, holy man!"
The Hermit crossed° his brow.
"Say quick," quoth he, "I bid thee say—
What manner of man art thou?"

Forthwith° this frame of mine was wrenched
With a woeful agony,
580 Which forced me to begin my tale;
And then it left me free.

Since then, at an uncertain hour,
That agony returns:
And till my ghastly tale is told,
585 This heart within me burns.

I pass, like night, from land to land;
I have strange power of speech;
That moment that his face I see,
I know the man that must hear me:
590 To him my tale I teach.

What loud uproar bursts from that door!
The wedding guests are there:
But in the garden bower the bride
And bridemaids singing are:
595 And hark the little vesper bell,
Which biddeth me to prayer!

O Wedding Guest! this soul hath been
Alone on a wide wide sea:
So lonely 'twas, that God himself
600 Scarce seemed there to be.

O sweeter than the marriage feast,
'Tis sweeter far to me,
To walk together to the kirk
With a goodly company!—

605 To walk together to the kirk,
And all together pray,
While each to his great Father bends,
Old men, and babes, and loving friends
And youths and maidens gay!

The ancient Mariner earnestly entreateth the Hermit to shrieve him; and the penance of life falls on him.

575. **crossed** *v.*: made the sign of the cross.
578. **forthwith** *adv.*: at once.

And ever and anon throughout his future life an agony constraineth him to travel from land to land;

Vocabulary
wrenched (rencht) *v.*: anguished; grief-stricken.

Samuel Taylor Coleridge   601

Direct Teaching

A Literary Focus

? Theme. What is the theme or moral message of the ballad? [Possible responses: Nature exacts its own revenge for crimes committed against it; it is essential to love all creatures.] These words are echoed in the first stanza of a Protestant hymn by C. F. Alexander composed in 1848:

> All things bright and beautiful
> All creatures great and small
> All things wise and wonderful
> The Lord God made them all.

B Reading Skills

? Expressing an opinion. How relevant is the poem's theme today? [Possible response: The theme of respect for all life is a lesson that humanity must continually relearn.]

Guided Practice

Monitoring students' progress. Guide the class in answering these questions.

Short Answer

1. Who narrates most of the story? [the Mariner]
2. To whom does the narrator tell his story? [the Wedding Guest]
3. What action taken by the Mariner seems to bring disaster on the crew? [He kills an albatross.]
4. Who "wins" the Mariner in the game of dice? [Life-in-Death]
5. What is the effect of the story on the person to whom it is told in the ballad? [At times the Wedding Guest is fearful, but he is mesmerized and ends up "a sadder and a wiser man."]

610

A
Farewell, farewell! but this I tell
To thee, thou Wedding Guest!
He prayeth well, who loveth well
Both man and bird and beast.

615
He prayeth best, who loveth best
All things both great and small;
For the dear God who loveth us,
He made and loveth all.

B
The Mariner, whose eye is bright,
620 Whose beard with age is hoar,
Is gone: and now the Wedding Guest
Turned from the bridegroom's door.

He went like one that hath been stunned,
And is of sense forlorn:°
A sadder and a wiser man,
625 He rose the morrow morn.

And to teach, by his own example, love and reverence to all things that God made and loveth.

623. forlorn v.: deprived.

"The Mariner, whose eye is bright, Whose beard with age is hoar, Is gone."

602   Collection 5   The Romantic Period

FAMILY/COMMUNITY ACTIVITY

Amazing travel tales. Have students ask members of their families or communities to relate the most interesting adventures they have had while traveling. Students might ask questions such as these:

- What is the most exotic place you've ever visited? What made it so unusual?
- Who is the most extraordinary person you've ever met while traveling? What made that person so special?
- What is the most amazing adventure you've ever had while traveling? How did it turn out?

Have students share these stories with the class. Then, ask them to compare and contrast the stories with the tale of the ancient Mariner.

PRIMARY SOURCE / LETTER

Joseph Cottle was a close friend of Coleridge and the first publisher of Lyrical Ballads.

Coleridge Describes His Addiction

TO JOSEPH COTTLE

April 26, 1814

You have poured oil in the raw and festering wound of an old friend's conscience, Cottle! but it is *oil of vitriol!* I but barely glanced at the middle of the first page of your letter, and have seen no more of it—not from resentment, God forbid! but from the state of my bodily and mental sufferings, that scarcely permitted human fortitude to let in a new visitor of affliction.

The object of my present reply is to state the case just as it is—first, that for ten years the anguish of my spirit has been indescribable, the sense of my danger staring, but the conscience of my GUILT worse, far worse than all! I have prayed with drops of agony on my brow, trembling not only before the justice of my Maker, but even before the mercy of my Redeemer. "I gave thee so many talents. What hast thou done with them?"

Secondly, overwhelmed as I am with the sense of my direful infirmity, I have never attempted to disguise or conceal the cause. On the contrary, not only to friends have I stated the whole case with tears, and the very bitterness of shame; but in two instances, I have warned young men, mere acquaintances, who had spoken of having taken laudanum, of the direful consequences, by an ample exposition of its tremendous effects on myself.

Thirdly, though before God I cannot lift up my eyelids, and only do not despair of his mercy, because to despair would be adding crime to crime, yet to my fellow men I may say, that I was seduced into the ACCURSED habit ignorantly. I had been almost bedridden for many months with swelling in the knees. In a medical journal I unhappily met with an account of a cure performed in a similar case, or what appeared to me so, by rubbing in of laudanum, at the same time taking a given dose internally. It acted like a charm, like a miracle! I recovered the use of my limbs, of my appetite, of my spirits, and this continued for near a fortnight. At length, the unusual stimulus subsided, the complaint returned—the supposed remedy was recurred to—but I cannot go through the dreary history. Suffice it to say, that effects were produced, which acted on me by terror and cowardice of PAIN and sudden death, not (so help me God!) by any temptation of pleasure, or expectation, or desire of exciting pleasurable sensations. On the very contrary, Mrs. Morgan and her sister will bear witness so far, as to say that the longer I abstained, the higher my spirits were, the keener my enjoyments—till the moment, the direful moment arrived, when my pulse began to fluctuate, my heart to palpitate, and such a dreadful falling abroad, as it were, of my whole frame, such intolerable restlessness and incipient bewilderment, that in the last of my several attempts to abandon the dire poison, I exclaimed in agony, what I now repeat in seriousness and solemnity, "I am too poor to hazard this!" Had I but a few hundred pounds, but £200, half to send to Mrs. Coleridge, and half to place myself in a private madhouse, where I could procure nothing but what a physician thought proper, and where a medical attendant could be constantly with me for two or three months (in less than that time, life or death would be determined) then there might be hope. Now there is none! O God! how willing would I place myself under Dr. Fox in his establishment; for my case is a species of madness, only that it is a derangement, an utter impotence of the volition, and not of the intellectual faculties. You bid me rouse myself: go, bid a man paralytic in both arms to rub them briskly together, and that will cure him. "Alas," he would reply, "that I cannot move my arms is my complaint and my misery."

Your affectionate, but most afflicted,

S. T. Coleridge

Connection

Summary ↔ *at grade level*

In this excerpt from a modern travel book, Bruce Chatwin tells of a harrowing 1593 voyage taken by John Davis that was similar in some respects to the one described in *The Rime of the Ancient Mariner*. An account of this voyage appeared in Richard Hakluyt's book, *The Principal Navigations, Voiages and Discoveries of the English Nation*, which some critics conjecture Coleridge was reading around the time he wrote his famous poem. Davis's ship, which was separated from the other ships in the fleet, sailed to Penguin Island. There the crew killed thousands of birds. The birds took their "revenge" through a "worme" that virtually destroyed the ship and killed almost everyone on board.

DIRECT TEACHING

A Reading Informational Text

Summarizing. How would you summarize the information provided so far? [Davis, the commander of the *Desire*, had begun a journey with Cavendish's fleet. He was separated from Cavendish near Port Desire; Cavendish then departed, believing that Davis had deserted him.]

B Content-Area Connections

Technology: Navigation
Only in recent centuries have navigational techniques been developed that allow ships to determine the position of known islands accurately. At one time, even if the crew of a sailing ship sighted land, they might be forced to wait weeks for favorable winds and then be unable to find suitable anchorage.

CONNECTION / TRAVEL BOOK

INFORMATIONAL TEXT

In this passage from his classic travel book, the writer Bruce Chatwin (1940–1989) tells a chilling story. Before this excerpt opens, Chatwin has said: "Albatrosses and penguins are the last birds I'd want to murder." He had been describing the penguin colony in Patagonia, on the south coast of Argentina. Now he flashes back to 1593.

from In Patagonia

Bruce Chatwin

On October 30, 1593, the ship *Desire*, of 120 tons, limping home to England, dropped anchor in the river at Port Desire, this being her fourth visit since Thomas Cavendish named the place in her, his flagship's, honor, seven years before.

The captain was now John Davis, a Devon man, the most skilled navigator of his generation. Behind him were three Arctic voyages in search of the Northwest Passage. Before him were two books of seamanship and six fatal cuts of a Japanese pirate's sword.

Davis had sailed on Cavendish's Second Voyage "intended for the South Sea." The fleet left Plymouth on August 26, 1591, the Captain-General in the galleon *Leicester;* the other ships were the *Roebuck*, the *Desire*, the *Dainty*, and the *Black Pinnace*. . . .

Cavendish was puffed up with early success, hating his officers and crew. On the coast of Brazil he stopped to sack the town of Santos. A gale scattered the ships off the Patagonian coast, but they met up, as arranged, at Port Desire.

The fleet entered the Magellan Strait with the southern winter already begun. A sailor's frostbitten nose fell off when he blew it. Beyond Cape Froward, they ran into northwesterly gales and sheltered in a tight cove with the wind howling over their mastheads. Reluctantly, Cavendish agreed to revictual in Brazil and return the following spring.

On the night of May 20, off Port Desire, the Captain-General changed tack without warning. At dawn, the *Desire* and the *Black Pinnace* were alone on the sea. Davis made for port, thinking his commander would join him as before, but Cavendish set course for Brazil and thence to St. Helena. One day he lay down in his cabin and died, perhaps of apoplexy, cursing Davis for desertion: "This villain that hath been the death of me."

Davis disliked the man but was no traitor. The worst of the winter over, he went south again to look for the Captain-General. Gales blew the two ships in among some undiscovered islands, now known as the Falklands.

This time, they passed the Strait and out into the Pacific. In a storm off Cape Pilar, the *Desire* lost the *Pinnace*, which went down with all hands. Davis was alone at the helm, praying for a speedy end, when the sun broke through the clouds. He took bearings, fixed his position, and so regained the calmer water of the Strait.

He sailed back to Port Desire, the crew scurvied and mutinous and lice lying in their flesh, "clusters of lice as big as peason, yea, and some as big as beans." He repaired the ship as best he could. The men lived off eggs, gulls, baby seals, scurvy grass, and the fish called *pejerrey*. On this diet they were restored to health.

Ten miles down the coast, there was an island, the original Penguin Island, where the sailors clubbed twenty thousand birds to death. They had no natural enemies and were

604 Collection 5 The Romantic Period

CONTENT-AREA CONNECTIONS

History: Navigation
The Strait of Magellan is a narrow waterway between the southernmost part of the South American mainland and the islands of Tierra del Fuego. Before the opening of the Panama Canal, this waterway was part of the shortest route between the Atlantic and the Pacific oceans. The strait was named for the Portuguese explorer Ferdinand Magellan, who led the first European expedition through the passage in his attempt to sail around the world in 1520.

unafraid of their murderers. John Davis ordered the penguins dried and salted and stowed fourteen thousand in the hold....

As they came up to the Equator, the penguins took their revenge. In them bred a "loathsome worme" about an inch long. The worms ate everything, iron only excepted—clothes, bedding, boots, hats, leather lashings, and live human flesh. The worms gnawed through the ship's side and threatened to sink her. The more worms the men killed, the more they multiplied.

Around the Tropic of Cancer, the crew came down with scurvy. Their ankles swelled and their chests, and their parts swelled so horribly that "they could neither stand nor lie nor go."

The Captain could scarcely speak for sorrow. Again he prayed for a speedy end. He asked the men to be patient; to give thanks to God and accept his chastisement. But the men were raging mad, and the ship howled with the groans and curses of the dying. Only Davis and a ship's boy were in health, of the seventy-six who left Plymouth. By the end there were five men who could move and work the ship.

And so, lost and wandering on the sea, with topsails and spritsails torn, the rotten hulk drifted, rather than sailed, into the harbor of Berehaven on Bantry Bay on June 11, 1593. The smell disgusted the people of that quiet fishing village....

"The Southern Voyage of John Davis" appeared in Hakluyt's edition of 1600. Two centuries passed and another Devon man, Samuel Taylor Coleridge, set down the 625 controversial lines of *The Ancient Mariner*, with its hammering repetitions and story of crime, wandering, and expiation.

John Davis and the Mariner have these in common: a voyage to the Black South, the murder of a bird or birds, the nemesis which follows, the drift through the tropics, the rotting ship, the curses of dying men. Lines 236–239 are particularly resonant of the Elizabethan voyage:

The many men, so beautiful!
And they all dead did lie:
And a thousand thousand slimy things
Lived on; and so did I.

In *The Road to Xanadu*, the American scholar John Livingston Lowes traced the Mariner's victim to a "disconsolate Black Albitross" shot by one Hatley, the mate of Captain George Shelvocke's privateer in the eighteenth century. Wordsworth had a copy of this voyage and showed it to Coleridge when the two men tried to write the poem together....

Lowes demonstrated how the voyages in Hakluyt and Purchas fueled Coleridge's imagination. "The mighty great roaring of ice" that John Davis witnessed on an earlier voyage off Greenland reappears in line 61: "It cracked and growled, and roared and howled." But he did not, apparently, consider the likelihood that Davis's voyage to the Strait gave Coleridge the backbone for his poem.

(Above) Engraving (1875) by Gustave Doré for Coleridge's *The Rime of the Ancient Mariner*.

DIRECT TEACHING

C Reading Skills

? Comparing and contrasting. How do the crew's action compare with the ancient Mariner's deed? [Possible response: The situations are different because the Mariner kills for no reason whereas these men kill the penguins to use as food.]

D Reading Skills

? Comparing and contrasting. How is the worm like—and unlike—the Polar Spirit in Coleridge's *Rime*? [Possible responses: The worm is a natural phenomenon; the Polar Spirit, though it causes suffering and death, embodies a supernatural force. Also, the worm has no intelligence or feeling; the Polar Spirit wills its actions.]

E Reading Skills

Recognizing word origins. Point out to students that *nemesis* refers to someone or something that pursues a person who has committed a crime to exact justice and impose punishment. In Greek mythology, Nemesis is a goddess who will stop at nothing to punish crimes. She personifies the ancient Greeks' anger at and desire to punish people who violated the community's laws and customs, especially those who brought misfortune on the community by offending the gods. Coleridge's Polar Spirit is a Romantic parallel to the Greek Nemesis.

Comparing and Contrasting Texts

Comparing setting, plot, characters, and theme. Did Coleridge use John Davis's voyage as the basis for his tale? What are the similarities between these accounts? What are the differences? Ask students to work in pairs comparing and contrasting the works. They might focus on these elements and add some of their own:

- setting
- kinds of suffering endured by the crew
- causes of death
- characteristics of the survivors
- the role of crime, punishment, and redemption

Then, ask students to work on their own to write a short persuasive essay on whether Coleridge used elements of Davis's tale in his poem.

Independent Practice

Response and Analysis

Reading Check

1. Students' time lines should include the following events: A storm drives the Mariner's ship toward the South Pole, where no living thing is seen; the crew are glad to see an albatross, which proves a good omen; the Mariner kills the bird; his shipmates criticize him and then praise him; the ship is becalmed; the albatross is avenged as a Spirit causes them distress; the crew hang the dead bird around the Mariner's neck; a skeleton ship, carrying Death and Life-in-Death, approaches the Mariner's ship; the Mariner's shipmates die; the Mariner is finally able to feel and express love for God's creatures, and the albatross drops from his neck; the bodies are "inspired," and the ship moves on with the help of angels; the Spirit continues to demand penance from the Mariner for his sin; the Mariner enters a trance, then awakens and begins his penance again; the curse is lifted, and the Mariner arrives back in his country.

2. The poem begins with an omniscient narrator, but from l. 41 on, the narrator is the ancient Mariner, speaking to the Wedding Guest.

3. The ship is becalmed; the Mariner and crew begin to suffer from heat and thirst.

4. A "wicked whisper" makes his heart "as dry as dust." When he turns his attention away from himself and blesses the water snakes, he is able to pray.

5. The Mariner says that he is destined to travel from land to land, telling his tale as penance for his sin.

Response and Analysis

Reading Check

1. Use a time line to summarize the **main events** of the Mariner's story. Here are the first and final events:

   The ancient Mariner stops the Wedding Guest and begins to tell his story.

   ↓

   The Wedding Guest leaves sadder and wiser.

2. Who is the **narrator** of the ballad? To whom is he telling his story?

3. In Part II, what consequences result from the Mariner's killing of the albatross?

4. In Part IV, why is the Mariner unable to pray? What happens to change this?

5. At the end of the ballad, how does the Mariner describe his current life?

Thinking Critically

6. Describe in detail the changing mental states of the Mariner in Part IV. Given the circumstances, are these changes believable?

7. Name three effects the Mariner's story has on the Wedding Guest. In your opinion, does each effect seem likely or unlikely? Explain.

8. What is the Mariner's "penance" (lines 408–409)? Does it seem fair to you that he should have to do any sort of penance? Why? (Refer to your Quickwrite notes for ideas.)

9. Explain in your own terms the Mariner's **moral** (lines 612–617). Does the story indicate that he ought to have added something to his moral conclusion? Explain.

10. This ballad is famous for its use of vivid **figurative language** and memorable sound devices. Find in the poem a striking example of each of the following: **simile, metaphor, personification, alliteration, assonance,** and **internal rhyme.**

11. For the most part, the form of the poem is the regular **ballad stanza.** Occasionally, however, Coleridge varies the **meter** of the lines and the length of the stanzas. Choose one irregular stanza, and explain how it differs from a regular one. What effects do these changes have on the poem?

12. What similarities and differences do you notice between Coleridge's tale of the ancient Mariner and the story described in the excerpt from Bruce Chatwin's *In Patagonia*? (See the **Connection** on page 604.)

13. Compare the Mariner's experiences to those of Coleridge as described in his letter to Joseph Cottle. (See the **Primary Source** on page 603.) What is the source of each man's guilt? What other states of mind or body do the two men share? What similar actions do they take?

14. Sometimes the archaic meaning of a word gives us a clue to the history of a word in current use. Look at the use of the word *jargoning* in line 362, for example. What does the word *jargon* mean today? What other examples of archaic words that are still in use today can you find? You might want to consult your reading notes.

15. There was a time in American history when almost every schoolchild could recite parts of *The Rime of the Ancient Mariner.* Find some stanzas that strike you as particularly quotable. What situations in contemporary life could you apply the lines to?

Extending and Evaluating

16. What do you think of Coleridge's sidenotes to the poem? Do you think reading them alters the meaning of the poem? Should they be consulted in a careful reading of the poem? Explain why or why not.

SKILLS FOCUS

Pages 606–607 cover
Literary Skills Analyze the characteristics of a literary ballad.
Reading Skills Analyze archaic words.
Writing Skills Write an essay analyzing a ballad.
Listening and Speaking Skills Give an oral presentation of a ballad.
Vocabulary Skills Understand word analogies.

Thinking Critically

6. Answers will vary. The Mariner begins by seeing himself as cursed and his surroundings as ugly. When he recognizes the beauty of the water snakes and blesses them, he begins to love, and the albatross falls from his neck. The changes are believable because his isolation helps him recognize his need for other living beings.

7. Answers will vary. When the Wedding Guest is accosted by the Mariner, he is irritated and frightened. Once the story is underway, the Wedding Guest is mesmerized. By the end of the tale, he is sadder and wiser. His responses—fear at being accosted by such a strange man, fascination at such a bizarre story, sadness and reflectiveness in reaction to the Mariner's fate and his message—seem plausible.

Literary Criticism

17. Coleridge once said that he would have preferred to write *The Rime of the Ancient Mariner* as a work of "pure imagination." He believed that it had "too much" of a moral, and that the moral was stated too openly. Do you agree or disagree with Coleridge about the message in his poem? Explain.

WRITING

Left Unsaid

Like many traditional ballads, this strange story of the ancient Mariner leaves some questions unanswered. For example, how could the Mariner tell that the Wedding Guest was a fit audience for his tale? Why did the Mariner shoot the albatross? How can the Mariner's punishment be regarded as fitting his crime? In a brief **essay, analyze** these or other questions that you think are unsatisfactorily resolved in the ballad. Suggest possible reasons for Coleridge's omission of the information.

Is It an Allegory?

An **allegory** is a narrative in which the characters, settings, and actions are symbolic: that is, they have both a literal and a figurative meaning. Could Coleridge's ballad have both a literal and an allegorical meaning? If so, what do the various elements in the ballad symbolize? What meaning would the tale have on an allegorical level? In a brief **essay, analyze** the ballad as an allegory. Be sure to consider the meaning of:
- the ancient Mariner
- the wedding
- the ship
- the albatross
- the sailors
- the moral lesson

LISTENING AND SPEAKING

The Mariner Live

Prepare for an **oral presentation** of this mysterious ballad. Before you start rehearsing, you will have to determine how many speakers you will need. The ballad is long and you might want to present a shortened form of the story. If so, be careful in deciding which scenes you will omit. You will have to keep key events so that the narrative makes sense to your audience. Decide how you will place your speakers on the stage. Will each speaker stand before a podium? Or will they sit on chairs or stools?

Vocabulary Development

Analogies

tyrannous   abated
dismal   wrenched
ghastly

On a separate sheet of paper, write the Vocabulary word from above that best completes each analogy.

1. JOYFUL : GLAD ::
   _____ : gloomy
2. LEARNED : SCHOLAR ::
   _____ : dictator
3. GATHERED : COLLECTED ::
   _____ : lessened
4. DEPRESSED : ECSTATIC ::
   _____ : unaffected
5. HOSTILE : UNFRIENDLY ::
   _____ : ghostly

Samuel Taylor Coleridge 607

---

tion of the storm; ll. 171–173—alliteration (repetition of "w"), which speeds up the rhythm and suggests the absent breeze; ll. 521–522—assonance (repetition of "o"), which enhances the lyrical quality of the stanza; l. 381—internal rhyme ("noon"/"tune"), which slows down the line to reflect the stopping of the ship.

11. Answers will vary. An example of an irregular stanza is ll. 248–252. The additional feet and rhythmic changes overturn the reader's expectations and draw attention to the events described.

12. Possible answers: In Coleridge's tale the bird is a single albatross, rather than thousands of penguins. The Mariner acts on the spur of the moment, without thinking; Davis's crew systematically killed thousands of animals. Coleridge's tale contains supernatural elements; Davis's ship and crew were ravaged by a real organism.

13. Answers will vary. Both Coleridge and the Mariner are wracked with physical pain and spiritual guilt. Coleridge is filled with shame and hovers on the verge of despair—but he refuses to sink into despair because he believes that that would be an even greater sin. Like the Mariner, he ultimately places his faith in God.

14. Jargon is language that is unintelligible or is specific to a professional group. Examples of archaic words still in use include *bower, vesper, self-same, aflame,* and *sere*.

15. Answers will vary but may include ll. 115–118 for the vivid simile, which expresses frustration at a lack of progress, and ll. 284–291, which convey the relief felt by someone letting go of a terrible burden and rediscovering happiness.

Extending and Evaluating

16. Answers will vary. The notes help summarize the plot. They
    (Continued)

---

8. Answers will vary. The Mariner's immediate penance is to suffer alone on the ship. His lifetime penance is to be an outcast, wandering and telling his story to relieve his agony. Some students may feel that the punishment imposed on the Mariner is excessive. On an allegorical level, however, the penance is fitting, as the albatross is a symbol of all living creatures.

9. Answers will vary. Possible answer: Loving all of God's creatures is the best form of prayer. To the Mariner this moral is sufficient, but students may suggest additional morals, such as "Think before you act."

10. Possible answers: ll. 33–34—simile likening the bride's beauty to that of a rose; ll. 185–194—metaphor describing Death and Life-in-Death; ll. 41–44—personifica-

do not alter the meaning but do add a critical voice, sometimes supplying helpful information. Students may feel that the notes are part of the poem and should be consulted, or they may feel that the poem should stand alone.

Literary Criticism

17. Some students may agree that the moral is unsuited to the tale or is too baldly stated; others may say that if the poem were a work of "pure imagination," it would be hard to understand and frustrating to read. Be sure that students support their answers.

Vocabulary Development

1. dismal
2. tyrannous
3. abated
4. wrenched
5. ghastly

Vocabulary Development

Practice

1. The clue "mournful tone" suggests the meaning of *lugubrious*.
2. A harbinger is a signal. The clue is the contrast between *sign of good fortune* and *harbinger of doom*.
3. To allay is to lessen. The context clue is the appositive *relieve*.
4. *Woeful* means "full of misery." The clue is the contrast with *joy*.
5. Terra firma is dry land. The clue is the contrast with *a long time at sea*.

Vocabulary Development

Using Context Clues
Sometimes you can determine the meaning of an unfamiliar word by looking for clues in the **context**—the surrounding words, phrases, and sentences. Below are some of the most useful types of context clues.

Restatement. A difficult word might be rephrased in more accessible language. Restatements may be signaled by specific words or phrases: *that is, or, in other words.* Look at punctuation—dashes and parentheses also serve as signals. Often a restatement will be an **appositive** set off by commas or an item in a series.

> Coleridge compares the sails on the ship to gossameres, or filmy cobwebs.

The word *gossameres* is defined in the sentence by the appositive *filmy cobwebs*.

Comparison. Compare an unfamiliar word with familiar words that surround it. Sometimes specific words and phrases may also signal a comparison context clue: *like, as, similar to.*

> And now the STORM-BLAST came, and he
> Was tyrannous and strong:
> He struck with his o'ertaking wings,
> And chased us south along.
> —from *The Rime of the Ancient Mariner*

Note all of the underlined words having to do with power. *Tyrannous* means "harsh; oppressive."

Contrast. An opposition might be set up. Certain key words and phrases signal a contrast context clue: *but, not, although, however, instead, on the other hand.*

> The sailors wanted desperately to quench their thirst; instead, they died with throats unslaked.

Unslaked, which is contrasted with "quenching thirst," means "unrelieved of thirst."

Vocabulary Skills
Use context clues.

Synonym. You might find a word nearby that has the same or nearly the same meaning as the unknown word.

> The sailors averred that the Mariner had sinned, asserting that killing the albatross would bring trouble.

Assert is a synonym for *aver*, "to claim."

Example. Sometimes the text provides an example. Certain words and phrases help you spot example context clues: *such as, including, especially, namely.*

> For his sin, the ancient Mariner does not perform common acts of penance such as prayer, fasting, and giving to the poor.

Prayer, fasting, and *giving to the poor* are all examples of types of *penance*—acts done in repentance for a sin or wrongdoing.

PRACTICE

Use context clues to help you determine the meaning of each boldface word.

1. **Lugubrious** tales such as *The Rime of the Ancient Mariner* appeal to readers despite their mournful tone.
2. The Ancient Mariner and his shipmates at first believed that the Albatross was a sign of good fortune, but the bird turned out to be a **harbinger** of doom.
3. The only way the Mariner could **allay**, or relieve, his agony was to tell his tale.
4. The joy of the wedding contrasts with the Mariner's **woeful** tale.
5. After a long time at sea, sailors returning home may find their legs shaky when they first walk on **terra firma**.

608 Collection 5 The Romantic Period

Assessment
- Holt Assessment: Literature, Reading, and Vocabulary

608 Collection 5 The Romantic Period

George Gordon, Lord Byron

(1788–1824)

Byron, Sixth Baron (detail) (late 18th to early 19th century) by Richard Westall.

Until one fateful day in 1794, George Gordon Byron seemed destined to grow up confined by the harsh Calvinism of Scotland. On that day, Byron's cousin was killed in battle and young George became first in line to be the sixth Baron Byron of Rochdale. Byron assumed the title when he was ten years old.

Byron's literary elevation came no less suddenly. In 1812, the midpoint of the Romantic period, Byron became a celebrity with the publication of the first two cantos of a poem called *Childe Harold's Pilgrimage,* based on his recent travels to Europe and Asia Minor. Byron "awoke one morning," as he later said, "and found myself famous."

Like his father (a sea captain, a psychopath, and a spender of women's fortunes), Byron was a larger-than-life figure. He seems to have had an obsessive determination to prove himself in every way. Extraordinarily handsome, he was born with a clubfoot, and in compensation he learned swimming, boxing, and horse riding. His lifestyle aggravated a glandular problem and a tendency toward obesity, so he would periodically go on brutal diets.

The shocking aspects of Byron's private life have become legendary as a result of his literary fame, not the reverse. But they are shocking, nevertheless—and sometimes rather sad. Scandal concerning his sexual affairs (including a relationship with his half sister Augusta), his scandalous separation from his wife, and his radical, pro-French political views made life in England uncomfortable. Byron left for the Continent in 1816, never to return.

Byron's literary career had begun modestly in 1807 with a small collection of short lyric pieces that was harshly reviewed by the *Edinburgh Review.* In response, Byron wrote the satire *English Bards and Scotch Reviewers* (1809), which reveals the vein of wit that helped cast Byron as a rebellious mocker of established conventions. His target in this satire is not only the *Edinburgh Review;* he also takes on such Romantic icons as Wordsworth and Coleridge.

When Byron left England in 1816, he was drawn into contact with Percy Shelley and his wife, Mary, in Switzerland. Because of the association with Shelley, Byron's writing life now began in earnest. It intensified when he moved to Italy. The Byron we glimpse in these years, despite the debauchery and the circuslike menagerie he kept about him in Venice, is a man who works very hard at his writing. His wildness and aristocratic ease obscure what was, in fact, a period of great literary productivity.

As a poet, Byron was not a Romantic in style. His masters, in fact, were the neoclassical writers whose wit and precision he admired. Yet throughout the nineteenth century, he was regarded as the incarnation of "Romantic." His premature death seemed to reinforce this image. Byron set sail for Greece in July 1823 to support the Greek nationalists in their struggle for independence from Turkey. In a marshy town in Greece called Missolonghi, he came down with fevers that took his life only a few months after his thirty-sixth birthday.

PRETEACHING

Summary ⇆ at grade level

> The speaker describes a beautiful woman he sees at a ball. She somehow combines the best aspects of both light and dark, and she projects sweetness, purity, innocence, and calm.

Selection Starter

Motivate. Ask students to imagine how they might compare a beautiful human being to something that would emphasize the person's beauty—an animal, a plant or flower, something on earth or in the heavens. Have students explain their choices.

VIEWING THE ART

> **Sir Frank Dicksee** (1853–1928) painted several works featuring literary characters. This painting depicts a character from Shakespeare's *The Tempest*.
>
> **Activity.** Ask students to talk about the features of the woman that they think make her beautiful, or not beautiful, as the case may be. [Students may cite her eyes, eyebrows, nose, mouth, hair, neck, and youth.] Dicksee probably used a model to paint this fictionalized character. Do you think the model was more beautiful than the painting or less beautiful? Why? [Possible responses: More—no painting can capture true human beauty; less—the artist idealized her features.]

Before You Read

She Walks in Beauty

Make the Connection

No matter how often we hear that beauty is only skin deep, we all know the undeniable allure of an extremely good-looking person. Beauty moves us. Often, we want to believe that outer appearances express inner qualities of goodness and beauty of character as well. Can a person's inward nature be accurately judged by his or her outward appearance?

Literary Focus

Simile

A **simile** is a figure of speech that makes an imaginative comparison between two seemingly unlike things by using a connective word such as *like, as, than,* or *resembles*. "He's as helpful as a doorknob on a bathtub" and "she plays flute better than the Pied Piper" are examples of similes. An **extended simile** continues the terms of the comparison as far as the writer wants to take it.

> A **simile** is a figure of speech that makes a comparison between two seemingly unlike things by using a connective word such as *like, as, than,* or *resembles*.
>
> For more on Simile, see the Handbook of Literary and Historical Terms.

Literary Skills Understand simile.

Background

"She Walks in Beauty," one of Byron's most famous poems, was supposedly inspired by Lady Wilmot Horton, a beautiful woman whom Byron saw at a ball, perhaps in the spring of 1814. Lady Horton was in mourning and, in the fashion of the times, was wearing a black dress decorated with glittering spangles.

Miranda (1878) by Sir Frank Dicksee.
The Maas Gallery, London.

610   Collection 5   The Romantic Period

DIFFERENTIATING INSTRUCTION

Learners Having Difficulty
Some students may have difficulty with Byron's metered verse. Have them work in groups of three. Each student should take a turn reading a stanza aloud to the group. The members can then discuss what the stanza means and work together to write a paraphrase or summary of it.

English-Language Learners
To prepare students for the poem's theme, arrange them in small mixed-ability groups to explore this question: "What makes someone or something beautiful?" Have students share their ideas and develop a list of beautifying characteristics that the group agrees on.

Advanced Learners
Remind students that Byron was inspired to write this poem by a woman, a quietly grieving widow, whom he saw once. Ask why Byron might have been inclined to idealize this unattainable woman.

She Walks in Beauty

George Gordon, Lord Byron

She walks in beauty, like the night
   Of cloudless climes° and starry skies;
And all that's best of dark and bright
   Meet in her aspect° and her eyes:
5 Thus mellowed to that tender light
   Which heaven to gaudy day denies.

One shade the more, one ray the less,
   Had half impaired the nameless grace
Which waves in every raven tress,
10   Or softly lightens o'er her face;
Where thoughts serenely sweet express
   How pure, how dear their dwelling place.

And on that cheek, and o'er that brow,
   So soft, so calm, yet eloquent,
15 The smiles that win, the tints that glow,
   But tell of days in goodness spent,
A mind at peace with all below,
   A heart whose love is innocent!

2. **climes** *n. pl.*: atmospheres; climates.
4. **aspect** *n.*: face; look.

Response and Analysis

Thinking Critically

1. What is the basic **simile** the speaker develops in the first stanza of the poem? What emotions does this simile evoke?
2. The words "dark and bright" in line 3 suggest a balance of opposites. How is this idea developed?
3. In line 6, what does the speaker imply about daytime when he calls it "gaudy"?
4. In stanzas 2 and 3, what conclusions does the speaker draw about the woman's character and personality?
5. What do you think the speaker means by "below" in line 17? Support your conclusion with evidence from the poem as a whole.

Extending and Evaluating

6. This poem has been criticized as sentimental and dependent on clichés. Which comparisons or conclusions might such critics have in mind? Do you agree? Why or why not?

WRITING

Only Skin Deep?

Imagine that the dark beauty described by Byron reads this poem and discovers that it was written about her. Write a letter from the woman to Byron, expressing what you think of the poem's portrayal of you. Are you flattered? embarrassed? outraged? Do you think the poem reveals the "real you"? In your response, quote specific lines from Byron's poem and respond to them. You may write your letter in the form of a poem.

Literary Skills
Analyze simile.

Writing Skills
Write a letter responding to a poem.

PRETEACHING

Summary 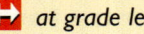 at grade level

The speaker expresses his love for nature, especially for the ocean. He notes that his poetic abilities are declining, but he hopes that his readers will remember something of what he wrote.

Selection Starter

Building background. The first two cantos of *Childe Harold's Pilgrimage* made Byron famous in his early twenties. He wrote Canto IV years later. No longer considered a prodigy, Byron was about thirty when the last part of the poem was published. Ask students as they read to think about the possible connection between the speaker's valediction and Byron's own sense of growing older.

Before You Read

from Childe Harold's Pilgrimage

Make the Connection

A quest may have a goal, but if the journey is long enough, the traveler may discover that the prize lies in the quest itself. What is explored, all alone on a journey, is the inner self. That may be true even when the pilgrim, like Byron's Childe Harold, cuts a spirited path through exotic lands. It is especially true when the pilgrim wanders, alone, in the vastness of glorious—but heartless—nature.

Literary Focus
Apostrophe

Apostrophe (ə·päs′trə·fē) is a figure of speech in which a speaker directly addresses an absent or dead person, an abstract quality, or something nonhuman as if it were present and capable of responding. Apostrophe was a popular device among the Romantic poets. Shelley, for example, apostrophizes the west wind (see page 622); Keats apostrophizes a nightingale and a Grecian urn (see pages 647, 652); and in this poem Byron apostrophizes the ocean.

> **Apostrophe** is a figure of speech in which a speaker directly addresses an absent or dead person, an abstract quality, or something nonhuman as if it were present and capable of responding.
>
> For more on Apostrophe, see the Handbook of Literary and Historical Terms.

Literary Skills
Understand apostrophe.

Reading Skills
Understand rhyme and rhythm.

Reading Skills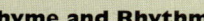
Reading Rhyme and Rhythm

In *Childe Harold's Pilgrimage,* Byron uses the **Spenserian stanza:** a tremendous undertaking of rhyme and rhythm invented by the Renaissance poet Edmund Spenser (c.1552–1599) for his epic poem *The Faerie Queene.* The Romantic poets Byron, Shelley, and Keats all employed this challenging verse form. It uses only three different end rhymes in each nine-line stanza for a rhyme scheme of *ababbcbcc.* The first eight lines of each stanza are written in **iambic pentameter,** and the ninth line adds a poetic foot to create an **alexandrine**—that is, a line of **iambic hexameter.** The alexandrine often sums up a stanza or finishes it off with a striking image. Punctuation serves as a guide for reading the poem aloud, with sentences often running over the end of a line. But each end rhyme should still be lightly emphasized to enhance the effect of the poem. As you read, watch also for the ways Byron uses the alexandrine to bring each stanza to a satisfying conclusion.

Background

In medieval times, *childe* likely meant a young noble awaiting knighthood; Byron uses it as a title, like Lord or Sir, for a youth of "gentle" birth. *Childe Harold's Pilgrimage* is a long, thinly disguised autobiographical poem about Byron's own journeys. Appearing from 1812 to 1818 in sections called cantos, it made Byron suddenly famous. The poem's pilgrim, Childe Harold, became the prototype for the moody, dashingly handsome character type who would eventually be dubbed the Byronic hero. In this excerpt from the final canto, the speaker addresses the ocean. The last two stanzas present Byron's personal conclusion to the whole poem. By this time, Byron said, he had ceased trying to separate himself from the figure of Childe Harold.

612   Collection 5   The Romantic Period

Wreckers off the Brittany Coast (1911) by Georges P. C. Maroniez.
Bonhams, London.

from Childe Harold's Pilgrimage, Canto IV

George Gordon, Lord Byron

1

There is a pleasure in the pathless woods,
There is a rapture on the lonely shore,
There is society, where none intrudes,
By the deep sea, and music in its roar:
5   I love not man the less, but Nature more,
From these our interviews, in which I steal°
From all I may be, or have been before,
To mingle with the Universe, and feel
What I can ne'er express, yet cannot all conceal.

6. **steal** *v.:* remove myself.

DIRECT TEACHING

A **Literary Focus**

❓ Apostrophe. What does the apostrophe add to the description? [Possible response: Urging the sea to "Roll on" depicts the sea's action. The repeated *roll* echoes the ocean's roar.]

B **Literary Focus**

❓ Word choice. What is the effect of the alliteration in this line? [Possible response: The repetition of *un–* stresses how insignificant humans seem when compared with nature.]

C **Reading Skills**

❓ Interpreting. What is the speaker's feeling for the ocean here? [Possible response: He seems nostalgic for when the ocean was his playmate and they had equal energy.]

D **Reading Skills**

❓ Making inferences. What is the "glow" that is "faint, and low"? [Possible response: the speaker's creative spark.]

E **Literary Focus**

❓ Apostrophe. What is the tone of the speaker's address to the reader? [Possible responses: dramatic; sorrowful.] Why might he make such an emphatic farewell? [Possible response: Byron may be telling the reader not to expect a Canto V.]

2

10 **A** Roll on, thou deep and dark blue Ocean—roll!
Ten thousand fleets sweep over thee in vain;
Man marks the earth with ruin—his control
Stops with the shore; upon the watery plain
The wrecks are all thy deed, nor doth remain
15 A shadow of man's ravage, save his own,
When, for a moment, like a drop of rain,
He sinks into thy depths with bubbling groan,
B Without a grave, unknelled,° uncoffined, and unknown.

3

And I have loved thee, Ocean! and my joy
20 Of youthful sports was on thy breast to be
Borne, like thy bubbles, onward: From a boy
I wantoned° with thy breakers—they to me
C Were a delight; and if the freshening° sea
Made them a terror—'twas a pleasing fear,
25 For I was as it were a child of thee,
And trusted to thy billows far and near,
And laid my hand upon thy mane—as I do here.

4

My task is done, my song hath ceased, my theme
Has died into an echo; it is fit
30 The spell should break of this protracted dream.
The torch shall be extinguished which hath lit
My midnight lamp—and what is writ, is writ;
Would it were worthier! but I am not now
That which I have been—and my visions flit
35 Less palpably° before me—and the glow
D Which in my spirit dwelt is fluttering, faint, and low.

5

Farewell! a word that must be, and hath been—
A sound which makes us linger;—yet—farewell!
Ye! who have traced the Pilgrim to the scene
40 Which is his last, if in your memories dwell
E A thought which once was his, if on ye swell
A single recollection, not in vain
He wore his sandal shoon and scallop shell;°
Farewell! with *him* alone may rest the pain,
45 If such there were—with *you,* the moral of his strain.°

---

18. unknelled (un·neld′) *v.*: without the traditional ringing of a church bell to announce his death.

22. wantoned *v.*: frolicked; played happily.
23. freshening *adj.*: becoming rough as the wind comes up.

35. palpably *adv.*: clearly.

43. sandal shoon . . . shell: *Shoon* is archaic for "shoes." Sandals and a scallop shell worn on a hat were traditional emblems of pilgrims. The scallop shell is a symbol of Saint James, whose shrine in Spain was a great attraction to pilgrims.
45. strain *n.*: passage of poetry or song.

---

614 Collection 5 The Romantic Period

CONTENT-AREA CONNECTIONS

Art: Creating Atmosphere
Have each student find a picture that reflects a powerful aspect of nature. Encourage students to browse in art books or to look at other works by the artists featured in this textbook. Students may share their findings in a discussion focusing on the vision of nature communicated by each artwork.

Geography: Coastal England
Individual activity. Have volunteers do research on one of the coastal areas of England. What is the landscape like, and is the water usually gentle or wild? How is the weather? Are there wide beaches where vacationers can enjoy themselves? Are there craggy cliffs that inspire awe and are also dangerous?

A CLOSER LOOK: SOCIAL INFLUENCES

INFORMATIONAL TEXT

An Irresistible Bad Boy: The Byronic Hero

"Mad, bad, and dangerous to know."
—Lady Caroline Lamb, speaking of Byron

"A man proud, moody, cynical, with defiance on his brow, and misery in his heart, a scorner of his kind, implacable in revenge, yet capable of deep and strong affection." This model of reckless, wounded manhood described by Thomas Babington Macaulay (1800–1859) became known as the Byronic hero. Both in his life and in his poetry, George Gordon, Lord Byron (1788–1824) gave his name to a type of hero who was devastatingly attractive yet fatally flawed.

Byron's personal charms and poetic talents offset a physical disability (a clubfoot), which embarrassed him terribly, and the complicated romantic entanglements that made him a social outcast. His heroes, whom he often invited his readers to identify with himself, were also passionate yet flawed individualists: intellectually searching, incapable of compromise, forever brooding over some mysterious past sin, painfully yet defiantly alone.

Byron, Sixth Baron (detail) (1835) by Thomas Phillips.
By Courtesy of the National Portrait Gallery, London.

Heroes for an unheroic age. The immense popularity of the Byronic hero and the Romantic-age celebration of his prototypes—Cain, Faust, Prometheus, and Napoleon—wasn't hard to understand. These were rash rebels, hailed or resurrected in reaction to a neoclassical world in which order and restraint ruled the day. Most of these daring figures, whose ambitions were doomed from the start, also embodied the deep pessimism of early nineteenth-century life.

Marlon Brando in Laslo Benedek's film *The Wild One* (1954).

James Dean in Nicholas Ray's film *Rebel Without a Cause* (1955).

The failure of the French Revolution had dampened idealism throughout Europe. And the labyrinthine restrictions of state, church, and society allowed no suitable outlets for the outsized energy of creative young men like Byron and his fictional heroes.

The American heirs. The model of a sensitive rebel continues to be an engaging one for popular heroes of recent time: In post–World War II America, for example, as society settled into a bland conformity, several searching, sensitive malcontents arrested the attention of moviegoers everywhere.

One version of the Byronic bad boy was played by Marlon Brando, who popularized motorcycles, leather jackets, and a sullen demeanor in the 1954 film *The Wild One.* The leader of a motorcycle gang, Brando is asked, "What are you rebelling against?" His response: "What have you got?" The actor James Dean personified youthful rebellion in both his brief film career and his tragically short life. In *Rebel Without a Cause* (1955), Dean's portrayal of Jim Stark, an alienated character searching for the meaning of manhood, made him a cult hero.

Like all Byronic heroes, these modern characters beckon their admirers to explore personal freedoms and to reject confining conventions. Because this freedom is achieved only by questioning accepted social behavior, these heroes are invariably lonely and misunderstood. And because this freedom often compels them to perform dangerous acts, the lives of these heroes can be much too short. Lord Byron died of a fever at age thirty-six, while fighting for Greek independence. James Dean died in an automobile accident at age twenty-four.

A CLOSER LOOK

This feature discusses George Gordon, Lord Byron's life and the concept of the Byronic hero and its influence on American culture.

DIRECT TEACHING

A Reading Skills

❓ **Recognizing archetypes.** What do all four figures have in common? [Possible response: They dared to go against convention by placing themselves above secular or religious authority.] How does each one of them fit the archetype of the Byronic hero? [In killing his brother, Cain is defiantly alone. Faust makes a bargain with the devil and is left remorseful after the death of a woman he has seduced. The gods punish Prometheus for stealing fire for humans. Napoleon was a power-hungry ruler who nonetheless instituted needed reforms.]

B Reading Informational Text

❓ **Analyzing patterns of organization.** The writer describes the Byronic hero and then compares him with two heroes of modern films. How does that two-part organization of the text about the Byronic hero help you to understand the concept? [Possible response: By comparing modern-day Byronic heroes with the prototypes, the text reinforces the definition of the Byronic hero and makes it more concrete.]

CONTENT-AREA CONNECTIONS

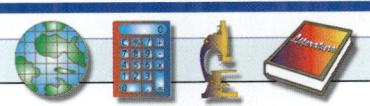

Culture: The Byronic Hero Today
Small-group activity. Have groups of students brainstorm to make lists of contemporary books and films with Byronic heroes. Have students share their lists with the class, then discuss one of these questions: How do the rebellious but sensitive heroes you discovered compare and contrast with Byron's heroes or their prototypes? If you found no Byronic figures, what do you think that reveals about our society today?

INDEPENDENT PRACTICE

Response and Analysis

Thinking Critically

1. Possible answers: The speaker finds a comfort in nature that he cannot find in society. The stanza agrees with the Romantic view that communing with nature is a healing experience.

2. Possible answer: Human beings destroy the earth. They can do little to the sea, but the sea can destroy them. A human being is like a "drop of rain" in the ocean—insignificant.

3. "And laid my hand upon thy mane." Possible answer: The comparison makes the speaker's and the sea's relationship more companionable, although the speaker acknowledges the sea's greater power.

4. Possible answer: its immensity.

5. Possible answer: It reveals the speaker's love of nature, especially for its power. He may also be drawn to danger.

6. *him*—the central character, Childe Harold; *you*—the reader. Possible answer: The references to *you* and *ye* in the final stanza are directed at readers who have been following the hero's adventures.

7. Possible answer: The two may be about to embark on the final journey—death.

8. Possible answers: self-knowledge; beauty; the meaning of life.

9. Students should identify the quality of the Spenserian stanza. The alexandrine puts a definitive end to the stanza, implying the power of the sea over humans.

10. Answers will vary. Students may choose to discuss how humans have affected nature adversely through overpopulation and pollution.

Response and Analysis

Thinking Critically

1. Restate the meaning of stanza 1 in a single sentence. How might the stanza serve as a general comment on the Romantic view of the relationship between human beings and nature?

2. In stanza 2, what does the speaker say man does to earth? What can man do to the sea—or the sea do to him? State the **simile** that expresses the relationship between man and sea.

3. In stanza 3, what **metaphor** compares the sea to a horse? What is the effect of this comparison?

4. What single aspect of the ocean does the speaker repeatedly emphasize?

5. In spite of the ocean's destructive aspects, the speaker professes that he loves it passionately. What does this tell you about his personality?

6. In lines 44 and 45, who are "*him*" and "*you*"? Explain your reasoning.

7. What link does the speaker imply between the pilgrim and himself in the final two stanzas?

8. From this brief excerpt, what would you guess the pilgrim was seeking?

9. Byron's verse form in *Childe Harold's Pilgrimage* is the challenging **Spenserian stanza**. How closely does stanza 2 adhere to the rhythms and rhyme scheme of that form? What purpose does the alexandrine of the final line fulfill? Refer to your reading notes for help.

10. Is Byron expressing a sensibility associated solely with the Romantic period, or do people today still identify with nature and experience moments of joy in its presence? Explain.

WRITING

Speaking to Nature

In stanzas 2 and 3 of this excerpt from *Childe Harold,* the speaker uses an **apostrophe** to address the sea. Write a prose apostrophe, or address, to some element of nature—sea, wind, fire, snow, thunderstorm, hail. Use stanzas 2 and 3 as a model for your address.

SKILLS FOCUS
Literary Skills Analyze apostrophe.
Reading Skills Analyze rhyme and rhythm.
Writing Skills Write a prose apostrophe.

The Junction of the Thames and the Medway (1807) by Joseph Mallord William Turner. Oil on canvas.

Widener Collection (1942. 9.87) Photograph © Board of Trustees, National Gallery of Art, Washington, D.C.

ASSESSING

Assessment
■ *Holt Assessment: Literature, Reading, and Vocabulary*

RETEACHING

For lessons reteaching author's tone and style, and poetic devices, see **Reteaching,** p. 1129A.

Percy Bysshe Shelley
(1792–1822)

Shelley Composing Prometheus Unbound (detail) (1845) by Joseph Severn.

When young Percy Shelley arrived at Oxford in 1810, his father introduced him to that bookish town's most important bookseller: "My son here," he said, "has a literary turn; he's already an author . . . do pray indulge him in his printing freaks." By spring, one of those "freaks"—an unsigned pamphlet on atheism—got Percy expelled and started a lifelong quarrel with his father. It was the first of many upheavals in the short, ill-fated life of an "author" who followed his "literary turn" wherever it led.

At nineteen, already estranged from his family, Shelley embarked on a career of courting the unconventional. To "rescue" her from a tyrannical father, he eloped with sixteen-year-old Harriet Westbrook, a classmate of his sisters'. Three years later he abandoned Harriet and ran away with seventeen-year-old Mary Godwin, the daughter of two of the most important radicals of the 1790s, Mary Wollstonecraft and William Godwin. Percy's alliance with Mary also involved responsibility for Mary's fifteen-year-old stepsister, Jane Clairmont (she soon changed her name to Claire), who accompanied the pair on their elopement to Switzerland. Claire's brief affair with Byron brought Shelley and Byron together in Switzerland in 1816 in one of the age's most important literary relationships.

Shortly after their return to England after a second trip to Switzerland, Mary's older half sister, Fanny, committed suicide. Then Harriet, only twenty-one, drowned herself in a pond in London's Hyde Park. Percy was now free to wed Mary, but was denied custody of his two children with Harriet.

Shelley and Mary fled their debts and notoriety in England and returned to the Continent. The next four years were Shelley's most productive, with one inspired work following another.

In 1822, when he was not yet even thirty, Shelley and a companion, Edward Williams, drowned when their sailing boat, the *Ariel*, sank in a storm off the northwestern coast of Italy. Almost two weeks later, Shelley's body washed ashore, a copy of Sophocles in one pocket and of Keats in the other. The body was burned in a pyre on the beach while friends (including Byron) stood by, and Shelley's ashes were buried in the Protestant cemetery in Rome.

It is said that the Italian sailors who encountered Shelley's boat in the storm on July 8, 1822, offered in vain to take Shelley and Williams on board. When this offer was refused, the sailors pleaded with the Englishmen to furl their sails. As Williams tried to do so, Shelley seized his arm and stopped him. We must certainly regret Shelley's untimely death, but at the same time, we can't help but wonder at his power to capture, and be captured by, the great dark forces that so fascinated him.

PRETEACHING

Summary ⇔ at grade level

Shelley's sonnet is a haunting reflection on the transience of earthly glory. The first speaker quotes a desert traveler who came upon the ruins of a monument to Ozymandias, a pharaoh of ancient Egypt. The traveler, in turn, quotes the ruler's boastful inscription on the monument's pedestal. Amid the ruins, the inscription becomes an ironic comment on the vanity of human ambition. All that now remains of Ozymandias is the broken statue, its inscription, and the scornful sneer that the sculptor captured on the statue's face. However, even this bit of art will be destroyed by the desert sand and wind, erasing the artist's own bid for immortality along with that of the pharaoh.

Selection Starter

Build background. Ask students what kind of monument a proud ruler would create to honor himself or herself. Write students' ideas on the chalkboard, and then review these suggestions after reading the poem.

Before You Read

Ozymandias

Make the Connection

Quickwrite

All human beings and all human beauty must perish, but can't our works survive us? We pass away, but isn't what we leave behind proof that our passage through life mattered? Like the poets of another restless age, the Renaissance, the Romantic poets posed these questions. How would you answer them? Jot down some thoughts about whether—and how—human beings can achieve immortality through their words and their works.

Literary Focus

Irony

Irony is a discrepancy between expectations and reality. This poem turns on a kind of irony called **situational irony,** which is created when the opposite of an expected event or outcome occurs. Even though "Ozymandias" is a short poem, several characters appear in its lines. Which of these characters expects one thing to happen, only to find that something else comes to pass? What might this ironic outcome have to do with Shelley's poem in particular, and with works of art in general?

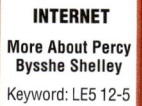

INTERNET
More About Percy Bysshe Shelley
Keyword: LE5 12-5

> **Irony** occurs when what actually happens is the opposite of what is expected or appropriate.
>
> *For more on Irony, see the Handbook of Literary and Historical Terms.*

Literary Skills
Understand irony and situational irony.

Background

Shelley wrote relatively few sonnets, and this one is certainly among his best. It is all the more interesting because it was written as part of a friendly and informal poetry competition in 1817. The poetic topic was Egypt, inspired by some extraordinary Egyptian fragments recently displayed at the British Museum in London. Some of these fragments were from the empire of Ramses II (ruled c. 1290–1224 B.C.) who left monuments all over Egypt, including the temples of Karnak and Luxor. Ozymandias is the Greek name for Ramses II. The Great Hall at Karnak is the greatest colonnaded hall ever constructed. It was so huge that one hundred men could stand on the capital of each column.

618 Collection 5 The Romantic Period

DIFFERENTIATING INSTRUCTION

Learners Having Difficulty
Invite learners having difficulty to read "Ozymandias" in interactive format in *The Holt Reader* and to use the sidenotes as aids to understanding the selection. The interactive version provides additional instruction, practice, and assessment of the literary skill taught in the Student Edition. Monitor students' responses to the selection, and correct any misconceptions that arise.

English-Language Learners
Some unconventional sentence structure may create problems for students. Explain that the clause "Which yet survive" refers to the passions of the pharaoh, as shown in the face of the statue. These passions have lasted longer than the mortal hands of the sculptor "that mocked" them and longer than the heart of the pharaoh that fueled them.

Special Education Students
For lessons designed for English-language learners and special education students, see *Holt Reading Solutions.*

Advanced Learners
Encourage students to report on Ramses' role in Egyptian and Hebrew history. (See Content-Area Connections on p. 619.)

Ozymandias

Percy Bysshe Shelley

I met a traveler from an antique land
Who said: Two vast and trunkless legs° of stone
Stand in the desert . . . Near them, on the sand,
Half sunk, a shattered visage° lies, whose frown,
5 And wrinkled lip, and sneer of cold command,
Tell that its sculptor well those passions read
Which yet survive, stamped on these lifeless things,
The hand that mocked them, and the heart° that fed;
And on the pedestal these words appear:
10 "My name is Ozymandias, king of kings,
Look on my works, ye Mighty, and despair!"
Nothing beside remains. Round the decay
Of that colossal wreck, boundless and bare
The lone and level sands stretch far away.

2. **trunkless legs:** that is, the legs without the rest of the body.
4. **visage** *n.:* face.

8. **hand . . . heart:** the hand of the sculptor who, with his art, derided the passions to which Ozymandias gave himself wholeheartedly.

Fragments of the Great Colossus of Memnonium, Thebes, from *Egypt and Nubia,* Vol. I (19th century) by David Roberts. Color lithograph.

Stapleton Collection, United Kingdom. The Bridgeman Art Library.

INDEPENDENT PRACTICE

Response and Analysis

Thinking Critically

1. Speakers include the original "I" who narrates the poem, the traveler who tells him about finding the statue, and Ozymandias himself telling his rivals to despair.

2. Possible answer: Ozymandias expected them to see his mighty works, but these works have almost disappeared. Now people see only this ruin and "despair" because it reminds them of glory's transience.

3. Possible answer: Pride is futile, and even art is destroyed by time. The message may be meant especially for Shelley's fellow artists.

4. Possible answer: The sculptor disliked the ruler. Shelley lets the sculptor editorialize by sculpting a "sneer of cold command."

5. Students may point to boastful dictators such as Saddam Hussein or to other discredited figures such as Ferdinand Marcos of the Philippines and Joseph Stalin of Soviet Russia.

ASSESSING

Assessment
- Holt Assessment: Literature, Reading, and Vocabulary

RETEACHING

For a lesson reteaching author's tone and style, see **Reteaching**, p. 1129A.

Response and Analysis

Thinking Critically

1. Even in the brief space of a sonnet, Shelley suggests a number of narrative frames. How many **speakers** do you hear in this poem? Summarize what each one says.

2. **Irony** is a discrepancy between expectations and reality. What did Ozymandias expect people to see when they looked at his "works"? What do they actually see?

3. Discuss your understanding of the poem's message about pride.

4. According to the poem, what was the sculptor's attitude toward the subject of his artwork?

5. What contemporary political figures who wield great power could this poem apply to? (Be sure to check your Quickwrite notes.)

WRITING

"So long lives this . . . ?"

In a brief **essay, compare and contrast** the message of "Ozymandias" with the message of Shakespeare's Sonnet 18 (see page 277). What does each sonnet say about the lasting power of art? Which sonnet do you agree with, and why?

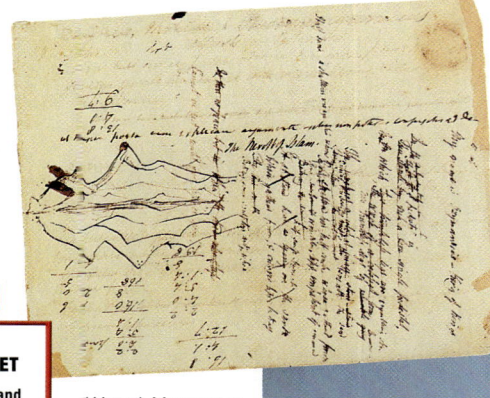

INTERNET
Projects and Activities
Keyword: LE5 12-5

SKILLS FOCUS

Literary Skills Analyze irony and situational irony.

Writing Skills Write an essay comparing and contrasting two poems.

(Above) Manuscript page from "Ozymandias" by Percy Bysshe Shelley.
MS. Shelley e. 4, fol. 85. The Bodleian Library, Oxford.

(Right) The Colossus of Ramses II, with his daughter Benta Anta in front of his legs, from the Great Temple of Amun (c. 1320–1200 B.C.).
Karnak, Egypt. The Bridgeman Art Library.

Before You Read

Ode to the West Wind

Make the Connection
Quickwrite
The faces of nature range from peaceful to terrifying, and the Romantics explored all of them. What attracted the Romantics to nature was the aspect philosophers call the sublime: the wildness, immensity, terror, and awesome grandeur of natural phenomena like the Alps or violent storms. To experience nature's power suddenly—whether by viewing Niagara Falls or by living through a hurricane—is, while terrible, also exhilarating, even transporting. Why do you think people find such displays of power so thrilling? What emotions are evoked? Jot down a few thoughts on this topic, or freewrite about a time when you experienced the sublime in nature.

Literary Focus
Ode
The **ode** was a favorite poetic form among the Romantics. A long, complex poem—usually a meditation on a serious topic—the ode provided the Romantics with a form suited to their introspective, philosophical subject matter. Like many Romantic odes, Shelley's "Ode to the West Wind" looks both outward and inward. It exalts an aspect of nature—the powerful yet invisible wind—and contemplates the movement of unseen forces in the poet's own mind and life.

> An **ode** is a complex, generally long lyric poem on a serious subject.
>
> *For more on the Ode, see the Handbook of Literary and Historical Terms.*

Windswept Landscape (c. 1870) by Camille Corot.
The Art Archive/Galleria d'Arte Moderna, Milan/Dagli Orti (A).

Background
This major lyric, written in late October 1819, was inspired by an oncoming storm near Florence, Italy, where Shelley was living. It marks, in his creative life, a temporary note of exaltation after a period of intense grief over the death of his three-year-old son, William. The ode demands to be read aloud.

INTERNET
More About Percy Bysshe Shelley
Keyword: LE5 12-5

Literary Skills
Understand the characteristics of an ode.

Percy Bysshe Shelley   621

PRETEACHING

Summary *at grade level*

Shelley's ode consists of five sonnets, each with a terza rima structure—three-line stanzas with the rhyme scheme *aba bcb cdc ded*—and a final couplet (*ee*). This ode is an extended apostrophe to the powerful west wind. After addressing the wind and describing its effects, the speaker characterizes the wind as both "Destroyer and preserver." He ends by asking the wind to share its power with him so that his words might spark new life in the world.

Selection Starter
Build background. In his famous essay *A Defense of Poetry*, Shelley describes how poetry is created by a divine imaginative spirit that works through humans: "Poetry is not like reasoning," he argues, "a power to be exerted according to the determination of will. A man cannot say, 'I will compose poetry.' . . . for the mind in creation is as a fading coal, which some invisible influence, like an inconstant wind, awakens to transitory brightness." As they read this poem, ask students to keep in mind Shelley's remarks about the "inconstant wind" that stirs the imagination.

Ode to the West Wind

Percy Bysshe Shelley

I

O wild West Wind, thou breath of Autumn's being,
Thou, from whose unseen presence the leaves dead
Are driven, like ghosts from an enchanter fleeing,

Yellow, and black, and pale, and hectic° red,
5 Pestilence-stricken multitudes: O thou,
Who chariotest to their dark wintry bed

The winged seeds, where they lie cold and low,
Each like a corpse within its grave, until
Thine azure° sister of the Spring shall blow

10 Her clarion° o'er the dreaming earth, and fill
(Driving sweet buds like flocks to feed in air)
With living hues and odors plain and hill:

Wild Spirit, which art moving everywhere;
Destroyer and preserver; hear, O, hear!

II

15 Thou on whose stream, 'mid the steep sky's commotion,
Loose clouds like earth's decaying leaves are shed,
Shook from the tangled boughs of Heaven and Ocean,

Angels of rain and lightning: there are spread
On the blue surface of thine aery° surge,
20 Like the bright hair uplifted from the head

Of some fierce Maenad,° even from the dim verge
Of the horizon to the zenith's height,
The locks of the approaching storm. Thou dirge°

Of the dying year, to which this closing night
25 Will be the dome of a vast sepulcher,
Vaulted with all thy congregated might

Of vapors, from whose solid atmosphere
Black rain, and fire, and hail will burst: O, hear!

III

Thou who didst waken from his summer dreams
30 The blue Mediterranean, where he lay,
Lulled by the coil of his crystalline streams,

---

4. **hectic** *adj.*: relating to the feverish flush caused by wasting diseases such as tuberculosis.

9. **azure** *adj.*: sky-blue.
10. **clarion** *n.*: type of trumpet.

19. **aery** *adj.*: archaic for "airy"; unsubstantial; seen only in the mind.
21. **Maenad** (mē'nad'): in Greek mythology, a woman who performs frenzied dances in the worship of Dionysus, the god of wine.
23. **dirge** *n.*: slow, solemn poem or song that expresses grief or mourning.

The Bard (1817) by John Martin.
Laing Art Gallery, Newcastle-upon-Tyne, England (Tyne and Wear Museums).

DIRECT TEACHING

VIEWING THE ART

John Martin (1789–1854) is remembered for his representations of sweeping landscapes and his ability to suggest dramatic narratives in a painting. *The Bard* illustrates the Romantic idea of the sublime—the fascination with strong emotions and awe-inspiring natural scenes. Martin's painting draws on an ode by Thomas Gray that tells the probably apocryphal story of how King Edward I put bards to death.

Activity. Why might a king want to destroy bards? [Possible response: He might feel threatened by bards who oppose his authority or who stir people to rebellion.] What does the painting suggest about the role of poets? [Possible response: Poets must oppose established order when it becomes tyranny.]

D Learners Having Difficulty

Breaking down difficult text. Tell students that the second stanza describes the wind's effect on clouds. Help students find Shelley's comparisons for the wind-swept cloud by looking for the word *like*. For instance, in ll. 16–17, the clouds are shaken from Heaven "*like . . . decaying leaves . . . shed*" from tree boughs. Line 20 also has *like*. Ask what effect these comparisons have. [Possible response: They convey impending doom or hysteria.]

E Literary Focus

Imagery. How does the poet describe the wind's effect on the sea? [Possible response: Stirring up huge waves, the wind disturbs the ocean as if waking someone from a dream.]

Advanced Learners

Have students discuss and write responses to one or more of these questions:
- How does the poem suggest the archetypal cycle of death and rebirth, both in the natural world and in the world of the poet?
- How might a poet periodically die and be reborn?
- What do you think Shelley meant by, "poets are the unacknowledged legislators of the world"?
- What value might a poet's creativity have for the rest of the world?

DIRECT TEACHING

A Literary Focus

Ode. What is the effect of the references in ll. 43–45 to the earlier parts of the poem? [Possible response: The references sum up the previous sections before moving on to something new.]

B Reading Skills

Expressing an opinion. Explain that Shelley's son had recently died. In l. 54, the speaker refers to the "thorns of life." This line is often quoted either to defend Shelley as the most sensitive of the Romantic poets or to mock his oversensitivity. Hold a discussion about each interpretation of this line.

C Literary Focus

Apostrophe. What requests does the speaker make in this section? [Possible response: He wants to be the wind's instrument—its lyre or trumpet.]

D Reading Skills

Contrasting. How has the speaker's view of himself changed in section V? [Possible response: He shifts from thinking of himself as a passive object of the wind to seeing himself as an instrument to convey a message to the world.]

Responses to Margin Questions

Lines 29–42. the sea
Lines 43–56. In l. 53 the speaker asks the wind to lift him, just as it has lifted leaves, waves, and clouds.
Lines 57–70. The speaker wishes to be turned into the wind's instrument, and he wants the wind to spread his thoughts throughout the universe. The last line could be interpreted as suggesting life ("Spring") after death ("Winter").

Beside a pumice° isle in Baiae's bay,°
And saw in sleep old palaces and towers
Quivering within the wave's intenser day,

35 All overgrown with azure moss and flowers
So sweet, the sense faints picturing them! Thou
For whose path the Atlantic's level powers

Cleave° themselves into chasms, while far below
The sea-blooms and the oozy woods which wear
40 The sapless foliage of the ocean, know

Thy voice, and suddenly grow gray with fear,
And tremble and despoil° themselves: O, hear!

IV

If I were a dead leaf thou mightest bear;
If I were a swift cloud to fly with thee;
45 A wave to pant beneath thy power, and share

The impulse of thy strength, only less free
Than thou, O uncontrollable! If even
I were as in my boyhood, and could be

The comrade of thy wanderings over Heaven,
50 As then, when to outstrip thy skiey° speed
Scarce seemed a vision; I would ne'er have striven

As thus with thee in prayer in my sore need.
Oh, lift me as a wave, a leaf, a cloud!

I fall upon the thorns of life! I bleed!

55 A heavy weight of hours has chained and bowed
One too like thee: tameless, and swift, and proud.

V

Make me thy lyre,° even as the forest is:
What if my leaves are falling like its own!
The tumult of thy mighty harmonies

60 Will take from both a deep, autumnal tone,
Sweet though in sadness. Be thou, Spirit fierce,
My spirit! Be thou me, impetuous° one!

Drive my dead thoughts over the universe
Like withered leaves to quicken a new birth!
65 And, by the incantation of this verse,

Scatter, as from an unextinguished hearth°
Ashes and sparks, my words among mankind!
Be through my lips to unawakened earth

The trumpet of a prophecy! O, Wind,
70 If Winter comes, can Spring be far behind?

---

32. pumice *n.*: light, porous volcanic stone. **isle in Baiae's bay:** in the Bay of Naples where pumice is found. These islands were once summer resorts for Roman nobility and, in Shelley's time, were notable for their ruins of ancient villas and monumental baths.

38. cleave *v.*: divide.

42. despoil *v.*: strip.

29–42. In sections I and II, the speaker describes the wind's powerful effect on the elements of earth and sky.
What third element is moved by the wind in this section?

50. skiey *adj.*: like the sky; also, coming from the sky.

43–56. *What direct request does the speaker make to the west wind? In which line is this request uttered?*

57. lyre *n.*: Aeolian (ē·ō′lē·ən) harp, a stringed instrument that emits sound when the wind blows across its strings.
62. impetuous *adj.*: forceful; rushing.
66. unextinguished hearth: from Shelley's "A Defense of Poetry": "The mind in creation is as a fading coal, which some invisible influence, like an inconstant wind, awakens to transitory brightness...."

57–70. *In your own words, describe what the speaker desires. How would you explain the meaning of the famous final line of the poem?*

Literary Criticism

Critic's Commentary: Mill
The philosopher John Stuart Mill (1806–1873) compared Shelley's imagery to Wordsworth's, finding that "Never did a fancy so teem with sensuous imagery as Shelley's. Wordsworth economizes an image and detains it until he had distilled all the poetry out of it, and it will not yield a drop more. Shelley lavishes his with a profusion which is unconscious because it is inexhaustible. The one, like a thrifty housewife, uses all his materials and wastes none; the other scatters them with a reckless prodigality of wealth of which perhaps there is no similar instance."

Activity. Ask students which kind of poetry they prefer—Wordsworth's or Shelley's—and why.

---

624 Collection 5 The Romantic Period

CRITICAL COMMENT

Shelley and the Ode

INFORMATIONAL TEXT

This ode is both an expression of Shelley's sense of purpose as a public poet, and a personal meditation on the role. In what a biographer calls a moment of both "triumph and defiance," Shelley copied a Greek phrase from the dramatist Euripides in his notebook after finishing the poem: "By virtuous power, I, a mortal, vanquish thee, a mighty god."

A genuine **ode** in its overall style and arrangement, the form of this poem is special. It consists of five sonnets in **terza rima**, with each section ending, as a **Shakespearean sonnet** does, with a couplet. Each group of three lines picks up the rhyme of the second line of the preceding three lines.

Shelley's admirers have been a little embarrassed by the exaggerated self-dramatization of "I fall upon the thorns of life! I bleed!" (line 54), but the poem is full of such heightened effects. They are consistent with the manner of the ode, with its large scale—the earth, the air, and the sea—with its imagery, and with the situation of the speaker, who is striving in "sore need" in prayer with a higher power.

"Ode to the West Wind" expresses Shelley's fascination with power and with those forces—both destroyers and preservers—that inspire the same powers within the poet.

Panorama of Florence (19th century) by J.M.W. Turner.
British Museum, London. © Scala/Art Resource, New York.

READING SKILLS REVIEW

Paraphrasing. Remind students that paraphrasing involves restating the ideas in a text in your own words. Paraphrasing is a good way for students to check their understanding of what they read.

Activity. Use annotation D on p. 623 to help students paraphrase section II of this poem. Then, form groups of three or four students and assign each group to work on a paraphrase of section III, IV, or V of the poem. Afterward, have each group read aloud their assigned section and then their paraphrase of it. Then, discuss how paraphrases can help readers understand a poem but cannot substitute for the experience of reading the original writing.

Critical Comment
This essay interprets the purpose of Shelley's "Ode to the West Wind" as being twofold—to define the poet's public responsibility and to communicate his own intense personal experience of being a poet.

DIRECT TEACHING

A Content-Area Connections
Literature: Euripides
Euripides (c. 480–406 B.C.) was the last of ancient Greece's great tragedians, after Aeschylus and Sophocles. He took no part in public affairs, preferring to sit in a cave and look out at the sea. His behavior earned him the reputation as an unsociable eccentric. His plays, of which nineteen survive, are famous for their psychological and moral insight.

B Literary Focus
Terza rima and the sonnet.
Make sure students understand the concept that each of the poem's sections is a complete, fourteen-line sonnet, with four three-line stanzas and one couplet. On the chalkboard, contrast this sonnet structure with the Shakespearean pattern of three quatrains ending with a couplet and with the Petrarchan pattern of an octave and a sestet. Discuss the different effects produced by different structures and rhyme schemes. Encourage students to notice that Shelley's terza rima structure, with its interlocking rhymes, has a powerful, driving momentum and is effective at creating echoing sounds and many vivid images, but may not be as conducive as the Shakespearean and Petrarchan patterns to reasoning out a complex train of thought.

INDEPENDENT PRACTICE

Response and Analysis

Thinking Critically

1. The images include blowing leaves and seeds, fleeting clouds, and the sea, which evoke exhilaration.
2. Possible answer: Instead of describing the wind's destructive and creative effects, the speaker asks for its power.
3. The wind scatters leaves (ll. 2–3) but also drops seeds (ll. 6–7).
4. Possible answer: He sees himself as "swift and proud" (l. 56) like the wind, and he longs to be as free as the wind is.
5. Possible answers: A smoldering hearth contains both dead ashes and fiery sparks. A poet's words are both dead (inert) and alive (inspiring). Shelley wants his inert words to inspire readers.
6. Possible answers: He asks the wind to let him be the voice of prophecy and expressive power.
7. Possible answer: Lines 53–56 express the speaker's pain, even as he hopes that his bowed spirit will rise again.

Literary Criticism

8. Possible answers: Agree—Shelley is attracted by the power of the wind, which fuels his poetry; disagree—Shelley actively sought a metaphor.

Literary Focus

Apostrophe

Possible answers: Shelley directly addresses the wind throughout the five stanzas. He asks to become the wind in l. 62.

Terza Rima and the Sonnet

1. Each section's rhyme scheme is *aba bcb cdc ded ee*; some rhymes are not exact.
2. The sections have no octaves, sestets, or quatrains, although their final couplets recall the Shakespearean sonnet. There are no distinct turns that answer questions or indicate a climax.

Response and Analysis

Thinking Critically

1. What is the central **image** in each of the first three sections? What emotions does this image evoke?
2. How are sections IV and V different in tone and emphasis from the first three?
3. How can the wind be both "destroyer and preserver" (line 14)? Cite lines to support your ideas.
4. Why do you think the speaker identifies with the wind so intensely?
5. How do you explain the **paradox**, or seeming contradiction, that words are like "ashes and sparks" (line 67)?
6. What do you think lines 68–70 mean? How would you paraphrase them?
7. What lines of this **ode** can you connect with the grief of a parent who has just seen a child die? What comfort does the parent find?

Literary Criticism

8. To some, this **ode** supports an argument that poetry is created only when the poet is inspired by an outside, greater force. Explain whether you agree or disagree with this idea of poetic inspiration.

WRITING

Why the West Wind?

Review your Quickwrite notes. Then, write a brief **essay** explaining why Shelley might shout to the wind, "Be thou me!" In the first part of the essay, explain why human beings are drawn to the sublime in nature. In the second part, **draw conclusions** about Shelley's own attraction to—and identification with—the west wind.

SKILLS FOCUS

Literary Skills Analyze the characteristics of an ode. Analyze apostrophe and terza rima rhyme scheme in sonnets.

Writing Skills Write an essay analyzing a poem.

Literary Focus

Apostrophe

An **apostrophe** is a figure of speech in which a writer directly addresses an absent or dead person, a personified inanimate object, or an abstract idea. Shelley's opening invocation, "O wild West Wind," is an apostrophe, and the device recurs repeatedly throughout the poem.

Perhaps the origins of the apostrophe lie in the repeated invocations of prayer, when the faithful call upon God to hear their prayers. Indeed, not only is the apostrophe a favorite Romantic device, but many Romantic poems are also titled or described as "hymns."

Analyzing apostrophe. The apostrophe also has an interesting connection with Romantic "empathy," or deep sympathy or identification with a person or object. In what lines of "Ode to the West Wind" does Shelley directly address the wind? Where does he ask to *become* what he apostrophizes?

Terza Rima and the Sonnet

In "Ode to the West Wind," Shelley adapts a rhyme scheme called **terza rima** to the sonnet form. Terza rima consists of sequences of three lines of interlocking rhyme.

Analyzing the ode's structure. Take Shelley's great ode apart to see how it works.

1. Identify Shelley's **rhyme scheme** in each fourteen-line section. Are the schemes all the same?
2. Each section is also a **sonnet**. Review sonnet forms (pages 275–277), and describe how Shelley has adapted them. Do Shelley's sonnets have **turns**?

Choral reading. Working in groups, prepare each section of the ode for choral reading. When you prepare your scripts, be sure to note passages that use **onomatopoeia** and **alliteration**.

ASSESSING

Assessment
- Holt Assessment: Literature, Reading, and Vocabulary

RETEACHING

For a lesson reteaching poetic devices, see **Reteaching,** p. 1129A.

Connecting to World Literature

The Golden Age of Chinese Poetry

You have just read many examples of Romantic poetry. In this Comparing to World Literature feature, you will read the following poems from China:

Tu Fu . . .	**Jade Flower Palace**	632
Tu Fu . . .	**Night Thoughts Afloat**	633
Li Po	**Quiet Night Thoughts**	637
Li Po	**Question and Answer Among the Mountains**	637
Li Po	**Letter to His Two Small Children**	638

Chinese civilization as a distinct and continuous culture has existed for more than three thousand years—longer than any other world culture. The art of writing developed in China between 2000 and 1000 B.C., and with it came the birth of a literary tradition that dwarfs all others. It has been estimated that more than half the books ever written have been written in Chinese.

Harmony and Balance

All Chinese literature, including poetry, is profoundly influenced by three schools of thought, dating to the sixth and fifth centuries B.C.: **Confucianism, Taoism,** and **Buddhism** (see pages 346–360). **Confucianism** emphasizes ethical values: honesty, loyalty, respect for elders, love of learning, and moral restraint. **Taoism** reveres nature as the great teacher and urges people to seek wisdom by contemplating the simplicity and power of natural forces. **Buddhism,** imported from India, stresses the importance of ridding oneself of earthly desires and of seeking ultimate peace and enlightenment through detachment. Many Chinese still incorporate elements of all three systems of thought in their spiritual lives.

Lyrical Imagery

Chinese poetry is almost exclusively lyrical and often focuses on contemplation of nature and the search for harmony between inner and outer forces or worlds. The very essence of Chinese poetry is its exploration of passing feelings and impressions and its appreciation of the interplay of opposites. Life is seen as a process of continual change in which opposing forces balance one another. Thus, Chinese poets muse about the changing seasons and phases of the moon, and they create vivid word pictures of scenes from nature, often recalled in moods of solitude, with imagery that tends to be spare and lean. This minimalist, or simplified, approach calls upon the reader to bring to the poem an appreciation of both evocative

A.D. 701–770
Li Po and Tu Fu live

c. 551–479 B.C.
Confucius teaches ethical principles known as Confucianism, recorded in his *Analects*

c. 500s B.C.
Teachings of Laotzu give rise to Taoism in China

c. 1500–1122 B.C.
Art of writing develops in China during the Shang dynasty

Pages 627–629 cover
Literary Skills
Understand Chinese poetry.
Compare and contrast Chinese poetry with Romantic poetry.

The Golden Age of Chinese Poetry **627**

Using the Time Line

Activity. Have students use reference sources to place the following events on the time line:
- Chou Dynasty [c. 1127–256 B.C.]
- construction of the Great Wall [c. 221–206 B.C.]
- invention of paper [c. A.D. 105]
- period of the Six Dynasties [A.D. 220–589]
- rule of Emperor T'ang Hsuan Tsung [A.D. 685–762]

Connecting to World Literature

SKILLS FOCUS, pp. 627–629

Grade-Level Skills

■ **Literary Skills**
Understand Chinese poetry.

■ **Literary Skills**
Compare Chinese poetry with Romantic poetry.

Elements of Literature: The Golden Age of Chinese Poetry

This essay discusses the philosophical traditions that are essential to Chinese poetry and introduces the two most prominent poets of the golden age of Chinese poetry, Tu Fu and Li Po.

DIRECT TEACHING

A Content-Area Connections

Philosophy: Confucianism and Education

During the reign of Emperor Wu Ti (140–87 B.C.) of the Han Dynasty, Confucians were given charge of the education that trained officials for government service. Here is a Confucian teaching: "Learning without thought is labor lost; thought without learning is perilous." Invite students to suggest contemporary examples of this teaching. [Possible responses: "learning without thought"—memorizing baseball statistics without understanding the game; "thought without learning"—coming up with an idea for a cleaning product without knowing that the chemicals explode when mixed together.]

SKILLS FOCUS, pp. 630–634

Grade-Level Skills

■ **Literary Skills**

Analyze the way mood achieves specific rhetorical or aesthetic purposes.

■ **Literary Skills**

Compare Chinese poetry with Romantic poetry.

More About the Writer

Background. A radical and innovative poet, Tu Fu tried to achieve the unexpected in his poetry by pairing unrelated images or by abruptly changing the focus from a distant view to a close-up. Admitting his passion for experimentation, Tu Fu wrote, "An odd weakness I have, for I dote on good verse, / I shall not die in peace until I have found what will startle the readers." Seeing Tu Fu grow haggard from his quest for artistic perfection, Li Po (p. 635) wrote, "How thin, wretchedly thin you have grown! / Have you been suffering from poetry again?" Translator Kenneth Rexroth remarked on Tu Fu's work by saying that it answers the question "What is the purpose of all art?"

Tu Fu
(712–770)

Tu Fu (dōō fōō) was born into a noble family of scholar-officials. As a youth he was confident of securing one of the imperial appointments that was the dream of every young aristocrat in the T'ang (tän) dynasty. So it was a bitter blow when, at the age of twenty-four, he failed the writing examinations in prose and poetry that were the means of gaining imperial positions.

Having failed the tests, Tu Fu spent most of his days wandering and moving in and out of minor government positions throughout the empire. Although he passed the imperial examinations much later in life, he did so without distinction. His failure kept him from realizing his youthful dream of becoming an advisor to the emperor.

Tu Fu's family connections and modest wealth nonetheless assured him a life of relative comfort until 755, when a violent rebellion ended the T'ang dynasty's days of glory. After that Tu Fu was often on the road, searching for a way to make a living. In 757, while Tu Fu was away seeking work, his young son died, possibly from starvation or plague. During the remaining years of his life, Tu Fu lived in hardship and poor health. He died in 770, on a houseboat on a river near Hangzhou.

The uncertain course of Tu Fu's life is reflected in his poetry, which is often marked by bitterness and melancholy. As a young man he wrote mainly about the beauty of nature and his own sorrows. As he grew older, however, Tu Fu's poems turned to more humanitarian themes. He became sensitive to people's sufferings and was the first Chinese poet to write at length about contemporary social concerns. After the bloody rebellion of 755, he wrote many poems condemning the folly of war—a common theme in Chinese poetry.

Although Tu Fu was neither well known nor especially well regarded as a poet during his own lifetime, he wrote in an elegant style that influenced Chinese poets for centuries after his death. His poetry is even more polished than that of Li Po (lē bō), the friend and fellow poet with whom he is often linked. To the Chinese, Li Po is the people's poet; Tu Fu is the poets' poet.

Portrait of Tu Fu from the Ch'ing dynasty. Rubbing from a Chinese carving, from *Travels of a Chinese Poet* by Florence Ayscough (1934).
General Research Division. New York Public Library, Astor, Lenox and Tilden Foundations.

630 Collection 5 The Romantic Period

RESOURCES: READING

Planning
■ *One-Stop Planner* CD-ROM with ExamView Test Generator

Differentiating Instruction
■ Holt Reading Solutions
■ The Holt Reader
■ Supporting Instruction in Spanish
■ Audio CD Library, Selections and Summaries in Spanish

Grammar and Language
■ Daily Language Activities

Assessment
■ Holt Assessment: Literature, Reading, and Vocabulary
■ *One-Stop Planner* CD-ROM with ExamView Test Generator
■ Holt Online Assessment

Internet
■ go.hrw.com (Keyword: LE5 12-5)
■ Elements of Literature Online

Media
■ Audio CD Library
■ Audio CD Library, Selections and Summaries in Spanish

Before You Read

Jade Flower Palace
Night Thoughts Afloat

Make the Connection
Have you ever wandered through an old, abandoned house—perhaps a ruin? Or have you ever found yourself totally apart from civilization, alone except for the whisperings of nature? If so, you may have noticed how, in the absence of human life, nature rushes in to fill the void. Animals move restlessly through shadows; weeds and trees reach upward toward the ancient, endless sky; the wind whispers like voices. The following poems by Tu Fu present a wistful view of two such encounters with places devoid of a human presence.

Literary Focus
Mood

Mood is the overall feeling or atmosphere in a work of literature. A poem's mood might be cheerful or gloomy, defiant or accepting. Writers usually establish a mood by using descriptive details and evocative language—words that call up particular images or feelings. In the traditional Chinese poetry of Tu Fu's time, a single mood usually characterized each poem. But Tu Fu broke new ground by including shifting moods within a single poem.

> **Mood** is the overall emotion created by a work of literature.
>
> For more on Mood, see the Handbook of Literary and Historical Terms.

Background
Perhaps the most respected of all the ancient Chinese poets, Tu Fu focused on the affairs of the world and the sufferings of his people. In stating his goal as a poet, Tu Fu once said, "If my words aren't startling, death itself has no rest."

Like many Chinese poets of his time, Tu Fu wrote in a variety of forms, but he was unequaled in his mastery of the difficult eight-line classical verse form called the *lü-shih* (lyoo′shə), meaning "regulated verse." This demanding form, somewhat like the Western *sonnet* (see page 275), was considered a showcase for a Chinese poet's classical technique.

The poems included here represent the poet's realistic and sometimes ironic outlook on life. As you read these poems, notice the vivid images and the concrete details that are hallmarks of Tu Fu's poetry.

Landscape (detail) (7th century) by Li Sixun. Ink and color on silk.
British Museum, London, UK/The Bridgeman Art Library.

Literary Skills
Understand mood.

The Golden Age of Chinese Poetry 631

PRETEACHING

Summary at grade level

In "Jade Flower Palace" the speaker describes the scene around the ruins of an old palace. The building is alive with memories and hints of past glory. The speaker wants to write a poem but is overcome by sad thoughts of the transience of all things.

In "Night Thoughts Afloat" the poet begins by painting a scene of the view from a boat on quiet water. However, he ends by mocking his own lack of achievement and low status, comparing himself to a gull hovering between sky and earth.

Selection Starter

Motivate. Ask students to think about the difference between a building that is not yet occupied and a building that was once lived in but is now empty. Why might some people find the old building particularly melancholy? Ask students for examples of such places in the community.

Build background. In conjunction with "Night Thoughts Afloat," remind students that Tu Fu spent the end of his life on a houseboat. Why might such a setting create conflicting emotions— a sense of peace and an awareness of failure?

DIFFERENTIATING INSTRUCTION

Learners Having Difficulty
Have students summarize what seems to have happened in the Jade Flower Palace. Encourage them to visualize the pictures of the ruins that Tu Fu paints.

Invite learners having difficulty to read "Jade Flower Palace" and "Night Thoughts Afloat" in interactive format in *The Holt Reader* and to use the sidenotes as aids to understanding the selections.

English-Language Learners
To help students empathize with the speaker's moods, show photographs of ruins of formerly beautiful places and nighttime river scenes. Ask students to discuss the feelings these pictures evoke. Make sure they understand that *it* in l. 18 of "Jade Flower Palace" refers to the palace ruins.

Special Education Students
For lessons designed for English-language learners and special education students, see *Holt Reading Solutions*.

Advanced Learners
Invite students to evaluate the imagery in Tu Fu's poems as they read. Challenge students to come up with other images that Tu Fu might have used.

The Golden Age of Chinese Poetry 631

A Keepsake from the Cloud Gallery (1750).
ADD Ms. 22689. By permission of the British Library, London.

Jade Flower Palace

Tu Fu
translated by **Kenneth Rexroth**

The stream swirls. The wind moans in
The pines. Gray rats scurry over
Broken tiles. What prince, long ago,
Built this palace, standing in
5 Ruins beside the cliffs? There are
Green ghost fires in the black rooms.
The shattered pavements are all
Washed away. Ten thousand organ
Pipes whistle and roar. The storm
10 Scatters the red autumn leaves.
His dancing girls are yellow dust.
Their painted cheeks have crumbled
Away. His gold chariots
And courtiers are gone. Only
15 A stone horse is left of his
Glory. I sit on the grass and
Start a poem, but the pathos of
It overcomes me. The future
Slips imperceptibly away.
20 Who can say what the years will bring?

632   Collection 5   The Romantic Period

Night Thoughts Afloat

Tu Fu
translated by **Arthur Cooper**

    By bent grasses
in a gentle wind
      Under straight mast
I'm alone tonight,

5   And the stars hang
above the broad plain
      But moon's afloat
in this Great River:

    Oh, where's my name
10 among the poets?
      Official rank?
"Retired for ill health."

    Drifting, drifting,
what am I more than
15   A single gull
between sky and earth?

Chinese landscape painting.
Private Collection/Art Resource, New York.

INDEPENDENT PRACTICE

Response and Analysis

Thinking Critically

1. Possible answer: The present reveals a crumbled past. The present and future share a similar fate.

2. Possible answers: *swirls* (l. 1) creates a feeling of excitement; *moans* (l. 1) creates a mournful tone; *crumbled* (l. 12) creates a sense of futility.

3. Possible answer: a gull hanging between sky and earth; the comparison suggests that he is not going anywhere, that he is caught between two larger forces.

4. Possible answer: The first two stanzas create a serene mood; the last two, a mood of frustration and bitterness.

Extending and Evaluating

5. Possible answer: In "Jade Flower Palace," ll. 1–17 create a gentle, melancholy mood. When the poet says he is overcome by pathos, the mood changes from melancholy to a paralyzing depression. The first part of "Night Thoughts Afloat" paints a tranquil, if lonely, scene. However, in l. 9, the poet breaks into a bitter lament. The shifts are startling. The poets destroy the beauty created in the first part of each poem, but they also add a human intensity, possibly making the poems more realistic.

Comparing Literature

6. Possible answer: Both poems focus on the ruins of a structure created by a powerful man. Tu Fu's poem is personal; the mood of Shelley's poem is ironic, with a somewhat detached tone. His speakers don't say how the ruins affect them, whereas Tu Fu's speaker is depressed.

Response and Analysis

Jade Flower Palace
Night Thoughts Afloat

Thinking Critically

1. In "Jade Flower Palace," Tu Fu contemplates the past, the present, and the future. **Summarize** his thoughts about each one.

2. Tu Fu uses vivid verbs to describe the scene before him in "Jade Flower Palace." Choose three of these verbs, and explain how each contributes to the **mood** of the poem.

3. To what does Tu Fu compare himself in "Night Thoughts Afloat"? What emotions do you think the poet is trying to express with this comparison?

4. The first two stanzas of "Night Thoughts Afloat" describe a scene, and the last two stanzas express the poet's feelings. What is the **mood** of the first two stanzas? of the last two?

Extending and Evaluating

5. In Tu Fu's time, a poem was expected to represent only one **mood, tone,** and **setting.** Tu Fu broke with tradition and often shifted moods, tones, and images within a poem. Find at least one shift in each of the two poems you have just read. How do these shifts affect your reading of each poem? Do you think the poems would be more effective if they focused on only one mood? Explain.

Comparing Literature

6. Tu Fu's poem "Jade Flower Palace" is similar in **theme** to Shelley's "Ozymandias" (see page 619). What theme do they share? In what other ways are the poems alike or different? You may want to consider the **mood, setting,** and **imagery** of each poem.

Literary Skills
Analyze mood. Compare and contrast Chinese poetry with Romantic poetry.

Writing Skills
Write a journal entry.

WRITING
Journal Entry

What concerns seem to preoccupy Tu Fu in the two poems you have read? Choose one of these poems, and **paraphrase** it in the form of a **journal entry.** Include details from the poem as well as the speaker's thoughts and emotions.

Japanese silkscreen with flowers (detail) (late 19th century).
© Christie's Images/CORBIS.

---

634   Collection 5   The Romantic Period

ASSESSING

Assessment
- Holt Assessment: *Literature, Reading, and Vocabulary*

RETEACHING

For a lesson reteaching author's tone and style, see **Reteaching,** p. 1129A.

Li Po
(701–762)

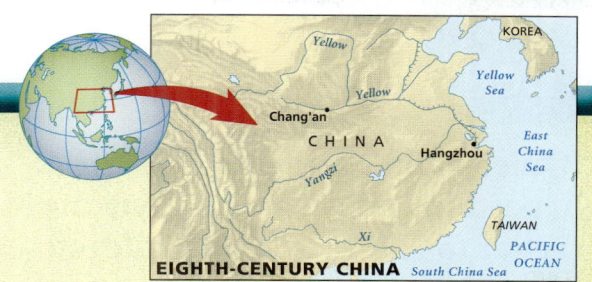

EIGHTH-CENTURY CHINA

Like Tu Fu, the Chinese poet Li Po (lē bō) lived during the T'ang (tän) dynasty (618–907), an age of great prosperity and cultural achievement. These two poets of contrasting dispositions and styles embody the highest poetic achievements of the T'ang dynasty. Tu Fu, a melancholy wanderer, wrote innovative poetry known for its elegance, realism, and social consciousness. Li Po, a free-spirited vagabond, wrote traditional lyric poetry characterized by its sense of playfulness, fantasy, and grace.

Although Li Po was probably born in central Asia, he grew up in the province of Sichuan (sē′chwän) in southwestern China. He was a well-educated youth from a good family who chose to forgo the test for imperial service taken by many young men of the upper classes. Instead, the young Li Po lived as a hermit and served as a wandering knight, a sword-wielding avenger of wrongs against women and children. At the age of twenty-five, he became a vagabond who wandered for most of his days.

As he traveled throughout China, Li Po wrote poetry and made many friends of government officials, fellow poets, and even hermits. He also married and lived with his wife's family for a short time before resuming life as a wanderer.

Li Po's travels in China served to spread his fame as a poet. Even the emperor admired him. In fact, Li Po abandoned his nomadic life for a time to serve the emperor as an imperial court poet. There Li Po delighted in a life of unaccustomed luxuries.

Sometime afterward Li Po entered into the service of a rebel prince. When the prince's bid for power failed, however, Li Po was imprisoned and then banished, a sentence that was revoked just as he was on his way into exile. Three years later the poet died suddenly. An appropriately romantic Chinese legend tells that he drowned one night as he leaned from his boat to embrace the watery reflection of the moon.

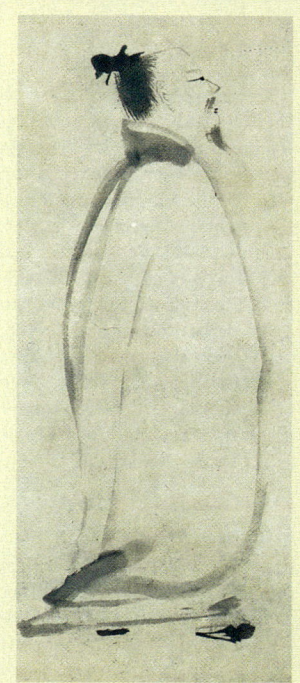

Li Po Chanting in Stroll (southern Sung dynasty, 13th century) by Liang Kai.
Tokyo National Museum.

SKILLS FOCUS, pp. 635–639

Grade-Level Skills

- **Literary Skills**
Analyze ways poets use poetic devices, including imagery.

- **Literary Skills**
Compare Chinese poetry with Romantic poetry.

More About the Writer

Background. Li Po wrote his first major poem in his teens with the incentive of winning favor at court. Shortly after composing the poem, however, he retreated to the mountains to live as a recluse. Reflecting on his life as a hermit, Li Po wrote, "I kept thousands of rare birds who came and ate out of my hand when I called to them, without any trace of fear or suspicion." His rapport with birds earned him fame as a person of unusual capacity and an invitation to court. Even though he did not succeed in political circles, Li Po was celebrated as a poet. He was considered to be a "Banished Immortal," someone whose disorderly conduct in Heaven resulted in a return to Earth.

RESOURCES: READING

Planning
- One-Stop Planner CD-ROM with ExamView Test Generator

Differentiating Instruction
- Supporting Instruction in Spanish
- Audio CD Library, Selections and Summaries in Spanish

Grammar and Language
- Daily Language Activities

Assessment
- Holt Assessment: Literature, Reading, and Vocabulary
- One-Stop Planner CD-ROM with ExamView Test Generator
- Holt Online Assessment

Internet
- go.hrw.com (Keyword: LE5 12-5)
- Elements of Literature Online

Media
- Audio CD Library
- Audio CD Library, Selections and Summaries in Spanish

PRETEACHING

Summary ⇔ at grade level

In powerful, deceptively simple images, the speaker in "Quiet Night Thoughts" meditates on what he sees from his bed: a patch of moonlight as white as frost. Then he looks back at the moon and dreams he is home far-away, implicitly connecting himself with the ray of moonlight, which is also far from its home.

"Question and Answer Among the Mountains" can be viewed as Li Po's defense of his reclusive, wandering life. A questioner asks how the speaker can live "in the green mountain," and the speaker's only reply is his smile, as he thinks how free his heart is, floating like a peach blossom down the stream, living "in a world apart that is not among men."

"Letter to His Two Small Children" is a beautiful, yearning evocation of the poet's faraway children. In the poem the speaker expresses his homesickness in delicate images. He imagines that his heart is in a peach tree near the home he left three years before. From the peach tree he sees his small daughter weeping for her father and his even smaller son sheltering with his sister under the tree's branches. He says that this dream made his wits "wild," so he wrote his letter, which he calls "this distant pang / From me to you. . . ."

Selection Starter

Motivate. Ask students what images from nature they associate with freedom. What images from nature do they associate with the idea of settling down or staying in one place?

Before You Read

Quiet Night Thoughts
Question and Answer Among the Mountains
Letter to His Two Small Children

Make the Connection
Quickwrite

In life we are often caught between two fundamental but opposing desires—to wander the world freely, experiencing all that life has to offer, and to settle into the stable security of a community and family. As you will see in the three works that follow, the Chinese poet Li Po was a restless spirit. He spent much of his life as a wanderer and a hermit, but his marriage and many friendships suggest that he also craved human connection and community. Would your ideal life emphasize solitude or fellowship—or some balance between the two? Jot down several sentences explaining your preferences.

Literary Focus
Imagery

Imagery is language that appeals to the senses—sight, hearing, smell, touch, and taste. The imagery a writer creates helps readers imagine a scene and respond emotionally to it. For example, a writer might describe an ocean as a "crashing gray tide" to build a feeling of fear, or as "rippling blue waves" to suggest tranquility. Li Po's poems rarely state an emotion directly; instead they allow the reader to extract the meaning of the poem by considering the emotional effect of the images.

Literary Skills Understand imagery.

> **Imagery** is language that appeals to the senses—sight, hearing, smell, touch, and taste.
>
> For more on Imagery, see the Handbook of Literary and Historical Terms.

Background

Like most of his contemporaries, Li Po wrote in a wide range of poetic forms. Yet according to Chinese critics, Li Po was at his best in concise four-line poems with five to seven words per line. His poem *Yeh-ssu* (ye·sə), translated here as "Quiet Night Thoughts," is a masterpiece of this form. (The English translation here has eight lines, twice as many as the original, in order to accommodate the rhythms of English verse.) A lifelong observer of nature, Li Po was renowned for creating vivid images of China's best-known mountains and streams, often recalled in a mood of solitude. The following three poems, though different in form, resonate with images of nature and the thoughts and emotions of the solitary poet.

636   Collection 5   The Romantic Period

DIFFERENTIATING INSTRUCTION

Learners Having Difficulty
Have students summarize each poem by focusing on what seems to be troubling the speaker, or, in the case of "Question and Answer," his questioner. What different attitudes toward staying in one place and being free to wander does each poem express?

English-Language Learners
The language in these poems is deceptively simple, but the way the language conveys feeling is more difficult to recognize. For example, in "Quiet Night Thoughts," the speaker sees a moonbeam on the ground, looks at the moon, and then dreams that he is home. Help students understand the unstated connection between these events: The moonbeam is far

Quiet Night Thoughts

Li Po
translated by **Arthur Cooper**

Before my bed
there is bright moonlight
  So that it seems
like frost on the ground:

5   Lifting my head
I watch the bright moon,
  Lowering my head
I dream that I'm home.

Landscape (detail) (1714) by Wang Yuan-Ch`i. Chinese ink heightened with colors on silk.
Réunion des Musées Nationaux. Art Resource, New York.

Question and Answer Among the Mountains

Li Po
translated by **Robert Kotewall** *and* **Norman L. Smith**

You ask me why I dwell in the green mountain;
I smile and make no reply for my heart is free of care.
As the peach-blossom flows down stream and is gone into
   the unknown,
I have a world apart that is not among men.

Letter to His Two Small Children

Li Po
translated by **Arthur Cooper**

Here in Wu° Land mulberry leaves are green,
Silkworms in Wu have now had three sleeps:

My family, left in Eastern Lu,
Oh, to sow now Turtle-shaded fields,
5 Do the Spring things I can never join,
Sailing Yangtze° always on my own—

Let the South Wind blow you back my heart,
Fly and land it in the Tavern court
Where, to the East, there are sprays and leaves
10 Of one peach tree, sweeping the blue mist;

This is the tree I myself put in
When I left you, nearly three years past;
A peach tree now, level with the eaves,
And I sailing cannot yet turn home!

15 Pretty daughter, P'ing-yang is your name,
Breaking blossom, there beside my tree,
Breaking blossom, you cannot see me
And your tears flow like the running stream;

And little son, Po-ch'in you are called,
20 Your big sister's shoulder you must reach
When you come there underneath my peach,
Oh, to pat and pet you too, my child!

I dreamt like this till my wits went wild,
By such yearning daily burned within;
25 So tore some silk, wrote this distant pang
From me to you living at Wen Yang . . .

1. **Wu** (wo͞o): river in central China.

6. **Yangtze** (yaŋk'sē): the longest river in China, flowing from Tibet to the East China Sea.

A dance scene (detail), from a series of book illustrations of the Miao customs.
Réunion des Musées Nationaux. Art Resource, New York.

Response and Analysis

Quiet Night Thoughts
Question and Answer Among the Mountains
Letter to His Two Small Children

Thinking Critically

1. What is the overall **mood**, or feeling, of "Quiet Night Thoughts"? How does the poet use **imagery** to convey that mood?

2. Like many Chinese poets, Li Po uses a form of **parallelism** in which pairs of lines follow the same basic sentence structure. Point out the parallelism in the last four lines of "Quiet Night Thoughts." What two ideas are contrasted in these two pairs of lines?

3. In "Question and Answer Among the Mountains," the speaker answers a question by not answering it. Explain this **paradox**, or seeming contradiction.

4. How does the poet use **images** of nature to emphasize his solitude in "Letter to His Two Small Children"? What emotions are evoked in this poem?

5. What central nature **image** occurs in both "Letter to His Two Small Children" and "Question and Answer Among the Mountains"? What very different emotions does this image evoke in each poem?

6. Find an example of **alliteration** in each translation of Li Po's poems. How do the repeated consonant sounds add to the effect of each poem?

Extending and Evaluating

7. In these poems the speakers express their feelings by using seasonal images of nature. Do you think this is an effective way to express one's emotions? Why or why not?

Comparing Literature

8. Compare Tu Fu's "Night Thoughts Afloat" (see page 633) and Li Po's "Quiet Night Thoughts." In particular, consider the poems' **images** and descriptive **details**. Do these images and details evoke similar emotions in each speaker? Explain.

9. Li Po's poems reflect the Taoist philosophy and religion, which teach that nature contains life's essence while the conventional human world, corrupted by materialism, is not true reality. Choose one poem by Li Po and one by the English Romantic poet William Wordsworth (see pages 550–564). How does each poem express the Taoist principle described above?

WRITING

Reflecting on Solitude

Write a short **reflective essay** about solitude. What ideal balance would you strike between being alone and being with others? Can you enjoy solitude in a city or must you be in a peaceful natural setting? What are the benefits of solitude? What are its challenges? Refer to your Quickwrite notes for ideas.

▶ Use "Writing a Reflective Essay," pages 656–663, for help with this assignment.

Literary Skills
Analyze imagery. Compare Chinese poetry with Romantic poetry.

Writing Skills
Write a reflective essay.

John Keats
(1795–1821)

John Keats by Charles Armitage Brown.
By courtesy of the National Portrait Gallery, London.

It is surprising that Keats became a poet at all, and surely a wonder that, when he died at the age of twenty-five, he had accomplished enough to become one of England's major poets.

John Keats's brief life was plagued with troubles, and he lacked most of the advantages a poet often needs to get started. His father, who ran a London stable, died when Keats was eight. His mother died of tuberculosis when he was fourteen, leaving the family finances tied up and inaccessible to the Keats children. After four years in a school where his literary interests were encouraged, he was apprenticed at the age of fifteen to learn medicine.

In 1816, not yet twenty-one, Keats completed his medical studies at Guy's Hospital in London. Before he could be legally licensed as a surgeon, he made the momentous decision to become a poet. Some harsh reviews of his first book of poetry (1817) stung him and added to the periodic doubts that made his dedication to poetry sometimes seem an awful burden. Now much of Keats's time was spent nursing his brother Tom, who was dying of tuberculosis.

After Tom's death in December 1818, Keats had a little more than two years to make what he could of his determination to lead a "literary life." Great passages and nearly perfect poems poured from him in that miraculous time. Already in failing health himself, he never knew the greatness of his achievements, which might have given him at least the consolation of literary success. He had also fallen in love—her name was Fanny Brawne—but his poor health and money problems kept him from marrying. "I am three and twenty," he wrote despairingly in March 1819, "with little knowledge and middling intellect. It is true that in the height of enthusiasm I have been cheated into some fine passages, but that is not the thing."

In the next six months, he wrote some of his most glorious poems. Yet, he lamented in a November letter to his brother George (who had immigrated to Kentucky in 1817), "Nothing could have in all circumstances fallen out worse for me than the last year has done, or could be more damping to my poetical talent." Three months later he coughed up blood. His medical training and his experience nursing Tom made the truth obvious: "That drop of blood is my death warrant." His only chance, a slim one, was to live in a warmer climate.

In late 1820, Keats and his friend Joseph Severn, an artist, travelled to Rome and settled into rooms in a house near the Spanish Steps. There Keats died in February 1821 and was buried in the Protestant cemetery—that "camp of death," as Shelley called it.

The stark sadness of Keats's life heightens our awareness of the qualities of his poems—not bleak, subdued, or heavy with resignation, but rich in sensuous detail and exciting representations of intense emotional experiences, full of courageous hope for what the imagination can seize and enjoy in life.

Before You Read

On First Looking into Chapman's Homer
When I Have Fears

Make the Connection
For all the Romantics, poetry was the true adventure. Imagination opened whole new worlds; the best poetry opened thrilling vistas of absolute newness. In the sonnet "On First Looking into Chapman's Homer," Keats addresses this theme of adventure through imagination. In the second sonnet you will read, "When I Have Fears," the young poet reflects upon the possibility that an untimely death may deny him many adventures of the mind—and the heart. How important do you think the life of the imagination is in the world today?

Literary Focus
Sonnet
Most poets who like the challenge of structure love to try the sonnet form. **Sonnets** always have fourteen lines, and they usually have two parts. The first part usually presents a problem, question, or idea that the second part resolves, answers, or emphasizes. Keats wrote "On First Looking into Chapman's Homer" in the Italian, or **Petrarchan,** form, dividing his thoughts into an octave and a sestet (see page 276). "When I Have Fears," however, uses the **Shakespearean** form—three four-line quatrains followed by a concluding couplet (see pages 276–277).

> A **sonnet** is a fourteen-line lyric poem, usually written in iambic pentameter, that has one of several rhyme schemes and structures.
>
> *For more on Sonnet, see the Handbook of Literary and Historical Terms.*

Reading Skills
Reading Inverted Syntax
Keats, like many other poets of his time, often inverts the **syntax,** or word order, of his sentences to meet the demands of meter and rhyme. The word order of a traditional English sentence is subject-verb-complement. Jot down the parts of Keats's syntax that give you trouble. Then, look for the subject and verb of each sentence.

Background
Keats wrote "On First Looking into Chapman's Homer" in 1816, just before his twenty-first birthday. The poem was inspired by an evening Keats spent with his favorite teacher, Charles Cowden Clarke. The two had stayed up all night reading a translation of Homer's *Iliad* by George Chapman, a contemporary of Shakespeare. Keats went home at dawn and by ten that morning sent Clarke this sonnet.

Keats's first Shakespearean sonnet, "When I Have Fears," was written in early 1818—a year fraught with disappointment in work and love and with the beginnings of the poet's ill health. The sonnet hauntingly anticipates Keats's ultimate doom in 1821 at the age of twenty-five.

By 1820, shortly before he died, Keats had published his new poems in "one of the richest volumes in the history of English poetry." He also hoped to nurture his "little dramatic skill" by writing a few more narrative poems to "nerve me up to the writing of a few fine plays—my greatest ambition." He longed to follow Shakespeare into "the fierce dispute / Betwixt damnation and impassioned clay."

Our wonder must be that none of the great poets who came before Keats—Chaucer, Shakespeare, Milton, Pope, or Wordsworth—would be found in this book if they had died at twenty-five.

INTERNET
More About
John Keats
Keyword: LE5 12-5

SKILLS FOCUS

Literary Skills
Understand the sonnet form.

Reading Skills
Understand inverted syntax.

John Keats 641

PRETEACHING

Summary *at grade level*

In "On First Looking into Chapman's Homer," the speaker recalls how a reading of Homer's *Iliad* in a translation by the Elizabethan George Chapman ignited his sympathetic imagination. He perceived the poetry so intensely that the moment matched the excitement explorers feel when gazing upon a planet or an ocean they have never seen before.

In "When I Have Fears," the speaker worries that an early death may prevent him from fulfilling his artistic promise and separate him from his beloved. These dreary thoughts cause him to question the ultimate importance of fame and love.

Skills Starter
Motivate. Invite volunteers to describe situations in which they have felt an overwhelming urge to express strong feelings about an event or an insight. Encourage students to explain how they used their creativity to express themselves.

Selection Starter
Build background. "On First Looking into Chapman's Homer" is Keats's first great poem. Written when he was twenty, it appeared in his first book of poetry, published in 1817. Keats and his friend Charles Clarke had stayed up all night reading Chapman's book. At daybreak, before going to sleep, Keats penned the sonnet in a remarkably short time.

DIFFERENTIATING INSTRUCTION

Learners Having Difficulty
Modeling. To help with the first poem, model the skill of reading inverted syntax. Say, "If we were writing the third line of the poem on p. 642, we'd probably write, 'I have been around many western islands.'" As students read Keats, encourage them to put each sentence into a subject-verb-complement order.

Invite learners having difficulty to read "When I Have Fears" in interactive format in *The Holt Reader* and to use the sidenotes as aids in understanding the selection.

English-Language Learners
For lessons designed for English-language learners and special education students, see *Holt Reading Solutions.*

Advanced Students
Have students work together to read various translations of a part of an epic poem by Homer. Ask them to decide which translation is most readable and why.

John Keats 641

On First Looking into Chapman's Homer

John Keats

Much have I traveled in the realms of gold,
   And many goodly states and kingdoms seen;
   Round many western islands have I been
Which bards in fealty to Apollo° hold.
5 Oft of one wide expanse had I been told
   That deep-browed Homer ruled as his demesne;°
   Yet did I never breathe its pure serene°
Till I heard Chapman speak out loud and bold:
Then felt I like some watcher of the skies
10 When a new planet swims into his ken;°
   Or like stout Cortez° when with eagle eyes
   He stared at the Pacific—and all his men
Looked at each other with a wild surmise—
Silent, upon a peak in Darien.

4. **bards in fealty to Apollo:** poets in loyal service (as feudal tenants to their lord) to Apollo, the Greek god of poetry.
6. **demesne** (di·mān′) *n.*: domain.
7. **serene** *n.*: archaic for "clear air."
10. **ken** *n.*: range of vision.
11. **Cortez:** sixteenth-century Spanish explorer. In this now famous mistake, Keats confuses Cortez with Balboa, another Spanish explorer. Balboa was actually the first European to see the eastern shore of the Pacific Ocean from the heights of Darien in Panama.

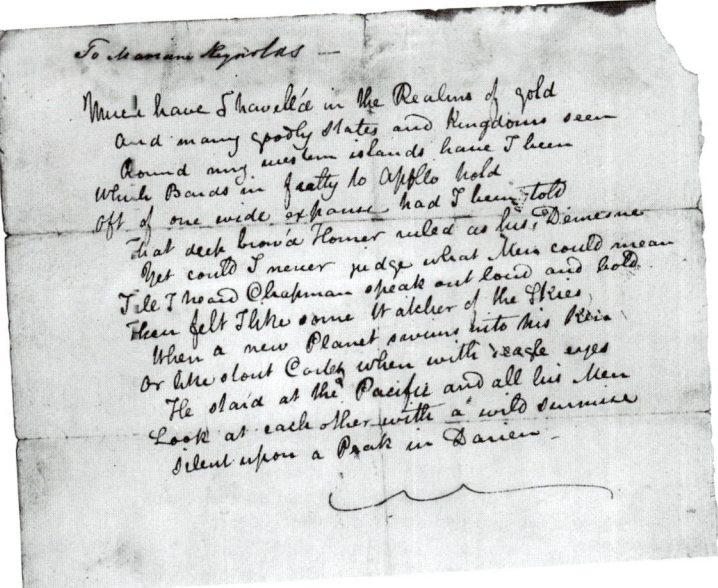

Manuscript of "On First Looking into Chapman's Homer" by John Keats.
MA.214, f.5. © The Pierpont Morgan Library, New York/Art Resource, New York.

The Poet's Theme (19th century) by John Callcott Horsley. Sotheby's Transparency Library, London.

When I Have Fears

John Keats

When I have fears that I may cease to be
   Before my pen has gleaned my teeming brain,
Before high-pilèd books, in charact'ry,°
   Hold like rich garners the full-ripened grain;
5 When I behold, upon the night's starred face,
   Huge cloudy symbols of a high romance,
And think that I may never live to trace
   Their shadows, with the magic hand of chance;
And when I feel, fair creature of an hour,
10   That I shall never look upon thee more,
Never have relish in the fairy° power
   Of unreflecting love!—then on the shore
Of the wide world I stand alone, and think
Till Love and Fame to nothingness do sink.

3. **charact'ry** *n.:* the characters of the alphabet.

11. **fairy** *adj.:* supernatural; unearthly.

INDEPENDENT PRACTICE

Response and Analysis

Thinking Critically

1. Possible answers: imaginary lands; parts of classical Greece and Rome.
2. Keats is speaking about the places to which he has "traveled" in his reading.
3. In ll. 9–10, Keats uses a simile to compare himself to an astronomer, or "watcher of the skies," who has just discovered a new planet. In ll. 11–12, he compares himself to a Spanish explorer discovering the Pacific Ocean. Both similes emphasize the excitement of a discovery that changes people's view of the world.
4. Possible answer: In the first part, the speaker describes his experiences with reading other books, from some of which he gains a general idea of Homer's writing. In the second part he describes the excitement he experienced when reading Chapman's translation of Homer.
5. Keats uses the simile of a harvest—"rich garners" filled with "full-ripened grain"—to described his unwritten literary works.
6. The speaker fears that he might never see his lover again or take joy in her unearthly beauty.
7. The speaker is addressing his lover; this is revealed in ll. 9–10.
8. The speaker begins with an anxious, melancholy, and somewhat regretful tone. By the end, the tone is more calm and resigned.
9. The turn occurs in the middle of l. 12.

Extending and Evaluating

10. Students might suggest that Keats's mistake adds to the impact of the poem; the error emphasizes the creative frenzy that seized Keats after reading the translation by Chapman.

644 Collection 5 The Romantic Period

Response and Analysis

On First Looking into Chapman's Homer
When I Have Fears

Thinking Critically

1. In "On First Looking into Chapman's Homer," what could "realms of gold" (line 1) be?
2. Keats saw something of his own country as a young man, but his only foreign travel was the desperate trip to Italy he made when he was dying. What then do you think Keats means in lines 1–4 of "On First Looking into Chapman's Homer," when he says that he has traveled much and seen many goodly states and kingdoms and western islands?
3. Keats uses two **extended similes** to describe how he felt when he read Chapman's translation of Homer. What are these two similes? What details in these similes suggest that reading Homer was like an act of discovery or exploration?
4. How would you sum up the two parts of "On First Looking into Chapman's Homer"?
5. In "When I Have Fears," what **simile** describes the books the speaker hopes to write?
6. One fear that the speaker of "When I Have Fears" expresses is that he will never be able to write the books he wishes to write. What else does he fear he will never do?
7. Whom does the speaker of "When I Have Fears" address? What line tells you this?
8. Describe the speaker's **tone** in "When I Have Fears." Do you think the tone is constant or does it change? Explain.
9. Where is the **turn** in "When I Have Fears"?

SKILLS FOCUS

Literary Skills
Analyze a sonnet.

Reading Skills
Analyze inverted syntax.

Writing Skills
Paraphrase a sonnet.

Extending and Evaluating

10. Think about the famous mistake in Keats's last simile in "On First Looking into Chapman's Homer." Does this mistake affect the power of the poem, or its quality? Explain your response.

WRITING

Keats in Your Own Words

Select one of these sonnets and **paraphrase** it, line by line, using your own words. Remember that in a paraphrase you should put inverted sentences in standard English word order. You should also rephrase figures of speech to make it clear that you understand them. Sometimes poets omit words; if that is the case in one of these sonnets, be sure to supply the missing words. Refer to your reading notes for help with any lines that give you difficulty. The first lines of "When I Have Fears" might be paraphrased like this:

> When I get worried that I might die before I have written all that is in my mind, which is teeming with ideas . . .

As you can see, a paraphrase is usually longer than the original and it is not nearly as interesting. But it forces you into the poem and sometimes challenges you to dig deep for meaning.

644 Collection 5 The Romantic Period

ASSESSING

Assessment

- Holt Assessment: Literature, Reading, and Vocabulary

PRIMARY SOURCE / LETTER

Keats's Last Letter

John Keats at Wentworth Place (1821–1823) by Joseph Severn. Oil.
The Granger Collection, New York.

Rome, 30 November 1820

My dear Brown,

'Tis the most difficult thing in the world to me to write a letter. My stomach continues so bad, that I feel it worse on opening any book, yet I am much better than I was in quarantine. Then I am afraid to encounter the pro-ing and con-ing of anything interesting to me in England. I have an habitual feeling of my real life having passed, and that I am leading a post-humous existence. God knows how it would have been—but it appears to me—however, I will not speak of that subject. I must have been at Bedhampton nearly at the time you were writing to me from Chichester—how unfortunate—and to pass on the river too! There was my star predominant! I cannot answer anything in your letter, which followed me from Naples to Rome, because I am afraid to look it over again. I am so weak (in mind) that I cannot bear the sight of any handwriting of a friend I love so much as I do you. Yet I ride the little horse, and, at my worst, even in quarantine, summoned up more puns, in a sort of desperation, in one week than in any year of my life. There is one thought enough to kill me; I have been well, healthy, alert, etc., walking with her, and now—the knowledge of contrast, feeling for light and shade, all that information (primitive sense) necessary for a poem, are great enemies to the recovery of the stomach. There, you rogue, I put you to the torture; but you must bring your philosophy to bear, as I do mine, really, or how should I be able to live? Dr. Clark is very attentive to me; he says, there is very little the matter with my lungs, but my stomach, he says, is very bad. I am well disappointed in hearing good news from George [Keats's brother], for it runs in my head we shall all die young. I have not written to Reynolds yet, which he must think very neglectful; being anxious to send him a good account of my health, I have delayed it from week to week. If I recover, I will do all in my power to correct the mistakes made during sickness; and if I should not, all my faults shall be forgiven. Severn is very well, though he leads so dull a life with me. Remember me to all friends, and tell Haslam I should not have left London without taking leave of him, but from being so low in body and mind. Write to George as soon you receive this, and tell him how I am, as far as you can guess; and also a note to my sister—who walks about my imagination like a ghost—she is so like Tom. I can scarcely bid you goodbye, even in a letter. I always made an awkward bow.

God bless you!
John Keats

Preteaching

Summary ⬆ above grade level

The speaker becomes intoxicated with a nightingale's song and the images it evokes in his mind. He wishes for poetic inspiration and for the freedom to fly away from the suffering that time and change inflict on people. He imagines that composing poetry could free him from his distress and that death would be a sweet release if the bird could sing him to his rest. As the last notes of the bird's song fade, the speaker returns to ordinary consciousness, wondering if his experience was only a dream.

Skills Starter

Motivate. Remind students that an ode typically addresses an object and then creates a relationship with it by praising it. Invite students to name special objects that they might like to praise in an ode. Ask them to suggest images that they might use to describe these objects.

Selection Starter

Build background. Keats was at an emotional low point when he wrote this ode, one of six odes completed in the spring and summer of 1819. His brother Tom had just died, despite Keats's efforts to nurse him. Worried about his own health, Keats didn't think he could survive another English winter. Poverty added to his despondency; although deeply in love with Fanny Brawn, he had no money, so marriage seemed impossible.

Before You Read

Ode to a Nightingale

Make the Connection
Quickwrite

From the first lines of this poem, you realize the speaker is passing into a reverie not wholly of the waking world. He is sharing an intense experience of extremes, a searching flight of the mind at once joyful and despairing, spiritual yet startlingly concrete. If you let yourself take this daring journey with Keats (as unfamiliar as it may seem at first), you will find yourself in a mysterious realm. Keats is not afraid of the dark.

How might the act of writing—a poem, a journal entry, or a story—help someone resolve or dispel feelings of depression or gloom? Write down your thoughts.

Literary Focus
Synesthesia

In the poetic device called **synesthesia** (sin'is·thē'zhə), one sense experience (such as smell) is described as another (such as touch). For example, in "Ode to a Nightingale" the speaker remarks that he "cannot see . . . what soft incense hangs upon the boughs" (lines 41–42). Incense, usually perceived through smell, is here described as both something that might be soft to the touch and something that might be seen. By inviting the reader to use his or her senses in unexpected ways, Keats brings a startling newness to common objects.

INTERNET
More About John Keats
Keyword: LE5 12-5

SKILLS FOCUS
Literary Skills
Understand synesthesia.

Synesthesia is a term used for descriptions of one kind of sensation in terms of another, as in describing a color as a sound or a sound as a taste.

For more on Synesthesia, see the Handbook of Literary and Historical Terms.

Background

When Keats was twenty-three, he spent a few months at the Hampstead home of his friend Charles Brown, who remembered:

❝ In the spring of 1819 a nightingale had built her nest near my house. Keats felt a tranquil and continual joy in her song, and one morning he took his chair from the breakfast table to the grass plot under a plum tree, where he sat for two or three hours. When he came into the house, I perceived he had some scraps of paper in his hand, and these he was quietly thrusting behind the books. On inquiry, I found those scraps, four or five in number, contained his poetic feeling on the song of our nightingale. ❞

There are no nightingales in North America. Their unearthly, sad, sweet song can only be heard in the British Isles, central and western Europe, and in Africa during the winter.

646 Collection 5 The Romantic Period

DIFFERENTIATING INSTRUCTION

Learners Having Difficulty
Have small groups slowly read each stanza aloud and then paraphrase what has happened and discuss how the speaker feels about his experience.

English-Language Learners
Place a blank transparency over "Ode to a Nightingale," and have students use markers to highlight sections they have difficulty understanding. Review these sections with students to ensure comprehension.

Ode to a Nightingale
John Keats

1

My heart aches, and a drowsy numbness pains
   My sense, as though of hemlock° I had drunk,
Or emptied some dull opiate to the drains°
   One minute past, and Lethewards° had sunk:
5 'Tis not through envy of thy happy lot,
   But being too happy in thine happiness—
     That thou, light-wingèd Dryad° of the trees,
       In some melodious plot
   Of beechen° green, and shadows numberless,
10   Singest of summer in full-throated ease.

2

O, for a draft of vintage!° that hath been
   Cooled a long age in the deep-delvèd earth,
Tasting of Flora° and the country green,
   Dance, and Provençal° song, and sunburnt mirth!
15 O for a beaker full of the warm South,
   Full of the true, the blushful Hippocrene,°
     With beaded bubbles winking at the brim,
       And purple-stainèd mouth;
   That I might drink, and leave the world unseen,
20   And with thee fade away into the forest dim:

3

Fade far away, dissolve, and quite forget
   What thou among the leaves hast never known,
The weariness, the fever, and the fret
   Here, where men sit and hear each other groan;
25 Where palsy° shakes a few, sad, last gray hairs,
   Where youth grows pale, and specter-thin, and dies;
     Where but to think is to be full of sorrow
       And leaden-eyed despairs,
   Where Beauty cannot keep her lustrous eyes,
30   Or new Love pine at them beyond tomorrow.

---

2. **hemlock** *n.*: poison.
3. **drains** *n. pl.*: dregs.
4. **Lethewards** (lē′thē·wərds): toward Lethe. In Greek and Roman mythology, Lethe is the river of forgetfulness that flows through the underworld.
7. **Dryad** (drī′ad′): in Greek mythology, nature goddess associated with trees.
9. **beechen** *adj.*: archaic for "pertaining to beech trees."
11. **vintage** *n.*: wine.
13. **Flora:** the richness of flowers. Flora is the Roman goddess of flowers.
14. **Provençal** (prō′vän·säl′): from Provence, a region in southern France known in the Middle Ages for its troubadors singing love songs.
16. **blushful Hippocrene** (hip′ō·krēn′): wine, which he would drink for inspiration. In Greek mythology, Hippocrene is the Muses' fountain, whose waters inspire the poets who drink from it.

25. **palsy** *n.*: a disease of the nervous system that causes partial paralysis and involuntary shaking.

Direct Teaching

VIEWING THE ART

John Atkinson Grimshaw (1836–1893) was an English landscape painter who used a camera obscura to project images onto his canvases before painting them.

Activity. Ask student to describe the mood of the painting and to identify elements that create that mood. [Students may discuss the solitary figure on the wooded path, the golden tone of the painting, the position of the sun and the long shadows suggesting late afternoon, and the bare branches suggesting winter.]

A Literary Focus

Tone. How does the tone change in ll. 31–33? [The tone becomes less melancholy and more hopeful, as the speaker announces that poetry will help him escape his pain.]

B Reading Skills

Comparing and contrasting. How are the images of the moon and stars different from the image of the earthly world below? [Possible response: The moon is imaginatively depicted as an enthroned queen surrounded by fairy stars; the earthly realm, however, is described as dark, gloomy, twisting, and mossy.]

Forge Valley, Scarborough (19th century) by John Atkinson Grimshaw.
Christopher Wood Gallery, London.

4

A   Away! away! for I will fly to thee,
       Not charioted by Bacchus and his pards,°
    But on the viewless wings of Poesy,°
       Though the dull brain perplexes and retards:
35 Already with thee! tender is the night,
       And haply the Queen-Moon is on her throne,
          Clustered around by all her starry Fays;°
B   But here there is no light,
       Save what from heaven is with the breezes blown
40   Through verdurous° glooms and winding mossy ways.

32. **not . . . pards:** not by getting drunk. Bacchus, the Roman god of wine, had a chariot pulled by leopards, shortened here to "pards."
33. **on . . . Poesy:** on the invisible wings of poetry; that is, by using his poetic imagination.
37. **Fays** *n. pl.*: fairies.
40. **verdurous** (vur′jər·əs) *adj.*: full of green foliage.

648   Collection 5   The Romantic Period

Literary Criticism

Critic's Commentary
The critics Cleanth Brooks and Robert Penn Warren offer this interpretation of Keats's ode: "The poem is essentially a reverie induced by the poet's listening to the song of the nightingale. In the first stanza the poet is just sinking into the reverie; in the last stanza he comes out of the reverie and back to a consciousness of the actual world in which he and all other human beings live. The first lines of the poem and the last, therefore, constitute a sort of frame for the reverie proper. . . . The poet has chosen to present his reverie largely in terms of imagery—imagery drawn from nature, the flowers and leaves, etc., actually associated with the bird physically, and imagery drawn from myth and literature. . . . The images are elaborate and decorative and the poet dwells upon them lovingly and leisurely, developing them in some detail as pictures. . . . The loving elaboration and slowed movement resembles the slowed movement of meditative trance, or dream, and therefore is appropriate to the general tone of this poem."

Whole-class activity. After students have finished reading the poem, ask them to comment on the critics' analysis.

648   Collection 5   The Romantic Period

5

I cannot see what flowers are at my feet,
    Nor what soft incense hangs upon the boughs,
But, in embalmèd° darkness, guess each sweet
    Wherewith the seasonable month endows
45 The grass, the thicket, and the fruit tree wild;
    White hawthorn, and the pastoral eglantine;°
      Fast fading violets covered up in leaves;
        And mid-May's eldest child,
    The coming° musk rose, full of dewy wine,
50   The murmurous haunt of flies on summer eves.

6

Darkling° I listen; and, for many a time
    I have been half in love with easeful Death,
Called him soft names in many a musèd rhyme,
    To take into the air my quiet breath;
55 Now more than ever seems it rich to die,
    To cease upon the midnight with no pain,
      While thou art pouring forth thy soul abroad
        In such an ecstasy!
    Still wouldst thou sing, and I have ears in vain—
60   To thy high requiem° become a sod.°

7

Thou wast not born for death, immortal Bird!
    No hungry generations tread thee down;
The voice I hear this passing night was heard
    In ancient days by emperor and clown:
65 Perhaps the self-same song that found a path
    Through the sad heart of Ruth,° when, sick for home,
      She stood in tears amid the alien corn;°
        The same that oft-times hath
    Charmed magic casements,° opening on the foam
70   Of perilous seas, in fairy lands forlorn.

8

Forlorn! the very word is like a bell
    To toll me back from thee to my sole self!
Adieu! the fancy° cannot cheat so well
    As she is famed to do, deceiving elf.
75 Adieu! adieu! thy plaintive° anthem fades
    Past the near meadows, over the still stream,
      Up the hillside; and now 'tis buried deep
        In the next valley glades:
    Was it a vision, or a waking dream?
80   Fled is that music:—Do I wake or sleep?

---

43. **embalmèd** *adj.:* perfumed.

46. **eglantine** (eg′lən·tīn′) *n.:* kind of rose.

49. **coming** *adj.:* soon to bloom.

51. **darkling** *adj.:* archaic for "in the dark."

60. **requiem** (rek′wē·əm) *n.:* Mass or song for the dead.
sod *n.:* piece of topsoil held together by the matted roots of living grasses.

66. **Ruth:** in the Bible, a young widow who left her own people to go with her mother-in-law to a strange land.
67. **corn** *n.:* British generic term for grain.
69. **casements** *n. pl.:* windows. Images of open windows intrigued Keats.
73. **fancy** *n.:* imagination.

75. **plaintive** *adj.:* sad; mournful.

DIRECT TEACHING

C Literary Focus
Synesthesia. In what way are ll. 41–43 examples of synesthesia? [The speaker tries to "see" the incense hanging on the trees, and he stands in perfumed darkness. Both descriptions juxtapose the sense of sight in terms of the sense of smell.]

D Literary Focus
Mood. What is the mood here? [Possible responses: morose, dispirited, passive.]

E Learners Having Difficulty
Interpreting. Although "half in love with easeful Death," the speaker here sees a flaw in choosing death. What is this flaw? [If he dies, he will not hear the bird's song or experience other beauties.]

F Literary Focus
Symbol. What might the bird symbolize for the speaker? [Possible responses: enduring art; the eternal beauty of nature.]

G Reading Skills
Determining author's purpose. Why do you think Keats uses *forlorn* in both l. 70 and l. 71? [The repetition emphasizes the speaker's mood and echoes tolling bells, which call the speaker back from his reverie to reality.]

H Literary Focus
Tone. What is the tone at the end of the poem? [Possible responses: reflective, resigned.]

DEVELOPING FLUENCY

Small-group activity. Ask a group of eight students to prepare an oral reading of "Ode to a Nightingale," with each student responsible for reading one stanza aloud. Ask the students to work together beforehand to prepare a reading that proceeds smoothly and effectively.

During the reading, allow students to play a musical selection that complements Keats's poetry. After the reading, ask each student to point out examples of rhymes, imagery, and other poetic devices in his or her stanza. Also ask each reader to discuss how he or she decided on the tone of voice to use in reading the stanza. Finally, have the group discuss what they like most about the poem as a whole.

Critical Comment

In this text the critic interprets Keats's "Ode" as the poet's exploration of his own poetic method.

DIRECT TEACHING

A Reading Informational Text

? Recognizing implicit assumptions. According to the commentary, what does the speaker feel poetry should celebrate? ["human life as a process of soul making"]

INDEPENDENT PRACTICE

Response and Analysis

Reading Check

1. The setting is the English countryside; the speaker is drowsy and depressed.
2. He'd like to drink enough wine to forget his troubles and share the nightingale's mirth.
3. The speaker wants to escape sickness, aging, and death. He escapes through poetry.
4. He is enamored of death, but the bird's song reminds him that he would miss beauty.
5. through the ages
6. The speaker is altered.

Thinking Critically

7. Possible answers: He wants to "ease" his troubles. He is "too happy" because of the bird's beautiful song.
8. The speaker yearns for wine that *tastes* of the "country green," "Provençal song," "sunburnt mirth." It heightens the mood of longing.
9. The speaker lives amid time and decay; the nightingale lives in an eternal realm.
10. Possible answer: There is no way to escape his "sole self."
11. Possible answers: The speaker's mood is less exalted because he saw in the nightingale an "ease" that he can never achieve. Or, the speaker's mood is more exalted because he sees poetry as a means to enduring beauty.
12. They suggest that the bird transcends time and place symbolizing eternity.

Extending and Evaluating

13. Its song may have reminded him of art's ability to transcend life.
14. Responses will vary.

CRITICAL COMMENT

Dialogue with the Soul

INFORMATIONAL TEXT

Keats's completed poem is not "about" or "on" the nightingale but, as the title tells us, "to" the nightingale. The speaker seems, as the poem opens, to have already passed beyond the limit of ordinary experience and become "too happy" in the experience conveyed in the nightingale's song. The poem consists of a series of propositions, each containing its own rejection as to how the speaker might imitate the "ease" of the song he hears—wine, poetry, even death are considered. Each time, the speaker in his humanness is drawn back to **A** his "sole self," to a preference for poetry as a celebration, not of "summer" but of human life as a process of soul making.

Response and Analysis

Reading Check

1. Describe the outward **setting** and the emotions of the speaker as they are portrayed in the first stanza.
2. According to the second stanza, what state of feeling does the speaker want to have?
3. What misfortunes does the speaker want to escape in the third stanza? What means of escape are considered in the fourth stanza?
4. What thoughts about death does the speaker have in stanza 6? How does he resolve these temptations?
5. Where does the speaker imagine the song of the nightingale has been heard in the seventh stanza?
6. What is happening in the final stanza?

Thinking Critically

SKILLS FOCUS

Literary Skills Analyze synesthesia.

Writing Skills Write an essay comparing two odes.

7. Why do you think the speaker wants to capture the nightingale's "ease"? Why is he "too happy in [its] happiness" (stanza 1)?
8. Find an example of **synesthesia** in stanza 2 of Keats's ode. What sensory experience does it describe? What feeling or **mood** does the device help to create?
9. What differences are emphasized between the realm (or experience) of the nightingale and that of the speaker?
10. What do you think the speaker realizes by the end of the poem?
11. How is the speaker's **mood** different at the poem's end than at its beginning?
12. Keats uses many **allusions** that conjure up several different historical and mythological periods. What is the effect of all these references?

Extending and Evaluating

13. Why do you think Keats chose the nightingale as the central **image** for this poem? Was it a good choice? Explain.
14. Review your Quickwrite notes. What do you think Keats's motivation or purpose was in writing this poem? Do you think he succeeded? Use evidence from the text to support your opinions.

WRITING

Poets on Poetry

Both Keats's "Ode to a Nightingale" and Shelley's "Ode to the West Wind" (see page 622) are concerned, at least partially, with the subject of poetic inspiration. In a brief **essay**, write a **comparison** of these two odes. Focus on how each poem treats the subject of poetic inspiration.

650 Collection 5 The Romantic Period

ASSESSING

Assessment

- Holt Assessment: Literature, Reading, and Vocabulary

RETEACHING

For a lesson reteaching poetic devices, see **Reteaching**, p. 1129A.

Before You Read

Ode on a Grecian Urn

Make the Connection
This poem is a work of art about the contemplation of a work of art—a Grecian urn, or jar. That means the ode is both concrete (descriptive) and contemplative (philosophical). It moves from rich images to abstract ideas about art versus life, permanence versus change, and body versus spirit.

Literary Focus
Metaphor
In the figure of speech known as **metaphor**, two seemingly unlike things are compared without the use of a connective word such as *like* or *as*. At the beginning of "Ode on a Grecian Urn," Keats uses three metaphors to describe the urn. For example, in line 1, he refers to the urn as "Thou still unravished bride of quietness . . ." By comparing the urn to a virgin bride, the poet implies that the urn has remained untouched throughout the ages, quietly awaiting contact with the human world. As you read, look for other metaphors that describe the urn.

> A **metaphor** is a figure of speech that makes a comparison between two seemingly unlike things without using a connective word such as *like, as, than,* or *resembles*.
>
> For more on Metaphor, see the Handbook of Literary and Historical Terms.

Reading Skills
Visualizing Imagery
Poets often use **imagery**—language that appeals to the senses—to bring their subject matter to life. Most images are visual, but images can also appeal to the senses of hearing, smell, taste, and touch. To better visualize the images presented in "Ode on a Grecian Urn," try reading the poem aloud. Stop after stanzas 1–3 and then after stanza 4, and write a few sentences describing the urn's decorations as you see them. Make sketches if you like.

Background
Antique Greek vases are usually black with reddish decorative painting, often depicting mythological subjects. Many vases show gods, goddesses, heroes, and mortals entangled in adventures. Traditionally, urns have been used as containers or for burial. No one knows exactly what urn Keats had in mind when he wrote this ode. Probably it is an imaginative combination of several vases he had seen, including two in the British Museum. The urn Keats describes has a series of scenes going around it, probably something like the one pictured on page 653.

INTERNET
More About John Keats
Keyword: LE5 12-5

Literary Skills
Understand metaphor.

Reading Skills
Visualize imagery.

Youth singing and playing the kithara, attributed to the Berlin Painter. Terra-cotta amphora (detail) (c. 490), said to be from Nola.
The Metropolitan Museum of Art, Fletcher Fund, 1956 (56.171.38).

PRETEACHING

Summary *above grade level*

> In this ode, the speaker addresses an antique Greek vase on which two painted scenes appear. In the first scene, gods or men pursue maidens in a forest setting while musicians play. In the second scene, a crowd of people and a priest lead a young cow toward an altar for a ritual sacrifice. The mood here is solemn and mournful in contrast with the feverish excitement of the first scene. In the final stanza, the speaker's aim is ambiguous: He may be celebrating the urn as a symbol of eternal art and idealized beauty, but he may be commenting on the limitations of art and the need to find fulfillment in living life.

Selection Starter

Build background. An important notion of the Romantic poets was that ancient Greek art promoted an ideal beauty and that this ideal was akin to the virtues of ancient Greece.

John Keats **651**

Ode on a Grecian Urn

John Keats

1

Thou still unravished bride of quietness,
    Thou foster child of silence and slow time,
Sylvan° historian, who canst thus express
    A flowery tale more sweetly than our rhyme:
5 What leaf-fringed legend haunts about thy shape
    Of deities or mortals, or of both,
        In Tempe or the dales of Arcady?°
    What men or gods are these? What maidens loath?°
What mad pursuit? What struggle to escape?
10   What pipes and timbrels?° What wild ecstasy?

2

Heard melodies are sweet, but those unheard
    Are sweeter; therefore, ye soft pipes, play on;
Not to the sensual ear, but, more endeared,
    Pipe to the spirit ditties° of no tone:
15 Fair youth, beneath the trees, thou canst not leave
    Thy song, nor ever can those trees be bare;
        Bold Lover, never, never canst thou kiss,
Though winning near the goal—yet, do not grieve;
    She cannot fade, though thou hast not thy bliss,
20   Forever wilt thou love, and she be fair!

3

Ah, happy, happy boughs! that cannot shed
    Your leaves, nor ever bid the Spring adieu;°
And, happy melodist, unwearied,
    Forever piping songs forever new;
25 More happy love! more happy, happy love!
    Forever warm and still to be enjoyed,
        Forever panting, and forever young;
All breathing human passion far above,
    That leaves a heart high-sorrowful and cloyed,°
30   A burning forehead, and a parching tongue.

4

Who are these coming to the sacrifice?
    To what green altar, O mysterious priest,
Lead'st thou that heifer lowing° at the skies,
    And all her silken flanks° with garlands dressed?

---

3. **sylvan** *adj.*: of the forest. (The urn is decorated with a rural scene.)
7. **Tempe** (tem′pē) ... **Arcady** (är′kə·dē): valleys in ancient Greece; ideal types of rural beauty.
8. **loath** *adj.*: reluctant.
10. **timbrels** *n. pl.*: tambourines.
14. **ditties** *n. pl.*: short, simple songs.
22. **adieu** (a·dyö′): French for "goodbye."
29. **cloyed** (kloid) *adj.*: satiated; wearied with excess.
33. **lowing** *v.*: mooing.
34. **flanks** *n. pl.*: sides between the ribs and the hips.

35 What little town by river or seashore,
       Or mountain-built with peaceful citadel,°
          Is emptied of this folk, this pious morn?
    And, little town, thy streets forevermore
       Will silent be; and not a soul to tell
40   Why thou art desolate, can e'er return.

                             5
    O Attic° shape! Fair attitude!° with brede°
       Of marble men and maidens overwrought,°
    With forest branches and the trodden weed;
       Thou, silent form, dost tease us out of thought
45 As doth eternity: Cold Pastoral!°
       When old age shall this generation waste,
          Thou shalt remain, in midst of other woe
    Than ours, a friend to man, to whom thou say'st,
       "Beauty is truth, truth beauty,"—that is all
50   Ye know on earth, and all ye need to know.

36. **citadel** (sit′ə·del′) *n*.: fortress.

41. **Attic**: Athenian; classically elegant. **attitude** *n*.: disposition or feeling conveyed by the postures of the figures on the urn. **brede** *n*.: interwoven design.
42. **overwrought** *adj*.: decorated to excess; also, in reference to the men and maidens, overexcited.
45. **Pastoral** *n*.: artwork depicting idealized rural life.

Attic vase painting showing transport of amphoras.
Louvre, Paris.

Primary Source

Keats: On Truth

Two years before writing "Ode on a Grecian Urn," Keats wrote the following lines to a friend: "I am certain of nothing but of the holiness of the Heart's affections, and the truth of the imagination. What the Imagination seizes as Beauty must be truth—whether it existed before or not—for I have the same idea of all our passions as of love: They are all in their sublimity, creative of essential beauty."

Advanced Learners
Before students read, have them reflect on the technique of apostrophe and list the technique's advantages and limitations. After they read, ask them to discuss how effectively Keats makes use of this technique.

Activity. Invite students to paraphrase Keats's comments. Then ask students to discuss how this primary source applies to the theme of "Ode on a Grecian Urn."

Critical Comment

In this passage a critic argues that in "Ode on a Grecian Urn" Keats finds that art is enlivened not so much by sensory experience as by the human imagination.

Response and Analysis

Reading Check

1. The urn can tell a tale more sweetly than his poetry.
2. He seems disenchanted by love, which has caused him suffering.
3. A priest leads a heifer to sacrifice, followed by a procession.
4. The urn will remain unchanged, proclaiming its message: "Beauty is truth, truth beauty."

Thinking Critically

5. The urn shows gods or men in an ancient glade, chasing maidens while musicians play. Two lovers are about to kiss.
6. Possible answer: "Thou foster child . . . " indicates that the urn has survived undisturbed for a long time; "Sylvan historian" suggests that it tells an old pastoral story.
7. Possible answer: They describe the consequences of excessive passion.
8. The "unheard" melodies depend on the imagination, not on the senses, and thus transcend time. Belief in the imagination's power over time is a Romantic idea.
9. Possible answer: It would be a state of mind beyond the material world of time and place.

Literary Criticism

10. Possible answer: If the entire couplet is enclosed in quotation marks, the urn is speaking for itself; if only "Beauty . . . beauty" is quoted, the conclusion is the speaker's. Students may choose the second version because it gives the poem ambiguity.

CRITICAL COMMENT

The Arc of Experience

INFORMATIONAL TEXT

This poem depicts a beautiful curve of emotion and engagement that begins and ends with detachment. At its center, it abandons all restraints, including those of art itself, to live in that world which is "happy" and "forever." By itself, the third stanza seems "overwrought" (a word used in the more detached fifth stanza)—so much so that we feel that all controls have been lost. But this is precisely the nature of the speaker's experience. Bit by bit, a miniature world of human passions comes alive, only to remind us that it is as dead as the clay on which it is represented. Keats has shown us that in the midst of change, art seems to provide the only truth. Yet this is a truth that depends not on sensory experience, but on the human imagination.

Response and Analysis

Reading Check

1. The urn is called a "sylvan historian" in line 3. What does the speaker say about the urn's ability to tell a tale?
2. What is suggested about the speaker's state by the last three lines of the third stanza?
3. Describe the picture on the urn according to the fourth stanza.
4. According to stanza 5, what will happen to the urn when the speaker is dead? What message does the urn give to people?

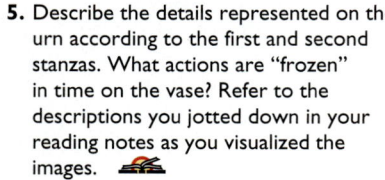

Thinking Critically

5. Describe the details represented on the urn according to the first and second stanzas. What actions are "frozen" in time on the vase? Refer to the descriptions you jotted down in your reading notes as you visualized the images.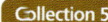
6. Discuss your understanding of the two **metaphors** for the urn in lines 2 and 3.
7. How do you interpret lines 28–30?
8. Why do you think "unheard" melodies (lines 11–14) are "sweeter" to the speaker? How would you relate this idea to Romanticism?
9. If the urn could "tease us out of thought" (line 44), what state would we be in? In what sense would this state be superior to thought?

Literary Criticism

10. A famous textual difficulty surrounds the poem's last two lines. Based on the manuscript, some scholars enclose the entire couplet within quotation marks. Explain how this could change the meaning of the lines. (Would the sentiments expressed in the couplet be the urn's or the poet's?) Which of the two meanings makes better sense when you consider the entire poem?

WRITING

Art Inspiration

Select a work of art reproduced in this book, and like Keats in "Ode on a Grecian Urn," directly address it. In a paragraph, tell what is happening in the work, pose questions about it, and describe your feelings.

654 Collection 5 The Romantic Period

ASSESSING

Assessment
- Holt Assessment: Literature, Reading, and Vocabulary

RETEACHING

For lessons reteaching poetic devices, see **Reteaching**, p. 1129A.

READ ON: FOR INDEPENDENT READING

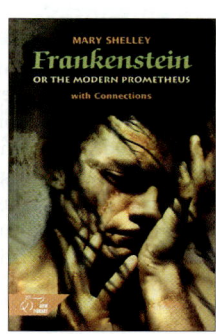

FICTION
Share the Terror
Mary Shelley said of her novel *Frankenstein* that she wanted to write a story that "would speak to the mysterious fears of our nature and awaken thrilling horror." She succeeded, writing an early science fiction novel as well as a vivid version of the Romantic mythology of the self.

This title is available in the HRW Library.

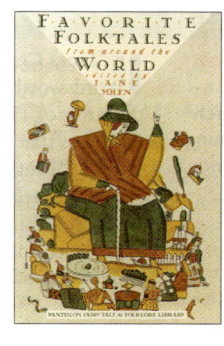

FICTION
Stories from Many Lands
The brothers Jacob and Wilhelm Grimm collected their famous fairy tales in the early part of the nineteenth century. Not everyone knows, however, that the fairy tale was a direct descendent of the folk tale—stories that were handed down orally through the ages. *Favorite Folktales from Around the World*, edited by Jane Yolen, features beautiful, highly readable translations of folk tales hailing from cultures as diverse as China, Africa, and Ireland.

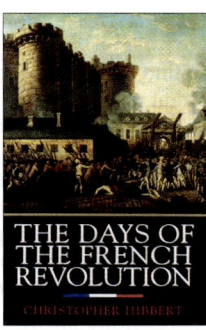

NONFICTION
Revolutionary Fever
Christopher Hibbert's *The Days of the French Revolution* brings all of the drama, turmoil, and bloodshed of the Reign of Terror to life. Here you will meet the principal players of the French Revolution—everyone from Robespierre to Marie Antoinette to Napoleon—and see their stories cast in a new light, though not at the expense of truth. Swiftly plotted and gripping from start to finish, Hibbert's historical narrative reads like a good novel.

FICTION
Love and Marriage
Originally published in 1813, Jane Austen's novel *Pride and Prejudice* is about five husband-hunting sisters in nineteenth-century England and the delicate tangles of love and courtship they ensnare themselves in. What struck people then, and still strikes us now, is Austen's ability to make commonplace people and events interesting. The superficially trivial content is deceptive; it masks a deeper irony that exposes the manners and customs of the period.

This title is available in the HRW Library.

Read On   655

DIFFERENTIATING INSTRUCTION

Estimated Word Counts and Reading Levels of Read On Books:

Fiction			Nonfiction		
Frankenstein	⇔	87,000	The Days of the French Revolution	⬆	107,700
Favorite Folktales from Around the World	⬇	197,600			
Pride and Prejudice	⇔	133,200			

KEY: ⬆ above grade level   ⇔ at grade level   ⬇ below grade level

Read On
For Independent Reading

If students enjoyed the themes and topics explored in this collection, you might recommend the following titles for independent reading.

Assessment Options
The following projects can help you evaluate and assess your students' outside reading.

- **Teach a class.** Ask student teams to prepare and teach a lesson about *Frankenstein*. They may give a brief introductory talk to establish context and setting and then ask classmates to read aloud predetermined selections from the novel. One objective of the lesson is for the student-teachers to encourage their classmates to formulate *5W-How?* questions about the novel based on the student-teachers' introductory comments and on excerpts students read aloud.

- **Stage a tale.** Have students prepare a readers' theater presentation inspired by one of the Grimm tales in the anthology edited by Jane Yolen. In addition to determining which parts of the tale are to be read by characters and one or more narrators, students may design sets and props. They should be able to discuss how their productions accentuate the theme of the Grimm brothers' tale.

- **Interview the author.** Pairs of students who have read *The Days of the French Revolution* may work together to plan and stage a hypothetical interview, in the style of a TV news-magazine show, with the author, Christopher Hibbert. Alternatively, students may interview a person about whom Hibbert writes. Suggest that students record the conversation on video or audiotape.

- **Write a poem.** Students may write a poem reflecting a theme they have encountered in *Pride and Prejudice*. Ask them to write in the style of one of the poets they encountered in this collection.

	(continued)
Second event	Finally, realizing I wasn't just going to stumble across my grandfather's name, I got the panel and line number from the information booth. When I found the panel, my view was obstructed by an older man busily doing a pencil rubbing of one of the names on the panel. When he finished, he looked at the paper sadly, then noticing me, held it up.
Narrative and descriptive details	
Dialogue	"The best friend I ever had," he said to me.
	I looked at the name—Randolph C. Rogers—and back at the man.
Thoughts and feelings	"That's . . . that's my grandfather's name," I said. What were the odds of my running into one of my grandfather's old friends at the Wall? Astronomical! There had to be a reason.
Hint at effect	"You're Randy Rogers' grandkid?" the man asked.
	"Yes, sir," I said, "but I never knew him."
	"Well, son, you're about to. Come sit down and let ol' Joe Weiss introduce you to your grandpa," he said in his loud, friendly voice.
Narrative and descriptive details	During the next two hours, Joe kept me spellbound with stories about my grandfather. Mixed in with many humorous tales were stories of courage and devotion to comrades and country. Joe told these stories as if they had happened the day before. My grandfather was becoming a real person to me.
Hint at significance and effect of the experience	
Narrative and descriptive details	Then, in a sober, quiet voice, Joe described what was very nearly his last mission: He and Grandfather were flying on patrol and had turned for home when Joe's plane was hit by ground fire. Joe ejected over enemy territory. My grandfather kept circling Joe's position, holding off enemy ground troops who were looking for Joe until the rescue helicopter arrived and whisked Joe away.
END	"Randy saved my life that day, no *if*'s, *and*'s, or *but*'s," Joe said, tears in his eyes. "He was quite a guy, the real deal. Three weeks later, a surface-to-air missile got him. He never knew what hit him."
Reflection Effect of experience	I've thought about the Wall, Joe, and my grandfather a lot since then. I think about the cynicism I once felt about ideas like courage, honor, sacrifice, and duty—cynicism that evaporated that day. The qualities possessed by my grandfather, Joe, and thousands of others are the qualities that make human existence worthwhile.
Insight gained into life	

INTERNET
More Writer's Models
Keyword: LE5 12-5

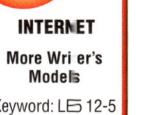 **PRACTICE & APPLY 2** Using the framework on page 659 and the Writer's Model above as guides, write the first draft of your essay. Remember to maintain a balance in narrating the events.

Revising

Evaluate and Revise Your Draft

A Polished Reflection A reflective essay is a personal kind of writing. You want it to reflect your complete experience with accuracy and flair. To make sure that it does, give it at least two more careful readings before you publish it. First, use the guidelines below to evaluate and revise your essay's content and organization. Then, use the guidelines on page 662 to evaluate and revise your essay's style.

PEER REVIEW Before you make your final revision, exchange essays with a classmate. Ask him or her for suggestions on how you could better engage readers' attention in your introduction.

▶ **First Reading: Content and Organization** Using the chart below, find ways to improve your reflective essay's content and organization. As you answer the evaluation questions, think about your intended **audience** and your **purpose** for writing the essay.

Rubric: Writing a Reflective Essay

Evaluation Questions	Tips	Revision Techniques
❶ Does the introduction provide necessary background information and engage readers' attention?	**Bracket** sentences that provide necessary background information. **Circle** the engaging opening.	**Add** background information. **Add** an engaging opener or **revise** existing sentences to make them more engaging.
❷ Does the introduction provide a hint about the significance or effect of the experience for the writer?	**Underline** the sentence or sentences in the introduction that hint at the significance or effect of the experience.	**Add** a sentence or two to hint at the significance or effect of the experience without revealing it entirely.
❸ Does the body use narrative and descriptive details to relate each event? Does it hint at the significance of the experience?	**Put a check mark** next to each narrative or descriptive passage. **Star** each hint at the significance or effect of the experience.	**Add** details or **elaborate** on events to make them clear. **Add** thoughts and feelings that hint at the significance or effect of the experience.
❹ Is the essay clearly organized? Do clue words point out any shifts from strict chronological order?	**Number** events in order. **Bracket** passages not in chronological order. **Highlight** clue words within the brackets.	If necessary, **rearrange** events in strict chronological order or **add** clue words to explain shifts in organization.
❺ Does the conclusion bring the narrative to a close and explicitly state the significance or effect of the experience?	**Highlight** the sentences that bring the narrative to a close. **Draw a wavy line** under the experience's significance or effect on the writer.	**Add** sentences that bring the narrative to a close. **Add** one or more sentences that explicitly state the experience's significance or effect.
❻ Does the conclusion reveal the insight into life gained by the writer?	**Draw a box** around the sentences that reveal the writer's insight into life.	**Add** one or more sentences that reveal the writer's insight into life.

Writing Workshop: Writing a Reflective Essay

DIFFERENTIATING INSTRUCTION

English-Language Learners
English-language learners might benefit from a class exchange in which you provide relevant examples of colloquialisms and ask volunteers to give the standard English version of each expression. Then, have speakers of other languages offer examples of colloquialisms from their languages with translations so that students can see how informal phrases appear in other languages.

GUIDED PRACTICE

Responding to the Revision Process

Answers
1. The addition of the colloquialism makes the dialogue more realistic and natural sounding.
2. The addition specifically identifies the experience's significance, which had only been hinted at before.

▶ **Second Reading: Style** Now, consider your style, or the way you express yourself in writing. One way to establish a fresh **tone** and make the dialogue in your essay sound natural is to use colloquialisms. **Colloquialisms** include the common sayings and expressions found in everyday speech, such as "You said it" or "Gimme a break." Use the guidelines in the chart below to evaluate your use of colloquialisms in your essay.

Style Guidelines

Evaluation Question	Tip	Revision Technique
● Does the dialogue in the reflective essay include colloquialisms that reflect natural, everyday speech?	▶ **Bracket** all the dialogue in the essay. **Underline** colloquialisms within the dialogue.	▶ **Add** colloquialisms to dialogue, or **replace** standard language with appropriate colloquialisms that an audience will understand.

ANALYZING THE REVISION PROCESS
Study these revisions, and answer the questions that follow.

> add
>
> "Randy saved my life that day*, no if's, and's, or but's,*" Joe said, tears in his eyes. "He was quite a guy, the real deal. Three weeks later, a surface-to-air missile got him. He never knew what hit him."
>
> I've thought about the Wall, Joe, and my grandfather a lot since then. I think about the cynicism I once felt about ideas like courage, honor, sacrifice, and duty—cynicism that
>
> add
>
> evaporated that day. *The qualities possessed by my grandfather, Joe, and thousands of others are the qualities that make human existence worthwhile.*

Responding to the Revision Process
1. What does the writer achieve by adding to the first sentence?
2. Why did the writer add a new sentence to the passage?

Writing Skills
Revise for content and style.

▶ **PRACTICE & APPLY 3** Using the guidelines on page 661 and above and feedback from peers, evaluate and revise the content, organization, and style of your essay.

Publishing

Proofread and Publish Your Essay

Polish Your Reflection Your reflective essay can have it all—an engaging subject, a natural and intimate style written in an intriguing voice, and a brilliant insight into what it means to be a human being—but if it is riddled with errors in grammar, usage, and mechanics, readers will be so distracted that they will stop reading out of frustration. You can avoid this dire conclusion to your efforts by carefully proofreading your essay.

Share the Wisdom Your reflective essay tells a story only you can tell. Now it's time to share the story with others. Here are ways to share your essay with an audience.

- Give an oral presentation of your reflection to classmates or family members. For more on **presenting a reflection,** see page 664.
- Trade essays with a classmate. After reading each other's essays, discuss shared experiences, feelings, and insights.
- With classmates, create a Web page about yourselves and the experiences that have influenced you.
- Give a copy of the essay to those who shared your experience, and compare their recollections of the experience with yours.

> **TIP** Thoroughly proofreading your paper will help you eliminate errors in the **conventions** of standard American English. As you proofread, be careful to check the punctuation of dialogue. For more on **using quotation marks,** see Quotation Marks, 13c–d, in the Language Handbook.

Reflect on Your Essay

What Did You Learn? Use the following questions to take stock of the choices you made while writing your reflective essay. Write a short response to each question, and keep your responses with your final draft in your portfolio.

- Have other experiences reinforced what you learned from the experience narrated in your essay? Explain.
- Have you had other experiences that contradicted what you learned from the experience narrated in your essay? Explain.
- What was the most difficult part of your reflection to put into words? Why do you think this part was so difficult?
- In what other kinds of writing might using narrative and descriptive details and quoting people's actual words be useful? Consider writing you might do both in this and other classes and outside of school, and explain how these strategies would enhance each type of writing.

PRACTICE & APPLY 4 Carefully proofread your essay for errors in standard American English grammar, usage, and mechanics. Then, publish your essay using one of the suggestions above. Finally, reflect on what you learned while writing your reflective essay by answering the questions above.

Writing Skills
Proofread, especially for correct use of quotation marks.

Writing Workshop: Writing a Reflective Essay   663

PRETEACHING

Motivate. Ask students to think of a time when they thought, "I have to tell someone about what happened to me." Then, ask if they have felt that an experience became more "real" after they had talked about it with someone. Provide five minutes for students to write down their thoughts. Allow volunteers to share their responses. Then, explain that the desire to share experiences as a way of processing them is natural. Tell them that they will adapt their reflective essays for oral presentation.

DIFFERENTIATING INSTRUCTION

Learners Having Difficulty
Students may be intimidated by the prospect of using different voices to deliver the dialogue of different speakers. Some may overact out of nervousness, and others may choose a monotone for all dialogue rather than attempt voice modulation. Have students work with a partner and try different, subtler techniques for delivering dialogue. For those who cannot manage to modify the pitch or sound of their voices, suggest they try delivering some speakers' dialogue slower, faster, or with more or less volume.

DIRECT TEACHING

Stage Your Presentation
You may want to provide students with examples of visuals they could use in their own presentations to help them show, rather than tell. For example, students may want to display maps since the locations of their experiences may be unfamiliar to others. Students may also display time lines if there are many different incidents that make up their experiences.

Listening & Speaking Workshop

Presenting a Reflection

Speaking Assignment
Adapt your reflective essay for oral presentation to an audience.

In the reflective essay you wrote earlier in this collection, you shared a significant experience in your life and told your readers how the experience affected you and what insight into life you gained from it. In this workshop you'll adapt your reflective essay for an oral presentation, which will allow you to use your voice and body language to bring the totality of the experience to life for your listeners.

Adapt Your Reflective Essay

Punch It Up The techniques of an oral presentation are different from the techniques of a written essay in some ways, but your **purpose** is the same—to narrate an experience and to explore the connection between the experience and an insight into life in general. Here are some suggestions for adapting your essay for an oral presentation.

- **Stage your presentation.** **Dialogue** is an important part of any presentation that involves narration and characters. In your oral presentation, imitate the voices of the people involved in your experience to bring them life. You can also act out your **movements, facial expressions,** and **gestures** and those of other people involved in your experience. Avoid overacting and exaggerated imitations, both of which can have a negative effect on your listeners. Also consider using **visuals** and **sound effects** to heighten the effect of your presentation; however, don't overdo it. Be sure that your experience remains the center of attention.

- **Explain yourself.** You can be subtle in writing, but in your oral presentation you must provide your audience with broad hints about the significance or effect of your experience. Plan to balance those hints with the narrative and descriptive details that describe each event. At the conclusion of your presentation, make sure your explicit statements about the significance or effect of the experience and the more general insight into life that you gained are clear enough for a listening audience.

- **Use effective language.** Effective language in a reflective presentation has clarity and force, and is **aesthetic,** or artistic and tasteful. Choose **concrete images** to narrate events and to describe places. Use rhetorical questions, parallelism, figurative language, and other **rhetorical devices** to enhance the effectiveness of your language. Where appropriate, use **irony,** which is especially effective in oral presentations because it can be communicated through your tone of voice as well as through your words. For example, the student

SKILLS FOCUS
Listening and Speaking Skills
Deliver an oral presentation of a reflective essay.

664 Collection 5 The Romantic Period

COLLECTION 5 RESOURCES: LISTENING & SPEAKING

Planning
- *One-Stop Planner* CD-ROM with ExamView Test Generator

Differentiating Instruction
- Workshop Resources: Writing, Listening, and Speaking
- Family Involvement Activities in English and Spanish
- Supporting Instruction in Spanish

Listening and Speaking
- Workshop Resources: Writing, Listening, and Speaking
- Daily Language Activities

who wrote the essay that begins on page 659 used tone of voice and a pause between contrasting ideas to make clear the irony of meeting in 2002 the grandfather who died in 1970: "I met my grandfather in 2002." [Pause.] "He was killed in Vietnam in 1970."

Rehearse Your Presentation

Naturally Speaking—Almost Reading a speech word for word usually sounds stiff and unnatural. Plan to present your reflection **extemporaneously** by creating brief note cards that remind you of the important events that make up your experience. Also include notes reminding you when in your presentation to use visuals, sound effects, gestures, and dialogue.

Words and Actions Sometimes the way you say something means as much as or more than what you say. An oral presentation gives you the opportunity to use both verbal and nonverbal techniques to mesmerize your audience. Here are some techniques to consider.

DELIVERY TECHNIQUES

Verbal Techniques	Nonverbal Techniques
Language: Use **standard American English** so that everyone will understand your presentation. In dialogue, however, use **informal expressions** to capture the uniqueness of the people involved in your experience.	**Eye Contact:** Give individuals in your listening audience the impression that you are speaking directly to them by making eye contact with as many of them as you can. This gives your presentation an intimate feeling.
Tone: Change the tone of your voice to reflect the nature of the events you're narrating or the person you're describing or quoting. Humorous events require a light tone. Somber events require a serious tone.	**Gestures:** Use gestures that match the events or movements you are portraying. Gestures should appear natural and unforced. Be aware that overly dramatic gestures can detract from the content of your presentation.
Volume: Vary the volume of your voice to fit the mood you want to create, but speak loudly enough to be heard.	**Facial Expressions:** Use facial expressions to express your feelings and to characterize people involved in your experience.

Practice, Practice, Practice An effective presentation requires practice. Using your note cards, rehearse your presentation until it feels completely natural to you. Rehearse in front of a mirror to check your gestures and facial expressions. Rehearse in front of family and friends, and ask for feedback that could help you improve your presentation. If possible, videotape a rehearsal. Then, watch the tape for ways you might improve your presentation.

PRACTICE & APPLY 5 Adapt your reflective essay for an oral presentation, and create note cards for rehearsal. After practicing your presentation, deliver it to an audience.

Listening and Speaking Skills
Rehearse your presentation. Use effective verbal and nonverbal delivery techniques.

Assessment
- *Holt Assessment: Writing, Listening, and Speaking*
- *One-Stop Planner* CD-ROM with ExamView Test Generator

Internet
- go.hrw.com (Keyword: LE5 12-5)
- *Elements of Literature Online*

Collection 5: Skills Review

Comparing Literature

SKILLS FOCUS, pp. 666–669

Grade-Level Skills

- **Literary Focus**

Compare literary works from different historical periods.

INTRODUCING THE SKILLS REVIEW

Use this review to assess students' ability to contrast works from different periods.

DIRECT TEACHING

A Literary Focus

? Theme. What are "mind-forged manacles"? [Possible response: narrow thinking that blocks insight.] **How is Blake's concern with these manacles typical of Romantic poets?** [The Romantics were eager for new experiences; they wanted to cast off old ways of thinking and gain more insight into truth.]

B Literary Focus

? Imagery. To what sense does most of the imagery in stanzas 2, 3, and 4 appeal? [Most of it appeals to the sense of hearing.]

C Literary Focus

? Theme. In what way does Blake's poem express a traditional Christian view? [Possible response: Evil is represented as a corruption of innocence.] **In what way is Blake's view more unorthodox?** [Possible response: Social institutions, including the church, are held responsible for evil.]

Collection 5: Skills Review
Comparing Literature

 The following two poems describe cities that—from the poets' perspectives—are on the verge of social ruin. William Blake's "London" depicts the poor living conditions of England in the early nineteenth century, a time when poverty and oppressive governmental policies contributed to a fractured society. Derek Walcott's "The Virgins" describes Frederiksted, one of the oldest port cities on the U.S. Virgin Island of St. Croix. Frederiksted is now a free port where tourists can purchase goods without paying customs duties. Its economy, once based on sugar cane, is now dependent on tourism.

DIRECTIONS: Read the two poems that follow. Then, read each multiple-choice question that follows, and write the letter of the best response.

London

William Blake

I wander through each chartered° street,
Near where the chartered Thames does flow,
And mark° in every face I meet
Marks of weakness, marks of woe.

5 In every cry of every man,
In every infant's cry of fear,
In every voice, in every ban,°
The mind-forged manacles I hear.

How the chimney sweeper's cry
10 Every blackning church appalls,°
And the hapless soldier's sigh
Runs in blood down palace walls.

But most through midnight streets I hear
How the youthful harlot's curse°
15 Blasts the newborn infant's tear
And blights with plagues the marriage hearse.

1. **chartered** *adj.:* controlled by law.

3. **mark** *v.:* notice.

7. **ban** *n.:* legal prohibition, public condemnation, or curse; also, a marriage announcement (spelled *bans*).

10. **appalls** *v.:* causes to lose color; also, dismays, terrifies, weakens.

14. **harlot's curse:** curse upon the harlot or prostitute by a hypocritical society that pushed women into prostitution and then condemned them for it; also, the curse the harlot utters in return. A very real form of the "curse" is disease.

Pages 666–669 cover
Literary Skills
Compare and contrast works from different literary periods.

666 Collection 5 The Romantic Period

ASSESSING

Assessment

- *Holt Assessment: Literature, Reading, and Vocabulary*

Collection 5: Skills Review

The Virgins
Derek Walcott

Down the dead streets of sun-stoned Frederiksted,
the first free port to die for tourism,
strolling at funeral pace, I am reminded
of life not lost to the American dream;
5   but my small-islander's simplicities
can't better our new empire's civilized
exchange of cameras, watches, perfumes, brandies
for the good life, so cheaply underpriced
that only the crime rate is on the rise
10 in streets blighted with sun, stone arches
and plazas blown dry by the hysteria
of rumor. A condominium drowns
in vacancy; its bargains are dusted,
but only a jeweled housefly drones
15 over the bargains. The roulettes spin
rustily to the wind—the vigorous trade
that every morning would begin afresh
by revving up green water round the pierhead
heading for where the banks of silver thresh.

---

1. In the first stanza of "London," the speaker is —
   A describing how he loves London
   B greeting fellow citizens of London
   C noticing other people's unhappiness
   D looking at the Thames

2. Which of the following is an **image** of oppression and restriction used in "London"?
   F the flowing Thames
   G the midnight streets
   H the soldier's sigh
   J the mind-forged manacles

DIRECT TEACHING

D Reading Skills
Comparing literature. How is the topic and the tone of "The Virgins" similar to those of Blake's "London"? [Both poets write about cities they know well and offer bitter comments about the conditions of these cities.]

E Reading Skills
Comparing literature. What does each speaker primarily blame for the conditions he sees in his society? [Blake blames the "mind-forged manacles," or the restrictive ways of thinking that limit people's understanding and trap them in negative behavior; Walcott mainly blames American economic expansionism and consumerism, as represented by widespread tourism and below-market prices.]

Answers and Model Rationales

1. **C** We can eliminate A because Blake is appalled by London. B and D contain incorrect information: The speaker does not greet his fellows and only briefly mentions the Thames.

2. **J** Manacles restrain prisoners, so "mind-forged manacles" is the best image of oppression. F is incorrect: London's river does not oppress. G and H are possible choices—the streets are controlled by the law and the soldier can be oppressed by rulers—but this is not the best answer.

Using Academic Language

Review of Literary Terms
Ask students to look back through the collection to find the meanings of the terms listed below. Then, have students show their grasp of the terms by citing passages from the collection that illustrate the meanings of those terms.
Romanticism (p. 529); **Symbol** (p. 536); **Parallelism** (p. 541); **Theme** (p. 547); **Blank Verse** (p. 551); **Personification** (p. 559); **Allusion** (p. 561); **Tanka** (p. 565); **Haiku** (p. 566); **Imagery** (pp. 567, 636); **Assonance** (p. 567); **Alliteration** (p. 574); **Literary Ballad** (p. 578); **Simile** (p. 610); **Apostrophe** (p. 612); **Irony** (p. 618); **Ode** (p. 621); **Mood** (p. 631); **Sonnet** (p. 641); **Synesthesia** (p. 646); **Metaphor** (p. 651).

3. **A** The palace is steeped in the blood of soldiers who die following orders. One can eliminate B (the speaker doesn't mention training), C (he doesn't extol patriotism), and D (he doesn't mention rebellion).

4. **H** The cries, sighs, and curses create a bitter tone. F is wrong: the speaker is not self-pitying. G is wrong: the tone and imagery are bold, not understated. J is wrong: the speaker is moved, not detached.

5. **D** The speaker states that the dream costs lives; he does not believe in it, so A is wrong. B is wrong: He blames tourism for killing the city. C is wrong: He does remember the earlier city.

6. **J** The speaker's tone is ironic; for example, he describes the killing influx of bargain seekers as "the good life." The other choices—onomatopoeia, allusion, and apostrophe—are not in evidence.

7. **C** Dryness and rustiness suggest death and decay. A is wrong: The speaker calls the streets dead, not dirty. B is wrong: "Plazas blown dry" has nothing to do with gambling. D is wrong: The plazas are not dry from drought.

8. **H** The severity of the conditions described in the poems implies that both cities are virtually beyond hope. F, G, and J are wrong: No images suggest that the cities have been or can be fixed or improved.

Collection 5: Skills Review

3. In lines 11–12 of "London," the speaker suggests that —
   A   the country's rulers are responsible for the deaths of soldiers
   B   all soldiers are poorly trained for battle
   C   patriotism is worth the loss of lives
   D   soldiers are rebelling

4. The overall **tone** of Blake's poem could best be described as —
   F   self-pitying
   G   understated
   H   bitter
   J   detached

5. In lines 1–4 of "The Virgins," the speaker implies that —
   A   he believes in the American dream
   B   he is pleased by what tourism has done for his city
   C   he doesn't remember what life was like before his city became a "new empire"
   D   he thinks the American dream can be destructive

6. Which of the following literary devices does Walcott use in "The Virgins"?
   F   onomatopoeia
   G   allusion
   H   apostrophe
   J   irony

7. What do such **images** as "plazas blown dry" and "the roulettes spin rustily" suggest about the setting Walcott is describing?
   A   The streets are not kept clean.
   B   The tourists are not in the mood for gambling.
   C   The city is dying and decaying.
   D   The city is suffering from a drought.

8. Like the speaker in "London," the speaker in "The Virgins" sees the living conditions of his city as being —
   F   recently improved
   G   easily fixed
   H   virtually beyond hope
   J   a source of hope for everyone

668   Collection 5   The Romantic Period

Collection 5: Skills Review

9. Unlike Blake, Walcott focuses more on which aspect of his city's plight?
   A desolation
   B people's hypocrisy
   C unfair treatment of women
   D disease and poverty

10. What is the major difference in **tone**, or attitude, between the speakers in both poems?
   F The speaker in "London" is more optimistic.
   G The speaker in "London" is more focused on the solution than the problem.
   H The speaker in "The Virgins" values the way his city used to be.
   J The speaker in "The Virgins" is not bothered by what he sees.

Essay Question

In an essay, compare and contrast these two poems, paying particular attention to the speakers' attitudes toward their cities. How do different literary devices enhance the meaning of each poem? Be sure to consider how Blake's poem reflects some key issues and characteristics of the English Romantic period and how Walcott's poem paints a complex and challenging portrait of contemporary life. Do some of the same issues and problems appear in both time periods? Explain.

---

9. **A** Walcott focuses more on the desolation by mentioning dead streets and vacant condominiums. B, C, and D are wrong: Blake focuses on all these things.

10. **H** The speaker in "The Virgins" indeed liked the simplicities of island life before tourists became numerous. F is wrong: The speaker in "London" is pessimistic. G is wrong: That speaker focuses on problems, not solution. J is wrong: The speaker is bothered by what he sees.

Essay Question

The speakers in both Blake's and Walcott's poems bemoan conditions in their native cities.

For Blake, London is nightmarish. He uses powerful images to depict the agony in the teeming streets. He sees humans, unable to think beyond their "mind-forged manacles," as doomed to a life of suffering.

Walcott depicts a dying Frederiksted, where traditional lifestyles have been sacrificed to the selling of luxury goods of questionable value. Taking an ironic view of the American dream, Walcott rails against consumerism and other economic forces.

Test-Taking Tips

Remind students that most multiple-choice questions about poetry will require them to make inferences. Explain that to answer multiple-choice questions about tone, mood, and theme, they must analyze word choices, images, and symbols. For more information, refer students to **Test Smarts**.

Collection 5: Skills Review

Vocabulary Skills

Multiple-Meaning Words

Modeling. Model the thought process of a reader answering item 1 by saying, "In this item, *set* has the meaning, 'put in the right place.' A is wrong; there, *set* is a noun meaning 'a group of related things.' B is wrong; there, *set* is part of the verb *set in*. C is a possibility; *set* here means 'to arrange or fix beforehand.' In D, however, *set* has the same meaning as it does in the quoted lines."

Answers and Model Rationales

1. **D** See rationale above.
2. **G** In F, *fast* is a verb meaning "to avoid eating." In G, *fast* has to do with speed as it does in the Coleridge sentence. The meaning of *fast* in H is "loyal," and in J, "soundly."
3. **A** In both the sentence and A, *cross* is a verb meaning "to go across." In B, *cross* means "annoyed." In C, *cross* means "oppose" or "go against." In D, *cross* means "mixture."
4. **G** In the sentence, *stand* means "to be upright on one's feet." In F, *stand* means a "moral position" or "stance." In H, *stand* means "something to place things on." In J, *stand* means "to undergo or be submitted to."
5. **B** In the sentence, *load* means "burden" or "what one is carrying." That's what *load* means in B.
6. **H** In the sentence, *frame* is a noun meaning "body." The word *frame* in H has this meaning. In F, *frame* is a verb meaning "place a border around something." In G, *frame* is a noun meaning "structure" or "system." In J, *frame* is a verb meaning "plan" or "put together."

Collection 5   The Romantic Period

Collection 5: Skills Review

Vocabulary Skills

Test Practice

Words with Multiple Meanings

DIRECTIONS: Choose the answer in which the underlined word is used in the same way as it is used in these sentences from *The Rime of the Ancient Mariner*.

1. "The guests are met, the feast is set: / Mays't hear the merry din."
   - A I'll need a new set of tools.
   - B Infection could set in if you don't clean the cut thoroughly.
   - C Did you set an appointment?
   - D The banquet room is set.

2. "The ship drove fast, loud roared the blast, / And southward aye we fled."
   - F The patient was asked to fast for twenty-four hours.
   - G The student learned fast.
   - H The two athletes became fast friends after they discovered they both liked tennis.
   - J Rocked by his father, the toddler fell fast asleep.

3. "At length did cross an Albatross, / Through the fog it came."
   - A You should only cross the creek at the shallow end.
   - B Ben's father was extremely cross when he found out Ben had locked the keys in the car.
   - C If you cross her, she'll resent it and may never forgive you.
   - D That dog is a cross between a German shepherd and a collie.

4. "The Hermit stepped forth from the boat, / And scarcely he could stand."
   - F The politician decided to take a firm stand on the issue.
   - G After an impressive performance, audience members generally stand and applaud.
   - H The sculptor put two of her statues on a marble stand.
   - J The defendants will stand trial for their accused crimes.

5. "For the sky and the sea, and the sea and the sky / Lay like a load on my weary eye"
   - A Our baseball team always tries to load the bases.
   - B Talking to someone can help you get a load off your mind.
   - C We had to load new software onto our computer before we could view the files.
   - D Don't load those heavy boxes by yourself.

6. "Forthwith this frame of mine was wrenched / With a woeful agony"
   - F He likes to frame his paintings.
   - G I have no frame of reference to help me understand you.
   - H Disease made his frame seem worn and frail.
   - J The lawyer had to frame her argument effectively.

Vocabulary Skills Understand words with multiple meanings.

670   Collection 5   The Romantic Period

Vocabulary Review

Use this activity to assess whether students have retained the collection Vocabulary.

Activity. Ask students to complete each of the analogies with a Vocabulary word from the box.

| dismal | ghastly | tyrannous |
| abated | wrenched | |

1. *Trustworthy* is to *statesman* as _____ is to *dictator*. [tyrannous]
2. *Ebbed* is to _____ as *flowed* is to *increased*. [abated]
3. *High-spirited* is to *mountaintop* as _____ is to *swamp*. [dismal]
4. *Amusing* is to *situation comedy* as _____ is to *horror movie*. [ghastly]
5. *Exhilarated* is to *ecstasy* as _____ is to *grief*. [wrenched]

Collection 5: Skills Review
Writing Skills

Test Practice

DIRECTIONS: Read the following paragraph from a draft of a student's reflective essay. Then, answer the questions below it.

(1) The automobile collision my mother and I were involved in was an unforgettable cataclysm. (2) She was driving me home from a late soccer tournament, and we were talking sleepily, trying to keep each other awake. (3) I guess I fell asleep, but I awoke suddenly to a terrible crunching of metal and to being slammed forward violently. (4) My mother had apparently fallen asleep, too, because our car was now off the road and smashed against a fence post. (5) After realizing that I was all right, I looked over at my mother and saw her eyes closed and her forehead bleeding. (6) My screams must have brought her to consciousness, because her eyes opened and a wave of relief flooded over me.

1. To express the significance of the experience, the writer could add
   A My mother and I should never have gone to that tournament.
   B Driving is a dangerous mode of transportation.
   C While I ended up with only minor injuries, my mother's were major.
   D The wreck made me realize how important my family is to me.

2. Which sentence could the writer add to express her insight about life?
   F I'll always remember this experience.
   G I've learned that life is fragile.
   H I've learned that accidents do happen.
   J I'll never drive when I'm tired.

3. To include more narrative details, the writer could
   A include the dialogue that occurred before the accident
   B describe the accident's setting
   C persuade others to learn from her mother's mistake
   D describe the damage to the car

4. Which sentence could replace sentence 1 to maintain an informal but appropriate tone?
   F The automobile accident was an unfortunate occurrence.
   G My mom and I had such a bad wreck; you wouldn't believe it.
   H My mother and I were once involved in an accident.
   J I'll never forget the day my mother and I got into a car wreck.

5. While presenting the passage orally, the speaker could
   A imitate the way the people in the experience really talk
   B keep her hands perfectly still
   C use her voice to reflect a humorous tone
   D look at her note cards to avoid getting nervous

SKILLS FOCUS

Writing Skills Write a reflective essay.

Collection 5: Skills Review **671**

Collection 6
The Victorian Period: 1832–1901

About Collection 6
In Collection 6, students will master the following skills:

- **Literary Skills:** Evaluate the philosophical, political, religious, ethical, and social influences of a historical period; analyze sound devices in poetry, dramatic monologue, Petrarchan sonnet, alliteration, assonance, mood, couplets, internal and external conflict, allegory, theme; compare and contrast realist works and works from different literary periods.
- **Reading Skills:** Analyze contrasting images, conflicts and resolutions, inferences; draw inferences from textual clues; make and revise predictions.
- **Vocabulary Skills:** Understand connotations; identify antonyms; analyze word analogies.
- **Writing Skills:** Develop, write, and revise an essay comparing and contrasting two literary works.

Minimum Course of Study
Most skills can be taught with a minimum number of selections and features. In the chart to the right, lessons **highlighted in green** constitute the minimum course of study that provides coverage of the skills taught in Collection 6.

Resource Manager
(see pp. 672E–672H)
Lesson and workshop resources are referenced in the Resource Manager on the pages that follow. These resources can be used to reinforce the skills taught in Collection 6, remediate students who are having difficulty, and provide supporting activities for English-language learners.

Scope and Sequence

Selection • Feature	Literary Skills
The Victorian Period: 1832–1901 by Donald Gray	• Evaluate the philosophical, political, religious, ethical, and social influences of a historical period
The Lady of Shalott by Alfred, Lord Tennyson — *at grade level*	• Analyze sound devices in poetry
Ulysses by Alfred, Lord Tennyson — *at grade level*	• Analyze theme
My Last Duchess by Robert Browning — *at grade level*	• Analyze a dramatic monologue
Sonnet 43 by Elizabeth Barrett Browning — *at grade level*	• Analyze a Petrarchan sonnet
Pied Beauty by Gerard Manley Hopkins — *at grade level*	• Analyze alliteration and assonance
Dover Beach by Matthew Arnold — *at grade level*	• Analyze mood
To an Athlete Dying Young by A. E. Housman — *at grade level*	• Analyze couplets
The Mark of the Beast by Rudyard Kipling — *at grade level*	• Analyze internal conflict and external conflict

Reading Skills	Vocabulary Skills	Writing ■ Grammar and Language ■ Listening and Speaking Skills
• Analyze contrasting images		• Write an essay analyzing a poem
		• Write an essay analyzing theme
• Draw inferences from textual clues		• Write a dramatic monologue • Deliver a dramatic reading
		• Write an essay comparing and contrasting two sonnets
		• Write a praise poem • Write an essay comparing and contrasting a poem with a psalm
		• Write a reflective essay • Write an essay analyzing a poem
		• Write an essay comparing and contrasting a poem with a song • Read a poem aloud
• Analyze conflicts and resolutions	• Understand connotations • Analyze word analogies	• Write a multimedia report

(continued)

Scope and Sequence

Selection • Feature	Literary Skills	Reading Skills
Connecting to World Literature: *The Rise of Realism*	• Evaluate the philosophical, political, religious, ethical, and social influences of a historical period • Compare realist works	
How Much Land Does a Man Need? *by* Leo Tolstoy ↔ *at grade level*	• Analyze allegory • Compare realist works	
The Bet *by* Anton Chekhov ↔ *at grade level*	• Analyze theme • Compare and contrast realist works	• Revise predictions
The Jewels *by* Guy de Maupassant ↔ *at grade level*	• Analyze theme • Compare and contrast realist works	• Analyze inferences
Writing Workshop: *Comparing and Contrasting Literature*		
Skills Review: *Literary Skills* *Vocabulary Skills* *Writing Skills*	• Compare and contrast works from different literary periods	

Vocabulary Skills	Writing ■ Grammar and Language ■ Listening and Speaking Skills
• Demonstrate word knowledge	• Write an essay supporting a claim • Use correct pronoun and antecedent agreement
• Demonstrate word knowledge • Identify antonyms	• Write an expository essay • Write a character analysis
	• Write an essay comparing and contrasting two literary works.
• Analyze word analogies	• Write an essay comparing and contrasting literary works

Resource Manager

Selection ■ Feature	Planning	Differentiating Instruction ■ Lesson Plans with ELL Strategies and Practice	Reading ■ Vocabulary
The Victorian Period: 1832–1901 *by* Donald Gray	• PowerNotes: The Victorian Period	• Holt Adapted Reader	• Holt Adapted Reader
The Lady of Shalott *by* Alfred, Lord Tennyson **Ulysses** *by* Alfred, Lord Tennyson	• One-Stop Planner with ExamView Test Generator	• The Holt Reader, pp. 206–210 • Holt Adapted Reader • Holt Reading Solutions, p. 139 • Supporting Instruction in Spanish, p. 37 • Audio CD Library, disc 11 • Audio CD Library, Selections and Summaries in Spanish	• The Holt Reader • Holt Adapted Reader • Holt Reading Solutions
My Last Duchess *by* Robert Browning	• One-Stop Planner with ExamView Test Generator	• The Holt Reader, pp. 211–215 • Holt Reading Solutions, p. 142 • Supporting Instruction in Spanish, p. 38 • Audio CD Library, disc 11 • Audio CD Library, Selections and Summaries in Spanish	• The Holt Reader • Holt Reading Solutions • PowerNotes: Making Inferences
Sonnet 43 *by* Elizabeth Barrett Browning	• One-Stop Planner with ExamView Test Generator	• The Holt Reader, pp. 216–218 • Holt Reading Solutions, p. 146 • Supporting Instruction in Spanish, p. 38 • Audio CD Library, disc 11 • Audio CD Library, Selections and Summaries in Spanish	• The Holt Reader • Holt Reading Solutions
Pied Beauty *by* Gerard Manley Hopkins	• One-Stop Planner with ExamView Test Generator	• Supporting Instruction in Spanish, p. 39 • Audio CD Library, disc 11 • Audio CD Library, Selections and Summaries in Spanish	
Dover Beach *by* Matthew Arnold	• One-Stop Planner with ExamView Test Generator	• The Holt Reader, pp. 219–223 • Holt Reading Solutions, p. 149 • Supporting Instruction in Spanish, p. 39 • Audio CD Library, disc 11 • Audio CD Library, Selections and Summaries in Spanish	• The Holt Reader • Holt Reading Solutions
To an Athlete Dying Young *by* A. E. Housman	• One-Stop Planner with ExamView Test Generator	• Supporting Instruction in Spanish, p. 39 • Audio CD Library, disc 11 • Audio CD Library, Selections and Summaries in Spanish	

Writing ■ Grammar and Language ■ Listening and Speaking	Assessment
• Daily Language Activities	• Holt Assessment: Literature, Reading, and Vocabulary • Holt Online Assessment • One-Stop Planner with ExamView Test Generator
• Daily Language Activities	• Holt Assessment: Literature, Reading, and Vocabulary • Holt Online Assessment • One-Stop Planner with ExamView Test Generator
• Daily Language Activities	• Holt Assessment: Literature, Reading, and Vocabulary • Holt Online Assessment • One-Stop Planner with ExamView Test Generator
• Daily Language Activities	• Holt Assessment: Literature, Reading, and Vocabulary • Holt Online Assessment • One-Stop Planner with ExamView Test Generator
• Daily Language Activities	• Holt Assessment: Literature, Reading, and Vocabulary • Holt Online Assessment • One-Stop Planner with ExamView Test Generator
• Daily Language Activities	• Holt Assessment: Literature, Reading, and Vocabulary • Holt Online Assessment • One-Stop Planner with ExamView Test Generator

(continued)

Technology

INTERNET
- go.hrw.com
- Holt Online Assessment
- Holt Online Essay Scoring
- Elements of Literature Online

MEDIA
- One-Stop Planner with ExamView Test Generator
- PowerNotes
- Audio CD Library, discs 11, 12, and 13
- Audio CD Library, Selections and Summaries in Spanish
- Visual Connections Videocassette Program, Segment 9
- Fine Art Transparencies, 13 and 14

 Transparency   Video

 CD-ROM   Audio CD

Resource Manager

Selection ■ Feature	Planning	Differentiating Instruction ■ Lesson Plans with ELL Strategies and Practice	Reading ■ Vocabulary
The Mark of the Beast *by* Rudyard Kipling	• One-Stop Planner with ExamView Test Generator	• Supporting Instruction in Spanish, p. 40 • Audio CD Library, disc 11 • Audio CD Library, Selections and Summaries in Spanish	• Vocabulary Development, p. 30
Connecting to World Literature: The Rise of Realism **How Much Land Does a Man Need?** *by* Leo Tolstoy **The Bet** *by* Anton Chekhov **The Jewels** *by* Guy de Maupassant	• One-Stop Planner with ExamView Test Generator	• The Holt Reader, pp. 225–235 • Holt Adapted Reader • Holt Reading Solutions, pp. 153–155 • Supporting Instruction in Spanish, pp. 41–43 • Audio CD Library, discs 12 and 13 • Audio CD Library, Selections and Summaries in Spanish	• The Holt Reader • Holt Adapted Reader • Holt Reading Solutions • Vocabulary Development, pp. 31, 32, 33
Writing Workshop: *Comparing and Contrasting Literature*	• One-Stop Planner with ExamView Test Generator	• Workshop Resources: Writing, Listening, and Speaking, pp. 61–69 • Family Involvement Activities in English and Spanish • Supporting Instruction in Spanish, p. 69	
Skills Review: *Literary Skills* *Vocabulary Skills* *Writing Skills*			

The Holt Reader

The Holt Reader is a consumable paperback book that can be used alone or to accompany *Elements of Literature*. It offers guided support throughout the reading process and encourages students to become active readers by circling, underlining, questioning, and jotting down responses as they read. *The Holt Reader* works well for homework, students who have missed class, additional instructional time, reteaching, and remediation.

Holt Reading Solutions (HRS)

Holt Reading Solutions pulls together reading resources in the *Elements of Literature* program to create a powerful tool for intervention and whole-class instruction. *HRS* includes diagnostic assessment tools, lesson plans for English-language learners and special education students, adaptations of selected reading selections, vocabulary and comprehension worksheets, information on phonics and decoding, and additional instruction and practice in remedial reading skills.

Writing ■ Grammar and Language ■ Listening and Speaking	Assessment
• Daily Language Activities	• Holt Assessment: Literature, Reading, and Vocabulary • Holt Online Assessment • One-Stop Planner with ExamView Test Generator
• Daily Language Activities • Language Workbook Worksheets, pp. 8, 9	• Holt Assessment: Literature, Reading, and Vocabulary • Holt Online Assessment • One-Stop Planner with ExamView Test Generator
• Daily Language Activities • Workshop Resources: Writing, Listening, and Speaking, pp. 61–69	• Holt Assessment: Writing, Listening, and Speaking • Holt Online Assessment • One-Stop Planner with ExamView Test Generator
	• Holt Assessment: Writing, Listening, and Speaking • One-Stop Planner with ExamView Test Generator

Technology

INTERNET
- go.hrw.com
- Holt Online Assessment
- Holt Online Essay Scoring
- Elements of Literature Online

MEDIA
 • One-Stop Planner with ExamView Test Generator
 • PowerNotes
- Audio CD Library, discs 11, 12, and 13
- Audio CD Library, Selections and Summaries in Spanish
- Visual Connections Videocassette Program, Segment 9
- Fine Art Transparencies, 13 and 14

 Transparency   Video

 CD-ROM   Audio CD

One-Stop Planner with ExamView Test Generator

The *One-Stop Planner* CD-ROM contains electronic versions of print-based teaching resources, clips from the video program, and valuable assessment tools. The *One-Stop Planner* resources are presented in easy-to-follow, point-and-click menu formats. To preview resources or print out worksheets and tests, you simply make a selection and click.

672H

Collection 6

INTRODUCING THE COLLECTION

The Victorian era was characterized by a spirit of inquiry and a reverence for stability and decorum. Students will gain an understanding and appreciation of this period by reading selections from the great Victorian poets in this collection. Robert and Elizabeth Browning, and A. E. Housman, and Alfred, Lord Tennyson, are among the poets who looked to both the past and the future for new ways of understanding love, grief, nature, and God. The collection concludes by giving students an opportunity to write an essay comparing two literary works from the same historical era.

VIEWING THE ART

William Powell Frith (1819–1909), whose lifetime spanned the Victorian age, was for a time the most popular artist in England. Some of his paintings in the Royal Gallery had to be roped off to protect them from the masses that swarmed around them. Ironically, the pictures themselves also teem with crowds. Frith strove for a photographic realism in his paintings, which offer a reliable guide to the daily lives and customs of his middle-class subjects.

Activity. Ask students, "What details in the painting create a sense of motion and activity?" [Possible responses: the sweeping lines of the women's dresses; the representation of the workmen carrying out their tasks.]

The Railway Station (detail) (19th century) by William Powell Frith.

COLLECTION 6 RESOURCES: READING

Planning
- *One-Stop Planner* CD-ROM with ExamView Test Generator

Differentiating Instruction
- Holt Reading Solutions
- The Holt Reader
- Holt Adapted Reader
- Family Involvement Activities in English and Spanish

- Supporting Instruction in Spanish
- Audio CD Library, Selections and Summaries in Spanish

Vocabulary
- Vocabulary Development

Grammar and Language
- Language Handbook Worksheets
- Daily Language Activities

Collection 6

The Victorian Period
1832–1901
Paradox and Progress

So many worlds, so much to do,
So little done, such things to be …

—Alfred, Lord Tennyson

A steam-driven threshing machine demonstrated in an open field at the Great London Exhibition (1851).
The Granger Collection, New York.

INTERNET
Collection Resources
Keyword: LE5 12-6

Assessment
- *Holt Assessment: Literature, Reading, and Vocabulary*
- *One-Stop Planner* CD-ROM with ExamView Test Generator
- Holt Online Assessment

Internet
- go.hrw.com (Keyword: LE5 12-6)
- *Elements of Literature Online*

Media
- *Audio CD Library*
- *Audio CD Library, Selections and Summaries in Spanish*
- *Fine Art Transparencies*
- *Visual Connections* Videocassette Program
- PowerNotes

THE QUOTATION
This quotation by Tennyson captures the mood of the times. How would you describe that mood? [Possible response: Tennyson is expressing an exuberant optimism and a vision of the world as a bright, busy place teeming with possibilities. The quotation suggests the faith in progress, scientific achievement, and social reform that characterized the Victorian age.]

The Victorian Period 1832–1901

Time Line

■ 1836
Texans Defeated at the Alamo

In 1835, Stephen Austin led Americans living in the Mexican province of Texas in a revolt for independence. Antonio Lopez de Santa Anna, who had helped Mexico win its independence from Spain in 1821, was president of the province at the time. Under Santa Anna's generalship the Mexican army besieged and defeated the Texas rebels at the Alamo, a mission in San Antonio, in 1836.

■ 1837–1838
Dickens Portrays Victorian Poverty

Charles Dickens depicts the poverty and the criminal underground in Victorian England in his novel *Oliver Twist*. Dickens may have drawn on his own memories when he wrote about Oliver's impoverished childhood. Dickens's father was thrown into debtors' prison for a time, and young Charles was forced to work in a shoe polish factory.

■ 1852
Sojourner Truth Speaks Out

The feminist and abolitionist Sojourner Truth delivered her famous "Ain't I a Woman?" speech at a women's rights convention in Akron, Ohio, in 1852. It was not until the twentieth century, however, that women in England and the United States won the right to vote.

■ 1854
Perry Opens Up Japan

In 1854, under enormous pressure from an American fleet under Commodore Perry, Japan reluctantly signed the Treaty of Kanagawa, which opened two Japanese ports to trade with American ships. Within a few years other Western powers also gained trading rights with Japan. Many Japanese were angered by what they saw as Western intrusion, and by 1867 the government had fallen.

LITERARY EVENTS

1832

1837–1838 Charles Dickens publishes *Oliver Twist* in periodical form

1840 Margaret Fuller helps found *The Dial*, a U.S. Transcendentalist journal that publishes Henry David Thoreau and Ralph Waldo Emerson

1842 Nikolai Gogol draws attention to the plight of Russian serfs with his comic epic *Dead Souls*

1843 William Wordsworth becomes poet laureate

1846 Elizabeth Barrett and Robert Browning elope; during their courtship she writes poems included in *Sonnets from the Portuguese*

1847

1847 Charlotte Brontë publishes *Jane Eyre*; Emily Brontë publishes *Wuthering Heights*

1848 Karl Marx and Friedrich Engels publish *The Communist Manifesto*

1850 Alfred, Lord Tennyson becomes poet laureate

1850 Nathaniel Hawthorne publishes *The Scarlet Letter*

1852 Sojourner Truth delivers her "Ain't I a Woman?" speech in Akron, Ohio

1857 Mary Ann Evans publishes stories in *Blackwood's Magazine*, using her pen name, George Eliot

1859 Charles Darwin publishes *On the Origin of Species by Means of Natural Selection*

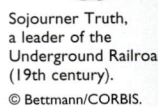

Sojourner Truth, a leader of the Underground Railroad (19th century).
© Bettmann/CORBIS.

POLITICAL AND SOCIAL EVENTS

Imperial state crown made for Victoria's coronation (1837).

1832

1832 First Reform Bill extends vote to men who own property worth ten pounds or more in annual rent

1836 Mexican army defeats Texans at the Alamo

1837 Victoria becomes queen of the United Kingdom of Great Britain and Ireland

1839 Reforms included in Custody Act allow divorced women legal access to their children

1842 First of what China terms "unequal treaties" makes Hong Kong a British colony

1845 Potato famine begins in Ireland; close to one million people die from starvation or famine-related diseases; massive emigration begins

1847

1847 Ten Hours Act limits the number of hours that women and children can work in factories

1848 In Seneca Falls, New York, women's rights convention is led by Elizabeth Cady Stanton and Lucretia Mott

1854 Japan opens trade to the West

1858 Change in laws allows Lionel de Rothschild to become first Jewish member of Parliament

1858 Medical Act closes loophole that briefly allowed women to become physicians in Great Britain

A cabin in Ballintober Bog, Roscommon, Ireland (19th century). Engraving.
The Bridgeman Art Library.

Using the Time Line

Activity. Have students use encyclopedias or other print or nonprint resources and databases to find the dates of the following events. Have them add the dates to the time line.

- Schubert's "Unfinished Symphony" is first performed. [1865]
- Halley's comet appears; Mark Twain is born. [1835]
- Charles Goodyear develops a process to make rubber commercially available. [1839]
- Sigmund Freud publishes *The Interpretation of Dreams*. [1899]
- The first skeletal remains of *archaeopteryx*, the evolutionary link between birds and reptiles, are discovered. [1861]
- Quantum theory is developed by Max Planck. [1900]

1860 – 1870

- **1862** In France, Victor Hugo publishes *Les Misérables*
- **1865** Lewis Carroll publishes *Alice's Adventures in Wonderland*
- **1868–1869** Louisa May Alcott publishes *Little Women*
- **1869** In Russia, **Leo Tolstoy** publishes the complete text of *War and Peace*
- **1884** Mark Twain's *Adventures of Huckleberry Finn* appears
- **1887** Arthur Conan Doyle introduces the world to Sherlock Holmes with *A Study in Scarlet*
- **1900** L. Frank Baum publishes *The Wonderful Wizard of Oz*

Sherlock Holmes and Dr. Watson on a train (c. 1901). Book illustration.
© Historical Picture Archive/CORBIS.

Illustration from *Alice in Wonderland* (c. 1900).
© Bettmann/CORBIS.

1860 – 1870

- **1861** U.S. Civil War begins
- **1861** Russian serfs are emancipated
- **1863** Abraham Lincoln's Emancipation Proclamation declares slavery illegal in Confederate territories
- **1867** Last Japanese shogun resigns; power returns to emperor
- **1867** Second Reform Act gives vote to most male industrial workers, doubling the number of voters
- **1868** Britain ends eighty-year practice of deporting convicts to Australia
- **1869** Debtors' prisons are abolished in England
- **1869** Suez Canal is opened
- **1869** Mohandas K. Gandhi is born in India
- **1879** Zulu War against British in South Africa begins
- **1879** Thomas Edison invents the incandescent lamp
- **1885** Indian National Congress is formed; begins agitating for Indian self-rule
- **1889** Emmeline Pankhurst forms Women's Franchise League, arguing for British women's suffrage
- **1893** Home Rule Bill (to create an Irish Parliament) defeated by British Parliament for second time
- **1898** French scientists Pierre and Marie Curie discover radium
- **1901** Queen Victoria dies

Mohandas Gandhi (1931).
© Hulton-Deutsch Collection/CORBIS.

■ 1868
Britain Ends Deportation of Convicts

The tens of thousands of convicts deported from England between 1788 and 1868 made up a large proportion of the Australian population for more than fifty years. Today Australia maintains strong ties with Great Britain; the two countries share a language, are close trading partners, and have similar legislative systems. During the Victorian period the English enjoyed books about Australia, such as Charles Rowcroft's *Tales of the Colonies* (1843) and Henry Kingsley's *The Recollections of Geoffrey Hamlyn* (1859). Convicts such as James Vaux published memoirs that told the stories of their new lives in Australia.

■ 1869
Suez Canal Is Opened

The French and the British both sought control over Egypt, which occupies a strategic position between the Mediterranean and the Red Sea. The Suez Canal was built with French financing, but Egypt also invested enormous resources in its construction. Those expenditures destabilized Egypt, enabling Britain to take control of the country in 1882. Britain did not yield control over Egypt and the canal until the 1950s.

■ 1870–1901
Europe Carves Up Africa

The European nations met at the Berlin Conference of 1884–1885 to divide up Africa among themselves. (No African ruler attended this meeting.) Within twenty years, all of Africa apart from Ethiopia and Liberia was claimed by European countries. The artificial borders created by the Europeans contributed to the destabilizing conflicts that developed within and between African countries after they regained their independence in the twentieth century.

Political and Social

Political and Social Milestones

Riots and Reforms, 1832–1848

During the 1840s, England's upper classes were gripped by an intense fear of revolution. After all, it was only fifty years since the French Revolution overturned the established order across the Channel, giving rise to decades of violence and war. To a British nation steeped in tradition, the newborn American democracy still seemed like an experiment. Many Britons saw it as a preposterous and dangerous attempt to elevate the vulgar mob to a level of social and political sophistication clearly beyond their reach. Charles Dickens's satirical novel *Martin Chuzzlewit* (1843–44) depicts the United States as a place of falsehood, corruption, vulgarity, violence, mediocrity, and slavery.

Prosperity, 1848–1870

In his book *Victorian People and Ideas,* Richard D. Altick evokes the prosperous mood of the time: "The fifties and sixties were boom times the like of which the nation had seldom known before; Great Britain found herself incomparably the richest nation on earth, the world's foremost banker, shipper, supplier of manufactured goods, and, through her navy, keeper of the peace in the mercantile sea lanes. Batteries of statistics (it was no accident that the Victorian period saw the development of the statistical science) told the proud story. The market value of British exports quadrupled between 1842 and 1870; by 1870 British foreign trade was to be three or four times larger than that of the United States. The tonnage of ships entering and leaving British ports doubled between the mid-forties and 1860.... The gross national income, £523,000,000 in 1851, would double by 1881."

Riots and Reforms, 1832–1848

As the Industrial Revolution put money into their pockets, members of the middle class demanded more power in the government. The Reform Bill of 1832 answered some of these demands, giving the vote to all males who owned property worth a certain amount. The growth of industry had also led to the rapid growth of cities—and of slums. Many factory workers lived poverty-stricken lives, sleeping in dirty, overcrowded rooms and working sixteen hours a day. When widespread unemployment and soaring bread prices gave way to a severe depression in the early 1840s, riots broke out. Fears of revolution spread among the upper classes. Finally, in 1845–1846, serious food shortages forced Parliament to repeal the tax on imported grains that had forced bread prices up. This measure came just in time to safeguard England from the wave of revolutions that spread across Europe in 1848.

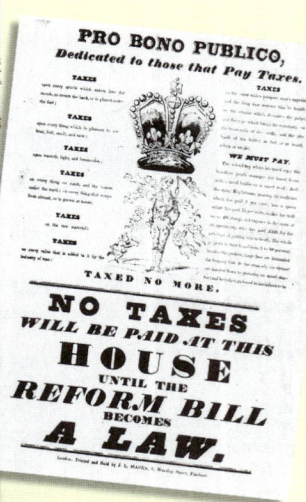

(Above) An 1832 placard announcing passive resistance, used to promote passage of the Reform Bill.
The Granger Collection, New York.

(Left) A riot at Newport, England, November 4, 1839. Wood engraving.
The Granger Collection, New York.

The Book Stall (detail) (1874) after Edwin Austin Abbey. Colored engraving.
The Granger Collection, New York.

Milestones 1832–1901

Prosperity, 1848–1870

A new spirit of optimism lifted the nation during the middle years of the century. Reason and courage, most Victorians believed, could overcome the problems that had festered in the 1840s. A new economic policy of free trade with European nations brought financial prosperity to the aristocracy and upper classes. A series of factory acts in Parliament gradually improved the squalor of working-class lives and gave the vote to even more men. Literacy spread, and the new reading public consumed scores of novels, newspapers, and magazines. The path of progress was being paved.

A Society of Propriety

Middle-class Victorian society was characterized by its elaborate code of respectability, decorum, and morality. This code probably developed in response to the political turmoil of previous decades. The Victorians were convinced that life would be improved if it were more refined, more rationally organized, and better policed. In addition, Victorian intellectuals believed that advances in science and technology would soon overcome all social problems.

(Above) An invention for cleaning tall buildings, observing military fortifications, and performing tree surgery (c. 1856).
© CORBIS.

(Below) *Ladies and Gentlemen Playing Croquet* (detail) (19th century) by William McConnell.
William Drummond, London, UK/The Bridgeman Art Library.

■ A Society of Propriety

Over the past several decades, historians and social psychologists have examined popular conceptions of Victorian society. The findings of scholars such as Matthew Sweet have led to a continuing reevaluation of the myth of Victorian respectability. In his book *Victoria's Heyday* (1972), the historian J. B. Priestley discusses the double standards in morality that prevailed in Victorian England. According to Priestley, many Victorians sought entertainment in the raucous nightlife, private clubs, and brothels of London.

VIEWING THE ART

> Croquet became a popular amusement among the leisured classes in England in the latter half of the nineteenth century. This scene shows a typical croquet party.
>
> **Activity.** From what standpoint does the viewer observe this scene? What effect does the viewpoint create? [Possible response: The viewer stands outside the scene and seems to be spying on the gathering. The viewer thus feels excluded from the scene and therefore more curious about it.]

The Victorian Period
1832–1901
by Donald Gray

PREVIEW

Think About...

The Victorian era was a time of overwhelming growth, prosperity, and progress in England. A sense of self-satisfaction characterized English society. The Victorians had unbounded confidence in progress—but this confidence led to uncomfortable questions. If progress and change are good, some Victorians wondered, should *all* things move forward and change? Should traditional values be questioned and updated? Should a government controlled by a landowning aristocracy be opened to the input of all? Much of the vast literature of this period grapples with these questions—sometimes critically, sometimes playfully, and sometimes mournfully—but always with an eye toward the paradoxes of the age.

As you read about this period, look for answers to these questions:
- What social and political factors affected life in Victorian England?
- What did Victorians value?
- How did discoveries in science affect people's religious beliefs?
- How did Victorian writers respond to issues of their time?

Collection introduction (pages 676–693) covers **Literary Skills** Evaluate the philosophical, political, religious, ethical, and social influences of a historical period.

Many Victorians thought of themselves as living in a time of great change. They were right, but the changes during Queen Victoria's long reign (1837–1901) occurred in a period of relative political and social stability, and many were the result of conditions that began before Victoria and most of her subjects were born.

Peace and Economic Growth: Britannia Rules

After Napoleon's defeat at Waterloo in 1815, Britain was not involved in a major European war until World War I began in 1914. The empire that had begun in the seventeenth and eighteenth centuries with British interests in India and North America grew steadily, until by 1900, Victoria was queen-empress of more than 200 million people living outside Great Britain.

The Opening of the Great Exhibition in Hyde Park, May 1, 1851 (detail) by Henry C. Selous. Oil on canvas. In the center are the queen, her husband, the Prince of Wales (in Highland dress), and other members of the royal family.
© Victoria and Albert Museum, London/Art Resource, New York.

The Victorian Period   679

DIRECT TEACHING

VIEWING THE ART

The Great Exhibition of the Works of Industry of All Nations, better known as the Crystal Palace Exhibition, was housed in an enormous glass and steel building erected in London's Hyde Park. The Crystal Palace became a symbol of the magnificence of industrial progress. It was dismantled during World War II because its glistening form made an easy target for German bombers. In *Gravity's Rainbow,* the American novelist Thomas Pynchon writes, "it will be a spectacle: the fall of a crystal palace," suggesting that the wars of the twentieth century helped destroy the values that defined the Victorian Age.

Activity. Have students write descriptions of a figure in the painting. Then, have them read their work aloud to see whether other students can determine which figure is being described.

---

terms they do not understand and to find the definitions in a dictionary or encyclopedia.

Special Education Students
For lessons designed for special education students, see *Holt Reading Solutions.*

Advanced Learners
Enrichment. Invite students to choose a historical or cultural topic, such as theater in the Victorian age or the orphans of Victorian London, and to supplement the information provided in the text with additional research. Encourage students to share their findings in oral reports, using visual aids if possible.

The Victorian Period   679

DIRECT TEACHING

VIEWING THE ART

Middle-class Victorians showed off their wealth in their drawing rooms or parlors, which were used mainly for entertaining guests. These rooms were lavishly decorated to create impressively elegant yet comfortable interiors.

A Content-Area Connections

Humanities: Thomas Bowdler Perhaps the most famous literary censor of all time was Thomas Bowdler, who is best known for changing hundreds of words and even cutting entire scenes from Shakespeare's plays. Bowdler's *Family Shakespeare* (1818) was embraced by Victorian readers. Bowdler's efforts have been immortalized in the verb *bowdlerize*. The word, which means "cut or modify a work," suggests prudery and violation of textual integrity.

B Literary Connections

Victims of Censorship: Hardy One of the most prominent victims of Victorian censorship was the novelist and poet Thomas Hardy. Magazine editors (who published novels in serial form) constantly rejected scenes from his novels or suggested alterations, mainly to eliminate any mention of sex. Hardy stubbornly resisted these efforts to change his work.

C Exploring the Culture
MALE AUTHORITY

According to the historian Daniel Pool, "When the husband and wife exchanged vows, they became one person, and, in the words of jurist William Blackstone, 'the husband is that person.'"

The Drawing Room (late 19th or early 20th century) by Paul Gustav Fischer.

I still cling fondly to the hope that some system of female instruction will be discovered, by which the young women of England may be sent from school to the homes of their parents, habituated to be on the watch for every opportunity of doing good to others; making it the first and the last inquiry of every day, "What can I do to make my parents, my brothers, or my sisters, more happy?... I hope to pursue the plan to which I have been accustomed, of seeking my own happiness only in the happiness of others."

—Sarah Stickney Ellis, essayist who argued that women's education should cultivate "the heart," not the mind

In art and popular fiction, sex, birth, and death were softened by sentimental conventions, made into tender courtships, joyous motherhoods, and deathbed scenes in which old people were saints and babies angels. In the real world, people were arrested for distributing information about sexually transmitted diseases. Victorian society regarded seduced or adulterous women (but not their male partners) as "fallen" and pushed them to the margins of society.

Authoritarian Values

Victorian decorum also supported powerful ideas about authority. Many Victorians were uneasy about giving strong authority to a central government. (The fundamental conservatism of British society is revealed in the fact that its version of the 1848 European revolutions was a peaceful gathering to petition Parliament.) In Victorian private lives, however, the autocratic father of middle-class households is a vivid figure in both fact (Elizabeth Barrett Browning's father, for example) and fiction.

Women were subject to male authority. Middle-class women especially were expected to marry and make their homes a comfortable refuge for their husbands from the male domains of business, politics, and the professions. Women who did not marry had few

SKILLS REVIEW

Generating relevant research questions. Remind students of the following criteria for research questions:

- Questions should interest you and your readers.
- Questions should help you discover new information.
- Questions should be limited enough to be manageable.
- A variety of sources of information on your topic should be available.

Activity. Ask students to use these criteria to formulate a research question on each of these topics:

1. the life of Charles Dickens
2. economic growth in Victorian Britain
3. the Pre-Raphaelite Brotherhood
4. the Great Famine in Ireland

Applicants for Admission to a Casual Ward (1874) by Luke Fildes. Oil on canvas.
Royal Holloway and Bedford New College, University of London.

occupations open to them. Working-class women could find jobs as servants in prosperous households, while unmarried middle-class ladies could become governesses or teachers. Many middle-class women remained unmarried because men often postponed marriage until they achieved financial security. Life for these unmarried, "redundant women," as they were called, was painful, although in literature, especially literature written by men, the figure of the middle-aged maiden was often played for comedy.

The excesses, cruelties, and hypocrisies of all these repressions were obvious to many Victorians. But the codes and barriers of decorum changed slowly because they were part of the ideology of progress. Prudery and social order were intended to control the immorality and sexual excesses that Victorians associated with the violent political revolutions of the eighteenth century and with the social corruption of the regency of George IV (1811–1820).

Intellectual Progress: The March of the Mind

The intellectual advances of the Victorian period were dramatically evident to those living in it. Humans began to understand more and more about the earth, its creatures, and its natural laws. Geologists worked out the history of the earth written in rocks and fossils. Based on countless observations, Charles Darwin and other biologists theorized about the evolution of species. The industrialization of England depended on and supported science and technology, especially chemistry (in the iron and textile industries) and engineering.

> Lady Bracknell. . . .
> *I do not approve of anything that tampers with natural ignorance. Ignorance is like a delicate exotic fruit; touch it and the bloom is gone. The whole theory of modern education is radically unsound. Fortunately in England, at any rate, education produces no effect whatsoever. If it did, it would prove a serious danger to the upper classes, and probably lead to acts of violence in Grosvenor Square.*
> —Oscar Wilde, from *The Importance of Being Earnest*

DIRECT TEACHING

A Reading Skills

? Interpreting. Who are the players in Huxley's chess game? [Possible response: The players are the individual human being and an omnipotent but fair God administering the laws of the physical universe.] How do you respond to his view of life? [Possible responses: Huxley's view is cold and terrifying, leaving no room for divine mercy and revealing little compassion; Huxley's view is somewhat sentimental because, like a Romantic, he personifies the forces that control nature.]

B Exploring the Historical Period
SCIENCE

S. C. Burchell writes that the period between the mid-1800s and the early 1900s "saw the formation of four of the major concepts on which modern science is based: the idea of evolution; the idea of conservation of energy; the idea of space as a continuum that is pervaded by fields of physical activity (such as electromagnetic fields); and the idea that all action is dependent on the existence of certain basic units—the atom in chemistry, the cell in biology, the quantum in physics and so on."

C Content-Area Connections

Philosophy: The "Laws" of History
The art critic and social reformer John Ruskin was one of these questioners. He wrote, "There is no law of history any more than of a kaleidoscope." Discuss with students the relevance of this quotation to the Victorian concept of order and progress.

Thomas Huxley and the Game of Science

Those who made and used scientific and technological knowledge had a confidence of their own. Thomas Huxley, a variously accomplished scientist who wrote and lectured frequently on the necessity of scientific education, imagined science as an exhilarating, high-stakes chess game with the physical universe.

Thomas Henry Huxley (c. 1870s).
© Hulton-Deutsch Collection/CORBIS.

> 66 The chessboard is the world, the pieces are the phenomena of the universe, the rules of the game are what we call the laws of Nature. The player on the other side is hidden from us. We know that his play is always fair, just, and patient. But also we know, to our cost, that he never overlooks a mistake, or makes the smallest allowance for ignorance. To the man who plays well, the highest stakes are paid, with that sort of overflowing generosity with which the strong shows delight in strength. And one who plays ill is checkmated—without haste, but without remorse. 99
>
> —Thomas Huxley, from *A Liberal Education*

Huxley resembles those confident Victorians who built railways and sewers, organized markets and schools, and pushed through electoral reforms and laws regulating the conditions of work. These reformers believed that the world offered a challenging set of problems that could be understood by human intelligence and solved by science, government, and other human institutions. Huxley made the game exciting by warning that humans could lose. But so long as the game is played in the material world, Huxley and others like him saw no reason that they would not win.

Questions and Doubts

Despite the confidence of the age, the Victorian period was filled with voices asking questions and raising doubts. Speaking for many of their contemporaries, and speaking to others they thought shallow and complacent, Victorian writers asked whether material comfort fully satisfied human needs and wishes. They questioned the cost of exploiting the earth and human beings to achieve such comfort. They protested or mocked codes of decorum and authority.

In the first half of the period, some writers complained that materialist ideas of reality completely overlooked the spirit or soul that made life beautiful and just. Later in the century, writers like Thomas Hardy and A. E. Housman thought that Macaulay's and Huxley's ideas of history and nature presupposed a coherence that did not really exist. Literature in Victorian culture often reassured its readers that, rightly perceived, the universe made sense. But some writers unsettled their readers by telling them that their understanding of the universe was wrong or by asking them to consider whether human life and the natural world made as much sense as they had once hoped.

The Popular Mr. Dickens

Charles Dickens, the most popular and most important figure in Victorian literature, is a case in point. The son of a debt-ridden clerk, Dickens lived out one of the favorite myths of the age. Through his own enormous talents and energy, he rose from poverty to become a wealthy and famous man. His was a peculiarly Victorian success. It was made possible by increasing affluence and literacy, which gave him a large reading public, and by improved printing and distribution, which made book publishing a big business.

The conventional happy endings of Dickens's novels satisfied his readers', and probably his own, conviction that things usually work out well for decent people. But many of Dickens's most memorable scenes show decent people neglected, abused, and exploited. Children, especially, endure terrible suffering. The hungry Oliver Twist begs for more gruel in the workhouse; the handicapped Tiny Tim in *A Christmas Carol* cheerfully hobbles toward his possible early death; and young David Copperfield is abused by his stepfather, the cold, dark Mr. Murdstone.

In his later novels, Dickens created characters and scenes to show that even the winners in the competition for material gain had reason to be as desperate and unhappy as the losers. In *Our Mutual Friend,* his last novel, Dickens describes a dinner party at the home of a family called the Veneerings, a name that emphasizes the family's superficial qualities. (A *veneer* is a thin layer of wood applied to cheap wood to make it look

Scene from *Oliver Twist* depicting Fagin's den of child thieves and a hungry Oliver.
© Bettmann/CORBIS.

Literary Criticism

Critic's Commentary: Dickens and Victorian Society
R. C. Churchill remarks that the common feature of Dickens's novels of the late 1840s and 1850s is "a criticism of Victorian society, which, like that of the workhouse chapters of *Oliver Twist,* goes deep enough to be a universal criticism of human nature."

Individual activity. Have students write a statement that can serve as both a criticism of Victorian society and a comment on human nature in general. [Possible response: People are so concerned with conformity to socially mandated roles that they fail to appreciate the qualities that make each individual wonderfully unique.]

DIRECT TEACHING

D Literary Connections
Oliver Twist as Social Commentary
The first few chapters of *Oliver Twist,* depicting Oliver in a workhouse, are among the finest Dickens ever wrote. Dickens attacks not just the poor conditions of the workhouse but the separate housing of family members.

E Reading Skills
? Interpreting denotation and connotation. Students might be interested in other clever character names in Dickens. For example, Mr. Gradgrind, the schoolmaster in *Hard Times,* displays all the roughness of manner that his name suggests. Other notably named characters include Mrs. Sparsit, Mr. Skimpole, Mr. Bumble, Mr. Sowerberry, and Mrs. Podsnap (see p. 690). Invite students to speculate on the personality and appearance of each of these characters.

VIEWING THE ART

In Charles Dickens's *Oliver Twist,* Fagin organizes and trains young orphans to work as pickpockets on the streets of Victorian London.

Activity. What does this illustration suggest we should think about Fagin and his gang of thieves? [Possible responses: Although Fagin is smiling, the thieves' tattered clothes reveal their poverty and desperation. The boys smoke pipes and wear men's clothing, implying that they have lost their childhood.]

DIRECT TEACHING

A Reading Skills
Recognizing rhetorical devices. Dickens often uses repetition for dramatic effect. Here the repetition of "Reflects" emphasizes that the Veneerings shed no "light" of their own; they merely reflect the false light of material wealth.

B Reading Skills
Using graphic aids. Remind students that boxed lists like this one summarize some of the most important ideas in the essay and enable students to review what they have read. Urge them to use the headings to focus their reading and to digest the content of each bulleted item fully before moving on to the next one. Encourage students to make summary lists like this one whenever they read informational material in textbooks and other sources.

A CLOSER LOOK

This feature examines the comic, satirical, and realistic drama of the Victorian era.

C Exploring the Culture
THE DRURY LANE THEATER

The Drury Lane Theater is the oldest theater in England still in use. It was first built in 1663 and was rebuilt several times.

FAST FACTS
Political Highlights
- By the end of the century, reform bills give most adult males the right to vote.
- A series of factory acts regulates the use of child labor and improves working conditions.
- Education is made compulsory and free by the end of the century, leading to a high national literacy rate.

---

more costly.) The Veneerings are the "new rich," "bran-new people in a bran-new house in a bran-new quarter of London":

> The great looking-glass above the sideboard reflects the table and the company. Reflects the new Veneering crest, in gold and eke in silver, frosted and also thawed, a camel of all work. The Herald's College found out a Crusading ancestor for Veneering who bore a camel on his shield (or might have done it if he had thought of it), and a caravan of camels take charge of the fruits and flowers and candles, and kneel down to be loaded with the salt. Reflects Veneering; forty, wavy-haired, dark, tending to corpulence, sly, mysterious, filmy. . . . Reflects Mrs. Veneering; fair, aquiline-nosed and fingered, not so much light hair as she might have, gorgeous in raiment and jewels. . . . Reflects Podsnap; prosperously feeding, two little light-colored wiry wings, one on either side of his else bald head, looking as like his hairbrushes as his hair. . . . Reflects Mrs. Podsnap; . . . quantity of bone, neck, and

---

A CLOSER LOOK: SOCIAL INFLUENCES

Victorian Drama: From Relief to Realism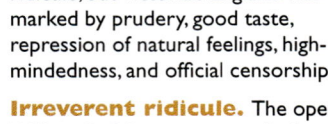

Though Queen Victoria, who came to the throne in 1837, loved the theater, it was she who once remarked, "We are not amused." And certainly the theater of the early part of her reign provided little to amuse anyone. Comedy must have license to explore, to expose, to look under the bed, and to ridicule, but Victoria's England was marked by prudery, good taste, repression of natural feelings, high-mindedness, and official censorship.

Irreverent ridicule. The operettas that William S. Gilbert wrote to Arthur Sullivan's music, beginning with *Trial by Jury* (1875), provided some delightful comic relief. Though today we think of these operettas (such as *The Pirates of Penzance* and *H.M.S. Pinafore*) merely as charming, tuneful, witty entertainments, in their period they irreverently ridiculed the law, the navy, the world of aesthetes, and the aristocracy.

Intrinsic to Gilbert and Sullivan operettas was a world-turned-on-its-head view of life that would influence both Oscar Wilde and Bernard Shaw. In

Interior of Drury Lane Theater, 1808 by Thomas Rowlandson and A. Pugin.
Guildhall Library, Corporation of London.

SKILLS REVIEW

Evaluating philosophical, political, religious, ethical, and social influences of the historical period. Numerous adaptations of novels by Charles Dickens are available on videotape. Some are feature films (such as *Oliver Twist* and *Great Expectations*); some are stage productions or films made for television (such as *Nicholas Nickleby*). Assign students to view one of these productions in small groups and to evaluate the accuracy of its depiction of philosophical, political, religious, ethical, and social aspects of the period. Students might formulate their own criteria to respond to the following questions:

1. Does the setting seem authentically Victorian? Why or why not?
2. Is the main character's philosophy of life authentically Victorian? Why or why not?
3. What political situation is described in the work? Is it presented in a historically accurate way?
4. What social, religious, or ethical issues do the characters face? How do Victorian beliefs and attitudes affect their decisions?

nostrils like a rocking horse, hard features, majestic head-dress in which Podsnap has hung golden offerings. . . . Reflects . . . mature young gentleman; with too much nose in his face, too much ginger in his whiskers, too much sparkle in his studs, his eyes, his buttons, his talk, and his teeth."

—Charles Dickens, from *Our Mutual Friend*

Attacks like Dickens's on the hollowness, glitter, superficiality, and excesses of Victorian affluence were common in Victorian literature. Dickens also raised questions about the costs of progress in his descriptions of the huddle and waste of cities and the smoke and fire of industrial landscapes. In 1871, the art historian and social critic John Ruskin noted a new phenomenon that we call smog; he called it the plague wind, or "the storm-cloud of the nineteenth century," and concluded, chillingly, ". . . [M]ere smoke would not blow to and fro in that wild way. It looks more to me as if it were made of dead men's souls."

FAST FACTS
Philosophical Views
- Victorians have confidence that all social and material problems can be solved by "progress." By the end of the century, however, the disruption and materialism of the era lead to a reevaluation of these views.
- Earlier Romantic views give way to spiritual doubt. Late Victorian intellectuals see human life as a struggle against indifferent natural forces.

Gilbert and Sullivan, "Things are seldom what they seem. / Skim milk masquerades as cream."

Moving toward realism. At the start of the era of Oscar Wilde and Bernard Shaw, drama was moving toward realism, which has remained the dominant dramatic mode for the last hundred years. In England and in Europe, fiction writers were dealing with the social realities of the time—Charles Dickens among others in England, Émile Zola in France. From Scandinavia came the revolutionary voices of Henrik Ibsen in plays such as *An Enemy of the People* (1882) and of August Strindberg in *Miss Julie* (1888).

While some playwrights were assimilating new points of view and style, theaters themselves were undergoing changes to accommodate the new plays. For years, London had been dominated by two huge theaters, Covent Garden and Drury Lane, each seating well over three thousand people—large theaters not congenial to intimate realistic drama.

Program cover for October 17, 1881, Savoy Theatre production of *Patience* by Sir W. S. Gilbert and Sir Arthur Sullivan.
Victoria and Albert Museum, London

In the early part of the nineteenth century, new, smaller theaters were built. The forestage, or apron, was removed, and gaslight (and soon electricity) took the place of candles once used to illuminate the stage. These changes cleared the way for the staging of smaller-scale realistic dramas, which an audience might view as though through an invisible "fourth wall," allowing the audience to eavesdrop on the action. In smaller theaters, on such stages with new lighting, playwrights could now achieve an illusion of reality.

The Victorian Period   691

Primary Source

Gilbert and Sullivan's Major-General
In *The Pirates of Penzance,* William S. Gilbert skewers the British military:

I am the very model of a modern Major-
   General,
I've information vegetable, animal, and
   mineral,
I know the kings of England, and I quote
   the fights historical
From Marathon to Waterloo, in order
   categorical;
I'm very well acquainted, too, with matters
   mathematical,
I understand equations, both the simple
   and quadratical,
About binomial theorem I'm teeming with
   a lot o' news,
With many cheerful facts about the square
   of the hypotenuse.

DIRECT TEACHING

D Content-Area Connections
Humanities: Ruskin
Point out that John Ruskin (1819–1900) wrote on social, political, and artistic subjects. Ruskin advocated individual responsibility and collective action to combat injustice, such as boycotting products made by industries that exploited workers.

E Literary Connections
Oscar Wilde
The Irish-born writer Oscar Wilde was known for his sparkling wit and flamboyant personality. Wilde wrote poetry, fiction, and literary criticism but is best known for his four comedies: *Lady Windermere's Fan* (1892), *A Woman of No Importance* (1893), *An Ideal Husband* (1895), and his masterpiece, *The Importance of Being Earnest* (1895).

F Literary Connections
George Bernard Shaw
The Irish-born playwright George Bernard Shaw (1856–1950) is considered by many to be the greatest British dramatist after Shakespeare. Like Wilde, he wrote late in the Victorian period, ridiculed Victorian values, and shocked the audiences of the time. In one of his early plays, *Mrs. Warren's Profession* (1893), Shaw takes on the topic of prostitution. Shaw continued writing plays well beyond the Victorian period. He published his famous play *Pygmalion* (the basis for the musical and the movie *My Fair Lady*) in 1913 and *Saint Joan* in 1923.

G Reading Skills
Speculating. Ask students to think of a Shakespearean play they have read. Then, ask them to imagine how nineteenth-century changes in theater design would have made a Victorian production of that play different from earlier productions.

The Victorian Period   691

SKILLS FOCUS, pp. 694–706

Grade-Level Skills

- **Literary Skills**

Analyze ways poets use sounds.

- **Literary Skills**

Analyze the way the theme of a selection represents a comment on life.

- **Reading Skills**

Identify contrasting images.

More About the Writer

Background. Tennyson was celebrated as much in his own day as some athletes and rock stars are today. His every action was reported in the press, and he was even stalked at home by devoted admirers. In *Tennyson: Aspects of His Life, Character, and Poetry,* Harold Nicolson says that in his later years, Tennyson's birthday had the status of a national celebration. People sent generous gifts, ranging from rolls of woven cloth to garden chairs. Lakes, cliffs, and roses were named in his honor. News about Tennyson's actions, clothes, and even his tobacco were standard newspaper fare.

Alfred, Lord Tennyson
(1809–1892)

Caricature of Alfred, Lord Tennyson (1872) by Frederick Waddy.

When Alfred Tennyson learned that Lord Byron had died while helping Greek nationalist rebels, he went to the woods and carved on a piece of sandstone, "Byron is dead." Tennyson was fourteen years old. He felt sure that he would be a poet, and he was already practicing the dramatic gestures of the Romantic poets he admired.

Tennyson's father, a clergyman of good family but little money, encouraged young Alfred's interest in poetry. At Cambridge University Alfred joined a group of young intellectuals, called the Apostles, who believed that their friend was destined to become the greatest poet of their generation.

In 1831, when his father died, lack of funds forced Tennyson to leave Cambridge, and he entered a troubled period. In 1832, he published his first significant book of poems, which some reviewers mocked for its melancholy themes and weak imitations of Keats's language. The next year Tennyson was devastated by the death of his closest friend, Arthur Henry Hallam. He became engaged to marry in 1836, but the marriage was postponed for fourteen years because of his uncertain financial prospects.

During this difficult period, when both his physical and mental health suffered, Tennyson apparently never considered any career but poetry. He polished his style to develop the melodious line and rich imagery of poems like "The Lady of Shalott." Tennyson published almost nothing in his "ten years' silence" from 1832 to 1842, but the friends to whom he read his poems remained convinced of his promise.

Gradually, Tennyson began to make his way. The two-volume *Poems* (1842) was favorably reviewed, and in 1845 the government granted him an annual pension of two hundred pounds. In 1850, he published *In Memoriam,* an elegy to Hallam that was immediately successful. It tells the story of his own recovery of faith in the immortality of the soul and of the harmony of creation—despite the new, unsettling discoveries of science and his deep sense of the unfairness of Hallam's death. That year, he was named poet laureate (after Wordsworth's death), and he finally married.

In the forty years before his death in 1892, Tennyson published nearly a dozen volumes of poems. His books sold like bestselling novels and made him rich. In 1884, he was made a peer of the realm and became Alfred, Lord Tennyson.

Tennyson never lost the melancholy and sense of chaos that friends and reviewers found in his early poems. He was immensely popular with his contemporaries because he spoke in a beautiful, measured language of their sense of the fragility and sadness of life. He also assured his readers that his own experience of sadness and disorder had taught him that everything was part of a benevolent plan in which eventually all losses would be made good.

694 Collection 6 The Victorian Period

RESOURCES: READING

Planning
- One-Stop Planner CD-ROM with ExamView Test Generator

Differentiating Instruction
- Holt Reading Solutions
- The Holt Reader
- Holt Adapted Reader
- Supporting Instruction in Spanish

- Audio CD Library, Selections and Summaries in Spanish

Grammar and Language
- Daily Language Activities

Assessment
- Holt Assessment: Literature, Reading, and Vocabulary
- One-Stop Planner CD-ROM with ExamView Test Generator

- Holt Online Assessment

Internet
- go.hrw.com (Keyword: LE5 12-6)
- Elements of Literature Online

Media
- Audio CD Library
- Audio CD Library, Selections and Summaries in Spanish

Before You Read

The Lady of Shalott

Make the Connection
Quickwrite
One of the main symbols in this dreamlike ballad is a mirror that the Lady uses as she weaves. Watch for how the mirror, with its reflected images, stands in opposition to the real world. This is only one opposition, or tension, in the world of the Lady of Shalott, of whom Tennyson said: "The newborn love for something, for someone in the wide world from which she had been so long secluded, takes her out of the region of shadows into that of realities."

What might Tennyson have meant by "the region of shadows" and the region of "realities"? Jot down a few ideas.

Literary Focus
Word Music
Ballads were originally songs, and indeed, Tennyson's ballad "The Lady of Shalott" almost begs to be sung. Its rhythms, cadences, and echoes are so strong that the ballad creates what is known as **word music**. Word music is created by the expert use of **meter** and by the regular and repetitive use of such elements as **rhyme, alliteration,** and **assonance.** Working together, these elements create an overall musical effect in a poem.

Be sure you read this poem aloud to hear the famous music of Tennyson's language. The first time you read the poem, enjoy the rhythmical power of the verse. On subsequent readings, try to identify the individual elements that contribute to the poem's musical quality.

For many years, students in both England and the United States could recite the mysterious story of the Lady of Shalott from memory. You might try to memorize the entire poem or parts of it.

> **Word music** is created when a poet uses a variety of elements such as **meter, rhyme, alliteration,** and **assonance** to generate an overall musical quality in a work.
>
> *For more on Meter, Rhyme, Alliteration, and Assonance, see the Handbook of Literary and Historical Terms.*

Reading Skills
Identifying Contrasting Images
"The Lady of Shalott" is brimming with contrasting images: the flat, flowing river and the upright, unchanging tower; the bustling lives of the villagers and the solitary life of the Lady; the weary whisper of the reaper and the robust song of Sir Lancelot. As you read the poem, be alert to such **oppositions**—the large and the small—in setting, actions, or imagery. Record the first example of each that you notice. Then, when Sir Lancelot appears in Part III, jot down at least one other contrast that he introduces.

Background
Tennyson wrote "The Lady of Shalott" in 1832 and then extensively revised it in 1842. He once commented: "I met the story first in some Italian novelle: but the web, mirror, island, etc., were my own." The symbol of Arthur's Camelot—an orderly, patriarchal kingdom in which beautiful, enchanted women languish—appealed to Tennyson, and to the Victorian imagination in general. Tennyson would return to this setting in such works as "Lancelot and Elaine" and the *Idylls of the King,* a series of twelve connected poems telling the story of King Arthur and the Knights of the Round Table.

INTERNET
More About Alfred, Lord Tennyson
Keyword: LE5 12-6

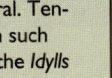

Literary Skills
Understand sound devices in poetry.

Reading Skills
Understand contrasting images.

Alfred, Lord Tennyson 695

DIRECT TEACHING

VIEWING THE ART

In this painting, **John William Waterhouse** (1849–1917) illustrates ll. 127–140 of "The Lady of Shalott" with an almost literal faithfulness. "Robed in snowy white," the Lady loosens the chain and sets out for Camelot. The broken reeds in the foreground and the fallen leaf in her lap may symbolize her imminent death.

Activity. In his painting, Waterhouse includes several objects not mentioned in Tennyson's poem to suggest that the Lady will die. What are they? [a crucifix and candles, objects one might see at a funeral]

The Lady of Shalott (1888) by John William Waterhouse.
Tate Gallery, London.

THE LADY OF SHALOTT

Alfred, Lord Tennyson

Part I

On either side the river lie
Long fields of barley and of rye,
That clothe the wold° and meet the sky;
And through the field the road runs by
5   To many-towered Camelot;°
And up and down the people go,
Gazing where the lilies blow°
Round an island there below,
    The island of Shalott.

10 Willows whiten,° aspens quiver,
Little breezes dusk and shiver
Through the wave that runs forever
By the island in the river
    Flowing down to Camelot.
15 Four gray walls, and four gray towers,
Overlook a space of flowers,
And the silent isle imbowers°
    The Lady of Shalott.

By the margin, willow-veiled,
20 Slide the heavy barges trailed
By slow horses; and unhailed
The shallop° flitteth silken-sailed
    Skimming down to Camelot:
But who hath seen her wave her hand?
25 Or at the casement seen her stand?
Or is she known in all the land,
    The Lady of Shalott?

Only reapers, reaping early
In among the bearded barley,

3. **wold** *n.*: rolling plain.
5. **Camelot**: legendary city, site of King Arthur's court and Round Table.
7. **blow** *v.*: blossom.
10. **whiten** *v.*: show the white undersides of their leaves when blown by the wind.
17. **imbowers** *n. pl.*: shelters with trees, gardens, and flowers.
22. **shallop** *n.*: small, open boat.

The Lady of Shalott (c. 1886–1905) by William Holman Hunt. Oil.

>   Hear a song that echoes cheerly°
>   From the river winding clearly,
>   Down to towered Camelot;
>   And by the moon the reaper weary,
>   Piling sheaves in uplands airy,
> 35   Listening, whispers "'Tis the fairy
>   Lady of Shalott."

Part II

>   There she weaves by night and day
>   A magic web with colors gay.
>   She has heard a whisper say,
> 40   A curse is on her if she stay
>   To look down to Camelot.
>   She knows not what the curse may be,
>   And so she weaveth steadily,
>   And little other care hath she,
> 45   The Lady of Shalott.

>   And moving through a mirror clear°
>   That hangs before her all the year,
>   Shadows of the world appear.
>   There she sees the highway near
> 50   Winding down to Camelot;
>   There the river eddy whirls,
>   And there the surly village churls,°
>   And the red cloaks of market girls,
>   Pass onward from Shalott.

> 55   Sometimes a troop of damsels glad,
>   An abbot on an ambling pad,°
>   Sometimes a curly shepherd lad,
>   Or long-haired page in crimson clad,
>   Goes by to towered Camelot;
> 60   And sometimes through the mirror blue
>   The knights come riding two and two:
>   She hath no loyal knight and true,
>   The Lady of Shalott.

>   But in her web she still delights
> 65   To weave the mirror's magic sights,
>   For often through the silent nights
>   A funeral, with plumes and lights

30. **cheerly** *adv.:* archaic for "cheerily."

46. **mirror clear:** Weavers worked on the back of the tapestry so that they could easily knot their yarns. To see the front of their designs, weavers looked in a mirror that reflected the front of the tapestry.
52. **churls** *n. pl.:* peasants; country folk.

56. **pad** *n.:* easy-gaited horse.

	And music, went to Camelot;
	Or when the moon was overhead,
70	Came two young lovers lately wed:
	"I am half sick of shadows," said
	The Lady of Shalott.

Part III

A bowshot from her bower eaves,
He rode between the barley sheaves,
75 The sun came dazzling through the leaves,
And flamed upon the brazen greaves°
    Of bold Sir Lancelot.
A red-cross knight° forever kneeled
To a lady in his shield,
80 That sparkled on the yellow field,
    Beside remote Shalott.

The gemmy° bridle glittered free,
Like to some branch of stars we see
Hung in the golden Galaxy.°
85 The bridle bells rang merrily
    As he rode down to Camelot;
And from his blazoned baldric° slung
A mighty silver bugle hung,
And as he rode his armor rung,
90   Beside remote Shalott.

All in the blue unclouded weather
Thick-jeweled shone the saddle leather,
The helmet and the helmet feather
Burned like one burning flame together,
95   As he rode down to Camelot;
As often through the purple night,
Below the starry clusters bright,
Some bearded meteor, trailing light,
    Moves over still Shalott.

100 His broad clear brow in sunlight glowed;
On burnished° hooves his war horse trode;
From underneath his helmet flowed
His coal-black curls as on he rode,
    As he rode down to Camelot.
105 From the bank and from the river
He flashed into the crystal mirror,
"Tirra lirra," by the river
    Sang Sir Lancelot.

---

76. greaves *n. pl.:* armor for the lower legs.

78. red-cross knight: The red cross is the emblem of Saint George, England's patron saint.

82. gemmy *adj.:* set with jewels.

84. Galaxy: Milky Way.

87. blazoned baldric: richly decorated sash worn across the chest diagonally.

101. burnished *adj.:* polished.

Direct Teaching

A Reading Skills

Analyzing tension and irony. How does Lancelot's arrival increase the narrative tension? [The Lady's desire to look at Lancelot causes her to defy the curse.] What is ironic about Lancelot's brief appearance? [He continues on his way to Camelot, never realizing the effect that he has had upon the Lady.]

B Literary Focus

Pathetic fallacy. A pathetic fallacy occurs when a writer assigns human emotions and moods to a force of nature. How does this stanza qualify as an example of a pathetic fallacy? [Possible response: The Lady knows that she is doomed. The disquiet of the wind and the river reflect her doom (or perhaps nature's protest against it); the sky seems to be mourning her fate.]

C Literary Focus

Imagery. What is the significance of the Lady's dressing in white? [Possible responses: The white robe resembles a shroud—the Lady knows she is doomed. It resembles a wedding dress—the Lady knows she will never be a bride.]

D Reading Skills

Identifying contrasting images. What contrasting images are presented in this stanza? [Possible response: The Lady is traveling to her death, yet she is singing. She is headed toward life (Camelot), yet she is dying.]

A
110 She left the web, she left the loom,
     She made three paces through the room,
     She saw the waterlily bloom,
     She saw the helmet and the plume,
          She looked down to Camelot.
     Out flew the web and floated wide;
115 The mirror cracked from side to side;
     "The curse is come upon me," cried
          The Lady of Shalott.

Part IV

B
     In the stormy east wind straining,
     The pale yellow woods were waning,
120 The broad stream in his banks complaining,
     Heavily the low sky raining
          Over towered Camelot;
     Down she came and found a boat
     Beneath a willow left afloat,
125 And round about the prow° she wrote
          The Lady of Shalott.

     And down the river's dim expanse
     Like some bold seër° in a trance,
     Seeing all his own mischance—
130 With a glassy countenance
          Did she look to Camelot.
     And at the closing of the day
     She loosed the chain, and down she lay;
     The broad stream bore her far away,
135   The Lady of Shalott.

C
     Lying, robed in snowy white
     That loosely flew to left and right—
     The leaves upon her falling light—
     Through the noises of the night
140   She floated down to Camelot;
     And as the boat head wound along
     The willowy hills and fields among,
     They heard her singing her last song,
          The Lady of Shalott.

D
145 Heard a carol, mournful, holy,
     Chanted loudly, chanted lowly,
     Till her blood was frozen slowly,
     And her eyes were darkened wholly,
          Turned to towered Camelot.

125. prow *n*.: front part of a boat.
128. seër *n*.: prophet.

The Lady of Shalott
(19th century) by John William Waterhouse.

Literary Criticism

Critic's Commentary: Word Music

In an essay called "Tennyson's Melody," the poet and critic John Hollander closely analyzes Tennyson's subtle blend of sound and image: "In the immediate context of mirroring, the doublings in *tirra lirra,* and of it by *river* are most prominent. The river is itself a mirror (the word rhyming with itself), the sound and light mirror each other, the 'tirra lirra' flashes into her hearing as Lancelot and Lancelot's image flash into the Lady's mirror.

"Sound thus answers sound, image answers image. . . . These doublings of sound and picture—shadow answering noise, echo mirroring image—seem to compose, throughout Tennyson's poetic world, a music of landscape."

150 For ere she reached upon the tide
     The first house by the waterside,
     Singing in her song she died,
          The Lady of Shalott.

     Under tower and balcony,
155 By garden wall and gallery,
     A gleaming shape she floated by,
     Dead-pale between the houses high,
          Silent into Camelot.
     Out upon the wharfs they came,
160 Knight and burgher,° lord and dame,
     And round the prow they read her name,
          The Lady of Shalott.

     Who is this? and what is here?
     And in the lighted palace near
165 Died the sound of royal cheer;
     And they crossed themselves for fear,
     All the knights at Camelot:
     But Lancelot mused a little space;
     He said, "She has a lovely face;
170 God in his mercy lend her grace,
          The Lady of Shalott."

160. **burgher** *n.*: townsperson.

CRITICAL COMMENT

INFORMATIONAL TEXT

Escaping a World of Shadows

Readers may differ in their interpretations of the meaning or moral of the simple story this richly ornamented and carefully wrought poem tells. As you learned before you read the poem, no one should disregard the clue offered by Tennyson himself: "The newborn love for something," he said of the Lady of Shalott, "for someone in the wide world from which she had been so long secluded, takes her out of the region of shadows into that of realities." He is referring particularly to the last lines of Part II when, having watched a young bride and groom in the moonlight, the Lady declares that she is "half sick of shadows."

Like the weaving that perpetually occupies the heroine—"A magic web with colors gay"—the narrative moves from scene to scene with a tapestried grace that quietly captures the romantic heart of the Age of Chivalry. The Lady is appropriately beautiful, wan, sequestered, and mysterious. Sir Lancelot, panoplied to the hilt with every object in the book of heraldry, is less a man than a vision of a man. And Camelot itself, "many-towered," exists like a little city afloat in time.

The "mirror clear" in line 46 is crucial both to the poem's narrative line and to its meaning. In the custom of weavers, the Lady has placed this mirror in a spot facing the loom from which she is able to see at a glance how her work is going. But, for the purposes of the story, the more important function of the mirror is to allow the Lady glimpses or "shadows" of the world in which she takes no part.

Alfred, Lord Tennyson   701

DIRECT TEACHING

E Literary Focus

Word music. What musical effects are used in the last two stanzas? [Possible responses: Alliteration is used in "gallery" and "garden," "houses" and "high"; consonance is used in repeated "l" sounds and blends; assonance is used in "high" and "silent," as well as in "out," "round," and "prow"; the continued regular meter, with its repeated rhymes, carries the reader to the end of the poem.]

CRITICAL COMMENT

This feature contrasts the world of shadows—the reflections in the mirror—with the real world from which the Lady is excluded.

F Reading Informational Text

Presenting an argument. How does the author present the argument in the first paragraph? [Possible response: The author presents the argument obliquely, referring the reader to Tennyson's quotation rather than making a direct statement.]

G Reading Informational Text

Recognizing rhetorical devices. What device does the author use to present the argument in the last paragraph? [Possible response: The author focuses on the image in l. 46. The reference to a crucial image in the text itself enhances the authority of the author's interpretation—that the mirror is the meeting place of reality and reflection.]

ASSESSING

Assessment
- Holt Assessment: *Literature, Reading, and Vocabulary*

RETEACHING

For a lesson reteaching poetic devices, see **Reteaching**, p. 1129A.

INDEPENDENT PRACTICE

Response and Analysis

Reading Check

1. The Lady lives on an island in a river upstream from Camelot.
2. To avoid the curse, she must not "look down to Camelot."
3. After she hears Lancelot singing, she leaves her loom and looks out the window. As a result, the mirror cracks and the curse descends upon her.

Thinking Critically

4. The Lady, threatened with a curse if she looks at Camelot, spends all her time weaving. One day she hears Lancelot singing nearby. The climax occurs as she looks at him and at Camelot, causing her mirror to break and the curse to be activated. She finds a boat and writes her name on it; then, singing, she drifts toward Camelot as she dies.
5. The sun flames on Lancelot's "brazen greaves"; his shield sparkles; his bridle glitters like a "branch of stars." In contrast, the Lady lives in a world of shadows; even her castle is gray. The contrast is between life and a pale reflection of life or between life and death.
6. The Lady notices two young lovers and feels envious. These feelings foreshadow her falling in love with Lancelot and her decision to leave her castle. Her complaint that she is "half sick of shadows" means that she is tired of isolation and wants to experience life firsthand.
7. Possible answers: The Lady lives alone in a world of shadows while the villagers and courtiers move in a bright, lively world. The poet suggests that participation in life is alluring but may be dangerous.
8. The poem is written mostly in iambic tetrameter. (The last line of each stanza is iambic trimeter.) Many lines are trochaic and open with a stressed syllable (ll. 7–8, 10–17). The rhyme scheme is aaaabcccb. The poem's lilt comes from alliteration, as in "Willows whiten" (l. 10) and "silken-sailed" (l. 22), and assonance, as in "Listening, whispers" (l. 35). The word music creates an intricate beauty, like that of a medieval tapestry, stylized and yet emotionally expressive.

Response and Analysis

Reading Check

1. Describe where the Lady of Shalott lives in relation to the city of Camelot.
2. What must the Lady of Shalott do to avoid the curse?
3. After she hears Sir Lancelot singing, what does the Lady do? What is the result of this action?

Thinking Critically

4. Summarize the main events in the **plot** of this narrative poem. What moment marks the poem's **climax**?
5. Point out **images** of dazzling light associated with Sir Lancelot in Part III. Find **contrasting images** associated with the Lady. What do you think Tennyson is trying to achieve through this contrast? Refer to your reading notes.

INTERNET
Projects and Activities
Keyword: LE5 12-6

SKILLS FOCUS

Literary Skills Analyze sound devices in poetry.
Reading Skills Analyze contrasting images.
Writing Skills Write an essay analyzing a poem.

6. Explain why lines 66–72 could **foreshadow,** or hint at, Lancelot's arrival and the Lady's actions in the second half of the poem. What yearning do you think the Lady expresses when she exclaims, "I am half sick of shadows" (line 71)?
7. How does Tennyson **contrast** the Lady's life with the lives of the villagers and court in Camelot? Do you think that Tennyson indicates a preference for any of these ways of life? Explain.
8. Scan the poem to find its **metrical form** and **rhyme scheme.** Then, locate examples of **alliteration** and **assonance** that contribute to the poem's haunting strains. How do these examples of **word music** make you feel?

Literary Criticism

9. When Tennyson published the first version of "The Lady of Shalott" in 1832, this is how the last stanza ended:

   The web was woven curiously
   The charm is broken utterly
   Draw near and fear not—this is I,
   The Lady of Shalott.

   Compare this scenario to what occurs in the last stanza of the version you've just read. What do you think of Tennyson's revision? Which ending do you find more moving? Explain.

WRITING

Shadows and Reality

In a short **essay, analyze** the theme of "The Lady of Shalott" in light of Tennyson's comment about the Lady: "The newborn love for something, for someone in the wide world from which she had been so long secluded, takes her out of the region of shadows into that of realities." Before you begin, gather details for your analysis in a chart like the one that follows:

What happens in the poem	
Key words	
Key images	
Key passages	
Significance of comment (see above)	
Theme of poem	

Be sure to check your Quickwrite notes as you decide what Tennyson means by "the region of shadows" and "that of realities."

Literary Criticism

9. Possible answers: The first version is superior because it suggests that the Lady does not die, that she survives the curse and will find happiness at Camelot; the revised version is better because it is true to the poem's melancholy spirit.

Before You Read

Ulysses

Make the Connection
Quickwrite

An old saying claims that youth is wasted on the young—that only older people have the experience and perspective to appreciate the joys of youthful health and exuberance. Stereotypes of "proper" activities for older adults often don't take into account the skills and talents developed over a lifetime of living. Tennyson's adventure-seeking Ulysses may be pursuing a young man's dream, but why should he abandon the passions of a lifetime merely because of his age?

Some famous singers, dancers, and athletes continue their careers long after their skills have peaked. What (besides money) do you think motivates them? Jot down some notes about whether you think you would behave the same way in their place.

Literary Focus
Theme

In their works of literature, most writers attempt to convey a central idea or insight about a subject. This idea is called the **theme** of a work. It is important to note that a **subject** and a theme are not the same. A subject can be summed up in a word or two—*love* or *change*, for example. A theme, however, is a complete idea that can be stated as a sentence—*True love is a mere illusion*, or *Change is painful, but can lead to growth and discovery*. As you will see, the subject of "Ulysses" is old age. While you read the poem, ask yourself what theme, or idea, Tennyson might be expressing about this subject. How might this theme represent a view on life?

> A **theme** is the central idea or insight of a work of literature.
>
> For more on Theme, see the Handbook of Literary and Historical Terms.

Background

Ulysses (*Odysseus* in Greek) is one of the Greek leaders who fought in the ten-year-long Trojan War. Homer's epic poem the *Odyssey* tells of his equally long journey home from Troy to Ithaca. In Tennyson's poem, Ulysses, now an old king, is at home with his wife and son, Telemachus (tə·lem′ə·kəs). After an exciting life of both marvels and horrors, the old king might finally rest—either thankfully or regretfully. But here, Ulysses wants to leave home yet again and embark on a final journey. He knows lost youth cannot be regained, but he seeks something else.

Tennyson said of this poem: "'Ulysses' was written soon after Arthur Hallam's death, and gave my feeling about the need of going forward, and braving the struggle of life perhaps more simply than anything in *In Memoriam*." (*In Memoriam* is Tennyson's famous elegy to his beloved friend.)

Soldiers in battle (detail from a Greek bowl).
Alinari/Art Resource, New York.

INTERNET
More About Alfred, Lord Tennyson
Keyword: LE5 12-6

Literary Skills
Understand theme.

Alfred, Lord Tennyson

PRETEACHING

Summary at grade level

The aging Ulysses recalls his past adventures, both happy and sad, and longs for the excitement of his younger days. He rejects the security of a settled life, preferring to keep testing his limits and expanding the boundaries of his experience. In the second half of the poem, Ulysses speaks of passing on his responsibilities as a ruler to his son, Telemachus. Ulysses realizes that his true soulmates are the mariners with whom he shared his toils and troubles. He longs to set sail again with them in search of "some work of noble note."

Selection Starter

Motivate. Discuss with students the archetype of the heroic quest. What makes people set out on perilous quests? What qualities are such people expected to have? Do heroes change over time? What happens when they grow old? What do they lose? What do they gain?

DIFFERENTIATING INSTRUCTION

Learners Having Difficulty
Ask students to stop after ll. 5, 17, 32, 43, and 57 and summarize what they have read. Be sure they understand how Ulysses feels at each point about his present and past experiences. When they finish reading, ask them to speculate about Ulysses' future.

Invite learners having difficulty to read "Ulysses" in interactive format in *The Holt Reader* and to use the sidenotes as aids to understanding the selection.

English-Language Learners
For lessons designed for English-language learners and special education students, see *Holt Reading Solutions*.

Advanced Learners
Enrichment. Have students relate "Ulysses" to "Do Not Go Gentle into That Good Night" (p. 1056), a poem written by Dylan Thomas a century after Tennyson wrote this poem. Ask students whether lines such as "Old age should burn and rave at close of day" and "Rage, rage against the dying of the light" apply to Tennyson's Ulysses.

DIRECT TEACHING

A Literary Focus

Theme. How do ll. 58–61 suggest the central theme of the poem? [Possible response: In these lines, Ulysses calls for action and asserts his determination to continue pursuing adventure.]

B Content-Area Connections

Humanities: Achilles
Achilles may represent Tennyson's beloved friend Arthur Hallam, the subject of his poem *In Memoriam A.H.H.*

C Literary Focus

Theme. State the theme of "Ulysses," as expressed in the final five lines of the poem. [Possible responses: Although time may rob us of strength, we must remain true to ourselves and never stop seeking knowledge and adventures; even as life fades away, the will to live never dies.]

INDEPENDENT PRACTICE

Response and Analysis

Thinking Critically

1. Possible answers: Ulysses' present life is dull and unsatisfying compared with his spectacular, heroic past. He prefers adventure, excitement, and struggle to security, serenity, and calm.

2. Ulysses describes experience as an arch through which he sees a boundless world to be explored. He means that no matter how far he goes, the horizon always seems to recede and draw him on.

3. Ulysses addresses his loyal sailors. He says he shares with them old age, a heroic heart, and a strong will.

'Tis not too late to seek a newer world.
Push off, and sitting well in order smite
The sounding furrows;° for my purpose holds
60 To sail beyond the sunset, and the baths
Of all the western stars, until I die.
It may be that the gulfs will wash us down;
It may be we shall touch the Happy Isles,°
And see the great Achilles,° whom we knew.
65 Though much is taken, much abides; and though
We are not now that strength which in old days
Moved earth and heaven, that which we are, we are,—
One equal temper of heroic hearts,
Made weak by time and fate, but strong in will
70 To strive, to seek, to find, and not to yield.

58–59. **smite . . . furrows:** row against the waves.

63. **Happy Isles:** in Greek mythology, Elysium (ē·liz′ē·əm), where dead heroes lived for eternity.

64. **Achilles** (ə·kil′ēz′): Greek warrior and leader in the Trojan War. (See page 57.)

Response and Analysis

Thinking Critically

1. How does Ulysses contrast his past and present lives? What conclusions can you draw about his values?

2. In lines 19–21, what does Ulysses mean by his metaphor describing "all experience"?

3. Whom does Ulysses address in the second half of the poem? In the concluding lines of the poem, what qualities does he say that he shares with his mariners?

4. **Personification** is a kind of metaphor in which a nonhuman thing or quality is talked about as if it were human. Find two examples of personification in the last verse paragraph of the poem. How does this use of personification make you feel?

5. Find Ulysses' references to his wife and son. What do you think his words reveal about his feelings toward them?

6. Choose several adjectives that you feel **characterize** Ulysses. Cite evidence from the poem.

INTERNET
Projects and Activities
Keyword: LE5 12-6

SKILLS FOCUS
Literary Skills Analyze theme.
Writing Skills Write an essay analyzing theme.

Extending and Evaluating

7. What do you think of Ulysses' decision to "sail beyond the sunset"? (It may help to review your Quickwrite notes.)

WRITING

"Not to Yield"
In an **essay, analyze** the theme of this poem—the central idea about human existence that you think it reveals. Be sure to use passages from the poem to support your statement of the theme. Before you write, gather your details in a chart like the following:

Theme	
Supporting passage	
Supporting passage	
Supporting passage	

At the end of your essay, describe your response to Ulysses' decision to leave home.

706 Collection 6 The Victorian Period

---

4. Ulysses declares that old age still has "his honor and his toil" (l. 50) and speaks of the deep (the sea) moaning "with many voices" (ll. 55–56). Ulysses' personification of old age and the sea makes them seem like old companions.

5. In l. 3, he calls his wife "aged," suggesting that he no longer finds her attractive. He says that he loves his son but implies that he is dull.

6. Possible answer: Ulysses is strong-willed, independent, adventurous, and curious about what the world has to offer. He may also be regarded as restless, selfish, and irresponsible because of his desire to leave Ithaca.

Extending and Evaluating

7. Students' opinions will vary.

Robert Browning
(1812–1889)

Robert Browning (1858) by Michele Gordigiani. Oil on canvas (29″ × 23″).
By Courtesy of the National Portrait Gallery, London.

Robert Browning wrote of his first published book, a long poem about the spiritual development of a poet, that it was part of a "foolish plan." He intended, he said, to write in many forms and under different names. Browning eventually gave up this idea, but he held on to his ambition of dazzling the world with his range and variety.

Browning's education allowed him to indulge his wide-ranging interests in music, art, the history of medicine, drama, literature, entomology, and other oddly assorted topics. Browning attended boarding school briefly but was mainly educated at home in a London suburb by tutors and by his wide reading in his banker-father's extensive library. As a teenager, Browning was brilliant, undisciplined, and determined to be a poet like his idol, Percy Bysshe Shelley. After a term at the University of London, he published (at his family's expense) several poems, plays, and pamphlets, but not until he began writing the short dramatic monologues of the 1840s—poems like "My Last Duchess" and "Porphyria's Lover"—did Browning find his proper form. While Browning struggled to gain recognition for his writing, he lived comfortably at home, supported by his parents, until he married at thirty-four.

In 1845, Browning wrote to Elizabeth Barrett, already an established poet: "I do . . . love these books with all my heart—and I love you too." Barrett was then a semi-invalid in her father's London house, where she submitted to his sternly protective care. Four months after the two poets began their correspondence, they met and fell in love. They secretly married in 1846, and a week later eloped to Italy. Mr. Barrett estranged himself from his famous daughter for the rest of his life.

Browning's happy marriage confirmed his belief that only by acting boldly can one wrest what is good from an imperfect world. "I was ever a fighter," he wrote in "Prospice." He liked to see himself in strenuous but joyous contests with difficulties. In his dramatic poems, he also liked to emphasize the error, weakness, and even the viciousness of his characters.

Browning lived in Italy until Elizabeth's death in 1861, when he returned to England with their twelve-year-old son. During the 1860s, his fame began to grow. Gradually, readers understood that by asking them to figure out and judge wicked men like the Duke in "My Last Duchess," Browning was really challenging them to discover what is virtuous and healthy, when love nourishes, and when and why it kills. Browning believed that human beings must act by a moral standard, just as he believed that those who act bravely will be rewarded.

By the time of his death in 1889, Browning had won a place next to Tennyson as the other great Victorian poet. Like Tennyson, he was read as a kind of sage who assured his contemporaries that "This world's no blot for us, / Nor blank; it means intensely, and means good" ("Fra Lippo Lippi").

Before You Read

Response and Analysis

Thinking Critically

1. According to the Duke, what happened to his last Duchess?
2. Identify the **characters** in this poem, their **relationships**, and their **motives**. (Refer to your reading notes.)
3. What impression do you think the Duke intends to create by his remarks to the Count's emissary? Why might he choose to present himself in this way?
4. Assume that the emissary is an insightful person. What impression is the Duke unintentionally making? (Be sure to refer to your Quickwrite notes.)
5. What do you think of the Duke's description of his last Duchess? Do you question his assessments? Why or why not?

Extending and Evaluating

6. Read the last sentence of the poem (lines 54–56). Do you find it an effective conclusion? What—if anything—might the speaker intend to convey with such a comment?
7. Many people like to read autobiographical details into literature. Can you see any connection between the marriage in this poem and the Brownings' own marriage? (See the **Connection** on page 711.)

Literary Criticism

8. Many critics see Robert Browning as a "psychological poet," one who is more modern to us than other Victorian writers. In what sense is "My Last Duchess" an exploration of abnormal psychology and human evil? Does Browning convincingly portray the complexity of human psychology in ways that make sense to us today? Explain.

SKILLS FOCUS

Literary Skills
Analyze a dramatic monologue.

Reading Skills
Draw inferences from textual clues.

Writing Skills
Write a dramatic monologue.

Listening and Speaking Skills
Deliver a dramatic reading.

WRITING

The Duchess Talks Back

Write a **dramatic monologue,** in prose, using the voice of the Duchess. Base your monologue on an imaginary incident that could have occurred between her and the Duke—or one that the Duke himself mentions—and take into account the personality portraits of both the Duchess and the Duke.

LISTENING AND SPEAKING

Performing a Dramatic Reading

Work with a partner to prepare two dramatic readings of Browning's poem, each one conveying a different interpretation of the Duke's **tone.** (For example, his words may sound sinister if read one way, but regretful or mournful if read another way.) Use facial expressions, gestures, and tone of voice to create two distinct impressions. Be sure to pay attention to performance details, such as clarity, force, and aesthetic effect, when you perform your dramatic readings for the class.

Victorian valentine with decorative envelope showing a "penny black" stamp.
Private Collection.

712   Collection 6   The Victorian Period

INDEPENDENT PRACTICE

Response and Analysis

Thinking Critically

1. The Duke says that he gave commands and so his wife stopped smiling entirely. Students will probably conclude that he had the Duchess killed.
2. Students might create a three-column chart showing the three characters (Duke, Duchess, and listener), their relationships, and their motives. The Duke is trying to intimidate and flatter the listener to win his next Duchess and her large dowry; he wanted to control and possess his last Duchess. The listener wants to negotiate the marriage on behalf of the Count; he would therefore be interested in what happened to the last Duchess. The Duchess may have feared her husband but tried to be happy despite her marriage.
3. The Duke intends to present himself as cultured, powerful, confident, and wealthy—a man who gets what he wants. He is probably trying to impress and intimidate the emissary as a negotiating tactic.
4. The Duke unwittingly comes off as arrogant and controlling, a man who has murdered his wife out of pride and jealousy.
5. The Duke represents the Duchess's conduct as improper and insubordinate. Students will probably question his judgment, since he took no interest in the Duchess's point of view. They may think that he misinterpreted her friendliness as infidelity.

Extending and Evaluating

6. Some students may feel that this reference to a statue of Neptune taming a seahorse confirms the Duke's need for mastery; others may think that the final lines detract from the impact of learning the Duchess's tragic fate. The Duke's intention may be to impress the listener with his wealth and culture and to show that he expects perfection in his possessions.
7. Possible answers: Robert Browning admired his wife's work and treated her with respect and affection; the Duke sees his wife as a possession and expects her to bend to his will. Whereas the Brownings' "quarreling" reflects their open communication, the Duke thinks that discussing problems with his wife would be "stooping." His arrogance and insecurity lead to estrangement and tragedy.

Literary Criticism

8. The Duke is a psychopath who either fails to realize the evil of his deeds or glories in that evil. The way Browning allows the Duke's words to reveal his true nature is psychologically realistic and typical of contemporary writing.

Elizabeth Barrett Browning
(1806–1861)

Elizabeth Barrett Browning (1858) by Michele Gordigiani. Oil on canvas (73.7 cm × 58.4 cm).
By Courtesy of the National Portrait Gallery, London.

Elizabeth Barrett Browning was one of the most famous poets of her day—more successful during her lifetime than her husband, Robert Browning. She is remembered today for her *Sonnets from the Portuguese*, of which "How Do I Love Thee?" is the best known.

During her lifetime, Barrett Browning was well known as a daring, versatile poet who frequently wrote on intellectual, religious, and political matters. As a girl, she studied Greek, Latin, French, Italian, history, and philosophy—an uncommon education for a woman in nineteenth-century England. She published long narratives, a novel in verse, translations of Greek plays, and poems that dealt with the abolition of slavery, the exploitation of children in factories, religious belief, and Italian nationalism.

Through the first half of her busy literary career, Elizabeth Barrett was a semi-invalid. Her illnesses have been variously diagnosed, but it is certain that their effect was intensified by the sometimes bullying protectiveness of her father, and perhaps by the drugs routinely prescribed in those days for a "nervous collapse." She wrote to Robert Browning during their courtship, "Papa says sometimes when he comes into this room unexpectedly and convicts me of having dry toast for dinner, . . . that obstinacy and dry toast have brought me to my present condition, and if I *pleased* to have porter and beefsteaks instead, I should be as well as ever I was, in a month!"

In 1845, she met Robert Browning, and the next year they married secretly and eloped to the Continent. Her father never forgave her for the marriage (he had forbidden all his children to marry), nor did he ever see her again. Barrett Browning flourished in Italy and bore a son when she was forty-three years old: her own "young Florentine" with "brave blue English eyes."

The Browning Readers
(late 19th or early 20th century)
by Sir William Rothenstein.
Bradford Galleries and Museums, London.

PRETEACHING

Summary ⇔ *at grade level*

This Petrarchan sonnet asks the question, "How do I love thee?" and answers with several paradoxical descriptions of the way the speaker feels about her beloved. The speaker's love is divine and everyday, childlike and mature; it will include tears as well as joy, exist through life, and persist after death.

Skills Starter

Build prerequisite skills. Remind students that the other major sonnet form, the Shakespearean sonnet, generally consists of three quatrains followed by a concluding couplet and commonly has the rhyme scheme *abab cdcd efef gg*. The progression of ideas usually follows the structure of the sonnet.

VIEWING THE ART

Sir Edward Burne-Jones once said, "I mean by a picture a beautiful romantic dream of something that never was, never will be—in a light better than ever shone—in a land that no one can define or remember."

Activity. In what way does Burne-Jones's statement apply to this painting? [Possible response: The conjunction of the ruins and the young couple gives the painting a romantic, dreamlike atmosphere.]

Before You Read

Sonnet 43

Make the Connection
Quickwrite

This poem expresses an ardent, joyful love—a truly transforming love—yet it is not a blind, infatuated love. Amid the fervor, you may find hints that love must weather more than joy. What do you think the most important emotional components of love are? Jot down your thoughts.

Literary Focus
Petrarchan Sonnet

All forty-four poems in *Sonnets from the Portuguese* are written in traditional **Petrarchan,** or Italian, **sonnet** form: an octave (eight lines) and sestet (six lines) in iambic pentameter, rhyming *abbaabba cdcdcd*. Sonnet 43 does not have the usual **turn,** or break in thought, at the sestet. Rather, the poem is broken into short units of thought.

> A **Petrarchan sonnet** is a fourteen-line poem that is divided into an eight-line **octave** and a six-line **sestet.**
>
> For more on the Sonnet, see the Handbook of Literary and Historical Terms.

Background

Elizabeth Barrett Browning wrote her sonnets before her marriage, but did not show them to her husband until two years later. Reluctant to publish the poems because they were so autobiographical, she deliberately gave them a title that suggested that they were a translation into English from an original Portuguese source.

SKILLS FOCUS
Literary Skills Understand the Petrarchan sonnet form.

Love Among the Ruins (1894) by Sir Edward Burne-Jones.

714 Collection 6 The Victorian Period

DIFFERENTIATING INSTRUCTION

Learners Having Difficulty
Because this sonnet contains few concrete details, students may have difficulty following the poet's train of thought. Have students work in pairs to "count the ways," creating a numbered list of "I love thee . . ." statements to form an outline of the poem. To make sure students comprehend Barrett Browning's meaning, have them put each statement into their own words.

Invite learners having difficulty to read Sonnet 43 in interactive format in *The Holt Reader* and to use the sidenotes as aids to understanding the selection.

English-Language Learners
Make sure students realize that the words "Being" and "Grace" (l. 4), "Right" (l. 7), and "Praise" (l. 8) are capitalized because they name abstract concepts. The poet refers to the ideals of justice and Christian faith to illustrate her profound love.

Advanced Learners
Enrichment. Invite students to compare and contrast this sonnet's form and meaning with those of another sonnet they have read on the subject of love. Suggest Shakespeare's in Collection 3. You might have students hold an informal panel discussion on which sonnets speak more wisely about love.

714 Collection 6 The Victorian Period

Sonnet 43

Elizabeth Barrett Browning

How do I love thee? Let me count the ways.
I love thee to the depth and breadth and height
My soul can reach, when feeling out of sight
For the ends of Being and ideal Grace.
5 I love thee to the level of everyday's
Most quiet need, by sun and candlelight.
I love thee freely, as men strive for Right;
I love thee purely, as they turn from Praise.
I love thee with the passion put to use
10 In my old griefs, and with my childhood's faith.
I love thee with a love I seemed to lose
With my lost saints°—I love thee with the breath,
Smiles, tears, of all my life!—and, if God choose,
I shall but love thee better after death.

12. **lost saints:** childhood faith.

Angel (detail), from a tomb in the municipal cemetery of Merida, Mexico.
© Pablo Corral V/CORBIS.

Response and Analysis

Thinking Critically

1. How many distinct ways does the speaker say that she loves her beloved?
2. What do you think the poem expresses about the speaker's religious faith?
3. How are the pauses in the last three lines different in **rhythm** from those in the rest of the poem? What is the emotional effect of this change in rhythm?
4. What examples of concrete and abstract words can you find in the poem? What different emotional effects do these different words produce?

Extending and Evaluating

5. In your opinion, has Barrett Browning described all of the important emotional aspects of love? Explain your response. (Refer to your Quickwrite notes for ideas.)

WRITING

Comparing and Contrasting Literature

In a brief **essay, compare and contrast** Sonnet 43 with Shakespeare's Sonnet 116 (see page 283). Focus on the similarities and differences in the ways in which the speakers express their love. Use passages from the poems to show how word choice and imagery work together to create a specific tone for each poem.

▶ Use "Comparing and Contrasting Literature," pages 784–791, for help with this assignment.

SKILLS FOCUS

Literary Skills
Analyze a Petrarchan sonnet.

Writing Skills
Write an essay comparing and contrasting two sonnets.

Elizabeth Barrett Browning   715

SKILLS FOCUS, pp. 716–719

Grade-Level Skills
- **Literary Skills**

Analyze ways poets use sounds, including alliteration and assonance.

More About the Writer

Background. Hopkins wrote "The Wreck of the *Deutschland*" as a seminarian in his early thirties. The poem was rejected by a Jesuit journal because it seemed too difficult for readers. Nevertheless, he was encouraged to write by his spiritual superiors. Hopkins dedicated himself to his priestly vocation by serving poor parishes, yet he suffered from his sense that he was an ineffective preacher. Hopkins continued to write poetry, and his poems continued to be rejected by publishers. During his last years, Hopkins felt isolated and discouraged, both as priest and poet, and yet he wrote poems that conveyed a sense of greater peace with himself and with the world.

In 1879, ten years before his death, Hopkins wrote to his friend Robert Bridges, "No doubt my poetry errs on the side of oddness." Thirty-nine years later, when Hopkins was long dead and Bridges finally published the first of his friend's poems, the times had changed. By 1918, the only "oddness" about Hopkins's work was the fact that such modern-sounding poems had been written by a man who lived in the Victorian period. What publishers had rejected in 1879 was considered admirable and innovative in 1918, especially in the context of poetry by Yeats, Pound, and Eliot.

Gerard Manley Hopkins
(1844–1889)

Hopkins was the eldest son of highly educated parents who were devoted to the Church of England. His father, British consul general of the Hawaiian Islands, sent the young Hopkins to Highgate, a London boarding school, where he won a poetry prize and later a scholarship to study classics at Oxford University. Hopkins intended to prepare himself for the Anglican ministry, but after much soul-searching, he converted to Roman Catholicism in 1866—a radical and shocking thing to do at the time.

In 1868, when he entered the Jesuit order, Hopkins burned almost all his poetry (a few poems remain) and "resolved to write no more, as not belonging to my profession, unless it were by the wish of my superiors." He wrote no poetry for seven years, but in 1875, he was asked to write an ode in memory of five Franciscan nuns who had drowned at sea. He sent "The Wreck of the *Deutschland*" to a Jesuit periodical. The poem's form was so eccentric that the editors "dared not print it."

Hopkins, an unusually conscientious man, was ordained as a Jesuit priest in 1877 and devoted himself to the immediate demands of the priesthood. He served in parishes in poor sections of English and Scottish cities, writing sermons and ministering to the sick. He also worked as a teacher of classics at a Jesuit seminary and later as a professor of Greek at the Roman Catholic university in Dublin. In 1889, at the age of forty-four, he died of typhoid fever in Dublin.

Hopkins published one of his poems in 1863, the year he entered college, but after that only a few insignificant poems appeared during his lifetime. He composed a small but very powerful body of poetry that he sent to his friends with careful instructions about how to understand them. In his letters, he elaborated on his ideas about using the stock of native English words for the diction of his verse. Hopkins's poems are also characterized by what he called **sprung rhythm,** and by **assonance, alliteration,** and **internal rhyme.**

Hopkins attempted in his sprung rhythm to imitate the sound of natural speech. He explained: "It consists in scanning by accents or stresses alone, . . . so that a foot may be but one strong syllable or it may be many light and one strong." In conventional metrics, a foot consists of a prescribed number of stressed and unstressed syllables (an *iamb*, for example, is an unstressed syllable followed by a stressed syllable). Sprung rhythm is not concerned with using only one kind of foot in a poem; in Hopkins's poems, a line may consist of many kinds of feet: iambs, trochees, dactyls, spondees, and so on.

For a while, literary critics regarded Hopkins as a twentieth-century poet—rather than a Victorian poet—because of his strongly individual language, compression of meaning, unconventional forms, and singular sound. But Hopkins is unmistakably rooted in the nineteenth century. In his almost ecstatic love of nature, his passionate conviction of a transcendental power, and his striving for individuality, Hopkins resembled the Romantic poets. In the "terrible sonnets" of his last four years, Hopkins expressed the doubts and spiritual anguish of many late-nineteenth-century writers.

Gerard Manley Hopkins (1880). Photograph by Forshaw and Coles.
By Courtesy of the National Portrait Gallery, London.

RESOURCES: READING

Planning
- One-Stop Planner CD-ROM with ExamView Test Generator

Differentiating Instruction
- Supporting Instruction in Spanish
- Audio CD Library, Selections and Summaries in Spanish

Grammar and Language
- Daily Language Activities

Assessment
- Holt Assessment: Literature, Reading, and Vocabulary
- One-Stop Planner CD-ROM with ExamView Test Generator
- Holt Online Assessment

Internet
- go.hrw.com (Keyword: LE5 12-6)
- Elements of Literature Online

Media
- Audio CD Library
- Audio CD Library, Selections and Summaries in Spanish

Before You Read

Pied Beauty

Make the Connection
Quickwrite
Perhaps not surprising from a poet as unconventional as Hopkins, "Pied Beauty" is a song of praise to God for all things that are *pied*—that is, covered with different-colored spots. Although its topic is unusual, the poem's form echoes that of a psalm—a praise song. (See page 337 for more about psalms.)

What examples of "spotted things" do you think Hopkins will include in his poem? Write down your own list of "spotted things," and include as many synonyms for *spotted* as you can think of. Then, as you read Hopkins's poem, see if he surprises you with any startling examples—or unusual synonyms.

Literary Focus
Alliteration and Assonance
In much of his poetry, Hopkins makes liberal use of two sound devices: **alliteration**, the repetition of consonant sounds, and **assonance**, the repetition of vowel sounds. In general, these devices account for the difficulty people have in reading Hopkins. (Like tongue-twisters, Hopkins's poems can prove challenging to read aloud!) In "Pied Beauty," the repeated sounds also serve a thematic purpose. Like the creatures' colorful spots, the sounds create points of connection between otherwise unlike things—"Fresh-firecoal chestnut-falls" and "finches' wings," for example, are united by the *f* sound they share. Consider the kinds of emotions these sounds conjure as you read the poem. Try reading it aloud.

> **Alliteration** is the repetition of similar consonant sounds in words that are close to one another.
> **Assonance** is the repetition of similar vowel sounds in words that are close together.
>
> *For more on Alliteration and Assonance, see the Handbook of Literary and Historical Terms.*

Background
Hopkins composed "Pied Beauty" in 1877, shortly before he was ordained a Roman Catholic priest. This period was also marked by Hopkins's enthusiastic return to poetry after a "seven-year silence," during which Hopkins had forsworn the craft in order to devote himself to his religious studies. However, the extensive journals he kept during those seven years provided material for much of the verse he would later write. The "Landscape plotted and pieced" in "Pied Beauty," for example, had first been viewed by Hopkins in 1872 during a vacation on the Isle of Man. There, he noted, the hillsides were "plotted and painted" with square, hedged-in fields.

Literary Skills
Understand alliteration and assonance.

PRETEACHING

Summary *at grade level*

In an awed, exuberant tone, the speaker praises God for his varied creation. In ll. 2–5 the speaker presents concrete visual images of a variety of dappled, or spotted, things. In ll. 7–9 he gives special praise to all that is unconventional, surprising, or unpredictable on earth. However, in l. 10, he points out that the father of creation—unlike his dappled, surprising creatures—possesses a transcendent, unchanging beauty. The final words state the poem's theme: praise of God.

Selection Starter
Building background. Explain that most hymns of praise focus on God's peerless, unchanging qualities—power, mercy, righteousness, perfection. It is unusual for a hymn of praise to focus on the things made by God, particularly the small, odd things that this poem celebrates. Ask students to think about the feelings about God the poet communicates by rejoicing in strange, surprising aspects of creation. Keep in mind Hopkins's own comment that his poetry "errs on the side of oddness."

DIFFERENTIATING INSTRUCTION

Learners Having Difficulty
Tell students that Hopkins meant for this poem to be a mouthful, with its surprising, unfamiliar words and twisting syntax. Like many of Hopkins's other poems, "Pied Beauty" is not supposed to flow easily; rather, it is meant to make the reader pause and focus on individual images and sounds. Go over the more difficult, archaic vocabulary, and help students see each vivid picture painted by the poet. Then, read the poem aloud to let students hear the wealth of sounds he brings together.

English-Language Learners
These learners will need help with Hopkins's unusual vocabulary and invented words. Have them work with more fluent students to make up lists of unfamiliar words, and to use context clues, glosses, and a dictionary to discover their meanings.

Advanced Learners
Enrichment. Invite students to research Hopkins's "sprung rhythm," an unusual metrical line that became popular with modern English poets. Have students present oral reports on Hopkins's rhythms in which they contrast Hopkins's poems with those of other poets' using more traditional meters.

Gerard Manley Hopkins 717

Pied Beauty

Gerard Manley Hopkins

Glory be to God for dappled things—
    For skies of couple-color as a brinded° cow;
        For rose-moles all in stipple° upon trout that swim;
Fresh-firecoal chestnut-falls;° finches' wings;
5   Landscape plotted and pieced°—fold, fallow, and plow;
      And áll trádes, their gear and tackle and trim.
All things counter, original, spare, strange;
    Whatever is fickle, freckled (who knows how?)
      With swift, slow; sweet, sour; adazzle, dim;
10 He fathers-forth° whose beauty is past change:
                      Praise him.

2. **brinded** *adj.:* archaic for "brindled"; streaked with a darker color.
3. **stipple** *n.:* random dots or spots.
4. **fresh-firecoal chestnut-falls:** freshly roasted chestnuts.
5. **pieced** *adj.:* parceled into fields.
10. **fathers-forth:** creates.

Evening Shadows (late 19th or early 20th century) by Viggo Christien Frederik Wilhelm Pedersen.

Response and Analysis

Thinking Critically

1. What is the purpose of Hopkins's poem? (How does the last line state the poet's purpose?)
2. What specific examples of "pied beauty" does the poet mention in lines 2–6?
3. What do you think the poet means by saying "all things counter" (line 7)?
4. How does Hopkins use **assonance** in line 5? What do these repeated sounds help you visualize and feel emotionally?
5. How does the poet combine **alliteration** with **antithesis** (opposites) in line 9?
6. In line 10, what contrast does the poet suggest between the beauty of the physical world and the beauty of God the creator?

Extending and Evaluating

7. A highly original text is always a challenge to evaluate. Is the text's newness a breakthrough to be admired, or is it merely odd (as it first seems)? Review "Pied Beauty," and find one example each of **inverted word order**, an **unusual compound**, and an **invented word**. What is the effect of Hopkins's unusual language?

WRITING

Celebrating Beauty

Hopkins catalogs a number of dappled, or pied, things whose beauty he celebrates. Starting from your Quickwrite notes, make your own list of things that are "original, spare, strange," in Hopkins's sense. Then, write a brief **praise poem** in which you catalog and describe a number of things whose beauty *you* want to celebrate.

Praise Poems

Find Psalm 8 in a Bible. In a brief **essay, compare and contrast** this psalm with Hopkins's poem. Gather details for your essay in a chart like the following one:

	Psalm	Hopkins
Purpose of poem		
Message of poem		
Images		
Key words or passages		
Tone of poem		

▶ Use "Comparing and Contrasting Literature," pages 784–791, for help with this assignment.

Autumn Leaves (1856) by Sir John Everett Millais. Oil on canvas (41 1/16" × 57 1/16").
© Manchester City Art Galleries, England.

INTERNET
Projects and Activities
Keyword: LE5 12-6

SKILLS FOCUS

Literary Skills
Analyze alliteration and assonance.

Writing Skills
Write a praise poem. Write an essay comparing and contrasting a poem with a psalm.

Gerard Manley Hopkins   719

SKILLS FOCUS, pp. 720–724

Grade-Level Skills

- **Literary Skills**

Analyze the way an author's style achieves specific aesthetic purposes, such as creating mood.

More About the Writer

Background. Arnold began "Dover Beach" on his honeymoon in 1851, but he did not publish it until some sixteen years later. His honeymoon travels in Europe inspired several other poems; he described them as "not merely an effort and a labor, but an actual tearing of oneself to pieces." Devoting most of his professional life to the work of educational reform, Arnold focused particularly on British secondary education. In defining his second career as a critic, Arnold said that the goal of criticism should be "to see the object as in itself it really is." He also said, "Poetry is nothing less than the most perfect speech of man, that in which he comes nearest to being able to utter the truth."

Matthew Arnold
(1822–1888)

Portrait of Matthew Arnold (1880) by George Frederic Watts.
By Courtesy of the National Portrait Gallery, London.

Unlike the other major Victorian poets, Matthew Arnold achieved fame as both a poet and a critic. He is as famous today for his essays of literary and social criticism as he is for his poetry. His poems stand with the achievements of Tennyson and Browning, their quiet tones and carefully shaped figures of speech expressing his reflections on what Victorian society was like, what it would become, and what it had cost.

Arnold had difficulty in his youth living up to the expectations of his famous father, Dr. Thomas Arnold, one of the leading thinkers of the Victorian era and headmaster of Rugby School. An uneven student at Rugby, Arnold nevertheless won a scholarship to Oxford University in 1841. Although he was less than enthusiastic as a student, he seemed to thoroughly enjoy playing the role of a dandy. His performance at Oxford was a failure by Rugby standards, and he graduated without knowing what he wanted to do.

Arnold had won prizes for his poetry at both Rugby and Oxford. In 1849, he published his first book of poetry, *The Strayed Reveller*, to mixed reviews. Two more volumes of poetry followed in 1852 and 1853, and as a result Arnold was elected an Oxford professor of poetry in 1857.

After his marriage in 1851, Arnold became a government inspector of schools for poor children, a job he held for thirty-five years. His work was exhausting, requiring him to travel all over England and write daily reports. Though he continued to write poetry in his free time, he found it increasingly difficult. In 1853, he told a friend, "I am past thirty, and three parts iced over—and my pen, it seems to me, is even stiffer and more cramped than my feeling."

After 1860, Arnold almost completely stopped writing poetry and began a second career as a critic. His travels and his work had given him firsthand knowledge of pressing social problems, and he became an energetic essayist and lecturer on literary, political, social, and religious questions. In his essays on literature and religion, Arnold urges his readers to acquire a knowledge of history and to study "the best that has been thought and known in the world"—the Greeks, Dante, and Shakespeare—in order to judge ideas and personal conduct. Without the steadying influence of what he called culture, Arnold warns, the nineteenth century's technological and political changes would accelerate into a grossly materialistic democracy.

All through his life, Arnold knew both the excitement of trying to change the temper of his age and the loneliness of not being comfortable in his own time.

RESOURCES: READING

Planning
- One-Stop Planner CD-ROM with ExamView Test Generator

Differentiating Instruction
- Holt Reading Solutions
- The Holt Reader
- Supporting Instruction in Spanish
- Audio CD Library, Selections and Summaries in Spanish

Grammar and Language
- Daily Language Activities

Assessment
- Holt Assessment: Literature, Reading, and Vocabulary
- One-Stop Planner CD-ROM with ExamView Test Generator
- Holt Online Assessment

Internet
- go.hrw.com (Keyword: LE5 12-6)
- Elements of Literature Online

Media
- Audio CD Library
- Audio CD Library, Selections and Summaries in Spanish

Before You Read

Dover Beach

Make the Connection
Quickwrite

Where do people look for answers in times of crisis? Do they look to science? to religion? to government? Enormous problems may seem to call for sweeping solutions. Instead of thinking big, however, what if we thought *small*? Arnold reminds people that they can also look to personal relationships to find the hope, love, and integrity that can make sense of a disordered world.

What do you think people cling to in troubled times? Write down a short list of people, places, or things you value and depend on the most when times are tough.

Literary Focus
Mood

Arnold creates a mood that shifts at certain points in the poem like the ebb and flow of the tide he describes. **Mood** is the feeling, or **atmosphere,** in a work created by the writer's choice of descriptive details, images, and sounds.

> **Mood** is the atmosphere in a literary work.
>
> *For more on Mood, see the Handbook of Literary and Historical Terms.*

At the Gallery (late 19th or early 20th century) by Paul Gustav Fischer.

Background
Arnold's first draft of "Dover Beach" dates from 1851, when he and his wife spent a night at Dover during their honeymoon trip on the English coast. Many of the beaches in the British Isles consist of round, gray pebbles, not sand. Arnold describes the sound of the sea receding over the pebbles as a "grating roar."

Literary Skills
Understand mood.

Matthew Arnold   721

PRETEACHING

Summary *at grade level*

The speaker is looking out at Dover Beach on the English coast. It is a moonlit night, and he calls his beloved to the window to breathe the sweet night air. He hears the endless roar of the waves, a sound that suggests eternal sadness. The speaker remarks that the ancient Greek dramatist Sophocles heard the same sound long ago, and it also reminded him of the ebb and flow of human misery. According to the speaker, the Sea of Faith, once full like the tide, is now retreating. He cries out to his beloved, imploring that they be true to one another. The world may seem beautiful and fresh but is actually full of cruelty, uncertainty, and meaningless conflict. Therefore, consolation can be found only in love.

Selection Starter

Build background. Explain that Arnold was writing at a time when scientific discoveries threatened to undermine traditional beliefs (the "Sea of Faith"). Political upheavals were also eroding social stability. In 1848, just three years before Arnold began writing this poem, several European countries were rocked by rebellions. Arnold may have been referring to these conflicts in "a darkling plain / Swept with confused alarms of struggle and flight, / Where ignorant armies clash by night." Arnold felt that art should unify a culture, a function traditionally served by religion. He proclaimed it the duty of the art critic "to make the best that has been thought and known in the world current everywhere."

DIFFERENTIATING INSTRUCTION

Learners Having Difficulty
Ask students to identify each complete thought in "Dover Beach" by disregarding the breaks at the ends of lines and by interpreting the semicolons and dash as periods. Also, ask students to clarify pronoun referents when they read by replacing the word "it" each time with the noun to which it refers. Invite learners having difficulty to read "Dover Beach" in interactive format in *The Holt Reader* and to use the sidenotes as aids to understanding the selection.

English-Language Learners
For lesson plans designed for English-language learners and special education students, see *Holt Reading Solutions*.

Matthew Arnold   721

Dover Beach

Matthew Arnold

The sea is calm tonight.
The tide is full, the moon lies fair
Upon the straits°—on the French coast the light
Gleams and is gone; the cliffs of England stand,
5   Glimmering and vast, out in the tranquil bay.
Come to the window, sweet is the night air!
Only, from the long line of spray
Where the sea meets the moon-blanched land,
Listen! you hear the grating roar
10 Of pebbles which the waves draw back, and fling,
At their return, up the high strand,°
Begin, and cease, and then again begin,
With tremulous cadence slow, and bring
The eternal note of sadness in.

15 Sophocles° long ago
Heard it on the Aegean,° and it brought
Into his mind the turbid ebb and flow
Of human misery; we
Find also in the sound a thought,
20 Hearing it by this distant northern sea.

The Sea of Faith
Was once, too, at the full, and round earth's shore
Lay like the folds of a bright girdle° furled.
But now I only hear
25 Its melancholy, long, withdrawing roar,
Retreating, to the breath
Of the night wind, down the vast edges drear
And naked shingles° of the world.

Ah, love, let us be true
30 To one another! for the world, which seems
To lie before us like a land of dreams,
So various, so beautiful, so new,
Hath really neither joy, nor love, nor light,
Nor certitude, nor peace, nor help for pain;
35 And we are here as on a darkling plain
Swept with confused alarms of struggle and flight,
Where ignorant armies clash by night.

---

3. straits *n. pl.*: Strait of Dover, a body of water separating southeastern England and northwestern France.

11. strand *n.*: shore.

15. Sophocles (säf'ə·klēz') (c. 496–406 B.C.): writer of tragedies in ancient Greece.
16. Aegean (ē·jē'ən): sea between Greece and Turkey.

23. girdle *n.*: belt.

28. shingles *n. pl.*: here, beaches covered with pebbles.

(Opposite) *Pegwell Bay, Kent—A Recollection of October 5, 1858* (1859–1860) by William Dyce.
Tate Gallery, London.

CRITICAL COMMENT

INFORMATIONAL TEXT

Love Is Itself a Faith

More than any other poem written in the nineteenth century, "Dover Beach" continues to echo through the consciousness of every new generation. To say why involves matters of both technique and meaning.

Compared with the characteristic product of the Romantic or Victorian poets, "Dover Beach" is low-keyed. The speaker's tone is largely that of quiet conversation. For all its conversational tone, however, the poem is remarkably ambitious in its claim to render a universal condition.

Unlike his predecessors and contemporaries, Arnold neither reaches for the sublime nor dwells on the sentimental in this poem. Instead, he writes a love poem that, incidentally, expresses the crisis of conscience brought about by the dwindling of religion—"the Sea of Faith"—and by the rise of science. Science has transformed human life through industrialism and through the mass warfare that scientific inventions have made possible. Against these bewildering developments, Arnold poses the notion that love is itself a faith to cling to and, by implication, that individual integrity and a humanistic vision broad enough to include the tragic conclusions of Sophocles are the only defenses against a world moving toward anarchy.

Comparing and Contrasting Texts

Arnold Versus Wordsworth. Have the students compare Wordsworth's "The World Is Too Much with Us" (p. 561) with Arnold's poem. Ask the following questions:

1. What similarities in outlook do you see in the poems? [Possible responses: nostalgia for an age in which people had faith; disgust with humanity's pettiness; the importance of the sea in recalling a time when human beings treasured the spiritual.]

2. What differences in outlook do you see in the poems? [Possible responses: Whereas Wordsworth's speaker is mainly distressed that people have lost the ability to find spiritual value in nature, Arnold seems distressed for the future of humanity; Wordsworth's speaker finds no consolation other than nostalgia for the past, whereas Arnold's speaker finds comfort in love.]

DIRECT TEACHING

CRITICAL COMMENT

This feature focuses on Arnold's faith, expressed in "Dover Beach," that love can provide comfort as religion did before science and industrialism transformed society.

E Reading Informational Text

❓ **Expressing an opinion.** Do you agree with this author's description of "Dover Beach" as a love poem? Why or why not? [Possible responses: Agree—the speaker's response to the sadness and uncertainty he sees is to reaffirm his love of one person; disagree—"Dover Beach" is only secondarily a love poem, since the speaker's primary concern is the spiritual emptiness of the modern era.]

F Reading Informational Text

❓ **Identifying the main idea.** What is the main idea of this Critical Comment? [Possible response: The speaker in "Dover Beach" seeks comfort from the torments of modern life in a faithful love.]

VIEWING THE ART

William Dyce (1806–1864) was a Scottish painter, designer, and writer who gained prominence in the 1840s. The setting of this painting is late afternoon. The weathered cliffs suggest the passage of time, whereas the figures on the shore remind the viewer how short human life is.

Activity. Ask students to describe the mood of the painting. [Possible response: The brown tones of the painting, the low tide, and the forlorn child with the shovel create a somber mood.]

INDEPENDENT PRACTICE

Response and Analysis

Thinking Critically

1. Possible answers: It is night in a room overlooking the sea in Dover, England. The speaker seems to be an educated man, addressing a loved one.

2. Possible answer: The mood is calm, peaceful, content. This mood is created by images of the calm sea, clear moonlight, and tall cliffs. This beginning establishes a context of beauty and serenity against which the chaos and ignorance of humanity play.

3. Possible answer: The "grating roar" and the sea flinging pebbles introduce a note of uneasiness, perhaps warning of danger.

4. Possible answer: The speaker says that Sophocles heard the sea's "eternal note of sadness." It reminded him of the "ebb and flow / Of human misery."

5. Possible answer: The "Sea of Faith" (a metaphor for religious belief) once surrounded the world, encompassing it like the folds of a bright belt that supported the earth and made it beautiful (a simile that extends the metaphor). These figures of speech evoke a deep nostalgia for something lost. The speaker's own faith has weakened, leaving him as barren and restless as the beaches he describes.

6. Possible answer: The speaker urges that he and his love be true to each other, as life is difficult, painful, and uncertain. His faith in love offers a possible solution to his unhappiness over the human condition. (Students may have listed similar consolations in their notes.)

7. Possible answer: The speaker sees the world as chaotic, painful, and joyless. This view is still relevant because of the struggles of competing nations and worldviews, complicated by the existence of weapons of mass destruction.

Response and Analysis

Thinking Critically

1. What is the **setting** of the first stanza? Who is the speaker, and whom is he addressing?

2. What **mood** do the first six lines evoke for you? What details in these lines establish that mood?

3. What **images** in the second half of the first stanza begin to change this mood? What emotions do these images evoke?

4. What does the speaker imagine Sophocles also heard long ago? What did the sound bring to Sophocles' mind?

5. Explain the **figure of speech** used to describe faith in lines 21–23. What do you think has happened to the speaker's faith, according to lines 24–28?

6. What does the speaker urge in the last stanza, and why? (How does the speaker's resolution compare with your Quickwrite notes?)

7. Describe the speaker's view of the world as it is presented in the last stanza. Is this view still relevant to today's world? Do "ignorant armies" still "clash by night"? Explain your response to this final image.

INTERNET
Projects and Activities
Keyword: LE5 12-6

SKILLS FOCUS

Literary Skills
Analyze mood.

Writing Skills
Write a reflective essay. Write an essay analyzing a poem.

Extending and Evaluating

8. When Arnold wrote his poem in the mid-1800s, industrialization and scientific advances had brought both improvements and problems. How does Arnold's poem express the paradox of progress felt by the Victorians? How is progress still a paradox for us today—that is, how does progress both help us and threaten or confuse us?

WRITING

Dover Beach Reflections

In a personal **essay**, reflect on a line or an image from "Dover Beach" that you think has special relevance to life today. In your essay, quote the line or image exactly. Be as specific as you can in your response to the quotation.

▶ Use "Writing a Reflective Essay," pages 656–663, for help with this assignment.

A World of Contrasts

Arnold begins his poem with a moonlit sea and ends it with a dark plain. Write a brief **essay** in which you **analyze** the contrasting imagery in "Dover Beach." Discuss how the contrasting images reinforce the theme of the poem.

Matthew Arnold (1871), illustration published in *Vanity Fair*.

Extending and Evaluating

8. Possible answer: The paradox seems to be that attempts to create a better world often result in a world that many people find alien and inhospitable. Examples today might include the conflict between developed and developing nations or between those advocating scientific innovation and those who fear that it is creating a less humane world.

ASSESSING

Assessment
- Holt Assessment: *Literature, Reading, and Vocabulary*

RETEACHING

For a lesson reteaching author's tone and style, see **Reteaching**, p. 1129A.

A. E. Housman
(1859–1936)

Alfred Edward Housman (1926) by Francis Dodd. Pencil drawing (14¾" × 10¾").

Housman said that he was careful not to think of poetry while he was shaving, for "if a line of poetry strays into my memory, my skin bristles so that the razor ceases to act." For Housman, poetry was all feeling. The feelings produced physical effects (shivers along the spine, tears, the sensation of being pierced by a spear) that came from what Housman said was the source of his own poems, "the pit of the stomach."

Housman's poetry is more restrained than his comments suggest. His poems evoke a narrow range of subdued feelings that are controlled by simple, tight verse forms and clear language and syntax.

Alfred Edward Housman was born in Worcestershire in western England, the oldest of seven children. He was close to his mother, who died on his twelfth birthday. His father, a lawyer, allowed his practice, money, and talent to dwindle away in despondency and drink. At sixteen, Housman won a scholarship to Oxford, where he prepared for a career as a scholar and teacher of classical literature. He attended classes irregularly, though, preferring to study on his own, and in the end failed his final examinations.

In 1882, Housman entered the civil service as a clerk in the patent office, determined to prove himself as a classical scholar despite his failure at Oxford. For the next ten years, he set himself a rigorous program: writing and publishing papers on Greek and Latin literature while working as a patent clerk. In 1892, his series of scholarly papers won him an appointment as professor of Latin at London University. He stayed until 1911, when he moved to Cambridge University as professor of Latin and fellow at Trinity College. Housman spent the rest of his life as a formal and rather aloof teacher and an authority in classical scholarship.

During his lifetime, Housman published only two books of poetry containing a little more than one hundred poems. His first collection, *A Shropshire Lad* (1896), became popular because its graceful recollection of youthful pleasures and their transience fit a late-century mood of disillusionment in a world that had "much good, but much less good than ill." In "Terence, This Is Stupid Stuff," Housman acknowledged that his poems could be dismissed as self-indulgent bellyaching. The test of poetry, he believed, is not what is said but how it is said. In the refined elegance of his poems, he expressed his pessimistic vision of a cold, empty world. Unlike the major Romantic and Victorian poets who preceded him, Housman saw no hope of improvement or change, but only the possibility of enduring and making bearable the painful conditions of human existence.

For Independent Reading

The following poems by Housman are among his most popular:
- "When I was One-and-Twenty"
- "Loveliest of Trees"

PRETEACHING

Summary 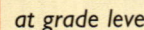 *at grade level*

The speaker addresses a young athlete who once received the townspeople's adulation and was carried aloft in victory. Now the young man's body is held high in a funeral procession. The speaker claims that the athlete is lucky to have died young, as he will never see his records surpassed or his name forgotten. Instead, he will amaze the "strengthless" dead with his unfading youth and glory.

Selection Starter

Motivate. Ask students to think of famous people who have died young (such as Princess Diana). Encourage them to discuss the feelings evoked by the news that someone young and famous has died: shock, sadness over the years not yet lived, awareness of the frailty of all human life. As they read this poem, ask students to speculate on the age of the speaker. Is he a contemporary of the young athlete being buried, or is he someone much older? How does the speaker's age affect the meaning and emotional power of the poem?

Before You Read

To an Athlete Dying Young

Make the Connection
Quickwrite

The strong, healthy athletes who earn fame and fortune seem to live charmed lives. But what happens when the cheering stops? When an athlete dies in the prime of life and at the peak of fame, devoted supporters discover a very sobering truth: Even these remarkable young men and women are not invincible.

At what age do you think you might be in the prime of your life—in top physical and mental condition? What do you hope to be doing at that time? Jot down a few thoughts.

Literary Focus
Couplet

"To an Athlete Dying Young" is written entirely in couplets. A **couplet** is a pair of lines, one after another, that rhyme. The lines in a couplet usually share the same meter as well. In Housman's poem, each couplet is joined with another to form a four-line stanza. The strong rhythm created by this pattern fits the poem's somber subject matter—death—and mimics the slow, mournful tempo of a funeral procession.

> A **couplet** consists of two consecutive lines of poetry that rhyme.
>
> *For more on Couplets, see the Handbook of Literary and Historical Terms.*

SKILLS FOCUS

Literary Skills Understand couplets.

Background

"To an Athlete Dying Young" appeared in 1896 in the first edition of *A Shropshire Lad,* a volume Housman himself paid to have published. The poet scarcely made a profit from this book of sixty-three verses, which often tell stories in the voice of a young soldier or farm boy. However, Housman lived to see his poems become enormously popular during the Boer War. Soldiers fighting in South Africa identified with the homesick lad from Shropshire and heard in his voice the echo of their own melancholy.

Speed skater racing at the 1994 Winter Olympics.
© Karl Weatherly/CORBIS.

726 Collection 6 The Victorian Period

DIFFERENTIATING INSTRUCTION

Learners Having Difficulty
The poem's somewhat archaic diction and sentence structure may be difficult for some readers, but the simple, touching subject—an athlete who has died young—is likely to appeal to them. Listening to a volunteer read the poem aloud will help their comprehension. Have students work in pairs to paraphrase what the speaker is saying to the dead athlete in each stanza.

English-Language Learners
Point out that l. 2 includes a noun converted into a verb: "chaired." Ask students to name other English verbs, such as *faxed, lunched,* and *videotaped,* that have developed from nouns. Then, explain the use of "shoulder-high." In l. 4, the athlete is carried on the townspeople's shoulders to celebrate his victory; in l. 5, his body is carried "home" to be buried.

Advanced Learners
Enrichment. Point out that Housman's poem contains several references to the classical world: the laurels worn by the victorious athlete (ll. 11, 25, and 28) and the ancient Greek concept of an afterlife in Hades (ll. 8 and 26). Encourage students to research the athletic customs of the ancient Greeks and Romans, as well as their concept of the afterlife.

TO AN ATHLETE DYING YOUNG

A. E. Housman

The time you won your town the race
We chaired you through the marketplace;
Man and boy stood cheering by,
And home we brought you shoulder-high.

5 Today, the road all runners come,
Shoulder-high we bring you home,
And set you at your threshold down,
Townsman of a stiller town.

Smart lad, to slip betimes° away
10 From fields where glory does not stay
And early though the laurel° grows
It withers quicker than the rose.

Eyes the shady night has shut
Cannot see the record cut,
15 And silence sounds no worse than cheers
After earth has stopped the ears:

Now you will not swell the rout
Of lads that wore their honors out,
Runners whom renown outran
20 And the name died before the man.

So set, before its echoes fade,
The fleet foot on the sill of shade,
And hold to the low lintel° up
The still-defended challenge cup.

25 And round that early-laureled head
Will flock to gaze the strengthless dead,
And find unwithered on its curls
The garland briefer than a girl's.

---

9. **betimes** *adv.:* archaic for "early."
11. **laurel** *n.:* classical symbol of victory. Victorious Greek and Roman athletes were crowned with laurel wreaths.
23. **lintel** *n.:* top of a door frame.

The Scottish athlete Eric Liddell (known as the Flying Scotsman) (1902–1945) winning the 440-yard race at the Amateur Athletics Association championships in 1924.
© Getty Images.

Connection

Summary 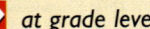 at grade level

This feature describes the elaborate rituals with which Victorians observed the death of loved ones. Customs included tolling bells and wearing mourning garments for fixed periods. At funerals, undertakers often provided professional mourners, called mutes, who were supposed to lend an air of melancholy to the proceedings.

DIRECT TEACHING

A Reading Skills

Synthesizing. What connection can you see between the custom of the "passing bell" and the famous line from John Donne's Meditation 17, "And therefore never send to know for whom the bell tolls; it tolls for thee"? [Possible response: The passing bell honors the dead and reminds the living that they too will die.]

B Reading Informational Text

Recognizing implicit assumptions. Why do you think the writer includes the information about the mutes? [Possible response: The writer probably expects that many readers will be unfamiliar with this custom.]

C Content-Area Connections

Culture: Mourning Customs
Ask students to identify vestiges of customary Victorian mourning dress in contemporary mourning practices. [Possible responses: People still tend to wear black clothes to funerals. Athletes often wear black armbands in honor of a deceased teammate.]

CONNECTION / HISTORY

Housman's poems somberly explore death. In the following excerpt, Daniel Pool explains the rituals the Victorians developed to respond to death.

Death and Other Grave Matters   INFORMATIONAL TEXT

Daniel Pool

Death—early death—was no stranger to the nineteenth-century English family, and perhaps that is why they loved to weep over the lingering demises of Dickens's small heroes and heroines. Certainly, they made a big production out of it in every other respect.

In some rural communities the ritual began even before one died, with the ringing of a "passing bell" in the parish church to signal that a member of the community lay on his or her deathbed. Characteristically, the bell tolled six times to indicate the passing of a woman, nine (the famous "nine tailors") to indicate the passing of a man, followed by a peal for each year of the dying person's life.

When a person died, a large funeral was held with everyone dressed in black (unless the deceased were a child or a young, unmarried girl, when the costume was white); mourners received black gloves and black scarfs. . . .

In most communities, funerals were an important social event, and propriety and due regard for the family's social standing necessitated that they be done right. . . . Characteristically, the undertaker would provide professional mourners, or "mutes," dressed in black to stand about and lend dignity to the affair. "There's an expression of melancholy in his face, my dear," says Mr. Sowerberry, the undertaker, to his wife when he takes on Oliver Twist as an apprentice, "which is very interesting. He would make a delightful mute, my love . . . I don't mean a regular mute to attend grown-up people, my dear, but only for children's practice. It would be very new to have a mute in proportion." When the body was actually brought to the gravesite for burial, there was often an additional tolling of the bells—the death knell—to let the parish know of the final laying to rest of the deceased. . . .

The departed were always to be mourned for specifically prescribed periods of time, which, in practice, affected mostly the clothes the survivors were permitted to wear and whether they could have fun or not. Men had it easy; they needed only to wear black armbands, a custom adopted from the military in the early years of the century. Women, however, were supposed to dress all in black. "My dear Celia," says Lady Catherine Chettam of Dorothea Casaubon [in George Eliot's novel *Middlemarch*] after her husband's death, "a widow must wear mourning at least a year." This meant an all-black wardrobe (the so-called widow's weeds), frequently of bombazine, a material especially favored because it did not gleam in light, and no jewelry or ornaments except for beads made of jet, a kind of coal. . . . A widow was expected to mourn her husband for two years, but she could moderate her funereal clothing a bit after a while to "half mourning," which consisted of pinstripe black. Parents and children were to be mourned for a year, a brother, sister, or grandparent for six months, an uncle or aunt for three months, and a first cousin got six weeks. (In-laws were mourned too, but for lesser periods of time.) Some women remained in their mourning garb for the rest of their lives. . . .

Of course, the lead in this fashionable mourning was set in part by the queen. After the death of her beloved Albert in 1861 until her own death in 1901, portraits generally show Victoria in the somber black and white attire suitable for honoring the memory of a late departed.

—from *What Jane Austen Ate and Charles Dickens Knew*

728   Collection 6   The Victorian Period

Response and Analysis

Thinking Critically

1. What parallel events are described in the first and second stanzas? What is the significance of repeating "shoulder-high"?
2. In line 9, why does the speaker call the athlete "smart"?
3. According to details in lines 13–20, what failures will the athlete miss, having died young? Do you think the speaker means what he says in lines 9–20? Explain.
4. What scene do you visualize in the last two stanzas of the poem? (Where is the athlete now?)
5. Think about the rituals described in the **Connection** on page 728. What emotions are the death rituals intended to express? Does "To an Athlete Dying Young" express similar sentiments or drastically different ones? Explain.
6. Poets can use **exact rhyme** (*June/moon*) or **half rhyme,** also called approximate rhyme (*moon/man*). Look at the end rhymes in Housman's poem. What pattern of rhyming sounds do you hear? Where do you hear half rhymes?
7. Housman also creates verbal music by using **alliteration,** the repetition of the same consonant sounds in words that are close together. Where do you hear alliteration in this poem?
8. The speaker suggests that it's best to die at one's peak, before glory begins to fade. Think about your Quickwrite notes, and then explain your response to this idea.

WRITING

Shakespeare's Influence

Renaissance poetry (see Collection 3) often dealt with the three timeless themes of love, death, and the ravages of time. Housman claimed that he was particularly influenced by Shakespeare's "Fear No More the Heat o' the Sun" (see page 288). In a short **essay, compare and contrast** the tone and message of Housman's poem with those of Shakespeare's song. Use details from the texts to support your comparisons.

▶ Use "Comparing and Contrasting Literature," pages 784–791, for help with this assignment.

LISTENING AND SPEAKING

Hearing Housman

Prepare this poem for a group reading. Before you read, decide how many readers you want to use. Also scan the poem before your reading to see what meter Housman uses. Where will you pause? Where will you make complete stops? How will you vary your reading so that the poem doesn't sound singsong?

Florence Griffith-Joyner (1959–1998) in action (1988).
© Duomo/CORBIS.

INTERNET
Projects and Activities
Keyword: LE5 12-6

SKILLS FOCUS

Literary Skills
Analyze couplets.

Writing Skills
Write an essay comparing and contrasting a poem with a song.

Listening and Speaking Skills
Read a poem aloud.

INDEPENDENT PRACTICE

Response and Analysis

4. Possible answer: The dead athlete is stepping over the threshold of the afterlife, where the spirits of the dead will gather to gaze upon him in wonder, since they lack his youth and strength.
5. Possible answer: "Death and Other Grave Matters" describes rituals meant to honor the dead and comfort the living. The writer displays a slightly irreverent attitude toward these rituals. Housman's poem mentions only the custom of the funeral procession. The comfort Housman offers is that everyone dies and most people die long after their achievements have been forgotten.
6. Each couplet ends with a rhyming sound. Half-rhymes appear in ll. 5–6: *come, home*.
7. Alliteration appears throughout the poem. Lines such as "Townsman of a stiller town" and "Runners whom renown outran" are good examples.
8. Some students may prefer a short, successful career of brilliant accomplishment; others may prefer to live a full span of years and experience both success and failure.

ASSESSING

Assessment
■ *Holt Assessment: Literature, Reading, and Vocabulary*

RETEACHING

For a lesson reteaching author's tone and style, see **Reteaching,** p. 1129A.

Thinking Critically

1. Possible answer: Both stanzas mention being brought home "shoulder-high" by a crowd. In the first case, the living athlete is carried on the shoulders of his rejoicing townsman; in the second case, pallbearers carry his body to the grave. The repetition emphasizes the ironic parallel between the two processions.
2. Possible answer: The speaker suggests that the athlete is clever to depart at the prime of life rather than lingering on after his glory has passed.
3. He will miss seeing his records broken and his achievements forgotten. Most students will feel that the speaker's words, although tinged with irony, are sincere.

DIRECT TEACHING

A Literary Focus

Style. What impression of the narrator do you get from the style of this passage describing the night of carousing at the station? [Possible response: He seems like a genial Englishman who is slightly cynical about the pros and cons of serving the Empire abroad and condescending toward the native people, as shown by his insulting reference to the "Fuzzies."]

B Reading Skills

Identifying conflicts and resolutions. What conflict is set in motion here? How might it be resolved? [Possible response: By putting his cigar out on the statue's forehead, Fleete commits a sacrilege against Hanuman, a Hindu divinity. Given the epigraph about Asian gods and devils, Fleete may suffer for committing this insult.]

C Literary Focus

Allusion. How is this direct allusion to the Book of Revelation related to the story at this point? [Possible response: It suggests, ironically, that Fleete—and not Hanuman—is the "beast," since Fleete has set his mark on the forehead of the statue.]

---

should lie They profited by their new security, for they tried to play pool with a curled-up hedgehog found in the garden, and one of them carried the marker round the room in his teeth. Half a dozen planters had come in from the south and were talking "horse" to the Biggest Liar in Asia, who was trying to cap all their stories at once. Everybody was there, and there was a general closing up of ranks and taking stock of our losses in dead or disabled that had fallen during the past year. It was a very wet night, and I remember that we sang "Auld Lang Syne" with our feet in the Polo Championship Cup, and our heads among the stars, and swore that we were all dear friends. Then some of us went away and annexed Burma, and some tried to open up the Sudan and were opened up by Fuzzies⁴ in that cruel scrub outside Suakim,⁵ and some found stars and medals, and some were married, which was bad, and some did other things which were worse, and the others of us stayed in our chains and strove to make money on insufficient experiences.

Fleete began the night with sherry and bitters, drank champagne steadily up to dessert, then raw, rasping Capri with all the strength of whiskey, took benedictine with his coffee, four or five whiskeys and sodas to improve his pool strokes, beer and bones⁶ at half-past two, winding up with old brandy. Consequently, when he came out, at half-past three in the morning, into fourteen degrees of frost, he was very angry with his horse for coughing, and tried to leapfrog into the saddle. The horse broke away and went to his stables; so Strickland and I formed a Guard of Dishonor to take Fleete home.

---

4. **Fuzzies:** Sudanese natives. British soldiers gave them this name because of their long, frizzy hair. In the poem "Fuzzy-Wuzzy" (1890), Kipling calls the Sudanese soldier "a first-class fightin' man."
5. **Suakim:** Suakin (swä′kən), Sudan; city on the Red Sea.
6. **bones:** *n. pl.:* dice.

734   Collection 6   The Victorian Period

Our road lay through the bazaar, close to a little temple of Hanuman, the Monkey-god, who is a leading divinity worthy of respect. All gods have good points, just as have all priests. Personally, I attach much importance to Hanuman, and am kind to his people—the great gray apes of the hills. One never knows when one may want a friend.

There was a light in the temple, and as we passed we could hear voices of men chanting hymns. In a native temple the priests rise at all hours of the night to do honor to their god. Before we would stop him, Fleete dashed up the steps, patted two priests on the back, and was gravely grinding the ashes of his cigar butt in to the forehead of the red stone image of Hanuman. Strickland tried to drag him out, but he sat down and said solemnly:

"Shee that? Mark of the B—beasht! *I* made it. Ishn't it fine?"

In half a minute the temple was alive and noisy, and Strickland, who knew what came of polluting gods, said that things might occur. He, by virtue of his official position, long residence in the country, and weakness for going among the natives, was known to the priests and he felt unhappy. Fleete sat on the ground and refused to move. He said that "good old Hanuman" made a very soft pillow.

Then, without any warning, a Silver Man came out of a recess behind the image of the god. He was perfectly naked in that bitter, bitter cold, and his body shone like frosted silver, for he was what the Bible calls "a leper as white as snow." Also he had no face, because he was a leper of some years' standing, and his disease was heavy upon him. We two stooped to haul Fleete up, and the temple was filling and filling with folk who seemed to spring from the earth, when the Silver Man ran in under our arms,

Vocabulary
divinity (də·vin′ə·tē) *n.:* god; sacred being.

CONTENT-AREA CONNECTIONS

Medicine: Leprosy
In the past, people with leprosy, a disease that corrodes human flesh, were forced to live in isolation from others for fear of contagion. Scientists today know that leprosy is only mildly contagious and can be treated, although a permanent cure is yet to be found. In Kipling's day, however, the fear of leprosy was intense and almost universal. In one particular type of leprosy, the mucous membranes of the eyes, nose, and throat become infected, and the voice may change dramatically. In addition, appendages such as the nose, fingers, and toes can become brittle and break off.
Individual activity. Ask students to research information about the recent developments in the treatment of leprosy.

making a noise exactly like the mewing of an otter, caught Fleete round the body and dropped his head on Fleete's breast before we could wrench him away. Then he retired to a corner and sat mewing while the crowd blocked all the doors.

The priests were very angry until the Silver Man touched Fleete. That nuzzling seemed to sober them.

At the end of a few minutes' silence one of the priests came to Strickland and said, in perfect English, "Take your friend away. He has done with Hanuman but Hanuman has not done with him." The crowd gave room and we carried Fleete into the road.

Strickland was very angry. He said that we might all three have been knifed, and that Fleete should thank his stars that he had escaped without injury.

Fleete thanked no one. He said that he wanted to go to bed. He was gorgeously drunk.

We moved on, Strickland silent and wrathful, until Fleete was taken with violent shivering fits and sweating. He said that the smells of the bazaar were overpowering, and he wondered why slaughterhouses were permitted so near English residences. "Can't you smell the blood?" said Fleete.

We put him to bed at last, just as the dawn was breaking, and Strickland invited me to have another whiskey and soda. While we were drinking he talked of the trouble in the temple, and admitted that it baffled him completely. Strickland hates being mystified by natives, because his business in life is to overmatch them with their own weapons. He has not yet succeeded in doing this, but in fifteen or twenty years he will have made some small progress.

"They should have mauled us," he said, "instead of mewing at us. I wonder what they meant. I don't like it one little bit."

I said that the Managing Committee of the temple would in all probability bring a criminal action against us for insulting their religion. There was a section of the Indian Penal Code which exactly met Fleete's offense. Strickland said he only hoped and prayed that they would do this. Before I left I looked into Fleete's room,

Indian fakir with green face. A fakir is a wandering beggar who is said to perform wonders.
© Lindsay Hebberd/Woodfin Camp & Associates.

and saw him lying on his right side, scratching his left breast. Then I went to bed cold, depressed, and unhappy, at seven o'clock in the morning.

At one o'clock I rode over to Strickland's house to inquire after Fleete's head. I imagined that it would be a sore one. Fleete was breakfasting and seemed unwell. His temper was gone, for he was abusing the cook for not supplying him with an underdone chop. A man who can eat raw meat after a wet night is a curiosity. I told Fleete this and he laughed.

"You breed queer mosquitoes in these parts," he said. "I've been bitten to pieces, but only in one place."

"Let's have a look at the bite," said Strickland. "It may have gone down since this morning."

While the chops were being cooked, Fleete

Rudyard Kipling   735

CONTENT-AREA CONNECTIONS

Culture: Hinduism

As stated in the text, the worship at Hindu temples does not occur at fixed times. The first act of the service is the opening of the temple door. Visitors to the temple may join in the chanting or place gifts of flowers, fruit, or perfume in front of the image or statue of the god. Visitors may also receive a small helping of the consecrated food. The priests are usually of the upper or Brahmin class, although the Silver Man, who is not a regular priest of the temple, is probably a wandering ascetic or fakir.

Paired activity. Have pairs of students report on aspects of Hindu worship. Possible topics include sacred animals such as cows, monkeys, tree squirrels, and some snakes; sacred rivers, especially the Ganges because it supposedly springs from the god Shiva's head; or the doctrine of reincarnation, the belief that a person may return to live many times in human, animal, or vegetable form.

DIRECT TEACHING

VIEWING THE ART

Queen Victoria instituted the Order of the Star of India on February 23, 1862, proclaiming that twenty-five knights would be styled Knights Grand Commanders.

Activity. The title *knight* was merely an honorary award after the Middle Ages. What might have motivated Queen Victoria to extend orders of knighthood in a colony? [The English monarchy wanted to create a hierarchy of authority and prestige among leaders of colonized countries to ensure allegiance to the Empire.]

A Content-Area Connections

Mythology: Scourges
The "mark of the beast," imposed upon those who defy the gods or defile their sacred places, is a theme with a long history. In ancient Greek mythology, Actaeon, a hunter, accidentally saw the virgin goddess Artemis bathing; as punishment, he was transformed into a stag and torn apart by his own hounds. Similarly, King Pentheus offended the god Dionysus by refusing to allow the god to be worshipped. As punishment, Pentheus was torn apart by maenads (frenzied women) who perceived him to be an animal. These tales remind people that denying or defiling the divine is an "inhuman" act—the act of an animal.

The First Investiture of the Star of India (detail) (1863), after William Simpson. The star of India was a merit award given to an order of knights.
The Bridgeman Art Library.

"Nonsense," said Fleete; "my mare will follow me like a dog." He went to her; she was in a loose box;⁸ but as he slipped the bars she plunged, knocked him down, and broke away into the garden. I laughed, but Strickland was not amused. He took his moustache in both fists and pulled at it till it nearly came out. Fleete, instead of going off to chase his property, yawned, saying that he felt sleepy. He went to the house to lie down, which was a foolish way of spending New Year's Day.

Strickland sat with me in the stables and asked if I had noticed anything peculiar in Fleete's manner. I said that he ate his food like a beast; but that this might have been the result of living alone in the hills out of the reach of society as refined and elevating as ours for instance. Strickland was not amused. I do not think that he listened to me, for his next sentence referred to the mark on Fleete's breast, and I said that it might have been caused by blister flies, or that it was possibly a birthmark newly born and now visible for the first time. We both agreed that it was unpleasant to look at, and Strickland found occasion to say that I was a fool.

"I can't tell you what I think now," said he, "because you would call me a madman; but you must stay with me for the next few days, if you can. I want you to watch Fleete, but don't tell me what you think till I have made up my mind."

"But I am dining out tonight," I said.

---
8. **loose box:** stall in which the horse is free to move about.

READING MINI-LESSON

Developing Word-Attack Skills
Y is the only letter that can be a consonant or a vowel. As a consonant, its sound is /y/, as in *year* and *yawned*. As a vowel occurring at the end of a word, it can stand for /ē/ or /ī/. Using the words *only, theory, necessary, my, story, any, entirely, by, heavy, excusably,* and *twenty,* help students recognize that final *y* most often stands for /ē/. It stands for /ī/ only when it is the principal vowel in a word.

Use these selection words to explore the sounds of medial *y*.

hydrophobia   strychnine
physically   asylum
paroxysm   hysteria

Help students recognize that when *y* occurs between two consonants, it can stand for /i/ or /ī/. Have them note the two words in which medial *y* stands for /ī/.

Activity. Have students group these words according to the sound of medial *y*. Encourage them to draw conclusions about when *y* stands for /i/ [s] and /ī/ [l].

cryptogram [s]   hyperbole [l]
hypertension [l]   paralysis [s]
dysentery [s]   analyst [s]

Students may conclude that /i/ is the more common sound, but particularly after *h*, medial *y* stands for /ī/.

"So am I," said Strickland, "and so is Fleete. At least if he doesn't change his mind."

We walked about the garden smoking, but saying nothing—because we were friends, and talking spoils good tobacco—till our pipes were out. Then we went to wake up Fleete. He was wide awake and fidgeting about his room.

"I say, I want some more chops," he said. "Can I get them?"

We laughed and said, "Go and change. The ponies will be round in a minute."

"All right," said Fleete. "I'll go when I get the chops—underdone ones, mind."

He seemed to be quite in earnest. It was four o'clock, and we had had breakfast at one; still, for a long time, he demanded those underdone chops. Then he changed into riding clothes and went out into the veranda. His pony—the mare had not been caught—would not let him come near. All three horses were unmanageable—mad with fear—and finally Fleete said that he would stay at home and get something to eat. Strickland and I rode out wondering. As we passed the Temple of Hanuman the Silver Man came out and mewed at us.

"He is not one of the regular priests of the temple," said Strickland. "I think I should peculiarly like to lay my hands on him."

There was no spring in our gallop on the racecourse that evening. The horses were stale, and moved as though they had been ridden out.

"The fright after breakfast has been too much for them," said Strickland.

That was the only remark he made through the remainder of the ride. Once or twice, I think, he swore to himself; but that did not count.

We came back in the dark at seven o'clock, and saw that there was no lights in the bungalow. "Careless ruffians my servants are!" said Strickland.

My horse reared at something on the carriage drive, and Fleete stood up under its nose.

"What are you doing, groveling about the garden?" said Strickland.

But both horses bolted and nearly threw us. We dismounted by the stables and returned to Fleete, who was on his hands and knees under the orange bushes.

"What the devil's wrong with you?" said Strickland.

"Nothing, nothing in the world," said Fleete, speaking very quickly and thickly. "I've been gardening—botanizing, you know. The smell of the earth is delightful. I think I'm going for a walk—a long walk—all night."

Then I saw that there was something excessively out of order somewhere, and I said to Strickland, "I am not dining out."

"Bless you!" said Strickland. "Here, Fleete, get up. You'll catch fever there. Come in to dinner and let's have the lamps lit. We'll dine at home."

Fleete stood up unwillingly, and said, "No lamps—no lamps. It's much nicer here. Let's dine outside and have some more chops—lots of 'em and underdone—bloody ones with gristle."

Now a December evening in Northern India is bitterly cold, and Fleete's suggestion was that of a maniac.

"Come in," said Strickland sternly. "Come in at once."

Fleete came, and when the lamps were brought, we saw that he was literally plastered with dirt from head to foot. He must have been rolling in the garden. He shrank from the light and went to his room. His eyes were horrible to look at. There was a green light behind them, not in them, if you understand, and the man's lower lip hung down.

Strickland said, "There is going to be trouble—big trouble—tonight. Don't you change your riding things."

We waited and waited for Fleete's reappearance, and ordered dinner in the meantime. We could hear him moving about his own room, but there was no light there. Presently from the room came the long-drawn howl of a wolf.

People write and talk lightly of blood running

Rudyard Kipling 739

CONTENT-AREA CONNECTIONS

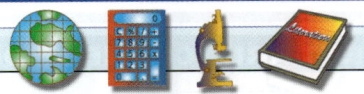

Music: Film Scores
Small-group activity. Have students form small groups to find or compose soundtrack music for a film of "The Mark of the Beast." They might choose a particular theme song for each character and use music to set the mood for different scenes. Have students play and explain their musical selections.

Film: Britain Seen Through an American Lens
Individual activity. Have students research how the British Empire has been portrayed in British and American films. They might prepare reports on such films as *Gunga Din, A Passage to India,* and *Gandhi,* as well as on the filmed version of Kipling's own work, *The Man Who Would Be King.*

Connecting to World Literature

SKILLS FOCUS, pp. 746–748

Grade-Level Skills

■ **Literary Skills**

Compare major literary forms of different historical periods.

■ **Literary Skills**

Evaluate the philosophical, political, religious, ethical, social, and philosophical influences of the historical period.

Literary Focus: The Rise of Realism

Invite students, as they read, to search for answers to the following questions:

- What is a triple-decker?
- Which aspects of Romanticism did Realists reject?
- How did realism differ in France, Russia, and the United States?

DIRECT TEACHING

Ⓐ Literary Connections
Victorian Novelists

Popular British novelists of the Victorian period included Charles Dickens (1812–1870); William Thackeray (1811–1863); the Brontë sisters, Charlotte (1816–1855) and Emily (1818–1848); George Eliot (Mary Ann Evans, 1819–1880); and Anthony Trollope (1815–1882).

Ⓑ Literary Connections
European Realists

Other seminal European realists included Norwegian dramatist Henrik Ibsen (*A Doll's House*), Russian novelists Ivan Turgenev (*Fathers and Sons*) and Fyodor Dostoevsky (*Crime and Punishment*), and French novelist Gustave Flaubert (*Madame Bovary*).

Connecting to World Literature
The Rise of Realism

You have just read "The Mark of the Beast" by Kipling. In this Connecting to World Literature feature, you will read three short stories from other countries that exemplify the style known as realism.

Leo Tolstoy	**How Much Land Does a Man Need?** Russia		751
Anton Chekhov	**The Bet**	Russia	767
Guy de Maupassant	**The Jewels**	France	776

The Tavern (detail) (19th century) by Écouard Manet.
Pushkin Museum of Fine Arts, Moscow.
© Scala/Art Resource, New York.

Pages 746–748 cover
Literary Skills
Evaluate the philosophical, political, religious, ethical, and social influences of a historical period. Compare realist works.

Ⓐ The Victorian era in England is famous for its magnificent storytelling—hefty three-volume novels of great passion, scope, and originality. Often these triple-deckers were serialized in magazines and read aloud by entire families. The genres ranged from historical fiction to suspenseful detective stories to explorations of social problems.

As a rule, Victorian popular novels suggested that solutions could be found to the complex social problems of the era. The novels also conveyed lessons in morality. By the latter half of the nineteenth century, however, serious writers were turning their hands to a less optimistic type of novel that expressed a literary philosophy called realism.

Realism: A Reaction to Romanticism

Realism was an attempt to produce an accurate portrayal of real life without filtering it through personal feelings or Romantic idealism. Noting that liberal reforms and the revolutions of the nineteenth century had failed to bring about an era of justice, realist writers rejected the century's earlier Romantic emotionalism, seeing it as an ineffective tool for reforming—or even describing—industrial society.

Realism concerned itself with more than just the details of daily life, however. It also sought to explain *why* ordinary people behave the way they do. Realist novelists often relied on the emerging sciences of human and animal behavior—biology, psychology, and sociology—as well as on their own insights and observations. Realists could be divided into several

Ⓑ different camps: Some emphasized social reform, others stressed scientific objectivity, and still others leaned toward social satire.

France: Scientific Objectivity

French realists, under the leadership of the novelist Gustave Flaubert, tried to make a science of their art by eliminating all sentimentality. They aimed simply to mirror life, without judgment or distortion. Yet a novel

The Potato Eaters (1885) by Vincent van Gogh.
Rijksmuseum Kroeller-Mueller, Otterlo, Netherlands. © Erich Lessing/Art Resource, New York.

like Flaubert's *Madame Bovary* is admired today not so much for its objectivity as for its perfect prose and its satire of the middle class.

Naturalism, a radical offshoot of realism, arose in the 1870s. Led by Émile Zola, naturalist writers considered free will an illusion and often showed their characters as helpless victims of heredity, fate, and environment. These writers tried to abolish the boundary between scientist and artist. Relying heavily on the growing scientific disciplines of psychology and sociology, they tried to dissect human behavior with as much objectivity as a scientist would dissect a frog or a cadaver. For naturalists, human life seemed a grim, losing battle against forces beyond the individual's control. The most talented naturalists, however, could not stay within the narrow ideology of their school. Guy de Maupassant (see page 774), for example, is sometimes called a naturalist, but his work is sharpened by irony and by a gift for choosing the right details.

Russia: Ultimate Questions

Realistic Russian novels began with those of Ivan Turgenev, whose ornate, lyrical prose brimmed with sympathy and warmth. Later Russian novelists, including Leo Tolstoy (see page 749) and Fyodor Dostoevsky, wrote gigantic, sprawling novels filled with violence, love, and family crises, and

The Rise of Realism   747

CONTENT-AREA CONNECTIONS

Science: Nineteenth-Century Advances
The late 1800s were scientific boom years. In 1859, Darwin had rocked a complacent world with *Origin of Species*. Only thirty years later, Marie and Pierre Curie discovered radium. Within that thirty-year span, the workings of the cell and the atom had been probed, electricity became available to the public, and advances in technology and medicine had opened new vistas. Small wonder, then that French naturalists strove to apply scientific principles in literature.

Small-group activity. Invite students to research information on one of these scientific advances and present their findings to the class.

DIRECT TEACHING

VIEWING THE ART

When **Vincent van Gogh** (1853–1890) began to treat art as a profession in 1880, he expressed his desire to help the poor by painting peasants and workers, most famously in *The Potato Eaters*. His goal in this painting was, he wrote, to capture the spirit of manual labor and show people who "have honestly earned their food."

Activity. Ask students how peasants and workers might be helped by such paintings. [The paintings might draw attention to the problems they face and prompt people to help them.] Have students describe elements in this painting that capture their attention.

C Literary Connections
Realism in France
French Romantic novelist Stendhal (Henri Beyle, 1783–1842) anticipated realism with his comment, "A novel is a mirror walking along the road." Guy de Maupassant (1850–1893), moving from realism to naturalism, maintained that, "The Realist, if he is an artist, will try not to show us a commonplace photograph of life, but to give us a more complete view of it, more striking, more convincing than reality itself."

D Literary Connections
Naturalism
Zola maintained that the novel should study "the machinery of [human] intellectual and sensory manifestations, under the influences of heredity and environment." His views set the stage for twentieth-century American naturalists such as Stephen Crane, Theodore Dreiser, and John Steinbeck.

The Rise of Realism   747

DIRECT TEACHING

VIEWING THE ART

This painting helped **Thomas Eakins** (1844–1916) acquire a reputation as a master of realism. The subject, however, was considered to be too shocking for a painting, and Eakins was mocked and spurned by some of his contemporaries for painting it.

Activity. Ask students to identify what might be considered repulsive and attractive about this painting. [Attractive elements might be Eakin's precise details of character, light, surgical tools, and so on; the body being operated on could repulse some people.]

A Exploring the Historical Period
TOLSTOY'S *WAR AND PEACE*

One of the great themes of Tolstoy's *War and Peace* is the devastation of Russia during the Napoleonic wars. When Napoleon invaded Russia in 1812, Czar Alexander I strategically withdrew northeastward, stripping the land and burning Moscow. As the Russian winter set in, Napoleon was forced to retreat, losing over 200,000 of his 600,000 soldiers. The czar's destruction of his own country, however, plunged Russia's serfs even deeper into misery.

B Literary Connections
Realism in Drama

As a playwright, Chekhov worked in the realist tradition pioneered by Henrik Ibsen. Ibsen had abandoned the grand scale of heroic drama to look into ordinary families and communities—and the things they didn't want said out loud. Chekhov's brilliant dramas *The Sea Gull, The Three Sisters, Uncle Vanya,* and *The Cherry Orchard* present his own brand of realism that explores the mediocrity and absurdity of Russia's pretentious, fading aristocrats.

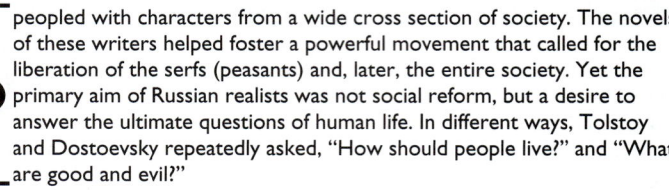

The Gross Clinic (1875) by Thomas Eakins. Oil on canvas.
Jefferson College, Philadelphia.
The Bridgeman Art Library.

A peopled with characters from a wide cross section of society. The novels of these writers helped foster a powerful movement that called for the liberation of the serfs (peasants) and, later, the entire society. Yet the primary aim of Russian realists was not social reform, but a desire to answer the ultimate questions of human life. In different ways, Tolstoy and Dostoevsky repeatedly asked, "How should people live?" and "What are good and evil?"

Unlike these two giants, the playwright and short-story writer Anton Chekhov (see page 765) worked on a much smaller scale. Chekhov found his subjects and themes in the common illusions and daily sufferings of unremarkable people. Like Tolstoy and Dostoevsky, however, Chekhov **B** dealt with the meanings of life and death. His stories and plays are about people's attempts—usually frustrated—to find meaning and purpose in their lives.

The Legacy of the Nineteenth Century

The literary styles of the nineteenth century—from the effusive poetry of the Romantics to the terse prose of the realists—still influence modern writing. Powerful expressions of feeling and realistic depictions of life are both now hallmarks of literary excellence. Realistic values, such as an emphasis on unflinching factual observation of ordinary people's lives, still exert a powerful influence on literature and thought.

Leo Tolstoy
(1828–1910)

When Count Leo Nikolayevich Tolstoy (lē'ō nē'kô·lä'ye·vich tôl'stoi') died of pneumonia at the age of eighty-two, he may have been the most famous man in the world. His death was front-page news in England and America. In addition to being the greatest living Russian novelist, Tolstoy was also a social and religious reformer.

Tolstoy was born to wealthy aristocratic parents, both of whom had died by the time he was nine. He, his three older brothers, and his younger sister were raised by aunts on the family estate. As Tolstoy grew older, he led an aimless life—as did many young men of the Russian aristocracy.

At nineteen, Tolstoy split his inheritance with his brothers and became the master of his family's estate and its three hundred serfs. Within three years, he managed to gamble away about one fourth of his inheritance. Looking for adventure, he joined the Russian army and fought bravely during the Crimean War. The suffering that he witnessed during the war helped bring out his serious, morally questioning nature.

In 1859, Tolstoy opened a school on his estate for his serfs' children. Soon after, he married Sonya Andreyevna Bers. In addition to bearing him thirteen children, Sonya recopied her husband's illegible manuscripts and took over the management of his estate. Tolstoy was thus free to write his greatest works, *War and Peace* (1869) and *Anna Karenina* (1877)—masterpieces of realistic fiction that capped his already immense reputation.

After years of moral questioning, Tolstoy underwent a spiritual conversion. Aspiring to be holy and to do good, he found his best models in Russia's self-sufficient Christian peasants. During the last thirty years of his life, his writings became fervent attacks on private ownership, capitalism, the Orthodox Church, and Russia's czarist government.

Though Tolstoy repudiated his early works for their bourgeois focus on the aristocracy, his reputation today rests on those early novels: *War and Peace,* a monumental telling of the lives of five aristocratic families during the Napoleonic Wars, and *Anna Karenina,* the tragic story of a woman who gives up her husband and child for what she thinks is true love.

Portrait of Leo Tolstoy (1873) by Ivan Nikolayevich Kramskoy.
© Getty Images.

SKILLS FOCUS, pp. 749–764

Grade-Level Skills

- **Literary Skills**

Analyze characteristics of subgenres used in short stories, including allegory.

More About the Writer

Background. Tolstoy's dramatic spiritual conversion at age fifty transformed the final thirty years of his life. The former aristocrat dressed in peasant clothing, became a vegetarian, labored in the fields alongside his former serfs, and refused royalties on his published writings. He became the leader of a utopian movement that championed the poor and fostered principles of community and social justice. Tolstoy's ideas inspired later pacifist reformers such as Mahatma Gandhi and Martin Luther King, Jr.

Tolstoy's final flight from his estate, Yasnaya Polyana (Clear Glade), was in part an attempt to simplify his life by escaping constant media attention. Ironically, however, his attempt attracted even more publicity. "LEO TOLSTOY LEAVES YASNAYA POLYANA," the headlines blared. As Tolstoy traveled, he followed the newspaper accounts of his journey. "Everything is known already," he complained. Journalists pursued him relentlessly, continually telegramming their editors with every shred of information they could glean. Even as Tolstoy lay dying in the stationmaster's house in Astopovo, frequent bulletins about his condition were released to the press. In a final irony, Tolstoy's rural grave became a major tourist attraction. His house in Moscow is now the Tolstoy Museum.

RESOURCES: READING

Planning
- *One-Stop Planner* CD-ROM with ExamView Test Generator

Differentiating Instruction
- Supporting Instruction in Spanish
- Audio CD Library, Selections and Summaries in Spanish

Vocabulary
- Vocabulary Development

Grammar and Language
- Daily Language Activities
- Language Handbook Worksheets

Assessment
- Holt Assessment: Literature, Reading, and Vocabulary
- *One-Stop Planner* CD-ROM with ExamView Test Generator
- Holt Online Assessment

Internet
- go.hrw.com (Keyword: LE5 12-6)
- Elements of Literature Online

Media
- Audio CD Library
- Fine Art Transparencies
- Audio CD Library, Selections and Summaries in Spanish

PRETEACHING

Summary ⇄ at grade level

In this parable, Pahom, a Russian peasant, overhears his wife and her sister arguing the merits of city life versus farm life. He boasts to himself that if he just had enough land, he would not even fear the Devil. The Devil hears the boast and plots to exploit Pahom's greed. Pahom soon succeeds in buying land, yet he quickly grows dissatisfied. He treats the local peasants as badly as he was once treated, and he continues to amass more land. When a traveling dealer tells Pahom about the region of the Bashkirs, where fertile land is available at low prices, Pahom travels there with his savings—one thousand rubles. The Bashkirs welcome him and agree to sell, for a thousand rubles, as much land as he can pace off in a day, as long as he returns before sunset to his starting point. Pahom walks a great distance, trying to encircle as much land as possible. In his mad rush back to the distant starting point, however, he collapses and dies. He ends up with six feet of land—enough for his grave.

Skills Starter

Build prerequisite skills. Ask students to list other familiar allegories, such as John Bunyan's *Pilgrim's Progress* (p. 313) and George Orwell's *Animal Farm,* and familiar parables, such as traditional Zen parables (p. 353) and "The Prodigal Son" from the Bible (p. 342). Remind students that allegories and parables, which work on two levels, allow authors to communicate ideas that otherwise would be difficult to convey. Then, ask students to identify some of the underlying ideas that are explored in the listed allegories and parables.

Before You Read

How Much Land Does a Man Need?

Make the Connection
Have you ever wanted something desperately and then gotten it? If so, perhaps you felt briefly satisfied. But how long did the satisfaction last? What feelings came afterward? In the following short story, Leo Tolstoy examines the vast difference between human wants and human needs. Getting what we *need,* Tolstoy suggests, allows us to live. Getting what we *want*—well, that can be another matter altogether.

Literary Focus
Allegory
Tolstoy's story "How Much Land Does a Man Need?" is often called a parable. A **parable** is a short, simple tale that is based on ordinary events and presents a moral lesson. Parables are related to a kind of writing called **allegory**—stories that operate on two different levels, the literal and the symbolic. The characters and events of an allegory can be understood both for what they are (the literal meaning) and for the abstract principles they represent (the symbolic meaning). As you read, try to guess what various elements of the story (such as Pahom, the Devil, and the land itself) stand for.

INTERNET
Vocabulary Practice
•
More About Leo Tolstoy
•
Keyword: LE5 12-6

An **allegory** is a story in which the characters, settings, and events stand for abstract ideas or moral concepts.

For more on Allegory, see the Handbook of Literary and Historical Terms.

SKILLS FOCUS

Literary Skills
Understand allegory.

Background
The nineteenth-century Russia that Leo Tolstoy describes in this story had just abandoned feudalism—a way of life dead in England since the Middle Ages. (See page 94.) Until Czar Alexander II ordered their emancipation in 1861, Russian peasants, called serfs, were virtual slaves of landowners and aristocrats: They could be bought or sold, and were not allowed to own property.

When Tolstoy wrote this story, serfs had already had twenty-five years of freedom and rights. No one, certainly not Tolstoy the reformer, would wish to see them thrust into bondage again. Yet in this parable he could wonder—with sharp, if somewhat black, humor—whether the peasants' progress had brought changes they would regret. As one character proclaims early on in the story, "Loss and gain are brothers twain."

Vocabulary Development

piqued (pēkt) v. used as adj.: provoked; resentful.

disparaged (di·spar'ijd) v.: belittled; spoke negatively of.

aggrieved (ə·grēvd') adj.: offended.

arable (ar'ə·bəl) adj.: fit to be farmed or cultivated.

haggled (hag'əld) v.: argued about a price.

prostrate (präs'trāt') adj.: lying flat.

(Opposite) *The Rainbow* by Arkhip Kuindzhi (1842–1910).
Russian State Museum, St. Petersburg. © Scala/Art Resource, New York.

750 Collection 6 The Victorian Period

Previewing Vocabulary

Ask student volunteers to act out the following chain of events.

1. Two customers <u>disparaged</u> the specialty of the house: eggplant. [Possible dialogue: "They say the eggplant is really awful here."]
2. The server grew visibly <u>aggrieved</u>. [Possible actions: scowling, sharp reply]
3. The customers used the word <u>arable</u> in criticizing the source of the eggplants. [Possible dialogue: "These eggplants were probably grown on land that's barely arable."]
4. The server's actions showed that he was <u>piqued</u>. [Possible actions: scowling, angry gestures]
5. When the bill came, the customers <u>haggled</u> with the manager. [Possible action: bickering]
6. The manager's response left them <u>prostrate</u> with astonishment. [Possible action: falling flat on the floor]

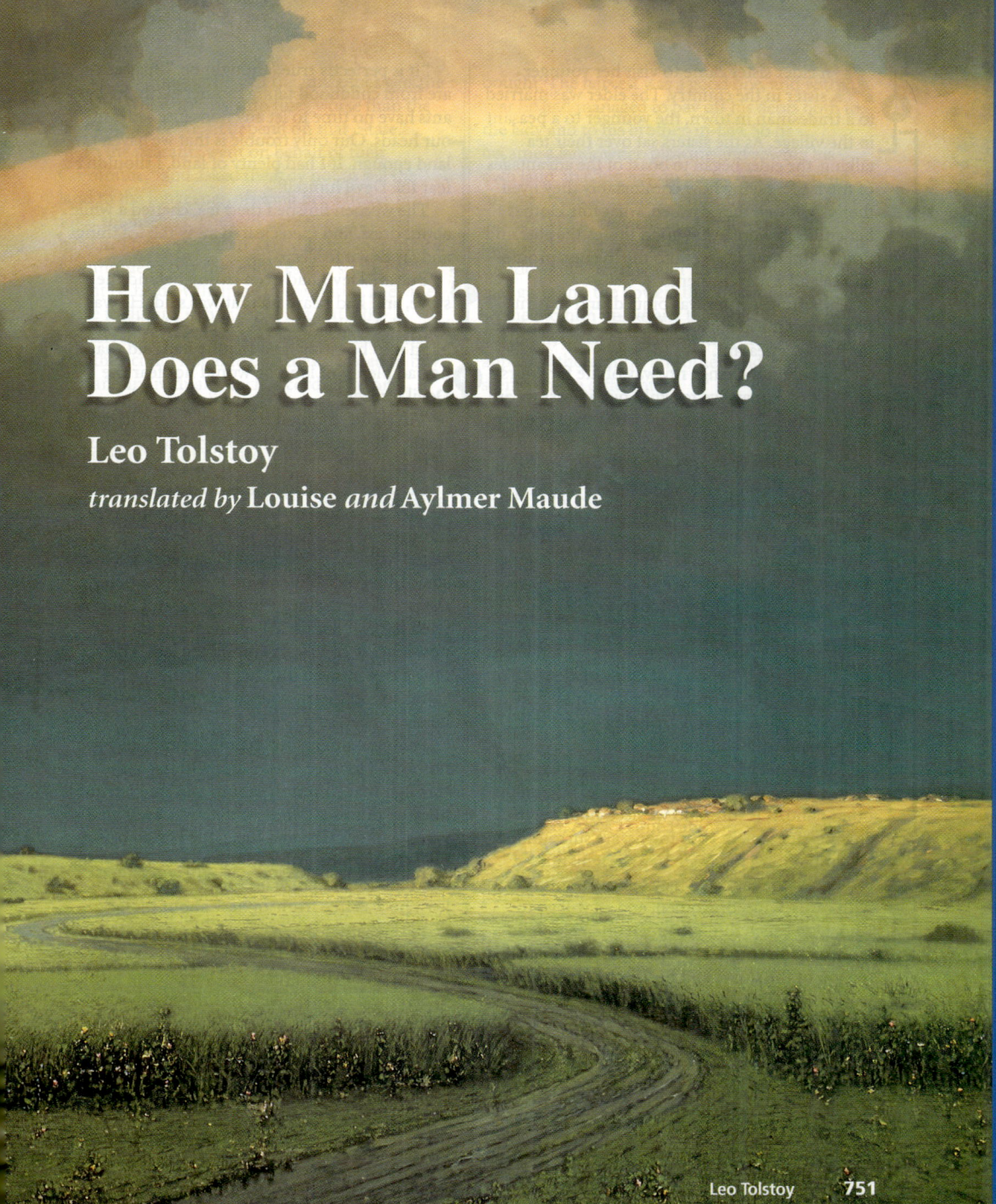

How Much Land Does a Man Need?

Leo Tolstoy

translated by Louise *and* Aylmer Maude

INDEPENDENT PRACTICE

Response and Analysis

Reading Check

1. They met at an office party, fell in love, and married. Lantin was happy, she was warm and attentive, and they lived well on his modest salary.
2. He objects to her love for the theater and for imitation jewelry.
3. It declines dramatically.

Thinking Critically

4. The statements are ironic. She is unfaithful.
5. He is ashamed to be revealed as a cuckold and a fool, but he takes the money because he is poor and hungry.
6. This virtuous wife makes him miserable. This detail suggests that morality means less to him than he thought or than it once did.
7. "The Jewels" reveals the vanity and complacency of the middle class. Possible theme: The middle class is easily fooled by appearances.

Comparing Literature

8. Tolstoy's Pahom and Maupassant's Lantin both envy the wealthy. For both, increased wealth brings moral degeneration. The richer Pahom grows, the greedier he becomes. When Lantin attains wealth, he greedily haggles with the jewelers, lies, and visits prostitutes. Pahom's greed kills him; Lantin's wealth fails to bring happiness. Both authors suggest that "progress" and "self-improvement" may be dangerous illusions.
9. Lantin would have left the necklace at the jewelers and would have been happy with his new wife.

Vocabulary Development

1. c 3. b 5. b
2. a 4. b

Response and Analysis

Reading Check

1. In two or three sentences, describe the Lantins' married life, including the way they met, their feelings about one another, and their economic circumstances.
2. What two tastes of Madame Lantin's does Monsieur Lantin object to?
3. How does the death of his wife affect Monsieur Lantin's standard of living?

Thinking Critically

4. People who know Madame Lantin say, "Happy the man who marries her. Nobody could find a better wife." Evaluate these statements based on what you have **inferred** about Madame Lantin by the end of the story. (Consult your reading notes for help.)
5. Monsieur Lantin suffers a **conflict** about whether to accept the eighteen thousand francs the jeweler offers for the necklace. Why do you think he hesitates? Why do you think he ultimately decides to take the money?
6. Re-read the last paragraph of the story. What is **ironic** about the fact that Monsieur Lantin is unhappy with his second wife? What might this seemingly offhand detail add to the meaning of the story?
7. Maupassant and his fellow realists were intent on using fiction to examine the issues of their day. What particular social problem does "The Jewels" reveal? What cynical idea or insight— what **theme**—does Maupassant express about this social problem?

Comparing Literature

8. Compare Tolstoy's character Pahom (in "How Much Land Does a Man Need?," page 751) with Maupassant's Monsieur Lantin. How does each character's personality contribute to his changing circumstances? What does each writer seem to suggest about nineteenth-century notions of progress and self-improvement?
9. How would this story have ended if it had been written by a Romantic or by a more sentimental writer, not a realist?

WRITING

A Close Look at Madame Lantin

We are told scarcely anything about Madame Lantin—not even her first name. However, Maupassant gives us some clues that help us to understand her personality, and we can make inferences about her motivations. Write a brief **analysis** of Madame Lantin's character. In your analysis, explain Madame Lantin's motivations, her behavior with her husband, and her seeming lack of guilt. Cite passages from the story to support your analysis.

SKILLS FOCUS

Literary Skills Analyze theme. Compare and contrast realist works.
Reading Skills Analyze inferences.
Writing Skills Write a character analysis.
Vocabulary Skills Identify antonyms.

Vocabulary Development
Antonyms

An **antonym** is a word that has the opposite or nearly the opposite meaning as another word. Choose the *best* antonym for each Vocabulary word.

1. **unpretentious:** (a) modest (b) unattractive (c) snobby
2. **assuage:** (a) upset (b) persuade (c) dismiss
3. **incurred:** (a) argued (b) avoided (c) started
4. **surreptitiously:** (a) forcefully (b) openly (c) cautiously
5. **contemptuous:** (a) tiresome (b) respectful (c) generous

---

ASSESSING

Assessment
- Holt Assessment: *Literature, Reading, and Vocabulary*

RETEACHING

For a lesson reteaching theme and meaning, see **Reteaching**, p. 1129A.

READ ON: FOR INDEPENDENT READING

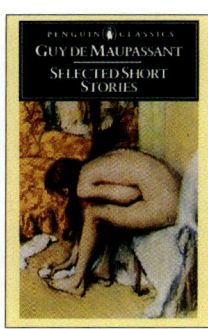

FICTION
Telling It Like It Is
Guy de Maupassant depicts all aspects of French society—from the hardships faced by the Norman peasantry to the private lives of the middle class—with unflinching clarity and accuracy. Rich in atmosphere and loaded with candor, his **Selected Short Stories** takes us from battlefield to parlor, featuring subjects that range from the Franco-Prussian War to domestic skirmishes, revealing a world that is still very recognizable today.

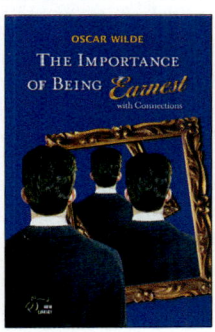

DRAMA
Found in a Handbag
Much of the satire in Oscar Wilde's play *The Importance of Being Earnest* is targeted at the British class system. Wilde openly defied Victorian ideas of respectability and presented his own philosophy as an alternative. The seemingly contradictory logic of the play is part of that philosophy: "The truth is rarely pure and never simple."

This title is available in the HRW Library.

NONFICTION
A Peek at Victorian Private Lives
Welcome to nineteenth-century England! In *What Jane Austen Ate and Charles Dickens Knew,* Daniel Pool gives new life to the daily routines of the Victorian period. Both the nitty-gritty details (How did they keep clean?) and the posh etiquette (How did one address a duke?) of the time are covered. Find out what the Victorians ate, what they wore, how they traveled, and whom they married.

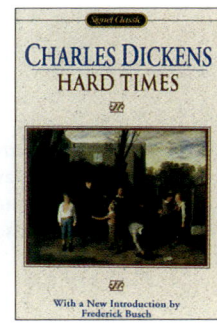

FICTION
Just the Facts
Set in Coketown, an imaginary industrial city in northern England, Charles Dickens's *Hard Times* is a harsh criticism of the dark side of the Industrial Revolution and of the materialist notion that concrete facts and things make up the only true reality. In this world that is populated by the likes of Professor Gradgrind and Mr. McChoakumchild, relentless lovers of facts, imagination is not tolerated. Gradgrind is forced to acknowledge the folly of his beliefs, however, as his children attempt to live up to his expectations and only make messes of their lives.

DIFFERENTIATING INSTRUCTION

Estimated Word Counts and Reading Levels of Read On Books:

Fiction
Hard Times	⇔	130,300
Selected Short Stories	⇩	130,500

Drama
The Importance of Being Earnest	⇔	36,200

Nonfiction
What Jane Austen Ate and Charles Dickens Knew	⇩	110,400

KEY: ⇧ *above grade level* ⇔ *at grade level* ⇩ *below grade level*

Read On
For Independent Reading
If students enjoyed the themes and topics explored in this collection, you might recommend the following titles for independent reading.

Assessment Options
The following projects can help you evaluate and assess your students' outside reading.

- **Create a silent dialogue.** Encourage pairs of students to respond to their reading of Guy de Maupassant's stories by assuming the identities of two characters from the same story or from different stories. Suggest that they create a silent dialogue by writing back and forth to each other, asking and replying to questions like the following: What obstacles did you have to overcome to achieve your goal? How did you deal with these obstacles? Did you succeed or fail in overcoming the obstacles?

- **Explore period propriety.** Ask a group of students to plan and present a panel discussion on the topic of propriety in Daniel Pool's book on daily life in nineteenth-century England and in Oscar Wilde's play *The Importance of Being Earnest.* As they discuss the works, encourage students to focus on what the authors set forth as proper behavior for the period and what they saw as the social results of propriety and impropriety.

- **Advertise a miniseries.** Ask individual students to imagine that Charles Dickens's *Hard Times* is being produced as a television miniseries. Have them decide how many episodes would be needed; then, have them write a summary of each segment for a television program guide and the copy for a television or newspaper advertisement promoting the series. A group of student writers and artists can also work together to plan a comprehensive advertising campaign for the series and then present their plans to the class.

Writing Workshop

Comparing and Contrasting Literature

Writing Assignment
Write an essay of 1,500 words in which you compare and contrast two pieces of literature from the same historical period.

Now that you've just read several literary works from the Victorian period (1832–1901), you've probably discovered that one of the best ways to become familiar with a particular era in history is to read its literature. Novels, short stories, poems, essays, and plays reflect in some ways the ideas and concerns of their times. In this workshop you'll write an essay **comparing and contrasting two literary works** from the same historical period and relating them to the major issues of their era.

Prewriting

Choose Your Subjects

Variations on a Theme What period in history intrigues you? What literature of a particular era invites your curiosity—the narratives of the Anglo-Saxon period, the poetry of the Renaissance, or the stories of prerevolutionary Russia? To choose a subject for your essay, first select a historical era for study by paging through the sections in this book, scanning a history book, or asking your teacher or librarian for ideas. Then, look through literature anthologies to find two works of literature from the same genre—short stories, poems, plays, or sections of novels—that belong to that historical time period. For example, one student chose to compare and contrast Leo Tolstoy's "How Much Land Does a Man Need?" (page 751) and Anton Chekhov's "The Bet" (page 767) because the authors of the two short stories were Russian contemporaries who wrote during a fascinating period of history.

Analyze the Literature

Break It Down Carefully read the works you've selected, and take notes on the **literary elements—setting, characters, plot,** and **theme.** Then, ask yourself, "How do the literary elements relate to a major issue of the historical time period?" (If you need to do research for information about the major issues of the time period, use the usual research sources—your textbooks, the library, or the Internet.) Chart your analysis to see similarities and differences in the two pieces of literature. For example, the chart on the next page shows how one student analyzed the literary elements of two short stories and speculated on an issue behind them. Notice that his speculation is related to the theme of the two works.

Writing Skills
Write an essay comparing and contrasting two literary works.

784   Collection 6   The Victorian Period

COLLECTION 6 RESOURCES: WRITING

Planning
- *One-Stop Planner* CD-ROM with ExamView Test Generator

Differentiating Instruction
- Workshop Resources: Writing, Listening, and Speaking
- Family Involvement Activities in English and Spanish
- Supporting Instruction in Spanish

Writing and Language
- Workshop Resources: Writing, Listening, and Speaking
- Daily Language Activities
- Language Handbook Worksheets

Assessment
- Holt Assessment: Writing, Listening, and Speaking

PRETEACHING

Skills Starter

Motivate. Ask students to imagine that they are participating in a time capsule project. Their task is to find a currently popular song that, when reviewed one hundred years in the future, will give insight into the cultural climate of their era. After the students have thought of a song, have them complete a journal entry in which they explain the cultural significance of the song. Does it comment on historical events? Social customs? Political issues? Have volunteers share their journal entries. Then, tell students that in this workshop they will compare and contrast two pieces of literature within the context of a particular historical period.

DIFFERENTIATING INSTRUCTION

English-Language Learners

Encourage English-language learners to select literature about their native countries or by authors from their native countries. If that is not possible, encourage students to select literature influenced by a social climate or historical event. For example, a student might choose literature written within the context of civil war whether it be the French Revolution, the Spanish Civil War, or the United States Civil War. These choices should help keep the assignment interesting for students from all countries.

Literary Element	"The Bet"	"How Much Land...?"
Setting	The home of a wealthy Russian banker	The countryside of southern Russia
Characters	A wealthy banker and a twenty-five-year-old lawyer	Pahom, a peasant in a village
Plot	After arguing over capital punishment versus life imprisonment, the banker and the lawyer make a wager of two million dollars.	Pahom, foolishly claiming that with enough land he would not fear the devil himself, becomes obsessed with land acquisition.
Theme	The quality of human life can't be measured by money, as both the banker and lawyer learn.	Unchecked greed produces a death of the human spirit and, as Pahom learns too late, sometimes a literal death.

Issue: Both stories, written during the end of czarist Russia, address the value of human possessions and wealth—an important issue in a country with such a vast difference between serfs (who owned nothing) and aristocrats (who owned everything).

Break It Down Even Further Nothing is ever as simple as it first seems, and the same is true for literary analysis. Writers incorporate **ambiguities** (lines or words that may have more than one interpretation), **nuances** (changes in tone), and **complexities** (rich but difficult ideas) into their prose and poetry. With literary analysis, readers unwrap layers of meaning with each reading. To help you discover the many dimensions of literature, analyze the **stylistic devices** in the works you're comparing. Examine how the writers use devices such as tone, imagery, figures of speech, concrete sensory details, repetition, and irony. Ask yourself, "What effects do these devices create, and how do these effects add to the development of the literary elements?" Chart your answers. For example, the student comparing the Russian short stories noted that irony is integral to the theme in each.

Reference Note
For more on **stylistic devices,** see page 391.

 DO THIS

Develop a Thesis

Make a Claim Look back over your notes about the literary elements and stylistic devices. Draw a conclusion about how three or more literary elements, stylistic devices, or a combination of elements and devices develop the historical issue you've identified. This conclusion will be your preliminary **thesis statement**—a statement that shows your comprehensive understanding of the significant ideas in the works and of the historical period.

Take a look at one student's thesis statement on the next page. His thesis statement not only identifies the elements and stylistic devices that develop the issue, it also makes clear that he'll focus on the similarities of the two works.

SKILLS FOCUS

Writing Skills
Analyze the literary works.
Develop a thesis statement.

- *One-Stop Planner* CD-ROM with ExamView Test Generator
- *Holt Online Assessment*
- *Holt Online Essay Scoring*

Internet
- go.hrw.com (Keyword: LE5 12-6)
- *Elements of Literature Online*

RETEACHING

TIP

To reteach the concept of literary present tense, display a poem using a projector. Write these three sentence stems on the chalkboard:
1) In this poem, the author explores _____. 2) For example, in the first (line, stanza) the author describes _____. 3) This point is illustrated in the line "_____."

Complete the first two sentences with input from the students. Then, underline the words *explores* and *describes* and emphasize that they are present tense. For the final sentence, copy a line or section of a line from the poem that contains a past-tense verb. Underline the verb, and tell students that when text is quoted directly, verb tenses remain the same.

CORRECTING MISCONCEPTIONS

Remind students that this assignment is not a research project, and that their essays do not need to include research elements.

PRACTICE & APPLY 1

Guided and Independent Practice

As students begin to compare and contrast the two works, suggest that they use a Venn diagram such as the following to organize their notes.

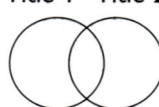

Title 1   Title 2

After students have finished comparing and contrasting the two works, have them complete **Practice and Apply 1** independently.

TIP Include in your thesis statement or in your introduction the titles and authors of the works you've analyzed. Also, use the **literary present** in your discussion. For more on the **literary present tense,** see Tenses and Their Uses, 3b–c, in the Language Handbook.

Reference Note
For more on **quotations, paraphrases, summaries,** and **documenting sources,** see pages 208, 209, and 211.

Both Chekhov's "The Bet" and Tolstoy's "How Much Land Does a Man Need?" use character, plot, and irony to bring out a similar theme—the human folly of acquiring possessions and wealth, an important issue in post-czarist Russia.

Gather Support

Proof Positive The literary elements, stylistic devices, or the combination you selected will be the key points of your essay. Develop and support these key points with accurate and detailed references to the texts. This **literary evidence** takes the form of **direct quotations** from the text, **paraphrases** of passages or scenes, and **summaries** of events. Add a page number in parentheses to document the source for each direct quotation. Although most of your literary evidence will come from the two works you're comparing and contrasting, you might consult additional sources for background information about the historical time period or for more facts about each writer. Document these additional sources also.

When you present your evidence, **elaborate** on it—tell what it means and how it proves your viewpoint. Look at the example below to see how one student elaborated on a piece of evidence.

Summary — In "The Bet," a young lawyer, only twenty-five years old, accepts a two-million-dollar bet that he will not be able to endure fifteen
Elaboration — years of willing imprisonment. His desire for money clouds his judgment and drives this sacrifice.

Organize Your Support

DO THIS

Get It in Order After you've gathered support, arrange the information so that you develop your perspective with strong organizational strategies. Make sure that the patterns and relationships of the information are clear to your readers. The two basic methods for organizing a comparison-contrast essay are the block method and the point-by-point method. In the **block method,** discuss all the key points of one literary piece, then all the key points of the other. In the **point-by-point method,** discuss each key point as it applies first to one literary piece, then the other. You may use one or the other or combine the two, but make sure you provide adequate transitions so that your readers can follow your line of reasoning.

Writing Skills
Gather and organize evidence.

PRACTICE & APPLY 1 Use the information on the previous pages to choose and analyze two literary works from the same historical era. Compare and contrast the two works; then, write a thesis statement. Gather support for your thesis, and organize it, providing transitions between your ideas.

Writing

Comparing and Contrasting Literature

A Writer's Framework

Introduction
- Provide background information for the historical period.
- Name the titles and authors of the literature.
- Use a clear thesis statement to identify the issue, key points, and your focus on similarities, differences, or both.

Body
- Develop each of the key points of your thesis.
- Use literary evidence and elaboration as support for each of your key points.
- Clarify your method of organization—block, point-by-point, or a combination.

Conclusion
- Summarize the key points about each work of literature.
- Restate your thesis.
- Close with a final, dramatic statement.

A Writer's Model

When a Man's Grasp Exceeds His Reach

The latter part of the nineteenth century was a time of dramatic change for Russia. Millions of serfs, who until 1861 were the property of landowners, were emancipated. The country's intellectuals celebrated this reform, as well as other reforms in society, politics, and the judicial system. Therefore, the literature of this period does more than entertain; it comments on society and offers moral instruction. Anton Chekhov (1860–1904), grandson of a serf, and Leo Tolstoy (1828–1910), aristocrat, were from opposite ends of the Russian economic spectrum; yet both writers felt very deeply the ironies that life had presented them. Both Chekhov's short story "The Bet" and Tolstoy's short story "How Much Land Does a Man Need?" use character, plot, and irony to bring out a similar theme—the human folly of acquiring possessions and wealth, an important issue in czarist Russia.

The main characters of both stories are willing to go to great extremes to obtain the things they think will make them happy. In "The Bet," a young lawyer, only twenty-five-years old, accepts a two-million-dollar bet that he will not be able to endure fifteen years of willing imprisonment. His desire for money clouds his judgment and drives this sacrifice. In "How Much Land Does a Man Need?" an ambitious, land-hungry peasant goes to great lengths to acquire more

(continued)

INTRODUCTION
Background information

Names of authors

Thesis statement
Titles of stories
Historical issue

BODY
Key point: Character
Evidence: Summary

Elaboration
Evidence: Summary

Collection 7
The Modern World: 1900 to the Present

About Collection 7
In Collection 7, students will master the following skills:

- **Literary Skills:** Evaluate the philosophical, political, religious, ethical, and social influences of a historical period; analyze figures of speech, allusion, political points of view on a topic, memoir, theme, irony, satire, epiphany, flashback, magic realism, paradox, foreshadowing, extended metaphor, lyric poetry; compare and contrast works from different literary periods.
- **Reading Skills:** Make inferences about theme and character motivation; compare main ideas across texts; evaluate historical context and an author's beliefs; identify and critique an author's argument; identify language structures and political influences; make, modify, and review predictions; compare and contrast aspects of a story; analyze point of view.
- **Vocabulary Skills:** Use synonyms and antonyms; complete word analogies; understand etymologies; analyze and find context clues.
- **Writing Skills:** Analyze strategies used by different forms of media.
- **Listening and Speaking Skills:** Prepare a persuasive speech.

Minimum Course of Study
Most skills can be taught with a minimum number of selections and features. In the chart to the right, lessons **highlighted in green** constitute the minimum course of study that provides coverage of the skills taught in Collection 7.

Scope and Sequence

Selection ■ Feature	Literary Skills
The Modern World: 1900 to the Present by John Leggett and David Adams Leeming	• Evaluate the philosophical, political, religious, ethical, and social influences of a historical period
A World at War	
Dulce et Decorum Est by Wilfred Owen ↔ at grade level	• Analyze figures of speech
The Hollow Men by T. S. Eliot ↑ above grade level	• Analyze allusion
Introducing Political Points of View: The Holocaust	• Analyze political points of view on a topic
Main Reading: **On the Bottom** from *Survival in Auschwitz* by Primo Levi ↔ at grade level	• Analyze the characteristics of a memoir
Connected Readings: • from **The War** by Marguerite Duras ↔ at grade level	• Understand an author's philosophical beliefs
• **Never Shall I Forget** by Elie Wiesel ↓ below grade level	
• **Blood, Sweat, and Tears** by Winston Churchill ↔ at grade level	
The Silver Fifty-Sen Pieces by Yasunari Kawabata ↔ at grade level	• Analyze theme
The Destructors by Graham Greene ↔ at grade level	• Analyze setting

Resource Manager
(see pp. 798I–798R)
Lesson and workshop resources are referenced in the Resource Manager on the pages that follow. These resources can be used to reinforce the skills taught in Collection 7, remediate students who are having difficulty, and provide supporting activities for English-language learners.

Reading Skills	Vocabulary Skills	Writing · Grammar and Language · Listening and Speaking Skills
		• Write an essay comparing and contrasting two poems
• Make inferences about an author's philosophical arguments		• Write an essay analyzing characters
• Compare main ideas across texts		• Write an essay analyzing political assumptions
• Evaluate historical context	• Use synonyms and antonyms	• Write an essay supporting an opinion
• Identify and critique an author's argument	• Complete word analogies	• Write a persuasive essay using logical, emotional, and ethical appeals
• Make inferences about theme	• Demonstrate word knowledge	• Write an essay explaining a critical comment • Use parallel structure correctly
• Make inferences about character motivation	• Demonstrate word knowledge	• Write an essay analyzing imagery

(continued)

Scope and Sequence

Selection ■ Feature	Literary Skills	Reading Skills
The Wild Swans at Coole by William Butler Yeats ↔ *at grade level*	• Analyze symbols	
Araby by James Joyce ↔ *at grade level*	• Analyze epiphany and irony	• Compare and contrast aspects of a story
The Rocking-Horse Winner by D. H. Lawrence ↔ *at grade level*	• Analyze symbols	
• **Lot's Wife** • **All the unburied ones** • **I am not one of those who left the land** by Anna Akhmatova ↔ *at grade level*	• Analyze theme	
The Demon Lover by Elizabeth Bowen ↔ *at grade level*	• Analyze flashback	• Make and modify predictions
Axolotl by Julio Cortázar ↑ *above grade level*	• Analyze the characteristics of magic realism	• Analyze point of view
The Book of Sand by Jorge Luis Borges ↔ *at grade level*	• Analyze paradox	• Review predictions
B. Wordsworth by V. S. Naipaul ↔ *at grade level*	• Analyze setting	
Half a Day by Naguib Mahfouz ↔ *at grade level*	• Analyze foreshadowing	
Digging by Seamus Heaney ↔ *at grade level*	• Analyze extended metaphor	
Ourselves Among Others		
The Doll's House by Katherine Mansfield ↔ *at grade level*	• Analyze symbols • Analyze a modern short story	
Musée des Beaux Arts by W. H. Auden ↔ *at grade level*	• Analyze diction	
Fear by Gabriela Mistral ↔ *at grade level*	• Analyze refrain	

Vocabulary Skills	Writing • Grammar and Language • Listening and Speaking Skills
	• Write an essay comparing two poems
• Create semantic charts	• Write a short story • Write an essay analyzing the narrator
	• Write an essay presenting evidence to support a claim • Write an interior monologue
	• Write journal entries in response to poems
• Create semantic charts	• Write a character description • Understand and use direct references and transitions
• Complete word analogies	• Write an essay analyzing the use of magic realism
• Identify synonyms	• Write a short story
• Create semantic charts	• Write an essay analyzing poetic vision
• Analyze context clues	• Write an essay comparing and contrasting two stories
	• Write a poem
• Find context clues	• Write an essay comparing and contrasting two characters • Understand and identify the use of active voice and passive voice
	• Write an essay comparing a poem and a painting with their myth source
	• Write a character analysis

(continued)

Scope and Sequence

Selection ■ Feature	Literary Skills	Reading Skills
Fern Hill *by* Dylan Thomas ↑ *above grade level*	• Analyze lyric poetry	
Do Not Go Gentle into That Good Night *by* Dylan Thomas ↔ *at grade level*	• Analyze an elegy • Analyze a villanelle	
Sonnet 79 / Soneto 79 *by* Pablo Neruda ↑ *above grade level*	• Analyze metaphor	
Like the Sun *by* R. K. Narayan ↔ *at grade level*	• Analyze situational irony	
Games at Twilight *by* Anita Desai ↔ *at grade level*	• Analyze imagery	• Analyze details
Next Term, We'll Mash You *by* Penelope Lively ↔ *at grade level*	• Analyze theme	
Introducing Political Points of View: Human Rights	• Analyze and compare political points of view on a topic	• Compare main ideas across tex
Main Reading: **Saboteur** *by* Ha Jin ↓ *below grade level* **Connected Readings:** • *from the* **Universal Declaration of Human Rights** *by* United Nations Commission on Human Rights • *from* **The Question of South Africa** *by* Desmond Tutu • *from* **Towards a True Refuge** *by* Aung San Suu Kyi ↔ *at grade level*	• Analyze irony	• Identify political influences
Media Workshop: *Analyzing and Using Media*		
Listening and Speaking Workshop: *Presenting and Analyzing Speeches*		
Skills Review: *Literary Skills* *Vocabulary Skills* *Writing Skills*	• Compare works from different literary periods	

Vocabulary Skills	Writing ■ Grammar and Language ■ Listening and Speaking Skills
	• Write an essay analyzing theme
	• Write a response to a poem
	• Write an essay comparing and contrasting two sonnets
• Complete word analogies	• Write a reflective essay
• Use synonyms • Analyze word analogies	• Write an essay comparing and contrasting two short stories
• Create semantic diagrams	• Write a character analysis
	• Prepare a multimedia presentation
• Use synonyms and antonyms	• Write a journal entry
	• Analyze strategies used by different forms of media
	• Prepare a persuasive speech
• Complete word analogies	• Write a persuasive essay

Resource Manager

Selection ■ Feature	Planning	Differentiating Instruction ■ Lesson Plans with ELL Strategies and Practice	Reading ■ Vocabulary
The Modern World: 1900 to the Present by John Leggett *and* David Adams Leeming	• PowerNotes: The 20th Century	• Holt Adapted Reader	• Holt Adapted Reader
A World at War			
Dulce et Decorum Est by Wilfred Owen	• One-Stop Planner with ExamView Test Generator	• Supporting Instruction in Spanish, p. 44 • Audio CD Library • Audio CD Library, Selections and Summaries in Spanish	
The Hollow Men by T. S. Eliot	• One-Stop Planner with ExamView Test Generator	• The Holt Reader, pp. 247–253 • Holt Reading Solutions, pp. 161–163 • Supporting Instruction in Spanish, p. 45 • Audio CD Library • Audio CD Library, Selections and Summaries in Spanish	• The Holt Reader • Holt Reading Solutions • PowerNotes: Making Inferences
Introducing Political Points of View: The Holocaust			
Main Reading: **On the Bottom** *from* **Survival in Auschwitz** by Primo Levi **Connected Readings:** • *from* **The War** by Marguerite Duras • **Never Shall I Forget** by Elie Wiesel	• One-Stop Planner with ExamView Test Generator	• Supporting Instruction in Spanish, pp. 45–46 • Audio CD Library • Audio CD Library, Selections and Summaries in Spanish	• Vocabulary Development, p. 36
Blood, Sweat, and Tears by Winston Churchill	• One-Stop Planner with ExamView Test Generator	• The Holt Reader, pp. 254–259 • Holt Reading Solutions, p. 166 • Supporting Instruction in Spanish, p. 47 • Audio CD Library • Audio CD Library, Selections and Summaries in Spanish	• The Holt Reader • Holt Reading Solutions • Vocabulary Development, p. 37
The Silver Fifty-Sen Pieces by Yasunari Kawabata	• One-Stop Planner with ExamView Test Generator	• Supporting Instruction in Spanish, p. 47 • Audio CD Library • Audio CD Library, Selections and Summaries in Spanish	• Vocabulary Development, p. 38 • PowerNotes: Making Inferences
The Destructors by Graham Greene	• One-Stop Planner with ExamView Test Generator	• Supporting Instruction in Spanish, p. 48 • Audio CD Library • Audio CD Library, Selections and Summaries in Spanish	• Vocabulary Development, p. 39 • PowerNotes: Making Inferences

Writing • Grammar and Language • Listening and Speaking	Assessment
• Daily Language Activities	• Holt Assessment: Literature, Reading, and Vocabulary • Holt Online Assessment • One-Stop Planner with ExamView Test Generator
• Daily Language Activities	• Holt Assessment: Literature, Reading, and Vocabulary • Holt Online Assessment • One-Stop Planner with ExamView Test Generator
• Daily Language Activities	• Holt Assessment: Literature, Reading, and Vocabulary • Holt Online Assessment • One-Stop Planner with ExamView Test Generator
• Daily Language Activities	• Holt Assessment: Literature, Reading, and Vocabulary • Holt Online Assessment • One-Stop Planner with ExamView Test Generator
• Daily Language Activities • Language Handbook Worksheets, p. 78	• Holt Assessment: Literature, Reading, and Vocabulary • Holt Online Assessment • One-Stop Planner with ExamView Test Generator
• Daily Language Activities	• Holt Assessment: Literature, Reading, and Vocabulary • Holt Online Assessment • One-Stop Planner with ExamView Test Generator

Technology

INTERNET
- go.hrw.com
- Holt Online Assessment
- Holt Online Essay Scoring
- Elements of Literature Online

MEDIA
- One-Stop Planner with ExamView Test Generator
- PowerNotes
- Audio CD Library, discs 14–20
- Audio CD Library, Selections and Summaries in Spanish
- Visual Connections Videocassette Program, Segments 10 and 11
- Fine Art Transparencies, 15, 16, 17, and 18

 Transparency   Video

 CD-ROM   Audio CD

(continued)

Resource Manager

Selection • Feature	Planning	Differentiating Instruction • Lesson Plans with ELL Strategies and Practice	Reading • Vocabulary
In the Shadow of War by Ben Okri	• One-Stop Planner with ExamView Test Generator	• The Holt Reader, pp. 261–268 • Holt Reading Solutions, pp. 170–172 • Supporting Instruction in Spanish, p. 48 • Audio CD Library • Audio CD Library, Selections and Summaries in Spanish	• The Holt Reader • Holt Reading Solutions • Vocabulary Development, p. 40
Clashes of Culture			
Shakespeare's Sister *from* **A Room of One's Own** by Virginia Woolf	• One-Stop Planner with ExamView Test Generator	• The Holt Reader, pp. 270–279 • Holt Adapted Reader • Holt Reading Solutions, pp. 175–177 • Supporting Instruction in Spanish, p. 49 • Audio CD Library • Audio CD Library, Selections and Summaries in Spanish	• The Holt Reader • Holt Adapted Reader • Holt Reading Solutions • Vocabulary Development, p. 41
Introducing Political Points of View: Colonialism			
Main Readings: • **Shooting an Elephant** by George Orwell	• One-Stop Planner with ExamView Test Generator	• The Holt Reader, pp. 281–291 • Holt Adapted Reader • Holt Reading Solutions, pp. 181–183 • Supporting Instruction in Spanish, p. 49 • Audio CD Library • Audio CD Library, Selections and Summaries in Spanish	• The Holt Reader • Holt Adapted Reader • Holt Reading Solutions • Vocabulary Development, p. 42
• **No Witchcraft for Sale** by Doris Lessing **Connected Readings:** • "I Believe in a British Empire" by Joseph Chamberlain • "The Noble Mansion of Free India" by Jawaharlal Nehru	• One-Stop Planner with ExamView Test Generator	• The Holt Reader, pp. 293–303 • Holt Reading Solutions, pp. 186–188 • Supporting Instruction in Spanish, p. 50 • Audio CD Library • Audio CD Library, Selections and Summaries in Spanish	• The Holt Reader • Holt Reading Solutions • Vocabulary Development, p. 43
Once upon a Time by Nadine Gordimer	• One-Stop Planner with ExamView Test Generator	• Supporting Instruction in Spanish, p. 51 • Audio CD Library • Audio CD Library, Selections and Summaries in Spanish	• Vocabulary Development, p. 44
Marriage Is a Private Affair by Chinua Achebe	• One-Stop Planner with ExamView Test Generator	• Supporting Instruction in Spanish, p. 51 • Audio CD Library • Audio CD Library, Selections and Summaries in Spanish	• Vocabulary Development, p. 45
Telephone Conversation by Wole Soyinka	• One-Stop Planner with ExamView Test Generator	• Supporting Instruction in Spanish, p. 52 • Audio CD Library • Audio CD Library, Selections and Summaries in Spanish	

Writing • Grammar and Language • Listening and Speaking	Assessment
• Daily Language Activities	• Holt Assessment: Literature, Reading, and Vocabulary • Holt Online Assessment • One-Stop Planner with ExamView Test Generator
• Daily Language Activities	• Holt Assessment: Literature, Reading, and Vocabulary • Holt Online Assessment • One-Stop Planner with ExamView Test Generator
• Daily Language Activities • Daily Language Activities	• Holt Assessment: Literature, Reading, and Vocabulary • Holt Online Assessment • One-Stop Planner with ExamView Test Generator
• Daily Language Activities	• Holt Assessment: Literature, Reading, and Vocabulary • Holt Online Assessment • One-Stop Planner with ExamView Test Generator
• Daily Language Activities • Language Handbook Worksheets, p. 39	• Holt Assessment: Literature, Reading, and Vocabulary • Holt Online Assessment • One-Stop Planner with ExamView Test Generator
• Daily Language Activities	• Holt Assessment: Literature, Reading, and Vocabulary • Holt Online Assessment • One-Stop Planner with ExamView Test Generator

Technology

INTERNET
- go.hrw.com
- Holt Online Assessment
- Holt Online Essay Scoring
- Elements of Literature Online

MEDIA

- One-Stop Planner with ExamView Test Generator

- PowerNotes

- Audio CD Library, discs 14–20

- Audio CD Library, Selections and Summaries in Spanish

- Visual Connections Videocassette Program, Segments 10 and 11

- Fine Art Transparencies, 15, 16, 17, and 18

 Transparency   Video

 CD-ROM   Audio CD

(continued)

Resource Manager

Selection • Feature	Planning	Differentiating Instruction • Lesson Plans with ELL Strategies and Practice	Reading • Vocabulary
Discoveries and Transformations			
• **The Second Coming** • **The Lake Isle of Innisfree** • **The Wild Swans at Coole** *by* William Butler Yeats	• One-Stop Planner with ExamView Test Generator	• The Holt Reader, pp. 306–308 • Holt Reading Solutions, p. 192 • Supporting Instruction in Spanish, pp. 52–53 • Audio CD Library • Audio CD Library, Selections and Summaries in Spanish	• The Holt Reader • Holt Reading Solutions
Araby *by* James Joyce	• One-Stop Planner with ExamView Test Generator	• The Holt Reader, pp. 310–319 • Holt Reading Solutions, pp. 195–199 • Supporting Instruction in Spanish, p. 53 • Audio CD Library • Audio CD Library, Selections and Summaries in Spanish	• The Holt Reader • Holt Reading Solutions • Vocabulary Development, p. 45
The Rocking-Horse Winner *by* D. H. Lawrence	• One-Stop Planner with ExamView Test Generator	• Supporting Instruction in Spanish, p. 54 • Audio CD Library • Audio CD Library, Selections and Summaries in Spanish	• Vocabulary Development, p. 47
• **Lot's Wife** • **All the unburied ones** • **I am not one of those who left the land** *by* Anna Akhmatova	• One-Stop Planner with ExamView Test Generator	• Supporting Instruction in Spanish, p. 55 • Audio CD Library • Audio CD Library, Selections and Summaries in Spanish	
The Demon Lover *by* Elizabeth Bowen	• One-Stop Planner with ExamView Test Generator	• Supporting Instruction in Spanish, p. 55 • Audio CD Library • Audio CD Library, Selections and Summaries in Spanish	• Vocabulary Development, p. 48
Axolotl *by* Julio Cortázar	• One-Stop Planner with ExamView Test Generator	• Supporting Instruction in Spanish, p. 56 • Audio CD Library • Audio CD Library, Selections and Summaries in Spanish	• Vocabulary Development, p. 49
The Book of Sand *by* Jorge Luis Borges	• One-Stop Planner with ExamView Test Generator	• Supporting Instruction in Spanish, p. 56 • Audio CD Library • Audio CD Library, Selections and Summaries in Spanish	• Vocabulary Development, p. 50
B. Wordsworth *by* V. S. Naipaul	• One-Stop Planner with ExamView Test Generator	• Supporting Instruction in Spanish, p. 57 • Audio CD Library • Audio CD Library, Selections and Summaries in Spanish	• Vocabulary Development, p. 51
Half a Day *by* Naguib Mahfouz	• One-Stop Planner with ExamView Test Generator	• Supporting Instruction in Spanish, p. 57 • Audio CD Library • Audio CD Library, Selections and Summaries in Spanish	• Vocabulary Development, p. 52

Writing ▪ Grammar and Language ▪ Listening and Speaking	Assessment
• Daily Language Activities	• Holt Assessment: Literature, Reading, and Vocabulary • Holt Online Assessment • One-Stop Planner with ExamView Test Generator
• Daily Language Activities	• Holt Assessment: Literature, Reading, and Vocabulary • Holt Online Assessment • One-Stop Planner with ExamView Test Generator
• Daily Language Activities	• Holt Assessment: Literature, Reading, and Vocabulary • Holt Online Assessment • One-Stop Planner with ExamView Test Generator
	• Holt Assessment: Literature, Reading, and Vocabulary • Holt Online Assessment • One-Stop Planner with ExamView Test Generator
• Daily Language Activities • Language Handbook Worksheets, pp. 99–104	• Holt Assessment: Literature, Reading, and Vocabulary • Holt Online Assessment • One-Stop Planner with ExamView Test Generator
• Daily Language Activities	• Holt Assessment: Literature, Reading, and Vocabulary • Holt Online Assessment • One-Stop Planner with ExamView Test Generator
• Daily Language Activities	• Holt Assessment: Literature, Reading, and Vocabulary • Holt Online Assessment • One-Stop Planner with ExamView Test Generator
• Daily Language Activities	• Holt Assessment: Literature, Reading, and Vocabulary • Holt Online Assessment • One-Stop Planner with ExamView Test Generator
• Daily Language Activities	• Holt Assessment: Literature, Reading, and Vocabulary • Holt Online Assessment • One-Stop Planner with ExamView Test Generator

Technology

INTERNET
- go.hrw.com
- Holt Online Assessment
- Holt Online Essay Scoring
- Elements of Literature Online

MEDIA
 • One-Stop Planner with ExamView Test Generator
 • PowerNotes
 • Audio CD Library, discs 14–20
 • Audio CD Library, Selections and Summaries in Spanish
 • Visual Connections Videocassette Program, Segments 10 and 11
 • Fine Art Transparencies, 15, 16, 17, and 18

 Transparency   Video

 CD-ROM   Audio CD

Resource Manager

Selection • Feature	Planning	Differentiating Instruction • Lesson Plans with ELL Strategies and Practice	Reading • Vocabulary
Digging by Seamus Heaney	• One-Stop Planner with ExamView Test Generator	• Supporting Instruction in Spanish, p. 58 • Audio CD Library • Audio CD Library, Selections and Summaries in Spanish	
Ourselves Among Others			
The Doll's House by Katherine Mansfield	• One-Stop Planner with ExamView Test Generator	• Holt Adapted Reader • Supporting Instruction in Spanish, p. 58 • Audio CD Library • Audio CD Library, Selections and Summaries in Spanish	• Holt Adapted Reader • Vocabulary Development, p. 53
Musée des Beaux Arts by W. H. Auden	• One-Stop Planner with ExamView Test Generator	• The Holt Reader, pp. 321–323 • Holt Reading Solutions, p. 201	• The Holt Reader • Holt Reading Solutions
Fear by Gabriela Mistral	• One-Stop Planner with ExamView Test Generator	• Supporting Instruction in Spanish, p. 59 • Audio CD Library • Audio CD Library, Selections and Summaries in Spanish	
Fern Hill **Do Not Go Gentle into That Good Night** by Dylan Thomas	• One-Stop Planner with ExamView Test Generator	• The Holt Reader, pp. 325–328 • Holt Reading Solutions, p. 205 • Supporting Instruction in Spanish, p. 59 • Audio CD Library • Audio CD Library, Selections and Summaries in Spanish	• The Holt Reader • Holt Reading Solutions
Sonnet 79 / Soneto 79 by Pablo Neruda	• One-Stop Planner with ExamView Test Generator		
Like the Sun by R. K. Narayan	• One-Stop Planner with ExamView Test Generator	• Supporting Instruction in Spanish, p. 60 • Audio CD Library • Audio CD Library, Selections and Summaries in Spanish	• Vocabulary Development, p. 54
Games at Twilight by Anita Desai	• One-Stop Planner with ExamView Test Generator	• The Holt Reader, pp. 330–340 • Holt Reading Solutions, pp. 209–211 • Supporting Instruction in Spanish, p. 60 • Audio CD Library • Audio CD Library, Selections and Summaries in Spanish	• The Holt Reader • Holt Reading Solutions • Vocabulary Development, p. 55
Next Term, We'll Mash You by Penelope Lively	• One-Stop Planner with ExamView Test Generator	• Supporting Instruction in Spanish, p. 61 • Audio CD Library • Audio CD Library, Selections and Summaries in Spanish	• Vocabulary Development, p. 56

Writing • Grammar and Language • Listening and Speaking	Assessment
• Daily Language Activities • Language Handbook Worksheets, p. 20	• Holt Assessment: Literature, Reading, and Vocabulary • Holt Online Assessment • One-Stop Planner with ExamView Test Generator
• Daily Language Activities	• Holt Assessment: Literature, Reading, and Vocabulary • Holt Online Assessment • One-Stop Planner with ExamView Test Generator
	• Holt Assessment: Literature, Reading, and Vocabulary • Holt Online Assessment • One-Stop Planner with ExamView Test Generator
• Daily Language Activities	• Holt Assessment: Literature, Reading, and Vocabulary • Holt Online Assessment • One-Stop Planner with ExamView Test Generator
• Daily Language Activities	• Holt Assessment: Literature, Reading, and Vocabulary • Holt Online Assessment • One-Stop Planner with ExamView Test Generator
• Daily Language Activities	• Holt Assessment: Literature, Reading, and Vocabulary • Holt Online Assessment • One-Stop Planner with ExamView Test Generator
• Daily Language Activities	• Holt Assessment: Literature, Reading, and Vocabulary • Holt Online Assessment • One-Stop Planner with ExamView Test Generator
• Daily Language Activities	• Holt Assessment: Literature, Reading, and Vocabulary • Holt Online Assessment • One-Stop Planner with ExamView Test Generator

Technology

INTERNET
- go.hrw.com
- Holt Online Assessment
- Holt Online Essay Scoring
- Elements of Literature Online

MEDIA

- One-Stop Planner with ExamView Test Generator

- PowerNotes

- Audio CD Library, discs 14–20

- Audio CD Library, Selections and Summaries in Spanish

- Visual Connections Videocassette Program, Segments 10 and 11

- Fine Art Transparencies, 15, 16, 17, and 18

 Transparency   Video

 CD-ROM   Audio CD

Resource Manager

Selection • Feature	Planning	Differentiating Instruction • Lesson Plans with ELL Strategies and Practice	Reading • Vocabulary
Introducing Political Points of View: Human Rights			
Main Reading: *Saboteur* by Ha Jin **Connected Readings:** • *from* **the Universal Declaration of Human Rights** by United Nations Commission on Human Rights • *from* **The Question of South Africa** by Desmond Tutu • *from* **Towards a True Refuge** by Aung San Suu Kyi	• One-Stop Planner with ExamView Test Generator	• Supporting Instruction in Spanish, pp. 62–63 • Audio CD Library • Audio CD Library, Selections and Summaries in Spanish	• Vocabulary Development, p. 57
Media Workshop: *Analyzing and Using Media*	• One-Stop Planner with ExamView Test Generator	• Workshop Resources: Writing, Listening, and Speaking, pp. 77–79 • Supporting Instruction in Spanish	
Listening and Speaking Workshop: *Presenting and Analyzing Speeches*	• One-Stop Planner with ExamView Test Generator	• Workshop Resources: Writing, Listening, and Speaking, pp. 86–87 • Supporting Instruction in Spanish, p. 109	
Skills Review: *Literary Skills* *Vocabulary Skills* *Writing Skills*			

The Holt Reader

The Holt Reader is a consumable paperback book that can be used alone or to accompany *Elements of Literature*. It offers guided support throughout the reading process and encourages students to become active readers by circling, underlining, questioning, and jotting down responses as they read. *The Holt Reader* works well for homework, students who have missed class, additional instructional time, reteaching, and remediation.

Holt Reading Solutions (HRS)

Holt Reading Solutions pulls together reading resources in the *Elements of Literature* program to create a powerful tool for intervention and whole-class instruction. *HRS* includes diagnostic assessment tools, lesson plans for English-language learners and special education students, adaptations of selected reading selections, vocabulary and comprehension worksheets, information on phonics and decoding, and additional instruction and practice in remedial reading skills.

Writing ■ Grammar and Language ■ Listening and Speaking	Assessment
	• Holt Assessment: Literature, Reading, and Vocabulary • Holt Online Assessment • One-Stop Planner with ExamView Test Generator
• Daily Language Activities	
• Daily Language Activities • Workshop Resources: Writing, Listening, and Speaking, pp. 77–79	• Holt Assessment: Writing, Listening, and Speaking • Holt Online Assessment • One-Stop Planner with ExamView Test Generator
• Workshop Resources: Writing, Listening, and Speaking, pp. 86–87	• Holt Assessment: Writing, Listening, and Speaking • Holt Online Assessment • One-Stop Planner with ExamView Test Generator
	• Holt Assessment: Writing, Listening, and Speaking • One-Stop Planner with ExamView Test Generator

Technology

INTERNET

- go.hrw.com
- Holt Online Assessment
- Holt Online Essay Scoring
- Elements of Literature Online

MEDIA

- One-Stop Planner with ExamView Test Generator

- PowerNotes
- Audio CD Library, discs 14–20
- Audio CD Library, Selections and Summaries in Spanish
- Visual Connections Videocassette Program, Segments 10 and 11
- Fine Art Transparencies, 15, 16, 17, and 18

 Transparency   Video

 CD-ROM   Audio CD

One-Stop Planner with ExamView Test Generator

The *One-Stop Planner* CD-ROM contains electronic versions of print-based teaching resources, clips from the video program, and valuable assessment tools. The *One-Stop Planner* resources are presented in easy-to-follow, point-and-click menu formats. To preview resources or print out worksheets and tests, you simply make a selection and click.

Collection 7

INTRODUCING THE COLLECTION

In this collection, students will read the works of many twentieth-century writers and learn about the historical events that influenced them. In Collection 7, students will revisit the Holocaust with Primo Levi, learn about colonialism with George Orwell, and get a glimpse of the human rights movement through the words of Desmond Tutu and Ha Jin. Students will analyze various themes and literary devices used by modern writers from different cultures. Finally, the collection concludes by providing students with opportunities to write a persuasive essay, analyze and use Media, and present speeches.

VIEWING THE ART

Henry Moore (1898–1986), one of the twentieth century's most important sculptors, sought to represent the interaction between his figures and the spaces they inhabit. In the sculpture shown here, Moore has hollowed out the abdomens of the parents, creating a cavity in which the baby is suspended. The interplay between the hollow space and the solid figures creates the impression that the two parents form a large lap into which their child eases.

Activity. What might Moore be trying to imply by representing two parents as one large lap? [Perhaps the sculpture symbolizes the togetherness that can be created in a harmonious family.]

Family Group (1948–1949) by Henry Moore. Bronze.
Henry Moore Foundation. Much Hadham, England. Reproduced by permission of the Henry Moore Foundation.

COLLECTION 7 RESOURCES: READING

Planning
- One-Stop Planner CD-ROM with ExamView Test Generator

Differentiating Instruction
- Holt Reading Solutions
- The Holt Reader
- Holt Adapted Reader
- Family Involvement Activities in English and Spanish

- Supporting Instruction in Spanish
- Audio CD Library, Selections and Summaries in Spanish

Vocabulary
- Vocabulary Development

Grammar and Language
- Language Handbook Worksheets
- Daily Language Activities

Collection 7

The Modern World
1900 to the Present

A Remarkable Diversity

> We are sharply cut off from our predecessors. A shift in the scale . . . has shaken the fabric from top to bottom, alienated us from the past and made us perhaps too vividly conscious of the present. Every day we find ourselves doing, saying, or thinking things that would have been impossible to our fathers.
>
> —Virginia Woolf

INTERNET
Collection Resources
Keyword: LE5 12-7

THE QUOTATION

Before World War I, Great Britain was probably the wealthiest and most powerful nation on earth, with a well-structured, class-conscious society at home and an empire that circled the globe. Ask students what events might have brought about the shift that Virginia Woolf describes in this comment written in the 1930s. [Possible responses: the huge loss of life during World War I; the economic turmoil and depression of the 1920s and 1930s.]

Assessment
- Holt Assessment: Literature, Reading, and Vocabulary
- One-Stop Planner CD-ROM with ExamView Test Generator
- Holt Online Assessment

Internet
- go.hrw.com (Keyword: LE5 12-7)
- Elements of Literature Online

Media
- Audio CD Library
- Audio CD Library, Selections and Summaries in Spanish
- Fine Art Transparencies
- Visual Connections Videocassette Program
- PowerNotes

Political and Social

Political and Social Milestones

The Great War, 1914–1918

The concentration of large forces in small areas and the strength of trench positions defended by machine guns and artillery led to a war of attrition between the Central Powers and the Allied forces.

The scale and duration of the struggle led to an unprecedented mobilization of national resources in Great Britain. The government was given extensive emergency powers, and most of the economy came under state direction. Even after two million men had volunteered, conscription had to be introduced for the first time in modern British history.

The defeat of Germany and Turkey gave Great Britain mandates over additional territories, including Egypt, Cyprus, Palestine, Jordan, Iraq, and the African countries of Tanganyika and Togo. However, the lingering strains and costs of the Great War, a deeply divided political situation in London, and, later, the Great Depression, left Great Britain unable to act effectively as a colonial power.

World War II, 1939–1945

Although the Second World War cost fewer British lives than did the First and spared the army the horrors of the trenches, the Nazis posed more of a threat to Great Britain than had the kaiser. With the British army driven from Europe in 1940 and British cities and ships under relentless Nazi air and submarine attack, Prime Minister Neville Chamberlain was considering a negotiated peace with Hitler. Winston Churchill, elected in 1940, was determined to continue fighting despite the bleak odds. British success that year in the Battle of Britain blunted German air power sufficiently to force Hitler to call off Operation Sealion, his planned invasion of Great Britain.

The Great War, 1914–1918

Imperial War Museum, London.

Rising nationalism among European countries, competition for colonies, growing military forces, advances in technology—these factors, among others, created an environment ripe for conflict in the early years of the twentieth century. When the Great War (later known as World War I) broke out in 1914, Great Britain allied itself with France and Russia against the Central Powers of Germany and Austria-Hungary. Scores of young, patriotic men rushed to the front lines. By its conclusion in 1918, the war had cost Great Britain 750,000 lives. It had also cost billions of dollars, sending England into debt and severely rocking the prosperity the nation had formerly enjoyed as a major world power. The confidence and optimism of the preceding era floundered as a wave of anxiety and uncertainty washed over the nation.

Over the Top, 1st Artists' Rifles at Marcoing (detail) (December 30, 1917) by John Northcote Nash.
Imperial War Museum, London.

Germany's invasion of the Soviet Union in June 1941 took the immediate pressure off the British, and the United States' entry into the war allied Great Britain with the world's most powerful economy. Although German submarines exacted a huge toll on British shipping, the Anglo-American alliance provided the strength to achieve victory.

Milestones

World War II, 1939–1945

In the 1930s, the Great Depression sent the United States and Europe into a crushing economic slump. Mass unemployment and poverty led to despair. In a world plagued by financial and emotional crises, dictators were able to rise to power in nations such as Germany, Italy, and Russia. When Hitler's armies invaded Poland in 1939, Great Britain and France took up arms against them, thus igniting World War II. After France fell to Germany, German troops moved on England, but Britain held firm. Finally, in 1945, the Allies—Great Britain, the United States, and the Soviet Union—defeated Germany and Japan. But the horrors of this war—particularly nuclear devastation and the Nazi concentration camps—had changed the world forever.

(Opposite) Children taking refuge in trenches during air raids in southeastern England.

Crowd at Nigerian independence ceremony in Lagos (1965).

The End of the Empire: New Nations Emerge

Before World War II, countries such as Australia, Canada, and South Africa had already separated from the British Empire. The end of World War II sealed the empire's fate. During the late 1940s and the 1950s, most of Britain's remaining colonies declared independence.

As a result of the decline of Western imperial powers after World War II, dozens of newly independent states emerged in Africa and Asia, and many older nations in Europe and Latin America were politically redefined. These nations and others began to assert their own identities and reclaim territories. This process of self-determination, however, was seldom achieved without conflict. In South Africa, Northern Ireland, Eastern Europe, the Middle East, and Central America, violence is still a common experience.

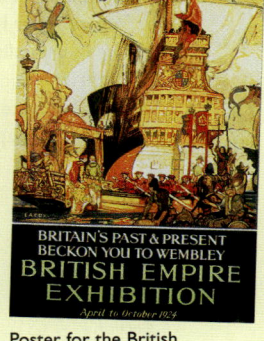

Poster for the British Empire Exhibition (1924) by E. A. Cox.
Victoria and Albert Museum, London.

■ The End of the Empire: New Nations Emerge

The loss of resources and prestige during World War II and the rise of nationalism among British colonies in Asia and Africa fatally weakened the British Empire. The British armies suffered humiliating losses in Singapore and Malaysia to the Japanese forces in the spring of 1942.

British control of India ended in 1947 after the rise of religious conflict, which resulted in the partitioning of the Indian subcontinent into India and Pakistan. Britain's Labour Party, which had unexpectedly taken power in 1945, also oversaw the country's withdrawal in 1948 from control of Burma, Ceylon, Trans-Jordan, Egypt (except the Suez Canal territory), and Palestine. The following year, Burma and Ceylon gained their independence.

The Suez Crisis of 1956 exposed further British weaknesses. When Gamel Abdul Nasser, the Arab nationalist leader of Egypt, moved to nationalize the Suez Canal, the takeover was opposed by British and French forces. Their poorly planned invasion, however, ended in an embarrassing withdrawal.

After Suez, many Britons became disillusioned with the empire. The colonies were expensive to administer and were a source of conflict with the Soviet Union and with the United States, which supported nationalist independence movements, especially in Africa. By 1969, none of Africa remained under British rule.

No longer a global territorial power and with a weakening domestic economy, Britain's status as a major power became increasingly precarious.

SKILLS FOCUS, pp. 804–818

Grade-Level Skills

■ **Literary Skills**

Evaluate the philosophical, political, religious, ethical, and social influences of the historical period.

Preview

Think About . . .

Ask students to preview the introduction, reading aloud the subheadings and commenting on the illustrations. Have students share what they know about the topics mentioned in the headings. Then, ask a volunteer to read aloud the four questions at the end of the preview. Direct students to take notes as they read in order to answer these questions.

The Modern World
1900 to the Present

by John Leggett *and* David Adams Leeming

PREVIEW

Think About . . .

"The center cannot hold," wrote poet William Butler Yeats in 1919. And indeed, in the early years of the twentieth century, the prosperity and stability of the Victorian era dissolved into chaos and conflict. The Great Britain of yesterday, ruled by the principles of order, industry, and self-control, was attacked on virtually every front—intellectual, social, economic, and political. Thinkers such as Sigmund Freud scandalized Victorian self-determinists by declaring that human beings are driven by unconscious, irrational desires. The theories of German philosopher Karl Marx led to the questioning of capitalism and eventually to the transformation of Great Britain into a socialist state. Two world wars and a major economic depression eroded Great Britain's political and economic power and brought a slow, painful death upon the once-mighty empire. Disenchanted with human institutions, the artists of the age turned their backs on the world, creating wildly new, experimental forms of expression—celebrating "art for art's sake."

As you read about this period, look for answers to these questions:

- How was English society changed by the Great War—World War I?
- What were some factors that led to the outbreak of World War II?
- What were the long-term effects of the two world wars on Great Britain?
- How did social and political events in the postwar world lead to a rich diversity of world literature?

Collection introduction (pages 802–818) covers **Literary Skills** Evaluate the philosophical, political, religious, ethical, and social influences of a historical period.

What a story of change, of the erosion of a proud, complacent, well-ordered society, is told by the early years of the twentieth century in Great Britain!

Change on the Horizon

If we had lived in the era of Victoria, which ended with the great queen's death in 1901, or during the nine-year reign of her son Edward VII, we would have believed that Britain, with its moral and economic dominance of the world, would sail on majestically forever. But of course that is the misconception of every stable age and society—that life will go on just as it always has.

DIFFERENTIATING INSTRUCTION

Learners Having Difficulty

As students read, have them take notes that they can use later as the basis for making generalizations about Great Britain in the twentieth century. Point out the section headings and the Fast Facts list (pp. 816–817), which summarizes ideas and events of the period. Remind students to form generalizations based on this text.

English-Language Learners

Make sure students understand that there are differences between British English and American English. Introduce the term *Briticism,* meaning "a word or phrase characteristic of British English." Share with students terms from British life that they may not know, such as *Labour Party, the House of Windsor, the royals,* and *dependencies.*

Special Education Students

For lessons designed for special education students, see *Holt Reading Solutions.*

The Arrival (1923–1924) by Christopher R. W. Nevinson.
Tate Gallery, London. © Tate, London 2002.

DIRECT TEACHING

VIEWING THE ART

Christopher R. W. Nevinson (1889–1946) became interested in futurism, an artistic movement founded on the celebration of technology and the dynamism of modern life. He painted *The Arrival* during his futurist period, though his war experience would lead him to eventually reject the tenets of the movement. The painting depicts the brave new world of industrialization and transportation.

Activity. Ask students to discuss the use of angles and geometric shapes in *The Arrival*. What seems "modern" about this style? [Fragmented images of the ship and port combine to suggest one entity.]

DIFFERENTIATING INSTRUCTION

Advanced Learners

Enrichment. Encourage students to read a recent work by Martin Amis, Margaret Drabble, A. S. Byatt, Anita Brookner, Graham Swift, Pat Barker, or another contemporary British novelist. Students might comment on what seems distinctively British in the work and what seems to be a product of a global culture.

DIRECT TEACHING

A Background
Sir Winston Churchill
Although he was defeated in the election after the war, Sir Winston Churchill served again as prime minister from 1951 to 1955. In 1953, he was awarded the Nobel Prize in literature for his many writings, including *The Second World War*, which is comprised of six volumes.

B Humanities Connections
Progress Toward Peace in Ireland
A few months after the referendum vote, John Hume, the Catholic head of the Social Democratic and Labor Party, and David Trimble, the Protestant leader of the Ulster Unionists, were awarded the 1998 Nobel Peace Prize.

C Exploring the Historical Period
INDEPENDENCE FOR INDIA
Call attention to the date of this quotation. Although full Indian independence was not achieved until 1947, the quotation proves that the seeds of discontent were growing much earlier. In the Great War, well over a million Indians had fought on behalf of the British; in return, they were promised a greater role in their own government. When this did not take place, acts of violence began to occur, prompting Gandhi's policy of nonviolent civil disobedience, the strategy that eventually led to self-rule for India.

Protest march in Belfast by Troops Out, a group calling for removal of British troops from Northern Ireland (1986).

> Little do town dwellers know how the semi-starved masses of India are slowly sinking to lifelessness. Little do they know that their miserable comfort represents the brokerage they get for the work they do for the foreign exploiter, that the profits and the brokerage are sucked from the masses. Little do they realize that the government established by law in British India is carried on for this exploitation of the masses. No sophistry, no jugglery in figures can explain away the evidence that the skeletons in many villages present to the naked eye. I have no doubt whatsoever that both England and the town dwellers of India will have to answer, if there is a God above, for this crime against humanity which is perhaps unequaled in history.
>
> —Mohandas K. Gandhi, 1922

Britain After World War II: The Sun Sets on the Empire

After the war ended in Europe, Winston Churchill and his Conservative party were defeated by the Labour party, and Britain was transformed into a welfare state. The government assumed responsibility for providing medical care and other basic benefits for its citizens. While recovering from the war and rebuilding its own economy, Great Britain could not hold on to its many colonies. Most of them—including India, the "jewel in the crown"—became independent nations, and the sun now set nightly on the British Empire.

In the spring of 1998, an end to thirty years of violent conflict over the status of the six British-controlled counties of Northern Ireland seemed near at hand. After years of fighting in the streets of Ulster and a bombing campaign by the Irish Republican Army (IRA) that at times extended into England, representatives of the Catholics and Protestants of Northern Ireland and the prime ministers of Great Britain and Ireland hammered out a promising formula for peace. An amazing 71 percent of the population of Northern Ireland and 94 percent of the population of the Republic of Ireland voted yes in a referendum on the historic agreement on May 24, 1998.

British Writing Today

One of the most influential literary figures in England before World War II was the poet W. H. Auden (see page 1045), who had an intellectual background and a left-wing, antifascist political point of view. After the war, however, a group of younger novelists and playwrights emerged who opposed the values of the Auden group. These writers, who became known as the Angry Young Men, criticized the pretensions of intellectuals and the bland lives of the newly prosperous mid-

---

SKILLS REVIEW

Evaluating sources of information on the Internet. Invite small groups of students to collaborate on an Internet search. Using a search engine, have each group conduct a keyword search on one of the topics in this introduction. Ask them to print out a list of the first twenty matches they find. Then, ask each group to divide up the work of evaluating those matches for credibility and usefulness and to apply the following criteria:

1. Evaluate the site.
   - What kind of site is this? For example, is it government (gov), education (edu), or commercial (com)? What do these terms tell you about the site?
   - Who contributes information to this site?

2. Evaluate the authorship.
   - Is the authorship stated? If so, who are the authors?
   - What is their purpose in posting this information on the net?
   - Are any credentials given? What are they?

3. Evaluate the information.

(Left) Lone protestor standing in front of tanks at Tiananmen Square (1989).

(Below) Students protesting apartheid in education, Johannesburg, South Africa.

creativity in her fiction. In *The Handmaid's Tale* (1985), the Canadian novelist Margaret Atwood (see page 1125) serves up a grim cautionary tale, warning readers of a possible future by creating a world in which a puritanical dictatorship seeks to repress and control women.

Never Forget: Responses to War and Government Repression

Since the beginning of the twentieth century, world history has been marked by periods of widespread warfare interspersed with periods of uneasy peace. Not surprisingly, then, much of modern world literature has been a direct and blistering response to war. In *All Quiet on the Western Front* (1928), the German author Erich Maria Remarque described the physical and psychological horrors of World War I with such vehemence that the novel was banned in Germany. But even this harrowing war novel paled beside the personal trauma of World War II's Holocaust as depicted by the Italian writer Primo Levi (see page 833), interned at Auschwitz, and the Romanian writer Elie Wiesel (see page 844), who has spent a lifetime serving as a witness to the atrocities of the Holocaust and has declared "Never shall I forget." The reclusive Polish poet Wisława Szymborska (see page 880), winner of the 1996 Nobel Prize in literature, uses the commonplaces of everyday life to explore the most profound human truths. Few modern Japanese writers could avoid addressing World War II, and "The Silver Fifty-Sen Pieces" by Yasunari Kawabata (see page 853) evokes the loss and pain that

FAST FACTS
Social Influences
- After World War I, in which nearly one million British soldiers die, many people in Great Britain develop a cynical attitude toward government and such values as national honor and glory.
- Writers from former British colonies and other parts of the world explore the effects of cultural domination, racism, sexism, and war.

DIRECT TEACHING

E Literary Connections
Margaret Atwood
Feminist novelist Margaret Atwood (1939–   ) treats a variety of contemporary themes in her novels, including the intrusive nature of mass society and the future of Canada and Canadian literature.

F Exploring the Culture
WORLD WARS AND SMALLER WARS
The twentieth century saw two major world wars but also a myriad of smaller wars fought by rival ethnic or religious groups or by followers of different ideologies within a country or region. Among these were the Chinese Civil War (1930s–1949), the Korean War (1950–1953), the Vietnam War (1964–1975), the Nigerian Civil War (1967–1970), and the Arab-Israeli conflicts, to name a few. No wonder so much of the past century's literature concerns the issue of war.

Check Test: Short Answer
Monitoring students' progress. Guide the class in answering the following questions.

1. Which three nineteenth-century thinkers had an enormous impact on twentieth-century developments? [Charles Darwin, Karl Marx, and Sigmund Freud]

2. What similar political development occurred in Italy, Germany, and Russia before World War II? [Dictators rose to power.]

3. What are some of the reasons for contemporary British literature's amazing diversity? [the influence of different social and philosophical movements; the influx of literature from Britain's former colonies; innovations in technology; the rise of feminism]

DIRECT TEACHING

A Literary Connections
Aleksandr Solzhenitsyn
Aleksandr Solzhenitsyn (1918–   ) was imprisoned in 1945 for criticizing Stalin. His early novel, *One Day in the Life of Ivan Denisovich* (1962), describes the grimness of the Soviet penal system. His later novels, highly critical of Russian society, were banned in the Soviet Union but published abroad. After accepting the Nobel Prize in literature in 1974, Solzhenitsyn lived in exile until 1994, when he returned to Russia.

B Exploring the Historical Period
TIANANMEN SQUARE MASSACRE
In spring 1989, thousands of pro-democracy demonstrators occupied Tiananmen Square, Beijing's central gathering place. They wanted an end to corruption in the ruling party, a greater say in government, and better conditions in universities. Thousands of students, ignoring government orders to leave the square, staged a hunger strike. In early June, Chinese leaders took action, sending in tanks and troops. Hundreds of protesters were killed and thousands were wounded in the ensuing massacre.

Review

Think About . . .

- English society was devastated by the Great War. Over 750,000 British soldiers died, and much of the nation's wealth was lost in the fighting. The country was weakened economically and disillusioned with its former social and political ideals.
- Resentments from World War I as well as the worldwide economic depression of the 1930s led to the rise of dictators in Germany, Italy, and Russia, who upset the balance of power in Europe.

I am cheered by a vital awareness of WORLD LITERATURE as of a single huge heart, beating out the cares and troubles of our world, albeit presented and perceived differently in each of its corners.
—Aleksandr Solzhenitsyn

A civilians endured. Writers in the former Soviet Union—such as Aleksandr Solzhenitsyn, who believes that literature "becomes the living memory of the nation," and Anna Akhmatova (see page 982), who was persecuted by the government for *not* writing on political themes (at least, the correct ones)—made an art out of defying government attempts to regulate their writing. And even though Communist China's government set out to "reeducate" its stubborn writers, some, like Ha Jin (see page 1089)—who left China after B seeing the Tiananmen Square massacre in 1989—explore the troubling, unequal relationships between the state and the individual.

A "Marvelous Capacity": The Promise of World Literature

In literature as in history, many different stories can proceed at the same time. Such a variety of writing can only broaden and deepen our understanding of the human condition. As Solzhenitsyn commented in his Nobel Prize acceptance speech, "The only substitute for what we ourselves have not experienced is art and literature. They have the marvelous capacity of transmitting from one nation to another—despite differences in language, customs, and social structure—practical experience, the harsh national experience of many decades never tasted by the other nation."

REVIEW

Talk About . . .
Turn back to the Think About questions posed at the start of this introduction (page 804). Get together with a group of classmates to discuss your views.

Write About . . .
Contrasting Literary Periods
Artistic (dis)order, then and now.
Many writers of the early twentieth century struggled to express the despair they felt living in an apparently meaningless, unpredictable world. Human institutions such as government and religion had proved unreliable and ineffective. The very notion of order was itself questioned and manipulated. Writers such as Virginia Woolf and D. H. Lawrence tampered with accepted forms and boundaries, abandoning chronological order and introducing topics that were once taboo. Shock value in art was all the rage. In your opinion, are we still "shockable" today? Does art continue to challenge norms and condemn human institutions? Or does it reflect a new stability in society? As you answer these questions, consider not just literature but other contemporary art forms, such as music, film, the visual arts, and dance.

- The combined effects of the two world wars weakened Great Britain, leaving the nation unable to maintain its empire. As a result, the nation gave its colonies independence and focused on becoming part of the European community.

- The independence of former British colonies fostered the emergence of writers with unique voices—writers whose works reflected both their complex heritage and a transcendence of natural boundaries.

Collection 7:
The Modern World:
1900 to the Present

A World at War

Owen
Sassoon
Eliot
Levi
Duras
Wiesel
Churchill
Kawabata
Greene
Okri
Szymborska

We are all of us made by war, twisted and warped by war, but we seem to forget it.
—Doris Lessing

British soldiers at Ypres, Belgium.
Imperial War Museum, London.

THE QUOTATION

Read the Doris Lessing quotation aloud and elicit responses. Ask students to suggest some ways in which a person might be affected by a current or past war, even if the person never personally fought in it. Elicit some long-term effects that a war, such as World War II or the Vietnam War, might have had on a nation's politics, culture, and economy. Ask students to discuss whether they think *twisted* and *warped* are the right verbs to describe these effects. Finally, have students discuss why it is a common tendency to forget a war and its effects.

Wilfred Owen
(1893–1918)
England

Wilfred Owen is one of the most poignant figures in modern literature. "The Poetry is in the pity," he said, and this famous remark could serve as his epitaph. Within the few adult years granted to him, Owen pursued a course of development that went from strength to strength. His interest in experimental techniques led him to master the use of half rhyme; this would become his most easily recognizable poetic signature. He also had a gift for lyricism that was bitterly tempered by "the truth un-told, / The pity of war, the pity war distilled." The result was a series of elegies and metrical statements as terse and stark as those carved on tombstones.

Like an apprentice determined to master his art, Owen immersed himself in the long history of English poetry. He chose for his model and mentor the poet John Keats (see page 640), whose astonishing life's work ended with his death at twenty-five (about the same age Shakespeare was when he began to write his plays). As a tutor in France for two years, Owen studied the French poets who were producing the tradition-shattering art that would become known as modernist. But all these literary influences were to become secondary to the devastating impact of a war Owen witnessed firsthand.

World War I broke out when Owen was twenty-one; he joined the British army, and the course of his life was determined. His progress in poetry was not made in the halls of an ancient university or in the country retreats where his literary forerunners were privileged to pursue their careers. His progress took place in the muddy purgatory of trench warfare and in the twilight existence of military hospitals.

In one of those hospitals, Craiglockhart, in Edinburgh, the young Owen met Siegfried Sassoon, a fellow officer and poet who had already distinguished himself for bravery in battle. Ironically, Sassoon was also the author of some of the most biting antiwar verses ever written (see page 823). Temperamentally, the two men were far apart. Owen was an idealistic youth thwarted by circumstance; Sassoon was an aristocrat appalled by the wartime complacency of his own class. Even so, they became friends and artistic colleagues at once. After Owen's death, Sassoon became the first important British writer to herald the younger man's genius and to call attention to what he had accomplished under the most appalling conditions.

In 1918, Owen was listed among those killed in action—a mere seven days before the war ended with a joyous ringing of bells and dancing in the streets.

Before You Read

Dulce et Decorum Est

Make the Connection
Quickwrite

In trench warfare, "no man's land" is the few hundred yards that separate one army's lines from another's. But for the group of writers who became known as the Trench Poets, the war itself was a no man's land: a dehumanizing, horrific experience that made a mockery of civilization. Wilfred Owen, like many other Trench Poets, died in the muddy trenches of World War I. But his words lived on, bringing to life the evils and obscenities of war for those back home.

What is your most vivid mental image of war? Recall impressions you've absorbed from film, photographs, the nightly news, literary works, the words of veterans, or other sources. Close your eyes. Think, "War," and then record in words what you see in your mind.

Literary Focus
Figures of Speech

Many readers of Owen's poetry had never visited the front lines, nor would they ever do so. To help his readers see, understand, and feel the foreign subject of war, Owen used figures of speech to describe war's images and events.

A **figure of speech** is a word or phrase that describes one thing in terms of another. Among the most common figures of speech are **similes**, **metaphors**, and **symbols**. Early in Owen's poem, for instance, the poet uses a simile to describe the speaker and his fellow soldiers who lurch forward "like old beggars under sacks" (line 1). Owen also uses **oxymoron**, a figure of speech that combines apparently contradictory ideas to create a strong emphasis. The word *bittersweet*, used to describe the feeling of being happy and sad at the same time, is an example of an oxymoron. (The phrases "tough love" and "cold comfort" are other examples of oxymorons.) In literature, "darkness visible" is a famous oxymoron used by Milton in *Paradise Lost* (see page 367). Owen and other Trench Poets found oxymorons useful in describing the unimaginable slaughter of trench warfare. As you read Owen's poem, see if you can identify several different kinds of figures of speech.

> A **figure of speech** is a word or phrase that describes one thing in terms of another and is not meant to be understood on a literal level.
>
> *For more on Figures of Speech, see the Handbook of Literary and Historical Terms.*

Background

This poem's title is taken from the Latin statement *Dulce et decorum est pro patria mori*, meaning "It is sweet and honorable to die for one's country." The statement originally appeared in an ode by the ancient Roman poet Horace and has been used for centuries as a morale builder—and as an epitaph, or gravestone inscription—for soldiers. Here the motto is given a bitter twist by a soldier-poet who cannot see how the sentiment it expresses matches the reality he has experienced.

After the introduction of poison gas as a battlefield weapon during World War I, every man in the trenches was equipped with a gas mask. This poem describes the horrible consequences of not getting the mask on in time.

Literary Skills
Understand figures of speech.

Wilfred Owen   821

PRETEACHING

Summary *at grade level*

> The speaker is marching with a group of battle-weary soldiers when a poison-gas shell explodes nearby. The soldiers scramble to don their gas masks, but one fails, and the others watch helplessly while the fumes choke him to death. The speaker says that, in all his dreams, he still sees the man dying. Then, he directly addresses the reader, asserting that if "you" could see that too, you would not teach children the vicious lie that it is sweet and honorable to die for one's country.

Skills Starter

Motivate. To encourage students to think about the contradictions of war, first have them make two lists of war-related words—one containing words with positive connotations, such as *honor, courage,* and *glory,* and the other containing words with negative connotations, such as *slaughter, violence,* and *gore.* Then have them create oxymorons by pairing words (or forms of words) taken from both lists—*glorious slaughter,* for example. Invite students to share the most striking oxymorons they created and to comment on the contradictory ideas contained in each.

DIFFERENTIATING INSTRUCTION

Learners Having Difficulty
Modeling. Have pairs of students take turns describing what they see in their mind's eye as they read "Dulce et Decorum Est." Model a description by saying, "I see a group of soldiers with packs on their backs, bent over like old men, coughing and cursing, as they try to move through mud."

English-Language Learners
For both this poem and the Connection that follows (p. 823), have students create a chart and record *who, what, where,* and *when.*

Wilfred Owen   821

Paths of Glory (1917) by Christopher R.W. Nevinson. Imperial War Museum, London.

Dulce et Decorum Est
Wilfred Owen

Bent double, like old beggars under sacks,
Knock-kneed, coughing like hags, we cursed through sludge,
Till on the haunting flares we turned our backs
And toward our distant rest began to trudge.
5 Men marched asleep. Many had lost their boots
But limped on, blood-shod. All went lame; all blind;
Drunk with fatigue; deaf even to the hoots
Of tired, outstripped Five-Nines° that dropped behind.

Gas! GAS! Quick, boys!—An ecstasy of fumbling,
10 Fitting the clumsy helmets just in time;
But someone still was yelling out and stumbling
And flound'ring like a man in fire or lime° . . .
Dim, through the misty panes and thick green light,
As under a green sea, I saw him drowning.

15 In all my dreams, before my helpless sight,
He plunges at me, guttering, choking, drowning.

If in some smothering dreams you too could pace
Behind the wagon that we flung him in,
And watch the white eyes writhing in his face,
20 His hanging face, like a devil's sick of sin;
If you could hear, at every jolt, the blood
Come gargling from the froth-corrupted lungs,
Obscene as cancer, bitter as the cud
Of vile, incurable sores on innocent tongues,—
25 My friend, you would not tell with such high zest
To children ardent for some desperate glory,
The old Lie: *Dulce et decorum est
Pro patria mori.*

8. **Five-Nines:** 5.9-caliber gas shells.

12. **lime** *n.:* powder produced from heat on limestone. It can cause severe skin irritations.

CONNECTION / POEM

In the battlefield trenches of World War I, enlisted men lived for weeks, sometimes years, in interconnected underground caverns infested by rats, with no drainage, poor ventilation, and only occasional dim shafts of natural light. In this poem, the "he" who recalls a grisly trench episode is the officer-poet, Siegfried Sassoon himself.

The Rear-Guard

Siegfried Sassoon

(Hindenburg Line,° April 1917.)
Groping along the tunnel, step by step,
He winked his prying torch° with patching glare
From side to side, and sniffed the unwholesome air.

Tins, boxes, bottles, shapes too vague to know,
5 A mirror smashed, the mattress from a bed;
And he, exploring fifty feet below
The rosy gloom of battle overhead.

Tripping, he grabbed the wall; saw someone lie
Humped at his feet, half-hidden by a rug,
10 And stooped to give the sleeper's arm a tug.
"I'm looking for headquarters." No reply.
"God blast your neck!" (For days he'd had no sleep.)

"Get up and guide me through this stinking place."
Savage, he kicked a soft, unanswering heap,
15 And flashed his beam across the livid face
Terribly glaring up, whose eyes yet wore
Agony dying hard ten days before;
And fists of fingers clutched a blackening wound.

Alone he staggered on until he found
20 Dawn's ghost that filtered down a shafted stair
To the dazed, muttering creatures underground
Who hear the boom of shells in muffled sound.
At last, with sweat of horror in his hair,
He climbed through darkness to the twilight air,
25 Unloading hell behind him step by step.

Hindenburg Line: German defensive barricade running across northern France. It was made of massive barbed-wire entanglements and deep trenches.
2. **torch** *n.*: flashlight.

Comparing and Contrasting Texts

Comparing sound effects. Both "The Rear-Guard" and "Dulce et Decorum Est" use rhythm and rhyme. Ask students how these elements add to or take away from the poems.

Small-group activity. Invite students to listen to the music of each poem as they read it aloud. Ask them to determine the ways in which the rhythms carry the reader forward and complement or contradict the message.

Connection

Summary ⇔ *at grade level*

During the grim trench warfare of World War I, a weary British officer prowls a tunnel fifty feet below ground while a battle rages overhead. He trips over a soldier and becomes abusive when the soldier does not respond to his demand for directions. Then the officer realizes that the soldier has been dead for days. He continues moving until he finds a stairway lit by a shaft of dawn's light and makes his way above ground.

DIRECT TEACHING

A English-Language Learners

Specialized vocabulary. Students may not know what a military rear-guard is. Ask a volunteer to explain. [A rear-guard is a detachment of troops that protects the rear of a military force.] Note that the wartime setting of this poem is not one of traditional, open battle and visible military formations but an underground one in which an isolated individual gropes his way along dark tunnels.

B Literary Focus

❓ **Figures of speech.** Why is "rosy gloom" a particularly disturbing oxymoron here? [It suggests a sky lit by explosives.]

C Reading Skills

❓ **Interpreting.** Where is the officer now headed, and how does he feel about it? How is this ironic? [Possible response: He is heading above ground and feels relief at leaving "hell behind him." The relief he feels is ironic, however, since he is emerging into the war zone.]

INDEPENDENT PRACTICE

Response and Analysis

Thinking Critically

1. The "misty panes" are the gas mask's panes of plastic that the wearer looks through; they are misty from the clouds of gas.

2. Possible answers: The oxymoron "an ecstasy of fumbling" evokes the anticipation of escaping death by donning a gas mask; "desperate glory" evokes the enthusiasm of enlisting in the military to die in patriotic sacrifice.

3. The "you" is collective. It can refer to anyone who might advocate simplistic patriotism.

4. Possible answers: The similes compare the soldier's dying to something "obscene" like cancer or the "cud" from an "incurable sore." They relate to the theme by suggesting that war is a hideous and obscene disease; that it corrupts and destroys the innocent; and that it reveals the lie that it is good, decorous, or sweet to die for one's country.

5. The rhyme scheme is *abab cdcd efef ghgh ijij klkl mnmn*. One half-rhyme is *glory/mori* (ll. 26 and 28). This strong, steady rhyme scheme heightens the disturbing mood of the poem by emphasizing the incongruity between romantic idealism and the harsh reality of war.

6. The tone is tormented and bitter. The tone of modern war movies and stories varies, but may be ironic as in the TV series *M*A*S*H*, elegiac as in the film *Gallipoli*, bitter as in the film *Welcome to Sarajevo*, or brutally realistic as in *Saving Private Ryan*.

Extending and Evaluating

7. A response should clearly state the student's position and support it with examples from the text and from personal observations.

Response and Analysis

Thinking Critically

1. What are the "misty panes" in line 13 through which the speaker glimpses the dying man?

2. An **oxymoron** is one kind of **figure of speech**. It combines apparently contradictory ideas, such as *wise fool*. What oxymorons can you find in the poem's second and last stanzas? What emotions or insights does a figure of speech that expresses contradiction evoke?

3. Who is the "you" addressed in the final stanza?

4. A **simile** is a **figure of speech** that compares two things using a word such as *like* or *as*. Explain the similes in lines 23–24. How do they relate to the **theme** of the poem?

5. What is the poem's **rhyme scheme**? Can you find any **half rhymes** (words that sound similar but do not rhyme exactly)? Describe the effect that this rhyme scheme has on the overall mood of the poem.

6. **Tone** is the attitude a writer takes toward the reader, a subject, or a character. Describe the speaker's **tone** in this poem. How does it compare with the tone of today's war stories or war movies? (Cite some examples in your answer.)

Extending and Evaluating

7. In the last lines of his poem, Owen refers to the traditional notion of an honorable death for one's country as "the old Lie." Do you agree that patriotism's high-minded idealism is a lie? Or is Owen perhaps stacking the deck by including so many gruesome battle details? In your response, relate Owen's poem to your own concepts of patriotism and warfare. Be sure to review your Quickwrite notes.

WRITING

Side-by-Side

In an **essay**, **analyze** the similarities and differences between Wilfred Owen's "Dulce et Decorum Est" and Siegfried Sassoon's poem "The Rear-Guard" (see the **Connection** on page 823). Identify the subject of each poem, and compare and contrast the speakers' attitudes toward their subjects. Analyze how each poet uses powerful imagery and figures of speech to evoke strong emotions in the reader. How does the language of each poem reinforce the speaker's attitude? Support your ideas by citing specific words and phrases from the texts.

SKILLS FOCUS

Literary Skills
Analyze figures of speech.

Writing Skills
Write an essay comparing and contrasting two poems.

Oppy Wood (1917) by John Northcote Nash.
Imperial War Museum, London.

ASSESSING

Assessment
- Holt Assessment: *Literature, Reading, and Vocabulary*

RETEACHING

For lessons reteaching author's tone and style, see **Reteaching**, p. 1129A.

824 Collection 7 The Modern World: 1900 to the Present

T. S. Eliot
(1888–1965)
America / England

Unlike poets whose long, outstanding careers eventually turn them into cultural monuments, T. S. Eliot was a monument who later became known as a man. Internationally famous at an early age, Eliot was the product of an aristocratic New England family that valued privacy and regarded self-exploitation and public exposure—even fame itself—as a form of vulgarity. Consequently, millions of readers knew T. S. Eliot less as a real personality than as a presence. Eliot was remote, disciplined, and self-possessed, a man whose sparse output was nevertheless the most celebrated and influential poetry written in English over a span of three decades.

Thomas Stearns Eliot was born in 1888 in St. Louis, Missouri, where his grandfather had established Washington University. In spite of this geographical displacement, the Eliots remained New Englanders. Eliot was educated at Harvard College, after which he did graduate studies at the Sorbonne in Paris. Like many other young American writers of his generation, he found life abroad so stimulating that he decided not to return home. Settling in London before World War I, he worked in a bank, married an Englishwoman, and became an editor and a publisher. Eliot made his expatriation complete by becoming a British citizen in 1927. In 1948, he was awarded the Nobel Prize. Not long before his death in 1965, on one of his several visits to the United States, so many people wanted to see and hear Eliot read his poetry that a football stadium had to be taken over to hold the audience.

Eliot had a vast influence as a poet. His techniques, along with those of his friend and fellow American expatriate, Ezra Pound, became the hallmarks of modern poetry. For over thirty years, in classrooms and in critical studies, Eliot's was *the* voice that expressed the dislocation and despair of the twentieth century. His world-weariness and his grave, restrained, and impersonal cadences—so much like the voices he heard in New England pulpits—were widely imitated and instantly recognized.

Eliot's critical studies were also far-reaching. He argued against the commonly held view that poets were romantics who had superior powers of observation and expression. Eliot regarded poets as craftspeople who used traditional literary materials not for personal revelations but for the creation of better-made poems. The poet, according to these theories, was like those anonymous master artisans who made individual contributions to the great medieval cathedrals but who remained personally unknown. Like these humble artisans, the poet was just part of the background. What is important is the poem (or the cathedral), not the worker who made it. This point of view criticized the notion that a search through the poet's life would give clues to the meaning of the work. The work, all-important, stood apart from its creator. Submitting to Eliot's instruction, poets, students, and critics for generations studied a poem not for its messages or meaning, but for its method and structure—for its architecture.

T. S. Eliot (1907) during his first year at Harvard, age nineteen.
By permission of the Houghton Library, Harvard University, Cambridge, MA (AC9.El464.Zzx Box 2, env. 3a).

SKILLS FOCUS, pp. 825–831

Grade-Level Skills
- **Literary Skills**
Analyze ways in which poets use allusions.
- **Reading Skills**
Make inferences about an author's philosophical arguments.

More About the Writer
Background. When Eliot became a British citizen in 1927, he also became a member of the Anglican Church. Deeply religious, Eliot affirmed the traditionalism, hierarchy, and conservatism of High Anglicanism—values extolled in his poems "The Journey of the Magi" (1927), "Ash-Wednesday" (1930), and the visionary *The Four Quartets* (1935–42). "The Hollow Men" also contains many references to religion, although the poet's objective here is not to affirm Christianity but rather to lament its apparent absence in the modern world.

RESOURCES: READING

Planning
- *One-Stop Planner* CD-ROM with ExamView Test Generator

Differentiating Instruction
- Holt Reading Solutions
- The Holt Reader
- Supporting Instruction in Spanish
- Audio CD Library, Selections and Summaries in Spanish

Grammar and Language
- Daily Language Activities

Assessment
- Holt Assessment: Literature, Reading, and Vocabulary
- *One-Stop Planner* CD-ROM with ExamView Test Generator
- Holt Online Assessment

Internet
- go.hrw.com (Keyword: LE5 12-7)
- Elements of Literature Online

Media
- Audio CD Library
- Fine Art Transparencies
- Audio CD Library, Selections and Summaries in Spanish

Preteaching

Summary ⬆ above grade level

The poem begins with two allusions to men who died in despair—Joseph Conrad's doomed protagonist Kurtz, and one of Britain's own doomed citizens Guy Fawkes. Part I of the poem introduces and describes "We . . . the hollow men . . . the stuffed men," and notes that those who have entered Paradise regard them not as violent, but as merely hollow. In Part II we learn that the speaker inhabits "death's dream kingdom," a realm of diverted gazes, empty voices, distance, and disguise. Part III extends the description of the "dead land," lamenting its stone-cold hardness, its lack of intimacy, and the futility of prayers uttered there. In Part IV, the inhabitants of this land, sightless and voiceless, gather to cross an archetypal river into absolute death. Part V presents in enigmatic and fragmented language the shadowy moment of death, which is, Eliot seems to say, the constant companion of the hollow man from birth, through life, and until the last, world-ending whimper.

Selection Starter

Background. Tell students that "The Hollow Men" was written in 1923. Ask them to recall what they can about this period in history. What major event had shaken the foundations of British society? Why was this once-powerful nation now overcome by cynicism and hopelessness? If necessary, remind students of the devastating impact of World War I on Great Britain: the hundreds of thousands lost in combat, the toppling of the old empire (and many of its traditions), and the birth of a new suspicion toward government. Encourage students to consider, as they read, how these historical conditions may have influenced Eliot's philosophical approach to "modern man."

Before You Read

The Hollow Men

Make the Connection

In 1925, when Eliot published "The Hollow Men," he believed that humanity was plagued by a loss of will and faith. His poem reveals a world of godless despair, an empty world without religion or the promise of salvation. How would you describe the condition of humanity today? Is it a world that matches Eliot's vision, or is your sense of the state of humanity today less bleak than his?

Literary Focus

Allusion

"The Hollow Men" opens with two quotations taken from different sources. The first line after the title is an **allusion,** or reference, to Joseph Conrad's famous short novel *Heart of Darkness*. This line refers to Kurtz, the book's main character, who journeys to the center of Africa and rapidly deteriorates. The line "Mistah Kurtz—he dead." strikes a note of futility that is echoed throughout Eliot's poem. The next line—"A penny for the Old Guy"—refers to one of the most notorious incidents in British history, the Gunpowder Plot. On November 5, 1605, a band of conspirators planned to kill King James I (and others) by placing barrels of gunpowder in the cellars of Parliament. The man chosen to light the fuse was a soldier named Guy Fawkes. But the plot failed; Fawkes was arrested and, in the cruel custom of the day, was sentenced to be hanged and drawn and quartered. To commemorate this grisly event, every year on November 5 huge bonfires are set all over England. When these fires are lit, straw-filled effigies of Fawkes that look like scarecrows—the "stuffed men" of the poem—go up in flames, lighting the skies. Children join the fun by carrying a "guy" and becoming beggars who ask passersby to give them "a penny for the guy" so that they can buy fireworks.

Eliot's poem is full of other allusions, especially to works by Shakespeare and Dante. As you read, think about the associations and emotions these different allusions evoke.

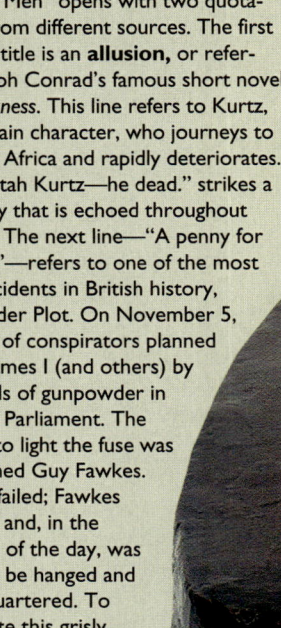

INTERNET
More About
T. S. Eliot
Keyword: LE5 12-7

SKILLS FOCUS

Literary Skills
Understand allusion.

Reading Skills
Make inferences about an author's philosophical arguments.

826 Collection 7 The Modern World: 1900 to the Present

An **allusion** is a reference to something in literature, history, or other subject areas that the reader should know in order to more fully understand the meaning of a work.

For more on Allusion, see the Handbook of Literary and Historical Terms.

Reading Skills
Analyzing the Author's Philosophical Arguments

In a 1923 essay, Eliot wrote of "the immense panorama of futility and anarchy which is contemporary history." As you read, make **inferences** (guesses based on evidence) about the hollow men, and analyze their character traits to show how effectively they reflect Eliot's opinion of human history. From the final four lines in the poem—among the most famous lines in modern poetry—what inferences do you think Eliot wants us to make about the fate of humanity?

DIRECT TEACHING

VIEWING THE ART

Swiss sculptor and painter **Alberto Giacometti** (1901–1966) is best known for his thin, attenuated human figures, which suggest a human consciousness pared down to its bare essence. In *City Square (La Place)*, anonymous figures are surrounded by empty space, each figure seemingly isolated from the others and reduced to its most fundamental form. Many people view Giacometti's works as visual metaphors of the postwar, anxiety-ridden world. His vision is of a world unable to recover from the horrors of war and the loss of faith.

Activity. Ask students how this sculpture reflects the world described by Eliot. Have them list lines or images by Eliot that might serve as an alternate title for this work. [Possible response: The barrenness of the sculpture, especially the gaunt human figures, reflects the "hollow" people and the bleak end of the world described in Eliot's poem. Possible alternate titles drawn from Eliot's poem are "shade without color," "twilight kingdom," "dead land," "cactus land," and "stone images."]

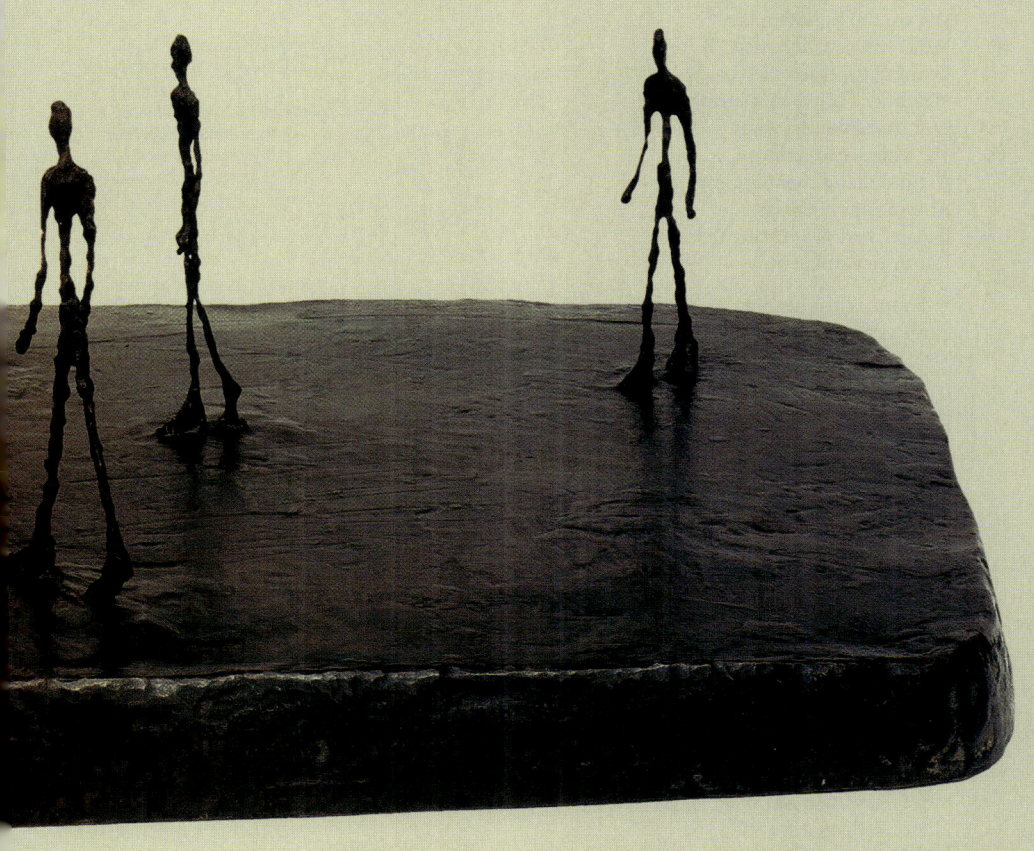

City Square (La Place) (1948) by Alberto Giacometti. Bronze (8½" × 25⅜" × 17¼") (21.6 × 64.5 × 43.8 cm).
The Museum of Modern Art, New York. Purchase (337.49).
© 2003 Artists Rights Society (ARS), New York/ADAGP, Paris.

DIRECT TEACHING

A Literary Focus
Allusion. This line from *Heart of Darkness* has various implications. Even before he physically dies, Kurtz is emotionally dead; in fact, he is described as "hollow at the core." (Incidentally, all the colonialists in the novel are described as "hollow men.") Kurtz comes to realize that evil is at the very heart of life, and his last chilling words are, "The horror! The horror!"

B Literary Focus
Allusion. The hollow men are like the souls who live in the first circle of Dante's *Inferno* in the *Divine Comedy*. These souls lived only for themselves, never committing to any principles. Beatrice, who represents the heavenly in the *Divine Comedy*, has "direct eyes." She is so holy—and so "whole"—that Dante cannot meet her gaze.

C Learners Having Difficulty
Summarizing. According to this stanza, what is "death's dream kingdom" like? [The realm of hollow men is eerie, obscure, and bleak.]

Responses to Margin Questions

Lines 1–10. It implies that the hollow men cannot think. Their "dried voices . . . quiet and meaningless" like "rats' feet over broken glass" further suggest the futility of their words and actions.

Lines 11–12. The paradoxes "shape without form," "shade without color," and "gesture without motion" suggest that the men are one-dimensional.

Lines 17–18. They are hollow in that they have no core or substance but are instead stuffed with dead matter.

The Hollow Men

T. S. Eliot

A *Mistah Kurtz—he dead.*

A penny for the Old Guy

I

We are the hollow men
We are the stuffed men
Leaning together
Headpiece filled with straw. Alas!
5   Our dried voices, when
We whisper together
Are quiet and meaningless
As wind in dry grass
Or rats' feet over broken glass
10 In our dry cellar.

   Shape without form, shade without color,
Paralyzed force, gesture without motion;

   Those who have crossed
With direct eyes, to death's other Kingdom°
15 Remember us—if at all—not as lost
Violent souls, but only
B As the hollow men
The stuffed men.

II

Eyes I dare not meet in dreams
20 In death's dream kingdom
These do not appear:
There, the eyes are
Sunlight on a broken column
C There, is a tree swinging
25 And voices are
In the wind's singing
More distant and more solemn
Than a fading star.

hollow men: allusion to Shakespeare's *Julius Caesar* (Act IV, Scene 2, lines 23–27): "hollow men . . . sink in the trial" (that is, fail when put to the test).

1–10. What does having a head filled with straw (line 4) imply about the hollow men? What other words and phrases in lines 1–10 give you clues about the character of the hollow men?

11–12. A **paradox** is an apparent contradiction that is actually true.
What paradoxes are listed in these lines? What do these paradoxes tell you about the hollow men?

13–14. Those . . . Kingdom: Those with "direct eyes" have crossed from the world of the hollow men into Paradise. The allusion is to Dante's *Paradiso*.

17–18. How can the hollow men be both "hollow" and "stuffed"?

DIFFERENTIATING INSTRUCTION

Learners Having Difficulty
Modeling. To help students read "The Hollow Men," model the reading skill of analyzing the author's philosophical arguments. Say, "The poem's title—'The Hollow Men'—gives you a clue about how Eliot views twentieth-century humanity: He believes that something essential is missing." Encourage students to ask themselves, "What is a hollow person lacking?"

Invite learners having difficulty to read "The Hollow Men" in interactive format in *The Holt Reader* and to use the sidenotes as aids to understanding the selection.

English-Language Learners
Have students listen to the audio recording, replaying it as many times as needed so that students form some idea of the poem's meaning before reading it on their own.

Let me be no nearer
30 In death's dream kingdom
Let me also wear
Such deliberate disguises
Rat's coat, crowskin, crossed staves°
In a field
35 Behaving as the wind behaves **D**
No nearer—

   Not that final meeting
In the twilight kingdom

III

This is the dead land
40 This is cactus land
Here the stone images
Are raised, here they receive
The supplication° of a dead man's hand
Under the twinkle of a fading star.

45 Is it like this
In death's other kingdom
Waking alone
At the hour when we are
Trembling with tenderness
50 Lips that would kiss
Form prayers to broken stone.

IV

The eyes are not here
There are no eyes here
In this valley of dying stars
55 In this hollow valley
This broken jaw of our lost kingdoms

   In this last of meeting places
We grope together
And avoid speech
60 Gathered on this beach of the tumid river°

   Sightless, unless
The eyes reappear
As the perpetual star
Multifoliate rose°
65 Of death's twilight kingdom
The hope only
Of empty men.

---

33. staves *n. pl.*: rods or staffs; "crossed staves / in a field" form a scarecrow.

37–38. What might the "final meeting / In the twilight kingdom" be? How might this explain what the speaker is afraid of?

43. supplication *n.*: humble plea.

39–44. What kind of **setting** is being described here? How is this setting appropriate to the nature of the hollow men?

41–51. In line 44, the image of the star is another **allusion** to Dante, who used the symbol of a star to represent God.

What do "stone images" make you think of? What would "prayers to broken stone" be?

60. tumid river: Hell's swollen river, the Acheron (ak′ər·än′), in Dante's *Inferno*. The damned must cross this river to enter the land of the dead.

64. multifoliate rose: Dante describes Paradise as a rose of many leaves (*Paradiso*, Canto 32).

T. S. Eliot **829**

DIRECT TEACHING

D Reading Skills

? Analyzing the author's philosophical arguments. How *does* the wind behave? [It blows in a random fashion; it is invisible and unpredictable.] What does this comparison suggest about Eliot's view of the hollow men? [He feels they are unseeing, insignificant, and unreliable.]

E Literary Focus

Allusion. Eliot's "stone images" alludes to the "graven images" of the Bible, in which the Lord commands, "You shall make for yourselves no idols and erect no graven image or pillar. . . ." (Leviticus 26:1). Ask students what Eliot's allusion suggests about the hollow men. [Possible responses: that they are alienated from God; that they worship idols.]

F Reading Skills

? Analyzing the author's philosophical arguments. What details in this passage suggest that all hope is not lost? [The hollow men are still capable of "trembling with tenderness" and desire.] What does this detail—which contrasts sharply with the general mood of hopelessness—tell you about Eliot's view of humanity? [Possible response: It suggests that Eliot believes humanity *can* be redeemed, even if it often seems unlikely.]

Responses to Margin Questions

Lines 37–38. It might be death or damnation.

Lines 39–44. The dead land reflects the barren interior of the hollow men.

Lines 41–51. "Stone images" alludes to the "graven images" of the Bible. "Prayers to broken stone" suggests both impotent pleas and impotent idols.

Advanced Learners

Enrichment. After they have read "The Hollow Men," ask students to comment on the allusions they recognize or have learned about by reading the glosses for the poem. Encourage students to work individually or in pairs to create a chart showing the borrowed lines—in other words, the lines that are direct quotations from other sources. Students should explain the ways in which these lines add meaning to the poem.

Direct Teaching

A Advanced Learners

Enrichment. Ask students to analyze ll. 72–90 in order to speculate about what Eliot means by "the Shadow." Suggest that students create two lists, one containing the first word or idea from each pair Eliot uses (*idea, motion,* and *conception,* for example) and another containing the second idea in each pair (*reality* and *act,* for example). Do the nouns in each list share any qualities? Which list of nouns, for example, seems more abstract? Which seems more concrete? What might occur in a person's life between his or her intent to do something and actually doing it? Have students explain to the rest of the class what they think Eliot is implying.

B Reading Skills

? Analyzing the author's philosophical arguments. Why do you think Eliot quotes only fragments of the Lord's Prayer? [Possible responses: to convey the fragmented nature of the modern psyche; to suggest that humanity is unfocused and disjointed; to underscore the idea that God, the fading star, seems to be withdrawing from the lives of humans.]

Responses to Margin Questions

Lines 68–71. The circular motion symbolizes a fruitless, repetitive existence. The prickly pear could be seen as threatening or foreboding.

Lines 95–98. A whimper is pathetic and hardly noticeable, supporting the idea that the hollow men's lives have no meaning. A "bang," on the other hand, might signify a victory or at least a dramatic defeat.

V

Here we go round the prickly pear°
Prickly pear prickly pear
70 Here we go round the prickly pear
At five o'clock in the morning.

Between the idea
And the reality
Between the motion
75 And the act°
Falls the Shadow
        For Thine is the Kingdom°

Between the conception
And the creation
80 Between the emotion
And the response
Falls the Shadow
        Life is very long

Between the desire
85 And the spasm
Between the potency°
And the existence
Between the essence
And the descent°
90 Falls the Shadow
        For Thine is the Kingdom

For Thine is
Life is
For Thine is the

95 This is the way the world ends
This is the way the world ends
This is the way the world ends
Not with a bang but a whimper.

---

68. prickly pear: cactus.

68–71. These lines are a parody of a children's rhyme that begins, "Here we go round the mulberry bush." The mulberry bush was traditionally a symbol of fertility. To go round and round means to never reach a destination; it is a pointless action.

? How would you interpret going round and round a prickly pear—a type of cactus?

74–75. between...act: reference to Shakespeare's *Julius Caesar:* "Between the acting of a dreadful thing / And the first motion, all the interim is / Like a phantasma or a hideous dream" (Act II, Scene 1, lines 63–65).

77. For...Kingdom: closing lines of the Lord's Prayer: "For thine is the kingdom, and the power, and the glory, forever and ever."

86. potency *n.:* strength; power.

88–89. between...descent: The Greek philosopher Plato defined "the essence" as an unattainable ideal and "the descent" as its imperfect expression in material or physical reality.

95–98. These lines are a continuation of the children's singsong rhyme, parodying the original words, "This is the way we clap our hands."

? What does it mean for the world to end with a "whimper" instead of with a "bang"?

---

830 Collection 7 The Modern World: 1900 to the Present

DEVELOPING FLUENCY

Small-group activity. Divide the class into five groups, and assign each group a section of "The Hollow Men" to read aloud. Have students concentrate on the sounds of the language. For example, be sure they evoke the variety of rhythms in the free verse in Part II; also be sure they create the singsong quality of the nursery rhyme and the haunting sound of the prayer in Part V. Groups may decide whether to read their section chorally or to assign parts to individuals. Offer groups the option of adding echoic effects, a beat, or even musical accompaniment. After the groups perform their sections, ask students to discuss which parts of the poem they found most dramatically musical.

Response and Analysis

Thinking Critically

1. In Section I, the hollow men are compared with the effigy of Guy Fawkes and contrasted with the historical Fawkes. What does this comparison and contrast tell you about the **character** of the hollow men?

2. What **mood** or emotional effect is conveyed by **imagery** using the words *dried* and *dry* in lines 5–10? How does the imagery convey a lack of passion, emotion, or excitement in the lives of the hollow men?

3. In Section III, what **mood** or emotional effect does the **imagery** convey?

4. In Section IV, what is the hope of the hollow men? What might regaining sight **symbolize,** and why do you think they are powerless to regain sight by themselves?

5. In Section V, what do you think Eliot means by "the Shadow" that intervenes between thought and action? Why do you think the speaker is unable to complete the Lord's Prayer?

6. Eliot **parodies** a nursery rhyme in the opening and closing lines of Section V. What is the effect of parodying serious content—the end of the world—in this way?

7. The last four lines of this poem are among the most famous in modern poetry. What is the difference between ending with a "bang" (as Guy Fawkes hoped to do) and ending with a "whimper"?

8. What is **ironic** about the hollow men being able to vividly describe their particular character traits and deficiencies?

9. How would you state the **theme** of this poem? How is this theme supported by the poem's **tone**? Use specific evidence from the text in your response.

Extending and Evaluating

10. In your opinion, does Eliot's use of **allusions** reinforce the meaning of the poem and its emotional impact, or does the extensive use of allusions make it more difficult for the reader to comprehend the main ideas and theme of the poem? How would the poem have been different if Eliot had used no allusions?

Literary Criticism

11. **Philosophical approach.** Do you think Eliot effectively demonstrates his argument that contemporary history is an "immense panorama of futility and anarchy"? Are the hollow men believable representatives of a particular type of human being? Support your opinion with evidence from the poem.

WRITING

Hollow Lives

In a brief **essay, analyze** the character of the hollow men as it is revealed through their appearance, words, actions, or lack of action. Use the following questions to guide your essay:

- What are the hollow men like socially, religiously, and personally?
- What are their values?
- How are they like or unlike most people?

Based on your analysis, what can you **infer** about Eliot's attitude toward the human condition? (You may want to consult your reading notes for help.)

SKILLS FOCUS

Literary Skills
Analyze allusion.

Reading Skills
Make inferences about an author's philosophical arguments.

Writing Skills
Write an essay analyzing characters.

Political Points of View

SKILLS FOCUS, pp. 832–847

Grade-Level Skills

■ **Literary Skills**

Analyze political points of view in a selection of literary works on a topic.

■ **Reading Skills**

Compare main ideas across texts.

Political Issue: The Holocaust

Explain that the term *holocaust,* which literally means "burned whole," originally referred to a religious offering that was completely burned up. Point out the capitalization of *Holocaust,* which links the term to nazism and World War II. Have students recall what they know about the Holocaust (drawing upon their Quickwrite notes, if you wish). Then, discuss why they think *Holocaust* is used to describe what happened to millions of Jews and various other groups of people under Nazi rule.

Skills Starter

Build review skills. Bring to class (or have students supply) several weekly news magazines or newspaper editorial pages. Ask students to read aloud letters from readers who are responding to the same news story or the same article from a previous issue. Call on volunteers to summarize the points of view presented. Then, discuss what clues about the writers' political assumptions appear in particular letters. For example, what reasons do the writers give for their views? What unstated ideas do the writers imply? What authorities might they cite for support? What buzzwords might suggest their allegiances?

Introducing Political Points of View

The Holocaust

Main Reading
Primo Levi . . . . *from* **Survival in Auschwitz** . . . . (Italy) 835

Connected Readings
Marguerite Duras . . . . *from* **The War** . . . . (France) 841
Elie Wiesel . . . . **"Never Shall I Forget"** . . . . (Romania) 845

You will be reading the three selections listed above in this Political Points of View feature on the Holocaust. In the top corner of the pages in this feature, you'll find three stars. Smaller versions of the stars appear next to the questions on page 839 that focus on the Holocaust. At the end of the feature (page 847), you'll compare the various points of view expressed in the selections.

Examining the Issue: The Holocaust

After Hitler became chancellor of Germany in 1933, the Nazi Party made strong political advances. With each German conquest, more Jews and other "undesirables"—Romanies, homosexuals, political dissidents, various religious groups, and people with disabilities, to name a few—fell into Nazi hands. The Nazis secretly began transporting many of these groups to concentration camps such as Auschwitz (oush′vits′) in Poland and Buchenwald (boo′kən·wôld′) in Germany. There, prisoners were shot by firing squads, executed in gas chambers, tortured in medical experiments, worked to death as slave laborers, or killed by starvation and disease. In all, about eleven million people were killed, nearly six million of them Jews.

Make the Connection
Quickwrite

The horrors of the Holocaust have been recorded in many books, movies, and television programs. Make some notes about what you most clearly remember about depictions of the Holocaust. What feelings did these facts and images evoke in you? Why might people think it so important to remember the unspeakable atrocities of the Holocaust?

SKILLS FOCUS

Pages 832–847 cover
Literary Skills Analyze political points of view on a topic.
Reading Skills Compare main ideas across texts.

Reading Skills

Comparing Main Ideas Across Texts

The first step in comparing texts is to identify and analyze the main idea or ideas of each text. After you have read each of the following selections, write down what you think are their main ideas. Then, compare the various points of view presented in these selections. Are these writers all saying the same things about the Holocaust?

Children behind a barbed-wire fence at Auschwitz concentration camp (c. 1945).
Getty Images.

832 Collection 7 The Modern World: 1900 to the Present

Primo Levi
(1919–1987)
Italy

Photograph by Jerry Bauer.

Primo Levi (prē'mō lā'vē) was a university student studying chemistry at the University of Turin (Italy) when World War II erupted in Europe. After the German army occupied northern Italy, Levi, a Jew, joined a resistance group, but he was soon arrested by Italian Fascists. Levi thought that he would wait out the war in a detention center, but when the Germans took over his detention camp, all Jews were immediately deported. In February 1944, Levi and 649 others were sent to Auschwitz (oush'vits'), the infamous Nazi death camp. Levi was one of only twenty-three of the group who survived until the camp was liberated less than a year later.

After liberation, Levi returned to Italy and resumed his work as a chemist. Soon, though, he felt compelled to record his nightmarish experiences at Auschwitz. His first book, *Survival in Auschwitz* (1947), tells of his eleven months in the hell of the death camp. Levi's next book, *The Reawakening* (1963), chronicles his eight-month return journey to Italy after liberation.

Levi did not confine his writing to Holocaust experiences. He also published poems, essays, short stories, novels, and memoirs; translated Kafka into Italian; and even dabbled in science fiction. Levi's last book, *The Drowned and the Saved* (1986), is a meditation on the meaning of the Nazi atrocities. To the critic Alexander Stille, who considered Levi's work "ultimately hopeful," this last book seemed pessimistic, causing the critic to speculate that "by the end of his life, Levi had become increasingly convinced that the lessons of the Holocaust were destined to be lost as it took a place among the routine atrocities of history."

On April 11, 1987, two days before the holiday of Passover, Levi fell to his death down the stairwell of his apartment. Some believe that the fall was an accident caused by illness and infirmity; others believe that Levi took his own life. Did Levi ultimately lose faith in humanity? That question may never be answered.

PRETEACHING

Summary ⇔ at grade level

Levi recalls his arrival at Buna, a workcamp that is part of the Auschwitz complex. Levi and the other men among the new arrivals, tired and thirsty, are told to remove and bundle their clothes. They are shaved and then locked in a shower room. As they wait, the men wonder aloud about what has happened to the women, but their translator refuses to pass along their questions. During the night, a fellow prisoner, the camp's dentist, visits them secretly; he tells them where they are and what kind of life they can expect at Buna. The new arrivals, however, do not get answers to many of their questions, and Levi is not sure if they can believe anything that the stranger tells them.

The showers finally go on; the prisoners bathe quickly and then are hustled off to dress. Afterward, Levi and the other prisoners are shocked at their phantom-like appearance. The excerpt concludes with Levi's reflections about having had everything taken from him—and about gaining a new understanding of the term *extermination camp* and the expression *to lie on the bottom*.

Skills Starter

Build review skills. Relate the power of memoir to students' lives by asking them to recall a historical event that has taken place within the past ten to fifteen years. Ask students which they would rather read—a newspaper article about the event or a firsthand account by someone who was involved in the event. Elicit that the blend of facts and firsthand impressions in a memoir can produce compelling reading.

Before You Read

On the Bottom
from Survival in Auschwitz

Political Points of View

At one time or another, most people have lost something that they treasured. But what exactly would you have to lose before you reached "rock bottom"—before your very identity was extinguished? In the following selection, Holocaust survivor Primo Levi describes his dehumanizing experience in a Nazi concentration camp in just these terms. "We had reached the bottom," Levi writes of himself and his fellow prisoners. "It is not possible to sink lower than this."

Literary Focus
Memoir

The word *memoir* comes from an Old French word meaning "memory." As this etymology suggests, a **memoir** records the memories of its author. In this way, it is a kind of autobiography, or writing about the self. Unlike an autobiography, however, a memoir usually focuses on one particular time period, often one of historical importance. The writer shares his or her experiences and gives the reader a personal glimpse into the way historical events impact people's lives.

INTERNET
Vocabulary Practice
Keyword: LE5 12-7

SKILLS FOCUS

Literary Skills
Analyze political points of view on a topic. Understand the characteristics of a memoir.

Reading Skills
Evaluate historical context.

> A **memoir** is a type of autobiography that usually focuses on a single time period or historical event.
>
> For more on Memoir, see the Handbook of Literary and Historical Terms.

Reading Skills
Evaluating Historical Context

As you read this excerpt from Levi's memoir, challenge yourself to think of experiences you've had or heard of or people you've known or heard about that even remotely resemble the people and events Levi writes about. Then, write responses to these questions: Is Levi describing an extreme version of what commonly happens in human history, or is he describing a singular, unforgettable atrocity? Would it be possible to understand this excerpt without knowledge of its historical context? As you read, take notes on the political, ethical, and social influences of the time that helped to shape Levi's memoir.

Background

Primo Levi wrote *Survival in Auschwitz* just after World War II ended, when the full horror of the Nazi extermination camps was not yet known to the world. The excerpt you are about to read begins after Levi and 649 other Jews have been packed into freight cars and sent to Poland with no food or water. When the doors of the boxcar finally open, the group is quickly divided into those who are able-bodied and those who are not. In Levi's convoy ninety-six men and twenty-nine women are selected to work in the labor camps of Auschwitz. All the others are murdered.

Vocabulary Development

tepid (tep′id) *adj.*: lukewarm.

taciturn (tas′ə·turn′) *adj.*: not talkative.

disconcerted (dis′kən·surt′id) *adj.*: frustrated; confused.

livid (liv′id) *adj.*: pale; colorless.

sordid (sôr′did) *adj.*: filthy; foul.

demolition (dem′ə·lish′ən) *n.*: destruction.

affinity (ə·fin′i·tē) *n.*: kinship; bond.

Previewing Vocabulary

Review the difference between a word's denotation (its dictionary meaning) and its connotation (images and emotions associated with the word). Discuss which Vocabulary words listed on p. 834 have positive connotations and which have negative connotations. [Only *affinity* has a positive connotation.] Challenge partners to compose sentences using the words as follows:

1. Compose a sentence using two of the negative words that relate to how something looks. [livid, sordid]

2. Compose a sentence using two of the negative words that relate to a person's attitude or behavior. [taciturn, disconcerted, tepid]

3. Compose a sentence using *affinity* and one of the negative words that you have not yet used.

On the Bottom
from Survival in Auschwitz

Primo Levi

translated by **Stuart Woolf**

The journey did not last more than twenty minutes. Then the lorry[1] stopped, and we saw a large door, and above it a sign, brightly illuminated (its memory still strikes me in my dreams): *Arbeit Macht Frei*,[2] work gives freedom.

We climb down, they make us enter an enormous empty room that is poorly heated. We have a terrible thirst. The weak gurgle of water in the radiators makes us ferocious; we have had nothing to drink for four days. But there is also a tap—and above it a card which says that it is forbidden to drink as the water is dirty. Nonsense. It seems obvious that the card is a joke, "they" know that we are dying of thirst and they put us in a room, and there is a tap, and *Wassertrinken Verboten*.[3] I drink and I incite my companions to do likewise, but I have to spit it out, the water is tepid and sweetish, with the smell of a swamp.

This is hell. Today, in our times, hell must be like this. A huge, empty room: we are tired, standing on our feet, with a tap which drips while we cannot drink the water, and we wait for something which will certainly be terrible, and nothing happens and nothing continues to happen. What can one think about? One cannot think any more; it is like being already dead. Someone sits down on the ground. The time passes drop by drop.

We are not dead. The door is opened and an SS[4] man enters, smoking. He looks at us slowly and asks, *"Wer kann Deutsch?"*[5] One of us whom I have never seen, named Flesch, moves forward; he will be our interpreter. The SS man makes a long, calm speech; the interpreter translates. We have to form rows of five, with intervals of two yards between man and man; then we have to undress and make a bundle of the clothes in a special manner, the woolen garments on one side, all the rest on the other; we must take off

(Top) Star of David cloth patch. The Nazi government required Jews to wear such patches.

(Bottom) Gates of the Auschwitz Concentration camp.

---

1. **lorry** (lôr′ē) *n.*: British for "truck."
2. **Arbeit Macht Frei** (är′bīt mäkht frī).
3. **Wassertrinken Verboten** (vä′ser trink′en fer·bō′ten): German for "Drinking water is forbidden."
4. **SS:** abbreviation for *Schutzstaffel* ("elite guard"), the Nazi units in charge of the extermination camps during World War II.
5. **Wer kann Deutsch?** (ver kän doich): German for "Who knows German?"

Vocabulary

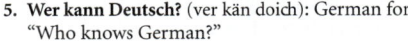
tepid (tep′id) *adj.*: lukewarm.

DIRECT TEACHING

A Political Issue

❓ **The Holocaust.** According to this paragraph, in what ways do both the prisoners and the Nazis feel that the victims of the Holocaust are less than human? [Possible response: The prisoners feel humiliated, abused, and "outside this world"; the German watches the prisoners' discomfort with mild interest, as if they were animals in some kind of experiment.]

B Political Issue

❓ **The Holocaust.** What information about concentration-camp life can you learn or infer from this paragraph? [Possible responses: Prisoners wore uniforms and were assigned numbers; prisoners were shaved; some prisoners worked for the camp authorities and received better treatment as a result; prisoners came from different nations and spoke different languages.]

C Literary Focus

❓ **Characterization.** Think about what Flesch, the translator, does and does not do. Think about what Levi says about him. Do you agree that Flesch is someone who deserves respect? Why or why not? [Possible responses: Yes, because Levi says that Flesch obviously does not want to translate the SS officer's crude jokes and that although Flesch suffered and fought for his country in World War I, he, too, is a prisoner here. No, there is more that Flesch could do to help the new arrivals, yet he refuses to do so.]

---

our shoes but pay great attention that they are not stolen.

Stolen by whom? Why should our shoes be stolen? And what about our documents, the few things we have in our pockets, our watches? We all look at the interpreter, and the interpreter asks the German, and the German smokes and looks him through and through as if he were transparent, as if no one had spoken.

I had never seen old men naked. Mr. Bergmann wore a truss[6] and asked the interpreter if he should take it off, and the interpreter hesitated. But the German understood and spoke seriously to the interpreter pointing to someone. We saw the interpreter swallow and then he said: "The officer says, take off the truss, and you will be given that of Mr. Coen." One could see the words coming bitterly out of Flesch's mouth; this was the German manner of laughing.

A Now another German comes and tells us to put the shoes in a certain corner, and we put them there, because now it is all over and we feel outside this world and the only thing is to obey. Someone comes with a broom and sweeps away all the shoes, outside the door in a heap. He is crazy, he is mixing them all together, ninety-six pairs, they will be all unmatched. The outside door opens; a freezing wind enters and we are naked and cover ourselves up with our arms. The wind blows and slams the door; the German reopens it and stands watching with interest how we writhe to hide from the wind, one behind the other. Then he leaves and closes it.

B Now the second act begins. Four men with razors, soapbrushes, and clippers burst in; they have trousers and jackets with stripes, with a number sewn on the front; perhaps they are the same sort as those others of this evening (this evening or yesterday evening?), but these are robust and flourishing. We ask many questions but they catch hold of us and in a moment we find ourselves shaved and sheared. What comic faces we have without hair! The four speak a language which does not seem of this world. It is certainly not German, for I understand a little German.

Finally another door is opened: here we are, locked in, naked, sheared and standing, with our feet in water—it is a shower room. We are alone. Slowly the astonishment dissolves, and we speak, and everyone asks questions and no one answers. If we are naked in a shower room, it means that we will have a shower. If we have a shower it is because they are not going to kill us yet. But why then do they keep us standing, and give us nothing to drink, while nobody explains anything, and we have no shoes or clothes, but we are all naked with our feet in the water, and we have been traveling five days and cannot even sit down.

And our women?

Mr. Levi asks me if I think that our women are like us at this moment, and where they are, and if we will be able to see them again. I say yes, because he is married and has a daughter; certainly we will see them again. But by now my belief is that all this is a game to mock and sneer at us. Clearly they will kill us, whoever thinks he is going to live is mad, it means that he has swallowed the bait, but I have not; I have understood that it will soon all be over, perhaps in this same room, when they get bored of seeing us naked, dancing from foot to foot and trying every now and again to sit down on the floor. But there are two inches of cold water and we cannot sit down.

C We walk up and down without sense, and we talk, everybody talks to everybody else, we make a great noise. The door opens, and a German enters; it is the officer of before. He speaks briefly, the interpreter translates. "The officer says you must be quiet, because this is not a rabbinical[7] school." One sees the words which are not his, the bad words, twist his mouth as they come out, as if he was spitting out a foul taste. We beg him to ask what we are waiting for, how long we will stay

---

6. **truss** *n.*: belt with a pad, worn to support a hernia, a rupture of the intestine through the abdominal wall.

7. **rabbinical** (rə·bin′i·kəl) *adj.*: of or relating to rabbis, teachers of Jewish law.

CONTENT-AREA CONNECTIONS

Music: Remembering the Holocaust

Many pieces of music have been written to commemorate the Holocaust, from film scores (such as Morton Gould's *Holocaust* and John Williams's *Schindler's List*) to classical works (such as Donald McCullough's *Holocaust Cantata* and Ronald Senator's *Holocaust Requiem—Kaddish for Terezin*). **Individual and collaborative-learning activity.** Invite students, working either individually or collaboratively, to find a recording of Holocaust-themed music to present to the class. As part of their presentation, they should give some background on the work and explain why they chose it. Challenge student listeners to try interpreting in words the emotional expression that each composer conveys with music.

here, about our women, everything; but he says no, that he does not want to ask. This Flesch, who is most unwilling to translate into Italian the hard, cold German phrases and refuses to turn into German our questions because he knows that it is useless, is a German Jew of about fifty, who has a large scar on his face from a wound received fighting the Italians on the Piave.[8] He is a closed, <u>taciturn</u> man, for whom I feel an instinctive respect as I feel that he has begun to suffer before us.

The German goes and we remain silent, although we are a little ashamed of our silence. It is still night and we wonder if the day will ever come. The door opens again, and someone else dressed in stripes comes in. He is different from the others, older, with glasses, a more civilized face, and much less robust. He speaks to us in Italian.

By now we are tired of being amazed. We seem to be watching some mad play, one of those plays in which the witches, the Holy Spirit, and the devil appear. He speaks Italian badly, with a strong foreign accent. He makes a long speech, is very polite, and tries to reply to all our questions.

We are at Monowitz, near Auschwitz, in Upper Silesia,[9] a region inhabited by both Poles and Germans. This camp is a workcamp, in German one says *Arbeitslager*,[10] all the prisoners (there are about ten thousand) work in a factory which produces a type of rubber called Buna,[11] so that the camp itself is called Buna.

We will be given shoes and clothes—no, not our own—other shoes, other clothes, like his. We are naked now because we are waiting for the shower and disinfection, which will take place immediately after the reveille,[12] because one cannot enter the camp without being disinfected.

Certainly there will be work to do; everyone must work here. But there is work and work: he, for example, acts as a doctor. He is a Hungarian doctor who studied in Italy and he is the dentist of the Lager.[13] He has been in the Lager for four and a half years (not in this one: Buna has only been open for a year and a half), but we can see that he is still quite well, not very thin. Why is he in the Lager? Is he Jewish like us? "No," he says simply, "I am a criminal."

We ask him many questions. He laughs, replies to some and not to others, and it is clear that he avoids certain subjects. He does not speak of the women: he says they are well, that we will see them again soon, but he does not say how or where. Instead he tells us other things, strange and crazy things, perhaps he too is playing with us. Perhaps he is mad—one goes mad in the Lager. He says that every Sunday there are concerts and football matches. He says that whoever boxes well can become cook. He says that whoever works well receives prize coupons with which to buy tobacco and soap. He says that the water is really not drinkable, and that instead a coffee substitute is distributed every day, but generally nobody drinks it as the soup itself is sufficiently watery to quench thirst. We beg him to find us something to drink, but he says he cannot, that he has come to see us secretly, against SS orders, as we still have to be disinfected, and that he must leave at once; he has come because he has a liking for Italians, and because, he says, he "has a little heart." We ask him if there are other Italians in the camp and he says there are some, a few, he does not know how

---

8. **Italians on the Piave** (pyä′vā): During World War I, Austria and Germany defeated 600,000 Italian troops in the Battle of Caporetto; the Italian forces were pushed back to the Piave River near Venice.
9. **Upper Silesia** (sī·lē′shə): region including parts of southwestern Poland, eastern Germany, and the northern Czech Republic. After World War I, Germany and Poland divided northern Silesia; southern Silesia fell under the rule of Czechoslovakia.
10. *Arbeitslager* (är′bīts·läg′ər).
11. **Buna** (boō′nə).
12. **reveille** (rev′ə·lē) *n.*: early-morning bugle call to waken military troops.
13. **Lager:** short for *Arbeitslager*.

Vocabulary
taciturn (tas′ə·tʉrn′) *adj.*: not talkative.

Primo Levi 837

DIRECT TEACHING

D Reading Skills

Comparing and contrasting. What do you think is the difference between a camp like Buna and the main camp in the Auschwitz complex? [Possible response: The purpose of a camp like Buna does not seem to have been to kill the prisoners; rather, it seems to have been to use them as unpaid, forced labor. The main camp, on the other hand, was primarily an extermination camp.]

E Reading Skills

Making inferences. Based on this information, what can you assume about the dentist's situation? [Possible responses: As the only dentist for ten thousand prisoners, he is overworked; he gets better treatment than many other prisoners, despite his criminal past, because the Nazis consider him useful.]

F Reading Skills

Speculating. Do you believe that the man who says he is the dentist of the Lager is telling the truth? Why or why not? [Possible responses: Yes, he is probably telling the truth because of the level of detail he provides. No, he looks too healthy and some of what he says sounds improbable—such as good boxers can become cooks.]

READING MINI-LESSON

Developing Word-Attack Skills
Direct attention to the selection word *disconcerted*. Help students recognize that the base word is the verb *concert*. Compare the pronunciation of *concert* when used as a verb /kən·sʉrt′/ and as a noun /kän′sərt/. Point out that *concert* is an example of words that are pronounced differently depending on their part of speech.

Activity. Each of these words can function as different parts of speech. Have volunteers use the words in oral sentences to illustrate the different parts of speech.

1. *articulate;* adjective and verb [adjective—/är·tik′yōō·lit/; verb—/är·tik′yōō·lāt/]
2. *abuse;* noun and verb [noun—/ə·byōōs′/; verb—/ə·byōōz′/]
3. *congregate;* verb and adjective [verb—/kän′grə·gāt′/; adjective—/kän′grə·git/]
4. *object;* noun and verb [noun—/äb′jikt/; verb—/əb·jekt′/]
5. *initiate;* noun and verb [noun—/i·nish′ē·it/; verb—/i·nish′ē·āt′/]
6. *reject;* noun and verb [noun—/rē′jekt/; verb—/re·jekt′/]
7. *alternate;* verb and noun [verb—/ôl′tər·nāt′/; noun—/ôl′tər·nit/]

Direct Teaching

A Reading Skills

? Evaluating influences upon characters. What do you think has influenced Levi to be so skeptical? [Possible responses: Levi may have been a skeptical person beforehand; Levi is not as quick as others to be broken by the Nazis' dehumanizing practices.]

B Political Issue

? The Holocaust. Have students relate this dressing scene to the earlier undressing scene. Why are the prisoners given substandard clothing? [Possible responses: Their captors plan to sell or reuse the clothing in which the prisoners arrived; the rags and shabby shoes are a further attempt to break the prisoners' spirits.]

C Literary Focus

? Memoir. Here Levi leaves the narrative to offer extended commentary. From his perspective, how is this moment more than just the completion of the entry process? [Possible response: It is the moment that the prisoners realize that they have become as hopeless, empty, and dehumanized as the Auschwitz prisoners they saw upon their arrival.]

D Reading Skills

? Tracing recurring themes. How would you use the ideas that Levi has repeated throughout his account to explain his concluding statement? [Possible response: The camp is a place of "extermination" in that it destroys the lives of some prisoners and the humanity of all prisoners; "to lie on the bottom" means to have everything taken away, even a sense of one's identity.]

many; and he at once changes the subject. Meanwhile a bell rang and he immediately hurried off and left us stunned and disconcerted. Some feel refreshed but I do not. I still think that even this dentist, this incomprehensible person, wanted to amuse himself at our expense, and I do not want to believe a word of what he said.

At the sound of the bell, we can hear the still dark camp waking up. Unexpectedly the water gushes out boiling from the showers—five minutes of bliss; but immediately after, four men (perhaps they are the barbers) burst in yelling and shoving and drive us out, wet and steaming, into the adjoining room which is freezing; here other shouting people throw at us unrecognizable rags and thrust into our hands a pair of broken-down boots with wooden soles; we have no time to understand and we already find ourselves in the open, in the blue and icy snow of dawn, barefoot and naked, with all our clothing in our hands, with a hundred yards to run to the next hut. There we are finally allowed to get dressed.

When we finish, everyone remains in his own corner and we do not dare lift our eyes to look at one another. There is nowhere to look in a mirror, but our appearance stands in front of us, reflected in a hundred livid faces, in a hundred miserable and sordid puppets. We are transformed into the phantoms glimpsed yesterday evening.[14]

Then for the first time we became aware that our language lacks words to express this offense, the demolition of a man. In a moment, with almost prophetic intuition, the reality was revealed to us: we had reached the bottom. It is not possible to sink lower than this; no human condition is more miserable than this, nor could it conceivably be so. Nothing belongs to us any more; they have taken away our clothes, our shoes, even our hair; if we speak, they will not listen to us, and if they listen, they will not understand. They will even take away our name: and if we want to keep it, we will have to find ourselves the strength to do so, to manage somehow so that behind the name something of us, of us as we were, still remains.

We know that we will have difficulty in being understood, and this is as it should be. But consider what value, what meaning is enclosed even in the smallest of our daily habits, in the hundred possessions which even the poorest beggar owns: a handkerchief, an old letter, the photo of a cherished person. These things are part of us, almost like limbs of our body; nor is it conceivable that we can be deprived of them in our world, for we immediately find others to substitute the old ones, other objects which are ours in their personification and evocation of our memories.

Imagine now a man who is deprived of everyone he loves, and at the same time of his house, his habits, his clothes, in short, of everything he possesses: he will be a hollow man, reduced to suffering and needs, forgetful of dignity and restraint, for he who loses all often easily loses himself. He will be a man whose life or death can be lightly decided with no sense of human affinity, in the most fortunate of cases, on the basis of a pure judgment of utility. It is in this way that one can understand the double sense of the term "extermination camp," and it is now clear what we seek to express with the phrase: "to lie on the bottom." ∎

---

14. **We are transformed . . . evening:** Levi is referring to the inmates at Auschwitz whom he and the other new prisoners witnessed briefly upon arriving at the camp on the previous evening.

Vocabulary

disconcerted (dis'kən·surt'id) *adj.*: frustrated; confused.
livid (liv'id) *adj.*: pale; colorless.
sordid (sôr'did) *adj.*: filthy; foul.
demolition (dem'ə·lish'ən) *n.*: destruction.
affinity (ə·fin'i·tē) *n.*: kinship; bond.

Check Test: True-False

Monitoring students' progress. Guide the class in answering these questions.

1. New arrivals are allowed to keep their shoes. [F]
2. When the interpreter translates the prisoners' questions, the Nazi ignores him. [T]
3. New arrivals spend hours in the bitter cold air. [F]
4. The Nazis' goal is to dehumanize the prisoners. [T]

Response and Analysis

Reading Check

1. When Levi arrives in Auschwitz, what factors lead him to conclude that this is "hell"?
2. What does the SS man tell Levi and the others to do with their shoes? What happens to all their shoes later?
3. When morning comes, what do the men have to do before they can finally get dressed? After they are dressed, why do they "not dare to lift their eyes"?
4. Describe the dehumanizing process that the prisoners go through.

Thinking Critically

5. Why does Levi first think that the sign saying not to drink the water is a joke? Why do you think the prisoners were put in a room with undrinkable water?
6. Why do you think Levi uses the phrase "second act" to describe what happens to the men after they undress? Why does he later say "We seem to be watching some mad play. . . ."?
7. What does it mean to be "hollow"? Why does Levi conclude that after a man has been made "hollow" it is easy to decide if such a man lives or dies? Explain whether you think the Nazis realized this and intentionally inflicted such a state on the prisoners.
8. How would you describe Levi's **tone**? Cite passages that illustrate this tone. What effect does the tone have on your perception of Levi's experiences?
9. How do you think some people were able to survive the inhuman treatment that Levi and the others received?

Literary Criticism

10. In writing this **memoir,** is Levi primarily sharing personal experiences, or is he viewing historical events through a particular political lens? Explain how important knowledge of the political, ethical, and social influences of the historical period is to understanding this selection. Explain. (You may want to consult your reading notes for help.)

WRITING

Never Again

Like many other survivors of the Holocaust, Levi felt the need to serve as a "witness" and to tell his story so that such events would never be repeated in human history. Do you think memoirs like Levi's can help stop something similar from happening again? In a brief **essay,** explain your thoughts, citing specific examples from Levi's text.

Vocabulary Development
Synonyms and Antonyms

tepid   sordid
taciturn   demolition
disconcerted   affinity
livid

On a separate piece of paper, use each Vocabulary word above to complete the exercise below.

1. _____ is a synonym for *pale.*
2. _____ is an antonym for *talkative.*
3. _____ is a synonym for *lukewarm.*
4. _____ is an antonym for *clean.*
5. _____ is a synonym for *connection.*
6. _____ is a synonym for *confused.*
7. _____ is an antonym for *construction.*

SKILLS FOCUS

Literary Skills
Analyze a memoir.

Reading Skills
Evaluate historical context.

Writing Skills
Write an essay supporting an opinion.

Vocabulary Skills
Use synonyms and antonyms.

Primo Levi 839

INDEPENDENT PRACTICE

Response and Analysis

6. Possible answer: Levi finds the situation so horrendous that he likens it to being in—or watching—a play. He may also sense that his captors are "watching" the suffering prisoners as if watching actors in a play.
7. Possible answer: A "hollow" man is a person who has lost everything, including his or her identity. It might be easy for a captor to view such a person as less than human and, as a result, to casually decide the person's fate.
8. Possible answer: Levi's tone is grim, even bitter. The tone is indicated by Levi's references to the events as a "mad" play and by his sense of loss.
9. Possible answers: Some people may have been able to survive through religious faith or through dedicating themselves to helping fellow prisoners.

Literary Criticism

10. Students may feel that Levi's account focuses on his personal experiences and that he makes no overt political statements.

Vocabulary Development

1. livid   5. affinity
2. taciturn   6. disconcerted
3. tepid   7. demolition
4. sordid

ASSESSING

Assessment

■ *Holt Assessment: Literature, Reading, and Vocabulary*

Reading Check

1. The men are thirsty, but the water is undrinkable; they are exhausted but are forced to stand and wait.
2. He tells them to take off their shoes and to make sure they are not stolen. Later, someone sweeps the shoes into a heap.
3. They must rush through a shower and then run naked across the snow to a hut where they may dress. To lift their eyes is to see themselves as "phantoms."
4. They are forced to disrobe and stand in the cold without water, food, or information about what will happen to them.

Thinking Critically

5. Possible answer: Levi thinks it is ridiculous that the water is undrinkable. The situation may have been set up to humiliate the new arrivals.

Connected Reading

Summary ⇨ *at grade level*

On the morning of May 12, 1945, Duras receives a phone call from François Morland. François has found her imprisoned husband, Robert, at the recently liberated Dachau concentration camp. Duras is to get word to two other members of the Resistance; they will disguise themselves as French army officers, go to Dachau, and try to bring Robert back to Paris. Only with great difficulty do they succeed in finding him, for he is so near death as to be unrecognizable. They sneak him out in another army uniform, but on the way to Paris, Robert expects to die and, as a result, spends much of the time "talking and telling his story."

When they arrive, Duras runs to meet them—but she is so horrified at Robert's appearance that she can only shriek hysterically. Calm soon returns, and a kindly doctor helps keep Robert from dying, but the painful knowledge of what Robert has gone through remains.

Selection Starter

Build background. Starting in the summer of 1944, Allied forces (the United States and England in the west and the Soviet Union in the east) began to drive Nazi troops back toward Germany. As the Allies advanced, the Nazis evacuated concentration camps on the outskirts of their territory and transported the prisoners to camps in areas still under Nazi control. Thousands died during the relocations, and the survivors found themselves in camps that were terribly overcrowded. One of these was Dachau, located about ten miles northwest of Munich. American forces liberated Dachau on April 29, 1945. Nine days after that, the war in Europe was officially over.

Connected Readings

The Holocaust

Marguerite Duras .... from **The War**
Elie Wiesel .... **"Never Shall I Forget"**

You have just read an excerpt from Primo Levi's memoir of the Holocaust and considered the ways in which memoirs present and interpret particular historical events. The next two selections you will read provide alternate insights into the horrors of the Holocaust. As you read, ask yourself how these insights are alike and different. After you read, you'll find questions on page 847 that ask you to compare all three selections.

INTERNET
Interactive Reading Model
Keyword: LE5 12-7

SKILLS FOCUS
Literary Skills
Understand an author's philosophical beliefs.

Political Points of View

Before You Read

The French writer Marguerite Duras was born in Indochina (now Vietnam) in 1914, just a few weeks before the eruption of World War I. By the time World War II began in 1939, Duras had returned to her parents' homeland, France, studied law at the Sorbonne, and begun a career with the French Ministry of Colonies. She had also married poet Robert Antelme, referred to in the following excerpt as "Robert L." Antelme, a member of the French Resistance—a group that worked secretly to resist Germany's presence in France—was arrested by the Nazis in 1944. He spent two years in concentration camps, surviving by only the slimmest of margins. This excerpt, which begins shortly after the end of the war in Europe, describes Antelme's return to Paris and to Duras herself.

As you will see in this excerpt, Duras's writing is characterized by unique rhythms and by a sparse, suggestive style. As one critic puts it, "Everything she feels, she writes, stringing the syllables together as an artist strings his pearls." During her lifetime, Duras published scores of novels, a dozen plays, and several screenplays. She came to be hailed as one of France's leading feminist writers, earning the prestigious Goncourt award in 1984 for her autobiographical novel *L'Amant*, or *The Lover*. Duras died in Paris in 1996.

Reading informational materials: Implicit and explicit beliefs and assumptions.
Although Duras's strong feelings about the horror of the Nazi concentration camps are unquestionable, her beliefs are not always **explicit**, or directly stated. Instead, she uses an accumulation of details to convey an **implicit**, or suggested, attitude toward her subject. Rather than directly stating how horrible the effects of a concentration camp were, Duras describes in an urgent, almost breathless style how Robert L. is taken from Dachau, what his physical condition is like, and how she and others react to the sight of him.

As you read, look for the details that reveal Duras's implicit beliefs about the horrors of the Holocaust. What techniques does Duras use to express these beliefs?

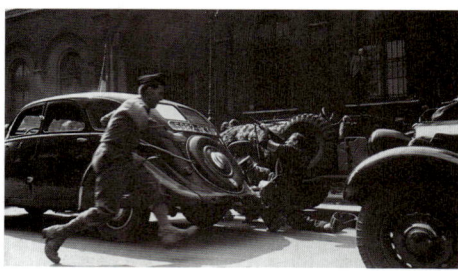

French soldier running to help a French resistance fighter who is taking aim at a German sniper (Paris, 1944). TimePix.

840 Collection 7 The Modern World: 1900 to the Present

MEMOIR
from The War

Marguerite Duras
translated by Barbara Bray

I can't remember what day it was, whether it was in April, no, it was a day in May when one morning at eleven o'clock the phone rang. It was from Germany, it was François Morland. He doesn't say hello, he's almost rough, but clear as always. "Listen carefully. Robert is alive. Now keep calm. He's in Dachau.[1] Listen very, very carefully. Robert is very weak, so weak you can't imagine. I have to tell you—it's a question of hours. He may live for another three days like that, but no more. D. and Beauchamp must start out today, this morning, for Dachau. Tell them this: they're to go straight to my office—the people there will be expecting them. They'll be given French officers' uniforms, passports, mission orders, gasoline coupons, maps, and permits. Tell them to go right away. It's the only way. If they tried to do it officially they'd arrive too late."

François Morland and Rodin were part of a mission organized by Father Riquet. They had gone to Dachau, and that was where they'd found Robert L. They had gone into the prohibited area of the camp, where the dead and the hopeless cases were kept. And there, one of the latter had distinctly uttered a name: "François." "François," and then his eyes had closed again. It took Rodin and Morland an hour to recognize Robert L. Rodin finally identified him by his teeth. They wrapped him up in a sheet, as people wrap up a dead body, and took him out of the prohibited part of the camp and laid him down by a hut in

---
1. **Dachau:** location of a German concentration camp that opened in 1933.

DIRECT TEACHING

A Reading Skills

? Evaluating influences on plot. According to Duras, why is the location of the American soldiers important? [Possible response: Because the soldiers stayed indoors, fearing typhoid, Beauchamp and D. had a chance to go where they wished to search for Robert.]

B Political Issue

? The Holocaust. How do you know that Robert suffered the same dehumanizing treatment as did Primo Levi and his Jewish colleagues? [Possible response: Like them, he was horribly weakened by his incarceration; like them, he was brainwashed to salute when seeing the SS huts.]

C Political Issue

? The Holocaust. Were you surprised by the orders the American soldiers were given to abandon prisoners who were beyond hope? Why or why not? [Many students will be surprised by these orders, but some will feel that the orders were necessary, given the shortage of medical help and supplies in the area at the time.]

D Reading Skills

? Analyzing philosophical assumptions. How clear does Robert make his philosophical views as he speaks? Explain. [Possible response: He is not very clear. In his weakened state, he blames only man in general and governments for what happened to him.]

E Political Issue

? The Holocaust. Why do you think that Robert would speak of the Holocaust in this way? [Possible responses: At places like Dachau, the absence of Christian charity was most obvious; Robert is charging "charitable" Christians with not having done more to stop the Holocaust; he is recalling incidents of charity among prisoners.]

A the survivors' part of the camp. They were able to do so because there were no American soldiers around. They were all in the guardroom, scared of the typhus.[2]

Beauchamp and D. left Paris the same day, early in the afternoon. It was May 12, the day of the peace. Beauchamp was wearing a colonel's uniform belonging to François Morland. D. was dressed as a lieutenant in the French army and carried his papers as a member of the Resistance,[3] made out in the name of D. Masse. They drove all night and arrived at Dachau the next morning. They spent several hours looking for Robert L.; then, as they were going past a body, they heard someone say D.'s name. It's my opinion they didn't recognize him; but Morland had warned us he was unrecognizable. They took him. And it was only afterward they must have recognized him. Under their clothes they had a third French **B** officer's uniform. They had to hold him upright, he could no longer stand alone, but they managed to dress him. They had to prevent him from saluting outside the SS[4] huts, get him through the guard posts, see that he wasn't given any of the vaccinations that would have killed him. The American soldiers, blacks for the most part, wore gas masks against typhus, the fear was so great. **C** Their orders were such that if they'd suspected the state Robert L. was really in, they'd have put him back immediately in the part of the camp where people were left to die. Once they got Robert L. out, the other two had to get him to walk to the Citroën II.[5] As soon as they'd stretched him out on the back seat he fainted. They thought it was all over, but no. The journey was very difficult, very slow. They had to stop every half hour

because of the dysentery.[6] As soon as they'd left Dachau behind, Robert L. spoke. He said he knew he wouldn't reach Paris alive. So he began to talk, so it should be told before he died. He didn't accuse any person, any race, any people. He **D** accused man. Emerging from the horror, dying, delirious, Robert L. was still able not to accuse anyone except the governments that come and go in the history of nations. He wanted D. and Beauchamp to tell me after his death what he had said. They reached the French frontier that night, near Wissemburg.[7] D. phoned me: "We've reached France. We've just crossed the frontier. We'll be back tomorrow by the end of the morning. Expect the worst. You won't recognize him." They had dinner in an officers' mess. Robert L. was still talking and telling his story. When he entered the mess all the officers stood up and saluted him. He didn't see. He never had seen that sort of thing. He spoke of the German martyrdom, of the martyrdom common to all men. He told what it was like. That evening he said he'd like to eat a trout before he died. In deserted Wissemburg they found a trout for Robert L. He ate a few mouthfuls. Then he started talking again. He spoke of charity. He'd heard some rhetorical phrases of Father Riquet's, and he **E** started to say these very obscure words: "When anyone talks to me of Christian charity, I shall say Dachau." But he didn't finish. That night they slept somewhere near Bar-sur-Aube.[8] Robert L. slept for a few hours. They reached Paris at the end of the morning. Just before they came to the rue Saint-Benoît, D. stopped to phone me again: "I'm ringing to warn you that it's more terrible than anything we've imagined . . . He's happy."

I heard stifled cries on the stairs, a stir, a clatter of feet. Then doors banging and shouts. It was them. It was them, back from Germany.

---

2. **typhus** *n.*: acute infectious fever, chiefly occurring in places where people live in unsanitary, crowded conditions.
3. **the Resistance:** underground organization that fought against Germans in occupied France during World War II.
4. **SS:** elite guard in the German military during the Nazi years.
5. **Citroën II:** model of car produced in France.

6. **dysentery** *n.:* diarrhea.
7. **Wissemburg:** town on the French side of the French-German border.
8. **Bar-sur-Aube:** town in northeast France.

---

842 Collection 7 The Modern World: 1900 to the Present

CONTENT-AREA CONNECTIONS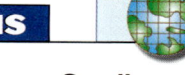

Science: Managing Disease
The occurrence of typhus, which is spread by lice, increased dramatically in the last few months of the war. Health workers entered Dachau shortly after its liberation, but they could not bring immediate relief; some 2,400 former prisoners died there within the next two weeks. Dachau was under quarantine for a time; some other camps were burned to keep the disease from spreading.

Small-group activity. Have students work together in small groups to research information about the treatment for such problems as typhus, malnutrition, and dysentery that existed in the camps. Students should try to find out if such treatments were available in 1945 and, if so, to what extent they were used by the liberating forces. Invite students to share their findings in an oral report.

I couldn't stop myself—I started to run downstairs, to escape into the street. Beauchamp and D. were supporting him under the arms. They'd stopped on the first-floor landing. He was looking up.

I can't remember exactly what happened. He must have looked at me and recognized me and smiled. I shrieked no, that I didn't want to see. I started to run again, up the stairs this time. I was shrieking, I remember that. The war emerged in my shrieks. Six years without uttering a cry. I found myself in some neighbors' apartment. They forced me to drink some rum, they poured it into my mouth. Into the shrieks.

I can't remember when I found myself back with him again, with him, Robert L. I remember hearing sobs all over the house; that the tenants stayed for a long while out on the stairs; that the doors were left open. I was told later that the concierge[9] had put decorations up in the hall to welcome him, and that as soon as he'd gone by she tore them all down and shut herself up alone in her lodge to weep.

In my memory, at a certain moment, the sounds stop and I see him. Huge. There before me. I don't recognize him. He looks at me. He smiles. Lets himself be looked at. There's a supernatural weariness in his smile, weariness from having managed to live till this moment. It's from this smile that I suddenly recognize him, but from a great distance, as if I were seeing him at the other end of a tunnel. It's a smile of embarrassment. He's apologizing for being here, reduced to such a wreck. And then the smile fades, and he becomes a stranger again. But the knowledge is still there, that this stranger is he, Robert L., totally.

He wanted to see around the apartment again. We supported him, and he toured the rooms.

---
9. **concierge** (kän'sē·erzh') *n.*: superintendent.

His cheeks creased, but didn't release his lips; it was in his eyes that we'd seen his smile. In the kitchen he saw the clafoutis[10] we'd made for him. He stopped smiling. "What is it?" We told him. What was it made with? Cherries—it was the height of the season. "May I have some?" "We don't know, we'll have to ask the doctor." He came back into the sitting room and lay down on the divan. "So I can't have any?" "Not yet." "Why?" "There have been accidents in Paris already from letting deportees eat too soon after they got back from the camps."

He stopped asking questions about what had happened while he was away. He stopped seeing us. A great, silent pain spread over his face because he was still being refused food, because it was still as it had been in the concentration camp. And, as in the camp, he accepted it in silence. He didn't see that we were weeping. Nor did he see that we could scarcely look at him or respond to what he said.

The doctor came. He stopped short with his hand on the door handle, very pale. He looked at us, and then at the form on the divan. He didn't understand. And then he realized: the form wasn't dead yet, it was hovering between life and death, and he, the doctor, had been called in to try to keep it alive. The doctor came into the room. He went over to the form and the form smiled at him. The doctor was to come several times a day for three weeks, at all hours of the day and night. Whenever we were too afraid we called him and he came. He saved Robert L. He too was caught up in the passionate desire to save Robert L. from death. He succeeded.

We smuggled the clafoutis out of the house while he slept. The next day he was feverish and didn't talk about food any more. ■

---
10. **clafoutis** *n.*: type of sponge cake with fruit in the center of it.

Primary Source

Liberator's Perspective

Lt. Col. Felix Sparks, the American who led the liberation of Dachau, provides this description of the conditions at the camp: "The first evidence of the horrors to come was a string of forty railroad cars on a railway spur leading into the camp. Each car was filled with emaciated human corpses, both men and women. A hasty search by the stunned infantry officers revealed no signs of life among the hundreds of still bodies, over 2,000 in all." (The final count was 2,310 men, women, and children, in 39 railroad cars.) "As we approached the confinement area, the scene numbed my senses. Dante's *Inferno* seemed pale compared to the real hell of Dachau. . . . While we were accustomed to death, we were not able to comprehend the type of death that we encountered at Dachau."

Connected Reading

Summary ⬇ below grade level

Using the refrain *Never shall I forget*, Wiesel presents a series of images relating to the Holocaust. He remembers how the "night" of his soul began with his arrival at a concentration camp and how children died there; he recalls the flames and nighttime silence that he associates with the place. Most of all, he always will remember—even if he lives forever—how the concentration camp destroyed his dreams, his religious faith, and his very desire to live.

Skills Starter

Build review skills. Explain that expressing political views can be similar to advertising: Sometimes a point can be more effectively made with a few statements or images than with an extended explanation. Call on volunteers to recall public service television commercials or print ads that leave powerful, memorable images. Discuss the message that each image conveys. Then urge students to look for a similar technique in "Never Shall I Forget."

Political Points *of* View

Before You Read

Elie Wiesel was only fifteen years old when he and all the other Jews in his Romanian village were deported to concentration camps in Poland and Germany. Together with his father, Wiesel was taken to Auschwitz, then to camps at Buna, Gleiwitz, and Buchenwald, where his father finally died of starvation and exposure. Wiesel also lost his mother and younger sister, both victims of the gas chambers. Against the odds, Wiesel and his two older sisters survived and were later reunited.

After the war, Wiesel spent several years in a French orphanage and then studied philosophy and literature at the Sorbonne. He also worked as a journalist. In 1955, after breaking a self-imposed vow never to write about the Holocaust, Wiesel poured his memories into a nine-hundred-page volume. This work was soon condensed and republished as *Night*. The following excerpt, "Never Shall I Forget," originally appeared as a prose passage in the condensed version. It is thought by some to be one of the most powerful passages in Holocaust literature.

Wiesel now lives in the United States, where he has served as the Chairman of the President's Commission on the Holocaust and where he was awarded the Congressional Gold Medal of Achievement. In 1986, Wiesel was awarded the Nobel Peace Prize. He continues to write and to advocate for the remembrance of the Holocaust and for the end of racism, hatred, and genocide.

Study C (detail) (1995) by Samuel Bak. Oil.
Courtesy Pucker Gallery, Boston, MA, 2002.

Conducting a Historical Investigation

Whole-class activity. In Wiesel's poem students will be reminded that children, too, suffered and died at the hands of the Nazis. Have students find Holocaust accounts (in words and pictures) from a child's point of view. You may want to have students read *Anne Frank: The Diary of a Young Girl;* below are a few other titles to consider.

- *Children in the Holocaust and World War II: Their Secret Diaries,* edited by Laurel Holiday
- *I Never Saw Another Butterfly: Children's Drawings and Poems from Terezin Concentration Camp 1942–1944,* edited by Hana Volavkova

Ask students to summarize the facts in each book, to give their opinion of the book, and to relate it to at least one of the selections in this Political Points of View feature.

POEM

Never Shall I Forget
Elie Wiesel

Never shall I forget that night,
the first night in the camp
which has turned my life into one long night,
seven times cursed and seven times sealed.

5 Never shall I forget that smoke.
Never shall I forget the little faces of the children
whose bodies I saw turned into wreaths of smoke
beneath a silent blue sky.

Never shall I forget those flames
10 which consumed my faith for ever.
Never shall I forget that nocturnal silence
which deprived me for all eternity of the desire to live.

Never shall I forget those moments
which murdered my God and my soul
15 and turned my dreams to dust.

Never shall I forget these things,
even if I am condemned to live
as long as God Himself.

Never.

Children and other prisoners liberated by the U.S. Third Army march from Buchenwald concentration camp in Germany in 1945. The freed prisoners are walking to an American-run hospital. The tall youth in line at the left, fourth from the front, is Elie Wiesel.
Associated Press.

Connection

Summary ⬇ *below grade level*

This page shows some of the historical information available at the Web site of the United States Holocaust Memorial Museum. Specifically, it summarizes the 1938 event known as *Kristallnacht* and explains how the event fits into the Holocaust as a whole.

DIRECT TEACHING

Ⓐ Content-Area Connections

History: Kristallnacht
Objects salvaged from Kristallnacht, such as a slashed and gouged wooden Torah ark from a destroyed Jewish synagogue, are on display at the Holocaust Museum. Also on display are hate posters used by the Nazis to inflame the public against the Jews and charts of eye and skin color and skull shape used by the Nazis to identify "undesirables."

Ⓑ Reading Informational Text

❓ Finding the main idea.
According to this Web page, why was *Kristallnacht* a turning point in the Holocaust? [Possible response: From this point on, the SS was in charge of the "Jewish Question," which it planned to solve through extermination. The night resulted in the death of ninety-one Jews and the first massive deportation of Jews to concentration camps.]

CONNECTION/WEB PAGE

The following Web page is from the United States Holocaust Memorial Museum Web site. This Washington, D.C., museum is a memorial to the millions of people who died in the Holocaust and is devoted to the continual study of the Holocaust. The Web page below is about one night of destruction and murder inflicted on German Jews by the Nazis. This night came to be known as Kristallnacht ("Night of Broken Glass") because of all the glass storefronts that the Nazis smashed. In the end, approximately 7,500 Jewish businesses were destroyed or damaged and at least ninety-one Jews were murdered. (Pogroms are organized, government-sanctioned persecutions.)

Location: http://www.ushmm.org/kristallnacht/menu.htm

On November 9, 1938, the Nazis unleashed a wave of pogroms against Germany's Jews. In the space of a few hours, thousands of synagogues and Jewish businesses and homes were damaged or destroyed. This event came to be called Kristallnacht ("Night of Broken Glass") for the shattered store windowpanes that carpeted German streets.

Ⓐ The pretext for this violence was the November 7 assassination of a German diplomat in Paris, Ernst vom Rath, by Herschel Grynszpan, a Jewish teenager whose parents, along with 17,000 other Polish Jews, had been recently expelled from the Reich. Though portrayed as spontaneous outbursts of popular outrage, these pogroms were calculated acts of retaliation carried out by the SA, SS, and local Nazi party organizations.

Ⓑ Storm troopers killed at least 91 Jews and injured many others. For the first time, Jews were arrested on a massive scale and transported to Nazi concentration camps. About 30,000 Jews were sent to Buchenwald, Dachau, and Sachsenhausen, where hundreds died within weeks of arrival. Release came only after the prisoners arranged to emigrate and agreed to transfer their property to "Aryans."

Kristallnacht culminated the escalating violence against Jews that began during the incorporation of Austria into the Reich in March 1938. It also signaled the fateful transfer of responsibility for "solving" the "Jewish Question" to the SS.

The burning of the synagogue in Ober Ramstadt during Kristallnacht. The local fire department prevented the fire from spreading to a nearby home but made no attempt to intervene in the synagogue fire.
Trudy Isenberg Collection, Courtesy of the USHMM Archives.

846 Collection 7 The Modern World: 1900 to the Present

Comparing and Contrasting Texts

Analyzing purposes of texts. Discuss these questions about the Web page with students:

- How is the purpose of this Web page different from the purpose of the account by Marguerite Duras? By Primo Levi? [Possible response: The Web page is meant to provide only facts, but Duras and Levi want to affect readers' emotions.]

- What kind of presentation might make use of both this Web page and Elie Wiesel's "Never Shall I Forget"? [Possible response: A multimedia production designed to teach facts about the Holocaust, to bear witness to the suffering of its victims, and to convince viewers to fight prejudice.]

Analyzing Political Points of View

The Holocaust

The questions on this page ask you to analyze the views on the Holocaust presented in the preceding three selections:

Primo Levi . . . . *from* **Survival in Auschwitz** . . . . . (Italy)
Marguerite Duras . . . . *from* **The War** . . . . (France)
Elie Wiesel . . . . **Never Shall I Forget** . . . . (Romania)

Comparing Political Assumptions

1. The authors of the three selections in this feature were directly connected to the events of the Holocaust. As a result, each piece of writing is **subjective**—that is, it tells about actual events from a very personal point of view. Describe the similarities and differences you find in these three points of view. As a point of comparison, contrast the subjective points of view in these selections with the objective, or factual, point of view of the **Connection** on page 846.

2. In your opinion, which selection could act as the most powerful deterrent against another Holocaust? Do you agree that keeping the memory of the Holocaust alive will make it less likely that such an event will occur again? (Review your Quickwrite notes on page 832.)

3. Loss of identity is a common theme in these three works. Describe what or who stripped these writers of their identities. Was it a single person? a group of people? Or was it a broader, more subtle idea or entity? Whom or what do you think each writer would point to as the enemy?

4. Choose two of the three selections you have read in this feature, and compare the speakers of the two selections. How would you describe each speaker's **tone**? Who seems closest to the events he or she describes? Who seems furthest removed? Explain.

WRITING

Analyzing Political Assumptions

In an **essay,** unearth the political assumptions that underlie these three selections, and then evaluate how clearly these assumptions are communicated. First, summarize the claim, or the main idea, that you believe each author wants to convey. (Consult your reading notes on page 832.) What idea *about* the Holocaust is each writer trying to express? Next, jot down specific details that help clarify this main idea. Finally, consider how all the texts work together to express a crucial idea, or assumption, about human nature and human experience. Use examples from the texts to illustrate and support your ideas.

Self-portrait with Jewish Identity Card (detail) (1943) by Felix Nussbaum. Oil on canvas.
Kulturgeschichtliches Museum Osnabrueck. © 2003 Artists Rights Society (ARS), New York/VG Bild-Kunst, Bonn.

SKILLS FOCUS

Literary Skills
Analyze and compare political points of view on a topic.

Reading Skills
Compare main ideas across texts.

Writing Skills
Write an essay analyzing political assumptions.

INDEPENDENT PRACTICE

Analyzing Political Points of View

2. Answers will vary, for all three pieces are emotionally charged. Many students will select "On the Bottom," deciding that its grim but vivid details create the most memorable images. Students may agree that remembering the Holocaust may make another such event less likely, but students may also realize that remembering, by itself, will not eliminate the threat.

3. Students should note that Duras's husband lost his identity but Duras herself did not. Possible answer: In each case, the loss of identity resulted most directly from the atrocities committed by individuals acting in accordance with the policies of Adolf Hitler. Ultimately, perhaps it was sheer racial hatred that did the most to destroy people's identities. Thus, the writers might agree that racism was the larger enemy.

4. Answers will vary. All of the speakers have a tone of shock, bitterness, and profound sadness. Levi reflects upon the loss of identity brought about by the Holocaust, and thus his tone is somewhat more intellectual: He is trying to understand. Duras focuses on her husband, and her love for him adds a tone of intimacy—which also conveys her shock upon realizing what the Nazis have done. Wiesel's tone is fiercely emotional but he may seem more repressed—ordered, controlled, and further removed—because he conveys his emotion in poetry instead of prose.

Comparing Political Assumptions

1. Answers will vary. Students should recognize that all three pieces have a bitter tone and convey a sense of outrage about the general suffering and individual dehumanization caused by the Holocaust. In addition, all three writers—as survivors (Levi and Wiesel) or as a witness (Duras)—are relating not only facts about the Holocaust but also their impressions and opinions after the fact. In contrast, the Web page from the Holocaust Museum is strictly factual. Its purpose is only to inform readers of the events of Kristallnacht: The writer is anonymous, and the text provides no personal impressions or opinions.

SKILLS FOCUS, pp. 848–852

Grade-Level Skills
- **Reading Skills**

Critique the validity, appeal, and truthfulness of an author's argument.

More About the Writer

Background. In a series of books on the history of the Second World War, Winston Churchill wrote about the blitz, which occurred after the fall of France and before the entry of the United States into the war. In *Their Finest Hour*, the volume of the series devoted to this period, Churchill stated the theme of the volume as follows:

> How the British people
> held the fort
> ALONE
> till those who
> hitherto had been half blind
> were half ready

Winston Churchill
1874–1965
England

Winston Churchill (soldier, statesman, man of letters, Nobel laureate and, in the eyes of many, savior of Britain) was born at Blenheim Palace. He was the son of Lord Randolph Churchill, a politician, and his wife Jennie Jerome. Of his early schooling, Churchill said, "I got into my bones the essential structure of the ordinary British sentence—which is a noble thing." Churchill's father, lacking confidence in his son's academic abilities, insisted that he prepare for a military career by entering Sandhurst Royal Military College.

Churchill emerged in 1895 a second lieutenant in the cavalry and volunteered to visit Cuba to observe Spain's tactics against Cuban rebels. He also went to write and send war dispatches to a British newspaper. On his return, he wrote an article about the conflict for the *Saturday Review*, and so began Churchill's simultaneous career as a writer with whatever profession—military or political—he undertook. Later, in 1897 while stationed in southern India, he joined a military action against Afghan tribesmen more than two thousand miles north at Malakand by becoming a war correspondent for the London *Daily Telegraph*. Officer casualties soon made it necessary for Churchill to drop his journalist role and take charge of troops, which he did zealously. Churchill wrote a history of the Malakand campaign, modestly mentioning himself only in a footnote.

In 1899, Churchill left the army and ran for a seat in Parliament, which he lost. The Boer War had started, and he sailed for South Africa as a war correspondent for the *Morning Post*. He was captured by the Boers but completed a daring escape that made him famous throughout Britain. He published two books on the war, one of which, *London to Ladysmith via Pretoria* (1900), was based on his press reports and sold 11,000 copies in fewer than six weeks. He was elected to Parliament in 1900.

By the time World War II began, Churchill had served in numerous government positions. For breadth of experience and energy, he had few peers when he became prime minister in 1940. He also had no equals in giving speeches that would rally the nation never to surrender, especially during the "blitz," when Germany bombed London for fifty-seven successive nights. Of the brave British fighter pilots who persevered night after night, he said, "Never in the field of human conflict has so much been owed by so many to so few." Few comments on war have been as poignant or memorable.

Following the war, Churchill published collections of his speeches and biographies and more books on military history. He was awarded the Nobel Prize for literature in 1953, when he was seventy-nine. But it was his leadership through the war that no one would forget and that prompted his daughter Mary to sum up his achievement by saying, "I owe you what every Englishman, woman and child does—Liberty itself."

RESOURCES: READING

Planning
- *One-Stop Planner* CD-ROM with ExamView Test Generator

Differentiating Instruction
- *Holt Reading Solutions*
- *The Holt Reader*
- *Supporting Instruction in Spanish*
- *Audio CD Library, Selections and Summaries in Spanish*

Vocabulary
- *Vocabulary Development*

Grammar and Language
- *Daily Language Activities*

Assessment
- *Holt Assessment: Literature, Reading, and Vocabulary*
- *One-Stop Planner* CD-ROM with ExamView Test Generator

- *Holt Online Assessment*

Internet
- go.hrw.com (Keyword: LE5 12-7)
- *Elements of Literature Online*

Media
- *Audio CD Library*
- *Audio CD Library, Selections and Summaries in Spanish*

Before You Read

Blood, Sweat, and Tears

Make the Connection
Quickwrite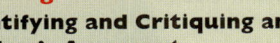

When a country faces war or natural disaster, its citizens look to their political leaders for assurance, guidance, and inspiration. Jot down your thoughts on what you would expect to hear from a government leader in a time of crisis.

Reading Skills

Identifying and Critiquing an Author's Argument

To persuade listeners or readers to agree with their arguments, speakers and writers often try to demonstrate their credibility through **logical appeals**. They may then try to engage their audience's support with **emotional appeals**. As you read, notice how Churchill begins his speech by listing the methodical, reasonable steps he has taken to form his government. He then arouses strong feelings in his audience by using emotionally charged words like "ordeal," "struggle," and "tyranny." What exactly is Churchill's purpose? As you read, try to define his purpose, and critique his effectiveness in accomplishing it.

Background

World War II officially began with Germany's invasion of Poland on September 1, 1939. On September 3, Britain declared war on Germany and started manufacturing arms, ships, and planes for both offense and defense. By the time Churchill gave his speech to Parliament on May 13, 1940, German troops had overrun Holland and Belgium and were driving deep into France. The Battle of Britain was imminent. As newly elected prime minister, Churchill had just formed a coalition government of Labour and Liberals and knew that he had to inspire the country with an unwavering belief in its ability to survive, triumph, and endure. No one who heard Churchill's radio speeches during the war ever forgot them.

Vocabulary Development

rigor (rig′ər) *n.*: extreme severity.

provision (prə·vizh′ən) *n.*: arrangement or preparation beforehand.

grievous (grēv′əs) *adj.*: outrageous; horrible.

lamentable (lə·men′tə·bəl) *adj.*: regrettable; unfortunate.

buoyancy (boi′ən·sē) *n.*: lightness of spirit; cheerfulness.

Our Heritage (1943) by Robert Austin. The poster first appeared in the London Underground.
London Transport Museum.

SKILLS FOCUS

Reading Skills
Identify and critique an author's argument.

Winston Churchill 849

PRETEACHING

Summary *at grade level*

Churchill's immediate audience for his first speech as prime minister was the House of Commons, but he clearly had a much wider audience in mind—not only other Britons but also the rest of the world, foes as well as friends. He devotes his first two paragraphs to appeals based on reason, establishing his credibility by explaining what he has accomplished since being named prime minister the previous Friday and what he plans to do next. Then, making the transition to emotional appeals, he uses repetition, parallelism, and personal references to convey the urgency of the situation, to declare his devotion to the tasks before him, and to exhort his listeners to unite in the cause of victory.

Selection Starter

Motivate. Remind students that Britain lost nearly a million soldiers in World War I, the so-called "war to end all wars." Before they read, ask them to speculate about how those who had been injured or had lost loved ones in that war might react to a speech committing the nation to another global war just twenty-two years later. What would it take to persuade them to unite behind Churchill?

Previewing Vocabulary

To reinforce students' understanding of the Vocabulary words on p. 849, have them complete the following analogies.

1. ADVISER : COUNSELOR :: _____ : prior arrangement [provision]
2. LOYAL : FAITHFUL :: _____ : regrettable [lamentable]
3. PUNISHMENT : FORGIVENESS :: _____ : flexibility [rigor]
4. WISDOM : FOOLISHNESS :: _____ : gloom [buoyancy]
5. REMOTE : DISTANT :: _____ : terrible [grievous]

Winston Churchill 849

INDEPENDENT PRACTICE

Response and Analysis

Reading Check

1. to the House of Commons
2. his new coalition government
3. to achieve victory

Thinking Critically

4. Possible answers: His decisive actions demonstrate competence; his ability to form a government shows credibility; his plans and his sense of urgency show command of the situation.
5. His tone is serious ("extreme urgency and rigor of events"); impassioned ("blood, toil, tears, and sweat"). Humor would be offensive; the nation is at war.
6. Possible answers: Parallelism emphasizes the gravity of the situation. The personal references stress the need for action. The final sentence is a deeply personal reference. He repeats "victory" and "no survival." The final sentence issues the call to action. His purpose is to unite the nation in defeating the Axis forces.
7. He is being honest with the nation about the suffering ahead and is stressing his own involvement.
8. Possible answer: He might have been trying to convince them that Britain would never surrender.

Extending and Evaluating

9. Responses will vary. Students should support their responses with examples from the text.
10. No; its brevity suits the situation.

Vocabulary Development

1. lamentable
2. grievous
3. rigor
4. buoyancy
5. provision

Response and Analysis

Reading Check
1. To whom is Churchill speaking?
2. What does he want approved?
3. What is the government's aim?

Thinking Critically
4. The credibility of a public figure is often revealed to an audience in public addresses. How would you **characterize** Churchill after reading his speech? In what ways does he convince you of his competence, credibility, and command of the situation?
5. How would you describe Churchill's **tone**—his attitude toward his audience? Find examples from the speech to support your judgment. Why do you suppose Churchill has avoided any humor or lightheartedness in his speech?
6. In the final two paragraphs, identify and analyze **rhetorical devices** that Churchill uses to arouse emotional reactions in his listeners. (Consider such techniques as emphasis, repetition, word choice, personal references, and call to action.) What is his purpose in these paragraphs? Refer to your reading notes.
7. How would you interpret Churchill's statement: "I have nothing to offer but blood, toil, tears, and sweat"? What does it reveal about Churchill and his argument?
8. Churchill knew that leaders of Germany would read his speech. What might he have been trying to convince the enemy of?

Extending and Evaluating
9. Did you find Churchill's speech persuasive and his arguments valid? Did he say the things you would expect a leader to say in a time of war? Support your responses with reasons and examples. (Be sure to consult your Quickwrite notes.)

SKILLS FOCUS

Reading Skills
Identify and critique an author's argument.

Writing Skills
Write a persuasive essay using logical, emotional, and ethical appeals.

Vocabulary Skills
Complete analogies.

10. Would Churchill's speech be more effective if it were longer and included more details, examples, and reasons to support his argument? Why or why not?

WRITING

Call to Action

Write a **persuasive essay** using **logical** and **emotional appeals** to convince your audience that they must take action on a particular issue affecting your school or community. To make your argument more convincing, use at least one **ethical appeal** to show that you are competent, sincere, trustworthy, fair, and knowledgeable.

▶ For help with this assignment, see "Writing a Persuasive Essay," pages 883–884.

Vocabulary Development
Analogies

rigor	lamentable
provision	buoyancy
grievous	

In an **analogy** the words in one pair relate to each other in the same way as the words in a second pair. On a separate sheet of paper, fill in each blank below with the Vocabulary word above that best completes the analogy.

1. ARID : DRY :: _____ : unfortunate
2. LIVELY : INACTIVE :: _____ : pleasant
3. FRIGID : COLD :: _____ : severity
4. WEALTH : POVERTY :: _____ : sadness
5. STRENGTH : VIGOR :: _____ : preparation

ASSESSING

Assessment

■ Holt Assessment: *Literature, Reading, and Vocabulary*

RETEACHING

For a lesson reteaching critiquing public documents, see **Reteaching**, p. 1129A.

Yasunari Kawabata
(1899–1972)
Japan

The concern with loneliness and death that pervades the novels and short stories of Yasunari Kawabata (yä·sü′nä·re kä′wä·bä′tä) may be a result of his childhood. His father died when Kawabata was three; the following year his mother died. Within the next five years his only sister and his grandmother died. At the age of fourteen, Kawabata began to record his thoughts and feelings when he saw that his grandfather, who had raised him for about six years, was growing very ill. These writings were published after his grandfather's death as *Diary of a Sixteen-Year-Old* (1925).

Born in Osaka, Kawabata attended Tokyo Imperial University, where he studied English literature and Japanese literature. In 1924, he joined with other students to found a literary magazine that became the mouthpiece of a new avant-garde literary movement called Neosensualism, which was influenced, in part, by haiku poetry. Neosensualist writers attempted to capture intense, immediate moments in life—images, sensations, and impressions. To achieve such immediacy in his novels, Kawabata placed one psychologically charged scene right after another, with no transitions. This technique gives the effect, one critic wrote, of "a series of brief flashes in a void."

Kawabata's novels include *The Izu Dancer* (1926), *The Snow Country* (1948), *Thousand Cranes* (1952), *The Sound of the Mountain* (1952), and *The House of the Sleeping Beauties* (1961). These novels, which focus on lonely men who try to find comfort in the beauty and goodness of women, are characterized by nostalgia and sadness. Although Kawabata is best known for his novels, he also wrote what he called *tanagokoro no shosetsu*, or "palm-of-the-hand stories." In their deceptive simplicity, these stories resemble haiku poetry (see pages 565–572). Just as a haiku offers brief, vivid images that rival the richness of a longer poem, so these little stories offer images and psychological insights that rival those of longer fiction.

Kawabata died alone in his studio in 1972, about a year and a half after his friend, the novelist Yukio Mishima, had committed ritual suicide for political reasons. Kawabata also took his own life, but he left no explanation of his motives.

In 1968, Kawabata became the first Japanese writer to be awarded the Nobel Prize in literature. In his acceptance speech he remarked on an aspect of traditional Japanese ink painting that applies, with startling accuracy, to his own work and to his life: "The heart [of it] is in space, abbreviation, what is left undrawn."

For Independent Reading
You may enjoy this story by Kawabata:
- "The Jay"

Before You Read

The Silver Fifty-Sen Pieces

PRETEACHING

Summary ⇨ at grade level

In the story's first scene, we learn that seventeen-year-old Yoshiko, who works in a Tokyo office, receives a monthly allowance from her mother. The only thing Yoshiko ever buys is a weekly loaf of French bread from a department store. Then one day in the store she is attracted to a glass paperweight embossed with the image of a dog. Ten days in a row she goes back to look at it, and then, feeling daring, she buys it. Her mother and older sister laugh at her for buying a "toy," but they both admit that it is lovely. The anecdote passes into family lore, evoking laughter whenever it comes up.

In the second scene, Yoshiko and her mother go shopping together. In the store's bargain basement, Yoshiko watches from the sidelines as her mother gets caught up in the thrill of the hunt. Finally, as the pair is heading out the door, the mother spots a display of inexpensive umbrellas. Uncharacteristically, Yoshiko herself enters the fray—until her mother calls a halt to the search.

In the third scene, set seven years later, in 1946, Yoshiko remembers the umbrella incident and misses her mother, who died in the bombing of Tokyo. The glass paperweight has survived Yoshiko's own brush with death in the bombing of Yokohama. Gazing at the glass dog, Yoshiko realizes with a shock that all the real dogs are gone from her burned-out neighborhood.

Selection Starter

Motivate. Ask students to consider this question as they read: What in life is lasting?

Make the Connection

Family members and groups of friends often cherish anecdotes about one another and embellish these stories through repeated telling. These anecdotes are often humorous and usually offer insight into the character of the person they are about. In the following story, Yasunari Kawabata describes the origins of one such family anecdote. This anecdote, as you will see, is about a small, beautiful treasure. By the story's end, however, we realize that the more striking treasure is the anecdote itself. Holding it up to the light, Kawabata shows us how a simple family story can reflect the hearts of those who share it.

Literary Focus
Theme

A **theme** is a literary work's central insight into human experience. Unlike a topic (such as *love* or *death*), a theme is a complete idea that usually takes the form of a sentence: *For a person to give love, he or she must first receive it.* As in this example, a theme does not reflect the specific content of a work. Rather, it moves beyond the work to express a general idea about life or human nature. Sometimes authors state a theme directly, but more often they imply or suggest it through the descriptive details, images, or symbols in the work itself.

INTERNET
Vocabulary Practice
Keyword: LE5 12-7

SKILLS FOCUS

A **theme** is the central idea or insight of a work of literature.

For more on Theme, see the Handbook of Literary and Historical Terms.

Literary Skills Understand theme.

Reading Skills Make inferences about theme.

Reading Skills
Making Inferences

Some works of literature are dominated by a particular **symbol,** something that stands for itself and also for something beyond itself. This symbol can give the reader a strong clue about the **theme** of the work—that is, it can help the reader make an **inference,** or an intelligent guess, about the work's underlying message. As you read "The Silver Fifty-Sen Pieces," try to identify the story's central symbol. Then, ask yourself: What abstract idea might this symbol represent? Next, try to figure out what Kawabata wants to convey about this abstract idea. When you have determined this, you will have inferred the story's theme.

Background

The protagonist of "The Silver Fifty-Sen Pieces" is a young woman living in Tokyo, Japan, in the years prior to and during Japan's war with China and Manchuria (1937–1945) and just after World War II (1939–1945). Young women living in their parents' households often held low-level jobs for several years before "retiring" to get married by age twenty-five.

Vocabulary Development

spurned (spurnd) *v.*: rejected.

exquisite (eks′kwiz·it) *adj.*: beautiful; delicate.

meticulous (mə·tik′yōō·ləs) *adj.*: precise; extremely concerned with details.

discrimination (di·skrim′i·nā′shən) *n.*: ability to make fine distinctions.

antipathy (an·tip′ə·thē) *n.*: strong dislike; aversion.

854 Collection 7 The Modern World: 1900 to the Present

Previewing Vocabulary

Have students explain what is wrong with each of the following sentences. Possible answers appear in brackets.

1. Look at that <u>exquisite</u> earthquake! [Destructive earthquakes are not delicate.]

2. His <u>antipathy</u> toward his lab partner was evident from his warm smile. [He wouldn't smile warmly at someone he didn't like.]

3. He <u>spurned</u> the dog's advances, unable to resist its pleading eyes and wagging tail. [If he truly spurned the dog, he would resist its appeals.]

4. Displaying her usual <u>discrimination</u>, Ella picked the bruised apple. [If Ella were truly discriminating, she would not have picked a bruised apple.]

5. These grimy windows prove how <u>meticulous</u> the cleaning crew was. [A cleaning crew that did precise work would not leave the windows dirty.]

The Silver Fifty-Sen Pieces

Yasunari Kawabata

translated by **Lane Dunlop** *and* **J. Martin Holman**

Rain at Yotsuya Mitsuke (1930) by Takashi Henmi.

It was a custom that the two-yen allowance that she received at the start of each month, in silver fifty-sen[1] pieces, be placed in Yoshiko's purse by her mother's own hand.

At that time, the fifty-sen piece had recently been reduced in size. These silver coins, which looked light and felt heavy, seemed to Yoshiko to fill up her small red leather purse with a solid dignity. Often, careful not to waste them, she kept them in her handbag until the end of the month. It was not that Yoshiko spurned such girlish pleasures as going out to a movie theater or a coffee shop with the friends she worked with; she simply saw those diversions as being

---

1. **two-yen, fifty-sen:** A fifty-sen piece is half of one yen, the basic monetary unit of Japan. (One hundred sen equal one yen.) Exchange rates vary, but one yen has usually been equivalent to an amount much less than one U.S. dollar.

Vocabulary
spurned (spurnd) *v.:* rejected.

DIRECT TEACHING

VIEWING THE ART

Despite a move toward industrialization in early twentieth-century Japan, the economy and culture of the country remained predominantly based on agriculture. Because its industrial growth depended on foreign trade, however, Japan suffered immensely in the worldwide depression of the 1930s. A feeling of hopelessness began to infect the nation, ultranationalist sentiment took hold, the military gained more power, and Japan was plunged into what came to be called "the dark valley" of militarism and war.

Activity. How does this print by **Yoshinobu Sakamoto** suggest Japan's modernization? [The print shows an urban scene with modern inventions such as a trolley, a van, and what may be a department store.]

A Reading Skills

Making inferences. What details suggest that buying the paperweight is significant for Yoshiko? [She returns to the store ten times before buying it, and when she does buy it, her heart beats fast.]

B Literary Focus

Characterization. How do the mother's and sister's initial reactions to the paperweight differ from Yoshiko's? [They consider it just a pretty toy, while Yoshiko considers it a work of art.] What do their reactions suggest about their attitude toward Yoshiko? [Possible responses: They consider her a child; they consider her foolish.]

Harimaya-chô (1935) by Yoshinobu Sakamoto.

outside her life. She had never experienced them, and so was never tempted by them.

Once a week, on her way back from the office, she would stop off at a department store and buy, for ten sen, a loaf of the seasoned French bread she liked so much. Other than that, there was nothing she particularly wanted for herself.

One day, however, at Mitsukoshi's, in the stationery department, a glass paperweight caught her eye. Hexagonal, it had a dog carved on it in relief.[2] Charmed by the dog, Yoshiko took the paperweight in her hand. Its thrilling coolness, its unexpected weightiness, suddenly gave her pleasure. Yoshiko, who loved this kind of delicately accomplished work, was captivated despite herself. Weighing it in her palm, looking at it from every angle, she quietly and reluctantly put it back in its box. It was forty sen.

The next day, she came back. She examined the paperweight again. The day after that, she came back again and examined it anew. After ten days of this, she finally made up her mind.

"I'll take this," she said to the clerk, her heart beating fast.

When she got home, her mother and older sister laughed at her.

"Buying this sort of thing—it's like a toy."

But when each had taken it in her hand and looked at it, they said, "You're right, it *is* rather pretty," and, "It's so ingenious."

They tried holding it up against the light. The polished clear glass surface and the misty surface, like frosted glass, of the relief, harmonized curiously. In the hexagonal facets,[3] too, there was an exquisite rightness, like the meter of a poem.

---

2. **relief** *n.:* sculptured shape raised from a flat background surface.

3. **facets** (fas′its) *n. pl.:* A facet is one surface of a many-sided solid figure.

Vocabulary

exquisite (eks′kwiz·it) *adj.:* beautiful; delicate.

DIFFERENTIATING INSTRUCTION

Advanced Learners

Enrichment. The power of Kawabata's palm-of-the-hand stories, like the power of haiku, arises from the unspoken feelings compressed into exact images. Challenge students to reduce the three scenes of this story to a series of haiku-like poems.

To Yoshiko, it was a lovely work of art.

Although Yoshiko hadn't hoped to be complimented on the deliberation with which she had made her purchase, taking ten days to decide that the paperweight was an object worth her possession, she was pleased to receive this recognition of her good taste from her mother and older sister.

Even if she was laughed at for her exaggerated carefulness—taking those ten days to buy something that cost a mere forty sen—Yoshiko would not have been satisfied unless she had done so. She had never had occasion to regret having bought something on the spur of the moment. It was not that the seventeen-year-old Yoshiko possessed such meticulous discrimination that she spent several days thinking about and looking at something before arriving at a decision. It was just that she had a vague dread of spending carelessly the silver fifty-sen pieces, which had sunk into her mind as an important treasure.

Years later, when the story of the paperweight came up and everybody burst out laughing, her mother said seriously, "I thought you were so lovable that time."

To each and every one of Yoshiko's possessions, an amusing anecdote of this sort was attached.

It was a pleasure to do their shopping from the top down, descending regularly from floor to floor, so first they went up to the fifth floor on the elevator. This Sunday, unusually allured by the charm of a shopping trip with her mother, Yoshiko had come to Mitsukoshi's.

Although their shopping for the day was done, when they'd descended to the first floor, her mother, as a matter of course, went on down to the bargain basement.

"But it's so crowded, Mother. I don't like it," grumbled Yoshiko, but her mother didn't hear her. Evidently the atmosphere of the bargain basement, with its competitive jockeying for position, had already absorbed her mother.

The bargain basement was a place set up for the sole purpose of making people waste their money, but perhaps her mother would find something. Thinking she'd keep an eye on her, Yoshiko followed her at a distance. It was air-conditioned so it wasn't all that hot.

First buying three bundles of stationery for twenty-five sen, her mother turned around and looked at Yoshiko. They smiled sweetly at each other. Lately, her mother had been pilfering Yoshiko's stationery, much to the latter's annoyance. Now we can rest easy, their looks seemed to say.

Drawn toward the counters for kitchen utensils and underwear, Yoshiko's mother was not brave enough to thrust her way through the mob of customers. Standing on tiptoe and peering over people's shoulders or putting her hand out through the small spaces between their sleeves, she looked but nevertheless didn't buy anything. At first unconvinced and then making up her mind definitely no, she headed toward the exit.

"Oh, these are just ninety-five sen? My . . ."

Just this side of the exit, her mother picked up one of the umbrellas for sale. Even after they'd burrowed through the whole heaped-up jumble, every single umbrella bore a price tag of ninety-five sen.

Apparently still surprised, her mother said, "They're so cheap, aren't they, Yoshiko? Aren't they cheap?" Her voice was suddenly lively. It was as if her vague, perplexed reluctance to leave without buying something more had found an outlet. "Well? Don't you think they're cheap?"

"They really are." Yoshiko, too, took one of the umbrellas in her hand. Her mother, holding hers alongside it, opened it up.

Japanese fifty-sen coins (pre–World War II).
HRW photo by Sam Dudgeon.

Vocabulary
meticulous (mə·tik′yoo·ləs) *adj.*: precise; extremely concerned with details.
discrimination (di·skrim′i·nā′shən) *n.*: ability to make fine distinctions.

READING MINI-LESSON

Developing Word-Attack Skills
Remind students that when the prefix *anti–* is added to a base word like *matter,* the two elements are combined without changes in stress.
/an′ti/ + /mat′ər/ = /an′ti·mat′ər/

When *anti–* is combined with a word part, there is often a change in stress. The selection word *antipathy* is an example. It is made up of the prefix *anti–* and the suffix *–pathy,* but it is not pronounced /an′ti·path′ē/; it is pronounced /an·tip′ə·thē/.

Activity. Have students read these words and identify the words that, like *antipathy,* have the greatest stress on the second syllable.

antimissile   antistatic   antiphonal
antiseptic   antipodes   antithesis

DIRECT TEACHING

C Literary Focus

? Theme. Because the money is a vital "treasure" to the main character of the story, Yoshiko, it is likely that the money is also central to the theme. At this point in the story, what insight into human nature might Kawabata be conveying? [Possible responses: When money is scarce, what you buy with it is especially precious. People sometimes attach important feelings to ordinary objects.]

D Reading Skills

? Making inferences. What does this comment suggest about her mother's feelings toward Yoshiko? [Possible responses: It suggests that she treasures the memory of that incident; it suggests that perhaps now she doesn't find Yoshiko as lovable as she used to.]

E Literary Focus

? Characterization. What do the details in these paragraphs reveal about Yoshiko's mother? [Possible responses: She enjoys competitive shopping but is not pushy; she feels free to use Yoshiko's stationery without asking and then expects Yoshiko's approval for buying some of her own.]

F Reading Skills

? Making inferences. Why do you think Yoshiko's mother is so anxious not to leave the store without buying something? [Possible response: Unlike Yoshiko, the enjoyment of buying or of getting a bargain is what matters to her—not the objects she buys.]

DIRECT TEACHING

A **Reading Skills**

Making inferences. Why is Yoshiko repelled by this search for a bargain? [Possible response: She is embarrassed and perhaps disgusted by her mother's acquisitiveness.]

B **Reading Skills**

Making inferences. Why does Yoshiko's mother call off the search for an umbrella so abruptly? [Possible responses: She realizes that Yoshiko is trying to be a dutiful daughter but that she is exasperated; Yoshiko's resentment is taking the fun out of shopping.]

C **Reading Skills**

Synthesizing. List the events and changes that have taken place in the last seven years. [Prices have risen enormously; Tokyo has been bombed; Yoshiko's mother has died; Yoshiko got married; the paperweight, the only object Yoshiko has from her family home, has survived.]

D **Literary Focus**

Theme. What does the paperweight symbolize? [Possible responses: It symbolizes Yoshiko's bygone youth and innocence; it symbolizes her life with her mother; it symbolizes the enduring nature of art.] How does it convey the theme of the story? [Possible responses: The paperweight, bought after such careful thought, conveys all the thoughts and emotions Yoshiko associates with the past, especially with her mother. It embodies the theme that memory and love can be recalled by ordinary material possessions.]

"Just the ribs alone would be cheap at the price. The fabric—well, it's rayon, but it's so well made, don't you think?"

How was it possible to sell such a respectable item at this price? As the question flashed through Yoshiko's mind, a strange feeling of antipathy welled up in her, as if she'd been shoved by a cripple. Her mother, totally absorbed, opening up one after the other, rummaged through the pile to find an umbrella suitable to her age. Yoshiko waited a while, then said, "Mother, don't you have an umbrella at home?"

"Yes, that's so, but . . ." Glancing quickly at Yoshiko, her mother went on, "It's ten years, no, more, I've had it fifteen years. It's worn out and old-fashioned. And, Yoshiko, if I passed this on to somebody, think how happy they would be."

"That's true. It's all right if it's for a gift."

"There's nobody who wouldn't be happy."

Yoshiko smiled. Her mother seemed to be choosing an umbrella with that "somebody" in mind. But it was not anybody close to them. If it were, surely her mother would not have said "somebody."

"What about this one, Yoshiko?"

"That looks good."

Although she gave an unenthusiastic answer, Yoshiko went to her mother's side and began searching for a suitable umbrella.

Other shoppers, wearing thin summer dresses of rayon and saying, "It's cheap, it's cheap," were casually snapping up the umbrellas on their way into and out of the store.

Feeling pity for her mother, who, her face set and slightly flushed, was trying so hard to find the right umbrella, Yoshiko grew angry at her own hesitation.

As if to say, "Why not just buy one, any one, quickly?" Yoshiko turned away from her mother.

"Yoshiko, let's stop this."

"What?"

A weak smile floating at the corners of her mouth, as if to shake something off, her mother put her hand on Yoshiko's shoulder and left the counter. Now, though, it was Yoshiko who felt some indefinable reluctance. But, when she'd taken five or six steps, she felt relieved.

Taking hold of her mother's hand on her shoulder, she squeezed it hard and swung it together with her own. Pressing close to her mother so that they were shoulder to shoulder, she hurried toward the exit.

This had happened seven years ago, in the year 1939.

When the rain pounded against the fire-scorched sheet-metal roof of the shack, Yoshiko, thinking it would have been good if they had bought that umbrella, found herself wanting to make a funny story of it with her mother. Nowadays, the umbrella would have cost a hundred or two hundred yen. But her mother had died in the firebombings of their Tokyo neighborhood of Kanda.[4]

Even if they had bought the umbrella, it probably would have perished in the flames.

By chance, the glass paperweight had survived. When her husband's house in Yokohama[5] had burned down, the paperweight was among those things that she'd frantically stuffed into an emergency bag. It was her one remembrance of life in her mother's house.

From evening on, in the alley, there were the strange-sounding voices of the neighborhood girls. They were talking about how you could make a thousand yen in a single night. Taking up the forty-sen paperweight, which, when she was those girls' age, she had spent ten days thinking about before deciding to buy, Yoshiko studied the charming little dog carved in relief. Suddenly, she realized that there was not a single dog left in the whole burned-out neighborhood. The thought came as a shock to her. ∎

---

4. **firebombings . . . Kanda:** For three years before the United States dropped atomic bombs on the Japanese cities of Hiroshima and Nagasaki in August 1945, incendiary (fire-making) bombs were used to devastate Tokyo and cripple its industry. Despite the fact that the bombs destroyed homes and landmarks and killed many people, the Japanese government would not surrender.
5. **Yokohama** (yō′kō·hä′mä): port city south of Tokyo on Tokyo Bay.

Vocabulary
antipathy (an·tip′ə·thē) *n.*: strong dislike; aversion.

---

858   Collection 7   The Modern World: 1900 to the Present

CONTENT-AREA CONNECTIONS

History: Raining Fire
Individual activity. Have students research and report on the bombing of Tokyo during World War II. Remind them to use reliable resources, to set the events in the context of the war as a whole, and to present their findings objectively.

FAMILY/COMMUNITY ACTIVITY

Encourage students to interview their parents, grandparents, and other older relatives and friends, asking what special items they took with them when they left home to go out on their own. Which of those items survive, and what do they mean to their owners? Provide class time for students to discuss the stories they gather and to relate them to the theme of "The Silver Fifty-Sen Pieces."

Response and Analysis

Reading Check
1. How does Yoshiko usually spend her two-yen allowance?
2. Describe the special object that Yoshiko finally buys. How long does she take to make up her mind? How do her mother and sister react to her purchase?
3. What items attract Yoshiko's mother in the bargain basement? Which of these items does she buy?
4. What details at the end of the story identify the time and location in which the story takes place?

Thinking Critically
5. Jot down details from the story that **characterize** Yoshiko and her mother. What contrast between their personalities do these details suggest?
6. What conclusions can you draw about the relationship between Yoshiko and her mother from Yoshiko's thoughts and reactions in the final scene?
7. What message or **main idea** does the author convey in the umbrella episode in the department store?
8. What do you think the paperweight **symbolizes** in the story? Why, in the final scene, does it give Yoshiko a shock?
9. Summarize the **theme** or central insight that this story suggests to you. Look at your reading notes and list the clues—the details, images, or events—that helped you **infer** the theme. What does this theme suggest about life?

Extending and Evaluating
10. Do you think the title "The Silver Fifty-Sen Pieces" is appropriate? Why or why not? What other title would you give this story? Explain.

WRITING
Overtones and Echoes
In regard to one of Kawabata's novels, a critic wrote that Kawabata returns again and again to a specific moment in time, creating "circles upon circles of memory, coincidence after coincidence, innocent themes followed by their sinister, scarcely audible overtones and echoes." In a brief **essay**, use details from the story to explain how this observation applies to "The Silver Fifty-Sen Pieces." Look closely at the final scene. How does the story's conclusion give the theme "sinister" echoes?

Vocabulary Development
What's Wrong with This Picture?

Explain what's wrong with each sentence below.

1. She spurned her mother, whom she loved dearly.
2. Those giant plastic garbage bags are simply exquisite!
3. A meticulous man, Harvey rarely proofreads his writing.
4. Lisa has a fine sense of discrimination. She frequently buys damaged goods.
5. Upon seeing him, her antipathy was so great that she flung herself into his arms.

SKILLS FOCUS

Literary Skills
Analyze theme.

Reading Skills
Make inferences about theme.

Writing Skills
Write an essay explaining a critical comment.

Vocabulary Skills
Demonstrate word knowledge.

Grammar Skills
Use parallel structure correctly.

INDEPENDENT PRACTICE

Response and Analysis
6. Possible answers: Yoshiko loved her mother and misses her. She regrets not helping her mother pick out an umbrella.
7. Possible answers: Seemingly minor events can create indelible memories; shared experiences outlast material goods.
8. Possible answers: The paperweight may symbolize memories, beauty, family, or the past. The dogs' absence brings home the devastation caused by the bombing and all the losses the Japanese have suffered.
9. Possible answers: Works of art endure and can prompt special memories. No matter what we lose, the past can live in our memory.

Extending and Evaluating
10. Possible answers: Yes, the title is appropriate because Yoshiko makes a deliberate decision to invest in the paperweight and to emotionally invest in her love for her mother. No, it is inappropriate because the symbolic value of the glass paperweight is more important than the money itself.

Vocabulary Development
Sample Answer
1. People don't reject those they love dearly.

Reading Check
1. Each week she bought a loaf of bread.
2. She buys a paperweight embossed with the figure of a dog. It takes her ten days to make up her mind. They laugh and call it a toy, but admit that it is pretty.
3. Drawn to the stationery, utensils, underwear, and umbrellas, she buys stationery.
4. It is 1946 in Japan. Yoshiko is in a shack in a bombed and burned-out neighborhood.

Thinking Critically
5. Possible answers: Yoshiko's careful handling of money indicates that she is disciplined, perhaps overly cautious; her attachment to the paperweight indicates that she is introspective. The mother's laughter at Yoshiko suggests insensitivity. However, her attempt to buy an umbrella shows her warm feelings for her daughter.

Grammar Link

Practice

Sample Answers

1. Japanese writers have been celebrated not only for their novels, poetry, and plays but also for their travel journals and diaries.

2. The *Manyoshu*, an eighth-century collection of more than 4,500 poems, consists of short poems, called *tanka*, and long poems of up to 150 lines in length, called *choka*.

3. The poetry anthology *Kokinshu* (*Collection from Ancient and Modern Times*), composed in A.D. 905, includes books of seasonal poems, mourning poems, and love poems.

4. Tenth-century Japanese writer Ki Tsurayuki is well-known as a contributor to the *Kokinshu* and as the author of the first "literary diary."

ASSESSING

Assessment

- Holt Assessment: Literature, Reading, and Vocabulary

RETEACHING

For a lesson reteaching theme and meaning, see **Reteaching**, p. 1129A.

Grammar Link

Effective Sentences: The Power of Parallelism

Good writers create **parallel structure** in a sentence by using the same grammatical form to express two or more equal, or parallel, ideas. Pairing adjectives with adjectives, prepositional phrases with prepositional phrases, and noun clauses with noun clauses emphasizes the relationship between the ideas. You can use parallel structure to link coordinate ideas, to compare or contrast ideas, and to link ideas with correlative conjunctions (such as *both...and, either...or*). Parallel structure can also make a passage rhythmic and memorable.

Compare the awkwardness of these examples of faulty parallelism with the clarity of phrasing in the parallel sentences from "The Silver Fifty-Sen Pieces."

FAULTY: Other shoppers, wearing thin summer dresses of rayon and who said, "It's cheap, it's cheap," were casually snapping up the umbrellas.... [participial phrase paired with adjective clause]

PARALLEL: Other shoppers, wearing thin summer dresses of rayon and saying, "It's cheap, it's cheap," were casually snapping up the umbrellas.... [participial phrase paired with participial phrase]

FAULTY: Yoshiko appreciated the paperweight both for its coolness and unexpected weightiness and because it was delicate. [prepositional phrase paired with adverb clause]

PARALLEL: Yoshiko appreciated the paperweight both for its coolness and unexpected weightiness and for its delicacy. [prepositional phrase paired with prepositional phrase]

PRACTICE

The following sentences are about Japanese literature. Rewrite each sentence to correct the nonparallel sentence structures.

1. Japanese writers have been celebrated not only for their novels, poetry, and plays but because they wrote travel journals and diaries.

2. The *Manyoshu*, an eighth-century collection of more than 4,500 poems, consists of short poems called tanka and choka, long poems of up to 150 lines.

3. The poetry anthology *Kokinshu* (*Collection from Ancient and Modern Times*), composed in A.D. 905, includes books of seasonal poems, mourning poems, and poems about love.

4. Tenth-century Japanese writer Ki Tsurayuki is well-known as a contributor to *Kokinshu* and because he wrote the first example of a "literary diary."

Apply to Your Writing

Review a writing assignment you are working on now or have already completed. Are there any nonparallel sentence structures? Revise to make them parallel sentence structures.

▶ For more help, see Using Parallel Structure, 9c, in the Language Handbook.

DIFFERENTIATING INSTRUCTION

Learners Having Difficulty

Write the following sentences on the chalkboard. Have students suggest revisions that will correct the nonparallel sentence structures. Possible answers are given.

1. Yoshiko works in an office and still living in her childhood home. [lives]

2. She likes both the paperweight's appearance and the way it feels heavy. [its weight]

3. Her mother and sister laugh at her not only for buying a "toy" but also because it took her so long to make up her mind. [for taking so long to make up her mind]

4. The story is told in three scenes, two of them set before Yoshiko's marriage and the third when the war is over. [after the war]

Graham Greene
(1904–1991)
England

For his serious idealistic novels dealing with contemporary moral dilemmas and for his light "entertainments" and thrillers, Graham Greene has won a rare combination of popular and critical admiration. His intention in his writing was always to tell the truth, which he saw as a primary duty of the artist. In his quest for truth, Greene often wrote about life's losers—at least those whom we conventionally think of as losers.

Henry Graham Greene was born to a comfortable family in Berkhamsted, Hertfordshire. His father was the headmaster of Berkhamsted School, which Greene attended as a child. For reasons that are not clear, as Greene grew into adolescence, he became increasingly depressed and unhappy at school, which he described as his first impression of hell. After he tried to run away, he was sent to London to undergo psychoanalysis. He would later recall those six months in London as among the happiest of his life.

While he was still at Berkhamsted, Greene had a story published by a local newspaper, and he recalled feeling a sense of true literary triumph "for the first and last time." The experience convinced him to become a professional writer. He attended Oxford University, wrote a novel that failed to find a publisher, and published a book of poems in 1925, the year he graduated.

In 1926, Greene became engaged to a Roman Catholic woman, Vivien Dayrell-Browning, and agreed to take instruction in her faith. Although he had been a confirmed atheist, he became convinced of "the probable existence of something we call God." His Catholic faith would turn out to be an important factor in his writing.

Greene took a job with the London *Times* and worked there until his first novel, *The Man Within*, was published in 1929. His next books were adventure stories, which received little attention. Greene began to come into his own with the thriller *Stamboul Train* (1932; also published under the title *Orient Express*). This story of a train journey to Istanbul was the first of Greene's works that were made into movies.

Greene brought his religious concerns into his fiction with the novel *Brighton Rock* (1938), in which he explored the nature of good and evil and the inexplicable workings of divine grace. Pursuing the theme further in *The Power and the Glory* (1940), Greene revealed an unorthodox kind of Catholicism in which naturally sinful men and women, living in a fallen world, are often given a last-minute chance at redemption.

Greene's novels came out steadily, among them *The Heart of the Matter* (1948), *The End of the Affair* (1951), and *A Burnt-Out Case* (1961). In the first volume of his autobiography, *A Sort of Life* (1971), Greene revealed his motives for writing fiction as "a desire to reduce the chaos of experience to some sort of order, and a hungry curiosity. We cannot love others, so the theologians teach, unless in some degree we can love ourselves, and curiosity too begins at home."

PRETEACHING

Summary ⇔ at grade level

T. (Trevor) takes the leadership of the Wormsley Common gang away from Blackie when he suggests the organized destruction of a historic house that survived the German blitz. While the house's owner, Mr. Thomas (whom the gang calls "Old Misery"), is away, the gang thoroughly demolishes the inside of the house. When the owner returns unexpectedly early, they lock him in his outhouse. During the night, the gang weakens the foundation of the house and rigs a truck parked nearby so that, on the next morning, the unwitting driver pulls down the house as he drives away. When the driver releases Mr. Thomas from the outhouse, Mr. Thomas is devastated by the loss of his house, but the driver cannot stop from laughing at the situation.

Selection Starter

Build background. Shortly after the war began in 1939, many young children were evacuated out of urban areas to the countryside. Some mothers went with their children, but more often, groups of children were sent off each with a suitcase and a gas mask to stay with older couples in the countryside. Many of the evacuees had returned to London by the time the blitz started in 1940. They, and others who had never been evacuated, spent many evenings sleeping in stations of the London Underground while bombs fell from the sky.

Before You Read

The Destructors

Make the Connection

This story is set in 1954, nine years after the end of World War II. During the war, London had been regularly "blitzed" by German planes dropping firebombs, and many of its buildings were destroyed. Years after the war, Londoners still walked among the rubble. More troubling than this physical destruction, though, was what many people saw as the moral destruction of society, the collapse of hope, especially among gangs of young people who had never known a reality other than war and its aftermath.

Literary Focus

Setting

The **setting** of this story reflects both political and social influences of the historical period: a drab corner of a city still reeling from war. This setting helps establish the story's pessimistic **mood**. As the story progresses, though, the setting becomes not just a backdrop, but rather a key plot element that helps to shape the characters. Greene's characteristic use of coarse **imagery** and language creates a seedy, drab world full of shabby violence.

INTERNET
Vocabulary Practice
Keyword: LE5 12-7

> The **setting** is the time and place of a story.
>
> For more on Setting, see the Handbook of Literary and Historical Terms.

SKILLS FOCUS

Literary Skills Understand setting.
Reading Skills Make inferences about character motivation.

Reading Skills

Inferring Motives

Each of the four numbered sections of this story gives you a bit more insight into the enigmatic main character, T. After each section, jot down how you see T., and note particular words and actions that you find most revealing. When you have finished reading the story, use these clues to make some **inferences** about the character. What do you think motivates T. to act as he does?

Background

In 1941, the London home of Graham Greene and his wife, Vivien, was blasted during an air raid. Vivien, who was devastated by the loss, later recalled "walk[ing] in tears on the edge of the front room [and] looking down at the deep frightening cavity two floors below. . . ." Graham, however, seemed less troubled. "It's sad because it was a pretty house," he wrote, "but oddly enough it leaves one very carefree." According to Vivien, Graham felt relieved of the burden of a house that had symbolized the couple's miserable marriage—and perhaps an even deeper misery in the writer himself.

Vocabulary Development

ignoble (ig·nō′bəl) adj.: shameful; degrading.

impromptu (im·prämp′tōō) adj.: unplanned.

exploit (eks′ploit) n.: daring act.

daunted (dônt′id) v. used as adj.: intimidated.

implacable (im·plak′ə·bəl) adj.: inflexible; relentless; stubborn.

fickleness (fik′əl·nis) n.: changeableness.

altruistic (al′trōō·is′tik) adj.: unselfish.

exhilaration (eg·zil′ə·rā′shən) n.: excitement; high spirits.

abstain (ab·stān′) v.: refrain from.

stealthy (stel′thē) adj.: secret; sly.

862   Collection 7   The Modern World: 1900 to the Present

Previewing Vocabulary

Have students collaborate to write original sentences using the Vocabulary words. After checking students' sentences, ask them to match each of these numbered words with its meaning.

1. altruistic [j]
2. implacable [c]
3. abstain [e]
4. daunted [h]
5. stealthy [d]
6. ignoble [a]
7. exhilaration [i]
8. fickleness [g]
9. exploit [f]
10. impromptu [b]

a. shameful
b. unplanned
c. inflexible
d. secret, sly
e. refrain from
f. daring act
g. changeableness
h. intimidated
i. high excitement
j. unselfish

THE DESTRUCTORS

Graham Greene

After the Blitz by L. S. Lowry.
Reproduced by kind permission of Miss Carol Lowry, copyright proprietor.

DIRECT TEACHING

VIEWING THE ART

Lawrence Stephen Lowry (1887–1976) painted this scene in response to the bombing of London by the Germans. For 57 nights, an average of 160 bombers attacked London. The raids, which were meant to break the will of the people, involved setting buildings on fire and killing civilians. During the raids, many inhabitants of London hid in the subways, railroad tunnels, or in other forms of municipal shelter.

Activity. Challenge students to find elements of hope in the painting. [The steeple, bathed in light, is showing; survivors are apparently working together in a communal effort to restore order.]

DIFFERENTIATING INSTRUCTION

Learners Having Difficulty
Encourage students to visualize the setting, events, and characters as they read. As an aid to this process, you might make available pictures of London after the blitz. Be sure students also understand what is meant by the "impromptu car-park." This helps explain the presence of the truck at the end of the story and its ability to inflict the final damage.

English-Language Learners
Explain that there are many Briticisms in this story, and be sure to define the most fundamental ones: *bank holiday* (a legal holiday, usually on a Monday to make a three-day weekend) and *common* (a shared open space). Point out the glosses that define and explain other Briticisms, such as *loo* (toilet) and *lorries* (trucks).

Direct Teaching

A **Literary Focus**

? Setting. What is the time and place? [It is August on the eve of a holiday. The place is Wormsley Common.] Note that the name *Wormsley* suggests something infested with worms; there is also a pun on the word *common*, which means both public land, such as a park, and ordinariness.

B **Reading Skills**

? Inferring motives. What might be the cause of T.'s "brooding silence" and seeming unpredictability? [Possible response: His family background suggests that T. has been raised in an atmosphere of conflict and resentment and, as a result, he may have a lot of pent-up anger.]

C **Content-Area Connections**

History: The Blitz
The word *blitz* is a shortened form of the German word *blitzkrieg*—literally "lightning war," an offensive strike, often of bombs from the air, launched with great violence and speed.

D **Literary Focus**

? Setting. In what ways is this already a setting of destruction? [Possible responses: Bomb blasts have demolished the buildings; number 3 is poorly supported and isolated.]

E **Reading Skills**

? Inferring motives. Note that some details about T. introduced here will be useful for understanding what motivates him later in the story. What are these details? [Possible responses: His father communicated the significance of a house by Wren to his son; T. deems the information about Wren to be worth both remembering and repeating.]

1

A It was on the eve of August Bank Holiday that the latest recruit became the leader of the Wormsley Common gang. No one was surprised except Mike, but Mike at the age of nine was surprised by everything. "If you don't shut your mouth," somebody once said to him, "you'll get a frog down it." After that Mike had kept his teeth tightly clamped except when the surprise was too great.

The new recruit had been with the gang since the beginning of the summer holidays, and there were possibilities about his brooding silence that all recognized. He never wasted a word even to tell his name until that was required of him by the rules. When he said "Trevor" it was a statement of fact, not as it would have been with the others a statement of shame or defiance. Nor did anyone laugh except Mike, who finding himself **B** without support and meeting the dark gaze of the newcomer opened his mouth and was quiet again. There was every reason why T., as he was afterward referred to, should have been an object of mockery—there was his name (and they substituted the initial because otherwise they had no excuse not to laugh at it), the fact that his father, a former architect and present clerk, had "come down in the world" and that his mother considered herself better than the neighbors. What but an odd quality of danger, of the unpredictable, established him in the gang without any ignoble ceremony of initiation?

The gang met every morning in an impromptu **C** car-park, the site of the last bomb of the first blitz. The leader, who was known as Blackie, claimed to have heard it fall, and no one was precise enough in his dates to point out that he would have been one year old and fast asleep on the down platform of Wormsley Common Underground[1] Station. On one side of the car-park leaned the first occupied house, number 3, of the shattered Northwood Terrace—literally **D** leaned, for it had suffered from the blast of the bomb and the side walls were supported on wooden struts. A smaller bomb and some incendiaries[2] had fallen beyond, so that the house stuck up like a jagged tooth and carried on the further wall relics of its neighbor, a dado,[3] the remains of a fireplace. T., whose words were almost confined to voting "Yes" or "No" to the plan of operations proposed each day by Blackie, once startled the whole gang by saying broodingly, "Wren[4] built that house, father says."

"Who's Wren?"

"The man who built St. Paul's."[5] **E**

"Who cares?" Blackie said. "It's only Old Misery's."

Old Misery—whose real name was Thomas—had once been a builder and decorator. He lived alone in the crippled house, doing for himself: Once a week you could see him coming back across the common with bread and vegetables, and once as the boys played in the car-park he put his head over the smashed wall of his garden and looked at them.

"Been to the loo,"[6] one of the boys said, for it was common knowledge that since the bombs fell something had gone wrong with the pipes of the house and Old Misery was too mean[7] to spend money on the property. He could do the redecorating himself at cost price, but he had never learned plumbing. The loo was a wooden shed at the bottom of the narrow garden with a star-shaped hole in the door: It had escaped the blast which had smashed the house next door and sucked out the window frames of number 3.

The next time the gang became aware of Mr. Thomas was more surprising. Blackie, Mike, and

---

1. **Underground** *n*.: British for "subway."
2. **incendiaries** *n*.: firebombs.
3. **dado** (dā′dō): wood paneling along the lower part of the walls of a room.
4. **Wren:** Sir Christopher Wren (1632–1723), a celebrated English architect.
5. **St. Paul's:** cathedral in London.
6. **loo:** British slang for "bathroom." *Loo* comes from the French word *lieux*, short for *les lieux d'aisances* (lā lyö de‑zäns′), which means "places of convenience."
7. **mean** *adj*.: stingy.

Vocabulary
ignoble (ig·nō′bəl) *adj*.: shameful; degrading.
impromptu (im·prämp′tōō) *adj*.: unplanned.

DIFFERENTIATING INSTRUCTION

Advanced Learners
Enrichment. T. and Mr. Thomas share some similarities, including their initial *T.* and the fact that T. is the child of an architect who would value a Christopher Wren building just as keenly as Old Misery (Mr. Thomas) does. What else unites these two characters? Is one Old Misery and the other "young misery"? In each one's world view, are there "only things"? Urge students to read with this focus in mind and to jot down their ideas.

Juvenile Counsel: Boys on a Doorstep (20th century) by Henry Lamb.
Private Collection. © Estate of Henry Lamb.

a thin yellow boy, who for some reason was called by his surname[8] Summers, met him on the common coming back from the market. Mr. Thomas stopped them. He said glumly, "You belong to the lot that play in the car-park?"

Mike was about to answer when Blackie stopped him. As the leader he had responsibilities. "Suppose we are?" he said ambiguously.

"I got some chocolates," Mr. Thomas said. "Don't like 'em myself. Here you are. Not enough to go round, I don't suppose. There never is," he added with somber conviction. He handed over three packets of Smarties.

The gang were puzzled and perturbed by this action and tried to explain it away. "Bet someone dropped them and he picked 'em up," somebody suggested.

"Pinched[9] 'em and then got in a bleeding funk," another thought aloud.

"It's a bribe," Summers said. "He wants us to stop bouncing balls on his wall."

"We'll show him we don't take bribes," Blackie said, and they sacrificed the whole morning to the game of bouncing that only Mike was young enough to enjoy. There was no sign from Mr. Thomas.

Next day T. astonished them all. He was late at the rendezvous, and the voting for that day's exploit took place without him. At Blackie's suggestion the gang was to disperse in pairs, take

---

8. **surname** *n.:* last name.

9. **pinched** *v.:* British for "stole."

Vocabulary
exploit (eks'ploit') *n.:* daring act.

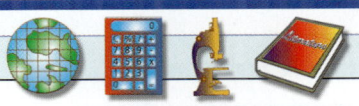

CONTENT-AREA CONNECTIONS

Architecture: Sir Christopher Wren
Mixed-ability group activity. Greene could have chosen any architect, but he chose Sir Christopher Wren. Why? Invite students to find out by researching Wren's career, influences, and philosophy. Form three mixed-ability groups, assign one of the three topics to each group, and have the groups report back to the whole class. Students will learn that Wren was a Renaissance man (who actually lived just after the Renaissance), gifted in mathematics and science (he was once a professor of astronomy) as well as in architecture. For the purposes of this story, however, the key facts are that Wren was most notably and consistently a church architect. He was obsessed with the way the strong clarity of geometry could create beauty and focus the public's thoughts on God.

DIRECT TEACHING

VIEWING THE ART

Henry Lamb's (1883–1960) paintings were included in the Second Post-Impressionist exhibition held in London in 1912. This painting shows boys lounging around a stoop.

Activity. How do the boys in the painting seem like or unlike the boys in Greene's story? [Possible response: The boys appear to be about the same age as the boys in Greene's story; they also seem to be enjoying idleness, as does the Wormsley gang—at least so far. The boys in the picture are fewer in number than the Wormsley gang.]

F Reading Skills

Inferring motives. Why do you think Mr. Thomas gives the boys candy? [Possible responses: He is lonely. He can see the boys are a tough group, and he would rather be on good terms with them. He hopes his kindness will do some good and perhaps help protect his property.]

G Reading Skills

Interpreting. What motives do the boys attach to Mr. Thomas's offer of candy? What does this suggest about their general attitude toward adults? [Possible responses: They guess that he found the candy somewhere, stole it, or is offering it as a bribe to stop them from bouncing balls on his wall. The boys are suspicious and distrusting of adults.]

DIRECT TEACHING

A Reading Skills

Making inferences. What kind of mischief does the Wormsley Common gang get into under Blackie's leadership, and what does this say about the boys' character? [The gang catches free rides on the city buses, not a serious infraction; this suggests that the gang is not truly evil.]

B Content-Area Connections

Culture: Class in British Culture
What details in this paragraph convey the distrust of the "common" boys for a higher-class world? [Possible responses: The fact that T. uses the word *beautiful* worries Blackie who was tempted to mock T.]

C Reading Skills

Inferring motives. What do you think has led T. to devise this destructive plan? [Possible responses: Since T. has come close to being ousted from the gang, he may be trying to prove that he is the gang's most determined member. His "disturbed" eyes suggest that he is beyond hope and conscience; seeing the beauty of the house has brought out an urge to destroy what he cannot have. Perhaps he has an unconscious urge to destroy something associated with his father—architecture.]

---

buses at random, and see how many free rides could be snatched from unwary conductors (the operation was to be carried out in pairs to avoid cheating). They were drawing lots for their companions when T. arrived.

"Where you been, T.?" Blackie asked. "You can't vote now. You know the rules."

"I've been *there*," T. said. He looked at the ground, as though he had thoughts to hide.

"Where?"

"At Old Misery's." Mike's mouth opened and then hurriedly closed again with a click. He had remembered the frog.

"At Old Misery's?" Blackie said. There was nothing in the rules against it, but he had a sensation that T. was treading on dangerous ground. He asked hopefully, "Did you break in?"

"No. I rang the bell."

"And what did you say?"

"I said I wanted to see his house."

"What did he do?"

"He showed it me."

"Pinch anything?"

"No."

"What did you do it for then?"

The gang had gathered round: It was as though an impromptu court were about to form and to try some case of deviation. T. said, "It's a beautiful house," and still watching the ground, meeting no one's eyes, he licked his lips first one way, then the other.

"What do you mean, a beautiful house?" Blackie asked with scorn.

"It's got a staircase two hundred years old like a corkscrew. Nothing holds it up."

"What do you mean, nothing holds it up. Does it float?"

"It's to do with opposite forces, Old Misery said."

"What else?"

"There's paneling."

"Like in the Blue Boar?"

"Two hundred years old."

"Is Old Misery two hundred years old?"

Mike laughed suddenly and then was quiet again. The meeting was in a serious mood. For the first time since T. had strolled into the car-park on the first day of the holidays his position was in danger. It only needed a single use of his real name and the gang would be at his heels.

"What did you do it for?" Blackie asked. He was just, he had no jealousy, he was anxious to retain T. in the gang if he could. It was the word "beautiful" that worried him—that belonged to a class world that you could still see parodied at the Wormsley Common Empire by a man wearing a top hat and a monocle,[10] with a haw-haw accent. He was tempted to say, "My dear Trevor, old chap," and unleash his hell hounds. "If you'd broken in," he said sadly—that indeed would have been an exploit worthy of the gang.

"This was better," T. said. "I found out things." He continued to stare at his feet, not meeting anybody's eye, as though he were absorbed in some dream he was unwilling—or ashamed—to share.

"What things?"

"Old Misery's going to be away all tomorrow and Bank Holiday."

Blackie said with relief, "You mean we could break in?"

"And pinch things?" somebody asked.

Blackie said, "Nobody's going to pinch things. Breaking in—that's good enough, isn't it? We don't want any court stuff."

"I don't want to pinch anything," T. said. "I've got a better idea."

"What is it?"

T. raised his eyes, as gray and disturbed as the drab August day. "We'll pull it down," he said. "We'll destroy it."

Blackie gave a single hoot of laughter and then, like Mike, fell quiet, daunted by the serious implacable gaze. "What'd the police be doing all the time?" he said.

"They'd never know. We'd do it from inside. I've found a way in." He said with a sort of

---

10. **monocle** *n.:* eyeglass for one eye.

Vocabulary
daunted (dônt'id) *v.* used as *adj.*: intimidated.
implacable (im·plak'ə·bəl) *adj.:* inflexible; relentless; stubborn.

Literary Criticism

Critic's Commentary: Greene on Evil
In his autobiographical essay "The Lost Childhood," Graham Greene describes the amazement he experienced as a result of reading, calling it "a key turned in a lock." The ideal characters of the fantastical tales he read as a child, however, failed to ring true after a while, and his adult reading revealed a startling truth. As Greene describes it, "Goodness has only once found a perfect incarnation in a human body and never will again, but evil can always find a home there. Human nature is not black and white but black and gray." Greene's writing is a lifelong study of these shadings.

moved around the inner walls worrying at the mortar between the bricks. They started too high, and it was Blackie who hit on the damp course[25] and realized the work could be halved if they weakened the joints immediately above. It was a long, tiring, unamusing job, but at last it was finished. The gutted house stood there balanced on a few inches of mortar between the damp course and the bricks.

There remained the most dangerous task of all, out in the open at the edge of the bomb site. Summers was sent to watch the road for passers by, and Mr. Thomas, sitting on the loo, heard clearly now the sound of sawing. It no longer came from his house, and that a little reassured him. He felt less concerned. Perhaps the other noises too had no significance.

A voice spoke to him through the hole. "Mr. Thomas."

"Let me out," Mr. Thomas said sternly.

"Here's a blanket," the voice said, and a long gray sausage was worked through the hole and fell in swathes over Mr. Thomas's head.

"There's nothing personal," the voice said. "We want you to be comfortable tonight."

"Tonight," Mr. Thomas repeated incredulously.

"Catch," the voice said. "Penny buns—we've buttered them, and sausage-rolls. We don't want you to starve, Mr. Thomas."

Mr. Thomas pleaded desperately. "A joke's a joke, boy. Let me out and I won't say a thing. I've got rheumatics. I got to sleep comfortable."

"You wouldn't be comfortable, not in your house, you wouldn't. Not now."

"What do you mean, boy?" but the footsteps receded. There was only the silence of night: no sound of sawing. Mr. Thomas tried one more yell, but he was daunted and rebuked by the silence—a long way off an owl hooted and made away again on its muffled flight through the soundless world.

At seven next morning the driver came to fetch his lorry. He climbed into the seat and tried to start the engine. He was vaguely aware of a voice shouting, but it didn't concern him. At last the engine responded and he backed the lorry until it touched the great wooden shore[26] that supported Mr. Thomas's house. That way he could drive right out and down the street without reversing. The lorry moved forward, was momentarily checked as though something were pulling it from behind, and then went on to the sound of a long rumbling crash. The driver was astonished to see bricks bouncing ahead of him, while stones hit the roof of his cab. He put on his brakes. When he climbed out the whole landscape had suddenly altered. There was no house beside the car-park, only a hill of rubble. He went round and examined the back of his car for damage, and found a rope tied there that was still twisted at the other end round part of a wooden strut.

The driver again became aware of somebody shouting. It came from the wooden erection which was the nearest thing to a house in that desolation of broken brick. The driver climbed the smashed wall and unlocked the door. Mr. Thomas came out of the loo. He was wearing a gray blanket to which flakes of pastry adhered. He gave a sobbing cry. "My house," he said. "Where's my house?"

"Search me," the driver said. His eye lit on the remains of a bath and what had once been a dresser and he began to laugh. There wasn't anything left anywhere.

"How dare you laugh," Mr. Thomas said. "It was my house. My house."

"I'm sorry," the driver said, making heroic efforts, but when he remembered the sudden check to his lorry, the crash of bricks falling, he became convulsed again. One moment the house had stood there with such dignity between the bomb sites like a man in a top hat, and then, bang, crash, there wasn't anything left—not anything. He said, "I'm sorry. I can't help it, Mr. Thomas. There's nothing personal, but you got to admit it's funny." ∎

---

25. **damp course:** layer of waterproof material placed between two layers of brick in a house's foundation to keep moisture from rising up through the walls.

26. **shore** *n.:* beam.

INDEPENDENT PRACTICE

Response and Analysis

Reading Check

1. Blackie; T. takes over when he proposes to wreck the house.
2. His father is a former architect "come down in the world"; his mother maintains a snobbish attitude.
3. It was built by a renowned architect; it is beautiful.
4. The gang first destroys the inside, then they destroy the structure itself by tying the key support to a truck, which pulls down the house when it drives away.

Thinking Critically

5. Possible answer: T. is not motivated by greed or by a desire to harm Mr. Thomas.
6. T. says that he neither loves nor hates. For him, life is "only things" to be destroyed.
7. Possible answer: The gang values risk-taking, amusement, destruction, and their reputation. These values may spring from postwar malaise or from their inability to find purpose in their lives.
8. Possible answers: The car-park is on the site of a bombing during the blitz. On one side, Mr. Thomas's house sticks up like a jagged tooth. Cars parked where houses once stood creates a bleak atmosphere, symbolizing moral desolation.
9. Possible answers: T. may be saying that having a reason would diminish the inexplicable joy of destruction. T.'s words also suggest that the alienation created by war can give rise to random crime.

Extending and Evaluating

10. Possible answer: Greene wants readers to see T. as a victim of the social upheaval caused by the war and the class system. The house represents what T. and his family have lost.

Response and Analysis

Reading Check

1. Who is the gang's leader at first? Who takes over? Why?
2. What is T.'s family background?
3. Why is Mr. Thomas's house valuable?
4. Describe how the house is destroyed.

Thinking Critically

5. T.'s **motives** for destroying Old Misery's house are important. What motives can you *eliminate* based on what T. says to Mr. Thomas and what the boys do with the money?
6. What are T.'s actual motives? Support your answer with details from the story. (Your reading notes will help.)
7. A gang is a social group with a shared set of values. What are this gang's values, and from where do you think they spring?
8. Describe the **setting** of the Wormsley Common car-park and its surroundings. How does the setting contribute to the story's emotional **atmosphere**? What larger idea or concept might the setting **symbolize**?
9. When Blackie asks T. whether he hates Mr. Thomas, T. answers, "Of course I don't.... There'd be no fun if I hated him." How would you explain T.'s answer? In what sense does T.'s response reveal what might happen to people—even children—in the aftermath of war?

Extending and Evaluating

10. How do you think Greene wants his readers to see T.—as a vicious criminal who should be punished, or as a disturbed victim of society who deserves understanding? In which way do you see him? Why? Evaluate T.'s **character** in light of the political and social influences that might have shaped him. Use evidence from the story to support your opinions.

Literary Criticism

11. One critic noted that the typical Greene character lives "on the border between love and hate, good and evil, heaven and hell." Which characters in this story live "on the border"? By the end of the story, have any of them fallen completely to one side or the other? Explain.

WRITING

Rotten to the Core?

Images of hollowness—of rotting from within—appear throughout this story. In the first part of a short **essay**, identify these **images** of hollowness and discuss how they apply to the house, to Wormsley Common, and even to the story's characters. In the second part of the essay, discuss the ways in which the setting of "The Destructors" connects with images in T. S. Eliot's "The Hollow Men" (see page 828). Explore the emotional effects of these various images on the reader.

SKILLS FOCUS

Literary Skills Analyze setting.

Reading Skills Make inferences about character motivation.

Writing Skills Write an essay analyzing imagery.

Vocabulary Skills Demonstrate word knowledge.

Vocabulary Development

Sentence Sense

ignoble	fickleness
impromptu	altruistic
exploit	exhilaration
daunted	abstain
implacable	stealthy

On a separate sheet of paper, use each Vocabulary word listed above in an original sentence based on the characters and events in "The Destructors."

Literary Criticism

11. All the characters seem "on the border" and remain so at the end of the story. Only a "thing" is destroyed.

Vocabulary Development

Sample Answer
"Although they should have been terrified, the boys were not daunted."

ASSESSING

Assessment

- Holt Assessment: Literature, Reading, and Vocabulary

Ben Okri
(1959–   )
Nigeria

Ben Okri grew up in the delta area of southern Nigeria. Although he later moved to London, his stories are set in Nigeria. Okri seems especially haunted by remembrances of the Nigerian Civil War (1967–1970), often called the Biafran War. This war began when the Ibo (ē′bō) people tried to secede from Nigeria and form their own state, called the Republic of Biafra. Thousands of people were killed in the civil war that ensued, and many more died of starvation. In fact, for years the very word *Biafra* conjured up images of swollen-bellied children holding up bowls and begging for food. The image of the starving child in Okri's story is a stark reminder of the horror of this war.

Okri first gained recognition in England with the publication of two novels, *Flowers and Shadows* (1980) and *The Landscapes Within* (1981), and a collection of short stories, *Incidents at the Shrine* (1986). "In the Shadow of War" is from *Stars of the New Curfew* (1988), Okri's first book to be published in the United States.

Okri's awards include the Commonwealth Writers' Prize for Africa and the *Paris Review* Aga Khan Prize for fiction. His 1991 novel, *The Famished Road*, received England's Booker Prize. *Songs of Enchantment*, a sequel to *The Famished Road*, appeared in 1993 and *Astonishing the Gods* in 1995.

Before You Read

In the Shadow of War

Make the Connection
Quickwrite

In some parts of the world, a state of war is almost constant, especially in places where ethnic and religious strife runs high. Like the author of the following story, the children of these lands struggle to come of age in a place where hostility is a given—where suspicion and paranoia infect every conversation and where random violence is common and often unprovoked.

Should children be protected from the knowledge of certain harsh realities, such as war and urban violence? What might be some of the positive and negative effects of shielding young people from harsh truths? Jot down your ideas.

Literary Focus
Point of View

Every writer tells a story from a particular **point of view,** or vantage point. Ben Okri was only eight years old when the Nigerian Civil War broke out, so it's not surprising that his main character, Omovo, is a child. Okri uses the **limited-third-person point of view** to tell the story only from Omovo's perspective. Through Omovo's eyes, we learn that war is a frightening, confusing time for children. Are the soldiers in this story good or evil? Is the veiled woman supernatural or mortal? Because Omovo's understanding is limited, the point of view from which this story is told deepens these mysteries.

SKILLS FOCUS

Pages 875–876 cover
Literary Skills
Understand the limited-third-person point of view.

Reading Skills
Make predictions.

SKILLS FOCUS, pp. 875–882

Grade-Level Skills
- **Literary Skills**
Analyze the way an author's use of point of view achieves specific rhetorical or aesthetic purposes.
- **Reading Skills**
Make predictions.

More About the Writer
Background. In interviews, Ben Okri rarely talks in detail about his youth. Instead, he directs readers curious about his childhood to his fiction. He admits that his youth had a significant impact on his writing, but he prefers to talk about his discovery of writing rather than about growing up in Nigeria. About that discovery at age 14, he says, "On this particular day, it rained, and this day changed my life. Everybody was out and I was in, alone. I was sitting in the living room and I took out a piece of paper and drew what was on the mantelpiece. That took me about an hour. Then I took another piece of paper and wrote a poem. That must have taken me ten minutes. I looked at the drawing and I looked at the poem. The drawing was dreadful and the poem was . . . tolerable, bearable. And it became clear to me that this was more my natural area."

RESOURCES: READING

Planning
- One-Stop Planner CD-ROM with ExamView Test Generator

Differentiating Instruction
- The Holt Reader
- Holt Reading Solutions
- Supporting Instruction in Spanish
- Audio CD Library, Selections and Summaries in Spanish

Vocabulary
- Vocabulary Development

Grammar and Language
- Daily Language Activities

Assessment
- Holt Assessment: Literature, Reading, and Vocabulary
- One-Stop Planner CD-ROM with ExamView Test Generator

- Holt Online Assessment

Internet
- go.hrw.com (Keyword: LE5 12-7)
- Elements of Literature Online

Media
- Audio CD Library
- Audio CD Library, Selections and Summaries in Spanish

PRETEACHING

Summary ⇔ at grade level

In a Nigerian village, during a civil war, soldiers offer a young boy, Omovo, a bribe to betray the whereabouts of a strange woman. He refuses. Later, Omovo follows the soldiers as they pursue the woman. Omovo sees her give supplies to starving people, probably refugees, who are living in a cave. The soldiers catch the woman as she returns; they interrogate, abuse, and kill her. Terrified, Omovo runs away, but he trips and falls, losing consciousness. When he wakes up, he finds himself back home, where he is shocked to find his father drinking with the soldiers. Omovo's father carries him to bed as Omovo tries in vain to tell what he has seen.

Selection Starter

Motivate. Have students discuss how, as children, they became aware of war. Was it through books, television, movies, or family experiences? Then, have them complete the Quickwrite.

Skills Starter

Build review skills. Review the term *point of view* with students and discuss the differences among first-person, limited-third-person, and omniscient points of view.

In **limited-third-person point of view,** the narrator is outside the story but tells the story from the vantage point of only one character.

For more on Point of View, see the Handbook of Literary and Historical Terms.

Reading Skills
Making Predictions

Instead of factual information (such as where and when the story takes place), the reader of this story is given a vivid picture of what the child, Omovo, sees and hears. Several key impressions are described early in the story—for example, Omovo's impressions of the soldiers; of his father's words and actions; and of the woman in the yellow smock. Use these details to make **predictions** about the characters you encounter—to look ahead and make educated guesses about what is likely to happen to them. Of whom should Omovo be suspicious? Which characters seem to present the most danger, and to whom? Jot down any predictions you make, and be prepared to explain why you made them. Adjust your predictions as necessary while you read.

INTERNET
Vocabulary Practice
Keyword: LE5 12-7

Background

This story takes place during the Nigerian Civil War (1967–1970). After Nigeria gained its independence from Great Britain in 1960, the nation struggled to fashion a stable government. But with over 250 distinct ethnic or tribal groups in Nigeria, the task proved formidable. In 1966, one of the major groups, the Hausa-Fulani, established a military power. Another major group, the Ibo, responded by declaring their homeland to be the independent Republic of Biafra. A bitter civil war ensued, during which thousands were killed or starved to death. The Biafrans surrendered in 1970.

Vocabulary Development

stupefying (stoo′pə·fī′in) *adj.*: dulling the mind and senses; bringing on a state of lethargy.

oppressive (ə·pres′iv) *adj.*: hard to bear.

succumbed (sə·kumd′) *v.*: yielded; gave way to.

ostentatious (äs′ten·tā′shəs) *adj.*: showy.

dementedly (dē·ment′id·lē) *adv.*: madly; wildly.

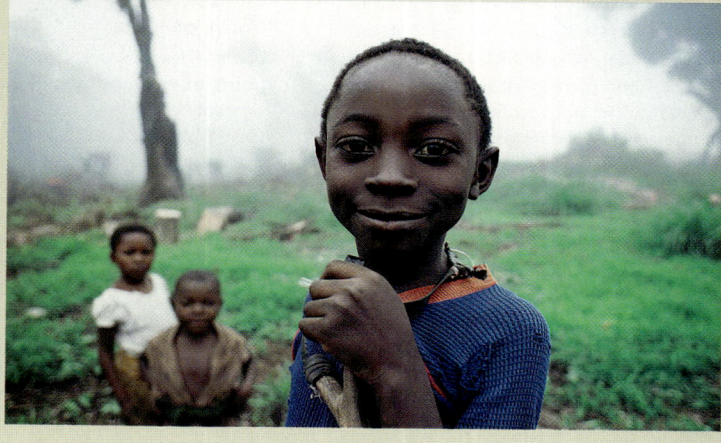

At Obudu Cattle Ranch on Sonkwala Mountain Nigeria (May 1989).

876 Collection 7 The Modern World: 1900 to the Present

Previewing Vocabulary

Have students complete these analogies with the five Vocabulary words listed on p. 876.

1. joke : comical :: burden : _____ [oppressive]
2. joyful : grim :: understated : _____ [ostentatious]
3. commandingly : imperiously :: crazily : _____ [dementedly]
4. traffic : yielded :: temptation : _____ [succumbed]
5. lively : stimulating :: dull : _____ [stupefying]

IN THE SHADOW OF WAR

Ben Okri

That afternoon three soldiers came to the village. They scattered the goats and chickens. They went to the palm-frond bar and ordered a calabash[1] of palm wine. They drank amidst the flies.

Omovo watched them from the window as he waited for his father to go out. They both listened to the radio. His father had bought the old Grundig[2] cheaply from a family that had to escape the city when the war broke out. He had covered the radio with a white cloth and made it look like a household fetish.[3] They listened to the news of bombings and air raids in the interior of the country. His father combed his hair, parted it carefully, and slapped some after-shave on his unshaven face. Then he struggled into the shabby coat that he had long outgrown.

Omovo stared out of the window, irritated with his father. At that hour, for the past seven days, a strange woman with a black veil over her head had been going past the house. She went up the village paths, crossed the Express road, and disappeared into the forest. Omovo waited for her to appear.

The main news was over. The radio announcer said an eclipse of the moon was expected that night. Omovo's father wiped the sweat off his face with his palm and said, with some bitterness:

"As if an eclipse will stop this war."

"What is an eclipse?" Omovo asked.

"That's when the world goes dark and strange things happen."

"Like what?"

His father lit a cigarette.

"The dead start to walk about and sing. So don't stay out late, eh."

Omovo nodded.

"Heclipses hate children. They eat them."

Omovo didn't believe him. His father smiled, gave Omovo his ten kobo[4] allowance, and said:

"Turn off the radio. It's bad for a child to listen to news of war."

Omovo turned it off. His father poured a libation[5] at the doorway and then prayed to his ancestors. When he had finished he picked up his briefcase and strutted out briskly. Omovo watched him as he threaded his way up the path to the bus stop at the main road. When a danfo bus[6] came, and his father went with it, Omovo turned the radio back on. He sat on the windowsill and waited for the woman. The last time he saw her she had glided past with agitated flutters of her yellow smock. The children stopped what they were doing and stared at her. They had said that she had no shadow. They had said that her feet never touched the ground.

---

1. **calabash** (kal′ə·bash′) *n*.: cup made from a calabash, a type of gourd.
2. **Grundig:** German brand of radio.
3. **fetish** (fet′ish) *n*.: object believed to have magical powers.
4. **kobo** (käb′ō) *n*.: Nigerian monetary unit.
5. **libation** (lī·bā′shən): liquid poured onto the ground as a sacrifice to the gods.
6. **danfo bus:** small bus. In the region surrounding Lagos, *danfo* means "in disrepair."

DIRECT TEACHING

A Literary Focus

Point of view. What clues show Omovo's limited understanding? [Possible responses: To him, the woman in yellow appears to be a blur, almost an apparition. He does not know who she is or why the other children throw things at her. He also does not know why the soldiers talk to the children and give them money.]

B Learners Having Difficulty

Monitoring students' progress. Make sure that students understand key elements in the plot by asking: Why are the soldiers interested in the woman? Why is Omovo interested in her? [Possible responses: The soldiers say she is a spy who helps their enemies. Omovo may be interested because she is out of the ordinary and because of what the soldiers said.]

C Advanced Learners

Comparing imagery. Compare the imagery used to describe the soldiers to the imagery used to describe the strange woman. What striking differences are there between these characters? [Possible responses: The soldiers are solid and earthy, persistent and intelligent. They sit and drink and then stumble in the heat. By contrast, the mysterious woman is an ethereal, veiled presence wafting through the town.]

D Literary Focus

Point of view. Using the limited-third-person point of view, the author permits the reader to see what Omovo sees without analyzing what it might mean. What do you think is going on in this region? [Possible response: The details indicate vestiges of colonialism and the effects of destruction brought on by war.]

As she went past the children began to throw things at her. She didn't flinch, didn't quicken her pace, and didn't look back.

The heat was stupefying. Noises dimmed and lost their edges. The villagers stumbled about their various tasks as if they were sleepwalking. The three soldiers drank palm wine and played draughts[7] beneath the sun's oppressive glare. Omovo noticed that whenever children went past the bar the soldiers called them, talked to them, and gave them some money. Omovo ran down the stairs and slowly walked past the bar. The soldiers stared at him. On his way back one of them called him.

"What's your name?" he asked.

Omovo hesitated, smiled mischievously, and said:

"Heclipse."

The soldier laughed, spraying Omovo's face with spit. He had a face crowded with veins. His companions seemed uninterested. They swiped flies and concentrated on their game. Their guns were on the table. Omovo noticed that they had numbers on them. The man said:

"Did your father give you that name because you have big lips?"

His companions looked at Omovo and laughed. Omovo nodded.

"You are a good boy," the man said. He paused. Then he asked, in a different voice:

"Have you seen that woman who covers her face with a black cloth?"

"No."

The man gave Omovo ten kobo and said:

"She is a spy. She helps our enemies. If you see her, come and tell us at once, you hear?"

Omovo refused the money and went back upstairs. He repositioned himself on the windowsill. The soldiers occasionally looked at him. The heat got to him and soon he fell asleep in a sitting position. The cocks, crowing dispiritedly, woke him up. He could feel the afternoon softening into evening. The soldiers dozed in the bar. The hourly news came on. Omovo listened without comprehension to the day's casualties. The announcer succumbed to the stupor, yawned, apologized, and gave further details of the fighting.

Omovo looked up and saw that the woman had already gone past. The men had left the bar. He saw them weaving between the eaves of the thatch houses, stumbling through the heat-mists. The woman was further up the path. Omovo ran downstairs and followed the men. One of them had taken off his uniform top. The soldier behind had buttocks so big they had begun to split his pants. Omovo followed them across the Express road. When they got into the forest the men stopped following the woman, and took a different route. They seemed to know what they were doing. Omovo hurried to keep the woman in view.

He followed her through the dense vegetation. She wore faded wrappers and a gray shawl, with the black veil covering her face. She had a red basket on her head. He completely forgot to determine if she had a shadow, or whether her feet touched the ground.

He passed unfinished estates, with their flaking, ostentatious signboards and their collapsing fences. He passed an empty cement factory: Blocks lay crumbled in heaps and the workers' sheds were deserted. He passed a baobab[8] tree, under which was the intact skeleton of a large animal. A snake dropped from a branch and slithered through the undergrowth. In the distance, over the cliff edge, he heard loud music and people singing war slogans above the noise.

He followed the woman till they came to a rough camp on the plain below. Shadowy figures moved about in the half-light of the cave. The

---

7. **draughts** (drafts) *n.:* British game of checkers.

8. **baobab** (bā′ō·bab′) *n.:* thick-trunked African tree; often called "upside-down tree" because its branches look like roots.

Vocabulary

stupefying (stōō′pə·fī′iŋ) *adj.:* dulling the mind and senses; bringing on a state of lethargy.
oppressive (ə·pres′iv) *adj.:* hard to bear.
succumbed (sə·kumd′) *v.:* yielded; gave way to.
ostentatious (äs′ten·tā′shəs) *adj.:* showy.

878 Collection 7 The Modern World: 1900 to the Present

DEVELOPING FLUENCY

Small-group activity. Okri's story moves rapidly, using many simple, straightforward narrative sentences one after the other. Have groups of three or four students choose a narrative passage without dialogue and prepare a choral reading of the passage to present to the whole class. Encourage students to make the sequence of events clear to the audience as they speak.

FAMILY/COMMUNITY ACTIVITY

Have students ask adults of different ages in their families what war or violent conflict they were aware of as children. Have students ask them how they, as children, acquired information about the war, and what effect they feel the war had on them. Have students share their findings with the class.

woman went to them. The figures surrounded her and touched her and led her into the cave. He heard their weary voices thanking her. When the woman reappeared she was without the basket. Children with kwashiorkor[9] stomachs and women wearing rags led her halfway up the hill. Then, reluctantly, touching her as if they might not see her again, they went back.

He followed her till they came to a muddied river. She moved as if an invisible force were trying to blow her away. Omovo saw capsized canoes and trailing, waterlogged clothes on the dark water. He saw floating items of sacrifice: loaves of bread in polythene[10] wrappings, gourds of food, Coca-Cola cans. When he looked at the canoes again they had changed into the shapes of swollen dead animals. He saw outdated currencies on the riverbank. He noticed the terrible smell in the air. Then he heard the sound of heavy breathing from behind him, then someone coughing and spitting. He recognized the voice of one of the soldiers urging the others to move faster. Omovo crouched in the shadow of a tree. The soldiers strode past. Not long afterward he heard a scream. The men had caught up with the woman. They crowded round her.

"Where are the others?" shouted one of them. The woman was silent.

"You dis witch! You want to die, eh? Where are they?"

She stayed silent. Her head was bowed. One of the soldiers coughed and spat toward the river.

"Talk! Talk!" he said, slapping her.

The fat soldier tore off her veil and threw it to the ground. She bent down to pick it up and stopped in the attitude of kneeling, her head still bowed. Her head was bald, and disfigured with a deep corrugation.[11] There was a livid gash along the side of her face. The bare-chested soldier pushed her. She fell on her face and lay still. The lights changed over the forest and for the first time Omovo saw that the dead animals on the river were in fact the corpses of grown men. Their bodies were tangled with riverweed and their eyes were bloated. Before he could react, he heard another scream. The woman was getting up, with the veil in her hand. She turned to the fat soldier, drew herself to her fullest height, and spat in his face. Waving the veil in the air, she began to howl dementedly. The two other soldiers backed away. The fat soldier wiped his face and lifted the gun to the level of her stomach. A moment before Omovo heard the shot a violent beating of wings just above him scared him from his hiding place. He ran through the forest screaming. The soldiers tramped after him. He ran through a mist which seemed to have risen from the rocks. As he ran he saw an owl staring at him from a canopy of leaves. He tripped over the roots of a tree and blacked out when his head hit the ground.

When he woke up it was very dark. He waved his fingers in front of his face and saw nothing. Mistaking the darkness for blindness he screamed, thrashed around, and ran into a door. When he recovered from his shock he heard voices outside and the radio crackling on about the war. He found his way to the balcony, full of wonder that his sight had returned. But when he got there he was surprised to find his father sitting on the sunken cane chair, drinking palm wine with the three soldiers. Omovo rushed to his father and pointed frantically at the three men.

"You must thank them," his father said. "They brought you back from the forest."

Omovo, overcome with delirium, began to tell his father what he had seen. But his father, smiling apologetically at the soldiers, picked up his son and carried him off to bed. ∎

---

9. **kwashiorkor** (kwä′shē·ôr′kôr′): severe disease of young children, caused by deficiency of protein and calories and marked by stunted growth and a protruding belly.
10. **polythene** (päl′i·thēn′): term used in most English-speaking countries other than the United States for *polyethylene* (päl′ē·eth′ə·lēn′), a synthetic substance used to make tough, lightweight plastics, films, and the like.
11. **corrugation** (kôr′ə·gā′shən) *n.*: groove or furrow.

Vocabulary
dementedly (dē·ment′id·lē) *adv.*: madly; wildly.

Ben Okri 879

Connection

Summary ⬇ below grade level

The speaker says that after every war someone has to "tidy up" so that the roads will be free for carts full of corpses. The cleaning up takes years after the "cameras have gone to other wars." Some will recall how it was, and some will listen to them, but others will be bored. Eventually, those who knew what the war was about die, and all is forgotten.

DIRECT TEACHING

A Literary Focus

Diction and tone. Point out the author's diction, especially the juxtaposition of the word *war* with the phrase *tidy up*. What does the diction suggest about the speaker's attitude toward war? [Possible responses: The phrase *tidy up* suggests someone cleaning a house. It is an ironic comment on the actual devastation caused by war. It may be suggesting that after a war is over, people forget its horrors too quickly.]

B Literary Focus

Imagery. How does this image contrast with the image of "tidying up" in the first stanza? [Possible response: This specific image of the horrors of war is a deliberate shock and a stark contrast with the idea of "tidying up."]

C Literary Focus

Theme. What is the speaker saying about war and its aftermath? [Possible response: Wars dominate the news, but comparatively little attention is paid to the undramatic work of recovering from a war, because the media moves on to cover violence elsewhere.]

CONNECTION/POEM

When Wisława Szymborska (vēs·wä′vä shĕm·bor′skä) was awarded the Nobel Prize in 1996, few people outside her native Poland had heard of her, but the resulting interest in Szymborska and her work has finally introduced her poetry to the world. She has been acclaimed for her ability to turn philosophical musings about subjects such as war, love, and suffering into poems that are complex yet clear. Szymborska's accessible style may be a response to the chaos and spiritual darkness she, as a twentieth-century Pole, has witnessed.

The End and the Beginning

Wisława Szymborska

translated by **Stanislaw Baranczak** and **Clare Cavanagh**

A After every war
someone's got to tidy up.
Things won't pick
themselves up, after all.

5 Someone's got to shove
the rubble to the roadsides
B so the carts loaded with corpses
can get by.

Someone's got to trudge
10 through sludge and ashes,
through the sofa springs,
the shards of glass,
the bloody rags.

Someone's got to lug the post
15 to prop the wall,
someone's got to glaze the window,
set the door in its frame.

No sound bites, no photo opportunities
C and it takes years.
20 All the cameras have gone
to other wars.

Comparing and Contrasting Texts

Examining points of view. The subject of war connects the short story "In the Shadow of War" and the poem "The End and the Beginning." However, each work provides a different perspective on the topic. The poem, though dotted with specific images of war and its aftermath, has an omniscient speaker who makes general pronouncements. The short story, told from a limited-third-person point of view, describes a specific incident in a specific war from the point of view of a child. Despite these differences, both works use images of death and destruction to underscore the horrors of war and its effects.

Mixed-ability group activity. Have small mixed-ability groups discuss the themes of the two works and how the point of view contributes to the development of each theme.

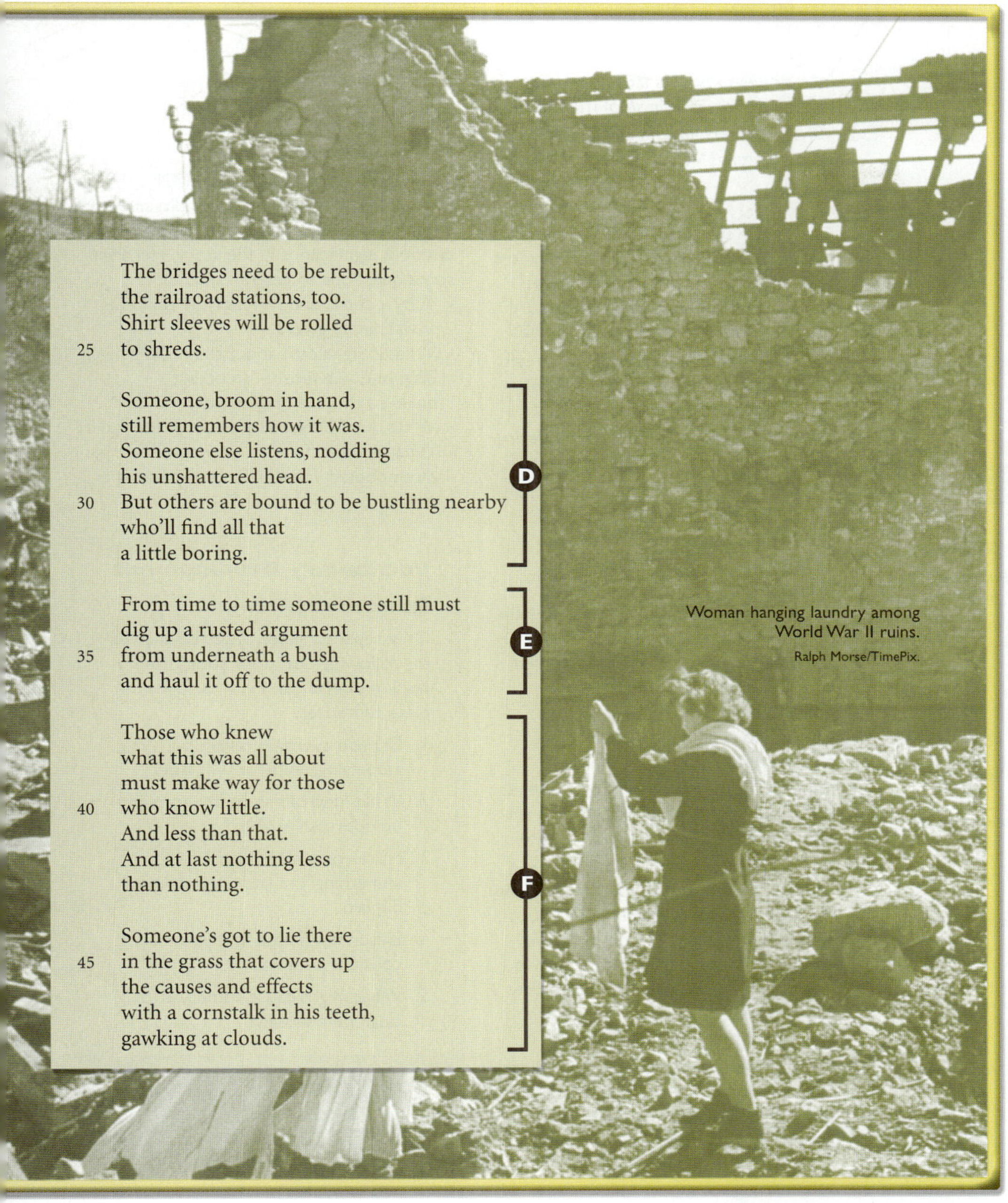

The bridges need to be rebuilt,
the railroad stations, too.
Shirt sleeves will be rolled
to shreds.

Someone, broom in hand,
still remembers how it was.
Someone else listens, nodding
his unshattered head.
But others are bound to be bustling nearby
who'll find all that
a little boring.

From time to time someone still must
dig up a rusted argument
from underneath a bush
and haul it off to the dump.

Those who knew
what this was all about
must make way for those
who know little.
And less than that.
And at last nothing less
than nothing.

Someone's got to lie there
in the grass that covers up
the causes and effects
with a cornstalk in his teeth,
gawking at clouds.

Woman hanging laundry among World War II ruins.
Ralph Morse/TimePix.

DIRECT TEACHING

D Learners Having Difficulty

Questioning. This stanza may seem confusing to students. Encourage them to clarify it by asking the following questions: Who is the first "someone" (l. 26)? [a person who remembers what the war was like] Who is the "someone" with the unshattered head (ll. 28–29)? [a person who did not experience the war firsthand] What is the "all that" that others find boring (ll. 31–32)? [war memories]

E Literary Focus

Theme. What view of war does this image suggest? [Possible response: The reasons people fight, which seem so important at the time, eventually lose significance. They become like discarded trash.]

F Reading Skills

Expressing an opinion. Do you think that the final stanzas of this poem present a positive or a negative view of humanity? Explain. [Possible responses: They present a negative view because they suggest that new generations of people don't know or remember anything about the sacrifices made by previous generations during war. The title of the poem might also suggest that the end of one war is the beginning of another.]

CONTENT-AREA CONNECTIONS

History: Poland in World War II

In 1795, Prussia, Russia, and Austria carved up Poland. The country did not achieve independence again until 1918, and that independence was short-lived. On August 23, 1939, Germany and the Soviet Union signed a nonaggression pact with a secret provision to divide Poland between them. On September 1, Germany invaded Poland, precipitating the beginning of World War II. On September 17, the Soviet Union invaded eastern Poland. For almost two years, the country was occupied jointly by Germany and the Soviet Union. In June 1941, however, Germany turned on its former ally and invaded the Soviet Union. Then Poland fell completely under the control of the Nazis, who brutally suppressed Polish resistance, including uprisings of the Polish underground and of Polish Jews living in the Warsaw ghetto. Throughout the course of the war, six million Poles were killed, including three million Jews who perished in death camps.

Whole-class activity. Wislawa Szymborska was born in 1923. Ask students to speculate on how events of her youth might have affected the views expressed in this poem.

INDEPENDENT PRACTICE

Response and Analysis

Reading Check

1. He says that the world might go dark, that the dead might walk, and that "heclipses" eat children.
2. The children believe that she is not human. She is captured, brutalized, and shot.

Thinking Critically

3. Possible answers: Omovo seems suspicious of the soldiers and sympathetic toward the woman. These feelings help predict that the soldiers will kill the woman.
4. Possible answers: Omovo's father wants his son out of harm's way. Omovo does not believe his father.
5. Possible answer: They want Omovo to reveal the woman's location. Omovo may refuse out of sympathy for the woman, distrust of the soldiers, or fear.
6. Possible answers: The details attest to the ravages of war. The details support the theme that the effects of war are unreasonable and destructive.
7. Possible answer: Details about the malnourished children suggest she is bringing food.
8. Possible answers: Okri's story is told from the point of view of a child; in the poem, war is seen from the point of view of an omniscient speaker. Omovo is terrified by war; the speaker in the poem uses irony to express resignation.
9. Answers will vary, but should be supported with examples from the text.

Vocabulary Development

Sample Answer

1. Television is stupefying because even when something boring is on air, it's difficult to find the willpower to turn it off.

Response and Analysis

Reading Check

1. What does Omovo's father say might happen during an eclipse of the moon?
2. What do the children believe about the veiled woman? What happens to her?

Thinking Critically

3. Early in the story, what are Omovo's feelings toward the soldiers? toward the woman? What later events do these feelings help you to **predict**? (Be sure to check your reading notes.)
4. Why do you think Omovo's father tells him what he does about the eclipse? How does Omovo react?
5. What is the soldier's motive for offering Omovo money? Why do you think Omovo refuses it?
6. The story's **limited-third-person point of view** allows us to see the action and setting through a child's eyes. How do you interpret details that Omovo sees on the riverbank—the unfinished estates, the empty factory, the skeleton, and the outdated currencies? Explain how Okri uses these details to create a child's-eye view of war and to support the underlying **theme** of the story.
7. What do you think the woman takes to the people in the cave? What clues are provided?
8. Both Okri's story and Szymborska's poem "The End and the Beginning" (see the **Connection** on page 880) concern war, but they are told from different **points of view**. Explain how the two points of view are different. How does Omovo feel about war? How does the speaker of the poem feel about it?
9. Re-read the final paragraph of the story. Might there be more than one explanation for the behavior of Omovo's father? (Review your Quickwrite notes.) If so, why might Okri choose to end on such an ambiguous note?

WRITING

Symbolic Object

The radio is a major **symbol** in Okri's story. Find all the references to the radio, and then write a short **essay** explaining its possible symbolic significance in the story. Here are some questions to get you started:

- Why is the brand name of the radio (a trivial detail) given?
- What is significant about the radio's being disguised as a fetish—an object believed to have magical powers?
- What does Omovo listen to on the radio?
- What is the difference between hearing a disembodied voice and actually seeing an event?

Vocabulary Development

Question and Answer

On a separate piece of paper, answer the following questions about the underlined Vocabulary words. Use complete sentences.

1. Do you ever find television stupefying? Why or why not?
2. What kind of environment might be oppressive? Why?
3. Have you ever succumbed to something and later regretted it? Explain.
4. Describe a home that you would consider ostentatious.
5. What might cause someone to laugh dementedly?

INTERNET
Projects and Activities
Keyword: LE5 12-7

SKILLS FOCUS

Literary Skills
Analyze the limited-third-person point of view.

Reading Skills
Make predictions.

Writing Skills
Write an essay explaining a symbol.

Vocabulary Skills
Demonstrate word knowledge.

ASSESSING

Assessment

- Holt Assessment: Literature, Reading, and Vocabulary

RETEACHING

For a lesson reteaching author's tone and style, see **Reteaching**, p. 1129A.

Mini-Workshop

Writing a Persuasive Essay

Creators of persuasive messages use reasons, appeals, and evidence to convince others to believe or do something—as Winston Churchill did in his "Blood, Sweat, and Tears" speech (page 850). In this workshop you'll use these tools to write a **persuasive essay** in which you develop a tightly reasoned argument for a particular audience.

Choose an Issue If you don't already have an **issue** (a topic about which reasonable people have opposing opinions) in mind for your essay, watch or listen to the news or read the newspaper for a few days. Is there an issue that inspires you to write or intrigues you? Look around you. Is there something in your school or community that you would like to see accomplished or changed? List several issues, and then use the following statements to evaluate each one. Make sure your final choice meets these criteria.

- The issue should be something you really care about.
- The issue should have clearly defined pro and con arguments.
- The issue should be narrow enough for you to argue successfully in a 1,500-word essay.

Identify Your Thesis and Call for Action Now that you have an issue, write a sentence that defines your **perspective,** or position, on that issue. This will be your **thesis statement,** sometimes called a position or opinion statement. One student created the following thesis statement, which identifies her opinion. Her thesis led her to develop her **call for action,** a sentence that tells her readers what she wants them to do.

> **Thesis:** The local animal shelter must change its euthanasia policy.
> **Call for Action:** We must write letters to our local animal shelter demanding a change in its policy of euthanizing animals.

Consider Purpose and Audience In order to succeed in your **purpose**—persuading your audience—you'll need to know something about them so that you can tailor your argument to their needs and interests. Use these questions to analyze your audience.

1. **What are their ages, interests, education levels, and values?** Use this information to determine what reasons, evidence, and language your readers will find most persuasive.
2. **What do they already know about the issue?** If your readers are not familiar with the issue, you'll need to give them enough background information to understand your argument.

Writing Assignment
Write a persuasive essay defending your position on an issue that is important to you.

Writing Skills
Write a persuasive essay.
Identify the thesis statement.
Determine purpose and audience.

COLLECTION 7 RESOURCES: WRITING

Planning
- *One-Stop Planner* CD-ROM with ExamView Test Generator

Differentiating Instruction
- *Workshop Resources: Writing, Listening, and Speaking*
- *Family Involvement Activities in English and Spanish*
- *Supporting Instruction in Spanish*

Writing and Language
- *Workshop Resources: Writing, Listening, and Speaking*
- *Daily Language Activities*
- *Language Handbook Worksheets*

PRETEACHING

Motivate. Ask students to think about a time when they persuaded someone to believe or do something. What techniques did they use? Explain that this workshop presents persuasive techniques that may improve their ability to convince others.

DIRECT TEACHING

Writing a Persuasive Essay
If such material is available in your school library, provide students with videotaped or audiotaped selections, or written examples read aloud, of famous speeches that make skillful use of the rhetorical devices listed on p. 884. Emphasize especially the power of analogies, repetition, and rhythm in speeches such as Winston Churchill's "Blood, Sweat, and Tears" speech, Martin Luther King, Jr.'s "I Have a Dream" speech, or Abraham Lincoln's Gettysburg Address. Students should concentrate on finding techniques and strategies they can use in their own persuasive messages.

RETEACHING

Identify Your Thesis and Call for Action
To help students develop their theses, have them analyze and evaluate the following sample position statements. Students should determine whether each statement focuses on a legitimate, arguable issue.

1. A national health plan is needed. [Acceptable. The topic is hotly debated, with strong points on each side.]
2. The federal government should continue to support research for the cure and prevention of cancer. [Unacceptable. Few people will disagree, so the statement is not arguable.]

SKILLS FOCUS, pp. 886–895

Grade-Level Skills

- **Literary Skills**

Analyze characteristics of the essay.

- **Reading Skills**

Analyze an author's philosophical assumptions and beliefs about a subject.

Review Skills

- **Reading Skills**

Identify the author's beliefs.

More About the Writer

Background. Although she was very well read, Virginia Woolf never had a formal education like her father and brothers, who attended Cambridge University. Woolf delivered an excerpt from *A Room of One's Own* as a speech at Cambridge's two women's colleges, Newham and Girton. Ironically, she spoke about the need for women's education at a school that she was unable to attend.

Virginia Woolf
(1882–1941)
England

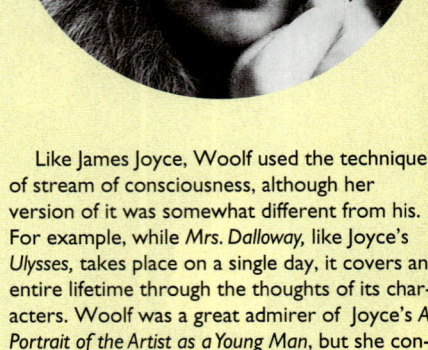

Virginia Woolf was born in Victorian London to the scholar and literary critic Sir Leslie Stephen and his artistic wife, Julia. In her youth, Woolf enjoyed all the advantages of a financially comfortable and intellectually challenging environment. Too frail to attend school regularly, she was privately tutored and given the luxury of access to her father's extensive library.

After her father's death in 1904, Virginia, her sister, Vanessa, and their two brothers moved to the area of London known as Bloomsbury. Soon they and their friends began to meet in what came to be called the Bloomsbury Group, an intellectual circle whose other prominent members included the writer E. M. Forster, the artist Duncan Grant, and the economist John Maynard Keynes. An informal gathering with the highest cultural standards, the Bloomsbury Group helped provide the right environment for Virginia Woolf's sensitive, experimental fiction. One member of the group was Leonard Woolf, a journalist and economist, whom Virginia married in 1912.

Woolf had been writing since she was fourteen and reviewing books since her early twenties, but it was not until she was thirty-three, in 1915, that her first novel, *The Voyage Out*, was published. The publication of *Jacob's Room* (1922) and *Mrs. Dalloway* (1925) established her position as one of the foremost writers of her time. With these novels—and with subsequent novels, such as *To the Lighthouse* (1927) and *The Waves* (1931)—Woolf pursued an experimental vision that emphasizes personal impressions over external events and focuses on the experience of life as it was being lived.

Like James Joyce, Woolf used the technique of stream of consciousness, although her version of it was somewhat different from his. For example, while *Mrs. Dalloway*, like Joyce's *Ulysses*, takes place on a single day, it covers an entire lifetime through the thoughts of its characters. Woolf was a great admirer of Joyce's *A Portrait of the Artist as a Young Man*, but she considered *Ulysses* an "illiterate, underbred book." Still, she worried that "what I am doing is probably being better done by Mr. Joyce."

Woolf also wrote a great many reviews and essays. In a number of them she explored the work of female writers, often focusing on a particular author who she felt had been neglected. In 1917, she and her husband established the Hogarth Press, which published many of the most important writers—male and female—of the day.

Troubled by sudden deaths and mental illness in her family, Woolf throughout her life suffered from bouts of depression and anxiety. These deepened with the German bombing raids over England in World War II, and in March 1941, she took her own life.

For Independent Reading

These are Woolf's two great novels:

- *Mrs. Dalloway*
- *To the Lighthouse*

886 Collection 7 The Modern World: 1900 to the Present

RESOURCES: READING

Planning
- One-Stop Planner CD-ROM

Differentiating Instruction
- Holt Reading Solutions
- The Holt Reader
- Holt Adapted Reader
- Supporting Instruction in Spanish
- Audio CD Library, Selections and Summaries in Spanish

Vocabulary
- Vocabulary Development

Grammar and Language
- Daily Language Activities

Assessment
- Holt Assessment: Literature, Reading, and Vocabulary
- One-Stop Planner CD-ROM with ExamView Test Generator

- Holt Online Assessment

Internet
- go.hrw.com (Keyword: LE5 12-7)
- Elements of Literature Online

Media
- Audio CD Library
- Audio CD Library, Selections and Summaries in Spanish
- Fine Art Transparencies

Before You Read

Shakespeare's Sister

Make the Connection
Quickwrite

Gender is perhaps the most basic difference between human beings in every culture. Beyond the biological differences are the social and cultural realities: the everyday concerns that men and women have and the work they are or are not able to accomplish. Virginia Woolf scrutinized those realities in her 1929 essay collection *A Room of One's Own*, from which this essay is taken.

In your opinion, what differences exist between opportunities available to men and those available to women in our society today? Why do you think these differences exist? Write down some of your thoughts.

Literary Focus
Essay

An **essay** is a short piece of nonfiction writing that explores a particular topic. Formal essays are usually impersonal in tone, and tend to be highly organized, logical, and full of facts. An **informal essay**, on the other hand, is highly subjective, usually dominated by the author's own feelings, beliefs, and biases. Even though informal essays can be humorous and casual in tone, they often reveal deeply held principles and touch upon controversial or troubling aspects of society. The following selection by Woolf is one such essay.

> An **essay** is a short piece of nonfiction writing that examines a single subject from a limited point of view.
>
> For more on the Essay, see the Handbook of Literary and Historical Terms.

Reading Skills
Identifying the Author's Beliefs

At the top of a sheet of paper, write "Virginia Woolf believes that . . ." and write the numbers 1–5 below this heading. Then, as you read, list some of the things that Woolf believes. (You may discover more or fewer than five.) Read carefully—some of Woolf's beliefs may be stated directly while others are only hinted at. When you are finished, place a checkmark next to the belief you think is most central to the essay.

Background

A Room of One's Own is considered a pioneering work of feminist criticism. The aims of feminist criticism include exposing sexist attitudes in or toward literature, reinterpreting earlier works from a feminist perspective, uncovering neglected women writers, and analyzing how gender affects a writer's subjects, themes, and even style.

Vocabulary Development

servile (sʉr′vīl) *adj.*: like or characteristic of a slave; submissive; yielding.

suppressed (sə·prest′) *v.* used as *adj.*: kept from being known.

propitious (prō·pish′əs) *adj.*: favorable.

prodigious (prō·dij′əs) *adj.*: enormous.

notorious (nō·tôr′ē·əs) *adj.*: widely but unfavorably known.

formidable (fôr′mə·də·bəl) *adj.*: difficult to handle or overcome.

guffaw (gə·fô′) *n.*: loud laughter.

INTERNET
Vocabulary Practice
•
More About Virginia Woolf
Keyword: LE5 12-7

Literary Skills Understand the characteristics of an essay.

Reading Skills Identify an author's beliefs.

PRETEACHING

Summary ⇄ at grade level

In this informal essay, Woolf imagines that William Shakespeare had a sister, Judith, who was as talented as her famous brother. Because Judith was a woman, Woolf believes, she would not have been allowed to develop or express her genius. Had she done so, she would have been rejected by her family and her society. Woolf expresses her belief that Judith would have committed suicide due to her frustrated ambition and unrecognized talent. Woolf also suggests that "Anonymous," the unknown author of many literary works, was a woman. Woolf describes the difficulties that a woman faced in the sixteenth century—and, by implication, still faced in the early twentieth century—in trying to succeed as a writer, artist, and creative public figure.

Skills Starter

Build review skills. Note that the term *essay* comes from a Latin word that has to do with weighing something. Suggest that the writer of an essay weighs or evaluates the importance of a topic as well as the arguments for and against the point of view that he or she presents. Point out that in this essay, Virginia Woolf is weighing the role and the potential of intelligent, ambitious women in society.

Previewing Vocabulary

Ask students to read the definitions of the Vocabulary words on p. 887 and then create a sentence that uses each word. Be sure students understand that the words are defined in the context of the essay and that they may have other meanings or connotations in different sentences. Then, present this exercise, and ask students to match each word to its antonym.

1. servile [c]
2. suppressed [e]
3. propitious [b]
4. prodigious [g]
5. notorious [f]
6. formidable [a]
7. guffaw [d]

a. manageable
b. unfavorable
c. domineering
d. sneer
e. disclosed
f. famous in a positive way
g. puny

laboring, uneducated, servile people. It was not born in England among the Saxons and the Britons. It is not born today among the working classes. How, then, could it have been born among women whose work began, according to Professor Trevelyan, almost before they were out of the nursery, who were forced to it by their parents and held to it by all the power of law and custom? Yet genius of a sort must have existed among women as it must have existed among the working classes. Now and again an Emily Brontë or a Robert Burns blazes out and proves its presence. But certainly it never got itself onto paper. When, however, one reads of a witch being ducked, of a woman possessed by devils, of a wise woman selling herbs, or even of a very remarkable man who had a mother, then I think we are on the track of a lost novelist, a suppressed poet, of some mute and inglorious[4] Jane Austen, some Emily Brontë who dashed her brains out on the moor or mopped and mowed about the highways crazed with the torture that her gift had put her to. Indeed, I would venture to guess that Anon, who wrote so many poems without signing them, was often a woman. It was a woman Edward Fitzgerald,[5] I think, suggested who made the ballads and the folk songs, crooning them to her children, beguiling her spinning with them, or the length of the winter's night.

This may be true or it may be false—who can say?—but what is true in it, so it seemed to me, reviewing the story of Shakespeare's sister as I had made it, is that any woman born with a great gift in the sixteenth century would certainly have gone crazed, shot herself, or ended her days in some lonely cottage outside the village, half witch, half wizard, feared and mocked at. For it needs little skill in psychology to be sure that a highly gifted girl who had tried to use her gift for poetry would have been so thwarted and hindered by other people, so tortured and pulled asunder by her own contrary instincts, that she must have lost her health and sanity to a certainty. No girl could have walked to London and stood at a stage door and forced her way into the presence of actor-managers without doing herself a violence and suffering an anguish which may have been irrational—for chastity may be a fetish invented by certain societies for unknown reasons—but were nonetheless inevitable. Chastity had then, it has even now, a religious importance in a woman's life, and has so wrapped itself round with nerves and instincts that to cut it free and bring it to the light of day demands courage of the rarest. To have lived a free life in London in the sixteenth century would have meant for a woman who was poet and playwright a nervous stress and dilemma which might well have killed her. Had she survived, whatever she had written would have been twisted and deformed, issuing from a strained and morbid imagination. And undoubtedly, I thought, looking at the shelf where there are no plays by women, her work would have gone unsigned. That refuge she would have sought certainly. It was the relic of the sense of chastity that dictated anonymity to women even so late as the nineteenth century. Currer Bell, George Eliot, George Sand,[6] all the victims of inner strife as their writings prove, sought ineffectively to veil themselves by using the name of a man. Thus they did homage to the convention, which if not implanted by the other sex was liberally encouraged by them (the chief glory of a

---

4. **mute and inglorious:** allusion to line 59 of Thomas Gray's poem "Elegy Written in a Country Churchyard."
5. **Edward Fitzgerald** (1809–1883): English translator and poet.
6. **Currer Bell, George Eliot, George Sand:** male pseudonyms for the female writers Charlotte Brontë, Mary Ann Evans, and Amantine-Aurore-Lucile Dupin.

Vocabulary
servile (sur′vil) *adj.:* like or characteristic of a slave; submissive; yielding.
suppressed (sə·prest′) *v.* used as *adj.:* kept from being known.

A Corner of the Artist's Room, Paris (late 19th or early 20th century) by Gwen John.
Sheffield City Art Galleries, England.
© 2003 Artists Rights Society (ARS), NY/DACS, London.

woman is not to be talked of, said Pericles,[7] himself a much-talked-of man), that publicity in women is detestable. Anonymity runs in their blood. The desire to be veiled still possesses them. They are not even now as concerned about the health of their fame as men are, and, speaking generally, will pass a tombstone or a signpost without feeling an irresistible desire to cut their names on it, as Alf, Bert, or Chas. must do in obedience to their instinct, which murmurs if it sees a fine woman go by, or even a dog, *Ce chien est à moi.*[8] And, of course, it may not be a dog, I thought, remembering Parliament Square, the Sieges Allee,[9] and other avenues; it may be a piece of land or a man with curly black hair. It is one of the great advantages of being a woman that one can pass even a very fine negress without wishing to make an Englishwoman of her. ❹

That woman, then, who was born with a gift of poetry in the sixteenth century, was an unhappy woman, a woman at strife against herself. All the conditions of her life, all her own instincts, were hostile to the state of mind which is needed to set free whatever is in the brain. But what is the state of mind that is most propitious to the act of creation, I asked. Can one come by any notion of the state that furthers and makes possible that strange activity? Here I opened the volume containing the Tragedies of Shakespeare. What was Shakespeare's state of mind, for instance, when he wrote *Lear* and *Antony and Cleopatra*? It was certainly the state of mind most favorable to poetry that there has ever existed. But Shakespeare himself said

---

7. **Pericles** (c. 495–429 B.C.): Athenian legislator and general.
8. *Ce chien est à moi* (sə shē·en′ ät ä mwä): French for "This dog is mine."
9. **Sieges Allee** (zē′gəs ä·lā′): busy thoroughfare in Berlin. The name—more commonly written as one word, *Siegesallee*—is German for "Avenue of Victory."

Vocabulary
propitious (prō·pish′əs) *adj.*: favorable.

❹ What impulse does Woolf attribute to men but not to women? What examples of this impulse does Woolf give?

nothing about it. We only know casually and by chance that he "never blotted a line." Nothing indeed was ever said by the artist himself about his state of mind until the eighteenth century perhaps. Rousseau[10] perhaps began it. At any rate, by the nineteenth century self-consciousness had developed so far that it was the habit for men of letters to describe their minds in confessions and autobiographies. Their lives also were written, and their letters were printed after their deaths. Thus, though we do not know what Shakespeare went through when he wrote *Lear,* we do know what Carlyle went through when he wrote *The French Revolution;* what Flaubert went through when he wrote *Madame Bovary;* what Keats was going through when he tried to write poetry against the coming of death and the indifference of the world.

And one gathers from this enormous modern literature of confession and self-analysis that to write a work of genius is almost always a feat of prodigious difficulty. Everything is against the likelihood that it will come from the writer's mind whole and entire. Generally material circumstances are against it. Dogs will bark; people will interrupt; money must be made; health will break down. Further, accentuating all these difficulties and making them harder to bear is the world's notorious indifference. It does not ask people to write poems and novels and histories; it does not need them. It does not care whether Flaubert finds the right word or whether Carlyle scrupulously verifies this or that fact. Naturally, it will not pay for what it does not want. And so the writer, Keats, Flaubert, Carlyle, suffers, especially in the creative years of youth, every form of distraction and discouragement. A curse, a cry of agony, rises from those books of analysis and confession. "Mighty poets in their misery dead"[11]—that is the burden of their song. If anything comes through in spite of all this, it is a miracle, and probably no book is born entire and uncrippled as it was conceived.

But for women, I thought, looking at the empty shelves, these difficulties were infinitely more formidable. In the first place, to have a room of her own, let alone a quiet room or a soundproof room, was out of the question, unless her parents were exceptionally rich or very noble, even up to the beginning of the nineteenth century. Since her pin money,[12] which depended on the goodwill of her father, was only enough to keep her clothed, she was debarred from such alleviations[13] as came even to Keats or Tennyson or Carlyle, all poor men, from a walking tour, a little journey to France, from the separate lodging which, even if it were miserable enough, sheltered them from the claims and tyrannies of their families. Such material difficulties were formidable; but much worse were the immaterial. The indifference of the world which Keats and Flaubert and other men of genius have found so hard to bear was in her case not indifference but hostility. The world did not say to her as it said to them, Write if you choose; it makes no difference to me. The world said with a guffaw, Write? What's the good of your writing? ∎

---

10. **Rousseau:** Jean-Jacques Rousseau (1712–1778), French author whose candid, autobiographical *Confessions* began a vogue in literature for confessional accounts.
11. **Mighty poets . . . dead:** line from William Wordsworth's poem "Resolution and Independence."
12. **pin money:** small allowance for personal expenses.
13. **alleviations** (ə·lē′vē·ā′shənz): *n. pl.:* things that lighten, relieve, or make easier to bear.

Vocabulary
prodigious (prō·dij′əs) *adj.:* enormous.
notorious (nō·tôr′ē·əs) *adj.:* widely but unfavorably known; infamous.
formidable (fôr′mə·də·bəl) *adj.:* difficult to handle or overcome.
guffaw (gə·fô′) *n.:* loud laughter.

SKILLS REVIEW

Analyzing structure and purpose. Use the following questions to analyze this essay.

1. What is Woolf's purpose for writing this essay? [Possible responses: to counter the argument that women do not have the same creative genius as men; to focus on the plight of female writers.]

2. How does the structure of Woolf's essay serve her purpose? [Possible response: Her opening example draws readers into her thesis; her hypothetical "life story" of Shakespeare's sister builds sympathy and reader identification; her conclusion sums up her argument.]

A CLOSER LOOK: POLITICAL INFLUENCES

Suffragists march in London (c. 1910).

INFORMATIONAL TEXT

Votes for Women!

In December 1913, during an opera about Joan of Arc staged especially for the British royal family, three elegantly dressed women stood and addressed the king through a megaphone. The crowd was thrown into a panic as the women likened their struggle for the vote to Joan of Arc's fifteenth-century fight for liberty. When the police finally removed them, other women, hidden in the balcony, showered the audience with suffragist pamphlets. The king, of course, did not respond. But the dramatic protest joined the suffragists to Joan and other brave women's rights forerunners, just as Virginia Woolf's portrait of Shakespeare's fictional sister drew on the past to spur change in her own time.

The vote—a right not granted to British women over the age of thirty until 1918, and not granted to women over twenty-one until 1928—was the key to meaningful change for

Virginia Woolf 893

SKILLS REVIEW

Relating a work to a historical period. Woolf's essay was published in 1929, only a year after the women of Britain had been granted universal suffrage. Challenge students to consider whether or not Woolf's essay remains relevant today. Would American culture today encourage a female genius like Shakespeare's sister, or would it thwart her? Encourage students to supply specific examples of both encouragement to and discouragement of talented women. Students also can discuss the extent to which they think genius is inherited (a matter of genetics) or nurtured (a matter of environment). Students' opinions on the nature versus nurture debate will affect their ideas about how culture encourages—or inhibits—individual achievement.

A CLOSER LOOK

This feature traces the history of the campaign for women's suffrage in Britain from the mid-1800s to 1914.

DIRECT TEACHING

VIEWING THE ART

This photograph shows the delivery of "human letters" to H. H. Asquith, the prime minister of Great Britain. Asquith had tried to defend the Liberal party's refusal to enfranchise women by saying that there was no proof that women actually wanted the vote. Women like the ones in the photograph responded not only by organizing suffrage rallies but also by walking to the prime minister's home carrying placards with the message "Votes for Women."

A Content-Area Connections

History: A Broad Range of Tactics
One suffragist was so determined to make an impression on Prime Minister Asquith that she had herself hoisted up to a dining-room window at a castle where he was vacationing. As he and his party were preparing to eat, she announced that women would continue to plague the prime minister until he gave them the vote.

B Reading Informational Text

Making assertions about an argument. Why might suffragists have chosen an opera about Joan of Arc to make their protest? [Possible response: Joan of Arc wanted to rescue France from its English conquerors. By identifying with her, the suffragists implied that they hoped for rescue from an oppressive English government.]

DIRECT TEACHING

C Reading Skills

? Identifying an author's beliefs. What is the writer's opinion of Virginia Woolf? What words and details support your inference? [Possible responses: The writer's use of the word *humble* proves that he or she admires Woolf's selfless devotion to the cause of women's suffrage. The writer feels that Woolf could have done more for the cause if she had been bolder.]

D Reading Informational Text

? Relating clarity to organizational patterns. How is the information in this passage organized? [chronological order] Why do you think the author selected this method of organization? [Possible response: Time order allows the author to show clearly how one event in the suffrage movement led to another.]

GUIDED PRACTICE

Monitoring students' progress. Guide the class in answering these comprehension questions. Direct students to locate passages in the text that support their responses.

Short Answer

1. For what purpose does Woolf invent Judith Shakespeare? [to show what she feels is the real reason that an Elizabethan woman could not have written plays of William Shakespeare's caliber]
2. According to Woolf, how does the world treat male writers? [with indifference]
3. According to Woolf, how does the world treat female writers? [with hostility]

---

women in Woolf's day. Woolf herself was among thousands of women who joined suffrage organizations during the first decade of the century. Although she could have written articles for publications such as *The Suffragette* or *Votes for Women*, she instead lent her support in more humble ways: She sat on the platform at public meetings and folded letters for countless mailings (she later recalled spending "hours writing names like Cowgill on envelopes"). Woolf was a pacifist, and her views on the use of physical force prevented her wholehearted involvement in the increasingly combative woman suffrage movement of the early 1900s.

A new phase in an old fight. Universal suffrage was not a new idea. Women and men had campaigned for it since the mid-1800s; in fact, the philosopher John Stuart Mill had brought a suffrage bill before the British Parliament in 1867. The fight entered a new phase in 1904, when the ardent suffragist Christabel Pankhurst strode off to the Manchester Free Trade Hall to challenge Winston Churchill on the subject of voting rights for women. Churchill refused to acknowledge Pankhurst's demands, and she was howled down by the crowd, but she counted it as her first "militant" step.

Afterward, members of the Women's Social and Political Union, which Pankhurst and her mother, Emmeline, had founded in 1903, were emboldened to take other steps: They held rallies and marches, staged suffrage plays at public meetings, broke the windows of government buildings, and interrupted Parliament by shouting "Votes for women!" from their enclosed seats in the "Ladies' Gallery." (Later, several women chained themselves to the metal grille that separated this gallery from the main chamber.) From 1906 to 1914, more than a thousand British suffragists were arrested and carted off to jail. Held in tiny cells and prohibited from speaking to one another, these women still found other ways to protest, mostly through hunger strikes. In answer the government force-fed the protesters until the procedure permanently damaged many women's health. Thereafter, in what came to be called Cat and Mouse licenses, hunger strikers were released from prison only until they regained their strength—then they were rearrested.

Success at last. The sight of "respectable" women getting roughed up by hostile crowds and held for months in prison did alter public opinion: Many people came to realize how badly women wanted the right to full citizenship. Yet protests continued without results until the beginning of World War I, when the Pankhursts and others abruptly turned their energies to the war effort. Ironically, many historians now think that women's work during the war, mostly as they filled the absent soldiers' jobs, was the turning point in the suffrage movement. When the war was over, most Britishers felt that women shouldn't—indeed couldn't—be deprived of the vote any longer.

Emmeline Pankhurst (second from left) with one of her daughters at a suffragist meeting (1908).

894 Collection 7 The Modern World: 1900 to the Present

FAMILY/COMMUNITY ACTIVITY

Encourage students to share this selection with a female community leader, such as a member of the school board, library board, or town government. Then, have students collaborate with their mentor to write an essay about a problem facing women in their community today, such as affordable childcare or elder care. Invite mentors to come to class, share their essays, and discuss parallels with Woolf's topic.

Response and Analysis

Reading Check
1. What happens to "Judith Shakespeare" when she goes to London?
2. According to Woolf, what general conditions make works of genius difficult to produce? What special conditions do women face in creating works of genius?

Thinking Critically
3. In her essay, Woolf says of women, "Anonymity runs in their blood." According to Woolf, why do women shy away from the limelight? What do you think of the reasons she gives for women's seeking anonymity?
4. How would you describe the **tone** of this essay? Is it conversational? angry? perplexed? ironic? What purpose does this tone serve? Support your ideas with examples from the text.
5. In this essay, Woolf expresses several beliefs—some quite strongly, others more subtly. In your opinion, which belief is most central to the **theme** of the essay? (Refer to the list you created while reading.) Do you share this belief? Explain.
6. Does Woolf make any **generalizations** in this essay that you think are unsupported by historical or contemporary evidence? Explain your response, citing as examples historical and political events.

Extending and Evaluating
7. Is Woolf's use of an invented biography of Judith Shakespeare convincing to you? Why might she use such a device? Cite reasons for your answer.

WRITING
The Gender Gap
Woolf's essay contains many ideas, both explicit and implicit, about gender roles. In a brief **essay,** (a) discuss how Woolf depicts men and women; (b) evaluate the fairness of these depictions; and (c) discuss how true or relevant these depictions are for men and women today. (Your Quickwrite notes may help you.)

▶ See "Analyzing Nonfiction," pages 941–942, for help with this assignment.

Vocabulary Development
What's the Difference?
Answer each of the following questions on a separate sheet of paper. (The underlined words are Vocabulary words.)

1. What's the difference between *servile* and *helpful*?
2. What's the difference between *suppressed* and *restrained*?
3. What's the difference between *propitious* and *foreboding*?
4. What's the difference between *prodigious* and *large*?
5. What's the difference between *notorious* and *famous*?
6. What's the difference between *formidable* and *unapproachable*?
7. What's the difference between *guffaw* and *laugh*?

INTERNET
Project and Activities
Keyword: LE5 12-7

SKILLS FOCUS

Literary Skills
Analyze an essay.

Reading Skills
Evaluate an author's beliefs.

Writing Skills
Write an essay analyzing a work of nonfiction.

Vocabulary Skills
Clarify word meanings.

Virginia Woolf 895

Reading Check
1. Men laugh at her desire to act. She is seduced by an acting company's manager, becomes pregnant, and commits suicide.
2. Difficulties include lack of privacy and free time as well as financial insecurity. Most women writers also face additional family responsibilities and the hostility of the public.

Thinking Critically
3. Woolf argues that women shun the limelight to avoid being ridiculed by men. Most students will agree there is some historical truth in Woolf's argument.
4. The tone is contemptuous irony, showing Woolf's distaste for the view that women do not have the creative capacity of men. The tone is especially evident when Woolf mentions the bishop and his views.

INDEPENDENT PRACTICE

Response and Analysis
5. Woolf's central idea is that women historically have been prevented from expressing creative genius by lack of opportunity, crippling stereotypes, and public rejection. Students will vary in their agreement with this view.
6. Most of Woolf's "evidence" is anecdotal and hypothetical, so unsupported generalizations occur throughout the essay.

Extending and Evaluating
7. Students who find the biography convincing may suggest that by creating a fictional biography, Woolf is able to present a sympathetic picture that adds emotional power to her argument. Students who disagree may argue that the technique is emotionally manipulative and based purely on conjecture.

Vocabulary Development
Sample Answer
Servile means "acting like a servant" and has negative connotations; *helpful* means "aiding" and has positive connotations.

ASSESSING

Assessment
- *Holt Assessment: Literature, Reading, and Vocabulary*

RETEACHING

For a lesson reteaching philosophical assumptions and beliefs, see **Reteaching,** p. 1129A.

Political Points of View

SKILLS FOCUS, pp. 896–921

Grade-Level Skills

■ **Literary Skills**
Analyze political points of view in a selection of literary works on a topic.

■ **Reading Skills**
Make reasonable assertions about an author's argument or purpose.

■ **Reading Skills**
Compare main ideas across texts.

Political Issue: Colonialism

Clearly, colonialism brought considerable benefits to Great Britain, including emigration opportunities, expanded trade, and greater resources. However, colonization undeniably had harmful effects on both the colonizer and the colonized: Cultures were radically altered, and people were brutally subjugated. Bitter hatreds ensued, often erupting into violence. Populations today still grapple with the legacy of oppression and resentment that colonialism created.

Skills Starter

Motivate. Present students with this assumption: "The potential for colonialism is inherent in a world comprised of countries in radically different stages of economic and technological development. The powerful invariably dominate the powerless." Then, divide the class in half to debate this question: Is colonialism inevitable?

Introducing Political Points of View

Colonialism

Main Readings			
George Orwell	**Shooting an Elephant**	(England)	899
Doris Lessing	**No Witchcraft for Sale**	(Zimbabwe)	909

Connected Readings			
Joseph Chamberlain	"I Believe in a British Empire"	(England)	917
Jawaharlal Nehru	"The Noble Mansion of Free India"	(India)	919

You will be reading the four selections listed above in this Political Points of View feature on colonialism. In the top corner of the pages in this feature, you'll find three stars. Smaller versions of the stars appear next to the questions on pages 905 and 915 that focus on colonialism. At the end of the feature, on page 921, you will be asked to compare the various points of view expressed in all four selections.

Examining the Issue: Colonialism

Colonialism refers to the rule of one nation over a group of people in a geographically distant land—usually for the purpose of maintaining control of that land's resources. Between the 1600s and the 1800s, Great Britain built a vast empire that included colonies in parts of Asia, Australia, Africa, and North America. Although the growth of the empire slowed significantly in the early 1800s, the rise of industrialization fueled Great Britain's need for raw materials, cheap labor, and worldwide markets. Through colonialism the British established a stronghold over millions of people, their lands, and their resources.

Make the Connection
Quickwrite

Think about impressions of British colonialism you have formed from your studies in history, from books you have read, or from movies you have seen. (Remember—the United States was once a British colony!) Make a list of some of these impressions. Then, based on your list, draw some conclusions about the ideals, principles, or beliefs behind British colonialism.

Pages 896–921 cover
Literary Skills Analyze political points of view on a topic.
Reading Skills Compare main ideas across texts.

Reading Skills
Comparing Main Ideas Across Texts

As you read each selection, try to identify its **main idea,** or theme. Ask yourself, "How does this writer feel about the issue of colonialism?" Write a few sentences in response to this question. Then, after reading all of the selections, compare your notes. What different ideas do these writers express about their common topic?

SKILLS REVIEW

Evaluating historical influences. Point out to students that an assessment of colonialism should include an analysis of changing historical circumstances. According to today's standards of behavior, for example, colonialism is inexcusable because it conflicts directly with the rights of national sovereignty and self-determination. Such rights, however, have been recognized only fairly recently.

Nineteenth-century empire builders believed they bore a moral responsibility to rule "backward peoples" and bring them the benefits of Western civilization. Ask students to find evidence (in statements of beliefs, attitudes, and official policies) that indicates in more detail the perspective on colonialism in the late nineteenth and early twentieth centuries and in the mid- to late twentieth century.

George Orwell
(1903–1950)
England

George Orwell was born Eric Blair in Bengal, India, where his British father was a member of the Indian civil service. A few years afterward, his family returned to England. A lonely child, Orwell spent a good deal of time making up stories and poems. He later wrote that from an early age he knew he was going to be a writer.

After graduating from Eton College, a prep school, Orwell joined the Indian Imperial Police, serving in Burma (now Myanmar) from 1922 to 1927, when he resigned to devote more time to writing. Returning to Europe, he taught and took part-time, ill-paying jobs in France and England. His first book, *Down and Out in Paris and London* (1933), is based on those experiences. He based his next novel, *Burmese Days* (1934), on his life in Burma.

Although he published journalistic pieces under his real name, with the publication of his earliest books he began to use the name George Orwell, and he continued to do so until his death. After publishing three novels, Orwell was asked to write a study of conditions among industrial workers in northern England for the socialist Left Book Club. This became *The Road to Wigan Pier* (1937), a moving portrait of the difficult lives of working-class people.

Deeply disturbed by the rise of fascism in the 1930s, Orwell fought against the Nationalists (Fascists) in the Spanish Civil War and published a book based on these experiences—*Homage to Catalonia* (1938). "The Spanish war," he wrote, "turned the scale and thereafter I knew where I stood. Every line of serious work that I have written since 1936 has been written, directly or indirectly, *against* totalitarianism and *for* democratic socialism."

His two most famous novels, *Animal Farm* (1945) and *1984* (1949), illustrate this point. *Animal Farm* is a political allegory that points out the dangers of totalitarianism, whether practiced by the left or the right. And *1984* has given us an entire vocabulary for the excesses of totalitarian regimes, including such terms as *newspeak* and *Big Brother*. In this book, Orwell stresses the connections between language, thought, and power, dramatizing in fiction the ideas he earlier explored in his famous essay "Politics and the English Language" (1946)—especially the idea that corrupt language can be used to promote political oppression.

For Independent Reading

You may enjoy the following works by Orwell:
- *1984* (novel)
- "A Hanging" (essay)

George Orwell making a radio broadcast for the BBC.

SKILLS FOCUS, pp. 897–906

Grade-Level Skills

- **Literary Skills**

Analyze political points of view on a topic.

- **Literary Skills**

Analyze the way irony achieves specific rhetorical or aesthetic purposes.

- **Reading Skills**

Make reasonable assertions about an author's argument or purpose.

More About the Writer

Background. Why do writers write? Orwell once offered this answer: "All writers are vain, selfish, and lazy, and at the very bottom of their motives there lies a mystery. Writing a book is a horrible, exhausting struggle, like a long bout of some painful illness. One would never undertake such a thing if one were not driven on by some demon that one can neither resist nor understand. For all one knows, that demon is merely the same instinct that makes a baby squall for attention. And yet it is also true that one can write nothing readable unless one constantly struggles to efface one's own personality. Good prose is like a windowpane."

RESOURCES: READING

Planning
- One-Stop Planner CD-ROM

Differentiating Instruction
- Holt Reading Solutions
- The Holt Reader
- Holt Adapted Reader
- Supporting Instruction in Spanish
- Audio CD Library, Selections and Summaries in Spanish

Vocabulary
- Vocabulary Development

Grammar and Language
- Daily Language Activities

Assessment
- Holt Assessment: Literature, Reading, and Vocabulary
- One-Stop Planner CD-ROM with ExamView Test Generator

- Holt Online Assessment

Internet
- go.hrw.com (Keyword: LE5 12-7)
- Elements of Literature Online

Media
- Audio CD Library
- Audio CD Library, Selections and Summaries in Spanish

PRETEACHING

Summary ↔ at grade level

Orwell recounts an experience he had while serving as a police officer of the British Empire in colonial Burma. One day, a frenzied elephant went on a rampage in a bazaar, killing one person. By the time Orwell arrives on the scene to deal with the matter, a large crowd of Burmese has gathered to watch. Although he hates his job (which he calls doing "the dirty work of the Empire") and does not want to kill the elephant, Orwell feels pressured by the crowd and his position to take action; otherwise, he will risk looking foolish. He therefore shoots the animal repeatedly and awkwardly, causing the elephant a protracted and agonizing death.

Skills Starter

Build review skills. Remind students that irony is based upon contrast—a contrast between expected words and situations and what actually is said or what actually happens. Ask volunteers to complete the following sentence in an unexpected way and then discuss the ironies in the resulting words and situations: *When I waved at the passing fire engine that afternoon, _____.* [Possible response: I never imagined that it would be putting out a fire at my house.] You may want to have students create other such ironic sentences.

As students read through "Shooting an Elephant," discuss how Orwell uses irony to underscore the difference between real power and the illusion of power.

Before You Read

Shooting an Elephant

Political Points of View

Wherever there were British colonies, there were British people who went there to live and to govern. No matter how long these people lived overseas, they generally remained outsiders, an alien minority holding power over a resentful people. As a police officer in British-controlled Burma (now Myanmar) in the 1920s, George Orwell did not just symbolize foreign rule—he was its agent. His awareness of being an enemy within another culture kindled enormous conflicts in him—and it propelled him to act against his conscience.

Literary Focus

Irony

The dominant literary mode in the twentieth century is **irony.** In this essay, Orwell uses several strategies to evoke a sense of irony. He uses **verbal irony**—saying one thing and meaning something else, often just the opposite. He also uses **situational irony,** in which something happens that is completely different from what we expect or what we think is appropriate.

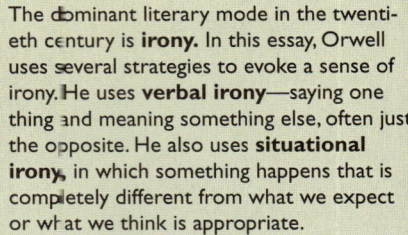

INTERNET

Vocabulary Practice

More About George Orwell

Keyword: LE5 12-7

Irony is a discrepancy between expectations and reality or between appearances and reality.

For more on Irony, see the Handbook of Literary and Historical Terms.

SKILLS FOCUS

Literary Skills Analyze political points of view on a topic. Understand irony.

Reading Skills Identify an author's purpose.

Reading Skills

Identifying the Author's Purpose

The purpose of an **informal essay**—such as this one by Orwell—is often to reveal the personality and opinions of its author. In the first sentence of the essay, Orwell admits that in Burma he "was hated by large numbers of people" because of the British tyranny he represented. This hatred controlled—and at times even tyrannized—Orwell himself. This ironic situation was not Orwell's alone; it was that of most British imperialists living abroad. In this essay, Orwell uses the term *imperialism* rather than *colonialism* to emphasize the tyrannical aspects of British rule. Imperialism connotes a powerful empire's control over another country's people and resources. Orwell's purpose here is twofold: to reveal his own personal dilemma and to reveal the cultural dilemma presented by colonialism itself. As you read, make note of words and phrases Orwell uses to describe these dilemmas.

Background

This essay is set in Burma, a country in Southeast Asia. After a series of wars with Great Britain during the 1800s, Burma finally came under British control in the 1880s. Although given some self-rule in 1937, Burma didn't become fully independent until 1948, after a harsh period of Japanese occupation during World War II. In 1989, the government changed the country's official name to the Union of Myanmar.

Vocabulary Development

supplant (sə·plant′) v.: replace; displace.

labyrinth (lab′ə·rinth′) n.: maze; complex or confusing arrangement.

squalid (skwäl′id) adj.: foul or unclean; wretched.

pretext (prē′tekst′) n.: excuse.

898 Collection 7 The Modern World: 1900 to the Present

Previewing Vocabulary

Ask pairs of students to read and discuss the definition of each of the Vocabulary words from p. 898. Then, suggest that students work together to create mnemonic devices for remembering word meanings or spellings. Sum up the preview by reading the following sentences and asking volunteers to choose the best Vocabulary word to complete each sentence.

1. Living conditions at the refugee camp are incredibly _____. [squalid]
2. I came up with some silly _____ for my lateness. [pretext]
3. Do you think that e-mail will totally _____ letter writing? [supplant]
4. The twisted streets of the Burmese village are like a _____. [labyrinth]

Shooting an Elephant

George Orwell

Elephants carrying men and goods across a river in Nepal (c. 1910).
Getty Images.

In Moulmein, in Lower Burma, I was hated by large numbers of people—the only time in my life that I have been important enough for this to happen to me. I was subdivisional police officer of the town, and in an aimless, petty kind of way anti-European feeling was very bitter. No one had the guts to raise a riot, but if a European woman went through the bazaars alone somebody would probably spit betel juice over her dress. As a police officer I was an obvious target and was baited whenever it seemed safe to do so. When a nimble Burman tripped me up on the football field and the referee (another Burman) looked the other way, the crowd yelled with hideous laughter. This happened more than once. In the end the sneering yellow faces of young men that met me everywhere, the insults hooted after me when I was at a safe distance, got badly on my nerves. The young Buddhist priests were the worst of all. There were several thousands of them in the town and none of them seemed to have anything to do except stand on street corners and jeer at Europeans.

All this was perplexing and upsetting. For at that time I had already made up my mind that imperialism was an evil thing and the sooner I chucked up my job and got out of it the better. Theoretically—and secretly, of course—I was all for the Burmese and all against their oppressors, the British. As for the job I was doing, I hated it more bitterly than I can perhaps make clear. In a job like that you see the dirty work of Empire at close quarters. The wretched prisoners huddling in the stinking cages of the lockups, the gray, cowed faces of the long-term convicts, the scarred buttocks of the men who had been flogged with

DIRECT TEACHING

A Literary Focus

? Irony. What is ironic about this statement? [Possible response: Orwell hates the notion of empire, with its built-in assumptions of power and superiority; in the same breath, however, he expresses a resentful and condescending attitude toward "the evil-spirited little beasts" that he helps to oppress.]

B Literary Focus

? Relating literature to its historical period. What do you learn about the setting here? [At this time, Burma is poor and undeveloped. People live in bamboo huts; fruit is sold in open-air stalls. The Burmese are unarmed.] What is Orwell's purpose in describing the historical setting? [Possible response: He wants to show that the Burmese depend on their British overlords for protection, perhaps even survival. This reality reinforces Orwell's conflicted feelings about colonialism.]

C English-Language Learners

Briticisms. Explain that *constables* is a British term for police officers.

Responses to Boxed Questions

1. The paradox is that Orwell sympathizes with the Burmese desire to be rid of their British oppressors yet he also hates the people who ridicule and abuse him.

2. The topic is the nature of imperialism. The essay will examine the true motives of colonists.

3. Orwell's tone is both humorous and suspenseful. He creates humor by having the mahout go off in the wrong direction; he creates suspense by showing that the Burmese are powerless.

bamboos—all these oppressed me with an intolerable sense of guilt. But I could get nothing into perspective. I was young and ill-educated and I had had to think out my problems in the utter silence that is imposed on every Englishman in the East. I did not even know that the British Empire is dying, still less did I know that it is a great deal better than the younger empires that are going to supplant it. All I knew was that I was stuck between my hatred of the empire I served and my rage against the evil-spirited little beasts who tried to make my job impossible. With one part of my mind I thought of the British Raj[1] as an unbreakable tyranny, as something clamped down, *in saecula saeculorum*,[2] upon the will of prostrate peoples; with another part I thought that the greatest joy in the world would be to drive a bayonet into a Buddhist priest's guts. Feelings like these are the normal by-products of imperialism; ask any Anglo-Indian official, if you can catch him off duty. ❶

One day something happened which in a roundabout way was enlightening. It was a tiny incident in itself, but it gave me a better glimpse than I had had before of the real nature of imperialism—the real motives for which despotic governments act. ❷ Early one morning the subinspector at a police station the other end of the town rang me up on the phone and said that an elephant was ravaging the bazaar. Would I please come and do something about it? I did not know what I could do, but I wanted to see what was happening and I got on to a pony and started out. I took my rifle, an old .44 Winchester and much too small to kill an elephant, but I thought the noise might be useful *in terrorem*.[3] Various Burmans stopped me on the way and told me about the elephant's doings. It was not, of course, a wild elephant, but a tame one which had gone "must."[4] It had been chained up, as tame elephants always are when their attack of "must" is due, but on the previous night it had broken its chain and escaped. Its mahout,[5] the only person who could manage it when it was in that state, had set out in pursuit, but had taken the wrong direction and was now twelve hours' journey away, and in the morning the elephant had suddenly reappeared in the town. The Burmese population had no weapons and were quite helpless against it. It had already destroyed somebody's bamboo hut, killed a cow, and raided some fruit stalls and devoured the stock; also it had met the municipal rubbish van and, when the driver jumped out and took to his heels, had turned the van over and inflicted violences upon it. ❸

The Burmese subinspector and some Indian constables were waiting for me in the quarter where the elephant had been seen. It was a very poor quarter, a labyrinth of squalid bamboo huts, thatched with palm leaf, winding all over a steep hillside. I remember that it was a cloudy,

> **❶ ?** What **paradox**, or seeming contradiction, does Orwell set up in these first two paragraphs?

> **❷ ?** What topic does Orwell identify for the story he is about to tell—and, by extension, for the entire essay?

> **❸ ?** Do you find Orwell's **tone** suspenseful, humorous, or both? Support your ideas with specific words and phrases from the text.

---

1. **Raj** (räj): rule over India. The word is derived from *rajya*, Hindi for "kingdom."
2. ***in saecula saeculorum*** (in sē′kōō·lə sē′kōō·lôr′əm): Latin for "forever and ever" (literally, "into ages of ages").
3. ***in terrorem*** (in ter·ôr′əm): Latin for "for terror." In other words, the gun might serve to frighten the elephant.
4. **must** *n.*: state of frenzy in animals. The word comes from *mast*, Hindi for "intoxicated."
5. **mahout** (mə·hout′) *n.*: elephant keeper. The word derives from *mahaut*, Hindi for "great in measure" and, thus, "important officer."

Vocabulary

supplant (sə·plant′) *v.*: replace; displace.
labyrinth (lab′ə·rinth′) *n.*: maze; complex or confusing arrangement.
squalid (skwäl′id) *adj.*: foul or unclean; wretched.

DIFFERENTIATING INSTRUCTION

Advanced Learners

Enrichment. Suggest that students consider this essay from the point of view of one of the Burmese bystanders (for example, the elephant's owner) and analyze how the essay's main idea changes when events are viewed from a radically different point of view. Students can then discuss how similar political events from current news might be interpreted from other points of view.

stuffy morning at the beginning of the rains. We began questioning the people as to where the elephant had gone and, as usual, failed to get any definite information. That is invariably the case in the East; a story always sounds clear enough at a distance, but the nearer you get to the scene of events the vaguer it becomes. Some of the people said that the elephant had gone in one direction, some said that he had gone in another, some professed not even to have heard of any elephant. I had almost made up my mind that the whole story was a pack of lies, when we heard yells a little distance away. There was a loud, scandalized cry of "Go away, child! Go away this instant!" and an old woman with a switch in her hand came round the corner of the hut, violently shooing away a crowd of naked children. Some more women followed, clicking their tongues and exclaiming; evidently there was something that the children ought not to have seen. I rounded the hut and saw a man's dead body sprawling in the mud. He was an Indian, a black Dravidian coolie,[6] almost naked, and he could not have been dead many minutes. The people said that the elephant had come suddenly upon him round the corner of the hut, caught him with its trunk, put its foot on his back, and ground him into the earth. This was the rainy season and the ground was soft, and his face had scored a trench a foot deep and a couple of yards long. He was lying on his belly with arms crucified and head sharply twisted to one side. His face was coated with mud, the eyes wide open, the teeth bared and grinning with an expression of unendurable agony. (Never tell me, by the way, that the dead look peaceful. Most of the corpses I have seen looked devilish.) The friction of the great beast's foot had stripped the skin from his back as neatly as one skins a rabbit. As soon as I saw the dead man I sent an orderly to a friend's house nearby to borrow an elephant rifle. I had already sent back the pony, not wanting it to go mad with fright and throw me if it smelled the elephant.

The orderly came back in a few minutes with a rifle and five cartridges, and meanwhile some Burmans had arrived and told us that the elephant was in the paddy fields below, only a few hundred yards away. As I started forward practically the whole population of the quarter flocked out of the houses and followed me. They had seen the rifle and were all shouting excitedly that I was going to shoot the elephant. They had not shown much interest in the elephant when he was merely ravaging their homes, but it was different now that he was going to be shot. It was a bit of fun to them, as it would be to an English crowd; besides they wanted the meat. It made me vaguely uneasy. I had no intention of shooting the elephant—I had merely sent for the rifle to defend myself if necessary—and it is always unnerving to have a crowd following you. I marched down the hill, looking and feeling a fool, with the rifle over my shoulder and an ever-growing army of people jostling at my heels. At the bottom, when you got away from the huts, there was a metaled[7] road and beyond that a miry waste of paddy fields a thousand yards across, not yet plowed but soggy from the first rains and dotted with coarse grass. The elephant was standing eight yards from the road, his left side toward us. He took not the slightest notice of the crowd's approach. He was tearing up bunches of grass, beating them against his knees to clean them, and stuffing them into his mouth.

I had halted on the road. As soon as I saw the elephant I knew with perfect certainty that I

---

6. **Dravidian** (drə·vid′ē·ən) **coolie:** *Dravidian* denotes any of several intermixed races living chiefly in southern India and northern Sri Lanka. A coolie is an unskilled laborer. The word is derived from *quli*, Hindi for "hired servant," and has become offensive.

7. **metaled** *v.* used as *adj.*: paved with cinders, stones, or the like.

Direct Teaching

A Literary Focus
Irony. By itself, this statement does not seem ironic. Invite comments about how the statement expresses Orwell's reasoning at that moment; then, have students refer to it as Orwell goes on to show how his reasoning is undermined and how the statement thus proves to be ironic.

B Reading Skills
? Identifying the author's purpose. How does the comparison of the narrator to a conjurer, or magician, help indicate the author's purpose? [Possible response: The narrator feels like people expect extraordinary and powerful action from him. He has come to embody the myth of the all-powerful Empire and cannot free himself from the role in which he has been cast. The comparison helps Orwell show the effect of colonialism on those empowered to carry it out.]

C Advanced Learners
? Recognizing pathos. In rhetoric an emotional appeal such as this one is known as pathos. Why might Orwell compare the elephant to a preoccupied grandmother? [He wants readers to understand his reluctance to shoot the animal.]

Responses to Boxed Questions

5. The elephant seems peaceful, which is ironic because readers have been prepared for a rampaging killer.

6. Possible response: Orwell is trapped because he must maintain the illusion of power invested in an official of the imperial government. To maintain this image, he must ignore his human instincts and shoot the "innocent" elephant.

---

ought not to shoot him. It is a serious matter to shoot a working elephant—it is comparable to destroying a huge and costly piece of machinery—and obviously one ought not to do it if it can possibly be avoided. And at that distance, peacefully eating, the elephant looked no more dangerous than a cow. I thought then and I think now that his attack of "must" was already passing off; in which case he would merely wander harmlessly about until the mahout came back and caught him. Moreover, I did not in the least want to shoot him. I decided that I would watch him for a little while to make sure that he did not turn savage again, and then go home. **5**

> **5** Once the elephant comes into view, what is Orwell's (and your) first impression of the creature? What is *ironic* about this description?

But at that moment I glanced round at the crowd that had followed me. It was an immense crowd, two thousand at the least and growing every minute. It blocked the road for a long distance on either side. I looked at the sea of yellow faces above the garish clothes—faces all happy and excited over this bit of fun, all certain that the elephant was going to be shot. They were watching me as they would watch a conjurer about to perform a trick. They did not like me, but with the magical rifle in my hands I was momentarily worth watching. And suddenly I realized that I should have to shoot the elephant after all. The people expected it of me and I had got to do it; I could feel their two thousand wills pressing me forward, irresistibly. And it was at this moment, as I stood there with the rifle in my hands, that I first grasped the hollowness, the futility of the white man's dominion in the East. Here was I, the white man with his gun, standing in front of the unarmed native crowd—seemingly the leading actor of the piece; but in reality I was only an absurd puppet pushed to and fro by the will of those yellow faces behind. I perceived in this moment that when the white man turns tyrant it is his own freedom that he destroys. He becomes a sort of hollow, posing dummy, the conventionalized figure of a sahib.[8] For it is the condition of his rule that he shall spend his life in trying to impress the "natives," and so in every crisis he has got to do what the "natives" expect of him. He wears a mask, and his face grows to fit it. I had got to shoot the elephant. I had committed myself to doing it when I sent for the rifle. A sahib has got to act like a sahib; he has got to appear resolute, to know his own mind and do definite things. To come all that way, rifle in hand, with two thousand people marching at my heels, and then to trail feebly away, having done nothing—no, that was impossible. The crowd would laugh at me. And my whole life, every white man's life in the East, was one long struggle not to be laughed at. **6**

> **6** Orwell began his essay by remarking that a tiny incident revealed to him the nature of imperialism.
> **?** What is the link between imperialism and shooting the elephant?

But I did not want to shoot the elephant. I watched him beating his bunch of grass against his knees, with that preoccupied grandmotherly air that elephants have. It seemed to me that it would be murder to shoot him. At that age I was not squeamish about killing animals, but I had never shot an elephant and never wanted to. (Somehow it always seems worse to kill a *large* animal.) Besides, there was the beast's owner to be considered. Alive, the elephant was worth at least a hundred pounds; dead, he would only be worth the value of his tusks, five pounds, possibly. But I had got to act quickly. I turned to some experienced-looking Burmans who had been there when we arrived, and asked them how the elephant had been behaving. They all said the same thing: He took no notice of you if

---

8. **sahib** (sä′ib′) *n.*: master; sir. In colonial India the title was used as a sign of respect for a European gentleman.

CONTENT-AREA CONNECTIONS

Geography: The British Empire
Small-group activity. Have students locate and examine a world map showing Britain's Empire in the 1920s. Then, challenge students to use this information to explain the once-famous saying "The sun never sets on the British Empire." Finally, have students offer reasons to explain how a small nation like Britain could have amassed such an empire.

Political Science: Colonialism
Individual activity. Urge students to explore another work by Orwell on a similar subject, such as the short essay "A Hanging" or the longer work *Burmese Days*. Ask students to give a report to the class analyzing what these works reveal about Orwell's attitude toward colonialism. Suggest that students consider whether or not Orwell's attitude changes over time.

you left him alone, but he might charge if you went too close to him.

It was perfectly clear to me what I ought to do. I ought to walk up to within, say, twenty-five yards of the elephant and test his behavior. If he charged, I could shoot; if he took no notice of me, it would be safe to leave him until the mahout came back. But also I knew that I was going to do no such thing. I was a poor shot with a rifle and the ground was soft mud into which one would sink at every step. If the elephant charged and I missed him, I should have about as much chance as a toad under a steamroller. But even then I was not thinking particularly of my own skin, only of the watchful yellow faces behind. For at that moment, with the crowd watching me, I was not afraid in the ordinary sense, as I would have been if I had been alone. A white man mustn't be frightened in front of "natives"; and so, in general, he isn't frightened. The sole thought in my mind was that if anything went wrong those two thousand Burmans would see me pursued, caught, trampled on, and reduced to a grinning corpse like that Indian up the hill. And if that happened it was quite probable that some of them would laugh. That would never do. There was only one alternative. I shoved the cartridges into the magazine and lay down on the road to get a better aim. 7

The crowd grew very still, and a deep, low, happy sigh, as of people who see the theater curtain go up at last, breathed from innumerable throats. They were going to have their bit of fun after all. The rifle was a beautiful German thing with cross-hair sights. I did not then know that in shooting an elephant one would shoot to cut an imaginary bar running from earhole to earhole. I ought, therefore, as the elephant was sideways on, to have aimed straight at his earhole; actually I aimed several inches in front of this, thinking the brain would be further forward.

When I pulled the trigger I did not hear the bang or feel the kick—one never does when a shot goes home—but I heard the devilish roar of glee that went up from the crowd. In that instant, in too short a time, one would have thought, even for the bullet to get there, a mysterious, terrible change had come over the

> 7. Describe Orwell's inner conflict and how he deals with it.

Elephants transporting munitions in Cambodia during the Indochinese War (1954).

DIRECT TEACHING

A Reading Skills

? Identifying the author's purpose. How do these details help Orwell achieve his purpose? [Possible response: The description of the elephant's painful death supports Orwell's negative feelings about colonialism.]

B Political Issue

? Colonialism. How does Orwell's detail about the owner's being "only an Indian" reveal his divided feelings about colonialism? [Possible responses: He quickly dismisses the Burmese as insignificant, yet he hates his job oppressing them. The remark might be ironic, showing Orwell's sympathy for the powerlessness of the colonized people.] How do his mixed emotions relate to the essay's main idea? [Possible response: Colonialism can create ambivalent emotions in the oppressor that are difficult to resolve.]

C Literary Focus

? Irony. Why is Orwell glad that the coolie died? [Possible response: Orwell is glad because it gives him a legal excuse for killing an animal that he killed only to avoid looking foolish.] How does the ending further Orwell's point? [It reconfirms the selfish motive for much of the colonial power's actions.]

Responses to Boxed Questions

8. Significant details include "suddenly stricken, shrunken, immensely old"; "an enormous senility"; and "like a huge rock toppling."

9. Often the law provides only a pretext; it does not ensure that the right thing is done.

elephant. He neither stirred nor fell, but every line of his body had altered. He looked suddenly stricken, shrunken, immensely old, as though the frightful impact of the bullet had paralyzed him without knocking him down. At last, after what seemed a long time—it might have been five seconds, I dare say—he sagged flabbily to his knees. His mouth slobbered. An enormous senility seemed to have settled upon him. One could have imagined him thousands of years old. I fired again into the same spot. At the second shot he did not collapse but climbed with desperate slowness to his feet and stood **A** weakly upright, with legs sagging and head drooping. I fired a third time. That was the shot that did for him. You could see the agony of it jolt his whole body and knock the last remnant of strength from his legs. But in falling he seemed for a moment to rise, for as his hind legs collapsed beneath him he seemed to tower upward like a huge rock toppling, his trunk reaching skyward like a tree. He trumpeted, for the first and only time. And then down he came, his belly toward me, with a crash that seemed to shake the ground even where I lay. **8**

8 ? What details in the description of the shooting seem most significant?

I got up. The Burmans were already racing past me across the mud. It was obvious that the elephant would never rise again, but he was not dead. He was breathing very rhythmically with long rattling gasps, his great mound of a side painfully rising and falling. His mouth was wide open—I could see far down into caverns of pale pink throat. I waited a long time for him to die, but his breathing did not weaken. Finally I fired my two remaining shots into the spot where I thought his heart must be. The thick blood welled out of him like red velvet, but still he did not die. His body did not even jerk when the shots hit him, the tortured breathing continued without a pause. He was dying, very slowly and in great agony, but in some world remote from me where not even a bullet could damage him further. I felt that I had got to put an end to that dreadful noise. It seemed dreadful to see the great beast lying there, powerless to move and yet powerless to die, and not even to be able to finish him. I sent back for my small rifle and poured shot after shot into his heart and down his throat. They seemed to make no impression. The tortured gasps continued as steadily as the ticking of a clock.

In the end I could not stand it any longer and went away. I heard later that it took him half an hour to die. Burmans were bringing dahs[9] and baskets even before I left, and I was told they had stripped his body almost to the bones by the afternoon.

Afterward, of course, there were endless **B** discussions about the shooting of the elephant. The owner was furious, but he was only an Indian and could do nothing. Besides, legally I had done the right thing, for a mad elephant has to be killed, like a mad dog, if its owner fails to control it. Among the Europeans opinion was divided. The older men said I was right, the younger men said it was a damn shame to shoot an elephant for killing a coolie, because an elephant was worth more than any damn Coringhee[10] coolie. And afterward I was very glad that the coolie had been killed; it put me legally in the right and it gave me a sufficient pretext for shooting the **C** elephant. I often wondered whether any of the others grasped that I had done it solely to avoid looking a fool. **9** ■

9 ? What implicit, or suggested, idea about the law does Orwell express?

---

9. **dahs** (däz) *n. pl.*: large carving knives.
10. **Coringhee** (kôr·iŋ'ē): port in southeastern India.

Vocabulary
pretext (prē'tekst') *n.*: excuse.

904   Collection 7   The Modern World: 1900 to the Present

Check Test: True-False

Monitoring students' progress. Guide the class in answering these questions.

1. The narrator enforces a colonial policy that he strongly supports. [F]
2. The narrator sends for an elephant rifle to protect himself against an animal that he thinks is dangerous. [T]
3. The Burmese protest the shooting of the elephant. [F]
4. Because the narrator is a good shot, he kills the elephant quickly and humanely. [F]

Response and Analysis

Reading Check
1. What problem is Orwell asked to solve?
2. About how big is the crowd following Orwell? Why does he say they have come along?
3. When Orwell finds the elephant, what two reasons does he give for not wanting to shoot it?
4. How does the animal react when shot?

Thinking Critically
5. What seems to be Orwell's attitude toward the Burmese? Do you think he embodies the perspective of a colonizer? Use the details you recorded in your reading notes as well as other evidence to support your answer.
6. Explain in your own words the meaning of Orwell's **ironic** insight that tyrants destroy their own freedom. Then, identify three other ironies contained in this essay.
7. What does this **essay** reveal about Orwell's code of ethics or behavior as a young police officer in Burma? What does it reveal about the true nature of colonialism? Are these insights related? Explain.
8. There are two Orwells in this essay: the one acting and the one looking back, narrating the action. Discuss the differences between the two observers, using examples from the text. How does the older Orwell feel about the younger one?
9. The elephant has tremendous symbolic importance in this essay. What political idea or assumption might the elephant **symbolize**? In other words, what political idea was the young Orwell confronted with, confused by, and ultimately weakened by? In your own words, explain your interpretation of the elephant as a political symbol. Cite details from the text to support your interpretation.

Extending and Evaluating
10. Orwell goes to great lengths to describe the shooting and the painfully slow death of the elephant. In your opinion, is such gruesome detail necessary? Why? What does it add to or take away from the essay?

WRITING

Words to Dwell On
Review Orwell's essay, and find one passage that you think is especially important, controversial, or even upsetting. Write a brief **essay** in which you cite the passage and explain why you have chosen it. In your essay, be sure to describe your response to the passage, and state whether you think it relates to any situation in today's society.

Vocabulary Development
True or False?

Identify each of the following statements as true or false, and briefly explain your answer:

1. It is a good idea to supplant unhealthy habits with healthy ones.
2. A direct route from one place to another is sometimes called a labyrinth.
3. A room that has been thoroughly cleaned would be described as squalid.
4. A pretext is usually offered by someone who is honest.

SKILLS FOCUS

Literary Skills
Analyze political points of view on a topic. Analyze irony.

Reading Skills
Identify an author's purpose.

Writing Skills
Write a response to an essay.

Vocabulary Skills
Demonstrate word knowledge.

INDEPENDENT PRACTICE

Response and Analysis

6. Tyrants become role-players who must act according to the expectations of those they oppress. Other examples of irony include Orwell's enforcing a political policy that he does not support; the crowd's not knowing that Orwell does not want to shoot the elephant; and Orwell's not knowing how to kill an elephant and thus botching the job.
7. Possible answer: Orwell has mixed feelings about imperialism and his role as its agent, yet he follows the rules and acts as he is directed. His actions suggest that imperialism is inherently contradictory.
8. The younger Orwell gets caught up in the situation; he is aware of the contradictions but cannot step outside the expectations of role and race. The narrator, the older Orwell, looks back with greater perspective and maturity and displays a keener awareness of the ironies of his position.
9. The elephant in its destructive romp may symbolize what the British Empire was doing to the parts of the world over which it held power—destroying parts of colonial culture as well as many of the colonized people.

Extending and Evaluating
10. Possible answer: By showing the elephant's protracted death, Orwell gains the reader's sympathy for his position.

Vocabulary Development
Possible Answers
1. T; *supplant* is a synonym for *replace*.
2. F; a *labyrinth* is a route so twisted as to be like a maze.
3. F; a *squalid* room is filthy and in need of cleaning.
4. F; a *pretext* is an excuse, something an honest person would probably avoid using.

Reading Check
1. He is asked to rid the bazaar of a mad (crazed) elephant.
2. At least two thousand people follow. Orwell says that they want the fun of seeing the elephant shot; they also want its meat.
3. To shoot a working elephant is like destroying expensive machinery; besides, the elephant's fit of madness has passed.
4. The elephant dies slowly and in such agony that Orwell cannot bear to watch.

Thinking Critically
5. Possible answer: Orwell does not believe that the British should rule the Burmese, but he is angry with individual Burmese who taunt him on the job. By referring to the Burmese as "little beasts," he shares the colonizers' perspective.

Vocabulary Development

Practice

- *Coup d'état,* from French, originally meant "blow to the head" and now means "a sudden and decisive action in politics, especially one effecting a change of government illegally or by force."

- *Détente,* from the French *detente,* originally meant "a loosening, to release." The word now means "an easing of tension between rivals."

- *Electorate* is from the Latin *electoratus.* During the Holy Roman Empire, the word referred to the rank or territory of an elector, a German prince entitled to help choose the emperor. *Electorate* now means "all those qualified to vote in an election."

- *Monarchy,* from French, originally meant "alone, first" and now means "a government ruled by a monarch or king."

- *Veto,* from Latin, originally meant "forbid" and now means "the power vested in one branch of government to cancel the decisions of another branch."

- *Fascist,* from the Italian *fascismo* and *fascio,* originally meant "bundles, group." Now *fascist* means "a person who believes in a dictatorial-type government."

Vocabulary Development

The Etymology of Political Science and Historical Terms

New words and phrases are introduced into our vocabulary almost every day. George Orwell's novel *1984* gave the world a number of now familiar political phrases, such as "thought police" and "Big Brother is watching you." Words coined by Orwell include *double-think,* which means "illogical thinking that distorts the truth to make it more acceptable," and *newspeak,* which means "deliberately ambiguous and deceptive talk used by government officials."

Many political science and historical terms have been borrowed from other languages. Consider the following terms:

Term	Word origin	Meaning
apartheid	Afrikaans, "the state of being separate"	official South African policy of strict racial segregation and discrimination (c. 1948–1991)
democracy	Greek (*demokratia*)	government in which all citizens take part and limit the power of rulers
constitution	Latin (*constituere*)	document outlining the fundamental laws and principles that govern a nation
capitalism	Latin (*capitalis*)	economic system in which private individuals invest money that is earned to produce profits
governor	Latin (*gubernator*), "a pilot"	elected head of a state in the United States
imperialism	Latin (*imperialis*), "empire"	domination of a powerful nation over the political, economic, and cultural affairs of another nation or region
parliament	Medieval English from French *parler,* "to speak"	national legislative body (as in Great Britain)
laissez-faire	French, "let people do as they please"	theory that opposes government regulation of economic matters

PRACTICE

Vocabulary Skills
Understand etymologies.

Use a dictionary to learn the history of the political science and historical terms listed below. Determine the language the word is borrowed from, its original meaning, and its current meaning.

coup d'état   détente   electorate
monarchy   veto   fascist

906 Collection 7 The Modern World: 1900 to the Present

ASSESSING

Assessment
- Holt Assessment: Literature, Reading, and Vocabulary

RETEACHING

For a lesson reteaching irony, see **Reteaching,** p. 1129A.

Doris Lessing
(1919–)
Zimbabwe

Doris Lessing was born in Persia (now Iran) to British parents who had fled England to escape what they saw as its narrowness and provincialism. When she was five, her father gave up his job running a bank, and the family moved to a three-thousand-acre farm in Southern Rhodesia (now Zimbabwe). The farm employed some thirty to fifty black African laborers, each of whom earned the equivalent of about $1.50 a month and who lived in mud huts with no sanitation.

In Africa, Lessing's mother was homesick for England and often ill, while her father grew increasingly eccentric. Lessing describes her own childhood as "hellishly lonely"; the nearest neighbor was miles away. Only as an adult did she appreciate that her solitude had fostered a fine education, since the lack of company allowed her to spend her time slowly reading the classics of European and American fiction.

At fourteen, Lessing left school and went to work in Salisbury, the capital of Rhodesia, first as a nursemaid and then as a stenographer and telephone operator. The city had a white population of about ten thousand and a larger black population that Lessing discovered "didn't count." When her first marriage collapsed, she entered radical politics. At twenty-six, she married a second time, but that marriage also ended in divorce.

"I can't remember a time when I didn't want to come to England," she later recalled. In 1949, she left Africa for England with her two-year-old son and the manuscript of her first novel, *The Grass Is Singing* (1950). Tracing a complex relationship between a white farmer's wife and her black servant, the book commanded attention as one of the earliest novels about Africa's racial problems. The short stories collected in Lessing's *African Stories* (1964) also take place in the Africa of her childhood.

Lessing's most widely read and discussed book is probably *The Golden Notebook* (1962), an ambitious, complexly structured work that combines fiction, parody, and factual reporting to explore Lessing's concerns with politics, mental illness, and the problems facing women in modern life. Another well-known book, *Briefing for a Descent into Hell* (1971), introduces readers to what Lessing calls "inner-space fiction," in which an individual mental breakdown is related to a wider social breakdown. Lessing also continues to write nonfiction works, and in 1994, she published *Under My Skin*, the first volume of her autobiography.

In all of Lessing's work, there is evidence of the responsibility she feels as a writer to be "an instrument of change." "It is not merely a question of preventing evil," she says, "but of strengthening a vision of a good which may defeat the evil."

For Independent Reading
The following stories by Lessing are classics:
- "A Sunrise on the Veld"
- "Through the Tunnel"

SKILLS FOCUS, pp. 907–915

Grade-Level Skills

■ **Literary Skills**
Analyze political points of view on a topic.

■ **Literary Skills**
Analyze the way the theme of a selection represents a comment on life.

■ **Reading Skills**
Identify historical context.

More About the Writer
Background. Lessing is convinced of the human ability to change, even though she expresses some short-term pessimism about human limitations. She says, "[Humans] are supremely equipped to survive, to adapt, and even in the long run to start thinking." In addition, Lessing has an abiding sense of the writer's responsibility. "Once a writer has a feeling of responsibility as a human being, for the other human beings he influences," she notes, ". . . he must become a humanist, and an instrument of change. . . ."

For Independent Reading

■ "A Sunrise on the Veld," another of Lessing's brilliantly crafted tales, explores the issue of taking responsibility for one's actions.

■ How do we prove our maturity? In "Through the Tunnel," Jerry sets a seemingly impossible test for himself. Will he survive?

RESOURCES: READING

Planning
- *One-Stop Planner* CD-ROM with ExamView Test Generator

Differentiating Instruction
- Holt Reading Solutions
- The Holt Reader
- Supporting Instruction in Spanish
- Audio CD Library, Selections and Summaries in Spanish

Vocabulary
- Vocabulary Development

Grammar and Language
- Daily Language Activities

Assessment
- Holt Assessment: Literature, Reading, and Vocabulary
- *One-Stop Planner* CD-ROM with ExamView Test Generator

- Holt Online Assessment

Internet
- go.hrw.com (Keyword: LE5 12-7)
- Elements of Literature Online

Media
- Audio CD Library
- Audio CD Library, Selections and Summaries in Spanish

PRETEACHING

Summary at grade level

The Farquars, a white couple living in South Africa, finally have a child, a son whom they name Teddy. Their black cook, Gideon, lovingly nurtures the boy. From the beginning, Gideon knows that there is an unbridgeable gap between Teddy and himself because of their races, but their friendship does not cool until the child dismisses Gideon's own son as being "only a black boy." One day, a snake spits in Teddy's eyes. As the boy begins to go blind, Gideon (who is the son of a famous medicine man) uses a root to cure him. When the story spreads, a white scientist arrives to ask Gideon to share the remedy for the benefit of humanity. To the family's consternation, Gideon at first refuses and then leads them to a plant that they have no confidence is the one that he used. The whites do not understand that Gideon's knowledge of herbal medicine is part of the inherited culture of his people and that the Farquars and the scientist are insulting him by expecting him to divulge it.

Selection Starter

Build background. Students will understand and appreciate the story better if they know the early colonial history of Rhodesia (now Zimbabwe). Explain that when British colonists arrived in the country they called Rhodesia (named for British financier Cecil Rhodes) in the late 1800s, they seized the country's most fertile, productive farmland for themselves. Africans were removed from their ancestral homelands to communal lands, where the soil was poor and raising crops was difficult. The displaced African farmers became a source of cheap labor in cities and mines. As a result, the white minority enjoyed a high standard of living while the black majority barely scraped by.

Before You Read

No Witchcraft for Sale

Political Points of View
Quickwrite

The upcoming story asks troubling, complex questions about cultural conflict. Some of its cultural clashes are obvious, some are bridged by the unifying force of deep affection, and some remain mysterious—for the people involved and perhaps for us. Do you think that some cultural differences cannot be bridged, no matter how much goodwill the parties bring to the encounter? Or do you think that with enough effort, people can truly understand and appreciate one another's grievances, beliefs, and aspirations? Write down a few of your thoughts on these questions.

Literary Focus
Theme

Stories can have many threads. A wide assortment of ideas may be conveyed through characters' attitudes, through conflicts and their outcomes, through symbols, or even through a title. Despite the variety of ideas a reader may glean from a story, one dominant, central idea, or **theme**, will unify the work.

INTERNET
Vocabulary Practice
Keyword: LE5 12-7

> A **theme** is the central idea, or insight, embodied in a work of literature.
>
> For more on Theme, see the Handbook of Literary and Historical Terms.

Literary Skills Understand theme.
Reading Skills Identify historical context.

Reading Skills
Identifying Historical Context

The time and place in which a writer lives often have a direct bearing on a work's themes, characters, and events—even if the work itself is set in a different time or place. This tale from Doris Lessing's *African Stories* takes place in Southern Rhodesia at a time when that South African country was still firmly under British rule. When Lessing wrote the story in 1964, however, Southern Rhodesia was demanding independence from Britain. The white minority in Southern Rhodesia was eager to establish its own government—a government that would continue the policy of denying rights to black citizens. Britain, which had come to support the voting rights of blacks in Southern Rhodesia, refused to grant independence. As you read, consider how the political climate in which Lessing wrote this story may have influenced her portrayal of the earlier time period. Record your ideas.

Background

Civil war tore apart the country of Southern Rhodesia after it declared independence from Britain in 1965. After years of fighting between black nationalists and government troops, Southern Rhodesia emerged as the republic of Zimbabwe under the leadership of a black African, Robert Mugabe (moo·gäb'ē), in 1980.

Vocabulary Development

reverently (rev'ə·rənt·lē) *adv.*: with deep respect, love, or awe, as for something sacred.

inevitable (in·ev'i·tə·bəl) *adj.*: certain to happen; unavoidable.

efficacy (ef'i·kə·sē) *n.*: ability to produce a desired effect; effectiveness.

perfunctory (pər·fuŋk'tə·rē) *adj.*: halfhearted; indifferent.

annulled (ə·nuld') *v.*: did away with; canceled.

perversely (pər·vurs'lē) *adv.*: disagreeably; contrarily.

908 Collection 7 The Modern World: 1900 to the Present

Previewing Vocabulary

Pair students and have them categorize the Vocabulary words on p. 908, perhaps by structural attributes such as affixes, parts of speech, or origin. Then, have students complete each of the following sentences with the appropriate Vocabulary word.

1. Teddy's apology was halfhearted and _____. [perfunctory]
2. Gideon expects his traditions to be treated respectfully, even _____. [reverently]
3. Disagreeably, Teddy was _____ rude to Gideon. [perversely]
4. Some insults cannot be _____ by apologies. [annulled]
5. It was _____ that someone would get hurt in the dangerous jungle. [inevitable]
6. The plant's _____ was proven when the wound healed. [efficacy]

No Witchcraft for Sale

Doris Lessing

The Farquars had been childless for years when little Teddy was born; and they were touched by the pleasure of their servants, who brought presents of fowls and eggs and flowers to the homestead when they came to rejoice over the baby, exclaiming with delight over his downy golden head and his blue eyes. They congratulated Mrs. Farquar as if she had achieved a very great thing, and she felt that she had—her smile for the lingering, admiring natives was warm and grateful.

Later, when Teddy had his first haircut, Gideon the cook picked up the soft gold tufts from the ground, and held them reverently in his hand. Then he smiled at the little boy and said: "Little Yellow Head." That became the native name for the child. Gideon and Teddy were great friends from the first. When Gideon had finished his work, he would lift Teddy on his shoulders to the shade of a big tree, and play with him there, forming curious little toys from twigs and leaves and grass, or shaping animals from wetted soil. When Teddy learned to walk it was often Gideon who crouched before him, clucking encouragement, finally catching him when he fell, tossing him up in the air till they both became breathless with laughter. Mrs. Farquar was fond of the old cook because of his love for her child.

There was no second baby; and one day Gideon said: "Ah, missus, missus, the Lord above sent this one; Little Yellow Head is the most good thing we have in our house." Because of that "we" Mrs. Farquar felt a warm impulse toward her cook; and at the end of the month she raised his wages. He had been with her now for several years; he was one of the few natives who had his wife and children in the compound and never wanted to go home to his kraal,[1] which was some hundreds of miles away. Sometimes a small piccanin[2] who had been born the same time as Teddy, could be seen peering from the edge of the bush, staring in awe at the little white boy with his miraculous fair hair and Northern blue eyes. The two little children would gaze at each other with a wide, interested gaze, and once Teddy put out his hand curiously to touch the black child's cheeks and hair.

Gideon, who was watching, shook his head wonderingly, and said: "Ah, missus, these are both children, and one will grow up to be a baas,[3] and one will be a servant"; and Mrs. Farquar smiled and said sadly, "Yes, Gideon, I was thinking the same." She sighed. "It is God's will," said Gideon, who was a mission boy.[4] The Farquars were very religious people; and this shared feeling about God bound servant and masters even closer together.

Teddy was about six years old when he was given a scooter, and discovered the intoxications of speed. All day he would fly around the homestead, in and out of flowerbeds, scattering squawking chickens and irritated dogs, finishing with a wide dizzying arc into the kitchen door. There he would cry: "Gideon, look at me!" And Gideon would laugh and say: "Very clever, Little Yellow Head." Gideon's youngest son, who was

---

1. **kraal** (kräl): South African village.
2. **piccanin** (pik′ə·nin): black African child. Derived from *pequeno* (pā·kā′nōō), Portuguese for "small," the term is often considered offensive.
3. **baas** (bäs): Afrikaans for "master." Afrikaans, a language developed from seventeenth-century Dutch, is spoken in South Africa.
4. **mission boy**: one educated by Christian missionaries.

Vocabulary
reverently (rev′ə·rənt·lē) *adv.*: with deep respect, love, or awe, as for something sacred.

DIRECT TEACHING

VIEWING THE ART

The culture of South Africa today includes both modern and traditional elements. For instance, some South African people utilize modern technology and retain a faith in sangomas, what westerners might call witch doctors.

Activity. A South African might immediately see the mixture of tradition and modernization in this picture, since Neverdie Mushwana, one of the most famous of the sangomas, is standing next to a car. What other elements in the photo suggest a mixture of the traditional and the modern? [Students may identify the snake wrapped around a man who looks like a medical doctor and the juxtaposition of the traditional-looking building and the printed sign indicating a post office box number.]

Neverdie Mushwana, a South African "witch doctor," in front of his home, with one of his snakes. Tzaneen, South Africa (March 1997).
Juhan KUUS/SIPA Press.

DIFFERENTIATING INSTRUCTION

English-Language Learners
Be sure students understand that Gideon's dialogue reflects the dialect of English spoken by black Rhodesians at the time that the story takes place. Direct students to the footnotes to learn the pronunciation and meaning of the dialect words. You may wish to begin reading the story aloud. Then, arrange students in small groups of mixed proficiency to continue reading aloud.

Special Education Students
For lessons designed for special education students, see *Holt Reading Solutions*.

now a herdsboy, came especially up from the compound to see the scooter. He was afraid to come near it, but Teddy showed off in front of him. "Piccanin," shouted Teddy, "get out of my way!" And he raced in circles around the black child until he was frightened, and fled back to the bush.

"Why did you frighten him?" asked Gideon, gravely reproachful.

Teddy said defiantly: "He's only a black boy," and laughed. Then, when Gideon turned away from him without speaking, his face fell. Very soon he slipped into the house and found an orange and brought it to Gideon, saying: "This is for you." He could not bring himself to say he was sorry; but he could not bear to lose Gideon's affection either. Gideon took the orange unwillingly and sighed. "Soon you will be going away to school, Little Yellow Head," he said wonderingly, "and then you will be grown up." He shook his head gently and said, "And that is how our lives go." He seemed to be putting a distance between himself and Teddy, not because of resentment, but in the way a person accepts something inevitable. The baby had lain in his arms and smiled up into his face: The tiny boy had swung from his shoulders and played with him by the hour. Now Gideon would not let his flesh touch the flesh of the white child. He was kind, but there was a grave formality in his voice that made Teddy pout and sulk away. Also, it made him into a man: With Gideon he was polite, and carried himself formally, and if he came into the kitchen to ask for something, it was in the way a white man uses toward a servant, expecting to be obeyed.

But on the day that Teddy came staggering into the kitchen with his fists to his eyes, shrieking with pain, Gideon dropped the pot full of hot soup that he was holding, rushed to the child, and forced aside his fingers. "A snake!" he exclaimed. Teddy had been on his scooter, and had come to a rest with his foot on the side of a big tub of plants. A tree snake, hanging by its tail from the roof, had spat full into his eyes. Mrs. Farquar came running when she heard the commotion. "He'll go blind," she sobbed, holding Teddy close against her. "Gideon, he'll go blind!" Already the eyes, with perhaps half an hour's sight left in them, were swollen up to the size of fists: Teddy's small white face was distorted by great purple oozing protuberances.[5] Gideon said: "Wait a minute, missus, I'll get some medicine." He ran off into the bush.

Mrs. Farquar lifted the child into the house and bathed his eyes with permanganate.[6] She had scarcely heard Gideon's words; but when she saw that her remedies had no effect at all, and remembered how she had seen natives with no sight in their eyes, because of the spitting of a snake, she began to look for the return of her cook, remembering what she heard of the efficacy of native herbs. She stood by the window, holding the terrified, sobbing little boy in her arms, and peered helplessly into the bush. It was not more than a few minutes before she saw Gideon come bounding back, and in his hand he held a plant.

"Do not be afraid, missus," said Gideon, "this will cure Little Yellow Head's eyes." He stripped the leaves from the plant, leaving a small white fleshy root. Without even washing it, he put the root in his mouth, chewed it vigorously, and then held the spittle there while he took the child forcibly from Mrs. Farquar. He gripped Teddy down between his knees, and pressed the balls of his thumbs into the swollen eyes, so that the child screamed and Mrs. Farquar cried out in protest: "Gideon, Gideon!" But Gideon took no notice.

---

5. **protuberances** (prō·tōō′bər·əns·iz) *n. pl.:* swellings; bulges.
6. **permanganate** (pər·maŋ′gə·nāt′) *n.:* dark purple chemical compound used as a disinfectant.

Vocabulary
inevitable (in·ev′i·tə·bəl) *adj.:* certain to happen; unavoidable.
efficacy (ef′i·kə·sē) *n.:* ability to produce a desired effect; effectiveness.

DIRECT TEACHING

A Literary Focus

Theme. This passage is central to the development of Lessing's theme. Why is this moment so significant? [Possible response: This is the most blatant example so far of racial conflict and injustice. Teddy's inability to apologize to Gideon shows that Teddy regards Gideon and his son as inferiors and shows the white Rhodesians' lack of concern for the ramifications of their behavior on the black population whose lands they have appropriated.] What theme does this incident reveal? [Possible response: In this setting, racial discrimination is learned early in life.]

B Literary Focus

Symbolism. Why do you think Lessing uses an injury to eyesight as the pivotal plot event? What might this incident symbolize? [Possible response: Physical blindness becomes a metaphor for racial blindness. The whites are blind to the humanity and dignity of the blacks, whom they have reduced to a servant class in their own homeland.]

C Reading Skills

Identifying historical context. How does this incident affect the accepted relationship, under colonialism, between Mrs. Farquar and Gideon? [Possible response: Mrs. Farquar, who usually is in a position of power over Gideon, suddenly is totally reliant upon her servant, for Gideon holds Teddy's eyesight in his hands.]

CONTENT-AREA CONNECTIONS

Science: Spitting Snakes
Paired activity. Partner students to research and share information about the species of spitting snake that attacked Teddy. Students should learn whether the snake's venom could cause blindness, and, if so, how. In addition, students may want to research information about various remedies for snakebite.

Culture: Traditional Healers
Individual activity. Explain that healers like Gideon did not disappear with Africa's decolonization. Invite students to research the role of traditional healers in modern Zimbabwe. What are some of the herbal medicines they dispense? What are some of the chronic illnesses they treat? How are they licensed?

DIRECT TEACHING

A Reading Skills

❓ Identifying historical context. Why might the Farquars feel unable to express their gratitude to Gideon? [Possible response: In their society, Gideon is their inferior. Giving him presents and an increase in wages just confirms his inferior position.]

B Literary Focus

❓ Theme. Why might the Africans withhold the truth about their plants' medicinal properties? [Possible responses: White people, in general, do not respect the Africans or their traditions, including those relating to healing. For the Africans, therefore, giving whites the knowledge of their healing plants would be like giving up part of their culture to those who would not appreciate the gift.]

C Reading Skills

❓ Comparing and contrasting. How does the scientist's motivation for finding the cure compare with the Farquars' motivation? [Possible response: The Farquars seem motivated simply by a desire to share the "miracle" cure, but the scientist is motivated by the desire to profit from it.]

A He knelt over the writhing child, pushing back the puffy lids till chinks of eyeball showed, and then he spat hard, again and again, into first one eye, and then the other. He finally lifted Teddy gently into his mother's arms, and said: "His eyes will get better." But Mrs. Farquar was weeping with terror, and she could hardly thank him: It was impossible to believe that Teddy could keep his sight. In a couple of hours the swellings were gone: The eyes were inflamed and tender but Teddy could see. Mr. and Mrs. Farquar went to Gideon in the kitchen and thanked him over and over again. They felt helpless because of their gratitude: It seemed they could do nothing to express it. They gave Gideon presents for his wife and children, and a big increase in wages, but these things could not pay for Teddy's now completely cured eyes. Mrs. Farquar said: "Gideon, God chose you as an instrument for His goodness," and Gideon said: "Yes, missus, God is very good."

   Now, when such a thing happens on a farm, it cannot be long before everyone hears of it. Mr. and Mrs. Farquar told their neighbors and the story was discussed from one end of the district to the other. The bush is full of secrets. No one can live in Africa, or at least on the veld,[7] without learning very soon that there is an ancient wisdom of leaf and soil and season—and, too, perhaps most important of all, of the darker tracts of the human mind—which is the black man's heritage. Up and down the district people were telling anecdotes, reminding each other of things that had happened to them.

   "But I saw it myself, I tell you. It was a puff-adder bite. The kaffir's[8] arm was swollen to the elbow, like a great shiny black bladder. He was groggy after half a minute. He was dying. Then suddenly a kaffir walked out of the bush with his hands full of green stuff. He smeared something on the place, and next day my boy was back at work, and all you could see was two small punctures in the skin."

   This was the kind of tale they told. And, as always, with a certain amount of exasperation, because while all of them knew that in the bush B of Africa are waiting valuable drugs locked in bark, in simple-looking leaves, in roots, it was impossible to ever get the truth about them from the natives themselves.

   The story eventually reached town; and perhaps it was at a sundowner party,[9] or some such function, that a doctor, who happened to be there, challenged it. "Nonsense," he said. "These things get exaggerated in the telling. We are always checking up on this kind of story, and we draw a blank every time."

   Anyway, one morning there arrived a strange car at the homestead, and out stepped one of the workers from the laboratory in town, with cases full of test tubes and chemicals.

   Mr. and Mrs. Farquar were flustered and pleased and flattered. They asked the scientist to lunch, and they told the story all over again, for the hundredth time. Little Teddy was there too, his blue eyes sparkling with health, to prove the truth of it. The scientist explained how humanity might benefit if this new drug could be offered for sale; and the Farquars were even C more pleased: They were kind, simple people, who liked to think of something good coming about because of them. But when the scientist began talking of the money that might result, their manner showed discomfort. Their feelings over the miracle (that was how they thought of it) were so strong and deep and religious, that it was distasteful to them to think of money. The scientist, seeing their faces, went back to his first

---

7. **veld** *n.*: in South Africa, open country with very few bushes or trees; grassland. *Veld*, also spelled *veldt*, is Afrikaans for "field."
8. **kaffir's** (kaf´ərz): *Kaffir* is a contemptuous term for a black African, derived from *kāfir*, Arabic for "infidel."
9. **sundowner party:** British colloquial term for "cocktail party." The term derives from the British custom of gathering for drinks at sunset.

912 Collection 7 The Modern World: 1900 to the Present

SKILLS REVIEW

Analyzing the relevance of setting. Remind students that the setting of a story includes not only the time and place but also the customs and attitudes of the characters. In the case of "No Witchcraft for Sale," the unjust colonial society has created a deep racial chasm between the "haves" (the white settlers) and the "have-nots" (the black natives). Discuss these questions about Lessing's setting:

- What are the place and time of this story? [Rhodesia in the mid-1960s] How important is this setting? [It is important because it explains why the characters from different races have difficulty communicating.]

- How does Teddy show that he is part of the "white" setting of the story? [At a young age, he learns to treat Gideon as a servant instead of a friend and he refers to Gideon's son as "only a black boy."]

- What customs that make up the story's setting create friction when the Big Doctor arrives? [the condescending way that the Big Doctor expects Gideon to reveal his secret; the fact that he offers Gideon a small present but he expects to make a lot of money]

point, which was the advancement of humanity. He was perhaps a trifle <u>perfunctory</u>: It was not the first time he had come salting the tail of a fabulous bush secret.[10]

Eventually, when the meal was over, the Farquars called Gideon into their living room and explained to him that this baas, here, was a Big Doctor from the Big City, and he had come all that way to see Gideon. At this Gideon seemed afraid; he did not understand; and Mrs. Farquar explained quickly that it was because of the wonderful thing he had done with Teddy's eyes that the Big Baas had come.

Gideon looked from Mrs. Farquar to Mr. Farquar, and then at the little boy, who was showing great importance because of the occasion. At last he said grudgingly: "The Big Baas want to know what medicine I used?" He spoke incredulously, as if he could not believe his old friends could so betray him. Mr. Farquar began explaining how a useful medicine could be made out of the root, and how it could be put on sale, and how thousands of people, black and white, up and down the continent of Africa, could be saved by the medicine when that spitting snake filled their eyes with poison. Gideon listened, his eyes bent on the ground, the skin of his forehead puckering in discomfort. When Mr. Farquar had finished he did not reply. The scientist, who all this time had been leaning back in a big chair, sipping his coffee and smiling with skeptical good humor, chipped in and explained all over again, in different words, about the making of drugs and the progress of science. Also, he offered Gideon a present.

There was silence after this further explanation, and then Gideon remarked indifferently that he could not remember the root. His face was sullen and hostile, even when he looked at the Farquars, whom he usually treated like old friends. They were beginning to feel annoyed;

---

10. **salting ... bush secret:** allusion to the ironic advice given to children, about catching a bird by putting salt on its tail. In other words, the scientist knows his search may be futile.

---

and this feeling <u>annulled</u> the guilt that had been sprung into life by Gideon's accusing manner. They were beginning to feel that he was unreasonable. But it was at that moment that they all realized he would never give in. The magical drug would remain where it was, unknown and useless except for the tiny scattering of Africans who had the knowledge, natives who might be digging a ditch for the municipality in a ragged shirt and a pair of patched shorts, but who were still born to healing, hereditary healers, being the nephews or sons of the old witch doctors whose ugly masks and bits of bone and all the uncouth properties of magic were the outward signs of real power and wisdom.

The Farquars might tread on that plant fifty times a day as they passed from house to garden, from cow kraal to mealie[11] field, but they would never know it.

But they went on persuading and arguing, with all the force of their exasperation; and Gideon continued to say that he could not remember, or that there was no such root, or that it was the wrong season of the year, or that it wasn't the root itself, but the spit from his mouth that had cured Teddy's eyes. He said all these things one after another, and seemed not to care they were contradictory. He was rude and stubborn. The Farquars could hardly recognize their gentle, lovable old servant in this ignorant, <u>perversely</u> obstinate African, standing there in

---

11. **mealie** *n.*: corn.

Vocabulary

perfunctory (pər·fuŋk′tə·rē) *adj.*: halfhearted; indifferent.
annulled (ə·nuld′) *v.*: did away with; canceled.
perversely (pər·vurs′lē) *adv.*: disagreeably; contrarily.

READING MINI-LESSON

Developing Word-Attack Skills
Remind students that breaking a word into parts is a useful strategy when dealing with long words. With some words, you can separate prefixes and suffixes and then deal with the word part with remains. Demonstrate this using the selection word *protuberance*.
- Identify *pro–* and *–ance*.
- Recognize that the word part *tuber* requires a long vowel sound: /tōō′bər/.
- Put the parts together to read the word: /prō·tōō′bər·əns/.

Activity. Have students divide these words into word parts to make them easier to read.
1. perfunctory [per funct ory]
2. indestructible [in de struct ible]
3. neocolonialism [neo colonial ism]
4. subarachnoid [sub arach noid]
5. procrastinate [pro cras ti nate]

Once upon a Time

Nadine Gordimer

Untitled (1982) by Jannis Kounellis. Feather River travertine, cast plaster, and steel.

Someone has written to ask me to contribute to an anthology of stories for children. I reply that I don't write children's stories; and he writes back that at a recent congress/book fair/seminar a certain novelist said every writer ought to write at least one story for children. I think of sending a postcard saying I don't accept that I "ought" to write anything.

And then last night I woke up—or rather was wakened without knowing what had roused me.

A voice in the echo chamber of the subconscious?

A sound.

A creaking of the kind made by the weight carried by one foot after another along a wooden floor. I listened. I felt the apertures of my ears distend with concentration. Again: the creaking. I was waiting for it; waiting to hear if it indicated that feet were moving from room to room, coming up the passage—to my door. I have no burglar bars, no gun under the pillow, but I have the same fears as people who do take these precautions, and my windowpanes are thin as rime,[1] could shatter like a wineglass. A woman was murdered (how do they put it) in broad daylight in a house two blocks away, last year, and the fierce dogs who guarded an old widower and his collection of antique clocks were strangled before he was knifed by a casual laborer he had dismissed without pay.

I was staring at the door, making it out in my mind rather than seeing it, in the dark. I lay quite still—a victim already—but the arrhythmia[2] of my heart was fleeing, knocking this way and that against its body-cage. How finely tuned the senses are, just out of rest, sleep! I could never listen intently as that in the distractions of the day; I was reading every faintest sound, identifying and classifying its possible threat.

But I learned that I was to be neither threatened nor spared. There was no human weight pressing on the boards, the creaking was a buckling, an epicenter[3] of stress. I was in it. The house that surrounds me while I sleep is built on undermined ground; far beneath my bed, the floor, the house's foundations, the stopes[4] and passages of gold mines have hollowed the rock, and when some face trembles, detaches, and falls, three

---
1. **rime** *n.*: frost.
2. **arrhythmia** (ə·rĭth′mē·ə) *n.*: irregular beating.
3. **epicenter** *n.*: central point.
4. **stopes** *n. pl.*: excavations.

Vocabulary
distend (di·stend′) *v.*: expand; swell.

thousand feet below, the whole house shifts slightly, bringing uneasy strain to the balance and counterbalance of brick, cement, wood, and glass that hold it as a structure around me. The misbeats of my heart tailed off like the last muffled flourishes on one of the wooden xylophones made by the Chopi and Tsonga[5] migrant miners who might have been down there, under me in the earth at that moment. The stope where the fall was could have been disused, dripping water from its ruptured veins; or men might now be interred there in the most profound of tombs.

I couldn't find a position in which my mind would let go of my body—release me to sleep again. So I began to tell myself a story; a bedtime story.

In a house, in a suburb, in a city, there were a man and his wife who loved each other very much and were living happily ever after. They had a little boy, and they loved him very much. They had a cat and a dog that the little boy loved very much. They had a car and a caravan trailer for holidays, and a swimming pool which was fenced so that the little boy and his playmates would not fall in and drown. They had a housemaid who was absolutely trustworthy and an itinerant gardener who was highly recommended by the neighbors. For when they began to live happily ever after they were warned, by that wise old witch, the husband's mother, not to take on anyone off the street. They were inscribed[6] in a medical benefit society, their pet dog was licensed, they were insured against fire, flood damage, and theft, and subscribed to the local Neighborhood Watch, which supplied them with a plaque for their gates lettered YOU HAVE BEEN WARNED over the silhouette of a would-be intruder. He was masked; it could not be said if he was black or white, and therefore proved the property owner was no racist.

It was not possible to insure the house, the swimming pool, or the car against riot damage. There were riots, but these were outside the city, where people of another color were quartered. These people were not allowed into the suburb except as reliable housemaids and gardeners, so there was nothing to fear, the husband told the wife. Yet she was afraid that some day such people might come up the street and tear off the plaque YOU HAVE BEEN WARNED and open the gates and stream in.... Nonsense, my dear, said the husband, there are police and soldiers and tear gas and guns to keep them away. But to please her—for he loved her very much and buses were being burned, cars stoned, and schoolchildren shot by the police in those quarters out of sight and hearing of the suburb—he had electronically controlled gates fitted. Anyone who pulled off the sign YOU HAVE BEEN WARNED and tried to open the gates would have to announce his intentions by pressing a button and speaking into a receiver relayed to the house. The little boy was fascinated by the device and used it as a walkie-talkie in cops and robbers play with his small friends.

The riots were suppressed, but there were many burglaries in the suburb and somebody's trusted housemaid was tied up and shut in a cupboard by thieves while she was in charge of her employers' house. The trusted housemaid of the man and wife and little boy was so upset by this misfortune befalling a friend left, as she herself often was, with responsibility for the possessions of the man and his wife and the little boy that she implored her employers to have burglar bars attached to the doors and windows of the house, and an alarm system installed. The wife said, She is right, let us take heed of her advice. So from every window and door in the house where they were living happily ever after they now saw the trees and sky through bars, and when the little boy's pet cat tried to climb in by the fanlight[7] to keep him company in his little bed at night, as it customarily had done, it set off the alarm keening[8] through the house.

---

5. **Chopi** (chō′pē) **and Tsonga** (tsän′gä): Bantu-speaking peoples of Mozambique in southeastern Africa. Tsonga is often spelled *Thonga*.
6. **inscribed** *v.:* enrolled.
7. **fanlight** *n.:* semicircular window over a door or a larger window.
8. **keening** *n.:* wailing.

Vocabulary
itinerant (ī·tin′ər·ənt) *adj.:* traveling.

DIRECT TEACHING

VIEWING THE ART

Nicolas de Staël (1914–1955) was a French painter born in Russia. In this painting, blocks of color collide and repeat one another.

Activity. Discuss the relevance of this painting (including its title) to the end of Gordimer's story. [Possible response: The colors and figures create a violent, discordant mood. Order has given way; chaos threatens. A red sky could suggest fire, warfare, and violence.]

Ⓐ Reading Skills

❓ **Interpreting.** Gordimer calls the security alarms "electronic harpies." Why are these alarms ineffective? [They go off so often that no one pays attention to them. Also, they make so much noise that they disguise the sounds of thieves intruding.]

Ⓑ Literary Focus

❓ **Parody.** What fairy tale elements are given an ironic twist here? [Possible response: The "wise old witch" appears again, apparently to help the family—but is she really making their life more secure? The specific gifts to the child suggest that he is being encouraged to ignore the real world—the dangerous world—around him.]

Le Ciel Rouge (The Red Sky) (1952) by Nicolas de Staël Oil on canvas.
Collection Walker Art Center, Minneapolis.
Gift of the T. B. Walker Foundation, 1954.
© 2003 Artists Rights Society (ARS), New York/ADAGP, Paris.

Ⓐ The alarm was often answered—it seemed—by other burglar alarms, in other houses, that had been triggered by pet cats or nibbling mice. The alarms called to one another across the gardens in shrills and bleats and wails that everyone soon became accustomed to, so that the din roused the inhabitants of the suburb no more than the croak of frogs and musical grating of cicadas'[9] legs. Under cover of the electronic harpies'[10] discourse intruders sawed the iron bars and broke into homes, taking away hi-fi equipment, television sets, cassette players, cameras and radios, jewelry and clothing, and sometimes were hungry enough to devour everything in the refrigerator or paused audaciously to drink the whiskey in the cabinets or patio bars. Insurance companies paid no compensation for single malt, a loss made keener by the property owner's knowledge that the thieves wouldn't even have been able to appreciate what it was they were drinking.

Then the time came when many of the people who were not trusted housemaids and gardeners hung about the suburb because they were unemployed. Some importuned for a job: weeding or painting a roof; anything, *baas*,[11] madam. But the man and his wife remembered the warning about taking on anyone off the street. Some drank liquor and fouled the street with discarded bottles. Some begged, waiting for the man or his wife to drive the car out of the electronically operated gates. They sat about with their feet in the gutters, under the jacaranda[12] trees that made a green tunnel of the street—for it was a beautiful suburb, spoiled only by their presence—and sometimes they fell asleep lying right before the gates in the midday sun. The wife could never see anyone go hungry. She sent the trusted housemaid out with bread and tea, but the trusted housemaid said these were loafers and *tsotsis*,[13] who would come and tie her up and shut her in a cupboard. The husband said, She's right. Take heed of her advice. You only encourage them with your bread and tea. They are looking for their chance.... And he brought the little boy's tricycle from the garden into the house every night, because if the house was surely secure, once locked and with the alarm set, someone might still be able to climb over the wall or the electronically closed gates into the garden.

You are right, said the wife, then the wall should be higher. And the wise old witch, the Ⓑ husband's mother, paid for the extra bricks as her Christmas present to her son and his wife—the little boy got a Space Man outfit and a book of fairy tales.

But every week there were more reports of intrusion: in broad daylight and the dead of night, in the early hours of the morning, and even in the lovely summer twilight—a certain family was at dinner while the bedrooms were being ransacked upstairs. The man and his wife, talking of the latest armed robbery in the suburb, were distracted by

---

9. **cicadas** (si·kā′dəz) *n. pl.*: Cicadas are large, flylike insects.
10. **harpies** *n. pl.*: Harpies are shrewish or grasping people. The word comes from the mythological harpies, hideous winged monsters that have the head and trunk of a woman and the tail, legs, and talons of a bird.
11. **baas** (bäs): Afrikaans for "master." Afrikaans, a language developed from seventeenth-century Dutch, is spoken in South Africa.
12. **jacaranda** (jak′ə·ran′də) *n.*: tropical American tree with large clusters of blue or lavender flowers.
13. **tsotsis** (tsät′sis): colloquial expression for "flashily dressed street thugs."

Vocabulary
audaciously (ô·dā′shəs·lē) *adv.*: boldly.

---

926   Collection 7   The Modern World: 1900 to the Present

Conducting a Historical Investigation

Mixed-ability group activity. Have students work in groups of five to eight students each to trace the history of apartheid in South Africa. Have students research the beginnings of the policy, its enforcement and challenges, its results, and its demise. Students should pay special attention to the efforts to abolish apartheid. Ask students to prepare a multimedia report to share their findings.

the sight of the little boy's pet cat effortlessly arriving over the seven-foot wall, descending first with a rapid bracing of extended forepaws down on the sheer vertical surface, and then a graceful launch, landing with swishing tail within the property. The whitewashed wall was marked with the cat's comings and goings; and on the street side of the wall there were larger red-earth smudges that could have been made by the kind of broken running shoes, seen on the feet of unemployed loiterers, that had no innocent destination.

When the man and wife and little boy took the pet dog for its walk round the neighborhood streets they no longer paused to admire this show of roses or that perfect lawn; these were hidden behind an array of different varieties of security fences, walls, and devices. The man, wife, little boy, and dog passed a remarkable choice: There was the low-cost option of pieces of broken glass embedded in cement along the top of walls, there were iron grilles ending in lance points, there were attempts at reconciling the aesthetics of prison architecture with the Spanish Villa style (spikes painted pink) and with the plastic urns of neoclassical façades (twelve-inch pikes finned like zigzags of lightning and painted pure white). Some walls had a small board affixed, giving the name and telephone number of the firm responsible for the installation of the devices. While the little boy and the pet dog raced ahead, the husband and wife found themselves comparing the possible effectiveness of each style against its appearance; and after several weeks when they paused before this barricade or that without needing to speak, both came out with the conclusion that only one was worth considering. It was the ugliest but the most honest in its suggestion of the pure concentration-camp style, no frills, all evident efficacy. Placed the length of walls, it consisted of a continuous coil of stiff and shining metal serrated into jagged blades, so that there would be no way of climbing over it and no way through its tunnel without getting entangled in its fangs. There would be no way out, only a struggle getting bloodier and bloodier, a deeper and sharper hooking and tearing of flesh. The wife shuddered to look at it. You're right, said the husband, anyone would think twice.... And they took heed of the advice on a small board fixed to the wall: Consult DRAGON'S TEETH The People For Total Security.

Next day a gang of workmen came and stretched the razor-bladed coils all round the walls of the house where the husband and wife and little boy and pet dog and cat were living happily ever after. The sunlight flashed and slashed, off the serrations, the cornice of razor thorns encircled the home, shining. The husband said, Never mind. It will weather. The wife said, You're wrong. They guarantee it's rustproof. And she waited until the little boy had run off to play before she said, I hope the cat will take heed.... The husband said, Don't worry, my dear, cats always look before they leap. And it was true that from that day on the cat slept in the little boy's bed and kept to the garden, never risking a try at breaching security.

One evening, the mother read the little boy to sleep with a fairy story from the book the wise old witch had given him at Christmas. Next day he pretended to be the Prince who braves the terrible thicket of thorns to enter the palace and kiss the Sleeping Beauty back to life: He dragged a ladder to the wall, the shining coiled tunnel was just wide enough for his little body to creep in, and with the first fixing of its razor teeth in his knees and hands and head he screamed and struggled deeper into its tangle. The trusted housemaid and the itinerant gardener, whose "day" it was, came running, the first to see and to scream with him, and the itinerant gardener tore his hands trying to get at the little boy. Then the man and his wife burst wildly into the garden and for some reason (the cat, probably) the alarm set up wailing against the screams while the bleeding mass of the little boy was hacked out of the security coil with saws, wire cutters, choppers, and they carried it—the man, the wife, the hysterical trusted housemaid, and the weeping gardener—into the house. ■

Vocabulary
aesthetics (es·thet′iks) *n*.: principles of beauty.
serrated (ser′āt′id) *v*. used as *adj*.: having jagged, sawlike notches along the edge.

Nadine Gordimer

INDEPENDENT PRACTICE

Response and Analysis

Reading Check

1. electronic gates, an alarm system, a higher wall, razor wire
2. Riots prompt the gates, burglaries prompt the alarm system, unemployed blacks prompt the higher wall, and suspected attempts at intrusion prompt the razor wire.
3. None of the security devices reassures the family of safety.
4. He is badly injured, perhaps killed, as he plays in the wire.

Thinking Critically

5. Humorous passages include descriptions of the "perfect" family and the son playing with the electronic gate. Gordimer's tone is ironic as she exposes the couple's futile attempts to insulate the family from those around them.
6. Fairy tale language elements include phrases such as "happily ever after"; the nameless couple; the "Dragon's Teeth" company; and the wise old witch. The parody emphasizes the gap between the real world that the family lives in and the fantasy of security that it tries to create. The overall effect is ironic.
7. The opening grounds the story in reality. Readers are reminded that nothing in the fairy tale is that long ago or far away.
8. The wall symbolizes racism, the true barrier in the story.
9. The moral of the story is that security cannot exist in a society that is based on inequality.
10. Possible answers: They can be seen as racists because they accept the racism of their society rather than trying to change it. They also can be seen as victims of a racist society that they did not create.

Response and Analysis

Reading Check

1. What four improvements to home security does the family make?
2. What events prompt each improvement?
3. How well does each improvement work?
4. What happens to the little boy at the end of the story?

Thinking Critically

5. Which passages in the story seem to have humorous intent? Did you find these passages funny or unsettling? Describe Gordimer's overall **tone** in this story.
6. Point out common **language structures** and other elements of the **fairy tale** genre used by Gordimer. In what sense has Gordimer created a **parody** of a fairy tale—an imitation meant to mock or amuse? How would you describe the effect of Gordimer's fairy tale parody? (Refer to your reading notes.)
7. Why do you think Gordimer uses a nonfiction introduction to her tale? How do you interpret the opening section after reading the story?
8. How can the security systems in the story—especially the wall—be seen as **symbols**? What do they symbolize?
9. **Fairy tales** often contain moral lessons. What is the moral of "Once upon a Time"? How does it contrast with the morals of traditional fairy tales you have read?
10. In your opinion, are the husband and wife in the story innocent homeowners who are merely trying to feel secure, or are they racists who cause their own tragedy? Explain your reasoning, using specific evidence from the text.

INTERNET
Projects and Activities
Keyword: LE5 12-7

SKILLS FOCUS

Literary Skills Analyze symbols.
Reading Skills Identify language structures.
Writing Skills Write an essay comparing and contrasting two literary works.
Vocabulary Skills Complete word analogies.

Extending and Evaluating

11. Some people might find this story to be overly brutal or violent. What do you think of this story's combination of ironic humor and a shocking ending? Why do you think Gordimer wrote her story this way? Compare your responses with those of your classmates and discuss them.

WRITING

The Great Divide
Both Gordimer's tale and George Orwell's "Shooting an Elephant" (see page 899) carry messages about cultural clashes. Write a short **essay comparing and contrasting** the two works in terms of their themes, genres, styles, and tones.

Vocabulary Development
Analogies

distend   aesthetics
itinerant   serrated
audaciously

In an **analogy** the words in one pair relate to each other in the same way as the words in a second pair. In each item below, identify the relationship between the words in the first pair. Then, complete the second pair with the Vocabulary word from the list above that expresses the same relationship.

1. CASUALLY : INFORMALLY :: _____ : boldly
2. GRITTY : SANDPAPER :: _____ : steak knife
3. TRY : ATTEMPT :: _____ : expand
4. TRIVIAL : IMPORTANT :: _____ : stay-at-home
5. BIOLOGY : THE NATURAL WORLD :: _____ : beauty

Extending and Evaluating

11. Students may argue that the brutality is necessary to make the author's point, or they may say that the description of the child's injury is gratuitously violent.

Vocabulary Development

1. audaciously   4. itinerant
2. serrated   5. aesthetics
3. distend

ASSESSING

Assessment
- Holt Assessment: Literature, Reading, and Vocabulary

Chinua Achebe
(1930–)
Nigeria

Nigerian author Chinua Achebe (chin'wä'ä·chā'bā) planned to study medicine, but literature and his country's nationalist movement forever changed his plans. As a student, he came to realize the destructive effects of colonialism and dedicated himself to redefining Africa, to telling the true story of Africans, including their achievements and failures. In his words, the European idea that "Africa was the Primordial Void, was sheer humbug; . . . Africa had a history, a religion, a civilization."

His novels, beginning with the celebrated *Things Fall Apart* (1958), focus on the changes in Nigerian life that occurred in the twentieth century. The novels trace life in Nigeria— sometimes presented as a fictionalized nation—from the arrival of early English missionaries, through years of colonial rule, to a post-independence era rife with corruption and political turmoil. Achebe believes that "Africa's meeting with Europe must be accounted a terrible disaster in this matter of human understanding and respect," yet his African characters are not idealized. They are held responsible for their private decisions and for solving the problems that threaten their nation's future.

Achebe is himself an Ibo, born in the eastern Nigerian town of Ogidi, where his father, a Christian convert, taught at the mission school. He has chosen to write in English, which he began to learn at age eight, in order to reach a wide audience.

During Nigeria's civil war of the late 1960s, Achebe worked for the cause of the secessionist Biafrans. Since then he has concentrated on teaching and encouraging and publishing promising young authors. Through his many works of fiction, nonfiction, and poetry, he has been a catalyst for an entire younger generation of African writers.

For Independent Reading

You may enjoy the following story by Achebe:
- "Dead Men's Path"

SKILLS FOCUS, pp. 929–936

Grade-Level Skills

■ **Literary Skills**

Analyze the way an author's style, including the use of irony, achieves specific rhetorical or aesthetic purposes.

More About the Writer

Background. Achebe is unusual among African novelists seeking their place in English letters because he has kept true to his own voice rather than following current fads in English literature. Achebe rejects the European notion "that art should be accountable to no one, and [needs] to justify itself to nobody," as he puts it in his book of essays *Morning Yet on Creation Day*. Instead, Achebe has centered his writing on the African oral tradition—that "art is, and always was, at the service of man. Our ancestors created their myths and told their stories for a human purpose," he explains. As a result, Achebe believes that "any good story, any good novel, should have a message, should have a purpose."

For Independent Reading

Students who enjoy "Marriage Is a Private Affair" also should appreciate "Dead Men's Path," in which the "modern methods" of a village school's new headmaster clash with the traditions of the villagers.

RESOURCES: READING

Planning
- *One-Stop Planner* CD-ROM with ExamView Test Generator

Differentiating Instruction
- *Supporting Instruction in Spanish*
- *Audio CD Library, Selections and Summaries in Spanish*

Vocabulary
- *Vocabulary Development*

Grammar and Language
- *Language Handbook Worksheets*
- *Daily Language Activities*

Assessment
- *Holt Assessment: Literature, Reading, and Vocabulary*
- *One-Stop Planner* CD-ROM with ExamView Test Generator
- *Holt Online Assessment*

Internet
- go.hrw.com (Keyword: LE5 12-7)
- *Elements of Literature Online*

Media
- *Audio CD Library*
- *Audio CD Library, Selections and Summaries in Spanish*

PRETEACHING

Summary ⬌ at grade level

A young Ibo man named Nnaemeka returns from the city of Lagos in Nigeria to the countryside in which he was born to tell his father that he plans to marry Nene, a young woman whom he has met in the city. Okeke, his father, refuses to accept the marriage because Nene is not an Ibo. Indeed, as tradition dictates, Nnaemeka's father has chosen an Ibo wife for him. Nnaemeka, however, is determined to marry the woman he loves, so he returns to Nene in the city. Equally adamant, Okeke returns the wedding picture that his son later sends, but he cuts Nene out of it. No reconciliation seems possible. Years later, however, Nene writes to Okeke that her two sons dearly want to meet their grandfather. At last, the old man regrets the barriers that he has placed between himself and his son's family, and he resolves to make up for lost time.

Selection Starter

Build background. Students will appreciate the story and grasp its theme better if they understand the importance of setting. Explain that the story has a dual setting: Lagos (Nigeria's largest city) and a traditional rural village. The dichotomy between cosmopolitan city life and conservative rural life dramatizes the clash between new and old, modern and traditional, Western and African. Point out that Achebe explores this cultural clash and how it affects the characters.

Before You Read

Marriage Is a Private Affair

Make the Connection
Quickwrite

Like the United States, many nations are collections of diverse peoples—and when people of different backgrounds come together, conflicts tend to arise. People may focus on differences in customs, religion, and ethnic heritage and fail to notice all the things they have in common.

These cultural distinctions, however, often become less significant when people expand their horizons. They travel, they read, they watch, they listen. They go beyond "their kind." This story focuses on entrenched cultural traditions about marriage and family. Jot down similarities and differences between your generation's attitudes toward love and marriage and those of your parents' generation. What qualities about marriage do you consider important? Is there any common ground in your points of view?

Literary Focus
Verbal Irony

Verbal irony occurs when a writer or speaker says one thing but means something else—usually the opposite of what is stated. If you tell a friend that you "just love being kept waiting in the rain," you are using verbal irony. A classic example of verbal irony occurs in Jonathan Swift's essay "A Modest Proposal" (see page 430), where he suggests that the Irish solve their social problems by selling their babies to their English landlords as food.

INTERNET
Vocabulary Practice
•
More About Chinua Achebe
•
Keyword: LE5 12-7

Literary Skills Understand verbal irony.

Verbal irony occurs when a writer or speaker says one thing but means something else—usually the opposite of what is stated.

For more on Irony, see the Handbook of Literary and Historical Terms.

Background

The West African nation of Nigeria has more than 250 ethnic groups. These groups speak different languages and frequently differ in religion, customs, and traditions. Both the Ibo and the Ibibio live in southeastern Nigeria but traditionally did not intermarry. In Achebe's story a young Ibo man and a young Ibibio woman have moved from their native regions to Lagos, a large, modern city in southwestern Nigeria.

Vocabulary Development

cosmopolitan (käz′mə·päl′ə·tən) *adj.*: worldly; sophisticated.

rash (rash) *adj.*: reckless.

commiserate (kə·miz′ər·āt′) *v.*: feel sorrow or pity for; sympathize.

persevered (pur′sə·vird′) *v.*: continued despite difficulty or opposition; persisted.

930 Collection 7 The Modern World: 1900 to the Present

Previewing Vocabulary

Have students work in pairs to study each of the Vocabulary words on p. 930 and its definition. Direct students to discuss any structural clues that help them decode the word's meaning. For example, students can focus on suffixes that signal parts of speech (such as *–an, –ate*) or tense (such as *–ed*); prefixes that signal meaning (such as *com–*), and roots (such as *cosmo*). Then, have students match each word to its meaning.

1. persevered [c]   a. reckless
2. commiserate [d]   b. worldly
3. rash [a]   c. kept on
4. cosmopolitan [b] d. sympathize

Marriage Is a Private Affair

Chinua Achebe

"Have you written to your dad yet?" asked Nene[1] one afternoon as she sat with Nnaemeka[2] in her room at 16 Kasanga Street, Lagos.[3]

"No. I've been thinking about it. I think it's better to tell him when I get home on leave!"

"But why? Your leave is such a long way off yet—six whole weeks. He should be let into our happiness now."

Nnaemeka was silent for a while, and then began very slowly as if he groped for his words: "I wish I were sure it would be happiness to him."

"Of course it must," replied Nene, a little surprised. "Why shouldn't it?"

"You have lived in Lagos all your life, and you know very little about people in remote parts of the country."

"That's what you always say. But I don't believe anybody will be so unlike other people that they will be unhappy when their sons are engaged to marry."

"Yes. They are most unhappy if the engagement is not arranged by them. In our case it's worse—you are not even an Ibo."[4]

This was said so seriously and so bluntly that Nene could not find speech immediately. In the cosmopolitan atmosphere of the city it had always seemed to her something of a joke that a person's tribe could determine whom he married.

At last she said, "You don't really mean that he will object to your marrying me simply on that account? I had always thought you Ibos were kindly disposed to other people."

---

1. **Nene** (nā′nā).
2. **Nnaemeka** ('n·nä·ä·mä′kə).
3. **Lagos** (lā′gōs'): former capital of Nigeria.
4. **Ibo** (ē′bō'): member of an African ethnic group living chiefly in southeastern Nigeria.

Old Ibibio mask.
Courtesy of The Trustees of the British Museum, London.

"So we are. But when it comes to marriage, well, it's not quite so simple. And this," he added, "is not peculiar to the Ibos. If your father were alive and lived in the heart of Ibibio-land[5] he would be exactly like my father."

"I don't know. But anyway, as your father is so fond of you, I'm sure he will forgive you soon enough. Come on then, be a good boy and send him a nice lovely letter . . ."

"It would not be wise to break the news to him by writing. A letter will bring it upon him with a shock. I'm quite sure about that."

"All right, honey, suit yourself. You know your father."

As Nnaemeka walked home that evening he turned over in his mind different ways of overcoming his father's opposition, especially now that he had gone and found a girl for him. He had thought of showing his letter to Nene but decided on second thoughts not to, at least for the moment. He read it again when he got home and couldn't help smiling to himself. He remembered Ugoye[6] quite well, an Amazon[7] of a girl who used to beat up all the boys, himself included, on the way to the stream, a complete dunce at school.

---

5. **Ibibio-land** (ĭb′ə·bē′ō′land): area of southeastern Nigeria that is the traditional homeland of the Ibibio, another African ethnic group.
6. **Ugoye** (ōō·gō′yā).
7. **Amazon:** tall, strong, aggressive woman. The term is taken from the name for the Amazons, a race of female warriors in Greek mythology.

Vocabulary
cosmopolitan (käz′mə·päl′ə·tən) *adj.*: worldly; sophisticated.

DIRECT TEACHING

VIEWING THE ART

Like masks in other parts of Africa, Nigerian masks are used in a variety of religious ceremonies and usually are worn by men. The design of each mask expresses the meaning and power of the spirit or ancestor that it depicts. Some masks are used in dramatic performances, as well.

Activity. What similarities and differences can you find in the masks on pp. 931 and 932? [The ears and eyes are similarly shaped; the overall triangular shape of the face is similar too, but the Ibibio mask is compressed, whereas the Ibo mask is elongated; head decorations are also different.]

A Learners Having Difficulty

❓ Finding sequence of events. The italicized text is part of a letter from Okeke (whose name we learn on the next page) to his son. When did this letter arrive, and what plot complication does it reveal? [The letter arrived before the story opens. It shows that Nnaemeka's father has already selected, from among the Ibo, the woman whom he wants his son to marry.]

B Content-Area Connections

Culture: Arranged Marriages Remind students that in cultures with arranged marriages, love is meant to grow after the marriage occurs.

C Reading Skills

❓ Speculating. Why might the father mispronounce Nene Atang's name? [Possible responses: Since her name is from another ethnic group, he might not know how to say it. By mispronouncing the name, he may wish to show that he does not respect his son's choice.]

Wood mask. Ibo, Nigeria (37 cm).
Courtesy of The Trustees of the British Museum, London.

I have found a girl who will suit you admirably—Ugoye Nweke,⁸ the eldest daughter of our neighbor, Jacob Nweke. She has a proper Christian upbringing. When she stopped schooling some years ago her father (a man of sound judgment) sent her to live in the house of a pastor where she has received all the training a wife could need. Her Sunday school teacher has told me that she reads her Bible very fluently. I hope we shall begin negotiations when you come home in December.

On the second evening of his return from Lagos, Nnaemeka sat with his father under a cassia tree. This was the old man's retreat where he went to read his Bible when the parching December sun had set and a fresh, reviving wind blew on the leaves.

"Father," began Nnaemeka suddenly, "I have come to ask for forgiveness."

"Forgiveness? For what, my son?" he asked in amazement.

"It's about this marriage question."

"Which marriage question?"

"I can't—we must—I mean it is impossible for me to marry Nweke's daughter."

"Impossible? Why?" asked his father.

"I don't love her."

"Nobody said you did. Why should you?" he asked.

"Marriage today is different . . ."

---

8. **Nweke** (ʾnwĕʹkä).

"Look here, my son," interrupted his father, "nothing is different. What one looks for in a wife are a good character and a Christian background."

Nnaemeka saw there was no hope along the present line of argument.

"Moreover," he said, "I am engaged to marry another girl who has all of Ugoye's good qualities, and who . . ."

His father did not believe his ears. "What did you say?" he asked slowly and disconcertingly.

"She is a good Christian," his son went on, "and a teacher in a girls' school in Lagos."

"Teacher, did you say? If you consider that a qualification for a good wife I should like to point out to you, Emeka, that no Christian woman should teach. St. Paul in his letter to the Corinthians⁹ says that women should keep silence." He rose slowly from his seat and paced forward and backward. This was his pet subject, and he condemned vehemently those church leaders who encouraged women to teach in their schools. After he had spent his emotion on a long homily he at last came back to his son's engagement, in a seemingly milder tone.

"Whose daughter is she, anyway?"

"She is Nene Atang."

"What!" All the mildness was gone again. "Did you say Neneataga, what does that mean?"

"Nene Atang from Calabar.¹⁰ She is the only girl I can marry." This was a very rash reply and Nnaemeka expected the storm to burst. But it did not. His father merely walked away into his room. This was most unexpected and perplexed Nnaemeka. His father's silence was infinitely more menacing than a flood of threatening speech. That night the old man did not eat.

When he sent for Nnaemeka a day later he applied all possible ways of dissuasion. But the young man's heart was hardened, and his father eventually gave him up as lost.

---

9. **St. Paul . . . Corinthians:** reference to a passage in the Bible (1 Corinthians 14:34).
10. **Calabar:** seaport city in southeastern Nigeria.

Vocabulary
rash (rash) *adj.*: reckless.

CONTENT-AREA CONNECTIONS

Culture: Marriage Practices
Remind students that the arranged marriage has been the traditional form of marriage throughout history. However, in the West, due to the rise of a middle class and the growth of democracy, love matches have supplanted the arranged marriage.

Paired activity. Have partners interview friends, parents, and grandparents to explore modern attitudes about marriage.

Culture: Nigeria Today
Individual activity. Invite students to research tensions in contemporary Nigeria between ethnic groups or between city dwellers and rural people. Ask students to consider questions such as these: Have relationships eased or intensified since independence? What steps have been taken to unite the country, and have they been effective? Students might present their findings in the form of an article for a magazine called *Nigeria Today*.

"I owe it to you, my son, as a duty to show you what is right and what is wrong. Whoever put this idea into your head might as well have cut your throat. It is Satan's work." He waved his son away.

"You will change your mind, Father, when you know Nene."

"I shall never see her," was the reply. From that night the father scarcely spoke to his son. He did not, however, cease hoping that he would realize how serious was the danger he was heading for. Day and night he put him in his prayers.

Nnaemeka, for his own part, was very deeply affected by his father's grief. But he kept hoping that it would pass away. If it had occurred to him that never in the history of his people had a man married a woman who spoke a different tongue, he might have been less optimistic. "It has never been heard," was the verdict of an old man speaking a few weeks later. In that short sentence he spoke for all of his people. This man had come with others to commiserate with Okeke[11] when news went round about his son's behavior. By that time the son had gone back to Lagos.

"It has never been heard," said the old man again with a sad shake of his head.

"What did Our Lord say?" asked another gentleman. "Sons shall rise against their Fathers; it is there in the Holy Book."

"It is the beginning of the end," said another.

The discussion thus tending to become theological, Madubogwu, a highly practical man, brought it down once more to the ordinary level.

"Have you thought of consulting a native doctor about your son?" he asked Nnaemeka's father.

"He isn't sick," was the reply.

"What is he then? The boy's mind is diseased and only a good herbalist can bring him back to his right senses. The medicine he requires is *Amalile*, the same that women apply with success to recapture their husbands' straying affection."

"Madubogwu is right," said another gentleman. "This thing calls for medicine."

---
11. Okeke (ō·kā′kā).

"I shall not call in a native doctor." Nnaemeka's father was known to be obstinately ahead of his more superstitious neighbors in these matters. "I will not be another Mrs. Ochuba. If my son wants to kill himself let him do it with his own hands. It is not for me to help him."

"But it was her fault," said Madubogwu. "She ought to have gone to an honest herbalist. She was a clever woman, nevertheless."

"She was a wicked murderess," said Jonathan, who rarely argued with his neighbors because, he often said, they were incapable of reasoning. "The medicine was prepared for her husband, it was his name they called in its preparation, and I am sure it would have been perfectly beneficial to him. It was wicked to put it into the herbalist's food, and say you were only trying it out."

Six months later, Nnaemeka was showing his young wife a short letter from his father:

It amazes me that you could be so unfeeling as to send me your wedding picture. I would have sent it back. But on further thought I decided just to cut off your wife and send it back to you because I have nothing to do with her. How I wish that I had nothing to do with you either.

When Nene read through this letter and looked at the mutilated picture her eyes filled with tears, and she began to sob.

"Don't cry, my darling," said her husband. "He is essentially good-natured and will one day look more kindly on our marriage." But years passed and that one day did not come.

For eight years, Okeke would have nothing to do with his son, Nnaemeka. Only three times (when Nnaemeka asked to come home and spend his leave) did he write to him.

"I can't have you in my house," he replied on one occasion. "It can be of no interest to me where or how you spend your leave—or your life, for that matter."

Vocabulary
commiserate (kə·miz′ər·āt′) v.: feel sorrow or pity for; sympathize.

Chinua Achebe 933

Literary Criticism

Critic's Commentary: Achebe's Communication

Critic Margaret Laurence discusses the theme of communication in Achebe's writing: "In Ibo villages, the men working on their farm plots in the midst of the rain forest often shout to one another—a reassurance, to make certain the other is still there . . . on the other side of the thick undergrowth. The writing of Chinua Achebe is like this. It seeks to send human voices through the thicket of our separateness."

Activity. Discuss these questions:
- What is the "separateness" in this story, and what caused it? [Possible response: The "separateness" is the rift between Nnaemeka and his father. They are divided over Nnaemeka's choice of a wife—an issue that touches upon cultural and age-related differences.]
- Based on Laurence's comment, how do you think Nnaemeka and Okeke might resolve their separateness? [Possible response: by trying harder to communicate.]

Vocabulary Development

1. commiserate
2. rash
3. cosmopolitan
4. persevered

Grammar Link

Practice

Possible Answers

1. Achebe, one of the founders of a new Nigerian literature based on oral traditions and changing society, has been praised by critics for writing novels portraying African communal life.
2. Since Achebe believes that artists should be accountable to society, he depicts characters realistically in his works.
3. The most populous country in Africa, Nigeria is home to more than 250 ethnic groups.
4. Ruled by a military government for sixteen years, Nigeria adopted a civilian government in 1999.
5. Nigeria is about twice the size of California, and three major native languages and more than one hundred dialects are spoken in the country.

ASSESSING

Assessment

- Holt Assessment: Literature, Reading, and Vocabulary

RETEACHING

For lessons reteaching author's tone and style, see **Reteaching**, p. 1129A.

Grammar Link

The Wrong Place at the Wrong Time: Dangling Modifiers

What would you think if you came across the following sentence in your reading?

> Having been raised in the city, marrying between tribes was perfectly acceptable.

Would you wonder who was raised in the city and who finds marrying between tribes acceptable? This sentence is confusing because it contains a **dangling modifier**—a word, phrase, or clause that does not sensibly, or reasonably, modify any word or group of words in a sentence. In the following sentence, the phrase *Having been raised in the city* now sensibly modifies *Nene*:

> Having been raised in the city, Nene thought marrying between tribes was perfectly acceptable.

There are three ways to correct dangling modifiers:

DANGLING   Dedicated to telling Africa's true story, Achebe's novels focus on details of twentieth-century Nigerian life. [Were Achebe's *novels* dedicated to telling Africa's true story?]

- Add a word that connects the dangling modifier to its object.

CORRECT   Dedicated to telling Africa's true story, Achebe writes novels that focus on details of twentieth-century Nigerian life.

- Add words to the modifier to make its meaning clear.

CORRECT   Since Achebe is dedicated to telling Africa's true story, his novels focus on details of twentieth-century Nigerian life.

- Reword the entire sentence.

CORRECT   Achebe is dedicated to telling Africa's true story, so he writes novels that focus on details of twentieth-century Nigerian life.

Grammar Skills Correct dangling modifiers.

PRACTICE

The following sentences are about Achebe and his homeland of Nigeria. Rewrite each sentence to correct the dangling modifiers.

1. One of the founders of a new Nigerian literature based on oral traditions and changing society, critics have praised his novels portraying African communal life.
2. Believing that artists should be accountable to society, Achebe's characters are depicted realistically in his works.
3. The most populous country in Africa, there are more than 250 ethnic groups in Nigeria.
4. Ruled by a military government for sixteen years, a civilian government was adopted in 1999 in Nigeria.
5. About twice the size of California, three major native languages and over one hundred dialects are spoken in Nigeria.

Apply to Your Writing

Review a writing assignment you are working on now or have already completed. Revise your sentences as necessary to correct any dangling modifiers.

▶ For more help, see Placement of Modifiers, 5h, in the Language Handbook.

936   Collection 7   The Modern World: 1900 to the Present

READING MINI-LESSON

Developing Word-Attack Skills

Use the selection words *annihilate* and *vehement* to introduce silent *h*. Point out that *h* is often silent at the beginning of words or syllables, but there are no strict guidelines for when *h* is silent or when it is pronounced. Display these words and have students identify the words in which the *h* is silent. Answers are underlined.

inhibit   prohibit   exhibit   cohort
exhort   hilarious   exhilarate

Point out that based on these examples, you might make the generalization that *h* is silent after the prefix *ex–*. Have students test the validity of this generalization with other words that have the prefix *ex–* before *h*: *exhale, exhaust,* and *exhume*. Help them recognize that *exhale* is an exception; the sound of *h* is heard in *exhale*. Explain that there are a finite number of words with silent *h*, and it is possible to memorize these instances.

Activity. Have students identify the words with silent *h*. Answers are underlined.

annihilate   halogen   horoscope
antihistamine   prohibition   hors d'oeuvre
cowherd   dihedral   posthumous
shepherd   inhibition   posthypnotic
nihilism   exhaustion   heir
nihility   exhibition   inherit
vehement   coheir   silhouette

Wole Soyinka
(1934–)
Nigeria

A voice of modern Africa, Wole Soyinka in 1986 became the first African to win the Nobel Prize in literature. Soyinka's favorite African deity is Ogun, god of both war and creative fire—a fitting muse for a multitalented writer and performer whose plays, songs, novels, and poetry combine political activism, universal themes, and African traditions.

Born Akinwande Oluwole Soyinka in a village in western Nigeria, Soyinka was the son of the principal of a Christian school and a teacher. His parents both supported European-style education, but his father also retained strong ties to his heritage as a member of the Yoruba tribe. Soyinka grew up respecting both traditions; his 1981 autobiography, *Aké: The Years of Childhood*, tells of his later struggle with this dual heritage.

After attending University College at Ibadan, Nigeria, Soyinka studied English literature in England at the University of Leeds. In London in the late 1950s, he wrote plays and poetry for theater and radio. During this period of African nationalism and pressure for independence, Soyinka's themes were racism, injustice, tyranny, and corruption, all treated with satiric wit. Also concerned with the collision of ancient traditions and modern realities, he peppered his plays with vivid Yoruba masquerade ritual.

Soyinka felt brutal despotism firsthand during Nigeria's civil war of the late 1960s, when he was imprisoned for two years for the so-called crime of meeting with secessionist leaders such as the writer Chinua Achebe (see page 929). He describes these experiences in *The Man Died: Prison Notes*, published in 1972. Since then he has continued to record and dramatize, with both passion and humor, the struggle and spirit of modern-day Africa and Africans.

PRETEACHING

Summary ⇿ at grade level

The black speaker is having a telephone conversation with a white landlady about renting an apartment. In an effort to save himself a wasted trip should the woman be racist, the speaker tells her that he is an African. She hesitates and then asks whether he is dark-skinned or light-skinned. Stunned, the speaker gives absurd details about his "color," in a flood of shame and fury that ends in a well-placed insult.

Skills Starter

Build review skills. Point out that satire is built on comedy; however, comedy aims to evoke mirth, whereas satire aims to correct lapses in human behavior through ridicule. Alexander Pope claimed that satire "heals with Morals what it hurts with wit."

VIEWING THE ART

The red British telephone booth, designed by Sir Giles Gilbert Scot in 1924 and replaced in 1985, is more than simply a telephone booth—it has become a cultural icon. Books have been written about it, most famously John Timpson's *Requiem For A Red Box,* and the booth appears among miniature souvenirs and in images on jigsaw puzzles.

Activity. How does the status attained by the telephone booth in British popular culture contribute to Soyinka's message? [Soyinka is suggesting that racism, like the telephone booth, is a conventional part of British life.]

Before You Read

Telephone Conversation

Make the Connection

Quickwrite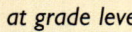

The following poem, written during Soyinka's college career in Britain in the late 1950s, records one of his own experiences with racial discrimination at a time when millions of people from former British colonies were arriving in England in search of economic and educational opportunities.

Think about the ways, both thoughtless and intentional, in which people practice discrimination. Then, jot down some examples. How might those who are discriminated against make others mindful of what they've suffered? Note any ideas that come to mind.

Literary Focus

Satire

Satire is a kind of writing that ridicules human folly, usually with the intention of bringing about awareness and possibly social reform. When writers use satire, they create an exaggerated or skewed picture of a common human vice, folly, or weakness. By making the vice appear foolish—even absurd—satirists hope to inspire people to recognize and shed the vice or to adopt the opposite behavior or attitude. In the following poem, Wole Soyinka uses satire to illustrate exactly how preposterous the human vice of racial discrimination really is.

> **Satire** is a kind of writing that ridicules human weakness, vice, or folly in order to bring about awareness and social reform.
>
> *For more on Satire, see the Handbook of Literary and Historical Terms.*

Literary Skills Understand satire.

Background

Soyinka's poem presents ideas primarily through a **dialogue.** The first speaker is talking from one of the red public telephone booths that were common in London years ago. Such phones had two buttons, A and B; pressing A put one through to the recipient of the call. In this poem the first speaker is a well-educated black African and the second a British woman who has property to rent. Soyinka's poem doesn't merely describe their exchange; it re-creates it.

Telephone Conversation

Wole Soyinka

The price seemed reasonable, location
Indifferent. The landlady swore she lived
Off premises. Nothing remained
But self-confession. "Madam," I warned,
5 "I hate a wasted journey—I am African."
Silence. Silenced transmission of
Pressurized good-breeding. Voice, when it came,
Lipstick coated, long gold-rolled
Cigarette-holder pipped. Caught I was, foully.

10 "HOW DARK?" . . . I had not misheard . . . "ARE YOU LIGHT
OR VERY DARK?" Button B. Button A. Stench
Of rancid breath of public hide-and-speak.
Red booth. Red pillar-box.° Red double-tiered
Omnibus° squelching tar. It *was* real! Shamed
15 By ill-mannered silence, surrender
Pushed dumbfoundment to beg simplification.
Considerate she was, varying the emphasis—

"ARE YOU DARK? OR VERY LIGHT?" Revelation came.
"You mean—like plain or milk chocolate?"
20 Her assent was clinical, crushing in its light
Impersonality. Rapidly, wavelength adjusted,
I chose. "West African sepia"—and as an afterthought,
"Down in my passport." Silence for spectroscopic
Flight of fancy,° till truthfulness clanged her accent
25 Hard on the mouthpiece. "WHAT'S THAT?" conceding,
"DON'T KNOW WHAT THAT IS." "Like brunette."

---

13. **pillar-box:** chiefly British for "mailbox."
13–14. **double-tiered omnibus:** bus with two decks, or tiers.
23–24. **spectroscopic** (spek′trō·skăp′ik) **. . . fancy:** wide range, or spectrum, of ideas.

INDEPENDENT PRACTICE

Response and Analysis

Thinking Critically

1. A black man phones a white woman about renting an apartment. When he mentions that he is African, she asks how dark he is. He answers with ironic humor, revealing his anger and humiliation. The theme is that racial prejudice is absurd.

2. Because the conversation (which should be relatively straightforward and businesslike) is sidetracked by a ludicrous discussion of how dark the speaker is, it might symbolize the psychological and social obstacles that people face in trying to communicate with each other.

3. Soyinka uses red to communicate anger; gold ("gold-rolled cigarette-holder") to communicate the landlady's gaudy pretentiousness; and sepia ("West-African sepia") to display the speaker's sophistication in contrast to the landlady's vulgarity.

4. The landlady's confession of ignorance contrasts ironically with the narrator's sophisticated use of language. In line 7, the presumption of "good-breeding" is flatly contradicted by the woman's bad manners.

5. Some students may see the speaker's description of his "colors" as the most satirical part, for he gives the landlady's ignorant question an answer that is both logical and absurd. Other students may cite the question that concludes the poem, since it uses humor to deflate the woman's pretensions and emphasizes her racism.

Extending and Evaluating

6. Students may find the speaker's last question a well-deserved retort or a cry of pain. It suggests how deeply prejudice can wound, in that the speaker stoops to the woman's level in flinging a polite translation of a vulgar retort at her.

7. Some students may say that the poem raises awareness and creates sympathy for the victims of prejudice; others may counter that political action is more effective than poetry.

"THAT'S DARK, ISN'T IT?" "Not altogether.
Facially, I am brunette, but madam, you should see
The rest of me. Palm of my hand, soles of my feet
30   Are a peroxide blonde. Friction, caused—
Foolishly, madam—by sitting down, has turned
My bottom raven black—One moment madam!"—sensing
Her receiver rearing on the thunderclap
About my ears—"Madam," I pleaded, "wouldn't you rather
35   See for yourself?"

Response and Analysis

Thinking Critically

1. Paraphrase what happens in this poem, and then state what you feel to be the poem's **theme**. How does this theme express a comment on life?

2. What might the telephone conversation itself—complete with all the inconveniences of an old-fashioned phone—**symbolize**? Explain.

3. This poem is full of colors—and not just of skin. What colors does Soyinka make his readers see in the poem? What ideas and emotions do you think he wants to communicate through these **images** of color?

4. What irony do you find in lines 23–26? What irony do you find in the description of the woman as an example of a well-bred person (line 7)?

5. In your opinion, which part of the poem is the most **satirical**? Quote the lines, and then explain why these lines are a good example of satire.

Extending and Evaluating

6. What do you think of the speaker's final question? What does it suggest about prejudice and discrimination?

7. Review your Quickwrite notes, and then think about whether Soyinka's poem is an effective way of making others aware of prejudice. Is it more or less effective than other ways? How so? Explain.

WRITING

Judging the Landlady

What kind of person is the landlady in Soyinka's poem? Write a brief **character analysis** of her. What do you learn about her from the speaker's assumptions, judgments, and tone, and from the woman's own words? How does the fact that she is a disembodied voice add to (or detract from) her character? Cite specific details from the poem to support your analysis.

INTERNET
Projects and Activities
Keyword: LE5 12-7

SKILLS FOCUS
Literary Skills
Analyze satire.
Writing Skills
Write a character analysis.

Nigerian bronze head, thought to be an Ife king (13th century).
The British Museum, London.

FAMILY/COMMUNITY ACTIVITY

From a legal standpoint, how easily could the speaker find an apartment in your community today? Have students research and report on local laws relating to discrimination in housing.

Mini-Workshop

Analyzing Nonfiction

At first glance, a nonfiction selection such as George Orwell's much anthologized essay "Shooting an Elephant" (page 899) might seem to convey only simple information about an event far removed from the experience of contemporary readers. A close analysis of the essay, however, reveals how carefully Orwell arranged the basic data of his experience to convey a **theme** that has significance beyond the essay's time and setting. In your **analysis of nonfiction**, you will examine the many layers of meaning that can make up an essay's theme, and you will share your insights with others.

Choose an Essay Find an essay whose subject matter intrigues you. You might scan the table of contents of this book for an essay you haven't yet read. You may also ask a librarian for suggestions of essay collections, or ask a teacher to recommend an essay you might enjoy.

Consider Purpose, Audience, and Tone Your **purpose** in analyzing an essay is to explain your interpretation of the essay's theme to an **audience** of your teacher or your peers. Use a serious, objective **tone** to show that you understand and respect the essay.

Gain an Overview Plan to read the essay at least twice. The first time through, read for general understanding and to note the organization of the essay. Take notes on the essay's **subject** and the author's **purpose**—informative, persuasive, expressive, or entertaining. Then, decide if the essay's **tone** is informal (personal) or formal (objective). You may need to do research to understand the context of the essay you are analyzing. Your research may include information on the author or on the topic of the essay.

Analyze the Theme To determine the **theme** of the essay, read back through the essay a second time for general statements about life or human nature, such as Orwell's declaration, "I perceived in this moment that when the white man turns tyrant it is his own freedom that he destroys" (902). Write down any **direct quotations** that you find, along with their page numbers. You may also **paraphrase** or **summarize** from the text to help you in your notetaking. Remember that while some essays state the theme, others imply a theme. If the theme isn't stated explicitly, ask yourself, "What do all my notes imply about the essay's statements on life or human nature? In answering that question, you'll be formulating your understanding of the essay's theme.

Look for Stylistic Devices Essayists often use stylistic devices to intensify the theme of the essay. As part of your analysis, you may want to include comments about the essay's use of **concrete sensory details, figures of speech, imagery,** or **irony**—verbal, dramatic, or situational. For example, one student noted that Orwell's figure of

Writing Assignment
Write an essay of at least 1,500 words in which you analyze the theme of a professional essay and support your analysis with textual evidence.

Writing Skills
Write an essay analyzing nonfiction. Determine purpose, audience, and tone.

PRETEACHING

Motivate. Have each student write a one-paragraph description of the classroom, and ask volunteers to share their descriptions with the class. Emphasize for students the variety of the results, especially given that all of the descriptions are of the same room. Lead students to discuss the ways in which nonfiction can be just as descriptive and artful as fiction.

DIRECT TEACHING

Analyze the Theme

If students analyze an essay in which the author does not clearly state a theme or main idea, they might ask additional questions such as these:
- How is the author's perspective on the subject unique and particular?
- What stylistic devices (such as repetition and imagery) give an idea of the author's main focus on the subject?

If students concentrate on what makes the essay unique, they will be better able to separate the subject from the author's thematic treatment of it.

COLLECTION 7 RESOURCES: WRITING

Planning
- *One-Stop Planner* CD-ROM with ExamView Test Generator

Differentiating Instruction
- *Workshop Resources: Writing, Listening, and Speaking*
- *Family Involvement Activities in English and Spanish*
- *Supporting Instruction in Spanish*

Writing and Language
- *Workshop Resources: Writing, Listening, and Speaking*
- *Daily Language Activities*
- *Language Handbook Worksheets*

Assessment
- *Holt Assessment: Writing, Listening, and Speaking*

- *One-Stop Planner* CD-ROM with ExamView Test Generator
- *Holt Online Assessment*
- *Holt Online Essay Scoring*

Internet
- go.hrw.com (Keyword: LE5 12-7)
- *Elements of Literature Online*

RETEACHING

Write a Thesis Statement
To reteach the skill of developing a thesis statement for an analytical essay, remind students of the stage children go through when they repeatedly ask the question "Why?" Point out to students that a good thesis statement similarly investigates the reasons beneath the surface: "How does Orwell reveal his view of imperialism in his essay?" "Why does he feel the way he does?"

DIFFERENTIATING INSTRUCTION

Advanced Learners
Enrichment. Because the themes of many pieces of nonfiction touch on wide-ranging philosophical or historical topics—George Orwell's "Shooting an Elephant," given its historical context and insight into human nature, is a good example—encourage students to cite one or two secondary sources in their essays. The secondary sources may provide important historical background or be used to elaborate on the ideas in the author's theme.

PRACTICE & APPLY

Guided and Independent Practice
Guide students in writing their analyses with these questions:
- How is the essay you have chosen relevant to issues current today? Introduce readers to your subject by relating it to a present-day event or concern.
- Does the author suggest something deep about the problem or hint at a possible answer? Conclude your essay by connecting the author's theme on the topic to the current issue you used in the introduction.

---

speech—"If the elephant charged and I missed him, I should have about as much chance as a toad under a steamroller" (903)—intensifies the drama of the moment and heightens Orwell's mixed feelings.

Write a Thesis Statement Sum up your ideas about the essay's theme in a sentence that will guide the rest of your analysis. The **thesis statement** should identify the theme you'll analyze and mention the stylistic device most important to the development of that theme. For example, one student's thesis statement identified the theme of Orwell's essay and hinted at the importance of irony to the development of that theme.

 TIP When drafting your essay, use **standard American English** for your analysis.

> In "Shooting an Elephant," George Orwell ironically describes an incident he experienced as a young police officer in colonial Burma to show that tyranny debases the oppressors as much as it debases the oppressed.

Gather Support To support your thesis statement, use three or more **key points**—reasons that readers should accept your interpretation of the theme. Then, use **evidence** you've gathered from the essay to support each of your key points. **Elaborate** by explaining how the evidence develops each key point. Here is the way one student developed a key point with evidence and elaboration.

DO THIS

TIP Remember to document direct quotations with page numbers in parentheses. For more on **documenting sources**, see page 211.

> **Key Point:** Orwell makes clear the irony of his situation in Burma: As a police officer, he was publicly required to carry out policy he did not believe in privately; privately, he despised the people who taunted him in public.
>
> **Evidence (paraphrase and direct quotation):** Orwell had decided that he favored the Burmese, as much as he disliked them, but as a representative of the British Empire his job required him to see "the dirty work of Empire at close quarters" (899).
>
> **Elaboration:** As an agent of the empire, he was required to enforce a system whose aims and methods he rejected. He understood and sympathized with the Burmese people's anti-European attitude, yet their behavior infuriated him.

Organize Your Essay Present your ideas in a logical manner—either **chronologically** or in the **order of importance.** Include background information and the author and title of the essay in your introduction. Close your essay with a restatement of thesis and a dramatic statement.

Writing Skills
Write a thesis statement. Gather support. Organize the essay.

PRACTICE & APPLY Use the instructions in this workshop to write an analysis of an essay. Share your essay with your classmates and, if possible, with a wider audience.

Collection 7:
The Modern World:
1900 to the Present

Discoveries and Transformations

Yeats
Rilke
Joyce
Lawrence
Akhmatova
Bowen
Cortázar
Borges
Naipaul
Mahfouz
Heaney

Life spends itself in the act of transformation, dissolving, bit by bit, the world as it appeared.
—Rainer Maria Rilke

Our Dream (1999) by Alfredo Castañeda. Oil on canvas.
Courtesy of Mary-Anne Martin/Fine Art, New York.

VIEWING THE ART

Born in Mexico, **Alfredo Castañeda** (1938–) is probably best known for his use of surreal imagery, something perfectly illustrated by *Our Dream*. This painting juxtaposes a realistic figure with a neon-like hat and a seascape-like beard.

Activity. Ask students to consider what the organization of the three disparate features of the painting suggests. [Possible response: Castañeda is suggesting that humans are progressively moving away from nature. The ocean represents the natural environment where scientists say life originated; the man represents the civilized world; and the neon-like hat represents the turn toward technology and the future.]

THE QUOTATION

Rainer Maria Rilke (1875–1926) was born to a German-speaking family in Prague, now the capital of the Czech Republic, when the area was still part of the Austro-Hungarian empire. He is considered one of the most original poets of the twentieth century. In this quotation, Rilke probes the transience of contemporary society, pointing out that everything is in the act of transformation.

SKILLS FOCUS, pp. 944–954

Grade-Level Skills

- **Literary Skills**

Analyze the way the theme of a selection represents a comment on life.

- **Literary Skills**

Analyze the way an author's style, including the use of symbol, assonance, and alliteration, achieves specific aesthetic purposes.

More About the Writer

Background. When the Abbey Theatre opened its doors in 1904, there were three plays in the repertory; two of them were by William Butler Yeats. Although Yeats's interest in drama waned after a few years, Lady Gregory, Yeats's partner in the venture, was a prolific, committed dramatist who wrote or translated more than forty plays. Yeats soon gave up an active role in the management of the Abbey, but the institution went on to play a critical role in the development of modern drama, showcasing such playwrights as John Millington Synge, Sean O'Casey, and George Bernard Shaw.

William Butler Yeats
(1865–1939)

Ireland

William Butler Yeats (detail) (20th century) by John Butler Yeats. Oil on canvas (77 cm × 64 cm). National Gallery of Ireland, Dublin.

Generally regarded as the twentieth century's greatest poet writing in English, William Butler Yeats (rhymes with *crates*) was born in Dublin, Ireland, the son of a well-known portrait painter. He arrived on the literary scene when the Pre-Raphaelite movement (see page 684) of the mid–nineteenth century was reviving.

The revival, called Art Nouveau, emphasized the mysterious and unfathomable—especially those recesses of the mind just then being scrutinized by the great pioneers in psychology, Sigmund Freud and Carl Jung. Particularly in poetry, the revival recommended suggestion above statement, symbols above facts, and musical measures above common speech. It was within this atmosphere that the young Yeats established a reputation as a lyricist of great delicacy and as a versifier of old tales drawn from Irish folklore and mythology. In a collection of his early poems, *The Wanderings of Oisin and Other Poems* (1889), Yeats was a romantic dreamer, evoking the mythic and heroic past of Ireland. At this stage of his career, he was a pioneer of the Celtic Revival, determined to make the Irish conscious of their heroic past.

In 1914, Yeats set out to create a stark, chiseled, and eloquently resonant kind of poetry. That same year, he published a volume aptly titled *Responsibilities*. The man who had once seen himself as the prophet-priest of Ireland's national destiny was now grappling with his own personal realities. For years, Yeats had idolized and yearned for Maud Gonne, the beautiful Irish political activist who rejected his hand and instead chose another, more politically radical suitor. Yeats finally accepted that rejection and in 1917, at fifty-two, married Georgie Hyde-Lees, an Englishwoman who would remain his "delight and comfort" for the next twenty-two years.

From 1922 to 1928, Yeats served as a senator of the newly formed Irish Free State. He also toured the United States, giving ritualized readings of the poems for which, in 1923, he was awarded the Nobel Prize in literature.

Yeats may be said to have carved out of English a language distinctly his own. Monumentally spare and unadorned, "cold and passionate as the dawn" in Yeats's own words, it confirms the basic definition of poetry as "heightened speech."

Yeats was also a dramatist, and in this role he helped his friend Lady Gregory establish Dublin's Abbey Theatre as a monument to Irish culture and high literary standards. Some audiences may agree with Yeats himself, who felt that some of his most memorable poems are embedded, like gems, in the scripts of his plays.

Nearly ten years after Yeats's death and burial in the south of France, his body was disinterred and sent back to Ireland. Like a primitive king, with full ceremony and military pomp, he returned on the deck of a battleship.

944 Collection 7 The Modern World: 1900 to the Present

RESOURCES: READING

Planning
- *One-Stop Planner* CD-ROM with ExamView Test Generator

Differentiating Instruction
- Holt Reading Solutions
- The Holt Reader
- Supporting Instruction in Spanish
- Audio CD Library, Selections and Summaries in Spanish

Grammar and Language
- Daily Language Activities

Assessment
- Holt Assessment: Literature, Reading, and Vocabulary
- *One-Stop Planner* CD-ROM with ExamView Test Generator
- Holt Online Assessment

Internet
- go.hrw.com (Keyword: LE5 12-7)
- Elements of Literature Online

Media
- Audio CD Library
- Audio CD Library, Selections and Summaries in Spanish

Before You Read

The Second Coming

Make the Connection
Quickwrite

This poem is Yeats's articulation of a feeling many of us have had—a feeling of anxiety and dread as one phase of life ends and another, more chaotic phase begins. Written after World War I, "The Second Coming" prophesies the passing of civilization from one era into the next. The change, Yeats predicts, will not be a pleasant one. Instead, it will be marked by violence, bloodshed, and the "rough beast" of totalitarianism, a form of government marked by authoritarianism and dictatorship.

Recall a major transition in your own life, especially one that you dreaded or resisted. Jot down a few sentences describing this transition. Then list four or five emotions that the transition triggered in you.

Literary Focus
Theme

The poem's title and many of its images allude to the Christian view of history—specifically, a prophecy from the Book of Revelation in the Bible. (An **allusion** is a reference to something that is known from literature, religion, politics, and so on.) In turn, the poem's **theme,** or central insight, relies upon this allusion—and turns it inside out. As you read, ask yourself why Yeats refers to this Christian idea of a just and peaceful end of time—especially in the context of the chaos just unleashed by World War I and the Russian Revolution of 1917. (Yeats wrote this poem in 1921.) What idea about the Second Coming—or about the security and comfort of Christian hope—might Yeats be attempting to express?

> The **theme** of a literary work is the central idea or insight it reveals about human experience.
>
> For more on Theme, see the Handbook of Literary and Historical Terms.

Background

In Christianity, the Second Coming refers to the belief that Jesus will one day return to earth and usher in an era of peace and justice. This Second Coming is prophesied in the Book of Revelation in the Bible. The "first coming" was the birth of Jesus in Bethlehem in Judea, just over two thousand years ago.

The poem addresses not only the Christian conception of the universe but also Yeats's personal view of history. As he explains in his book *A Vision,* Yeats saw human history as cyclical. Each cycle, known as a gyre, begins in a rational state and then gradually dissolves into chaos and irrationality. "What if the irrational returns?" Yeats asks in his poem *A Vision.* That question is repeated poetically in the work you are about to read.

INTERNET
More About William Butler Yeats
Keyword: LE5 12-7

Literary Skills
Understand theme.

PRETEACHING

Summary *at grade level*

Although this poem's title alludes to the traditional Christian belief in the Second Coming of Jesus, the speaker ironically reverses our expectations. As the Second Coming is described in the poem, humanity will experience a ghastly new era of warfare and savagery. Using an ominously ironic tone, the speaker juxtaposes the "rocking cradle" at Bethlehem with the advent of a "rough beast" that symbolizes a dark and pitiless epoch to come.

Selection Starter

Motivate. Ask students to speculate about the state of the world ten years from now. Will human beings have made much progress toward ending warfare, feeding the hungry, curing diseases, and eliminating poverty? How do students think that they might personally contribute to such efforts?

VIEWING THE ART

Yeats's father, **John Butler Yeats** (1839–1922), was a distinguished portrait painter.

Activity. Before students read Yeats's poems, ask them what they can infer about the poet's personality from his posture and facial expression in the portrait by his father on p. 944. [Possible responses: He is sensitive, pleasant-natured, scholarly.]

DIFFERENTIATING INSTRUCTION

Learners Having Difficulty
Make sure students understand the many allusions in this poem, including the title, references to an Egyptian sphinx, the beast of the Apocalypse in the Bible, and the "rocking cradle."

Invite learners having difficulty to read "The Second Coming" in interactive format in *The Holt Reader* and to use the sidenotes as aids to understanding the selection.

English-Language Learners
For lessons designed for English-language learners and special education students, see *Holt Reading Solutions.*

The Second Coming

William Butler Yeats

Turning and turning in the widening gyre
The falcon cannot hear the falconer;
Things fall apart; the center cannot hold;
Mere anarchy is loosed upon the world,
5   The blood-dimmed tide is loosed, and everywhere
The ceremony of innocence is drowned;
The best lack all conviction, while the worst
Are full of passionate intensity.

Surely some revelation is at hand;
10 Surely the Second Coming is at hand.
The Second Coming! Hardly are those words out
When a vast image out of Spiritus Mundi°
Troubles my sight: somewhere in sands of the desert
A shape with lion body and the head of a man,
15 A gaze blank and pitiless as the sun,
Is moving its slow thighs, while all about it
Reel shadows of the indignant desert birds.
The darkness drops again; but now I know
That twenty centuries of stony sleep
20 Were vexed to nightmare by a rocking cradle,
And what rough beast, its hour come round at last,
Slouches towards Bethlehem to be born?

---

12. **Spiritus Mundi:** Latin for "the world's soul or spirit"; for Yeats, the collective reservoir of human memory from which artists draw their images.

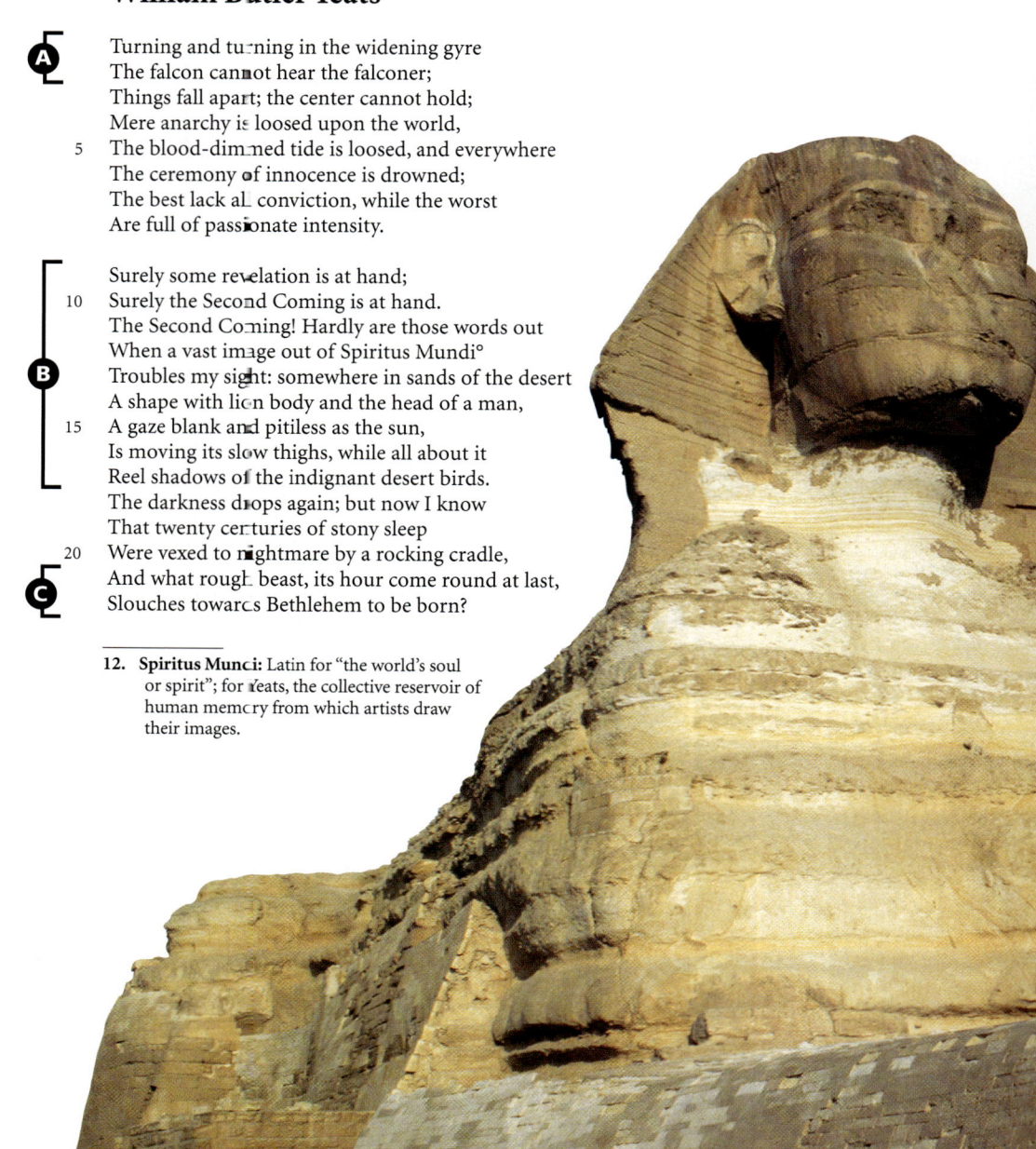

Response and Analysis

Thinking Critically

1. The first two lines of the poem present an **image**—that of a falconer who is unable to limit the flight of his released hawk as it spirals out of control. How does this image help to convey one of the poem's central **themes**? (Consider the poem's historical context—the time during which it was written—in your response.)

2. What do you think the poet means by the word *center* in line 3? What condition is being described by the phrase "the center cannot hold"?

3. What might the "blood-dimmed tide" in line 5 refer to? What could the "ceremony of innocence" in line 6 mean?

4. What **image** of the Second Coming troubles the speaker in the second half of the poem? List some of the specific words that make this image especially vivid.

5. **Irony** is a discrepancy between what is expected and what actually happens. How does the idea of the Second Coming become **ironic** in the second stanza? In what sense is this irony frightening?

6. Comment on the poet's use of each of the following words: *mere* (line 4), *pitiless* (line 15), *indignant* (line 17), *stony* (line 19), and *slouches* (line 22). Think about the **connotations** of each word. What idea or emotion does each word help to convey? How vivid or forceful do you find each word in its particular context?

7. If you had to name one dominant emotion expressed by the speaker of this poem, what would it be? Check your Quickwrite notes for ideas before you respond.

Extending and Evaluating

8. Why might Yeats have ended the poem with a question? In your opinion, can this question be answered? Explain.

WRITING

Yesterday and Today

This poem was written after the horrors of World War I. Yeats asks, "Have we, like the falconer, lost control of the means to halt our descent into chaos?" Is Yeats's question still relevant today? In a brief **essay,** explain how "The Second Coming" reflects—or does not reflect—your own ideas about human progress and the shape of the future. Use quotations from the poem in your response.

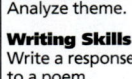

Literary Skills
Analyze theme.

Writing Skills
Write a response to a poem.

Thinking Critically

1. The image supports the theme of society spinning out of control, which seemed accurate in the aftermath of World War I.

2. Possible answers: The word *center* suggests order, rationality, spiritual conviction, or moral behavior. The phrase "the center cannot hold" suggests that evil or chaos is gaining the upper hand.

3. The "blood-dimmed tide" may refer to warfare. The "ceremony of innocence" may refer to baptism, the ritual of initiation into Christianity, or, more generally, to peacefulness or morality.

INDEPENDENT PRACTICE

Response and Analysis

4. The main image is of a threatening, semi-human creature slowly stirring in the desert. Details include "A shape with lion body and the head of a man," "A gaze blank and pitiless," "slow thighs," and "Slouches."

5. Instead of the promise of peace and justice suggested by the biblical allusion, Yeats ironically prophesies a future of beastliness, savagery, and chaos. The image threatens belief in Christianity.

6. *Mere* (l. 4) is verbally ironic when coupled with *anarchy*; *pitiless* (l. 15) denotes absence of mercy and connotes danger; *indignant* (l. 17) suggests that nature itself is outraged; *stony* (l. 19) suggests heartlessness; *slouches* (l. 22) suggests disorder, menace, or contempt. Students may find these words particularly vivid in the context.

7. Possible answers: dread, terror, outrage.

Extending and Evaluating

8. Possible answer: The question reinforces the prevailing mood of terror. The question cannot be answered, because it concerns the future.

ASSESSING

Assessment
- *Holt Assessment: Literature, Reading, and Vocabulary*

RETEACHING

For a lesson reteaching author's tone and style, see **Reteaching,** p. 1129A.

William Butler Yeats

PRETEACHING

Summary ⇔ at grade level

In a lyric that is both decisive and dreamlike, the speaker determines that he will leave his urban home and go to the lake island of Innisfree. There he will build a cabin and live alone in harmony with nature. He looks forward to the peace and transcendent natural beauty of the island. He states that one reason for his departure is that he constantly hears, deep in his heart, the sound of the lake water lapping along the shoreline.

Selection Starter

Motivate. Since this poem alludes to Henry David Thoreau's *Walden*, call on volunteers to share their knowledge about that work and about Thoreau. Point out that Yeats wrote this poem set in Ireland many years after Thoreau's death. However, the poem can be regarded, in some measure at least, as Yeats's response to Thoreau's deep-seated wish to live in harmony with nature.

Before You Read

The Lake Isle of Innisfree

Make the Connection
Quickwrite

Imagination can help us visualize what we want to create or accomplish—what we hope to make real. But imagination can also transport us *out* of reality, into a distant place or state of mind that renews our energy and restores our spirit. As you read this poem by Yeats, ask yourself whether the poem is more concerned with a broad vision of a life the poet wishes to create for himself than with an immediate momentary escape from the daily grind.

When your life becomes hectic or stressful, do you imagine a place or a time in which you could feel calm and free? Describe what this place is like or might be like. How does imagining this place make you feel?

Literary Focus
Assonance and Alliteration

As a young poet, Yeats inherited much of the vocabulary and poetic conventions of his nineteenth-century predecessors. Thus, some of the phrases in this poem—"veils of the morning," "midnight's all a glimmer"—are right out of the old-fashioned Victorian vocabulary. Innisfree itself is one of those impossibly idyllic, great good places that industrial-era Victorians yearned for. Nevertheless, this poem rises above its more mundane counterparts.

Yeats's lyrical skills, especially his haunting use of **assonance** and **alliteration,** create a poem whose verbal music has echoed in readers' memories for over a hundred years. The lilting rhythms of the poem and the repetition of both vowel sounds (assonance) and consonant sounds (alliteration) work together to soothe and transport the reader, much as a lullaby does a child.

INTERNET
More About
William
Butler Yeats
Keyword: LE5 12-7

SKILLS FOCUS

Literary Skills
Understand
assonance and
alliteration.

Assonance is the repetition of similar vowel sounds in words that are close together.

Alliteration is the repetition of similar consonant sounds in words that are close together.

For more on Assonance and Alliteration, see the Handbook of Literary and Historical Terms.

Background

Innisfree is a real island in Sligo, the beautiful county in the west of Ireland where Yeats spent many summers as a child, visiting his grandparents. Yeats once said that the poem came to him when he was in London on a dreary day. He passed a store display that used dripping water in a fountain, and he thought at once of the lake island of his childhood. Yeats's father had once read Thoreau's *Walden* to him. The bean rows and cabin in this poem are straight from Thoreau's account of his life in the Walden Woods of Massachusetts.

948 Collection 7 The Modern World: 1900 to the Present

The Lake Isle of Innisfree

William Butler Yeats

I will arise and go now, and go to Innisfree,
And a small cabin build there, of clay and wattles° made:
Nine bean-rows will I have there, a hive for the honey-bee,
And live alone in the bee-loud glade.

5   And I shall have some peace there, for peace comes dropping slow,
Dropping from the veils of the morning to where the cricket sings;
There midnight's all a glimmer, and noon a purple glow,
And evening full of the linnet's° wings.

I will arise and go now, for always night and day
10 I hear lake water lapping with low sounds by the shore;
While I stand on the roadway, or on the pavements gray,
I hear it in the deep heart's core.

2. wattles *n. pl.:* interwoven twigs or branches.

8. linnet's: A linnet is a European songbird.

Lakeside Cottages (c. 1929) by Paul Henry. Oil on canvas (16" × 24").
Hugh Lane Municipal Gallery of Modern Art, Dublin.

INDEPENDENT PRACTICE

Response and Analysis

Thinking Critically

1. He will go to Innisfree, build a small cabin, and live in it alone. He does not actually do this within the bounds of the poem, but he imaginatively hears the sound of the lake in the city.
2. He describes the buzzing of bees, a cricket singing, and lake water lapping the shore.
3. Peace is like the fall of morning dew.
4. The island is beautiful, natural, and tranquil; the speaker's actual location has roadways and gray pavements.
5. Possible answer: He evidently loves the peace and quiet of life away from the city.
6. Possible answers: The tone is lyrical, nostalgic, and muted. Because the speaker seems to value the beauty of nature, the poem could be called a Romantic work.

Extending and Evaluating

7. Possible answers: He refers so often to himself because his intentions and emotions are highly personal. Many students will agree that the repetition of the long *i* sound is soothing.

Literary Focus: Assonance and Alliteration

1. The dominant vowel sounds are long *i* (*I, arise, nine, hive*), long *o* (*go, rows, alone*), long *e* (*Innisfree, bean, bee*), and long *a* (*clay, made, glade*).
2. The rhyming words emphasize the long *a, e,* and *o* sounds and the short *i* sound.

Response and Analysis

Thinking Critically

1. In the first stanza, what does the speaker say he will do? Does he do this? Explain.
2. What sounds does the speaker describe in the poem?
3. To what does the speaker compare peace?
4. How do the surroundings of the lake island contrast with the speaker's actual location?
5. Why do you think the speaker cannot find peace in the city setting?
6. How would you describe the **tone** of this poem? Do you think it could be called a Romantic poem? Explain why or why not.

Extending and Evaluating

7. The pronoun *I* is repeated seven times in this short, twelve-line poem. In your opinion, why does the speaker so often insert himself into the scene he describes? Does this intrusion make the poem more or less soothing to you, the reader? Explain.

Lough Gill, County Sligo (20th century) by Jack Butler Yeats. Watercolor on paper.
National Gallery of Ireland, Dublin. © A. P. Watt Ltd on behalf of Michael B. Yeats.

Literary Skills Analyze assonance and alliteration.
Writing Skills Write a poem or a paragraph describing a place.

WRITING

A Place of Peace

The first line of "The Lake Isle of Innisfree" is often quoted. Write your own **poem** or **paragraph** beginning with the words "I will arise and go now. . ." Then, go on to describe your own ideal place of peace. You should refer to your Quickwrite notes before you begin.

Literary Focus

Assonance and Alliteration

The music of this poem comes in part from Yeats's use of **assonance,** the repetition of similar vowel sounds in nearby words. The poem is also notable for a famous line (line 10) of **alliteration**—the repetition of similar consonant sounds in nearby words.

1. What vowel sounds dominate the first stanza?
2. What vowel sounds are emphasized by the rhyming words?
3. Explain how alliteration helps the reader visualize the imagery of line 10.
4. How would you describe the total effect of the vowel sounds in the poem? (How would the poem have been different if the poet had used more hard consonants, such as *k, d,* or *p*?)

3. The liquid, repeated *l* sound in *lake, lapping,* and *low* helps the reader "see" the scene by the shore and "hear" the gently moving water.
4. The repeated vowel sounds make the poem musical and haunting. Harder consonants would have produced a harsher, less airy, and less lyrical effect.

Assessment
- Holt Assessment: Literature, Reading, and Vocabulary

RETEACHING

For a lesson reteaching author's tone and style, see **Reteaching,** p. 1129A.

Before You Read

The Wild Swans at Coole

Make the Connection
Quickwrite

Yeats first saw the scene described in this poem when he was thirty-two. He wrote the poem at the age of fifty-one. How might the passage of time transform a person's response to something familiar—be it a person, a place, or a thing?

Think of a familiar scene to which you have returned over the years. In a short paragraph, describe how time has affected your responses to the scene.

Literary Focus
Symbol

A **symbol** is something that can be understood literally (for what it is) and also figuratively (as a representative of something beyond itself). Yeats's swans can be regarded as symbols, but what do they represent? As you read this poem, keep in mind that symbols, by their very nature, are open-ended: Their meanings are various and open to interpretation.

> A **symbol** is a figure of speech in which a person, place, thing, or event stands both for itself and for something beyond itself.
>
> *For more on Symbol, see the Handbook of Literary and Historical Terms.*

Background

Yeats's good friend and fellow writer Lady Gregory lived on an estate known as Coole Park in Ireland's County Galway. When Yeats first visited there in 1897, he was in love with Maud Gonne, the beautiful activist for Irish independence, who was more interested in politics than in marriage. This poem, written in 1916, recalls Yeats's first view of the swans; now, nineteen years later, he realizes that "All's changed."

The swans are wild, or migratory. Like the poet, they return annually to familiar places. Yeats knew that swans are monogamous, that "lover by lover" they continue to live in a state of mated bliss denied to him. But the larger meanings of the poem lie in the relationship between memory, time, loss, and the inflexible patterns of natural life represented by the swans.

INTERNET
More About William Butler Yeats
Keyword: LE5 12-7

SKILLS FOCUS

Literary Skills Understand symbols.

William Butler Yeats 951

PRETEACHING

Summary ⟷ at grade level

On a lakeshore in Coole Park, in an October twilight, the speaker counts fifty-nine swans. He recalls counting them nineteen years before and remarks that "their hearts have not grown old" and they have remained faithful to their mates. The speaker, however, has a sore heart, and he acknowledges that much has changed in his life since he first saw the swans.

Selection Starter

Build background. Over an extended period of time, Yeats's love for Maud Gonne inspired many of his works besides "The Wild Swans at Coole." These works include poems from the collection *The Wind among the Reeds* (1899), the dramatic plays *The Wanderings of Oisin* (1889) and *The Shadowy Waters* (1906), and the plays *The Land of Heart's Desire* (1894), *On Baile's Strand* (1904), and *Deirdre* (1907).

DIFFERENTIATING INSTRUCTION

Learners Having Difficulty
Have small groups of students write a paraphrase of one of the five stanzas and present it to the class.

Advanced Learners
Enrichment. Encourage students to read the poem in light of the following events: World War I was raging; the Easter Rising of 1916 had ended in defeat; Maud Gonne had given Yeats a final rebuff.

The Wild Swans at Coole

William Butler Yeats

The trees are in their autumn beauty,
The woodland paths are dry,
Under the October twilight the water
Mirrors a still sky;
5 Upon the brimming water among the stones
Are nine-and-fifty swans.

The nineteenth autumn has come upon me
Since I first made my count;
I saw, before I had well finished,
10 All suddenly mount
And scatter wheeling in great broken rings
Upon their clamorous wings.

I have looked upon those brilliant creatures,
And now my heart is sore.
15 All's changed since I, hearing at twilight,
The first time on this shore,
The bell-beat of their wings above my head,
Trod with a lighter tread.

Unwearied still, lover by lover,
20 They paddle in the cold
Companionable streams or climb the air;
Their hearts have not grown old;
Passion or conquest, wander where they will,
Attend upon them still.

25 But now they drift on the still water,
Mysterious, beautiful;
Among what rushes will they build,
By what lake's edge or pool
Delight men's eyes when I awake some day
30 To find they have flown away?

DIRECT TEACHING

A Vocabulary Development

Multiple meanings. Yeats uses *still* in l. 4 to mean "motionless" or "tranquil." *Still* can also be used as an adverb to mean "up to this or that time." How is *still* used in ll. 19, 24, and 25? [In ll. 19 and 24, *still* means "up to this or that time"; in l. 25, it means "motionless."]

B Reading Skills

Making inferences. What is the speaker's mood in the third stanza? [Possible responses: regretful; nostalgic; disappointed.] Why do you think that viewing the swans elicits such a mood? [It reminds him of a happier time nineteen years earlier, when he first viewed the swans.]

C Reading Skills

Interpreting. In the fourth stanza, what does the speaker suggest about himself in contrast to the swans? [Possible response: He suggests that he is alone and weary and that his own heart has grown old.]

D Literary Focus

Symbol. In order to serve as a symbol, the swans must possess qualities that allow them to stand not only for themselves but also for something else. What words in ll. 25–29 help establish the swans' status as symbols? ["Mysterious, beautiful"; "Delight men's eyes"]

CONTENT-AREA CONNECTIONS

Music: Swan Song
Ask students to locate a recording or to invent a melody that captures the essence of this poem. Point out that the tone and mood of the poem change as it progresses, and then suggest that the music they choose or create should reflect these changes. Students may want to play their musical selections as they read the poem to the class.

History: Maud Gonne MacBride
Individual activity. Maud Gonne, object of Yeats's unrequited love, embraced Irish Republicanism and worked tirelessly in the slums of Dublin and the poverty-stricken west. The man she preferred to Yeats was John MacBride, a leader of the organization that was to become Sinn Fein. Encourage students to research this fascinating woman and present their findings to the class in an oral report.

CONNECTION / POEM

The poet Rainer Maria Rilke (ri′nər mä • rē′ä ril′kə) (1875–1926), who wrote in German, was among the most original writers of the twentieth century. One of his greatest influences was the French sculptor Auguste Rodin, with whom Rilke worked. One day, Rilke confided to Rodin that he was suffering from writer's block. Rodin suggested a cure: Go to the zoo, he said, and observe an animal until you can truly see it. Rilke took the unusual advice, concentrated on a panther, and soon after produced the first of his "thing poems"—poems that seek to communicate both the concrete outward appearance of a thing (an animal, for example) and its abstract, invisible inner vitality and spirit—its "inward nature." In "The Swan," Rilke makes an elegant extended comparison using the concrete image of a swan to explore a concept that is anything but concrete.

The Swan

Rainer Maria Rilke
translated by **Robert Bly**

This clumsy living that moves lumbering
as if in ropes through what is not done
reminds us of the awkward way the swan walks.

And to die, which is a letting go
5   of the ground we stand on and cling to every day,
is like the swan when he nervously lets himself down

into the water, which receives him gaily
and which flows joyfully under
and after him, wave after wave,
10 while the swan, unmoving and marvelously calm,
is pleased to be carried, each minute more fully grown,
more like a king, composed, farther and farther on.

Comparing and Contrasting Texts

Evaluating symbolic meanings. In both Yeats's "The Wild Swans at Coole" and Rilke's "The Swan," swans are symbolically linked to beauty, mystery, and grace. However, Rilke also describes the awkward gait of the swan on land. Whereas a melancholy atmosphere marks Yeats's poem, the mood in Rilke's poem is joyful, especially in the last stanza. Yeats sadly alludes to themes of old age, decline, and mortality, but for Rilke, death is a fulfillment or a consummation, affording human beings the full achievement of their identity.

Small-group activity. Have small groups of students discuss the possible symbolic meanings of another animal: for example, an elephant, a lion, a tiger, a giraffe, a peacock, or a honeybee. Encourage students to explore any variations or ambiguities among their perspectives on those symbols.

Connection

Summary *at grade level*

The speaker compares the way we live to the awkward walk of a swan on land. Dying, which he sees as a "letting go," resembles the anxious descent of the swan into water. Just as it is only in water that the swan achieves its true identity, it is only in death that human beings truly find themselves.

DIRECT TEACHING

A Reading Skills

Comparing and contrasting. In ll. 1–3, to what does the speaker compare "this clumsy living"? [to the awkward way a swan walks]

B Reading Skills

Speculating. What are some of the things in life—"the ground we stand on"—that people tend to "cling to"? [Possible responses: relationships, creature comforts, careers.] When people let go of such things, do they tend to be nervous, like the swan? Why or why not? [Possible response: Yes, because of the intense investment of their time and emotions, and because of habit.]

C Literary Focus

Symbol. What might the swan symbolize in the poem? [calm, serenity, beauty, the full attainment of one's own nature; the peaceful state of death]

INDEPENDENT PRACTICE

Response and Analysis

Thinking Critically

1. He feels melancholy. Line 18 suggests that nineteen years ago, he felt more carefree.

2. Hints include the nineteen autumns (l. 7), which reveal that he is now much older. His "sore" heart (l. 14) suggests that he has undergone a sad or sobering experience. Lines 15–18 suggest that he wishes his life hadn't changed in the ways it has. Lines 22–24 imply that his heart has grown old; perhaps he has lost a lover or his ability to love.

3. Possible answer: Where will the swans go, and where will they build nests and delight others' eyes when they leave here?

4. Possible answers: He envies their beauty, faithfulness, timelessness, enduring passion, mystery, and ability to delight, perhaps because he has lost those qualities or never possessed them. The swans might symbolize timeless beauty, permanence, or perfect love.

5. The melancholy mood is reinforced by the setting, a twilight in autumn; both the time of day and the season are symbols for advancing age.

6. Possible answer: The word might suggest that the speaker's life is as fleeting as a dream; thus the word *awake*, paradoxically, could imply the speaker's death, and it could point to themes of mortality and lost passion.

7. Elegies are characterized by imagery drawn from nature, formal language and structure, and a solemn tone, all of which appear in this poem. The poem is more similar to "The Seafarer" (p. 82) and "Break, Break, Break" (p. 84)—especially in its mourning for time past—than it is to elegies that focus on someone who has died.

Extending and Evaluating

8. Possible answers: *sore, changed, mysterious, beautiful, awake,* and *away*. Students should be able to present persuasive reasons for their choice.

Response and Analysis

Thinking Critically

1. How does the speaker feel as he gazes at the swans? How did he feel nineteen years earlier when he heard the beating of their wings?

2. The second, third, and fourth stanzas offer hints about the personal experience that underlies the poem. What are those hints? Why do you think the speaker's heart is "sore" (line 14)? Reviewing your Quickwrite notes may help you understand the speaker's feeling.

3. **Paraphrase,** or state in your own words, the question the speaker asks in the last stanza.

4. What qualities of the swans do you think the speaker envies? Why? What might the swans **symbolize** to the speaker?

5. How are the time of year and the time of day in this poem appropriate to its **mood**?

6. The word *awake* in the next-to-last line is mysterious at first reading. Do you think it signifies that the poem has all been a dream? Or could it mean something else? How might this word offer a clue to the **theme** of the poem?

7. An **elegy** is a poem that mourns the death of a person or laments something that has been lost, such as beauty or times past. In what sense might this poem be thought of as an elegy? How does the poem relate in **theme, tone,** and **imagery** to any of the other famous elegies in this book (see pages 319, 727, and 1057)?

SKILLS FOCUS

Literary Skills
Analyze symbols.

Writing Skills
Write an essay comparing two poems.

Extending and Evaluating

8. In your opinion, what is the most important word or phrase in this poem? Be sure to compare your response with the responses of other readers. Be able to defend your choice with evidence from the poem.

WRITING

Birds of a Feather

In a brief **essay, compare** "The Wild Swans at Coole" with Rilke's "The Swan" (see the **Connection** on page 953). Use this graphic to collect details for your composition.

	Yeats	Rilke
Imagery		
Symbols		
Theme		

Japanese Footbridge and Water Lily Pool, Giverny (1899) by Claude Monet.
© Philadelphia Museum of Art/CORBIS.

954 Collection 7 The Modern World: 1900 to the Present

ASSESSING

Assessment

- Holt Assessment: Literature, Reading, and Vocabulary

James Joyce
(1882–1941)
Ireland

James Joyce (1934) by Jacques-Émile Blanche.
© Courtesy of the National Gallery of Ireland, Dublin. © 2003 Artists Rights Society (ARS), New York/ADAGP, Paris.

James Joyce's controversial masterpiece, *Ulysses* (1922), has probably had a greater effect on twentieth-century fiction than any other work of our times. Based on Homer's *Odyssey*, Joyce's *Ulysses* describes the events of a single day in Dublin, the city where Joyce grew up. And just as Homer's epic interpreted the world of the ancient Greeks, so does Joyce's epic mirror and interpret for us our own lives in the twentieth century.

Joyce was born in Rathgar, Ireland, a Dublin suburb. One of ten children in a fairly impoverished family, he was educated at a series of Roman Catholic schools, but by the time he entered University College, Dublin, he had lost his faith. After graduating, he went to Paris and existed frugally by giving English lessons and writing book reviews.

In 1903, Joyce returned home to be at his dying mother's bedside. Afterward he lived briefly in a Martello Tower (a former military fortification) on the coast near Dublin, a site that has now become the James Joyce Museum. There he began an autobiographical novel, *Stephen Hero*, and also wrote some of the stories later published in *Dubliners* (1914).

In June 1904, Joyce met and fell in love with a Galway girl named Nora Barnacle. The date of their first walk, June 16, 1904, was later immortalized as Bloomsday, the date on which the action of *Ulysses* takes place. When Joyce's debts mounted, he persuaded Nora to leave Ireland with him; Joyce was never to live in Ireland again.

The penniless couple settled first in the Italian city of Trieste, where their two children, George and Lucia, were born. Joyce's luck began to turn after 1914, when the influential American poet Ezra Pound reviewed *Dubliners* favorably and persuaded a British magazine to serialize *A Portrait of the Artist as a Young Man*, Joyce's rewritten version of *Stephen Hero*.

When Italy entered World War I in 1915, the Joyces left Trieste for Zurich, where Joyce worked on the early chapters of *Ulysses*. Because of sizable gifts from anonymous patrons, Joyce's financial troubles had begun to ease, but his physical problems increased. Between 1917 and 1930, he endured twenty-five operations for glaucoma and cataracts. Sometimes he was totally blind, yet he continued work on *Ulysses*.

British printers found *Ulysses* so scandalous that they refused to set it in type. In 1922, however, Sylvia Beach, the American owner of a bookstore in Paris called Shakespeare & Co., agreed to put out an edition of one thousand copies. Many of the reviews were favorable, but the book was banned in both Britain and the United States. Not until 1934, after a famous court case, was *Ulysses* published in America. A British edition soon followed, and the book's fame spread rapidly worldwide.

The Joyces, who had been living in Paris, returned to Zurich in 1940, when France fell to Nazi Germany. There Joyce became increasingly ill, his eye troubles complicated by a duodenal ulcer. He died on January 13, 1941, one month short of his fifty-ninth birthday.

PRETEACHING

Summary ⇄ at grade level

The young narrator has a crush on a neighborhood girl. The girl tells him she longs to go to Araby, a visiting bazaar, but cannot. The narrator decides to go and bring her something from what he imagines will be a thrillingly romantic place. After a series of frustrations, he arrives late, as the bazaar is closing. Instead of fulfilling his dreams of exotic luxury, Araby is dreary. It features cheap trinkets and is staffed by ordinary workers. The narrator has a desultory conversation with a young vendor. He leaves feeling disillusioned and ashamed of his vain dreams.

Selection Starter

Motivate. Have students think about an occasion when their hopes for an event, a place, or an experience were disappointed. How did they feel? What did they learn from the experience? Invite volunteers to tell about their experiences.

Before You Read

Araby

Make the Connection

When a person embarks upon a quest for the unknown—or for the deeply desired—he or she may suddenly see life in glowing terms. In place of the former, predictable routine there is a sense of endless possibilities in a fascinating world where anything can happen. Unfortunately, this "anything" is often something other than the anticipated outcome.

Literary Focus
Epiphany

Joyce called the moments of insight, or revelation, that his characters experience "epiphanies." Before Joyce used the word in this way, an **epiphany** referred solely to a religious experience, a moment during which a human being felt an intense connection with the divine or understood a spiritual truth he or she hadn't before. Although Joyce gave the word a modern, literary meaning, you will see that the main character's epiphany is described with the help of religious language and imagery.

INTERNET
Vocabulary Practice
•
More About James Joyce
•
Keyword: LE5 12-7

> In fiction, an **epiphany** is a moment of sudden insight or revelation experienced by a character.
>
> For more on Epiphany, see the Handbook of Literary and Historical Terms.

Reading Skills
Comparing and Contrasting

In "Araby" the main character has a vivid imagination that sometimes causes him to misunderstand the realities of his life. As you read the story, look for differences between the way the character imagines things to be and the way they really are. List these differences in a two-column comparison-contrast chart like the one here.

Imagination	Reality

Background

On May 14, 1894, a five-day charity bazaar came to the city of Dublin. The bazaar was called Araby, a reference to Arabia, where bazaars—markets with long rows of stalls or shops—are common. For the children of Dublin, Arabia seemed a mysterious, exotic place, very different from the streets of the dreary city in which they lived.

The house in this story is based on one in which Joyce and his family actually lived. It stood on the same blind (dead-end) street as the Christian Brothers' School Joyce attended.

Vocabulary Development

imperturbable (im′pər·tur′bə·bəl) *adj.*: calm; impassive.

somber (säm′bər) *adj.*: gloomy.

impinge (im·pinj′) *v.*: strike; touch.

annihilate (ə·nī′ə·lāt′) *v.*: destroy; make nonexistent.

monotonous (mə·nät″n·əs) *adj.*: unvarying.

garrulous (gar′ə·ləs) *adj.*: talkative.

improvised (im′prə·vīzd′) *v.* used as *adj.*: made for the occasion from whatever is handy.

pervades (pər·vādz′) *v.*: spreads throughout.

Literary Skills
Understand epiphany.

Reading Skills
Compare and contrast aspects of a story.

956 Collection 7 The Modern World: 1900 to the Present

Previewing Vocabulary

To reinforce understanding of the Vocabulary words on p. 956, have student pairs take turns choosing a Vocabulary word and then using it correctly in a sentence. When student pairs have finished selecting and using all the Vocabulary words, have students match every word in the following exercise with its definition.

1. improvised [e]
2. impinge [g]
3. annihilate [c]
4. monotonous [h]
5. imperturbable [d]
6. pervades [b]
7. somber [f]
8. garrulous [a]

a. talkative
b. spreads throughout
c. destroy
d. calm
e. made on the spot
f. dreary
g. strike
h. unvarying

Araby

James Joyce

North Richmond Street, being blind, was a quiet street except at the hour when the Christian Brothers' School set the boys free. An uninhabited house of two stories stood at the blind end, detached from its neighbors in a square ground. The other houses of the street, conscious of decent lives within them, gazed at one another with brown imperturbable faces.

The former tenant of our house, a priest, had died in the back drawing-room. Air, musty from having been long enclosed, hung in all the rooms, and the waste room behind the kitchen was littered with old useless papers. Among these I found a few paper-covered books, the pages of which were curled and damp: *The Abbot,* by Walter Scott, *The Devout Communicant,* and *The Memoirs of Vidocq.*[1] I liked the last best because its leaves were yellow. The wild garden behind the house contained a central apple-tree and a few straggling bushes under one of which I found the late tenant's rusty bicycle-pump. He had been a very charitable priest; in his will he had left all his money to institutions and the furniture of his house to his sister.

When the short days of winter came dusk fell before we had well eaten our dinners. When we met in the street the houses had grown somber. The space of sky above us was the color of ever-changing violet and toward it the lamps of the street lifted their feeble lanterns. The cold air stung us and we played till our bodies glowed. Our shouts echoed in the silent street. The career[2] of our play brought us through the dark muddy lanes behind the houses where we ran the gauntlet[3] of the rough tribes from the cottages, to the back doors of the dark dripping gardens where odors arose from the ashpits, to the dark odorous stables where a coachman smoothed and combed the horse or shook music from the buckled harness. When we returned to the street light from the kitchen windows had filled the areas. If my uncle was seen turning the corner we hid in the shadow until we had seen him safely housed. Or if Mangan's sister came out on the doorstep to call her brother in to his tea we watched her from our shadow peer up and down the street. We waited to see whether she would remain or go in and, if she remained, we left our shadow and walked up to Mangan's steps resignedly. She was waiting for us, her figure defined by the light from the half-opened door. Her brother always teased her before he obeyed and I stood by the railings looking at her. Her dress swung as she moved her body and the soft rope of her hair tossed from side to side.

Every morning I lay on the floor in the front parlor watching her door. The blind was pulled down to within an inch of the sash so that I could not be seen. When she came out on the doorstep my heart leaped. I ran to the hall, seized my books, and followed her. I kept her brown figure always in my eye and, when we came near the point at which our ways diverged, I quickened my pace and passed her. This happened morning after morning. I had

---

1. *The Abbott . . . Vidocq* (vē·duk′): in order, a historical romance about Mary, Queen of Scots, by Sir Walter Scott; an 1813 religious manual written by a Franciscan friar; and the memoirs (though not actually written by François Vidocq) of a French criminal who later became a detective.
2. **career** *n.:* course; path.
3. **gauntlet** (gônt′lit) *n.:* series of challenges. Derived from *gatlopp,* Swedish for "running down a lane," the term originally referred to a form of military punishment in which a wrongdoer had to run between two rows of soldiers who struck him as he passed.

Vocabulary
imperturbable (im′pər·tur′bə·bəl) *adj.:* calm; impassive.
somber (säm′bər) *adj.:* gloomy.

James Joyce 957

DIRECT TEACHING

VIEWING THE ART

In the second half of the nineteenth century, Irish artists began to look to continental Europe, rather than to England, for their training and inspiration. **Walter Osborne** (1859–1903) was among these artists. He moved to Antwerp, Belgium, to develop his craft and later moved to France where he became greatly influenced by French Impressionism. Osborne far surpassed his Irish contemporaries in his ability to employ European artistic techniques to create a uniquely Irish art. This picture, with its young boy walking through a market street playing a flute, captures the look and feel of Dublin in the late Victorian period.

Activity. How does the boy fit into the environment? [Possible response: The market is somewhat desolate, yet the boy walks down the street, engrossed in his music. It thereby suggests that he is somehow apart from the scene he is passing through.]

St Patrick's Close, Dublin by Walter Osborne.
© Courtesy of The National Gallery of Ireland.

DIFFERENTIATING INSTRUCTION

English-Language Learners
Students may be confused by the word *bazaar,* the meaning of which varies from culture to culture. Explain that in this story the word is used to mean "fair" or "carnival." Then, invite students to describe comparable events that take place in their own culture.

Special Education Students
For lessons designed for special education students, see *Holt Reading Solutions*.

Advanced Learners
Enrichment. The narrator imagines the Araby bazaar as a place of Eastern enchantment and mystery. Ask students to note other passages in the text in which the narrator romanticizes someone or something. What does this tendency reveal about the boy?

never spoken to her, except for a few casual words, and yet her name was like a summons to all my foolish blood.

Her image accompanied me even in places the most hostile to romance. On Saturday evenings when my aunt went marketing I had to go to carry some of the parcels. We walked through the flaring streets, jostled by drunken men and bargaining women, amid the curses of laborers, the shrill litanies[4] of shop-boys who stood on guard by the barrels of pigs' cheeks, the nasal chanting of street-singers, who sang a *come-all-you* about O'Donovan Rossa,[5] or a ballad about the troubles in our native land. These noises converged in a single sensation of life for me: I imagined that I bore my chalice[6] safely through a throng of foes. Her name sprang to my lips at moments in strange prayers and praises which I myself did not understand. My eyes were often full of tears (I could not tell why) and at times a flood from my heart seemed to pour itself out into my bosom. I thought little of the future. I did not know whether I would ever speak to her or not or, if I spoke to her, how I could tell her of my confused adoration. But my body was like a harp and her words and gestures were like fingers running upon the wires.

One evening I went into the back drawing-room in which the priest had died. It was a dark rainy evening and there was no sound in the house. Through one of the broken panes I heard the rain impinge upon the earth, the fine incessant needles of water playing in the sodden beds. Some distant lamp or lighted window gleamed below me. I was thankful that I could see so little. All my senses seemed to desire to veil themselves and, feeling that I was about to slip from them, I pressed the palms of my hands together until they trembled, murmuring: *O love! O love!* many times.

At last she spoke to me. When she addressed the first words to me I was so confused that I did not know what to answer. She asked me was I going to *Araby.* I forget whether I answered yes or no. It would be a splendid bazaar, she said; she would love to go.

—And why can't you? I asked.

While she spoke she turned a silver bracelet round and round her wrist. She could not go, she said, because there would be a retreat that week in her convent.[7] Her brother and two other boys were fighting for their caps and I was alone at the railings. She held one of the spikes, bowing her head toward me. The light from the lamp opposite our door caught the white curve of her neck, lit up her hair that rested there and, falling, lit up the hand upon the railing. It fell over one side of her dress and caught the white border of a petticoat, just visible as she stood at ease.

—It's well for you,[8] she said.

—If I go, I said, I will bring you something.

What innumerable follies laid waste my waking and sleeping thoughts after that evening! I wished to annihilate the tedious intervening days. I chafed against the work of school. At night in my bedroom and by day in the classroom her image came between me and the page I strove to read. The syllables of the word *Araby* were called to me through the silence in which my soul luxuriated and cast an Eastern enchantment over me. I asked for leave to go to the bazaar on Saturday night. My aunt was surprised and hoped it was

---

4. **litanies** *n. pl.:* repeated sales cries. Literally, a litany is a prayer composed of a series of specific invocations and responses.
5. **come-all-you . . . Rossa:** A come-all-you (kum·al′yə) is a type of Irish ballad that usually begins "Come all you [young lovers, rebels, Irishmen, and so on]." O'Donovan Rossa was Jeremiah O'Donovan (1831–1915) from County Cork. He was active in Ireland's struggle against British rule in the mid–nineteenth century.
6. **chalice** (chal′is) *n.:* cup; specifically, the cup used for Holy Communion wine. Joyce's use of the term evokes the image of a young man on a sacred mission.
7. **retreat . . . convent:** temporary withdrawal from worldly life by the students and teachers at the convent school, to devote time to prayer, meditation, and studies.
8. **It's well for you:** "You're lucky" (usually said enviously).

Vocabulary

impinge (im·pinj′) *v.:* strike; touch.
annihilate (ə·nī′ə·lāt′) *v.:* destroy; make nonexistent.

James Joyce 959

Direct Teaching

A **Reading Skills**

? Making inferences. Why does the cold gloom of the empty rooms cheer the boy? [Possible responses: The solitude allows him to be alone with his thoughts of Mangan's sister. He feels free of the obligations and routines of his everyday life.]

B **Reading Skills**

? Analyzing character. How would you characterize the aunt and the uncle and their relationship with the boy? [Possible responses: The aunt is religious and thoughtful; the uncle is self-absorbed and forgetful. They both seem to care for the boy but are somewhat distant from him. Their understanding of him is superficial.]

---

not some Freemason[9] affair. I answered few questions in class. I watched my master's face pass from amiability to sternness; he hoped I was not beginning to idle. I could not call my wandering thoughts together. I had hardly any patience with the serious work of life which, now that it stood between me and my desire, seemed to me child's play, ugly monotonous child's play.

On Saturday morning I reminded my uncle that I wished to go to the bazaar in the evening. He was fussing at the hallstand, looking for the hat-brush, and answered me curtly:

—Yes, boy, I know.

As he was in the hall I could not go into the front parlor and lie at the window. I left the house in bad humor and walked slowly toward the school. The air was pitilessly raw and already my heart misgave me.

When I came home to dinner my uncle had not yet been home. Still it was early. I sat staring at the clock for some time and, when its ticking began to irritate me, I left the room. I mounted the staircase and gained the upper part of the house. The high cold empty gloomy rooms liberated me and I went from room to room singing. From the front window I saw my companions playing below in the street. Their cries reached me weakened and indistinct and, leaning my forehead against the cool glass, I looked over at the dark house where she lived. I may have stood there for an hour, seeing nothing but the brown-clad figure cast by my imagination, touched discreetly by the lamplight at the curved neck, at the hand upon the railings and at the border below the dress.

When I came downstairs again I found Mrs. Mercer sitting at the fire. She was an old garrulous woman, a pawnbroker's widow, who collected used stamps for some pious purpose. I had to endure the gossip of the tea-table. The meal was prolonged beyond an hour and still my uncle did not come. Mrs. Mercer stood up to go:

She was sorry she couldn't wait any longer, but it was after eight o'clock and she did not like to be out late, as the night air was bad for her. When she had gone I began to walk up and down the room, clenching my fists. My aunt said:

—I'm afraid you may put off your bazaar for this night of Our Lord.

At nine o'clock I heard my uncle's latchkey in the halldoor. I heard him talking to himself and heard the hallstand rocking when it had received the weight of his overcoat. I could interpret these signs. When he was midway through his dinner I asked him to give me the money to go to the bazaar. He had forgotten.

—The people are in bed and after their first sleep now, he said.

I did not smile. My aunt said to him energetically:

—Can't you give him the money and let him go? You've kept him late enough as it is.

My uncle said he was very sorry he had forgotten. He said he believed in the old saying: *All work and no play makes Jack a dull boy*. He asked me where I was going and, when I had told him a second time he asked me did I know *The Arab's Farewell to his Steed*.[10] When I left the kitchen he was about to recite the opening lines of the piece to my aunt.

I held a florin[11] tightly in my hand as I strode down Buckingham Street toward the station. The sight of the streets thronged with buyers and glaring with gas recalled to me the purpose of my journey. I took my seat in a third-class carriage of a deserted train. After an intolerable delay the train moved out of the station slowly. It crept onward among ruinous houses and over the twinkling river. At Westland Row Station a crowd of people pressed to the carriage doors; but the porters moved them back, saying that it

---

9. **Freemason:** The Freemasons are a secret society whose practices were originally drawn from those of British medieval stonemasons' guilds; its members, almost exclusively Protestant, were often hostile to Catholics. The aunt apparently associates the exotic bazaar with the mysterious practices of Freemasonry.

10. *The Arab's . . . Steed:* popular sentimental poem by the English writer Caroline Norton (1808–1877).

11. **florin** *n.*: British coin worth at the time the equivalent of about fifty cents.

Vocabulary

monotonous (mə·nät′′n·əs) *adj.*: unvarying.
garrulous (gar′ə·ləs) *adj.*: talkative.

READING MINI-LESSON

Developing Word-Attack Skills
Use these pairs of words to review the effect of final *e* on the vowel sound in words. Final *e* signals that the vowel sound is long.

pat, pate   slop, slope
them, theme sum, consume
slim, slime bus, abuse

Then, have students compare the sounds in these pairs of words.

sooth, soothe   stag, stage
tic, entice   ping, impinge

Help students make the following generalizations about the effect of final *e* on the preceding consonant sound.

- unvoiced *th*, as in *sooth*, becomes voiced *th*, as in *soothe*
- hard *c* /k/, as in *tic*, becomes soft *c* /s/, as in *entice*
- hard *g* /g/, as in *stag*, becomes soft *g* /j/, as in *stage*
- the digraph *ng* /ng/, as in *ping*, becomes /nj/, as in *impinge*

Activity. Have students identify the two words in each of the following sentences that demonstrate the effect of final *e* on the preceding consonant sound.

Fairground, Tottenham (1925) by Allan Gwynne-Jones. Watercolor.
Waterman Fine Art Ltd., London, UK.
© Courtesy of the estate of Allan Gwynne-Jones.

was a special train for the bazaar. I remained alone in the bare carriage. In a few minutes the train drew up beside an improvised wooden platform. I passed out on to the road and saw by the lighted dial of a clock that it was ten minutes to ten. In front of me was a large building which displayed the magical name.

I could not find any sixpenny entrance and, fearing that the bazaar would be closed, I passed in quickly through a turnstile, handing a shilling to a weary-looking man. I found myself in a big hall girdled at half its height by a gallery. Nearly all the stalls were closed and the greater part of the hall was in darkness. I recognized a silence like that which pervades a church after a service. I walked into the center of the bazaar timidly. A few people were gathered about the stalls which were still open. Before a curtain, over which the words *Café Chantant*[12] were written in colored lamps, two men were counting money on a salver.[13] I listened to the fall of the coins.

Remembering with difficulty why I had come I went over to one of the stalls and examined porcelain vases and flowered tea-sets. At the door of the stall a young lady was talking and laughing with two young gentlemen. I remarked their English accents and listened vaguely to their conversation.

—O, I never said such a thing!
—O, but you did!
—O, but I didn't!
—Didn't she say that?
—Yes. I heard her.
—O, there's a . . . fib!

Observing me the young lady came over and asked me did I wish to buy anything. The tone of her voice was not encouraging; she seemed to have spoken to me out of a sense of duty. I looked humbly at the great jars that stood like eastern guards at either side of the dark entrance to the stall and murmured:

—No, thank you.

The young lady changed the position of one of the vases and went back to the two young men. They began to talk of the same subject. Once or twice the young lady glanced at me over her shoulder.

I lingered before her stall, though I knew my stay was useless, to make my interest in her wares seem the more real. Then I turned away slowly and walked down the middle of the bazaar. I allowed the two pennies to fall against the sixpence in my pocket. I heard a voice call from one end of the gallery that the light was out. The upper part of the hall was now completely dark.

Gazing up into the darkness I saw myself as a creature driven and derided by vanity; and my eyes burned with anguish and anger. ■

Vocabulary
improvised (im′prə·vīzd′) v. used as *adj.*: made for the occasion from whatever is handy.
pervades (pər·vādz′) v.: spreads throughout.

---

12. *Café Chantant* (kȧ·fā′ shän′tän′): The name refers to a coffeehouse with musical entertainment.
13. salver (sal′vər) n.: serving tray.

James Joyce 961

DIRECT TEACHING

VIEWING THE ART

Allan Gwynne-Jones (1892–1982) captured the excitement of a fair in this image.

Activity. Ask students how they think the painting relates to the narrator's experience of Araby in fantasy and in reality. [Possible response: The scene probably comes close to what the boy imagines Araby to be like before he actually sees it.]

C Literary Focus

Irony. In what way is Araby different from the place the boy may have imagined? [Possible response: Araby is dark, silent, and ominous. The boy probably expected a brightly lit, crowded bazaar.]

D Reading Skills

Comparing and contrasting. What emotions overwhelm the boy? [humiliation, futility, disillusionment] How do they differ from the emotions he expected to feel? [He expected to feel triumphant and valued.]

E Literary Focus

Epiphany. What does the boy realize about himself? [Possible responses: He realizes that his hopes were unrealistic; he sees himself as vain—that is, useless and naive—for having had such high hopes.]

---

1. The door hangs heavy on its hinges.
2. One day a strange visitor rang the bell.
3. Clothed in light, frothy garments, she opened the door.
4. She breathed in the chill air blowing in from the heath.
5. Now she cringes whenever the doorbell rings.

Check Test: True-False

Monitoring students' progress. Guide the class in answering the following questions.

1. The former tenant of the narrator's house was a priest. [T]
2. The narrator goes to the fair to buy a present for his aunt. [F]
3. The word *Araby* suggests romance to the narrator. [T]
4. Araby turns out to be everything the narrator hoped it would be. [F]

INDEPENDENT PRACTICE

Literary Focus

Irony

Possible Answers

1. *Verbal irony*—Your friend is wearing unattractive clothes, and you say, "Nice outfit."
2. *Situational irony*—You wake up late for school, madly get your clothes on, tear out of the house, and arrive at school only to realize it is a holiday.
3. *Dramatic irony*—In *Oedipus Rex*, the audience knows that Oedipus has killed his father and married his mother, but he does not; this makes his promise to punish the murderer highly ironic.

Students will probably agree that there is still a discrepancy between social ideals and reality. For example, one social ideal is that criminals are jailed and innocent people are exonerated; in reality, however, guilty people sometimes go free while innocent people are convicted.

ASSESSING

Assessment

- *Holt Assessment: Literature, Reading, and Vocabulary*

RETEACHING

For a lesson reteaching author's tone and style, see **Reteaching, p. 1129A**.

---

that comes to nothing. The protagonist fails to reach the goal he has been struggling to achieve, and in the end he is revealed to himself as the very opposite of the person he dreamed he was. "Araby" is ironic—both in its form and in many of its details.

In Greek comedy, an *eiron* was a character who was not what he appeared to be. From that Greek term comes *irony*, which in all its varieties also refers to things that are not what they appear to be.

1. **Verbal irony.** The most common form of irony is **verbal irony**, in which you say the opposite of what you really mean. We often use verbal irony in conversation. When asked how you feel after a really terrible day, you might say, for example, "I feel just great." We would know by the tone of your voice that you are being ironic—in reality, you feel anything but great. **Sarcasm** is a very broad and cutting form of verbal irony.

2. **Situational irony.** Another form of irony is **situational irony,** in which things turn out differently from what is expected. In its simplest form, this can involve a cartoon character laughing so hard at someone who has slipped on a banana peel that she herself walks right into an open manhole. In its most sophisticated form, as in Sophocles' *Oedipus Rex*, the hero, Oedipus, in trying to escape a curse, brings it down upon himself. Surprise endings invariably feature situational irony.

3. **Dramatic irony.** A third form of irony, dramatic irony, occurs when readers or an audience knows something that a character does not know. In "Little Red Riding Hood," we know the wolf has dressed in the grandmother's clothes, but Red Riding Hood does not. This discrepancy between what we know and what the characters know creates a sense of irony and a degree of dramatic tension.

4. **Romance versus reality.** In "Araby" almost all of the irony stems from the discrepancy between the narrator's romantic view of things and the way things really are. The boy's love for Mangan's sister is obviously overblown, an adolescent crush on someone he does not actually know. In pursuit of his love, he seeks some exotic gift from Araby, but this, too, becomes an ironic quest: In reality, he has simply taken a suburban train to a charity bazaar and returned empty-handed. In addition, through the aunt and uncle, the story shows that love in the real world—at least married love in Dublin—is not the ideal the boy imagines. It is, rather, marriage between an ineffectual woman and a man who comes home late and drunk.

But the ironies in "Araby" go still further. The hero's love and the quest he undertakes are directly associated with religion: "I imagined that I bore my chalice safely through a throng of foes. Her name sprang to my lips at moments in strange prayers and praises which I myself did not understand." Worshiping Mangan's sister is as much a religious act as an emotional one, and when his romantic dreams are shattered, his disillusion is not just with love, but with all of his spiritual values. Just as the aunt and uncle represent the reality of love, the reality of the religious part of the narrator's quest is represented by the dead priest and his rusty bicycle pump.

For Joyce, modern Ireland—its society, religion, and culture—was in a state of decay. The gap between the ideals of Ireland's past and the reality of its present was the chief source of his sense of irony.

Finding examples of irony. Illustrate the three types of irony described here with examples of your own. Your examples might be drawn from actual life, books, plays, films, personal experience, or your imagination. Do you think there is still a discrepancy between social ideals and reality today?

DIFFERENTIATING INSTRUCTION

Learners Having Difficulty

Students may find it easier to handle the material presented in the Literary Focus feature if they take notes as they read, organizing them into a chart like the one that follows:

Type of Irony	Definition	Example
Verbal		
Situational		
Dramatic		

D. H. Lawrence
(1885–1930)
England

David Herbert Lawrence was born in the English Midlands, the frailest child of a coal miner and a former schoolteacher. An able scholar, he too chose to become a teacher, for he resented the physical and spiritual ugliness that mining had brought about in the Midlands.

While he was teaching, Lawrence began publishing poems and stories in magazines. In 1912, a year after publishing his first novel, Lawrence called on his former professor, Ernest Weekley, and became enchanted with Weekley's German-born wife, Frieda. Within weeks, Frieda Weekley had left her husband and three children and fled with Lawrence to Germany. For the next two years the couple traveled through Austria and Italy. During this short time, Lawrence finished his novel *Sons and Lovers* (1913) and began work on two others, *The Rainbow* (1915) and *Women in Love* (1920).

Reviews of *Sons and Lovers* were cautiously favorable, but the moral controversy over Lawrence's work was already heating up. While in Italy, Lawrence began to see industrialized England as corrosive and oppressive and the Victorian world he had known as overcivilized and prudish. He embraced a belief in "blood knowledge," in putting one's animal self in balance with one's intellect. Returning to England in 1914, he announced that "the source of all life and knowledge is in man and woman, and the source of all living is in the interchange and the meeting and mingling of these two." When a privately printed edition of Lawrence's novel *Women in Love* was published in 1920, one London critic judged it "a loathsome study of sex depravity leading youth to unspeakable disaster."

Around this time a wealthy American writer, Mabel Dodge Luhan, who deeply admired Lawrence's work, invited him to come to Taos, New Mexico. Lawrence found New Mexico gorgeous, but he had his doubts about Americans, calling them "a host of people who must all have a sense of inferiority complex somewhere, striving to make good over everybody else." Meanwhile, in New York, those Lawrence called "the vice people" had been trying to suppress publication of *Women in Love*. Lawrence rejoiced to learn that a magistrate had declared that his novels were not obscene and in fact made a "distinct contribution to the literature of the present day."

By now, however, Lawrence was growing used to the attacks his work provoked on each publication day. But then he learned that he had incurable tuberculosis. Knowing he had only a few years remaining, Lawrence left the United States and returned to Italy. He now wrote continually, producing *Lady Chatterley's Lover* (1928), the work for which he is best remembered. The book drew new waves of anger from the censors. U.S. customs officers seized copies as they arrived on the docks, and the novel was banned in Britain.

Giving in at last to doctors' advice, Lawrence retreated in early 1930 to a sanitarium in southern France, where he wrote every day until the end of his life. On March 2, 1930, with Frieda at his bedside, Lawrence died. He is buried at Taos.

SKILLS FOCUS, pp. 967–981

Grade-Level Skills
- **Literary Skills**

Analyze various literary devices, including symbolism.

More About the Writer
Background. In his restless fascination with travel, D. H. Lawrence prefigured later generations of peripatetic, global novelists, including Graham Greene, V. S. Naipaul, and Paul Theroux. Besides his extended visits to Italy and New Mexico, Lawrence also spent time in Mexico, where his novel *The Plumed Serpent* (1926) is set, and in Australia, which is the setting for his novel *Kangaroo* (1925).

For Independent Reading
- *Sons and Lovers,* like many fine first novels, is strongly colored by autobiographical elements. Like D. H. Lawrence, Paul Morel, the novel's hero, grows up in a conflicted, working-class family in the English Midlands. The novel explores the loving but possessive relationship between Paul and his mother.

RESOURCES: READING

Planning
- *One-Stop Planner* CD-ROM with ExamView Test Generator

Differentiating Instruction
- *Supporting Instruction in Spanish*
- *Audio CD Library, Selections and Summaries in Spanish*

Vocabulary
- *Vocabulary Development*

Grammar and Language
- *Daily Language Activities*

Assessment
- *Holt Assessment: Literature, Reading, and Vocabulary*
- *One-Stop Planner* CD-ROM with ExamView Test Generator
- *Holt Online Assessment*

Internet
- go.hrw.com (Keyword: LE5 12-7)
- *Elements of Literature Online*

Media
- *Audio CD Library*
- *Audio CD Library, Selections and Summaries in Spanish*

PRETEACHING

Summary ⟷ at grade level

Paul, a young British boy, desperately wants to gain the love of his mother, who is distant and depressed. When he asks her why their family always seems short of money, she tells him about the family's need for "luck." The confused but determined boy discovers that when he rides his rocking horse in a mad frenzy, he can foresee the winners of actual horse races. Paul uses these uncanny revelations to change the family's fortunes. Working with the gardener and Uncle Oscar, the boy makes a great deal of money and has it turned over to his mother through the family lawyer. He hopes the money will finally stop the mysterious voices in the house from "whispering" for more money; however, the voices only "whisper" more madly. Finally, in order to predict the winner of the Derby, Paul makes a last, frenzied rocking-horse ride. He successfully predicts the winner, after which he collapses. Critically ill, Paul is informed by the gardener that he has won over seventy thousand pounds. After asserting to his mother that he is lucky, the boy dies in the night, leaving her to contemplate what she has gained and what she has lost.

Before You Read

The Rocking-Horse Winner

Make the Connection
Quickwrite

The old saying that "the love of money is the root of all evil" dates back to the Bible. Over the centuries, immeasurable evil—hatred, war, murder—has sprung from the desire for riches. Even on the most personal level—wife to husband, parent to child, friend to friend—the craving for wealth can have devastating effects.

Jot down some associations about money—and what people will do to get it—that come to mind.

Literary Focus
Symbol

Beginning with the title, the image of a child's rocking horse dominates this story. The horse is associated with every important development in the plot. As the story's tragedy unfolds, the horse seems to take on more than its literal meaning as a child's toy. It is slowly transformed into a **symbol**, richly suggestive of emotions, themes, and meanings for the story as a whole.

INTERNET
Vocabulary Practice
Keyword: LE5 12-7

SKILLS FOCUS

Literary Skills Understand symbols.

> A **symbol** is a person, place, thing, or event that stands both for itself and for something beyond itself.
>
> *For more on Symbol, see the Handbook of Literary and Historical Terms.*

Background

Lawrence saw men and women as torn between the promptings of their instincts (which he saw as natural and therefore good) and the demanding voices of their upbringing and education (which he saw as destructive). As you read "The Rocking-Horse Winner," which is told like a modern fable, notice which voices are most dominant in the house and what effects these voices have on the characters.

Vocabulary Development

asserted (ə·surt′id) v.: declared.

obscure (əb·skyoor′) adj.: little-known.

reiterated (rē·it′ə·rāt′id) v.: repeated.

uncanny (un·kan′ē) adj.: strange; eerie; weird.

iridescent (ir′i·des′ənt) adj.: showing rainbowlike colors.

overwrought (ō′vər·rôt′) adj.: overly excited.

remonstrated (ri·män′strāt′id) v.: protested.

arrested (ə·rest′id) v. used as adj.: checked or halted in motion.

968   Collection 7   The Modern World: 1900 to the Present

Previewing Vocabulary

Have students in small groups read the Vocabulary words and their definitions. Then have a volunteer from each group present a sentence from which one of the Vocabulary words is left out. Have the other students try to figure out the missing word. The student who answers should devise another incomplete sentence for another Vocabulary word.

Then ask students to complete each analogy with a Vocabulary word.

1. FAVORED : HATED :: continued : _____ [arrested]
2. WEARY : ENERGETIC :: famous : _____ [obscure]
3. FARCE : AMUSING :: ghost : _____ [uncanny]
4. STROLLED : AMBLED :: restated : _____ [reiterated]
5. TACITURN : TALKATIVE :: monochromatic : _____ [iridescent]
6. PUSHED : PULLED :: denied : _____ [asserted]
7. THREATENED : MENACED :: objected : _____ [remonstrated]
8. OVERDONE : SIMPLE :: calm : _____ [overwrought]

The Rocking-Horse Winner

D. H. Lawrence

DIRECT TEACHING

A Literary Focus

Situational irony. This opening paragraph reveals a conflict between appearance and reality. How does this conflict reveal itself? [Possible response: The woman appears to love her children, but in actuality she cannot feel love for anybody.]

B Content-Area Connections

Literature: Lady Cynthia Asquith Lawrence wrote this story for his friend Lady Cynthia Asquith. Cynthia was born into the upper class of British society, the daughter of the eleventh Earl of Wemyss. She married a man with too little money and was always short of cash. Her sons found her to be a neglectful mother whose love was conditional, depending on their successes. Lawrence translated his impressions of the Asquith family into "The Rocking-Horse Winner."

C Literary Focus

Symbol. Why is the pervasive "whispering" in the house an effective symbol for the family's financial problem? [Possible response: The problem is persistent, troubling, and never spoken of openly.]

A There was a woman who was beautiful, who started with all the advantages, yet she had no luck. She married for love, and the love turned to dust. She had bonny children, yet she felt they had been thrust upon her, and she could not love them. They looked at her coldly, as if they were finding fault with her. And hurriedly she felt she must cover up some fault in herself. Yet what it was that she must cover up she never knew. Nevertheless, when her children were present, she always felt the center of her heart go hard. This troubled her, and in her manner she was all the more gentle and anxious for her children, as if she loved them very much. Only she herself knew that at the center of her heart was a hard little place that could not feel love, no, not for anybody. Everybody else said of her: "She is such a good mother. She adores her children." Only she herself, and her children themselves, knew it was not so. They read it in each other's eyes.

There were a boy and two little girls. They lived in a pleasant house, with a garden, and they had discreet servants, and felt themselves superior to anyone in the neighborhood.

B Although they lived in style, they felt always an anxiety in the house. There was never enough money. The mother had a small income,[1] and the father had a small income, but not nearly enough for the social position which they had to keep up. The father went into town to some office. But though he had good prospects, these prospects never materialized. There was always the grinding sense of the shortage of money, though the style was always kept up.

At last the mother said: "I will see if *I* can't make something." But she did not know where to begin. She racked her brains, and tried this thing and the other, but could not find anything successful. The failure made deep lines come into her face. Her children were growing up, they would have to go to school. There must be more money, there must be more money. The father, who was always very handsome and expensive in his tastes, seemed as if he never *would* be able to do anything worth doing. And the mother, who had a great belief in herself, did not succeed any better, and her tastes were just as expensive.

C And so the house came to be haunted by the unspoken phrase: *There must be more money! There must be more money!* The children could hear it all the time, though nobody said it aloud. They heard it at Christmas, when the expensive and splendid toys filled the nursery. Behind the shining modern rocking horse, behind the smart doll's house, a voice would

---
1. **income** *n.*: money from an inheritance or investments—not a salary.

DIFFERENTIATING INSTRUCTION

Learners Having Difficulty
Ask students to note each time the rocking horse is mentioned in the story and to ask themselves what it symbolizes. Have students review the definition of *symbol*, if necessary.

English-Language Learners
To keep students actively engaged in reading the text, have them read in small groups and make predictions about what is to come. Students should stop at least six times as they read and jot down what they believe will be the next major development in the plot. (For example, they might stop just before the conversation between Paul and his mother begins.) Once students complete the story, they can evaluate their predictions.

start whispering: "There *must* be more money! There *must* be more money!" And the children would stop playing, to listen for a moment. They would look into each other's eyes, to see if they had all heard. And each one saw in the eyes of the other two that they too had heard. "There *must* be more money! There *must* be more money!"

It came whispering from the springs of the still-swaying rocking horse, and even the horse, bending his wooden, champing head, heard it. The big doll, sitting so pink and smirking in her new pram,[2] could hear it quite plainly, and seemed to be smirking all the more self-consciously because of it. The foolish puppy, too, that took the place of the teddy bear, he was looking so extraordinarily foolish for no other reason but that he heard the secret whisper all over the house: "There *must* be more money!"

Yet nobody ever said it aloud. The whisper was everywhere, and therefore no one spoke it. Just as no one ever says: "We are breathing!" in spite of the fact that breath is coming and going all the time.

"Mother," said the boy Paul one day, "why don't we keep a car of our own? Why do we always use uncle's, or else a taxi?"

"Because we're the poor members of the family," said the mother.

"But why *are* we, mother?"

"Well—I suppose," she said slowly and bitterly, "it's because your father has no luck."

The boy was silent for some time.

"Is luck money, mother?" he asked, rather timidly.

"No, Paul. Not quite. It's what causes you to have money."

"Oh!" said Paul vaguely. "I thought when Uncle Oscar said *filthy lucker*, it meant money."

"*Filthy lucre*[3] does mean money," said the mother. "But it's lucre, not luck."

"Oh!" said the boy. "Then what is luck, mother?"

"It's what causes you to have money. If you're lucky you have money. That's why it's better to be born lucky than rich. If you're rich, you may lose your money. But if you're lucky, you will always get more money."

"Oh! Will you? And is father not lucky?"

"Very unlucky, I should say," she said bitterly.

The boy watched her with unsure eyes.

"Why?" he asked.

"I don't know. Nobody ever knows why one person is lucky and another unlucky."

"Don't they? Nobody at all? Does *nobody* know?"

"Perhaps God. But He never tells."

"He ought to, then. And aren't you lucky either, mother?"

"I can't be, if I married an unlucky husband."

"But by yourself, aren't you?"

"I used to think I was, before I married. Now I think I am very unlucky indeed."

"Why?"

"Well—never mind! Perhaps I'm not really," she said.

The child looked at her to see if she meant it. But he saw, by the lines of her mouth, that she was only trying to hide something from him.

"Well, anyhow," he said stoutly, "I'm a lucky person."

"Why?" said his mother, with a sudden laugh.

He stared at her. He didn't even know why he had said it.

---

2. **pram** *n.*: chiefly British for "baby carriage." The word is short for *perambulator*.

3. **filthy lucre** (lōō′kər): riches (a derogatory usage).

DIRECT TEACHING

A Reading Skills

? Making inferences. What does the boy want from his mother, but not get? [Possible responses: attention; warmth; love; security.]

B Reading Skills

? Understanding cause and effect. What effect does the conversation with his mother have on Paul? [Paul desperately seeks "luck" to please his mother.] What evidence suggests that this effect is not a positive one? [Possible responses: Paul becomes heedless of others, self-absorbed, and sly. Words and phrases such as "charging madly," "frenzy," "wildly," and "strange glare" suggest a somewhat sinister and dangerous aspect to Paul's rides.]

C Vocabulary Development

? Connotations. What do the words *mad* and *furious* suggest about how Paul rides the rocking horse? [Possible responses: He rides it without pleasure, in a frenzy, with no thought for his own welfare. He seems possessed by his quest.]

D Reading Skills

? Drawing conclusions. What state does Paul appear to be in when he is riding the rocking horse? [Possible response: He appears to be in a trance or to be hypnotized.]

"God told me," he asserted, brazening it out.[4]

"I hope He did, dear!" she said, again with a laugh, but rather bitter.

"He did, mother!"

"Excellent!" said the mother, using one of her husband's exclamations.

The boy saw she did not believe him; or rather, that she paid no attention to his assertion. This angered him somewhere, and made him want to compel her attention.

He went off by himself, vaguely, in a childish way, seeking for the clue to "luck." Absorbed, taking no heed of other people, he went about with a sort of stealth, seeking inwardly for luck. He wanted luck, he wanted it, he wanted it. When the two girls were playing dolls in the nursery, he would sit on his big rocking horse, charging madly into space, with a frenzy that made the little girls peer at him uneasily. Wildly the horse careered,[5] the waving dark hair of the boy tossed, his eyes had a strange glare in them. The little girls dared not speak to him.

When he had ridden to the end of his mad little journey, he climbed down and stood in front of his rocking horse, staring fixedly into its lowered face. Its red mouth was slightly open, its big eye was wide and glassy-bright.

"Now!" he would silently command the snorting steed. "Now, take me to where there is luck! Now take me!"

And he would slash the horse on the neck with the little whip he had asked Uncle Oscar for. He *knew* the horse could take him to where there was luck, if only he forced it. So he would mount again and start on his furious ride, hoping at last to get there. He knew he could get there.

"You'll break your horse, Paul!" said the nurse.

"He's always riding like that! I wish he'd leave off!" said his elder sister Joan.

But he only glared down on them in silence. Nurse gave him up. She could make nothing of him. Anyhow, he was growing beyond her.

One day his mother and his Uncle Oscar came in when he was on one of his furious rides. He did not speak to them.

"Hallo, you young jockey! Riding a winner?" said his uncle.

"Aren't you growing too big for a rocking horse? You're not a very little boy any longer, you know," said his mother.

But Paul only gave a blue glare from his big, rather close-set eyes. He would speak to nobody when he was in full tilt. His mother watched him with an anxious expression on her face.

At last he suddenly stopped forcing his horse into the mechanical gallop and slid down.

"Well, I got there!" he announced fiercely, his blue eyes still flaring, and his sturdy long legs straddling apart.

"Where did you get to?" asked his mother.

"Where I wanted to go," he flared back at her.

"That's right, son!" said Uncle Oscar. "Don't you stop till you get there. What's the horse's name?"

"He doesn't have a name," said the boy.

"Gets on without all right?" asked the uncle.

"Well, he has different names. He was called Sansovino last week."

"Sansovino, eh? Won the Ascot.[6] How did you know this name?"

"He always talks about horse races with Bassett," said Joan.

The uncle was delighted to find that his small nephew was posted with all the racing news. Bassett, the young gardener, who had been wounded in the left foot in the war and had got his present job through Oscar Cresswell, whose batman[7] he had been, was a perfect blade of the "turf."[8] He lived in the racing events, and the small boy lived with him.

Oscar Cresswell got it all from Bassett.

"Master Paul comes and asks me, so I can't do more than tell him, sir," said Bassett, his face

---

4. **brazening it out:** acting boldly.
5. **careered** *v.:* rushed.
6. **Ascot:** famous horse race held annually at Ascot Heath in England. Several traditional British races are mentioned in the story.
7. **batman** *n.:* officer's personal attendant.
8. **blade of the "turf":** stylish young racing fan.

Vocabulary
asserted (ə·surt′id) *v.:* declared.

972   Collection 7   The Modern World: 1900 to the Present

DEVELOPING FLUENCY

As students read, ask them to note that Lawrence uses more exclamations as Paul persists in his riding. The result is an increasingly desperate tone.

Individual activity. Have students rewrite the following paragraph, adding exclamation points to achieve variety and emphasis. Then, have them compare their decisions by reading the paragraph aloud.

She reached the top of the hill and looked down. The sidewalk stretched away, a concrete ribbon unfurling to the street below. Seeing it filled the child with both delight and dread. She started down, skates making their familiar low-level grating. Down and down. Trees and houses became a blur. Cars zipped by, indistinguishable in the speed of her racing. Vainly, she wondered where the bottom was.

terribly serious, as if he were speaking of religious matters.

"And does he ever put anything on a horse he fancies?"

"Well—I don't want to give him away—he's a young sport, a fine sport, sir. Would you mind asking him himself? He sort of takes a pleasure in it, and perhaps he'd feel I was giving him away, sir, if you don't mind."

Bassett was serious as a church.

The uncle went back to his nephew and took him off for a ride in the car.

"Say, Paul, old man, do you ever put anything on a horse?" the uncle asked.

The boy watched the handsome man closely.

"Why, do you think I oughtn't to?" he parried.

"Not a bit of it! I thought perhaps you might give me a tip for the Lincoln."

The car sped on into the country, going down to Uncle Oscar's place in Hampshire.

"Honor bright?" said the nephew.

"Honor bright, son!" said the uncle.

"Well, then, Daffodil."

"Daffodil! I doubt it, sonny. What about Mirza?"

"I only know the winner," said the boy. "That's Daffodil."

"Daffodil, eh?"

There was a pause. Daffodil was an <u>obscure</u> horse comparatively.

"Uncle!"

"Yes, son?"

"You won't let it go any further, will you? I promised Bassett."

"Bassett be damned, old man! What's he got to do with it?"

"We're partners. We've been partners from the first. Uncle, he lent me my first five shillings, which I lost. I promised him, honor bright, it was only between me and him; only you gave me that ten-shilling note I started winning with, so I thought you were lucky. You won't let it go any further, will you?"

The boy gazed at his uncle from those big, hot, blue eyes, set rather close together. The uncle stirred and laughed uneasily.

"Right you are, son! I'll keep your tip private. Daffodil, eh? How much are you putting on him?"

"All except twenty pounds," said the boy. "I keep that in reserve."

The uncle thought it a good joke.

"You keep twenty pounds in reserve, do you, you young romancer?[9] What are you betting, then?"

"I'm betting three hundred," said the boy gravely. "But it's between you and me, Uncle Oscar! Honor bright?"

The uncle burst into a roar of laughter.

"It's between you and me all right, you young Nat Gould,"[10] he said, laughing. "But where's your three hundred?"

"Bassett keeps it for me. We're partners."

"You are, are you! And what is Bassett putting on Daffodil?"

"He won't go quite as high as I do, I expect. Perhaps he'll go a hundred and fifty."

"What, pennies?" laughed the uncle.

"Pounds," said the child, with a surprised look at his uncle. "Bassett keeps a bigger reserve than I do."

---

9. **romancer** *n.*: imaginative storyteller.
10. **Nat Gould:** famous British authority on racing.

Vocabulary
obscure (əb·skyoor′) *adj.*: little-known.

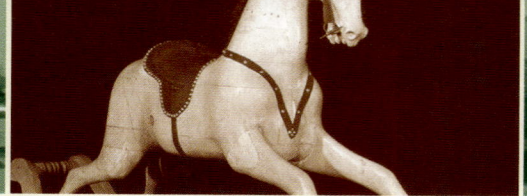

DIRECT TEACHING

A Reading Skills

❓ Comparing and contrasting. How does Uncle Oscar's attitude toward Paul's tips differ from Bassett's? [Uncle Oscar is amused and skeptical, while Bassett firmly believes in Paul's predictions.]

B Reading Skills

❓ Making inferences. Why is Paul so anxious that his uncle not get anyone else involved in the betting partnership? [Possible response: He is afraid that another partner might be unlucky and ruin the winning streak.]

C Reading Skills

❓ Speculating. Why do you think that Bassett is so quick to attribute Paul's knowledge to the supernatural? [Possible responses: As a man with little education, Bassett cannot imagine any other source for Paul's knowledge. A religious man, Bassett believes Paul to be divinely inspired. Gamblers are often superstitious.]

D Vocabulary Development

Understanding idioms. The British idiom *as sure as eggs* (which, in its full version, is *as sure as eggs is eggs*) is uncommon. Explain that the origin of the phrase is obscure, but it figuratively means "something is certain" or "will definitely happen."

A Between wonder and amusement Uncle Oscar was silent. He pursued the matter no further, but he determined to take his nephew with him to the Lincoln races.

"Now, son," he said, "I'm putting twenty on Mirza, and I'll put five on for you on any horse you fancy. What's your pick?"

"Daffodil, uncle."

"No, not the fiver on Daffodil!"

"I should if it was my own fiver," said the child.

"Good! Good! Right you are! A fiver for me and a fiver for you on Daffodil."

The child had never been to a race meeting before, and his eyes were blue fire. He pursed his mouth tight and watched. A Frenchman just in front had put his money on Lancelot. Wild with excitement, he flayed his arms up and down, yelling "*Lancelot! Lancelot!*" in his French accent.

Daffodil came in first, Lancelot second, Mirza third. The child flushed and with eyes blazing, was curiously serene. His uncle brought him four five-pound notes, four to one.

"What am I to do with these?" he cried, waving them before the boy's eyes.

"I suppose we'll talk to Bassett," said the boy. "I expect I have fifteen hundred now; and twenty in reserve; and this twenty."

His uncle studied him for some moments.

"Look here, son!" he said. "You're not serious about Bassett and that fifteen hundred, are you?"

"Yes, I am. But it's between you and me, uncle. Honor bright?"

"Honor bright all right, son! But I must talk to Bassett."

B "If you'd like to be a partner, uncle, with Bassett and me, we could all be partners. Only, you'd have to promise, honor bright, uncle, not to let it go beyond us three. Bassett and I are lucky, and you must be lucky, because it was your ten shillings I started winning with...."

Uncle Oscar took both Bassett and Paul into Richmond Park for an afternoon, and there they talked.

"It's like this, you see, sir," Bassett said. "Master Paul would get me talking about racing events, spinning yarns, you know, sir. And he was always keen on knowing if I'd made or if I'd lost. It's about a year since, now, that I put five shillings on Blush of Dawn for him: And we lost. Then the luck turned, with that ten shillings he had from you: That we put on Singhalese. And since that time, it's been pretty steady, all things considering. What do you say, Master Paul?"

"We're all right when we're sure," said Paul. "It's when we're not quite sure that we go down."

"Oh, but we're careful then," said Bassett.

C "But when are you *sure*?" smiled Uncle Oscar.

D "It's Master Paul, sir," said Bassett in a secret, religious voice. "It's as if he had it from heaven. Like Daffodil, now, for the Lincoln. That was as sure as eggs."

"Did you put anything on Daffodil?" asked Oscar Cresswell.

"Yes, sir. I made my bit."

"And my nephew?"

Bassett was obstinately silent, looking at Paul.

"I made twelve hundred, didn't I, Bassett? I told uncle I was putting three hundred on Daffodil."

"That's right," said Bassett, nodding.

"But where's the money?" asked the uncle.

"I keep it safe locked up, sir. Master Paul he can have it any minute he likes to ask for it."

"What, fifteen hundred pounds?"

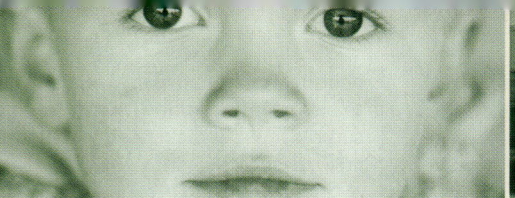

"And twenty! And *forty*, that is, with the twenty he made on the course."

"It's amazing!" said the uncle.

"If Master Paul offers you to be partners, sir, I would, if I were you: if you'll excuse me," said Bassett.

Oscar Cresswell thought about it.

"I'll see the money," he said.

They drove home again, and sure enough, Bassett came round to the garden house with fifteen hundred pounds in notes. The twenty pounds reserve was left with Joe Glee, in the Turf Commission[11] deposit.

"You see, it's all right, uncle, when I'm *sure*! Then we go strong, for all we're worth. Don't we, Bassett?"

"We do that, Master Paul."

"And when are you sure?" said the uncle, laughing.

"Oh, well, sometimes I'm *absolutely* sure, like about Daffodil," said the boy; "and sometimes I have an idea; and sometimes I haven't even an idea, have I, Bassett? Then we're careful, because we mostly go down."

"You do, do you! And when you're sure, like about Daffodil, what makes you sure, sonny?"

"Oh, well, I don't know," said the boy uneasily. "I'm sure, you know, uncle; that's all."

"It's as if he had it from heaven, sir." Bassett reiterated.

"I should say so!" said the uncle.

But he became a partner. And when the Leger was coming on Paul was "sure" about Lively Spark, which was a quite inconsiderable horse.

The boy insisted on putting a thousand on the horse, Bassett went for five hundred, and Oscar Cresswell two hundred. Lively Spark came in first, and the betting had been ten to one against him. Paul had made ten thousand.

"You see," he said, "I was absolutely sure of him."

Even Oscar Cresswell had cleared two thousand.

"Look here, son," he said, "this sort of thing makes me nervous."

"It needn't, uncle! Perhaps I shan't be sure again for a long time."

"But what are you going to do with your money?" asked the uncle.

"Of course," said the boy, "I started it for mother. She said she had no luck, because father is unlucky, so I thought if *I* was lucky, it might stop whispering."

"What might stop whispering?"

"Our house. I *hate* our house for whispering."

"What does it whisper?"

"Why—why"—the boy fidgeted—"why, I don't know. But it's always short of money, you know, uncle."

"I know it, son, I know it."

"You know people send mother writs,[12] don't you, uncle?"

"I'm afraid I do," said the uncle.

"And then the house whispers, like people laughing at you behind your back. It's awful, that is! I thought if I was lucky——"

---

11. **Turf Commission:** committee of the Jockey Club, the chief governing body for horse racing. This committee operates a bank in which bettors can deposit money for future bets.

12. **writs** *n. pl.*: legal papers; here, those demanding payment.

Vocabulary
reiterated (rē·it′ə·rāt′id) *v.*: repeated.

Secondary Source

Critic's Commentary: Paul as Hero and Symbol

This discussion of some elements in "The Rocking-Horse Winner" is excerpted from "A Rocking Horse: The Symbol, the Pattern, the Way to Live" by W. D. Snodgrass: "[The] story resembles many well-known fairy tales or magical stories in which the hero bargains with evil powers for personal advantages or forbidden knowledge. These bargains are always 'rigged' so that the hero, after his apparent triumphs, will lose in the end—this being, in itself, the standard 'moral.' . . . So, in some sense, Paul *is* demonic, yet a poor devil; though he has compacted with evil, his intentions were good and he has destroyed only himself. At first metaphorically, in the end literally, he has committed suicide. But that may be, finally, the essence of evil. . . . Paul is destroyed, we have said, by his desire to 'know.' It is not only that he has chosen wrong ways of knowing or wrong things to know. The evil is that he *has* chosen to know, to live by intellection. In a letter, Lawrence wrote: '. . . Paul is a symbol of civilized man, whipping himself on in a nervous endless "mechanical gallop," an "arrested prance," in chase of something which will destroy him if he ever catches it, and which he never really wanted anyway.'"

DIRECT TEACHING

A **Reading Skills**

❓ **Expressing an opinion.** Paul fears his mother would stop him from betting, while his uncle does not think she would. Who do you think is right? Why? [Possible responses: Paul, because his mother would find his betting an embarrassment; Uncle Oscar, because Paul's mother would be so happy to get the money that she wouldn't care where it came from.]

B **Reading Skills**

❓ **Analyzing character.** Why does Paul's mother work secretly? [Possible responses: She thinks working is beneath her; she fears she will not succeed.] What does her dissatisfaction reveal about her? [Possible responses: She wants big rewards without working for them; she is very competitive and cannot stand being anywhere but at the top.]

C **Reading Skills**

❓ **Hypothesizing.** If you were Paul, how would your mother's reaction to the gift make you feel? [Possible responses: disappointed; confused; hurt; angry.]

D **Literary Focus**

❓ **Symbol.** In annotation C on p. 970, the pervasive whispering in the house is read as a symbol for the family's financial problems. Why does the whispering increase at this point in the story? [Possible response: It mirrors the mother's neurosis—the more she has, the more she needs.] What human foible might the whispering symbolize? [Possible responses: greed; insecurity; materialism.]

"You might stop it," added the uncle.

The boy watched him with big blue eyes, that had an <u>uncanny</u> cold fire in them, and he said never a word.

"Well, then!" said the uncle. "What are we doing?"

A "I shouldn't like mother to know I was lucky," said the boy.

"Why not, son?"

"She'd stop me."

"I don't think she would."

"Oh!"—and the boy writhed in an odd way—"I *don't* want her to know, uncle."

"All right, son. We'll manage it without her knowing."

They managed it very easily. Paul, at the other's suggestion, handed over five thousand pounds to his uncle, who deposited it with the family lawyer, who was then to inform Paul's mother that a relative had put five thousand pounds into his hands, which sum was to be paid out a thousand pounds at a time, on the mother's birthday, for the next five years.

"So she'll have a birthday present of a thousand pounds for five successive years," said Uncle Oscar. "I hope it won't make it all the harder for her later."

Paul's mother had her birthday in November. The house had been "whispering" worse than ever lately, and, even in spite of his luck, Paul could not bear up against it. He was very anxious to see the effect of the birthday letter, telling his mother about the thousand pounds.

When there were no visitors, Paul now took his meals with his parents, as he was beyond the nursery control. His mother went into town nearly every day. She had discovered that she had an odd knack of sketching furs and dress materials, so she worked secretly in the studio of a friend who was the chief "artist" for the

B leading drapers.[13] She drew the figures of ladies in furs and ladies in silk and sequins for the newspaper advertisements. This young woman artist earned several thousand pounds a year, but Paul's mother only made several hundreds,

---

13. **drapers** *n. pl.:* dealers in cloth and dry goods.

---

and she was again dissatisfied. She so wanted to be first in something, and she did not succeed, even in making sketches for drapery advertisements.

She was down to breakfast on the morning of her birthday. Paul watched her face as she read her letters. He knew the lawyer's letter. As his

C mother read it, her face hardened and became more expressionless. Then a cold, determined look came on her mouth. She hid the letter under the pile of others, and said not a word about it.

"Didn't you have anything nice in the post for your birthday, mother?" said Paul.

"Quite moderately nice," she said, her voice cold and absent.

She went away to town without saying more.

But in the afternoon Uncle Oscar appeared. He said Paul's mother had had a long interview with the lawyer, asking if the whole five thousand could not be advanced at once, as she was in debt.

"What do you think, uncle?" said the boy.

"I leave it to you, son."

"Oh, let her have it, then! We can get some more with the other," said the boy.

"A bird in the hand is worth two in the bush, laddie!" said Uncle Oscar.

"But I'm sure to *know* for the Grand National; or the Lincolnshire; or else the Derby. I'm sure to know for *one* of them," said Paul.

So Uncle Oscar signed the agreement, and Paul's mother touched the whole five thousand. Then something very curious happened. The voices in the house suddenly went mad, like a chorus of frogs on a spring evening. There were

D certain new furnishings, and Paul had a tutor. He was *really* going to Eton,[14] his father's school, in the following autumn. There were flowers in the winter, and a blossoming of the luxury Paul's mother had been used to. And yet the voices in the house, behind the sprays of

---

14. **Eton:** Eton College, a private prep school for boys, near London.

Vocabulary

uncanny (un·kan′ē) *adj.:* strange; eerie; weird.

mimosa and almond blossom, and from under the piles of iridescent cushions, simply trilled and screamed in a sort of ecstasy: "There *must* be more money! Oh-h-h; there must be more money. Oh, now, now-w! Now-w-w—there *must* be more money!—more than ever! More than ever!"

It frightened Paul terribly. He studied away at his Latin and Greek with his tutor. But his intense hours were spent with Bassett. The Grand National had gone by: He had not "known," and had lost a hundred pounds. Summer was at hand. He was in agony for the Lincoln. But even for the Lincoln he didn't "know," and he lost fifty pounds. He became wild-eyed and strange, as if something were going to explode in him.

"Let it alone, son! Don't you bother about it!" urged Uncle Oscar. But it was as if the boy couldn't really hear what his uncle was saying.

"I've got to know for the Derby! I've got to know for the Derby!" the child reiterated, his big blue eyes blazing with a sort of madness.

His mother noticed how overwrought he was.

"You'd better go to the seaside. Wouldn't you like to go now to the seaside, instead of waiting? I think you'd better," she said, looking down at him anxiously, her heart curiously heavy because of him.

But the child lifted his uncanny blue eyes.

"I couldn't possibly go before the Derby, mother!" he said. "I couldn't possibly!"

"Why not?" she said, her voice becoming heavy when she was opposed. "Why not? You can still go from the seaside to see the Derby with your Uncle Oscar, if that's what you wish. No need for you to wait here. Besides, I think you care too much about these races. It's a bad sign. My family has been a gambling family, and you won't know till you grow up how much damage it has done. But it has done damage. I shall have to send Bassett away, and ask Uncle Oscar not to talk racing to you, unless you promise to be reasonable about it: Go away to the seaside and forget it. You're all nerves!"

"I'll do what you like, mother, so long as you don't send me away till after the Derby," the boy said.

"Send you away from where? Just from this house?"

"Yes," he said, gazing at her.

"Why, you curious child, what makes you care about this house so much, suddenly? I never knew you loved it."

He gazed at her without speaking. He had a secret within a secret, something he had not

Vocabulary
iridescent (ir′i·des′ənt) *adj.:* showing rainbowlike colors.
overwrought (ō′vər·rôt′) *adj.:* overly excited.

DIRECT TEACHING

A Literary Focus

? Irony. How does this passage show the irony in the relationship between mother and son? [Possible responses: He is trying to reassure her, but he doesn't realize that he is destroying himself in order to satisfy her insatiable need for money. She senses that he is in danger but does nothing about it except warn him not to let his nerves "go to pieces."]

B Reading Skills

? Understanding cause and effect. Paul's mother has felt anxious about him before but has been able to ignore her apprehensions. Why can she no longer ignore her anxiety? [Possible responses: Her son is looking and behaving very oddly. She senses some crisis is at hand; she may be beginning to feel some responsibility for his altered state.]

C Reading Skills

? Determining author's purpose. Why do you think Lawrence hardly mentions the father? [Possible response: Although the father is a remote, ineffectual figure, Lawrence seems to blame the family's problems on the mother's greed and social pretensions.]

---

divulged, even to Bassett or to his Uncle Oscar.

But his mother, after standing undecided and a little bit sullen for some moments, said:

"Very well, then! Don't go to the seaside till after the Derby, if you don't wish it. But promise me you won't let your nerves go to pieces. Promise you won't think so much about horse racing and *events*, as you call them!"

"Oh no," said the boy casually, "I won't think much about them, mother. You needn't worry. I wouldn't worry, mother, if I were you."

"If you were me and I were you," said his mother, "I wonder what we *should* do!"

"But you know you needn't worry, mother, don't you?" the boy repeated.

"I should be awfully glad to know it," she said wearily.

"Oh, well, you *can*, you know. I mean, you *ought* to know you needn't worry," he insisted.

"Ought I? Then I'll see about it," she said.

Paul's secret of secrets was his wooden horse, that which had no name. Since he was emancipated from a nurse and a nursery-governess, he had had his rocking horse removed to his own bedroom at the top of the house.

"Surely you're too big for a rocking horse!" his mother had remonstrated.

"Well, you see, mother, till I can have a *real* horse, I like to have *some* sort of animal about," had been his quaint answer.

"Do you feel he keeps you company?" she laughed.

"Oh yes! He's very good, he always keeps me company, when I'm there," said Paul.

So the horse, rather shabby, stood in an arrested prance in the boy's bedroom.

The Derby was drawing near, and the boy grew more and more tense. He hardly heard what was spoken to him, he was very frail, and his eyes were really uncanny. His mother had sudden strange seizures of uneasiness about him. Sometimes, for half an hour, she would feel a sudden anxiety about him that was almost anguish. She wanted to rush to him at once, and know he was safe.

Two nights before the Derby, she was at a big party in town, when one of her rushes of anxiety about her boy, her firstborn, gripped her heart till she could hardly speak. She fought with the feeling, might and main, for she believed in common sense. But it was too strong. She had to leave the dance and go downstairs to telephone to the country. The children's nursery-governess was terribly surprised and startled at being rung up in the night.

"Are the children all right, Miss Wilmot?"

"Oh yes, they are quite all right."

"Master Paul? Is he all right?"

"He went to bed as right as a trivet. Shall I run up and look at him?"

"No," said Paul's mother reluctantly. "No! Don't trouble. It's all right. Don't sit up. We shall be home fairly soon." She did not want her son's privacy intruded upon.

"Very good," said the governess.

It was about one o'clock when Paul's mother and father drove up to their house. All was still. Paul's mother went to her room and slipped off her white fur cloak. She had told her maid not to wait up for her. She heard her husband downstairs, mixing a whiskey and soda.

Vocabulary
remonstrated (ri·män′strāt′id) v.: protested.
arrested (ə·rest′id) v. used as *adj.*: checked or halted in motion.

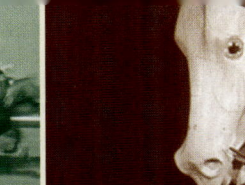

And then, because of the strange anxiety at her heart, she stole upstairs to her son's room. Noiselessly she went along the upper corridor. Was there a faint noise? What was it?

She stood, with arrested muscles, outside his door, listening. There was a strange, heavy, and yet not loud noise. Her heart stood still. It was a soundless noise, yet rushing and powerful. Something huge, in violent, hushed motion. What was it? What in God's name was it? She ought to know. She felt that she knew the noise. She knew what it was.

Yet she could not place it. She couldn't say what it was. And on and on it went, like a madness.

Softly, frozen with anxiety and fear, she turned the door handle.

The room was dark. Yet in the space near the window, she heard and saw something plunging to and fro. She gazed in fear and amazement.

Then suddenly she switched on the light, and saw her son, in his green pajamas, madly surging on the rocking horse. The blaze of light suddenly lit him up, as he urged the wooden horse, and lit her up, as she stood, blonde, in her dress of pale green and crystal, in the doorway.

"Paul!" she cried. "Whatever are you doing?"

"It's Malabar!" he screamed in a powerful, strange voice. "It's Malabar!"

His eyes blazed at her for one strange and senseless second, as he ceased urging his wooden horse. Then he fell with a crash to the ground, and she, all her tormented motherhood flooding upon her, rushed to gather him up.

But he was unconscious, and unconscious he remained, with some brain fever. He talked and tossed, and his mother sat stonily by his side.

"Malabar! It's Malabar! Bassett, Bassett, I *know*! It's Malabar!"

So the child cried, trying to get up and urge the rocking horse that gave him his inspiration.

"What does he mean by Malabar?" asked the heart-frozen mother.

"I don't know," said the father stonily.

"What does he mean by Malabar?" she asked her brother Oscar.

"It's one of the horses running for the Derby," was the answer.

And, in spite of himself, Oscar Cresswell spoke to Bassett, and himself put a thousand on Malabar: at fourteen to one.

The third day of the illness was critical: They were waiting for a change. The boy, with his rather long, curly hair, was tossing ceaselessly on the pillow. He neither slept nor regained consciousness, and his eyes were like blue stones. His mother sat, feeling her heart had gone, turned actually into a stone.

In the evening, Oscar Cresswell did not come, but Bassett sent a message, saying could he come up for one moment, just one moment? Paul's mother was very angry at the intrusion, but on second thoughts she agreed. The boy was the same. Perhaps Bassett might bring him to consciousness.

The gardener, a shortish fellow with a little brown moustache and sharp little brown eyes, tiptoed into the room, touched his imaginary cap to Paul's mother, and stole to the bedside, staring with glittering, smallish eyes at the tossing, dying child.

"Master Paul!" he whispered. "Master Paul! Malabar came in first all right, a clean win. I did

Comparing and Contrasting Texts

Lawrence also wrote the following on the subject of materialism: "I don't want to own a house, nor land, nor a motor-car, nor shares in anything. I don't want a fortune—not even an assured income. . . . There is deep inside one a revolt against the fixed thing, fixed society, fixed money, fixed homes, even fixed love."

Small-group activity. After students have read Lawrence's thoughts about natural human energy and money in his letter to Rolf Gardiner in the Primary Source on p. 980, ask them to look for evidence of his ideas in "The Rocking-Horse Winner." Working in small groups, they might pursue their analysis by developing and answering questions such as the following:

- How might being "simple and direct, and a bit free from oneself above all" have helped Paul and his mother?
- How does Lawrence portray the evil of "money-fear" and "money-lust" in the story?
- How applicable are Lawrence's ideas to modern society in general?

DIRECT TEACHING

A Reading Skills

? Synthesizing. Of what other characters in literature do the boy's ravings remind you? [Possible responses: Faust, Macbeth. Like them, Paul seems to have made a pact with a supernatural force.]

B Literary Focus

? Theme. Why does Uncle Oscar think Paul is better off dead? [Possible response: He realizes Paul was mad and feels Paul has been saved from a life of agony.] How does his comment relate to the theme of the story? [It underscores Lawrence's view that materialism is destructive.]

Primary Source

In this excerpt from a letter to Rolf Gardiner, Lawrence reveals the philosophical belief that contributes to the theme of "The Rocking-Horse Winner."

C Reading Informational Text

? Finding the main idea. What does Lawrence want young people to avoid doing? [making money their chief goal]

D Reading Informational Text

? Analyzing philosophical assumptions. What outlook on life does Lawrence suggest here? [Possible response: To get the most out of life, people must learn to celebrate life, and to cooperate with and love one another.]

---

as you told me. You've made over seventy thousand pounds, you have; you've got over eighty thousand. Malabar came in all right, Master Paul."

"Malabar! Malabar! Did I say Malabar, mother? Did I say Malabar? Do you think I'm lucky, mother? I knew Malabar, didn't I? Over eighty thousand pounds! I call that lucky, don't you, mother? Over eighty thousand pounds! I knew, didn't I know I knew? Malabar came in all right. If I ride my horse till I'm sure, then I tell you, Bassett, you can go as high as you like. Did you go for all you were worth, Bassett?"

"I went a thousand on it, Master Paul."

"I never told you, mother, that if I can ride my horse, and *get there*, then I'm absolutely sure—oh, absolutely! Mother, did I ever tell you? I *am* lucky!"

"No, you never did," said his mother.

But the boy died in the night.

And even as he lay dead, his mother heard her brother's voice saying to her: "My God, Hester, you're eighty-odd thousand to the good, and a poor devil of a son to the bad. But, poor devil, poor devil, he's best gone out of a life where he rides his rocking horse to find a winner." ■

PRIMARY SOURCE / LETTER

D. H. Lawrence on Money

A theme that runs through nearly all Lawrence's works is the celebration of life—the human energy and force that express the joy of existence. Opposing this natural energy is materialism, which Lawrence believed misdirects our energies and warps the soul.

Rolf Gardiner, one of Lawrence's first admirers, managed a large farm in Dorset. In 1926, Lawrence wrote to Gardiner: "And don't be too earnest—earnest—how does one spell it?—nor overburdened by a mission: neither too self-willed. One must be simple and direct, and a bit free from oneself above all."

In another letter to Gardiner, Lawrence makes a rare brief mention of the evils of materialism.

Villa Mirenda, Scandicci
Florence
18 Dec., 1927

Dear Rolf Gardiner,

. . . If I were talking to the young, I should say only one thing to them: Don't you live just to make money, either for yourself or for anybody else. Don't look on yourself as a wage slave. Try to find out what life itself is, and live. Repudiate the money idea.

And then I'd teach 'em, if I could, to dance and sing together. The togetherness is important.

But they must first overthrow in themselves the money-fear and money-lust. . . .

Check Test: True-False

Monitoring students' progress. Guide the class in answering these questions.

1. Paul's mother wishes she had more children. [F]
2. Paul believes that what the family needs is luck. [T]
3. As he rides his rocking horse, Paul is content. [F]
4. Uncle Oscar's attitude toward Paul's death is resignation. [T]

Response and Analysis

Reading Check

1. The opening, written in the style of a fairy tale, tells of a woman who "had no luck." How has she been unlucky? What else does the writer tell us directly about the mother's **character**?
2. How does Paul's mother define *luck* when Paul asks her what it means? What is Paul's confusion about the word *luck*?
3. What step does Paul take to ease his mother's anxiety over the family's debts? How does she react when she learns of her birthday surprise?
4. Who is Bassett? Why does he keep Paul's secret?
5. Does Paul solve his mother's problem? Why or why not?

Thinking Critically

6. How do you explain the ever louder voices in the house? In your opinion, why do only Paul and his sisters hear and react to the voices?
7. How would you describe what happens to Paul at the end of the story?
8. What might the rocking horse **symbolize**?
9. State the **theme**, or meaning, of the story in a sentence, using the words *love* and *money*. How does this theme apply to life today? Consult your Quickwrite notes for help.
10. How would you describe the **tone** of the story?

Extending and Evaluating

11. What do you think of Lawrence's decision to end the story as he did? In what ways is the story's ending a distortion of the usual fairy-tale ending? How does this ending support Lawrence's views on money and materialism as stated in the *Primary Source* on page 980?

WRITING

Keeping Up with the Joneses

"The mother's extravagance results partly from social pressure—the need to keep up appearances." Find evidence in the story to support this statement, and write a brief **essay** in which you present that evidence.

Inside His Mind

Review **stream of consciousness** as a narrative form (see pages 962–963), and write an **interior monologue** in which you reveal the workings of Paul's mind as he rides his rocking horse to that tragic victory. What thoughts, feelings, and associations run through his mind?

Vocabulary Development
Rating Connotations

Connotations are the feelings associated with a word—feelings that go beyond a word's strict dictionary definition, or **denotation**. Often, connotations show shades of meaning or intensity. On a separate sheet of paper, use the symbols "+," "−," or "=" to show how the words in each of the following pairs compare in intensity. Use "+" if the vocabulary word on the left seems stronger, "−" if it seems weaker, and "=" if it seems equivalent in meaning to the word on the right.

1. asserted ( )   stated
2. obscure ( )   unknown
3. reiterated ( )   repeated
4. uncanny ( )   mysterious
5. iridescent ( )   rainbowlike
6. overwrought ( )   hysterical
7. remonstrated ( )   complained
8. arrested ( )   stopped

INTERNET
Projects and Activities
Keyword: LE5 12-7

Literary Skills
Analyze symbols.

Writing Skills
Write an essay presenting evidence to support a claim. Write an interior monologue.

Vocabulary Skills
Understand and evaluate connotations.

D. H. Lawrence 981

Reading Check

1. The woman's love has turned to dust; she finds herself unable to love her children; she feels flawed. She is ambitious and eager for social position; she is not as rich as she hoped to be and is never satisfied.
2. She says that luck is what causes people to have money. Paul is confused because he believes luck and money are the same thing. He doesn't realize that one can be lucky in other ways.
3. Paul bets on horses and wins a great deal of money. He asks his uncle to make an anonymous birthday present to his mother of a thousand pounds a year for five years. His mother is disappointed because she wants the whole amount right away.
4. Bassett is the gardener and Paul's gambling partner. Bassett keeps the secret because he feels that Paul's talent is somehow divine; they are making money; and as an employee, Bassett must obey Paul.

INDEPENDENT PRACTICE

Response and Analysis

5. Paul fails to solve his mother's problem because her problem stems from false values or feelings of inadequacy, not simply from the lack of money or luck.

Thinking Critically

6. Possible answers: The voices represent his mother's materialism and the family's debts. The children sense the anxiety.
7. Possible answers: He becomes possessed; he wills himself into a psychic frenzy.
8. Possible answers: greed; temptation; an instrument of supernatural forces; Paul's desire for his mother's love.
9. Possible answer: The love of money leads to death. Many people today are slaves to money.
10. Possible answers: ominous, mystical, satirical.

Extending and Evaluating

11. The typical fairy tale ends happily, but here Paul dies and his mother is left with the consequences of her greed. This outcome stresses Lawrence's point about the evils of materialism.

Vocabulary Development

1. +   3. =   5. +   7. +
2. −   4. +   6. −   8. +

ASSESSING

Assessment

- Holt Assessment: Literature, Reading, and Vocabulary

Lot's Wife

Anna Akhmatova
translated by **Richard Wilbur**

The just man followed then his angel guide
Where he strode on the black highway, hulking and bright;
But a wild grief in his wife's bosom cried,
Look back, it is not too late for a last sight

5 *Of the red towers of your native Sodom, the square
Where once you sang, the gardens you shall mourn,
And the tall house with empty windows where
You loved your husband and your babes were born.*

She turned, and looking on the bitter view
10 Her eyes were welded shut by mortal pain;
Into transparent salt her body grew,
And her quick feet were rooted in the plain.

Who would waste tears upon her? Is she not
The least of our losses, this unhappy wife?
15 Yet in my heart she will not be forgot
Who, for a single glance, gave up her life.

Head of Akhmatova (1913) by Natan Altman.
Museum Ludwig Köln.

All the unburied ones

Anna Akhmatova
translated by **Judith Hemschemeyer**

All the unburied ones—I buried them,
I mourned for them all, but who will mourn for me?

I am not one of those who left the land

Anna Akhmatova
translated by **Stanley Kunitz**

I am not one of those who left the land
to the mercy of its enemies.
Their flattery leaves me cold,
my songs are not for them to praise.

5   But I pity the exile's lot.
Like a felon, like a man half-dead,
dark is your path, wanderer;
wormwood° infects your foreign bread.

But here, in the murk of conflagration,°
10 where scarcely a friend is left to know,
we, the survivors, do not flinch
from anything, not from a single blow.

Surely the reckoning will be made after
the passing of this cloud.
15 We are the people without tears,
straighter than you . . . more proud . . .

---

8. **wormwood** *n.:* herb that produces a bitter oil. The word can also refer to something that produces feelings of bitterness.
9. **conflagration** (kän′flə·grā′shən) *n.:* fire.

Farmwoman in a Field (1931) by Konstantin Rozhdestvyenski.
Museum Ludwig Köln.

Independent Practice

Response and Analysis

Thinking Critically

1. Possible answers: It is her home. "Mortal pain" suggests that we should be sympathetic, for her attitude is very human.

2. Possible answer: The story of an unwilling exile probably had strong emotional associations for Akhmatova. At the time, Akhmatova was strongly tempted to flee the Soviet Union's totalitarian regime. However, she chose to remain.

3. Possible answers: The theme is that the homeland is precious and separation from it is painful. This view of life suggests that people have undeniable roots. The historical paroxysm of Stalin's Soviet Union made such a view especially poignant and topical.

4. Possible answers: The tone is mournful. The speaker is compassionate toward the victims of tyranny; she then agonizes over who will mourn for her if she also becomes a victim.

5. The two groups are those who abandoned the homeland and those who chose to remain. The speaker feels sorry for the exiles but asserts that those who stayed are "more proud."

6. Some students may argue that both poems address the theme of loving one's homeland—either as a patriot who refuses to leave ("I am not one. . . . ") or as an exile who longs to return ("Lot's Wife"). Akhmatova's firsthand experience of Stalin's tyranny shaped her compassion for the situation of both the patriot and the exile. Nevertheless, as one who refused to leave the Soviet Union, she values the experience of the patriot over that of the exile.

7. Answers will vary.

Response and Analysis

Lot's Wife
All the unburied ones
I am not one of those who left the land

Thinking Critically

1. What, in general, makes Lot's wife care about Sodom, despite its evils? What does the phrase "mortal pain" (line 10) suggest about how we should view her attitude?

2. Re-read the biography of Akhmatova on page 982 and the Background on page 983. Then, explain how "Lot's Wife" might have been shaped by the events of Akhmatova's life and by the political situation in Russia at the time she wrote the poem.

3. How would you state the **theme** of "Lot's Wife"? What view of life does this theme reflect, and how is this view of life shaped by historical influences?

4. What is the **tone** of "All the unburied ones"? What attitude does the speaker express, and toward whom?

5. What two groups of people are contrasted in "I am not one of those who left the land"? Paraphrase what the speaker says about each group.

6. How is the **theme** of "I am not one. . ." different from that of "Lot's Wife"? Again, consider Akhmatova's historical circumstances. What do you think accounts for the difference in the two poems?

7. Review your Quickwrite notes. Do any of Akhmatova's poems echo your feelings about leaving home during troubled times? Do any of them compel you to rethink your ideas? Explain.

SKILLS FOCUS
Literary Skills Analyze theme.
Writing Skills Write journal entries in response to poems.

Extending and Evaluating

8. Recall that Akhmatova helped found a poetic movement known as **acmeism**. Acmeists strove to eliminate ambiguous symbols from their work and instead emphasized the clear communication of ideas. They also organized their thoughts into **stanzas**—line groupings that followed a rhyme scheme and that often expressed a single idea. Of the three poems you have read, which do you think is the best example of acmeism? Why? Use examples from the poem to support your opinion.

WRITING

Through a Poet's Eyes
Imagine that you are Anna Akhmatova. Write three **journal entries,** each one expressing, in prose, the ideas conveyed in each of the three poems. When you are finished, swap journal entries with a classmate. How are your entries similar? How are they different?

Woman with a Rake (1928–1932) by Kasimir Malevich.
Tretyakov Gallery, Moscow.

Extending and Evaluating

8. Possible answer: Students may choose "I am not one of those who left the land" as the clearest example of an acmeist poem since it is well-organized into four-line stanzas, contains vivid language, and expresses an unambiguous theme without using symbols.

ASSESSING

Assessment
- *Holt Assessment: Literature, Reading, and Vocabulary*

RETEACHING

For a lesson reteaching theme and meaning, see **Reteaching,** p. 1129A.

Elizabeth Bowen
(1899–1973)
Ireland

Photograph by Robin Adler.

Elizabeth Bowen was born in Dublin and spent her early years in Ireland's County Cork, on her family's splendid country estate, Bowen's Court. As Bowen later wrote, her family strove "to live as though living gave them no trouble." An only child, Bowen was looked after by a governess, taken to the Anglican church on Sundays, and taught to dance, wear gloves, and pay attention to manners. On her mother's orders she was not taught to read until she was seven. When Bowen's father, a lawyer, was confined to a mental hospital, Elizabeth was not allowed to dwell on it. By her twelfth year her father had recovered, but her mother had contracted fatal cancer. ("Good news," her mother is reported to have remarked, with her characteristic optimism. "Now I'm going to see what Heaven's like.") Elizabeth was not allowed to attend her mother's funeral or to mourn her.

Bowen's fiction clearly bears the stamp of her early years. Much of her writing is concerned with the processes of growing up, of losing innocence, of coming to terms with reality. Her main characters are often wealthy, sensitive, and well-mannered women; yet her novels also reveal a sense that life cannot be trusted, that existence is a struggle.

At seventeen, after attending a boarding school in England, Bowen moved to London to write stories. There she attended readings at the Poetry Bookshop, where she made the first of the literary friendships that were to become the fabric of her life. Among these literary friends were Edith Sitwell and Ezra Pound.

In 1923, Bowen published her first collection of stories, *Encounters,* to little notice. She also married Alan Cameron, a teacher. For most of the next ten years, the couple lived in the university town of Oxford, where Cameron taught and his wife wrote industriously. She produced story collections regularly and wrote nearly a novel a year.

In 1935, the couple moved back to London, where Bowen became a notable hostess of the literary world. During World War II, with its nightly air raids on London, Bowen was a dedicated air-raid warden, but she also went right on giving parties. Once, while entertaining guests on her balcony, she took no notice of the magnesium flares, but when she had gathered everyone inside, she said, in a typical understatement, "I feel I should apologize for the noise." During that period, she was writing the stories published in 1945 in *The Demon Lover,* a collection she called a "diary" of her reactions to the war.

After the war, Bowen and her husband returned to Bowen's Court but had barely begun this new, serene era when Cameron died of a heart attack. Predictably, Bowen became more active than ever.

Although she had been irrepressibly healthy all her life, a persistent cough proved to be a symptom of lung cancer. She died in 1973 and is buried in an Irish churchyard.

PRETEACHING

Summary ⇄ at grade level

During World War II, a married woman in her forties returns to her closed-up London house to collect a few items. Entering the house, she discovers a recent letter from a soldier she promised to marry twenty-five years earlier, a man reported lost in action in France during World War I. In the letter, the man reminds the woman that she made a promise to him; he claims he is confident she will keep their appointment. In a flashback to 1916, the woman recalls their loveless affair and the man's intimidating ways. To escape the memory, she rushes from the empty house and enters the only cab at the taxi stand. When the driver turns to face her, she screams, apparently recognizing him as the dreaded former fiancé. She beats on the closed windows as the driver speeds away into the empty streets.

Selection Starter

Motivate. Call on volunteers to share their impressions of ghost stories from films, novels, or television shows. Encourage students to discuss why such stories are perennially popular.

Before You Read

The Demon Lover

Make the Connection

Ghost stories can be mesmerizing, even when they're scaring us to death. Part of why we're so drawn to them is that they make us think about which events are real and which are happening only in our imagination, or in the imagination of a character. See how well you can figure out what's real and what's not in this story. Is it a ghost story at all?

Literary Focus

Flashback

A **flashback** is a scene in a narrative or dramatic work that interrupts the present action to tell what happened at an earlier time. "The Demon Lover" uses a **flashback** to provide important background information about the main character, Mrs. Drover. To recognize where the flashback begins, look for the sudden appearance of a verb in the past perfect tense (that is, preceded by the helping verb *had*).

INTERNET
Vocabulary Practice
Keyword: LE5 12-7

> A **flashback** is a scene in a narrative that interrupts the present action to "flash backward" and tell what happened at an earlier time.
>
> For more on Flashback, see the Handbook of Literary and Historical Terms.

Reading Skills

Modifying Your Predictions

Think about the title of this story. Then, freewrite for a few minutes, predicting what you think this story will be about. As you read, **modify**, or adjust, your predictions based on what happens in the story. Note which details lead you to modify a prediction.

Literary Skills Understand flashback.

Reading Skills Make and modify predictions.

Background

"The Demon Lover" takes place in London in the early 1940s during World War II, when frequent German air raids over the city drove many Londoners to find temporary lodgings in the country.

The title of the story comes from a version of a British ballad sometimes called "The House Carpenter." In the ballad a woman's husband, who has been missing at sea for seven years, returns to take her back to "the banks of Italy." The woman, who has married a house carpenter in the meantime and had children with him, is lured by the first husband's wealth (he now owns eight ships) and goes to sea with him—only to find that he has a demon's cloven foot. The demon lover then breaks the ship in two, sinking it, so that he and his wife can go together to the place they are destined for—hell.

Vocabulary Development

prosaic (prō·zā′ik) *adj.*: ordinary; dull.

refracted (ri·frakt′id) *v.* used as *adj.*: bent by its passage from one medium to another.

assent (ə·sent′) *n.*: acceptance.

intermittent (in′tər·mit′'nt) *adj.*: starting and stopping at intervals; periodic.

precipitately (pri·sip′ə·tit·lē) *adv.*: suddenly.

emanated (em′ə·nāt′id) *v.*: flowed; came forth.

impassively (im·pas′iv·lē) *adv.*: calmly; indifferently.

aperture (ap′ər·chər) *n.*: opening.

988 Collection 7 The Modern World: 1900 to the Present

Previewing Vocabulary

Have students in small groups study the Vocabulary words listed on p. 988. Then, have a volunteer in each group start a game of Password by giving a clue to the meaning of one of the Vocabulary words. As the other members try to guess the word, another clue is added after each wrong guess. The person who correctly identifies the word begins providing clues for another word.

In the following exercise, choose the word that fits in each blank.

1. She gave her _____ to the plan. [assent]
2. The cat pounced _____, startling its prey. [precipitately]
3. The aloof star _____ greeted her fans. [impassively]
4. Light is _____ in water. [refracted]
5. Delicious smells _____ from the kitchen. [emanated]
6. The _____ flashing of the light gave me a headache. [intermittent]
7. The student thought the article was _____ and repetitive. [prosaic]
8. I peered through the _____ in the wall. [aperture]

The Demon Lover
Elizabeth Bowen

Toward the end of her day in London Mrs. Drover went round to her shut-up house to look for several things she wanted to take away. Some belonged to herself, some to her family, who were by now used to their country life. It was late August; it had been a steamy, showery day: At the moment the trees down the pavement glittered in an escape of humid yellow afternoon sun. Against the next batch of clouds, already piling up ink-dark, broken chimneys and parapets[1] stood out. In her once familiar street, as in any unused channel, an unfamiliar queerness had silted up; a cat wove itself in and out of railings, but no human eye watched Mrs. Drover's return. Shifting some parcels under her arm, she slowly forced round her latchkey in an unwilling lock, then gave the door, which had warped, a push with her knee. Dead air came out to meet her as she went in.

The staircase window having been boarded up, no light came down into the hall. But one door, she could just see, stood ajar, so she went quickly through into the room and unshuttered the big window in there. Now the prosaic woman, looking about her, was more perplexed than she knew by everything that she saw, by traces of her long former habit of life—the yellow smoke stain up the white marble mantelpiece, the ring left by a vase on the top of the escritoire;[2] the bruise in the wallpaper where, on the door being thrown open widely, the china handle had always hit the wall. The piano, having gone away to be stored, had left what looked like claw marks on its part of the parquet.[3] Though not much dust had seeped in, each object wore a film of another kind; and, the only ventilation being the chimney, the whole drawing room smelled of the cold hearth. Mrs. Drover put down her parcels on the escritoire and left the room to proceed upstairs; the things she wanted were in a bedroom chest.

She had been anxious to see how the house was—the part-time caretaker she shared with some neighbors was away this week on his holiday, known to be not yet back. At the best of times he did not look in often, and she was never

---
1. **parapets** (par′ə·pets′) *n. pl.*: low walls around rooftops.
2. **escritoire** (es′kri·twär′) *n.*: writing table.
3. **parquet** (pär·kā′) *n.*: wood floor made of boards arranged in geometric patterns.

Vocabulary
prosaic (prō·zā′ik) *adj.*: ordinary; dull.

DIRECT TEACHING

VIEWING THE ART

Edward Bawden (1903–1989) was an English graphic designer, illustrator, and painter who produced covers, illustrations, posters, ads, and calendars. As an official war artist during World War II, he also painted a number of large-scale murals. *Cat on a Pile of Blankets* displays his typically simple lines and touches of wit.

Activity. Ask students to speculate on the identity of the figure in the mirror and why it appears only as a shadow or silhouette. What emotions do the mirror, the shadow, and the cat arouse? [Possible response: The figure in the mirror is the cat's fantasy of its absent or deceased owner. The objects create a sense of mystery, foreboding, and loss.]

Ⓐ Reading Skills

❓ Making inferences. What is mysterious about the arrival of the letter? [It is inside the house; the caretaker is away; it bears no stamp.] How do you think it was delivered? [Possible responses: Perhaps the caretaker hand-delivered it; an intruder left it and is waiting somewhere in the house; a supernatural being somehow got inside the house.]

Cat on a Pile of Blankets (1985) by Edward Bawden.
The Fine Art Society, London. © The Edward Bawden Estate.

sure that she trusted him. There were some cracks in the structure, left by the last bombing, on which she was anxious to keep an eye. Not that one could do anything—

A shaft of refracted daylight now lay across the hall. She stopped dead and stared at the hall table—on this lay a letter addressed to her.

Ⓐ She thought first—then the caretaker *must* be back. All the same, who, seeing the house shuttered, would have dropped a letter in at the box? It was not a circular, it was not a bill. And the post office redirected, to the address in the country, everything for her that came through the post. The caretaker (even if he *were* back) did not know she was due in London today—her call here had been planned to be a surprise—so his negligence in the manner of this letter, leaving it to wait in the dusk and the dust, annoyed her. Annoyed, she picked up the letter, which bore no stamp. But it cannot be important, or they would know . . . She took the letter rapidly upstairs with her, without a stop to look

Vocabulary
refracted (ri·frakt′id) *v.* used as *adj.*: bent by its passage from one medium to another.

990   Collection 7   The Modern World: 1900 to the Present

DIFFERENTIATING INSTRUCTION

Advanced Learners
Enrichment. Have students discuss how war can change people. Ask them to refer to books they have read, movies they have seen, or personal or family experiences with war that they would like to share. As they read the story, ask students to note whether or not any of the main points brought up in the discussion apply to the main character, and if so, to what extent. Students might also consider Graham Greene's short story "The Destructors" (p. 863), which is also set in London during World War II.

at the writing till she reached what had been her bedroom, where she let in light. The room looked over the garden and other gardens: The sun had gone in; as the clouds sharpened and lowered, the trees and rank lawns seemed already to smoke with dark. Her reluctance to look again at the letter came from the fact that she felt intruded upon—and by someone contemptuous of her ways. However, in the tenseness preceding the fall of rain she read it: It was a few lines.

> Dear Kathleen: You will not have forgotten that today is our anniversary, and the day we said. The years have gone by at once slowly and fast. In view of the fact that nothing has changed, I shall rely upon you to keep your promise. I was sorry to see you leave London, but was satisfied that you would be back in time. You may expect me, therefore, at the hour arranged. Until then ...   K.

Mrs. Drover looked for the date: It was today's. She dropped the letter onto the bedsprings, then picked it up to see the writing again—her lips, beneath the remains of lipstick, beginning to go white. She felt so much the change in her own face that she went to the mirror, polished a clear patch in it, and looked at once urgently and stealthily in. She was confronted by a woman of forty-four, with eyes starting out under a hat brim that had been rather carelessly pulled down. She had not put on any more powder since she left the shop where she ate her solitary tea.[4] The pearls her husband had given her on their marriage hung loose round her now rather thinner throat, slipping in the V of the pink wool jumper her sister knitted last autumn as they sat round the fire. Mrs. Drover's most normal expression was one of controlled worry, but of assent. Since the birth of the third of her little boys, attended by a quite serious illness, she had had an intermittent muscular flicker to the left of her mouth, but in spite of this she could always sustain a manner that was at once energetic and calm.

Turning from her own face as precipitately as she had gone to meet it, she went to the chest where the things were, unlocked it, threw up the lid, and knelt to search. But as rain began to come crashing down she could not keep from looking over her shoulder at the stripped bed on which the letter lay. Behind the blanket of rain the clock of the church that still stood struck six—with rapidly heightening apprehension she counted each of the slow strokes. "The hour arranged ... My God," she said, "*what* hour? How should I ...? After twenty-five years ..."

The young girl talking to the soldier in the garden had not ever completely seen his face. It was dark; they were saying goodbye under a tree. Now and then—for it felt, from not seeing him at this intense moment, as though she had never seen him at all—she verified his presence for these few moments longer by putting out a hand, which he each time pressed, without very much kindness, and painfully, on to one of the breast buttons of his uniform. That cut of the button on the palm of her hand was, principally, what she was to carry away. This was so near the end of a leave from France that she could only wish him already gone. It was August 1916. Being not kissed, being drawn away from and looked at intimidated Kathleen till she imagined spectral glitters in the place of his eyes. Turning away and looking back up the lawn she saw, through branches of trees, the drawing-room window alight: She caught a breath for the moment when she could go running back there into the safe arms of her mother and sister, and cry: "What shall I do, what shall I do? He has gone."

Hearing her catch her breath, her fiancé said, without feeling: "Cold?"

---

4. **tea:** in Britain, a light, late-afternoon meal, served with tea.

Vocabulary
assent (ə·sent′) *n.:* acceptance.
intermittent (in′tər·mit″nt) *adj.:* starting and stopping at intervals; periodic.
precipitately (pri·sip′ə·tit·lē) *adv.:* suddenly.

Elizabeth Bowen 991

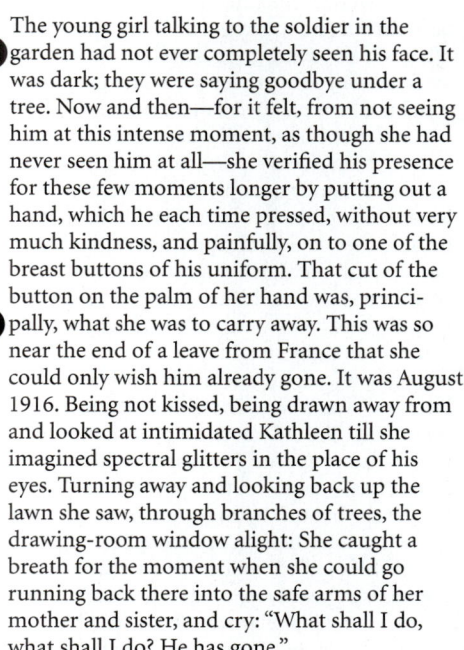

DIRECT TEACHING

B Reading Skills
Modifying your predictions. Have students look at the predictions they made after reading the title of the story. Give them the opportunity to change their predictions at this point, and ask them to make new predictions concerning the meaning of the letter.

C Reading Skills
Making inferences. What does the change in Mrs. Drover's coloring suggest about the letter or its writer? [Possible response: She recognizes the handwriting and is shocked or frightened by it.]

D English-Language Learners
Reading elliptical constructions. Ellipses are used when words are omitted. Sometimes a writer uses ellipses to help indicate a character's state of mind. Read the elliptical sentences aloud. What do you think is Mrs. Drover's state of mind? [Possible responses: She cannot seem to complete a thought. She is nervous, upset, and fearful as she tries to remember something from her past.]

E Literary Focus
Flashback. What are the signals that a flashback begins here? [There is an abrupt shift of setting and characters. The girl is young, and the reader can assume that she is Mrs. Drover. The space between paragraphs indicates a shift in time from the main action.]

CONTENT-AREA CONNECTIONS

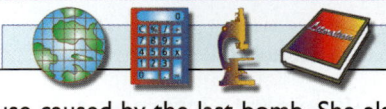

Psychology: The Bombing of London
The Germans relentlessly bombed London from September 6 through October 12, 1940. During this time, 12,696 London civilians were killed by bombs. In September alone, the Germans dropped more than ten thousand bombs on the city. Throughout this story, Bowen obliquely refers to the bombing. For instance, Mrs. Drover has returned to London to check on cracks in the structure of the house caused by the last bomb. She also listens to the clock in the church "that was still standing" strike six. Such references remind readers of the damage inflicted on both property and people.

Individual activity. These attacks resulted in psychological trauma as well as physical damage. Have students research the psychological effects of the bombing on London citizens at the time.

DIRECT TEACHING

A Reading Skills

? Speculating. Why does Kathleen feel free when the soldier is gone? Why has she made the "unnatural promise," and why is it a "sinister" betrothal? [Possible responses: She feels free of the intimidation with which he extracted the promise. She made the promise out of fear, or perhaps because she couldn't bring herself to refuse a man about to go off to war.]

B Reading Skills

? Interpreting. Why do you think Kathleen does not attract men? [Possible responses: She appears unapproachable because she recalls the "unnatural promise" she made and worries that the soldier will return "sooner or later." She feels a "complete dislocation from everything," so she can't focus on romance.]

C Literary Focus

? Flashback. Some flashbacks end abruptly, while others flow right back into the present. How does this flashback end? What signal returns the story to the present? [The events in Mrs. Drover's life are summarized up to the present, after which the words "As things were" signal a return to the present.]

D Reading Skills

? Modifying your predictions. Provide students with another opportunity to modify their predictions. Also, ask them to make a new prediction about what they think will happen to Mrs. Drover. Will her former fiancé come to get her? Will the whole incident prove to be a figment of her imagination? Or will the story be resolved in some other manner?

"You're going away such a long way."

"Not so far as you think."

"I don't understand?"

"You don't have to," he said. "You will. You know what we said."

"But that was—suppose you—I mean, suppose."

"I shall be with you," he said, "sooner or later. You won't forget that. You need do nothing but wait."

Only a little more than a minute later she was free to run up the silent lawn. Looking in through the window at her mother and sister, who did not for the moment perceive her, she already felt that unnatural promise drive down between her and the rest of all humankind. No other way of having given herself could have made her feel so apart, lost and forsworn.[5] She could not have plighted a more sinister troth.[6]

Kathleen behaved well when, some months later, her fiancé was reported missing, presumed killed. Her family not only supported her but were able to praise her courage without stint[7] because they could not regret, as a husband for her, the man they knew almost nothing about. They hoped she would, in a year or two, console herself—and had it been only a question of consolation things might have gone much straighter ahead. But her trouble, behind just a little grief, was a complete dislocation from everything. She did not reject other lovers, for these failed to appear: For years she failed to attract men—and with the approach of her thirties she became natural enough to share her family's anxiousness on this score. She began to put herself out,[8] to wonder; and at thirty-two she was very greatly relieved to find herself being courted by William Drover. She married him, and the two of them settled down in this quiet, arboreal[9] part of Kensington: In this house the years piled up, her children were born, and they all lived till they were driven out by the bombs of the next war. Her movements as Mrs. Drover were circumscribed, and she dismissed any idea that they were still watched.

As things were—dead or living the letter writer sent her only a threat. Unable, for some minutes, to go on kneeling with her back exposed to the empty room, Mrs. Drover rose from the chest to sit on an upright chair whose back was firmly against the wall. The desuetude[10] of her former bedroom, her married London home's whole air of being a cracked cup from which memory, with its reassuring power, had either evaporated or leaked away, made a crisis—and at just this crisis the letter writer had, knowledgeably, struck. The hollowness of the house this evening canceled years on years of voices, habits, and steps. Through the shut windows she only heard rain fall on the roofs around. To rally herself, she said she was in a mood—and for two or three seconds shutting her eyes, told herself that she had imagined the letter. But she opened them—there it lay on the bed.

On the supernatural side of the letter's entrance she was not permitting her mind to dwell. Who, in London, knew she meant to call at the house today? Evidently, however, this had been known. The caretaker, *had* he come back, had had no cause to expect her: He would have taken the letter in his pocket, to forward it, at his own time, through the post. There was no other sign that the caretaker had been in—but, if not? Letters dropped in at doors of deserted houses do not fly or walk to tables in halls. They do not sit on the dust of empty tables with the air of certainty that they will be found. There is needed some human hand—but nobody but the caretaker had a key. Under circumstances she did not care to consider, a house can be entered without a key. It was possible that she was not alone now. She might be being waited for, downstairs. Waited for—until when? Until "the

---

5. **forsworn** (fôr·swôrn′) *adv.:* having lied under oath; perjured.
6. **plighted . . . troth:** made a more sinister promise of marriage.
7. **stint** *n.:* limitation.
8. **put herself out:** vex or distress herself.
9. **arboreal** (är·bôr′ē·əl) *adj.:* full of trees.
10. **desuetude** (des′wi·tōōd′) *adj.:* disuse.

SKILLS REVIEW

Making inferences to interpret subtleties in the text. Remind students that an inference is an educated guess based on information in the text and on the reader's prior knowledge and experience. Encourage them to back up their inferences with specific details from the text. Remind them that when they make inferences about a character, they should pay close attention to the character's speech, appearance, thoughts, and actions, as well as to what others say and think about the character.

Activity. As they read, have students list clues to Mrs. Drover's character suggested by her appearance, thoughts, and actions. Next to each clue, have them write what they infer about Mrs. Drover from the clue. Then have students form groups to discuss their inferences and to consider how Mrs. Drover's character contributes to her dilemma.

Rainy Weather (late 19th or early 20th century) by Vilhelm Hammershoi.

Elizabeth Bowen 993

DIRECT TEACHING

VIEWING THE ART

Vilhelm Hammershoi (1864–1916) was a Danish artist who painted quiet interiors. Gray tones and a few strong accents provide the ingredients of his atmospheric scenes. In *Rainy Weather* a woman gazes out the window. She is seen from the back, so we are unable to discern her emotional state; instead, a mood is established by the room's light and the dark weather.

Activity. Ask students to describe the atmosphere of the room. How does Bowen's story influence what they see? [The atmosphere is dismal, melancholy, and forlorn. Students may project Mrs. Drover's anxiety onto the woman in the picture.]

READING MINI-LESSON

Developing Word-Attack Skills
Explain that over the centuries, English has borrowed words freely from other languages. As a result, the regular letter-sound relationships of English do not apply to all the words in the language.

Remind students of the phonogram *—et*. Words with this phonogram were probably some of the first words students learned to read—for example, *get, let, met, net, pet, wet*. Point out that the phonogram *—et* appears in two words in the selection: *parapet* and *parquet*. Write the words on the chalkboard and compare the pronunciations. Explain that although both words have French origins, *parapet* has taken on a typically English pronunciation, whereas in *parquet*, *—et* retains the French sound /ā/.

Activity. Have students read the following sentences and identify the words in which *et* stands for /ā/.

1. From the garret, she watched them play croquet on the lawn.
2. Her gimlet eye spotted his white beret.
3. His way of handling the mallet had a certain cachet.
4. A bouquet from him graced the spinet.
5. They dined on filet of beef and claret.

Elizabeth Bowen 993

DIRECT TEACHING

A Reading Skills

❓ **Expressing an opinion.** What would you do if you were in Mrs. Drover's position at this point in the story? [Possible responses: Get out of the house immediately. Telephone her husband or a friend.]

B Reading Skills

❓ **Speculating.** How do you think the soldier convinced Mrs. Drover to make her dreadful promise? [Possible response: He probably pressured her psychologically.] Why can't she remember her former fiancé's face? [Possible responses: The thought of him is so distressing that she has developed a mental block. Time has dulled her memory.]

C Reading Skills

Modifying your predictions. After students have read these lines, ask them to modify their predictions again.

D Reading Skills

❓ **Speculating.** Who might be leaving the house? [Possible responses: The caretaker, who may have been there all along; the ghost of Mrs. Drover's presumed-dead fiancé or the living man himself; nobody—her imagination is playing tricks on her.]

---

hour arranged." At least that was not six o'clock: Six has struck.

She rose from the chair and went over and locked the door.

The thing was, to get out. To fly? No, not that: She had to catch her train. As a woman whose utter dependability was the keystone of her family life she was not willing to return to the country, to her husband, her little boys, and her sister, without the objects she had come up to fetch. Resuming work at the chest she set about making up a number of parcels in a rapid, fumbling-decisive way. These, with her shopping parcels, would be too much to carry; these meant a taxi—at the thought of the taxi her heart went up and her normal breathing resumed. I will ring up the taxi now; the taxi cannot come too soon: I shall hear the taxi out there running its engine, till I walk calmly down to it through the hall. I'll ring up—But no: the telephone is cut off . . . She tugged at a knot she had tied wrong.

The idea of flight . . . He was never kind to me, not really. I don't remember him kind at all. Mother said he never considered me. He was set on me, that was what it was—not love. Not love, not meaning a person well. What did he do, to make me promise like that? I can't remember—But she found that she could.

She remembered with such dreadful acuteness that the twenty-five years since then dissolved like smoke and she instinctively looked for the weal[11] left by the button on the palm of her hand. She remembered not only all that he said and did but the complete suspension of *her* existence during that August week. I was not myself—they all told me so at the time. She remembered—but with one white burning blank as where acid has dropped on a photograph: *Under no conditions* could she remember his face.

So, wherever he may be waiting, I shall not know him. You have no time to run from a face you do not expect.

---

11. **weal** (wēl) *n.*: lump; welt.

The thing was to get to the taxi before any clock struck what could be the hour. She would slip down the street and round the side of the square to where the square gave on the main road. She would return in the taxi, safe, to her own door, and bring the solid driver into the house with her to pick up the parcels from room to room. The idea of the taxi driver made her decisive, bold: She unlocked her door, went to the top of the staircase, and listened down.

She heard nothing—but while she was hearing nothing the *passé*[12] air of the staircase was disturbed by a draft that traveled up to her face. It emanated from the basement: Down there a door or window was being opened by someone who chose this moment to leave the house.

The rain had stopped; the pavements steamily shone as Mrs. Drover let herself out by inches from her own front door into the empty street. The unoccupied houses opposite continued to meet her look with their damaged stare. Making toward the thoroughfare and the taxi, she tried not to keep looking behind. Indeed, the silence was so intense—one of those creeks of London silence exaggerated this summer by the damage of war—that no tread could have gained on hers unheard. Where her street debouched[13] on the square where people went on living, she grew conscious of, and checked, her unnatural pace. Across the open end of the square two buses impassively passed each other: Women, a perambulator,[14] cyclists, a man wheeling a barrow signalized, once again, the ordinary flow of life. At the square's most populous corner should be—and was—the short taxi rank. This evening, only one taxi—but this, although it

---

12. ***passé*** (pä·sā') *adj.*: no longer fresh; rather old.
13. **debouched** (dē·bōōshd') *v.*: came out; emerged.
14. **perambulator** (pər·am'byōō·lāt'ər) *n.*: chiefly British for "baby carriage." The word is often shortened to *pram*.

Vocabulary

emanated (em'ə·nāt'id) *v.*: flowed; came forth.
impassively (im·pas'iv·lē) *adv.*: calmly; indifferently.

---

994 Collection 7 The Modern World: 1900 to the Present

Check Test: True-False

Monitoring students' progress. Guide the class in answering these questions.

1. The closed-up house unsettles Mrs. Drover. [T]
2. The letter is dated the same day she finds it. [T]
3. She dearly loved the letter writer many years ago. [F]
4. A friendly taxi driver calms Mrs. Drover. [F]

presented its blank rump, appeared already to be alertly waiting for her. Indeed, without looking round the driver started his engine as she panted up from behind and put her hand on the door. As she did so, the clock struck seven. The taxi faced the main road: To make the trip back to her house it would have to turn—she had settled back on the seat and the taxi *had* turned before she, surprised by its knowing movement, recollected that she had not "said where." She leaned forward to scratch at the glass panel that divided the driver's head from her own.

The driver braked to what was almost a stop, turned round, and slid the glass panel back: The jolt of this flung Mrs. Drover forward till her face was almost into the glass. Through the aperture driver and passenger, not six inches between them, remained for an eternity eye to eye. Mrs. Drover's mouth hung open for some seconds before she could issue her first scream. After that she continued to scream freely and to beat with her gloved hands on the glass all round as the taxi, accelerating without mercy, made off with her into the hinterland of deserted streets. ■

Vocabulary
aperture (ap'ər·chər) *n.*: opening.

Response and Analysis

Reading Check
Using the following chart, create a story map for "The Demon Lover":

Situation	
Characters	
Conflict	
Event	
Event	
Event [etc.]	
Climax	
Resolution	

Thinking Critically

1. In some stories, descriptions of the **setting** provide much more than the physical background—they also create a particular **mood**. List the **images** in the story's first paragraph that help create an unsettling mood.

2. Why has the Drover family left their London home? Cite two places in the text that make the reason clear. For what purpose has Mrs. Drover returned?

3. What details in the lovers' last meeting **foreshadow** a sinister, threatening reunion? What do we learn about Mrs. Drover's fiancé that explains why she is terrified of him?

4. The use of an **omniscient narrator** allows Bowen to give readers information about Mrs. Drover's psychological makeup that Mrs. Drover herself is not consciously aware of. Identify several such passages in the text. How do you interpret Mrs. Drover's psychological state?

INTERNET
Projects and Activities
Keyword: LE5 12-7

Literary Skills
Analyze flashback.

Reading Skills
Make and modify predictions.

Writing Skills
Write a character description.

Vocabulary Skills
Create semantic charts.

Elizabeth Bowen 995

DIRECT TEACHING

E Reading Skills
? Modifying your predictions. How do you think the ending will resolve the story's tension? [Possible response: The cab driver will turn out to be the "demon lover."]

F Literary Focus
? Theme. Is this story strictly for entertainment, or does it offer a comment on life and human behavior? [The ghost story is entertaining, but it also explores the memories, guilt, and anxiety of the central character and comments on the destructive effects of war.]

INDEPENDENT PRACTICE

Response and Analysis

dark"; "broken chimneys"; the warped door; and the dead air in the home.

2. Bombings caused the Drovers to leave their home. There are "cracks . . . left by the last bombing" (p. 990) and Mrs. Drover hears "creeks of London silence exaggerated . . . by the damage of war" (p. 994). Mrs. Drover has returned to collect things for her family.

3. The lover hurts Kathleen's hand; she imagines "spectral glitters" in place of his eyes (p. 991); he says threateningly, "I shall be with you sooner or later" (p. 992). Mrs. Drover reflects, "He was never kind to me. . . . He was set on me, that was what it was—not love. Not love, not meaning a person well" (p. 994).

4. Possible answer: She is generally anxious and sometimes "perplexed" (p. 989); she normally wears an expression of "controlled worry" (991). Her elliptical phrases and "intermittent muscular flicker" (p. 991) suggest that she is emotionally unstable.

Elizabeth Bowen 995

Reading Check
Sample Story Map
Basic situation—Mrs. Drover has returned to her London house to retrieve some items. *Characters*—Mrs. Drover and her former fiancé. *Conflict*—She fears harm from her former fiancé or from his ghost. *Event*—Mrs. Drover finds a letter from her former fiancé, a soldier who supposedly died during World War I. The letter indicates that he is holding her to her promise of marriage and will arrive for their appointment. *Event*—Mrs. Drover recalls their loveless affair and the man's cruelty and coldness. *Climax*—Afraid, she hurries from the house and escapes into a waiting taxicab. *Resolution*—When the driver turns, she recognizes her former fiancé and screams as the taxi speeds away.

Thinking Critically

1. Possible answers: The shut-up house; the "steamy, showery day"; the "humid . . . yellow sun"; the clouds that pile up "ink-

INDEPENDENT PRACTICE

5. The reader may suspect that the taxi driver is the demon lover; Mrs. Drover does not. Even though she is unnerved by the letter and is afraid her lover may return, she feels safe in the taxi until the driver turns around.

6. Possible answers: During the destruction of wartime, people experience "complete dislocation from everything," even love. The theme suggests a sober, even pessimistic outlook on the effects of war.

Extending and Evaluating

7. Possible answers: The abrupt shift to Mrs. Drover's past is effective, given her disorientation and anxious frame of mind. The abrupt shift is confusing because the reader doesn't see the connection between Mrs. Drover and the young girl until well into the flashback.

Literary Criticism

8. Responses will vary, but students should support their interpretation with evidence from the text. The hallucination theory, which must cover the letter as well as the taxi, is supported by all the references to the damage and dislocation of war. The ghost story theory is supported by the description of the house, by the letter's mysterious appearance, and by Mrs. Drover's reaction to the taxi driver.

---

5. **Dramatic irony** occurs when a reader or an audience is aware of something that a character does not know. What is the central dramatic irony of the story? Did you predict the story would turn out the way it does? Check your reading notes.

6. The two world wars bracket this story like bookends. During each war, Mrs. Drover experiences dislocation and confusion. During each war, the demon lover is part of her life. Yet he doesn't appear during the intervening twenty-five years. Use these strands of the story—war, Mrs. Drover's inner turmoil, and the lover's appearances—to develop your understanding of the story's **theme**. What view of life does this theme suggest?

Extending and Evaluating

7. Contributing to the story's richness and depth is the interplay between present and past. Think about the **flashback** that tells what happened earlier in Mrs. Drover's life. Do you think the abrupt shift into the past is effective or merely confusing? Why?

Literary Criticism

8. Some readers believe that Mrs. Drover's experience is a hallucination: Her powers of imagination have combined with the pressures of wartime life to transform everyday reality into a waking nightmare. Other readers consider the story to be an out-and-out ghost story. Which interpretation do you favor, or do you have another? Support your interpretation with evidence from the text.

WRITING

No Prince Charming

At no time in the story are we given a description of the demon lover's face. At the end of the story, however, when Mrs. Drover is finally within six inches of his face, she begins to scream. In a few **paragraphs**, describe what you imagine Mrs. Drover sees. You might also create a drawing or painting of the demon lover.

Vocabulary Development
Word Information Charts

prosaic   intermittent   impassively
refracted precipitately   aperture
assent   emanated

The chart below organizes some basic information about the word *prosaic*. Using a dictionary, make similar charts for the rest of the Vocabulary words listed above.

prosaic
Meaning: ordinary; dull
Origin: Latin, "prose"
Synonym and/or Antonym: commonplace (synonym); exciting (antonym)
Examples: Grocery lists are prosaic; doing laundry is prosaic.

Vocabulary Development
Sample Answer
refracted. *Meaning*—bent. *Origin*—Latin, "back" + "broken." *Synonym*—bent. *Antonym*—straightened. *Examples*—The prism refracted the ray of light; the sunlight was refracted by the water.

Grammar Link

Building Coherence: Connecting Ideas

In a coherent composition, ideas are clearly connected, and every paragraph flows smoothly and sensibly from one to the next. You can connect ideas within and between paragraphs with **direct references** and **transitions**.

You use **direct references** naturally in writing—for example, using *she* to refer to Elizabeth Bowen in the sentences that follow.

> At seventeen, Elizabeth Bowen moved to London to write stories. There she became friends with other young writers.

You can improve coherence by employing direct references purposefully.

- Refer to a noun or pronoun used earlier
- Repeat a word used earlier
- Substitute a synonym for words used earlier

Transitions show *how* ideas are connected. Often these expressions show chronological or spatial relationships. They may also show relationships of cause and effect, definition, or contrast.

> During the Blitz, the German Luftwaffe targeted London. Therefore, many residents of London fled the city. [*Therefore* indicates a cause-and-effect relationship.]

Note the different purposes of the types of transitions in the chart below:

Transitions that compare ideas	again, also, and, besides, both, each of, furthermore, in addition, likewise, moreover, similarly, too
Transitions that contrast ideas	although, but, however, in spite of, instead, neither . . . nor, nevertheless, still, yet
Transitions that indicate time or position	above, afterward, before, eventually, first (second, etc.), meanwhile, nearby, next
Transitions that indicate purpose, cause, or effect	as, because, consequently, for, just as . . . so, since, so, so that, then, therefore
Transitions that indicate a summary, a conclusion, or an example	as a result, for example, for instance, in conclusion, in fact, in other words, on the whole, overall, therefore, thus

PRACTICE

Turn the sentences below into a clear paragraph by inserting direct references or effective transitions.

"The Demon Lover" by Elizabeth Bowen is set during World War II. World War II played an integral part in Elizabeth Bowen's life and writings. Many people fled to the country to escape the German air raids over London. Bowen remained in London. Bowen continued to write. Bowen incorporated her experiences in wartime England into her novels.

Apply to Your Writing

Look over a writing assignment you are working on now or have already completed. Revise your work by adding direct references and transitions to make your sentences and paragraphs flow smoothly.

▶ For more help, see Sentence Combining, 10a–d, in the Language Handbook.

Grammar Skills
Understand and use direct references and transitions.

Grammar Link

Practice

Sample Revision
"The Demon Lover" by Elizabeth Bowen is set during World War II. This conflict played an integral part in Bowen's life and writings. Although many people fled to the country to escape the German air raids over London, Bowen remained in the city. She continued to write and incorporated her wartime experiences into her novels.

ASSESSING

Assessment
- *Holt Assessment: Literature, Reading, and Vocabulary*

DIFFERENTIATING INSTRUCTION

Learners Having Difficulty
Write the following pairs of sentences on the chalkboard. Have students use direct references or effective transitions (or both) to combine each pair. Sample answers are given in brackets.

1. Mrs. Drover turned the key in the lock. Mrs. Drover pushed the door with her knee. [Mrs. Drover turned the key in the lock and then pushed the door with her knee.]

2. She stared at the hall table. On the table was a letter for her. [She stared at the hall table because a letter for her was on it.]

3. She quickly took the letter upstairs and kept walking. She reached her bedroom. [She quickly took the letter upstairs and kept walking until she reached her bedroom.]

4. Mrs. Drover checked the date on the letter. Mrs. Drover saw that the date was that day's. [When Mrs. Drover checked the date on the letter, she saw that it was that day's.]

SKILLS FOCUS, pp. 998–1005

Grade-Level Skills

- **Literary Skills**

Analyze characteristics of magic realism.

- **Reading Skills**

Analyze point of view.

Review Skills

- **Literary Skills**

Analyze various literary devices, including figurative language, imagery, allegory, and symbolism.

More About the Writer

Background. Cortázar has been compared to the great Argentine writer Jorge Luis Borges, especially because both authors tend to write about metaphysical themes such as life, death, the nature of reality, and the power of the imagination. Cortázar was employed as a translator for UNESCO after moving to Paris in 1951. He wrote a number of novels, several collections of short stories, and a book of poetry that was published posthumously.

For Independent Reading

- "House Taken Over" describes how unseen invaders take over the home of an elderly Argentine brother and sister.
- "The Night Face Up" is a suspenseful tale in which the victim of a motorcycle accident drifts in and out of lucidity, imagining that he has been transported back in time and has become the sacrificial victim in an Aztec ritual ceremony.

Julio Cortázar
(1914–1984)
Argentina

A visitor to an aquarium is transformed into a salamander; a rich Argentine woman discovers and changes places with her exact double, who is a beggar in Budapest; a man finds himself vomiting rabbits, which gradually destroy his apartment. Welcome to the world of Julio Cortázar.

For Cortázar the fantastic is not something supernatural but "something very simple, that can happen in the midst of everyday reality, during this sunny midday, now, between you and I, or on the subway. . . ." Cortázar's views of the fantastic are heavily influenced by French surrealism and the writings of Edgar Allan Poe, whose works Cortázar translated into Spanish.

Born in Belgium to Argentine parents, Julio Cortázar grew up in a suburb of Buenos Aires. Throughout his childhood he read voraciously and wrote his own imaginative tales. After high school, Cortázar qualified as a teacher of French literature, but he gave up university studies in order to take a teaching job to support his family. While he taught, he wrote stories, but he didn't publish his first collection, *Bestiary*, until 1951.

That year was a turning point in another way: Disillusioned by the regime of the Argentine dictator Juan Perón, Cortázar accepted a French government grant to study in Paris. Though he lived in exile most of his life—mainly in France, working as a freelance translator for the United Nations and for various publishers—Cortázar always considered himself a Latin American.

Cortázar once said that a writer's job is "to set fire to language," and the Argentine writer did just that in 1963, when he astounded the publishing world with *Hopscotch,* a long, structurally innovative novel whose chapters can be read in several different sequences.

Cortázar—who was influenced by jazz and classical music, Zen Buddhism, detective novels, and movies—kept the fun-loving, youthful side of his nature alive to the end of his days. "He liberated us all with a new, airy, humorous, and mysterious language, both everyday and mythical," the Mexican novelist Carlos Fuentes said in a tribute to his friend shortly after Cortázar's death from leukemia in 1984.

For Independent Reading

You may enjoy the following stories by Cortázar:

- "House Taken Over"
- "The Night Face Up"

998   Collection 7   The Modern World: 1900 to the Present

RESOURCES: READING

Planning
- *One-Stop Planner* CD-ROM with ExamView Test Generator

Differentiating Instruction
- Supporting Instruction in Spanish
- Audio CD Library, Selections and Summaries in Spanish

Vocabulary
- Vocabulary Development

Grammar and Language
- Daily Language Activities

Assessment
- Holt Assessment: Literature, Reading, and Vocabulary
- *One-Stop Planner* CD-ROM with ExamView Test Generator
- Holt Online Assessment

Internet
- go.hrw.com (Keyword: LE5 12-7)
- Elements of Literature Online

Media
- Audio CD Library
- Audio CD Library, Selections and Summaries in Spanish

Before You Read

Axolotl

Make the Connection

Fantastic occurrences are often the stuff of sleep. Surreal images and irrational happenings flood our dreams, yet during the day, our lives seem ordered, routine, rational. What happens when these two worlds overlap or intersect—when we can't distinguish between them?

Literary Focus

Magic Realism

The term **magic realism** (*lo real maravilloso*) was coined in 1949 by the Cuban novelist, essayist, and musicologist Alejo Carpentier. He used the term to describe a blurring of the lines that usually separate what seems real to the reader from what seems imagined or unreal to the same reader. Carpentier believed that by incorporating magic, myth, imagination, and religion into literature, we can expand our rigid concept of reality.

In "Axolotl," as in all **magic realism**, the impossible and the possible—fantasy and reality—are set in opposition. Cortázar introduces some surrealistic element or extraordinary event into an otherwise entirely realistic environment, and the two different worlds become so intertwined that neither character nor reader can separate them.

> **Magic realism** is literature that combines incredible events with realistic details and relates them all in a matter-of-fact tone.
>
> For more on Magic Realism, see the Handbook of Literary and Historical Terms.

Reading Skills

Identifying Point of View

As you read "Axolotl," try to determine the **point of view,** or the vantage point from which the writer tells the story. Who or what is narrating the story? Jot down clues that might reveal the identity of the narrator. Why do you think Cortázar chose this particular point of view?

Background

In Cortázar's fantastic stories—among the best of **magic realism**—daily life is often mysteriously subverted by unknown forces. This "invasion by the imaginary," as he called it, creates a tension that can both invigorate and disturb.

The creatures shown on pages 1001 and 1002 are not from a sci-fi movie. They are real axolotls (ak′sə·lät″lz)—a type of Mexican salamander.

> **Vocabulary Development**
>
> **translucent** (trans·lōō′sənt) *adj.*: partially transparent.
>
> **diminutive** (də·min′yōō·tiv) *adj.*: very small.
>
> **tentative** (ten′tə·tiv) *adj.*: hesitant; uncertain.
>
> **proximity** (präk·sim′ə·tē) *n.*: closeness.

INTERNET
Vocabulary Practice
Keyword: LE5 12-7

Literary Skills Understand the characteristics of magic realism.

Reading Skills Identify point of view.

Julio Cortázar 999

AXOLOTL

Julio Cortázar
translated by Paul Blackburn

There was a time when I thought a great deal about the axolotls. I went to see them in the aquarium at the Jardin des Plantes[1] and stayed for hours watching them, observing their immobility, their faint movements. Now I am an axolotl.

I got to them by chance one spring morning when Paris was spreading its peacock tail after a wintry Lent. I was heading down the boulevard Port-Royal, then I took Saint-Marcel and L'Hôpital and saw green among all that gray and remembered the lions. I was friend of the lions and panthers, but had never gone into the dark, humid building that was the aquarium. I left my bike against the gratings and went to look at the tulips. The lions were sad and ugly and my panther was asleep. I decided on the aquarium, looked obliquely at banal fish until, unexpectedly, I hit it off with the axolotls. I stayed watching them for an hour and left, unable to think of anything else.

In the library at Sainte-Geneviève, I consulted a dictionary and learned that axolotls are the larval stage (provided with gills) of a species of salamander of the genus *Ambystoma*. That they were Mexican I knew already by looking at them and their little pink Aztec faces and the placard at the top of the tank. I read that specimens of them had been found in Africa capable of living on dry land during the periods of drought, and continuing their life under water when the rainy season came. I found their Spanish name, *ajolote*, and the mention that they were edible, and that their oil was used (no longer used, it said) like cod-liver oil.

I didn't care to look up any of the specialized works, but the next day I went back to the Jardin des Plantes. I began to go every morning, morning and afternoon some days. The aquarium guard smiled perplexedly taking my ticket. I would lean up against the iron bar in front of the tanks and set to watching them. There's nothing strange in this, because after the first minute I knew that we were linked, that something infinitely lost and distant kept pulling us together. It had been enough to detain me that first morning in front of the sheet of glass where some bubbles rose through the water. The axolotls huddled on the wretched narrow (only I can know how narrow and wretched) floor of moss and stone in the tank. There were nine specimens, and the majority pressed their heads against the glass, looking with their eyes of gold at whoever came near them. Disconcerted, almost ashamed, I felt it a lewdness to be peering at these silent and immobile figures heaped at the bottom of the tank. Mentally I isolated one, situated on the right and somewhat apart from the others, to study it better. I saw a rosy little body, translucent (I thought of those Chinese

---

1. **Jardin des Plantes** (zhär·dan' dā plänt): Paris botanical garden, part of the French National Museum of Natural History. The name means "garden of plants" in French.

Vocabulary
translucent (trans·lōō'sənt) *adj.*: partially transparent.

Julio Cortázar

DIRECT TEACHING

VIEWING THE ART

The axolotl is a larval salamander indigenous to Central America. Unlike other salamanders, it remains in its aquatic larva stage for life, rather than metamorphosing into an amphibious adult. Human modernization has threatened the axolotl with extinction. The organism has proved unable to accommodate itself to modern pollutants and is threatened by predators artificially introduced into its environment to provide sport for fishermen.

Activity. How does this image compare with the author's description on pp. 999–1002? [Students should identify as many features as possible, based on the text.] What bearing on the story might the endangered status of the axolotls have? [The narrator's identification with the axolotl suggests that he may be alienated from the world.]

DIRECT TEACHING

VIEWING THE ART

To the Aztecs, axolotls (whose name derives from the Aztec word *Xolotl*, the name of an ancient deity) were mystical creatures, living disciples of the god of games who also guided the dead to heaven.

Activity. How does this image increase your understanding of the appearance of an axolotl, compared to the image on p. 1001? [The elongated body and the position of the external "gills" are clearer in this image.]

A Reading Skills

Identifying point of view. In this passage, the point of view shifts back and forth from that of the observer to that of the observed. Where do these shifts occur? [The passage begins with the narrator observing an axolotl but then shifts to the narrator speaking as if he were one of the species, saying "the most sensitive part of *our* body." A second shift occurs with the sentence beginning "It's that we. . . ." The shift here is signaled by the change from the first-person singular pronoun, *I*, to the first-person plural pronoun, *we*.]

figurines of milky glass), looking like a small lizard about six inches long, ending in a fish's tail of extraordinary delicacy, the most sensitive part of our body. Along the back ran a transparent fin which joined with the tail, but what obsessed me was the feet, of the slenderest nicety, ending in tiny fingers with minutely human nails. And then I discovered its eyes, its face. Inexpressive features, with no other trait save the eyes, two orifices, like brooches, wholly of transparent gold, lacking any life but looking, letting themselves be penetrated by my look, which seemed to travel past the golden level and lose itself in a diaphanous² interior mystery. A very slender black halo ringed the eye and etched it onto the pink flesh, onto the rosy stone of the head, vaguely triangular, but with curved and irregular sides which gave it a total likeness to a statuette corroded by time. The mouth was masked by the triangular plane of the face, its considerable size would be guessed only in profile; in front a delicate crevice barely slit the lifeless stone. On both sides of the head where the ears should have been, there grew three tiny sprigs red as coral, a vegetal outgrowth, the gills, I suppose. And they were the only thing quick about it; every ten or fifteen seconds the sprigs pricked up stiffly and again subsided. Once in a while a foot would barely move, I saw the diminutive toes poise mildly on the moss. It's that we don't enjoy moving a lot, and the tank is so cramped—we

---

2. **diaphanous** *adj.*: transparent.

Vocabulary
diminutive (də·min′yōō·tiv) *adj.*: very small.

1002 Collection 7   The Modern World: 1900 to the Present

CONTENT-AREA CONNECTIONS

Science: The Axolotl
Individual activity. Ask students to research the axolotl, a member of the genus *Ambystoma,* and write a report in which they answer the following questions: Where does it live? What does it eat? What are its natural enemies? Does it live in groups or alone? [Some details are provided in Viewing the Art on p. 1001.]

Art: The Metamorphosis
Small-group activity. Have students work in small groups to create illustrations for this story. Encourage them to try to depict the transformation of the man into an axolotl. Does the change happen gradually or suddenly? Perhaps it happens only in the narrator's mind. Ask students how they will resolve this issue before they begin their illustrations.

barely move in any direction and we're hitting one of the others with our tail or our head—difficulties arise, fights, tiredness. The time feels like it's less if we stay quietly.

It was their quietness that made me lean toward them fascinated the first time I saw the axolotls. Obscurely I seemed to understand their secret will, to abolish space and time with an indifferent immobility. I knew better later; the gill contraction, the tentative reckoning of the delicate feet on the stones, the abrupt swimming (some of them swim with a simple undulation[3] of the body) proved to me that they were capable of escaping that mineral lethargy in which they spent whole hours. Above all else, their eyes obsessed me. In the standing tanks on either side of them, different fishes showed me the simple stupidity of their handsome eyes so similar to our own. The eyes of the axolotls spoke to me of the presence of a different life, of another way of seeing. Glueing my face to the glass (the guard would cough fussily once in a while), I tried to see better those diminutive golden points, that entrance to the infinitely slow and remote world of these rosy creatures. It was useless to tap with one finger on the glass directly in front of their faces; they never gave the least reaction. The golden eyes continued burning with their soft, terrible light; they continued looking at me from an unfathomable depth which made me dizzy.

And nevertheless they were close. I knew it before this, before being an axolotl. I learned it the day I came near them for the first time. The anthropomorphic[4] features of a monkey reveal the reverse of what most people believe, the distance that is traveled from them to us. The absolute lack of similarity between axolotls and human beings proved to me that my recognition was valid, that I was not propping myself up with easy analogies. Only the little hands . . . But an eft,[5] the common newt, has such hands also, and we are not at all alike. I think it was the axolotls' heads, that triangular pink shape with the tiny eyes of gold. That looked and knew. That laid the claim. They were not *animals*.

It would seem easy, almost obvious, to fall into mythology. I began seeing in the axolotls a metamorphosis which did not succeed in revoking a mysterious humanity. I imagined them aware, slaves of their bodies, condemned infinitely to the silence of the abyss, to a hopeless meditation. Their blind gaze, the diminutive gold disc without expression and nonetheless terribly shining, went through me like a message: "Save us, save us." I caught myself mumbling words of advice, conveying childish hopes. They continued to look at me, immobile; from time to time the rosy branches of the gills stiffened. In that instant I felt a muted pain; perhaps they were seeing me, attracting my strength to penetrate into the impenetrable thing of their lives. They were not human beings, but I had found in no animal such a profound relation with myself. The axolotls were like witnesses of something, and at times like horrible judges. I felt ignoble in front of them; there was such a terrifying purity in those transparent eyes. They were larvas, but larva means disguise and also phantom. Behind those Aztec faces, without expression but of an implacable cruelty, what semblance was awaiting its hour?

I was afraid of them. I think that had it not been for feeling the proximity of other visitors and the guard, I would not have been bold enough to remain alone with them. "You eat them alive with your eyes, hey," the guard said, laughing; he likely thought I was a little cracked. What he didn't notice was that it was they devouring me slowly with their eyes, in a cannibalism of gold. At any distance from the aquarium, I had only to think of them, it was as though I were being affected from a distance. It got to the point that I was going every day, and at night I thought of them immobile in the

---

3. **undulation** *n.*: wavelike movement.
4. **anthropomorphic** *adj.*: having human shape or characteristics; humanlike.
5. **eft** *n.*: archaic for "newt," kind of amphibious salamander.

Vocabulary
tentative (ten′tə·tiv) *adj.*: hesitant; uncertain.
proximity (präk·sim′ə·tē) *n.*: closeness.

Julio Cortázar 1003

DIRECT TEACHING

A Reading Skills

Analyzing motivation. Why does the narrator want to prove that the axolotls do not really possess consciousness? [Possible response: Frightened by his train of thought, part of him is trying to cling to rationality.]

B Reading Skills

Synthesizing. Throughout, the narrator has repeatedly declared that nothing is strange, not even the fact that he has become an axolotl. Why does he finally admit that there is one strange thing? [Possible response: Cortázar inverts the narrator's refrain to highlight the moment of the narrator's surreal transformation.]

C Literary Focus

Magic realism. In what sense can the narrator be both an axolotl in the tank and a man looking into the tank? [Possible responses: The narrator's consciousness is inside the axolotl, but his body remains outside the tank. The point of view has shifted from that of the man to that of the axolotl.]

GUIDED PRACTICE

Monitoring students' progress. Guide the class in answering these questions.

True-False

1. The story is written in the first person. [T]
2. The narrator believes that the axolotls are suffering. [T]
3. The narrator-turned-axolotl hopes his story will be told. [T]

---

darkness, slowly putting a hand out which immediately encountered another. Perhaps their eyes could see in the dead of night, and for them the day continued indefinitely. The eyes of axolotls have no lids.

I know now that there was nothing strange, that that had to occur. Leaning over in front of the tank each morning, the recognition was greater. They were suffering, every fiber of my body reached toward that stifled pain, that stiff torment at the bottom of the tank. They were lying in wait for something, a remote dominion destroyed, an age of liberty when the world had been that of the axolotls. Not possible that such a terrible expression which was attaining the overthrow of that forced blankness on their stone faces should carry any message other than one of pain, proof of that eternal sentence, of that liquid hell they were undergoing. Hopelessly, I wanted to prove to myself that my own sensibility was projecting a nonexistent consciousness upon the axolotls. They and I knew. So there was nothing strange in what happened. My face was pressed against the glass of the aquarium, my eyes were attempting once more to penetrate the mystery of those eyes of gold without iris, without pupil. I saw from very close up the face of an axolotl immobile next to the glass. No transition and no surprise, I saw my face against the glass, I saw it on the outside of the tank, I saw it on the other side of the glass. Then my face drew back and I understood.

Only one thing was strange: to go on thinking as usual, to know. To realize that was, for the first moment, like the horror of a man buried alive awaking to his fate. Outside, my face came close to the glass again, I saw my mouth, the lips compressed with the effort of understanding the axolotls. I was an axolotl and now I knew instantly that no understanding was possible. He was outside the aquarium, his thinking was a thinking outside the tank. Recognizing him, being him himself, I was an axolotl and in my world. The horror began—I learned in the same moment—of believing myself prisoner in the body of an axolotl, metamorphosed into him with my human mind intact, buried alive in an axolotl, condemned to move lucidly among unconscious creatures. But that stopped when a foot just grazed my face, when I moved just a little to one side and saw an axolotl next to me who was looking at me, and understood that he knew also, no communication possible, but very clearly. Or I was also in him, or all of us were thinking humanlike, incapable of expression, limited to the golden splendor of our eyes looking at the face of the man pressed against the aquarium.

He returned many times, but he comes less often now. Weeks pass without his showing up. I saw him yesterday, he looked at me for a long time and left briskly. It seemed to me that he was not so much interested in us any more, that he was coming out of habit. Since the only thing I do is think, I could think about him a lot. It occurs to me that at the beginning we continued to communicate, that he felt more than ever one with the mystery which was claiming him. But the bridges were broken between him and me, because what was his obsession is now an axolotl, alien to his human life. I think that at the beginning I was capable of returning to him in a certain way—ah, only in a certain way—and of keeping awake his desire to know us better. I am an axolotl for good now, and if I think like a man it's only because every axolotl thinks like a man inside his rosy stone semblance. I believe that all this succeeded in communicating something to him in those first days, when I was still he. And in this final solitude to which he no longer comes, I console myself by thinking that perhaps he is going to write a story about us, that, believing he's making up a story, he's going to write all this about axolotls. ■

DIFFERENTIATING INSTRUCTION

Advanced Learners

Enrichment. After students have finished reading the selection, ask how the narrator's reality is transformed. [The narrator's imagination transforms him into an axolotl.] Then have students discuss the following question: While the actual transformation may not be believable, is there something that is believable in the story? [Possible responses: It is possible that the narrator suffers, just as he imagines the axolotl does. It is believable that he identifies with the axolotl, an odd creature that is isolated and incapable of communication, one that seems to see and understand everything but can do nothing with its knowledge.]

Response and Analysis

Reading Check
1. What is an axolotl?
2. Where are the axolotls kept?
3. How does the narrator feel about axolotls?
4. What happens to the narrator?

Thinking Critically
5. Describe the **character** of the narrator as he relates his numerous trips to the aquarium. Is he well balanced psychologically? How do you know?
6. Identify at least three strong images that show how the narrator views the axolotls. How does the narrator's **imagery** describing the axolotls give the animals a surreal or otherworldly quality?
7. It is one thing to project feelings or thoughts onto an animal but quite another to become that animal and retain human consciousness. With the above sentence in mind, how would you state the **theme** or central idea of the story? What view of life does this theme represent?
8. What effect does the **point of view** have on how convincing, rational, or logical the story sounds? Refer to your reading notes.
9. As the story ends, the axolotl says, "I console myself by thinking that perhaps he is going to write a story about us. . . ." Why is this a consolation to the axolotl?
10. Describe the **tone** of the story. Is it completely serious, or is there an undercurrent of sly humor in the story? Explain.

Extending and Evaluating
11. In one of the very first sentences of the story, the narrator matter-of-factly confides, "Now I am an axolotl." As he tells his story, he alternates between the past (himself as a human fascinated by axolotls) and the present (himself as an axolotl in the tank). In your opinion, would the story have been less or more effective if it had been told in a traditional way, with the transformation into an axolotl presented as a surprise ending? In general, how do you feel about the way **magic realism** blurs the distinction between fantasy and reality in such a calm, accepting way?

WRITING
Finding Realism in the Magic
In a brief **essay**, **analyze** Cortázar's use of **magic realism** in "Axolotl." You may want to create a chart in which you list fantastic details on one side and realistic details on the other. As you write, keep the following questions in mind: What does magic realism allow Cortázar to express about the human condition? How does Cortázar use magic realism to comment on mundane aspects of reality?

Vocabulary Development
Analogies

translucent   tentative
diminutive   proximity

In an **analogy** the words in one pair relate to each other in the same way as the words in a second pair. On a separate sheet of paper, identify the Vocabulary word from above that completes each analogy below.

1. MOVING : STAGNANT :: _____ : opaque.
2. LAUGHTER : TEARS :: _____ : distance.
3. LAVISH : MEAGER :: _____ : certain.
4. TALL : GIRAFFE :: _____ : flea.

Literary Skills
Analyze the characteristics of magic realism.

Reading Skills
Analyze point of view.

Writing Skills
Write an essay analyzing the use of magic realism.

Vocabulary Skills
Complete word analogies.

Julio Cortázar   1005

INDEPENDENT PRACTICE

Response and Analysis

6. *Images*—"little pink Aztec faces"; "rosy" little bodies; "tiny fingers with minutely human nails"; "transparent" golden eyes; and "three tiny sprigs red as coral." The exotic imagery makes the creatures seem unique.
7. Possible answers: Genuine communication is unattainable. Intense thought can cause the mind to blur reality and fantasy.
8. Possible answer: The nearly seamless shifts in viewpoint make the story more convincing.
9. Possible answer: The axolotl hopes that the story will show how the inability to communicate causes suffering.
10. Possible answer: The tone is matter-of-fact. Examples of sly humor and irony include the send-up of evolutionary theory and the closing remarks of the narrator-turned-axolotl, who hopes that his human "self" will write a story about him.

Extending and Evaluating
11. Many students may feel that the mingling of fantasy and reality makes the story more intriguing.

Vocabulary Development
1. translucent   3. tentative
2. proximity   4. diminutive

ASSESSING

Assessment
- Holt Assessment: Literature, Reading, and Vocabulary

Reading Check
1. It is the larval stage of a species of salamander.
2. The axolotls are kept at the aquarium in the Jardin des Plantes in Paris.
3. He is fascinated by them.
4. He believes he has been transformed into an axolotl.

Thinking Critically
5. Possible answers: He is eccentric, visiting the aquarium obsessively. His use of the pronouns *we* and *our* to refer to himself and the axolotls suggests that he may not be well-balanced.

VIEWING THE ART

Though known primarily for his sculpture, **Alberto Giacometti** (1901–1966) also painted. In his mature work, he became fascinated by the interplay between the mediums in which he worked and the forms that he wanted to create. Giacometti's paintings use expressionistic, interwoven lines to build up the forms of three dimensional figures, often isolating them in an empty space.

Activity. How does the contrast between the face and the background affect your experience of the face? [Possible response: The face seems alive because of the flatness of the space that surrounds it, but it also looks isolated from reality by the void of the background.]

DIFFERENTIATING INSTRUCTION

Learners Having Difficulty
Modeling. To help students read "The Book of Sand," model the reading skill of making predictions. Say, "Suppose you read that the current owner of the Book of Sand appears melancholy, or sad, and calls the book 'diabolic,' or wicked. Knowing this, you might predict that if the narrator buys the book, it will somehow make him melancholy, too."

Encourage students to look for clues in the selection that help them make predictions.

The Book of Sand

Jorge Luis Borges *translated by* **Andrew Hurley**

> . . . thy rope of sands . . .
> —George Herbert (1593–1623)

The line consists of an infinite number of points; the plane, of an infinite number of lines; the volume, of an infinite number of planes; the hypervolume, of an infinite number of volumes . . . No—this, *more geometrico*,[1] is decidedly not the best way to begin my tale. To say that the story is true is by now a convention of every fantastic tale; mine, nevertheless, *is* true.

I live alone, in a fifth-floor apartment on Calle Belgrano.[2] One evening a few months ago, I heard a knock at my door. I opened it, and a stranger stepped in. He was a tall man, with blurred, vague features, or perhaps my nearsightedness made me see him that way. Everything about him spoke of honest poverty: he was dressed in gray, and carried a gray valise. I immediately sensed that he was a foreigner. At first I thought he was old; then I noticed that I had been misled by his sparse hair, which was blond, almost white, like the Scandinavians'. In the course of our conversation, which I doubt lasted more than an hour, I learned that he hailed from the Orkneys.[3]

I pointed the man to a chair. He took some time to begin talking. He gave off an air of melancholy, as I myself do now.

"I sell Bibles," he said at last.

"In this house," I replied, not without a somewhat stiff, pedantic note, "there are several English Bibles, including the first one, Wyclif's.[4] I also have Cipriano de Valera's,[5] Luther's[6] (which is, in literary terms, the worst of the lot), and a Latin copy of the Vulgate. As you see, it isn't exactly Bibles I might be needing."

After a brief silence he replied.

"It's not only Bibles I sell. I can show you a sacred book that might interest a man such as yourself. I came by it in northern India, in Bikaner."

He opened his valise and brought out the book. He laid it on the table. It was a cloth-bound octavo[7] volume that had clearly passed through many hands. I examined it; the unusual heft[8] of it surprised me. On the spine was printed *Holy Writ,* and then *Bombay.*

"Nineteenth century, I'd say," I observed.

"I don't know," was the reply. "Never did know."

I opened it at random. The characters were unfamiliar to me. The pages, which seemed worn and badly set, were printed in double columns, like a Bible. The text was cramped, and composed into versicles.[9] At the upper

---

1. ***more geometrico*:** in the geometrical manner.
2. **Calle Belgrano:** street in Buenos Aires.
3. **Orkneys:** group of islands off the northern coast of Scotland.

(Opposite) *Head of a Man (Diego)* (1964) by Alberto Giacometti.
Konsthaus Zürich, Switzerland. © 2003 Artists Rights Society (ARS), New York/ADAGP, Paris.

4. **Wyclif's Bible:** first English translation of the Bible. John Wycliff (c. 1330–1384) took charge of the project and perhaps did some translating.
5. **Cipriano de Valera's:** Spanish translation of the Bible; Casiodoro de Reina (1520–1594) translated the Bible, and Cipriano de Valera (1531–1602) edited it.
6. **Luther's:** German translation of the Bible. Martin Luther (1483–1546) was the German priest who set in motion the Protestant Reformation.
7. **octavo** *n.*: book, the pages of which have been made from sheets of paper that have been folded eight times.
8. **heft** *adj.*: heaviness.
9. **versicles** *n. pl.*: little verses.

Vocabulary
pedantic (pi·dan′tik) *adj.*: showing an exaggerated concern for books, learning, and rules.

Direct Teaching

A Reading Skills

? Making predictions. From these curious features of the book, and from what you know of the narrator's character, what do you predict the narrator will do about the book? [Possible responses: The narrator will try to acquire the book to solve its mysterious puzzles; he will become obsessed with the book.]

B Literary Focus

? Symbol. What does this curious fact, as well as the name of the book, suggest about the volume? [Possible response: The book's name and its seeming ability to "grow" new pages suggest that the book itself is infinite.] What might the Book of Sand symbolize? [Possible response: It may be a symbol of the infinite aspects of learning, of history, of the imagination, or of the universe itself.]

C Reading Skills

? Interpreting. Why do you think the stranger calls the book "diabolic"? [Possible responses: The book may have affected the stranger's life adversely; he may feel that the book violates his Christian beliefs.]

A corner of each page were Arabic numerals. I was struck by an odd fact: the even-numbered page would carry the number 40,514, let us say, while the odd-numbered page that followed it would be 999. I turned the page; the next page bore an eight-digit number. It also bore a small illustration, like those one sees in dictionaries: an anchor drawn in pen and ink, as though by the unskilled hand of a child.

It was at that point that the stranger spoke again.

"Look at it well. You will never see it again."

There was a threat in the words, but not in the voice.

I took note of the page, and then closed the book. Immediately I opened it again. In vain I searched for the figure of the anchor, page after page. To hide my discomfiture, I tried another tack.

"This is a version of Scripture in some Hindu language, isn't that right?"

"No," he replied.

Then he lowered his voice, as though entrusting me with a secret.

"I came across this book in a village on the plain, and I traded a few rupees[10] and a Bible for it. The man who owned it didn't know how to read. I suspect he saw the Book of Books as an amulet.[11] He was of the lowest caste; people could not so much as step on his shadow without being defiled. He told me his book was called the Book of Sand because neither sand nor this book has a beginning or an end."

He suggested I try to find the first page.

B I took the cover in my left hand and opened the book, my thumb and forefinger almost touching. It was impossible: several pages always lay between the cover and my hand. It was as though they grew from the very book.

"Now try to find the end."

I failed there as well.

---

10. **rupees** *n. pl.:* basic monetary unit of many Asian countries, including India, Pakistan, and Nepal.
11. **amulet** *n.:* ornament often inscribed with a magical incantation or symbol to protect the wearer from evil.

"This can't be," I stammered, my voice hardly recognizable as my own.

"It can't be, yet it *is*," the Bible peddler said, his voice little more than a whisper. "The number of pages in this book is literally infinite. No page is the first page; no page is the last. I don't know why they're numbered in this arbitrary way, but perhaps it's to give one to understand that the terms of an infinite series can be numbered any way whatever."

Then, as though thinking out loud, he went on.

"If space is infinite, we are anywhere, at any point in space. If time is infinite, we are at any point in time."

His musings irritated me.

"You," I said, "are a religious man, are you not?"

C "Yes, I'm Presbyterian. My conscience is clear. I am certain I didn't cheat that native when I gave him the Lord's Word in exchange for his diabolic book."

I assured him he had nothing to reproach[12] himself for, and asked whether he was just passing through the country. He replied that he planned to return to his own country within a few days. It was then that I learned he was a Scot, and that his home was in the Orkneys. I told him I had great personal fondness for Scotland because of my love for Stevenson and Hume.[13]

"And Robbie Burns,"[14] he corrected.

---

12. **reproach** *v.:* criticize or censure.
13. **Stevenson and Hume:** Robert Louis Stevenson (1850–1894), Scottish author; David Hume (1711–1776), Scottish philosopher.
14. **Robbie Burns:** Robert Burns (1759–1796), Scottish poet.

Vocabulary
discomfiture (dis·kum′fi·chər) *n.:* frustration; embarrassment.
caste (kast) *n.:* social class.
defiled (dē·fīld′) *v.:* made unclean.
diabolic (dī′ə·bäl′ik) *adj.:* of or having to do with evil or the devil.

1010   Collection 7   The Modern World: 1900 to the Present

Differentiating Instruction

Learners Having Difficulty
Make sure students understand that in most of his writing, Borges explores the shifting nature of reality. Tell students that the curious, seemingly impossible characteristics of the book are deliberately included to provoke the narrator's—and also the reader's—imagination. You might discuss some visual analogues to the story: for example, a hall of mirrors or a painting by M. C. Escher.

Advanced Learners
Enrichment. Scottish philosopher David Hume was a skeptic who believed that absolute knowledge of the world is impossible and that what human beings interpret as cause and effect is merely the mind's linking of ideas and impressions. Challenge students to find out more about Hume's philosophy and to discuss how it relates to the idea of an endlessly shifting universe that Borges explores in "The Book of Sand."

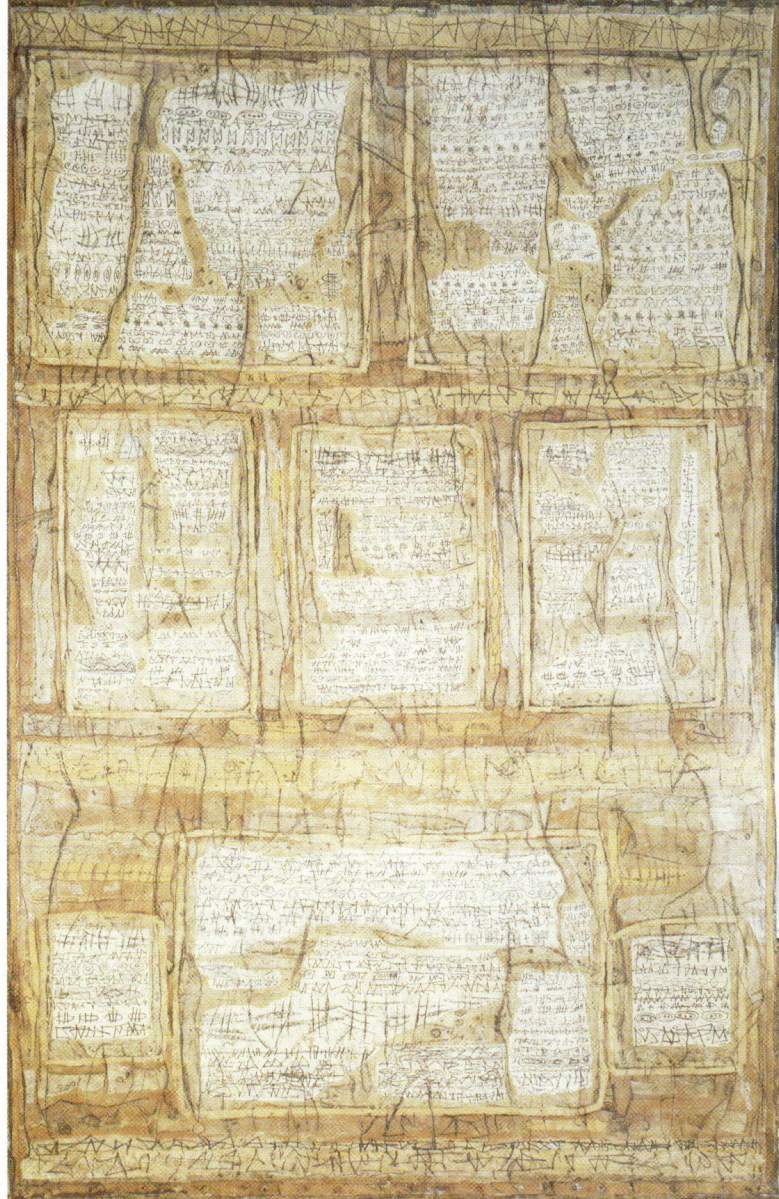

Layered Song (1980) by Clyde Connell.
Courtesy of Arthur Rogers Gallery, New Orleans.

DIRECT TEACHING

VIEWING THE ART

Clyde Connell (1901–1998), an artist from Louisiana, made sculptures and paintings for years in obscurity until she finally gained recognition in the 1970s. The stone-colored shapes with scribblings that mimic primitive script in this image are typical of her paintings. The "writing" is particularly interesting, as it is not true language, but represents the human desire to create symbols and bring meaning to the world.

Activity. Compare or contrast the themes evoked by Connell's art and Borges' story. [Possible responses: The writing in Connell's *Layered Song* is very dense, giving the impression of infinite complexity. Borges' story explores the theme that for humans, the appearance of infinity is potentially dangerous because of the way it seizes the attention and the imagination. Connell's art also captures human fascination with the infinite, but not its danger to the mind.]

DIRECT TEACHING

A **Reading Skills**

❓ Finding details. What details in this passage reveal that the narrator is really very eager to acquire the Book of Sand? [Possible responses: the phrases "feigned indifference" and "devised my plan."]

B **Literary Focus**

❓ Irony. How does this passage illustrate situational irony? [Possible response: The narrator thought he was being crafty, but the peddler intended to sell him the book all along.]

C **Reading Skills**

❓ Making predictions. Now that the narrator has acquired the book, what do you think will happen? [Possible responses: He will be tortured by the book's mysteries; he will go insane.]

D **Reading Skills**

❓ Speculating. The narrator says that he "tried" not to notice exactly where he left the book. What does this suggest about his future? [Possible response: The word *tried* suggests that he did not succeed; he may be drawn back to it over and over again, ad infinitum.]

As we talked I continued to explore the infinite book.

"Had you intended to offer this curious specimen to the British Museum, then?" I asked with feigned indifference.

"No," he replied, "I am offering it to you," and he mentioned a great sum of money.

I told him, with perfect honesty, that such an amount of money was not within my ability to pay. But my mind was working; in a few moments I had devised my plan.

"I propose a trade," I said. "You purchased the volume with a few rupees and the Holy Scripture; I will offer you the full sum of my pension, which I have just received, and Wyclif's black-letter[15] Bible. It was left to me by my parents."

"A black-letter Wyclif!" he murmured.

I went to my bedroom and brought back the money and the book. With a bibliophile's zeal he turned the pages and studied the binding.

"Done," he said.

I was astonished that he did not haggle. Only later was I to realize that he had entered my house already determined to sell the book. He did not count the money, but merely put the bills into his pocket.

We chatted about India, the Orkneys, and the Norwegian jarls[16] that had once ruled those islands. Night was falling when the man left. I have never seen him since, nor do I know his name.

I thought of putting the Book of Sand in the space left by the Wyclif, but I chose at last to hide it behind some imperfect volumes of the *Thousand and One Nights*.

I went to bed but could not sleep. At three or four in the morning I turned on the light. I took out the impossible book and turned its pages. On one, I saw an engraving of a mask. There was a number in the corner of the page—I don't remember now what it was—raised to the ninth power.

I showed no one my treasure. To the joy of possession was added the fear that it would be stolen from me, and to that, the suspicion that it might not be truly infinite. Those two points of anxiety aggravated my already habitual misanthropy. I had but few friends left, and those, I stopped seeing. A prisoner of the Book, I hardly left my house. I examined the worn binding and the covers with a magnifying glass, and rejected the possibility of some artifice. I found that the small illustrations were spaced at two-thousand-page intervals. I began noting them down in an alphabetized notebook, which was very soon filled. They never repeated themselves. At night, during the rare intervals spared me by insomnia,[17] I dreamed of the book.

Summer was drawing to a close, and I realized that the book was monstrous. It was cold consolation to think that I, who looked upon it with my eyes and fondled it with my ten flesh-and-bone fingers, was no less monstrous than the book. I felt it was a nightmare thing, an obscene thing, and that it defiled and corrupted reality.

I considered fire, but I feared that the burning of an infinite book might be similarly infinite, and suffocate the planet in smoke.

I remembered reading once that the best place to hide a leaf is in the forest. Before my retirement I had worked in the National Library, which contained nine hundred thousand books; I knew that to the right of the lobby a curving staircase descended into the shadows of the basement, where the maps and periodicals are kept. I took advantage of the librarians' distraction to hide the Book of Sand on one of the library's damp shelves; I tried not to notice how high up, or how far from the door.

I now feel a little better, but I refuse even to walk down the street the library's on. ■

---

15. **black-letter** *n.*: typeset used in early printed books.
16. **jarls** *n. pl.*: Scandinavian nobles ranking directly below a king.
17. **insomnia** *n.*: inability to sleep.

Vocabulary

bibliophile (bib'lē•ə•fīl) *n.*: one who loves books.
misanthropy (mi•san'thrə•pē) *n.*: hatred for humankind.
artifice (ärt'ə•fis) *n.*: trickery; deception.

Response and Analysis

Reading Check
1. You are the narrator of "The Book of Sand." Immediately after getting rid of the book, you run into an old friend. Tell him or her about your strange adventure, recounting all the **main events** of the story from beginning to end.

Thinking Critically
2. Why does the narrator come to feel that the book is "monstrous"?
3. Write two brief descriptions of the main character, one at the beginning of the story and the other at the end. What accounts for the differences in his outlook and personality? (Your response should go beyond "the book.")
4. The main character is a self-declared bibliophile, or book lover. Does he read people as skillfully as he reads books? Use evidence from the story to support your opinion.
5. A **paradox** is a seeming contradiction that nevertheless holds true. For example, the illustrations in the Book of Sand are both there and not there. How would you explain this paradox? Identify and explain another paradox in the story. Explain how these paradoxes made you feel as you read the story.
6. What dependable realities does Borges question in this story? Did the story succeed in making you think about how you take realities for granted? Why or why not? Be sure to check your Quickwrite notes.
7. Why do you think Borges gave his story the same title as the book *in* the story? Was it simply a matter of telling what the story was about? Or do the two texts share some of the same qualities? (Consider Borges' fascination with puzzles, paradoxes, and literary mystery before you respond.)

Extending and Evaluating
8. How satisfied are you with the **resolution** of the story? Why? Looking back at the **predictions** you made while reading may help you decide how you feel about the ending.

WRITING
A Never-Ending Story
Predict what happens next to the Book of Sand. Write a **story** about another adventure in the weird book's history. (Imagine, for example, what would happen if someone really did try to burn it.) Introduce new characters, a new setting, and several new events.

Vocabulary Development
Substitute Sentences

pedantic	diabolic
discomfiture	bibliophile
caste	misanthropy
defiled	artifice

Imagine that you have been assigned to read "The Book of Sand" to a group of twelve-year-olds. You're worried that Borges's vocabulary is too difficult for them, so you decide to retell the story in simpler language.

Find the sentences in the story in which the Vocabulary words listed above appear, and copy the sentences onto a sheet of paper. Then, rewrite each sentence to make it easier, substituting more commonly known words or phrases for the Vocabulary words. To locate **synonyms**—words with similar meanings—use a **thesaurus** or a **synonym finder**.

SKILLS FOCUS

Literary Skills
Analyze paradox.

Reading Skills
Review predictions.

Writing Skills
Write a short story.

Vocabulary Skills
Identify synonyms.

Jorge Luis Borges 1013

INDEPENDENT PRACTICE

Response and Analysis
5. Possible answers: In addition to the paradox of the illustrations, the book appears to have no beginning or end. The book may symbolize an infinitely shifting reality or the infinitely varied imagination. Some students may be intrigued by the paradoxes; others may find them irritating or baffling.
6. Borges questions the concept of sequence (the page numbers) and the idea that objective reality is predictable (the illustrations). Students may say the story made them realize that they take certain realities for granted.
7. Possible answer: Borges wanted to suggest that the texts share the qualities of mystery, paradox, and infinitude.

Extending and Evaluating
8. Possible answers: The resolution is satisfying because the narrator finally gets rid of the book; it is not satisfying because the philosophical questions raised by the book remain unresolved.

Vocabulary Development
Sample Answer
- "In this house," I replied, not without a somewhat stiff, fussy tone, "there are several English Bibles. . . ." (p. 1009)

ASSESSING

Assessment
- *Holt Assessment: Literature, Reading, and Vocabulary*

Reading Check
1. **Sample Answer**
   Some months ago a salesman showed me what he claimed was a sacred book from India, called The Book of Sand. The pages were oddly numbered; the book seemed to have no beginning or end. When I tried to find an illustration I'd seen, I couldn't locate it again. I bought the volume and became obsessed with it. I soon cut myself off from all human contact to focus on the book's mysteries. The book began to seem monstrous. Finally, I hid it in the library.

Thinking Critically
2. Possible answer: He thinks that his obsession has brought out the worst in him.
3. At first the narrator seems self-assured, even smug. At the end he has become a recluse, obsessed with the book even after it is gone. The book has altered his view of the universe.
4. No; for example, he fails to discern the peddler's plan to unload the book on him.

B. Wordsworth

V. S. Naipaul

Three beggars called punctually every day at the hospitable houses in Miguel Street. At about ten an Indian came in his dhoti[1] and white jacket, and we poured a tin of rice into the sack he carried on his back. At twelve an old woman smoking a clay pipe came and she got a cent. At two a blind man led by a boy called for his penny.

Sometimes we had a rogue.[2] One day a man called and said he was hungry. We gave him a meal. He asked for a cigarette and wouldn't go until we had lit it for him. That man never came again.

The strangest caller came one afternoon at about four o'clock. I had come back from school and was in my home clothes. The man said to me, "Sonny, may I come inside your yard?"

He was a small man and he was tidily dressed. He wore a hat, a white shirt, and black trousers.

I asked, "What you want?"

He said, "I want to watch your bees."

We had four small gru-gru palm trees[3] and they were full of uninvited bees.

I ran up the steps and shouted, "Ma, it have a man outside here. He say he want to watch the bees."

My mother came out, looked at the man, and asked in an unfriendly way, "What you want?"

The man said, "I want to watch your bees."

His English was so good, it didn't sound natural, and I could see my mother was worried. She said to me, "Stay here and watch him while he watch the bees."

The man said, "Thank you, Madam. You have done a good deed today."

He spoke very slowly and very correctly as though every word was costing him money.

We watched the bees, this man and I, for about an hour, squatting near the palm trees.

The man said, "I like watching bees. Sonny, do you like watching bees?"

I said, "I ain't have the time."

He shook his head sadly. He said, "That's what I do, I just watch. I can watch ants for days. Have you ever watched ants? And scorpions, and centipedes, and *congorees*[4]—have you watched those?"

I shook my head.

I said, "What you does do, mister?"

He got up and said, "I am a poet."

I said, "A good poet?"

He said, "The greatest in the world."

"What your name, mister?"

"B. Wordsworth."

"B for Bill?"

"Black. Black Wordsworth. White Wordsworth was my brother. We share one heart. I can watch a small flower like the morning glory and cry."

I said, "Why you does cry?"

"Why, boy? Why? You will know when you grow up. You're a poet, too, you know. And when you're a poet you can cry for everything."

I couldn't laugh.

He said, "You like your mother?"

"When she not beating me."

He pulled out a printed sheet from his hip pocket and said, "On this paper is the greatest poem about mothers and I'm going to sell it to you at a bargain price. For four cents."

---

1. **dhoti** (dō'tē) *n.*: loincloth worn by many Hindu men.
2. **rogue** (rōg) *n.*: archaic for "wandering beggar."
3. **gru-gru** (grōō'grōō') **palm trees**: spiny-trunked West Indian palm trees.
4. **congorees** (käŋ'gə-rēz') *n. pl.*: conger eels; long, scaleless eels found in the warm waters of the West Indies.

Papiamento (1987) by Julio Larraz. Oil on canvas.

I went inside and I said, "Ma, you want to buy a poetry for four cents?"

My mother said, "Tell that blasted man to haul his tail away from my yard, you hear."

I said to B. Wordsworth, "My mother say she ain't have four cents."

B. Wordsworth said, "It is the poet's tragedy." And he put the paper back in his pocket. He didn't seem to mind.

I said, "Is a funny way to go round selling poetry like that. Only calypsonians[5] do that sort of thing. A lot of people does buy?"

---
5. **calypsonians** (kə·lip′sō′nē·ənz) *n. pl.*: West Indian folk musicians who traditionally perform satirical, syncopated songs that are improvised, or composed on the spot. *Calypso* possibly comes from *kaiso*, a Trinidadian dialect word meaning "town crier."

He said, "No one has yet bought a single copy."

"But why you does keep on going round, then?"

He said, "In this way I watch many things, and I always hope to meet poets."

I said, "You really think I is a poet?"

"You're as good as me," he said.

And when B. Wordsworth left, I prayed I would see him again.

About a week later, coming back from school one afternoon, I met him at the corner of Miguel Street.

He said, "I have been waiting for you for a long time."

I said, "You sell any poetry yet?"

DIRECT TEACHING

A Literary Focus

Setting. How does the tropical setting of Trinidad help form B. Wordsworth's ideas about life? [Possible response: B. Wordsworth appreciates the beauty of the island's insects, flowers, and fruits, and he takes the time to enjoy them.]

B Reading Skills

Drawing conclusions. What Romantic attitudes are stressed in Naipaul's description of B. Wordsworth's home? [Possible responses: a love of nature in its wild state; a dislike of urban life.]

C Learners Having Difficulty

Re-reading. Re-read these two paragraphs to try to identify the narrator's feelings. Why does looking at the sky help him? [Possible responses: It makes him forget his problems; he realizes that he and his troubles are insignificant; he feels connected to something beautiful that is larger than himself.]

D Reading Skills

Interpreting. Why does B. Wordsworth want to keep his friendship with the boy a secret? [Possible responses: He realizes that boys value secrets; he feels this secret will solidify their friendship.]

He shook his head.

He said, "In my yard I have the best mango tree in Port-of-Spain.[6] And now the mangoes are ripe and red and very sweet and juicy. I have waited here for you to tell you this and to invite you to come and eat some of my mangoes."

He lived in Alberto Street in a one-roomed hut placed right in the center of the lot. The yard seemed all green. There was the big mango tree. There was a coconut tree and there was a plum tree. The place looked wild, as though it wasn't in the city at all. You couldn't see all the big concrete houses in the street.

He was right. The mangoes were sweet and juicy. I ate about six, and the yellow mango juice ran down my arms to my elbows and down my mouth to my chin and my shirt was stained.

My mother said when I got home, "Where you was? You think you is a man now and could go all over the place? Go cut a whip for me."

She beat me rather badly, and I ran out of the house swearing that I would never come back. I went to B. Wordsworth's house. I was so angry, my nose was bleeding.

B. Wordsworth said, "Stop crying, and we will go for a walk."

I stopped crying, but I was breathing short. We went for a walk. We walked down St. Clair Avenue to the Savannah[7] and we walked to the racecourse.

B. Wordsworth said, "Now, let us lie on the grass and look up at the sky, and I want you to think how far those stars are from us."

I did as he told me, and I saw what he meant. I felt like nothing, and at the same time I had never felt so big and great in all my life. I forgot all my anger and all my tears and all the blows.

When I said I was better, he began telling me the names of the stars, and I particularly remembered the constellation of Orion the Hunter,[8] though I don't really know why. I can spot Orion even today, but I have forgotten the rest.

Then a light was flashed into our faces, and we saw a policeman. We got up from the grass.

The policeman said, "What you doing here?"

B. Wordsworth said, "I have been asking myself the same question for forty years."

We became friends, B. Wordsworth and I. He told me, "You must never tell anybody about me and about the mango tree and the coconut tree and the plum tree. You must keep that a secret. If you tell anybody, I will know, because I am a poet."

I gave him my word and I kept it.

I liked his little room. It had no more furniture than George's front room,[9] but it looked cleaner and healthier. But it also looked lonely.

One day I asked him. "Mister Wordsworth, why you does keep all this bush in your yard? Ain't it does make the place damp?"

He said, "Listen, and I will tell you a story. Once upon a time a boy and girl met each other and they fell in love. They loved each other so much they got married. They were both poets. He loved words. She loved grass and flowers and trees. They lived happily in a single room, and then one day, the girl poet said to the boy poet, 'We are going to have another poet in the family.' But this poet was never born, because the girl died, and the young poet died with her, inside her. And the girl's husband was very sad, and he said he would never touch a thing in the girl's garden. And so the garden remained, and grew high and wild."

I looked at B. Wordsworth, and as he told me this lovely story, he seemed to grow older. I understood his story.

---

6. **Port-of-Spain:** seaport on the island of Trinidad; capital of Trinidad and Tobago.
7. **Savannah** (sə·van′ə): two-hundred-acre park in the center of Port-of-Spain. The racecourse is located there.
8. **Orion** (ō·rī′ən) **the Hunter:** constellation named for a hunter in Greek and Roman mythology whom Diana—the goddess of the moon and of hunting—loves but accidentally kills.
9. **George's front room:** George is a character in another story in Naipaul's book *Miguel Street*.

READING MINI-LESSON

Developing Word-Attack Skills
Explain that George Bernard Shaw once observed that English spelling is so irregular that *fish* could be spelled *ghoti*—*gh* for /f/, as in *cough*; *o* for /i/, as in *women*; *ti* for /sh/, as in *action*. The Hindu word *dhoti* /dō′tē/, which appears in this selection, is very similar in spelling to *ghoti* and contains two common but not regular letter-sound correspondences: silent *h* and *i* for long *e*. Silent *h* has been dealt with in an earlier mini-lesson. Explore with students words in which *i* stands for /ē/.

Activity. Have students study the words that follow, on p. 1019, and identify those in which *i* stands for /ē/. Then, ask students to develop some general rules about when *i* stands for /ē/.

We went for long walks together. We went to the Botanical Gardens and the Rock Gardens. We climbed Chancellor Hill in the late afternoon and watched the darkness fall on Port-of-Spain, and watched the lights go on in the city and on the ships in the harbor.

He did everything as though he were doing it for the first time in his life. He did everything as though he were doing some church rite.

He would say to me, "Now, how about having some ice cream?"

And when I said, yes, he would grow very serious and say, "Now, which café shall we patronize?" As though it were a very important thing. He would think for some time about it, and finally say, "I think I will go and negotiate the purchase with that shop."

The world became a most exciting place. One day, when I was in his yard, he said to me, "I have a great secret which I am now going to tell you."

I said, "It really secret?"

"At the moment, yes."

I looked at him, and he looked at me. He said, "This is just between you and me, remember. I am writing a poem."

"Oh." I was disappointed.

He said, "But this is a different sort of poem. This is the greatest poem in the world."

I whistled.

He said, "I have been working on it for more than five years now. I will finish it in about twenty-two years from now, that is, if I keep on writing at the present rate."

"You does write a lot, then?"

He said, "Not any more. I just write one line a month. But I make sure it is a good line."

I asked, "What was last month's good line?"

He looked up at the sky, and said, "*The past is deep.*"

I said, "It is a beautiful line."

B. Wordsworth said, "I hope to distill the experiences of a whole month into that single line of poetry. So, in twenty-two years, I shall have written a poem that will sing to all humanity."

I was filled with wonder.

Our walks continued. We walked along the sea wall at Docksite one day, and I said, "Mr. Wordsworth, if I drop this pin in the water, you think it will float?"

He said, "This is a strange world. Drop your pin, and let us see what will happen."

The pin sank.

I said, "How is the poem this month?"

But he never told me any other line. He merely said, "Oh, it comes, you know. It comes."

Or we would sit on the sea wall and watch the liners come into the harbor.

But of the greatest poem in the world I heard no more.

I felt he was growing older.

"How you does live, Mr. Wordsworth?" I asked him one day.

He said, "You mean how I get money?"

When I nodded, he laughed in a crooked way.

He said, "I sing calypsos in the calypso season."

"And that last you the rest of the year?"

"It is enough."

"But you will be the richest man in the world when you write the greatest poem?"

He didn't reply.

One day when I went to see him in his little house, I found him lying on his little bed. He looked so old and so weak, that I found myself wanting to cry.

He said, "The poem is not going well."

He wasn't looking at me. He was looking through the window at the coconut tree, and he was speaking as though I wasn't there. He said, "When I was twenty I felt the power within

Vocabulary
botanical (bə·tan′i·kəl) *adj.*: of plants or plant life; connected to the science of botany.
rite (rīt) *n.*: formal ceremony.
patronize (pā′trən·īz′) *v.*: be a customer of.
distill (di·stil′) *v.*: draw out the essence of.

The Trial (1986) by Julio Larraz. Oil on canvas.
© Julio Larraz, Private Collection, Courtesy Nohra Haime Gallery, New York City.

myself." Then, almost in front of my eyes, I could see his face growing older and more tired. He said, "But that—that was a long time ago."

And then—I felt it so keenly, it was as though I had been slapped by my mother. I could see it clearly on his face. It was there for everyone to see. Death on the shrinking face.

He looked at me, and saw my tears and sat up.

He said, "Come." I went and sat on his knees.

He looked into my eyes, and he said, "Oh, you can see it, too. I always knew you had the poet's eye."

He didn't even look sad, and that made me burst out crying loudly.

He pulled me to his thin chest, and said, "Do you want me to tell you a funny story?" and he smiled encouragingly at me.

But I couldn't reply.

He said, "When I have finished this story, I want you to promise that you will go away and never come back to see me. Do you promise?"

I nodded.

He said, "Good. Well, listen. That story I told you about the boy poet and the girl poet, do you remember that? That wasn't true. It was something I just made up. All this talk about poetry and the greatest poem in the world, that wasn't true, either. Isn't that the funniest thing you have heard?"

But his voice broke.

I left the house, and ran home crying, like a poet, for everything I saw.

I walked along Alberto Street a year later, but I could find no sign of the poet's house. It hadn't vanished, just like that. It had been pulled down, and a big, two-storied building had taken its place. The mango tree and the plum tree and the coconut tree had all been cut down, and there was brick and concrete everywhere.

It was just as though B. Wordsworth had never existed. ■

Comparing and Contrasting Texts

Evaluating philosophical assumptions. The English Romantic poet William Wordsworth did his part to glorify childhood in his "Ode: Intimations of Immortality from Recollections of Early Childhood." In this poem, Wordsworth asserts that children come freshly from God, trailing clouds of glory from heaven. As they mature and become engrossed in the mundane tasks of daily life, however, the glory fades. Wordsworth views childhood as a state distinct from adulthood. This state fades gradually as people mature, but it leaves a significant mark on the rest of their lives. What would B. Wordsworth say about the distinctions between childhood and adulthood?

Response and Analysis

Reading Check
1. How does the boy meet B. Wordsworth?
2. Who does B. Wordsworth say he is?
3. What secret does B. Wordsworth share with the boy?
4. What does B. Wordsworth reveal to the boy at the end of the story?

Thinking Critically
5. How does the boy feel about B. Wordsworth? What does he learn from him?
6. Do you think B. Wordsworth's tragic story about the boy poet and the girl poet is true? If true, why would he deny it? If not, why did he tell it in the first place?
7. Consider what B. Wordsworth says to the policeman who asks, "What you doing here?" What deeper significance do you see in B. Wordsworth's reply? (Is that what poets also seek to know?)
8. Consider the contrast in the story between the mother's no-nonsense ways and the poetic vision of B. Wordsworth. Then, find some of B. Wordsworth's statements about poetry in the story. What might Naipaul want to express about the nature of poetry and the role of the poet in society? Consider whether you agree with these assessments. (You may want to review your Quickwrite notes for ideas.)
9. What specific pictures of the **setting** are most vivid in your mind? If you were going to illustrate the story, what **images** would you concentrate on?
10. If we think of the narrator in the story as the author's recollection of himself at that age, what does the story suggest about the influences (historical, political, cultural) that made Naipaul a writer? What does it suggest about his view of the poet's position and role in society?

Extending and Evaluating
11. In your opinion, why does Naipaul set up such a sharp contrast between the language of the two characters in the story? If both characters spoke the same dialect, would the story be stronger or weaker? Explain.

WRITING
Seeing Things Differently
Near the end of the story, the poet pays the boy the highest of compliments, saying, "I always knew you had the poet's eye." In a brief **essay,** explain what you think the poet's eye sees. How is poetic vision different from an everyday perspective? Use examples from the story to illustrate the two different kinds of vision and to support your claims.

Vocabulary Development
Question and Answer Charts

botanical   patronize
rite   distill

Work with a group to make up two questions about each Vocabulary word above, and organize your answers in a chart. (An example is shown below.) After you have completed charts for all the words, invite another group to answer some of your questions.

botanical	
Questions	Answers
What might you learn from a book containing botanical information?	You might learn how different plants are structured, how they grow, where they are found, and so on.

INTERNET
Projects and Activities
Keyword: LE5 12-7

Literary Skills
Analyze setting.

Writing Skills
Write an essay analyzing poetic vision.

Vocabulary Skills
Create semantic charts.

V. S. Naipaul   1021

Reading Check
1. He asks to watch bees in the boy's yard.
2. He says he is the world's greatest poet and brother of poet W. Wordsworth.
3. He tells him the secret of the mango tree, the coconut tree, and the plum tree.
4. He reveals that he made up the story about the girl poet and her baby, as well as his claim to be writing the world's greatest poem.

Thinking Critically
5. The boy likes B. Wordsworth. He learns sensitivity to the world.
6. Possible answers: The story is true; he denies it because he doesn't want the boy to be saddened by his death. Or, the story is not true; he tells it to inspire the boy's imagination.

INDEPENDENT PRACTICE

Response and Analysis
7. Possible answer: He is questioning the purpose of his life. Many poets seek to understand the purpose of life.
8. Possible answers: Poetry involves observation, enjoyment, sharing, questioning, experimenting, and remembering experience. Poetry touches all aspects of life.
9. Possible answers: the palm trees humming with bees; the poet's yard; the starry skies, including the constellation Orion.
10. The story suggests that the inspiration of natural beauty and the frustration of poverty and colonialism all played a part in Naipaul's becoming a writer. Naipaul believes that poets play a crucial role in affirming nature's beauty and confirming the potential of human beings.

Extending and Evaluating
11. The contrast emphasizes the boy's limited educational opportunities in a colonial town. Without the contrast, the story would be weaker; B. Wordsworth's educated speech emphasizes that he has much to teach the boy.

Vocabulary Development
Sample Question and Answer
- rite—What might a rite of passage be? [a ceremony marking a transition from one stage of life to another]

ASSESSING

Assessment
- Holt Assessment: Literature, Reading, and Vocabulary

SKILLS FOCUS, pp. 1022–1027

Review Skills
- **Literary Skills**

Analyze the development of time and sequence, including the use of foreshadowing and flashback.

More About the Writer

Background. It took Naguib Mahfouz almost two decades to win acclaim in his homeland. Even after the Arabic-speaking world, including Egypt, had recognized him as its greatest novelist, the non-Arabic world barely acknowledged his literary gifts. Mahfouz was over seventy years old when he won the Nobel Prize in literature in 1988, and many of his works are now being translated into English for the first time. Small wonder, then, that among his friends Mahfouz is known as Al-Sabir, or "the patient one."

Despite his interest in world literature, Mahfouz remains the quintessential Egyptian writer: His fiction depicts the experiences of the average Egyptian. Mahfouz's fame as a Nobel laureate has not changed his habits; he still visits downtown Cairo's Ali Baba cafe every morning at 7:00 A.M. to read his newspaper and to catch up on the gossip.

In 1994, a failed attempt was made on Mahfouz's life for what some say are his anti-Islamic works and for his support of Egypt's 1979 peace treaty with Israel.

Naguib Mahfouz
(1911–   )
Egypt

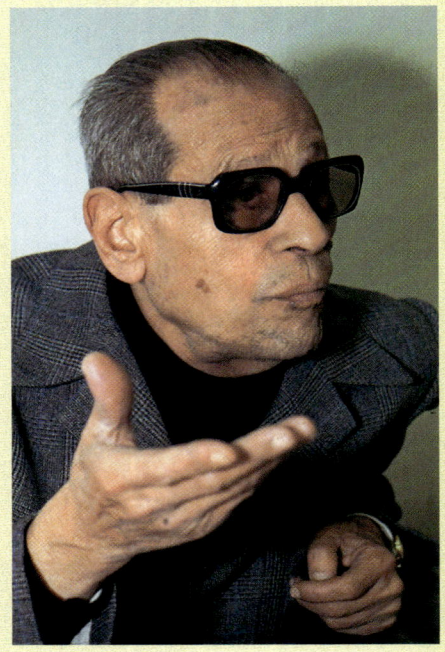

As a boy in Cairo's picturesque old quarter, Naguib Mahfouz (nä·zhēb′ mä′fo͞oz) encountered many unusual characters who would influence his life and work. Among them was the journalist El-Muwaylili, who was experimenting with new forms of fiction. At the time the novel form was virtually unknown in Arabic literature, where poetry and nonfiction were stressed. El-Muwaylili's efforts inspired Mahfouz to write full-fledged novels. Eventually Mahfouz would become the best-known fiction writer in the Arabic language and the first Arabic author to win the Nobel Prize in literature.

Interested in both philosophy and literature, Mahfouz attended Cairo University, where classes were conducted in English and French. His growing proficiency in those languages allowed him to read many European classics and to familiarize himself with the novel and short story forms. Still uncertain of his future, Mahfouz submitted a short story to a Cairo magazine. He considers the day it was accepted the most important day of his life.

The course of Mahfouz's writing career seems to recapitulate two centuries of literary movements. His early historical novels, set in the time of the pharaohs, display the idealistic nationalism of Romantic-era authors like Johann Wolfgang von Goethe. In the chaotic period leading up to World War II, Mahfouz turned to social realism in books like *New Cairo* (1946) and *Midaq Alley* (1947), which vividly evoke his boyhood neighborhood and the effects of war on the average Egyptian. Mahfouz continued in this realistic vein with his masterful Cairo trilogy—*Palace Walk* (1956), *The Palace of Desire* (1957), and *Sugar Street* (1957)—about three generations of a Cairo family who symbolize Egyptian experience in modern times. In the 1960s, Mahfouz began to experiment with stream of consciousness (see pages 962–963), as well as with the more indirect symbolism associated with modernism. His preoccupation with the individual facing spiritual and emotional crises was prompted in part by the growing Arab-Israeli conflict and Egypt's bitter defeat in the 1967 Six-Day War.

RESOURCES: READING

Planning
- *One-Stop Planner* CD-ROM with ExamView Test Generator

Differentiating Instruction
- Supporting Instruction in Spanish
- Audio CD Library, Selections and Summaries in Spanish

Vocabulary
- Vocabulary Development

Grammar and Language
- Daily Language Activities

Assessment
- Holt Assessment: Literature, Reading, and Vocabulary
- *One-Stop Planner* CD-ROM with ExamView Test Generator
- Holt Online Assessment

Internet
- go.hrw.com (Keyword: LE5 12-7)
- Elements of Literature Online

Media
- Audio CD Library
- Audio CD Library, Selections and Summaries in Spanish

Before You Read

Half a Day

Make the Connection
Quickwrite

Albert Einstein theorized that time is relative. While scientists might disagree about the objective truth of this theory, most people would agree that their *perception* of time often fluctuates. Indeed, any given minute, hour, or day might seem eternal to one person but utterly fleeting to the next.

Can you recall an event or experience during which you felt that time either raced or dragged? Jot down a few sentences describing this memory. What explanation can you provide for the way you perceived time?

Literary Focus
Foreshadowing

When a writer uses **foreshadowing,** he or she provides clues that suggest what might happen later in the story. Sometimes those clues take the form of specific events that work together to create a strong sense of suspense in the story. In other cases, though, the clues are quite subtle, adding up to a certain **mood** or atmosphere that is only later revealed to have significance to the plot. As you read "Half a Day," try to determine which kind of foreshadowing Mahfouz uses.

> **Foreshadowing** is the use of clues that hint at what will happen later in the story.
>
> *For more on Foreshadowing, see the Handbook of Literary and Historical Terms.*

Background

Because so much of Egypt is desert, the majority of Egyptians have always lived on the fertile banks of the Nile River. Since World War II, more and more people from rural areas along the Nile have moved to Egypt's major cities, also located on the river. The largest of these cities is Cairo, Egypt's capital, where Mahfouz grew up and where "Half a Day" is set. Cairo's population has changed dramatically since Mahfouz was a boy, and many of the city's fields and gardens have given way to tall modern buildings, raucous crowds, and some of the world's worst traffic jams.

Vocabulary Development

unmarred (ən·märd′) *adj.:* undamaged; unspoiled.

pitiable (pit′ē·ə·bəl) *adj.:* lamentable; regrettable.

intricate (in′tri·kit) *adj.:* full of elaborate details or parts.

avail (ə·vāl′) *n.:* benefit; advantage.

refuse (ref′yo͞os) *n.:* trash.

View of Cairo.

INTERNET
Vocabulary Practice
Keyword: LE5 12-7

Literary Skills
Understand foreshadowing.

1023

PRETEACHING

Summary ⇔ *at grade level*

The narrator recalls his father accompanying him on his first day of school, advising him to be a good example to others and to be a man. The narrator makes friends and participates in the school's rich variety of activities. However, pleasure mingles with pain because of unexpected accidents and harsh rivalries. At the end of the day when the bell rings, the narrator looks around for his father. Not finding him after a long wait, he decides to return home on his own. A middle-aged passerby greets him. Then the narrator notices how changed the streets look, with their hordes of people and high buildings. The narrator becomes dazed with confusion. While he waits anxiously to cross a street to reach his home, a young lad comes up to him, stretches out his arm, and says, "Grandpa, let me take you across."

Selection Starter

Motivate. Have students share anecdotes about a childhood memory: perhaps their first day of school, a birthday party, or another memorable occasion. Like Mahfouz in "Half a Day," they might play tricks with time to make a point about time's passage.

Previewing Vocabulary

Have students in small groups study the Vocabulary words on p. 1023 and their definitions. Then, use the following exercise to reinforce their understanding of the words in context.

1. After the wrecked car was overhauled, its finish looked glossy and _____. [unmarred]
2. The abandoned kittens were in _____ condition. [pitiable]
3. Opening the back of the clock, I was impressed when I saw its numerous, _____ parts. [intricate]
4. We tried to secure the loan at a local bank, but to no _____. [avail]
5. Laws against littering are strictly enforced here, since no one likes to see streets strewn with _____. [refuse]

Naguib Mahfouz 1023

DIRECT TEACHING

A Reading Skills

? Finding the main idea. Which sentence expresses the main idea of this paragraph? [the last] What is the effect of this placement? [Withholding the narrator's destination creates suspense and adds emphasis.]

B Literary Focus

? Figurative language. The father's remarks contain a figure of speech. To what does he compare school? [a factory] What kind of figurative language is this? [a metaphor]

C Reading Skills

? Evaluating. Do you think that Mahfouz does a good job of capturing a child's feelings on the first day of school? Why or why not? [Students should compare the details of the story to details from their personal experiences.]

D Literary Focus

? Foreshadowing. Why might this exchange be significant for the narrator? [Possible response: Judging from the story's opening, this exchange may be the narrator's first glimpse of misfortune.] After students finish the story, return to this passage. How does the exchange foreshadow the story's ending? [Possible response: By the end, the narrator is an old man whose father is almost certainly dead.]

E Learners Having Difficulty

Finding sequence of events. Help students recognize the shift in scope and tone in this passage: Earlier the focus was a young boy's sensory impressions; here a maturing narrator begins to reflect on the value of his experiences.

Half a Day

Naguib Mahfouz
translated by **Denys Johnson-Davies**

A I proceeded alongside my father, clutching his right hand, running to keep up with the long strides he was taking. All my clothes were new: the black shoes, the green school uniform, and the red tarboosh.[1] My delight in my new clothes, however, was not altogether unmarred, for this was no feast day[2] but the day on which I was to be cast into school for the first time.

My mother stood at the window watching our progress, and I would turn toward her from time to time, as though appealing for help. We walked along a street lined with gardens; on both sides were extensive fields planted with crops, prickly pears, henna trees, and a few date palms.

"Why school?" I challenged my father openly. "I shall never do anything to annoy you."

B "I'm not punishing you," he said, laughing. "School's not a punishment. It's the factory that makes useful men out of boys. Don't you want to be like your father and brothers?"

I was not convinced. I did not believe there was really any good to be had in tearing me away from the intimacy of my home and throwing me into this building that stood at the end of the road like some huge, high-walled fortress, exceedingly stern and grim.

When we arrived at the gate we could see the courtyard, vast and crammed full of boys and girls. "Go in by yourself," said my father, "and join them. Put a smile on your face and be a good example to others."

C I hesitated and clung to his hand, but he gently pushed me from him. "Be a man," he said. "Today you truly begin life. You will find me waiting for you when it's time to leave."

---

1. **tarboosh** (tär·boosh′) *n.*: brimless cloth cap worn by Muslim men.
2. **feast day:** holiday.

I took a few steps, then stopped and looked but saw nothing. Then the faces of boys and girls came into view. I did not know a single one of them, and none of them knew me. I felt I was a stranger who had lost his way. But glances of curiosity were directed toward me, and one boy approached and asked, "Who brought you?"

"My father," I whispered.

D "My father's dead," he said quite simply.

I did not know what to say. The gate was closed, letting out a pitiable screech. Some of the children burst into tears. The bell rang. A lady came along, followed by a group of men. The men began sorting us into ranks. We were formed into an intricate pattern in the great courtyard surrounded on three sides by high buildings of several floors; from each floor we were overlooked by a long balcony roofed in wood.

"This is your new home," said the woman. "Here, too, there are mothers and fathers. Here there is everything that is enjoyable and beneficial to knowledge and religion. Dry your tears and face life joyfully."

E We submitted to the facts, and this submission brought a sort of contentment. Living beings were drawn to other living beings, and from the first moments my heart made friends with such boys as were to be my friends and fell in love with such girls as I was to be in love with, so that it seemed my misgivings had had no basis. I had never imagined school would have this rich variety. We played all sorts of different

Vocabulary
unmarred (ən·märd′) *adj.*: undamaged; unspoiled.
pitiable (pit′ē·ə·bəl) *adj.*: lamentable; regrettable.
intricate (in′tri·kit) *adj.*: full of elaborate details or parts.

1024 Collection 7 The Modern World: 1900 to the Present

DIFFERENTIATING INSTRUCTION

Learners Having Difficulty
Remind students that the theme of a literary work is a generalization about human life or behavior that can be derived from details within the work. To identify the theme of a literary work, students should ask themselves the following question: What do the details suggest about human life or human nature *in general*? For a work of fiction, students should consider such elements as characterization, conflict, outcome or resolution, the title of the work, and any symbolism that the work may contain. Suggest that students keep the title "Half a Day" in mind as they read Mahfouz's story.

games: swings, the vaulting horse,[3] ball games. In the music room we chanted our first songs. We also had our first introduction to language. We saw a globe of the Earth, which revolved and showed the various continents and countries. We started learning the numbers. The story of the Creator of the universe was read to us, we were told of His present world and of His Hereafter, and we heard examples of what He said. We ate delicious food, took a little nap, and woke up to go on with friendship and love, play and learning.

As our path revealed itself to us, however, we did not find it as totally sweet and unclouded as we had presumed. Dust-laden winds and unexpected accidents came about suddenly, so we had to be watchful, at the ready, and very patient. It was not all a matter of playing and fooling around. Rivalries could bring about pain and hatred or give rise to fighting. And while the lady would sometimes smile, she would often scowl and scold. Even more frequently she would resort to physical punishment.

In addition, the time for changing one's mind was over and gone and there was no question of ever returning to the paradise of home. Nothing lay ahead of us but exertion, struggle, and perseverance. Those who were able took advantage of the opportunities for success and happiness that presented themselves amid the worries.

The bell rang announcing the passing of the day and the end of work. The throngs of children rushed toward the gate, which was opened again. I bade farewell to friends and sweethearts and passed through the gate. I peered around but found no trace of my father, who had promised to be there. I stepped aside to wait. When I had waited for a long time without avail, I decided to return home on my own. After I had taken a few steps, a middle-aged man passed by,

3. **vaulting horse:** that is, the horse one leaps over in gymnastics.

Vocabulary
avail (ə·vāl′) *n.*: benefit; advantage.

CONTENT-AREA CONNECTIONS

Historical Landmarks: Cairo
Small-group activity. Cairo is one of the most important and historic cities in Africa and in the Islamic world. It consists of two cities: Modern Cairo facing the Nile and Old Cairo running east from Place Ezbekieh to Muski Street, the site of Egypt's most famous bazaar. Have students work in small groups to compile a collage of illustrations of Cairo's landmarks, ranging from the citadel of the Muslim ruler Saladin to El Azhar University and the Egyptian Museum. Students' collages can be displayed in the classroom. Each group might appoint a spokesperson to deliver a brief commentary on the elements of the collage.

DIRECT TEACHING

A **Reading Skills**

? Interpreting. What is unusual about the way in which the middle-aged man behaves toward the narrator? [He treats the narrator as an adult.]

B **Literary Focus**

? Foreshadowing. What do the many changes suggest has happened? [Possible response: More time has passed than seems apparent to the narrator.] What ending might these details foreshadow? [Responses will vary. Encourage students to discuss their ideas with their classmates.]

C **Literary Focus**

? Theme. What do the young man's remark and actions indicate has happened to the narrator? [He has become an old man.] What theme does this surprise ending suggest about human life? [It passes very quickly.]

Cairo street scene.

and I realized at once that I knew him. He came toward me, smiling, and shook me by the hand, saying, "It's a long time since we last met—how are you?"

With a nod of my head, I agreed with him and in turn asked, "And you, how are you?"

"As you can see, not all that good, the Almighty be praised!"

Again he shook me by the hand and went off. I proceeded a few steps, then came to a startled halt. Good Lord! Where was the street lined with gardens? Where had it disappeared to? When did all these vehicles invade it? And when did all these hordes of humanity come to rest upon its surface? How did these hills of refuse come to cover its sides? And where were the fields that bordered it? High buildings had taken over, the street surged with children, and disturbing noises shook the air. At various points stood conjurers[4] showing off their tricks and making snakes appear from baskets. Then there was a band announcing the opening of a circus, with clowns and weight lifters walking in front. A line of trucks carrying central security troops crawled majestically by. The siren of a fire engine shrieked, and it was not clear how the vehicle would cleave its way to reach the blazing fire. A battle raged between a taxi driver and his passenger, while the passenger's wife called out for help and no one answered. Good God! I was in a daze. My head spun. I almost went crazy. How could all this have happened in half a day, between early morning and sunset? I would find the answer at home with my father. But where was my home? I could see only tall buildings and hordes of people. I hastened on to the crossroads between the gardens and Abu Khoda.[5] I had to cross Abu Khoda to reach my house, but the stream of cars would not let up. The fire engine's siren was shrieking at full pitch as it moved at a snail's pace, and I said to myself, "Let the fire take its pleasure in what it consumes."[6] Extremely irritated, I wondered when I would be able to cross. I stood there a long time, until the young lad employed at the ironing shop on the corner came up to me. He stretched out his arm and said gallantly, "Grandpa, let me take you across." ■

---

4. **conjurers** n.: magicians.

5. **Abu Khoda:** (ä·bo͞o′ kō′dä).
6. **Let the fire ... consumes:** Egyptian proverb.

Vocabulary
refuse (ref′yo͞os) n.: trash.

Check Test: Short Answer

Monitoring students' progress. Guide the class in answering the following questions.

1. As the story opens, for what event is the narrator all dressed up? [his first day of school]
2. What does the father promise before leaving the narrator? [to be waiting for him when it's time to leave]
3. When the narrator tells the other boy that his father brought him, what does the other boy say? [that his own father is dead]
4. What does the young man from the ironing shop call the narrator? ["Grandpa"]

Response and Analysis

Reading Check

1. As the story opens, where is the narrator's father taking him for the first time? What advice does the father give?
2. Identify four things the narrator likes about his new experience and two things he dislikes.
3. As the narrator walks home alone, what does a middle-aged man on the street do?
4. List three questions the narrator asks himself while walking home.
5. What does the "young lad" do and say at the busy intersection?

Thinking Critically

6. What surprise was revealed at the end of the story? Did you have any idea that the story might end in this way? Explain.
7. Re-read the story, and identify three details that **foreshadow** the surprise ending.
8. Describe what you thought about the narrator's identity and state of mind when you first read the story. Now, upon reviewing the story, what can you say about the narrator and his state of mind? Has Mahfouz, the writer, merely played a literary trick, or has he realistically portrayed the way a person might perceive reality? Explain.
9. What **theme** about time—and about life in general—does the ending help express? (You may want to refer to your Quickwrite notes.) How is the title of the story relevant to this theme? Support your response with examples from the text.
10. A **symbol** is a person, place, thing, or event that stands both for itself and for something beyond itself. What might the following elements in the story **symbolize**? Support your ideas with evidence from the text.

- the father
- the woman at the school
- the school
- home
- the story's title

WRITING

What's Real?

Both Mahfouz's "Half a Day" and Cortázar's "Axolotl" (see page 1000) play with the idea of identity and self-perception. In a brief **essay, compare and contrast** these stories. How are the narrators in the two stories alike and different? How are their experiences similar and dissimilar? Use examples from both texts to support your ideas and opinions. What does each story have to say about the nature of reality?

Vocabulary Development
Analyzing Context Clues

Explain why the **context clues** in the following sentences are wrong. (The underlined words are Vocabulary words from the selection.)

1. Mia was extremely upset to learn that her new car had been unmarred by the hailstorm.
2. The most pitiable moment of the field trip was when Jackson found fifty dollars lying on the sidewalk.
3. The directions to my house are very intricate: Just walk straight for two blocks.
4. To no avail, I asked the waiter for another napkin, and within seconds he had returned with one.
5. "What a joy to see your bedroom brimming with refuse!" Mom cried.

SKILLS FOCUS

Literary Skills
Analyze foreshadowing.

Writing Skills
Write an essay comparing and contrasting two stories.

Vocabulary Skills
Analyze context clues.

Naguib Mahfouz 1027

Reading Check

1. His father is taking him to school. He tells him to smile, to set a good example for the other children, and to "be a man."
2. He likes friends, love, games, and music; he dislikes rivalries and scoldings.
3. The man greets him as a fellow adult.
4. He wants to know where the street went; where the people came from; and how the hills of refuse came into existence.
5. Respectfully calling the narrator "Grandpa," he offers to help him cross the busy street.

Thinking Critically

6. The narrator is old; answers will vary.
7. Possible answers: The father's absence; the middle-aged man's attitude; the many changes on the streets.

INDEPENDENT PRACTICE

Response and Analysis

8. Possible answer: The narrator's first day of school is recalled so vividly that the story seems told from a child's point of view. Mahfouz then gradually shifts the narrator's perspective so that the storyline symbolically parallels the narrator's seemingly fast maturation and growth into old age. In the story, real time is unrealistically sped up, but the sense of perceived time passing quickly seems real.
9. Possible answer: Life is fleeting; the title implies that at its end, even a long life may seem to have passed in mere hours.
10. Possible answers: The father may symbolize security; the woman at the school, life's triumphs and failures, or the inevitability of change; the school, life itself; home, security or the afterlife; the story's title, life's brevity.

Vocabulary Development
Possible Answers

1. A new-car owner would be pleased, not upset, that the hail didn't damage her car.
2. Most people would be happy to find money.
3. Walking straight is simple, not complicated.
4. The request was not in vain; it brought a result.
5. Most mothers want their children to clean their rooms.

ASSESSING

Assessment

- Holt Assessment: Literature, Reading, and Vocabulary

SKILLS FOCUS, pp. 1028–1030

Grade-Level Skills
- **Literary Skills**

Analyze ways in which poets use figures of speech, including extended metaphors.

More About the Writer

Background. Much of Heaney's poetry reflects his rural Ulster upbringing and the extended sectarian conflict in Northern Ireland. Heaney analyzes the internecine violence in unique terms, protesting the unwillingness of both sides to speak out freely. As the speaker in "Digging" asserts, Heaney feels that through his writing, generations of his rural ancestors will find a voice.

PRETEACHING

Summary *at grade level*

In this poem, the speaker meditates on his father digging in his flower garden. The sight reminds him of his father digging potatoes twenty years earlier and of his grandfather, who could cut more peat in a day than any other farmer in the area. The speaker comments that he has no spade to dig as his father and grandfather did, but he will dig up meaning with his pen.

Seamus Heaney
(1939–   )
Ireland

Seamus Heaney was born to Roman Catholic parents in largely Protestant Northern Ireland. His boyhood on a farm in County Derry contributed profoundly to his identity as a poet, though Heaney never promoted himself as a rustic or regarded his work as an expression of regionalism. He earned his education as a scholarship student, first at a Catholic preparatory school and then at Queens University in Belfast, where, still in his mid-twenties, he was appointed lecturer in English.

Instead of leading him away from his roots in Irish soil, Heaney's studies—particularly those having to do with the history and psychology of myth—opened for him a way of seeing anew not only the misty grandeur of his native landscape, but also the figures in it who, unknowingly, unite the past with the present. Heaney is an acute observer of rural life and of life lived on the industrial margins of cities, and he deals with both without romanticizing them.

The American poet Robert Lowell regarded Heaney as "the best Irish poet since William Butler Yeats." In 1995, commended for his works "of lyrical beauty and ethical depth, which exalt everyday miracles and the living past," Heaney was awarded the Nobel Prize in literature. In 1999, Heaney's new translation of the Anglo-Saxon epic *Beowulf* (see page 33) accomplished what seemed to be impossible. The ancient epic beat out *Harry Potter and the Prisoner of Azkaban* for Britain's coveted Whitbread Book of the Year Award.

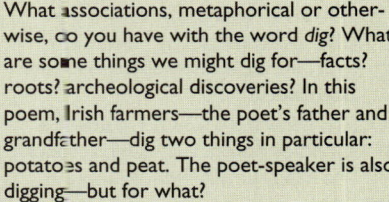

Digging

Make the Connection
What associations, metaphorical or otherwise, do you have with the word *dig*? What are some things we might dig for—facts? roots? archeological discoveries? In this poem, Irish farmers—the poet's father and grandfather—dig two things in particular: potatoes and peat. The poet-speaker is also digging—but for what?

Literary Skills
Understand extended metaphor.

Literary Focus
Extended Metaphor
Up until the poem's last line, you may not realize that "Digging" contains an **extended metaphor**. In this case, the comparison between the father's work and the poet's work resonates throughout the poem. As you read, try to identify the connections between the two kinds of digging.

> An **extended metaphor** is a comparison developed over a few lines or throughout an entire poem.
>
> *For more on Metaphor, see the Handbook of Literary and Historical Terms.*

RESOURCES: READING

Planning
- *One-Stop Planner* CD-ROM with ExamView Test Generator

Differentiating Instruction
- *Supporting Instruction in Spanish*
- *Audio CD Library, Selections and Summaries in Spanish*

Grammar and Language
- *Daily Language Activities*

Assessment
- *Holt Assessment: Literature, Reading, and Vocabulary*
- *One-Stop Planner* CD-ROM with ExamView Test Generator
- *Holt Online Assessment*

Internet
- go.hrw.com (Keyword: LE5 12-7)
- *Elements of Literature Online*

Media
- *Audio CD Library*
- *Audio CD Library, Selections and Summaries in Spanish*

Digging

Seamus Heaney

Between my finger and my thumb
The squat pen rests; snug as a gun.

Under my window, a clean rasping sound
When the spade sinks into gravelly ground:
5   My father, digging. I look down

Till his straining rump among the flowerbeds
Bends low, comes up twenty years away
Stooping in rhythm through potato drills°
Where he was digging.

10 The coarse boot nestled on the lug,° the shaft
Against the inside knee was levered firmly.
He rooted out tall tops, buried the bright edge deep
To scatter new potatoes that we picked
Loving their cool hardness in our hands.

15 By God, the old man could handle a spade.
Just like his old man.

My grandfather cut more turf in a day
Than any other man on Toner's bog.
Once I carried him milk in a bottle
20 Corked sloppily with paper. He straightened up
To drink it, then fell to right away
Nicking and slicing neatly, heaving sods
Over his shoulder, going down and down
For the good turf. Digging.

25 The cold smell of potato mould, the squelch and slap
Of soggy peat, the curt cuts of an edge
Through living roots awaken in my head.
But I've no spade to follow men like them.

Between my finger and my thumb
30 The squat pen rests.
I'll dig with it.

---

8. **drills** *n. pl.:* furrows or rows of planted seeds.
10. **lug** *n.:* earlike prong or projection by which a spade is supported.

INDEPENDENT PRACTICE

Response and Analysis

Thinking Critically

1. The speaker sees his father stooping to dig with a spade.
2. The phrase signals the speaker's shift from the present moment to his memories of the past. Students may have expected *feet, yards,* or *rows.*
3. He compares his pen to a gun and to a spade. The gun comparison suggests the power of the written word. The spade comparison links the speaker's heritage to his present occupation.
4. The speaker compares his work as a writer to that of his ancestors. Just as they dug the earth to produce food and fuel, he intends to dig into human experience for spiritual and emotional sustenance.
5. Examples of alliteration— l. 2 ("squat . . . snug"); l. 4 ("spade sinks," "gravelly ground"); l. 5 ("digging . . . down"); l. 12 ("tall tops"); l. 14 ("hardness . . . hands"); l. 22 ("nicking . . . neatly"); l. 23 ("down . . . down"); l. 25 ("squelch . . . slap"); l. 26 ("curt cuts"). Examples of rhyme—ll. 1–2 (approximate rhyme); ll. 3–5; and ll. 17 and 21.
6. Possible answers: Digging to cultivate the soil might be regarded as intruding on or injuring the natural environment. "Digging" into people's experiences and emotions might be regarded as intrusive or even offensive.
7. Possible answers: Other violent images include "rooted out tall tops" and "buried the bright edge deep" (l. 12) and "nicking and slicing neatly"(l. 22). The poet may be suggesting that creation too requires boldness, determination, and precision.

Response and Analysis

Thinking Critically

1. Describe what the speaker sees from his window.
2. Why do you think the father comes up "twenty *years* away" in line 7? (What word did you expect to find there?)
3. What different things does the speaker compare his pen to? What significance can you find in these comparisons, particularly the one in the last stanza?
4. Explain the **extended metaphor** in the poem. What kind of digging does the speaker intend to do?
5. What examples of **alliteration** (or repeated consonant sounds) and **rhyme** can you find in the poem?
6. In lines 25–27, the spade cuts through the "living roots." How might digging, either the kind done by the speaker's father or the kind done by the speaker himself, be seen as an act of violence?
7. Identify other **images** of violence or destruction in the poem. What point might the poet be making about the relationship between creation and destruction?

WRITING

Do Your Own Digging

Seamus Heaney once wrote that in "Digging" he truly found his own voice: "Finding a voice means that you can get your own feeling into your own words and that your words have the feel of you about them." Beginning with the last three lines of Heaney's poem, write your own **poem,** being careful to do your "digging" with words that suit your own voice. You might want to begin by recalling something about your parents, guardians, grandparents, or other older family members.

Portrait of Seamus Heaney (1973) by Edward McGuire. Oil on canvas (56" × 44").
Reproduced with the kind permission of the Trustees of the Ulster Museum, Belfast.

Literary Skills Analyze extended metaphor.
Writing Skills Write a poem.

ASSESSING

Assessment
- Holt Assessment: Literature, Reading, and Vocabulary

RETEACHING

For a lesson reteaching poetic devices, see **Reteaching,** p. 1129A.

Mini-Workshop

Writing a Short Story

V. S. Naipaul's B. Wordsworth lives only in the world of a short story, remembered by the narrator (and, of course, the reader) for his sad one line of poetry: "The past is deep" (page 1019). In writing **short stories**—short, imaginative, fictional narratives—you, too, can create a world in which characters, such as B. Wordsworth, will live and speak their memorable lines.

Find a Story Idea Short story topics are everywhere, if you just know where to look. One way to find an idea for a story is to remember important events in your own life and imagine what might have happened if you had made another decision. You can also observe everyday people and imagine a story about an interesting-looking person, or tell a story about a person in your family's old photo albums.

Consider Audience and Purpose As you choose a story idea, think about your purpose, audience, tone, and form. Your **purpose** for writing a short story is to develop an entertaining and interesting story for an **audience** of your classmates. To create a **tone**—serious, humorous, or ironic—use language creatively to reveal your attitude toward the subject. The usual **form** for a short story is a prose narrative; therefore, use well-formed, expressive sentences and paragraphs.

Establish the Setting Locate your story in a specific place, or **setting**. For example, in Naipaul's "B. Wordsworth," the main character lives "in a one-roomed hut placed right in the center of the lot. The yard seemed all green. There was the big mango tree. There was a coconut tree and there was a plum tree" (page 1018).

Develop Characters Create one or two main characters and only one or two supporting characters. To create complex, **dynamic** main characters—characters that grow and change over the course of your story—use a combination of direct and indirect characterization techniques. Use primarily indirect characterization to allow your readers to make their own judgments about the characters.

Writing Assignment
Write a short story of at least 1,500 words with an interesting plot and well-developed characters.

TIP Use **concrete sensory details**—the sights, sounds, and smells—to create a scene the reader won't easily forget.

CHARACTERIZATION TECHNIQUES

Direct characterization *tells* readers what the character is like.

Indirect characterization *shows* readers what the character is like through
- **dialogue**—what the character says and how he or she says it
- **thoughts and feelings**—what the character thinks or feels; show thoughts and feelings through **interior monologue**—telling "out loud" what the character is thinking
- **actions**—what the character does
- **reactions**—how a character responds to another character

---

COLLECTION 7 RESOURCES: WRITING

Planning
- *One-Stop Planner* CD-ROM with ExamView Test Generator

Differentiating Instruction
- *Workshop Resources: Writing, Listening, and Speaking*
- *Family Involvement Activities in English and Spanish*
- *Supporting Instruction in Spanish*

Writing and Language
- *Workshop Resources: Writing, Listening, and Speaking*
- *Daily Language Activities*
- *Language Handbook Worksheets*

Assessment
- *Holt Assessment: Writing, Listening, and Speaking*

PRETEACHING

Motivate. Ask students to consider what makes a story good—not just a published, literary story, but one they would want to tell to their friends. Lead students to discuss connections they find between the stories they read and those they tell: the insights into human nature, the ironies, the surprises. After students have decided what they think makes a good tale, tell them to keep these elements in mind as they create their own short stories.

DIRECT TEACHING

Find a Story Idea

Tell students that some of the most effective story ideas arise from characterization. For example, who could forget a man so vengeful that he would chase a white whale halfway around the world? or a young boy so fed up with civilized ways that he would set off on a raft down the Mississippi? Give students these tips in developing their main characters:

- **Make your character intense.** Good friends tend to be dependable and well-balanced, but good characters have only to be interesting. Is a character too much in love? too mean? too nice? That lack of balance can propel a plot.
- **Make your character react.** Most people wouldn't dream of chasing down a bank robber, for very good reasons. However, fiction is a place in which the improbable can become reality. A good character pushes the boundaries.
- **Give your character a desire.** Sometimes—when faced with a menu, for example—it is hard to decide what one wants. An interesting character usually knows exactly what he or she wants and is prepared to work toward that goal.

RETEACHING

Determine Point of View

To reteach the importance of consistency in point of view, ask students how they would react to a story in which an animal that escapes from the city zoo is first described as an elephant, then as a lion, and finally as a flock of flamingos. Point out to students that such inconsistency can confuse a reader about the plot and meaning of a story. In the same way, if a student begins a story with first-person point of view but shifts to third-person point of view, the reader will probably also be confused.

DIFFERENTIATING INSTRUCTION

Learners Having Difficulty

Students may focus too much on the various elements of storytelling, such as the techniques of irony, and forget that their basic mission is to tell an interesting story. Students can overcome this problem by telling their story ideas to a partner. Partners can ask questions such as "And then what happened?" and "How did the character feel then?" to keep the writers on track.

PRACTICE & APPLY

Guided and Independent Practice

Guide students by making sure each one has a story idea exciting to him or her. If students have difficulty thinking of an idea for which they have enthusiasm, they should ask themselves these questions:

- What events would my readers *not* expect to happen?
- How would the character *want* to act? What would be the consequences of that action?
- What events or decisions by the character would cause a crisis?

DO THIS

TIP The third-person-omniscient narrator's point of view can relate a story from **shifting perspectives;** that is, the narrator can tell how two or more characters perceive the same events.

SKILLS FOCUS

Writing Skills
Write a short story. Determine audience and purpose. Establish setting and develop characters. Develop plot and point of view. Express the theme. Use various stylistic devices.

Develop a Plot The things that happen in a short story—the **sequence of events**—make up the plot. Unlike the sprawl of a novel's plot, the plot for a short story has to be compressed. Follow the steps below to develop the plot of your short story.

1. Initiate the **conflict,** or the struggle between opposing forces. An **external conflict** is a conflict between two characters, between a character and an outside force, or between a character and a situation. An **internal conflict** is a conflict within a character.
2. Develop **complications,** or rising actions. These are the consequences of a character's actions or decisions.
3. Lead to a **climax,** the point at which the complications have reached their most intense moment and the conflict is resolved.
4. Resolve the conflict in the **denouement,** or falling action, that reveals the significance of the story's events for the characters.

Organize the Events Most short stories are told in chronological order. However, to highlight the significance of events, use flashbacks or flash-forwards. Vary the **pace** of your story, the rate at which events occur, to show changes in time, place, or mood.

Determine Point of View The **point of view** from which you tell your story determines what your narrator—or **speaker**—in your short story can and cannot tell your audience. You can choose from three basic points of view—a first-person narrator, a third-person-limited narrator, and a third-person-omniscient narrator. Once you choose a point of view, use it consistently.

Use Stylistic Devices Writers use **style**—the creative use of language—for specific aesthetic purposes. Style distinguishes one writer's story from another's. For example, one author's use of **imagery, concrete sensory details,** and **figures of speech** is an important part of the author's particular style. Use stylistic devices in your short story.

Sometimes an author will use **irony**—the contrast between appearance and reality—for a specific purpose. **Verbal irony** occurs when a character says one thing and means another. **Situational irony** occurs when what happens is opposite of what is expected or appropriate. **Dramatic irony** occurs when the readers know something that the character does not.

Indicate the Significance Most professional short story writers do not directly express the significance, or **theme,** of their story. Instead they *show* readers the significance through the details of their short story and their style, and sometimes by writing a clever last line of the story. For example, the last line of Naipaul's "B. Wordsworth" captures the significance of the story: "It was just as though B. Wordsworth had never existed" (page 1020). Try distilling the theme of your story into one dramatic line, and use it as your last sentence.

PRACTICE & APPLY Follow the instructions in this workshop to write a short story to share with your class.

COLLECTION 7 RESOURCES: WRITING

(continued from p. 1031)
- *One-Stop Planner* CD-ROM with ExamView Test Generator
- Holt Online Assessment
- Holt Online Essay Scoring

Internet
- go.hrw.com (Keyword: LE5 12-7)
- *Elements of Literature Online*

The Caplan Collection of the Children's Museum of Indianapolis.

Collection 7:
The Modern World:
1900 to the Present

Ourselves Among Others

Mansfield
Auden
Mistral
Thomas
Neruda
Narayan
Desai
Lively
Jin
Tutu
Aung San Kyi

All paths lead to the same goal: to convey to others what we are. And we must pass through solitude and difficulty, isolation and silence, in order to reach forth to the enchanted place where we can dance our clumsy dance and sing our sorrowful song.

—Pablo Neruda

VIEWING THE ART

This cotton appliqué wall hanging created by **Felicitas Ramos** in Lima, Peru, in 1983, depicts a bustling market scene with three-dimensional dolls. It is part of the Caplan Collection at the Children's Museum of Indianapolis, a large collection of folk art and hand-made toys from across the world.

THE QUOTATION

This quotation was taken from the Chilean poet Pablo Neruda's Nobel Prize acceptance speech. In it, he expresses his view that the purpose of life and of poetry is to share "what we are" with others. Ask students how experiences of "solitude and difficulty" might help us to communicate. [Possible responses: Such experiences are universal and make compassion for ourselves and others possible. Being alone and facing obstacles helps us gain self-knowledge, which is essential to true communication with others.]

The Modern World: 1900 to the Present **1033**

PRETEACHING

Selection Starter

Motivate. Invite students to study the elaborate doll's house in the picture and imagine how a child who received it would feel. Then, ask students to remember themselves as they were at a much younger age—perhaps between eight and ten years old. Did they or their playmates receive any special toys or equipment, such as a beautiful doll, a fancy bicycle, or a motorized toy vehicle, that all the other children coveted and wanted to play with? Call on volunteers to share their memories of these special objects. How did having such an object affect its owner's status and popularity?

The Doll's House

Katherine Mansfield

DIFFERENTIATING INSTRUCTION

Learners Having Difficulty
Suggest that students jot down all the references to rank, class, status, and hierarchy in the story. For example, it is important to Isabel that she be the first to tell about the doll's house. Have students meet in groups to compare their notes, and then list the references chronologically (as they appear in the story) on the chalkboard to show the development of this central motif in the story.

English-Language Learners
To help these students understand the characters in the story, pair them with readers who are proficient in English. Ask each pair to choose two characters and create a "silent dialogue." Have the pairs assume the personae of their chosen characters and pass notes back and forth as a means of communicating with each other. For example, each might write what the doll's house means to her.

1036 Collection 7 The Modern World: 1900 to the Present

When dear old Mrs. Hay went back to town after staying with the Burnells, she sent the children a doll's house. It was so big that the carter[1] and Pat carried it into the courtyard, and there it stayed, propped up on two wooden boxes beside the feed-room door. No harm could come of it; it was summer. And perhaps the smell of paint would have gone off by the time it had to be taken in. For, really, the smell of paint coming from that doll's house ("Sweet of old Mrs. Hay, of course; most sweet and generous!")—but the smell of paint was quite enough to make anyone seriously ill, in Aunt Beryl's opinion. Even before the sacking was taken off. And when it was . . .

There stood the doll's house, a dark, oily, spinach green, picked out with bright yellow. Its two solid little chimneys, glued onto the roof, were painted red and white, and the door, gleaming with yellow varnish, was like a little slab of toffee. Four windows, real windows, were divided into panes by a broad streak of green. There was actually a tiny porch, too, painted yellow, with big lumps of congealed paint hanging along the edge.

But perfect, perfect little house! Who could possibly mind the smell? It was part of the joy, part of the newness.

"Open it quickly, someone!"

The hook at the side was stuck fast. Pat pried it open with his penknife, and the whole housefront swung back, and—there you were, gazing at one and the same moment into the drawing room and dining room, the kitchen and two bedrooms. That is the way for a house to open! Why don't all houses open like that? How much more exciting than peering through the slit of a door into a mean little hall with a hatstand and two umbrellas! That is—isn't it?—what you long to know about a house when you put your hand on the knocker. Perhaps it is the way God opens houses at dead of night when He is taking a quiet turn with an angel . . .

"O-oh!" The Burnell children sounded as though they were in despair. It was too marvelous; it was too much for them. They had never seen anything like it in their lives. All the rooms were papered. There were pictures on the walls, painted on the paper, with gold frames complete. Red carpet covered all the floors except the kitchen; red plush chairs in the drawing room, green in the dining room; tables, beds with real bedclothes, a cradle, a stove, a dresser with tiny plates, and one big jug. But what Kezia liked more than anything, what she liked frightfully, was the lamp. It stood in the middle of the dining-room table, an exquisite little amber lamp with a white globe. It was even filled all ready for lighting, though, of course, you couldn't light it. But there was something inside that looked like oil, and that moved when you shook it.

The father and mother dolls, who sprawled very stiff as though they had fainted in the drawing room, and their two little children asleep upstairs, were really too big for the doll's house. They didn't look as though they belonged. But the lamp was perfect. It seemed to smile at Kezia, to say, "I live here." The lamp was real.

The Burnell children could hardly walk to school fast enough the next morning. They burned to tell everybody, to describe, to—well—to boast about their doll's house before the school bell rang.

"I'm to tell," said Isabel, "because I'm the eldest. And you two can join in after. But I'm to tell first."

There was nothing to answer. Isabel was bossy, but she was always right, and Lottie and Kezia knew too well the powers that went with being eldest. They brushed through the thick buttercups at the road edge and said nothing.

"And I'm to choose who's to come and see it first. Mother said I might."

For it had been arranged that while the doll's house stood in the courtyard they might ask the girls at school, two at a time, to come and look.

Vocabulary
congealed (kən·jēld′) v. used as adj.: thickened.

---
1. **carter** n.: delivery person.

Katherine Mansfield 1037

DIRECT TEACHING

VIEWING THE ART

Peter Vilhelm Ilsted (1861–1933) was a Danish painter whose work reveals the influence of his brother-in-law, the painter Vilhelm Hammershoi (see p. 993). *Girl Sitting on the Steps* is typical of Ilsted's subdued, restrained style.

Activity. Ask students to compare this painting by Ilsted with his painting shown on p. 772. Have students speculate about the sequence of events that could be associated with the two images. What mood is common to both paintings? [Possible response: a somber, pensive, quiet mood.]

 Content-Area Connections

Culture: Afternoon Tea
In many countries influenced by British culture, afternoon tea was a fashionable ritual during the nineteenth century. It provided the newly prosperous with a pleasant way of socializing with friends and family while signaling their leisured status. Served between 3:00 and 5:00 P.M., afternoon tea usually consisted of strong tea, crustless sandwiches, scones, pastries, and cakes.

B Literary Focus

Implied metaphor. The "ring" of girls around Isabel, which the writer compares to a royal court, symbolizes the unbridgeable gap between the classes. Just as a British commoner would not approach the queen of England, so the Kelveys dare come only within earshot of the upper-class Burnells. This is another example of the story's focus on the theme of social stratification.

Girl Sitting on the Steps (late 19th or early 20th century) by Peter Vilhelm Ilsted. Colored mezzotint.

A Not to stay to tea, of course, or to come traipsing[2] through the house. But just to stand quietly in the courtyard while Isabel pointed out the beauties, and Lottie and Kezia looked pleased . . .

But hurry as they might, by the time they had reached the tarred palings[3] of the boys' playground the bell had begun to jangle. They only just had time to whip off their hats and fall into line before the roll was called. Never mind. Isabel tried to make up for it by looking very important and mysterious and by whispering behind her hand to the girls near her, "Got something to tell you at playtime."

Playtime came and Isabel was surrounded. The girls of her class nearly fought to put their arms round her, to walk away with her, to beam flatteringly, to be her special friend. She held quite a court under the huge pine trees at the side of the playground. Nudging, giggling together, B the little girls pressed up close. And the only two who stayed outside the ring were the two who were always outside, the little Kelveys. They knew better than to come anywhere near the Burnells.

For the fact was, the school the Burnell children went to was not at all the kind of place their parents would have chosen if there had been any choice. But there was none. It was the only school for miles. And the consequence was all the children in the neighborhood, the Judge's little girls, the doctor's daughters, the storekeeper's children, the milkman's, were forced to mix together. Not to speak of there being an equal number of rude, rough little boys as well. But the line had to be drawn somewhere. It was drawn at the Kelveys.

2. **traipsing** (trāps′·ŋ) *v.* used as *adj.*: colloquial for "wandering."
3. **palings** (pāl′·ŋz) *n. pl.*: fence stakes.

1038 Collection 7   The Modern World: 1900 to the Present

CONTENT-AREA CONNECTIONS

Geography: New Zealand
Mixed-ability group activity. Encourage students to learn more about the island nation of New Zealand, the setting of Mansfield's story. Have them work in small groups collecting information on New Zealand's population distribution, topography, and geography. Then, have them present their findings in an audiovisual format.

Art and Architecture: A Doll's House
Mixed-ability group activity. Encourage students to draw or build their own versions of the doll's house in the story. Have small groups work together to render the exterior, the interior, or one room of the house. Suggest that students begin by doing research on Victorian and early-twentieth-century homes and domestic furnishings.

Many of the children, including the Burnells, were not allowed even to speak to them. They walked past the Kelveys with their heads in the air, and as they set the fashion in all matters of behavior, the Kelveys were shunned by everybody. Even the teacher had a special voice for them, and a special smile for the other children when Lil Kelvey came up to her desk with a bunch of dreadfully common-looking flowers.

They were the daughters of a spry, hardworking little washerwoman, who went about from house to house by the day. This was awful enough. But where was Mr. Kelvey? Nobody knew for certain. But everybody said he was in prison. So they were the daughters of a washerwoman and a jailbird. Very nice company for other people's children! And they looked it. Why Mrs. Kelvey made them so conspicuous was hard to understand. The truth was they were dressed in "bits" given to her by the people for whom she worked. Lil, for instance, who was a stout, plain child, with big freckles, came to school in a dress made from a green art-serge[4] tablecloth of the Burnells', with red plush sleeves from the Logans' curtains. Her hat, perched on top of her high forehead, was a grown-up woman's hat, once the property of Miss Lecky, the postmistress. It was turned up at the back and trimmed with a large scarlet quill. What a little guy[5] she looked! It was impossible not to laugh. And her little sister, our Else, wore a long white dress, rather like a nightgown, and a pair of little boy's boots. But whatever our Else wore she would have looked strange. She was a tiny wishbone of a child, with cropped hair and enormous solemn eyes—a little white owl. Nobody had ever seen her smile; she scarcely ever spoke. She went through life holding on to Lil, with a piece of Lil's skirt screwed up in her hand. Where Lil went our Else followed. In the playground, on the road going to and from school, there was Lil marching in front and our Else holding on behind. Only when she wanted anything, or when she was out of breath, our Else gave Lil a tug, a twitch, and Lil stopped and turned round. The Kelveys never failed to understand each other.

Now they hovered at the edge; you couldn't stop them listening. When the little girls turned round and sneered, Lil, as usual, gave her silly, shamefaced smile, but our Else only looked.

And Isabel's voice, so very proud, went on telling. The carpet made a great sensation, but so did the beds with real bedclothes, and the stove with an oven door.

When she finished Kezia broke in. "You've forgotten the lamp, Isabel."

"Oh, yes," said Isabel, "and there's a teeny little lamp, all made of yellow glass, with a white globe that stands on the dining-room table. You couldn't tell it from a real one."

"The lamp's best of all," cried Kezia. She thought Isabel wasn't making half enough of the little lamp. But nobody paid any attention. Isabel was choosing the two who were to come back with them that afternoon and see it. She chose Emmie Cole and Lena Logan. But when the others knew they were all to have a chance, they couldn't be nice enough to Isabel. One by one they put their arms round Isabel's waist and walked her off. They had something to whisper to her, a secret. "Isabel's *my* friend."

Only the little Kelveys moved away forgotten; there was nothing more for them to hear.

Days passed, and as more children saw the doll's house, the fame of it spread. It became the one subject, the rage. The one question was, "Have you seen Burnells' doll's house? Oh, ain't it lovely!" "Haven't you seen it? Oh, I say!"

Even the dinner hour was given up to talking about it. The little girls sat under the pines eating their thick mutton sandwiches and big slabs of johnny cake spread with butter. While always,

---

4. **art-serge** (ärt·sûrj): type of woven wool fabric.
5. **guy** *n.*: British for "an odd-looking person." The word comes from the name of Guy Fawkes, an English conspirator executed for taking part in the 1605 Gunpowder Plot to bomb the king and the houses of Parliament. In England, handmade likenesses of Guy Fawkes are burned annually on November 5—Guy Fawkes Day.

Vocabulary
conspicuous (kən·spik′yōō·əs) *adj.:* attracting attention.

Katherine Mansfield 1039

Primary Source

Katherine Mansfield: On Being a Writer

The following quotations are from *The Letters and Journals of Katherine Mansfield: A Selection*, edited by C. K. Stead. The first is a journal entry; the second is from a letter to a friend, Richard Murry.

"30 May 1917. To be alive and to be a 'writer' is enough. Sitting at my table just now I saw one person turning to another, smiling, putting out his hand—speaking. And suddenly I clenched my fist and brought it down on the table and called out—There is *nothing* like it!"

"20 June 1921. . . . About the old masters. What I feel about them (all of them—writers too, of course) is the more one *lives* with them the better it is for one's work. It's almost a case of living *into* one's ideal world—the world that one desires to express. Do you know what I mean? For this reason I find that if I stick to men like Chaucer and Shakespeare and Marlowe and even Tolstoy, I keep much nearer what I want to do than if I confuse things with reading a lot of lesser men. I'd like to make the old masters my *daily* bread—in the sense in which it's used in the Lord's Prayer, really—to make them a kind of essential nourishment. All the rest is—well—it comes *after*."

DIRECT TEACHING

A Reading Skills

Drawing conclusions. How do the girls' lunches illustrate the distance between the Kelveys and the other children? [Possible response: The Kelveys have only jam sandwiches, while the other children have thick meat sandwiches and buttered johnny cakes, revealing the difference in wealth between the Kelvey family and the others.]

B Literary Focus

Motivation. Why does Kezia want to invite the Kelveys to look at the doll's house? [Possible responses: She wants to share her joy with them; she sympathizes with them and feels that it is wrong to exclude them.]

C Reading Skills

Making inferences. Why, on this particular day, do the girls decide to be spiteful to the Kelveys? [Possible response: The girls are bored because they have already seen the doll's house. Now they must find new ways to amuse themselves and assert their superiority.]

D Reading Skills

Identifying cause and effect. Why do the girls have so much energy after they insult Lil and Else? [Possible responses: They feel powerful and superior when they belittle others; they are invigorated by what they see as Lena's daring.]

E Vocabulary Development

Connotations. Why do you think Mansfield chose to use "clambered" rather than *climbed* to describe Kezia's action? [Possible response: "Clambered"—in both its meaning and its awkward sound—suggests the clumsiness and difficulty of Kezia's movement.]

Bethnal Green Museum, London/The Bridgeman Art Library.

as near as they could get, sat the Kelveys, our Else holding on to Lil, listening too, while they chewed their jam sandwiches out of a newspaper soaked with large red blobs . . .

"Mother," said Kezia, "can't I ask the Kelveys just once?"

"Certainly not, Kezia."

"But why not?"

"Run away, Kezia; you know quite well why not."

At last everybody had seen it except them. On that day the subject rather flagged. It was the dinner hour. The children stood together under the pine trees, and suddenly, as they looked at the Kelveys eating out of their paper, always by themselves, always listening, they wanted to be horrid to them. Emmie Cole started the whisper.

"Lil Kelvey's going to be a servant when she grows up."

"O-oh, how awful!" said Isabel Burnell, and she made eyes at Emmie.

Emmie swallowed in a very meaning way and nodded to Isabel as she'd seen her mother do on those occasions.

"It's true—it's true—it's true," she said.

Then Lena Logan's little eyes snapped. "Shall I ask her?" she whispered.

"Bet you don't," said Jessie May.

"Pooh, I'm not frightened," said Lena. Suddenly she gave a little squeal and danced in front of the other girls. "Watch! Watch me! Watch me now!" said Lena. And sliding, gliding, dragging one foot, giggling behind her hand, Lena went over to the Kelveys.

Lil looked up from her dinner. She wrapped the rest quickly away. Our Else stopped chewing. What was coming now?

"Is it true you're going to be a servant when you grow up, Lil Kelvey?" shrilled Lena.

Dead silence. But instead of answering, Lil only gave her silly, shamefaced smile. She didn't seem to mind the question at all. What a sell[6] for Lena! The girls began to titter.

Lena couldn't stand that. She put her hands on her hips; she shot forward. "Yah, yer father's in prison!" she hissed, spitefully.

This was such a marvelous thing to have said that the little girls rushed away in a body, deeply, deeply excited, wild with joy. Someone found a long rope, and they began skipping. And never did they skip so high, run in and out so fast, or do such daring things as on that morning.

In the afternoon Pat called for the Burnell children with the buggy and they drove home. There were visitors. Isabel and Lottie, who liked visitors, went upstairs to change their pinafores.[7] But Kezia thieved out at the back. Nobody was about; she began to swing on the big white gates of the courtyard. Presently, looking along the road, she saw two little dots. They grew bigger, they were coming toward her. Now she could see that one was in front and one close behind. Now she could see that they were the Kelveys. Kezia stopped swinging. She slipped off the gate as if she was going to run away. Then she hesitated. The Kelveys came nearer, and beside them walked their shadows, very long, stretching right across the road with their heads in the buttercups. Kezia clambered back on the gate; she had made up her mind; she swung out.

"Hullo," she said to the passing Kelveys.

---

6. **sell** *n.*: slang for "trick."
7. **pinafores** (pin′ə·fôrz′) *n. pl.*: sleeveless, apronlike garments that young girls wear over dresses.

Vocabulary

flagged (flagd) *v.*: declined; lost strength or interest.
clambered (klam′bərd) *v.*: climbed clumsily.

1040 Collection 7 The Modern World: 1900 to the Present

CONTENT-AREA CONNECTIONS

Psychology: Character's Inner Thoughts

Individual activity. Have students imagine what Kezia is thinking at various times in the story and record her thoughts as journal entries. Remind students to study Kezia's actions, reactions, and dialogue in the text, and suggest that they draw on their own experiences to imagine Kezia's feelings.

Social Science: Status Systems

Small-group activity. Ask students to research the way status is assigned in various societies. Direct them to the work of social anthropologists and sociologists. Prompt them with these questions: Do all societies engage in social ranking? What is the status system in the United States? Are there universal markers of high status? Is status a true valuation of personal or social worth?

1040 Collection 7 The Modern World: 1900 to the Present

They were so astounded that they stopped. Lil gave her silly smile. Our Else stared.

"You can come and see our doll's house if you want to," said Kezia, and she dragged one toe on the ground. But at that Lil turned red and shook her head quickly.

"Why not?" asked Kezia.

Lil gasped, then she said, "Your ma told our ma you wasn't to speak to us."

"Oh, well," said Kezia. She didn't know what to reply. "It doesn't matter. You can come and see our doll's house all the same. Come on. Nobody's looking."

But Lil shook her head still harder.

"Don't you want to?" asked Kezia.

Suddenly there was a twitch, a tug at Lil's skirt. She turned round. Our Else was looking at her with big, imploring eyes; she was frowning; she wanted to go. For a moment Lil looked at our Else very doubtfully. But then our Else twitched her skirt again. She started forward. Kezia led the way. Like two little stray cats they followed across the courtyard to where the doll's house stood.

"There it is," said Kezia.

There was a pause. Lil breathed loudly, almost snorted; our Else was still as a stone.

"I'll open it for you," said Kezia kindly. She undid the hook and they looked inside.

"There's the drawing room and the dining room, and that's the—"

"Kezia!"

Oh, what a start they gave!

"Kezia!"

It was Aunt Beryl's voice. They turned round. At the back door stood Aunt Beryl, staring as if she couldn't believe what she saw.

"How dare you ask the little Kelveys into the courtyard?" said her cold, furious voice. "You know as well as I do, you're not allowed to talk to them. Run away, children, run away at once. And don't come back again," said Aunt Beryl. And she stepped into the yard and shooed them out as if they were chickens.

"Off you go immediately!" she called, cold and proud.

They did not need telling twice. Burning with shame, shrinking together, Lil huddling along

National Trust Photographic Library/Nadia Mackenzie/The Bridgeman Art Library.

like her mother, our Else dazed, somehow they crossed the big courtyard and squeezed through the white gate.

"Wicked, disobedient little girl!" said Aunt Beryl bitterly to Kezia, and she slammed the doll's house to.

The afternoon had been awful. A letter had come from Willie Brent, a terrifying, threatening letter, saying if she did not meet him that evening in Pulman's Bush, he'd come to the front door and ask the reason why! But now that she had frightened those little rats of Kelveys and given Kezia a good scolding, her heart felt lighter. That ghastly pressure was gone. She went back to the house humming.

When the Kelveys were well out of sight of Burnells', they sat down to rest on a big red drainpipe by the side of the road. Lil's cheeks were still burning; she took off the hat with the quill and held it on her knee. Dreamily they looked over the hay paddocks,[8] past the creek, to the group of wattles[9] where Logan's cows stood waiting to be milked. What were their thoughts?

Presently our Else nudged up close to her sister. But now she had forgotten the cross lady. She put out a finger and stroked her sister's quill; she smiled her rare smile.

"I seen the little lamp," she said, softly.

Then both were silent once more. ■

---

8. **paddocks** (pad′əks) *n. pl.*: fenced pieces of land.
9. **wattles** (wät″lz) *n. pl.*: acacia trees.

Katherine Mansfield 1041

DEVELOPING FLUENCY

Small-group activity. Help students prepare a group reading of a scene from "The Doll's House." First, help them choose a scene and determine how many readers are needed. Then, have them prepare a script and provide each reader with a copy. Tell students to try out different ways of interpreting their characters' feelings and delivering their lines. Before the final reading, have students rehearse before a small group and ask for an evaluation of their performance.

DIRECT TEACHING

F Literary Focus

Symbol. What does Kezia *not* get to point out? [the lamp] What might Aunt Beryl's appearance at this moment suggest on a symbolic level? [Possible response: To Kezia the lamp is the most important feature of the doll's house, the detail that makes it human and welcoming; Aunt Beryl's coldness contrasts with the warmth of the lamp.]

G Reading Skills

Tracing recurring themes. How does Aunt Beryl's behavior recall an earlier part of the story? [Possible response: Aunt Beryl gains a sense of power by humiliating the Kelveys. Her actions recall those of the girls who taunt Lil in the schoolyard.]

H Literary Focus

Symbol. The story ends with the symbol of the lamp, emphasizing once again its centrality to the story. It is the lamp that moves the silent Else to smile and speak. What has the lamp come to mean for both Else and the reader? [Possible responses: The lamp represents the light of kindness that briefly shone out of Kezia; it might represent the warmth of inclusion and belonging.]

GUIDED PRACTICE

Monitoring students' progress. Guide the class in answering the following items. Have students find passages that support their answers.

True-False

1. The doll's house is an all-white Victorian wonder. [F]
2. The Burnells are eager to tell about the new doll's house. [T]
3. Kezia's favorite part of the doll's house is the cradle. [F]
4. Kezia invites the Kelveys to see the doll's house. [T]

INDEPENDENT PRACTICE

Response and Analysis

Reading Check

1. The furniture is realistic and consists of chairs, tables, beds with bedclothes, a cradle, a stove, a dresser, a jug, and a lamp. The dolls are too large for the house and look as though they do not belong in it.

2. Possible answers: Kezia, who seems to ignore class distinctions and is comfortable with all kinds of people; Else, who seems to look at the world squarely as it is.

Thinking Critically

3. Isabel wants to show off. Kezia invites Lil and Else possibly because she wants to rebel against her family's snobbishness or share the lamp's "light" of belonging.

4. Else depends on and defers to the older Lil. Students may say that because Else rarely speaks, her words in the last line carry weight: Her silence and her way of absorbing events create the impression that she is wise and perceptive.

5. Possible answers: The doll's house is a status symbol—a toy that represents wealth and social standing. To Kezia the lamp may symbolize hospitality or fellowship. To Else the lamp may represent hope, kindness, or a world illuminated by justice instead of prejudice. The lamp is the more powerful symbol because its significance is deeper.

6. Possible answer: One theme is the desire for status, as gauged by material possessions and the power to impress and control others. The Burnell girls wish to feel superior and use their family's status to lord it over others.

7. Possible answer: The girls' cruelty is disturbing but believable. The children have apparently absorbed snobbish attitudes from their elders.

1042 Collection 7 The Modern World: 1900 to the Present

Response and Analysis

Reading Check

1. Review the description of the doll's house. What do the furniture and the dolls themselves look like?
2. Review the descriptions of the characters in the story. Who among them appears comfortable, or truly to "belong" in the world?

Thinking Critically

3. Why does Isabel invite friends to see the doll's house? Why does Kezia invite Lil and Else to see it?
4. Describe the relationship between Lil and Else. Is it significant that Else speaks the last line of dialogue in the story? Why?
5. What do you think the doll's house might **symbolize** in the story? What in particular do you think the little lamp symbolizes? (Recall Else's comment at the end of the story—"I seen the little lamp.") In your opinion, which symbol evokes the strongest emotions in the reader? Explain.
6. How would you state this story's **theme**? What does the story reveal about cruelty, status, families, and outsiders? Use textual evidence to support your interpretation of theme.
7. How do you feel about the extraordinary meanness shown by Lil and Else's classmates? How do you account for it?
8. Look back at your Quickwrite notes about status and competition. What similarities, if any, exist between our world and the world of the story?

Extending and Evaluating

9. The narrator of "The Doll's House" enters the minds of different characters at different points in the story. Explain whether you think the narrator's **omniscient point of view** adds to the power of the story or makes the narrative confusing. Support your opinion with specific passages.

WRITING

Burnell versus Kelvey

Choose two of the children from the story—one Burnell and one Kelvey—and write an **essay comparing and contrasting** them. In your essay, focus on one or two of each character's actions or statements. What do these actions or words reveal about the character? In your opinion, what moved the character to act or speak in such a way? Conclude by suggesting what Mansfield might have wanted her readers to realize about each of these young figures.

INTERNET
Projects and Activities
Keyword: LE5 12-7

SKILLS FOCUS

Literary Skills
Analyze symbols. Analyze a modern short story.

Writing Skills
Write an essay comparing and contrasting two characters.

Vocabulary Skills
Find context clues.

Grammar Skills
Understand and identify the use of active voice and passive voice.

Vocabulary Development
Finding Context Clues

congealed   flagged
conspicuous   clambered

Go back to the text and locate each of the Vocabulary words in the list above. On a separate sheet of paper, make note of any context clues that would help you define the word (if it weren't already defined at the bottom of the page). The first word is done for you.

Word: congealed (verb used as an adjective): "thickened" (p. 1037).

Clues: The sentence says that there were "big lumps" of paint "hanging" from the edge of the porch. Thin, wet paint wouldn't hang in lumps, but thick dried globs of paint would.

---

8. Possible answer: Status is still important to many people, although the sources of status may have changed.

Extending and Evaluating

9. Possible answer: The use of an omniscient narrator is effective because it clarifies the characters' motives and makes their actions understandable. For example, the description of Aunt Beryl's feelings about the letter helps explain her cruelty to the Kelveys.

Vocabulary Development

Word: conspicuous: "tending to attract attention" (p. 1039). **Clues:** The girls are described as being oddly dressed.
Word: flagged: "declined" (p. 1040). **Clues:** Interest in the doll's house is fading, since everyone except the Kelveys has seen it.
Word: clambered: "climbed clumsily" (p. 1040). **Clues:** Kezia has "made up her mind" and hastily climbs back on the gate.

Literary Focus

The Modern Short Story

People have been telling stories since the first campfire, but the short story as a distinct literary form is really an invention of the nineteenth century. A number of factors probably contributed to the rise of the short story at roughly the same time in France, Germany, and the United States. Growing literacy, the consequent popularity of magazines, and the form's flexibility and appeal to a wide variety of writers were doubtless responsible for its success.

The American critic and writer Edgar Allan Poe created the most influential theoretical foundations for the short story in his 1842 review of Nathaniel Hawthorne's *Twice-Told Tales.* In his review, Poe claimed that the story should be considered superior to the novel because, since a story could be read in one sitting, it could have a more unified aesthetic effect on the reader. To Poe, a unified effect was the most important literary goal. "A skillful artist," he wrote, "having conceived a certain *single effect* . . . then combines such events . . . as may best serve him in establishing this preconceived effect. . . . [T]here should be no word written of which the tendency, direct or indirect, is not to the one pre-established design." The effect that Poe aimed for in most of his own stories was shock or horror.

The stories of Poe and other nineteenth-century writers frequently involved people in extreme states—physical, emotional, or both. It was not unusual for characters to go mad or die at the end. Such grand events satisfied both writers' and readers' need for **closure,** or the feeling that one has reached a satisfactory conclusion. Some writers, such as Guy de Maupassant in France and O. Henry in the United States, provided this closure through the use of a surprising twist, or **trick ending.**

Realism, a literary movement that developed in the latter part of the nineteenth century, tried to portray life as it really is, not as we might wish or fear it could be. Some realists, such as the Russian Anton Chekhov, often wrote stories that had no strong beginning or end, but merely portrayed the events of daily life. These **slice-of-life** stories provided readers with snapshots of life in a variety of places and social classes. The American writer Henry James faithfully depicted his characters' perceptions and motivations in a style called **psychological realism.**

The modern story more often aims not at a sensory effect *on* the reader but at revelation *to* the reader—the revelation of some essential truth implicit in the story. The main character of the story may remain ignorant of this truth even at the end, and **dramatic irony,** the result of the reader's knowing more than the character does, is a common element in modern fiction. Though readers may clearly see dramatic irony in "The Doll's House," the story doesn't at first appear to have the unity of form that Poe championed. But closer examination reveals a coherence of language, theme, and imagery, in this case all related to the central symbol of the doll's house.

In a general sense we can say three things about the modern short story:

1. It is more likely to be concerned with explorations of character than with the construction of a fast-paced plot.
2. It is more apt to imply important facts and psychological truths than to state them directly.
3. It is more likely to move toward a revelation of truth than toward a single emotional effect.

Analyzing a modern short story. With some classmates, choose a story from a recent periodical or short story collection. Then, collaborate in writing a critique of the story for the entire class. As part of the critique, consider to what extent the story demonstrates the characteristics of the modern short story listed above.

Grammar Link

Practice

1. Passive voice. The Burnell children admired the beautiful doll house.
2. Passive voice. Isabel gave the children a description of the doll house.
3. Active voice. Lil and Else were invited into the courtyard by Kezia.
4. Passive voice. Aunt Beryl chastised Kezia for inviting the Kelveys into the courtyard.
5. Passive voice. Critics often debate the symbolism of the lamp in Katherine Mansfield's "The Doll's House."

ASSESSING

Assessment
- Holt Assessment: Literature, Reading, and Vocabulary

Grammar Link

Active-Voice Verbs and Passive-Voice Verbs

Here are two ways to convey the same information:

> Katherine Mansfield uses very specific details to describe daily life in New Zealand.

> Very specific details are used by Katherine Mansfield to describe daily life in New Zealand.

Each sentence uses a different voice. The first sentence, which uses the **active voice,** expresses an action done *by* the subject (Katherine Mansfield). The second sentence, which uses the **passive voice,** expresses an action done *to* the subject (*very specific details*). The second sentence is awkward.

In general the active voice is preferable because it presents ideas directly and emphasizes the doer of the action. Bring your writing to life, and capture your audience's attention by using active-voice verbs whenever possible.

Use passive-voice verbs when you want to emphasize the receiver of an action rather than the performer or when you don't know the identity of the performer. Remember, however, that passive-voice verbs can be less direct and less concise than the active-voice verbs. Overusing passive-voice verbs can make it difficult for the reader to follow the action.

Doll's house nursery with toys.
Bethnal Green Museum, London/Bridgeman Art Library.

PRACTICE

Label the following sentences passive or active. Then, revise the sentences by changing passive-voice verbs to active or active-voice verbs to passive.

1. The beautiful doll house was admired by the Burnell children.
2. A description of the doll house was given by Isabel to the children.
3. Kezia invited Lil and Else into the courtyard.
4. Kezia was chastised by Aunt Beryl for inviting the Kelveys into the courtyard.
5. The symbolism of the lamp in Katherine Mansfield's "The Doll's House" is often debated by critics.

Apply to Your Writing

Take out a writing assignment you are working on now or have already completed. Highlight all the *be* verbs or verb phrases. (*Be* verbs can signal an unnecessary use of the passive voice.) If necessary, replace passive-voice verbs with active-voice verbs.

▶ For more help, see Active Voice and Passive Voice, 3d–3e, in the Language Handbook.

1044   Collection 7   The Modern World: 1900 to the Present

DIFFERENTIATING INSTRUCTION

Learners Having Difficulty
Write the following sentences on the chalkboard. Have students identify the verb in each sentence as either active or passive voice.

1. The children were given a doll's house by Mrs. Hay. [passive voice]
2. Isabel Burnell wanted to impress her classmates with the new doll's house. [active voice]
3. Else Kelvey was captivated by the little amber lamp. [passive voice]
4. Aunt Beryl did not consider the feelings of others. [active voice]
5. The causes and effects of snobbery are explored by Katherine Mansfield in "The Doll's House." [passive voice]

W. H. Auden
(1907–1973)
England / America

TimePix.

Wystan Hugh Auden gave a name to his times—the Age of Anxiety—and he lived to see the day when his influence was so broad and deep that, as far as poetry was concerned, that same era could have been called the Age of Auden.

Auden was born in York, a city in northern England near the city of Leeds. He was the son of a physician and a nurse who encouraged his early interest in science and engineering. But in his adolescence, Auden discovered poetry, and he studied, with an analytical eye, all its forms, from Chaucer onward. By the time he entered Oxford, he was as much a teacher as he was a student, and he quickly gathered about himself other young poets, who accepted him as their leader.

Auden as a poet was difficult to classify, and he remains so to this day. In spite of their virtuosity, uniform excellence, and formal variety, Auden's poems—lyrics, oratorios, ballads—tend to cohere as a body of work rather than to distinguish themselves as separate entities. For this reason, Auden is often regarded less as the author of certain individual poems than as the creator of a climate in which all things Audenesque thrive in an atmosphere uniquely his own.

Auden put his indelible stamp on the poetry of the 1930s, establishing his preeminence among the brilliant group of poets that included Stephen Spender, Louis MacNeice, and Cecil Day-Lewis. Auden caused his British compatriots shock and dismay when, in the critical year of 1939, as Hitler's divisions were about to march into Poland and ignite World War II, he decided to make his home in the United States. Auden had come to feel that, as the rise of fascism made war in Europe inevitable, his chances of enjoying creative freedom and of making a livelihood were greatest in America. From 1939 to 1942, he taught at the University of Michigan and various other American universities. In 1946, he became a U.S. citizen.

For the next ten years, Auden lived mostly in New York City and California. He spent his summers in Kirchstetten, Austria, in a house he bought in 1957 with profits from his extensive reading tours—the first, and last, home of his own. This retreat, not far from Vienna, provided him with much-needed privacy and the opportunity to experience firsthand the culture of central Europe.

In England, Auden's emigration to the United States was, at the time, widely regarded as a defection, if not an outright betrayal. But the British eventually welcomed him back—first by electing him professor of poetry at Oxford and later by making it possible for him to live on the campus of Christ Church College as a guest of Oxford University whenever he returned to England.

For Independent Reading
You may enjoy the following poem by Auden:
- "The Unknown Citizen"

PRETEACHING

Summary ⇄ *at grade level*

The speaker states that the Old Masters understood that even the most dramatic suffering is often met with indifference. He discusses *The Fall of Icarus,* a painting by Pieter Bruegel the Elder in which a farmer is shown tranquilly plowing a field as Icarus falls to his death a short distance away. The routines of everyday life go on in the presence of suffering and death.

Skills Starter

Motivate. Write the following nouns on the chalkboard: *suffering, blues, anguish, heartache, desolation, distress.* Although the words are synonyms, they are not interchangeable. Call on volunteers to identify the nouns appropriate for formal writing (an essay, a speech, a poem) and those appropriate for informal or casual writing (song lyrics, dialogue, a diary entry). Point out that writers use diction, or word choice, to create different effects.

VIEWING THE ART

The Flemish painter **Pieter Bruegel the Elder** (c. 1525–1569) depicted the vigor and coarseness of country life in rich detail, often adding a humanist moral.

Activity. Ask students how *The Fall of Icarus* frustrates viewers' expectations. [They expect the painting to focus on Icarus.] Using Bruegel's painting as an example, ask students how an artist can convey a message by *refraining* from saying or showing something.

Before You Read

Musée des Beaux Arts

Make the Connection
Quickwrite

Every generation sees imperfections and injustices in the way things are. For Auden, during what he termed the Age of Anxiety, people had grown indifferent to human suffering, and society no longer treasured the individual. Auden felt that this indifference to the plight of others and disregard for the value of individuality were symptoms of a society in need of reform.

To what extent do you think people today are indifferent to human suffering? Jot down your thoughts, and include some examples to support your viewpoint.

Literary Focus
Diction

Many of Auden's poems combine eloquent poetic language with **colloquial** words—the down-to-earth language of everyday life. This use of contrasting **diction,** or word choice, has several effects. It works to surprise the reader, who may be trained to expect only lofty, dignified language in poetry. It also creates a casual, offhand tone that unnerves the reader by mirroring the randomness of the "real world." Auden hoped that by unsettling his readers through language, he might move them to take positive action—to seek or show compassion in a seemingly indifferent world.

> **Diction** is a writer's or speaker's choice of words.
>
> *For more on Diction, see the Handbook of Literary and Historical Terms.*

The Fall of Icarus (16th century) by Pieter Bruegel the Elder.
Musées Royaux des Beaux-Arts, Brussels, Belgium.

SKILLS FOCUS
Literary Skills
Understand diction.

1046 Collection 7 The Modern World: 1900 to the Present

DIFFERENTIATING INSTRUCTION

Learners Having Difficulty
Explain that the inversion in the first line, which would read more naturally as "They were never wrong about suffering," puts the focus on the word "suffering" right at the opening of the poem. Also point out that each stanza of the poem consists of one long sentence, made up of complete thoughts linked by semicolons. Have students paraphrase each complete thought. Then, invite them to read "Musée des Beaux Arts" in interactive format in *The Holt Reader,* using the sidenotes as aids to understanding the selection.

The source and inspiration for this poem are found in the famous painting by the Renaissance artist Pieter Bruegel showing Icarus drowning, permanently on display in the Musée des Beaux Arts (myo͞o·zā′ dā bō zàr′), or Fine Arts Museum, in Brussels, Belgium. The painting depicts a dramatic moment in the Greek legend of Daedalus and his son, Icarus. According to the legend, the two were imprisoned on the island of Crete. In order to escape, Daedalus constructed wings of feathers and wax. Together they managed to take off from the island, but Icarus flew so high that the sun's heat melted the wax in his wings, causing him to fall into the sea and drown.

According to one critic, the painting represents "the greatest conception of indifference" in the history of art. The indifference, whether it is the artist's attitude or merely a strategy of technique, lies in its unexpected focus. The painting's center of interest is not Icarus, but a peasant plowing a field. He is handsomely dressed—in medieval rather than ancient Greek costume—and the furrows he tills are richly realistic. In the lower right-hand corner of the painting, almost as an afterthought, Icarus is seen splashing into the water not far from a passing ship.

Study the painting, and find the figure of the boy falling into the sea. Then, read the poem to see how Auden interprets the painting. Has he confirmed in words what the painter expressed with paint?

Musée des Beaux Arts

W. H. Auden

About suffering they were never wrong,
The Old Masters: how well they understood
Its human position; how it takes place
While someone else is eating or opening a window or just walking dully along;
5   How, when the aged are reverently, passionately waiting
For the miraculous birth, there always must be
Children who did not specially want it to happen, skating
On a pond at the edge of the wood:
They never forgot
10 That even the dreadful martyrdom must run its course
Anyhow in a corner, some untidy spot
Where the dogs go on with their doggy life and the torturer's horse
Scratches its innocent behind on a tree.

In Bruegel's *Icarus*, for instance: how everything turns away
15 Quite leisurely from the disaster; the plowman may
Have heard the splash, the forsaken cry,
But for him it was not an important failure; the sun shone
As it had to on the white legs disappearing into the green
Water; and the expensive delicate ship that must have seen
20 Something amazing, a boy falling out of the sky,
Had somewhere to get to and sailed calmly on.

CONTENT-AREA CONNECTIONS

Culture: Mythology and History

Bruegel uses the myth of Icarus, which he transplants to the sixteenth-century Dutch lowlands, to dramatize the theme of the world's indifference to the fate of individuals. Auden, in turn, uses Bruegel's interpretation of the myth as inspiration for his own poetic commentary on 1930s Europe, where traditional values were being shaken by fascism. Although Auden wrote the poem in part as a response to the events of his time, the theme of the world's indifference to individual suffering resonates in all ages.

Response and Analysis

INDEPENDENT PRACTICE

DIRECT TEACHING

VIEWING THE ART

Alexei von Jawlensky (1864–1941) was a Russian-born German artist. In his portraits he reduced facial features to simple, colorful forms, which recall Russian Orthodox icons, reflecting his spiritual approach to art.

Activity. Mistral's poem makes an association between fear and being a princess. Does Jawlensky's painting suggest a similar fear? Explain. [Possible responses: Yes, the princess may be about to use the fan to keep from seeing something frightening. No, the painting seems whimsical.]

A Literary Focus

? Refrain. What refrain does the poet use? What effect does it create? [Possible response: The refrain is "I don't want them to turn [make] / my little girl. . . ." The refrain creates a songlike effect, making the poem sound like a sad lullaby.]

B Literary Focus

? Imagery. Why do you think the speaker moves from the image of a bird to that of a princess? [Possible response: The succession of images suggests the child's becoming more sophisticated and worldly and growing away from her mother.]

C Literary Focus

? Repetition. What effect does the combination of refrain and progressive imagery create? [Possible response: The repetitive quality of the refrain holds the poem together and gives it a songlike quality. The progression from "swallow" to "princess" to "queen" suggests the process of growing up.]

Fairy Tale Princess with Fan (1912) by Alexei von Jawlensky. Oil on cardboard.
Museum Ludwig Köln.
© 2003 Artists Rights Society (ARS), NY/VG Bild-Kunst, Bonn

Fear

Gabriela Mistral
translated by **Doris Dana**

I don't want them to turn
my little girl into a swallow.
She would fly far away into the sky
and never fly again to my straw bed,
5   or she would nest in the eaves
where I could not comb her hair.
I don't want them to turn
my little girl into a swallow.

I don't want them to make
10   my little girl a princess.
In tiny golden slippers
how could she play on the meadow?
And when night came, no longer
would she sleep at my side.
15   I don't want them to make
my little girl a princess.

And even less do I want them
one day to make her queen.
They would put her on a throne
20   where I could not go to see her.
And when nighttime came
I could never rock her . . .

I don't want them to make
my little girl a queen!

1050   Collection 7   The Modern World: 1900 to the Present

DIFFERENTIATING INSTRUCTION

English-Language Learners
Be sure students recognize that "them," an unidentified group, has no antecedent in the poem. Help students see that by leaving the identity of "them" vague, the poet makes "them" seem less like actual people and more like some inevitable process or unstoppable force.

Advanced Learners
Encourage students to think about possible symbolic meanings for the "little girl." For example, the little girl might symbolize a part of the poet herself or the poet's writings. The mother's fear may represent the author's own concern about becoming famous or losing her gift for poetry.

Response and Analysis

Thinking Critically

1. Who is the **speaker** in this poem? What is this speaker concerned about?

2. A swallow is a bird that migrates, usually nesting in widely separated summer and winter regions. Given this information, why do you think Mistral uses the specific **image** of a swallow, rather than simply any bird?

3. What does the image of a "straw bed" tell you about the social or economic situation of the speaker? What else might that image suggest?

4. In the second stanza the speaker evokes the **image** of "tiny golden slippers" "on the meadow" as incongruous or out of place. In what other way would the slippers be incongruous for her daughter?

5. In the third stanza, why do you think the speaker fears that she could no longer see her own daughter if she were made a queen? (In your answer, consider the **connotations** of the words *queen* and *throne*.)

6. What is **ironic** about a mother fearing that her daughter will become a "queen"—someone who lives a life untouched by common cares and daily concerns?

7. In a sentence, state the **theme** of the poem. What comment on life does this theme make?

8. Explain how the **refrain** helps reveal the speaker's emotional state. What effect does it have on the **tone** of the poem?

9. Why do you think this poem is titled "Fear"? Does the poem match your idea of what a poem with this title would be about? Explain.

Extending and Evaluating

10. We are not told who the "them" of the poem are. Who do you think they are? Would the emotional impact of the poem be increased or reduced if the speaker identified "them"? Explain your response.

WRITING

Separation Anxiety

Write a brief **character analysis** of the speaker in the poem. In your analysis, consider these questions: Is she rich or poor? Why is she so fearful of being separated from her daughter—and do these fears seem justified? (Refer to your Quickwrite notes.) What seem to be the mother's values? What adjectives other than *fearful* can you use to describe her?

Mother and Child (1926) by Diego Rivera.
Private Collection. © 2003 Banco de Mexico Diego Rivera & Frida Kahlo Museums Trust. Reproduction authorized by: Instituto Nacional de Bellas Artes Y Literatura, Mexico.

SKILLS FOCUS

Literary Skills
Analyze refrain.

Writing Skills
Write a character analysis.

INDEPENDENT PRACTICE

Response and Analysis

7. Possible answer: The theme of the poem is that parents sometimes find it hard to accept a child's growing up. This theme suggests that as a child's life goes on, the outside world and the family exert competing pulls.

8. Possible answer: The repetition creates the effect of an incantation, as if the speaker, unable to stop the separation process in any other way, is repeating a prayer to keep her child with her. It gives the poem a childlike tone.

9. Possible answer: The poem is a response to a parent's fear of being separated from her child. Rather than describing the fear, the poem represents an attempt, probably futile, to keep it at bay.

Extending and Evaluating

10. Possible answer: The "them" in the poem might be the forces that cause a child to grow away from his or her parents and become independent. The emotional power of the poem would be reduced if the speaker identified "them," because leaving their identity unknown suggests a childlike, irrational anxiety. A faceless enemy is more menacing than one who is identified.

ASSESSING

Assessment

- *Holt Assessment: Literature, Reading, and Vocabulary*

Thinking Critically

1. a mother who fears losing her child

2. Possible answer: The swallow suggests greater separation.

3. Possible answers: It suggests that the speaker is poor and lives in a rural setting; it might also suggest the simple, intimate bond between mother and child.

4. Possible answer: Gold slippers might be incongruous in a poor, rural community.

5. Possible answer: The mother may fear that her daughter would not want to see someone as poor as she, or that she would not be allowed by "them" to see her daughter.

6. Possible answer: One might expect the mother to be happy for her daughter's success; instead, she focuses on the way her daughter's elevation would create distance between them.

SKILLS FOCUS, pp. 1052–1058

Grade-Level Skills
- **Literary Skills**

Analyze characteristics of subgenres used in poetry, including lyric poetry, elegies, and villanelles.

More About the Writer

Background. At the age of twenty, Thomas moved to London and became involved in broadcasting, filmmaking, and publishing. He threw himself into life in the big city and developed the drinking problem that eventually led to his death.

The photographs on pp. 1054 and 1057 were taken by Rollie McKenna, a photographer who visited the Thomases in Wales just two months before the poet died in New York City. McKenna was accompanied on that final visit by John Malcolm Brinnin, one of the authors of this series, who was then director of the Poetry Center at New York's YMHA. Brinnin's mission, which proved unsuccessful, was to dissuade Thomas from undertaking another American tour because of its potentially destructive effects on the poet's health. Shortly after this visit, the poet set off for that journey from which he would not return.

Dylan Thomas
(1914–1953)
Wales

Born in Swansea, Wales, Dylan Thomas was a prodigy—a supremely gifted young man who wrote some of his most famous works before he was twenty. Largely self-educated, he chose the rough-and-tumble life of a newspaper reporter over the comparative serenity of a university education. His recognition by the leading poets and critics of Britain and the United States came early, and with it came international fame. Neither was enough to prevent him from living on the edge of poverty until his death.

The only son of parents who lived by a code of "good appearances" among their neighbors, Thomas as a child was continually torn between a deep-seated wish to live up to the expectations of his schoolmaster father and an equally strong impulse to please his doting mother. At the same time, he rejected both parents' pretensions to gentility. This conflict was later intensified by a strangely childish self-indulgence that continually defeated his attempts to be a devoted husband to his wife, Caitlin, and a loving father to their three children. The temporary solace he found in alcohol led to that "insult [damage] to the brain" that caused his early and sudden death in St. Vincent's Hospital in New York City. At the time, Thomas was making his fourth visit to the United States and preparing to collaborate on an opera with the composer Igor Stravinsky.

A man of magical presence, with an endless flow of wit and a transparent hunger for affection, Thomas charmed both his British and his American contemporaries. When he first came to America in 1950, he was regarded as the most charismatic British visitor since Oscar Wilde in 1885. His first reading tour of American colleges and universities was followed by ever more extensive trips, on which he crisscrossed the continent from Florida to British Columbia. Those who attended Thomas's readings responded to his personal magnetism. But they also heard something new in modern poetry—a kind of expression combining the oratorical *hywl*, or chanting eloquence, of the Welsh chapel service with the theatrical delivery of the Victorian actors who once thrilled American audiences with thunderous recitations from Shakespeare and Marlowe. Thomas's poems are a mixture of intricate language and preacherlike eloquence, of sonorous solemnity combined with a playful use of language apparent even in his most serious works.

In his last years, Thomas found that the concentration needed to write poetry was more and more difficult to achieve. Consequently, he turned to less demanding forms of expression and produced two works that became familiar around the world: *Under Milk Wood* (1954), which he called a "play for voices," and his lyrical memoir *A Child's Christmas in Wales* (1955), now a holiday classic.

Celebrated by critics, sought after by American lecture agencies, and idolized almost like a rock star, Thomas died at the height of a fame he could neither accept nor enjoy. "Once I was lost and proud," he told a reporter from *The New York Times;* "now I'm found and humble. I prefer that other."

For Independent Reading
You may enjoy the following works by Thomas:
- "In my craft or sullen art" (poem)
- *A Child's Christmas in Wales* (memoir)

RESOURCES: READING

Planning
- **One-Stop Planner** CD-ROM with ExamView Test Generator

Differentiating Instruction
- Holt Reading Solutions
- The Holt Reader
- Supporting Instruction in Spanish
- Audio CD Library, Selections and Summaries in Spanish

Grammar and Language
- Daily Language Activities

Assessment
- Holt Assessment: Literature, Reading, and Vocabulary
- **One-Stop Planner** CD-ROM with ExamView Test Generator
- Holt Online Assessment

Internet
- go.hrw.com (Keyword: LE5 12-7)
- Elements of Literature Online

Media
- Audio CD Library
- Audio CD Library, Selections and Summaries in Spanish

Before You Read

Fern Hill

Make the Connection
Quickwrite
Childhood is often remembered as a time of carefree innocence. Most of us have some memory of an idyllic moment from childhood, when the world was a glorious place and everything seemed just right.

Freewrite about one happy childhood memory of your own. Then, list three adjectives besides *happy* that describe the emotions you associate with this memory.

Literary Focus
Lyric Poetry
Lyric poetry focuses on expressing emotions or thoughts rather than on telling a story. In the lyric poem "Fern Hill," Dylan Thomas uses a full range of sound effects and **figures of speech** to convey vivid memories of a young boy's enchanted life in the Welsh countryside. Although the speaker's memories are colored by reflection and experience, it is the exuberance of his feelings, above all, that claims our attention.

> Lyric poetry focuses on expressing thoughts or emotions, rather than on telling a story.
>
> For more on Lyric Poetry, see the Handbook of Literary and Historical Terms.

Background
As a child, Thomas spent his summers among relatives who worked on a farm that, in his poem, he calls Fern Hill. Set in an apple orchard, the farmhouse is made of the whitewashed stucco typical of Wales and has a number of outlying barns for livestock and hay storage. Not far from the sea, Fern Hill looks down upon enormous tidal flats, in an ever-changing seascape that provides a bountiful habitat for thousands of water birds.

"Fern Hill" is a memory of childhood joy, a vision of an earthly paradise as well as of the playground of a boy for whom every day is an enchanted adventure. Yet, typical of Thomas, joy is never unshadowed. At the end of this extended song of praise, "time" holds him not, as we might expect, "green and growing," but "green and dying." Here we have a variation on one of Thomas's persistent themes—the lurking presence of death in life, of the worm in the seed.

SKILLS FOCUS

Literary Skills Understand the characteristics of lyric poetry.

Portrait of Dylan Thomas by Augustus John.
National Museum of Wales, Cardiff. © Courtesy of the Estate of Augustus John.

Dylan Thomas   1053

PRETEACHING

Summary ⬆ above grade level

The speaker recalls his idyllic childhood at Fern Hill, the Welsh farm where he spent his younger days in carefree, imaginative play. To him Fern Hill was like the Garden of Eden, a place where he was the lord of nature, exuberant, independent, and unaware of the passage of time. He concludes by musing that he did not know then, as he does now, that time would take him from that magical place and reveal to him his mortality.

Selection Starter
Motivate. Ask students which is their favorite season of the year now, and which was their favorite as children. Point out that many people have noted that time seems to last longer when one is a child. Ask them why they think this might be so. After the discussion, have students complete the Quickwrite.

VIEWING THE ART

Augustus John (1878–1961), a prominent English portrait artist, painted portraits of many leading writers, including James Joyce and W. B. Yeats.

Activity. After students read and discuss "Fern Hill," ask them whether they see a contrast in the painting like that in the poem. [Possible response: Thomas's boyish, even childlike features—red lips, unruly hair—contrast with his intense, serious expression.]

DIFFERENTIATING INSTRUCTION

English-Language Learners
Explain that part of what makes this poem so haunting is the way Thomas plays with syntax and idioms to create new and arresting expressions. For example, point out the phrase "once below a time" in l. 7. The standard expression that begins fairy tales in English is "Once upon a time," meaning "long ago." Thomas uses "once below a time" to mean "long ago," but by changing the preposition *upon* to *below,* he adds a new layer of meaning, and suggests both the dominance of time and the child's lack of awareness of time. Encourage students to find and interpret other unconventional expressions—for example, the "whinnying green stable" (l. 35); "All the sun long" (l. 19) instead of "All the day long"; and "the house high hay" (l. 41).

Dylan Thomas   1053

PRETEACHING

Summary ⬆ above grade level

The speaker begins the poem by asking his love to "tie" her heart to his. He goes on to evoke, by means of surreal images, the fearful mystery of night and sleep. He also suggests that love—specifically his love—can connect him "to a purer motion," a "constancy" that answers questions and unlocks doors.

Selection Starter

Motivate. Write "Sleep is a(n) _____" on the chalkboard, and ask students to complete the sentence with a figure of speech that they think captures an aspect of sleep. You might turn the students' responses into a poem, each line introducing a new metaphor. Then, explain that Neruda's poem builds a series of metaphors about night and sleep.

VIEWING THE ART

Romanian sculptor **Constantin Brancusi** (1876–1957) was among the most influential sculptors of the twentieth century. Inspired by non-Western art, he radically pared down forms throughout his career, making his sculptures increasingly abstract. *The Kiss* was carved directly out of a single block of stone, so that the kissing couple appear to be a single figure.

Activity. Why do you think Brancusi used a single block of stone to make *The Kiss*? [By doing so, the material itself emphasizes the couple's unity.]

Before You Read

Sonnet 79 / Soneto 79

Make the Connection
Quickwrite
Poets often declare that love unites or completes a couple so that they seem to act as one person. Jot down your thoughts on whether or not such a state is preferable to being alone or independent.

Literary Focus
Metaphor
Poets use **metaphors** to make comparisons between unlike things, to convey emotion, and to suggest more than is possible with a literal statement. For example, in the first line of this sonnet, when Neruda says "tie your heart to mine," he is comparing his lover's heart to a boat that can be moored safely or secured to his heart (the Spanish word *amarra* means "moor"). But in the English translation, *tie* can also suggest the joining of musical notes, especially in the context of the "double drum" in line 3. Readers fluent in both Spanish and English can expect a heightened emotional impact from the poem in its two versions.

INTERNET
More About
Pablo Neruda
Keyword: LE5 12-7

Metaphor is a figure of speech that makes a comparison between two seemingly unlike things without using a connective word such as *like, as, than,* or *resembles.*

For more on Metaphor, see the Handbook of Literary and Historical Terms.

Background
Mention the Renaissance poets, and the word *love* comes to mind almost immediately. Their sonnets resonate with the passion born of true love, but the Renaissance poets do not hold exclusive rights to this often mysterious emotion. Modern poets also write about the experience of love—in every language and culture. Sonnet 79 comes from Neruda's *One Hundred Love Sonnets,* a book that he wrote for his wife, Matilde Urrutia. In the book's dedication to her, Neruda uses the following **metaphor** to compare writing sonnets to building houses: "I built up these lumber piles of love, and with fourteen boards each I built little houses, so that your eyes, which I adore and sing to, might live in them. Now that I have declared the foundations of my love, I surrender this century to you: wooden sonnets that rise only because you gave them life." The book is divided into four parts—morning, afternoon, evening, and night—each corresponding to a different stage in a person's life. As you read Sonnet 79, try to determine which stage of life it refers to.

The Kiss (c. 1940) by Constantin Brancusi.
Musée National d'Art Moderne, Paris.
© 2003 Artists Rights Society (ARS), New York/ADAGP, Paris.

Literary Skills Understand metaphor.

1060 Collection 7

DIFFERENTIATING INSTRUCTION

Learners Having Difficulty
Some students may find the images and figures of speech in this poem difficult to visualize or to connect with the subject of love. Ask them how a "double drum" might be able to "defeat the darkness" and what this struggle says about the power of love to overcome life's anxieties. The description of sleep in the second stanza is particularly challenging. Explain that the images are not literal, point-for-point comparisons but rather dreamlike associations, each one slipping into the next. For example, the "earth's grapes," whose threads are snipped by sleep, may be the concrete realities of the day that we leave behind when we sleep; the comparison of sleep to a "headlong train" suggests a relentless force carrying us from consciousness into the world of dreams.

1060 Collection 7 The Modern World: 1900 to the Present

Sonnet 79

Pablo Neruda
translated by **Stephen Tapscott**

By night, Love, tie your heart to mine, and the two
together in their sleep will defeat the darkness
like a double drum in the forest, pounding
against the thick wall of wet leaves.

5   Night travel: black flame of sleep
that snips the threads of the earth's grapes,
punctual as a headlong train that would haul
shadows and cold rocks, endlessly.

Because of this, Love, tie me to a purer motion,
10 to the constancy that beats in your chest
with the wings of a swan underwater,

so that our sleep might answer all the sky's
starry questions with a single key,
with a single door the shadows had closed.

Soneto 79

De noche, amada, amarra tu corazón al mío
y que ellos en el sueño derroten las tinieblas
como un doble tambor combatiendo en el bosque
contra el espeso muro de las hojas mojadas.

5   Nocturna travesía, brasa negra del sueño
interceptando el hilo de las uvas terrestres
con la puntualidad de un tren descabellado
que sombra y piedras frías sin cesar arrastrara.

Por eso, amor, amárrame al movimiento puro,
10 a la tenacidad que en tu pecho golpea
con las alas de un cisne sumergido,

para que a las preguntas estrelladas del cielo
responda nuestro sueño con una sola llave,
con una sola puerta cerrada por la sombra.

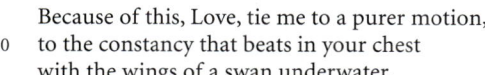

The Lover's Rock (1963) by David Alfaro Siqueiros.
Mixed media on masonite (80 cm × 60 cm).
Private Collection. Courtesy of Galería Arvil, Mexico City, Mexico. Reproduction authorized by: Instituto Nacional de Bellas Artes y Literatura, Mexico. © Estate of David Alfaro Siqueiros/Licensed by VAGA, New York, NY.

INDEPENDENT PRACTICE

Response and Analysis

Thinking Critically

Possible Answers

1. The lovers will never be isolated or alone; they can support each other in the struggle against "the darkness."

2. The darkness may symbolize death, the uncertainties of life, or the speaker's inner demons.

3. The simile compares the lovers' hearts beating together to a double drum sounding in the forest. It conveys both fear of the dark and the consolation of companionship.

4. "Night travel" might mean facing one's terrors, such as the fear of mortality. The extended metaphor conveys awe at the way sleep annihilates consciousness.

5. The lover's heartbeat is a small, steady, reliable motion that is "purer" than large gestures. It is compared to "wings of a swan underwater," something submerged or only partly visible but powerful and beautiful nonetheless.

6. They might be humanity's perennial questions: "Why are we here? Is there a purpose for living?" or those of an individual: "Will I be happy? What will my life be like?"

7. The turn is at l. 9, the first line of the sestet. The speaker's focus shifts from fear of the night to the comfort and security that his love offers.

Extending and Evaluating

8. *Brasa* literally means "ember." Translating it as "flame" creates the image of something powerful and destructive rather than something that may flare up or die out.

9. Other poems: Shakespeare's Sonnets 29 (p. 279) and 116 (p. 283); Donne's "Valediction Forbidding Mourning" (p. 305); and Arnold's "Dover Beach" (p. 722).

Response and Analysis

Thinking Critically

1. The central **metaphor** of the poem is that of the lovers' hearts being tied together. What will this accomplish for the lovers?

2. Why is the speaker so fearful of "the darkness"?

3. Explain the **simile** in line 3. What feeling or emotion does it convey?

4. "Night travel" is Neruda's **image** for sleep, but to what else might it refer? What emotions or feelings does the **extended metaphor** of sleep as a "black flame . . . that snips . . ." convey?

5. Why do you think Neruda calls the "constancy that beats in your chest" (literally, his beloved's heartbeat) a "purer motion"? Interpret the remarkable visual **image** in line 11.

6. Explain what the "sky's starry questions" might mean.

7. This sonnet follows the form of the **Italian**, or **Petrarchan**, **sonnet** (see page 276), though it doesn't follow its traditional rhyme scheme. Neruda's nontraditional sonnet does, however, contain the abrupt turns of thought of the classic sonnet. Identify the change, or **turn**, in Sonnet 79.

Extending and Evaluating

8. Work with a classmate who speaks or reads Spanish, and evaluate the effectiveness and accuracy of the English translation. (For example, why does the translator render "brasa negra" as "black flame"?)

9. What do you think of the idea that love completes people—that it unites them so that they can be seen as one person? (Refer to your Quickwrite notes.) In what other poems in this book have you encountered this idea?

SKILLS FOCUS

Literary Skills
Analyze metaphor.

Writing Skills
Write an essay comparing and contrasting two sonnets.

1062   Collection 7   The Modern World: 1900 to the Present

Literary Criticism

10. The poet and novelist Stephen Dobyns noted that by the 1960s, in Chile, Neruda's first collection of love poetry was still being "discussed, wondered over, and dreamt with. Despite having been written in the twenties, it seemed of the moment. . . . My wife and her friends felt no doubt about what the poems meant. They had no need for critics. The poems were being spoken directly to them." Does the Neruda sonnet you have just read reflect contemporary views of romantic love? Is Neruda closer in spirit to the metaphysical Renaissance poets (see page 301) or to the Romantic poets (see pages 522–533)—or does he represent a much more modern sensibility? Explain.

WRITING

What Is Love?

Review one of the Renaissance love sonnets you studied in Collection 3 and, in a brief **essay, compare and contrast** it with Neruda's sonnet. In your essay, explore these points:

- the form of each sonnet (Petrarchan or Shakespearean)
- the speaker's intention in each sonnet
- what you learn about the person to whom each sonnet is addressed
- the theme of each sonnet
- the poet's use of figures of speech
- how the views of love presented in the two sonnets differ from each other

---

Literary Criticism

10. Neruda's sonnet views love as a compensation for existential confusion and suffering, an idea also found in the works of the metaphysical poets. Neruda's complex imagery also recalls the works of these poets, but the dreamlike shifting of metaphors in his poetry is modern. Whereas a metaphysical poet would develop a conceit over a number of lines, Neruda moves from metaphor to metaphor quickly (as in ll. 5–8).

ASSESSING

Assessment

- *Holt Assessment: Literature, Reading, and Vocabulary*

RETEACHING

For a lesson reteaching poetic devices, see **Reteaching**, p. 1129A.

1062   Collection 7   The Modern World: 1900 to the Present

R. K. Narayan
(1906–2001)
India

R.K. Narayan (nə·rī′yen), considered one of India's greatest writers, was born in Madras, India, into a large, middle-class family. His father was a prominent teacher, and Narayan too was groomed for a career in education, though he hated school. In spite of his dislike for academics, Narayan graduated from Maharajah's College in Mysore and served a brief stint as a village teacher. For Narayan, however, teaching proved to be a short-lived profession; he soon settled into his career as a writer.

Due to his mother's poor health and his father's itinerant career, Narayan was raised primarily by his grandmother, a strong woman sought after by neighbors for her marital advice, astrological readings, and healing remedies. She taught him traditional Indian tales and prayers and greatly fueled his interest in writing. Through her, Narayan developed an intense curiosity about the lives of so-called ordinary people.

In his first novel, *Swami and Friends* (1935), Narayan introduced the imaginary city of Malgudi, based on his hometown, Mysore, in southern India. In subsequent works, Narayan returns again and again to this fictional place and its eccentric and lovable characters. Whether writing about the timeless inhabitants of Malgudi or retelling ancient stories from the Sanskrit epics *The Mahabharata* and *The Ramayana,* Narayan based all his writings on his concept of the universality of human nature.

Narayan lived to see most of the twentieth century. He saw India dominated by political clashes, social conflicts, and historic upheavals. However, these tumultuous events did not alter his fictional world, and some critics have condemned him for seeming to ignore India's turbulent history in his writing. To such criticisms, Narayan said, "I write primarily for myself. And I write about what interests me, human beings and human relationships. . . . Only the story matters; that's all."

For Independent Reading
You may enjoy the following story by Narayan:
- "An Astrologer's Day"

PRETEACHING

Summary ⇄ at grade level

Sekhar, a teacher, believes that just as people avoid staring straight at the sun, they also avoid facing the truth. He realizes that people temper what they say to avoid shocking others. As an experiment, he sets aside one day on which he will give and take only the truth, no matter what the consequences. He begins by telling his wife what he really thinks of her cooking; later he tells a colleague what he thinks of someone who has just died. Then his headmaster, who has secretly spent a fortune on music lessons, asks Sekhar to evaluate his singing. Sekhar's opinion on musical matters is highly respected. The headmaster's performance is terrible, and, bravely but anxiously, Sekhar tells him so. The next day, to Sekhar's surprise, the headmaster thanks him for telling the truth. However, he insists that Sekhar grade one hundred test papers in a single night. A small price to pay for telling the truth, thinks Sekhar.

Skills Starter

Build review skills. Remind students that irony is expressed in many different tones and is influenced by the author's beliefs and emotional stance. Irony can be gentle and humorous, as in "Like the Sun." It can be objective, dispassionate, or coldly analytical. It can also be angry, bitter, or even cruel.

Before You Read

Like the Sun

Make the Connection
Quickwrite
The expression *The truth hurts* doesn't make clear who is being hurt: the person to whom the truth is told or the truth-teller. Write down what you think might happen if, on one day each year, you told the truth no matter whose feelings were hurt.

Literary Focus
Irony
Situational irony involves a contrast between expectation and reality. In "Like the Sun," Narayan fashions a situation in which a character's obsession with telling people the truth leads to ironic consequences (people rarely want to hear the truth about themselves) and creates humor.

> **Situational irony** occurs when what actually happens is the opposite of what is expected or appropriate.
>
> *For more on Irony, see the Handbook of Literary and Historical Terms.*

INTERNET
Vocabulary Practice
Keyword: LE5 12-7

Literary Skills
Understand situational irony.

Vocabulary Development

tempering (tem′pər·iŋ) v. used as n.: moderating; toning down.

resolve (ri·zälv′) n.: determination; firm purpose.

culinary (kul′ə·ner′ē) adj.: related to cooking.

wince (wins) v.: flinch; draw back.

shirked (shurkt) v.: neglected or avoided a task or duty.

inclinations (in′klə·nā′shənz) n. pl.: likings; tendencies.

incessantly (in·ses′ənt·lē) adv.: constantly; unendingly.

ingratiating (in·grā′shē·āt·iŋ) v. used as adj.: purposely trying to gain favor.

assailed (ə·sāld′) v.: assaulted; attacked.

sullen (sul′ən) adj.: resentful; gloomy.

1064 Collection 7 The Modern World: 1900 to the Present

Previewing Vocabulary

Have students read the definitions of the Vocabulary words listed on p. 1064. Then, reinforce their understanding of the words by having them respond to the following items.

1. What might someone say who is <u>tempering</u> her criticism of a bad movie?
2. Why does a young writer need <u>resolve</u>?
3. What is your greatest <u>culinary</u> accomplishment?
4. Name two things that make you <u>wince</u>.
5. What should the punishment be for politicians who have <u>shirked</u> their responsibilities?
6. Do your natural <u>inclinations</u> lead you to exercise or to watch television?
7. In nature, what physical processes occur <u>incessantly</u>?
8. When is <u>ingratiating</u> behavior appropriate?
9. Who <u>assailed</u> the British troops at Concord Bridge?
10. How can you tell if someone is feeling <u>sullen</u>?

1064 Collection 7 The Modern World: 1900 to the Present

Like the Sun

R. K. Narayan

Selection Starter

Motivate. Tell students that the title "Like the Sun" comes from the first sentence of the story, in which the main character, Sekhar, compares truth to the sun. Ask students to discuss the simile. In what way might the sun and truth be alike? [Possible response: The sun sheds light on an object, as the truth can illuminate an idea.] How might the looking straight at the sun be like facing the truth? [Possible response: Facing the truth, like staring straight at the sun, can be painful and overwhelming.] Invite students to read "Like the Sun" to see how the simile applies to the story.

DIFFERENTIATING INSTRUCTION

Learners Having Difficulty
Point out that Sekhar's experience is embodied in popular sayings, such as "Put your money where your mouth is" and "If you talk the talk, you'd better walk the walk." Discuss with students the pros and cons of trying to put principles into practice in the real world.

English-Language Learners
Students may need help understanding such idioms as "spent a fortune," "to forget himself," "smooth sailing," and "in store for him."

Advanced Learners
Enrichment. You may wish to ask students to research and report on an episode in the life of a philosopher who put ideals to the test in the real world. Possible choices include Socrates, Marcus Aurelius, Jean Jacques Rousseau, and Henry David Thoreau.

Direct Teaching

A Reading Skills

? Predicting. Judging from Sekhar's reflections, what do you think is going to happen to him? Give at least one reason to support your prediction. [Possible responses: He is going to hurt someone by telling the truth; he is going to learn a hard lesson because he plans to "take" truth as well as give it.]

B Literary Focus

Irony. Explain the irony in the episode with Sekhar's wife. [Possible response: The irony lies in Sekhar's expectation that always telling the truth will make life "worth living." The reality is that he is unnecessarily hurting the person he loves most.]

C Literary Focus

? Allusion and irony. Explain that the allusion in this sentence is to the sword of Damocles, a courtier of ancient Syracuse who was seated at a feast under a sword hanging by a single hair. Why is the allusion ironic? [Possible response: The allusion is ironic because Sekhar does not realize that the real sword hanging over his head is the consequence of his experiment in truth telling.]

D Literary Focus

? Irony. Why is the headmaster's statement ironic? [Possible response: For Sekhar the surprise is different from what the headmaster imagines. It is ironic that the headmaster should seek Sekhar's opinion on a sensitive matter on the very day that Sekhar has decided to tell the absolute truth.]

A Truth, Sekhar reflected, is like the sun. I suppose no human being can ever look it straight in the face without blinking or being dazed. He realized that, morning till night, the essence of human relationships consisted in tempering truth so that it might not shock. This day he set apart as a unique day—at least one day in the year we must give and take absolute Truth whatever may happen. Otherwise life is not worth living. The day ahead seemed to him full of possibilities. He told no one of his experiment. It was a quiet resolve, a secret pact between him and eternity.

B The very first test came while his wife served him his morning meal. He showed hesitation over a tidbit, which she had thought was her culinary masterpiece. She asked, "Why, isn't it good?" At other times he would have said, considering her feelings in the matter, "I feel full up, that's all." But today he said, "It isn't good. I'm unable to swallow it." He saw her wince and said to himself, Can't be helped. Truth is like the sun.

His next trial was in the common room when one of his colleagues came up and said, "Did you hear of the death of so and so? Don't you think it a pity?" "No," Sekhar answered. "He was such a fine man—" the other began. But Sekhar cut him short with: "Far from it. He always struck me as a mean and selfish brute."

During the last period when he was teaching geography for Third Form A,[1] Sekhar received a note from the headmaster: "Please see me before you go home." Sekhar said to himself: It must be about these horrible test papers. A hundred papers in the boys' scrawls; he had shirked this **C** work for weeks feeling all the time as if a sword were hanging over his head.

The bell rang and the boys burst out of the class.

Sekhar paused for a moment outside the headmaster's room to button up his coat; that was another subject the headmaster always sermonized about.

He stepped in with a very polite "Good evening, sir."

---

1. **Third Form A:** equivalent to ninth-grade classes in the United States.

The headmaster looked up at him in a very friendly manner and asked, "Are you free this evening?"

Sekhar replied, "Just some outing which I have promised the children at home—"

"Well, you can take them out another day. Come home with me now."

"Oh . . . yes, sir, certainly . . ." And then he added timidly, "Anything special, sir?"

"Yes," replied the headmaster, smiling to himself . . . "You didn't know my weakness for music?"

"Oh, yes, sir . . ."

"I've been learning and practicing secretly, and now I want you to hear me this evening. I've engaged a drummer and a violinist to accompany me—this is the first time I'm doing it full-dress and I want your opinion. I know it will be valuable."

Sekhar's taste in music was well-known. He was one of the most dreaded music critics in the town. **D** But he never anticipated his musical inclinations would lead him to this trial. . . . "Rather a surprise for you, isn't it?" asked the headmaster. "I've spent a fortune on it behind closed doors. . . ." They started for the headmaster's house. "God hasn't given me a child, but at least let him not deny me the consolation of music," the headmaster said, pathetically, as they walked. He incessantly chattered about music: how he began one day out of sheer boredom; how his teacher at first laughed at him, and then gave him hope; how his ambition in life was to forget himself in music.

At home the headmaster proved very ingratiating. He sat Sekhar on a red silk carpet, set before him several dishes of delicacies, and fussed over him as if he were a son-in-law of the house. He even said, "Well, you must listen with a

---

Vocabulary

tempering (tem′pər·iŋ) v. used as n.: moderating; toning down.
resolve (ri·zälv′) n.: determination; firm purpose.
culinary (kul′ə·ner′ē) adj.: related to cooking.
wince (wins) v.: flinch; draw back.
shirked (shurkt) v.: neglected or avoided a task or duty.
inclinations (in′klə·nā′shənz) n. pl.: likings; tendencies.
incessantly (in·ses′ənt·lē) adv.: constantly; unendingly.
ingratiating (in·grā′shē·āt·iŋ) v. used as adj.: purposely trying to gain favor.

Comparing and Contrasting Texts

Comparing philosophical ideas. The *Bhagavad-Gita* (see p. 350) has long been a treasured source of philosophical reflection and spiritual discipline. Among the subjects discussed in its didactic verses are the ways a person can reach "the pure calm of infinity."

Have students choose a line, a verse, or an idea from the *Bhagavad-Gita* and apply it to Sekhar in Narayan's "Like the Sun." What could Sekhar have learned from the *Bhagavad-Gita*? Students might focus on the line "Be forever lucid" in verse 45 or on the concepts of action and discipline.

DIRECT TEACHING

Content-Area Connections
Music: Indian Classical Music
Indian classical music is basically melodic rather than harmonic; a melody is usually played or sung against the background of a drone, a sustained tone or group of tones. Melodies are often traditional or may be improvised. In India the singing voice is considered the most beautiful melodic instrument.

READING MINI-LESSON

Developing Word-Attack Skills
Remind students that final e is usually a signal that the preceding vowel sound is long (as in *brute, daze, suppose,* and *absolute*). But when e appears in the middle of a word, it may have a different effect. Have students compare these pairs of words:

outrage   outrageous
mole   molecule
line   linear
muse   museum

In *outrageous*, e has the same function as in the base word *outrage*. In *molecule*, which is related to *mole*, e stands for the unstressed vowel sound /ə/. In *linear* (which is related to *line*) and *museum* (which is related to *muse*), e has the sound /ē/.

Activity. Have students categorize these words by the function of medial e. Does it signal a long vowel, stand for /ə/, or have the sound /ē/?

1. malefactor [/ə/]
2. mileage [long vowel]
3. caveat [/ē/]
4. category [/ə/]
5. placebo [/ē/]
6. homeopathic [/ē/]
7. rarefy [/ə/]
8. paleolith [/ē/]
9. valediction [/ə/]
10. primeval [/ē/]

DIRECT TEACHING

A Literary Focus

Tone. How is the tone of these three similes different from the tone of the simile that begins the story? [Possible response: The tone of the opening simile is serious, whereas the tone of these similes is humorous.]

B Reading Skills

Making inferences. What does the relief of the drummer and violinist suggest? [Possible response: It suggests that Sekhar's evaluation of the headmaster's performance is accurate.]

C Literary Focus

Irony. What is ironic about Sekhar's reflection? [Possible response: He realizes that the actual experience of telling the truth is very different from the *idea* of telling the truth.]

D Literary Focus

Irony. Explain the irony of this twist in the plot. [Possible response: The headmaster says that he appreciates Sekhar's honesty—not the response Sekhar expected. Nevertheless, the headmaster—in a natural human response—retaliates.]

GUIDED PRACTICE

Monitoring students' progress. Guide the class in answering these questions.

True-False

1. Sekhar is kind to his wife when he tells her the truth. [F]
2. The headmaster values Sekhar's opinion. [T]
3. Sekhar tells the truth, even though it may hurt his career. [T]
4. Sekhar learns that it is not always right to tell the truth. [F]

---

free mind. Don't worry about these test papers." He added half humorously, "I will give you a week's time."

"Make it ten days, sir," Sekhar pleaded.

"All right, granted," the headmaster said generously. Sekhar felt really relieved now—he would attack them at the rate of ten a day and get rid of the nuisance.

The headmaster lighted incense sticks. "Just to create the right atmosphere," he explained. A drummer and a violinist, already seated on a Rangoon[2] mat, were waiting for him. The headmaster sat down between them like a professional at a concert, cleared his throat, and began an alapana,[3] and paused to ask, "Isn't it good Kalyani?"[4] Sekhar pretended not to have heard the question. The headmaster went on to sing a full song composed by Thyagaraja[5] and followed it with two more. All the time the headmaster was singing, Sekhar went on commenting within himself, He croaks like a dozen frogs. He is bellowing like a buffalo. Now he sounds like loose window shutters in a storm.

The incense sticks burnt low. Sekhar's head throbbed with the medley of sounds that had assailed his eardrums for a couple of hours now. He felt half stupefied. The headmaster had gone nearly hoarse, when he paused to ask, "Shall I go on?" Sekhar replied, "Please don't, sir, I think this will do. . . ." The headmaster looked stunned. His face was beaded with perspiration. Sekhar felt the greatest pity for him. But he felt he could not help it. No judge delivering a sentence felt more pained and helpless. Sekhar noticed that the headmaster's wife peeped in from the kitchen, with eager curiosity. The drummer and the violinist put away their burdens with an air of relief. The headmaster removed his spectacles, mopped his brow, and asked, "Now, come out with your opinion."

"Can't I give it tomorrow, sir?" Sekhar asked tentatively.

"No. I want it immediately—your frank opinion. Was it good?"

"No, sir . . ." Sekhar replied.

"Oh! . . . Is there any use continuing my lessons?"

"Absolutely none, sir . . ." Sekhar said with his voice trembling. He felt very unhappy that he could not speak more soothingly. Truth, he reflected, required as much strength to give as to receive.

All the way home he felt worried. He felt that his official life was not going to be smooth sailing hereafter. There were questions of increment and confirmation and so on, all depending upon the headmaster's goodwill. All kinds of worries seemed to be in store for him. . . . Did not Harischandra[6] lose his throne, wife, child, because he would speak nothing less than the absolute Truth whatever happened?

At home his wife served him with a sullen face. He knew she was still angry with him for his remark of the morning. Two casualties for today, Sekhar said to himself. If I practice it for a week, I don't think I shall have a single friend left.

He received a call from the headmaster in his classroom next day. He went up apprehensively.

"Your suggestion was useful. I have paid off the music master. No one would tell me the truth about my music all these days. Why such antics at my age! Thank you. By the way, what about those test papers?"

"You gave me ten days, sir, for correcting them."

"Oh, I've reconsidered it. I must positively have them here tomorrow. . . ." A hundred papers in a day! That meant all night's sitting up! "Give me a couple of days, sir . . ."

"No. I must have them tomorrow morning. And remember, every paper must be thoroughly scrutinized."

"Yes, sir," Sekhar said, feeling that sitting up all night with a hundred test papers was a small price to pay for the luxury of practicing Truth. ∎

---

2. **Rangoon:** capital of Myanmar; it is now called Yangon.
3. **alapana** *n*.: performance of Indian melody.
4. **Kalyani** *n*.: Hindustani melody.
5. **Thyagaraja:** (1767–1847) one of India's foremost composers.
6. **Harischandra:** ancient Hindu king known for his love of truth.

Vocabulary

assailed (ə·sāld′) *v*.: assaulted; attacked.
sullen (sul′ən) *adj*.: resentful; gloomy.

FAMILY/COMMUNITY ACTIVITY

Encourage students to ask members of different professions how they define "telling the truth," on the basis of the criteria of their professions. The following professions may provide a variety of responses: lawyer, politician, doctor, nurse, psychologist or psychiatrist, scientist, accountant, writer or artist, journalist, historian, police officer, clergyman, sales representative, advertising copywriter, public relations agent, real estate agent. Have students gather the responses, compare them, and discuss the strengths and weaknesses of each.

Response and Analysis

Reading Check

1. What does Sekhar resolve to do on the day of the story?
2. Why does Sekhar dread going to the headmaster's home?
3. What does Sekhar tell the headmaster?
4. How does the headmaster repay Sekhar for his truthfulness?

Thinking Critically

5. Describe the **character** of Sekhar and the sources of his **conflict**. What is **ironic** about such a character's resolve to tell the "absolute Truth"?
6. Why do you think Sekhar is devoting only one day to his truth-telling?
7. Explain the **situational irony** that occurs the day after Sekhar tells the headmaster that his singing is no good.
8. How can you tell that the headmaster was not entirely pleased with Sekhar's truthfulness?
9. In one sentence, state the **theme** of the story. Does the theme reinforce or contradict common ideas about truth?
10. How would you describe Narayan's attitude toward Sekhar and the subject of truth? (Consider whether Narayan is serious, admiring, slightly mocking, poking fun or ridiculing, or something else.) What point is Narayan trying to make? Explain how Narayan uses **tone** to enhance his point.
11. Humor often turns on unexpected events. How does the story's **irony** create a comic effect?

Extending and Evaluating

12. Did you find the story believable? Why or why not?

WRITING

Is Honesty the Best Policy?

Is telling the truth easy? Is it always the right thing to do? Write a brief **reflective essay** in which you share your thoughts about the expected—or unexpected—consequences of telling the truth. Use examples from your own experiences if possible. Refer to your Quickwrite notes for ideas.

▶ See "Writing a Reflective Essay," pages 656–663, for help with this assignment.

Vocabulary Development

Analogies

tempering	inclinations
resolve	incessantly
culinary	ingratiating
wince	assailed
shirked	sullen

On a separate sheet of paper, complete each analogy below with a Vocabulary word from the list above.

1. EMPLOYED : HIRED :: _____ : neglected
2. EXCITING : DULL :: _____ : gleeful
3. EXPLOITING : USING :: _____ : moderating
4. STABILITY : SECURITY :: _____ : firmness
5. BOTANICAL : PLANTS :: _____ : cooking
6. GRIEF : SADNESS :: _____ : preferences
7. QUICKLY : SWIFTLY :: _____ : constantly
8. WARY : CAUTIOUS :: _____ : charming
9. NONCHALANT : CONCERNED :: _____ : retreated
10. HARM : HURT :: _____ : flinch

Literary Skills Analyze situational irony.

Writing Skills Write a reflective essay.

Vocabulary Skills Complete word analogies.

Games at Twilight

Anita Desai

Two young girls, Rajasthan, India.

It was still too hot to play outdoors. They had had their tea, they had been washed and had their hair brushed, and after the long day of confinement in the house that was not cool but at least a protection from the sun, the children strained to get out. Their faces were red and bloated with the effort, but their mother would not open the door, everything was still curtained and shuttered in a way that stifled the children, made them feel that their lungs were stuffed with cotton wool and their noses with dust and if they didn't burst out into the light and see the sun and feel the air, they would choke.

"Please, ma, please," they begged. "We'll play in the veranda and porch—we won't go a step out of the porch."

"You will, I know you will, and then——"

"No—we won't, we won't," they wailed so horrendously that she actually let down the bolt of the front door so that they burst out like seeds from a crackling, overripe pod into the veranda, with such wild, maniacal yells that she retreated to her bath and the shower of talcum powder and the fresh sari that were to help her face the summer evening.

They faced the afternoon. It was too hot. Too bright. The white walls of the veranda glared stridently in the sun. The bougainvillea[1] hung about it, purple and magenta, in livid balloons. The garden outside was like a tray made of beaten brass, flattened out on the red gravel and the stony soil in all shades of metal—aluminum, tin, copper, and brass. No life stirred at this arid time of day—the birds still drooped, like dead fruit, in the papery tents of the trees; some squirrels lay limp on the wet earth under the garden tap. The outdoor dog lay stretched as if dead on the veranda mat, his paws and ears and tail all reaching out like dying travelers in search of water. He rolled his eyes at the children—two white marbles rolling in the purple sockets, begging for sympathy—and attempted to lift his tail in a wag but could not. It only twitched and lay still.

Then, perhaps roused by the shrieks of the children, a band of parrots suddenly fell out of the eucalyptus tree, tumbled frantically in the still, sizzling air, then sorted themselves out into battle formation and streaked away across the white sky.

The children, too, felt released. They too began tumbling, shoving, pushing against each other, frantic to start. Start what? Start their business. The business of the children's day which is—play.

"Let's play hide-and-seek."
"Who'll be It?"
"You be It."
"Why should I? You be——"
"You're the eldest——"
"That doesn't mean——"

The shoves became harder. Some kicked out. The motherly Mira intervened. She pulled the boys roughly apart. There was a tearing sound of cloth, but it was lost in the heavy panting and angry grumbling, and no one paid attention to the small sleeve hanging loosely off a shoulder.

"Make a circle, make a circle!" she shouted, firmly pulling and pushing till a kind of vague circle was formed. "Now clap!" she roared, and, clapping, they all chanted in melancholy unison: "Dip, dip, dip—my blue ship——" and every now and then one or the other saw he was safe by the way his hands fell at the crucial moment—palm on palm, or back of hand on palm—and dropped out of the circle with a yell and a jump of relief and jubilation.

Raghu was It. He started to protest, to cry "You cheated—Mira cheated—Anu cheated———" but it was too late, the others had all already streaked away. There was no one to hear when he called out, "Only in the veranda—the porch—Ma said—Ma *said* to stay in the porch!" No one had stopped to listen, all he saw were their brown legs flashing through the dusty shrubs, scrambling up brick walls, leaping over compost heaps and hedges, and then the porch stood empty in the purple shade of the bougainvillea, and the garden was empty as before; even the limp squirrels had whisked away, leaving everything gleaming, brassy, and bare.

Only small Manu suddenly reappeared, as if he had dropped out of an invisible cloud or from a bird's claws, and stood for a moment in the center of the yellow lawn, chewing his finger and near to tears as he heard Raghu shouting, with his head pressed against the veranda wall, "Eighty-three, eighty-five, eighty-nine, ninety . . ." and then made off in a panic, half of him wanting to fly north, the other half counseling south. Raghu turned just in time to see the flash of his white shorts and the uncertain skittering of his red sandals, and charged after him with such

---

1. **bougainvillea** (boo′gən·vil′ē·ə) *n.*: woody, tropical vine with showy, purplish leaves.

Vocabulary
maniacal (mə·nī′ə·kəl) *adj.*: crazed; wildly enthusiastic.
stridently (strīd′′nt·lē) *adv.*: harshly; sharply.

Anita Desai   1073

Literary Criticism

Critical Comment: A Writer's Writer
In her review of the collection *Games at Twilight*, Victoria Glendinning calls the title story a "jewel." She believes that it "recounts something that has happened in one way or another to nearly everyone in childhood. . . . Mrs. Desai is a writer's writer in that anyone who has ever set pen to paper must ask himself just what it is about the writing that makes the story so memorable, and there is, naturally, no simple answer to the question."

Small-group activity. Prompt students to discuss the quotation. Ask:
- Do you agree that Desai is recounting something that has happened "to nearly everyone in childhood"? How would you describe that experience?
- What do *you* think makes the story memorable?

DIRECT TEACHING

C Reading Skills
? **Analyzing details.** Desai deliberately puts the evocative words "wailed," "wild," and "maniacal" into the same sentence. What are the long *a* and *i* sounds intended to evoke? [Possible response: They evoke the sound of the children's cries.]

D Literary Focus
? **Imagery.** What images does Desai use to create the impression of oppressive heat? [Possible responses: glaring white walls; hanging bougainvillea; garden like a tray of beaten brass; drooping birds; limp squirrels; stretched-out dog.] What does the appearance of the animals suggest? [death]

E Reading Skills
? **Evaluating.** Do the language and behavior of the children seem believable to you? Why or why not? [Possible response: Yes, the interruptions, rough play, and self-centeredness seem convincing.]

F Reading Skills
Analyzing details. Point out to students the sense of action created by the words "flashing," "scrambling," and "leaping," followed by the abrupt stop of "and then the porch stood empty." Explain that Desai uses diction and sentence structure to suggest physical action.

G Reading Skills
? **Determining author's purpose.** Point out the poignancy in this scene with Manu. What effect do you think the author intends to create by including it? [Possible responses: Desai wants readers to recall the intense emotions they felt in similar situations as children.]

Anita Desai   1073

Direct Teaching

Ⓐ Reading Skills

❓ **Analyzing details.** Does Ravi actually wait a long time, or does he just feel that it has been a long time? How do you know? [He waits a long time; the afternoon light has turned to gray, and Ravi hears the gardener watering the lawn.]

Ⓑ Reading Skills

❓ **Analyzing details.** What feelings are evoked by the details in this passage? [Possible responses: Loneliness and isolation are evoked by the shadows of the shed and by the distant house. The growing darkness of the foliage evokes the overall gloom of the dying day. "Homing" is applied to the sparrows, but sadly and ironically, Ravi is not at home.]

Ⓒ Literary Focus

❓ **Imagery.** What visual imagery does Desai use here to help you picture the children? [In the light of dusk, the children's faces are pale, like death masks, and the vegetation is as dark as ink, casting long shadows.] How does the imagery help you understand Ravi's emotions at this moment? [Possible response: The children look like ghosts, and the atmosphere is tomblike. The children are "dead" to Ravi, just as he has been forgotten by them.]

Ⓐ It grew darker in the shed as the light at the door grew softer, fuzzier, turned to a kind of crumbling yellow pollen that turned to yellow fur, blue fur, gray fur. Evening. Twilight. The sound of water gushing, falling. The scent of earth receiving water, slaking its thirst in great gulps and releasing that green scent of freshness, coolness. Through the crack Ravi saw the long purple shadows of the shed and the garage lying still across the yard. Beyond that, the white walls of the house. The bougainvillea had lost its lividity, hung in dark bundles that quaked and twittered and seethed with masses of homing sparrows. The lawn was shut off from his view. Could he hear the children's voices? It seemed to him that he could. It seemed to him that he could hear them chanting, singing, laughing. But what about the game? What had happened? Could it be over? How could it when he was still not found?

Ⓑ It then occurred to him that he could have slipped out long ago, dashed across the yard to the veranda, and touched the "den." It was necessary to do that to win. He had forgotten. He had only remembered the part of hiding and trying to elude the seeker. He had done that so successfully, his success had occupied him so wholly, that he had quite forgotten that success had to be clinched by that final dash to victory and the ringing cry of "Den!"

With a whimper he burst through the crack, fell on his knees, got up, and stumbled on stiff, benumbed legs across the shadowy yard, crying heartily by the time he reached the veranda so that when he flung himself at the white pillar and bawled, "Den! Den! Den!" his voice broke with rage and pity at the disgrace of it all, and he felt himself flooded with tears and misery.

Ⓒ Out on the lawn, the children stopped chanting. They all turned to stare at him in amazement. Their faces were pale and triangular in the dusk. The trees and bushes around them stood inky and sepulchral, spilling long shadows across them. They stared, wondering at his reappearance, his passion, his wild animal howling. Their mother rose from her basket chair and came toward him, worried, annoyed, saying, "Stop it, stop it, Ravi. Don't be a baby. Have you hurt yourself?" Seeing him attended to, the children went back to clasping their hands and chanting, "The grass is green, the rose is red. . . ."

But Ravi would not let them. He tore himself out of his mother's grasp and pounded across the lawn into their midst, charging at them with his head lowered so that they scattered in surprise. "I won, I won, I won," he bawled, shaking his head so that the big tears flew. "Raghu didn't find me. I won, I won——"

It took them a minute to grasp what he was saying, even who he was. They had quite forgotten him. Raghu had found all the others long ago. There had been a fight about who was to be It next. It had been so fierce that their mother had emerged from her bath and made them change to another game. Then they had played another and another. Broken mulberries from the tree and eaten them. Helped the driver wash the car when their father returned from work. Helped the gardener water the beds till he roared at them and swore he would complain to their parents. The parents had come out, taken up their positions on the cane chairs. They had begun to play again, sing and chant. All this time no one had remembered Ravi. Having disappeared from the scene, he had disappeared from their minds. Clean.

"Don't be a fool," Raghu said roughly, pushing him aside, and even Mira said, "Stop howling, Ravi. If you want to play, you can stand at the end of the line," and she put him there very firmly.

The game proceeded. Two pairs of arms reached up and met in an arc. The children trooped under it again and again in a <u>lugubrious</u> circle, ducking their heads and <u>intoning</u>

Vocabulary
lugubrious (lə·gōō′brē·əs) *adj.*: very solemn or mournful, especially in a way that seems exaggerated or ridiculous.

Comparing and Contrasting Texts

Comparing treatments of a theme. The theme of the loss of innocence is powerful and universal. As they mature, children confront the indifference of nature and of other people, and they become aware of cruelty and evil and death. For many people this awakening is a painful experience. Have students compare the treatment of this theme in Desai's "Games at Twilight" with that in James Joyce's "Araby" (p. 957). Ask them to focus on the main characters' expectations and the way those expectations are disappointed, and to speculate on effects of those experiences.

If All the World Were Paper and All the Waters Ink (1962) by Jess.
The Fine Arts Museums of San Francisco, California. Courtesy of the Odyssia Gallery, New York.

"The grass is green,
The rose is red;
Remember me
When I am dead, dead, dead, dead . . ."

And the arc of thin arms trembled in the twilight, and the heads were bowed so sadly, and their feet tramped to that melancholy refrain so mournfully, so helplessly, that Ravi could not bear it. He would not follow them, he would not be included in this funereal game. He had wanted victory and triumph—not a funeral. But he had been forgotten, left out, and he would not join them now. The ignominy of being forgotten—how could he face it? He felt his heart go heavy and ache inside him unbearably. He lay down full length on the damp grass, crushing his face into it, no longer crying, silenced by a terrible sense of his insignificance. ■

Vocabulary
ignominy (ig′nə·min′ē) *n.*: shame; dishonor.

INDEPENDENT

SKILLS FOCUS, pp. 1080–1087

Grade-Level Skills
- **Literary Skills**

Analyze the way the theme of a selection represents a comment on life.

More About the Writer

Background. Lively's seventh novel, *Moon Tiger* (1987), won the prestigious Booker Prize. It depicts life in England and World War II action in Egypt from the point of view of a dying woman. Through flashbacks, the book shows how the protagonist's life has been affected by past events and how emotion connects memories. She declares that "a lifetime is not linear but instant. . . . Inside the head, everything happens at once."

Lively's own childhood in Egypt undoubtedly had a powerful effect on her view of life-shaping events. In her remarkable memoir, *Oleander, Jacaranda: A Childhood Perceived,* she recalls her experiences in Cairo when World War II was raging. The blend of cultures—Greek, Egyptian, British, French—and the momentous events serve as a backdrop for her observations of people and nature. Ultimately Lively is concerned with what we perceive and who we become because of those perceptions.

Response and Analysis

Penelope Lively
(1933–   )
England

Penelope Lively was born in Cairo, Egypt, where her father, a bank manager, and her mother left her upbringing to Lucy, her nursemaid and governess. Lively says of Lucy: "She had stern moral values—a general code of truthfulness and honesty and kindness spiced with fervent patriotism. All this rubbed off on me except the patriotism. . . ." Lucy as tutor helped Lively become a free-ranging, unrestrained, ravenous reader who was required to retell or write about everything that she read. Lively returned to England in 1945 and entered boarding school, where sports were favored over literature. Her copy of a poetry anthology was confiscated, and the school's headmistress later returned it with a rebuke: "There is no need for you to read this sort of thing in your spare time, Penelope. You will be *taught* all that." Lively then notes: "She went on to point out that my lacrosse skills were abysmally below par."

Lively survived boarding school and went on to Oxford, where she graduated "equipped both for everything and nothing." She worked briefly as a research assistant for a sociology professor, then married and raised her two children at home where, she says, "I read my way through twentieth-century literature as it were, stirring the baby food with one hand and holding a book in the other." The day her youngest child started school, Lively began writing children's fiction. Her first novel, *Astercote* (1970), has a supernatural plot, and its theme of the persistence of memory and the reality of the past as an influence on the present would pervade her later novels. She went on to write a number of successful books for children and young adults, including *The Whispering Knights* (1971), *The Driftway* (1972), and the Whitbread Award-winning *A Stitch in Time* (1976).

Lively's first novel for adults, *The Road to Lichfield* (1977), treats the complexities and difficulties of marriage, the ways that the present repeats or parallels the past, and the relationships we have with the past. In one part of the novel, a character loses her job as a history teacher because she teaches "what actually happened."

Lively believes that her thematic interest in the past influencing the present had something to do with growing up in Egypt—a place where remnants from several different eras and civilizations exist side by side, making the progression of time difficult to pinpoint.

Lively has also written numerous short stories, and in one of her unpublished lectures says, "In its very structure the short story has an eerie relationship with the processes of memory. . . . It holds up for inspection an incident, a relationship, a situation. . . ." Her comment fits "Next Term, We'll Mash You."

RESOURCES: READING

Planning
- *One-Stop Planner* CD-ROM with ExamView Test Generator

Differentiating Instruction
- Supporting Instruction in Spanish
- Audio CD Library, Selections and Summaries in Spanish

Vocabulary
- Vocabulary Development

Grammar and Language
- Daily Language Activities

Assessment
- Holt Assessment: Literature, Reading, and Vocabulary
- *One-Stop Planner* CD-ROM with ExamView Test Generator
- Holt Online Assessment

Internet
- go.hrw.com (Keyword: LE5 12-7)
- Elements of Literature Online

Media
- Audio CD Library
- Audio CD Library, Selections and Summaries in Spanish

Before You Read

Next Term, We'll Mash You

Make the Connection
Quickwrite

Have you ever been suddenly put in a new social situation, such as enrolling in a new school, going to a camp for the first time, or moving to a different town? Jot down four or five tips that you would give someone to help him or her adjust to such a new situation and avoid problems.

Literary Focus
Theme

A **theme** is the central idea or insight in a work of literature. It is different from the subject of a work, which can be expressed in a word or two such as love, revenge, or growing up. The theme of a story is stated in a sentence as the generalization about human behavior or life that the writer is trying to dramatize or convey. Writers rarely state the theme of a story explicitly or tack it on as a moral; instead, they imply the theme by revealing it through the title, the central conflict, a symbol, or their characters' thoughts and actions. Often the key to figuring out a theme is to first understand the characters in a story—what they value and what motivates them.

> **Theme** is the central idea or insight of a work of literature.
>
> *For more on Theme, see the Handbook of Literary and Historical Terms.*

Background

Private schools in England (called public schools there) are often expensive, exclusive, highly conscious of class distinctions, and set up as boarding schools where children live and are subjected to guidance and discipline by older students. Every spring, parents take their children to visit and inspect schools where they may be enrolled in the fall. The word *mash* in the title is a colloquial term meaning "smash" or "beat up."

Vocabulary Development

subdued (səb·dōōd′) *adj.*: quiet; controlled.

geniality (jē′nē·al′ə·tē) *n.*: friendliness; cordiality.

untainted (ən·tānt′id) *adj.*: untarnished; without a trace of anything offensive.

condescension (kän′di·sen′shən) *n.*: behavior that is patronizing.

indulgent (in·dul′jənt) *adj.*: lenient; permissive.

amiable (ā′mē·ə·bəl) *adj.*: friendly; likeable.

inaccessible (in·ak·ses′ə·bəl) *adj.*: not accessible; impossible to enter or reach.

haggard (hag′ərd) *adj.*: gaunt; worn and exhausted from anxiety.

Cricket match at the Vine Cricket Ground, Kent, England.

Literary Skills Understand theme.

Penelope Lively 1081

PRETEACHING

Summary *at grade level*

Mr. and Mrs. Manders drive with their son Charles to St. Edwards, an expensive boarding school in the Sussex countryside, to decide whether to enroll Charles. When they arrive, the parents note the beautiful grounds, the maid's uniform, and the elegant furnishings. They remark on the high tone of the school and the connections they might make with other parents. Mrs. Spokes, the headmaster's wife, greets them and serves sherry, while Mrs. Manders silently assesses her clothing and jewelry. They make polite conversation until the headmaster enters. Like his wife, he is genial and inspires quiet confidence. Mrs. Spokes takes Charles out and introduces him to the Lower Third class. When she leaves, the students surround Charles and overwhelm him with questions. He stares silently, sights and sounds swirling around him. Out of the noise, one voice says clearly, "Next term, we'll mash you." A bell rings, the children leave, and the headmaster's wife returns Charles to his parents. Back in the car, the parents decide that they will send Charles to the school. Mrs. Manders asks Charles whether the boys told him about the swimming pool. Charles does not answer. He is "haggard with anticipation."

Previewing Vocabulary

To reinforce students' understanding of the Vocabulary words, have partners work together on the following activities. You may want to monitor students' efforts to determine if their behavior demonstrates an understanding of the underlined words.

1. Have a conversation in which one person is lively and one is <u>subdued</u>.
2. Explain why <u>geniality</u> is important—or not important—in a teacher.
3. Use <u>untainted</u> in a sentence about a politician.
4. Demonstrate treating someone with <u>condescension</u>.
5. Explain the effects of <u>indulgent</u> parents on children.
6. Suggest an <u>amiable</u> thing you might say to a new student.
7. Describe how some movie stars are more <u>inaccessible</u> than others.
8. Name an activity that might make you appear <u>haggard</u>.

Penelope Lively 1081

PRETEACHING

VIEWING THE ART

The English school system is very different from the American. English high school students, or secondary students, as they are called in England, do not struggle to pass classes every term. Rather, they are required to take two sets of exams. They enter the first phase of secondary education during what we would call seventh grade and study up to ten subjects for five years. They then take exams known as O-levels ("Ordinary"). If they pass, they receive a General Certificate of Secondary Education. At this point, students are allowed to quit school or to go on to a technical training college or vocational school. If they want to go to a university, they must study for two more years and then pass an exam known as the A-level ("Advanced").

Skills Starter

Motivate. Remind students that the title of a story often suggests the theme. Ask, "From the title alone, what do you think might be the theme of the story?" Students may say that the theme probably deals with a threat, violence, or conflict. Then, ask, "What do the title and the photograph together suggest?" Students may say that they suggest a feeling of menace. The boys present a united front. They may be bullies. They may be determined to crush the opposition.

Motivate. Ask students what they think are children's greatest fears. Do parents pay enough attention to children's unspoken anxieties? Call on volunteers to offer examples and reasons for their responses.

Next Term, We'll Mash You

Penelope Lively

The photographs on pages 1082, 1085, and 1086 were taken at the five-hundredth anniversary of Eton College (1990).
© Graham Tim/CORBIS Sygma.

1082 Collection 7 The Modern World: 1900 to the Present

Inside the car it was quiet, the noise of the engine even and subdued, the air just the right temperature, the windows tight-fitting. The boy sat on the back seat, a box of chocolates, unopened, beside him, and a comic, folded. The trim Sussex[1] landscape flowed past the windows: cows, white-fenced fields, highly priced period houses. The sunlight was glassy, remote as a colored photograph. The backs of the two heads in front of him swayed with the motion of the car.

His mother half-turned to speak to him. "Nearly there now, darling."

The father glanced downwards at his wife's wrist. "Are we all right for time?"

"Just right. Nearly twelve."

"I could do with a drink. Hope they lay something on."[2]

"I'm sure they will. The Wilcoxes say they're awfully nice people. Not really the schoolmaster-type at all, Sally says."

The man said, "He's an Oxford chap."

"Is he? You didn't say."

"Mmn."

"Of course, the fees are that much higher than the Seaford place."

"Fifty quid[3] or so. We'll have to see."

The car turned right, between white gates and high, dark, tight-clipped hedges. The whisper of the road under the tires changed to the crunch of gravel. The child, staring sideways, read black lettering on a white board: "St. Edward's Preparatory School. Please Drive Slowly." He shifted on the seat, and the leather sucked at the bare skin under his knees, stinging.

The mother said, "It's a lovely place. Those must be the playing fields. Look, darling, there are some of the boys." She clicked open her handbag, and the sun caught her mirror and flashed in the child's eyes; the comb went through her hair and he saw the grooves it left, neat as distant ploughing.

"Come on, then, Charles, out you get."

The building was red brick, early nineteenth century, spreading out long arms in which windows glittered blackly. Flowers, trapped in neat beds, were alternate red and white. They went up the steps, the man, the woman, and the child two paces behind.

The woman, the mother, smoothing down a skirt that would be ridged from sitting, thought: I like the way they've got the maid all done up properly. The little white apron and all that. She's foreign, I suppose. Au pair.[4] Very nice. If he comes here, there'll be Speech Days and that kind of thing. Sally Wilcox says it's quite dressy—she got that cream linen coat for coming down here. You can see why it costs a bomb. Great big grounds and only an hour and a half from London.

They went into a room looking out into a terrace. Beyond, dappled lawns, gently shifting trees, black and white cows grazing behind iron railings. Books, leather chairs, a table with magazines—*Country Life, The Field, The Economist*. "Please, if you would wait here. The Headmaster won't be long."

Alone, they sat, inspected. "I like the atmosphere, don't you, John?"

"Very pleasant, yes." Four hundred a term, near enough. You can tell it's a cut above the Seaford place, though, or the one at St. Albans. Bob Wilcox says quite a few City people send their boys here. One or two of the merchant bankers, those kind of people. It's the sort of contact that would do no harm at all. You meet someone, get talking at a cricket[5] match or what have you . . . Not at all a bad thing.

---

1. **Sussex:** county on the southeast coast of England.
2. **lay something on:** have a reception with drinks and/or snacks.
3. **quid** *n.*: slang for pounds, British monetary unit.
4. **au pair** *n.*: foreign person who does domestic work for room and board and for an opportunity to learn the language of her employers.
5. **cricket** *n.*: team sport played with balls and flat wooden bats.

Vocabulary
subdued (səb·dōōd′) *adj.*: quiet; controlled.

Direct Teaching

A **Literary Focus**

? Theme. Sometimes a theme is conveyed by what characters do not say. What do the parents not discuss? What does that suggest about the theme? [Possible response: They do not discuss Charles's education or his separation anxiety. The theme may be the emotional gulf between parents and child.] What might Charles's silence suggest about the theme? [Possible response: He is full of anxiety and may feel that he is being abandoned. The theme may be the unrecognized fears of children.]

B **Literary Focus**

? Irony. Explain the irony in this remark. [Possible responses: The parents *have* forgotten about Charles—or at least about his feelings. They *do* seem to be choosing a school for their own social and financial concerns rather than for Charles's best interests.]

C **Literary Focus**

? Character. What does this passage reveal about the father? [Possible responses: Like his wife, he assesses the headmaster's wife, but for her physical attractiveness and voice. He values the money it took to produce her voice and manner.]

A "All right, Charles? You didn't get sick in the car, did you?"

The child had black hair, slicked down smooth to his head. His ears, too large, jutted out, transparent in the light from the window, laced with tiny, delicate veins. His clothes had the shine and crease of newness. He looked at the books, the dark brown pictures, his parents, said nothing.

"Come here, let me tidy your hair."

The door opened. The child hesitated, stood up, sat, then rose again with his father.

"Mr. and Mrs. Manders? How very nice to meet you—I'm Margaret Spokes, and will you please forgive my husband who is tied up with some wretch who broke the cricket pavilion window and will be just a few more minutes. We try to be organized but a schoolmaster's day is always just that bit unpredictable. Do please sit down and what will you have to revive you after that beastly drive? You live in Finchley,[6] is that right?"

"Hampstead,[7] really," said the mother. "Sherry would be lovely." She worked over the headmaster's wife from shoes to hairstyle, pricing and assessing. Shoes old but expensive—Russell and Bromley. Good skirt. Blouse could be Marks and Sparks—not sure. Real pearls. Super Victorian ring. She's not gone to any particular trouble—that's just what she'd wear anyway. You can be confident, with a voice like that, of course. Sally Wilcox says she knows all sorts of people.

The headmaster's wife said, "I don't know how much you know about us. Prospectuses[8] don't tell you a thing, do they? We'll look round everything in a minute, when you've had a chat with my husband. I gather you're friends of the Wilcoxes, by the way. I'm awfully fond of Simon—he's down for Winchester, of course, but I expect you know that."

The mother smiled over her sherry. Oh, I know that all right. Sally Wilcox doesn't let you forget that.

B "And this is Charles? My dear, we've been forgetting all about you! In a minute I'm going to borrow Charles and take him off to meet some of the boys because after all you're choosing a school for him, aren't you, and not for you, so he ought to know what he might be letting himself in for and it shows we've got nothing to hide."

The parents laughed. The father, sherry warming his guts, thought that this was an amusing woman. Not attractive, of course, a bit homespun, but impressive all the same. Partly **C** the voice, of course; it takes a bloody expensive education to produce a voice like that. And other things, of course. Background and all that stuff.

"I think I can hear the thud of the Fourth Form coming in from games, which means my husband is on the way, and then I shall leave you with him while I take Charles off to the common-room."

For a moment the three adults centered on the child, looking, judging. The mother said, "He looks so hideously pale, compared to those boys we saw outside."

"My dear, that's London, isn't it? You just have to get them out, to get some color into them. Ah, here's James. James—Mr. and Mrs. Manders. You remember, Bob Wilcox was mentioning at Sports Day . . ."

The headmaster reflected his wife's style, like paired cards in Happy Families. His clothes were mature rather than old, his skin well-scrubbed, his shoes clean, his <u>geniality</u> <u>untainted</u> by the least <u>condescension</u>. He was genuinely sorry to have kept them waiting, but in this business one lurches from one minor

---

6. **Finchley:** part of the London borough of Barnet.
7. **Hampstead:** part of the London borough of Camden—and a much more desirable place to live.
8. **prospectuses** *n. pl.*: advertisements.

Vocabulary

geniality (jē′nē·al′ə·tē) *n.*: friendliness; cordiality.
untainted (ən·tānt′id) *adj.*: untarnished; without a trace of anything offensive.
condescension (kän′di·sen′shən) *n.*: behavior that is patronizing.

Primary Source

Penelope Lively at Boarding School

Until Lively was twelve, her only teacher was her governess. In her memoir *Oleander, Jacaranda,* Lively describes her first experience of school. Her account suggests that she drew on firsthand experience to portray Charles's feelings: "When eventually I went to my first school, in England, I was well up to standard in all areas except Math and Latin, both of which needed some urgent repair work. But I was woefully short on social skills. The disadvantages of all that indulgent one-to-one attention are obvious. I had never learned alongside another child, indeed had had very little to do with other children. I was introspective and good at being alone—not qualities that come in handy at an English girls' boarding school. Flung into that fetid jungle, I was lost. I knew none of the strategies of survival. Alternatively exhilarated and alarmed by the sudden exposure to this horde, I flailed around like an untrained puppy, and invited dislike. Children sense an outsider, and I was that, all right. Eventually I learned a stoical endurance, but where learning was concerned, the sun had now gone in."

crisis to the next . . . And this is Charles? Hello, there, Charles. His large hand rested for a moment on the child's head, quite extinguishing the thin, dark hair. It was as though he had but to clench his fingers to crush the skull. But he took his hand away and moved the parents to the window, to observe the mutilated cricket pavilion, with indulgent laughter.

And the child is borne away by the headmaster's wife. She never touches him or tells him to come, but simply bears him away like some relentless tide, down corridors and through swinging glass doors, towing him like a frail craft, not bothering to look back to see if he is following, confident in the strength of magnetism, or obedience.

And delivers him to a room where boys are scattered among inky tables and rungless chairs and sprawled on a mangy carpet. There is a scampering, and a rising, and a silence falling, as she opens the door.

"Now this is the Lower Third, Charles, who you'd be with if you come to us in September. Boys, this is Charles Manders, and I want you to tell him all about things and answer any questions he wants to ask. You can believe about half of what they say, Charles, and they will tell you the most fearful lies about the food, which is excellent."

The boys laugh and groan; amiable, exaggerated groans. They must like the headmaster's

Vocabulary
indulgent (in·dul′jənt) *adj.*: lenient; permissive.
amiable (ā′mē·ə·bəl) *adj.*: friendly; likeable.

Penelope Lively 1085

DIRECT TEACHING

D Literary Focus

? Theme. What does this shocking passage convey about the theme? [Possible responses: The headmaster is genial, yet his hand obliterates the top of Charles's head as if he were a giant or an ogre. The possibility that he might crush Charles's skull apparently occurs only to Charles, emphasizing the theme of the adults' blindness to the child's terror.]

E Reading Skills

? Analyzing details. What do these details suggest about life at St. Edward's? [Possible responses: The headmaster's wife banters with the boys and their responses are "amiable." The details suggest that St. Edward's is a good school that the students enjoy.]

READING MINI-LESSON

Developing Word-Attack Skills
Direct students' attention to this passage on p. 1083: "the comb went through her hair and he saw the grooves it left, as neat as distant ploughing." Point out the two words spelled with *ough*—*through* and *ploughing*—and discuss the sounds that the letters stand for in each word. In *through*, *ough* stands for /o͞o/; in *ploughing*, which is a variant spelling for *plowing*, *ough* stands for /ou/.

Have students suggest other words containing the sequence *ough*. Together, identify the sounds represented by *ough* in each word. Possibilities include these:

bough /ou/   slough /o͞o/
cough /ôf/   slough /uf/
dough /ō/   though /ō/
lough /äk/   tough /uf/
rough /uf/   trough /ôf/

Activity. Ask if the two words spelled with *ough* in each sentence have the same sound.

1. The waves are never rough in the lough. [different: /uf/, /äk/]
2. They moved slowly through the slough. [same: /o͞o/]
3. A bough had fallen into the trough. [different: /ou/, /ôf/]
4. A loofa will help slough off rough skin. [same: /uf/]

Penelope Lively 1085

DIRECT TEACHING

A Literary Focus

? Character. What is actually happening in the classroom? [The children gather around Charles, all talking at once.] What does Charles *feel* is happening? [Possible response: He is overwhelmed by the crowd of children. He retreats into himself, the scene swirls around him, and he grows dizzy.]

B Literary Focus

? Theme. The repetition of the title suggests that these words encapsulate the theme. How does the threat point up the divide between the children's and the adults' worlds? [Possible responses: Charles's terror and the threat of next term's violence are secret and unobserved by the adults.]

C Literary Focus

? Theme. How does the word *haggard* help to convey the theme? [Possible responses: The word is rarely applied to children and suggests that fear has aged him prematurely, that his innocence has been lost.] What ironic twist does the word *anticipation* add to the theme? [Possible response: What Charles anticipates is quite different from what his parents anticipate.]

GUIDED PRACTICE

Monitoring students' progress. Guide the class in answering these questions.

True-False

1. The story's title refers to an upcoming sports competition. [F]
2. The Manders don't ask about the school's educational standing. [T]
3. The headmaster of St. Edward's is a cruel, violent man. [F]
4. Charles likes the school. [F]

---

wife: There is licensed repartee.⁹ They look at her with bright eyes in open, eager faces. Someone leaps to hold the door for her, and close it behind her. She is gone.

A The child stands in the center of the room, and it draws in around him. The circle of children contracts, faces are only a yard or so from him; strange faces, looking, assessing.

Asking questions. They help themselves to his name, his age, his school. Over their heads he sees beyond the window an inaccessible world of shivering trees and high racing clouds and his voice which has floated like a feather in the dusty schoolroom air dies altogether and he becomes mute, and he stands in the middle of them with shoulders humped, staring down at feet: grubby plimsolls¹⁰ and kicked brown sandals. There is a noise in his ears like rushing water, a torrential din out of which voices boom, blotting each other out so that he cannot always hear the words. Do you? they say, and Have you? and What's your? and the faces, if he looks up, swing into one another in kaleidoscopic patterns and the floor under his feet is unsteady, lifting and falling.

B And out of the noises comes one voice that is complete, that he can hear. "Next term, we'll mash you," it says. "We always mash new boys."

And a bell goes, somewhere beyond doors and down corridors, and suddenly the children are all gone, clattering away and leaving him there with the heaving floor and the walls that shift and swing, and the headmaster's wife comes back and tows him away and he is with his parents again, and they are getting into the car, and the high hedges skim past the car windows once more, in the other direction, and the gravel under the tires changes to black tarmac.

"Well?"

"I liked it, didn't you?" The mother adjusted the car around her, closing windows, shrugging into her seat.

"Very pleasant, really. Nice chap."

---

9. **licensed repartee:** approved banter.
10. **plimsolls** *n. pl.:* sneakers.

"I liked him. Not quite so sure about her."

"It's pricey, of course."

"All the same . . ."

"Money well spent, though. One way and another."

"Shall we settle it, then?"

"I think so. I'll drop him a line."

The mother pitched her voice a notch higher to speak to the child in the back of the car. "Would you like to go there, Charles? Like Simon Wilcox. Did you see that lovely gym, and the swimming pool? And did the other boys tell you all about it?"

C The child does not answer. He looks straight ahead of him, at the road coiling beneath the bonnet of the car. His face is haggard with anticipation. ■

Vocabulary

inaccessible (in·ak·ses′ə·bəl) *adj.:* not accessible; impossible to enter or reach.

haggard (hag′ərd) *adj.:* gaunt; worn and exhausted from anxiety.

Comparing and Contrasting Texts

Comparing portrayals of children. Both Penelope Lively's "Next Term, We'll Mash You" and Anita Desai's "Games at Twilight" center on the minds and hearts of children. Have students compare the two stories. Encourage them to formulate specific questions about both stories. They might also use the following questions:

- How are Charles and Ravi alike? How are they different? What conflicts and obstacles does each boy face?
- How convincing are the portrayals of the children in each story?
- Are the themes of the stories similar? Why or why not?
- Which story packs a more powerful emotional punch? Why?

Response and Analysis

Reading Check
1. Why are Charles and his parents going to the prep school?
2. Who takes Charles to see some of the students?
3. What do the students plan to do to Charles?
4. At the end of the story, what do Charles's parents plan to do?

Thinking Critically
5. How are Mr. and Mrs. Manders **characterized**? What is important to them, and what do you think motivates their actions? Use specific evidence from the text.
6. What does the condescending treatment of Charles by the headmistress and her husband reveal about their **characters**?
7. How does the brief description of the red brick school and its garden convey a sinister **atmosphere**?
8. How does Lively reveal Charles's **character**? In a brief paragraph, sum up his emotional **conflict**—that is, how he probably feels about his parents and the school. Use evidence from the text to support your opinion.
9. What point do you think the writer is trying to make by setting up the **ironic** contrast between the parents' approval of the school and Charles's silent dread of it?
10. What do you think is the **theme** of the story—its comment on life? Does this theme relate to the tips you listed in your Quickwrite notes? Explain.
11. Do you think Charles's parents love their son? Explain.

Extending and Evaluating
12. Do you find it believable that Charles doesn't answer his parents' questions or tell them what is going to happen to him next term? Explain your answer.

WRITING
Family Traits
Write a brief **character analysis** of the Manders family. You should show how their character is revealed through dialogue, action, and the reactions of other characters. Also, consider these questions: What adjectives will you use to describe the Manderses? What motivates them? Are they believable characters? What are their conflicts? Show how their characterization points to the theme of the story. Be sure to state the **theme** as a generalization about human behavior that goes beyond specifics of the story.

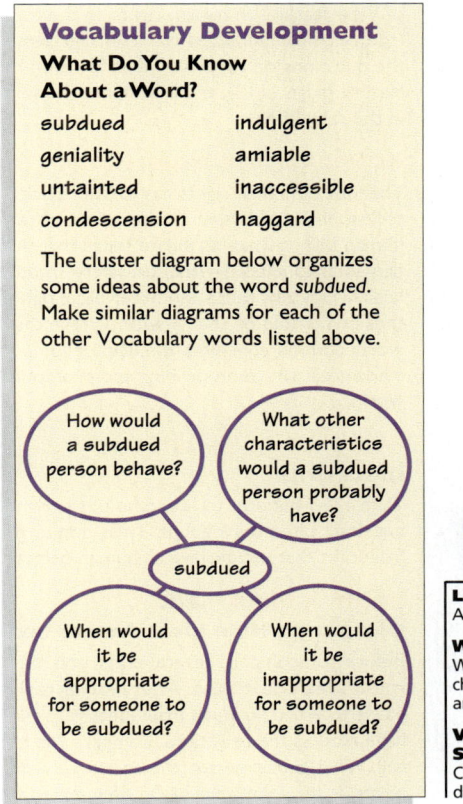

Vocabulary Development
What Do You Know About a Word?

subdued indulgent
geniality amiable
untainted inaccessible
condescension haggard

The cluster diagram below organizes some ideas about the word *subdued*. Make similar diagrams for each of the other Vocabulary words listed above.

SKILLS FOCUS

Literary Skills Analyze theme.
Writing Skills Write a character analysis.
Vocabulary Skills Create semantic diagrams.

INDEPENDENT PRACTICE

Response and Analysis

6. Possible answers: They treat Charles with polite authority, suggesting they are competent, confident, and firm. They are distant to Charles, unaware of his fears, and not reassuring. They are concerned with running a school, not with providing emotional nurturing.
7. Possible answer: The building is old and its long "arms" stretch out as if to grasp. The black windows suggest menacing eyes. The flowers, perhaps like students, are "trapped."
8. Possible answers: She reveals Charles's character through his sensations and thoughts. His conflict may be a fear of separation from his parents or a realization that he is already distant from them. His conflict may be facing up to his fear of the students.
9. Possible answer: The contrast points up the emotional distance and lack of understanding that marks the family.
10. Possible answers: Parents are often unaware of the conflicts and terrors their children endure. Parents' concerns are often at odds with their children's emotional needs.
11. Possible answers: Yes, they want the best for him, although they are not emotionally engaged with him. No, they choose a school based on what is best for them, not him.

Extending and Evaluating
12. Possible answers: Yes, because they are unlikely to understand. No, because his fear would force him to say something.

Vocabulary Development
Students' cluster diagrams may vary.

Reading Check
1. They are looking at the school to decide whether to enroll Charles.
2. The headmaster's wife takes Charles to see some of the students.
3. The students plan to "mash," or beat up, Charles next term.
4. The parents plan to send Charles to St. Edward's.

Thinking Critically
5. Possible answers: They are materialistic (the cost of school) and status conscious (what their friends think). They assess people and things according to appearances (maid's uniform, school grounds), monetary value (Mrs. Spokes's jewelry), and usefulness (social and business connections).

Political Points of View

SKILLS FOCUS, pp. 1088–1110

Grade-Level Skills

■ **Literary Skills**

Analyze political points of view in a selection of literary works on a topic.

■ **Reading Skills**

Compare main ideas across texts.

Political Issue: Human Rights

You might approach the issue of human rights by discussing with students a news article on human rights violations. Students should identify the violations and their causes and give their opinions on possible solutions. Ask students to recall other recent news stories involving human rights. After students finish their Quickwrites, have the class compile two lists of rights and freedoms, one headed "Freedom from . . . " (torture, prejudice, and so on) and one headed "Freedom to . . ." (work, practice one's religion, live and travel freely, and so on.)

Skills Starter

Build review skills. To help students identify political assumptions, pose these questions:

- Fred gets a speeding ticket and plans to challenge it in court. What assumptions is Fred making about his rights? [that he has a right to a fair hearing; that he has a right to be considered innocent until proven guilty]

- What assumptions or beliefs might impel someone to brutalize another person? [the belief that some people have fewer rights than others; the belief that some people deserve to be attacked]

Help students conclude that a political assumption is a belief about the rights, characteristics, or responsibilities of government, society, or a member of a society.

Introducing Political Points of View

Human Rights

Main Reading			
Ha Jin	**Saboteur**	(China)	1091
Connected Readings			
United Nations Commission on Human Rights . . . *from the* **Universal Declaration of Human Rights**			1101
Desmond Tutu . . . . *from* **The Question of South Africa**		(South Africa)	1103
Aung San Suu Kyi . . . *from* **Towards a True Refuge**		(Myanmar)	1107

You will be reading the four selections listed above in this Political Points of View feature on human rights. In the top corner of the pages in this feature, you'll find three stars. Smaller versions of the stars appear next to the questions on page 1099 that focus on human rights. At the end of the feature (page 1110), you'll compare the various points of view expressed in the selections.

Examining the Issue: Human Rights

The idea of human rights has existed since the beginning of civilization. As philosophers and other thinkers have observed throughout history, human beings share an innate sense that they are entitled to certain fundamental conditions—shelter, safety, freedom from slavery, and even life itself. Tragically, these and other basic rights are often cruelly violated by those who hold or seek power. Within the last century, however, the world community—with the help of some very strong individuals—has made great strides in defining and promoting human rights throughout the world.

Make the Connection
Quickwrite ✏️

Take a few minutes to list some of the rights and freedoms that you enjoy but don't often think about. Then, add to the list any other rights and freedoms that you believe all human beings should share.

Pages 1088–1110 cover
Literary Skills Analyze political points of view on a topic.
Reading Skills Compare main ideas across texts.

Reading Skills
Comparing Main Ideas Across Texts

Before you compare several texts, you must identify and analyze the **main idea** of each one. After reading each of the following selections, pause to write down its main ideas regarding human rights. When you have read all the selections, compare the notes you have taken. Ask yourself, *What distinct perspective does each writer bring to the issue? On what points do the writers agree? On what points do they disagree?*

1088 Collection 7 The Modern World: 1900 to the Present

Ha Jin
(1956–)
China

Jin Xuefei (whose name means "golden flying snow") was born in Liaoning Province, China, where his father was an army officer. At fourteen, Jin joined the People's Liberation Army (part of China's armed forces) and for five years was stationed near the Russian border awaiting a possible invasion: "I knew there might be a war, and so we were ready and knew if we had to die, we'd die. We were quite happy . . . because everything was new: big guns and trucks. And I was young." The Cultural Revolution—the government's violent attempt at social change which included destruction of "old" art, historic buildings, and books (especially those that seemed to contradict the teachings of China's leader Mao Zedong)—had begun in 1966. Colleges were closed until 1977, when Jin entered Heilongjiang University to study English.

In 1985, Jin left China for graduate studies at Brandeis University in Massachusetts, with every intention of returning home. But after the 1989 student uprising and massacre in Tiananmen Square, Jin says, "I realized that if I wanted to be a writer, I would have to stay in the States because it would be impossible for me to write honestly in Chinese in China. So it was a painful decision, but it took a year for me to decide to write English exclusively and to stay as immigrant." He decided to use the pen name Ha Jin for the poetry and fiction books that he started publishing in 1990, barely twelve years after he formally began studying English. Jin's stories and novels dramatize life in China under a repressive government: "I guess we are compelled to write about what has hurt us most." He is a painstaking writer who revises drafts of stories and novels at least thirty times.

Jin's first novel, the comic *In the Pond* (1998), depicts an artist, who, reduced to working in a fertilizer plant, taunts his superiors with unflattering cartoons and, ironically, is promoted to a propaganda office. His second novel, *Waiting* (1999), which won the National Book Award, is about a couple who must wait eighteen years before marrying. It opens with the unforgettable sentence: "Every summer Lin Kong returned to Goose Village to divorce his wife, Shuyu."

Jin's collection of short stories, *The Bridegroom* (2000), includes "Saboteur," a story that shows how even the most tyrannized and frustrated individual can still wreak devastating revenge on a community.

PRETEACHING

Summary ⬇ below grade level

As this troubling story unfolds, its main character, carefully described as an individual, gains an added dimension as a symbol of his society. Mr. Chiu is a university lecturer recovering from hepatitis. He and his wife are lunching outside a train station in Muji, on their way home from their honeymoon, when a police officer inconsiderately dumps his tea near them, soaking their shoes. Mr. Chiu complains; the police rough him up and jail him as a saboteur, accusing him of disrupting public order. As police officials pressure Chiu to admit his "crime," he feels his hepatitis worsening. Still, he stands on his rights, resists police bullying, and demands an apology. He holds out for two days, his illness intensifying steadily. On the third day, he wakens to see a man handcuffed to a tree in the exercise yard. It is one of Chiu's former students, now a lawyer, whom Chiu's wife has sent to help. Soon the police begin torturing the young man. To spare him, Chiu signs the "confession" the snickering officers have prepared. By now he is dreaming of murdering their families, and his liver hurts so much that he can hardly stand. After he and the lawyer are released, Chiu leads the young man on a round of visits to eateries near the police station, sampling a little food at each. Then Chiu and the lawyer board the train home. Within a month, eight hundred people in Muji mysteriously develop hepatitis. Two of the dead are children.

Before You Read

Saboteur

Political Points of View

A *saboteur* is a person who commits sabotage, or purposely undermines the work of an opposing power. The word first came into use in the 1800s, when frustrated French laborers threw their wooden shoes, or *sabots*, into factory machines to protest the inhumane conditions under which they worked. Ha Jin personalizes the idea of sabotage by posing the following questions: *Is it possible to sabotage a person's humanity? If so, how would this "sabotaged" person behave?*

Literary Focus

Irony

The **irony** at work in "Saboteur" becomes apparent early on: Both the reader and the protagonist quickly learn that what *should* happen and what *will* happen are entirely different things. Ha Jin's irony, though, goes beyond the realm of fiction. It shows us that, in the real world, the discrepancy between what should and what does happen is frequently experienced as a painful injustice.

INTERNET
Vocabulary Practice
•
More About Ha Jin
•
Keyword: LE5 12–7

> **Irony** is a discrepancy between expectations and reality or between appearances and reality.
>
> For more on Irony, see the Handbook of Literary and Historical Terms.

SKILLS FOCUS

Literary Skills
Analyze political points of view on a topic. Understand irony.

Reading Skills
Identify political influences.

Reading Skills

Identifying Political Influences

"Saboteur" is set in contemporary China, long after the end of Mao's Cultural Revolution. However, the story critiques the oppressive conditions that continue to plague China. As you read the story, take note of symbols and characters that represent China's political heritage. What does Ha Jin seem to be saying about the fate of human rights in a society that is governed by force?

Background

In 1949, the Communists established the People's Republic of China under their military hero Mao Zedong (also spelled Mao Tse-tung). During Mao's Cultural Revolution, many political figures were removed from power, imprisoned, and sometimes executed. Today, China remains a communist nation, but it is gradually opening its doors to Western notions of human rights.

Vocabulary Development

coherent (kō·hir′ənt) *adj*.: logical; orderly; understandable.

propagating (präp′ə·gāt′iŋ) *v*.: publicizing; spreading.

induced (in·dōōst′) *v*.: caused.

contemptuously (kən·temp′chōō·əs·lē) *adv*.: with contempt or scorn.

precedent (pres′ə·dənt) *n*.: first occurrence of something that can later be used as an example or standard.

profusely (prō·fyōōs′lē) *adv*.: abundantly; excessively.

reactionary (rē·ak′shə·ner′ē) *adj*.: characterized by strong resistance to change or progress.

razed (rāzd) *v*.: torn down.

1090   Collection 7   The Modern World: 1900 to the Present

Previewing Vocabulary

Have students use the Vocabulary words to solve the following acrostic. Letters with double underlines spell a word that describes some of the characters in "Saboteur."

1. r _ _ _ _ _ o _ _ r _ (resistant to progress)
2. _ _ d _ c _ _ (caused)
3. _ o _ e _ _ _ t (logical)
4. _ r _ _ _ _ _ _ y (abundantly)
5. _ _ n _ _ _ p _ u _ _ s _ _ (with scorn)
6. p _ _ _ _ g _ _ _ _ g (spreading)
7. _ r _ c _ _ _ _ t (first example)
8. _ a _ _ d (torn down)

[1. reactionary   5. contemptuously
2. induced   6. propagating
3. coherent   7. precedent
4. profusely   8. razed

Hidden word: *inhumane*]

1090   Collection 7   The Modern World: 1900 to the Present

Saboteur

Ha Jin

Mr. Chiu and his bride were having lunch in the square before Muji Train Station.[1] On the table between them were two bottles of soda spewing out brown foam and two paper boxes of rice and sautéed cucumber and pork. "Let's eat," he said to her, and broke the connected ends of the chopsticks. He picked up a slice of streaky pork and put it into his mouth. As he was chewing, a few crinkles appeared on his thin jaw.

To his right, at another table, two railroad policemen were drinking tea and laughing; it seemed that the stout, middle-aged man was telling a joke to his young comrade, who was tall and of athletic build. Now and again they would steal a glance at Mr. Chiu's table.

The air smelled of rotten melon. A few flies kept buzzing above the couple's lunch. Hundreds of people were rushing around to get on the platform or to catch buses to downtown. Food and fruit vendors were crying for customers in lazy voices. About a dozen young women, representing the local hotels, held up placards which displayed the daily prices and words as large as a palm, like FREE MEALS, AIR-CONDITIONING, and ON THE RIVER. In the center of the square stood a concrete statue of Chairman Mao, at whose feet peasants were napping, their backs on the warm granite and their faces toward the sunny sky. A flock of pigeons perched on the Chairman's raised hand and forearm.

The rice and cucumber tasted good, and Mr. Chiu was eating unhurriedly. His sallow face showed exhaustion. He was glad that the honeymoon was finally over and that he and his bride were heading back for Harbin.[2] During the two weeks' vacation, he had been worried about his liver, because three months ago he had suffered from acute hepatitis;[3] he was afraid he might have a relapse. But he had had no severe symptoms, despite his liver being still big and tender. On the whole he was pleased with his health, which could endure even the strain of a honeymoon; indeed, he was on the course of recovery. He looked at his bride, who took off her wire glasses, kneading the root of her nose with her fingertips. Beads of sweat coated her pale cheeks.

"Are you all right, sweetheart?" he asked.

"I have a headache. I didn't sleep well last night."

"Take an aspirin, will you?"

"It's not that serious. Tomorrow is Sunday and I can sleep in. Don't worry."

As they were talking, the stout policeman at the next table stood up and threw a bowl of tea in their direction. Both Mr. Chiu's and his bride's sandals were wet instantly.

"Hooligan!" she said in a low voice.

Mr. Chiu got to his feet and said out loud, "Comrade Policeman, why did you do this?" He stretched out his right foot to show the wet sandal.

"Do what?" the stout man asked huskily, glaring at Mr. Chiu while the young fellow was whistling.

"See, you dumped tea on our feet."

"You're lying. You wet your shoes yourself."

"Comrade Policeman, your duty is to keep order, but you purposely tortured us common

---

1. **Muji Train Station:** train station in Muji City, a provincial town in central China.
2. **Harbin:** city in northeast China on the Songhua river.
3. **hepatitis** *n.*: disease marked by inflammation of the liver. It can be highly contagious.

DIRECT TEACHING

A Literary Focus

? Irony. What is ironic about the officer's calling Mr. Chiu a saboteur? [Possible responses: The other officer, not Mr. Chiu, is the offender. The police are the ones "disrupting public order" by baiting an innocent person and then pouncing on him when he protests.]

B Political Issue

? Human rights. How do the police violate Mr. Chiu's basic human rights? [Possible responses: They use brutality; they arrest him unjustly for criticizing an officer's bad manners.]

citizens. Why violate the law you are supposed to enforce?" As Mr. Chiu was speaking, dozens of people began gathering around.

With a wave of his hand, the man said to the young fellow, "Let's get hold of him!"

A They grabbed Mr. Chiu and clamped handcuffs around his wrists. He cried, "You can't do this to me. This is utterly unreasonable."

"Shut up!" The man pulled out his pistol. "You can use your tongue at our headquarters."

The young fellow added, "You're a saboteur, you know that? You're disrupting public order."

The bride was too petrified to say anything coherent. She was a recent college graduate, had majored in fine arts, and had never seen the police make an arrest. All she could say was, "Oh, please, please!"

The policemen were pulling Mr. Chiu, but he refused to go with them, holding the corner of the table and shouting, "We have a train to catch. We already bought the tickets."

The stout man punched him in the chest. "Shut up. Let your ticket expire." With the pistol **B** butt he chopped Mr. Chiu's hands, which at once released the table. Together the two men were dragging him away to the police station.

Realizing he had to go with them, Mr. Chiu turned his head and shouted to his bride, "Don't wait for me here. Take the train. If I'm not back by tomorrow morning, send someone over to get me out."

She nodded, covering her sobbing mouth with her palm.

Vocabulary

coherent (kō·hir′ənt) *adj.:* logical; orderly; understandable.

DIFFERENTIATING INSTRUCTION

Advanced Learners

Enrichment. Encourage students to learn more about China during the 1980s and 1990s and to share their findings as sources of additional insights into "Saboteur." They might research government, education, lifestyles, Communist Party membership, or details about the city of Harbin, Mr. Chiu's home.

After removing his belt, they locked Mr. Chiu into a cell in the back of the Railroad Police Station. The single window in the room was blocked by six bars; it faced a spacious yard, in which stood a few pines. Beyond the trees, two swings hung from an iron frame, swaying gently in the breeze. Somewhere in the building a cleaver was chopping rhythmically. There must be a kitchen upstairs, Mr. Chiu thought.

He was too exhausted to worry about what they would do to him, so he lay down on the narrow bed and shut his eyes. He wasn't afraid. The Cultural Revolution was over already, and recently the Party had been propagating the idea that all citizens were equal before the law. The police ought to be a law-abiding model for common people. As long as he remained cool-headed and reasoned with them, they probably wouldn't harm him.

Late in the afternoon he was taken to the Interrogation Bureau on the second floor. On his way there, in the stairwell, he ran into the middle-aged policeman who had manhandled him. The man grinned, rolling his bulgy eyes and pointing his fingers at him as if firing a pistol. Egg of a tortoise! Mr. Chiu cursed mentally.

The moment he sat down in the office, he burped, his palm shielding his mouth. In front of him, across a long desk, sat the chief of the bureau and a donkey-faced man. On the glass desktop was a folder containing information on his case. He felt it bizarre that in just a matter of hours they had accumulated a small pile of writing about him. On second thought he began to wonder whether they had kept a file on him all the time. How could this have happened? He lived and worked in Harbin, more than three hundred miles away, and this was his first time in Muji City.

The chief of the bureau was a thin, bald man who looked serene and intelligent. His slim hands handled the written pages in the folder in the manner of a lecturing scholar. To Mr. Chiu's left sat a young scribe, with a clipboard on his knee and a black fountain pen in his hand.

"Your name?" the chief asked, apparently reading out the question from a form.
"Chiu Maguang."
"Age?"
"Thirty-four."
"Profession?"
"Lecturer."
"Work unit?"
"Harbin University."
"Political status?"
"Communist Party member."

The chief put down the paper and began to speak. "Your crime is sabotage, although it hasn't induced serious consequences yet. Because you are a Party member, you should be punished more. You have failed to be a model for the masses and you—"

"Excuse me, sir," Mr. Chiu cut him off.
"What?"
"I didn't do anything. Your men are the saboteurs of our social order. They threw hot tea on my feet and on my wife's feet. Logically speaking, you should criticize them, if not punish them."

"That statement is groundless. You have no witness. Why should I believe you?" the chief said matter-of-factly.

"This is my evidence." He raised his right hand. "Your man hit my fingers with a pistol."

"That doesn't prove how your feet got wet. Besides, you could have hurt your fingers yourself."

"But I am telling the truth!" Anger flared up in Mr. Chiu. "Your police station owes me an apology. My train ticket has expired, my new leather sandals are ruined, and I am late for a conference in the provincial capital. You must compensate me for the damage and losses. Don't mistake me for a common citizen who would tremble when you sneeze. I'm a scholar, a philosopher, and an expert in dialectical

Vocabulary
propagating (präp′ə·gāt′iŋ) *v.:* publicizing; spreading.
induced (in·doost′) *v.:* caused; brought about.

CONTENT-AREA CONNECTIONS

Science: Hepatitis

Small-group activity. *Hepatitis* refers to any swelling of the liver. Acute viral hepatitis, the disease from which Mr. Chiu suffers, is caused by a contagious virus. Have interested students form groups to do research on hepatitis A, B, C, and D and report on symptoms, means of transmission, and treatment. After each group has reported, challenge the class to decide which form of viral hepatitis Mr. Chiu probably has.

DIRECT TEACHING

C Content-Area Connections

History: China's Cultural Revolution
The Cultural Revolution (1966–1976) was Mao Zedong's attempt to close the economic and social gap between peasants and urban professionals. He shut down schools and urged former students to join groups called Red Guards to "overturn the old order." Chaos and violence ensued as Red Guards persecuted intellectuals and professionals. Economic collapse followed, and Mao was forced to call in China's military to restore order. Distrust of intellectuals and of "bourgeois" lifestyles lingered, however.

D Reading Skills

Identifying political influences. To what two political influences does this sentence allude? [the Cultural Revolution and the Communist Party] What seems to be the effect of each on Mr. Chiu? [The sentence suggests that if the Cultural Revolution were still in force, Mr. Chiu would be afraid. He seems to believe that the Party's power is such that everyone must accept the ideas it promotes—then, he thinks, his rights will be respected.]

E Reading Skills

Identifying political influences. Mr. Chiu is a university lecturer—an intellectual. Why might he have felt fearful if the Cultural Revolution were still in progress? [During the revolution, intellectuals were prime targets for violence.]

F Literary Focus

Irony. Mr. Chiu holds fast to his belief that the police "owe" him an apology and "must" compensate him. How likely is it that events will turn out as he expects? [Possible response: Chances are slim. The policemen seem confident that they can use brutality without being held accountable.]

DIRECT TEACHING

A Literary Focus

? Irony. Apparently many people whom Mr. Chiu hadn't even noticed made statements against him. What might explain this surprising turn of events? [Possible responses: The witnesses missed part of the incident and assumed that Mr. Chiu was at fault; they truly believe that criticizing the police is wrong; the police pressured them; the police fabricated the statements.]

B Political Issue

? Human rights. The police declare Mr. Chiu guilty without a trial. Do you consider this a human rights violation? Why or why not? [Possible responses: Yes, because everyone deserves a fair chance to defend himself or herself. No, because it's just a minor incident, and the police do listen to him before dismissing his claims.]

C Literary Focus

? Irony. What threat might the chief's words and behavior imply? [Possible response: His actions—blowing smoke in Mr. Chiu's face and using sinister phrases such as "comply with our wishes"—hint at the possibility of further brutality.]

materialism. If necessary, we will argue about this in *The Northeastern Daily,* or we will go to the highest People's Court in Beijing. Tell me, what's your name?" He got carried away with his harangue,[4] which was by no means trivial and had worked to his advantage on numerous occasions.

"Stop bluffing us," the donkey-faced man broke in. "We have seen a lot of your kind. We can easily prove you are guilty. Here are some of the statements given by eyewitnesses." He pushed a few sheets of paper toward Mr. Chiu.

Mr. Chiu was dazed to see the different handwritings, which all stated that he had shouted in the square to attract attention and refused to obey the police. One of the witnesses had identified herself as a purchasing agent from a shipyard in Shanghai. Something stirred in Mr. Chiu's stomach, a pain rising to his rib. He gave out a faint moan.

"Now you have to admit you are guilty," the chief said. "Although it's a serious crime, we won't punish you severely, provided you write out a self-criticism and promise that you won't disrupt the public order again. In other words, your release will depend on your attitude toward this crime."

"You're daydreaming," Mr. Chiu cried. "I won't write a word, because I'm innocent. I demand that you provide me with a letter of apology so I can explain to my university why I'm late."

Both the interrogators smiled <u>contemptuously</u>. "Well, we've never done that," said the chief, taking a puff at his cigarette.

"Then make this a <u>precedent</u>."

"That's unnecessary. We are pretty certain that you will comply with our wishes." The chief blew a column of smoke toward Mr. Chiu's face.

At the tilt of the chief's head, two guards stepped forward and grabbed the criminal by the arms. Mr. Chiu meanwhile went on saying,

---

4. **harangue** *n.:* ranting speech.

"I shall report you to the Provincial Administration. You'll have to pay for this! You are worse than the Japanese military police."

They dragged him out of the room.

After dinner, which consisted of a bowl of millet[5] porridge, a corn bun, and a piece of pickled turnip, Mr. Chiu began to have a fever, shaking with a chill and sweating <u>profusely</u>. He knew that the fire of anger had gotten into his liver and that he was probably having a relapse. No medicine was available, because his briefcase had been left with his bride. At home it would have been time for him to sit in front of their color TV, drinking jasmine tea and watching the evening news. It was so lonesome in here. The orange bulb above the single bed was the only source of light, which enabled the guards to keep him under surveillance at night. A moment ago he had asked them for a newspaper or a magazine to read, but they turned him down.

Through the small opening on the door noises came in. It seemed that the police on duty were playing cards or chess in a nearby office; shouts and laughter could be heard now and then. Meanwhile, an accordion kept coughing from a remote corner in the building. Looking at the ballpoint and the letter paper left for him by the guards when they took him back from the Interrogation Bureau, Mr. Chiu remembered the old saying, "When a scholar runs into soldiers, the more he argues, the muddier his point becomes." How ridiculous this whole thing was. He ruffled his thick hair with his fingers.

---

5. **millet** *n.* used as *adj.:* grass cultivated for its grain.

Vocabulary

contemptuously (kən·temp′choo·əs·lē) *adv.:* with contempt or scorn.

precedent (pres′ə·dənt) *n.:* first occurrence of something that can later be used as an example or standard.

profusely (prō·fyoos′lē) *adv.:* abundantly; excessively.

1094 Collection 7 The Modern World: 1900 to the Present

CONTENT-AREA CONNECTIONS

Philosophy: Dialectical Materialism
Small-group activity. Mr. Chiu calls himself an expert on dialectical materialism, the philosophy developed by Karl Marx and Friedrich Engels. Invite interested students to research and report on dialectical materialism. Have them provide a definition, some background on dialectics, and a short explanation of Mao's application of dialectical materialism in building Communist China.

History: Mao Zedong
Small-group activity. Few national leaders have influenced the course of history, for better or worse, as much as China's Mao Zedong (1893–1976). Encourage interested students to present a biography of Mao. They might cover his early life, his rise to power, his defeat of the Kuomintang, his actions during World War II and the Korean War, the "Hundred Flowers" movement, the "Great Leap Forward," the Cultural Revolution, his death, and subsequent Chinese leaders' views on his leadership.

He felt miserable, massaging his stomach continually. To tell the truth, he was more upset than frightened, because he would have to catch up with his work once he was back home—a paper that was due at the printers next week, and two dozen books he ought to read for the courses he was going to teach in the fall.

A human shadow flitted across the opening. Mr. Chiu rushed to the door and shouted through the hole, "Comrade Guard, Comrade Guard!"

"What do you want?" a voice rasped.

"I want you to inform your leaders that I'm very sick. I have heart disease and hepatitis. I may die here if you keep me like this without medication."

"No leader is on duty on the weekend. You have to wait till Monday."

"What? You mean I'll stay in here tomorrow?"

"Yes."

"Your station will be held responsible if anything happens to me."

"We know that. Take it easy, you won't die."

It seemed illogical that Mr. Chiu slept quite well that night, though the light above his head had been on all the time and the straw mattress was hard and infested with fleas. He was afraid of ticks, mosquitoes, cockroaches—any kind of insect but fleas and bedbugs. Once, in the countryside, where his school's faculty and staff had helped the peasants harvest crops for a week, his colleagues had joked about his flesh, which they said must have tasted nonhuman to fleas. Except for him, they were all afflicted with hundreds of bites.

More amazing now, he didn't miss his bride a lot. He even enjoyed sleeping alone, perhaps because the honeymoon had tired him out and he needed more rest.

The backyard was quiet on Sunday morning. Pale sunlight streamed through the pine branches. A few sparrows were jumping on the ground, catching caterpillars and ladybugs. Holding the steel bars, Mr. Chiu inhaled the morning air, which smelled meaty. There must

Chinese soldiers blocking student demonstrators (1989).

have been an eatery or a cooked-meat stand nearby. He reminded himself that he should take this detention with ease. A sentence that Chairman Mao had written to a hospitalized friend rose in his mind: "Since you are already in here, you may as well stay and make the best of it."

His desire for peace of mind originated in his fear that his hepatitis might get worse. He tried to remain unperturbed. However, he was sure that his liver was swelling up, since the fever still persisted. For a whole day he lay in bed, thinking about his paper on the nature of contradictions. Time and again he was overwhelmed by anger,

DIRECT TEACHING

A Literary Focus

? Irony. Mr. Chiu still assumes that justice will prevail. Which details in the story suggest to you that it may not? [Possible responses: police indifference to his threats and complaints; the number of people who were willing to sign statements against him; the absence of help from the university so far.]

B Literary Focus

? Irony. What irony is there in Mrs. Chiu's choice of a rescuer for her husband? [Possible response: Fenjin was once Mr. Chiu's student; Fenjin has no power and can apparently be of little help; the police have already put him in a worse situation than Mr. Chiu is in.]

C Literary Focus

? Irony. How would you trace the changes in Mr. Chiu's feelings for his wife since the story opened? [Possible response: At first he seemed to care about her (he was concerned about her headache); the previous night he was indifferent; now he finds her useless and stupid.]

D Learners Having Difficulty

? Summarizing. Mr. Chiu faces an ethical dilemma. How would you summarize it? [Possible response: He doesn't want to get involved with Fenjin but feels that he must, since Fenjin came to help him.]

E Political Issue

? Human rights. What human rights violations do you find in the treatment of Fenjin? [Possible responses: He is chained, hit, tortured, denied protection from the elements and toilet facilities, and humiliated.]

---

cursing aloud, "A bunch of thugs!" He swore that once he was out, he would write an article about his experience. He had better find out some of the policemen's names.

A It turned out to be a restful day for the most part; he was certain that his university would send somebody to his rescue. All he should do now was remain calm and wait patiently. Sooner or later the police would have to release him, although they had no idea that he might refuse to leave unless they wrote him an apology. Damn those hoodlums, they had ordered more than they could eat!

When he woke up on Monday morning, it was already light. Somewhere a man was moaning; the sound came from the backyard. After a long yawn, and kicking off the tattered blanket, Mr. Chiu climbed out of bed and went to the window. In the middle of the yard, a young man was fastened to a pine, his wrists handcuffed around the trunk from behind. He was wriggling and swearing loudly, but there was no sight of anyone else in the yard. He looked familiar to Mr. Chiu.

Mr. Chiu squinted his eyes to see who it was. To his astonishment, he recognized the man, who was Fenjin, a recent graduate from the Law Department at Harbin University. Two years ago Mr. Chiu had taught a course in Marxist materialism, in which Fenjin had enrolled. Now, how on earth had this young devil landed here?

B Then it dawned on him that Fenjin must have been sent over by his bride. What a stupid **C** woman! A bookworm, who only knew how to read foreign novels! He had expected that she would contact the school's Security Section, which would for sure send a cadre⁶ here. Fenjin held no official position; he merely worked in a private law firm that had just two lawyers; in fact, they had little business except for some detective work for men and women who sus-

---

6. **cadre** *n*.: group of officers or personnel.

pected their spouses of having extramarital affairs. Mr. Chiu was overcome with a wave of nausea.

Should he call out to let his student know he was nearby? He decided not to, because he didn't know what had happened. Fenjin must **D** have quarreled with the police to incur such a punishment. Yet this could never have occurred if Fenjin hadn't come to his rescue. So no matter what, Mr. Chiu had to do something. But what could he do?

It was going to be a scorcher. He could see purple steam shimmering and rising from the ground among the pines. Poor devil, he thought, as he raised a bowl of corn glue⁷ to his mouth, sipped, and took a bite of a piece of salted celery.

When a guard came to collect the bowl and the chopsticks, Mr. Chiu asked him what had happened to the man in the backyard. "He called our boss 'bandit,'" the guard said. "He claimed he was a lawyer or something. An arrogant son of a rabbit."

Now it was obvious to Mr. Chiu that he had to do something to help his rescuer. Before he could figure out a way, a scream broke out in the backyard. He rushed to the window and saw a tall policeman standing before Fenjin, an iron bucket on the ground. It was the same young fellow who had arrested Mr. Chiu in the square two days before. The man pinched Fenjin's nose, then raised his hand, which stayed in the **E** air for a few seconds, then slapped the lawyer across the face. As Fenjin was groaning, the man lifted up the bucket and poured water on his head.

"This will keep you from getting sunstroke, boy. I'll give you some more every hour," the man said loudly.

Fenjin kept his eyes shut, yet his wry face showed that he was struggling to hold back from cursing the policeman, or, more likely, that he

---

7. **corn glue:** edible paste.

1096 Collection 7 The Modern World: 1900 to the Present

DEVELOPING FLUENCY

Individual activity. After students read "Saboteur," ask them to re-read it, this time assuming that Mr. Chiu symbolizes Chinese society and that his illness symbolizes the "ill effects" of decades of government-sanctioned brutality. Before they re-read, have students scan the text for the following:

- details about Mr. Chiu that make symbolic or metaphorical statements about the impact of human rights violations on society as a whole
- clues that foreshadow Mr. Chiu's behavior at the end of the story

was sobbing in silence. He sneezed, then raised his face and shouted, "Let me go take a piss."

"Oh yeah?" the man bawled. "Pee in your pants."

Still Mr. Chiu didn't make any noise, gripping the steel bars with both hands, his fingers white. The policeman turned and glanced at the cell's window; his pistol, partly holstered, glittered in the sun. With a snort he spat his cigarette butt to the ground and stamped it into the dust.

Then the door opened and the guards motioned Mr. Chiu to come out. Again they took him upstairs to the Interrogation Bureau.

The same men were in the office, though this time the scribe was sitting there empty-handed. At the sight of Mr. Chiu the chief said, "Ah, here you are. Please be seated."

After Mr. Chiu sat down, the chief waved a white silk fan and said to him, "You may have seen your lawyer. He's a young man without manners, so our director had him taught a crash course in the backyard."

"It's illegal to do that. Aren't you afraid to appear in a newspaper?"

"No, we are not, not even on TV. What else can you do? We are not afraid of any story you make up. We call it fiction. What we do care about is that you cooperate with us. That is to say, you must admit your crime."

"What if I refuse to cooperate?"

"Then your lawyer will continue his education in the sunshine."

A swoon swayed Mr. Chiu, and he held the arms of the chair to steady himself. A numb pain stung him in the upper stomach and nauseated him, and his head was throbbing. He was sure that the hepatitis was finally attacking him. Anger was flaming up in his chest; his throat was tight and clogged.

The chief resumed, "As a matter of fact, you don't even have to write out your self-criticism. We have your crime described clearly here. All we need is your signature."

Holding back his rage, Mr. Chiu said, "Let me look at that."

With a smirk the donkey-faced man handed him a sheet, which carried these words:

I hereby admit that on July 13 I disrupted public order at Muji Train Station, and that I refused to listen to reason when the railroad police issued their warning. Thus I myself am responsible for my arrest. After two days' detention, I have realized the reactionary nature of my crime. From now on, I shall continue to educate myself with all my effort and shall never commit this kind of crime again.

A voice started screaming in Mr. Chiu's ears, "Lie, lie!" But he shook his head and forced the voice away. He asked the chief, "If I sign this, will you release both my lawyer and me?"

"Of course, we'll do that." The chief was drumming his fingers on the blue folder—their file on him.

Mr. Chiu signed his name and put his thumbprint under his signature.

"Now you are free to go," the chief said with a smile, and handed him a piece of paper to wipe his thumb with.

Mr. Chiu was so sick that he couldn't stand up from the chair at first try. Then he doubled his effort and rose to his feet. He staggered out of the building to meet his lawyer in the backyard, having forgotten to ask for his belt back. In his chest he felt as though there were a bomb. If he were able to, he would have razed the entire police station and eliminated all their families. Though he knew he could do nothing like that, he made up his mind to do something.

"I'm sorry about this torture, Fenjin," Mr. Chiu said when they met.

Vocabulary

reactionary (rē·ak′shə·ner′ē) *adj.*: characterized by strong resistance to change or progress.
razed (rāzd) *v.*: torn down.

DIRECT TEACHING

A Content-Area Connections
Social Studies: International Cuisine
Tree ears, a kind of mushroom that grows on tree trunks, are an Asian delicacy.

B Literary Focus
❓ Irony. Mr. Chiu's hepatitis has turned his face yellowish, blotchy, and "ugly." In what ways is his behavior also ugly? [Possible responses: He seems possessed by spite and thoughts of revenge; he grits his teeth, snarls, and mutters imprecations.]

C Advanced Learners
❓ Enrichment. In your opinion, how much responsibility do the Muji railroad police bear for the hepatitis deaths? [Possible responses: None—Mr. Chiu is solely responsible for his own actions. Some—if they had not brutalized Mr. Chiu and Fenjin, Mr. Chiu would not have turned vengeful and spread his hepatitis.]

GUIDED PRACTICE

Monitoring students' progress. Guide students in making two lists: one of injustices done to Mr. Chiu, and one of injustices that Mr. Chiu commits. [Injustices done to Mr. Chiu: He is arrested on a trumped-up charge, brutalized, denied medical care, denied a fair hearing, denied compensation for losses, and forced to sign a false confession. Injustices Mr. Chiu commits: He purposely spreads a life-threatening illness; he indirectly kills four adults and two children.]

"It doesn't matter. They are savages." The lawyer brushed a patch of dirt off his jacket with trembling fingers. Water was still dribbling from the bottoms of his trouser legs.

"Let's go now," the teacher said.

The moment they came out of the police station, Mr. Chiu caught sight of a tea stand. He grabbed Fenjin's arm and walked over to the old woman at the table. "Two bowls of black tea," he said and handed her a one-yuan note.

After the first bowl, they each had another one. Then they set out for the train station. But before they walked fifty yards, Mr. Chiu insisted on eating a bowl of tree-ear soup at a food stand. Fenjin agreed. He told his teacher, "You mustn't treat me like a guest."

"No, I want to eat something myself."

As if dying of hunger, Mr. Chiu dragged his lawyer from restaurant to restaurant near the police station, but at each place he ordered no more than two bowls of food. Fenjin wondered why his teacher wouldn't stay at one place and eat his fill.

Mr. Chiu bought noodles, wonton, eight-grain porridge, and chicken soup, respectively, at four restaurants. While eating, he kept saying through his teeth, "If only I could kill all the bastards!" At the last place he merely took a few sips of the soup without tasting the chicken cubes and mushrooms.

Fenjin was baffled by his teacher, who looked ferocious and muttered to himself mysteriously, and whose jaundiced[8] face was covered with dark puckers. For the first time Fenjin thought of Mr. Chiu as an ugly man.

Within a month over eight hundred people contracted acute hepatitis in Muji. Six died of the disease, including two children. Nobody knew how the epidemic had started. ∎

---

8. **jaundiced** *adj.*: spiteful; also, yellowish pigment of the skin caused by disease, often of the liver (in this case, hepatitis).

FAMILY/COMMUNITY ACTIVITY

You might invite a local expert on disease control to visit the class and discuss precautions your community takes to guard against outbreaks of viral hepatitis. Encourage students to summarize "Saboteur" for your guest and to ask him or her about the likelihood that actions such as Mr. Chiu's could start a deadly epidemic.

Response and Analysis

Reading Check

1. With whom is Mr. Chiu dining in the Muji train station?
2. Describe the incident that leads to a conflict between Mr. Chiu and the nearby policemen.
3. From what ailment does Mr. Chiu suffer?
4. Why does Mr. Chiu finally sign the statement of his guilt?
5. How does Mr. Chiu exact revenge for the injustice done to him?

Thinking Critically

6. The central **irony** in this story—the difference between what should and what does happen—revolves around an injustice done to the main character. Explain what this irony is. How does the end of the story reveal yet another irony and yet another injustice?
7. Prior to the incident in the train station, do you find Mr. Chiu to be a sympathetic character? Why or why not?
8. Throughout most of his ordeal, Mr. Chiu remains optimistic that justice will prevail. Provide two or three examples of this attitude. How does Mr. Chiu's optimism help create the story's ominous **mood**?
9. What might the statue of Chairman Mao, described early in the story, represent? Might this symbol serve an **ironic** purpose in the story? Explain why or why not.
10. How, in your opinion, did the political history of China influence the plot or the characters of "Saboteur"? (Review your reading notes, the biography of Ha Jin on page 1089, and the information in the Background on page 1090 before you respond.) What message or **theme** about politics and human rights can be drawn from the story?

WRITING

You Can Never Go Home Again

Re-read the second-to-last paragraph of the story. Then, imagine that you are Mr. Chiu on the evening that he returns to his home and his new bride. Write a **journal entry** that describes what has happened to you and that also reflects how you have been changed by the experience.

Vocabulary Development
Synonyms and Antonyms

In items 1–4 below, choose the best **synonym** for each capitalized Vocabulary word. In items 5–8, choose the best **antonym**. Write your answers on a separate sheet of paper.

Synonyms

1. COHERENT: (a) brief (b) logical (c) disorganized (d) creative
2. PROPAGATING: (a) spreading (b) adding (c) concealing (d) beginning
3. PRECEDENT: (a) example (b) requirement (c) presentation (d) award
4. REACTIONARY: (a) influential (b) excessive (c) sudden (d) resistant

Antonyms

5. INDUCED: (a) admitted (b) caused (c) intimidated (d) halted
6. CONTEMPTUOUSLY: (a) angrily (b) sorrowfully (c) kindly (d) heartily
7. PROFUSELY: (a) loudly (b) scarcely (c) suspiciously (d) delicately
8. RAZED: (a) comforted (b) stunned (c) erected (d) interfered

SKILLS FOCUS

Literary Skills Analyze political points of view on a topic. Analyze irony.

Reading Skills Identify political influences.

Writing Skills Write a journal entry.

Vocabulary Skills Use synonyms and antonyms.

Ha Jin 1099

INDEPENDENT PRACTICE

Response and Analysis

8. Mr. Chiu's optimism lets him demand apologies, relax in his cell, and trust that the university will send rescuers. It reinforces the ominous mood by underscoring the difference between the way things should be and the way they actually are.
9. The statue of Mao with the peasants leaning against it may represent people being protected by his regime. The symbol serves an ironic purpose: Mao's oppressive policies cause people to be brutalized.
10. Possible answer: China's suppression of human rights underlies the nonchalant police brutality and the outrage that causes Chiu to act cruelly. Unfair police tactics sabotage Chiu's humanity, and he in turn sabotages the health of a population. Possible themes: Inhumane treatment causes inhumane behavior; a political system that suppresses human rights erodes its citizens' capacity for compassion.

Vocabulary Development

1. b   4. d   7. b
2. a   5. d   8. c
3. a   6. c

ASSESSING

Assessment
- *Holt Assessment: Literature, Reading, and Vocabulary*

Reading Check

1. He is with his bride.
2. One officer dumps his leftover tea, soaking the Chius' new sandals.
3. He suffers from hepatitis.
4. He signs it to spare his young lawyer further torture.
5. He purposely starts a hepatitis epidemic.

Thinking Critically

6. The central irony is the difference between the way the police should treat Mr. Chiu—protecting his rights—and the unjust, brutal way they do treat him. In another irony at the end of the story, Mr. Chiu becomes a "saboteur" because of the false charges of sabotage leveled against him.
7. Some students will find Mr. Chiu unsympathetic because he seems concerned more about his liver than about his bride. Some students may find him sympathetic, noting that he is concerned about his bride's headache and at first protests reasonably to the police about their actions.

Connected Reading

Summary ⇔ at grade level

The Preamble to the United Nations' 1948 "Universal Declaration of Human Rights" states why the Declaration is needed: Granting every human being equal rights is a vital prerequisite to achieving world peace, freedom, and social and economic progress. These rights must be specified, protected by law, promoted through education, and supported by all UN member nations.

Selection Starter

Build background. Eleanor Roosevelt (1884–1962) chaired the UN Commission on Human Rights from 1946 to 1951. A social activist since her high school years, she became one of America's most respected and effective advocates for the causes of racial and gender equality and humanitarian aid to the destitute. Her energetic leadership helped to shape the Declaration of Human Rights, and it was largely due to her efforts that the UN member nations adopted the Declaration unanimously.

Today, the UN Commission on Human Rights attempts to ensure human rights worldwide and to monitor complaints of human rights violations. The Commission is not empowered to send peacekeeping troops to protect human rights; it can rely only on the impact of international publicity. The Commission does, however, have the power to hold International Criminal Tribunals for war crimes.

Connected Readings

United Nations Commission on Human Rights .... *from the* **Universal Declaration of Human Rights**
Desmond Tutu .... *from* **The Question of South Africa**
Aung San Suu Ky .... *from* **Towards a True Refuge**

You have just read Ha Jin's short story "Saboteur" and considered the ways in which societies and individuals can be shaped by the denial of human rights. The next three selections you will read also make strong statements about the inherent rights of human beings—and the crucial need for respecting those rights. As you read, ask yourself how the insights presented in these selections are alike and different from Ha Jin's. After you read, you'll find questions on page 1110 asking you to compare all four selections.

Political Points *of* View

Before You Read

In the years following World War II, a movement to recognize and clarify the inalienable rights of human beings began to gather force. This movement was propelled by the horror people felt as they discovered the atrocities that had been committed against millions of innocent people in Nazi Germany. But who would address the issue of human rights? What group or nation could assume such a huge responsibility? With the formation of the United Nations in 1945, the creation of a universal statement of human rights became a possibility. Under the guidance of this organization—and, more specifically, of the U.S. First Lady Eleanor Roosevelt, Chairperson of the UN Commission on Human Rights—such a document was formulated, revised, and finally adopted by the UN General Assembly on December 10, 1948.

The Preamble to the United Nations' Universal Declaration of Human Rights appears on page 1101. You will notice that the Preamble consists of a series of statements beginning "Whereas. . . ." These statements provide a rationale for the declaration; that is, they say *why* such a declaration is necessary. After the Preamble comes a list (which does not appear with this selection) of thirty articles that specify the rights of all humans, in all times and in all countries. The thirty articles address such specific human rights issues as equal protection under the law, the prohibition of slavery, the right to be "presumed innocent until proved guilty," and the right to "freedom of thought, conscience, and religion," among many other rights. The document, which celebrated its fiftieth anniversary in 1998, continues to guide the leaders of nations as they envision and try to realize a world characterized by peace, justice, and unity.

United Nations, New York.

POLITICAL STATEMENT

from the Universal Declaration of Human Rights

United Nations Commission on Human Rights

Preamble

Whereas recognition of the inherent dignity and of the equal and inalienable rights of all members of the human family is the foundation of freedom, justice and peace in the world,

Whereas disregard and contempt for human rights have resulted in barbarous acts which have outraged the conscience of mankind, and the advent of a world in which human beings shall enjoy freedom of speech and belief and freedom from fear and want has been proclaimed as the highest aspiration of the common people, ❶

Whereas it is essential, if man is not to be compelled to have recourse, as a last resort, to rebellion against tyranny and oppression, that human rights should be protected by the rule of law, ❷

Whereas it is essential to promote the development of friendly relations between nations,

Whereas the people of the United Nations have in the Charter reaffirmed their faith in fundamental human rights, in the dignity and worth of the human person and in the equal rights of men and women and have determined to promote social progress and better standards of life in larger freedom, ❸

Whereas Member States° have pledged themselves to achieve, in co-operation with the United Nations, the promotion of universal respect for and observance of human rights and fundamental freedoms,

Whereas a common understanding of these rights and freedoms is of the greatest importance for the full realization of this pledge, ❹

° **Member States:** When the United Nations was formed in 1945, there were fifty-one member states. As of 2000, there were 189.

Margin questions:

❶ What assumptions about human needs and desires underlie these two opening paragraphs? What freedoms are identified as fundamental to human rights?

❷ Why is it "essential" to protect human rights through law?

❸ What values and goals does the Charter of the United Nations set forth?

❹ What have the Member States pledged? What is identified here as most important for the "full realization" of this pledge?

DIRECT TEACHING

Ⓐ Political Issue

❓ Human rights. Why is it crucial, according to this document, to recognize that every human being has equal rights? [There can be no freedom, justice, or world peace until universal human rights are recognized.]

Ⓑ Reading Skills

❓ Identifying political influences. World War II raged from 1939 to 1945; this document was written between 1946 and 1948. To what wartime atrocities does the term "barbarous acts which have outraged the conscience of mankind" most likely allude? [the Holocaust; Japanese war crimes in China.]

Responses to Margin Questions

1. The opening assumes that people are created equal and have certain basic human rights. Identified as fundamental are freedom of speech, freedom of belief, freedom from fear, and freedom from want.

2. Legal recourse is essential to prevent desperate people from resorting to violence when human rights are violated.

3. Values include faith in basic human rights, in the worth of each person, and in the equality of men and women. Goals include social progress, improved standards of living, and greater freedom.

4. Member States have pledged to promote "universal respect for and observance of human rights and fundamental freedoms." Most important is "a common understanding of these rights and freedoms."

DIFFERENTIATING INSTRUCTION

Learners Having Difficulty

Modeling. You might have students read the Preamble's last clause first (p. 1102), beginning with "*Now, Therefore,* THE GENERAL ASSEMBLY *proclaims*...." Model the reading skill of paraphrasing this clause by saying, "The General Assembly has decided that everyone should teach, observe, and respect these basic rights and freedoms for all human beings." Then, remind students that the seven introductory clauses, each beginning with "Whereas," list the reasons for the General Assembly's decision. Encourage students to paraphrase each of these clauses. (Each paraphrase might begin with "Because.")

DIRECT TEACHING

Response to Margin Question

5. Human rights can be achieved through education that promotes respect for these rights and through the "progressive measures" of UN Member States to "secure their recognition and observance" in their own countries and in territories under their control.

Connected Reading

Summary ⬌ *at grade level*

> In this 1984 speech to the UN Security Council, Desmond Tutu draws an ironic contrast between the beauty and bounty of South Africa and the brutal human rights violations that are a part of daily life under apartheid; he eloquently asks the Security Council's help in ending apartheid and minimizing the violence that seems almost inevitable.

More About the Writer

Background. In 1995, Desmond Tutu resigned as Archbishop of Cape Town to chair the Truth and Reconciliation Commission, established by the newly restructured post-apartheid government to investigate human rights violations under apartheid. Commission members pledged to recommend reparations for atrocities and to consider amnesty for anyone who confessed to committing them. Tutu presided over two years of testimony from victims and offenders, learning that atrocities had been committed by all major political organizations and even a former South African president. Despite opposition, Tutu kept the humanitarian promise of amnesty.

Now, Therefore,
THE GENERAL ASSEMBLY
proclaims

THIS UNIVERSAL DECLARATION OF HUMAN RIGHTS as a common standard of achievement for all peoples and all nations, to the end that every individual and every organ of society, keeping this Declaration constantly in mind, shall strive by teaching and education to promote respect for these rights and freedoms and by progressive measures, national and international, to secure their universal and effective recognition and observance, both among the peoples of Member States themselves and among the peoples of territories under their jurisdiction. ❺

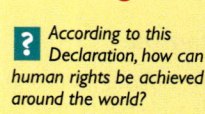

❺ According to this Declaration, how can human rights be achieved around the world?

Political Points *of* View

Before You Read

Desmond Tutu (opposite page) is one of the best-known civil rights leaders in the world. He was born in 1931 in Klerksdorp, South Africa, not far from the South African capital of Johannesburg. Under South Africa's strict racial segregation policy, known as apartheid (ə·pär′tāt′), Tutu was educated in all-black schools. He later received a bachelor's degree in arts from the University of South Africa and, after teaching for a short while, entered the Anglican ministry. Tutu was ordained in 1961 and went on to become the first black archbishop of Capetown—the head of the Anglican Church in South Africa.

From this position of leadership, Tutu worked to end apartheid and to create a just South African government. He met with world leaders and asked them to restrict their business dealings with South Africa. These negotiations created international pressure on South Africa to abolish its unjust racial laws. Gradually and painfully, the laws of apartheid were dismantled by the end of 1991.

In 1984, in the midst of his crusade, Tutu was awarded the Nobel Peace Prize. Tutu gave the speech that begins on the next page to the United Nations Security Council shortly after receiving the prestigious award.

SPEECH

from The Question of South Africa
Desmond Tutu

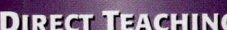

I speak out of a full heart, for I am about to speak about a land that I love deeply and passionately; a beautiful land of rolling hills and gurgling streams, of clear starlit skies, of singing birds, and gamboling lambs; a land God has richly endowed with the good things of the earth, a land rich in mineral deposits of nearly every kind; a land of vast open spaces, enough to accommodate all its inhabitants comfortably; a land capable of feeding itself and other lands on the beleaguered[1] continent of Africa, a veritable breadbasket; a land that could contribute wonderfully to the material and spiritual development and prosperity of all Africa and indeed of the whole world. It is endowed with enough to satisfy the material and spiritual needs of all its peoples.

And so we would expect that such a land, veritably flowing with milk and honey, should be a land where peace and harmony and contentment reigned supreme. Alas, the opposite is the case. For my beloved country is wracked by division, by alienation, by animosity, by separation, by injustice, by avoidable pain and suffering. It is a deeply fragmented society, ridden by fear and anxiety, covered by a pall of despondency and a sense of desperation, split up into hostile, warring factions.

It is a highly volatile[2] land, and its inhabitants sit on a powder keg with a very short fuse indeed, ready to blow us all up into kingdom come. There is endemic[3] unrest, like a festering sore that will not heal until not just the symptoms are treated but the root causes are removed.

South African society is deeply polarized. Nothing illustrates this more sharply than the events of the past week. While the black community was in the seventh heaven of delight because of the decision of that committee in Oslo, and while the world was congratulating the recipient of the Nobel Peace Prize[4], the white government and most white South Africans, very sadly, were seeking to devalue that prize. An event that should have been the occasion of uninhibited joy and thanksgiving revealed a sadly divided society.

1. How does Tutu describe the social and political conditions in South Africa? Why are these conditions "opposite" to what one might expect to find?

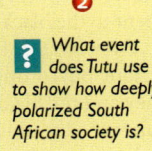

2. What event does Tutu use to show how deeply polarized South African society is?

Before I came to this country in early September to go on sabbatical, I visited one of the trouble spots near Johannesburg.... In this black township, we met an old lady who told us that she was looking after her grandchildren and the children of neighbors while they were at work. On the day about which she was speaking, the police had been chasing black schoolchildren in that street, but the children had eluded the police, who then drove down the street past the old lady's house. Her wards[5] were playing in front of

---

1. **beleaguered** adj.: stressed; threatened.
2. **volatile** adj.: explosive.
3. **endemic** adj.: native.
4. **committee ... Prize:** The committee is the Nobel Committee and the recipient is Tutu himself.
5. **wards** n. pl.: children who have been placed in the care of others because their parents are dead or incapable of caring for them.

DIRECT TEACHING

A Literary Focus

Irony. What nonviolent techniques are black students and miners using to protest apartheid? [Students are boycotting school; miners are striking from work.] What is the ironic result of these nonviolent protests? [Many boycotters and strikers have been killed.]

B Reading Skills

Identifying political influences. The "road of reform" that Tutu alludes to was Prime Minister P. W. Botha's policy of making limited changes to the government while maintaining apartheid. In 1984, Botha opened the previously all-white national parliament to Asian and mixed-race representatives—but not to blacks, who make up a majority of the population.

C Literary Focus

Irony. Notice Tutu's humorously ironic understatement describing himself: ". . . a bishop in the church, some would say reasonably responsible. . . ." What effect might this humor have on his listeners? [Possible response: It wins their sympathy by revealing the absurdity of his plight.]

Responses to Boxed Questions

3. Tutu's examples include the murder of a black child, a white infant, and black officials. Tutu shows fairness in deploring the violent deaths of both blacks and whites.

4. Contributing problems include high unemployment caused by drought and a worldwide recession, and the government's increasing the prices of food and rent in black townships.

5. The world is not taking action because there are not large numbers of "casualties" at any one time. The "root cause" he identifies is the policy of apartheid.

---

the house, in the yard. She was sitting in the kitchen at the back, when her daughter burst in, calling agitatedly for her. She rushed out into the living room. A grandson had fallen just inside the door, dead. The police had shot him in the back. He was six years old. Recently, a baby, a few weeks old, became the first white casualty of the current uprisings. Every death is one too many. Those whom the black community has identified as collaborators with a system that oppresses them and denies them the most elementary human rights have met cruel death, which we deplore as much as any others. They have rejected these people operating within the system, whom they have seen as lackies[6] and stooges, despite their titles of town councilors, and so on, under an apparently new dispensation[7] extending the right of local government to the blacks. **③**

> **③** What tragic examples does Tutu use here to illustrate that his nation is "a sadly divided society"? How can you tell that Tutu is fair to both sides?

Over 100,000 black students are out of school, boycotting—as they did in 1976—what they and the black community perceive as an inferior education designed deliberately for inferiority. An already highly volatile situation has been ignited several times and, as a result, over 80 persons have died. There has been industrial unrest, with the first official strike by black miners taking place, not without its toll of fatalities among the blacks.

Some may be inclined to ask: But why should all this unrest be taking place just when the South African government appears to have embarked on the road of reform? . . .

There is little freedom in this land of plenty. There is little freedom to disagree with the determinations of the authorities. There is large-scale unemployment because of the drought and the recession that has hit most of the world's economy. And it is at such a time that the authorities have increased the prices of various foodstuffs and also of rents in black townships—measures designed to hit hardest those least able to afford the additional costs. It is not surprising that all this has exacerbated an already tense and volatile situation. **④**

> **④** What problems contribute to the "tense and volatile situation"?

So the unrest is continuing, in a kind of war of attrition, with the casualties not being large enough at any one time to shock the world sufficiently for it to want to take action against the system that is the root cause of all this agony. We have warned consistently that unrest will be endemic in South Africa until its root cause is removed. And the root cause is apartheid—a vicious, immoral and totally evil, and unchristian system. . . . **⑤**

> **⑤** According to Tutu, why isn't the world doing anything about the situation in his country? What does he identify as the "root cause" of his country's ills?

As blacks we often run the gauntlet of roadblocks on roads leading into our townships, and these have been manned by the army in what are actually described as routine police operations. When you use the army in this fashion, who is the enemy?

The authorities have not stopped stripping blacks of their South African citizenship. Here I am, 53 years old, a bishop in the church, some would say reasonably responsible; I travel on a document that says of my nationality that it is "undeterminable at present." The South African government is turning us into aliens in the land of our birth. It continues unabated with its vicious policy of forced population removals. It is threatening to remove the people of Kwa

---

6. **lackies** *n. pl.*: submissive followers.
7. **dispensation** *n.*: an exemption from an impediment.

1104 Collection 7 The Modern World: 1900 to the Present

DEVELOPING FLUENCY

Mixed-ability group activity. This excerpt from "The Question of South Africa" is a powerful choice for choral reading. Written to be spoken, it gains its fullest impact from oral presentation. First, ask the class as a whole to identify natural breaks in the speech and to group the sixteen paragraphs into three to five main sections. Then, divide students into mixed-ability groups, assigning one section to each group. Have groups practice reading their sections aloud, deciding how to most effectively emphasize rhythms and parallel structures. Finally, have groups perform their sections, in order, in a class presentation.

Archbishop Desmond Tutu (1986).

Ngema. It treats carelessly the women in the KTC squatter camp near Cape Town[8] whose flimsy plastic coverings are destroyed every day by the authorities; and the heinous crime of those women is that they want to be with their husbands, with the fathers of their children. **6**

White South Africans are not demons; they are ordinary human beings, scared human beings, many of them; who would not be, if they were outnumbered five to one? Through this lofty body I wish to appeal to my white fellow South Africans to share in building a new society, for blacks are not intent on driving whites into the sea but on claiming only their rightful place in the sun in the land of their birth.

We deplore all forms of violence, the violence of an oppressive and unjust society and the violence of those seeking to overthrow that society, for we believe that violence is not the answer to the crisis of our land.

We dream of a new society that will be truly nonracial, truly democratic, in which people count because they are created in the image of God. **7**

> **6** What examples does Tutu use to show that the South African government is turning its black population into "aliens" in their own country?

> **7** How can you tell that Tutu wants justice and fairness for both sides? How does he try to assure white South Africans that he is not advocating a violent overthrow of their rule?

---

8. KTC squatter camp near Cape Town: Cape Town is a city on the southwestern coast of South Africa; the KTC squatter camp was where low-paid black South Africans, unable to afford real homes, were obliged to live in flimsy shacks. These shacks were divided by gender.

DIRECT TEACHING

D Advanced Learners

Enrichment. Tutu selectively repeats the word *violence*. What effect does this repetition create? [Possible response: It emphasizes the prevalence of violence in South Africa.]

Responses to Boxed Questions

6. Tutu cites denials of people's right to travel freely by citing the stripping of his own citizenship; he gives examples of the government's forced population removals and the destruction of shelters for poor blacks.

7. Tutu sympathizes with the fears of whites who are outnumbered five to one, and he deplores the violence committed by both sides. He invites all South Africans to join in creating a new, nonracial society.

CONTENT-AREA CONNECTIONS

Political Science: The UN Versus Apartheid

Every year, beginning in 1952, the UN General Assembly urged South Africa to end racial discrimination. After a 1960 police massacre of anti-apartheid demonstrators, the UN imposed sanctions on South Africa, and in 1974 it suspended South Africa from the General Assembly. Still, the UN stopped short of calling for international boycotts or pressuring South Africa to accept the presence of peacekeeping forces.

Small-group activity. Suggest that interested students research information about the efforts of the UN and the international community in the 1970s and 1980s to oppose apartheid. They might also explore the effectiveness of Desmond Tutu's speech in spurring the UN to stronger action. Have students share their findings with the class.

DIRECT TEACHING

Response to Boxed Question

8. Tutu is asking the Security Council to pressure the South African government to formally negotiate with opponents of apartheid. His ultimate hope is to end apartheid and create a new society through peaceful means.

Connected Reading

Summary ⇔ *at grade level*

> In this speech, Suu Kyi shows why peace and prosperity must begin with protecting human rights and educating people to value dialogue, compromise, and altruism.

More About the Writer

Background. Aung San Suu Kyi (soo·che) left Myanmar at fifteen when her mother became ambassador to India. In high school in New Delhi, Suu Kyi studied the nonviolent philosophy of Gandhi; years later, she would meld this with the tenets of Buddhism to guide her National League for Democracy (NLD) in Myanmar. First, however, she earned a degree from Oxford, worked in the UN, and began graduate studies. Her mother's illness recalled her to Myanmar in 1988, just before dictator Ne Win resigned. Suu Kyi began pressing for open elections and founded the NLD. The military group that seized power soon arrested her but could not silence her. Her husband, British scholar Michael Aris, published a collection of her writings, *Freedom From Fear*, in 1991. In the same year, since she was still under house arrest, her teenage sons accepted her Nobel Peace Prize and delivered her acceptance speech. In May 2002, Myanmar's military government granted Aung San Suu Kyi freedom to travel both within and outside her country.

We are committed to work for justice, for peace, and for reconciliation. We ask you, please help us; urge the South African authorities to go to the conference table with the . . . representatives of all sections of our community. I appeal to this body to act. I appeal in the name of the ordinary, the little people of South Africa. I appeal in the name of the squatters in crossroads and in the KTC camp. I appeal on behalf of the father who has to live in a single-sex hostel as a migrant worker, separated from his family for 11 months of the year. I appeal on behalf of the students who have rejected this travesty of education made available only for blacks. I appeal on behalf of those who are banned arbitrarily, who are banished, who are detained without trial, those imprisoned because they have had a vision of this new South Africa. I appeal on behalf of those who have been exiled from their homes.

I say we will be free, and we ask you: Help us, that this freedom comes for all of us in South Africa, black and white, but that it comes with the least possible violence, that it comes peacefully, that it comes soon. **8**

> **8** What is Tutu asking of the United Nations Security Council? What is his ultimate hope for his country?

Political Points *of* View

Before You Read

Aung San Suu Kyi (opposite page) is the leader of the pro-democracy movement in the southeast Asian nation of Myanmar (formerly Burma). Her father, General Aung San Kyi, fought for Burmese independence from Great Britain in the 1940s and was assassinated in 1947. Like her father, Aung San Suu Kyi has been persecuted as an opponent of an established government.

After studying at Oxford University, marrying, and living in England for many years, she returned to Myanmar in 1988 and began to agitate for political reform. In that year the State Law and Order Restoration Council (SLORC), a militant, dictatorial body, seized control of the Burmese government. Since then SLORC has used force and suppression to govern and control the Burmese people

Living conditions in Myanmar are among the worst in the world, and poverty is rampant. Four out of ten children are malnourished and according to the United Nations, the government spends only twenty-eight cents per student in public schools. The SLORC is also known to use slave labor, including children, for public projects. Many of its laws are explicitly designed to strip individuals of their rights. It is illegal, for example, for people to gather in groups larger than four or even to own a computer.

In 1990, SLORC allowed general elections, but when Aung San Suu Kyi's party won, the government refused to acknowledge the results. Aung San Suu Kyi had been placed under house arrest shortly before the election, and she remained a captive until 1995. During the years of her confinement, when she was unable to leave her home or see her family, she wrote many books and speeches promoting democracy, human rights, and world peace. She received the Nobel Peace Prize in 1991. The following excerpt is taken from a speech written by Aung San Suu Kyi during her house arrest. It was delivered by her husband at Oxford University in 1993.

1106 Collection 7 The Modern World: 1900 to the Present

Primary Source

Aung San Suu Kyi: More About "Towards a True Refuge"

Suu Kyi wrote this speech for an Oxford University meeting on issues relating to refugees. In her introductory remarks, she explains the title of the speech:

"[T]he Burmese expression for *refugee* is *dukkha-the*, 'one who has to bear *dukkha*, suffering.' In that sense, none of us can avoid knowing what it is to be a refugee. The refuge we all seek is protection from forces which wrench us away from the security and comfort, physical and mental, which give dignity and meaning to human existence."

SPEECH

from Towards a True Refuge
Aung San Suu Kyi

It is perfectly natural that all people should wish for a secure refuge. It is unfortunate that in spite of strong evidence to the contrary, so many still act as though security would be guaranteed if they fortified themselves with an abundance of material possessions. The greatest threats to global security today come not from the economic deficiencies of the poorest nations but from religious, racial (or tribal) and political dissensions raging in those regions where principles and practices which could reconcile the diverse instincts and aspirations of mankind have been ignored, repressed or distorted. ❶ Man-made disasters are made by dominant individuals and cliques which refuse to move beyond the autistic[1] confines of partisan[2] interest. An eminent development economist has observed that the best defense against famine is an accountable government. It makes little political or economic sense to give aid without trying to address the circumstances that render aid ineffectual. No amount of material goods and technological know-how will compensate for human irresponsibility and viciousness. ❷

Developed and developing nations alike suffer as a result of policies removed from a framework of values which uphold minimum standards of justice and tolerance. The rapidity with which the old Soviet Union splintered into new states, many of them stamped with a fierce racial assertiveness, illustrates that decades of authoritarian rule may have achieved uniformity and obedience but could not achieve long-term harmony or stability. Nor did the material benefits enjoyed under the relatively successful post-totalitarian state of Yugoslavia succeed in dissipating the psychological impress of brooding historical experience that has now led to some of the worst religious and ethnic violence the Balkans[3] have ever witnessed. Peace, stability and unity cannot be bought or coerced; they have to be nurtured by promoting a sensitivity to human needs and respect for the rights and opinions of others. Diversity and dissent need not inhibit the emergence of strong, stable societies, but inflexibility, narrowness and unadulterated materialism can prevent healthy growth. And when attitudes have been allowed to harden to the point that otherness becomes a sufficient reason for nullifying[4] a person's claim to be treated as a fellow human being, the trappings of modern civilization crumble with frightening speed. ❸

In the most troubled areas of the world reserves of tolerance and compassion disappear,

> ❶ What does Aung San Suu Kyi identify as the "greatest threats to global security today"?

> ❷ According to Aung San Suu Kyi, why is simply giving material aid to a nation ultimately ineffective?

> ❸ Identify the problem that plagues both developing and developed nations. How can "peace, stability, and unity" ultimately be achieved? What can cause a civilization to "crumble"?

---
1. **autistic** *adj.*: in this context, "self-centered."
2. **partisan** *adj.*: factional; biased.
3. **Balkans:** countries occupying the Balkan Peninsula in southeastern Europe.
4. **nullifying** *v.*: invalidating; canceling.

security becomes nonexistent and creature comforts are reduced to a minimum—but stockpiles of weapons abound. As a system of values this is totally mad. By the time it is accepted that the only way out of an impasse[5] of hate, bloodshed and social and economic chaos created by men is for those men to get together to find a peaceful solution through dialogue and compromise, it is usually no longer easy to restore sanity. Those who have been conditioned by systems which make a mockery of the law by legalizing injustices and which attack the very foundations of harmony by perpetuating social, political and economic imbalances cannot adjust quickly—if at all—to the concept of a fair settlement which places general well-being and justice above partisan advantage.

What "system of values" does Aung San Suu Kyi identify as "totally mad"? In contrast, what can you infer is her system of values?

During the Cold War the iniquities[6] of ruthless governments and armed groups were condoned for ideological[7] reasons. The results have been far from happy. Although there is greater emphasis on justice and human rights today, there are still ardent advocates in favor of giving priority to political and economic expediency[8]—increasingly the latter. It is the old argument: achieve economic success and all else will follow. But even long-affluent[9] societies are plagued by formidable social ills which have provoked deep anxieties about the future. And newly rich nations appear to be spending a significant portion of their wealth on arms and armies. Clearly there is no inherent link between greater prosperity and greater security and peace—or even the expectation of greater peace. Both prosperity and peace are necessary for the happiness of mankind, the one to

---

5. **impasse** *n.:* deadlock.
6. **iniquities** *n. pl.:* sins.
7. **ideological** *adj.:* conceptual.
8. **expediency** *n.:* suitability, advantageousness.
9. **affluent** *adj.:* wealthy.

Aung San Suu Kyi (1996).

alleviate suffering, the other to promote tranquillity. Only policies that place equal importance on both will make a truly richer world, one in which men can enjoy *chantha*[10] of the body and of the mind. The drive for economic progress needs to be tempered with an awareness of the dangers of greed and selfishness which so easily lead to narrowness and inhumanity. If peoples and nations cultivate a generous spirit which welcomes the happiness of others as an enhancement of the happiness of the self, many seemingly insoluble problems would prove less intractable.[11] **⑤**

Those who have worked with refugees are in the best position to know that when people have been stripped of all their material supports, there only remain to sustain them the values of their cultural and spiritual inheritance. A tradition of sharing instilled by age-old beliefs in the joy of giving and the sanctity of compassion will move a homeless destitute to press a portion of his meagre ration on strangers with all the grace and delight of one who has ample riches to dispense. On the other hand, predatory traits honed by a long-established habit of yielding to "every urge of nature which made self-serving the essence of human life" will lead men to plunder fellow sufferers of their last pathetic possessions. And of course the great majority of the world's refugees are seeking sanctuary from situations rendered untenable[12] by a dearth[13] of humanity and wisdom. **⑥**

The dream of a society ruled by lovingkindness, reason and justice is a dream as old as civilized man. Does it have to be an impossible dream? Karl Popper,[14] explaining his abiding optimism in so troubled a world as ours, said that the darkness had always been there but the light was new. Because it is new it has to be tended with care and diligence. It is true that even the smallest light cannot be extinguished by all the darkness in the world because darkness is wholly negative. It is merely an absence of light. But a small light cannot dispel acres of encircling gloom. It needs to grow stronger, to shed its brightness further and further. And people need to accustom their eyes to the light to see it as a benediction[15] rather than a pain, to learn to love it. We are so much in need of a brighter world which will offer adequate refuge to all its inhabitants. **⑦**

> **⑤** What "old argument" does Aung San Suu Kyi identify in this paragraph? What is she saying about the link between "prosperity" on one hand and "peace" on the other? In your own words, state the main idea of this paragraph.

> **⑥** What values can sustain the impoverished and homeless—the refugees of the world? On the other hand, what attitude gives rise to "predatory traits"?

> **⑦** What is the age-old "dream" of society? In your own words, identify what you think Aung San Suu Kyi means by "light" and "darkness." How can light grow enough to overcome darkness?

---

10. *chantha* n.: prosperity and general happiness.
11. *intractable* adj.: inflexible; stubborn.
12. *untenable* adj.: indefensible.
13. *dearth* n.: scarcity.
14. **Karl Popper** (1902–1994): a Viennese born philosopher who became a British subject.
15. *benediction* n.: blessing.

DIRECT TEACHING

B Content-Area Connections

Literature: Sacred Texts
The quotation comes from a Judaic scholarly commentary on the *Torah*, the sacred text of Judaism: "In morals, holiness negatively demanded resistance to every urge of nature which made self-serving the essence of human life; and positively, submission to an ethic which placed service to others at the center of its system."

Responses to Boxed Questions

5. The "old argument" is that a nation's priority should be economic success, because it will lead to other good things. She is saying that prosperity alone will not bring peace. Her main idea is that economic progress must be linked with policies that protect human rights and educate people to move beyond self-interest toward altruism.

6. Refugees can be sustained by the values of generosity and compassion. A selfish attitude gives rise to "predatory traits."

7. The dream is of a society "ruled by loving kindness, reason, and justice." Students may say that by "light" she means peace, justice, equality, and compassion; by "darkness" she means violence, inhumanity, greed, and oppression.

Conducting a Historical Investigation

Invite students to use online or print resources to learn more about the history of Myanmar (formerly Burma) after British rule. Students might choose topics such as the contributions of General Aung San, father of Suu Kyi; Myanmar under U Nu; the Nonaligned Movement; the Ne Win regime; or changes in the SLORC since 1997.

Direct students to present their findings in essays, oral reports, or audiovisual presentations.

PRETEACHING

Skills Starter

Motivate. Ask students how they obtain coverage of their favorite sports. For example, do they enjoy reading in the newspaper about last night's basketball games, do they watch the games live on TV, or do they listen to them on the radio? Discuss with students how the various media differ in covering a sporting event. Then, ask students how media differ in covering a news event.

MODELING AND DEMONSTRATION

Media Literacy Concepts

Use the questions in the **Media Literacy Concepts** chart and the examples in the **Media Strategies** chart to model for students the process of analyzing a media message. Answer the first chart's questions in reference to a newspaper story (the more objective-seeming the better), and point out examples in the news story of strategies listed in the second chart. Then, ask for volunteers to demonstrate using the same questions and strategy descriptions to analyze another media message of their choice.

Media Workshop

Analyzing and Using Media

Assignment
Analyze media purposes, strategies, and techniques; then, create and deliver a multimedia presentation of your own.

INTERNET
Media Tutorials
Keyword: LE5 12-7

Which do you think would have a greater impact on you: reading the text from Desmond Tutu's speech "The Question of South Africa" (page 1103) or seeing and hearing him deliver the speech? Each medium—print, film, video, radio, television, or the Internet—has distinct characteristics that shape the way you experience its message. Understanding how you are being affected by each medium and its message is an important skill to learn. In this workshop you'll first analyze how different media shape your experiences of their messages. Then, you'll also create and deliver your own **multimedia presentation**, using words, images, and sounds.

Analyzing Media

Media Sources Imagine a day with no media messages: no radio, television, or newspaper in the morning; no billboards on the way to school; and no posters in the school hallways. Obviously, receiving and decoding media messages are a part of daily life. These messages reach their intended audiences through two categories of **media sources**.

- **Print media sources** include books, newspapers, magazines, pamphlets, advertising fliers, billboards, and posters.
- **Electronic media sources** include films, television, the Internet, radio, and CD-ROMs.

Media Literacy Concepts Critical readers and viewers use **media literacy concepts** to analyze, interpret, and evaluate media messages. The left column of the following chart will help you understand basic media literacy concepts. The questions in the right column will help you analyze the media messages you receive.

MEDIA LITERACY CONCEPTS

Concept	Analysis Questions
1. **All media messages are created by someone.** Individuals—alone or in groups—write, edit, select, illustrate, or compose every media message. They decide what to include in the message, what to omit, and how to sequence the elements.	What words, images, or sounds were used to create the message? What may have been omitted?
2. **Media messages are not reality**—they are *representations of reality* that reflect one point of view. Even an eyewitness news account of a flood has been edited to show only a few images and words for the nightly news.	What is the point of view or experience of the message maker? How does this message affect the way I think about this topic?

(continued)

1112   Collection 7   The Modern World: 1900 to the Present

COLLECTION 7 RESOURCES: MEDIA

Planning
- One-Stop Planner CD-ROM with ExamView Test Generator

Differentiating Instruction
- Workshop Resources: Writing, Listening, and Speaking
- Family Involvement Activities in English and Spanish
- Supporting Instruction in Spanish

Writing and Language
- Workshop Resources: Writing, Listening, and Speaking
- Daily Language Activities

Assessment
- Holt Assessment: Writing, Listening, and Speaking
- One-Stop Planner CD-ROM with ExamView Test Generator

(continued)

3. **Individuals interpret media messages differently.** Your interpretation of a media message is based on your knowledge of the world in which you live.	What does the message make me think of? How does the message make me feel?
4. **People create media messages for many purposes**—informing, persuading, entertaining, gaining power, expressing ideas, transmitting culture, and making money.	Who created this message? What is the purpose of this message? Is there more than one purpose?
5. **Each mass medium has unique characteristics.** Media producers shape messages according to the characteristics of the medium through which the message will be presented.	Through what medium is the message delivered? How does the form affect the message?

Media Strategies Media producers use certain strategies to achieve their purposes and to shape their messages for their intended audiences. For you to be an effective media consumer, you should be able to **interpret** and **evaluate** the use of these strategies. The chart below describes some of the most common **media strategies**.

MEDIA STRATEGIES

Strategy	Examples
Language is often the main strategy by which a media purpose is accomplished. It can be tailored to suit any purpose, audience, or message.	A children's educational television show might use simple, direct language to inform its young viewers. An activist's persuasive speech might use powerful, emotional language to prompt listeners to take action.
Visual representations, such as art, photographs, charts, and maps, present information that a reader or viewer can understand or respond to instantly.	A graph in a newspaper might give information about the stock market's recent performance. An advertising photo of a tropical island might elicit in the consumer a desire to travel.
Special effects, including graphics, lighting, and sound, highlight specific details and create illusions.	A film producer might use special visual effects to entertain an audience by making an actor seem to perform superhuman feats.
Stereotypes are generalized beliefs based on misinformation or insufficient evidence about an entire group of individuals.	An advertisement might use the stereotype of the overworked mother to promote a home-cleaning service.

Visual Image Makers **Visual image makers** use the media strategies shown in the chart above as well as other strategies unique to their fields to present events and communicate information. Here are the most common types of visual image makers and their strategies.

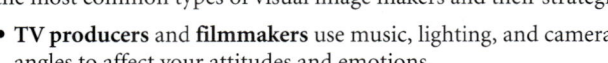
Listening and Speaking Skills
Analyze strategies used by different forms of media.

- **TV producers** and **filmmakers** use music, lighting, and camera angles to affect your attitudes and emotions.

Media Workshop: Analyzing and Using Media 1113

Internet
- go.hrw.com (Keyword: LE5 12-7)
- *Elements of Literature Online*

DIFFERENTIATING INSTRUCTION

English-Language Learners

Students more familiar with the politics of their native countries may not recognize the examples given for the ways in which media have affected the democratic process in the United States. Discuss the concepts with students, and have them share with the class examples from their native countries. All students might benefit from the various perspectives.

Advanced Learners

Enrichment. Ask students to research specific historical instances in which the media have influenced the democratic process in the United States, either in the course of an election or in the swaying of public opinion about government policies. Allow students time in class to make brief presentations of their findings to the class.

PRACTICE & APPLY 1

Guided and Independent Practice

Guide students by offering these strategies to help them choose interesting topics:
- Is there a major news story that currently holds your attention? Find messages that give different perspectives on the story.
- Do you have a favorite sport or hobby? Locate sources that promote or criticize it.
- Is there a person or place in the news that interests you? That person or place can be your topic.

- **Graphic artists** use computer software that alters photographs to create images that look real but aren't. In addition, software allows graphic artists to create moving, three-dimensional images.
- **Illustrators** draw or paint images, often to explain or decorate stories or texts.
- **News photographers** take pictures of current events, shaping information by deciding which images to use and by selecting the angle, distance, lighting, and composition of a shot.

Keep in mind that these media producers design their messages for specific audiences. They familiarize themselves with their intended audiences, consider what the audiences already know, and determine how they want the audiences to be affected by their messages.

Media Effects Interpreting and analyzing media messages can enhance your enjoyment and boost your understanding. Your ability to recognize the powerful, direct impact that media have on the democratic process will help you make informed decisions as a voter and as a citizen. Notice the ways media affect the democratic process at the local, state, and national levels.

- Media **influence elections** by reaching the voter directly. Politicians solicit votes and campaign donations by using TV, radio, newspaper advertisements, and direct mailings to voters' homes. Effective or ineffective use of the media can alter the outcome of elections. For example, a candidate uses direct phone calls to voters, asking them to vote—especially for himself. In a tight election, these votes could determine the final outcome.
- Media **create images of leaders,** often through campaign advertisements. For example, by showing a candidate dressed in work clothes and toiling at a community project, an advertisement portrays her as someone who works hard for a worthy cause.
- Media **shape attitudes** through the amount of attention given to an issue. The more a certain issue is covered, the more importance people begin to attach to it. For example, media coverage of the effects of pollution has inspired people to petition their representatives to support environmental protection initiatives.

Listening and Speaking Skills
Analyze the impact of the media.

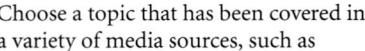 Choose a topic that has been covered in a variety of media sources, such as employment opportunities for high school versus college graduates. Find media messages on that topic in four different media sources, including two each from both print and electronic sources. For each message, take notes on (1) its intended purpose or purposes, (2) how the message is shaped for its intended audience, and (3) how the message uses media strategies. Finally, evaluate the effectiveness of each message in a paragraph by answering the question, "How well does each message achieve its intended purpose for its intended audience?"

Create and Deliver a Multimedia Presentation

Choose a Topic With the information you've studied about analyzing and evaluating media, you're ready to affect others with your own **multimedia presentation**—a presentation that combines a spoken part with text, images, and sounds. Multimedia presentations are similar to speeches and oral presentations. A speech or an oral presentation may occasionally use text, images, or sounds to enhance the spoken part. However, multimedia presentations integrate text, images, and sounds throughout the presentation more fully, balancing the media with the spoken words.

To begin creating your presentation, choose a topic. Do that by reading and considering the contemporary literature of a country or culture that intrigues you. You may already be interested in a particular country and know of pieces of literature from that country. If not, look through this book and world literature anthologies, read magazines or newspapers, listen to radio shows, search the Internet, or ask your teacher or librarian for suggestions.

TIP Consider the **purpose** and **audience** when selecting a topic. When you know why and for whom you are writing, you should be better able to focus your thoughts and establish a direction for your presentation. In this workshop your purpose will be to inform, and your audience will be your teacher and classmates.

Research Your Topic Once you've selected a topic, you're ready to locate, access, and analyze information about the literature you've read and the country or culture of its origin. You'll use the information you collect to create the spoken part of your presentation. Use the following guidelines to help you research your topic.

- Choose one or more pieces of literature that reflect the culture or country you've chosen. One student chose an Egyptian short story—Naguib Mahfouz's "Half a Day" (page 1024).
- Analyze the literature, and decide what cultural ideas it reflects. The student who chose "Half a Day" decided that the story reflects the same ideas about change and modernization that many Egyptians might feel.
- Draw information about the culture from many sources—both print and electronic. Take careful notes on any facts, examples, or quotations that you might use in your presentation.
- Document all your sources. Your audience members can then refer to your list of documented sources for further information. You will also avoid the serious academic offense of **plagiarism**—using someone else's words, images, or sounds without giving proper credit. (For more on **documenting sources,** see page 211.)

Writing Skills
Create a multimedia presentation.

Media Workshop: Analyzing and Using Media **1115**

DIRECT TEACHING

Choose a Topic

Ask a school librarian to set aside a number of anthologies that include literature from other cultures and countries. You may also want to display a world map on the wall of the classroom and label the regions students choose in order to encourage students to cover a broad range of countries and cultures.

If students use the Internet to help them choose a topic, please be aware that Internet resources are sometimes public forums, and that their content can be unpredictable.

RETEACHING

Choose a Topic

Students may have trouble thinking of a topic on which they could give a presentation and may benefit from working together to find a suitable subject. Students can help each other brainstorm for names of contemporary authors from various countries and can pool their resources while researching. Partners can also help each other define the purpose and audience of their presentations.

CORRECTING MISCONCEPTIONS

Students may make the mistake of drawing broad conclusions or generalizations about a culture with which they are not familiar. Tell students that they should be able to cite at least two sources for any such conclusions that they reach in order to prevent making snap judgments.

Media Workshop: Analyzing and Using Media **1115**

DIRECT TEACHING

Develop a Thesis Statement
Remind students that their thesis statements may change as they research their topics, and point out that many different thesis statements are possible on a single topic. A possible alternative to the thesis statement given might be, "In Egypt, as in other countries, change due to modernization is inevitable, and the older one gets, the faster the changes seem to happen." Remind students to keep their audience in mind as they construct their thesis statements.

Select Media
Students working on the same or similar topics (two famous writers from the same culture or country, for example) may benefit by working together to share ideas for possible media, sources for obtaining different media, and ideas for what does and does not work for their presentations.

If students look for information online, be aware that Internet resources are sometimes public forums, and that their content can be unpredictable.

Reference Note
For more on writing a thesis statement, see page 210.

DO THIS

Develop a Thesis Statement Next, review the information you've gathered, and decide on what you want to say about the literature and its originating culture or country. Write a clear **thesis statement** that encompasses your ideas and presents your focus. Developing your thesis statement for your spoken content provides the blueprint for your multimedia presentation. Here is one student's thesis statement for her presentation on Egypt and Naguib Mahfouz's "Half a Day."

> Modernization in Egypt over the last several decades has resulted in marked cultural changes—population growth, urban expansion, and a disregard for tradition—changes lamented in Naguib Mahfouz's symbolic short story "Half a Day."

Select Media Choose text, images, and sounds that elaborate on the spoken content and that add to your presentation's **aesthetic appeal** and **effectiveness.** Incorporate information from a wide range of media sources, including films, newspapers, magazines, CD-ROMs, online information, television, videos, and electronic media-generated images. As you review these media sources, consider the different effects of each, and decide what type of support is appropriate for each part of your presentation and appropriate for your audience.

Use the following chart as a guide for choosing the most appealing and effective medium for each element of your presentation. The right-hand column of the chart shows examples used by the student creating a presentation on Egyptian culture.

USING MEDIA

Media	Uses	Student Examples
Text—any words that appear on a poster, the screen of a video, a computer slide, and so on	to emphasize or enhance key points or their support, and to provide captions for images	• a definition of *modernization* • quotations from "Half a Day"
Images—visual representations such as photos, illustrations, charts, video or film clips, and computer-generated animation	to provide visual impressions of people, places, and things relevant to the topic, and to appeal to the audience's emotions	• a collage of Egyptian images • a video clip from a documentary about Egypt • a map of Egypt and surrounding areas • a photograph of Naguib Mahfouz
Sounds—sound files or other recordings of music, speeches, literary readings, and sound effects	to enhance and support a key point, to create a mood, and to appeal to the audience's emotions	• recordings of traditional and electronic Egyptian music • a recording of Naguib Mahfouz reading from his works

Maximize Your Impact The most appropriate text, image, or sound effect might seem ineffective and even distracting if it isn't designed properly. Pay close attention to the quality of the material you choose. Think carefully about how to incorporate it into your presentation. Use the following design principles to create the maximum impact on your audience.

- **Text** Limit the amount of text that you expect your audience to read. For each screen or slide, use a maximum of six lines, with six words per line. Write large and clearly, or, if you are using a computer program, choose a plain font and a large font size (36 to 48 points). If you decide to emphasize with color, boldface, italics, or underscoring, do so sparingly. Combining too many of these treatments distracts and confuses an audience.

- **Images** Because images should enhance, not compete with, the spoken material in your presentation, use them only when needed. Be sure images are large enough and clear enough to be seen by everyone in the room. Cue video clips so that they show only the most significant material.

- **Sounds** Adjust the sound level according to purpose. For example, a sound whose purpose is to inform, such as a recording of a speech, should be loud enough for everyone in the audience to hear. Background music or sounds that contribute to mood, however, should be soft and not intrusive.

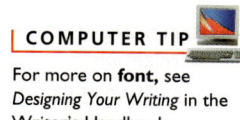

COMPUTER TIP
For more on **font**, see *Designing Your Writing* in the Writer's Handbook.

Organize Your Presentation To help ensure that the audience finds your presentation easy to follow, plan its organization carefully. Follow the steps in the chart below to help you effectively combine the spoken content and the multimedia support you've chosen.

ORGANIZING A MULTIMEDIA PRESENTATION

1. Create **note cards** for the key points and supporting details in the spoken part of your presentation (as you would do when presenting a speech).

2. Group cards for key points and details together, and arrange the groups by **order of importance**. Begin with the most important key point and end with the least important one, or vice versa.

3. Make a note card for each piece of multimedia support you plan to use. Use a different color card from the note cards for your spoken content so that you can balance the media support you are using with your spoken content. You might even use a different color card for each type of support, such as peach for text, blue for images, and yellow for sound.

4. Insert each media card before the spoken content card that it will support.

5. Use your note cards to create an **outline** of your presentation. Check that your organization makes sense and that multimedia support is properly integrated into the presentation.

PRETEACHING

Motivate. Ask students if they have ever felt so strongly about a cause, event, or issue that they wanted to tell their opinion to everyone they knew—and maybe even to people they didn't know. Discuss with students contemporary situations in which one would find persuasive speaking—at a student council meeting, for example. Then, encourage students to begin thinking of a topic on which they could deliver a persuasive speech.

DIRECT TEACHING

Preparing a Persuasive Speech

Point out to students that the audience they are trying to convince will be the people who hold the opposing viewpoint. In order for students to reach this audience successfully, they must first understand its members. As soon as students choose a topic, have them freewrite on the subject of their opposition: Who are they? Why do they hold the opposing viewpoint? In what ways could their opinion be swayed? Students should keep these questions and their possible answers in mind as they develop their speeches.

Listening & Speaking Workshop

Presenting and Analyzing Speeches

Speaking Assignment
Prepare a formal persuasive speech, and deliver it to an audience. Then, listen to and evaluate the persuasive speeches of others.

Multimedia presentations often have a persuasive purpose. The purpose of a **persuasive speech** is almost always obvious to listeners. In this workshop you will experience persuasion from both sides—as a speaker using the techniques of persuasion and as a listener analyzing the techniques of a persuasive speaker.

Preparing a Persuasive Speech

A Hot Topic You might already have a special topic for a persuasive speech. If not, choose a topic that is controversial, or arguable, and that you have strong feelings about. For example, if you're convinced that a controversial freeway proposed for your neighborhood will destroy the neighborhood's character, you might have a good topic for a persuasive speech. It's difficult to deliver a successful persuasive speech on a topic that isn't important to you or the audience.

TIP Keep in mind that your reasoning will be evaluated as you present your speech. Therefore, avoid faulty logic and the use of propaganda. For more on **logical fallacies** and **propaganda,** see page 1123.

Pointed Persuasion You know the general **purpose** of your persuasive speech—to convince listeners to act or think in a certain way. Now, write down your specific position or perspective on the topic you've selected as a clear **opinion statement,** like the one below.

> The proposed freeway should not be built because it would destroy the peace and safety of a family neighborhood.

INTERNET
Speeches
Keyword: LE5 12-?

Listening and Speaking Skills
Prepare a persuasive speech. Understand and identify logical fallacies and propaganda techniques. Use effective rhetorical devices.

Bull's-Eye Your next consideration should be your target **audience.** If audience members are receptive to your ideas, use your speech to reinforce those feelings and move them to action. If you think they are resistant to your ideas, anticipate and address their **counterarguments** and convince them that your perspective is a reasonable one. If you anticipate an indifferent audience, show them the importance of your topic.

Perfect Aim To convince others to accept your opinion, support your opinion statement with **reasons** that include logical, emotional, or ethical appeals.

- **Logical appeals** influence a listener's rational judgment by giving reasons supported by evidence in the form of facts, examples, statistics, or expert opinions.
- **Emotional appeals** use strong and vivid language, anecdotes, and stories to arouse feelings.

1120 Collection 7 The Modern World: 1900 to the Present

COLLECTION 7 RESOURCES: LISTENING & SPEAKING

Planning
- *One-Stop Planner* CD-ROM with ExamView Test Generator

Differentiating Instruction
- *Workshop Resources: Writing, Listening, and Speaking*
- *Family Involvement Activities in English and Spanish*
- *Supporting Instruction in Spanish*

Listening and Speaking
- *Workshop Resources: Writing, Listening, and Speaking*
- *Daily Language Activities*

Assessment
- *Holt Assessment: Writing, Listening, and Speaking*
- *One-Stop Planner* CD-ROM with ExamView Test Generator

- **Ethical appeals** target a listener's sense of right and wrong. Speakers who use ethical appeals must be credible.

Logical appeals are generally preferred in more formal arguments because they are based on concrete and provable facts.

The Right Approach You want your speech to be **focused** and **coherent**. There are two classic approaches—deductive and inductive—to presenting persuasive arguments. The best method for your speech will depend upon your assessment of your audience's attitude toward your opinion statement.

- **The Deductive Approach:** Deductive reasoning moves from the general to the specific. For a neutral or favorable audience, begin with your opinion statement and then move to the particular reasons—the logical, emotional, and ethical appeals that support your opinion.

- **The Inductive Approach:** Inductive reasoning moves from specific to general. For an audience reluctant to agree with you, start with your reasons and end with your opinion statement.

Language Power To achieve clarity, force, and an aesthetic, or artistic and tasteful, effect in your persuasive speech, use the **rhetorical devices** listed below to emphasize and enhance your appeals.

 **TIP** No matter which of these approaches you decide to take, you still have to arrange your reasons in a logical progression. **Order of importance,** usually least important to most important, is the most effective arrangement because it is often the most dramatic.

RHETORICAL DEVICES

Device	Example
Repetition is the repeated use of words, phrases, or clauses for emphasis.	The proposed freeway will destroy houses, will destroy our neighborhood, and will destroy our way of life.
Restatement is the repetition of an idea using different language.	Traffic congestion on the proposed freeway will foul our air. We will choke on the freeway pollution.
Parallelism is the rhythmic repetition of grammatical forms or parts of speech.	The proposed freeway will destroy our peace and quiet; it will foul our air; it will endanger the lives of our children; it will destroy the value of our property.
Rhetorical questions are asked for effect. They do not require a response.	Do you think the people who will use the freeway care about the peace and quiet of our neighborhood?
Argument by analogy shows a parallel between basically dissimilar events or situations.	As far as noise is concerned, building a freeway would be similar to building a jet runway through the middle of our neighborhood. Both would cause an increase in sound levels and sonic vibrations.
Irony is the contrast between expectation and reality. **Verbal irony** is most often used in speech. It is the contrast between what a speaker says and what he or she means.	Of course we believe proponents of the freeway when they tell us the freeway will be an economic boon—just ask the residents of what used to be City Heights about their so-called economic boon.

Internet
- go.hrw.com (Keyword: LE5 12-7)
- *Elements of Literature Online*

Collection 7: Skills Review

Comparing Literature

SKILLS FOCUS, pp. 1124–1127

Grade-Level Skills

■ **Literary Skills**
Compare major literary forms of different historical periods.

INTRODUCING THE SKILLS REVIEW

Use this review to assess students' ability to contrast works from different periods.

DIRECT TEACHING

A Reading Skills
Understanding the speaker's point of view. Have students re-read the first stanza of the poem. Make sure they understand that the speaker is not describing events he has witnessed but that he is imagining in vivid detail a legend that has a strong hold upon his imagination.

B Literary Focus
? Imagery. How does the tone of the imagery change in the last two stanzas? What is the emotional effect of that change? [Possible response: The images describing the boatman's enchantment and death are abrupt and violent, contrasting with the beauty and gentle melancholy of earlier images. The contrast shocks the reader and reinforces the dual nature of the Lorelei: beautiful but deadly.]

C Literary Focus
? Characteristics of major literary periods. What characteristics of Romanticism can you find in this poem? [Possible responses: Nature is seen as a mirror of human emotions and events; the speaker is strongly influenced by his imagination.]

1124 | Collection 7 | The Modern World: 1900 to the Present

Collection 7: Skills Review
Comparing Literature

Test Practice

The following poems allude to two closely related legends. "The Lorelei," by the German poet Heinrich Heine (1797–1856), describes a steep, rocky cliff on the Rhine River in Germany. According to legend, the spirit of a woman sits on these rocks at night, combing her hair, singing, and luring boatmen to their deaths. The contemporary poem "Siren Song," by Canadian writer Margaret Atwood (1939–   ), takes its inspiration from the sirens of Greek myth—those mysterious women who tempted Odysseus and his sailors with their sweet singing.

DIRECTIONS: Read the two poems that follow. Then, read each multiple-choice question that follows, and write the letter of the best response.

The Lorelei

Heinrich Heine
translated by Louis Untermeyer

I cannot tell why this imagined
   Despair has fallen on me;
The ghost of an ancient legend
   That will not let me be:

5 The air is cool, and twilight
   Flows down the quiet Rhine;
A mountain alone in the high light
   Still holds the faltering shine.

The last peak rosily gleaming
10   Reveals, enthroned in air,
A maiden, lost in dreaming,
   Who combs her golden hair.

Combing her hair with a golden
   Comb in her rocky bower,°
15 She sings the tune of an olden
   Song that has magical power.

The boatman has heard; it has bound him
   In throes of a strange, wild love;
Blind to the reefs that surround him,
20   He sees but the vision above.

And lo, hungry waters are springing—
   Boat and boatman are gone. . . .
Then silence. And this, with her singing,
   The Lorelei has done.

---

14. **bower** *n.*: enclosed place or retreat, usually a lady's bedroom or private room. It can also refer to any natural enclosure.

SKILLS FOCUS
Pages 1124–1127 cover
Literary Skills Compare and contrast works from different literary periods.

1124   Collection 7   The Modern World: 1900 to the Present

READING MINI-LESSON

Reviewing Word-Attack Skills
Activity. Have students identify the syllable that is said with greatest stress in each word. Answers are underlined.

1. <u>par</u>entage
2. <u>par</u>ental
3. <u>con</u>cert
4. discon<u>cert</u>ed
5. illus<u>tra</u>tion
6. il<u>lus</u>trative
7. <u>par</u>asite
8. para<u>sit</u>ic
9. <u>mal</u>efactor
10. ma<u>lev</u>olent

Activity. Have students identify the word in each of the following pairs that has a silent *h*.

1. vehement, behemoth [vehement]
2. antihistamine, annihilate [annihilate]

Collection 7: Skills Review

DIRECT TEACHING

A Reading Skills

Identifying the speaker's point of view. Who is the speaker? [the mythical Siren] What clues does Atwood give to the speaker's identity? [Possible responses: The speaker's assertion that she knows the siren song; her description of being on an island in a "bird suit"; looking "picturesque and mythical" along with two other "feathery maniacs."]

B Literary Focus

Characteristics of major literary periods. In what ways does this contemporary poem differ from "The Lorelei"? [Possible responses: "Siren Song" is more fragmented and less literal in its narrative than "The Lorelei." The characters in "Siren Song" are not directly identified; the reader must use clues in the text to infer the identity of the speaker and of the person she is addressing. "The Lorelei" takes a traditional view of the myth by retelling it from the point of view of the male speaker, who identifies with the Lorelei's victim; Atwood tells her story from the point of view of the female predator, the Siren.]

Siren Song

Margaret Atwood

This is the one song everyone
would like to learn: the song
that is irresistible:

5   the song that forces men
to leap overboard in squadrons
even though they see the beached
skulls

the song nobody knows
because anyone who has heard it
is dead, and the others can't
remember.

10   Shall I tell you the secret
and if I do, will you get me
out of this bird suit?

I don't enjoy it here
squatting on this island
15   looking picturesque and mythical

with these two feathery maniacs,
I don't enjoy singing
this trio, fatal and valuable.

I will tell the secret to you,
20   to you, only to you.
Come closer. This song

is a cry for help: Help me!
Only you, only you can,
you are unique

25   at last. Alas
it is a boring song
but it works every time.

---

3. exhaust, exhale [exhaust]
4. inhibitions, prohibitions [prohibitions]
5. posthumous, posthypnotic [posthumous]

Activity. Have students tell if the pronunciations of the underlined words in these sentences are the same or different.

1. A more <u>articulate</u> person could <u>articulate</u> this better.
[different; /är·tik′yə·lit/, /är·tik′yə·lāt′/]

2. That <u>excuse</u> will not <u>excuse</u> you.
[different; /ek·sky⎯oos′/, /ek·sky⎯ooz′/]

3. We can <u>appropriate</u> <u>appropriate</u> gear.
[different; /ə·prō′prē·āt′/, /ə·prō′prē·it/]

4. The <u>initiate</u> will <u>initiate</u> the ceremony.
[different; /i·nish′ē·it/, /i·nish′ē·āt′/]

5. Lecturers rarely <u>associate</u> with the <u>associate</u> professors.
[different; /ə·sō′shē·āt′/, /ə·sō′shē·it/]

---

nineteenth-century trait: the glorification of the myth and legend of the pre-industrial era

tasy, while the narrator's moral ambiguity challenges the reader's assumptions. Heine is

Collection 7: Skills Review

Have students read the rest of the speech and look for other passages in which Nehru uses powerful persuasive devices to reach his audience. Draw on the chalkboard a chart like the one below, and fill it in with examples of persuasive passages that students identify. Or, if you prefer, provide them with the passage and have them identify the persuasive device that Nehru uses and its effect on the audience. (Possible responses appear in brackets.)

Passage	Device	Effect
["when we step out ..., when an age ends, and when the soul of a nation ..."]	[parallelism]	[underscores the importance of the occasion; creates a memorable rhythm, which holds the audience's attention]
["At the dawn of history, India started on her unending quest ... has never lost sight of that quest or forgotten the ideals which gave her strength.... India discovers herself again."]	[figurative and emotional language]	[appeals to patriotism and idealism; acknowledges past suffering and offers hope for a better future]
["Before the birth of freedom we have endured all the pains of labor ...."]	[metaphor]	[links a political experience to a highly personal experience (giving birth), stirring emotions of joy, hope, and identification]
["to wipe every tear from every eye"]	[emotional language and parallelism]	[stirs feelings of sympathy and solidarity; creates a pleasing, musical rhythm]
["so is freedom, so is prosperity now, and so also is disaster in this One World...."]	[parallelism]	[emphasizes important ideas; balances good and bad experiences, thereby appealing to reason and emotion]
["We have to build the noble mansion of free India...."]	[metaphor]	[equates the new nation with high-mindedness, spaciousness, beauty, and wealth; appeals to feelings of pride, hope, and idealism]

Independent Practice: **Evaluating rhetorical devices.** Assign students in small groups to locate recent speeches made by local or national politicians, such as the most recent State of the Union address by the president. Ask groups to read the speech or sections of it and identify the speaker's purpose. Ask, "What does he or she want to convince the audience to think or do?" Then, have students work together to identify and evaluate the rhetorical devices the speaker uses to try to persuade the audience. Encourage students to organize their ideas on a chart like the one in the Guided Practice. When they have completed their charts, have a class discussion about the effective use of persuasive devices and the relative power of appeals to reason and emotion. Urge students to support their opinions with examples from their group work.

1129C Public Documents

Patterns of Organization

Objective: To analyze the way repetition of the main ideas, patterns of organization, and word choice affect the meaning of a text.

Direct Teaching: Share the following information with students.

When writers sit down to write, their thoughts don't instantly flow onto the page in clear and easy-to-understand sentences and paragraphs. On the contrary, good writers work hard to present their ideas in organized patterns that readers can recognize and follow. For example, writers can organize events, actions, or steps in a process in chronological order, the order in which the events or steps occurred. Writers also can present events and actions in cause-and-effect order: Event A brings about Event B, or Event B is the result of Event A. When writers are presenting ideas, they are likely to organize their presentation around a main idea that is followed by supporting details. These supporting details can take the form of reasons, facts, or examples. This type of organization is often used when a writer is making an assertion or advancing an argument and wishes to convince the reader of his or her opinion.

Writers also seek to make their ideas clear and memorable by repeating key words and phrases. Parallel structure is a very polished form of repetition in which grammatically similar words, phrases, clauses, or sentences are repeated for emphasis or emotional effect. Lincoln's formulation "government of the people, by the people, for the people" is a famous example of parallel structure. Word choice also affects clarity. A precise word makes meaning instantly clear; a vague one obscures it. In general, specific words have greater impact than general ones, and figurative and sensory language make a stronger impression than literal or abstract word choices. For example, "a summer soldier" or "sunshine patriot" is a far more powerful choice of words than "an unreliable participant."

Guided Practice: Analyzing patterns of organization and word choice. Have a volunteer read aloud the first passage from Margaret Cavendish's "Female Orations" (p. 332). Ask the class, "What is the purpose of the passage?" Help them to see that as a participant in a fictional debate, the speaker is trying to convince her listeners to adopt her point of view on women's position in society. Next, work with students to identify the speaker's assertions and the support she offers for those opinions in the form of reasons, facts, or examples. As students volunteer assertions, write them in the first column of a chart like the one on p. 1129E. If the class is having difficulty, you may want to provide the assertions and have students find the supporting details. (Possible responses appear in brackets.)

When students have finished analyzing the patterns of assertion and support, ask them to look again at the passages they identified for examples of effective sentence structure and vivid word choice. Write these in the third column of the chart, and discuss with students how these words and sentences make the speaker's ideas clearer and more convincing. If students are having trouble appreciating Cavendish's use of repetition and figurative language, rephrase some of her passages in less rhythmic and more abstract prose so they can hear the difference.

Assertion	Support	Sentence Structure and Word Choice
["I have been industrious to assemble you together"]	[Reason: "that we may unite in prudent counsels, to make ourselves as free, happy, and famous as men"]	[Parallel structure: "free, happy, and famous"]
["for men are happy, and we women are miserable"]	[Examples: "they possess all the ease, rest, pleasure, wealth, power, and fame; whereas women are restless with labor, easeless with pain, melancholy for want of pleasures, helpless for want of power, and die in oblivion, for want of fame."]	[Parallel structure: "women are restless with labor, easeless with pain, melancholy for want of pleasures, helpless for want of power, and die in oblivion, for want of fame."]
["...men are so unconscionable and cruel against us that they...bar us of all sorts of liberty"]	[Examples: "will not suffer us freely to associate amongst our own sex...would fain bury us in their houses or beds, as in a grave...we live like bats or owls, labor like beasts, and die like worms."]	[Figurative language and parallel structure: "bury us in their houses or beds, *as in a grave* (simile); ...we live *like bats or owls*, labor *like beasts*, and die *like worms* (similes)."]

Independent Practice: Analyzing writing for clarity. Have individual students continue studying Cavendish's patterns of organization, sentence structure, and word choice by applying the same technique of analysis begun in the Guided Practice to the remaining passages from "Female Orations." Have them organize their ideas on a chart and bring their charts to class for a general discussion of Cavendish's methods. Also, encourage students to consider alternative patterns of organization that Cavendish or another speaker might have used to make clear and convincing arguments about the position of women.

As an alternative, have students read and analyze John Donne's sermon Meditation 17 (p. 308), charting how Donne makes use of assertion and support, parallel structure, rhetorical questions, figurative language, and other powerful word choices. Ask students to use their charts to write a brief essay on Donne's organizational patterns, sentence structure, and word choice, explaining how these contributed to the clarity and effectiveness of his argument.

Analyzing an Author's Arguments

Objective: To make reasonable assertions about an author's arguments by using elements of the text to defend interpretations.

Direct Teaching: Share the following ideas with students.

Whether you are reading fiction or nonfiction, reading is not a passive task. When reading fiction, you will need to activate your imagination to make the characters, setting, and events come alive. To get the most out of reading nonfiction, you will need to question and evaluate the ideas presented to you. One of the best ways to evaluate informative or persuasive prose is first to identify the author's main idea and then find the evidence, reasoning, or examples the author uses to support this idea. The next step is to form opinions, make inferences, and draw conclusions about the case the writer has made for the main idea or argument. You can apply this process by using these questions:

- What assertions, or statements, can I make about the writer's arguments?

- How can I support these assertions with direct quotations, paraphrases, or other evidence from the text itself?

Reader assertions include generalizations characterizing the writer's point of view, such as a statement declaring that a writer's ideas are too pessimistic. An assertion may also take the form of an overall evaluation of the writer's persuasiveness, such as a conclusion that the support is insufficient to prove the point.

Guided Practice: Analyzing an author's arguments. If needed, review the process of finding the main idea and identifying supporting details. Remind students that an author's main idea or argument is sometimes stated directly in a sentence somewhere near the beginning or end of the text. Just as often, however, the main idea is not summed up in any one statement in the text and must be inferred from the overall weight of the evidence presented. Be sure students understand that to assert an idea, they must express it in a clear and positive statement. To be convincing, an assertion about an author's argument—whether in the form of an evaluation, an opinion, or a conclusion—must be supported with facts, examples, or other evidence from the text.

Have students read Virginia Woolf's "Shakespeare's Sister" (p. 887). After students have reviewed the entire selection, ask them to identify the purpose of Woolf's essay. [to persuade] Next, have a volunteer read the first column of text aloud while students listen for the sentence in which Woolf sums up her main idea or argument. Draw on the chalkboard a flowchart like the one on p. 1129G, and fill in student responses as the discussion progresses. (Possible responses appear in brackets.) When students have located Woolf's main idea, ask them to discuss the kind of support she offers to persuade readers to accept her argument. Guide students to see that Woolf primarily offers inferences or suppositions about the life of a hypothetical sister of Shakespeare. Her inferences, however, are based on known facts about women's lives in Shakespeare's day. Then, have students provide examples of Woolf's supporting arguments and write these on the chart. Finally, help students to make an assertion about the nature or effectiveness of the case Woolf makes to support her main idea.

Main Idea

["It would have been impossible, completely and entirely, for any woman to have written the plays of Shakespeare in the age of Shakespeare."]

Support

[Shakespeare's sister would not have received any formal education.]

[Her days would have been filled with tiring domestic duties.]

[She probably would have had to write secretly and would have hidden or destroyed her writing.]

[She would have been forced to marry very young or run away to London.]

[In London, she would have been unable to support herself and would have been taken advantage of by men.]

[A gifted female, without any outlet for her talent, she would have ended up frustrated, maybe mentally ill, or even suicidal.]

Reader Assertion

[Woolf convincingly supports her argument because the imagined life she creates for Shakespeare's sister is based on known facts about women's lives in the sixteenth century and is presented in such vivid, lively, and plausible detail that readers find it believable.]

You may want to continue the class discussion by raising this question: *Do you think Virginia Woolf makes a convincing case that women writers in her day face difficulties like those of "Shakespeare's sister"?* Ask students to look at the selection to see how Woolf supports this assertion, and have them discuss the effectiveness of her reasoning. Remind students that they should assess Woolf's effectiveness in supporting her ideas, not express their own views on the struggles of women writers.

Independent Practice: Analyzing an author's arguments. Have students read Joseph Chamberlain's speech "I Believe in a British Empire" (p. 917). Then, have them work in pairs to identify Chamberlain's main idea and the arguments he presents to support his thesis, using direct quotations from or paraphrases of the text. Next, have them evaluate the effectiveness of the case Chamberlain makes for his main idea or claim and assert their evaluation in a formal statement. To organize their ideas, encourage students to use a flowchart like the one in the Guided Practice. (Possible responses appear in brackets on the chart that follows.)

Alternatively, students may want to work in pairs to prepare a rebuttal to Chamberlain's main idea. Remind them that they will have to assert a counterargument and support it with reasons, facts, inferences, or appeals to logic and emotion. They may want to imagine themselves as editorial writers for a London newspaper or as members of the opposition party in Parliament in the early 1900s, preparing to speak out against Chamberlain's view of the empire.

Main Idea

["I believe in a British Empire, in an Empire which, though it should be its first duty to cultivate friendship with all the nations of the world, should yet, even if alone, be self-sustaining and self-sufficient, able to maintain itself against the competition of all its rivals."]

Support

[The old isolationism "went very far to dry and even to sap the loyalty of our colonial brethren."]

["The Empire is in its infancy . . . we can mold [it and] . . . decide its future destinies."]

["I want you to consider the infinite importance of this not only to yourselves but to your descendants."]

["think what it means to your power and influence as a country . . . to your position among the nations of the world . . . to your trade and commerce. . . ."]

["if we were . . . face to face some day . . . with some great coalition of hostile nations . . . there is nothing within the power of these self-governing colonies they would not do to come to our aid."]

Reader Assertion

[Chamberlain's reasons for advocating a strong Empire are unconvincing because they are based more on appeals to narrow self-interest and wishful thinking about the loyalty and self-government of the colonies than on hard evidence.]

Critiquing Public Documents

Objective: To critique the validity, appeal, and truthfulness of arguments in public documents.

Direct Teaching: Share the following ideas with students.

Many public documents—such as speeches, debates, and policy statements—are prepared for political purposes. Although they provide information, they are basically statements of opinion or calls to action, designed to win audience support for the author's ideas and plans. Politicians almost always have a persuasive purpose when they address people. Therefore, when we read or listen to political statements or speeches, whether from the past or present, it is important to decide exactly what the writer or speaker wants the audience to believe or do. Then, we can go on to examine how he or she goes about trying to convince the audience. We can expect to find appeals to the minds and hearts of listeners in every persuasive message, and these techniques can be either effective or ineffective, depending on the soundness of the reasoning and the power of the emotional appeal. We also find many appeals to authority, status, or expertise. The opinions of experts and authorities generally carry more weight than those of the untrained and undistinguished. Also, effective persuaders often try to anticipate and address what they know to be the doubts and concerns of their audience and to counter the objections opponents are likely to raise. For example, a speaker who is trying to persuade voters to support an increase in the local school budget may counter fears of increased property taxes by assuring listeners that a better school system will increase the resale value of their homes.

Guided Practice: Critiquing public documents. Review with students the difference between logical and emotional appeals. Remind them that emotional appeals often carry charged or heightened language, which is designed to stir the audience to feelings of affection, loyalty, patriotism, fear, or pity. Speakers can also appeal to an audience's desire for reward or their fear of punishment or hardship. Remind students that the most effective persuaders foresee and address the concerns of their audience, giving a sense that they understand the immediate and long-range effects of what they are proposing and the impact their proposals will have on the interested parties.

Now, have students read Queen Elizabeth I's "Tilbury Speech" (p. 330). Explain that the speech was delivered in 1588 just before news of the defeat of the Spanish fleet (which was attempting to invade England) was received. Make sure students understand that Elizabeth was expecting an invasion and that her purpose was to rally the army and the people for a vigorous defense of the nation. Ask students what kinds of concerns the English people might have had on the eve of the supposed invasion. [Possible responses: whether the queen, a woman, was ready for leading the nation in a time of war; who would be called on to fight and die; why any subject should risk his or her life for queen and country; how aware the queen was of the effects of her call to arms on her subjects.] Write the concerns on the chalkboard as students offer them, and ask them if and how these concerns are addressed in the "Tilbury Speech."

After students have read the speech, draw on the chalkboard a chart like the one on p. 1129L. Read aloud each excerpt in the first column. Next, discuss with students whether the passage appeals to logic, emotion, authority, or all three, and what, if any, audience concern or objection the passage addresses. Work with students to be as specific as possible in identifying Elizabeth's persuasive techniques. (Possible responses appear in brackets.)

Passage	Persuasive Techniques
"My loving people . . ."	[appeals primarily to listeners' emotions—their sense of affection and loyalty to the queen as an individual and a symbol of the nation]
"We have been persuaded by some that are careful of our safety to take heed how we commit ourself to armed multitudes for fear of treachery, but I assure you I do not desire to distrust my faithful and loving people."	[a subtle appeal to both logic and emotion, calling attention to the queen's personal courage and trust in her subjects in order to persuade her audience to show similar courage and trust in her]
"Let tyrants fear. I have always so behaved myself that, under God, I have placed my chiefest strength and safeguard in the loyal hearts and goodwill of my subjects."	[appeals to logic, emotion, and authority, reminding the audience of the queen's exemplary conduct as a monarch and her subjection to God, the highest authority, with the implication that her subjects now owe her their complete loyalty]
"I know I have the body but of a weak and feeble woman, but I have the heart and stomach of a king—and of a king of England too—and think foul scorn that Parma, or Spain, or any prince of Europe should dare to invade the borders of my realm. . . . I myself shall take up arms, I myself will be your general, judge, and rewarder. . . ."	[appeals to emotion by stirring up the audience's feelings of patriotism, indignation, and fear in the face of an invasion; addresses the subjects' doubts on the fitness and resolve of their female monarch and warns would-be invaders that they shall face opposition]
"I know already for your forwardness you have deserved rewards and crowns, and we do assure you, in the word of a prince, they shall be duly paid to you."	[appeals to the audience's desire for rewards and to the people's respect for the queen's authority to make good on her promises; reveals the queen's understanding of the practical concerns of her people, which she addresses by promising material rewards for their loyal service]

After discussing the persuasive appeals of particular passages, lead students in a general discussion of the overall effectiveness of Queen Elizabeth's speech. Ask questions like the following:

- Do you think most of the queen's audience would have supported her call to arms?

- Which of her appeals do you think would have been most effective?

- What factors beyond the persuasiveness of this particular speech would have played a part in her audience's response to her message?

- How would the speech of the president of a contemporary democracy facing invasion be similar to or different from Queen Elizabeth's speech?

Ask students to explain their responses. Help them to see that much of the force of Queen Elizabeth's arguments was based on her personal record as a benign monarch and on the general respect for the monarchy that existed in England in her day. A contemporary president might appeal less to personal loyalty and affection and more to the self-interest and nationalism of the citizens.

Independent Practice: Critiquing public documents. Have students working in pairs read aloud Winston Churchill's speech "Blood, Sweat and Tears" (p. 850). Then, ask them to identify the policy or course of action that Churchill is asking his audience to support. [Possible response: As prime minister, Churchill is seeking government and popular support for his plans to wage all-out war to save the British Empire.] Next, have the pairs work together to prepare an oral report in which they critique Churchill's persuasive techniques and compare and contrast them with those of Queen Elizabeth I in the "Tilbury Speech." (They may want to organize their analysis of Churchill's techniques in a chart like the one used for the Guided Practice.) Suggest that students pay attention not only to what Churchill and Elizabeth I say but also to how they deliver their message—that is, their use of language. Remind students that although the two speeches were inspired by similar circumstances (the threat of war and invasion), one was given by a hereditary monarch in the sixteenth century and the other by an elected leader of a democratic nation four centuries later.

Theme and Meaning

Objective: To analyze the way in which the theme of a selection represents a comment on life, using evidence from the text to support your claim.

Direct Teaching: Share the following information with students.

The theme of a literary work is its central idea or general comment on human life and experience. A work's theme expresses the insights of the author, but it also may offer clues to the views or values of the culture or period to which the author belongs. The theme is not the same as the subject or topic of a selection. For example, friendship may be the subject of many stories and poems, but writers' insights into the meaning of friendship will differ from work to work. Writers rarely state their themes directly in their stories and poems. Rather, they leave it to readers and critics to weigh all the literary elements in a work and come up with a generalization that summarizes the writer's take on the subject. Such a generalization is called a theme statement. "Friendship is more enduring than romance because it is based on reason, not passion" is an example of a theme statement on the subject of friendship. To determine this statement, a reader would have to look at how individual literary elements—like characterization, setting, symbolism, conflict, and resolution—combine and interact in a work to suggest this general meaning. Discovering the theme, then, is a process of reflection and integration, which requires careful reading and often re-reading of the text.

Guided Practice: Analyzing themes. Ask students to form small reading groups and read Ben Okri's "In the Shadow of War" (p. 875). On the chalkboard draw a web like the one at the bottom of this page. Use the web to help students gather and organize evidence from the story that will help them to develop a theme statement for "In the Shadow of War." (Possible responses appear in brackets on the web.) Begin by asking students to identify the subject of the story. Write their responses on the web. Follow up with discussions of the story's main character, setting, symbolism, conflict, and resolution.

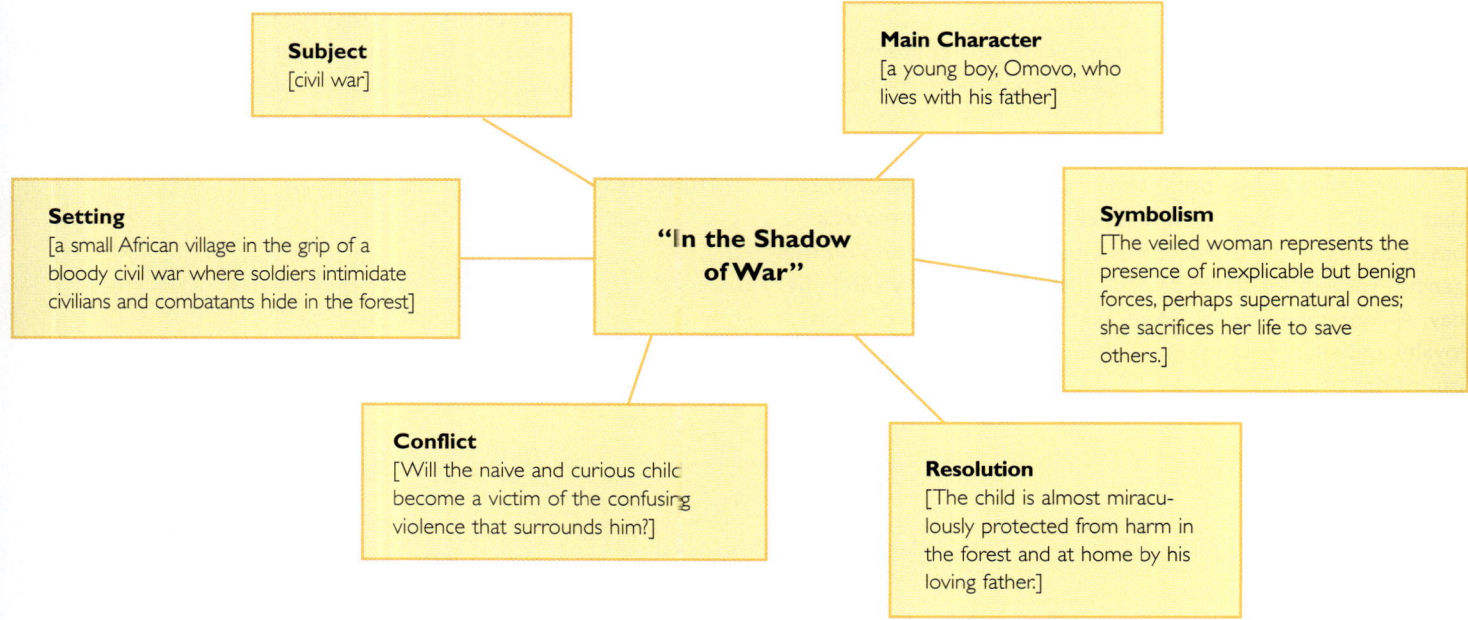

When you have filled in the web with all the evidence they have gathered from the story, ask students to reflect on what they have discovered and discuss what comment on human experience they think Ben Okri is making in this story. Tell them that there is more than one way to state Okri's theme and that various interpretations are valid as long as they can be supported with evidence from the text. Then, write several student theme statements on the chalkboard. [Possible theme statements: Even in time of war, innocence is sometimes protected by mysterious forces; the evils of war and its pervasive cruelty are counterbalanced by deeds of bravery, love, and self-sacrifice; in civil war, it is hard to know who are one's enemies and who are one's friends.] **Ask students to evaluate each one, referencing the story and their own prior knowledge.**

Independent Practice: Analyzing themes. Have students working in pairs read A. E. Housman's poem "To an Athlete Dying Young" (p. 726) or another poem in the Student Edition. Then, have them work together to gather evidence from the poem that will help them to discover the comment on life that the poet is making. Encourage them to organize their evidence on a web like the one below. (Possible responses appear in brackets.) Ask the partners to use their charts to write a short essay, stating the writer's theme as they see it and explaining the process they used to arrive at their conclusion. Have them share their essays with students who analyzed the same poem and compare and contrast the various theme statements. [Possible theme statements: It is better to die young when success and happiness are fresh than to grow old, stale, and disillusioned; all human achievement ends in death, so it matters little whether we die young or old.]

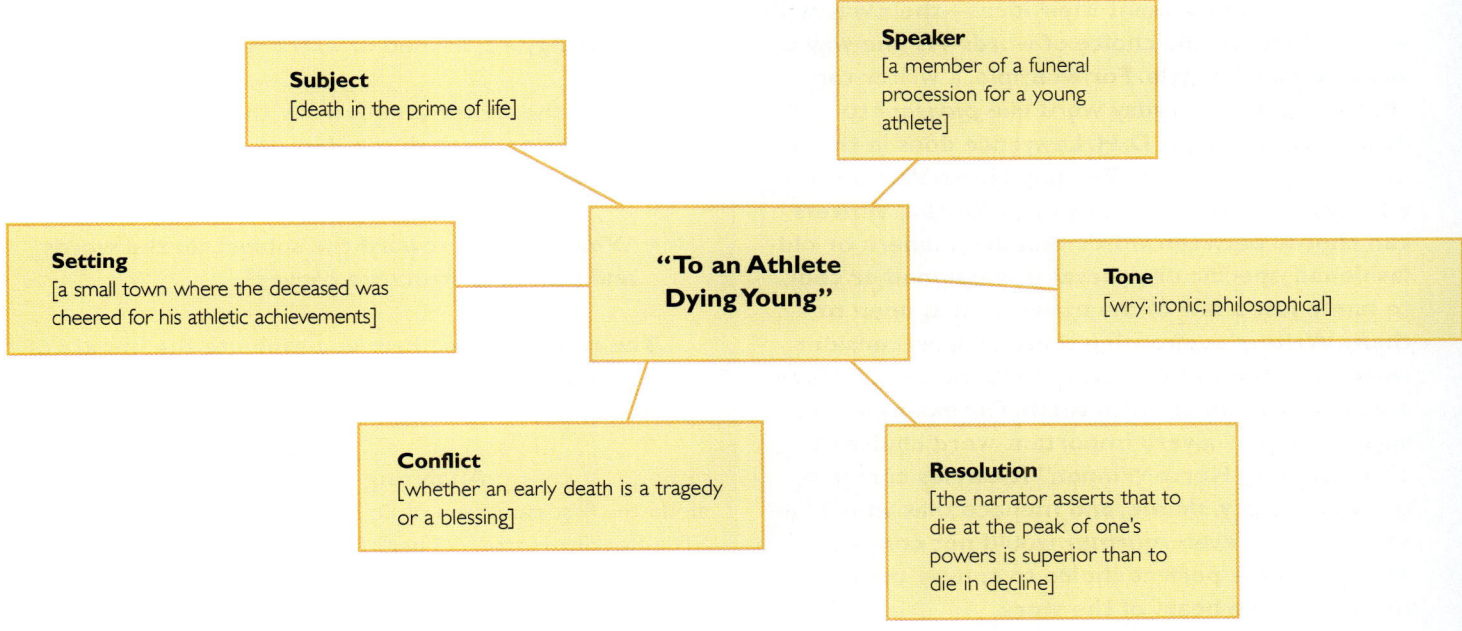

Irony, Tone, and Author's Style

Objective: To analyze the ways irony, tone, and the author's style achieve specific purposes.

Direct Teaching: Share the following ideas with students.

When we talk about an author's style we mean the way in which he or she writes, rather than what he or she writes about. Style is the distinctive manner in which writers present their ideas—their way with words. Diction—the choice of words—is one way a writer creates a style. For example, a writer can choose a plain, everyday word like *pleasant* to describe a house (as D. H. Lawrence does in the second paragraph of "The Rocking-Horse Winner") or a fancier one, like *charming* or *delightful.* Writers can choose between words that are modern or old-fashioned, specific or general, impassioned or cool, to name just a few of the many choices open to them. Writers confronting these choices consider words' connotations—that is, the emotions, images, and ideas associated with them. For example, the verb *whisper* is a very important word choice in "The Rocking-Horse Winner." It carries connotations of secrecy, shame, and menace that words like *say, speak,* or even *murmur* would not convey. *Whisper* is the perfect choice to convey the dark mystery at the heart of the story.

The use of irony is another technique that affects the tone or attitude the writer takes toward the subject. Irony is a discrepancy between what is expected and what actually happens or between what is true and what appears to be true.

Sentence structure is another important component of style. The unique rhythm—the pattern of repeated sounds—of a passage is created by the way its words, phrases, and clauses are strung together. Sequences of short, simple sentences, for example, create one effect while strings of long, complex sentences create another.

As you read, pay careful attention to the writer's word choices and to the rhythm created by the sentence structure. Look to see if the words and sentences create an overall tone or attitude. A tone can be described in words such as *lighthearted, mournful, detached, disillusioned.* To assess style, ask yourself questions like these:

- Are most of the words simple or elaborate, formal or slangy, restrained or extravagant?

- Does the writer create irony through word choices or through the depiction of characters and events?

- What attitude toward the subject do the words and sentence structure convey?

The responses will help you evaluate the impact of the author's style on the tone and message of the work.

Guided Practice: Analyzing irony, tone, and style. Read aloud the first paragraph of D. H. Lawrence's short story "The Rocking-Horse Winner" (p. 970). Begin an analysis of Lawrence's style in this passage by calling students' attention to the following examples of Lawrence's diction: "a woman who was beautiful"; "started with all the advantages"; "had no luck"; "married for love"; "love turned to dust"; and "felt the center of her heart go hard." Ask students how they would describe these word choices. [Possible responses: plain, straightforward, understated, unadorned.] If students are having difficulty characterizing the diction, give them some alternatives such as "a woman who was as brilliant as summer lightning" or "love curdled like sour milk." These examples should help them to see that Lawrence makes little use of figurative or flowery language.

Next, review irony with students. Encourage them to consult the Handbook of Literary and Historical Terms (p. 1181) for detailed definitions of verbal, dramatic, and situational irony. Guide them to study the examples provided in the handbook.

Then, draw on the chalkboard a chart like the one below. Write in the chart the following instances of irony from Lawrence's first paragraph. Work with students to identify the type of irony in each example and to explain the nature of the ironic contrast. Write students' responses on the chart. (Possible responses appear in brackets.)

Ask students to look at the sentence structure of the first paragraph. Point out that the passage consists of a series of compound and compound-complex sentences that seem to go on and on without much subordination of one idea to the next. Everything seems of equal importance. Ask students what effect this kind of sentence structure creates. Guide them to see that the sentence structure in the first paragraph creates a sense of confusion or mystification—no one, certainly not the reader, seems to know exactly what is going on in this family.

Examples of Irony	Type of Irony
"started with all the advantages, yet she had no luck"	[situational: what happens is the opposite of what is expected]
"She married for love, and the love turned to dust."	[situational: what happens is the opposite of what is expected]
"She had bonny children . . . and she could not love them."	[situational: what happens is the opposite of what is expected]
"And hurriedly she felt she must cover up some fault in herself. Yet what it was that she must cover up she never knew."	[dramatic: the reader knows something the character doesn't]
"In her manner she was all the more gentle and anxious for her children, as if she loved them very much."	[situational: a contrast between what the character does and what she feels]
"Everybody else said of her: 'She is such a good mother. She adores her children.'"	[verbal: a contrast between what is said and what is known to be true; may also be construed as dramatic irony, since one character, the mother, and the audience know that what is being said is untrue, even if the people saying it believe it to be true]

Independent Practice: Analyzing style and tone. When students have finished working with you on the Guided Practice, ask them to read the entire text of "The Rocking-Horse Winner" as homework and use what they have learned about Lawrence's diction, use of irony, and sentence structure in the first paragraph to analyze the rest of the story. Have them write a short essay or oral report on the overall style and tone of Lawrence's story. You may also want to challenge some students by asking them to compare Lawrence's style and tone with that of Nadine Gordimer in "Once upon a Time" (p. 923) or V. S. Naipaul in "B. Wordsworth" (p. 1015).

Poetic Devices

Objective: To analyze the ways poets use imagery, personification, figures of speech, and sounds.

Direct Teaching: Share the following ideas with students.

When someone mentions the word *poetry*, what do you think of? Do you think of a lullaby or nursery rhyme, the words to your favorite song, a Shakespearean sonnet, or a humorous limerick? All of these are poetry. What sets poetry apart from ordinary prose is its ability to excite readers with new sensations, ideas, and feelings and make the familiar seem fresh and alive again. What is even more amazing is that poets achieve these effects with words alone, by making use of a variety of poetic devices. These devices include imagery, figures of speech, and various sound effects. Imagery is the use of words to make vivid sense impressions on readers' imaginations. Imagery makes it possible for readers to see, hear, smell, and feel what the writer wants them to experience. Figurative language links objects or experiences that seem at first to have no similarity but turn out to be connected in some unexpected and revealing way. T. S. Eliot, for example, linked fog and cats in "The Love Song of J. Alfred Prufrock" when he wrote that a yellow fog "rubs its back upon the window-panes" and "Curled once about the house, and fell asleep." Sound effects—like alliteration, assonance, and rhyme—are what give poetry its musical quality. Imagery, figures of speech, and sound effects all work together to stir readers' emotions and imaginations at levels deeper than ordinary prose can reach.

Guided Practice: Identifying poetic devices. Review with students the definitions of the terms *simile, metaphor, personification, alliteration, assonance,* and *rhyme* in the Handbook of Literary and Historical Terms (p. 1181). Go over the provided examples with students, and ask them to offer additional examples from their favorite poems. Remind them that poems are meant to be read aloud and listened to carefully and that more than one reading is usually needed to notice many of their devices. Then, have volunteers read aloud John Donne's "Death be not proud" (p. 312) and William Wordsworth's "Composed upon Westminster Bridge" (p. 559). As the volunteers are reading the poems, draw on the chalkboard charts like the one below and the one on p. 1129R. Explain that the first column of the charts includes examples of the use of poetic devices from the two poems they have just heard. Have students take turns identifying the device(s) used in each passage. Be sure to tell them that many passages display more than one of the devices you have been discussing. Write their responses in the second column of the charts. (Responses appear in brackets.)

"Death be not proud"		
Passage from Poem	**Poetic Device**	**Emotional Effect**
"Die not, poor Death, nor yet canst thou kill me."	[personification (of Death); alliteration ("Die not, poor Death . . . canst thou kill me")]	[makes Death seem real rather than abstract; alliteration adds emphasis and a tone of determination]
"Thou art slave to fate, chance, kings, and desperate men"	[personification (of death); assonance ("slave to fate")]	[assonance emphasizes the feeling of inevitability]
"One short sleep past, we wake eternally"	[metaphor (sleep and death are linked); alliteration ("short sleep . . . we wake")]	[stirs feelings of promise and hope]

"Composed upon Westminster Bridge"		
Passage from Poem	**Poetic Device**	**Emotional Effect**
"This City now doth, like a garment, wear / The beauty of the morning; silent, bare"	[imagery (visual, auditory); personification (City wears a garment); alliteration (<u>c</u>ity / <u>s</u>ilent, <u>b</u>eauty / <u>b</u>are); end rhyme]	[helps one to imagine a quiet city just before dawn]
"Never did sun more beautifully steep / In his first splendor, valley, rock, or hill"	[imagery (visual); personification (of the sun); alliteration (<u>s</u>un / <u>s</u>teep / <u>s</u>plendor)]	[creates a picture of sun-drenched nature and stirs feelings of joy and elation]
"the very houses seem asleep; / and all that mighty heart is lying still!"	[personification (of house); metaphor (city is compared to a slumbering organism); assonance (m<u>i</u>ghty / l<u>y</u>ing)]	[creates a picture of power in repose and stirs feelings of both peace and excitement]

Independent Practice: Analyzing poetic devices' emotional effects. Add a third column to the chart as shown on this page. For each example, have student pairs discuss how the poetic devices make them feel or help them imagine an experience in the poem. (Possible responses appear in brackets.) When partners have finished their discussions, have students regroup as a class and compare and contrast their responses.

For further practice, ask students to read Tu Fu's "Jade Flower Palace" (p. 631). For homework, have them find examples of the poetic devices they have been studying and analyze them, using a three-column chart like the one in this lesson. When they have completed their charts, ask them to write a short essay on the emotional effects that Tu Fu creates by means of his poetic devices.

Archetypes

Objective: To analyze archetypes drawn from myth and tradition.

Direct Teaching: Share the following information with students.

The English word *archetype* comes from a Greek word meaning "original," which in turn came from the Greek root word for "stamp" or "model." A literary archetype, then, is a pattern, which becomes the model for many different but related versions of a character, plot, setting, or object. Since myths, religious texts, and folk tales are among the earliest forms of literature, they are the source for many of the archetypal patterns on which so much later literature is based. Archetypes are also used in political speeches, films, television shows, and advertisements. The larger-than-life hero of the Greek myths is an example of an archetypal character and his or her quest to overcome evil or regain a lost paradise is an archetypal plot. This same character and plot structure recur in the literature and popular culture of many nations, times, and places. The details change, but the core remains the same, suggesting that human beings everywhere share the same concerns and use their imaginations in similar ways.

Guided Practice: Identifying archetypes. Draw on the chalkboard a web like the one below. Help students to think of examples of the four kinds of archetypes, and write their examples in the web. (Possible responses appear in brackets.) Remind students that archetypes are still being used in movies, such as fantasy or science fiction films, and in other forms of popular media, such as television series, music videos, and advertisements. Give them a few examples to start them off.

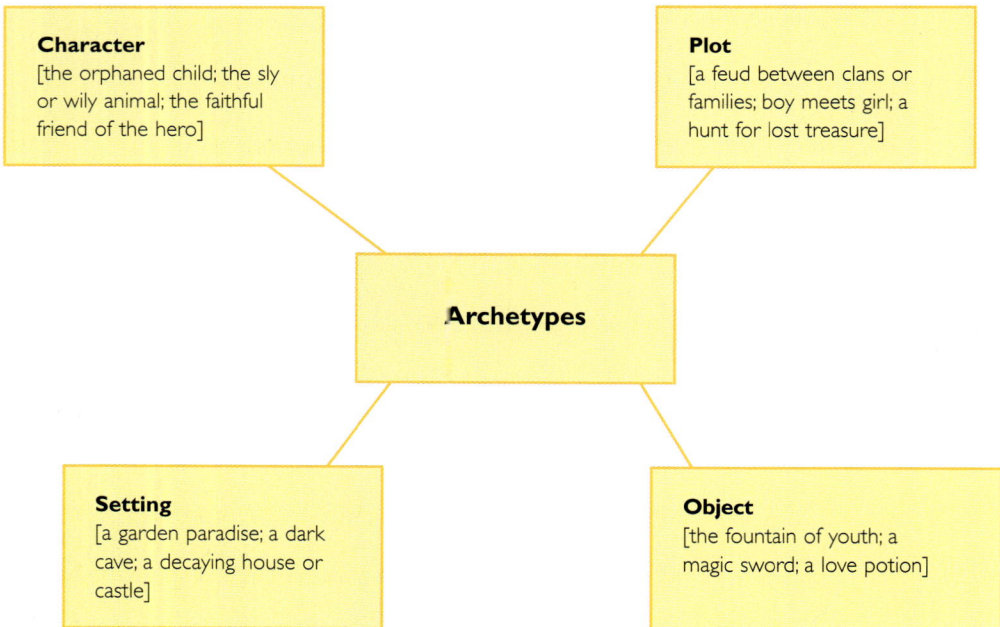

1129S   Archetypes

Have students read the excerpt from "The Third Voyage of Sindbad the Sailor" (p. 180). Ask students to keep the four kinds of archetypes in mind as they read and look for examples of each. Draw another web for the Sindbad selection like the one on this page, and write in any appropriate examples of archetypes that students identify. (Possible responses appear in brackets.)

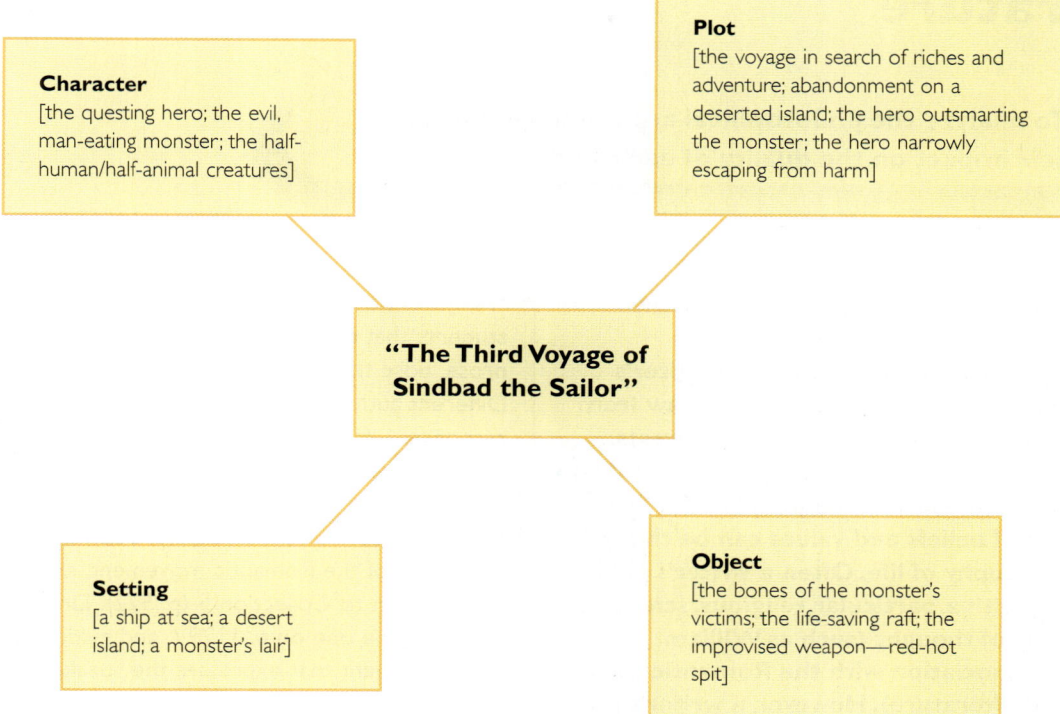

After you have competed the web, lead students in a general discussion of the role of archetypes in literature by asking questions such as these:

- Was the story of Sindbad more or less interesting because it was based on archetypal patterns? Explain.

- What other stories, movies, or television programs do you know based on similar patterns?

- Why do you think these patterns keep reappearing in texts from different authors, times, and cultures?

- What have you learned or could you learn from such stories?

Help students understand that archetypes recur because human beings everywhere face similar problems, devise similar solutions, and have similar feelings in the face of adversity.

Independent Practice: Analyzing archetypes. Have students read "The Battle with Grendel" (p. 20) or "The Monster's Mother" (p. 26). Next, assign partners to read the same excerpt from *Beowulf* and work together to identify archetypes in the text. [Possible responses: the superhuman hero, the good king, the man-eating monster, the monster's lair, the battle between good and evil, the magic sword, the descent to the underworld, the hidden treasure.] Have students compare and contrast the *Beowulf* excerpt with "The Third Voyage of Sindbad the Sailor" and prepare an oral report to be given in class. Encourage partners to use a two-column chart or a Venn diagram to organize their analysis of the works' similarities and differences. Students can refer to their charts or diagrams when giving their reports. Then, lead a class discussion of why these archetypal battles between heroes and monsters keep recurring and how cultural or religious differences may account for some of the variations in the basic plot. Be sure students give examples of contemporary movies and television shows that dramatize these epic battles between the good brave hero and the evil monster or villain.

Reteaching Lessons

Archetypes **1129T**

Philosophical Approach to Literature

> **Objective:** To analyze the philosophical arguments in literary works and their impact on the quality of each work.

Direct Teaching: Share the following ideas with students.

The ideas that form the foundation of a writer's work come from many sources. Writers draw from their own knowledge, experiences, and interests. Their writing also reflects what they understand and believe about the world and the people in it. This overall pattern of beliefs and values can be thought of as their philosophy of life. Often a writer's philosophy coincides with a particular religious, scientific, or literary body of thought (such as William Wordsworth's association with the Romantic movement in English literature). However, a writer's philosophy may stem from a very personal set of beliefs, which do not conform to any one philosophical system (such as the ideas of William Blake). Writers' philosophies affect how they write about issues, such as war, materialism, self-sacrifice, and the importance of art or spirituality in human life. Careful readers will look to see if writers have successfully integrated their philosophical beliefs into their works and will evaluate whether characters and other details "ring true" or function merely as mouthpieces for the writers' philosophical positions.

Guided Practice: Analyzing philosophical positions. Tell students that many works of literature, both in poetry and prose, pose the question, "What is really important in life?" Different authors in different times and places have different responses—from human love to faith in the unseen—but whatever response they offer will reflect their personal philosophy and values. Read aloud William Wordsworth's poem "The World Is Too Much with Us" (p. 562), and review with students the tenets of the Romantic movement, as presented in the introduction to Collection 5 (p. 522). Draw on the chalkboard a chart like the one on p. 1129V, and guide students in formulating a statement that expresses the speaker's belief about what is most important in life. (A possible response appears in brackets.) As students volunteer statements, ask them to provide details from the poem that support their conclusions, and write these at the bottom of the chart. Keep the discussion going until all agree on a single statement of the speaker's highest value.

Next, ask students if they think William Wordsworth, through his speaker, made a good case for his philosophical point of view. Tell students that they do not have to accept a belief in order to judge whether a writer has made a convincing case for it. Rather, they need only evaluate the strength of the evidence—in this case, the power of Wordsworth's diction and imagery.

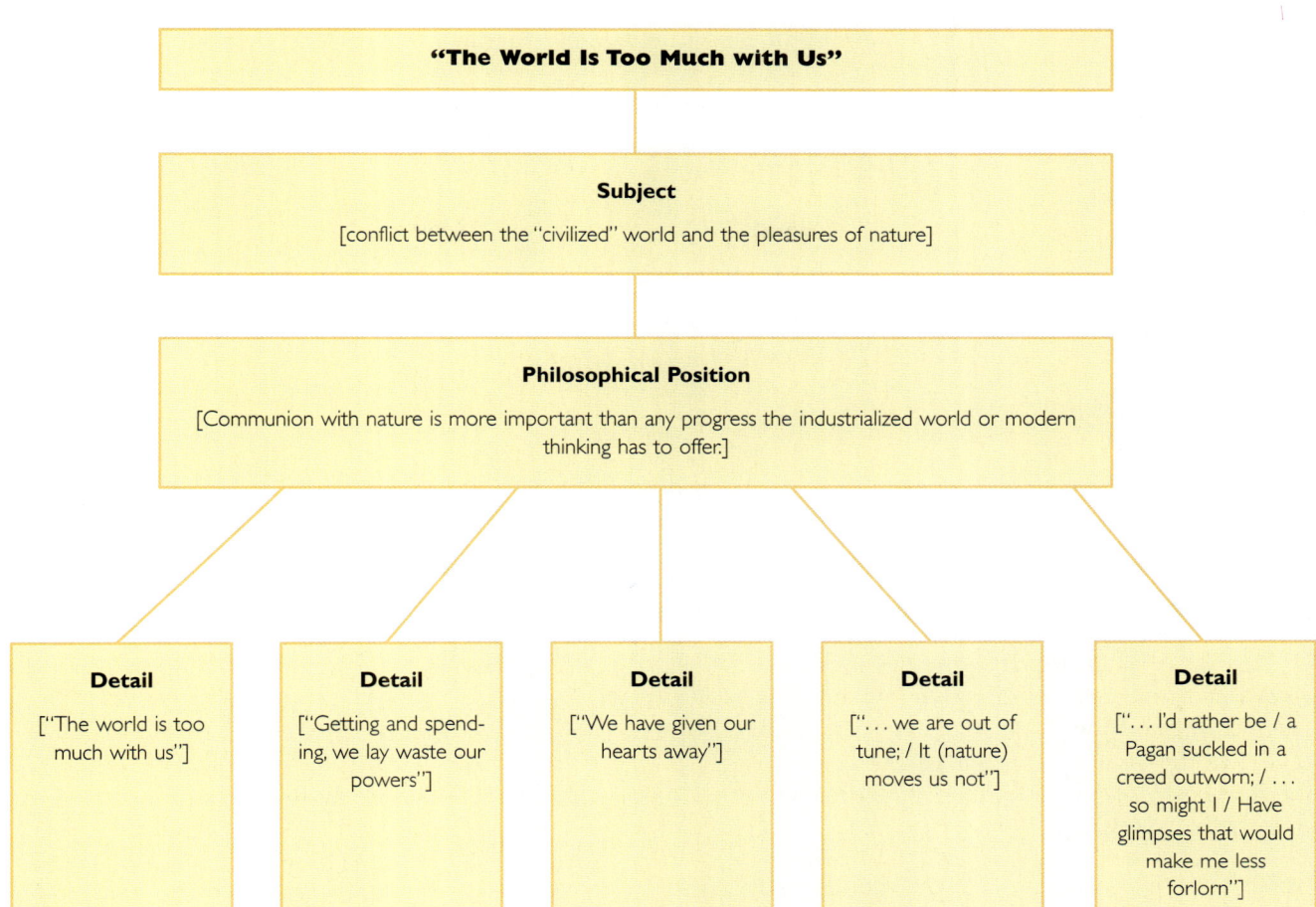

Independent Practice: Analyzing philosophical positions in literature. Ask students to read Boccaccio's "Federigo's Falcon" (p. 186), or Leo Tolstoy's "How Much Land Does a Man Need?" (p. 750). Have pairs who have read the same selection work together to discover how the author, through his characters and plot, answers the question "What is most important in life?" To gain insight into the author's background and general philosophy of life, urge students to read the biographical information on the author that precedes each selection. Then, ask the partners to make a chart for their story like the one used in the Guided Practice. They can use it to write a short essay that explains what they have learned from the story about the author's philosophy and values. Remind students that authors do not necessarily agree with the actions or choices of all their characters, but they often reveal their beliefs by the way they work out their plots. Therefore, it is important for students to identify what the values of the main characters are, how far the characters are willing to go to get what they want, and what the outcomes of their choices are. [Possible responses: Boccaccio values love, loyalty, and self-sacrifice over personal gain, since Monna and Federigo are ultimately rewarded for acting out of love. Tolstoy values life and freedom over material wealth, since Pahom dies as a result of his obsessive greed.] Finally, conduct a class discussion of partners' conclusions about the authors' values and an evaluation of the two works. Ask, "Which writer do you think illustrates his philosophical position more effectively, and why?" Remind students to consider whether the fates of the main characters seem believable in the contexts of the stories or merely contrived for the purpose of emphasizing the authors' philosophical points.

Resource Center

Reading Matters by Kylene Beers **1133**	Handbook of Literary and Historical Terms **1181**
The World of Work **1147**	Language Handbook **1205**
Writer's Handbook **1153**	Glossary **1243**
Test Smarts **1165**	Spanish Glossary **1249**

The Parisian Novels (The Yellow Books), Vincent van Gogh, 1888.

Reading Matters

When the Text Is Tough

Remember the reading you did back in first, second, and third grades? Big print. Short texts. Easy words. In high school, however, the texts you read are often filled with small print, long chapters, and complicated plots or topics. Also, you now find yourself reading a variety of material—from your driver's-ed handbook to college applications, from job applications to income-tax forms, from e-mail to e-zines, from classics to comics, from textbooks to checkbooks.

Doing something every day that you find difficult and tedious isn't much fun—and that includes reading. So this section of this book is designed for you, to show you what to do when the text gets tough. Let's begin to look at some reading matters—because after all, reading *matters*.

READING UP CLOSE: HOW TO USE THIS SECTION

- **This section is for you.** Turn to it whenever you need to remind yourself about what to do when the text gets tough. Don't wait for your teacher to assign this section for you to read. It's your handbook. Use it.

- **Read the sections that you need.** You don't have to read every word. Skim the headings, and find the information you need.

- **Use this information to help you with reading for other classes,** not just for the reading you do in this book.

- **Don't be afraid to *re-read* the information** you find in Reading Matters. The best readers constantly re-read information.

- **If you need more help, then check the index.** The index will direct you to other pages in this book with information on reading skills and strategies.

Using Reading Matters with the Student Edition

Introduce Reading Matters to students early in the school year, so that they can apply the strategies to improve both their reading comprehension and their speed as the school year proceeds. Begin by previewing the section, noting each lesson's content, headings, and Reading Up Close boxes. Tell students that the strategies apply to both literary and informational texts. If possible, model each strategy in class.

You may decide to use a particular reading strategy as preteaching instruction for a selection or a collection. Or you may choose to use this section only with students who need remediation. You can also use strategy lessons for reteaching and review.

Using This Lesson

Twelfth-graders don't need to be convinced; they *know* that reading matters. By this point in their high school education, they have probably had both good and bad experiences with standardized tests whose critical-reading sections measure their comprehension. They are well aware that such tests determine in part whether they will graduate from high school and whether they will be admitted to college. Explain that the strategies and tips in Reading Matters have been designed to improve both their comprehension and their speed.

Reading Up Close

You might briefly go over the Reading Up Close box in class. Point out that Reading Matters is a resource that students can consult when they are having difficulty understanding a text or when they simply want to improve their reading proficiency. Be sure to emphasize that they will not be tested on the material.

Improving Your Comprehension

This lesson, the heart of Reading Matters, gives students strategies for improving comprehension of literary and informational texts. Assure students that these reading strategies will help them understand the types of texts—for example, college or job applications—that will play a crucial part in their lives.

Reading Up Close

Have students work in small groups to decide on creative ways to use each of the symbols. Emphasize that there are no right answers.

Possible Responses

1. A fork-in-the-road sign might mark a point where the text has two levels of meaning, as in an allegory.
2. A dead-end sign might indicate a point at which the reader is confused by the text.
3. A winding-road sign might indicate that the text requires special attention.
4. The no-U-turn sign might indicate a point where the reader resists the temptation to re-read and continues with the hope of understanding the text better after finishing it.
5. A yield sign might indicate a point in the text where the writer's ideas or opinions run contrary to the reader's beliefs.
6. A U-turn sign might indicate a point in the text where the reader has to re-read a passage to improve comprehension.
7. A falling-rocks sign might signal difficult vocabulary, unfamiliar allusions, or complex ideas.
8. A stop sign might indicate a point where the reader pauses to summarize the text or to note questions or comments.
9. A person-working sign might indicate a point where the reader thinks the writer needs to clarify some aspect of the text.
10. The railroad-crossing sign might indicate a point that requires re-reading (see p. 1138).

Improving Your Comprehension

Comprehension, your ability to understand what you read, is a critical part of the reading process. Your comprehension can be affected by many factors. Think about each of the following types of texts, and rate your comprehension of each from 1 (*never understand*) to 5 (*always understand*):

A. notes from friends
B. e-mail messages from friends
C. college applications
D. job applications
E. magazines
F. computer manuals
G. Internet sites
H. school textbooks
I. novels you choose
J. novels your teachers choose for you

You probably didn't rate yourself the same for each type of text. Factors such as your interest level and the text's vocabulary level will cause your ratings to differ from text to text. Now, go back, and look specifically at items H, I, and J. How did you rate there? If you think your comprehension of those materials is low, then you'll want to study the next few pages carefully. They are filled with tips to help you improve your comprehension.

Visualizing the text. The ability to visualize—or see in your mind—what you are reading is important for comprehension. To understand how visualizing makes a difference, try this quick test. At home, turn on a television to a program you enjoy. Then, turn your back to the television set. How long will you keep "watching" the program that way? Probably not long. Why not? Because it would be boring if you couldn't see what was happening. The same is true of reading: If you can't see in your mind what is happening on the page, then you probably will tune out quickly. You can improve your ability to visualize a text by practicing the following strategies:

READING UP CLOSE

▶ Monitoring Your Comprehension

Skilled readers often pay more attention to what they don't understand than to what they do. Here are some symbols you could put on self-sticking notes and place on texts as you are reading so that you can keep up with what's confusing you. Decide how you would use each symbol.

What reading problem could each sign indicate?

Using the Visualizing the Text Strategy

The **Visualizing the Text strategy** applies to literary texts, biographies, autobiographies, and informational essays, as well as some science and nature writing. All of these texts contain sensory details and images that students can visualize. Emphasize that this strategy applies to all kinds of sensory details, not just those that appeal to the sense of sight.

Have students work with a partner or in a small group to practice the four numbered strategies. When they've finished reading, ask them to describe how well the strategies worked.

1. **Read a few sentences; then pause, and describe what is happening on the page.** Forcing yourself to describe the scene will take some time at first, but doing that will help in the long run.
2. **On a sheet of paper or a stick-on note, make a graphic representation of what is happening as you are reading.** For instance, if two characters are talking, draw two stick figures with arrows pointing between them to show yourself that they are talking.
3. **Discuss a scene or a part of a chapter with a partner.** Talk about what you "saw" as you were reading.
4. **Read aloud.** You might be having trouble visualizing the text because you aren't "hearing" it. Try reading a portion of your text aloud, using good expression and phrasing. As you hear the words, you may find it easier to see the scenes.

READING UP CLOSE

▶ **Visualizing What You Read**

Read the following excerpt from "The Day of Destiny" (see page 194), and discuss what you "see":

> Then, on the night of Trinity Sunday, Arthur was vouchsafed a strange dream:
>
> He was appareled in gold cloth and seated in a chair which stood on a pivoted scaffold. Below him, many fathoms deep, was a dark well, and in the water swam serpents, dragons, and wild beasts. Suddenly the scaffold tilted and Arthur was flung into the water, where all the creatures struggled toward him and began tearing him limb from limb.
>
> Arthur cried out in his sleep and his squires hastened to waken him.

How's your metacognition? Your attention wanders for a moment as you are reading something, but your eyes don't quit moving from word to word. After a few minutes you realize you are several pages beyond the last point at which you can remember thinking about what you were reading. Then you know you need to back up and start over. This ability to think about your thinking—or, in this case, your lack of thinking—is called **metacognition**.

Metacognition refers to your ability to analyze what you are doing as you try to make sense of texts. A critical part of metacognition is paying attention to what you are reading. It's normal to find that your attention *sometimes* wanders while reading. If it always wanders, though, then try one of the following activities: (1) Keep paper and pen close, and jot down notes as you read; (2) read for a set amount of time (five minutes), and then stop and review what's happened since the last time you stopped. Lengthen this time as you find yourself able to focus longer. Take the following quiz to see what your metacognition level is:

Reading Up Close

As students read the passage from "The Day of Destiny," have them jot down details that appeal to the senses. [Possible responses: *Sight*—"appareled in gold cloth"; "a chair which stood on a pivoted scaffold"; "dark well." *Sound*—"cried out."]

Using the Metacognition Strategy

When it comes to movies and TV, students choose to watch fast-moving, action-packed drama, so it's no wonder that when they are required to read literary texts with a slow-moving plot, their attention is likely to wander. Older literary texts with long sentences, difficult syntax, and a heavy vocabulary load present special problems in maintaining attention. For some students the difficulty arises mainly while reading informational texts, such as textbooks, reference books, and newspaper and magazine articles.

You might review this lesson before students read the excerpt from "The Day of Destiny" (p. 194) or any of the Renaissance poems in Collection 3.

Go over the two numbered activities in class. The first advises students to take notes as they read; the second advises that they stop to review and summarize the paragraphs they've just read.

Reading Up Close

This survey is designed to help students measure how well they pay attention to what they read.

Point out that students' responses to the survey will vary according to the type of text they are reading. For example, students' attention may never wander when they are reading a poem by their favorite writer, but it may wander a lot when they are reading their science textbook to prepare for an exam. Suggest that students complete the survey for each type of text they read during the school year.

Using the Think-Aloud Strategy

The **Think-Aloud strategy** requires that students monitor their understanding of a text and, as a result, helps them stay focused as they read. Some students will have difficulty classifying their partner's comments. Emphasize that such classification isn't essential. The purpose of the Think-Aloud strategy is to help students become active readers, who are aware of their thoughts, responses, and questions.

You may wish to model a Think-Aloud in class by reading aloud a challenging poem or prose passage, making comments as you read. Be sure to demonstrate a wide variety of Think-Aloud comments, and point out that it isn't necessary to comment on every sentence or line.

READING UP CLOSE

▶ **Measuring Your Attention Quotient**

The lower the score, the less you pay attention to what you are reading. The higher the score, the more you pay attention.

When I read, I

A. **let my mind wander a lot**

1	2	3
most of the time	sometimes	almost never

B. **forget what I'm reading**

1	2	3
most of the time	sometimes	almost never

C. **get confused and stay confused or don't even realize I am confused**

1	2	3
most of the time	sometimes	almost never

D. **discover I've turned lots of pages and don't have a clue as to what I've read**

1	2	3
most of the time	sometimes	almost never

E. **rarely finish whatever I'm supposed to be reading**

1	2	3
most of the time	sometimes	almost never

Try Think-Aloud. Comprehension problems don't appear only after you *finish* reading. Confusion occurs *as* you read. Therefore, don't wait until you complete your reading assignment to try to understand the text; instead, work on comprehending while reading by becoming an active reader.

Active readers **predict, connect, clarify, question,** and **visualize** as they read. If you don't do those things, you need to pause while you read to

- make **predictions**
- make **connections**
- **clarify** in your own thoughts what you are reading
- **question** what you don't understand
- **visualize** the text

Use the Think-Aloud strategy to practice your active-reading skills. Here is how Think-Aloud works: Read a selection of text aloud to a partner. As you read, pause to make comments and ask questions. Your partner's job is to tally your comments and classify each one according to the list at the top of this page.

READING UP CLOSE

▶ **One Student's Think-Aloud**

Here's Steve's Think-Aloud for Shakespeare's Sonnet 130 (page 284):

After reading entire sonnet once: I don't get it. This is like he's saying the woman he loves is ugly. Why would he say these things? **(Question)**

After reading sonnet a second time: He isn't saying very nice things about her. At the end he still says his love is rare, so I think he does love her. **(Comment/Clarification)**

After reading sonnet a third time: You know, maybe this is a joke about love: like, it's always supposed to be perfect, you know—coral red lips and eyes like the sun—but even if she doesn't have those things, he still loves her. I think it's those last two lines that are important, you know, showing that someone you love doesn't have to be perfect. This is like realizing that even if your car isn't the coolest car in the lot, it's your car, and so you still love it. **(Connection)**

Question the text. This scenario may be familiar: You've just finished reading one of the selections in this book. Then you look at the questions that you'll be discussing tomorrow in class. You realize that you don't know the answers. In frustration you decide to give up on the questions.

While giving up is one way to approach the problem, it's not the best approach. In fact, what you need to do is focus *more* on questions—and focus on them while reading the text, not just at the end. This doesn't mean memorizing study questions before you read so that as you are reading you are thinking only about those questions. What it means is constantly asking yourself questions about characters, plot, point of view, setting, conflict, and even vocabulary while reading. You'll find that the more you question the text while reading, the more prepared you'll be to answer the questions at the end of the text.

READING UP CLOSE

▶ **Asking Questions While Reading**

Here is a list of questions you can use as you read literary selections. You should recopy this list on note cards and keep it close as you read.

Character Questions

1. Who is the central character? Is this character the narrator? What are the greatest strengths and greatest weaknesses of this character? What does this character discover by the story's end? Has he or she changed?

(continued)

Reading Up Close

Tell students that Steve's comments about Shakespeare's Sonnet 130 (p. 284) are only a sample of the many comments and questions that he could have recorded. Point out that Steve read the sonnet three times (using the Re-reading strategy—see p. 1138) and that each re-reading led to a deeper understanding of the sonnet.

You might ask students to work with a partner to try out the Think-Aloud strategy with a challenging text, such as John Milton's "The Fall of Satan" from *Paradise Lost* (p. 367) or the excerpt from John Bunyan's *The Pilgrim's Progress* (p. 384).

Using the Question the Text Strategy

Question the Text combines aspects of the Metacognition (p. 1135) and Think-Aloud (p. 1136) strategies but is much more analytic. This reading strategy focuses on the elements of literature students are used to discussing.

Reading Up Close

The questions in the Reading Up Close box will seem familiar to students because they resemble the questions that follow the literary selections in the Student Edition. Advise students that they can use these questions to analyze any unfamiliar short story, novel, or play.

The questions in the Reading Up Close box do not apply to poetry, nonfiction, or informational material. If you have time, suggest that students work with a partner or a small group to develop a list of analytical questions for a different type of writing, such as poetry, essays, biographies and autobiographies, or informational materials. See whether groups working on the same genre can reach a consensus on important questions to ask.

Using the Re-reading and Rewording Strategies

Re-reading. The difference between the **Re-reading strategy** and an ordinary second reading of a text lies in the level of the reader's awareness. When readers apply the Re-reading strategy, they focus on passages, sentences, or words that puzzle them, and they actively try to untangle these puzzles. Re-reading is an easy strategy and works well with all types of literary and informational texts.

You might ask a volunteer to model the Re-reading strategy in class. Have the student read aloud a difficult passage from a historical text, such as the introductory essays in Collections 1 or 2, while applying the Think-Aloud strategy. By reading the passage a second time and completing a Think-Aloud again, the student will demonstrate how the strategy allows the reader to answer questions that were identified the first time around.

As practice, you might have student apply this strategy to the excerpts from *Gilgamesh* (p. 48) or the *Iliad* (p. 57).

Rewording. Suggest that students consult a college dictionary and a thesaurus when they set out to apply the **Rewording strategy**. For students who need occasional practice with rewording, you might assign short passages from informational or literary texts that contain difficult words, complex ideas, or both.

(continued)

2. Is the narrator telling the story while it is happening or while looking back? Can you trust this narrator? What if the narrator were a different character? How would the story change? What point of view does the narrator have—first person, limited third person, omniscient—and how does that point of view affect the narrator's authority?

3. Who are the other characters? What makes them important to the central character? What do their actions reveal about their personalities? How do your thoughts about the characters change as you read the story? Can you find specific points in the text where your feelings about characters shift? Could any character have been omitted from the story?

4. Which character do you like the best? What do you have in common with this character?

Plot, Setting, and Conflict Questions

1. What are the major events in the plot? Which events are mandatory in order for the story to reach the conclusion it does? What prior knowledge is necessary for understanding the plot?

2. How does the setting affect the story? Could you change the location or the historical context and have the same story? How does the author situate the reader in the setting? Is the setting believable?

3. What event creates the conflict? How does the central character react to the conflict? How do other characters react? How is the conflict resolved?

Re-reading and rewording. The best way to improve your comprehension is simply to **re-read**. The first time you read something, you get the basic idea of the text. The next time you read it, you revise your understanding. Try thinking of your first reading as a draft—like the first draft of an essay. As you revise your essay, you are improving your writing. As you revise your reading, you are improving your comprehension.

Sometimes, as you re-read, you find some specific sentences or even passages that you just don't understand. When that's the case, you need to spend some time closely studying those sentences. One effective way to tackle tough text is to **reword** the text:

1. On a piece of paper, write down the sentences that are confusing you.
2. Leave a few blank lines between each line that you write.
3. Then, choose the difficult words, and reword them in the space above.

While you wouldn't want to reword every line of a long text—or even a short one—this is a powerful way to help your understanding of key sentences.

READING UP CLOSE

▶ **One Student's Rewording**

Thomas tried rewording some of "The Fall of Satan" (page 367, lines 1–6). Because word order is as confusing as word choice, Thomas combined reordering with rewording. Open your book to page 367, and read the original lines there. Then, see Thomas's changes below. Also, note that he has combined a Think-Aloud (see page 1136) with his rewording.

> This first part seems backwards. Look, I think he's asking this muse—what's a muse? OK, the sidenote says it's a muse of poetry; I think this is like a Greek mythology character—so I think he's asking this muse to sing—not a real song, but just to tell him something. So it really could start by saying Heavenly Muse, tell me about "man's first disobedience, and the fruit of that forbidden tree." Well, that would be in the Garden of Eden. So he's saying to the Muse,
>
> Tell me about when man first sinned in the Garden of Eden by eating the apple that brought death to the world and all our problems because now we don't live in Eden, until Christ brings us back to that blissful—that would be like perfect—seat.

Summarizing narrative text. Understanding a long piece of text is easier if you can summarize chunks of it. If you are reading a **narrative,** or a story (including a biography or an autobiography), then use a strategy called **Somebody Wanted But So** (**SWBS**) for help writing a summary of what you are reading.

SWBS is a powerful way to think about the characters in a narrative and to note what each does, what conflict each faces, and what the resolution is. As you write an SWBS statement for different characters or subjects within the same narrative, you are forcing yourself to rethink the narrative from different **points of view.**

Here are the steps for writing SWBS statements:

1. Write the words *Somebody, Wanted, But,* and *So* across the top of four columns.
2. Under the "Somebody" column, write a character's name.
3. Then, under the "Wanted" column, write what that character wanted to do.
4. Next, under the "But" column, explain what happened that kept the character from doing what he or she wanted.
5. Finally, under the "So" column, explain the eventual outcome.

If you're making an SWBS chart for a long story or novel, you might need to write several SWBS statements at different points in the story.

Reading Up Close

Point out that the first part of the box presents Thomas's Think-Aloud on ll. 1–6 of John Milton's "The Fall of Satan" (p. 367); his rewording is the indented passage at the end. You might ask students to compare carefully Thomas's rewording with the original text and then to apply the Rewording strategy to another passage from Milton's poem.

Using the SWBS Strategy: Summarizing Narrative Text

The **SWBS (Somebody Wanted But So) strategy** helps students clarify and organize their thinking about a narrative text, such as a story, novel, or play. Remind students that long, complex narratives often require several SWBS statements to summarize the plot adequately. As students read the numbered steps for writing an SWBS statement, point out that they are focusing on a single character and his or her conflict.

Reading Up Close

The following is a sample SWBS statement from the point of view of one of the merchants in the excerpt from *The Pilgrim's Progress* (p. 384): *Somebody*—merchants. *Wanted*—to sell their vanities to the pilgrims. *But*—the pilgrims did not care to buy the vanities. *So*—a great hubbub ensued.

For further practice, have students use the SWBS strategy with any of the stories or the play excerpt in the Student Edition.

Using the GIST Strategy: Summarizing Expository Text

The **GIST (Generating Interactions between Schemata and Text) strategy** requires that students write a summary statement that is exactly twenty words long—not an easy task. Each GIST statement summarizes the main idea of its section and all preceding sections.

Tell students that they will probably have to try out many different GIST statements until they find one that is both accurate and the right length.

Reading Up Close

Have students turn to p. 1103 to compare the text and the GIST statements, and ask them to suggest improvements or other wordings. [Possible response: Until South Africa's problems are addressed and the root causes removed, racial division and political unrest are sure to worsen.]

The GIST strategy works well for nonfiction selections or informational material. You might have students practice this strategy on one of the selections in Political Points of View: "Education and Equality" (p. 322) in Collection 3 or the excerpt from Mary Wollstonecraft's *A Vindication on the Rights of Woman* (p. 487) in Collection 4.

READING UP CLOSE

▶ **One Student's SWBS Chart**

Read this SWBS statement of the excerpt from *The Pilgrim's Progress* (page 384). This statement includes information up through the break on page 386. Try writing an SWBS statement from the point of view of one of the merchants at Vanity Fair.

Somebody	Wanted	But	So
Christian	did not want to buy the merchandise at Vanity Fair,	but the merchants kept pushing wares on him,	so he was taken to prison and put on trial.

Summarizing expository text. If summarizing the information in a text is difficult, try a strategy called GIST.

1. Choose three or four sections of text you want to summarize.
2. Read the first section of text.
3. Draw twenty blank lines on a sheet of paper.
4. Write a summary of the first section of text using exactly twenty words—one word for each blank.
5. Read the next section of text.
6. Now, in your next set of twenty blanks, write a new summary statement that combines your first summary with whatever you want to add from this second section of text. You still have only twenty blanks to fill in, not forty.

Repeat this process one or two more times, depending on how many more sections of text you have to read. When you are finished, you'll have a twenty-word statement that gives you the gist, or overall idea, of the entire text.

READING UP CLOSE

▶ **One Student's GIST**

Study the GIST statements for the first four paragraphs of text from Desmond Tutu's speech "The Question of South Africa" found on page 1103. Then, try your hand at creating the third GIST.

GIST 1 (for the first column of text)
South Africa has enough resources to provide for its people and should be peaceful, but social unrest is dividing it.

GIST 2 (adding the second column of text)
South Africa is divided because of the repressive policies of the white government; unemployment and higher prices have worsened things.

GIST 3 (adding the first column of text on page 1104)
___ ___ ___ ___ ___ ___ ___ ___ ___

Using question maps. Most readers at some point will struggle with a text. Some readers find reading poetry a struggle, but they can breeze through computer magazines. Others find the technical language in computer magazines difficult but read poetry easily. It's not whether you struggle with texts that matters; instead, what matters is what you *do* when you struggle.

If you are an independent reader, then you know how to find the answers on your own—independently—to whatever causes you to struggle. If you are a dependent reader, you expect others to do the explaining for you. Dependent readers often say, "I don't get it," and give up. Independent readers, by contrast, know what they don't get and then figure out how to get it.

If you think you are a dependent reader, try using a question map like the one below. As you complete the chart, you'll be mapping your way toward independent reading.

1. In the first column, **list your questions** as you are reading.
2. In the second column, **make notes about each question.** For instance, jot down what made you think about the question or what page you are on in the text.
3. In the third column, **list possibilities for finding answers.** Remember that re-reading the text is always a good idea. Other places to find answers include dictionaries (especially if you have questions about vocabulary), your own mind (sometimes the text gives you part of the information, and you must figure out the rest), or other parts of the book (especially if you are reading a science, math, or history book).
4. In the final column, **jot down answers to your questions** only after you've made notes about them and thought out where to find answers to them. If you can't answer your questions at this point, then it's time to see your teacher.

READING UP CLOSE

▶ **One Student's Question Map**

Here is a part of Denise's question map for "The Mark of the Beast" (page 733):

Questions	Notes	Places to find answers	Answers
1. Why is *Providence* capitalized?	p. 733, 4th line	Ask teacher	making luck be like a person
2. Who is Hanuman?	p. 734, 2nd line	dictionary or encyclopedia	a god in Hindu mythology

Using the Question Maps Strategy

The **Question Maps strategy** is intended to guide dependent readers through the process of independently answering the questions that confront them as they read a difficult text. Readers generate a list of questions, figure out how to answer the questions, and then answer them—without relying on others to do the answering for them.

Many students already read independently and do not need to make question maps, but encourage everyone to practice the strategy at least once. Students will find question maps particularly useful with older literary texts, such as those in Collections 1 and 2.

Reading Up Close

In class, go over Denise's question map for "The Mark of the Beast" (p. 733). If students have already read this selection, ask them to continue the question map, adding their own questions and answers. To practice this strategy, students might make a question map for the next selection they're assigned to read.

Using the Smart Words Strategy

The **Smart Words strategy** provides students with a vocabulary that is critical to their evaluation of literary texts. Students will find the words useful when they write about or discuss literary texts. Note that the first two sections, "Words and Phrases to Describe the Plot" and "Words and Phrases to Describe the Characters," apply only to fiction and drama. The second two sections, "Words to Describe the Theme" and "Words and Phrases to Describe the Author's Style of Writing," can be applied to both fiction and nonfiction.

These word lists are not exhaustive. Ask students to suggest other "smart words" to add to each list. You might also assign small groups the task of creating additional lists of smart words for evaluating poems or informational material.

Reading Up Close

Before students begin this exercise, you might have them bring to class a critical review of a novel—a review they have written or a review they've found in a newspaper or magazine or on the Internet. As they go over their review with a partner, have them keep track of the smart words the writer uses to evaluate the novel. Ask students to determine whether the review is favorable or unfavorable. Also, have students identify the words and phrases that reveal the writer's opinion.

Know some smart words. Sometimes you understand what you've read, but when it comes time to talk about or write about the selection, you can't find the words you want to use to discuss the plot, characters, theme, or author's writing style. Here's a list of words and phrases that can serve as a springboard to discussion. They are beginning points—you still must be able to explain why you chose those words or phrases.

Words and Phrases to Describe the Plot

Positive	Negative
realistic	unrealistic
good pace from scene to scene	plodding
suspenseful	predictable
well-developed ideas	sketchy ideas

Words and Phrases to Describe the Characters

Positive	Negative
original	stereotyped
well-rounded	flat
dynamic; able to change	static; unable to change

Words to Describe the Theme

Positive	Negative
subtle	obvious
unique	overworked
powerful	trivial

Words and Phrases to Describe the Author's Style of Writing

Positive	Negative
descriptive; filled with figurative language	boring; lacking imagery
original	filled with clichés
lively; full of action	plodding; slow-moving
poetic; lyrical	stilted

READING UP CLOSE

▶ **Using Smart Words**

Choose one of the stories you've read in *Elements of Literature* this semester and, using some of the words and phrases in the above list, describe the plot, characters, theme, and author's writing style. Remember to support your word choices with examples from the story.

Improving Your Reading Rate

If your reading concerns are more about getting through the words than figuring out the meaning, then this part of Reading Matters is for you.

If you think you are a slow reader, then reading can seem overwhelming. However, you can change your **reading rate**—the pace at which you read. All you have to do is practice. The point isn't to read so that you just rush over words—the I'mgoingtoreadsofastthatallthewordsruntogether approach. Instead, the goal is to find a pace that keeps you moving comfortably through the pages. Why is it important to establish a good reading rate? Let's do a little math to see why your silent-reading rate counts.

MATH PROBLEM!
If you read 40 words per minute (wpm) and there are 400 words on a page, how long will it take you to read 1 page? 5 pages? How long will it take if you read 80 wpm? 100 wpm? 200 wpm?

Words per Minute (wpm)	1 page @400 words/page	5 pages @400 words/page
40 wpm	10 minutes	50 minutes
80 wpm	5 minutes	25 minutes
100 wpm	4 minutes	20 minutes
200 wpm	2 minutes	10 minutes

Reading rate and homework. Now, assume that with literature homework, science homework, and social studies homework, you have forty pages to read in one night. If you are reading at 40 wpm, you are spending more than six *hours* just reading the information; but at 100 wpm, you spend only two hours and forty minutes. At 200 wpm, you'd finish in one hour and twenty minutes.

Figuring out your reading rate. To determine your silent-reading rate, you'll need three things: a watch or clock with a second hand, a book, and someone who will watch the time for you. Then, complete the following steps:

1. Have your friend time you as you begin reading to yourself.
2. Read at your normal rate. Don't speed just because you're being timed.
3. Stop when your friend tells you that one minute is up.
4. Count the number of words you read in that minute. Write down that number.

Example

1st minute	180 words
2nd minute	215 words
3rd minute	190 words
	585 words ÷ 3 = 195 wpm

Reading Matters

Improving Your Reading Rate

Review this brief lesson early in the school year so that students have ample time to benefit from improving their reading rate. You might ask everyone to do a base-line reading-rate score and to retest themselves several times throughout the year. Stress that reading speed varies with the kind of text and the reader's purpose. Ask students to identify some kinds of texts they read quickly (for example, e-mail, a sports or entertainment magazine, a murder mystery) and some types of texts they read much more slowly (a physics textbook, an encyclopedia article, a difficult poem, technical directions).

Reading Rate and Homework

Seniors will appreciate anything that lessens the time they have to spend on homework. The math problem and the chart should convince them that increasing their reading rate means more free time.

Figuring Out Your Reading Rate

Select a long passage from the essay "The Middle Ages" (p. 94), and have students read for one minute. Caution students not to sacrifice comprehension for speed; they need to pay attention to what they are reading. Have them figure out their own reading rates, and ask a few Reading Check questions about the content, such as:

- Who was William the Conqueror?
- Why did William invade England?
- How did the Norman invasion change England and its language?

Reading Rate Reminders

In class, review the three steps to faster reading. If any of your students have the bad reading habits described in items 1 and 2, assure them that they can change; others have done it. Whenever they read, they need to try consciously to stop reading one word at a time, sounding words aloud, and pointing to each word. You might suggest that they keep a reading log to record their efforts and successes.

---

5. Repeat this process several more times, using different passages.
6. Then, add the number of words together, and divide by the number of times you timed yourself. That's your average number of words per minute.

Reading Rate Reminders

1. **Make sure you aren't reading one word at a time with a pause between each word.** For instance, read the following rhyme. The first time you read it, pause between each word; the second time, pause only where you see the slash marks. Hear the difference the phrasing makes?

> Mary had a little lamb, / Its fleece was white as snow. / Everywhere that Mary went, / The lamb was sure to go.

Word-at-a-time reading is much slower than phrase reading.

2. **Make sure when you are reading silently that you really are reading silently.** As you read, avoid moving your lips or reading aloud softly. Also, don't use your finger to point to words as you read. Instead, use a bookmark to stay on the correct line while you practice your phrase reading.

3. **As you practice your fluency, remember that the single best way to improve your reading rate is simply to read more.** You won't get better at what you never do. Also, always remember that your rate will vary as your purpose for reading varies. Don't rush to read fast if that means understanding less.

Vocabulary Development

Fluency, reading rate, and comprehension are all connected to how quickly you recognize words and know what they mean. No matter how many words you study in school, you can't learn all the words you'll ever encounter. So you need to understand how words work—what *prefixes, suffixes,* and *roots* mean—so that when you encounter new words, you can see their components and figure out their meanings.

LATIN AND GREEK ROOTS, PREFIXES, AND SUFFIXES

Prefixes	Meaning	Examples
ad–	to	adapt, addict, adhere, admit
amphi–	both; around	amphibian, amphitheater
an–	without	anarchy, anesthesia, anonymous, anorexia
auto–	self	autobiography, autograph, automatic, automobile
co–	together	coauthor, cognate, coincide, cooperate
de–	opposite	deactivate, deform, degrade, deplete, descend
dis–	opposite	disagree, disarm, discontinue, disgust, dishonest
for–	not	forbid, forget, forgo
il–	not	illegal, illegible, illegitimate, illiterate, illogical
im–	not	imbalance, immaculate, immature
in–	not	inaccurate, inactive, inadvertent, incognito
ir–	not	irreconcilable, irregular, irresponsible
mal–	bad	maladjusted, malaise, malevolent, malice
pro–	before	progeny, prognosis, program, prologue
pro–	forward	proceed, produce, proficient, progress
re–	again	reappear, redistribute, redo, repaint, rewrite
sub–	under	subcontract, subject, submarine, subordinate
trans–	across	transatlantic, transcend, transcribe, transfer
un–	not	unable, uncertain, uncomfortable, unhappy

Roots	Meaning	Examples
–act–	do	action, actor, enact, react, transact
–aud–	hear	audible, audience, audition, auditorium
–cred–	believe	credit, credulous, discredit, incredible
–dic–	speak	contradict, dictate, diction, predict, verdict
–graph–	write	autograph, paragraph, phonograph, photograph
–loc–	place	allocate, dislocate, locate, location

(continued)

Vocabulary Development

Emphasize to students that a familiarity with the Latin and Greek roots, prefixes, and suffixes will give them an advantage when taking standardized tests. Point out that when they encounter a word they have never seen—in a difficult selection that tests reading comprehension, for example—they can figure out the meaning using context clues together with their knowledge of the roots, prefixes, and suffixes. This knowledge can help students answer difficult analogy questions.

(continued)

–man–	hand	manipulate, manual, manufacture, manuscript
–mot–	move	demote, motion, motor, promote
–ped–	foot	pedal, pedestal, pedestrian
–pop–	people	populace, popular, population
–port–	carry	export, import, portable, porter, transport
–sign–	mark	insignia, signal, signature, significant
–spec–	see	inspect, respect, spectacle, spectator, suspect
–tract–	pull; drag	attract, contract, detract, subtract, traction, tractor
–vid–	see	evidence, provide, providence, video
–volve–	roll	evolve, involve, revolution, revolve, revolver

Suffixes	Meaning	Examples
–ade	action or process	blockade, escapade, parade
–age	action or process	marriage, pilgrimage, voyage
–ant	one who	assistant, defendant, immigrant, merchant, servant
–cle	small	corpuscle, cubicle, particle
–dom	state or quality of	boredom, freedom, martyrdom, wisdom
–ent	one who	parent, resident, regent, superintendent
–ful	full of	careful, fearful, joyful, thoughtful
–ic	relating to	comic, historic, poetic, public
–less	without	ageless, careless, thoughtless, tireless
–let	small	islet, leaflet, owlet, rivulet
–ly	resembling	fatherly, helpfully, motherly, scholarly
–ly	every	daily, monthly, weekly, yearly
–ment	action or process	development, embezzlement, government
–ment	state or quality of	amazement, amusement, predicament
–ment	product or thing	fragment, instrument, ornament
–or	one who	actor, auditor, doctor, donor

Word Family Tree

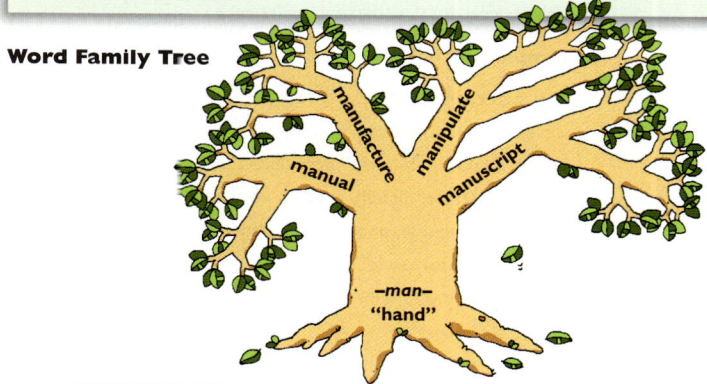

The World of Work

The ability to read critically and write effectively is your driver's license to navigating today's world. Without strong reading and writing skills, you will feel as frustrated and powerless as you do in a traffic jam. A future college student must be able to write application essays and understand scholarship guidelines. A mechanic must be able to read instruction manuals to use new equipment. A renter must understand a lease before getting an apartment. A supervisor must be able to write an effective memo to present ideas. In your life and in the world of work, you will rely on reading and writing skills to learn new information, communicate effectively, and get the results you want.

Reading

To avoid getting stranded in life and in the world of work, you will need to learn to read **informative documents** and **persuasive documents.**

Informative Documents

Informative documents are like road maps: They provide facts and information. They can also be good places to check when you want to verify or clarify information from other sources. If a friend writes down directions that you're uncertain about, you consult a map to verify the directions. Likewise, if you read on a Web site an angry customer's complaint about repairs on a computer you just bought, you could review the warranty to see if the information is valid. Two kinds of common informative documents are consumer documents and workplace documents.

Consumer Documents You've probably already made thousands of buying decisions in your life. As you get older, however, buying decisions often carry bigger consequences. Should you sign a six- or a twelve-month apartment lease? Should you buy or lease a car? Being informed about the details of major purchases can help you avoid costly mistakes. This information can be found in **consumer documents,** such as warranties, contracts, product information, and instruction manuals.

- **Warranties** describe what happens if the product doesn't work properly or breaks down. Warranties note how long the product is covered for repair or replacement, which repairs the warranty does and does not cover, and how to receive repair service.

```
The SureFocus digital camera is
guaranteed to be free of defects
in material or workmanship under
normal use for a period of one
(1) year from the date of pur-
chase. Equipment covered by the
warranty will be repaired by
SureFocus Repair Members WITHOUT
CHARGE, except for insurance,
transportation, and handling
charges. A copy of this warranty
card and proof of purchase must
be enclosed when returning equip-
ment for warranty service. The
warranty does not apply in the
following cases:
```
- the camera has been damaged through abuse
- leaking batteries or other liquids have caused damage to the camera
- unauthorized repair technicians have attempted to service the camera

- **Contracts** give details about an agreement that a buyer enters into with a company. A lease for an apartment or a car is a contract that defines the terms of the lease, including how long it lasts, what the responsibilities of the customer—also known as the lessee— and the landlord or car company are, how to end the lease, and what the penalties for breaking the lease are. A lease always includes a space for the customer's signature, which signifies agreement with the terms of the contract. Below is a portion of a typical apartment lease.

> This apartment lease is entered into by <u>Althea Brown</u>, hereinafter "Lessee," and Sun Valley Apartments.
> 1. **Grant of Lease:** Sun Valley Apartments does hereby lease unto Lessee Apartment #<u>B-2</u>, located at <u>101 Saguaro Drive, El Cajon, CA</u>.
> 2. **Term of Lease:** This lease shall begin on the <u>first</u> day of <u>August, 2003</u>, and extend until the <u>first</u> day of <u>August, 2004</u>, after which the lessee can extend the lease month to month until terminated according to the terms described below.
> 3. **Rental Payments:** Lessee agrees to pay as rent the sum of <u>$800</u> per month each month during the term of this lease before the <u>fifth</u> day of each month.

- **Product information** describes the basic features and materials of a product. A suit label would tell whether the suit is 100 percent wool or a blend of materials and would give cleaning instructions. Product information on the box of a cordless telephone would tell the frequency, number of channels, and whether it has automatic redial, memory, caller ID, voice-mail indicator light, and other features.
- **Instruction manuals** tell the owner how to set up, operate, and troubleshoot problems with a product. Instruction manuals also include safety precautions, diagrams, and descriptions of the product's features.

Workplace Documents Two common workplace documents—**procedure manuals** and **memoranda**—can tell you how to do your job and how to stay informed so you are both knowledgeable and effective.

- **Procedure manuals** are the step-by-step directions that tell employees how to serve customers, operate machinery, report problems, request vacation, or do anything that the company wants performed in a certain way. Procedure manuals are often used to train new employees and to clarify procedures for existing employees. As you read a procedure manual, pay attention to the specific instructions so you know exactly how to carry out the procedures.
- **Memoranda**—or memos—are the standard form of communication in many businesses. Memos are concise messages, generally covering only one topic. For example, an employee might send a memo to a supervisor reporting on the status of a project, or a supervisor might send a brief summary of discussions and decisions made in a meeting. To read a memo effectively, first check the subject line at the top to learn the topic of the memo. As you read, notice the pattern of organization in the body of the memo. Headings or bullets may indicate the main ideas. Pay attention to the purpose of the memo to decide whether and how to respond. Is the memo summarizing information, requesting action, or providing facts, such as dates and prices?

Persuasive Documents While informative documents are like road maps, persuasive documents are like travel brochures, trying to influence a reader's destination. Persuasive documents try to persuade readers to believe or act in a certain way. It's important for you to be able to distinguish between informative and persuasive public documents. For example, a policy statement from a county commission about recycling might quote facts, but its primary purpose is to influence citizens to support the commission's position. By critically reading persuasive public documents, you can evaluate whether you agree or disagree. Persuasive public documents include **policy statements, political platforms, speeches,** and **debates**.

- A **policy statement** outlines a person's or group's position on an issue and sometimes provides the rationale for that position. For example, the mayor might issue a policy statement explaining why she supports or opposes a tax increase for school construction. The policy statement gives the main points for the mayor's position and may provide facts or use rhetorical devices to support the position. A policy statement may also include a **call to action,** or a request for readers to take a specific action. Some organizations issue policy statements to endorse specific legislation, hoping to win the support of the voting public or of the lawmakers who can create the legislation.

- A **political platform** outlines a political candidate's position on a variety of issues so voters know where the candidate stands. It may also set forth the candidate's goals and describe the beliefs that guide his or her positions. The positions and goals are known as the *planks* of the platform. The audience for a political platform is usually friendly to the candidate, and the platform is intended to rouse support and to persuade undecided voters. Sometimes a platform will also address and rebut opposing viewpoints. Below is an excerpt from the political platform of a city council candidate about the issue of noise pollution.

> Rocky Mount is a quiet and peaceful place that does not need more intrusion from the local government to reduce noise levels. We are not close to a major airport, so we do not hear the regular drone of airplanes. Concertgoers hear Beethoven and Mozart, not the loud rock groups that play in larger cities. Noise pollution is an occasional, not regular or excessive, problem that can be handled without more city ordinances. Therefore, I do not support the development of laws to address the nonexistent issue of noise pollution.

- A **persuasive speech** is designed to change an audience's attitudes or beliefs or to move an audience to action. A speaker may make persuasive arguments and address audience counterclaims by using reasoning and rhetorical devices such as repetition. (For more on **persuasive speaking,** see page 1120.)

- A **debate** involves two teams who take turns discussing a controversial topic. The topic under discussion is called the *proposition*. One side argues for the proposition, and the other side argues against it. Each side also refutes, or argues against, its opponent's case.

Critiquing Persuasive Documents

Persuasive documents use logical, emotional, and ethical appeals to be convincing. Notice how these appeals are used to help you critique a document's validity and truthfulness.

The World of Work

- **Logical appeals** are based on reasons and supporting evidence. As you read, notice whether the evidence is based on reliable facts that can be confirmed through other, unbiased sources. If you are unsure, consult informative public documents, such as state laws, to verify the evidence. Notice whether the appeal makes sense and avoids fallacies, such as hasty generalizations or circular reasoning. A **hasty generalization** is a conclusion based on insufficient evidence. **Circular reasoning** occurs when the reason for an opinion is simply the opinion stated in different words.

- **Emotional appeals** rely on strong feelings to persuade readers. The writer may use examples that tug on heartstrings or arouse anger. Vivid language may make either positive or negative associations with the topic. Evaluate emotional appeals based on all of the evidence. If an argument is based primarily on emotion, the case may be weak. Watch out for signs of bias and stereotypes—including words such as *always* and *never*—that suggest the reasoning is unsound.

- **Ethical appeals** rely on the reader's sense of right and wrong. For example, a writer might persuade an audience to share a certain view by implying that the opposing position is unpatriotic or selfish.

Critique a persuasive document by seeing how fairly the writer treats the topic. Does the writer use credible evidence? Does he or she know enough about the topic to be believed?

PRACTICE & APPLY 1 Choose a persuasive public document, and critique its effectiveness and validity. Identify the appeals and the call to action, if any. Consult at least one informative public document to verify information presented in the persuasive document.

Writing

Writing is your passport to exciting places in life. A powerful résumé can win you the job of your dreams. A memo proposing cost-saving measures can earn you a promotion. A letter to your city council can lead to a new soccer field for a recreational league. Clear, effective writing is one of the best skills you can have as you enter the world of work.

Job Applications and Résumés One of the first places you will use writing beyond school will be in a job application or résumé. To fill out a **job application** completely and accurately, first read the instructions carefully. Type or write neatly in blue or black ink. Include all information requested. If a question does not apply to you, write *N/A* or *not applicable* in the blank. Proofread your completed form and neatly correct any errors. Finally, submit the form to the correct person.

A **résumé** summarizes your skills, education, achievements, and work experience. Prepare a résumé to use when you apply for a job or when you seek admission to a college or special program. Keep in mind that a résumé should be tailored to match the target audience. Select and highlight the skills and experiences that would most appeal to the employer or college reading the résumé. For a college or academic program, for example, you would highlight a strong GPA, successful class projects, and involvement in school clubs. The language would create a sophisticated, but not artificial, tone. For an employer, on the other hand, you would highlight work experience, both paid and volunteer, and the skills you learned on the job, using clear and direct language.

Here are some more tips to help you create a résumé:

- Give complete information about work experience, including job title, dates of employment, company, and location.

- Do not use *I;* instead, use short, parallel phrases that describe duties and activities.
- Proofread carefully. Mistakes on a résumé make the writer seem careless—not a positive quality for an employee.

Workplace Documents Memos are the standard form of communication in many businesses. To write a concise, easy-to-understand memo, you must first understand your main purpose for writing. Are you writing to provide information or to make a request? Memos should provide all essential information—*who, what, when, where, why,* and *how*—and get quickly to the point. If you are asking for action and information, include a deadline. Memos follow a standard format that includes the date, the recipient, the sender, and the subject at the top of the document. Notice how the following memo gets right to the point and communicates information clearly and directly.

```
Date:      February 25, 2003
To:        Sophia Cervenka
From:      Cole Hurley
Subject:   Computer Training

Training on the new software will
begin Monday, March 10, 2003.
Members of your department who are
interested in receiving training
should call me at extension 4390
by Friday, March 7, to sign up.
Training will last from 8:00
A.M.-3:00 P.M. The next training
session will be held on March 18.
```

Word-Processing Features A clear message is essential in workplace communication, but the appearance of workplace documents also counts. Learn to use word-processing features to your advantage by making documents that are easy on both the eyes and the mind.

- **Margins** are the space that surrounds the text on a page. Most word-processing programs automatically set side and top margins. You can adjust these default margins to suit your purpose.
- A **font** is a complete set of characters (including letters, numbers, and punctuation marks) in a particular size and design. For most workplace documents, use a font that is businesslike and easy to read. For more on **fonts,** see page 1162.
- **Line spacing** is the white space between lines of text. Most letters and memos are single-spaced to conserve space, but longer reports are often double-spaced to allow room for handwritten edits and comments.

Integrating Databases, Graphics, and Spreadsheets Workplace documents often integrate databases, graphics, and spreadsheets into text. For example, a pie chart or a spreadsheet can show budget expenses, or a list of customers in a specific ZIP Code might be integrated from a database into a report. Add features such as these to communicate your ideas more effectively. Place a graphic close to the related text, and explain the graphic's context. For help in integrating visuals and other components into documents, consult the Help section of your word-processing program or ask your teacher to help you.

Résumé Format Word-processing features can help you create an attractive format for your résumé. Here are some guidelines to remember:

- Make sure the résumé is not cluttered. Use wide margins for the top, bottom, and sides, and use double-spacing between sections to make the résumé easy to scan for information.
- Consider using a different font, boldface, and a larger point size for your name and for headings. Be sure all the fonts are easy to read.

The following résumé was written by a student interested in a sales job. He highlighted skills and experiences that show his interpersonal skills and initiative and used an attractive, easy-to-read format.

MIGUEL GUERRERO
1902 Greig Street
Santa Rosa, CA 95403
(707) 555-0085
E-mail: mguerrero@fhs.k12.ca.us

EDUCATION
   Senior, Forsythe High School
   Grade-point average: 3.3 (B)

WORK EXPERIENCE
Summer 2001–present
   Waiter, Starlite Restaurant
   - Serve customers quickly and efficiently
   - Train new employees in effective customer service
   - Twice awarded Star Employee

Summer 2000
   Campaign Volunteer, Antonio Suarez Campaign for Mayor
   - Assisted in door-to-door campaigns
   - Collected and input data for mailing list
   - Organized teen volunteers to distribute flyers

SKILLS
   Communication: Telephone sales, oral presentations
   Computers: Word processing, Web design

ACTIVITIES
   Debate team, soccer team, student government representative

REFERENCES
   Janet Matteson, Owner   David Cho, Principal
   Starlite Restaurant   Forsythe High School
   (707) 555-0146   (707) 555-0013

PRACTICE & APPLY 2 Create a résumé for your dream job. Think about what experiences and skills you have that would appeal to a potential employer. Present this information in a clear, concise, and eye-catching way.

Writer's Handbook

The Writing Process

Effective writing involves a process. The steps in this process, called a **recursive** process because you may repeat them several times, are like those of a spiral staircase—you must travel around and around, yet with each revolution you ascend toward your goal. While each writer's process is slightly different, most effective writers follow the steps below.

STAGES OF THE WRITING PROCESS

Prewriting
- Identify your purpose and audience.
- Choose a topic and an appropriate form.
- Formulate your thesis, or main idea, about the topic.
- Gather information about the topic.
- Organize information in a preliminary plan.

Writing
- Draft an introduction that seizes your readers' attention and provides necessary background information.
- State your thesis clearly and assertively.
- Develop body paragraphs that elaborate on key ideas.
- Follow an organizational plan.
- Draft a conclusion that restates your thesis and leaves readers with something to think about.

Revising
- Evaluate your draft.
- Revise to improve its content, organization, and style.

Publishing
- Proofread your draft, and correct errors in spelling, punctuation, grammar, and usage.
- Share your final draft with readers.
- Reflect on your writing experience.

Throughout the writing process, make sure you do the following:

- **Keep your ideas coherent and focused.** Keep your specific purpose in mind to help you present a tightly reasoned argument. Evaluate every idea to make sure it will focus your readers on your main point, and make that point clear in your thesis statement.

- **Share your own perspective.** You bring your own ideas to every piece you write. Share not only information you've gathered but also your viewpoint on your topic. Let your natural voice shine through to readers.

- **Keep your audience in mind.** Consider your readers' backgrounds and interests. If your form is not assigned, choose a form that will grab your readers, such as a song, editorial, screenplay, or letter.

- **Plan to publish.** Labor over every piece as though it will be published or shared with an audience. Enlist the help of a classmate when you proofread a finished piece, and use the questions in the chart below. The numbers in parentheses indicate the sections in the Language Handbook that contain instruction on each concept.

QUESTIONS FOR PROOFREADING

1. Is every sentence complete, not a fragment or run-on? (8a, 9d–e)
2. Are punctuation marks used correctly? (12a–r, 13a–o)
3. Are the first letters of sentences, proper nouns, and proper adjectives capitalized? (11a, c)
4. Does each verb agree in number with its subject? (2a) Are verb forms and tenses used correctly? (3b–c)
5. Are subject and object forms of personal pronouns used correctly? (4a–e) Does every pronoun agree with a clear antecedent in number and gender? (2j)

When revising and proofreading, use the symbols below.

SYMBOLS FOR REVISING AND PROOFREADING

Symbol	Example	Meaning of Symbol
≡	805 Linden avenue	Capitalize a lowercase letter.
/	the First of May	Lowercase a capital letter.
∧	one ^of my friends	Insert a missing word, letter, or punctuation mark.
⟶	at the beginning (onset)	Replace a word.
⌿	Give me a a number	Delete a word, letter, or punctuation mark.
∽	beleive	Change the order of letters.
¶	¶ "Yes," she answered.	Begin a new paragraph.

1154 Resource Center Writer's Handbook

Paragraphs

The Parts of a Paragraph

Paragraphs can be as different as oak trees are from pines. Some paragraphs are a single word; others run several pages. Their uses differ, too: A paragraph may present a main idea, connect one idea to another, emphasize an idea, or simply give the reader's eyes a rest in a long passage.

Many paragraphs in essays and other types of nonfiction, including workplace writing, develop one main idea. A main-idea paragraph is often built from a **topic sentence, supporting sentences,** and a **clincher sentence.**

PARTS OF A PARAGRAPH

Topic Sentence
- an explicit statement of the paragraph's main idea or central focus
- often the first or second sentence in a paragraph, but may appear at the end to emphasize or summarize

Supporting Sentences
- provide elaboration by supporting, building, or proving the main idea
- often include details of the following types:
  - *sensory details*: information about sight, sound, taste, smell, and texture
  - *facts*: details that can be proved true
  - *examples*: specific instances that illustrate a general idea
  - *anecdotes*: brief stories about people or events that illustrate a main idea
  - *analogies*: comparisons between ideas familiar to readers and unfamiliar concepts being explained

Clincher Sentence
- may restate the topic sentence, summarize supporting details, offer a final thought, or help readers refocus on the main idea of a long paragraph

TIP Not every paragraph has, or needs, a topic sentence. In fiction, paragraphs rarely have topic sentences. Paragraphs presenting time sequences (how-to instructions or histories, for example) may also lack topic sentences—the steps or events themselves focus the reader's mind. Finally, a paragraph may imply, or suggest, its main idea without directly stating it in a topic sentence. In your school writing, however, topic sentences are a help: They keep *you* focused on each paragraph's topic.

TIP Not every paragraph needs a clincher sentence. Use one for a strong or dramatic touch or for renewing a main idea in a lengthy or complicated paragraph.

Paragraphs 1155

Writer's Handbook

CONNECTING IDEAS

Type of Connection	How to Use It
Direct References, or Repetition of Ideas	• Refer to a noun or pronoun used earlier in the paragraph. • Repeat a word used earlier. • Substitute synonyms for words used earlier.
Transitional Expressions	• Compare ideas (*also, and, another, in the same way, just, like, likewise, moreover, similarly, too*). • Contrast ideas (*although, but, however, in spite of, instead, nevertheless, on the other hand, still, yet*). • Show cause and effect (*accordingly, as a result, because, consequently, for, since, so, so that, therefore*). • Indicate time (*after, at last, before, early, eventually, first, later, next, then, thereafter, until, when, while*). • Show place (*above, across, adjacent, behind, beside, beyond, down, here, in, near, over, there*). • Show importance (*first, last, less significant, mainly, more important, to begin with*).
Parallelism	• Use the same grammatical forms or structures to balance related ideas in a sentence. • Sparingly, use the same sentence structures to show connections between related ideas in a paragraph or composition.

PRACTICE & APPLY Develop two paragraphs on a single topic that interests you. First, choose two primary methods of organizing ideas on the topic (keeping in mind that you may use a combination of orders). Then, plan a topic sentence, a variety of supporting details, and a clincher sentence for each of your two paragraphs. Finally, draft your paragraphs, clearly organizing and connecting ideas and eliminating any ideas that detract from your focus.

The Writer's Language

Revising often focuses on a piece's content and organization. However, to communicate ideas effectively, you must work just as carefully to revise a piece's **style**—how you express those ideas. When revising your style, fine-tune your writing's **sound, word choice,** and **sentence variety,** and use **rhetorical devices** to grab reader attention and make your ideas clear and interesting.

A Sound Style Keep your **audience** and **purpose** in mind to help you choose a suitable **voice, tone,** and **level of formality** for a piece of writing.

Voice In writing, voice is your unique personality on paper. Just as you recognize a friend's spoken voice, you can recognize the work of favorite writers by the unique way they express ideas. To evaluate your own writing voice, read your work out loud. If your writing doesn't sound natural, revise it to bring your personality to life.

Tone Tone reveals your attitude toward a topic and audience. Always use an appropriate tone for your audience and purpose. For example, if your purpose is to persuade readers to share your view on an important issue, your tone should be serious and respectful.

Level of Formality You wouldn't don formal wear for a beach party, and neither should you use a casual, informal style for a serious essay on a subject about which you care deeply. Match the level of formality to your subject, your audience, and your purpose. Look at these examples.

INFORMAL   Some people shouldn't own pets. Period.

FORMAL   Certain people should not own pets under any circumstances.

Word Choice Make sure your words express the ideas you want them to express. Every word should help create a clear, vivid picture of what you mean and communicate the connotation you want.

Precise Language Replace vague language in your writing with words that are distinct and strong. For example, you might describe a big boulder you saw on a hike as being as *huge as a car* or as *mammoth as a double-decker bus.* You could mention that the boulder *rumbled* down the hill or *squatted* by the path. Using **precise verbs, nouns,** and **adjectives** like these will make your writing clearer and more interesting.

Connotations As you choose words, notice their **connotations**—the emotional effects they create. For instance, the word *cheap* means "economical," but it also has the negative connotation of being poor in quality. The word *inexpensive* expresses the same idea as *cheap* but in a more positive way. Choose words carefully by considering their effects.

Writer's Handbook

Reference Note
For more on **revising to add variety,** see **Revising for Variety,** 9g–i, in the Language Handbook.

Sentence Variety Readers can become bored with writing that uses the same types of sentences over and over. Create variety by varying the beginnings of your sentences and mixing simple, compound, and complex sentences.

Rhetorical Devices To give your ideas a greater impact, use the rhetorical devices of **parallelism, repetition,** and **analogy.**

Parallelism Just as a train stays on its tracks because they're parallel, readers will stay on track if your written ideas are grammatically parallel.

NOT PARALLEL	More lives are saved when **drivers wear seatbelts** and **motorcyclists are wearing helmets.**
PARALLEL	More lives are saved when **drivers wear seatbelts** and **motorcyclists wear helmets.**

You can also use parallelism for effect by using similar sentence structures to express related ideas.

Repetition Repeating important words or phrases can create an emotional response or underscore their significance. Use this technique sparingly to make your key ideas resonate with readers.

Analogy An analogy illustrates an idea by comparing it to something with similar characteristics. For example, you could say, "The politician worked the crowd as if he were selling the Fountain of Youth."

A Stylish Model Read the following passage, noting the writer's sound, word choice, sentence variety, and rhetorical devices.

A Writer's Model

Voice/tone

Repetition
Analogy
Connotation

Precise verbs

> Credit cards are a ticket to an unpleasant lesson for college freshmen. One in five college students will rack up $10,000 in credit card debt by graduation. That's right—$10,000! Some people use credit as recklessly as play money. Unfortunately, the consequences for misusing credit cards are staggering. A $5,000 credit card debt can take up to 30 years and $15,000 to pay off—three times the value of the items purchased. Credit cards only look good until the bill comes due. I encourage students to stand firm and refuse the temptations dangled before them by credit card companies.

PRACTICE & APPLY Revise the paragraph below to improve its style. Add your own ideas as appropriate.

I think students should be allowed to bring cell phones to school. What if we need to call someone? Students have rights too. I think the school staff should quit treating us like babies. This rule just isn't fair and should be changed.

Designing Your Writing

A document must be designed to convey information in a way that is easy to understand and remember. In other words, the text arrangement and appearance and any visuals must support the content. You can create effective design and visuals by hand, or you can use advanced publishing software and graphics programs to design pages and to integrate other features into your word-processed documents.

Page Design

Lay It on the Line If you want your documents to catch readers' attention, you must design them to be visually appealing and easy to read. Use the following design elements to improve readability.

- **Columns** arrange text in separate sections printed vertically side by side. Text in reference books and newspapers usually appears in columns. A **block** is a rectangle of text shorter than a page. The text in advertisements is usually set in blocks so that it may be read quickly. Blocks and columns are separated from each other by white space.

- A **bullet** (•) is a symbol used to highlight information in a text. Bullets separate information into lists like this one. Bullets attract attention and help readers remember information.

- A **heading** appears at the beginning of a section of text to tell readers what that section is about. A **subheading** indicates a smaller section within a heading. Headings and subheadings may be set off from other text in large, **boldface,** or *italic* type or in a different font.

- **White space** is any area on a page where there is little or no text or graphics. Usually, white space is limited to the margins and the spaces between words, lines, and columns. Advertisements usually have more white space than do books or articles.

- A **caption** appears under a photograph or illustration to explain its meaning and connect it to the text. Captions may appear in italics or in a smaller type size than the main text.

- **Contrast** refers to the balance of light and dark areas on a page. Dark areas contain blocks of text or graphics. Light areas have little type. A page with high contrast, or roughly balanced light and dark areas, is easier to read than a page with low contrast.

- **Emphasis** is how a page designer indicates to a reader which information on a page is most important. Because readers' eyes are drawn naturally to color, large and bold print, and graphics, these elements are commonly used to create emphasis.

Type

Letter Perfect The basic material of your document is the type. Your choice of different **cases** and **fonts** can pull the reader into the text, provide emphasis, and make your document easy to read.

Case The two cases of type are uppercase, or capital, letters and lowercase, or small, letters. You can vary case in these ways:

- **Uppercase letters** Text in all uppercase letters attracts readers' attention and may be used in headings or titles. Because text in all capital letters can be difficult to read, use all capitals only for emphasis, not for large bodies of text.
- **Small caps** Small caps are uppercase letters that are reduced in size. They are used in abbreviations of time, such as 9:00 A.M. and A.D. 1500. Small caps may be combined with capital letters for an artistic effect.

Font A font is one complete set of characters (such as letters, numbers, and punctuation marks) of a given size and design. The three types of fonts are explained in the chart below.

Quick guide

CATEGORIES OF FONTS

Category	Explanation	Uses
decorative, or **script,** fonts	elaborately designed characters that convey a distinct mood or feeling	Decorative fonts are difficult to read and should be used in small amounts for an artistic effect.
serif fonts	characters with small strokes (serifs) at each end, such as the main type on this page	Because the strokes on serif characters help guide the reader's eyes from letter to letter, serif type is often used for large bodies of type.
sans serif fonts	characters such as these, formed of straight lines with no serifs	Sans serif fonts are easy to read and are used as headings, subheadings, and captions.

- **Font size** The size of the type in a document is called the font size or point size. In general, newspapers and textbooks use type measured at 12 points. Type for headings and headlines is larger, while captions are usually smaller.
- **Font style** Most text is set in roman (not slanted) style. *Italic*, or slanted, style is used for captions or book titles. Underscored or boldface type can be used for emphasis.

1162 Resource Center Writer's Handbook

Visuals

Show, Don't Tell If you wanted to tell about the weekly expenses and income from your summer lawn-care business, it would be more effective to show the information in a table than to list it in a paragraph. Visuals, or graphics, such as this must be accurate and appropriate. You can create visuals by hand or by using technology, such as advanced computer software and graphics programs. You can also add to a document's impact by integrating a database or spreadsheet into it. Here are some useful visuals.

- **Graphs** present numeric information and can show trends or changes over time or how one thing changes in relation to another. A **bar graph** can also compare quantities at a glance, or note the parts of a whole. A **line graph** can compare trends or show how two or more variables interact, as in this example.

> **TIP** Consider copying and pasting information from databases into your documents. For example, if you were writing a letter to your school administration proposing a senior class trip to a national park, you could paste information from a database comparing costs and available activities at several parks in your area. (Always give credit to your sources for such data.)

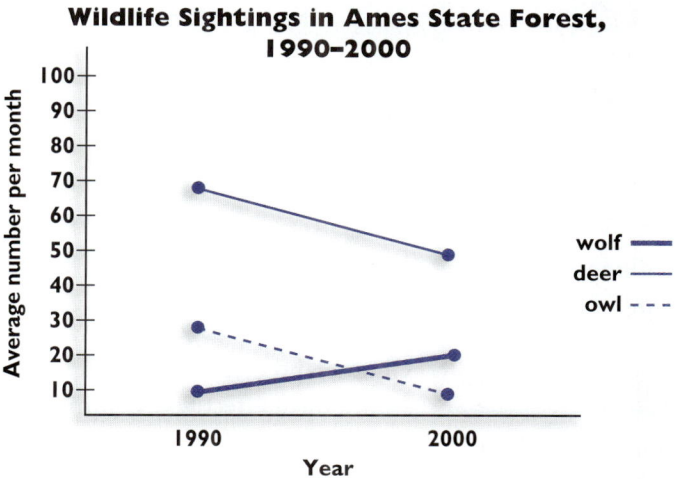

- **Tables** use rows and columns to provide detailed information arranged in an accessible way. A **spreadsheet** is a special kind of table created on a computer. The cells of a spreadsheet are associated with mathematical equations. Spreadsheets are especially useful for budgets or schedules in which the numbers are variables in an equation. In the spreadsheet below, the last column of each row calculates the average of the figures to the left of it.

First Quarter Grades					
Name	Essay	Test	Speech	Project	Average
Cooper, L.	84	78	81	92	84
Nguyen, H.	90	86	88	95	90
Torres, B.	88	94	91	90	91
Watt, K.	96	90	93	88	92

Designing Your Writing **1163**

- **Pictures,** such as drawings and photographs, can show how something works, what something or someone looks like, or something new, unfamiliar, or indescribable. You can scan a copyright-free picture on the computer or paste it manually into your document. Place it near the reference in the text, and include a caption.

- **Charts** show relationships among ideas or data. A **flowchart** uses geometric shapes linked by arrows to show the sequence of events in a process. A **pie chart** is a circle divided into wedges. Each wedge represents a certain percentage of the total, as in this example.

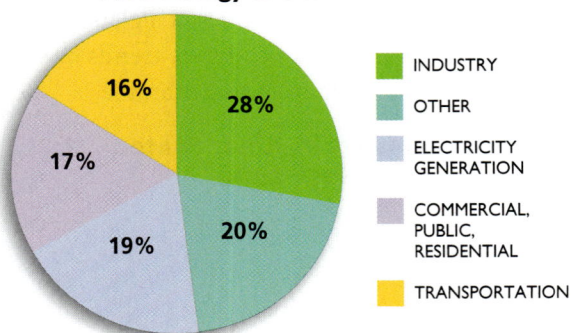

How Energy Is Used Worldwide

- **Time lines** identify the events that have taken place over a given period of time. (For an example of a time line, see page 2.)

PRACTICE & APPLY Choose and create the visual you think would most effectively communicate the following information using the guidelines in this section.

The estimated expenses for the Sanger High senior class trip are as follows: bus rental, $1,000; gas, $200; hotel, ten rooms at $45 per room for five days, or $2,250; food, $30 a day per person (ten people for five days), or $1,500. The total trip cost is $4,950.

Test Smarts

by **Flo Ota De Lange** *and* **Sheri Henderson**

Strategies for Taking Multiple-Choice Tests

Senior year. You're on the homestretch and on your way to—maybe you don't know yet exactly where you're headed. Whatever you do, be sure to pick up that diploma. A high school diploma will open doors whatever you choose to do, and the skills you acquire in earning your diploma are ones you'll need for lifelong learning.

To graduate, you still need to pass a lot of tests. You'll have plenty of quizzes, midterm exams, and finals to get through. You'll take the state's standardized tests, and if you plan to go on to college, you'll need to tackle the *Scholastic Assessment Test (SAT)* or the *American College Testing Program (ACT)*.

The following pages can help you prepare for all your standardized tests. They are designed to help you with three goals:

- to become familiar with the different types of questions you will be asked
- to learn some strategies for approaching the questions
- to discover the kinds of questions that give you trouble

Once you have met those goals, you will want to practice answering the kinds of questions that give you trouble until you feel comfortable with them. Here are some basic strategies that will help you approach your multiple-choice tests with confidence:

Stay Calm
You have studied the material, and you know your stuff, but you're still nervous. That's OK. A little nervousness will help you focus, but so will a calm body. **Take a few deep breaths** before you begin.

Track Your Time
First, take a few minutes to estimate how much time you have for each question. Then, set checkpoints for yourself—how many questions should be completed at a quarter of the time, half of the time, and so on. That way you can **pace yourself** as you work through the test.

Master the Directions
Read the directions carefully so you know exactly what to do and how to do it. If you are supposed to fill in a bubble, fill it in carefully. Be careful to match each question's number to the number on the answer sheet.

Study the Questions
Read each question once, twice, three times—until you are absolutely certain you know what the question is asking. Watch out for words like *not* and *except:* They tell you to look for choices that are false, different, or opposite.

Anticipate Answers
Once you are sure you understand the question, **anticipate the answer** before you read the choices. If the answer you guessed is there, it is probably correct. To be sure, though, check out each choice. If you understand the question but don't know the answer, eliminate any choices you think are wrong. Then, make an educated—not a wild—guess to choose one of the remaining choices. **Avoid distracters,** answer choices that are true but don't fit the question.

Don't Give Up
If you are having a hard time with a test, take a deep breath and **keep on going.** On most tests

the questions do not get more difficult as you go, and an easier question is probably coming up soon. The last question on a test is worth just as many points as the first, so give it your all—all the way to the end.

Types of Test Questions

You will feel a lot more confident if you are familiar with the kinds of questions given on a test. The following pages describe and give examples of and tips for answering the different types of multiple-choice questions you'll find on many standardized tests.

Critical-Reading Questions

The critical-reading section of a test seeks to determine how well you can think analytically about what you read. This is not news to you. That is the purpose of every reading test you have ever taken. Although challenging tests may give you long, difficult readings and complicated questions, it helps to remember that you will find everything you need—including the answers—right there on the page.

Strategies for Critical-Reading Questions

Here are some tips for answering critical-reading questions.

- **Look for main ideas.** In this kind of test, pay special attention to the **introductory and concluding paragraphs,** in which writers often state their main idea. Read all footnotes or margin notes. As you read the passage, look for **key words, phrases,** and **ideas.** If you are allowed to write on the test, circle or underline them.
- **Look for structure.** Try to determine how the logic of a passage is developed by paying attention to **transition words** and the **pattern of organization.** Does the author build an argument brick by brick, using words and phrases such as *also, and, as well as, furthermore*? Does the author instead offer an argument with contrasts, using words and phrases such as *however, although, in spite of, nevertheless*? And finally, **what is the writer's point?**
- **Eliminate obviously wrong answer choices.** If the questions are long and complicated, it often helps to translate them into plain English to be sure you understand what's being asked. Then, anticipate the possible answers. When you have eliminated the obviously wrong choices, put your finger on the choice you think is correct, and go back to the passage. **Check it.** Do not rely on memory. This is particularly important for vocabulary-in-context questions.
- **Watch out for traps.** Be wary of choices that use extreme words, like *always* and *never*. Look out for choices that are true but do not correctly answer the question—these are called *distracters*. Remember that questions using *except* or *least* or *not* are asking you to find the false answer. Trust your common sense.

We'll use the reading selection below to discuss a few of the most common kinds of critical-reading questions:

> **DIRECTIONS:** Read the passage below. Then, read the questions that follow, and write the letter of the best answer.
>
> *from* Acceptance and Nobel Lecture—1993
> Nelson Mandela
>
> We speak here of the challenge of the dichotomies of war and peace, violence and nonviolence, racism and human dignity, oppression and repression and liberty and human rights, poverty and freedom from want.
>
> We stand here today as nothing more than a representative of the millions of our people who dared to rise up against a social system whose very essence is war, violence, racism, oppression and repression, and the impoverishment of an entire people.
>
> I am also here today as a representative of the millions of people across the globe, the antiapartheid movement, the governments and organizations that joined with us not to fight against South Africa as a country or
>
> *(continued)*

(continued)

20 any of its peoples but to oppose an inhuman system and sue for a speedy end to the apartheid crime against humanity.

25 These countless human beings, both inside and outside our country, had the nobility of spirit to stand in the path of tyranny and injustice without seeking selfish gain. They recognized that an injury to one is an injury
30 to all and therefore acted together in defense of justice and a common human decency. Because of their courage and persistence for many years, we can, today, even set the dates
35 when all humanity will join together to celebrate one of the outstanding human victories of our century.

When that moment comes, we shall, together, rejoice in a common
40 victory over racism.

VOCABULARY-IN-CONTEXT QUESTIONS ask you to define words within the context of the reading. If the word is fairly common, look out! A word's meaning in the reading may be an unusual or uncommon one. If it is a really tough word, read several lines above and several lines below the line in which the word is found. The meaning will be in there somewhere. Whatever you do, **always go back and check the reading** for vocabulary-in-context questions. Always.

1. The word *dichotomies* in line 2 is used to describe—
   A a separation of social classes
   B the establishment of groups
   C an ordering of topics
   D a division into opposites
   E a medieval hierarchy

Answer: All the choices refer to some kind of structure. Based on the context clue of the sets of opposites that follow the word *dichotomies*, you can figure out that **D** is the correct answer. If you've taken science courses, you have another clue in the Greek prefix *di–*, which means "twice; double" in words such as *dioxide*.

PARAPHRASING or RESTATING QUESTIONS ask you to choose the best restatement of an idea, detail, or fact in the selection. You are not asked to make any judgments about the idea; instead, like an interpreter, you are simply asked to report accurately what the writer said. If the question is long and complex, put it into your own words **before** you read the choices. The answer is easier to find if you know what is being asked.

2. When Mandela speaks of "the apartheid crime against humanity" (lines 22–23), he is referring to how—
   A a social system that injures some injures all
   B like any social system, apartheid has its pros and cons
   C apartheid leads to crime
   D apartheid is a crime because it is illegal in South Africa
   E humanity has committed crimes against apartheid

Answer: Even if you didn't know that apartheid was the South African social and legal system of segregation, the sentence tells you that it is a "crime against humanity." Only **choice A** refers to this concept. **B, C,** and **D** do not paraphrase the speaker's meaning, and **E** says the opposite of his meaning.

INFERENCE QUESTIONS ask you to read between the lines, to connect clues from the ideas in selections. You compile hints and key bits of information to arrive at the answer. Inference questions require careful reading in order to glean what is implied rather than stated outright.

3. The speaker would most likely agree that—

   A South Africans alone are responsible for South Africa's problems

   B apartheid could be overturned by a response from the world community

   C there is a bright side to everything

   D the law is the law and must be obeyed

   E apartheid does not favor any one racial group over another

Answer: First, rule out any choices that are not true according to what is said in the speech. Choices **C, D,** and **E** can all be eliminated because they are contrary to what Mandela states directly. Choice **A** seems possible, and so does **B**. Re-read the speech. See that the third and fourth paragraphs make clear that the speaker believes apartheid is a world problem, not just South Africa's. Therefore, **choice B is the best answer.**

TONE or MOOD QUESTIONS ask you to infer the writer's attitude toward the subject. Pay attention to the descriptions of the subject. Are they positive, neutral, or negative? Is the writer hopeful, sad, admiring, wishy-washy, sarcastic? (A standardized test might use more difficult vocabulary words for those same words: *sanguine, melancholy, reverent, ambivalent, sardonic.*)

4. Which of the following words best describes Mandela's attitude toward his subject?

   A amused   D bewildered

   B resigned   E diplomatic

   C impassioned

Answer: Mandela is clearly neither amused **(A)**, resigned **(B)**, nor bewildered **(D)**. His subject is serious, and he speaks with conviction about change. Although a Nobel Peace Prize acceptance speech is an occasion that may call for diplomacy **(E)**, Mandela is evidently passionate about his subject. Since *impassioned* is a synonym for *passionate*, **C is the best choice.**

MAIN-IDEA or BEST-TITLE QUESTIONS ask you to consider the big picture, much as you might do when you step back from a still-life painting to focus on the entire effect rather than zoom in on the individual fruits and objects that create that effect. Ask yourself:

- What is the subject?
- What aspect of the subject does the writer address?
- What does the writer want me to understand about this aspect?

Main ideas are often found at the beginning or end of a selection. In choosing your answers, be wary of those that may be true but are either too specific or too general to reflect the message of *this* selection.

5. Which of the following titles is best for Nelson Mandela's speech?

   A "Racism Defeated"

   B "Apartheid in South Africa"

   C "South Africa United"

   D "Millions of People Unite"

   E "A Stand Against Injustice"

Answer: **The best answer is E** since Mandela talks about the stand he and millions of others have taken against the injustice of apartheid. Racism has not yet been defeated, so **A** is not right. **B** and **D** are too general. **C** is irrelevant.

EVALUATING-THE-WRITER'S-CRAFT QUESTIONS ask you to look at the selection's organization, logic, and argumentative techniques. They often look like this:

6. In his speech the speaker makes his central point primarily by—

   A attacking the specific persons responsible for apartheid

   B praising the efforts of many people to combat apartheid

   C warning the world against future apartheids

   D counting the gains of apartheid

   E describing in detail crimes against humanity

1168   Resource Center   Test Smarts

Answer: **The best answer is B;** the third through fifth paragraphs praise those who fight against apartheid. Choice **A** seems possible, but the word *specific* signals that it's not the right answer—Mandela never mentions any specific persons. You can eliminate **E** because although he mentions crimes against humanity, Mandela does not describe them in detail. Choices **C** and **D** do not relate to the speech.

Vocabulary Questions

You will encounter several types of vocabulary questions on standardized tests. They all test your knowledge of word meanings, both in and out of context.

SENTENCE-COMPLETION, or FILL-IN-THE-BLANK, QUESTIONS look easy, but they require your full attention. Here's a step-by-step way to approach each question:

- **Cover up the answer choices, and read the entire sentence carefully.** Most sentences contain clues to the intended meaning and thus to the word you want. Ask yourself, "What is this blank about?" and "What else does the sentence say about the subject of the blank?"
- **Look for clue words.** Pay special attention to words that change the direction of a sentence. Look for words that **reverse** the sentence's main idea, such as *no, not, although, however, but.* Look also for words that indicate that a **synonym** is wanted: *and, also, in addition, likewise, moreover.* Finally, look for words that suggest **cause and effect:** *thus, therefore, because, since, so.*
- **Anticipate answers.** Think of words that might best fill the blank.
- **Look at the choices.** If the word you guessed is there, it is probably the correct choice. You can double-check by eliminating any choices that are obviously wrong. Then, try *each* choice in the blank, and re-read the sentence *each* time to find the best fit. Take no shortcuts on this step.

Here are four fill-in-the-blank questions:

7. Biologists say meeting a Noah's ark-like emergency today would require an ocean freighter to hold the ten million species weighing a total of one thousand tons, says Clifford Pickover in "Keys to Infinity," but successfully preserving them from extinction would still be _____ because at least fifty members of a species are required to maintain genetic health.

   A feasible **D** dubious
   B inappropriate **E** effortless
   C abstruse

Answer: You are looking for a word that means "unlikely." How do you know that? Your clue lies in the part of the sentence that follows the word *because,* which tells you that it will take fifty times the two-by-two formula to keep the animals in good genetic shape. (Of course, a difficult test like the *SAT* will not give you a word as easy as *unlikely* as a choice.)

Let's imagine for a moment that those choices are all unfamiliar words, and maybe they are to you. You can still think them through. **Use what you know to eliminate incorrect answers.** You can eliminate **B** and **E**—the task described is neither inappropriate nor easy enough to be called effortless. Cross out **C** (*abstruse,* which means "difficult to understand"), because it doesn't fit the context either. **A** (*feasible,* which means "doable") and **D** (*dubious*) are the remaining choices. Choice **A** suggests the meaning that is opposite the context, so **D is the best answer.**

8. If it were possible to _____ a car body in a vat of human stomach acid, the acid would eat the car body, given enough time and assuming you could keep the vat from dissolving.

   A vacillate **D** ostracize
   B vilify **E** refurbish
   C immerse

Answer: **C is the correct answer,** the only choice that makes sense in the sentence. You have a great clue in the second half of this sentence, which tells you that the car would dissolve *in* the acid. This would, of course, require the car to be *in* the acid. Thus, you would look for a word like *soak* to fill the blank, so *immerse,* which means "plunge into a liquid," is your best choice.

Two Blanks to Fill In

Some sentence-completion questions have two blanks. The trick is to find the choice that fits both blanks correctly—in the order given. **As a shortcut, determine the choices that fit *one* blank, whichever blank seems easier to you. Cross out all the choices that don't fit. Then, consider *only* the remaining choices when filling in the other blank.**

9. Researchers have determined that the ability to wiggle one's ears and curl one's tongue is _____, much to the disappointment of kids who have spent hours trying to _____ these skills.

   A genetic, achieve

   B complicated, procure

   C unreliable, sustain

   D inherited, flaunt

   E acquired, relinquish

Answer: Before you look at the choices, make sense of the sentence. One clue lies in the word *disappointment,* which tells you that the kids are not successful in learning the skill. Another clue lies in the word *researchers,* which suggests that the blank word will be scientific. Since the kids couldn't learn the skills, the skills must be *inborn.*

Now, look at the choices. **You can immediately eliminate any first-blank choices that do not reflect the sentence's meaning**—in this case, eliminate any first-blank choices that do not mean "inborn." Strike out **E** (*acquired,* an antonym), **B** (*complicated*), and **C** (*unreliable*). Both **A** (*genetic*) and **D** (*inherited*) could fill the first blank.

Now, go on to the second blank, checking only the choices that fit the first blank—in this case, **A** and **D**. In this half of the sentence, you know you are looking for a verb that means "get; learn." **A** (*achieve*) is a possibility, but **D** (*flaunt*) doesn't work since it is not possible to flaunt what has not been acquired. Thus, **A is your best answer.**

10. Elephants, which are the largest animals walking the earth today, can _____ a number of human _____, including seasickness, colds, pneumonia, mumps, and diabetes.

    A recollect, infirmities

    B diagnose, junctures

    C acquire, tendencies

    D contract, maladies

    E atrophy, ailments

Answer: You know that the second blank will mean "illnesses" because the second half of the sentence lists quite a few human illnesses. The first blank will therefore mean something akin to the word *catch.*

For this question it might be easier to begin with the second blank. Remember that you are looking for a word that means "illnesses," so you can quickly eliminate **B** and **C**. Choices **A** (*infirmities*), **D** (*maladies*), and **E** (*ailments*) all fit the second blank.

Your next step is to check the first blank for choices **A, D,** and **E,** the only choices that fit the second blank. Which of them has a first-blank choice that means "catch"? Only **choice D** (*contract*) fits the meaning you need. (Yes, *acquire* also means "catch," but you've already eliminated **C** because the second blank doesn't fit.) **D is the best answer.**

Finally, try out the sentence to make sure that both words in choice D make sense.

ANALOGY QUESTIONS require that you figure out the relationship between one pair of words and then select another pair with the same relationship. Analogies use many kinds of relationships, including **cause and effect, part and whole, performer and related object, performer and related action, person or object, quality, synonym, antonym, characteristic, degree.** (For more about analogies, see pages 444, 514, 607, 745 1079.)

The more comprehensive your vocabulary, the better off you will be when you face an analogy question. If you are stumped, try breaking an unfamiliar word into its prefix, suffix, and root. In some tests the analogy questions get harder as you go, but don't give up. Everyone's vocabulary is different, and a word that seems difficult to others may be easy for you. Let's try one out:

> 11. TEACHER : STUDENTS : :
>
> **A** actor : playwrights
>
> **B** speaker : audience
>
> **C** horse : corrals
>
> **D** business owner : stocks
>
> **E** enemy : airplanes

Begin by turning the first pair of words (the stem words) into a sentence that defines their relationship. Your sentence should begin with the first word in the pair and end with the second word; you fill in the middle. A sentence for item 11 might be *A teacher's job is to educate or inspire students*. Now, try each choice out within the same sentence: An actor's job is to educate or inspire playwrights? A speaker's job is to educate or inspire an audience? A horse's job is to educate or inspire corrals? (No way.) A business owner's job is to educate or inspire stocks? An enemy's job is to educate or inspire airplanes?

Answer: **B is the best answer** because it preserves the relationship and the kind of comparison being made. Both a teacher and a speaker are kinds of people. Students and audiences listen to them and—the teacher and the speaker hope—become educated or inspired as a result of what they hear. None of the other choices show the same relationship.

You may already have noticed that words in vocabulary questions are anything but commonplace. What's a student to do in the face of such *egregious, inordinate,* and *maliciously pedantic* word choices? Study them. Study them. Study them. The best way, though, to learn vocabulary words is to read. Read many different kinds of materials. Don't just skim over words you don't know: Look them up. Then, think about the meaning they add to the passage you are reading. If you follow those suggestions, you'll increase your vocabulary *exponentially,* and questions on vocabulary tests will be much less *formidable*.

In the analogy questions that follow, the first uses easy words only; the second throws in some challenging words.

> 12. SHEEP : FLOCK : :
>
> **A** milk : water
>
> **B** street : road
>
> **C** car : truck
>
> **D** trees : orchard
>
> **E** telephone : receiver

Answer: To define the relationship in the stem words, you might make up this sentence: *Sheep are part of a group called a flock*. Then, try out that same sentence with all of the choices. You can eliminate **A, B,** and **C** because none of them make sense in your sentence. **D** makes sense: Trees are part of a group called an orchard. **E** might have made sense if the words were in reverse order (a receiver is part of a telephone)—but they're not. **So D is the correct answer.** The analogy is based on the relationship of a part to a whole.

> 13. LUMINOUS : GLOWING : :
>
> **A** burnished : beautiful
>
> **B** murky : dark
>
> **C** weathered : new
>
> **D** distraught : erroneous
>
> **E** inane : sagacious

Answer: **The answer is B.** The relationship in this analogy is that of synonyms: *Luminous* means the same as *glowing*. You can eliminate choices **C** and **E** (the word pairs are antonyms, not synonyms) as well as **D,** in which the words seem totally unrelated. The words in **A** aren't synonyms either (*burnished* means "bright," not "beautiful"), so that leaves only **B,** whose words (*murky, dark*) are indeed synonyms.

Test Smarts

Multiple-Choice Writing Questions

Multiple-choice writing questions are designed to test your knowledge of standard written English. Some questions ask you to spot errors in a sentence's grammar or punctuation. Some ask you to spot the best written form of a sentence. Some ask when a paragraph is (or isn't) properly developed. You will need to know the rules of punctuation and grammar. Here are some question formats you might encounter:

IDENTIFYING-SENTENCE-ERROR QUESTIONS

ask you to look at underlined sections of a sentence and choose the section that includes an error. You are *not* expected to correct the error.

> 14. The average person knows about 50,000 of
>   **A**
>
> the 150,000 words in a standard college dictionary, have learned most of them by
>   **B**   **C**
>
> high school, which means 3,000 words per
>   **D**
>
> year or eight every day. No error.
>   **E**

Answer: **The correct answer is B.** Replace the verb phrase *have learned* with the present participle *having learned*. The phrase *having learned most of them by high school* is a participial phrase that modifies *person*. Remember, however, that you are asked only to *find* the error, not to correct it or explain why it's wrong. By the way, have you picked up your eight words today?

IMPROVING-SENTENCES QUESTIONS

ask you to correct an underlined section by choosing the best version offered. It is helpful to find the error before you look at the answer choices. Then, anticipate how it could best be corrected. The answers to questions like those are often confusing to read because they are long and very poorly written (remember that all but one of them are wrong). Take some time with such questions.

> 15. Over an average person's life span, his or her heart will pump about 50 million gallons, <u>which equals enough to fill a million bathtubs or filling fifty 10-ft-deep swimming pools being as big as football fields.</u>
>
> **A** which equals enough to fill a million bathtubs or to fill fifty 10-foot-deep swimming pools as big as football fields.
>
> **B** enough to fill a million bathtubs or fifty 10-foot-deep swimming pools as big as football fields.
>
> **C** which means a million bathtubs or fifty 10-foot-deep swimming pools as big as football fields will be filled by it.
>
> **D** enough to fill a million bathtubs with 10-foot-deep swimming pools being as big as football fields.
>
> **E** which is a million bathtubs, 10-foot-deep swimming pools, and football fields.

Answer: **The best answer is B.** Your next-best choice, **A**, says the same thing but with less economy. **C** is awkward and unnecessarily switches verb tenses; **D** and **E** totally garble the information.

IMPROVING-THE-PARAGRAPH QUESTIONS

present a paragraph followed by questions. You may be asked to pick a choice that combines or rewrites portions of sentences. You may be asked to decide which sentences could be added or removed from the paragraph. You may be asked which sentence could be used to strengthen the argument of the writer, or you may be asked to choose a thesis statement for the paragraph.

DIRECTIONS: Read the paragraph below. Then, find the best answer to the following questions.

(1) An initially beneficial chemical whose use had unintended consequences is DDT. (2) Beginning in 1939, this pesticide was used throughout the United States to exterminate disease-carrying and crop-eating insects. (3) This powerful chemical also helped India. (4) It helped India reduce cases of malaria from 75 million to fewer than five million. (5) In 1962, scientists began to realize that the chemical was passing through the food chain and harming some types of birds. (6) As a result of high concentrations of DDT in the birds' tissue, many species began laying thin-shelled eggs that cracked easily. (7) One result of widespread DDT spraying was the decline of some bird populations.

16. Which of the following choices represents the *best* way to combine sentences 3–4?

   A This powerful chemical also helped India, it reduced cases of malaria from 75 million to fewer than five million.

   B This powerful chemical also helped India by helping India to reduce cases of malaria from 75 million to fewer than five million.

   C India also was helped by this powerful chemical, which had the effect of India's reducing cases of malaria from 75 million to fewer than five million.

   D This powerful chemical also helped India to reduce cases of malaria from 75 million to fewer than five million.

   E This powerful chemical also helped India: reduce cases of malaria from 75 million to fewer than five million.

Answer: You are looking for the sentence that contains all of the important information with the *least* amount of repetition. It takes careful reading to figure out that **the best answer is D,** which cuts the clutter and maintains the meaning. Answer **A** is a run-on sentence, so that's out. **B** is awkwardly repetitious; **C** makes the verb passive, increasing wordiness. The difference between choices **D** and **E** is slight—only a colon and the word *to*. That's enough to make **E** wrong (the rest of the sentence doesn't go with the colon) and **D** smooth, streamlined, and the only correct answer.

17. Which of the words below could *best* be inserted in sentence 5 immediately after "In 1962,"?

   A also   **D** and
   B however   **E** because
   C but

Answer: **The best answer is B,** the only choice that makes sense in the context of the paragraph. Choice **B** (*however*) reflects the reversed direction of sentence 5, which clearly states that—unlike the information given in the preceding sentences—not everything about DDT was good.

Strategies for Taking Writing Tests

Writing a Response to Literature

When you are asked to respond to a literary passage on a writing test, the passage may be a short story, a novel excerpt, a poem, or a section of a play. No matter the type of passage, you'll need to understand not only its literal meaning, but also the deeper point the writer is making. Follow the steps below to write a response to a passage from a play. The sample responses provided are based on the prompt to the right. (The excerpt from *Macbeth* appears on page 295.)

> **Prompt**
>
> *Macbeth* follows the title character's murderous and deceitful ascent to the throne of Scotland. Macbeth gives the "Tomorrow, and tomorrow, and tomorrow" speech as his scheme begins to unravel. In an essay, explain the meaning of the speech and the deeper point you think Shakespeare is making in it.

THINKING IT THROUGH — Writing a Response to Literature

STEP 1 **Carefully read the prompt and the selection.** Be sure you can identify the task and the surface meaning of the passage.

I need to explain both what the passage means and the writer's deeper point. Macbeth is saying he thinks life is short and meaningless.

STEP 2 **Draw a conclusion about the deeper meaning of the piece, and gather support for that conclusion.** Base your conclusion on your own knowledge and on details that seem important in the selection.

It seems like Macbeth's life will be short and meaningless because of what he has done, but maybe other people's lives can be more than just one day after another if they do more important and better things than Macbeth did. Words like "petty," "fools," "poor," "idiot," and "nothing" seem to indicate how Macbeth feels about himself after realizing what he has done. In my own experience, life only seems like a series of tomorrows when you're not doing anything that matters.

STEP 3 **Develop a thesis statement for your essay based on your conclusion and your evidence.**

The "Tomorrow, and tomorrow, and tomorrow" speech from *Macbeth* explains how empty Macbeth's life has become, but it also points to another, better path.

STEP 4 **Write your response.** Explain how examples you use from the text relate to each other and to your thesis. Write with a serious, authoritative tone, and use precise language to explain the conclusion you have drawn. End your response by emphasizing your thesis in a memorable way. Proofread your finished response, and correct any errors in English-language conventions.

Writing a Response to Expository Text

Expository text provides information. A written **response to expository text** should demonstrate your understanding of the information provided and the organization of that information. To write a response to expository text for a test, use the steps below. The sample responses provided are based on the prompt to the right. ("Life in 999: A Grim Struggle" begins on page 30.)

> **Prompt**
>
> The article "Life in 999: A Grim Struggle" explains what life was like for most Europeans over 1,000 years ago. Using examples from the article, explain in an essay the main ways in which daily life then differed from life now.

THINKING IT THROUGH

Writing a Response to Expository Text

▶ **STEP 1 Carefully read the prompt and the selection.** Make sure you understand what tasks the prompt calls for.

I need to pick out the main categories of differences between life in Europe in the year 999 and life now, and give examples of those differences.

▶ **STEP 2 Decide on your general answer, and identify your main supporting points.** Skim the selection to identify the main points you will make to support your answer to the prompt.

The article explains what people ate, where people lived, physical problems people faced, and how time was marked.

▶ **STEP 3 Develop a thesis statement for your essay.** Your thesis statement will sum up your main points and draw a conclusion about your topic.

Life in 999 was much different from life today, when we have better food and housing, fewer physical problems, and a clearer idea of how time passes.

▶ **STEP 4 Gather support for your thesis.** Choose details and examples from the selection that will provide strong support, and elaborate on them.

I can compare the limited foods people ate with the selection in a typical mall food court, and I can compare the simple huts people lived in with modern housing that has electricity and running water. I can explain how much longer life expectancy is now and how crowded some cities are. Finally, I can compare the way people in 999 might not have known what month it was with all the devices people use now to identify the passage of time.

▶ **STEP 5 Write your essay.** Begin with an attention-getter, such as a question or a surprising statement. Organize ideas clearly and logically, using transitions to show readers the links among those ideas. Then, find and correct any errors in English-language conventions in your draft.

Writing a Biographical Narrative

Writing a **biographical narrative** requires you to do more than simply retell an event from someone's life. Through vivid descriptions and explanations, you must make readers feel that they, too, witnessed the event. To give a biographical narrative meaning, share a significant conclusion about the person involved in the event. To write a biographical narrative in response to a test prompt, follow the steps below. The sample responses provided are based on the prompt to the right.

Prompt

While everyone makes mistakes, some people handle them better than others. In a narrative, relate how someone you witnessed handled making a mistake, including the consequences of the way the mistake was handled. Note what this tells you about the person and how witnessing this event affected you.

THINKING IT THROUGH — Writing a Biographical Narrative

▶ **STEP 1 Carefully read the prompt, and choose a subject.**

I need to explain what someone I saw make a mistake did—how they handled the mistake and what the consequences were. I'll tell about when my government teacher said something negative about a political candidate during class.

▶ **STEP 2 Identify the parts of the event you will relate.** Outline in sequence the smaller events that make up your chosen event.

A student mentioned who he planned to vote for in the upcoming election. Mrs. Jackson made a joke about the candidate that offended the student. Mrs. Jackson apologized and explained that she had strong opinions because she liked politics so much—that's why she became a government teacher—and she hoped we would also develop strong opinions, but express them more appropriately. Her apology started a great discussion.

▶ **STEP 3 Identify important details about the people, events, and setting.** Details should be relevant and specific to bring the incident to life.

Mrs. Jackson's expressions and tone of voice are important, as are those of the student whose candidate she insulted.

▶ **STEP 4 Draw a conclusion based on the details.** Decide why the incident is significant; this conclusion will be the basis for your narrative's thesis.

Mrs. Jackson showed what a good teacher she is by admitting her mistake and turning it into a thought-provoking lesson. I'll be careful now to back up my opinions rather than insulting someone else's position.

▶ **STEP 5 Write your narrative.** Provide context for readers in your introduction. Make your point of view clear and consistent, and make sure every detail you include helps support your thesis or bring the event to life. Finally, correct any errors in grammar, usage, and mechanics.

Writing an Expository Composition

Expository compositions explain. You might write an expository composition to tell how to do something, define a topic, compare and contrast two things, or explain causes and effects. No matter the task, expository writing should anticipate readers' questions and clear up any potential misunderstandings or biases about the topic. Use the steps below to write an effective expository composition for a test.

> **Prompt**
>
> Consider an important, recent event in your community or in the larger world. In an essay, discuss what you think are the primary cause and the most important effect of the event. Support the cause and effect you identify with examples.

THINKING IT THROUGH: Writing an Expository Composition

STEP 1 Carefully read the prompt, and choose a topic you know well.

I need to explain the main cause and effect of an event. I'll pick the collapse that happened last month of the old two-lane bridge over Town Creek.

STEP 2 Identify the major parts of the topic.

The parts are one cause and one effect. There were lots of causes, including increased truck traffic and a recent flood, but the main cause is lack of funding for repairs. The main effect is increased traffic on the only other bridge over the creek.

STEP 3 Brainstorm background information and details about each part of the topic. Your essay will need to answer potential questions and clear up any misunderstandings or biases readers might have.

Voters opposed funding needed for repairs a few years ago because many thought that since the bridge had stood for so many years, the repairs were only cosmetic, not structural. Now those voters are paying the price with longer drives to cross the other bridge in heavy traffic while the old bridge is being rebuilt—at greater expense than the proposed repairs would have entailed.

STEP 4 Synthesize your ideas to plan a thesis. Draft a thesis sentence explaining the point made by all of your information about your topic.

The collapse of Old Town Creek Bridge was the result of an attempt to save money; now it is costing drivers both time and money as they are diverted to the only other bridge over the creek.

STEP 5 Write your essay. Don't just string together ideas in your draft. Instead, provide insight into your topic by thoroughly explaining your major points. Organize ideas in an easy-to-follow way, and connect them with transitional expressions to help guide readers. Finally, proofread and correct any errors in English-language conventions.

Writing a Persuasive Composition

In a **persuasive composition** written for a test, you must quickly identify a position and strong reasons and evidence that support that position. To make the most of your time, follow the steps below. The sample responses provided are based on the prompt to the right. Notice that in some cases it is faster and easier to develop a strong argument for a position that doesn't fit your views; your goal on a test is simply to write the best essay you can.

> **Prompt**
>
> Many states are considering enacting graduated driver's license laws, which limit such things as the time of day when teenagers may drive or the number of passengers they may carry. In an essay, explain whether you agree or disagree with such laws, and back up your position with evidence.

THINKING IT THROUGH — Writing a Persuasive Composition

▶ **STEP 1 Carefully read the prompt, analyzing the situation and the task.**

The laws limit when teenagers can drive or how many people can ride with them. I have to decide based on evidence whether these laws are a good idea.

▶ **STEP 2 Draft an opinion statement.** Choose the easiest position to defend.

Personally, I don't want my rights limited, but I think I can use stronger evidence if I pick the position in favor of graduated licenses. My opinion statement will be: Graduated license laws, while unpopular with teenagers, are a good idea.

▶ **STEP 3 Identify reasons and evidence.** Use the acronym MATH (**M**oney, **A**ttitudes, **T**ime, **H**ealth/safety) to identify reasons and counterclaims.

Money: Graduated licenses will be more expensive to issue and enforce, but they might reduce expenses resulting from accidents caused by teen drivers.

Attitude: I have a friend who's a terrible driver but feels like he has the right to drive however he wants. These limits might change that attitude.

Time: Parents will waste time picking up teenagers from jobs if they have to work later than they're allowed to drive, but this is a minor problem.

Health/safety: Keeping teens from driving late at night or with a carload of friends might prevent a lot of accidents.

▶ **STEP 4 Choose your two or three strongest reasons.** Use reasons and responses to readers' potential counterclaims that relate to the prompt.

I'll focus on the most important issues related to these laws—safety and money.

▶ **STEP 5 Write your essay.** Write with a convincing, knowledgeable voice, and thoroughly explain your reasons and evidence. Organize your ideas in order of importance, finishing with your strongest reason to leave a lasting impression. Then, proofread your draft, and correct any errors in English-language conventions.

Writing an Analytical Composition

On a writing test, you may be asked to write an **analytical composition**. To do so, you must show insight in analyzing a statement, idea, or situation. Usually you will form a generalization and support it with evidence. Follow the steps below. The sample responses provided are based on the prompt to the right.

> **Prompt**
>
> Consider the following statement, and write an essay in which you analyze its meaning: "Novelty is too often mistaken for progress." Use examples from history or science as well as from your own experience to support your analysis.

THINKING IT THROUGH: Writing an Analytical Composition

STEP 1 Read the prompt, and identify your general response to it. Make sure you understand any quotations or important ideas in the prompt.

The statement means that people often see that something is different and automatically think it's better even though it may not be.

STEP 2 Identify two or three pieces of strong supporting evidence.

The Edsel was supposed to be an innovative car in the 1950s, but it turned out to have a lot of problems and was a failure.

Another example is the designated hitter rule in baseball. People thought having a designated hitter batting in place of the pitcher would make the game more exciting, but it wound up making the games longer and making pitchers less well-rounded players.

STEP 3 Synthesize your ideas to plan a thesis statement. Draft a sentence or two explaining how your examples support your analysis.

When progress takes the form of a stylish new car that runs poorly or a new sports rule that winds up hurting the game, it isn't progress at all, but only novelty.

STEP 4 Organize your support. Depending on your topic, consider using order of importance, comparison and contrast, cause and effect, chronological order, or a combination of orders.

First, I'll discuss the Edsel because its problems were so obvious. Then, I'll explain the less obvious problems with the designated hitter rule. That order can lead into a final statement about how people should consider not only obvious problems but also more subtle ones when they're deciding whether something is truly progress or only novelty.

STEP 5 Draft your essay. Clearly explain what you think quotations or important ideas in the prompt mean, and state your thesis. Connect your ideas with transitional expressions, and elaborate on those ideas with details. Conclude by restating your thesis, and close with a memorable comment. Finally, correct any errors in grammar, usage, and mechanics.

Handbook of Literary and Historical Terms

ALEXANDRINE A line of poetry made up of six iambs—that is, a line written in iambic hexameter. The following alexandrine is from Lord Byron's *Childe Harold's Pilgrimage* (Collection 5):

> Without a grave, unknelled, uncoffined, and unknown.

See page 612.

ALLEGORY A story in which the characters, settings, and events stand for abstract or moral concepts. Allegories thus have two meanings: a literal meaning and a symbolic meaning. Allegories were a popular literary form during the Middle Ages. The best-known English allegory is John Bunyan's *The Pilgrim's Progress* (Collection 3), which recounts the adventures of a character named Christian. The hero's journey to the Celestial City brings him up against many trials that symbolize the pitfalls facing the Christian traveling through this world toward the spiritual world.

See pages 342, 383, 750.

ALLITERATION The repetition of consonant sounds in words that are close to one another. Alliteration occurs most often at the beginning of words, as in "rough and ready." But consonants within words sometimes alliterate, as in "baby blue." The echoes that alliteration creates can increase a poem's rhythmic and musical effects and make its lines especially memorable. In this line from Shakespeare's Sonnet 30 (page 280), the *w* sounds emphasize the melancholy tone:

> And with old woes new wail my dear time's waste.

Alliteration is an essential feature of Anglo-Saxon poetry; in most lines, two or three of the four stressed syllables alliterate.

See pages 41, 280, 281, 574, 717, 948, 950.

"Basil, do you think the center is going to hold?"

Drawing by Booth; ©1984 The New Yorker Magazine, Inc.

ALLUSION A reference to a statement, person, place, event, or thing that is known from literature, history, religion, mythology, politics, sports, science, or popular culture. The concluding lines of Wilfred Owen's poem "Dulce et Decorum Est" (Collection 7) are *"Dulce et decorum est / Pro patria mori."* ("It is sweet and proper to die for one's country"). These lines allude to a line from an ode by the Latin poet Horace. The title of William Faulkner's *The Sound and the Fury* is an allusion to a line from Shakespeare's *Macbeth* (Collection 3). The cartoon above alludes to William Butler Yeats's poem "The Second Coming" (Collection 7).

See pages 379, 561, 826.

ANALOGY A comparison of two things to show that they are alike in certain respects. Writers often make analogies to show how something unfamiliar is like something well-known or widely experienced. For example, people often draw an analogy between creating a work of art and giving birth to a child.

See pages 376, 444, 745, 1079.

Handbook of Literary and Historical Terms

ANECDOTE A brief and sometimes witty story that focuses on a single interesting incident or event, often in order to make a point or teach a moral lesson. Sometimes an anecdote reveals the character of a famous person. Taoists, Zen Buddhists, and Sufis, among others, use anecdotes to convey indirectly the teachings of their philosophies.

See pages 347, 357.

ANIMISM A belief that spirits or souls are present in all living things. This belief was at the heart of the ancient Celtic religion, and it can be found in many other ancient religions.

See page 7.

ANTAGONIST The character or force that opposes or blocks the protagonist, or main character, in a narrative. Usually the antagonist is human, like Sir Modred, the villainous rebel who destroys the Round Table in Sir Thomas Malory's *Le Morte d'Arthur* (Collection 2) or the schoolgirls who mercilessly taunt the Kelvey sisters in Katherine Mansfield's "The Doll's House" (Collection 7). Sometimes the antagonist is supernatural, like Satan, who opposes God in John Milton's *Paradise Lost* (Collection 3).

ANTICLIMAX See *Climax*.

ANTITHESIS A contrast of ideas expressed in a grammatically balanced statement. In the following line from Canto III of *The Rape of the Lock* (Collection 4), Alexander Pope balances noun against noun and verb against verb:

> And wretches hang that jurymen may dine.

See page 446.

APHORISM A concise, sometimes witty saying that expresses a principle, truth, or observation about life. Alexander Pope's poetry contains some of the most famous aphorisms in the English language, as in this example from *An Essay on Criticism* (Collection 4):

> To err is human, to forgive, divine.

APOSTROPHE A figure of speech in which a speaker directly addresses an absent or dead person, an abstract quality, or something nonhuman as if it were present and capable of responding. Apostrophe was a popular device with the Romantic poets: Wordsworth, for example, apostrophizes the river Wye in his "Tintern Abbey" (Collection 5). Among the second-generation Romantics, Shelley apostrophized the west wind; Byron apostrophized the ocean; and Keats apostrophized a nightingale and a Greek urn (all in Collection 5).

See pages 612, 626.

ARCHETYPE A pattern that appears in literature across cultures and is repeated through the ages. An archetype can be a character, a plot, an image, or a setting. All stories or myths that contain a quest, for example, share certain features, suggesting that each quest-story has been formed from a master pattern. Similarly, all epic heroes have a number of common characteristics, though each one also has culturally specific characteristics. Ignoring the culturally specific characteristics of a particular epic hero will allow you to perceive what the archetype of the epic hero is.

See pages 20, 45, 179, 184, 198, 201.

ASIDE Private words that a character in a play speaks to the audience or to another character and that are not supposed to be overheard by others onstage. Stage directions usually tell when a speech is an aside.

ASSONANCE The repetition of similar vowel sounds followed by different consonant sounds in words that are close together. Assonance differs from exact rhyme in that it does not repeat the consonant sound following the vowel. The words *face* and *base* rhyme, while the words *face* and *fade* are assonant. Like alliteration, assonance can create musical and rhythmic effects. In this line from Alfred, Lord Tennyson's "The Lady of Shalott" (Collection 6), the repetition of the short *a* sounds creates a rhythmic effect that mimics the action being described:

> An abbot on an ambling pad,

See pages 717, 948, 950.

ATMOSPHERE **The mood or feeling in a literary work.** Atmosphere is usually created through descriptive details and evocative language. For example, Ben Okri sets the mood of his short story "In the Shadow of War" (Collection 7) with a dreamlike description of the war-torn forest around Lagos, Nigeria.

See pages 631, 721.

AUGUSTAN **Similar to the reign of Emperor Augustus (63 B.C.–A.D. 14) or having qualities or tastes that are associated with classical Rome.** In English literary history the Augustan Age dates from the Restoration to the middle of the eighteenth century. Perhaps more than anyone else, Alexander Pope (Collection 4) exhibits Augustan literary tastes in his poetry.

See page 414.

AUTOBIOGRAPHY **A written account of the author's own life.** Unlike **diaries, journals,** and letters, autobiographies are unified narratives usually prepared for a public audience. And unlike **memoirs,** which often focus on famous events and people, autobiographies are usually quite introspective. George Orwell's "Shooting an Elephant" (Collection 7) is a well-known autobiographical essay.

See also *Memoir*.

BALLAD **A song or songlike poem that tells a story.** Most ballads have a regular pattern of **rhythm** and **rhyme,** and they use simple language with a great deal of repetition. Ballads generally have a **refrain**—lines or words that are repeated at regular intervals. They usually tell sensational stories of tragedy, adventure, betrayal, revenge, and jealousy. **Folk ballads** are composed by anonymous singers and are passed down orally from generation to generation before they are written down (often in several different versions). "Lord Randall" (Collection 2) is an example of a folk ballad. **Literary ballads,** on the other hand, are composed and written down by known poets, usually in the style of folk ballads. Samuel Taylor Coleridge's *The Rime of the Ancient Mariner* (Collection 5) is a famous literary ballad.

The typical ballad stanza is a quatrain with the rhyme scheme *abcb*. The first and third lines have four stressed syllables, and the second and fourth lines have three. The number of unstressed syllables in each line may vary, but often the meter is primarily **iambic.**

See pages 108, 111, 578.

BIOGRAPHY **An account of a person's life written by another person.** The *Life of Samuel Johnson* by James Boswell is one of the most famous biographies ever written.

BLANK VERSE **Poetry written in unrhymed iambic pentameter.** "Blank" means that the poetry is unrhymed. "Iambic pentameter" means that each line contains five iambs, or metrical feet, each consisting of an unstressed syllable followed by a stressed syllable (˘ ´). Blank verse is the most important metrical form used in English dramatic and epic poetry. It is the verse line used in Shakespeare's plays and John Milton's *Paradise Lost* (Collection 3). One of the reasons blank verse has been so popular, even among modern poets, is that it combines the naturalness of unrhymed verse with the structure of metrical verse. Except for **free verse,** it is the poetic form that sounds the most like natural speech. It also lends itself easily to slight variations within the basic pattern. Like most of the English Romantic poets, William Wordsworth made extensive use of blank verse, as in these lines from "Tintern Abbey" (Collection 5):

> ˘ ´ ˘ ´ ˘ ´ ˘ ´ ˘ ´
> And now, with gleams of half-extinguished thought,
> ˘ ´ ˘ ´ ˘ ´ ˘ ´ ˘ ´
> With many recognitions dim and faint,
> ˘ ´ ˘ ´ ˘ ´ ˘ ´ ˘ ´
> And somewhat of a sad perplexity,
> ˘ ´ ˘ ´ ˘ ´ ˘ ´ ˘ ´
> The picture of the mind revives again:

See pages 376, 551, 564.

CADENCE **The natural rise and fall of the voice.** Poets who write in **free verse** try to imitate the natural cadences of spoken language.

See also *Rhythm*.

CAESURA **A pause or break within a line of poetry, usually indicated by the natural rhythm of the language.** A midline, or medial, caesura is a characteristic of Anglo-Saxon poetry; it divides the four-beat line in half. Later poets use the caesura less predictably, as in the following lines from Wilfred Owen's "Dulce et Decorum Est" (Collection 7). Here, the caesuras are indicated by the symbol ||.

> Bent double, || like old beggars under sacks,
> Knock-kneed, || coughing like hags, || we cursed through sludge

See page 41.

CANTO A subdivision in a long poem, corresponding to a chapter in a book. Poems divided into cantos include Pope's *The Rape of the Lock* (Collection 4) and Byron's *Childe Harold's Pilgrimage* (Collection 5). Not all major subdivisions of long poems are called cantos: Milton's *Paradise Lost* (Collection 3) is divided into books, and Coleridge's *The Rime of the Ancient Mariner* (Collection 5) into parts.

The word *canto* comes from a Latin word for "song" and originally designated a section of a narrative poem that a minstrel could sing in one session.

See page 453.

CAPITALISM An economic philosophy that advocates the idea that the means of production and distribution should be owned and controlled by private individuals. Adam Smith, an eighteenth-century economist, is one of the great theorists of capitalism, a system which helped to foster the conditions that produced the Industrial Revolution in England and the technological advances of the nineteenth and twentieth centuries.

See also *Laissez Faire*.

CARPE DIEM A Latin phrase that literally means "seize the day"—that is, "make the most of present opportunities." The *carpe diem* theme is common in seventeenth-century English poetry, as in this famous line from Robert Herrick's "To the Virgins, to Make Much of Time": "Gather ye rosebuds while ye may." The theme is also forcefully expressed in Andrew Marvell's "To His Coy Mistress" (both in Collection 3).

See page 263.

CHARACTER An individual in a story or play. A character always has human traits, even if the character is an animal, like the heron and the crab in "Right-Mind and Wrong-Mind" (Collection 2) or the ravens in "The Twa Corbies" (Collection 2); or a god, as in the *Iliad* (Collection 1); or a monster, as in *Beowulf* (Collection 1). A character may also be a human with superhuman powers, like Gilgamesh (Collection 1). But most characters are ordinary human beings, like Geoffrey Chaucer's colorful pilgrims in *The Canterbury Tales* (Collection 2) and the boy in James Joyce's "Araby" (Collection 7).

The process by which the writer reveals the personality of a character is called **characterization.** A writer can reveal a character in the following ways:

1. by telling us directly what the character is like: humble, ambitious, vain, easily manipulated, and so on
2. by describing how the character looks and dresses
3. by letting us hear the character speak
4. by revealing the character's private thoughts and feelings
5. by revealing the character's effect on other people—showing how other characters feel or behave toward the character
6. by showing the character's actions

The first method of revealing a character is called **direct characterization.** When a writer uses this method, we do not have to figure out what a character's personality is like—the writer tells us directly. The other five methods of revealing a character are known as **indirect characterization.** When a writer uses these methods, we have to exercise our own judgment, putting clues together to figure out what a character is like—just as we do in real life when we are getting to know someone.

Characters can be classified as static or dynamic. A **static character** is one who does not change much in the course of a story. A **dynamic character,** on the other hand, changes in some important way as a result of the story's action. Characters can also be classified as flat or round. **Flat characters** have only one or two personality traits. They are one-dimensional—they can be summed up by a single phrase. In contrast, **round characters** have more dimensions to their personalities—they are complex, solid, and multifaceted, like real people.

See pages 118, 144, 155, 291.

CHIVALRY The system of ideals and social codes governing the behavior of knights and gentlewomen in feudal times. The ideal knight was meant to be brave, honorable, and courteous; gentlewomen were meant to be chaste. The code of chivalry is reflected in medieval romance literature, particularly in Malory's *Le Morte d'Arthur* (Collection 2).

See page 100.

CLASSICISM A movement in art, literature, and music that advocates imitating the principles manifested in the art and literature of ancient ("classical") Greece and Rome. Classicism emphasizes reason, clarity, balance, harmony, restraint, order, and universal themes. Classicism is often placed in direct opposition to **Romanticism,** with its emphasis on unrestrained emotions and personal themes. However, this opposition should be approached with caution, as it is sometimes exaggerated for effect. Classicism was particularly admired in art in the eighteenth century and is exemplified in Alexander Pope's mock heroic epic, *The Rape of the Lock* (Collection 4).

See page 414.

See also *Neoclassicism, Romanticism.*

CLICHÉ An expression that was fresh and apt when it was first coined but is now so overused that it has become hackneyed and stale. "Busy as a bee" and "fresh as a daisy" are two examples. Clichés are often likened to dead metaphors—figures of speech ("leg of a chair," "mouth of a river") whose power to surprise has now been completely lost.

CLIMAX The point of greatest emotional intensity or suspense in a plot when the outcome of the conflict becomes known. In Shakespeare's plays, the climax usually occurs in the last act, just before the final scene. Following the climax, the story is **resolved,** or closed.

Some critics talk of more than one climactic moment in a long work (though usually the greatest climax occurs near the end of the plot). In drama, one such climactic moment is called the **turning point,** or **crisis.** At the turning point, something happens that seals the fate of the hero. In Shakespeare's plays, this moment usually occurs in the third act. At the turning point the hero's fortunes begin to decline or improve. All the action leading up to this turning point is **rising action,** and all the action following it is **falling action.** The turning point in Guy de Maupassant's "The Jewels" (Collection 6) occurs when Madame Lantin dies, leaving her husband alone and ravaged by grief. From that point onward, it is downhill for Monsieur Lantin—everything goes wrong, culminating in the story's climax, when Lantin, attempting to sell his wife's necklace, discovers that she has been deceptive. The sale of the jewels brings about the ironic resolution of the story: Lantin becomes wealthy and remarries, choosing a wife who is virtuous but makes him very unhappy.

In contrast, when something trivial or comical occurs at the point in a narrative when one expects something important or serious, the accompanying deflation is called an **anticlimax.** James Joyce's "Araby" (Collection 7) contains such an anticlimactic moment.

See also *Plot.*

COMEDY In general, a story that ends happily. The hero of a comedy is usually an ordinary character who overcomes a series of obstacles that block what he or she wants. Often a comedy pits two young people who wish to marry against parental blocking figures who want to prevent the marriage. The wedding that concludes these comedies suggests the formation of a new society and a renewal of life. Comedy is distinct from **tragedy,** in which a great person comes to an unhappy or disastrous end, usually through some lapse in judgment or character flaw. Comedies are often, but not always, intended to make us laugh. Two famous comedies are Oscar Wilde's play *The Importance of Being Earnest* and George Bernard Shaw's *Pygmalion.* Even though it contains some of the darker elements of tragedy, Shakespeare's *The Tempest* (Collection 3) is considered a comedy because harmony and reconciliation are achieved by the end of the play.

See also *Farce, Tragedy.*

COMMUNISM A philosophy that advocates the creation of a classless and stateless society in which economic goods are distributed equally. The most famous communist government is, of course, the now dissolved Soviet Union, a country which one could say perverted the ideals of communism, since it had a ruling class which was better off than the working class. Human nature seems to prevent people from bringing into being a perfect communist society. George Orwell's novel *Animal Farm* satirizes the ideals of communism, showing the ruination of a farm which has been taken over by radical animal reformers. Ha Jin's "Saboteur" (Collection 7) is set in communist China and focuses on issues of human rights under totalitarian regimes.

See page 810.

CONCEIT A fanciful and elaborate figure of speech that makes a surprising connection between two seemingly dissimilar things. A conceit may be a brief metaphor, or it may form the framework of an entire poem. Two particularly important types of conceits are the **Petrarchan conceit** and the **metaphysical conceit.**

Petrarchan conceits get their name from the fourteenth-century Italian poet Petrarch, who developed their use in his influential sonnet sequence. Poets influenced by Petrarch used these conceits to describe the beauty of the lady for whom they wrote. She invariably had hair of gold, lips of cherry red, and teeth of oriental pearl. In Sonnet 130 (Collection 3), Shakespeare ridicules the use of such conceits. Petrarchan conceits were also used to describe a paradoxical state.

The metaphysical conceit is so called because it was widely used by the seventeenth-century metaphysical poets. This type of conceit is especially startling, complex, and ingenious. A famous example is John Donne's comparison of separated lovers to the legs of a compass in "A Valediction: Forbidding Mourning" (Collection 3).

See page 304.

CONFLICT A struggle or clash between opposing characters, forces, or emotions. In an **external conflict,** a character struggles against some outside force: another character, society as a whole, or some natural force. An **internal conflict,** on the other hand, is a struggle between opposing needs, desires, or emotions within a single character. Many works, especially longer ones, contain both internal and external conflicts. For example, in Ha Jin's "Saboteur" (Collection 7), Mr. Chiu undergoes an internal conflict between his desire to stick to his principles and his desire to be released from jail. In Doris Lessing's "No Witchcraft for Sale" (Collection 7), the conflict between Gideon and the scientist reflects larger cultural conflicts.

See page 731.
See also *Plot.*

CONNOTATIONS All the meanings, associations, or emotions that have come to be attached to a word. For example, an expensive restaurant might prefer to advertise its "delicious cuisine" rather than its "delicious cooking." *Cuisine* and *cooking* have the same literal meaning—"prepared food." But *cuisine* has connotations of elegance and sophistication, while *cooking* does not. The same restaurant would certainly not describe its food as "great grub."

Notice the difference between the following pairs of words: *young/immature, ambitious/cutthroat, uninhibited/shameless, lenient/lax.* We might describe ourselves using the first words but someone else using the second ones. The English philosopher Bertrand Russell once gave a classic example of the different connotations of words: "I am firm. You are obstinate. He is a pigheaded fool."

See page 443.
See also *Denotation.*

CONSONANCE The repetition of final consonant sounds after different vowel sounds. The words *east* and *west, dig* and *dog, turn* and *torn,* and Shakespeare's famous *"struts* and *frets"* (from *Macbeth,* in Collection 3) are examples of consonance. The term is also sometimes used to refer to repeated consonant sounds in the middle of words, as in *solemn stillness.* (Consonance, when loosely defined, can be a form of **alliteration.** Strictly speaking, however, alliteration is the repetition of initial consonant sounds.) Like **assonance,** consonance is one form of **approximate rhyme.**

See also *Alliteration, Assonance.*

COUPLET Two consecutive lines of poetry that rhyme. The couplet has been widely used since the Middle Ages, especially to provide a sense of closure. A couplet that presents a completed thought is called a closed couplet. Shakespeare used closed couplets to end his sonnets, as in this example from Sonnet 29 (Collection 3):

> For thy sweet love remembered such wealth brings
> That then I scorn to change my state with kings.

A couplet written in **iambic pentameter** is called a **heroic couplet.** Although the heroic couplet has been used in English literature since Chaucer, it was perfected during the eighteenth century. Here is an example from Pope's *An Essay on Man* (Collection 4):

> Alike in ignorance, his reason such,
> Whether he thinks too little, or too much:

See pages 167, 278, 446, 726.

COURTLY LOVE **A conventional medieval code of behavior that informed a knight of the proper way to treat his lady.** The code was first developed by the troubadours (lyric poets) of southern France and extensively employed in European literature from the twelfth century throughout the medieval period.

See page 100.

DEISM **The belief that God, after creating the universe, ceased to interfere with the laws of nature and society.** Influenced by Newton's description of the universe as a great clock that was set in motion by the Creator, the deists of the mid-eighteenth century argued that people could only gain an understanding of the laws of nature and society by using their reason.

See page 416.

DENOTATION **The literal, dictionary definition of a word.** For example, a denotation, or dictionary definition, of the word *star* (as in "movie star") is an "eminent actor or actress," but the **connotation** is that of an actor or actress who is adored by fans and who leads a fascinating and glamorous life.

See also *Connotation*.

DENOUEMENT See *Plot*.

DEUS EX MACHINA **Any artificial or contrived device used at the end of a plot to resolve or untangle the complications.** The term is Latin and means "god from a machine." The phrase refers to a device used in ancient Greek and Roman drama: At the conclusion of the play, a god would be lowered onto the stage by a mechanical device so that he could save the hero and end the story happily. The term now refers to any device that resolves a plot in a forced or implausible way: An orphan finds that he has inherited a fortune just as he is being packed off to the poorhouse; a hero is saved because the villain has forgotten to load his gun. Oscar Wilde's *The Importance of Being Earnest* and Charles Dickens's *Oliver Twist* both contain examples of *deus ex machina*.

DIALECT **A way of speaking that is characteristic of a particular region or group of people.** A dialect may have a distinct vocabulary, pronunciation system, and grammar. In the Middle Ages, when Latin was the "literary" language of Europe, writers such as Geoffrey Chaucer (Collection 2) began writing for middle-class audiences in their own regional languages, or what are now interchangeably called **dialects** or **vernaculars.** Today one dialect usually becomes accepted as the standard for a country or culture. In the United States, the dialect used in formal writing and spoken by most TV and radio announcers is known as standard English.

Writers often use other dialects, however, to establish character or to create local color. For example, V. S. Naipaul (Collection 7) has used the dialect spoken by Trinidad's Asian Indian population in many of his works. The East London cockney dialect, and the lower-class background it betrays, are at the very heart of George Bernard Shaw's famous play *Pygmalion*. In this excerpt from the play, Henry Higgins, with his friend Colonel Pickering in attendance, begins to instruct the flower girl Eliza Doolittle in how to speak "proper" English:

> **Higgins.** Say your alphabet.
> **Liza.** I know my alphabet. Do you think I know nothing? I dont need to be taught like a child.
> **Higgins.** *(thundering).* Say your alphabet.
> **Pickering.** Say it, Miss Doolittle. You will understand presently. Do what he tells you; and let him teach you in his own way.
> **Liza.** Oh well, if you put it like that—Ahyee, bəyee, cəyee, dəyee—
> **Higgins.** *(with the roar of a wounded lion).* Stop. Listen to this, Pickering. . . . *(To Eliza)* Say A, B, C, D.
> **Liza.** *(almost in tears).* But I'm saying it. Ahyee, Bəe, Cə-ee—

DIALOGUE **Conversation between two or more people.** Writers use dialogue to advance the action of a plot, to present an interplay of ideas and personalities, and to reveal the background, occupation, or social level of the characters through **tone** and **dialect.**

DICTION **A writer's or speaker's choice of words.** Speakers and writers use different types of words depending on the audience they're addressing, the subject they're discussing, and the effect they're trying to produce. For example, slang that would be suitable in a casual conversation with a friend ("He's a total nerd") would be unsuitable in a political debate. Similarly, the language that a nutritionist would use to describe a meal would be different from the language that a restaurant reviewer or a novelist would use.

Diction is an essential element of a writer's **style.** A writer's diction can be simple or flowery *(shop/ boutique),* modern or old-fashioned *(pharmacy/ apothecary),* general or specific *(sandwich/grilled cheese on rye).* Notice that the **connotations** of words (rather than their strict, literal meanings or **denotations**) are an important aspect of diction.

See pages 365, 1046.

DIDACTIC LITERATURE Literary works that are meant to instruct, give advice, or convey a philosophy or moral message. Much didactic literature derives from religious teaching, as is the case with "The Parable of The Prodigal Son" (Collection 3) and the Taoist anecdotes (Collection 3). Secular works such as fables, folk tales and maxims are also didactic in intent.

See pages 346, 349, 351.
See also *Fable, Parable.*

DISSONANCE (dis′ə·nəns) **A harsh, discordant combination of sounds.** The opposite of **euphony** (yo͞o′fə·nē), a pleasant, harmonious combination of sounds, dissonance is usually created by the repetition of harsh consonant sounds. Dissonance is often used in poetry to communicate energy. Dissonance is also called **cacophony** (kə·käf′ə·nē).

DRAMATIC MONOLOGUE A poem in which a character addresses one or more listeners who remain silent or whose replies are not revealed. The occasion is usually a critical one in the speaker's life. Tennyson's "Ulysses" and Browning's "My Last Duchess" (both in Collection 6) are famous dramatic monologues.

See page 708.

DRAMATIC SONG A poem found in a play that serves to establish mood, reveal character, or advance action. The songs in Shakespeare's plays are the best songs of this kind (Collection 3). Employing a variety of techniques and forms and relying heavily on **onomatopoeia,** Shakespeare wrote songs that can be read alone, but which are best understood within the context of the plays in which they appear.

See page 286.

ELEGY A poem that mourns the death of a person or laments something lost. Elegies may lament the passing of life and beauty, or they may be meditations on the nature of death. A type of **lyric,** an elegy is usually formal in language and structure and solemn or even melancholy in tone. Much of English poetry is elegiac, from the Anglo-Saxon lyric "The Seafarer" (Collection 1) to A. E. Housman's "To an Athlete Dying Young" (Collection 6) and Dylan Thomas's "Do Not Go Gentle into That Good Night" (Collection 7).

See pages 288, 1056.

END-STOPPED LINE A line of poetry in which the meter and the meaning conclude with the end of the line. Often the end-of-line pause is marked with punctuation, though it need not be. These lines from Alexander Pope's *An Essay on Man* (Collection 4) are end-stopped:

> Know then thyself, presume not God to scan;
> The proper study of mankind is man.

See also *Run-on line.*

ENLIGHTENMENT or THE AGE OF REASON One of the names historians have applied to the eighteenth century. The period has been called the Enlightenment and the Age of Reason because at that time, people began to rely on reason and experience, rather than superstition and church authority, to gain an understanding of the world.

See page 414.

EPIC A long narrative poem that relates the great deeds of a larger-than-life hero who embodies the values of a particular society. Most epics include elements of myth, legend, folklore, and history. Their tone is serious and their language grand. Most **epic heroes** undertake quests to achieve something of tremendous value to themselves or their society. Homer's *Odyssey* and *Iliad* (Collection 1) and Virgil's *Aeneid* are the best-known epics in the Western tradition. The two most important English epics are the Anglo-Saxon poem *Beowulf* (Collection 1) and John Milton's *Paradise Lost* (Collection 3).

Many epics share standard characteristics and formulas known as **epic conventions,** which the oral poets drew upon to help them recall the stories they were recounting and which the writers of literary epics draw upon to establish the epic quality of their poems. The conventions include: an **invocation,** or formal plea for aid, to a deity or some other spiritual power; action that begins *in medias res* (literally "in the middle of things") and then **flashes back** to events that take place before the narrative's current time setting; **epic similes,** or elaborately extended comparisons relating heroic events to simple, everyday events; a consistently predictable **metrical structure;** and **stock epithets,** or descriptive adjectives or phrases used repeatedly with—or in place of—a noun or proper name.

See pages 20, 44, 71.
See also *Literary Epic.*

EPIGRAM **A brief, clever, and usually memorable statement.** Alexander Pope's writings are **epigrammatic** in style. Here is an example from his *Essay on Criticism:*

> We think our fathers fools, so wise we grow,
> Our wiser sons, no doubt, will think us so.

See pages 172, 177, 318, 450.
See also *Maxim, Proverb.*

EPIPHANY **In a literary work, a moment of sudden insight or revelation that a character experiences.** The word comes from the Greek and can be translated as "manifestation" or "showing forth." The term has religious meanings that have been transferred to literature by modern writers. James Joyce first gave the word its literary meaning in an early draft of *A Portrait of the Artist as a Young Man.* In Joyce's story "Araby" (Collection 7), the narrator experiences an epiphany at the end of the story when he recognizes the cheap vulgarity of the bazaar and the emptiness of his dream.

See page 956.

EPITAPH **An inscription on a tombstone or a commemorative poem written about a person who has died.** Epitaphs range from the solemn to the farcical. Ben Jonson's "On My First Son" (Collection 3) contains a famously poignant epitaph.

See page 319.

EPITHET **An adjective or other descriptive phrase that is regularly used to characterize a person, place, or thing.** Phrases such as "Peter the Great," "Richard the Lion-Hearted," and "America the Beautiful" are epithets. Homer created so many descriptive epithets in his *Iliad* (Collection 1) and *Odyssey* that his name has been permanently associated with a type of epithet. The **Homeric epithet** consists of a compound adjective that is regularly used to modify a particular noun. Famous examples are "the wine-dark sea," "the gray-eyed goddess Athena," and the "rosy-fingered dawn."

See also *Kenning.*

ESSAY **A short piece of nonfiction prose that examines a single subject from a limited point of view.** There are two major types of essays. **Informal essays** (also called **personal essays**) generally reveal a great deal about the personalities and feelings of their authors. They tend to be loosely structured, conversational, sometimes even humorous, in tone; and usually highly subjective. **Formal essays** (also called **traditional essays**) are usually serious and impersonal in tone. Because they are written to inform or persuade, they are expected to be factual, logical, and tightly organized.

In the European literary tradition the essay began in France with Michel de Montaigne, who sought to test his own judgment by analyzing it in a series of short prose pieces, which he called *essais,* a common sixteenth-century spelling of the French word *assay,* which means "trial" or "attempt." Sir Francis Bacon, who published his *Essays* (see "Of Studies" Collection 3) in the late sixteenth and early seventeenth century, brought the form into England and pioneered what we now call the formal essay. Notable twentieth-century English essayists include Virginia Woolf and George Orwell (both in Collection 7).

See page 887.

EXAGGERATION See *Hyperbole.*

FABLE **A very brief story in prose or verse that teaches a moral, or a practical lesson about life.** The characters in most fables are animals that behave and speak like humans. Some of the most popular fables are those attributed to Aesop, who was supposed to have been a slave in ancient Greece. Several of the pilgrims' tales in Geoffrey Chaucer's *The Canterbury Tales* (Collection 2) also contain fables. Other popular and widely influential fables include those collected in the Panchatantra, like "Right-Mind and Wrong-Mind" (Collection 2).

See page 172.
See also *Parable*.

FALLING ACTION See *Climax*.

FARCE A type of comedy in which ridiculous and often stereotyped characters are involved in far-fetched, silly situations. The humor in farce is based on crude physical action, slapstick, and clowning. Characters may slip on banana peels, get pies thrown in their faces, and knock one another on the head with ladders. The movies featuring Abbott and Costello, Laurel and Hardy, and the Marx brothers are all examples of farces.

The word *farce* comes from a Latin word for "stuffing," and in fact farces were originally used to fill in the waiting time between the acts of a serious play. Even in tragedies, farcical elements are often included to provide **comic relief**, or a break from the pervading tension. Shakespeare frequently lets his "common" characters engage in farcical actions.

FASCISM A nationalistic philosophy that advocates rule by a single charismatic dictator. Fascism properly speaking refers to the philosophy of Benito Mussolini's political party, which was founded in 1919 to oppose communism in Italy. The word, however, was soon used to describe the philosophies of similar repressive, nationalistic political parties in other countries. The German Nazis were fascists. The regimes of Francisco Franco in Spain and Juan Peron in Argentina were fascistic.

See page 810.

FEUDALISM The economic, political, and social system of medieval Europe. This system was basically composed of three classes: the feudal lords, who were powerful landowners; vassals, who did work or military service for the feudal lords in exchange for land; and serfs, who were servants to the lords and vassals and who were bound to their masters' land.

See pages 93, 97.

FIGURE OF SPEECH A word or phrase that describes one thing in terms of another, dissimilar thing, and is not meant to be understood on a literal level. Some 250 different types of figures of speech have been identified, but the most common are the **simile** ("My love is like a red, red rose"), the **metaphor** ("The Lord is my shepherd"), and **personification** ("Death, be not proud"). These involve a comparison between unlike things, but not all figures of speech involve comparison. When one refers to the king using the word *crown,* one is not comparing the crown to the king, but associating the crown with the king.

See page 821.
See also *Hyperbole, Metaphor, Metonymy, Oxymoron, Personification, Simile, Symbol.*

FLASHBACK A scene in a movie, play, short story, novel, or narrative poem that interrupts the present action of the plot to "flash backward" and tell what happened at an earlier time. "The Demon Lover" by Elizabeth Bowen (Collection 7) includes a flashback that describes Mrs. Drover's farewell to her fiancé twenty-five years before the main action of the story takes place.

See page 988.

FOIL A character who sets off another character by strong contrast. This contrast emphasizes the differences between two characters, bringing out the distinctive qualities in each. In the *Epic of Gilgamesh* (Collection 1), Enkidu is a foil to Gilgamesh.

See page 47.

FORESHADOWING The use of clues to hint at what is going to happen later in the plot. Foreshadowing arouses the reader's curiosity and builds up **suspense.** Foreshadowing occurs in Elizabeth Bowen's "The Demon Lover" (Collection 7) when Mrs. Drover imagines "spectral glitters in the place of" her fiancé's eyes, and when we learn that she made an "unnatural promise" to him—that she "could not have plighted a more sinister troth."

See page 1023.
See also *Suspense.*

FRAME STORY An introductory narrative within which one or more of the characters proceed to tell individual stories. Perhaps the best-known example of stories contained in a frame story is the Persian collection called *The Thousand and One Nights* (Collection 2). In English literature, Geoffrey

Chaucer's *The Canterbury Tales* (Collection 2) uses a frame story involving a group of people on a pilgrimage; within the narrative frame, each of the pilgrims then tells his or her own story. Giovanni Boccaccio's *Decameron* (Collection 2) contains another notable example of the frame-story device.

See pages 115, 118, 169, 172, 186.

FREE VERSE **Poetry that has no regular meter or rhyme scheme.** Free verse usually relies on the natural **rhythms** of ordinary speech. Poets writing in free verse may use **alliteration, internal rhyme, onomatopoeia,** and other musical devices to achieve their effects. They may also place great emphasis on **imagery.** Matthew Arnold's "Dover Beach" (Collection 6) is an early example of free verse, and T. S. Eliot's poems, including "The Hollow Men" (Collection 7), are especially fine and famous examples.

GOTHIC **A term used to describe literary works that contain primitive, medieval, wild, mysterious, or natural elements.** Such elements were frowned upon by eighteenth-century neoclassicists but hailed by the Romantic writers of the following era. The **Gothic novel,** a genre popular in the late eighteenth and early nineteenth centuries, is chiefly characterized by gloomy settings and an atmosphere of terror and mystery. Mary Wollstonecraft Shelley's *Frankenstein* is one of the most widely known Gothic novels.

See page 530.

HAIKU **A brief, unrhymed, three-line poem developed in Japan in the 1600s.** The first and third lines of a traditional haiku have five syllables each, and the middle line has seven. Haiku generally juxtapose familiar images and present them in a compressed form, forcing the reader to make an imaginative leap to understand the connection between them.

See page 565.

HUMANISM **An intellectual movement of the Renaissance that restored the study of the classics and focused on examining human life here and now.** Though humanists were still interested in theology and religious questions, the focus of their interest expanded to include earthly matters as well. Famous humanists include Sir Thomas More and Erasmus.

See page 242.

HYPERBOLE **A figure of speech that uses exaggeration to express strong emotion or create a comic effect.** While hyperbole (also known as **overstatement**) does not express the *literal* truth, it is often used in the service of truth to capture a sense of intensity or to emphasize the essential nature of something. For instance, if you claim that it was 250 degrees in the shade, you are using hyperbole to express the truth that it was miserably hot.

See pages 271, 301.

IAMBIC PENTAMETER **A line of poetry made up of five iambs.** An **iamb** is a metrical foot, or unit of measure, consisting of an unstressed syllable followed by a stressed syllable (˘ ′). The word *suggest,* for example, is made up of one iamb. *Pentameter* derives from the Greek words *penta* (five) and *meter* (measure). Here are two lines from John Keats's "Ode to a Nightingale" (Collection 5) that are written in iambic pentameter:

> Forlorn! the very word is like a bell
> To toll me back from thee to my sole self!

Iambic pentameter is by far the most common verse line in English poetry. Shakespeare's sonnets and plays, for example, are written primarily in this meter. Many modern poets, such as W. H. Auden (Collection 7), have continued to use iambic pentameter. Other than **free verse,** it is the poetic meter that sounds the most like natural speech.

See page 278.
See also *Blank Verse.*

IMAGERY **Language that appeals to the senses.** Most images are visual—that is, they appeal to the sense of sight. But imagery can also appeal to the senses of hearing, touch, taste, or smell. While imagery is an element in all types of writing, it is especially important in poetry.

See pages 32, 144, 567, 636, 651, 1071.

INCREMENTAL REPETITION **A device widely used in ballads whereby a line or lines are repeated with slight variations from stanza to**

stanza. Each repetition advances the plot of the narrative. Incremental repetition is used in the folk ballad "Lord Randall" (Collection 2).

See page 111.

INDUSTRIAL REVOLUTION **The period of social and economic change following the replacement of hand tools by machines and power tools, which allowed manufacturers to increase their production and save money.** The perfection of the steam engine in the last half of the eighteenth century signaled the arrival of the age of the machine. The Industrial Revolution began on a small scale among textile manufacturers in the middle of the eighteenth century, but soon spread rapidly. Most textile products were produced by steam-engine-powered machines by the early nineteenth century. As the nineteenth century progressed, other industries began to use steam engines to produce their goods. George Eliot used the Industrial Revolution as the backdrop for *Silas Marner* (1861), and Charles Dickens satirizes its social effects in *Hard Times* (1854).

See page 527.

IN MEDIAS RES **The technique of starting a story in the middle and then using a flashback to tell what happened earlier.** *In medias res* is Latin for "in the middle of things." Epics traditionally begin *in medias res*. For example, John Milton's *Paradise Lost* (Collection 3) opens with Satan and his cohorts in Hell, after the war in Heaven and their fall, events that are recounted later in a flashback.

See page 71.

IRONY **A contrast or discrepancy between expectation and reality—between what is said and what is really meant, between what is expected and what really happens, or between what appears to be true and what really is true.**

Verbal irony occurs when a writer or speaker says one thing but really means something quite different—often the opposite of what he or she has said. If you tell your friend that you "just love being kept waiting in the rain," you are using verbal irony. A classic example of verbal irony is Jonathan Swift's suggestion in *A Modest Proposal* (Collection 4) that the Irish solve their poverty and overpopulation problems by selling their babies as food to their English landlords.

Situational irony occurs when what actually happens is the opposite of what is expected or appropriate. In James Joyce's story "Araby" (Collection 7), the boy hears about a bazaar called Araby and imagines that it will be a splendid, exotic place. Yet when he arrives, he finds that in reality the Araby bazaar is cheap and commonplace.

Dramatic irony occurs when the audience or the reader knows something important that a character in a play or story does not know. Dramatic irony occurs at the end of Elizabeth Bowen's "The Demon Lover" (Collection 7), when Mrs. Drover is riding in the taxi. The reader suspects that the taxi driver is the demon lover even though Mrs. Drover does not. Dramatic irony is a powerful device in William Blake's "The Chimney Sweeper" from *Songs of Innocence* (Collection 5). The speaker is a child who believes what he has been told—that "if all do their duty they need not fear harm." But the reader, who is not so innocent, realizes that this is not so.

See pages 145, 186, 428, 618, 898, 930, 966, 1064, 1090.

KENNING **In Anglo-Saxon poetry, a metaphorical phrase or compound word used to name a person, place, thing, or event indirectly.** *Beowulf* (Collection 1) includes the kennings "whale-road" for the sea and "shepherd of evil" for Grendel.

See page 42.
See also *Epithet*.

LAISSEZ FAIRE (les′ā fer′) **An economic policy based on the idea that economic forces should be allowed to operate freely and without government regulation.**

See page 528.

LITERARY EPIC **Literary epics are epics that have been composed by individual writers, often following earlier models.** Unlike an **oral epic** or a **primary epic**, which is performed by generations of anonymous storytellers and modified slightly with each retelling, a literary epic is the product of a single imagination working within the epic tradition.

See page 363.
See also *Epic*.

LYRIC POETRY **Poetry that focuses on expressing emotions or thoughts, rather than on telling a story.** Most lyrics are short, and they usually imply rather than directly state a single strong emotion. The term *lyric* comes from the Greek. In ancient Greece, lyric poems were recited to the accompaniment of a stringed instrument called the lyre. Today, poets still try to make their lyrics melodious, but they rely only on the musical effects they can create with words (such as **rhyme, rhythm, alliteration,** and **onomatopoeia**). Samuel Taylor Coleridge's "Kubla Khan," William Wordsworth's "Tintern Abbey" (both in Collection 5), and Matthew Arnold's "Dover Beach" (Collection 6) are all lyric poems.

See page 1053.

MAGIC REALISM **A literary style that combines incredible events with realistic details and relates them all in a matter-of-fact tone.** Magic realism originated in Latin America, where writers such as Gabriel García Márquez and Julio Cortázar (Collection 7) drew on elements of surrealism and local folklore to create a style that is both timeless and innovative.

See pages 816, 999.

MATERIALISM **A belief that nothing exists except matter and that the operations of everything, including thought, will, and feeling, are caused by material agencies.**

MAXIM **A brief, direct statement that expresses a basic rule of human conduct or a general truth about human behavior.** "It is better to give than to receive" is an example of a well-known maxim.

See pages 355, 356.
See also *Epigram, Moral Tale, Proverb.*

MEMOIR **A type of autobiography that usually focuses on a single time period or historical event.** *Survival in Auschwitz* by Primo Levi (Collection 7) is a memoir about the author's experience at the death camp in 1944–1945.

See page 834.

METAPHOR **A figure of speech that makes a comparison between two seemingly unlike things without using a connective word such as *like, as, than,* or *resembles*.** You are using a metaphor if you say you're "at the end of your rope" or describe two political candidates as "running neck and neck."

Some metaphors are **directly** stated, like Percy Bysshe Shelley's comparison "My soul is an enchanted boat." (If he had written, "My soul is *like* an enchanted boat," he would have been using a **simile.**) Other metaphors are **implied,** like John Suckling's line "Time shall molt away his wings." The words *molt* and *wings* imply a comparison between time and a bird shedding its feathers.

An **extended metaphor** is a metaphor that is extended, or developed, over several lines of writing or even throughout an entire poem.

A **dead metaphor** is a metaphor that has become so common that we no longer even notice that it is a figure of speech. Our everyday language is filled with dead metaphors, such as *foot of the bed, bone of contention,* and *mouth of the river.*

A **mixed metaphor** is the incongruous mixture of two or more metaphors. Mixed metaphors are usually unintentional and often conjure up ludicrous images: "If you put your money on that horse, you'll be barking up the wrong tree."

See pages 280, 341, 651, 1028, 1060.

METAPHYSICAL POETRY **A term applied to the poetry of John Donne, Andrew Marvell, and other seventeenth-century poets who wrote in a difficult and abstract style.** Metaphysical poetry is intellectual and detached. It is characterized by ingenious, obscure imagery, philosophical meditation, verbal wit, and it often uses rough-sounding meter.

See pages 301, 303.

METER **A generally regular pattern of stressed and unstressed syllables in poetry.** When we want to indicate the metrical pattern of a poem, we mark the stressed syllables with the symbol ′ and the unstressed syllables with the symbol ˘. Indicating the metrical pattern of a poem in this way is called **scanning** the poem, or **scansion.** Here is how to scan these lines from William Blake's "The Tyger" (Collection 5):

> ′˘ ′˘ ′˘ ′
> Tyger! Tyger! burning bright
> ′˘ ′˘ ′˘ ′
> In the forests of the night

Meter is measured in units called feet. A **foot** usually consists of one stressed syllable and one or more unstressed syllables. The basic metrical feet used in

English poetry are the **iamb** (as in cŏnvínce), the **trochee** (as in bórrŏw), the **anapest** (as in cŏntrădíct), the **dactyl** (as in áccŭratĕ), and the **spondee** (as in séawéed). A poem is described as iambic, trochaic, anapestic, dactylic, or spondaic according to what kind of foot appears most often in its lines.

A complete description of a metrical line indicates both the type and number of feet the line contains. For example, a line of iambic pentameter consists of five iambs, while a line of trochaic tetrameter consists of four trochees.

See page 278.

METONYMY (mə·tän′ə·mē) **A figure of speech in which something closely related to a thing or suggested by it is substituted for the thing itself.** You are using metonymy if you call the judiciary "the bench," the king "the crown," the president (or presidential staff) "the White House," or the race track "the turf."

See also *Synecdoche*.
See page 291.

MOCK EPIC A comic narrative poem that parodies the epic by treating a trivial subject in a lofty, grand manner. A mock epic uses dignified language, elaborate figures of speech, and supernatural intervention. The style of the mock epic is called **mock heroic** (and short mock epics are often called mock heroics). Alexander Pope's *The Rape of the Lock* (Collection 4) is considered the supreme mock epic in the English language.

See page 451.

MODERNISM A broad trend in literature and other arts, from approximately 1890 to 1940, that reflected the impact of works like Sigmund Freud's writings on psychology. In general, modernist writers rejected the forms and values of the past and sought new forms to reflect the fragmentation and uncertainty that they felt characterized modern life. Many modern poets, for example, rejected traditional poetic meters and wrote **free verse.** Novelists such as James Joyce employed a technique called **stream of consciousness** to record the randomness and free associations of their characters' thoughts.

See page 810.

MONOLOGUE A long, formal speech made by a character in a play. A monologue may be directed at another character or the audience. Shakespeare's soliloquies (Collection 3) can also be called monologues.

See page 292.
See also *Soliloquy*.

MOOD See *Atmosphere*.

MORAL TALE A tale that teaches a lesson about life. Several of the pilgrims' tales in Geoffrey Chaucer's *The Canterbury Tales* (Collection 2) are moral tales.

See pages 154, 177.

MOTIF In literature, a word, a character, an object, an image, a metaphor, or an idea that recurs in a work or in several works. The rose is a motif that runs through many love poems. *Beowulf* (Collection 1) contains many of the traditional motifs associated with heroic literature from all over the world, including a hero who does great deeds in battle or undertakes an extraordinary journey and a supernatural or fantastic being that takes part in the action. These motifs, along with others common to heroic literature, also appear in epics such as the *Iliad* (Collection 1) and Milton's *Paradise Lost* (Collection 3). A motif almost always bears an important relationship to the **theme** of a work of literature.

MOTIVATION The reasons for or forces behind the action of a character. Motivation is revealed through a combination of the character's desires and moral nature with the circumstances in which he or she is placed. In James Joyce's "Araby" (Collection 7), the narrator's crush on Mangan's sister and his romanticized view of the world combine to provide his motivation for attending the bazaar.

See also *Character*.

MYTH An anonymous traditional story, rooted in a particular society, that usually serves to explain the mysteries of nature and a society's beliefs and customs. Most myths grew out of religious rituals, and almost all of them involve the exploits of gods and heroes. Myths helped people to understand and cope with things beyond human control. Every culture has its own **mythology,** but in the Western world the most important myths have been those of ancient Greece and Rome. In twentieth-century literature, **allusions** to myths are often **ironic,** intended to reveal how diminished humanity has become in comparison with grand mythological figures.

NARRATOR **One who tells, or narrates, a story.** In fiction the narrator occupies any one of a variety of relations to the events described: from the center of the action to a distant, even objective, observer. A narrator may also be reliable or unreliable—if unreliable, the reader is made aware that the narrator's perceptions and interpretations of the action are different from those of the author. Such unreliable narrators can be deceitful or bumbling, but are often just naive or highly impressionable characters. The narrator at the beginning of James Joyce's "Araby" (Collection 7), for example, is an impressionable boy, and the story is, in part, about how the boy's point-of-view changes and becomes more reliable.

See page 155.
See also *Point of View.*

NEOCLASSICISM **The revival of classical standards and forms during the late seventeenth and eighteenth centuries.** The neoclassicists valued the classical ideals of order, reason, balance, harmony, clarity, and restraint. In particular, they studied and tried to emulate the Latin poets Horace and Virgil. Alexander Pope (Collection 4) is one of the most celebrated English neoclassical poets.

See page 414.

NOVEL **A long fictional prose narrative, usually of more than fifty thousand words.** In general, the novel uses the same basic literary elements as the short story: **plot, character, setting, theme,** and **point of view.** The novel's length usually permits these elements to be more fully developed than they are in the short story. However, this is not always true of the modern novel. Some modern novels are basically character studies, with only the barest plot structures. Others reveal little about their characters and concentrate instead on setting or tone or even the language of the novel itself.

Some of the greatest novels ever written are *Tom Jones* by Henry Fielding, *Pride and Prejudice* by Jane Austen, *Jane Eyre* by Charlotte Brontë, *Bleak House* and *Great Expectations* by Charles Dickens, *The Brothers Karamazov* by Fyodor Dostoyevsky, *Madame Bovary* by Gustave Flaubert, *Middlemarch* by George Eliot, *Jude the Obscure* by Thomas Hardy, *War and Peace* by Leo Tolstoy, *Lord Jim* by Joseph Conrad, *Sons and Lovers* by D. H. Lawrence, *Ulysses* by James Joyce, and *One Hundred Years of Solitude* by Gabriel García Márquez.

See page 424.

OCTAVE **An eight-line stanza or poem or the first eight lines of an Italian, or Petrarchan, sonnet.** The usual rhyme scheme of the octave in this type of sonnet is *abbaabba*. The octave, which is sometimes called the **octet,** is followed by a six-line **sestet** with the rhyme scheme *cdecde* or *cdcdcd*.

See page 276.
See also *Sonnet.*

ODE **A complex, generally long lyric poem on a serious subject.** In English poetry, there are basically two types of odes. One is highly formal and dignified in style and is generally written for ceremonial or public occasions. This type of ode derives from the choral odes of the classical Greek poet Pindar. The other type of ode derives from those written by the Latin poet Horace, and it is much more personal and reflective. In English poetry, it is exemplified by the intimate, meditative odes of such Romantic poets as Wordsworth, Keats, and Shelley (Collection 5).

See pages 563, 621.

ONOMATOPOEIA (än′ō·mat′ō·pē′ə) **The use of a word whose sound imitates or suggests its meaning.** Many familiar words, such as *clap, squish, sizzle,* and *wheeze* are onomatopoeic. In poetry, onomatopoeia can reinforce meaning while creating evocative and musical effects. The word "lapping," in the following lines from W. B. Yeats's "The Lake Isle of Innisfree" (Collection 7), is onomatopeic.

> I will arise and go now, for always night and day
> I hear lake water lapping with low sounds by the shore;

See page 286.

OTTAVA RIMA An eight-line stanza in iambic pentameter with the rhyme scheme *abababcc*. The form was developed in Italy and was popularized by the fourteenth-century Italian poet Giovanni Boccaccio (Collection 2). The most famous example of ottava rima in English poetry is Lord Byron's *Don Juan*. William Butler Yeats's "Sailing to Byzantium" is another notable example.

OXYMORON A figure of speech that combines apparently contradictory or incongruous ideas. "Bittersweet," "cruel kindness," and "eloquent silence" are oxymorons. The classic oxymoron "wise fool" is almost a literal translation of the term from the Greek—*oxys* means "sharp" or "keen," and *moros* means "foolish." A famous oxymoron in literature is John Milton's description of Hell in *Paradise Lost* (Collection 3):

> No light, but rather darkness visible. . .

See pages 375, 821.

PARABLE A short, allegorical story that teaches a moral or religious lesson about life. The most famous parables in Western literature are those like "The Parable of the Prodigal Son" (Collection 3) told by Jesus in the Gospels of the Bible.

See pages 342, 347, 353.

PARADOX An apparent contradiction that is actually true. A paradox may be a statement or a situation; as a statement, it is a figure of speech. The metaphysical poets of the seventeenth century (Collection 3) made brilliant use of paradoxes, as in this famous example from John Donne's "Death be not proud" (Collection 3):

> One short sleep past, we wake eternally,
> And death shall be no more; Death, thou shalt die.

The speaker in the cartoon above doesn't understand the famous series of paradoxes that open *A Tale of Two Cities* by Charles Dickens.

See pages 312, 1007.

"I wish you would make up your mind, Mr. Dickens. Was it the best of times or was it the worst of times? It could scarcely have been both."

Drawing by Handelsman; ©1987 The New Yorker Magazine, Inc.

PARALLELISM The repetition of words, phrases, or sentences that have the same grammatical structure or that restate a similar idea. Parallelism is often used in literature meant to be spoken aloud, such as poetry, drama, and speeches, because it can help make lines emotional, rhythmic, and memorable. It is also one of the most important techniques used in Biblical poetry. The parallelism in the following lines from Psalm 23 (Collection 3) heightens the emotional effect and enacts a meditative tone:

> He maketh me to lie down in green pastures:
> He leadeth me beside the still waters.
> He restoreth my soul:
> He leadeth me in the paths of righteousness for
>   his name's sake.

See pages 324, 338, 360, 541.

PARODY The imitation of a work of literature, art, or music for amusement or instruction. Parodies usually use exaggeration or inappropriate subject matter to make a serious style seem ridiculous. Alexander Pope's *The Rape of the Lock* (Collection 4) is a parody of such serious and sweeping epics as the *Iliad* (Collection 1) and the *Aeneid*. Cervantes' *Don Quixote* (Collection 4) is a parody of medieval romances.

See pages 463, 474.

PASTORAL **A type of literature that depicts country life in idyllic, idealized terms.** The term *pastoral* comes from the Latin word for shepherd, and originally, pastorals were about shepherds, nymphs, and rural life. Today, the term has a looser meaning and refers to any literary work that portrays an idyllic rural setting or that expresses nostalgia for an age or place of lost innocence. The most famous traditional English pastoral is Christopher Marlowe's "The Passionate Shepherd to His Love," which is satirized in Sir Walter Raleigh's "The Nymph's Reply to the Shepherd" (both in Collection 3).

See page 257.

PERSONIFICATION **A kind of metaphor in which a nonhuman or nonliving thing or quality is talked about as if it were human or had life.** In these lines, from William Wordsworth's "The World Is Too Much with Us" (Collection 5), the sea is given human form and the wind is given a voice:

> This Sea that bares her bosom to the moon;
> The winds that will be howling at all hours,

See pages 316, 559.
See also *Apostrophe, Figure of Speech, Metaphor*.

PLOT **The series of related events that make up a story or drama.** The plot is the underlying structure of a story. Most plots are built on these "bare bones": A **basic situation,** or **exposition,** introduces the characters, setting, and, usually, the story's major **conflict.** Out of this basic situation, **complications** develop that intensify the conflict. **Suspense** mounts until a **climax**—the tensest or most exciting part of the plot—is reached, where something happens to determine the outcome of the conflict. Finally, all the problems or mysteries of the plot are unraveled in the **resolution,** or **denouement.**

See page 184.
See also *Climax*.

POINT OF VIEW **The vantage point from which a writer tells a story.** There are three main points of view: **first person, limited third person,** and **omniscient third person.**

In the **first-person point of view,** the narrator is a character in the story. Using the pronoun *I*, this narrator tells us his or her own experiences but cannot reveal the private thoughts of other characters. When we read a story told in the first person, we hear and see only what the narrator hears and sees. We may have to interpret what this narrator says because a first-person narrator may or may not be objective, honest, or perceptive. For example, in James Joyce's "Araby" (Collection 7), the narrator is a boy who is, in the beginning of the story, a youth whose point of view is romantic, and the story is about his giving up this view.

In the **limited-third-person point of view,** the narrator is outside the story—like an omniscient narrator—but tells the story from the vantage point of only one character. The narrator can enter the mind of this chosen character but cannot tell what any other characters are thinking except by observation. This narrator also can go only where the chosen character goes. For example, "In the Shadow of War" by Ben Okri (Collection 7) is told entirely from the point of view of Omovo, the main character. We experience the stupefying summer heat, the mysteriousness of the veiled woman, and the horror of the gruesome river scene through Omovo's eyes alone.

In the **omniscient** (or **"all-knowing"**) **point of view,** the person telling the story knows everything that's going on in the story. This omniscient narrator is outside the story, a godlike observer who can tell us what all the characters are thinking and feeling, as well as what is happening anywhere in the story. For example, in "The Rocking-Horse Winner" by D. H. Lawrence (Collection 7), the narrator enters into the thoughts and secrets of every character, revealing both the "hard little place" in the mother's heart and Paul's determination to "compel her attention" by being lucky.

See pages 875, 999.
See also *Narrator, Stream of Consciousness*.

POSTMODERNISM **A trend in art and philosophy that reflects the late-twentieth-century distrust in the idea that there is a legitimate and true system of thought that can be used to understand the world and our place in it.**

Postmodernists, like the modernists, see contemporary life as fragmentary, but rather than regard the fragmentary condition of our world with horror, as for instance T. S. Eliot had done in "The Hollow Men" (Collection 7), postmodernists look upon the fragments as materials that can be plundered and combined in new ways to create works of art. Postmodern writing typically experiments with nontraditional forms and allows for multiple meanings. The lines between real and imaginary worlds are often blurred, as is the boundary between fiction and nonfiction. Other characteristics of postmodern literature are cultural diversity and an often playful self-consciousness; that is, an acknowledgment that literature is not a mirror that accurately reflects the world, but a created world unto itself. Gabriel García Márquez's *One Hundred Years of Solitude,* in which reality and fantasy are blended, is an exemplary postmodern novel.

See page 813.

PROTAGONIST **The main character in fiction, drama, or narrative poetry.** The protagonist is the character we focus our attention on—the person whose conflict sets the plot in motion. (The character or force that blocks the protagonist is called the **antagonist.**) In *Beowulf* (Collection 1), the title character is the protagonist and the monster Grendel his antagonist. Most protagonists are **rounded, dynamic** characters who change in some important way by the end of the story. Whatever the protagonist's weaknesses, we still usually identify with his or her conflict and care about how it is resolved.

PROVERB **A short saying that expresses a common truth or experience, usually about human failings and the ways that people interact with one another.** Proverbs often incorporate such literary elements as **metaphor, alliteration, parallelism,** and **rhyme.**

See page 359.
See also *Epigram, Maxim.*

PUN **A play on the multiple meanings of a word or on two words that sound alike but have different meanings.** Many jokes and riddles are based on puns. ("Why was Cleopatra so negative? Answer: Because she was the queen of denial.") Shakespeare was one of the greatest punsters of all time. Dylan Thomas uses a pun in his poem, "Do Not Go Gentle into That Good Night" (Collection 7)

> Do not go gentle into that good night,
> Old age should burn and rave at the close of day;
> Rage, rage against the dying of the light.

The casual farewell "good night" also means death.

QUATRAIN **A four-line stanza or poem or a group of four lines unified by a rhyme scheme.** The quatrain is the most common verse unit in English poetry. This quatrain from John Donne's "A Valediction: Forbidding Mourning" (Collection 3) has the rhyme scheme *abab:*

> As virtuous men pass mildly away,
>   And whisper to their souls, to go,
> Whilst some of their sad friends do say,
>   The breath goes now, and some say, no:

See page 278.

RATIONALISM **A philosophy that advocates the idea that one should use reason rather than emotion when one is attempting to discover the truth.** Rationalists believe that one must follow reason to determine what opinions are correct and what course of action one should take in any given situation. Opposed to rationalism is Romanticism, which places emphasis on the value of intuition and emotion in arriving at truth.

REALISM **In literature and art, the attempt to depict people and things as they really are, without idealization.** Realism as a movement developed during the mid–nineteenth century as a reaction against Romanticism. Realist writers believed that fiction should truthfully depict the harsh, gritty reality of everyday life without beautifying, sentimentalizing, or romanticizing it. The Norwegian playwright Henrik Ibsen was among the first to introduce realism to the stage. The English novelists Charles Dickens, George Eliot, Thomas Hardy, and Joseph Conrad are also considered realists.

See pages 746, 1043.
See also *Romanticism.*

REFRAIN **A repeated word, phrase, line, or group of lines.** While refrains are most common in poetry and songs, they are sometimes used in prose, particularly speeches. Refrains are used to create rhythm, build suspense, or emphasize important words or ideas.

See pages 108, 111, 1049.

REFORMATION **The break from Catholicism and the authority of the pope that resulted in the establishment of the Protestant churches in the sixteenth century.** Most scholars date the beginning of the Reformation to 1517, the year Martin Luther nailed his *Ninety-five Theses* to the door of a church in Wittenburg, Germany. The *Theses* criticized the Catholic Church's abuse of indulgences and called for reform. In response the Church leaders condemned Luther, and he was forced to break from the Catholic Church and begin his own religious movement.

See page 246.

RENAISSANCE **A French word meaning "rebirth," used to designate the period in European history beginning in Italy in the fourteenth century and ending in the seventeenth century when scientific truths began to challenge long-accepted religious beliefs.** The Renaissance was characterized by a renewal of interest in classical learning and a focus on the study of human life on earth, not only on God and eternity.

See page 240.

RESOLUTION See *Plot*.

RHYME **The repetition of accented vowel sounds and all sounds following them in words that are close together in a poem.** *Park* and *bark* rhyme, as do *sorrow* and *borrow*. The most common type of rhyme, **end rhyme,** occurs at the ends of lines. **Internal rhyme** occurs within lines. Both types are used throughout *The Rime of the Ancient Mariner* by Samuel Taylor Coleridge (Collection 5), contributing to the poem's bouncy, songlike rhythm:

> The fair breeze blew, the white foam flew,
> The furrow followed free;
> We were the first that ever burst
> Into that silent sea.

When words sound similar but do not rhyme exactly, they are called **approximate rhymes** (or **half rhymes, slant rhymes,** or **imperfect rhymes**).

The pattern of rhymed lines in a poem is called its **rhyme scheme.** A rhyme scheme is indicated by giving each new rhyme a new letter of the alphabet. For example, the rhyme scheme of Coleridge's lines is *abcb*.

See page 167.

RHYTHM **The alternation of stressed and unstressed syllables in language.** Rhythm occurs naturally in all forms of spoken and written language. The most obvious kind of rhythm is produced by **meter,** the regular pattern of stressed and unstressed syllables found in some poetry. Writers can also create less structured rhythms by using rhyme, repetition, pauses, and variations in line length and by balancing long and short words or phrases. (Poetry that is written without any regular meter or rhyme scheme is called **free verse.**)

See also *Free Verse, Meter*.

ROMANCE **Historically, a medieval verse narrative chronicling the adventures of a brave knight or other hero who must undertake a quest and overcome great danger for love of a noble lady or high ideal.** Such a heroic character is bound by the code of **chivalry,** which emphasizes loyalty to his lord and ready service to the oppressed. He also must adhere to the philosophy of **courtly love,** an idealized view of the relationship between the sexes in which a knight performs brave deeds to win the approval of his lady.

Today the term *romance* has come to mean any story that presents a world of wish-fulfillment, a world that is happier, more perfect, or more heroic than the real world. Characters in romances "live happily ever after" in a world where good always triumphs over evil. Many of today's most popular novels, movies, TV shows, and even cartoons are essentially romances. *Sir Gawain and the Green Knight* and Sir Thomas Malory's *Le Morte d'Arthur* (Collection 2) are famous English romances.

See pages 101, 193.

ROMANTICISM **A literary, artistic, and philosophical movement that developed as a reaction against neoclassicism in the late eighteenth century and dominated the early nineteenth century.** While classicism and neoclassicism emphasize reason, order, harmony, and restraint, Romanticism emphasizes emotion, imagination, intuition, freedom, personal experience, the beauty of nature, the primitive, the exotic, and even the grotesque. However, many critics feel that the traditional opposition between Romanticism and classicism is all too often forced and exaggerated.

In English literature, William Blake, Samuel Taylor Coleridge, William Wordsworth, Percy Bysshe Shelley, John Keats, Lord Byron (all in Collection 5), Mary Wollstonecraft Shelley, and Sir Walter Scott are the leading Romantic writers.

See page 529.

RUN-ON LINE **A line of poetry that does not contain a pause or conclusion at the end, but rather continues on to the next line.** Run-on lines force the reader on to the next line. Only with the next line do they form a grammatical unit and thus make complete sense. Such lines are said to exhibit **enjambment** (French for "striding over"). The following lines from Margaret Atwood's "Siren Song" (Collection 7) are run-on lines:

> This is the one song everyone
> would like to learn: the song
> that is irresistible:

See also *End-stopped Line.*

SARCASM **A kind of particularly cutting irony, in which praise is used tauntingly to indicate its opposite in meaning.** The speaker's tone of voice can be an important clue in understanding this kind of irony. When a mud-soaked, windblown friend arrives for dinner, one might say sarcastically, "Why, don't you look lovely!"

See page 966.

SATIRE **A kind of writing that ridicules human weakness, vice, or folly in order to bring about social reform.** Satires often try to persuade the reader to do or believe something by showing the opposite view as absurd or—even more forcefully—vicious and inhumane. Among the most brilliant satirists in English literature are Geoffrey Chaucer, Alexander Pope, John Dryden, Jonathan Swift, Jane Austen, George Bernard Shaw, and Evelyn Waugh.

See pages 462, 466, 938.

SCANSION See *Meter.*

SCOP **An Anglo-Saxon minstrel or poet.** Scops are the Anglo-Saxon equivalents to the ancient Celtic bards.

See page 14.

SESTET **A six-line stanza or poem or the last six lines of an Italian, or Petrarchan, sonnet.** The usual rhyme scheme of the sestet in an Italian sonnet is *cdecde* or *cdcdcd*. It follows an eight-line **octave** with the rhyme scheme *abbaabba*.

See page 276.

SETTING **The time and place of a story or play.** Usually the setting is established early in a story. It may be presented immediately through descriptive details, as in Anita Desai's "Games at Twilight" (Collection 7), or it may be revealed more gradually, as in Rudyard Kipling's "The Mark of the Beast" (Collection 6). Setting often contributes greatly to a story's emotional effect. The exotic setting of V. S. Naipaul's "B. Wordsworth" (Collection 7) sets the tone for its eccentric characters, while the green valley in William Wordsworth's "Tintern Abbey" (Collection 5) creates a contemplative calm. Setting may also play a role in a story's conflict, as the fortresslike suburban houses do in Nadine Gordimer's "Once upon a Time" (Collection 7). Two of the most important functions of setting are to reveal character and to suggest a theme, as the setting of blitzed London does in Graham Greene's "The Destructors" (Collection 7).

See pages 862, 1015.
See also *Atmosphere*.

SHORT STORY **A brief work of fiction.** The short story generally has a simpler plot than a novel and often reveals character through significant moments, or **epiphanies,** rather than through the accretion of many incidents or detailed descriptions.

See page 1043.

SIMILE **A figure of speech that makes a comparison between two seemingly unlike things by using a connective word such as *like*, *than*, or *resembles*.** The following simile, from George Gordon, Lord Byron's "She Walks in Beauty" (Collection 5), is one of the most famous in English literary history:

> She walks in beauty, like the night
> Of cloudless climes and starry skies;

An **epic simile,** also called a **Homeric simile,** is an extended simile in which many parallels are made between two dissimilar things.

See pages 56, 71, 376, 610.
See also *Figure of Speech, Metaphor*.

SOCIAL DARWINISM **The notion that, in society, only the fittest will survive.** This idea is an extension of Darwin's scientific theories of natural selection—though Darwin was not involved in its development. Social Darwinism was used to justify rigid class distinctions, indifference to social ills, and doctrines of racial superiority.

See page 806.

SOCIALISM **A political movement that advocates the idea that the ownership and operation of the means of production and distribution should be owned by the community rather than by private individuals.** This political movement is related to communism in that it seeks to eliminate class distinctions within society.

SOLILOQUY **A long speech in which a character who is usually alone onstage expresses his or her private thoughts or feelings.** The soliloquy is an old dramatic convention that was particularly popular in Shakespeare's day. Perhaps the most famous soliloquy is the "To be, or not to be" speech (Collection 3) in Shakespeare's play *Hamlet*. Another major soliloquy occurs in *Macbeth*, when Macbeth bewails his wife's death in the celebrated "Tomorrow, and tomorrow, and tomorrow" speech (Collection 3).

See page 292.
See also *Monologue*.

SONNET **A fourteen-line lyric poem, usually written in iambic pentameter, that has one of several rhyme schemes.** There are two major types of sonnets. The oldest sonnet form is the **Italian sonnet,** also called the **Petrarchan sonnet** (after the fourteenth-century Italian poet Petrarch, who popularized the form). The Petrarchan sonnet is divided into two parts: an eight-line **octave** with the rhyme scheme *abbaabba* and a six-line **sestet** with the rhyme scheme *cdecde* or *cdcdcd*. The octave usually presents a problem, poses a question, or expresses an idea, which the sestet then resolves, answers, or drives home. The transition from octave to sestet is known as the **turn.** Louise Labé's Sonnet 23 (Collection 3), Elizabeth Barrett Browning's Sonnet 43 (Collection 6), and John Keats's "On First Looking into Chapman's Homer" (Collection 5) are written in the Petrarchan form.

The other major sonnet form, which was widely used by Shakespeare, is called the **Shakespearean sonnet,** or the **English sonnet** (Collection 3). It has three four-line units, or **quatrains,** followed by a concluding two-line unit, or **couplet.** The organization of thought in the Shakespearean sonnet usually corresponds to this structure. The three quatrains often express related ideas or examples, while the couplet sums up the poet's conclusion or message found in the first three. The turn in the Shakespearean sonnet usually occurs during the transition from the third quatrain to the couplet. The rhyme scheme of the Shakespearean sonnet is *abab cdcd efef gg*.

A third type of sonnet, the **Spenserian sonnet,** was developed by Edmund Spenser. Like the Shakespearean sonnet, the Spenserian sonnet is divided into three quatrains and a couplet, but it uses a rhyme scheme that links the quatrains: *abab bcbc cdcd ee*.

A group of sonnets on a related theme is called a **sonnet sequence** or a **sonnet cycle.**

See pages 276, 278, 563, 641, 714.

Handbook of Literary and Historical Terms **1201**

SPEAKER **The imaginary voice, or persona, assumed by the author of a poem.** This voice is often not identified immediately or directly. Rather, the reader gradually comes to understand that a unique voice is speaking and that this speaker's characteristics must be interpreted as they are revealed. This process is an especially important part of reading a **lyric poem.**

SPEECH **A more or less formal address delivered to an audience or assembly or the written or printed copy of this address.** The use of the word *speech* to designate an address to an audience seems to have entered into the English language in the sixteenth century.

Speeches are most commonly delivered by politicians, political activists, and other public figures. For an eloquent example of a twentieth-century political speech, see Desmond Tutu's "The Question of South Africa" (Collection 7).

SPENSERIAN STANZA **A nine-line stanza with the rhyme scheme** *ababbcbcc.* The first eight lines of the stanza are in iambic pentameter, and the ninth line is an **alexandrine**—that is, a line of iambic hexameter. The form was created by Edmund Spenser for his long poem *The Faerie Queene*. Several English Romantic poets have used the Spenserian stanza, including John Keats, Percy Bysshe Shelley, Lord Byron (all in Collection 5), and Robert Burns.

See page 612.

SPRUNG RHYTHM **A term coined by Gerard Manley Hopkins (Collection 6) to designate his unconventional use of poetic meter.** Instead of the regular, musical **meter** of most poetry, Hopkins uses sounds that impede smooth reading and echo the sound of Anglo-Saxon poetry, which greatly influenced him. Sprung rhythm is based on the stressed syllables in a line without regard for the number of unstressed syllables; it also makes frequent use of **alliteration** and inverted syntax.

See page 716.

STANZA **A group of consecutive lines in a poem that form a single unit.** A stanza in a poem is something like a paragraph in prose: It often expresses a unit of thought. A stanza may consist of only one line or of any number of lines beyond that. The word *stanza* is Italian for "stopping place" or "place to rest."

STREAM OF CONSCIOUSNESS **A writing style that tries to depict the random flow of thoughts, emotions, memories, and associations running through a character's mind.** The term *interior monologue* is often used interchangeably with "stream of consciousness." James Joyce and Virginia Woolf (both in Collection 7) were among the first to experiment with the stream-of-consciousness style in their novels.

See page 809.

STYLE **The manner in which writers or speakers say what they wish to say.** An author's style simultaneously expresses his or her ideas and reveals his or her unique way of expressing them. Style is closely connected to **diction,** or word choice, and, depending on what the author wants to communicate, can be formal or casual, plain or ornate, abstract or concrete, as well as comic, poetic, forceful, journalistic, and so on. Sir Francis Bacon (Collection 3) and James Joyce (Collection 7) are both often studied for their styles.

See pages 365, 376.
See also *Diction.*

SUSPENSE **The uncertainty or anxiety we feel about what is going to happen next in a story.** Writers often create suspense by dropping hints or clues that something—especially something bad—is going to happen. In "The Demon Lover" by Elizabeth Bowen (Collection 7), we begin to feel suspense when Mrs. Drover receives a mysterious letter that makes her lips "go white"; our anxiety increases sharply when the flashback reveals that the letter writer is her old fiancé; and our suspense reaches a climax when she escapes into a taxi and we discover who the driver is.

SYMBOL **A person, place, thing, or event that stands both for itself and for something beyond itself.** Many symbols have become widely recognized: A lion is a symbol of power; a dove is a symbol of peace. These established symbols are sometimes called **public symbols.** But writers often invent new, personal symbols whose meaning is revealed in their work. For example, the old house in Graham Greene's "The Destructors" (Collection 7) is a symbol of civilization and beauty.

See pages 536, 923, 951, 968, 1035.

SYMBOLISM **A literary movement that began in France during the late nineteenth century and advocated the use of highly personal symbols to suggest ideas, emotions, and moods.** The French symbolists believed that emotions are fleeting, individual, and essentially inexpressible—and that the poet is, therefore, forced to suggest meaning rather than directly express it. Many twentieth-century writers were influenced by the symbolists, including T. S. Eliot, William Butler Yeats, James Joyce, Dylan Thomas, and Virginia Woolf (all in Collection 7).

See page 792.

SYNECDOCHE (si·nek′də·kē) **A figure of speech in which a part represents the whole.** The capital city of a nation, for example, is often spoken of as though it were the government: "Washington is claiming popular support for its position." Another example is "our daily bread" meaning food. Synecdoche is closely related to **metonymy.**

See also *Metonymy.*

SYNESTHESIA (sin′əs·thē′zhə) **In literature, a term used for descriptions of one kind of sensation in terms of another.** For example, color may be described as sound (a "loud" yellow), sound as taste (how "sweet" the sound), odor as tangible (a "sharp" smell), and so on.

See page 646.

TANKA **A traditional five-line form of Japanese poetry.** The tanka follows a strict form: The first and third lines have five syllables each, and the second, fourth, and fifth lines have seven syllables each.

See page 565.

TERCET **A triplet, or stanza of three lines, in which each line ends with the same rhyme.** It is also either of the two three-line groups forming the sestet of a **sonnet.**

TERZA RIMA **An interlocking, three-line stanza form with the rhyme scheme *aba bcb cdc ded* and so on.** Terza rima is an Italian verse form originally devised by Dante for *The Divine Comedy.* Among the many English poems that borrowed the form, Shelley's "Ode to the West Wind" (Collection 5) is one of the most famous.

See page 626.

THEME **The central idea or insight about human experience revealed in a work of literature.** A theme is not the same as the subject of a work, which can usually be expressed in a word or two: old age, ambition, love. The theme is the idea the writer wishes to convey about that subject—the writer's view of the world or revelation about human nature. For example, one theme of James Joyce's "Araby" (Collection 7) might be stated this way: One of the painful aspects of growing up is that some of our dreams turn out to be illusions.

A theme may also be different from a **moral,** which is a lesson or rule about how to live. The theme of "Araby" stated above, for example, would not make sense as a moral.

While some stories, poems, and plays have themes that are directly stated, most themes are **implied.** It is up to the reader to piece together all the clues the writer has provided about the work's total meaning.

See pages 547, 703, 766, 775, 854, 908, 945, 983, 1081.

TONE **The attitude a writer takes toward the reader, a subject, or a character.** Tone is conveyed through the writer's choice of words and details. For example, Jonathan Swift's *A Modest Proposal* (Collection 4) is satiric in tone, while the tone of "Pied Beauty" by Gerard Manley Hopkins (Collection 6) might be described as awed.

See pages 281, 307, 485.

TOTALITARIANISM **A system of government that advocates the rule of an absolute dictator or a single political party.** Totalitarian governments forbid any opposition to the government party or ruler to emerge within the state. Consequently, free speech and other liberties guaranteed in democracies are denied to those living under a totalitarian government. George Orwell's *Animal Farm* explores the consequences of a totalitarian regime.

TRAGEDY **A play, novel, or other narrative depicting serious and important events, in which the main character comes to an unhappy end.** In a tragedy, the main character is usually dignified, courageous, and often high ranking. This character's downfall may be caused by a **tragic flaw**—an error in judgment or a character weakness—or the downfall may result from forces beyond his or her control. The **tragic hero** usually wins some self-knowledge and wisdom, even though he or she suffers defeat, possibly even death. Tragedy is distinct from **comedy,** in which an ordinary character overcomes obstacles to get what he or she wants. *Beowulf* (Collection 1), Shakespeare's *Macbeth* (Collection 3), and John Milton's *Paradise Lost* (Collection 3) are all tragedies.

See also *Comedy.*

TURN See *Sonnet.*

UNDERSTATEMENT A figure of speech that consists of saying less than what is really meant or saying something with less force than is appropriate. Understatement is the opposite of **hyperbole** and is a form of **irony.** You are using understatement if you come in from a torrential downpour and say, "It's a bit wet out there," or if you describe a Great Dane as "not exactly a small dog." Understatement can be used to create a kind of deadpan humor, but it can also function as a sustained ironic tone throughout a work, as in Wole Soyinka's "Telephone Conversation" (Collection 7).

See also *Hyperbole, Irony.*

VERNACULAR See *Dialect.*

VILLANELLE A nineteen-line poem divided into five tercets (three-line stanzas), each with the rhyme scheme *aba,* and a final quatrain with the rhyme scheme *abaa.* Line 1 is repeated entirely to form lines 6, 12, and 18, while line 3 is repeated as lines 9, 15, and 19. Thus, there are only two rhymes in the poem, and the two lines used as **refrains** (lines 1 and 3) are paired as the final couplet. The villanelle was originally used in French pastoral poetry. Dylan Thomas's "Do Not Go Gentle into That Good Night" (Collection 7) is an example of a modern villanelle.

See page 1058.

WIT A quality of speech or writing that combines verbal cleverness with keen perception, especially of the incongruous. The definition of *wit* has undergone dramatic changes over the centuries. In the Middle Ages it meant "common sense"; in the Renaissance it meant "intelligence"; and in the seventeenth century it meant "originality of thought." The modern meaning of *wit* began to develop during the seventeenth and eighteenth centuries with the writings of John Dryden and Alexander Pope (Collection 4). In his *Essay on Criticism,* Pope said:

> True wit is Nature to advantage dressed:
> What oft was thought, but ne'er so well expressed

Perhaps the best examples of more modern wit can be found in the works of Oscar Wilde and George Bernard Shaw.

See page 423.

Language Handbook

CONTENTS

The Parts of Speech	1206
Agreement	1207
Using Verbs	1209
Using Pronouns	1211
Using Modifiers	1213
Phrases	1214
Clauses	1216
Sentence Structure	1217
Sentence Style	1220
Sentence Combining	1223
Capitalization	1224
Punctuation	1227, 1230
Spelling	1235
Glossary of Usage	1237

Resources

Grammar and Language

- *Language Handbook Worksheets,* pp. 1–4

Language Handbook

1 THE PARTS OF SPEECH

PART OF SPEECH	DEFINITION	EXAMPLES
NOUN	Names person, place, thing, or idea	writer, Ben Okri, Anglo-Saxons, family, country, Wales, poem, "My Last Duchess," Romanticism
PRONOUN	Takes the place of one or more nouns or pronouns	
Personal	Refers to one(s) speaking (first person), spoken to (second person), spoken about (third person)	I, me, my, mine, we, us, our, ours, you, your, yours, he, him, his, she, her, hers, it, its, they, them, their, theirs
Reflexive	Refers to subject and directs action of verb back to subject	myself, ourselves, yourself, yourselves, himself, herself, itself, themselves
Intensive	Refers to and emphasizes noun or another pronoun	(See Reflexive.)
Demonstrative	Refers to specific one(s) of group	this, that, these, those
Interrogative	Introduces question	what, which, who, whom, whose
Relative	Introduces subordinate clause and refers to noun or pronoun outside that clause	that, which, who, whom, whose
Indefinite	Refers to one(s) not specifically named	all, any, anyone, both, each, either, everybody, many, none, nothing
ADJECTIVE	Modifies noun or pronoun by telling *what kind, which one, how many,* or *how much*	**a** paperback book, **an** Anglo-Saxon law, **this** one, **the seven brave** warriors, **less** space
VERB	Shows action or state of being	
Action	Expresses physical or mental activity	describe, travel, fight, believe, consider, remember
Linking	Connects subject with word identifying or describing it	appear, be, seem, become, feel, look, smell, sound, taste
Helping (Auxiliary)	Assists another verb in expressing time, voice, or mood	be, have, may, can, shall, must, would
ADVERB	Modifies verb, adjective, or adverb by telling *how, when, where,* or *to what extent*	walks **slowly**, **quite** different, **somewhat** boldly, coming **here soon**
PREPOSITION	Relates noun or pronoun to another word	about, at, by, for, from, in, on, according to, along with, because of
CONJUNCTION	Joins words or word groups	
Coordinating	Joins words or word groups used in the same way	and, but, for, nor, or, so, yet

1206  Language Handbook

Correlative	A pair of conjunctions that join parallel words or word groups	both . . . and, either . . . or, neither . . . nor, not only . . . but (also)
Subordinating	Begins a subordinate clause and connects it to an independent clause	although, as if, because, since, so that, unless, when, where, while
INTERJECTION	Expresses emotion	ah, wow, ugh, whew

2 AGREEMENT

AGREEMENT OF SUBJECT AND VERB

2a. **A verb should agree with its subject in number. Singular subjects take singular verbs. Plural subjects take plural verbs.**

SINGULAR He **lives** in Camelot.
PLURAL They **live** in Camelot.

2b. **The number of the subject is not changed by a phrase or a clause following the subject.**

EXAMPLE
The **Lilliputians,** a nation of tiny people, **capture** Gulliver.

2c. **Indefinite pronouns may be singular, plural, or either.**

(1) The following indefinite pronouns are singular: *anybody, anyone, anything, each, either, everybody, everyone, everything, neither, nobody, no one, nothing, one, somebody, someone,* and *something.*

EXAMPLE
One of the most beautiful places in England **is** the Lake District.

(2) The following indefinite pronouns are plural: *both, few, many,* and *several.*

EXAMPLE
Both of the epics **were written** by John Milton.

(3) The indefinite pronouns *all, any, most, none,* and *some* are singular when they refer to singular words and are plural when they refer to plural words.

SINGULAR **None** of the equipment **was damaged.** [*None* refers to *equipment.*]
PLURAL **None** of the machines **were damaged.** [*None* refers to *machines.*]

2d. **A *compound subject* may be singular, plural, or either.**

(1) Subjects joined by *and* usually take a plural verb.

EXAMPLE
After rehearsal, **Juan, Anita,** and **Marcus are going** out to dinner.

A compound subject that names only one person or thing takes a singular verb.

EXAMPLE
His **wife** and **partner** in crime **is** Lady Macbeth.

(2) Singular subjects joined by *or* or *nor* take a singular verb.

EXAMPLE
Jill or **Jorge plans** to write a character analysis of Macduff.

(3) When a singular subject and a plural subject are joined by *or* or *nor,* the verb agrees with the subject nearer the verb.

EXAMPLE
Neither the **dancers** nor the **choreographer was** pleased with the routine.

2e. **The verb agrees with its subject even when the verb precedes the subject, as in sentences beginning with *here, there,* or *where.***

SINGULAR Where **is** [*or* where's] **Malcolm**?
PLURAL Here **are** [*not* here's] **Malcolm** and his **brother.**

2f. **A *collective noun* (such as *audience, flock,* or *team*) is singular in form but names a group of persons or things. A collective noun takes a singular verb when the noun refers to the group as a unit and takes a plural verb when the noun refers to the parts or members of the group.**

Language Handbook **1207**

Resources

Grammar and Language
- *Language Handbook Worksheets,* pp. 5–11

SINGULAR	The tour **group is** on the bus. [The group as a unit is on the bus.]	
PLURAL	The tour **group are talking** about their plans. [The members of the group are talking to one another.]	

2g. An expression of an amount (a length of time, a statistic, or a fraction, for example) is singular when the amount is thought of as a unit or when it refers to a singular word and plural when the amount is thought of as many parts or when it refers to a plural word.

SINGULAR	**Fifty years is** how long Beowulf rules Geatland. [one unit]
PLURAL	**One fourth** of the seniors **are working** on a production of *Macbeth*. [The fraction refers to *seniors*.]

Expressions of measurement (length, weight, capacity, area) are usually singular.

EXAMPLE
Four and seven-tenths inches is the diameter of a compact disc.

2h. The title of a creative work (such as a book, song, film, or painting) or the name of an organization, a country, or a city (even if it is plural in form) takes a singular verb.

EXAMPLES
"**Tears, Idle Tears**" **was written** by Alfred, Lord Tennyson.
The **United Nations was formed** in 1945.
Has the **Netherlands been flooded** recently?

2i. A verb agrees with its subject, not with its predicate nominative.

SINGULAR	The **subject** of the lecture **was** epic heroes.
PLURAL	Epic **heroes were** the subject of the lecture.

AGREEMENT OF PRONOUN AND ANTECEDENT

A pronoun usually refers to a noun or another pronoun. The word to which a pronoun refers is called its *antecedent*.

2j. A pronoun agrees with its antecedent in number and gender. Singular pronouns refer to singular antecedents. A few singular pronouns also indicate gender (feminine, masculine, or neuter). Plural pronouns refer to plural antecedents.

EXAMPLES
Alfred, Lord Tennyson published *Idylls of the King* after **he** became poet laureate. [singular, masculine]
Lady Macbeth helps **her** husband. [singular, feminine]
The **Lilliputians** gave **their** captive food. [plural]

2k. Indefinite pronouns may be singular, plural, or either.

(1) Singular pronouns are used to refer to the indefinite pronouns *anybody, anyone, anything, each, either, everybody, everyone, everything, neither, nobody, no one, nothing, one, somebody, someone,* and *something*. The gender of any of these pronouns is determined by the word or words that the pronoun refers to.

EXAMPLES
Each of the **boys** has learned **his** part in *Macbeth*.
One of the **girls** has injured **herself**.

If the antecedent may be either masculine or feminine, use both the masculine and feminine pronouns to refer to it.

EXAMPLE
Anyone who is going on the field trip needs to bring **his** or **her** lunch.

(2) Plural pronouns are used to refer to the indefinite pronouns *both, few, many,* and *several*.

EXAMPLE
Many of the spectators leapt from **their** seats and cheered.

(3) Singular or plural pronouns may be used to refer to the indefinite pronouns *all, any, most, none,* and *some*. These indefinite pronouns are singular when they refer to singular words and are plural when they refer to plural words.

SINGULAR	**None** of the renovated theater matches **its** original beauty. [*None* refers to the singular noun *theater*.]
PLURAL	**None** of the geese have left on **their** annual migration. [*None* refers to the plural noun *geese*.]

2l. A plural pronoun is used to refer to two or more singular antecedents joined by *and*.

EXAMPLE
Malcolm and Donalbain left Scotland soon after **their** father was killed.

2m. A singular pronoun is used to refer to two or more singular antecedents joined by *or* or *nor*.

EXAMPLE
Neither **Malcolm nor Donalbain** felt **he** was safe.

2n. A collective noun (such as *club* or *family*) takes a singular pronoun when the noun refers to the group as a unit and takes a plural pronoun when the noun refers to the parts or members of the group.

SINGULAR The **jury** reached **its** decision less than one hour later. [The jury decided as a unit.]

PLURAL The **jury** disagree on how much importance **they** should give to one of the defendant's statements. [The members of the jury disagree.]

2o. The title of a creative work (such as a book, song, film, or painting) or the name of an organization, a country, or a city (even if it is plural in form) takes a singular pronoun.

EXAMPLES
I read ***Gulliver's Travels*** and wrote a report on **it**.
The **United Arab Emirates** generates most of **its** revenue from the sale of oil.

3 USING VERBS

THE PRINCIPAL PARTS OF VERBS

Every verb has four basic forms called the *principal parts*: the *base form*, the *present participle*, the *past*, and the *past participle*. A verb is classified as *regular* or *irregular* depending on the way it forms its past and past participle.

3a. A *regular verb* forms the past and past participle by adding *–d* or *–ed* to the base form. An *irregular verb* forms the past and the past participle in some other way.

COMMON REGULAR AND IRREGULAR VERBS

The following examples include *is* and *have* in italics to show that helping verbs (forms of *be* and *have*) are used with the present participle and past participle forms.

BASE FORM	PRESENT PARTICIPLE	PAST	PAST PARTICIPLE
REGULAR			
attack	*is* attacking	attacked	*have* attacked
drown	*is* drowning	drowned	*have* drowned
occur	*is* occurring	occurred	*have* occurred
risk	*is* risking	risked	*have* risked
try	*is* trying	tried	*have* tried
use	*is* using	used	*have* used
IRREGULAR			
be	*is* being	was, were	*have* been
bring	*is* bringing	brought	*have* brought
burst	*is* bursting	burst	*have* burst
come	*is* coming	came	*have* come
eat	*is* eating	ate	*have* eaten
go	*is* going	went	*have* gone
lead	*is* leading	led	*have* led
pay	*is* paying	paid	*have* paid
see	*is* seeing	saw	*have* seen
sing	*is* singing	sang	*have* sung
steal	*is* stealing	stole	*have* stolen
take	*is* taking	took	*have* taken
throw	*is* throwing	threw	*have* thrown

NOTE If you are not sure about the principal parts of a verb, look in a dictionary. Entries for irregular verbs give the principal parts. If no principal parts are listed, the verb is a regular verb.

TENSES AND THEIR USES

3b. The *tense* of a verb indicates the time of the action or state of being that is expressed by the verb.

(1) The **present tense** is used mainly to express an action or a state of being that is occurring now.

EXAMPLE
The article **compares** Beowulf with other epic heroes.

Resources

Grammar and Language
- Language Handbook Worksheets, pp. 12–23

The present tense is also used
- to show a customary or habitual action or state of being
- to convey a general truth—something that is always true
- to make a historical event seem current (such use is called the **historical present**)
- to summarize the plot or subject matter of a literary work or to refer to an author's relationship to his or her work (such use is called the **literary present**)
- to express future time

EXAMPLES
Every Friday, our teacher **gives** us a vocabulary quiz. [customary action]
Reptiles **are** coldblooded. [general truth]
The Greeks **establish** separate city-states, which **war** among themselves. [historical present]
In the land of the Lilliputians, Gulliver **appears** gigantic. [literary present]
The two-week seminar on Shakespeare **begins** on Monday. [future time]

(2) The **past tense** is used to express an action or state of being that occurred in the past but did not continue into the present.

EXAMPLE
An expert on T. S. Eliot's poetry **spoke** to our class.

(3) The **future tense** (will or shall + base form) is used to express an action or a state of being that will occur.

EXAMPLE
Laurie **will play** the part of Lady Macbeth.

 NOTE Shall and will are both acceptable in forming the future tense.

(4) The **present perfect tense** (have or has + past participle) is used to express an action or a state of being that occurred at some indefinite time in the past.

EXAMPLE
Kenneth Branagh **has played** the roles of Henry V and of Iago.

The present perfect tense is also used to express an action or a state of being that began in the past and continues into the present.

EXAMPLE
Herot **has stood** empty for twelve years.

(5) The **past perfect tense** (had + past participle) is used to express an action or state of being completed in the past before some other past occurrence.

EXAMPLE
The kingdom **had suffered** before Beowulf arrived. [The suffering occurred before the arriving.]

Be sure to use the past perfect tense in "if" clauses that express the earlier of two past actions.

EXAMPLE
If you **had read** [not read or would have read] the article, you would have learned about Sutton Hoo.

(6) The **future perfect tense** (will have or shall have + past participle) is used to express an action or state of being that will be completed in the future before some other future occurrence.

EXAMPLE
By this time tomorrow, I **will** [or shall] **have memorized** "The Seafarer."

3c. Avoid unnecessary shifts in tense.

INCONSISTENT	Wiglaf discovered the dragon's treasure and then brings it to Beowulf. [shift from past to present tense]
CONSISTENT	Wiglaf **discovered** the dragon's treasure and then **brought** it to Beowulf. [past tense]
CONSISTENT	Wiglaf **discovers** the dragon's treasure and then **brings** it to Beowulf. [present tense]

When describing events that occur at different times, use verbs in different tenses to show the order of events.

EXAMPLE
She **taught** school for several years, but now she **works** for a publishing company. [Because she taught at a specific time in the past, the past tense *taught* is correct. Because she works at the present time, the present tense *works* is correct.]

ACTIVE VOICE AND PASSIVE VOICE

3d. **Voice** is the form a transitive verb takes to indicate whether the subject of the verb performs or receives the action.

A verb is in the **active voice** when its subject performs the action (its object receives the action).

ACTIVE VOICE William Shakespeare **wrote** more than thirty-five plays.

A verb is in the **passive voice** whenever its subject receives the action (the verb has no object). A passive verb is always a verb phrase that includes a form of *be* and the past participle of an action verb.

PASSIVE VOICE More than thirty-five plays **were written** by William Shakespeare.

1210 Resource Center Language Handbook

3e. **Use the passive voice sparingly.**

In general, the passive voice is less direct and less forceful than the active voice. In some cases, the passive voice also may sound awkward.

AWKWARD PASSIVE	The sleeping grooms are smeared with King Duncan's blood by Lady Macbeth.
ACTIVE	Lady Macbeth **smears** the sleeping grooms with King Duncan's blood.

Although you generally will want to use active voice rather than passive voice, the passive voice is not less correct than the active voice. In fact, the passive voice is useful in the following situations:

1. when you do not know the performer of the action

EXAMPLE
The Globe **was built** in 1599.

2. when you do not want to reveal the performer of the action

EXAMPLE
The actor **was criticized** for his portrayal of Macbeth.

3. when you want to emphasize the receiver of the action

EXAMPLE
King Duncan **was murdered** while he was asleep.

4 USING PRONOUNS

CASE

Case is the form that a noun or a pronoun takes to indicate its use in a sentence. In English, there are three cases: *nominative*, *objective*, and *possessive*. Most personal pronouns have a different form for each case.

The Nominative Case

4a. **A subject of a verb is in the nominative case.**

EXAMPLES
They built the tower near the sea as **he** had requested. [*They* is the subject of the verb *built*. *He* is the subject of the verb *had requested*.]

4b. **A predicate nominative is in the nominative case.**

EXAMPLE
The only students who auditioned for the part of King Arthur were **he** and **Carlos**. [*He* and *Carlos* are predicate nominatives that follow the linking verb *were* and identify the subject *students*.]

PERSONAL PRONOUNS

SINGULAR

	NOMINATIVE	OBJECTIVE	POSSESSIVE
FIRST PERSON	I	me	my, mine
SECOND PERSON	you	you	your, yours
THIRD PERSON	he, she, it	him, her, it	his, her, hers, its

PLURAL

	NOMINATIVE	OBJECTIVE	POSSESSIVE
FIRST PERSON	we	us	our, ours
SECOND PERSON	you	you	your, yours
THIRD PERSON	they	them	their, theirs

NOTE The form of a noun is the same for both the nominative case and the objective case. A noun changes its form for the possessive case, usually by adding an apostrophe and an *s* to most singular nouns and only an apostrophe to most plural nouns.

For more information about forming possessives of nouns, see 13f.

Resources

Grammar and Language

- Language Handbook Worksheets, pp. 24–35

The Objective Case

4c. An object of a verb is in the objective case.

EXAMPLES
The knight's answer pleases **her.** [*Her* is a direct object that tells *whom* the answer pleases.]
The Pardoner tells **them** a story about three greedy rioters. [*Them* is an indirect object that tells *to whom* the Pardoner tells a story.]

4d. An object of a preposition is in the objective case.

EXAMPLE
Are the Lilliputians afraid of **him**? [*Him* is the object of the preposition *of*.]

The Possessive Case

4e. A noun or a pronoun preceding a gerund is in the possessive case.

EXAMPLE
We were all thrilled by **Joetta's** [*or her*] scoring in the top 5 percent. [*Joetta's* or *her* modifies *scoring*, a gerund used as the object of the preposition *by*.]

Do not confuse a gerund with a present participle, which is a verb form that ends in *–ing* and may function as an adjective.

EXAMPLE
Macbeth found **them** [*not their*] standing around a caldron. [*Them* is modified by the participial phrase *standing around a caldron*.]

SPECIAL PRONOUN PROBLEMS

4f. An appositive is in the same case as the noun or pronoun to which it refers.

EXAMPLES
Duncan's sons, **Malcolm and he,** leave Scotland. [The compound appositive *Malcolm and he* refers to the subject, *sons*.]
Macduff suspects both of them, **Malcolm and him.** [The compound appositive *Malcolm and him* refers to *them*, the object of the preposition *of*.]

4g. A pronoun following *than* or *as* in an elliptical construction is in the same case as it would be if the construction were completed.

An **elliptical construction** is a clause from which words have been omitted.

NOMINATIVE I see him more often **than she.** [I see him more often *than she sees him*. *She* is the subject in the elliptical construction.]
OBJECTIVE I see him more often **than her.** [I see him more often *than I see her*. *Her* is the direct object in the elliptical construction.]

4h. A pronoun ending in *–self* or *–selves* should not be used in place of a personal pronoun.

EXAMPLE
Everyone except John and **me** [*not myself*] has read *Don Juan*.

4i. The pronoun *who* (*whoever*) is in the nominative case. The pronoun *whom* (*whomever*) is in the objective case.

EXAMPLES
Who wrote "Ozymandias"? [*Who* is the subject of the verb *wrote*.]
With **whom** did Wordsworth write *Lyrical Ballads*? [*Whom* is the object of the preposition *with*.]

CLEAR PRONOUN REFERENCE

The word that a pronoun stands for or refers to is called the **antecedent** of the pronoun.

4j. A pronoun should always refer clearly to its antecedent.

Avoid an ambiguous, a general, a weak, or an indefinite reference by

1. rephrasing the sentence, or
2. replacing the pronoun with an appropriate noun, or
3. giving the pronoun a clear antecedent.

AMBIGUOUS When the Green Knight was talking to Sir Gawain, he was holding his head in his hand. [The antecedent of *he* and *his* is unclear. Was the Green Knight holding Sir Gawain's head or his own?]
CLEAR The Green Knight was holding his head in his hand when he was talking to Sir Gawain.
GENERAL Macbeth will become king. This is one of the witches' prophecies. [*This* has no specific antecedent.]
CLEAR That Macbeth will become king is one of the witches' prophecies.

WEAK	Our dog Hank is jealous of my new baby sister. To help him get over it, I try to give him extra attention. [The antecedent of *it* is not expressed.]
CLEAR	To help our dog Hank get over his jealousy of my new baby sister, I try to give him extra attention.
INDEFINITE	In this book it includes pictures of artifacts from the Sutton Hoo ship burial. [*It* is not necessary to the meaning of the sentence.]
CLEAR	This book includes pictures of artifacts from the Sutton Hoo ship burial.

5 USING MODIFIERS

A *modifier* is a word or group of words that limits the meaning of another word or group of words. The two kinds of modifiers are *adjectives* and *adverbs*.

5a. Use an *adjective* to limit the meaning of a noun or a pronoun. Use an *adverb* to limit the meaning of a verb, an adjective, or another adverb.

COMPARISON OF MODIFIERS

5b. *Comparison* refers to the change in the form of an adjective or an adverb to show increasing or decreasing degrees in the quality the modifier expresses.

The three degrees of comparison are *positive*, *comparative*, and *superlative*.

1. Most one-syllable modifiers form the comparative and superlative degrees by adding –*er* and –*est*.

2. Some two-syllable modifiers form the comparative and superlative degrees by adding –*er* and –*est*. Other two-syllable modifiers form the comparative and superlative degrees by using *more* and *most*.

3. Modifiers of more than two syllables form the comparative and superlative degrees by using *more* and *most*.

4. To show a decrease in the qualities they express, all modifiers form the comparative by using *less* and the superlative by using *least*.

POSITIVE	COMPARATIVE	SUPERLATIVE
soft	softer	softest
thirsty	thirstier	thirstiest
slowly	more slowly	most slowly
skillfully	less skillfully	least skillfully

 For information about adding suffixes such as –*er* and –*est* to words, see 14e–j.

5. Some modifiers form the comparative and superlative degrees in other ways.

POSITIVE	COMPARATIVE	SUPERLATIVE
bad (ill)	worse	worst
far	farther (further)	farthest (furthest)
good (well)	better	best
little	less	least
many (much)	more	most

5c. Use the comparative degree when comparing two things. Use the superlative degree when comparing more than two.

COMPARATIVE	After reading *King Lear* and *The Winter's Tale*, I can understand why *King Lear* is the **more popular** play. [comparison of two plays]
SUPERLATIVE	Of the three plays I saw, I think *Macbeth* was the **most powerful**. [comparison of three plays]

5d. Avoid a double comparison or a double negative. A *double comparison* is the use of two comparative forms (usually –*er* and *more* or *less*) or two superlative forms (usually –*est* and *most* or *least*) to modify the same word. A *double negative* is the use of two negative words where one is enough.

EXAMPLES
Who is the **noblest** [*not* most noblest] of King Arthur's knights?
I know **nothing** [*not* don't know nothing] about the Wars of the Roses.

Resources

Grammar and Language

- *Language Handbook Worksheets,* pp. 36–42

5e. Include the word *other* or *else* when comparing one member of a group with the rest of the group.

ILLOGICAL Wiglaf is bolder than any of Beowulf's followers. [Wiglaf is one of Beowulf's followers. Logically, Wiglaf cannot be bolder than himself.]

LOGICAL Wiglaf is bolder than any of Beowulf's **other** followers.

5f. Avoid comparing items that cannot logically be compared.

ILLOGICAL I think Olivier's portrayal of Hamlet is more compelling than any other actor. [The sentence makes an illogical comparison between a portrayal and an actor.]

LOGICAL I think Olivier's portrayal of Hamlet is more compelling than any other actor's [portrayal]. [The sentence makes a logical comparison between portrayals.]

PLACEMENT OF MODIFIERS

5g. Avoid using a *misplaced modifier*—a modifying word, phrase, or clause that sounds awkward because it modifies the wrong word or group of words.

To correct a misplaced modifier, place the word, phrase, or clause as close as possible to the word or words you intend it to modify.

MISPLACED The old man told the three young rioters under a tree they would find Death. [What occurred under a tree: the telling or the finding?]

CLEAR The old man told the three young rioters they would find Death **under a tree.**

MISPLACED The anxious hunter watched the raging lion come charging at him as he readied his bow and arrow.

CLEAR **As he readied his bow and arrow,** the anxious hunter watched the raging lion come charging at him.

5h. Avoid using a *dangling modifier*—a modifying word, phrase, or clause that does not sensibly modify any word or words in a sentence.

You may correct a dangling modifier by
- adding a word or words that the dangling word, phrase, or clause can sensibly refer to
- adding a word or words to the dangling word, phrase, or clause
- rewording the sentence

DANGLING After becoming poet laureate, "The Charge of the Light Brigade" was written. [Who became poet laureate?]

CLEAR After becoming poet laureate, Alfred, Lord Tennyson wrote "The Charge of the Light Brigade."

CLEAR Alfred, Lord Tennyson wrote "The Charge of the Light Brigade" after he became poet laureate.

6 PHRASES

WHAT IS A PHRASE?

6a. A *phrase* is a group of related words that is used as a single part of speech and that does not contain a verb and its subject.

EXAMPLE
The Rime of the Ancient Mariner, **Coleridge's best-known poem**, *was published in 1798.* [*Coleridge's best-known poem* functions as a noun, *was published* is a verb, and *in 1798* functions as an adverb.]

THE PREPOSITIONAL PHRASE

6b. A *prepositional phrase* begins with a preposition and ends with the *object of the preposition*, a word or word group that functions as a noun.

EXAMPLE
From the rafters of Herot hung one **of Grendel's arms.** [The noun *rafters* is the object of the preposition *from*. The noun *Herot* is the object of the preposition *of*. The noun *arms* is the object of the preposition *of*.]

An object of a preposition may be compound.

EXAMPLE
The three men ignored the warnings **of the tavern-knave and the publican.** [Both *tavern-knave* and *publican* are objects of the preposition *of.*]

(1) An **adjective phrase** is a prepositional phrase that modifies a noun or a pronoun. An adjective phrase tells *what kind* or *which one.*

EXAMPLE
The three rioters found eight bushels **of gold coins.** [*Of gold coins* modifies the noun *bushels.*]

An adjective phrase usually follows the word it modifies. That word may be the object of another preposition.

EXAMPLE
They told stories on their journey **to Canterbury.** [*To Canterbury* modifies *journey,* the object of the preposition *on.*]

More than one adjective phrase may modify the same word.

EXAMPLE
Chaucer's trips **to Italy on important diplomatic missions** broadened his knowledge. [The phrases *to Italy* and *on important diplomatic missions* modify the noun *trips.*]

(2) An **adverb phrase** is a prepositional phrase that modifies a verb, an adjective, or an adverb. An adverb phrase tells *how, when, where, why,* or *to what extent* (*how long* or *how far*).

As you can see in the example below, more than one adverb phrase can modify the same word. The example also shows that an adverb phrase, unlike an adjective phrase, can precede the word it modifies.

EXAMPLE
In 1799, Wordsworth returned **with his sister to the Lake District.** [Each phrase modifies the verb *returned. In 1799* tells *when,* *with his sister* tells *how,* and *to the Lake District* tells *where.*]

VERBALS AND VERBAL PHRASES

A *verbal* is a form of a verb used as a noun, an adjective, or an adverb. A *verbal phrase* consists of a verbal and its modifiers and complements.

Participles and Participial Phrases

 6c. A *participle* is a verb form that is used as an adjective. A *participial phrase* consists of a participle and all the words related to the participle.

The two kinds of participles are the *present participle* and the *past participle.*

(1) Present participles end in *–ing.*

EXAMPLE
Sir Gawain heard the Green Knight **sharpening his ax.** [The participial phrase modifies the noun *Green Knight.* The noun *ax* is the direct object of the present participle *sharpening.*]

(2) Most **past participles** end in *–d* or *–ed.* Others are irregularly formed.

EXAMPLE
Tormented by her guilt, Lady Macbeth lost her sanity. [The participial phrase modifies the noun *Lady Macbeth.* The adverb phrase *by her guilt* modifies the past participle *tormented.*]

Gerunds and Gerund Phrases

6d. A *gerund* is a verb form ending in *–ing* that is used as a noun. A *gerund phrase* consists of a gerund and all the words related to the gerund.

EXAMPLES
For Gulliver, **living in Brobdingnag** is quite different from **living in Lilliput.** [*Living in Brobdingnag* is the subject of the verb *is. Living in Lilliput* is the object of the preposition *from.* The adverb phrases *in Brobdingnag* and *in Lilliput* modify the gerund *living.*]

The Miller enjoys **playing the bagpipes.** [*Playing the bagpipes* is the direct object of the verb *enjoys. Bagpipes* is the direct object of the gerund *playing.*]

Infinitives and Infinitive Phrases

6e. An *infinitive* is a verb form that can be used as a noun, an adjective, or an adverb. An infinitive usually begins with *to.* An *infinitive phrase* consists of an infinitive and all the words related to the infinitive.

EXAMPLES
The three rioters vow **to kill Death.** [The infinitive phrase acts as a noun and is the direct object of the verb *vow. Death* is the direct object of the infinitive *to kill.*]

She had a great desire **to visit Stratford-on-Avon.** [The infinitive phrase acts as an adjective and modifies the noun *desire. Stratford-on-Avon* is the direct object of the infinitive *to visit.*]

Macbeth goes to the witches' haunt **to talk to them.**
[The infinitive phrase acts as an adverb and modifies the verb *goes*. The adverb phrase *to them* modifies the infinitive *to talk.*]

Lady Macbeth helps her husband **become king.**
[The sign of the infinitive, *to*, is omitted. The infinitive has a subject, *husband*, making the entire construction an *infinitive clause*. The infinitive clause acts as a noun and is the direct object of the verb *helps*.]

APPOSITIVES AND APPOSITIVE PHRASES

6f. An *appositive* is a noun or a pronoun placed beside another noun or pronoun to identify or explain it. An *appositive phrase* consists of an appositive and its modifiers.

An appositive or appositive phrase usually follows the word it identifies or explains.

EXAMPLES
Have you read Coleridge's poem **"Kubla Khan"**?
[The appositive *"Kubla Khan"* identifies the noun *poem*.]

Shakespeare was born in Stratford-on-Avon, **a market town about eighty miles from London.**
[The entire appositive phrase *a market town about eighty miles from London* identifies the noun *Stratford-on-Avon*.]

For emphasis, however, an appositive or an appositive phrase may precede the word that it explains or identifies.

EXAMPLE
A riot of colorful sights, intriguing aromas, and surprising noises, a Cairo bazaar is great fun to visit. [The appositive phrase explains why a Cairo bazaar is fun to visit.]

7 CLAUSES

7a. A *clause* is a group of words that contains a verb and its subject and that is used as part of a sentence. There are two kinds of clauses: the *independent clause* and the *subordinate clause*.

THE INDEPENDENT CLAUSE

7b. An *independent* (or *main*) *clause* expresses a complete thought and can stand by itself as a sentence.

EXAMPLE
          SUBJECT   VERB
William Shakespeare wrote more than 150 sonnets. [one independent clause]

THE SUBORDINATE CLAUSE

7c. A *subordinate* (or *dependent*) *clause* does not express a complete thought and cannot stand alone as a sentence.

EXAMPLE
         SUBJECT   VERB
that **Lord Byron swam** across the Hellespont

The thought expressed by a subordinate clause becomes complete when the clause is combined with an independent clause to create a complete sentence.

EXAMPLE
I read **that Lord Byron swam across the Hellespont.**

The Adjective Clause

7d. An *adjective clause* is a subordinate clause that modifies a noun or a pronoun.

An adjective clause always follows the word or words that it modifies. Usually, an adjective clause begins with a *relative pronoun* (such as *that, which, who, whom, whose*). A relative pronoun both relates an adjective clause to the word or words the clause modifies and performs a function within its own clause by serving as a subject, an object of a verb, an object of a preposition, or a modifier.

EXAMPLES
Mary Shelley, **who wrote *Frankenstein,*** liked reading ghost stories with her friends. [The relative pronoun *who* relates the adjective clause to the noun *Mary Shelley* and serves as the subject of the verb *wrote*.]

Resources
Grammar and Language
- *Language Handbook Worksheets,* pp. 51–65

The knight **for whom Sir Gawain is searching** is the Knight of the Green Chapel. [The relative pronoun *whom* relates the adjective clause to the noun *knight* and serves as the object of the preposition *for*.]

An adjective clause may begin with a *relative adverb,* such as *when* or *where.*

EXAMPLES
My uncle Robert told us about the time **when he backpacked across the island of Luzon.** [The adjective clause modifies the noun *time*.]
Malcolm flees to England, **where he raises an army to attack Macbeth.** [The adjective clause modifies the noun *England*.]

The Noun Clause

7e. A *noun clause* is a subordinate clause that may be used as a subject, a predicate nominative, a direct object, an indirect object, or an object of a preposition.

Words that are commonly used to introduce noun clauses include *how, that, what, whether, who, whoever,* and *why.*

EXAMPLES
That Fleance escapes the murderers troubles Macbeth. [subject]
Power is **what Macbeth desires.** [predicate nominative]
Banquo suspected **that Macbeth had murdered Duncan.** [direct object]
The teacher will give **whoever can recite the soliloquy** ten points. [indirect object]
The teacher will give ten points to **whoever can recite the soliloquy.** [object of a preposition]

The word that introduces a noun clause may or may not have another function in the clause.

EXAMPLES
Do you know **who wrote *Don Juan*?** [The word *who* introduces the noun clause and serves as the subject of the verb *wrote*.]
The witches predict **that Macbeth will become king.** [The word *that* introduces the noun clause but does not have any function within the noun clause.]

The Adverb Clause

7f. An *adverb clause* 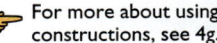 is a subordinate clause that modifies a verb, an adjective, or an adverb.

An adverb clause, which may come before or after the word or words it modifies, tells *how, when, where, why, to what extent,* or *under what condition.* An adverb clause is introduced by a *subordinating conjunction*—a word or word group that relates the adverb clause to the word or words the clause modifies.

EXAMPLES
He acted **as though he had seen a ghost.** [The adverb clause modifies the verb *acted,* telling *how* he acted.]
Jane is taller **than her grandmother is.** [The adverb clause modifies the adjective *taller,* telling *to what extent* Jane is tall.]
They stayed longer **than I thought they would.** [The adverb clause modifies the adverb *longer,* telling *to what extent* their stay was longer.]

The Elliptical Clause

7g. Part of a clause may be left out when the meaning can be understood from the context of the sentence. Such a clause is called an *elliptical clause.*

EXAMPLES
While [he was] painting, Rembrandt concentrated completely on his work.
Ken may ride with us **if he wants to** [ride with us].
This job took longer **than the last one** [took].

 For more about using pronouns in elliptical constructions, see 4g.

8 SENTENCE STRUCTURE

SENTENCE OR FRAGMENT?

8a. A *sentence* is a group of words that has a subject and a verb and expresses a complete thought.

EXAMPLES
"My Last Duchess" is an example of a dramatic monologue.
For how many years was Winston Churchill the prime minister of Britain?
What an ambitious man Macbeth was!

Resources

Grammar and Language
- *Language Handbook Worksheets,* pp. 66–75

Only a sentence should begin with a capital letter and end with a period, a question mark, or an exclamation point. Do not be misled by a group of words that looks like a sentence but that either does not have a subject and a verb or does not express a complete thought. Such a word group is called a *sentence fragment.*

FRAGMENT	Awakens and finds himself surrounded by people six inches tall.
SENTENCE	Gulliver awakens and finds himself surrounded by people six inches tall.

SUBJECT AND PREDICATE

8b. A sentence consists of two parts: a subject and a predicate. A *subject* tells *whom* or *what* the sentence is about. A *predicate* tells something about the subject.

In the following examples, all the words labeled *subject* make up the **complete subject,** and all the words labeled *predicate* make up the **complete predicate.**

EXAMPLES

SUBJECT	PREDICATE
My sister and I	enjoyed *Gulliver's Travels.*

PREDICATE	SUBJECT	PREDICATE
For fifty years	Beowulf	ruled Geatland.

The Simple Subject

8c. A *simple subject* is the main word or group of words that tells *whom* or *what* the sentence is about.

EXAMPLE
The first **leader** of the gang was Blackie. [The complete subject is *the first leader of the gang.*]

The Simple Predicate

8d. A *simple predicate* is a verb or verb phrase that tells something about the subject.

EXAMPLE
Have you **read** "The Seafarer"? [The complete predicate is *have read "The Seafarer."*]

The Compound Subject and the Compound Verb

8e. A *compound subject* consists of two or more subjects that are joined by a conjunction—usually *and* or *or*—and that have the same verb.

EXAMPLE
A **nun** and three **priests** accompany the Prioress on the pilgrimage.

8f. A *compound verb* consists of two or more verbs that are joined by a conjunction—usually *and, but,* or *or*—and that have the same subject.

EXAMPLE
Truth **enlightens** the mind, **frees** the spirit, and **strengthens** the soul.

How to Find the Subject of a Sentence

8g. To find the subject of a sentence, ask *Who?* or *What?* before the verb.

(1) The subject of a sentence is never within a prepositional phrase.

EXAMPLES
A **group** of pilgrims gathered at the Tabard. [Who gathered? Group gathered. *Pilgrims* is the object of the preposition *of.*]
Out of the stillness came the loud **sound** of laughter. [What came? Sound came. *Stillness* is the object of the preposition *out of. Laughter* is the object of the preposition *of.*]

(2) The subject of a sentence expressing a command or a request is always understood to be *you,* although *you* may not appear in the sentence.

COMMAND	Name the pilgrim accompanying the Plowman. [Who is being told to name? *You* is understood.]

The subject of a command or a request is *you* even when the sentence also contains a **noun of direct address**—a word that names or identifies the one or ones spoken to.

REQUEST	Marla, [you] please read the first stanza of "To a Skylark."

(3) The subject of a sentence expressing a question usually follows the verb or a part of the verb phrase. Turning the question into a statement will often help you find the subject.

QUESTION	Have you read Lord Byron's poem "She Walks in Beauty"?
STATEMENT	**You** have read Lord Byron's poem "She Walks in Beauty." [Who has read? You have read.]

QUESTION	Were Shakespeare's plays popular during his own lifetime?
STATEMENT	Shakespeare's plays were popular during his own lifetime. [What were popular? Plays were popular.]

(4) The word *there* or *here* is never the subject of a sentence.

EXAMPLES
There is Canterbury Cathedral. [What is there? Canterbury Cathedral is there.]
Here are my drawings of Chaucer's pilgrims. [What are here? Drawings are here.]

COMPLEMENTS

8h. A *complement* is a word or a group of words that completes the meaning of a verb or a verbal. The four main kinds of complements are *direct objects, indirect objects, objective complements,* and *subject complements.*

The Direct Object and the Indirect Object

8i. A *direct object* is a noun, a pronoun, or a word group that functions as a noun and tells *who* or *what* receives the action of a transitive verb.

EXAMPLES
Banquo definitely suspected him. [Suspected whom? him]
Beethoven composed sonatas and symphonies. [Composed what? sonatas and symphonies—compound direct object]

8j. An *indirect object* is a word or word group that comes between a transitive verb and a direct object. An indirect object, which may be a noun, a pronoun, or a word group that functions as a noun, tells *to whom, to what, for whom,* or *for what* the action of the verb is done.

EXAMPLES
The Wife of Bath told the other pilgrims an interesting story. [Told to whom? pilgrims]
We should give practicing for the concert our full attention. [Should give our full attention to what? practicing for the concert]

The Objective Complement

8k. An *objective complement* is a word or word group that helps complete the meaning of a transitive verb by identifying or modifying the direct object. An objective complement, which may be a noun, a pronoun, an adjective, or a word group that functions as a noun or an adjective, usually follows the direct object.

EXAMPLES
Macduff called Malcolm king. [The noun *king* identifies the direct object *Malcolm.*]
He believed the money his. [The pronoun *his* modifies the direct object *money.*]
Everyone considered him chivalrous. [The adjective *chivalrous* modifies the direct object *him.*]

 NOTE A *transitive verb* is an action verb that takes an object, which tells who or what receives the action.

The Subject Complement

8l. A *subject complement* is a word or a word group that completes the meaning of a linking verb or a verbal and that identifies or modifies the subject. The two kinds of subject complements are *predicate nominatives* and *predicate adjectives.*

(1) A *predicate nominative* is a word or group of words that follows a linking verb and refers to the same person, place, thing, or idea as the subject of the verb. A predicate nominative may be a noun, a pronoun, or a word group that functions as a noun.

EXAMPLES
Of these three poets, Wordsworth was the most prolific one. [The pronoun *one* refers to the subject *Wordsworth.*]
The main characters are Paul and his mother. [The two nouns *Paul* and *mother* are a compound predicate nominative that refers to the subject *characters.*]

(2) A *predicate adjective* is an adjective that follows a linking verb and that modifies the subject of the verb.

EXAMPLES
Did King Hrothgar feel powerless? [The adjective *powerless* modifies the subject *King Hrothgar.*]
Iago is sly and scheming. [The two adjectives *sly* and *scheming* are a compound predicate adjective that modifies the subject *Iago.*]

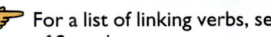 For a list of linking verbs, see Part 1: The Parts of Speech.

Language Handbook

SENTENCES CLASSIFIED ACCORDING TO STRUCTURE

8m. According to their structure, sentences are classified as *simple, compound, complex,* and *compound-complex.*

(1) A *simple sentence* has one independent clause and no subordinate clauses.

EXAMPLE
"Not Waving but Drowning" is one of my favorite poems.

(2) A *compound sentence* has two or more independent clauses but no subordinate clauses.

EXAMPLES
Othello is a great man, but his character is flawed.
Agatha Christie was a prolific writer; she wrote more than eighty books in less than sixty years.

(3) A *complex sentence* has one independent clause and at least one subordinate clause.

EXAMPLE
The poet who wrote "Ode on a Grecian Urn" is John Keats. [The independent clause is *the poet is John Keats*. The subordinate clause is *who wrote "Ode on a Grecian Urn."*]

(4) A *compound-complex* sentence has two or more independent clauses and at least one subordinate clause.

EXAMPLE
After Macbeth killed their father, Malcolm fled to England, and Donalbain escaped to Ireland. [The two independent clauses are *Malcolm fled to England* and *Donalbain escaped to Ireland*. The subordinate clause is *after Macbeth killed their father*.]

SENTENCES CLASSIFIED ACCORDING TO PURPOSE

8n. According to their purpose, sentences are classified as *declarative, interrogative, imperative,* and *exclamatory.*

(1) A *declarative sentence* makes a statement. It is followed by a period.

EXAMPLE
The lock on the front door is broken.

(2) An *interrogative sentence* asks a question. It is followed by a question mark.

EXAMPLE
Have you read Dylan Thomas's "Fern Hill"?

(3) An *imperative sentence* makes a request or gives a command. It is usually followed by a period. A very strong command, however, is followed by an exclamation point.

EXAMPLES
Please return this book to the library.
Give me the name of the warrior who succeeds Beowulf.
Stop making that noise!

(4) An *exclamatory sentence* expresses strong feeling or shows excitement. It is followed by an exclamation point.

EXAMPLES
What a talented writer she was!
We won!

 For more information about using end marks, see 12a–e.

9 SENTENCE STYLE

WAYS TO ACHIEVE CLARITY

Coordinating Ideas

9a. To *coordinate* two or more ideas, or to give them equal emphasis, link them with a connecting word, an appropriate mark of punctuation, or both.

EXAMPLE
I read the novel *Frankenstein*, **and** then I saw the film.

Subordinating Ideas

9b. To *subordinate* an idea, or to show that one idea is related to but less important than another, use an adverb clause or an adjective clause.

EXAMPLES
Sir Gawain accepts the magic sash **because he wants it to protect him from the Green Knight.** [adverb clause]
Hrunting is the name of the sword **that Unferth gives Beowulf.** [adjective clause]

Resources

Grammar and Language
- *Language Handbook Worksheets,* pp. 76–90

Using Parallel Structure

9c. Use the same grammatical form (*parallel structure*) to express ideas of equal importance.

(1) Use parallel structure when you link coordinate ideas.

EXAMPLE
In the winter I usually like **to ski** and **to skate**. [infinitive paired with infinitive]

(2) Use parallel structure when you compare or contrast ideas.

EXAMPLE
Einstein liked mathematical **research** more than laboratory **supervision**. [noun contrasted with noun]

(3) Use parallel structure when you link ideas with correlative conjunctions (*both . . . and, either . . . or, neither . . . nor,* or *not only . . . but also*).

EXAMPLE
Virginia Woolf was not only **a novelist** but also **an essayist**. [Note that the correlative conjunctions come directly before the parallel terms.]

When you revise for parallel structure, you may need to add an article, a preposition, or a pronoun before each of the parallel terms.

UNCLEAR	I admire the poems of Byron more than Wordsworth.
CLEAR	I admire the poems of Byron more than **those of** Wordsworth.

OBSTACLES TO CLARITY

Sentence Fragments

9d. Avoid using a *sentence fragment*—a word or word group that either does not contain a subject and a verb or does not express a complete thought.

 For more information about sentence fragments, see 8a.

Here are two common ways to correct a sentence fragment.

1. Add words to make the thought complete.

FRAGMENT	Twelve Geats around Beowulf's tower. [The verb is missing.]
SENTENCE	Twelve Geats **rode** around Beowulf's tower.

2. Attach the fragment to the sentence that comes before or after it.

FRAGMENT	A doctor and a gentlewoman see Lady Macbeth. Walking in her sleep. [participial phrase]
SENTENCE	A doctor and a gentlewoman see Lady Macbeth **walking in her sleep**.

 NOTE Sentence fragments can be effective when used in expressive and creative writing and in informal writing.

Run-on Sentences

9e. Avoid using a *run-on sentence*—two or more complete thoughts that are run together as if they were one complete thought.

The two kinds of run-on sentences are *fused sentences* and *comma splices*. A **fused sentence** has no punctuation or connecting word at all between the complete thoughts. A **comma splice** has just a comma between the complete thoughts.

FUSED SENTENCE	Wiglaf helps Beowulf the other warriors retreat in fear.
COMMA SPLICE	Wiglaf helps Beowulf, the other warriors retreat in fear.

You can correct run-on sentences in several ways.

1. Make two sentences.

EXAMPLE
Wiglaf helps Beowulf**.** **T**he other warriors retreat in fear.

2. Use a comma and a coordinating conjunction.

EXAMPLE
Wiglaf helps Beowulf**, but** the other warriors retreat in fear.

3. Change one of the independent clauses to a subordinate clause.

EXAMPLE
Wiglaf helps Beowulf**, while the other warriors retreat in fear.**

4. Use a semicolon.

EXAMPLE
Wiglaf helps Beowulf**;** the other warriors retreat in fear.

5. Use a semicolon and a conjunctive adverb.

EXAMPLE
Wiglaf helps Beowulf**; however,** the other warriors retreat in fear.

Unnecessary Shifts in Sentences

9f. Avoid making unnecessary shifts in subject, in tense, and in voice.

AWKWARD Grandma goes to the farmers' market, where the freshest produce is. [shift in subject]

BETTER **Grandma** goes to the farmers' market, where **she** finds the freshest produce.

AWKWARD Macbeth sees Banquo's ghost, but no one else did. [shift in tense]

BETTER Macbeth **sees** Banquo's ghost, but no one else **does**.

AWKWARD Lyle spent four hours at the library, but no books on his research topic were found. [shift in voice]

BETTER Lyle **spent** four hours at the library, but he **found** no books on his research topic.

REVISING FOR VARIETY

9g. Use a variety of sentence beginnings.

Putting the subject first in a declarative sentence is not wrong, but starting every sentence with the subject can make your writing boring. To add variety to your sentences, rearrange sentence parts to vary the beginnings. The following examples show how a writer can revise sentences to avoid beginning with the subject every time.

SUBJECT FIRST	Lady Macbeth is cunning and ruthless and goads her husband into committing murder.
SINGLE-WORD MODIFIERS FIRST	**Cunning** and **ruthless,** Lady Macbeth goads her husband into committing murder.
SUBJECT FIRST	*In Memoriam,* which was published in 1850, is Alfred, Lord Tennyson's elegy for his friend Arthur Hallam.
PARTICIPIAL PHRASE FIRST	**Published in 1850,** *In Memoriam* is Alfred, Lord Tennyson's elegy for his friend Arthur Hallam.
APPOSITIVE PHRASE FIRST	**An elegy for Alfred, Lord Tennyson's friend Arthur Hallam,** *In Memoriam* was published in 1850.

1222 Resource Center Language Handbook

Varying Sentence Structure

9h. Use a mix of simple, compound, complex, and compound-complex sentences in your writing.

EXAMPLE
The three "weird sisters" greet Macbeth and Banquo with prophecies. [simple] According to the witches, Macbeth will become king, but Banquo will not, though his descendants will. [compound-complex] When Macbeth asks the witches to tell him more, they vanish. [complex] The subsequent conversation between Banquo and Macbeth lends insight into each man's character. [simple] That is, Banquo is skeptical of the witches' prophecies; however, Macbeth believes in them. [compound]

 For information about the four kinds of sentence structure, see 8m.

Revising to Reduce Wordiness

9i. Avoid using unnecessary words in your writing.

The following guidelines suggest some ways to revise wordy sentences.

1. Take out a whole group of unnecessary words.

    WORDY Grendel's mother carried Beowulf to her home where she lived.

    IMPROVED Grendel's mother carried Beowulf to her home.

2. Replace pretentious words and expressions with straightforward ones.

    WORDY In *Lord of the Flies,* a group of males, all of whom are under thirteen years of age, is stranded on a land mass surrounded by water and totally free of inhabitants.

    IMPROVED In *Lord of the Flies,* a group of **young boys** is stranded on an **uninhabited island.**

3. Reduce a clause to a phrase.

    WORDY Sir Lancelot falls in love with Queen Guinevere, who is the wife of King Arthur.

    IMPROVED Sir Lancelot falls in love with Queen Guinevere, **King Arthur's wife.**

4. Reduce a phrase or a clause to one word.

    WORDY At that point in time, Mr. Thomas returns.

    IMPROVED **Then,** Mr. Thomas returns.

10 Sentence Combining

COMBINING BY INSERTING WORDS AND PHRASES

10a. Combine related sentences by taking a key word (or using another form of the key word) from one sentence and inserting it into another sentence.

ORIGINAL	The famous magician Harry Houdini performed impossible escapes. The escapes only seemed impossible.
COMBINED	The famous magician Harry Houdini performed **seemingly** impossible escapes. [The verb *seemed* becomes the adverb *seemingly*.]

10b. Combine related sentences by taking (or creating) a phrase from one sentence and inserting it into another.

ORIGINAL	Have you read the poem "The Hollow Men"? It was written by T. S. Eliot.
COMBINED	Have you read the poem "The Hollow Men" **by T. S. Eliot**? [prepositional phrase]

COMBINING BY COORDINATING IDEAS

10c. Combine related sentences whose ideas are equally important by using coordinating conjunctions (*and, but, or, nor, for, so, yet*) or correlative conjunctions (*both . . . and, either . . . or, neither . . . nor, not only . . . but also*).

The relationship of the ideas determines which connective will work best. When joined, the coordinate ideas form compound elements.

ORIGINAL	*Paradise Lost* was written by John Milton. *Paradise Regained* was also written by him.
COMBINED	*Paradise Lost* **and** *Paradise Regained* were written by John Milton. [compound subject]
ORIGINAL	*Adonais* is one of Shelley's best-known poems. Many critics think that *Prometheus Unbound* is his masterpiece.
COMBINED	*Adonais* is one of Shelley's best-known poems**, but** many critics think that *Prometheus Unbound* is his masterpiece. [compound sentence]

Another way to form a compound sentence is to link independent clauses with a semicolon or with a semicolon and a conjunctive adverb (such as *however, likewise,* or *therefore*) followed by a comma.

EXAMPLES
She was willing to compromise**;** he was not.
They moved to Dorsetshire**; however,** they stayed there only a few months.

COMBINING BY SUBORDINATING IDEAS

10d. Combine related sentences whose ideas are not equally important by placing the less important idea in a subordinate clause (adjective clause, adverb clause, or noun clause).

ORIGINAL	I read about the life of Queen Victoria. She ruled Great Britain from 1837 to 1901.
COMBINED	I read about the life of Queen Victoria, **who ruled Great Britain from 1837 to 1901.** [adjective clause]

or

COMBINED	Queen Victoria, **whose life I read about,** ruled Great Britain from 1837 to 1901. [adjective clause]
ORIGINAL	Grendel's mother attacks Herot. King Hrothgar once again asks Beowulf for help.
COMBINED	**When Grendel's mother attacks Herot,** King Hrothgar once again asks Beowulf for help. [adverb clause]
ORIGINAL	They will find Death under an oak tree. An old man tells the three rioters that this will happen.
COMBINED	An old man tells the three rioters **that they will find Death under an oak tree.** [noun clause]

☞ For more information about subordinate clauses and subordinating ideas, see 7c–g and 9b.

Resources

Grammar and Language

- *Language Handbook Worksheets,* pp. 91–104

Resources

Grammar and Language

- Language Handbook Worksheets, pp. 105–112

11 Capitalization

11a. Capitalize the first word in every sentence.

EXAMPLE
The warrior who succeeds Beowulf as king is Wiglaf.

(1) Capitalize the first word of a sentence following a colon.

EXAMPLE
Mrs. Kelley asked me this question: How old is Beowulf when he fights Grendel?

(2) Capitalize the first word of a direct quotation.

EXAMPLE
After winning, Brian said, "We couldn't have done it without the support of the good people of Raleigh."

When quoting from another writer's work, capitalize the first word of the quotation only if the writer has capitalized it in the original work.

EXAMPLE
After winning, Brian acknowledged "the support of the good people of Raleigh."

(3) Traditionally, the first word of a line of poetry is capitalized.

EXAMPLES
If all the world and love were young,
And truth in every shepherd's tongue,
These pretty pleasures might me move
To live with thee and be thy love.
    —Sir Walter Raleigh, "The Nymph's
       Reply to the Shepherd"

NOTE Some writers do not follow this rule. Whenever you quote from a writer's work, always use capital letters exactly as the writer uses them.

11b. Capitalize the first word in the salutation and the closing of a letter.

EXAMPLES
Dear John,   Dear Sir or Madam: Sincerely,

11c. Capitalize proper nouns and proper adjectives.

A *common noun* is a general name for a person, a place, a thing, or an idea. A *proper noun* names a particular person, place, thing, or idea. A *proper adjective* is formed from a proper noun. Common nouns are capitalized only if they begin a sentence (also, in most cases, a line of poetry), begin a direct quotation, or are part of a title.

COMMON NOUNS	PROPER NOUNS	PROPER ADJECTIVES
dramatist	Shakespeare	Shakespearean performer
country	Russia	Russian diplomat
mountains	the Alps	Alpine flora

In most proper nouns made up of two or more words, do not capitalize articles (*a*, *an*, *the*), short prepositions (those with fewer than five letters, such as *at*, *of*, *for*, *to*, *with*), the mark of the infinitive (*to*), and coordinating conjunctions (*and*, *but*, *for*, *nor*, *or*, *so*, *yet*).

EXAMPLES
Speaker of the House of Representatives
American Society for the Prevention of Cruelty
    to Animals

 NOTE When you're not sure whether to capitalize a word, check a dictionary.

(1) Capitalize the names of most persons and animals.

GIVEN NAMES	Virginia	Geoffrey
SURNAMES	Woolf	Chaucer
ANIMALS	Lassie	Rocinante

 NOTE Some names contain more than one capital letter. Usage varies in the capitalization of *van*, *von*, *du*, *de la*, and other parts of many multiword names. Always verify the spelling of a name with the person, or check the name in a reference source.

EXAMPLES
La Fontaine   O'Connor   al-Khansa   McEwen
Van Doren   Ibn Ezra   van Gogh   de Vega

(2) Capitalize the names of nationalities, races, and peoples.

EXAMPLES
Japanese   Caucasian   Hispanic   Celt

(3) Capitalize brand names. Notice that the noun that follows a brand name is not capitalized.

EXAMPLES
Sealtest milk   Wonder bread   Crest toothpaste

1224   Resource Center   Language Handbook

(4) Capitalize geographical names.

TYPE OF NAME	EXAMPLES	
Towns, Cities	Stratford-on-Avon Rio de Janeiro	Dublin South Bend
Counties, Townships	Marion County Brooklyn Borough	Alexandria Township Lafayette Parish
States, Territories	Oklahoma Yucatán	North Carolina Yukon Territory
Regions	the Middle East Western Hemisphere	the Lake District the Southwest
Countries	England	Costa Rica
Continents	South America	Europe
Islands	Long Island	British Isles
Mountains	Himalayas Pikes Peak	Mount Rainier Sierra Nevada
Other Landforms and Features	Cape of Good Hope Death Valley	Isthmus of Corinth Black Forest
Bodies of Water	Indian Ocean Bering Strait	Red Sea San Francisco Bay
Parks	Hawaii Volcanoes National Park Point Reyes National Seashore	
Roads, Highways, Streets	Route 42 Interstate 75	King Avenue Thirty-fourth Street

NOTE Words such as *city*, *state*, and *county* are often capitalized in official documents such as proclamations. In general usage, however, these words are not capitalized.

OFFICIAL USAGE
the State of Iowa

GENERAL USAGE
the state of Iowa

NOTE Words such as *north*, *western*, and *southeast* are not capitalized when they indicate direction.

EXAMPLES
north of London
heading southwest

NOTE The second word in a hyphenated number begins with a small letter.

EXAMPLE
Forty-second Street

(5) Capitalize the names of organizations, teams, business firms, institutions, buildings and other structures, and government bodies.

TYPE OF NAME	EXAMPLES
Organizations	Disabled American Veterans Professional Photographers of America
Teams	River City Eastside Bombers Harlem Globetrotters
Business Firms	Aaron's Carpets National Broadcasting Corporation
Institutions	Oxford University Southern Christian Leadership Conference
Buildings and Other Structures	Lincoln Center for the Performing Arts the Great Wall of China
Government Bodies	United States Congress House of Commons

NOTE Do not capitalize words such as *democratic*, *republican*, and *socialist* when they refer to principles or forms of government. Capitalize such words only when they refer to specific political parties.

EXAMPLES
The citizens demanded democratic reforms.
Who will be the Republican nominee for governor?

NOTE Do not capitalize words such as *building, hospital, theater, high school,* and *post office* unless they are part of a proper noun.

Language Handbook **1225**

(6) Capitalize the names of historical events and periods, special events, holidays and other calendar items, and time zones.

TYPE OF NAME	EXAMPLES	
Historical Events and Periods	Middle Ages	Reign of Terror
Special Events	Super Bowl	Pan-American Games
Holidays and Other Calendar Items	Monday November	Memorial Day National Book Week
Time Zones	Eastern Daylight Time (EDT) Central Mountain Time (CMT)	

NOTE Do not capitalize the name of a season unless it is being personified or used as part of a proper noun.

EXAMPLES
We moved here last fall.
This month Fall begins painting the leaves in brilliant hues.
The Fall Festival is next week.

(7) Capitalize the names of ships, trains, aircraft, spacecraft, monuments, awards, planets and other heavenly bodies, and any other particular places and things.

TYPE OF NAME	EXAMPLES	
Ships	Merrimac	U.S.S. Nautilus
Trains	Zephyr	Hill Country Flyer
Aircraft	Enola Gay	Spruce Goose
Spacecraft	Columbia	Magellan
Monuments	Mount Rushmore National Memorial Effigy Mounds National Monument	
Awards	Nobel Prize	Medal of Freedom
Planets and Other Heavenly Bodies	Neptune Big Dipper	Polaris Cassiopeia
Other Particular Places and Things	Hurricane Alma Marshall Plan	Silk Route Union Jack

NOTE Do not capitalize the words *sun* and *moon*. Do not capitalize the word *earth* unless it is used along with the proper names of other particular places, things, or events.

EXAMPLES
The equator is an imaginary circle around the earth.
Is Mercury closer to the sun than Earth is?

☞ For more information about the names of particular places and things, see the discussion of proper nouns in 11c.

11d. Do not capitalize the names of school subjects, except names of languages and course names followed by a number.

EXAMPLES
French   art   Algebra I

11e. Capitalize titles.

(1) Capitalize a title belonging to a particular person when it comes before the person's name.

EXAMPLES
General Patton   Dr. Sanchez   President Clinton

In general, do not capitalize a title used alone or following a name. Some titles, however, are by tradition capitalized. If you are unsure about capitalizing a title, check in a dictionary.

EXAMPLES
Who is the prime minister of Britain?
When was Ann Richards governor of Texas?
The Prince of Wales met earlier today with European leaders.

A title is usually capitalized when it is used alone in direct address.

EXAMPLE
Good afternoon, Sir [*or* sir], may I help you?

(2) Capitalize a word showing a family relationship when the word is used before or in place of a person's name, unless a possessive comes before the word.

EXAMPLES
I asked Mom if Uncle Bob is named after her uncle Roberto.

(3) Capitalize the first and last words and all important words in titles of books, periodicals, poems, stories, essays, speeches, plays, historical documents, movies, radio and television programs, works of art, musical compositions, and cartoons.

TYPE OF NAME	EXAMPLES	
Books	*A Tale of Two Cities*	*Gulliver's Travels*
Periodicals	*National Geographic*	*Time*
Poems	"She Walks in Beauty"	"To His Coy Mistress"
Stories	"The Rocking-Horse Winner"	"Games at Twilight"
Essays and Speeches	"A Modest Proposal"	the Gettysburg Address
Plays	*The Tragedy of Macbeth*	*Pygmalion*
Historical Documents	Magna Carta	Treaty of Versailles
Movies	*Robin Hood: Prince of Thieves*	*Clueless*
Radio and TV Programs	*Adventures in World Music*	*Nova*
Works of Art	*The Kiss*	*March of Humanity*
Musical Compositions	*War Requiem*	"Tears in Heaven"
Cartoons	*For Better or Worse*	*Jump Start*

NOTE Unimportant words in a title include articles (*a, an, the*), short prepositions (those with fewer than five letters, such as *of, to, in, for, from, with*), and coordinating conjunctions (*and, but, for, nor, or, so, yet*).

☞ For information about which titles should be italicized and which should be enclosed in quotation marks, see 13b and 13d.

11f. Capitalize the names of religions and their followers, holy days and celebrations, holy writings, and specific deities and venerated beings.

TYPE OF NAME	EXAMPLES	
Religions and Followers	Christianity Muslim	Buddhist Judaism
Holy Days and Celebrations	Easter Passover	Ramadan Holy Week
Holy Writings	Bible Talmud	Koran I Ching
Specific Deities and Venerated Beings	Allah Dalai Lama	God Jehovah

NOTE The words *god* and *goddess* are not capitalized when they refer to mythological deities. The names of specific mythological deities are capitalized, however.

EXAMPLES
The Greek god of the sea was Poseidon.

12 PUNCTUATION

END MARKS

12a. A statement (or declarative sentence) is followed by a period.

EXAMPLE
The Ancient Mariner told an amazing tale.

12b. A question (or interrogative sentence) is followed by a question mark.

EXAMPLE
Do you know who played the leading role in the first movie version of *Hamlet*?

Resources

Grammar and Language
- *Language Handbook Worksheets,* pp. 113–124

12c. A request or command (or imperative sentence) is followed by either a period or an exclamation point.

EXAMPLES
Turn the music down, please. [request]
Name the poet who wrote "The Lady of Shalott." [mild command]
Watch out! [strong command]

12d. An exclamation (or exclamatory sentence) is followed by an exclamation point.

EXAMPLE
What an interesting story "My Oedipus Complex" is!

TYPE OF ABBREVIATION	EXAMPLES
Personal Names	Howard G. Chua-Eoan W. H. Auden
Organizations, Companies	Co. Inc. Ltd.
Titles Used with Names	Ms. Sr. Dr.
Times of Day	A.M. (or a.m.) P.M. (or p.m.)
Years	B.C. (written after the date) A.D. (written before the date)
Addresses	St. Blvd. P. O. Box
States	S.C. Calif.

12e. An abbreviation is usually followed by a period.

If an abbreviation with a period ends a sentence, do not add another period. However, do add a question mark or an exclamation point if one is needed.

EXAMPLES
The store opens at 10 A.M.
Does the store open at 10 A.M.?

Some abbreviations, including those for most units of measurement, are written without periods.

EXAMPLES
AM/FM, CIA, CNN, PC, NASA, SOS,
cc, ft, lb, kw, ml, psi, rpm [*but* in. *for* inch]

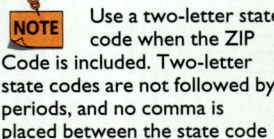 **NOTE** Use a two-letter state code when the ZIP Code is included. Two-letter state codes are not followed by periods, and no comma is placed between the state code and the ZIP Code.

EXAMPLE
Lexington, **KY** 40505

COMMAS

12f. Use commas to separate items in a series.

EXAMPLE
Virginia Woolf, James Joyce, and D. H. Lawrence are among the writers we are studying.

If all the items in a series are linked by *and*, *or*, or *nor*, do not use commas to separate them.

EXAMPLE
Byron **and** Shelley **and** Keats were contemporaries.

12g. Use a comma to separate two or more adjectives preceding a noun.

EXAMPLE
Gawain is the most gallant, honorable knight.

When the last adjective before a noun is thought of as part of the noun, the comma before the adjective is omitted.

EXAMPLE
I've finally found a decent, affordable used car.
[*Used car* is thought of as one unit.]

12h. Use a comma before *and, but, or, nor, for, so,* and *yet* when they join independent clauses.

EXAMPLE
I read Seamus Heaney's "The Grauballe Man," and now I want to read more of his poems.

You may omit the comma before *and, but, or,* or *nor* if the clauses are very short and there is no chance of misunderstanding.

12i. Use commas to set off nonessential clauses and nonessential participial phrases.

A *nonessential* clause or phrase is one that can be left out without changing the meaning of the sentence.

NONESSENTIAL CLAUSE	W. H. Auden, **who was born in York, England,** became an American citizen in 1946.
NONESSENTIAL PHRASE	The little blue sports car, **leaving all the others far behind,** forged into the lead.

☞ For more information about phrases, see 6a–f. For more on clauses, see 7a–g.

1228   Resource Center   Language Handbook

An *essential* clause or phrase is one that cannot be left out without changing the meaning of the sentence. Essential clauses and phrases are *not* set off by commas.

ESSENTIAL CLAUSE	The writer **who received the Nobel Prize in literature in 1923** was William Butler Yeats.
ESSENTIAL PHRASE	The pilgrims **riding along with the Knight** are the Squire and the Yeoman.

12j. Use commas after certain introductory elements.

(1) Use a comma after a one-word adverb such as *first, next, yes,* or *no* or after any mild exclamation such as *well* or *why* at the beginning of a sentence.

EXAMPLE
Yes, I have read *Don Juan.*

(2) Use a comma after an introductory participial phrase.

EXAMPLE
Looking calm, Jill walked to the podium.

(3) Use a comma after two or more introductory prepositional phrases or after a single long one.

EXAMPLE
With the help of Wiglaf, he killed the dragon.

(4) Use a comma after an introductory adverb clause.

EXAMPLE
After I had locked the car door, I remembered that the keys were still in the ignition.

12k. Use commas to set off elements that interrupt a sentence.

(1) Appositives and appositive phrases are usually set off by commas.

EXAMPLES
George Bernard Shaw's first play, ***Widowers' Houses,*** was published in 1893.
Is that she, **the one holding the sunflowers**?

Sometimes an appositive is so closely related to the word or words near it that it should not be set off by commas. Such an appositive is called a *restrictive appositive.*

EXAMPLE
The poet **Edmund Spenser** died suddenly in 1599.

(2) Words used in direct address are set off by commas.

EXAMPLE
Your research paper, **Dylan,** is quite interesting.

(3) Parenthetical expressions are set off by commas.

Parenthetical expressions are remarks that add incidental information or that relate ideas to each other. Some common parenthetical expressions are *for example, I think, moreover,* and *on the other hand.*

EXAMPLE
Macbeth is superstitious and sensitive; Lady Macbeth, **on the other hand,** is logical and bold.

 NOTE A contrasting expression introduced by *not, rather than,* or a similar term is parenthetical. Set it off by commas.

EXAMPLE
Percy Bysshe Shelley, **not John Keats,** wrote "Ode to the West Wind."

12l. Use a comma in certain conventional situations.

(1) Use a comma to separate items in dates and addresses.

EXAMPLES
On April 23, 1616, William Shakespeare died.
My grandparents' address is 505 King Street, Austin, TX 78701.

(2) Use a comma after the salutation of a personal letter and after the closing of any letter.

EXAMPLES
Dear Alicia,   Yours truly,

(3) Use commas to set off abbreviations such as *Jr., Sr., RN, M.D., Ltd.,* or *Inc.*

EXAMPLES
Is Jorge Rivera, Jr., in your class?
She is the owner of Flowers by Arthurine, Inc.

SEMICOLONS

12m. Use a semicolon between independent clauses that are closely related in thought and are not joined by *and, but, for, nor, or, so,* or *yet.*

EXAMPLE
The rain had finally stopped; a few rays of sunshine were pushing through breaks in the clouds.

12n. Use a semicolon between independent clauses joined by a conjunctive adverb or a transitional expression.

A *conjunctive adverb*—such as *furthermore, however,* or *nevertheless*—or a *transitional expression*—such

Language Handbook **1229**

as *for instance, in fact,* or *that is*—indicates the relationship of the independent clauses that it joins.

EXAMPLE
The snow made traveling difficult; **nevertheless,** we arrived home safely.

12o. Use a semicolon (rather than a comma) before a coordinating conjunction to join independent clauses that contain commas.

EXAMPLE
During the seventeenth century—the era of such distinguished prose writers as Sir Thomas Browne, John Donne, and Jeremy Taylor—the balanced compound sentence using commas and semicolons reached a high degree of perfection and popularity; but the tendency today is to use a fast-moving style with shorter sentences, fewer commas, and fewer semicolons. [commas within the clauses]

12p. Use a semicolon between items in a series if the items contain commas.

EXAMPLE
The summer reading list includes *Jude the Obscure,* by Thomas Hardy; *Lord Jim,* by Joseph Conrad; and *Lord of the Flies,* by William Golding.

COLONS

12q. Use a colon to mean "note what follows."

(1) Use a colon before a list of items, especially after expressions such as *as follows* and *the following.*

EXAMPLE
Collection 8 includes poems by the following authors: Robert Burns, William Blake, William Wordsworth, and Samuel Taylor Coleridge.

 NOTE Do not use a colon before a list that directly follows a verb or a preposition.

EXAMPLES
Collection 8 includes poems by Robert Burns, William Blake, William Wordsworth, and Samuel Taylor Coleridge. [The list directly follows the preposition *by*.]
The main characters in Charles Dickens's *A Tale of Two Cities* are Dr. Manette, Lucie Manette, Charles Darnay, and Sydney Carton. [The list directly follows the verb *are*.]

(2) Use a colon before a quotation that lacks a speaker tag such as *he said* or *she remarked.*

EXAMPLE
His father's response surprised him: "I'm proud of you, son."

 For information about punctuating quotations that do have speaker tags, see 13c.

(3) Use a colon before a long, formal statement or quotation.

EXAMPLE
When he awoke, Gulliver found himself tied down: "I could only look upward; the sun began to grow hot, and the light offended my eyes. I heard a confused noise about me, but in the posture I lay, could see nothing except the sky."

12r. Use a colon in certain conventional situations.

EXAMPLES
12:01 A.M. [between the hour and the minute]
Mark 3:10 [between chapter and verse in referring to passages from the Bible]
To Whom It May Concern: [after the salutation of a business letter]
"A Valediction: Forbidding Mourning" [between a title and a subtitle]

13 PUNCTUATION

ITALICS

Italics are printed characters that *slant to the right like this.* To indicate italics in handwritten or typewritten work, use underlining.

13a. Use italics (underlining) for words, letters, and symbols referred to as such and for foreign words that have not been adopted into English.

EXAMPLES
The words *hiss* and *clang* are examples of onomatopoeia.
You typed *ie* instead of *ei.*
The motto *e pluribus unum* appears on all United States coins.

Resources

Grammar and Language
- *Language Handbook Worksheets,* pp. 125–132

1230 Resource Center Language Handbook

13b. Use italics (underlining) for titles of books, plays, long poems, periodicals, newspapers, works of art, films, television series, long musical compositions, recordings, comic strips, computer software, court cases, trains, ships, aircraft, and spacecraft.

TYPE OF NAME	EXAMPLE
Books	*The Canterbury Tales*
Plays	*The Taming of the Shrew*
Long Poems	*The Rime of the Ancient Mariner*
Periodicals	*Sports Illustrated*
Newspapers	*The Boston Globe*
Works of Art	*The Persistence of Memory*
Films	*It's a Wonderful Life*
TV Series	*American Playhouse*
Long Musical Compositions	*The Planets*
Recordings	*Unforgettable*
Comic Strips	*Doonesbury*
Computer Software	*Lotus 1-2-3*
Court Cases	*Marbury v. Madison*
Trains, Ships, Aircraft, and Spacecraft	*Orient Express* *Queen Elizabeth 2* *Enola Gay* *Apollo 13*

NOTE The article *the* before the title of a book, periodical, or newspaper is neither italicized nor capitalized unless it is part of the official title. The official title of a book appears on the book's title page. The official title of a periodical or newspaper is the name on its masthead, usually found on the editorial page.

EXAMPLES
What role does fate play in "The Seafarer"?
I found this information in *The New York Times*.
My mom looks through the *Sun-Times* every morning.

☞ For a list of titles that are enclosed in quotation marks, see 13d. For information about capitalizing titles, see 11e(3).

QUOTATION MARKS

13c. Use quotation marks to enclose a *direct quotation*—a person's exact words.

(1) A direct quotation usually begins with a capital letter.

EXAMPLE
Sir Francis Bacon wrote, "**K**nowledge is power."

However, when the quotation is only a part of a sentence, do not begin it with a capital letter.

EXAMPLE
In Act 1, Scene 5, Lady Macbeth describes her husband's nature as "**t**oo full o' th' milk of human kindness."

Do not use quotation marks to enclose an *indirect quotation* (a rewording of a direct quotation).

DIRECT QUOTATION	Al said, "I'm going fishing today."
INDIRECT QUOTATION	Al said that he is going fishing today.

(2) When the expression identifying the speaker divides a quoted sentence, the second part begins with a lowercase letter.

EXAMPLE
"All good moral philosophy," according to Sir Francis Bacon, "**i**s but the handmaid to religion."
[Notice that each part of a divided quotation is enclosed in quotation marks.]

When the second part of a divided quotation is a new sentence, the first word begins with a capital letter.

EXAMPLE
"On his first voyage, Gulliver finds himself in Lilliput," explained Ms. Chávez. "**T**he people there are only six inches tall."

(3) When used with quotation marks, other marks of punctuation are placed according to the following rules.

- Commas and periods are always placed inside the closing quotation marks.

EXAMPLES
"Read these lines**,**" he said, "and tell me what you think they mean**.**"

- Semicolons and colons are always placed outside the closing quotation marks.

EXAMPLES
Gloria promised, "I'll go to the dance with you"; however, she said that several weeks ago.
Find examples of the following figures of speech in Wordsworth's poem "I Wandered Lonely as a Cloud": personification, metaphor, and simile.

- Question marks and exclamation points are placed inside the closing quotation marks if the quotation itself is a question or an exclamation. Otherwise, they are placed outside.

EXAMPLES
Did Keats write "Ode on a Grecian Urn"?
"What an imagination you have!" exclaimed Beth.

(4) When quoting a passage that consists of more than one paragraph, put quotation marks at the beginning of each paragraph and at the end of only the last paragraph in the passage.

EXAMPLE
  "At Mr. Bowyers's, a great deal of company; some I knew, others I did not. Here we stayed upon the leads and below till it was late, expecting to see the fireworks; but they were not performed tonight. Only, the City had a light like a glory round about it, with bonfires.
  "At last I went to King Street; and there sent Crockford to my father's and my house to tell them I could not come home tonight, because of the dirt and a coach could not be had."
  —Samuel Pepys, *The Diary of Samuel Pepys*

(5) Use single quotation marks to enclose a quotation within a quotation.

EXAMPLE
Ms. Markham asked us, "What do you think John Donne meant when he said, 'No man is an island, entire of itself'?"

(6) When writing *dialogue* (a conversation), begin a new paragraph every time the speaker changes, and enclose each speaker's words in quotation marks.

EXAMPLE
  This frighted the fellow that attended about the work; but after some pause John Hayward, recovering himself, said, "Lord, bless us! There's somebody in the cart not quite dead!"
  So another called to him and said, "Who are you?"
  The fellow answered, "I am the poor piper. Where am I?"
  "Where are you?" says Hayward. "Why, you are in the dead-cart, and we are going to bury you."
  —Daniel Defoe, *A Journal of the Plague Year*

13d. Use quotation marks to enclose titles of short works, such as short stories, poems, essays, articles, songs, episodes of television series, and chapters and other parts of books.

TYPE OF NAME	EXAMPLE
Short Stories	"The Doll's House" "Games at Twilight"
Poems	"Ode to a Nightingale" "Thoughts of Hanoi"
Essays	"Shakespeare's Sister" "The Myth of Sisyphus"
Articles	"How to Improve Your Grades"
Songs	"Wind Beneath My Wings" "Frankie and Johnny"
TV Episodes	"Tony's Surprise Party" "Inside the Earth"
Chapters of a Book	"The Age of Reform" "How Ecosystems Change"

 NOTE Neither italics nor quotation marks are used for the titles of major religious texts or for the titles of historical or legal documents.

EXAMPLES
the Bible
Code of Hammurabi
Bill of Rights
Monroe Doctrine

 For a list of titles that are italicized, see 13b.

ELLIPSIS POINTS

13e. Use three spaced periods called *ellipsis points* (. . .) to mark omissions from quoted material and pauses in a written passage.

ORIGINAL At last she spoke to me. When she addressed the first words to me I was so confused that I did not know what to answer. She asked me was I going to *Araby*. I forget whether I answered yes or no. It would be a splendid bazaar, she said; she would love to go.
  —James Joyce, "Araby"

(1) If the quoted material that comes before the ellipsis points is not a complete sentence, use three ellipsis points with a space before the first point.

EXAMPLE
Of his conversation with Mangan's sister, the narrator says, "When she addressed the first words to me . . . I did not know what to answer."

(2) If the quoted material that comes before the ellipsis points is a complete sentence, use an end mark before the ellipsis points.

EXAMPLE
According to Mangan's sister, "It would be a splendid bazaar. . . ."

(3) If one sentence or more is omitted, ellipsis points follow any end mark that precedes the omitted material.

EXAMPLE
The narrator recalls his encounter with Mangan's sister: "At last she spoke to me. . . . She asked me was I going to *Araby*."

(4) To show that a full line or more of poetry has been omitted, use a line of spaced periods that is as long as the line of poetry above it.

ORIGINAL It fell about the Martinmas time,
        And a gay time it was then,
        When our goodwife got puddings to make,
        And she's boild them in the pan.
            —Traditional, "Get Up and Bar the Door"

ONE LINE It fell about the Martinmas time,
OMITTED   . . . .
        When our goodwife got puddings to make,
        And she's boild them in the pan.

APOSTROPHES

Possessive Case

13f. The *possessive case* of a noun or a pronoun indicates ownership or relationship. Use an apostrophe in forming the possessive case of nouns and indefinite pronouns.

(1) To form the possessive of a singular noun, add an apostrophe and an *s*.

EXAMPLES
Beowulf's shield   the principal's office

 When forming the possessive of a singular noun that ends in an *s* sound, add only an apostrophe if the addition of *'s* will make the noun awkward to pronounce. Otherwise, add *'s*.

EXAMPLES
Ms. Rodgers' class   the witness's testimony

(2) To form the possessive of a plural noun ending in *s*, add only the apostrophe.

EXAMPLES
the players' uniforms   the volunteers' efforts

(3) Form the possessive of only the last word in a compound word, in the name of an organization or business, or in a word group showing joint possession.

EXAMPLES
brother-in-law's car
Ralph Merrill and Company's products
Macbeth and Lady Macbeth's plan

 When a possessive pronoun is part of a word group showing joint possession, each noun in the word group is also possessive.

EXAMPLE
Chen's, Ramona's, and **my** project

(4) Form the possessive of each noun in a word group showing individual possession of similar items.

EXAMPLE
Byron's, Shelley's, and Keats's poems

(5) Possessive forms of words indicating time, such as *minute, day, month,* and *year,* and words indicating amounts in cents or dollars require apostrophes.

EXAMPLES
four weeks' vacation   a dollar's worth

(6) To form the possessive of an indefinite pronoun, add an apostrophe and an *s*.

EXAMPLES
no one's fault   somebody else's jacket

Contractions

13g. Use an apostrophe to show where letters, words, or numbers have been omitted in a contraction.

EXAMPLES
let us . . . . **let's**   she would . . . . . **she'd**
you will . . . . . **you'll**   1998 . . . . **'98**

The word *not* can be shortened to *–n't* and added to a verb, usually without changing the spelling of the verb.

EXAMPLES
do not . . . . **don't**   should not . . . **shouldn't**
EXCEPTION
will not . . . **won't**

Language Handbook **1233**

Plurals

13h. Use an apostrophe and an *s* to form the plurals of all lowercase letters, some uppercase letters, numerals, and some words referred to as words.

EXAMPLES
There are two *c*'s and two *m*'s in *accommodate*.
Try not to use so many *I*'s in your cover letter.
[Without the apostrophe, the plural of the pronoun *I* would spell *Is*.]

NOTE You may add only an *s* to form the plurals of words, numerals, and capital letters if the plural forms will not cause misreading. However, it is never wrong to use an apostrophe in such cases and is usually a good idea to do so.

EXAMPLE
James I ruled England during the early **1600s** [*or* 1600's].

HYPHENS

13i. Use a hyphen to divide a word at the end of a line.

- Do not divide a one-syllable word.

EXAMPLE
Did the Green Knight know that Sir Gawain had **kissed** [*not* kis-sed] his wife?

- Divide a word only between syllables.

EXAMPLE
First, Macbeth was killed; then he was **decapi-tated** [*not* decapita-ted].

- Divide an already hyphenated word at the hyphen.

EXAMPLE
Queen Elizabeth I was ruler of England for **forty-five** [*not* for-ty-five] years.

- Do not divide a word so that one letter stands alone.

EXAMPLE
Paradise Lost by John Milton is a famous English **epic** [*not* e-pic].

13j. Use a hyphen with compound numbers from twenty-one to ninety-nine and with fractions used as modifiers.

EXAMPLES
thirty-seven
a **three-fourths** majority [*but* three fourths of the voters]

DASHES

13k. Use dashes to set off abrupt breaks in thought.

EXAMPLE
The playwright handles her material—I should say lack of material—quite well.

13l. Use dashes to set off appositives or parenthetical expressions that contain commas.

EXAMPLE
Several of the British Romantic poets—Shelley, Keats, and Byron, for example—led fascinating lives.

13m. Use a dash to set off an introductory list or group of examples.

EXAMPLE
Alliteration, caesuras, and kennings—these are features of Anglo-Saxon poetry.

PARENTHESES

13n. Use parentheses to enclose informative or explanatory material of minor importance.

EXAMPLES
A *roman à clef* **(**literally, "novel with a key"**)** is a novel about real people to whom the novelist has assigned fictitious names.
The Globe **(**see the drawing on page 284**)** was built in 1599. [The *s* in *see* is lowercase because the parenthetical sentence is within a complete sentence.]
The Globe was built in 1599. **(**See the drawing on page 284.**)** [The *S* in *See* is capitalized and a period follows *page 284* because the parenthetical sentence is not within another sentence but instead stands on its own.]

BRACKETS

13o. Use brackets to enclose an explanation within quoted or parenthetical material.

EXAMPLE
The newspaper article stated that "at the time of that Democratic National Convention **[**in Chicago in 1968**]** there were many protest groups operating in the United States."

14 Spelling

UNDERSTANDING WORD STRUCTURE

Many English words are made up of roots and affixes (prefixes and suffixes).

Roots

The **root** of a word is the part that carries the word's core meaning.

ROOT	MEANING	EXAMPLES
–fin–	end, limit	final, infinite
–gram–	write, writing	grammar, epigram
–tract–	pull, draw	tractor, extract
–vit–	life	vitamin, vital

Prefixes

A **prefix** is one or more letters or syllables added to the beginning of a word or word part to create a new word.

PREFIX	MEANING	EXAMPLES
contra–	against	contradict, contrast
inter–	between, among	interstate, interact
mis–	not, wrongly	misfire, misspell
re–	back, again	reflect, refinance

Suffixes

A **suffix** is one or more letters or syllables added to the end of a word or word part to create a new word.

SUFFIX	MEANING	EXAMPLES
–fy	make, cause	verify, pacify
–ish	suggesting, like	smallish, childish
–ist	doer, believer	artist, humanist
–ty	quality, state	cruelty, certainty

SPELLING RULES

 Always keep in mind that the best way to be sure you have spelled a word correctly is to look the word up in a dictionary.

ie and *ei*

14a. Write *ie* when the sound is long *e*, except after *c*.

EXAMPLES
relieve   chief   field   conceit   deceive

EXCEPTIONS
either   leisure   neither   seize   protein

14b. Write *ei* when the sound is not long *e*.

EXAMPLES
reign   foreign   their   sovereign   weight

EXCEPTIONS
ancient   view   friend   mischief   conscience

 Rules 14a and 14b apply only when the *i* and the *e* are in the same syllable.

–cede, –ceed, and *–sede*

14c. The only English word ending in *–sede* is *supersede*. The only words ending in *–ceed* are *exceed, proceed,* and *succeed.* Most other words with this sound end in *–cede.*

EXAMPLES
con**cede**   pre**cede**   re**cede**   se**cede**

Adding Prefixes

14d. When adding a prefix, do not change the spelling of the original word.

EXAMPLES
over + run = **over**run   mis + spell = **mis**spell

Adding Suffixes

14e. When adding the suffix *–ness* or *–ly,* do not change the spelling of the original word.

EXAMPLES
gentle + ness = gentle**ness**   final + ly = final**ly**

Language Handbook 1235

Resources

Grammar and Language
- *Language Handbook Worksheets,* pp. 133–140

affect, effect *Affect* is a verb meaning "to influence." *Effect* may be either a verb meaning "to bring about or to accomplish" or a noun meaning "the result [of an action]."

EXAMPLES
How did the murder of King Duncan **affect** Lady Macbeth? [verb]
In this dispute, management and labor should be able to **effect** a compromise. [verb]
What far-reaching **effects** did the *Brown* v. *Board of Education of Topeka* decision have? [noun]

all ready, already *All ready* means "all prepared." *Already* means "previously."

EXAMPLES
Are you **all ready** for the audition?
We have **already** read "The Seafarer."

all right *All right* means "satisfactory," "unhurt; safe," "correct," or, in reply to a question or to preface a remark, "yes." *Alright* is a misspelling.

EXAMPLES
Does this look **all right** [*not* alright]?
Oh, **all right** [*not* alright], you can go.

all the farther, all the faster Avoid using these expressions in formal situations. Use *as far as* or *as fast as*.

EXAMPLE
Is that **as fast as** [*not* all the faster] Chris can run?

all together, altogether *All together* means "everyone in the same place." *Altogether* means "entirely."

EXAMPLES
The knights were **all together** for the celebration.
Sir Gawain was not **altogether** honest with the Green Knight.

allusion, illusion An *allusion* is an indirect reference to something. An *illusion* is a mistaken idea or a misleading appearance.

EXAMPLES
The speaker made an **allusion** to Emily Brontë's *Wuthering Heights*.
Before selecting a career, he had to abandon some of his **illusions** about his own abilities.
The director chose certain colors to create an **illusion** of depth on the small stage.

a lot Avoid this expression in formal situations by using *many* or *much*.

EXAMPLE
Many [*not* a lot] of my friends work part time after school and on weekends.

already See **all ready, already**.

altogether See **all together, altogether**.

among See **between, among**.

and etc. *Etc.* stands for the Latin words *et cetera*, meaning "and others" or "and so forth." Always avoid using *and* before *etc.* In general, avoid using *etc.* in formal situations. Use one of its meanings instead.

EXAMPLE
We are comparing the main female characters in Shakespeare's tragedies: Lady Macbeth, Cleopatra, Juliet, **and others** [*or* etc. *but not* and etc.].

any one, anyone The expression *any one* specifies one member of a group. *Anyone* means "one person, no matter which."

EXAMPLES
Any one of you could win the poetry contest.
Anyone who finishes the test early may leave.

as See **like, as**.

as if See **like, as if**.

at Avoid using *at* after a construction beginning with *where*.

NONSTANDARD Where was Beowulf at when Grendel's mother attacked?
STANDARD **Where** was Beowulf when Grendel's mother attacked?

a while, awhile *A while* means "a period of time." *Awhile* means "for a short time."

EXAMPLES
Herot remained empty for quite **a while**.
They stayed there **awhile**.

bad, badly *Bad* is an adjective. *Badly* is an adverb. In standard English, *bad* should follow a sense verb, such as *feel, look, sound, taste,* or *smell,* or other linking verb.

EXAMPLE
The prospects for fair weather look **bad** [*not* badly].

because In formal situations, do not use the construction *reason . . . because*. Instead, use *reason . . . that*.

EXAMPLE
The **reason** Sir Gawain accepts the green sash is **that** [*not* because] he thinks it will protect him from the Green Knight.

being as, being that Avoid using either of these expressions for *since* or *because*.

EXAMPLE
Because [*not* being as *or* being that] Sir Gawain is a knight, we expect him to behave chivalrously.

beside, besides   *Beside* means "by the side of" or "next to." *Besides* means "in addition to" or "other than" or "moreover."

EXAMPLES
The Geats built Beowulf's tomb **beside** the sea.
No one **besides** Wiglaf helped Beowulf battle the dragon.
I have decided that I do not want to take journalism; **besides,** I cannot fit it into my schedule.

between, among   Use *between* to refer to only two items or to more than two when comparing each item individually to each of the others.

EXAMPLES
The reward money will be divided **between** Chang and Marta.
Sasha explained the difference **between** assonance, consonance, and alliteration. [Each item is compared individually to each of the others.]

Use *among* to refer to more than two items when you are not considering each item in relation to each other item individually.

EXAMPLE
The reward money will be divided **among** the four girls.

bring, take   *Bring* means "to come carrying something." *Take* means "to go carrying something."

EXAMPLES
I'll **bring** my copy of *Gulliver's Travels* when I come over.
Please **take** the model of the Globe Theater to the library.

bust, busted   Avoid using these words as verbs. Instead, use a form of *break* or *burst,* depending on the meaning.

EXAMPLES
The window is **broken** [*not* busted].
The water main has **burst** [*not* busted] open.

can, may   Use *can* to express ability. Use *may* to express possibility.

EXAMPLES
Can you play the guitar?
It **may** rain later.

cannot (can't) help but   Avoid using *but* and the infinitive form of a verb after the expression *cannot (can't) help.* Instead, use a gerund alone.

NONSTANDARD	I can't help but laugh when I look at that photograph.
STANDARD	I can't help **laughing** when I look at that photograph.

compare, contrast   Used with *to, compare* means "to look for similarities between." Used with *with, compare* means "to look for both similarities and differences between." *Contrast* is always used to point out differences.

EXAMPLES
The simile at the end of the poem **compares** the eagle's fall **to** a thunderbolt.
We **compared** Shakespeare's style **with** that of Christopher Marlowe.
The tour guide also **contrasted** the two castles' provisions for defense.

could of   See **of.**

double subject   Avoid using an unnecessary pronoun after the subject of a sentence.

EXAMPLE
George Bernard Shaw [*not* George Bernard Shaw he] wrote *Pygmalion.*

due to   Avoid using *due to* for "because of" or "owing to."

EXAMPLE
All schools were closed **because of** [*not* due to] inclement weather.

effect   See **affect, effect.**

either, neither   *Either* usually means "one or the other of two." In referring to more than two, use *any one* or *any* instead. *Neither* usually means "not one or the other of two." In referring to more than two, use *none* instead.

EXAMPLES
Either of the two quotations would be appropriate to use at the beginning of your speech.
You should be able to find ample information about **any one** of those four poets.
Neither of the Perez twins is in school today.
None of the seniors have voted yet.

etc.   See **and etc.**

every day, everyday   *Every day* means "each day." *Everyday* means "daily," "ordinary," or "usual."

EXAMPLES
Every day presents its own challenges.
The party will be casual; wear **everyday** clothes.

every one, everyone   *Every one* specifies every single person or thing of those named. *Everyone* means "everybody, all of the people named."

EXAMPLES
Elizabeth Bowen wrote **every one** of these stories.
Did **everyone** read "The Demon Lover"?

except See **accept, except.**

farther, further Use *farther* to express physical distance. Use *further* to express abstract relationships of degree or quantity.

EXAMPLES
Your house is **farther** from school than mine is.
The United Nations members decided that **further** debate was unnecessary.

fewer, less Use *fewer* to modify a plural noun and *less* to modify a singular noun.

EXAMPLES
Fewer students are going out for football this year.
Now I spend **less** time watching TV.

good, well Avoid using the adjective *good* to modify an action verb. Instead, use the adverb *well*, meaning "capably" or "satisfactorily."

EXAMPLE
We did **well** [*not* good] on the exam.

Used as an adjective, *well* means "in good health" or "satisfactory in appearance or condition."

EXAMPLES
I feel **well**.
It's eight o'clock, and all is **well**.

had of See **of.**

had ought, hadn't ought Do not use *had* or *hadn't* with *ought*.

EXAMPLES
Your application **ought** [*not* had ought] to have been sent in earlier.
She **ought not** [*not* hadn't ought] to swim so soon after eating lunch.

illusion See **allusion, illusion.**

imply, infer *Imply* means "to suggest indirectly." *Infer* means "to interpret" or "to draw a conclusion."

EXAMPLES
The speaker of "To a Skylark" **implies** that the skylark is a divine being.
I **inferred** from her speech that she would support a statewide testing program.

in, in to, into *In* generally shows location. In the construction *in to*, *in* is an adverb followed by the preposition *to*. *Into* generally shows direction.

EXAMPLES
Rudyard Kipling was born **in** Bombay.
He found the treasure and turned it **in to** his king.
Sir Gawain rode **into** the wilderness to find the Green Knight.

infer See **imply, infer.**

irregardless, regardless *Irregardless* is nonstandard. Use *regardless* instead.

EXAMPLE
Regardless [*not* irregardless] of the danger, he continued his journey.

its, it's *Its* is the possessive form of *it*. *It's* is the contraction of *it is* or *it has*.

EXAMPLES
The community is proud of **its** school system.
It's [it is] a symbol of peace.
It's [it has] been cooler today.

kind of, sort of In formal situations, avoid using these terms for the adverb *somewhat* or *rather*.

INFORMAL	Macbeth appeared to be kind of worried.
FORMAL	Macbeth appeared to be **rather** [*or* **somewhat**] worried.

kind of a(n), sort of a(n) In formal situations, omit the *a(n)*.

INFORMAL	What kind of a poem is "The Passionate Shepherd to His Love"?
FORMAL	What **kind of** poem is "The Passionate Shepherd to His Love"?

kind(s), sort(s), type(s) With the singular form of each of these nouns, use *this* or *that*. With the plural form, use *these* or *those*.

EXAMPLES
This type of engine performs more economically than any of **those types.**

less See **fewer, less.**

lie, lay The verb *lie* means "to rest" or "to stay, to recline, or to remain in a certain state or position." Its principal parts are *lie, lying, lay,* and *lain*. *Lie* never takes an object. The verb *lay* means "to put [something] in a place." Its principal parts are *lay, laying, laid,* and *laid*. *Lay* usually takes an object.

EXAMPLES
Gulliver was **lying** on his back and could hardly move. [no object]
The Lilliputians **laid** baskets of food near Gulliver's mouth. [*Baskets* is the object of *laid*.]

like, as In formal situations, do not use *like* for *as* to introduce a subordinate clause.

INFORMAL	John looks like his father looked twenty years ago.
FORMAL	John looks **as** his father looked twenty years ago.

like, as if   In formal situations, avoid using the preposition *like* for the compound conjunction *as if* or *as though* to introduce a subordinate clause.

INFORMAL   The heavy footsteps sounded like they were coming nearer.

FORMAL   The heavy footsteps sounded **as if** [*or* **as though**] they were coming nearer.

might of, must of   See **of.**

neither   See **either, neither.**

nor   See **or, nor.**

of   *Of* is a preposition. Do not use *of* in place of *have* after verbs such as *could, should, would, might, must,* and *ought* [*to*]. Also, do not use *had of* for *had.*

EXAMPLES
If I **had** [*not* had of] known about the shortcut, I **would have** [*not* would of] been here sooner.

Avoid using *of* after other prepositions such as *inside, off,* and *outside.*

EXAMPLE
Flimnap fell **off** [*not* off of] the tightrope.

off, off of   Do not use *off* or *off of* for *from.*

EXAMPLE
You can get a program **from** [*not* off of] the usher.

on to, onto   In the expression *on to, on* is an adverb and *to* is a preposition. *Onto* is a preposition.

EXAMPLES
The lecturer moved **on to** her next main idea.
She walked **onto** the stage.

or, nor   Use *or* with *either*; use *nor* with *neither*.

EXAMPLES
The list of authors does not include **either** James Joyce **or** [*not* nor] D. H. Lawrence.
Neither James Joyce **nor** D. H. Lawrence is on the list of authors.

ought   See **had ought, hadn't ought.**

ought to of   See **of.**

raise   See **rise, raise.**

reason . . . because   See **because.**

refer back   Since the prefix *re–* in *refer* means "back," adding *back* is generally unnecessary.

EXAMPLE
The writer is **referring** [*not* referring back] to the years when he lived in Ireland.

rise, raise   The verb *rise* means "to go up" or "to get up." Its principal parts are *rise, rising, rose,* and *risen. Rise* never takes an object. The verb *raise* means "to cause [something] to rise" or "to lift up." Its principal parts are *raise, raising, raised,* and *raised. Raise* usually takes an object.

EXAMPLES
Her blood pressure **rose** as she waited. [no object]
The Green Knight **raised** the ax above his head. [*Ax* is the object of *raised.*]

should of   See **of.**

sit, set   The verb *sit* means "to rest in an upright, seated position." Its principal parts are *sit, sitting, sat,* and *sat. Sit* seldom takes an object. The verb *set* means "to put [something] in a place." Its principal parts are *set, setting, set,* and *set. Set* usually takes an object.

EXAMPLES
Banquo's ghost **sits** in Macbeth's place. [no object]
Please **set** the groceries on the table. [*Groceries* is the object of *set.*]

some, somewhat   In formal situations, avoid using *some* to mean "to some extent." Use *somewhat.*

EXAMPLE
The Wedding Guest was somewhat shaken [*not* shaken some] by the Ancient Mariner's gaze and appearance.

sort(s)   See **kind(s), sort(s), type(s)** and **kind of a(n), sort of a(n).**

sort of   See **kind of, sort of.**

take   See **bring, take.**

than, then   *Than* is a conjunction used in comparisons. *Then* is an adverb meaning "at that time" or "next."

EXAMPLES
Is King Macbeth more superstitious **than** Lady Macbeth?
First, we will read "The Lamb"; **then**, we will read "The Tyger."

that   See **who, which, that.**

their, there, they're   *Their* is a possessive form of *they.* As an adverb, *there* means "at that place." *There* is also used to begin a sentence. *They're* is the contraction of *they are.*

EXAMPLES
They built a tomb for **their** fallen leader.
Macduff was not **there** at the time.
There is very little time left.
They're waiting for Banquo.

theirs, there's   *Theirs* is a possessive form of the pronoun *they*. *There's* is the contraction of *there is*.

EXAMPLES
The treasure is **theirs** now.
There's an allusion to the Bible in the poem.

them   Do not use *them* as an adjective. Use *those*.

EXAMPLE
Have you seen **those** [*not* them] murals by Judith Baca at the art museum?

then   See **than, then**.

there   See **their, there, they're**.

there's   See **theirs, there's**.

they're   See **their, there, they're**.

this here, that there   Avoid using *here* or *there* after *this* or *that*.

EXAMPLE
This [*not* this here] poem was written by Robert Browning.

try and, try to   Use *try to*, not *try and*.

EXAMPLE
I will **try to** [*not* try and] finish reading *The Diary of Samuel Pepys* tonight.

type, type of   Avoid using the noun *type* as an adjective. Add *of* after *type*.

EXAMPLE
What **type of** [*not* type] character is the knight in "The Wife of Bath's Tale"?

type(s)   See **kind(s), sort(s), type(s)**.

ways   Use *way*, not *ways*, when referring to distance.

EXAMPLE
Is Canterbury a long **way** [*not* ways] from the Tabard Inn?

well   See **good, well**.

when, where   Do not use *when* or *where* to begin a definition.

NONSTANDARD   A caesura is where you break or pause in a line of poetry.
STANDARD   A caesura is **a break or pause in a line of poetry**.

where   Do not use *where* in place of *that*.

EXAMPLE
I read **that** [*not* where] you won a scholarship.

where . . . at   See **at**.

who, which, that   *Who* refers to persons only. *Which* refers to things only. *That* may refer to either persons or things.

EXAMPLES
Sir Gawain was the knight **who** [*or* that] accepted the Green Knight's challenge.
The Globe, **which** was built in 1599, burned down in 1613.
Is this the only poem **that** Sir Walter Raleigh ever wrote?

who's, whose   *Who's* is the contraction of *who is* or *who has*. *Whose* is the possessive form of *who*.

EXAMPLES
Well, look **who's** [who is] here!
Who's [who has] read all of the play?
Whose treasure is it?

would of   See **of**.

your, you're   *Your* is a possessive form of *you*. *You're* is the contraction of *you are*.

EXAMPLES
Is that **your** car?
I can see that **you're** tired.

Glossary

The glossary that follows is an alphabetical list of words found in the selections in this book. Use this glossary just as you would use a dictionary—to find out the meanings of unfamiliar words. (Some technical, foreign, and more obscure words in this book are not listed here but instead are defined for you in the footnotes that accompany many of the selections.)

Many words in the English language have more than one meaning. This glossary gives the meanings that apply to the words as they are used in the selections in this book. Words closely related in form and meaning are usually listed together in one entry (for instance, compassion and compassionate), and the definition is given for the first form.

The following abbreviations are used:

adj.	adjective
adv.	adverb
n.	noun
v.	verb

Each word's pronunciation is given in parentheses. A guide to the pronunciation symbols appears at the bottom of every other page. For more information about the words in this glossary or for information about words not listed here, consult a dictionary.

A

abate (ə·bāt′) v.: lessen.
abominable (ə·bäm′ə·nə·bəl) adj.: disgusting; hateful.
abrogate (ab′rə·gāt) v.: abolish; repeal. —**abrogated** v. used as adj.
absolve (ab·zälv′) v.: forgive; make free from blame.
abstain (ab·stān′) v.: refrain from.
accrue (ə·kroō′) v.: increase over time.
adversary (ad′vər·ser′ē) n.: enemy.
aesthetic (es·thet′ik) n.: principle of beauty.
affectation (af′ek·tā′shən) n.: artificial behavior designed to impress others.
affinity (ə·fin′i·tē) n.: kinship; bond.
affliction (ə·flik′shən) n.: suffering.
aggrieved (ə·grēvd′) adj.: offended.
agility (ə·jil′ə·tē) n.: ability to move quickly and easily.
allure (ə·loor′) v.: tempt; attract.
altruistic (al′troō·is′tik) adj.: unselfish.
amiable (ā′mē·ə·bəl) adj.: friendly; likeable.
animosity (an′ə·mäs′ə·tē) n.: hostility; violent hatred or resentment.
annihilate (ə·nī′ə·lāt′) v.: destroy; make nonexistent.
annul (ə·nul′) v.: do away with; cancel.
antipathy (an·tip′ə·thē) n.: strong dislike; aversion
aperture (ap′ər·chər) n.: opening.
approbation (ap′rə·bā′shən) n.: approval.
arable (ar′ə·bəl) adj.: fit to be farmed or cultivated.
arbitrate (är′bə·trāt′) v.: settle or decide by listening to both sides of an argument.
arrest (ə·rest′) v.: check or halt in motion. —**arrested** v. used as adj.
artifice (ärt′ə·fis) n.: trickery; deception.
assail (ə·sāl′) v.: attack; assault.
assent (ə·sent′) n.: acceptance.
assert (ə·surt′) v.: declare.
assuage (ə·swāj′) v.: ease; calm.
audacious (ô·dā′shəs) adj.: bold. —**audaciously** adv.
austere (ô·stir′) adj.: restrained; spare; very plain.
avail (ə·vāl′) n.: benefit; advantage.
avarice (av′ə·ris) n.: too great a desire for wealth.

B

benign (bi·nīn′) adj.: kind; gracious.
bequest (bē·kwest′) n.: gift left by means of a will.
bibliophile (bib′lē·ə·fīl) n.: one who loves books.

---

at, āte, cär; ten, ēve; is, īce; gō, hôrn, look, tool; oil, out; up, fur; ə for unstressed vowels, as a in ago, u in focus; ′ as in Latin (lat′'n); chin; she; thin; the; ŋ as in ring (riŋ); zh as in azure (azh′ər)

Glossary 1243

suppress (sə·pres′) v.: keep from being known. —**suppressed** v. used as adj.
surreptitious (sur′əp·tish′əs) adj.: sneaky or stealthy. —**surreptitiously** adv.
sustenance (sus′tə·nəns) n.: food or money to support life.

T

taciturn (tas′ə·turn′) adj.: not talkative.
temerity (tə·mer′ə·tē) n.: foolish or rash boldness; recklessness.
temper (tem′pər) v.: moderate; tone down. —**tempering** v. used as adj.
temporal (tem′pə·rəl) adj.: limited to this world; not spiritual.
tentative (ten′tə·tiv) adj.: hesitant; uncertain.
tepid (tep′id) adj.: lukewarm.
titillate (tit″l·āt′) v.: excite; stimulate. —**titillating** v. used as adj.
transcend (tran·send′) v.: exceed; surpass.
transfigure (trans·fig′yər) v.: change the form of.
transgress (trans·gres′) v.: sin against; violate a limit.
translucent (trans·lōō′sənt) adj.: partially transparent.
tyrannous (tir′ə·nəs) adj.: harsh; oppressive.

U

uncanny (un·kan′ē) adj.: strange; eerie; weird.
unmarred (ən·märd′) adj.: undamaged; unspoiled.
unpretentious (ən·prē·ten′shəs) adj.: modest.
untainted (ən·tānt′id) adj.: untarnished; without a trace of anything offensive.

V

vehement (vē′ə·mənt) adj.: violent. —**vehemently** adv.
victuals (vit″lz) n.: provisions; pieces of food.
vigil (vij′əl) n.: staying watchfully awake.
vitiate (vish′ē·āt) v.: impair; weaken; spoil.
vivacity (vī·vas′ə·tē) n.: liveliness; high-spiritedness.

W

wince (wins) v.: flinch; draw back.
wrenched (rencht) v.: anguished; grief-stricken.

Z

zealous (zel′əs) adj.: fervent; devoted. —**zealously** adv.

Spanish Glossary

A

abate/reducir v. disminuir; aminorar; atenuar.
abominable/abominable adj. espantoso; detestable; horrible.
abrogate/abrogar v. abolir; invalidar; revocar.
absolve/absolver v. perdonar; indultar; dispensar.
abstain/abstenerse v. privarse; renunciar; callarse.
accrue/acumularse v. incrementar con el tiempo; crecer.
adversary/adversario s. enemigo; contrincante; antagonista.
aesthetic/estético s. artístico, fundamento de la belleza.
affectation/afectación s. simulación; comportamiento artificial con el fin de impresionar a los demás.
affinity/afinidad s. simpatía; atracción.
affliction/aflicción s. pesar; angustia; consternación.
aggrieved/agraviado adj. resentido; ofendido; maltratado.
agility/agilidad s. ligereza; velocidad; prontitud; presteza.
allure/atraer v. seducir; cautivar; conquistar.
altruistic/altruista adj. generoso; filántropo; sin egoísmo.
amiable/amable adj. afable; simpático; cordial.
animosity/animosidad s. antipatía; rencor; aversión; hostilidad.
annihilate/aniquilar v. destruir; exterminar.
annul/anular v. abolir; cancelar; revocar.
antipathy/antipatía s. hostilidad; repugnancia; aversión.
aperture/abertura s. rendija; grieta.
approbation/aprobación s. asentimiento; conformidad; adhesión.
arable/arable adj. cultivable; labradero.
arbitrate/arbitrar v. mediar; interceder; resolver; juzgar.
arrest/arrestar v. detener; interrumpir; demorar; retrasar; permanecer quieto.
artifice/artificio s. engaño; ardid; astucia.
assail/asaltar v. atacar; acometer un ataque; abrumar con preguntas.
assent/asentimiento n. afirmación; consentimiento; confirmación; aceptación.
assert/afirmar v. aseverar; asegurar; sostener.
assuage/aliviar v. mitigar; calmar; apaciguar.
audacious/audaz adj. atrevido; intrépido; osado.
assailant/asaltante s. atracador; agresor.
austere/austero adj. sobrio; riguroso; serio; sin adornos.
avail/servir v. sacar partido de; valerse de; utilizar.
avarice/avaricia s. codicia; egoísmo.

B

benign/benigno adj. favorable; sano; propicio; clemente.
bequest/legado s. cesión; herencia; obsequio realizado mediante un testamento.
bibliophile/bibliófilo adj. coleccionista de, o experto en libros; amante de los libros.
botanical/botánico adj. que trata de las plantas; asociado con la ciencia de la botánica.
brandish/blandir v. esgrimir; empuñar; aferrar.
brevity/brevedad s. laconismo; concisión; abreviación.
buoyancy/júbilo s. ligereza de espíritu; alegría; estar por las nubes.

C

candor/sinceridad s. franqueza; imparcialidad; candidez; ingenuidad.
capacity/capacidad s. facultad; volumen; aptitud.
caprice/capricho s. deseo repentino; extravagancia; antojo.
caste/casta s. clase social; casta; linaje.
censure/censurar v. condemnar; criticar; desaprobar.
clamber/encaramarse v. subir a gatas; ascender; trepar.
clemency/clemencia s. piedad; misericordia; compasión.

Spanish Glossary

clamor/clamor s. estruendo; ruido; fragor.
coherent/coherente adj. lógico; claro; razonable.
commiserate/compadecer adj. expresar simpatía; apiadarse; conmoverse.
compensate/compensar v. indemnizar; remediar; igualar.
compulsory/obligatorio adj. requerido por una regla o por la ley; forzoso.
concede/conceder v. otorgar; conferir; asignar; agraciar.
condescension/condescendencia s. consentimiento; tolerancia; complacencia.
confounded/confundido adj. desconcertado; confuso.
congeal/congelar v. cuajar; solidificar; coagular; solidificar.
console/consolar v. tranquilizar; calmar; dar sosiego.
conspicuous/visible adj. obvio; llamativo; notable; patente; que llama la atención.
consternation/consternación s. abatimiento; aturdimiento tras un susto o un disgusto.
contemptuous/despreciativo adj. peyorativo; frío; indiferente.
contention/contienda s. disputa; controversia; discusión.
contortion/contorsión s. encogimiento; espasmo; forma o movimiento torcido.
contrive/lograr v. idear; inventar; ingeniárselas; conseguir.
corpulent/corpulento adj. gordo; voluminoso; enorme.
cosmopolitan/cosmopolita adj. internacional; vividor; mundano.
credential/credencial s. título; comprobante; justificante; cédula.
culinary/culinario adj. nutricio; alimenticio; asociado con la cocina.
cursory/precipitado adj. rápido; superficial.

D

daunt/intimidar v. desanimar; desalentar.
decree/decreto s. orden; mandato; ley.
deference/deferencia s. atención; respeto; educación.
defile/ensuciar v. manchar; contaminar; calumniar.
deject/descorazonar v. acobardar; desalentar; desmoralizar.
delusion/engaño s. error; confusión; espejismo.
demented/demente adj. ido; loco; tocado.
demolition/demolición s. desmoronamiento; derrumbe; destrucción.
desist/desistir v. renunciar; dimitir; ceder.
desolation/desolación s. tristeza; congoja; ruina; devastación.
diabolic/diabólico adj. perverso; infernal; malo; maléfico.
digress/desviarse v. apartarse del tema principal.
diligence/diligencia s. encargo; esmero; atención.
diminutive/diminuto adj. minúsculo; pequeño.
dire/terrible adj. espantoso; horrible; medida extrema o necesidad urgente.
discern/discernir v. comprender; distinguir; reconocer la diferencia.
discomfiture/desconcierto s. confusión; sorpresa; turbación.
disconcerted/desconcertado adj. trastornado; perturbado; alterado.
disconsolate/desconsolado adj. que causa tristeza o depresión; afligido; dolorido.
discourse/discurso s. alocución; oración.
discrimination/discriminación s. destreza en realizar distinciones finas.
dismal/deprimente adj. triste; patético; penoso.
disparage/menospreciar v. desdeñar; deslucir; rebajar.
dispassionate/desapasionado adj. imparcial; objetivo; falto de emoción. —**dispassionately/desapasionadamente** adv. imparcialmente; fríamente.
disperse/dispersar v. desordenar; desmontar.
disposition/disposición s. inclinación; carácter; tendencia.
dissuade/disuadir v. impedir; prohibir.
distend/distender v. hinchar; dilatar; alargar.
distill/destilar v. condensar; sublimar; extraer una esencia.
distraught/turbado adj. loco; enloquecido; trastornado.
divinity/divinidad s. Dios; deidad; ente sagrado.
dogged/tenaz adj. persistente; obstinado; terco.
duress/coerción s. coacción; imposición; tiranía.

E

efficacy/eficacia s. capacidad; destreza en producir el efecto deseado.
emanate/emanó v. procedió; derivó; brotó de una fuente.
eminent/eminente adj. ilustre; excepcional; notable.

endow/dotar *v.* hacer una donación; proporcionar; equipar; abastecer.
enmity/enemistad *s.* hostilidad; odio; antipatía.
ethereal/etéreo *adj.* celeste; sutil; impalpable; que no es de la tierra; espiritual.
exhilaration/exaltación *v.* entusiasmo; alegría; regocijo.
expedient/conveniencia *s.* utilidad; provecho.
exploit/hazaña *s.* proeza; gesta; iniciativa.
exquisite/exquisito *adj.* delicado; fino; elegante; distinguido.
extol/alabar *v.* encomiar; ensalzar; glorificar.
extort/extorsionar *v.* despojar; obtener mediante amenazas o violencia.
exult/exultar *v.* no caber en sí; gozar; exaltarse.

F

fastidious/melindroso *adj.* delicado; quisquilloso; caprichoso.
fawning/adulador *adj.* servil; lisonjero; halagador.
fickleness/inconstancia *s.* veleidad; informalidad.
flaccid/flácido *adj.* fofo; lacio; caído.
flag/flaquear *v.* aflojar; desistir.
formidable/formidable *adj.* tremendo; terrible; impresionante; que inspira la admiración de otros; que causa pavor.
frivolous/frívolo *adj.* de poco peso; mundano; trivial; de poca importancia.
frugal/frugal *adj.* sobrio; parco; abstinente.
furl/plegar *v.* aferrar las velas; poner una bandera a media asta; enrollar.

G

gallant/galante *adj.* atento; noble; rendido.
garrulous/locuaz *adj.* parlanchín; indiscreto; que habla mucho de temas poco importantes.
genial/simpático *adj.* afable; cordial.
geniality/simpatía *s.* amistad; afinidad.
ghastly/horroroso *adj.* espantoso; repulsivo; horrible.
glut/saciar *v.* inundar; hartar; saturar.
grievous/doloroso *adj.* penoso; cruel; lamentable.
grisly/horroroso *adj.* espantoso; aterrador; grotesco.
grovel/arrastrarse *v.* humillarse; someterse; mortificarse.
guffaw/carcajada *s.* risotada; carcajada; risa.
guile/engaño *s.* astucia; ardid; disimulo.

H

haggard/ojeroso *adj.* pálido; exangüe; agotado; marchito.
haggle/regatear *v.* debatir un precio.

I

ignoble/innoble *s.* vil; indigno; infame.
ignominy/ignominia *s.* infamia; deshonor; bajeza.
illusory/ilusorio *adj.* ficticio; irreal; imaginario; inexistente.
impassive/impasible *adj.* inalterable; inmutable.
impediment/impedimento *s.* obstáculo; dificultad; estorbo.
imperturbarble/imperturbable *adj.* inalterable; tranquilo; sereno.
impetuous/impetuoso *adj.* impulsivo; precipitado.
impinge/tocar *v.* tropezar con; chocar.
implacable/implacable *adj.* inclemente; severo; inflexible; que no cambia.
impromptu/improvisado *adj.* espontáneo; imprevisto; intuitivo.
improvise/improvisar *v.* crear; inventar; ingeniárselas con lo que hay.
inaccessible/inaccesible *adj.* impenetrable; cerrado; que no se puede acceder.
incessant/incesante *adj.* constante; continuo; perpetuo.
incliniation/inclinación *s.* predisposición; índole; tendencia.
incur/contraer *v.* incurrir en gastos; sufrir.
indiscriminate/indistinto *adj.* sin criterio; confuso; indeterminado.
induce/inducir *v.* persuadir; convencer; incitar.
indulgent/indulgente *adj.* tolerante; complaciente; blando.
inevitable/inevitable *adj.* necesario; irremediable; fijo.
infallible/infalible *adj.* seguro; incontestable; positivo; indudable.
infernal/infernal *adj.* diabólico; maléfico; endiablado.
ingratiating/zalamero *adj.* lisonjero; alabador.
initiative/iniciativa *s.* decisión; ingenio; atrevimiento.
insipid/insípido *adj.* soso; aburrido; incoloro.
intermittent/intermitente *adj.* esporádico; ocasional; que ocurre o aparece alternamente.
intoxicate/embriagar *v.* arrebatar; extasiar; encantar; entusiasmar.
intricate/intrincado *adj.* complejo; enrevesado; lleno de detalles espinosos.

iridescente/iridiscente *adj.* irisado; con los colores del arco iris; resplandeciente; brillante.
itinerant/itinerante *adj.* ambulante; de viaje; errante; nómada.

L

labyrinth/laberinto *s.* meandro; embrollo; enredo.
lamentable/lamentable *adj.* triste; deplorable; calamitoso.
lavish/pródigo *adj.* generoso; extravagante; profuso.
lethargy/letargo *s.* sopor; modorra; somnolencia.
livid/lívido *adj.* pálido; descolorido; exangüe; demacrado.
lugubrious/lúgubre *adj.* sombrío; tétrico; exageradamente solemne.

M

malice/malicia *s.* picardía; perfidia; deseo de hacer el mal.
maniacal/maníaco *adj.* trastornado; locamente entusiasta; desatinado; frenético
meticulous/meticuloso *adj.* minucioso; exacto; concienzudo.
misanthropy/misantropía *s.* misoginia; ascetismo; desdén por la raza humana.
monotonous/monótono *adj.* aburrido; continuo; iterativo; sin variación.

N

nimble/ágil *adj.* vivo; ligero.
notorious/célebre *adj.* famoso; popular; conocido; renombrado; un criminal notorio.

O

obscure/oscurecer *adj.* oscuro; desconocido; humilde; retirado.
obstinate/obstinado *adj.* terco; testarudo.
oppressive/opresivo *adj.* angustioso; difícil de soportar.
ostentatious/ostentoso *adj.* aparatoso; teatral; grandioso.
overwrought/sobreexcitado *adj.* emocionado; alterado; estimulado; conmovido.

P

pallor/palidez *s.* anemia; lividez.
partial/parcial *adj.* un juicio arbitrario; improcedente.
patronize/patronizar *v.* ser cliente de; favorecer; proteger.
pedantic/pedante *adj.* fatuo; afectado; que demuestra un interés desmesurado en los libros, la educación y las reglas.
pensive/pensativo *adj.* meditabundo; ensimismado; absorto.
perfunctory/negligente *adj.* descuidado; superficial; somero.
persevere/perseverar *v.* persistir; empeñarse; obstinarse.
pervade/extenderse *v.* difundirse; propagarse; esparcirse.
perverse/perverso *adj.* perjudicial; contrario; nocivo.
pestilence/pestilencia *s.* plaga; peste; epidemia.
pique/pique *s.* resentimiento; disgusto; molestia.
piteous/patético *adj.* lastimoso; lúgubre; lloroso.
pitiable/lastimoso *adj.* lamentable; deplorable; penoso.
posterity/posteridad *s.* descendencia; sucesión; porvenir; generaciones futuras.
precedent/precedente *s.* antecedente; primer ocurrencia de algo que servirá de norma en el futuro; referencia.
precipitate/precipitado *adj.* lanzado; atolondrado.
preliminary/preliminar *adj.* preparatorio; inicial; básico.
presumption/presunción *s.* engreimiento; jactancia; petulancia.
pretext/pretexto *s.* evasiva; excusa; justificación.
prevail/prevalecer *v.* triunfar; vencer.
procure/proporcionar *v.* obtener; conseguir; lograr.
prodigious/prodigioso *adj.* maravilloso; enorme; fuera de serie.
prodigy/prodigio *s.* fenómeno; niño dotado de un talento extraordinario.
profuse/profuso *adj.* abundante; pródigo; copioso.
propagate/propagar *v.* irradiar; difundir; popularizar.
propensity/propensión *s.* preferencia; inclinación; tendencia.
propitious/propicio *adj.* favorable; próspero; ventajoso.
prosaic/prosaico *adj.* insulso; mediocre; ordinario; soso.
prostrate/postrado *adj.* tumbado boca abajo; abatido; humillado.

provision/disposición s. arreglo; acuerdo; suministro.
proximity/proximidad s. cercanía; contacto; linde.
prudent/prudente adj. sensato; moderado; cauteloso.

R

rash/incauto adj. imprudente; precipitado; audaz.
raze/arrasar v. asolar; allanar; aplanar; talar.
reactionary/reaccionario adj. retrógrado; apegado; opositor de cambios y del progreso.
recess/recinto s. cercado; nicho; alcoba.
refract/refractar v. torcer pasando de un medio a otro.
refuse/basura s. desperdicios; desechos.
reiterate/reiterar v. repetir; insistir; confirmar; reincidir.
remonstrate/protestar v. amonestar; reprender; sermonear.
renounce/renunciar v. desistir; dimitir; declinar.
repast/comida s. colación; banquete; cena.
reproach/reprender v. condenar; criticar; censurar.
reproachful/reprobador adj. reparador; censurador.
reprove/censurar v. condenar; criticar; reprender.
residue/residuo s. resto; sobra; saldo.
resolute/resuelto adj. determinado; decidido; audaz; temerario.
resolve/resolución s. decisión; propósito; valor.
respite/respiro s. tregua; pausa; postergación.
reverent/reverente adj. respetuoso; considerado; que siente gran devoción por algo sagrado.
righteous/recto adj. honrado; moral.
rigor/rigor s. dureza; precisión; severidad.
rite/rito s. ceremonia; culto; acto.

S

scourge/látigo s. castigo; azote.
scrupulous/escrupuloso adj. cuidadoso; esmerado; aplicado.
serrated/serrado adj. dentado; apuntado.
servile/servil adj. bajo; esclavo; sumiso.
shirk/eludir v. esquivar; zafarse de un deber; rehuir.
sloth/pereza s. flojera; dejadez; lentitud.
solicitude/solicitud s. cuidado; preocupación; atención; deferencia.
somber/sombrío adj. oscuro; triste; lúgubre.
sordid/sórdido adj. mezquino; indecoroso; vil.

specious/especioso adj. artificioso; fingido; simulado.
spurn/despreciar v. rechazar; menospreciar; desfavorecer; desdeñar.
squalid/escuálido adj. mugrente; sucio; repugnante.
squall/ráfaga s. racha; borrasca; violenta tormenta de poca duración.
stealthy/cauteloso adj. sigiloso; secreto; disimulado.
strident/estridente adj. ruidoso; llamativo; chillón.
stupefying/estupefaciente adj. que atonta; aturdidor; soporífero; pesado.
subdued/sojuzgado adj. sometido; dominado; sumiso.
succor/socorro s. ayuda, sosiego; auxilio; refuerzo.
succumb/sucumbir v. ceder; rendirse; capitular.
sullen/hosco adj. ceñudo; resentido; huraño; arisco.
supercilious/arrogante adj. altanero; desdeñoso; altivo.
superfluity/superfluidad s. exceso; futilidad.
supplant/suplantar v. suplir; reemplazar; sustituir.
suppress/suprimir v. contener; evitar que se divulgue; reprimir; ocultar.
surreptitious/subrepticio adj. clandestino; disimulado.
sustenance/sustento s. alimento; subsistencia; nutrición.

T

taciturn/taciturno adj. abatido; silencioso; huraño.
temerity/temeridad s. imprudencia; osadía.
temper/templar v. suavizar; moderar; temperar.
temporal/temporal adj. transitorio; pasajero.
tentative/indeciso adj. vacilante; irresoluto; tímido.
tepid/tibio adj. templado; ni caliente ni frío.
titillating/excitante adj. apasionante; intrigante.
transcend/superar v. ir más allá de; exceder; rebasar; sobrepasar.
transfigure/transfigurar v. mudar; transformar.
transgress/transgredir v. infringir; desobedecer; contravenir.
translucent/translúcido adj. transparente; claro; diáfano.
tyrannous/tirano s. déspota; dictador; opresor.

U

uncanny/extraño adj. insólito; misterioso; raro.
unmarred/intacto adj. indemne; ileso; limpio; entero.

unpretentious/modesto *adj.* humilde; sencillo; moderado.
untainted/fresco *adj.* no contaminado; no corrompido.

V

vehement/vehemente *adj.* violento; apasionado; elocuente.
victuals/vituallas *s.* provisiones; víveres.
vigil/vela *s.* vigilia; vigilancia durante las horas de sueño.
vitiate/viciar *v.* corromper; invalidar; debilitar.
vivacity/vivacidad *s.* energía; vigor; brío.

W

wince/estremecerse *v.* hacer una mueca de dolor.
wrenched/angustiado *adj.* afligido; acongojado.

Z

zealous/celoso *adj.* entusiasta; apasionado.

Acknowledgments

For permission to reprint copyrighted material, grateful acknowledgment is made to the following sources:

Ardis Publishers: "Raven doth to raven fly" from *Alexander Pushkin: Collected Narrative and Lyrical Poetry*, translated by Walter Arndt. Copyright © 1984 by Walter Arndt.

Bantam Books, a division of Random House, Inc.: From "The Second Teaching: Philosophy and Spiritual Decline" from *The Bhagavad-Gita*, translated by Barbara Stoler Miller. Translation copyright © 1986 by Barbara Stoler Miller. From "Give Us This Day Our Daily Bread" from *Shakespeare Alive* by Joseph Papp and Elizabeth Kirkland. Copyright © 1988 by the New York Shakespeare Festival.

Darhansoff and Verrill Literary Agency: "I Am Not One of Those Who Left the Land . . ." from *Poems of Akhmatova* by Anna Akhmatova, translated by Stanley Kunitz and Max Hayward. Copyright © 1967, 1968, 1972, 1973 by Stanley Kunitz and Max Hayward.

Joan Daves Agency/Writer's House, Inc., New York, on behalf of the proprietors: "Fear" from *Selected Poems of Gabriela Mistral: A Bilingual Edition*, translated by Doris Dana. Copyright © 1961, 1964, 1970, 1971 by Doris Dana. Published by The Johns Hopkins University Press, Baltimore, 1971.

Anita Desai c/o Rogers, Coleridge & White Ltd., 20 Powis Mews, London W11 1JN: From "Games at Twilight" from *Games at Twilight and Other Stories* by Anita Desai. Copyright © 1978 by Anita Desai.

Doubleday, a division of Random House, Inc.: "Marriage Is a Private Affair" from *Girls at War and Other Stories* by Chinua Achebe. Copyright © 1972, 1973 by Chinua Achebe. "A morning-glory vine" by Kobayashi Issa from *An Introduction to Haiku*, translated by Harold G. Henderson. Copyright © 1958 by Harold G. Henderson. "Half a Day" from *The Time and the Place and Other Stories* by Naguib Mahfouz, translated by Denys Johnson-Davies. Copyright © 1991 by the American University in Cairo Press.

Dutton Signet, a division of Penguin Group (USA) Inc.: "Le Morte D'Arthur" from *Le Morte D'Arthur* by Sir Thomas Malory, translated by Keith Baines. Copyright © 1962 by Keith Baines; copyright renewed © 1990 by Francesca Evans. Introduction copyright © 1962 by Robert Graves; copyright renewed © 1990 by Beryl Graves. From *Beowulf*, translated by Burton Raffel. Copyright © 1963 and renewed © 1991 by Burton Raffel. From "The Unfed Dervish," "Information and Knowledge," "The Elephant-Keeper," "Safety and Riches," and "The Fox and the Camels" from *The Way of the Sufi* by Idries Shah. Copyright © 1968 by Idries Shah.

Faber and Faber Ltd., an affiliate of Farrar, Straus and Giroux, LLC: From *Wit* by Margaret Edson. Copyright © 1993, 1999 by Margaret Edson.

Farrar, Straus and Giroux, LLC: "Once upon a Time" from *Jump and Other Stories* by Nadine Gordimer. Copyright © 1991 by Felix Licensing, B.V. "Digging" from *Selected Poems 1966–1987* by Seamus Heaney. Copyright © 1990 by Seamus Heaney. "The Virgins" from *Sea Grapes* by Derek Walcott. Copyright © 1976 by Derek Walcott.

The Gale Group: Quote by Chinua Achebe from *Contemporary Novelists, Fifth Edition*, edited by Lesley Henderson. Copyright © 1991 by Gale Group.

Grove/Atlantic, Inc.: "Next Term, We'll Mash You" from *Pack of Cards and Other Stories* by Penelope Lively. Copyright © 1978 by Penelope Lively.

Harcourt, Inc.: "The Hollow Men" from *Collected Poems 1909–1962* by T. S. Eliot. Copyright 1936 by Harcourt, Inc.; copyright © 1963, 1964 by T. S. Eliot. "Shooting an Elephant" from *Shooting an Elephant and Other Essays* by George Orwell. Copyright © 1936 by George Orwell. From *Mrs. Dalloway* by Virginia Woolf. Copyright © 1925 by Harcourt, Inc.; copyright renewed © 1953 by Leonard Woolf. From "Shakespeare's Sister" and from page 64 from *A Room of One's Own* by Virginia Woolf. Copyright 1929 by Harcourt, Inc.; copyright renewed © 1957 by Leonard Woolf.

HarperCollins Publishers, Inc.: "The Swan" from *Selected Poems of Rainer Maria Rilke*, edited and translated by Robert Bly. Copyright © 1981 by Robert Bly. "8 The supreme good is like water" from *Tao Te Ching by Lao Tzu, A New English Version*, translated by Stephen Mitchell. Translation copyright © 1988 by Stephen Mitchell.

Hill and Wang, a division of Farrar, Straus & Giroux, LLC: "Never Shall I Forget" from *Night* by Elie Wiesel, translated by Stella Rodway. Copyright © 1958 by Les Editions de Minuit; English translation copyright © 1960 by MacGibbon & Kee, renewed © 1988 by The Collins Publishing Group. All rights reserved.

Houghton Mifflin Company: "Siren Song" from *Selected Poems, 1965–1975* by Margaret Atwood. Copyright © 1976 by Margaret Atwood. All rights reserved. From *Gilgamesh: A Verse Narrative* by Herbert Mason. Copyright © 1970 by Herbert Mason. All rights reserved. From "The Seventh Elegy" from *Duino Elegies: The Sonnets to Orpheus* by Rainer Maria Rilke, translated by Robert Hunter. Translation copyright © 1987, 1993 by Robert Hunter. All rights reserved.

Melanie Jackson Agency, L.L.C.: "Telephone Conversation" by Wole Soyinka from *Reflections: Nigerian Prose and Verse*, edited by Frances Ademola. Copyright © 1962, 1990 by Wole Soyinka.

Alfred A. Knopf, a division of Random House, Inc.: "The Demon Lover" from *The Collected Stories of Elizabeth Bowen*. Copyright 1946 and renewed © 1974 by Elizabeth Bowen. Excerpt (retitled "Trojan Gold") from *Gods, Graves and Scholars* by C. W. Ceram. Copyright 1951, © 1967 by Alfred A. Knopf, Inc. From *Grendel* by John Gardner. Copyright © 1971 by John Gardner. "The Doll's House" from *The Short Stories of Katherine Mansfield*. Copyright 1923 by Alfred A. Knopf, Inc.; copyright renewed 1951 by John Middleton Murry. "B. Wordsworth" from *Miguel Street* by V. S. Naipaul. Copyright © 1959 by V. S. Naipaul.

Edmund Morris: From "A Visit with Nadine Gordimer" by Edmund Morris from *The New York Times Book Review*, June 7, 1981. Copyright © 1981 by Edmund Morris.

Navajivan Trust: "Speech, March 23, 1922" by Mohandas Gandhi.

Jawaharlal Nehru Memorial Fund: From speech by Jawaharlal Nehru, August 14, 1947.

New Directions Publishing Corporation: "Dulce et Decorum Est" and "Strange Meeting" from *The Collected Poems of Wilfred Owen*. Copyright © 1963 by Chatto & Windus, Ltd. "Do Not Go Gentle into That Good Night" and "Fern Hill" from *The Poems of Dylan Thomas*. Copyright © 1952 by Dylan Thomas. "Jade Flower Palace" by Tu Fu from *One Hundred Poems from the Chinese*, translated by Kenneth Rexroth. Copyright © 1971 by Kenneth Rexroth.

The New Press, www.thenewpress.com: From *The War* by Marguerite Duras, translated by Barbara Bray. Copyright © 1986 by Barbara Bray.

The New York Times Company: From "Scenes from a Modern Marriage" by Julia Markus from *The New York Times*, February 14, 1995. Copyright © 1995 by The New York Times Company.

The Nobel Foundation: From Nobel Peace Prize acceptance speech by Nelson Mandela. Copyright © 1993 by The Nobel Foundation.
North Point Press, a division of Farrar, Straus & Giroux, LLC: "The Silver Fifty-Sen Pieces" from *Palm-of-the-Hand Stories* by Yasunari Kawabata, translated by Lane Dunlop and J. Martin Holman. Translation copyright © 1988 by Lane Dunlop and J. Martin Holman.
W. W. Norton & Company, Inc.: "Fifth Day, Ninth Story" (retitled "Federigo's Falcon") from *The Decameron* by Giovanni Boccaccio, translated by Mark Musa and Peter Bondanella. Translation copyright © 1982 by Mark Musa and Peter Bondanella. From *Beowulf*, translated by Seamus Heaney. Copyright © 2000 by Seamus Heaney.
Oxford University Press, Inc.: From "The Troglodyte World" from *The Great War and Modern Memory* by Paul Fussell. Copyright © 1975 by Oxford University Press, Inc.
Pantheon Books, a division of Random House, Inc.: "A Clever Judge" by Chang Shih-nan and "Gold, Gold" by Lieh Tzu from *Chinese Fairy Tales and Fantasies*, translated and edited by Moss Roberts. Copyright © 1979 by Moss Roberts. "Axolotl" from *End of the Game and Other Stories* by Julio Cortázar, translated by Paul Blackburn. Copyright © 1967 by Random House, Inc. "Saboteur" from *The Bridegroom: Stories by Ha Jin*. Copyright © 2000 by Ha Jin.
Peter Pauper Press, Inc.: From *African Proverbs* compiled by Charlotte and Wolf Leslau. Copyright © 1962, 1985 by Peter Pauper Press. "Even stones in streams" by Uejima Onitsura from *Haiku Harvest: Japanese Haiku, Series IV*, translated by Peter Beilenson and Harry Behn. Copyright © 1962 by Peter Pauper Press, Inc.
Penguin Books Ltd.: "I waited and I" by Princess Nukada, "The end of my journey" by Oshikochi Mitsune, "Now, I cannot tell" by Ki Tsurayuki, "How helpless my heart! " by Ono Komachi, and "Every single thing" by Priest Saigyo from *The Penguin Book of Japanese Verse*, translated by Geoffrey Bownas and Anthony Thwaite (Penguin Classics, 1964). Translation copyright © 1964 by Geoffrey Bownas and Anthony Thwaite. "The Prologue," "The Pardoner's Prologue and Tale," and "The Wife of Bath's Prologue and Tale" from *The Canterbury Tales* by Geoffrey Chaucer, translated by Nevill Coghill (Penguin Classics 1951, Fourth Revised Edition 1977). Copyright © 1951, 1958, 1960, 1975, 1977 by Nevill Coghill. "Night" from *The Koran*, translated by N. J. Dawood (Penguin Classics 1956, Fifth Revised Edition 1990). Copyright © 1956, 1959, 1966, 1968, 1974, 1990 by N. J. Dawood. "The Third Voyage of Sindbad the Sailor" from *The Thousand and One Nights*, translated by N. J. Dawood (Penguin Classics 1957). Translation copyright © 1957 by N. J. Dawood. "The Jewels" from *Selected Short Stories* by Guy de Maupassant, translated by Roger Colet (Penguin Classics, 1971). Copyright © 1971 by Roger Colet. "Quiet Night Thoughts" and "Letter to His Two Small Children" by Li Po and "Night Thoughts Afloat" by Tu Fu from *Li Po and Tu Fu*, translated by Arthur Cooper (Penguin Classics, 1973). Copyright © 1973 by Arthur Cooper. "Question and answer among the mountains" by Li Po from *The Penguin Book of Chinese Verse*, translated by Robert Kotewall and Norman L. Smith (Penguin Books, 1962). Translation copyright © 1962 by N. L. Smith and R. H. Kotewall.
Pollinger Limited and the Estate of Frieda Lawrence Ravagli: From "Letter to Rolf Gardiner, 18 December 1927," "Letter to Earl Brewster, 22 September 1922," and from "Letter to Rolf Gardiner, 17 July 1926" from *The Letters of D. H. Lawrence*, vol. V–VI. Copyright 1932 by the Estate of D. H. Lawrence; copyright 1934 by Frieda Lawrence; copyright 1933, 1948, 1953, 1954, © 1956, 1957, 1958, 1959, 1960, 1961, 1962, 1967, 1969 by Stefano Ravagli and R. G. Seaman, executors of the Estate of Frieda Lawrence Ravagli; copyright © 1987 by the Estate of Frieda Lawrence Ravagli. Published by Cambridge University Press.
The Random House Group Limited: From "William Caxton, Printer" from *The Story of Britain* by Sir Roy Strong. Copyright © 1996 by Oman Productions Ltd. Originally published by Julia McRae.

Random House, Inc.: "Musée des Beaux Arts" from *W. H. Auden: Collected Poems* by W. H. Auden, edited by Edward Mendelson. Copyright 1940 and renewed © 1968 by W. H. Auden. "Sonnet 42: The spring returns, the spring wind softly blowing" from *The Sonnets of Petrarch*, translated by Joseph Auslander. Copyright © 1931 by Longmans, Green and Co.
The Saturday Review: From "Black Man's Burden" by Maxwell Geismar from *The Saturday Review*, March 8, 1975. Copyright © 1979 by General Media International, Inc.
Schocken Books, a division of Random House, Inc.: "Sonnet XXIII" by Louise Labé from *A Book of Women Poets from Antiquity to Now*, edited by Willis Barnstone and Aliki Barnstone. Copyright © 1980, 1992 by Schocken Books.
Scribner, an imprint of Simon & Schuster Adult Publishing Group: From *In Patagonia* by Bruce Chatwin. Copyright © 1977 by Bruce Chatwin. Number 17 from Book II, numbers 15 and 21 from Book VII, and number 23 from Book XV from *The Analects of Confucius*, translated by Arthur Waley. Copyright © 1938 George Allen & Unwin, Ltd. "Death and Other Grave Matters" from *What Jane Austen Ate and Charles Dickens Knew* by Daniel Pool. Copyright © 1993 by Daniel Pool.
Simon & Schuster, Inc.: "No Witchcraft for Sale" from *African Stories* by Doris Lessing. Copyright © 1951, 1953, 1954, 1957, 1958, 1962, 1963, 1964, 1965, 1972, 1981 by Doris Lessing.
Wislawa Szymborska: "The End and the Beginning" by Wislawa Szymborska, translated by Stanislaw Baranczak and Clare Cavanagh from *The New Republic*, January 18, 1993. Copyright © 1993 by Wislawa Szymborska.
Time Inc.: From "Life in 999: A Grim Struggle" by Howard G. Chua-Eoan from *Time*, vol. 140, no. 27, October 15, 1992. Copyright © 1992 by Time Inc.
Charles E. Tuttle Co., Inc., Boston, MA, and Tokyo, Japan: "The First Principle," "The Gates of Paradise," "The Moon Cannot Be Stolen," and "Temper" from *Zen Flesh, Zen Bones: A Collection of Zen and Pre-Zen Writings*, compiled by Paul Reps. Copyright © 1957 by Charles E. Tuttle Co., Inc.
United Nations Publication Board: Preamble to the Universal Declaration of Human Rights, United Nations, December 10, 1948. Copyright © 1948 by United Nations. From "The Question of Africa" by Desmond Tutu from a speech to the United Nations Security Council, October 23, 1984. Copyright © 1984 by United Nations.
United States Holocaust Memorial Museum: From "Historic Overview" from *U. S. Holocaust Memorial Museum – Kristallnacht* Web site, accessed November 15, 2001, at http://www.ushmm.org/kristallnacht/frame.htm. Copyright © by United States Holocaust Memorial Museum.
University College, Dublin, Head, Department of Irish Folklore: Excerpt from *Memories of the Famine* by Maire ni Grianna from Main Manuscript Collection IFC 1074:279-83 from the collections of the Department of Irish Folklore, University College, Dublin.
University of California Press: Excerpts (retitled "The First Day of the Great Fire of London") from *The Diary of Samuel Pepys*, vol. VII, edited by Robert Latham and William Matthews. Copyright © 1972 by the University of California Press.
The University of Chicago Press: From *The Panchatantra*, translated from the Sanskrit by Arthur William Ryder. Copyright 1925 by the University of Chicago Press.
University of Texas Press and Agencia Literaria Carmen Balcells: "Sonnet 79/Soneto 79" from *100 Love Sonnets/Cien sonetos de amor* by Pablo Neruda, translated by Stephen Tapscott. Copyright © 1959 by Pablo Neruda and Fundación Pablo Neruda; translation copyright © 1986 by University of Texas Press.
Laurence S. Untermeyer on behalf of The Estate of Louis Untermeyer, Norma Anchin Untermeyer c/o Professional Publishing Services Company: "The Lorelei" from *Heinrich Heine: Paradox and Poet* by Louis Untermeyer. Copyright 1937 by Louis Untermeyer.

Viking Penguin, a division of Penguin Group (USA) Inc.: From "The Book of Sand" from *Collected Fictions* by Jorges Luis Borges, translated by Andrew Hurley. Copyright © 1998 by Maria Kodama; translation copyright © 1998 by Penguin Putnam Inc. "Top of the Food Chain" from *Without A Hero* by T. Coraghessan Boyle. Copyright © 1993 by T. Coraghessan Boyle. From *Don Quixote* by Miguel de Cervantes Saavedra, translated by Samuel Putnam. Copyright 1949 by The Viking Press, Inc. "The Destructors" from *Collected Stories of Graham Greene*. Copyright © 1955, 1983 by Graham Greene. "The Death of Hector" and "The Rage of Achilles" from *The Iliad* by Homer, translated by Robert Fagles. Copyright © 1990 by Robert Fagles. "The Rocking-Horse Winner" from *Complete Short Stories of D. H. Lawrence*. Copyright 1933 by the Estate of D. H. Lawrence; copyright renewed © 1961 by Angelo Ravagli and C. M. Weekley, Executors of the Estate of Frieda Lawrence Ravagli. "On the Bottom" from *If This Is a Man (Survival in Auschwitz)* by Primo Levi, translated by Stuart Woolf. Copyright © 1958 by Guilio Einaudi editore S.P.A.; copyright © 1959 by Orion Press, Inc. "Like the Sun" from *Under the Banyan Tree* by R. K. Narayan. Copyright © 1985 by R. K. Narayan. "In the Shadow of War" from *Stars of the New Curfew* by Ben Okri. Copyright © 1988 by Ben Okri. From "Towards a True Refuge" from *Freedom from Fear and Other Writings*, Revised Edition by Aung San Suu Kyi, foreword by Vaclav Havel, translated by Michael Aris. Copyright © 1991, 1995 by by Aung San Suu Kyi and Michael Aris.

Wiley Publishing, Inc.: From *Webster's New World™ College Dictionary, Fourth Edition*. Copyright © 1999, 2000 by Wiley Publishing, Inc. All rights reserved.

Yale University Press: From "The Seafarer" from *Poems from the Old English*, translated by Burton Raffel. Copyright © 1960, 1964, 1998 by Burton Raffel.

Zephyr Press: From "All the Unburied Ones . . ." from *The Complete Poems of Anna Akhmatova, vol. II*, translated by Judith Hemschemeyer, edited by Roberta Reeder. Translation copyright © 1983, 1984, 1985, 1986, 1987, 1988, 1989 by Judith Hemschemeyer.

Sources Cited

From "Marguerite Duras, The unspeakable, she said . . ." by Jean-Louis Arnaud from *Label France*, no. 24, June 1996, Web site accessed June 27, 2001, at http://www.france.diplomatie.fr/label_france/ENGLISH/LETTRES/DURAS/duras.html.

Picture Credits

The illustrations and/or photographs on the Contents pages are picked up from pages in the textbook. Credits for those works can be found either on the textbook page on which they appear or in the list below.

Page A2: (top left, bottom right) © Michael Holford; (bottom left) The Art Archive; **A3:** (top left) Bridgeman Art Library; (bottom) Erich Lessing/Art Resource, NY; **A4:** (top) The Huntington Library, Art Collections, and Botanical Gardens, San Marino, California/SuperStock; (bottom) Bridgeman Art Library; **A5** (top): Harry Ransom Humanities Research Center, The University of Texas at Austin; **A6:** (left center) Art Resource, NY; (bottom) © The Cleveland Museum of Art, 2002, Gift from various donors and by Exchange (1960.176); **A7:** (top) Victoria & Albert Museum, London/Art Resource, NY; (bottom) © Ted Spiegel; **A8:** (top) Philadelphia Museum of Art, Purchased Edith H. Bell Fund (75-23-1); (bottom) Werner Forman Archive; **A9:** (right) Courtesy of the Fogg Art Museum, Harvard University Art Museums, Gift of W. A. White, © President and Fellows of Harvard College. Photo by Rick Stafford; **A9** (left), **A10** (top left): Bridgeman Art Library; **A10** (bottom): The Illustrated London News Picture Library; **A11:** (top) Bridgeman Art Library; (left center) Eric Kamp/Index Stock Imagery/PictureQuest; **A12:** (top left) Library of Congress, Washington, D.C./Bridgeman Art Library; (bottom) Bridgeman Art Library; **A14:** © Scala/Art Resource, NY; **A15** (bottom): Art Resource, NY; **A16:** (left) AKG London; (right) © Scala/Art Resource, NY; **A17:** The Museum of Modern Art, New York. Purchase. © 2003 Artists Rights Society (ARS), New York/ADAGP, Paris. Photograph © 2003 The Museum of Modern Art, New York; **A18:** (top) © HRW, photo by Sam Dudgeon; (left) Permission of Angelica Garnett. Sotheby's Transparency Library, London; **A19:** (top) Collection Walker Art Center, Minneapolis. Gift of the T. B. Walker Foundation, 1954. © 2003 Artists Rights Society (ARS), New York/ADAGP, Paris; (left) Courtesy of The Trustees of the British Museum, London; **A20:** © Julio Larraz, Private Collection, Courtesy Nohra Haime Gallery, New York; **A21:** © Joseph Sohm, ChromoSohm Inc./CORBIS; **A28:** © Bruce Paton; **A29:** © CORBIS; **A31:** Bridgeman Art Library; **A33:** © CORBIS; **A35:** The Maas Gallery, London, UK/Bridgeman Art Library; **A37:** AP/Wide World Photos; **xx:** Art Resource, NY; **3:** (bottom left) © Justin Kerr Photography; (bottom right) The Pierpont Morgan Library, NY/Art Resource, NY; **4–5:** (bottom) Bridgeman Art Library; **7:** © David Parker/Science Photo Library/Photo Researchers, Inc.; **9:** Bridgeman Art Library; **10:** © Michael Holford; **11:** © Erich Lessing/Art Resource, NY; **13:** © Werner Forman/Art Resource, NY; **16:** Art Resource, NY; **17:** Bridgeman Art Library; **18:** © Michael Holford; **20:** © Werner Forman/Art Resource, NY; **21:** Photo: Eirik Irgens Johnsen; **22:** © Werner Forman/Art Resource, NY; **23:** © Michael Holford; **24:** © Werner Forman/Art Resource, NY; **25:** Boltin Picture Library; **32:** Courtesy of Ted Spiegel; **33:** (background) British Library, London, UK/The Art Archive; **34:** (background) detail, © Werner Forman/Art Resource, NY; **39:** © Werner Forman/Art Resource, NY; **43:** © Erich Lessing/Art Resource, NY; **48:** © Giraudon/Art Resource, NY; **49, 50, 51, 52, 53:** (bottom borders) Bildarchiv Steffens/Bridgeman Art Library; **52, 54:** Bildarchiv Steffens; **73:** (top left) Cover from *The Hobbit* and *The Lord of the Rings* by J.R.R. Tolkien. Copyright © 1982 by Christopher R. Tolkien, Michael H. R. Tolkien, John F. R. Tolkien and Priscilla M.A.R. Tolkien. Cover art by Michael Herring. Used by permission of Ballantine Books, a division of Random House, Inc.; (top right) Cover from *Grendel* by John Gardner. Copyright © 1971 by John Gardner. Cover illustration by Mark Penbenhy. Used by permission of Vintage Books, a division of Random House, Inc.; (bottom left) Cover from *Mythology: The Voyage of the Hero* by David Adams Leeming. Copyright © 1998 by David Adams Leeming. Used by permission of Oxford University Press; (bottom right) Cover painting courtesy Professor Donal Cruise O'Brien; **89:** Bibliothèque Nationale de France; **90:** (top left) © Giraudon/Art Resource, NY; (bottom right) Bridgeman Art Library, London/New York; **91:** (top) © Giraudon/Art Resource, NY; (bottom left) Bibliothèque Nationale/AKG London; (bottom right) Photograph by Schecter Lee/Photo © 1986 The Metropolitan Museum of Art; **93:** (top and bottom) The Bridgeman Art Library; **97:** Robert Harding Picture Library; **99:** Art Resource, NY; **107:** The Bridgeman Art Library; **110:** Photo AKG London; **112:** The Bridgeman Art Library; **115, 116** (bottom): SuperStock; **121:** Bridgeman Art Library, London/New York; **122, 123, 124, 126, 129, 130, 131, 132, 134, 135, 136, 138, 139, 143, 146:** SuperStock; **149:** Photograph © 1991 The Metropolitan Museum of Art; **156:** SuperStock; **158:** G. Dagli Orti/The Art Archive; **161:** © Bettmann/CORBIS; **165:** Bridgeman Art Library, London/New York; **167:** G. Dagli Orti/The Art Archive; **168:** The Bridgeman Art Library; **185:** © Scala/Art Resource, NY; **189:** © Giraudon/Art Resource, NY; **196–197, 200:** Bridgeman Art Library; **203:** (top left) Cover from *The Arabian Nights,* translated by Hussain Haddawy. Based on the text edited by Muhsin Mahdi. Cover illustration by Dia Azzawi. Copyright © 1990 by W. W. Norton & Company; (top right) *Life in a Medieval Castle* by Joseph and Frances Gies. Copyright © 1974 by Joseph and Frances Gies. HarperCollins Publishers; (bottom left) From *The Hitchhiker's Guide to the Galaxy* by Douglas Adams, copyright © 1979 by Douglas Adams. Used by permission of Harmony Books, a division of Random House, Inc.; (bottom right) Cover (Ace Edition) from *The Once and Future King* by T. H. White, copyright 1938, 1939, 1940, © 1958 by T. H. White, renewed. Used by permission of G. P. Putnam's Sons, a division of Penguin Putnam, Inc.; **234:** (top) Bridgeman Art Library, London/New York; (center) Bridgeman Art Library; (bottom) © Bettmann/CORBIS; **235:** (top) © Erich Lessing/Art Resource, NY; (bottom left) Photo AKG London; (bottom right) Bridgeman Art Library, London/New York; **236:** (left) © Scala/Art Resource, NY; **240** (bottom): Bridgeman Art Library, London/New York; **244** (right): © Erich Lessing/Art Resource, NY; **249, 255, 256, 261:** Bridgeman Art Library, London/New York; **263:** (left) Erica Lansner/Black Star Publishing/PictureQuest; (right) Bridgeman Art Library; **265:** Christie's, London/Art Resource, NY; **269:** Bridgeman Art Library, London/New York; **270:** Sotheby's Transparency Library, London; **274:** Martha Swope/© Time, Inc.; **275:** Bridgeman Art Library, London/New York; **280:** David Young-Wolff/PhotoEdit; **282:** © 1985 Jose Azel/AURORA/PictureQuest; **290:** Pictor International, Ltd./PictureQuest; **292:** Collections/Julian Nieman; **297, 298:** © Michal Daniel; **300, 302:** Bridgeman Art Library, London/New York; **303:** James P. Blair/Words & Pictures/PictureQuest; **304:** Art Resource, NY; **306:** Bridgeman Art Library, London/New York; **308:** © Woodmansterne Limited Watford; **310:** Pictor International, Ltd./PictureQuest; **316:** Photograph © 1979

The Metropolitan Museum of Art; **319:** Bridgeman Art Library, London/New York; **320:** © Getty Images; **321, 323:** Bridgeman Art Library, London/New York; **326, 327:** G. Dagli Orti/The Art Archive; **329:** Collections/Alain Le Garsmeur; **331:** © Ted Spiegel; **336, 337:** Art Resource, NY; **339:** Foto Marburg/Art Resource, NY; **350:** Photograph © 1989 The Metropolitan Museum of Art; **354:** © Ben Simmons/CORBIS/The Stock Market; **358:** Photograph © 1978 The Metropolitan Museum of Art; **361:** Photograph © 1983 The Metropolitan Museum of Art; **366:** Bridgeman Art Library, London/New York; **373:** Art Resource, NY; **379:** Dennis MacDonald/PhotoEdit/ PictureQuest; **389:** (top left) *The Enlightened Mind* by Stephen Mitchell. Cover design © 1992 by David Bullen. HarperCollins Publishers; (top right) Used by permission of William Morrow & Company; (bottom left) From *Shakespeare Alive!* (jacket cover) by Joseph Papp and Elizabeth Kirkland. Used by permission of Bantam Books, a division of Random House, Inc.; (bottom right) *The Tragedy of Macbeth* by William Shakespeare. Cover, © HRW. Cover art by Joe Melomo; **406:** Bridgeman Art Library, London/New York; **408:** (right) Bolton Picture Library; (bottom left) Mansell/© Time, Inc.; **409:** (right) © Photothèque des Musées de la Ville de Paris; (bottom left) Bridgeman Art Library, London/New York; **410** (left): Bolton Museum and Art Gallery, Lancashire, UK/Bridgeman Art Library; **411:** (left middle) Victoria and Albert Museum, London, UK/Bridgeman Art Library; (bottom middle) Mary Evans Picture Library; **413:** Derby Museum and Art Gallery, Derbyshire, UK/ Bridgeman Art Library; **415, 416:** Bridgeman Art Library, London/ New York; **417** (top): © Bettmann/CORBIS; **419:** Culver Pictures, Inc.; **420** (top), **421:** Bridgeman Art Library, London/New York; **422:** Max A. Polster Archive; **423:** Bridgeman Art Library, London/New York; **424:** Roger-Viollet, Paris/Bridgeman Art Library; **425:** North Wind Picture Archives; **426:** Bridgeman Art Library, London/New York; **430, 431:** The Illustrated London News Picture Library; **445:** Bridgeman Art Library, London/New York; **446:** Yale Center for British Art, Paul Mellon Collection, USA/Bridgeman Art Library; **448:** Bridgeman Art Library, London/New York; **452:** Hermitage, St. Petersburg/Bridgeman Art Library; **456:** Robert Halsband Collection; **465:** North Wind Picture Archives; **467, 470, 471:** © Martha Swope/TimePix; **473:** Bridgeman Art Library; **475:** Collection Kharbine-Tapabor, Paris, France/Bridgeman Art Library; **486–487:** Victoria and Albert Museum, London, UK/Bridgeman Art Library; **491:** National Gallery, London, UK/Bridgeman Art Library; **494:** Eric Kamp/Index Stock Imagery/PictureQuest; **496:** National Gallery, London, UK/Bridgeman Art Library; **499:** (top left) *The Misanthrope and Tartuffe* by Molière. Cover illustration by Mark English. Used by permission of Harcourt Publishers; (top right) From *Robinson Crusoe* by Daniel Defoe. Used by permission of Bantam Books, a division of Random House, Inc.; (bottom left) *Isaac Newton and the Scientific Revolution* by Gale E. Christianson. © 1996 by Gale E. Christianson. Cover used courtesy of Oxford University Press; (bottom right) *Animal Farm* by George Orwell. Cover © HRW, art by Fred Lynch; **517:** © Getty Images; **518:** (left) © Bettmann/CORBIS; **523:** Bridgeman Art Library, London/New York; **524:** Photo Bulloz, Paris; **525:** © Giraudon/Art Resource, NY; **526:** Bridgeman Art Library, London/New York; **527:** (top) © Getty Images; (bottom) Fine Art Photographic Library Ltd.; **528** (top): Mary Evans Picture Library; **533** (detail): The Bridgeman Art Library; **536:** Art Resource, NY; **537:** Bridgeman Art Library, London/New York; **538:** Tate Gallery, London/Art Resource, NY; **539:** Bridgeman Art Library; **541:** © Getty Images; **547:** Larry Lefever from Grant Heilman Photography, Inc.; **548:** Bridgeman Art Library, London/New York; **549:** The Pierpont Morgan Library, New York/Art Resource, NY; **553, 554–555:** Bridgeman Art Library, London/New York; **558:** © Michael Jenner/Robert Harding Picture Library; **560:** Sotheby's Transparency Library, London; **561:** © Erich Lessing/Art Resource, NY; **581:** © W. Perry Conway/CORBIS; **609:** Sotheby's Transparency Library, London; **610, 613:** Bridgeman Art Library, London/ New York; **615** (center): © Getty Images; **616:** Photo by Richard Carafelli; **617:** Robert Harding Picture Library; **628** (background): © Frank Lane Picture Agency/CORBIS; **630:** Photographer: Robert Rubic; **635:** Bridgeman Art Library, London/New York; **642:** The Pierpont Morgan Library/Art Resource, NY; **643:** Sotheby's Transparency Library, London; **646:** © Eric and David Hosking/ CORBIS; **648:** Bridgeman Art Library, London/New York; **651:** Photograph © 1989 The Metropolitan Museum of Art; **653:** © Scala/Art Resource, NY; **655:** (top left) *Frankenstein, Or the Modern Prometheus* by Mary Shelley. Cover © HRW, illustration by Cliff Nielsen; (top right) Cover illustration © Philippe Weisbecker. Used by permission of Riley Illustration; (bottom left) Used by permission of William Morrow & Company, an imprint of HarperCollins Publishers; (bottom right) From *Pride and Prejudice* by Jane Austen. Used by permission of Bantam Books, a division of Random House, Inc.; **672:** Fine Art Photographic Library Ltd.; **674** (center): Crown copyright. Historic Royal Palaces, Hampton Court Palace, East Molesey, Surrey; **682:** © Getty Images; **684, 685:** Art Resource, NY; **686:** Fine Art Photographic Library Ltd.; **687** (top), **690:** Bridgeman Art Library, London/New York; **691:** Victoria and Albert Museum, London/Art Resource, NY; **692:** Bridgeman Art Library; **693** (detail), **696–697:** Art Resource, NY; **700:** Mary Evans Picture Library; **704–705, 708:** © Erich Lessing/Art Resource, NY; **712:** The Art Archive; **713** (bottom): Bridgeman Art Library, London/New York; **714:** Photo by Derrick E. Witty; **715:** © Pablo Corral Vega/CORBIS; **717:** © Getty Images; **718:** © Fine Art Photographic Library, London/Art Resource, NY; **721:** Sotheby's Transparency Library, London; **722–723:** © Tate Gallery, London/Art Resource, NY; **723** (top): © Getty Images; **724:** Mary Evans Picture Library; **726:** © Karl Weatherly/CORBIS; **727:** © Getty Images; **732:** © Bernard-Pierre Wolf/Magnum Photos; **735:** © Lindsay Hebberd/Woodfin Camp & Associates; **749** (bottom): © Getty Images; **751, 754–755:** © Scala/Art Resource, NY; **764** (detail): AKG London; **765:** Sovfoto/Eastfoto; **769:** © Scala/Art Resource, NY; **781:** Bridgeman Art Library; **783:** (top left) Cover from *Selected Short Stories* by Guy de Maupassant. Cover art: *After the Bath* by Edgar Degas (1834–1917). Pastel on cardboard. Photo: Jean Schormans. Musée d'Orsay, Paris, France. © Réunion des Musées Nationaux/Art Resource, NY; (top right) Reprinted with permission of Simon & Schuster from *What Jane Austen Ate and Charles Dickens Knew: From Fox Hunting to Whist—The Facts of Daily Life in 19th-Century England* by Daniel Pool. Copyright © 1993 by Daniel Pool; (bottom left) *The Importance of Being Earnest* by Oscar Wilde. Cover © HRW, photo by Scott Van Osdol; (bottom right) Cover from *Hard Times* by Charles Dickens. Cover art: *The Fight Interrupted*, 1815–1816, by William Mulready (1786–1863). © Victoria & Albert Museum, London/Art Resource, NY; **799:** © Michael Hart/Getty Images; **800:** (bottom left) Bridgeman Art Library, London/New York; (center right) © Bettmann/CORBIS; **801:** (top) © Giraudon/ Art Resource, NY; (center left) © Max Nauta/Bettmann/CORBIS; (center right) The Kobal Collection/United Artists; (bottom) NASA; **802:** (bottom left) Bridgeman Art Library; (right) © Topham/The Image Works; **803:** (bottom right) Bridgeman Art Library; (top) © Marilyn Silverstone/Magnum Photos, Inc.; **805:** Tate Gallery, London/Art Resource, NY; **806:** (left) © Bettmann/CORBIS; (right) Culver Pictures, Inc.; **807:** Photothèque R. Magritte-ADAGP/Art Resource, NY; **808:** (left) © Getty Images; (right) The Kobal Collection/Universal; **809:** © The Museum of Modern Art/Licensed by Scala/Art Resource, NY; **810:** © Bettmann/CORBIS; **811:** Bridgeman Art Library; **812:** © Bill Pierce/TimePix; **813:** (bottom) Manu Sassoonian/Art Resource, NY; (top) Tate Gallery, London/Art Resource. © Bridget Riley; **814:** © Margaret Courtney-Clark/ CORBIS; **815** (top): © Hans Georg Roth/CORBIS; **816:** AP/Wide World Photos; **817:** (left) © Charlie Cole/SIPA Press; (right) © Paul Velasco; Gallo Images/CORBIS; **818:** (bottom) © Tate Gallery/Art Resource, NY; (top) © Bettmann/CORBIS; **820:** © Getty Images;

Picture Credits / Illustrations 1259

822: Bridgeman Art Library, London/New York; **823:** © Getty Images; **826–827:** Photograph © The Museum of Modern Art/Licensed by Scala/Art Resource, NY; **832:** © Getty Images; **833:** (bottom) Courtesy of Touchstone Book, Published by Simon & Schuster. Cover painting *Just*, oil on canvas by Mindy Weisel, 1989; (top) © Jerry Bauer; **835:** (bottom) © Ira Nowinski/CORBIS; (top) Private Collection/Bridgeman Art Library; **840:** © Ralph Morse/TimePix; **841:** © Mascolo Jean/CORBIS Sygma; **845:** (bottom right) AP/Wide World Photos; **848:** AP/Wide World Photos; **850:** AP/Wide World Photos; **853:** Kyodo News International Inc.; **857, 859:** Sam Dudgeon; **860:** Detail of *Rain at Yotsuya Mitsuke*, 1930, Takashi Henmi. Courtesy of the Trustees of the British Museum, London; **861:** © Bettmann/CORBIS; **865, 867:** Bridgeman Art Library, London/New York; **870:** The Fine Arts Society, London, UK/Bridgeman Art Library; **875:** © Syndicated Features Ltd/The Image Works; **876:** © Bruce Paton; **878, 879:** © CORBIS; **880–881:** © Ralph Morse/TimePix; **885:** © Thomas Haley/SIPA Press; **886:** AP/Wide World Photos; **888:** Permission of Angelica Garnett/Sotheby's Transparency Library, London; **891:** Bridgeman Art Library, London/New York; **893:** © Getty Images; **894:** © Hulton-Deutsch Collection; **897:** Globe Photos, Inc.; **899:** © Getty Images; **903:** SIPA Press; **908:** © Bettmann/CORBIS; **909:** © Hans Reinhard/Bruce Coleman, Inc.; **910:** © Juhan Kuus/SIPA Press; **913:** © Hans Reinhard/Bruce Coleman, Inc.; **916:** © Michael Nicholson/CORBIS; **919:** AP/Wide World Photos; **920:** © Bill Ellzey/National Geographic Image Collection; **922, 929:** AP/Wide World Photos; **934:** Photographer: Richard Todd (X65.7994); **937:** © Wyman Ira/CORBIS Sygma; **938–939:** © Masa Uemura/Getty Images; **940:** © Werner Forman Archive/Art Resource, NY; **946:** © Steve Vidler/Estock Photo; **951:** © Clive Druett; Papilio/CORBIS; **952:** © George Lepp/CORBIS; **952–953:** © Jon Sparks/CORBIS; **954:** © Philadelphia Museum of Art/CORBIS; **961:** Bridgeman Art Library, London/New York; **963, 967:** © Bettmann/CORBIS; **969:** © Derek P. Redfearn/Getty Images; **970:** (left center) © Anna Palma/CORBIS; (top) AP/Wide World Photos; **971:** AP/Wide World Photos; **973:** Private Collection/Bridgeman Art Library; **974:** (top, center) Private Collection/Bridgeman Art Library; (top right, left) AP/Wide World Photos; **975:** (top center) © Anna Palma/CORBIS; (top right, left) AP/Wide World Photos; **977:** AP/Wide World Photos; **978:** (top center) AP/Wide World Photos; (top left) Private Collection/Bridgeman Art Library, (top right) © Anna Palma/CORBIS; **979:** (top center) AP/Wide World Photos; (top left) @ Anna Palma/CORBIS; (top right) Private Collection/Bridgeman Art Library; **982:** © Topham Picturepoint/The Image Works; **984:** © Rheinisches Bildarchiv/Stadt Köln; **985:** © Rheinisches Bildarchiv/Stadt Köln; **986:** Bridgeman Art Library, London/New York; **987:** © Syndicated Features Ltd/The Images Works; **990:** Bridgeman Art Library, London/New York; **993:** Sotheby's Transparency Library, London; **998:** © Bettmann/CORBIS; **1001:** Jane Burton/Bruce Coleman, Inc.; **1002:** © Stephen Dalton/Photo Researchers, Inc.; **1006:** © Nancy Crampton; **1011:** Neil Johnson Photo, Shreveport, LA; **1014:** © Bettmann/CORBIS; **1022:** AP/Wide World Photos; **1023:** © Christie's Images/CORBIS; **1025:** © SIPA Press; **1026:** © Gary John Norman/Panos Pictures; **1028:** © Smith Richard Frank/CORBIS Sygma; **1029:** © Nicholas Devore III/Bruce Coleman, Inc.; **1034:** © Liaison Agency/Getty Images; **1035, 1036:** The Art Archive; **1038:** Bridgeman Art Library, London/New York; **1040:** Bethnal Green Museum, London/Bridgeman Art Library; **1041:** Nadia Mackenzie/National Trust Photographic Library/Bridgeman Art Library; **1044:** Bethnal Green Museum, London/Bridgeman Art Library; **1045:** © Rollie McKenna; **1046:** © Scala/Art Resource, NY; **1050:** © Rheinisches Bildarchiv/Stadt Köln; **1051:** Photo: © Art Resource, NY. © 2003 Banco de Mexico Diego Rivera & Frida Khalo Museums Trust, Av. Cinco de Mayo No. 2, Col. Centro, Del. Cuauhtemoc 06059, Mexico. D.F.; **1053:** Bridgeman Art Library; **1054:** © Hulton Archive/Getty Images; **1056:** Bridgeman Art Library; **1057:** © Rollie McKenna; **1059:** © Bettmann/CORBIS; **1060:** CNAC/MNAM/Dist. Réunion des Musées Nationaux/Art Resource, NY; **1063:** AP/Wide World Photos; **1064:** © Michael S. Yamashita/CORBIS; **1065:** © Ron Miller/Photonica; **1065:** (background) © Michael Freeman/CORBIS; **1067:** © Michael Boys/CORBIS; **1070:** © Timothy Greenfield-Sanders/CORBIS OUTLINE; **1072:** © Jon Hicks/Estock Photo; **1077:** Museum purchase, Roscoe and Margaret Oaks Income Fund, Museum Society Auxiliary, Mr. and Mrs. John N. Rosekrans, Jr., Walters H. and Phyllis J. Shorestein Foundation Fund, Mrs. Paul L. Wattis, Bobbie and Mike Wilsey, Mr. and Mrs. Steven MacGregor Read, Mr. and Mrs. Gorham B. Knowles, Mrs. Edward T. Harrison, Mrs. Nan Tucker McEvoy, Harry and Ellen Parker in honor of Steven Nash, Katherine Doyle Spann, Mr. and Mrs. William E. Steen, Mr. and Mrs. Leonard E. Kingsley, George Hopper Fitch, Princess Ranieri de San Faustino, Mr. and Mrs. Richard Madden (1994.32); **1080:** © Miriam Berkley; **1081:** © Michael Busselle/CORBIS; **1082, 1085, 1086:** Graham Tim/CORBIS Sygma; **1089:** AP/Wide World Photos; **1092:** © Dean Conger/CORBIS; **1095:** © Peter Turnley/CORBIS; **1098:** © Dermot Tatlow/Panos Pictures; **1100:** © Joseph Sohm; ChromoSohm Inc./CORBIS; **1105:** © David Turnley/CORBIS; **1108:** AP/Wide World Photos; **1109:** (top left) From *Testament of Youth* by Vera Brittain, copyright © 1933 by Vera Brittain. Used by permission of Penguin, a division of Penguin Putnam, Inc.; (top right) *Brave New World* by Aldous Huxley. Copyright © 1932, 1946 by Aldous Huxley. Cover design © Marc Cohen. Cover photo © Jeffery Zaruba/Photonica; (bottom left) *One Hundred Years of Solitude* by Gabriel Garcia Márquez. Cover design © 1998 by Marc Cohen. Cover painting © Cathleen Toelke. HarperCollins Publishers; (bottom right) *Things Fall Apart* by Chinua Achebe. Cover, © HRW, art by Earl Keleny.

Illustrations

Costello, Chris, A5, 193, 194

Sawchuk, Peter, 451, 453, 457, 948

Maps

The British Isles, A44–A45
Map of the World, A46–A47
Ancient Mesopotamia, 46
Ancient Greece, 55
India, 171

Medieval Arabia, 178
Early Renaissance Italy, 185
France, 465
Renaissance Spain, 473
Medieval Japan, 568

Sixteenth-Century Japan, 570
Eighth-Century China, 630, 635
Nineteenth-Century Russia, 749, 765
Nineteenth-Century France, 774

Index of Skills

The boldface page numbers indicate an extensive treatment of the topic.

LITERARY SKILLS

Acmeism, 982, 986
Allegory, **342**, 345, **383**, 388, **750**, 763, **1181**
Allusion, 364, **379**, 381, **561**, 563, 650, 731, 744, **826–827**, 829, 831, 945, **1181**
Ambiguity, 766, 882
Analogy
  extended, 326
  literary, 376, 496, **1181**
Analysis questions (Interpretations), 32, 40, 54, 69, 111, 143, 154, 166, 177, 184, 191, 201, 262, 271, 279, 280, 281, 282, 283, 284, 291, 299, 303, 306, 310, 316, 321, 328, 341, 345, 360, 375, 381, 388, 442, 450, 460, 471, 480, 492, 540, 546, 548, 558, 560, 563, 572, 577, 606, 611, 616, 620, 626, 634, 639, 644, 650, 654, 702, 706, 712, 715, 719, 724, 729, 744, 763, 773, 782, 824, 831, 839, 852, 859, 874, 882, 895, 905, 915, 928, 935, 940, 947, 950, 954, 964, 981, 986, 995–996, 1005, 1013, 1021, 1027, 1030, 1042, 1048, 1051, 1055, 1058, 1062, 1069, 1078, 1087, 1099
Anecdote, 347, 357, 854, **1182**
Antagonist, **1182**
Antithesis, **446**, 450, 719, **1182**
Aphorism, 347, **1182**
Apostrophe, 563 **612**, **626**, **1182**
  analyzing, 626
Apostrophizing, 563
Approximate rhyme, 167, 729
Archetype, 20, 32, 35, 45, 46, **179**, 184, 198, 201, **1182**
Aside, **1182**
Assonance, 567, 578, 606, 695, 702, **717**, 719, **948**, 950, **1182**
Atmosphere, 721, 874, 1087, **1183**
Autobiography, **1183**
Axiom, 327, 347
Ballad, 101, **108**, **111–112**, **1183**
  folk, 578
  literary, **578**
Ballad stanza, 606
Beat, simple, 112
Biography, **1183**
Blank verse, 364, 376, **551**, 558, 564, **1183**
Cadence, **1183**

Caesura, 41, **1183**
Canto, 453, **1184**
Carpe diem, 259, **263**, 265, **1184**
Character, 118, 143, 144, 155, 166, 291, 388, 708, 712, 831, 874, 981, 1005, 1069, 1087, **1184**
  imagery and, **144**
Characterization, **118**, 706, 859, 935, 1087
Chronological order, 460, 1078
Cliché, **1185**
Climax, 702, **1185**
Closed couplet, 447
Closure, 1043
Comparing Literature, 54, 70, 82–85, 177, 184, 191, 226–229, 360, 400–403, 472, 480, 510–513, 572, 634, 639, 666–669, 763, 773, 782, 792–795, 964, 1124–1127
Conceits, 284, 306, **1185**
  metaphysical, **304**
Conflict, **731**, 744, 763, 782, 935, 964, 1069, 1087, **1186**
  external, **731**, 744
  internal, **731**, 744
Connecting to World Literature
Chinese poetry, 627–629
  epics, 44–45
  frame story, 169–170
  realism, 746–748
  satire, 462–464
  tanka and haiku, 565–566
  wisdom literature, 346–348
Connotation, 443, 485, 947, 964, 1051, **1186**
Consonance, **1186**
Contrast, 702, 719, 928,
Contrasting images, 702
Conventional phrases, 112
Conventions, epic, 71
Couplet, **167**, 278, 284, 460, 563, **726**, **1186**
  closed, 447
  heroic, 446, 447
Denotation, **1187**
Denouement, **1187**
Details, 328, 639, 964, 1078
  omission of, 111
Dialect, **1187**
Dialogue, 938, 1015, **1187**
Diction, 365, **1046**, 1048, **1187**
Didactic literature, **349**, **1188**
Didactic verse, 351
Dirge, 288
Dramatic irony, 375, **966**, 1043
Dramatic monologue, **708**, **1188**
Dramatic song, **286**, **1188**

Elegy, 38, 288, 423, 954, **1056**, 1058, **1188**
Elevated style, 363
Ending, trick, 1043
End-stopped line, **1188**
English sonnet, 278
Epic, 20, **44–45**, 71, **1188**
  literary, 363
  mock, **451**, 458, 460
Epic conventions, 71
Epic hero, **20**, 32, 37, **44–45**, 54
Epic simile, **56**, 69, 71, 364, **376**, 460
Epigram, 172, 177, **318**, **450**, **1189**
Epiphany, **956**, 964, **1189**
Epitaph, 319, 321, **1189**
Epithet, **1189**
  stock, **71**
Essay, **887**, 895, 905, **1189**
  formal, 887
  informal, 887
Evaluation questions, 32, 54, 69, 111, 166, 262, 271, 316, 328, 360, 375, 388, 442, 450, 471, 540, 548, 558, 560, 563, 577, 606, 611, 634, 639, 644, 650, 706, 712, 715, 719, 724, 744, 782, 824, 831, 839, 852, 859, 874, 895, 905, 928, 935, 940, 947, 950, 954, 964, 981, 986, 996, 1005, 1013, 1021, 1042, 1048, 1051, 1062, 1069, 1078, 1087
Exact rhyme, 729
Exaggeration, 471, 480, **1189**. See also Hyperbole.
Exemplum, 145
Extended metaphor, 341, **1028**, 1030, 1062
Extended simile, 610, 644
External conflict, **731**, 744
Fable, 171, **172**, 177, **1189**
Fairy tale, 928
Figurative language, 606
Figures of speech, 42, 54, 346, 724, **821**, 824, 1053, **1190**
  hyperbole, 271, 301, 303, **1191**
  metonymy, 291, **1194**
  oxymoron, 375, 821, 824, **1196**
  personification, 154, 283, 291, 316, **559**, 560, 563, 606, 706, 1055, **1197**
  pun, 1058, **1198**
  symbol, 32, 40, 154, 345, **536**, 537, 548, 572, 577, 821, 831, 854, 859, 874, 905, **923**, 928, 935, 940, **951**, 954, **968**, 981, 1027, **1035**, 1042, **1202**
  See also Conceits, Metaphor, Simile.
First-person point of view, 964
Flashback, 71, **988**, 996, **1190**

Foil, **47**, 480, **1190**
Folk ballad, 578
Foreshadowing, 22, 702, 763, 995, **1023**, 1027, **1190**
Formal essay, 887
Frame story, 115, **118**, 143, 169–170, 171, 172, 178, 186, **1190**
Free verse, **1191**
Generalization, 895
Graphic organizers
　archetype chart, 201
　main-event time line, 606
　plot chart, 184
　satire chart, 471
　story map, 995
Haiku, **565–566**, 572, **1191**
Half rhyme, 167, 729, 824
Hero, 615
　epic, **20**, 32, 37, 44–45, 54
　romance, 193
Heroic couplet, 446, 447
Homeric simile, **56**, 71
Humorous imitation, 480
Hyperbole, 271, 301, 303, **1191**. See also Exaggeration.
Iamb, 376
Iambic hexameter, 612
Iambic pentameter, 114, 278, 447, 551, **1191**
Idea
　explicit, 335
　implicit, 335
　main, 310, 328, 558, 859
Imagery, 32, 40, 144, 271, 282, 306, 540, 548, 560, **567**, 572, 577, 626, 634, **636**, 639, 650, 651, 667, 668, 702, 724, 831, 862, 940, 947, 954, 995, 1005, 1015, 1021, 1030, 1051, 1062, **1071**, 1078, 1127, **1191**
　character and, 144
Implicit idea, 335
Incongruity, 480
Incremental repetition, 111, **1191**
Inference, 335, 782, 859
Informal essay, 887
In medias res, **71**, **1192**
Internal conflict, **731**, 744
Internal rhyme, 578, 606
Invocation, **71**
Irony, 111, **145**, 154, 166, 281, 442, 460, **618**, 620, 831, **898**, 902, 905, 940, 947, **965–966**, 1051, **1064**, 1069, 1087, **1090**, 1099, **1192**
　dramatic, 375, **966**, 996, 1043
　situational, **145**, 186, 191, 618, 898, **966**, **1064**, 1069
　verbal, **145**, **428**, 480, 898, **930**, 935, **966**
Italian sonnet, 276, 563, 641, 714, 1062. See also Petrarchan sonnet.
Kennings, **42**, **1192**
Language
　figurative, 606
　persuasive, 299
Language structures, 928
Limited-third-person point of view, **875–876**, 882

Literary ballad, 578
Literary Criticism, 40, 69, 184, 306, 345, 375, 388, 492, 607, 626, 654, 702, 712, 744, 831, 874, 915, 996, 1055, 1058, 1062
Literary epic, 363, **1192**
Literature
　comparing, 54, 70, 82–85, 177, 184, 191, 226–229, 360, 400–403, 472, 480, 510–513, 572, 634, 639, 666–669, 763, 773, 782, 792–795, 964, 1124–1127
　didactic, **349**
　postcolonial, 813
　wisdom, 346–348
　See also Connecting to World Literature.
Lyric forms, Romantic, **563–564**
Lyric poetry, **1053**, 1055, **1192**
Magic realism, 816, **999**, **1005**, **1193**
Main events, 606, 1013
Main idea, 310, 328, 558, 859
Maxim, 347, 355, 356, **1193**
Meditative poem, **563–564**
Memoir, **834**, 839, **1193**
Metaphor, 280, 282, 283, 299, 310, 321, 341, 347, 360, 606, 616, **651**, 654, 821, 1058, **1060**, 1062, **1193**
　extended, 341, **1028**, 1030, 1062
Metaphysical conceits, **304**, 306
Metaphysical poetry, **301**, **303**, **1193**
Meter, 278, 577, 578, 606, 695, 702, **1193**
Metonymy, 291, **1194**
Mock epic, **451**, 458, 460, **1194**
Modernism, 810, **1194**
Modern short story, **1043–1044**
Monologue, **292**, **1194**
　dramatic, **708**
Mood, 281, 560, 572, **631**, 634, 639, 650, **721**, 724, 831, 862, 954, 964, 995, 1023, 1078, 1099, 1126, 1194
Moral, 154, 177, 606
　lesson, 177, 546
　tale, 1194
Motif, 18, **1194**
Motivation, 712, 773, 874, **1194**
Myth, **1194**
Narrator, **155**, 166, 606, 915, 964, **1195**
　omniscient, 995
Naturalism, 747
Negritude, 814
Octave, 276, 714, **1195**
Ode, 424, **563**, **621**, 626, **1195**
Omniscient narrator, 995
Omniscient point of view, 1042
Onomatopoeia, 286, 1055, **1195**
Oral tradition, 346
Ottava rima, **1196**
Oxymoron, 375, 821, 824, **1196**
Parable, **342**, 345, 347, 353, 360, 381, **750**, **1196**
Paradox, **312**, 316, 328, 375, 491, 560, 626, 639, 828, 900, **1007**, 1013, 1055, **1196**
Parallelism, **324**, 328, 337, **338**, 341, 346, 348, 360, **541**, 546, 548, 639, **1196**

Paraphrasing, 271, 282, 321, 450, 546, 954, 986
Parody, 463, 471, **474**, 480, 481, 831, 928, **1196**
Pastoral, **257**, 259, 262, **1197**
Personification, 154, 283, 291, 316, **559**, 560, 563, 606, 706, 1055, **1197**
Persuasive language, 299
Petrarchan sonnet, 276, 284, 316, 563, 641, **714**, 1062. See also Italian sonnet.
Plot, 111, 184, 915, **1197**
Poem, meditative, **563–564**
Poetry
　alexandrine, 612, **1181**
　alliteration, **41–42**, 280, 281, 291, 348, **574**, 577, 606, 639, 695, 702, **717**, 719, 729, **948**, 950, 1030, 1055, **1181**
　assonance, 567, 578, 606, 695, 702, **717**, 719, **948**, 950, **1182**
　blank verse, 364, 376, **551**, 558, 564, **1183**
　caesura, 41, **1183**
　canto, 453, **1184**
　carpe diem, 259, **263**, 265, **1184**
　didactic verse, 351
　haiku, **565–566**, 572, **1191**
　iamb, 376
　iambic hexameter, 612
　iambic pentameter, 114, 278, 447, 551, **1191**
　lyric, **1053**, 1055, **1192**
　metaphysical, **301**, **303**, **1192**
　meter, 278, 577, 578, 606, 695, **1193**
　octave, 276, 714, **1195**
　ode, 424, **563**, **621**, 626, **1195**
　onomatopoeia, 286, 1055, **1195**
　pastoral, **257**, 259, 262, **1197**
　quatrain, 278, **1198**
　refrain, 108, 111, **1049**, 1051, **1198**
　rhyme scheme, 577, 578, 626, 702, 824
　rhythm, 715, **1199**
　run-on lines, 558, **1200**
　sestet, 276, 714, **1200**
　tanka, **565–566**, 572, **1203**
　tercet, **1203**
　terza rima, 625, 626, **1203**
　triplet, 447
　turn, 277, 279, 280, 281, 282, 283, 626, 714, 1062, 1204
　villanelle, **1058**, **1204**
　volta, 276
　See also Couplet, Rhyme, Sonnet, Stanza.
Point of view, 328, 744, 935, 999, 1005, **1197**
　first person, 964
　limited third person, **875–876**, 882
　omniscient, 1042
　See also Political Points of View.
Political Points of View
　analyzing, 335, 498, 847, 921, 1110
　colonialism, 896–921
　education and equality, 322–335
　Holocaust, the, 832–847
　human rights, 1088–1110

introducing, 322, 482–483, 832, 896, 1088
  women's rights, 482–498
Postcolonial literature, 813
Postmodernism, 813, **1197**
Proverb, 347, 359, **1198**
Psychological realism, 1043
Pun, 1058, **1198**
Quatrain, 278, **1198**
Reading Comprehension (Reading Check), 32, 40, 54, 69, 111, 143, 154, 166, 177, 184, 191, 201, 328, 345, 375, 388, 442, 460, 471, 480, 492, 558, 606, 650, 654, 702, 744, 763, 773, 782, 852, 859, 874, 882, 895, 905, 915, 928, 935, 964, 981, 995, 1005, 1013, 1021, 1027, 1042, 1069, 1078, 1087, 1099
Realism, 746–748, 1043, **1198**
  magic, 816, **999**, 1005, **1193**
  psychological, 1043
Refrain, 108, 111, **1049**, 1051, **1199**
Repetition, 337, 346
  incremental, 111
Resolution, 28, 763, 1013, **1199**
Rhyme, 167, 348, 695, 1030, **1199**
  approximate, 167
  exact, 729
  half, 167, 729, 824
  internal, 578, 606
Rhyme scheme, 577, 578, 626, 702, 824
Rhythm, 715, **1199**
Romance, 101, 193, **1199**
Romance hero, **193**
Romantic lyric forms, **563–564**
Run-on lines, 558, **1200**
Sarcasm, 966, **1200**
Satire, 143, 154, 424, 442, 460, **462–464, 466**, 471, 492, **938**, 940, **1200**
  chart, 471
Scansion, **1200**
Sestet, 276, 714, **1200**
Setting, 634, 650, 724, 829, **862**, 874, 964, 995, **1015**, 1021, **1200**
Shakespearean sonnet, **276, 278**, 316, 563, 625, 641
Short story, **1043, 1201**
Simile, 279, 291, 306, 606, **610**, 611, 616, 644, 821, 824, 1062, **1201**
  epic, **56**, 69, 71, 364, **376**, 460
  extended, 610, 644
  homeric, **56**, 71
Situational irony, **145, 186**, 191, 618, 898, **966, 1064**, 1069
Soliloquy, **292**, 1201
Song, dramatic, **286**, **1188**
Sonnet, **276–277**, 563, 626, **641, 1201**
  English, 278
  Italian, 276, 563, 641, 714, 1062
  Petrarchan, 276, 284, 316, 563, 641, **714**, 1062
  Shakespearean, **276, 278**, 316, 563, 625, 641
Sound effects, 291, 1053
Speaker, 271, 303, 306, 540, 564, 620, 1051, 1062, 1127, **1202**
Speech, **1202**

Spenserian stanza, 612, 616, **1202**
Sprung rhythm, 716, **1202**
Stanza, 986, **1202**
  ballad, 606
  Spenserian, 612, 616, **1202**
Stock epithet, **71**
Story
  frame, 115, **118**, 143, 169–170, 171, 172, 178, 186, **1190**
  literal, 383, 388
  map, 995
  slice-of-life, 1043
  symbolic, 383, 388
  See also Modern short story.
Stream of consciousness, 962, **1202**
Style, **365, 376, 1202**
  elevated, 363
Subjective point of view, 847
Suspense, **1203**
Symbol, 32, 40, 154, 345, **536**, 537, 548, 572, 577, 821, 831, 854, 859, 874, 905, **923**, 928, 935, 940, **951**, 954, **968**, 981, 1027, **1035**, 1042, **1203**
Symbolism, **1203**
Synecdoche, **1203**
Synesthesia, **646**, 650, **1203**
Syntax, 365
Tanka, **565–566**, 572, **1203**
Tercet, **1203**
Terza rima, 625, 626, **1203**
Theme, 40, 291, 345, 460, **547**, 548, 560, 563, 572, 634, **703**, 744, 763, **766**, 773, **775**, 782, 831, **854**, 859, 882, 895, **908**, 915, 935, 940, **945**, 947, 954, 981, **983**, 986, 996, 1005, 1027, 1042, 1048, 1051, 1069, 1078, **1081**, 1087, 1099, 1126, **1203**
Time and sequence
  chronological order, 460, 1078
  flashback, 71, **988**, 996, **1190**
  foreshadowing, 22, 702, 763, 995, **1023**, 1027, **1190**
Title, 1078
Tone, 262, 279, 281, 303, **307**, 310, 316, 442, 460, **485**, 492, 546, 563, 564, 634, 644, 668, 669, 824, 839, 847, 895, 900, 928, 950, 954, 964, 981, 986, 1005, 1048, 1051, 1069, 1126, 1127, **1203**
Tragedy, **1204**
Trick ending, 1043
Triplet, 447
Turn, 277, 279, 280, 281, 282, 283, 626, 714, 1062, 1204
Understatement, 271, **1204**
Verbal irony, **145, 428**, 480, 898, **930**, 935, **966**
Vernacular, 113, 1204
Verse
  blank, 364, 376, **551**, 558, 564, **1183**
  didactic, 351
Villanelle, **1058, 1204**
Volta, 276
Wisdom literature, 346–348
Word music, **695**, 702
World Literature, connecting to. See Connecting to World Literature.

VOCABULARY SKILLS

Affixes,
  Anglo-Saxon, **43**
  Greek, 378, **1145–1146**
  Latin, 378, **1145–1146**
Analogy, **177, 444**, 514, **607**, 796, **852, 928, 1005**, 1069, 1128.
  action and related object, 1079
  analyzing, **444**, 745, 1079
  cause and effect, 745
  characteristic, 745
  classification, 745
  location, 1079
  part and whole, 1079
  performer and related action, 1079
  reading, 1079
  solving, 1079
Analyzing
  analogy, **444**, 745, 1079
  context clues, **915, 1027**
Anglo-Saxon affixes, **43**
Anglo-Saxon prefixes, **43**
Anglo-Saxon suffixes, **43**
Anglo-Saxon words, **43**
Antonym, 444, 514, **782**, 839, 1099
  map, 144
Appositive, 608
Archaic words, reading, **578**
Cluster diagram, 1087
Comparison, **608**
Connotation, **443**
  rating, **744, 981**
Context clues, 86, 1042
  using, **608, 915, 1027**
Contrast, **608**
Denotation, 744, 981
Diction, 443
Etymology, 168, **191, 201**
  map, **461**
  of political science and historical terms, **906**
Graphic organizers
  antonym map, 144
  cluster diagram, 1087
  etymology chart, 168, 191, 201
  etymology map, **461**
  intensity scale, 443
  question and answer chart, **481, 1021**
  semantic map, 184
  Venn diagrams, **388**
  word chart, 70
  word information chart, **472, 965, 996**
  word-origin chart, 906
Greek affixes, 378, **1145–1146**
Greek roots, **377**, 906, **1145–1146**
Historical terms, etymology of, **906**
Identifying word relationships, **376**
Intensity Scale, 443
Latin affixes, 378, **1145–1146**
Latin roots, **377**, 906, **1145–1146**
Mathematical words derived from Greek and Latin, **377–378**
Multiple-choice tests
  analogy questions, **1170**
  sentence-completion, or fill-in-the-blank, questions, **1169**

Index of Skills   **1263**

Multiple meanings, words with, **168**, 230, 670
Political science terms, etymology of, **906**
Prefixes, Anglo-Saxon, **43**
Rating connotations, **744**, **981**
Reading
   archaic words, **578**
   word analogy, 1079
Scientific words derived from Greek and Latin, **377–378**
Semantic mapping, **184**
Solving word analogy, 1079
Suffixes, Anglo-Saxon, **43**
Synonym, 404, 444, 514, **608**, 839, 1013, 1099
Test Practice, 86, 230, 404, 514, 670, 796, 1128
Using context clues, **608**, **915**, **1027**
Venn diagrams, **388**
Vocabulary Development, 20, 41, 43, 47, 54, 56, 70, 86, 118, 144, 145, 154, 155, 167, 168, 172, 177, 179, 184, 186, 191, 193, 201, 230, 324, 328, 365, 376, 377–378, 383, 388, 404, 429, 443, 444, 451, 461, 466, 472, 474, 481, 485, 492, 514, 579, 607, 608, 670, 731, 744, 745, 750, 763, 766, 773, 775, 782, 796, 834, 839, 849, 852, 859, 862, 874, 876, 882, 887, 895, 898, 905, 906, 908, 915, 923, 928, 930, 935, 956, 965, 968, 981, 988, 996, 999, 1005, 1007, 1013, 1021, 1023, 1027, 1035, 1042, 1064, 1069, 1071, 1078, 1079, 1081, 1087, 1090, 1099, 1128
Word chart, 70
Word information chart, **472**, **965**, **996**
Word knowledge, 41, 54, 154, 167, 328, **481**, 492, 763, 773, 859, 874, 882, 895, 905, 1013, 1021, 1087
Word origins, 168, 906
Word relationships, identifying, **376**
Words with multiple meanings, **168**, 230, 670

READING SKILLS

Alexandrine, **612**, 616
Analyzing
   arguments, **324**, **827**, 831
   details, **1071**, 1078
   rhetorical devices, **483**, 498
   style, **118**
Anecdote, illustrative, **483**
Appeal to authority, **483**
Archaic words, reading, **578**
Argument by analogy, **483**
Arguments
   analyzing, **324**, **827**, 831
   critiquing, **849**
   identifying, **849**
Author's argument. *See* Arguments.
Author's purpose. *See* Purpose.
Author's stance.
   identifying, **446**
   See also Purpose.

Before You Read. *See* Setting a purpose for reading.
Beliefs, identifying, **887**
Bias, 495
Character, 118, 143, **708**, 712,
   interpreting, **155**, 166
Comparing and contrasting, **956**
   main ideas across texts, **832**, **896**, **1088**
Comprehension, improving your, **1134**
Conflict, identifying, **731**, **744**
Connotation, 443, 485
Context clues, 365
Contrasting, comparing and, **956**
Contrasting images, identifying, **695**, 702
Counterargument, **483**
Critiquing arguments, **849**
Details, 988
   analyzing, **1071**, 1078
   key, 118
Drawing inferences, **322**, 335
   from textual clues, **708**
Emotional appeals, **428**, 442, 849, 852
Essay, 905
Ethical appeals, **428**, 437, 442
Evaluating historical context, **186**, **834**
Example, illustrative, **483**
Explicit belief, 335, 840
GIST, **1140**
Graphic organizers
   comparison-contrast chart, 956
   conflict chart, 731
Historical allusion, **483**
Historical context
   evaluating, **186**, **834**, **908**
Identifying
   arguments, **849**
   author's stance, **446**
   beliefs, **887**
   conflicts and resolutions, **731**, **744**
   contrasting images, **695**, 702
   language structures, **923**, 928
   point of view, **999**, 1005
   political influences, **1090**
   purpose, **898**
Illustrative anecdote or example, **483**
Imagery, 1078
   visualizing, **651**
   contrasting, identifying, **695**, 702
Implicit belief, 335, 840
Independent Reading, 73, 203, 274, 317, 389, 427, 499, 655, 725, 730, 765, 774, 783, 853, 886, 897, 907, 922, 929, 998, 1006, 1045, 1052, 1059, 1063, 1070, 1111
Inferences, 322, 335, **708**, 766, 782, 827
   making, **322**, 335, **708**, **775**, 782, **854**, 859
   of motivation, **862**, 874
Interpreting character, **155**, 166
Inverted syntax, reading, **641**
Key details, 118
Language structures, identifying, **923**, 928
Logical appeals, **428**, 442, 849, 852
Main ideas, 324, 328, 896, **1088**,
   comparing, across texts, **832**, **896**, **1088**
Making inferences, **775**, 782, **854**, 859

Making predictions, **766**, **876**, **882**, **1007**, 1013
Metacognition, **1135**
Milton's style, **365**, **376**
Modifying predictions, **988**
Motivation, 708, 712
   inference of, **862**, 874
Multiple-choice tests
   critical-reading questions, **1166**
   evaluating-the-writer's-craft questions, **1168**
   inference questions, **1167**
   main-idea or best-title questions, **1168**
   paraphrasing or restating questions, **1167**
   strategies for taking, **1165**
   tone or mood questions, **1168**
   vocabulary-in-context questions, **1167**
Narrator, 915
Noting patterns of organization, **485**, 551
Organization, patterns of. *See* Patterns of organization.
Parallelism, **324**, 328
Paraphrasing, 450
Patterns of organization, noting, **485**, 551
Persuasive techniques, recognizing, **428**
Point of view, 328, 495, **1139**
   identifying, **999**, 1005
Political influences, identifying, **1090**
Predictions, 766, 1007
   making, **766**, **876**, **882**, **1007**, 1013
   modifying, **988**, 996
Purpose, 442, 446
   identifying, **898**
Question maps, **1141**
Reading
   archaic words, **578**
   inverted syntax, **641**
   matters, 1133–1146
   rate, **1143**
   rhyme and rhythm, **612**
Recognizing, persuasive techniques, **428**
Repetition, **483**
Rephrasing. *See* Paraphrasing.
Re-reading, **1138**
Resolution, identifying, **731**
Restatement, **483**
Rewording, **1138**
Rhetoric, 310
Rhetorical devices, analyzing, **483**, 498
Rhetorical questions, **483**
Rhyme, reading, **612**
Rhythm, reading, **612**
Setting a purpose for reading (Before You Read), 20, 47, 56, 108, 118, 145, 155, 172, 179, 186, 193, 257, 263, 278, 286, 292, 301, 304, 307, 312, 318, 324, 330, 332, 338, 342, 349, 365, 379, 383, 428, 446, 451, 466, 474, 485, 494, 495, 536, 541, 547, 551, 559, 561, 567, 574, 578–579, 610, 612, 618, 621, 631, 636, 641, 646, 651, 695, 703, 708, 714, 717, 721, 726, 731, 750, 766, 775, 821, 826–827, 834, 839, 840, 844, 849, 854, 862, 875–876, 887, 898, 908, 916, 923, 930, 938, 945,

948, 951, 956, 968, 983, 988, 999, 1007, 1015, 1023, 1028, 1035, 1046, 1049, 1053, 1056, 1060, 1064, 1071, 1081, 1088, 1090, 1100, 1102, 1106
Setting a purpose for reading (Reading Informational Materials), 324, 330, 332, 428, 446, 485, 494, 495, 834, 840, 849, 898, 916, 919, 1088, 1090, 1100, 1102, 1106
Somebody wanted but so, 1139
Speaker, 708
Style
   analyzing, 118
   Milton's, **365, 376**
Subjective point of view, 847
Summarizing
   expository text, **1140**
   narrative text, **1139**
Syntax, inverted, reading, **641**
Textual clues, drawing inferences from, **708**
Think-aloud, **1136**
Visualizing
   imagery, **651**
   text, **1134**
Writer. See Author's entries.

WRITING SKILLS

Actions, 75, 76, 658, 1031, 1087
Adapting essay, 81
Address to a work of art, 654
Address to nature, 616
Advice column letter, 481
Aesthetic appeal, 1116
Allegory, 345, 388, 607
Alliteration, 391
Allusion, 563
Ambiguity, 391, 785
American Psychological Association (APA) format, 207
Analogy, 884, 1160
Analysis of literature (poetry), **390–397**
   choosing and analyzing a poem for, 390–392
   evaluating and revising, 395–396
   peer review of, 395
   prewriting, 390–392
   proofreading, 397
   publishing, 397
   reflecting on writing, 397
   stating your thesis and gathering support for, 392
   writer's framework, 393
   writer's model, 393–394
   writing first draft of, 393–394
Analysis of nonfiction, **941–942**
   analyzing the theme for, 941
   choosing an essay for, 941
   considering purpose, audience, and tone for, 941
   gaining an overview for, 941
   gathering support for, 942
   looking for stylistic devices for, 941–942
   organizing your essay for, 942
   writing a thesis statement for, 942
Analytical composition, 1179

Analyzing
   ballad, 607
   character, 40, 782, 831
   humor, 472
   imagery, 724
   literary works for literary essay, 500–501
   the literature for comparison and contrast of literature (short story), 784–785
   magic realism, 1005
   media for multimedia presentation, 1112–1114
   poetry, 824
   questions, 607
   research information for report of literary research, 210
   theme, 702, 706
   the theme for analysis of nonfiction, 941
Anecdote, 884
Apostrophe, 616
Appearance, 658
Art, 1113
Attitude, 191, 1125
Audience, 75, 205, 656, 852, 883, 941, 1031, 1032, 1114, 1115, 1117, 1119, 1159
Audiovisual equipment, 1119
Background information, 883, 942
Background music, 1117
Ballad, analyzing, 607
Bar graph, 1163
Beginning of reflective essay, 659
Bibliography, 207, 213
Bibliography card, 207
Biographical narrative, 1176
Blank verse, 558
Block method of organization, 285, 403, 786
Body
   of analysis of literature (poetry), 393
   of comparison and contrast of literature (short story), 787
   of descriptive essay, 77
   of literary essay, 503
   of report of literary research, 216
Bold face, 1161, 1163
Brainstorming, 75, 507
Bullet, 1161
Business memo, 481
Call for action, 883
Call number, 208
Caption, 1161
Card catalog, 206
Carpe diem song, 271
Case, 1162
   small caps, 1162
   uppercase letters, 1162
Catalog, 719
CD-ROMs, 206, 1114
Character, 40, 712, 784, 785, 1013, 1087
   analyzing, 782, 831
Character analysis, 40, 154, 940, 1051, 1087
Characterization, 1031, 1087
Charts, 1113, 1164
The Chicago Manual of Style format, 207

Choosing
   and analyzing a poem for analysis of literature (poetry), 390–392
   a character for descriptive essay, 74
   an essay for analysis of nonfiction, 941
   an experience for reflective essay, 656
   an issue for persuasive essay, 883
   and narrowing a research topic for report of literary research, 204–205
   a topic for multimedia presentation, 1115
   your subjects for comparison and contrast of literature (short story), 784
Chronological order, 76, 211, 392, 502, 658, 942, 1032, 1157
Circular reasoning, 1150
Claim, evaluating, 577
Climax, 1032
Clincher sentence, 1155
Coherence, 1156
Colleges, 206
Colloquialisms, 662
Color, 1117
Columns, 1161
Community resources, 206
Comparing
   messages, 1048
   sonnets, 285
Comparison-and-contrast essay
   attitudes, 693, 824
   ballads, 229
   characters, 191, 1042
   elegies, 85
   epics, 461
   heroes, 70, 201
   messages, 620, 928
   odes, 650
   personification, 316
   perspectives, 915
   poems, 271, 403, 669, 795, 824, 955, 1125
   psalm and poem, 719
   psalms, 341
   sonnets, 282, 715, 1062
   stories, 1027, 1078
   tastes, 426
   technological revolutions, 254
   tone and message, 729
   tragedies, 513
   versions of poem, 540
   views of life, 345
Comparison and contrast of literature (short story), **784–791**
   analyzing the literature for, 784–785
   choosing your subjects for, 784
   developing a thesis for, 785–786
   evaluating and revising, 789–790
   organizing your support for, 786
   peer review of, 789
   prewriting, 784–786
   proofreading, 791
   publishing, 791
   reflecting on writing, 791
   writer's framework, 787
   writer's model, 787–788
   writing first draft of, 787–788
Complexity, 391, 785

Index of Skills   **1265**

Complications, 1032
Concerns, 656
Conclusion
 of analysis of literature (poetry), 393
 of comparison and contrast of literature (short story), 787
 of descriptive essay, 77
 of literary essay, 503
 of report of literary research, 216
Conclusions, drawing, 626, 896
Concrete images, 657
Concrete sensory details, 785, 941, 1031, 1032
Conditions, 656
Conflict, 915, 935, 1032, 1087
Connotations, 1159
Considering audience and purpose
 for analysis of nonfiction, 941
 for descriptive essay, 75
 for persuasive essay, 883–884
 for report of literary research, 205
 for short story, 1031
 and tone
Consumer documents, 1147
 contracts, 1148
 instruction manuals, 1148
 product information, 1148
 warranties, 1147
Contest, 791
Contracts, 1148
Contrast, 1161
Contrasting literary periods, 17, 107, 254, 426, 533, 693, 818
Conventions of good writing, 81
Conversation poem, 558
Couplets, 279
Cover page, 791
Creating and delivering a multimedia presentation, 1115–1119
Creating images of leaders, 1114
Debate, 1149
Delivery, 1119
Denouement, 1032
Description, 40, 205, 284, 461, 560, 657, 996
 descriptive essay, **74–81**
Descriptive details, 75, 76, 658
Descriptive essay, **74–81**
 choosing a character for, 74
 considering audience and purpose for, 75
 evaluating and revising, 79–80
 gathering, evaluating, and organizing support for, 75–76
 peer review of, 79
 prewriting, 74–76
 proofreading, 81
 publishing, 81
 reflecting on writing, 81
 writer's framework, 77
 writer's model, 77–78
 writing first draft of, 77–78
 writing your thesis statement for, 76
Designing Your Writing, 1161–1164
Details, 40, 154, 201, 492, 546, 634, 702, 706, 719, 729, 763, 795, 847, 859, 915, 940, 955, 1055

chart, 40, 271, 341, 702, 706, 719, 954
cluster diagram, 154
Determining point of view for short story, 1032
Developing
 characters for short story, 1031
 main ideas, 210
 a plot for short story, 1032
 a thesis for comparison and contrast of literature (short story), 785–786
 a thesis statement for multimedia presentation, 1116
Dialogue, 54, 388, 658, 1031, 1087
Diction, 391, 502, 795
Direct characterization, 1031
Direct quotations, 786, 941
 recording, 208–209
Direct references, 1157–1158
Documenting
 exact words and phrases, 75
 for report of literary research, 211–215
 sources, 392, 786, 942, 1115
Dramatic irony, 1032
Dramatic monologue, 712
Drawing conclusions, 626, 896
Dynamic characters, 1031
Editor in Charge: Content and Organization
 analysis of literature (poetry), 395
 comparison and contrast of literature (short story), 789
 descriptive essay, 79
 literary essay, 505
 reflective essay, 661
 report of literary research, 221
Editor in Charge: Style Guidelines
 analysis of literature (poetry), 396
 comparison and contrast of literature (short story), 790
 descriptive essay, 80
 literary essay, 506
 reflective essay, 662
 report of literary research, 222
Effectiveness, 1116
Elaborating, 392, 942
 evidence, 501, 502, 786
Electronic media-generated images, 1116
Electronic media sources, 1112
Elements, chart, 345
E-mail, 81
Emotional appeal, 852, 874, 884, 1150
Emphasis, 1162
Encyclopedia, 204, 206
Endnotes, 212
End of reflective essay, 659
Epic, 461
Episode, 184
Essay, 17, 40, 262, 310, 328, 345, 375, 381, 450, 472, 492, 498, 548, 563, 607, 626, 702, 706, 724, 763, 773, 831, 839, 847, 859, 874, 882, 895, 905, 935, 947, 965, 981, 1005, 1021, 1048, 1055, 1058
 comparison-and-contrast. See Comparison-and-contrast essay.
Establishing a setting for short story, 1031
Ethical appeal, 852, 884, 1150

Evaluating
 claim, 577
 media, 1113
 writing. See Revising.
Events, 656, 657, 1013
Evidence, 70, 501, 883, 884, 942, 965, 981
 chart, 884
 elaborating, 501, 502, 786
 literary, 392, 501, 502, 786
Exact words and phrases, documenting, 75
Exaggeration, 303, 443, 481
Examples, 201, 328, 492, 577, 847, 884, 1021, 1027
 precise and relevant, 501
Experiences, personal, 656
Expert testimony, 884
Explanation, 657
Exposition, 205
 analysis of literature (poetry), **390–397**
 analysis of nonfiction, **941–942**
 comparison and contrast of literature (short story), **784–791**
 literary essay, **500–507**
 multimedia presentation, 1108, **1112–1119**
 report of literary research, **204–223**
Expository composition, 1175
Extended metaphor, 310
External conflict, 1032
Eye contact, 1119
Facial expressions, 1119
Facts, 884
Feedback, 81, 397, 1119
 chart, 1119
Feelings, 75, 76
Feelings and thoughts, 1031
Figurative language, 75, 76, 282, 391, 403, 502
Figures of speech, 299, 376, 644, 785, 824, 941, 1032, 1062
Film, 1112, 1116
Filmmakers, 1113
Finding a story idea for short story, 1031
First-person point of view, 54, 546, 965, 1032
5W-How? questions, 111, 205
Flashback, 658, 1032
Flash-forward, 658, 1032
Flowchart, 1164
Font, 1117, 1151, 1162
 decorative, 1162
 sans serif, 1162
 script, 1162
 serif, 1162
 size of, 1163
 style of, 1163
Footnotes, 212
Form
 of argument, 884
 of description, 75
 of short story, 1031
Formal outline, 210, 211
Formality, level of, 1159
Frame story, 143
Freewriting, 567, 988, 1053
Gaining an overview for analysis of nonfiction, 941

Gathering
   evaluating, and organizing support for descriptive essay, 75–76
   and recording details for reflective essay, 657–658
   support for analysis of nonfiction, 942
Generalization, 1087
Genre, 928
Gestures, 1119
Government offices, 206
Graphic artists, 1114
Graphic organizers
   cluster diagram, 154
   details chart, 40, 271, 341, 702, 706, 719, 954
   evidence chart, 884
   feedback chart, 1119
   line graph, 1163
   magic-realism chart, 1005
   major-point chart, 501
   media-chart format, 1118
   pie chart, 1164
   sonnet-comparison chart, 285
   spreadsheet, 1163
   update chart, 345
Graphics, 223, 397, 1113
Graphs, 1163
Haiku, 572
Hasty generalization, 1150
Heading, 1161
Headings from outlines, 211
Headlines, 111
Historical background, 501
Historical report, 167
Historical societies, 206
Humor, 388
   analyzing, 472
Humorous imitation, 481
I. See First-person point of view.
Identifying your thesis and calling for action for persuasive essay, 883
Illustrators, 1114
Imagery, 282, 391, 502, 572, 715, 785, 795, 824, 941, 954, 1032
   analyzing, 724
Images, 563, 874, 1116, 1117
Imitation, 303
   humorous, 481
Incongruity, 481
Indexes to newspapers, essays, and articles, 206
Indicating the significance for short story, 1032
Indirect characterization, 1031
Inference, 782, 831
Influencing elections, 1114
Information resources, 206
Informative documents, 1147
   consumer documents, 1147
   workplace documents, 1148
Instruction manuals, 1148
Interior monologue, 54, 658, 981, 1031
Internal conflict, 1032
Internet, 74, 204, 206, 254, 397, 784, 1112, 1115
Interpretation, 210
   of character, 291

Interpreting media, 1113
Introducing quotations, 506
Introduction
   of analysis of literature (poetry), 393
   of ballad, 112
   of comparison and contrast of literature (short story), 787
   of descriptive essay, 77
   of literary essay, 503
   of report of literary research, 216
Irony, 443, 502, 785, 795, 941, 1032
Issue, 883
Italic, 1161, 1165
Job application, 1150
Journal entry, 634, 986, 1099
Key points, 392, 942
Keywords, 74
Language, 391, 1113
Letter, 306, 321, 335, 611, 1058
Library, 784
Library resources, 206
Lighting, 1113
Line graph, 1163
Line spacing, 1151
Literary analysis, 390
Literary elements, 390–391, 784, 785
Literary essay, **500–507**
   analyzing literary works for, 500–501
   choosing a topic for, 500
   evaluating and revising, 505–506
   organizing your essay for, 502
   peer review of, 505
   prewriting, 500–502
   proofreading, 507
   publishing, 507
   reflecting on writing, 507
   writer's framework, 503
   writer's model, 503–504
   writing a thesis statement for, 501
   writing first draft of, 503–504
Literary evidence, 392, 501, 502, 786
Literary magazines, 81
   online, 507
Literary periods, contrasting, 17, 107, 254, 426, 533, 693, 818
Literary research, 204
Literary trends, 500
Logical appeal, 852, 884, 1150
Logical order, 211, 1157
Looking for stylistic devices for analysis of nonfiction, 941–942
Lyric poetry, 563
Lyrics, 271
Magazines, 1116
   literary. See Literary magazines.
Magic realism, analyzing, 1005
   chart, 1005
Main character, 1031
Main ideas, developing, 210
Maintaining balance, 658
Major point, 501, 502
   chart, 501
Making
   an outline for report of literary research, 211
   a research plan for report of literary research, 205–206

Mapping story details, 184
Maps, 1113
Margins, 1151
Maximizing your impact for multimedia presentation, 1117
Media-chart format, 1118
Media effects, 1114
Media literacy concepts, **1112–1113**
Media messages, 1112–1113, 1114
Media sources, 1112
Media strategies, 1113
Media Workshop: multimedia presentation, **1112–1119**
Mementos, 657
Memoir, 481
Memoranda, 1148
Messages, 403, 729
   comparing, 1048
Metaphor, 310, 391
Meter, 403
Microfilm or microfiche, 206
Middle of reflective essay, 659
Mini-Workshops
   analysis of nonfiction, **941–942**
   persuasive essay, **883–884**
   short story, **1031–1032**
Mock epic, 461
Mock-heroic writing, 461
Models. See Writer's Models.
Modern Language Association of America (MLA) format, 207
Mood, 572, 1032
Motivation, 782, 1087
Multimedia presentation, 1108, **1112–1119**
   analyzing media for, 1112–1114
   choosing a topic for, 1115
   creating and delivering a, 1115–1119
   developing a thesis statement for, 1116
   maximizing your impact for, 1117
   organizing your presentation for, 1117–1118
   practicing your presentation for, 1119
   researching your topic for, 1115
   selecting media for, 1116
Multimedia report, 744
Multiple-choice test, 481
Museums, 206
Narration, 205
   reflective essay, 639, **656–663**, 1069
   short story, 964–965, **1031–1032**
Narrative, 657
Narrative details, 75, 76, 658
Narrator, 143, 965, 1032
Newspapers, 1116
News photographers, 1114
News story, 111
Nonverbal behavior, 1119
Note cards, 208, 1117
Noting sources for report of literary research, 207–208
Nuance, 391, 785
Online catalog, 206
Online databases, 206
Online information, 1116
Online literary magazines, 507
Online periodical indexes, 206

Index of Skills   1267

Online services, 206
Online sources, 921
Onomatopoeia, 391
Opinion, 375, 533, 818, 915, 1027, 1042
Oral presentation, 1115
Order of importance, 76, 211, 392, 658, 884, 942, 1117, 1157
Organizational patterns, 211
Organizing
   for analysis of nonfiction, 942
   for comparison and contrast of literature (short story), 786
   your essay
   the events for short story, 1032
   for literary essay, 502
   for persuasive essay, 884
   your presentation for multimedia presentation, 1117–1118
   for reflective essay, 658
   your support
Outline, 211
   formal, 210, 211
Outlining, 1117
Pace of short story, 1032
Page design, 397, 791, 1161
Pamphlet, 397
Parable, 345
Paragraphs, 950, 996
   parts of, 1155
   qualities of, 1156
Parallelism, 790, 884, 1157–1158, 1160
Paraphrase, 209, 299, 376, 634, 644, 786, 941
Parenthetical citations, 212, 501–502
Parody, 461, 481
Peer review
   of analysis of literature (poetry), 395
   of comparison and contrast of literature (short story), 789
   of descriptive essay, 79
   of literary essay, 505
   of reflective essay, 661
   of report of literary research, 221
Personal experiences, 656
Personification, 316, 560
Perspectives, 883
   relevant, 207
Persuasion
   persuasive essay, 852, **883–884**
Persuasive documents, 1147, 1149
   critiquing, 1149–1150
   debate, 1149
   persuasive speech, 1149
   policy statement, 1149
   political platform, 1149
Persuasive essay, 852, **883–884**
   choosing an issue for, 883
   considering purpose and audience for, 883–884
   identifying your thesis and calling for action for, 883
   organizing your support for, 884
   supporting your position for, 884
Persuasive composition, 1178
Persuasive speech, 1149
Persuasive strategies, 657
Petrarchan sonnet, 1062

Photographs, 1111
Physical appearance, 75, 76
Pictures, 1164
Pie chart, 1164
Plagiarizing, 209, 1115
Plot, 75, 784, 785, 1032
Poem, 279, 611, 950, 1030, 1058
Poetry, analyzing, 824
Point-by-point method of organization, 786
Point of view, 1032
Policy statement, 1149
Political campaign speech, 481
Political platform, 1149
Practicing your presentation for multimedia presentation, 1117
Praise poem, 719
Precise examples, 501
Precise language
   adjectives, nouns, and verbs, 1159
Predictions, 1015
Prewriting
   analysis of literature (poetry), 390–392
   comparison and contrast of literature (short story), 784–786
   descriptive essay, 74–76
   literary essay, 500–502
   reflective essay, 656–658
   report of literary research, 204–215
Primary sources, 207
Print media, 1112
Print media sources, 1112
Print sources, 921
Procedure manuals, 1148
Production information, 1148
Prologue, 143
Proofreading
   analysis of literature (poetry), 397
   comparison and contrast of literature (short story), 791
   descriptive essay, 81
   literary essay, 507
   questions for, 1154
   reflective essay, 663
   report of literary research, 223
   symbols for, 1154
Proposal, 443
Prose apostrophe, 616
Prose narrative, 546
Proverb, 345
Publishing
   analysis of literature (poetry), 397
   comparison and contrast of literature (short story), 791
   descriptive essay, 81
   literary essay, 507
   reflective essay, 663
   report of literary research, 223
Purpose, 75, 205, 656, 883, 941, 1031, 1115, 1159
Questions, analyzing, 607
Quick guide!
   ambiguities, nuances, and complexities, 391
   audience feedback, 1119
   characterization techniques, 1031
   guidelines for giving credit within a paper, 212

   guidelines for note cards, 208
   information resources, 206
   literary elements, 390–391
   media literacy concepts, 1112–1113
   media strategies, 1113
   narrative and descriptive details, 658
   organizing a multimedia presentation, 1117
   questions for proofreading, 1154
   reflecting on a subject, 657
   sample entries for *Works Cited* list, 213–215
   stages of the writing process, 1153
   symbols for revising and proofreading, 1154
   types of order, 1157
   using media, 1116
Quickwrite, 20, 32, 47, 54, 56, 69, 155, 166, 304, 306, 312, 316, 322, 324, 328, 335, 342, 345, 379, 381, 451, 460, 482, 498, 541, 546, 547, 548, 561, 563, 567, 572, 574, 577, 578, 606, 618, 620, 621, 626, 636, 644, 646, 650, 695, 702, 703, 706, 708, 712, 714, 715, 717, 719, 721, 724, 726, 729, 766, 773, 821, 824, 832, 847, 849, 852, 875, 882, 887, 895, 896, 908, 915, 921, 930, 935, 938, 940, 945, 947, 948, 950, 951, 954, 968, 981, 983, 986, 1007, 1013, 1015, 1021, 1023, 1027, 1035, 1042, 1046, 1048, 1049, 1051, 1053, 1055, 1056, 1058, 1060, 1062, 1064, 1069, 1071, 1078, 1081, 1087, 1088, 1108
Quotations, 1108
   direct, recording, 208–209
   introducing, 506
   long, 209
Radio, 206, 1112
Reactions, 75, 76, 1031, 1087
Readers' Guide to Periodical Literature, 206
Reasons, 884, 942
References, 392
Reflecting on writing
   analysis of literature (poetry), 397
   comparison and contrast of literature (short story), 791
   descriptive essay, 81
   literary essay, 507
   reflective essay, 663
   report of literary research, 223
Reflecting on your subject for reflective essay, 656–657
Reflection questions, 657
Reflective essay, 639, **656–663**, 1069
   choosing an experience for, 656
   evaluating and revising, 661–662
   gathering and recording details for, 657–658
   organizing for, 658
   peer review of, 661
   prewriting, 656–658
   proofreading, 663
   publishing, 663
   reflecting on writing, 663
   reflecting on your subject for, 656–657
   thinking about purpose for, 656

writer's framework, 659
writer's model, 659–660
writing first draft of, 659–660
Rehearsing, 1119
Relevant examples, 501
Relevant perspectives, 207
Reliability of sources, 207
Repetition, 785, 884, 1160
Reply, 284
Report, 921
Report of literary research, **204–223**
   analyzing research information for, 210
   choosing and narrowing a research topic for, 204–205
   considering purpose, audience, and tone for, 205
   documenting sources for, 211–215
   evaluating and revising, 221–222
   making an outline for, 211
   making a research plan for, 205–206
   noting sources for, 207–208
   peer review of, 221
   prewriting, 204–215
   proofreading, 223
   publishing, 223
   reflecting on writing, 223
   researching and taking notes for, 208–209
   writer's framework, 216
   writer's model, 216–220
   writing a thesis statement for, 210
   writing first draft of, 216–220
Research, 167, 443, 921, 1108
Researching
   and taking notes for report of literary research, 208–209
   your topic for multimedia presentation, 1115
Research questions, 205–206
Research report, 167
Research strategies, 207
Resources, 507
Response, 17, 107, 284, 303, 328, 450, 492, 611, 724, 905, 947, 1058
   to expository text, 1175
   to literature, 1174
Résumé, 1150–1151
Retelling, 111
Revising, 1119, 1159–1160
   analysis of literature (poetry), 395–396
   comparison and contrast of literature (short story), 789–790
   descriptive essay, 79–80
   literary essay, 505–506
   reflective essay, 661–662
   report of literary research, 221–222
   symbols for, 1154
Rewriting, 345
Rhetorical devices, 884, 1159, 1160
Rhyme, 391
Rhythm, 391, 884
Roman, 1163
Satire, 388, 472, 502
Schools, 206
Secondary sources, 207
Selecting media for multimedia presentation, 1116

Sensory details, 40, 75, 76
   concrete, 1031, 1032
Sentence variety, 1159, 1160
Sequence of events, 1032
Setting, 658, 784, 785, 874, 1013, 1031
Shakespearean sonnet, 1062
Shaping attitudes, 1114
Short story, 964–965, **1031–1032**
   considering audience and purpose for, 1031
   determining point of view for, 1032
   developing a plot for, 1032
   developing characters for, 1031
   establishing a setting for, 1031
   finding a story idea for, 1031
   indicating the significance for, 1032
   organizing the events for, 1032
   using stylistic devices for, 1032
Significant ideas, 391
Simile, 391
Situational irony, 1032
Sonnet, 1062
Sonnet form, 279
Sound, 1113, 1116, 1117, 1159
Sound effects, 282, 403
Source cards, 207
   annotating, 208
Sources, 206
   documenting, 392, 786, 942
   numbering, 207
   reliability and validity of, 207
Spatial order, 76, 658, 1157
Speaker, 390, 403, 548, 884, 1032
Special effects, 1113
Specialized reference books, 206
Speech, 1115
Spreadsheet, 1163–1164
Stages of the writing process, 1153
Stating your thesis and gathering support for analysis of literature (poetry), 392
Statistics, 884
Stereotypes, 1113
Story, 184, 1013
Story details, mapping, 184
Stream of consciousness, 981
Structure of arguments, 502
Style, 80, 222, 396, 506, 662, 790, 928, 1032, 1159
Stylistic devices, 391, 502, 785
Subheading, 1161
Subject, 941
Summarizing, 209, 392, 498, 847, 941
Summary, 299, 786
Supporting characters, 1031
Supporting your position for persuasive essay, 884
Supporting sentences, 1155
Symbol, 882, 954
Synthesis, 205
Table of contents, 211
Tables, 1163
Tanka, 572
Television, 206, 1112, 1116
Test Practice, 87, 231, 405, 515, 671, 797, 1127
Test Smarts
   analytical composition, 1179

biographical narrative, 1176
expository composition, 1175
persuasive composition, 1178
response to expository text, 1175
response to literature, 1174
Text, 1116, 1117
Theme, 391, 548, 563, 784, 785, 795, 928, 941, 954, 1032, 1055, 1062, 1078, 1087
   analyzing, 702, 706
Thesis, 76
Thesis statement, 76, 210, 392, 501, 785–786, 883, 942, 1116
Thinking about purpose for reflective essay, 656
Third-person-limited point of view, 1032
Third-person-omniscient point of view, 1032
Thoughts, 75, 76, 658
Thoughts and feelings, 1031
Time lines, 1164
Title, 328
Tone, 662, 715, 729, 785, 928, 941, 1031, 1078, 1125, 1159
   of paper, 205
   of poem, 282, 391, 403
Topic list, 443
Topic sentence, 1155
Transitional expressions, 1157–1158
Transitions, 1118
TV producers, 1113
Type, 397, 791
Update, 345, 360, 376
   chart, 345
Unity, 1156
Using stylistic devices for short story, 1032
Validity of sources, 207
Verbal irony, 481, 1032
Video, 1112, 1116
Video stores, 206
Villanelle, 1058
Visual image makers, 1113
Visualizing, 657
Visual representations, 1113
Visuals, 223, 397, 1163
Voice, 712, 1159
Warranties, 1147
Web page, 663
Web site, 81, 207, 223, 397, 507
White space, 1161
Word choice, 715, 1159
Word processing and desktop publishing. See Designing Your Writing.
   font, 1117
   graphics and visuals, 223
   page design and type, 791
   page design, type, and visuals, 397
Workplace documents, 1148, 1151
   integrating databases, graphics, and spreadsheets, 1151
   memoranda, 1148
   procedure manuals, 1148
   word-processing features, 1151
Works Cited list, 207, 212, 213
   sample, 219–220
   sample entries for, 213–215
World Wide Web, 206

Writer's Models
    analysis of literature (poetry), 393–394
    comparison and contrast of literature (short story), 787–788
    descriptive essay, 77–78
    literary essay, 503–504
    reflective essay, 659–660
    report of literary research, 216–220
Writing first draft
    of analysis of literature (poetry), 393–394
    of comparison and contrast of literature (short story), 787–788
    of descriptive essay, 77–78
    of literary essay, 503–504
    of reflective essay, 659–660
    of report of literary research, 216–220
Writing sample, 223, 791
Writing a thesis statement
    for analysis of nonfiction, 942
    for descriptive essay, 76
    for literary essay, 501
    for report of literary research, 210
Writing Workshops
    analysis of literature (poetry), **390–397**
    comparison and contrast of literature (short story), **784–791**
    descriptive essay, **74–81**
    literary essay, **500–507**
    reflective essay, **656–663**
    report of literary research, **204–223**

LANGUAGE (GRAMMAR, USAGE, AND MECHANICS) SKILLS

Accept, except, 1237
Active voice, **1044**
Active-voice verbs, **1044**
Adjective(s), 1206, 1228
    clauses, **311**, 1216
    phrases, 1215
    proper, 1224
Adverb(s), 1206
    clauses, **311**, 1217
    conjunctive, 1229
    phrases, 1215
Affect, effect, 1238
Agreement
    of pronoun and antecedent, **764**, 1208–1209
    of subjects and verbs, **493**, 1207
All ready, already, 1238
All together, altogether, 1238
Allusion, illusion, 1238
A lot, 1238
American English, standard, using, 942
Among, between, 1239
Antecedent, 764
    agreement with pronoun, **764**
Any one, anyone, 1238
Apostrophes
    with contractions, 1233
    with plurals, 1234
    with possessive case, 1233
Appositives, 1216, 1229
As if, like, 1241

As, like, 1240
At, 1238
A while, awhile, 1238
Bad, badly, 1238
Because, 1238
Being as, being that, 1238
Beside, besides, 1239
Between, among, 1239
Brackets, 209, 1234
Bring, take, 1239
Bust, busted, 1239
Can, may, 1239
Cannot (can't) help but, 1239
Capitalization, 81, 1224–1227
Clauses, 1216–1217
    adjective, 1216
    adverb, 1217
    elliptical, 1217
    independent, 1216, 1228, 1229, 1230
    noun, 1217
    subordinate, 1216
Coherence, building, **997**
Colons, 1230
Combining sentences, **202**
Commas, 311, 316
    with interrupters, 1229
    with introductory words, phrases, and clauses, 1228–1229
    with items in a series, 1228
    with quotation marks, 1231
Compare, contrast, 1239
Complements
    indirect objects, 1219
    objective complements, 1219
    subject complements, 1219
        predicate adjectives, 1219
        predicate nominatives, 1219
Compound subjects, 493
Compound word, unusual, 719
Conjunctions, 1206–1207, 1229
    coordinating, 1206, 1230
    correlative, 1207
    subordinating, 1207
Consistency, verb tense, 549
Coordinating conjunctions, **202**
Dangling modifiers, 223, **936**
Dashes, 1234
Dialogue, punctuating, 663, 1231–1232
Direct references, **997**
Double negative, 1213
Double subject 1239
Due to, 1239
Effect, affect, 1238
Either, neither, 1239
Ellipsis points, 209, 1232–1233
End marks, 1227–1228
Etc., 1238
Every day, everyday, 1239
Every one, everyone, 1239
Except, accept, 1237
Fewer, less, 1240
Gender, agreement in, 764
Gerund, 1212, 1215
Good, well, 1240
Graphic organizers, transitions chart, 997
Had ought, hadn't ought, 1240
Hyphens, 1234

Illusion, allusion, 1238
Imply, infer, 1240
In, in to, into, 1240
Indefinite pronouns, 764
Invented word, 719
Inverted word order, 719
Inverting syntax, 376
Irregardless, regardless, 1240
Irregular syntax, 376
Italics, 1230–1231
Its, it's, 1240
Kind of, sort of, 1240
Less, fewer, 1240
Lie, lay, 1240
Like, as, 1240
Like, as if, 1241
Literary present tense, 502, 786, 1210
Modifiers, 1213–1214
    comparative and superlative forms of, 1213
    dangling, 223, **936**
    misplaced, 1214
Neither, either, 1239
Nonrestrictive clauses, **311**
Nor, or, 1241
Noun(s), 1206
    clauses, 1217
    collective, 1207, 1209
    plural, 1236–1237
    possessive, 1211, 1212, 1233
    proper, 1224
Number, agreement in, 764
Of, 1241
Off, off of, 1241
Omitting words, 376
On to, onto, 1241
Or, nor, 1241
Parallel structure, 790, 791, **860,** 1221
Parallelism, 790, 791, **860,** 1221
Parentheses, 1234
Parenthetical expressions, 1229
Parts of speech, 1206–1207
Passive voice, **1044**
Passive-voice verbs, **1044**
Person, agreement in, 764
Phrases, 1214–1216
    adjective, 1215
    adverb, 1215
    appositive, 1216, 1229
    gerund, 1215
    infinitive, 1215–1216
    participial, 1215, 1228
    prepositional, 1214–1215
    verbal, 1215–1216
Plural subjects and verbs, **493**
Possessives, 1212, 1233
Prefixes, 1235
Prepositional phrases, 1214–1215
Prepositions, 1206
Present tense, literary, 502, 786, 1210
Pronouns, 764, 1206, 1208–1209, 1211–1213
    agreement with antecedent, **764**
    case of
        nominative, 1211, 1212
        objective, 1212
        possessive, 1212

demonstrative, 1206
interrogative, 1206
personal, 1206, 1211
plural, 1208
reference with, 1212–1213
reflexive and intensive, 1206
relative, 1206
special problems with
  and appositives, 1212
  and elliptical construction, 1212
  and *–self* or *–selves,* 1212
  and *who* and *whom,* 1212
Punctuation, 1227–1234
  dialogue, 663, 1231–1232
  quotations, 397
  titles, 507, 1231–1232
Quotation marks, 209, 397, 507, 663, 1231–1232
Quotations, punctuating, 397, 1231–1232
Reason . . . because, reason . . . that, 1238
Refer back, 1241
Regardless, irregardless, 1240
Restrictive clauses, 311
Rise, raise, 1241
Roots, 1235
Run-on sentences, **72**
Semicolon, 72, 316, 1229–1230
Sentence fragments, **72**
Sentences, 1217–1223
  classified by purpose, 1220
  classified by structure
    complex, 1220
    compound, 1220
    compound-complex, 1220
    simple, 1220
  combining, **202,** 1223
  effective, **860**
  versus fragments, 1221
  improving the style of, 1220–1222
  revising wordy, 1222
  run-on, **72,** 1221
  subject and predicate in, 1218–1219
    compound subjects, 1207
    compound verbs, 1218
    finding the subject, 1218–1219
    simple predicates, 1218
    simple subjects, 1218
  varying the structure of, 1222
  writing clear, 1220–1221
Singular subjects and verbs, **493**
Sit, set, 1241
Some, somewhat, 1241
Sort of, kind of, 1240
Spelling, 1235–1237
  –cede, –ceed, and *–sede,* 1235
  ie and *ei,* 1235
  noun plurals, 1236–1237
  prefixes, 1235
  suffixes, 1235–1236
  word parts, 1235
    prefixes, 1235
    roots, 1235
    suffixes, 1235
Standard American English, using, 942
Subject, 376
  compound, 493
Subject-verb agreement, **493**

Subordinating conjunctions, **202**
Suffixes, 1235–1236
Syntax, irregular, 376
Take, bring, 1239
Tense consistency, verb, **549**
Than, then, 1241
That, who, which, 1242
Theirs, there's, 1242
Their, there, they're, 1241
This here, that there, 1242
Titles, punctuating, 507, 1231–1232
Transitional words and phrases, 396, 1229
Transitions, **997**
  chart, 997
Try and, try to, 1242
Type, type of, 1242
Verbs, 376, 1206
  action, 1206
  active and passive voice of, **1044,** 1210–1211
  agreement of subjects and, **493**
  helping (auxiliary), 1206
  linking, 1206
  principal parts of, 1209
  regular and irregular, 1209
  tense consistency of, **549**
Way, ways, 1242
Well, good, 1240
When, where, 1242
Who's, whose, 1242
Who, which, that, 1242
Word, invented, 719
Word order, inverted, 719
Word parts, 1235
Your, you're, 1242

LISTENING AND SPEAKING SKILLS

Adapting
  a play, 472
  your literary research paper for research presentation, 224
  your reflective essay for reflective presentation, 664–665
  your written essay for literary response presentation, 508
Aesthetic appeal, 1116
Aesthetic effect, 111, 712
Aesthetic language, 664
Alliteration, 450, 626
Ambiguity, 508
American English, standard, 509, 665
Analogy, argument by, 1121
Analyzing media for multimedia presentation, 1112–1114
Anecdote, 224
Antitheses, 450
Appeal
  aesthetic, 1116
  emotional, 1120, 1123
  ethical, 1121, 1123
  logical, 1120, 1121, 1123
Aptness, 398
Argument by analogy, 1121
Art, 1113
Artistic merit, 398

Artistic staging, 399
Attack *ad hominem,* 1123
Audience, 111, 177, 224, 225, 299, 397, 399, 507, 607, 664, 665, 1114, 1115, 1117, 1119, 1120, 1121, 1122, 1123
Audiovisual equipment, 1119
Background music, 1117
Ballad performance, 111
Ballad presentation, 607
Bandwagon effect, 1123
Body language, 399, 664
Body of literary response presentation, 508
Book of ballads, collecting, 112
Books, 1108
Cartoon, 154
CD-ROMs, 1116
Character, 299, 472
Charts, 225, 1113
Choosing a topic for multimedia presentation, 1115
Choral reading, 291, 626
Chorus, 291
Coherent speech, 1121
Colloquialisms, 509, 1122
Color, 1117
Complexity, 508
Concise notes, 509
Conclusion
  of literary response presentation, 508
  of research presentation, 224
  of syllogism, 1122
Concrete images, 664
Contractions, 1122
Counterarguments, 1120
Couplet reading, 450
Creating and delivering a multimedia presentation, 1115–1119
Creating images of leaders, 1115
Deductive approach, 1121
Delivering
  your recitation for recitation of literature, 399
  your speech for persuasive speech evaluation and presentation, 1122
Delivery, 41, 321, 1119
  formal, 1122
Delivery techniques, 509, 665
Description, 224
Developing a thesis statement for multimedia presentation, 1116
Dialogue, 472, 664
Diction, 225, 1123
Discussing, 17, 69, 85, 107, 254, 279, 391, 426, 533, 572, 693, 773, 818, 928, 1071
Documenting sources, 1115
Dramatic reading, 41, 712
Drawing, 996, 1078
Effective language, 664
Effectiveness, 1116
Electronic media-generated images, 1116
Electronic media sources, 1112
Emotional appeal, 1120, 1123
Emphasis, 225, 291, 299, 509
English, standard American, 509, 665
Enunciation, 509

Index of Skills **1271**

Ethical appeal, 1121, 1123
Evaluating media, 1113
Evidence, 509, 1123
  literary, 508
Exhibits, 225
Expert testimony, 1123
Exposition, 224
Expository strategies
  literary response presentation, **508–509**
  multimedia presentation, 1112–1119
  research presentation, **224–225**
Extemporaneous presentation, 225
Extemporaneous speech, 509, 665
Eye contact, 225, 509, 665, 1119, 1122
Fable performance, 177
Facial expressions, 225, 299, 399, 509, 664, 665, 712, 1119
Facts, 1123
False causality, 1123
Feedback, 509, 665, 1119
  chart, 1119
Film, 1112, 1116
Filmmakers, 1113
Film presentation, 81
Film programs, 744
Focused speech, 1121
Font, 1117
Formal delivery, 1122
Gestures, 41, 225, 299, 399, 509, 664, 665, 712, 1119, 1122
Government publications, 1108
Graphic artists, 1114
Graphic organizers
  feedback chart, 1119
  media-chart format, 1118
Graphics, 1113
Graphs, 225
Group reading, 291, 729
Group work, 81, 107, 111, 177, 254, 291, 426, 481, 533, 572, 626, 663, 693, 729, 773, 791, 818, 954, 1021, 1044, 1119
Illustration, 81, 154, 184
Illustrators, 1114
Images, 1116, 1117
Inductive approach, 1121
Influencing elections, 1114
Informal expressions, 665
Integrating quotations, 224
Internet, 1112, 1115
Interpretation, 398
Interpreting media, 1113
Interpretive techniques, 399
Interviewing, 921
Introduction
  of literary response presentation, 508
  of recitation of literature, 399
  of research presentation, 224
Irony, 664, 1121
  verbal, 1121
Language, 665, 1113
  aesthetic, 664
  body, 399, 664
  effective, 664
Lighting, 1113
Listening and Speaking Workshops

literary response presentation, **508–509**
persuasive speech evaluation and presentation, **1120–1123**
recitation of literature, **398–399**
reflective presentation, **664–665**
research presentation, **224–225**
Listening to a persuasive speech for persuasive speech evaluation and presentation, 1122–1123
Literary evidence, 508
Literary response presentation, **508–509**
  adapting your written essay for, 508
  rehearsing and delivering your oral response for, 509
Logical appeal, 1120, 1121, 1123
Logical fallacies, 1120, 1123
Magazines, 1108, 1116
Major premise of syllogism, 1122
Maps, 1113
Maximizing your impact for multimedia presentation, 1117
Media
  evaluating, 1113
  interpreting, 1113
  print, 1112
Media-chart format, 1118
Media effects, 1114
Media literacy concepts, **1112–1113**
Media messages, 1112–1113, 1114
Media sources, 1112
Media strategies, 1113
Media Workshop: multimedia presentation, **1112–1119**
Memorizing, 1122
Meter, 729
Minor premise of syllogism, 1122
Monologue, 299
Mood, 399
Movements, 399, 664
Multimedia presentation, 1108, **1112–1119**
  analyzing media for, 1112–1114
  choosing a topic for, 1115
  creating and delivering a, 1115–1119
  developing a thesis statement for, 1116
  maximizing your impact for, 1117
  organizing your presentation for, 1117–1118
  practicing your presentation for, 1119
  researching your topic for, 1115
  selecting media for, 1116
Multimedia report, 744
Narration, 224
Narrative strategies
  recitation of literature, **398–399**
  reflective presentation, **664–665**
Newspapers, 1108, 1116
News photographers, 1114
Nonverbal behavior, 1119
Nonverbal techniques, 665
Note cards, 225, 509, 665, 1117
Notes, concise, 509
Nuance, 508
Octave, 381
Online information, 1116
Onomatopoeia, 626

Opinion statement, 1120, 1123
Oral performance, 712
Oral presentation, 177, 224, 450, 607, 663, 729, 1115
Oral reading, 321, 381
Oral response to literature, 507, 508
Order of importance, 1117, 1121
Organizing your presentation for multimedia presentation, 1117–1118
Originality, 398
Outlining, 1117
Overgeneralization, 1123
Painting, 996
Parallelism, 508, 1121
Paraphrasing, 398
Partner work, 17, 79, 177, 221, 299, 395, 396, 481, 505, 507, 661, 663, 712, 789, 986, 1035, 1062
Pauses, 41, 225, 291, 321, 381, 399, 509, 1122
Performance techniques, 225
Perspectives, relevant, 224
Persuasive speech evaluation and presentation, **1120–1123**
  delivering your speech for, 1122
  listening to a persuasive speech for, 1122–1123
  preparing a persuasive speech for, **1120–1122**
Persuasive strategies
  persuasive speech evaluation and presentation, **1120–1123**
Photographs, 225, 1113
Pitch of voice, 399, 1122
Plagiarism, 1115
Play adaptation, 472
Podium, 607
Poetry recital, 321
Practicing your presentation for multimedia presentation, 1119
Preparing
  a persuasive speech for persuasive speech evaluation and presentation, **1120–1122**
  your recitation for recitation of literature, 398
Primary sources, 224
Print media, 1112
Print media sources, 1112
Professional recitations, 399
Pronunciation, 509
Propaganda, 1120, 1123
Proposition of fact, 1122
Proposition of policy, 1122
Proposition of problem, 1123
Proposition of value, 1123
Purpose, 224, 664, 1115, 1120
Quick guide!
  audience feedback, 1119
  delivery techniques, 509, 665
  logical fallacies and propaganda techniques, 1123
  marking text for delivery, 399
  media literacy concepts, 1112–1113
  media strategies, 1113
  organizing a multimedia presentation, 1117

performance techniques, 225
rhetorical devices, 1121
selecting criteria for a recitation, 398
using media, 1116
Quotations, 1108
  integrating, 224
  writing, 509
Radio, 1112
Radio transcripts, 1108
Rate of speaking, 399
Reading aloud, 42, 202, 280, 324, 341, 376, 450, 551, 558, 564, 572, 621, 651, 695, 717
Reasons, 1120
Recitation, 321, 397, 398
  delivering your recitation for, 399
  of literature, **398–399**
  preparing your recitation for, 398
  professional, 399
Recording, song, 154
Red herring, 1123
Reflective presentation, **664–665**
  adapting your reflective essay for, 664–665
  rehearsing your presentation for, 665
Refrain, 291
Rehearsing, 41, 177, 225, 399, 450, 509, 607, 665, 1119, 1122
  and delivering your oral response for literary response presentation, 509
  your presentation
  for reflective presentation, 665
  for research presentation, 225
Relevance, 398
Relevant perspectives, 224
Repetition, 508, 1121
Re-reading, 41, 75, 221, 291, 324, 375, 376, 390, 433, 564, 661, 708, 744, 779, 782, 882, 915, 941, 986, 1027, 1048, 1099
Research, 224, 398, 1108
Researching your topic for multimedia presentation, 1115
Research presentation, **224–225**
  adapting your literary research paper for, 224
  rehearsing your presentation for, 225
Restatement, 1121
Revising, 1119
Rhetorical devices, 508, 664, 1121
Rhetorical questions, 508, 1120
Rhymes, 450
Scanning, 729
Seating, onstage, 607
Secondary sources, 224
Selecting media for multimedia presentation, 1116
Selection criteria, 398
Sentence structure, 381
Sestet, 381
Sets, 472
Shaping attitudes, 1114
Slang, 509, 1122
Soliloquy, 299
Solo reading, 291
Song recording, 154
Sonnet presentation, 381

Sound, 1113, 1116, 1117
Sound effects, 41, 664
Soundtrack, 81
Sources
  documenting, 1115
  electronic media, 1112
  media, 1112
  primary, 224
  print media, 1112
  secondary, 224
Speakers, 381, 607
Special effects, 1113
Speech, 1115
Speech performance, 299
Staging, 607
  artistic, 399
Staging presentation, 664
Standard American English, 509, 665
Statistics, 1123
Stereotypes, 1113
Stress of voice, 399
Stylistic devices, 508
Syllogism, 1122
Syntax, 1123
Television, 1112, 1116
Television programs, 744
Text, 1116, 1117
Themes, universal, 508
Thesis, 224
Thesis statement, 508, 1116
Tone, 321, 1122
Tone of voice, 399, 664–665, 665, 712
Transitions, 1118
TV producers, 1113
Unique aspects, 508
Universal themes, 508
Verbal irony, 1121
Verbal techniques, 665
Video, 1112, 1116
Video presentation, 81
Videotaping, 225, 665
Visual image makers, 1113
Visual representations, 1113
Visuals, 225, 664
Voice, 291, 299, 321, 399, 664
  pitch of, 399, 1122
  stress of, 399
  tone of, 399, 664–665, 665, 712
  volume of, 399, 665, 1122
Volume of voice, 399, 665, 1122
Web sites, 1108
Writing quotations, 509

INDEPENDENT READING

Animal Farm, 499
Arabian Nights, The, 203
"Astrologer's Day, An," 1063
"Borges and Myself," 1006
Brave New World, 1109
Captains Courageous, 730
"Child's Christmas in Wales, A," 1052
"Chip of Glass Ruby, A," 922
"Darling, The," 765
Days of the French Revolution, The, 655
"Dead Men's Path," 929

"Devoted Son, A," 1070
Enlightened Mind: An Anthology of Sacred Prose, The, 389
Favorite Folktales from Around the World, 655
Frankenstein, 655
"Gooseberries," 765
Grendel, 73
Gulliver's Travels, 427
Hamlet, 274
Hard Times, 783
Hitchhiker's Guide to the Galaxy, The, 203
Hobbit, The, 73
"House Taken Over," 998
Importance of Being Earnest, The, 783
"In my craft or sullen art," 1052
Isaac Newton and the Scientific Revolution, 499
"Jay, The," 853
Kim, 730
"Lady with a Dog, The," 765
Life in a Medieval Castle, 203
Lord of the Rings, The, 73
"Loveliest of Trees," 725
Macbeth, 274, 389
"Mandalay," 730
"Man Who Would Be King, The," 730
"Meeting, The," 1006
Midsummer Night's Dream, A, 274
Misanthrope, The, 499
Mrs. Dalloway, 886
Mythology: The Voyage of the Hero, 73
"Necklace, The," 774
"Night Face Up, The," 998
1984, 897
"Ode to My Socks," 1059
"Ode to Walt Whitman," 1059
Once and Future King, The, 203
One Hundred Love Sonnets, 1059
One Hundred Years of Solitude, 1109
"On My First Daughter," 317
Othello, 274
"Piece of Yarn, The," 774
Pride and Prejudice, 655
Robinson Crusoe, 499
Selected Short Stories, 783
Shakespeare Alive!, 389
"Six Feet of the Country," 922
"Soldier of Urbina, A," 1006
"Song: Still to be Neat," 317
"Studies in the Park," 1070
Sundiata: An Epic of Old Mali, 73
"Sunrise on the Veld, A," 907
Tartuffe, 499
Tempest, The, 274
Testament of Youth, 1109
Things Fall Apart, 1109
"Through the Tunnel," 907
To the Lighthouse, 886
"Train from Rhodesia, The," 922
"Two Friends," 774
"Unknown Citizen, The," 1045
What Jane Austen Ate and Charles Dickens Knew, 783
"When I was One-and-Twenty," 725
Zen and the Art of Motorcycle Maintenance, 389

Index of Art

A. S.
  An Early London Coffeehouse (detail), 409, 410–411
Abbey, Edwin Austin (after)
  The Book Stall, 676–677
Agnese of Venice, Battista
  World map from the *Portolan Atlas of the World,* 235
Alexander Pope, 417, 449
Alfaro Siqueiros, David
  The Lover's Rock, 1061
Alice in Wonderland, illustration for, 675
All Quiet on the Western Front (poster), 808
al-Rahim, Mirza Abd (Mughal School)
  Tamarind tree (detail), 176
Altman, Natan
  Head of Akhmatova, 984
American Spelling Book, The, title page of, 519
Ancient Babylon, ruins from, 340
Ancient Troy (map), 60
Andrea del Castagno (Andrea di Bartolo)
  Boccaccio, 185
Andrew Marvell, 266
"And on the bay the moonlight lay . . ." (illustration for *The Rime of the Ancient Mariner*), 596
Angel (detail of carving for a tomb), 715
Anglo-Saxon Chronicle (detail of manuscript), 17
Anglo-Saxon silver knife mount, 37
Animal head from Viking ship, 21
Anne Boleyn, from *Memoirs of the Court of Queen Elizabeth,* 247
"Araby in Dublin" (poster), 965
Arming a man for fighting on foot (detail of illustration for *Ordinances of Armory*), 99
Arthur is mortally wounded (detail of illustration for *Roman du Saint Graal*), 196–197
Ascent of the Prophet Mohammed to Heaven, The (manuscript illustration), 349
Ashanti head, 359
Athena (coin), 59
Attack on a fortress (detail of illustration), 96
Audubon, John James
  Scarlet Ibis, 519
"Auguries of Innocence," from the Pickering, or Ballads, manuscript, 549

August: Departure for the Hunt with Falcons (illustration for *Très riches heures du duc de Berry*), 189
Austin, Robert
  Our Heritage, 849
Bacon, Francis
  Study for Portrait V, 1056
Bak, Samuel
  Study C (detail), 844–845
Battle between King Arthur and Modred (illustration for *St. Alban's Chronicle*), 195
Bawden, Edward
  Cat on a Pile of Blankets, 990
Bayeux Tapestry (details)
  The battle in which King Harold is killed, 4–5; The coronation of King Harold, 11; William the Conqueror's invasion fleet, 92; Norman horsemen chasing defeated English soldiers, 95
Beardsley, Aubrey
  Lady of the Lake (illustration for *Morte d'Arthur*), 198
Bedivere returning Excalibur to the lake upon the death of Arthur (illustration for *Roman du Saint Graal*), 200
Bell, Vanessa
  Virginia Woolf in a Deck Chair, 888
Beowulf (manuscript), 21, 33
Beraud, Jean
  Outside the Theatre du Vaudeville (detail), 781
Beyond the Valley of the Kasbahs, 577
Blake, William
  Chaucer's Canterbury Pilgrims, 116–117, 168 (detail); *Winter,* 287; *The Angel of Divine Presence* (detail), 366; *The Angel Michael Binding Satan,* 370; *Satan in His Original Glory,* 373; *The Ghost of Samuel Appearing to Saul,* 535; *Elohim Creating Adam,* 536; *The Tyger,* from *Songs of Experience,* 537; *The Agony in the Garden* (detail), 538; *The Lamb,* from *Songs of Innocence and of Experience,* 539; "The Chimney Sweeper," from *Songs of Innocence and of Experience,* 543; *A Poison Tree,* from *Songs of Experience,* 548
Blanche, Jacques-Émile
  James Joyce, 955
Blyenberch, Abraham van (after)
  Benjamin Jonson, 317
Bondel, Carl

A Wooded Landscape at Evening (detail), 306
Booth
  "Basil, do you think the center is going to hold?" 1181
Bouvier, J.
  Dressing the young civilian (engraving from *Anglo Indians*), 742
Brancusi, Constantin
  The Kiss (sculpture), 1060
Braun, Georg
  Bird's-eye view of London, from *Atlas Civitatis Orbis Terrarum,* 245
Breu the Elder, Jorg
  Summer (detail), 270
Bridget O'Donnel of West Cork and her children (illustration), 430
British School (possibly after Lucas de Heere)
  An Allegory of the Tudor Succession: The Family of Henry VIII, 247
"Britons" (World War I poster), 802
Brown, Charles Armitage
  John Keats, 640
Bruegel the Elder, Pieter
  The Fall of Icarus, 1046
Burne-Jones, Philip
  Rudyard Kipling, 730
Burne-Jones, Sir Edward
  The Sleeping Princess, 528; *Love Among the Ruins,* 714
Cabin in Ballintober Bog, Roscommon, Ireland (engraving), 674
Canaletto
  Interior of Henry VII's Chapel, Westminster Abbey, 415
Candide, program for, 472
Canterbury Tales, The (Ellesmere manuscript), 115
  Figure thought to be Chaucer, 116, 143; Decorative border, 119; The Knight, 122; The Squire, 123; The Canon Yeoman, 123; The Prioress, 124; The Nun's Priest, 124; The Friar, 126; The Clerk of Oxford, 129; The Franklin, 130; The Cook, 131; The Physician, 132; The Parson, 134; The Miller, 135; The Manciple, 136; The Reeve, 136; The Summoner, 138; The Pardoner, 139, 146; The Wife of Bath, 156
Capon, William
  The First Opera House in the Haymarket, 421
Card makers (illustration), 527

Cartoon mocking huge wigs worn by rich women, 417
Castañeda, Alfredo; *Our Song,* 815; *Our Dream,* 943
Celtic cross, 5
Celtic shield, 38
Central soup depot, Cork, Ireland (illustration), 428–429
Chagall, Marc
  The Prodigal Son, 343, 344 (detail)
Chardin, Jean-Baptiste
  The Young Schoolmistress, 496
Charioteer of Delphi (detail) (statue), 70
Chariot race (amphora), 63
Chef, The (woodcut), 110
Children pushing a coal cart through a mine shaft (illustration), 528
Children at work in a cotton factory (engraving), 545
Child working in a brick factory (illustration), 521
Chinese landscape painting, 633
Chinese porcelain jar, 91
Claesz, Pieter
  Still Life—Vanitas, 316
Clay, Alfred Barron
  The Return of Charles II to Whitehall in 1660, 410
Cole, George Vicat
  A Surrey Cornfield, 527
Colossus of Ramses II, with his daughter, from the Great Temple of Amun, 620
Comes Litoris Saxon per Britaniam (map), 2
Confucius (stele), 355
Connell, Clyde
  Layered Song, 1011
Constable, John
  A Country Road with Trees and Figures, 562; *Study of Sky and Trees,* 564
Coronation of Charlemagne by Pope Leo III (miniature), 3
Corot, Camille
  Windswept Landscape, 621
Couple courting, from a Bible manuscript, 286
Cox, E. A.
  "Britain's Past & Present" (poster for the British Empire Exhibition), 803
Cranach the Elder, Lucas
  Martin Luther's sermon (detail of triptych), 234; *Martin Luther,* 246
Crusaders' 1153 attack on Ascalon (detail of illustration for *Passages d'Outremer*), 102
Daguerre, Louis Jacques Mandé
  The Ruins of Holyrood Chapel, 313
Daily Life in London During the Great Plague (woodcut), 106
Dance scene (one in a series of illustrations of the Miao customs) (detail), 638

Danes attacking an East Anglian town (illustration), 3
Daniel Defoe, 495
d'Annonay, Charles E. Bizet
  A Still Life with Books (details), 326, 327
Darhwal School
  Arjuna and His Charioteer Lord Krsna Confront Carna (detail), 352
Death with his spear (illustration for "The Pardoner's Tale"), 151
Delaroche, Hippolyte (Paul)
  Napoleon in his study, 518
Diary of Samuel Pepys, opening page of, 408
Dicksee, Sir Frank
  Miranda, 610
Dictionary of the English Language, A, definition from, 411
Dodd, Francis
  Alfred Edward Housman, 725
Dollhouses, 1035 (detail), 1036, 1040 (detail), 1041 (detail), 1044 (detail)
Domesday Book, 90
Doré, Gustave
  The Fallen Angels on the Wing, 369; Don Quixote and Sancho setting out (detail), 475; The adventure with the windmills, 478; Don Quixote and the windmill (detail), 480–481; Illustration for *The Rime of the Ancient Mariner,* 605
Dragonhead from a Viking horse collar (detail), 22
Dragon-shaped brooch, 27
Dragon ship (detail of manuscript illustration), 4
Dulac, Edmund
  The Princess in the Kitchens (illustration for *The Arabian Nights*), 178; Illustration for *Sindbad the Sailor and Other Stories,* 183
Dürer, Albrecht
  Three Peasants (detail), 269
Dyce, William
  Pegwell Bay, Kent—A Recollection of October 5, 1858, 722–723
Eakins, Thomas
  The Gross Clinic, 748
Elephant painting, 171
Elizabeth Vernon, countess of Southampton, 255
Emblems and Devices of Love, illustration for (detail), 275
Embroidered wall hanging (detail), 261
English School
  English Ships and the Spanish Armada, August 1588 (detail), 252; Lettice Knollys, daughter of Sir Henry Knollys (detail), 256; Lady with a large ruff, 302; Margaret Cavendish, duchess of Newcastle, 333; *The Pilgrim's Progress,* frontispiece for, 386–387

Escher, Maurits Cornelius
  Bond of Union, 301
Execution of King Charles I . . . , The (woodcut), 414
Execution of Mary, Queen of Scots (detail), 251
Fagin's den of child thieves and a hungry Oliver (illustration for *Oliver Twist*), 689
Faithorne, William
  John Milton, 361
Fang, Shih-shu
  Small bridge over flowing stream (folding fan), 629
February, from *The Grimani Breviary* (detail), 31
February: Man warming himself (illustration for *Breviaire d'amour*), 101
Feyen-Perrin, Francois Nicolas Augustin
  Guy de Maupassant, 774
Figure of a man from the Square Temple at Tell Asmar, 50
Fildes, Luke
  Applicants for Admission to a Casual Ward, 687
Fischer, Paul Gustav
  The Drawing Room, 686; *At the Gallery,* 721
Florence Nightingale tending the wounded during the Crimean War (illustration), 682
Food coupon issued by the British Ministry of Food during World War I, 800
Forshaw and Coles
  Gerard Manley Hopkins, 716
Fragments of the Great Colossus of Memnonium, Thebes (illustration for *Egypt and Nubia*), 618–619
French bracelets, 778
French Revolution button, 409
French School
  Reputed portrait of Christopher Marlowe, 258
Friedrich, Caspar David
  Wanderer Above the Sea of Clouds, The, 523; *Two Men Contemplating the Moon,* 531; *View of a Harbour,* 580
Frith, William Powell
  The Railway Station (detail), 672; *Many Happy Returns of the Day,* 692
Gainsborough, Thomas
  A Woman in Blue (Portrait of the Duchess of Beaufort), 452
Galileo's telescopes, 241
Gemini, Thomas
  English astrolabe, 234
Geoffrey Chaucer, 113
Germanic hero Weland and the adoration of the Magi (Franks casket), 28
German School
  Nicolaus Copernicus (detail), 235
Ghirlandaio, Domenico (Domenico Bigordi)
  St. Jerome in His Study (detail), 236

Giacometti, Alberto
   City Square (*La Place*) (sculpture), 826–827; *Head of a Man* (*Diego*), 1008
Gilbert, Sir John
   Worcester (details), 516, 533; *Brickmakers*, 517
Giles, Catherine
   The Blackened Ruins, City of London, 870
Gilgamesh between two demigods supporting the sun (detail of monument), 49
Gilgamesh depicted on Chaldean seal, 51
Gilgamesh holding a lion (relief), 48
Goddess Athena (statue), 57
God Odin being eaten by the wolf Fenrir (carving), 13
Gogh, Vincent van
   The Potato Eaters, 747
   The Parisian Novels (*The Yellow Books*), 1131
Gold and enamel jewel thought to have belonged to King Alfred, 10
Gold and silver brooch with diamonds and emeralds, 776
Golf Book of Hours, scene from (detail), 88
Gordigiani, Michele
   Robert Browning, 707; *Elizabeth Barrett Browning*, 713
Gower, George (attributed to)
   The Armada portrait of Elizabeth I, 250
Gower, George, circle of
   Mary Denton, née Martyn, 256
Goya y Lucientes, Francisco de
   Colossus, 181
Granting of land to two knights (illustration for *Life of the Noble Princes of Hainaut*), 98
Great ax, with depiction of bird-animal, 37
Great Fire of London, The, 408
Great Harry, The, from the Anthony Roll manuscript (detail), 248
Grimani Breviary, The (details), 318
Grimshaw, John Atkinson
   Forge Valley, Scarborough, 648
Grimshaw, Louis H.
   Westminster Bridge, London (detail), 560
Guillotine, 521
Gulliver awakens in Lilliput (illustration for *Gulliver's Travels*), 411
Gulliver's Travels, title page for, 411
Gundestrup caldron, 43
God, perhaps with sacrificial victims, 8
Gwynne-Jones, Allan
   Fairground, Tottenham, 961
Hadrian's Wall, 4
"'Ha! ha!' quoth he . . ." (illustration for *The Rime of the Ancient Mariner*), 600
Hammershoi, Vilhelm
   Rainy Weather, 993
Handelsman
   "I wish you would make up your mind, Mr. Dickens. . . . ," 1196
Hauschild, W.
   Woman reading *Tristan und Isolde*, 334
Haydon, Benjamin Robert
   William Wordsworth, 550
Head of Humbaba carved to resemble intestines, 53
Hector and Menelaus fight over the body of Euphorbos, 58
Henmi, Takashi
   Rain at Yotsuya Mitsuke, 855, 860 (detail)
Henry, Paul
   Lakeside Cottages, 949
Hercules slaying the centaur Eurytion (detail of sculpture), 44–45
Hernando Cortés meeting Montezuma II (illustration), 235
Highmore, Joseph
   Mr. B. Finds Pamela Writing (illustration for *Pamela, or Virtue Rewarded*), 486–487
Hilliard, Nicholas
   Queen Elizabeth within the Armada jewel, 234; Young man leaning against a tree among roses, 259; *Sir Walter Raleigh*, 260; *Portrait*, 278; *Man aged twenty-four*, 281
Hines, Lewis
   Cartoon protesting child labor, 680
HMS *Beagle*, 519
Hoefnagel, J.
   A Marriage Fête at Bermondsey, 239
Hogarth, William
   Night, 419; *The Laughing Audience*, 422; *Marriage à la Mode: The Marriage Contract*, 491
Hoitsu, Sakai
   Hanging Scroll Depicting the Autumnal Moon (detail), 569
Holbein the Younger, Hans
   The Ambassadors, 232; *King Henry VIII*, 236; *Sir Thomas More* (detail), 244; *Erasmus of Rotterdam* (detail), 244; *Mrs. Pemberton*, 304
Homage to the First Principle (detail), 357
Hooke, Robert
   Eye of a Fly (illustration for *Micrographia*), 438; *Blue Fly* (illustration for *Micrographia*), 439
Hooper, Willoughby Wallace, and George Western
   English officer attended by his Indian servant, 741
Horsley, John Callcott
   The Poet's Theme, 643
Hours of the Duchess of Burgandy, illustration for, 91
Hunt, William Holman
   The Lady of Shalott, 698
Ibibio mask, 931
Ibo mask, 932
"I dreamt that they were filled with dew . . ." (illustration for *The Rime of the Ancient Mariner*), 592
Igbo mural painting depicting a cassava beetle (detail), 814
Iknega headdress, 934
Illuminated P, from a Flemish Bible (detail), 337
Ilsted, Peter Vilhelm
   The Verandah at Liselund, 767 (detail), 772; *Girl Sitting on the Steps*, 1038
Imperial state crown made for Victoria's coronation, 674
Interior of a coal mine in South Staffordshire, England (illustration), 521
Invasion of Danes under Hinguar and Hubba, detail of illustration for *Life, Passion, and Miracles of St. Edmund*, A48
Invention for cleaning tall buildings, observing military fortifications, and performing tree surgery (illustration), 677
Irish cabin (illustration), 433
Irish peasant (illustration), 434
Italian School
   The Outdoor Concert (detail), 263
"It is an ancient Mariner . . ." (illustration for *The Rime of the Ancient Mariner*), 582
"It reached the ship, it split the bay . . ." (illustration for *The Rime of the Ancient Mariner*), 599
Jane Austen, 518
Japanese fifty-sen coins, 857, 859
Japanese silkscreen with flowers (detail), 634
Jawlensky, Alexei von
   Fairy Tale Princess with Fan, 1050
Jervas, Charles
   Jonathan Swift, 427
Jess
   If All the World Were Paper and All the Waters Ink, 1077
John, Augustus
   Portrait of Dylan Thomas, 1053
John, Gwen
   A Corner of the Artist's Room, Paris, 891
John Donne, 300
John Donne in his shroud (marble), 307
John Lydgate and the Canterbury pilgrims leaving Canterbury (illustration for Lydgate's poems), 121
Judy O'Donnel's "home" under the bridge (illustration), 437
Keepsake from the Cloud Gallery, A, 632
King, Charles Bird (lithograph by Lehman and Duval, after)
   Sequoyah, 519
King James Bible, title page for, 336
Kingston brooch, 3
King Sweyn and his Danish troops arrive in England (manuscript illustration), 9, 17 (detail)

1276   Index of Art

Knight and his lady feeding a falcon (manuscript illustration), 109
Knight and Old Lady (manuscript illustration), 160
Koran, leaf from, 350
Kounellis, Jannis
   Untitled, 924
Kramskoy, Ivan Nikolayevich
   Leo Tolstoy, 749
Kublai Khan, 574
Kuindzhi, Arkhip
   The Rainbow, 751
Lamb, Henry
   Juvenile Counsel: Boys on a Doorstep, 865, 867 (detail)
Landseer, Sir Edwin Henry
   King Charles Spaniels (detail), 460
Larkin, William, earl of
   Lady said to be Lady Style, 255
Larraz, Julio
   Papiamento, 1017; *The Trial*, 1020
Le Franc, Martin
   The Nine Muses, 112
Leonardo da Vinci
   The Lady with the Ermine, 284
Leslie, C. R.
   Sir Plume Demands . . . the Lock, 459
Levine, David
   Jonathan Swift, 464
Liang Kai
   Li Po Chanting in Stroll, 635
Life of Confucius and his disciples, scene from, 347
Li Sixun
   Landscape (detail), 631
Lowry, L. S.
   After the Blitz, 863
McConnell, William
   Ladies and Gentlemen Playing Croquet (detail), 677
McGuire, Edward
   Portrait of Seamus Heaney, 1030
Magna Carta (document), 104
Magritte, René
   Le Faux Miroir (The False Mirror), 807
Makowski, Wladimir Jegorowitsch
   Man in the Field, 761, 764 (detail)
Malevich, Kasimir
   Woman with a Rake, 986
Man and his wife on horseback (book of hours illustration), 90
Man and woman (illustration for the *Aeneid*), 158, 167 (detail)
Man and woman on horseback, detail of illustration for *The Devonshire Hunting Tapestries*, 165
Man carrying a goat (bas relief), 52
Manet, Édouard
   The Tavern (detail), 746
Marco Polo in Beijing (illustration), 91
Marie Antoinette, queen of France, 518
Marie de France, 90
"Mariner, whose eye is bright . . . , The" (illustration for *The Rime of the Ancient Mariner*), 602

Maroniez, Georges P. C.
   Wreckers off the Brittany Coast, 613
Martin, John
   The Fallen Angels Entering Pandemonium (illustration for *Paradise Lost*), 363; *The Bard*, 623
Martineau, Robert Braithwaite
   A Lady with a Gold Chain and Earrings, 709
Martyrdom of Thomas Becket (detail of manuscript illustration), 103
Mary Tudor, 249
Master with his carpenter and stonemason (illustration), 93
Matthew Arnold (illustration in *Vanity Fair*), 724
Mayan figure holding tortillas, 3
Medieval knight in armor (manuscript illustration), 99
Medieval knight on horseback (illustration), 161
Michelangelo
   Creation of Adam, from the Sistine Chapel ceiling (detail), 242
Miguel de Cervantes, 473
Millais, John Everett
   Christ in the House of His Parents, 684; *Autumn Leaves*, 719
Modest Proposal, A, title page of, 428
Mollison, James
   Voltaire, 465
Monet, Claude
   Japanese Footbridge and Water Lily Pool, Giverny, 954
Montas, Antoine
   Haitian village scene, 813
Moore, Henry
   Family Group (sculpture), 798; *Two Apprehensive Shelterers*, 811
Mosaic from the palace of Attalos II (detail), 48
Mosaic of Tritons, Nereids, and a sea antelope, 561
Motto of the Republic of France, 520
Mountain landscape (silk scroll), 356
Mounted knight arrayed in helmet and shirt of mail and carrying a shield (relief), 105
Mughal School
   Peacocks and cranes beside a river (illustration for *Baburnama*), 175
Munkácsy, Mihály
   The Blind Milton Dictating Paradise Lost *to His Daughters*, 380
Munn, Paul Sandby
   Bedlam Furnace, Madeley Dale, Shropshire, 526
Muryu
   Birds on a Snowy Plum Bough, 566
"Musée des Beaux Arts" (manuscript), 1048
Nash, John Northcote
   Over the Top, 1st Artists' Rifles at Marcoing (detail), 802; *Oppy Wood*, 824

Nasmyth, Patrick
   Landscape (detail), 554–555
Nebot, Balthasar
   Covent Garden with St. Paul's Church, 420
Netherlands School
   Launch of Fireships Against the Armada, 237
Nevinson, Christopher R. W.
   The Arrival, 805, 818 (detail); *Paths of Glory*, 822
Newton's reflecting telescope, 416
Nigerian head, thought to be an Ife king, 940
Noblewomen watching a tournament (manuscript illustration), 101
Nussbaum, Felix
   Self-portrait with Jewish Identity Card (detail), 847
Off for a day of haying, a peasant pushes his wife to work in a wheelbarrow (manuscript illustration), 100
Old Fleet Prison, The, illustration for (detail), 407
Oliver, Isaac (attributed to)
   The Rainbow Portrait (Elizabeth I), 331
"On First Looking into Chapman's Homer" (manuscript), 642
Opie, John
   Mary Wollstonecraft Godwin, 484
Osborne, Walter
   St. Patrick's Close, Dublin, 958
"Ozymandias" (manuscript), 620
Palace of Kublai Khan at Peking (illustration for *Livre des Merveilles*), 575
Parker, Henry Perlee
   Pitmen at Play (detail), 692
Patience (cover of operetta program), 691
Peake the Elder, Robert
   Portrait of a boy, 319
Pedersen, Viggo Christien Frederik Wilhelm
   Evening Shadows, 718
Phillips, Thomas
   William Blake (detail), 534; *Byron, Sixth Baron* (detail), 615
Picasso, Pablo
   Guernica, 801; *Les Demoiselles d'Avignon*, 809
Picture stone from Gotland, Sweden (detail), 32
Pisano, Andrea
   Grammar students with their teacher (bas relief), 233
Plan of the road from the City of Destruction to the Celestial City (engraving for *The Pilgrim's Progress*), 384
Poems on Various Subjects, Religious and Moral, frontispiece for, 409
Portrait of a Young Woman (detail), 285

Index of Art   **1277**

Priam begging Achilles to give him the body of Hector (detail of drinking vessel), 64
"Pro Bono Publico" (placard promoting passage of the Reform Bill), 676
Prow of the Oseberg ship, 19
Ran-ku
  Bashō (sculpture), 570
Renoir, Auguste
  Jeanne Samary in a Scoop Neckline Dress (detail), 776
Ricci, Arturo
  The Art Class, 483
Richardson, Jonathan (attributed to)
  Alexander Pope and Dog Bounce (detail), 445
Rigaud, Jean
  View Across Greenwich Park Toward London (detail), 448
Riley, Bridget
  Nataraja, 813
Riot at Newport, England, November 4, 1839 (engraving), 676
Rivera, Diego
  Mother and Child, 1051
Robert, Hubert
  Italian Landscape, 312
Robinson Crusoe, cover of, 424
Romance of the Rose, scene from, 97
Roman du roi Arthur et les compagnons de la Table Ronde, Le, illustration for (detail), 192
Roman helmet, 2
Rossetti, Dante Gabriel
  Proserpine, 685
Rothenstein, Sir William
  The Browning Readers, 713
Rowlandson, Thomas
  Tom Jones Refused Admittance by the Nobleman's Porter (illustration for Tom Jones), 425; The Author and His Publisher, 446; The Royal Academy Exhibition, 463
Rowlandson, Thomas, and A. Pugin
  Interior of Drury Lane Theater, 1808, 690
Rozhdestvyenski, Konstantin
  Farmwoman in a Field, 985
Saint John dictating to the Venerable Bede (miscellany illustration), 15
St. Matthew's Gospel, opening page of, from the Lindisfarne Gospels, 16
Sakamoto, Yoshinobu
  Harimaya-chô, 856
Sampson, Richard
  Motets, 321
Sarto, Andrea del (Andrea d'Agnolo)
  Study of Hands, 241
Schiavonetti
  Robert Herrick, 264
Seated Buddha (sculpture), 2
Seger, William
  Gilbert Talbot, seventh earl of Shrewsbury, 256

Selous, Henry C.
  Opening of the Great Exhibition in Hyde Park, May 1, 1851, The (details), 679, 693
Serov, Valentin
  Portrait of the Painter Konstantin Alekseevich Korovin, 769
Severn, Joseph
  Shelley Composing Prometheus Unbound (detail), 617; John Keats at Wentworth Place, 645
Shah Jahan, who ruled India during the Mughal dynasty, 173
Shepherds, from Chartres Cathedral (bas relief), 339
Sherlock Holmes and Dr. Watson on a train (illustration), 675
Shrine to the monkey-god in Chamundi Hill Temple, Mysore, India, 732
Shunman, Kubo
  Illustration from Illustrated Collection of Butterflies, 572
Sigurd kills the dragon (detail) (church portal), 39
Silver and gold brooch with amber ornaments, 26
Simpson, William (after)
  The First Investiture of the Star of India (detail), 738
Sindbad the Sailor being carried by a sea monster (illustration for One Thousand and One Nights), 179
Sindbad the Sailor entertains a group with stories of his seven fantastic voyages (illustration for The Thousand and One Nights), 170
Sintzenich, Gustave Ellinthorpe
  View of Strawberry Hill, Middlesex, 530
Sir Francis Bacon, 240
Sir Winston Churchill, 801
Sittou, M.
  Catherine of Aragon, 249
Sojourner Truth, 674
Soldiers in battle (detail of a bowl), 703
Song of Roland (stained-glass window), 90
Sphinx, 946–947
Staël, Nicolas de
  Le Ciel Rouge (The Red Sky), 926
Star of David cloth patch, 835
Steam-driven threshing machine demonstrated at the Great London Exhibition, 673
Stonehenge, 1, 7
Stoop, Dirck
  Coronation Procession of Charles II to Westminster from the Tower of London (details), 406, 426
Storming of the Bastille, 525
Sumerian bull's head (detail of musical instrument or piece of furniture), 54
Superman (comic-strip character), 44–45
Survival in Auschwitz, cover for, 833

Sutton Hoo ship treasure
  Helmet fragment, 12; Replica of a six-stringed instrument, 14; Sutton Hoo helmet, 18; Eagle shield ornament, 23; Anglo-Saxon gold buckle, 25; Shoulder clasp, 33; Bronze stag atop ceremonial scepter, 36
"Tale of the Wife of Bath" (opening page of the Kelmscott Chaucer), 162
Taylor, John (attributed to)
  William Shakespeare, 272
Teacher and his pupil, from the Coburg Pentateuch, 348
Thomas Babington Macaulay, 680
Three Living, the Three Dead, The, from the Psalter and Prayer Book of Bonne of Luxembourg, 149
Three-ringed gold collar (detail), 24
Three standing figures (Odin, Thor, and Freyr) in tunics (tapestry), 13
"Through utter drought all dumb we stood!" (illustration for The Rime of the Ancient Mariner), 587
Time (tapestry), 288 (detail), 289
Tintern Abbey ruins, 558
Titian (Tiziano Vecellio)
  Man with Glove, 708
Tragic End of Louis XVI, 524
Transport of amphoras (vase), 653
Treatise on Falconry, illustration for (detail), 187
Trumbull, John
  The Death of General Mercer at the Battle of Princeton (detail), 520
Tu Fu (rubbing of carving, from Travels of a Chinese Poet), 630
Turkish portrait of a dervish, 358
Turner, J.M.W. (Joseph Mallord William)
  View of Hampton Court, Herefordshire, 454; Tintern Abbey, 553; The Junction of the Thames and the Medway, 616; Panorama of Florence, 625; Ulysses Deriding Polyphemus, 704–705
Turtle-shaped Ashanti emblem, 408
Two lovers (detail of Italian plate), 268
Two men observe the construction of a house (illustration), 93
"Upon the whirl, where sank the ship . . ." (illustration for The Rime of the Ancient Mariner), 600
Upper part of buildings discovered below a temple of Athena, illustration from Troy and Its Remains, 68
Valkenborch, Lucas van
  Spring (detail), 265
van der Straet, Jan
  Printing Shop, 243, 254 (detail)
Vandyke, Peter
  Samuel Taylor Coleridge, 573
van Somer, Paul
  Nobleman in garter robes, said to be the seventh earl of Shrewsbury,

255; *Sir Francis Bacon, Viscount of St. Albans*, (detail), 323
Vasilyev, Fiodor
   Road in the Woods (detail), 754–755
Verheyden, Isidore
   The Gleaners, 758
Victorian valentine, envelope, and "penny black" stamp, 712
Viking coin minted in England, 20
Viking sword handles, 34
Vredeman de Vries, Paulus
   Ladies and Gentlemen Dancing in a Sumptuous Interior, 240
Waddy, Frederick
   Caricature of Alfred, Lord Tennyson, 694
Wallcousins, E.
   Nebuchadnezzar admires the Hanging Gardens of Babylon (illustration for *Myths of Babylonia and Assyria*), 338
Wang Yuan-Ch`i
   Landscape (detail), 637
Warriors (detail of vase), 66
Waterhouse, John William
   The Lady of Shalott, 696–697; *The Lady of Shalott*, 700
Watts, George Frederic
   The Irish Famine, 681; *Portrait of Matthew Arnold*, 720
Westall, Richard
   Byron, Sixth Baron (detail), 609
Westminster Bridge (engraving), 559
Whitby Abbey ruins, 12
White, Robert
   John Bunyan, 382
William Congreve, English dramatist and poet, 420
William the Conquerer (coin), 96
William of Orange receiving his crown (illustration), 418
W;t, jacket for, 315
"With my crossbow / I shot the ALBATROSS." (illustration for *The Rime of the Ancient Mariner*), 579
Woman possibly personifying Summer (detail) (embroidery), 257
Worcester teapot, 461
Wright of Derby, Joseph
   The Orrery, 413; *Mr. and Mrs. William Chase*, 423
Yeats, Jack Butler
   Lough Gill, County Sligo, 950
Yeats, John Butler
   William Butler Yeats (detail), 944
Yoshitoshi, Tsukioka
   Lady Chiyo, 571
Young English chimney sweep covered with soot (drawing), 542
Young English chimney sweep sitting on top of a chimney, reading (engraving), 546
Young musician (illustration for *De Musica*), 108
Youth singing and playing the kithara (detail of amphora), attributed to the Berlin Painter, 651

Index of Authors and Titles

Page numbers in italic type refer to the pages on which author biographies appear.

Achebe, Chinua, *929*, 931
African Proverbs, 359
Akhmatova, Anna, *982*, 984, 985
Aldington, Richard, 467
All the Unburied Ones, 985
Analects of Confucius, The, from, 355
Annals, The, from, 510
Araby, 957–961
Arndt, Walter, 227
Arnold, Matthew, *720*, 722
Ashdown, Ellen, 39
Atwood, Margaret, 1125
Auden, W. H., *1045*, 1047
Aung San Suu Kyi, 1107
Auslander, Joseph, 276
Axioms, 327
Axolotl, 1000–1004

Bacon, Sir Francis, 240, 242, *323*, 325, 327
Baines, Keith, 194
Bait, The, 262
Baranczak, Stanislaw, 880
Barnstone, Willis, 285
Bashō, Matsuo, *570*, 571
Bay Psalm Book, from, 341
Behn, Harry, 571
Beilenson, Peter, 571
Beowulf, Part I, from, 21–28
Beowulf, Part II, from, 33–38
Bet, The, 767–772
Bhagavad-Gita, from the, 351
Blackburn, Paul, 1000
Blake, William, 517, 531, 532, *534*, 537, 539, 542, 543, 547, 549, 666
"Blake Is a Real Name . . .," 538
Blood, Sweat, and Tears, 850–851
Blow, Blow, Thou Winter Wind, 287
Bly, Robert, 953
Boccaccio, Giovanni, *185*, 187
Bondanella, Peter, 187
Book of Sand, The, 1009–1012
Borges, Jorge Luis, *1006*, 1009
Bowen, Elizabeth, *987*, 989
Bownas, Geoffrey, 569
Boyle, T. Coraghessan, 438
Bray, Barbara, 841
Break, Break, Break, 84
Browning, Elizabeth Barrett, *713*, 715
Browning, Robert, *707*, 709
Bunyan, John, *382*, 384

Burning of Rome, The, from, 510–511
Buson, Taniguchi, 570, 571
B. Wordsworth, 1016–1020
Byron, George Gordon, Lord, *609*, 611, 613

Caesar, Julius, 7
Candide, from, 467–470
Cantor, Norman F., 89
Canterbury Tales, The, from, 120–142
    Pardoner's Tale, The, from, 146–153
    Prologue, The, 120–142
    Wife of Bath's Tale, The, from, 156–166
Carlyle, Thomas, 525
Cavanagh, Clare, 880
Cavendish, Margaret, 332
Ceram, C. W., 67
Cervantes, Miguel de, *473*, 475
Chamberlain, Joseph, 917
Chang Shih-nan, 357
Chatwin, Bruce, 604
Chaucer, Geoffrey, *113–114*, 120, 146, 156
Chekhov, Anton, *765*, 767
Childe Harold's Pilgrimage, Canto IV, from, 613–614
Chimney Sweeper, The (from Songs of Innocence), 542
Chimney Sweeper, The (from Songs of Experience), 543
Chua-Eoan, Howard G., 30
Chudleigh, Mary, Lady, 494
Churchill, Winston, 8, *811*, *848*, 850
Clever Judge, A, 357
Coghill, Nevill, 120, 146, 156
Coleridge, Samuel Taylor, *573*, 575, 581, 603
Coleridge Describes His Addiction, 603
Colet, Roger, 776
Composed upon Westminster Bridge, 560
Cooper, Arthur, 633, 637, 638
Cortázar, Julio, *998*, 1000
D. H. Lawrence on Money, 980
Dana, Doris, 1050
Dawood, N. J., 180, 350
Day of Destiny, The, 194–200
Death and Other Grave Matters, 728
Death be not proud, 313
Death of Hector, The, from, 57–66
Decameron, from the, 187
Defoe, Daniel, 407, 495
Demon Lover, The, 989–995
Denby, David, 69
Desai, Anita, *1070*, 1072
Destructors, The, 863–873

Diary of Samuel Pepys, The, from, 511–512
Dickens, Charles, 524
Digging, 1029
Doll's House, The, 1036–1041
Donne, John, 262, *300*, 302, 305, 308, 313
Do Not Go Gentle into That Good Night, 1057
Don Quixote, from, 475–479
Dover Beach, 722
Drummer Hodge, 792–793
Dryden, John, 421
Dulce et Decorum Est, 822
Dunlop, Lane, 855
Duras, Marguerite, 841

Edson, Margaret, 314
Education of Women, The, from, 495–497
Eliot, T. S., *825*, 828
Elizabeth I, 250, 253, 330
Ellis, Sarah Stickney, 686
End and the Beginning, The, 880–881
Engels, Friedrich, 806
Essay on Man, An, from, 449
Essays, from the, 327
Evidence Given Before the Sadler Committee, from, 544–545

Fagles, Robert, 57, 71
Fall of Satan, The, 367–374
Fear, 1050
Fear No More the Heat o' the Sun, 288–289
Federigo's Falcon, 187–190
Female Orations, from, 332–334
Fern Hill, 1054–1055
Freud, Sigmund, 806
Full Fathom Five, 290
Fury of the Northmen, The, 39
Fussell, Paul, 808

Games at Twilight, 1072–1077
Gandhi, Mohandas K., 812
Gardner, John, 29
Garnett, Constance, 767
George III, 414
Get Up and Bar the Door, 110
Gilgamesh, from, 48–53
Give Us This Day Our Daily Bread, 269–270
Gods, Graves, and Scholars, from, 67
Gold, Gold, 357

1280 Index of Authors and Titles

Gordimer, Nadine, *922*, 924
Greene, Graham, *861*, 863
Grendel, from, 29
Grianna, Marie ni, 681

Haiku, 571
Half a Day, 1024–1026
Hamlet, from, 293
Hardy, Thomas, 792
Heaney, Seamus, 33, *1028*, 1029
Heine, Heinrich, 1124
Hemschemeyer, Judith, 985
Henderson, Harold G., 571
Henry V, from, 296
Henry VIII, 247
Heroic Couplets, 447–448
Herrick, Robert, *264*, 265
Hollow Men, The, 828–830
Holman, J. Martin, 855
Homer, 57
Hooke, Robert, 415
Hopkins, Gerard Manley, *716*, 718
Housman, A. E., *725*, 727
How Much Land Does a Man Need?, 751–762
Hurault, André, 252
Hurley, Andrew, 1009

I am not one of those who left the land, 985
"I Believe in a British Empire," 917–918
Iliad, from the, 57–66
In Patagonia, from, 604–605
In the Shadow of War, 877–879
Issa, Kobayashi, *570*, 571

Jade Flower Palace, 632
Jewels, The, 776–781
Jin, Ha, *1089*, 1091
Johnson-Davies, Denys, 1024
Jonson, Ben, *317*, 319, 320
Joyce, James, *810*, *955*, 957

Kawabata, Yasunari, *853*, 855
Keats, John, *640*, 642, 643, 645, 647, 652
Keats's Last Letter, 645
King James Bible, from, 339, 340, 344
Kingsley, Charles, *682*, 683
Kipling, Rudyard, *730*, 733
Kirkland, Elizabeth, 269
Komachi, Ono, *568*, 569
Koran, from the, 350
Kotewall, Robert, 637
Kubla Khan, 575–576
Kunitz, Stanley, 985

Labé, Louise, 285
Lady of Shalott, The, 697–701
Lake Isle of Innisfree, The, 949
Lamb, Charles, 538
Lamb, The, 539
Laotzu, 356
Lawrence, D. H., *809*, *967*, 969, 980
Le Morte d'Arthur, from, 194
Leslau, Charlotte and Wolf, 359

Lessing, Doris, *819*, *907*, 909
Letter to His Two Small Children, 638
Levi, Primo, *833*, 835
Lewisohn, Ludwig, 793
Lieh Tzu, 357
Life in 999: A Grim Struggle, 30–31
Like the Sun, 1065–1068
Lines Composed a Few Miles Above Tintern Abbey, 552–557
Li Po, *635*, 637, 638
Lively, Penelope, *1080*, 1082
London, 666
London, 1802, 526
Lord Randall, 109
Lorelei, The, 1124
Lot's Wife, 984
Luther, Martin, 246

Macaulay, Thomas Babington, 680
Macbeth, from, 295
Mahfouz, Naguib, *1022*, 1024
Malory, Sir Thomas, *192*, 194
Mandela, Nelson, 1166
Mansfield, Katherine, *1034*, 1036
Mark of the Beast, The, 733–743
Markus, Julia, 711
Marlowe, Christopher, *258*, 259
Marriage Is a Private Affair, 931–934
Marvell, Andrew, *266*, 267
Marx, Karl, 806
Mason, Herbert, 48
Maude, Louise and Aylmer, 751
Maupassant, Guy de, *774*, 776
Meade, Margaret, 885
Meditation 17, 308–309
Mill, John Stuart, 684
Miller, Barbara Stoler, 351
Milton, John, *361–362*, 367, 375, 380
Mistral, Gabriela, *1049*, 1050
Mitchell, Stephen, 356
Mitsune, Oshikochi, *568*, 569
Modest Proposal, A, 430–437
Musa, Mark, 187
Musée des Beaux Arts, 1047
My Last Duchess, 709–710

Naipaul, V. S., *1014*, 1016
Narayan, R. K., *1063*, 1065
Nehru, Jawaharlal, 919
Neruda, Pablo, 1033, *1059*, 1061
Never Shall I Forget, 845
Next Term, We'll Mash You, 1082–1086
Night, 350
Night Thoughts Afloat, 633
"Noble Mansion of Free India, The," 919–920
No Witchcraft for Sale, 909–914
Nukada, Princess, *568*, 569
Nymph's Reply to the Shepherd, The, 261

Ode on a Grecian Urn, 652–653
Ode to a Nightingale, 647–649
Ode to the West Wind, 622–624
Of Studies, 325–326

Okri, Ben, *875*, 877
Once upon a Time, 924–927
On First Looking into Chapman's Homer, 642
Onitsura, Uejima, *570*, 571
On My First Son, 319
On the Bottom, 835–838
Orwell, George, *897*, 899
Our revels now are ended, 298
Owen, Wilfred, *820*, 822
Ozymandias, 619

Panchatantra, from the, 173
Papp, Joseph, 269
Parable of the Prodigal Son, The, 344
Paradise Lost, from, 367
Pardoner's Tale, The, from, 146–153
Passionate Shepherd to His Love, The, 259
Pepys, Samuel, 511
Petrarch, Francesco, 276
Philosophy and Spiritual Discipline, from, 351–352
Pied Beauty, 718
Pilgrim's Progress, The, from, 384–387
Poison Tree, A, 547
Pool, Daniel, 728
Pope, Alexander, *417*, *445*, 447, 449, 450, 453
Pound, Ezra, 628
Prelude, The, from, 529, 533
Psalm 23 (Bay Psalm Book), 341
Psalm 23 (King James Bible), 339
Psalm 137, 340
Pushkin, Alexander, 227
Putnam, Samuel, 475

Question and Answer Among the Mountains, 637
Question of South Africa, The, from, 1103–1106
Quiet Night Thoughts, 637

Raffel, Burton, 1, 21, 42, 82
Raleigh, Sir Walter, 250, *260*, 261
Ramsay, George Gilbert, 510
Rape of the Lock, The, from, 453–459
Raven doth to raven fly, 227
Rear-Guard, The, 823
Reps, Paul, 353
Rexroth, Kenneth, 632
Right-Mind and Wrong-Mind, 173–176
Rilke, Rainer Maria, *943*, 953
Rimbaud, Arthur, 793
Rime of the Ancient Mariner, The, 581–602
Roberts, Moss, 357
Rocking-Horse Winner, The, 969–980
Ronsard, Pierre de, 400
Room of One's Own, A, from, 888
Ryder, Arthur William, 173

Saboteur, 1091–1098
Saigyo, *568*, 569
Saint Crispin's Day Speech, 296–297
Sassoon, Siegfried, 823

Index of Authors and Titles   **1281**

Sayings of Saadi, 358
Scenes from a Modern Marriage, 711
Seafarer, The, from, 82–83
Second Coming, The, 946
Shah, Idries, 358
Shakespeare, William, 233, 272–274, 277, 279, 280, 281, 282, 283, 284, 287, 288, 290, 293, 295, 296, 298
Shakespeare Alive!, from, 269
Shakespeare's Sister, 888–892
Shelley, Percy Bysshe, *617,* 619, 622
Sheridan, Richard, 422
She Walks in Beauty, 611
Shooting an Elephant, 899–904
Silver Fifty-Sen Pieces, The, 855–858
Siren Song, 1125
Sleeper of the Valley, The, 793
Smith, Norman L., 637
Solzhenitsyn, Aleksandr, 818
Soneto 79, 1061
Song, 302
Song: To Celia, 320
Songs of Experience, from, 537, 543, 547
Songs of Innocence, from, 539, 542
Sonnet 18 (Shakespeare), 277
Sonnet 23 (Labé), 285
Sonnet 29 (Shakespeare), 279
Sonnet 30 (Shakespeare), 280
Sonnet 42 (Petrarch), 276
Sonnet 43 (Browning), 715
Sonnet 71 (Shakespeare), 281
Sonnet 73 (Shakespeare), 282
Sonnet 79 (Neruda), 1061
Sonnet 116 (Shakespeare), 283
Sonnet 130 (Shakespeare), 284
Soyinka, Wole, *937,* 939
Stalin, Joseph, 811
Survival in Auschwitz, from, 835
Swan, The, 953

Swift, Jonathan, *427,* 430
Szymborska, Wisława, 880

Tacitus, 510
Tanka, 569
Taoist Anecdotes, 357
Tao Te Ching, from the, 356
Tapscott, Stephen, 1061
Telephone Conversation, 939–940
Tempest, The, from, 298
Tennyson, Alfred, Lord, 84, 673, *694, 697,* 704
Third Voyage of Sindbad the Sailor, The, from, 180–183
Thomas, Dylan, *1052,* 1054, 1057
Thousand and One Nights, The, from, 180
Thwaite, Anthony, 569
Tilbury Speech, 330
To an Athlete Dying Young, 727
To be, or not to be, 293–294
To His Coy Mistress, 267–268
Tolstoy, Leo, 749, 751
Tomorrow, and tomorrow, and tomorrow, 295
Top of the Food Chain, 438–441
To the Ladies, 494
To the Virgins, to Make Much of Time, 265
Towards a True Refuge, from, 1107–1109
Trojan Gold, 67–68
Tsurayuki, Ki, *568,* 569
Tu Fu, *630,* 632, 633
Tutu, Desmond, 1103
Twa Corbies, The, 226
Tyger, The, 537

Ulysses (Tennyson), 704–706
United Nations Commission on Human Rights, 1101

United States Holocaust Memorial Museum Web site, 846
Universal Declaration of Human Rights, from the, 1101–1102
Untermeyer, Louis, 1124

Valediction: Forbidding Mourning, A, 305
Vindication of the Rights of Woman, A, from, 487–491
Virgins, The, 667
Voltaire, *465,* 467

Walcott, Derek, 667
Waley, Arthur, 355
War, The, from, 841–843
When I consider how my light is spent, 380
When I Have Fears, 643
When You Are Old (Ronsard), 400
When You Are Old (Yeats), 401
Wiesel, Elie, 845
Wife of Bath's Tale, The, from, 156–166
Wilbur, Richard, 984
Wilde, Oscar, 687
Wild Swans at Coole, The, 952
W;t, from, 314–315
Wolfe, Humbert, 400
Wollstonecraft, Mary, 484, 487
Woolf, Stuart, 835
Woolf, Virginia, 799, *886,* 888
Wordsworth, William, 526, 529, 533, 550, 552, 560, 562
World Is Too Much with Us, The, 562
Wynkfielde, Robert, 251

Yeats, William Butler, 401, *944,* 946, 949, 952

Zen Parables, 353–354

For permission to reprint copyrighted material, grateful acknowledgment is made to the following sources:

Addison-Wesley Educational Publishers, Inc.: From *Chaucer's Poetry: An Anthology for the Modern Reader*, Selected and Edited by E. T. Donaldson. Copyright © 1958, 1975 by The Ronald Press Company.

Aitken Stone Ltd.: Quotes by V. S. Naipaul from *Words and Their Masters* by Israel Shenker. Copyright © 1974 by V.S. Naipaul.

Georges Borchardt, Inc.: From *The Life and Times of Chaucer* by John Gardner. Copyright © 1977 by Boskydell Artist, Ltd. From *The Poetry of Chaucer* by John Gardner. Copyright © 1977 by Boskydell Artist Ltd.

Cambridge University Press: From "Art, Drama, and the People" from *Tolstoy: A Critical Introduction* by R. F. Christian. Copyright © 1969 by Cambridge University Press. From "Cervantes" from *The Literature of the Spanish People*, 2nd Edition, by Gerald Brenan. Copyright 1951 by Cambridge University Press.

Rosica Colin Ltd.: From *The Decameron* by Giovanni Boccaccio, translated by Richard Aldington. Copyright © 1957, 1985 by the Estate of Richard Aldington.

The Gale Group: From *The Canterbury Tales: A Literary Pilgrimage* by David Williams. Copyright 1987 by Twayne Publishers.

Martin Gardner: From *The Annotated Ancient Mariner*, with Introduction and notes by Martin Gardner. Copyright © 1965 by Martin Gardner.

Harcourt, Inc.: From "Why I Write" from *Such, Such Were the Joys* by George Orwell. Copyright 1953 by Sonia Brownell Orwell, copyright renewed © 1981 by Mrs. George Perutz, Mrs. Miriam Gross, and Dr. Michael Dickson, Executors of the Estate of Sonia Brownell Orwell.

Henry Holt and Company, LLC: From *Jonathan Swift: A Portrait* by Victoria Glendinning. Copyright © 1998 by Victoria Glendinning.

Kay & Boose LLP for The Maugham Trust: From Introduction from *Tellers of Tales: 100 Short Stories from the United States, England, France, Russia, and Germany*, edited by Somerset Maugham. Copyright 1939 by Somerset Maugham.

Alfred A. Knopf, a division of Random House, Inc.: Quotes by Pablo Neruda from *Seven Voices: Seven Latin American Writers Talk to Rita Guibert*, translated by Frances Partridge. Copyright © 1972 by Alfred A. Knopf, a division of Random House, Inc.

James L. Matterer: From "A Chaucerian Cookery" from *Godecookery* Web site. Accessed on February 4, 2002 at http://www.godecookery.com/chaucer/ccookery.htm. Copyright © 2000 by James L. Matterer.

Jawaharlal Nehru Memorial Fund: From *Eulogy for Gandhi* by Jawaharlal Nehru, February 2, 1948.

W. W. Norton & Company, Inc.: From *Victorian People and Ideas: A Companion for the Modern Reader of Victorian Literature* by Richard Altick. Copyright © 1973 by W. W. Norton & Company, Inc. From *The Hidden Wordsworth* by Kenneth R. Johnston. Copyright © 1998 by Kenneth Richard Johnston. From *Alexander Pope: A Life* by Maynard Mack. Copyright © 1986 by Maynard Mack.

Palgrave Macmillan: From *Twentieth-Century English Literature* by Harry Blamires. Copyright © 1982 by Harry Blamires. From *A History of Japan: Stone Age to Superpower* by Kenneth G. Henshall. Copyright © 1999 by Kenneth G. Henshall.

Simon & Schuster Adult Publishing Group: From Introduction from *Pope: A Collection of Critical Essays*, edited by J. V. Guerinot. Copyright © 1972 by Prentice-Hall, Inc. From *Literature of the Western World*, vol. 1, edited by Brian Wilkie and James Hurt. Copyright © 1984 by Prentice-Hall, Inc.

W. D. Snodgrass: From "A Rocking-Horse: The Symbol, the Pattern, the Way to Live" by W. D. Snodgrass from *The Hudson Review*, XI, Summer 1958. Copyright © 1958 by W. D. Snodgrass.

University of California Press: From *The Idea of The Canterbury Tales* by Donald R. Howard. Copyright © 1976 by University of California Press.

Sources Cited

From *William Wordsworth: A Poetic Life* by John L. Mahoney. Published by Fordham University Press, New York, 1997.

From *Japanese Literature: An Introduction for Western Readers* by Donald Keene. Published by Grove Press, New York, 1955.

From *The Song of the Earth* by Jonathan Bate. Published by Harvard University Press, Cambridge, MA, 2000.

From Introduction by Salman Rushdie from *Mirrorwork,* edited by Salman Rushdie and Elizabeth West. Published by Henry Holt and Company, LLC, New York, 1997.

Letter to James Joyce, April 12, 1927, from *James Joyce's Letters to Sylvia Beach, 1921–1940,* edited by Melissa Banta and Oscar A. Silverman. Published by Indiana University Press, Bloomington, 1987.

From "Chaucer's Pardoner, the Scriptural Eunuch, and the Pardoner's Tale" by Robert P. Miller from *Speculum,* XXX, 1955. Published by the Medieval Academy of America, 1955.

From "Chaucer the Pilgrim" by E. Talbot Donaldson from *Publications of the Modern Language Association,* LXIX, 1954.

From "Talking with Ben Okri: Shakespeare Is an African Writer" by Alan Ryan from *Newsday,* July 19, 1992.

From quote by Felix L. Sparks given at the U.S. Holocaust Memorial Museum, May 8, 1995, from the *remember.og* Web site, accessed February 6, 2002 at htp://remember.org/witness/sparks.html.

From *Disowned by Memory: Wordsworth's Poetry of the 1790s* by David Bromwich. Published by The University of Chicago Press, 1998.

From "Tennyson's Mody" by John Hollander from *The Georgia Review 3,* vol. 29, Fall 1975. Published by University of Georgia, 1975.